AF861803

# Smith and Roberson's Business Law

MANN | ROBERTS

CENGAGE Learning

Australia • Brazil • Japan • Korea • Mexico • Singapore • Spain • United Kingdom • United States

CENGAGE Learning

**Smith and Roberson's Business Law**

Executive Editors:
Maureen Staudt
Michael Stranz

Senior Project Development Manager:
Linda deStefano

Marketing Specialist:
Courtney Sheldon

Senior Production/Manufacturing Manager:
Donna M. Brown

Production Editorial Manager:
Kim Fry

Sr. Rights Acquisition Account Manager:
Todd Osborne

Smith and Roberson's Business Law, 15th Edition
Richard A. Mann, Barry S. Roberts



For product information and technology assistance, contact us at
**Cengage Learning Customer & Sales Support, 1-800-354-9706**
For permission to use material from this text or product,
submit all requests online at **cengage.com/permissions**
Further permissions questions can be emailed to
**permissionrequest@cengage.com**

This book contains select works from existing Cengage Learning resources and was produced by Cengage Learning Custom Solutions for collegiate use. As such, those adopting and/or contributing to this work are responsible for editorial content accuracy, continuity and completeness.



ISBN-13: 978-1-285-14190-9

ISBN-10: 1-285-14190-3

**Cengage Learning**
5191 Natorp Boulevard
Mason, Ohio 45040
USA

Cengage Learning is a leading provider of customized learning solutions with office locations around the globe, including Singapore, the United Kingdom, Australia, Mexico, Brazil, and Japan. Locate your local office at: **international.cengage.com/region.**

Cengage Learning products are represented in Canada by Nelson Education, Ltd.

For your lifelong learning solutions, visit **www.cengage.com/custom.**
Visit our corporate website at **www.cengage.com.**

Printed in the United States of America

# Brief Contents

# PART 1
# The Legal Environment of Business

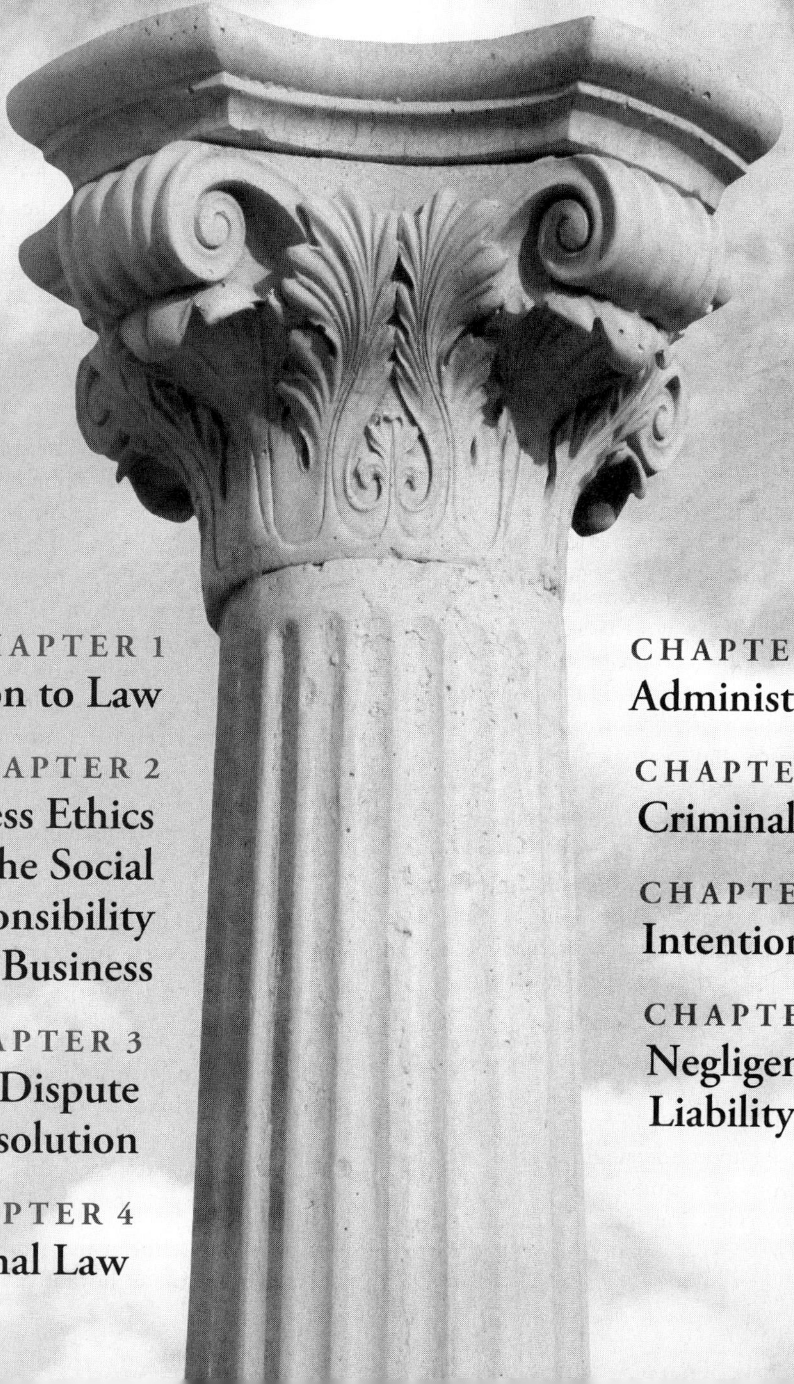

# CHAPTER 1
# Introduction to Law

Law concerns the relations of individuals with one another as such relations affect the social and economic order. It is both the product of civilization and the means by which civilization is maintained. As such, law reflects the social, economic, political, religious, and moral philosophy of society. The laws of the United States influence the lives of every U.S. citizen. At the same time, the laws of each State influence the lives of its citizens and the lives of many noncitizens as well. The rights and duties of all individuals, as well as the safety and security of all people and their property, depend upon the law.

The law is pervasive. It interacts with and influences the political, economic, and social systems of every civilized society. It permits, forbids, or regulates practically every known human activity and affects all persons either directly or indirectly. Law is, in part, prohibitory: certain acts must not be committed. For example, one must not steal; one must not murder. Law is also partly mandatory: certain acts must be done or be done in a prescribed way. Taxes must be paid; corporations must make and file certain reports with State authorities; traffic must keep to the right. Finally, law is permissive: individuals may choose to perform or not to perform certain acts. Thus, one may or may not enter into a contract; one may or may not dispose of one's estate by will.

Because the areas of law are so highly interrelated, an individual who intends to study the several branches of law known collectively as business law should first consider the nature, classification, and sources of law as a whole. This enables the student not only to comprehend better any given branch of law but also to understand its relation to other areas of law.

## NATURE OF LAW

The law has evolved slowly, and it will continue to change. It is not a pure science based upon unchanging and universal truths. Rather, it results from a continuous effort to balance, through a workable set of rules, the individual and group rights of a society. In *The Common Law*, Oliver Wendell Holmes writes,

> The life of the law has not been logic; it has been experience. The felt necessities of the time, the prevalent moral and political theories, avowed or unconscious, even the prejudices which judges share with their fellowmen, have had a good deal more to do than the syllogism in determining the rules by which men should be governed. The law embodies the story of a nation's development through many centuries, and it cannot be dealt with as if it contained only the axioms and corollaries of a book of mathematics.

### DEFINITION OF LAW

A fundamental but difficult question regarding law is this: what is it? Numerous philosophers and jurists (legal scholars) have attempted to define it. American jurists and Supreme Court Justices Oliver Wendell Holmes and Benjamin Cardozo defined law as predictions of the way that a court will decide specific legal questions. William Blackstone, an English jurist, on the other hand, defined law as "a rule of civil conduct prescribed by the supreme power in a state, commanding what is right, and prohibiting what is wrong." Similarly, Austin, a nineteenth-century English jurist, defined law as a general command that a state or sovereign makes to those who are subject to its authority by laying down a course of action enforced by judicial or administrative tribunals.

Because of its great complexity, many legal scholars have attempted to explain the law by outlining its essential characteristics. Roscoe Pound, a distinguished American jurist and former dean of the Harvard Law School, described law as having multiple meanings:

> First, we may mean the legal order, that is, the regime of ordering human activities and relations through systematic application of the force of politically organized society, or through social pressure in such a society backed by such force. We use the term "law" in this sense when we speak of "respect for law" or for the "end of law."
>
> Second, we may mean the aggregate of laws or legal precepts; the body of authoritative grounds of judicial and

administrative action established in such a society. We may mean the body of received and established materials on which judicial and administrative determinations proceed. We use the term in this sense when we speak of "systems of law" or of "justice according to law."

Third, we may mean what Mr. Justice Cardozo has happily styled "the judicial process." We may mean the process of determining controversies, whether as it actually takes place, or as the public, the jurists, and the practitioners in the courts hold it ought to take place.

## FUNCTIONS OF LAW

At a general level the primary function of law is to maintain stability in the social, political, and economic system while simultaneously permitting change. The law accomplishes this basic function by performing a number of specific functions, among them dispute resolution, protection of property, and preservation of the state.

Disputes, which inevitably arise in a society as complex and interdependent as ours, may involve criminal matters, such as theft, or noncriminal matters, such as an automobile accident. Because disputes threaten the stability of society, the law has established an elaborate and evolving set of rules to resolve them. In addition, the legal system has instituted societal remedies, usually administered by the courts, in place of private remedies such as revenge.

The recognition of private ownership of property is fundamental to our economic system, based as it is upon the exchange of goods and services among privately held units of consumption. Therefore, a second crucial function of law is to protect the owner's use of property and to facilitate voluntary agreements (called contracts) regarding exchanges of property and services. Accordingly, a significant portion of law, as well as this text, involves property and its disposition, including the law of property, contracts, sales, commercial paper, and business associations.

A third essential function of the law is preservation of the state. In our system, law ensures that changes in leadership and the political structure are brought about by political actions such as elections, legislation, and referenda, rather than by revolution, sedition, and rebellion.

## LEGAL SANCTIONS

A primary function of the legal system is to make sure that legal rules are enforced. **Sanctions** are the means by which the law enforces the decisions of the courts. Without sanctions, laws would be ineffectual and unenforceable.

An example of a sanction in a civil (noncriminal) case is the seizure and sale of the property of a debtor who fails to pay a court-ordered obligation, called a judgment. Moreover, under certain circumstances a court may enforce its order by finding an offender in contempt and sentencing him to jail until he obeys the court's order. In criminal cases, the principal sanctions are the imposition of a fine, imprisonment, and capital punishment.

## LAW AND MORALS

Although moral and ethical concepts greatly influence the law, morals and law are not the same. They may be considered as two intersecting circles, as shown in *Figure 1-1*. The more darkly shaded area common to both circles includes the vast body of ideas that are both moral and legal. For instance, "Thou shall not kill" and "Thou shall not steal" are both moral precepts and legal constraints.

◆ **FIGURE 1-1: Law and Morals**

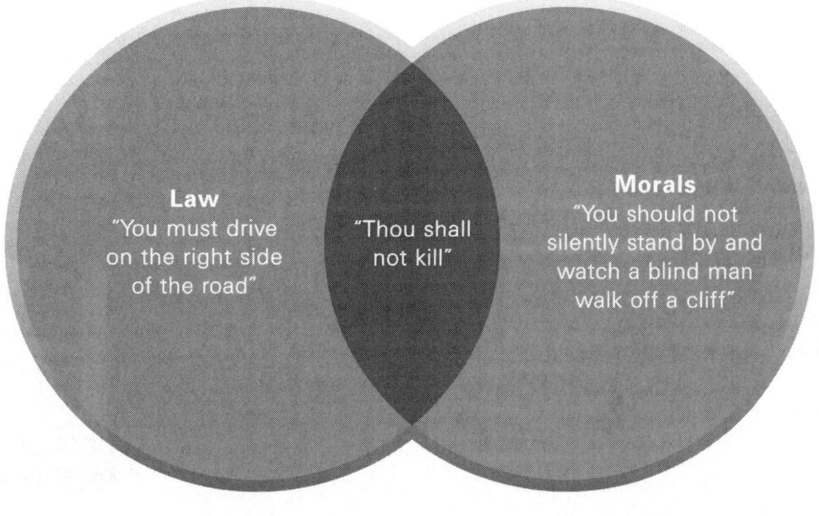

On the other hand, that part of the legal circle which does not intersect the morality circle includes many rules of law that are completely unrelated to morals, such as the rules stating that you must drive on the right side of the road and that you must register before you can vote. Likewise, the portion of the morality circle which does not intersect the legal circle includes moral precepts not enforced by law, such as the moral prohibition against silently standing by and watching a blind man walk off a cliff or foreclosing a poor widow's mortgage.

◆ **SEE FIGURE 1-1: Law and Morals**

### LAW AND JUSTICE

Law and justice represent separate and distinct concepts. Without law, however, there can be no justice. Although justice has at least as many definitions as law does, justice may be defined as fair, equitable, and impartial treatment of the competing interests and desires of individuals and groups with due regard for the common good.

On the other hand, law is no guarantee of justice. Some of history's most monstrous acts have been committed pursuant to "law." For example, the Nazis acted "legally" under German law during the 1930s and 1940s. Totalitarian societies often have shaped formal legal systems around the atrocities they have sanctioned.

## CLASSIFICATION OF LAW

Because the subject is vast, classifying the law into categories is helpful. Though a number of classifications are possible, the most useful categories are (1) substantive and procedural, (2) public and private, and (3) civil and criminal.

Basic to understanding these classifications are the terms *right* and *duty*. A **right** is the capacity of a person, with the aid of the law, to require another person or persons to perform, or to refrain from performing, a certain act. Thus, if Alice sells and delivers goods to Bob for the agreed price of $500 payable at a certain date, Alice has the capability, with the aid of the courts, of enforcing the payment by Bob of the $500. A **duty** is the obligation the law imposes upon a person to perform, or to refrain from performing, a certain act. Duty and right are correlatives: no right can rest upon one person without a corresponding duty resting upon some other person or, in some cases, upon all other persons.

◆ **SEE FIGURE 1-2: Classification of Law**

### SUBSTANTIVE AND PROCEDURAL LAW

**Substantive law** creates, defines, and regulates legal rights and duties. Thus, the rules of contract law that determine when a binding contract is formed are rules of substantive law. This book is principally concerned with substantive law. On the other hand, **procedural law** establishes the rules for enforcing those rights that exist by reason of substantive law. Thus, procedural law defines the method by which one may obtain a remedy in court.

### PUBLIC AND PRIVATE LAW

**Public law** is the branch of substantive law that deals with the government's rights and powers in its political or sovereign capacity and in its relation to individuals or groups. Public law consists of constitutional, administrative, and criminal law. **Private law** is that part of substantive law governing individuals and legal entities (such as corporations) in

◆ **FIGURE 1-2: Classification of Law**

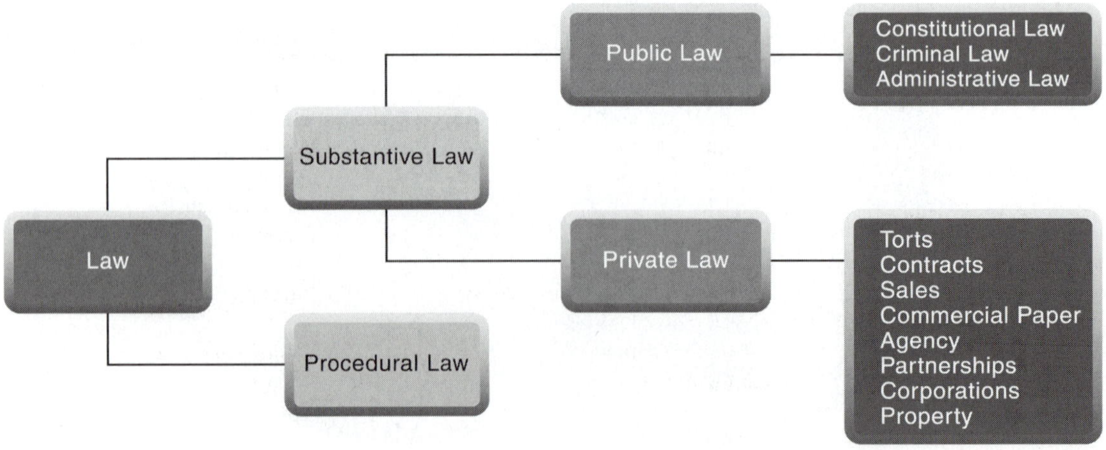

their relations with one another. Business law is primarily private law.

### CIVIL AND CRIMINAL LAW

The **civil law** defines duties the violation of which constitutes a wrong against the party injured by the violation. In contrast, the **criminal law** establishes duties the violation of which is a wrong against the whole community. Civil law is a part of private law, whereas criminal law is a part of public law. (The term *civil law* should be distinguished from the concept of a civil law *system*, which is discussed later in this chapter.) In a civil action the injured party **sues** to recover **compensation** for the damage and injury he has sustained as a result of the defendant's wrongful conduct. The party bringing a civil action (the **plaintiff**) has the burden of proof, which he must sustain by a **preponderance** (greater weight) of the evidence. Whereas the purpose of criminal law is to punish the wrongdoer, the purpose of civil law is to compensate the injured party. The principal forms of relief the civil law provides are a judgment for money damages and a decree ordering the defendant to perform a specified act or to desist from specified conduct.

A crime is any act or omission that public law prohibits in the interest of protecting the public and that the government makes punishable in a judicial proceeding brought (**prosecuted**) by it. The government must prove criminal guilt **beyond a reasonable doubt**, which is a significantly higher burden of proof than that required in a civil action. The government prohibits and punishes crimes upon the ground of public policy, which may include the safeguarding of the government itself, human life, or private property. Additional purposes of criminal law include deterrence and rehabilitation.

◆ **SEE FIGURE 1-3: Comparison of Civil and Criminal Law**

## SOURCES OF LAW

The sources of law in the U.S. legal system are the Federal and State constitutions, Federal treaties, interstate compacts, Federal and State statutes and executive orders, the ordinances of countless local municipal governments, the rules and regulations of Federal and State administrative agencies, and an ever-increasing volume of reported Federal and State court decisions.

The *supreme law* of the land is the U.S. Constitution. The Constitution provides that Federal statutes and treaties shall be the supreme law of the land. Federal legislation and treaties are, therefore, paramount to State constitutions and statutes. Federal legislation is of great significance as a source of law. Other Federal actions having the force of law are executive orders of the President and rules and regulations of Federal administrative officials, agencies, and commissions. The Federal courts also contribute considerably to the body of law in the United States.

The same pattern exists in every State. The paramount law of each State is contained in its written constitution. (Although a State constitution cannot deprive citizens of Federal constitutional rights, it can guarantee rights beyond those provided in the U.S. Constitution.) State constitutions tend to be more specific than the U.S. Constitution and, generally, have been amended more frequently. Subordinate to the State constitution are the statutes that the State's legislature enacts and the case law that its judiciary develops. Likewise, State administrative agencies issue rules and regulations having the force of law, as do executive orders promulgated by the governors of most States. In addition, cities, towns, and villages have limited legislative powers within their respective municipal areas to pass ordinances and resolutions.

◆ **SEE FIGURE 1-4: Hierarchy of Law**

◆ FIGURE 1-3: **Comparison of Civil and Criminal Law**

| | Civil Law | Criminal Law |
|---|---|---|
| **Commencement of Action** | Aggrieved individual (plaintiff) sues | State or federal government prosecutes |
| **Purpose** | Compensation<br>Deterrence | Punishment<br>Deterrence<br>Rehabilitation<br>Preservation of peace |
| **Burden of Proof** | Preponderance of the evidence | Beyond a reasonable doubt |
| **Principal Sanctions** | Monetary damages<br>Equitable remedies | Capital punishment<br>Imprisonment<br>Fines |

**FIGURE 1-4: Hierarchy of Law**

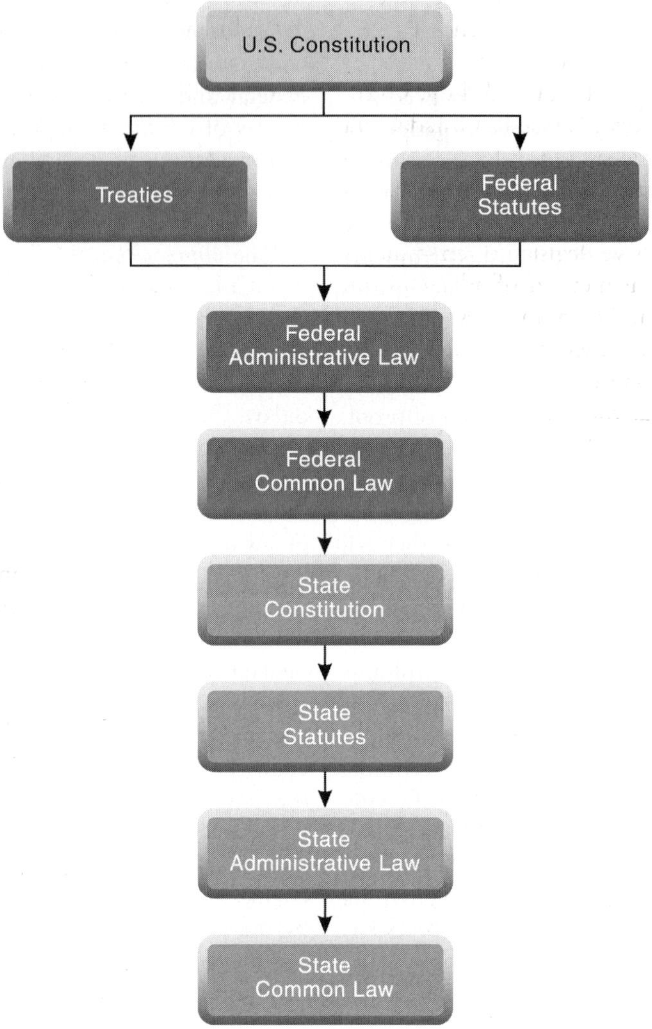


## CONSTITUTIONAL LAW

A **constitution**—the fundamental law of a particular level of government—establishes the governmental structure and allocates power among the levels of government, thereby defining political relationships. One of the fundamental principles on which our government is founded is that of separation of powers. As detailed in the U.S. Constitution, this means that the government consists of three distinct and independent branches: the Federal judiciary, the Congress, and the executive branch.

A constitution also restricts the powers of government and specifies the rights and liberties of the people. For example, the Constitution of the United States not only specifically states what rights and authority are vested in the national government but also specifically enumerates certain rights and liberties of the people. Moreover, the Ninth Amendment to the U.S. Constitution makes it clear that this enumeration of rights does not in any way deny or limit other rights that the people retain.

All other law in the United States is subordinate to the Federal Constitution. No law, Federal or State, is valid if it violates the Federal Constitution. Under the principle of **judicial review**, the Supreme Court of the United States determines the constitutionality of *all* laws.

## JUDICIAL LAW

The U.S. legal system is a **common law system**, first developed in England. It relies heavily on the judiciary as a source of law and on the **adversary system** for the adjudication of disputes. In an adversary system the parties, not the court, must initiate and conduct litigation. This approach is based upon the belief that the truth is more likely to emerge from the investigation and presentation of evidence by two opposing parties, both motivated by self-interest, than from judicial investigation motivated only by official duty. Other English-speaking countries, including England, Canada, and Australia, also use the common law system.

In distinct contrast to the common law system are civil law systems, which are based on Roman law. **Civil law systems** depend on comprehensive legislative enactments (called codes) and an inquisitorial method of adjudication. In the **inquisitorial system**, the judiciary initiates litigation, investigates pertinent facts, and conducts the presentation of evidence. The civil law system prevails in most of Europe, Scotland, the State of Louisiana, the province of Quebec, Latin America, and parts of Africa and Asia.

**Common Law** The courts in common law systems have developed a body of law, known as "case law," "judge-made law," or "common law," that serves as precedent for determining later controversies. In this sense, common law is distinguished from other sources of law such as legislation and administrative rulings.

To evolve steadily and predictably, the common law has developed by application of *stare decisis* (to stand by the decisions). Under the principle of ***stare decisis***, courts, in deciding cases, adhere to and rely on rules of law that they or superior courts announced and applied in prior decisions involving similar cases. Judicial decisions thus have two uses: (1) to determine with finality the case currently being decided and (2) to indicate how the courts will decide similar cases in the future. *Stare decisis* does not, however, preclude courts from correcting erroneous decisions or from choosing among conflicting precedents. Thus, the doctrine allows sufficient flexibility for the common law to change.

The strength of the common law is its ability to adapt to change without losing its sense of direction. As Justice Cardozo said, "The inn that shelters for the night is not the journey's end. The law, like the traveler, must be ready for the morrow. It must have a principle of growth."

**Equity** As the common law developed in England, it became overly rigid and beset with technicalities. Consequently, in many cases the courts provided no remedies because the judges insisted that a claim must fall within one of the recognized forms of action. Moreover, courts of common law could provide only limited remedies; the principal type of relief obtainable was a monetary judgment. Consequently, individuals who could not obtain adequate relief from monetary awards began to petition the king directly for justice. He, in turn, came to delegate these petitions to his chancellor.

Gradually, there evolved a supplementary system of judicial relief for those who had no adequate remedy at common law. This new system, called **equity**, was administered by a court of chancery presided over by a chancellor. The chancellor, deciding cases on "equity and good conscience," afforded relief in many instances where common law judges had refused to act or where the remedy at law was inadequate. Thus, two systems of law administered by different tribunals developed side by side: the common law courts and the courts of equity.

An important difference between law and equity was that the chancellor could issue a **decree**, or order, compelling a defendant to do or refrain from doing a specific act. A defendant who did not comply with the order could be held in contempt of court and punished by fine or imprisonment. This power of compulsion available in a court of equity opened the door to many needed remedies not available in a court of common law.

Equity jurisdiction, in some cases, recognized rights that were enforceable at common law but for which equity provided more effective remedies. For example, in a court of equity, for breach of a land contract the buyer could obtain a decree of **specific performance** commanding the defendant seller to perform his part of the contract by transferring title to the land. Another powerful and effective remedy available only in the courts of equity was the **injunction**, a court order requiring a party to do or refrain from doing a specified act. Still another remedy not available elsewhere was **reformation**, where, upon the ground of mutual mistake, contracting parties could bring an action to reform or change the language of a written agreement to conform to their actual intentions. Finally, an action for **rescission** of a contract allowed a party to invalidate a contract under certain circumstances.

Although courts of equity provided remedies not available in courts of law, they granted such remedies only at their discretion, not as a matter of right. The courts exercised this discretion according to the general legal principles, or **maxims**, that they formulated over the years. A few of these familiar maxims of equity are the following: Equity will not suffer a wrong to be without a remedy. Equity regards the substance rather than the form. Equity abhors a forfeiture. Equity delights to do justice and not by halves. He who comes into equity must come with clean hands. He who seeks equity must do equity.

In nearly every jurisdiction in the United States, courts of common law and courts of equity have united to form a single court that administers both systems of law. Vestiges of the old division remain, however. For example, the right to a trial by jury applies only to actions at law but not, under Federal law and in almost every State, to suits filed in equity.

**Restatements of Law** The common law of the United States results from the independent decisions of the State and Federal courts. The rapid increase in the number of decisions by these courts led to the establishment of the American Law Institute (ALI) in 1923. The ALI was composed of a distinguished group of lawyers, judges, and law teachers who set out to prepare "an orderly restatement of the general common law of the United States, including in that term not only the law developed solely by judicial decision, but also the law that has grown from the application by the courts of statutes that were generally enacted and were in force for many years." Wolkin, "Restatements of the Law: Origin, Preparation, Availability," 21 *Ohio B.A.Rept.* 663 (1940).

Regarded as the authoritative statement of the common law of the United States, the Restatements cover many important areas of the common law, including torts, contracts, agency, property, and trusts. Although not law in themselves, they are highly persuasive and frequently have been used by courts in support of their opinions. Because they state much of the common law concisely and clearly, relevant portions of the Restatements are frequently relied upon in this book.

## LEGISLATIVE LAW

Since the end of the nineteenth century, legislation has become the primary source of new law and ordered social change in the United States. The annual volume of legislative law is enormous. Justice Felix Frankfurter's remarks to the New York City Bar in 1947 are even more appropriate in the twenty-first century:

> Inevitably the work of the Supreme Court reflects the great shift in the center of gravity of law-making. Broadly speaking, the number of cases disposed of by opinions has not changed from term to term. But even as late as 1875 more than 40 percent of the controversies before the Court were common-law litigation, fifty years later only 5 percent, while today cases not resting on statutes are reduced almost to zero. It is therefore accurate to say that courts have ceased to be the primary makers of law in the sense in which they "legislated" the common law. It is certainly true of the Supreme Court that almost every case has a statute at its heart or close to it.

This modern emphasis upon legislative or statutory law has occurred because common law, which develops evolutionarily and haphazardly, is not well suited for making drastic or comprehensive changes. Moreover, courts tend to be hesitant about overruling prior decisions, whereas legislatures frequently repeal prior enactments. In addition, legislatures are independent and able to choose the issues they wish to address, while courts may deal only with issues that arise in actual cases. As a result, legislatures are better equipped to make the dramatic, sweeping, and relatively rapid changes in the law that enable it to respond to numerous and vast technological, social, and economic innovations.

While some business law topics, such as contracts, agency, property, and trusts, still are governed principally by the common law, most areas of commercial law have become largely statutory, including partnerships, corporations, sales, commercial paper, secured transactions, insurance, securities regulation, antitrust, and bankruptcy. Because most States enacted statutes dealing with these branches of commercial law, a great diversity developed among the States and hampered the conduct of commerce on a national scale. The increased need for greater uniformity led to the development of a number of proposed uniform laws that would reduce the conflicts among State laws.

The most successful example is the **Uniform Commercial Code** (UCC), which was prepared under the joint sponsorship and direction of the National Conference of Commissioners on Uniform State Laws (NCCUSL) and the ALI. (Selected provisions of the Code are set forth in Appendix B of this book.) All fifty States (although Louisiana has adopted only part of it), the District of Columbia, and the Virgin Islands have adopted the UCC. The underlying purposes and policies of the Code are as follows:

1. simplify, clarify, and modernize the law governing commercial transactions;
2. permit the continued expansion of commercial practices through custom, usage, and agreement of the parties; and
3. make uniform the law among the various jurisdictions.

The NCCUSL has drafted more than 250 uniform laws, including the Uniform Partnership Act, the Uniform Limited Partnership Act, and the Uniform Probate Code. The ALI has developed a number of model statutory formulations, including the Model Code of Evidence, the Model Penal Code, a Model Land Development Code, and a proposed Federal Securities Code. In addition, the American Bar Association has promulgated the Model Business Corporation Act.

**Treaties** A treaty is an agreement between or among independent nations. Article II of the U.S. Constitution authorizes the President to enter into treaties with the advice and consent of the Senate, "providing two thirds of the Senators present concur."

Only the Federal government, not the States, may enter into treaties. A treaty signed by the President and approved by the Senate has the legal force of a Federal statute. Accordingly, a Federal treaty may supersede a prior Federal statute, while a Federal statute may supersede a prior treaty. Like statutes, treaties are subordinate to the Federal Constitution and subject to judicial review.

**Executive Orders** In addition to his executive functions, the President of the United States also has authority to issue laws, which are called **executive orders**. Typically, Federal legislation specifically delegates this authority. An executive order may amend, revoke, or supersede a prior executive order. An example of an executive order is the one issued by President Johnson in 1965 prohibiting discrimination by Federal contractors on the basis of race, color, sex, religion, or national origin in employment on any work the contractor performed during the period of the Federal contract.

The governors of most States enjoy comparable authority to issue executive orders.

### ADMINISTRATIVE LAW

**Administrative law** is the branch of public law that is created by administrative agencies in the form of rules, regulations, orders, and decisions to carry out the regulatory powers and duties of those agencies. Administrative functions and activities concern matters of national safety, welfare, and convenience, including the establishment and maintenance of military forces, police, citizenship and naturalization, taxation, coinage of money, elections, environmental protection, and the regulation of transportation, interstate highways, waterways, television, radio, trade and commerce, and, in general, public health, safety, and welfare.

To accommodate the increasing complexity of the social, economic, and industrial life of the nation, the scope of administrative law has expanded enormously. Justice Jackson stated that "the rise of administrative bodies has been the most significant legal trend of the last century, and perhaps more values today are affected by their decisions than by those of all the courts, review of administrative decisions apart." *Federal Trade Commission v. Ruberoid Co.,* 343 U.S. 470 (1952). This is evidenced by the great increase in the number and activities of Federal government boards, commissions, and other agencies. Certainly, agencies create more legal rules and adjudicate more controversies than all the legislatures and courts combined.

## LEGAL ANALYSIS

Decisions in State trial courts generally are not reported or published. The precedent a trial court sets is not sufficiently weighty to warrant permanent reporting. Except in New York and a few other States where selected trial court opinions are published, decisions in trial courts are simply filed in the office of the clerk of the court, where they are available for public inspection. Decisions of State courts of appeals are published in consecutively numbered volumes called "reports." Court decisions are found in the official State reports of most States. In addition, West Publishing Company publishes State reports in a regional reporter, called the National Reporter System, composed of the following: Atlantic (A. or A.2d); South Eastern (S.E. or S.E.2d); South Western (S.W., S.W.2d, or S.W.3d); New York Supplement (N.Y.S. or N.Y.S.2d); North Western (N.W. or N.W.2d); North Eastern (N.E. or N.E.2d); Southern (So., So.2d, or So.3d); and Pacific (P., P.2d, or P.3d). At least twenty States no longer publish official reports and have designated a commercial reporter as the authoritative source of State case law. After they are published, these opinions, or "cases," are referred to ("cited") by giving (1) the name of the case; (2) the volume, name, and page of the official State report, if any, in which it is published; (3) the volume, name, and page of the particular set and series of the National Reporter System; and (4) the volume, name, and page of any other selected case series. For instance, *Lefkowitz v. Great Minneapolis Surplus Store, Inc.,* 251 Minn. 188, 86 N.W.2d 689 (1957) indicates that the opinion in this case may be found in Volume 251 of the official Minnesota Reports at page 188; and in Volume 86 of the North Western Reporter, Second Series, at page 689.

The decisions of courts in the Federal system are found in a number of reports. U.S. District Court opinions appear in the Federal Supplement (F.Supp. or F.Supp.2d). Decisions of the U.S. Court of Appeals are found in the Federal Reporter (Fed., F.2d, or F.3d), while the U.S. Supreme Court's opinions are published in the U.S. Supreme Court Reports (U.S.), Supreme Court Reporter (S.Ct.), and Lawyers Edition (L.Ed.). While all U.S. Supreme Court decisions are reported, not every case decided by the U.S. District Courts and the U.S. Courts of Appeals is reported. Each circuit has established rules determining which decisions are published.

In reading the title of a case, such as "*Jones v. Brown,*" the "v." or "vs." means "versus" or "against." In the trial court, Jones is the **plaintiff**, the person who filed the suit, and Brown is the **defendant**, the person against whom the suit was brought. When a case is appealed, some, but not all, courts of appeals place the name of the party who appeals, or the **appellant**, first, so that "*Jones v. Brown*" in the trial court becomes, if Brown loses and becomes the appellant, "*Brown v. Jones*" in the appellate court. But because some appellate courts retain the trial court order of names, determining from the title itself who was the plaintiff and who was the defendant is not always possible. The student must read the facts of each case carefully and clearly identify each party in her mind to understand the discussion by the appellate court. In a criminal case, the caption in the trial court will first designate the prosecuting governmental unit and then will indicate the defendant, as in *"State v. Jones"* or *"Commonwealth v. Brown."*

The study of reported cases requires the student to understand and apply legal analysis. Normally, the reported opinion in a case sets forth (1) the essential facts, the nature of the action, the parties, what happened to bring about the controversy, what happened in the lower court, and what pleadings are material to the issues; (2) the issues of law or fact; (3) the legal principles involved; (4) the application of these principles; and (5) the decision.

A serviceable method by which students may analyze and brief cases after reading and comprehending the opinion is to write a brief containing the following:

1. the facts of the case
2. the issue or question involved
3. the decision of the court
4. the reasons for the decision

By way of example, the edited case of *Ryan v. Friesenhahn* (see *Case 1-1*) is presented after the chapter summary and then briefed using the suggested format.

◆ **SEE CASE 1-1**

## CHAPTER SUMMARY

**NATURE OF LAW**

**Definition of Law** "a rule of civil conduct prescribed by the supreme power in a state, commanding what is right, and prohibiting what is wrong" (William Blackstone)

**Functions of Law** to maintain stability in the social, political, and economic system through dispute resolution, protection of property, and the preservation of the state, while simultaneously permitting ordered change

**Legal Sanctions** are means by which the law enforces the decisions of the courts

**Law and Morals** are different but overlapping; law provides sanctions, while morals do not

**Law and Justice** are separate and distinct concepts; justice is the fair, equitable, and impartial treatment of competing interests with due regard for the common good

**CLASSIFICATION OF LAW**

**Substantive and Procedural Law**

- ***Substantive Law*** law creating rights and duties
- ***Procedural Law*** rules for enforcing substantive law

**Public and Private Law**

- ***Public Law*** law dealing with the relationship between government and individuals
- ***Private Law*** law governing the relationships among individuals and legal entities

**Civil and Criminal Law**

- ***Civil Law*** law dealing with rights and duties the violation of which constitutes a wrong against an individual or other legal entity
- ***Criminal Law*** law establishing duties which, if violated, constitute a wrong against the entire community

**SOURCES OF LAW**

**Constitutional Law** fundamental law of a government establishing its powers and limitations

**Judicial Law**

- ***Common Law*** body of law developed by the courts that serves as precedent for determination of later controversies
- ***Equity*** body of law based upon principles distinct from common law and providing remedies not available at law

**Legislative Law** statutes adopted by legislative bodies

- ***Treaties*** agreements between or among independent nations
- ***Executive Orders*** laws issued by the President or by the governor of a State

**Administrative Law** body of law created by administrative agencies to carry out their regulatory powers and duties

# CASES

## CASE 1-1

## RYAN v. FRIESENHAHN

Court of Appeals of Texas, 1995
911 S.W.2d 113

**Rickhoff, J.**

This is an appeal from a take-nothing summary judgment granted the defendants in a social host liability case. Appellants' seventeen-year-old daughter was killed in a single-car accident after leaving appellees' party in an intoxicated condition. While we hold that the appellants were denied an opportunity to amend their pleadings, we also find that their pleadings stated a cause of action for negligence and negligence per se. We reverse and remand.

Todd Friesenhahn, son of Nancy and Frederick Friesenhahn, held an "open invitation" party at his parents' home that encouraged guests to "bring your own bottle." Sabrina Ryan attended the party, became intoxicated, and was involved in a fatal accident after she left the event. According to the Ryans' petition, Nancy and Frederick Friesenhahn were aware of this activity and of Sabrina's condition.

Sandra and Stephen Ryan, acting in their individual and representative capacities, sued the Friesenhahns for wrongful death, negligence, and gross negligence. * * *

* * *

***a. The Petition*** The Ryans pled, in their third amended petition, that Todd Friesenhahn planned a "beer bust" that was advertised by posting general invitations in the community for a party to be held on the "Friesenhahn Property." The invitation was open and general and invited persons to "B.Y.O.B." (bring your own bottle). According to the petition, the Friesenhahns had actual or constructive notice of the party and the conduct of the minors in "possessing, exchanging, and consuming alcoholic beverages."

The Ryans alleged that the Friesenhahns were negligent in (1) allowing the party to be held on the Friesenhahn property; (2) directly or indirectly inviting Sabrina to the party; (3) allowing the party to continue on their property "after they knew that minors were in fact possessing, exchanging, and consuming alcohol"; (4) failing "to provide for the proper conduct at the party"; (5) allowing Sabrina to become intoxicated and failing to "secure proper attention and treatment"; (6) and allowing Sabrina to leave the Friesenhahn property while driving a motor vehicle in an intoxicated state. * * *

***b. Negligence Per Se*** Accepting the petition's allegations as true, the Friesenhahns were aware that minors possessed and consumed alcohol on their property and specifically allowed Sabrina to become intoxicated. The Texas Alcoholic Beverage Code provides that one commits an offense if, with criminal negligence, he "makes available an alcoholic beverage to a minor." [Citation.] The exception for serving alcohol to a minor applies only to the minor's adult parent. [Citation.]

An unexcused violation of a statute constitutes negligence per se if the injured party is a member of the class protected by the statute. [Citation.] The Alcoholic Beverage Code was designed to protect the general public and minors in particular and must be liberally construed. [Citation.] We conclude that Sabrina is a member of the class protected by the Code.

In viewing the Ryans' allegations in the light most favorable to them, we find that they stated a cause of action against the Friesenhahns for the violation of the Alcoholic Beverage Code.

***c. Common Law Negligence*** The elements of negligence include (1) a legal duty owed by one person to another; (2) breach of that duty; and (3) damages proximately caused by the breach. [Citation.] To determine whether a common law duty exists, we must consider several factors, including risk, foreseeability, and likelihood of injury weighed against the social utility of the defendant's conduct, the magnitude of the burden of guarding against the injury and consequences of placing that burden on the defendant. [Citation.] We may also consider whether one party has superior knowledge of the risk, and whether one party has the right to control the actor whose conduct precipitated the harm. [Citation.]

As the Supreme Court in [citation] explained, there are two practical reasons for not imposing a third-party duty on social hosts who provide alcohol to adult guests: first, the host cannot reasonably know the extent of his guests' alcohol consumption level; second, the host cannot reasonably be expected to control his guests' conduct. [Citation.] The Tyler court in [citation] relied on these principles in holding that a minor "had no common law duty to avoid making alcohol available to an intoxicated guest [another minor] who he knew would be driving." [Citation.]

We disagree with the Tyler court because the rationale expressed [by the Supreme Court] in [citation] does not apply to the relationship between minors, or adults and minors. The adult social host need not estimate the extent of a minor's alcohol consumption because serving minors any amount of alcohol is a criminal offense. [Citation.] Furthermore, the social host may control the minor, with whom there is a special relationship, analogous to that of parent-child. [Citation.]

* * *

As this case demonstrates, serving minors alcohol creates a risk of injury or death. Under the pled facts, a jury could find that the Friesenhahns, as the adult social hosts, allowed open invitations to a beer bust at their house and they could foresee, or reasonably should have foreseen, that the only means of arriving at their property would be by privately operated vehicles; once there, the most likely means of departure would be by the same means. That adults have superior knowledge of the risk of drinking should be apparent from the legislature's decision to allow persons to become adults on their eighteenth birthday for all purposes but the consumption of alcohol. [Citations.]

While one adult has no general duty to control the behavior of another adult, one would hope that adults would exercise special diligence in supervising minors—even during a simple swimming pool party involving potentially dangerous but legal activities. We may have no special duty to watch one adult to be sure he can swim, but it would be ill-advised to turn loose young children without insuring they can swim. When the "party" is for the purpose of engaging in dangerous and illicit activity, the consumption of alcohol by minors, adults certainly have a greater duty of care. [Citation.]

* * * Accordingly, we find that the Ryans' petition stated a common-law cause of action.

* * *

We reverse and remand the trial court's summary judgment.

## Brief of Ryan v. Friesenhahn

***I. Facts***

Todd Friesenhahn, son of Nancy and Frederick Friesenhahn, held an open invitation party at his parents' home that encouraged guests to bring their own bottle. Sabrina Ryan attended the party, became intoxicated, and was involved in a fatal accident after she left the party. Sandra and Stephen Ryan, Sabrina's parents, sued the Friesenhahns for negligence, alleging that the Friesenhahns were aware of underage drinking at the party and of Sabrina's condition when she left the party. The trial court granted summary judgment for the Friesenhahns.

***II. Issue***

Is a social host who serves alcoholic beverages to a minor liable in negligence for harm suffered by the minor as a result of the minor's intoxication?

***III. Decision***

In favor of the Ryans. Summary judgment reversed and case remanded to the trial court.

***IV. Reasons***

Accepting the Ryans' allegations as true, the Friesenhahns were aware that minors possessed and consumed alcohol on their property and specifically allowed Sabrina to become intoxicated. The Texas Alcoholic Beverage Code provides that a person commits an offense if, with criminal negligence, he "makes available an alcoholic beverage to a minor." A violation of a statute constitutes negligence per se if the injured party is a member of the class protected by the statute. Since the Alcoholic Beverage Code was designed to protect the general public and minors in particular, Sabrina is a member of the class protected by the Code. Therefore, we find that the Ryans stated a cause of action against the Friesenhahns for the violation of the Alcoholic Beverage Code.

In considering common-law negligence as a basis for social host liability, the Texas Supreme Court has held that there are two practical reasons for not imposing a third-party duty on social hosts who provide alcohol to adult guests: first, the host cannot reasonably know the extent of his guests' alcohol consumption level; second, the host cannot reasonably be expected to control his guests' conduct. However, this rationale does not apply where the guest is a minor. The adult social host need not estimate the extent of a minor's alcohol consumption because serving minors any amount of alcohol is a criminal offense. Furthermore, the social host may control the minor, with whom there is a special relationship, analogous to that of parent-child.

# QUESTIONS

1. Identify and describe the basic functions of law.
2. Distinguish between law and justice.
3. Distinguish between law and morals.
4. Define and discuss substantive and procedural law.
5. Distinguish between public and private law.
6. Distinguish between civil and criminal law.
7. Identify and describe the sources of law.
8. Distinguish between law and equity.
9. Explain the principle of *stare decisis*.
10. Identify and define four remedies available in equity.

C H A P T E R 3

# Civil Dispute Resolution

As discussed in *Chapter 1*, substantive law establishes the rights and duties of individuals and other legal entities while procedural law determines the means by which these rights are asserted. Procedural law attempts to accomplish two competing objectives: (1) to be fair and impartial, and (2) to operate efficiently. The judicial process in the United States represents a balance between these two objectives as well as a commitment to the adversary system.

The first part of this chapter describes the structure and function of the Federal and State court systems. The second part of this chapter deals with jurisdiction; the third part discusses civil dispute resolution, including the procedure in civil lawsuits.

## THE COURT SYSTEM

Courts are impartial tribunals (seats of judgment) established by governmental bodies to settle disputes. A court may render a binding decision only when it has jurisdiction over the dispute and the parties to that dispute; that is, when it has a right to hear and make a judgment in a case. The United States has a dual court system: The Federal government has its own independent system, as does each of the fifty States plus the District of Columbia.

### THE FEDERAL COURTS

Article III of the U.S. Constitution states that the judicial power of the United States shall be vested in one Supreme Court and such lower courts as Congress may establish. Congress has established a lower Federal court system consisting of a number of special courts, district courts, and courts of appeals. The Federal court system is staffed by judges who receive lifetime appointments from the President, subject to confirmation by the Senate.

◆ SEE FIGURE 3-1: **Federal Judicial System**

◆ FIGURE 3-1: **Federal Judicial System**

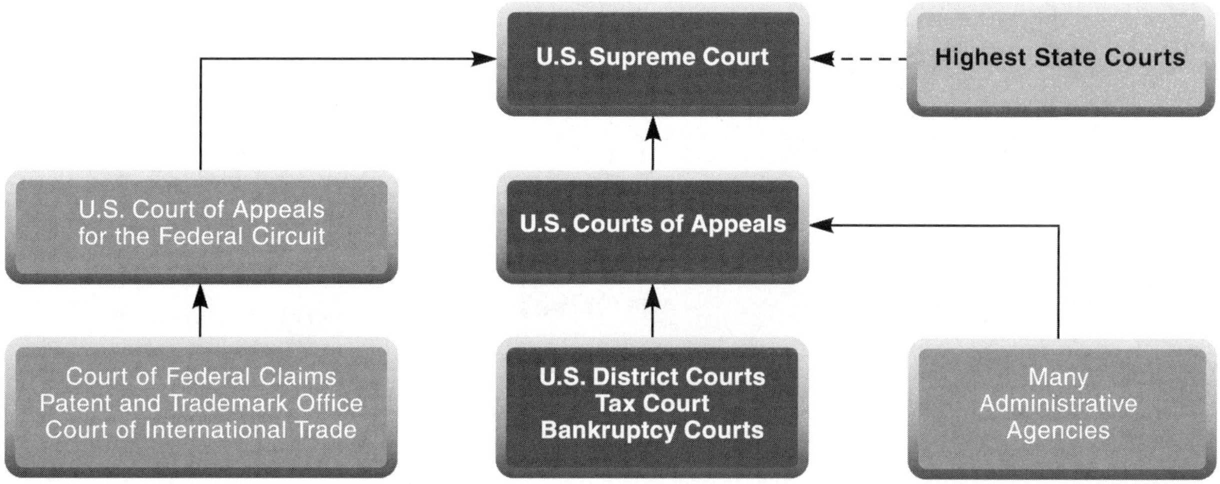

### DISTRICT COURTS

The district courts are the general trial courts in the Federal system. Most cases begin in a district court, and it is here that issues of fact are decided. The district court is generally presided over by *one* judge, although in certain cases three judges preside. In a few cases, an appeal from a judgment or decree of a district court is taken directly to the Supreme Court. In most cases, however, appeals go to the Circuit Court of Appeals of the appropriate circuit, the decision of which is, in most cases, final.

Congress has established ninety-four judicial districts, each of which is located entirely in a particular State. All States have at least one district, while certain States contain more than one. For instance, New York has four districts, Illinois has three, and Wisconsin has two, while a number of less populated States each make up a single district.

### COURTS OF APPEALS

Congress has established twelve judicial circuits (eleven numbered circuits plus the D.C. Circuit), each having a court known as the Court of Appeals, which primarily hears appeals from the district courts located within its circuit. In addition, these courts review decisions of many administrative agencies, the Tax Court, and the Bankruptcy Court. Congress has also established the U.S. Court of Appeals for the Federal Circuit, which is discussed in the section on "Special Courts." The U.S. Courts of Appeals generally hear cases in panels of *three* judges, although in some instances all of the judges of the circuit will sit *en banc* to decide a case.

The function of appellate courts is to examine the record of a case on appeal and to determine whether the trial court committed prejudicial error. If so, the appellate court will **reverse** or **modify** the judgment and if necessary **remand** it (send it back) to the lower court for further proceeding. If no prejudicial error exists, the appellate court will **affirm** the decision of the lower court.

◆ SEE FIGURE 3-2: **Circuit Courts of the United States**

### THE SUPREME COURT

The nation's highest tribunal is the U.S. Supreme Court, which consists of nine justices (a Chief Justice and eight Associate Justices) who sit as a group in Washington, D.C. A quorum consists of any six justices. In certain types of cases, the U.S. Supreme Court has original jurisdiction

◆ FIGURE 3-2: **Circuit Courts of the United States**

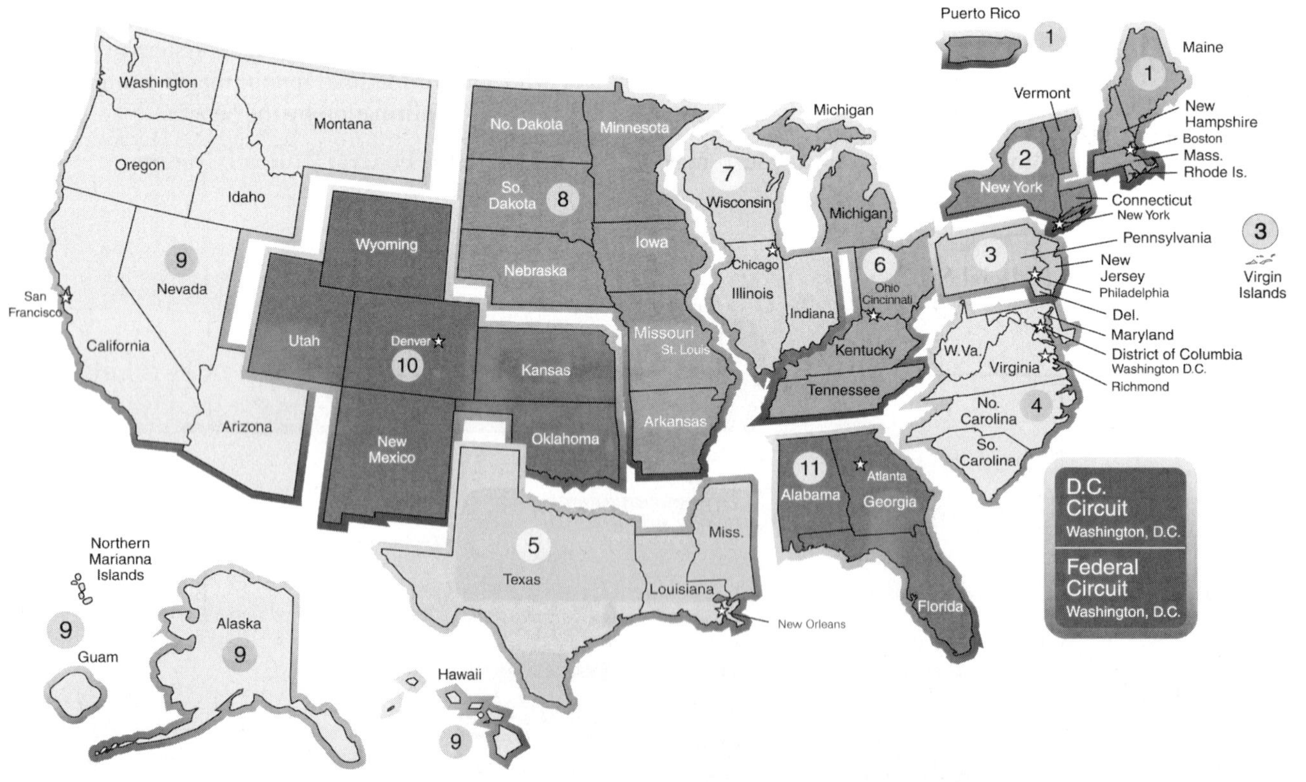


Source: Administrative Office of The United States Courts, January 1983

(the right to hear a case first). The Court's principal function, nonetheless, is to review decisions of the Federal Courts of Appeals and, in some instances, decisions involving Federal law made by the highest State courts. Cases reach the Supreme Court under its appellate jurisdiction by one of two routes. Very few come by way of **appeal by right**—cases the Court must hear should a party request the review. In 1988, Congress enacted legislation that almost completely eliminated the right to appeal to the U.S. Supreme Court.

The second way in which the Supreme Court may review a decision of a lower court is by the discretionary **writ of *certiorari***, which requires a lower court to produce the records of a case it has tried. Now almost all cases reaching the Supreme Court come to it by means of writs of *certiorari.* The Court uses the writ as a device to choose the cases it wishes to hear. The Court grants writs for cases involving a Federal question of substantial importance or a conflict in the decisions of the U.S. Circuit Courts of Appeals. Only a small percentage of the petitions to the Supreme Court for review by *certiorari* are granted, however. The vote of four justices is required to grant a writ.

### SPECIAL COURTS

The special courts in the Federal judicial system include the U.S. Court of Federal Claims, the U.S. Tax Court, the U.S. Bankruptcy Courts, and the U.S. Court of Appeals for the Federal Circuit. These courts have jurisdiction over particular subject matter. The U.S. Court of Federal Claims has national jurisdiction to hear claims against the United States. The U.S. Tax Court has national jurisdiction over certain cases involving Federal taxes. The U.S. Bankruptcy Courts have jurisdiction to hear and decide certain matters under the Federal Bankruptcy Act, subject to review by the U.S. District Court. The U.S. Court of Appeals for the Federal Circuit has nationwide jurisdiction and reviews decisions of the Court of Federal Claims, the Patent and Trademark Office, patent cases decided by the U.S. District Court, the U.S. Court of International Trade, the Merit Systems Protection Board, and the U.S. Court of Veterans Appeals.

## STATE COURTS

Each of the fifty States and the District of Columbia has its own court system. In most States the voters elect judges for a stated term.

◆ SEE FIGURE 3-3: **State Court System**

### INFERIOR TRIAL COURTS

At the bottom of the State court system are the **inferior trial courts**, which decide the least serious criminal and civil matters. Usually, inferior trial courts do not keep a complete written record of trial proceedings. Such courts, which are referred to as municipal courts, justice of the peace courts, or traffic courts, hear minor criminal cases such as traffic offenses. They also conduct preliminary hearings in more serious criminal cases.

**Small claims courts** are inferior trial courts which hear civil cases involving a limited amount of money. Usually there is no jury, the procedure is informal, and neither side employs an attorney. An appeal from small claims court is

◆ FIGURE 3-3: **State Court System**

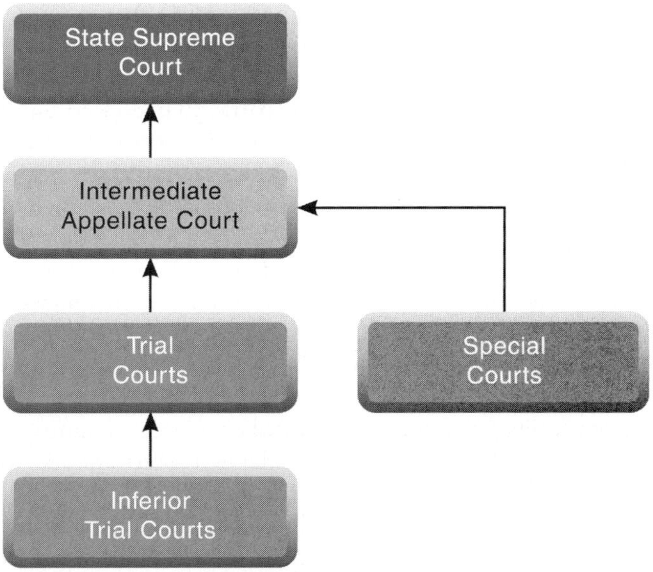

taken to the trial court of general jurisdiction, where a new trial (called a trial *de novo*), in which the small claims court's decision is given no weight, is begun.

### TRIAL COURTS

Each State has trial courts of general jurisdiction, which may be called county, district, superior, circuit, or common pleas courts. (In New York the trial court is called the Supreme Court.) These courts do not have a dollar limitation on their jurisdiction in civil cases and hear all criminal cases other than minor offenses. Unlike the inferior trial courts, these trial courts of general jurisdiction maintain formal records of their proceedings as procedural safeguards.

### SPECIAL COURTS

Many States have special courts that have jurisdiction over particular areas. For example, many States have probate courts with jurisdiction over the administration of wills and estates. Many States also have family courts, which have jurisdiction over divorce and child custody cases. Appeals from these special courts go to the general State appellate courts.

### APPELLATE COURTS

At the summit of the State court system is the State's court of last resort, a reviewing court generally called the Supreme Court of the State. Except for those cases in which review by the U.S. Supreme Court is available, the decision of the highest State tribunal is final. Most States also have created intermediate appellate courts to handle the large volume of cases seeking review. Review by such a court is usually by right. Further review is in most cases at the highest court's discretion.

## JURISDICTION

**Jurisdiction** means the power or authority of a court to hear and decide a given case. To resolve a lawsuit, a court must have two kinds of jurisdiction. The first is subject matter jurisdiction. Where a court lacks jurisdiction over the subject matter of a case, no action it takes in the case will have legal effect.

The second kind of jurisdiction is over the parties to a lawsuit. This jurisdiction is required for the court to render an enforceable judgment that affects the rights and duties of the parties to the lawsuit. A court usually may obtain jurisdiction over the defendant if she lives and is present in the court's territory or the transaction giving rise to the case has a substantial connection to the court's territory. The court obtains jurisdiction over the plaintiff when he voluntarily submits to the court's power by filing a complaint with the court.

## SUBJECT MATTER JURISDICTION

**Subject matter jurisdiction** refers to the authority of a particular court to adjudicate a controversy of a particular kind. Federal courts have *limited* subject matter jurisdiction, as set forth in the U.S. Constitution, Article III, Section 2. State courts have jurisdiction over *all* matters that the Constitution or Congress has not given exclusively to the Federal courts or expressly denied the State courts.

### FEDERAL JURISDICTION

The Federal courts have, to the exclusion of the State courts, subject matter jurisdiction over some areas. Such jurisdiction is called **exclusive Federal jurisdiction**. Federal jurisdiction is exclusive only if Congress so provides, either explicitly or implicitly. If Congress does not so provide and the area is one over which Federal courts have subject matter jurisdiction, they share this jurisdiction with the State courts. Such jurisdiction is known as **concurrent Federal jurisdiction**.

**Exclusive Federal Jurisdiction** The Federal courts have exclusive jurisdiction over Federal criminal prosecutions; admiralty, bankruptcy, antitrust, patent, trademark, and copyright cases; suits against the United States; and cases arising under certain Federal statutes that expressly provide for exclusive Federal jurisdiction.

**Concurrent Federal Jurisdiction** There are two types of concurrent Federal jurisdiction: Federal question jurisdiction and diversity jurisdiction. The first arises whenever there is a Federal question over which the Federal courts do not have exclusive jurisdiction. A **Federal question** is any case arising under the Constitution, statutes, or treaties of the United States. For a case to be treated as "arising under" Federal law, either Federal law must create the plaintiff's cause of action or the plaintiff's right to relief must depend upon the resolution of a substantial question of Federal law in dispute between the parties. There is no minimum dollar requirement in Federal question cases. When a State court hears a concurrent Federal question case, it applies Federal substantive law, but its own procedural rules.

Diversity jurisdiction arises where there is "diversity of citizenship" and the amount in controversy exceeds $75,000. Then private litigants may bring an action in a Federal district court or a State court. **Diversity of citizenship** exists (1) when the plaintiffs are all citizens of a State or States different from the State or States of which the defendants are citizens; (2) when a foreign country brings an action against citizens of the United States; or (3) when the controversy is between citizens of a State and citizens of a foreign country. The citizenship of an individual litigant is the State in which the litigant resides or is domiciled, whereas that of a corporate litigant is both the State of incorporation and the State in which its principal place of business is located. For example, if the amount in controversy exceeds $75,000, then diversity of citizenship jurisdiction would be satisfied if Ada, a citizen of California, sues Bob, a citizen of Idaho. If, however, Carol, a citizen of Virginia, and Dianne, a citizen of North Carolina, sue Evan, a citizen of Georgia, and Farley, a citizen of North Carolina, diversity of citizenship would not exist because both Dianne, a plaintiff, and Farley, a defendant, are citizens of North Carolina.

The $75,000 jurisdictional requirement is satisfied if the plaintiff makes a good faith claim to the amount in the complaint, unless it is clear to a legal certainty that the claim does not exceed the required amount.

◆ SEE CASE 3-1

When a Federal district court hears a case solely under diversity of citizenship jurisdiction, no Federal question is involved, and, accordingly, the Federal court must apply substantive State law. The conflict of laws rules of the State in which the district court is located determine which State's substantive law the court will use. (Conflict of laws is discussed later.) Federal courts apply Federal procedural rules in diversity cases.

In any case involving concurrent jurisdiction, the plaintiff has the choice of bringing the action in either an appropriate Federal court or State court. If the plaintiff brings the case in a State court, however, the defendant usually may have it **removed** (shifted) to a Federal court for the district in which the State court is located.

## STATE JURISDICTION

**Exclusive State Jurisdiction** The State courts have exclusive jurisdiction over *all other matters* not granted to the Federal courts in the Constitution or by Congress. Accordingly, exclusive State jurisdiction would include cases involving diversity of citizenship where the amount in controversy is $75,000 or less. In addition, the State courts have exclusive jurisdiction over all cases to which Federal judicial power does not reach. These matters include, but are by no means limited to, property, torts, contracts, agency, commercial transactions, and most crimes.

◆ SEE FIGURE 3-4: **Federal and State Jurisdiction**

◆ SEE FIGURE 3-5: **Subject Matter Jurisdiction**

**Choice of Law in State Courts** A court in one State may be a proper forum for a case even though some or all of the relevant events occurred in another State. For example, a California plaintiff may sue a Washington defendant in Washington over a car accident that occurred in Oregon. Because of Oregon's connections to the accident, Washington may choose, under its **conflict of laws rules**, to apply the substantive law of Oregon. Conflict of laws rules vary from State to State.

## *STARE DECISIS* IN THE DUAL COURT SYSTEM

The doctrine of *stare decisis* presents certain problems when there are two parallel court systems. Consequently, in the United States, *stare decisis* functions approximately as follows:

1. The U.S. Supreme Court has never held itself to be bound rigidly by its own decisions, and lower Federal courts and State courts have followed that course with respect to their own decisions.
2. A decision of the U.S. Supreme Court on a Federal question is binding on all other courts, Federal or State.
3. On a Federal question, although a decision of a Federal court other than the Supreme Court may be persuasive in a State court, the decision is not binding.

◆ FIGURE 3-4: **Federal and State Jurisdiction**

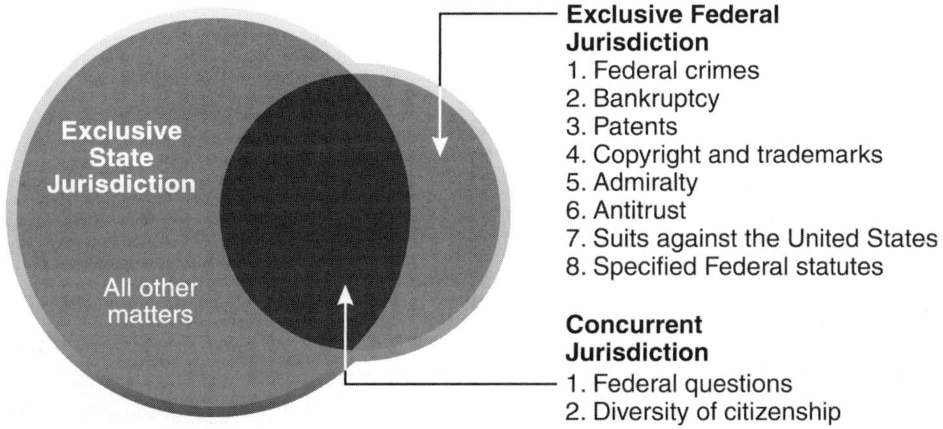

FIGURE 3-5: **Subject Matter Jurisdiction**

| Types of Jurisdiction | Court | Substantive Law Applied | Procedural Law Applied |
|---|---|---|---|
| **Exclusive Federal** | Federal | Federal | Federal |
| **Concurrent: Federal Question** | Federal<br>State | Federal<br>Federal | Federal<br>State |
| **Concurrent: Diversity** | Federal<br>State | State<br>State | Federal<br>State |
| **Exclusive State** | State | State | State |

4. A decision of a State court may be persuasive in the Federal courts, but it is not binding except where Federal jurisdiction is based on diversity of citizenship. In such a case the Federal courts must apply State law as determined by the highest State tribunal.
5. Decisions of the Federal courts (other than the U.S. Supreme Court) are not binding upon other Federal courts of equal or inferior rank, unless the latter owe obedience to the deciding court. For example, a decision of the Fifth Circuit Court of Appeals binds district courts in the Fifth Circuit but binds no other Federal court.
6. A decision of a State court is binding upon all courts inferior to it in its jurisdiction. Thus, the decision of the supreme court in a State binds all other courts in that State.
7. A decision of a State court is not binding on courts in other States except in cases in which the latter courts are required, under their conflict of laws rules, to apply the law of the former State as determined by the highest court in that State. For example, if a North Carolina court is required to apply Virginia law, it must follow decisions of the Virginia Supreme Court.

SEE FIGURE 3-6: ***Stare Decisis* in the Dual Court System**

## JURISDICTION OVER THE PARTIES

The second essential type of jurisdiction a court must have is the power to bind the parties involved in the dispute. The court obtains jurisdiction over the *plaintiff* when she voluntarily submits to the court's power by filing a complaint with the court. With respect to the defendant, a court may meet the requirements for this type of jurisdiction, called jurisdiction over the parties, in any of three ways: (1) *in personam* jurisdiction, (2) *in rem* jurisdiction, or (3) attachment jurisdiction. In addition, the exercise of jurisdiction must satisfy the constitutionally imposed requirements of due process: reasonable notification and a reasonable opportunity to be heard.

FIGURE 3-6: ***Stare Decisis* in the Dual Court System**

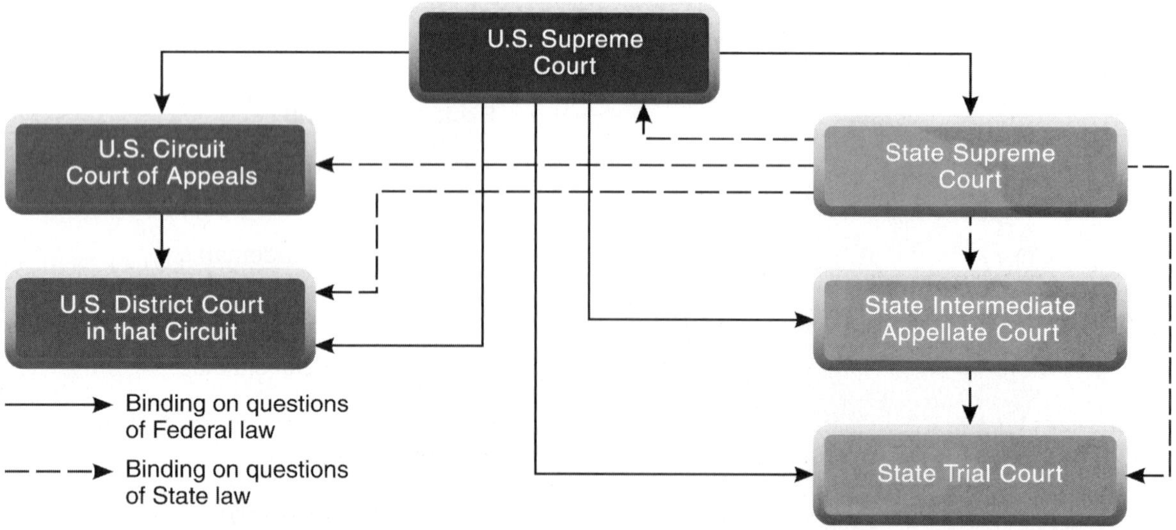

Moreover, the court's exercise of jurisdiction is valid under the Due Process Clause of the U.S. Constitution only if the defendant has minimum contacts with the State sufficient to prevent the court's assertion of jurisdiction from offending "traditional notions of fair play and substantial justice." For a court constitutionally to assert jurisdiction over a defendant, the defendant must have engaged in either purposeful acts in the State or acts outside the State that are of such a nature that the defendant could reasonably foresee being sued in that State. This overriding limitation on jurisdictional power is imposed upon the Federal and State courts through the U.S. Constitution, as discussed more fully in *Chapter 4*.

What notice is due depends on several factors but generally must be "notice reasonably calculated, under the circumstances, to apprise interested parties of the pendency of the action and afford them the opportunity to present their objections."

◆ **SEE CASE 3-2**

### *IN PERSONAM* JURISDICTION

*In personam* jurisdiction, or **personal jurisdiction**, is jurisdiction of a court over the parties to a lawsuit, in contrast to jurisdiction over their property. A court obtains *in personam* jurisdiction over a defendant either (1) by serving process on the party within the State in which the court is located, or (2) by reasonable notification to a party outside the State in those instances where a "long-arm statute" applies. To *serve process* means to deliver a summons, which is an order to respond to a complaint lodged against a party. (The terms *summons* and *complaint* are explained more fully later in this chapter.)

Personal jurisdiction may be obtained by personally serving a person within a State if that person is domiciled in that State. The U.S. Supreme Court has held that a State may exercise personal jurisdiction over a nonresident defendant who is temporarily present if the defendant is personally served in that State. Personal jurisdiction may also arise from a party's consent. For example, parties to a contract may agree that any dispute concerning that contract will be subject to the jurisdiction of a specific court.

Most States have adopted **long-arm statutes** to expand their jurisdictional reach beyond those persons who may be personally served within the State. These statutes allow courts to obtain jurisdiction over nonresident defendants whose contacts with the State in which the court is located are such that the exercise of jurisdiction does not offend traditional notions of fair play and substantial justice. The typical long-arm statute permits a court to exercise jurisdiction over a defendant, even though process is served beyond its borders, if the defendant (1) has committed a tort (civil wrong) within the State, (2) owns property within the State and that property is the subject matter of the lawsuit, (3) has entered into a contract within the State, or (4) has transacted business within the State and that business is the subject matter of the lawsuit.

### *IN REM* JURISDICTION

Courts in a State have the jurisdiction to adjudicate claims to property situated within the State if the plaintiff gives those persons who have an interest in the property reasonable notice and an opportunity to be heard. Such jurisdiction over property is called ***in rem*** jurisdiction, from the Latin word *res*, which means "thing." For example, if Carpenter and Miller are involved in a lawsuit over property located in Kansas, then an appropriate court in Kansas would have *in rem* jurisdiction to adjudicate claims with respect to this property so long as both parties are given notice of the lawsuit and a reasonable opportunity to contest the claim.

### ATTACHMENT JURISDICTION

Attachment jurisdiction, or **quasi *in rem* jurisdiction**, is jurisdiction over property rather than over a person. Attachment jurisdiction is invoked by seizing the defendant's property located within the State to obtain payment of a claim against the defendant that is *unrelated* to the property seized. For example, Allen, a resident of Ohio, has obtained a valid judgment in the amount of $20,000 against Bradley, a citizen of Kentucky. Allen can attach Bradley's automobile, which is located in Ohio, to satisfy his court judgment against Bradley.

◆ **SEE FIGURE 3-7: Jurisdiction**

### VENUE

Venue, which often is confused with jurisdiction, concerns the geographical area in which a lawsuit *should* be brought. The purpose of venue is to regulate the distribution of cases within a specific court system and to identify a convenient forum. In the Federal court system, venue determines the district or districts in a given State in which a suit may be brought. State rules of venue typically require that a suit be initiated in a county where one of the defendants resides. In matters involving real estate, most venue rules require that a suit be initiated in the county where the property is situated. A defendant may, however, object to the venue for various reasons.

## CIVIL DISPUTE RESOLUTION

As mentioned in *Chapter 1*, one of the primary functions of law is to provide for the peaceful resolution of disputes. Accordingly, our legal system has established an elaborate set of governmental mechanisms to settle disputes. The most prominent of these is judicial dispute resolution, called *litigation*. The rules of civil procedure, discussed in the first part

◆ FIGURE 3-7: **Jurisdiction**

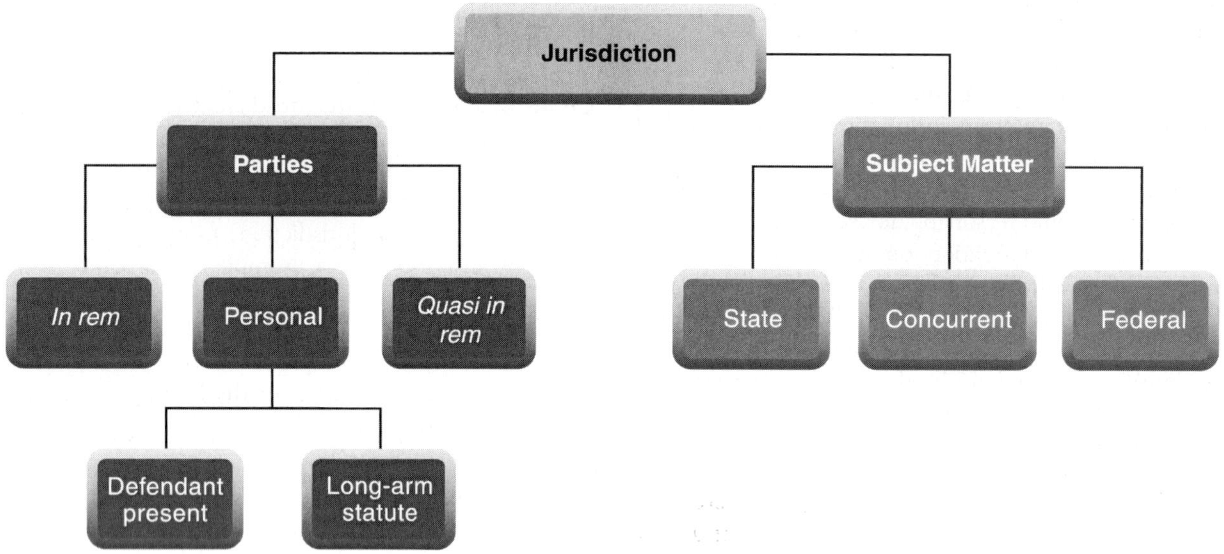


of this section, govern judicial resolution of civil disputes. Judicial resolution of criminal cases is governed by the rules of criminal procedure, which are covered in *Chapter 6*. Dispute resolution by administrative agencies, which is also common, is discussed in *Chapter 5*.

As an alternative to governmental dispute resolution, several nongovernmental methods of dispute resolution, such as arbitration, have developed. These are discussed in the second part of this section.

## CIVIL PROCEDURE

Civil disputes that enter the judicial system must follow the rules of civil procedure. These rules are designed to resolve the dispute justly, promptly, and inexpensively.

To acquaint the student with civil procedure, it will be helpful to carry a hypothetical action through the trial court to the highest court of review in the State. Although there are technical differences in trial and appellate procedure among State and Federal courts, the following example will provide a general understanding of the trial and appeal of cases. Assume that Pam Pederson, a pedestrian, while crossing a street in Chicago, is struck by an automobile driven by David Dryden. Pederson suffers serious personal injuries, incurs heavy medical and hospital expenses, and is unable to work for several months. Pederson desires that Dryden pay her for the loss and damages she sustained. After attempts at settlement fail, Pederson brings an action at law against Dryden. Pederson is the plaintiff, and Dryden the defendant. Each is represented by a lawyer. Let us follow the progress of the case.

### THE PLEADINGS

The **pleadings** are a series of responsive, formal, written statements in which each side to a lawsuit states its claims and defenses. The purpose of pleadings is to give notice and to establish the issues of fact and law that the parties dispute. An "issue of fact" is a dispute between the parties regarding the events that gave rise to the lawsuit. In contrast, an "issue of law" is a dispute between the parties as to what legal rules apply to these facts. Issues of fact are decided by the jury, or by the judge when there is no jury, whereas issues of law are decided by the judge.

**COMPLAINT AND SUMMONS** A lawsuit commences when Pederson, the plaintiff, files with the clerk of the trial court a **complaint** against Dryden which contains (1) a statement of the claim and supporting facts showing that she is entitled to relief, and (2) a demand for that relief. Pederson's complaint alleges that while exercising due and reasonable care for her own safety, she was struck by Dryden's automobile, which was negligently being driven by Dryden, causing her personal injuries and damages of $50,000, for which Pederson requests judgment.

Once the plaintiff has filed a complaint, the clerk issues a **summons** to be served upon the defendant to notify him that a suit has been brought against him. If the defendant has contacts with the State sufficient to show that the State's assertion of jurisdiction over him is constitutional, proper service of the summons establishes the court's jurisdiction over the person of the defendant. The sheriff of the county or a deputy sheriff serves a summons and a copy of the complaint upon Dryden, the defendant, commanding him to file his appearance and answer with the clerk of the court within a specific time, usually thirty days from the date the summons was served. A number of States permit the server to leave a copy of the summons at the defendant's home with a person of "suitable age and discretion." Most long-arm statutes allow service of the summons to be sent to out-of-state defendants by registered mail. If the defendant is a corporation, the statutes typically authorize actual service to the company's general or managing agent. When direct methods of notifying the defendant are unavailable, service by publication may be allowed.

**RESPONSES TO COMPLAINT** At this point Dryden has several options. If he fails to respond at all, a **default judgment** will be entered against him for the relief the court determines in a hearing. He may make **pretrial motions** contesting the court's jurisdiction over him or asserting that the action is barred by the statute of limitations, which requires suits to be brought within a specified time. Dryden also may move that the complaint be made more definite and certain, or that the complaint be dismissed for failure to state a claim upon which the court may grant relief. Such a motion, sometimes called a **demurrer**, essentially asserts that even if all of Pederson's allegations were true, she still would not be entitled to the relief she seeks, and that, therefore, there is no need for a trial of the facts. The court rules on this motion as a matter of law. If it rules in favor of the defendant, the plaintiff may appeal the ruling.

If he does not make any pretrial motions, or if they are denied, Dryden will respond to the complaint by filing an **answer**, which may contain admissions, denials, affirmative defenses, and counterclaims. Thus, Dryden might answer the complaint by denying its allegations of negligence and stating, on the other hand, that he, Dryden, was driving his car at a low speed and with reasonable care (a **denial**) when his car struck Pederson (an **admission**), who had dashed across the street in front of Dryden's car without looking in any direction to see whether cars or other vehicles were approaching; that, accordingly, Pederson's injuries were caused by her own negligence (an **affirmative defense**); and that, therefore, she should not be permitted to recover any damages. Dryden might further state that Pederson caused damages to his car and request a judgment for $2,000 (a **counterclaim**). These pleadings create an issue of fact regarding whether Pederson or Dryden, or both, failed to exercise due and reasonable care under the circumstances and were thus negligent and liable for their carelessness.

If the defendant counterclaims, the plaintiff must respond by a **reply**, which may also contain admissions, denials, and affirmative defenses.

## PRETRIAL PROCEDURE

**JUDGMENT ON PLEADINGS** After the pleadings, either party may move for **judgment on the pleadings**, which requests the judge to rule as a matter of law whether the facts as alleged in the pleadings, which for the purpose of the motion are taken to be as the nonmoving party alleges them, form a sufficient basis to warrant granting the requested relief.

**DISCOVERY** In preparation for trial and even before completion of the pleadings stage, each party has the right to obtain relevant evidence, or information that may lead to evidence, from the other party. This procedure is known as **discovery**. It includes (1) pretrial **depositions** consisting of sworn testimony, taken out of court, of the opposing party or other witnesses; (2) sworn answers by the opposing party to **written interrogatories**; (3) **production** of documents and physical objects in the possession of the opposing party or, by a court-ordered subpoena, in the possession of nonparties; (4) a relevant court-ordered physical and/or mental **examination**, by a physician, of the opposing party; and (5) admissions of facts obtained by a **request for admissions** submitted to the opposing party. By properly using discovery, each party may become fully informed of relevant evidence and avoid surprise at trial. Another purpose of this procedure is to encourage and facilitate settlements by providing both parties with as much relevant information as possible.

**PRETRIAL CONFERENCE** Also furthering these objectives is the **pretrial conference** between the judge and the attorneys representing the parties. The basic purposes of the pretrial conference are (1) to simplify the issues in dispute by amending the pleadings, admitting or stipulating facts, and identifying witnesses and documents to be presented at trial; and (2) to encourage settlement of the dispute without trial. (More than 90 percent of all cases are settled before going to trial.) If no settlement occurs, the judge will enter a pretrial order containing all of the amendments, stipulations, admissions, and other matters agreed to during the pretrial conference. The order supersedes the pleadings and controls the remainder of the trial.

**SUMMARY JUDGMENT** The evidence disclosed by discovery may be so clear that a trial to determine the facts becomes unnecessary. Thus, after discovery, either party may move for a summary judgment, which requests the judge to rule that, because there are no issues of fact to be determined by trial, the party thus moving should prevail as a matter of law. A **summary judgment** is a final binding determination on the merits made by the judge before a trial.

◆ **SEE CASE 3-3**

## TRIAL

In all Federal civil cases at common law involving more than $20, the U.S. Constitution guarantees the right to a jury trial. In addition, nearly every State constitution provides a similar right. In addition, Federal and State statutes may authorize jury trials in cases not within the constitutional guarantees. Under Federal law and in almost all States, jury trials are *not* available in equity cases. Even in cases in which a jury trial is available, the parties may waive (choose not to have) a trial by jury. When a trial is conducted without a jury, the judge serves as the fact finder and will make separate findings of fact and conclusions of law. When a trial is conducted with a jury, the judge determines issues of law and the jury determines questions of fact.

**JURY SELECTION** Assuming a timely demand for a jury has been made, the trial begins with the selection of a jury. The jury selection process involves a ***voir dire***, an examination by the parties' attorneys (or, in some courts, by the judge) of the potential jurors. Each party may make an unlimited number of **challenges for cause**, which prevent a prospective juror from serving if the juror is biased or cannot be fair and impartial. In addition, each party has a limited number of **peremptory challenges**, which allow the party to disqualify a prospective juror without showing cause. The Supreme Court has held that the U.S. Constitution prohibits discrimination in jury selection on the basis of race or gender.

**CONDUCT OF TRIAL** After the jury has been selected, both attorneys make an **opening statement** concerning the facts that they expect to prove in the trial. The plaintiff and her witnesses then testify upon **direct examination** by the plaintiff's attorney. Each is then subject to **cross-examination** by the defendant's attorney. Thus, in our hypothetical case, the plaintiff and her witnesses testify that the traffic light at the street intersection where Pederson was struck was green for traffic in the direction in which Pederson was crossing but changed to yellow when she was about one-third of the way across the street.

During the trial the judge rules on the admission and exclusion of evidence on the basis of its relevance and reliability. If the judge does not allow certain evidence to be introduced or certain testimony to be given, the attorney may preserve the question of admissibility for review on appeal by making an **offer of proof**. The law does not regard the offer of proof as evidence, and the offer, which consists of oral statements of counsel or witnesses showing for the record the substance of the evidence which the judge has ruled inadmissible, is not heard by the jury.

After cross-examination, followed by redirect examination of each of her witnesses, Pederson rests her case. At this point, Dryden may move for a directed verdict in his favor. A **directed verdict** is a final binding determination on the merits made by the judge after a trial but before the jury renders a verdict. If the judge concludes that the evidence introduced by the plaintiff, which is assumed for the purposes of the motion to be true, would not be sufficient for the jury to find in favor of the plaintiff, then the judge will grant the directed verdict in favor of the defendant. In some States, the judge will deny the motion for a directed verdict if there is *any* evidence on which the jury might possibly render a verdict for the plaintiff. If a directed verdict is reversed on appeal, a new trial is necessary.

If the judge denies the motion for a directed verdict, the defendant then has the opportunity to present evidence. The defendant and his witnesses testify that Dryden was driving his car at a low speed when it struck Pederson and that Dryden at the time had the green light at the intersection.

After the defendant has presented his evidence, the plaintiff and the defendant may be permitted to introduce rebuttal evidence. Once both parties have rested (concluded), either party may move for a directed verdict. By this motion the party contends that the evidence is so clear that reasonable persons could not differ as to the outcome of the case. If the judge grants the motion for a directed verdict, he takes the case away from the jury and enters a judgment for the party making the motion.

If the judge denies the motion, the plaintiff's attorney makes a **closing argument** to the jury, reviewing the evidence and urging a verdict in favor of Pederson. Dryden's attorney then makes a closing argument, summarizing the evidence and urging a verdict in favor of Dryden. Pederson's attorney is permitted to make a short argument in rebuttal.

**JURY INSTRUCTIONS** The attorneys previously have tendered possible written **jury instructions** on the applicable law to the trial judge, who gives to the jury those instructions he approves and denies those he considers incorrect. The judge also may give the jury instructions of his own. These instructions (called "charges" in some States) advise the jury of the particular rules of law that apply to the facts the jury determines from the evidence.

**VERDICT** The jury then retires to the jury room to deliberate and to reach a **general verdict** in favor of one party or the other. If it finds the issues in favor of the defendant, its verdict is that the defendant is not liable. If, however, it finds the issues for the plaintiff and against the defendant, its verdict will hold the defendant liable and will specify the amount of the plaintiff's damages. In this case, the jury found that Pederson's damages were $35,000. Upon returning to the jury box, the foreman either announces the verdict or hands it in written form to the clerk to give to the judge, who reads the general verdict in open court. In some jurisdictions, the jury must reach a **special verdict** by making specific written findings on each factual issue. The judge then applies the law to these findings and renders a judgment. In the United States the prevailing litigant is ordinarily *not* entitled to collect attorneys' fees from the losing party, unless otherwise provided by statute or an enforceable contract allocating attorney's fees.

**MOTIONS CHALLENGING THE VERDICT** The unsuccessful party may then file a written motion for a new trial or for judgment notwithstanding the verdict. The judge may grant a **motion for a new trial** if (1) the judge committed prejudicial error during the trial, (2) the verdict is against the weight of the evidence, (3) the damages are excessive, or (4) the trial was not fair. The judge has the discretion to grant a motion for a new trial (on grounds 1, 3, or 4 above) even if substantial evidence supports the verdict. On the other hand, he must deny the motion for judgment notwithstanding the verdict (also called a judgment n.o.v.) if any substantial evidence supports the verdict. This motion is similar to a motion for a directed verdict, only it is made *after* the jury's verdict. To grant the **motion for judgment notwithstanding the verdict**, the judge must decide that the evidence is so clear that reasonable people could not differ as to the outcome of the case. If a judgment n.o.v. is reversed on appeal, a new trial is *not* necessary, and the jury's verdict is entered. If the judge denies the motions for a new trial and for a judgment n.o.v., he enters **judgment on the verdict** for $35,000 in favor of Pederson.

## APPEAL

The purpose of an appeal is to determine whether the trial court committed prejudicial error. Most jurisdictions permit an appeal only from a final judgment. As a general rule, an appellate court reviews only errors of law. Errors of law include the judge's decisions to admit or exclude evidence; the judge's instructions to the jury; and the judge's actions in denying or granting a motion for a demurrer, a summary judgment, a directed verdict, or a judgment n.o.v. Appellate courts review errors of law *de novo*. An appellate court will reverse errors of fact only if they are so clearly erroneous that the court considers them to constitute an error of law.

Assume that Dryden directs his attorney to appeal. The attorney files a notice of appeal with the clerk of the trial court within the prescribed time. Later, Dryden, as appellant, files in the reviewing court the record on appeal, which contains the pleadings, transcript of the testimony, rulings by the judge on motions made by the parties, arguments of counsel, jury instructions, the verdict, posttrial motions, and the judgment from which the appeal is taken. In States having an intermediate court of appeals, such court will usually be the reviewing court. In States having no intermediate courts of appeal, a party may appeal directly from the trial court to the State supreme court.

Dryden, as appellant, is required to prepare a condensation of the record, known as an abstract, or pertinent excerpts from the record, which he files with the reviewing court together with a brief and argument. His **brief** contains a statement of the facts, the issues, the rulings by the trial court which Dryden contends are erroneous and prejudicial, grounds for reversal of the judgment, a statement of the applicable law, and arguments on his behalf. Pederson, the appellee, files an answering brief and argument. Dryden may, but is not required to, file a reply brief. The case is now ready for consideration by the reviewing court.

The appellate court does not hear any evidence; rather, it decides the case upon the record, abstracts, and briefs. After **oral argument** by the attorneys, if the court elects to hear one, the court takes the case under advisement and makes a decision based upon majority rule, after which the court prepares a written opinion containing the reasons for its decision, the applicable rules of law, and its judgment. The judgment may **affirm** the judgment of the trial court, or, if the appellate court finds that reversible error was committed, the judgment may be **reversed**, or the case may be **reversed and remanded** for a new trial. In some instances the appellate court will affirm the lower court's decision in part and reverse it in part. The losing party may file a petition for rehearing, which is usually denied.

If the reviewing court is an intermediate appellate court, the party losing in that court may decide to seek a reversal of its judgment by filing within a prescribed time a notice of appeal, if the appeal is by right, or a petition for leave to appeal to the State supreme court, if the appeal is by discretion. This petition corresponds to a petition for a writ of *certiorari* in the U.S. Supreme Court. The party winning in the appellate court may file an answer to the petition for leave to appeal. If the petition is granted or if the appeal is by right, the record is certified to the state supreme court, where each party files a new brief and argument. Oral argument may be held, and the case is taken under advisement. If the supreme court concludes that the judgment of the appellate court is correct, it affirms. If it decides otherwise, it reverses the judgment of the appellate court and enters a reversal or an order of remand. The unsuccessful party may again file a petition for a rehearing, which is likely to be denied. Barring the remote possibility of an application for still further review by the U.S. Supreme Court, the case either has reached its termination or, upon remand, is about to start its second journey through the courts, beginning, as it did originally, in the trial court.

## ENFORCEMENT

If Dryden does not appeal or if the reviewing court affirms the judgment if he does appeal and Dryden does not pay the judgment, the task of enforcement remains. Pederson must request the clerk to issue a **writ of execution**, demanding payment of the judgment, which is served by the sheriff upon the defendant. If the writ is returned "unsatisfied," Pederson may post bond or other security and order a levy on and sale of specific nonexempt property belonging to Dryden, which is then seized by the sheriff, advertised for sale, and sold at public sale under the writ of execution. If the proceeds of the sale do not produce sufficient funds to pay the judgment, plaintiff Pederson's attorney may institute a supplementary proceeding in an attempt to locate money or other property belonging to Dryden. In an attempt to collect the judgment, Pederson's attorney also may proceed by **garnishment** against

Dryden's employer to collect from Dryden's wages or against a bank in which Dryden has an account.

If Pederson cannot satisfy the judgment with Dryden's property located within Illinois (the State where the judgment was obtained), Pederson will have to bring an action on the original judgment in other States where Dryden owns property. Because the U.S. Constitution requires each State to accord judgments of other States **full faith and credit**, Pederson will be able to obtain a local judgment that may be enforced by the methods described above.

◆ SEE FIGURE 3-8: **Stages in Civil Procedure**

## ALTERNATIVE DISPUTE RESOLUTION

Litigation is complex, time-consuming, and expensive. Furthermore, court adjudications involve long delays, lack special expertise in substantive areas, and provide only a limited range of remedies. In addition, the litigation process offers little opportunity for compromise and often causes or exacerbates animosity between the disputants. Consequently, in an attempt to overcome some of the disadvantages of litigation, several nonjudicial methods of dealing with disputes have developed. The most important of these alternatives to litigation is arbitration. Others include conciliation, mediation, "mini-trials," and summary jury trials.

The various techniques differ in a number of ways, including (1) whether the process is voluntary, (2) whether the process is binding, (3) whether the disputants represent themselves or are represented by attorneys, (4) whether the decision is made by the disputants or by a third party, (5) whether the procedure used is formal or informal, and (6) whether the basis for the decision is law or some other criterion.

Which method of civil dispute resolution—litigation or one of the nongovernmental methods—is better for a particular dispute depends on several factors, including the financial circumstances of the disputants, the nature of their relationship (commercial or personal, ongoing or limited), and the urgency of their need for a quick resolution. Alternative dispute resolution methods are especially suitable where privacy, speed, preservation of continuing relations, and control over the process—including the flexibility to compromise—are important to the parties. Nevertheless, the disadvantages of using alternative dispute mechanisms may make court adjudication more appropriate. For example, except for arbitration, only courts can compel participation and provide a binding resolution. In addition, only courts can establish precedents and create public duties. Furthermore, the courts provide

◆ FIGURE 3-8: **Stages in Civil Procedure**

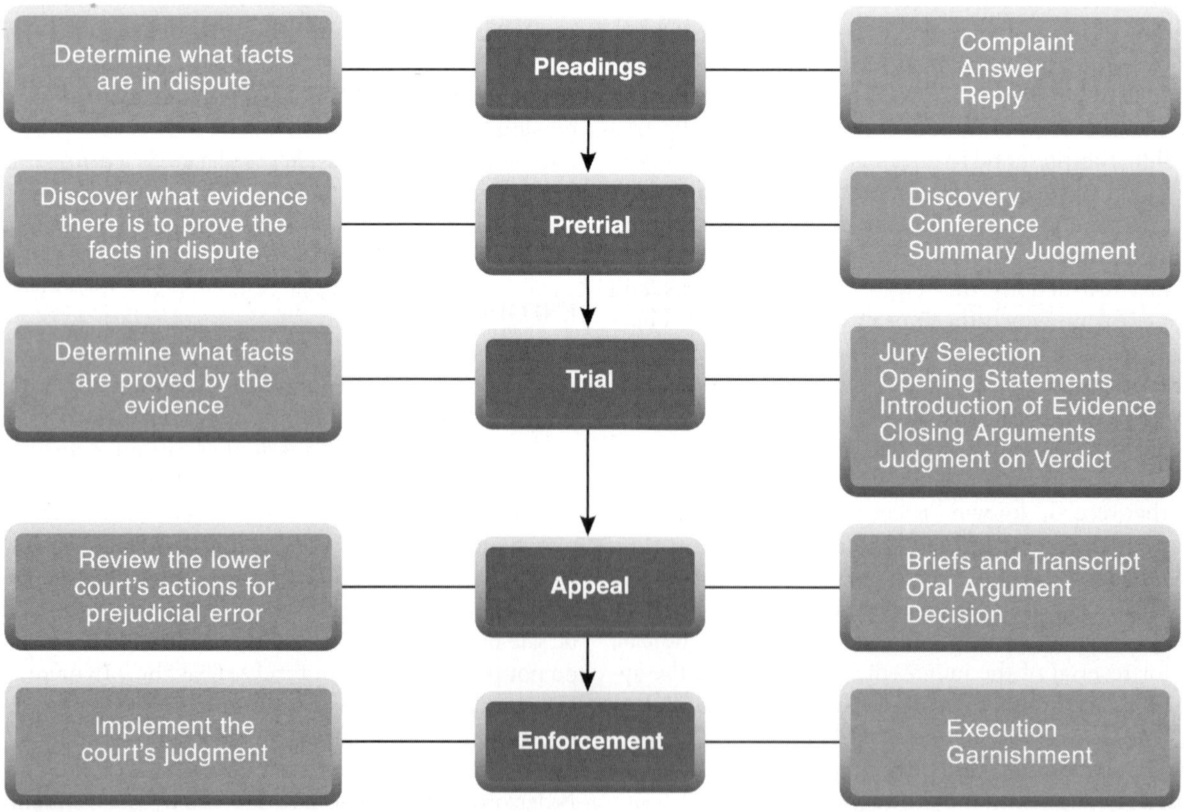

greater due process protections and uniformity of outcome. Finally, the courts are independent of the disputants and are publicly funded.

◆ SEE FIGURE 3-9: **Comparison of Adjudication, Arbitration, and Mediation/Conciliation**

## ARBITRATION

In **arbitration**, the parties select a neutral third person or persons (the arbitrator[s]) who render(s) a binding decision after hearing arguments and reviewing evidence. Because the presentation of the case is less formal and the rules of evidence are more relaxed, arbitration usually takes less time and costs less than litigation. Moreover, in many arbitration cases the parties are able to select an arbitrator with special expertise concerning the subject of the dispute. Thus, the quality of the arbitrator's decision may be higher than that available through the court system. In addition, arbitration normally is conducted in private, which enables the parties to avoid unwanted publicity. Arbitration is commonly used in commercial and labor management disputes.

**Types of Arbitration** Arbitration is of two basic types—consensual, which is by far the most common, and compulsory. **Consensual arbitration** occurs whenever the parties to a dispute agree to submit the controversy to arbitration. They may do this in advance by agreeing in their contract that disputes arising out of the contract will be resolved by arbitration. Or, after a dispute arises, they may agree to submit the dispute to arbitration. In either instance, such agreements are enforceable under the Federal Arbitration Act (FAA) and statutes in more than forty States. The great majority of these States have adopted the Uniform Arbitration Act (UAA); the others have adopted substantially similar legislation. (In 2000, the National Conference of Commissioners on Uniform State Laws promulgated the Revised UAA to provide State legislatures with a more up-to-date statute to resolve disputes through arbitration. To date, twelve States have adopted the Revised UAA.) In **compulsory arbitration**, which is relatively infrequent, a Federal or State statute requires arbitration for specific types of disputes, such as those involving public employees like police officers, teachers, and firefighters.

**Procedure** Usually the parties' agreement to arbitrate specifies how the arbitrator or arbitrators will be chosen. If it does not, the FAA and State statutes provide methods for selecting arbitrators. Although the requirements for arbitration hearings vary from State to State, they generally consist of opening statements, case presentation, and closing statements. Case presentations may include witnesses, documentation, and site inspections. The parties may cross-examine witnesses and the parties may be represented by attorneys.

The decision of the arbitrator, called an **award**, is binding on the parties. Nevertheless, it is subject to very limited judicial review. Under the FAA and the Revised UAA, grounds for review include (1) the award was procured by corruption, fraud, or other undue means; (2) the arbitrators were partial or corrupt; (3) the arbitrators were guilty of misconduct prejudicing the rights of a party to the arbitration proceeding; and (4) the arbitrators exceeded their powers. Historically, the courts were unfriendly to arbitration; now, however, they favor the procedure.

**International Arbitration** Arbitration is a commonly used means for resolving international disputes. The United Nations Committee on International Trade Law (UNCITRAL) and

◆ FIGURE 3-9: **Comparison of Adjudication, Arbitration, and Mediation/Conciliation**

| | Court Adjudication | Arbitration | Mediation/Conciliation |
|---|---|---|---|
| **Advantages** | Binding<br>Public norms<br>Precedents<br>Uniformity<br>Publicly funded<br>Compels participation | Binding<br>Parties control process<br>Privacy<br>Special expertise<br>Speedy resolution | Preserves relations<br>Parties control process<br>Privacy<br>Flexible |
| **Disadvantages** | Expensive<br>Time-consuming<br>Long delays<br>Limited remedies<br>Lacks special expertise<br>No compromise<br>Disrupts relationships<br>Publicity | No public norms<br>No precedent<br>No uniformity | Not binding<br>Lacks finality<br>No compelled participation<br>No precedent<br>No uniformity |

*Source:* Adapted from Table 4 of *Report of the Ad Hoc Panel on Dispute Resolution and Public Policy*, prepared by the National Institute for Dispute Resolution.

the International Chamber of Commerce have promulgated arbitration rules that have won broad international adherence. The FAA has provisions implementing the United Nations Convention on the Recognition and Enforcement of Foreign Arbitral Awards. A number of States have enacted laws specifically governing international arbitration; some of the statutes have been based on the Model Law on International Arbitration drafted by UNCITRAL.

**Court-Annexed Arbitration** A growing number of Federal and State courts have adopted court-annexed arbitration in civil cases in which the parties seek limited amounts of damages. The arbitrators are usually attorneys. Appeal from this type of *nonbinding* arbitration is by trial *de novo*.

Many States have enacted statutes requiring the arbitration of medical malpractice disputes. Some States provide for mandatory nonbinding arbitration before bringing a case to court. Other States provide for voluntary but binding arbitration agreements, which patients sign before receiving medical treatment.

◆ **SEE CASE 3-4**

### CONCILIATION

**Conciliation** is a nonbinding, informal process in which the disputing parties select a neutral third party (the conciliator) who attempts to help them reach a mutually acceptable agreement. The duties of the conciliator include improving communications, explaining issues, scheduling meetings, discussing differences of opinion, and serving as an intermediary between the parties when they are unwilling to meet.

### MEDIATION

**Mediation** is a process in which a neutral third party (the mediator) selected by the disputants helps them to resolve their disagreement. In addition to employing conciliation techniques to improve communications, the mediator, unlike the conciliator, proposes possible solutions for the parties to consider. Like the conciliator, the mediator lacks the power to render a binding decision. Mediation is commonly used by the judicial system in such tribunals as small claims courts, housing courts, family courts, and neighborhood justice centers. In 2001 the National Conference of Commissioners on Uniform State Laws promulgated the Uniform Mediation Act, which was amended in 2003. The Act establishes a privilege of confidentiality for mediators and participants. To date ten States have adopted it.

Sometimes the techniques of arbitration and mediation are combined in a procedure called "med-arb." In med-arb, the neutral third party serves first as a mediator. If all issues are not resolved through such mediation, she then serves as an arbitrator authorized to render a binding decision on the remaining issues.

### MINI-TRIAL

A mini-trial is a structured settlement process that combines elements of negotiation, mediation, and trials. Mini-trials are most commonly used when both disputants are corporations. In a mini-trial, attorneys for the two corporations conduct limited discovery and then present evidence to a panel consisting of managers from each company, as well as a neutral third party, who may be a retired judge or other attorney. After the lawyers complete their presentations, the managers try to negotiate a settlement without the attorneys. The managers may consult the third party on how a court might resolve the issues in dispute.

### SUMMARY JURY TRIAL

A summary jury trial is a mock trial in which the parties present their case to an advisory jury. Though not binding, the jury's verdict does influence the negotiations in which the parties must participate following the mock trial. If the parties do not reach a settlement, they may have a full trial *de novo*.

### NEGOTIATION

Negotiation is a consensual bargaining process in which the parties attempt to reach an agreement resolving their dispute. Negotiation differs from other methods of alternate dispute resolution in that no third parties are involved.

## CHAPTER SUMMARY

### THE COURT SYSTEM

**FEDERAL COURTS**

**District Courts** trial courts of general jurisdiction that can hear and decide most legal controversies in the Federal system

**Courts of Appeals** hear appeals from the district courts and review orders of certain administrative agencies

**The Supreme Court** the nation's highest court, whose principal function is to review decisions of the Federal Courts of Appeals and the highest State courts

**Special Courts** have jurisdiction over cases in a particular area of Federal law and include the U.S. Court of Federal Claims, the U.S. Tax Court, the U.S. Bankruptcy Courts, and the U.S. Court of Appeals for the Federal Circuit

**STATE COURTS**

**Inferior Trial Courts** hear minor criminal cases, such as traffic offenses, and civil cases involving small amounts of money; conduct preliminary hearings in more serious criminal cases
**Trial Courts** have general jurisdiction over civil and criminal cases
**Special Courts** trial courts, such as probate courts and family courts, having jurisdiction over a particular area of State law
**Appellate Courts** include one or two levels; the highest court's decisions are final except in those cases reviewed by the U.S. Supreme Court

## JURISDICTION

**SUBJECT MATTER JURISDICTION**

**Definition** authority of a court to decide a particular kind of case
**Federal Jurisdiction**
- ***Exclusive Federal Jurisdiction*** Federal courts have sole jurisdiction over Federal crimes, bankruptcy, antitrust, patent, trademark, copyright, and other specified cases
- ***Concurrent Federal Jurisdiction*** authority of more than one court to hear the same case; State and Federal courts have concurrent jurisdiction over (1) Federal question cases (cases arising under the Constitution, statutes, or treaties of the United States) that do not involve exclusive Federal jurisdiction, and (2) diversity of citizenship cases involving more than $75,000

**State Jurisdiction** State courts have exclusive jurisdiction over all matters to which the Federal judicial power does not reach

**JURISDICTION OVER THE PARTIES**

**Definition** the power of a court to bind the parties to a suit
***In Personam* Jurisdiction** jurisdiction based upon claims against a person, in contrast to jurisdiction over the person's property
***In Rem* Jurisdiction** jurisdiction based on claims against property
**Attachment Jurisdiction** jurisdiction over a defendant's property to obtain payment of a claim not related to the property
**Venue** geographical area in which a lawsuit should be brought

## CIVIL DISPUTE RESOLUTION

**CIVIL PROCEDURE**

**The Pleadings** a series of statements that give notice and establish the issues of fact and law presented and disputed
- ***Complaint*** initial pleading by the plaintiff stating his case
- ***Summons*** notice given to inform a person of a lawsuit against her
- ***Answer*** defendant's pleading in response to the plaintiff's complaint
- ***Reply*** plaintiff's pleading in response to the defendant's answer

**Pretrial Procedure** process requiring the parties to disclose what evidence is available to prove the disputed facts; designed to encourage settlement of cases or to make the trial more efficient
- ***Judgment on Pleadings*** a final ruling in favor of one party by the judge based on the pleadings
- ***Discovery*** right of each party to obtain evidence from the other party
- ***Pretrial Conference*** a conference between the judge and the attorneys to simplify the issues in dispute and to attempt to settle the dispute without trial
- ***Summary Judgment*** final ruling by the judge in favor of one party based on the evidence disclosed by discovery

**Trial** determines the facts and the outcome of the case
- ***Jury Selection*** each party has an unlimited number of challenges for cause and a limited number of peremptory challenges
- ***Conduct of Trial*** consists of opening statements by attorneys, direct and cross-examination of witnesses, and closing arguments
- ***Directed Verdict*** final ruling by the judge in favor of one party based on the evidence introduced at trial
- ***Jury Instructions*** judge gives the jury the particular rules of law that apply to the case
- ***Verdict*** the jury's decision based on those facts the jury determines the evidence proves
- ***Motions Challenging the Verdict*** include motions for a new trial and a motion for judgment notwithstanding the verdict

**Appeal** determines whether the trial court committed prejudicial error
**Enforcement** plaintiff with an unpaid judgment may resort to a writ of execution to have the sheriff seize property of the defendants and to garnishment to collect money owed to the defendant by a third party

---

**ALTERNATIVE DISPUTE RESOLUTION**

**Arbitration** a nonjudicial proceeding in which a neutral party selected by the disputants renders a binding decision (award)
**Conciliation** a nonbinding process in which a third party acts as an intermediary between the disputing parties
**Mediation** a nonbinding process in which a third party acts as an intermediary between the disputing parties and proposes solutions for them to consider
**Mini-Trial** a nonbinding process in which attorneys for the disputing parties (typically corporations) present evidence to managers of the disputing parties and a neutral third party, after which the managers attempt to negotiate a settlement in consultation with the third party
**Summary Jury Trial** mock trial followed by negotiations
**Negotiation** consensual bargaining process in which the parties attempt to reach an agreement resolving their dispute without the involvement of third parties

## CASES

## CASE 3-1

### Concurrent Federal Jurisdiction
### WHITE v. FCI USA, INC.

United States Court of Appeals for the Fifth Circuit, 2003
319 F.3d 672
http://caselaw.lp.findlaw.com/data2/circs/5th/0250890p.pdf

**Per Curiam:**
Plaintiff-Appellant Regina White ("White") brought suit against Defendant-Appellee FCI USA, Inc. ("FCI"), White's former employer, for wrongful termination on March 29, 2001, in the 246th Judicial District Court of El Paso County, Texas ("state court"). White based her suit upon [citation], which permits suits for wrongful termination where the employee was terminated for refusal to perform illegal acts.

In her Original Petition, White prayed that the judgment include punitive damages, attorney's fees, pre-judgment interest, court costs, and compensatory damages for lost pay, lost fringe benefits, front pay, loss of wage earning capacity, harm to White's credit and credit reputation, and mental anguish and emotional distress (both past and future). The Original Petition did not specify how much monetary relief White was seeking.

FCI removed on May 25, 2001, asserting removal jurisdiction on the basis of diversity. In its Notice of Removal, FCI asserted that the amount in controversy exceeded $75,000.

White filed a Motion to Remand, but the U.S. District Court for the Western District of Texas ("district court") denied her motion. The district court concluded that

FCI had set forth facts sufficient to show by a preponderance of the evidence that the $75,000 amount-in-controversy requirement was met.

* * *

Diversity jurisdiction under [citation] only exists where the parties are citizens of different states and the amount in controversy exceeds $75,000. [Citation.] White correctly notes that the amount in controversy should be determined at the time of filing. [Citation.] However, White never specified the total amount of monetary relief she was seeking.

Where the plaintiff fails to allege a specific amount of damages, this Court has prescribed a procedure for determining the amount in controversy:

> * * * [W]hen a complaint does not allege a specific amount of damages, the party invoking federal jurisdiction must prove by a preponderance of the evidence that the amount in controversy exceeds the jurisdictional amount. The district court must first examine the complaint to determine whether it is "facially apparent" that the claims exceed the jurisdictional amount. If it is not thus apparent, the court may rely on "summary judgment-type" evidence to ascertain the amount in controversy. [Citation.]

The district court examined the Original Petition on its face and evaluated the evidence presented by FCI. The district court concluded it was "more probable than not" that the lengthy list of compensatory and punitive damages sought by White, when combined with attorney's fees, would exceed $75,000. [Citation.] In fact, the district court concluded that the compensatory damages or punitive damages alone would "in all likelihood" exceed $75,000. [Citation.] The district court also noted White's admission that her damages "[did] not yet equal" $75,000 but "it [was] possible that [they] will exceed $75,000.00 at the time of trial." On the basis of this evidence and analysis, the district court found that the amount-in-controversy requirement was met.

* * *

In its Requests for Admission, FCI asked White to admit or deny that she was seeking damages of $75,000 or more. White admitted that her damages "[did] not yet equal" $75,000 but "it [was] possible that [they] will exceed $75,000.00 at the time of trial." Through this language, White implied that the amount in controversy was not limited to the damages she suffered before her filing. Instead, White indicated that she was seeking continuing and future damages as well.

* * *

This Court has held that "the jurisdictional facts that support removal must be judged at the time of the removal." [Citation.] At the time of removal, it was apparent from the face of the Original Petition and the evidence presented by FCI that the amount in controversy exceeded $75,000. The preponderance of the evidence thus indicated that the amount-in-controversy requirement was met. This Court has held that "once a defendant is able to show that the amount in controversy exceeds the jurisdictional amount, removal is proper, provided plaintiff has not shown that it is legally certain that his recovery will not exceed the amount stated." [Citation.] White failed to specify an amount of damages less than $75,000 or to present any substantive evidence in support of her motion to remand. White thus failed to show that it was legally certain that her recovery will not exceed $75,000.

Based on the preponderance of evidence, this Court affirms the district court's conclusion that the amount-in-controversy requirement was met.

---

CASE 3-2

## Jurisdiction
## WORLD-WIDE VOLKSWAGEN CORP. v. WOODSON

Supreme Court of the United States, 1980
444 U.S. 286, 100 S.Ct 559, 62 L.Ed.2d 490
http://laws.findlaw.com/us/444/286.html

**White, J.**

The issue before us is whether, consistently with the Due Process Clause of the Fourteenth Amendment, an Oklahoma court may exercise *in personam* jurisdiction over a nonresident automobile retailer and its wholesale distributor in a products-liability action, when the defendants' only connection with Oklahoma is the fact that an automobile sold in New York to New York residents became involved in an accident in Oklahoma.

Respondents Harry and Kay Robinson purchased a new Audi automobile from petitioner Seaway Volkswagen, Inc. (Seaway), in Massena, N.Y., in 1976. The following year the Robinson family, who resided in New York, left that State for a new home in Arizona. As they passed through the State of Oklahoma, another car struck their Audi in the rear, causing a fire which severely burned Kay Robinson and her two children.

The Robinsons subsequently brought a products-liability action in the District Court for Creek County, Okla., claiming that their injuries resulted from defective design and placement of the Audi's gas tank and fuel system. They joined as defendants the automobile's manufacturer, Audi NSU Auto Union

Aktiengesellschaft (Audi); its importer, Volkswagen of America, Inc. (Volkswagen); its regional distributor, petitioner World-Wide Volkswagen Corp. (World-Wide); and its retail dealer, petitioner Seaway. Seaway and World-Wide entered special appearances, claiming that Oklahoma's exercise of jurisdiction over them would offend the limitations on the State's jurisdiction imposed by the Due Process Clause of the Fourteenth Amendment.

The facts presented to the District Court showed that World-Wide is incorporated and has its business office in New York. It distributes vehicles, parts, and accessories, under contract with Volkswagen, to retail dealers in New York, New Jersey, and Connecticut. Seaway, one of these retail dealers, is incorporated and has its place of business in New York. Insofar as the record reveals, Seaway and World-Wide are fully independent corporations whose relations with each other and with Volkswagen and Audi are contractual only. Respondents adduced no evidence that either World-Wide or Seaway does any business in Oklahoma, ships or sells any products to or in that State, has an agent to receive process there, or purchases advertisements in any media calculated to reach Oklahoma. In fact, as respondents' counsel conceded at oral argument, [citation], there was no showing that any automobile sold by World-Wide or Seaway has ever entered Oklahoma with the single exception of the vehicle involved in the present case.

* * *

The Supreme Court of Oklahoma [held] that personal jurisdiction over petitioners was authorized by Oklahoma's "long-arm" statute, [citation]. * * *

* * *

The Due Process Clause of the Fourteenth Amendment limits the power of a state court to render a valid personal judgment against a nonresident defendant. [Citation.] A judgment rendered in violation of due process is void in the rendering State and is not entitled to full faith and credit elsewhere. [Citation.] Due process requires that the defendant be given adequate notice of the suit, [citation], and be subject to the personal jurisdiction of the court, [citation]. In the present case, it is not contended that notice was inadequate; the only question is whether these particular petitioners were subject to the jurisdiction of the Oklahoma courts.

As has long been settled, and as we reaffirm today, a state court may exercise personal jurisdiction over a nonresident defendant only so long as there exist "minimum contacts" between the defendant and the forum State. [Citation.] The concept of minimum contacts, in turn, can be seen to perform two related, but distinguishable, functions. It protects the defendant against the burdens of litigating in a distant or inconvenient forum. And it acts to ensure that the States, through their courts, do not reach out beyond the limits imposed on them by their status as coequal sovereigns in a federal system.

The protection against inconvenient litigation is typically described in terms of "reasonableness" or "fairness." We have said that the defendant's contacts with the forum State must be such that maintenance of the suit "does not offend 'traditional notions of fair play and substantial justice.'" [Citation.] The relationship between the defendant and the forum must be such that it is "reasonable * * * to require the corporation to defend the particular suit which is brought there." [Citation.] Implicit in this emphasis on reasonableness is the understanding that the burden on the defendant, while always a primary concern, will in an appropriate case be considered in light of other relevant factors, including the forum State's interest in adjudicating the dispute, [citation]; the plaintiff's interest in obtaining convenient and effective relief, [citation], at least when that interest is not adequately protected by the plaintiff's power to choose the forum, [citation]; the interstate judicial system's interest in obtaining the most efficient resolution of controversies; and the shared interest of the several States in furthering fundamental substantive social policies, [citation].

* * *

Thus, the Due Process Clause "does not contemplate that a state may make binding a judgment *in personam* against an individual or corporate defendant with which the state has no contacts, ties, or relations." [Citation.]

* * *

Applying these principles to the case at hand, we find in the record before us a total absence of those affiliating circumstances that are a necessary predicate to any exercise of state-court jurisdiction. Petitioners carry on no activity whatsoever in Oklahoma. They close no sales and perform no services there. They avail themselves of none of the privileges and benefits of Oklahoma law. They solicit no business there either through salespersons or through advertising reasonably calculated to reach the State. Nor does the record show that they regularly sell cars at wholesale or retail to Oklahoma customers or residents or that they indirectly, through others, serve or seek to serve the Oklahoma market. In short, respondents seek to base jurisdiction on one, isolated occurrence and whatever inferences can be drawn therefrom: the fortuitous circumstance that a single Audi automobile, sold in New York to New York residents, happened to suffer an accident while passing through Oklahoma.

* * *

Because we find that petitioners have no "contacts, ties, or relations" with the State of Oklahoma, [citation], the judgment of the Supreme Court of Oklahoma is Reversed.

CASE 3-3

## Pretrial Procedure: Summary Judgment
## PARKER v. TWENTIETH CENTURY-FOX CORP.

Supreme Court of California, 1970
3 Cal.3d 176, 89 Cal.Rptr. 737, 474 P.2d 689

**Burke, J.**

Defendant Twentieth Century-Fox Film Corporation appeals from a summary judgment granting to plaintiff [Shirley MacLaine Parker] the recovery of agreed compensation under a written contract for her services as an actress in a motion picture. As will appear, we have concluded that the trial court correctly ruled in plaintiff's favor and that the judgment should be affirmed.

Plaintiff is well known as an actress, and in the contract between plaintiff and defendant is sometimes referred to as the "Artist." Under the contract, dated August 6, 1965, plaintiff was to play the female lead in defendant's contemplated production of a motion picture entitled "Bloomer Girl." The contract provided that defendant would pay plaintiff a minimum "guaranteed compensation" of $53,571.42 per week for 14 weeks commencing May 23, 1966, for a total of $750,000. Prior to May 1966 defendant decided not to produce the picture and by a letter dated April 4, 1966, it notified plaintiff of that decision and that it would not "comply with our obligations to you under" the written contract.

By the same letter and with the professed purpose "to avoid any damage to you," defendant instead offered to employ plaintiff as the leading actress in another film tentatively entitled "Big Country, Big Man" (hereinafter, "Big Country"). The compensation offered was identical, as were 31 of the 34 numbered provisions or articles of the original contract. Unlike "Bloomer Girl," however, which was to have been a musical production, "Big Country" was a dramatic "western type" movie. "Bloomer Girl" was to have been filmed in California; "Big Country" was to be produced in Australia. Also, certain terms in the proffered contract varied from those of the original. Plaintiff was given one week within which to accept; she did not and the offer lapsed. Plaintiff then commenced this action seeking recovery of the agreed guaranteed compensation.

The complaint sets forth two causes of action. The first is for money due under the contract; the second, based upon the same allegations as the first, is for damages resulting from defendant's breach of contract. Defendant in its answer admits the existence and validity of the contract, that plaintiff complied with all the conditions, covenants and promises and stood ready to complete the performance, and that defendant breached and "anticipatorily repudiated" the contract. It denies, however, that any money is due to plaintiff either under the contract or as a result of its breach, and pleads as an affirmative defense to both causes of action plaintiff's allegedly deliberate failure to mitigate damages, asserting that she unreasonably refused to accept its offer of the leading role in "Big Country."

Plaintiff moved for summary judgment under Code of Civil Procedure section 437c, the motion was granted, and summary judgment for $750,000 plus interest was entered in plaintiff's favor. This appeal by defendant followed.

The familiar rules are that the matter to be determined by the trial court on a motion for summary judgment is whether facts have been presented which give rise to a triable factual issue. The court may not pass upon the issue itself. Summary judgment is proper only if the affidavits or declarations in support of the moving party would be sufficient to sustain a judgment in his favor and his opponent does not by affidavit show facts sufficient to present a triable issue of fact. The affidavits of the moving party are strictly construed, and doubts as to the propriety of summary judgment should be resolved against granting the motion. Such summary procedure is drastic and should be used with caution so that it does not become a substitute for the open trial method of determining facts. The moving party cannot depend upon allegations in his own pleadings to cure deficient affidavits, nor can his adversary rely upon his own pleadings in lieu or in support of affidavits in opposition to a motion; however, a party can rely on his adversary's pleadings to establish facts not contained in his own affidavits. [Citations.] Also, the court may consider facts stipulated to by the parties and facts which are properly the subject of judicial notice. [Citations.]

* * *

Applying the foregoing rules to the record in the present case, with all intendments in favor of the party opposing the summary judgment motion—here, defendant—it is clear that the trial court correctly ruled that plaintiff's failure to accept defendant's tendered substitute employment could not be applied in mitigation of damages because the offer of the "Big Country" lead was of employment both different and inferior, and that no factual dispute was presented on that issue. The mere circumstance that "Bloomer Girl" was to be a musical review calling upon plaintiff's talents as a dancer as well as an actress, and was to be produced in the City of Los Angeles, whereas "Big Country" was a straight dramatic role in a "Western type" story taking place in an opal mine in Australia, demonstrates the difference in kind between the two employments; the female lead as a dramatic actress in a western style motion picture can by no stretch of imagination be considered the equivalent of or substantially similar to the lead in a song-and-dance production.

Additionally, the substitute "Big Country" offer proposed to eliminate or impair the director and screenplay approvals accorded to plaintiff under the original "Bloomer Girl" contract * * * and thus constituted an offer of inferior employment. No expertise or judicial notice is required in order to hold that the deprivation or infringement of an employee's rights held under an original employment contract converts the available "other employment" relied upon by the employer to mitigate damages, into inferior employment which the employee need not seek or accept. [Citation.]

* * *

The judgment is affirmed.

## CASE 3-4

### Arbitration
### VADEN v. DISCOVER BANK

Supreme Court of the United States, 2009

556 U.S. ___, 129 S.Ct. 1262, 173 L.Ed.2d 2

http://www.supremecourtus.gov/opinions/08pdf/07-773.pdf

**Ginsburg, J.**

This case originated as a garden-variety, state-law-based contract action: Discover sued its cardholder, [Betty] Vaden, in a Maryland state court to recover arrearages amounting to $10,610.74, plus interest and counsel fees. [Court's footnote: Discover apparently had no access to a federal forum for its suit against Vaden on the basis of diversity-of-citizenship jurisdiction. Under that head of federal-court jurisdiction, the amount in controversy must "excee[d] … $75,000."] Vaden's answer asserted usury as an affirmative defense. Vaden also filed several counterclaims, styled as class actions. Like Discover's complaint, Vaden's pleadings invoked only state law: Vaden asserted that Discover's demands for finance charges, interest, and late fees violated Maryland's credit laws. [Citation.] Neither party invoked—by notice to the other or petition to the state court—the clause in the credit card agreement providing for arbitration of "any claim or dispute between [Discover and Vaden]." [Citation.]

Faced with Vaden's counterclaims, Discover sought federal-court aid. It petitioned the United States District Court for the District of Maryland for an order, pursuant to § 4 of the Federal Arbitration Act (FAA or Act), [citation], compelling arbitration of Vaden's counterclaims. Although those counterclaims were framed under state law, Discover urged that they were governed entirely by federal law, specifically, § 27(a) of the Federal Deposit Insurance Act (FDIA), [citation], prescribes the interest rates state-chartered, federally insured banks like Discover can charge, "notwithstanding any State constitution or statute which is hereby preempted." This provision, Discover maintained, was completely preemptive, *i.e.,* it superseded otherwise applicable Maryland law, and placed Vaden's counterclaims under the exclusive governance of the FDIA. On that basis, Discover asserted, the District Court had authority to entertain the § 4 petition pursuant to [citation], which gives federal courts jurisdiction over cases "arising under" federal law.

[The District Court agreed and ordered arbitration. Reasoning that a Federal court has jurisdiction over a § 4 petition if the parties' underlying dispute presents a Federal question, the Fourth Circuit eventually affirmed. Vaden sought review by the U.S. Supreme Court, which granted *certiorari.*]

* * *

In 1925, Congress enacted the FAA [Federal Arbitration Act] "[t]o overcome judicial resistance to arbitration," [citation], and to declare "'a national policy favoring arbitration' of claims that parties contract to settle in that manner," [citation]. To that end, § 2 provides that arbitration agreements in contracts "involving commerce" are "valid, irrevocable, and enforceable." [Citation.] Section 4—the section at issue here—provides for United States district court enforcement of arbitration agreements. Petitions to compel arbitration, § 4 states, may be brought before "any United States district court which, save for such agreement, would have jurisdiction under title 28 [of the U.S. Code] of the subject matter of a suit arising out of the controversy between the parties." [Citation.]

The "body of federal substantive law" generated by elaboration of FAA § 2 is equally binding on state and federal courts. [Citations.] "As for jurisdiction over controversies touching arbitration," however, the Act is "something of an anomaly" in the realm of federal legislation: It "bestow[s] no federal jurisdiction but rather requir[es] [for access to a federal forum] an independent jurisdictional basis" over the parties' dispute. [Citation.] * * *

The independent jurisdictional basis Discover relies upon in this case is 28 U.S.C. § 1331, which vests in federal district courts jurisdiction over "all civil actions arising under the Constitution, laws, or treaties of the United States." Under the longstanding well-pleaded complaint rule, however, a suit "arises under" federal law "only when the plaintiff's statement of his own cause of action shows that it is based upon [federal law]." [Citation.] Federal jurisdiction cannot be predicated on an actual or anticipated defense: "It is not enough that the plaintiff alleges some anticipated defense to his cause of action and asserts that the defense is invalidated by some provision of [federal law]." [Citation.]

* * *

A *complaint* purporting to rest on state law, we have recognized, can be recharacterized as one "arising under" federal law if the law governing the complaint is exclusively federal. [Citation.] Under this so-called "complete preemption doctrine," a plaintiff's "state cause of action [may be recast] as a federal claim for relief, making [its] removal [by the defendant] proper on the basis of federal question jurisdiction." [Citation.] A state-law-based *counterclaim,* however, even if similarly susceptible to recharacterization, would remain nonremovable. Under our precedent construing § 1331, as just explained, counterclaims, even if they rely exclusively on federal substantive law, do not qualify a case for federal-court cognizance.

Attending to the language of the FAA and the above-described jurisdictional tenets, we approve the "look through" approach to this extent: A federal court may "look through" a § 4 petition to determine whether it is predicated on an action that "arises under" federal law; in keeping with the well-pleaded complaint rule as amplified in [citation] however, a federal court may not entertain a § 4 petition based on the contents, actual or hypothetical, of a counterclaim.

The text of § 4 drives our conclusion that a federal court should determine its jurisdiction by "looking through" a § 4 petition to the parties' underlying substantive controversy.

* * *

The phrase "save for [the arbitration] agreement" indicates that the district court should assume the absence of the arbitration agreement and determine whether it "would have jurisdiction under title 28" without it. [Citation.] * * *

* * *

Having determined that a district court should "look through" a § 4 petition, we now consider whether the court "would have [federal-question] jurisdiction" over "a suit arising out of the controversy" between Discover and Vaden. [Citation.] As explained above, § 4 of the FAA does not enlarge federal-court jurisdiction; rather, it confines federal courts to the jurisdiction they would have "save for [the arbitration] agreement." [Citation.] Mindful of that limitation, we read § 4 to convey that a party seeking to compel arbitration may gain a federal court's assistance only if, "save for" the agreement, the entire, actual "controversy between the parties," as they have framed it, could be litigated in federal court. We conclude that the parties' actual controversy, here precipitated by Discover's state-court suit for the balance due on Vaden's account, is not amenable to federal-court adjudication. Consequently, the § 4 petition Discover filed in the United States District Court for the District of Maryland must be dismissed.

* * *

Discover, we note, is not left without recourse. Under the FAA, state courts as well as federal courts are obliged to honor and enforce agreements to arbitrate. [Citations.] Discover may therefore petition a Maryland court for aid in enforcing the arbitration clause of its contracts with Maryland cardholders.

* * *

For the reasons stated, the District Court lacked jurisdiction to entertain Discover's § 4 petition to compel arbitration. The judgment of the Court of Appeals affirming the District Court's order is therefore reversed, and the case is remanded for further proceedings consistent with this opinion.

## QUESTIONS

1. List and describe the courts in the Federal court system and in a typical State court system.
2. Distinguish between appeal by right and writ of *certiorari.*
3. Distinguish between subject matter jurisdiction and jurisdiction over the parties.
4. Distinguish between exclusive and concurrent Federal jurisdiction. Identify the two types of Federal concurrent jurisdiction.
5. Define and describe a typical long-arm statute.
6. List and distinguish among the three types of jurisdiction over the parties.
7. Describe the purpose of pleadings.
8. List and explain the various stages of a civil proceeding.
9. Compare and contrast the following: demurrer, judgment on the pleadings, summary judgment, directed verdict, and judgment notwithstanding the verdict.
10. Compare and contrast litigation, arbitration, conciliation, and mediation.

# PROBLEMS

**1.** On June 15, a newspaper columnist predicted that the coast of State X would be flooded on the following September 1. Relying on this pronouncement, Gullible quit his job and sold his property at a loss so as not to be financially ruined. When the flooding did not occur, Gullible sued the columnist in a State X court for damages. The court dismissed the case for failure to state a cause of action under applicable State law. On appeal, the State X Supreme Court upheld the lower court. Three months after this ruling, the State Y Supreme Court heard an appeal in which a lower court had ruled that a reader could sue a columnist for falsely predicting flooding.

**(a)** Must the State Y Supreme Court follow the ruling of the State X Supreme Court as a matter of *stare decisis*?

**(b)** Should the State Y lower court have followed the ruling of the State X Supreme Court until the State Y Supreme Court issued a ruling on the issue?

**(c)** Once the State X Supreme Court issued its ruling, could the U.S. Supreme Court overrule the State X Supreme Court?

**(d)** If the State Y Supreme Court and the State X Supreme Court rule in exactly opposite ways, must the U.S. Supreme Court resolve the conflict between the two courts?

**2.** State Senator Bowdler convinced the legislature of State Z to pass a law requiring all professors to submit their class notes and transparencies to a board of censors to be sure that no "lewd" materials were presented to students at State universities. Professor Rabelais would like to challenge this law as violating his First Amendment rights under the U.S. Constitution.

**(a)** May Professor Rabelais challenge this law in the State Z courts?

**(b)** May Professor Rabelais challenge this law in a Federal district court?

**3.** While driving his car in Virginia, Carpe Diem, a resident of North Carolina, struck Butt, a resident of Alaska. As a result of the accident, Butt suffered more than $60,000 in medical expenses. Butt would like to know, if he personally serves the proper papers to Diem, whether he can obtain jurisdiction against Diem for damages in the following courts:

**(a)** Alaska State trial court

**(b)** Federal Circuit Court of Appeals for the Ninth Circuit (includes Alaska)

**(c)** Virginia State trial court

**(d)** Virginia Federal district court

**(e)** Federal Circuit Court of Appeals for the Fourth Circuit (includes Virginia and North Carolina)

**(f)** Virginia equity court

**(g)** North Carolina State trial court

**4.** Sam Simpleton, a resident of Kansas, and Nellie Naive, a resident of Missouri, each bought $85,000 in stock at local offices in their home States from Evil Stockbrokers, Inc. ("Evil"), a business incorporated in Delaware, with its principal place of business in Kansas. Both Simpleton and Naive believe that they were cheated by Evil Stockbrokers and would like to sue Evil for fraud. Assuming that no Federal question is at issue, assess the accuracy of the following statements:

**(a)** Simpleton can sue Evil in a Kansas State trial court.

**(b)** Simpleton can sue Evil in a Federal district court in Kansas.

**(c)** Naive can sue Evil in a Missouri State trial court.

**(d)** Naive can sue Evil in a Federal district court in Missouri.

**5.** The Supreme Court of State A ruled that, under the law of State A, pit bull owners must either keep their dogs fenced or pay damages to anyone bitten by the dogs. Assess the accuracy of the following statements:

**(a)** It is likely that the U.S. Supreme Court would issue a writ of *certiorari* in the "pit bull" case.

**(b)** If a case similar to the "pit bull" case were to come before the Supreme Court of State B in the future, the doctrine of *stare decisis* would leave the court no choice but to rule the same way as the "pit bull" case.

**6.** The Supreme Court of State G decided that the U.S. Constitution requires professors to warn students of their right to remain silent before questioning the students about cheating. This ruling directly conflicts with a decision of the Federal Court of Appeals for the circuit that includes State G.

**(a)** Must the Federal Circuit Court of Appeals withdraw its ruling?

**(b)** Must the Supreme Court of State G withdraw its ruling?

**7.** Thomas Clements brought an action to recover damages for breach of warranty against defendant Signa Corporation. (A warranty is an obligation that the seller of goods assumes with respect to the quality of the goods sold.) Clements had purchased a motorboat from Barney's Sporting Goods, an Illinois corporation. The boat was manufactured by Signa Corporation, an Indiana corporation with its principal place of business in Decatur, Indiana. Signa has no office in Illinois and no agent authorized to do business on its behalf within Illinois. Clements saw Signa's boats on display at the Chicago Boat Show. In addition, literature on Signa's boats was distributed at the Chicago Boat Show. Several boating magazines, delivered to Clements in Illinois, contained advertisements for Signa's boats. Clements also had seen Signa's boats on display at Barney's Sporting Goods Store in Palatine, Illinois, where he eventually purchased the boat. A written warranty issued by Signa was delivered to Clements in Illinois. Although Signa was served with a summons, it failed to enter an appearance in this case. The court entered a default order and, subsequently, a judgment of $6,220 against Signa. Signa appealed. Decision?

**8.** Mariana Deutsch worked as a knitwear mender and attended a school for beauticians. The sink in her apartment collapsed on her foot, fracturing her big toe and making it painful for her to stand. She claims that as a consequence of the injury she was compelled to abandon her plans to become a beautician because that job requires long periods of standing. She also asserts that she was unable to work at her current job for a month. She filed a tort claim against Hewes Street Realty for negligence in failing properly to maintain the sink. She brought the suit in Federal district court, claiming damages of $25,000. Her medical expenses and actual loss of salary were less than $1,500; the rest of her alleged damages were for loss of future earnings as a beautician. Hewes Street moved to dismiss the suit on the basis that Deutsch's claim fell short of the jurisdictional requirement, which then was $10,000, and that the Federal court therefore lacked subject matter jurisdiction over her claim. Decision?

**9.** Vette sued Aetna under a fire insurance policy. Aetna moved for summary judgment on the basis that the pleadings and discovered evidence showed a lack of an insurable interest in Vette. (An "insurable interest" exists where the insured derives a monetary benefit or advantage from the preservation or continued existence of the property or would sustain an economic loss from its destruction.) Aetna provided ample evidence to infer that Vette had no insurable interest in the contents of the burned building. Vette also provided sufficient evidence to put in dispute this factual issue. The trial court granted the motion for summary judgment. Vette appealed. Decision?

**10.** Mark Womer and Brian Perry were members of the U.S. Navy and were stationed in Newport, Rhode Island. On April 10, Womer allowed Perry to borrow his automobile so that Perry could visit his family in New Hampshire. Later that day, while operating Womer's vehicle, Perry was involved in an accident in Manchester, New Hampshire. As a result of the accident, Tzannetos Tavoularis was injured. Tavoularis brought action against Womer in a New Hampshire superior court, contending that Womer was negligent in lending the automobile to Perry when he knew or should have known that Perry did not have a valid driver's license. Womer sought to dismiss the action on the ground that the New Hampshire courts lacked jurisdiction over him, citing the following facts: (a) he lived and worked in Georgia; (b) he had no relatives in New Hampshire; (c) he neither owned property nor possessed investments in New Hampshire; and (d) he had never conducted business in New Hampshire. Did the New Hampshire courts have jurisdiction?

**11.** Kenneth Thomas brought suit against his former employer, Kidder, Peabody & Company, and two of its employees, Barclay Perry and James Johnston, in a dispute over commissions on sales of securities. When he applied to work at Kidder, Peabody & Company, Thomas had filled out a form, which contained an arbitration agreement clause. Thomas had also registered with the New York Stock Exchange (NYSE). Rule 347 of the NYSE provides that any controversy between a registered representative and a member company shall be settled by arbitration. Kidder, Peabody & Company is a member of the NYSE. Thomas refused to arbitrate, relying on Section 229 of the California Labor Code, which provides that actions for the collection of wages may be maintained "without regard to the existence of any private agreement to arbitrate." Perry and Johnston filed a petition in a California State court to compel arbitration under Section 2 of the Federal Arbitration Act. Should the petition of Perry and Johnston be granted?

**12.** Steven Gwin bought a lifetime Termite Protection Plan for his home from the local office of Allied-Bruce, a franchise of Terminix International Company. The plan provided that Allied-Bruce would "protect" Gwin's house against termite infestation, reinspect periodically, provide additional treatment if necessary, and repair damage caused by new termite infestations. Terminix International guaranteed the fulfillment of these contractual provisions. The plan also provided that all disputes arising out of the contract would be settled exclusively by arbitration. Four years later Gwin had Allied-Bruce reinspect the house in anticipation of selling it. Allied-Bruce gave the house a "clean bill of health." Gwin then sold the house and transferred the Termite Protection Plan to Dobson. Shortly thereafter, Dobson found the house to be infested with termites. Allied-Bruce attempted to treat and repair the house, using materials from out of state, but these efforts failed to satisfy Dobson. Dobson then sued Gwin, Allied-Bruce, and Terminix International in an Alabama state court. Allied-Bruce and Terminix International asked for a stay of these proceedings until arbitration could be carried out as stipulated in the contract. The trial court refused to grant the stay. The Alabama Supreme Court upheld that ruling, citing a state statute that makes predispute arbitration agreements unenforceable. The court found that the Federal Arbitration Act, which preempts conflicting state law, did not apply to this contract because its connection to interstate commerce was too slight. Was the Alabama Supreme Court correct? Explain.

# CHAPTER 4
# Constitutional Law

As mentioned in *Chapter 1*, public law is that branch of substantive law which deals with the rights and powers of government in its political or governing capacity and in its relation to individuals or groups. Public law consists of constitutional law, administrative law, and criminal law. The first is discussed in this chapter; *Chapter 5* addresses administrative law, and *Chapter 6* covers criminal law.

As the fundamental and organic law of particular jurisdictions, constitutions serve a number of critical functions. They are the supreme law of their respective jurisdictions. In addition, they establish the structure of and allocate power among the various levels of government. They also impose restrictions upon the powers of government and enumerate the rights and liberties of the people.

The Constitution of the United States (reprinted in *Appendix A*) was adopted on September 17, 1787, by representatives of the thirteen newly created States. Its purpose is stated in the preamble:

> We the People of the United States, in Order to form a more perfect Union, establish Justice, insure domestic Tranquility, provide for the common defence, promote the general Welfare, and secure the Blessings of Liberty to ourselves and our Posterity, do ordain and establish this Constitution for the United States of America.

Although the framers of the U.S. Constitution enumerated precisely what rights and authority were vested in the new national government, they considered it unnecessary to list those liberties the people were to reserve for themselves. As Alexander Hamilton, a coauthor of *The Federalist*, explained, "Here in strictness the people surrender nothing; and as they retain everything, they have no need of particular reservations." Nonetheless, during the State conventions to ratify the Constitution, people expressed fear that the Federal government might abuse its powers. To calm these concerns, the first Congress approved ten amendments to the U.S. Constitution, now known as the Bill of Rights, which were adopted on December 15, 1791.

The Bill of Rights restricts the powers and authority of the Federal government and establishes many of the civil and political rights enjoyed in the United States, including the right to due process of law and freedoms of speech, press, religion, assembly, and petition. Although the Bill of Rights does not apply directly to the States, the Supreme Court has held that the Fourteenth Amendment incorporates most of the principal guarantees of the Bill of Rights, thus making them applicable to the States.

This chapter will discuss constitutional law as it applies to business and commerce. It will begin by surveying some of the basic principles of constitutional law. Then it will examine the allocation of power between the Federal and State governments with respect to the regulation of business. Finally, it will discuss the constitutional restrictions on the power of government to regulate business.

## BASIC PRINCIPLES OF CONSTITUTIONAL LAW

The delegates to the constitutional convention desired a stronger national government but feared the accumulation of governmental power in the hands of one person or group. These two concerns underlie several principles basic to the U.S. Constitution: Federalism, Federal supremacy, judicial review, and separation of powers. An additional basic principle of constitutional law is State action.

### FEDERALISM

Federalism is the division of governing power between the Federal government and the States. The U.S. Constitution enumerates the powers of the Federal government and specifically reserves to the States or the people the powers it does not expressly delegate to the Federal government. Accordingly, the Federal government is a government of enumerated, or limited, powers, and a specified power must authorize each of its acts. The doctrine of enumerated powers does not, however, significantly limit the Federal government because a number of the enumerated powers, in particular the power to regulate interstate and foreign commerce, have been broadly interpreted.

Furthermore, the Constitution grants Congress not only specified powers but the power "[t]o make all Laws which shall be necessary and proper for carrying into Execution the foregoing Powers, and all other Powers vested by this Constitution in the Government of the United States, or in any Department or Officer thereof." In the Supreme Court's view, the Necessary and Proper Clause enables Congress to legislate in areas not mentioned in the list of enumerated powers as long as such legislation reasonably relates to some enumerated power. As Chief Justice John Marshall noted in the landmark case of *McCulloch v. Maryland*, 17 U.S. (4 Wheat.) 316 (1819), "[l]et the end be legitimate, let it be within the scope of the constitution, and all means which are appropriate, which are plainly adapted to that end, which are not prohibited, but consist with the letter and spirit of the constitution, are constitutional."

## FEDERAL SUPREMACY AND PREEMPTION

Although under our Federalist system the States retain significant powers, the **Supremacy Clause** of the U.S. Constitution provides that, within its own sphere, Federal law is supreme and State law must, in case of conflict, yield. Accordingly, any State constitutional provision or law that conflicts with the U.S. Constitution or valid Federal laws or treaties is unconstitutional and may not be given effect. In *McCulloch v. Maryland*, Chief Justice Marshall stated, "This great principle is, that the Constitution and the laws made in pursuance thereof are supreme; that they control the Constitution and laws of the respective states, and cannot be controlled by them."

Under the Supremacy Clause, whenever Congress enacts legislation within its constitutional powers, the Federal action **preempts** (overrides) any conflicting State legislation. Even a State regulation that is not obviously in conflict must give way if Congress clearly has intended that its enactment should preempt the field. In such an instance, nonconflicting State legislation would be prohibited. This intent may be expressly stated in the legislation or inferred from the pervasiveness of the Federal regulation, the need for uniformity, or the danger of conflict between concurrent Federal and State regulation.

When Congress has not intended to displace all State legislation, then nonconflicting State legislation is permitted. When Congress has not acted, the fact that it has the power to act does not prevent the States from acting. Until Congress exercises its power to preempt, State regulation is permitted.

◆ **SEE CASES 3-4 AND 4-1**

## JUDICIAL REVIEW

**Judicial review** describes the process by which the courts examine governmental actions to determine whether they conform to the U.S. Constitution. If governmental action violates the U.S. Constitution, under judicial review the courts will invalidate that action. Judicial review extends to legislation, acts of the executive branch, and the decisions of inferior courts. Such review scrutinizes actions of both the Federal and State governments and applies to both the same standards of constitutionality. The U.S. Supreme Court is the final authority as to the constitutionality of any Federal and State law. The U.S. Constitution does not expressly provide for judicial review, but in 1803 Chief Justice John Marshall, speaking for the Court, declared the existence of such authority in the landmark case of *Marbury v. Madison*, 5 U.S. (1 Cranch) 137 (1803).

## SEPARATION OF POWERS

Another fundamental principle on which our government is founded is that of separation of powers. The U.S. Constitution vests power in three distinct and independent branches of government: the executive, legislative, and judicial branches. The doctrine of separation of powers prevents excessive power from concentrating in any group or branch of government. Basically, the legislative branch is granted the power to make the law, the executive branch to enforce the law, and the judicial branch to interpret the law. The separation of powers is not complete, however, and in some instances two or more branches share power. For example, the executive branch has veto power over legislation enacted by Congress; the legislative branch must approve many executive appointments; and the judicial branch may declare both legislation and executive actions unconstitutional. Nevertheless, shared powers usually operate as checks and balances on the power of the branches sharing them.

◆ **SEE FIGURE 4-1: Separation of Powers: Checks and Balances**

## STATE ACTION

Most of the protections provided by the U.S. Constitution and its amendments apply only to Federal or State governmental action, collectively referred to as state action. Only the Thirteenth Amendment, which abolishes slavery or involuntary servitude, applies to the actions of private individuals. By statute, however, the government may extend to private activity some or all of the protections that guard against state action. **State action** includes any actions of the Federal and State governments, as well as their subdivisions, such as city or county governments and agencies. For example, when a legislature, executive officer, or court takes some official action against an individual, state action has occurred.

◆ **FIGURE 4-1: Separation of Powers: Checks and Balances**

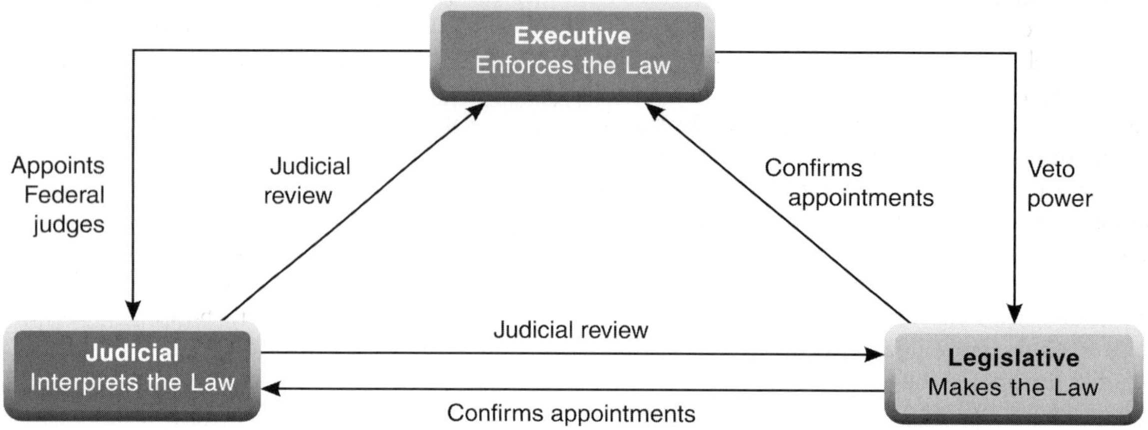


In addition, action taken by private citizens may constitute state action if the State exercised coercive power over the challenged private action, encouraged the action significantly, or was substantially entangled with the action. For example, the Supreme Court found state action when the Supreme Court of Missouri ordered a lower court to enforce an agreement among white property owners that prohibited the transfer of their property to nonwhites. *Shelley v. Kraemer*, 334 U.S. 1 (1948). Moreover, if "private" individuals or entities engage in public functions, their actions may be considered state action subject to constitutional limitations. For example, in *Marsh v. Alabama*, 326 U.S. 501 (1946), the Supreme Court held that a company town was subject to the First Amendment because the State had allowed the company to exercise all of the public functions and activities usually conducted by a town government. Since that case, the Supreme Court has been less willing to find state action based upon the performance of public functions by private entities; the Court now limits such findings to functions "traditionally exclusively reserved to the State." For instance, in *Jackson v. Metropolitan Edison Co.*, 419 U.S. 345 (1974), the Court held that a privately owned electric utility was *not* subject to the Due Process Clause, even though the State had granted the utility a monopoly, because operating a utility is *not* state action. In reaching this conclusion, the Court held that the fact that the State could have operated its own utilities did not make the activity of providing electric services state action.

◆ **SEE CASE 4-2**

## POWERS OF GOVERNMENT

As previously stated, the U.S. Constitution created a Federal government of enumerated powers. Moreover, as the Tenth Amendment declares, "[t]he powers not delegated to the United States by the Constitution, nor prohibited by it to the States, are reserved to the States respectively, or to the people." Consequently, legislation Congress enacts must be based on a specified power granted to the Federal government by the Constitution or be reasonably necessary to carry out an enumerated power.

Some governmental powers may be exercised only by the Federal government. These exclusive Federal powers include the power to establish laws regarding bankruptcy, to establish post offices, to grant patents and copyrights, to coin currency, to wage war, and to enter into treaties. Other governmental powers are concurrent and may be exercised by both the Federal government and the States. Concurrent powers include taxation, spending, and the exercise of police power (regulation of public health, safety, and welfare).

This part of the chapter examines the sources and extent of the powers of the Federal government—as well as the residual power of the States—to regulate business and commerce.

### FEDERAL COMMERCE POWER

The U.S. Constitution provides that "[t]he Congress shall have Power.... To regulate Commerce with foreign Nations, and among the several States...." Article I, Section 8. This Commerce Clause has two important effects: (1) it provides the Federal government with a broad source of power for regulating the economy, and (2) it restricts State regulations that obstruct or unduly burden interstate commerce. As the U.S. Supreme Court has stated, "The Clause is both a prolific sourc[e] of national power and an equally prolific source of conflict with legislation of the state[s]." This section will discuss the first of these effects; the next section will discuss the second effect.

The U.S. Supreme Court interprets the Commerce Clause as granting virtually complete power to Congress to regulate the economy and business. More specifically, under the Commerce Clause, Congress has the power to regulate (1) the channels of interstate commerce, (2) the instrumentalities of interstate commerce, and (3) those activities having a substantial relation to interstate commerce. A court may invalidate legislation enacted under the Commerce Clause only if it is clear either (1) that there is no rational basis for a congressional finding that the regulated activity affects interstate commerce, *or* (2) that there is no reasonable connection between the selected regulatory means and the asserted ends.

Because of the broad and permissive interpretation of the commerce power, Congress currently regulates a vast range of activities. Many of the activities discussed in this text are regulated by the Federal government through its exercise of the commerce power, including Federal crimes, consumer warranties and credit transactions, electronic funds transfers, trademarks, unfair trade practices, other consumer transactions, residential real estate transactions, consumer and employee safety, labor relations, civil rights in employment, transactions in securities, and environmental protection.

## STATE REGULATION OF COMMERCE

The Commerce Clause, as previously discussed, specifically grants to Congress the power to regulate commerce among the States. In addition to acting as a broad source of Federal power, the clause also implicitly restricts the States' power to regulate activities if the result obstructs or unduly burdens interstate commerce.

**Regulations** The Supreme Court ultimately decides the extent to which State regulation may affect interstate commerce. In doing so, the Court weighs and balances several factors: (1) the necessity and importance of the State regulation, (2) the burden it imposes upon interstate commerce, and (3) the extent to which it discriminates against interstate commerce in favor of local concerns. The application of these factors involves case-by-case analysis. In general, where a State statute regulates evenhandedly to accomplish a legitimate State interest and its effects on interstate commerce are only incidental, the Court will uphold the statute unless the burden imposed on interstate commerce is clearly excessive compared with the local benefits. The Court will uphold a discriminatory regulation only if no other reasonable method of achieving a legitimate local interest exists.

◆ **SEE CASE 4-3**

**Taxation** The Commerce Clause, in conjunction with the Import-Export Clause, also limits the power of the States to tax. The Import-Export Clause provides: "No State shall, without the Consent of the Congress, lay any Imposts or Duties on Imports or Exports." Article I, Section 10. Together, the Commerce Clause and the Import-Export Clause exempt from State taxation goods that have entered the stream of commerce, whether they are interstate or foreign, imports or exports. The purpose of this immunity is to protect goods in commerce from both discriminatory and cumulative State taxes. Once the goods enter the stream of interstate or foreign commerce, the power of the State to tax ceases and does not resume until the goods are delivered to the purchaser or the owner terminates the movement of the goods through commerce.

The Due Process Clause of the Fourteenth Amendment also restricts the power of States to tax. Under the Due Process Clause, for a State tax to be constitutional, sufficient nexus must exist between the State and the person, thing, or activity to be taxed.

## FEDERAL FISCAL POWERS

The Federal government exerts a dominating influence over the national economy through its control of financial matters. Much of this impact, as previously discussed, results from the exercise of its regulatory powers under the Commerce Clause. In addition, the government derives substantial influence from powers that are independent of the Commerce Clause. These include (1) the power to tax, (2) the power to spend, (3) the power to borrow and coin money, and (4) the power of eminent domain.

**Taxation** The Federal government's power to tax, although extremely broad, is subject to three major limitations: (1) direct taxes other than income taxes must be apportioned among the States, (2) all custom duties and excise taxes must be uniform throughout the United States, and (3) no duties may be levied upon exports from any State.

Besides raising revenues, taxes also have regulatory and socioeconomic effects. For example, import taxes and custom duties can protect domestic industry from foreign competition. Graduated or progressive tax rates and exemptions may further social policies seeking to redistribute wealth. Tax credits encourage investment in favored enterprises, to the disadvantage of unfavored ones. The Court will uphold a tax that does more than just raise revenue "so long as the motive of Congress and the effect of its legislative action are to secure revenue for the benefit of the general government…." *J.W. Hampton Co. v. United States*, 276 U.S. 394 (1928).

**Spending Power** The Constitution authorizes the Federal government to pay debts and to spend for the common defense and general welfare of the United States. Article I, Section 8. The spending power of Congress, which is extremely broad, will be upheld so long as it does not violate a specific constitutional limitation upon Federal power.

Furthermore, through its spending power, Congress may accomplish indirectly what it may not do directly. For example, in *South Dakota v. Dole*, 483 U.S. 203 (1987), the Supreme Court held that Congress could condition a State's receipt of Federal highway funds on that State's mandating twenty-one as the minimum drinking age, even though the Twenty-first Amendment grants the States significant powers with respect to alcohol consumption within their respective borders. As the Court noted, "Constitutional limitations on Congress when exercising its spending power are less exacting than those on its authority to regulate directly."

**Borrowing and Coining Money** The U.S. Constitution also grants Congress the power to borrow money on the credit of the United States and to coin money. Article I, Section 8. These two powers have enabled the Federal government to establish a national banking system, the Federal Reserve System, and specialized Federal lending programs such as the Federal Land Bank. Through these and other institutions and agencies, the Federal government wields extensive control over national fiscal and monetary policies and exerts considerable influence over interest rates, the money supply, and foreign exchange rates.

**Eminent Domain** The government's power to take private property for public use, known as the power of **eminent domain**, is recognized as one of the inherent powers of government in the U.S. Constitution and in the constitutions of the States. Nonetheless, the power is carefully limited. The Fifth Amendment to the Constitution contains a Takings Clause that specifies that "nor shall private property be taken for public use, without just compensation." Although this amendment applies only to the Federal government, the Supreme Court has held that the Takings Clause is incorporated through the Fourteenth Amendment and is therefore applicable to the States. Moreover, similar or identical provisions are found in State constitutions.

As the language of the Takings Clause indicates, the taking must be for a public use. Public use has been held to be synonymous with public purpose. Thus, private entities such as railroads and housing authorities may use the government's power of eminent domain so long as the entity's use of the property benefits the public. When the government or a private entity properly takes property under the power of eminent domain, the owners of the property must receive just compensation, which has been interpreted as the fair market value of the property.

The Supreme Court has held that the Takings Clause requires just compensation only if a governmental taking actually occurs, not if governmental regulation only reduces the value of the property. If, however, a regulation deprives the owner of all economic use of the property, then a taking has occurred. Eminent domain is discussed further in *Chapter 50*.

◆ **SEE CASE 50-2**

◆ **SEE FIGURE 4-2: Powers of Government**

◆ FIGURE 4-2: **Powers of Government**

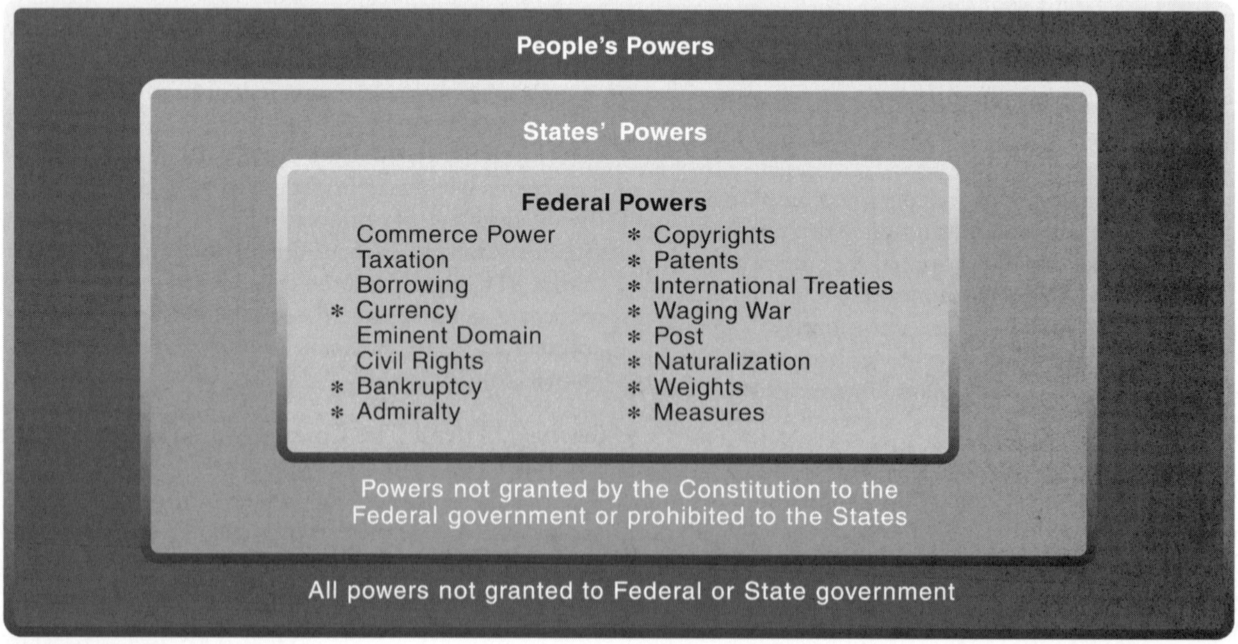


*Exclusive power

## LIMITATIONS ON GOVERNMENT

The Constitution of the United States grants certain enumerated powers to the Federal government while reserving other powers, without enumeration, to the States. The Constitution and its amendments, however, impose limits on the powers of both the Federal government and the States. This part of the chapter will discuss those limitations most applicable to business: (1) the Contract Clause, (2) the First Amendment, (3) due process, and (4) equal protection. The first of these—the Contract Clause—applies only to the actions of State governments, whereas the other three apply to both the Federal government and the States.

None of these restrictions operates as an absolute limitation but instead triggers scrutiny by the courts to determine whether the governmental power exercised encroaches impermissibly upon the interest the Constitution protects. The U.S. Supreme Court has used different levels of scrutiny, depending on the interest affected and the nature of the governmental action. Although the Court has differentiated levels of scrutiny most thoroughly in the area of equal protection, such differentiation also occurs in other areas, including substantive due process and protection of free speech.

The least rigorous level of scrutiny is the **rational relationship test**, which requires that governmental action conceivably bear some rational relationship to a legitimate governmental interest that the governmental action proposes to further. The most exacting level of scrutiny is the **strict scrutiny test**, which requires that the governmental action be necessary to promote a compelling governmental interest. Finally, under the **intermediate test**, the governmental action must have a substantial relationship to an important governmental objective. These standards will be more fully explained later.

◆ SEE FIGURE 4-3: **Limitations on Government**

### CONTRACT CLAUSE

Article I, Section 10, of the Constitution provides: "No State shall … pass any … Law impairing the Obligation of Contracts…." The Supreme Court has used this clause to restrict States from retroactively modifying public charters and private contracts. For example, the Contract Clause protects against impairing the charter of a corporation formed under a State incorporation statute. Although the Contract Clause does not apply to the Federal government, due process limits the Federal government's power to impair contracts.

Moreover, the Supreme Court has held that the Contract Clause does not preclude the States from exercising eminent domain or their police powers. As the Supreme Court stated, "No legislature can bargain away the public health or the public morals." *Stone v. Mississippi*, 101 U.S. (11 Otto) 814 (1879).

### FIRST AMENDMENT

The First Amendment states:

> Congress shall make no law respecting an establishment of religion, or prohibiting the free exercise thereof; or abridging the freedom of speech, or of the press; or the right of the people peaceably to assemble, and to petition the Government for a redress of grievances.

The First Amendment's protection of free speech is not absolute. Some forms of speech, such as obscenity, receive no protection. Most forms of speech, however, are protected by the strict or exacting scrutiny standard, which requires the existence of a compelling and legitimate State interest to justify a restriction of speech. In furthering such an interest, the State must use means that least restrict free speech. This section will examine the application of the First Amendment's guarantee of free speech to (1) corporate political speech, (2) commercial speech, and (3) defamation.

**Corporate Political Speech** Freedom of speech is indispensable to the discovery and spread of political truth; indeed, "the best test of truth is the power of the thought to get itself accepted in the competition of the market." *Abrams v. United States*, 250 U.S. 616 (1919) (Holmes's dissent). To

◆ FIGURE 4-3: **Limitations on Government**

| Test/Interest | Equal Protection | Substantive Due Process | Free Speech |
|---|---|---|---|
| **Strict Scrutiny** | Fundamental Rights<br>Suspect Classifications | Fundamental Rights | Protected Noncommercial Speech |
| **Intermediate** | Gender<br>Legitimacy | | Commercial Speech |
| **Rational Relationship** | Economic Regulation | Economic Regulation | Nonprotected Speech |

promote this competition of ideas, the First Amendment's guarantee of free speech applies not only to individuals but also to corporations. Accordingly, corporations may not be prohibited from speaking out on political issues. For example, in *First National Bank v. Bellotti*, 435 U.S. 765 (1978), the Supreme Court held unconstitutional a Massachusetts criminal statute that prohibited banks and business corporations from making contributions and expenditures with regard to most referenda issues. The Court in *Bellotti* held that if speech is otherwise protected, the fact that the speaker is a corporation does not alter the speech's protected status.

The Supreme Court retreated somewhat from its holding in *Bellotti* when it upheld a State statute prohibiting corporations, except media corporations, from using general treasury funds to make independent expenditures in elections for public office but permitting such expenditures from segregated funds used solely for political purposes. The Court held that the statute did not violate the First Amendment because the burden on corporations' exercise of political expression was justified by a compelling State interest in preventing corruption in the political arena: "the corrosive and distorting effects of immense aggregations of wealth that are accumulated with the help of the corporate form and that have little or no correlation to the public's support for the corporations' political ideas." The Court held that the statute was sufficiently narrowly tailored because it "is precisely targeted to eliminate the distortion caused by corporate spending while also allowing corporations to express their political views" by making expenditures through segregated funds. *Austin v. Michigan Chamber of Commerce*, 494 U.S. 652 (1990).

In a recent landmark five-to-four decision, *Citizens United v. Federal Election Commission*, 558 U.S. ___ (2010), the U.S. Supreme Court explicitly overruled the *Austin* case. *Citizens United* involved a First Amendment challenge to a Federal law that prohibited corporations and unions from using their general funds to make independent expenditures for speech defined as an "electioneering communication" or for speech expressly advocating the election or defeat of a candidate. (An electioneering communication is "any broadcast, cable, or satellite communication" that "refers to a clearly identified candidate for Federal office" and is made within thirty days of a primary election.) The Supreme Court invalidated these provisions as conflicting with the First Amendment, holding: "We return to the principle established in … *Bellotti* that the Government may not suppress political speech on the basis of the speaker's corporate identity. No sufficient governmental interest justifies limits on the political speech of nonprofit or for-profit corporations."

**COMMERCIAL SPEECH** Commercial speech is expression related to the economic interests of the speaker and her audience, such as advertisements for a product or service. Since the mid-1970s, U.S. Supreme Court decisions have eliminated the doctrine that commercial speech is wholly outside the protection of the First Amendment. Instead, the Court has established the principle that speech proposing a commercial transaction is entitled to protection which, though extensive, is less considerable than that accorded political speech. Protection is accorded commercial speech because of the interest such communication holds for the advertiser, consumer, and general public. Advertising and similar messages convey important information for the proper and efficient distribution of resources in our free market system. At the same time, commercial speech is less valuable and less vulnerable than other varieties of speech and therefore does not merit complete First Amendment protection.

In commercial speech cases, a four-part analysis has developed. First, the court must determine whether the expression is protected by the First Amendment. For commercial speech to come within that provision, such speech, at the least, must concern lawful activity and not be misleading. Second, the court must determine whether the asserted governmental interest is substantial. If both inquiries yield positive answers, then, third, the court must determine whether the regulation directly advances the governmental interest asserted and, fourth, whether or not the regulation is more extensive than is necessary to serve that interest. The Supreme Court recently held that governmental restrictions of commercial speech need not be absolutely the least severe so long as they are "narrowly tailored" to achieve the governmental objective.

Because the constitutional protection extended to commercial speech is based on the informational function of advertising, governments may regulate or suppress commercial messages that do not accurately inform the public about lawful activity. "The government may ban forms of communication more likely to deceive the public than to inform it, or commercial speech related to illegal activity." *Central Hudson Gas and Electric Corp. v. Public Service Commission*, 447 U.S. 557 (1980). Therefore, governmental regulation of false and misleading advertising is permissible under the First Amendment.

◆ **SEE CASE 4-4**

**DEFAMATION** Defamation is a civil wrong or tort that consists of disgracing or diminishing a person's reputation through the communication of a false statement. An example would be the publication of a false statement that a person had committed a crime or had a loathsome disease. For further discussion of defamation, see *Chapter 7*.

Because defamation involves a communication, it receives the protection extended to speech by the First Amendment. Moreover, the case of *New York Times Co. v. Sullivan*, 376 U.S. 254 (1964), held that a public official who was defamed in regard to his conduct, fitness, or role as public official could not recover in a defamation action unless the statement was made with *actual malice*, which requires clear and convincing proof that the defendant had knowledge of the falsity of the communication or acted in reckless disregard of its truth or falsity. This restriction upon the right to recover for defamation is based on "a profound national commitment to the principle that debate on public issues should be uninhibited, robust and wide-open, and that it may well include vehement, caustic and sometimes unpleasantly sharp attacks on government and public officials." The communication may deal with the official's qualifications for and his performance in office, which would likely include most aspects of character and public conduct.

In addition, the Supreme Court has extended the same rule to public figures and candidates for public office. Though the Court has not precisely defined the term public figure, examples of persons held to be public figures have included a well-known football coach of a State university and a retired army general who had taken a prominent and controversial position regarding racial segregation. In *Gertz v. Robert Welch, Inc.*, 418 U.S. 323 (1974), the Court explained:

> For the most part [public figures are] those who attain this status [by assuming] roles of especial prominence in the affairs of society. Some occupy positions of such persuasive power and influence that they are deemed public figures for all purposes. More commonly, those classed as public figures have thrust themselves to the forefront of particular public controversies in order to influence the resolution of the issues involved.

Thus, the public official or public figure must prove that the defendant published the defamatory and false comment about him with knowledge or in reckless disregard of the comment's falsity and its defamatory character. In a defamation suit brought by a private person (one who is neither a public official nor a public figure), the plaintiff must prove that the defendant published the defamatory and false comment with malice *or* negligence.

## DUE PROCESS

The Fifth and Fourteenth Amendments prohibit the Federal and State governments, respectively, from depriving any person of life, liberty, or property without due process of law. Due process has two different aspects: *substantive* due process and *procedural* due process. As discussed in *Chapter 1*, substantive law creates, defines, or regulates legal rights, whereas procedural law establishes the rules for enforcing those rights. Accordingly, **substantive due process** concerns the compatibility of a law or governmental action with fundamental constitutional rights such as free speech. In contrast, **procedural due process** involves the review of the decision-making process that enforces substantive laws and results in depriving a person of life, liberty, or property.

**Substantive Due Process** Substantive due process, which involves a court's determination of whether a particular governmental action is compatible with individual liberties, addresses the constitutionality of the substance of a legal rule, not the fairness of the process by which the rule is applied. From 1885 until 1937, the Supreme Court viewed substantive due process as authorization to act as a "super legislature," invalidating any law it considered unwise. Since 1937, the Court has abandoned this approach and no longer overturns legislation affecting economic and social interests, so long as the legislation relates rationally to legitimate governmental objectives.

Nonetheless, the Court will carefully scrutinize legislation that affects the fundamental rights of individuals under the Constitution to determine whether such legislation is necessary to promote a compelling or overriding State interest. Included among the fundamental rights that trigger the strict scrutiny standard of substantive due process are (1) the First Amendment rights of freedom of speech, religion, press, peaceful assembly, and petition; (2) the right to engage in interstate travel; (3) the right to vote; (4) the right to privacy; and (5) the right to marry.

◆ **SEE CASE 7-1**

**Procedural Due Process** Procedural due process pertains to the governmental decision-making process that results in depriving a person of life, liberty, or property. As the Supreme Court has interpreted procedural due process, the government is required to provide an individual with a fair procedure if, but only if, the person faces deprivation of life, liberty, or property. When governmental action adversely affects an individual but does not deny life, liberty, or property, the government is not required to give the person any hearing at all.

**Liberty**, for the purposes of procedural due process, generally includes the ability of individuals to engage in freedom of action and choice regarding their personal lives. Any significant physical restraint constitutes a deprivation of liberty, which requires procedural safeguards. The most important and common examples of proceedings involving deprivation of liberty are criminal proceedings, discussed more fully in *Chapter 6*. In addition, civil proceedings that result in depriving a person of freedom of action are subject to the requirements of procedural due process. Liberty also includes an individual's right to engage in the fundamental rights described above.

**Property**, for the purposes of procedural due process, includes not only all forms of real and personal property but also certain entitlements conferred by the government, such as social security payments and food stamps. In *Logan v. Zimmerman Brush Co.*, 455 U.S. 422 (1982), the Supreme Court stated, "The hallmark of property … is an individual entitlement grounded in state law, which cannot be removed except 'for cause.'" Under this interpretation of property, the Court has, for example, found protected property interests in high school education, when attendance is required; welfare benefits, when the individual has previously been found to meet the statutory requirements; social security payments; and a driver's license. On the other hand, if a public employee's job is terminable at any time, he has no property interest in his employment; accordingly, he may lose his job without any procedural due process protections.

When applicable, procedural due process requires that the procedure be fundamentally fair and impartial in resolving the factual and legal basis for the governmental actions that result in the deprivation of life, liberty, or property. The Supreme Court generally considers three factors in determining which procedures are required: the importance of the individual interest involved; the adequacy of the existing procedural protections and the probable value, if any, of additional safeguards; and the governmental interest in fiscal and administrative efficiency.

◆ **SEE CASES 3-2 AND 7-1**

## EQUAL PROTECTION

The Fourteenth Amendment states that "nor shall any State … deny to any person within its jurisdiction the equal protection of the laws." Although this amendment applies only to the actions of State governments, the Supreme Court has interpreted the Due Process Clause of the Fifth Amendment to subject Federal actions to the same standards of review. Basically, the guarantee of equal protection requires that government action provide similar treatment for similarly situated persons. Since 1937, when the Supreme Court abandoned substantive due process as a critical check on legislation, the equal protection guarantee has become the most important constitutional concept protecting individual rights.

When governmental action involves the classification of people, the equal protection guarantee comes into play. In determining whether governmental action satisfies the equal protection guarantee, the Supreme Court uses one of three standards of review, depending on the nature of the right involved: (1) the rational relationship test, (2) the strict scrutiny test, or (3) the intermediate test.

**Rational Relationship Test** The rational relationship test, which applies to economic regulation, requires that the classification conceivably bear some rational relationship to a legitimate governmental interest that the classification proposes to further. Under this standard of review, governmental action is permitted to attack part of the evil to which the action is addressed. Moreover, there is a strong presumption that the action is constitutional. Therefore, the courts will overturn the governmental action only if clear and convincing evidence shows that there is no reasonable basis justifying the action.

**Strict Scrutiny Test** The strict scrutiny test is far more exacting than the rational relationship test. Under this test, the courts do not defer to the government; rather, they independently determine whether a classification of persons is constitutionally permissible. This determination requires that the classification be necessary to promote a compelling or overriding governmental interest.

The strict scrutiny test is applied when governmental action affects fundamental rights or involves suspect classifications. Fundamental rights include most of the provisions of the Bill of Rights and some other rights, such as interstate travel, voting, and access to criminal justice. Suspect classifications include those made on the basis of race or national origin. A classic and important example of strict scrutiny applied to classifications based upon race is the 1954 school desegregation case, *Brown v. Board of Education of Topeka*, 347 U.S. 483, in which the Supreme Court ruled that segregated public school systems violated the equal protection guarantee. Subsequently, the Court has invalidated segregation in public beaches, buses, parks, public golf courses, and courtroom seating.

A recent U.S. Supreme Court case again addressed the application of strict scrutiny to public schools. School districts in Seattle, Washington, and metropolitan Louisville, Kentucky, had voluntarily adopted student assignment plans that relied on race to determine which schools certain children may attend. In a five-to-four decision the Court held that public school systems may not seek to achieve or maintain integration through measures that take explicit account of a student's race. The Court reaffirmed that when the government distributes burdens or benefits on the basis of individual racial classifications, that action is reviewed under strict scrutiny requiring the most exact connection between justification and classification. Therefore, the school districts must demonstrate that the use of individual racial classifications in their school assignment plans is narrowly tailored to achieve a compelling government interest. In reversing the lower courts' decisions upholding the schools' plans, the Court held: "The [school] districts have also failed to show that they considered methods other than explicit racial classifications to achieve their stated goals. Narrow tailoring requires 'serious, good faith consideration of workable race-neutral alternatives.'" *Parents Involved in Community Schools v. Seattle School District No. 1*, 551 U.S. 701 (2007).

requirements for Phenergan because [Wyeth ] could have warned against IV-push administration without prior FDA approval, and because federal labeling requirements create a floor, not a ceiling, for state regulation." * * *

The importance of the pre-emption issue * * * persuaded us to grant Wyeth's petition for certiorari. [Citation.] The question presented by the petition is whether the FDA's drug labeling judgments "preempt state law product liability claims premised on the theory that different labeling judgments were necessary to make drugs reasonably safe for use." [Citation.]

* * *

Our answer * * * must be guided by two cornerstones of our pre-emption jurisprudence. First, "the purpose of Congress is the ultimate touchstone in every pre-emption case." [Citations.] Second, "[i]n all pre-emption cases, and particularly in those in which Congress has 'legislated ... in a field which the States have traditionally occupied,'... we 'start with the assumption that the historic police powers of the States were not to be superseded by the Federal Act unless that was the clear and manifest purpose of Congress.'" [Citation.]

* * *

Wyeth first argues that Levine's state-law claims are pre-empted because it is impossible for it to comply with both the state-law duties underlying those claims and its federal labeling duties. [Citation.] The FDA's premarket approval of a new drug application includes the approval of the exact text in the proposed label. [Citation.] Generally speaking, a manufacturer may only change a drug label after the FDA approves a supplemental application. There is, however, an FDA regulation that permits a manufacturer to make certain changes to its label before receiving the agency's approval. Among other things, this "changes being effected" (CBE) regulation provides that if a manufacturer is changing a label to "add or strengthen a contraindication, warning, precaution, or adverse reaction" or to "add or strengthen an instruction about dosage and administration that is intended to increase the safe use of the drug product," it may make the labeling change upon filing its supplemental application with the FDA; it need not wait for FDA approval. [Citation.]

* * *

* * * Wyeth suggests that the FDA, rather than the manufacturer, bears primary responsibility for drug labeling. Yet through many amendments to the FDCA [Food, Drug and Cosmetic Act] and to FDA regulations, it has remained a central premise of federal drug regulation that the manufacturer bears responsibility for the content of its label at all times. It is charged both with crafting an adequate label and with ensuring that its warnings remain adequate as long as the drug is on the market. [Citations.]

Indeed, prior to 2007, the FDA lacked the authority to order manufacturers to revise their labels. [Citation.] When Congress granted the FDA this authority, it reaffirmed the manufacturer's obligations and referred specifically to the CBE regulation, which both reflects the manufacturer's ultimate responsibility for its label and provides a mechanism for adding safety information to the label prior to FDA approval. [Citations.] Thus, when the risk of gangrene from IV-push injection of Phenergan became apparent, Wyeth had a duty to provide a warning that adequately described that risk, and the CBE regulation permitted it to provide such a warning before receiving the FDA's approval.

Of course, the FDA retains authority to reject labeling changes made pursuant to the CBE regulation in its review of the manufacturer's supplemental application, just as it retains such authority in reviewing all supplemental applications. But absent clear evidence that the FDA would not have approved a change to Phenergan's label, we will not conclude that it was impossible for Wyeth to comply with both federal and state requirements.

* * *

Wyeth also argues that requiring it to comply with a state-law duty to provide a stronger warning about IV-push administration would obstruct the purposes and objectives of federal drug labeling regulation. Levine's tort claims, it maintains, are pre-empted because they interfere with "Congress's purpose to entrust an expert agency to make drug labeling decisions that strike a balance between competing objectives." [Citation.] We find no merit in this argument, which relies on an untenable interpretation of congressional intent and an overbroad view of an agency's power to pre-empt state law.

* * * Building on its 1906 Act, Congress enacted the FDCA [Federal Food, Drug and Cosmetic Act of 1938] to bolster consumer protection against harmful products. [Citation.] Congress did not provide a federal remedy for consumers harmed by unsafe or ineffective drugs in the 1938 statute or in any subsequent amendment. Evidently, it determined that widely available state rights of action provided appropriate relief for injured consumers. It may also have recognized that state-law remedies further consumer protection by motivating manufacturers to produce safe and effective drugs and to give adequate warnings.

If Congress thought state-law suits posed an obstacle to its objectives, it surely would have enacted an express pre-emption provision at some point during the FDCA's 70-year history. But despite its 1976 enactment of an express pre-emption provision for medical devices, [citation], Congress has not enacted such a provision for prescription drugs. [Citation.] * * *

Despite this evidence that Congress did not regard state tort litigation as an obstacle to achieving its purposes, Wyeth nonetheless maintains that, because the FDCA requires the FDA to determine that a drug is safe and effective under the conditions set forth in its labeling, the agency must be presumed to have performed a precise balancing of risks and benefits and to have established a specific labeling standard that leaves no room for different state-law judgments. In advancing this argument, Wyeth relies not on any statement by Congress, but instead on the preamble to a 2006 FDA regulation governing the content and format of prescription drug labels. [Citation.] In that preamble, the FDA declared that the FDCA establishes "both a 'floor' and a 'ceiling,'" so that "FDA approval of labeling … preempts conflicting or contrary State law." [Citation.] It further stated that certain state-law actions, such as those involving failure-to-warn claims, "threaten FDA's statutorily prescribed role as the expert Federal agency responsible for evaluating and regulating drugs." [Citation.]

This Court has recognized that an agency regulation with the force of law can pre-empt conflicting state requirements. [Citation.] In such cases, the Court has performed its own conflict determination, relying on the substance of state and federal law and not on agency proclamations of pre-emption. * * *

* * *

In keeping with Congress' decision not to pre-empt common-law tort suits, it appears that the FDA traditionally regarded state law as a complementary form of drug regulation. The FDA has limited resources to monitor the 11,000 drugs on the market, and manufacturers have superior access to information about their drugs, especially in the postmarketing phase as new risks emerge. State tort suits uncover unknown drug hazards and provide incentives for drug manufacturers to disclose safety risks promptly. They also serve a distinct compensatory function that may motivate injured persons to come forward with information. Failure-to-warn actions, in particular, lend force to the FDCA's premise that manufacturers, not the FDA, bear primary responsibility for their drug labeling at all times. Thus, the FDA long maintained that state law offers an additional, and important, layer of consumer protection that complements FDA regulation. The agency's 2006 preamble represents a dramatic change in position.

* * *

In short, Wyeth has not persuaded us that failure-to-warn claims like Levine's obstruct the federal regulation of drug labeling. Congress has repeatedly declined to pre-empt state law, and the FDA's recently adopted position that state tort suits interfere with its statutory mandate is entitled to no weight. Although we recognize that some state-law claims might well frustrate the achievement of congressional objectives, this is not such a case.

We conclude that it is not impossible for Wyeth to comply with its state and federal law obligations and that Levine's common-law claims do not stand as an obstacle to the accomplishment of Congress' purposes in the FDCA. Accordingly, the judgment of the Vermont Supreme Court is affirmed.

CASE 4-2

## State Action
## BRENTWOOD ACADEMY v. TENNESSEE SECONDARY SCHOOL ATHLETIC ASSOCIATION

Supreme Court of the United States, 2001
531 U.S. 288, 121 S.Ct. 924, 148 L.Ed.2d 807
http://laws.findlaw.com/us/000/99-901.html

**Souter, J.**

The issue is whether a statewide association incorporated to regulate interscholastic athletic competition among public and private secondary schools may be regarded as engaging in state action when it enforces a rule against a member school. The association in question here includes most public schools located within the State, acts through their representatives, draws its officers from them, is largely funded by their dues and income received in their stead, and has historically been seen to regulate in lieu of the State Board of Education's exercise of its own authority. We hold that the association's regulatory activity may and should be treated as state action owing to the pervasive entwinement of state school officials in the structure of the association, there being no offsetting reason to see the association's acts in any other way.

Respondent Tennessee Secondary School Athletic Association (Association) is a not-for-profit membership corporation organized to regulate interscholastic sport among the public and private high schools in Tennessee that belong to it. No school is forced to join, but without any other authority actually regulating interscholastic athletics, it enjoys the memberships of almost all the State's public high schools (some 290 of them or 84% of the Association's voting membership), far outnumbering the 55 private schools that belong. A member school's team may play or scrimmage only against the team of another member, absent a dispensation.

The Association's rulemaking arm is its legislative council, while its board of control tends to administration. The voting membership of each of these nine-person committees is limited under the Association's bylaws to high school principals, assistant principals, and superintendents elected by the member schools, and the public school administrators who so serve typically attend meetings during regular school hours. Although the Association's staff members are not paid by the State, they are eligible to join the State's public retirement system for its employees. Member schools pay dues to the Association, though the bulk of its revenue is gate receipts at member teams' football and basketball tournaments, many of them held in public arenas rented by the Association.

The constitution, bylaws, and rules of the Association set standards of school membership and the eligibility of students to play in interscholastic games. Each school, for example, is regulated in awarding financial aid, most coaches must have a Tennessee state teaching license, and players must meet minimum academic standards and hew to limits on student employment. Under the bylaws, "in all matters pertaining to the athletic relations of his school," [citation], the principal is responsible to the Association, which has the power "to suspend, to fine, or otherwise penalize any member school for the violation of any of the rules of the Association or for other just cause," [citation].

* * *

The action before us responds to a 1997 regulatory enforcement proceeding brought against petitioner, Brentwood Academy, a private parochial high school member of the Association. The Association's board of control found that Brentwood violated a rule prohibiting "undue influence" in recruiting athletes, when it wrote to incoming students and their parents about spring football practice. The Association accordingly placed Brentwood's athletic program on probation for four years, declared its football and boys' basketball teams ineligible to compete in playoffs for two years, and imposed a $3,000 fine. When these penalties were imposed, all the voting members of the board of control and legislative council were public school administrators.

Brentwood sued the Association and its executive director in federal court * * * claiming that enforcement of the Rule was state action and a violation of the First and Fourteenth Amendments. The District Court entered summary judgment for Brentwood and enjoined the Association from enforcing the Rule. [Citation.] * * *

The United States Court of Appeals for the Sixth Circuit reversed. [Citation.] It recognized that there is no single test to identify state actions and state actors but applied three criteria * * *, and found no state action under any of them. It said the District Court was mistaken in seeing a symbiotic relationship between the State and the Association, it emphasized that the Association was neither engaging in a traditional and exclusive public function nor responding to state compulsion * * *

We granted certiorari, 528 U.S. 1153 (2000), to resolve the conflict and now reverse.

* * * Thus, we say that state action may be found if, though only if, there is such a "close nexus between the State and the challenged action" that seemingly private behavior "may be fairly treated as that of the State itself." [Citation.]

* * *

Our cases have identified a host of facts that can bear on the fairness of such an attribution. We have, for example, held that a challenged activity may be state action when it results from the State's exercise of "coercive power," [citation], when the State provides "significant encouragement, either overt or covert," [citation], or when a private actor operates as a "willful participant in joint activity with the State or its agents," [citation]. We have treated a nominally private entity as a state actor when it is controlled by an "agency of the State," [citation], when it has been delegated a public function by the State, [citations], when it is "entwined with governmental policies" or when government is "entwined in [its] management or control," [citation].

* * *

* * * [T]he "necessarily fact-bound inquiry," [citation], leads to the conclusion of state action here. The nominally private character of the Association is overborne by the pervasive entwinement of public institutions and public officials in its composition and workings, and there is no substantial reason to claim unfairness in applying constitutional standards to it.

The Association is not an organization of natural persons acting on their own, but of schools, and of public schools to the extent of 84% of the total. Under the Association's bylaws, each member school is represented by its principal or a faculty member, who has a vote in selecting members of the governing legislative council and board of control from eligible principals, assistant principals and superintendents.

Although the findings and prior opinions in this case include no express conclusion of law that public school officials act within the scope of their duties when they represent their institutions, no other view would be rational, * * *. Interscholastic athletics obviously play an integral part in the public education of Tennessee, where nearly every public high school spends money on competitions among schools. Since a pickup system of interscholastic games would not do, these public teams need some mechanism to produce rules and regulate competition. The mechanism is an organization overwhelmingly composed of public school officials who select representatives (all of them public officials at the time in question here), who in turn adopt and enforce the rules that make the system work. Thus, by giving these jobs to the Association, the 290 public schools of Tennessee belonging to it can sensibly be seen as exercising their own authority to meet their own responsibilities. * * *

In sum, to the extent of 84% of its membership, the Association is an organization of public schools represented by their officials acting in their official capacity to provide an integral element of secondary public schooling. There would be no recognizable Association, legal or tangible, without the public school officials, who do not merely control but overwhelmingly perform all but the purely ministerial acts by which the Association exists and functions in practical terms. * * *

To complement the entwinement of public school officials with the Association from the bottom up, the State of Tennessee has provided for entwinement from top down. State Board members are assigned ex officio to serve as members of the board of control and legislative council, and the Association's ministerial employees are treated as state employees to the extent of being eligible for membership in the state retirement system.

* * *

The entwinement down from the State Board is therefore unmistakable, just as the entwinement up from the member public schools is overwhelming. Entwinement will support a conclusion that an ostensibly private organization ought to be charged with a public character and judged by constitutional standards; entwinement to the degree shown here requires it.

* * *

The judgment of the Court of Appeals for the Sixth Circuit is reversed, and the case is remanded for further proceedings consistent with this opinion.

It is so ordered.

## CASE 4-3

### State Regulation of Commerce
### DEPARTMENT OF REVENUE OF KENTUCKY v. DAVIS, ET AL.

United States Supreme Court, 2008

553 U.S. 328, 128 S.Ct. 1801, 170 L.Ed.2d 685

http://www.law.cornell.edu/supct/html/06-666.ZS.html

**Souter, J.**

Like most other States, the Commonwealth of Kentucky taxes its residents' income. [Citation.] The tax is assessed on "net income," which excludes "interest on any State or local bond" ("municipal bond," for short), [citation]. Kentucky piggybacks on this exclusion, but only up to a point: it adds "interest income derived from obligations of sister states and political subdivisions thereof" back into the taxable net. [Citation.] Interest on bonds issued by Kentucky and its political subdivisions is thus entirely exempt, whereas interest on municipal bonds of other States and their subdivisions is taxable. (Interest on bonds issued by private entities is taxed by Kentucky regardless of the private issuer's home.)

The ostensible reason for this regime is the attractiveness of tax-exempt bonds at "lower rates of interest … than that paid on taxable … bonds of comparable risk." [Citation.] Under the Internal Revenue Code, for example, [citation], "if the market rate of interest is 10 percent on a comparable corporate bond, a municipality could pay only 6.5 percent on its debt and a purchaser in a 35 percent marginal tax bracket would be indifferent between the municipal and the corporate bond, since the after-tax interest rate on the corporate bond is 6.5 percent." [Citation.] The differential tax scheme in Kentucky works the same way; the Commonwealth's tax benefit to residents who buy its bonds makes lower interest rates acceptable, while limiting the exception to Kentucky bonds raises in-state demand for them without also subsidizing other issuers.

The significance of the scheme is immense. Between 1996 and 2002, Kentucky and its subdivisions issued $7.7 billion in long-term bonds to pay for spending on transportation, public safety, education, utilities, and environmental protection, among other things. [Citation.] Across the Nation during the same period, States issued over $750 billion in long-term bonds, with nearly a third of the money going to education, followed by transportation (13%) and utilities (11%). [Citation.] Municipal bonds currently finance roughly two-thirds of capital expenditures by state and local governments. [Citation.]

Funding the work of government this way follows a tradition going back as far as the 17th century. [Citation.] * * *

* * *

The Commerce Clause empowers Congress "[t]o regulate Commerce … among the several States," Art. I, § 8, cl. 3, and although its terms do not expressly restrain "the several States" in any way, we have sensed a negative implication in the provision since the early days, [citation]. The modern law of what has come to be called the dormant Commerce Clause is driven by concern about "economic protectionism—that is, regulatory measures designed to benefit in-state economic interests by burdening out-of-state competitors." [Citation.] The point is to "effectuat[e] the Framers' purpose to 'prevent a State from retreating into [the] economic isolation,'" [citation], "that had plagued relations among the Colonies and later among the States under the Articles of Confederation," [citation].

* * *

Under the resulting protocol for dormant Commerce Clause analysis, we ask whether a challenged law discriminates against interstate commerce. [Citation.] A discriminatory law is "virtually *per se* invalid," [citation], and will survive only if it "advances a legitimate local purpose that cannot be adequately served by reasonable nondiscriminatory alternatives," [citation]. Absent discrimination for the forbidden purpose, however, the law "will be upheld unless the burden imposed on [interstate] commerce is clearly excessive in relation to the putative local benefits." *Pike v. Bruce Church, Inc.*, [citation]. State laws frequently survive this *Pike* scrutiny, [citation], though not always, as in *Pike* itself, [citation].

Some cases run a different course, however, and an exception covers States that go beyond regulation and themselves "participat[e] in the market" so as to "exercis[e] the right to favor [their] own citizens over others." [Citation.] This "market participant" exception reflects a "basic distinction ... between States as market participants and States as market regulators," [citation], "[t]here [being] no indication of a constitutional plan to limit the ability of the States themselves to operate freely in the free market," [citations].

Our most recent look at the reach of the dormant Commerce Clause came just last Term, in a case decided independently of the market participation precedents. *United Haulers* upheld a "flow control" ordinance requiring trash haulers to deliver solid waste to a processing plant owned and operated by a public authority in New York State. We found "[c]ompelling reasons" for "treating [the ordinance] differently from laws favoring particular private businesses over their competitors." [Citation.] State and local governments that provide public goods and services on their own, unlike private businesses, are "vested with the responsibility of protecting the health, safety, and welfare of [their] citizens," [citation], and laws favoring such States and their subdivisions may "be directed toward any number of legitimate goals unrelated to protectionism," [citation]. That was true in *United Haulers*, where the ordinance addressed waste disposal, "both typically and traditionally a local government function." [Citation.] And if more had been needed to show that New York's object was consequently different from forbidden protectionism, we pointed out that "the most palpable harm imposed by the ordinances—more expensive trash removal—[was] likely to fall upon the very people who voted for the laws," rather than out-of-state interests. [Citation.] Being concerned that a "contrary approach ... would lead to unprecedented and unbounded interference by the courts with state and local government," [citation], we held that the ordinance did "not discriminate against interstate commerce for purposes of the dormant Commerce Clause," [citation].

It follows *a fortiori* from *United Haulers* that Kentucky must prevail. In *United Haulers,* we explained that a government function is not susceptible to standard dormant Commerce Clause scrutiny owing to its likely motivation by legitimate objectives distinct from the simple economic protectionism the Clause abhors, [citations]. This logic applies with even greater force to laws favoring a State's municipal bonds, given that the issuance of debt securities to pay for public projects is a quintessentially public function, with the venerable history we have already sketched, [citation]. By issuing bonds, state and local governments "sprea[d] the costs of public projects over time," [citation], much as one might buy a house with a loan subject to monthly payments. Bonds place the cost of a project on the citizens who benefit from it over the years, * * * and they allow for public work beyond what current revenues could support. [Citation.] Bond proceeds are thus the way to shoulder the cardinal civic responsibilities listed in *United Haulers:* protecting the health, safety, and welfare of citizens. It should go without saying that the apprehension in *United Haulers* about "unprecedented ... interference" with a traditional government function is just as warranted here, where the Davises would have us invalidate a century-old taxing practice, [citation], presently employed by 41 States, [citation], and affirmatively supported by all of them, [citation].

* * * [T]he Kentucky tax scheme parallels the ordinance upheld in *United Haulers:* it "benefit[s] a clearly public [issuer, that is, Kentucky], while treating all private [issuers] exactly the same." [Citation.]

* * * Kentucky's tax exemption favors a traditional government function without any differential treatment favoring local entities over substantially similar out-of-state interests. This type of law does "not 'discriminate against interstate commerce' for purposes of the dormant Commerce Clause." [Citation.]

* * *

A look at the specific markets in which the exemption's effects are felt both confirms the conclusion that no traditionally forbidden discrimination is underway and points to the distinctive character of the tax policy. The market as most broadly conceived is one of issuers and holders of all fixed-income securities, whatever their source or ultimate destination. In this interstate market, Kentucky treats income from municipal bonds of other States just like income from bonds privately issued in Kentucky or elsewhere; no preference is given to any local issuer, and none to any local holder, beyond what is entailed in the preference Kentucky grants itself when it engages in activities serving public objectives. * * * These facts suggest that no State perceives any local advantage or disadvantage beyond the permissible ones open to a government and to those who deal with it when that government itself enters the market. [Citation.]

* * *

In sum, the differential tax scheme is critical to the operation of an identifiable segment of the municipal financial market as it currently functions, and this fact alone demonstrates that the unanimous desire of the States to preserve the tax feature is a far cry from the private protectionism that has driven the development of the dormant Commerce Clause. * * *

The judgment of the Court of Appeals of Kentucky is reversed, and the case is remanded for further proceedings not inconsistent with this opinion.

## CASE 4-4

First Amendment

## THOMPSON v. WESTERN STATES MEDICAL CENTER

Supreme Court of the United States, 2002
535 U.S. 357, 122 S.Ct. 1497, 152 L.Ed.2d 563
http://laws.findlaw.com/us/000/01-344.html

**O'Connor, J.**

Section 503A of the Food and Drug Administration Modernization Act of 1997 (FDAMA or Act), [citation], exempts "compounded drugs" from the Food and Drug Administration's standard drug approval requirements as long as the providers of those drugs abide by several restrictions, including that they refrain from advertising or promoting particular compounded drugs. Respondents, a group of licensed pharmacies that specialize in compounding drugs, sought to enjoin enforcement of the subsections of the Act dealing with advertising and solicitation, arguing that those provisions violate the First Amendment's free speech guarantee. The District Court agreed with respondents and granted their motion for summary judgment, holding that the provisions do not meet the test for acceptable government regulation of commercial speech set forth in *Central Hudson Gas & Elec. Corp. v. Public Serv. Comm'n of N. Y.*, [citation]. * * * The Court of Appeals for the Ninth Circuit affirmed in [relevant] part * * * agreeing that the provisions regarding advertisement and promotion are unconstitutional. * * * We conclude, as did the courts below, that §503A's provisions regarding advertisement and promotion amount to unconstitutional restrictions on commercial speech, and we therefore affirm.

### I

Drug compounding is a process by which a pharmacist or doctor combines, mixes, or alters ingredients to create a medication tailored to the needs of an individual patient. Compounding is typically used to prepare medications that are not commercially available, such as medication for a patient who is allergic to an ingredient in a mass-produced product. It is a traditional component of the practice of pharmacy, [citation], and is taught as part of the standard curriculum at most pharmacy schools, [citation]. Many States specifically regulate compounding practices as part of their regulation of pharmacies. * * *

The Federal Food, Drug, and Cosmetic Act of 1938 (FDCA), [citation], regulates drug manufacturing, marketing, and distribution. Section 505(a) of the FDCA, [citation], provides that "no person shall introduce or deliver for introduction into interstate commerce any new drug, unless an approval of an application filed [with the Food and Drug Administration] * * * is effective with respect to such drug." * * *

* * * The FDAMA, which amends the FDCA, exempts compounded drugs from the FDCA's "new drug" requirements and other requirements provided the drugs satisfy a number of restrictions. * * * Finally, and most relevant for this litigation, the prescription must be "unsolicited," §353a (a), and the pharmacy, licensed pharmacist, or licensed physician compounding the drug may "not advertise or promote the compounding of any particular drug, class of drug, or type of drug." §353a(c). The pharmacy, licensed pharmacist, or licensed physician may, however, "advertise and promote the compounding service." *Ibid.*

Respondents are a group of licensed pharmacies that specialize in drug compounding. They have prepared promotional materials that they distribute by mail and at medical conferences to inform patients and physicians of the use and effectiveness of specific compounded drugs. Fearing that they would be prosecuted under the FDAMA if they continued to distribute those materials, respondents filed a complaint in the United States District Court for the District of

Nevada, arguing that the Act's requirement that they refrain from advertising and promoting their products if they wish to continue compounding violates the Free Speech Clause of the First Amendment. Specifically, they challenged the requirement that prescriptions for compounded drugs be "unsolicited," §353a(a), and the requirement that pharmacists "not advertise or promote the compounding of any particular drug, class of drug, or type of drug," §353a(c). * * *

* * *

## II

The parties agree that the advertising and soliciting prohibited by the FDAMA constitute commercial speech.

In *Virginia Bd. of Pharmacy v. Virginia Citizens Consumer Council, Inc.*, [citation], the first case in which we explicitly held that commercial speech receives First Amendment protection, we explained the reasons for this protection: "It is a matter of public interest that [economic] decisions, in the aggregate, be intelligent and well-informed. To this end, the free flow of commercial information is indispensable." * * *

Although commercial speech is protected by the First Amendment, not all regulation of such speech is unconstitutional. [Citation.] In *Central Hudson*, [citation], we articulated a test for determining whether a particular commercial speech regulation is constitutionally permissible. Under that test we ask as a threshold matter whether the commercial speech concerns unlawful activity or is misleading. If so, then the speech is not protected by the First Amendment. If the speech concerns lawful activity and is not misleading, however, we next ask "whether the asserted governmental interest is substantial." [Citation.] If it is, then we "determine whether the regulation directly advances the governmental interest asserted," and, finally, "whether it is not more extensive than is necessary to serve that interest." [Citation.] Each of these latter three inquiries must be answered in the affirmative for the regulation to be found constitutional.

* * *

## III

* * *

The Government asserts that three substantial interests underlie the FDAMA. The first is an interest in "preserving the effectiveness and integrity of the FDCA's new drug approval process and the protection of the public health that it provides." [Citation.] The second is an interest in "preserving the availability of compounded drugs for those individual patients who, for particularized medical reasons, cannot use commercially available products that have been approved by the FDA." [Citation.] Finally, the Government argues that "achieving the proper balance between those two independently compelling but competing interests is itself a substantial governmental interest." [Citation.]

* * *

Preserving the effectiveness and integrity of the FDCA's new drug approval process is clearly an important governmental interest, and the Government has every reason to want as many drugs as possible to be subject to that approval process. The Government also has an important interest, however, in permitting the continuation of the practice of compounding so that patients with particular needs may obtain medications suited to those needs. And it would not make sense to require compounded drugs created to meet the unique needs of individual patients to undergo the testing required for the new drug approval process. Pharmacists do not make enough money from small-scale compounding to make safety and efficacy testing of their compounded drugs economically feasible, so requiring such testing would force pharmacists to stop providing compounded drugs. Given this, the Government needs to be able to draw a line between small-scale compounding and large-scale drug manufacturing. That line must distinguish compounded drugs produced on such a small scale that they could not undergo safety and efficacy testing from drugs produced and sold on a large enough scale that they could undergo such testing and therefore must do so.

The Government argues that the FDAMA's speech-related provisions provide just such a line, *i.e.*, that, in the terms of *Central Hudson*, they "directly advance the governmental interests asserted." [Citation.] Those provisions use advertising as the trigger for requiring FDA approval—essentially, as long as pharmacists do not advertise particular compounded drugs, they may sell compounded drugs without first undergoing safety and efficacy testing and obtaining FDA approval. If they advertise their compounded drugs, however, FDA approval is required. * * *

* * * Assuming it is true that drugs cannot be marketed on a large scale without advertising, the FDAMA's prohibition on advertising compounded drugs might indeed "directly advance" the Government's interests. *Central Hudson*, [citation]. Even assuming that it does, however, the Government has failed to demonstrate that the speech restrictions are "not more extensive than is necessary to serve [those] interests." [Citation.] In previous cases addressing this final prong of the Central Hudson test, we have made clear that if the Government could achieve its interests in a manner that does not restrict speech, or that restricts less speech, the Government must do so. * * *

Several non-speech-related means of drawing a line between compounding and large-scale manufacturing might be possible here. * * *

* * *

Even if the Government had argued that the FDAMA's speech-related restrictions were motivated by a fear that advertising compounded drugs would put people who do not need such drugs at risk by causing them to convince their doctors to prescribe the drugs anyway, that fear would fail to justify the restrictions. Aside from the fact that this concern rests on the questionable assumption that doctors would prescribe unnecessary medications * * * this concern amounts to a fear that people would make bad decisions if given truthful information about compounded drugs. * * * We have previously rejected the notion that the Government has an interest in preventing the dissemination of truthful commercial information in order to prevent members of the public from making bad decisions with the information. * * *

* * *

If the Government's failure to justify its decision to regulate speech were not enough to convince us that the FDAMA's advertising provisions were unconstitutional, the amount of beneficial speech prohibited by the FDAMA would be. Forbidding the advertisement of compounded drugs would affect pharmacists other than those interested in producing drugs on a large scale. It would prevent pharmacists with no interest in mass-producing medications, but who serve clienteles with special medical needs, from telling the doctors treating those clients about the alternative drugs available through compounding. * * *

Accordingly, we affirm the Court of Appeals' judgment that the speech-related provisions of FDAMA §503A are unconstitutional.

So ordered.

---

CASE 4-5

## Equal Protection
## BROWN v. BOARD OF EDUCATION OF TOPEKA

Supreme Court of the United States, 1954
347 U.S. 483, 74 S.Ct. 686, 98 L.Ed. 873
http://laws.findlaw.com/US/347/483.html

**Warren, C. J.**

These cases come to us from the States of Kansas, South Carolina, Virginia, and Delaware. They are premised on different facts and different local conditions, but a common legal question justifies their consideration together in this consolidated opinion.

In each of the cases, minors of the Negro race, through their legal representatives, seek the aid of the courts in obtaining admission to the public schools of their community on a nonsegregated basis. In each instance, they have been denied admission to schools attended by white children under laws requiring or permitting segregation according to race. This segregation was alleged to deprive the plaintiffs of the equal protection of the laws under the Fourteenth Amendment. In each of the cases other than the Delaware case, a three-judge federal district court denied relief to the plaintiffs on the so-called "separate but equal" doctrine announced by this Court in *Plessy v. Ferguson*, [citation]. Under that doctrine, equality of treatment is accorded when the races are provided substantially equal facilities, even though these facilities be separate. In the Delaware case, the Supreme Court of Delaware adhered to that doctrine, but ordered that the plaintiffs be admitted to the white schools because of their superiority to the Negro schools.

The plaintiffs contend that segregated public schools are not "equal" and cannot be made "equal" and that hence they are deprived of the equal protection of the laws. Because of the obvious importance of the question presented, the Court took jurisdiction. * * *

Reargument was largely devoted to the circumstances surrounding the adoption of the Fourteenth Amendment in 1868. It covered exhaustively consideration of the Amendment in Congress, ratification by the states, then existing practices in racial segregation, and the views of proponents and opponents of the Amendment. This discussion and our own investigation convince us that, although these sources cast some light, it is not enough to resolve the problem with which we are faced. At best, they are inconclusive. The most avid proponents of the post-War Amendments undoubtedly intended them to remove all legal distinctions among "all persons born or naturalized in the United States." Their opponents, just as certainly, were antagonistic to both the letter and the spirit of the Amendments and wished them to have the most limited effect. What others in Congress and the state legislatures had in mind cannot be determined with any degree of certainty.

An additional reason for the inconclusive nature of the Amendment's history, with respect to segregated schools, is the status of public education at that time. In the South, the movement toward free common schools, supported by general taxation, had not yet taken hold. Education of white children was largely in the hands of private groups. Education of Negroes was almost nonexistent, and practically all of the race were illiterate. In fact, any education of Negroes was forbidden by law in some states. Today, in contrast, many Negroes have achieved outstanding success in the arts and sciences as well as in the business and professional world. It is true that public school education at the time of the Amendment had advanced further in the North, but the effect of the Amendment on Northern States was generally ignored in the congressional debates. Even in the North, the conditions of public education did not approximate those existing today. The curriculum was usually rudimentary; ungraded schools were common in rural areas; the school term was but three months a year in many states; and compulsory school attendance was virtually unknown. As a consequence, it is not surprising that there should be so little in the history of the Fourteenth Amendment relating to its intended effect on public education.

In the first cases in this Court construing the Fourteenth Amendment, decided shortly after its adoption, the Court interpreted it as proscribing all state-imposed discriminations against the Negro race. The doctrine of "separate but equal" did not make its appearance in this Court until 1896 in the case of *Plessy v. Ferguson*, involving not education but transportation. American courts have since labored with the doctrine for over half a century. In this Court, there have been six cases involving the "separate but equal" doctrine in the field of public education. * * * In none of these cases was it necessary to reexamine the doctrine to grant relief to the Negro plaintiff. And in *Sweatt v. Painter*, [citation], the Court expressly reserved decision on the question whether *Plessy v. Ferguson* should be held inapplicable to public education.

In the instant cases, that question is directly presented. Here, unlike *Sweatt v. Painter*, there are findings below that the Negro and white schools involved have been equalized, or are being equalized, with respect to buildings, curricula, qualifications and salaries of teachers, and other "tangible" factors. Our decision, therefore, cannot turn on merely a comparison of these tangible factors in the Negro and white schools involved in each of the cases. We must look instead to the effect of segregation itself on public education.

* * *

Today, education is perhaps the most important function of state and local governments. Compulsory school attendance laws and the great expenditures for education both demonstrate our recognition of the importance of education to our democratic society. It is required in the performance of our most basic public responsibilities, even service in the armed forces. It is the very foundation of good citizenship. Today it is a principal instrument in awakening the child to cultural values, in preparing him for later professional training, and in helping him to adjust normally to his environment. In these days, it is doubtful that any child may reasonably be expected to succeed in life if he is denied the opportunity of an education. Such an opportunity, where the state has undertaken to provide it, is a right which must be made available to all on equal terms.

We come then to the question presented: Does segregation of children in public schools solely on the basis of race, even though the physical facilities and other "tangible" factors may be equal, deprive the children of the minority group of equal educational opportunities? We believe that it does.

In *Sweatt v. Painter*, [citation], in finding that a segregated law school for Negroes could not provide them equal educational opportunities, this Court relied in large part on "those qualities which are incapable of objective measurement but which make for greatness in a law school." In *McLaurin v. Oklahoma State Regents*, [citation], the Court in requiring that a Negro admitted to a white graduate school be treated like all other students, again resorted to intangible considerations: " * * * his ability to study, to engage in discussions and exchange views with other students, and, in general, to learn his profession." Such considerations apply with added force to children in grade and high schools. To separate them from others of similar age and qualifications solely because of their race generates a feeling of inferiority as to their status in the community that may affect their hearts and minds in a way unlikely ever to be undone. The effect of this separation on their educational opportunities was well stated by a finding in the Kansas case by a court which nevertheless felt compelled to rule against the Negro plaintiffs:

> Segregation of white and colored children in public schools has a detrimental effect upon the colored children. The impact is greater when it has the sanction of the law, for the policy of separating the races is usually interpreted as denoting the inferiority of the Negro group. A sense of inferiority affects the motivation of a child to learn. Segregation with the sanction of law, therefore, has a tendency to (retard) the educational and mental development of Negro children and to deprive them of some of the benefits they would receive in a racial(ly)-integrated school system.

Whatever may have been the extent of psychological knowledge at the time of *Plessy v. Ferguson*, this finding is amply supported by modern authority. Any language in *Plessy v. Ferguson* contrary to this finding is rejected.

We conclude that in the field of public education the doctrine of "separate but equal" has no place. Separate educational facilities are inherently unequal. Therefore, we hold that the plaintiffs and others similarly situated for whom the actions have been brought are, by reason of the segregation complained of, deprived of the equal protection of the laws guaranteed by the Fourteenth Amendment. This disposition makes unnecessary any discussion whether such segregation also violates the Due Process Clause of the Fourteenth Amendment.

## QUESTIONS

1. List and distinguish the basic principles of constitutional law.
2. Describe the sources and extent of the power of the Federal and State governments to regulate business and commerce.
3. Distinguish the three levels of scrutiny used by the courts to determine the constitutionality of governmental action.
4. Explain the effect of the First Amendment upon (a) corporate political speech, (b) commercial speech, and (c) defamation.
5. Explain the difference between substantive and procedural due process.

## PROBLEMS

**1.** In May, Patricia Allen left her automobile on the shoulder of a road in the city of Erehwon after the car stopped running. A member of the Erehwon city police department came upon the car later that day and placed on it a sticker that stated that unless the car was moved, it would be towed. After a week the car had not been removed, and the police department authorized Baldwin Auto Wrecking Co. to tow it away and store it on its property. Allen was told by a friend that her car was at Baldwin's. Allen asked Baldwin to allow her to take possession of her car, but Baldwin refused to relinquish the car until the $70 towing fee was paid. Allen could not afford to pay the fee, and the car remained at Baldwin's for six weeks. At that time, Baldwin requested that the police department issue a permit to dispose of the automobile. After the police department tried unsuccessfully to telephone Allen, the department issued the permit. In late July, Baldwin destroyed the automobile. Allen brings an action against the city and Baldwin for damages for loss of the vehicle, arguing that she was denied due process. Decision?

**2.** In 1967, large oil reserves were discovered in the Prudhoe Bay area of Alaska. As a result, State revenues increased from $124 million in 1969 to $3.7 billion in 1981. In 1980, the State legislature enacted a dividend program that would distribute annually a portion of these earnings to the State's adult residents. Under the plan, each citizen eighteen years of age or older receives one unit for each year of residency subsequent to 1959, the year Alaska became a State. Crawford, a resident since 1978, brings suit challenging the dividend distribution plan as violative of the equal protection guarantee. Did the dividend program violate the Equal Protection Clause of the Fourteenth Amendment? Explain.

**3.** Maryland enacted a statute prohibiting any producer or refiner of petroleum products from operating retail service stations within the State. The statute also required that any producer or refiner discontinue operating its company-owned retail service stations. Approximately 3,800 retail service stations in Maryland sell more than twenty different brands of gasoline. All of this gasoline is brought in from other States, as no petroleum products are produced or refined in Maryland. Only 5 percent of the total number of retailers are operated by a producer or refiner. Maryland enacted the statute because a survey conducted by the State comptroller indicated that gasoline stations operated by producers or refiners had received preferential treatment during periods of gasoline shortage. Seven major producers and refiners bring an action challenging the statute on the ground that it discriminated against interstate commerce in violation of the Commerce Clause of the U.S. Constitution. Are they correct? Explain.

**4.** The Federal Aviation Act of 1958 provides that "the United States of America is declared to possess and exercise complete and exclusive national sovereignty in the airspace of the United States." The city of Orion adopted an ordinance that makes it unlawful for jet aircraft to take off from its airport between 11:00 P.M. of one day and 7:00 A.M. of the next day. Jordan Airlines, Inc., is adversely affected by this ordinance and brings suit challenging it under the Supremacy Clause of the U.S. Constitution as conflicting with the Federal Aviation Act or preempted by it. Is the ordinance valid? Explain.

**5.** The Public Service Commission of State X issued a regulation completely banning all advertising that "promotes the use of electricity" by any electric utility company in State X. The commission issued the order to conserve energy. Central Electric Corporation of State X challenges the order in the State courts, arguing that the commission has restrained commercial speech in violation of the First Amendment. Was the corporation's freedom of speech unconstitutionally infringed? Explain.

**6.** E–Z–Rest Motel is a motel with 216 rooms located in the center of a large city in State Y. It is readily accessible from two interstate highways and three major State highways. The motel solicits patronage from outside of State Y through various national advertising media, including magazines of national circulation. It accepts convention trade from outside State Y, and approximately 75 percent of its registered guests are from out of State Y. An action under the Federal Civil Rights Act of 1964 has been brought against E–Z–Rest Motel alleging that the motel discriminates on the basis of race and color. The motel contends that the statute cannot be applied to it because it is not engaged in interstate commerce. Can the Federal government regulate this activity under the Interstate Commerce Clause? Why?

**7.** State Z enacted a Private Pension Benefits Protection Act requiring private employers with one hundred or more employees to pay a pension funding charge upon terminating a pension plan or closing an office in State Z. Acme Steel Company closed its offices in State Z, whereupon the State assessed the company $185,000 under the vesting provisions of the act. Acme challenged the constitutionality of the act under the Contract Clause (Article I, Section 10) of the U.S. Constitution. Was the act constitutional? Explain.

**8.** A State statute empowered public school principals to suspend students for up to ten days without any notice or hearing. A student who was suspended for ten days challenges the constitutionality of his suspension on the ground that he was denied due process. Was due process denied? Explain.

**9.** Iowa enacted a statute prohibiting the use of sixty-five-foot double-trailer-truck combinations. All of the other midwestern and western States permit such trucks to be used on their roads. Despite these restrictions, Iowa's statute permits cities abutting the State line to enact local ordinances adopting the length limitations of the adjoining State. Where a city has exercised this option, otherwise oversized trucks are permitted within the city limits and in nearby commercial zones. Consolidated Freightways is adversely affected by this statute and brings suit against Iowa, alleging that the statute violates the Commerce Clause. The District Court found that the evidence established that sixty-five-foot doubles were as safe as the shorter truck units. Does the statute violate the Commerce Clause? Explain.

**10.** Metropolitan Edison Company is a privately owned and operated Pennsylvania corporation subject to extensive regulation by the Pennsylvania Public Utility Commission. Under a provision of its general tariff filed with the commission, Edison had the right to discontinue electric service to any customer on reasonable notice of nonpayment of bills. Catherine Jackson had been receiving electricity from Metropolitan Edison when her account was terminated because of her delinquency in payments. Edison later opened a new account for her residence in the name of James Dodson, another occupant of Jackson's residence. In August of the following year, Dodson moved away and no further payments were made to the account. Finally, in October, Edison disconnected Jackson's service without any prior notice. Jackson brought suit claiming that her electric service could not be terminated without notice and a hearing. She further argued that such action, allowed by a provision of Edison's tariff filed with the commission, constituted "state action" depriving her of property in violation of the Fourteenth Amendment's guarantee of due process of law. Should Edison's actions be considered state action? Explain.

**11.** Miss Horowitz was admitted as an advanced medical student at the University of Missouri–Kansas City. During the spring of her first year, several faculty members expressed dissatisfaction with Miss Horowitz's clinical performance, noting that it was below that of her peers, that she was erratic in attendance at her clinical sessions, and that she lacked a critical concern for personal hygiene. Upon the recommendation of the school's Council on Evaluation, she was advanced to her second and final year on a probationary basis. After subsequent unfavorable reviews during her second year and a negative evaluation of her performance by seven practicing physicians, the council recommended that Miss Horowitz be dismissed from the school for her failure to meet academic standards. The decision was approved by the dean and later affirmed by the provost after an appeal by Miss Horowitz. She brought suit against the school's Board of Curators, claiming that her dismissal violated her right to procedural due process under the Fourteenth Amendment and deprived her of "liberty" by substantially impairing her opportunities to continue her medical education or to return to employment in a medically related field. Is her claim correct? Explain.

**12.** The McClungs own Ollie's Barbecue, a restaurant located a few blocks from the interstate highway in Birmingham, Alabama, with dining accommodations for whites only and a takeout service for blacks. In the year preceding the passage of the Civil Rights Act of 1964, the restaurant had purchased a substantial portion of the food it served from outside the state. The restaurant has refused to serve blacks since its original opening in 1927 and asserts that if it were required to serve blacks it would lose much of its business. The McClungs sought a declaratory judgment to render unconstitutional the application of the Civil Rights Act to their restaurant because their admitted racial discrimination did not restrict or significantly impede interstate commerce. Decision?

**13.** Alabama law imposes a fee of $97.60 per ton for hazardous wastes generated outside the state and disposed of at a commercial facility in Alabama. The fee for hazardous wastes generated within Alabama is $25.60 per ton. Chemical Waste Management, Inc., which operates a commercial hazardous waste land disposal facility in Emelle, Alabama, filed suit requesting a declaratory judgment that the Alabama law violated the Commerce Clause of the U.S. Constitution. Alabama argued that the additional fee of $72.00 served a legitimate local purpose related to its citizens' health and safety, given recent large increases in the hazardous waste received into the state and the possible adverse effects of such waste. Judgment? Explain.

# CHAPTER 5
# Administrative Law

Administrative law is the branch of public law that is created by administrative agencies in the form of rules, regulations, orders, and decisions to carry out the regulatory powers and duties of those agencies. Administrative agencies are governmental entities—other than courts and legislatures—having authority to affect the rights of private parties through their operations. Such agencies, often referred to as commissions, boards, departments, administrations, government corporations, bureaus, or offices, regulate a vast array of important matters involving national safety, welfare, and convenience. For instance, Federal administrative agencies are charged with responsibility for national security, citizenship and naturalization, law enforcement, taxation, currency, elections, environmental protection, consumer protection, regulation of transportation, telecommunications, labor relations, trade, commerce, and securities markets, as well as with providing health and social services.

Because of the increasing complexity of the social, economic, and industrial life of the nation, the scope of administrative law has expanded enormously. Justice Jackson stated that "the rise of administrative bodies has been the most significant legal trend of the last century, and perhaps more values today are affected by their decisions than by those of all the courts, review of administrative decisions apart." *Federal Trade Commission v. Ruberoid Co.*, 343 U.S. 470 (1952). This observation is even more true today, as evidenced by the dramatic increase in the number and activities of Federal government boards, commissions, and other agencies. Certainly, agencies create more legal rules and adjudicate more controversies than all of the nation's legislatures and courts combined.

State agencies also play a significant role in the functioning of our society. Among the more important State boards and commissions are those that supervise and regulate banking, insurance, communications, transportation, public utilities, pollution control, and workers' compensation.

Countless administrative agencies establish much of the Federal, State, and local law in this country. These agencies, which many label the "fourth branch of government," possess tremendous power and have long been criticized as being "in reality miniature independent governments … [which are] a haphazard deposit of irresponsible agencies." 1937 Presidential Task Force Report.

Despite the criticism against them, these agencies clearly play a significant and necessary role in our society. Administrative agencies relieve legislatures of the impossible burden of fashioning legislation that deals with every detail of a specific problem. As a result, Congress can enact legislation, such as the Federal Trade Commission Act, which prohibits unfair and deceptive trade practices, without having to define such practices specifically or to anticipate all the particular problems that may arise. Instead, Congress may enact an **enabling statute** that creates an agency—in this example, the Federal Trade Commission (FTC)—to which it can delegate the power to issue rules, regulations, and guidelines to carry out the statutory mandate. In addition, the establishment of separate, specialized bodies enables administrative agencies to be staffed by individuals with expertise in the field being regulated. Administrative agencies can thus develop the knowledge and devote the time necessary to provide continuous and flexible solutions to evolving regulatory problems.

This chapter will focus on Federal administrative agencies, which can be classified as either independent or executive. Executive agencies are those housed within the executive branch of government, whereas independent agencies are not. Many Federal agencies are discussed in other parts of this text. More specifically, the FTC and the Justice Department are discussed in *Chapter 41*; the FTC and the Consumer Product Safety Commission (CPSC) in *Chapter 42*; the Department of Labor, the National Labor Relations Board (NLRB), and the Equal Employment Opportunity Commission (EEOC) in *Chapter 43*; the Securities and Exchange Commission (SEC) in *Chapters 44* and *45*; and the Environmental Protection Agency (EPA) in *Chapter 46*.

## OPERATION OF ADMINISTRATIVE AGENCIES

Most administrative agencies perform three basic functions: (1) rulemaking, (2) enforcement, and (3) adjudication. The term administrative process refers to the activities in which administrative agencies engage while carrying out their rulemaking, enforcement, and adjudicative functions. Administrative agencies exercise powers that the Constitution has allocated to the three separate branches of government. More specifically, agencies exercise legislative power when they make rules, executive power when they enforce their enabling statutes and their rules, and judicial power when they adjudicate disputes. This concentration of power has raised questions regarding the propriety of having the same bodies which establish the rules also act as prosecutors and judges in determining whether those rules have been violated. To address this issue and bring about certain additional procedural reforms, Congress enacted the Administrative Procedure Act (APA) in 1946.

### RULEMAKING

Rulemaking is the process by which an administrative agency enacts or promulgates rules of law. Under the APA, a rule is "the whole or a part of an agency statement of general or particular applicability and future effect designed to implement, interpret, or process law or policy." Section 551(4). Once promulgated, rules are applicable to all parties. Moreover, the rulemaking process notifies all parties that the agency is considering the impending rule and provides concerned individuals with an opportunity to be heard. Administrative agencies promulgate three types of rules: legislative rules, interpretative rules, and procedural rules.

**Legislative Rules** Legislative rules, often called *regulations*, are in effect "administrative statutes." **Legislative rules** are those issued by an agency that is able, under a legislative delegation of power, to make rules having the force and effect of law. For example, the FTC has rulemaking power with which to elaborate upon its enabling statute's prohibition of unfair or deceptive acts or practices. Legislative rules, which are immediately binding, generally receive greater deference from reviewing courts than do interpretative rules.

Legislative rules have the force of law if they are constitutional, within the power granted to the agency by the legislature, and issued according to proper procedure. To be constitutional, regulations must not violate any provisions of the U.S. Constitution, such as due process or equal protection. In addition, they may not involve an unconstitutional delegation of legislative power from the legislature to the agency. To be constitutionally permissible, the enabling statute granting power to an agency must establish reasonable standards to guide the agency in implementing the statute. Statutes have met this requirement through such language as "to prohibit unfair methods of competition," "fair and equitable," "public interest, convenience, and necessity," and other equally broad expressions. In any event, an agency may not exceed the actual authority granted by its enabling statute.

Legislative rules must be promulgated in accordance with the procedural requirements of the APA, although the enabling statute may impose more stringent requirements. Most legislative rules are issued in accordance with the **informal rulemaking** procedures of the APA, which require that the agency provide the following:

1. prior notice of a proposed rule, usually by publication in the *Federal Register*;
2. an opportunity for interested parties to participate in the rulemaking; and
3. publication of a final draft containing a concise general statement of the rule's basis and purpose at least thirty days before its effective date. Section 553.

In some instances the enabling statute requires that an agency make certain rules only after providing the opportunity for a hearing. This formal rulemaking procedure, which is far more complex than the informal procedures, is governed by the same APA provisions that govern an adjudication, discussed later. In **formal rulemaking**, when an agency makes rules, it must consider the record of the trial-type agency hearing and include a statement of "findings and conclusions, and the reasons or basis therefore, on all the material issues of fact, law, or discretion presented on the record." Section 557(c).

Some enabling statutes direct that the agency, in making rules, follow certain procedures that are more formal than those the agency uses in informal rulemaking but do not compel the full hearing that formal rulemaking requires. This intermediate procedure, known as **hybrid rulemaking**, results from combining the informal procedures of the APA with additional procedures specified by the enabling statute. For example, an agency may be required to conduct a legislative-type hearing (formal) that permits no cross-examination (informal).

In 1990 Congress enacted the Negotiated Rulemaking Act to encourage the involvement of affected parties in the initial stages of the policy-making process prior to the publication of notice of a proposed rule. The Act authorizes agencies to use negotiated rulemaking but does not require it. If an agency decides to use negotiated rulemaking, the affected parties and the agency develop an agreement and offer it to the agency. If accepted, the agreement becomes a basis for the proposed regulation, which is then published for comment.

**Interpretative Rules** Interpretative rules are agency-issued statements that explain how the agency construes its governing statute. For instance, the SEC "renders administrative interpretations of the law and regulations there-under to members of the public, prospective registrants and others, to help them decide legal questions about the application of the law and the regulations to particular situations and to aid them in complying with the law." *The Work of the SEC* (1980).

Interpretative rules, which are exempt from the APA's procedural requirements of notice and comment, are not automatically binding on private parties the agency regulates or on the courts, although they are given substantial weight. As the Supreme Court has stated, "The weight of such [an interpretative rule] in a particular case will depend upon the thoroughness evident in its consideration, the validity of its reasoning, its consistency with earlier and later pronouncements, and all those factors which give it power to persuade." *Skidmore v. Swift & Co.*, 323 U.S. 134 (1944).

**Procedural Rules** Procedural rules are also exempt from the notice and comment requirements of the APA and are not law. These rules establish rules of conduct for practice before the agency, identify an agency's organization, and describe its method of operation. For example, the SEC's Rules of Practice deal with such matters as who may appear before the commission; business hours and notice of proceedings and hearings; settlements, agreements, and conferences; the presentation of evidence and taking of depositions and interrogatories; and the review of hearings.

## ENFORCEMENT

Agencies also investigate to determine whether certain conduct has violated the statute or the agency's legislative rules. In carrying out this executive function, the agencies traditionally have been accorded great discretion to compel the disclosure of information, subject to constitutional limitations. These limitations require that (1) the investigation be authorized by law and undertaken for a legitimate purpose, (2) the information sought be relevant, (3) the demand for information be sufficiently specific and not unreasonably burdensome, and (4) the information sought not be privileged.

The following explains some of the SEC's investigative and enforcement functions:

> Most of the Commission's investigations are conducted privately. Facts are developed to the fullest extent possible through informal inquiry, interviewing witnesses, examining brokerage records and other documents, reviewing and trading data, and similar means. The Commission is empowered to issue subpoenas requiring sworn testimony and the production of books, records, and other documents pertinent to the subject matter under investigation. In the event of refusal to respond to a subpoena, the Commission may apply to a Federal court for an order compelling obedience. The Work of the SEC (1986).

## ADJUDICATION

After concluding an investigation, the agency may use informal or formal methods to resolve the matter. Because the caseload of administrative agencies is vast, far greater than that of the judicial system, agencies adjudicate most matters informally. Informal procedures include advising, negotiating, and settling. In 1990 Congress enacted the Administrative Dispute Resolution Act to authorize and encourage Federal agencies to use mediation, conciliation, arbitration, and other techniques for the prompt and informal resolution of disputes. The Act does not, however, require agencies to use alternative dispute resolution, and the affected parties must consent to its use.

The formal procedure by which an agency resolves a matter (called **adjudication**) involves finding facts, applying legal rules to the facts, and formulating orders. An **order** "means the whole or a part of a final disposition, whether affirmative, negative, injunctive or declaratory in form, of an agency." APA Section 551(6). In essence an administrative trial, adjudication is used when required by the enabling statute.

The procedures the administrative agencies employ to adjudicate cases are nearly as varied as the agencies themselves. Nevertheless, the APA does establish certain mandatory standards for those Federal agencies the Act covers. For example, under the Act, an agency must give notice of a hearing. The APA also requires that the agency give all interested parties the opportunity to submit and consider "facts, arguments, offers of settlement, or proposals of adjustment." Section 554(c). In many cases this involves testimony and cross-examination of witnesses. If no settlement is reached, a hearing must be held.

The hearing is presided over by an administrative law judge (ALJ) and is prosecuted by the agency. The agency appoints ALJs through a professional merit selection system and may remove them only for good cause. There are more than twice as many ALJs as there are Federal judges. Hearings never use juries; thus, the agency serves as both the prosecutor and decision maker. To reduce the potential for a conflict of interest, the APA provides for a separation of functions between those agency members engaged in investigation and prosecution from those involved in decision making. Section 544(d). Oral and documentary evidence may be introduced by either party, and the agency must base all sanctions, rules, and orders upon "consideration of the whole record or those parts cited by a party and supported by and in accordance with the reliable, probative, and substantial evidence." Section 556(d). All decisions must include a statement of findings of fact and conclusions of law and the reasons or bases for them, as well as a statement of the appropriate rule, order, sanction, or relief.

If authorized to do so by law and within its delegated jurisdiction, an agency may impose in its orders sanctions such as penalties; fines; the seizure of property; the assessment of damages, restitution, compensation, or fees; and the requirement, revocation, or suspension of a license. Sections 551(10) and 558(b). In most instances orders are final unless appealed, and failure to comply with an order subjects the party to a statutory penalty. If the order is appealed, the governing body of the agency may decide the case *de novo*. Section 557(b). Thus, the agency may hear additional evidence and arguments in deciding whether to revise the findings and conclusions made in the initial decision.

Although administrative adjudications mirror to a large extent the procedures of judicial trials, the two differ substantially:

> Agency hearings, especially those dealing with rulemaking, often tend to produce evidence of general conditions as distinguished from facts relating solely to the respondent. Administrative agencies in rulemaking and occasionally in formal adversarial adjudications more consciously formulate policy than do courts. Consequently, administrative adjudications may require that the administrative law judge consider more consciously the impact of his decision upon the public interest as well as upon the particular respondent.... An administrative hearing is tried to an administrative law judge and never to a jury. Since many of the rules governing the admission of proof in judicial trials are designed to protect the jury from unreliable and possibly confusing evidence, it has long been asserted that such rules need not be applied at all or with the same vigor in proceedings solely before an administrative law judge.... Consequently, the technical common law rules governing the admissibility of evidence have generally been abandoned by administrative agencies. McCormick on Evidence, 4th ed., Section 350, p. 605.

◆ **SEE CASE 5-1**

## LIMITS ON ADMINISTRATIVE AGENCIES

An important and fundamental part of administrative law is the limits judicial review imposes upon the activities of administrative agencies. On matters of policy, however, courts are not supposed to substitute their judgment for that of an agency. Additional limitations arise from the legislature and the executive branch, which, unlike the judiciary, may address the wisdom and correctness of an agency's decision or action. Moreover, legally required disclosure of agency actions provides further protection for the public.

◆ **SEE FIGURE 5-1: Limits on Administrative Agencies**

◆ **FIGURE 5-1: Limits on Administrative Agencies**

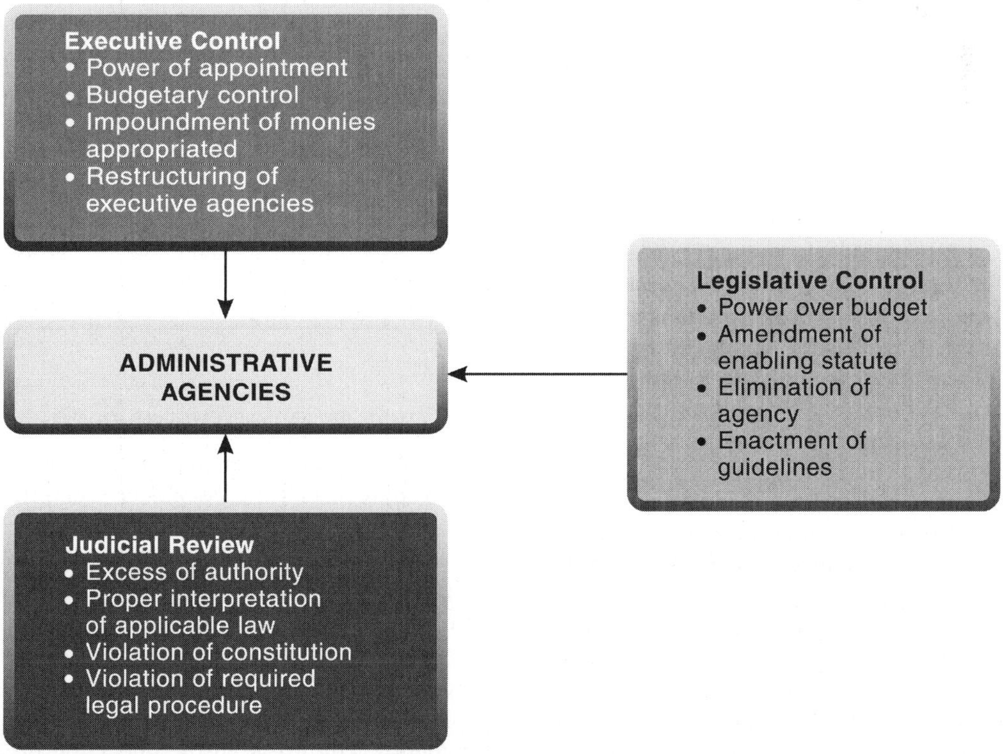

## JUDICIAL REVIEW

As discussed in *Chapter 4*, judicial review describes the process by which the courts examine governmental action. Judicial review, which is available unless a statute precludes such review or the agency action is committed to agency discretion by law, acts as a control or check on a particular rule or order of an administrative agency. Section 701.

**General Requirements** Parties seeking to challenge agency action must have standing and must have exhausted their administrative remedies. Standing requires that the agency action injure the party in fact and that the party assert an interest that is in the "zone of interests to be protected or regulated by the statute in question." Judicial review is ordinarily available only for *final* agency action. Section 704. Accordingly, if a party seeks review while an agency proceeding is in progress, a court will usually dismiss the action because the party has failed to exhaust his administrative remedies.

◆ **SEE CASE 5-2**

In exercising judicial review, the court may decide either to compel agency action unlawfully withheld or to set aside impermissible agency action. In making its determination the court must review the whole record and may set aside agency action only if the error is prejudicial.

**Questions of Law** When conducting a review, a court decides all relevant questions of law, interprets constitutional and statutory provisions, and determines the meaning or applicability of the terms of an agency action. This review of questions of law includes determining whether the agency has (1) exceeded its authority, (2) properly interpreted the applicable law, (3) violated any constitutional provision, or (4) acted contrary to the procedural requirements of the law.

**Questions of Fact** When reviewing factual determinations, the courts use one of three different standards. Where informal rulemaking or informal adjudication has occurred, the standard generally is the **arbitrary and capricious** test, which requires only that the agency had a rational basis for reaching its decision. Where an agency has held a formal hearing, the **substantial evidence** test usually applies. It also applies to informal or hybrid rulemaking, if the enabling statute so requires. The substantial evidence test requires that the agency support its conclusions with "such relevant evidence as a reasonable mind might accept as adequate to support a conclusion." *Consolidated Edison Co. v. NLRB*, 305 U.S. 197 (1938). Finally, in rare instances the reviewing court may apply the **unwarranted by the facts** standard, which permits the court to try the facts *de novo*. This strict review is available only when the enabling statute so provides, when the agency has conducted an adjudication with inadequate fact-finding procedures, or when issues that were not before the agency are raised in a proceeding to enforce nonadjudicative agency action.

◆ **SEE CASE 5-3**

## LEGISLATIVE CONTROL

The legislature may exercise control over administrative agencies in various ways. Through its budgetary power, it may greatly restrict or expand an agency's operations. Congress may amend an enabling statute to increase, modify, or decrease an agency's authority. Even more drastically, it may completely eliminate an agency. Or Congress may establish general guidelines to govern agency action, as it did by enacting the APA. Moreover, it may reverse or change an agency rule or decision through specific legislation. In addition, each house of Congress has oversight committees that review the operations of administrative agencies. Finally, the Senate has the power of confirmation over some high-level appointments to administrative agencies.

In 1996 Congress enacted the Congressional Review Act, which subjects most rules to a new, extensive form of legislative control. With limited exceptions, the Act requires agencies to submit newly adopted rules to each house of Congress before they can take effect. If the rule is a major rule, it does not become final until Congress has had an opportunity to disapprove it. A **major rule** is any rule that the Office of Management and Budget (OMB) finds has resulted in or is likely to result in (1) an annual effect on the economy of at least $100 million, (2) a major increase in costs or prices, or (3) a significant adverse effect on competition, employment, investment, productivity, innovation, or international competitiveness of U.S. enterprises. If the rule is not a major rule it takes effect as it otherwise would have after its submission to Congress and it is subject to possible disapproval by Congress. All rules covered by the Act shall not take effect if Congress adopts a joint resolution of disapproval. The President may veto the joint resolution, but Congress may then vote to override the veto. A rule that has been disapproved is treated as though it had never taken effect.

## CONTROL BY EXECUTIVE BRANCH

By virtue of their power to appoint and remove their chief administrators, U.S. Presidents have significant control over administrative agencies housed within the executive branch. With respect to independent agencies, however, the President has less control because commissioners serve for a fixed term that is staggered with the President's term of office. Nevertheless, his power to appoint agency chairs and to fill vacancies confers considerable control, as does his power to remove commissioners for statutorily defined cause. The President's central role in the budgeting process of agencies also enables him to exert great control over agency policy and operations. Even more extreme is the President's power to impound monies appropriated to an agency by Congress. In addition, the President may radically alter, combine, or even abolish agencies of the executive branch unless either house of Congress disapproves such an action within a prescribed time.

## DISCLOSURE OF INFORMATION

Requiring administrative agencies to disclose information about their actions makes them more accountable to the public. Accordingly, Congress has enacted disclosure statutes to enhance public and political oversight of agency activities. These statutes include the Freedom of Information Act (FOIA), the Privacy Act, and the Government in the Sunshine Act.

**Freedom of Information Act** First enacted in 1966, FOIA gives the public access to most records in the files of Federal administrative agencies. Once a person has requested files, an agency must indicate within ten working days whether it intends to comply with the request and must within a reasonable time respond to the request. The agency may charge a fee for providing the records.

FOIA permits agencies to deny access to nine categories of records: (1) records specifically authorized in the interest of national defense or foreign policy to be kept secret; (2) records that relate solely to the internal personnel rules and practices of an agency; (3) records specifically exempted by statute from disclosure; (4) trade secrets and commercial or financial information that is privileged or confidential; (5) inter- or intra-agency memorandums; (6) personnel and medical files the disclosure of which would constitute a clearly unwarranted invasion of personal privacy; (7) investigatory records compiled for law enforcement purposes; (8) records that relate to the regulation or supervision of financial institutions; and (9) certain geological and geophysical information and data.

The Electronic Freedom of Information Act Amendments of 1996 require agencies to provide public access to information in an electronic format. Agencies must, within one year after their creation, make records available by computer telecommunications or other electronic means.

**Privacy Act** The Privacy Act of 1974 protects certain government records pertaining to individuals that a Federal agency maintains and retrieves by an individual's name or other personal identifier, including social security number. In general, the Privacy Act prohibits unauthorized disclosures of those records covered by the Act. It also gives individuals the right to review and copy records about themselves, to find out whether these records have been disclosed, and to request corrections or amendments of these records, unless the records are legally exempt. It also requires agencies to maintain in their records only that information about an individual that is relevant and necessary to accomplish an agency function and to collect information to the greatest extent practicable directly from the individual.

**Government in the Sunshine Act** The Government in the Sunshine Act requires meetings of many Federal agencies to be open to the public. This Act applies to multimember bodies whose members the President appoints with the advice and consent of the Senate, such as the SEC, the FTC, the Federal Communications Commission (FCC), the CPSC, and the Commodity Futures Trading Commission (CFTC). The Act does not cover executive agencies such as the EPA, the Food and Drug Administration (FDA), and the National Highway Traffic Safety Administration (NHTSA).

Agencies generally may close meetings on the same grounds on which they may refuse disclosure of records under FOIA. In addition, agencies such as the SEC and the Federal Reserve Board may close meetings to protect information the disclosure of which would lead to financial speculation or endanger the stability of financial institutions. The Sunshine Act also permits agencies to close meetings that concern agency participation in pending or anticipated litigation.

## CHAPTER SUMMARY

**OPERATION OF ADMINISTRATIVE AGENCIES**

**Rulemaking** process by which an administrative agency promulgates rules of law
- ***Legislative Rules*** substantive rules issued by an administrative agency under the authority delegated to it by the legislature
- ***Interpretative Rules*** statements issued by an administrative agency indicating how it construes its governing statute
- ***Procedural Rules*** rules issued by an administrative agency establishing its organization, method of operation, and rules of conduct for practice before the agency

**Enforcement** process by which agencies determine whether their rules have been violated
**Adjudication** formal methods by which an agency resolves disputes

---

**LIMITS ON ADMINISTRATIVE AGENCIES**

**Judicial Review** acts as a control or check by a court on a particular rule or order of an administrative agency
**Legislative Control** includes control over the agency's budget and enabling statute
**Control by Executive Branch** includes the President's power to appoint members of the agency
**Disclosure of Information** congressionally required public disclosure enhances oversight of agency activities

# CASES

CASE 5-1

## Adjudication
## AMERICAN AIRLINES, INCORPORATED v. DEPARTMENT OF TRANSPORTATION

United States Court of Appeals, Fifth Circuit, 2000
202 F.3d 788
http://laws.findlaw.com/5th/9960008cv0v3.html

**Garza, J.**

This consolidated appeal involves respondent Department of Transportation's ("DOT's") interpretation of federal law governing airline service at Love Field airport. Petitioners Dallas Fort Worth International Airport Board ("DFW Board"), City of Fort Worth ("Fort Worth"), American Airlines, Inc. ("American"), City of Dallas ("Dallas"), Southwest Airlines Company ("Southwest"), and Love Field Citizens Action Committee (the "Committee") petition for review of DOT's declaratory, procedural, and reconsideration orders. Legend Airlines, Inc. ("Legend"), Continental Airlines, Inc. ("Continental"), and Continental Express, Inc. ("Continental Express") have intervened. For the reasons set forth below, we affirm.

Prior to 1968, Dallas and Fort Worth operated independent and competing airports. One of Dallas's airports was Love Field. DOT's predecessor agency, the Civil Aeronautics Board ("CAB"), found that the competition between Dallas's and Fort Worth's airports was harmful. Accordingly, in 1964 CAB ordered the cities to build a jointly operated airport that would serve as the region's primary airport. The cities responded by creating the DFW Board and by jointly adopting the 1968 Regional Airport Concurrent Bond Ordinance (the "Ordinance"). The Ordinance authorized the issuance of bonds to finance the Dallas-Fort Worth Airport ("DFW"). Of critical importance here is section 9.5 of the Ordinance, which contained the cities' agreement to "take such steps as may be necessary, appropriate and legally permissible * * * to provide for the orderly, efficient and effective phase-out at Love Field, Redbird, GSIA and Meacham Field, of any and all Certificated Air Carrier Services, and to transfer such activities to the [DFW] Regional Airport."

The eight CAB-certified air carriers who were using the Dallas and Fort Worth airports * * * [agreed] to move their air services to DFW as specified in the Ordinance. Southwest, which was solely running intrastate flights from Love Field and thus was exempt from CAB certification and pressure, refused to move to DFW and did not sign [the] agreement. Litigation ensued over efforts to force Southwest from Love Field, terminating with our statement that "Southwest Airlines Co. has a federally declared right to the continued use of and access to Love Field, so long as Love Field remains open." [Citation.]

Congress deregulated the airline industry in 1978. Shortly thereafter, Southwest applied for permission to provide interstate service between Love Field and New Orleans. CAB granted the application, concluding that it lacked power to deny it. This prompted Congress to intervene by enacting the Wright Amendment. [Citation.] The Wright Amendment generally bans interstate service from Love Field. However, it provides certain exemptions from this ban, two of which are significant here: (1) the commuter airline exemption allows interstate "air transportation provided by commuter airlines operating aircraft with a passenger capacity of 56 passengers or less"; and (2) the contiguous state exemption allows flights to and from Louisiana, Arkansas, Oklahoma, and New Mexico, if the flights do not "provide any through service or ticketing with another air carrier" and do not "offer for sale transportation to or from * * * any point which is outside any such State." [Citation.]

The Shelby Amendment [enacted in 1997] * * * expanded the contiguous states exemption to allow direct flights between Love Field and airports within Kansas, Alabama, and Mississippi. [Citation.]

The parties in this case responded in various ways to the Shelby Amendment. Southwest began offering flights between Love Field and Mississippi and Alabama. Legend has announced plans to offer long-haul service to states outside the Love Field service area using large aircraft reconfigured to have less than 57 seats. Continental Express plans to use regional jets with less than 57 seats to fly between Love Field and Cleveland. Continental Express and American offer intrastate flights from Love Field to their hubs, in Houston and Austin respectively.

In response, Fort Worth sued Dallas, the DFW Board, Legend, Continental, and Continental Express in Texas state court to block the proposed additional service from Love Field. * * *

* * *

At the urging of several of the parties, and while both the federal and state actions were pending, DOT initiated the interpretative proceeding that is the subject of this petition for review. DOT issued an order informing the parties in this action that it intended to rule on four "federal law issues" and allowing the parties an opportunity to submit comments on these issues. Subsequently, in response to the parties' initial comments, * * * DOT ultimately issued a "Declaratory Order" resolving the * * * questions it had set forth. Specifically, DOT ruled that:

> (i) the City of Fort Worth may not enforce any commitment by the City of Dallas * * * to limit operations at Love Field authorized by federal law, and the proprietary powers of the City of Dallas do not allow it to restrict services at Love Field authorized by federal law; (ii) the ability of the City of Dallas to limit the type of airline service operated at Love Field is preempted by the Wright and Shelby Amendments; (iii) any airline operating aircraft with a passenger capacity of no more than 56 passengers and a gross aircraft weight of no more than 300,000 pounds may operate service with any type of equipment and flights of any length from or to Love Field, notwithstanding any claim that such service violates any agreement between the Cities of Dallas and Fort Worth; (iv) the Dallas-Fort Worth International Airport Board may not enforce any contract provision that allegedly bars an airline from operating interstate airline service at another airport in the Dallas-Fort Worth metropolitan area; and (v) any airline may offer through service between Love Field and any other point to passengers using a flight between Love Field and another point within Texas operated under subsection (a) of the Wright Amendment, as amended by the Shelby Amendment. * * *

[Citation.] In an accompanying "Procedural Order," DOT rejected various procedural objections raised by the parties. DOT subsequently reaffirmed its rulings on reconsideration.

* * *

Several of the parties challenge DOT's declaratory order on procedural grounds * * * that: DOT violated the Administrative Procedure Act ("APA"). * * *

Fort Worth and the DFW Board argue that DOT's ruling violated the APA in various ways. See § 706 (directing a reviewing court to "hold unlawful and set aside agency action, findings, and conclusions found to be * * * without observance of procedure required by law"). Although DOT has already rejected some of these challenges in its earlier rulings, we review *de novo* DOT's interpretation and application of the APA. [Citation.]

Several parties contend that DOT failed to provide them with sufficient notice as required under § 554(b) or, alternatively, § 553, of the APA. We exercise plenary review over whether DOT complied with applicable procedures. [Citation.]

DOT issued its declaratory order after conducting an informal adjudication, pursuant to its authority under § 554(e) to "issue a declaratory ruling to terminate a controversy or remove uncertainty." [Citations.] Several parties object to DOT's failure to adhere to the APA's notice requirements for formal adjudications. However, in the absence of a statute requiring an agency to conduct its adjudication "on the record after opportunity for agency hearing," [citation], an agency can define its own procedures for conducting an informal adjudication. [Citation.]

While the APA does not expressly require notice in informal adjudications, courts have inferred a requirement that there be "some sort of procedures for notice [and] comment * * * as a necessary means of carrying out our responsibility for a thorough and searching review [of agency action]." [Citation.] Here, DOT issued an order in which it specified the legal issues on which it would rule, allowed the parties to submit comments on these issues, and extended the comment period at the request of several parties. It then ruled on precisely the issues that it identified. We find that DOT's actions satisfied the minimum procedural notice requirements. [Citation.]

Fort Worth contends that DOT failed to comply with § 554(b) by neglecting to notify parties that DOT would also be considering a factual issue: the effect of increased service at Love Field on DFW Airport. This argument fails for two reasons. First, as noted, the formal notice requirement of § 554(b) does not apply to an informal adjudication. Second, the parties were effectively on notice of this issue since it was one that they could reasonably expect to arise given the issues of which DOT gave notice. [Citation.] The fact that Dallas, Continental Express, and Legend all submitted factual evidence to DOT should also have put Fort Worth on notice that it could submit its own factual evidence.

We also note the absence of anything in the record to indicate that Fort Worth possesses any information bearing on the impact of increased service at Love Field. Fort Worth has had three opportunities to present or identify such evidence—during the comment period, in its motion for reconsideration, and in its brief on appeal—but has not demonstrated that it possesses relevant factual information not considered by DOT. This continued failure to identify the evidence it would have submitted indicates that Fort Worth was not prejudiced by any inadequacy in DOT's notice. [Citations.]

We also reject the DFW Board's argument that DOT's order amounts to a substantive rule subject to the notice and comment provision of § 553. Agencies have discretion to choose between adjudication and rulemaking as a means of setting policy. [Citation.] In determining whether an agency action constituted adjudication or rulemaking, we look to the product of the agency action. We also accord significant deference to an agency's characterization of its own action. [Citation.] Since the APA defines "adjudication" as the "agency process for formulating an order," § 551(7), and DOT classifies its ruling as a declaratory order, we find that the agency engaged in adjudication rather than rulemaking. Furthermore, because DOT's order interpreted the rights of a small number of parties properly before it, DOT did not abuse its discretion by acting through an adjudicatory proceeding. [Citation.]

* * *

For the foregoing reasons, we DENY the petitions for review and AFFIRM DOT's orders.

CASE 5-2

## Judicial Review: Standing
## SUMMERS v. EARTH ISLAND INSTITUTE

Supreme Court of the United States, 2009
555 U.S. ___, 129 S.Ct. 1142, 173 L.Ed. 1
http://www.supremecourtus.gov/opinions/08pdf/07-463.pdf

**Scalia, J.**

Respondents are a group of organizations dedicated to protecting the environment. (We will refer to them collectively as "Earth Island.") They seek to prevent the United States Forest Service from enforcing regulations that exempt small fire-rehabilitation and timber-salvage projects from the notice, comment, and appeal process used by the Forest Service for more significant land management decisions. We must determine whether respondents have standing to challenge the regulations in the absence of a live dispute over a concrete application of those regulations.

### I

In 1992, Congress enacted the Forest Service Decisionmaking and Appeals Reform Act (Appeals Reform Act or Act), [citation]. Among other things, this required the Forest Service to establish a notice, comment, and appeal process for "proposed actions of the Forest Service concerning projects and activities implementing land and resource management plans developed under the Forest and Rangeland Renewable Resources Planning Act of 1974." [Citation.]

The Forest Service's regulations implementing the Act provided that certain of its procedures would not be applied to projects that the Service considered categorically excluded from the requirement to file an environmental impact statement (EIS) or environmental assessment (EA). [Citation.] Later amendments to the Forest Service's manual of implementing procedures, adopted by rule after notice and comment, provided that fire-rehabilitation activities on areas of less than 4,200 acres, and salvage-timber sales of 250 acres or less, did not cause a significant environmental impact and thus would be categorically exempt from the requirement to file an EIS or EA. [Citation.] This had the effect of excluding these projects from the notice, comment, and appeal process.

In the summer of 2002, fire burned a significant area of the Sequoia National Forest. In September 2003, the Service issued a decision memo approving the Burnt Ridge Project, a salvage sale of timber on 238 acres damaged by that fire. Pursuant to its categorical exclusion of salvage sales of less than 250 acres, the Forest Service did not provide notice in a form consistent with the Appeals Reform Act, did not provide a period of public comment, and did not make an appeal process available.

In December 2003, respondents filed a complaint in the Eastern District of California, challenging the failure of the Forest Service to apply to the Burnt Ridge Project § 215.4(a) of its regulations implementing the Appeals Reform Act (requiring prior notice and comment), and

§ 215.12(f) of the regulations (setting forth an appeal procedure). * * *

The District Court granted a preliminary injunction against the Burnt Ridge salvage-timber sale. Soon thereafter, the parties settled their dispute over the Burnt Ridge Project and the District Court concluded that "the Burnt Ridge timber sale is not at issue in this case." [Citation.] The Government argued that, with the Burnt Ridge dispute settled, and with no other project before the court in which respondents were threatened with injury in fact, respondents lacked standing to challenge the regulations; and that absent a concrete dispute over a particular project a challenge to the regulations would not be ripe. The District Court proceeded, however, to adjudicate the merits of Earth Island's challenges. It invalidated five of the regulations (including §§ 215.4(a) and 215.12(f)), [citation], and entered a nationwide injunction against their application, [citation].

The Ninth Circuit held that Earth Island's challenges to regulations not at issue in the Burnt Ridge Project were not ripe for adjudication because there was "not a sufficient 'case or controversy'" before the court to sustain a facial challenge. [Citation.] It affirmed, however, the District Court's determination that §§ 215.4(a) and 215.12(f), which were applicable to the Burnt Ridge Project, were contrary to law, and upheld the nationwide injunction against their application.

The Government sought review of the question whether Earth Island could challenge the regulations at issue in the Burnt Ridge Project, and if so whether a nationwide injunction was appropriate relief. We granted certiorari, [citation].

## II

In limiting the judicial power to "Cases" and "Controversies," Article III of the Constitution restricts it to the traditional role of Anglo-American courts, which is to redress or prevent actual or imminently threatened injury to persons caused by private or official violation of law. Except when necessary in the execution of that function, courts have no charter to review and revise legislative and executive action. [Citations.] This limitation "is founded in concern about the proper—and properly limited—role of the courts in a democratic society." [Citations.]

The doctrine of standing is one of several doctrines that reflect this fundamental limitation. It requires federal courts to satisfy themselves that "the plaintiff has 'alleged such a personal stake in the outcome of the controversy' as to warrant *his* invocation of federal-court jurisdiction." [Citation.] He bears the burden of showing that he has standing for each type of relief sought. [Citation.] To seek injunctive relief, a plaintiff must show that he is under threat of suffering "injury in fact" that is concrete and particularized; the threat must be actual and imminent, not conjectural or hypothetical; it must be fairly traceable to the challenged action of the defendant; and it must be likely that a favorable judicial decision will prevent or redress the injury. [Citation.] This requirement assures that "there is a real need to exercise the power of judicial review in order to protect the interests of the complaining party." [Citation.] Where that need does not exist, allowing courts to oversee legislative or executive action "would significantly alter the allocation of power ... away from a democratic form of government," [citation].

The regulations under challenge here neither require nor forbid any action on the part of respondents. The standards and procedures that they prescribe for Forest Service appeals govern only the conduct of Forest Service officials engaged in project planning. "[W]hen the plaintiff is not himself the object of the government action or inaction he challenges, standing is not precluded, but it is ordinarily 'substantially more difficult' to establish." [Citation.] Here, respondents can demonstrate standing only if application of the regulations by the Government will affect *them* in the manner described above.

It is common ground that the respondent organizations can assert the standing of their members. To establish the concrete and particularized injury that standing requires, respondents point to their members' recreational interests in the National Forests. While generalized harm to the forest or the environment will not alone support standing, if that harm in fact affects the recreational or even the mere esthetic interests of the plaintiff, that will suffice. [Citation.]

Affidavits submitted to the District Court alleged that organization member Ara Marderosian had repeatedly visited the Burnt Ridge site, that he had imminent plans to do so again, and that his interests in viewing the flora and fauna of the area would be harmed if the Burnt Ridge Project went forward without incorporation of the ideas he would have suggested if the Forest Service had provided him an opportunity to comment. The Government concedes this was sufficient to establish Article III standing with respect to Burnt Ridge. [Citation.] Marderosian's threatened injury with regard to that project was originally one of the bases for the present suit. After the District Court had issued a preliminary injunction, however, the parties settled their differences on that score. Marderosian's injury in fact with regard to that project has been remedied, and it is, as the District Court pronounced, "not at issue in this case." [Citation.] We know of no precedent for the proposition that when a plaintiff has sued to challenge the lawfulness of certain action or threatened action but has settled that suit, he retains standing to challenge the basis for that action (here, the regulation in the abstract), apart from any concrete application that threatens imminent harm to his interests. Such a holding would fly in the face of Article III's injury-in-fact requirement. [Citation.]

Respondents have identified no other application of the invalidated regulations that threatens imminent and concrete harm to the interests of their members. * * *

Respondents argue that they have standing to bring their challenge because they have suffered procedural injury, namely that they have been denied the ability to file comments on some Forest Service actions and will continue to be so denied. But deprivation of a procedural right without some concrete interest that is affected by the deprivation—a procedural right *in vacuo*—is insufficient to create Article III standing. Only a "person who has been accorded a procedural right to protect *his concrete interests* can assert that right without meeting all the normal standards for redressability and immediacy." [Citation.] * * *

The judgment of the Court of Appeals is reversed in part and affirmed in part.

CASE 5-3

## Judicial Review: Questions of Fact
## FCC v. FOX TELEVISION STATIONS

Supreme Court of the United States, 2009
556 U.S. ____, 129 S.Ct. 1800, 173 L.Ed.2d 738
http://www.law.cornell.edu/supct/html/07-582.ZO.html

**Scalia, J.**

Federal law prohibits the broadcasting of "any … indecent … language," [citation], which includes expletives referring to sexual or excretory activity or organs, see [citation]. This case concerns the adequacy of the Federal Communications Commission's explanation of its decision that this sometimes forbids the broadcasting of indecent expletives even when the offensive words are not repeated.

* * *

* * * Congress has given the Commission various means of enforcing the indecency ban, including civil fines, see § 503(b)(1), and license revocations or the denial of license renewals, [citation].

The Commission first invoked the statutory ban on indecent broadcasts in 1975, declaring a daytime broadcast of George Carlin's "Filthy Words" monologue actionably indecent. [Citation.] At that time, the Commission announced the definition of indecent speech that it uses to this day, prohibiting "language that describes, in terms patently offensive as measured by contemporary community standards for the broadcast medium, sexual or excretory activities or organs, at times of the day when there is a reasonable risk that children may be in the audience." [Citation.]

* * *

In the ensuing years, the Commission took a cautious, but gradually expanding, approach to enforcing the statutory prohibition against indecent broadcasts. * * *

Although the Commission had expanded its enforcement beyond the "repetitive use of specific words or phrases," it preserved a distinction between literal and nonliteral (or "expletive") uses of evocative language. [Citation.] The Commission explained that each literal "description or depiction of sexual or excretory functions must be examined in context to determine whether it is patently offensive," but that "deliberate and repetitive use … is a requisite to a finding of indecency" when a complaint focuses solely on the use of nonliteral expletives. [Citation.]

* * *

In 2004, the Commission took one step further by declaring for the first time that a nonliteral (expletive) use of the F- and S-Words could be actionably indecent, even when the word is used only once. The first order to this effect dealt with an NBC broadcast of the Golden Globe Awards, in which the performer Bono commented, "'This is really, really, f* * *ing brilliant.'" * * *

* * *

This case concerns utterances in two live broadcasts aired by Fox Television Stations, Inc., and its affiliates prior to the Commission's Golden Globes Order. The first occurred during the 2002 Billboard Music Awards, when the singer Cher exclaimed, "I've also had critics for the last 40 years saying that I was on my way out every year. Right. So f* * * 'em." [Citation.] The second involved a segment of the 2003 Billboard Music Awards, during the presentation of an award by Nicole Richie and Paris Hilton, principals in a Fox television series called "The Simple Life." Ms. Hilton began their interchange by reminding Ms. Richie to "watch the bad language," but Ms. Richie proceeded to ask the audience, "Why do they even call it 'The Simple Life?' Have you ever tried to get cow s* * * out of a Prada purse? It's not so f* * *ing simple." [Citation.] Following each of these broadcasts, the Commission received numerous complaints from parents whose children were exposed to the language.

On March 15, 2006, the Commission released Notices of Apparent Liability for a number of broadcasts that the

Commission deemed actionably indecent, including the two described above. [Citation.] * * *

The order first explained that both broadcasts fell comfortably within the subject-matter scope of the Commission's indecency test because the 2003 broadcast involved a literal description of excrement and both broadcasts invoked the "F-Word," which inherently has a sexual connotation. [Citation.] The order next determined that the broadcasts were patently offensive under community standards for the medium. Both broadcasts, it noted, involved entirely gratuitous uses of "one of the most vulgar, graphic, and explicit words for sexual activity in the English language." * * *

* * *

The order explained that the Commission's prior "strict dichotomy between 'expletives' and 'descriptions or depictions of sexual or excretory functions' is artificial and does not make sense in light of the fact that an 'expletive's' power to offend derives from its sexual or excretory meaning." * * * Although the Commission determined that Fox encouraged the offensive language by using suggestive scripting in the 2003 broadcast, and unreasonably failed to take adequate precautions in both broadcasts, [citation], the order * * * declined to impose any forfeiture or other sanction for either of the broadcasts, [citation].

* * * The [Second Circuit] Court of Appeals reversed the agency's orders, finding the Commission's reasoning inadequate under the Administrative Procedure Act. [Citation.] The majority was "skeptical that the Commission [could] provide a reasoned explanation for its 'fleeting expletive' regime that would pass constitutional muster," but it declined to reach the constitutional question. [Citation.] We granted certiorari, [citation].

The Administrative Procedure Act, [citation], which sets forth the full extent of judicial authority to review executive agency action for procedural correctness, [citation], permits (insofar as relevant here) the setting aside of agency action that is "arbitrary" or "capricious," [citation]. Under what we have called this "narrow" standard of review, we insist that an agency "examine the relevant data and articulate a satisfactory explanation for its action." *Motor Vehicle Mfrs. Assn. of United States, Inc. v. State Farm Mut. Automobile Ins. Co.*, [citation]. We have made clear, however, that "a court is not to substitute its judgment for that of the agency," [citation], and should "uphold a decision of less than ideal clarity if the agency's path may reasonably be discerned," [citation].

In overturning the Commission's judgment, the Court of Appeals here relied in part on Circuit precedent requiring a more substantial explanation for agency action that changes prior policy. The Second Circuit has interpreted the Administrative Procedure Act and our opinion in *State Farm* as requiring agencies to make clear "'why the original reasons for adopting the [displaced] rule or policy are no longer dispositive'" as well as "'why the new rule effectuates the statute as well as or better than the old rule.'" [Citation.] * * *

We find no basis in the Administrative Procedure Act or in our opinions for a requirement that all agency change be subjected to more searching review. The Act mentions no such heightened standard. And our opinion in *State Farm* neither held nor implied that every agency action representing a policy change must be justified by reasons more substantial than those required to adopt a policy in the first instance. * * *

To be sure, the requirement that an agency provide reasoned explanation for its action would ordinarily demand that it display awareness that it *is* changing position. An agency may not, for example, depart from a prior policy *sub silentio* or simply disregard rules that are still on the books. [Citation.] And of course the agency must show that there are good reasons for the new policy. But it need not demonstrate to a court's satisfaction that the reasons for the new policy are *better* than the reasons for the old one; it suffices that the new policy is permissible under the statute, that there are good reasons for it, and that the agency *believes* it to be better, which the conscious change of course adequately indicates. This means that the agency need not always provide a more detailed justification than what would suffice for a new policy created on a blank slate. Sometimes it must—when, for example, its new policy rests upon factual findings that contradict those which underlay its prior policy; or when its prior policy has engendered serious reliance interests that must be taken into account. [Citation.] It would be arbitrary or capricious to ignore such matters. In such cases it is not that further justification is demanded by the mere fact of policy change; but that a reasoned explanation is needed for disregarding facts and circumstances that underlay or were engendered by the prior policy.

Judged under the above described standards, the Commission's new enforcement policy and its order finding the broadcasts actionably indecent were neither arbitrary nor capricious. First, the Commission forthrightly acknowledged that its recent actions have broken new ground, taking account of inconsistent "prior Commission and staff action" and explicitly disavowing them as "no longer good law." [Citation.] * * * There is no doubt that the Commission knew it was making a change. That is why it declined to assess penalties * * *.

Moreover, the agency's reasons for expanding the scope of its enforcement activity were entirely rational. * * * Even isolated utterances can be made in "pander[ing,] … vulgar and shocking" manners, [citation], and can constitute harmful "'first blow[s]'" to children, [citation]. It is surely rational (if not inescapable) to believe that a safe harbor for single words would "likely lead to more widespread use of the offensive language." [Citation.]

* * *

The Second Circuit did not definitively rule on the constitutionality of the Commission's orders, but respondents nonetheless ask us to decide their validity under the First Amendment. This Court, however, is one of final review, "not of first view." [Citation.] * * * We see no reason to abandon our usual procedures in a rush to judgment without a lower court opinion. We decline to address the constitutional questions at this time.

The judgment of the United States Court of Appeals for the Second Circuit is reversed, and the case is remanded for further proceedings consistent with this opinion.

## QUESTIONS

1. List and explain the three basic functions of administrative agencies.
2. List and distinguish among the three types of rules promulgated by administrative agencies.
3. Explain the difference between formal and informal methods of adjudication.
4. Identify and explain (a) the questions of law determined by a court in conducting a review of a rule or order of an administrative agency, and (b) the three standards of judicial review of factual determinations made by administrative agencies.
5. Describe the limitations imposed on administrative agencies by the legislative branch, the executive branch, and the legally required disclosure of information.

## PROBLEMS

**1.** In 1942, Congress passed the Emergency Price Control Act in the interest of national defense and security. The stated purpose of the Act was "to stabilize prices and to prevent speculative, unwarranted and abnormal increases in prices and rents." The Act established the Office of Price Administration, which was authorized to establish maximum prices and rents that were to be "generally fair and equitable and [were to] effectuate the purposes of this Act." Convicted for selling beef at prices in excess of those set by the agency, Stark appeals on the ground that the Act unconstitutionally delegated to the agency the legislative power of Congress to control prices. Is Stark correct in this contention?

**2.** The Secretary of Commerce (Secretary) published notice in the *Federal Register* inviting comments regarding flammability standards for mattresses. Statistical data were compiled, consultant studies were conducted, and seventy-five groups submitted comments. The Secretary then determined that all mattresses, including crib mattresses, must pass a cigarette test, consisting of bringing a mattress in contact with a burning cigarette. The department's staff supported this position by stating: "Exemption of youth and crib mattresses is not recommended. While members of these age groups do not smoke, their parents frequently do, and the accidental dropping of a lighted cigarette on these mattresses while attending to a child is a distinct possibility." Bunny Bear, Inc., now challenges the cigarette flammability test, asserting that the standard was not shown to be applicable to crib mattresses, because "infants and young children obviously do not smoke." Bunny Bear argues that the Secretary has not satisfied the burden of proof justifying the inclusion of crib mattresses within this general safety standard. Is Bunny Bear correct? Explain.

**3.** Reagan National Airport in Washington, D.C., is one of the busiest and most crowded airports in the nation. Accordingly, the Federal Aviation Administration (FAA) has restricted the number of commercial landing and takeoff slots at National to forty per hour. Allocation of the slots among the air carriers serving National had been by voluntary agreement through an airline scheduling committee (ASC). When a new carrier requested twenty slots during peak hours, National's ASC was unable to agree on a slot allocation schedule. The FAA engaged in informal rulemaking and invited public comment as a means to solve the slot allocation dilemma. The FAA then issued Special Federal Aviation Regulation 43 (SFAR 43) based on public comments and a proposal made at the last National ASC meeting, thereby decreasing the number of slots held by current carriers and shifting some slots to less desirable times. SFAR 43 also granted eighteen slots to the new carrier. More specifically, SFAR 43 requires five carriers to give up one or more slots in specific hours during the day, requires twelve carriers to shift one slot to the latest hour of operations, and then reserves and allocates the yielded slots among the new entrants and several other carriers. Northwest Airlines seeks judicial review of SFAR 43, claiming that it is arbitrary, capricious, and not a product of reasoned decision making, and that it capriciously favors the Washington–New York market as well as the new carrier. What standard would apply to the agency's actions? Should Northwest prevail? Explain.

**4.** Bachowski was defeated in a United Steelworkers of America union election. After exhausting his union remedies, Bachowski filed a complaint with Secretary of Labor Dunlop. Bachowski invoked the Labor-Management Reporting and Disclosure Act, which required Dunlop to investigate the complaint and determine whether to bring a court action to set aside the election. Dunlop decided such action was unwarranted. Bachowski then filed an action in a Federal district court to order Dunlop to file suit to set aside the election. What standard of review would apply and what would Bachowski have to prove to prevail under that standard?

**5.** The Federal Crop Insurance Corporation (FCIC) was created as a wholly government-owned corporation to insure wheat producers against unavoidable crop failure. As required by law, the FCIC published in the *Federal Register* conditions for crop insurance. Specifically, the FCIC published that spring wheat reseeded on winter wheat acreage was ineligible for coverage. When farmer Merrill applied for insurance on his wheat crop, he informed the local FCIC agent that 400 of his 460 acres of spring wheat were reseeded on the winter wheat acreage. The agent advised Merrill that his entire crop was insurable. When drought destroyed Merrill's wheat, Merrill tried to collect the insurance, but the FCIC refused to pay, asserting that Merrill is bound by the notice provided by publication of the regulation in the *Federal Register.* Is the FCIC correct? Explain.

**6.** The Department of Energy (DOE) issued a subpoena requesting information regarding purchases, sales, exchanges, and other transactions in crude oil from Phoenix Petroleum Company (Phoenix). The aim of the DOE audit was to uncover violations of the Emergency Petroleum Allocation Act of 1973 (EPAA), which provided for summary, or expedited, enforcement of DOE decisions. However, after the subpoena was issued, but before Phoenix had responded, the EPAA expired. The EPAA provided that "[t]he authority to promulgate and amend any regulation, or to issue any order under this Chapter shall expire at midnight September 30, 1981, but such expiration shall not affect any action or pending proceedings, administrative, civil or criminal action or proceeding, whether or not pending, based upon any act committed or liability incurred prior to such expiration date." Using the summary enforcement provisions of the now-defunct EPAA, the DOE sues to enforce the subpoena. Phoenix argues that because the EPAA has expired, the DOE lacks the authority either to issue the subpoena or to use the summary enforcement provisions. Is Phoenix correct? Why?

**7.** Under the Communications Act of 1934 the Federal Communications Commission may not impose common carrier obligations on cable operators. A common carrier is one that "makes a public offering to provide [communication facilities] whereby all members of the public who choose to employ such facilities may communicate or transmit." In May 1976, the Commission issued rules requiring cable television systems of a designated size (a) to develop a minimum twenty-channel capacity by 1986, (b) to make available on a first-come, nondiscriminatory basis certain channels for access by third parties, and (c) to furnish equipment and facilities for such access. The purpose of these rules was to ensure public access to cable systems. Midwest Video Corporation claimed that the access rules exceeded the Commission's jurisdiction granted it by the Communications Act of 1934, because the rules infringe upon the cable systems' journalistic freedom by in effect treating the cable operators as "common carriers." The Commission contended that its expansive mandate under the Communications Act to supervise and regulate broadcasting encompassed the access rules. Did the Commission exceed its authority under the Act?

**8.** Congress enacted the National Traffic and Motor Vehicle Safety Act of 1966 (the Act) for the purpose of reducing the number of traffic accidents that result in death or personal injury. The Act directs the Secretary of Transportation to issue motor vehicle safety standards in order to improve the design and safety features of cars. The Secretary has delegated authority to promulgate safety standards to the National Highway Traffic Safety Administration (NHTSA) under the informal rulemaking procedure of the APA. The Act also authorizes judicial review under the provisions of the Administrative Procedure Act (APA) of all orders establishing, amending, or revoking a Federal motor vehicle safety standard issued by the NHTSA.

Pursuant to the Act, the NHTSA issued Motor Vehicle Safety Standard 208, which required all cars made after September 1982 to be equipped with passive restraints (either automatic seatbelts or airbags). The cost of implementing the standard was estimated to be around $1 billion. However, early in 1981, due to changes in economic circumstances and particularly due to complaints from the automotive industry, the NHTSA rescinded Standard 208. The NHTSA had originally assumed that car manufacturers would install airbags in 60 percent of new cars and passive seatbelts in 40 percent. However, by 1981 it appeared that manufacturers were planning to install seatbelts in 99 percent of all new cars. Moreover, the majority of passive seatbelts could be easily and permanently detached by consumers. Therefore, the NHTSA felt that Standard 208 would not result in any significant safety benefits.

State Farm Mutual Automobile Insurance Company (State Farm) and the National Association of Independent Insurers (NAII) filed petitions in Federal court for review of the NHTSA's rescission of Standard 208. What standard of review would apply to the rescission? Should it be set aside? Explain.

**9.** David Diersen filed a complaint against the Chicago Car Exchange (CCE), an automobile dealership, alleging that the CCE fraudulently furnished him an inaccurate odometer reading when it sold him a 1968 Dodge Charger, in violation of the Vehicle Information and Cost Savings Act (the Odometer Act or the Act). The Odometer Act requires all persons transferring a motor vehicle to give an accurate, written odometer reading to the purchaser or recipient of the transferred vehicle. Under the Act, those who disclose an inaccurate odometer reading with the intent to defraud are subject to a private cause of action by the purchaser and may be held liable for treble damages or $1,500, whichever is greater. The CCE had purchased the vehicle from Joseph Slaski, who certified to the CCE that the mileage was approximately 22,600. The CCE did not suspect that the odometer reading was inaccurate. After purchasing the vehicle, Diersen conducted an extensive investigation and discovered that the vehicle's title documents previously listed its mileage as 75,000. Before Diersen filed this lawsuit, the CCE offered to have Diersen return the car for a complete refund. Diersen refused this offer and decided instead to sue the CCE under the Act. The district court granted the defendant's motion for summary judgment, relying upon a regulation promulgated by the National Highway Traffic Safety Administration (NHTSA) which purports to exempt vehicles that are at least ten years old (such as the one Diersen purchased from the CCE) from the Act's odometer disclosure requirements. Diersen then filed a motion for reconsideration of the court's summary judgment order, arguing that the older-car exemption created by the NHTSA lacked any basis in the Act and was therefore invalid. Should Dierson's motion for reconsideration be granted? Explain.

**10.** Section 7 (a)(2) of the Endangered Species Act of 1973 (ESA) provides (in relevant part) that "[e]ach Federal agency shall, in consultation with and with the assistance of the Secretary (of the Interior), insure that any action authorized, funded, or carried out by such agency … is not likely to jeopardize the continued existence of any endangered species or threatened species or result in the destruction or adverse modification of habitat of such species which is determined by the Secretary, after consultation as appropriate with affected States, to be critical." In 1978, the Fish and Wildlife Service and the National Marine Fisheries Service, on behalf of the Secretary of the Interior and the Secretary of Commerce, respectively, promulgated a joint regulation stating that the obligations imposed by Section 7(a)(2) extend to actions taken in foreign nations. In 1983, the Interior Department proposed a revised joint regulation that would require consultation only for actions taken in the United States or on the high seas. Shortly thereafter, Defenders of Wildlife and other organizations filed an action against the Secretary of the Interior, seeking a declaratory judgment that the new regulation is in error as to the geographic scope of Section 7(a)(2) and an injunction requiring the Secretary to promulgate a new regulation restoring the initial interpretation. Do the plaintiffs have standing to bring this action? Explain.

# C H A P T E R 7
# Intentional Torts

All forms of civil liability are either (1) voluntarily assumed, as by contract, or (2) involuntarily assumed, as imposed by law. Tort liability is of the second type. Tort law gives persons redress from civil wrongs or injuries to their person, property, and economic interests. Examples include assault and battery, automobile accidents, professional malpractice, and products liability. The law of torts has three principal objectives: (1) to compensate persons who sustain harm or loss resulting from another's conduct, (2) to place the cost of that compensation only on those parties who should bear it, and (3) to prevent future harms and losses. The law of torts therefore reallocates losses caused by human misconduct. In general, a tort is committed when:

**1.** a duty owed by one person to another
**2.** is breached and
**3.** proximately causes
**4.** injury or damage to the owner of a legally protected interest.

Each person is legally responsible for the damages his tortious conduct proximately causes. Moreover, as discussed in *Chapter 20*, businesses that conduct their business activities through employees are also liable for the torts their employees commit in the course of employment. The tort liability of employers makes the study of tort law essential to business managers.

Injuries may be inflicted intentionally, negligently, or without fault (strict liability). This chapter will discuss intentional torts; the following chapter will cover negligence and strict liability.

The same conduct may, and often does, constitute both a crime and a tort. An example would be an assault and battery committed by Johnson against West. For the commission of this crime, the State may take appropriate action against Johnson. In addition, however, Johnson has violated West's right to be secure in his person and so has committed a tort against West, who may, regardless of the criminal action by the State against Johnson, bring a civil action against Johnson for damages. On the other hand, an act may be criminal without being tortious, and, by the same token, an act may be a tort but not a crime.

In a tort action, the injured party *sues* to recover *compensation* for the injury sustained as a result of the defendant's wrongful conduct. The primary purpose of tort law, unlike criminal law, is to compensate the injured party, not to punish the wrongdoer. In certain cases, however, courts may award **punitive** or exemplary damages, which are damages over and above the amount necessary to compensate the plaintiff. Where the defendant's tortious conduct has been intentional—or, in some States, reckless—and outrageous, exhibiting "malice" or a fraudulent or evil motive, most courts permit a jury to award punitive damages. The allowance of punitive damages is designed to deter others from similar conduct by punishing and making an example of the defendant.

◆ **SEE CASE 7-1**

Tort law is primarily common law. The Restatement of Torts provides an orderly presentation of this law. From 1934 to 1939, the American Law Institute (ALI) adopted and promulgated the first Restatement. Since then, the Restatement has served as a vital force in shaping the law of torts. Between 1965 and 1978, the institute adopted and promulgated a second edition of the Restatement of Torts, which revises and supersedes the first Restatement. This text will refer to the second Restatement simply as the Restatement.

In 1996, the ALI approved the development of a new Restatement, called Restatement Third, Torts: Liability for Physical and Emotional Harm, which addresses the general or basic elements of the tort action for liability for accidental personal injury, property damage, and emotional harm but does not cover liability for economic loss. This work will replace comparable provisions in the Restatement Second, Torts. The final work will be published in two volumes. Volume 1 is now available and covers liability for negligence causing physical harm, duty, strict liability, factual cause, and scope of liability (traditionally called proximate cause). Volume 2 will cover affirmative duties, emotional harm, landowner liability, and liability of actors who retain independent contractors. Volume 2 is expected to be published in 2011.

Because this new Restatement applies to nonintentional torts, it will be covered extensively in the next chapter and it will be cited as the "Third Restatement." A few of its provisions, however, do apply to intentional torts and will be included in this chapter. Comment c to Section 5 of the Third Restatement provides that the Second Restatement remains largely authoritative in explaining the details of specific intentional torts and their related defenses.

The Institute's Restatement Third, Torts: Economic Torts and Related Wrongs will update coverage on torts that involve economic loss or pecuniary harm *not* resulting from physical harm or physical contact to a person or property. The Institute began this project in 2004, but as of 2010 no part of the work has been approved. In late 2007 the project's Reporter left the project; the project is in abeyance until a successor Reporter is appointed.

State legislatures and, to a lesser extent, courts have actively assessed the need for **tort reform**. In general, tort reform has focused on limiting liability by restricting damages or narrowing claims. The majority of States have enacted at least one piece of legislation that falls into the broad category of tort reform, but these States have enacted different changes or different combinations of changes affecting specific aspects of tort law. Approaches to tort reform that have been taken at the State level include the following:

1. Laws that address specific types of claims; for example, limits on medical malpractice awards or on the liability of providers of alcohol.
2. Laws abolishing joint and several liability or limiting the application of this rule. Where joint and several liability is abolished, each one of the several defendants is liable only for his share of the plaintiff's damages.
3. Laws adding defenses to certain types of tort actions.
4. Laws capping noneconomic damages—so-called pain and suffering awards.
5. Laws to abolish or limit punitive damages, or to raise the standard of proof beyond the preponderance of the evidence.
6. Laws aimed at attorneys' fees; for example, laws that directly regulate contingent fees.

## INTENT

Intent, as used in tort law, does not require a hostile or evil motive; rather, the term denotes either that the actor desires to cause the consequences of his act *or* that he believes that those consequences are substantially certain to result from it. Restatement, Section 8A. The Third Restatement provides that "[a] person acts with the intent to produce a consequence if: (a) the person acts with the purpose of producing that consequence; or (b) the person acts knowing that the consequence is substantially certain to result." Section 1.

The following examples illustrate the definition of intent: (1) If A fires a gun in the middle of the Mojave Desert, he intends to fire the gun; but when the bullet hits B, who is in the desert without A's knowledge, A does not intend that result. (2) A throws a bomb into B's office to kill B. A knows that C is in B's office and that the bomb is substantially certain to injure C, although A has no desire to harm C. A, nonetheless, is liable to C for any injury caused C. A's intent to injure B is *transferred* to C.

Infants (persons who have not reached the age of majority, which is eighteen years in almost all States) are held liable for their intentional torts. The infant's age and knowledge, however, are critical in determining whether the infant had sufficient intelligence to form the requisite intent. Incompetents, like infants, are generally held liable for their intentional torts.

A number of established and specifically named torts protect an individual from various intentional interferences with his person, dignity, property, and economic interests. Because the law of torts is dynamic, new forms of relief continue to develop. To guide the courts in determining when they should impose liability for intentionally inflicted harm that does not fall within the requirements of an established tort, Section 870 of the Restatement provides a general catchall intentional tort:

> One who intentionally causes injury to another is subject to liability to the other for that injury, if his conduct is generally culpable and not justifiable under the circumstances. This liability may be imposed although the actor's conduct does not come within a traditional category of tort liability.

This section also provides a unifying principle both for long-established torts and for those that have developed more recently. The Third Restatement has a similar provision. Section 5.

◆ **SEE FIGURE 7-1: Intent**

## HARM TO THE PERSON

The law provides protection against intentional harm to the person. The primary interests protected by these torts are freedom from bodily contact (by the tort of battery), freedom from apprehension (assault), freedom from confinement (false imprisonment), and freedom from mental

◆ FIGURE 7-1: **Intent**

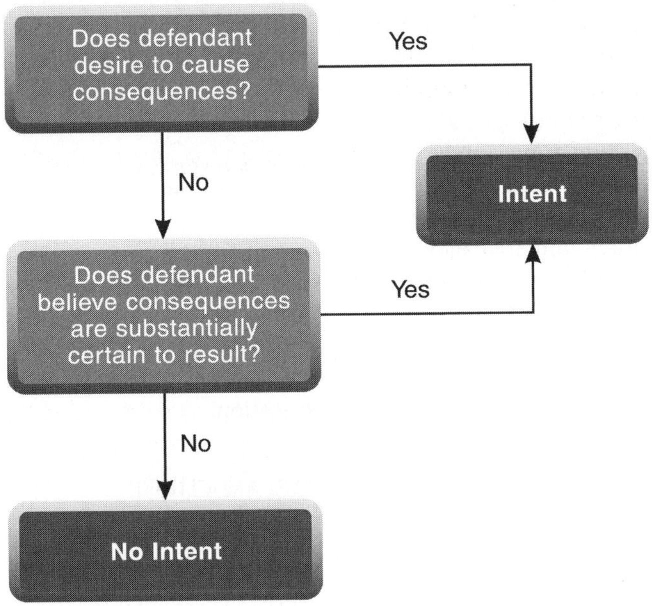


distress (infliction of emotional distress). Generally, intentional torts to the person entitle the injured party to recover damages for bodily harm, emotional distress, loss or impairment of earning capacity, reasonable medical expenses, and harm the tortious conduct caused to property or business.

## BATTERY

**Battery** is an intentional infliction of harmful or offensive bodily contact. It may consist of contact causing serious injury, such as a gunshot wound or a blow to the head with a club. Or it may involve contact causing little or no physical injury, such as knocking a hat off of a person's head or flicking a glove in another's face. Bodily contact is offensive if it would offend a reasonable person's sense of dignity, even if the defendant intended the conduct only as a joke or a compliment. Restatement, Section 19. For instance, kissing another without permission would constitute a battery. Bodily contact may be accomplished by the use of objects, such as Arthur's throwing a rock at Bea with the intention of hitting her. If the rock hits Bea or any other person, Arthur has committed a battery. Nonetheless, in a densely populated society one cannot expect complete freedom from personal contact with others. Accordingly, neither casually bumping into another in a congested area nor gently tapping that other on the shoulder to get her attention would constitute a battery.

## ASSAULT

**Assault** is intentional conduct by one person directed at another that places the other in apprehension of imminent (immediate) bodily harm or offensive contact. It is usually committed immediately preceding a battery, but if the intended battery fails, the assault remains. Assault is principally a mental rather than a physical intrusion. Accordingly, damages for assault may include compensation for fright and humiliation. The person in danger of immediate bodily harm must have *knowledge* of the danger and be apprehensive of its imminent threat to his safety. For example, if Joan aims a loaded gun at Kelly's back, but Pat subdues her before Kelly becomes aware of the danger, Joan has not committed an assault upon Kelly.

Historically, it has been said that words alone do not constitute an assault. Nonetheless, spoken words must be taken in context, and if as taken cause apprehension, these spoken words will constitute an assault. On the other hand, words sometimes will negate an apparent threat so that there is no assault. This does not mean that a defendant can avoid liability for an assault by making his threat conditional. The threat "If you do not give me your book, I will break your arm" constitutes an assault.

## FALSE IMPRISONMENT

The tort of **false imprisonment**, or false arrest, is the intentional confining of a person against her will within fixed boundaries if the person is conscious of the confinement or is harmed by it. Merely obstructing a person's freedom of movement is not false imprisonment so long as a reasonable alternative exit is available. False imprisonment may be brought about by physical force, by the threat of physical force (both express and implied), by physical barriers, or by force directed against the plaintiff's property. For instance, an individual who remains in a store after his wallet is confiscated or who remains on a train after the conductor refuses to allow her suitcase to be removed are both examples of false imprisonment through the use of force against personal property. Damages for false imprisonment may include compensation for loss of time, physical discomfort, inconvenience, physical illness, and mental suffering.

Merchants occasionally encounter potential liability for false imprisonment when they seek to question a suspected shoplifter. A merchant who detains an innocent person may face a lawsuit for false imprisonment. Nonetheless, most States have statutes protecting the merchant, provided she detains the suspect upon probable cause, in a reasonable manner, and for not more than a reasonable time.

◆ **SEE CASE 7-2**

### INFLICTION OF EMOTIONAL DISTRESS

One of the more recently recognized torts is that of intentional *or reckless* infliction of emotional distress. The Restatement, Section 46, states the rule as follows:

> One who by extreme and outrageous conduct intentionally or recklessly causes severe emotional distress to another is subject to liability for such emotional distress, and if bodily harm to the other results from it, for such bodily harm.

**Recklessness** is conduct that evidences a conscious disregard of or an indifference to the consequences of the act committed. The Third Restatement provides a more detailed definition:

> A person acts recklessly in engaging in conduct if: (a) the person knows of the risk of harm created by the conduct or knows facts that make the risk obvious to another in the person's situation, and (b) the precaution that would eliminate or reduce the risk involves burdens that are so slight relative to the magnitude of the risk as to render the person's failure to adopt the precaution a demonstration of the person's indifference to the risk. Section 2.

Under this tort, the courts impose liability for conduct exceeding all bounds usually tolerated by society when such conduct intentionally or recklessly causes serious mental distress. Many courts allow recovery even in the absence of physical injury. This cause of action does not protect a person from abusive language or rudeness, but rather from atrocious, intolerable conduct beyond all bounds of decency. Examples of this tort would include leading to a person's home, when he is present, a noisy demonstrating mob yelling threats to lynch him unless he leaves town, or placing a rattlesnake in another's bed as a practical joke. Other examples would include sexual harassment on the job and outrageous, prolonged bullying tactics employed by creditors or collection agencies attempting to collect a debt or by insurance adjusters trying to force a settlement of an insurance claim.

◆ **SEE CASE 7-2**

## HARM TO THE RIGHT OF DIGNITY

The law also protects a person against intentional harm to his right of dignity. This protection includes a person's reputation, privacy, and right to freedom from unjustifiable litigation.

### DEFAMATION

The tort of defamation is a false communication that injures a person's reputation by disgracing him and diminishing the respect in which he is held. An example would be the publication of a false statement that a person had committed a crime or had a loathsome disease. In *Beckman v. Dunn*, 276 Pa.Super. 527, 419 A.2d 583 (1980), the court stated,

> A communication is defamatory if it tends to harm the reputation of another so as to lower him in the estimation of the community or deter third persons from associating or dealing with him, and necessarily involves the idea of disgrace.

**Elements of Defamation** The elements of a defamation action are (1) a false and defamatory statement concerning another; (2) an unprivileged publication (communication) to a third party; (3) depending on the status of the defendant, negligence or recklessness on her part in knowing or failing to ascertain the falsity of the statement; and (4) in some cases, proof of special harm caused by the publication. Restatement, Section 558. The burden of proof is on the plaintiff to prove the falsity of the defamatory statement.

If a defamatory communication is handwritten, typewritten, printed, pictorial, or in another medium with like communicative power, such as a television or radio broadcast, it is designated **libel**. If it is spoken or oral, it is designated **slander**. Restatement, Sections 568 and 568A. In either case, it must be communicated to a person or persons other than the one who is defamed, a process referred to as *publication*. If Maurice hands or mails to Pierre a defamatory letter he has written about Pierre's character, this is not a publication, as it is intended only for Pierre. The publication must have been intentional or the result of the defendant's negligence.

Any living person, as well as corporations, partnerships, and unincorporated associations, may be defamed. Restatement, Sections 561 and 562. Unless a statute provides otherwise, no action may be brought for defamation of a deceased person. Restatement, Section 560.

A significant trend affecting business has been the bringing of defamation suits against former employers by discharged employees. It has been reported that such suits account for approximately one-third of all defamation lawsuits.

◆ SEE CASE 7-3

**Defenses to Defamation** **Privilege** is immunity from tort liability granted when the defendant's conduct furthers a societal interest of greater importance than the injury inflicted upon the plaintiff. Three types of privileges apply to defamation: absolute, conditional, and constitutional.

**Absolute privilege** protects the defendant regardless of his motive or intent. This type of privilege, which has been confined to those few situations in which public policy clearly favors complete freedom of speech, includes (1) statements made by participants in a judicial proceeding regarding that proceeding; (2) statements made by members of Congress on the floor of Congress and by members of State and local legislative bodies; (3) statements made by certain executive branch officers in the discharge of their governmental duties; and (4) statements regarding a third party made between spouses when they are alone.

Qualified or **conditional privilege** depends upon proper use of the privilege. A person has conditional privilege to publish defamatory matter to protect his own legitimate interests or, in some cases, the interests of another. Conditional privilege also extends to many communications in which the publisher and the recipient have a common interest, such as in letters of reference. A publisher who acts in an excessive manner, without probable cause, or for an improper purpose forfeits conditional privilege.

The First Amendment to the U.S. Constitution guarantees freedom of speech and freedom of the press. The U.S. Supreme Court has applied these rights to the law of defamation by extending a form of constitutional privilege to defamatory and false statements regarding public officials or public figures so long as it is done without malice. Restatement, Section 580A. For these purposes, *malice* is not ill will but clear and convincing proof of the publisher's knowledge of falsity or reckless disregard of the truth. Thus, under **constitutional privilege** the public official or public figure must prove that the defendant published the defamatory and false comment with knowledge or in reckless disregard of the comment's falsity and its defamatory character. In a defamation suit brought by a private person (one who is neither a public official nor a public figure) the plaintiff must prove that the defendant published the defamatory and false comment with malice *or* negligence.

Congress enacted Section 230 of the **Communications Decency Act of 1996 (CDA)**, granting immunity to Internet service providers (ISPs) from liability for defamation when publishing information originating from a third party. A court has interpreted this provision of the CDA as immunizing an ISP that refused to remove or retract an allegedly defamatory posting made on its bulletin board. The immunity granted by the CDA to ISPs has spawned a number of lawsuits urging ISPs to reveal the identities of subscribers who have posted allegedly defamatory statements. To date, ISPs have complied, generating additional litigation by angry ISP patrons attempting to keep their identities protected by asserting that their right to free speech is being compromised.

Because Section 230 of the CDA grants immunity only to ISPs, there is the possibility that employers will be held liable for some online defamatory statements made by an employee. Section 577(2) of the Restatement of Torts provides that a person who intentionally and unreasonably fails to remove defamatory matter that she knows is exhibited on property in her possession or under her control is liable for its continued publication. Therefore, employers in control of e-forums, such as electronic bulletin boards and chat rooms, should act quickly to remove any defamatory statement brought to their attention.

## INVASION OF PRIVACY

The invasion of a person's right to privacy actually consists of four distinct torts: (1) appropriation of a person's name or likeness; (2) unreasonable intrusion upon the seclusion of another; (3) unreasonable public disclosure of private facts; or (4) unreasonable publicity that places another in a false light in the public eye. Restatement, Section 652A.

It is entirely possible and not uncommon for a person to invade another's right of privacy in a manner entailing two or more of these related torts. For example, Cindy forces her way into Ozzie's hospital room, takes a photograph of Ozzie, and publishes it to promote Cindy's cure for Ozzie's illness along with false statements about Ozzie that a reasonable person would consider highly objectionable. Ozzie would be entitled to recover on any or all of the four torts comprising invasion of privacy.

◆ SEE FIGURE 7-2: Privacy

**Appropriation** Appropriation is the unauthorized use of the plaintiff's name or likeness for the defendant's benefit, as, for example, in promoting or advertising a product or service. Restatement, Section 652C. The tort of appropriation, also known as the **right of publicity**, seeks to protect the individual's right to the exclusive use of his identity. In the earlier example, Cindy's use of Ozzie's photograph to promote Cindy's business constitutes the tort of appropriation.

◆ FIGURE 7-2: **Privacy**

| | Appropriation | Intrusion | Public Disclosure | False Light |
|---|---|---|---|---|
| **Publicity** | Yes | No | Yes | Yes |
| **Private facts** | No | Yes | Yes | No |
| **Offensiveness** | No | Yes | Yes | Yes |
| **Falsity** | No | No | No | Yes |

◆ SEE CASE 7-4

**Intrusion** Intrusion is the unreasonable and highly offensive interference with the solitude or seclusion of another. Restatement, Section 652B. Such unreasonable interference would include improper entry into another's dwelling, unauthorized eavesdropping upon another's private conversations, and unauthorized examination of another's private papers and records. The intrusion must be highly offensive or objectionable to a reasonable person and must involve matters that are private. Thus, there is no liability if the defendant examines public records or observes the plaintiff in a public place. This form of invasion of privacy is committed once the intrusion occurs, as publicity is not required.

**Public Disclosure of Private Facts** Under the tort of public disclosure of private facts, the courts impose liability for publicity given to private information about another if the matter made public would be highly offensive and objectionable to a reasonable person. Like intrusion, this tort applies only to private, not public, information regarding an individual; unlike intrusion, it requires publicity. Under the Restatement, the publicity required differs in degree from the "publication" required under the law of defamation. This tort requires that private facts be communicated to the public at large or that they become public knowledge, whereas publication of a defamatory statement need only be made to a single third party. Section 652D, Comment a. Some courts, however, have allowed recovery where the disclosure was made to only one person. Thus, under the Restatement approach, Kathy, a creditor of Gary, will not invade Gary's privacy by writing a letter to Gary's employer to inform the employer of Gary's failure to pay a debt, but Kathy would be liable if she posted in the window of her store a statement that Gary will not pay the debt he owes to her. Also, unlike defamation, this tort applies to truthful private information if the matter published would be offensive and objectionable to a reasonable person of ordinary sensibilities.

**False Light** The tort of false light imposes liability for publicity that places another in a false light that is highly offensive if the defendant *knew* or acted in *reckless disregard* of the fact that the matter publicized was false. Restatement, Section 652E. For example, Linda includes Keith's name and photograph in a public "rogues' gallery" of convicted criminals. Because Keith has never been convicted of any crime, Linda is liable to him for placing him in a false light. Other examples include publicly and falsely attributing to a person an opinion, statement, or written work, as well as the unauthorized use of a person's name on a petition or on a complaint in a lawsuit.

Like defamation, the matter must be untrue; unlike defamation, it must be "publicized," not merely "published." Restatement, Section 652D, Comment a. Although the matter must be objectionable to a reasonable person, it need not be defamatory. In many instances, the same facts will give rise to actions both for defamation and for false light.

**Defenses** The defenses of absolute, conditional, and constitutional privilege apply to publication of any matter that is an invasion of privacy to the same extent that such defenses apply to defamation.

### MISUSE OF LEGAL PROCEDURE

Three torts comprise the misuse of legal procedure: malicious prosecution, wrongful civil proceedings, and abuse of process. Each protects an individual from being subjected to unjustifiable litigation. Malicious prosecution and wrongful civil proceedings impose liability for damages caused by improperly brought proceedings, including harm to reputation, credit, or standing; emotional distress; and the expenses incurred in defending against the wrongfully brought lawsuit. Abuse of process is a tort consisting of the use of a legal proceeding (criminal or civil) to accomplish a purpose for which the proceeding is not designed. Abuse of process applies even when there is probable cause or when the plaintiff or prosecution succeeds in the litigation.

## HARM TO PROPERTY

The law also provides protection against invasions of a person's interests in property. Intentional harm to property includes the torts of (1) trespass to real property, (2) nuisance, (3) trespass to personal property, and (4) conversion.

### REAL PROPERTY

**Real property** is land and anything attached to it, such as buildings, trees, and minerals. The law protects the possessor's rights to the exclusive use and quiet enjoyment of the land. Accordingly, damages for harm to land include compensation for the resulting diminution in the value of the land, the loss of use of the land, and the discomfort caused to the possessor of the land. Restatement, Section 929.

**Trespass** Section 158 of the Restatement provides:

> One is subject to liability to another for trespass, irrespective of whether he thereby causes harm to any legally protected interest of the other, if he intentionally
>
> **(a)** enters land in the possession of the other, or causes a thing or a third person to do so, or
> **(b)** remains on the land, or
> **(c)** fails to remove from the land a thing which he is under a duty to remove.

It is no defense that the intruder acted under the mistaken belief of law or fact that he was not trespassing. If the intruder intended to be upon the particular property, his reasonable belief that he owned the land or had permission to enter upon the land is irrelevant. Restatement, Section 164. An intruder is not liable if his own actions do not cause his presence on the land of another. For example, if Carol throws Ralph onto Tim's land, Ralph is not liable to Tim for trespass, although Carol is.

A trespass may be committed on, beneath, or above the surface of the land, although the law regards the upper air, above a prescribed minimum altitude for flight, as a public highway. Therefore, no aerial trespass occurs unless the aircraft enters into the lower reaches of the airspace and substantially interferes with the landowner's use and enjoyment. Restatement, Section 159.

**Nuisance** A nuisance is a nontrespassory invasion of another's interest in the private use and enjoyment of land. Restatement, Section 821D. In contrast to trespass, nuisance does not require interference with another's right to exclusive possession of land, but rather imposes liability for significant and unreasonable harm to another's use or enjoyment of land. Examples of nuisances include the emission of unpleasant odors, smoke, dust, or gas, as well as the pollution of a stream, pond, or underground water supply. In one case, a computer's serious disturbance of a television retailer's signal reception was considered a nuisance.

### PERSONAL PROPERTY

**Personal property**, or chattel, is any type of property other than an interest in land. The law protects a number of interests in the possession of personal property, including an interest in the property's physical condition and usability, an interest in the retention of possession, and an interest in its availability for future use.

**Trespass** Trespass to personal property consists of the intentional dispossession or unauthorized use of the personal property of another. Though the interference with the right to exclusive use and possession may be direct or indirect, liability is limited to instances in which the trespasser (1) dispossesses the other of the property; (2) substantially impairs the condition, quality, or value of the property; (3) deprives the possessor of the use of the property for a substantial time; or (4) causes harm to the possessor or to some person or thing in which the possessor has a legally protected interest. Restatement, Section 218. For example, Albert parks his car in front of his house. Ronald pushes Albert's car around the corner. Albert subsequently looks for his car but cannot find it for several hours. Ronald is liable to Albert for trespass.

**Conversion** Conversion is an intentional exercise of dominion or control over another's personal property that so seriously interferes with the other's right of control as to justly require the payment of full value for the property. Restatement, Section 222A. Thus, all conversions are trespasses, but not all trespasses are conversions.

Conversion may consist of the intentional destruction of personal property or the use of property in an unauthorized manner. For example, Ken entrusts an automobile to Barbara, a dealer, for sale. After she drives the car 8,000 miles on her own business, Barbara is liable to Ken for conversion. On the other hand, in the example in which Ronald pushed Albert's car around the corner, Ronald would *not* be liable to Albert for conversion. Moreover, a person who buys stolen property is liable to the rightful owner for conversion even if the buyer acquires the property in good faith and without knowledge that it was stolen. Restatement, Section 229.

## HARM TO ECONOMIC INTERESTS

Economic interests account for a fourth set of interests the law protects against intentional interference. Economic or pecuniary interests include a person's existing and prospective contractual relations, a person's business reputation, a person's name and likeness (previously discussed under the section titled "Appropriation"), and a person's freedom from deception. Business torts—those torts that protect a person's economic interests—are discussed in this section under the following headings: (1) interference with contractual relations, (2) disparagement, and (3) fraudulent misrepresentation.

## INTERFERENCE WITH CONTRACTUAL RELATIONS

To conduct business it is necessary to establish trade relations with employees, suppliers, and customers. Though these relations may or may not be contractual, those that are, or are capable of being established by contract, receive legal protection against interference. Section 766 of the Restatement provides:

> One who intentionally and improperly interferes with the performance of a contract (except a contract to marry) between another and a third person by inducing or otherwise causing the third person not to perform the contract, is subject to liability to the other for the pecuniary loss resulting to the other from the failure of the third person to perform the contract.

The law imposes similar liability for intentional and improper interference with another's prospective contractual relation, such as a lease renewal or financing for construction. Restatement, Section 766B.

In either case, the rule requires that a person act with the purpose or motive of interfering with another's contract or with the knowledge that such interference is substantially certain to occur as a natural consequence of her actions. The interference may occur by threats or by prevention through the use of physical force. Frequently, interference is accomplished through inducement, such as the offer of a better contract. For instance, Edgar may offer Doris, an employee of Frank, a salary of $5,000 more per year than the contractual arrangement between Doris and Frank. If Edgar is aware that a contract exists between Doris and Frank and of the fact that his offer to Doris will interfere with that contract, then Edgar is liable to Frank for intentional interference with contractual relations.

To be distinguished is the situation in which the contract may be terminated at will or in which the contractual relation is only prospective. In these cases, competition is a proper basis for interference; for if one party is pursuing a contractual relation, others also are free to pursue a similar arrangement. For example, Amos and Brenda are competing distributors of transistors. Amos induces Carter, a prospective customer of Brenda, to buy transistors from Amos instead of Brenda. Amos has no liability to Brenda because his interference with Brenda's prospective contract with Carter is justified on the basis of competition, so long as Amos does not use predatory means such as physical violence, fraud, civil suits, or criminal prosecution to persuade Carter to deal with him.

Damages for interference with contractual relations include the pecuniary loss of the benefits of the contract, consequential losses caused by the interference, and emotional distress or actual harm to reputation. Restatement, Section 774A. In one case, Pennzoil had orally entered into a contract to merge with Getty Oil. Before the merger was consummated, however, Texaco induced Getty to merge with Texaco instead. Pennzoil sued Texaco for tortious interference with the merger contract and was awarded $7.53 billion in compensatory damages and $3 billion in punitive damages. *Texaco, Inc. v. Pennzoil, Co.*, 729 S.W.2d 768 (1987).

## DISPARAGEMENT

The tort of **disparagement** or injurious falsehood imposes liability upon a person who publishes a false statement that results in harm to another's interests which have pecuniary value, if the publisher knows that the statement is false or acts in reckless disregard of its truth or falsity. This tort most commonly involves false statements that the publisher intends to cast doubt upon the title or quality of another's property or products. Thus, Adam, while contemplating the purchase of merchandise that belongs to Barry, reads a newspaper advertisement in which Carol falsely asserts she owns the merchandise. Carol has disparaged Barry's property in the goods. Similarly, Marlene, knowing her statement to be false, tells Lionel that Matthew, an importer of wood, does not deal in mahogany. As a result, Lionel, who had intended to buy mahogany from Matthew, buys it elsewhere. Marlene is liable to Matthew for disparagement.

Absolute, conditional, and constitutional privileges apply to the same extent to the tort of disparagement as they do to defamation. In addition, a competitor has conditional privilege to compare her products favorably with those of a rival, even though she does not believe that her products are superior. No privilege applies, however, if the comparison contains false assertions of specific unfavorable facts about the competitor's property. For example, a manufacturer who advertises that his goods are the best in the market, even though he knows that a competitor's product is better, is not liable for disparagement. If he goes further, however, by falsely stating that his product is better because his competitor uses shoddy materials, then his disparagement would no longer be privileged, and he would be liable to his competitor for disparagement.

The pecuniary loss an injured person may recover is that which directly and immediately results from impairment of the marketability of the property disparaged. The injured party also may recover damages for expenses necessary to counteract the false publication, including litigation expenses, the cost of notifying customers, and the cost of publishing denials. Thus, Ursula publishes in a magazine an untrue statement that cranberries grown during the current season in a particular area are unwholesome. Shortly thereafter, the business of Victor, a jobber who has contracted to buy the entire output of cranberries grown in this area, falls off by 50 percent. If no other facts account for this decrease in his business, Victor is entitled to recover the amount of his loss from Ursula, plus the expenses necessary to counteract the misinformation published.

### FRAUDULENT MISREPRESENTATION

With respect to intentional, or fraudulent, misrepresentation, Section 525 of the Restatement provides:

> One who fraudulently makes a misrepresentation of fact, opinion, intention, or law for the purpose of inducing another to act or to refrain from action in reliance upon it, is subject to liability to the other in deceit for pecuniary loss caused to him by his justifiable reliance upon the misrepresentation.

For example, Smith represents to Jones that a tract of land in Texas is located in an area where oil drilling had recently commenced. Smith makes this statement knowing it to be false. In reliance upon the statement, Jones purchases the land from Smith, who is liable to Jones for fraudulent misrepresentation. Although fraudulent misrepresentation is a tort action, it is closely connected with contractual negotiations; the effects of such misrepresentation on assent to a contract are discussed in *Chapter 11*.

◆ SEE FIGURE 7-3: **Intentional Torts**

## DEFENSES TO INTENTIONAL TORTS

Even though the defendant has intentionally invaded the interests of the plaintiff, the defendant will not be liable if such conduct was privileged. A defendant's conduct is privileged if it furthers an interest of such social importance that the law confers immunity from tort liability for the damage the conduct causes to others. Examples of privilege include self-defense, defense of property, and defense of others. In addition, the plaintiff's consent to the defendant's conduct is a defense to intentional torts.

### CONSENT

If one consents to conduct resulting in damage or harm to his own person, dignity, property, or economic interests, no liability will generally attach to the intentional infliction of injury. **Consent**, which signifies that one is willing for an act to occur, negates the wrongfulness of the act. A person may manifest consent expressly or impliedly, by words or by conduct.

Consent must be given by an individual with capacity to do so. Consent given by a minor, mental incompetent, or intoxicated individual is invalid if he is not capable of appreciating the nature, extent, or probable consequences of the conduct to which he has consented. Consent is not effective

◆ FIGURE 7-3: **Intentional Torts**

| Interest Protected | Tort |
|---|---|
| **Person** | |
| Freedom from contact | Battery |
| Freedom from apprehension | Assault |
| Freedom of movement | False imprisonment |
| Freedom from distress | Infliction of emotional distress |
| **Dignity** | |
| Reputation | Defamation |
| Privacy | Appropriation |
| | Intrusion |
| | Public disclosure of private facts |
| | False light |
| Freedom from wrongful legal actions | Misuse of legal procedure |
| **Property** | |
| Real | Trespass |
| | Nuisance |
| Personal | Trespass |
| | Conversion |
| **Economic** | |
| Contracts | Interference with contractual rights |
| Goodwill | Disparagement |
| Freedom from deception | Fraudulent misrepresentation |

if given under duress, by which one constrains another's will by compelling that other to give consent unwillingly.

### PRIVILEGE

A person who would otherwise be liable for a tort is *not* liable if he acts pursuant to and within the limits of a privilege. Restatement, Section 890. Conditional privileges, as discussed in the section on defamation, depend upon proper use of the privilege. Absolute privilege, on the other hand, protects the defendant regardless of his purpose. Examples of absolute privilege include untrue, defamatory statements made by participants during the course of judicial proceedings, by legislators, by certain governmental executives, and between spouses. Absolute immunity also protects a public prosecutor from civil liability for malicious prosecution.

One conditional privilege—self-defense—entitles an individual to injure another's person without the other's consent. The law created the privilege of **self-defense** to enable an individual to protect himself against tortious interference. By virtue of this privilege an individual may inflict or impose what would otherwise constitute battery, assault, or false imprisonment.

Section 63 of the Restatement provides:

> An actor is privileged to use reasonable force, not intended or likely to cause death or serious bodily harm, to defend himself against unprivileged harmful or offensive contact or other bodily harm which he reasonably believes that another is about to inflict intentionally upon him.

The privilege of self-defense exists whether or not the danger actually exists, provided that the defendant reasonably believed self-defense was necessary. The reasonableness of the defendant's actions is based upon what a person of average courage would have thought under the circumstances. A possessor of property is also permitted to use reasonable force, not intended or likely to cause death or serious bodily harm, to protect his real and personal property.

## CHAPTER SUMMARY

| | |
|---|---|
| **HARM TO THE PERSON** | **Battery** intentional infliction of harmful or offensive bodily contact<br>**Assault** intentional infliction of apprehension of immediate bodily harm or offensive contact<br>**False Imprisonment** intentional confining of a person against her will<br>**Infliction of Emotional Distress** extreme and outrageous conduct intentionally or recklessly causing severe emotional distress |
| **HARM TO THE RIGHT OF DIGNITY** | **Defamation** false communication that injures a person's reputation<br>• ***Libel*** written or electronically transmitted defamation<br>• ***Slander*** spoken defamation<br>• ***Defenses*** truth, absolute privilege, conditional privilege, and constitutional privilege are defenses to a defamation action<br>**Invasion of Privacy**<br>• ***Appropriation*** unauthorized use of a person's identity<br>• ***Intrusion*** unreasonable and highly offensive interference with the seclusion of another<br>• ***Public Disclosure of Private Facts*** highly offensive publicity of private information<br>• ***False Light*** highly offensive and false publicity about another<br>**Misuse of Legal Procedure** torts that protect an individual from unjustifiable litigation |
| **HARM TO PROPERTY** | **Real Property** land and anything attached to it<br>• ***Trespass*** wrongfully entering on land of another<br>• ***Nuisance*** a nontrespassory interference with another's use and enjoyment of land |

| | |
|---|---|
| | **Personal Property** any property other than land<br>• ***Trespass*** an intentional taking or use of another's personal property<br>• ***Conversion*** intentional exercise of control over another's personal property |
| **HARM TO ECONOMIC INTERESTS** | **Interference with Contractual Relations** intentionally causing one of the parties to a contract not to perform<br>**Disparagement** publication of false statements about another's property or products<br>**Fraudulent Misrepresentation** a false statement, made with knowledge of its falsity, intended to induce another to act |
| **DEFENSES TO INTENTIONAL TORTS** | **Consent** a person may not recover for injury to which he willingly and knowingly consents<br>**Self-Defense** a person may take appropriate action to prevent harm to himself where time does not allow resort to the law |

# CASES

## CASE 7-1

### Punitive Damages

## PHILIP MORRIS USA v. WILLIAMS

Supreme Court of the United States, 2007

549 U.S. 346, 127 S.Ct. 1057, 166 L.Ed.2d 940

http://www.law.cornell.edu/supct/pdf/05-1256P.ZS

**Breyer, J.**

This lawsuit arises out of the death of Jesse Williams, a heavy cigarette smoker. Respondent [plaintiff at trial], Williams' widow, represents his estate in this state lawsuit for negligence and deceit against Philip Morris, the manufacturer of Marlboro, the brand that Williams favored. A jury found that Williams' death was caused by smoking; that Williams smoked in significant part because he thought it was safe to do so; and that Philip Morris knowingly and falsely led him to believe that this was so. The jury ultimately found that Philip Morris was negligent (as was Williams) and that Philip Morris had engaged in deceit. In respect to deceit, the claim at issue here, it awarded compensatory damages of about $821,000 (about $21,000 economic and $800,000 noneconomic) along with $79.5 million in punitive damages.

The trial judge subsequently found the $79.5 million punitive damages award "excessive," [citation], and reduced it to $32 million. Both sides appealed. The Oregon Court of Appeals rejected Philip Morris' arguments and restored the $79.5 million jury award. Subsequently, [the State Supreme Court rejected Philip Morris' arguments that the trial court should have instructed the jury that it could not punish Philip Morris for injury to persons not before the court, and that the roughly 100-to-1 ratio the $79.5 million award bore to the compensatory damages amount indicated a "grossly excessive" punitive award].

* * *

Philip Morris then sought certiorari. It asked us to consider, among other things, (1) its claim that Oregon had unconstitutionally permitted it to be punished for harming nonparty victims; and (2) whether Oregon had in effect disregarded "the constitutional requirement that punitive damages be reasonably related to the plaintiff's harm." [Citation.] We granted certiorari limited to these two questions.

* * *

This Court has long made clear that "punitive damages may properly be imposed to further a State's legitimate interests in punishing unlawful conduct and deterring its repetition." [Citations.] At the same time, we have emphasized the need to avoid an arbitrary determination of an award's amount. Unless a State insists upon proper standards that will cabin the jury's discretionary authority, its punitive damages system may deprive a defendant of "fair notice … of the severity of the penalty that a State may impose,"[citation]; it may threaten "arbitrary punishments," *i.e.*, punishments that reflect not an "application of law" but "a decision maker's caprice," [citation]; and, where the amounts are sufficiently large, it may impose one State's (or one jury's)"policy choice," say as to the conditions under which (or even whether) certain products can be sold, upon "neighboring States" with different public policies, [citation].

For these and similar reasons, this Court has found that the Constitution imposes certain limits, in respect both to procedures for awarding punitive damages and to amounts forbidden as "grossly excessive." [Citation] (requiring judicial review of the size of punitive awards); [citation] (review must be de novo); [citation] (excessiveness decision depends upon the reprehensibility of the defendant's conduct, whether the award bears a reasonable relationship to the actual and potential harm caused by the defendant to the plaintiff, and the difference between the award and sanctions "authorized or imposed in comparable cases"); [citation] (excessiveness more likely where ratio exceeds single digits). Because we shall not decide whether the award here at issue is "grossly excessive," we need now only consider the Constitution's procedural limitations.

In our view, the Constitution's Due Process Clause forbids a State to use a punitive damages award to punish a defendant for injury that it inflicts upon nonparties or those whom they directly represent, *i.e.*, injury that it inflicts upon those who are, essentially, strangers to the litigation. For one thing, the Due Process Clause prohibits a State from punishing an individual without first providing that individual with "an opportunity to present every available defense." [Citation.] Yet a defendant threatened with punishment for injuring a nonparty victim has no opportunity to defend against the charge, by showing, for example in a case such as this, that the other victim was not entitled to damages because he or she knew that smoking was dangerous or did not rely upon the defendant's statements to the contrary.

* * *

Finally, we can find no authority supporting the use of punitive damages awards for the purpose of punishing a defendant for harming others. We have said that it may be appropriate to consider the reasonableness of a punitive damages award in light of the *potential* harm the defendant's conduct could have caused. But we have made clear that the potential harm at issue was harm potentially caused *the plaintiff*. [Citation] ("We have been reluctant to identify concrete constitutional limits on the ratio between harm, or potential harm, *to the plaintiff* and the punitive damages award"). * * *

* * * Evidence of actual harm to nonparties can help to show that the conduct that harmed the plaintiff also posed a substantial risk of harm to the general public, and so was particularly reprehensible—although counsel may argue in a particular case that conduct resulting in no harm to others nonetheless posed a grave risk to the public, or the converse. Yet for the reasons given above, a jury may not go further than this and use a punitive damages verdict to punish a defendant directly on account of harms it is alleged to have visited on nonparties.

* * * We therefore conclude that the Due Process Clause requires States to provide assurance that juries are not asking the wrong question, *i.e.*, seeking, not simply to determine reprehensibility, but also to punish for harm caused strangers.

* * *

The instruction that Philip Morris said the trial court should have given distinguishes between using harm to others as part of the "reasonable relationship" equation (which it would allow) and using it directly as a basis for punishment. The instruction asked the trial court to tell the jury that "you *may* consider the extent of harm suffered by others *in determining what [the] reasonable relationship is*" between Philip Morris' punishable misconduct and harm caused to Jesse Williams, "*[but] you are not to punish the defendant for the impact of its alleged misconduct on other persons, who may bring lawsuits of their own* in which other juries can resolve their claims…." [Citation.] And as the Oregon Supreme Court explicitly recognized, Philip Morris argued that the Constitution "prohibits the state, acting through a civil jury, from using punitive damages to punish a defendant for harm to nonparties." [Citation.]

* * *

As the preceding discussion makes clear, we believe that the Oregon Supreme Court applied the wrong constitutional standard when considering Philip Morris' appeal. We remand this case so that the Oregon Supreme Court can apply the standard we have set forth. Because the application of this standard may lead to the need for a new trial, or a change in the level of the punitive damages award, we shall not consider whether the award is constitutionally "grossly excessive." We vacate the Oregon Supreme Court's judgment and remand the case for further proceedings not inconsistent with this opinion.

It is so ordered.

CASE 7-2

## False Imprisonment/Infliction of Emotional Distress

## FERRELL V. MIKULA

Court of Appeals of Georgia, 2008, reconsideration denied, 2008

295 Ga.App. 326, 672 S.E.2d

http://scholar.google.com/scholar_case?case=12901711244406213270&hl=en&as_sdt=2&as_vis=1&oi=scholarr

**Barnes, C. J.**

Racquel Ferrell and the parents of Kristie Ferrell sued Ruby Tuesday, Inc. and its manager Christian Mikula for false imprisonment, intentional infliction of emotional distress, * * *. After extensive discovery, the defendants moved for summary judgment on all counts. In a one-page order stating only that no genuine issues as to any material fact existed, the trial court granted the motion, and the Ferrells' appeal. For the reasons that follow, we affirm the trial court's grant of summary judgment to the defendants on the Ferrells' claim for intentional infliction of emotional distress * * * but reverse the grant on the false imprisonment claim.

* * *

* * * [T]he evidence shows that on Friday night, August 6, 2006, 18-year-old Racquel Ferrell and 13-year-old Kristie Ferrell went to Ruby Tuesday. After they ate and paid their bill, the girls left the restaurant, got into their car, and drove out of the parking lot. As they began to enter the highway, Racquel noticed a black truck following her very closely with its headlights on high. She could not see well out of her rear-view mirror with the bright lights behind her, so she changed lanes, but the truck changed lanes with her and stayed close behind. She switched lanes again, and the truck did too. A marked police car by the side of the road pulled onto the highway between the girls' car and the following truck and pulled the car over. After asking Racquel if she had any drugs or weapons, the officer pulled her out of the car, placed her in handcuffs, and put her in the back seat of his patrol car. Another officer removed Kristie from the car, placed her in handcuffs, and put her in the back of another patrol car.

All of the police officers gathered to talk to the driver of the truck that had been following the Ferrells, who turned out to be a uniformed off-duty police officer working as a security guard for Ruby Tuesday. The officer who arrested Racquel returned to the patrol car where she was being held and told her if she had not paid her Ruby Tuesday bill she was going to jail. She protested, and the officer conferred again with the other officers, then returned to the car and said, "It was a mistake." He explained that the manager at the restaurant had sent the off-duty officer after them because he said the girls had not paid their bill, but they did not fit the description of the two people who had walked out without paying. The officers removed the handcuffs from Racquel and Kristie and returned them to their car. After asking for Racquel's driver's license and obtaining information about both girls, the officer told them they were free to go.

Mikula had been an assistant manager for about a month, and was the only manager at Ruby Tuesday that night. One of the servers, Robert, reported that his customers at Table 24 had a complaint, so Mikula talked to the couple and told them he would "take care of" the food item in question. The customers were a man and a woman in their late 20s to early 30s. Mikula left the table to discuss the matter with Robert, after which server Aaron told Mikula that the patrons at Table 24 had left without paying. Mikula looked at the table, confirmed they had not left any money for the bill, and went out the main entrance. He saw a car pulling out of the parking lot, and said to the off-duty officer, "Hey, I think they just left without paying." The officer said, "Who, them?" Mikula said, "I think so," and the officer got up and went to his vehicle.

* * *

Mikula knew the officer was going to follow the people in the car and would stop them, but did not ask the officer if he had seen who got into the car. He did not give the officer a description of the people at Table 24, and did not know the race, age, gender, or number of people in the car being followed. He did not know if there were people in any of the other cars in the parking lot. He did not ask any other people in the restaurant if they had seen the people at Table 24 leave the building, which had two exits. He did not know how long the people had been gone before Aaron told him they left, or whether another customer had picked up money from Table 24. He could have tried to obtain more information to determine whether the people in the car he pointed out were the people who had been sitting at Table 24, but did not do so.

* * *

In this case, the Ferrells were detained without a warrant, and thus have a claim for false imprisonment * * *. [Citation.] "False imprisonment is the unlawful detention of the person of another, for any length of time, whereby such person is deprived of his personal liberty." [Citation.] "The only essential elements of the action being the detention and its unlawfulness, malice and the want of probable cause need not be shown." [Citations.]

The evidence in this case clearly establishes that the Ferrells were detained. "* * * under modern tort law an individual may be imprisoned when his movements are restrained in the open street, or in a traveling automobile." [Citation.] Ruby Tuesday does not argue otherwise, but instead argues that the evidence established sufficient probable cause and the plaintiffs failed to establish that Mikula acted with malice. But malice is not an element of false imprisonment, * * *. Further, * * * the mere existence of probable cause standing alone has no real defensive bearing on the issue of liability [for false imprisonment]. [Citation.]

* * *

Arresting or procuring the arrest of a person without a warrant constitutes a tort, "unless he can justify under some of the exceptions in which arrest and imprisonment without a warrant are permitted by law, [citations]." Generally, one "who causes or directs the arrest of another by an officer without a warrant may be held liable for false imprisonment, in the absence of justification, and the burden of proving that such imprisonment lies within an exception rests upon the person … causing the imprisonment." [Citations.] * * *

Accordingly, as the Ferrells have established an unlawful detention, the next issue to consider is whether Mikula "caused" the arrest. Whether a party is potentially liable for false imprisonment by "directly or indirectly urg[ing] a law enforcement official to begin criminal proceedings" or is not liable because he "merely relates facts to an official who then makes an independent decision to arrest" is a factual question for the jury. [Citation.] The party need not expressly request an arrest, but may be liable if his conduct and acts "procured and directed the arrest." [Citation.]

* * *

Here, Mikula told the officer that the car leaving the parking lot contained people who left without paying for their food, although he did not know or try to ascertain who was in the car. He also knew the officer was going to detain the people in the car and could have tried to stop him, but made no attempt to do so. Accordingly, the trial court erred in granting summary judgment to the defendants on the plaintiffs' false imprisonment claim.

* * *

The Ferrells also contend that the trial court erred in granting summary judgment to the defendants on their claim for intentional infliction of emotional distress. The elements of a cause of action for intentional infliction of emotional distress are: (1) intentional or reckless conduct; (2) that is extreme and outrageous; (3) a causal connection between the wrongful conduct and the emotional distress; and (4) severe emotional distress. [Citation.] Further,

> [l]iability for this tort has been found only where the conduct has been so outrageous in character, and so extreme in degree, as to go beyond all possible bounds of decency, and to be regarded as atrocious, and utterly intolerable in a civilized community. Generally, the case is one in which the recitation of the facts to an average member of the community would arouse his resentment against the actor, and lead him to exclaim, "Outrageous!"

[Citation.]

In this case, the action upon which the Ferrells base their emotional distress claim is being stopped by the police, placed in handcuffs, and held in a patrol car for a short period of time before being released. While this incident was unfortunate, the question raised by the evidence was whether the restaurant manager's actions were negligent, not whether he acted maliciously or his conduct was extreme, atrocious, or utterly intolerable. Accordingly, the trial court did not err in granting the defendants' motion for summary judgment on the Ferrells' claim for intentional infliction of emotional distress.

* * *

Judgment affirmed in part and reversed in part.

## CASE 7-3

### Defamation
### FRANK B. HALL & CO., INC. v. BUCK

Court of Appeals of Texas, Fourteenth District, 1984
678 S.W.2d 612, cert. denied, 472 U.S. 1009, 105 S.Ct. 2704, 86 L.Ed.2d 720 (1985)

**Junell, J.**

Larry W. Buck (Buck or appellee) sued his former employer, Frank B. Hall & Co. (Hall or appellant), for damages for defamation of character, * * *. By unanimous verdict, a jury found damages for * * * defamation of character and exemplary damages. The court entered judgment for appellee for $1,905,000.00 in damages, plus interest, attorney's fees and costs of court. For the reasons set forth below we affirm.

Appellee, an established salesman in the insurance business, was approached in the spring of 1976 by a representative of Hall with a prospective job offer. Appellee was then an executive vice-president of the insurance firm of Alexander & Alexander, and in the previous year he generated approximately $550,000.00 in commissions for the firm. He was the top producer in Alexander's Houston office and was ranked nationally among the top five salesmen for Alexander. After several meetings, Buck accepted Hall's offer of employment and began working for Hall on June 1, 1976. Hall agreed to pay Buck an annual salary of $80,000.00 plus additional compensation equal to seven and one-half percent of net retained commissions for each year to a maximum commission of $600,000.00, plus fringe benefits. The agreement was to be for a three year period. Several Alexander employees followed Buck to Hall's office. During the next several months Buck generated substantial commission income for Hall and succeeded in bringing several major accounts to the firm.

In October, 1976, Mendel Kaliff, then president of Frank B. Hall & Co. of Texas, held a meeting with Buck and Lester Eckert, Hall's office manager and a former Alexander employee. Kaliff informed Buck his salary was being reduced to $65,000.00 and that Hall was eliminating Buck's incentive and profit sharing benefits. Kaliff told Buck these measures were being taken because of Buck's failure to produce sufficient income for Hall. However, Kaliff added that if Buck could generate $400,000.00 net commission income by June 1, 1977, his salary and benefits would be reinstated retroactively.

On March 31, 1977, at another impromptu meeting, Kaliff and Eckert abruptly fired Buck and instructed him not to return to Hall's offices. Buck sought employment with several other insurance firms, but his efforts were fruitless. Distraught at having lost his job and being unable to find suitable employment in the insurance business, Buck hired an investigator, Lloyd Barber, in an attempt to discover Hall's true reasons for firing him. This suit is based upon statements made by Hall employees to Lloyd Barber and to Charles Burton, a prospective employer, and upon a note written by Virginia Hilley, a Hall employee. Appellant brings eighty points of error, which will be grouped in thirteen categories.

* * *

Lloyd Barber contacted Mendel Kaliff, Lester Eckert and Virginia Hilley and told them that he was an investigator, Buck was being considered for a position of trust and responsibility, and Barber was seeking information about Buck's employment with Frank B. Hall & Co. Barber testified that he had interviewed Kaliff, Eckert and Hilley on separate occasions in September and October of 1977, and had tape-recorded the conversations. Appellee introduced into evidence Barber's properly authenticated investigative reports, which were based on these taped interviews. The report shows Kaliff remarked several times that Buck was untrustworthy, and not always entirely truthful; he said Buck was disruptive, paranoid, hostile and was guilty of padding his expense account. Kaliff said he had locked Buck out of his office and had not trusted him to return. He charged that Buck had promised things he could not deliver. Eckert told Barber that Buck was horrible in a business sense, irrational, ruthless, and disliked by office personnel. He described Buck as a "classical sociopath," who would verbally abuse and embarrass Hall employees. Eckert said Buck had stolen files and records from Alexander & Alexander. He called Buck "a zero," "a Jekyll and Hydeperson" who was "lacking in compucture (sic) or scruples."

Virginia Hilley told Barber that Buck could have been charged with theft for materials he brought with him to Hall from Alexander & Alexander.

Any act wherein the defamatory matter is intentionally or negligently communicated to a third person is a publication. In the case of slander, the act is usually the speaking of the words. Restatement (Second) Torts §577 comment a (1977). There is ample support in the record to show that these individuals intentionally communicated disparaging remarks to a third person. The jury was instructed that "Publication means to communicate defamatory words to some third person in such a way that he understands the words to be defamatory. A statement is not published if it was authorized, invited or procured by Buck and if Buck knew in advance the contents of the invited communication." In response to special issues, the jury found that the slanderous statements were made and published to Barber.

Hall argues that Buck could and should have expected Hall's employees to give their opinion of Buck when requested to do so. Hall is correct in stating that a plaintiff may not recover for a publication to which he has consented, or which he has authorized, procured or invited, [citation]; and it may be true that Buck could assume that Hall's employees would give their opinion when asked they do so. However, there is nothing in the record to indicate that Buck knew Hall's employees would defame him when Barber made the inquiries. The accusations made by Kaliff, Eckert and Hilley were not mere expressions of opinion but were false and derogatory statements of fact.

* * *

A defamer cannot escape liability by showing that, although he desired to defame the plaintiff, he did not desire to defame him to the person to whom he in fact intentionally published the defamatory communication. The publication is complete although the publisher is mistaken as to the identity of the person to whom the publication is made. Restatement (Second) of Torts §577 comment 1 (1977). Likewise, communication to an agent of the person defamed is a publication, unless the communication is invited by the person defamed or his agent. Restatement §577 comment e. We have already determined that the evidence is sufficient to show that Buck did not know what Kaliff, Eckert or Hilley would say and that he did not procure the defamatory statements to create a lawsuit. Thus, the fact that Barber may have been acting at Buck's request is not fatal to Buck's cause of action. There is absolutely no proof that Barber induced Kaliff, Eckert or Hilley to make any of the defamatory comments.

* * *

When an ambiguity exists, a fact issue is presented. The court, by submission of proper fact issues, should let the jury render its verdict on whether the statements were fairly susceptible to the construction placed thereon by the plaintiff. [Citation.] Here, the jury found (1) Eckert made a statement calculated to convey that Buck had been terminated because of serious misconduct; (2) the statement was slanderous or libelous; (3) the statement was made with malice; (4) the statement was published; and (5) damage directly resulted from the statement. The jury also found the statements were not substantially true. The jury thus determined that these statements, which were capable of a defamatory meaning, were understood as such by Burton.

* * *

We hold that the evidence supports the award of actual damages and the amount awarded is not manifestly unjust. Furthermore, in responding to the issue on exemplary damages, the jury was instructed that exemplary damages must be based on a finding that Hall "acted with ill will, bad intent, malice or gross disregard to the rights of Buck." Although there is no fixed ratio between exemplary and actual damages, exemplary damages must be reasonably apportioned to the actual damages sustained. [Citation.] Because of the actual damages [$605,000] and the abundant evidence of malice, we hold that the award of punitive damages [$1,300,000] was not unreasonable. * * *

The judgment of the trial court is affirmed.

## CASE 7-4

### Appropriation
## WHITE v. SAMSUNG ELECTRONICS AMERICA, INC.

United States Court of Appeals, Ninth Circuit, 1992

971 F.2d 1395, cert. denied, 508 U.S. 951, 113 S.Ct. 2443, 124 L.Ed.2d 660 (1993)

**Goodwin, J.**

This case involves a promotional "fame and fortune" dispute. In running a particular advertisement without Vanna White's permission, defendants Samsung Electronics America, Inc. (Samsung) and David Deutsch Associates, Inc. (Deutsch) attempted to capitalize on White's fame to enhance their fortune. White sued, alleging infringement of various intellectual property rights, but the district court granted summary judgment in favor of the defendants. We affirm in part, reverse in part, and remand.

Plaintiff Vanna White is the hostess of "Wheel of Fortune," one of the most popular game shows in television history. An estimated forty million people watch the program daily. Capitalizing on the fame which her participation in the show has bestowed on her, White markets her identity to various advertisers.

The dispute in this case arose out of a series of advertisements prepared for Samsung by Deutsch. The series ran in at least half a dozen publications with widespread, and in some cases national, circulation. Each of the advertisements in the series followed the same theme. Each depicted a current item from popular culture and a Samsung electronic product. Each was set in the twenty-first century and conveyed the message that the Samsung product would still be in use by that time. By hypothesizing outrageous future outcomes for the cultural items, the ads created humorous effects. For example, one lampooned current popular notions of an unhealthy diet by depicting a raw steak with the caption: "Revealed to be health food, 2010 A.D." Another depicted irreverent "news"-show host Morton Downey Jr. in front of an American flag with the caption: "Presidential candidate. 2008 A.D."

The advertisement which prompted the current dispute was for Samsung videocassette recorders (VCRs). The ad depicted a robot, dressed in a wig, gown, and jewelry which Deutsch consciously selected to resemble White's hair and dress. The robot was posed next to a game board which is instantly recognizable as the Wheel of Fortune game show set, in a stance for which White is famous. The caption of the ad read: "Longest running game show. 2012 A.D." Defendants referred to the ad as the "Vanna White" ad. Unlike the other celebrities used in the campaign, White neither consented to the ads nor was she paid.

Following the circulation of the robot ad, White sued Samsung and Deutsch in federal district court under: * * * the California common law right of publicity; * * *. The district court granted summary judgment against White on each of her claims. White now appeals.

* * *

White * * * argues that the district court erred in granting summary judgment to defendants on White's common law right of publicity claim. In *Eastwood v. Superior Court*, [citation], the California court of appeal stated that the common law right of publicity cause of action "may be pleaded by alleging (1) the defendant's use of the plaintiff's identity; (2) the appropriation of plaintiff's name or likeness to defendant's advantage, commercially or otherwise; (3) lack of consent, and (4) resulting injury." [Citation.] The district court dismissed White's claim for failure to satisfy *Eastwood*'s second prong, reasoning that defendants had not appropriated White's "name or likeness" with their robot ad. We agree that the robot ad did not make use of White's name or likeness. However, the common law right of publicity is not so confined.

The *Eastwood* court did not hold that the right of publicity cause of action could be pleaded only by alleging an appropriation of name or likeness. *Eastwood* involved an unauthorized use of photographs of Clint Eastwood and of his name. Accordingly, the *Eastwood* court had no occasion to consider the extent beyond the use of name or likeness to which the right of publicity reaches. That court held only that the right of publicity cause of action "may be" pleaded by alleging, *inter alia*, appropriation of name or likeness, not that the action may be pleaded only in those terms.

The "name or likeness" formulation referred to in *Eastwood* originated not as an element of the right of publicity cause of action, but as a description of the types of cases in which the cause of action had been recognized. The source of this formulation is Prosser, *Privacy*, 48 Cal.L.Rev. 383, 401–07 (1960), one of the earliest and most enduring articulations of the common law right of publicity cause of action. In looking at the case law to that point, Prosser recognized that right of publicity cases involved one of two basic factual scenarios: name appropriation, and picture or other likeness appropriation. [Citation.]

Even though Prosser focused on appropriations of name or likeness in discussing the right of publicity, he noted that "[i]t is not impossible that there might be appropriation of the plaintiff's identity, as by impersonation, without use of either his name or his likeness, and that this would be an invasion of his right of privacy." [Citation.] At the time Prosser wrote, he noted however, that "[n]o such case appears to have arisen." [Citation.]

Since Prosser's early formulation, the case law has borne out his insight that the right of publicity is not limited to the appropriation of name or likeness. In *Motschenbacher v. R.J. Reynolds Tobacco Co.*, [citation], the defendant had used a photograph of the plaintiff's race car in a television commercial. Although the plaintiff appeared driving the car in the photograph, his features were not visible. Even though the defendant had not appropriated the plaintiff's name or likeness, this court held that plaintiff's California right of publicity claim should reach the jury.

In *Midler*, this court held that, even though the defendants had not used Midler's name or likeness, Midler had stated a claim for violation of her California common law right of publicity because "the defendants * * * for their own profit in selling their product did appropriate part of her identity" by using a Midler sound-alike. [Citation.]

In *Carson v. Here's Johnny Portable Toilets, Inc.*, [citation], the defendant had marketed portable toilets under the brand name "Here's Johnny"—Johnny Carson's signature "Tonight Show" introduction—without Carson's permission. The district court had dismissed Carson's Michigan common law right of publicity claim because the defendants had not used Carson's "name or likeness." [Citation.] In reversing the district court, the sixth circuit found "the district court's conception of the right of publicity * * * too narrow" and held that the right was implicated because the defendant had appropriated Carson's identity by using, *inter alia*, the phrase "Here's Johnny." [Citation.]

These cases teach not only that the common law right of publicity reaches means of appropriation other than name or likeness, but that the specific means of appropriation are relevant only for determining whether the defendant has in fact appropriated the plaintiff's identity. The right of publicity does not require that appropriations of identity be accomplished through particular means to be actionable. It is noteworthy that the *Midler* and *Carson* defendants not only avoided using the plaintiff's name or likeness, but they also avoided appropriating the celebrity's voice, signature, and photograph. The photograph in *Motschenbacher* did include the plaintiff, but because the plaintiff was not visible the driver could have been an actor or dummy and the analysis in the case would have been the same.

Although the defendants in these cases avoided the most obvious means of appropriating the plaintiffs' identities, each of their actions directly implicated the commercial interests which the right of publicity is designed to protect. As the *Carson* court explained,

> [t]he right of publicity has developed to protect the commercial interest of celebrities in their identities. The theory of the right is that a celebrity's identity can be valuable in the promotion of products, and the celebrity has an interest that may be protected from the unauthorized commercial exploitation of that identity. * * * If the celebrity's identity is commercially exploited, there has been an invasion of his right whether or not his "name or likeness" is used.

[Citation.] It is not important how the defendant has appropriated the plaintiff's identity, but whether the defendant has done so. *Motschenbacher*, *Midler*, and *Carson* teach the impossibility of treating the right of publicity as guarding only against a laundry list of specific means of appropriating identity. A rule which says that the right of publicity can be infringed only through the use of nine different methods of appropriating identity merely challenges the clever advertising strategist to come up with the tenth.

Indeed, if we treated the means of appropriation as dispositive in our analysis of the right of publicity, we would not only weaken the right but effectively eviscerate it. The right would fail to protect those plaintiffs most in need of its protection. Advertisers use celebrities to promote their products. The more popular the celebrity, the greater the number of people who recognize her, and the greater the visibility for the product. The identities of the most popular celebrities are not only the most attractive for advertisers, but also the easiest to evoke without resorting to obvious means such as name, likeness, or voice.

Consider a hypothetical advertisement which depicts a mechanical robot with male features, an African-American complexion, and a bald head. The robot is wearing black hightop Air Jordan basketball sneakers, and a red basketball uniform with black trim, baggy shorts, and the number 23 (though not revealing "Bulls" or "Jordan" lettering). The ad depicts the robot dunking a basketball one-handed, stiff-armed, legs extended like open scissors, and tongue hanging out. Now envision that this ad is run on television during professional basketball games. Considered individually, the robot's physical attributes, its dress, and its stance tell us little. Taken together, they lead to the only conclusion that any sports viewer who has registered a discernible pulse in the past five years would reach: the ad is about Michael Jordan.

Viewed separately, the individual aspects of the advertisement in the present case say little. Viewed together, they leave little doubt about the celebrity the ad is meant to depict. The female-shaped robot is wearing a long gown, blond wig, and large jewelry. Vanna White dresses exactly like this at times, but so do many other women. The robot is in the process of turning a block letter on a game-board. Vanna White dresses like this while turning letters on a game-board but perhaps similarly attired Scrabble-playing women do this as well. The robot is standing on what looks to be the Wheel of Fortune game show set. Vanna White dresses like this, turns letters, and does this on the Wheel of Fortune game show. She is the only one. Indeed, defendants themselves referred to their ad as the "Vanna White" ad. We are not surprised.

Television and other media create marketable celebrity identity value. Considerable energy and ingenuity are expended by those who have achieved celebrity value to exploit it for profit. The law protects the celebrity's sole right to exploit this value whether the celebrity has achieved her fame out of rare ability, dumb luck, or a combination thereof. We decline Samsung and Deutsch's invitation to permit the evisceration of the common law right of publicity through means as facile as those in this case. Because White has alleged facts showing that Samsung and Deutsch had appropriated her identity, the district court erred by rejecting, on summary judgment, White's common law right of publicity claim.

## QUESTIONS

1. Identify and define the torts that protect against intentional harm to personal rights.
2. Explain the application of the various privileges to defamation suits and how they are affected by whether the plaintiff is (a) a public figure, (b) a public official, or (c) a private person.
3. Distinguish the four torts comprising invasion of privacy.
4. Identify and describe the torts that protect against harm to property.
5. Distinguish by example among interference with contractual relations, disparagement, and fraudulent misrepresentation.

## PROBLEMS

**1.** The Penguin intentionally hits Batman with his umbrella. Batman, stunned by the blow, falls backwards, knocking Robin down. Robin's leg is broken in the fall, and he cries out, "Holy broken bat bones! My leg is broken." Who, if anyone, is liable to Robin? Why?

**2.** CEO was convinced by his employee, M. Ploy, that a co-worker, A. Cused, had been stealing money from the company. At lunch that day in the company cafeteria, CEO discharges Cused from her employment, accuses her of stealing from the company, searches through her purse over her objections, and finally forcibly escorts her to his office to await the arrival of the police, which he has his secretary summon. Cused is indicted for embezzlement but subsequently is acquitted upon establishing her innocence. What rights, if any, does Cused have against CEO?

**3.** Ralph kisses Edith while she is asleep but does not waken or harm her. Edith sues Ralph for battery. Has a battery been committed?

**4.** Claude, a creditor seeking to collect a debt, calls on Dianne and demands payment in a rude and insolent manner. When Dianne says that she cannot pay, Claude calls Dianne a deadbeat and says that he will never trust her again. Is Claude liable to Dianne? If so, for what tort?

**5.** Lana, a ten-year-old child, is run over by a car negligently driven by Mitchel. Lana, at the time of the accident, was acting reasonably and without negligence. Clark, a newspaper reporter, photographs Lana while she is lying in the street in great pain. Two years later, Perry, the publisher of a newspaper, prints Clark's picture of Lana in his newspaper as a lead to an article concerning the negligence of children. The caption under the picture reads: "They ask to be killed." Lana, who has recovered from the accident, brings suit against Clark and Perry. What result?

**6.** In 1963 the *Saturday Evening Post* featured an article entitled "The Story of a College Football Fix," characterized in the subtitle as "A Shocking Report of How Wally Butts and Bear Bryant

Rigged a Game Last Fall." Butts was athletic director of the University of Georgia, and Bryant was head coach of the University of Alabama. The article was based on a claim by one George Burnett that he had accidentally overheard a long-distance telephone conversation between Butts and Bryant in the course of which Butts divulged information on plays Georgia would use in the upcoming game against Alabama. The writer assigned to the story by the *Post* was not a football expert, did not interview either Butts or Bryant, and did not personally see the notes Burnett had made of the telephone conversation. Butts admitted that he had a long-distance telephone conversation with Bryant but denied that any advance information on prospective football plays was given. Has Butts been defamed by the *Post*?

**7.** Joan, a patient confined in a hospital, has a rare disease that is of great interest to the public. Carol, a television reporter, requests Joan to consent to an interview. Joan refuses, but Carol, nonetheless, enters Joan's room over her objection and photographs her. Joan brings a suit against Carol. Is Carol liable? If so, for what tort?

**8.** Owner has a place on his land where he piles trash. The pile has been there for three months. John, a neighbor of Owner and without Owner's consent or knowledge, throws trash onto the trash pile. Owner learns that John has done this and sues him. What tort, if any, has John committed?

**9.** Chris leaves her car parked in front of a store. There are no signs that say Chris cannot park there. The store owner, however, needs the car moved to enable a delivery truck to unload. He releases the brake and pushes Chris's car three or four feet, doing no harm to the car. Chris returns and sees that her car has been moved and is very angry. She threatens to sue the store owner for trespass to her personal property. Can she recover?

**10.** Carr borrowed John's brand-new car for the purpose of going to the store. He told John he would be right back. Carr then decided, however, to go to the beach while he had the car. Can John recover from Carr the value of the automobile? If so, for what tort?

**11.** Marcia Samms claimed that David Eccles had repeatedly and persistently called her at various hours, including late at night, from May to December, soliciting her to have illicit sexual relations with him. She also claimed that on one occasion Eccles came over to her residence to again solicit sex and indecently exposed himself to her. Mrs. Samms had never encouraged Eccles but had continuously repulsed his "insulting, indecent, and obscene" proposals. She brought suit against Eccles, claiming she suffered great anxiety and fear for her personal safety and severe emotional distress, demanding actual and punitive damages. Can she recover? If so, for what tort?

**12.** National Bond and Investment Company sent two of its employees to repossess Whithorn's car after he failed to complete the payments. The two repossessors located Whithorn while he was driving his car. They followed him and hailed him down to make the repossession. Whithorn refused to abandon his car and demanded evidence of their authority. The two repossessors became impatient and called a wrecker. They ordered the driver of the wrecker to hook Whithorn's car and move it down the street while Whithorn was still inside the vehicle. Whithorn started the car and tried to escape, but the wrecker lifted the car off the road and progressed seventy-five to one hundred feet until Whithorn managed to stall the wrecker. Has National Bond committed the tort of false imprisonment?

**13.** In March, William Proxmire, a U.S. senator from Wisconsin, initiated the "Golden Fleece of the Month Award" to publicize what he believed to be wasteful government spending. The second of these awards was given to the Federal agencies that had for seven years funded Dr. Hutchinson's research on stress levels in animals. The award was made in a speech Proxmire gave in the Senate; the text was also incorporated into an advance press release that was sent to 275 members of the national news media. Proxmire also referred to the research in two subsequent newsletters sent to one hundred thousand constituents and during a television interview. Hutchinson then brought this action alleging defamation resulting in personal and economic injury. Assuming that Hutchinson proved that the statements were false and defamatory, would he prevail?

**14.** Capune was attempting a trip from New York to Florida on an eighteen-foot-long paddleboard. The trip was being covered by various media to gain publicity for Capune and certain products he endorsed. By water, Capune approached a pier owned by Robbins, who had posted signs prohibiting surfing and swimming around the pier. Capune was unaware of these notices and attempted to continue his journey by passing under the pier. Robbins ran up yelling and threw two bottles at Capune. Capune was frightened and tried to maneuver his paddleboard to go around the pier. Robbins then threw a third bottle that hit Capune in the head. Capune had to be helped out of the water and taken to the hospital. He suffered a physical wound that required twenty-four sutures and, as a result, had to discontinue his trip. Capune brought suit in tort against Robbins. Is Robbins liable? If so, for which tort or torts?

**15.** Ralph Nader, who has been a critic of General Motors Corp. for several years, claims that when General Motors learned that Nader was about to publish a book entitled *Unsafe at Any Speed*, criticizing one of its automobiles, it decided to conduct a campaign of intimidation against him. Specifically, Nader claims that GMC (a) conducted a series of interviews with Nader's acquaintances, questioning them about his political, social, racial, and religious views; (b) kept him under surveillance in public places for an unreasonable length of time, including close observation of him in a bank; (c) caused him to be accosted by women for the purpose of entrapping him into illicit relationships; (d) made threatening, harassing, and obnoxious telephone calls to him; (e) tapped his telephone and eavesdropped by means of mechanical and electronic equipment on his private conversations with others; and (f) conducted a "continuing" and harassing investigation of him. Nader brought suit against GMC for invasion of privacy. Which, if any, of the alleged actions would constitute invasion of privacy?

**16.** Bill Kinsey was charged with murdering his wife while working for the Peace Corps in Tanzania. After waiting six months in jail, he was acquitted at a trial that attracted wide publicity. Five years later, while a graduate student at Stanford University, Kinsey had a brief affair with Mary Macur. He abruptly ended the affair by telling Macur he would no longer be seeing her because another woman, Sally Allen, was coming from England to live with him. A few months later, Kinsey and Allen moved to Africa and were subsequently married. Soon after Bill ended their affair, Macur began a letter-writing campaign designed to expose Bill and his mistreatment of her. Macur sent several letters to both Bill and Sally Kinsey, their parents, their neighbors, their parents' neighbors, members of Bill's dissertation committee, other faculty, and the president of Stanford University. The letters contained statements accusing Bill of murdering his first wife, spending six months in jail for the crime, being a rapist, and other questionable behavior. The Kinseys brought an action for invasion of privacy, seeking damages and a permanent injunction. Will the Kinseys prevail? If so, for what tort?

**17.** The Brineys (defendants) owned a large farm on which was located an abandoned farmhouse. For a ten-year period the house had been the subject of several trespassings and housebreakings. In an attempt to stop the intrusions, Briney boarded up the windows and doors and posted "no trespassing" signs. After one break-in, however, Briney set a spring gun in a bedroom. It was placed over the bedroom window so that the gun could not be seen from outside, and no warning of its presence was posted. The gun was set to hit an intruder in the legs. Briney loaded the gun with a live shell, but he claimed that he did not intend to injure anyone.

Katko (plaintiff) and a friend, McDonough, had broken into the abandoned farmhouse on an earlier occasion to steal old bottles and fruit jars for their antique collection. They returned for a second time after the spring gun had been set, and Katko was seriously wounded in the leg when the gun discharged as he entered the bedroom. He then brought action for damages. Decision?

**18.** Plaintiff, John W. Carson, was the host and star of *The Tonight Show*, a well-known television program broadcast by the National Broadcasting Company. Carson also appeared as an entertainer in nightclubs and theaters around the country. From the time he began hosting *The Tonight Show*, he had been introduced on the show each night with the phrase "Here's Johnny." The phrase "Here's Johnny" is still generally associated with Carson by a substantial segment of the television viewing public. To earn additional income, Carson began authorizing use of this phrase by outside business ventures.

Defendant, Here's Johnny Portable Toilets, Inc., is a Michigan corporation engaged in the business of renting and selling "Here's Johnny" portable toilets. Defendant's founder was aware at the time he formed the corporation that "Here's Johnny" was the introductory slogan for Carson on *The Tonight Show*. He indicated that he coupled the phrase with a second one, "The World's Foremost Commodian," to make "a good play on a phrase." Carson brought suit for invasion of privacy. Should Carson recover? If so, for which tort?

**19.** Susan Jungclaus Peterson was a twenty-one-year-old student at Moorhead State University who had lived most of her life on her family farm in Minnesota. Though Susan was a dean's list student during her first year, her academic performance declined after she became deeply involved in an international religious cult organization known locally as The Way of Minnesota, Inc. The cult demanded an enormous psychological and monetary commitment from Susan. Near the end of her junior year, her parents became alarmed by the changes in Susan's physical and mental well-being and concluded that she had been "reduced to a condition of psychological bondage by The Way." They sought help from Kathy Mills, a self-styled "deprogrammer" of minds brainwashed by cults.

On May 24, Norman Jungclaus, Susan's father, picked up Susan at Moorhead State. Instead of returning home, they went to the residence of Veronica Morgel, where Kathy Mills attempted to deprogram Susan. For the first few days of her stay, Susan was unwilling to discuss her involvement. She lay curled in a fetal position in her bedroom, plugging her ears and hysterically screaming and crying while her father pleaded with her to listen. By the third day, however, Susan's demeanor changed completely. She became friendly and vivacious and communicated with her father. Susan also went roller-skating and played softball at a nearby park over the following weekend. She spent the next week in Columbus, Ohio, with a former cult member who had shared her experiences of the previous week. While in Columbus, she spoke daily by telephone with her fiancé, a member of The Way, who begged her to return to the cult. Susan expressed the desire to get her fiancé out of the organization, but a meeting between them could not be arranged outside the presence of other members of The Way. Her parents attempted to persuade Susan to sign an agreement releasing them from liability for their actions, but Susan refused. After nearly sixteen days of "deprogramming" Susan left the Morgel residence and returned to her fiancé and The Way. Upon the direction of The Way ministry, she brought this action against her parents for false imprisonment. Will Susan prevail? Explain.

**20.** Debra Agis was a waitress in a restaurant owned by the Howard Johnson Company. On May 23, Roger Dionne, manager of the restaurant, called a meeting of all waitresses at which he informed them that "there was some stealing going on." Dionne also stated that the identity of the party or parties responsible was not known and that he would begin firing all waitresses in alphabetical order until the guilty party or parties were detected. He then fired Debra Agis, who allegedly "became greatly upset, began to cry, sustained emotional distress, mental anguish, and loss of wages and earnings." Mrs. Agis brought a complaint against the Howard Johnson Company and Roger Dionne, alleging that the defendants acted recklessly and outrageously, intending to cause emotional distress and anguish. The defendants argued that damages for emotional distress are not recoverable unless physical injury occurs as a result of the distress. Will Agis be successful on her complaint?

**21.** The plaintiff, Edith Mitchell, was forcibly stopped as she exited a Wal-Mart (defendant) store. The plaintiff, accompanied by her thirteen-year-old daughter, went through the checkout and purchased several items at the store. As she exited, the plaintiff passed through an electronic antitheft device, which sounded an alarm. Robert Canady, employed by the defendant as a "people greeter" and security guard, forcibly stopped the plaintiff at the exit, grabbed the plaintiff's bag, and told her to step back inside, but never touched the plaintiff or her daughter and never threatened to touch either of them. Nevertheless, the plaintiff described the security guard's actions in her affidavit as "gruff, loud, rude behavior." This security guard removed every item the plaintiff had just purchased and ran it through the security gate. One of the items still had a security code unit on it, which an employee admitted could have been overlooked by the cashier. When the security guard finished examining the contents of the plaintiffs' bag, he put it on the checkout counter. This examination of her bag took ten or fifteen minutes. Once her bag had been checked, no employee of the defendant ever told the plaintiff she could not leave. The plaintiff was never threatened with arrest. The plaintiff brought a tort action against the Wal-Mart alleging false imprisonment, assault, battery, and intentional infliction of emotional distress. Is the defendant liable for any of these torts? Explain.

**22.** On July 31, Amanda Vaughn and Jason Vaughn accompanied their mother, Emma Simpson Vaughn, to a Wal-Mart store. Amanda's friend, Kimberly Dickerson, was also with them. Once they entered the store, Mrs. Vaughn and Jason went into separate areas of the store. The two girls remained together in the front of the store and selected a stamp album to purchase. Kimberly took the album to the checkout register, and while she was at the register, she also selected a pack of gum. Once Kimberly paid for her two items, they were placed in a bag and she was given her change. Kimberly testified that she did not immediately put the change in her wallet while she was at the register. Instead, Kimberly walked back into the merchandise area where Amanda had remained. Kimberly was in the merchandise area, away from the registers, when she placed her change in her purse. Kimberly proceeded to place her hand in the Wal-Mart bag to retrieve the gum she had just purchased.

At this time, Ms. Clara Lynn Neal, a customer service manager, observed Kimberly's hand coming out of her Wal-Mart bag. According to Ms. Neal, because the two girls were in a somewhat secluded area of the store, Ms. Neal walked past the two girls twice to observe them before she walked over to them.

Ms. Neal testified that she asked Kimberly if she could see her bag and her receipt and that Kimberly voluntarily gave her the bag. Plaintiffs alleged that Ms. Neal "detained the girls, snatched Kimberly's bag from her, searched the bag, discovered a receipt, tied the bag, and then personally escorted the girls to an area near the front door away from the registers." However, Kimberly's testimony stated that "[Ms. Neal] said she was going to have to check my bag because she doesn't know if I'm stealing something. So I didn't say anything. I didn't really give it to her because I was shocked. So she took it, and she was like searching through it."

Once Ms. Neal checked the purchases with the receipt, the girls were told to go to the front of the store and wait for their party. The girls were never told that they could not leave the store and the girls were not detained by anyone else. According to all parties, from the time Ms. Neal walked up to the girls, verified the purchases, and returned the bag to Kimberly, the entire incident only lasted about one minute. While the girls were waiting at the front of the store, Jason was asked by his mother to inform the girls that she was ready to go. Jason approached the girls, and they responded that they could not leave. When Jason reported to his mother that the girls stated they could not leave the area, Mrs. Vaughn then went to the front of the store to investigate. Before Mrs. Vaughn took the children home, she explained to a store manager what had occurred. Do the girls have a cause of action against Wal-Mart?

C H A P T E R 8

# Negligence and Strict Liability

Whereas intentional torts deal with conduct that has a substantial certainty of causing harm, negligence involves conduct that creates an unreasonable risk of harm. The basis of liability for negligence is the failure to exercise reasonable care, under given circumstances, for the safety of another person or his property, which failure causes injury to such person or damage to his property, or both. Thus, if the driver of an automobile intentionally runs down a person, she has committed the intentional tort of battery. If, on the other hand, the driver hits and injures a person while driving without reasonable regard for the safety of others, she is negligent.

Strict liability is not based upon the negligence or intent of the defendant but rather upon the nature of the activity in which he is engaging. Under this doctrine, defendants who engage in certain activities, such as keeping animals or carrying on abnormally dangerous conditions, are held liable for the injuries they cause, even if they have exercised the utmost care. The law imposes this liability to effect a just reallocation of loss, given that the defendant engaged in the activity for his own benefit and is in a better position to manage, by insurance or otherwise, the risk inherent in the activity.

As mentioned in *Chapter 7*, in 1996 the American Law Institute (ALI) approved the development of a new Restatement, called Restatement Third, Torts: Liability for Physical and Emotional Harm, which addresses the general or basic elements of the tort action for liability for accidental personal injury, property damage, and emotional harm but does not cover liability for economic loss. This work will replace comparable provisions in the Restatement Second, Torts. The final work will be published in two volumes. Volume 1 is now available and covers liability for negligence causing physical harm, duty, strict liability, factual cause, and scope of liability (traditionally called proximate cause). Volume 2 will cover affirmative duties, emotional harm, landowner liability, and liability of actors who retain independent contractors. Volume 2 is expected to be published in 2011. "Physical harm" is defined as bodily harm (physical injury, illness, disease, and death) or property damage (physical impairment of real property or tangible personal property). The provisions of Volume 1 will be covered extensively in this chapter and will be cited as the "Third Restatement."

The Institute's Restatement Third, Torts: Economic Torts and Related Wrongs will update coverage on torts that involve economic loss or pecuniary harm *not* resulting from physical harm or physical contact to a person or property. The Institute began this project in 2004, but as of 2010 no part of the work has been approved. In late 2007 the project's Reporter left the project; the project is in abeyance until a successor Reporter is appointed.

## NEGLIGENCE

A person acts negligently if the person does not exercise reasonable care under all the circumstances. Third Restatement, Section 3. Moreover, the general rule is that a person is under a duty to all others at all times to exercise reasonable care for the safety of the others' person and property. Third Restatement, Section 7.

An action for negligence consists of five elements, each of which the plaintiff must prove:

1. **Duty of care**: that a legal duty required the defendant to conform to the standard of conduct established for the protection of others;
2. **Breach of duty**: that the defendant failed to exercise reasonable care;
3. **Factual cause**: that the defendant's failure to exercise reasonable care in fact caused the harm the plaintiff sustained;
4. **Harm**: that the harm sustained is of a type protected against negligent conduct; and
5. **Scope of liability**: that the harm sustained is within the "scope of liability," which historically has been referred to

as "proximate cause." Third Restatement, Section 6, comments.

The first two elements will be discussed in the next section, "Breach of Duty of Care"; the last three elements will be covered in subsequent sections.

## BREACH OF DUTY OF CARE

Negligence consists of conduct that creates an unreasonable risk of harm. In determining whether a given risk of harm was unreasonable, the law considers the following factors: (1) the foreseeable probability that the person's conduct will result in harm, (2) the foreseeable gravity or severity of any harm that may follow, and (3) the burden of taking precautions to eliminate or reduce the risk of harm. Third Restatement, Section 3. Thus, the standard of conduct, which is the basis for the law of negligence, is usually determined by a cost-benefit or risk-benefit analysis.

### REASONABLE PERSON STANDARD

The duty of care imposed by law is measured by the degree of carefulness that a reasonable person would exercise in a given situation. The reasonable person is a fictitious individual who is always careful and prudent and never negligent. What the judge or jury determines a reasonable person would have done in light of the facts disclosed by the evidence in a particular case sets the standard of conduct for that case. The reasonable person standard is thus external and *objective*, as described by Justice Holmes:

> If, for instance, a man is born hasty and awkward, is always hurting himself or his neighbors, no doubt his congenital defects will be allowed for in the courts of Heaven, but his slips are no less troublesome to his neighbors than if they sprang from guilty neglect. His neighbors accordingly require him, at his peril, to come up to their standard, and the courts which they establish decline to take his personal equation into account. Holmes, The Common Law.

**Children** A child is a person below the age of majority, which in almost all States has been lowered from twenty-one to eighteen. The standard of conduct to which a child must conform to avoid being negligent is that of a reasonably careful person of the same age, intelligence, and experience under all the circumstances. Third Restatement, Section 10. For example, Alice, a five-year-old girl, was walking with her father on the crowded sidewalk along Main Street when he told her that he was going to take her to Disney World for her birthday next week. Upon hearing the news, Alice became so excited that she began to jump up and down and run around. During this fit of exuberance, Alice accidentally ran into and knocked down an elderly woman who was passing by. Alice's liability, if any, would be determined by whether a reasonable five-year-old person of like age, intelligence, and experience under like circumstances would have the capacity and judgment to understand the increased risk her enthusiastic display of joy caused to others.

The law applies an individualized test because children do not possess the judgment, intelligence, knowledge, and experience of adults. Moreover, children as a general rule do not engage in activities entailing high risk to others, and their conduct normally does not involve a potential for harm as great as that of adult conduct. A child who engages in a dangerous activity that is characteristically undertaken by adults, however, such as flying an airplane or driving a boat or car, is held in almost all States to the standard of care applicable to adults. Finally, some States modify this individualized test by holding that under a minimum age, most commonly the age of seven, a child is incapable of committing a negligent act. The Third Restatement further provides that a child less than five years of age is incapable of negligence. Section 10.

**Physical Disability** If a person is ill or otherwise physically disabled, the standard of conduct to which he must conform to avoid being negligent is that of a reasonably careful person with the same disability. Third Restatement, Section 11(a). Thus, a blind man must act as a reasonable man who is blind, and a woman with multiple sclerosis must act as a reasonable woman with multiple sclerosis. However, the conduct of a person during a period of sudden incapacitation or loss of consciousness resulting from physical illness is negligent only if the sudden incapacitation or loss of consciousness was reasonably foreseeable to the actor. Examples of sudden incapacitation include heart attack, stroke, epileptic seizure, and diabetes. Third Restatement, Section 11(b).

**Mental Disability** A person's mental or emotional disability is not considered in determining whether conduct is negligent unless the person is a child. Third Restatement, Section 11(c). The defendant is held to the standard of conduct of a reasonable person who is *not* mentally or emotionally disabled, even though the defendant is, in fact, incapable of conforming to the standard. Thus, an adult with the mental acumen of a six-year-old will be held liable for his negligent conduct if he fails to act as carefully as a reasonable adult of normal intelligence. In this case the law may demand more of the individual than his mental limitations permit him to accomplish. When a person's intoxication is voluntary, it is not considered as an excuse for conduct that is otherwise lacking in reasonable care. Third Restatement, Section 12, Comment c.

**Superior Skill or Knowledge** If a person has skills or knowledge beyond those possessed by most others, these skills or knowledge are circumstances to be taken into account in determining whether the person has acted with reasonable care. Third Restatement, Section 12. Thus, persons who are qualified and who practice a profession or trade that calls for special skill and expertise are required to exercise that care and skill that members in good standing of their profession or trade normally possess. This standard applies to such professionals as physicians, surgeons, dentists, attorneys, pharmacists, architects, accountants, and engineers and to those who perform skilled trades, such as airline pilots, electricians, carpenters, and plumbers. A member of a profession or skilled trade who possesses greater skill than that common to the profession or trade is required to exercise that skill.

**Emergencies** An emergency is a sudden and unexpected event that calls for immediate action and permits no time for deliberation. In determining whether a defendant's conduct is reasonable, the law takes into consideration the fact that he was at the time confronted with a sudden and unexpected emergency. Third Restatement, Section 9. The standard is still that of a reasonable person under the circumstances—the emergency is simply part of the circumstances. If, however, the defendant's own negligent or tortious conduct created the emergency, he is liable for the consequences of this conduct even if he acted reasonably in the resulting emergency situation. Moreover, failure to anticipate an emergency may itself constitute negligence.

**Violation of Statute** The reasonable person standard of conduct may be established by legislation or administrative regulation. Third Restatement, Section 14. Some statutes expressly impose civil liability upon violators. Absent such a provision, courts may adopt the requirements of the statute as the standard of conduct if the statute is designed to protect against the type of accident the defendant's conduct causes and the accident victim is within the class of persons the statute is designed to protect.

If the statute is found to be applicable, the majority of the courts hold that an unexcused violation is **negligence *per se***; that is, the violation conclusively constitutes negligent conduct. In a minority of States, the violation is considered merely to be evidence of negligence. In either event, the plaintiff must also prove legal causation and injury.

For example, a statute enacted to protect employees from injuries requires that all factory elevators be equipped with specified safety devices. Arthur, an employee in Freya's factory, and Carlos, a business visitor to the factory, are injured when the elevator fails because the safety devices have not been installed. The court may adopt the statute as a standard of conduct as to Arthur and hold Freya negligent *per se* to Arthur, but not as to Carlos, because Arthur, not Carlos, is within the class of persons the statute is intended to protect. Carlos would have to establish that a reasonable person in the position of Freya under the circumstances would have installed the safety device.

On the other hand, compliance with a legislative enactment or administrative regulation does not prevent a finding of negligence if a reasonable person would have taken additional precautions. Third Restatement, Section 16. For instance, driving at the speed limit may not constitute due care when traffic or road conditions require a lower speed. Legislative or administrative rules normally establish *minimum* standards.

◆ **SEE FIGURE 8-1: Negligence and Negligence *Per Se***

◆ **SEE CASE 1-1**

## DUTY TO ACT

As stated above, the general rule is that a person is under a duty to all others at all times to exercise reasonable care for the safety of the others' person and property. On the other hand, except in special circumstances, a person who has not created risk of harm to others ordinarily has no duty of care to another. Third Restatement, Section 37. This rule applies even though the person may be in a position to help another in peril. As William Prosser, an authority on tort law, has stated, "The law has persistently refused to recognize the moral obligation of common decency and common humanity, to come to the aid of another human being who is in danger, even though the outcome is to cost him his life." For example, Toni, an adult standing at the edge of a steep cliff, observes a baby carriage with a crying infant in it slowly rolling toward the edge and certain doom. Toni could easily prevent the baby's fall at no risk to her own safety. Nonetheless, Toni does nothing, and the baby falls to his death. Toni is under no legal duty to act and, therefore, incurs no liability for failing to do so.

Nonetheless, special relations between the parties may impose a duty of reasonable care upon the defendant to aid or protect the other with respect to risks that arise within the scope of the relationship. Thus, if in the example above, Toni were the baby's mother or babysitter, Toni would be under a duty to act and therefore would be liable for not taking action. The special relations giving rise to the duty to aid or protect another include (1) a common carrier with its passengers, (2) an innkeeper with its guest, (3) an employer with its employees, (4) a school with its students, (5) a landlord with its tenants with respect to common areas under the landlord's control, (6) a business open to the public with its customers, and (7) a custodian with those in its custody including parents with their children. Third Restatement, Section 40.

In addition, when a person's prior conduct, even though not tortious, creates a continuing risk of physical harm, the

◆ FIGURE 8-1: **Negligence and Negligence *Per Se***

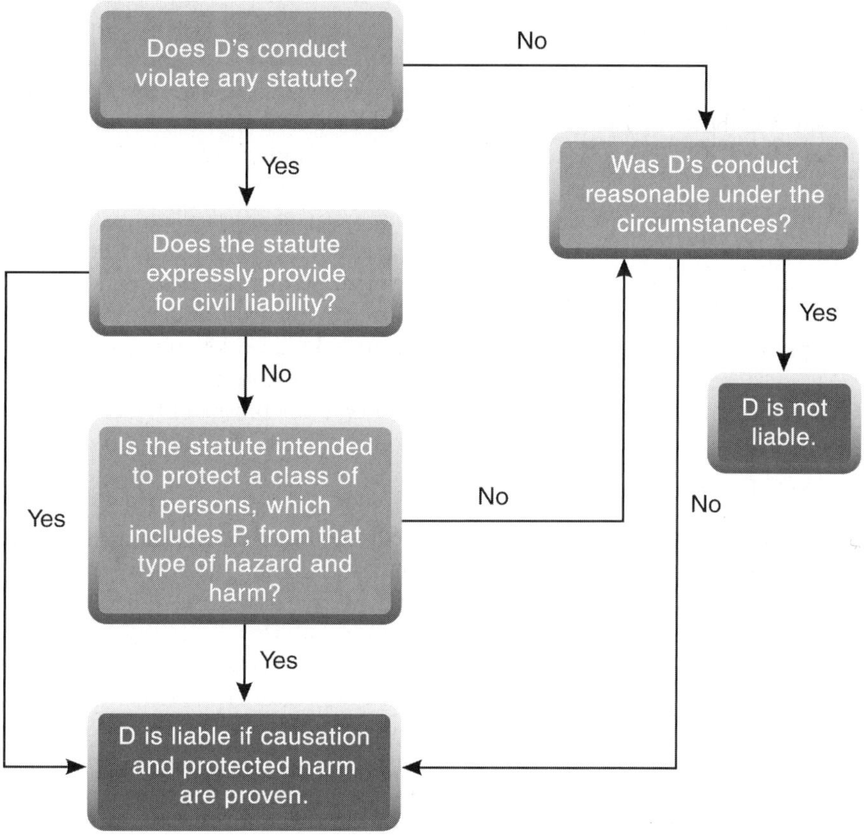


person has a duty to exercise reasonable care to prevent or minimize the harm. Third Restatement, Section 39. For example, Dale innocently drives her car into Bob, rendering him unconscious. Dale leaves Bob lying in the middle of the road, where he is run over by a second car driven by Chen. Dale is liable to Bob for the additional injuries inflicted by Chen.

Moreover, a person who voluntarily begins a rescue by taking charge of another who is imperiled and unable to protect himself incurs a duty to exercise reasonable care under the circumstances. Furthermore, a person who discontinues aid or protection is under a duty of reasonable care not to leave the other in a worse position. Third Restatement, Section 44. For example, Ann finds Ben drunk and stumbling along a dark sidewalk. Ann leads Ben halfway up a steep and unguarded stairway, where she abandons him. Ben attempts to climb the stairs but trips and falls, suffering serious injury. Ann is liable to Ben for having left him in a worse position. Most States have enacted Good Samaritan statutes to encourage voluntary emergency care. These statutes vary considerably, but they typically limit or disallow liability for some rescuers under specified circumstances.

There are special relationships in which one person has some degree of control over another person, including (1) a parent with dependent children, and (2) an employer with employees when the employment facilitates the employee's causing harm to third parties. The parent and the employer each owe a duty of reasonable care under the circumstances to third persons with regard to foreseeable risks that arise within the scope of the relationship. Third Restatement, Section 41. Depending upon the circumstances, reasonable care may require controlling the activities of the other person or merely providing a warning. Generally, the duty of parents is limited to dependent children; thus when children reach majority or are no longer dependent, parents no longer have control and the duty of reasonable care ceases.

The duty of employers includes the duty to exercise reasonable care in the hiring, training, supervision, and retention of employees. This duty of employers is independent of the vicarious liability of an employer for an employee's tortious conduct during the course of employment, and extends to conduct by the employee that occurs both inside and outside the scope of employment so long as the employment facilitates the employee causing harm to third parties.

The Third Restatement provides the following example of an employer's duty:

> Don is employed by Welch Repair Service, which knows that Don had several episodes of assault in his previous employment. Don goes to Traci's residence, where he had previously been dispatched by Welch, and misrepresents to Traci that he is there on Welch business to check repairs that had previously been made in Traci's home. After Traci admits Don, he assaults Traci. Welch is subject to a duty under this subsection with regard to Don's assault on Traci.

◆ **SEE CASE 8-1**

## DUTIES OF POSSESSORS OF LAND

The right of possessors of land to use that land for their own benefit and enjoyment is limited by their duty to do so in a reasonable manner; that is, by the use of their land, they cannot cause unreasonable risks of harm to others. Liability for breach of this obligation may arise from conduct in any of the three areas of torts discussed in this and the preceding chapter: intentional harm, negligence, or strict liability. Most of these cases fall within the classification of negligence.

In conducting activities on her land, the possessor of land is required to exercise reasonable care to protect others who are not on her property. For example, a property owner who constructs a factory on her premises must take reasonable care that it is not unreasonably dangerous to people off the site.

The duty of a possessor of land to persons who come upon the land depends on whether those persons are trespassers, licensees, or invitees. A few States have abandoned these distinctions, however, and simply apply ordinary negligence principles of foreseeable risk and reasonable care. The Third Restatement will include provisions on landowner liability, but the ALI has not yet approved them.

**Duty to Trespassers** A trespasser is a person who enters or remains on the land of another without permission or privilege to do so. The lawful possessor of the land is not liable to adult trespassers for her failure to maintain the land in a reasonably safe condition. Nonetheless, trespassers are not criminals, and the lawful possessor is not free to inflict intentional injury on them. Moreover, most courts hold that upon discovering the presence of trespassers on her land, the lawful possessor is required to exercise reasonable care for their safety in carrying on her activities and to warn the trespassers of potentially highly dangerous conditions that the trespassers are not likely to discover.

**Duty to Licensees** A licensee is a person who is privileged to enter or remain upon land only by virtue of the lawful possessor's consent. Restatement, Section 330. Licensees include members of the possessor's household, social guests, and salespersons calling at private homes. A licensee will become a trespasser, however, if he enters a portion of the land to which he is not invited or remains upon the land after his invitation has expired.

The possessor, who owes a higher duty of care to licensees than to trespassers, must warn a licensee of dangerous activities and conditions (1) of which the possessor has knowledge or has reason to know and (2) which the licensee does not and is not likely to discover. A licensee who is not warned may recover if the activity or dangerous condition resulted from the possessor's failure to exercise reasonable care to protect him from the danger. Restatement, Section 342. To illustrate: Jose invites a friend, Julia, to his place in the country at 8:00 P.M. on a winter evening. Jose knows that a bridge in his driveway is in a dangerous condition that is not noticeable in the dark. Jose does not inform Julia of this fact. The bridge gives way under Julia's car, causing serious harm to Julia. Jose is liable to Julia.

Some States have extended to licensees the same protection traditionally accorded invitees. A number of States have included social guests in the invitee category.

**Duty to Invitees** An invitee is either a public invitee or a business visitor. Restatement, Section 332. A **public invitee** is a person invited to enter or remain on land as a member of the public for a purpose for which the land is held open to the public. Such invitees include those who use public parks, beaches, or swimming pools, as well as those who use governmental facilities, such as a post office or office of the Recorder of Deeds, where business with the public is transacted openly. A **business visitor** is a person invited to enter or remain on the premises for a purpose directly or indirectly concerning business dealings with the possessor of the land, such as one who enters a store or a tradesperson who enters a residence to make repairs.

With respect to the condition of the premises, the possessor of land is under a duty to exercise reasonable care to protect invitees against dangerous conditions they are unlikely to discover. This liability extends not only to those conditions of which the possessor knows but also to those she would discover by the exercise of reasonable care. Restatement, Section 343. For example, at the front of Tilson's supermarket is a large glass front door that is well lit and plainly visible. Johnson, a customer, nonetheless mistakes the glass for an open doorway and walks into it, injuring himself. Tilson is not liable to Johnson. If, on the other hand, the glass was difficult to see and a person might foreseeably mistake the glass for an open doorway, then Tilson would be liable to Johnson if Johnson crashed into the glass while exercising reasonable care.

◆ **SEE FIGURE 8-2: Duties of Possessors of Land**

◆ **SEE CASE 8-2**

FIGURE 8-2: **Duties of Possessors of Land**

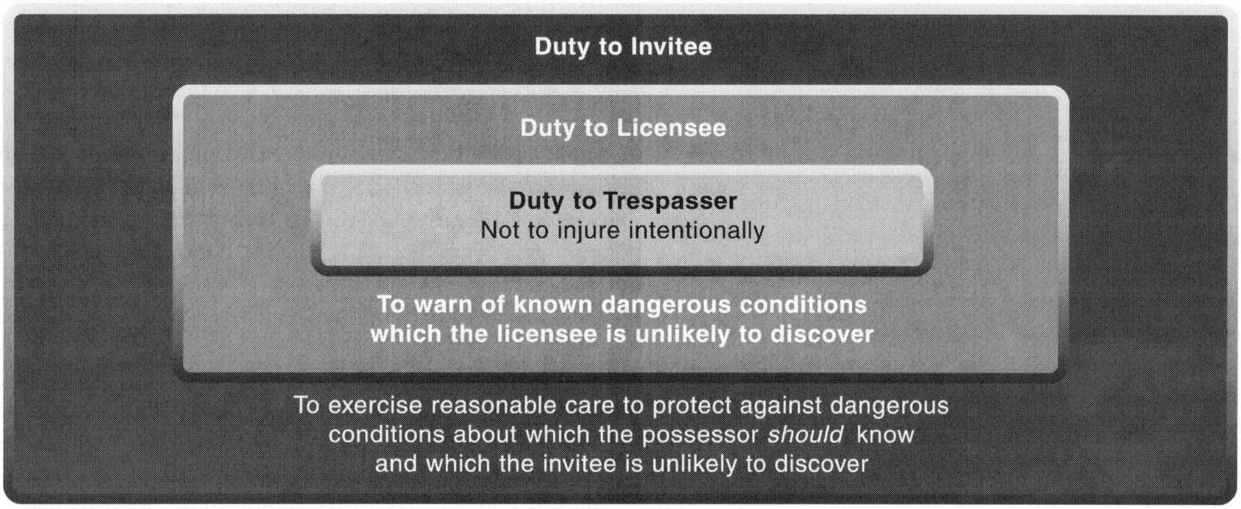


### *RES IPSA LOQUITUR*

A rule of circumstantial evidence has developed that permits the jury to infer both negligent conduct and causation from the mere occurrence of certain types of events. This rule, called ***res ipsa loquitur***, meaning "the thing speaks for itself," applies "when the accident causing the plaintiff's physical harm is a type of accident that ordinarily happens as a result of the negligence of a class of actors of which the defendant is the relevant member." Third Restatement, Section 17.

For example, Abrams rents a room in Brown's motel. During the night a large piece of plaster falls from the ceiling and injures Abrams. In the absence of other evidence, the jury may infer that the harm resulted from Brown's negligence in permitting the plaster to become defective. Brown is permitted, however, to introduce evidence to contradict the inference of negligence.

## FACTUAL CAUSE

Liability for the negligent conduct of a defendant requires that the conduct in fact caused harm to the plaintiff. The Third Restatement states: "Tortious conduct must be a factual cause of physical harm for liability to be imposed." Section 26. A widely applied test for causation in fact is the **but-for test**: A person's conduct is a cause of an event if the event would not have occurred *but for* the person's negligent conduct. That is, conduct is a factual cause of harm when the harm would not have occurred absent the conduct. Third Restatement, Section 26. For instance, Arnold fails to erect a barrier around an excavation. Doyle is driving a truck when its accelerator becomes stuck, and he and the truck plummet into the excavation. Arnold's negligence is not a cause in fact of Doyle's death if the runaway truck would have crashed through the barrier that Arnold could have erected. Similarly, the failure to install a proper fire escape on a hotel is not the cause in fact of the death of a person who is suffocated by smoke while sleeping in bed during a hotel fire.

If the tortious conduct of Adam is insufficient by itself to cause Paula's harm, but when Adam's conduct is combined with the tortious conduct of Barry, the combined conduct is sufficient to cause Paula's harm, then Adam and Barry are each considered a factual cause of Paula's harm. Third Restatement, Section 26, Comment c.

The but-for test, however, is not satisfied when there are two or more causes, each of which is sufficient to bring about the harm in question and each of which is active at the time the harm occurs. For example, Wilson and Hart negligently set fires that combine to destroy Kennedy's property. Either fire would have destroyed the property. Under the but-for test, either Wilson or Hart, or both, could argue that the fire caused by the other would have destroyed the property and that he, therefore, is not liable. The Third Restatement addresses this problem of multiple *sufficient* causes by providing, "If multiple acts exist, each of which alone would have been a factual cause under [the but-for test] of the physical harm at the same time, each act is regarded as a factual cause of the harm." Section 27. Under this rule, the conduct of both Wilson and Hart would be found to be a factual cause of the destruction of Kennedy's property.

## SCOPE OF LIABILITY (PROXIMATE CAUSE)

As a matter of social policy, legal responsibility has not followed all the consequences of a negligent act. Tort law does not impose liability on a defendant for all harm factually caused by the defendant's negligent conduct. Liability has been limited—to a greater extent than with intentional torts—to those harms that result from the risks that made the defendant's conduct tortious. Third Restatement, Section 29. This "risk standard" limitation on liability also applies to strict liability cases. Section 29, Comment l. The Third Restatement provides the following example:

> Richard, a hunter, finishes his day in the field and stops at a friend's house while walking home. His friend's nine-year-old daughter, Kim, greets Richard, who hands his loaded shotgun to her as he enters the house. Kim drops the shotgun, which lands on her toe, breaking it. Although Richard was negligent for giving Kim his shotgun, the risk that made Richard negligent was that Kim might shoot someone with the gun, not that she would drop it and hurt herself (the gun was neither especially heavy nor unwieldy). Kim's broken toe is outside the scope of Richard's liability, even though Richard's tortious conduct was a factual cause of Kim's harm.

### FORESEEABILITY

Determining the liability of a negligent defendant for unforeseeable consequences has proved to be troublesome and controversial. The Second Restatement and many courts have adopted the following position:

1. If the actor's conduct is a substantial factor in bringing about harm to another, the fact that the actor neither foresaw nor should have foreseen the extent of the harm or the manner in which it occurred does **not** prevent him from being liable.
2. The actor's conduct may be held not to be a legal cause of harm to another where, after the event and looking back from the harm to the actor's negligent conduct, it appears to the court highly extraordinary that it should have brought about the harm. Restatement, Section 435.

Comment j to Section 29 of the Third Restatement explains that

> the foreseeability test for proximate cause is essentially consistent with the standard set forth in this Section. Properly understood, both the risk standard and a foreseeability test exclude liability for harms that were sufficiently unforeseeable at the time of the actor's tortious conduct that they were not among the risks—potential harms—that made the actor negligent. Negligence limits the requirement of reasonable care to those risks that are foreseeable.

For example, Albert, while negligently driving an automobile, collides with a car carrying dynamite. Albert is unaware of the contents of the other car and has no reason to know about them. The collision causes the dynamite to explode, shattering glass in a building a block away. The shattered glass injures Betsy, who is inside the building. The explosion also injures Calvin, who is walking on the sidewalk near the collision. Albert would be liable to Calvin because Albert should have realized that his negligent driving might result in a collision that would endanger pedestrians nearby. Betsy's harm, however, was beyond the risks posed by Albert's negligent driving and he, accordingly, is not liable to Betsy.

◆ **SEE CASE 8-3**

### SUPERSEDING CAUSE

An intervening cause is an event or act that occurs after the defendant's negligent conduct and, together with the defendant's negligence, causes the plaintiff's harm. If the intervening cause is deemed a superseding cause, then it relieves the defendant of liability for harm to the plaintiff caused in fact by both the defendant's negligence and the intervening event or act. For example, Carol negligently leaves in a public sidewalk a substantial excavation without a fence or warning lights, into which Gary falls at night. Darkness is an intervening, but not a superseding, cause of harm to Gary because it is a normal consequence of the situation caused by Carol's negligence. Therefore, Carol is liable to Gary. In contrast, if Carol negligently leaves an excavation in a public sidewalk into which Barbara intentionally shoves Gary, under the Second Restatement as a matter of law, Carol is not liable to Gary because Barbara's conduct is a superseding cause that relieves Carol of liability. The Third Restatement rejects this exception to liability, stating,

> Whether Gary's harm is within the scope of Carol's liability for her negligence is an issue for the factfinder. The factfinder will have to determine whether the appropriate characterization of the harm to Gary is falling into an unguarded excavation site or being deliberately pushed into an unguarded excavation site and, if the latter, whether it is among the risks that made Carol negligent. Section 34, Comment e.

An intervening cause that is a foreseeable or normal consequence of the defendant's negligence is not a superseding cause. Thus, a person who negligently places another person or his property in imminent danger is liable for the injury sustained by a third-party rescuer who attempts to aid the imperiled person or his property. Third Restatement, Section 32. The same is true of attempts by the endangered person to escape the peril, as, for example, when a person swerves off the road to avoid a head-on collision with an automobile driven negligently on the wrong side of the road. It is commonly held that a negligent defendant is liable for the results of necessary medical treatment of the injured party, even if the treatment itself is negligent. Third Restatement, Section 35.

## HARM

The plaintiff must prove that the defendant's negligent conduct proximately caused harm to a legally protected interest. Certain interests receive little or no protection against such conduct, while others receive full protection. The courts determine the extent of protection for a particular interest as a matter of law on the basis of social policy and expediency. For example, negligent conduct that is the proximate cause of harmful contact with the person of another is actionable. Thus, if Bob, while driving his car, negligently runs into Julie, a pedestrian who is carefully crossing the street, Bob is liable for physical injuries Julie sustains as a result of the collision. On the other hand, if Bob's careless driving causes the car's side-view mirror to brush Julie's coat but results in no physical injuries to her or damage to the coat, thus causing only offensive contact with Julie's person, Bob is not liable because Julie did not sustain harm to a legally protected interest.

The courts traditionally have been reluctant to allow recovery for negligently inflicted emotional distress. Nevertheless, this view has changed gradually during this century, and the majority of courts now hold a person liable for negligently causing emotional distress if bodily harm—such as a heart attack—results from the distress. Restatement, Section 436. In the great majority of States, a defendant is not liable for negligent conduct resulting solely in emotional disturbance. Restatement, Section 436A. A few courts, however, have recently allowed recovery of damages for negligently inflicted emotional distress even in the absence of resultant physical harm. The Third Restatement will include provisions on liability for emotional harm, but the ALI has not yet approved them.

Most courts do not award damages for mental distress suffered by those who have witnessed injury to a closely related person caused by the negligence of another. A number of courts, however, recently have done so.

## DEFENSES TO NEGLIGENCE

A plaintiff who has established by the preponderance of the evidence all the required elements of a negligence action may, nevertheless, be denied recovery if the defendant proves a valid defense. As a general rule, any defense to an intentional tort is also available in an action in negligence. In addition, contributory negligence, comparative negligence, and assumption of risk are three defenses available in negligence cases that are not defenses to intentional torts.

### CONTRIBUTORY NEGLIGENCE

The Restatement, Section 463, defines contributory negligence as "conduct on the part of the plaintiff which falls below the standard to which he should conform for his own protection, and which is a legally contributing cause cooperating with the negligence of the defendant in bringing about the plaintiff's harm." The Third Restatement's definition of negligence as the failure of a person to exercise reasonable care under all the circumstances applies to the contributory negligence of the plaintiff. Section 3, Comment b. In those few States that have not adopted comparative negligence (Alabama, Maryland, North Carolina, and Virginia, as well as Washington, D.C.), the contributory negligence of the plaintiff, whether slight or extensive, prevents him from recovering *any* damages from the defendant.

Notwithstanding the contributory negligence of the plaintiff, if the defendant had a **last clear chance** to avoid injury to the plaintiff but did not avail himself of such chance, the plaintiff's contributory negligence does not bar his recovery of damages. Restatement, Section 479.

### COMPARATIVE NEGLIGENCE

The harshness of the contributory negligence doctrine has caused all but a few States to reject its all-or-nothing rule and to substitute the doctrine of comparative negligence, which is also called comparative fault or comparative responsibility. (In States adopting comparative negligence, the doctrine of last clear chance has also been abandoned.) Approximately a dozen States have judicially or legislatively adopted "pure" comparative negligence systems. (The ALI's recently promulgated Third Restatement of Torts: Apportionment of Liability advocates this form of comparative negligence.) Under **pure comparative negligence**, the law apportions damages between the parties in proportion to the degree of fault or negligence found against them. For instance, Matthew negligently drives his automobile into Nancy, who is crossing against the light. Nancy sustains damages in the amount of $10,000 and sues Matthew. If the trier of fact determines that Matthew's negligence contributed 70 percent to Nancy's injury and that Nancy's contributory negligence contributed 30 percent to her injury, then Nancy would recover $7,000.

Most States have adopted the doctrine of "modified" comparative negligence. Under modified comparative negligence the plaintiff recovers as in pure comparative negligence unless her contributory negligence was "as great as" or "greater than" that of the defendant, in which case the plaintiff recovers nothing. Thus, in the example above, if the trier of fact determined that Matthew's negligence contributed 40 percent to Nancy's injury and Nancy's contributory negligence contributed 60 percent, then Nancy would recover nothing from Matthew.

## ASSUMPTION OF RISK

A plaintiff who has *voluntarily* and *knowingly* assumed the risk of harm arising from the negligent or reckless conduct of the defendant cannot recover from such harm. Restatement, Section 496A. In **express** assumption of the risk, the plaintiff expressly agrees to assume the risk of harm from the defendant's conduct. Usually, but not always, such an agreement is by contract. Courts usually construe these exculpatory contracts strictly and will hold that the plaintiff has assumed the risk only if the terms of the agreement are clear and unequivocal. Moreover, some contracts for assumption of risk are considered unenforceable as a matter of public policy. See *Chapter 13*.

In **implied** assumption of the risk, the plaintiff voluntarily proceeds to encounter a known danger. Thus, a spectator entering a baseball park may be regarded as consenting that the players may proceed with the game without taking precautions to protect him from being hit by the ball. Most States have abolished or modified the defense of implied assumption of risk. Some have abandoned it entirely while others have merged implied assumption of risk into their comparative negligence systems.

Reflecting this general trend, the Third Restatement of Torts: Apportionment of Liability has abandoned the doctrine of implied voluntary assumption of risk: it is no longer a defense that the plaintiff was aware of a risk and voluntarily confronted it. But if a plaintiff's conduct in the face of a known risk is unreasonable, it might constitute contributory negligence, thereby reducing the plaintiff's recovery under comparative negligence. This new Restatement limits the defense of assumption of risk to express assumption of risk, which consists of a contract between the plaintiff and another person to absolve the other person from liability for future harm. Section 2. Contractual assumption of risk may occur by written agreement, express oral agreement, or conduct that creates an implied-in-fact contract, as determined by the applicable rules of contract law. Some contractual assumptions of risk, however, are not enforceable under other areas of substantive law or as against public policy.

◆ SEE FIGURE 8-3: Defenses to a Negligence Action

◆ SEE CASE 8-4

◆ FIGURE 8-3: **Defenses to a Negligence Action**

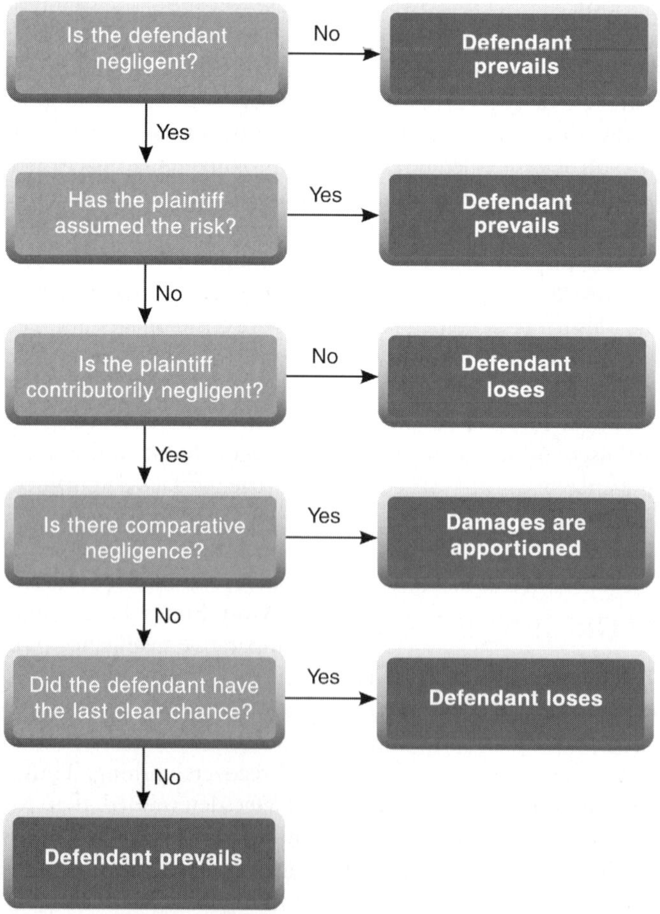

## STRICT LIABILITY

In some instances, people may be held liable for injuries they have caused even though they have not acted intentionally or negligently. Such liability is called strict liability, absolute liability, or liability without fault. The law has determined that because certain types of otherwise socially desirable activities pose sufficiently high risks of harm regardless of how carefully they are conducted, those who perform these activities should bear the cost of any harm they cause. The doctrine of strict liability is not predicated upon any particular fault of the defendant, but rather upon the nature of the activity in which he is engaging.

## ACTIVITIES GIVING RISE TO STRICT LIABILITY

The following activities giving rise to strict liability will be discussed in this section: (1) activities that are, in themselves, abnormally dangerous, and (2) the keeping of animals. In addition, strict liability is imposed upon other activities. Nearly all States have imposed a limited form of strict product liability upon manufacturers and merchants who sell goods in a *defective condition* unreasonably dangerous to the user or consumer. This topic is covered in *Chapter 24*. All States have enacted workers' compensation statutes that make employers liable to employees for injuries arising out of the course of employment. Because the law imposes this liability without regard to the employer's negligence, it is a form of strict liability. Workers' compensation is discussed in *Chapter 43*. Moreover, the liability imposed upon an employer for torts that employees commit in the scope of their employment is a type of strict liability, as discussed in *Chapter 20*. Additional instances of strict liability include carriers and innkeepers (*Chapter 48*), innocent misrepresentation (*Chapter 11*), and some violations of the securities laws (*Chapter 44*).

### ABNORMALLY DANGEROUS ACTIVITIES

A person who carries on an abnormally dangerous activity is subject to strict liability for physical harm resulting from the activity. Third Restatement, Section 20(a). "An activity is abnormally dangerous if: (1) the activity creates a foreseeable and highly significant risk of physical harm even when reasonable care is exercised by all actors; and (2) the activity is not one of common usage." Third Restatement, Section 20(b). The court determines whether an activity is abnormally dangerous by applying these factors. Activities to which the rule has been applied include collecting water or sewage in such quantity and location as to make it dangerous; storing explosives or flammable liquids in large quantities; blasting or pile driving; crop dusting; drilling for or refining oil in populated areas; and emitting noxious gases or fumes into a settled community. On the other hand, courts have refused to apply the rule where the activity is a "natural" use of the land, such as drilling for oil in the oil fields of Texas, collecting water in a stock watering tank, or transmitting gas through a gas pipe or electricity through electric wiring.

◆ **SEE CASE 8-5**

### KEEPING OF ANIMALS

Strict liability for harm caused by animals existed at common law and continues today with some modification. As a general rule, those who possess animals for their own purposes do so at their peril and must protect against the harm those animals may cause to people and property.

**TRESPASSING ANIMALS** Owners and possessors of animals, except for dogs and cats, are subject to strict liability for physical harm their animals cause by trespassing on the property of another. Third Restatement, Section 21. There are two exceptions to this rule: (1) keepers of animals are not strictly liable if those animals incidentally stray upon land immediately adjacent to a highway on which they are being lawfully driven, although the owner may be liable for negligence if he fails to properly control them; and (2) keepers of farm animals, typically cattle, in some western States are not strictly liable for harm caused by their trespassing animals that are allowed to graze freely.

**NONTRESPASSING ANIMALS** Owners and possessors of wild animals are subject to strict liability for physical harm caused by such animals, whether they are trespassing or not. Third Restatement, Section 22(b). Accordingly the owner or possessor is liable even if she has exercised reasonable care in attempting to restrain the wild animal. **Wild animals** are defined as those that, in the particular region in which they are kept, are known to be likely to inflict serious damage and cannot be considered safe, no matter how domesticated they become. The Third Restatement has a similar definition: "A wild animal is an animal that belongs to a category of animals that have not been generally domesticated and that are likely, unless restrained, to cause personal injury." Section 22(b). The court determines whether a category of animals is wild. Animals that have been determined to be wild include bears, lions, elephants, monkeys, tigers, wolves, zebras, deer, and raccoons. On the other hand, iguanas, pigeons, and manatees are not considered wild animals because they do not pose a risk of causing substantial personal injury. Third Restatement, Section 22, Comment b.

**Domestic animals** are those that are traditionally devoted to the service of humankind and that as a class are considered safe. Examples of domestic animals are dogs, cats, horses, cattle, and sheep. Owners and possessors of domestic animals are subject to strict liability if they knew, or had reason to know, of an animal's dangerous tendencies abnormal for the animal's category. Restatement, Section 509; Third Restatement, Section 23. The animal's dangerous propensity must be the cause of the harm. For example, merely because he knows that a dog has a propensity to fight with other dogs, a keeper is not liable when the dog bites a human. On the other hand, a person whose 150-pound sheepdog has a propensity to jump enthusiastically on visitors would be liable for any damage caused by the dog's playfulness. About half of the States statutorily impose strict liability in dog cases even where the owner or possessor does not know, and did not have reason to know, of the dog's dangerous tendencies.

## DEFENSES TO STRICT LIABILITY

This section will discuss the availability in a strict liability action for abnormally dangerous activities and keeping of animals of the following defenses: (1) contributory negligence, (2) comparative negligence, and (3) assumption of risk.

### CONTRIBUTORY NEGLIGENCE

Because the strict liability of one who carries on an abnormally dangerous activity or keeps animals is not based on his negligence, the ordinary contributory negligence of the plaintiff is not a defense to such liability. In imposing strict liability, the law places on the defendant the full responsibility for preventing harm. For example, Adrian negligently fails to observe a sign on a highway warning of a blasting operation conducted by Benjamin. As a result, Adrian is injured by these operations; nonetheless, he may recover from Benjamin.

### COMPARATIVE NEGLIGENCE

Despite the rationale that disallows contributory negligence as a defense to strict liability, some States apply the doctrine of comparative negligence to some types of strict liability. The Third Restatement provides that if the plaintiff has been contributorily negligent in failing to take reasonable precautions, the plaintiff's recovery in a strict-liability claim for physical harm caused by abnormally dangerous activities or keeping of animals is reduced in accordance with the share of comparative responsibility assigned to the plaintiff. Section 25.

### ASSUMPTION OF RISK

Under the Second Restatement of Torts voluntary assumption of risk is a defense to an action based upon strict liability. If the owner of an automobile knowingly and voluntarily parks the vehicle in a blasting zone, he may not recover for harm to his automobile. The assumption of risk, however, must be voluntary. For example, the possessor of land located near a blasting operation is not required to move away; she may, in fact, recover for harm she suffers because of the operation.

The Third Restatement of Torts: Apportionment of Liability has abandoned the doctrine of implied voluntary assumption of risk in tort actions generally: it is no longer a defense that the plaintiff was aware of a risk and voluntarily confronted it. This new Restatement limits the defense of assumption of risk to express assumption of risk, which consists of a contract between the plaintiff and another person to absolve the other person from liability for future harm. Section 2.

The Third Restatement: Liability for Physical and Emotional Harm recognizes a limitation on strict liability for abnormally dangerous activities and keeping of animals when the victim suffers harm as a result of exposure to the animal or activity resulting from the victim's securing some benefit from that exposure. Section 24(a). The Third Restatement gives the following example: "if the plaintiff is a veterinarian or a groomer who accepts an animal such as a dog from the defendant, the plaintiff is deriving financial benefits from the acceptance of the animal, and is beyond the scope of strict liability, even if the dog can be deemed abnormally dangerous."

## CHAPTER SUMMARY

## NEGLIGENCE

**BREACH OF DUTY OF CARE**

**Definition of Negligence** conduct that falls below the standard established by law for the protection of others against unreasonable risk of harm

**Reasonable Person Standard** degree of care that a reasonable person would exercise under all the circumstances

- ***Children*** must conform to conduct of a reasonable person of the same age, intelligence, and experience under all the circumstances
- ***Physical Disability*** a disabled person's conduct must conform to that of a reasonable person under the same disability
- ***Mental Disability*** a mentally disabled person is held to the reasonable person standard

- ***Superior Skill or Knowledge*** if a person has skills or knowledge beyond those possessed by most others, these skills or knowledge are circumstances to be taken into account in determining whether the person has acted with reasonable care
- ***Emergencies*** the reasonable person standard applies, but an unexpected emergency is considered part of the circumstances
- ***Violation of Statute*** if the statute applies, the violation is negligence *per se* in most States

**Duty to Act** a person is under a duty to all others at all times to exercise reasonable care for the safety of the others' person and property; however, except in special circumstances, no one is required to aid another in peril

**Duties of Possessors of Land**

- ***Duty to Trespassers*** not to injure intentionally
- ***Duty to Licensees*** to warn of known dangerous conditions licensees are unlikely to discover for themselves
- ***Duty to Invitees*** to exercise reasonable care to protect invitees against dangerous conditions possessor should know of but invitees are unlikely to discover

***Res Ipsa Loquitur*** permits the jury to infer both negligent conduct and causation

---

**FACTUAL CAUSE AND SCOPE OF LIABILITY**

**Factual Cause** the defendant's conduct is a factual cause of the harm when the harm would not have occurred absent the conduct

**Scope of Liability (Proximate Cause)** liability is limited to those harms that result from the risks that made the defendant's conduct tortious

- ***Foreseeability*** excludes liability for harms that were sufficiently unforeseeable at the time of the defendant's tortious conduct that they were not among the risks that made the defendant negligent
- ***Superseding Cause*** an intervening act that relieves the defendant of liability

---

**HARM**

**Harm to Legally Protected Interest** courts determine which interests are protected from negligent interference

**Burden of Proof** plaintiff must prove that defendant's negligent conduct caused harm to a legally protected interest

---

**DEFENSES TO NEGLIGENCE**

**Contributory Negligence** failure of a plaintiff to exercise reasonable care for his own protection, which in a few States prevents the plaintiff from recovering anything

**Comparative Negligence** damages are divided between the parties in proportion to their degree of negligence; applies in almost all States

**Assumption of Risk** plaintiff's express consent to encounter a known danger; some States still apply implied assumption of the risk

---

## STRICT LIABILITY

---

**ACTIVITIES GIVING RISE TO STRICT LIABILITY**

**Definition of Strict Liability** liability for nonintentional and nonnegligent conduct

**Abnormally Dangerous Activity** strict liability is imposed for any activity that (1) creates a foreseeable and highly significant risk of harm and (2) is not one of common usage

**Keeping of Animals** strict liability is imposed for wild animals and usually for trespassing domestic animals

---

**DEFENSES TO STRICT LIABILITY**

**Contributory Negligence** is not a defense to strict liability

**Comparative Negligence** some States apply this doctrine to some strict liability cases

**Assumption of Risk** express assumption of risk is a defense to an action based upon strict liability; some States apply implied assumption of risk to strict liability cases

## CASES

CASE 8-1

### Duty to Act
### SOLDANO v. O'DANIELS

California Court of Appeal, Fifth District, 1983
141 Cal.App.3d 443, 190 Cal.Rptr. 310

**Andreen, J.**

Does a business establishment incur liability for wrongful death if it denies use of its telephone to a good samaritan who explains an emergency situation occurring without and wishes to call the police?

This appeal follows a judgment of dismissal of the second cause of action of a complaint for wrongful death upon a motion for summary judgment. The motion was supported only by a declaration of defense counsel. Both briefs on appeal adopt the defense averments:

> This action arises out of a shooting death occurring on August 9, 1977. Plaintiff's father [Darrell Soldano] was shot and killed by one Rudolph Villanueva on that date at defendant's Happy Jack's Saloon. This defendant owns and operates the Circle Inn which is an eating establishment located across the street from Happy Jack's. Plaintiff's second cause of action against this defendant is one for negligence.

Plaintiff alleges that on the date of the shooting, a patron of Happy Jack's Saloon came into the Circle Inn and informed a Circle Inn employee that a man had been threatened at Happy Jack's. He requested the employee either call the police or allow him to use the Circle Inn phone to call the police. That employee allegedly refused to call the police and allegedly refused to allow the patron to use the phone to make his own call. Plaintiff alleges that the actions of the Circle Inn employee were a breach of the legal duty that the Circle Inn owed to the decedent.

We were advised at oral argument that the employee was the defendant's bartender. The state of the record is unsatisfactory in that it does not disclose the physical location of the telephone—whether on the bar, in a private office behind a closed door or elsewhere. The only factual matter before the trial court was a verified statement of the defense attorney which set forth those facts quoted above. Following normal rules applicable to motions for summary judgment, we strictly construe the defense affidavit. [Citation.] Accordingly, we assume the telephone was not in a private office but in a position where it could be used by a patron without inconvenience to the defendant or his guests. We also assume the call was a local one and would not result in expense to defendant.

There is a distinction, well rooted in the common law, between action and nonaction. [Citation.] It has found its way into the prestigious Restatement Second of Torts (hereafter cited as "Restatement"), which provides in section 314:

> The fact that the actor realizes or should realize that action on his part is necessary for another's aid or protection does not of itself impose upon him a duty to take such action.

* * *

As noted in [citation], the courts have increased the instances in which affirmative duties are imposed not by direct rejection of the common law rule, but by expanding the list of special relationships which will justify departure from that rule. * * *

* * *

Section 314A of the Restatement lists other special relationships which create a duty to render aid, such as that of a common carrier to its passengers, an innkeeper to his guest, possessors of land who hold it open to the public, or one who has a custodial relationship to another. A duty may be created by an undertaking to give assistance. [Citation.]

Here there was no special relationship between the defendant and the deceased. It would be stretching the concept beyond recognition to assert there was a relationship between the defendant and the patron from Happy Jack's Saloon who wished to summon aid. But this does not end the matter.

It is time to re-examine the common law rule of nonliability for nonfeasance in the special circumstances of the instant case.

* * *

We turn now to the concept of duty in a tort case. The [California] Supreme Court has identified certain factors to be considered in determining whether a duty is owed to third persons. These factors include:

> the foreseeability of harm to the plaintiff, the degree of certainty that the plaintiff suffered injury, the closeness of the connection between the defendant's conduct and the injury suffered, the moral blame attached to the defendant's conduct, the policy of preventing future harm, the extent of the burden to the defendant and consequences to the community of imposing a duty to exercise care with resulting liability for breach, and the availability, cost, and prevalence of insurance for the risk involved. [Citation.]

We examine those factors in reference to this case. (1) The harm to the decedent was abundantly foreseeable; it was imminent. The employee was expressly told that a man had been threatened. The employee was a bartender. As such he knew it is foreseeable that some people who drink alcohol in the milieu of a bar setting are prone to violence. (2) The certainty of decedent's injury is undisputed. (3) There is arguably a close connection between the employee's conduct and the injury: the patron wanted to use the phone to summon the police to intervene. The employee's refusal to allow the use of the phone prevented this anticipated intervention. If permitted to go to trial, the plaintiff may be able to show that the probable response time of the police would have been shorter than the time between the prohibited telephone call and the fatal shot. (4) The employee's conduct displayed a disregard for human life that can be characterized as morally wrong: he was callously indifferent to the possibility that Darrell Soldano would die as the result of his refusal to allow a person to use the telephone. Under the circumstances before us the bartender's burden was minimal and exposed him to no risk: all he had to do was allow the use of the telephone. It would have cost him or his employer nothing. It could have saved a life. (5) Finding a duty in these circumstances would promote a policy of preventing future harm. A citizen would not be required to summon the police but would be required, in circumstances such as those before us, not to impede another who has chosen to summon aid. (6) We have no information on the question of the availability, cost, and prevalence of insurance for the risk, but note that the liability which is sought to be imposed here is that of employee negligence, which is covered by many insurance policies. (7) The extent of the burden on the defendant was minimal, as noted.

* * *

We acknowledge that defendant contracted for the use of his telephone, and its use is a species of property. But if it exists in a public place as defined above, there is no privacy or ownership interest in it such that the owner should be permitted to interfere with a good faith attempt to use it by a third person to come to the aid of another.

* * *

We conclude that the bartender owed a duty to the plaintiff's decedent to permit the patron from Happy Jack's to place a call to the police or to place the call himself.

It bears emphasizing that the duty in this case does not require that one must go to the aid of another. That is not the issue here. The employee was not the good samaritan intent on aiding another. The patron was.

* * *

We conclude there are sufficient justiciable issues to permit the case to go to trial and therefore reverse.

## CASE 8-2

### Duty to Invitees

### LOVE v. HARDEE'S FOOD SYSTEMS, INC.

Court of Appeals of Missouri, Eastern District, Division Two, 2000

16 S.W.3d 739

http://caselaw.lp.findlaw.com/scripts/getcase.pl?court=mo&vol=/appeals/052000/&invol=5050200_2000

**Crane, J.**

At about 3:15 P.M. on November 15, 1995, plaintiff, Jason Love, and his mother, Billye Ann Love, went to the Hardee's Restaurant in Arnold, Missouri, which is owned by defendant, Hardee's Food Systems, Inc. There were no other customers in the restaurant between 3:00 P.M. and 4:00 P.M., but two or three workmen were in the back doing construction. The workmen reported that they did not use the restroom and did not see anyone use the restroom. After eating his lunch, plaintiff, who was wearing rubber-soled boat shoes, went to use the restroom. He opened the restroom door, took one step in, and, upon taking his second step, slipped on water on the restroom floor. Plaintiff fell backwards, hit his head, and felt a shooting pain down his right leg. He found himself lying in an area of dirty water, which soaked his clothes. There were no barricades, warning cones, or anything else that would either restrict access to the bathroom or warn of the danger.

Plaintiff crawled up to the sink to pull himself up and made his way back to the table and told his mother that his back and leg were "hurting pretty bad." His mother reported the fall to another employee. Plaintiff's mother went back to the men's restroom and looked at the water on the floor. She observed that the water was dirty. The restaurant supervisor came out and interviewed plaintiff and viewed the water in the restroom. * * * The supervisor then filled out an accident report form, which reported that the accident occurred at 3:50 P.M. The supervisor testified that the water appeared to have come from someone shaking his hands after washing them. The supervisor told plaintiff he could not recall the last time the restroom had been checked. Plaintiff was taken to a hospital emergency room. As a result of his injuries, plaintiff underwent two back surgeries, missed substantial time from work, and suffered from continuing pain and limitations on his physical activities.

Defendant had a policy requiring that the restroom was to be checked and cleaned every hour by a maintenance man. The maintenance man was scheduled to work until 3:00 P.M., but normally left at 1:00 P.M. The supervisor could not recall whether the maintenance man left at 1:00 P.M. or 3:00 P.M. on November 15. The time clock activity report would show when the maintenance man clocked out, but defendant was unable to produce the time clock report for November 15.

It was also a store policy that whenever employees cleaned the tables, they would check the restroom. The restrooms were used by customers and employees. If an employee had to use the restroom, then that employee was also supposed to check the restroom. The restaurant supervisor did not ask if any employees had been in the restroom, or if they had checked it in the hour prior to the accident, and did not know if the restroom was actually inspected or cleaned at 3:00 P.M.

The restaurant had shift inspection checklists on which the manager would report on the cleanliness of the restrooms and whether the floors were clean and dry. However, the checklists for November 15 were thrown away. * * *

Plaintiff subsequently filed the underlying lawsuit against defendant to recover damages for negligence. The jury returned a verdict in plaintiff's favor in the amount of $125,000. * * *

* * * [Defendant] argues that plaintiff failed to make a submissible case of negligence because plaintiff failed to prove that defendant had actual or constructive notice of the water on the restroom floor in that there was no evidence showing the source of the water or the length of time the water had been on the floor.

* * *

In order to have made a submissible case, plaintiff had to show that defendant knew or, by using ordinary care, could have known of the dangerous condition and failed to use ordinary care to remove it, barricade it, or warn of it, and plaintiff sustained damage as a direct result of such failure. [Citation.]

"In order to establish constructive notice, the condition must have existed for a sufficient length of time or the facts must be such that the defendant should have reasonably known of its presence." [Citation.] [Prior] cases * * * placed great emphasis on the length of time the dangerous condition had been present and held that times of 20 or 30 minutes, absent proof of other circumstances, were insufficient to establish constructive notice as a matter of law. [Citations.]

* * *

Defendant's liability is predicated on the foreseeability of the risk and the reasonableness of the care taken, which is a question of fact to be determined by the totality of the circumstances, including the nature of the restaurant's business and the method of its operation. [Citations.]

In this case the accident took place in the restaurant's restroom which is provided for the use of employees and customers. The cause of the accident was water, which is provided in the restroom. The restaurant owner could reasonably foresee that anyone using the restroom, customers or employees, would use the tap water provided in the restroom and could spill, drop, or splash water on the floor. Accordingly, the restaurant owner was under a duty to use due care to guard against danger from water on the floor.

There was substantial evidence to support submissibility. First, there was evidence from which the jury could infer that the water came from the use of the restroom. It was on the floor of the restroom and the supervisor testified it appeared that someone had shaken water from his hands on the floor.

Next, there was evidence from which the jury could infer that, if the water was caused by a non-employee, the water was on the floor for at least 50 minutes, or longer, because there was evidence that no other customers were in the store to use the restroom after 3:00 P.M. and the workmen on the site advised that they had not used the restroom.

In addition, plaintiff adduced evidence from which the jury could have found that defendants' employees had the opportunity to observe the hazard. The restroom was to be used by the employees and was supposed to be checked by them when they used it; employees cleaning tables were supposed to check the restroom when they cleaned the tables; and a maintenance man was supposed to check and clean the restroom every hour.

There was evidence from which the jury could have inferred that the maintenance man charged with cleaning the restroom every hour did not clean the restroom at 3:00 P.M. as scheduled on the day of the accident. There was testimony that the maintenance man usually left at 1:00 P.M. The supervisor could not recall what time the maintenance man left that day and defendant was unable to produce the time clock reports for that day which would have shown when the maintenance man clocked out. This could have created a span of 2 hours and 50 minutes during which there was no employee working at the restaurant whose primary responsibility was to clean the restroom. [Citation.]

There was also evidence from which the jury could have inferred that the restroom was not inspected by any employee who had the responsibility to inspect it during that same time period. The supervisor testified that he could not recall the last time the restroom had been checked and did not ask any employees if they had been in the restroom or had checked it in the hour before the accident. * * *

* * *

The judgment of the trial court is affirmed.

CASE 8-3

## Scope of Liability (Proximate Cause)

## PALSGRAF v. LONG ISLAND RAILROAD CO.

Court of Appeals of New York, 1928

248 N.Y. 339, 162 N.E. 99

**Cardozo, C. J.**

Plaintiff was standing on a platform of defendant's railroad after buying a ticket to go to Rockaway Beach. A train stopped at the station, bound for another place. Two men ran forward to catch it. One of the men reached the platform of the car without mishap, though the train was already moving. The other man, carrying a package, jumped aboard the car, but seemed unsteady as if about to fall. A guard on the car, who had held the door open, reached forward to help him in, and another guard on the platform pushed him from behind. In this act, the package was dislodged, and fell upon the rails. It was a package of small size, about fifteen inches long, and was covered by a newspaper. In fact it contained fireworks, but there was nothing in its appearance to give notice of its contents. The fireworks when they fell exploded. The shock of the explosion threw down some scales at the other end of the platform many feet away. The scales struck the plaintiff, causing injuries for which she sues.

The conduct of the defendant's guard, if a wrong in its relation to the holder of the package, was not a wrong in its relation to the plaintiff, standing far away. Relatively to her it was not negligence at all. Nothing in the situation gave notice that the falling package had in it the potency of peril to persons thus removed. Negligence is not actionable unless it involves the invasion of a legally protected interest, the violation of a right. "Proof of negligence in the air, so to speak, will not do." [Citations.] "Negligence is the absence of care, according to the circumstances." [Citations.]

* * *

If no hazard was apparent to the eye of ordinary vigilance, an act innocent and harmless, at least to outward seeming, with reference to her, did not take to itself the quality of a tort because it happened to be a wrong, though apparently not one involving the risk of bodily insecurity, with reference to someone else. "In every instance, before negligence can be predicated of a given act, back of the act must be sought and found a duty to the individual complaining, the observance of which would have averted or avoided the injury." [Citations.]

* * *

A different conclusion will involve us, and swiftly too, in a maze of contradictions. A guard stumbles over a package which has been left upon a platform. It seems to be a bundle of newspapers. It turns out to be a can of dynamite. To the eye of ordinary vigilance, the bundle is abandoned waste, which may be kicked or trod on with impunity. Is a passenger at the other end of the platform protected by the law against the unsuspected hazard concealed beneath the waste? If not, is the result to be any different, so far as the distant passenger is concerned, when the guard stumbles over a valise which a truckman or a porter has left upon the walk? The passenger far away, if the victim of a wrong at all, has a cause of action, not derivative, but original and primary. His claim to be protected against invasion of his bodily security is neither greater nor less because the act resulting in the invasion is a wrong to another far removed. In this case, the rights that are said to have been violated, the interests said to have been invaded, are not even of the same order. The man was not injured in his person nor even put in danger. The purpose of the act, as well as its effect, was to make his person safe. If there was a wrong to him at all, which may very well be doubted, it was a wrong to a property interest only, the safety of his package. Out of this wrong to property, which threatened injury to nothing else, there has passed, we are told, to the plaintiff by derivation or succession a right of action for the invasion of an interest of another order, the right to bodily security. The diversity of interests emphasizes the futility of the effort to build the plaintiff's right upon the basis of a wrong to someone else. * * * One who jostles one's neighbor in a crowd does not invade the rights of others standing at the outer fringe when the unintended contact casts a bomb upon the ground. The wrongdoer as to them is the man who carries the bomb, not the one who explodes it without suspicion of the danger. Life will have to be made over, and human nature transformed, before prevision so extravagant can be accepted as the norm of conduct, the customary standard to which behavior must conform.

* * *

The judgment of the Appellate Division and that of the Trial Term should be reversed, and the complaint dismissed, with costs in all courts.

CASE 8-4

## Contributory Negligence
## MOORE v. KITSMILLER

Court of Appeals of Texas, Twelfth District, Tyler, 2006
201 S.W.3d 147, review denied
http://www.12thcoa.courts.state.tx.us/opinions/HTMLopinion.asp?OpinionID=7549

**Worthen, C. J.**

In the spring of 2001, Kitsmiller purchased a house in Van Zandt County to use as rental property. In mid-June, he hired B&H Shaw Company, Inc. ("B&H") to install a replacement septic tank in the back yard. The septic tank was located about two or three feet from a concrete stoop at the back door of the garage. B&H mounded dirt over the septic tank and the lateral lines going out from it upon completion. Sometime after B&H installed the septic tank, Kitsmiller smoothed out the mounds of dirt over the septic tank and lateral lines using the box blade on his tractor. Kitsmiller then leased the property to Moore and his wife on July 27. Kitsmiller testified that he viewed the back yard about a week or ten days prior to leasing the property to the Moores and stated that the dirt around the septic system looked firm.

On August 7, the Moores moved in. On August 11, Moore and his wife ventured into the back yard for the first time, carrying some trash bags to a barrel. Moore testified that his wife led the way and he followed her about a foot and a half behind. Moore testified that at the time, his right arm was in a sling and a bag of trash was in his left hand. He stated that as he stepped off the stoop, he was unable to see the ground and could only see his wife and the bag of trash in his left arm. His wife testified that the ground looked flat as she walked toward the barrel. Moore testified that he had only taken a few steps off the stoop when his left leg sank into a hole, causing him to fall forward into his wife. As he tried to steady himself with his right foot, it hung and then sank, causing him to fall backward on his head and back. Moore testified that the injury to his back required surgery and affected his ability to earn a living.

Moore filed suit against Kitsmiller and B&H. He sought damages for past and future pain and suffering, past and future mental anguish, past and future physical impairment, and past and future loss of earning capacity. In their answers to Moore's suit, both Kitsmiller and B&H pleaded the affirmative defense of contributory negligence. [Citation.] B&H specifically pleaded that Moore was negligent for not having kept a proper lookout when stepping into the back yard and looking for obstructions, such as erosion or soft soil.

During the jury trial, Moore testified Kitsmiller should have notified him where the septic tank and lateral lines were located and that the dirt should have remained mounded over the tank and lines. On August 13, Moore asked Ken Martin to inspect the site of the fall (the "occurrence"). Martin is an on-site septic tank complaint investigator for both the Texas Commission on Environmental Quality and Van Zandt County. Martin testified that dirt should have been mounded over the septic tank and lateral lines, so that when the dirt settled, there would be no holes in the ground around the septic tank or lateral lines. However, there was no dirt mounded over the septic tank or lines when he inspected the site. Martin's photographs of the site also indicated that there were no mounds of dirt over the septic tank. Further, the photographs showed sunken ground around the septic tank, including, but not limited to, the area where Moore fell. Martin testified that it was common for sinkholes to develop around a septic tank. He also testified that he had observed situations where dirt around a septic tank or lateral line looked to be solid, but sank when a person stepped on it. Martin testified that the photographs showed an obvious depression around the septic tank. Bill Shaw, president of B&H, testified that Moore should have been watching where he was going as he stepped into the back yard. Shaw stated that Martin's photographs indicated to him that the depressions in the ground around the septic tank were visible at the time of the occurrence.

The first question for the jury was whose negligence caused the occurrence. The jury responded that both Kitsmiller and Moore were negligent, but B&H was not. In the second question, the jury determined that Kitsmiller was 51% negligent and Moore was 49% negligent. In the third question, the jury determined that Moore was entitled to $210,000.00 in damages. On September 29, 2004, the trial court entered a judgment in favor of Moore and against Kitsmiller in the amount of $210,000.00 plus interest and costs.

On October 14, 2004, Kitsmiller asked that the trial court modify the judgment to $107,100.00 based upon Moore's contributory negligence. The trial court entered a modified final judgment on November 1, 2004 awarding Moore $107,100.00 plus interest and costs. On November 23, 2004, a partial satisfaction and release of judgment filed with the court showed that Kitsmiller had paid the amount awarded in the modified judgment to Moore. However, Moore reserved the right to appeal all issues involving his contributory negligence to this court. Moore then timely filed his notice of appeal.

* * *

* * * Moore contends the evidence is legally insufficient to support the judgment. Moore argues that his wife and Kitsmiller testified that the back yard was flat at the time of the occurrence. He contends that no one could have anticipated

any danger from walking into the yard. Therefore, Moore argues that there is no evidence in the record to support the jury's determination that he was contributorily negligent.

Contributory negligence contemplates an injured person's failure to use ordinary care regarding his or her own safety. [Citation.] This affirmative defense requires proof that the plaintiff was negligent and that the plaintiff's negligence proximately caused his or her injuries. [Citation.] Negligence requires proof of proximate cause. [Citation.] Proximate cause requires proof of both cause in fact and foreseeability. [Citation.] The test for cause in fact is whether the negligent act or omission was a substantial factor in bringing about an injury without which the harm would not have occurred. [Citation.] Foreseeability requires that a person of ordinary intelligence should have anticipated the danger created by a negligent act or omission. [Citation.]

Because comparative responsibility involves measuring the party's comparative fault in causing the plaintiff's injuries, it necessitates a preliminary finding that the plaintiff was in fact contributorily negligent. [Citation.] The standards and tests for determining contributory negligence ordinarily are the same as those for determining negligence, and the rules of law applicable to the former are applicable to the latter. [Citation.] The burden of proof on the whole case is on the plaintiff. [Citation.] However, on special issues tendered by the defendant presenting an affirmative defense such as contributory negligence, the burden of proof is on the defendant to prove the defense by a preponderance of the evidence. [Citation.]

When attacking the legal sufficiency of an adverse finding on an issue on which the party did not have the burden of proof, that party must demonstrate there is no evidence to support the adverse finding. [Citation.] To evaluate the legal sufficiency of the evidence to support a finding, we must determine whether the proffered evidence as a whole rises to a level that would enable reasonable and fair minded people to differ in their conclusions. [Citation.] We sustain a no evidence issue only if there is no more than a scintilla of evidence proving the elements of the claim. [Citation.] In making this determination, we must view the evidence in the light most favorable to the verdict, crediting favorable evidence if reasonable jurors could and disregarding contrary evidence unless reasonable jurors could not. [Citation.] The trier of fact may draw reasonable and logical inferences from the evidence. [Citation.] It is within the province of the jury to draw one reasonable inference from the evidence although another inference could have been made. [Citation.]

* * *

Moore testified that when he stepped off the stoop into the back yard for the first time on August 11, 2001, he could only see his wife and the plastic bag of trash he was carrying in his left hand. The jury was allowed to draw an inference from this evidence that Moore was not watching where he was walking. An individual must keep a proper lookout where he is walking, and a jury is allowed to make a reasonable inference that failure to do so was the proximate cause of his injuries. [Citation.] It was reasonable for the jury to make an inference from Moore's testimony that his failure to keep a proper lookout where he was walking contributed to the occurrence.

Moore contends that the only reasonable inference the jury could have made was that, even if he had been watching where he was walking, he would not have been able to avoid stepping in the holes because they were not visible to the naked eye. The jury could have made that inference, but chose not to do so. Shaw's testimony that Martin's photographs showed the depressions could have been present at the time of the occurrence could have led the jury to believe that Moore's contention was not a reasonable inference. We conclude that the jury made a reasonable inference from the evidence in finding Moore contributorily negligent.

* * *

* * * [T]he judgment of the trial court is affirmed.

## CASE 8-5

### Abnormally Dangerous Activities
### KLEIN v. PYRODYNE CORPORATION

Supreme Court of Washington, 1991
117 Wash.2d 1, 810 P.2d 917

**Guy, J.**

The plaintiffs in this case are persons injured when an aerial shell at a public fireworks exhibition went astray and exploded near them. The defendant is the pyrotechnic company hired to set up and discharge the fireworks. The issue before this court is whether pyrotechnicians are strictly liable for damages caused by fireworks displays. We hold that they are.

Defendant Pyrodyne Corporation (Pyrodyne) is a general contractor for aerial fireworks at public fireworks displays. Pyrodyne contracted to procure fireworks, to provide pyrotechnic operators, and to display the fireworks at the Western Washington State Fairgrounds in Puyallup, Washington, on July 4, 1987. All operators of the fireworks display were Pyrodyne employees acting within the scope of their employment duties.

As required by Washington statute, Pyrodyne purchased a $1,000,000 insurance policy prior to the fireworks show. The policy provided $1,000,000 coverage for each occurrence of bodily injury or property damage liability. Plaintiffs allege that Pyrodyne failed to carry out a number of the other statutory and regulatory requirements in preparing for and setting off the fireworks. For example, they allege that Pyrodyne failed to properly bury the mortar tubes prior to detonation, failed to provide a diagram of the display and surrounding environment to the local government, failed to provide crowd control monitors, and failed to keep the invitees at the mandated safe distance.

During the fireworks display, one of the 5-inch mortars was knocked into a horizontal position. From this position a shell inside was ignited and discharged. The shell flew 500 feet in a trajectory parallel to the earth and exploded near the crowd of onlookers. Plaintiffs Danny and Marion Klein were injured by the explosion. Mr. Klein's clothing was set on fire, and he suffered facial burns and serious injury to his eyes.

The parties provide conflicting explanations of the cause of the improper horizontal discharge of the shell. Pyrodyne argues that the accident was caused by a 5-inch shell detonating in its aboveground mortar tube without ever leaving the ground. Pyrodyne asserts that this detonation caused another mortar tube to be knocked over, ignited, and shot off horizontally. In contrast, the Kleins contend that the misdirected shell resulted because Pyrodyne's employees improperly set up the display. They further note that because all of the evidence exploded, there is no means of proving the cause of the misfire.

The Kleins brought suit against Pyrodyne under theories of products liability and strict liability. Pyrodyne filed a motion for summary judgment, which the trial court granted as to the products liability claim. The trial court denied Pyrodyne's summary judgment motion regarding the Kleins' strict liability claim, holding that Pyrodyne was strictly liable without fault and ordering summary judgment in favor of the Kleins on the issue of liability. Pyrodyne appealed the order of partial summary judgment to the Court of Appeals, which certified the case to this court. Pyrodyne is appealing solely as to the trial court's holding that strict liability is the appropriate standard of liability for pyrotechnicians. A strict liability claim against pyrotechnicians for damages caused by fireworks displays presents a case of first impression in Washington.

## Analysis

***Fireworks Displays as Abnormally Dangerous Activities***

The Kleins contend that strict liability is the appropriate standard to determine the culpability of Pyrodyne because Pyrodyne was participating in an abnormally dangerous activity. * * *

The modern doctrine of strict liability for abnormally dangerous activities derives from *Fletcher v. Rylands*, [citation], in which the defendant's reservoir flooded mine shafts on the plaintiff's adjoining land. *Rylands v. Fletcher* has come to stand for the rule that "the defendant will be liable when he damages another by a thing or activity unduly dangerous and inappropriate to the place where it is maintained, in the light of the character of that place and its surroundings." [Citation.]

The basic principle of *Rylands v. Fletcher* has been accepted by the Restatement (Second) of Torts (1977). [Citation.] Section 519 of the Restatement provides that any party carrying on an "abnormally dangerous activity" is strictly liable for ensuing damages. The test for what constitutes such an activity is stated in section 520 of the Restatement. Both Restatement sections have been adopted by this court, and determination of whether an activity is an "abnormally dangerous activity" is a question of law. [Citations.]

Section 520 of the Restatement lists six factors that are to be considered in determining whether an activity is "abnormally dangerous." The factors are as follows: (a) existence of a high degree of risk of some harm to the person, land or chattels of others; (b) likelihood that the harm that results from it will be great; (c) inability to eliminate the risk by the exercise of reasonable care; (d) extent to which the activity is not a matter of common usage; (e) inappropriateness of the activity to the place where it is carried on; and (f) extent to which its value to the community is outweighed by its dangerous attributes. Restatement (Second) of Torts §520 (1977). As we previously recognized in [citation], the comments to section 520 explain how these factors should be evaluated: Any one of them is not necessarily sufficient of itself in a particular case, and ordinarily several of them will be required for strict liability. On the other hand, it is not necessary that each of them be present, especially if others weigh heavily. Because of the interplay of these various factors, it is not possible to reduce abnormally dangerous activities to any definition. The essential question is whether the risk created is so unusual, either because of its magnitude or because of the circumstances surrounding it, as to justify the imposition of strict liability for the harm that results from it, even though it is carried on with all reasonable care. Restatement (Second) of Torts §520, Comment f (1977). Examination of these factors persuades us that fireworks displays are abnormally dangerous activities justifying the imposition of strict liability.

We find that the factors stated in clauses (a), (b), and (c) are all present in the case of fireworks displays. Any time a person ignites aerial shells or rockets with the intention of sending them aloft to explode in the presence of large crowds of people, a high risk of serious personal injury or property damage is created. That risk arises because of the possibility that a shell or rocket will malfunction or be misdirected. Furthermore, no matter how much care pyrotechnicians exercise, they cannot entirely eliminate the high risk inherent in setting off powerful explosives such as fireworks near crowds.

* * *

The factor expressed in clause (d) concerns the extent to which the activity is not a matter "of common usage." The Restatement explains that "[a]n activity is a matter of common usage if it is customarily carried on by the great mass of mankind or by many people in the community." Restatement (Second) of Torts §520, Comment i (1977). As examples of activities that are not matters of common usage, the Restatement comments offer driving a tank, blasting, the manufacture, storage, transportation, and use of high explosives, and drilling for oil. The deciding characteristic is that few persons engage in these activities. Likewise, relatively few persons conduct public fireworks displays. Therefore, presenting public fireworks displays is not a matter of common usage.

* * *

The factor stated in clause (e) requires analysis of the appropriateness of the activity to the place where it was carried on. In this case, the fireworks display was conducted at the Puyallup Fairgrounds. Although some locations—such as over water—may be safer, the Puyallup Fairgrounds is an appropriate place for a fireworks show because the audience can be seated at a reasonable distance from the display. Therefore, the clause (e) factor is not present in this case.

The factor stated in clause (f) requires analysis of the extent to which the value of fireworks to the community outweighs its dangerous attributes. We do not find that this factor is present here. This country has a long-standing tradition of fireworks on the 4th of July. That tradition suggests that we as a society have decided that the value of fireworks on the day celebrating our national independence and unity outweighs the risks of injuries and damage.

In sum, we find that setting off public fireworks displays satisfies four of the six conditions under the Restatement test; that is, it is an activity that is not "of common usage" and that presents an ineliminably high risk of serious bodily injury or property damage. We therefore hold that conducting public fireworks displays is an abnormally dangerous activity justifying the imposition of strict liability.

* * *

***Conclusion***

We hold that Pyrodyne Corporation is strictly liable for all damages suffered as a result of the July 1987 fireworks display. Detonating fireworks displays constitutes an abnormally dangerous activity warranting strict liability * * *. This establishes the standard of strict liability for pyrotechnicians. Therefore, we affirm the decision of the trial court.

## QUESTIONS

1. List and briefly describe the three required elements of an action for negligence.
2. Explain the duty of care that is imposed upon (a) adults, (b) children, (c) persons with a physical disability, (d) persons with a mental deficiency, (e) persons with superior knowledge, and (f) persons acting in an emergency.
3. Differentiate among the duties that possessors of land owe to trespassers, licensees, and invitees.
4. Identify the defenses that are available to a tort action in negligence and those that are available to a tort action in strict liability.
5. Identify and discuss those activities giving rise to a tort action in strict liability.

## PROBLEMS

**1.** A statute requiring railroads to fence their tracks is construed as intended solely to prevent animals that stray onto the right-of-way from being hit by trains. B&A Railroad Company fails to fence its tracks. Two of Calvin's cows wander onto the track. Nellie is hit by a train. Elsie is poisoned by weeds growing beside the track. For which cow(s), if any, is B&A Railroad Company liable to Calvin? Why?

**2.** Martha invites John to come to lunch. Though she knows that her private road is dangerous to travel, having been heavily eroded by recent rains, Martha doesn't warn John of the condition, reasonably believing that he will notice the deep ruts and exercise sufficient care. While John is driving over, his attention is diverted from the road by the screaming of his child, who has been stung by a bee. He fails to notice the condition of the road, hits a rut, and skids into a tree. If John is not contributorily negligent, is Martha liable to John?

**3.** Nathan is run over by a car and left lying in the street. Sam, seeing Nathan's helpless state, places him in his car for the purpose of taking him to the hospital. Sam drives negligently into a ditch, causing additional injury to Nathan. Is Sam liable to Nathan?

**4.** Led Foot drives his car carelessly into another car. The second car contains dynamite, which Led had no way of knowing. The collision causes an explosion, which shatters a window of a building half a block away on another street. The flying glass inflicts serious cuts on Sally, who is working at a desk near the window. The explosion also harms Vic, who is walking on the sidewalk near the point of the collision. Toward whom is Led Foot negligent?

**5.** A statute requires all vessels traveling on the Great Lakes to provide lifeboats. One of Winston Steamship Company's boats is sent out of port without a lifeboat. Perry, a sailor, falls overboard in a storm so strong that had there been a lifeboat, it could not have been launched. Perry drowns. Is Winston liable to Perry's estate?

**6.** Lionel is negligently driving an automobile at excessive speed. Reginald's negligently driven car crosses the centerline of the highway and scrapes the side of Lionel's car, damaging its fenders. As a result, Lionel loses control of his car, which goes into the ditch. Lionel's car is wrecked, and Lionel suffers personal injuries. What, if anything, can Lionel recover?

**7.** Ellen, the owner of a baseball park, is under a duty to the entering public to provide a reasonably sufficient number of screened seats to protect those who desire such protection against the risk of being hit by batted balls. Ellen fails to do so.

**(a)** Frank, a customer entering the park, is unable to find a screened seat and, although fully aware of the risk, sits in an unscreened seat. Frank is struck and injured by a batted ball. Is Ellen liable?

**(b)** Gretchen, Frank's wife, has just arrived from Germany and is viewing baseball for the first time. Without asking any questions, she follows Frank to a seat. After the batted ball hits Frank, it caroms into Gretchen, injuring her. Is Ellen liable to Gretchen?

**8.** Negligent in failing to give warning of the approach of its train to a crossing, CC Railroad thereby endangers Larry, a blind man who is about to cross. Mildred, a bystander, in a reasonable effort to save Larry, rushes onto the track to push Larry out of danger. Although Mildred acts as carefully as possible, she is struck and injured by the train.

**(a)** Can Mildred recover from Larry?

**(b)** Can Mildred recover from CC Railroad?

**9.** Vance was served liquor while he was an intoxicated patron of the Clear Air Force Station Non-Commissioned Officers' Club. He later injured himself as a result of his intoxication. An Alaska State statute makes it a crime to give or to sell liquor to intoxicated persons. Vance has brought an action seeking damages for the injuries he suffered. Could Vance successfully argue that the United States was negligent *per se* by its employee's violation of the statute?

**10.** Timothy keeps a pet chimpanzee, which is thoroughly tamed and accustomed to playing with its owner's children. The chimpanzee escapes, despite every precaution to keep it upon its owner's premises. It approaches a group of children. Wanda, the mother of one of the children, erroneously thinking the chimpanzee is about to attack the children, rushes to her child's assistance. In her hurry and excitement, she stumbles and falls, breaking her leg. Can Wanda recover for her personal injuries?

**11.** Hawkins slipped and fell on a puddle of water just inside the automatic door to the H. E. Butt Grocery Company's store. The water had been tracked into the store by customers and blown through the door by a strong wind. The store manager was aware of the puddle and had mopped it up several times earlier in the day. Still, no signs had been placed to warn store patrons of the danger. Hawkins brought an action to recover damages for injuries sustained in the fall. Was the store negligent in its conduct?

**12.** Escola, a waitress, was injured when a bottle of Coca-Cola exploded in her hand while she was putting it into the restaurant's cooler. The bottle came from a shipment that had remained under the counter for thirty-six hours after being delivered by the bottling company. The bottler had subjected the bottle to the method of testing for defects commonly used in the industry, and there is no evidence that Escola or anyone else did anything to damage the bottle between its delivery and the explosion. Escola brought an action against the bottler for damages. As she is unable to show any specific acts of negligence on its part, she seeks to rely on the doctrine of *res ipsa loquitur*. Should she be able to recover on this theory? Explain.

**13.** Hunn injured herself when she slipped and fell on a loose plank while walking down some steps. The night before, while entering the hotel, she had noticed that the steps were dangerous, and although she knew from her earlier stays at the hotel that another exit was available, she chose that morning to leave via the dangerous steps. The hotel was aware of the hazard, as one of the other guests who had fallen that night had reported his accident to the desk clerk then on duty. Still, there were no cautionary signs on the steps to warn of the danger, and they were not roped off or otherwise excluded from use. Hunn brought an action against the hotel for injuries she sustained as a result of her fall. Should she recover? Explain.

**14.** Fredericks, a hotel owner, had a dog named "Sport" that he had trained as a watchdog. When Vincent Zarek, a guest at the hotel, leaned over to pet the dog, it bit him. Although Sport had never bitten anyone before, Fredericks was aware of the dog's violent tendencies and, therefore, did not allow it to roam around the hotel alone. Vincent brought an action for injuries sustained when the dog bit him. Is Fredericks liable for the actions of his dog? Explain.

**15.** Two thugs in an alley in Manhattan held up an unidentified man. When the thieves departed with his possessions, the man quickly gave chase. He had almost caught one when the thief managed to force his way into an empty taxicab stopped at a traffic light. The Peerless Transport Company owned the cab. The thief pointed his gun at the driver's head and ordered him to drive on. The driver started to follow the directions while closely pursued by a posse of good citizens, but then suddenly jammed on the brakes and jumped out of the car to safety. The thief also jumped out, but the car traveled on, injuring Mrs. Cordas and her two children. The Cordases then brought an action for damages, claiming that the cab driver was negligent in jumping to safety and leaving the moving vehicle uncontrolled. Was the cab driver negligent? Explain.

**16.** A foul ball struck Marie Uzdavines on the head while she was watching the Metropolitan Baseball Club ("The Mets") play the Philadelphia Phillies at the Mets' home stadium in New York. The ball came through a hole in a screen designed to protect spectators sitting behind home plate. The screen contained several holes that had been repaired with baling wire lighter in weight than the wire used in the original screen. Although the manager of the stadium makes no formal inspections of the screen, his employees do try to repair the holes as they find them. Weather conditions, rust deterioration, and baseballs hitting the screen are the chief causes of these holes. The owner of the stadium, the city of New York, leases the stadium to "The Mets" and replaces the entire screen every two years. Uzdavines sued The Mets for negligence under the doctrine of *res ipsa loquitur*. Is this an appropriate case for *res ipsa loquitur*? Explain.

**17.** Two-year-old David Allen was bitten by Joseph Whitehead's dog while he was playing on the porch at the Allen residence. Allen suffered facial cuts, a severed muscle in his left eye, a hole in his left ear, and scarring over his forehead. Through his father, David sued Whitehead, claiming that, as owner, Whitehead is responsible for his dog's actions. Whitehead admitted that (1) the dog was large, mean looking, and frequently barked at neighbors; (2) the dog was allowed to roam wild; and (3) the dog frequently chased and barked at cars. He stated, however, that (1) the dog was friendly and often played with his and neighbors' children; (2) he had not received previous complaints about the dog; (3) the dog was neither aggressive nor threatening; and (4) the dog had never bitten anyone before this incident. Is Whitehead liable?

**18.** Larry VanEgdom, in an intoxicated state, bought alcoholic beverages from the Hudson Municipal Liquor Store in Hudson, South Dakota. An hour later, VanEgdom, while driving a car, struck and killed Guy William Ludwig, who was stopped on his motorcycle at a stop sign. Lela Walz, as special administrator of Ludwig's estate, brought an action against the city of Hudson, which operated the liquor store, for the wrongful death of Ludwig. Walz alleged that the store employee was negligent in selling intoxicating beverages to VanEgdom when he knew or could have observed that VanEgdom was drunk. Decision?

**19.** The *MacGilvray Shiras* was a ship owned by the Kinsman Transit Company. During the winter months, when Lake Erie was frozen, the ship and others moored at docks on the Buffalo River. As oftentimes happened, one night an ice jam disintegrated upstream, sending large chunks of ice downstream. Chunks of ice began to pile up against the *Shiras*, which at that time was without power and manned only by a shipman. The ship broke loose when a negligently constructed "deadman" to which one mooring cable was attached pulled out of the ground. The "deadman" was operated by Continental Grain Company. The ship began moving down the S-shaped river stern first and struck another ship, the *Tewksbury*. The *Tewksbury* also broke loose from its mooring, and the two ships floated down the river together. Although the crew manning the Michigan Avenue Bridge downstream had been notified of the runaway ships, they failed to raise the bridge in time to avoid a collision because of a mix-up in the shift changeover. As a result, both ships crashed into the bridge and were wedged against the bank of the river. The two vessels substantially dammed the flow of the river, causing ice and water to back up and flood installations as far as three miles upstream. The injured parties brought this action for damages against Kinsman, Continental, and the city of Buffalo. Who, if any, is liable? Explain.

**20.** Carolyn Falgout accompanied William Wardlaw as a social guest to Wardlaw's brother's camp. After both parties had consumed intoxicating beverages, Falgout walked onto a pier that was then only partially completed. Wardlaw had requested that she not go on the pier. Falgout said, "Don't tell me what to do," and proceeded to walk on the pier. Wardlaw then asked her not to walk past the completed portion of the pier. She ignored his warnings and walked to the pier's end. When returning to the shore, Falgout got her shoe caught between the boards. She fell, hanging by her foot, with her head and arms in the water. Wardlaw rescued Falgout, who had seriously injured her knee and leg. She sued Wardlaw for negligence. Decision?

**21.** Joseph Yania, a coal strip-mine owner, and Boyd Ross visited a coal strip-mining operation owned by John Bigan to discuss a business matter with Bigan. On Bigan's property there were several cuts and trenches he had dug to remove the coal underneath. While there, Bigan asked the two men to help him pump water from one of these cuts in the earth. This particular cut contained water eight to ten feet in depth with sidewalls or embankments sixteen to eighteen feet in height. The two men agreed, and the process began with Ross and Bigan entering the cut and standing at the point where the pump was located. Yania stood at the top of one of the cut's sidewalls. Apparently, Bigan taunted Yania into jumping into the water from the top of the sidewall—a height of sixteen to eighteen feet. As a result, Yania drowned. His widow brought a negligence action against Bigan. She claims that Bigan was negligent "(1) by urging, enticing, taunting, and inveigling Yania to jump into the water; (2) by failing to warn Yania of a dangerous condition on the land; and (3) by failing to go to Yania's rescue after he jumped into the water." Was Bigan negligent?

**22.** Rebecca S. Dukat arrived at Mockingbird Lanes, a bowling alley in Omaha, Nebraska, at approximately 6:00 P.M. to bowl in her league game. The bowling alley's parking lot and adjacent sidewalk were covered with snow and ice. Dukat proceeded to walk into the bowling alley on the only sidewalk provided in and out of the building. She testified that she noticed the sidewalk was icy. After bowling three games and drinking three beers, Dukat left the bowling alley at approximately 9:00 P.M. She retraced her steps on the same sidewalk, which was still ice-covered and in a condition that, according to Frank Jameson, general manager of Mockingbird Lanes, was "unacceptable" if the bowling alley were open to customers. As Dukat proceeded along the sidewalk to her car, she slipped, attempted to catch herself by reaching toward a car, and fell. She suffered a fracture of both bones in her left ankle as well as a ruptured ligament. Dukat sued Leiserv, Inc., doing business as Mockingbird Lanes, alleging that Leiserv was negligent in failing to keep the sidewalk in a reasonably safe condition, in failing to warn her of a dangerous condition, and in failing to take adequate and reasonable measures to protect her. Leiserv alleged two affirmative defenses: (1) Dukat was contributorily negligent, and (2) Dukat had assumed the risk of injury. Decision?

PART 2

# Contracts

# CHAPTER 9
# Introduction to Contracts

It is impossible to overestimate the importance of contracts in the field of business. Every business, whether large or small, must enter into contracts with its employees, its suppliers, and its customers to conduct its business operations. Contract law is, therefore, an important subject for the business manager. Contract law is also basic to other fields of law treated in other parts of this book, such as agency, partnerships, corporations, sales of personal property, commercial paper, and secured transactions.

Even the most common transaction may involve a multitude of contracts. For example, in a typical contract for the sale of land, the seller promises to transfer title to the land, and the buyer promises to pay an agreed-upon purchase price. In addition, the seller may promise to pay certain taxes or assessments; the buyer may promise to assume a mortgage on the property or may promise to pay the purchase price to a creditor of the seller. If attorneys represent the parties, they very likely do so on a contractual basis. If the seller deposits the proceeds of the sale in a bank, he enters into a contract with the bank. If the buyer leases the property, he enters into a contract with the tenant. When one of the parties leaves his car in a parking lot to attend to any of these matters, he assumes a contractual relationship with the proprietor of the lot. In short, nearly every business transaction is based upon contract and the expectations the agreed-upon promises create. Knowing the legal requirements for making binding contracts is, therefore, essential.

## DEVELOPMENT OF THE LAW OF CONTRACTS

That law arises from social necessity is clearly true of the law of contracts. The vast and complicated institution of business can be conducted efficiently and successfully only upon the certainty that promises will be fulfilled. Business must be assured not only of supplies of raw materials or manufactured goods, but also of labor, management, capital, and insurance as well. Common experience has shown that promises based solely on personal honesty or integrity do not have the reliability essential to business. Hence the development of the law of contracts, which is the law of enforceable promises.

Contract law, like law as a whole, is not static. It has undergone—and is still undergoing—enormous changes. In the nineteenth century virtually absolute autonomy in forming contracts was the rule. The law imposed contract liability only where the parties strictly complied with the required formalities. The same principle also dictated that once a contract was formed it should be enforced according to its terms and that neither party should be lightly excused from performance.

During the twentieth century, contract law experienced tremendous changes. As will be discussed in the next ten chapters, many of the formalities of contract formation were relaxed. Today, the law usually recognizes contractual obligations whenever the parties manifest an intent to be bound. In addition, an increasing number of promises are now enforced in certain circumstances, even though they do not comply strictly with the basic requirements of a contract. While in the past contract liability was absolute and escape from liability, once assumed, was rare, presently the law allows a party to be excused from contractual duties where fraud, duress, undue influence, mistake, unconscionability, or impossibility is present. The law has expanded the nineteenth century's narrow view of contract damages to grant equitable remedies and restitution as remedies for breach of contract. The older doctrine of privity of contract, which sharply restricted which parties could enforce contract rights, has given way to the current view that permits intended third-party beneficiaries to sue in their own right.

In brief, the twentieth century left its mark on contract law by limiting the absolute freedom of contract and, at the same time, by relaxing the requirements of contract formation. Accordingly, it is now considerably easier to get into a contract and correspondingly less difficult to get out of one.

### COMMON LAW

Contracts are primarily governed by State common law. An orderly presentation of this law is found in the Restatements of the Law of Contracts. The American Law Institute adopted and promulgated the first Restatement on May 6, 1932. On May 17, 1979, the institute adopted and promulgated a revised edition of the Restatement—the Restatement, Second, Contracts—which will be referred to as the Restatement. Regarded as a valuable authoritative reference work for more than seventy years, the Restatements have been extensively relied upon and quoted in reported judicial opinions.

### THE UNIFORM COMMERCIAL CODE

The sale of personal property forms a substantial portion of commercial activity. Article 2 of the Uniform Commercial Code (the Code, or UCC) governs sales in all States except Louisiana. (Selected provisions of the UCC are set forth in *Appendix B* of this text.) A **sale** consists of the passing of title to goods from a seller to a buyer for a price. Section 2–106. A contract for sale includes both a present sale of goods and a contract to sell goods at a future time. Section 2–106. The Code essentially defines goods as movable personal property. Section 2–105(1). **Personal property** is any type of property other than an interest in real property (land). For example, the purchase of a television set, automobile, or textbook is considered a sale of goods. All such transactions are governed by Article 2 of the Code, but, where the Code has not specifically modified general contract law, the common law of contracts continues to apply. Section 1–103. In other words, the law of sales is a specialized part of the general law of contracts, and the law of contracts governs unless specifically displaced by the Code.

Amendments to Article 2 were promulgated in 2003 to accommodate electronic commerce and to reflect development of business practices, changes in other law, and interpretive difficulties of practical significance. To date no States have adopted them. However, at least thirty-seven States have adopted the 2001 Revisions to Article 1, which applies to all of the articles of the Code.

◆ SEE FIGURE 9-1: **Law Governing Contracts**

◆ SEE CASE 21-2

### TYPES OF CONTRACTS OUTSIDE THE CODE

General contract law governs all contracts outside the scope of the Code. Such contracts play a significant role in commercial activities. For example, the Code does *not* apply to employment contracts, service contracts, insurance contracts, contracts involving **real property** (land and anything attached to it, including buildings), and contracts for the sale of intangibles such as patents and copyrights. These transactions continue to be governed by general contract law.

◆ SEE CASE 9-1

## DEFINITION OF A CONTRACT

A **contract** is a binding agreement that the courts will enforce. Section 1 of the Restatement more precisely defines a contract as "a promise or a set of promises for the breach of which the law gives a remedy, or the performance of which the law in some way recognizes as a duty." The Restatement provides further insight by defining a **promise** as "a manifestation of the intention to act or refrain from acting in a specified way." Restatement, Section 2.

Those promises that meet all of the essential requirements of a binding contract are contractual and will be enforced. All other promises are not contractual, and usually no legal remedy is available for a **breach** (a failure to perform

◆ FIGURE 9-1: **Law Governing Contracts**

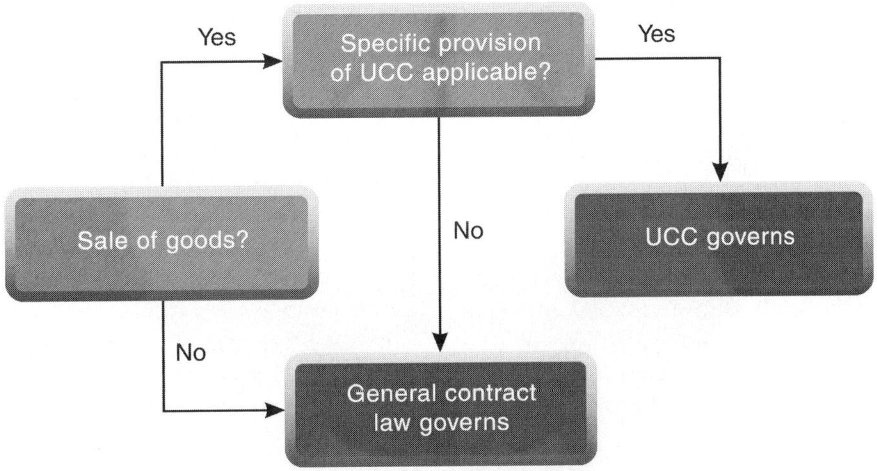

properly) of these promises. The remedies provided for breach of contract (discussed in *Chapter 18*) include compensatory damages, equitable remedies, reliance damages, and restitution. Thus, a promise may be contractual (and therefore binding) or noncontractual. In other words, all contracts are promises, but not all promises are contracts.

◆ SEE FIGURE 9-2: **Contractual and Noncontractual Promises**

◆ SEE CASE 9-2

## REQUIREMENTS OF A CONTRACT

The four basic requirements of a contract are as follows:

1. **Mutual Assent**. The parties to a contract must manifest by words or conduct that they have agreed to enter into a contract. The usual method of showing mutual assent is by offer and acceptance.
2. **Consideration**. Each party to a contract must intentionally exchange a legal benefit or incur a legal detriment as an inducement to the other party to make a return exchange.
3. **Legality of Object**. The purpose of a contract must not be criminal, tortious, or otherwise against public policy.
4. **Capacity.** The parties to a contract must have contractual capacity. Certain persons, such as those adjudicated (judicially declared) incompetent, have no legal capacity to contract, while others, such as minors, incompetent persons, and intoxicated persons, have limited capacity to contract. All others have full contractual capacity.

In addition, though occasionally a contract must be evidenced by a writing to be enforceable, in most cases an oral contract is binding and enforceable. If all of these essentials are present, the promise is contractual and legally binding. If any is absent, however, the promise is noncontractual. These requirements will be separately considered in succeeding chapters.

◆ SEE FIGURE 9-3: **Validity of Agreements**

◆ SEE CASE 9-2

## CLASSIFICATION OF CONTRACTS

Contracts can be classified according to various characteristics, such as method of formation, content, and legal effect. The standard classifications are (1) express or implied contracts; (2) unilateral or bilateral contracts; (3) valid, void, voidable, or unenforceable contracts; (4) executed or executory contracts; and (5) formal or informal contracts. These classifications are not mutually exclusive. For example, a contract may be express, bilateral, valid, executory, and informal.

### EXPRESS AND IMPLIED CONTRACTS

Parties to a contract may indicate their assent either by express language or by conduct that implies such willingness. Thus, a contract may be (1) entirely oral; (2) partly oral and partly written; (3) entirely written; (4) partly oral or written and partly implied from the conduct of the parties; and (5) wholly implied from the conduct of the parties. The first three are known as express contracts, and the last two as implied

◆ FIGURE 9-2: **Contractual and Noncontractual Promises**

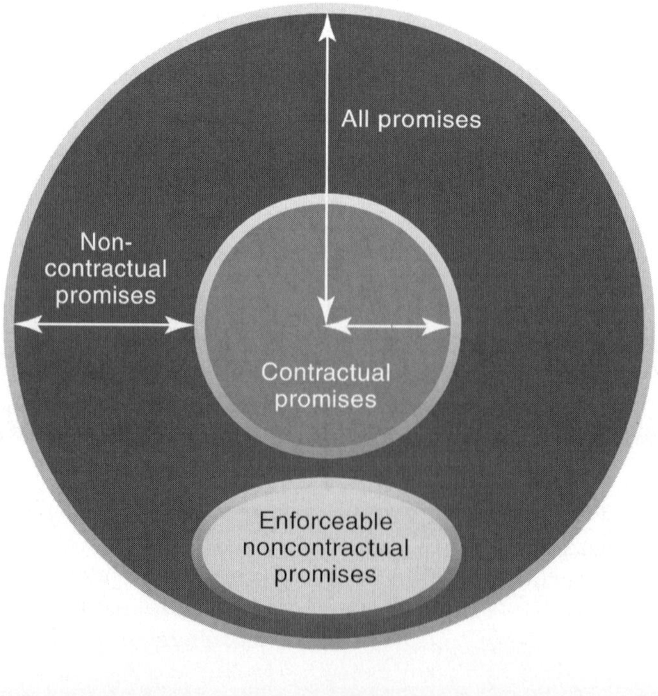

◆ FIGURE 9-3: **Validity of Agreements**

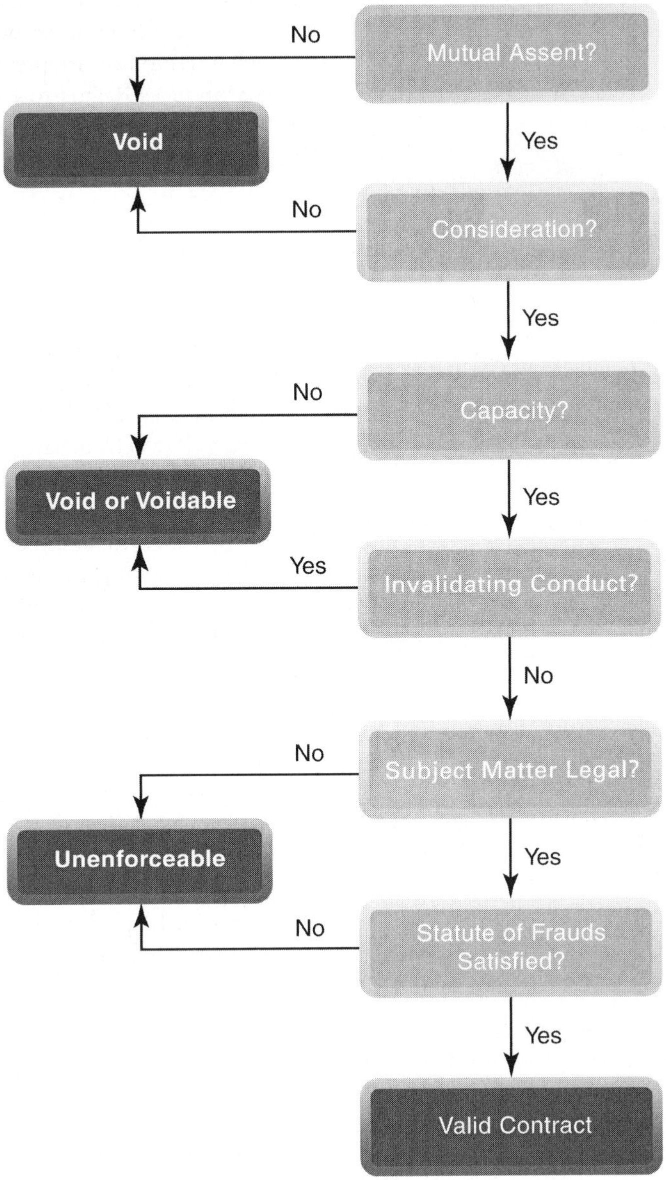


contracts. Both express and implied contracts are genuine contracts, equally enforceable. The difference between them is merely the manner in which the parties manifest assent.

An **express contract** is therefore one in which the parties have manifested their agreement by oral or written language, or both.

An **implied contract** is one that is inferred from the parties' conduct, not from spoken or written words. Implied contracts are also called implied in fact contracts. Thus, if Elizabeth orders and receives a meal in Bill's restaurant, a promise is implied on Elizabeth's part to pay Bill the price stated in the menu or, if none is stated, Bill's customary price. Likewise, when a passenger boards a bus, a wholly implied contract is formed by which the passenger undertakes to pay the customary fare and the bus company undertakes to provide the passenger transportation.

◆ **SEE CASE 9-1**

## UNILATERAL AND BILATERAL CONTRACTS

In the typical contractual transaction, each party makes at least one promise. For example, if Ali says to Ben, "If you promise to mow my lawn, I will pay you ten dollars," and Ben agrees to mow Ali's lawn, Ali and Ben have made mutual promises, each undertaking to do something in exchange for the promise of the other. When a contract comes into existence by the exchange of promises, each party is under a duty to the other. This kind of contract is called a

**bilateral contract**, because each party is both a *promisor* (a person making a promise) and a *promisee* (the person to whom a promise is made).

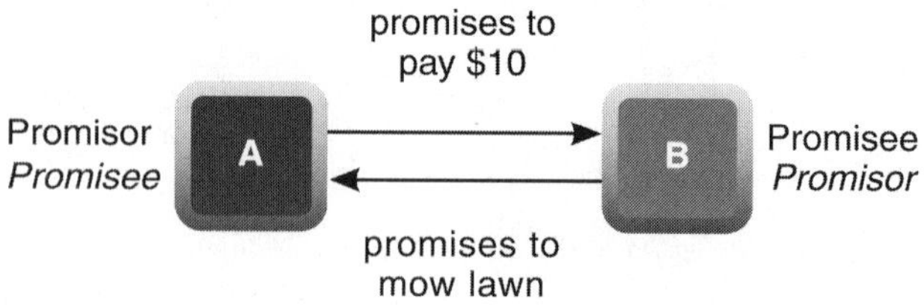


But suppose that only one of the parties makes a promise. Ali says to Ben, "If you will mow my lawn, I will pay you ten dollars." A contract will be formed when Ben has finished mowing the lawn and not before. At that time, Ali becomes contractually obligated to pay $10.00 to Ben. Ali's offer was in exchange for Ben's act of mowing the lawn, not for his promise to mow it. Because he never made a promise to mow the lawn, Ben was under no duty to mow it. This is a **unilateral contract** because only one of the parties made a promise.

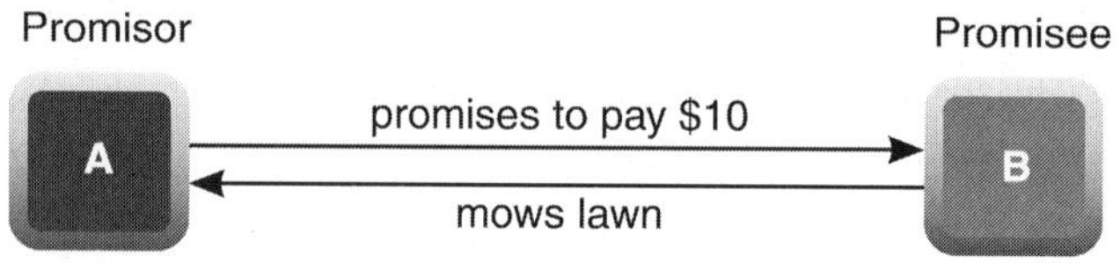


Thus, whereas a bilateral contract results from the exchange of a promise for a return promise, a unilateral contract results from the exchange of a promise either for an act or for a forbearance (refraining) from acting. If a contract is not clearly unilateral or bilateral, the courts presume that the parties intended a bilateral contract. Thus, in the above example, if Ali says to Ben, "I will pay you ten dollars if you will mow my lawn," and Ben replies, "OK, I will mow your lawn," a bilateral contract is formed.

## VALID, VOID, VOIDABLE, AND UNENFORCEABLE CONTRACTS

By definition, a **valid contract** is one that meets all of the requirements of a binding contract. It is an enforceable promise or agreement.

A **void contract** is an agreement that does not meet all of the requirements of a binding contract. Thus, it is no contract at all; it is merely a promise or an agreement having no legal effect. An example of a void agreement is an agreement entered into by an adjudicated incompetent.

A voidable contract, on the other hand, is not wholly lacking in legal effect. A **voidable contract** is a contract, but because of the manner in which it was formed or a lack of capacity of a party to it, the law permits one or more of the parties to avoid the legal duties the contract creates. Restatement, Section 7. If the contract is avoided, both parties are relieved of their legal duties under the agreement. For instance, through intentional misrepresentation of a material fact (*fraud*), Thomas induces Regina to enter into a contract. Regina may, upon discovery of the fraud, notify Thomas that by reason of the misrepresentation she will not perform her promise, and the law will support Regina. Though not void, the contract induced by fraud is voidable at the election of Regina, the defrauded party. Thomas, the fraudulent party, has no such election. If Regina elects to avoid the contract, Thomas will be released from his promise under the agreement, although he may be liable under tort law for damages for fraud.

A contract that is neither void nor voidable may, nonetheless, be unenforceable. An **unenforceable contract** is one for the breach of which the law provides no remedy. Restatement, Section 8. For example, a contract may be unenforceable because of a failure to satisfy the requirements of the Statute of Frauds, which requires certain kinds of contracts to be evidenced by a writing to be enforceable. Also, the running of the time within which a suit may be filed, as provided in the Statute of Limitations, bars the right to bring a lawsuit for breach of contract. After that period has run, the contract is referred to as unenforceable, rather than void or voidable.

## EXECUTED AND EXECUTORY CONTRACTS

The terms *executed* and *executory* pertain to the state of performance of a contract. A contract fully performed by all of the parties to it is an **executed contract**. Strictly, an executed contract is in the present tense no contract, as all duties under it have been performed; but it is useful to have a term for a completed contract. (The word *executed* is also used to mean "signed," as in to execute or sign a certain document.)

The term **executory**, which means "unperformed," applies to situations in which one or more promises by any party to the contract are as yet unperformed or where the contract is wholly unperformed by one or more of the parties. Thus, David and Carla make a contract under which David is to sell and deliver certain goods to Carla in ten days and Carla is to pay the agreed price in thirty days. Prior to the delivery of the goods by David on the tenth day, the contract is wholly executory. Upon David's delivery of the goods to Carla, the contract is executed as to David and executory as to Carla. When Carla duly pays for the goods, the contract is wholly executed and thereby completely fulfilled.

## FORMAL AND INFORMAL CONTRACTS

A **formal contract** depends upon a particular form, or mode of expression, for its legal existence. For example, at common law a promise under seal (a particular symbol that serves to authenticate an instrument) is enforceable without anything more. Another formal contract is a negotiable instrument, such as a check, which has certain legal attributes resulting solely from the special form in which it is made. A letter of credit (a promise to honor drafts or other demands for payment) is also a formal contract. Recognizances, or formal acknowledgments of indebtedness made in court, are another example of formal contracts. All other contracts, whether oral or written, are simple or **informal contracts**, as they do not depend upon formality for their legal validity.

## PROMISSORY ESTOPPEL

As a general rule, promises are unenforceable if they do not meet all the requirements of a contract. Nevertheless, to avoid injustice, in certain circumstances courts enforce noncontractual promises under the doctrine of promissory estoppel. A noncontractual promise is enforceable when it is made under circumstances that should lead the promisor reasonably to expect that the promise would induce the promisee to take definite and substantial action or forbearance in reliance on the promise, and the promisee does take such action or forbearance. See *Figure 9-2*. Section 90 of the Restatement provides:

> A promise which the promisor should reasonably expect to induce action or forbearance on the part of the promisee or a third person and which does induce such action or forbearance is binding if injustice can be avoided only by enforcement of the promise. The remedy granted for breach may be limited as justice requires.

For example, Gordon promises Constance not to foreclose for a period of six months on a mortgage Gordon owns on Constance's land. Constance then expends $100,000 to construct a building on the land. His promise not to foreclose is binding on Gordon under the doctrine of promissory estoppel.

◆ SEE FIGURE 9-4: **Contracts, Promissory Estoppel, and Quasi Contracts**

◆ SEE CASE 9-3

## QUASI CONTRACTS

In addition to implied in fact contracts, there are implied in law, or quasi, contracts, which were not included in the foregoing classification of contracts because a quasi (meaning "as if") contract is not a contract at all but based in restitution. The term *quasi contract* is used because the remedy granted for quasi contract is similar to one of the remedies available for breach of contract.

A quasi contract is *not* a contract because it is based on neither an express nor an implied promise. A **contract implied in law** or quasi contract is an obligation imposed by law to avoid injustice. For example, Anna by mistake delivers to Robert a plain, unaddressed envelope containing $100 intended for Claudia. Robert is under no contractual obligation to return it. However, Anna is permitted to recover the $100 from Robert. The law imposes a quasi-contractual obligation upon Robert to prevent his unjust enrichment at Anna's expense. The elements of such a recovery are (1) a benefit conferred upon the defendant (Robert) by the plaintiff (Anna); (2) an appreciation or knowledge by the defendant (Robert) of the benefit; and (3) acceptance or retention by the defendant (Robert) of the benefit under circumstances rendering inequitable the defendant's (Robert's) retention of the benefit without compensating the plaintiff for its value.

One court has summarized the doctrine of quasi contract as follows:

> Quasi contracts are not contracts at all, although they give rise to obligations more akin to those stemming from contract than from tort. The contract is a mere fiction, a form imposed in order to adapt the case to a given remedy.... Briefly stated, a quasi-contractual obligation is one imposed by law where there has been no agreement or expression of assent, by word or act, on the part of either party involved. The law creates it, regardless of the intention of the parties, to assure a just and equitable result. *Bradkin v. Leverton*, 26 N.Y.2d 192, 309 N.Y.S.2d 192, 257 N.E.2d 643 (1970).

◆ FIGURE 9-4: **Contracts, Promissory Estoppel, and Quasi Contracts**

| | Contract | Promissory Estoppel | Quasi Contract |
|---|---|---|---|
| **Type of Promise** | Contractual | Noncontractual | None<br>Void<br>Unenforceable<br>Invalidated |
| **Requirements** | All of the essential elements of a contract | Detrimental and justifiable reliance | Benefit conferred and knowingly accepted |
| **Remedies** | Equitable<br>Compensatory<br>Reliance<br>Restitution | Promise enforced to the extent necessary to avoid injustice | Reasonable value of benefit conferred |

Not infrequently, courts use quasi contracts to provide a remedy when the parties have entered into a void contract, an unenforceable contract, or a voidable contract that is avoided. In such a case, the law of quasi contracts will determine the recovery permitted for any performance rendered by the parties under the invalid, unenforceable, or invalidated agreement.

◆ SEE FIGURE 9-4: Contracts, Promissory Estoppel, and Quasi Contracts

## CHAPTER SUMMARY

### LAW OF CONTRACTS

**Definition of Contract** a binding agreement that the courts will enforce
**Common Law** most contracts are governed primarily by State common law, including contracts involving employment, services, insurance, real property (land and anything attached to it), patents, and copyrights
**Uniform Commercial Code** Article 2 of the UCC governs the sales of goods
- ***Sale*** the transfer of title from seller to buyer
- ***Goods*** tangible personal property (personal property is all property other than an interest in land)

### REQUIREMENTS OF A CONTRACT

**Mutual Assent** the parties to a contract must manifest by words or conduct that they have agreed to enter into a contract
**Consideration** each party to a contract must intentionally exchange a legal benefit or incur a legal detriment as an inducement to the other party to make a return exchange
**Legality of Object** the purpose of a contract must not be criminal, tortious, or otherwise against public policy
**Capacity** the parties to a contract must have contractual capacity

### CLASSIFICATION OF CONTRACTS

**Express and Implied Contracts**
- ***Express Contract*** an agreement that is stated in words, either orally or in writing
- ***Implied in Fact Contract*** a contract in which the agreement of the parties is inferred from their conduct

**Unilateral Bilateral and Contracts**
- ***Bilateral Contract*** a contract in which both parties exchange promises
- ***Unilateral Contract*** a contract in which only one party makes a promise

**Valid, Void, Voidable, and Unenforceable Contracts**
- ***Valid Contract*** one that meets all of the requirements of a binding contract
- ***Void Contract*** no contract at all; without legal effect
- ***Voidable Contract*** a contract capable of being made void
- ***Unenforceable Contract*** a contract for the breach of which the law provides no remedy

**Executed and Executory Contracts**
- ***Executed Contract*** a contract that has been fully performed by all of the parties
- ***Executory Contract*** a contract that has yet to be fully performed

**Formal and Informal Contracts**
- ***Formal Contract*** an agreement that is legally binding because of its particular form or mode of expression
- ***Informal Contracts*** all contracts other than formal contracts

### PROMISSORY ESTOPPEL

**Definition** a doctrine enforcing some noncontractual promises
**Requirements** a promise made under circumstances that should lead the promisor reasonably to expect that the promise would induce the promisee to take definite and substantial action, and the promisee does take such action
**Remedy** a court will enforce the promise to the extent necessary to avoid injustice

**QUASI CONTRACTS** **Definition** an obligation not based on contract that is imposed to avoid injustice
**Requirements** a court will impose a quasi contract when (1) the plaintiff confers a benefit upon the defendant, (2) the defendant knows or appreciates the benefit, and (3) the defendant's retention of the benefit is inequitable
**Remedy** the plaintiff recovers the reasonable value of the benefit she conferred upon the defendant

## CASES

CASE 9-1

### Contracts Outside the Code/Express and Implied Contracts
### FOX v. MOUNTAIN WEST ELECTRIC, INC.

Supreme Court of Idaho, 2002
137 Idaho 703, 52 P.3d 848 2002, rehearing denied, 2002
http://caselaw.lp.findlaw.com/data2/idahostatecases/sc/1026/fox8.pdf

**Walters, J.**

Lockheed Martin Idaho Technical Company ("LMITCO") requested bids for a comprehensive fire alarm system in its twelve buildings located in Idaho Falls. At a prebid meeting, MWE [Mountain West Electric, Inc.] and Fox met and discussed working together on the project. MWE was in the business of installing electrical wiring, conduit and related hookups and attachments. Fox provided services in designing, drafting, testing and assisting in the installation of fire alarm systems, and in ordering specialty equipment necessary for such projects. The parties concluded that it would be more advantageous for them to work together on the project than for each of them to bid separately for the entire job, and they further agreed that Fox would work under MWE. The parties prepared a document defining each of their roles entitled "Scope and Responsibilities."

Fox prepared a bid for the materials and services that he would provide, which was incorporated into MWE's bid to LMITCO. MWE was the successful bidder and was awarded the LMITCO fixed price contract. In May 1996, Fox began performing various services at the direction of MWE's manager. During the course of the project, many changes and modifications to the LMITCO contract were made.

A written contract was presented to Fox by MWE on August 7, 1996. A dispute between MWE and Fox arose over the procedure for the compensation of the change orders. MWE proposed a flow-down procedure, whereby Fox would receive whatever compensation LMITCO decided to pay MWE. This was unacceptable to Fox. Fox suggested a bidding procedure to which MWE objected. On December 5, 1996, Fox met with MWE to discuss the contract. No compensation arrangement was agreed upon by the parties with respect to change orders. Fox left the project on December 9, 1996, after delivering the remaining equipment and materials to MWE. MWE contracted with Life Safety Systems ("LSS") to complete the LMITCO project.

Fox filed a complaint in July 1998 seeking monetary damages representing money due and owing for materials and services provided by Fox on behalf of MWE. MWE answered and counterclaimed seeking monetary damages resulting from the alleged breach of the parties' agreement by Fox.

Following a court trial, the district court found that an implied-in-fact contract existed between the parties based on the industry standard's flow-down method of compensation. The court found in favor of MWE. * * * Fox appeals.

* * *

#### Implied-in-Fact Contract

* * *

This Court has recognized three types of contractual relationships:

> First is the express contract wherein the parties expressly agree regarding a transaction. Secondly, there is the implied in fact contract wherein there is no express agreement, but the conduct of the parties implies an agreement from which an obligation in contract exists. The third category is called an implied in law contract, or quasi contract. However, a contract implied in law is not a contract at all, but an obligation imposed by law for the purpose of bringing about justice and equity without reference to the intent or the agreement of the parties and, in some cases, in spite of an agreement between the parties. It is a non-contractual obligation that is to be treated procedurally as if it were a contract, and is often refered (sic) to as quasi contract, unjust enrichment, implied in law contract or restitution.
>
> [Citation.]

"An implied in fact contract is defined as one where the terms and existence of the contract are manifested by the conduct of the parties with the request of one party and the performance by the other often being inferred from the circumstances attending the performance." [Citation.] The implied-in-fact contract is grounded in the parties' agreement and tacit understanding. [Citation.] "The general rule is that where the conduct of the parties allows the dual inferences that one performed at the other's request and that the requesting party promised payment, then the court may find a contract implied in fact." [Citations.]

[UCC §] 1–205(1) defines "course of dealing" as "a sequence of previous conduct between the parties to a particular transaction which is fairly to be regarded as establishing a common basis of understanding for interpreting their expressions and other conduct."

* * *

Although the procedure was the same for each change order, in that MWE would request a pricing from Fox for the work, which was then presented to LMITCO, each party treated the pricings submitted by Fox for the change orders in a different manner. This treatment is not sufficient to establish a meeting of the minds or to establish a course of dealing when there was no "common basis of understanding for interpreting [the parties'] expressions" under [UCC §] 1–205(1).

* * * After a review of the record, it appears that the district court's findings are supported by substantial and competent, albeit conflicting, evidence. This Court will not substitute its view of the facts for the view of the district court.

Using the district court's finding that pricings submitted by Fox were used by MWE as estimates for the change orders, the conclusion made by the district court that an implied-in-fact contract allowed for the reasonable compensation of Fox logically follows and is grounded in the law in Idaho. [Citation.]

This Court holds that the district court did not err in finding that there was an implied-in-fact contract using the industry standard's flow-down method of compensation for the change orders rather than a series of fixed price contracts between MWE and Fox.

***Uniform Commercial Code***

Fox contends that the district court erred by failing to consider previous drafts of the proposed contract between the parties to determine the terms of the parties' agreement. Fox argues the predominant factor of this transaction was the fire alarm system, not the methodology of how the system was installed, which would focus on the sale of goods and, therefore, the Uniform Commercial Code ("UCC") should govern. Fox argues that in using the UCC various terms were agreed upon by the parties in the prior agreement drafts, including terms for the timing of payments, payments to Fox's suppliers and prerequisites to termination.

MWE contends that the UCC should not be used, despite the fact that goods comprised one-half of the contract price, because the predominant factor at issue is services and not the sale of goods. MWE points out that the primary issue is the value of Fox's services under the change orders and the cost of obtaining replacement services after Fox left the job. MWE further argues that the disagreement between the parties over material terms should prevent the court from using UCC gap fillers. Rather, MWE contends the intent and relationship of the parties should be used to resolve the conflict.

This Court in [citation], pointed out "in determining whether the UCC applies in such cases, a majority of courts look at the entire transaction to determine which aspect, the sale of goods or the sale of services, predominates." [Citation.] It is clear that if the underlying transaction to the contract involved the sale of goods, the UCC would apply. [Citation.] However, if the contract only involved services, the UCC would not apply. [Citation.] This Court has not directly articulated the standard to be used in mixed sales of goods and services, otherwise known as hybrid transactions.

The Court of Appeals in *Pittsley v. Houser,* [citation], focused on the applicability of the UCC to hybrid transactions. The court held that the trial court must look at the predominant factor of the transaction to determine if the UCC applies. [Citation.]

> The test for inclusion or exclusion is not whether they are mixed, but, granting that they are mixed, whether their predominant factor, their thrust, their purpose, reasonably stated, is the rendition of service, with goods incidentally involved (e.g., contract with artist for painting) or is a transaction of sale, with labor incidentally involved (e.g., installation of a water heater in a bathroom). This test essentially involves consideration of the contract in its entirety, applying the UCC to the entire contract or not at all.

[Citation.] This Court agrees with the Court of Appeals' analysis and holds that the predominant factor test should be used to determine whether the UCC applies to transactions involving the sale of both goods and services.

One aspect that the Court of Appeals noted in its opinion in *Pittsley,* in its determination that the predominant factor in that case was the sale of goods, was that the purchaser was more concerned with the goods and less concerned with the installation, either who would provide it or the nature of the work. MWE and Fox decided to work on this project together because of their differing expertise. MWE was in the business of installing electrical wiring, while Fox designed, tested and assisted in the installation of fire alarm systems, in addition to ordering specialty equipment for fire alarm projects.

The district court found that the contract at issue in this case contained both goods and services; however, the predominant factor was Fox's services. The district court found that the goods provided by Fox were merely incidental to the services he provided, and the UCC would provide no assistance in interpreting the parties' agreement.

This Court holds that the district court did not err in finding that the predominant factor of the underlying transaction was services and that the UCC did not apply.

* * *

This Court affirms the decision of the district court.

CASE 9-2

## Definition and Requirements of a Contract
## STEINBERG v. CHICAGO MEDICAL SCHOOL

Illinois Court of Appeals, 1976
41 Ill.App.3d 804, 354 N.E.2d 586

**Dempsey, J.**

In December 1973 the plaintiff, Robert Steinberg, applied for admission to the defendant, the Chicago Medical School, as a first-year student for the academic year 1974–75 and paid an application fee of $15. The Chicago Medical School is a private, not-for-profit educational institution, incorporated in the State of Illinois. His application for admission was rejected and Steinberg filed a[n] * * * action against the school, claiming that it had failed to evaluate his application * * * according to the academic entrance criteria printed in the school's bulletin. Specifically, his complaint alleged that the school's decision to accept or reject a particular applicant for the first-year class was primarily based on such nonacademic considerations as the prospective student's familial relationship to members of the school's faculty and to members of its board of trustees, and the ability of the applicant or his family to pledge or make payment of large sums of money to the school. The complaint further alleged that, by using such unpublished criteria to evaluate applicants, the school had breached the contract which Steinberg contended was created when the school accepted his application fee.

* * *

The defendant filed a motion to dismiss, arguing that the complaint failed to state a cause of action because no contract came into existence during its transaction with Steinberg inasmuch as the school's informational publication did not constitute a valid offer. The trial court sustained [ruled in favor of] the motion to dismiss and Steinberg appeals from this order.

* * *

A contract is an agreement between competent parties, based upon a consideration sufficient in law, to do or not do a particular thing. It is a promise or a set of promises for the breach of which the law gives a remedy, or the performance of which the law in some way recognizes as a duty. [Citation.] A contract's essential requirements are: competent parties, valid subject matter, legal consideration, mutuality of obligation and mutuality of agreement. Generally, parties may contract in any situation where there is no legal prohibition, since the law acts by restraint and not by conferring rights. [Citation.] However, it is basic contract law that in order for a contract to be binding the terms of the contract must be reasonably certain and definite. [Citation.]

A contract, in order to be legally binding, must be based on consideration. [Citation.] Consideration has been defined to consist of some right, interest, profit or benefit accruing to one party or some forbearance, disadvantage, detriment, loss or responsibility given, suffered, or undertaken by the other. [Citation.] Money is a valuable consideration and its transfer or payment or promises to pay it or the benefit from the right to its use, will support a contract.

In forming a contract, it is required that both parties assent to the same thing in the same sense [citation] and that their minds meet on the essential terms and conditions. [Citation.] Furthermore, the mutual consent essential to the formation of a contract must be gathered from the language employed by the parties or manifested by their words or acts. The intention of the parties gives character to the transaction, and if either party contracts in good faith he is entitled to the benefit of his contract no matter what may have been the secret purpose or intention of the other party. [Citation.]

Steinberg contends that the Chicago Medical School's informational brochure constituted an invitation to make an offer; that his subsequent application and the submission of his $15 fee to the school amounted to an offer; that the school's voluntary reception of his fee constituted an acceptance and because of these events a contract was created between the school and himself. He contends that the school was duty bound under the terms of the contract to evaluate his application according to its stated standards and that the deviation from these standards not only breached the contract, but amounted to an arbitrary selection which constituted a violation of due process and equal protection. He concludes that such a breach did in fact take place each and every time during the past ten years that the school evaluated applicants according to their relationship to the school's faculty members or members of its board of trustees, or in accordance with their ability to make or pledge large sums of money to the school. Finally, he asserts that he is a member and a proper representative of the class that has been damaged by the school's practice.

The school counters that no contract came into being because informational brochures, such as its bulletin, do not constitute offers, but are construed by the courts to be general proposals to consider, examine and negotiate. The school points out that this doctrine has been specifically applied in Illinois to university informational publications.

* * *

We agree with Steinberg's position. We believe that he and the school entered into an enforceable contract; that the school's obligation under the contract was stated in the school's bulletin in a definitive manner and that by accepting his application fee—a valuable consideration—the school bound itself to fulfill its promises. Steinberg accepted the school's promises in good faith and he was entitled to have his application judged according to the school's stated criteria.

* * *

[Reversed and remanded.]

CASE 9-3

## Promissory Estoppel
## SKEBBA v. KASCH

Court of Appeals of Wisconsin, 2006

2006 WI App 232, 724 N.W.2d 408; review denied, 2007 WI 59

http://caselaw.lp.findlaw.com/scripts/getcase.pl?court=wi&vol=2006%5C26899&invol=2

**Kessler, J.**

Skebba, a salesman, worked for many years for a company that eventually experienced serious financial difficulties. Kasch, with his brother, owned M.W. Kasch Co. Kasch hired Skebba as a sales representative, and over the years promoted him first to account manager, then to customer service manager, field sales manager, vice president of sales, senior vice president of sales and purchasing and finally to vice president of sales. Kasch's father was the original owner of the business, and had hired Skebba's father. Skebba's father mentored Kasch.

When M.W. Kasch Co. experienced serious financial problems in 1993, Skebba was solicited by another company to leave Kasch and work for them. When Skebba told Kasch he was accepting the new opportunity, Kasch asked what it would take to get him to stay, and noted that Skebba's leaving at this time would be viewed very negatively within the industry. Shortly thereafter, Skebba told Kasch that he needed security for his retirement and family and would stay if Kasch agreed to pay Skebba $250,000 if one of these three conditions occurred: (1) the company was sold; (2) Skebba was lawfully terminated; or (3) Skebba retired. Skebba reports, and the jury apparently found, that Kasch agreed to this proposal and Kasch promised to have the agreement drawn up. Skebba turned down the job opportunity and stayed with Kasch from December 1993 (when this discussion occurred) through 1999 when the company assets were sold.

Over the years, Skebba repeatedly asked Kasch for a written summary of this agreement; however, none was forthcoming. Eventually, Kasch sold the business. Kasch received $5.1 million dollars for his fifty-one percent share of the business when it was sold. Upon the sale of the business, Skebba asked Kasch for the $250,000 Kasch had previously promised to him, but Kasch refused, and denied ever having made such an agreement. Instead, Kasch gave Skebba a severance agreement which had been drafted by Kasch's lawyers in 1993. This agreement promised two years of salary continuation on the sale of the company, but only if Skebba was not hired by the successor company and the severance agreement required a set-off against the salary continuation of any sums Skebba earned from any activity during the two years of the severance agreement. Skebba sued, alleging breach of contract and promissory estoppel.

The jury found there was no contract, but that Kasch had made a promise upon which Skebba relied to his detriment, that the reliance was foreseeable, and that Skebba was damaged in the amount of $250,000. The trial court concluded that, based on its reading of applicable case law, it could not specifically enforce the promise the jury found Kasch made to Skebba because there were other ways to measure damages. In motions after verdict, the trial court struck the jury's answer on damages, concluding that under *Hoffman* [*v. Red Owl Food Stores*], because Skebba did not prove what he would have earned had he taken the job with the other company, he could not establish what he had lost by relying on Kasch's promise and, therefore, had not proved his damages. We conclude that the trial court misread *Hoffman*.* * *

Kasch did *not* promise to pay Skebba more than Skebba would have earned at the job Skebba turned down. Kasch did *not* promise that total income to Skebba would be greater than in the turned-down job, no matter how long he remained with Kasch. Kasch *only* promised that if Skebba stayed, Kasch would pay Skebba $250,000 (the sum Skebba wanted for his retirement), at the earliest of (1) Kasch selling the business, (2) Skebba retiring, or (3) Skebba being lawfully terminated. Skebba stayed. Kasch sold the business while Skebba was still employed by Kasch. Kasch refused to pay as promised.

The purpose of promissory estoppel is to enforce promises where the failure to do so is unjust. *U.S. Oil Co., Inc. v. Midwest Auto Care Servs.*, [citation]. In this case, the trial court specifically relied on parts of *Hoffman* in determining that specific performance of the promise could not be awarded and in concluding that Skebba had not properly established damages. *Hoffman* was the first case in Wisconsin to adopt promissory estoppel. * * * [T]he *Hoffman* court explained its adoption of a cause of action based on promissory estoppel as grounded in section 90 of the Restatement of Contracts which:

> does not impose the requirement that the promise giving rise to the cause of action must be so comprehensive in scope as to meet the requirements of an offer that would ripen into a contract if accepted by the promisee. Rather the conditions imposed are:
>
> **1.** Was the promise one which the promisor should reasonably expect to induce action or forbearance of a definite and substantial character on the part of the promisee?
> **2.** Did the promise induce such action or forbearance?
> **3.** Can injustice be avoided only by enforcement of the promise?
>
> [Citation.]

The *Hoffman* court explains that the first two of these requirements are facts to be found by a jury or other fact-finder, while the third is a policy decision to be made by the court. [Citations.] In making this policy decision, a court must consider a number of factors in determining whether injustice can only be avoided by enforcement of the promise. *U.S. Oil*, [citation]. The court in *U.S. Oil* adopted those considerations set forth in the Restatement (Second) of Contracts §139(2), (1981):

> (a) the availability and adequacy of other remedies, particularly cancellation and restitution;
> (b) the definite and substantial character of the action or forbearance in relation to the remedy sought;
> (c) the extent to which the action or forbearance corroborates evidence of the making and terms of the promise, or the making and terms are otherwise established by clear and convincing evidence;
> (d) the reasonableness of the action or forbearance; [and]
> (e) the extent to which the action or forbearance was foreseeable by the promisor.
>
> [Citation.]

The record does not indicate that the trial court here applied the considerations our supreme court announced in *U.S. Oil*. Instead, the trial court apparently relied on the *Hoffman* court's discussion of various damage theories that the court explained might be appropriate once the determination had been made to enforce the promise by application of promissory estoppel. * * *

* * *

A court, in fashioning a remedy, can consider any equitable *or* legal remedy which will "prevent injustice." * * *

As later commentators have noted, Wisconsin, with its landmark *Hoffman* decision, is one of a small group of states which recognizes that to fulfill the purpose of promissory estoppel—*i.e.*, prevent injustice—a court must be able to fashion a remedy that restores the promisee to where he or she would be if the promisor had fulfilled the promise. [Citation.] In this case, Skebba performed—he remained at M.W. Kasch—in reliance on Kasch's promise to pay $250,000 to him if one of three conditions occurred. Kasch enjoyed the fruits of Skebba's reliance—he kept on a top salesperson to help the company through tough financial times and he avoided the damage that he believed Skebba's leaving could have had on M.W. Kasch's reputation in the industry. Accordingly, to prevent injustice, the equitable remedy for Skebba to receive is Kasch's specific performance promised payment of the $250,000.

The record in this case, considered in light of the *U.S. Oil* tests and the jury's findings, compels specific performance of the promise because otherwise Kasch will enjoy all of the benefits of induced reliance while Skebba will be deprived of that which he was promised, with no other available remedy to substitute fairly for the promised reward. * * * In short, every factor this court requires to be considered supports enforcement of the promise through promissory estoppel. The trial court submitted the promissory estoppel cause of action to the jury. The jury concluded that the promise had been made, that Skebba relied on the promise to his detriment, and that such reliance was foreseeable by Kasch. The jury also found that Skebba's damages were the amount Skebba testified Kasch promised to pay Skebba if he was still employed when the company was sold, that is, $250,000. * * *

* * * In this case, specific performance *is* the *necessary* enforcement mechanism to prevent injustice for Skebba's reliance on the promise the jury found Kasch had made to him.

Accordingly, we conclude that the trial court erred in holding that specific performance was not available on this promissory estoppel claim. We further conclude that the trial court erred in its application of *Hoffman* to the facts of this case. We reverse and remand for further proceedings consistent with this opinion.

Order reversed and cause remanded.

## QUESTIONS

1. Distinguish between contracts that are covered by the Uniform Commercial Code and those covered by common law.
2. List the requirements of a contract.
3. Distinguish among (a) express and implied contracts, (b) unilateral and bilateral contracts, (c) valid, void, voidable, and unenforceable contracts, (d) executed and executory contracts, and (e) formal and informal contracts.
4. Explain the doctrine of promissory estoppel.
5. Identify the three elements of an enforceable quasi contract and explain how it differs from a contract.

## PROBLEMS

**1.** Owen telephones an order to Hillary's store for certain goods, which Hillary delivers to Owen. Neither party says anything about the price or payment terms. What are the legal obligations of Owen and Hillary?

**2.** Minth is the owner of the Hiawatha Supper Club, which he leased for two years to Piekarski. During the period of the lease, Piekarski contracted with Puttkammer for the resurfacing of the access and service areas of the supper club. Puttkammer performed the work satisfactorily. Minth knew about the contract and the performance of the work. The work, including labor and materials, had a reasonable value of $2,540, but Puttkammer was never paid because Piekarski went bankrupt. Puttkammer brought an action against Minth to recover the amount owed to him by Piekarski. Will Puttkammer prevail? Explain.

**3.** Jonathan writes to Willa, stating "I'll pay you $150 if you reseed my lawn." Willa reseeds Jonathan's lawn as requested. Has a contract been formed? If so, what kind?

**4.** Calvin uses fraud to induce Maria to promise to pay money in return for goods he has delivered to her. Has a contract been formed? If so, what kind? What are the rights of Calvin and Maria?

**5.** Anna is about to buy a house on a hill. Prior to the purchase she obtains a promise from Betty, the owner of the adjacent property, that Betty will not build any structure that would block Anna's view. In reliance on this promise Anna buys the house. Is Betty's promise binding? Why or why not?

**6.** Mary Dobos was admitted to Boca Raton Community Hospital in serious condition with an abdominal aneurysm. The hospital called upon Nursing Care Services, Inc., to provide around-the-clock nursing services for Mrs. Dobos. She received two weeks of in-hospital care, forty-eight hours of postrelease care, and two weeks of at-home care. The total bill was $3,723.90. Mrs. Dobos refused to pay, and Nursing Care Services, Inc., brought an action to recover. Mrs. Dobos maintained that she was not obligated to render payment in that she never signed a written contract, nor did she orally agree to be liable for the services. The necessity for the services, reasonableness of the fee, and competency of the nurses were undisputed. After Mrs. Dobos admitted that she or her daughter authorized the forty-eight hours of postrelease care, the trial court ordered compensation of $248 for that period. It did not allow payment of the balance, and Nursing Care Services, Inc., appealed. Decision?

**7.** St. Charles Drilling Co. contracted with Osterholt to install a well and water system that would produce a specified quantity of water. The water system failed to meet its warranted capacity, and Osterholt sued for breach of contract. Does the Uniform Commercial Code (UCC) apply to this contract?

**8.** Helvey brought suit against the Wabash County REMC (REMC) for breach of implied and express warranties. He alleged that REMC furnished electricity in excess of 135 volts to Helvey's home, damaging his 110-volt household appliances. This incident occurred more than four years before Helvey brought this suit. In defense, REMC pleads that the Uniform Commercial Code's Article 2 statute of limitations of four years has passed, thereby barring Helvey's suit. Helvey argues that providing electrical energy is not a transaction in goods under the UCC but rather a furnishing of services that would make applicable the general contract six-year statute of limitations. Is the contract governed by the UCC? Why?

**9.** Jack Duran, president of Colorado Carpet Installation, Inc., began negotiations with Fred and Zuma Palermo for the sale and installation of carpeting, carpet padding, tile, and vinyl floor covering in their home. Duran drew up a written proposal that referred to Colorado Carpet as "the seller" and to the Palermos as "the customer." The proposal listed the quantity, unit cost, and total price of each item to be installed. The total price of the job was $4,777.75. Although labor was expressly included in this figure, Duran estimated the total labor cost at $926. Mrs. Palermo in writing accepted Duran's written proposal soon after he submitted it to her. After Colorado Carpet delivered the tile to the Palermo home, however, Mrs. Palermo had a disagreement with Colorado

Carpet's tile man and arranged for another contractor to perform the job. Colorado Carpet brought an action against the Palermos for breach of contract. Does the UCC apply to this contract?

**10.** On November 1, the Kansas City Post Office Employees Credit Union merged into the Kansas City Telephone Employees Credit Union to form the Communications Credit Union (Credit Union). Systems Design and Management Information (SDMI) develops computer software programs for credit unions, using Burroughs (now Unisys) hardware. SDMI and Burroughs together offered to sell to Credit Union both a software package, called the Generic System, and Burroughs hardware. Later in November, a demonstration of the software was held at SDMI's offices, and the Credit Union agreed to purchase the Generic System software. This agreement was oral. After Credit Union was converted to the SDMI Generic System, major problems with the system immediately became apparent, so SDMI filed suit against Credit Union to recover the outstanding contract price for the software. Credit Union counterclaimed for damages based upon breach of contract and negligent and fraudulent misrepresentation. Does the UCC apply to this contract?

**11.** Richardson hired J. C. Flood Company, a plumbing contractor, to correct a stoppage in the sewer line of her house. The plumbing company's "snake" device, used to clear the line leading to the main sewer, became caught in the underground line. To release it, the company excavated a portion of the sewer line in Richardson's backyard. In the process, the company discovered numerous leaks in a rusty, defective water pipe that ran parallel with the sewer line. To meet public regulations, the water pipe, of a type no longer approved for such service, had to be replaced either then or later, when the yard would have to be redug for such purpose. The plumbing company proceeded to repair the water pipe. Though Richardson inspected the company's work daily and did not express any objection to the extra work involved in replacing the water pipe, she refused to pay any part of the total bill after the company completed the entire operation. J. C. Flood Company then sued Richardson for the costs of labor and material it had furnished. Richardson argued that she only requested correction of a sewer obstruction and had never agreed to the replacement of the water pipe. Is Richardson correct in her assertion? Explain.

**12.** Insul-Mark is the marketing arm of Kor-It Sales, Inc. Kor-It manufactures roofing fasteners, and Insul-Mark distributes them nationwide. Kor-It contracted with Modern Materials, Inc., to have large volumes of screws coated with a rust-proofing agent. The contract specified that the coated screws must pass a standard industry test and that Kor-It would pay according to the pound and length of the screws coated. Kor-It had received numerous complaints from customers that the coated screws were rusting, and Modern Materials unsuccessfully attempted to remedy the problem. Kor-It terminated its relationship with Modern Materials and brought suit for the deficient coating. Modern Materials counterclaimed for the labor and materials it had furnished to Kor-It. The trial court held that the contract (a) was for performance of a service, (b) not governed by the UCC, (c) governed by the common law of contracts, and (d) therefore, barred by a two-year statute of limitations. Insul-Mark appealed. Decision?

**13.** In March, William Tackaberry, a real estate agent for Weichert Co. Realtors, informed Thomas Ryan, a local developer, that he knew of property Ryan might be interested in purchasing. Ryan indicated he was interested in knowing more about the property. Tackaberry disclosed the property's identity and the seller's proposed price. Tackaberry also stated that the purchaser would have to pay Weichert a 10 percent commission. Tackaberry met with the property owner and gathered information concerning the property's current leases, income, expenses, and development plans. Tackaberry also collected tax and zoning documents relevant to the property. In a face-to-face meeting on April 4, Tackaberry gave Ryan the data he had gathered and presented Ryan with a letter calling for a 10 percent finder's fee to be paid to Weichert by Ryan upon "successfully completing and closing of title." Tackaberry arranged a meeting, held three days later, where Ryan contracted with the owner to buy the land. Ryan refused, however, to pay the 10 percent finder's fee to Weichert. Weichert sues Ryan for the finder's fee. To what, if anything, is Weichert entitled to recover? Explain.

**14.** Max E. Pass, Jr., and his wife, Martha N. Pass, departed in an aircraft owned and operated by Mr. Pass from Plant City, Florida, bound for Clarksville, Tennessee. Somewhere over Alabama the couple encountered turbulence, and Mr. Pass lost control of the aircraft. The plane crashed killing both Mr. and Mrs. Pass. Approximately four and a half months prior to the flight in which he was killed, Mr. Pass had taken his airplane to Shelby Aviation, an aircraft service company, for inspection and service. In servicing the aircraft, Shelby Aviation replaced both rear wing attach point brackets on the plane. Three and one half years after the crash, Max E. Pass, Sr., father of Mr. Pass and administrator of his estate, and Shirley Williams, mother of Mrs. Pass and administratrix of her estate, filed suit against Shelby Aviation. The lawsuit alleged that the rear wing attach point brackets sold and installed by Shelby Aviation were defective because they lacked the bolts necessary to secure them properly to the airplane. The plaintiffs asserted claims against the defendant for breach of express and implied warranties under Article 2 of the UCC, which governs the sale of goods. Shelby Aviation contended that the transaction with Mr. Pass had been primarily for the sale of services, rather than of goods, and that consequently Article 2 of the UCC did not cover the transaction. Does the UCC apply to this transaction? Explain.

# CHAPTER 10 Mutual Assent

Although each of the requirements for forming a contract is essential to its existence, mutual assent is so basic that frequently a contract is referred to as the agreement between the parties. The Restatement, Section 3, provides this definition: "An agreement is a manifestation of mutual assent on the part of two or more parties." Enforcing the contract means enforcing the agreement; indeed, the agreement between the parties is the very core of the contract.

The manner in which parties usually show mutual assent is by **offer** and **acceptance**. One party makes a proposal (offer) by words or conduct to the other party, who agrees by words or conduct to the proposal (acceptance). A contractual agreement always involves either a promise exchanged for a promise (*bilateral contract*) or a promise exchanged for an act or forbearance to act (*unilateral contract*), as manifested by what the parties communicate to one another.

An implied contract may be formed by conduct. Thus, though there may be no definite offer and acceptance, or definite acceptance of an offer, a contract exists if both parties have acted in a manner that manifests (indicates) a recognition by each of them of the existence of a contract. It may be impossible to determine the exact moment at which a contract was made.

To form the contract, the parties must manifest their agreement objectively. The important thing is what the parties indicate to one another by spoken or written words or by conduct. The law applies an **objective standard** and is, therefore, concerned only with the assent, agreement, or intention of a party as it reasonably appears from his words or actions. The law of contracts is not concerned with what a party may have actually thought or the meaning that he intended to convey, even if his subjective understanding or intention differed from the meaning he objectively indicated by word or conduct. For example, if Leslie seemingly offers to sell to Sam her Chevrolet automobile but intends to offer and believes that she is offering her Ford automobile, and Sam accepts the offer, reasonably believing it was for the Chevrolet, a contract has been formed for the sale of the Chevrolet. Subjectively, there is no agreement as to the subject matter, but objectively there is a manifestation of agreement, and the objective manifestation is binding.

The Uniform Commercial Code's (UCC or Code) treatment of mutual assent is covered in greater detail in *Chapter 21*.

## OFFER

An offer is a definite proposal or undertaking made by one person to another which manifests a willingness to enter into a bargain. The person making the proposal is the **offeror**. The person to whom it is made is the **offeree**. Upon receipt, the offer confers on the offeree the power of acceptance, by which the offeree expresses her willingness to comply with the terms of the offer.

The communication of an offer to an offeree does not of itself confer any rights or impose any duties on either of the parties. The offeror, by making his offer, simply confers upon the offeree the power to create a contract by accepting the offer. Until the offeree exercises this power, the outstanding offer creates neither rights nor liabilities.

An offer may take several forms: (1) It may propose a promise for a promise. (This is an offer to enter into a bilateral contract.) An example is an offer to sell and deliver goods in thirty days in return for the promise to pay a stipulated amount upon delivery of the goods. If the offeree accepts this offer, the resulting contract consists of the parties' mutual promises, each made in exchange for the other. (2) An offer may be a promise for an act. (This is an offer to enter into a unilateral contract.) A common example is an offer of a reward for certain information or for the return of lost property. The offeree can accept such an offer only by the performance of the act requested. (3) An offer may be in the form of an act for a promise. (This is an offer to enter into an "inverted" unilateral contract.) For example, Maria offers the stated price to a clerk in a theater ticket office and asks for a ticket for a certain performance. The clerk can accept this offer of an act only by delivery of the requested ticket, which amounts, in effect, to the theater owner's promise to admit Maria to the designated performance.

## ESSENTIALS OF AN OFFER

An offer need not take any particular form to have legal validity. To be effective, however, it must (1) be communicated to the offeree, (2) manifest an intent to enter into a contract, and (3) be sufficiently definite and certain. If these essentials are present, an offer that has not terminated gives the offeree the power to form a contract by accepting the offer.

### COMMUNICATION

To have the mutual assent required to form a contract, the offeree must have knowledge of the offer; he cannot agree to something of which he has no knowledge. Accordingly, the offeror must communicate the offer, in an intended manner, to the offeree.

For example, Andy signs a letter containing an offer to Bonnie and leaves it on top of the desk in his office. Later that day, Bonnie, without prearrangement, goes to Andy's office, discovers that Andy is away, notices the letter on his desk, reads it, and writes on it an acceptance which she dates and signs. No contract is formed because the offer never became effective; Andy never communicated it to Bonnie. If Andy had mailed the letter, and it had gone astray in the mail, the offer would likewise never have become effective.

Not only must the offer be communicated to the offeree, but the communication must also be made or authorized by the offeror. For instance, if Joanne tells Karlene that she plans to offer Larry $600 for his piano, and Karlene promptly informs Larry of this proposal, no offer has been made. There was no authorized communication of any offer by Joanne to Larry. By the same token, if Lance should offer to sell his diamond ring to Ed, an acceptance of this offer by Dianne would not be effective, because Lance made the offer to Ed, not to Dianne.

An offer need not be stated or communicated by words. Conduct from which a reasonable person may infer a proposal in return for either an act or a promise amounts to an offer.

An offer may be made to the general public. No person, however, can accept such an offer until and unless he has knowledge that the offer exists. For example, if a person, without knowing of an advertised reward for information leading to the return of a lost watch, gives information that leads to its return, he is not entitled to the reward. His act was not an acceptance of the offer because he could not accept something of which he had no knowledge.

### INTENT

To have legal effect an offer must manifest an intent to enter into a contract. The intent of an offer is determined objectively from the words or conduct of the parties. The meaning of either party's manifestation is based upon what a reasonable person in the other party's position would have believed. The courts sometimes consider subjective intention in interpreting the parties' communications (the interpretation of contracts is discussed in *Chapter 16*).

Occasionally, a person exercises her sense of humor by speaking or writing words that—taken literally and without regard to context or surrounding circumstances—a promisee could construe as an offer. The promisor intends the promise as a joke, however, and the promisee as a reasonable person should understand it to be such. Therefore, it is not an offer. Because the person to whom it is made realizes or should realize that it is not made in earnest, it should not create a reasonable expectation in his mind. No contractual intent exists on the part of the promisor, and the promisee is or reasonably ought to be aware of that fact. If, however, the intended jest is so successful that the promisee as a reasonable person under all the circumstances believes that the joke is in fact an offer, and so believing accepts, the objective standard applies and the parties have entered into a contract.

A promise made under obvious excitement or emotional strain is likewise not an offer. For example, Charlotte, after having her month-old Cadillac break down for the third time in two days, screams in disgust, "I will sell this car to anyone for $10.00!" Lisa hears Charlotte and hands her a ten-dollar bill. Under the circumstances, Charlotte's statement was not an offer, if a reasonable person in Lisa's position would have recognized it merely as an overwrought, nonbinding utterance.

It is important to distinguish language that constitutes an offer from that which merely solicits or invites offers. Such proposals, although made in earnest, lack intent and are therefore not deemed offers. As a result, a purported acceptance does not bring about a contract but operates only as an offer to accept. These proposals include preliminary negotiations, advertisements, and auctions.

◆ **SEE CASE 10-1**

**Preliminary Negotiations** If a communication creates in the mind of a reasonable person in the position of the offeree an expectation that his acceptance will conclude a contract, then the communication is an offer. If it does not, then the communication is a preliminary negotiation. Initial communications between potential parties to a contract often take the form of preliminary negotiations, through which the parties either request or supply the terms of an offer that may or may not be given. A statement that may indicate a willingness to make an offer is not in itself an offer. If Terri writes to Susan, "Will you buy my automobile for $3,000?" and Susan replies "Yes," no contract exists. Terri has not made an offer to sell her automobile to Susan for $3,000. The offer or must manifest an intent to enter into a contract, not merely a willingness to enter into negotiation.

**Advertisements** Merchants desire to sell their merchandise and thus are interested in informing potential customers about the goods, terms of sale, and the price. But if they make widespread promises to sell to each person on their mailing list, the number of acceptances and resulting contracts might conceivably exceed their ability to perform. Consequently, a merchant might refrain from making offers by merely announcing that he has goods for sale, describing the goods, and quoting prices. He is simply inviting his customers and, in the case of published advertisements, the public, to make offers to him to buy the goods. His advertisements, circulars, quotation sheets, and merchandise displays are *not* offers because (1) they do not contain a promise and (2) they leave unexpressed many terms that would be necessary to the making of a contract. Accordingly, his customers' responses are not acceptances because he has made no offer to sell.

Nonetheless, a seller is not free to advertise goods at one price and then raise the price once demand has been stimulated. Although, as far as contract law is concerned, the seller has made no offer, such conduct is prohibited by the Federal Trade Commission as well as by legislation in many States. (See *Chapter 42*.)

Moreover, in some circumstances a public announcement or advertisement may constitute an offer if the advertisement or announcement contains a definite promise of something in exchange for something else and confers a power of acceptance upon a specified person or class of persons. The typical offer of a reward is an example of a definite offer, as was shown in *Lefkowitz v. Great Minneapolis Surplus Store, Inc.* In this case, the court held that a newspaper advertisement was an offer because it contained a promise of performance in definite terms in return for a requested act.

◆ **SEE CASE 10-2**

**Auction Sales** The auctioneer at an auction sale does *not* make offers to sell the property that is being auctioned but invites offers to buy. The classic statement by the auctioneer is, "How much am I offered?" The persons attending the auction may make progressively higher bids for the property, and each bid or statement of a price or a figure is an offer to buy at that figure. If the bid is accepted—this customarily is indicated by the fall of the hammer in the auctioneer's hand—a contract results. A bidder is free to withdraw his bid at any time prior to its acceptance. The auctioneer is likewise free to withdraw the goods from sale *unless* the sale is advertised or announced to be without reserve.

If the auction sale is advertised or announced in explicit terms to be **without reserve**, the auctioneer may not withdraw an article or lot put up for sale unless no bid is made within a reasonable time. Unless so advertised or announced, the sale is with reserve. A bidder at either type of sale may retract his bid at any time prior to acceptance by the auctioneer. Such retraction, however, does not revive any previous bid.

## DEFINITENESS

The terms of a contract, all of which the offer usually contains, must be reasonably certain so as to provide a court with a basis for determining the existence of a breach and for giving an appropriate remedy. Restatement, Section 33. It is a fundamental policy that contracts should be made by the parties and not by the courts; accordingly, remedies for breach must have their basis in the parties' contract.

However, where the parties have intended to form a contract, the courts will attempt to find a basis for granting a remedy. Missing terms may be supplied by course of dealing, usage of trade, or inference. Thus, uncertainty as to incidental matters will seldom be fatal so long as the parties intended to form a contract. Nevertheless, the more terms the parties leave open, the less likely it is that they have intended to form a contract. Because of the great variety of contracts, the terms essential to all contracts cannot be stated. In most cases, however, material terms would include the parties, subject matter, price, quantity, quality, and time of performance.

◆ **SEE CASE 10-3**

**Open Terms** With respect to agreements for the sale of goods, the Code provides standards by which omitted terms may be determined, provided the parties intended to enter into a binding contract. The Code provides missing terms in a number of instances, where, for example, the contract fails to specify the price, the time or place of delivery, or payment terms. Sections 2–204(3), 2–305, 2–308, 2–309, and 2–310. The Restatement, Section 34, has adopted an approach similar to the Code's in supplying terms the parties have omitted from their contract.

Under the Code, an offer for the purchase or sale of goods may leave open particulars of performance to be specified by one of the parties. Any such specification must be made in good faith and within limits set by commercial reasonableness. Section 2–311(1). **Good faith** is defined as honesty in fact in the conduct or transaction concerned. Section 1–201(19). Under the 2001 Revised UCC Article 1, good faith means honesty in fact and the observance of reasonable commercial standards of fair dealing. Section 1–201(20). Commercial reasonableness is a standard determined in terms of the business judgment of reasonable persons familiar with the practices customary in the type of transaction involved and in terms of the facts and circumstances of the case.

If the price is to be fixed otherwise than by agreement and is not so fixed through the fault of one of the parties, the other party has an option to treat the contract as cancelled or to fix a reasonable price in good faith for the goods. However, where the parties intend not to be bound unless the price is fixed or agreed upon as provided in the agreement, and it is not so fixed or agreed upon, the Code provides in accordance with the parties' intent that no contractual liability exists. In such case the seller must refund to the buyer any portion of the price she has received, and the buyer must return the goods to the seller or, if unable to do so, pay the reasonable value of the goods. Section 2–305(4).

◆ **SEE CASE 12-4**

**Output and Requirements Contracts** A buyer's agreement to purchase the entire output of a seller's factory for a stated period, or a seller's agreement to supply a buyer with all his requirements for certain goods, may appear to lack definiteness and mutuality of obligation. Such an agreement does not specify the exact quantity of goods; moreover, the seller may have some control over her output and the buyer over his requirements. Nonetheless, under the Code and the Restatement such agreements are enforceable by the application of an objective standard based upon the good faith of both parties. Thus, a seller who operated her factory for eight hours a day before entering an output agreement cannot operate her factory twenty-four hours a day and insist that the buyer take all of the output. Nor can the buyer expand his business abnormally and insist that the seller still supply all of his requirements.

## DURATION OF OFFERS

An offer confers upon the offeree a power of acceptance, which continues until the offer terminates. The ways in which an offer may be terminated, *other than by acceptance*, are through (1) lapse of time; (2) revocation; (3) rejection; (4) counteroffer; (5) death or incompetency of the offeror or offeree; (6) destruction of the subject matter to which the offer relates; and (7) subsequent illegality of the type of contract the offer proposes.

### LAPSE OF TIME

The offeror may specify the time within which the offer is to be accepted, just as he may specify any other term or condition in the offer. He may require that the offeree accept the offer immediately or within a **specified** period, such as a week or ten days. Unless otherwise terminated, the offer remains open for the specified period. Upon the expiration of that time, the offer no longer exists and cannot be accepted. Any subsequent purported acceptance will serve as a new offer.

If the offer states no time within which the offeree must accept, the offer will terminate after a **reasonable** time. Determining a "reasonable" period of time is a question of fact, depending on the nature of the contract proposed, the usages of business, and other circumstances of the case (including whether the offer was communicated by electronic means). Restatement, Section 41. For instance, an offer to sell a perishable good would be open for a far shorter time than an offer to sell undeveloped real estate.

◆ **SEE CASE 10-4**

### REVOCATION

An offeror generally may withdraw an offer at any time before it has been accepted, even though he has definitely promised to keep it open for a stated time. To be effective, notice of revocation of the offer must actually reach the offeree before she has accepted. If the offeror originally promises that the offer will be open for thirty days, but after five days wishes to terminate it, he may do so merely by giving the offeree notice that he is withdrawing the offer. Notice, which may be given by any means of communication, effectively terminates the offer when **received** by the offeree. A very few States, however, have adopted a rule that treats revocations the same as acceptances, thus making them effective upon dispatch. An offeror, however, may revoke an offer made to the general public only by giving to the revocation publicity equivalent to that given the offer.

Notice of revocation may be communicated indirectly to the offeree through reasonably reliable information from a third person that the offeror has disposed of the goods which he has offered for sale or has otherwise placed himself in a position which indicates an unwillingness or inability to perform the promise contained in the offer. Restatement, Section 43. For example, Jane offers to sell her portable television set to Bruce and tells Bruce that he has ten days in which to accept. One week later, Bruce observes the television set in Carl's house and is informed that Carl had purchased it from Jane. The next day Bruce sends to Jane an acceptance of the offer. There is no contract, because Jane's offer was effectively revoked when Bruce learned of Jane's inability to sell the television set to him because she had sold it to Carl.

Certain limitations, however, restrict the offeror's power to revoke the offer at any time prior to its acceptance. These limitations apply to the following five situations.

#### OPTION CONTRACTS

An option is a contract by which the offeror is bound to hold open an offer for a specified period of time. It must comply with all of the requirements of a contract, including *consideration* being given to the offeror by the offeree. (Consideration is discussed in *Chapter 12*.) For example, if Ann, in return for the payment of $500 to her by Bobby, grants Bobby an option, exercisable at any time within thirty days, to buy Blackacre at a price of $80,000, Ann's offer is irrevocable. Ann is legally bound to keep the offer open for thirty days, and any communication by Ann to Bobby giving notice of withdrawal of the offer is ineffective. Bobby is not bound to accept the offer, but the option contract entitles him to thirty days in which to accept.

◆ **SEE CASE 12-4**

**FIRM OFFERS UNDER THE CODE** The Code provides that a *merchant* is bound to keep an offer to buy or sell **goods** open for a stated period (or, if no time is stated, for a reasonable time) not exceeding three months, if the merchant gives assurance in a **signed writing** that the offer will be held open. Section 2–205. The Code, therefore, makes a merchant's written promise not to revoke an offer for a stated period enforceable even though no consideration is given to the offeror for that promise. A **merchant** is defined as a person (1) who is a dealer in goods of a given kind, (2) who by his occupation holds himself out as having knowledge or skill peculiar to the goods or practices involved, or (3) who employs an agent or broker whom he holds out as having such knowledge or skill. Section 2–104.

**STATUTORY IRREVOCABILITY** Certain offers, such as bids made to the State, municipality, or other governmental body for the construction of a building or some other public work, are made irrevocable by statute. Another example is preincorporation stock subscription agreements, which are irrevocable for a period of six months under many State incorporation statutes. See Section 6.20 of the Model Business Corporation Act (Appendix D).

**IRREVOCABLE OFFERS OF UNILATERAL CONTRACTS** Where an offer contemplates a unilateral contract, that is, a promise for an act, injustice to the offeree may result if revocation is permitted after the offeree has started to perform the act requested in the offer and has substantially but not completely accomplished it. Traditionally, such an offer is not accepted and no contract is formed until the offeree has *completed* the requested act. By simply commencing performance, the offeree does not bind himself to complete performance; nor, historically, did he bind the offeror to keep the offer open. Thus, the offeror could revoke the offer at any time prior to the offeree's completion of performance. For example, Linda offers Tom $300 if Tom will climb to the top of the flagpole in the center of campus. Tom commences his ascent, and when he is five feet from the top, Linda yells to him, "I revoke."

The Restatement deals with this problem by providing that where the performance of the requested act necessarily requires the offeree to expend time and effort, the offeror is obligated not to revoke the offer for a reasonable time. This obligation arises when the offeree begins performance. If, however, the offeror does not know of the offeree's performance and has no adequate means of learning of it within a reasonable time, the offeree must exercise reasonable diligence to notify the offeror of the performance.

**PROMISSORY ESTOPPEL** As discussed in the previous chapter, a noncontractual promise may be enforced when it is made under circumstances that should lead the promisor reasonably to expect that the promise will induce the promisee to take action in reliance on it. This doctrine has been used in some cases to prevent an offeror from revoking an offer prior to its acceptance. The Restatement provides the following rule:

> An offer which the offeror should reasonably expect to induce action or forbearance of a substantial character on the part of the offeree before acceptance and which does induce such action or forbearance is binding as an option contract to the extent necessary to avoid injustice. Restatement, Section 87(2).

Thus, Ramanan Plumbing Co. submits a written offer for plumbing work to be used by Resolute Building Co. as part of Resolute's bid as a general contractor. Ramanan knows that Resolute is relying on Ramanan's bid, and in fact Resolute submits Ramanan's name as the plumbing subcontractor in the bid. Ramanan's offer is irrevocable until Resolute has a reasonable opportunity to notify Ramanan that Resolute's bid has been accepted.

## REJECTION

An offeree is at liberty to accept or reject the offer as he sees fit. If the offeree decides not to accept it, he is not required to reject it formally but may simply wait until the offer terminates by the lapse of time. Through a **rejection** of an offer, the offeree manifests his unwillingness to accept. A communicated rejection terminates the power of acceptance. From the effective moment of rejection, which is the **receipt** of the rejection by the offeror, the offeree may no longer accept the offer. Rejection by the offeree may consist of express language or may be implied from language or from conduct.

## COUNTEROFFER

A **counteroffer** is a counterproposal from the offeree to the offeror that indicates a willingness to contract but upon terms or conditions different from those contained in the offer. It is not an unequivocal acceptance of the original offer and, by indicating an unwillingness to agree to the terms of the offer, it operates as a rejection. It also operates as a new offer. For instance, assume that Jordan writes Chris a letter stating that he will sell to Chris a secondhand color television set for $300. Chris replies that she will pay Jordan $250 for the set. This is a counteroffer that, upon **receipt** by Jordan, terminates the original offer. Jordan may, if he wishes, accept the counteroffer and thereby create a contract for $250. If, on the other hand, Chris states in her reply that she wishes to consider the $300 offer but is willing to pay $250 at once for the set, she is making a counteroffer that does *not* terminate Jordan's original offer. In the first instance, after making the $250 counteroffer, Chris may not accept the $300 offer. In the second instance she may do so, as the manner in which she stated the counteroffer did not indicate an unwillingness to accept the original offer, and Chris therefore did not terminate it. In addition, a mere inquiry about the possibility of obtaining different or new terms is not a counteroffer and does not terminate the offer.

Another common type of counteroffer is the **conditional acceptance**, which purports to accept the offer but expressly makes the acceptance conditional upon the offeror's assent to additional or different terms. Nonetheless, it is a counteroffer and terminates the original offer. The Code's treatment of acceptances containing terms that vary from the offer are discussed later in this chapter.

### DEATH OR INCOMPETENCY

The death or incompetency of either the offeror or the offeree ordinarily terminates an offer. Upon his death or incompetency the offeror no longer has the legal capacity to enter into a contract; thus, all his outstanding offers are terminated. Death or incompetency of the offeree likewise terminates the offer, because an ordinary offer is not assignable (transferable) and may be accepted only by the person to whom it was made. When the offeree dies or ceases to have legal capability to enter into a contract, no one else has the power to accept the offer. Therefore, the offer terminates.

The death or incompetency of the offeror or offeree, however, does *not* terminate an offer contained in an option.

### DESTRUCTION OF SUBJECT MATTER

Destruction of the specific subject matter of an offer terminates the offer. The impossibility of performance prevents a contract from being consummated and thus terminates all outstanding offers with respect to the destroyed property. Suppose that Martina, owning a Buick automobile, offers to sell the car to Worthy and allows Worthy five days in which to accept. Three days later the car is destroyed by fire. On the following day, Worthy, without knowledge of the car's destruction, notifies Martina that he accepts her offer. There is no contract. Martina's offer was terminated by the destruction of the car.

### SUBSEQUENT ILLEGALITY

One of the four essential requirements of a contract, as previously mentioned, is legality of purpose or subject matter. If performance of a valid contract is subsequently made illegal, the obligations of both parties under the contract are discharged. Illegality taking effect after the making of an offer but prior to acceptance has the same effect: the offer is legally terminated.

## ACCEPTANCE

The acceptance of an offer is essential to the formation of a contract. Once an acceptance has been given, the contract is formed. An acceptance can only be made by an offeree. Acceptance of an offer for a bilateral contract requires some overt act by which the offeree manifests his assent to the terms of the offer, such as speaking or sending a letter, a telegram, or other explicit or implicit communication to the offeror. If the offer is for a unilateral contract, the offeree may refrain from acting as requested or may signify acceptance through performance of the requested act with the intention of accepting. For example, if Joy publishes an offer of a reward to anyone who returns the diamond ring which she has lost (a unilateral contract offer), and Steven, with knowledge of the offer, finds and returns the ring to Joy, Steven has accepted the offer. If, however, Steven returns the ring to Joy but in doing so disclaims the reward and says that he does not accept the offer, there is no contract. Without the intention of accepting the offer, merely doing the act requested by the offeror is not sufficient to form a contract.

A late or defective acceptance does not create a contract. After the offer has expired, it cannot be validly accepted. A late or defective acceptance, however, does manifest the offeree's willingness to enter into a contract and therefore constitutes a new offer. To create a contract based upon this offer, the original offeror must accept the new offer by manifesting his assent.

## COMMUNICATION OF ACCEPTANCE

### GENERAL RULE

Because acceptance manifests the offeree's assent to the offer, the offeree must communicate this acceptance to the offeror. This is the rule as to all offers to enter into bilateral contracts. In the case of an offer to enter into a unilateral contract, however, notice of acceptance to the offeror is usually not required. If, however, the offeree in a unilateral contract has reason to know that the offeror has no adequate means of learning of the performance with reasonable promptness and certainty, then the offeree must make reasonable efforts to notify the offeror of acceptance or lose the right to enforce the contract. Restatement, Section 54.

◆ **FIGURE 10-1: Mutual Assent**

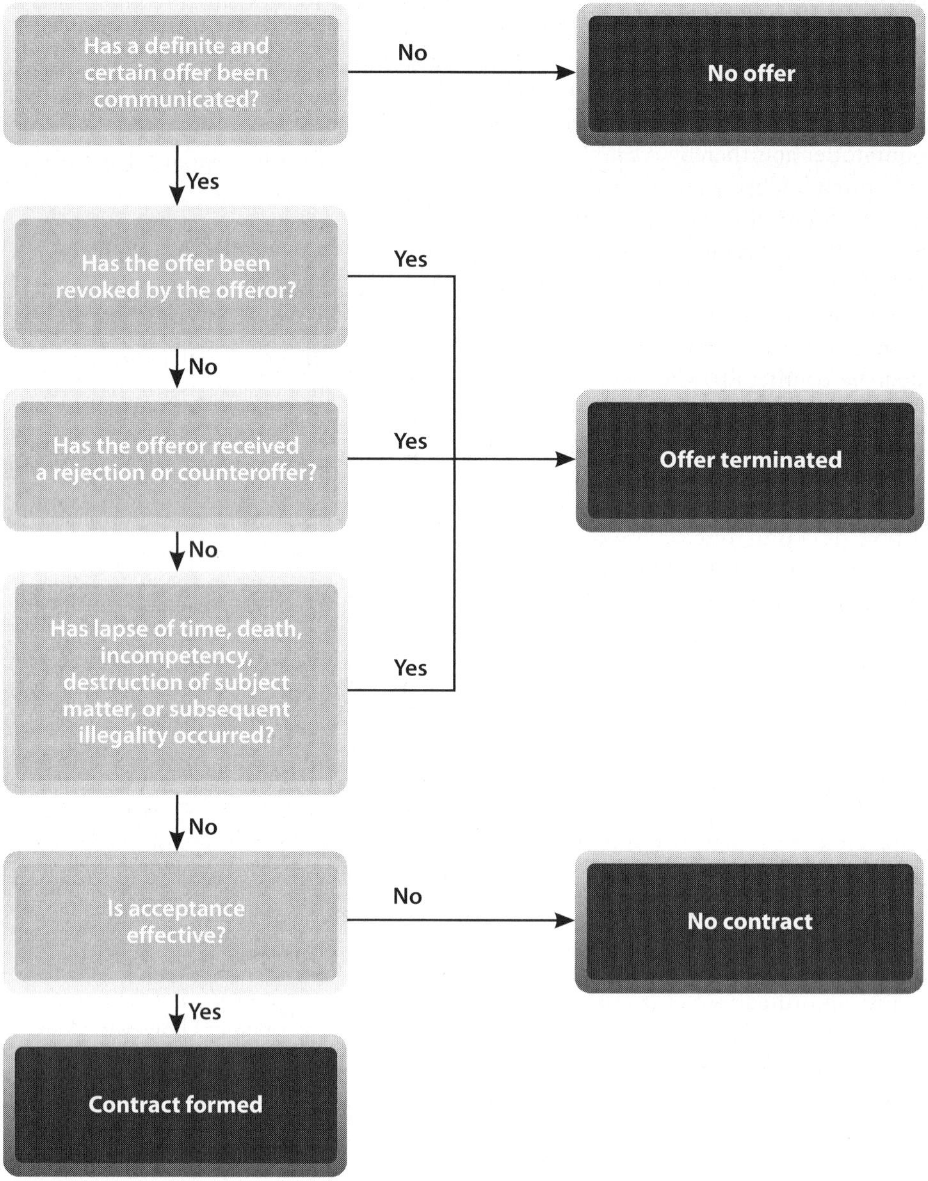


## SILENCE AS ACCEPTANCE

An offeree is generally under no legal duty to reply to an offer. Silence or inaction, therefore, does *not* indicate acceptance of the offer. By custom, usage, or course of dealing, however, silence or inaction by the offeree may operate as an acceptance.

Thus, the silence or inaction of an offeree who fails to reply to an offer operates as an acceptance and causes a contract to be formed. Through previous dealings, the offeree has given the offeror reason to understand that the offeree will accept all offers unless the offeree sends notice to the contrary. Another example of silence operating as an acceptance occurs when the prospective member of a mail-order club agrees that his failure to return a notification card rejecting offered goods will constitute his acceptance of the club's offer to sell the goods.

Furthermore, if an offeror sends unordered or unsolicited merchandise to a person stating that she may purchase the goods at a specified price and that the offer will be deemed to have been accepted unless the goods are returned within a stated period of time, the offer is one for an inverted unilateral contract (i.e., an act for a promise). This practice led to abuse, however, which has prompted the Federal government as well as most States to enact statutes which provide that in such cases the offeree-recipient of the goods may keep them as a gift and is under no obligation either to return them or to pay for them.

## EFFECTIVE MOMENT

As previously discussed, an offer, a revocation, a rejection, and a counteroffer are effective when they are *received*. An acceptance, on the other hand, is generally effective upon **dispatch**. This is true unless the offer specifically provides otherwise, the offeree uses an unauthorized means of communication, or the acceptance follows a prior rejection.

**Stipulated Provisions in the Offer** If the offer specifically stipulates the means of communication the offeree is to use, the acceptance, to be effective, must conform to that specification. Thus, if an offer states that acceptance must be made by registered mail, any purported acceptance not made by registered mail would be ineffective. Moreover, the rule that an acceptance is effective when dispatched or sent does not apply where the offer provides that the offeror must receive the acceptance. If the offeror states that a reply must be received by a certain date or that he must hear from the offeree or uses other language indicating that the acceptance must be received by him, the effective moment of the acceptance is when the offeror receives it, not when the offeree sends or dispatches it.

**Authorized Means** Historically, an authorized means of communication was the means the offeror expressly authorized in the offer, or, if none was authorized, it was the means the offeror used. For example, if in reply to an offer by mail, the offeree places in the mail a letter of acceptance properly stamped and addressed to the offeror, a contract is formed at the time and place that the offeree mails the letter. This assumes, of course, that the offer at that time was open and had not been terminated by any of the methods previously discussed. The reason for this rule is that the offeror, by using the mail, impliedly authorized the offeree to use the same method of communication. It is immaterial if the letter of acceptance goes astray in the mail and is never received.

The Restatement, Section 30, and the Code, Section 2–206(1)(a), both now provide that where the language in the offer or the circumstances do not otherwise indicate, an offer to make a contract shall be construed as authorizing acceptance in any **reasonable** manner. These provisions are intended to allow flexibility of response and the ability to keep pace with new modes of communication.

◈ SEE FIGURE 10-1: **Mutual Assent**

◆ SEE CASE 10-3

**Unauthorized Means** When the offeree uses an unauthorized method of communication, the traditional rule is that acceptance is effective when and if received by the offeror, provided that he receives it within the time during which the authorized means would have arrived. The Restatement, Section 67, provides that if these conditions are met, the effective time for the acceptance relates back to the moment of dispatch.

**Acceptance Following a Prior Rejection** An acceptance sent after a prior rejection is not effective when sent by the offeree, but is only effective when and if the offeror receives it before he receives the rejection. Thus, when an acceptance follows a prior rejection, the first communication to be received by the offeror is the effective one. For example, Anna in New York sends by mail to Fritz in San Francisco an offer that is expressly stated to be open for one week. On the fourth day, Fritz sends to Anna by mail a letter of rejection that is delivered on the morning of the sixth day. At noon on the fifth day, however, Fritz had dispatched a telegram of acceptance that is received by Anna before the close of business on that day. A contract was formed when Anna received Fritz's telegram of acceptance, as it was received before the letter of rejection.

◈ SEE FIGURE 10-2: **Offer and Acceptance**

# VARIANT ACCEPTANCES

A variant acceptance—one that contains terms different from or additional to those in the offer—receives distinctly different treatment under the common law and the Code.

◈ FIGURE 10-2: **Offer and Acceptance**

| | Time Effective | Effect |
|---|---|---|
| **Communications by Offeror** | | |
| • Offer | Received by offeree | Creates power to form a contract |
| • Revocation | Received by offeree | Terminates offer |
| **Communications by Offeree** | | |
| • Rejection | Received by offeror | Terminates offer |
| • Counteroffer | Received by offeror | Terminates offer |
| • Acceptance | Sent by offeree | Forms a contract |
| • Acceptance after prior rejection | Received by offeror | If received before rejection forms a contract |

### COMMON LAW

An acceptance must be *positive* and *unequivocal.* In that it may not change, add to, subtract from, or qualify in any way the provisions of the offer, it must be the **mirror image** of the offer. Any communication by the offeree that attempts to modify the offer is not an acceptance but is a counter-offer, which does not create a contract.

### CODE

The Code modifies the common law "mirror image" rule, by which the acceptance cannot vary or deviate from the terms of the offer. This modification is necessitated by the realities of modern business practices. A vast number of business transactions use standardized business forms. For example, a merchant buyer sends to a merchant seller on the buyer's order form a purchase order for 1,000 dozen cotton shirts at $60.00 per dozen, with delivery by October 1 at the buyer's place of business. On the reverse side of this standard form are twenty-five numbered paragraphs containing provisions generally favorable to the buyer. When the seller receives the buyer's order, he agrees to the quantity, price, and delivery terms and sends to the buyer on his acceptance form an unequivocal acceptance of the offer. However, on the back of his acceptance form, the seller has thirty-two numbered paragraphs generally favorable to himself and in significant conflict with the buyer's form. Under the common law's *mirror image* rule, no contract would exist, for the seller has not accepted unequivocally all the material terms of the buyer's offer.

The Code in Section 2–207 attempts to alleviate this **battle of the forms** by focusing upon the intent of the parties. If the offeree expressly makes her acceptance conditioned upon assent to the additional or different terms, no contract is formed. If the offeree does not expressly make her acceptance conditional upon the offeror's assent to the additional or different terms, a contract is formed. The issue then becomes whether the offeree's different or additional terms may become part of the contract. If both offeror and offeree are merchants, such *additional* terms may become part of the contract, provided they do not materially alter the agreement and are not objected to either in the offer itself or within a reasonable period of time. If both parties are not merchants or if the additional terms materially alter the offer, then the additional terms are merely construed as proposals to the contract. *Different* terms proposed by the offeree will not become part of the contract unless the offeror accepts them. The courts are divided over what terms a contract includes when those terms differ or conflict. Some courts hold that the offeror's terms govern; other courts, holding that the terms cancel each other out, look to the Code to provide the missing terms. Some follow a third alternative and apply the additional terms test to different terms. (See *Figure 21-4* in *Chapter 21.*)

To apply Section 2–207 to the example above: because both parties are merchants and the acceptance was not conditional upon assent to the additional or different terms, (1) the contract will be formed without the seller's different terms unless the buyer specifically accepts them; (2) the contract will be formed without the seller's additional terms unless (a) the buyer specifically accepts them or (b) they do not materially alter the offer and the buyer does not object; and (3) depending upon the jurisdiction, either (a) the buyer's conflicting terms are included in the contract or (b) the Code provides the missing terms, as the conflicting terms cancel each other out, or (c) the additional terms test is applied.

## CHAPTER SUMMARY

### OFFER

**ESSENTIALS OF AN OFFER**

**Definition** indication of willingness to enter into a contract
**Communication** offeree must have knowledge of the offer and the offer must be made by the offeror to the offeree
**Intent** determined by an objective standard of what a reasonable offeree would have believed
**Definiteness** offer's terms must be clear enough to provide a court with a basis for giving an appropriate remedy

**DURATION OF OFFERS**

**Lapse of Time** offer remains open for the time period specified or, if no time is stated, for a reasonable period of time
**Revocation** generally, an offer may be terminated at any time before it is accepted, subject to the following exceptions

- ***Option Contract*** contract that binds offeror to keep an offer open for a specified time
- ***Firm Offer*** a merchant's irrevocable offer to sell or buy goods in a signed writing ensures that the offer will not be terminated for up to three months

- ***Statutory Irrevocability*** offer made irrevocable by statute
- ***Irrevocable Offer of Unilateral Contract*** a unilateral offer may not be revoked for a reasonable time after performance is begun
- ***Promissory Estoppel*** noncontractual promise that binds the promisor because she should reasonably expect that the promise will induce the promisee (offeree) to take action in reliance on it

**Rejection** refusal to accept an offer terminates the power of acceptance
**Counteroffer** counterproposal to an offer that generally terminates the original offer
**Death or Incompetency** of either the offeror or the offeree terminates the offer
**Destruction of Subject Matter** of an offer terminates the offer
**Subsequent Illegality** of the purpose or subject matter of the offer terminates the offer

## ACCEPTANCE OF OFFER

**REQUIREMENTS**

**Definition** positive and unequivocal expression of a willingness to enter into a contract on the terms of the offer
**Mirror Image Rule** except as modified by the Code, an acceptance cannot deviate from the terms of the offer

**COMMUNICATION OF ACCEPTANCE**

**General Rule** acceptance effective upon dispatch unless the offer specifically provides otherwise or the offeree uses an unauthorized means of communication
**Stipulated Provisions** the communication of acceptance must conform to the specification in the offer
**Authorized Means** the Restatement and the Code provide that unless the offer provides otherwise, acceptance is authorized to be in any reasonable manner
**Unauthorized Means** acceptance effective when received, provided that it is received within the time within which the authorized means would have arrived
**Acceptance Following a Prior Rejection** first communication received by the offeror is effective
**Defective Acceptance** does not create a contract but serves as a new offer

# CASES

## CASE 10-1

### Objective Standard
### CATAMOUNT SLATE PRODUCTS, INC. v. SHELDON

Supreme Court of Vermont, 2004
2003 VT 112, 845 A.2d 324
http://dol.state.vt.us/gopher_root3/supct/current/2002-487.op

**Skoglund, J.**

Catamount Slate Products, Inc. and its principals the Reed family appeal from a Rutland Superior Court ruling enforcing what appellees characterize as a binding, mediated settlement agreement. The trial court concluded that, at the end of their September 5, 2000 mediation, the parties had reached a binding settlement agreement. Because the Reeds lacked the requisite intent to be bound to the settlement agreement in the absence of a writing, we hold that no binding agreement was reached. * * *

The Reeds own and operate Catamount Slate, a slate quarry and mill, on 122 acres in Fair Haven, Vermont. The appellees, the Sheldons, are also Fair Haven property owners and the Reeds' neighbors. Since 1997, the parties have been litigating the Reeds' right to operate their slate business and to use the access road leading to the quarry. In 2000, with several legal actions pending, the parties agreed to try to resolve their disputes in a state-funded mediation with retired judge Arthur O'Dea serving as mediator.

Prior to the mediation, Judge O'Dea sent each party a Mediation Agreement outlining the rules governing the mediation. Paragraph nine of the Mediation Agreement stated that:

> i. all statements, admissions, confessions, acts, or exchange * * * are acknowledged by the parties to be

> offers in negotiation of settlement and compromise, and as such inadmissible in evidence, and not binding upon either party unless reduced to a final agreement of settlement. Any final agreement of settlement must be in writing and signed by every party sought to be charged.

* * *

The mediation was held on September 5, 2000. Judge O'Dea began the session by reaffirming the statements made in the Mediation Agreement. After ten hours, the parties purportedly reached an agreement on all major issues. Judge O'Dea then orally summarized the terms of the resolution with the parties and counsel present. The attorneys took notes on the terms of the agreement with the understanding that they would prepare the necessary documents for signature in the coming days.

The resolution required the Reeds to pay the Sheldons $250 a month for the right to use the access road, while the Sheldons agreed to be coapplicants on Catamount Slate's pending Act 250 permit. Payments were to commence on October 1, 2000. The parties also agreed to a series of terms governing the operation of the slate quarry, including, among other things, hours of operation, number of truck trips permitted on the access road, the amount and frequency of blasting, and the location of seismic measurements. These terms were to be memorialized in two distinct documents, a Lease Agreement and a Settlement Agreement.

On September 7, 2000, two days after the mediation, the Sheldons' attorney, Emily Joselson, drafted a letter outlining the terms of the settlement and sent copies to James Leary, the Reeds' attorney, and Judge O'Dea. Within a week, Leary responded by letter concurring in some respects and outlining the issues on which the Reeds disagreed with Joselson's characterization of the settlement.

* * *

On October 1, 2000, the Reeds began paying the $250 monthly lease payments, but, since the settlement agreement was not final, the parties agreed that the money would go into an escrow account maintained by the Sheldons' counsel. The check was delivered to the Sheldons' attorney with a cover memo stating, "This check is forwarded to you with the understanding that the funds will be disbursed to your clients only after settlement agreement becomes final. Of course, if the settlement agreement does not come to fruition, then the funds must be returned to my clients." The parties continued to exchange letters actively negotiating the remaining details of the Lease and Settlement Agreements for the better part of the next five months. Although there were others along the way, by early 2001 the only remaining issues in dispute were the location of seismic measurements and the definition of "over blast."

In February 2001, while drafts were still being exchanged, Christine Stannard, the Reeds' daughter, saw a deed and map in the Fair Haven Town Clerk's Office which led her to believe that the disputed road was not owned by the Sheldons, but was a town highway. The Reeds then refused to proceed any further with negotiating the settlement agreement. A written settlement agreement was never signed by either party.

The Sheldons responded by filing a motion to enforce the settlement agreement. * * * The trial court granted the motion, finding that the attorneys' notes taken at the end of the mediation and the unsigned drafts of the Lease and Settlement Agreements sufficiently memorialized the agreement between the parties and thus constituted an enforceable settlement agreement. * * *

The question before us is whether the oral agreement reached at mediation, when combined with the unexecuted documents drafted subsequently, constituted a binding, enforceable settlement agreement. Parties are free to enter into a binding contract without memorializing their agreement in a fully executed document. See Restatement (Second) of Contracts §4 (1981). In such an instance, the mere intention or discussion to commit their agreement to writing will not prevent the formation of a contract prior to the document's execution. [Citations.]

"On the other hand, if either party communicates an intent not to be bound until he achieves a fully executed document, no amount of negotiation or oral agreement to specific terms will result in the formation of a binding contract." [Citation.] The freedom to determine the exact moment in which an agreement becomes binding encourages the parties to negotiate as candidly as possible, secure in the knowledge that they will not be bound until the execution of what both parties consider to be a final, binding agreement.

We look to the intent of the parties to determine the moment of contract formation. [Citation.] Intent to be bound is a question of fact. [Citation.] "To discern that intent a court must look to the words and deeds [of the parties] which constitute objective signs in a given set of circumstances." [Citation.] In [citation], the Second Circuit articulated four factors to aid in determining whether the parties intended to be bound in the absence of a fully executed document. [Citation.] The court suggested that we "consider (1) whether there has been an express reservation of the right not to be bound in the absence of a writing; (2) whether there has been partial performance of the contract; (3) whether all of the terms of the alleged contract have been agreed upon; and (4) whether the agreement at issue is the type of contract that is usually committed to writing." [Citations.]

The language of the parties' correspondence and other documentary evidence presented reveals an intent by the mediation participants not to be bound prior to the execution of a final document. First, the Mediation Agreement Judge O'Dea sent to the parties prior to the mediation clearly contemplates that any settlement agreement emanating from the mediation would be binding only after being put in writing and signed. Paragraph nine of the Agreement expressly stated that statements made during mediation would not be "binding upon either party unless reduced to a final agreement of settlement" and that "any final agreement of settlement [would] be in writing and signed by every party sought to be charged." Further, Judge O'Dea reminded the parties of these ground rules at the outset of the mediation. The Reeds testified that they relied on these statements and assumed that, as indicated, they would not be bound until they signed a written agreement.

* * *

Even more compelling evidence of the Reeds' lack of intent to be bound in the absence of a writing is the statement in the cover letter accompanying the Reeds' $250 payments to the Sheldons' attorney saying, "This check is forwarded to you with the understanding that the funds will be disbursed to your clients only after settlement agreement becomes final. Of course, if the settlement agreement does not come to fruition, then the funds must be returned to my clients." This factor weighs in favor of finding that the Reeds expressed their right not to be bound until their agreement was reduced to a final writing and executed.

Because there was no evidence presented of partial performance of the settlement agreement, we next consider the third factor, whether there was anything left to negotiate. * * *

As stated by the Second Circuit in [citation], "the actual drafting of a written instrument will frequently reveal points of disagreement, ambiguity, or omission which must be worked out prior to execution. Details that are unnoticed or passed by in oral discussion will be pinned down when the understanding is reduced to writing." (internal quotations and citations omitted). [Citation.] This case is no exception. A review of the lengthy correspondence in this case makes clear that several points of disagreement and ambiguity arose during the drafting process. Beyond the location of seismic measurements and the definition of "over blast," correspondence indicates that the parties still had not reached agreement on the term and width of the lease, acceptable decibel levels and notice provisions for blasts, the definition of "truck trips," and whether all claims would be dismissed without prejudice after the execution of the agreement. Resolution of these issues was clearly important enough to forestall final execution until the language of the documents could be agreed upon. In such a case, where the parties intend to be bound only upon execution of a final document, for the court to determine that, despite continuing disagreement on substantive terms, the parties reached a binding, enforceable settlement agreement undermines their right to enter into the specific settlement agreement for which they contracted.

The fourth and final factor, whether the agreement at issue is the type of contract usually put into writing, also weighs in the Reeds' favor. Being a contract for an interest in land, the Lease Agreement is subject to the Statute of Frauds and thus generally must be in writing. * * *

* * *

In conclusion, three of the four factors indicate that the parties here did not intend to be bound until the execution of a final written document, and therefore we hold that the parties never entered into a binding settlement agreement. * * * Accordingly, the order enforcing the settlement is reversed and the case is remanded for further proceedings.

## CASE 10-2

Invitations Seeking Offers

**LEFKOWITZ v. GREAT MINNEAPOLIS SURPLUS STORE, INC.**

Supreme Court of Minnesota, 1957

251 Minn. 188, 86 N.W.2d 689

**Murphy, J.**

This is an appeal from an order of * * * judgment award[ing] the plaintiff the sum of $138.50 as damages for breach of contract.

This case grows out of the alleged refusal of the defendant to sell to the plaintiff a certain fur piece which it had offered for sale in a newspaper advertisement. It appears from the record that on April 6, 1956, the defendant published the following advertisement in a Minneapolis newspaper:

Saturday 9 AM Sharp
3 Brand New
Fur Coats
Worth to $100.00
First Come First Served
$1 Each

On April 13, the defendant again published an advertisement in the same newspaper as follows:

Saturday 9 AM
2 Brand New Pastel
Mink 3-Skin Scarfs
Selling for $89.50
Out they go
Saturday. Each ... $1.00
1 Black Lapin Stole

Beautiful,
worth $139.50 ... $1.00
First Come First Served

The record supports the findings of the court that on each of the Saturdays following the publication of the above-described ads the plaintiff was the first to present himself at the appropriate counter in the defendant's store and on each occasion demanded the coat and the stole so advertised and indicated his readiness to pay the sale price of $1. On both occasions, the defendant refused to sell the merchandise to the plaintiff, stating on the first occasion that by a "house rule" the offer was intended for women only and sales would not be made to men, and on the second visit that plaintiff knew defendant's house rules. * * *

The defendant contends that a newspaper advertisement offering items of merchandise for sale at a named price is a "unilateral offer" which may be withdrawn without notice. He relies upon authorities which hold that, where an advertiser publishes in a newspaper that he has a certain quantity or quality of goods which he wants to dispose of at certain prices and on certain terms, such advertisements are not offers which become contracts as soon as any person to whose notice they may come signifies his acceptance by notifying the other that he will take a certain quantity of them. Such advertisements have been construed as an invitation for an offer of sale on the terms stated, which offer, when received, may be accepted or rejected and which therefore does not become a contract of sale until accepted by the seller; and until a contract has been so made, the seller may modify or revoke such prices or terms. [Citations.] * * * On the facts before us we are concerned with whether the advertisement constituted an offer, and, if so, whether the plaintiff's conduct constituted an acceptance.

* * *

The test of whether a binding obligation may originate in advertisements addressed to the general public is "whether the facts show that some performance was promised in positive terms in return for something requested."

* * *

Whether in any individual instance a newspaper advertisement is an offer rather than an invitation to make an offer depends on the legal intention of the parties and the surrounding circumstances. [Citations.] We are of the view on the facts before us that the offer by the defendant of the sale * * * was clear, definite, and explicit, and left nothing open for negotiation. The plaintiff, having successfully managed to be the first one to appear at the seller's place of business to be served, as requested by the advertisement, and having offered the stated purchase price of the article, was entitled to performance on the part of the defendant. We think the trial court was correct in holding that there was in the conduct of the parties a sufficient mutuality of obligation to constitute a contract of sale.

* * *

Affirmed.

## CASE 10-3

## Effective Moment
## OSPREY L.L.C. v. KELLY-MOORE PAINT CO., INC.

Supreme Court of Oklahoma, 1999
1999 OK 50, 984 P.2d 194
http://caselaw.findlaw.com/scripts/getcase.pl?court=OK&vol=/supreme/1999/&invol=1999OK50

**Kauger, J.**

The first impression question presented is whether a faxed or facsimile delivery of a written notice renewing a commercial lease is sufficient to exercise timely the renewal option of the lease. Under the facts presented, we hold that it is.

The appellant, Osprey, an Oklahoma limited liability company (Osprey), owns commercial property in Edmond, Oklahoma. On March 18, 1977, the appellee, Kelly-Moore Paint Company (Kelly-Moore), a California corporation, negotiated a fifteen-year lease for its Edmond, Oklahoma, store with Osprey's predecessors James and Victoria Fulmer. The lease contained two five-year renewal options which required that the lessee give notice of its intent to renew the lease at least six months prior to its expiration date. The lease also provided that all notices "shall be given in writing and may be delivered either personally or by depositing the same in United States mail, first class postage prepaid, registered or certified mail, return receipt requested."

It is undisputed that after the first fifteen years, Kelly-Moore timely informed Osprey's predecessors by certified letter of its intent to extend the lease an additional five years. The first five-year extension was due to expire on August 31, 1997. According to the property manager of Kelly-Moore, she telephoned one of the owners of

Osprey in January of 1997, to inform him that Kelly-Moore intended to extend its lease for the remaining five-year period. On Friday, February 28, 1997, the last day of the six-month notification deadline, Kelly-Moore faxed a letter of renewal notice to Osprey's office at 5:28 P.M., Oklahoma time. Kelly-Moore also sent a copy of the faxed renewal notice letter by Federal Express the same day.

Although the fax activity report and telephone company records confirm that the fax was transmitted successfully and that it was sent to Osprey's correct facsimile number, Osprey denies ever receiving the fax. The Federal Express copy of the notice was scheduled for delivery on Saturday, March 1, 1997. However, Osprey actually received it on Monday, March 3, 1997. In a letter dated March 6, 1997, Osprey acknowledged that it had received Kelly-Moore's Federal Express notice; denied that the notice was timely according to the terms of the lease; and it rejected the notice as untimely. In July of 1997, Osprey wrote Kelly-Moore reminding it to vacate the premises by August 31, 1997. Kelly-Moore refused to vacate, insisting that it had effectively extended the lease term for the remaining five years.

On September 2, 1997, Osprey filed an action for forcible entry and detainer in the district court of Oklahoma County. * * * Kelly-Moore argued that it was entitled to possession of the property because of its timely renewal of the lease. After a trial on the merits, the trial court granted judgment in favor of Kelly-Moore, finding that the faxed notice was effective. Osprey appealed. The Court of Civil Appeals reversed, determining that the plain language of the lease required that it be renewed for an additional term by delivering notice either personally or by mail, and that Kelly-Moore had done neither. We granted certiorari on April 13, 1999, to address the question of first impression.

UNDER THE FACTS PRESENTED, THE FAXED DELIVERY OF THE WRITTEN NOTICE OF RENEWAL TIMELY EXERCISED THE RENEWAL OPTION OF THE LEASE.

The precise issue of whether a faxed or facsimile delivery of a written notice to renew a commercial lease is sufficient to exercise timely the renewal option of the lease is one of first impression in Oklahoma. Neither party has cited to a case from another jurisdiction which has decided this question, or to any case which has specifically defined "personal delivery" as including facsimile delivery.

* * *

Osprey argues that: (1) the lease specifically prescribed limited means of acceptance of the option, and it required that the notice of renewal be delivered either personally or sent by United States mail, registered or certified; (2) Kelly-Moore failed to follow the contractual requirements of the lease when it delivered its notice by fax; and (3) because the terms for extending the lease specified in the contract were not met, the notice was invalid and the lease expired on August 31, 1997. Kelly-Moore counters that: (1) the lease by the use of the word "shall" mandates that the notice be written, but the use of the word "may" is permissive; and (2) although the notice provision of the lease permits delivery personally or by United States mail, it does not exclude other modes of delivery or transmission which would include delivery by facsimile. * * *

A lease is a contract and in construing a lease, the usual rules for the interpretation of contractual writings apply. * * *

Language in a contract is given its plain and ordinary meaning, unless some technical term is used in a manner meant to convey a specific technical concept. A contract term is ambiguous only if it can be interpreted as having two different meanings. * * * The lease does not appear to be ambiguous. "Shall" is ordinarily construed as mandatory and "may" is ordinarily construed as permissive. The contract clearly requires that notice "shall" be in writing. The provision for delivery, either personally or by certified or registered mail, uses the permissive "may" and it does not bar other modes of transmission which are just as effective.

The purpose of providing notice by personal delivery or registered mail is to insure the delivery of the notice, and to settle any dispute which might arise between the parties concerning whether the notice was received. A substituted method of notice which performs the same function and serves the same purpose as an authorized method of notice is not defective. Here, the contract provided that time was of the essence. Although Osprey denies that it ever received the fax, the fax activity report and telephone company records confirm that the fax was transmitted successfully, and that it was sent to Osprey's correct facsimile number on the last day of the deadline to extend the lease. The fax provided immediate written communication similar to personal delivery and, like a telegram, would be timely if it were properly transmitted before the expiration of the deadline to renew. Kelly-Moore's use of the fax served the same function and the same purpose as the two methods suggested by the lease and it was transmitted before the expiration of the deadline to renew. Under these facts, we hold that the faxed or facsimile delivery of the written notice to renew the commercial lease was sufficient to exercise timely the renewal option of the lease.

* * *

Court of Civil Appeals opinion vacated; trial court AFFIRMED.

## CASE 10-4

# Duration of Offers
# SHERROD v. KIDD

Court of Appeals of Washington, Division 3, 2007
155 P.3d 976
http://www.courts.wa.gov/opinions/index.cfm?fa=opinions.showOpinionTextOnly&filename=254984MAJ&printOnly=y

**Sweeney, C. J.**

* * *

David and Elizabeth Kidd's dog bit Mikaila Sherrod. Mikaila through her guardian ad litem (GAL) made a claim for damages. On June 14, 2005, the Kidds offered to settle the claim for $31,837. On July 12, Mikaila through her GAL sued the Kidds. On July 20, the Kidds bumped their offer to $32,843.

The suit was subject to mandatory arbitration. The parties proceeded to arbitration on April 28, 2006. On May 5, the arbitrator awarded Mikaila $25,069.47. On May 9, the GAL wrote to the Kidds and purported to accept their last offer of $32,843, made the year before.

The GAL on Mikaila's behalf moved to enforce the settlement agreement. The court concluded the offer was properly accepted because it had not been withdrawn. And it entered judgment in the amount of the first written offer.

* * *

The Kidds contend that the trial court did not consider that implicit in its settlement offer was the GAL's forbearance in proceeding with the arbitration to its conclusion. The GAL argues that the offer was not conditioned upon the arbitration proceeding in any manner. And the offer provided no time limit for its acceptance. The GAL further claims that the consideration to create an enforceable agreement—her promise to dismiss her lawsuit—was the same when she accepted it as when it was offered. Her consideration included relinquishing her right to request a trial de novo.

An offer to form a contract is open only for a reasonable time, unless the offer specifically states how long it is open for acceptance. [Citations.] "[I]n the absence of an acceptance of an offer … within a reasonable time (where no time limit is specified), there is no contract." [Citation.]

How much time is reasonable is usually a question of fact. [Citation.] But we can decide the limits of a reasonable time if the facts are undisputed. [Citation.] And here the essential facts are not disputed.

A reasonable time "is the time that a reasonable person in the exact position of the offeree would believe to be satisfactory to the offeror." [Citation.] "The purpose of the offeror, to be attained by the making and performance of the contract, will affect the time allowed for acceptance, if it is or should be known to the offeree. In such case there is no power to accept after it is too late to attain that purpose." [Citation.] A reasonable time for an offeree to accept an offer depends on the "nature of the contract and the character of the business in which the parties were engaged." [Citation.]

Implicit in an offer (and an acceptance) to settle a personal injury suit is the party's intent to avoid a less favorable result at the hands of a jury, a judge or, in this case, an arbitrator. The defendant runs the risk that the award might be more than the offer. The plaintiff, of course, runs the risk that the award might be less than the offer. Both want to avoid that risk. And it is those risks that settlements avoid.

* * *

* * * Here, the value of this claim was set after arbitration. It was certainly subject to appeal but nonetheless set by a fact finder.

This offer expired when the arbitrator announced the award and was not subject to being accepted.

We reverse the decision of the trial judge to the contrary.

## QUESTIONS

1. Identify the three necessary essentials of an offer and discuss briefly the requirements associated with each.
2. Identify and discuss briefly seven ways by which an offer may be terminated other than by acceptance.
3. Compare briefly the traditional and modern theories of definiteness of acceptance of an offer as shown by the common law "mirror image" rule and by the rule of the Uniform Commercial Code.
4. Discuss the five situations limiting an offeror's right to revoke her offer.
5. Explain the various rules that determine when an acceptance takes effect.

# PROBLEMS

**1.** Ames, seeking business for his lawn maintenance firm, posted the following notice in the meeting room of the Antlers, a local lodge: "To the members of the Antlers—Special this month. I will resod your lawn for two dollars per square foot using Fairway brand sod. This offer expires July 15."

The notice also included Ames's name, address, and signature, and specified that the acceptance was to be in writing.

Bates, a member of the Antlers, and Cramer, the janitor, read the notice and became interested. Bates wrote a letter to Ames saying he would accept the offer if Ames would use Putting Green brand sod. Ames received this letter July 14 and wrote to Bates saying he would not use Putting Green sod. Bates received Ames's letter on July 16 and promptly wrote Ames that he would accept Fairway sod. Cramer wrote to Ames on July 10, saying he accepted Ames's offer.

By July 15, Ames had found more profitable ventures and refused to resod either lawn at the specified price. Bates and Cramer brought an appropriate action against Ames for breach of contract. Decisions as to the respective claims of Bates and Cramer?

**2.** Garvey owned four speedboats named *Porpoise*, *Priscilla*, *Providence*, and *Prudence*. On April 2, Garvey made written offers to sell the four boats in the order named for $4,200 each to Caldwell, Meens, Smith, and Braxton, respectively, allowing ten days for acceptance. In which, if any, of the following four situations described was a contract formed?

(a) Five days later, Caldwell received notice from Garvey that he had contracted to sell *Porpoise* to Montgomery. The next day, April 8, Caldwell notified Garvey that he accepted Garvey's offer.

(b) On the third day, April 5, Meens mailed a rejection to Garvey which reached Garvey on the morning of the fifth day. But at 10:00 A.M. on the fourth day, Meens sent an acceptance by telegram to Garvey, who received it at noon on the same day.

(c) Smith, on April 3, replied that she was interested in buying *Providence* but declared the price asked appeared slightly excessive and wondered if, perhaps, Garvey would be willing to sell the boat for $3,900. Five days later, having received no reply from Garvey, Smith, by letter, accepted Garvey's offer and enclosed a certified check for $4,200.

(d) Braxton was accidentally killed in an automobile accident on April 9. The following day, the executor of Braxton's estate mailed an acceptance of Garvey's offer to Garvey.

**3.** Alpha Rolling Mill Corporation, by letter dated June 8, offered to sell Brooklyn Railroad Company two thousand to five thousand tons of fifty-pound iron rails upon certain specified terms, adding that, if the offer was accepted, Alpha Corporation would expect to be notified prior to June 20. Brooklyn Company, on June 16, by telegram, referring to Alpha Corporation's offer of June 8, directed Alpha Corporation to enter an order for 1,200 tons of fifty-pound iron rails on the terms specified. The same day, June 16, Brooklyn Company, by letter to Alpha Corporation, confirmed the telegram. On June 18, Alpha Corporation, by telegram, declined to fill the order. Brooklyn Company, on June 19, telegraphed Alpha Corporation: "Please enter an order for 2,000 tons of rails as per your letter of the eighth. Please forward written contract. Reply." In reply to Brooklyn Company's repeated inquiries regarding whether the order for two thousand tons of rails had been entered, Alpha denied the existence of any contract between Brooklyn Company and itself. Thereafter, Brooklyn Company sued Alpha Corporation for breach of contract. Decision?

**4.** On April 8, Burchette received a telephone call from Bleluck, a truck dealer, who told Burchette that a new model truck in which Burchette was interested would arrive in one week. Although Bleluck initially wanted $10,500, the conversation ended after Bleluck agreed to sell and Burchette agreed to purchase the truck for $10,000, with a $1,000 down payment and the balance upon delivery. The next day, Burchette sent Bleluck a check for $1,000, which Bleluck promptly cashed.

One week later, when Burchette called Bleluck and inquired about the truck, Bleluck informed Burchette he had several prospects looking at the truck and would not sell for less than $10,500. The following day, Bleluck sent Burchette a properly executed check for $1,000 with the following notation thereon: "Return of down payment on sale of truck." After notifying Bleluck that she will not cash the check, Burchette sues Bleluck for damages. Should Burchette prevail? Explain.

**5.** On November 15, I. Sellit, a manufacturer of crystalware, mailed to Benny Buyer a letter stating that Sellit would sell to Buyer one hundred crystal "A" goblets at $100 per goblet and that "the offer would remain open for fifteen (15) days." On November 18, Sellit, noticing the sudden rise in the price of crystal "A" goblets, decided to withdraw her offer to Buyer and so notified Buyer. Buyer chose to ignore Sellit's letter of revocation and gleefully watched as the price of crystal "A" goblets continued to skyrocket. On November 30, Buyer mailed to Sellit a letter accepting Sellit's offer to sell the goblets. The letter was received by Sellit on December 4. Buyer demands delivery of the goblets. What result?

**6.** On May 1, Melforth Realty Company offered to sell Greenacre to Dallas, Inc., for $1 million. The offer was made by telegraph and stated that the offer would expire on May 15. Dallas decided to purchase the property and sent a registered letter to Melforth on May 10, accepting the offer. Due to unexplained delays in the postal service, Melforth did not receive the letter until May 22. Melforth wishes to sell Greenacre to another buyer, who is offering $1.2 million for the tract of land. Has a contract resulted between Melforth and Dallas?

**7.** Rowe advertised in newspapers of wide circulation and otherwise made known that she would pay $5,000 for a complete set consisting of ten volumes of certain rare books. Ford, not knowing of the offer, gave Rowe all but one of the set of rare books as a Christmas present. Ford later learned of the offer, obtained the one remaining book, tendered it to Rowe, and demanded the $5,000. Rowe refused to pay. Is Ford entitled to the $5,000?

**8.** Scott, manufacturer of a carbonated beverage, entered into a contract with Otis, owner of a baseball park, whereby Otis rented to Scott a large signboard on top of the center field wall. The contract provided that Otis should letter the sign as Scott desired and would change the lettering from time to time within forty-eight hours after receipt of written request from Scott. As directed by Scott, the signboard originally stated in large letters that Scott would pay $1,000 to any ballplayer hitting a home run over the sign.

In the first game of the season, Hume, the best hitter in the league, hit one home run over the sign. Scott immediately served written notice on Otis instructing Otis to replace the offer on the signboard with an offer to pay $500 to every pitcher who pitched a no-hit game in the park. A week after receipt of Scott's letter, Otis had not changed the wording on the sign. On that day, Perry, a pitcher for a scheduled game, pitched a no-hit game while Todd, one of his teammates, hit a home run over Scott's sign. Scott refuses to pay any of the three players. What are the rights of Scott, Hume, Perry, and Todd?

**9.** Barnes accepted Clark's offer to sell to him a portion of Clark's coin collection. Clark forgot that his prized $20 gold piece at the time of the offer and acceptance was included in the portion which he offered to sell to Barnes. Clark did not intend to include the gold piece in the sale. Barnes, at the time of inspecting the offered portion of the collection, and prior to accepting the offer, saw the gold piece. Is Barnes entitled to the $20 gold piece?

**10.** Small, admiring Jasper's watch, asked Jasper where and at what price he had purchased it. Jasper replied, "I bought it at West Watch Shop about two years ago for around $85, but I am not certain as to that." Small then said, "Those fellows at West are good people and always sell good watches. I'll buy that watch from you." Jasper replied, "It's a deal." The next morning Small telephoned Jasper and said he had changed his mind and did not wish to buy the watch. Jasper sued Small for breach of contract. In defense, Small has pleaded that he made no enforceable contract with Jasper (a) because the parties did not agree on the price to be paid for the watch, and (b) because the parties did not agree on the place and time of delivery of the watch to Small. Are either, or both, of these defenses good?

**11.** Jeff says to Brenda, "I offer to sell you my PC for $900." Brenda replies, "If you do not hear otherwise from me by Thursday, I have accepted your offer." Jeff agrees and does not hear from Brenda by Thursday. Does a contract exist between Jeff and Brenda? Explain.

**12.** On November 19, Hoover Motor Express Company sent to Clements Paper Company a written offer to purchase certain real estate. Sometime in December, Clements authorized Williams to accept. Williams, however, attempted to bargain with Hoover to obtain a better deal, specifically that Clements would retain easements on the property. In a telephone conversation on January 13 of the following year, Williams first told Hoover of his plan to obtain the easements. Hoover replied, "Well, I don't know if we are ready. We have not decided; we might not want to go through with it." On January 20, Clements sent a written acceptance of Hoover's offer. Hoover refused to buy, claiming it had revoked its offer through the January 13 phone conversation. Clements then brought suit to compel the sale or obtain damages. Did Hoover successfully revoke its offer?

**13.** Walker leased a small lot to Keith for ten years at $1,000 a month, with a right for Keith to extend the lease for another ten-year term under the same terms except as to rent. The renewal option provided:

> Rental will be fixed in such amount as shall actually be agreed upon by the lessors and the lessee with the monthly rental fixed on the comparative basis of rental values as of the date of the renewal with rental values at this time reflected by the comparative business conditions of the two periods.

Keith sought to exercise the renewal right and, when the parties were unable to agree on the rent, brought suit against Walker. Who prevails? Why?

**14.** The Brewers contracted to purchase Dower House from McAfee. Then, several weeks before the May 7 settlement date for the purchase of the house, the two parties began to negotiate for the sale of certain items of furniture in the house. On April 30, McAfee sent the Brewers a letter containing a list of the furnishings to be purchased at specified prices; a payment schedule, including a request for a $3,000 payment, due on acceptance; and a clause reading, "If the above is satisfactory, please sign and return one copy with the first payment."

On June 3, the Brewers sent a letter to McAfee stating that enclosed was a $3,000 check; that the original contract had been misplaced and could another be furnished; that they planned to move into Dower House on June 12; and that they wished the red desk to be included in the contract. McAfee then sent a letter dated June 8 to the Brewers, listing the items of furniture purchased.

The Brewers moved into Dower House in the middle of June. Soon after they moved in, they tried to contact McAfee at his office to tell him that there had been a misunderstanding relating to their purchase of the listed items. They then refused to pay him any more money, and he brought action to recover the balance outstanding. Will McAfee be able to collect the additional money from the Brewers?

**15.** The Thoelkes were owners of real property located in Orange County, which the Morrisons agreed to purchase. The Morrisons signed a contract for the sale of that property and mailed it to the Thoelkes in Texas on November 26. The next day the Thoelkes executed the contract and placed it in the mail addressed to the Morrisons' attorney in Florida. After the executed contract was mailed but before it was received in Florida, the Thoelkes called the Morrisons' attorney in Florida and attempted to repudiate the contract. Does a contract exist between the Thoelkes and the Morrisons? Discuss.

**16.** Lucy and Zehmer met while having drinks in a restaurant. During the course of their conversation, Lucy apparently offered to buy Zehmer's 471.6-acre farm for $50,000 cash. Although Zehmer claims that he thought the offer was made in jest, he wrote the following on the back of a pad: "We hereby agree to sell to W. O. Lucy the Ferguson Farm complete for $50,000, title satisfactory to buyer." Zehmer then signed the writing and induced his wife Ida to do the same. She claims, however, that she signed only after Zehmer assured her that it was only a joke. Finally, Zehmer claims that he was "high as a Georgia pine" at the time but admits that he was not too drunk to make a valid contract. Decision?

**17.** Lee Calan Imports advertised a used Volvo station wagon for sale in the *Chicago Sun-Times*. As part of the information for the advertisement, Lee Calan Imports instructed the newspaper to print the price of the car as $1,795. However, due to a mistake made by the newspaper, without any fault on the part of Lee Calan Imports, the printed ad listed the price of the car as $1,095. After reading the ad and then examining the car, O'Brien told a Lee Calan Imports salesperson that he wanted to purchase the car for the advertised price of $1,095. Calan Imports refuses to sell the car to O'Brien for $1,095. Is there a contract? If so, for what price?

**18.** On May 20, cattle rancher Oliver visited his neighbor Southworth, telling him, "I know you're interested in buying the land I'm selling." Southworth replied, "Yes, I do want to buy that land, especially as it adjoins my property." Although the two men did not discuss the price, Oliver told Southworth he would determine the value of the property and send that information to him, so that Southworth would have "notice" of what Oliver "wanted for the land." On June 13, Southworth called Oliver to ask if he still planned to sell the land. Oliver answered, "Yes, and I should have the value of the land determined soon." On June 17, Oliver sent a letter to Southworth listing a price quotation of $324,000.

Southworth then responded to Oliver by letter on June 21, stating that he accepted Oliver's offer. However, on June 24 Oliver wrote back to Southworth, saying, "There has never been a firm offer to sell, and there is no enforceable contract between us." Oliver maintains that a price quotation alone is not an offer. Southworth claims a valid contract has been made. Who wins? Discuss.

**19.** On December 23, Wyman, a lawyer representing First National Bank & Trust (defendant), wrote to Zeller (plaintiff) stating that he had been instructed to offer a building to Zeller for sale at a price of $240,000. Zeller had previously expressed an interest in purchasing the building for $240,000. The letter also set forth details concerning interest rates and loan fees.

After receiving the letter, Zeller instructed his attorney, Jamma, to send Wyman a written counteroffer of $230,000 with varying interest and loan arrangements. Jamma sent the written counteroffer as instructed on January 10. On the same day, Jamma telephoned Wyman and informed him of the counteroffer. Jamma then tried to telegraph acceptance of the original offer to Wyman. When Wyman refused to sell the property to him, Zeller brought this action to seek enforcement of the alleged contract. The trial court entered summary judgment against Zeller, and he appealed. Decision?

**20.** First Development Corporation of Kentucky (FDCK) sought to purchase a fifteen-acre parcel of riverfront property owned by Martin Marietta. On May 9, FDCK made an offer to purchase the property for $300,000, which it submitted to Coldwell Banker, Martin Marietta's real estate agent. This offer was accompanied by an earnest money deposit evidenced by a $1,000 check payable to Coldwell Banker. The deposit was fully refundable if transfer of title to FDCK was not completed for any reason except FDCK's failure to perform. After this offer expired without being accepted, FDCK asked Don Gilmour, Coldwell Banker's account agent, to seek a counteroffer. In a letter to Gilmour, dated September 7, Martin Marietta agreed to sell the property for $550,000. The counteroffer stated it was to remain open for thirty days. Gilmour informed Pollitt, president of FDCK, of the counteroffer by telephone on September 7 and sent a copy of the letter to Pollitt, which was received on September 12.

Within days of the expiration of FDCK's original offer, Bill Harvey, president of Harmony Landing, a development company, initiated direct negotiations with Martin Marietta to purchase the riverfront parcel. These negotiations resulted in a contract being executed on September 21 or 22. During a September 21 phone call, Gilmour advised Pollitt of Harmony Landing's interest in buying the property, but Pollitt remained noncommittal during the conversation. Later that day, Pollitt, along with his partner and engineer, visited the property and discussed various studies and arrived at a decision to accept the September 7 offer from Martin Marietta. However, Pollitt did not convey this acceptance to Gilmour. Rather, he consulted his attorneys regarding a contract to accept Martin Marietta's offer.

After consulting with his attorneys, Pollitt prepared an acceptance of Martin Marietta's offer but did not put it in the mail. The next morning, Pollitt placed the acceptance in his office suite's mail depository. However, after being informed by Gilmour that Martin Marietta had accepted Harmony Landing's option on the river property, Pollitt retrieved the acceptance and personally delivered it to Gilmour at 4:15 P.M. The acceptance was returned to Pollitt and he subsequently initiated this action for temporary and permanent injunction and specific performance. The district court ruled that the $1,000 check, payable to and in the possession of Coldwell Banker during the period of this controversy was, by operation of law, converted into consideration for a thirty-day irrevocable option in favor of FDCK to purchase the riverfront property in accordance with the terms of Martin Marietta's letter of September 7. Does a contract exist between Martin Marietta and FDCK?

**21.** On August 12, Mr. and Mrs. Mitchell, the owners of a small secondhand store, attended Alexander's Auction, where they bought a used safe for $50. The safe, part of the Sumstad estate, contained a locked inside compartment. Both the auctioneer and the Mitchells knew this fact. Soon after the auction, the Mitchells had the compartment opened by a locksmith, who discovered $32,207 inside. The Everett Police Department impounded the money. The city of Everett brought an action against the Sumstad estate and the Mitchells to determine the owner of the money. Who should receive the money? Why?

**22.** Irwin Schiff is a self-styled "tax rebel" who has made a career, and substantial profit, out of his tax protest activities. On February 7, Schiff appeared live on CBS News *Nightwatch*, a late-night program with a viewer participation format. During the broadcast Schiff repeated his assertion that nothing in the Internal Revenue Code stated that an individual was legally required to pay federal income tax. Schiff then challenged, "If anybody calls this show—I have the Code—and cites any section of this Code that says an individual is required to file a tax return, I will pay them $100,000." Call-in telephone numbers were periodically flashed on the screen. John Newman, an attorney, did not see Schiff's live appearance on *Nightwatch*. Newman did, however, see a two-minute videotaped segment, including Schiff's challenge, which was rebroadcast several hours later on the *CBS Morning News*. Newman researched the matter that same day, and on the following day, February 9, placed a call using directory assistance to *CBS Morning News* stating that the call was performance of the consideration requested by Mr. Schiff in exchange for his promise to pay $100,000. When Schiff refused to pay, Newman sued. Should Newman prevail? Explain.

C H A P T E R 1 1

# Conduct Invalidating Assent

The preceding chapter considered one of the essential requirements of a contract, namely, the objective manifestation of mutual assent by each party to the other. In addition to requiring that the offer and acceptance be satisfied, the law demands that the agreement be voluntary and knowing. If these requirements are not met, then the agreement is either voidable or void. This chapter deals with situations in which the consent manifested by one of the parties to the contract is not effective because it was not knowingly and voluntarily given. These situations are considered under the headings of duress, undue influence, fraud, nonfraudulent misrepresentation, and mistake.

## DURESS

A person should not be held to an agreement into which she has not entered voluntarily. Accordingly, the law will not enforce any contract induced by **duress**, which in general is any wrongful or unlawful act or threat that overcomes the free will of a party.

### PHYSICAL COMPULSION

There are two basic types of duress. The first occurs when one party compels another to manifest assent to a contract through actual **physical force**, such as pointing a gun at a person or taking a person's hand and compelling him to sign a written contract. This type of duress, while extremely rare, renders the agreement **void**. Restatement, Section 174(1).

### IMPROPER THREATS

The second type of duress involves the use of improper threats or acts, *including economic and social coercion*, to compel a person to enter into a contract. The threat may be explicit or may be inferred from words or conduct; in either case, it must leave the victim with no reasonable alternative. This type of duress makes the contract **voidable** at the option of the coerced party. Restatement, Section 175(2). For example, if Lance, a landlord, induces Tamara, an infirm, bedridden tenant, to enter into a new lease on the same apartment at a greatly increased rent by wrongfully threatening to terminate Tamara's lease and evict her, Tamara can escape or *avoid* the new lease by reason of the duress exerted upon her.

With respect to the second and more common type of duress, the fact that the act or threat would not affect a person of average strength and intelligence is not determinative if it places the particular person in fear and induces him to perform an action against his will. The test is *subjective*, and the question is, did the threat actually induce assent on the part of the person claiming to be the victim of duress? Threats that would suffice to induce assent by one person may not suffice to induce assent by another. All circumstances must be considered, including the age, background, and relationship of the parties. Restatement, Section 175. Indeed, as Comment c to this section of the Restatement states,

> Persons of a weak or cowardly nature are the very ones that need protection; the courageous can usually protect themselves. Timid and inexperienced persons are particularly subject to threats, and it does not lie in the mouths of the unscrupulous to excuse their imposition on such persons on the ground of their victims' infirmities.

Ordinarily, the acts or threats constituting duress are themselves crimes or torts. But this is not true in all cases. The acts need not be criminal or tortious to be *wrongful*; they merely need to be contrary to public policy or morally reprehensible. For example, if the threat involves a breach of a contractual duty of good faith and fair dealing or the use of the civil process in bad faith, it is improper.

Moreover, the courts have generally held that contracts induced by threats of criminal prosecution are voidable, regardless of whether the coerced party had committed an unlawful act. Likewise, threatening the criminal prosecution of a near relative, such as a son or husband, is duress, regardless of the guilt or innocence of the relative.

To be distinguished from such threats of prosecution are threats to resort to ordinary civil remedies to recover a debt due from another. Threatening to bring a civil suit against an individual to recover a debt is not wrongful. What is prohibited is threatening to bring a civil suit when bringing such a suit would be abuse of process.

◆ **SEE CASE 11-1**

## UNDUE INFLUENCE

Undue influence is the unfair persuasion of a person by a party generally in a dominant position based upon a **confidential relationship**. The law very carefully scrutinizes contracts between those in a relationship of trust and confidence that is likely to permit one party to take unfair advantage of the other. Examples are the relationships of guardian-ward, trustee-beneficiary, principal-agent, spouses to each other, parent-child, attorney-client, physician-patient, and clergy-parishioner.

A transaction induced by unfair influence on the part of the dominant party is **voidable**. The ultimate question in undue influence cases is whether the dominant party induced the transaction by influencing a freely exercised and competent judgment or by dominating the mind or emotions of a submissive party. The weakness or dependence of the person persuaded is a strong indicator of the fairness or unfairness of the persuasion. For example, Ronald, a person without business experience, has for years relied in business matters on the advice of Nancy, who is experienced in business. Nancy, without making any false representations of fact, induces Ronald to enter into a contract with Nancy's confederate, George. The contract, however, is disadvantageous to Ronald, as both Nancy and George know. The transaction is voidable on the grounds of undue influence.

Undue influence, as previously mentioned, generally arises in the context of relationships in which one person is in a position of dominance, or is likely to be. Where such a relationship exists at the time of the transaction, and it appears that the dominant party has gained at the other party's expense, the transaction is presumed to be voidable. For example, in a legally challenged contract between a guardian and his ward, the law presumes that advantage was taken by the guardian. It is, therefore, incumbent upon the guardian to rebut this presumption. Important factors in determining whether a contract is fair are (1) whether the dominant party made full disclosure of all relevant information known to him, (2) whether the consideration was adequate, and (3) whether the dependent party received competent and independent advice before completing the transaction. Without limitation, in every situation in which a confidential relationship exists, the dominant party is held to utmost good faith in his dealings with the other.

◆ **SEE CASE 11-2**

## FRAUD

Another factor affecting the validity of consent given by a contracting party is fraud, which prevents assent from being knowingly given. There are two distinct types of fraud: fraud in the execution and fraud in the inducement.

### FRAUD IN THE EXECUTION

Fraud in the execution, which is extremely rare, consists of a misrepresentation that deceives the defrauded person as to the very nature of the contract. Such fraud occurs when a person does not know, or does not have reasonable opportunity to know, the character or essence of a proposed contract because the other party misrepresents its character or essential terms. Fraud in the execution renders the transaction **void**.

For example, Abigail delivers a package to Boris, requests that Boris sign a receipt for it, holds out a simple printed form headed "Receipt," and indicates the line on which Boris is to sign. This line, which to Boris appears to be the bottom line of the receipt, is actually the signature line of a promissory note cleverly concealed underneath the receipt. Boris signs where directed without knowing that he is signing a note. This is fraud in the execution. The note is void and of no legal effect because Boris has not actually given his assent, even though his signature is genuine and appears to manifest his assent to the terms of the note. The nature of Abigail's fraud precluded consent to the signing of the note because it prevented Boris from reasonably knowing what he was signing.

### FRAUD IN THE INDUCEMENT

Fraud in the inducement, generally referred to as fraud or deceit, is an intentional misrepresentation of material fact by one party to the other, who consents to enter into a contract in justifiable reliance upon the misrepresentation. Fraud in the inducement renders the contract **voidable** by the defrauded party. For example, Ada, in offering to sell her dog to Ben, tells Ben that the dog won first prize in its class in a recent national dog show. In fact, the dog had not even been entered in the show. Nonetheless, Ada's statement induces Ben to accept the offer and pay a high price for the dog. A contract exists, but it is voidable by Ben because of Ada's fraud, which induced his assent.

The requisites for fraud in the inducement are as follows:

1. a false representation
2. of a fact
3. that is material and

4. made with knowledge of its falsity and the intention to deceive (scienter) and
5. which representation is justifiably relied upon.

**False Representation** A basic element of fraud is a false representation or misrepresentation; that is, an assertion not in accord with the facts, made through positive statement or conduct that misleads. **Concealment** is an action intended or known to be likely to keep another from learning of a fact of which he otherwise would have learned. Active concealment is a form of misrepresentation that can form the basis for fraud, as where a seller puts heavy oil or grease in a car engine to conceal a knock. Truth may be suppressed by concealment as much as by misrepresentation.

Expressly denying knowledge of a fact which a party knows to exist is a misrepresentation if it leads the other party to believe that the facts do not exist or cannot be discovered. Moreover, a statement of misleading half-truth is considered the equivalent of a false representation.

As a general rule, **silence** or nondisclosure alone does *not* amount to fraud. A seller generally is not obligated to tell a purchaser everything he knows about the subject of a sale. Thus, it is not fraud when a buyer possesses advantageous information about the seller's property, of which he knows the seller to be ignorant, and does not disclose such information to the seller. Likewise, a buyer is under no duty to inform a seller of the greater value or other advantages of his property. Assume that Sid owns a farm that, as a farm, is worth $10,000. Brenda knows that there is oil under Sid's farm and knows that Sid is ignorant of this fact. Brenda, without disclosing this information to Sid, makes an offer to Sid to buy the farm for $10,000. Sid accepts the offer, and a contract is duly made. Sid, on later learning the facts, can do nothing about the matter, either at law or in equity. As one case puts it, "a purchaser is not bound by our laws to make the man he buys from as wise as himself."

Although nondisclosure usually does not constitute a misrepresentation, in certain situations it does. One such situation arises when (1) a person fails to disclose a fact known to him, (2) he knows that the disclosure of that fact would correct a mistake of the other party as to a basic assumption on which that party is making the contract, and (3) nondisclosure of the fact amounts to a failure to act in a good faith and in accordance with reasonable standards of fair dealing. Restatement, Section 161. Accordingly, if the property at issue in the contract possesses a substantial latent (hidden) defect, one that the buyer would not discover by an ordinary examination, the seller may be obliged to reveal it. Suppose, for example, that Judith owns a valuable horse, which Judith knows is suffering from a disease only a competent veterinary surgeon might detect. Judith offers to sell this horse to Curt, but does not inform Curt about the condition of the horse. Curt makes a reasonable examination of the horse and, finding it in apparently normal condition, purchases it from Judith. Curt, on later discovering the disease in question, can have the sale set aside. Judith's silence, under the circumstances, was a misrepresentation.

There are other situations in which the law imposes a duty of disclosure. For example, one may have a duty of disclosure because of prior representations, innocently made before entering into the contract, which are later discovered to be untrue. Another instance in which silence may constitute fraud is a transaction involving a fiduciary. A **fiduciary** is a person in a confidential relationship who owes a duty of trust, loyalty, and confidence to another. For example, an agent owes a fiduciary duty to his principal, as does a trustee to the beneficiary of a trust and a partner to her copartners. A fiduciary may not deal at *arm's length* but rather owes a duty to make full disclosure of all relevant facts when entering into a transaction with the other party to the relationship. In contrast, in most everyday business or market transactions, the parties are said to deal at "arm's length," meaning that they deal with each other on equal terms.

**Fact** The basic element of fraud is the misrepresentation of a material fact. A **fact** is an event that actually took place or a thing that actually exists. Suppose that Dale induces Mike to purchase shares in a company unknown to Mike at a price of $100 per share by representing that she had paid $150 per share for them during the preceding year, when in fact she had paid only $50. This representation of a past event is a misrepresentation of fact.

Actionable fraud rarely can be based on what is merely a statement of **opinion**. A representation is one of opinion if it expresses only the uncertain belief of the representer as to the existence of a fact or his judgment as to quality, value, authenticity, or other matters of judgment.

The line between fact and opinion is not an easy one to draw and in close cases presents an issue for the jury. The solution will often turn on the superior knowledge of the person making the statement and the information available to the other party. Thus, if Dale said to Mike that the shares were "a good investment," she is merely stating her opinion, and in the usual case Mike ought to regard it as no more than that. Other common examples of opinion are statements of value, such as "This is the best car for the money in town" or "This deluxe model will give you twice the wear of a cheaper model." Such exaggerations and commendations of articles offered for sale are to be expected from dealers, who are merely puffing their wares with sales talk. If, however, the representer is a professional advising a client, the courts are more likely to regard as actionable an untrue statement of opinion. When the person expressing the opinion is one who holds himself out as having expert knowledge, the tendency is to grant relief to those who have sustained loss through reasonable reliance upon the expert evaluation.

Also to be distinguished from a representation of fact is a **prediction** of the future. Predictions, which are similar to opinions in that no one can know with certainty what will happen in the future, normally are not regarded as factual statements. Likewise, promissory statements ordinarily do not constitute a basis of fraud, as a breach of promise does not necessarily indicate that the promise was fraudulently made. A promise that the promisor, at the time of making, had no intention of keeping, however, is a misrepresentation of fact. Most courts take the position that a misrepresented state of mind "is as much a fact as the state of a person's digestion." *Edgington v. Fitzmaurice,* 29 Ch.D. 459 (1885). If a dealer promises, "I will service this machine free for the next year," but at the time has no intention of doing so, his conduct is actionable if the other elements of fraud are present.

Historically, courts held that representations of **law** were not statements of fact but rather of opinion. The present trend is to recognize that a statement of law may have either the effect of a statement of fact or a statement of opinion. Restatement, Torts, Section 545. For example, a statement of law asserting that a particular statute has been enacted or repealed has the effect of a statement of fact. On the other hand, a statement as to the legal consequences of a particular set of facts is a statement of opinion. Nonetheless, such a statement may imply that the facts known to the maker are consistent with the legal conclusion stated. For example, an assertion that a company has the legal right to do business in a State may include the assurance that the company has taken all the steps required to be duly qualified. Moreover, a statement by one who is learned in the law, such as a practicing attorney, may be considered a statement of fact.

◆ **SEE CASE 11-3**

**Materiality** In addition to being a misrepresentation of fact, a misrepresentation also must be material. A misrepresentation is **material** if (1) it would be likely to induce a reasonable person to manifest his assent or (2) the maker knows that it would be likely to induce the recipient to do so. Restatement, Section 162. In the sale of a racehorse, whether a certain jockey rode the horse in its most recent race may not be material, but its running time for the race probably would be. The Restatement of Contracts provides that a contract justifiably induced by a misrepresentation is voidable if the misrepresentation is either fraudulent *or* material. Therefore, a fraudulent misrepresentation does not have to be material for the recipient to obtain rescission, but it must be material if she is to recover damages. Restatement, Section 164; Restatement, Torts, Section 538.

◆ **SEE CASE 11-4**

**Knowledge of Falsity and Intention to Deceive** To establish fraud, the misrepresentation must have been known by the one making it to be false and must have been made with an intent to deceive. This element of fraud is known as ***scienter***. Knowledge of falsity can consist of (1) actual knowledge, (2) lack of belief in the statement's truthfulness, or (3) reckless indifference as to its truthfulness.

**Justifiable Reliance** A person is not entitled to relief unless he has justifiably relied upon the misrepresentation. If the misrepresentation in no way influenced the complaining party's decision, he must abide by the terms of the contract. He is not deceived if he does not rely. Justifiable reliance requires that the misrepresentation contribute substantially to the misled party's decision to enter into the contract. If the complaining party knew or it was obvious that the defendant's representation was untrue, but he still entered into the contract, he has not justifiably relied. Moreover, where the misrepresentation is fraudulent, the party who relies on it is entitled to relief even though he does not investigate the statement or is contributorily negligent in relying on it. Restatement, Torts, Sections 540, 545A. Not knowing or discovering the facts before making a contract does not constitute unjustified reliance unless it amounts to a failure to act in good faith and in accordance with reasonable standards of fair dealing. Restatement, Section 172. Thus, most courts will not allow a person who concocts a deliberate and elaborate scheme to defraud—one that the defrauded party should readily detect—to argue that the defrauded party did not justifiably rely upon the misrepresentation.

## NONFRAUDULENT MISREPRESENTATION

Nonfraudulent misrepresentation is a material, false statement that induces another to rely justifiably but is made without *scienter.*

**Negligent misrepresentation** is a false representation that is made without due care in ascertaining its truthfulness. **Innocent misrepresentation** is a false representation made without knowledge of its falsity but with due care. To obtain relief for nonfraudulent misrepresentation, all of the other elements of fraud must be present *and* the misrepresentation must be material. The remedies that may be available for nonfraudulent misrepresentation are rescission and damages (see *Chapter 18*).

◆ **SEE CASE 11-5**

◆ **SEE FIGURE 11-1: Misrepresentation**

## MISTAKE

A **mistake** is a belief that is not in accord with the facts. Where the mistaken facts relate to the basis of the parties' agreement, the law permits the adversely affected party to

◆ FIGURE 11-1: **Misrepresentation**

| | Fraudulent | Negligent | Innocent |
|---|---|---|---|
| **False statement of fact** | Yes | Yes | Yes |
| **Materiality** | Yes for damages<br>No for rescission | Yes | Yes |
| **Fault** | Scienter | Without due care (knowledge and intent) | Without due care and knowledge |
| **Reliance** | Yes | Yes | Yes |
| **Injury** | Yes for damages<br>No for rescission | Yes for damages<br>No for rescission | Yes for damages<br>No for rescission |
| **Remedies** | Damages<br>Rescission | Damages<br>Rescission | Damages<br>Rescission |

avoid or reform the contract under certain circumstances. But because permitting avoidance for mistake undermines the objective approach to mutual assent, the law has experienced considerable difficulty in specifying those circumstances that justify permitting the subjective matter of mistake to invalidate an otherwise objectively satisfactory agreement. As a result, establishing clear rules to govern the effect of mistake has proven elusive.

The Restatement and modern cases treat mistakes of law in existence at the time of making a contract no differently than mistakes of fact. For example, Susan contracts to sell a parcel of land to James with the mutual understanding that James will build an apartment house on the land. Both Susan and James believe that such a building is lawful. Unknown to them, however, the town in which the land is located had enacted an ordinance precluding such use of the land three days before they entered into the contract. This mistake of law, which the courts would treat as a mistake of fact, would lead to the consequences discussed below.

## MUTUAL MISTAKE

**Mutual mistake** occurs when *both* parties are mistaken as to the same set of facts. If the mistake relates to a basic assumption on which the contract is made and has a material effect on the agreed exchange, then it is **voidable** by the adversely affected party unless he bears the risk of the mistake. Restatement, Section 152.

Usually, market conditions and the financial situation of the parties are not considered basic assumptions. Thus, if Gail contracts to purchase Pete's automobile under the belief that she can sell it at a profit to Jesse, she is not excused from liability if she is mistaken in this belief. Nor can she rescind the agreement simply because she was mistaken as to her estimate of what the automobile was worth. These are the ordinary risks of business, and courts do not undertake to relieve against them. But suppose that the parties contract upon the assumption that the automobile is a 1993 Cadillac with fifteen thousand miles of use, when in fact the engine is that of a cheaper model and has been run in excess of fifty thousand miles. Here, a court would likely allow a rescission because of mutual mistake of a material fact. Another example of mutual mistake of fact was presented in a California case where a noted violinist purchased two violins from a collector for $8,000, the bill of sale reading, "I have on this date sold to Mr. Efrem Zimbalist one Joseph Guarnerius violin and one Stradivarius violin dated 1717." Actually, unknown to either party, neither violin was genuine. Taken together they were worth no more than $300. The sale was voidable by the purchaser for mutual mistake. In a New Zealand case, the plaintiff purchased a "stud bull" at an auction. There were no express warranties as to "sex, condition, or otherwise." Actually, the bull was sterile. Rescission was allowed, with the court observing that it was a "bull in name only."

◆ **SEE CASE 11-5**

## UNILATERAL MISTAKE

Unilateral mistake occurs when only one of the parties is mistaken. Courts have been hesitant to grant relief for unilateral mistake even though it relates to a basic assumption on which the party entered into the contract and has a material effect on the agreed exchange. Nevertheless, relief will be granted where the nonmistaken party knows, or reasonably should know, that such a mistake has been made (palpable unilateral mistake) or where the mistake was caused by the fault of the nonmistaken party. For example, suppose a building contractor makes a serious error in his computations and as a result submits a bid on a job that is one-half the amount it should be. If the other party knows that he made such an error, or reasonably should have known, she cannot, as a general rule, take advantage of the other's mistake by accepting the offer. In addition, many courts and the Restatement allow rescission where the effect of the unilateral mistake makes enforcement of the contract unconscionable. Section 153.

### ASSUMPTION OF RISK OF MISTAKE

A party who has undertaken to bear the risk of a mistake will be unable to avoid the contract, even though the mistake (which may be either mutual or unilateral) otherwise would have permitted her to do so. This allocation of risk may occur by agreement of the parties. For instance, a ship at sea may be sold "lost or not lost." In such case the buyer is liable whether the ship was lost or not lost at the time the contract was made. There is no mistake; instead, there is a conscious allocation of risk.

Conscious ignorance may serve to allocate the risk of mistake when the parties recognize that they have limited knowledge of the facts. For example, the Supreme Court of Wisconsin refused to set aside the sale of a stone for which the purchaser paid one dollar, but which was subsequently discovered to be an uncut diamond valued at $700. The parties did not know at the time of sale what the stone was and knew they did not know. Each consciously assumed the risk that the value might be more or less than the selling price.

### EFFECT OF FAULT UPON MISTAKE

The Restatement provides that a mistaken party's fault in not knowing or discovering a fact before making a contract does not prevent him from avoiding the contract "unless his fault amounts to a failure to act in good faith and in accordance with reasonable standards of fair dealing." Restatement, Section 157. This rule does not, however, apply to a failure to read a contract. As a general proposition, a party is held to what she signs. Her signature authenticates the writing, and she cannot repudiate that which she has voluntarily approved. Generally, one who assents to a writing is presumed to know its contents and cannot escape being bound by its terms merely by contending that she did not read them; her assent is deemed to cover unknown as well as known terms. Restatement, Section 157, Comment b.

### MISTAKE IN MEANING OF TERMS

Somewhat related to mistakes of facts is the situation in which the parties misunderstand the meaning of one another's manifestations of mutual assent. A famous case involving this problem is *Raffles v. Wichelhaus,* 2 Hurlstone & Coltman 906 (1864), popularly known as the "*Peerless* Case." A contract of purchase was made for 125 bales of cotton to arrive on the *Peerless* from Bombay. It happened, however, that there were two ships by the name of *Peerless*, each sailing from Bombay, one in October and the other in December. The buyer had in mind the ship that sailed in October, while the seller reasonably believed the agreement referred to the *Peerless* sailing in December. Neither party was at fault, but both believed in good faith that a different ship was intended. The English court held that no contract existed. The Restatement, Section 20, is in accord.

There is no manifestation of mutual assent in cases in which the parties attach materially different meanings to their manifestations and neither party knows or has reason to know the meaning attached by the other. If blame can be ascribed to either party, however, that party will be held responsible. Thus, if the seller knew of two ships by the name of *Peerless* sailing from Bombay, then he would be at fault, and the contract would be for the ship sailing in October as the buyer expected. If neither party is to blame or both are to blame, there is no contract at all; that is, the agreement is void.

## CHAPTER SUMMARY

| | |
|---|---|
| DURESS | **Definition** wrongful or unlawful act or threat that overcomes the free will of a party<br>**Physical Compulsion** coercion involving physical force renders the agreement void<br>**Improper Threats** improper threats or acts, including economic and social coercion, render the contract voidable |
| UNDUE INFLUENCE | **Definition** taking unfair advantage of a person by reason of a dominant position based on a confidential relationship<br>**Effect** renders a contract voidable |
| FRAUD | **Fraud in the Execution** a misrepresentation that deceives the other party as to the nature of a document evidencing the contract renders the agreement void |

**Fraud in the Inducement** renders the agreement voidable if the following elements are present:
- ***False Representation*** positive statement or conduct that misleads
- ***Fact*** an event that occurred or thing that exists
- ***Materiality*** of substantial importance
- ***Knowledge of Falsity and Intention to Deceive*** called *scienter* and includes (1) actual knowledge, (2) lack of belief in statement's truthfulness, or (3) reckless indifference to its truthfulness
- ***Justifiable Reliance*** a defrauded party is reasonably influenced by the misrepresentation

**NONFRAUDULENT MISREPRESENTATION**

**Negligent Misrepresentation** misrepresentation made without due care in ascertaining its truthfulness; renders agreement voidable

**Innocent Misrepresentation** misrepresentation made without knowledge of its falsity but with due care; renders contract voidable

**MISTAKE**

**Definition** an understanding that is not in accord with existing fact

**Mutual Mistake** both parties have a common but erroneous belief forming the basis of the contract; renders the contract voidable by either party

**Unilateral Mistake** courts are unlikely to grant relief unless the error is known or should be known by the nonmistaken party

**Assumption of Risk** a party may assume the risk of a mistake

**Effect of Fault upon Mistake** not a bar to avoidance unless the fault amounts to a failure to act in good faith

# CASES

## CASE 11-1

### Duress
### BERARDI v. MEADOWBROOK MALL COMPANY

Supreme Court of Appeals of West Virginia, 2002
212 W.Va. 377, 572 S.E.2d 900
http://www.state.wv.us/wvsca/docs/fall02/30517.htm

**Per Curiam:**

Jerry A. Berardi (hereinafter referred to as "Mr. Berardi"), Betty J. Berardi, and Bentley Corporation, plaintiffs below/appellants (hereinafter collectively referred to as "the Berardis"), seek reversal of a summary judgment granted to Meadowbrook Mall Company, an Ohio Limited Partnership, and the Cafaro Company (hereinafter referred to as "Cafaro Company"), an Ohio Corporation, defendants below/appellees (hereinafter collectively referred to as "Meadowbrook" or * * * "Cafaro Company"). * * *

**I**

***Facts and Procedural History***

Between 1985 and 1987, the Berardis leased space for three restaurants from Meadowbrook. In 1990, the Berardis were delinquent in their rent. Cafaro Company, an affiliate of Meadowbrook, sent a letter dated October 1, 1990, to Mr. Berardi citing the arrearages. The letter informed him that a lawsuit would be filed in Ohio requesting judgment for the total amount of the arrearages. The letter proposed that after filing the suits, a consent judgment would be forwarded to Mr. Berardi granting judgment for the full amount of arrearages. Once the consent judgment was signed by both parties and filed with the court, the letter pledged, no steps to enforce the judgment would be undertaken providing the Berardis continued to operate their three restaurants consistent with the then present payment arrangement. Mr. Berardi signed the letter on October 5, 1990. In April 1996, Meadowbrook caused to be filed in the Circuit Court of Harrison County, West Virginia, [the] * * * judgment of the Ohio lawsuits. * * * [Meadowbrook received a] lien on the Goff Building [which was owned by the Berardis, and which] impeded the refinancing [of the building by the Berardis].

Correspondence was exchanged between counsel for the parties. * * * The correspondence ultimately led, in June 1997, to the Berardis and Anthony Cafaro (an authorized agent for Meadowbrook) signing a "Settlement Agreement and Release" settling the 1990 Ohio judgments. In this document, the Berardis acknowledged the validity of the 1990 Ohio judgments and that the aggregate due under them, plus interest and leasehold charges, was $814,375.97. The Berardis agreed to pay Meadowbrook $150,000 on the date the Goff Building refinancing occurred, and also to pay Meadowbrook $100,000 plus 8.5% interest per year on the third anniversary of the initial $150,000 payment. These payments would discharge the Berardis from all other amounts due and owing. The payment of the initial $150,000 would also result in Meadowbrook releasing the lien against the Goff Building.

The agreement additionally recited:

> Berardis hereby release and forever discharge Meadowbrook, its employees, agents, successors, and assigns from any and all claims, demands, damages, actions, and causes of action of any kind or nature that have arisen or may arise as a result of the leases, or Guaranties whether said claims are known or unknown, contingent, or liquidated, from the beginning of time to the effective date of the agreement. Berardis acknowledge there was no unethical behavior on behalf of Meadowbrook Mall Company, its employees, agents.

Nevertheless, on October 2, 2000, the Berardis filed a complaint against Meadowbrook alleging that Meadowbrook breached the October 1990 agreement by attempting to enforce the 1990 Ohio judgments, that Meadowbrook extorted by duress and coercion the 1997 agreement, and that Meadowbrook and other business entities had conspired to enter into extortionate agreements with their tenants. Meadowbrook filed a motion to dismiss under the 1997 settlement. * * * Meadowbrook sought summary judgment, which the circuit court granted. From this summary judgment, Berardi now appeals.

* * *

## III
### *Discussion*

The Berardis contend that because the 1997 agreement was coerced by economic duress, the circuit erred in finding it was enforceable. * * *

Meadowbrook retorts that the 1997 settlement agreement is valid and was not the result of economic duress in a legal sense. It contends the release was an arms-length transaction between sophisticated business people represented by counsel which is indisputably valid.

* * *

"We begin our discussion of this issue by reiterating, at the outset, that settlements are highly regarded and scrupulously enforced, so long as they are legally sound." [Citation.] "The law favors and encourages the resolution of controversies by contracts of compromise and settlement rather than by litigation; and it is the policy of the law to uphold and enforce such contracts if they are fairly made and are not in contravention of some law or public policy." [Citations.] Those who seek to avoid a settlement "face a heavy burden" [citation] and "since * * * settlement agreements, when properly executed, are legal and binding, this Court will not set aside such agreements on allegations of duress * * * absent clear and convincing proof of such claims." [Citation.]

The Berardis contend the 1997 settlement is invalid as it was procured by "economic duress:"

> The concept of "economic or business duress" may be generally stated as follows: Where the plaintiff is forced into a transaction as a result of unlawful threats or wrongful, oppressive, or unconscionable conduct on the part of the defendant which leaves the plaintiff no reasonable alternative but to acquiesce, the plaintiff may void the transaction and recover any economic loss.
>
> [Citation.] In [citation], we emphasized that
>
> [t]here appears to be general acknowledgment that duress is not shown because one party to the contract has driven a hard bargain or that market or other conditions now make the contract more difficult to perform by one of the parties or that financial circumstances may have caused one party to make concessions.

"Duress is not readily accepted as an excuse" to avoid a contract. [Citation.] Thus, to establish economic duress, "in addition to their own * * * statements, the plaintiffs must produce objective evidence of their duress. The defense of economic duress does not turn only upon the subjective state of mind of the plaintiffs, but it must be reasonable in light of the objective facts presented." [Citation.]

Mr. Berardi is a sophisticated businessman who has operated a number of commercial enterprises. As of 1997, the Berardis had substantial assets and a considerable net worth. While economic duress may reach large business entities as well as the "proverbial little old lady in tennis shoes," [citation], when the parties are sophisticated business entities, releases should be voided only in "'extreme and extraordinary cases.'" [Citation.] Indeed, "where an experienced businessman takes sufficient time, seeks the advice of counsel and understands the content of what he is signing he cannot claim the execution of the release was a product of duress." [Citation.] While the presence of counsel will not *per se* defeat a claim of economic duress, "a court must determine if the attorneys had an opportunity for meaningful input under the circumstances." [Citation.]

Here, the Berardis were represented by Attorneys John Farmer and Louis E. Enderle, Jr. in negotiations leading up to the June 1997 agreement. These negotiations apparently commenced at least as of April 22 and culminated in the June 1997 agreement. It also appears Mr. Berardi communicated with Attorney Enderle during negotiations. * * * Mr. Enderle stated in his deposition that he was unaware of any reason why the 1997 settlement agreement was unenforceable. The Berardis testified in their depositions they understood they would be bound by the terms of the agreement. * * *

Further, Mr. Berardi testified at his deposition that he never became aware of any new facts relative to the 1997 agreement that prompted him to sue Meadowbrook. The Berardis stated in their answers to Meadowbrook's requests for admission that there were no new facts which came to light after the 1997 agreement.

> "No case can be found, we apprehend, where a party who, without force or intimidation and with full knowledge of all the facts of the case, accepts on account of an unlitigated and controverted demand a sum less than what he claims and believes to be due him, and agrees to accept that sum in full satisfaction, has been permitted to avoid his act on the ground that this is duress."

[Citations.]

Moreover, the Berardis did not file their complaint until October 2, 2000. A party seeking to repudiate a release must act promptly in disavowing it once the putative duress ends or else the party will be deemed to have ratified the agreement. [Citations.] * * *

Finally, we do not believe that any relative economic inequality between the Berardis and Meadowbrook sufficiently factor into the summary judgment calculation. We have recognized that, "in most commercial transactions it may be assumed that there is some inequality of bargaining power. * * * " [Citation.] Indeed, even when one sophisticated business entity enjoys "a decided economic advantage" over another such entity, economic duress is extremely circumscribed:

> "Because an element of economic duress is * * * present when many contracts are formed or releases given, the ability of a party to disown his obligations under a contract or release on that basis is reserved for extreme and extraordinary cases. Otherwise, the stronger party to a contract or release would routinely be at risk of having its rights under the contract or release challenged long after the instrument became effective."

[Citation.]

Given the facts, the law's disfavor of economic duress, its approbation of settlements, the sophisticated nature of the parties, and the extremely high evidentiary burden the Berardis must overcome, we harbor no substantial doubt nor do we believe the circuit court abused its discretion.

* * *

## IV
### *Conclusion*

The judgment of the Circuit Court of Harrison County is affirmed.

---

# CASE 11-2

## Undue Influence
## REA v. PAULSON

Court of Appeals of Oregon, 1994
131 Or.App. 743, 887 P.2d 355

**Buttler, J.**

Plaintiff (Ken Rea), as personal representative of his mother's estate, brought this action to set aside a deed from his mother to defendant Paulson (Larry), a son of decedent by a second marriage, and a deed from Larry to defendant Brady executed after this action had been commenced. Brady, in turn, filed a cross-claim against Larry for damages in the event plaintiff prevailed in setting aside the deed to him. The trial court, sitting in equity, found in favor of plaintiff on his complaint, and in favor of Brady on her cross-complaint. Brady, alone, appeals from the resulting judgment.

* * *

Decedent died on January 31, 1988, leaving four children: Ken, Donald, Barbara and Larry. She had purchased a home in Rainier, the property that is the subject of this lawsuit, in 1983, for $21,300. At that time, she had a will that she had executed in 1967, leaving all of her property to her four children in equal shares. That will was never changed. After she moved into the house in Rainier, Ken and his wife, and Barbara and Don, helped decedent, who suffered from arthritis in both hands, renal failure, congestive heart failure and diabetes, as a result of which she had trouble getting around and, during the last part of her life, used an electric cart. She was taking several medications, * * *, and was receiving insulin daily and dialysis an average of three times a week. Although there is no evidence that she was mentally incompetent, the medications and treatments made her drowsy, tired and depressed, and caused mood swings. It is undisputed that she was dependent on the help of others in her daily living.

Larry was not in the Rainier area when his mother moved there and did not visit her. The other children and her neighbor helped her. The other children re-roofed the house for her, picked fruit and stored it and mowed the lawn; her daughter helped her with her finances and had a joint account with her, which the daughter never used. All of those children visited her frequently, and at least one of them saw her every day. Decedent expressed concern about losing the house because of her medical bills, and suggested that she put the house in Ken's name; he and Barbara looked into the situation and concluded that it was not necessary, and so advised their mother. At some point, it is not clear when, Larry was told by state welfare authorities, as Ken and Barbara had learned, that so long as his mother maintained her house as her primary residence and was not receiving Medicaid, she was not in danger of losing her house to the state. There is no evidence that decedent was receiving Medicaid, although she did receive Social Security benefits and Medicare.

Some time in early 1987, Larry and his then girlfriend (later his wife) moved in with decedent and took over her care. Larry expressed his concern to his mother that the state might take her house. Not long thereafter, Larry rented a house in Longview in his name and persuaded his mother to move in with him, his girlfriend and her child. After decedent moved to Longview, she rented her house in Rainier; the rent was used to maintain the house in Longview. At that time decedent had a savings account with approximately $2,000 in it; Larry held his mother's power of attorney. At the time of her death in January, 1988, that account was exhausted, although her medical expenses were being paid by Medicare. Larry admitted that he used some of that money to buy a bicycle and a guitar. He had also used her credit card, on which there was a substantial balance after her death, which he did not pay. He said that that debt "died with his mother." On numerous occasions, Larry expressed to his mother his concern that the state would take her house if she kept it in her name. She was fearful of that, in spite of what she had been told by Ken and Barbara. Larry told her that they were wrong, and frequently urged her to make up her mind "about the deed."

Decedent was hospitalized three times during 1987: February 13 to 18, August 2 to 10 and November 11 to 30. She was in a nursing home following her first hospitalization and again shortly before her death.

Finally, on September 30, 1987, Larry suggested to his mother that they go to a title company in Rainier to get a deed. He took her, along with his then wife and her child, to the title company where he obtained a statutory form of warranty deed and filled it out in his handwriting, using the property description provided by the title company. For no explained reason, he then drove to Longview to a notary public, where decedent signed the deed after the notary explained to her that when she signed it she would be giving up all of her rights in the property. Larry then had it recorded on October 22, 1987. He did not mention it to any of his half-brothers or -sister until two months later when he boasted of it to his half-sister.

Clearly, decedent had trust and confidence in Larry and was completely dependent on him in her daily life. He helped her with her finances and held her power of attorney. She was unable to write checks; Larry wrote them for her, and "she signed them as best she could." She was unable to come and go as she wished; after she moved in with Larry, she depended on him to take her places. Because Larry made it clear to decedent's other children that they were not welcome in his home, he succeeded in driving a wedge between them and their mother, with whom they had had a very close relationship until he appeared on the scene and took control of her life. He did not advise them of her death. We conclude that there was a confidential relationship between decedent and Larry and that, under the circumstances, he held a position of dominance over her; he was, literally, in the driver's seat. [Citation.]

Although one who claims that another has asserted undue influence has the burden to prove it, an inference of undue influence arises when, in addition to a confidential relationship, there are suspicious circumstances. [Citation.] That inference, if unexplained, may be sufficient, although the burden of proof remains with the one asserting undue influence. [Citation.] Circumstances that give rise to suspicions of undue influence are set out in [citation], and several are present here. Larry took his mother to the title company in St. Helens, where he procured the deed, filled it out in his own handwriting and then took his mother to Longview, where she signed it before a notary public. He not only procured the deed, he also participated in its preparation. Although he contends that it was his mother's idea, if it was, it was the result of his having persuaded her that she would lose the house if she did not deed the property to him, and of his repeatedly telling her to make up her mind "about the deed." At that time, Larry knew that the state would not take her home away from her as long as it was her primary residence, even if she was receiving Medicaid. Therefore, his persistence in raising the question was false, and he knew it was false. He did not argue that, because the Rainier house was no longer her primary residence, there was a risk that the state would take it. That argument would have been disingenuous, given that it was he who had suggested that she rent her house and move in with him.

Another important factor is the absence of independent advice. Although Ken and Barbara had advised decedent long before the deed was executed that she would not lose her house to the state if she maintained it in her name instead of deeding it to Ken, as she was contemplating at the time, Larry had persuaded her that Ken was wrong and that she should deed it to him. Under the circumstances, independent advice was essential, and Larry breached his fiduciary duty to her by not seeing to it that she get independent advice.

We also consider the change in attitude of decedent toward her other children after Larry took charge of his mother. Larry conceded that he had little good to say to his mother about his half-brothers and -sister. More than that, the record shows that he told them that they were not welcome at his home, and that when Barbara tried to call her mother on the telephone, he would get on another line to interfere with the call. As a result, the relations between decedent and her other children deteriorated after Larry took over the care of their mother.

We have no reason to doubt that decedent was grateful to Larry for his having helped her during her final days, or that she loved him. However, the circumstances leading up to the conveyance, and the preparation and signing of the deed, lead us to conclude that it was the product of undue influence exerted by Larry on his mother.

* * *

Affirmed.

---

CASE 11-3

Fraud: Fact

## MAROUN v. WYRELESS SYSTEMS, INC.

Supreme Court of Idaho, 2005

141 Idaho 604, 114 P.3d 974

http://caselaw.lp.findlaw.com/data2/idahostatecases/sc/1055/maroun.pdf

**Trout, J.**

* * *

Tony Y. Maroun (Maroun) was employed by Amkor when he accepted an offer to work for Wyreless, a start-up company. On November 20, 2000, a letter was sent from Bradley C. Robinson, president of Wyreless, to Maroun setting forth the terms of their employment agreement. The pertinent portions of the letter were as follows:

* * *

- Annual salary of $300,000.
- $300,000 bonus for successful organization of Wyreless Systems, Inc.
- 15% of the issued equity in Wyreless Systems, Inc.
- The equity and "organization bonus" will need to be tied to agreeable milestones (e.g., acquisition of Matricus, organization of management team, etc).
- Full medical benefits.
- Position of Chief Executive Officer, President and a position on the Board.
- Bonuses and incentives will need to be determined by the Board and you after the business plan has been agreed by all parties.

* * *

I would like you to have an understanding of the fund raising status. I was able to get a commitment from two investors today for a minimum of $250,000 for arrival into the WSI bank account early next week. I believe we will be able to raise an additional $350,000 during the following week. * * * If we are not successful in raising the required capital for the business the funds remaining in the account on May 1, 2001 will be release[d] to you and Jen Gadelman (sic) as compensation beyond salaries and expenses for your efforts in developing the business.

I anticipate a starting date of employment of December 1, 2000 or as soon you (sic) can reasonably and professional (sic) resolve your responsibilities with Amkor.

Thereafter, Maroun started working for Wyreless but his employment was terminated in February 2001. Maroun then filed suit (the Wyreless suit), alleging he had not received two salary payments totaling $23,077, had not received 15% of issued equity and had not received the remainder of the $600,000 in bank account funds, alleged to be a balance of $429,145. * * * Maroun also claimed Wyreless' corporate shell should be set aside and the shareholders of Wyreless should be jointly and severally liable for any damages Wyreless caused to him. * * * After Maroun filed a motion for partial summary judgment against Wyreless on the basis that there was no dispute Maroun was owed $23,077 in unpaid wages, the parties stipulated to entry of a judgment in favor of Maroun in the amount of $23,077.

* * *

In the fall of 2002, * * * Wyreless filed a motion for summary judgment on the remaining portions of Maroun's wage claim, which included the claim for 15% of Wyreless shares and the alleged $429,145 balance of the Wyreless fund account. The district court granted the motion. * * * Maroun appealed.

* * *

Maroun argues the district court erred in granting summary judgment in favor of Robinson on the fraud claim. Fraud requires: (1) a statement or a representation of fact; (2) its falsity; (3) its materiality; (4) the speaker's knowledge of its falsity; (5) the speaker's intent that there be reliance; (6) the hearer's ignorance of the falsity of the statement; (7) reliance by the hearer; (8) justifiable reliance; and (9) resultant injury. [Citation.] In opposition to the defendants' motion for summary judgment, Maroun filed an affidavit that stated Robinson made the following representations to Maroun:

**(1)** That Wyreless was to be a corporation of considerable size, with initial net revenues in excess of several hundred million dollars.
**(2)** That Robinson would soon acquire one and one-half million dollars in personal assets, which Robinson would make available to personally guaranty payment of my compensation from Wyreless.
**(3)** That he would have no difficulty in obtaining the initial investments required to capitalize Wyreless as a large, world leading corporation with initial net revenues in excess of several hundred million dollars.
**(4)** That he had obtained firm commitments from several investors and that investment funds would be received in Wyreless' bank account in the near future.

"An action for fraud or misrepresentation will not lie for statements of future events." [Citation.] "[T]here is a general rule in [the] law of deceit that a representation consisting of [a] promise or a statement as to a future event will not serve as [a] basis for fraud...." [Citation.] Statements numbered one and two both address future events. Robinson allegedly stated Wyreless "was to be" and that he "would soon acquire." "[T]he representation forming the basis of a claim for fraud must concern past or existing material facts." [Citation.] Neither of these statements constitutes a statement or a representation of past or existing fact. A "promise or statement that an act will be undertaken, however, is actionable, if it is proven that the speaker made the promise without intending to keep it." [Citation.] There is no indication in the record that Robinson did not intend to fulfill those representations to Maroun at the time he made the statements.

"Opinions or predictions about the anticipated profitability of a business are usually not actionable as fraud." [Citation.] Statement number three appears to be merely Robinson's opinion. As to statement number four, no evidence was submitted that Robinson had not received commitments at the time he made the statement to Maroun. Accordingly, the district court's grant of summary judgment against Maroun on the fraud claim is affirmed.

* * *

[The district court's ruling on this issue is affirmed.]

## CASE 11-4

### Fraud: Materiality
### REED v. KING

California Court of Appeals, 1983
145 Cal.App.3d 261, 193 Cal.Rptr. 130

**Blease, J.**

In the sale of a house, must the seller disclose it was the site of a multiple murder?

Dorris Reed purchased a house from Robert King. Neither King nor his real estate agents (the other named defendants) told Reed that a woman and her four children were murdered there 10 years earlier. However, it seems "truth will come to light; murder cannot be hid long." (Shakespeare, *Merchant of Venice*, act II, scene II.) Reed learned of the gruesome episode from a neighbor after the sale. She sues seeking rescission and damages. King and the real estate agent defendants successfully demurred to her first amended complaint for failure to state a cause of action. Reed appeals the ensuing judgment of dismissal. We will reverse the judgment.

* * * King and his real estate agent knew about the murders and knew the event materially affected the market value of the house when they listed it for sale. They represented to Reed the premises were in good condition and fit for an "elderly lady" living alone. They did not disclose the fact of the murders. At some point King asked a neighbor not to inform Reed of that event. Nonetheless, after Reed moved in neighbors

informed her no one was interested in purchasing the house because of the stigma. Reed paid $76,000, but the house is only worth $65,000 because of its past.

* * *

Does Reed's pleading state a cause of action? Concealed within this question is the nettlesome problem of the duty of disclosure of blemishes on real property which are not physical defects or legal impairments to use.

Reed seeks to state a cause of action sounding in contract, i.e., rescission, or in tort, i.e., deceit. In either event her allegations must reveal a fraud. [Citation.] "The elements of actual fraud, whether as the basis of the remedy in contract or tort, may be stated as follows: There must be (1) a *false representation* or concealment of a material fact (or, in some cases, an opinion) susceptible of knowledge, (2) made with *knowledge* of its falsity or without sufficient knowledge on the subject to warrant a representation, (3) with the *intent* to induce the person to whom it is made to act upon it; and such person must (4) act in *reliance* upon the representation (5) to his *damage*." (Original italics.) [Citation.]

The trial court perceived the defect in Reed's complaint to be a failure to allege concealment of a material fact. * * *

Concealment is a term of art which includes mere nondisclosure when a party has a duty to disclose. [Citation.] Rest.2d Contracts, § 161; Rest.2d Torts, § 551; Reed's complaint reveals only nondisclosure despite the allegation King asked a neighbor to hold his peace. There is no allegation the attempt at suppression was a cause in fact of Reed's ignorance. [Citations.] Accordingly, the critical question is: does the seller have a duty to disclose here? Resolution of this question depends on the materiality of the fact of the murders.

In general, a seller of real property has a duty to disclose: "where the seller knows of facts *materially* affecting the value or desirability of the property which are known or accessible only to him and also knows that such facts are not known to, or within the reach of the diligent attention and observation of the buyer, the seller is under a duty to disclose them to the buyer. [Citation.] This broad statement of duty has led one commentator to conclude: "The ancient maxim *caveat emptor* ('let the buyer beware') has little or no application to California real estate transactions." [Citation.]

Whether information "is of sufficient materiality to affect the value or desirability of the property * * * depends on the facts of the particular case." [Citation.] Materiality "is a question of law, and is part of the concept of right to rely or justifiable reliance." [Citation.] * * * Three considerations bear on this legal conclusion; the gravity of the harm inflicted by nondisclosure; the fairness of imposing a duty of discovery on the buyer as an alternative to compelling disclosure, and the impact on the stability of contracts if rescission is permitted.

Numerous cases have found nondisclosure of physical defects and legal impediments to use of real property are material. [Citation.] However, to our knowledge, no prior real estate sale case has faced an issue of nondisclosure of the kind presented here.

* * *

The murder of innocents is highly unusual in its potential for so disturbing buyers they may be unable to reside in a home where it has occurred. This fact may foreseeably deprive a buyer of the intended use of the purchase. Murder is not such a common occurrence that *buyers* should be charged with anticipating and discovering this disquieting possibility.

Accordingly, the fact is not one for which a duty of inquiry and discovery can sensibly be imposed upon the buyer. Reed alleges the fact of the murders has a quantifiable effect on the market value of the premises. We cannot say this allegation is inherently wrong and, in the pleading posture of the case, we assume it to be true. If information known or accessible only to the seller has a significant and measurable effect on market value and, as is alleged here, the seller is aware of this effect, we see no principled basis for making the duty to disclose turn upon the character of the information. Physical usefulness is not and never has been the sole criterion of valuation. * * *

Reputation and history can have a significant effect on the value of realty. "George Washington slept here" is worth something, however physically inconsequential that consideration may be. Ill repute or "bad will" conversely may depress the value of property. * * *

Whether Reed will be able to prove her allegation the decade-old multiple murder has a significant effect on market value we cannot determine. If she is able to do so by competent evidence she is entitled to a favorable ruling on the issues of materiality and duty to disclose. Her demonstration of objective tangible harm would still the concern that permitting her to go forward will open the floodgates to rescission on subjective and idiosyncratic grounds.

* * *

The judgment is reversed.

CASE 11-5

## Mistake/Innocent Misrepresentation
## LESHER v. STRID

Court of Appeals of Oregon, 2000
165 Or.App. 34, 996 P.2d 988
http://caselaw.findlaw.com/scripts/getcase.pl?court=OR&vol=A99602&invol=1

**Wollheim, J.**

Defendant appeals from a judgment of the trial court granting plaintiff's request for rescission of a contract for the sale of real property. As relevant to this appeal, plaintiffs Vernon and Janene Lesher, purchasers of an 18-acre parcel of property in Josephine County (the subject property), sought rescission of the contract under theories of a mutual mistake of fact or an innocent misrepresentation of fact regarding the existence of water rights appurtenant [belongs to] to the property. The trial court granted rescission on those grounds. * * * [W]e affirm.

In May 1995, plaintiffs agreed to purchase the subject property from defendant with the intention of using it to raise horses. In purchasing the subject property, they relied on their impression that at least four acres of the subject property had a right to irrigation from Slate Creek. The earnest money agreement to the contract provided:

> "**Water Rights** are being conveyed to Buyer at the close of escrow. * * * Seller will provide Buyer with a written explanation of the operation of the irrigation system, water right certificates, and inventory of irrigation equipment included in sale." (Bold in original.)

The earnest money agreement also provided:

> **"THE SUBJECT PROPERTY IS BEING SOLD 'AS IS'** subject to the Buyer's approval of the tests and conditions as stated herein. Buyer declares that Buyer is not depending on any other statement of the Seller or licensees that is not incorporated by reference in this earnest money contract." (Bold in original.)

Before signing the earnest money agreement, defendants presented to plaintiffs, through their mutual realtor, a 1977 Water Resources Department water rights certificate and a map purporting to show an area of the subject property to be irrigated ("area to be irrigated" map). The 1977 water rights certificate * * * [showed that the property] carries a four-acre water right with a priority of 1892. * * *

Vernon Lesher testified that, at the time plaintiffs purchased the subject property, he believed that the subject property carried four acres of appurtenant water rights by virtue of the 1977 certificate and "area to be irrigated" map. Defendant's representative, Sally Doss, agreed that, at the time of the conveyance, Doss believed that a 1892 four-acre irrigation right was appurtenant to the subject property and that, if it was not, she was mistaken. Vernon testified that before buying the subject property, plaintiffs owned property with two irrigated acres. Vernon testified that plaintiffs intended to and, in fact, did sell the two-acre water right property and sought the subject property to expand their ability to raise horses. In particular, plaintiffs needed to have adequate acreage for pasturing the horses. Vernon testified that irrigation was necessary for creating pasture. He stated that, without a right to irrigate four acres, plaintiffs would not have purchased the property. * * *

After purchasing the subject property and before establishing a pasture, plaintiffs learned that the property might not carry a four-acre water right. * * *

* * *

* * * [The trial court] found that both plaintiffs and defendant believed at the time of the sale that the right was appurtenant to the property and that the supply of adequate irrigated land was an essential part of the bargain for plaintiffs. In the alternative, the court found that defendant innocently misrepresented to plaintiffs that those rights existed appurtenant to the subject property. It found that plaintiffs reasonably relied on the representations and documents provided to plaintiffs pertaining to the water rights, and that plaintiffs' belief about the water rights was a material inducement to their purchase of the subject property. The trial court found that a mutual mistake of a material fact by plaintiffs and defendant "and/or" an innocent misrepresentation of fact by defendant merited rescission of the contract.

On appeal, defendant argues that plaintiffs are not entitled to rescission, because they have not proven by clear and convincing evidence that a mistake of fact occurred about the water rights. In the alternative, defendant argues that plaintiffs unjustifiably relied on defendant's representation about the water rights because defendant's representation was extrinsic to the contract and because plaintiffs were grossly negligent in relying on the 1977 certificate and the "area to be irrigated" map to conclude that four acres of irrigation water rights with an 1892 priority date were appurtenant to the subject property.

Grounds for rescission on the basis of a mutual mistake of fact or innocent misrepresentation must be proved by clear and convincing evidence. [Citations.] An innocent misrepresentation of fact renders a contract voidable by a party if the party's "manifestation of assent is induced by * * * a material misrepresentation by the other party upon which the recipient is justified in relying[.]" [Citations.] A mutual mistake of fact renders a contract voidable by the adversely affected party, "where the parties are mistaken as to the facts existing at the time of the contract, if the mistake is so fundamental that it frustrates the purpose of the contract," [citation], and where the adversely affected party does not bear the risk of the mistake, [citation]. A mistake "is a state of mind which is not in accord with the facts." [Citation].

Even though it appears that the trial court did not apply the clear and convincing standard, * * * , we find that plaintiffs' evidence meets that standard. Both defendant and plaintiffs testified that they believed that the four acres of water rights were appurtenant to the subject property. Defendant does not dispute that the 1977 water rights certificate and the "area to be irrigated" map are her representation about the water right.

* * *

Plaintiffs also established by clear and convincing evidence that the existence of the four-acre water right was material and essential to the contract. Vernon testified that the motivation for the purchase was to expand his ability to raise horses from property they already owned where they had a two-acre irrigation right and that the subject property's water right was essential to the contract. Certainly, a smaller water right would limit, not expand, plaintiffs' ability to raise horses. The mistake, therefore, goes to the very essence of the contract.

We next consider defendant's arguments that plaintiffs bore the risk of that mistake. The Restatement (Second) of Contracts § 154 explains that a party bears the risk of a mistake, in part, if the risk is allocated to the party by agreement of the parties, or if the risk is allocated to the party "by the court on the ground that it is reasonable in the circumstances to do so." We find nothing in the contract that would allocate to plaintiffs the risk of a mistake as to the existence of a four-acre water right.

Defendant argues in the alternative that plaintiffs' mistake of fact is the result of defendant's misrepresentation, on which plaintiffs could not reasonably rely. An "innocent misrepresentation may support a claim for rescission of a real estate agreement if the party who relied on the misrepresentations of another establishes a right to have done so." [Citations.]

Defendant argues that her representations about the four-acre water right were extrinsic to the contract and that the contract's "as is" clause expressly excluded reliance on such extrinsic representations. * * * The "as is" clause specifically contemplated reliance on any statements by the seller that were "incorporated by reference" in the earnest money agreement. The earnest money agreement specifically referred to the conveyance of water rights.

* * *

Plaintiffs have established that both a mutual mistake of fact and an innocent misrepresentation of fact entitle them to rescission of the deed of sale.

Affirmed.

## QUESTIONS

1. Identify the types of duress and discuss the legal effect of each.
2. Identify the types of fraud and the elements that must be shown to establish the existence of each.
3. Discuss undue influence and identify some of the situations giving rise to a confidential relationship.
4. Identify and discuss the situations involving voidable mistakes.
5. Define the two types of nonfraudulent misrepresentation.

## PROBLEMS

1. Anita and Barry were negotiating, and Anita's attorney prepared a long and carefully drawn contract, which was given to Barry for examination. Five days later and prior to its execution, Barry's eyes became so infected that it was impossible for him to read. Ten days thereafter and during the continuance of the illness, Anita called upon Barry and urged him to sign the contract, telling him that time was running out. Barry signed the contract despite the fact he was unable to read it. In a subsequent action by Anita, Barry claimed that the contract was not binding upon him because it was impossible for him to read and he did not know what it contained prior to his signing it. Should Barry be held to the contract?
2. **(a)** Johnson tells Davis that he paid $150,000 for his farm in 2007, and that he believes it is worth twice that at the present time. Relying upon these statements, Davis buys the farm from Johnson for $225,000. Johnson did pay $150,000 for the farm in 2007, but its value has increased only slightly, and it is presently not worth $300,000. On discovering this, Davis offers to reconvey the farm to Johnson and sues for the return of his $225,000. Result?

**(b)** Modify the facts in (a) by assuming that Johnson had paid $100,000 for the property in 2007. What result?

**3.** On September 1, Adams in Portland, Oregon, wrote a letter to Brown in New York City, offering to sell to Brown one thousand tons of chromite at $48 per ton, to be shipped by *S.S. Malabar* sailing from Portland, Oregon, to New York City via the Panama Canal. Upon receiving the letter on September 5, Brown immediately mailed to Adams a letter stating that she accepted the offer. There were two ships by the name of *S.S. Malabar* sailing from Portland to New York City via the Panama Canal, one sailing in October and the other sailing in December. At the time of mailing her letter of acceptance Brown knew of both sailings and further knew that Adams knew only of the December sailing. Is there a contract? If so, to which *S.S. Malabar* does it relate?

**4.** Adler owes Panessi, a police captain, $500. Adler threatens that unless Panessi discharges him from the debt, Adler will disclose the fact that Panessi has on several occasions become highly intoxicated and has been seen in the company of certain disreputable persons. Panessi, induced by fear that such a disclosure would cost him his position or in any event lead to social disgrace, gives Adler a release but subsequently sues to set it aside and recover on his claim. Will Adler be able to enforce the release?

**5.** Harris owned a farm that was worth about $600 per acre. By false representations of fact, Harris induced Pringle to buy the farm at $1,500 per acre. Shortly after taking possession of the farm, Pringle discovered oil under the land. Harris, on learning this, sues to have the sale set aside on the ground that it was voidable because of fraud. Result?

**6.** On February 2, Phillips induced Miller to purchase from her fifty shares of stock in the XYZ Corporation for $10,000, representing that the actual book value of each share was $200. A certificate for fifty shares was delivered to Miller. On February 16, Miller discovered that the book value on February 2 was only $50 per share. Will Miller be successful in a lawsuit against Phillips? Why?

**7.** Doris mistakenly accused Peter's son, Steven, of negligently burning down her barn. Peter believed that his son was guilty of the wrong and that he, Peter, was personally liable for the damage, as Steven was only fifteen years old. Upon demand made by Doris, Peter paid Doris $2,500 for the damage to her barn. After making this payment, Peter learned that his son had not caused the burning of Doris's barn and was in no way responsible for its burning. Peter then sued Doris to recover the $2,500 he had paid her. Will he be successful?

**8.** Jones, a farmer, found an odd-looking stone in his fields. He went to Smith, the town jeweler, and asked him what he thought it was. Smith said he did not know but thought it might be a ruby. Jones asked Smith what he would pay for it, and Smith said $200, whereupon Jones sold it to Smith for $200. The stone turned out to be an uncut diamond worth $3,000. Jones brought an action against Smith to recover the stone. On trial, it was proved that Smith actually did not know the stone was a diamond when he bought it, but he thought it might be a ruby. Can Jones void the sale? Explain.

**9.** Decedent Judith Johnson, a bedridden, lonely woman of eighty-six years, owned outright Greenacre, her ancestral estate. Ficky, her physician and friend, visited her weekly and was held in the highest regard by Johnson. Johnson was extremely fearful of suffering and depended upon Ficky to ease her anxiety and pain. Several months before her death, she deeded Greenacre to Ficky for $5,000. The fair market value of Greenacre at this time was $125,000. Johnson was survived by two children and six grandchildren. Johnson's children challenged the validity of the deed. Should the deed be declared invalid due to Ficky's undue influence? Explain.

**10.** Dorothy and John Huffschneider listed their house and lot for sale with C. B. Property. The asking price was $165,000, and the owners told C. B. that the size of the property was 6.8 acres. Dean Olson, a salesman for C. B., advertised the property in local newspapers as consisting of six acres. James and Jean Holcomb signed a contract to purchase the property through Olson after first inspecting the property with Olson and being assured by Olson that the property was at least 6.6 acres. The Holcombs never asked for or received a copy of the survey. In actuality, the lot was only 4.6 acres. The Holcombs now seek to rescind the contract. Decision?

**11.** In February, Gardner, a schoolteacher with no experience in running a tavern, entered into a contract to purchase for $40,000 the Punjab Tavern from Meiling. The contract was contingent upon Gardner's obtaining a five-year lease for the tavern's premises and a liquor license from the State. Prior to the formation of the contract, Meiling had made no representations to Gardner concerning the gross income of the tavern. Approximately three months after the contract was signed, Gardner and Meiling met with an inspector from the Oregon Liquor Control Commission (OLCC) to discuss transfer of the liquor license. Meiling reported to the agent, in Gardner's presence, that the tavern's gross income figures for February, March, and April were $5,710, $4,918, and $5,009, respectively. The OLCC granted the required license, the transaction was closed, and Gardner took possession on June 10. After discovering that the tavern's income was very low and that the tavern had very few female patrons, Gardner contacted Meiling's bookkeeping service and learned that the actual gross income for those three months had been approximately $1,400 to $2,000. Will a court grant Gardner rescission of the contract? Explain.

**12.** Christine Boyd was designated as the beneficiary of a life insurance policy issued by Aetna Life Insurance Company on the life of Christine's husband, Jimmie Boyd. The policy insured against Jimmie's permanent total disability and also provided for a death benefit to be paid on Jimmie's death. Several years after the policy was issued, Jimmie and Christine separated. Jimmie began to travel extensively, and Christine therefore was unable to keep track of his whereabouts or his state of health. Jimmie, however, continued to pay the premiums on the policy until Christine tried to cash in the policy to alleviate her financial distress. A loan previously had been made on the policy, however, leaving its cash surrender value, and thus the amount that Christine received, at only $4.19. Shortly thereafter, Christine learned that Jimmie had been permanently and totally disabled before the surrender of the policy. Aetna also was unaware of Jimmie's condition, and Christine requested that the surrendered policy be reinstated and that the disability payments be made. Jimmie died soon thereafter, and Christine then requested that Aetna pay the death benefit. Decision?

**13.** Plaintiff, Gibson, entered into negotiation with W. S. May, president of Home Folks Mobile Home Plaza, Inc., to buy Home Plaza Corporation. Plaintiff visited the mobile home park on several occasions, at which time he noted the occupancy, visually inspected the sewer and water systems, and asked May numerous questions concerning the condition of the business. Plaintiff, however, never requested to see the books, nor did May try to conceal them. May admits making the following representations to the plaintiff: (a) the water and sewer systems were in good condition and no major short-term expenditures would be needed; (b) the park realized a 40 percent profit on natural gas sold to tenants; and (c) usual park vacancy was 5 percent. In addition, May gave plaintiff the park's accountant-prepared income statement, which showed a net income of $38,220 for the past eight months. Based on these figures, plaintiff projected an annual net profit of $57,331.20. Upon being asked whether this figure accurately represented income of the business for the past three years, May stated by letter that indeed it did.

Plaintiff purchased the park for $275,000. Shortly thereafter, plaintiff spent $5,384 repairing the well and septic systems. By the time plaintiff sold the park three years later, he had expended $7,531 on the wells and $8,125 on the septic systems. Furthermore, in the first year, park occupancy was nowhere near 95 percent. Even after raising rent and the charges for natural gas, plaintiff still operated at a deficit. Plaintiff sued defendant, alleging that May, on behalf of defendant, made false and fraudulent statements on which plaintiff relied when he purchased the park. Decision?

**14.** Columbia University brought suit against Jacobsen on two notes signed by him and his parents. The notes represented the balance of tuition he owed the University. Jacobsen counterclaimed for money damages due to Columbia's deceit or fraudulent misrepresentation. Jacobsen argues that Columbia fraudulently misrepresented that it would teach wisdom, truth, character, enlightenment, and similar virtues and qualities. He specifically cites as support the Columbia motto: "*in lumine tuo videbimus lumen*" ("In your light we shall see light"); the inscription over the college chapel: "Wisdom dwelleth in the heart of him that hath understanding"; and various excerpts from its brochures, catalogues, and a convocation address made by the University's president. Jacobsen, a senior who was not graduated because of poor scholastic standing, claims that the University's failure to meet its promises made through these quotations constituted fraudulent misrepresentation or deceit. Decision?

**15.** Frank Berryessa stole funds from his employer, the Eccles Hotel Company. His father, W. S. Berryessa, learned of his son's trouble and, thinking the amount involved was about $2,000, gave the hotel a promissory note for $2,186 to cover the shortage. In return, the hotel agreed not to publicize the incident or notify the bonding company. (A bonding company is an insurer that is paid a premium for agreeing to reimburse an employer for thefts by an employee.) Before this note became due, however, the hotel discovered that Frank had actually misappropriated $6,865. The hotel then notified its bonding company, Great American Indemnity Company, to collect the entire loss. W. S. Berryessa claims that the agent for Great American told him that unless he paid them $2,000 in cash and signed a note for the remaining $4,865, Frank would be prosecuted. Berryessa agreed, signed the note, and gave the agent a cashier's check for $1,500 and a personal check for $500. He requested that the agent not cash the personal check for about a month. Subsequently, Great American sued Berryessa on the note. He defends against the note on the grounds of duress and counterclaims for the return of the $1,500 and the cancellation of the uncashed $500 check. Who should prevail? Explain.

**16.** Jane Francois married Victor H. Francois. At the time of the marriage, Victor was a fifty-year-old bachelor living with his elderly mother, and Jane was a thirty-year-old, twice-divorced mother of two. Victor had a relatively secure financial portfolio; Jane, on the other hand, brought no money or property to the marriage.

The marriage deteriorated quickly over the next couple of years, with disputes centered on financial matters. During this period, Jane systematically gained a joint interest in and took control of most of Victor's assets. Three years after they married, Jane contracted Harold Monoson, an attorney, to draw up divorce papers. Victor was unaware of Jane's decision until he was taken to Monoson's office, where Monoson presented for Victor's signature a "Property Settlement and Separation Agreement." Monoson told Victor that he would need an attorney, but Jane vetoed Victor's choice. Monoson then asked another lawyer, Gregory Ball, to come into the office. Ball read the agreement and strenuously advised Victor not to sign it because it would commit him to financial suicide. The agreement transferred most of Victor's remaining assets to Jane. Victor, however, signed it because Jane and Monoson persuaded him that it was the only way that his marriage could be saved. In October of the following year, Jane informed Victor that she had sold most of his former property and that she was leaving him permanently. Can Victor have the agreement set aside as a result of undue influence?

**17.** Iverson owned Iverson Motor Company, an enterprise engaged in the repair as well as the sale of Oldsmobile, Rambler, and International Harvester Scout automobiles. Forty percent of the business's sales volume and net earnings came from the Oldsmobile franchise. Whipp contracted to buy Iverson Motors, which Iverson said included the Oldsmobile franchise. After the sale, however, General Motors refused to transfer the franchise to Whipp. Whipp then returned the property to Iverson and brought this action seeking rescission of the contract. Should the contract be rescinded? Explain.

**18.** On February 10, Mrs. Sunderhaus purchased a diamond ring from Perel & Lowenstein for $6,990. She was told by the company's salesperson that the ring was worth its purchase price, and she also received at that time a written guarantee from the company attesting to the diamond's value, style, and trade-in value. When Mrs. Sunderhaus went to trade the ring for another, however, she was told by two jewelers that the ring was valued at $3,000 and $3,500, respectively. Mrs. Sunderhaus knew little about the value of diamonds and claims to have relied on the oral representation of the Perel & Lowenstein's salesperson and the written representation as to the ring's value. She seeks rescission of the contract or damages in the amount of the sales price over the ring's value. Decision?

**19.** Division West Chinchilla Ranch advertised on television that a five-figure income could be earned by raising chinchillas with an investment of only $3.75 per animal per year and only thirty minutes of maintenance per day. The minimum investment was $2,150 for one male and six female chinchillas. Division West represented to plaintiffs that chinchilla ranching would be easy and that no experience was required to make ranching profitable. Plaintiffs, who had no experience raising chinchillas, each invested $2,150 or more to purchase Division's chinchillas and supplies. After three years without earning a profit, plaintiffs sue Division for fraud. Do these facts sustain an action for fraud in the inducement?

**20.** William Schmalz entered into an employment contract with Hardy Salt Company. The contract granted Schmalz six months' severance pay for involuntary termination but none for voluntary separation or termination for cause. Schmalz was asked to resign from his employment. He was informed that if he did not resign, he would be fired for alleged misconduct. When Schmalz turned in his letter of resignation, he signed a release prohibiting him from suing his former employer as a consequence of his employment. Schmalz consulted an attorney before signing the release and upon signing it received $4,583.00 (one month's salary) in consideration. Schmalz now sues his former employer for the severance pay, claiming that he signed the release under duress. Is Schmalz correct in his assertion?

**21.** Treasure Salvors and the State of Florida entered into a series of four annual contracts governing the salvage of the *Nuestra Senora de Atocha*. The *Atocha* is a Spanish galleon that sank in 1622, carrying a treasure now worth well over $250 million. Both parties had contracted under the impression that the seabed on which the *Atocha* lay was land owned by Florida. Treasure Salvors agreed to relinquish 25 percent of the items recovered in return for the right to salvage on State lands. In accordance with these contracts, Treasure Salvors delivered to Florida its share of the salvaged artifacts. Subsequently, the U.S. Supreme Court held that the part of the continental shelf on which the *Atocha* was resting had *never* been owned by Florida. Treasure Salvors then brought suit to rescind the contracts and to recover the artifacts it had delivered to the State of Florida. Should Treasure Salvors prevail?

**22.** International Underwater Contractors, Inc. (IUC), entered into a written contract with New England Telephone and Telegraph Company (NET) to assemble and install certain conduits under the Mystic River for a lump sum price of $149,680. Delays caused by NET forced IUC's work to be performed in the winter months instead of during the summer as originally bid, and as a result, a major change had to be made in the system from that specified in the contract. NET repeatedly assured IUC that it would pay the cost if IUC would complete the work. The change cost IUC an additional $811,810.73; nevertheless, it signed a release settling the claim for a total sum of $575,000. IUC, which at the time was in financial trouble, now seeks to recover the balance due, arguing that the signed release is not binding because it was signed under economic duress. Is IUC correct?

**23.** Conrad Schaneman was a Russian immigrant who could neither read nor write the English language. In 2006 Conrad deeded (conveyed) a farm he owned to his eldest son, Laurence, for $23,500, which was the original purchase price of the property in 1976. The value of the farm in 1976 was between $145,000 and $160,000. At the time he executed the deed, Conrad was an eighty-two-year-old invalid, severely ill, and completely dependent on others for his personal needs. He weighed between 325 and 350 pounds, had difficulty breathing, could not walk more than fifteen feet, and needed a special jackhoist to get in and out of the bathtub. Conrad enjoyed a long-standing, confidential relationship with Laurence, who was his principal adviser and handled Conrad's business affairs. Laurence also obtained a power of attorney from Conrad and made himself a joint owner of Conrad's bank account and $20,000 certificate of deposit. Conrad brought this suit to cancel the deed, claiming it was the result of Laurence's undue influence. The district court found that the deed was executed as a result of undue influence, set aside the deed, and granted title to Conrad. Laurence appealed. Decision?

**24.** At the time of her death, Olga Mestrovic was the owner of a large number of works of art created by her late husband, Ivan Mestrovic, an internationally known sculptor and artist whose works were displayed throughout Europe and the United States. By the terms of Olga's will, all the works of art created by her husband were to be sold and the proceeds distributed to members of the Mestrovic family. Also included in the estate of Olga Mestrovic was certain real property that 1st Source Bank (the Bank), as personal representative of the estate of Olga Mestrovic, agreed to sell to Terrence and Antoinette Wilkin. The agreement of purchase and sale made no mention of any works of art, although it did provide for the sale of such personal property as a dishwasher, drapes, and French doors stored in the attic. Immediately after closing on the real estate, the Wilkins complained to the Bank of the clutter left on the premises; the Bank gave the Wilkins an option of cleaning the house themselves and keeping any personal property they desired, to which the Wilkins agreed. At the time these arrangements were made, neither the Bank nor the Wilkins suspected that any works of art remained on the premises. During cleanup, however, the Wilkins found eight drawings and a sculpture created by Ivan Mestrovic to which the Wilkins claimed ownership based upon their agreement with the Bank that, if they cleaned the real property, they could keep such personal property as they desired. Who is entitled to ownership of the artwork?

**25.** Ronald D. Johnson is a former employee of International Business Machines Corporation (IBM). As part of a downsizing effort, IBM discharged Johnson. In exchange for an enhanced severance package, Johnson signed a written release and covenant not to sue IBM. IBM's downsizing plan provided that surplus personnel were eligible to receive benefits, including outplacement assistance, career counseling, job retraining, and an enhanced separation allowance. These employees were eligible, at IBM's discretion, to receive a separation allowance of two weeks' pay. However, employees who signed a release could be eligible for an enhanced severance allowance equal to one week's pay for each six months of accumulated service with a maximum of twenty-six weeks' pay. Surplus employees could also apply for alternate, generally lower-paying, manufacturing positions. Johnson opted for the release and received the maximum twenty-six weeks' pay. He then alleged, among other claims, that IBM subjected him to economic duress when he signed the release and covenant-not-to-sue, and he sought to rescind both. What will Johnson need to show in order to prove his cause of action?

**26.** Mrs. Audrey E. Vokes, a widow of fifty-one years and without family, purchased fourteen separate dance courses from J. P. Davenport's Arthur Murray, Inc., School of Dance. The fourteen courses totaled in the aggregate 2,302 hours of dancing lessons at a cost to Mrs. Vokes of $31,090.45. Mrs. Vokes was induced continually to reapply for new courses by representations made by Mr. Davenport that her dancing ability was improving, that she was responding to instruction, that she had excellent potential, and that they were developing her into an accomplished dancer. In fact, she had no dancing ability or aptitude and had trouble "hearing the musical beat." Mrs. Vokes brought action to have the contracts set aside. Should she prevail on her claim? Explain.

# CHAPTER 12
# Consideration

Consideration is the primary—but not the only—basis for the enforcement of promises in our legal system. Consideration is the inducement to make a promise enforceable. The doctrine of consideration ensures that promises are enforced only in cases in which the parties have exchanged something of value in the eye of the law. Gratuitous (gift) promises, accordingly, are legally enforceable only under certain circumstances, which are discussed later in the chapter.

Consideration, or that which is exchanged for a promise, is present only when the parties intend an exchange. The consideration exchanged for the promise may be an act, a forbearance to act, or a promise to do either of these. In like manner, Section 71 of the Restatement defines consideration for a promise as (1) an act other than a promise, (2) a forbearance, (3) the creation, modification, or destruction of a legal relation, or (4) a return promise if any of these are bargained for and given in exchange for the promise.

Thus, consideration comprises two basic elements: (1) legal sufficiency (something of value) and (2) bargained-for exchange. Both must be present to satisfy the requirement of consideration. The consideration may be given to the promisor or to some other person; likewise, it may be given by the promisee or by some other person.

## LEGAL SUFFICIENCY

To be legally sufficient, the consideration exchanged for the promise must be either a legal detriment to the promisee *or* a legal benefit to the promisor. In other words, in return for the promise the promisee must give up something of legal value or the promisor must receive something of legal value.

**Legal detriment** means (1) doing (or undertaking to do) that which the promisee was under no prior legal obligation to do or (2) refraining from doing (or the undertaking to refrain from doing) that which he was previously under no legal obligation to refrain from doing. On the other hand, **legal benefit** means the obtaining by the promisor of that which he had no prior legal right to obtain. Most, if not all, cases involving legal detriment to the promisee also will involve a legal benefit to the promisor. Nonetheless, the presence of either is sufficient.

◆ **SEE CASE 12-1**

### ADEQUACY

Legal sufficiency has nothing to do with adequacy of consideration. Restatement, Section 79. The subject matter that the parties agree to exchange does not need to have the same or equal value; rather, the law will regard consideration as adequate if the parties have freely agreed to the exchange. The requirement of legally sufficient consideration is, therefore, not at all concerned with whether the bargain was good or bad, or whether one party received disproportionately more or less than what he gave or promised in exchange. Such facts, however, may be relevant to the availability of certain defenses (such as fraud, duress, or undue influence) or certain remedies (such as specific performance). The requirement of legally sufficient consideration is simply (1) that the parties have agreed to an exchange and (2) that, with respect to each party, the subject matter exchanged, or promised in exchange, either imposed a legal detriment upon the promisee or conferred a legal benefit upon the promisor. If the purported consideration is clearly without value, however, such that the transaction is a sham, many courts would hold that consideration is lacking.

### UNILATERAL CONTRACTS

In a unilateral contract, a promise is exchanged for a completed act or a forbearance to act. Because only one promise exists, only one party, the **offeror**, makes a promise and is therefore the **promisor** while the other party, the **offeree**, is the person receiving the promise and thus is the **promisee**. For example, A promises to pay B $2,000 if B paints A's house. B paints A's house.

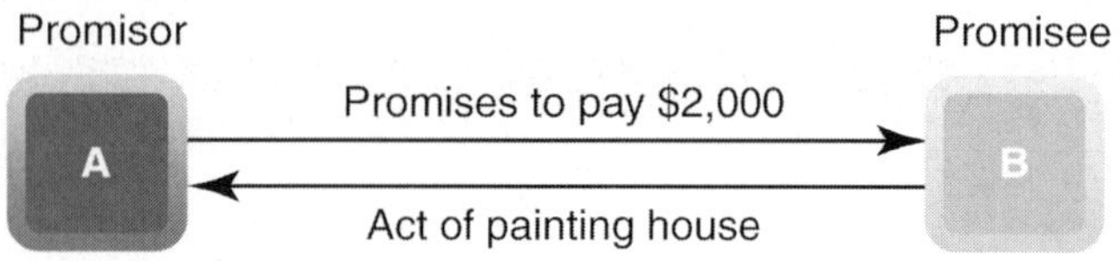


For A's promise to be binding, it must be supported by consideration consisting of either a legal detriment to B, the promisee (offeree), or a legal benefit to A, the promisor (offeror). B's having painted the house is a legal detriment to B, the promisee, because she was under no prior legal duty to paint A's house. Also, B's painting A's house is a legal benefit to A, the promisor, because A had no prior legal right to have his house painted by B.

A unilateral contract may also consist of a promise exchanged for a forbearance. To illustrate, A negligently injures B, for which B may recover damages in a tort action. A promises to pay B $5,000 if B forbears from bringing suit. B accepts by not filing suit.

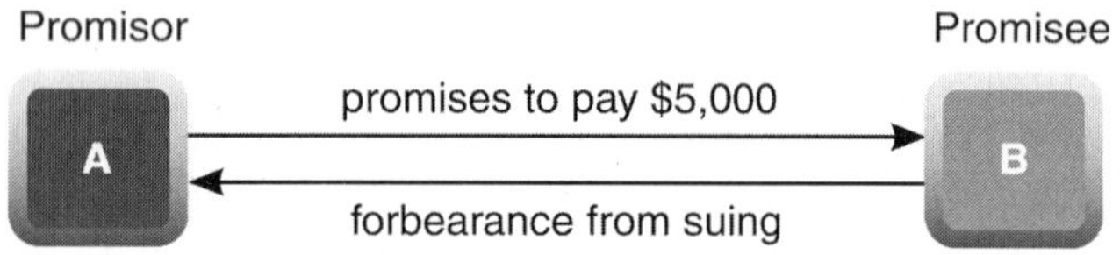


A's promise to pay B $5,000 is binding because it is supported by consideration: B, the promisee (offeree), has incurred a legal detriment by refraining from bringing suit, which he was under no prior legal obligation to refrain from doing. A, the promisor (offeror), has received a legal benefit because she had no prior legal right to B's forbearance from bringing suit.

## BILATERAL CONTRACTS

In a bilateral contract, the parties exchange promises. Thus, each party is *both* a promisor and a promisee. For example, if A (the offeror) promises (offers) to purchase an automobile from B (the offeree) for $15,000 and B promises to sell the automobile to A for $15,000 (accepts the offer), the following relationship exists:

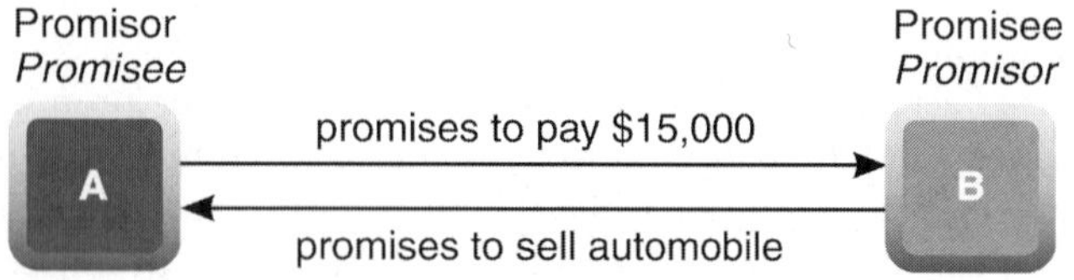


**A's promise** (the offer) to pay B $15,000 is binding and therefore enforceable by B, if that promise is supported by legal consideration from B (offeree), which may consist of either a legal detriment to B, the promisee, or a legal benefit to A, the promisor. B's promise to sell A the automobile is a legal detriment to B because he was under no prior legal duty to sell the automobile to A. Moreover, B's promise is also a legal benefit to A because A had no prior legal right to that automobile. Consequently, A's promise to pay $15,000 to B is supported by consideration and is enforceable.

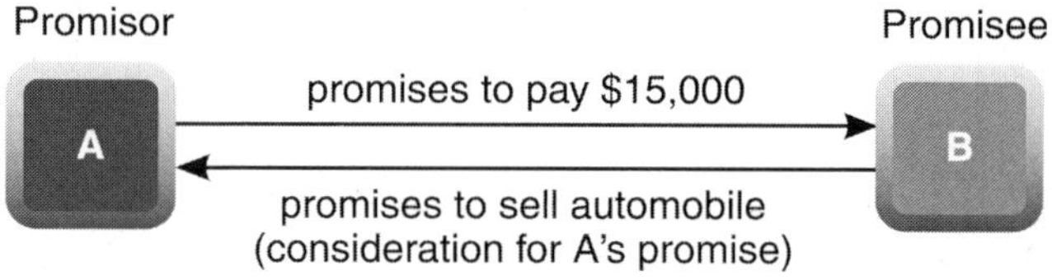


For **B's promise** (the acceptance) to sell the automobile to A to be binding, it likewise must be supported by consideration from A (offeror), which may be either a legal detriment to A, the promisee, or a legal benefit to B, the promisor. A's promise to pay B $15,000 is a legal detriment to A because he was under no prior legal duty to pay $15,000 to B. At the same time, A's promise is also a legal benefit to B because B had no prior legal right to the $15,000. Thus, B's promise to sell the automobile is supported by consideration and is enforceable.

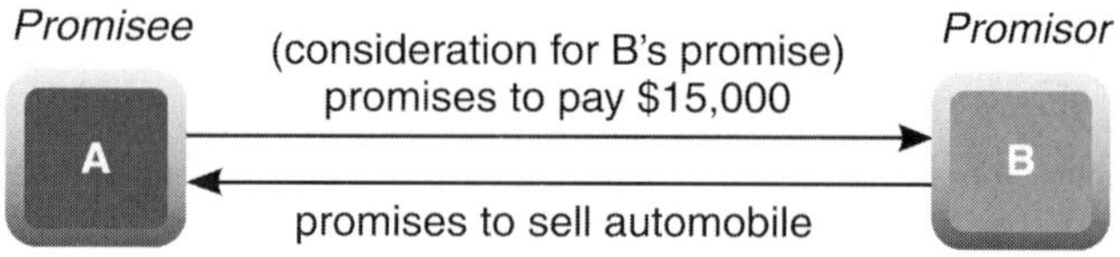


To summarize, for A's promise to B to be binding, B must support the promise with legally sufficient consideration, which requires that the promise A receives in exchange from B provide either a legal benefit to A (the promisor) or a legal detriment to B (the promisee). A, in turn, must support B's return promise with consideration for that promise to be binding on B.

Thus, in a bilateral contract each promise is the consideration for the other, a relationship that has been referred to as **mutuality of obligation**. A general consequence of mutuality of obligation is that each promisor in a bilateral contract must be bound, or neither is bound.

◆ SEE CASE 12-2

◆ SEE FIGURE 12-1: **Consideration in Unilateral and Bilateral Contracts**

◆ FIGURE 12-1: **Consideration in Unilateral and Bilateral Contracts**

| Type of Contract | Offer | Acceptance | Consideration |
|---|---|---|---|
| **Unilateral** | Promise by A | Performance of requested act or forbearance by B | *Promise* by A<br>*Performance* of requested act or forbearance by B |
| **Bilateral** | Promise by A | Return promise by B to perform requested act or forbearance | *Promise* by A<br>Return *promise* by B to perform requested act or forbearance |

## ILLUSORY PROMISES

Words of promise that make the performance of the purported promisor entirely optional constitute no promise at all. Consequently, they cannot serve as consideration. In this section, such illusory promises will be distinguished from promises that impose obligations of performance upon the promisor and thus can be legally sufficient consideration. An **illusory promise** is a statement that is in the form of a promise but imposes no obligation upon the maker of the statement. An illusory promise is not consideration for a return promise. Thus, a statement committing the promisor to purchase such quantity of goods as she may "desire," "want," or "wish to buy" is an illusory promise because its performance is entirely optional. For example, if ExxonMobil, Inc., agrees to sell to Barnes Co. as many barrels of oil as Barnes shall choose at $40 per barrel, there would be no consideration: Barnes may wish or desire to buy none of the oil, yet in buying none it would fulfill its promise. An agreement containing such a promise as that made by Barnes, although accepted by both parties, does not create a contract because the promise is illusory—performance by Barnes is entirely optional, and the offer places no constraint upon its freedom. Barnes is not bound to do anything, nor can Ames reasonably expect to receive any performance. Thus, Barnes, by its promise, suffers no legal detriment and confers no legal benefit. Consequently, Barnes's promise does not provide legally sufficient consideration for ExxonMobil's promise; thus, ExxonMobil's promise is not binding upon ExxonMobil.

Many courts have transformed otherwise illusory promises into actual promises by implying an obligation of good faith or fair dealing. Under this approach, courts have held to be nonillusory a promise "to spend such time as he personally sees fit in developing" a business and a clause "specifying that leases 'satisfactory' to plaintiff must be secured before he would be bound to perform."

**Output and Requirements Contracts** A seller's agreement to sell her entire production to a particular purchaser is called an **output contract**. It affords the seller an ensured market for her product. Conversely, a **requirements contract**, or a purchaser's agreement to buy from a particular seller all the materials of a particular kind he needs, ensures the buyer of a ready source of inventory or supplies. These contracts may or may not be accompanied by an estimate of the quantity to be sold or to be purchased. Nevertheless, these promises are not illusory. The buyer under a requirements contract does not promise to buy as much as she desires to buy but, rather, to buy as much as she *needs*. Similarly, under an output contract the seller promises to sell to the buyer the seller's entire production, not merely as much as the seller desires.

Furthermore, the Code, Section 2–306(1), imposes a good faith limitation upon the quantity to be sold or purchased under an output or requirements contract. Thus, a contract of this type involves such actual output or requirements as may occur in good faith, except that no quantity unreasonably disproportionate to any stated estimate or, in the absence of a stated estimate, to any normal prior output or requirements may be tendered or demanded. Therefore, after contracting to sell to Adler, Inc., its entire output, Benevito Company cannot increase its production from one eight-hour shift per day to three eight-hour shifts per day.

**Exclusive Dealing Contracts** Where a manufacturer of goods grants an exclusive right to a distributor to sell its products in a designated territory, unless otherwise agreed, the manufacturer is under an implied obligation to use its best efforts to supply the goods, and the distributor must use his best efforts to promote their sale. Uniform Commercial Code (UCC) Section 2–306(2). The obligations that arise upon acceptance of an **exclusive dealing agreement** are sufficient consideration to bind both parties to the contract.

**Conditional Promises** A conditional promise is a promise the performance of which depends upon the happening or nonhappening of an event not certain to occur (the condition). A conditional promise is sufficient consideration *unless* the promisor knows at the time of making the promise that the condition cannot occur. Restatement, Section 76.

Thus, if Debbie offers to pay John $8,000 for John's automobile, provided that Debbie receives such amount as an inheritance from the estate of her deceased uncle, and John accepts the offer, the duty of Debbie to pay $8,000 to John is *conditioned* upon her receiving $8,000 from her deceased uncle's estate. The consideration moving from John to Debbie is the promise to transfer title to the automobile. The consideration moving from Debbie to John is the promise of $8,000 subject to the condition.

## PREEXISTING OBLIGATION

The law does not regard the performance of, or the promise to perform, a preexisting legal duty, public or private, as either a legal detriment to the party under the prior legal obligation or a benefit to the other party. A **public duty** does not arise out of a contract; rather, it is imposed upon members of society by force of the common law or by statute. As illustrated in the law of torts, public duty includes the duty not to commit an assault, battery, false imprisonment, or defamation. The criminal law also imposes numerous public duties. Thus, if Cleon promises to pay Spike, the village ruffian, $100 not to abuse him physically, Cleon's promise is unenforceable because both tort and criminal law impose on Spike a preexisting public obligation to refrain from so acting.

By virtue of their public office, public officials, such as the mayor of a city, members of a city council, police officers, and firefighters, are under a preexisting obligation to perform their duties.

The performance of, or the promise to perform, a **preexisting contractual duty**, a duty the terms of which are neither doubtful nor the subject of honest dispute, is also legally insufficient consideration because the doing of what one is legally bound to do is neither a detriment to the promisee nor a benefit to the promisor. For example, Leigh and Associates employs Jason for one year at a salary of $2,000 per month and at the end of six months promises Jason that, in addition to the salary, it will pay him $3,000 if he remains on the job for the remainder of the period originally agreed upon. Leigh's promise is not binding because Jason's promise does not constitute legally sufficient consideration. If Jason's duties were changed in nature or amount, however, Leigh's promise would be binding because Jason's new duties are a legal detriment.

◆ SEE CASE 12-2

**Modification of a Preexisting Contract** A modification of a contract occurs when the parties to the contract mutually agree to change one or more of its terms. Under the common law, a modification of an existing contract must be supported by mutual consideration to be enforceable. In other words, the modification must be supported by some new consideration beyond that which is already owing (thus, there must be a separate and distinct modification contract). For example, Fred and Jodie agree that Fred shall put in a gravel driveway for Jodie at a cost of $2,000. Subsequently, Jodie agrees to pay an additional $1,000 if Fred will blacktop the driveway. Because Fred was not bound by the original contract to provide blacktopping, he would incur a legal detriment in doing so and is therefore entitled to the additional $1,000.

The Code has modified the common law rule for contract modification by providing that the parties can effectively modify a contract for the sale of goods without new consideration, though the Comments to this section make the modification subject to the requirement of good faith. Moreover, the Restatement has moved toward this position by providing that a modification of an executory contract is binding if it is fair and equitable in light of surrounding facts that the parties did not anticipate when the contract was made. Restatement, Section 89. A few States have followed the Code's rule by statutorily providing that the parties need provide no new consideration when modifying any contract. These States vary, however, as to whether the modification must be in writing and whether the original contract must be executory.

◆ SEE CASE 12-3

◆ SEE FIGURE 12-2: **Modification of a Preexisting Contract**

**Substituted Contracts** A substituted contract results when the parties to a contract mutually agree to rescind their original contract and enter into a new one. This situation involves separate contracts: the original contract, the agreement of rescission, and the substitute contract. Substituted contracts are perfectly valid, allowing the parties effectively to discharge the original contract and to impose obligations under the new one. The rescission is binding in that each party, by giving up his rights under the original contract, has provided consideration to the other, as long as each party still has rights under the original contract. Where the rescission and new agreement are simultaneous, the effect is the same as a contractual modification. The Restatement takes the position that the substitute contract is *not* binding unless it is fair and equitable in view of circumstances the parties did not anticipate when they made the original contract. Section 89, Comment b.

**Settlement of a Liquidated Debt** A **liquidated debt** is an obligation the existence or amount of which is undisputed. Under the common law, the partial payment of a sum of money in consideration of a promise to discharge a fully matured, undisputed debt is legally *insufficient* to support the promise of discharge. To illustrate, assume that Pamela

◆ FIGURE 12-2: **Modification of a Preexisting Contract**

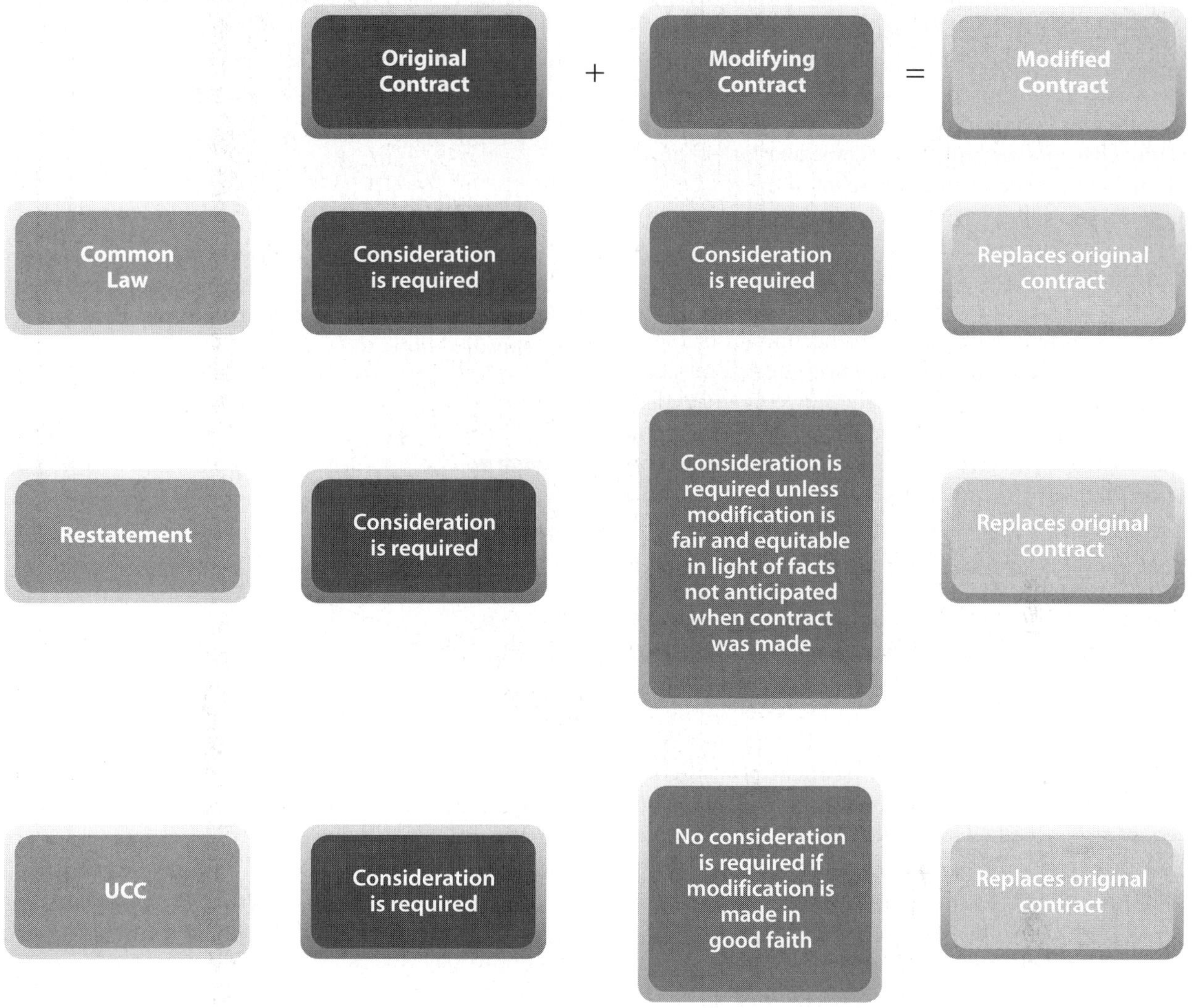


owes Julie $100, and in consideration of Pamela's paying Julie $50, Julie agrees to discharge the debt. In a subsequent suit by Julie against Pamela to recover the remaining $50, at common law Julie is entitled to judgment for $50 on the ground that Julie's promise of discharge is not binding because Pamela's payment of $50 was no legal detriment to the promisee, Pamela, as she was under a preexisting legal obligation to pay that much and more. Consequently, the consideration for Julie's promise of discharge was legally insufficient, and Julie is not bound on her promise. If, however, Julie had accepted from Pamela any new or different consideration, such as the sum of $40 and a fountain pen worth $10 or less, or even the fountain pen with no payment of money, in full satisfaction of the $100 debt, the consideration moving from Pamela would be legally sufficient inasmuch as Pamela was under no legal obligation to give a fountain pen to Julie. In this example, consideration would also exist if Julie had agreed to accept $50 before the debt became due, in full satisfaction of the debt. Pamela was under no legal obligation to pay any of the debt before its due date. Consequently, Pamela's early payment would represent a legal detriment to Pamela as well as a legal benefit to Julie. The law is not concerned with the amount of the discount, as that is simply a question of adequacy for the courts to decide. Likewise, Pamela's payment of a lesser amount on the due date at an agreed-upon different place of payment would be legally sufficient consideration. The Restatement requires that the new consideration "differs from what was required by the duty in a way which reflects more than a pretense of bargain." Section 73.

Settlement of an Unliquidated Debt An **unliquidated debt** is an obligation disputed as to either its existence or its amount. A promise to settle a validly disputed claim in exchange for an agreed payment or other performance is supported by consideration. Where the dispute is based upon contentions that are nonmeritorious or not made in good faith, however, the debtor's surrender of such a claim is no legal detriment to the claimant. The Restatement adopts a different position by providing that the settlement of a claim that proves invalid is consideration if at the time of the settlement (1) the claimant honestly believed that the claim was valid, or (2) the claim was in fact doubtful because of uncertainty as to the facts or the law. Section 74.

For example, where a person has requested professional services from an accountant or a lawyer and the parties reached no agreement with respect to the amount of the fee to be charged, the accountant or lawyer is entitled to receive from her client a reasonable fee for the services rendered. As no definite amount has been agreed upon, the client's obligation is uncertain; nevertheless, his legal obligation is to pay the reasonable worth of the services performed. When the accountant or lawyer sends the client a bill for services rendered, even though the amount stated in the bill is an estimate of the reasonable value of the services, the debt does not become undisputed until and unless the client agrees to pay the amount of the bill. If the client honestly disputes the amount that is owed and tenders in full settlement an amount less than the bill, acceptance of the lesser amount by the creditor discharges the debt. Thus, if Ted sends to Betty, an accountant, a check for $120 in payment of his debt to Betty for services rendered, which services Ted considered worthless but for which Betty billed Ted $600, Betty's acceptance of the check releases Ted from any further liability. Ted has given up his right to dispute the billing further, while Betty has forfeited her right to further collection. Thus, there is mutuality of consideration.

## BARGAINED-FOR EXCHANGE

The central idea behind consideration is that the parties have intentionally entered into a bargained exchange with one another and have given to each other something in exchange for a promise or performance. "A performance or return promise is bargained for if it is sought by the promisor in exchange for his promise and is given by the promisee in exchange for that promise." Restatement, Section 71. Thus, a promise to give someone a birthday present is without consideration, as the promisor received nothing in exchange for his promise of a present.

### PAST CONSIDERATION

Consideration is the inducement for a promise or performance. The element of bargained-for exchange is absent where a promise is given for a past transaction. Therefore, unbargained-for past events are not consideration, despite their designation as "past consideration." A promise made on account of something that the promisee has already done is not enforceable. For example, Noel gives emergency care to Tim's adult son while the son is ill. Tim subsequently promises to pay Noel for her services, but his promise is not binding because there is no bargained-for exchange.

◆ **SEE CASE 12-4**

### THIRD PARTIES

Consideration to support a promise may be given to a person other than the promisor if the promisor bargains for that exchange. For example, A promises to pay B $15 if B delivers a specified book to C.

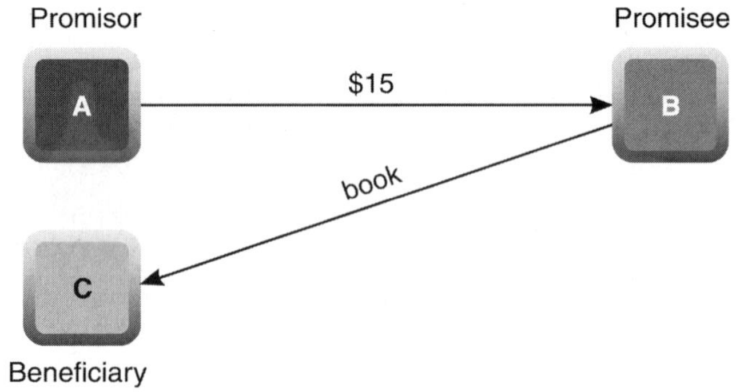


A's promise is binding because B incurred a legal detriment by delivering the book to C, as B was under no prior legal obligation to do so, and A had no prior legal right to have the book given to C. A and B have bargained for A to pay B $15 in return for B's delivering the book to C. A's promise to pay $15 is also consideration for B's promise to give the book to C.

Conversely, consideration may be given by some person other than the promisee. For example, A promises to pay B $25 in return for D's promise to give a radio to A.

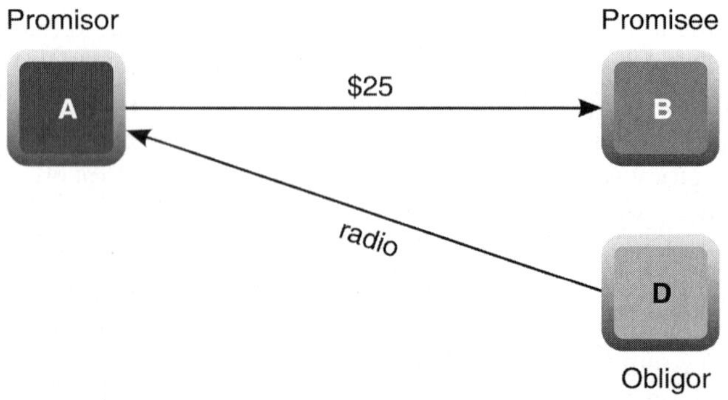


A's promise to pay $25 to B is consideration for D's promise to give a radio to A and vice versa.

## CONTRACTS WITHOUT CONSIDERATION

Certain transactions are enforceable even though they are not supported by consideration. Such transactions include (1) promises to perform prior unenforceable obligations, (2) promises that induce detrimental reliance (promissory estoppel), (3) promises made under seal, and (4) promises made enforceable by statute.

### PROMISES TO PERFORM PRIOR UNENFORCEABLE OBLIGATIONS

In certain circumstances the courts will enforce new promises to perform an obligation that originally was not enforceable or has become unenforceable by operation of law. These situations include promises to pay debts barred by the statute of limitations, debts discharged in bankruptcy, and voidable obligations. In addition, as previously indicated, some courts will enforce promises to pay moral obligations.

**PROMISE TO PAY DEBT BARRED BY THE STATUTE OF LIMITATIONS** Every State has a statute of limitations, which provides that legal actions must be initiated within a prescribed period after the right to bring the action arose. Actions not commenced within the specified time period, which varies among the States and also with the nature of the legal action, will be dismissed.

An exception to the past consideration rule extends to promises to pay all or part of a contractual or quasi-contractual debt barred by the statute of limitations. The new promise is binding according to its terms without consideration for a second statutory period. Any recovery under the new promise is limited to the terms contained in the new promise. Most States require that new promises falling under this rule, except those indicated by part payment, be in writing to be enforceable.

**PROMISE TO PAY DEBT DISCHARGED IN BANKRUPTCY** Another exception to the requirement that consideration be given in exchange for a promise to make it binding is a promise to pay a debt that has been discharged in bankruptcy. Restatement, Section 83. The Bankruptcy Act, however, imposes a number of requirements before a promise to pay a debt discharged in bankruptcy may be enforced. These requirements are discussed in *Chapter 39*.

**VOIDABLE PROMISES** Another promise that is enforceable without new consideration is a new promise to perform a voidable obligation that has not previously been avoided. Restatement, Section 85. The power of avoidance may be based on lack of capacity, fraud, misrepresentation, duress, undue influence, or mistake. For instance, a promise to perform an antecedent obligation made by a minor upon reaching the age of majority is enforceable without new consideration. To be enforceable, the promise itself must not be voidable. For example, if the new promise is made without knowledge of the original fraud or by a minor before reaching the age of majority, then the new promise is not enforceable.

**MORAL OBLIGATION** Under the common law, a promise made to satisfy a preexisting moral obligation is made for past consideration and therefore is unenforceable for lack of consideration. Instances involving such obligations include promises to pay for board and lodging previously furnished to a needy relative of the promisor, promises to pay debts owed by a relative, and an employer's promises to pay a completely disabled former employee a sum of money in addition to an award the employee has received under a workers' compensation statute. Although in many cases the moral obligation may be strong by reason of the particular facts and circumstances, no liability generally attaches to the promise.

The Restatement and a minority of States give considerable recognition to moral obligations as consideration. The Restatement provides that a promise made for "a benefit previously received by the promisor from the promisee is binding to the extent necessary to prevent injustice." Section 86. For instance, Tim's subsequent promise to Noel to reimburse her for the expenses she incurred in rendering emergency services to Tim's son is binding even though it is not supported by new consideration.

The Restatement also provides for enforcement of a moral obligation when a person promises to pay for a mistakenly conferred benefit. For example, Pam hires Elizabeth to pave her driveway, and Elizabeth mistakenly paves Chuck's driveway next door. Chuck subsequently promises to pay Pam $1,000 for the benefit conferred. Under the Restatement, Chuck's promise to pay the $1,000 is binding.

### PROMISSORY ESTOPPEL

As discussed in *Chapter 9*, in certain circumstances in which detrimental reliance has occurred, the courts will enforce noncontractual promises under the doctrine of promissory estoppel. When applicable, the doctrine makes gratuitous promises enforceable to the extent necessary to avoid injustice. The doctrine applies when a promise that the promisor reasonably should expect to induce detrimental reliance does induce such action or forbearance.

Promissory estoppel does not mean that every gratuitous promise is binding simply because it is followed by a change of position on the part of the promisee. To create liability, the promisee must make the change of position in justifiable reliance on the promise. For example, Smith promises to Barclay not to foreclose on a mortgage Smith holds on Barclay's factory for a period of six months. In justifiable reliance on Smith's promise, Barclay expends $900,000 on expanding the factory. Smith's promise not to foreclose is binding on Smith under the doctrine of promissory estoppel.

The most common application of the doctrine of promissory estoppel is to charitable subscriptions. Numerous churches, memorials, college buildings, hospitals, and other structures used for religious, educational, and charitable purposes have been built with the assistance of contributions fulfilling pledges or promises to contribute to particular worthwhile causes. Although the pledgor regards herself as making a gift for a charitable purpose and gift promises generally are not enforceable, the courts tend to enforce charitable subscription promises. Numerous reasons and theories have been advanced in support of liability: the most accepted argues that the subscription has induced a change of position by the promisee (the church, school, or charitable organization) in reliance on the promise. The Restatement, moreover, has relaxed the reliance requirement for charitable subscriptions so that actual reliance need not be shown; the probability of reliance is sufficient.

◆ **SEE CASE 12-4**

## PROMISES MADE UNDER SEAL

Under the common law, when a person desired to bind himself by bond, deed, or solemn promise, he executed his promise under seal. He did not have to sign the document, his delivery of a document to which he had affixed his seal being sufficient. No consideration for his promise was necessary. In some States the courts still hold a promise under seal to be binding without consideration.

Nevertheless, most States have abolished by statute the distinction between contracts under seal and written unsealed contracts. In these States, the seal is no longer recognized as a substitute for consideration. The Code has also adopted this position, specifically eliminating the use of seals in contracts for the sale of goods.

## PROMISES MADE ENFORCEABLE BY STATUTE

Some gratuitous promises that otherwise would be unenforceable have been made binding by statute. Most significant among these are (1) contract modifications, (2) renunciations, and (3) irrevocable offers.

**Contract Modifications** As mentioned previously, the UCC has abandoned the common law rule requiring that a modification of an existing contract be supported by consideration to be valid. The Code provides that a contract for the sale of goods can be effectively modified without new consideration, provided the modification is made in good faith. Section 2–209.

**Renunciation** Under the Code, Section 1–107, any claim or right arising out of an alleged breach of contract can be discharged in whole or in part without consideration by a written waiver or renunciation signed and delivered by the aggrieved party. Under the 2001 Revised UCC Article 1, a claim or right arising out of an alleged breach may be discharged in whole or in part without consideration by agreement of the aggrieved party in an authenticated record. Section 1–306. This section is subject to the obligation of good faith and, as with all sections of Article 1, applies to a transaction to the extent that it is governed by one of the other article of the UCC. Section 1–102.

**Irrevocable Offers** Under the Code, a *firm offer*, a written offer signed by a merchant offeror promising to keep open an offer to buy or sell goods, is not revocable for lack of consideration during the time stated, not to exceed three months, or if no time is stated, for a reasonable time. Section 2–205.

## CHAPTER SUMMARY

**CONSIDERATION**

**Definition** the inducement to enter into a contract
**Elements** legal sufficiency and bargained-for exchange

**LEGAL SUFFICIENCY**

**Definition** consists of either a benefit to the promisor or a detriment to the promisee
- ***Legal Benefit*** obtaining something to which one had no prior legal right
- ***Legal Detriment*** doing an act one is not legally obligated to do or not doing an act that one has a legal right to do

**Adequacy** not required where the parties have freely agreed to the exchange
**Illusory Promise** promise that imposes no obligation on the promisor; the following promises are *not* illusory:
- ***Output Contract*** agreement to sell all of one's production to a single buyer
- ***Requirements Contract*** agreement to buy all of one's needs from a single producer
- ***Exclusive Dealing Contract*** grant to a franchisee or licensee by a manufacturer of the sole right to sell goods in a defined market
- ***Conditional Promise*** a contract in which the obligations are contingent upon the occurrence of a stated event

**Preexisting Public Obligations** public duties such as those imposed by tort or criminal law are neither a legal detriment nor a legal benefit

**Preexisting Contractual Obligation** performance of a preexisting contractual duty is not consideration

- ***Modification of a Preexisting Contract*** under the common law a modification of a preexisting contract must be supported by mutual consideration; under the Code a contract can be modified without new consideration
- ***Substituted Contracts*** the parties agree to rescind their original contract and to enter into a new one; rescission and new contract are supported by consideration
- ***Settlement of an Undisputed Debt*** payment of a lesser sum of money to discharge an undisputed debt (one whose existence or amount is not contested) does not constitute legally sufficient consideration
- ***Settlement of a Disputed Debt*** payment of a lesser sum of money to discharge a disputed debt (one whose existence or amount is contested) is legally sufficient consideration

---

**BARGAINED-FOR EXCHANGE**

**Definition** a mutually agreed-upon exchange

**Past Consideration** an act done before the contract is made is not consideration

---

**CONTRACTS WITHOUT CONSIDERATION**

**Promises to Perform Prior Unenforceable Obligations**

- ***Promise to Pay Debt Barred by the Statute of Limitations*** a new promise by the debtor to pay the debt renews the running of the statute for a second statutory period
- ***Promise to Pay Debt Discharged in Bankruptcy*** may be enforceable without consideration
- ***Voidable Promises*** a new promise to perform a voidable obligation that has not been previously avoided is enforceable
- ***Moral Obligation*** a promise made to satisfy a preexisting moral obligation is generally unenforceable for lack of consideration

**Promissory Estoppel** doctrine that prohibits a party from denying her promise when the promisee takes action or forbearance to his detriment reasonably based upon the promise

**Promises under Seal** where still recognized, the seal acts as a substitute for consideration

**Promises Made Enforceable by Statute** some gratuitous promises have been made enforceable by statute; the Code makes enforceable (1) contract modifications, (2) renunciations, and (3) firm offers

# CASES

## CASE 12-1

### Legal Sufficiency
### PEARSALL v. ALEXANDER

District of Columbia Court of Appeals, 1990
572 A.2d 113

**Newman, J.**

In what must be a common development wherever there are state-sponsored lotteries, this is the story of two friends who split the price of a ticket only to have the ticket win and split their friendship.

Harold Pearsall appeals from the dismissal of his complaint against Joe Alexander, in which Pearsall claimed breach of an agreement to share the proceeds of a winning D.C. Lottery ticket worth $20,000. The trial court found that such an agreement did, in fact, exist, but determined that the agreement was invalid under §1 of the Statute of Anne [a statute outlawing certain forms of wagering or gaming], as enacted in D.C. Code §16–1701 [citation]. We conclude that the trial court erred in applying §16–1701 to the Pearsall-Alexander agreement and, therefore, we reverse and remand with instructions to enter judgment for the appellant.

## I

Harold Pearsall and Joe Alexander were friends for over twenty-five years. About twice a week they would get together after work, when Alexander would meet Pearsall at the Takoma Metro station in his car. The pair would then proceed to a liquor store, where they would purchase what the two liked to refer to as a "package"—a half-pint of vodka, orange juice, two cups, and two lottery tickets—before repairing to Alexander's home. There they would "scratch" the lottery tickets, drink screwdrivers, and watch television. On occasion these lottery tickets would yield modest rewards of two or three dollars, which the pair would then "plow back" into the purchase of additional lottery tickets. According to Pearsall, the two had been sharing D.C. Lottery tickets in this fashion since the Lottery began.

On the evening of December 16, 1982, Pearsall and Alexander visited the liquor store twice, buying their normal "package" on each occasion. The first package was purchased when the pair stopped at the liquor store on the way to Alexander's home from the Metro station. Pearsall went into the store alone, and when he returned to the car, he said to Alexander, in reference to the tickets, "Are you in on it?" Alexander said "Yes." When Pearsall asked Alexander for his half of the purchase price of the tickets, Alexander replied that he had no money. When they reached Alexander's home, Alexander, expressing his anxiety that Pearsall might lose the tickets, demanded that Pearsall produce them, snatched them from Pearsall's hand, and "scratched" them, only to find that both were worthless.

At about 8:00 p.m. that same evening, Alexander, who apparently had come by some funds of his own, returned to the liquor store and bought a second "package." This time Pearsall, who had been offended by Alexander's conduct earlier in taking both tickets, snatched the two tickets from Alexander and announced that he would be the one to "scratch" them. Intending only to bring what he regarded as Alexander's childish behavior to Alexander's attention, Pearsall immediately relented and gave over one of the tickets to Alexander. Each man then "scratched" one of the tickets. Pearsall's ticket proved worthless; Alexander's was a $20,000 winner.

Alexander became very excited about the ticket and began calling friends to announce the good news. Fearing that Alexander might lose the ticket, Pearsall told Alexander to sign his name on the back of the ticket. Subsequently, Alexander cashed in the ticket and received the winnings; but, when Pearsall asked for his share, Alexander refused to give Pearsall anything.

Pearsall brought suit against Alexander, claiming breach of an agreement to share the proceeds of the winning ticket. * * *

The trial court dismissed Pearsall's complaint on the public policy grounds raised by Alexander, finding that "the enforcement of contracts arising from gaming transactions is barred by the Statute of Anne, as enacted in D.C. Code" §16–1701, even when such contracts concern legalized gambling. * * *

[The court then held that the agreement involved in this case was not a gaming contract as defined in the statute.] * * *

## III

The record supports the trial court's finding that an agreement existed between Pearsall and Alexander to share equally in the proceeds of the winning ticket at issue.

The conduct of the two men on the evening of December 16, 1982, when the ticket was purchased, clearly demonstrates a meeting of the minds. After purchasing the first pair of tickets, Pearsall asked Alexander if he was "in on it." Not only did Alexander give his verbal assent, but later, when the two reached Alexander's home, Alexander, who had contributed nothing to the purchase price of the tickets, snatched *both* tickets from Pearsall and anxiously "scratched" them. It is evident from this that Alexander considered himself "in on" an agreement to share in the fortunes of the tickets purchased by his friend. It is equally clear that in giving over tickets he had purchased, Pearsall gave his assent to the agreement he had proposed earlier in the car. Moreover, this conduct took place within the context of a long-standing pattern of similar conduct, analogous to a "course of conduct" as described in the Uniform Commercial Code, which included their practice of "plowing back" small returns from winning tickets into the purchase of additional tickets.

It is also clear to us that, by exchanging mutual promises to share in the proceeds of winning tickets, adequate consideration was given by both parties. An exchange of promises is consideration, so long as it is bargained-for. [Citation.] Moreover, consideration may consist of detriment to the promisee. [Citation.] The giving over of one-half of the proceeds of a winning ticket would be a detriment to either man. Therefore, Pearsall's promise to share, as expressed in his question to Alexander, "Are you in on it?" induced a detriment in Alexander. Likewise, Alexander's promise to share, as contained in his assent, induced a detriment in Pearsall.

* * *

## IV

In conclusion, we find that there was a valid, enforceable agreement between Pearsall and Alexander to share in the proceeds of the $20,000 ticket purchased by Alexander on the evening of December 16, 1982. Therefore, we reverse and remand with instructions to enter judgment in favor of the appellant.

Reversed and remanded.

# CASE 12-2

## Preexisting Obligation
## DENNEY v. REPPERT

Court of Appeals of Kentucky, 1968
432 S. W.2d 647

**Myre, Special Commissoner**

The sole question presented in this case is which of several claimants is entitled to an award for information leading to the apprehension and conviction of certain bank robbers.

* * *

On June 12th or 13th, 1963, three armed men entered the First State Bank, Eubank, Kentucky, and with a display of arms and threats robbed the bank of over $30,000. Later in the day they were apprehended by State Policemen Garret Godby, Johnny Simms, and Tilford Reppert, placed under arrest, and the entire loot was recovered. Later all of the prisoners were convicted and Garret Godby, Johnny Simms, and Tilford Reppert appeared as witnesses at the trial.

The First State Bank of Eubank was a member of the Kentucky Bankers Association which provided and advertised a reward of $500.00 for the arrest and conviction of each bank robber. Hence the outstanding reward for the three bank robbers was $1,500.00. Many became claimants for the reward and the Kentucky State Bankers Association, being unable to determine the merits of the claims for the reward, asked the circuit court to determine the merits of the various claims and to adjudge who was entitled to receive the reward or share in it. All of the claimants were made defendants in the action.

At the time of the robbery the claimants Murrell Denney, Joyce Buis, Rebecca McCollum, and Jewell Snyder were employees of the First State Bank of Eubank and came out of the grueling situation with great credit and glory. Each one of them deserves approbation and an accolade. They were vigilant in disclosing to the public and the peace officers the details of the crime, and in describing the culprits, and giving all the information that they possessed that would be useful in capturing the robbers. Undoubtedly, they performed a great service. It is in the evidence that the claimant Murrell Denney was conspicuous and energetic in his efforts to make known the robbery, to acquaint the officers as to the personal appearance of the criminals, and to give other pertinent facts.

The first question for determination is whether the employees of the robbed bank are eligible to receive or share in the reward. The great weight of authority answers in the negative. * * *

> To the general rule that, when a reward is offered to the general public for the performance of some specified act, such reward may be claimed by any person who performs such act, is the exception of agents, employees, and public officials who are acting within the scope of their employment or official duties. * * *

* * *

At the time of the robbery the claimants Murrell Denney, Joyce Buis, Rebecca McCollum, and Jewell Snyder were employees of the First State Bank of Eubank. They were under duty to protect and conserve the resources and moneys of the bank, and safeguard every interest of the institution furnishing them employment. Each of these employees exhibited great courage and cool bravery, in a time of stress and danger. The community and the county have recompensed them in commendation, admiration, and high praise, and the world looks on them as heroes. But in making known the robbery and assisting in acquainting the public and the officers with details of the crime and with identification of the robbers, they performed a duty to the bank and the public, for which they cannot claim a reward.

The claims of Corbin Reynolds, Julia Reynolds, Alvie Reynolds, and Gene Reynolds also must fail. According to their statements they gave valuable information to the arresting officers. However, they did not follow the procedure as set forth in the offer of reward in that they never filed a claim with the Kentucky Bankers Association. It is well established that a claimant of a reward must comply with the terms and conditions of the offer of reward. [Citation.]

State Policemen Garret Godby, Johnny Simms, and Tilford Reppert made the arrest of the bank robbers and captured the stolen money. All participated in the prosecution. At the time of the arrest, it was the duty of the state policemen to apprehend the criminals. Under the law they cannot claim or share in the reward and they are interposing no claim to it.

This leaves the defendant, Tilford Reppert the sole eligible claimant. The record shows that at the time of the arrest he was a deputy sheriff in Rockcastle County, but the arrest and recovery of the stolen money took place in Pulaski County. He was out of his jurisdiction, and was thus under no legal duty to make the arrest, and is thus eligible to claim and receive the reward. In *Kentucky Bankers Ass'n et al. v. Cassady* [citation], it was said:

> It is * * * well established that a public officer with the authority of the law to make an arrest may accept an

offer of reward or compensation for acts or services performed outside of his bailiwick or not within the scope of his official duties. * * *

* * *

It is manifest from the record that Tilford Reppert is the only claimant qualified and eligible to receive the reward. Therefore, it is the judgment of the circuit court that he is entitled to receive payment of the $1,500.00 reward now deposited with the clerk of this court.

The judgment is affirmed.

---

## CASE 12-3

## Modification of a Preexisting Contract
## NEW ENGLAND ROCK SERVICES, INC. v. EMPIRE PAVING, INC.

Appellate Court of Connecticut, 1999

53 Conn.App. 771, 731 A.2d 784cert. denied, 250 Conn. 921, 738 A.2d 658

**Schaller, J.**

The defendants, Empire Paving, Inc. (Empire), and its bonding company, American Insurance Company, doing business as Fireman's Fund Insurance Company (Fireman's Fund), appeal from the judgment of the trial court awarding damages to the named plaintiff, New England Rock Services, Inc. (Rock Services), under a contract between the parties. The principal issue on appeal is whether the trial court improperly concluded that an agreement made by the parties on December 9, 1995, modified an earlier contract executed by them on October 26, 1995. We affirm the judgment of the trial court.

The following facts are relevant to the disposition of this appeal. On October 26, 1995, Empire entered into a contract with Rock Services under which Rock Services would provide drilling and blasting services as a subcontractor on the Niles Hill Road sewer project on which Empire was the general contractor and the city of New London was the owner. Pursuant to the contract, Rock Services agreed to drill and blast a certain amount of rock encountered on the sewer project. In return, Rock Services was to be paid an agreed upon price of $29 per cubic yard with an estimated amount of 5000 cubic yards, or on a time and materials basis, whichever was less.

On October 31, 1995, Rock Services commenced work on the project. From the beginning, Rock Services experienced a number of problems with the project. The primary obstacle was the presence of a heavy concentration of water on the site. The water problem hindered Rock Services' ability to complete its work as anticipated. The trial court found that it was the custom and practice in the industry for the general contractor to control the water on the site and that, on this particular job, Empire failed to control the water on the site properly. In an effort to mitigate the water problem, Rock Services attempted to "load behind the drill," a process that allows a blaster to load the drilled hole with a charge immediately after the hole is drilled, before water has the opportunity to seep into the hole. The city fire marshall, however, refused to allow Rock Services to employ this method of drilling. Thereafter, in order to complete its work, Rock Services was compelled to use the more costly and time consuming method of casing the blasting hole, a process that requires the blaster to drive a plastic casing down into the drilled hole to prevent seepage.

In late November, 1995, Rock Services advised Empire that it would be unable to complete the work as anticipated because of the conditions at the site and requested that Empire agree to amend the contract to allow Rock Services to complete the project on a time and materials basis. On December 8, 1995, Empire signed a purchase order that modified the original agreement. The modification required Empire to pay for the blasting work on a time and materials basis for the remainder of the project. Rock Services, thereafter, completed its work on the project.

Upon completion of the work, Empire refused to pay Rock Services for the remaining balance due on the time and materials agreement in the amount of $58,686.63, and Rock Services instituted this action. The trial court concluded that the later purchase order was a valid and enforceable modification of the earlier contract. The trial court found that the parties intended the purchase order to modify the earlier agreement and that Empire's assent to the modification was not made under duress but, rather, was a calculated business decision. After finding Empire's withholding of the amount due to Rock Services wrongful, the trial court awarded Rock Services damages in the amount of $58,686.63, plus interest and costs. This appeal followed.

On appeal, Empire claims that the trial court improperly found that the later purchase order was a valid and enforceable modification of the earlier contract. Specifically, Empire claims that the later agreement lacked the requisite consideration to be a valid and enforceable modification of the earlier contract. We disagree.

* * *

In concluding that the modification was valid and enforceable, the trial court determined that the later agreement was supported by sufficient consideration. * * *

> "The doctrine of consideration is fundamental in the law of contracts, the general rule being that in the absence of consideration an executory promise is unenforceable." [Citation.] While mutual promises may be sufficient consideration to bind parties to a modification; [citations] a promise to do that which one is already bound by his contract to do is not sufficient consideration to support an additional promise by the other party to the contract. [Citations.]"
>
> "A modification of an agreement must be supported by valid consideration and requires a party to do, or promise to do, something further than, or different from, that which he is already bound to do. [Citations.] It is an accepted principle of law in this state that when a party agrees to perform an obligation for another to whom that obligation is already owed, although for lesser remuneration, the second agreement does not constitute a valid, binding contract. [Citations.] The basis of the rule is generally made to rest upon the proposition that in such a situation he who promises the additional [work] receives nothing more than that to which he is already entitled and he to whom the promise is made gives nothing that he was not already under legal obligation to give. [Citations.]"

Our Supreme Court in [citation], however, articulated an exception to the preexisting duty rule: "'[W]here a contract must be performed under burdensome conditions not anticipated, and not within the contemplation of the parties at the time when the contract was made, and the promisee measures up to the right standard of honesty and fair dealing, and agrees, in view of the changed conditions, to pay what is then reasonable, just, and fair, such new contract is not without consideration within the meaning of that term, either in law or in equity.'" * * * "'What unforeseen difficulties and burdens will make a party's refusal to go forward with his contract equitable, so as to take the case out of the general rule and bring it within the exception, must depend upon the facts of each particular case. They must be substantial, unforeseen, and not within the contemplation of the parties when the contract was made. They need not be such as would legally justify the party in his refusal to perform his contract, unless promised extra pay, or to justify a court of equity in relieving him from the contract; for they are sufficient if they are of such a character as to render the party's demand for extra pay manifestly fair, so as to rebut all inference that he is seeking to be relieved from an unsatisfactory contract, or to take advantage of the necessities of the opposite party to coerce from him a promise for further compensation. Inadequacy of the contract price which is the result of an error of judgment, and not of some excusable mistake of fact, is not sufficient.'" [Citation.] * * * Empire argues strenuously that the water conditions on the site cannot qualify as a new circumstance that was not anticipated at the time the original contract was signed. * * *

Empire's argument, however, is misplaced. Rock Services does not argue that it was unaware of the water conditions on the site but, rather, that Empire's failure to control or remove the water on the site constituted the new or changed circumstance. Rock Services argues that Empire's duty to control or remove the water on the job site arose in accordance with the custom and practice in the industry and, therefore, Empire's failure to control or remove the water on the site constituted a new circumstance that Rock Services did not anticipate at the time the original contract was signed. * * *

The judgment is affirmed.

---

CASE 12-4

Past Condition/Promissory Estoppel

## DILORENZO v. VALVE AND PRIMER CORPORATION

Appellate Court of Illinois, First District, Fifth Division, 2004

807 N.E.2d 673, 283 Ill.Dec. 68

http://www.state.il.us/court/Opinions/AppellateCourt/2003/1stDistrict/June/Html/1012803.htm

**Reid, J.**

### Background

DiLorenzo was an officer, director and shareholder of 100 shares of stock of Valve & Primer. M. Chris Dickson was the chief executive officer and majority shareholder of Valve & Primer. DiLorenzo was employed by Valve & Primer for approximately 40 years prior to the events that led to this lawsuit.

According to DiLorenzo, on or about May 12, 1987, he informed Valve & Primer that he wanted incentives in any future employment agreements. DiLorenzo claims that, through Dickson, Valve & Primer offered him a 10-year stock option that would allow DiLorenzo to purchase an additional 300 shares at the fixed price of $250 per share. Dickson and the board of directors allegedly favorably voted on the agreement at a meeting held on June 8, 1987.

DiLorenzo claims he received a copy of the minutes of that meeting. DiLorenzo also claims that in reliance on the minutes of the special board meeting, which were never altered or revoked by the board of directors during the time he remained employed by Valve & Primer, he stayed in his job for over nine additional years. According to DiLorenzo, while he was working for Valve & Primer, in reliance upon the minutes of the special board meeting, when he was approached by other companies with employment opportunities he did not follow up on any of these recruitment offers.

Valve & Primer claims the 1987 employment agreement between it and DiLorenzo did not contain a stock purchase agreement. The only purported proof of the agreement is an unsigned copy of board meeting minutes of which DiLorenzo had the only copy. Valve & Primer claimed the purported minutes were inconsistent in subject matter and format from other corporate minutes it produces in the ordinary course of business.

In January 1996, DiLorenzo entered into a semi-retirement agreement with Valve & Primer. Valve & Primer claims he attempted to tender his remaining 100 shares pursuant to a stock redemption agreement. According to Valve & Primer, DiLorenzo demanded $4,000 per share for the remaining 100 shares. It claims DiLorenzo admitted he came up with the proposed share value himself and that no one of any expertise valued the stock. DiLorenzo responded that he had corporate accountants review financial statements before valuing the company's shares. Valve & Primer declined to purchase the shares at DiLorenzo's price. This resulted in a dispute between DiLorenzo and Valve & Primer through Dickson. Shortly thereafter, Valve & Primer fired DiLorenzo. After the termination, DiLorenzo claims he attempted to exercise the purported stock purchase agreement.

In addition to DiLorenzo, George Christofidis, another long-time employee, attempted to exercise the stock option. * * * In the alternative, DiLorenzo argued before the trial court that, even if the purported agreement was not found to be valid, it should be enforced along promissory estoppel grounds.

* * *

## Analysis

DiLorenzo argues on appeal that the trial court misapplied the law in finding there was insufficient consideration to support the stock option agreement. He argues that substantial continued employment is sufficient consideration for agreements entered into in the employment setting. DiLorenzo argues that he has provided consideration for the stock option. It was as an incentive for continued employment. He also argues that, even if there was an initial lack of consideration, performance may ameliorate an initial lack of consideration, if the performance was clearly invited. He claims his continued employment for nine years in reliance on the agreement satisfied the condition of the performance being invited. Here he claims Valve & Primer benefitted both from the pre-1987 employment and the post-1987 work. DiLorenzo argues that he was not promising to do something he was already obligated to do, which he concedes would not be valid consideration.

Valve & Primer responds that the trial court correctly granted it summary judgment because DiLorenzo failed to show any consideration to support the alleged stock option. Valve & Primer, without admitting that the board meeting minutes are genuine, argues that they indicate that the alleged stock option was given to "reward" him for his long service to the company. Valve & Primer's position is that, if the alleged consideration for a promise has been conferred prior to the promise upon which the alleged agreement is based, then no contract is formed. Valve & Primer also argues that the argument that the option was based, at least in part, on his claimed continued employment must fail because it relies on something DiLorenzo was already obligated to do. According to Valve & Primer, because DiLorenzo contends that the stock option vested immediately, only past performance could serve as consideration. As the trial court noted, that is insufficient consideration. * * *

In reply, DiLorenzo contends that there is sufficient consideration to support the stock option. He argues that whether the 1987 corporate minutes are authentic is not an issue on appeal. Since the trial court took the minutes as true, the appellate court should do likewise. * * *

The purported minutes of the June 8, 1987, special meeting contain the following relevant language:

> "That in order to *retain and reward* such dedication George Christofidis be given an option to purchase additional shares not to exceed 300; and that Ralph DiLorenzo be given an option to purchase additional shares not to exceed 300. Said option to be exercised within 10 years from below date at the price of $250.00 per share. Each share was to be restricted wherein the share must first be offered to Valve and Primer Corporation to be paid by Valve and Primer Corporation and held as Treasury Stock. Valve and Primer Corporation would be given 45 days to consummate the purchase. In the event that Valve and Primer Corporation did not choose to purchase, said stock would be offered to the existing shareholders on a pro rate basis also to be purchased within 45 days. And in the event the shareholders did not purchase said shares, the shares could be sold to any interested person or persons. Purchase price of shares would be based upon the book value pursuant to a certified audit of the worth of the Corporation at the time of sale."

We begin by addressing whether there was consideration for the stock options. "A stock option is the right to buy a share or shares of stock at a specified price or within a specified period." [Citation.] In order to evaluate the nature and scope of the stock options issued to DiLorenzo, we must assume, for purposes of this portion of our discussion, that DiLorenzo's corporate minutes are valid.

"A contract, to be valid, must contain offer, acceptance, and consideration; to be enforceable, the agreement must also be sufficiently definite so that its terms are reasonably certain and able to be determined." [Citation.] "A contract is sufficiently definite and certain to be enforceable if the court is able from its terms and provisions to ascertain what the parties intended, under proper rules of construction and applicable principles of equity." [Citation.] "A contract may be enforced even though some contract terms may be missing or left to be agreed upon, but if essential terms are so uncertain that there is no basis for deciding whether the agreement has been kept or broken, there is no contract." [Citation.] A bonus promised to induce an employee to continue his employment is supported by adequate consideration if the employee is not already bound by contract to continue. [Citation.] Because we are assuming the validity of the document issuing the stock options, we now turn to whether the underlying option is supported by valid consideration so as to make it a proper contract.

"Consideration is defined as the bargained-for exchange of promises or performances and may consist of a promise, an act or a forbearance." [Citation.]

> "The general principles applicable to option contracts have been long established. An option contract has two elements, an offer to do something, or to forbear, which does not become a contract until accepted; and an agreement to leave the offer open for a specified time [citation], or for a reasonable time [citation]. An option contract must be supported by sufficient consideration; and if not, it is merely an offer which may be withdrawn at any time prior to a tender of compliance. [Citation.] If a consideration of 'one dollar' or some other consideration is stated but which has, in fact, not been paid, the document is merely an offer which may be withdrawn at any time prior to a tender of compliance. The document will amount only to a continuing offer which may be withdrawn by the offer or at any time before acceptance. [Citation.] The consideration to support an option consists of 'some right, interest, profit or benefit accruing to one party, or some forbearance, detriment, loss or responsibility given, suffered or undertaken by the other' [citation]; or otherwise stated, 'Any act or promise which is of benefit to one party or disadvantage to the other * * *.'" [Citation.]

"The preexisting duty rule provides that where a party does what it is already legally obligated to do, there is no consideration because there has been no detriment." [Citation.]

Focusing on the lack of a detriment to the employee, the trial court found no valid consideration. Based upon our view of the discussion in [citation], the trial court was correct in concluding that the option contract is merely an offer which may be withdrawn at any time prior to a tender of compliance. DiLorenzo could have exercised the option the moment it was purportedly made, then immediately quit, thereby giving nothing to the employer. Though the exercise of the option would require the transfer of money for the stock, the option itself carries with it no detriment to DiLorenzo. Therefore, there was no consideration for the option.

* * *

We next address DiLorenzo's claim that he is entitled to the value of the shares of stock based upon the theory of promissory estoppel. DiLorenzo argues that the trial court misapplied the law in finding that there was insufficient reliance to support a claim for promissory estoppel. He claims that, once the trial court decided there was insufficient consideration to support the option contract, promissory estoppel should have been applied by the court to enforce the agreement as a matter of equity. DiLorenzo argues that he detrimentally relied upon Valve & Primer's promise in that he worked at Valve & Primer for an additional period in excess of nine years in reliance on the stock option agreement. * * *

Valve & Primer responds that the trial court was correct in finding insufficient reliance to support the promissory estoppel claim. Valve & Primer argues that the DiLorenzo could not satisfy the detrimental reliance prong of the promissory estoppel elements. Though DiLorenzo claimed he did not act upon offers of employment he claims were made by other companies during the course of his employment with Valve & Primer, he presented to the trial court nothing but his own testimony in support of his claim. Valve & Primer argues that, since DiLorenzo essentially is claiming his stock option vested immediately, he cannot contend that he detrimentally relied upon the purported agreement in the corporate minutes by turning down those other opportunities. * * * For purposes of promissory estoppel, if DiLorenzo's allegations are taken as true, and the purported option vested immediately, it required nothing of him in order to be exercised other than the payment of $250 per share.

"Promissory estoppel arises when (1) an unambiguous promise was made, (2) the defendant relied on the promise, (3) the defendant's reliance on the promise was reasonable, and (4) the defendant suffered a detriment." [Citation.] Whether detrimental reliance has occurred is determined according to the specific facts of each case. [Citation.]

While we would accept that, under certain circumstances, it may be possible for a relinquishment of a job offer to constitute consideration sufficient to support a contract, this is not such a case. There is nothing in the language of the corporate minutes or any other source to be found in this record to suggest that Valve & Primer conditioned the alleged stock option on DiLorenzo's promise to remain in his employment. While the corporate minutes say the alleged grant of the stock option was intended to "retain and reward," it contains no mechanism making the retention mandatory. Since the corporate minutes lack a mandatory obligation on which DiLorenzo could have reasonably detrimentally relied, and he could have elected to buy the shares of stock immediately, DiLorenzo's decision to remain on the job for the additional period of over nine years must be viewed as a voluntary act. Under those circumstances, promissory estoppel would not apply. It was, therefore, not an abuse of discretion to grant Valve & Primer's motion for summary judgment on that issue.

* * *

Affirmed.

## QUESTIONS

1. Define consideration and what is meant by legal sufficiency.
2. Discuss illusory promises, output contracts, requirements contracts, exclusive dealing contracts, and conditional contracts.
3. Explain whether preexisting public and contractual obligations satisfy the legal requirement of consideration.
4. Explain the concept of bargained-for exchange. Is this element present with past consideration or third-party beneficiaries? Explain.
5. Identify and discuss those contracts that are enforceable even though they are not supported by consideration.

## PROBLEMS

**1.** In consideration of $1,800 paid to him by Joyce, Hill gave Joyce a written option to purchase his house for $180,000 on or before April 1. Prior to April 1, Hill verbally agreed to extend the option until July 1. On May 18, Hill, known to Joyce, sold the house to Gray, who was ignorant of the unrecorded option. On May 20 Joyce sent an acceptance to Hill who received it on May 25. Is there a contract between Joyce and Hill? Explain.

**2.** **(a)** Ann owed $2,500 to Barry for services Barry rendered to Ann. The debt was due June 30, 2010. In March 2011, the debt was still unpaid. Barry was in urgent need of ready cash and told Ann that if she would pay $1,500 of the debt at once, Barry would release her from the balance. Ann paid $1,500 and stated to Barry that all claims had been paid in full. In August 2011, Barry demanded the unpaid balance and subsequently sued Ann for $1,000. Result?

**(b)** Modify the facts in (a) by assuming that Barry gave Ann a written receipt stating that all claims had been paid in full. Result?

**(c)** Modify the facts in (a) by assuming that Ann owed Barry the $2,500 on Ann's purchase of a motorcycle from Barry. Result?

**3.** **(a)** Judy orally promises her daughter, Liza, that she will give her a tract of land for her home. Liza, as intended by Judy, gives up her homestead and takes possession of the land. Liza lives there for six months and starts construction of a home. Is Judy bound to convey the real estate?

**(b)** Ralph, knowing that his son, Ed, desires to purchase a tract of land, promises to give him the $25,000 he needs for the purchase. Ed, relying on this promise, buys an option on the tract of land. Can Ralph rescind his promise?

**4.** George owed Keith $800 on a personal loan. Neither the amount of the debt nor George's liability to pay the $800 was disputed. Keith had also rendered services as a carpenter to George without any agreement as to the price to be paid. When the work was completed, an honest and reasonable difference of opinion developed between George and Keith with respect to the value of Keith's services. Upon receiving from Keith a bill of $600 for the carpentry services, George mailed in a properly stamped and addressed envelope his check for $800 to Keith. In an accompanying letter, George stated that the enclosed check was in full settlement of both claims. Keith indorsed and cashed the check. Thereafter, Keith unsuccessfully sought to collect from George an alleged unpaid balance of $600. May Keith recover the $600 from George?

**5.** The Snyder Mfg. Co., being a large user of coal, entered into separate contracts with several coal companies. In each contract it was agreed that the coal company would supply coal during the entire year in such amounts as the manufacturing company might desire to order, at a price of $41 per ton. In February the Snyder Company ordered one thousand tons of coal from Union Coal Company, one of the contracting parties. Union Coal Company delivered five hundred tons of the order and then notified Snyder Company that no more deliveries would be made and that it denied any obligation under the contract. In an action by Union Coal to collect $41 per ton for the five hundred tons of coal delivered, Snyder files a counterclaim, claiming damages of $1,500 for failure to deliver the additional five hundred tons of the order and damages of $4,000 for breach of agreement to deliver coal during the balance of the year. What contract, if any, exists between Snyder and Union?

**6.** On February 5, Devon entered into a written agreement with Gordon whereby Gordon agreed to drill a well on Devon's property for the sum of $5,000 and to complete the well on or before April 15. Before entering into the contract, Gordon made test borings and had satisfied himself as to the character of the subsurface. After two days of drilling, Gordon struck hard rock. On February 17, Gordon removed his equipment and advised Devon that the project had proved unprofitable and that he would not continue. On March 17, Devon went to Gordon and told Gordon that he would assume the risk of the enterprise and would pay Gordon $100 for each day required to drill the well, as compensation for labor, the use of Gordon's equipment, and Gordon's services in supervising the work, provided Gordon would furnish certain special equipment designed to cut through hard rock. Gordon said that the proposal was satisfactory. The work was continued by Gordon and completed in an additional fifty-eight days. Upon completion of the work, Devon failed to pay, and Gordon brought an action to recover $5,800. Devon answered that he had never become obligated to pay $100 a day and filed a counterclaim for damages in the amount of $500 for the month's delay based on an alleged breach of contract by Gordon. Decision?

**7.** Discuss and explain whether there is valid consideration for each of the following promises:

**(a)** A and B entered into a contract for the purchase and sale of goods. A subsequently promised to pay a higher price for the goods when B refused to deliver at the contract price.

**(b)** A promised in writing to pay a debt, which was due from B to C, on C's agreement to extend the time of payment for one year.

**(c)** A orally promised to pay $150 to her son, B, solely in consideration of past services rendered to A by B, for which there had been no agreement or request to pay.

**8.** Alan purchased shoes from Barbara on open account. Barbara sent Alan a bill for $10,000. Alan wrote back that two hundred pairs of the shoes were defective and offered to pay $6,000 and give Barbara his promissory note for $1,000. Barbara accepted the offer, and Alan sent his check for $6,000 and his note, in accordance with the agreement. Barbara cashed the check, collected on the note, and one month later sued Alan for $3,000. Is Barbara bound by her acceptance of the offer?

**9.** Nancy owed Sharon $1,500, but Sharon did not initiate a lawsuit to collect the debt within the time prescribed by the statute of limitations. Nevertheless, Nancy promises Sharon that she will pay the barred debt. Thereafter, Nancy refuses to pay. Sharon brings suit to collect on this new promise. Is Nancy's new promise binding? Explain.

**10.** Anthony lends money to Frank. Frank dies without having paid the loan. Frank's widow, Carol, promises Anthony to repay the loan. Upon Carol's refusal to pay the loan, Anthony brings suit against Carol for payment of the loan. Is Carol bound by her promise to pay the loan?

**11.** The parties entered into an oral contract in June, under which plaintiff agreed to construct a building for defendant on a time and materials basis, at a maximum cost of $56,146, plus sales tax and extras ordered by defendant. When the building was 90 percent completed, defendant told plaintiff he was unhappy with the whole job as "the thing just wasn't being run right." The parties then on October 17 signed a written agreement lowering the maximum cost to $52,000 plus sales tax. Plaintiff thereafter completed the building at a cost of $64,155. The maximum under the June oral agreement, plus extras and sales tax, totaled $61,040. Defendant contended that he was obligated to pay only the lower maximum fixed by the October 17 agreement. Decision?

**12.** Taylor assaulted his wife, who then took refuge in Ms. Harrington's house. The next day, Mr. Taylor entered the house and began another assault on his wife, who knocked him down and, while he was lying on the floor, attempted to cut his head open or decapitate him with an ax. Harrington intervened to stop the bloodshed, and the ax, as it was descending, fell upon her hand, mutilating it badly, but sparing Taylor his life. Afterwards, Taylor orally promised to compensate Harrington for her injury. Is Taylor's promise enforceable? Explain.

**13.** Jonnel Enterprises, Inc., contracted to construct a student dormitory at Clarion State College. On May 6, Jonnel entered into a written agreement with Graham and Long as electrical contractors to perform the electrical work and to supply materials for the dormitory. The contract price was $70,544.66. Graham and Long claim that they believed the May 6 agreement obligated them to perform the electrical work on only one wing of the building, but that three or four days after work was started, a second wing of the building was found to be in need of wiring. At that time Graham and Long informed Jonnel that they would not wire both wings of the building under the present contract, so a new contract was orally agreed upon by the parties. Under the new contract Graham and Long were obligated to wire both wings and were to be paid only $65,000, but they were relieved of the obligations to supply entrances and a heating system. Graham and Long resumed their work, and Jonnel made seven of the eight progress payments called for. When Jonnel did not pay the final payment, Graham and Long brought this action. Jonnel claims that the May 6 contract is controlling. Is Jonnel correct in its assertion? Why?

**14.** Baker entered into an oral agreement with Healey, the State distributor of Ballantine & Sons liquor products, that Ballantine would supply Baker with its products on demand and that Baker would have the exclusive agency for Ballantine within a certain area of Connecticut. Shortly thereafter the agreement was modified to give Baker the right to terminate at will. Eight months later, Ballantine & Sons revoked its agency. May Baker enforce the oral agreement? Explain.

**15.** PLM, Inc., entered into an oral agreement with Quaintance Associates, an executive "headhunter" service, for the recruitment of qualified candidates to be employed by PLM. As agreed, PLM's obligation to pay Quaintance did not depend on PLM's actually hiring a qualified candidate presented by Quaintance. After several months Quaintance sent a letter to PLM, admitting that it had so far failed to produce a suitable candidate, but included a bill for $9,806.61, covering fees and expenses. PLM responded that Quaintance's services were worth only $6,060.48, and that payment of the lesser amount was the only fair way to handle the dispute. Accordingly, PLM enclosed a check for $6,060.48, writing on the back of the check "IN FULL PAYMENT OF ANY CLAIMS QUAINTANCE HAS AGAINST PLM, INC." Quaintance cashed the check and then sued PLM for the remaining $3,746.13. Decision?

**16.** Red Owl Stores told the Hoffman family that, upon the payment of approximately $518,000, a grocery store franchise would be built for them in a new location. Upon the advice of Red Owl, the Hoffmans bought a small grocery store in their hometown in order to get management experience. After the Hoffmans operated at a profit for three months, Red Owl advised them to sell the small grocery, assuring them that Red Owl would find them a larger store elsewhere. Although selling at that point would cost them much profit, the Hoffmans followed Red Owl's directions. In addition, to raise the money required for the deal, the Hoffmans sold their bakery business in their hometown. The Hoffmans also sold their house, and moved to a new home in the city where their new store was to be located. Red Owl then informed the Hoffmans that it would take $624,100, not $518,000, to complete the deal. The family scrambled to find the additional funds. However, when told by Red Owl that it would now cost them $654,000 to get their new franchise, the Hoffmans decided to sue instead. Should Red Owl be held to its promises? Explain.

**17.** Plaintiff, Brenner, entered into a contract with the defendant, Little Red School House, Ltd., which stated that in return for a nonrefundable tuition of $1,080 Brenner's son could attend defendant's school for a year. When Brenner's ex-wife refused to enroll their son, plaintiff sought and received a verbal promise of a refund. Defendant now refuses to refund plaintiff's money for lack of consideration. Did mutual consideration exist between the parties? Explain.

**18.** Ben Collins was a full professor with tenure at Wisconsin State University in 2006. In March 2006 Parsons College, in an attempt to lure Dr. Collins from Wisconsin State, offered him a written contract promising him the rank of full professor with tenure and a salary of $55,000 for the 2006–07 academic year. The contract further provided that the College would increase his salary by $2,000 each year for the next five years. In return, Collins was to teach two trimesters of the academic year beginning in October 2006. In addition, the contract stipulated, by reference to the College's faculty bylaws, that tenured professors could be dismissed only for just cause and after written charges were filed with the Professional Problems Committee. The two parties signed the contract, and Collins resigned his position at Wisconsin State.

In February 2008, the College tendered a different contract to Collins to cover the following year. This contract reduced his salary to $45,000 with no provision for annual increments, but left his rank of full professor intact. It also required that Collins waive any and all rights or claims existing under any previous employment contracts with the College. Collins refused to sign this new contract, and Parsons College soon notified him that he would not be employed the following year. The College did not give any grounds for his dismissal; nor did it file charges with the Professional Problems Committee. As a result, Collins was forced to take a teaching position at the University of North Dakota at a substantially reduced salary. He sued to recover the difference between the salary Parsons College promised him until 2011 and the amount he earned. Decision? Will Collins prevail? Explain.

**19.** Anna Feinberg began working for the Pfeiffer Company in 1965 at age seventeen. By 2002 she had attained the position of bookkeeper, office manager, and assistant treasurer. In appreciation for her skill, dedication, and long years of service, the Pfeiffer Board of Directors resolved to increase Feinberg's monthly salary to $1,400 and to create for her a retirement plan. The plan allowed that Feinberg would be given the privilege of retiring from active duty at any time she chose and that she would receive retirement pay of $700 per month, although the Board expressed the hope that Feinberg would continue to serve the company for many years. Feinberg, however, chose to retire two years later, in 2004. The Pfeiffer Company paid Feinberg her retirement pay until 2011. The company discontinued payments, alleging that no contract had been made by the Board of Directors as there had been no consideration paid by Feinberg, and that the resolution was merely a promise to make a gift. Feinberg sued. Is the promise supported by consideration? Is the promise enforceable? Explain.

**20.** Rodney and Donna Mathis (Mathis) filed a wrongful death action against St. Alexis Hospital and several physicians, arising out of the death of their mother, Mary Mathis. Several weeks before trial, an expert consulted by Mathis notified the trial court and Mathis's counsel that, in his opinion, Mary Mathis's death was not proximately caused by the negligence of the physicians. Shortly thereafter, Mathis voluntarily dismissed the wrongful death action. Mathis and St. Alexis entered into a covenant-not-to-sue in which Mathis agreed not to pursue any claims against St. Alexis or its employees in terms of the medical care of Mary Mathis. St. Alexis, in return, agreed not to seek sanctions, including attorneys' fees and costs incurred in defense of the previously dismissed wrongful death action. Subsequently, Mathis filed a second wrongful death action against St. Alexis Hospital, among others. Mathis asked the court to rescind the covenant-not-to-sue, arguing that because St. Alexis was not entitled to sanctions in connection with the first wrongful death action, there was no consideration for the covenant-not-to-sue. Are they correct in this contention? Explain.

# CHAPTER 13
# Illegal Bargains

An essential requirement of a binding promise or agreement is legality of objective. When the formation or performance of an agreement is criminal, tortious, or otherwise contrary to public policy, the agreement is illegal and unenforceable (as opposed to being void). The law does not provide a remedy for the breach of an unenforceable agreement and thus "leaves the parties where it finds them." It is preferable to use the term *illegal bargain* or *illegal agreement* rather than *illegal contract*, because the word *contract*, by definition, denotes a legal and enforceable agreement. The illegal bargain is made unenforceable (1) to discourage such undesirable conduct and (2) to preclude the inappropriate use of the judicial process in carrying out such socially undesirable bargains.

The Restatement avoids defining the term *illegal bargain*, instead focusing upon whether public policy should bar enforcement of the agreement. By relying upon the concept of public policy, the Restatement provides the courts with greater flexibility in determining the enforceability of questioned agreements by weighing the strength of legally recognized policies against the effect that declaring a particular bargain to be against public policy would have on the contracting parties and on the public.

This chapter will discuss (1) agreements in violation of a statute, (2) agreements contrary to public policy, and (3) the effect of illegality upon agreements.



## VIOLATIONS OF STATUTES

The courts will not enforce an agreement declared illegal by statute. For example, wagering or gambling contracts are specifically declared unenforceable in most States. In addition, an agreement to violate a statute prohibiting crimes, such as murder, robbery, embezzlement, forgery, and price fixing, is unenforceable. Likewise, an agreement that is induced by criminal conduct will not be enforced. For example, if Alice enters into an agreement with Brent Co. through the bribing of Brent Co.'s purchasing agent, the agreement would be unenforceable.

### LICENSING STATUTES

Every jurisdiction has laws requiring a license for those who engage in certain trades, professions, or businesses. Common examples are licensing statutes which apply to lawyers, doctors, dentists, accountants, brokers, plumbers, and contractors. Some licensing statutes mandate schooling and/or examination, while others require only financial responsibility and/or good moral character. Whether or not a person may recover for services rendered if he has failed to comply with a licensing requirement depends upon the terms or type of licensing statute. This rule pertains only to the rights of the unlicensed party to enforce the obligations of the other party.

The statute itself may expressly provide that an unlicensed person engaged in a business or profession for which a license is required shall not recover for services rendered. Absent such statutory provision, the courts commonly distinguish between those statutes or ordinances that are **regulatory** in character and those that are enacted merely to raise **revenue** through the issuance of licenses. If the statute is regulatory, a person cannot recover for professional services unless he has the required license, as long as the public policy behind the regulatory purpose clearly outweighs the person's interest in being paid for his services. Restatement, Section 181. Some courts have gone further by balancing the penalty the unlicensed party suffers against the benefit the other party receives. In contrast, if the law is for revenue purposes only, agreements for such services are enforceable.

A regulatory license, including those issued under statutes prescribing standards for those wishing to practice law or medicine, is a measure designed to protect the public against unqualified persons. A revenue license, on the other hand, does not seek to protect against incompetent or unqualified practitioners but simply to furnish revenue. An example is a statute requiring a license of plumbers but not establishing standards of competence for those who seek to follow the trade. The courts regard such legislation as a taxing measure lacking any expression of legislative intent to preclude unlicensed plumbers from enforcing their business contracts.

◆ **SEE CASE 13-1**

### GAMBLING STATUTES

In a wager the parties stipulate that one shall win and the other lose depending upon the outcome of an event in which their sole "interest" arises from the possibility of such gain or loss. All States have legislation pertaining to gambling or wagering, and U.S. courts generally refuse to recognize the enforceability of a gambling agreement. Thus, if Arnold makes a bet with Bernice on the outcome of a ball game, the agreement is unenforceable by either party. Some States, however, now permit certain kinds of regulated gambling. Wagering conducted by governmental agencies, principally State-operated lotteries, has come to constitute an increasingly important source of public revenues.

To be distinguished from wagers are ordinary insurance contracts in which the insured, having an "insurable interest" (discussed in *Chapter 49*), pays a certain sum of money or premium in exchange for an insurance company's promise to pay a larger amount upon the occurrence of some event, such as a fire, which causes loss to the insured. Here, the agreement compensates for loss under an existing risk; it does not create an entirely new risk. In a wager, the parties contemplate gain through mere chance, whereas in an insurance contract they seek to distribute possible loss. Furthermore, most games at fast-food restaurants and grocery store drawings have been upheld because the participants need not make a purchase to be eligible for the prize.

### USURY STATUTES

A **usury statute** is a law establishing a maximum rate of permissible interest for which a lender and borrower of money may contract. Though, historically, every State had a usury law, a recent trend has been to limit or relax usury statutes. The maximum rates permitted vary greatly from State to State and among types of transactions. These statutes typically are general in their application, although certain specified types of transactions are exempted. For example, numerous States impose no limit on the rate of interest that may be charged on loans to corporations. Furthermore, some States permit the parties to contract for any rate of interest on loans made to individual proprietorships or partnerships for the purpose of carrying on a business. Moreover, there are not many protections remaining for typical consumer transactions, including those involving credit cards. (More than half of the States have no interest rate limits on credit card transactions.)

In addition to the exceptions accorded certain designated types of borrowers, a number of States have exempted specific lenders. For example, the majority of the States have enacted installment loan laws, which permit eligible lenders a return on installment loans that is higher than the applicable general interest statute would permit. These specific lender usury statutes, which have all but eliminated general usury statutes, vary greatly but generally have included small consumer loans, corporate loans, loans by small lenders, real estate mortgages, and numerous other transactions.

For a transaction to be usurious, courts usually require evidence of the following factors: (1) a loan or forbearance (2) of money (3) which is repayable absolutely and in all events (4) for which an interest charge is exacted in excess of the interest rate allowed by law. Transactions that are really loans may not be clothed with the trappings of a sale for the purpose of avoiding the usury laws.

The legal effect to be given a usurious loan varies from State to State. In a few States, the lender forfeits both principal and interest. In some jurisdictions, the lender can recover the principal but forfeits all interest. In other States, only that portion of interest exceeding the permitted maximum is forfeited. In several States, the amount forfeited is a multiple (double or treble) of the interest charged. Disposition of usurious interest already paid also varies. Some States do not allow any recovery of usurious interest paid; others allow recovery of such interest or a multiple of it.

### SUNDAY STATUTES

In the absence of a statutory prohibition, the common law does not prohibit entering into contracts on Sunday. Some States, however, have legislation, referred to as **Blue Laws**, modifying this common law rule and prohibiting certain types of commercial activity on Sunday. Even in a State which prohibits contracts on Sunday, a court nonetheless will enforce a subsequent weekday ratification of a loan made on Sunday or a promise to pay for goods sold and delivered on Sunday. In addition, Blue Laws usually do not apply to activities of "necessity" and "charity."

## VIOLATIONS OF PUBLIC POLICY

The reach of a statute may extend beyond its language. Sometimes, the courts, by analogy, use the statute and the policy it seeks to serve as a guide in determining the private contract rights of one harmed by a violation of the statute. In addition, the courts must frequently articulate the "public policy" of the State without significant help from statutory sources. This judicially declared public policy is very broad in scope, it often being said that agreements having "a tendency to be injurious to the public or the public good" are contrary to public policy. Thus, the term *public policy* eludes precise definition. Contracts raising questions of public policy include agreements that (1) restrain trade, (2) exempt or exculpate a party from liability for his own tortious conduct, (3) are unconscionable, (4) involve tortious conduct, (5) tend to obstruct the administration of justice, (6) tend to corrupt public officials or impair the legislative process, or (7) impair family relationships. This section will focus on the first four of these types of agreements.

## COMMON LAW RESTRAINT OF TRADE

A **restraint of trade** is any contract or agreement that eliminates or tends to eliminate competition or otherwise obstructs trade or commerce. One type of restraint is a **covenant not to compete**, which is an agreement to refrain from entering into a competing trade, profession, or business.

An agreement to refrain from a particular trade, profession, or business is enforceable if (1) the purpose of the restraint is to protect a property interest of the promisee and (2) the restraint is no more extensive than is reasonably necessary to protect that interest. Restraints typically arise in two situations: the sale of a business and employment contracts.

**Sale of a Business** As part of an agreement to sell a business, the seller frequently promises not to compete in that particular type of business in a *defined area* for a stated *time*. To protect the business's goodwill (an asset that the buyer has purchased), the buyer must be allowed to enforce such a covenant (promise) by the seller not to compete with the purchaser within reasonable limitations. Most litigation on this subject has involved the requirement that the restraint be no greater than is reasonably necessary. Whether the restraint is reasonable or not depends on the geographic area it covers, the time period for which it is to be effective, and the hardship it imposes on the promisor and the public.

For example, the promise of a person selling a service station business in Detroit not to enter the service station business in Michigan for the next twenty-five years is unreasonable, both as to area and time. The business interest to be protected would not include the entire State, so it is not necessary to the protection of the purchaser that the seller be prevented from engaging in the service station business in the entire State or perhaps, for that matter, in the entire city of Detroit. Limiting the area to the neighborhood in which the station is located or to a radius of a few miles probably would be adequate.

The same type of inquiry must be made about time limitations. In the sale of a service station, a twenty-five-year ban on competition from the seller would be unreasonable; a one-year ban probably would not. The court, in determining what is reasonable under particular circumstances, must consider each case on its own facts.

**Employment Contracts** Salespeople, management personnel, and other employees frequently are required to sign employment contracts prohibiting them from competing with their employers during their time of employment and for some additional stated period after termination. The same is also frequently true among corporations or partnerships involving professionals, such as accountants, lawyers, investment brokers, stockbrokers, or doctors. Although the courts readily enforce a covenant not to compete during the period of employment, the promise not to compete after termination is subjected to an even stricter test of reasonableness than that applied to noncompetition promises included in a contract for the sale of a business. One reason for this is that the employer is in a stronger bargaining position than the employee.

A court order enjoining a former employee from competing in a described territory for a stated time is the usual method by which an employer seeks to enforce the employee's promise not to compete. Before granting such injunctions, the courts insist that the employer demonstrate that the restriction is *necessary* to protect his legitimate interests, such as trade secrets or customer lists. Because issuing the injunction may place the employee out of work, the courts must carefully balance the public policy favoring the employer's right to protect his business interests against the public policy favoring full opportunity for individuals to gain employment.

Thus, one court has held unreasonable a covenant in a contract requiring a travel agency employee, after termination of her employment, to refrain from engaging in a like business in any capacity in either of two named towns or within a sixty-mile radius of those towns for two years. There was no indication that the employee had enough influence over customers to cause them to move their business to her new agency, nor was it shown that any trade secrets were involved. *United Travel Service, Inc. v. Weber*, 108 Ill. App.2d 353, 247 N.E.2d 801 (1969). Instead of refusing to enforce an unreasonable covenant, some courts, considering the action justifiable under the circumstances of the case, will reform the agreement to make it reasonable and enforceable.

Due to the rapid evolution of business practices in the Internet industry, it has been argued that noncompete agreements for Internet company employees need their own rules. *National Business Services, Inc. v. Wright* addressed the geographic scope of an Internet noncompete agreement, upholding a one-year time restriction and a territorial clause that prevented the employee from taking another Internet-related job anywhere in the United States. The court stated, "Transactions involving the Internet, unlike traditional 'sales territory' cases, are not limited by state boundaries."

◆ **SEE CASE 13-2**

## EXCULPATORY CLAUSES

Some contracts contain an exculpatory clause that excuses one party from liability for her own tortious conduct. The courts generally agree that exculpatory clauses relieving a person from tort liability for harm caused intentionally or recklessly are unenforceable as violating public policy. On the other hand, exculpatory clauses that excuse a party from liability for harm caused by negligent conduct are scrutinized carefully by the courts, which often require that the clause be conspicuously placed in the contract and clearly written. Accordingly, an exculpatory clause on the reverse side of a parking lot claim check, which attempts to relieve the parking lot operator of liability for negligently damaging the customer's automobile, will generally be held unenforceable as against public policy.

The Restatement provides that exculpatory clauses excusing negligent conduct are unenforceable on grounds of public policy if they exempt (1) an employer from liability to an employee, (2) a public service business (such as a common carrier) from liability to a customer, or (3) a person from liability to a party who is a member of a protected class. Restatement, Section 195. For example, a railroad company will not be permitted to avoid liability for the negligent operation or maintenance of its trains.

A similar rule applies to a contractual provision unreasonably exempting a party from the legal consequences of a misrepresentation. Restatement, Section 196. Such a term is unenforceable on the grounds of public policy with respect to both fraudulent and nonfraudulent misrepresentations.

Further, where the superior bargaining position of one party has enabled him to impose upon the other party such a provision, the courts are inclined to nullify the provision. Such a situation may arise in residential leases exempting a landlord from liability for his negligence. Moreover, an exculpatory clause may be unenforceable for unconscionability.

◆ **SEE CASE 13-3**

## UNCONSCIONABLE CONTRACTS

The court may scrutinize every contract of sale to determine whether it is, in its commercial setting, purpose, and effect, **unconscionable**. The court may refuse to enforce an unconscionable contract in its entirety or any part it finds to be unconscionable. Section 2–302 of the UCC provides:

> If the court as a matter of law finds the contract or any clause of the contract to have been unconscionable at the time it was made the court may refuse to enforce the contract, or it may enforce the remainder of the contract without the unconscionable clause, or it may so limit the application of any unconscionable clause as to avoid any unconscionable result.

Similarly, Section 208 of the Restatement parallels this provision and provides:

> If a contract or term thereof is unconscionable at the time the contract is made a court may refuse to enforce the contract, or may enforce the remainder of the contract without the unconscionable term, or may so limit the application of any unconscionable term as to avoid any unconscionable result.

Neither the Code nor the Restatement defines the word *unconscionable*; however, the *New Webster's Dictionary* (Deluxe Encyclopedic Edition) defines the term as "contrary to the dictates of conscience; unscrupulous or unprincipled; exceeding that which is reasonable or customary; inordinate, unjustifiable."

The doctrine of unconscionability has been justified on the basis that it permits the courts to resolve issues of unfairness explicitly as regards that unfairness without recourse to formalistic rules or legal fictions. In policing contracts for fairness, the courts have again demonstrated their willingness to limit freedom of contract to protect the less advantaged from overreaching by dominant contracting parties. The doctrine of unconscionability has evolved through its application by the courts to include both procedural and substantive unconscionability.

**Procedural unconscionability** involves scrutiny for the presence of "bargaining naughtiness." In other words, was the negotiation process fair, or were there procedural irregularities, such as burying important terms of the agreement in fine print or obscuring the true meaning of the contract with impenetrable legal jargon?

**Substantive unconscionability**, which involves the actual terms of the contract, consists of oppressive or grossly unfair provisions, such as an exorbitant price or an unfair exclusion or limitation of contractual remedies. An all-too-common example is that involving a necessitous buyer in an unequal bargaining position with a seller, who consequently obtains an exorbitant price for his product or service. In one case, a court held unconscionable a price of $749 ($920 on time) for a vacuum cleaner that cost the seller $140. In another case the buyers, welfare recipients, purchased by time payment contract a home freezer unit for $900 which, when added to time credit charges, credit life insurance, credit property insurance, and sales tax, amounted to $1,235. The purchase resulted from a visit to the buyer's home by a salesman representing Your Shop At Home Service, Inc.; the maximum retail value of the freezer unit at time of purchase was $300. The court held the contract unconscionable and reformed it by reducing the price to the total payment ($620) the buyers had managed to make.

Some courts hold that in order for a contract to be unenforceable both substantive and procedural unconscionability must be present. Nevertheless, they need not exist to the same degree; the more oppressive one is, the less evidence of the other is required.

Closely akin to the concept of unconscionability is the doctrine of contracts of adhesion. A standard-form contract prepared by one party, an **adhesion contract** generally involves the preparer's offering the other party the contract on a "take-it-or-leave-it" basis. Such contracts are not automatically unenforceable but are subject to greater scrutiny for procedural or substantive unconscionability.

◆ **SEE CASE 13-4**

### TORTIOUS CONDUCT

"A promise to commit a tort or to induce the commission of a tort is unenforceable on grounds of public policy." Restatement, Section 192. The courts will not permit contract law to violate the law of torts. Any agreement attempting to do so is considered contrary to public policy. For example, Andrew and Barlow Co. enter into an agreement under which Andrew promises Barlow that in return for $5,000 he will disparage the product of Barlow Co.'s competitor Cosmo, Inc., in order to provide Barlow Co. with a competitive advantage. Andrew's promise is to commit the tort of disparagement and is unenforceable as contrary to public policy.

## EFFECT OF ILLEGALITY

As a general rule, illegal contracts are unenforceable. In a few instances, however, one of the parties may be permitted to enforce all or part of the contract; whereas, under other circumstances, the courts will allow one party to recover in restitution for his performance of the illegal contract.

### GENERAL RULE: UNENFORCEABILITY

In most cases when an agreement is illegal, neither party can successfully sue the other for breach or recover for any performance rendered. Whichever party is plaintiff is immaterial to the courts. As is frequently said in these cases, the court will leave the parties where it finds them.

### EXCEPTIONS

The courts recognize several exceptions to the general rule regarding the effect of illegality on a contract and may, after considering the circumstances surrounding a particular contract, grant relief to one of the parties, though not to the other. The following sections will consider these exceptions.

**Party Withdrawing before Performance** A party to an illegal agreement may, prior to performance, withdraw from the transaction and recover whatever she has contributed, if the party has not engaged in serious misconduct. Restatement, Section 199. A common example is recovery of money left with a stakeholder pursuant to a wager before it is paid over to the winner.

**Party Protected by Statute** Sometimes an agreement is illegal because it violates a statute designed to protect persons in the position of one of the parties. For example, State "Blue Sky Laws" prohibiting the sale of unregistered securities are designed primarily for the protection of investors. In such cases, even though there is an unlawful agreement, the statute usually expressly gives the purchaser the right to rescind the sale and recover the money paid.

**Party Not Equally at Fault** Where one of the parties is less at fault than the other, he will be allowed to recover payments made or property transferred. Restatement, Section 198. For example, this exception would apply where one party induces the other to enter into an illegal bargain through fraud, duress, or undue influence.

**Excusable Ignorance** An agreement that appears on its face to be entirely permissible may, nevertheless, be illegal by reason of facts and circumstances of which one of the parties is completely unaware. For example, a man and woman make mutual promises to marry, but unknown to the woman, the man is already married. This is an agreement to commit the crime of bigamy, and the marriage, if entered into, is void. In such case the courts permit the party who is ignorant of the illegality to maintain a lawsuit against the other party for damages.

A party may also be excused for ignorance of relatively minor legislation. Restatement, Section 180. For instance, Jones and Old South Building Co. enter into a contract to build a factory that contains specifications in violation of the town's building ordinance. Jones did not know of the violation and had no reason to know. Old South's promise to build would not be rendered unenforceable on grounds of public policy, and Jones would have a claim against Old South for damages for breach of contract.

**Partial Illegality** A contract may be partly unlawful and partly lawful. The courts view such a contract in one of two ways. First, the partial illegality may be held to taint the entire contract with illegality, so that it is wholly unenforceable. Second, it may be possible to separate the illegal from the legal part, in which case the court will hold the illegal part unenforceable but will enforce the legal part. For example, if a contract contains an illegal covenant not to compete, the covenant will not be enforced, though the rest of the contract may be.

## CHAPTER SUMMARY

| | |
|---|---|
| **VIOLATIONS OF STATUTES** | **General Rule** the courts will not enforce agreements declared illegal by statute<br>**Licensing Statutes** require formal authorization to engage in certain trades, professions, or businesses<br>• ***Regulatory License*** licensing statute that is intended to protect the public against unqualified persons; an unlicensed person may not recover for services she has performed<br>• ***Revenue License*** licensing statute that seeks to raise money; an unlicensed person may recover for services he has performed<br>**Gambling Statutes** prohibit wagers, which are agreements that one party will win and the other lose depending upon the outcome of an event in which their only interest is the gain or loss<br>**Usury Statutes** establish a maximum rate of interest<br>**Sunday Statutes** prohibition of certain types of commercial activity on Sunday (also called Blue Laws) |
| **VIOLATIONS OF PUBLIC POLICY** | **Common Law Restraint of Trade** unreasonable restraints of trade are not enforceable<br>• ***Sale of a Business*** the promise by the seller of a business not to compete in that particular business in a reasonable geographic area for a reasonable period of time is enforceable<br>• ***Employment Contracts*** an employment contract prohibiting an employee from competing with his employer for a reasonable period following termination is enforceable provided the restriction is necessary to protect legitimate interests of the employer<br>**Exculpatory Clauses** the courts generally disapprove of contractual provisions excusing a party from liability for her own tortious conduct<br>**Unconscionable Contracts** unfair or unduly harsh agreements are not enforceable<br>• ***Procedural Unconscionability*** unfair or irregular bargaining<br>• ***Substantive Unconscionability*** oppressive or grossly unfair contractual terms<br>**Tortious Conduct** an agreement that requires a person to commit a tort is unenforceable<br>**Corrupting Public Officials** agreements that corrupt public officials are not enforceable |
| **EFFECT OF ILLEGALITY** | **Unenforceability** neither party may recover under an illegal agreement where both parties are *in pari delicto* (in equal fault)<br>**Exceptions** permit one party to recover payments<br>• ***Party Withdrawing before Performance***<br>• ***Party Protected by Statute***<br>• ***Party Not Equally at Fault***<br>• ***Excusable Ignorance***<br>• ***Partial Illegality*** |

# CASES

CASE 13-1

## Licensing Statutes
## PACIFIC CUSTOM POOLS, INC. v. TURNER CONSTRUCTION COMPANY

Court of Appeal, Second District, Division 4, California, 2000
79 Cal.App.4th 1254, 94 Cal.Rptr.2d 756
http://caselaw.lp.findlaw.com/data2/CaliforniaStateCases/B122853.doc

**Berle, J.**

On this * * * appeal, Pacific Custom Pools, Inc., challenges the trial court's granting of summary judgment based on the failure of Pacific Custom Pools to substantially comply with the contractor's licensing requirements, * * *. We hold that the trial court properly granted summary judgment * * *.

### Factual Background and Procedural History

Universal City Studios, Inc. ("Universal") entered into a general contract with Turner Construction Company ("Turner") for the construction of the Jurassic Park ride (the "project") at the theme park in Universal City, California. In turn, Turner entered into a subcontract ("the Agreement") on the project with Pacific Custom Pools, Inc. ("PCP"), pursuant to which PCP agreed to furnish and install all water treatment work for the project for the contract price of $959,131. PCP further subcontracted its work to Harrington Industrial Plastics, Inc. ("Harrington") and Pacific Engineered Projects ("PEP") for those companies to provide materials and supplies on the project. PCP performed work on the project from April 1995 until June 1996 for which it was paid $897,719. During the period of October 12, 1995 to March 14, 1996, PCP's contractor's license was under suspension, and although the license had also expired as of January 31, 1996, it was not renewed until May 5, 1996.

[PCP brought suit against Universal and Turner, the defendants, for the remainder of the contract price. The trial court granted the defendants' motion for summary judgment on the basis that PCP had not been licensed in California and thus could not bring suit. PCP appealed.]

* * *

### *Doctrine of Substantial Compliance with Licensing Requirements*

Section 7031, subdivision (a) provides that a contractor may not maintain an action for the recovery of compensation for the performance of work requiring a license unless it was "a duly licensed contractor at all times during the performance of that" work. In *Hydrotech Systems, Ltd. v. Oasis Waterpark* (1991) [citation] the [California] Supreme Court set forth the social policy underpinning section 7031:

> The purpose of the licensing law is to protect the public from incompetence and dishonesty in those who provide building and construction services. [Citation.] The licensing requirements provide minimal assurance that all persons offering such services in California have the requisite skill and character, understand applicable local laws and codes, and know the rudiments of administering a contracting business. [Citation.]
>
> "Section 7031 advances this purpose by withholding judicial aid from those who seek compensation for unlicensed contract work. The obvious statutory intent is to discourage persons who have failed to comply with the licensing law from offering or providing their unlicensed services for pay.
>
> "Because of the strength and clarity of this policy, it is well settled that section 7031 applies despite injustice to the unlicensed contractor. 'Section 7031 represents a legislative determination that the importance of deterring unlicensed persons from engaging in the contracting business outweighs any harshness between the parties, and that such deterrence can best be realized by denying violators the right to maintain any action for compensation in the courts of this state. [Citation.]' * * *"

Through a series of cases beginning in 1966, the courts attempted to alleviate the severity of the application of section 7031 by allowing recovery to a contractor who has substantially complied with the licensing statutory scheme. [Citations.]

In reaction to this development in the law, the Legislature amended section 7031 in 1989 to add a subsection (d) which provided that the substantial compliance doctrine shall not apply to that statute. [Citations.] In 1991, the Legislature further amended section 7031 to provide an exception to the prohibition of the substantial compliance doctrine where noncompliance with licensure requirements was the result of inadvertent clerical error or other error or delay not caused by the negligence of the licensee. [Citation.]

* * *

An unlicensed contractor may thus avoid the consequences of the prohibition against the substantial compliance doctrine under section 7031, subd. (d) if the contractor proves that it had been licensed before performing work, acted reasonably in trying to maintain a license and did not know or reasonably should not have known that it was not licensed. The parties concur that PCP was licensed before commencing work on the project. However, the parties dispute whether PCP acted reasonably and in good faith to maintain its license, and whether PCP knew or should have reasonably known that it was not licensed.* * *

In * * * the case at bar: (a) PCP was aware in November 1995 that its license was suspended for failure to file a judgment bond and that the deadline date for license renewal was January 31, 1996; (b) PCP knew shortly after February 23, 1996 that a renewal application sent in February 1996 was untimely; and (c) that PCP was advised on April 22, 1996 that its license had not been renewed because PCP's filing fee check had been dishonored. These facts do not suggest that PCP acted reasonably or in good faith to maintain licensure or that PCP did not know or reasonably should not have known that it was not duly licensed, to support a claim of substantial compliance within the meaning of section 7031.

* * *

The summary judgment is affirmed * * *.

## CASE 13-2

Restraint of Trade

## PAYROLL ADVANCE, INC. v. YATES

Missouri Court of Appeals, 2008

270 S.W.3d 428

http://caselaw.findlaw.com/mo-court-of-appeals/1038798.html

**Barney, J.**

Payroll Advance, Inc. ("Appellant") appeals from the judgment of the trial court entered in favor of Barbara Yates ("Respondent") on Appellant's petition for injunctive relief and breach of contract of an "Employment Agreement" ("the Employment Agreement") which contains a covenant not to compete. * * *

* * *

[T]he record reveals that Appellant, a foreign corporation, is licensed to transact business in the State of Missouri and has numerous locations throughout the state, including a branch located in Kennett, Missouri. [Footnote: Appellant is "a payday loan company. [It] gives loans to clients out in the community." As best we discern the record, loans are made for short periods of time at high rates of interest. Appellant's manager testified that a payday loan company such as Appellant's is not like a bank because banks "normally [do not do] short-term loans." She also distinguished Appellant's entity from a title loan company or a debt consolidation concern.] It is customary for each of Appellant's branch offices to employ a sole employee at each branch and that sole employee is typically referred to as the manager of that particular branch. In June of 1998, Respondent was hired as the manager of the branch office in Kennett. On November 19, 1999, as a condition of her continued employment, Appellant presented Respondent with the Employment Agreement which included * * *, a provision entitled "NON-COMPETE" ("the covenant not to compete"). This provision set out:

> [Respondent] agrees not to compete with [Appellant] as owner, manager, partner, stockholder, or employee in any business that is in competition with [Appellant] and within a 50 mile radius of [Appellant's] business for a period of two (2) years after termination of employment or [Respondent] quits or [Respondent] leaves employment of [Appellant].

Respondent was employed with Appellant from June of 1998 through November 8, 2007, when Respondent was apparently fired for cause.

Approximately thirty-two days after being terminated by Appellant, Respondent became employed with Check Please, one of the approximately fourteen other payday loan establishments in the area. At Check Please, Respondent performed basically the same duties such as office management and customer care as she had when employed with Appellant.

On February 7, 2008, Appellant filed its "First Amended Petition for Injunctive Relief and Breach of Contract." In this petition, Appellant brought Count I for injunctive relief to prevent Respondent from soliciting its clients for her new employer, and to stop her from using client information she purportedly obtained from her time with Appellant. Count II of the petition was for damages for breach of contract for violation of the covenant not to compete together with attorney fees and costs.

* * *

On February 14, 2008, the trial court entered its judgment which found "[n]o evidence exists that, following [Appellant's] termination of [Respondent's] ten year period of employment, [Respondent] removed any customer list or other documents from [Appellant's] place of business [or] ... made any personal or other contact with any previous or present customer of [Appellant's] business or intends to do so." The trial court further determined that that if the covenant not to compete was enforced as requested, Respondent will be prohibited from engaging in employment with any payday loan business in at least 126 cities situated in Missouri, Arkansas and Tennessee ([p]resumably [Respondent] also would be prohibited from such employment within a 50-mile radius of [Appellant's] 17 other locations scattered throughout the State of Missouri. Further, [Respondent] arguably also would be prohibited from employment at a bank, savings and loan company, credit union, pawn shop or title-loan company within such geographical areas....)

Accordingly, in its discretion, the trial court found "the above result would be unreasonable under the facts and circumstances of the particular industry, agreement, and geographic location here involved." The trial court then ruled in favor of Respondent and against Appellant. The trial court also denied Respondent's request for attorney's fees and costs. This appeal followed.

* * *

"Generally, because covenants not to compete are considered to be restraints on trade, they are presumptively void and are enforceable only to the extent that they are demonstratively reasonable." [Citations.] "Non-competition agreements are not favored in the law, and the party attempting to enforce a noncompetition agreement has the burden of demonstrating both the necessity to protect the claimant's legitimate interests and that the agreement is reasonable as to time and space." [Citation.]

> There are at least four valid and conflicting concerns at issue in the law of non-compete agreements. First, the employer needs to be able to engage a highly trained workforce to be competitive and profitable, without fear that the employee will use the employer's business secrets against it or steal the employer's customers after leaving employment. Second, the employee must be mobile in order to provide for his or her family and to advance his or her career in an ever-changing marketplace. This mobility is dependent upon the ability of the employee to take his or her increasing skills and put them to work from one employer to the next. Third, the law favors the freedom of parties to value their respective interests in negotiated contracts. And, fourth, contracts in restraint of trade are unlawful. [Citation.]

"Missouri courts balance these concerns by enforcing non-compete agreements in certain limited circumstances." [Citation.] "Non-compete agreements are typically enforceable so long as they are reasonable. In practical terms, a non-compete agreement is reasonable if it is no more restrictive than is necessary to protect the legitimate interests of the employer." [Citation.] Furthermore, "[n]on-compete agreements are enforceable to the extent they can be narrowly tailored geographically and temporally." [Citation.] Lastly, it is not "necessary for the employer to show that actual damage has occurred, in order to obtain an injunction. The actual damage might be very hard to determine, and this is one reason for granting equitable relief." [Citation.]

Here, viewing the evidence in a light most favorable to the trial court's holding, [citation], it is clear the trial court took umbrage with the covenant's restrictive provisions and geographical limitations on Respondent's [Yates'] ability to find employment.

* * *

The question of reasonableness of a restraint is to be determined according to the facts of the particular case and hence requires a thorough consideration of all surrounding circumstances, including the subject matter of the contract, the purpose to be served, the situation of the parties, the extent of the restraint, and the specialization of the business.

* * *

Here, the covenant not to compete grandly declares that Respondent cannot "compete with Appellant [Payroll] as owner, manager, partner, stockholder, or employee *in any business* that is in competition with [Appellant] and within a 50 mile radius of [Appellant's] business...." (Emphasis added.) There was evidence from Appellant's representative at trial that Appellant has seventeen branch offices in Missouri and still other locations in Arkansas. If this Court interprets the plain meaning of the covenant not compete as written, the covenant not to compete would prevent Respondent not only from working at a competing business within 50 miles of the branch office in Kennett, Missouri, but Respondent would also be barred from working in a competing business within 50 miles of *any* of Appellant's branch offices. Under this interpretation, Respondent would be greatly limited in the geographic area she could work.

Additionally, the covenant not to compete bars Respondent from working at "any business that is in competition with [Appellant]." Yet, it fails to set out with precision what is to be considered a competing business and certainly does not specify that it only applies to other payday loan businesses. In that Appellant is in the business of making loans, it could be inferred that in addition to barring Respondent's employment at a different payday loan establishment the covenant not to compete also bars her from being employed anywhere loans are made including banks, credit unions, savings and loan organizations, title-loan companies, pawn shops, and other financial organizations. Such a restraint on the geographic scope of Respondent's employment and upon her type of employment is unduly burdensome and unreasonable. [Citation.]

* * *

Appellant's second point relied on asserts the trial court erred in denying its petition because [t]he trial court erroneously applied the law in failing to modify the covenant not to compete to a geographic scope it found to be reasonable in that the court found the geographic scope to be unreasonable for the payday loan industry but failed to modify the covenant not to compete to reflect a geographic scope that would be reasonable and enforceable.

* * * This Court "recognize[s] that an unreasonable restriction against competition in a contract may be modified and enforced to the extent that it is reasonable, regardless of the covenant's form of wording." * * *

Having reviewed the record in this matter, it appears the record is devoid of a request by Appellant for modification of the covenant not to compete either in its pleadings, at trial, or in its motion for new trial before the trial court. It is settled law that "'appellate courts are merely courts of review for trial court errors, and there can be no review of matter which has not been presented to or expressly decided by the trial court.'" [Citation.]

* * *

The judgment of the trial court is affirmed.

## CASE 13-3

### Exculpatory Clauses

### ANDERSON v. MCOSKAR ENTERPRISES, INC.

Court of Appeals of Minnesota, 2006

712 N.W.2d 796

http://caselaw.findlaw.com/mn-court-of-appeals/1324756.html

**Shumaker, J.**

* * *

Respondent McOskar Enterprises, Inc. owns and operates a fitness and health club in Monticello known as "Curves for Women." [Plaintiff/] Appellant Tammey J. Anderson joined the club on April 2, 2003.

As part of the registration requirements, Anderson read an "AGREEMENT AND RELEASE OF LIABILITY," initialed each of the three paragraphs in the document, and dated and signed it. The first paragraph purported to release Curves from liability for injuries Anderson might sustain in participating in club activities or using club equipment:

> In consideration of being allowed to participate in the activities and programs of Curves for Women® and to use its facilities, equipment and machinery in addition to the payment of any fee or charge, I do hereby waive, release and forever discharge Curves International Inc., Curves for Women®, and their officers, agents, employees, representatives, executors, and all others (Curves® representatives) from any and all responsibilities or liabilities from injuries or damages arriving [sic] out of or connected with my attendance at Curves for Women®, my participation in all activities, my use of equipment or machinery, or any act or omission, including negligence by Curves® representatives.

The second paragraph provided for Anderson's acknowledgment that fitness activities "involve a risk of injury" and her agreement "to expressly assume and accept any and all risks of injury or death."

After completing the registration, Anderson began a workout, primarily with machines, under the supervision of a trainer. About 15 or 20 minutes later, having used four or five machines, Anderson developed a headache in the back of her head. She contends that she told the trainer, who suggested that the problem was likely just a previous lack of use of certain muscles and that Anderson would be fine.

Anderson continued her workout and developed pain in her neck, shoulder, and arm. She informed the trainer but continued to exercise until she completed the program for that session.

The pain persisted when Anderson returned home. She then sought medical attention, eventually had a course of physical therapy, and, in June 2003, underwent a cervical diskectomy. She then started this lawsuit for damages, alleging that Curves had been negligent in its acts or omissions during her workout at the club.

Curves moved for summary judgment on the ground that Anderson had released the club from liability for negligence. The district court agreed and granted the motion. Anderson challenges the court's ruling on appeal.

* * *

It is settled Minnesota law that, under certain circumstances, "parties to a contract may, without violation of public policy, protect themselves against liability resulting from their own negligence." [Citation.] The "public interest in freedom of contract is preserved by recognizing [release and exculpatory] clauses as valid." [Citation.]

Releases of liability are not favored by the law and are strictly construed against the benefited party. [Citation.] "If the clause is either ambiguous in scope or purports to release the benefited party from liability for intentional, willful or wanton acts, it will not be enforced." [Citation.] Furthermore, even if a release clause is unambiguous in scope and is limited only to negligence, courts must still ascertain whether its enforcement will contravene public policy. On this issue, a two-prong test is applied:

> Before enforcing an exculpatory clause, both prongs of the test are examined, to-wit: (1) whether there was a disparity of bargaining power between the parties (in terms of a compulsion to sign a contract containing an unacceptable provision and the lack of ability to negotiate elimination of the unacceptable provision) … and (2) the types of services being offered or provided (taking into consideration whether it is a public or essential service).
>
> [Citation.]

The two-prong test describes what is generally known as a "contract of adhesion," more particularly explained in *Schlobohm*:

> It is a contract generally not bargained for, but which is imposed on the public for *necessary* service on a "take it or leave it" basis. Even though a contract is on a printed form and offered on a "take it or leave it" basis, those facts alone do not cause it to be an adhesion contract. There must be a showing that the parties were greatly disparate in bargaining power, that there was no opportunity for negotiation *and* that the services could not be obtained elsewhere.
>
> [Citation.]

* * *

* * * There is nothing in the Curves release that expressly exonerates the club from liability for any intentional, willful, or wanton act. Thus, we consider whether the release is ambiguous in scope.

* * *

Anderson argues that the release is ambiguous because it broadly exonerates Curves from liability for "any act or omission, including negligence…." * * *

* * *

The vice of ambiguous language is that it fails precisely and clearly to inform contracting parties of the meaning of their ostensible agreement. Because ambiguous language is susceptible of two or more reasonable meanings, each party might carry away from the agreement a different and perhaps contradictory understanding. In the context of a release in connection with an athletic, health, or fitness activity, the consumer surely is entitled to know precisely what liability is being exonerated. A release that is so vague, general, or broad as to fail to specifically designate the particular nature of the liability exonerated is not enforceable. [Citation.]

* * * It is clear from this release that Anderson agreed to exonerate Curves from liability for negligence, that being part of the express agreement that Anderson accepted and it is solely negligence of which Curves is accused.

The unmistakable intent of the parties to the Curves agreement is that Curves at least would not be held liable for acts of negligence. * * *

* * *

Even if a release is unambiguously confined to liability for negligence, it still will be unenforceable if it contravenes public policy. Anderson contends that the Curves contract is one of adhesion characterized by such a disparity in bargaining power that she was compelled to sign it without any ability to negotiate.

But her argument is unpersuasive in view of the *Schlobohm* holding that "an adhesion contract is … forced upon an unwilling and often unknowing public for services that cannot readily be obtained elsewhere." [Citation.] It is, according to *Schlobohm*, a contract "imposed on the public for *necessary* service on a 'take it or leave it' basis." *Schlobohm* involved a "gym or health spa" known as Spa Petite. Similar to Curves, it offered fitness services and required members to sign a contract that provided for a release of liability for negligence. The supreme court found no disparity in bargaining power between Spa Petite and the litigating member; found that there had been no showing that the spa's services were necessary or that they could not have been obtained elsewhere; and found that health and fitness clubs ordinarily are not within the public-service or public-necessity classification that make their services of great public importance and necessary for the public to obtain.

Even if there was a disparity of bargaining ability here—which has not been demonstrated—there was no showing that the services provided by Curves are necessary and unobtainable elsewhere. * * *

The Curves release did not contravene public policy, and we adopt the supreme court's conclusion in *Schlobohm*: "Here there is no special legal relationship and no overriding public interest which demand that this contract provision, voluntarily entered into by competent parties, should be rendered ineffectual." [Citation.]

* * *

The district court did not err in granting respondent's motion for summary judgment on the ground that appellant signed and agreed to a release of respondent's liability for negligence. We affirm.

## CASE 13-4

### Unconscionable Contract
### SANCHEZ v. WESTERN PIZZA ENTERPRISES, INC.

Court of Appeal, Second District, California., 2009
90 Cal.Rptr.3d 818, 172 Cal.App.4th 154
http://www.lawlink.com/research/CaseLevel3/86571

**Croskey, J.**

* * * [Octavio] Sanchez works as a delivery driver at a Domino's Pizza restaurant owned by Western Pizza. He drives his own car in making deliveries. His hourly wage has ranged from the legal minimum wage to approximately 50 cents above minimum wage. Western Pizza reimburses him at a fixed rate of 80 cents per delivery regardless of the number of miles driven or actual expenses incurred.

Sanchez and Western Pizza are parties to an undated arbitration agreement. The record does not indicate when the parties signed the agreement. The agreement states that the execution of the agreement "is not a mandatory condition of employment." It states that any dispute that the parties are unable to resolve informally will be submitted to binding arbitration before an arbitrator "selected from the then-current Employment Arbitration panel of the Dispute Eradication Services," and that the arbitrator must be approved by both parties. It states that the parties waive the right to a jury trial. It also states that the arbitration fees will be borne by Western Pizza and, "Except as otherwise required by law, each party shall bear its own attorney fees and costs."

The arbitration agreement states that the arbitrator "shall be responsible for resolving any disputes over the interpretation or application of this Arbitration Agreement." It also states, "[e]xcept as expressly provided, the interpretation, scope and enforcement of this ADR Agreement and all procedural issues shall be governed by the procedural and substantive provisions of the Federal Arbitration Act * * *.

The arbitration agreement also provides a procedure for small claims: "If either Party asserts that a dispute involves an amount in controversy that is too small to warrant resolution by standard arbitration procedures, the claim may be resolved by a summary small claims procedure (the 'Small Claims Procedure'). The Parties shall meet and confer to agree on whether the use of a Small Claims Procedure is appropriate in light of the nature and amount of the claim and, if so, what dispute resolution procedures are most appropriate. To the extent the Parties are unable to agree, the Arbitrator shall decide whether and to what extent a Small Claims Procedure shall apply. The Small Claims Procedure may involve relaxed rules of evidence, the use of broad principles of equity in place of strict application of law, telephonic hearings, and such other economic procedures as the Arbitrator deems appropriate under the circumstances of the dispute and consistent with due process. In no event, however, shall the Arbitrator utilize a Small Claims Procedure for a dispute involving a claim in excess of $50,000."

The arbitration agreement includes a waiver of class arbitration, stating: "the Arbitrator shall not consolidate or combine the resolution of any claim or dispute between the two Parties to this ADR Agreement with the resolution of any claim by any other party or parties, including but not limited to any employee of the Company. * * *

* * *

Sanchez filed a putative class action complaint against Western Pizza in August 2007. He alleges that Western Pizza does not record the number of miles driven by its delivery drivers but instead reimburses them at the rate of 80 cents per delivery. He alleges that the drivers not only are not adequately reimbursed for their expenses incurred in the performance of their job duties, but also as a result are paid less than the legal minimum wage. * * *

Western Pizza asked Sanchez, through their respective counsel, if he would submit the dispute to binding arbitration and provided a copy of the arbitration agreement. Sanchez's counsel responded that the class arbitration waiver was unenforceable, that the agreement impermissibly restricted the right to discovery, and that the agreement purported to require the use of an arbitrator whose website included a testimonial by a former colleague of the defendant's counsel who stated that the arbitrator had persuaded the plaintiff to "'settle for a very small sum.'" Sanchez's counsel stated that Sanchez would submit to arbitration only if the class arbitration waiver and the provisions for small claims and a referee were stricken from the agreement and the arbitration proceeded as a class arbitration before JAMS or AAA.

Western Pizza moved to compel arbitration and stay the action. * * *

Western Pizza argued in reply that only an arbitrator could determine the enforceability of the class arbitration waiver or the unconscionability of the arbitration agreement as a whole, that the class arbitration waiver was not unenforceable under [citation] and that the arbitration agreement was not unconscionable.

The trial court at the hearing on the motion * * * stated, "we have an individual plaintiff with a small claim who would otherwise be unable to afford legal services, and the class action would be an appropriate mechanism by which he could, in effect, bundle his claim with other claims and make it more efficient and expedient." The court also stated that the "small claims procedure" did not allow discovery in cases where the amount in dispute was up to $50,000, and that the agreement waived other rights and was procedurally and substantively unconscionable. * * * Western Pizza timely appealed the order.

* * *

Western Pizza contends * * * the arbitration agreement is neither procedurally nor substantively unconscionable.

* * *

Procedural and substantive unconscionability must both be present to justify the refusal to enforce a contract or clause based on unconscionability. [Citation.] Procedural unconscionability focuses on oppression or unfair surprise, while substantive unconscionability focuses on overly harsh or one-sided terms. [Citations.] The more procedural unconscionability is present, the less substantive unconscionability is required to justify a determination that a contract or clause is unenforceable. Conversely, the less procedural unconscionability is present, the more substantive unconscionability is required to justify such a determination. [Citation.]

"[A] finding of procedural unconscionability does not mean that a contract will not be enforced, but rather that courts will scrutinize the substantive terms of the contract to ensure they are not manifestly unfair or one-sided. [Citation.] … [T]here are degrees of procedural unconscionability. At one end of the spectrum are contracts that have been freely negotiated by roughly equal parties, in which there is no procedural unconscionability. Although certain terms in these contracts may be construed strictly, courts will not find these contracts substantively unconscionable, no matter how one-sided the terms appear to be. [Citation.] Contracts of adhesion that involve surprise or other sharp practices lie on the other end of the spectrum. [Citation.] Ordinary contracts of adhesion, although they are indispensable facts of modern life that are generally enforced [citation], contain a degree of procedural unconscionability even without any notable surprises, and 'bear within them the clear danger of oppression and overreaching.'" [Citation.]

> Thus, a conclusion that a contract contains no element of procedural unconscionability is tantamount to saying that, no matter how one-sided the contract terms, a court will not disturb the contract because of its confidence that the contract was negotiated or chosen freely, that the party subject to a seemingly one-sided term is presumed to have obtained some advantage from conceding the term or that, if one party negotiated poorly, it is not the court's place to rectify these kinds of errors or asymmetries. [Citation.]

Unconscionability under California law is a generally applicable contract defense and therefore applies to arbitration agreements regardless of whether the FAA [Federal Arbitration Act] applies. [Citations.]

* * *

### The Arbitration Agreement Is Procedurally Unconscionable

Procedural unconscionability focuses on oppression or unfair surprise, as we have stated. Oppression results from unequal bargaining power when a contracting party has no meaningful choice but to accept the contract terms. [Citation.] Unfair surprise results from misleading bargaining conduct or other circumstances indicating that a party's consent was not an informed choice. [Citation.]

* * *

The arbitration agreement [in this case] states that the purpose of the agreement is "to resolve any disputes that may arise between the Parties in a timely, fair and individualized manner," but otherwise does not extol the benefits of arbitration. The arbitration agreement does not limit the limitations periods, the remedies available, or the amount of punitive damages. It states, "Except as otherwise required by law, each party shall bear its own attorney fees and costs," and therefore incorporates any statutory right to recover fees rather than creating a presumption against a fee recovery. Thus, the arbitration agreement neither contains the same types of disadvantages for employees as were present in [citation] nor fails to mention such disadvantageous terms. Moreover, the arbitration agreement expressly states that the agreement "is not a mandatory condition of employment."

We conclude, however, that the record indicates a degree of procedural unconscionability in two respects. First, * * * the inequality in bargaining power between the low-wage employees and their employer makes it likely that the employees felt at least some pressure to sign the arbitration agreement. Second, the arbitration agreement suggests that there are multiple arbitrators to choose from ("the then-current Employment Arbitration panel of the Dispute Eradication Services") and fails to mention that the designated arbitration provider includes only one arbitrator. This renders the arbitrator selection process illusory and creates a significant risk that Western Pizza as a "repeat player" before the same arbitrator will reap a significant advantage. [Citation.] These circumstances indicate that the employees' decision to enter into the arbitration agreement likely was not a free and informed decision but was marked by some degree of oppression and unfair surprise, i.e., procedural unconscionability. We therefore must scrutinize the terms of the arbitration agreement to determine whether it is so unfairly one-sided as to be substantively unconscionable.

### The Arbitrator Selection Provision Is Substantively Unconscionable

"Substantively unconscionable terms may take various forms, but may generally be described as unfairly one-sided." [Citation.] "Given the lack of choice and the potential disadvantages that even a fair arbitration system can harbor for employees, we must be particularly attuned to claims that employers with superior bargaining power have imposed one-sided, substantively unconscionable terms as part of an arbitration agreement. 'Private arbitration may resolve disputes faster and cheaper than judicial proceedings. Private arbitration, however, may also become an instrument of injustice imposed on a "take it or leave it" basis. The courts must distinguish the former from the latter, to ensure that private arbitration systems resolve disputes not only with speed and economy but also with fairness.'"[Citation.]

Sanchez contends the arbitration agreement is substantively unconscionable in several respects. He cites the class arbitration waiver, the small claims provision, the absence of any provision requiring a written arbitration award, the designation of an arbitration provider consisting of a single arbitrator, and the absence of any express provision for discovery. In light of our conclusion that the trial court properly decided that the class arbitration waiver is contrary to public policy and therefore unenforceable, we need not decide whether that provision is unconscionable. [Citation.]

* * *

* * * We conclude that the absence of express provisions requiring a written arbitration award and allowing discovery does not render the arbitration agreement unconscionable. Rather, those terms are implied as a matter of law as part of the agreement. [Citation.]

* * * We conclude that the matters authorized under the small claims provision are an ordinary incident of arbitration and that the small claims provision is not substantively unconscionable.

Finally, an arbitration agreement must provide for a neutral arbitrator. * * * In our view, the designation of a "panel" of arbitrators consisting of a single arbitrator selected by Western Pizza created a false appearance of mutuality in the selection of an arbitrator. Moreover, the effective designation of a single arbitrator in what appears to be a standard arbitration agreement applicable to a large number of corporate employees gives rise to a significant risk of financial interdependence between Western Pizza and the arbitrator, and an opportunity for Western Pizza to gain an advantage through its knowledge of and experience with the arbitrator. * * * We conclude that this provision is unfairly one-sided and substantively unconscionable.

### The Entire Arbitration Agreement Is Unenforceable

A trial court may either sever an unconscionable or otherwise unlawful provision from an arbitration agreement and enforce the remainder, restrict the application of the provision so as to avoid unconscionable results, or refuse to enforce the entire agreement. [Citation.] Although a court has some discretion in this regard, a court may refuse to enforce the entire agreement only if the central purpose of the agreement is tainted by illegality. [Citation.] * * *

Whether a contract is severable in this regard is primarily a question of contract interpretation. "'Whether a contract is entire or separable depends upon its language and subject matter, and this question is one of construction to be determined by the court according to the intention of the parties.'" [Citation.] Questions of contract interpretation are subject to de novo review unless the interpretation turns on the credibility of extrinsic evidence. [Citation.]

* * *

The arbitration agreement here includes a class arbitration waiver that is contrary to public policy and an unconscionable arbitrator selection clause, as we have stated. These are important provisions that, if they were not challenged in litigation, could create substantial disadvantages for an employee seeking to arbitrate a modest claim. Although it may be true that neither of these provisions alone would justify the refusal to enforce the entire arbitration agreement [citation], we believe that these provisions considered together indicate an effort to impose on an employee a forum with distinct advantages for the employer. [Thus,] * * * we conclude that the arbitration agreement is permeated by an unlawful purpose. Accordingly, the denial of the motion to compel arbitration was proper.

## QUESTIONS

1. Identify and explain the types of contracts that may violate a statute, and distinguish between the two types of licensing statutes.
2. Describe when a covenant not to compete will be enforced, and discuss the two situations in which these types of covenants most frequently arise.
3. Explain when exculpatory agreements, agreements involving the commission of a tort, and agreements involving public officials will be held to be illegal.
4. Distinguish between procedural and substantive unconscionability.
5. Explain the usual effects of illegality and the major exceptions to this rule.

## PROBLEMS

**1.** Johnson and Wilson were the principal shareholders in XYZ Corporation, located in the city of Jonesville, Wisconsin. This corporation was engaged in the business of manufacturing paper novelties, which were sold over a wide area in the Midwest. The corporation was also in the business of binding books. Johnson purchased Wilson's shares of the XYZ Corporation and, in consideration thereof, Wilson agreed that for a period of two years he would not (a) manufacture or sell in Wisconsin any paper novelties of any kind that would compete with those sold by the XYZ Corporation or (b) engage in the bookbinding business in the city of Jonesville. Discuss the validity and effect, if any, of this agreement.

**2.** Wilkins, a resident of and licensed by the State of Texas as a certified public accountant (CPA), rendered service in his professional capacity in Louisiana to Coverton Cosmetics Company. He was not registered as a CPA in Louisiana. His service under his contract with the cosmetics company was not the only occasion on which he had practiced his profession in that State. The company denied liability and refused to pay him, relying upon a Louisiana statute declaring it unlawful for any person to perform or offer to perform services as a CPA for compensation until he has been registered by the designated agency of the State and holds an unrevoked registration card. Provision is made for issuance of a certificate as a CPA without examination to any applicant who holds a valid unrevoked certificate as a CPA under the laws of any other State. The statute provides further that rendition of services of the character performed by Wilkins, without registration, is a misdemeanor punishable by a fine or imprisonment in the county jail, or both. Discuss whether Wilkins would be successful in an action against Coverton seeking to recover a fee in the amount of $1,500 as the reasonable value of his services.

**3.** Michael is interested in promoting the passage of a bill in the State legislature. He agrees with Christy, an attorney, to pay Christy for her services in drawing up the required bill, procuring its introduction in the legislature, and making an argument for its passage before the legislative committee to which it will be referred. Christy renders these services. Subsequently, upon Michael's refusal to pay her, Christy sues Michael for damage for breach of contract. Will Christy prevail? Explain.

**4.** Anthony promises to pay McCarthy $10,000 if McCarthy reveals to the public that Washington is a Communist. Washington is not a Communist and never has been. McCarthy successfully persuades the media to report that Washington is a Communist and now seeks to recover the $10,000 from Anthony, who refuses to pay. McCarthy initiates a lawsuit against Anthony. What result?

**5.** The Dear Corporation was engaged in the business of making and selling harvesting machines. It sold everything pertaining to its business to the ABC Company, agreeing "not again to go into the manufacture of harvesting machines anywhere in the United States." The seller, which had national and international goodwill in its business, now begins the manufacture of such machines contrary to its agreement. Should the court enjoin it?

**6.** Charles Leigh, engaged in the industrial laundry business in Central City, employed Tim Close, previously employed in the home laundry business, as a route salesperson on July 1. Leigh rents linens and industrial uniforms to commercial customers; the soiled linens and uniforms are picked up at regular intervals by route drivers and replaced with clean ones. Every employee is assigned a list of customers. The contract of employment stated that in consideration of being employed, upon termination of his employment, Close would not "directly or indirectly engage in the linen supply business or any competitive business within Central City, Illinois, for a period of one year from the date when his employment under this contract ceases." On May 10 of the following year, Leigh terminated Close's employment for valid reasons. Thereafter, Close accepted employment with Ajax Linen Service, a direct competitor of Leigh in Central City. He commenced soliciting former customers whom he had called on for Leigh and obtained some of them as customers for Ajax. Will Leigh be able to enforce the provisions of the contract?

**7.** On April 30, 2010, Barack and George entered into a bet on the outcome of the 2010 Kentucky Derby. On January 28, 2011, Barack, who bet on the winner, approached George, seeking to collect the $3,000 George had wagered. George paid Barack the $3,000 wager but now seeks to recover the funds from Barack. Result?

**8.** Carl, a salesman for Smith, comes to Benson's home and sells him a complete set of "gourmet cooking utensils" that are worth approximately $300. Benson, an eighty-year-old man living alone in a one-room efficiency apartment, signs a contract to buy the utensils for $1,450, plus a credit charge of $145, and to make payment in ten equal monthly installments. Three weeks after Carl leaves with the signed contract, Benson decides he cannot afford the cooking utensils and has no use for them. What can Benson do? Explain.

**9.** Consider the same facts as in problem 8, but assume that the price was $350. Benson, nevertheless, wishes to avoid the contract based on the allegation that Carl befriended and tricked him into the purchase. Discuss.

**10.** Adrian rents a bicycle from Barbara. The bicycle rental contract Adrian signed provides that Barbara is not liable for any injury to the renter caused by any defect in the bicycle or the negligence of Barbara. Injured when she is involved in an accident due to Barbara's improper maintenance of the bicycle, Adrian sues Barbara for her damages. Will Barbara be protected from liability by the provision in their contract?

**11.** Merrill Lynch employed Post and Maney as account executives. Both men elected to be paid a salary and to participate in the firm's pension and profit-sharing plans rather than take a straight commission. Thirteen years later, Merrill Lynch terminated the employment of both Post and Maney. Both men began working for a competitor of Merrill Lynch. Merrill Lynch then informed them that all of their rights in the company-funded pension plan had been forfeited pursuant to a provision of the plan that permitted forfeiture in the event an employee directly or indirectly competed with the firm. Is Merrill Lynch correct in its assertion?

**12.** Tovar applied for the position of resident physician in Paxton Community Memorial Hospital. The hospital examined his background and licensing and assured him that he was qualified for the position. Relying upon the hospital's promise of permanent employment, Tovar resigned from his job and began work at the hospital. He was discharged two weeks later, however, because he did not hold a license to practice medicine in Illinois as required by State law. He had taken the examination but had never passed it. Tovar claims that the hospital promised him a position of permanent employment and that by discharging him it breached their employment contract. Discuss.

**13.** Carolyn Murphy, a welfare recipient with very limited education and with four minor children, responded to an advertisement that offered the opportunity to purchase televisions without a deposit or credit history. She entered into a rent-to-own contract for a twenty-five-inch console color television set that required seventy-eight weekly payments of $16 (a total of $1,248, which was two and one-half times the retail value of the set). Under the contract, the renter could terminate the agreement by returning the television and forfeiting any payments already made. After Murphy had paid $436 on the television, she read a newspaper article criticizing the lease plan. She stopped payment and sued the television company. The television company has attempted to take possession of the set. Decision?

**14.** Albert Bennett, an amateur cyclist, participated in a bicycle race conducted by the United States Cycling Federation. During the race, Bennett was hit by an automobile. He claims that employees of the Federation improperly allowed the car onto the course. The Federation claims that it cannot be held liable to Bennett because Bennett signed a release exculpating the Federation from responsibility for any personal injury resulting from his participation in the race. Is the exculpatory clause effective?

**15.** In February, Brady contracted to construct a house for Fulghum for $106,850. Brady began construction on March 13. Neither during the negotiation of this contract nor when he began performance was Brady licensed as a general contractor as required by North Carolina law. Brady was awarded his builder's license on October 22, having passed the examination on his second attempt. At that time, he had completed two-thirds of the work on Fulghum's house. Fulghum paid Brady $104,000. Brady brought suit, seeking an additional $2,850 on the original contract and $28,926 for "additions and changes" Fulghum requested during construction. Is Fulghum liable to Brady? Explain.

**16.** Robert McCart owned and operated an H&R Block tax preparation franchise. When Robert became a district manager for H&R Block, he was not allowed to continue operating a franchise. So, in accordance with company policy, he signed over his franchise to his wife June. June signed the new franchise agreement, which included a covenant not to compete for a two-year period within a fifty-mile radius of the franchise territory should the H&R Block franchise be terminated, transferred, or otherwise disposed of. June and Robert were both aware of the terms of this agreement, but June chose to terminate her franchise agreement anyway. Shortly thereafter, June sent out letters to H&R Block customers, criticizing H&R Block's fees and informing them that she and Robert would establish their own tax preparation services at the same address as the former franchise location. Each letter included a separate letter from Robert detailing the tax services to be offered by the McCarts' new business. Should H&R Block be able to obtain an injunction against June? Against Robert?

**17.** Michelle Marvin and actor Lee Marvin began living together, holding themselves out to the general public as man and wife without actually being married. The two orally agreed that while they lived together they would share equally any and all property and earnings accumulated as a result of their individual and combined efforts. In addition, Michelle promised to render her services as "companion, homemaker, housekeeper and cook" to Lee. Shortly thereafter, she gave up her lucrative career as an entertainer in

order to devote her full time to being Lee's companion, homemaker, housekeeper, and cook. In return he agreed to provide for all of her financial support and needs for the rest of her life. After living together for six years, Lee compelled Michelle to leave his household but continued to provide for her support. One year later, however, he refused to provide further support. Michelle sued to recover support payments and half of their accumulated property. Lee contends that their agreement is so closely related to the supposed "immoral" character of their relationship that its enforcement would violate public policy. The trial court granted Lee's motion for judgment on the pleadings. Decision?

**18.** Richard Brobston was hired by Insulation Corporation of America (ICA) in 1999. Initially, he was hired as a territory sales manager but was promoted to national account manager in 2003 and to general manager in 2007. In 2009, ICA was planning to acquire computer-assisted design (CAD) technology to upgrade its product line. Prior to acquiring this technology, ICA required that Brobston and certain other employees sign employment contracts that contained restrictive covenants or be terminated and changed their employment status to "at will" employees. These restrictive covenants provided that in the event of Brobston's termination for any reason, Brobston would not reveal any of ICA's trade secrets or sales information and would not enter into direct competition with ICA within three hundred miles of Allentown, Pennsylvania, for a period of two years from the date of termination. The purported consideration for Brobston's agreement was a $2,000 increase in his base salary and proprietary information concerning the CAD system, customers, and pricing.

Brobston signed the proffered employment contract. In October 2009, Brobston became vice president of special products, which included responsibility for sales of the CAD system products as well as other products. Over the course of the next year, Brobston failed in several respects to properly perform his employment duties and on August 13, 2010, ICA terminated Brobston's employment. In December 2010, Brobston was hired by a competitor of ICA who was aware of ICA's restrictive covenants. Can ICA enforce the employment agreement by enjoining Brobston from disclosing proprietary information about ICA and by restraining him from competing with ICA? If so, for what duration and over what geographic area?

**19.** Henrioulle, an unemployed widower with two children, received public assistance in the form of a rent subsidy. He entered into an apartment lease agreement with Marin Ventures that provided, "INDEMNIFICATION: Owner shall not be liable for any damage or injury to the tenant, or any other person, or to any property, occurring on the premises, or any part thereof, and Tenant agrees to hold Owner harmless for any claims for damages no matter how caused." Henrioulle fractured his wrist when he tripped over a rock on a common stairway in the apartment building. At the time of the accident, the landlord had been having difficulty keeping the common areas of the apartment building clean. Will the exculpatory clause effectively bar Henrioulle from recovery? Explain.

**20.** Emily was a Java programmer employed with Sun Microsystems in Palo Alto, California. Upon beginning employment, Emily signed a contract that included a noncompete clause that prevented her from taking another Java programming position with any of five companies Sun listed as "direct competitors" within three months of terminating her employment. Later that year Emily resigned and two months later accepted a position with Hewlett-Packard (HP) in Houston, Texas. HP was listed in Emily's contract as a "direct competitor," but she argues that due to the significant geographic distance between both jobs, the contract is not enforceable. Explain whether the contract is enforceable.

**21.** EarthWeb provided online products and services to business professionals in the information technology (IT) industry. EarthWeb operated through a family of websites offering information, products, and services for IT professionals to use for facilitating tasks and solving technology problems in a business setting. EarthWeb obtained this content primarily through licensing agreements with third parties. Schlack began his employment with EarthWeb in its New York City office. His title at EarthWeb was Vice President, Worldwide Content, and he was responsible for the content of all of EarthWeb's websites. Schlack's employment contract stated that he was an employee at will and included a section titled "Limited Agreement Not To Compete." That section provided:

> (c) For a period of twelve (12) months after the termination of Schlack's employment with EarthWeb, Schlack shall not, directly or indirectly:
>
> (1) work as an employee … or in any other … capacity for any person or entity that directly competes with EarthWeb. For the purpose of this section, the term "directly competing" is defined as a person or entity or division on an entity that is
>
> (i) an online service for Information Professionals whose primary business is to provide Information Technology Professionals with a directory of third party technology, software, and/or developer resources; and/or an online reference library, and or
>
> (ii) an online store, the primary purpose of which is to sell or distribute third party software or products used for Internet site or software development.

About one year later, Schlack tendered his letter of resignation to EarthWeb. Schlack revealed at this time that he had accepted a position with ITworld.com, a subsidiary of IDG. EarthWeb sought to enforce the noncompete agreement in Schlack's employment agreement. Discuss who should prevail and why.

**22.** Between 2005 and 2010, Williams purchased a number of household items on credit from Walker-Thomas Furniture Co., a retail furniture store. Walker-Thomas retained the right in its contracts to repossess an item if Williams defaulted on an installment payment. Each contract also provided that each installment payment by Williams would be credited *pro rata* to all outstanding accounts or bills owed to Walker-Thomas. As a result of this provision, an unpaid balance would remain on every item purchased until the entire balance due on all items, whenever purchased, was paid in full. Williams defaulted on a monthly installment payment in 2010, and Walker-Thomas sought to repossess all the items that Williams had purchased since 2005. Discuss.

# CHAPTER 14
# Contractual Capacity

A binding promise or agreement requires that the parties to the agreement have contractual capacity. Everyone is regarded as having such capacity unless the law for reasons of public policy holds that the individual lacks such capacity. This essential ingredient of a contract will be discussed by considering those classes and conditions of persons who are legally limited in their capacity to contract: (1) minors, (2) incompetent persons, and (3) intoxicated persons.

## MINORS

A **minor**, also called an infant, is a person who has not attained the age of legal majority. At common law, a minor was a person who was under twenty-one years of age. Today the age of majority has been changed in nearly all jurisdictions by statute, usually to age eighteen. Almost without exception, a minor's contract, whether executory or executed, is **voidable** at his or his guardian's option. Restatement, Section 14. Thus, the minor is in a favored position by having the option to disaffirm the contract or to enforce it. The adult party to the contract cannot avoid her contract with a minor. Even an "emancipated" minor, one who because of marriage or other reason is no longer subject to strict parental control, may avoid contractual liability in most jurisdictions. Consequently, businesspeople deal at their peril with minors and in situations of consequence generally require an adult to cosign or guarantee the performance of the contract. Nevertheless, most States recognize special categories of contracts that cannot be avoided (such as student loans or contracts for medical care) or that have a lower age for capacity (such as bank account, marriage, and insurance contracts).

### LIABILITY ON CONTRACTS

A minor's contract is not entirely void and of no legal effect; rather, it is *voidable* at the minor's option. The exercise of this power of avoidance, called a **disaffirmance**, ordinarily releases the minor from any liability on the contract. On the other hand, after the minor becomes of age, she may choose to adopt or **ratify** the contract, in which case she surrenders her power of avoidance and becomes bound.

**Disaffirmance** As previously stated, a minor's contract is voidable at his or his guardian's option, conferring upon him a power to avoid liability. He, or in some jurisdictions his guardian, may, through words or conduct manifesting an intention not to abide by the contract, exercise the power to disaffirm.

In general, a minor's disaffirmance must come either during his minority or within a reasonable time after he reaches majority, as long as he has not already ratified the contract. In most States, defining a reasonable time depends upon such circumstances as the nature of the transaction, whether either party has caused the delay, and the extent to which either party has been injured by the delay. Some States, however, statutorily prescribe a time period, generally one year, in which the minor may disaffirm the contract.

A notable exception is that a sale of land by a minor cannot be disaffirmed until after he reaches his majority. But must he disaffirm immediately upon becoming an adult? In the case of a sale of land, there is a strong precedent that the minor may wait until the period of the statute of limitations has expired, if the sale involves no questions of fairness and equity.

Disaffirmance may be either *express* or *implied.* No particular form of words is essential, so long as they show an intention not to be bound. This intention also may be manifested by acts or by conduct. For example, a minor agrees to sell property to Alice and then sells that property to Brian. The sale to Brian would constitute a disaffirmance of the contract with Alice.

A troublesome yet important problem in this area, upon which the courts are not in agreement, pertains to the minor's duty upon disaffirmance. The majority hold that the minor must return any property he has received from the other party, provided he has it in his possession at the time of disaffirmance. Nothing more is required. If the minor disaffirms the purchase of an automobile and the vehicle has been wrecked, he need only return the wrecked vehicle. Other States require at least the payment of a reasonable amount for the use of the property or the amount of its depreciation while in the hands of the minor. A few States, either by statute or court ruling, recognize a duty upon the part of the minor to make *restitution*, that is, return an equivalent of what has been received in order to place the seller in approximately the same position she would have occupied had the sale not occurred.

Finally, can a minor disaffirm and recover property that his buyer has transferred to a good faith purchaser for value? Traditionally, the minor could avoid the contract and recover the property, despite the fact that the third person gave value for it and had no notice of the minority. Thus, in the case of the sale of real estate, a minor may rescind her deed of conveyance even against a good faith purchaser of the land who did not know of the minority. Regarding the sale of goods, however, this principle has been changed by Section 2–403 of the Uniform Commercial Code (UCC), which provides that a person with voidable title (e.g., the person buying goods from a minor) has power to transfer valid title to a good faith purchaser for value. For example, a minor sells his car to an individual who resells it to a used car dealership, a good faith purchaser for value. The used car dealer would acquire legal title even though he bought the car from a seller who had only voidable title.

◆ **SEE CASE 14-1**

**Ratification** A minor has the option of ratifying a contract after reaching the age of majority. Ratification makes the contract binding *ab initio* (from the beginning). That is, the result is the same as if the contract had been valid and binding from its inception. Ratification, once effected, is final and cannot be withdrawn. Further, it must be in total, validating the entire contract. The minor can ratify the contract only as a whole, both as to burdens and benefits. He cannot, for example, ratify so as to retain the consideration he received and escape payment or other performance on his part, nor can he retain part of the contract and disaffirm the rest.

Ratification may be express, implied from conduct, or result from the failure to make a timely disaffirmance. Suppose that a minor makes a contract to buy property from an adult. The contract is voidable by the minor, and she can escape liability. But suppose that after reaching her majority, she promises to go through with the purchase. Because she has *expressly* ratified the contract she entered when she was a minor, her promise is binding, and the adult can recover for breach upon her failure to perform. In the absence of a statutory provision to the contrary, an express ratification may be oral.

Note that a minor has no power to ratify a contract while he remains a minor. A ratification cannot be based on words or conduct occurring while a minor is still underage, for his ratification at that time would be no more effective than his original contractual promise. The ratification must take place after the individual has acquired contractual capacity by attaining his majority.

Ratification, as previously stated, need not be express; it may be *implied* from the minor's conduct. Suppose that the minor, after attaining her majority, uses the property involved in the contract, undertakes to sell it to someone else, or performs some other act showing an intention to affirm the contract. She may not thereafter disaffirm the contract but is bound by it. Perhaps the most common form of implied ratification occurs when a minor, after attaining her majority, continues to use the property which she purchased as a minor. This use is obviously inconsistent with the nonexistence of the contract, and whether the contract is performed or still partly executory, it will amount to a ratification and prevent a disaffirmance by the minor. Simply keeping the goods for an unreasonable time after attaining majority also has been construed as a ratification. Although the courts are divided on the issue, payments by the minor upon reaching majority, either on principal or interest or on the purchase price of goods, have been held to amount to a ratification. Some courts require additional evidence of an intention to abide by the contract, such as an express promise to that effect or the actual use of the subject matter of the contract.

◆ **SEE CASE 14-2**

## LIABILITY FOR NECESSARIES

Contractual incapacity does not excuse a minor from an obligation to pay for necessaries, those things that suitably and reasonably supply his personal needs, such as food, shelter, medicine, and clothing. Even here, however, the minor is liable not for the agreed price but for the *reasonable* value of the items furnished. Recovery is based on quasi contract. Thus, if a clothier sells a minor a suit that the minor needs, the clothier can successfully sue the minor. The clothier's recovery is limited, however, to the reasonable value of the suit, even if this amount is much less than the agreed-upon selling price.

Defining necessaries is a difficult problem. In general, the States regard as **necessary** those things that the minor needs to maintain himself in his particular station in life. Items necessary for subsistence and health—such as food, lodging, clothing, medicine, and medical services—are obviously included. But other less essential items, such as textbooks, school instruction, and legal advice, may be included as well. Further, many States enlarge the concept of necessaries to include articles of property and services that a minor needs to earn the money required to provide the necessities of life for himself and his dependents. Nevertheless, many States limit necessaries to items that are not provided to the minor. Thus, if a minor's guardian provides her with an adequate wardrobe, a blouse the minor purchased would not be considered a necessary. In addition, a minor is *not* liable for anything on the grounds that it is necessary unless it has been actually furnished to him and used or consumed by him. In other words, a minor may disaffirm his executory contracts for necessaries and refuse to accept the clothing, lodging, or other items or services.

Ordinarily, luxury items such as cameras, tape recorders, stereo equipment, television sets, and motorboats seldom qualify as necessaries. Whether automobiles and trucks are necessaries has caused considerable controversy, but some courts have recognized that under certain circumstances an automobile may be necessary when it is used by the minor for his business activities.

◆ **SEE CASE 14-3**

### LIABILITY FOR MISREPRESENTATION OF AGE

The States do not agree on whether a minor who has fraudulently misrepresented her age when entering into contract has the power to disaffirm. Suppose a contracting minor says that she is eighteen years of age (or twenty-one if that is the year of attaining majority) and actually looks that old or even older. By the prevailing view in this country, the minor may nevertheless disaffirm the contract. Some States, however, prohibit disaffirmance if a minor misrepresents her age and the adult party, in good faith, reasonably relied upon the misrepresentation. Other States not following the majority rule either (1) require the minor to restore the other party to the position she occupied before the making of the contract or (2) allow the defrauded party to recover damages against the minor in tort.

### LIABILITY FOR TORT CONNECTED WITH CONTRACT

It is well settled that minors are generally liable for their torts. There is, however, a legal doctrine providing that if a tort and a contract are so "interwoven" that the court must enforce the contract to enforce the tort action, the minor is not liable in tort. Thus, if a minor rents an automobile from an adult, he enters into a contractual relationship obliging him to exercise reasonable care and diligence to protect the property from injury. By negligently damaging the automobile, he breaches that contractual undertaking. But his contractual immunity protects him from an action by the adult based on the contract. Can the adult nonetheless recover damages on a tort theory? By the majority view, he cannot. For, it is reasoned, a tort recovery would, in effect, be an enforcement of the contract and would defeat the protection that contract law affords the minor.

A different result arises, however, when the minor departs from the terms of the agreement, as by using a rental automobile for an unauthorized purpose and in so doing negligently causing damage to the automobile. In that event, most courts would hold that the tort is independent, and the adult can collect from the minor. Such a situation would not involve the breach of a contractual duty, but rather the commission of a tort while performing an activity completely beyond the scope of the rental agreement.

## INCOMPETENT PERSONS

This section discusses the contract status of incompetent persons who are under court-appointed guardianship and those who are not adjudicated incompetents.

### PERSON UNDER GUARDIANSHIP

If a person is under guardianship by court order, her contracts are void and of no legal effect. Restatement, Section 13. A *guardian* is appointed by a court, generally under the terms of a statute, to control and preserve the property of a person (the *ward*) whose impaired capacity prevents her from managing her own property. Nevertheless, a party dealing with an individual under guardianship may be able to recover the fair value of any necessaries provided to the incompetent. Moreover, the contracts of the ward may be ratified by her guardian or by herself upon termination of the guardianship.

◆ **SEE CASE 14-4**

### MENTAL ILLNESS OR DEFECT

A contract is a consensual transaction; therefore, for a contract to be valid, it is necessary that the parties have a certain level of mental capacity. If a person lacks such capacity (is mentally incompetent), he may avoid liability under the agreement (because the contract is **voidable**).

Under the traditional, cognitive ability test, a person who is lacking in sufficient mental capacity to enter into a contract is one unable to comprehend the subject of the contract, its nature, and probable consequences. To avoid the contract, he need not be proved permanently incompetent, but his mental defect must be something more than a weakness of intellect or a lack of average intelligence. In short, a person is competent unless he is unable to understand the nature and effect of his act in entering a contract. Restatement, Section 15. In this situation, the incompetent may disaffirm the contract even if the other party did not know, or had no reason to know, of the incompetent's mental condition.

A second type of mental incompetence recognized by the Restatement and some States is a mental condition that impairs a person's ability to act in a reasonable manner. Section 15. In other words, the person understands what he is doing but cannot control his behavior in order to act in a reasonable and rational way. If the contract he enters is entirely executory or grossly unfair, it is voidable. If, however, the contract is executed and fair, and the competent party had no reason to suspect the incompetency of the other, the incompetent must restore the competent party to the *status quo* by returning the consideration he has received or its equivalent in money. If restoration to the *status quo* is impossible, avoidance will depend upon the equities of the situation.

Like minors and persons under guardianship, an incompetent person is liable for necessaries furnished him on the principle of quasi contract, the amount of recovery being the reasonable value of the goods or services. Moreover, an incompetent person may ratify or disaffirm his voidable contracts when he becomes competent or during a lucid period.

## INTOXICATED PERSONS

A person may avoid any contract that he enters into if the other party has reason to know that, because of intoxication, he is unable either to understand the nature and consequences of his actions or to act in a reasonable manner. Restatement, Section 16. Such contracts are voidable, although they may be ratified when the intoxicated person regains his capacity. Slight intoxication will not destroy one's contractual capacity, but neither is it essential that one be so drunk as to be totally without reason or understanding.

The effect of intoxication on contractual capacity is similar to that accorded contracts that are voidable because of the second type of incompetency, although the courts are even more strict with contracts a party enters while intoxicated, given the idea that the condition is voluntary. Most courts, therefore, require that the intoxicated person on regaining his capacity must act promptly to disaffirm and must generally offer to restore the consideration received. Individuals who are taking prescribed medication or who are involuntarily intoxicated are treated the same as those who are incompetent under the cognitive ability test. As with incompetent persons, intoxicated persons are liable in quasi contract for necessaries furnished them during their incapacity.

*Figure 14-1* summarizes the voidability of contracts made by persons with contractual incapacity.

◆ **SEE FIGURE 14-1: Incapacity: Minors, Nonadjudicated Incompetents, and Intoxicated**

◆ **SEE CASE 14-4**

◆ **FIGURE 14-1: Incapacity: Minors, Nonadjudicated Incompetents, and Intoxicated**

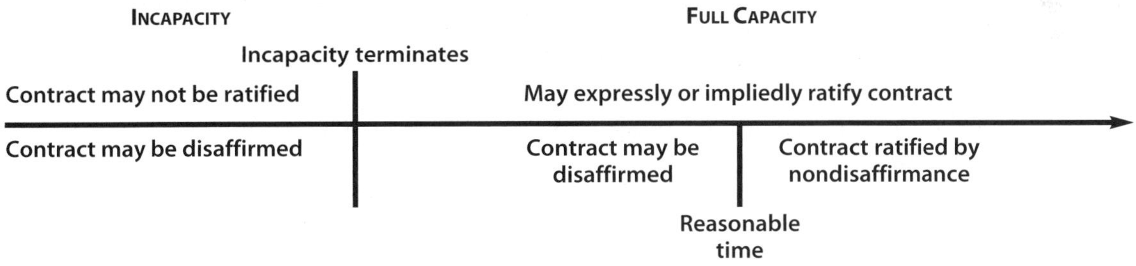


# CHAPTER SUMMARY

**MINORS**

**Definition** persons who are under the age of majority (usually 18 years)

**Liability on Contracts** a minor's contracts are voidable at the minor's option

- ***Disaffirmance*** avoidance of the contract; may be done during minority and for a reasonable time after reaching majority
- ***Ratification*** affirmation of the entire contract; may be done upon reaching majority

**Liability for Necessaries** a minor is liable for the reasonable value of necessary items (those that reasonably supply a person's needs)

**Liability for Misrepresentation of Age** prevailing view is that a minor may disaffirm the contract
**Liability for Tort Connected with Contract** if a tort and a contract are so intertwined that to enforce the tort the court must enforce the contract, the minor is not liable in tort

---

**INCOMPETENT AND INTOXICATED PERSONS**

**Person under Guardianship** contracts made by a person placed under guardianship by court order are void
**Mental Illness or Defect** a contract entered into by a mentally incompetent person (one who is unable to understand the nature and consequences of his acts) is voidable
**Intoxicated Persons** a contract entered into by an intoxicated person (one who cannot understand the nature and consequence of her actions) is voidable

# CASES

## CASE 14-1

### Minors: Disaffirmance
### BERG v. TRAYLOR

Court of Appeal, Second District, Division 2, California, 2007
148 Cal.App.4th 809, 56 Cal.Rptr.3d 140
http://www.lawlink.com/research/caselevel3/84225

**Todd, J.**

Appellants Meshiel Cooper Traylor (Meshiel) and her minor son Craig Lamar Traylor (Craig) appeal the judgment confirming an arbitration award in favor of Craig's former personal manager, respondent Sharyn Berg (Berg), for unpaid commissions under a contract between Berg, Meshiel and Craig and unrepaid loans from Berg. * * *

On January 18, 1999, Berg entered into a two-page "Artist's Manager's Agreement" (agreement) with Meshiel and Craig, who was then 10 years old. Meshiel signed the agreement and wrote Craig's name on the signature page where he was designated "Artist." Craig did not sign the agreement. Pursuant to the agreement, Berg was to act as Craig's exclusive personal manager in exchange for a commission of 15 percent of all gross monies or other consideration paid to him as an artist during the three-year term of the agreement, as well as income from merchandising or promotional efforts or offers of employment made during the term of the agreement, regardless of when Craig received such monies. The agreement expressly provided that any action Craig "may take in the future pertaining to disaffirmance of this agreement, whether successful or not," would not affect Meshiel's liability for any commissions due Berg. The agreement also provided that any disputes concerning payment or interpretation of the agreement would be determined by arbitration in accordance with the rules of Judicial Arbitration and Mediation Services, Inc. (JAMS).

* * *

On or about June 13, 2001, Craig obtained a recurring acting role on the Fox Television Network show "Malcolm in the Middle" (show). On September 11, 2001, four months prior to the expiration of the agreement, Meshiel sent a certified letter to Berg stating that while she and Craig appreciated her advice and guidance, they no longer needed her management services and could no longer afford to pay Berg her 15 percent commission because they owed a "huge amount" of taxes. On September 28, 2001, Berg responded, informing appellants that they were in breach of the agreement.

* * *

In 2004, Berg filed suit against Meshiel and Craig for breach of the agreement, breach of the implied covenant of good faith and fair dealing, breach of an oral loan agreement, conversion and declaratory relief. * * *

* * *

The arbitration hearing commenced on February 7, 2005. * * * Though Meshiel and Craig's counsel failed to appear at the hearing, Meshiel personally appeared with Craig's talent agent, Steven Rice. Craig did not appear. * * *

On February 11, 2005, the arbitrator issued his award, which was served on the parties on February 14, 2005. * * * The arbitrator awarded Berg commissions and interest of $154,714.15, repayment of personal loans and interest of $5,094, and attorney fees and costs of $13,762. He also awarded Berg $405,000 "for future earnings projected on a minimum of 6 years for national syndication earnings," and stated that this part of the award would "vest and become final, as monies earned after February 7, 2005, become due and payable." On February 20, 2005, the arbitrator served a clarification of the award, stating that "all monies earned by Craig Traylor, pursuant to the contract with Ms. Berg, are paid directly to Ms. Berg ...."

After deduction of fees and commissions, etc., the balance of the funds shall be forwarded to the client."

[The defendants then filed a petition with the State trial court to vacate the arbitration award. Following a hearing, the trial court trial court entered a judgment in favor of Berg against Meshiel and Craig consistent with the arbitrator's award.]

* * *

Simply stated, one who provides a minor with goods and services does so at her own risk. [Citation.] The agreement here expressly contemplated this risk, requiring that Meshiel remain obligated for commissions due under the agreement regardless of whether Craig disaffirmed the agreement. Thus, we have no difficulty in reaching the conclusion that Craig is permitted to and did disaffirm the agreement and any obligations stemming therefrom, while Meshiel remains liable under the agreement and resulting judgment. Where our difficulty lies is in understanding how counsel, the arbitrator, and the trial court repeatedly and systematically ignored Craig's interests in this matter. From the time Meshiel signed the agreement, her interests were not aligned with Craig's. That no one—counsel, the arbitrator, or the trial court—recognized this conflict and sought appointment of a guardian *ad litem* for Craig is nothing short of stunning. It is the court's responsibility to protect the rights of a minor who is a litigant in court. [Citation.]

* * *

"As a general proposition, parental consent is required for the provision of services to minors for the simple reason that minors may disaffirm their own contracts to acquire such services." [Citation.] According to Family Code section 6700, "a minor may make a contract in the same manner as an adult, subject to the power of disaffirmance". * * * In turn, Family Code section 6710 states: "Except as otherwise provided by statute, a contract of a minor may be disaffirmed by the minor before majority or within a reasonable time afterwards or, in case of the minor's death within that period, by the minor's heirs or personal representative." Sound policy considerations support this provision:

> The law shields minors from their lack of judgment and experience and under certain conditions vests in them the right to disaffirm their contracts. Although in many instances such disaffirmance may be a hardship upon those who deal with an infant, the right to avoid his contracts is conferred by law upon a minor 'for his protection against his own improvidence and the designs of others.' It is the policy of the law to protect a minor against himself and his indiscretions and immaturity as well as against the machinations of other people and to discourage adults from contracting with an infant. Any loss occasioned by the disaffirmance of a minor's contract might have been avoided by declining to enter into the contract. [Citation.]

Berg offers two reasons why the plain language of Family Code section 6710 is inapplicable, neither of which we find persuasive. First, she argues that a minor may not disaffirm an agreement signed by a parent. * * * [This is not in accord with the law as stated in numerous cases.]

Second, Berg argues that Craig cannot disaffirm the agreement because it was for his and his family's necessities. Family Code section 6712 provides that a valid contract cannot be disaffirmed by a minor if all of the following requirements are met: the contract is to pay the reasonable value of things necessary for the support of the minor or the minor's family, the things have actually been furnished to the minor or the minor's family, and the contract is entered into by the minor when not under the care of a parent or guardian able to provide for the minor or the minor's family. These requirements are not met here. The agreement was not a contract to pay for the necessities of life for Craig or his family. While such necessities have been held to include payment for lodging [citation] and even payment of attorneys' fees [citation], we cannot conclude that a contract to secure personal management services for the purpose of advancing Craig's acting career constitutes payment for the type of necessity contemplated by Family Code section 6712. Nor is there any evidence that Meshiel was unable to provide for the family in 1999 at the time of the agreement. As such, Family Code section 6712 does not bar the minor's disaffirmance of the contract.

No specific language is required to communicate an intent to disaffirm. "A contract (or conveyance) of a minor may be avoided by any act or declaration disclosing an unequivocal intent to repudiate its binding force and effect." [Citation.] Express notice to the other party is unnecessary. [Citation.] We find that the "Notice of Disaffirmance of Arbitration Award by Minor" filed on August 8, 2005 was sufficient to constitute a disaffirmance of the agreement by Craig. * * *

We find that Craig was entitled to and did disaffirm the agreement which, among other things, required him to arbitrate his disputes with Berg. On this basis alone, therefore, the judgment confirming the arbitration award must be reversed.

* * *

Appellants do not generally distinguish their arguments between mother and son, apparently assuming that if Craig disaffirms the agreement and judgment, Meshiel would be permitted to escape liability as well. But a disaffirmance of an agreement by a minor does not operate to terminate the contractual obligations of the parent who signed the agreement. [Citation.] The agreement Meshiel signed provided that Craig's disaffirmance would not serve to void or avoid Meshiel's obligations under the agreement and that Meshiel remained liable for commissions due Berg regardless of Craig's disaffirmance. Accordingly, we find no basis for Meshiel to avoid her independent obligations under the agreement.

The judgment is reversed as to Craig and affirmed as to Meshiel.

CASE 14-2

## Minors: Ratification
## IN RE THE SCORE BOARD, INC.

United States District Court, D. New Jersey, 1999
238 B.R. 585
http://lawlibrary.rutgers.edu/fed/html/ca99-259-1.html

**Irenas, J.**

During the Spring of 1996, Appellant Kobe Bryant ("Bryant"), then a seventeen-year old star high school basketball player, declared his intention to forego college and enter the 1996 lottery draft of the National Basketball Association. On May 8, 1996, The Score Board Inc. ("Debtor"), then a New Jersey based company in the business of licensing, manufacturing and distributing sports and entertainment-related memorabilia, contacted Bryant's Agent, Arn Tellem ("Tellem" or "Agent") in anticipation of making a deal with Bryant.

* * *

In early July 1996, after the above [initial] negotiations, Debtor prepared and forwarded a signed written licensing agreement ("agreement") to Bryant. The agreement granted Debtor the right to produce licensed products, such as trading cards, with Bryant's image. Bryant was obligated to make two personal appearances on behalf of Debtor and provide between a minimum of 15,000 and a maximum of 32,500 autographs. Bryant was to receive a $2.00 stipend for each autograph, after the first 7,500. Under the agreement, Bryant could receive a maximum of $75,000 for the autographs.

In addition to being compensated for the autographs, Bryant was entitled to receive base compensation of $10,000. Moreover, Debtor agreed to pay Bryant $5,000, of the $10,000, within ten days following receipt of the fully executed agreement. Finally, Bryant was entitled to a $5,000 bonus if he returned the agreement within six weeks.

Bryant rejected the above agreement, and on July 11, 1996, while still a minor, Bryant made a counter-offer ("counter-offer"), signed it and returned it to Debtor. The counter-offer made several changes to Debtor's agreement, including the number of autographs. Bryant also changed the amount of prepaid autographs from 7,500 to 500.

Balser claimed that he signed the counter-offer and placed it into his files. The copy signed by Debtor was subsequently misplaced, however, and has never been produced by Debtor during these proceedings. Rather, Debtor has produced a copy signed only by Bryant.

On August 23, 1996, Bryant turned eighteen. Three days later, Bryant deposited a check for $10,000 into his account from Debtor.

On or about September 1, 1996, Bryant began performing his obligations under the agreement, including autograph signing sessions and public appearances. He subsequently performed his contractual duties for about a year and a half.

By late 1997, Bryant grew reluctant to sign any more autographs under the agreement and his Agent came to the conclusion that a fully executed contract did not exist. By this time, Tellem became concerned with Debtor's financial condition because it failed to make certain payments to several other players. Debtor claims that the true motivation for Bryant's reluctance stems from his perception that he was becoming a "star" player, and that his autograph was "worth" more than $2.00.

* * *

On March 17, 1998, Debtor sent Bryant a check for $1,130 as compensation for unpaid autographs. Bryant alleges that he was entitled to $10,130, not $1,130. The Bankruptcy Court found that Bryant was owed $10,130 and the check for $1,130 was based on a miscalculation.

On March 18, 1998, Debtor filed a voluntary *Chapter 11* bankruptcy petition. On March 23, 1998, Tellem returned the $1,130 check upon learning of Debtor's financial trouble. Included with the check was a letter that questioned the validity of the agreement between Bryant and Debtor.

* * * On April 20, 1998, Tellem stated that no contract existed because the counter-offer was never signed by Debtor and there was never a meeting of the minds. Tellem added that the counter-offer expired and that Kobe Bryant withdrew from the counter-offer.

Subsequently, Debtor began to sell its assets, including numerous executory contracts with major athletes, including Bryant. Bryant argued that Debtor could not do this, because he believed that a contract never existed. In the alternative, if a contract was created, Bryant contended that it was voidable because it was entered into while he was a minor. * * *

On December 21, 1998, the Honorable Gloria M. Burns ruled in her memorandum opinion that Debtor accepted Bryant's counter-offer and, therefore, a valid contract existed between Bryant and Debtor. In the alternative, the Bankruptcy Court held that even if Bryant's counter-offer was not signed by Debtor, the parties' subsequent conduct demonstrated their acceptance of the contractual obligation by performance, thereby creating an enforceable contract. Judge Burns denied Bryant's claims of mutual mistake, infancy and his motion for stay relief.

* * *

On February 2, 1999, the Bankruptcy Court entered its final orders: (1) granting Debtor's motion to assume its executory contract with Bryant and assign it to Oxxford; and (2) overruling Bryant's objection to the sale.

Bryant challenges the Bankruptcy Court's finding that he ratified the agreement upon attaining majority. Contracts made during minority are voidable at the minor's election within a reasonable time after the minor attains the age of majority. [Citations]

The right to disaffirm a contract is subject to the infant's conduct which, upon reaching the age of majority, may amount to ratification. [Citation.] "Any conduct on the part of the former infant which evidences his decision that the transaction shall not be impeached is sufficient for this purpose." [Citation.]

On August 23, 1996, Bryant reached the age of majority, approximately six weeks after the execution of the agreement. On August 26, 1996, Bryant deposited the $10,000 check sent to him from Debtor. Bryant also performed his contractual duties by signing autographs.

The Bankruptcy Court did not presume ratification from inaction as Bryant asserts. It is clear that Bryant ratified the contract from the facts, because Bryant consciously performed his contractual duties.

Bryant asserts that he acted at the insistence of his Agent, who believed that he was obligated to perform by contract. Yet, neither Bryant nor his Agent disputed the existence of a contract until the March 23, 1998, letter by Tellem. That Bryant may have relied on his Agent is irrelevant to this Court's inquiry and is proper evidence only in a suit against the Agent. To the contrary, by admitting that he acted because he was under the belief that a contract existed, Bryant confirms the existence of the contract. Moreover, it was Bryant who deposited the check, signed the autographs, and made personal appearances.

For the above reasons, Bryant's appeal of the Bankruptcy Court's orders finding that a valid and enforceable contract exists is denied.

# CASE 14-3

## Minors: Liability for Necessaries

## ZELNICK v. ADAMS

Supreme Court of Virginia, 2002

263 Va. 601, 561 S.E.2d 711

http://caselaw.findlaw.com/va-supreme-court/1227337.html

**Lemons, J.**

In this appeal, we consider whether a contract for legal services entered into on behalf of a minor is voidable upon a plea of infancy or subject to enforcement as an implied contract for necessaries and, if enforceable, the basis for determining value of services rendered.

### Facts and Proceedings Below

Jonathan Ray Adams ("Jonathan") was born on April 5, 1980, the natural child of Mildred A. Adams ("Adams" or "mother") and Cecil D. Hylton, Jr. ("Hylton" or "father"). Jonathan's parents were never married to each other. On September 8, 1995, after highly contested litigation, an agreed order ("paternity order") was entered in Dade County, Florida, establishing Hylton's paternity of Jonathan.

Jonathan's grandfather, Cecil D. Hylton, Sr. ("Hylton Sr."), died testate [with a will] on August 25, 1989. His will established certain trusts and provided that the trustees had sole discretion to determine who qualified as "issue" under the will.

The will created two separate trusts for Hylton Sr.'s grandchildren: the First Grandchildren's Charitable Trust and the Second Grandchildren's Charitable Trust ("the trusts"). Hylton Sr.'s grandchildren and great grandchildren would potentially receive distributions from the trusts in the years 2014 and 2021. * * *

On July 11, 1996, Adams met with an attorney, Robert J. Zelnick ("Zelnick"), about protecting Jonathan's interest as a beneficiary of the trusts. She had received information leading her to believe that distributions were being made from the trusts to some of Hylton Sr.'s grandchildren. Adams told Zelnick that she contacted Jonathan's father about these alleged distributions, but she had not received a response from him. Adams explained that she had also contacted the law firm that had prepared Hylton Sr.'s will and the trustees, and no one would provide her any information about the distributions or whether the Estate would recognize Jonathan as a beneficiary. * * *

Adams explained that she could not afford to pay Zelnick's hourly fee and requested legal services on her son's behalf on a contingency fee basis. At the conclusion of the meeting, Zelnick told Adams that he was unsure whether he would take the case, but that he would investigate the matter.

Zelnick next spoke with Adams during a telephone conversation on July 18, 1996. He informed her that he had obtained a copy of the will and reviewed it, and that he was willing to accept the case "to help her have Jonathan declared a beneficiary of the estate." Adams went to Zelnick's office the next day, July 19, 1996, where Zelnick explained that the gross amount of the estate was very large. According to Zelnick, he "wanted to make sure that she had some understanding of the size of the estate before she entered into this agreement." * * * On July 19, 1996, Adams signed a retainer agreement ("the contract") for Zelnick's firm to represent Jonathan on a one-third contingency fee basis "in his claim against the estate of Cecil D. Hylton."

In May 1997, Zelnick filed a bill of complaint for declaratory judgment, accounting and other relief on Jonathan's behalf to have Jonathan recognized as the grandchild and "issue" of Hylton Sr. for the purposes of the will and trusts. * * * A consent decree was entered on January 23, 1998, which ordered that Jonathan was "declared to be the grandchild and issue of Cecil D. Hylton" and was "entitled to all bequests, devises, distributions and benefits under the Last Will and Testament of Cecil D. Hylton and the trusts created thereunder that inure to the benefit of the grandchildren and issue of Cecil D. Hylton."

In March 1998, Jonathan's father brought a bill of complaint for declaratory judgment against Adams and Zelnick, on Jonathan's behalf, to have the contract with Zelnick declared void. Upon reaching the age of majority, Jonathan filed a petition to intervene, wherein he disaffirmed the contract. * * *

On April 6, 2000, Jonathan filed a motion for summary judgment. He asserted that the contract was "void as a matter of law" because it was not a contract for necessaries. Jonathan argued that the 1997 suit was unnecessary due to the Florida paternity decree which conclusively established Hylton's paternity. He further argued that the 1997 suit was unnecessary because the trusts could not distribute any funds until the years 2014 and 2021 and the issue was not "ripe for determination." Finally, Jonathan claimed that the contingency fee agreement was unreasonable.

The trial court granted Jonathan's motion for summary judgment and ruled that the contingency fee agreement was void. The trial court held that the contract was not binding on Jonathan because he was "in his minority" when the contract was executed. Furthermore, according to the trial court, the doctrine of necessaries did not apply to the contract "because the matter could have been adjudicated after the majority of [Jonathan], who was within a few years of his majority at the time that all of this came out."

Nonetheless, the trial court held that Zelnick was entitled to a fee under the theory of quantum meruit. * * * Zelnick testified that he spent approximately 150 to 200 hours on the case, and that in 1996–1997, his hourly rate was $200 an hour.

* * *

The trial court entered judgment in favor of Zelnick in the amount of $60,000. * * * Both Zelnick and Jonathan have appealed the judgment of the trial court. * * *

## Analysis

* * *

Under well and long-established Virginia law, a contract with an infant is not void, only voidable by the infant upon attaining the age of majority. [Citation.] This oft-cited rule is subject to the relief provided by the doctrine of necessaries which received thorough analysis in the case of *Bear's Adm'x v. Bear*, [citation].

In *Bear*, we explained that when a court is faced with a defense of infancy, the court has the initial duty to determine, as a matter of law, whether the "things supplied" to the infant under a contract may fall within the general class of necessaries. [Citation.] The court must further decide whether there is sufficient evidence to allow the finder of fact to determine whether the "things supplied" were in fact necessary in the instant case. If either of these preliminary inquiries is answered in the negative, the party who provided the goods or services to the infant under the disaffirmed contract cannot recover. If the preliminary inquiries are answered in the affirmative, then the finder of fact must decide, under all the circumstances, whether the "things supplied" were actually necessary to the "position and condition of the infant." If so, the party who provided the goods or services to the infant is entitled to the "reasonable value" of the things furnished. In contracts for necessaries, an infant is not bound on the express contract, but rather is bound under an implied contract to pay what the goods or services furnished were reasonably worth. [Citation.]

"Things supplied," which fall into the class of necessaries, include "board, clothing and education." [Citation.] Things that are "necessary to [an infant's] subsistence and comfort, and to enable [an infant] to live according to his real position in society" are also considered part of the class of necessaries. [Citation.] * * *

Certainly, the provision of legal services may fall within the class of necessaries for which a contract by or on behalf of an infant may not be avoided or disaffirmed on the grounds of infancy. Generally, contracts for legal services related to prosecuting personal injury actions, and protecting an infant's personal liberty, security, or reputation are considered contracts for necessaries. [Citation.] "Whether attorney's services are to be considered necessaries or not depends on whether or not there is a necessity therefor. If such necessity exists, the infant may be bound. * * * If there is no necessity for services, there can be no recovery" for the services. [Citation.]

The Supreme Court of Appeals of West Virginia recently addressed this issue in a paternity action against the estate of an infant's father, brought by the infant's mother on the infant's behalf. [Citation.] The court held that contracts for legal services by infants should be regarded as contracts for necessaries in some instances because "if minors are not required to pay for legal representation, they will not be able to protect their various interests." [Citation.]

Other states have also broadened the definition of "necessaries" to include contracts for legal services for the protection of an infant's property rights. * * *

In determining whether the doctrine of necessaries may be applied to defeat an attempt to avoid or disaffirm a contract on the grounds of infancy, the trial court must first determine as a matter of law if the class of "things supplied" falls within the "general classes of necessaries." We hold that a contract for legal services falls within this class. However, the inquiry does not end with this determination. The ultimate determination is an issue of fact. The trier of fact must conclude that "under all the circumstances, the things furnished were actually necessary to the position and condition of the infant * * * and whether the infant was already sufficiently supplied." [Citation.] If the contract does not fall within the "general classes of necessaries," the trial court must, as a matter of law, sustain the plea of infancy and permit the avoidance of the contract. Similarly, if the contract does fall within the "general classes of necessaries," but upon consideration of all of the circumstances, the trier of fact determines that the provision of the particular services or things was not actually necessary, the plea of infancy must be sustained. Where there is a successful avoidance of the contract, the trial court may not circumvent the successful plea of infancy by affording a recovery to the claimant on the theory of quantum meruit. However, if the plea of infancy is not sustained, the claimant is not entitled to enforcement of the express contract. Rather, as we have previously held, "even in contracts for necessaries, the infant is not bound on the express contract but on the implied contract to pay what they are reasonably worth." [Citation.]

* * *

Upon review of the record, we hold that the * * * reason stated by the trial court for holding that the necessaries doctrine did not apply, namely that the contract "was conducted while he was in his minority and he's not bound by that," is an error of law. We hold that a contract for legal services is within the "general classes of necessaries" that may defeat a plea of infancy. * * *

* * *

The trial court's determination that the necessaries doctrine did not apply was made upon motion for summary judgment filed by Jonathan. Nowhere in Jonathan's motion for summary judgment is the issue raised that the services were unnecessary at the time rendered. * * * Although Jonathan argues that the services were not necessary at all because he alleges that the Florida litigation resolved the question of his inclusion as a beneficiary under the will of Hylton Sr., the timing of the services was not even mentioned as an issue, much less as a reason for granting summary judgment. * * *

Because the trial court erred in its determination, on this record, on summary judgment, that the doctrine of necessaries did not apply, we will reverse the judgment of the trial court and remand for further proceedings, including the taking of evidence on the issue of the factual determination of necessity "under all of the circumstances." Consistent with this opinion, should the trial court upon remand hold that the doctrine of necessaries does not apply because the evidence adduced does not support the claim, the contract is avoided and no award shall be made.

Should the trial court upon remand hold that the evidence is sufficient to defeat Jonathan's plea of infancy, the trial court shall receive evidence of the reasonable value of the services rendered. * * *

Reversed and remanded.

---

CASE 14-4

Intoxicated Persons/Incompetent Persons

## FIRST STATE BANK OF SINAI v. HYLAND

Supreme Court of South Dakota, 1987

399 N.W.2d 894

**Henderson, J.**

Plaintiff-appellant First State Bank of Sinai (Bank) sued defendant-appellee Mervin Hyland (Mervin) seeking to hold him responsible for payment on a promissory note which he cosigned. * * * [T]he circuit court entered * * * judgment holding Mervin not liable for the note's payment. Bank appeals, advocating that the court erred when it ruled that

1. Mervin was incompetent to transact business when he signed the note;
2. Mervin's obligation to Bank was void; and
3. Mervin did not subsequently accept/ratify the obligation.

* * *

On March 10, 1981, Randy Hyland (Randy) and William Buck (Buck), acting for Bank, executed two promissory notes. One note was for $6,800 and the other note was for $3,000. Both notes became due on September 19, 1981.

The notes remained unpaid on their due date and Bank sent notice to Randy informing him of the delinquencies.

On October 20, 1981, Randy came to the Bank and met with Buck. Buck explained to Randy that the notes were past due. Randy requested an extension. Buck agreed, but on the condition that Randy's father, Mervin, act as cosigner. One $9,800 promissory note dated October 20, 1981 (the two notes of $6,800 and $3,000 were combined) was created. Randy was given the note for the purpose of obtaining his father's signature. According to Randy, Mervin signed the note on October 20 or 21, 1981.

Mervin had transacted business with Bank since 1974. Previously, he executed approximately 60 promissory notes with Bank. Mervin was apparently a good customer and paid all of his notes on time. Buck testified that he knew Mervin drank, but that he was unaware of any alcohol-related problems.

Randy returned to the Bank about one week later. Mervin had properly signed the note. In Buck's presence, Randy signed the note, which had an April 20, 1982 due date.

On April 20, 1982, the note was unpaid. Buck notified Randy of the overdue note. On May 5, 1982, Randy appeared at the Bank. He brought a blank check signed by Mervin with which the interest on the note was to be paid. Randy filled in the check amount at the Bank for $899.18 (the amount of interest owing). Randy also requested that the note be extended. Buck agreed, but required Mervin's signature as a prerequisite to any extension. A two-month note for $9,800 with a due date of July 2, 1982, was prepared and given to Randy.

Randy did not secure his father's signature on the two-month note, and Mervin testified that he refused to sign that note. On June 22, 1982, Randy filed for bankruptcy which later resulted in the total discharge of his obligation on the note.

On July 14, 1982, Buck sent a letter to Randy and Mervin informing them of Bank's intention to look to Mervin for the note's payment. On December 19, 1982, Bank filed suit against Mervin, requesting $9,800 principal and interest at the rate of 17 percent until judgment was entered. Mervin answered on January 14, 1983. His defense hinged upon the assertion that he was incapacitated through the use of liquor when he signed the note. He claimed he had no recollection of the note, did not remember seeing it, discussing it with his son, or signing it.

Randy testified that when he brought the note home to his father, the latter was drunk and in bed. Mervin then rose from his bed, walked into the kitchen, and signed the note. Later, Randy returned to the Bank with the signed note.

The record reveals that Mervin was drinking heavily from late summer through early winter of 1981. During this period, Mervin's wife and son accepted responsibilities for managing the farm. Mervin's family testified that his bouts with liquor left him weak, unconcerned with regard to family and business matters, uncooperative, and uncommunicative. When Mervin was drinking, he spent most of his time at home, in bed.

Mervin's problems with alcohol have five times resulted in his involuntary commitment to hospitals. Two of those commitments occurred near the period of the October 1981 note. On September 10, 1981, Mervin was involuntarily committed to the Human Services Center at Yankton. He was released on September 19, 1981. On November 20, 1981, he was involuntarily committed to River Park at Pierre.

Between the periods of his commitments, September 19, 1981 until November 20, 1981, Mervin did transact some business himself. * * *

A trial was held on October 4, 1985. Mervin was found to be entirely without understanding (as a result of alcohol consumption) when he signed the October 20, 1981 promissory note. The court pointed to Mervin's lack of personal care and nonparticipation in family life and farming business as support for finding the contractual relationship between the parties void at its inception. It was further held that Bank had failed to show Mervin's subsequent ratification of the contract. Bank appeals.

* * *

Historically, the void contract concept has been applied to nullify agreements made by mental incompetents who have contracted * * * after a judicial determination of incapacity had been entered. [Citations.] * * *

Mervin had numerous and prolonged problems stemming from his inability to handle alcohol. However, he was not judicially declared incompetent during the note's signing.

* * *

Contractual obligations incurred by intoxicated persons may be voidable. [Citation.] Voidable contracts (contracts other than those entered into following a judicial determination of incapacity) * * * may be rescinded by the previously disabled party. [Citation.] However, disaffirmance must be prompt, upon the recovery of the intoxicated party's mental abilities, and upon his notice of the agreement, if he had forgotten it. [Citation.] * * *

A voidable contract may also be ratified by the party who had contracted while disabled. Upon ratification, the contract becomes a fully valid legal obligation. [Citation.] Ratification can either be express or implied by conduct. [Citations.] In addition, failure of a party to disaffirm a contract over a period of time may, by itself, ripen into a ratification, especially if rescission will result in prejudice to the other party. [Citations.]

Mervin received both verbal notice from Randy and written notice from Bank on or about April 27, 1982, that the note was overdue. On May 5, 1982, Mervin paid the interest owing with a check which Randy delivered to Bank. This by itself could amount to ratification through conduct. If

Mervin wished to avoid the contract, he should have then exercised his right of rescission. We find it impossible to believe that Mervin paid almost $900 in interest without, in his own mind, accepting responsibility for the note. His assertion that paying interest on the note relieved his obligation is equally untenable in light of his numerous past experiences with promissory notes.

* * *

We conclude that Mervin's obligation to Bank is not void. * * * Mervin's obligation on the note was voidable and his subsequent failure to disaffirm (lack of rescission) and his payment of interest (ratification) then transformed the voidable contract into one that is fully binding upon him.

We reverse and remand.

## QUESTIONS

1. Define a necessary and explain how it affects the contracts of a minor.
2. How and when may a minor ratify a contract?
3. What is the liability of a minor who disaffirms a contract?
4. Distinguish between the legal capacity of a person under guardianship and a mentally incompetent person who is not under guardianship.
5. What is the rule governing an intoxicated person's capacity to enter into a contract?

## PROBLEMS

**1.** Michael, a minor, operates a one-man automobile repair shop. Anderson, having heard of Michael's good work on other cars, takes her car to Michael's shop for a thorough engine overhaul. Michael, while overhauling Anderson's engine, carelessly fits an unsuitable piston ring on one of the pistons, with the result that Anderson's engine is seriously damaged. Michael offers to return the sum that Anderson paid him for his work, but refuses to pay for the damage. Can Anderson recover from Michael in tort for the damage to her engine? Why?

**2.** On March 20, Andy Small became seventeen years old, but he appeared to be at least twenty-one.

**(a)** On April 1, he moved into a rooming house in Chicago where he orally agreed to pay the landlady $300 a month for room and board, payable at the end of each month. On April 30, he refused to pay his landlady for his room and board for the month of April.

**(b)** On April 4, he went to Honest Hal's Carfeteria and signed a contract to buy a used car on credit with a small down payment. He made no representation as to his age, but Honest Hal represented the car to be in A-1 condition, which it subsequently turned out not to be. On April 25, he returned the car to Honest Hal and demanded a refund of his down payment.

**(c)** On April 7, Andy sold and conveyed to Adam Smith a parcel of real estate that he owned. On April 28, he demanded that Adam Smith reconvey the land although the purchase price, which Andy received in cash, had been spent in riotous living. Explain the outcome of each transaction.

**3.** Jones, a minor, owned a 2009 automobile. She traded it to Stone for a 2010 car. Jones went on a three-week trip and found that the 2010 car was not as good as the 2009 car. She asked Stone to return the 2009 car but was told that it had been sold to Tate. Jones thereupon sued Tate for the return of the 2009 car. Is Jones entitled to regain ownership of the 2009 car? Explain.

**4.** On May 7, Roy, a minor, a resident of Smithton, purchased an automobile from Royal Motors, Inc., for $18,750 in cash. On the same day, he bought a motor scooter from Marks, also a minor, for $750 and paid him in full. On June 5, two days before attaining his majority, Roy disaffirmed the contracts and offered to return the car and the motor scooter to the respective sellers. Royal Motors and Marks each refused the offers. On June 16, Roy brought separate appropriate actions against Royal Motors and Marks to recover the purchase price of the car and the motor scooter. By agreement on July 30, Royal Motors accepted the automobile. Royal then filed a counterclaim against Roy for the reasonable rental value of the car between June 5 and July 30. The car was not damaged during this period. Royal knew that Roy lived twenty-five miles from his place of employment in Smithton and that he would probably drive the car, as he did, to provide himself transportation. Decision as to (a) Roy's action against Royal Motors, Inc., and its counterclaim against Roy; and (b) Roy's action against Marks?

**5.** On October 1, George Jones entered into a contract with Johnson Motor Company, a dealer in automobiles, to buy a used car for $10,850. He paid $1,100 down and, under the agreement, was to make monthly payments thereafter of $325 each. Although Jones was seventeen years old at the time he made the contract, he represented to the company that he was twenty-one years old because he was afraid that if the company knew his real age, it would not sell the car to him. His appearance was that of a man of twenty-one years of age. After making the first payment on November 1, he failed to make any more payments. On December 15, the company repossessed the car under the terms provided in the contract. At that time, the car had been damaged and was in need of repairs. On December 20, George Jones became of age and at once disaffirmed the contract and demanded the return of the $1,425 he had paid on it. On refusal of the company to do so, George Jones brought an action to recover the $1,425, and the company set up a counterclaim for $1,500 for expenses it incurred in repairing the car. Who will prevail? Why?

**6.** Rebecca entered into a written contract to sell certain real estate to Mary, a minor, for $80,000, payable $4,000 on the execution of the contract and $800 on the first day of each month thereafter until paid. Mary paid the $4,000 down payment and eight monthly installments before attaining her majority. Thereafter, Mary made two additional monthly payments and caused the contract to be recorded in the county where the real estate was located. Mary was then advised by her attorney that the contract was voidable. After being so advised, Mary immediately tendered the contract to Rebecca, together with a deed reconveying all of Mary's interest in the property to Rebecca. Also, Mary demanded that Rebecca return the money she had paid under the contract. Rebecca refused the tender and declined to repay any portion of the money paid to her by Mary. Can Mary cancel the contract and recover the amount paid to Rebecca? Explain.

**7.** Anita sold and delivered an automobile to Marvin, a minor. Marvin, during his minority, returned the automobile to Anita, saying that he disaffirmed the sale. Anita accepted the automobile and said she would return the purchase price to Marvin the next day. Later in the day, Marvin changed his mind, took the automobile without Anita's knowledge, and sold it to Chris. Anita had not returned the purchase price when Marvin took the car. On what theory, if any, can Anita recover from Marvin? Explain.

**8.** Ira, who in 2008 had been found innocent of a criminal offense because of insanity, was released from a hospital for the criminally insane during the summer of 2009 and since that time has been a reputable and well-respected citizen and businessperson. On February 1, 2010, Ira and Shirley entered into a contract in which Ira would sell his farm to Shirley for $100,000. Ira now seeks to void the contract. Shirley insists that Ira is fully competent and has no right to avoid the contract. Who will prevail? Why?

**9.** Daniel, while under the influence of alcohol, agreed to sell his 2003 automobile to Belinda for $8,000. The next morning, when Belinda went to Daniel's house with the $8,000 in cash, Daniel stated that he did not remember the transaction but that "a deal is a deal." One week after completing the sale, Daniel decides that he wishes to avoid the contract. What result?

**10.** Langstraat, age seventeen, owned a motorcycle that he insured against liability with Midwest Mutual Insurance Company. He signed a notice of rejection attached to the policy indicating that he did not desire to purchase uninsured motorists' coverage from the insurance company. Later he was involved in an accident with another motorcycle owned and operated by a party who was uninsured. Langstraat now seeks to recover from the insurance company, asserting that his rejection was not a valid rejection because he is a minor. Can Langstraat recover from Midwest? Explain.

**11.** G.A.S. married his wife, S.I.S., on January 19, 2000. He began to suffer mental health problems in 2006, during which year he was hospitalized at the Delaware State Hospital for eight weeks. Similar illnesses occurred in 2008 and the early part of 2010, with G.A.S. suffering from such symptoms as paranoia and loss of a sense of reality. In early 2011, G.A.S. was still committed to the Delaware State Hospital, attending a regular job during the day and returning to the hospital at night. During this time, he entered into a separation agreement prepared by his wife's attorney. G.A.S., however, never spoke with the attorney about the contents of the agreement; nor did he read it prior to signing. Moreover, G.A.S. was not independently represented by counsel when he executed this agreement. Can G.A.S. disaffirm the separation agreement? Explain.

**12.** A fifteen-year-old minor was employed by Midway Toyota, Inc. On August 18, 2009, the minor, while engaged in lifting heavy objects, injured his lower back. In October 2009 he underwent surgery to remove a herniated disk. Midway Toyota paid him the appropriate amount of temporary total disability payments ($53.36 per week) from August 18, 2009, through November 15, 2010. In February 2011 a final settlement was reached for 150 weeks of permanent partial disability benefits totaling $6,136.40. Tom Mazurek represented Midway Toyota in the negotiations leading to the agreement and negotiated directly with the minor and his mother, Hermione Parrent. The final settlement agreement was signed by the minor only. Mrs. Parrent, who was present at the time, did not object to the signing, but neither she nor anyone else of "legal guardian status" co-signed the agreement. The minor later sought to disaffirm the agreement and reopen his workers' compensation case. The workers' compensation court denied his petition, holding that Mrs. Parrent "participated fully in consideration of the offered final settlement and ... ratified and approved it on behalf of her ward ... to the same legal effect as if she had actually signed [it] ..." The minor appealed. Decision?

**13.** Rose, a minor, bought a new Buick Riviera from Sheehan Buick. Seven months later, while still a minor, he attempted to disaffirm the purchase. Sheehan Buick refused to accept the return of the car or to refund the purchase price. Rose, at the time of the purchase, gave all the appearance of being of legal age. The car had been used by him to carry on his school, business, and social activities. Can Rose successfully disaffirm the contract?

**14.** L. D. Robertson bought a pickup truck from King and Julian, doing business as the Julian Pontiac Company. Robertson, at the time of purchase, was seventeen years old, living at home with his parents, and driving his father's truck around the county to different construction jobs. According to the sales contract, he traded in a passenger car for the truck and was given $2,723 credit toward the truck's $6,743 purchase price, agreeing to pay the remainder in monthly installments. After he paid the first month's installment, the truck caught fire and was rendered useless. The insurance agent, upon finding that Robertson was a minor, refused to deal with him. Consequently, Robertson sued to exercise his right as a minor to rescind the contract and to recover the purchase price he had already paid ($2,723 credit for the car plus the one month's installment). The defendants argue that Robertson, even as a minor, cannot rescind the contract as it was for a necessary item. Are they correct?

**15.** Haydocy Pontiac sold Jennifer Lee an automobile for $21,552, of which $20,402 was financed with a note and security agreement. At the time of the sale Lee, age twenty, represented to Haydocy that she was twenty-one years old, the age of majority, and capable of contracting. After receiving the car, Lee allowed John Roberts to take possession of it. Roberts took the car and has not returned. Lee has failed to make any further payments on the car. Haydocy has sued to recover on the note, but Lee disaffirms the contract, claiming that she was too young to enter into a valid contract. Can Haydocy recover the money from Lee? Explain.

**16.** Carol White ordered a $225 pair of contact lenses through an optometrist. White, an emancipated minor, paid $100 by check and agreed to pay the remaining $125 at a later time. The doctor ordered the lenses, incurring a debt of $110. After the lenses were ordered, White called to cancel her order and stopped payment on the $100 check. The lenses could be used by no one but White. The doctor sued White for the value of the lenses. Will the doctor be able to recover the money from White? Explain.

**17.** Williamson, her mortgage in default, was threatened with foreclosure on her home. She decided to sell the house. The Matthewses learned of this and contacted her about the matter. Williamson claims that she offered to sell her equity for $17,000 and that the Matthewses agreed to pay off the mortgage. The Matthewses contend that the asking price was $1,700. On September 27, the parties signed a contract of sale, which stated the purchase price to be $1,800 (an increase of $100 to account for furniture in the house) plus the unpaid balance of the mortgage. The parties met again on October 10 to sign the deed. Later that day, Williamson, concerned that she had not received her full $17,000 consideration, contacted an attorney. Can Williamson set aside the sale based upon inadequate consideration and mental weakness due to intoxication?

**18.** Halbman, a minor, purchased a used Oldsmobile from Lemke for $11,250. Under the terms of the contract, Halbman would pay $1,000 down and the balance in $125 weekly installments. Upon making the down payment, Halbman received possession of the car, but Lemke retained the title until the balance was paid. After Halbman had made his first four payments, a connecting rod in the car's engine broke. Lemke denied responsibility, but offered to help Halbman repair it if Halbman would provide the parts. Halbman, however, placed the car in a garage where the repairs cost $637.40. Halbman never paid the repair bill.

Hoping to avoid any liability for the vehicle, Lemke transferred title to Halbman even though Halbman never paid the balance owed. Halbman returned the title with a letter disaffirming the contract and demanded return of the money paid. Lemke refused. Because the repair bill remained unpaid, the garage removed the car's engine and transmission and towed the body to Halbman's father's house. Vandalism during the period of storage rendered the car unsalvageable. Several times Halbman requested Lemke to remove the car. Lemke refused. Halbman sued Lemke for the return of his consideration, and Lemke countersued for the amount still owed on the contract. Decision?

**19.** On June 11, Chagnon bought a used Buick from Keser for $9,950. Chagnon, who was then a minor, obtained the contract by falsely advising Keser that he was over the age of majority. On September 25, two months and four days after reaching his majority, Chagnon disaffirmed the contract and, ten days later, returned the Buick to Keser. He then brought suit to recover the money he had paid for the automobile. Keser counterclaimed that he suffered damages as the direct result of Chagnon's false representation of his age. A trial was brought to the court, sitting without a jury, all of which culminated in a judgment in favor of Chagnon against Keser in the sum of $6,557.80. This particular sum was arrived at by the trial court in the following manner: the trial court found that Chagnon initially purchased the Buick for the sum of $9,950 and that he was entitled to the return of his $9,950; and then, by way of setoff, the trial court subtracted from the $9,950 the sum of $3,392.20, apparently representing the difference between the purchase price paid for the vehicle and the reasonable value of the Buick on October 5, the date when the Buick was returned to Keser. Is this legally correct? Do you agree? Why?

**20.** On April 29, 2010, Kirsten Fletcher and John E. Marshall III jointly signed a lease to rent an apartment for the term beginning on July 1, 2010, and ending on June 30, 2011, for a monthly rent of $525 per month. At the time the lease was signed, Marshall was not yet eighteen years of age. Marshall turned eighteen on May 30, 2010. Two weeks later, the couple moved into the apartment. About two months later, Marshall moved out to attend college, but Fletcher remained. She paid the rent herself for the remaining ten months of the lease and then sought contribution for Marshall's share of the rent plus court costs in the amount of $2,500. Can Fletcher collect from Marshall?

**21.** Rogers was a nineteen-year-old (the age of majority then being twenty-one) high school graduate pursuing a civil engineering degree when he learned that his wife was expecting a child. As a result, he quit school and sought assistance from Gastonia Personnel Corporation in finding a job. Rogers signed a contract with the employment agency providing that he would pay the agency a service charge if it obtained suitable employment for him. The employment agency found him such a job, but Rogers refused to pay the service charge, asserting that he was a minor when he signed the contract. Gastonia sued to recover the agreed-upon service charge from Rogers. Should Rogers be liable under his contract? If so, for how much?

C H A P T E R 15

# Contracts in Writing

An **oral** contract, that is, one not written, is in every way as enforceable as a written contract unless otherwise provided by statute. Although most contracts are not required to be in writing to be enforceable, it is highly desirable that significant contracts be written. Written contracts avoid the numerous problems that proving the terms of oral contracts inevitably involves. The process of setting down the contractual terms in a written document also tends to clarify the terms and to reveal problems the parties might not otherwise foresee. Moreover, the terms of a written contract do not change over time, while the parties' recollections of the terms might.

When the parties do reduce their agreement to a complete and final written expression, the law (under the parol evidence rule) honors this document by not allowing the parties to introduce any evidence in a lawsuit that would alter, modify, or vary the terms of the written contract. Nevertheless, the parties may differ as to the proper or intended meaning of language contained in the written agreement where such language is ambiguous or susceptible to different interpretations. To ascertain the proper meaning requires an interpretation, or construction, of the contract. The rules of construction permit the parties to introduce evidence to resolve ambiguity and to show the meaning of the language employed and the sense in which both parties used it.

This chapter will examine (1) the types of contracts that must be in writing to be enforceable, (2) the parol evidence rule, and (3) the rules of contractual interpretation.

## STATUTE OF FRAUDS

The statute of frauds requires that certain designated types of contracts be evidenced by a writing to be enforceable. The original statute became law in 1677, when the English Parliament adopted "An Act for Prevention of Frauds and Perjuries," commonly referred to as the statute of frauds. From the early days of U.S. history practically every State had and continues to have a statute of frauds patterned upon the original English statute.

The statute of frauds has no relation whatever to any kind of fraud practiced in the making of contracts. The common law rules relating to such fraud are discussed in *Chapter 11*. The purpose of the statute is to prevent perjured testimony in court from creating fraud in the proof of certain oral contracts, which purpose the statute accomplishes by requiring that certain contracts be evidenced by a signed writing. On the other hand, the statute does not prevent the performance of oral contracts if the parties are willing to perform. In brief, the statute relates only to the proof or evidence of a contract. It has nothing to do with the circumstances surrounding the making of a contract or with a contract's validity.

### CONTRACTS WITHIN THE STATUTE OF FRAUDS

Many more types of contracts are *not* subject to the statute of frauds than are subject to it. Most oral contracts, as previously indicated, are as enforceable and valid as a written contract. If, however, a given contract is subject to the statute of frauds, the contract is said to be **within** the statute; to be enforceable, it must comply with the statute's requirements. All other types of contracts are said to be "not within" or "outside" the statute and need not comply with its requirements to be enforceable.

The following kinds of contracts are within the original English statute and remain within most State statutes; compliance requires a writing signed by the party to be charged (the party against whom the contract is to be enforced).

1. Promises to answer for the duty of another
2. Promises of an executor or administrator to answer personally for a duty of the decedent whose funds he is administering
3. Agreements upon consideration of marriage
4. Agreements for the transfer of an interest in land
5. Agreements not to be performed within one year

A sixth type of contract within the statute applied to contracts for the sale of goods. Section 2–201 of the Uniform Commercial Code (UCC) now governs the enforceability of contracts of this kind.

The various provisions of the statute of frauds apply independently. Accordingly, a contract for the sale of an interest in land may also be a contract in consideration of marriage, a contract not to be performed in one year, *and* a contract for the sale of goods.

In addition to those contracts specified in the original statute, most States require that other contracts be evidenced by a writing as well; for example, a contract to make a will, to authorize an agent to sell or purchase real estate, or to pay a commission to a real estate broker. Moreover, Article 1 of the UCC requires that a contract for the sale of securities, contracts creating certain types of security interests, and contracts for the sale of other personal property for more than $5,000 also be in writing. The 2001 Revision to Article 1 has deleted this requirement.

## ELECTRONIC RECORDS

One significant impediment to e-commerce has been the questionable enforceability of contracts entered into through electronic means such as the Internet or e-mail because of the writing requirements under contract and sales law (statute of frauds). In response, the **Uniform Electronic Transactions Act (UETA)** was promulgated by the National Conference of Commissioners on Uniform State Laws (NCCUSL) in July 1999, and has been adopted by almost all of the States and introduced in a number of others. UETA applies only to transactions between parties each of which has agreed to conduct transactions by electronic means. It gives full effect to electronic contracts, encouraging their widespread use, and develops a uniform legal framework for their implementation. UETA protects electronic signatures and contracts from being denied enforcement because of the statute of frauds. Section 7 of UETA accomplishes this by providing the following:

1. A record or signature may not be denied legal effect or enforceability solely because it is in electronic form.
2. A contract may not be denied legal effect or enforceability solely because an electronic record was used in its formation.
3. If a law requires a record to be in writing, an electronic record satisfies the law.
4. If a law requires a signature, an electronic signature satisfies the law.

Section 14 of UETA further validates contracts formed by machines functioning as electronic agents for parties to a transaction: "A contract may be formed by the interaction of electronic agents of the parties, even if no individual was aware of or reviewed the electronic agents' actions or the resulting terms and agreements." The Act excludes from its coverage wills, codicils, and testamentary trusts as well as all Articles of the UCC except Articles 2 and 2A.

In addition, Congress in 2000 enacted the **Electronic Signatures in Global and National Commerce (E-Sign)**. The Act, which uses language very similar to that of UETA, makes electronic records and signatures valid and enforceable across the United States for many types of transactions in or affecting interstate or foreign commerce. E-Sign does not generally preempt UETA. E-Sign does not require any person to agree to use or accept electronic records or electronic signatures. The Act defines transactions quite broadly to include the sale, lease, exchange, and licensing of personal property and services, as well as the sale, lease, exchange, or other disposition of any interest in real property. E-Sign defines an electronic record as "a contract or other record created, generated, sent, communicated, received, or stored by electronic means." It defines an electronic signature as "an electronic sound, symbol, or process, attached to or logically associated with a contract or other record and executed or adopted by a person with the intent to sign the record." Like UETA, E-Sign ensures that Internet and e-mail agreements will not be unenforceable because of the statute of frauds by providing that

1. a signature, contract, or other record relating to such transaction may not be denied legal effect, validity, or enforceability solely because it is in electronic form; and
2. a contract relating to such transaction may not be denied legal effect, validity, or enforceability solely because an electronic signature or electronic record was used in its formation.

To protect consumers, E-Sign provides that they must consent *electronically* to conducting transactions with electronic records after being informed of the types of hardware and software required. Prior to consent, consumers must also receive a "clear and conspicuous" statement informing consumers of their right to (1) have the record provided on paper or in nonelectronic form; (2) after consenting to electronic records, receive paper copies of the electronic record; and (3) withdraw consent to receiving electronic records.

As defined by E-Sign, an electronic agent is a computer program or other automated means used independently to initiate an action or respond to electronic records or performances in whole or in part without review or action by an individual at the time of the action or response. The Act validates contracts or other records relating to a transaction in or affecting interstate or foreign commerce formed by electronic agents so long as the action of each electronic agent is legally attributable to the person to be bound.

E-Sign specifically excludes certain transactions, including (1) wills, codicils, and testamentary trusts; (2) adoptions, divorces, and other matters of family law; and (3) the UCC other than sales and leases of goods.

### SURETYSHIP PROVISION

The **suretyship** provision applies to a contractual promise by a surety (*promisor*) to a **creditor** (*promisee*) to perform the duties or obligations of a third person (**principal debtor**) if the principal debtor does not perform. Thus, if a mother tells a merchant to extend $1,000 worth of credit to her son and says, "If he doesn't pay, I will," the promise must be in writing (or have a sufficient electronic record) to be enforceable. The factual situation can be reduced to the simple statement, "If X doesn't pay, I will." The promise is said to be **collateral**, in that the promisor is not primarily liable. The mother does not promise to pay in any event; her promise is to pay only if the one primarily obligated, her son, defaults.

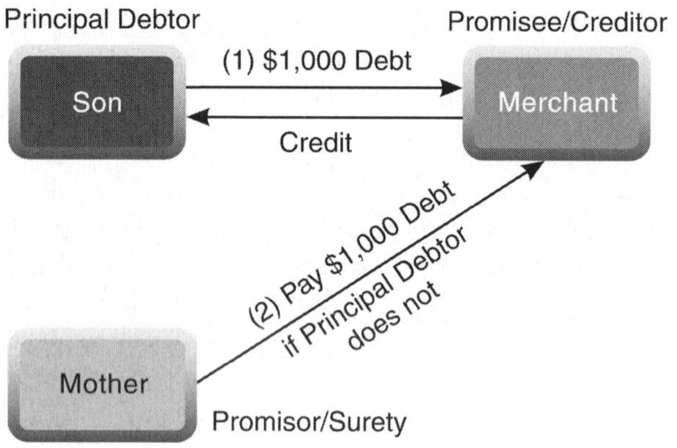


The rule applies only to cases involving three parties and two contracts. The primary contract, between the principal debtor and the creditor, creates the indebtedness. The collateral contract is made by the third person (surety) directly with the creditor, whereby the surety promises to pay the debt to the creditor in case the principal debtor fails to do so. For a complete discussion of suretyship see *Chapter 38*.

**Original Promise** If the promisor makes an **original promise** by undertaking to become primarily liable, then the statute of frauds does not apply. For example, a father tells a merchant to deliver certain items to his daughter and says, "I will pay $400 for them." The father is not promising to answer for the debt of another; rather, he is making the debt his own. It is to the father, and the father alone, that the merchant extends credit; only from the father may the creditor seek payment. The statute of frauds does not apply, and the promise may be oral.

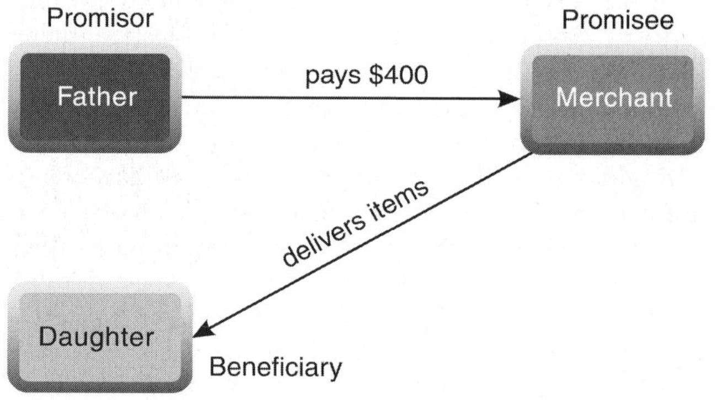


**Main Purpose Doctrine** The courts have developed an exception to the suretyship provision based on the purpose or object of the promisor, called the "main purpose doctrine" or "leading object rule." Where the object or purpose of the promisor is to obtain an economic benefit for himself, the promise is *not* within the statute. Restatement, Section 116. The expected benefit to the surety "must be such as to justify the conclusion that his main purpose in making the promise is to advance his own interest." Restatement, Section 116, Comment b. The fact that the surety received consideration for his promise or that he might receive a slight and indirect advantage is insufficient to bring the promise within the main purpose doctrine.

Suppose that a supply company has refused to furnish materials upon the credit of a building contractor. Facing a possible slowdown in the construction of his building, the owner of the land promises the supplier that if he will extend credit to the contractor, the owner will pay if the contractor does not. Here, the primary purpose of the promisor is to serve his own economic interest, even though the performance of the promise would discharge the duty of another. The intent to benefit the contractor is at most incidental, and courts will uphold oral promises of this type.

◆ **SEE CASE 15-1**

**Promise Made to Debtor** The suretyship provision has been interpreted not to include promises made to a debtor. For example, D owes a debt to C. S promises D that she will pay D's debt in return for valid consideration from D. Because S made the promise to the debtor (D), not the creditor, the promise may be oral. The promise is not a collateral promise to pay C if D fails to pay and thus is not a promise to discharge the obligation of another.

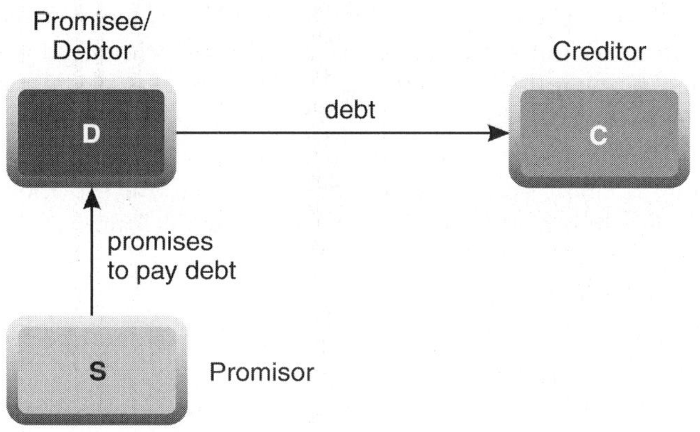


## EXECUTOR-ADMINISTRATOR PROVISION

The executor-administrator provision applies to the contractual promises of an executor of a decedent's will, or to those of the administrator of his estate if the decedent dies without a will, to answer personally for a duty of the decedent. An **executor** or **administrator** is a person appointed by a court to carry on, subject to order of court, the administration of the estate of a deceased person. If the will of a decedent nominates a certain person as executor, the court customarily appoints that person. (For a more detailed discussion of executors and administrators, see *Chapter 52*.) If an executor or administrator promises to pay personally a debt of the decedent, the promise must be in writing—or in proper electronic form—to be enforceable. For example, Brian, who is Ann's son and executor of her will, recognizing that Ann's estate will not provide funds sufficient to pay all of her debts, orally promises Curtis, one of Ann's creditors, that he, Brian, will personally pay all of his mother's creditors in full in return for valid consideration from Curtis. Brian's oral promise is not enforceable. This provision does not apply to promises to pay debts of the deceased out of assets of the estate.

The executor-administrator provision is thus a specific application of the suretyship provision. Accordingly, the exceptions to the suretyship provision apply to this provision as well.

## MARRIAGE PROVISION

The notable feature of the marriage provision is that it does *not* apply to mutual promises to marry. The provision applies only if a promise to marry is made in consideration for some promise other than a reciprocal promise to marry. Restatement, Section 124. If, for example, Greg and Betsy each orally promise and agree to marry each other, their agreement is not within the statute and is a binding contract between them. If, however, Greg promises to convey title to a certain farm to Betsy if she accepts his proposal of marriage, their agreement would fall within the statute of frauds.

## LAND CONTRACT PROVISION

The land contract provision covers promises to transfer "any interest in land," which includes any right, privilege, power, or immunity in real property. Restatement, Section 125. Thus, all promises to transfer, buy, or pay for an interest in land, including ownership interests, leases, mortgages, options, and easements, are within the provision.

The land contract provision does not include contracts to transfer an interest in personal property. It also does not cover short-term leases, which by statute in most States are those for one year or less; contracts to build a building on a piece of land; contracts to do work on the land; or contracts to insure a building on the land.

The courts may enforce an oral contract for the transfer of an interest in land if the party seeking enforcement has so changed his position in reasonable reliance upon the contract that injustice can be prevented only by enforcing the contract. Restatement, Section 129. In applying this **part performance** exception, many States require that the transferee has paid a portion or all of the purchase price *and* either has taken possession of the real estate or has started to make valuable improvements on the land. For example, Aaron orally agrees to sell land to Barbara for $30,000. With Aaron's consent, Barbara takes possession of the land, pays Aaron $10,000, builds a house on the land, and occupies it. Several years later, Aaron repudiates the contract. The courts will enforce the contract against Aaron. On the other hand, the courts will not enforce the promise unless equity so demands.

An oral promise by a purchaser is also enforceable if the seller fully performs by conveying the property to the purchaser. As previously indicated, however, payment of part or all of the price is not sufficient in itself to remove the contract from the scope of the statute.

## ONE-YEAR PROVISION

The statute of frauds requires all contracts that *cannot* be fully performed within one year of their making to be in writing or in proper electronic form. Restatement, Section 130.

**The Possibility Test** To determine whether a contract can be performed within a year, the courts ask whether it is *possible* to complete its performance within a year. The **possibility test** does not ask whether the agreement is likely to be performed within one year from the date it was formed; nor does it ask whether the parties think that performance will be within the year. The enforceability of the contract depends not on probabilities or on the actuality of subsequent events but on whether the terms of the contract make it possible for performance to occur within one year. For example, an oral contract between Alice and Bill for Alice to build a bridge, which should reasonably take three years, is enforceable if it is possible, although extremely unlikely and difficult, for Alice to perform the contract in one year. Similarly, if Alice agrees to employ Bill for life, this contract also is not within the statute of frauds. Given the possibility that Bill may die within the year (in which case the contract would be completely performed), the contract is therefore one that is *fully performable* within a year. Contracts of indefinite duration are likewise excluded from the provision. On the other hand, an oral contract to employ another person for thirteen months could not possibly be performed within a year and is unenforceable.

◆ **SEE CASE 15-2**

**Computation of Time** The year runs from the time the agreement is made, not from the time when the performance is to begin. For example, on January 1, 2010, A orally hires B to work for eleven months starting on May 1, 2010. That contract will be fully performed on March 31, 2011, which is more than one year after January 1, 2010, the date the contract was made. Consequently, it is *within* the statute of frauds and unenforceable as it is oral.

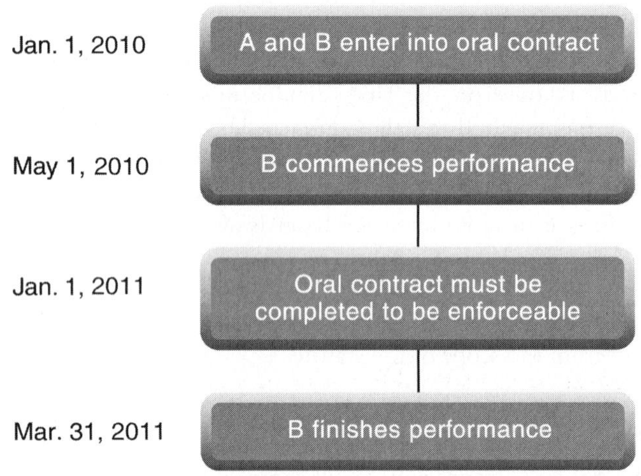


Similarly, a contract for a year's performance, which is to begin three days after the date on which the contract is made, is within the statute and, if oral, is unenforceable. If, however, the performance is to begin the following day or, under the terms of the agreement, could have begun the following day, the contract is not within the statute and need not be in writing, as the one year's performance would be completed on the anniversary date of the making of the contract.

**Full Performance by One Party** Where one party to a contract has fully performed, most courts hold that the promise of the other party is enforceable, even though by its terms the performance of the contract was not possible within the period of a year. Restatement, Section 130. For example, Vince borrows $4,800 from Julie, orally promising to pay Julie $4,800 in three annual installments of $1,600. Vince's promise is enforceable, notwithstanding the one-year provision, because Julie has fully performed by making the loan.

## SALE OF GOODS

The original statute of frauds, which applied to contracts for the sale of goods, has been used as a prototype for the UCC Article 2 statute of frauds provision. Section 2–201 of the UCC provides that a contract for the sale of goods for the price of **$500 or more** is not enforceable unless there is some writing or record sufficient to indicate that the parties have made a contract for sale. **Goods**, as previously indicated, are defined as movable personal property. Section 2–105(1). The definition expressly includes growing crops and unborn animals.

**Admission** The Code permits an oral contract for the sale of goods to be enforced against a party who in his pleading, testimony, or otherwise in court admits that a contract was made, but limits enforcement to the quantity of goods so admitted. Section 2–201(3)(b). The language "otherwise in court" may include pretrial deposition and written interrogatories of the defendant. Some courts now apply this exception to other statute of frauds provisions.

**Specially Manufactured Goods** The Code permits a seller to enforce an oral contract for goods specially manufactured for a buyer, but only if evidence indicates that the goods were made for the buyer and the seller can show that he made a *substantial beginning* of their manufacture prior to receiving any notice of repudiation. Section 2–201(3)(a). If goods manufactured on special order are nonetheless readily marketable in the ordinary course of the seller's business, this exception does not apply.

For example, if Jim brings an action against Robin alleging breach of an oral contract under which Robin agreed to purchase from Jim three million balloons with Robin's trademark imprinted on them at a price of $30,000, the action is not subject to the defense of the statute of frauds unless Robin can show (1) that the balloons are suitable for sale to other buyers, which is highly improbable in view of the trademark, or (2) that Jim received notice of repudiation before he had made a substantial start on the production of the balloons or had otherwise substantially committed himself to procuring them.

◆ **SEE CASE 15-3**

**Delivery or Payment and Acceptance** Prior to the Code, delivery and acceptance of part of the goods or payment of part of the price made the entire oral contract enforceable

◆ FIGURE 15-1: **The Statute of Frauds**

| Contracts within the Statute of Frauds | Exceptions |
|---|---|
| **Suretyship—a promise to answer for the duty of another** | • Main purpose rule<br>• Original promise<br>• Promise made to debtor |
| **Executor-Administrator—a promise to answer personally for debt of decedent** | • Main purpose rule<br>• Original promise<br>• Promise made to debtor |
| **Agreements made upon consideration of marriage** | • Mutual promises to marry |
| **Agreements for the transfer of an interest in land** | • Part performance plus detrimental reliance<br>• Seller conveys property |
| **Agreements not to be performed within one year** | • Full performance by one party<br>• Possibility of performance within one year |
| **Sale of goods for $500 or more** | • Admission<br>• Specially manufactured goods<br>• Delivery or payment acceptance |

against the buyer who had received part delivery or against the seller who had received part payment. Under the Code, such "partial performance" validates the contract only for the goods that have been accepted or for which payment has been accepted. Section 2–201(3)(c). To illustrate, Johnson orally agrees to buy one thousand watches from Barnes for $15,000. Barnes delivers three hundred watches to Johnson, who receives and accepts the watches. The oral contract is enforceable to the extent of three hundred watches ($4,500)—those received and accepted—but is unenforceable to the extent of seven hundred watches ($10,500).

But what if the contract, such as one for the sale of an automobile, is indivisible so that the making of part payment creates only a choice between not enforcing the contract or enforcing it as a whole? Presently, authority is divided on this issue, although the better rule appears to be that such part payment and acceptance makes the entire contract enforceable.

◆ SEE FIGURE 15-1: **The Statute of Frauds**

## MODIFICATION OR RESCISSION OF CONTRACTS WITHIN THE STATUTE OF FRAUDS

Oral contracts modifying previously existing contracts are unenforceable if the resulting contract is within the statute of frauds. The reverse is also true: an oral modification of a prior contract is enforceable if the new contract is not within the statute. Thus, examples of unenforceable oral contractual modifications include an oral promise to guarantee additional duties of another, an oral agreement to substitute different land for that described in the original contract, and an oral agreement to extend an employee's contract for six months to a total of two years. On the other hand, an oral agreement to modify an employee's contract from two years to six months at a higher salary is not within the statute of frauds and is enforceable.

By extension, an oral rescission is effective and discharges all unperformed duties under the original contract. For example, Linda and Donald enter into a written contract of employment for a two-year term. Later they orally agree to rescind the contract. The oral agreement is effective, and the written contract is rescinded. Where, however, land has been transferred, an agreement to rescind the transaction constitutes a contract to retransfer the land and is within the statute of frauds.

Under the UCC, the decisive point is the contract price *after* the modification. Section 2–209(3). If the parties enter into an oral contract to sell for $450 a motorcycle to be delivered to the buyer and later, prior to delivery, orally agree that the seller shall paint the motorcycle and install new tires and that the buyer shall pay a price of $550, the modified contract is unenforceable. Conversely, if the parties have a written contract for the sale of two hundred bushels of wheat at a price of $4 per bushel and later orally agree to decrease the quantity to one hundred bushels at the same price per bushel, the agreement, as modified, is for a total price of $400 and thus is enforceable.

## COMPLIANCE WITH THE STATUTE OF FRAUDS

Even though a contract is within the statute of frauds, a sufficient *writing*, *memorandum*, or *record* may justify its enforcement. The writing or record need not be in any specific form, nor be an attempt by the parties to enter into a binding contract, nor represent their entire agreement: it need only comply with the requirements of the statute of frauds.

### GENERAL CONTRACTS PROVISIONS

The English statute of frauds and most modern statutes of frauds require that the agreement be evidenced by a writing or record to be enforceable. The note, memorandum, or record, which may be formal or informal, must

1. specify the parties to the contract;
2. specify with reasonable certainty the subject matter and the essential terms of the unperformed promises; and
3. be signed by the party to be charged or by his agent.

The statute's purpose in requiring a writing or record is to ensure that the parties have entered into a contract. The writing or record, therefore, need not exist at the time of the litigation; showing that the memorandum once existed is sufficient.

The memorandum may be a receipt or a check. It may be such that the parties themselves view the memorandum as having no legal significance whatever, as, for example, a personal letter between the parties, an interdepartmental communication, an advertisement, or the record books of a business. The writing or record need not have been delivered to the party who seeks to take advantage of it, and it may even contain a repudiation of the oral agreement. For example, Adrian and Joseph enter into an oral agreement that Adrian will sell Blackacre to Joseph for $5,000. Adrian subsequently receives a better offer and sends Joseph a signed letter, which begins by reciting all the material terms of the oral agreement. The letter concludes, "Since my agreement to sell Blackacre to you for $5,000 was oral, I am not bound by my promise. I have since received a better offer and will accept that one." Adrian's letter constitutes a sufficient memorandum for Joseph to enforce Adrian's promise to sell Blackacre. It should be recognized that because Joseph did not sign the memorandum, the writing does not bind him. Thus, a contract may be enforceable against only one of the parties.

The "signature" may be initials or may even be typewritten or printed, so long as the party intended it to authenticate the writing or record. Furthermore, the signature need not be at the bottom of the page or at the customary place for a signature. The memorandum may consist of *several* papers or documents, none of which would be sufficient by itself. The several memoranda, however, must together satisfy all of the requirements of a writing or record to comply with the statute of frauds and must clearly indicate that they relate to the same transaction. Restatement, Section 132. The latter requirement can be satisfied if (1) the writings are physically attached, (2) the writings refer to each other, or (3) an examination of the writings shows them to be in reference to each other.

◆ **SEE CASE 15-4**

### SALE OF GOODS

The statute of frauds provision under Article 2 is more liberal. For a sale of goods, Section 2–201 of the Code requires merely some writing or record

1. sufficient to indicate that a contract has been made between the parties;
2. specifying the quantity of goods to be sold; and
3. signed by the party against whom enforcement is sought or by her authorized agent or broker.

The writing or record is sufficient even if it omits or incorrectly states an agreed-upon term; however, where the quantity term is misstated, the contract can be enforced only to the extent of the quantity stated in the writing or record.

As with general contracts, several related documents may satisfy the writing or record requirement. Moreover, the signature again may be by initials or even typewritten or printed, so long as the party intended thereby to authenticate the writing or record.

In addition, the Code provides relief to a merchant who, within a reasonable time after entering into the oral contract, confirms the contract for the sale of goods by a letter or signed writing to the other party if he too is a merchant. As between **merchants**, the **written confirmation**, if sufficient against the sender, is also sufficient against the recipient unless he gives written notice of his objection within ten days after receiving the confirmation. Section 2–201(2). This means that if these requirements have been met, the recipient of the writing or record is in the same position he would have assumed by signing it; and the confirmation, therefore, is enforceable against him.

For example, Brown Co. and ATM Industries enter into an oral contract that provides that ATM will deliver twelve thousand shirts to Brown at $6 per shirt. Brown sends a letter to ATM acknowledging the agreement. The letter, containing the quantity term but not the price, is signed by

Brown's president and is mailed to ATM's vice president for sales. Brown was bound by the contract once its authorized agent signs the letter; ATM cannot raise the defense of the statute of frauds if ATM does not object to the letter within ten days after receiving it. Therefore, it is extremely important for merchants to examine their mail carefully and promptly to make certain that any written confirmations conform to their understanding of their outstanding contractual agreements.

## EFFECT OF NONCOMPLIANCE

The English statute provided that "no action shall be brought" upon a contract to which the statute of frauds applied *and* which did not comply with its requirements. The Code, by comparison, states that the contract "is not enforceable by way of action or defense." Despite the difference in language the basic legal effect is the same: a contracting party has a defense to an action by the other party to enforce an oral contract that is within the statute and that does not comply with its requirements. In short, the oral contract is **unenforceable**.

For example, if Tia, a painter, and James, a homeowner, make an oral contract under which James is to give Tia a certain tract of land in return for her painting his house, the contract is unenforceable under the statute of frauds. It is a contract for the sale of an interest in land. Either party can repudiate and has a defense to an action by the other to enforce the contract.

### FULL PERFORMANCE

After all the promises of an oral contract have been performed by all the parties, the statute of frauds no longer applies. Accordingly, neither party can have the contract set aside on the grounds that it should have been in writing. The purpose of the statute is not to prohibit the performance of oral contracts but simply to exclude oral evidence of contracts within its provisions. Courts, in other words, will not "unscramble" a fully performed contract merely because it was not in writing or a proper record. In short, the statute applies to executory contracts only.

### RESTITUTION

A party to a contract that is unenforceable because of the statute of frauds may have, nonetheless, acted in reliance upon the contract. In such a case the party may recover in restitution the benefits he conferred upon the other in relying upon the unenforceable contract. Thus, if Wilton makes an oral contract to furnish services to Rochelle that are not to be performed within a year and Rochelle discharges Wilton after three months, Wilton may recover as restitution the value of the services he rendered during the three months. Most courts require, however, that the party seeking restitution not be in default.

### PROMISSORY ESTOPPEL

A growing number of courts have used the doctrine of promissory estoppel to displace the requirement of a writing by enforcing oral contracts within the statute of frauds where the party seeking enforcement has reasonably and foreseeably relied upon a promise in such a way that injustice can be avoided only by enforcing the promise. Restatement, Section 139. This section is essentially identical to Section 90 of the Restatement, which, as discussed in *Chapter 12*, dispenses with the requirement of consideration, although the comments to Section 139 state that "the requirement of consideration is more easily displaced than the requirement of a writing." The remedy granted is limited, as justice requires, and depends upon such factors as the availability of other remedies; the foreseeability, reasonableness, and substantiality of the reliance; and the extent to which reliance corroborates evidence of the promise.

# PAROL EVIDENCE RULE

A contract reduced to writing and signed by the parties is frequently the result of many conversations, conferences, proposals, counterproposals, letters, and memoranda and sometimes is the product of negotiations conducted, or partly conducted, by agents of the parties. Any given stage in the negotiations may have produced tentative agreements that were superseded (or regarded as such by one of the parties) by subsequent negotiations. Offers may have been made and withdrawn, either expressly or by implication, or forgotten in the give-and-take of negotiations. Ultimately, though, the parties prepare and sign a final draft of the written contract, which may or may not include all of the points that were discussed and agreed upon during the negotiations. By signing the agreement, however, the parties have declared it to be their contract; and the terms it contains represent the contract they have made. As a rule of substantive law, neither party is later permitted to show that the contract they made differs from the terms and provisions that appear in the written agreement. This rule, which also applies to wills and deeds, is called the parol evidence rule.

## THE RULE

When a contract is expressed in a writing that is intended to be the complete and final expression of the rights and duties of the parties, parol evidence of *prior* oral or written negotiations or agreements of the parties, or their *contemporaneous* oral agreements that vary or change the written contract, are not admissible. The word *parol* means literally "speech" or "words." The term **parol evidence** refers to any evidence, whether oral or in writing, which is outside the written contract and not incorporated into it either directly or by reference.

The parol evidence rule applies only to an *integrated* contract; that is, one contained in a certain writing or writings to which the parties have assented as the statement of the complete agreement or contract between them. When a contract is thus integrated, the courts will not permit parol evidence of any prior or contemporaneous agreement to vary, change, alter, or modify any of the terms or provisions of the written contract. Restatement, Section 213.

A writing may contain a **merger clause**, which states that the writing is intended to be the complete and final expression of the agreement between the parties. Most courts consider a merger clause to be conclusive proof of an integrated contract, while a few courts view a merger clause only as evidence of an integrated contract.

The reason for the parol evidence rule is that the parties, by reducing their entire agreement to writing, are regarded as having intended the writing that they signed to include the whole of their agreement. The terms and provisions contained in the writing are there because the parties intended them to be there. Conversely, any provision not in the writing is regarded as having been omitted because the parties intended that it should not be a part of their contract. In safeguarding the contract as made by the parties, the rule excluding evidence that would tend to change, alter, vary, or modify the terms of a written agreement applies to all integrated written contracts and deals with what terms are part of the contract. The rule differs from the statute of frauds, which governs what contracts must be evidenced by a writing to be enforceable.

◆ **SEE CASE 15-4**

◆ **SEE CASE 15-5**

## SITUATIONS TO WHICH THE RULE DOES NOT APPLY

The parol evidence rule, in spite of its name, is neither an exclusionary rule of evidence nor a rule of construction or interpretation; rather, it is a rule of substantive law that defines the limits of a contract. Bearing this in mind, as well as the reason underlying the rule, it should be clear that the rule does **not** apply to any of the following:

1. A contract that is partly written and partly oral; that is, one in which the parties do not intend the writing to be their entire agreement.
2. A clerical or *typographical error* that obviously does not represent the agreement of the parties. Where, for example, a written contract for the services of a skilled mining engineer provides that his rate of compensation is to be $7 per day, a court of equity would permit reformation (correction) of the contract to rectify the mistake upon a showing that both parties intended the rate to be $700 per day.
3. Evidence showing the lack of *contractual capacity* of one of the parties, such as proof of minority, intoxication, or mental incompetency. Such evidence would not tend to vary, change, or alter any of the terms of the written agreement, but rather would show that the written agreement was voidable or void.
4. A *defense* of fraud, misrepresentation, duress, undue influence, mistake, illegality, or unconscionability. Though evidence establishing any of these defenses would not purport to vary, change, or alter any of the terms of the written agreement, it would show such agreement to be voidable, void, or unenforceable.
5. A *condition precedent* to which the parties agreed orally at the time they executed the written agreement and to which they made the entire agreement subject. Again, such evidence does not tend to vary, alter, or change any of the terms of the agreement, but rather shows whether the entire written agreement, unchanged and unaltered, ever became effective. For example, if John signs a subscription agreement to buy stock in a corporation to be formed and delivers the agreement to Thompson with the mutual understanding that it is not to be binding unless the other persons financially responsible under it shall each agree to buy at least an equivalent amount of such stock, John is permitted to show by parol evidence this condition.
6. A *subsequent mutual rescission or modification* of the written contract. Parol evidence of a later agreement does not tend to show that the integrated writing did not represent the contract between the parties at the time it was made. Parties to an existing contract, whether written or oral, may agree to change the terms of their contract as they see fit, or to cancel it completely, if they so desire.
7. Parol evidence is admissible to explain *ambiguous* terms in the contract. To enforce a contract, it is necessary to understand its intended meaning. Nevertheless, such interpretation is not to alter, change, or vary the terms of the contract.
8. The rule does not prevent a party from proving the existence of a separate, distinct contract between the same parties.

## SUPPLEMENTAL EVIDENCE

Although a written agreement may not be contradicted by evidence of a prior agreement or of a contemporaneous agreement, under the Restatement, Section 216, and the Code, Section 2–202, a written contract may be explained or supplemented by (1) course of dealing between the parties, (2) usage of trade, (3) course of performance, or (4) evidence of consistent additional terms, unless the parties intended the writing to be a complete and exclusive statement of their agreement.

A **course of dealing** is a sequence of previous conduct between the parties under an agreement that the court reasonably may

◆ **FIGURE 15-2: Parol Evidence Rule**

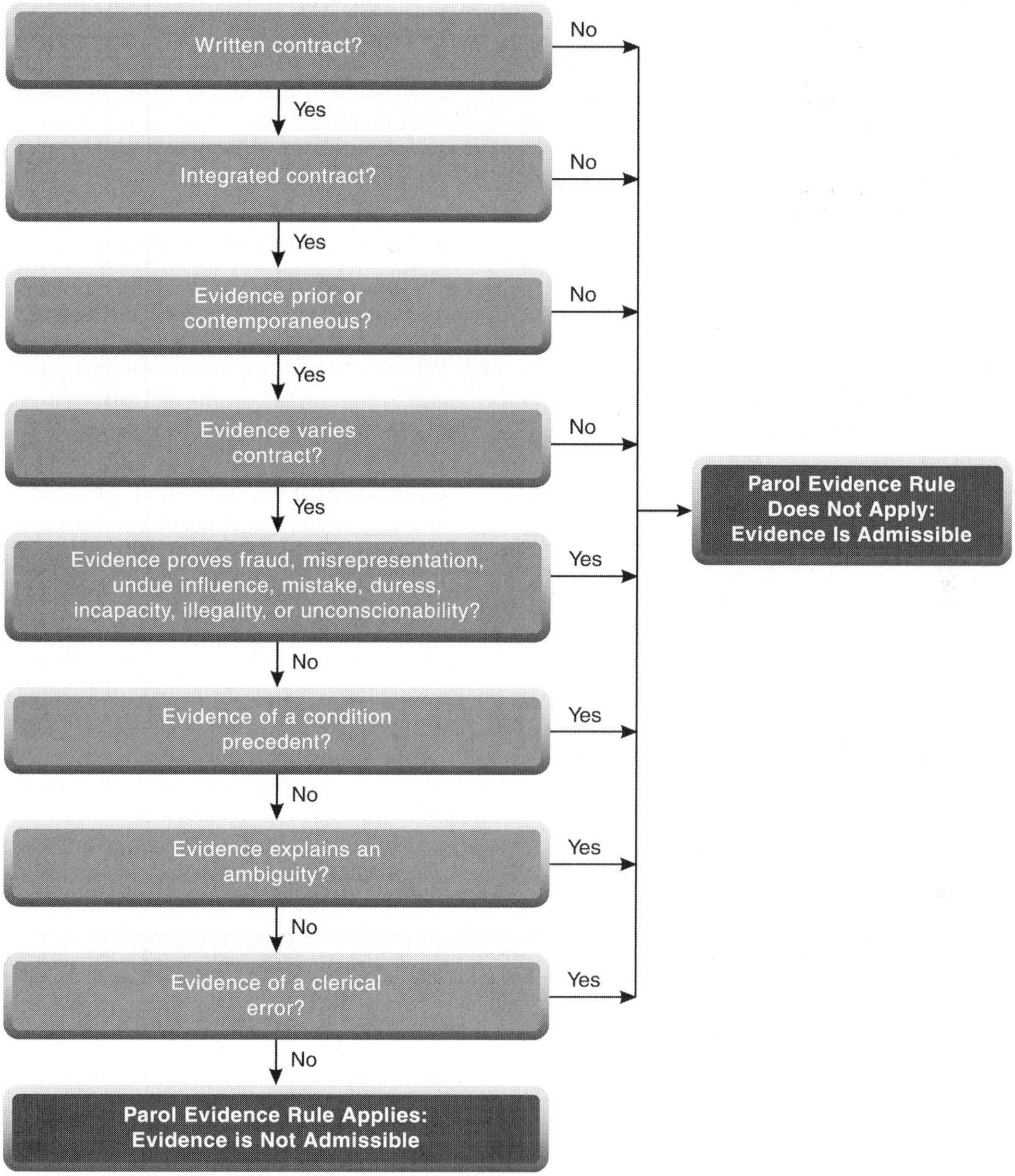


regard as establishing a common basis of understanding for interpreting their expressions and other conduct.

A **usage of trade** is a practice or method of dealing, regularly observed and followed in a place, vocation, or trade.

**Course of performance** refers to the manner and extent to which the respective parties to a contract have accepted without objection successive tenders of performance by the other party.

The Restatement and the Code permit *supplemental consistent evidence* to be introduced into a court proceeding, but only if it does not contradict a term or terms of the original agreement and would probably not have been included in the original contract.

◆ SEE FIGURE 15-2: **Parol Evidence Rule**

## INTERPRETATION OF CONTRACTS

Although the written words or language in which the parties embodied their agreement or contract may not be changed by parol evidence, the ascertainment (determination) of the meaning to be given the written language is outside the scope of the parol evidence rule. Though written words embody the terms of the contract, words are but symbols. If their meaning is unclear, the courts may clarify this meaning by applying rules of interpretation or construction and by using extrinsic (external) evidence, where necessary.

The Restatement, Section 200, defines **interpretation** as the ascertainment of the meaning of a promise or agreement or a term of the promise or agreement. Where the language in a contract is unambiguous, the courts will not accept extrinsic evidence tending to show a meaning different from that which the words clearly convey. Its function being to interpret and construe written contracts and documents, the court adopts rules of interpretation to apply a legal standard to the words contained in the agreement. The courts will attempt to interpret a contract in accordance with the intent of the parties. If the subjective intent of the parties fails to provide a clear interpretation, the courts will make an objective interpretation. Among the rules that aid interpretation are the following:

1. Words and other conduct are interpreted in the light of all the circumstances, and the principal purpose of the parties, if ascertainable, is given great weight.
2. A writing is interpreted as a whole, and all writings that are part of the same transaction are interpreted together.
3. Unless a different intention is manifested, language that has a commonly accepted meaning is interpreted in accordance with that meaning.
4. Unless a different intention is manifested, technical terms and words of art are given their technical meanings.
5. Wherever reasonable, the manifestations of intention of the parties to a promise or agreement are interpreted as consistent with each other and with any relevant course of performance, course of dealing, or usage of trade.
6. An interpretation that gives a reasonable, lawful, and effective meaning to all the terms is preferred over an interpretation that leaves a part unreasonable, unlawful, or of no effect.
7. Specific terms and exact terms are given greater weight than general language.
8. Separately negotiated or added terms are given greater weight than standardized terms or other terms not separately negotiated.
9. Express terms, course of performance, course of dealing, and usage of trade are weighted in that order.
10. Where a term or promise has several possible meanings, it will be interpreted against the party who supplied the contract or the term. Restatement, Sections 201, 202, and 203.
11. Where written provisions are inconsistent with typed or printed provisions, the written provision is given preference. Likewise, typed provisions are given preferences to printed provisions.
12. If the amount payable is set forth in both figures and words and the amounts differ, the words control the figures.

It may be observed that, through the application of the parol evidence rule (where properly applicable) and the above rules of interpretation and construction, the law not only enforces a contract but, in so doing, exercises great care that the contract being enforced is the one the parties made and that the sense and meaning of the parties' intentions are carefully ascertained and given effect.

# CHAPTER SUMMARY

## STATUTE OF FRAUDS

### CONTRACTS WITHIN THE STATUTE OF FRAUDS

**Rule** contracts within the statute of frauds must be evidenced by a writing to be enforceable

**Electronic Records** full effect is given to electronic contracts and signatures

**Suretyship Provision** applies to promises to pay the debts of others

- ***Promise Must Be Collateral*** promisor must be secondarily, not primarily, liable
- ***Main Purpose Doctrine*** if primary object is to provide an economic benefit to the surety, then the promise is not within the statute

**Executor-Administrator Provision** applies to promises to answer personally for duties of decedents

**Marriage Provision** applies to promises made in consideration of marriage but not to mutual promises to marry

**Land Contract Provision** applies to promises to transfer any rights, privileges, powers, or immunities in real property

**One-Year Provision** applies to contracts that cannot be performed within one year

- ***The Possibility Test*** the criterion is whether it is possible, not likely, for the agreement to be performed within one year
- ***Computation of Time*** the year runs from the time the agreement is made

| | |
|---|---|
| | • ***Full Performance by One Party*** makes the promise of the other party enforceable under majority view<br>**Sale of Goods** a contract for the sale of goods for the price of $500 or more must be evidenced by a writing or record to be enforceable<br>• ***Admission*** an admission in pleadings, testimony, or otherwise in court makes the contract enforceable for the quantity of goods admitted<br>• ***Specially Manufactured Goods*** an oral contract for specially manufactured goods is enforceable<br>• ***Delivery or Payment and Acceptance*** validates the contract only for the goods that have been accepted or for which payment has been accepted<br>**Modification or Rescission of Contracts within the Statute of Frauds** oral contracts modifying existing contracts are unenforceable if the resulting contract is within the statute of frauds |
| **METHODS OF COMPLIANCE** | **General Contract Law** the writing(s) or record must<br>• specify the parties to the contract<br>• specify the subject matter and essential terms<br>• be signed by the party to be charged or by her agent<br>**Sale of Goods** provides a general method of compliance for all parties and an additional one for merchants<br>• ***Writing(s) or Record*** must (1) be sufficient to indicate that a contract has been made between the parties, (2) be signed by the party against whom enforcement is sought or by her authorized agent, and (3) specify the quantity of goods to be sold<br>• ***Written Confirmation*** between merchants, a written confirmation that is sufficient against the sender is also sufficient against the recipient unless the recipient gives written notice of his objection within ten days |
| **EFFECT OF NONCOMPLIANCE** | **Oral Contract within Statute of Frauds** is unenforceable<br>**Full Performance** statute does not apply to executed contracts<br>**Restitution** is available in quasi contract for benefits conferred in reliance on the oral contract<br>**Promissory Estoppel** oral contracts will be enforced where the party seeking enforcement has reasonably and justifiably relied on the promise and the court can avoid injustice only by enforcement |

## PAROL EVIDENCE RULE AND INTERPRETATION OF CONTRACTS

| | |
|---|---|
| **PAROL EVIDENCE RULE** | **Statement of Rule** when parties express a contract in a writing that they intend to be the complete and final expression of their rights and duties, evidence of their prior oral or written negotiations or agreements of their contemporaneous oral agreements that vary or change the written contract are not admissible<br>***Situations to Which the Rule Does Not Apply***<br>• a contract that is not an integrated document<br>• correction of a typographical error<br>• showing that a contract was void or voidable<br>• showing whether a condition has in fact occurred<br>• showing a subsequent mutual rescission or modification of the contract<br>**Supplemental Evidence** may be admitted<br>• ***Course of Dealing*** previous conduct between the parties<br>• ***Usage of Trade*** practice engaged in by the trade or industry<br>• ***Course of Performance*** conduct between the parties concerning performance of the particular contract<br>• ***Supplemental Consistent Evidence*** |

**INTERPRETATION OF CONTRACTS**

**Definition** the ascertainment of the meaning of a promise or agreement or a term of the promise or agreement

**Rules of Interpretation** include the following:

- all the circumstances are considered and the principal purpose of the parties is given great weight
- a writing is interpreted as a whole
- commonly accepted meanings are used unless the parties manifest a different intention
- wherever possible, the intentions of the parties are interpreted as consistent with each other and with course of performance, course of dealing, or usage of trade
- technical terms are given their technical meaning
- specific terms are given greater weight than general language
- separately negotiated terms are given greater weight than standardized terms or those not separately negotiated
- the order for interpretation is express terms, course of performance, course of dealing, and usage of trade
- where a term has several possible meanings, the term will be interpreted against the party who supplied the contract or term
- written provisions are given preference over typed or printed provisions, and typed provisions are given preference over printed provisions
- if an amount is set forth in both words and figures and they differ, words control figures

# CASES

## CASE 15-1

### Suretyship/Main Purpose Rule
### ROSEWOOD CARE CENTER, INC., v. CATERPILLAR, INC.

Supreme Court of Illinois, 2007
226 Ill.2d 559, 877 N.E.2d 1091, 315 Ill.Dec. 762
http://caselaw.findlaw.com/il-supreme-court/1066308.html

**Burke, J.**

On January 3, 2002, Caterpillar contacted HSM Management Services (HSM), the management agent for Rosewood, a skilled nursing facility. Caterpillar requested that Rosewood admit Cook on a "managed care basis (fixed rate)." HSM advised Caterpillar that Rosewood would not admit Cook on those terms.

Shortly thereafter, on January 10, Dr. Norma Just, Caterpillar's employee in charge of medical care relating to workers' compensation claims, contacted HSM. Just told HSM that Cook had sustained a work-related injury and was receiving medical care at Caterpillar's expense under the workers' compensation laws. Just requested that Cook be admitted to Rosewood for skilled nursing care and therapy, and stated that the cost of Cook's care would be 100% covered and paid directly by Caterpillar to Rosewood with a zero deductible and no maximum limit. Just further advised HSM that Cook had been precertified for four weeks of care. Just asked that Rosewood send the bills for Cook's care to Caterpillar's workers' compensation division.

That same day, HSM faxed a letter to Dr. Just confirming their conversation. In this letter, HSM requested Just to acknowledge that she had agreed to (1) a "SNF admission for Cook," (2) four weeks of treatment, and (3) the need for further evaluation in connection with the length of care Cook would require. Just signed the fax, acknowledging her agreement, and returned it the next day.

On January 20, "Sue" from Dr. Just's office telephoned HSM and confirmed approval for Cook's transfer from the hospital to Rosewood. On January 30, Sue reconfirmed, via telephone, Caterpillar's authorization for Cook's care and treatment in accordance with the January 10 agreement, except that Sue now advised HSM that Cook was precertified for two weeks of care instead of the original four weeks.

On January 30, Cook was admitted to Rosewood. Upon her admission, Cook signed a document entitled

"Assignment of Insurance Benefits" as required by law. In this document, Cook assigned any insurance benefits she might receive to Rosewood and acknowledged her liability for any unpaid services.

Caterpillar, through its health-care management company, continued to orally "authorize" care for Cook and did so on February 8, February 25, March 11, March 21, April 8, April 18, May 16, and June 4. Cook remained at Rosewood until June 13, 2002. The total of Rosewood's charges for Cook's care amounted to $181,857.

Rosewood billed Caterpillar on a monthly basis on February 12, March 11, April 15, May 14, June 10, and July 15. Caterpillar never objected to the bills being sent to it for Cook's care, nor did it ever advise Rosewood that treatment was not authorized. However, Caterpillar ultimately refused to pay for services rendered to Cook.

Rosewood filed a * * * complaint against both Caterpillar and Cook. Relevant here, count III of Rosewood's complaint stated a claim for breach of contract against Caterpillar, * * * Rosewood averred that it only admitted Cook based on Caterpillar's promise. Rosewood further averred that it would not have admitted Cook without Caterpillar's promise to pay.

Caterpillar moved to dismiss the breach of contract count (count III). * * * Caterpillar argued that these claims were barred because its alleged agreement to take responsibility for the cost of Cook's care was not in writing, as required by the statute of frauds. * * *

On April 4, 2005, the trial court granted Caterpillar's motion to dismiss the breach of contract * * * and, thus, barred Rosewood's claims. * * *

On appeal, the appellate court reversed and remanded.

* * *

In general, the statute of frauds provides that a promise to pay the debt of another, i.e., a suretyship agreement, is unenforceable unless it is in writing. * * *

* * *

> The plain object of the statute is to require higher and more certain evidence to charge a party, where he does not receive the substantial benefit of the transaction, and where another is primarily liable to pay the debt or discharge the duty; and thereby to afford greater security against the setting up of fraudulent demands, where the party sought to be charged is another than the real debtor, and whose debt or duty, on performance of the alleged contract by such third person, would be discharged. [Citation.]

* * *

## II. "Main Purpose" or "Leading Object" Rule

* * * According to Rosewood, Caterpillar's promise falls outside the statute of frauds pursuant to the "main purpose" or "leading object" rule. Under this rule, when the "main purpose" or "leading object" of the promisor/surety is to subserve or advance its own pecuniary or business interests, the promise does not fall within the statute. [Citation.] As section 11 of the Restatement (Third) of Suretyship & Guaranty states:

> A contract that all or part of the duty of the principal obligor to the obligee shall be satisfied by the secondary obligor is not within the Statute of Frauds as a promise to answer for the duty of another if the consideration for the promise is in fact or apparently desired by the secondary obligor mainly for its own economic benefit, rather than the benefit of the principal obligor. [Citation.]

The reason for the "main purpose" or "leading object" rule has been explained:

> Where the secondary obligor's main purpose is its own pecuniary or business advantage, the gratuitous or sentimental element often present in suretyship is eliminated, the likelihood of disproportion in the values exchanged between secondary obligor and obligee is reduced, and the commercial context commonly provides evidentiary safeguards. Thus, there is less need for cautionary or evidentiary formality than in other secondary obligations. [Citations.]

* * *

It is clear * * * that the "main purpose" or "leading object" rule, as set out in the Restatements, has been a part of Illinois law since 1873. We note that the majority of jurisdictions have adopted this rule as well. [Citations.]

Applying this rule in the case at bar, Caterpillar denies that the "main purpose" for its alleged promise to Rosewood was to promote its own interest. Caterpillar also denies that it received any benefit from the agreement. Alternatively, Caterpillar argues that we should remand this cause for further proceedings to determine the "main purpose" or "leading object" of its promise.

Whether the "main purpose" or "leading object" of the promisor is to promote a pecuniary or business advantage to it is generally a question for the trier of fact. [Citation.] * * *

Here, a decision on what was Caterpillar's "main purpose" or "leading object" in making the promise cannot be made based on the allegations in the complaint. * * * The determination must be made by the trier of fact based on evidence to be presented by the parties. * * *

## III. Whether a Suretyship Was Created in This Case

Rosewood makes a final argument for why Caterpillar's promise is not within the statute of frauds. Rosewood argues that no suretyship was created by Caterpillar's promise. According to Rosewood, Caterpillar contracted directly with Rosewood, became liable for its own commitment, and received benefits as a result.

A suretyship exists when one person undertakes an obligation of another person who is also under an obligation or duty to the creditor/obligee. [Citation.] Specifically, "[a] contract is not within the Statute of Frauds as a contract to answer for the duty of another unless the promisee is an obligee of the other's duty, the promisor is a surety for the other, and the promisee knows or has reason to know of the suretyship relation." [Citation.] Moreover:

> Where promises of the same performance are made by two persons for a consideration which inures to the benefit of only one of them, the promise of the other is within the Statute of Frauds as a contract to answer for the duty of another, whether or not the promise is in terms conditional on default by the one to whose benefit the consideration inures, unless
>
> (a) the other is not a surety for the one to whose benefit the consideration inures; or * * *
>
> (c) the promisee neither knows nor has reason to know that the consideration does not inure to the benefit of both promisors. [Citation.]

* * *

The question of whether Caterpillar's promise was a suretyship or not, like the question regarding Caterpillar's "main purpose" or "leading object," cannot be determined on the basis of allegations in Rosewood's complaint. This question is a factual one to be made based on evidence to be presented by the parties. Accordingly, this issue must also be resolved by the circuit court on remand.

## CASE 15-2

### One-Year Provision
### IACONO v. LYONS

Court of Appeals of Texas, 2000
962 S.W.2d 268, rehearing denied

**O'Connor, J.**

Mary Iacono, the plaintiff below and appellant here, appeals from a take-nothing summary judgment rendered in favor of Carolyn Lyons, the defendant below and appellee here. We reverse and remand.

#### Background

The plaintiff and defendant had been friends for almost 35 years. In late 1996, the defendant invited the plaintiff to join her on a trip to Las Vegas, Nevada. There is no dispute that the defendant paid all the expenses for the trip, including providing money for gambling.

The plaintiff contended she was invited to Las Vegas by the defendant because the defendant thought the plaintiff was lucky. Sometime before the trip, the plaintiff had a dream about winning on a Las Vegas slot machine. The plaintiff's dream convinced her to go to Las Vegas, and she accepted the defendant's offer to split "50-50" any gambling winnings.

In February 1997, the plaintiff and defendant went to Las Vegas. They started playing the slot machines at Caesar's Palace. The plaintiff contends that, after losing $47, the defendant wanted to leave to see a show. The plaintiff begged the defendant to stay, and the defendant agreed on the condition that she (the defendant) put the coins into the machines because doing so took the plaintiff too long. The plaintiff agreed, and took the defendant to a dollar slot machine that looked like the machine in her dream. The machine did not pay on the first try. The plaintiff then said, "Just one more time," and the defendant looked at the plaintiff and said, "This one's for you, Puddin."

The slot machine paid $1,908,064. The defendant refused to share the winnings with the plaintiff, and denied they had an agreement to split any winnings. The defendant told Caesar's Palace she was the sole winner and to pay her all the winnings.

The plaintiff sued the defendant for breach of contract. The defendant moved for summary judgment on the grounds that any oral agreement was unenforceable under the statute of frauds or was voidable for lack of consideration. The trial court rendered summary judgment in favor of the defendant. * * *

* * *

#### Consideration

The defendant asserted the agreement, if any, was unenforceable under the statute of frauds because it could not be performed within one year. There is no dispute that the winnings were to be paid over a period of 20 years.

* * *

[The one year provision of the statute of frauds] does not apply if the contract, from its terms, could possibly be performed within a year—however improbable performance within one year may be. [Citations.]

To determine the applicability of the statute of frauds with indefinite contracts, this Court may use any reasonably clear method of ascertaining the intended length of performance. [Citation.] The method is used to determine the parties' intentions at the time of contracting. [Citation.] The fact that the entire performance within one year is not required, or expected, will not bring an agreement within the statute. [Citations.]

Assuming without deciding that the parties agreed to share their gambling winnings, such an agreement possibly could have been performed within one year. For example, if the plaintiff and defendant had won $200, they probably would have received all the money in one pay-out and could have split the winnings immediately. * * *

Therefore, the defendant was not entitled to summary judgment based on her affirmative defense of the statute of frauds.

* * *

We reverse the trial court's judgment and remand for further proceedings.

---

CASE 15-3

## Specially Manufactured Goods
## KALAS v. COOK

Appellate Court of Connecticut, 2002

70 Conn.App. 477, 800 A.2d 553, 47 U.C.C. Rep.Serv.2d 1307

http://www.jud.state.ct.us/external/supapp/Cases/AROap/70ap412.pdf

**Peters, J.**

Pursuant to a long-standing oral agreement, a print shop manufactured and delivered written materials designed by the buyer for the buyer's use and sale. After the buyer's death, the executor of her estate refused to pay for the last deliveries of these materials to the buyer. The principal issue in this appeal is whether the statute of frauds, as codified in the Uniform Commercial Code, [citation], bars enforcement of the oral agreement. * * * [W]e agree with the [trial] court's conclusion that, under the circumstances of this case, the seller is entitled to be paid.

The plaintiff, Barbara H. Kalas, owner of the print shop, filed a complaint against the defendant, Edward W. Cook, executor of the estate of the buyer, Adelma G. Simmons. The plaintiff alleged that the defendant, in breach of the obligations contained in an oral contract with Simmons for the sale of goods, had refused to pay for goods delivered to her. The defendant denied these allegations and interposed a number of special defenses, including a defense under the statute of frauds. * * *

The trial court held that the transaction between the plaintiff and the deceased was a sale of goods as that term is defined in [UCC] §2–105. That determination has not been challenged on appeal. As a contract for the sale of goods, its enforcement was not precluded by the statute of frauds provision. * * * Accordingly, the court rendered a judgment in favor of the plaintiff in the amount of $24,599.38. The defendant has appealed.

The facts found by the trial court, which are currently uncontested, establish the background for the court's judgment. The plaintiff, doing business as Clinton Press of Tolland, operated a printing press and, for several decades, provided written materials, including books and pamphlets for Simmons. Simmons ordered these materials for use and sale at her farm, known as Caprilands Herb Farm (Caprilands). The defendant has not suggested that these materials could have been sold on the open market.

Due to limited space at Caprilands, the plaintiff and Simmons agreed that the written materials would remain stored at the plaintiff's print shop until Simmons decided that delivery was necessary. The materials were delivered either routinely, based on Simmons' ordinary need for materials, or upon her request for a special delivery. After each delivery, the plaintiff sent an invoice requesting payment by Simmons. These invoices were honored.

In 1991, the town of Tolland acquired the land on which the plaintiff resided. In early 1997, the plaintiff was notified that she would have to vacate the property by the end of that calendar year. Upon receiving that notice, the plaintiff decided to close her business. The plaintiff and Simmons agreed that the materials printed for Caprilands and stored at the plaintiff's print shop would be delivered on an accelerated basis. * * *

On December 3, 1997, after several months of deterioration of her physical health, Simmons died. * * * The plaintiff submitted a claim against the estate for $24,599.38 for unpaid deliveries to Caprilands. These deliveries took place from February 12, 1997 to December 11, 1997, with the last two deliveries occurring after Simmons' death.

* * *

On appeal, the defendant argues that the oral contract was invalid * * * because a writing was required by [UCC] §2–201. This argument is unpersuasive. * * *

* * *

* * * Contracts for the sale of goods * * * are governed by §2–201. [Citations.]

Under §2–201, oral agreements for the sale of goods at a price of $500 or more are presumptively unenforceable. [Citations.] The applicable provisions in this case, however, are other subsections of §2–201.

Under §2–201 (3) (a), an oral contract for the sale of goods is enforceable if the goods in question are "specially manufactured." In determining whether the specially manufactured goods exception applies, courts generally apply a four part standard: "(1) the goods must be specially made for the buyer; (2) the goods must be unsuitable for sale to others in the ordinary course of the seller's business; (3) the seller must have substantially begun to have manufactured the goods or to have a commitment for their procurement; and (4) the manufacture or commitment must have been commenced under circumstances reasonably indicating that the goods are for the buyer and prior to the seller's receipt of notification of contractual repudiation." [Citation.] In applying this standard, "courts have traditionally looked to the goods themselves. The term 'specially manufactured,' therefore, refers to the nature of the particular goods in question and not to whether the goods were made in an unusual, as opposed to the regular, business operation or manufacturing process of the seller." [Citations.]

Printed material, particularly that, as in this case, names the buyer, has been deemed by both state and federal courts to fall within the exception set out for specially manufactured goods. [Citations.]

It is inherent in the court's findings that the printed materials in the present case were specially manufactured goods. The materials were printed specifically for Caprilands. The materials included brochures and labels with the Caprilands name, as well as books that were written and designed by Simmons. The plaintiff testified that the books were printed, as Simmons had requested, in a rustic style with typed inserts and hand-drawn pictures. Therefore, none of these materials was suitable for sale to others. It is undisputed that, at the time of breach of the alleged contract, goods printed for Simmons already had been produced.

We conclude that, in light of the nature of the goods at issue * * * this case falls within the exception for specially manufactured goods. To be enforceable, the agreement for their production was, therefore, not required to be in writing under §2–201 (3) (a). Accordingly, we affirm the judgment of the court. * * * [Citations.]

CASE 15-4

Writing/Parol Evidence

## ESTATE OF JACKSON v. DEVENYNS

Supreme Court of Wyoming, 1995

892 P.2d 786

**Golden, J.**

Appellants, personal representatives of the estate of George Herbert Jackson, appeal the probate court's order of conveyance in favor of appellees. Appellants claim a writing signed by George Jackson purporting to sell seventy-nine acres, reserve approximately one acre, and sell machinery is unenforceable because the agreement does not sufficiently describe the property as required by * * * the statute of frauds. Following appellees' petition * * *, the probate court determined the writing satisfied the statute of frauds, was enforceable, and ordered the estate's personal representatives to perform the contract.

We hold the agreement's property description is insufficient to meet the requirements of the statute of frauds and reverse the order of conveyance.

* * *

### Facts

On February 9, 1993, George Jackson (Jackson) and his neighbors, Karen and Steve Devenyns (Devenyns), drafted and signed a document which reads as follows:

> George Jackson agrees to sell 79 acres and machinery to Steve and Karen Devenyns for $120,000.00
>
> **1.** 2 annual down payments of 12,500 starting in 93 $75000.00 will be carried for 13 years at 7% interest payable in yearly payments starting 1995.
>
> **2.** On the seventh year 2001 20,000.00 will be added to the balance of the mortgage payable at 7% interest.
>
> **3.** George has complete right to farm 79 acres for 3 yrs or less. He pays all water & farming expenses for the first year. Devenyns splits farming and water for 2-3rd yr. but can have hay
>
> **4.** Devenyns begins paying taxes in 93 for 79 acres.
>
> **5.** George has right to use 9 acres for 6 yrs and at the end of the 6th year the $20,000 is added to mortgage.
>
> **6.** As far as mineral rights each party will retain 50% of mineral rights with any leasing to be done by mutual consent.
>
> **7.** Pumphouse and waterline remain property of George and he shall have easement to pumphouse.
>
> **8.** Devenyns agree [ ] not to sell 9 acres which contains pumphouse at least until after place is paid for—15 years.
>
> George want[s] to keep yard intact which is area 66' × 114' as well as area around house approximately 1.3 acres 168' × 325'.

Devenyns ha[ve] first option to buy on property George will provide title insurance and survey house and approximately 1.3 acre from total. This survey can be done within 5 months.

These matters were discussed by both parties on 2/9/93 and agreed upon
Steve Devenyns
George H. Jackson

Jackson died on May 8, 1993. After the attorney for Jackson's estate refused the Devenyns' request to honor the contract, the Devenyns petitioned for an order of conveyance. * * *

The estate objected to the petition, contending the property description did not comply with the statute of frauds' requirement that the document itself sufficiently describe the property to be conveyed. The estate filed a motion, * * * objecting to proposed testimony as violative of the parol evidence rule, the statute of frauds. * * * However, the probate court heard testimony from witnesses for the Devenyns and considered parol evidence to determine whether the document satisfied the statute of frauds.

* * *

From parol evidence, the probate court determined that Jackson had used words of ownership referring to the eighty acres of real property he owned in Park County, Wyoming, and that Jackson did not own any other real property in the world. The probate court further found that Jackson had conveyed his seventy-nine acre farm, but had reserved out an approximate one acre parcel containing Jackson's house and yard. The probate court held that the reserved one acre could be satisfactorily determined by a surveyor using the dimensions found on page two of the agreement, and the sketch found on page three, as well as from assistance of witnesses who testified at the hearing that they could point out the specific area based on conversations with Jackson. The probate court held the agreement was enforceable and ordered conveyance by the estate to the Devenyns. This appeal followed.

## Discussion

### *Statute of Frauds*

* * *

A written memorandum purporting to convey real estate must sufficiently describe the property so as to comply with the requirements of the statute of frauds and permit specific performance. [Citation.] Wyoming [statute of frauds] states:

> (a) In the following cases every agreement shall be void [unenforceable in most states] unless such agreement, or some note or memorandum thereof be in writing, and subscribed by the party to be charged therewith:
>
> * * *
>
> (v) Every agreement or contract for the sale of real estate, or the lease thereof, for more than one (1) year[.]

The question of what constitutes a memorandum sufficient to satisfy the statute of frauds is set forth in Restatement (Second) of Contracts, §131 (1979) as follows:

> §131. General Requisites of a Memorandum
>
> Unless additional requirements are prescribed by the particular statute, a contract within the Statute of Frauds is enforceable if it is evidenced by any writing, signed by or on behalf of the party to be charged, which
>
> (a) reasonably identifies the subject matter of the contract,
> (b) is sufficient to indicate that a contract with respect thereto has been made between the parties or offered by the signer to the other party, and
> (c) states with reasonable certainty the essential terms of the unperformed promises in the contract.

* * * This Court's decision in [citation] concluded that a valid contract to convey land must expressly contain a description of the land, certain in itself or capable of being rendered certain by reference to an extrinsic source which the writing itself designates. [Citation.] Noland expressly prohibited supplying the writing's essential provisions by inferences or presumptions deduced from oral testimony. [Citation.]

### *Parol Evidence*

The parties both recognize that the central issue is the adequacy of the property description supplied in the agreement to satisfy the statute of frauds. The estate contends the probate court improperly relied upon parol evidence in deciding the document had sufficiently described Jackson's property in satisfaction of the statute of frauds. The general rule for Wyoming is that parol evidence is admissible to identify described property, but parol evidence may not supply a portion of the description. [Citation.]

This writing insufficiently describes the property it purports to convey, to reserve, and for which it grants an option to purchase. All three of these land transactions fall under the statute of frauds and each must be sufficiently definite in description to satisfy the statute of frauds or, as a matter of law, the contract is void because an essential term has been omitted. [Citation.] We also note that if the description of the property reserved out of the tract to be conveyed is indefinite and uncertain, then the general description of the land to be conveyed is indefinite and the entire conveyance must fail. [Citation.]

* * *

Nevertheless, the Devenyns urge the writing's use of words such as "remain," "retain," and "keep" was correctly found by the probate court to indicate that Jackson was selling property he owned at that time and that these words are a "key" or "index finger" which, under Noland, permits parol evidence that Jackson only owned this property in all of the world and, therefore, the location of conveyed property is described. However, Noland determined that Wyoming required greater certainty in the description provided by the writing before extrinsic evidence is permitted to supplement. [Citation.] * * *

When a writing only states the total acreage without any description of the location of the land involved, the statute of frauds' requirement that the subject matter be reasonably certain is not satisfied and the contract is void. [Citation.] Without the prohibited supplied inference of ownership, the present description only provides the total acreage, does not provide any certainty that this particular tract was intended to be conveyed and, consequently, is too uncertain to be enforced. [Citations.]

The descriptions for the property reserved and for the option also fail to satisfy the statute of frauds. The reserved property boundaries can only be ascertained by witnesses actually directing a surveyor on-site according to the witnesses' memory of Jackson's boundary description. Parol evidence cannot supply a portion of the description. [Citation.] The option granted in the document does not provide any description at all, leaving unclear for what property an option was granted.

### Conclusion

The parol evidence received in this case reveals that fraud is not a concern and leaves no doubt as to the identity of the property involved, but the property was not described in the agreement and the agreement cannot be enforced. The legislative policy justifying the statute of frauds requires this Court to test not what the parties to the contract know, but what they put in the contract as the description. A description cannot be supplied by parol proof because that allows in the harm which the statute was intended to prevent. The probate court erred as a matter of law in accepting parol evidence to describe the land.

In view of our decision that the contract is unenforceable under the statute of frauds, * * * [t]he order of conveyance is reversed.

---

CASE 15-5

## Parol Evidence
## JENKINS v. ECKERD CORPORATION

District Court of Appeal of Florida, First District, 2005
913 So.2d 43
http://caselaw.findlaw.com/fl-district-court-of-appeal/1180876.html

**Van Nortwick, J.**

In January 1991, Sandhill and K & B Florida Corporation (K & B), a pharmaceutical retailer, entered into the subject lease (K & B Lease) providing for the rental of a parcel of real property located in the Gulf Breeze Shopping Center in Gulf Breeze, Florida. Shortly before the execution of the K & B Lease, Sandhill had leased space in the shopping center to Delchamps, Inc., a regional supermarket chain, as a so-called "anchor" tenant in the shopping center. Article 2B of the K & B Lease referred to the Delchamps lease and provided, in pertinent part, as follows:

### Article 2

* * *

B. Lessor represents to Lessee that Lessor has entered into leases with the following named concerns: with Delchamps, Inc. (Delchamps) for a minimum of 45,000 square feet for supermarket grocery store and that Lessor will construct and offer for lease individual retail shops for a minimum of 21,000 square feet for various retail uses, all located and dimensioned shown on the attached Plot Plan, ... Lessor further represents that said Delchamps lease is for leasing and paying rent by Delchamps as designated hereinabove in the Shopping Center, all as shown on the Plot Plan, Exhibit "A", * * * *The continued leasing and payment of rent for their store in the Shopping Center by Delchamps is part of the consideration to induce Lessee to lease and pay rent for its store, as hereinafter described on the Leased Premises as a part of the Shopping Center. Accordingly, should Delchamps fail or cease to lease and pay rent for its store in the Shopping Center during the Lease Term as hereinafter set out, Lessee shall have the right and privilege of: (a) cancelling this Lease and of terminating all of its obligations hereunder at any time thereafter upon written notice* by Lessee to Lessor, and such cancellation and termination shall be effective ninety (90) days after the mailing of such written notice; ... It is specifically understood that Lessor shall be obligated to immediately notify Lessee in writing should Delchamps fail or cease to lease and pay rent for such a store in the Shopping Center during the primary term of this Lease, but any failure of Lessor to notify Lessee thereof shall in no way deprive Lessee of its privilege of cancelling this Lease and terminating all of its obligation hereunder. [Emphasis in original].

Article 29A of the K & B Lease contained an integration clause which provided that "[t]his lease contains all of the agreements made between the parties hereto and may not be modified orally or in any manner other than by an agreement in writing signed by the parties hereto or their heirs, legal representatives, successors, transferees, or assigns." The Delchamps lease included an assignment provision which granted Delchamps "the right, at any time after the commencement of the term hereof, to assign this lease ..."

In August 1997, Rite Aid, Incorporated (Rite Aid), another drugstore operator, acquired K & B and continued to operate the drugstore in the shopping center under the K & B Lease as a Rite Aid store. In September 1997, Jitney Jungle Stores of America, Inc. (Jitney Jungle), another grocery store operator, acquired the capital stock of Delchamps and continued the operation of the Delchamps grocery store in the shopping center. In 1998, Eckerd acquired certain drugstore properties from Rite Aid, including the drugstore in the shopping center. The K & B Lease was assigned to Eckerd, which began operating an Eckerd drugstore in the leased premises. In October 1999, Jitney Jungle, and its affiliates, including Delchamps, filed for bankruptcy protection under Chapter 11 of the United States Bankruptcy Code. Thereafter, an order was entered in the bankruptcy proceeding approving Delchamps' assignment of its lease in the shopping center to Bruno's Supermarkets, Inc. (Bruno's). Since the assignment, Bruno's has occupied the leased premises under the assigned Delchamps lease and has operated a Bruno's grocery store there. Sandhill failed to provide notice to, or obtain consent from, Eckerd of this assignment.

On June 14, 2001, Eckerd notified Sandhill that Eckerd intended to close the drugstore it operated in the leased premises and that it had retained the services of an agent to locate a suitable subtenant for the space. Eckerd indicated that its agent would be available to negotiate should Sandhill be interested in early termination of the lease. On June 22, 2001, Eckerd notified Sandhill that, because Delchamps had ceased to lease and pay rent for its store in the shopping center, pursuant to article 2B of the K & B Lease, Eckerd was cancelling its lease effective September 20, 2001. Eckerd continued to pay rent due under the lease through October 2001.

In December 2001, Sandhill filed suit against Eckerd for an alleged breach of the shopping center lease, seeking damages for rent, taxes, and common-area maintenance (CAM) charges for the period of November 2001 to the date of trial. In its answer, Eckerd alleged that it terminated its lease obligations pursuant to article 2B of the lease promptly upon learning that Delchamps no longer leased the grocery store in the Gulf Breeze Shopping Center. Eckerd counterclaimed for return of rent and CAM charges it paid to Sandhill for the period of July 2001 through October 2001. The case proceeded to nonjury trial.

At trial, Sandhill sought to introduce testimony relating to its negotiations of the K & B Lease to explain the parties' intent in drafting the allegedly ambiguous language of article 2B. The trial court sustained Eckerd's parol evidence and relevancy objections to the admission of extrinsic evidence pertaining to the parties' intent when entering into the original agreement. [The district court thus prohibited the introduction of oral evidence relating to explain the parties' intent in drafting the "ambiguous language."]

* * *

At the close of Sandhill's case, Eckerd moved for, and the trial court granted, a directed verdict in favor of Eckerd. The trial court ruled:

> I am going to grant the motion for a directed verdict. I think the language of the lease speaks for itself ... It's not ambiguous. It's probably very fortuitous for Eckerd that it coincided with the time they were moving down the highway, but I don't think that it has a valid reason not to enforce the terms of the language of the lease as it's written. So I am going to grant the motion for directed verdict in favor of Eckerd. A judgment will be for Eckerd.

The trial court also awarded Eckerd $16,026.04 in damages reflecting the amount of rent payments made by Eckerd for the period from September 20, 2001, to October 31, 2001. This appeal ensued.

* * *

It is a fundamental rule of contract interpretation that a contract which is clear, complete, and unambiguous does not require judicial construction. [Citations.]

* * *

In the case on appeal, the trial court concluded, and we agree, that article 2B of the K & B Lease clearly and unambiguously gave the lessee the option to cancel the lease if Delchamps ceased to lease and pay rent for the use of its store. As is clear from article 2B itself, the subject language was an inducement for the drugstore tenant to lease in the shopping center. * * *

* * *

Sandhill argues that the trial court erred in applying the parol evidence rule and refusing to allow the introduction of extrinsic evidence in interpreting article 2B of the K & B Lease. Sandhill correctly acknowledges that, if a contract provision is "clear and unambiguous," a court may not consider extrinsic or "parol" evidence to change the plain meaning set forth in the contract. [Citation.] Sandhill contends that parol evidence was admissible below since the lease is incomplete and contains a latent ambiguity. [Citations.] A latent ambiguity arises when a contract on its face appears clear and unambiguous, but fails to specify the rights or duties of the parties in certain situations. [Citation.] Sandhill submits that, while the reference in article 2B of the K & B Lease to the Delchamps lease may be "unambiguous" when read literally, this reference was not "clear" or "complete" with regard to the operation of the lease should the Delchamps lease be assigned. We cannot agree.

The operation of the parol evidence rule encourages parties to embody their complete agreement in a written contract and fosters reliance upon the written contract. "The parol evidence rule serves as a shield to protect a valid, complete and unambiguous written instrument from any verbal assault that would contradict, add to, or subtract from it, or affect its construction." [Citation.] The parol evidence rule presumes that the written agreement that is sought to be modified or explained is an integrated agreement; that is, it represents the complete and exclusive instrument setting forth the parties' intended agreement. [Citation.] The concept of integration is based on a presumption that the parties to a written contract intended that writing "to be the sole expositor of their agreement." [Citation.] The terms of an integrated written contract can be varied by extrinsic evidence only to the extent that the terms are ambiguous and are given meaning by the extrinsic evidence. [Citation.]

Here, * * * the K & B Lease contains a so-called merger or integration clause. Although the existence of a merger clause does not *per se* establish that the integration of the agreement is total, [citation], a merger clause is a highly persuasive statement that the parties intended the agreement to be totally integrated and generally works to prevent a party from introducing parol evidence to vary or contradict the written terms. * * * Here, we find that the K & B Lease is an integrated agreement complete in all essential terms.

Further, Article 2B is not in the least unclear or incomplete. It contains no latent or patent ambiguity. Although article 2B does not mention assignment by Delchamps, it unambiguously grants the lessee the right to terminate the K & B Lease if Delchamps ceases to lease and pay rent for its store in the shopping center *for any reason.* * * * Accordingly, the trial court correctly ruled that it could not admit extrinsic evidence.

* * *

Affirmed.

## QUESTIONS

1. Identify and discuss the five types of general contracts covered by the statute of frauds and the contracts covered by the Uniform Commercial Code (UCC) statute of frauds' provisions.
2. Describe the writing that is required to satisfy the statute of frauds under general contract law and the UCC.
3. Identify and discuss the other methods of complying with the statute of frauds under general contract law and the UCC.
4. Explain the parol evidence rule and identify the situations to which the rule does not apply.
5. Discuss the rule that aids in the interpretation of a contract.

## PROBLEMS

**1.** Rafferty was the principal shareholder in Continental Corporation, and, as a result, he received the lion's share of Continental's dividends. Continental Corporation was eager to close an important deal for iron ore products to use in its business. A written contract was on the desk of Stage Corporation for the sale of the iron ore to Continental. Stage Corporation, however, was cautious about signing the contract; and it did not sign until Rafferty called Stage Corporation on the telephone and stated that if Continental Corporation did not pay for the ore, he would. Business reversals struck Continental Corporation, and it failed. Stage Corporation sues Rafferty. What defense, if any, has Rafferty?

**2.** Green was the owner of a large department store. On Wednesday, January 26, he talked to Smith and said, "I will hire you as sales manager in my store for one year at a salary of $48,000; you are to begin work next Monday." Smith accepted and started work on Monday, January 31. At the end of three months, Green discharged Smith. On May 15, Smith brings an action against Green to recover the unpaid portion of the $28,000 salary. Is Smith's employment contract enforceable?

**3.** Rowe was admitted to the hospital suffering from a critical illness. He was given emergency treatment and later underwent surgery. On at least four occasions, Rowe's two sons discussed with the hospital the payment for services it was to render. The first of these four conversations took place the day after Rowe was admitted. The sons informed the treating physician that their father had no financial means but that they themselves would pay for such services. During the other conversations, the sons authorized whatever treatment their father needed, assuring the hospital that they would pay for the services. After Rowe's discharge, the hospital brought this action against the sons to recover the unpaid bill for the services rendered to their father. Are the sons' promises to the hospital enforceable? Explain.

**4.** Ames, Bell, Cain, and Dole each orally ordered LCD televisions from Marvel Electronics Company, which accepted the orders. Ames's television was to be encased in a specially designed ebony cabinet. Bell, Cain, and Dole ordered standard televisions described as "Alpha Omega Theatre." The price of Ames's television was $1,800, and the televisions ordered by Bell, Cain, and Dole were $700 each. Bell paid the company $75 to apply on his purchase; Ames, Cain, and Dole paid nothing. The next day, Marvel sent Ames, Bell, Cain, and Dole written confirmations captioned "Purchase Memorandum," numbered 12345, 12346, 12347, and 12348, respectively, containing the essential terms of the oral agreements. Each memorandum was sent in duplicate with the request that one copy be signed and returned to the company. None of the four purchasers returned a signed copy. Ames promptly called the company and repudiated the oral contract, which it received before beginning manufacture of the set for Ames or making commitments to carry out the contract. Cain sent the company a letter reading in part, "Referring to your Contract No. 12347, please be advised I have canceled this contract. Yours truly, (Signed) Cain." The four televisions were duly tendered by Marvel to Ames, Bell, Cain, and Dole, all of whom refused to accept delivery. Marvel brings four separate actions against Ames, Bell, Cain, and Dole for breach of contract. Decide each claim.

**5.** Moriarity and Holmes enter into an oral contract by which Moriarity promises to sell and Holmes promises to buy Blackacre for $100,000. Moriarity repudiates the contract by writing a letter to Holmes in which she states accurately the terms of the bargain, but adds "our agreement was oral. It, therefore, is not binding upon me, and I shall not carry it out." Thereafter, Holmes sues Moriarity for specific performance of the contract. Moriarity interposes the defense of the statute of frauds, arguing that the contract is within the statute and, hence, unenforceable. What result? Discuss.

**6.** On March 1, Lucas called Craig on the telephone and offered to pay him $190,000 for a house and lot that Craig owned. Craig accepted the offer immediately on the telephone. Later in the same day, Lucas told Annabelle that if she would marry him, he would convey to her the property he then owned, which was the subject of the earlier agreement. On March 2, Lucas called Penelope and offered her $25,000 if she would work for him for the year commencing March 15, and she agreed. Lucas and Annabelle were married on June 25. By this time, Craig had refused to convey the house to Lucas. Thereafter, Lucas renounced his promise to convey the property to Annabelle. Penelope, who had been working for Lucas, was discharged without cause on July 5; Annabelle left Lucas and instituted divorce proceedings.

What rights, if any, have (a) Lucas against Craig for his failure to convey the property; (b) Annabelle against Lucas for failure to convey the house to her; and (c) Penelope against Lucas for discharging her before the end of the agreed term of employment?

**7.** Clay orally promises Trent to sell him five crops of potatoes to be grown on Blackacre, a farm in Minnesota, and Trent promises to pay a stated price for them on delivery. Is the contract enforceable?

**8.** Grant leased an apartment to Epstein for the term May 1, 2010, to April 30, 2011, at $750 a month "payable in advance on the first day of each and every month of said term." At the time the lease was signed, Epstein told Grant that he received his salary on the tenth of the month and that he would be unable to pay the rent before that date each month. Grant replied that would be satisfactory. On June 2, due to Epstein's not having paid the June rent, Grant sued Epstein for such rent. At the trial, Epstein offered to prove the oral agreement as to the date of payment each month. Is the oral evidence admissible?

**9.** Rachel bought a car from the Beautiful Used Car Agency under a written contract. She purchased the car in reliance on Beautiful's agent's oral representations that it had never been in a wreck and could be driven at least two thousand miles without adding oil. Thereafter, Rachel discovered that the car had, in fact, been previously wrecked and rebuilt, that it used excessive quantities of oil, and that Beautiful's agent was aware of these facts when the car was sold. Rachel brings an action to rescind the contract and recover the purchase price. Beautiful objects to the introduction of oral testimony concerning representations of its agent, contending that the written contract alone governed the rights of the parties. Decision on the objection?

**10.** In a contract drawn up by Booke Company, it agreed to sell and Yermack Contracting Company agreed to buy wood shingles at $6.50. After the shingles were delivered and used, Booke Company billed Yermack Company at $6.50 per bunch of nine hundred shingles. Yermack Company refused to pay because it thought the contract meant $6.50 per thousand shingles. Booke Company brought action to recover on the basis of $6.50 per bunch. The evidence showed that there was no applicable custom or usage in the trade and that each party held its belief in good faith. Decision?

**11.** Halsey, a widower, was living without family or housekeeper in his house in Howell, New York. Burns and his wife claim that Halsey invited them to give up their house and business in Andover, New York, to live in his house and care for him. In return, they allege, he promised them the house and its furniture upon his death. Acting upon this proposal, the Burnses left Andover, moved into Halsey's house, and cared for him until he died five months later. No deed, will, or memorandum exists to authenticate Halsey's promise. McCormick, the administrator of the estate, claims the oral promise is unenforceable under the statute of frauds. Explain whether McCormick is correct.

**12.** Amos orally agrees to hire Elizabeth for an eight-month trial period. Elizabeth performs the job magnificently, and after several weeks Amos orally offers Elizabeth a six-month extension at a salary increase of 20 percent. Elizabeth accepts the offer. At the end of the eight-month trial period, Amos discharges Elizabeth, who brings suit against Amos for breach of contract. Is Amos liable? Why?

**13.** Ethel Greenberg acquired the ownership of the Carlyle Hotel on Miami Beach. Having had little experience in the hotel business, she asked Miller to participate in and counsel her operation of the hotel, which he did. He claims that because his efforts produced a substantial profit, Ethel made an oral agreement for the continuation of his services. Miller alleges that in return for his services, Ethel promised to marry him and to share the net income resulting from the operation of the hotel. Miller maintains that he rendered his services to Ethel in reliance upon her promises. The couple planned to wed in the fall, but Ethel, due to physical illness, decided not to marry. Miller sued for damages for Ethel's breach of their agreement. Is the oral contract enforceable? Discuss.

**14.** Dean was hired on February 12 as a sales manager of the Co-op Dairy for a minimum period of one year with the dairy agreeing to pay his moving expenses. By February 26, Dean had signed a lease, moved his family from Oklahoma to Arizona, and reported for work. After he worked for a few days, he was fired. Dean then brought this action against the dairy for his salary for the year, less what he was paid. The dairy argues that the statute of frauds bars enforcement of the oral contract because the contract was not to be performed within one year. Is the dairy correct in its assertion?

**15.** Alice solicited an offer from Robett Manufacturing Company to manufacture certain clothing that Alice intended to supply to the government. Alice contends that in a telephone conversation Robett made an oral offer that she immediately accepted. She then received the following letter from Robett, which, she claims, confirmed their agreement:

> Confirming our telephone conversation, we are pleased to offer the 3,500 shirts at $4.00 each and the trousers at $3.80 each with delivery approximately ninety days after receipt of order. We will try to cut this to sixty days if at all possible.
>
> This, of course, as quoted f.o.b. Atlanta and the order will not be subject to cancellation, domestic pack only.
>
> Thanking you for the opportunity to offer these garments, we are
>
> Very truly yours,
> Robett Manufacturing Co., Inc.

Is the agreement enforceable against Robett?

**16.** David and Nancy Songer planned to travel outside the United States and wanted to acquire medical insurance prior to departure. They spoke with an agent of Continental who requested that Nancy Songer undergo a medical examination based on a statement that she had a heart murmur. She promptly complied, and the Songers later met with the agent to complete the application. David Songer signed the application and tendered a check for the first six months' premium. The Songers also claim that the agent stated that a "binder" was in effect such that policy coverage was available immediately. The agent subsequently denied making this statement, relying, instead, on a clause in the contract that required home office acceptance. The Songers left the United States and sixty days later inquired as to the status of their application. At approximately the same time, Continental denied the application and sent a refund to the Songers. Nancy Songer was then severely injured in an automobile accident. When Continental refused to honor the policy, the Songers claimed that the oral representation constituted part of the contract due to the vagueness of the policy "acceptance" language. Is the evidence regarding the oral representations admissible?

**17.** Yokel, a grower of soybeans, had sold soybeans to Campbell Grain and Seed Company and other grain companies in the past. Campbell entered into an oral contract with Yokel to purchase soybeans from him. Promptly after entering into the oral contract, Campbell signed and mailed to Yokel a written confirmation of the oral agreement. Yokel received the written confirmation but neither signed it nor objected to its content. Campbell now brings this action against Yokel for breach of contract upon Yokel's failure to deliver the soybeans. Should Yokel be considered a merchant and thus bound by Campbell's written confirmation?

**18.** Presti claims that he reached an oral agreement with Wilson by telephone in October 2010 to buy a horse for $60,000. Presti asserts that he sent Wilson a bill of sale and a postdated check, which Wilson retained. Presti also claims that Wilson told him that he wished not to consummate the transaction until January 1, 2011, for tax reasons. The check was neither deposited nor negotiated. Wilson denies that he ever agreed to sell the horse or that he received the check and bill of sale from Presti. Presti's claim is supported by a copy of his check stub and by the affidavit of his executive assistant, who says that he monitored the telephone call and prepared and mailed both the bill of sale and the check. Wilson argues that the statute of frauds governs this transaction, and because there was no writing, the contract claim is barred. Is Wilson correct? Explain.

**19.** Louie E. Brown worked for the Phelps Dodge Corporation under an oral contract for approximately twenty-three years. In 2010, he was suspended from work for unauthorized possession of company property. In 2011, Phelps Dodge fired Brown after discovering that he was using company property without permission and building a trailer on company time. Brown sued Phelps Dodge for benefits under an unemployment benefit plan. According to the plan, "in order to be eligible for unemployment benefits, a laid-off employee must: (1) Have completed 2 or more years of continuous service with the company, and (2) Have been laid off from work because the company had determined that work was not available for him." The trial court held that the wording of the second condition was ambiguous and should be construed against Phelps Dodge, the party who chose the wording. A reading of the entire contract, however, indicates that the plan was not intended to apply to someone who was fired for cause. What is the correct interpretation of this contract?

**20.** Katz offered to purchase land from Joiner, and, after negotiating the terms, Joiner accepted. On October 13, over the telephone, both parties agreed to extend the time period for completing and mailing the written contract until October 20. Although the original paperwork deadline in the offer was October 14, Katz stated he had inserted that provision "for my purpose only." All other provisions of the contract remained unchanged. Accordingly, Joiner completed the contract and mailed it on October 20. Immediately after, however, Joiner sent Katz an overnight letter stating that "I have signed and returned contract, but have changed my mind. Do not wish to sell property." Joiner now claims an oral modification of a contract within the statute of frauds is unenforceable. Katz counters that the modification is not material and therefore does not affect the underlying contract. Explain who is correct.

**21.** When Mr. McClam died, he left the family farm, heavily mortgaged, to his wife and children. To save the farm from foreclosure, Mrs. McClam planned to use insurance proceeds and her savings to pay off the debts. She was unwilling to do so, however, unless she had full ownership of the property. Mrs. McClam wrote her daughter, stating that the daughter should deed over her interest in the family farm to her mother and promising that all the children would inherit the farm equally upon their mother's death. The letter further explained that if foreclosure occurred, each child would receive very little, but if they complied with their mother's plan, each would eventually receive a valuable property interest upon her death. Finally, the letter stated that all the other children had agreed to this plan. Consequently, the daughter also agreed. Years later, Mrs. McClam tries to convey the farm to her son Donald. The daughter challenges, arguing that the mother is contractually bound to convey the land equally to all of the children. Donald says this was an oral agreement to sell land and is unenforceable. The daughter argues that the letter satisfies the statute of frauds, making the contract enforceable. Who gets the farm? Explain.

**22.** Butler Brothers Building Company sublet all of the work in a highway construction contract to Ganley Brothers, Inc. Soon thereafter, Ganley brought this action against Butler for fraud in the inducement of the contract. The contract, however, provided: "The contractor [Ganley] has examined the said contracts ..., knows all the requirements, and is not relying upon any statement made by the company in respect thereto." Can Ganley introduce into evidence the oral representations made by Butler?

**23.** Shane Quadri, contacted Don Hoffman, an employee of Al J. Hoffman & Co. (Hoffman Agency), to procure car insurance. Later, Quadri's car was stolen on October 25 or 26. Quadri contacted Hoffman, who arranged with Budget Rent-a-Car for a rental car for Quadri until his car was recovered. Hoffman authorized Budget Rent-a-Car to bill the Hoffman Agency. Later, when the stolen car was recovered, Hoffman telephoned Goodyear and arranged to have four new tires put on Quadri's car to replace those damaged during the theft. Budget and Goodyear sued Hoffman for payment of the car rental and tires. Is Hoffman liable on his oral promise to pay for the car rental and the four new tires?

**24.** Stuart Studio, an art studio, prepared a new catalog for the National School of Heavy Equipment, a school run by Gilbert and Donald Shaw. When the artwork was virtually finished, Gilbert Shaw requested Stuart Studio to purchase and supervise the printing of twenty-five thousand catalogs. Shaw told the art studio that payment of the printing costs would be made within ten days after billing and that if the "National School would not pay the full total that he would stand good for the entire bill." Shaw was chairman of the board of directors of the school, and he owned 100 percent of its voting stock and 49 percent of its nonvoting stock. The school became bankrupt, and Stuart Studio was unable to recover the sum from the school. Stuart Studio then brought this action against Shaw on the basis of his promise to pay the bill. Is Shaw obligated to pay the debt in question? Explain.

**25.** Thomson Printing Company is a buyer and seller of used machinery. On April 10, the president of the company, James Thomson, went to the surplus machinery department of B.F. Goodrich Company in Akron, Ohio, to examine some used equipment that was for sale. Thomson discussed the sale, including a price of $9,000, with Ingram Meyers, a Goodrich employee and agent. Four days later, on April 14, Thomson sent a purchase order to confirm the oral contract for purchase of the machinery and a partial payment of $1,000 to Goodrich in Akron. The purchase order contained Thomson Printing's name, address, and telephone number, as well as certain information about the purchase, but did not specifically mention Meyers or the surplus equipment department. Goodrich sent copies of the documents to a number of its divisions, but Meyers never learned of the confirmation until weeks later, by which time the equipment had been sold to another party. Thomson Printing brought suit against Goodrich for breach of contract. Goodrich claimed that no contract had existed and that at any rate the alleged oral contract could not be enforced because of the statute of frauds. Is the contract enforceable? Why?

**26.** On July 5, 2000, Richard Price signed a written employment contract as a new salesman with the Mercury Supply Company. The contract was of indefinite duration and could be terminated by either party for any reason upon fifteen days' notice. Between 2000 and 2008, Price was promoted several times. In 2005, Price was made vice president of sales. In September 2008, however, Price was told that his performance was not satisfactory and that if he did not improve he would be fired. In February 2011, Price received notice of termination. Price claims that in 2005 he entered into a valid oral employment contract with Mercury Supply Company wherein he was made vice president of sales for life or until he should retire. Is the alleged oral contract barred by the one-year provision of the statute of frauds?

**27.** Plaintiffs leased commercial space from the defendant to open a florist shop. After the lease was executed, the plaintiffs learned that they could not place a freestanding sign along the highway to advertise their business because the Deschutes County Code allowed only one freestanding sign on the property, and the defendant already had one in place. The plaintiffs filed this action, alleging that defendant had breached the lease by failing to provide them with space in which they could erect a freestanding sign. Paragraph 16 of the lease provides as follows: "Tenant shall not erect or install any signs visible from outside the leased premises with out [*sic*] the previous written consent of the Landlord." Explain whether this evidence is admissible.

**28.** Jesse Carter and Jesse Thomas had an auto accident with a driver insured by Allstate. Carter and Thomas hired attorney Joseph Onwuteaka to represent them. Mr. Onwuteaka sent a demand letter for settlement of plaintiffs' claims to Allstate's adjustor, Ms. Gracie Weatherly. Mr. Onwuteaka claims Ms. Weatherly made, and he orally accepted, settlement terms on behalf of the plaintiffs. When Allstate did not honor the agreements, Carter and Thomas filed a suit for breach of contract. Discuss the enforceability of the oral agreement.

# CHAPTER 16

# Third Parties to Contracts

Whereas prior chapters considered contractual situations essentially involving only two parties, this chapter deals with the rights or duties of third parties, namely, persons who are not parties to the contract but who have a right to, or an obligation for, its performance. These rights and duties arise either by (1) an assignment of the rights of a party to the contract, (2) a delegation of the duties of a party to the contract, or (3) the express terms of a contract entered into for the benefit of a third person. In an assignment or delegation, the third party's rights or duties arise after the contract is made, whereas in the third situation, the third-party beneficiary's rights arise at the time the contract was formed. We will consider these three situations in that order.

## ASSIGNMENT OF RIGHTS

Every contract creates both rights and duties. A person who owes a duty under a contract is an **obligor**, while a person to whom a contractual duty is owed is an **obligee**. For instance, Ann promises to sell to Bart an automobile for which Bart promises to pay $10,000 in monthly installments over the next three years. Ann's right under the contract is to receive payment from Bart, whereas Ann's duty is to deliver the automobile. Bart's right is to receive the automobile; his duty is to pay for it.

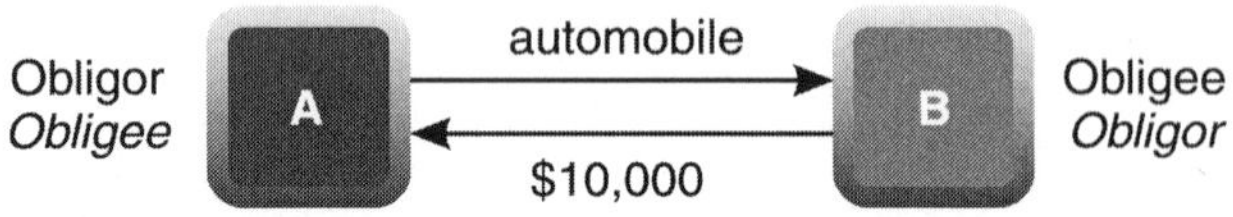


An **assignment of rights** is the voluntary transfer to a third party of the rights arising from the contract. In the above example, if Ann were to transfer her right under the contract (the installment payments due from Bart) to Clark for $8,500 in cash, this would constitute a valid assignment of rights. In this case, Ann would be the **assignor**, Clark would be the **assignee**, and Bart would be the **obligor**.

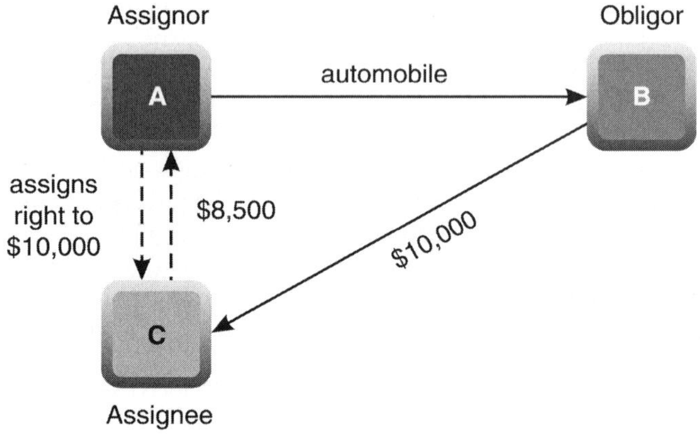


An effective assignment terminates the assignor's right to receive performance by the obligor. After an assignment, only the assignee has a right to the obligor's performance.

On the other hand, if Ann and Doris agree that Doris should deliver the automobile to Bart, this would constitute a delegation, not an assignment, of duties between Ann and Doris. A **delegation of duties** is a transfer to a third party of a contractual obligation. In this instance, Ann would be the **delegator**, Doris would be the **delegatee**, and Bart would be the **obligee**. Delegations of duties are discussed later in this chapter.

### LAW GOVERNING ASSIGNMENTS

The law governing assignments arises principally from the common law of contracts, Article 2 of the Uniform Commercial Code (UCC), and Article 9 of the UCC. Article 2 applies to assignments of rights under a contract for the sale of goods. Article 9 covers all assignments made to secure the performance of an obligation *and* all assignments involving rights to payment for goods sold or leased or for services rendered.

## REQUIREMENTS OF AN ASSIGNMENT

The Restatement defines an assignment of a right as a "manifestation of the assignor's intention to transfer it by virtue of which the assignor's right to performance by the obligor is extinguished in whole or in part and the assignee acquires a right to such performance." Section 317(1). No special form or particular words are necessary to create an assignment. Any words that fairly indicate an intention to make the assignee the owner of the right are sufficient. For instance, Eve delivers to Harold a writing addressed to Mary stating, "Pay Harold for his own use $1,000 out of the amount you owe me." This writing is a legally sufficient assignment. Restatement, Section 325, Illustration 1.

Unless otherwise provided by statute, an assignment may be oral. The UCC imposes a writing requirement on all assignments beyond $5,000. Section 1–206. The 2001 Revision to Article 1, however, has deleted this requirement. In addition, Article 9 requires certain assignments to be in writing.

Consideration is not required for an effective assignment. Consequently, gratuitous assignments are valid and enforceable. By giving value for the assignment, the assignee manifests his assent to the assignment as part of the bargained-for exchange. On the other hand, when the assignment is gratuitous, the assignee's assent is not always required. Any assignee who has not assented to an assignment may, however, disclaim the assignment within a reasonable time after learning of its existence and terms. Restatement, Section 327. No particular formality is required for the disclaimer, which renders the assignment inoperative from the beginning.

**Revocability of Assignments** When the assignee gives consideration in exchange for an assignment, a contract exists between the assignor and the assignee. Consequently, the assignor may not revoke the assignment without the assignee's assent. A gratuitous assignment, in contrast, is revocable by the assignor and is terminated by her death, incapacity, or subsequent assignment of the right, unless she has made an effective delivery of the assignment to the assignee by transferring a deed or other document evidencing the right, such as a stock certificate or savings passbook. Delivery may also consist of physically delivering a signed, written assignment of the contract right.

A gratuitous assignment is also rendered irrevocable if, prior to the attempted revocation, the donee-assignee receives payment of the claim from the obligor, obtains a judgment against the obligor, or obtains a new contract with the obligor. For example, Nancy owes Howard $50,000. Howard signs a written statement granting Paul a gratuitous assignment of his rights from Nancy but dies prior to delivering to Paul the signed, written assignment of the contract right. The assignment is terminated and therefore ineffective. On the other hand, had Howard delivered the signed, written assignment to Paul before he died, the assignment would have been effective and irrevocable.

**Partial Assignments** A partial assignment is a transfer of a portion of the contractual rights to one or more assignees. Although partial assignments were not enforceable at early common law, such assignments now are permitted and are enforceable. The obligor, however, may require all the parties entitled to the promised performance to litigate the matter in one action, thus ensuring that all parties are present and thereby avoiding the undue hardship of multiple lawsuits. For example, Jack owes Richard $2,500. Richard assigns $1,000 to Mildred. Neither Richard nor Mildred can maintain an action against Jack if Jack objects, unless the other is joined in the lawsuit against Jack.

## RIGHTS THAT ARE ASSIGNABLE

As a general rule, most contract rights, including rights under an option contract, are assignable. The most common contractual right that may be assigned is the right to the payment of money, such as an account receivable or interest due or to be paid. The right to property other than money, such as goods or land, is also frequently assignable.

## RIGHTS THAT ARE NOT ASSIGNABLE

To protect the obligor or the public interest, some contract rights are not assignable. These nonassignable contract rights include those that (1) materially change the obligor's duty or materially increase the risk or burden upon the obligor, (2) transfer highly personal contract rights, (3) are validly prohibited by the contract, or (4) are prohibited by statute or public policy. Restatement, Section 317(2).

**Assignments That Materially Increase the Duty, Risk, or Burden** An assignment is ineffective where performance by the obligor to the assignee would differ materially from her performance to the assignor; that is, where the assignment would significantly change the nature or extent of the obligor's duty. Thus, an automobile liability insurance policy issued to Alex is not assignable by Alex to Betty. The risk assumed by the insurance company was liability for Alex's negligent operation of the automobile. Liability for operation of the same automobile by Betty would be a risk entirely different from the one that the insurance company had assumed. Similarly, Alex would not be allowed to assign to Cynthia, the owner of a twenty-five-room mansion, his contractual right to have Betty paint his small, two-bedroom house. Clearly, such an assignment would materially increase Betty's duty of performance. By comparison, the right to receive monthly payments under a contract may be assigned; for mailing the check to the assignee costs no more than mailing it to the assignor. Moreover, if a contract explicitly provides that it may be assigned, then rights under it are assignable even if the assignment would change the duty, risk, or burden of performance on the obligor. Restatement, Section 323(1).

**Assignments of Personal Rights** Where the rights under a contract are highly personal, in that they are limited to the person of the obligee, such rights are not assignable. An extreme example of such a contract is an agreement of two persons to marry one another. The prospective groom obviously cannot transfer to some third party the prospective bride's promise to marry him. A more typical example of a contract involving personal rights would be a contract between a teacher and a school. The teacher could not assign to another teacher her right to a faculty position. Similarly, a student who is awarded a scholarship cannot assign his right to some other person.

◆ **SEE CASE 16-1**

**Express Prohibition against Assignment** Contract terms prohibiting assignment of rights under the contract are strictly construed. Moreover, most courts interpret a general prohibition against assignments as a mere promise not to assign. As a consequence, the prohibition, if violated, gives the obligor a right to damages for breach of the terms forbidding assignment but does *not* render the assignment ineffective.

Section 322(1) of the Restatement provides that, unless circumstances indicate the contrary, a contract term prohibiting assignment of the contract bars only the delegation to the assignee (delegatee) of the assignor's (delegator's) duty of performance, not the assignment of rights. Thus, Abe and Bill contract for the sale of land by Bill to Abe for $30,000 and provide in their contract that Abe may not assign his rights under it. Abe pays Bill $30,000 and thereby fully performs his obligations under the contract. Abe then assigns his rights to Cheryl, who is entitled to receive the land from Bill (the obligor) despite the contractual prohibition of assignment.

UCC Section 2–210(2) provides that a right to damages for breach of the whole contract or a right arising out of the assignor's due performance of his entire obligation can be assigned despite a contractual provision to the contrary. UCC Section 2–210(3) provides that, unless circumstances indicate the contrary, a contract term prohibiting assignment of the contract bars only the delegation to the assignee (delegatee) of the assignor's (delegator's) duty of performance, not the assignment of rights. UCC Section 9-408 makes ineffective any term in a contract prohibiting the assignment of a security interest arising out of a sale of any right to payment for goods sold or leased or for services rendered.

◆ **SEE CASE 16-2**

**Assignments Prohibited by Law** Various Federal and State statutes, as well as public policy, prohibit or regulate the assignment of certain types of contract rights. For instance, assignments of future wages are subject to statutes, some of which prohibit such assignments altogether while others require them to be in writing and subject to certain restrictions. Moreover, an assignment that violates public policy will be unenforceable even in the absence of a prohibiting statute.

## RIGHTS OF THE ASSIGNEE

**Obtains Rights of Assignor** The general rule is that an assignee **stands in the shoes** of the assignor. He acquires the rights of the assignor, but no new or additional rights, and takes the assigned rights with all of the defenses, defects, and infirmities to which they would be subject, were the assignor to bring an action against the obligor. Thus, in an action brought by the assignee against the obligor, the obligor may plead fraud, duress, undue influence, failure of consideration, breach of contract, or any other defense against the assignor arising out of the original contract. The obligor also may assert rights of setoff or counterclaim arising against the assignor out of entirely separate matters, provided they arose prior to his receiving notice of the assignment.

The Code permits the buyer under a contract of sale to agree as part of the contract that he will not assert against an assignee any claim or defense that the buyer may have against the seller if the assignee takes the assignment for value, in good faith, and without notice of conflicting claims or of certain defenses. UCC Section 9–403. Such a provision in an agreement renders the seller's rights more marketable. The Federal Trade Commission, however, has invalidated such waiver of defense provisions in consumer credit transactions. (This rule is discussed more fully in *Chapter 28*.) Article 9 reflects this rule by essentially rendering waiver-of-defense clauses ineffective in consumer transactions. UCC Section 9–403(d). Most States also have statutes protecting buyers in consumer transactions by prohibiting waiver of defenses.

**Notice** To be valid, notice of an assignment does not have to be given to the obligor. Nonetheless, giving such notice is advisable because an assignee will lose his rights against an obligor who pays the assignor without notice of the assignment: to compel an obligor to pay a claim a second time, when she was not notified that a new party was entitled to payment would be unfair. For example, Donald owes Gary $1,000 due on September 1. Gary assigns the debt to Paula on August 1, but neither he nor Paula informs Donald. On September 1, Donald pays Gary. Donald is fully discharged from his obligation, whereas Gary is liable for $1,000 to Paula. On the other hand, if Paula had given notice of the assignment to Donald before September 1 and Donald had paid Gary nevertheless, Paula would then have the right to recover the $1,000 from either Donald or Gary.

Furthermore, notice cuts off any defenses based on subsequent agreements between the obligor and assignor. Moreover, as already indicated, notice precludes subsequent setoffs and counterclaims of the obligor that arise out of entirely separate matters.

### IMPLIED WARRANTIES OF ASSIGNOR

An implied warranty is an obligation imposed by law upon the transfer of property or contract rights. In the absence of an express intention to the contrary, an assignor who receives value makes the following implied warranties to the assignee with respect to the assigned right:

1. that he will do nothing to defeat or impair the assignment;
2. that the assigned right actually exists and is subject to no limitations or defenses other than those stated or apparent at the time of the assignment;
3. that any writing evidencing the right delivered to the assignee or exhibited to him as an inducement to accept the assignment is genuine and what it purports to be; and
4. that the assignor has no knowledge of any fact that would impair the value of the assignment.

Thus, Eric has a right against Julia and assigns it for value to Gwen. Later, Eric gives Julia a release. Gwen may recover damages from Eric for breach of the first implied warranty.

### EXPRESS WARRANTIES OF ASSIGNOR

An **express warranty** is an explicitly made contractual promise regarding property or contract rights transferred. The assignor is further bound by any express warranties he makes to the assignee with respect to the right assigned. The assignor does not, however, guarantee that the obligor will pay the assigned debt or otherwise perform, unless such a guarantee is explicitly stated.

### SUCCESSIVE ASSIGNMENTS OF THE SAME RIGHT

The owner of a right could conceivably make successive assignments of the same claim to different persons. Assume that B owes A $1,000. On June 1, A for value assigns the debt to C. Thereafter, on June 15, A assigns it to D, who in good faith gives value and has no knowledge of the prior assignment by A to C. If the assignment is subject to Article 9, then that article's priority rules will control, as discussed in *Chapter 38*. Otherwise, the priority is determined by the common law. The majority rule in the United States is that the **first assignee in point of time** (here, C) prevails over subsequent assignees. By comparison, in England and in a minority of the States, the first assignee to notify the obligor prevails.

The Restatement adopts a third view: a prior assignee is entitled to the assigned right and its proceeds to the exclusion of a subsequent assignee, *except* where the prior assignment is revocable or voidable by the assignor or where the subsequent assignee in good faith and without knowledge of the prior assignment gives value and obtains one of the following: (1) payment or satisfaction of the obligor's duty, (2) a judgment against the obligor, (3) a new contract with the obligor, or (4) possession of a writing of a type customarily accepted as a symbol or evidence of the right assigned. Restatement, Section 342.

## DELEGATION OF DUTIES

As indicated, contractual duties are *not* assignable, but their performance generally may be *delegated* to a third person. A **delegation of duties** is a transfer of a contractual obligation to a third party. For example, A promises to sell B a new automobile, for which B promises to pay $10,000 by monthly installments over the next three years. If A and D agree that D should deliver the automobile to B, this would not constitute an assignment but would be a delegation of duties between A and D. In this instance, A would be the **delegator**, D would be the **delegatee**, and B would be the **obligee**.

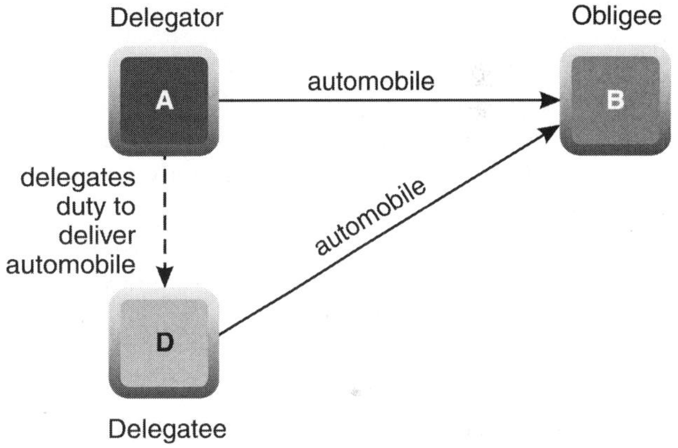


A delegation of duty does not extinguish the delegator's obligation to perform, because A remains liable to B. When the delegatee accepts, or assumes, the delegated duty, both the delegator and delegatee are held liable to the obligee for performance of the contractual duty.

### DELEGABLE DUTIES

Although contractual duties generally are delegable, a delegation will not be permitted if

1. the nature of the duties is personal in that the obligee has a substantial interest in having the delegator perform the contract;
2. the performance is expressly made nondelegable; or
3. the delegation is prohibited by statute or public policy.

Restatement, Section 318 and UCC Section 2–210. The courts will examine a delegation more closely than an assignment because a delegation compels the nondelegating party to the contract (the obligee) to receive performance from a party with whom she has not dealt.

For example, a schoolteacher may not delegate her performance to another teacher, even if the substitute is equally competent; for this is a contract that is personal in nature. In the frequently quoted words of an English case: "You have a right to the benefit you contemplate from the character, credit and substance of the person with whom you contract." On the other hand, under a contract in which performance involves no peculiar or special skill and in which no personal trust or confidence is involved, the party may delegate the performance of his duty. For example, the duty to pay money, to deliver fungible goods such as corn, or to mow a lawn is usually delegable.

◆ **SEE CASE 16-3**

### DUTIES OF THE PARTIES

Even when permitted, a delegation of a duty to a third person still leaves the delegator bound to perform. If the delegator desires to be discharged of the duty, she is allowed to enter into an agreement by which she obtains the consent of the obligee to substitute a third person (the delegatee) in her place. This is a **novation**, whereby the delegator is discharged and the third party becomes directly bound upon his promise to the obligee.

Though a delegation authorizes a third party to perform a duty for the delegator, a delegatee becomes liable for performance only if he assents to perform the delegated duties. Thus, if Frank owes a duty to Grace, and Frank delegates that duty to Henry, Henry is not obligated to either Frank or Grace to perform the duty unless Henry agrees to do so. Nevertheless, if Henry promises either Frank (the delegator) or Grace (the obligee) that he will perform Frank's duty, Henry is said to have **assumed the delegated duty** and becomes liable to both Frank and Grace for nonperformance. Accordingly, when duties are both delegated and assumed, both the delegator and the delegatee are liable to the obligee for proper performance of the original contractual duty. The delegatee's promise to perform creates contract rights in the obligee who may bring an action against the delegatee as a third party beneficiary of the contract between the delegator and the delegatee. (Third-party contracts are discussed later in this chapter.)

The question of whether a delegatee has assumed delegated duties frequently arises in the following ambiguous situation: Marty and Carol agree to an assignment of Marty's contract with Bob. The Code clearly resolves this ambiguity by providing that, unless the language or circumstances indicate the contrary, an assignment of "the contract," or of "all my rights under the contract," or an assignment in similar general terms is an assignment of rights *and* a delegation of performance of the assignor's duties; its acceptance by the assignee constitutes a promise by her to perform those duties. Section 2–210(4). The Restatement, Section 328, has also adopted this position. For example, Cooper Oil Co. has a contract to deliver oil to Halsey. Cooper Oil Co. delivers to Lowell Oil Co. a writing assigning to Lowell Oil Co. "all Cooper Oil Co.'s rights under the contract." Lowell Oil Co. is under a duty to Halsey to deliver the oil called for by the contract, and Cooper Oil Co. is liable to Halsey if Lowell Oil Co. does not perform. It should also be recalled that the Restatement and the Code provide that a clause prohibiting an assignment of "the contract" is to be construed as barring only the delegation to the assignee (delegatee) of the assignor's (delegator's) performance, unless the circumstances indicate the contrary.

## THIRD-PARTY BENEFICIARY CONTRACTS

A contract in which a party (the **promisor**) promises to render a certain performance not to the other party (the **promisee**) but to a third person (the **beneficiary**) is called a third-party beneficiary contract. The third person is not a party to the contract but is merely a beneficiary of it. Such contracts may be divided into two types: (1) intended beneficiary and (2) incidental beneficiary. An **intended beneficiary** is intended by the two parties to the contract (the promisor and promisee) to receive a benefit from the performance of their agreement. Accordingly, the courts generally permit intended beneficiaries to enforce third-party contracts. For example, Abbott promises Baldwin to deliver an automobile to Carson if Baldwin promises to pay $10,000. Carson is the intended beneficiary.

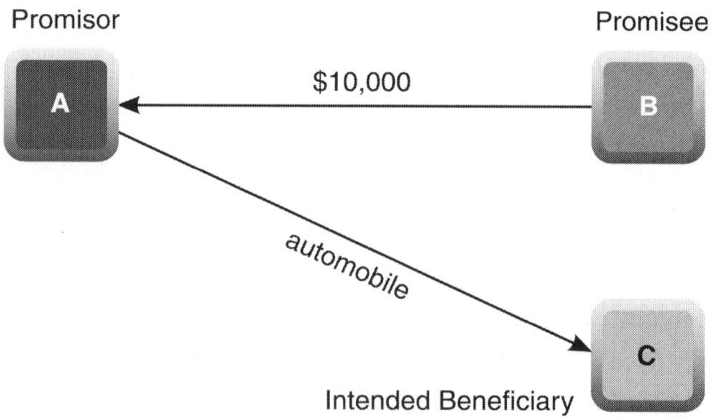


In an **incidental beneficiary** contract, the third party is not intended to receive a benefit under the contract. Accordingly, courts do not enforce the third party's right to the benefits of the contract. For example, Abbott promises to purchase and deliver to Baldwin an automobile for $10,000. In all probability, Abbott would acquire the automobile from Davis. Davis would be an incidental beneficiary and would have no enforceable rights against either Abbott or Baldwin.

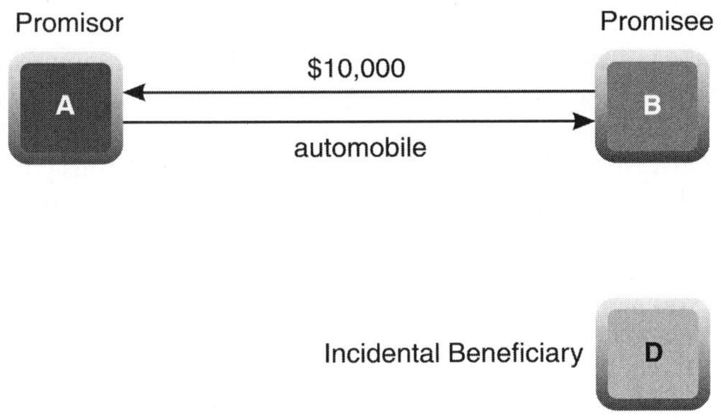


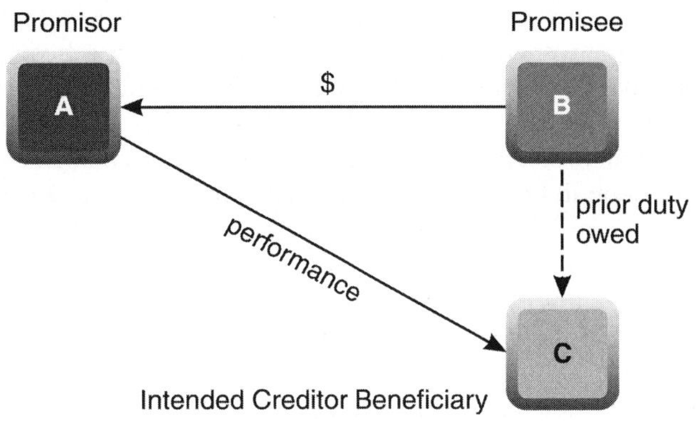


## INTENDED BENEFICIARY

Unless otherwise agreed between the promisor and promisee, a beneficiary of a promise is an intended beneficiary if the parties intended this to be the result of their agreement. Restatement, Section 302. There are two types of intended beneficiaries: (1) donee beneficiaries and (2) creditor beneficiaries.

**Donee Beneficiary** A third party is an intended donee beneficiary if the promisee's purpose in bargaining for and obtaining the agreement with the promisor is to make a gift of the promised performance to the beneficiary. The ordinary life insurance policy illustrates this type of contract. The insured (the promisee) makes a contract with an insurance company (the promisor) that promises, in consideration of premiums paid to it by the insured, to pay upon the death of the insured a stated sum of money to the named beneficiary, who is an intended donee beneficiary.

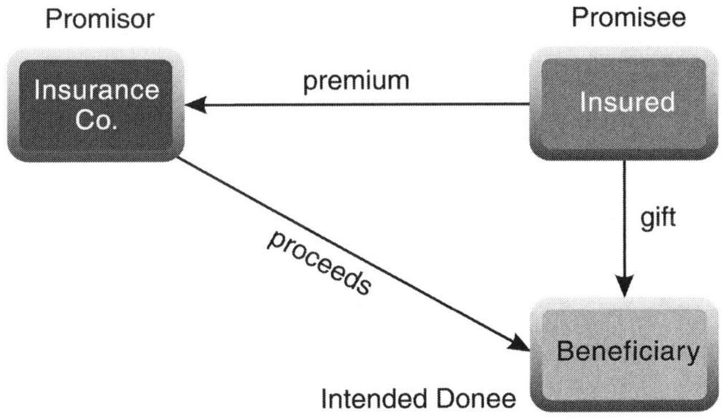


**Creditor Beneficiary** A third person is also an intended beneficiary if the promisee intends the performance of the promise to satisfy a legal duty he owes to the beneficiary, who is a creditor of the promisee. The contract involves consideration moving from the promisee to the promisor in exchange for the promisor's engaging to pay a debt or to discharge an obligation the promisee owes to the third person.

To illustrate, in a contract for the sale by Wesley of his business to Susan, Susan promises Wesley that she will pay all of his outstanding business debts, as listed in the contract. Here, Wesley's creditors are creditor beneficiaries. Similarly, in the classic *Lawrence v. Fox*, 20 N.Y. 268 (1859), Holly loaned Fox $300 in consideration for Fox's promise to pay that sum to Lawrence, a creditor of Holly. Fox failed to pay Lawrence, who sued Fox for the $300. The court held for Lawrence, who was permitted to recover as a third-party creditor beneficiary to the contract between Holly and Fox.

◆ **SEE CASE 16-4**

**Rights of Intended Beneficiary** An intended *donee* beneficiary may enforce the contract only against the promisor. He cannot maintain an action against the promisee, as the promisee was under no legal obligation to him. An intended *creditor* beneficiary, however, may enforce the contract against either or both parties. If Willard owes Lola $500, and Julie contracts with Willard to pay this debt to Lola, Willard is not thereby relieved of his liability to Lola. If Julie breaks the contract, Lola, as a creditor beneficiary, may sue her. In addition, Lola may sue Willard as her debtor. If Lola should obtain judgments against both Julie and Willard, she is, of course, entitled to collect only one judgment. If Lola recovers against Willard, Willard has a right of reimbursement from Julie, the promisor. Restatement, Section 310.

**Vesting of Rights** A contract for the benefit of an intended beneficiary confers upon that beneficiary rights that she may enforce. Until these rights **vest** (take effect), however, the promisor and promisee may, by later agreement, vary or completely discharge them. The States vary considerably as to when vesting occurs. Some hold that vesting takes place immediately upon the making of the contract. In others, vesting occurs when the third party learns of the contract and assents to it. In another group of States, vesting requires the third party to change his position in reliance upon the promise made for his benefit. The Restatement has adopted the following position: If the contract between the promisor and promisee provides that they may not vary its terms without the consent of the beneficiary, such a provision is effective. Otherwise, the parties to the contract may rescind or vary the contract unless the intended beneficiary (1) has brought an action upon the promise, (2) has changed her position in reliance upon it, or (3) has assented to the promise at the request of the promisor or promisee. Restatement, Section 311.

On the other hand, the promisor and promisee may provide that the benefits will *never* vest. For example, Mildred purchases an insurance policy on her own life, naming her husband as beneficiary. Her policy, as such policies commonly do, reserves to Mildred the right to change the beneficiary or even to cancel the policy entirely.

**Defenses against Beneficiary** In an action by the intended beneficiary of a third-party contract to enforce the promise, the promisor may assert any defense that would be available to her if the action had been brought by the promisee. The rights of the third party are based upon the promisor's contract with the promisee. Thus, the promisor may assert the absence of mutual assent or consideration, lack of capacity, fraud, mistake, and the like against the intended beneficiary. Once an intended beneficiary's rights have vested, however, the promisor may not assert the defense of contractual modification or rescission.

### INCIDENTAL BENEFICIARY

An incidental third-party beneficiary is a person whom the parties to a contract did not intend to benefit but who nevertheless would derive some benefit from its performance. For instance, a contract to raze an old, unsightly building and replace it with a costly, modern house would benefit the owner of the adjoining property by increasing his property's value. He would have no rights under the contract, however, as the benefit to him would be unintended and incidental.

A third person who may benefit incidentally from the performance of a contract to which he is not a party has no rights under the contract. Neither the promisee nor the promisor intended that the third person benefit. Assume that for a stated consideration George promises Kathy that he will purchase and deliver to Kathy a brand-new Sony television of the latest model. Kathy pays in advance for the television. George does not deliver the television to Kathy. As an incidental beneficiary, Cosmos Appliances, Inc., the local exclusive Sony dealer, has no rights under the contract, although performance by George would produce a sale from which Cosmos would benefit.

## CHAPTER SUMMARY

### ASSIGNMENT OF RIGHTS

**Definition of Assignment** voluntary transfer to a third party of the rights arising from a contract so that the assignor's right to performance is extinguished
- ***Assignor*** party making an assignment
- ***Assignee*** party to whom contract rights are assigned
- ***Obligor*** party owing a duty to the assignor under the original contract
- ***Obligee*** party to whom a duty of performance is owed under a contract

**Requirements of an Assignment** include intent but not consideration
- ***Revocability of Assignment*** when the assignee gives consideration, the assignor may not revoke the assignment without the assignee's consent
- ***Partial Assignment*** transfer of a portion of contractual rights to one or more assignees

**Assignability** most contract rights are assignable, except
- assignments that materially increase the duty, risk, or burden upon the obligor
- assignments of personal rights
- assignments expressly forbidden by the contract
- assignments prohibited by law

**Rights of Assignee** the assignee stands in the shoes of the assignor
- ***Defenses of Obligor*** may be asserted against the assignee
- ***Notice*** is not required but is advisable

**Implied Warranty** obligation imposed by law upon the assignor of a contract right

**Express Warranty** explicitly made contractual promise regarding contract rights transferred

**Successive Assignments of the Same Right** the majority rule is that the first assignee in point of time prevails over later assignees; minority rule is that the first assignee to notify the obligor prevails

**DELEGATION OF DUTIES**

**Definition of Delegation** transfer to a third party of a contractual obligation
- ***Delegator*** party delegating his duty to a third party
- ***Delegatee*** third party to whom the delegator's duty is delegated
- ***Obligee*** party to whom a duty of performance is owed by the delegator and delegatee

**Delegability** most contract duties may be delegated, *except*
- duties that are personal
- duties that are expressly nondelegable
- duties whose delegation is prohibited by statute or public policy

**Duties of the Parties**
- ***Delegation*** delegator is still bound to perform original obligation
- ***Novation*** contract, to which the obligee is a party, substituting a new promisor for an existing promisor, who is consequently no longer liable on the original contract and is not liable as a delegator

**THIRD-PARTY BENEFICIARY CONTRACTS**

**Definition** a contract in which one party promises to render a performance to a third person (the beneficiary)

**Intended Beneficiaries** third parties intended by the two contracting parties to receive a benefit from their contract
- ***Donee Beneficiary*** a third party intended to receive a benefit from the contract as a gift
- ***Creditor Beneficiary*** a third person intended to receive a benefit from the agreement to satisfy a legal duty owed to her
- ***Rights of Intended Beneficiary*** an intended donee beneficiary may enforce the contract against the promisor; an intended creditor beneficiary may enforce the contract against either or both the promisor and the promisee
- ***Vesting of Rights*** if the beneficiary's rights vest, the promisor and promisee may not thereafter vary or discharge these vested rights
- ***Defenses against Beneficiary*** in an action by the intended beneficiary of a third-party contract to enforce the promise, the promisor may assert any defense that would be available to her if the action had been brought by the promisee

**Incidental Beneficiary** third party whom the two parties to the contract have no intention of benefiting by their contract and who acquires no rights under the contract

# CASES

## CASE 16-1

### Rights That Are Not Assignable: Personal Rights

### REISER v. DAYTON COUNTRY CLUB COMPANY

United States Court of Appeals, Sixth Circuit, 1992
972 F.2d 689

**Joiner, J.**

In this case we are asked to review an order barring a trustee in bankruptcy under Chapter 7 from assuming and assigning a golf membership in a country club as an executory contract, pursuant to section 365 of the Bankruptcy Code. [Citation.]

The Dayton Country Club is an organization, in the form of a corporation, consisting of several hundred individuals who have joined together for recreation and entertainment. Its shares of stock may be held only by the members of the club and may not be accumulated in any substantial amount by one member.

The club offers social events, dining facilities, tennis courts, a swimming pool, and a golf course. It became apparent over a period of time that each of these diverse programs could be enjoyed to full advantage by a different number of members. For example, since there was only one 18-hole golf course available, and because of the nature of the game, the maximum number of members eligible to play golf needed to be limited in order to make the playing of the game enjoyable to those playing. There was no need to so limit the number of members who could use the tennis courts, the pool, the restaurants, or who could enjoy the social events of the club. The club developed within its membership a special membership category for those who had full golfing privileges. This category was limited to 375 members. Detailed rules, procedures, and practices were developed to ensure the fair selection of golfing members. These rules, procedures, and practices define how this additional privilege is allocated, how the number of members is maintained at 375, how vacancies occur, how they are filled, and what additional fees are charged.

The record reflects that members of the club are entitled to play, eat, and socialize in all activities of the club except golf. If, in addition to these activities, a member desires to play golf, he or she asks to become a golfing member in one of several golf membership categories. When he or she makes this request, an additional substantial fee is paid to the club and the individual is placed on a waiting list. At the time the record was made in this case, there were about 70 persons on that list. When a vacancy occurs because of a failure to pay dues or a resignation, the first person on the waiting list is given the option to become a golfing member by paying an additional substantial fee. Upon becoming a golfing member, the monthly dues also increase substantially. If the person at the top of the waiting list declines the membership, then that person is placed at the bottom of the list and the next person on the list is given the opportunity to become a golfing member. There is no provision for any person to assign or sell the golf membership to any other person or for any person to become a golfing member in any other way except in two intimate and personal situations dealt with in discrete ways. When the death of a golfing member occurs, a spouse (who had been enjoying the hospitality of the club) may take the deceased member's place. If a divorce occurs, the member may designate his or her spouse as the golfing member. The club also has a program to encourage the younger generation of member families to become golfing members. Golfing members are permitted also to invite guests. Through its membership committee, the club makes the rules and establishes the procedures to describe whom among its larger membership list may be golfing members.

The nature of the golf membership within the overall club membership is the heart of this case. We are not dealing with the right to be a member of the club and there is nothing in this case relating to laws and social policies against discrimination. The issues in this case relate solely to the rights, duties, and privileges of the club and its members arising from the club's effort to provide golfing privileges to some but not all of its members, and the effect of the bankruptcy laws upon that effort.

This matter involves appeals from separate orders entered in the bankruptcies of debtors Magness and Redman, both of whom were golfing members of the Dayton Country Club. The trustee in bankruptcy sought to assume and assign, through sale, the rights under these memberships to (1) members on the waiting list, (2) other club members, or (3) the general public, provided that the purchaser first obtains membership in the Dayton Country Club. In other words, the trustee seeks to increase the value of the bankruptcy estate by taking value for and assigning to others a relationship between the bankrupt and the club. The assignment would be to the detriment of other club members who had paid for and acquired the right to become golfing members in due course. The question is whether the trustee has the right to make the assignment.

The arrangement between the members of the club, including Magness and Redman, and the Dayton Country Club, is a complex one involving rights, privileges, and duties, all of which are bound up in what is loosely called the contract for "full golf membership." At the least, this contract involves (1) an executed portion, the achievement of "full golf membership," and the payment of the nonrefundable fee the club charges for that membership in accordance with the rules, procedures, and practices prescribed by the club; (2) the rights of other club members to apply for golf membership as set out in the rules, procedures, and practices of the club; (3) the rights of those in the club who have applied for and have been accepted and have made substantial payments for full golf membership; (4) the obligation of the members to pay monthly dues; and (5) the obligation of the club to provide recreational facilities called for in its charter and bylaws. In other words, this contract between the debtors and the club and others is neither a simple contract to buy and sell a product or a service nor is it a lease.

Not only is it appropriate to cast these complex relationships in terms of both executed and executory contracts, it is not inappropriate to think of these contracts as creating a type of property interest. The full golf membership and the rights that come from that relationship with the club can be described as a property right of that member, the parameters of which are defined by the rules, procedures, and practices of the club. These rules, procedures, and practices, and therefore the extent of the members' property interest, do not extend to any right on the members' part to pass on the membership to others, except in the two situations described above (death or divorce). The persons on the waiting list also can be described as having a type of property interest in the relationship described in their contracts with the club. Theirs is a lesser interest than that of the full golfing members, but a real one nonetheless. They have paid the club for the right to be considered in the numbered order on the list to become full golfing members as vacancies occur. They, like the full golfing members, have a status defined by the various rules, procedures, and practices pertaining to filling the membership roster.

The bankruptcy courts found, and the district court affirmed, that the full golf memberships are executory contracts under §365 of the Bankruptcy Code. [Citation.] Section 365(f)(1) of the Bankruptcy Code provides that executory contracts may be assigned notwithstanding non-assignment provisions in the contract or the law. * * *

Section 365(c)(1) contains an exception to section 365(f)'s bar to enforcement of non-assignment provisions:

> (c) The trustee may not assume or assign any executory contract or unexpired lease of the debtor, whether

or not such contract or lease prohibits or restricts assignment of rights or delegation of duties, if—

(1)(A) applicable law excuses a party, other than the debtor, to such contract or lease from accepting performance from or rendering performance to an entity other than the debtor or the debtor in possession, whether or not such contract or lease prohibits or restricts assignment of rights or delegation of duties; and (B) such party does not consent to such assumption or assignment. * * * [Citation.]

The bankruptcy courts found that the trustee was barred from assigning the full golf memberships by Ohio law under §365(c). The courts concluded that the club's rules were, in effect, anti-assignment provisions, and that Ohio law excused the club from accepting performance by others. The court thus gave effect to the provisions. * * *

The trustee appealed these rulings to the district court. * * *

The district court affirmed the order barring assignment of Magness' full golf membership on the basis of the bankruptcy court's reasoning, and observed as well that the case did not involve "the legal equivalent of a long-term commercial lease" but rather "a non-commercial dispute over the possession of a valuable membership in a recreational and social club."

The trustee then appealed to this court. * * * We conclude that the decision of the district court was correct. * * * We now affirm.

* * *

As stated earlier in this opinion, the contracts involve complex issues and multiple parties: the members of the club, in having an orderly procedure for the selection of full golfing members; the club itself, in demonstrating to all who would become members that there is a predictable and orderly method of filling vacancies in the golfing roster; and more particularly, persons on the waiting list who have deposited substantial sums of money based on an expectation and a developed procedure that in due course they, in turn, would become full golfing members.

If the trustee is permitted to assume and assign the full golf membership, the club would be required to breach its agreement with the persons on the waiting list, each of whom has contractual rights with the club. It would require the club to accept performance from and render performance to a person other than the debtor. * * *

* * *

The contracts creating the complex relationships among the parties and others are not in any way commercial. They create personal relationships among individuals who play golf, who are waiting to play golf, who eat together, swim and play together. They are personal contracts and Ohio law does not permit the assignment of personal contracts. [Citation.]

So-called personal contracts, or contracts in which the personality of one of the parties is material, are not assignable. Whether the personality of one or both parties is material depends on the intention of the parties, as shown by the language which they have used, and upon the nature of the contract.

The claim that the assignment will be made only to those who are already members of the club is not relevant. "Nor would the fact that a particular person it attempted to designate [assign] was personally unexceptionable affect the nature of the contract." [Citation.]

Therefore, we believe that the trustee's motion to assign the full golf membership should be denied. We reach this conclusion because the arrangements for filling vacancies proscribe assignment, the club did not consent to the assignment and sale, and applicable law excuses the club from accepting performance from or rendering performance to a person other than the debtor.

CASE 16-2

## Express Prohibition of Assignment
## ALDANA v. COLONIAL PALMS PLAZA, INC.

District Court of Appeal of Florida, Third District, 1991
591 So.2d 953

**Per Curiam**

The appellant, Robert Aldana, appeals an adverse summary judgment in favor of appellee, Colonial Palms Plaza, Inc. and an order awarding Colonial Palms Plaza, Inc. attorney's fees pursuant to the offer of judgment rule. We reverse.

Colonial Palms Plaza, Inc. [Landlord], entered into a lease agreement with Abby's Cakes On Dixie, Inc. [Tenant] for commercial space in a shopping center. The lease included a provision in which Landlord agreed to pay Tenant a construction allowance of up to $11,250 after Tenant satisfactorily completed certain improvements to the rented premises.

Prior to the completion of the improvements, Tenant assigned its right to receive the first $8,000 of the construction allowance to Robert Aldana [Assignee]. In return, Assignee loaned Tenant $8,000 to finance the construction. Assignee recorded the assignment and sent notice to the assignment by certified mail to Landlord.

When Tenant completed the improvements to the rented premises, Landlord ignored the assignment and paid Tenant the construction allowance. Assignee sued Landlord for the money due pursuant to the assignment. The trial court granted Landlord's motion for summary judgment.

The trial court also awarded Landlord attorney's fees pursuant to the offer of judgment rule, [citation], and costs pursuant to [citation].

Landlord relies on an anti-assignment clause in the lease agreement to argue that the assignment was void and unenforceable. The clause states in part:

> TENANT agrees not to assign, mortgage, pledge, or encumber this Lease, in whole or in part, or to sublet the whole or any part of the DEMISED PREMISES, or to permit the use of the whole or any part of the DEMISED PREMISES by any licensee or concessionaire, without first obtaining the prior, specific written consent of LANDLORD at LANDLORD'S sole discretion. * * * Any such assignment, encumbrance or subletting without such consent shall be void and shall at LANDLORD'S option constitute a default.

* * *

Assignee argues * * * that under ordinary contract principles, the lease provision at issue here does not prevent the assignment of the right to receive contractual payments. We agree.

So far as pertinent here, the lease provides that "TENANT agrees not to assign * * * this Lease, in whole or in part. * * *" Tenant did not assign the lease, but instead assigned a right to receive the construction allowance.

The law in this area is summarized in Restatement (Second) of Contracts, §322(1), as follows:

> Unless the circumstances indicate the contrary, a contract term prohibiting assignment of "the contract" bars only the delegation to an assignee of the performance by the assignor of a duty or condition.

As a rule of construction, in other words, a prohibition against assignment of the contract (or in this case, the lease) will prevent assignment of contractual duties, but does not prevent assignment of the right to receive payments due—unless the circumstances indicate the contrary. [Citations.]

Landlord was given notice of the assignment. Delivery of the notice of the assignment to the debtor fixes accountability of the debtor to the assignee. [Citation.] Therefore, Landlord was bound by the assignment. [Citation.] The trial court improperly granted final summary judgment in favor of Landlord and the judgment must be reversed. Consequently, the trial court's award of attorney's fees and costs to Landlord must also be reversed. The cause is remanded for further proceedings consistent herewith.

Reversed and remanded.

CASE 16-3

## Delegation of Duties
## PUBLIC SERVICE COMMISSION OF MARYLAND v. PANDA-BRANDYWINE, L.P.

Court of Appeals of Maryland, 2003

375 Md. 185, 825 A.2d 462

http://caselaw.findlaw.com/md-court-of-appeals/1006511.html

**Wilner, J.**

PEPCO [Potomac Electric Power Company] is an electric utility serving the metropolitan Washington, D.C. area. Panda [Panda-Brandywine, L.P.] is a "qualified facility" (QF) under the Public Utility Regulatory Policies Act of 1978 [citation]. * * *

* * *

In August, 1991, PEPCO and Panda entered into a PPA [power purchase agreement] calling for (1) the construction by Panda of a new 230-megawatt cogenerating power plant in Prince George's County, (2) connection of the facility to PEPCO's high voltage transmission system by transmission facilities to be built by Panda but later transferred without cost to PEPCO, and (3) upon commencement of the commercial operation of the plant, for PEPCO to purchase the power generated by that plant for a period of 25 years. The plant was built at a cost of $215 million, financed mostly through loans.

The PPA is 113 pages in length, single-spaced, and is both detailed and complex. In it, PEPCO was given substantial authority to review, influence, and, in some instances, determine important aspects of both the construction and operation of the Panda facility. * * *

* * *

Section 19.1 of the PPA provided, with certain exceptions not relevant here, that "neither this Agreement, nor any of the rights or obligations hereunder, may be assigned, transferred, or delegated by either Party, without the express prior written consent of the other Party, which consent shall not be unreasonably withheld…" * * *

* * *

In 1999, the General Assembly passed the Electric Consumer Choice and Competition Act of 1999 [citation], calling for the restructuring of the electric industry in an effort to promote competition in the generation and delivery of electricity * * * PEPCO's proposed restructuring involved a complete divestiture of its electric generating assets and its various PPAs, to be accomplished by an auction. * * *

The sale to the winning bidder was to be accomplished by an Asset Purchase and Sale Agreement (APSA) that included a number of PPAs to which PEPCO was a party and specifically the PPA with Panda. * * *

* * *

[Under the APSA] the buyer was authorized to take all actions that PEPCO could lawfully take under the PPA without further approval from PEPCO * * *.

* * *

* * * on June 7, 2000, SEI was declared the winning bidder. On September 27, 2000, the PSC [Public Service Commission] entered an order (Order No. 76472) declaring, among other things, that the provisions in the APSA did not constitute an assignment or transfer within the meaning of §19.1 of the Panda PPA, that PEPCO was not assigning "significant obligations and rights under the PPA," that Panda would not be harmed by the transaction, and that the APSA did not "fundamentally alter[]" the privity of contract between Panda and PEPCO. It thus concluded that Panda's consent to the proposed APSA was not required. * * *

Panda sought judicial review in the Circuit Court for Montgomery County. That court found that the APSA * * * effected an assignment of Panda's PPA. It reversed the PSC order * * *.

* * *

* * * PEPCO appealed [and the] court concluded that, through the APSA, PEPCO effectively and improperly delegated its duties under the PPA to SEI. It added that the APSA amounted to an assignment because it extinguished PEPCO's right to performance from Panda—a right that was transferred to SEI. * * *We granted cross-petitions for *certiorari* to consider whether the Court of Special Appeals erred * * *.

* * *

By prohibiting both nonconsensual assignment and delegation, the PPA recognizes a nuance, or distinction, that is occasionally overlooked. In a bilateral contract, each party ordinarily has both rights and duties—the right to expect performance from the other party to the contract and the duty to perform what the party has agreed to perform. Although both are often the subject of transfer, the law does distinguish between them, using the term "assignment" to refer to the transfer of contractual rights and the term "delegation" to refer to the transfer of contractual duties. * * *

Restatement §317 defines the assignment of a right as "a manifestation of the assignor's intention to transfer it by virtue of which the assignor's right to performance by the obligor is extinguished in whole or in part and the assignee acquires a right to such performance." Section 317(2) permits a contractual right to be assigned unless (a) "the substitution of a right of the assignee for the right of the assignor would materially change the duty of the obligor, or materially increase the burden or risk imposed on him by his contract, or materially impair his chance of obtaining return performance, or materially reduce its value to him," (b) the assignment is forbidden by statute or is inoperative on grounds of public policy, or (c) "*assignment is validly precluded by contract.*" (Emphasis added).

Section 318 speaks to the delegation of performance. Section 318(1) allows an obligor to delegate the performance of a contractual duty "unless the delegation is contrary to public policy *or the terms of his promise.*" (Emphasis added.) Section 318(2) provides that, unless otherwise agreed, a promise requires performance by a particular person "only to the extent that the obligee has a substantial interest in having that person perform or control the acts promised." Finally, §318(3) states that, "unless the obligee agrees otherwise, neither delegation of performance nor a contract to assume the duty made with the obligor by the person delegated discharges any duty or liability of the delegating obligor."

Although using somewhat different language, we have adopted those principles. In *Macke Co. v. Pizza of Gaithersburg,* [citation], we held that "in the absence of a contrary provision ... rights and duties under an executory bilateral contract may be assigned and delegated, subject to the exception that duties under a contract to provide personal services may never be delegated, nor rights be assigned under a contract where *delectus personae* was an ingredient of the bargain."

These general statements, both in §§317 and 318 and in *Macke* regarding the extent to which rights may be assigned and duties of performance may be delegated are, as noted, subject to any valid contractual provision prohibiting assignment or delegation. Section 19.1 of the PPA very clearly prohibits both the assignment of rights and the delegation of duties of performance, absent express written consent. The issue, then, is not whether PEPCO can make such an assignment or delegation but only whether it has, in fact, done so. The answer to that lies in the effect that the [provisions of the APSA] have on the contractual relationship between PEPCO and Panda.

* * * [Under the APSA] SEI was expressly authorized to take all actions that PEPCO could lawfully take under the PPA, without further approval by PEPCO, including the right to perform all obligations of PEPCO in respect to the PPA, to deal directly with Panda "with respect to all matters arising under the ... PPA," to "monitor [Panda's] performance" under the PPA, to review and audit all bills and related documentation rendered by Panda, with some restrictions to enter into amendments to the PPA, and to delegate any or all of those functions to any third party.

* * * [The APSA] permitted SEI, rather than PEPCO, to determine how much of Panda's output it could sell on the open market pursuant to the 1997 letter agreement. * * * It gives SEI a substantial measure of control over Panda's operations.

* * *

* * * The APSA involves a great deal more than merely a resale of electricity purchased from Panda and even more than the effective substitution of one customer for another. Much of Panda's control over its own facility and business was subject to the approval and cooperation of PEPCO; indeed, to a large extent, the operation of the facility was, in many important respects, almost a joint venture. In agreeing to that kind of arrangement, Panda necessarily was relying on its perceptions of PEPCO's competence and managerial style. One does not ordinarily choose a business partner by auction or lottery, and there is no evidence that Panda did so in this case. Paraphrasing §318(2) of the Restatement, Panda has "a substantial interest in having [PEPCO] perform or control the acts promised." Under [the APSA], that control has been delegated irrevocably to SEI—a stranger to Panda—with the ability of SEI to delegate it to others.

* * * Virtually none of the rights and responsibilities transferred to SEI under [the APSA] are permitted under §19.1 of the PPA. * * * We hold that [the APSA] constitutes an assignment of rights and obligations under the PPA in contravention of §19.1 of that agreement and that it is therefore invalid and unenforceable.

* * *

[Judgment affirmed.]

## CASE 16-4

Intended Beneficiary

## STINE v. STEWART

Supreme Court of Texas, 2002

80 S.W.3d 586

http://caselaw.lp.findlaw.com/scripts/getcase.pl?court=tx&vol=/sc/010896&invol=1

**Per Curiam**

On April 26, 1984, [Mary] Stine loaned her daughter [Mary Ellen Stewart] and son-in-law [William] Stewart $100,000 to purchase a home. In return, the Stewarts jointly executed a promissory note for $100,000, payable on demand to Stine. The note required interest payments at a floating rate adjusted every six months to one percent below the prime rate. It also required the Stewarts to pay the interest on the first of each month as it accrued on the unpaid principal. The Stewarts did not give a security interest or mortgage to secure the note. The Stewarts eventually paid $50,000 on the note, leaving $50,000, together with unpaid accrued interest, due.

The Stewarts divorced on October 2, 1992. The couple executed an Agreement Incident to Divorce * * * which disposed of marital property, including the home the agreement identifies as the Lago Vista property. The agreement provides that Stewart could lease the house, but if Stewart sold it, he agreed that "any monies owing to [Stine] are to be paid in the current principal sum of $50,000.00." The agreement further states:

> The parties agree that with regard to the note to Mary Nelle Stine, after application of the proceeds of the [Lago Vista property], if there are any amounts owing to [Stine] the remaining balance owing to her will be appropriated 50% to NANCY KAREN STEWART and 50% to WILLIAM DEAN STEWART, JR. and said 50% from each party will be due and payable upon the determination that the proceeds from the sale of said residence are not sufficient to repay said $50,000.00 in full.

Stine did not sign the agreement.

On November 17, 1995, Stewart sold the Lago Vista property for $125,000, leaving $6,820.21 in net proceeds. Stewart did not pay these proceeds to Stine and did not make any further payments on the $50,000 principal. Consequently, on July 27, 1998, Stine sued Stewart for breaching the agreement. * * *

After a bench trial, the trial court concluded that Stine was an intended third-party beneficiary of the agreement and that Stewart breached the agreement when he refused to pay Stine as the agreement required. The trial court awarded Stine $28,410 in damages * * * from Stewart.

The court of appeals reversed the judgment and rendered judgment for Stewart. [Citation.] The court of appeals concluded that, because the agreement does not show that the Stewarts intended to confer a gift to Stine, Stine was not an intended third-party donee beneficiary of the agreement. [Citation.] Additionally, the court of appeals concluded that Stine was not an intended third-party creditor beneficiary of the agreement. [Citation.] * * *

A third party may recover on a contract made between other parties only if the parties intended to secure a benefit to that third party, and only if the contracting parties entered into the contract directly for the third party's benefit. [Citation.] A third party does not have a right to enforce the contract if she received only an incidental benefit. [Citation.] "A court will not create a third-party beneficiary contract by implication." [Citation.] Rather, an agreement must clearly and fully express an intent to confer a direct benefit to the third party. [Citation.] To determine the parties' intent, courts must examine the entire agreement when interpreting a contract and give effect to all the contract's provisions so that none are rendered meaningless. [Citation.]

To qualify as an intended third-party beneficiary, a party must show that she is either a "donee" or "creditor" beneficiary of the contract. [Citation.] An agreement benefits a "donee" beneficiary if, under the contract, "the performance promised will, when rendered, come to him as a pure donation." [Citation]; *see also* RESTATEMENT (SECOND) OF CONTRACTS §302(1)(b). In contrast, an agreement benefits a "creditor" beneficiary if, under the agreement, "that performance will come to him in satisfaction of a legal duty owed to him by the promisee." [Citation]; *see also* RESTATEMENT (SECOND) OF CONTRACTS §302(1)(a). This duty may be an indebtedness, contractual obligation or other legally enforceable commitment owed to the third party. [Citation.]

Stine contends that she has standing to sue for breach of the agreement as a third-party beneficiary, because the Stewarts intended to secure a benefit to her—that is, the payment of the remaining balance under the note. Stine also argues that whether or not limitations expired on enforcing the note, she was still a third-party creditor beneficiary because the debt remained an existing, legal obligation. Moreover, Stine contends, the agreement "acknowledges" the$50,000 debt owed to her because it recognizes that the note exists and requires the Stewarts to pay any amounts due under the note when Stewart sells the Lago Vista property. * * *

Stewart responds that Stine does not have standing to sue under the agreement, because she is only an incidental beneficiary. Stewart argues that the agreement was not entered into directly and primarily for Stine's benefit, and the agreement does not fully and clearly express the intent to confer a benefit to Stine. * * * Moreover, Stewart contends that the agreement does not acknowledge the original note, because it does not contain unequivocal language that revives the expired debt. * * *

We agree with the court of appeals' determination that Stine was not an intended third-party donee beneficiary of the agreement. [Citation.] But, we conclude that Stine is a third-party creditor beneficiary. The agreement expressly provides that the Stewarts intended to satisfy an obligation to repay Stine the $50,000 that the Stewarts owed her. Specifically, the agreement refers to the monies owed to Stine as "the current principal sum of $50,000." Then, the agreement states that Stewart agreed to pay the property sale net proceeds "with regard to the note" to Stine. The agreement further provides that, if the property sale net proceeds did not cover the amount owed to Stine, the remainder would be immediately due and payable from the Stewarts, with each owing one half. Thus, the agreement expressly requires the Stewarts to satisfy their existing obligation to pay Stine. [Citation.]

* * *

Furthermore, contrary to Stewart's argument, a third-party beneficiary does not have to show that the signatories executed the contract *solely* to benefit her as a non-contracting party. Rather, the focus is on whether the contracting parties intended, at least in part, to discharge an obligation owed to the third party. [Citation.] Here, the entire agreement is obviously not for Stine's sole benefit. However, certain provisions in the agreement expressly state the Stewarts' intent to pay Stine the money due to her.

* * *

The agreement's language clearly shows that Stewart intended to secure a benefit to Stine as a third-party creditor beneficiary. The agreement also acknowledges the existence of a legal obligation owed to Stine and thus revives it as an enforceable obligation. Consequently, Stewart breached the agreement when he refused to pay Stine the money owed to her as the agreement requires. * * * Accordingly, we reverse the court of appeals' judgment and remand this case to the trial court to render judgment consistent with this opinion. [Citation.]

## QUESTIONS

1. Distinguish between an assignment of rights and a delegation of duties.
2. Identify
   **(a)** the requirements of an assignment of contract rights and
   **(b)** those rights that are not assignable.
3. Identify those situations in which a delegation of duties is not permitted.
4. Distinguish between an intended beneficiary and an incidental beneficiary.
5. Explain when the rights of an intended beneficiary vest.

## PROBLEMS

**1.** On December 1, Euphonia, a famous singer, contracted with Boito to sing at Boito's theater on December 31 for a fee of $25,000 to be paid immediately after the performance.

**(a)** Euphonia, for value received, assigns this fee to Carter.

**(b)** Euphonia, for value received, assigns this contract to sing to Dumont, an equally famous singer.

**(c)** Boito sells his theatre to Edmund and assigns his contract with Euphonia to Edmund. State the effect of each of these assignments.

**2.** The Smooth Paving Company entered into a paving contract with the city of Chicago. The contract contained the clause "contractor shall be liable for all damages to buildings resulting from the work performed." In the process of construction, one of the bulldozers of the Smooth Paving Company struck and broke a gas main, causing an explosion and a fire that destroyed the house of John Puff. Puff brought an action for breach of the paving contract against the Smooth Paving Company to recover damages for the loss of his house. Can Puff recover under this contract? Explain.

**3.** Anne, who was unemployed, registered with the Speedy Employment Agency. A contract was then made under which Anne, in consideration of such position as the Agency would obtain for her, agreed to pay the Agency one-half of her first month's salary. The contract also contained an assignment by Anne to the Agency of one-half of her first month's salary. Two weeks later, the Agency obtained a permanent position for Anne with the Bostwick Co. at a monthly salary of $1,900. The agency also notified Bostwick of the assignment by Anne. At the end of the first month, Bostwick paid Anne her salary in full. Anne then quit and disappeared. The Agency now sues Bostwick Co. for $950 under the assignment. Who will prevail? Explain.

**4.** Georgia purchased an option on Greenacre from Pamela for $10,000. The option contract contained a provision by which Georgia promised not to assign the option contract without Pamela's permission. Georgia, without Pamela's permission, assigns the contract to Michael. Michael seeks to exercise the option, and Pamela refuses to sell Greenacre to him. Must Pamela sell the land to Michael?

**5.** Julia contracts to sell to Hayden, an ice cream manufacturer, the amount of ice Hayden may need in his business for the ensuing three years to the extent of not more than 250 tons a week at a stated price per ton. Hayden makes a corresponding promise to Julia to buy such an amount of ice. Hayden sells his ice cream plant to Clark and assigns to Clark all Hayden's rights under the contract with Julia. Upon learning of the sale, Julia refuses to furnish ice to Clark. Clark sues Julia for damages. Decision?

**6.** Brown enters into a written contract with Ideal Insurance Company under which, in consideration of her payment of the premiums, the insurance company promises to pay State College the face amount of the policy, $100,000, on Brown's death. Brown pays the premiums until her death. Thereafter, State College makes demand for the $100,000, which the insurance company refuses to pay upon the ground that State College was not a party to the contract. Can State College successfully enforce the contract?

**7.** Grant and Debbie enter into a contract binding Grant personally to do some delicate cabinetwork. Grant assigns his rights and delegates performance of his duties to Clarence.

**(a)** On being informed of this, Debbie agrees with Clarence, in consideration of Clarence's promise to do the work, that Debbie will accept Clarence's work, if properly done, instead of the performance promised by Grant. Later, without cause, Debbie refuses to allow Clarence to proceed with the work, though Clarence is ready to do so, and makes demand on Grant that Grant perform. Grant refuses. Can Clarence recover damages from Debbie? Can Debbie recover from Grant?

**(b)** Instead, assume that Debbie refuses to permit Clarence to do the work, employs another carpenter, and brings an action against Grant, claiming as damages the difference between the contract price and the cost to employ the other carpenter. Explain whether Debbie will prevail.

**8.** Rebecca owes Lewis $2,500 due on November 1. On August 15, Lewis assigns this right for value received to Julia, who gives notice on September 10 of the assignment to Rebecca. On August 25, Lewis assigns the same right to Wayne, who in good faith gives value and has no prior knowledge of the assignment by Lewis to Julia. Wayne gives Rebecca notice of the assignment on August 30. What are the rights and obligations of Rebecca, Lewis, Julia, and Wayne?

**9.** Lisa hired Jay in the spring, as she had for many years, to set out in beds the flowers Lisa had grown in her greenhouses during the winter. The work was to be done in Lisa's absence for $300. Jay became ill the day after Lisa departed and requested his friend, Curtis, to set out the flowers, promising to pay Curtis $250 when Jay received his payment. Curtis agreed. Upon completion of the planting, an agent of Lisa's, who had authority to dispense the money, paid Jay, and Jay paid Curtis. Within two days it became obvious that the planting was a disaster. Everything set out by Curtis had died of water rot because he had operated Lisa's automatic watering system improperly.

May Lisa recover damages from Curtis? May she recover damages from Jay? If so, does Jay have an action against Curtis?

**10.** Caleb, operator of a window-washing business, dictated a letter to his secretary addressed to Apartments, Inc., stating, "I will wash the windows of your apartment buildings at $4.10 per window to be paid upon completion of the work." The secretary typed the letter, signed Caleb's name, and mailed it to Apartments, Inc. Apartments, Inc., replied, "Accept your offer."

Caleb wrote back, "I will wash them during the week commencing July 10 and direct you to pay the money you will owe me to my son, Bernie. I am giving it to him as a wedding present." Caleb sent a signed copy of the letter to Bernie.

Caleb washed the windows during the time stated and demanded payment to him of $8,200 (two thousand windows at $4.10 each), informing Apartments, Inc., that he had changed his mind about having the money paid to Bernie. What are the rights of the parties?

**11.** McDonald's has an undeviating policy of retaining absolute control over who receives new franchises. McDonald's granted to

Copeland a franchise in Omaha, Nebraska. In a separate letter, it also granted him a right of first refusal for future franchises to be developed in the Omaha-Council Bluffs area. Copeland then sold all rights in his six McDonald's franchises to Schupack. When McDonald's offered a new franchise in the Omaha area to someone other than Schupack, Schupack attempted to exercise the right of first refusal. McDonald's would not recognize the right in Schupack, claiming that it was personal to Copeland and, therefore, nonassignable without its consent. Schupack brought an action for specific performance, requiring McDonald's to accord him the right of first refusal. Is Schupack correct in his contention?

**12.** In 1952, the estate of George Bernard Shaw granted to Gabriel Pascal Enterprises, Limited, the exclusive rights to produce a musical play and a motion picture based on Shaw's play *Pygmalion*. The agreement contained a provision terminating the license if Gabriel Pascal Enterprises did not arrange for well-known composers, such as Lerner and Loewe, to write the musical and produce it within a specified time. George Pascal, owner of 98 percent of the Gabriel Pascal Enterprise's stock, attempted to meet these requirements but died in July 1954 before negotiations had been completed. In February 1954, however, while the license had two years yet to run, Pascal sent a letter to Kingman, his executive secretary, granting to her certain percentages of his share of the profits from the expected stage and screen productions of *Pygmalion*. Subsequently, Pascal's estate arranged for the writing and production of the highly successful *My Fair Lady*, based on Shaw's *Pygmalion*. Kingman then sued to enforce Pascal's gift assignment of the future royalties. Decision?

**13.** Northwest Airlines leased space in the terminal building at the Portland Airport from the Port of Portland. Crosetti entered into a contract with the Port to furnish janitorial services for the building, which required Crosetti to keep the floor clean, to indemnify the Port against loss due to claims or lawsuits based upon Crosetti's failure to perform, and to provide public liability insurance for the Port and Crosetti. A patron of the building who was injured by a fall caused by a foreign substance on the floor at Northwest's ticket counter brought suit for damages against Northwest, the Port, and Crosetti. Upon settlement of this suit, Northwest sued Crosetti to recover the amount of its contribution to the settlement and other expenses on the grounds that Northwest was a third-party beneficiary of Crosetti's contract with the Port to keep the floors clean and, therefore, within the protection of Crosetti's indemnification agreement. Will Northwest prevail? Why?

**14.** Tompkins-Beckwith, as the contractor on a construction project, entered into a subcontract with a division of Air Metal Industries. Air Metal procured American Fire and Casualty Company to be surety on certain bonds in connection with contracts it was performing for Tompkins-Beckwith and others. As security for these bonds, on January 3, Air Metal executed an assignment to American Fire of all accounts receivable under the Tompkins-Beckwith subcontract. On November 26 of that year, Boulevard National Bank lent money to Air Metal. To secure the loans, Air Metal purported to assign to the bank certain accounts receivable it had under its subcontract with Tompkins-Beckwith.

In June of the following year, Air Metal defaulted on various contracts bonded by American Fire. On July 1, American Fire served formal notice on Tompkins-Beckwith of Air Metal's assignment. Tompkins-Beckwith acknowledged the assignment and agreed to pay. In August Boulevard National Bank notified Tompkins-Beckwith of its assignment. Tompkins-Beckwith refused to recognize the bank's claim and, instead, paid all remaining funds that had accrued to Air Metal to American Fire. The bank then sued to enforce its claim under Air Metal's assignment. Is the assignment effective? Why?

**15.** The International Association of Machinists (the union) was the bargaining agent for the employees of Powder Power Tool Corporation. On August 24, the union and the corporation executed a collective bargaining agreement providing for retroactively increased wage rates for the corporation's employees effective as of April 1. Three employees who were working for Powder before and for several months after April 1, but who were not employed by the corporation when the agreement was executed on August 24, were paid to the time their employment terminated at the old wage scale. The three employees assigned their claims to Springer, who brought this action against the corporation for the extra wages. Decision?

**16.** In March, Adrian Saylor sold government bonds owned exclusively by him and with $6,450 of the proceeds opened a savings account in a bank in the name of "Mr. or Mrs. Adrian M. Saylor." In June of the following year, Saylor deposited the additional sum of $2,132 of his own money in the account. There were no other deposits and no withdrawals prior to Saylor's death a year later. Is the balance of the account on Saylor's death payable wholly to Adrian Saylor's estate, wholly to his widow, or half to each?

**17.** Linda King was found liable to Charlotte Clement as the result of an automobile accident. King, who was insolvent at the time, declared bankruptcy and directed her attorney, Prestwich, to list Clement as an unsecured creditor. The attorney failed to carry out this duty, and consequently King sued him for legal malpractice. When Clement pursued her judgment against King, she received a written assignment of King's legal malpractice claim against Prestwich. Clement has attempted to bring the claim, but Prestwich alleges that a claim for legal malpractice is not assignable. Decision?

**18.** Rensselaer Water Company contracted with the city of Rensselaer to provide water to the city for use in homes, public buildings, industry, and fire hydrants. During the term of the contract, a building caught fire. The fire spread to a nearby warehouse and destroyed it and its contents. The water company knew of the fire but failed to supply adequate water pressure at the fire hydrant to extinguish the fire. The warehouse owner sued the water company for failure to fulfill its contract with the city. Can the warehouse owner enforce the contract? Explain.

**19.** While under contract to play professional basketball for the Philadelphia 76ers, Billy Cunningham negotiated a three-year contract with the Carolina Cougars, another professional basketball team. The contract with the Cougars was to begin at the expiration of the contract with the 76ers. In addition to a signing bonus of $125,000, Cunningham was to receive under the new contract a salary of $100,000 for the first year, $110,000 for the second, and $120,000 for the third. The contract also stated that Cunningham "had special, exceptional and unique knowledge, skill and ability as a basketball player" and that Cunningham therefore agreed the Cougars could enjoin him from playing basketball for any other team for the term of the contract. In addition, the contract contained a clause prohibiting its assignment to another club without Cunningham's consent. In 1971 the ownership of the Cougars changed, and Cunningham's contract was assigned to Munchak Corporation, the new owners, without his consent. When Cunningham refused to play for the Cougars, Munchak Corporation sought to enjoin his playing for any other team. Cunningham asserts that his contract was not assignable. Was the contract assignable? Explain.

**20.** Pauline Brown was shot and seriously injured by an unknown assailant in the parking lot of National Supermarkets. Pauline and George Brown brought a negligence action against National, Sentry Security Agency, and T. G. Watkins, a security guard and Sentry employee. Sentry had a security contract with National. The Browns maintained that the defendants have a legal duty to protect National's customers both in the store and in the parking lot, and that this duty was breached. The defendants denied this allegation. What will the Browns have to prove to prevail? Explain.

**21.** On April 1, members of Local 100, Transport Workers Union of America (TWU), began an 11-day mass transit strike that paralyzed the life and commerce of the city of New York. Plaintiffs are engaged in the practice of law as a profession, maintaining offices in Manhattan. Plaintiffs sue both individually and on behalf of all other professional and business entities (the class) that were damaged as a consequence of the defendants' willful disruption of the service provided by the public transportation system of the City of New York. The law firm sought to recover as a third-party beneficiary of the collective bargaining agreement between the union and New York City. The agreement contains a no-strike clause and states that the TWU agreed to cooperate with the city to provide a safe, efficient, and dependable mass transit system. As a member of the public which depends on the public transit system and which employs dozens of persons who need the public transit system to get to and from work, plaintiffs argue that they are within the class of persons for whose benefit the TWU has promised to provide "dependable transportation service." Are the members of the class action suit entitled to recover? Explain.

**22.** On behalf of himself and other similarly situated options investors, Rick Lockwood sued defendant, Standard & Poor's Corporation (Standard & Poor's), for breach of contract. Lockwood alleged that he and other options investors suffered lost profits on certain options contracts because Standard & Poor's failed to correct a closing stock index value. Standard & Poor's compiles and publishes two composite stock indexes, the "S&P 100" and the "S&P 500" (collectively the S&P indexes). The S&P indexes are weighted indexes of common stocks primarily listed for trading on the New York Stock Exchange (NYSE). Standard & Poor's licenses its S&P indexes to the Chicago Board Options Exchange (CBOE) to allow the trading of securities options contracts (S&P index options) based on the S&P indexes (the license agreement). S&P index options are settled by the Options Clearing Corporation (OCC). The exercise settlement values for S&P index options are the closing index values for the S&P 100 and S&P 500 stock market indexes as reported by Standard & Poor's to OCC following the close of trading on the day of exercise.

In his complaint, Lockwood alleged that at approximately 4:12 P.M. on Friday, December 15, 1989, the last trading day prior to expiration of the December 1989 S&P index options contracts, the NYSE erroneously reported a closing price for Ford Motor Company common stock. Ford Motor Company was one of the composite stocks in both the S&P 100 and S&P 500. At approximately 4:13 P.M., Standard & Poor's calculated and disseminated closing index values for the S&P 100 and S&P 500 stock market indexes based on the erroneous price for Ford stock. The NYSE reported a corrected closing price for Ford Motor at approximately 4:18 P.M. Standard & Poor's corrected the values of the S&P 100 and S&P 500 stock market indexes the following Monday, December 18, 1989. In the meantime, however, OCC automatically settled all expiring S&P index options according to the expiration date of Saturday, December 16, 1989. OCC used the uncorrected closing index values to settle all expiring S&P index options. Due to the error, Lockwood alleges that the S&P 100 index was overstated by 0.15 and he lost $105. Lockwood claimed investors in S&P 500 index options suffered similar losses. Lockwood filed a class action on behalf of "all holders of long put options and all sellers of short call options on the S&P 100 or S&P 500 ... which were settled based on the closing index values for December 15, 1989, as reported by Standard & Poor's," claiming that the options holders could recover in contract as third-party beneficiaries of the license agreement between Standard & Poor's and the CBOE. Are the members of the class action suit entitled to recover? Explain.

**23.** Pizza of Gaithersburg and The Pizza Shops contracted with Virginia Coffee Service to have vending machines installed in each of their pizza establishments. One year later, the Macke Company purchased Virginia's assets, and the vending machine contracts were assigned to Macke. When The Pizza Shops attempted to terminate their contracts for vending services, Macke brought suit for damages for breach of contract. The Pizza Shops argued that they had dealt with Macke before but had chosen Virginia because they preferred the way it conducted its business. They contended that because there was a material difference between the performance of Virginia and that of Macke, they were justified in refusing to recognize Virginia's delegation of its duties to Macke. Who should prevail?

# CHAPTER 17
# Performance, Breach, and Discharge

The subject of discharge of contracts concerns the termination of contractual duties. In earlier chapters we have seen how parties may become bound to a contract. It is also important to know how a person may become unbound from a contract. For although contractual promises are made for a purpose, and the parties reasonably expect this purpose to be fulfilled by performance, performance of a contractual duty is only one method of discharge.

Whatever causes a binding promise to cease to be binding constitutes a discharge of the contract. In general, there are four kinds of discharge: (1) performance by the parties, (2) material breach by one or both of the parties, (3) agreement of the parties, and (4) operation of law. Moreover, many contractual promises are not absolute promises to perform but rather are conditional; that is, they are dependent upon the happening or nonhappening of a specific event. After a discussion of conditions, the four kinds of discharge will be covered.

## CONDITIONS

A **condition** is an event whose happening or nonhappening affects a duty of performance under a contract. Some conditions must be satisfied before any duty to perform arises; others terminate the duty to perform; still others either limit or modify the duty to perform. A promisor inserts conditions into a contract for her protection and benefit. Furthermore, the more conditions to which a promise is subject, the less content the promise has. For example, a promise to pay $8,000, provided that such sum is realized from the sale of an automobile, provided the automobile is sold within sixty days, and provided that the automobile, which has been stolen, can be found, is clearly different from, and worth considerably less than, an unconditional promise by the same promisor to pay $8,000.

A fundamental difference exists between the breach or nonperformance of a contractual promise and the failure or nonhappening of a condition. A breach of contract subjects the promisor to liability. It may or may not, depending upon its materiality, excuse nonperformance by the nonbreaching party of his duty under the contract. The happening or nonhappening of a condition, on the other hand, either prevents a party from acquiring a right to performance by the other party or deprives him of such a right, but subjects neither party to any liability.

Conditions may be classified by *how* they are imposed: express conditions, implied-in-fact conditions, or implied-in-law conditions (also called constructive conditions). They also may be classified by *when* they affect a duty of performance: conditions concurrent, conditions precedent, or conditions subsequent. These two ways of classifying conditions are not mutually exclusive; for example, a condition may be constructive and concurrent or express and precedent.

### EXPRESS CONDITION

An **express condition** is explicitly set forth in language. No particular form of words is necessary to create an express condition, so long as the event to which the performance of the promise is made subject is clearly expressed. An express condition is usually preceded by such words as "provided that," "on condition that," "if," "subject to," "while," "after," "upon," or "as soon as."

The basic rule applied to express conditions is that they must be fully and literally performed before the conditional duty to perform arises. Where application of the full and literal performance test would result in a forfeiture, however, the courts usually apply to the completed portion of the condition a *substantial satisfaction* test, as discussed later in this chapter under the section titled "Substantial Performance."

**Satisfaction of a Contracting Party** The parties to a contract may agree that performance by one of them will be to the satisfaction of the other, who will not be obligated to pay for such performance unless he is satisfied. This is an express condition to the duty to pay for the performance. Assume that tailor Melissa contracts to make a suit of clothes to Brent's satisfaction, and that Brent promises to pay Melissa $350 for the suit if he is satisfied with it when completed. Melissa completes the suit using materials ordered by Brent. Though the suit fits Brent beautifully, he tells Melissa that he is not satisfied with it and refuses to acceptor pay for it. If Brent's dissatisfaction is honest and in good faith, even if it is unreasonable, Melissa is not entitled to recover $350 or any amount from Brent by reason of the nonhappening of the express condition. Where satisfaction relates to a matter of personal taste, opinion, or judgment, the law applies the **subjective satisfaction** standard: if the promisor in good faith is dissatisfied, the condition has not occurred.

If the contract does not clearly indicate that satisfaction is subjective, or if the performance contracted for relates to mechanical fitness or utility, the law assumes an **objective satisfaction** standard. For example, the objective standard would apply to the sale of a building or standard goods, such as steel, coal, or grain. In such cases, the question would not be whether the promisor was actually satisfied with the performance by the other party but whether, as a reasonable person, he ought to be satisfied.

◆ SEE CASE 17-1

Satisfaction of a Third Party A contract may condition the duty of one contracting party to accept and pay for the performance of the other contracting party upon the approval of a third party who is not a party to the contract. For example, building contracts commonly provide that before the owner is required to pay, the builder shall furnish a certificate of the architect stating that the building has been constructed according to the plans and specifications. For although the owner is paying for the building, not for the certificate, he must have both the building and the certificate before he is obligated to pay. The duty of payment was made expressly conditional upon the presentation of the certificate.

## IMPLIED-IN-FACT CONDITIONS

**Implied-in-fact conditions** are similar to express conditions, in that they must fully and literally occur and in that the parties understand them to be part of the agreement. They differ in that they are not stated in express language; rather, they are necessarily inferred from the terms of the contract, the nature of the transaction, or the conduct of the parties. Thus, if Fernando, for $750, contracts to paint Peggy's house any color Peggy desires, it is necessarily implied in fact that Peggy will inform Fernando of the desired color before Fernando begins to paint. The notification of choice of color is an implied-in-fact condition, an operative event that must occur before Fernando is subject to the duty of painting the house.

## IMPLIED-IN-LAW CONDITIONS

An **implied-in-law condition**, or a **constructive condition**, is imposed by law to accomplish a just and fair result. It differs from an express condition and an implied-in-fact condition in two ways: (1) it is not contained in the language of the contract or necessarily inferred from the contract, and (2) it need only be substantially performed. For example, Melinda contracts to sell a certain tract of land to Kelly for $18,000, but the contract is silent as to the time of delivery of the deed and payment of the price. The law will imply that the respective performances are not independent of one another; consequently, the courts will treat the promises as mutually dependent and will therefore hold that a delivery or tender of the deed by Melinda to Kelly is a condition to Kelly's duty to pay the price. Conversely, Melinda's duty to deliver the deed to Kelly is conditioned upon the payment or tender of $18,000 by Kelly to Melinda. If the contract specifies a sale on credit, however, giving Kelly thirty days after delivery of the deed within which to pay the price, these conditions are not implied by law because the parties have expressly agreed to make their respective duties of performance independent of each other.

## CONCURRENT CONDITIONS

**Concurrent conditions** occur when the mutual duties of performances are to take place simultaneously. As indicated in the previous section, in the absence of an agreement to the contrary, the law assumes that the respective performances under a contract are concurrent conditions.

## CONDITIONS PRECEDENT

A **condition precedent** is an event that must occur before performance under a contract is due. For instance, if Gail is to deliver shoes to Mike on June 1, with Mike's duty to pay for the shoes on July 15, Gail's delivery of the shoes is a condition precedent to Mike's performance. Similarly, if Seymour promises to buy Edna's land for $50,000, provided Seymour can obtain financing in the amount of $40,000 at 10 percent interest or less for thirty years within sixty days of signing the contract, Seymour's obtaining the specified financing is a condition precedent to his duty. If the condition is satisfied, Seymour is bound to perform; if it is not, he is not so bound. Seymour, however, is under an implied-in-law duty to use his best efforts to obtain financing under these terms.

## CONDITIONS SUBSEQUENT

A **condition subsequent** is an event that terminates an existing duty. For example, where goods are sold under terms of "sale or return," the buyer has the right to return the goods to the seller within a stated period but is under an immediate duty to pay the price unless she and the seller have agreed upon credit. A return of the goods, which operates as a condition subsequent, terminates the duty to pay the price. Conditions subsequent occur very infrequently in contract law, while conditions precedent are quite common.

## DISCHARGE BY PERFORMANCE

Discharge by performance is undoubtedly the most frequent method of discharging a contractual duty. If a promisor exactly performs his duty under the contract, he is no longer subject to that duty.

Every contract imposes upon each party a duty of good faith and fair dealing in its performance and its enforcement. Restatement, Section 205. As discussed in *Chapter 21*, the Uniform Commercial Code (UCC) imposes a comparable duty. Section 1–203; Revised Section 1–304.

**Tender** is an offer by one party—who is ready, willing, and able to perform—to the other party to perform his obligation according to the terms of the contract. Under a bilateral contract, the refusal or rejection of a tender of performance may be treated as a repudiation that excuses or discharges the tendering party from further duty of performance under the contract. For example, on the due date of contractual performance, George arrives at Thelma's house prepared to do plumbing work under their contract. Thelma, however, refuses to allow George to enter the premises. George is therefore discharged from performing the contract and has a legal claim against Thelma for material breach.

If a debtor owes money on several accounts and tenders to his creditor less than the total amounts due, the debtor has the right to designate the account or debt to which the payment is to be applied, and the creditor must accept this direction. If the debtor does not direct the application of the payment, the creditor may apply it to any account owing to him by the debtor or distribute it among several such accounts.

## DISCHARGE BY BREACH

**Breach** of contract is the unexcused failure of a party to perform her promise. While breach of contract always gives rise to a cause of action for damages by the aggrieved (injured) party, it may have a more important effect: an uncured (uncorrected) *material* breach by one party operates as an excuse for nonperformance by the other party and discharges the aggrieved party from any further duty under the contract. If, on the other hand, the breach is not material, the aggrieved party is not discharged from the contract, although she may recover money damages. Under the Code, *any* deviation discharges the aggrieved party.

### MATERIAL BREACH

An unjustified failure to perform *substantially* the obligations promised in a contract constitutes a **material breach**. The key is whether, despite the breach, the aggrieved party obtained substantially what he bargained for or whether the breach significantly impaired his rights under the contract. A material breach discharges the aggrieved party from his duty of performance. For instance, Esta orders a custom-made, tailored suit from Stuart to be made of wool; but Stuart instead makes the suit of cotton. Assuming that the labor component of this contract predominates and thus the contract is not considered a sale of goods, Stuart has materially breached the contract. Consequently, Esta not only is discharged from her duty to pay for the suit but may also recover money damages from Stuart due to his breach.

Although there are no clear-cut rules as to what constitutes a material breach, the Restatement, Section 241, lists a number of relevant factors:

> In determining whether a failure to render or to offer performance is material, the following circumstances are significant:
>
> (a) the extent to which the injured party will be deprived of the benefit which he reasonably expected;
> (b) the extent to which the injured party can be adequately compensated for the part of that benefit of which he will be deprived;
> (c) the extent to which the party failing to perform or to offer to perform will suffer forfeiture;
> (d) the likelihood that the party failing to perform or to offer to perform will cure his failure, taking account of all the circumstances including any reasonable assurances;
> (e) the extent to which the behavior of the party failing to perform or to offer to perform comports with standards of good faith and fair dealing.

An *intentional* breach of contract is generally held to be material. Moreover, a failure to perform a promise promptly is a material breach if "**time is of the essence**," that is, if the parties have clearly indicated that a failure to perform by the stated time is material; otherwise, the aggrieved party may recover damages only for the loss caused by the delay.

Finally, the parties to a contract may, within limits, specify what breaches are to be considered material.

◆ **SEE CASE 17-2**

**PREVENTION OF PERFORMANCE** One party's substantial interference with or **prevention of performance** by the other generally constitutes a material breach that discharges the other party to the contract. For instance, Craig prevents an architect from giving Maud a certificate that is a condition to Craig's liability to pay Maud a certain sum of money. Craig may not then use Maud's failure to produce a certificate as an excuse for his nonpayment. Likewise, if Harold has contracted to grow a certain crop for Rafael, and Rafael plows the field and destroys the seedlings after Harold has planted the seed, his interference with Harold's performance discharges Harold from his duty under the contract. It does not, however, discharge Rafael from his duty under the contract.

**Perfect Tender Rule** The Code greatly alters the common law doctrine of material breach by adopting what is known as the **perfect tender rule**. This rule, which is discussed more fully in *Chapter 22*, essentially provides that *any* deviation from the promised performance in a sales contract under the Code constitutes a material breach of the contract and discharges the aggrieved party from his duty of performance. Thus, if a seller of camera accessories delivers to a buyer ninety-nine of the one hundred ordered pieces, or ninety-nine correct accessories and one incorrect accessory, the buyer may rightfully reject the improper delivery.

### SUBSTANTIAL PERFORMANCE

If a party substantially, but not completely, performs her obligations under a contract, the common law generally will allow her to obtain the other party's performance, less any damages caused by the partial performance. Thus, in the specially ordered suit illustration discussed in the previous section, if Stuart, the tailor, used the correct fabric but improperly used black buttons instead of blue, Stuart would be permitted to collect from Esta the contract price of the suit less the damage, if any, caused to Esta by the substitution of the wrongly colored buttons. The doctrine of substantial performance assumes particular importance in the construction industry in cases in which a structure is built on the aggrieved party's land. Consider the following: Kent Construction Co. builds a $300,000 house for Martha but deviates from the specifications, causing Martha $10,000 in damages. If this breach were considered material, then Martha would not have to pay for the house that is now on her land. This would clearly constitute an unjust forfeiture on Kent's part. Therefore, because Kent's performance is substantial, the courts would probably not deem the breach material. As a result, Kent would be able to collect $290,000 from Martha.

### ANTICIPATORY REPUDIATION

A breach of contract, as previously discussed, is a failure to perform the terms of a contract. Although it is logically and physically impossible to fail to perform a duty before the date on which that performance is due, a party nonetheless may announce before the due date that she will not perform, or she may commit an act that makes her unable to perform. Either act repudiates the contract, which notifies the other party that a breach is imminent. Such repudiation before the performance date fixed by the contract is called an **anticipatory repudiation**. The courts, as shown in the leading case of *Hochster v. De La Tour*, view it as a breach that discharges the nonrepudiating party's duty to perform and permits her to bring suit immediately. Nonetheless, the nonbreaching party may wait until the time the performance is due, to see whether the repudiator will retract his repudiation and perform his contractual duties. To be effective, the retraction must come to the attention of the injured party before she materially changes her position in reliance on the repudiation or before she indicates to the repudiator that she considers the repudiation to be final. If the retraction is effective and the repudiator does perform, then there is a discharge by performance; if he does not perform, there is a material breach.

◆ **SEE CASE 17-3**

### MATERIAL ALTERATION OF WRITTEN CONTRACT

An unauthorized alteration or change of any of the material terms or provisions of a written contract or document is a discharge of the entire contract. To be a discharge, the alteration must be material and fraudulent and must be the act of a party to the contract or someone acting on his behalf. An alteration is material if it would vary any party's legal relations with the maker of the alteration or would adversely affect that party's legal relations with a third person. Restatement, Section 286. An unauthorized change in the terms of a written contract by a person who is not a party to the contract does not discharge the contract.

## DISCHARGE BY AGREEMENT OF THE PARTIES

The parties to a contract may by agreement discharge each other from performance under the contract. They may do this by rescission, substituted contract, accord and satisfaction, or novation.

### MUTUAL RESCISSION

A **mutual rescission** is an agreement between the parties to terminate their respective duties under the contract. Literally a contract to end a contract, it must contain all the essentials of a contract. In rescinding an executory, bilateral contract, each party furnishes consideration in giving up his rights under the contract in exchange for the other party's relinquishment of his rights under the contract. Where one party has already fully performed, a mutual rescission may not be binding at common law because of lack of consideration.

### SUBSTITUTED CONTRACT

A **substituted contract** is a new contract accepted by both parties in satisfaction of their duties under the original contract. Restatement, Section 279. A substituted contract immediately discharges the original duty and imposes new obligations. For example, the Restatement, Section 279, gives the following illustration:

> A and B make a contract under which A promises to build on a designated spot a building, for which B promises to pay $100,000. Later, before this contract is performed, A and B make a new contract under which A is to build on the same spot a different building, for which B is to pay $200,000. The new contract is a substituted contract and the duties of A and B under the original contract are discharged.

### ACCORD AND SATISFACTION

An **accord** is a contract by which an obligee promises to accept a stated performance in satisfaction of the obligor's existing contractual duty. Restatement, Section 281. The performance of the accord is called a **satisfaction**, and it discharges the original duty. Thus, if Ted owes Alan $500 and the parties agree that Ted shall paint Alan's house in satisfaction of the debt, the agreement is an accord. The debt, however, is not discharged until Ted performs the accord by painting Alan's house.

◆ **SEE CASE 17-2**

### NOVATION

A **novation** is a substituted contract that involves an agreement among *three* parties to substitute a new promisee for the existing promisee, or to replace the existing promisor with a new one. Restatement, Section 280. A novation discharges the old obligation by creating a new contract in which there is either a new promisee or a new promisor. Thus, if B owes A $500, and A, B, and C agree that C will pay the debt and B will be discharged, the novation is the substitution of the new promisor C for B. Alternatively, if the three parties agree that B will pay $500 to D instead of to A, the novation is the substitution of a new promisee (D for A). In each instance, the debt B owes to A is discharged.

## DISCHARGE BY OPERATION OF LAW

This chapter has considered various ways by which contractual duties may be discharged. In all of these cases, the discharge resulted from the action of one or both of the parties to the contract. This section examines discharge brought about by the operation of law.

### IMPOSSIBILITY

"Contract liability is strict liability … [and an] obligor is therefore liable for in damages breach of contract even if he is without fault and even if circumstances have made the contract more burdensome or less desirable than he had anticipated." Restatement, Introductory Note to Chapter 11. Historically, the common law excused a party from contractual duties for **objective impossibility**; that is, where no one could render the performance. If, by comparison, a particular contracting party is unable to perform because, for instance, of financial inability or lack of competence, this **subjective impossibility** does not excuse the promisor from liability for breach of contract. For example, the Christys entered into a written contract to purchase an apartment house from Pilkinton for $30,000. Pilkinton tendered a deed to the property and demanded payment of the unpaid balance of $29,000 due on the purchase price. Because of a decline in their used car business, the Christys, who did not possess and could not borrow the unpaid balance, asserted that it was impossible for them to perform their contract. The court held for Pilkinton, identifying a distinction between objective impossibility, which amounts to saying, "the thing cannot be done," and subjective impossibility—"I cannot do it." The latter, which is illustrated by a promisor's financial inability to pay, does not discharge the contractual duty. *Christy v. Pilkinton*, 224 Ark. 407, 273 S.W.2d 533 (1954).

The **death** or **incapacity** of a person who has contracted to render *personal services* discharges his contractual duty due to objective impossibility. Restatement, Section 262. For example, a singer unable to perform a contractual engagement because of a severe cold is excused from performance, as is a pianist or violinist who is unable to perform because of a hand injury.

**Destruction of Subject Matter** Destruction of the subject matter or of the agreed-upon means of performance of a contract, without the fault of the promisor, is also excusable impossibility. "Subject matter" here means specific subject matter. Suppose that Alice contracts to sell to Gary five office chairs at an agreed price. Alice has one hundred of these chairs in stock, out of which she expects to deliver five to Gary. Before she can do so, fire destroys the entire stock of one hundred chairs. Though not at fault, Alice is not excused from performance. This was not a contract for the sale of specific goods; consequently, Alice could perform the contract by delivering to Gary any five chairs of the kind and grade specified in the contract. Her failure to do so will render her liable to Gary for breach of contract. Suppose, now, that Alice and Gary make a contract for Alice to manufacture these five chairs in her factory but that prior to their manufacture, fire destroys the factory. Again, Alice is not at fault. Although the chairs are available from other manufacturers, the destruction of the factory discharges Alice's duty to deliver the chairs. Suppose further that Alice and Gary enter into a contract under which Alice is to sell to Gary the particular desk that she uses in her private office. This desk, and no other, is the specific subject matter of the contract. If, before the sale is completed, this desk is destroyed by fire without Alice's fault, it is then impossible for Alice to perform. The contract is therefore discharged.

**Subsequent Illegality** If the performance of a contract that was legal when formed becomes illegal or impractical by reason of a subsequently enacted law, the duty of performance is discharged. Restatement, Section 264. For example, Jill contracts to sell and deliver to Fred ten cases of a certain whiskey each month for one year. A subsequent prohibition law makes the manufacture, transportation, or sale of intoxicating liquor unlawful. The contractual duties that Jill has yet to perform are discharged.

**Frustration of Purpose** Where, after a contract is made, a party's principal purpose is substantially frustrated without his fault by the occurrence of an event the nonoccurrence of which was a basic assumption on which the contract was made, his remaining duties to render performance are discharged, unless the party has assumed the risk. Restatement, Second 265. This rule developed from the so-called coronation cases. When, upon the death of his mother, Queen Victoria, Edward VII became King of England, impressive coronation ceremonies were planned, including a procession along a designated route through certain streets in London. Owners and lessees of buildings along the route made contracts to permit the use of rooms with a view on the date scheduled for the procession. The King, however, became ill, and the procession did not take place. The purpose for using the rooms having failed, the rooms were not used. Numerous suits were filed, some by landowners seeking to hold the would-be viewers liable on their promises, and some by the would-be viewers seeking to recover money they paid in advance for the rooms. The principle involved was novel, but from these cases evolved the **frustration of purpose doctrine**, under which a contract is discharged if supervening circumstances make impossible the fulfillment of the purpose that both parties had in mind, unless one of the parties has contractually assumed that risk.

**Commercial Impracticability** The Restatement, Section 261, and the Code, Section 2–615, have relaxed the traditional test of objective impossibility by providing that performance need not be actually or literally impossible, but that commercial impracticability will excuse nonperformance. This does not mean mere hardship or an unexpectedly increased cost of performance. A party will be discharged from performing his duty only when a supervening event not caused by his fault makes his performance impracticable. Moreover, the nonoccurrence of the subsequent event must have been a "basic assumption" both parties made when entering into the contract, neither party having assumed the risk that the event would occur. Commercial impracticability could include

> a severe shortage of raw materials or of supplies due to a contingency such as war, embargo, local crop failure, unforeseen shutdown of major sources of supply or the like, which either causes a marked increase in cost or altogether prevents the seller from securing supplies necessary to his performance. UCC Section 2–615, Comment 4.

◆ **SEE CASE 17-4**

## BANKRUPTCY

**Bankruptcy** is a discharge of a contractual duty by operation of law available to a debtor who, by compliance with the requirements of the Bankruptcy Code, obtains an order of discharge by the bankruptcy court. It is applicable only to obligations that the Code provides are dischargeable in bankruptcy. The subject of bankruptcy is treated in *Chapter 39*.

## STATUTE OF LIMITATIONS

At common law a plaintiff was not subject to any time limitation within which to bring an action. Now, however, all States have statutes providing such a limitation. The majority of courts hold that the running of the period of the statute of limitations does not operate to discharge the obligation, but only to bar the creditor's right to bring an action.

◆ **SEE FIGURE 17-1: Discharge of Contracts**

◆ FIGURE 17-1: **Discharge of Contracts**

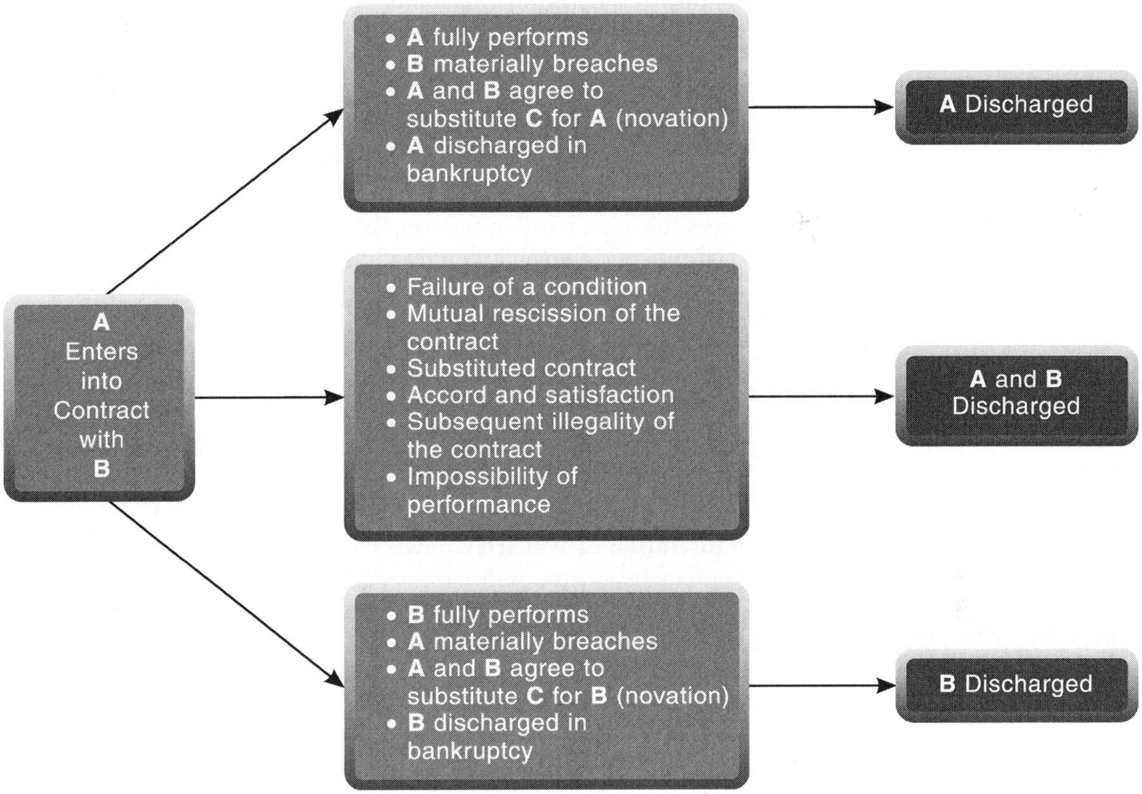


## CHAPTER SUMMARY

**CONDITIONS**

**Definition of a Condition** an event whose happening or nonhappening affects a duty of performance

**Express Condition** contingency explicitly set forth in language

- ***Satisfaction*** express condition making performance contingent upon one party's approval of the other's performance
- ***Subjective Satisfaction*** approval based upon a party's honestly held opinion
- ***Objective Satisfaction*** approval based upon whether a reasonable person would be satisfied

**Implied-in-Fact Conditions** contingency understood by the parties to be part of the agreement, though not expressed

**Implied-in-Law Conditions** contingency not contained in the language of the contract but imposed by law; also called a constructive condition

**Concurrent Conditions** conditions that are to take place at the same time

**Conditions Precedent** an event that must or must not occur before performance is due

**Conditions Subsequent** an event that terminates a duty of performance

**DISCHARGE BY PERFORMANCE**

**Discharge** termination of a contractual duty

**Performance** fulfillment of a contractual obligation resulting in a discharge

| | |
|---|---|
| **DISCHARGE BY BREACH** | **Definition of Breach** a wrongful failure to perform the terms of a contract that gives rise to a right to damages by the injured party<br>**Material Breach** nonperformance that significantly impairs the injured party's rights under the contract and discharges the injured party from any further duty under the contract<br>• ***Prevention of Performance*** one party's substantial interference with or prevention of performance by the other; constitutes a material breach and discharges the other party to the contract<br>• ***Perfect Tender Rule*** standard under the Uniform Commercial Code that a seller's performance under a sales contract must strictly comply with contractual duties and that any deviation discharges the injured party<br>**Substantial Performance** performance that is incomplete but that does not defeat the purpose of the contract; does not discharge the injured party but entitles him to damages<br>**Anticipatory Repudiation** an inability or refusal to perform, before performance is due, that is treated as a breach, allowing the nonrepudiating party to bring suit immediately<br>**Material Alteration of Written Contract** a material and fraudulent alteration of a written contract by a party to the contract; discharges the entire contract |
| **DISCHARGE BY AGREEMENT OF THE PARTIES** | **Mutual Rescission** an agreement between the parties to terminate their respective duties under the contract<br>**Substituted Contract** a new contract accepted by both parties in satisfaction of the parties' duties under the original contract<br>**Accord and Satisfaction** substituted duty under a contract (accord) and the discharge of the prior contractual obligation by performance of the new duty (satisfaction)<br>**Novation** a substituted contract involving a new third-party promisor or promisee |
| **DISCHARGE BY OPERATION OF LAW** | **Impossibility** performance of contract cannot be done<br>• ***Subjective Impossibility*** the promisor—but not all promisors—cannot perform; does not discharge the promisor<br>• ***Objective Impossibility*** no promisor is able to perform; generally discharges the promisor<br>• ***Destruction of Subject Matter*** will discharge contract if it occurs without the promisor's fault<br>• ***Subsequent Illegality*** if performance becomes illegal or impractical as a result of a change in the law, the duty of performance is discharged<br>• ***Frustration of Purpose*** principal purpose of a contract cannot be fulfilled because of a subsequent event<br>• ***Commercial Impracticability*** where performance can be accomplished only under unforeseen and unjust hardship, the contract is discharged under the Code and the Restatement<br>**Bankruptcy** discharge available to a debtor who obtains an order of discharge by the bankruptcy court<br>**Statute of Limitations** after the statute of limitations has run, the debt is not discharged, but the creditor cannot maintain an action against the debtor |

## CASES

# CASE 17-1

## Express Conditions: Satisfaction
## SILVESTRI v. OPTUS SOFTWARE, INC.

Supreme Court of New Jersey, 2003
175 N.J. 113, 814 A.2d 602
http://lawlibrary.rutgers.edu/courts/supreme/a-95-01.opn.html

**LaVecchia, J.**

This is a breach of contract action. Defendant Optus Software, Inc. ("Optus" or "the company"), a small computer software company, hired plaintiff Michael Silvestri as its Director of Support Services, responsible for supervising the provision of technical support services to the company's customers. Silvestri's two-year employment contract [commencing on January 4, 1999 at an annual salary of $70,000] contained a clause that reserved to the company the right to terminate his employment for failure to perform to the company's satisfaction (the "satisfaction clause").

Nine months into the contract, Silvestri was terminated under the satisfaction clause by the chief executive officer of Optus, Joseph Avellino. Silvestri filed this action, contending that the company's dissatisfaction was objectively unreasonable and that therefore his termination was a breach of the employment contract. The trial court granted summary judgment to the company. The Appellate Division reversed, however, holding that an employer must meet an objective standard for satisfaction in order to invoke a right to terminate pursuant to a satisfaction clause in an employment contract.

The question presented then is whether the employer's satisfaction is subject to an objective or subjective evaluation. We conclude that, absent language to the contrary, a subjective assessment of personal satisfaction applies and that the trial court's grant of summary judgment to the company was appropriate. * * *

* * * Silvestri was charged with supervision of the support services staff, responsibility for communication with resellers of the Optus computer software to end-users, and coordination of ongoing training for support staff and resellers of the company's products in order to maintain their proficiency in assisting end-users. * * *

The record indicates that Silvestri enjoyed the full support of Avellino during the first six months of his employment. Avellino's communications within and without the organization praised Silvestri's abilities and underscored his role as leader of the support services group. As late as July 16, 1999, Avellino sent an e-mail message to all members of the group, exhorting them to support their new supervisor. The e-mail referred to the problems Optus had been having in providing technical support to resellers and end-users, stressed that Optus had hired Silvestri to help alleviate those problems, and again asked the staff to support Silvestri.

Although Avellino repeatedly expressed his belief in Silvestri's ability and efforts during those early months, his attitude started to change during the summer months of 1999. In June, July, and August, several clients and resellers communicated to Avellino their disappointment with the performance and attitude of the support services staff generally, and several complaints targeted Silvestri specifically. Avellino informed Silvestri of those criticisms. As the criticisms mounted, Avellino's concerns and frustrations grew, as evidenced by his e-mail exchanges with Silvestri and others. Finally, on September 3, 1999, Avellino told Silvestri that they needed to have a "heart-to-heart" talk about his performance. On September 17, 1999, Silvestri was terminated.

* * *

* * * Avellino explained that he terminated Silvestri because Silvestri had failed to "exhibit the leadership and management skills necessary to perform his duties to the Company's satisfaction." He cited the objective evidence of the complaints received from the various customers and resellers as well as the concerns and frustrations he communicated to Silvestri at the time those complaints increased. The implication of the certification was that Avellino's dissatisfaction was not an after-the-fact justification for termination. The relationship had been deteriorating over time and finally reached a breaking point after Silvestri failed, in the company's judgment, to respond adequately to the numerous customer complaints. Optus is a small company in the business of customer services, and difficulty with support to resellers and end-users of Optus's products carries the potential for significant consequences in such a business.

Silvestri did not assert that there was any reason for his termination other than Avellino's genuine dissatisfaction with his performance. Rather, Silvestri challenged the reasonableness of that dissatisfaction. He portrayed Avellino as a meddling micro-manager who overreacted to any customer criticism and thus could not reasonably be satisfied. * * *

* * *

Agreements containing a promise to perform in a manner satisfactory to another, or to be bound to pay for satisfactory performance, are a common form of enforceable contract. [Citation.] Such "satisfaction" contracts are generally divided into two categories for purposes of review: (1) contracts that involve matters of personal taste, sensibility, judgment, or convenience; and (2) contracts that contain a requirement of satisfaction as to mechanical fitness, utility, or marketability. [Citation.] The standard for evaluating satisfaction depends on the type of contract. Satisfaction contracts of the first type are interpreted on a subjective basis, with satisfaction dependent on the personal, honest evaluation of the party to be satisfied. [Citation.] Absent language to the contrary, however, contracts of the second type—involving operative fitness or mechanical utility—are subject to an objective test of reasonableness, because in those cases the extent and quality of performance can be measured by objective tests. [Citation]; Restatement (Second) of Contracts §228; [citation].

A subjective standard typically is applied to satisfaction clauses in employment contracts because "there is greater reason and a greater tendency to interpret [the contract] as involving personal satisfaction," rather than the satisfaction of a hypothetical "reasonable" person. [Citations.]

In the case of a high-level business manager, a subjective test is particularly appropriate to the flexibility needed by the owners and higher-level officers operating a competitive enterprise. [Citation.] When a manager has been hired to share responsibility for the success of a business entity, an employer is entitled to be highly personal and idiosyncratic in judging the employee's satisfactory performance in advancing the enterprise. [Citations.]

The subjective standard obliges the employer to act "honestly in accordance with his duty of good faith and fair dealing," [citation], but genuine dissatisfaction of the employer, honestly held, is sufficient for discharge. [Citation.]

Although broadly discretionary, a satisfaction-clause employment relationship is not to be confused with an employment-at-will relationship in which an employer is entitled to terminate an employee for any reason, or no reason, unless prohibited by law or public policy. [Citation.] In a satisfaction clause employment setting, there must be honest dissatisfaction with the employee's performance. The employer may not claim "dissatisfaction" as the reason for termination when another reason is the actual motivation, even if that other reason is neither discriminatory nor contrary to public policy and would therefore pass muster as the basis for discharge of an at-will employee. Moreover, the dissatisfaction with the discharged employee must be honest and genuine. If, however, the employer's dissatisfaction is honest and genuine, even if idiosyncratic, its reasonableness is not subject to second guessing under a reasonable-person standard. * * *

* * *

We hold that a subjective test of performance governs the employer's resort to a satisfaction clause in an employment contract unless there is some language in the contract to suggest that the parties intended an objective standard. There is no such language here. * * * We are, moreover, persuaded that in the circumstances before us, application of another's notion of satisfactory performance would undermine recognized and accepted notions of business judgment and individualized competitive strategy, as well as principles of freedom of contract. Idiosyncratic judgments as to what constitutes satisfactory performance are expected and should be permitted. The employer, not some hypothetical reasonable person, is best suited to determine if the employee's performance is satisfactory. * * *

Turning then to application of the subjective test in this setting, * * * we conclude that the entry of summary judgment in favor of defendants was appropriate. The only issue available to Silvestri is whether the dissatisfaction with his performance was genuine, and he has failed to make a prima facie showing that it was not. * * *

The judgment of the Appellate Division is reversed and the matter remanded for entry of summary judgment in favor of defendants.

## CASE 17-2

### Material Breach/Accord and Satisfaction
### ASSOCIATED BUILDERS, INC. v. WILLIAM M. COGGINS ET AL.

Supreme Judicial Court of Maine, 1999
1999 ME 12, 722 A.2d 1278
http://caselaw.findlaw.com/me-supreme-judicial-court/1340879.html

**Dana, J.**

Associated Builders, Inc. appeals from a grant of a summary judgment entered in the Superior Court * * * in favor of the defendants William M. Coggins and Benjamin W. Coggins, d/b/a Ben & Bill's Chocolate Emporium. Associated contends that the court erred when it held that despite a late payment by the Cogginses, an accord and satisfaction relieved the Cogginses of a contractual liability. The Cogginses argue that the three-day delay in payment was not a material breach of the accord and, even if the breach was material, Associated waived its right to enforce the forfeiture. We agree with the Cogginses and affirm the judgment. Associated provided labor and materials to the Cogginses to complete a structure on Main Street in Bar Harbor. After a dispute arose regarding compensation, Associated and the Cogginses executed an agreement stating that there existed an outstanding balance of $70,005.54 and setting forth the following terms of repayment:

> It is agreed that, two payments will be made by [the Cogginses] to [Associated] as follows: Twenty Five Thousand Dollars ($25,000.00) on or before June 1, 1996 and Twenty Five Thousand

> Dollars ($25,000.00) on or before June 1, 1997. No interest will be charged or paid providing payments are made as agreed. If the payments are not made as agreed then interest shall accrue at 10% [ ] per annum figured from the date of default. There will be no prepayment penalties applied. It is further agreed that Associated Builders will forfeit the balance of Twenty Thousand and Five Dollars and Fifty Four Cents ($20,005.54) providing the above payments are made as agreed.

The Cogginses made their first payment in accordance with the agreement. The second payment, however, was delivered three days late on June 4, 1997. Claiming a breach of the contract, Associated filed a complaint demanding the balance of $20,005.54, plus interest and cost. The Cogginses answered the complaint raising the affirmative defense of an accord and satisfaction and waiver. Both parties moved for a summary judgment. The court granted the Cogginses' motion and Associated appealed.

* * *

"An accord 'is a contract under which an obligee promises to accept a substituted performance in future satisfaction of the obligor's duty.'" [Citation.] Settlement of a disputed claim is sufficient consideration for an accord and satisfaction. [Citation.] Here, the court correctly found the June 15, 1995 agreement to be an accord.

Satisfaction is the execution or performance of the accord. See RESTATEMENT (SECOND) OF CONTRACTS §281(1) (1981). If the obligor breaches the accord, the obligee may enforce either the original duty or any duty pursuant to the accord. [Citations.] The obligor's breach of the accord, however, must be material. [Citations.] The question before the court, therefore, was whether the Cogginses' late payment constituted a material breach of the accord. The court found that it was not.

We apply traditional contract principles to determine if a party has committed a material breach. [Citation.] A material breach "is a nonperformance of a duty that is so material and important as to justify the injured party in regarding the whole transaction as at an end." [Citation]; see RESTATEMENT (SECOND) OF CONTRACTS §241 (1981). [Court's footnote: The Restatement lists five factors as significant in determining if a failure to render performance is material: (a) the extent to which the injured party will be deprived of the benefit which he reasonably expected; (b) the extent to which the injured party can be adequately compensated for the part of the benefit of which he will be deprived; (c) the extent to which the party failing to perform * * * will suffer forfeiture; (d) the likelihood that the party failing to perform * * * will cure his failure * * *; (e) the extent to which the behavior of the party failing to perform or to offer to perform comports with standards of good faith and fair dealing.]

"Time of performance is merely one element in determining whether a defective or incomplete or belated performance is substantial [performance]." [Citation.] Applying these principles, courts have found that a slight delay of payment that causes no detriment or prejudice to the obligee is not a material breach. [Citations.]

We discern no error in the Superior Court's finding that the Cogginses' payment to Associated after a three-day delay was not a material breach and, therefore, satisfied the June 15, 1995 accord. [Citation.] By receiving the second and final payment of $25,000, Associated was not deprived of the benefit that it reasonably expected. See RESTATEMENT (SECOND) OF CONTRACTS §241(a) (1981). Moreover, Associated has not alleged any prejudice from this three-day delay. [Citations.] Further, the Cogginses' late payment was not made in bad faith. [Citations.] Finally, neither the purpose of the June 15, 1995 accord nor the language of the accord suggests that time was of the essence. [Citation.] Because the late payment was not a material breach of the June 15, 1995 accord, the Cogginses have complied with the June 15, 1995 agreement relieving them of further liability to Associated.

* * *

Judgment affirmed.

## CASE 17-3

### Anticipatory Breach
### HOCHSTER v. DE LA TOUR

Queen's Bench of England, 1853
2 Ellis and Blackburn Reports 678

**Lord Campbell, C. J.**

[On April 12, 1852, Hochster contracted with De La Tour to serve as a guide for De La Tour on his three-month trip to Europe, beginning on June 1 at an agreed-upon salary. On May 11, De La Tour notified Hochster that he would not need Hochster's services. He also refused to pay Hochster any compensation. Hochster brings this action to recover damages for breach of contract.]

On this motion * * * the question arises, Whether, if there be an agreement between A. and B., whereby B. engages to employ A. on and from a future day for a given period of time, to travel with him into a foreign country as a [guide], and to start with him in that capacity on that day, A. being to receive a monthly salary during the continuance of such service, B. may, before the day, refuse to perform the agreement and break and renounce it, so as to entitle A. before the day to commence an action against B. to recover damages for breach of the agreement; A. having been ready and willing to perform it, till it was broken and renounced by B.

* * *

If the plaintiff has no remedy for breach of the contract unless he treats the contract as in force, and acts upon it down to the 1st June, 1852, it follows that, till then, he must enter into no employment which will interfere with his promise "to start with the defendant on such travels on the day and year" and that he must then be properly equipped in all respects as a [guide] for a three months' tour on the continent of Europe. But it is surely much more rational, and more for the benefit of both parties, that, after the renunciation of the agreement by the defendant, the plaintiff should be at liberty to consider himself absolved from any future performance of it, retaining his right to sue for any damage he has suffered from the breach of it. Thus, instead of remaining idle and laying out money in preparations which must be useless, he is at liberty to seek service under another employer, which would go in mitigation of the damages to which he would otherwise be entitled for a breach of the contract. It seems strange that the defendant after renouncing the contract, and absolutely declaring that he will never act under it, should be permitted to object that faith is given to his assertion, and that an opportunity is not left to him of changing his mind. * * *

* * * The man who wrongfully renounces a contract into which he has deliberately entered cannot justly complain if he is immediately sued for a compensation in damage by the man whom he has injured: and it seems reasonable to allow an option to the injured party, either to sue immediately, or to wait till the time when the act was to be done, still holding it as prospectively binding for the exercise of this option, which may be advantageous to the innocent party, and cannot be prejudicial to the wrongdoer.

Judgment for plaintiff.

## CASE 17-4

### Impossibility
### NORTHERN CORP. v. CHUGACH ELECTRICAL ASSOCIATION

Supreme Court of Alaska, 1974
518 P.2d 76

**Boochever, J.**

[Northern Corporation entered into a contract with Chugach in August 1966 to repair and upgrade the upstream face of Cooper Lake Dam in Alaska. The contract required Northern to obtain rock from a quarry site at the opposite end of the lake and to transport the rock to the dam during the winter across the ice on the lake. In December 1966, Northern cleared the road on the ice to permit deeper freezing, but thereafter water overflowed on the ice, preventing the use of the road. Northern complained of the unsafe condition of the lake ice, but Chugach insisted on performance. In March 1967, one of Northern's loaded trucks broke through the ice and sank. Northern continued to encounter difficulties and ceased operations with the approval of Chugach. On January 8, 1968, Chugach notified Northern that it would be in default unless all rock was hauled by April 1. After two more trucks broke through the ice, causing the deaths of the drivers, Northern ceased operations and notified Chugach that it would make no more attempts to haul across the lake. Northern advised Chugach it considered the contract terminated for impossibility of performance and commenced suit to recover the cost incurred in attempting to complete the contract.]

* * *

The focal question is whether the * * * contract was impossible of performance. The September 27, 1966 directive specified that the rock was to be transported "across Cooper Lake to the dam site when such lake is frozen to a sufficient depth to permit heavy vehicle traffic thereon," and * * * specified that the hauling to the dam site would be done during the winter of 1966–67. It is therefore clear that the parties contemplated that the rock would be transported across the frozen lake by truck. Northern's repeated efforts to perform the contract by this method during the winter of 1966–67 and subsequently in February 1968, culminating in the tragic loss of life, abundantly support the trial court's findings that the contract was impossible of performance by this method.

Chugach contends, however, that Northern was nevertheless bound to perform, and that it could have used means other than hauling by truck across the ice to transport the rock. The answer to Chugach's contention is that * * * the parties contemplated that the rock would be hauled by truck once the ice froze to a sufficient depth to support the weight of the vehicles. The specification of this particular method of performance presupposed the existence of ice frozen to the requisite depth. Since this expectation of the parties was never fulfilled, and since the provisions relating to the means of performance was clearly material, Northern's duty to perform was discharged by reason of impossibility.

There is an additional reason for our holding that Northern's duty to perform was discharged because of impossibility. It is true that in order for a defendant to prevail under the original common law doctrine of impossibility, he had to show that no one else could have performed the contract. However, this harsh rule has gradually been eroded, and the Restatement of Contracts has departed from the early common law rule by recognizing the principle of "commercial impracticability." Under this doctrine, a party is discharged from his contract obligations, even if it is technically possible to perform them, if the costs of performance would be so disproportionate to that reasonably contemplated by the parties as to make the contract totally impractical in a commercial sense. * * * Removed from the strictures of the common law, "impossibility" in its modern context has become a coat of many colors, including among its hues the point argued here—namely, impossibility predicated upon "commercial impracticability." This concept—which finds expression both in case law * * * and in other authorities * * * is grounded upon the assumption that in legal contemplation something is impracticable when it can only be done at an excessive and unreasonable cost. As stated in *Transatlantic Financing Corp. v. United States* [citation]

> * * * The doctrine ultimately represents the ever-shifting line, drawn by courts hopefully responsive to commercial practices and mores, at which the community's interest in having contracts enforced according to their terms is outweighed by the commercial senselessness of requiring performance. * * *

* * *

In the case before us the detailed opinion of the trial court clearly indicates that the appropriate standard was followed. There is ample evidence to support its findings that "[t]he ice haul method of transporting riprap ultimately selected was within the contemplation of the parties and was part of the basis of the agreement which ultimately resulted in amendment No. 1 in October 1966," and that that method was not commercially feasible within the financial parameters of the contract. We affirm the court's conclusion that the contract was impossible of performance.

## QUESTIONS

1. Identify and distinguish among the various types of conditions.
2. Distinguish between full performance and tender of performance.
3. Explain the difference between material breach and substantial performance. Explain how the Uniform Commercial Code's perfect tender rule differs.
4. Distinguish among a mutual rescission, substituted contract, accord and satisfaction, and novation.
5. Identify and discuss the ways discharge may be brought about by operation of law.

# PROBLEMS

**1.** A–1 Roofing Co. entered into a written contract with Jaffe to put a new roof on the latter's residence for $1,800, using a specified type of roofing, and to complete the job without unreasonable delay. A–1 undertook the work within a week thereafter, but when all the roofing material was at the site and the labor 50 percent completed, the premises were totally destroyed by fire caused by lightning. A–1 submitted a bill to Jaffe for $1,200 for materials furnished and labor performed up to the time of the destruction of the premises. Jaffe refused to pay the bill, and A–1 now seeks payment from Jaffe. Should A–1 prevail? Explain.

**2.** By contract dated January 5, Rebecca agreed to sell to Nancy, and Nancy agreed to buy from Rebecca, a certain parcel of land then zoned commercial. The specific intent of Nancy, which was known to Rebecca, was to erect a manufacturing plant on the land; and the contract stated that the agreement was conditioned upon Nancy's ability to construct such a plant upon the land. The closing date for the transaction was set for April 1. On February 15, the city council rezoned the land from commercial to residential, which precluded the erection of the plant. As the closing date drew near, Nancy made it known to Rebecca that she did not intend to go through with the purchase because the land could no longer be used as intended. On April 1, Rebecca tendered the deed to Nancy, who refused to pay Rebecca the agreed purchase price. Rebecca brought an action against Nancy for breach of their contract. Can Rebecca enforce the contract?

**3.** The Perfection Produce Company entered into a written contract with Hiram Hodges for the purchase of three hundred tons of potatoes to be grown on Hodge's farm in Maine at a stipulated price per ton. Although the land would ordinarily produce one thousand tons and the planting and cultivation were properly done, Hodges was able to deliver only one hundred tons because an unprecedented drought caused a partial crop failure. Perfection accepted the one hundred tons but paid only 80 percent of the stipulated price per ton. Hodges sued the produce company to recover the unpaid balance of the agreed price for the one hundred tons of potatoes accepted by Perfection. Perfection counterclaimed against Hodges for his failure to deliver the remaining two hundred tons. Who will prevail? Why?

**4.** On November 23, Sylvia agreed to sell to Barnett her Pontiac automobile for $7,000, delivery and payment to be made on December 1. On November 26, Barnett informed Sylvia that he wished to rescind the contract and would pay Sylvia $350 if Sylvia agreed. She agreed and took the $350 cash. On December 1, Barnett tendered to Sylvia $6,650 and demanded that she deliver the automobile. Sylvia refused and Barnett initiated a lawsuit. May Barnett enforce the original contract?

**5.** Webster, Inc., dealt in automobile accessories at wholesale. Although he manufactured a few items in his own factory, among them windshield wipers, Webster purchased most of his inventory from a large number of other manufacturers. In January, Webster entered into a written contract to sell Hunter two thousand windshield wipers for $4,900, delivery to be made June 1. In April, Webster's factory burned to the ground, and Webster failed to make delivery on June 1. Hunter, forced to buy windshield wipers elsewhere at a higher price, is now trying to recover damages from Webster. Will Hunter be successful in its claim?

**6.** Erwick Construction Company contracted to build a house for Charles. The specifications called for the use of Karlene Pipe for all plumbing. Erwick, however, got a better price on Boynton Pipe and substituted the equally good Boynton Pipe for Karlene Pipe. Upon inspection, Charles discovered the change, and he now refuses to make the final payment. The contract price was for $200,000, and the final payment is $20,000. Erwick now brings suit seeking the $20,000. Will Erwick succeed in its claim?

**7.** Green owed White $3,500, which was due and payable on June 1. White owed Brown $3,500, which was due and payable on August 1. On May 25, White received a letter signed by Green stating, "If you will cancel my debt to you, in the amount of $3,500, I will pay, on the due date, the debt you owe Brown, in the amount of $3,500." On May 28, Green received a letter signed by White stating, "I received your letter and agree to the proposals recited therein. You may consider your debt to me canceled as of the date of this letter." On June 1, White, needing money to pay his income taxes, made a demand upon Green to pay him the $3,500 due on that date. Is Green obligated to pay the money demanded by White?

**8.** By written contract Ames agreed to build a house on Bowen's lot for $165,000, commencing within ninety days of the date of the contract. Prior to the date for beginning construction, Ames informed Bowen that he was repudiating the contract and would not perform. Bowen refused to accept the repudiation and demanded fulfillment of the contract. Eighty days after the date of the contract, Bowen entered into a new contract with Curd for $162,000. The next day, without knowledge or notice of Bowen's contract with Curd, Ames began construction. Bowen ordered Ames from the premises and refused to allow him to continue. Will Ames be able to collect damages from Bowen? Explain.

**9.** Judy agreed in writing to work for Northern Enterprises, Inc., for three years as superintendent of Northern's manufacturing establishment and to devote herself entirely to the business, giving it her whole time, attention, and skill, for which she was to receive $72,000 per annum, in monthly installments of $6,000. Judy worked and was paid for the first twelve months, when, through no fault of her own or Northern's, she was arrested and imprisoned for one month. It became imperative for Northern to employ another, and it treated the contract with Judy as breached and abandoned, refusing to permit Judy to resume work upon her release from jail. What rights, if any, does Judy have under the contract?

**10.** The Park Plaza Hotel awarded its valet and laundry concession to Larson for a three-year term. The contract contained the following provision: "It is distinctly understood and agreed that the services to be rendered by Larson shall meet with the approval of the Park Plaza Hotel, which shall be the sole judge of the sufficiency and propriety of the services." After seven months, the hotel gave a month's notice to discontinue services based on the failure of the services to meet its approval. Larson brought an action against the hotel, alleging that its dissatisfaction was unreasonable. The hotel defended upon the ground that subjective or personal satisfaction may be the sole justification for termination of the contract. Who is correct? Explain.

**11.** Schlosser entered into an agreement to purchase a cooperative apartment from Flynn Company. The written agreement contained the following provision:

> This entire agreement is conditioned on Purchaser's being approved for occupancy by the board of directors of the Cooperative. In the event approval of the Purchaser shall be denied, this agreement shall thereafter be of no further force or effect.

When Schlosser unilaterally revoked her "offer," Flynn sued for breach of contract. Schlosser claims the approval provision was a condition precedent to the existence of a binding contract and, thus, she was free to revoke. Decision?

**12.** Jacobs, owner of a farm, entered into a contract with Earl Walker in which Walker agreed to paint the buildings on the farm. As authorized by Jacobs, Walker acquired the paint from Jones with the bill to be sent to Jacobs. Before the work was completed, Jacobs without good cause ordered Walker to stop. Walker made offers to complete the job, but Jacobs declined to permit Walker to fulfill his contract. Explain whether Jones and Walker will be successful in an action against Jacobs for breach of contract.

**13.** On August 20, Hildebrand entered into a written contract with the city of Douglasville whereby he was to serve as community development project engineer for three years at an "annual fee" of $19,000. This salary figure could be changed without affecting the other terms of the contract. One of the provisions for termination of the contract was written notice by either party to the other at any time at least ninety days prior to the intended date of termination. The contract listed a substantial number of services and duties Hildebrand was to perform for the city; among the lesser duties were (1) keeping the community development director (Hildebrand's supervisor) informed at all times of his whereabouts and how he could be contacted, and (2) attending meetings at which his presence was requested. Two years later, on September 20, by which time Hildebrand's annual fee had risen to $1,915.83 per month, the city fired Hildebrand effective immediately, citing "certain material breaches … of the … agreement." The city specifically charged that he did not attend the necessary meetings although requested to do so and seldom if ever kept his supervisor informed of his whereabouts and how he could be contacted. Will Hildebrand prevail in a suit against the mayor and city for damages in the amount of $5,747.49 because of the city's failure to give him ninety days' notice prior to termination?

**14.** Walker & Co. contracted to provide a sign for Harrison to place above his dry cleaning business. According to the contract, Harrison would lease the sign from Walker, making monthly payments for thirty-six months. In return, Walker agreed to maintain and service the sign at its own expense. Walker installed the sign in July, and Harrison made the first rental payment. Shortly thereafter, someone hit the sign with a tomato. Harrison also claims he discovered rust on its chrome and little spider webs in its corners. Harrison repeatedly called Walker for the maintenance work promised under the contract, but Walker did not respond immediately. Harrison then telegraphed Walker that due to Walker's failure to perform the maintenance services, he held Walker in material breach of the contract. A week later, Walker sent out a crew, which did all of the requested maintenance services. Has Walker committed a material breach of contract? Explain.

**15.** Barta entered into a written contract to buy the K&K Pharmacy, located in the local shopping center. Included in the contract was a provision stating that "this Agreement shall be contingent upon Buyer's ability to obtain a new lease from Landlord for the premises presently occupied by Seller. In the event Buyer is unable to obtain a lease satisfactory to Buyer, this Agreement shall be null and void." Barta planned to sell "high traffic" grocery items such as bread, milk, and coffee to attract customers to his drugstore. A grocery store in the local shopping center, however, held the exclusive right to sell grocery items. Barta, therefore, could not obtain a leasing agreement meeting his approval. Barta refused to close the sale. In a suit by K&K Pharmacy against Barta for breach of contract, who will prevail? Explain.

**16.** Victor Packing Co. (Victor) contracted to supply Sun Maid Raisin Growers 1,800 tons of raisins from the current year's crop. After delivering 1,190 tons of raisins by August, Victor refused to supply any more. Although Victor had until the end of the crop season to ship the remaining 610 tons of raisins, Sun Maid treated Victor's repeated refusals to ship any more raisins as a repudiation of the contract. To prevent breaching its own contracts, Sun Maid went into the marketplace to "cover" and bought the raisins it needed. Unfortunately, between the time Victor refused delivery and Sun Maid entered the market, disastrous rains had caused the price of raisins to skyrocket. May Sun Maid recover from Victor the difference between the contract price and the market price before the end of the current crop year?

**17.** In May, Watts was awarded a construction contract, based on its low bid, by the Cullman County Commission. The contract provided that it would not become effective until approved by the State director of the Farmers Home Administration (now part of the U.S. Department of Agriculture Rural Development Office). In September construction still had not been authorized, and Watts wrote to the County Commission requesting a 5 percent price increase to reflect seasonal and inflationary price increases. The County Commission countered with an offer of 3.5 percent. Watts then wrote the commission, insisting on a 5 percent increase and stating that if this was not agreeable, it was withdrawing its original bid. The commission obtained another company to perform the project, and on October 14, informed Watts that it had accepted the withdrawal of the bid. Watts sued for breach of contract. Explain whether Watts will prevail and why or why not.

**18.** K&G Construction Co. was the owner of and the general contractor for a housing subdivision project. Harris contracted with the company to do excavating and earth-moving work on the project. Certain provisions of the contract stated that (1) K&G was to make monthly progress payments to Harris; (2) no such payments were to be made until Harris obtained liability insurance; and (3) all of Harris's work on the project must be performed in a workmanlike manner. On August 9, a bulldozer operator, working for Harris, drove too close to one of K&G's houses, causing the collapse of a wall and other damage. When Harris and his insurance carrier denied liability and refused to pay for the damage, K&G refused to make the August monthly progress payment. Harris, nonetheless, continued to work on the project until mid-September, when the excavator ceased its operations due to K&G's refusal to make the progress payment. K&G had another excavator finish the job at an added cost of $1,450. It then sued Harris for the bulldozer damage, alleging negligence, and also for the $1,450 damages for breach of contract. Harris claims that K&G defaulted first, having no legal right to refuse the August progress payment. Did K&G default first? Explain.

**19.** Mountain Restaurant Corporation (Mountain) leased commercial space in the ParkCenter Mall to operate a restaurant called Zac's Grill. The lease specified that the lessee shall "at all times have a non exclusive and non revocable right, together with the other tenants and occupants of ... the shopping center, to use the parking area ... for itself, its customers and employees." Zac's Grill was to be a fast-food restaurant where tables were anticipated to "turn over" twice during lunch. Zac's operated successfully until parking close to the restaurant became restricted. Two other restaurants opened and began competing for parking spaces, and the parking lot would become full between 12:00 and 12:30 p.m. Parking, however, was always available at other areas of the mall. Business declined for Zac's, which fell behind on the rent due to ParkCenter until finally the restaurant closed. Mountain claims that it was discharged from its obligations under the lease because of material breach. Is Mountain correct? Explain.

**20.** In late 2007 or early 2008, the plaintiff, Lan England, agreed to sell 258,363 shares of stock to the defendant, Eugene Horbach, for $2.75 per share, resulting in a total price of $710,498.25. Although the purchase money was to be paid in the first quarter of 2008, the defendant made periodic payments on the stock at least through September 2008. The parties met in May of 2009 to finalize the transaction. At this time, the plaintiff believed that the defendant owed at least $25,000 of the original purchase price. The defendant did not dispute that amount. The parties then reached a second agreement whereby the defendant agreed to pay to the plaintiff an additional $25,000 and to hold in trust 2 percent of the stock for the plaintiff. In return, the plaintiff agreed to transfer the stock and to forego his right to sue the defendant for breach of the original agreement.

In December 2010, the plaintiff made a demand for the 2 percent stock, but the defendant refused, contending that the 2 percent agreement was meant only to secure his payment of the additional $25,000. The plaintiff sued for breach of the 2 percent agreement. Prior to trial, the defendant discovered additional business records documenting that he had, before entering into the second agreement, actually overpaid the plaintiff for the purchase of the stock. The defendant asserts the plaintiff could not enforce the second agreement as an accord and satisfaction because (1) it was not supported by consideration, and (2) it was based upon a mutual mistake that the defendant owed additional money on the original agreement. Is the defendant correct in his assertions? Explain.

**21.** An artist once produced a painting now called *The Plains of Meudon*. For a while, the parties in this case thought that the artist was Theodore Rousseau, a prominent member of the Barbizon school, and that the painting was quite valuable. With this idea in mind, the Kohlers consigned the painting to Leslie Hindman, Inc. (Hindman), an auction house. Among other things, the consignment agreement between the Kohlers and Hindman defined the scope of Hindman's authority as agent. First, Hindman was obliged to sell the painting according to the conditions of sale spelled out in the auction catalog. Those conditions provided that neither the consignors nor Hindman made any warranties of authenticity. Second, the consignment agreement gave Hindman extensive and exclusive discretionary authority to rescind sales if in its "sole discretion" it determined that the sale subjected the company or the Kohlers to any liability under a warranty of authenticity.

Despite having some doubts about its authenticity, Thune was still interested in the painting but wanted to have it authenticated before committing to its purchase. Unable to obtain an authoritative opinion about its authenticity before the auction, Leslie Hindman and Thune made a verbal agreement that Thune could return the painting within approximately thirty days of the auction if he was the successful bidder and if an expert then determined that Rousseau had not painted it. Neither Leslie Hindman nor anyone else at Hindman told the Kohlers about the questions concerning the painting or about the side agreement between Thune and Hindman. At the auction, Thune prevailed in the bidding with a high bid of $90,000, and he took possession of the painting without paying. He then sent it to an expert in Paris who decided that it was not a Rousseau. Thune returned the painting to Hindman within the agreed upon period. Explain whether the Kohlers would be successful in a lawsuit against either Hindman, Inc., or Thune.

COLUMN: © PHOTOGRAPHEROLYMPUS CLOUDS: © KERTLIS

# CHAPTER 18
# Contract Remedies

When one party to a contract breaches the contract by failing to perform his contractual duties, the law provides a remedy for the injured party. Although the primary objective of contract remedies is to compensate the injured party for the loss resulting from the breach, it is impossible for any remedy to equal the promised performance. To an injured party a court can give as relief what it regards as an equivalent of the promised performance.

This chapter will examine the most common judicial remedies available for breach of contract: (1) monetary damages, (2) the equitable remedies of specific performance and injunction, and (3) restitution. Sales of goods are governed by Article 2 of the Uniform Commercial Code (UCC), which provides specialized remedies that are discussed in *Chapter 25*.

## INTERESTS PROTECTED BY CONTRACT REMEDIES

Contract remedies are available to protect one or more of the following interests of the injured party:

1. the **expectation interest**, which is his interest in having the benefit of his bargain by being put in a position as good as the one he would have occupied had the contract been performed;
2. the **reliance interest**, which is his interest in being reimbursed for loss caused by reliance on the contract by being put in a position as good as the one he would have been in had the contract not been made; or
3. the **restitution interest**, which is his interest in having restored to him any benefit that he has conferred on the other party. Restatement, Section 344.

The expectation interest is protected by the contract remedies of compensatory damages, specific performance, and injunction. The reliance interest is protected by the contractual remedy of reliance damages, while the restitution interest is protected by the contractual remedy of restitution.

## MONETARY DAMAGES

A judgment awarding monetary damages is the most frequently granted judicial remedy for breach of contract. Monetary damages, however, will be awarded only for losses that are foreseeable, established with reasonable certainty, and unavoidable. The equitable remedies discussed in this chapter are discretionary and are available only if monetary damages are inadequate.

### COMPENSATORY DAMAGES

The right to recover compensatory money damages for breach of contract is always available to the injured party. Restatement, Section 346. The purpose in allowing **compensatory damages** is to place the injured party in a position as good as the one she would have occupied had the other party performed under the contract. This involves compensating the injured party for the dollar value of the benefits she would have received had the contract been performed less any savings she experienced by not having to perform her own obligations under the contract. Because these damages are intended to protect the injured party's expectation interest, or the value he expected to derive from the contract, the amount of compensatory damages is generally computed as follows:

**Loss of value**
\+ **Incidental damages**
\+ **Consequential damages**
− **Loss or cost avoided by injured party**
= **Compensatory damages**

**Loss of Value** In general, loss of value is the *difference between the value of the promised performance* of the breaching party *and the value of the actual performance* rendered by the breaching party.

**Value of promised performance**
− **Value of actual performance**
= **Loss of value**

If the breaching party renders no performance at all, then the loss of value is the value of the promised performance. If defective or partial performance is rendered, the loss of value is the difference between the value that the full performance would have had and the value of the performance actually rendered. Thus, where there has been a breach of warranty, the injured party may recover the difference between the value the goods would have had, if they had been as warranted, and the value of the goods in the condition in which the buyer received them. To illustrate, Victor sells an automobile to Joan and expressly warrants that it will get forty-five miles per gallon, but the automobile gets only twenty miles per gallon. The automobile would have been worth $14,000 had it been as warranted, but it is worth only $10,000 as delivered. Joan would recover $4,000 in damages for loss of value.

In addition to loss of value, the injured party may also recover for all other losses actually suffered, subject to the limitation of foreseeability discussed below. These damages include incidental and consequential damages.

Incidental Damages **Incidental damages** are damages that arise directly out of the breach, such as costs incurred to acquire the nondelivered performance from some other source. For example, Agnes employs Benton for nine months for $40,000 to supervise construction of a factory, but fires him without cause after three weeks. Benton, who spends $850 in reasonable fees attempting to find comparable employment, may recover $850 in incidental damages, in addition to any other actual loss he may suffer.

Consequential Damages **Consequential damages** include lost profits and injury to person or property resulting from defective performance. Thus, if Tracy leases to Sean a defective machine that causes him $40,000 in property damage and $120,000 in personal injuries, Sean may recover, in addition to damages for loss of value and incidental damages, $160,000 as consequential damages.

Cost Avoided The recovery by the injured party, however, is reduced by any cost or loss she has avoided by not having to perform. For example, Clinton agrees to build a hotel for Debra for $11,250,000 by September 1. Clinton breaches by not completing construction until October 1. As a consequence, Debra loses revenues for one month in the amount of $400,000 but saves operating expenses of $60,000. She therefore may recover damages for $340,000. Similarly, in a contract in which the injured party has not fully performed, the injured party's recovery is reduced by the value to him of the performance he promised but did not render. For example, Clinton agrees to convey land to Debra in return for Debra's promise to work for Clinton for two years, but she repudiates the contract before Clinton has conveyed the land. Clinton's recovery for loss from Debra is reduced by the value to Clinton of the land.

### NOMINAL DAMAGES

An action to recover damages for breach of contract may be maintained even though the plaintiff has not sustained or cannot prove any injury or loss resulting from the breach. Restatement, Section 346. In such a case, he will be permitted to recover **nominal damages**—a small sum fixed without regard to the amount of loss. For example, Edward contracts to sell and deliver goods to Florence for $1,000. Edward refuses to deliver the goods as agreed, and so breaks the contract. Florence, however, is able to purchase goods of the same kind and quality elsewhere for $1,000 without incurring any incidental damages. As a result, although Edward has violated Florence's rights under the contract, Florence has suffered no actual loss. Consequently, if Florence, as she may, should sue Edward for breach of contract, she would recover a judgment for nominal damages only. Nominal damages are also available where loss is actually sustained but cannot be proved with reasonable certainty.

### RELIANCE DAMAGES

As an alternative to compensatory damages, the injured party may seek reimbursement for foreseeable loss caused by his reliance upon the contract. The purpose of **reliance damages** is to place the injured party in a position as good as the one he would have held, had the contract *not been made*. Reliance damages include expenses incurred in preparing to perform, in actually performing, or in forgoing opportunities to enter into other contracts. An injured party may prefer damages for reliance to compensatory damages when he is unable to establish his lost profits with reasonable certainty. For example, Donald agrees to sell his retail store to Gary, who spends $750,000 acquiring inventory and fixtures. Donald then repudiates the contract, and Gary sells the inventory and fixtures for $735,000. Neither party can establish with reasonable certainty what profit Gary would have made; Gary, therefore, may recover from Donald as damages the loss of $15,000 he sustained on the sale of the inventory and fixtures plus any other costs he incurred in entering into the contract. An injured party may choose reliance damages instead of compensatory damages when the contract is itself unprofitable. In such a case, however, if the breaching party can prove with reasonable certainty the amount of the loss, it will be subtracted from the injured party's reliance damages.

### DAMAGES FOR MISREPRESENTATION

The basic remedy for misrepresentation is rescission (avoidance) of the contract, though when appropriate, the courts also will require restitution. At common law, an alternative remedy to rescission is a suit for damages. The Code liberalizes the common law by not restricting a defrauded party to an election of remedies; that is, the injured party may both rescind the contract by restoring the other party to the status quo and recover damages or obtain any other remedy available under the Code. UCC Section 2–721. In most States, the measure of damages for misrepresentation depends upon whether the misrepresentation was fraudulent or nonfraudulent.

**Fraud** A party induced by fraud to enter into a contract may recover general damages in a tort action. A minority of States allows the injured party to recover, under the "**out-of-pocket**" rule, general damages equal to the difference between the value of what she has received and the value of what she has given for it. The great majority of States, however, under the "**benefit-of-the-bargain**" rule, permits the intentionally defrauded party to recover general damages that are equal to the difference between the value of what she has received and the value of the fraudulent party's performance as represented. The Restatement of Torts provides the fraudulently injured party with the option of either out-of-pocket or benefit-of-the-bargain damages. Section 549. To illustrate, Emily intentionally misrepresents the capabilities of a printing press and thereby induces Melissa to purchase the machine for $20,000. The value of the press as delivered is $14,000, but if the machine had performed as represented, it would be worth $24,000. Under the out-of-pocket rule, Melissa would recover $6,000, whereas under the benefit-of-the-bargain rule, she would recover $10,000.

In addition to a recovery of general damages under one of the measures just discussed, consequential damages may be recovered to the extent they are proved with reasonable certainty and to the extent they do not duplicate general damages. Moreover, where the fraud is gross, oppressive, or aggravated, punitive damages are permitted.

◆ **SEE CASE 18-1**

**Nonfraudulent Misrepresentation** Where the misrepresentation is negligent, the deceived party may recover general damages—under the out-of-pocket measure—and consequential damages. Restatement of Torts, Section 552B. Some States, however, permit the recovery of general damages under the benefit-of-the-bargain measure for negligent misrepresentation. Where the misrepresentation is neither fraudulent nor negligent, however, the Restatement limits damages to the out-of-pocket measure. Section 552C.

## PUNITIVE DAMAGES

**Punitive damages** are monetary damages in addition to compensatory damages awarded to a plaintiff in certain situations involving willful, wanton, or malicious conduct. Their purpose is to punish the defendant and thus discourage him and others from similar wrongful conduct. The purpose of allowing contract damages, on the other hand, is to compensate the plaintiff for the loss that he has sustained because of the defendant's breach of contract. Accordingly, the Restatement provides that punitive damages are *not* recoverable for a breach of contract unless the conduct constituting the breach is also a tort for which the plaintiff may recover punitive damages. Restatement, Section 355.

◆ **SEE CASE 18-1**

## LIQUIDATED DAMAGES

A contract may contain a **liquidated damages** provision by which the parties agree in advance to the damages to be paid in event of a breach. Such a provision will be enforced if it amounts to a reasonable forecast of the loss that may or does result from the breach. If, however, the sum agreed upon as liquidated damages bears no reasonable relationship to the amount of probable loss that may or does result from breach, it is unenforceable as a penalty. (A penalty is a contractual provision designed to deter a party from breaching her contract and to punish her for doing so.) Restatement, Section 356, Comment a states,

> The parties to a contract may effectively provide in advance the damages that are to be payable in the event of breach as long as the provision does not disregard the principle of compensation. The enforcement of such provisions for liquidated damages saves the time of courts, juries, parties and witnesses and reduces the expense of litigation. This is especially important if the amount in controversy is small. However, the parties to a contract are not free to provide a penalty for its breach. The central objective behind the system of contract remedies is compensatory, not punitive.

By examining the substance of the provision, the nature of the contract, and the extent of probable harm to the promisee that a breach may reasonably be expected to cause, the courts will determine whether the agreed amount is proper as liquidated damages or unenforceable as a penalty. If a liquidated damage provision is not enforceable, the injured party nevertheless is entitled to the ordinary remedies for breach of contract.

To illustrate, Reliable Construction Company contracts with Equerry to build a grandstand at Equerry's racecourse at a cost of $1,330,000, to have it completed by a certain date, and to pay Equerry, as liquidated damages, $5,000 per day for every day's delay beyond that date in completing the grandstand. The stipulated sum for delay is liquidated damages and not a penalty because the amount is reasonable. If, instead, the sum stipulated had been $40,000 per day, it would obviously have been unreasonable and therefore a penalty. Provisions for liquidated damages are sometimes found in contracts for the sale of a business, in which the seller agrees not to reenter the same business within a reasonable geographic area and time period. Actual damages resulting from the seller's breach of his agreement would ordinarily be difficult to ascertain, and the sum stipulated, if reasonable, would be enforced as liquidated damages.

◆ **SEE CASE 18-2**

## LIMITATIONS ON DAMAGES

To accomplish the basic purposes of contract remedies, the law imposes the limitations of foreseeability, certainty, and mitigation upon monetary damages. These limitations are intended to ensure that damages can be taken into account at the time of contracting, that damages are compensatory and not speculative, and that damages do not include loss that could have been avoided by reasonable efforts.

**Foreseeability of Damages** A contracting party is generally expected to consider foreseeable risks when entering into the contract. Therefore, compensatory or reliance damages are recoverable only for loss that the party in breach had reason to foresee as a *probable* result of such breach when the contract was made; conversely, the breaching party is not liable for loss that was not foreseeable when the parties entered into the contract. The test of foreseeability is *objective*, based upon what the breaching party had reason to foresee. Loss may be deemed foreseeable as a probable result of a breach by following from the breach (1) in the ordinary course of events or (2) as a result of special circumstances, beyond the ordinary course of events, which the party in breach had reason to know. Restatement, Section 351(2). Moreover, "[a] court may limit damages for foreseeable loss by excluding recovery for loss of profits, by allowing recovery only for loss incurred in reliance, or otherwise if it concludes that in the circumstances justice so requires in order to avoid disproportionate compensation." Restatement, Section 351(3).

The leading case on the subject of foreseeability of damages is *Hadley v. Baxendale*, decided in England in 1854. In this case, the plaintiffs operated a flour mill at Gloucester. Their mill was compelled to cease operating because of a broken crankshaft attached to the steam engine that furnished power to the mill. It was necessary to send the broken shaft to a foundry located at Greenwich so that a new shaft could be made. The plaintiffs delivered the broken shaft to the defendants, who were common carriers, for immediate transportation from Gloucester to Greenwich, but did not inform the defendants that operation of the mill had ceased because of the nonfunctioning crankshaft. The defendants received the shaft, collected the freight charges in advance, and promised to deliver the shaft for repairs the following day. The defendants, however, did not make delivery as promised; as a result, the mill did not resume operations for several days, causing the plaintiffs to lose profitable sales. The defendants contended that the loss of profits was too remote, and therefore unforeseeable, to be recoverable. Nonetheless, the jury, in awarding damages to the plaintiffs, was permitted to take into consideration the loss of these profits. The appellate court reversed the decision and ordered a new trial on the ground that the plaintiffs had never communicated to the defendants the special circumstances that caused the loss of profits, namely, the continued stoppage of the mill while awaiting the return of the repaired crankshaft. A common carrier, the court reasoned, would not reasonably have foreseen that the plaintiffs' mill would be shut down as a result of delay in transporting the broken crankshaft.

On the other hand, if the defendants in *Hadley v. Baxendale* had been informed that the shaft was necessary for the operation of the mill, or otherwise had reason to know this fact, they would be liable for the plaintiffs' loss of profit during that period of the shutdown caused by their delay. Under these circumstances, the loss would be the "foreseeable" and "natural" result of the breach.

Should a plaintiff's expected profit be extraordinarily large, the general rule is that the breaching party will be liable for such special loss only if he had reason to know of it. In any event, the plaintiff may recover for any ordinary loss resulting from the breach. Thus, if Madeline breaches a contract with Jane, causing Jane, due to special circumstances, $10,000 in damages where ordinarily such a breach would result in only $6,000 in damages, Madeline would be liable to Jane for $6,000, not $10,000, provided that Madeline was unaware of the special circumstances causing Jane the unusually large loss.

**Certainty of Damages** Damages are not recoverable for loss beyond an amount that the injured party can establish with reasonable certainty. Restatement, Section 352. If the injured party cannot prove a particular element of her loss with reasonable certainty, she nevertheless will be entitled to recover the portion of her loss that she can prove with reasonable certainty. The certainty requirement creates the greatest challenge for plaintiffs seeking to recover consequential damages for lost profits on related transactions. Those attempting to prove lost profits caused by breach of a contract to produce a sporting event or to publish a new book experience similar difficulties.

**Mitigation of Damages** Under the doctrine of mitigation of damages, the injured party may not recover damages for loss that he could have avoided with reasonable effort and without undue risk, burden, or humiliation. Restatement, Section 350. Thus, if James is under a contract to manufacture goods for Kathy, and Kathy repudiates the contract after James has commenced performance, James will not be allowed to recover for losses he sustains by continuing to manufacture the goods if to do so would increase the amount of damages. The amount of loss that James could reasonably have avoided is deducted from the amount that would otherwise be recoverable as damages. On the other hand, if the goods were almost completed when Kathy repudiated the contract, completing the goods might mitigate the damages, because the finished goods may be resalable whereas the unfinished goods may not. UCC Section 2–704(2).

Similarly, if Harvey contracts to work for Olivia for one year for a weekly salary and is wrongfully discharged by Olivia after two months, Harvey must use reasonable efforts to mitigate his damages by seeking other employment. If, after such efforts, he cannot obtain other employment of the same general character, he is entitled to recover full pay for the contract period that he is unemployed. He is not obliged to accept a radically different type of employment or to accept work at a distant place. For example, a person employed as a schoolteacher or accountant who is wrongfully discharged is not obliged, in order to mitigate damages, to accept available employment as a chauffeur or truck driver. If Harvey does *not* seek other employment, then if Olivia proves with reasonable certainty that employment of the same general character was available, Harvey's damages are reduced by the amount he could have earned.

◆ **SEE CASE 3-3**

## REMEDIES IN EQUITY

At times, damages based on the expectation interest, reliance interest, or restitution interest will not adequately compensate an injured party. In these cases, equitable relief in the form of specific performance or an injunction may be available to protect the injured party's interest.

The remedies of specific performance and an injunction are not a matter of right but rest in the discretion of the court. Consequently, they will not be granted where:

1. there is an adequate remedy at law;
2. it is impossible to enforce them, as where the seller has already conveyed the subject matter of the contract to an innocent third person;
3. the terms of the contract are unfair;
4. the consideration is grossly inadequate;
5. the contract is tainted with fraud, duress, undue influence, mistake, or unfair practices;
6. the terms of the contract are not sufficiently certain; or
7. the relief would cause unreasonable hardship.

A court may grant specific performance or an injunction despite a provision for liquidated damages. Restatement, Section 361. Moreover, a court will grant specific performance or an injunction even though a term of the contract prohibits equitable relief, if denying such relief would cause unreasonable hardship to the injured party. Restatement, Section 364(2).

Another equitable remedy is **reformation**, a process whereby the court "rewrites" or "corrects" a written contract to make it conform to the true agreement of the parties. The purpose of reformation is not to make a new contract for the parties but rather to express adequately the contract they have made for themselves. The remedy of reformation is granted when the parties agree on a contract but write it in a way that inaccurately reflects their actual agreement. For example, Acme Insurance Co. and Bell agree that for good consideration Acme will issue an annuity paying $500 per month. Through a clerical error, the annuity policy is issued for $50 per month. A court of equity, upon satisfactory proof of the mistake, will reform the policy to provide for the correct amount—$500 per month. In addition, as discussed in *Chapter 13*, where a covenant not to compete is unreasonable, some courts will reform the agreement to make it reasonable and enforceable.

### SPECIFIC PERFORMANCE

**Specific performance** is an equitable remedy that compels the defaulting party to perform her contractual obligations. Ordinarily, where a seller breaches her contract for the sale of **personal property**, the buyer has a sufficient remedy at law. If, however, the personal property contracted for is rare or unique, this remedy is inadequate. Examples of such property would include a famous painting or statue, an original manuscript or a rare edition of a book, a patent, a copyright, shares of stock in a closely held corporation, or an heirloom. Articles of this kind cannot be purchased elsewhere. Accordingly, should the seller breach her contract for the sale of any such article, money damages will not adequately compensate the buyer. Consequently, in these instances, the buyer may avail herself of the equitable remedy of specific performance.

Although courts of equity will grant specific performance in connection with contracts for the sale of personal property only in exceptional circumstances, they will always grant it in cases involving breach of contract for the sale of **real property**. The reason for this is that every parcel of land is considered unique. Consequently, if the seller refuses to convey title to the real estate contracted for, the buyer may seek the aid of a court of equity to compel the seller to convey the title. Most courts of equity will likewise compel the buyer in a real estate contract to perform at the suit of the seller. Courts of equity will not grant specific performance of contracts for personal services. In the first place, enforcing such a decree may be difficult if not impossible. In the second place, it is against the policy of the courts to force one person to work for or to serve another against his will, even though the person has contracted to do so, in that such enforcement would closely resemble involuntary servitude. For example, if Carmen, an accomplished concert pianist, agrees to appear at a certain time and place to play a specified program for Rudolf, a court would not issue a decree of specific performance upon her refusal to appear.

◆ **SEE CASE 18-3**

### INJUNCTIONS

The **injunction**, as used as a contract remedy, is a formal court order enjoining (commanding) a person to refrain from doing a specific act or to cease engaging in specified conduct. A court of equity, at its discretion, may grant an injunction against breach of a contractual duty where damages for a breach would be inadequate. For example, Clint enters into a written contract to give Janice the right of first refusal on a tract of land he owns. Clint, however, subsequently offers the land to Blake without first offering it to Janice. A court of equity may properly enjoin Clint from selling the land to Blake. Similarly, valid covenants not to compete may be enforced by an injunction.

An employee's promise of exclusive personal services may be enforced by an injunction against serving another employer as long as the probable result will not be to deprive the employee of other reasonable means of making a living. Restatement, Section 367. Suppose, for example, that Allan makes a contract with Marlene, a famous singer, under which Marlene agrees to sing at Allan's theater on certain dates for an agreed fee. Before the date of the first performance, Marlene makes a contract with Craig to sing for Craig at his theater on the same dates. Although, as already discussed, Allan cannot secure specific performance of his contract by Marlene, a court of equity will, on suit by Allan against Marlene, issue an injunction against her, ordering her not to sing for Craig.

Where the services contracted for are not unusual or extraordinary, the injured party cannot obtain injunctive relief. His only remedy is an action at law for damages.

◆ **SEE CASE 18-4**

## RESTITUTION

One remedy that may be available to a party to a contract is restitution. **Restitution** is the act of returning to the aggrieved party the consideration, or its value, which he gave to the other party. The purpose of restitution is to restore the injured party to the position he occupied before the contract was made. Therefore, the party seeking restitution must return what he has received from the other party.

Restitution is available in several contractual situations: (1) as an alternative remedy for a party injured by breach; (2) for a party in default; (3) for a party who may not enforce a contract because of the statute of frauds; and (4) for a party wishing to rescind (avoid) a voidable contract.

### PARTY INJURED BY BREACH

A party is entitled to restitution if the other party totally breaches the contract by nonperformance or repudiation. Restatement, Section 373. For example, Benedict agrees to sell land to Beatrice for $60,000. After Beatrice makes a partial payment of $15,000, Benedict wrongfully refuses to transfer title. As an alternative to damages or specific performance, Beatrice may recover the $15,000 in restitution.

### PARTY IN DEFAULT

Where a party, after having partly performed, commits a breach by nonperformance or repudiation that discharges the other party's duty to perform, the party in default is entitled to restitution for any benefit she has conferred in excess of the loss she has caused by her breach. Restatement, Section 374. For example, Nathan agrees to sell land to Lilly for $60,000, and Lilly makes a partial payment of $15,000. Lilly then repudiates the contract. Nathan sells the land to Murray in good faith for $55,000. Lilly may recover from Nathan in restitution the part payment of the $15,000 *less* the $5,000 damages Nathan sustained because of Lilly's breach, which equals $10,000.

### STATUTE OF FRAUDS

A party to a contract that is unenforceable because of the statute of frauds may, nonetheless, have acted in reliance upon the contract. In such a case, that party may recover in restitution the benefits she conferred upon the other in relying upon the unenforceable contract. In most States, the party seeking restitution must not be in default. Thus, if Wilton makes an oral contract to furnish services to Rochelle that are not to be performed within a year, and Rochelle discharges Wilton after three months, Wilton may recover as restitution the value of the services he rendered during the three months.

### VOIDABLE CONTRACTS

A party who has rescinded or avoided a contract for lack of capacity, duress, undue influence, fraud in the inducement, nonfraudulent misrepresentation, or mistake is entitled to restitution for any benefit he has conferred upon the other party. Restatement, Section 376. For example, Samuel fraudulently induces Edith to sell land for $60,000. Samuel pays the purchase price, and Edith conveys the land. Discovering the fraud, Edith may disaffirm the contract and recover the land as restitution. Generally, the party seeking restitution must return any benefit that he has received under the agreement; however, as discussed in *Chapter 14* (which deals with contractual capacity), this is not always the case.

◆ **SEE FIGURE 18-1: Contract Remedies**

## LIMITATIONS ON REMEDIES

### ELECTION OF REMEDIES

If a party injured by a breach of contract has more than one remedy available to him, his manifesting a choice of one of them, such as bringing suit, does not prevent him from

◆ **FIGURE 18-1: Contract Remedies**

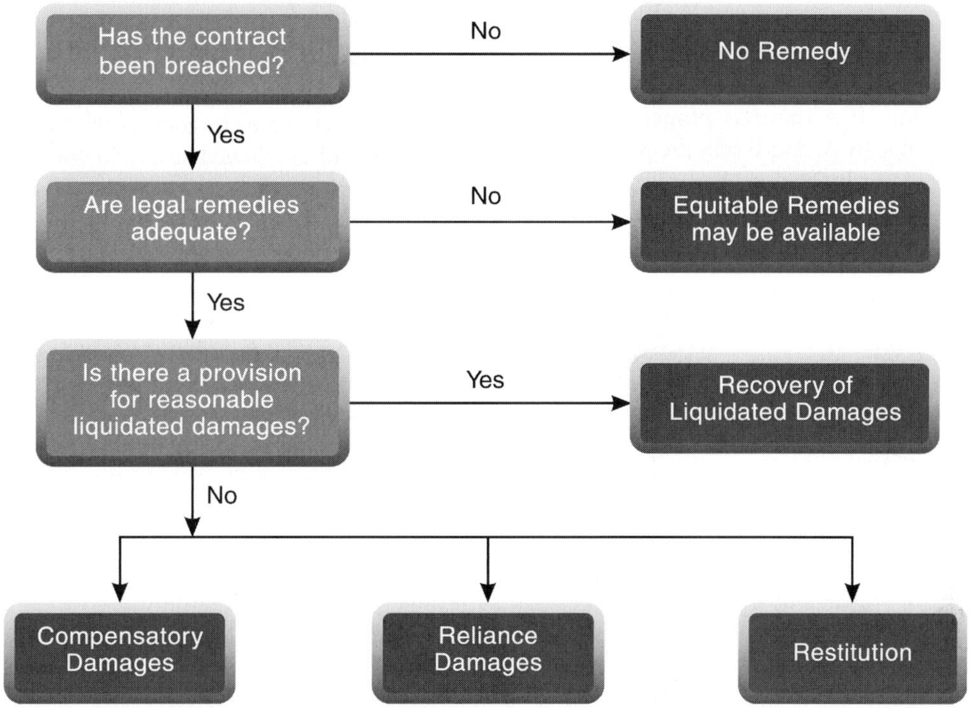


seeking another remedy unless the remedies are inconsistent and the other party materially changes his position in reliance on the manifestation. Restatement, Section 378. For example, a party who seeks specific performance, an injunction, or restitution may be entitled to incidental damages for delay in performance. Damages for *total breach*, however, are inconsistent with the remedies of specific performance, injunction, and restitution. Likewise, the remedy of specific performance or an injunction is inconsistent with that of restitution.

With respect to contracts for the sale of goods, the Code rejects any doctrine of election of remedies. Thus, the remedies it provides are essentially cumulative, including all of the available remedies for breach. Whether one remedy precludes another depends on the facts of the individual case. UCC Section 2–703, Comment 1.

◆ **SEE CASE 18-1**

## LOSS OF POWER OF AVOIDANCE

A party with a power of avoidance for lack of capacity, duress, undue influence, fraud, misrepresentation, or mistake may lose that power if (1) she affirms the contract; (2) she delays unreasonably in exercising the power of disaffirmance; or (3) the rights of third parties intervene.

**Affirmance** A party who has the power to avoid a contract for lack of capacity, duress, undue influence, fraud in the inducement, nonfraudulent misrepresentation, or mistake will lose that power by affirming the contract. Affirmance occurs when the party, with full knowledge of the facts, either declares his intention to proceed with the contract or takes some other action from which such intention may reasonably be inferred. Thus, suppose that Pam was induced to purchase a ring from Sally through Sally's fraudulent misrepresentation. If, after learning the truth, Pam undertakes to sell the ring to Janet or else does something that is consistent only with her ownership of the ring, she may no longer rescind the transaction with Sally. In the case of incapacity, duress, or undue influence, affirmance is effective only after the circumstances that made the contract voidable cease to exist. Where there has been fraudulent misrepresentation, the defrauded party may affirm only after he knows of the misrepresentation. If the misrepresentation is nonfraudulent or a mistake is involved, the defrauded or mistaken party may affirm only after he knows or should know of the misrepresentation or mistake.

**Delay** The power of avoidance may be lost if the party who has the power does not rescind within a reasonable time after the circumstances that made the contract voidable have ceased to exist. Determining a reasonable time depends upon all the circumstances, including the extent to which the delay enables the party with the power of avoidance to speculate at the other party's risk. To illustrate, a defrauded purchaser of stock cannot wait unduly to see if the market price or value of the stock appreciates sufficiently to justify retaining the stock.

**Rights of Third Parties** The intervening rights of third parties further limit the power of avoidance and the accompanying right to restitution. If A transfers property to B in a transaction that is voidable by A, and B sells the property to C (a good faith purchaser for value) before A exercises her power of avoidance, A will lose the right to recover the property.

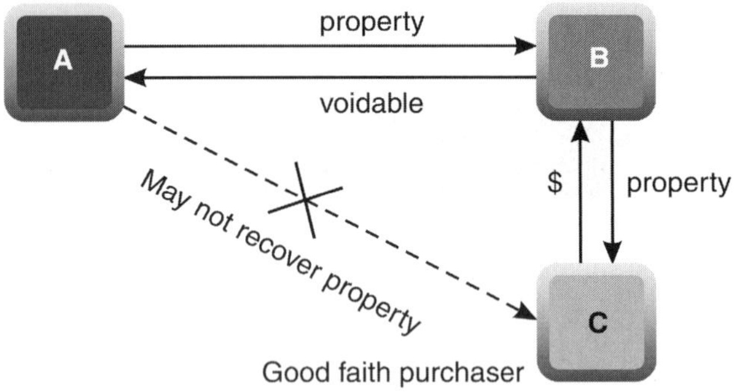


Thus, if C, a third party who is a good faith purchaser, acquires an interest in the subject matter of the contract before A has elected to rescind, no rescission is permitted. Because the transaction is voidable, B acquires a voidable title to the property. Upon a sale of the property by B to C, who is a purchaser in good faith and for value, C obtains good title and is allowed to retain the property. As both A and C are innocent, the law will not disturb the title held by C, the good faith purchaser. In this case, as in all cases in which rescission is not available, A's only recourse is against B.

The one notable exception to this rule is the situation involving a sale, *other than a sale of goods*, by a minor who subsequently wishes to avoid the transaction, in which the property has been retransferred to a good faith purchaser. Under this special rule, a good faith purchaser is deprived of the protection generally provided such third parties. Therefore, the third party in a transaction not involving goods, real property being the primary example, is no more protected from the minor's disaffirmance than is the person dealing directly with the minor.

## CHAPTER SUMMARY

**MONETARY DAMAGES**

**Compensatory Damages** contract damages placing the injured party in a position as good as the one he would have held had the other party performed; equals loss of value minus loss avoided by injured party plus incidental damages plus consequential damages
- ***Loss of Value*** value of promised performance minus value of actual performance
- ***Cost Avoided*** loss or costs the injured party avoids by not having to perform
- ***Incidental Damages*** damages arising directly out of a breach of contract
- ***Consequential Damages*** damages not arising directly out of a breach but arising as a foreseeable result of the breach

**Nominal Damages** a small sum awarded where a contract has been breached but the loss is negligible or unproved

**Reliance Damages** contract damages placing the injured party in as good a position as she would have been in had the contract not been made

**Damages for Misrepresentation**
- ***Benefit-of-the-Bargain Damages*** difference between the value of the fraudulent party's performance as represented and the value the defrauded party received
- ***Out-of-Pocket Damages*** difference between the value given and the value received

**Punitive Damages** are generally *not* recoverable for breach of contract

**Liquidated Damages** reasonable damages agreed to in advance by the parties to a contract

**Limitations on Damages**
- ***Foreseeability of Damages*** potential loss that the party now in default had reason to know of when the contract was made
- ***Certainty of Damages*** damages are not recoverable beyond an amount that can be established with reasonable certainty
- ***Mitigation of Damages*** injured party may not recover damages for loss he could have avoided by reasonable effort

**REMEDIES IN EQUITY**

**Availability** only in cases in which there is no adequate remedy at law
**Types**
- ***Specific Performance*** court decree ordering breaching party to render promised performance
- ***Injunction*** court order prohibiting a party from doing a specific act
- ***Reformation*** court order correcting a written contract to conform with the original intent of the contracting parties

**RESTITUTION**

**Definition of Restitution** restoration of the injured party to the position she was in before the contract was made
**Availability**
- ***Party Injured by Breach*** if the other party totally breaches the contract by nonperformance or repudiation
- ***Party in Default*** for any benefit conferred in excess of the loss caused by the breach
- ***Statute of Frauds*** where a contract is unenforceable because of the statute of frauds, a party may recover the benefits conferred on the other party in reliance on the contract
- ***Voidable Contracts*** a party who has avoided a contract is entitled to restitution for any benefit conferred on the other party

**LIMITATIONS ON REMEDIES**

**Election of Remedies** if remedies are not inconsistent, a party injured by a breach of contract may seek more than one
**Loss of Power of Avoidance** a party with the power to avoid a contract may lose that power by
- affirming the contract
- delaying unreasonably in exercising the power of avoidance
- being subordinated to the intervening rights of third parties

## CASES

### CASE 18-1

### Election of Remedies/Punitive Damages
### MERRITT v. CRAIG

Court of Special Appeals of Maryland, 2000
130 Md.App. 350, 746 A.2d 923, certiorari denied, 359 Md. 29, 753 A.2d 2
http://caselaw.findlaw.com/md-court-of-special-appeals/1417322.html

**Davis, J.**
In the fall of 1995, during their search for a new residence, appellants [Benjamin K. and Julie S. Merritt] inspected Craig's property located at Pergin Farm Road in Garrett County [Maryland]. After viewing the residence, appellants advised Craig that they were interested in purchasing the property; however, their offer was contingent upon a satisfactory home inspection. On November 5, 1995, appellants, their inspector, and appellee's husband Mark Craig conducted an inspection of the basement area of the residence, during which there was an examination of cistern and water supply pipes. The examination revealed that the cistern had been used to store a water supply reserve, but was not currently utilized.

The inspector advised appellants that the system he had observed was one which utilized a submersible pump in the well from which water flowed to a pressure tank in the basement. The pressure tank distributed water through the internal piping system of the house. There were also two water lines that entered into the basement area. One of the lines came from an 800-foot well that was located on the property, and the other line came from a well located on the adjacent property. The well located on the adjacent property supplied water to both appellants' residence and a guest house owned by Craig. The existence of the adjacent well was not disclosed to appellants.

On December 2, 1995, a contract of sale for the property was executed between appellants and Craig, along with a "Disclosure Statement" signed by Craig on June 9, 1994, and acknowledged by appellants on November 2, 1995, affirming that there were no problems with the water supply to the dwelling. Between November 5, 1995 and June 1996, Craig caused the water line from the guest house to appellants' residence to be cut, and the cistern reactivated to store water from the existing well on appellants' lot. On May 18, 1996, Craig's husband advised Dennis Hannibal, one of the real estate agents involved in the deal, that he had spent $4,196.79 to upgrade the water system on appellants' property and to restore the cistern and remove appellants' house from the second well on Craig's guest house property. On June 14, 1996, appellants and Craig had settlement on the property. Later that afternoon, Craig's husband, without appellants' knowledge, excavated the inside wall of appellants' house and installed a cap to stop a leaking condition on the water line that he had previously cut.

Subsequently, appellants, while attempting to fill a water bed, noticed that the water supply in their well had depleted. On July 13, 1996, appellants met with Craig to discuss a solution to the water failure problem, believing that Craig was responsible for cutting a water line to their house. Appellants agreed with Craig to conduct a flow test to the existing well and contribute money for the construction of a new well. On October 29, 1996, the well was drilled and produced only one half gallon of water per minute. On December 13, 1996, appellants paid for the drilling of a second well on their property, but it failed to produce water. In January 1997, appellants contacted a plumber, Robert Warnick, who confirmed that the line from the guest house well to appellants' residence had been cut flush with the inside surface of the basement wall and cemented closed. Appellants continued to do further work on the house in an effort to cure the water problem.

On February 11, 1997, appellants brought suit against Craig and other appellees in the Circuit Court for Garrett County, seeking rescission of the deed to the property and contract of sale, along with compensatory and punitive damages. During the course of the trial, the judge dismissed appellants' claim for rescission on the ground that they had effectively waived their right to rescission. * * * At the close of trial, the jury returned a verdict in favor of appellants and awarded compensatory damages in the amount of $42,264.76. Appellants were also awarded punitive damages in the amount of $150,000. Subsequently, appellants filed a motion to alter or amend the judgment requesting the court to grant rescission of the contract of sale and the deed, which the circuit court denied on June 17, 1998. Craig moved for judgment notwithstanding the verdict on May 8, 1998, which was also denied by the circuit court. Following the circuit court action, this appeal ensued.

* * *

* * * Under Maryland law, when a party to a contract discovers that he or she has been defrauded, the party defrauded has either "a right to retain the contract and collect damages for its breach, or a right to rescind the contract and recover his or her own expenditures," not both. [Citations.] "These rights [are] inconsistent and mutually exclusive, and the discovery put[s] the purchaser to a prompt election." [Citation.] "A plaintiff seeking rescission must demonstrate that he [or she] acted promptly after discovery of the ground for rescission," otherwise the right to rescind is waived. [Citations.] * * *

In the case *sub judice* [before the court], appellants claim that they were entitled to a rescission of the subject contract of sale and deed and incidental damages. Appellants also claim that they were entitled to compensatory and punitive damages arising from Craig's actions. Appellants, however, may not successfully rescind the contract while simultaneously recovering compensatory and punitive damages. Restitution is "a party's unilateral unmaking of a contract for a legally sufficient reason, such as the other party's material breach" and it in effect "restores the parties to their precontractual position." [Citation.] The restoration of the parties to their original position is incompatible with the circumstance when the complaining party is, at once, relieved of all obligations under the contract while simultaneously securing the windfall of compensatory and punitive damages beyond incidental expenses.

* * *

In sum, although whether appellants promptly repudiated the contract was not squarely before the court, we are not persuaded by appellees' assertion that appellants did not seek rescission in a timely fashion. We hold that, under the facts of this case, appellants must elect the form of relief, i.e., damages or rescission * * *

* * *

We hold that * * * the appellants are entitled to be awarded punitive damages resulting from Craig's actions. A "[p]laintiff seeking to recover punitive damages must allege in detail in the complaint the facts that indicate the entertainment by defendant of evil motive or intent." [Citation.] The Court of Appeals has held that "punitive damages may only be awarded in such cases where 'the plaintiff has established that the defendant's conduct was characterized by evil motive, intent to injure, ill will or fraud. * * * '" [Citation.] In cases of fraud that arise out of a contractual relationship, the plaintiff would have to establish actual malice to recover punitive damages. [Citation.] Finally, we have stated that "actual or express malice requires an intentional or willful act (or omission) * * * and 'has been characterized as the performance of an act without legal justification or excuse, but with an evil or rancorous motive influenced by hate, the purpose being to deliberately and willfully injure the plaintiff.'" [Citation.]

* * *

The jury believed that the representations made by Craig were undertaken with actual knowledge that the representations were false and with the intention to deceive appellants. * * * Moreover, the record reflects that the jury could reasonably infer Craig's intention to defraud appellants by her representation in the Disclosure Statement that there were no problems with the water supply, and by subsequently making substantial changes in the water system by cutting off a water line which supplied water to appellants' residence immediately after appellants' inspector examined the system. Therefore, we hold that the circuit court was not in error in finding facts from the record sufficient to support an award of punitive damages.

Craig also challenges the punitive damages award on the basis that the amount of the award was excessive. * * *

In the case at hand, the trial judge undertook the appropriate review of the jury's award. It is clear from the court's comments at the hearing that the court's decision not to disturb the jury's verdict was based on the evidence presented at trial and was not excessive. * * * Craig's conduct toward appellants was reprehensible and fully warranted punitive damages. Her conduct in willfully misrepresenting the condition of the water system in the Disclosure Statement, coupled with her actions and those of her husband in interfering and diverting the water flow subsequent to the inspection and sale of the property, constitute egregious conduct. As a result of Craig's conduct, appellants were forced to employ extreme water conservation practices due to an insufficient water supply and they attempted to ameliorate the problem by having two new wells drilled on the property which proved to be unproductive. Moreover, the lack of water supply to appellants' property clearly reduced its market value. * * *

* * *

* * * Consequently, should appellants seek compensatory and punitive damages on remand, appellants' actual knowledge, coupled with the intent to deceive, is a sufficient factual predicate for submission of punitive damages to the jury.

Judgement of the circuit court reversed; case remanded for further proceedings consistent with this opinion.

## CASE 18-2

### Liquidated Damages

### ARROWHEAD SCHOOL DISTRICT NO. 75, PARK COUNTY, MONTANA, v. JAMES A. KLYAP, JR.

Supreme Court of Montana, 2003
318 Mont. 103, 79 P.3d 250
http://caselaw.findlaw.com/mt-supreme-court/1246054.html

**Nelson, J.**

Arrowhead School District No. 75 (District) is located in Park County south of Livingston [Montana]. The District consists of one school, Arrowhead School (School).

For the 1997–98 school year, the School employed about eleven full-time teachers and several part-time teachers. During that school year, the School employed Klyap as a new teacher instructing math, language arts, and physical education for the sixth, seventh, and eighth grades. In addition, Klyap, through his own initiative, helped start a sports program and coached flag football, basketball, and volleyball.

* * * the School offered Klyap a contract for the 1998– 99 school year on or about June 15, 1998, which he accepted by signing on or about June 30, 1998. This contract provided for a $20,500 salary and included the liquidated damages clause at issue here. The clause calculated liquidated damages as a percentage of annual salary determined by the date of breach; a breach of contract after July 20, 1998, required payment of 20% of salary as damages. Klyap also signed a notice indicating he accepted responsibility for familiarizing himself with the information in the teacher's handbook which also included the liquidated damages clause.

* * *

* * * On August 12, [Klyap] informed the School that he would not be returning for the 1998-99 school year even though classes were scheduled to start on August 26. As a result of Klyap's decision not to teach at the School, the School sought to enforce the liquidated damages clause in Klyap's teaching contract for the stipulated amount of $4,100, 20% of the $20,500 salary. * * *

After Klyap resigned, the School attempted to find another teacher to take Klyap's place. Although at the time that Klyap was offered his contract the School had 80 potential applicants, only two viable applicants remained available. Right before classes started, the School was able to hire one of those applicants, a less experienced teacher, at a salary of $19,500.

* * * After a bench trial, the District Court determined the clause was enforceable * * * because the damages suffered by the School [were] impractical and extremely difficult to fix. Specifically, the court found the School suffered damages because it had to spend additional time setting up an interview committee, conducting interviews, training the new, less experienced teacher, and reorganizing the sports program. The District Court also found that all these activities took away from the other school and administrative duties that had been scheduled for that time and that the new teacher missed all the staff development training earlier that year. Finally, the court found that such clauses are commonly used in Montana and that the School had routinely and equitably enforced the clause against other teachers. After concluding that the School took appropriate steps to mitigate its damages, the court awarded judgment in favor of the School in the amount of $4,100. * * *

* * *

The fundamental tenet of modern contract law is freedom of contract; parties are free to mutually agree to terms governing their private conduct as long as those terms do not conflict with public laws. [Citation.] This tenet presumes that parties are in the best position to make decisions in their own interest. Normally, in the course of contract interpretation by a court, the court simply gives effect to the agreement between the parties in order to enforce the private law of the contract. [Citation.] When one party breaches the contract, judicial enforcement of the contract ensures the nonbreaching party receives expectancy damages, compensation equal to what that party would receive if the contract were performed. [Citations.] By only awarding expectancy damages rather than additional damages intended to punish the breaching party for failure to perform the contract, court enforcement of private contracts supports the theory of efficient breach. In other words, if it is more efficient for a party to breach a contract and pay expectancy damages in order to enter a superior contract, courts will not interfere by requiring the breaching party to pay more than was due under their contract. [Citation.]

Liquidated damages are, in theory, an extension of these principles. Rather than wait until the occurrence of breach, the parties to a contract are free to agree in advance on a specific damage amount to be paid upon breach. [Citation.] This amount is intended to predetermine expectancy damages. Ideally, this predetermination is intended to make the agreement between the parties more efficient. Rather than requiring a post-breach inquiry into damages between the parties, the breaching party simply pays the nonbreaching party the stipulated amount. Further, in this way, liquidated damages clauses allow parties to estimate damages that are impractical or difficult to prove, as courts cannot enforce expectancy damages without sufficient proof.

* * *

In order to determine whether a clause should be declared a penalty, courts attempt to measure the reasonableness of a liquidated damages clause. * * * As indicated by * * * §356 of the RESTATEMENT (SECOND) OF CONTRACTS (1965) (hereinafter RESTATEMENT §356), the threshold indicator of reasonableness is whether the situation involves damages of a type that are impractical or extremely difficult to prove. * * *

According to RESTATEMENT §356 and other treatises, damages must be reasonable in relation to the damages the parties anticipated when the contract was executed or in relation to actual damages resulting from the breach.

* * *

* * * Liquidated damages in a personal service contract induce performance by an employee by predetermining compensation to an employer if the employee leaves. However, the employer clearly prefers performance by the specific employee because that employee was chosen for hire. The preference for performance by a specific person is reflected in the rule that personal service contracts are not assignable. Further, because personal service contracts are not enforceable by specific performance, [citation], liquidated damages are an appropriate way for employers to protect their interests. * * *

* * *

After reviewing the facts of this case, we hold that while the 20% liquidated damages clause is definitely harsher than most, it is still within Klyap's reasonable expectations and is not unduly oppressive. First, as the School pointed out during testimony, at such a small school teachers are chosen in part depending on how their skills complement those of the other teachers. Therefore, finding someone who would provide services equivalent to Klyap at such a late date would be virtually impossible. This difficulty was born out when only two applicants remained available and the School hired a teacher who was less experienced than Klyap. As a teacher, especially one with experience teaching at that very School, Klyap would have to be aware of the problem finding equivalent services would pose.

Second, besides the loss of equivalent services, the School lost time for preparation for other activities in order to attempt to find equivalent services. * * * Further, the new teacher missed all the staff development training earlier that year so individual training was required. And finally, because Klyap was essential to the sports program, the School had to spend additional time reorganizing the sports program as one sport had to be eliminated with Klyap's loss. These activities all took away from the other school and administrative duties that had been scheduled for that time. * * *

Finally, although the School testified it had an intent to secure performance and avoid the above damages by reason of the clause, * * *, such an intent does not turn a liquidated damages clause into a penalty unless the amount is unreasonably large and therefore not within reasonable expectations. * * *

Therefore, because as a teacher Klyap would know teachers are typically employed for an entire school year and would know how difficult it is to replace equivalent services at such a small rural school, it was within Klyap's reasonable expectations to agree to a contract with a 20% of salary liquidated damages provision for a departure so close to the start of the school year.

* * * Accordingly, we hold the District Court correctly determined that the liquidated damages provision was enforceable.

[Affirmed.]

---

## CASE 18-3

### Specific Performance
## REAL ESTATE ANALYTICS, LLC v. VALLAS

Court of Appeal, Fourth District, Division 1, California, 2008
160 Cal.App.4th 463, 72 Cal.Rptr.3d 835, review denied 2008
http://caselaw.findlaw.com/data2/californiastatecases/D049161.pdf

**Haller, J.**

Real Estate Analytics, LLC (REA) is a limited liability company formed by Troy Shadian. In January 2004, Shadian and his business partner, Roshan Bhakta, became interested in [Theodore Tee] Vallas's 14.13-acre property (the Lanikai Lane property) located in Carlsbad [California] near the Pacific Coast Highway. The property contained a mobilehome park with 147 individual mobilehomes and numerous amenities, including a pool, playground, laundry facilities, and a long winding street. Vallas leased the property to a mobilehome park operator, which managed the park and subleased the spaces to residents who owned their mobilehomes. The lease began in 1951 and terminates in 2013.

* * *

* * * [I]n March 2004, REA and Vallas entered into a written purchase and sale agreement. Under the agreement, the sales price was $8.5 million, with REA to pay an immediate $100,000 deposit, and then pay $2.9 million at closing. In return, Vallas agreed to finance the remaining $5.5 million, with the unpaid balance to be paid over a five-year period, with the balance due on April 1, 2009.

REA's primary goal in purchasing the property was to make a profit for its investors. One proposed business model was to subdivide the property and sell the subdivided lots to the property's mobilehome park residents. Shadian and Bhakta intended to make a substantial monetary profit through this investment.

* * *

[On June 14 Vallas cancelled the contract. The next day REA brought a breach of contract action seeking specific performance. The court, sitting without a jury, found Vallas breached the contract but refused to grant specific performance and instead awarded REA damages of $500,000, reflecting the difference between the contract price and the fair market value at the time of the breach.]

* * * [T]he court declined to award specific performance based on its finding that damages would provide REA adequate relief. * * * [T]he court found specific performance was not appropriate because REA purchased the property "solely as a commodity" to earn "money for their investors," and not because of the "uniqueness" of the property itself.

* * *

REA contends the court erred in refusing to order specific performance of the parties' real estate contract.

* * *

To obtain specific performance after a breach of contract, a plaintiff must generally show: (1) the inadequacy of his legal remedy; (2) an underlying contract that is both reasonable and supported by adequate consideration; (3) the existence of a mutuality of remedies; (4) contractual terms which are sufficiently definite to enable the court to know what it is to enforce; and (5) a substantial similarity of the requested performance to that promised in the contract. [Citations.] * * *

In this case, the court refused to specifically enforce the contract based on its finding that the first element (inadequacy of legal remedy) was not satisfied because REA sought to purchase the property as an investment, and not for some particular use of the land. REA contends this finding was incorrect as a matter of law and, alternatively, unsupported by the evidence.

It is a familiar legal principle that a damage award is generally an inadequate remedy for a breach of real estate contract, and therefore courts routinely grant a plaintiff's request for specific performance. [Citation.] This rule arose in medieval England where land ownership was a primary indicator of the owner's social status and voting rights. [Citations.] * * *

Although these historical reasons no longer apply, most jurisdictions have continued the rules requiring special treatment of land sale contracts, reflecting the enduring view that: (1) each parcel of land is unique and therefore there can be no adequate replacement after a breach; and (2) monetary damages are difficult to calculate after a party refuses to complete a land sales contract, particularly expectation damages. (See Rest.2d Contracts, § 360.) * * * [L]egislatures and the courts have largely adhered to the rule that specific performance is the appropriate remedy upon a breach of a real estate contract.

In California, these principles are embodied in section 3387. Section 3387 states:

> It is to be presumed that the breach of an agreement to transfer real property cannot be adequately relieved by pecuniary compensation. In the case of a single-family dwelling which the party seeking performance intends to occupy, this presumption is conclusive. In all other cases, this presumption is a presumption affecting the burden of proof.

By imposing a conclusive presumption for certain residential transactions, the Legislature decided that monetary damages can never be satisfactory compensation for a buyer who intends to live at a single-family home, regardless of the circumstances. But by establishing a rebuttable presumption with respect to other property, the Legislature left open the possibility that damages can be an adequate remedy for a breach of a real estate contract. The rebuttable presumption shifts the burden of proof to the breaching party to prove the adequacy of the damages. By so doing, the Legislature intended that a damages remedy for a nonbreaching party to a commercial real estate contract is the exception rather than the rule.

* * *

* * * By imposing a rebuttable presumption on the inadequacy of remedy element for certain types of purchases, the Legislature necessarily contemplated that there may be circumstances when the presumption that damages are inadequate can be overcome. * * *

But the specific issue presented here is not whether a defendant can ever rebut the inadequacy of remedy presumption. The issue is whether Vallas did so in this case. And on this issue, we agree with REA that Vallas did not make a sufficient evidentiary showing to establish damages were adequate to compensate REA for the breach. * * * Although it did not need to do so, REA produced strong evidence to support the presumption. This evidence showed that the Lanikai Lane property is unique in terms of its size, location, and existing use—it consists of 14.13 acres near the Pacific Ocean and contains an established mobilehome community. The property has ocean views and is close to several desirable local beaches, two major vacation resorts, the Del Mar racetrack, expensive neighborhoods, and major transportation routes. REA's evidence also showed that Lanikai Lane is unique in terms of the potential profits resulting from ownership because of its existing use (mobilehome park) on a long-term lease that would terminate in 2013, and the fact that existing residents would like to obtain ownership interests in the property. REA purchased the property for investment purposes, and it intended to obtain the highest return on this investment by subdividing the property and selling it to the existing residents of the park, which could result in substantial profits.

Given the statutory presumption that damages were inadequate and the largely undisputed evidence strongly supporting this presumption, Vallas had a high threshold to satisfy his burden to show damages would be an adequate remedy. * * *

* * *

* * * Thus, although REA did not necessarily intend to benefit from its personal or commercial *use* of the land, the land did have a particular unique value because of the manner in which it could be used to earn profits upon a resale. * * * Missing from the court's analysis was the recognition that to rebut the presumption that damages are an inadequate remedy, the defendant must come forward with evidence showing that damages will fully compensate the plaintiff for the breach. The record in this case was bereft of any such evidence.

Judgment reversed. The court is ordered to enter a new judgment granting specific performance and to strike the alternate damages remedy. * * *

CASE 18-4

Injunctions

## MADISON SQUARE GARDEN CORP., ILL. v. CARNERA

United States Court of Appeals, Second Circuit, 1931
52 F.2d 47

**Chase, J.**

Suit by plaintiff, Madison Square Garden Corporation, against Primo Carnera, defendant. From an order granting an injunction against defendant, defendant appeals.

On January 13, 1931, the plaintiff and defendant by their duly authorized agents entered into the following agreement in writing:

1. Carnera agrees that he will render services as a boxer in his next contest (which contest, hereinafter called the "First Contest," shall be with the winner of the proposed Schmeling-Stribling contest, or, if the same is drawn, shall be with Schmeling, and shall be deemed to be a contest for the heavyweight championship title; provided, however, that, in the event of the inability of the Garden to cause Schmeling or Stribling, as the case may be, to perform the terms of his agreement with the Garden calling for such contest, the Garden shall be without further liability to Carnera) exclusively under the auspices of the Garden, in the United States of America, or the Dominion of Canada, at such time, not, however, later than midnight of September 30, 1931, as the Garden may direct. * * *

**9.** Carnera shall not, pending the holding of the First Contest, render services as a boxer in any major boxing contest, without the written permission of the Garden in each case had and obtained. A major contest is understood to be one with Sharkey, Baer, Campolo, Godfrey, or like grade heavyweights, or heavyweights who shall have beaten any of the above subsequent to the date hereof. If in any boxing contest engaged in by Carnera prior to the holding of the First Contest, he shall lose the same, the Garden shall at its option, to be exercised by a two weeks' notice to Carnera in writing, be without further liability under the terms of this agreement to Carnera. Carnera shall not render services during the continuance of the option referred to in paragraph 8 hereof for any person, firm or corporation other than the Garden. Carnera shall, however, at all times be permitted to engage in sparring exhibitions in which no decision is rendered and in which the heavyweight championship title is not at stake, and in which Carnera boxes not more than four rounds with any one opponent. * * *

Thereafter the defendant, without the permission of the plaintiff, written or otherwise, made a contract to engage in a boxing contest with the Sharkey mentioned in paragraph 9 of the agreement above quoted, and by the terms thereof the contest was to take place before the first contest mentioned in the defendant's contract with the plaintiff was to be held.

The plaintiff then brought this suit to restrain the defendant from carrying out his contract to box Sharkey, and obtained the preliminary injunction order, from which this appeal was taken. Jurisdiction is based on diversity of citizenship and the required amount is involved.

The District Court has found on affidavits which adequately show it that the defendant's services are unique and extraordinary. A negative covenant in a contract for such personal services is enforceable by injunction where the damages for a breach are incapable of ascertainment. [Citations.]

The defendant points to what is claimed to be lack of consideration for his negative promise, in that the contract is inequitable and contains no agreement to employ him. It is true that there is no promise in so many words to employ the defendant to box in a contest with Stribling or Schmeling, but the agreement read as a whole binds the plaintiff to do just that, providing either Stribling or Schmeling becomes the contestant as the result of the match between them and can be induced to box the defendant. The defendant has agreed to "render services as a boxer" for the plaintiff exclusively, and the plaintiff has agreed to pay him a definite percentage of the gate receipts as his compensation for so doing. The promise to employ the defendant to enable him to earn the compensation agreed upon is implied to the same force and effect as though expressly stated. * * * [Citations.]

As we have seen, the contract is valid and enforceable. It contains a restrictive covenant which may be given effect. Whether a preliminary injunction shall be issued under such circumstances rests in the sound discretion of the court. [Citations.] The District Court, in its discretion, did issue the preliminary injunction and required the plaintiff as a condition upon its issuance to secure its own performance of the contract in suit with a bond for $25,000 and to give a bond in the sum of $35,000 to pay the defendant such damages as he may sustain by reason of the injunction. Such an order is clearly not an abuse of discretion.

Order affirmed.

## QUESTIONS

1. Explain how compensatory and reliance damages are computed.
2. Define
   - (a) nominal damages,
   - (b) incidental damages,
   - (c) consequential damages,
   - (d) foreseeability of damages,
   - (e) punitive damages,
   - (f) liquidated damages, and
   - (g) mitigation of damages.
3. Define the various types of equitable relief and discuss when the courts will grant such relief.
4. Explain how restitutionary damages are computed and identify the situations in which restitution is available as a contractual remedy.
5. Identify and explain the limitations on contractual remedies.

## PROBLEMS

**1.** Edward, a candy manufacturer, contracted to buy one thousand barrels of sugar from Marcia. Marcia failed to deliver, and Edward was unable to buy any sugar in the market. As a direct consequence he was unable to make candies to fulfill unusually lucrative contracts for the Christmas trade.

**(a)** What damages is Edward entitled to recover?

**(b)** Would it make any difference if Edward had told Marcia that he wanted the sugar to make candies for the Christmas trade and that he had accepted lucrative contracts for delivery for the Christmas trade?

**2.** Daniel agreed to erect an apartment building for Steven for $12 million and that Daniel would suffer a deduction of $12,000 per day for every day of delay. Daniel was twenty days late in finishing the job, losing ten days because of a strike and ten days because the material suppliers were late in furnishing materials. Daniel claims that he is entitled to payment in full (a) because the agreement as to $12,000 a day is a penalty and (b) because Steven has not shown that he has sustained any damage. Discuss each contention and decide.

**3.** Sharon contracted with Jane, a shirtmaker, for one thousand shirts for men. Jane manufactured and delivered five hundred shirts, which were paid for by Sharon. At the same time, Sharon notified Jane that she could not use or dispose of the other five hundred shirts and directed Jane not to manufacture any more under the contract. Nevertheless, Jane proceeded to make up the other five hundred shirts and tendered them to Sharon. Sharon refused to accept the shirts, and Jane then sued for the purchase price. Is she entitled to the purchase price? If not, is she entitled to any damages? Explain.

**4.** Stuart contracts to act in a comedy for Charlotte and to comply with all theater regulations for four seasons. Charlotte promises to pay Stuart $1,800 for each performance and to allow Stuart one benefit performance each season. It is expressly agreed "Stuart shall not be employed in any other production for the period of the contract." During the first year of the contract, Stuart and Charlotte have a terrible quarrel. Thereafter, Stuart signs a contract to perform in Elaine's production and ceases performing for Charlotte. Charlotte seeks (a) to prevent Stuart from performing for Elaine, and (b) to require Stuart to perform his contract with Charlotte. What result?

**5.** Louis leased a building to Pam for five years at a rental of $1,000 per month, Pam depositing $10,000 as security for performance of all her promises in the lease, which was to be retained by Louis in case of any breach on Pam's part. Pam defaulted in the payment of rent for the last two months of the lease. Louis refused to return any of the deposit, claiming it as liquidated damages. Pam sued Louis to recover $8,000 (the $10,000 deposit less the amount of rent due Louis for the last two months). What amount of damages should Pam be allowed to collect from Louis? Explain.

**6.** In which of the following situations is specific performance available as a remedy?

**(a)** Mary and Anne enter into a written agreement under which Mary agrees to sell and Anne agrees to buy for $100 per share one hundred shares of the three hundred shares outstanding of the capital stock of the Infinitesimal Steel Corporation, whose shares are not listed on any exchange and are closely held. Mary refuses to deliver when tendered the $10,000.

**(b)** Modifying (a) above, assume that the subject matter of the agreement is stock of the United States Steel Corporation, which is traded on the New York Stock Exchange.

**(c)** Modifying (a) above, assume that the subject matter of the agreement is undeveloped farmland of little commercial value.

**7.** On March 1, Joseph sold to Sandra fifty acres of land in Oregon, which Joseph at the time represented to be fine black loam, high, dry, and free of stumps. Sandra paid Joseph the agreed price of $140,000 and took from him a deed to the land. Subsequently discovering that the land was low, swampy, and not entirely free of stumps, Sandra nevertheless undertook to convert the greater part of the land into cranberry bogs. After one year of cranberry culture, Sandra became entirely dissatisfied, tendered the land back to Joseph, and demanded from Joseph the return of the $140,000. Upon Joseph's refusal to repay the money, Sandra brings an action against him to recover the $140,000. What judgment?

**8.** James contracts to make repairs to Betty's building in return for Betty's promise to pay $12,000 upon completion of the repairs. After partially completing the repairs, James is unable to continue. Betty refuses to pay James and hires another builder, who completes the repairs for $5,000. The building's value to Betty has increased by $10,000 as a result of the repairs by James, but Betty has lost $500 in rents because of the delay caused by James's breach. James sues Betty. How much, if any, may James recover in restitution from Betty?

**9.** Linda induced Sally to enter into a purchase of a home theater receiver by intentionally misrepresenting the power output to be seventy-five watts when in fact the unit delivered only forty watts. Sally paid $450 for the receiver. Receivers producing forty watts generally sell for $200, whereas receivers producing seventy-five watts generally sell for $550. Sally decides to keep the receiver and sue for damages. How much may Sally recover in damages from Linda?

**10.** Virginia induced Charles to sell his boat to her by misrepresentation of material fact upon which Charles reasonably relied. Virginia promptly sold the boat to Donald, who paid fair value for it and knew nothing concerning the transaction between Virginia and Charles. Upon discovering the misrepresentation, Charles seeks to recover the boat. What are Charles's rights against Virginia and Donald?

**11.** Felch was employed as a member of the faculty of Findlay College under a contract that permitted dismissal only for cause. He was dismissed by action of the President and Board of Trustees, which did not comply with a contractual provision for dismissal that requires a hearing. Felch requested the court to grant specific performance of the contract and require Findlay College to continue Felch as a member of the faculty and to pay him the salary agreed upon. Is Felch entitled to specific performance? Explain.

**12.** Copenhaver, the owner of a laundry business, contracted with Berryman, the owner of a large apartment complex, to allow Copenhaver to own and operate the laundry facilities within the apartment complex. Berryman subsequently terminated the five-year contract with Copenhaver with forty-seven months remaining. Within six months, Copenhaver placed the equipment into use in other locations and generated at least as much income as he would have earned at Berryman's apartment complex. He then filed suit, claiming that he was entitled to conduct the laundry operations for an additional forty-seven months and that through such operations he would have earned a profit of $13,886.58, after deducting Berryman's share of the gross receipts and other operating expenses. Decision?

**13.** Billy Williams Builders and Developers (Williams) entered into a contract with Hillerich under which Williams agreed to sell to Hillerich a certain lot and to construct on it a house according to submitted plans and specifications. The house built by Williams was defectively constructed. Hillerich brought suit for specific performance of the contract and for damages resulting from the defective construction and delay in performance. Williams argued that Hillerich was not entitled to have both specific performance and damages for breach of the contract because the remedies were inconsistent and Hillerich had to elect one or the other. Explain whether Williams is correct in this assertion.

**14.** Developers under a plan approved by the city of Rye had constructed six luxury cooperative apartment buildings and were to construct six more. In order to obtain certificates of occupancy for the six completed buildings, the developers were required to post a bond with the city to ensure completion of the remaining buildings. The developers posted a $100,000 bond upon which the defendant, Public Service Mutual Insurance Company, as guarantor or surety, agreed to pay $200 for each day after the contractual deadline that the remaining buildings were not completed. After the contractual deadline, more than five hundred days passed without completion of the buildings. The city claims that its inspectors and employees will be required to devote more time to the project than anticipated because it has taken extra years to complete. It also claims that it will lose tax revenues for the years the buildings are not completed. Should the city prevail in its suit against the developers and the insurance company to recover $100,000 on the bond? Explain.

**15.** Kerr Steamship Company sent a telegram at a cost of $26.78 to the Philippines through the Radio Corporation of America. The telegram, which contained instructions in unintelligible code for loading cargo on one of Kerr's ships, was mislaid and never delivered. Consequently, the ship was improperly loaded and the cargo was lost. Kerr sued the Radio Corporation for $6,675.29 in profits lost on the cargo because of the Radio Corporation's failure to deliver the telegram. Should Kerr be allowed to recover damages from Radio? Explain.

**16.** El Dorado Tire Company fired Bill Ballard, a sales executive. Ballard had a five-year contract with El Dorado but was fired after only two years of employment. Ballard sued El Dorado for breach of contract. El Dorado claimed that any damages due to breach of the contract should be mitigated because of Ballard's failure to seek other employment after he was fired. El Dorado did not provide any proof showing the availability of comparable employment. Explain whether El Dorado is correct in its contention.

**17.** California and Hawaiian Sugar Company (C and H) is an agricultural cooperative in the business of growing sugarcane in Hawaii and transporting the raw sugar to its refinery in California for processing. Because of the seasonal nature of the sugarcane crop, availability of ships to transport the raw sugar immediately after harvest is imperative. After losing the services of the shipping company it had previously used, C and H decided to build its own ship, a Macababoo, which had two components, a tug and a barge. C and H contracted with Halter Marine to build the tug and with Sun Ship to build the barge. In finalizing the contract for construction of the barge, both C and H and Sun Ship were represented by senior management and by legal counsel. The resulting contract called for a liquidated damages payment of $17,000 per day that delivery of the completed barge was delayed. Delivery of both the barge and the tug were significantly delayed. Sun Ship paid the $17,000 per day liquidated damages amount and then sued to recover it, claiming that without the liquidated damages provision, C and H's legal remedy for money damages would have been significantly less than that paid by Sun Ship pursuant to the liquidated damages provision. Decision?

**18.** Bettye Gregg offered to purchase a house from Head & Seeman, Inc. (seller). Though she represented in writing that she had between $15,000 and $20,000 in equity in another home that she would pay to the seller after she sold the other home, she knew that she did not have such equity. In reliance upon these intentionally fraudulent representations, the seller accepted Gregg's offer and the parties entered into a land contract. After taking occupancy, Gregg failed to make any of the contract payments. The seller's investigations then revealed the fraud. Head & Seeman then brought suit seeking rescission of the contract, return of the real estate, and restitution. Restitution was sought for the rental value for the five months of lost use of the property and the seller's out-of-pocket expenses made in reliance upon the bargain. Gregg contends that under the election of remedies doctrine, the seller cannot both rescind the contract and recover damages for its breach. Is Gregg correct? Explain.

**19.** Watson agreed to buy Ingram's house for $355,000. The contract provided that Watson deposit $15,000 as earnest money and that "in the event of default by the Buyer, earnest money shall be forfeited to Seller as liquidated damages, unless Seller elects to seek actual damages or specific performance." Because Watson did not timely comply with all of the terms of the contract, nine months after the Watson sale was to occur, Ingram sold the house to a third party for $355,000. Is Ingram entitled to Watson's $15,000 earnest money as liquidated damages? Explain.

**20.** Sanders agreed in writing to write, direct, and produce a motion picture on the subject of lithography for the Tamarind Lithography Workshop. After the completion of this film, *Four Stones for Kanemitsu*, litigation arose concerning the parties' rights and obligations under their agreement. Tamarind and Sanders resolved this dispute by a written settlement agreement, whereby Tamarind promised to provide Sanders a screen credit stating: "A Film by Terry Sanders." Tamarind did not comply with this agreement and failed to include the screen credit for Sanders in the prints it subsequently distributed. Sanders sued Tamarind seeking damages for breach of the settlement agreement and specific performance to compel Tamarind's compliance with its obligation to provide the screen credit. To what remedies is Sanders entitled? Explain.

# PART 3
# Agency

## CHAPTER 19
Relationship of Principal and Agent

## CHAPTER 20
Relationship with Third Parties

# CHAPTER 19

# Relationship of Principal and Agent

By using agents, one person (the principal) may enter into any number of business transactions as though he had personally carried them out, thus multiplying and expanding his business activities. The law of agency, like the law of contracts, is basic to almost every other branch of business law. Practically every type of contract or business transaction can be created or conducted through an agent. Therefore, the place and importance of agency in the practical conduct and operation of business cannot be overemphasized.

This is particularly true in the case of partnerships, corporations, and other business associations. Partnership is founded on the agency of the partners. Each partner is an agent of the partnership and, as such, has the authority to represent and bind the partnership in all usual transactions of the partnership. A corporation, being an artificial legal entity, must act through the agency of its officers and employees. Limited liability companies act through the actions of their members, managers, or both. Thus, practically and legally, agency is an essential part of partnerships, corporations, and other business associations. In addition, sole proprietors also may employ agents in the operations of their business. Business, therefore, is largely conducted not by owners themselves but by their agents or representatives.

The law of agency divides broadly into two main and somewhat overlapping parts: the internal and the external. An agent functions as an agent by dealing with third persons, thereby establishing legal relationships between the principal and those third persons. These relationships, which constitute the external part of agency law, are discussed in the next chapter. This chapter will cover the internal relationship between principal and agent, including the nature of agency, the creation of an agency, the duties of agent to principal, the duties of principal to agent, and the termination of agency.

Agency is primarily governed by State common law. An orderly presentation of this law was found in the Restatement (Second) of the Law of Agency, published in 1958 by the American Law Institute (ALI). Regarded as a valuable authoritative reference work, the Restatement is extensively cited and quoted in reported judicial opinions and by legal scholars. In 2006, the ALI published the Restatement of the Law Third, Agency, which completely replaced the ALI's Restatement Second of Agency. This chapter and the next chapter will refer to the Third Restatement as the Restatement.

## NATURE OF AGENCY

**Agency** is a consensual relationship in which one person (the agent) acts as a representative of or otherwise acts on behalf of another person (the principal) with power to affect the legal rights and duties of the principal. Moreover, the principal has a right to control the actions of the agent. Restatement, Section 1.01.

An agent, therefore, is one who represents another, the principal, in business dealings with a third person; the operation of agency therefore involves three persons: the principal, the agent, and a third person who deals with the agent. In dealing with a third person, the agent acts for and in the name and place of the principal, who, along with the third person, is, if properly entered into, a party to the transaction. When the agent is dealing with the third person, the principal, in legal effect, is present in the person of the agent; and the result of the agent's functioning is exactly the same as if the principal had dealt directly with the third person. If, moreover, the existence and identity of the principal are disclosed, the agent acts not as a party but simply as an intermediary.

Within the scope of the authority granted to her by her principal, the agent may negotiate the terms of contracts with others and bind her principal to such contracts. In addition, the negligence of an agent who is an employee in conducting the business of her principal exposes the principal to tort liability for injury and loss suffered by third persons. The old maxim "*qui facit per alium, facit per se*" (he who acts through another, acts himself) accurately describes the relationship between principal and agent. The rights and liabilities of the parties where an agent enters into a contract with a third party or commits a tort against a third party are discussed in the next chapter.

### SCOPE OF AGENCY PURPOSES

As a general rule, a person may do through an agent whatever business activity he may accomplish personally. Conversely, whatever he cannot legally do himself, he cannot authorize another to do for him. Thus, a person may not validly authorize another to commit an illegal act or crime. Any such agreement is illegal and therefore unenforceable. Also, a person may not appoint an agent to perform acts that are so personal that their performance may not be delegated to another, as in the case of a contract for personal services. For example, Howard, a painter, contracts to paint a portrait of Doris. But Howard has one of his students execute the painting and tenders it to Doris. This is not a valid tender because the duty to paint Doris's portrait is not delegable.

### OTHER LEGAL RELATIONSHIPS

Two other legal relationships overlap with agency: employer-employee and principal-independent contractor. In the **employment relationship** (historically referred to as the master-servant relationship), for the purposes of vicarious liability discussed in the next chapter, an employee is an agent whose principal controls or has the right to control the manner and means of the agent's performance of work. Restatement, Section 7.07(3). All employees are agents, even those employees not authorized to contract on behalf of the employer or otherwise to conduct business with third parties. Thus, an assembly-line worker in a factory is an agent of the company employing her since she is subject to the employer's control, thereby consenting to act "on behalf" of the principal, but she does not have the right to bind the principal in contracts with third parties.

Although all employees are agents, not all agents are employees. Agents who are not employees are generally referred to as **independent contractors**. (The Third Restatement does not use this term.) In these cases, although the principal has the right of control over the agent, the principal does not control the manner and means of the agent's performance. For instance, an attorney retained to handle a particular transaction would be an independent contractor-agent regarding that particular transaction because the attorney is hired by the principal to perform a service, but the manner of the attorney's performance is not controlled by the principal. Other examples are auctioneers, brokers, and factors.

Finally, not all independent contractors are agents because the person hiring the independent contractor has no right of control over the independent contractor. For example, a taxicab driver hired to carry a person to the airport is not an agent of that person. Likewise, if Pam hires Bill to build a stone wall around her property, Bill is an independent contractor who is not an agent.

In determining whether an agent is an employee, the courts consider numerous factors, including the following:

**(a)** the extent of control that the agent and the principal have agreed the principal may exercise—or has exercised in practice—over details of the work;
**(b)** whether the agent is engaged in a distinct occupation or business;
**(c)** whether the type of work done by the agent is customarily done under a principal's direction or without supervision;
**(d)** the skill required in the agent's occupation;
**(e)** whether the agent or the principal supplies the tools and other instrumentalities required for the work and the place in which to perform it;
**(f)** the length of time during which the agent is engaged by a principal;
**(g)** whether the agent is paid by the job or by the time worked;
**(h)** whether the agent's work is part of the principal's regular business;
**(i)** whether the principal and the agent believe that they are creating an employment relationship; and
**(j)** whether the principal is or is not in business.

Restatement, Section 7.07.

The distinction between employee and independent contractor has several important legal consequences. For example, as discussed in the next chapter, a principal is liable for the torts committed by an employee within the scope of his employment but ordinarily is not liable for torts committed by an independent contractor. In addition, the obligations of a principal under numerous Federal and State statutes apply only to agents who are employees. These statutes cover such matters as labor relations, employment discrimination, disability, employee safety, workers' compensation, social security, minimum wage, and unemployment compensation. These and other statutory enactments affecting the employment relationship are discussed in *Chapter 43*.

◆ **SEE CASE 19-1**

## CREATION OF AGENCY

As previously stated, agency is a consensual relationship that the principal and agent may form by contract *or* agreement. The Restatement defines an agency relationship as "the fiduciary relationship that arises when one person (a 'principal') manifests assent to another person (an 'agent') that the agent shall act on the principal's behalf and subject to the principal's control, and the agent manifests assent or otherwise consents so to act." Section 1.01. Thus the agency relationship involves three basic elements: assent, control by the principal, and the agent's acting on behalf of the principal. A person can manifest assent or intention through written or spoken words or other conduct. Restatement, Section 1.03. Thus, whether an agency relationship has been created is determined by an *objective test.* If the principal requests another to act for him with respect to a matter and indicates that the other is to act without further communication, and the other consents to act, the relation of principal and agent exists. For example, Paula writes to Austin, a factor whose business is purchasing goods for others, telling him to select described goods and ship them at once to Paula. Before answering Paula's letter, Austin does as directed, charging the goods to Paula. He is authorized to do this because an agency relationship exists between Paula and Austin.

The principal has the right to control the conduct of the agent with respect to the matters entrusted to the agent. Restatement, Section 1.01.

The principal's right to control continues throughout the duration of the agency relationship. The relationship of principal and agent is consensual and not necessarily contractual; therefore, it may exist without consideration. Restatement, Section 1.04(3). Even though the agency relationship is consensual, how the parties label the relationship does not determine whether it is an agency. Section 1.02. An agency created without an agent's right to compensation is a **gratuitous agency**. For example, Patti asks her friend Andrew to return for credit goods recently purchased from a store. If Andrew consents, a gratuitous agency has been created. The power of a gratuitous agent to affect the principal's relationships with third persons is the same as that of a paid agent, and his liabilities to and rights against third persons also are the same. Nonetheless, agency by contract, the most usual method of creating the relationship, must satisfy all the requirements of a contract.

In some circumstances a person is held liable as a principal, even though no actual agency has been created, in order to protect third parties who justifiably rely on a reasonable belief that a person is an agent and who act on that belief to their detriment. Called **agency by estoppel**, apparent agency, or ostensible agency, this liability arises when (1) a person ("principal") intentionally or carelessly causes a third party to believe that another person (the "agent") has authority to act on the principal's behalf; (2) the principal has notice of the third party's belief and does not take reasonable steps to notify the third party; (3) the third party reasonably and in good faith relies on the appearances created by the principal; and (4) the third party justifiably and detrimentally changes her position in reliance on the agent's apparent authority. Restatement, Section 2.05. When these requirements are met, the principal is liable to the third party for the loss the third party suffered by changing her position. The doctrine is applicable when the person against whom estoppel is asserted has made no manifestation that an actor has authority as an agent but is responsible for the third party's belief that an actor is an agent, and the third party has justifiably been induced by that belief to undergo a detrimental change in position. Restatement, Section 2.05.

◆ **SEE CASE 19-2**

## FORMALITIES

As a general rule, a contract of agency requires no particular formality. Usually the contract is express or inferred from the conduct of the principal. In some cases, however, the contract must be in writing. For example, the appointment of an agent for a period of more than a year comes within the one-year clause of the statute of frauds and thus must be in writing to be enforceable. In some States, the authority of an agent to sell land must be stated in a writing signed by the principal. Many States have "equal dignity" statutes providing that a principal must grant his agent in a written instrument the authority to enter into any contract required to be in writing. Restatement, Section 3.02. See *Chapter 15* for a discussion of State and Federal legislation giving electronic records and signatures the legal effect of traditional writings and signatures.

A **power of attorney** is an instrument that states an agent's authority. Restatement, Section 1.04(7). A power of attorney is a formal manifestation from principal to agent, who is known as "an attorney in fact," as well as to third parties that evidences the agent's appointment and the nature or extent of the agent's authority. Under a power of attorney, a principal may, for example, appoint an agent not only to execute a contract for the sale of the principal's real estate, but also to execute the deed conveying title to the real estate to the third party. A number of States have created an optional statutory short-form power of attorney based on the Uniform Statutory Form Power of Attorney Act. In 2006, a new Uniform Power of Attorney Act was promulgated to replace the Uniform Statutory Form Power of Attorney Act. To date, only five States have adopted the 2006 Act.

## CAPACITY

The capacity of an individual to be a principal, and thus to act through an agent, depends upon the capacity of the principal to do the act herself. Restatement, Section 3.04(1). For example, contracts entered into by a minor or an incompetent not under a guardianship are voidable. Consequently, the appointment of an agent by a minor or an incompetent not under a guardianship and any resulting contracts are voidable, regardless of the agent's contractual capacity. The capacity of a person that is not an individual, such as a government or business association, is determined by the law governing that entity. Restatement, Section 3.04(2).

Almost all of the States have adopted the Uniform Durable Power of Attorney Act providing for a durable power of attorney under which an agent's power survives or is triggered by the principal's loss of mental competence. (In 2006, a new Uniform Power of Attorney Act was promulgated to replace Uniform Durable Power of Attorney Act. To date, only five States have adopted the 2006 Act.) A **durable power of attorney** is a written instrument that expresses the principal's intention that the agent's authority will not be affected by the principal's subsequent incapacity or that the agent's authority will become effective upon the principal's subsequent incapacity.

Any person able to act, including individuals, corporations, partnerships, and other associations, ordinarily has the capacity to act as an agent. Restatement, Section 3.05. Because the act of the agent is considered the act of the principal, the incapacity of an agent to bind himself by contract does not disqualify him from making a contract that is binding on his principal. The agent's liability, however, depends upon the agent's capacity to contract. Thus, although the contract of agency may be voidable, an authorized contract between the principal and the third person who dealt with the agent is valid.

An "electronic agent" is a computer program or other automated means used independently to initiate an action or respond to electronic records or performances in whole or in part without review or action by an individual. Electronic agents are not persons and, therefore, are not considered agents. In 2000, Congress enacted the Electronic Signatures in Global and National Commerce (E-Sign). The Act makes electronic records and signatures valid and enforceable across the United States for many types of transactions in or affecting interstate or foreign commerce. The Act validates contracts or other records relating to a transaction in or affecting interstate or foreign commerce formed by electronic agents so long as the action of each electronic agent is legally attributable to the person to be bound. E-Sign specifically excludes certain transactions, including (1) wills, codicils, and testamentary trusts; (2) adoptions, divorces, and other matters of family law; and (3) the Uniform Commercial Code other than sales and leases of goods.

## DUTIES OF AGENT TO PRINCIPAL

The duties of the agent to the principal are determined by the express and implied terms of any contract between the agent and the principal. Restatement, Section 8.07. In addition to these contractual duties, the agent is subject to various other duties imposed by law, unless the parties agree otherwise. Normally, a principal bases the selection of an agent on the agent's ability, skill, and integrity. Moreover, the principal not only authorizes and empowers the agent to bind her on contracts with third persons, but also frequently places the agent in possession of her money and other property. As a result, the agent is in a position, either through negligence or dishonesty, to injure the principal. Accordingly, an agent as a **fiduciary** (a person in a position of trust and confidence) owes his principal the duties of obedience, good conduct, diligence, and loyalty; the duty to inform; and the duty to provide an accounting. Moreover, the agent is subject to liability for loss caused to the principal by any breach of duty.

A gratuitous agent is subject to the same duty of loyalty that is imposed upon a paid agent and is liable to the principal for the harm he causes by his careless performance. Although the lack of consideration usually places a gratuitous agent under no duty to perform for the principal, such an agent may be liable to the principal for failing to perform a promise on which the principal has relied if the agent should have realized that his promise would induce reliance. Restatement, Section 8.07, comment c.

### DUTY OF OBEDIENCE

The duty of obedience requires the agent to act in the principal's affairs only as actually authorized by the principal and to obey all lawful instructions and directions of the principal. Restatement, Section 8.09. If an agent exceeds her actual authority, she is subject to liability to the principal for loss caused the principal. An agent is also liable to the principal for unauthorized acts that are the result of the agent's unreasonable interpretations of the principal's directions. An agent is not, however, under a duty to follow orders to perform illegal or tortious acts, such as misrepresenting the quality of his principal's goods or those of a competitor. Still, he may be subject to liability to his principal for breach of the duty of obedience (1) because he entered into an unauthorized contract for which his principal is liable, (2) because he has improperly delegated his authority, or (3) because he has committed a tort for which the principal is liable. Thus, an agent who sells on credit in violation of his principal's explicit instructions has breached the duty of obedience and is liable to the principal for any amounts the purchaser does not pay. Moreover, an agent who violates his duty of obedience materially breaches the agency contract and loses his right to compensation.

### DUTY OF GOOD CONDUCT

An agent has a duty, within the scope of the agency relationship, to act reasonably and to avoid conduct that is likely to damage the principal's interests. Restatement, Section 8.10. This duty reflects the fact that the conduct of agents can have a significant effect on the principal's reputation. A breach of this duty makes the agent liable to the principal and subject to rightful discharge or termination.

## DUTY OF DILIGENCE

Subject to any agreement with the principal, an agent has a duty to the principal to act with the care, competence, and diligence normally exercised by agents in similar circumstances. Special skills or knowledge possessed by an agent are circumstances to be taken into account in determining whether the agent acted with due care and diligence. Moreover, if the agent claims to possess special skill or knowledge, the agent has a duty to act with the care, competence, and diligence normally exercised by agents with such skill or knowledge. Restatement, Section 8.08. By failing to exercise the required care, competence, and diligence, she is liable to the principal for any resulting harm. For example, Peg appoints Alvin as her agent to sell goods in markets where the highest price can be obtained. Although by carefully obtaining information he could have obtained a higher price in a nearby market, Alvin sells goods in a glutted market, receiving only a low price. Consequently, he is liable to Peg for breach of the duty of diligence.

A gratuitous agent owes a standard of care that is reasonable to expect under the circumstances, which include the skill and experience that the agent possesses. Thus, providing a service gratuitously may subject an agent to duties of competence and diligence to the principal that do not differ from the duties owed by a compensated agent. Restatement, Section 8.08, comment e.

## DUTY TO INFORM

An agent has a duty to use reasonable effort to provide the principal with facts that the agent knows, has reason to know, or should know if (1) the agent knows, or has reason to know, that the principal would wish to have the facts; or (2) the facts are material to the agent's duties to the principal. However, this duty does not apply to facts if providing them to the principal would violate a superior duty owed by the agent to another person. Restatement, Section 8.11. The rule of agency providing that notice to an agent is notice to his principal makes this duty imperative. Restatement, Section 5.02. An agent who breaches this duty is subject to liability to the principal for loss caused the principal by the agent's breach and may also be subject to termination of the agency relationship. Moreover, if the agent's breach of this duty constitutes a breach of the contract between the agent and the principal, the agent is also liable for breach of contract.

Examples of information that an agent is under a duty to communicate to his principal include the following: (1) that a customer of the principal has become insolvent; (2) that a debtor of the principal has become insolvent; (3) that a partner of a firm with which the principal has previously dealt, and with which the principal or agent is about to deal, has withdrawn from the firm; or (4) that property which the principal has authorized the agent to sell at a specified price can be sold at a higher price.

## DUTY TO ACCOUNT

Subject to any agreement with the principal, an agent has a duty to keep and render accounts to the principal of money or other property received or paid out on the principal's account. Moreover, the agent may not mingle the principal's property with any other person's property and may not deal with the principal's property so that it appears to be the agent's property. Restatement, Section 8.12.

## FIDUCIARY DUTY

A **fiduciary duty** arises out of a relationship of trust and confidence and requires the utmost loyalty and good faith. An agent has a fiduciary duty to act loyally for the principal's benefit in all matters connected with the agency relationship. Restatement, Section 8.01. This duty is imposed by law upon the agent and is also owed by an employee to his employer. The principal may agree that conduct by an agent that would otherwise constitute a breach of the fiduciary duty shall not constitute a breach of that duty provided that in obtaining the principal's consent, the agent (1) acts in good faith, (2) discloses all material facts that the agent knows, has reason to know, or should know would reasonably affect the principal's judgment, and (3) otherwise deals fairly with the principal. Restatement, Section 8.06.

An agent's fiduciary duty to a principal generally begins with the formation of the agency relationship and ends with its termination. Restatement, Section 8.01. However, as discussed below, an agent may be subject to duties after termination applicable to the agent's use of the principal's property and confidential information provided by the principal.

The fiduciary duty arises most frequently in the following situations involving principals and their agents although it is by no means limited to these situations.

**Conflicts of Interest** An agent has a duty not to deal with the principal as, or on behalf of, an adverse party in a transaction connected with the agency relationship. Restatement, Section 8.03. An agent must act solely in the interest of his principal, not in his own interest or in the interest of another. In addition, an agent may not represent his principal in any transaction in which the agent has a personal interest. Nor may he act on behalf of adverse parties to a transaction without both principals' approval to the dual agency. An agent may take a position that conflicts with the interest of his principal only if the principal, with full knowledge of all of the facts, consents. For example, A, an agent of P who desires to purchase land, agrees with C, who represents B, a seller of land, that A and C will endeavor to effect a transaction between their principals and will pool their commissions. A and C have committed a breach of fiduciary duty to P and B.

**Self-Dealing** An agent has a duty not to deal with the principal as an adverse party in a transaction connected with the agency relationship. Restatement, Section 8.03. The courts closely scrutinize transactions between an agent and her principal. Because the agent may not deal at arm's length with her principal, she thus owes her principal a duty of full disclosure of all relevant facts that affect the transaction. Moreover, the transaction must be fair. Thus, an agent who is employed to buy may not buy from himself without the principal's consent. Restatement, Section 8.06. For example, Penny employs Albert to purchase for her a site suitable for a shopping center. Albert owns such a site and sells it to Penny at the fair market value, but does not disclose to Penny that he had owned the land. Penny may rescind the transaction. An agent who is employed to sell may not become the purchaser nor may he act as agent for the purchaser without the consent of the principal. The agent's loyalty must be undivided, and he must devote his actions exclusively to represent and promote the interests of his principal.

◆ **SEE CASE 19-3**

**Duty Not to Compete** During the agency relationship an agent must not compete with his principal or act on behalf or otherwise assist any of the principal's competitors. Restatement, Section 8.04. After the agency terminates without breach by the agent, however, unless otherwise agreed, the agent may compete with his former principal. The courts will enforce by injunction a contractual agreement by the agent not to compete after the agency terminates if the restriction is reasonable as to time and place and is necessary to protect the principal's legitimate interest. Contractual agreements not to compete are discussed in *Chapter 13* where it is noted that such noncompete contracts may be subject to different standards for Internet companies and their employees.

◆ **SEE CASE 13-2**

**Misappropriation** An agent may not use property of the principal for the agent's own purposes or for the benefit of a third party. Restatement, Section 8.05(1). Unless the principal consents, an agent who has possession of the principal's property has a duty to use it only on the principal's behalf even if the agent's use of the property does not cause harm to the principal. An agent is liable to the principal for any profit the agent made while using the principal's property or for the value of the agent's use of the principal's property. An agent's duties regarding the principal's property continue after the agency terminates, and a former agent has a duty to return any of the principal's property she still possesses.

**Confidential Information** An agent may not use or disclose confidential information obtained in the course of the agency for his own benefit or those of a third party. Restatement, Section 8.05(2). Confidential information is information that, if disclosed, would harm the principal's business or that has a value because it is not generally known. Such information includes unique business methods, trade secrets, business plans, personnel, nonpublic financial results, and customer lists. An agent may, however, reveal confidential information that the principal is committing, or is about to commit, a crime. Many statutes provided protection to employees who "whistle-blow."

Unless otherwise agreed, even after the agency terminates, the agent may not use or disclose to third persons confidential information. The agent may, however, utilize the generally known skills, knowledge, and information she acquired during the agency relationship.

**Duty to Account for Financial Benefits** Unless otherwise agreed, an agent has a duty not to acquire any financial or other material benefits in connection with transactions conducted on behalf of the principal. Restatement, Section 8.02. Such benefits would include bribes, kickbacks, and gifts. Moreover, an agent may not profit secretly from any transaction subject to the agency. All material benefits, including secret profits, belong to the principal, to whom the agent must account. In addition, the principal may recover any damages caused by the agent's breach. Thus, if an agent, authorized to sell certain property of his principal for $1,000, sells it for $1,500, he may not secretly pocket the additional $500. Further, suppose Peabody employs real estate broker Anderson to sell his land for a commission of 6 percent of the sale price. Anderson, knowing that Peabody is willing to sell for $20,000, agrees secretly with a prospective buyer who is willing to pay $22,000 for the land that he will endeavor to obtain Peabody's consent to sell for $20,000, in which event the buyer will pay Anderson $1,000, or one-half of the amount that the buyer believes she is saving on the price. The broker has violated his fiduciary duty and must pay to Peabody the secret profit of $1,000. Furthermore, Anderson loses the right to any commission on the transaction.

**Principal's Remedies** An agent who violates his fiduciary duty is liable to his principal for breach of contract, in tort for losses caused and possibly punitive damages, and in restitution for profits he made or property he received in breach of the fiduciary duty. Moreover, he loses the right to compensation. The principal may avoid a transaction in which the agent breached his fiduciary duty, even though the principal suffered no loss. A breach of fiduciary duty may also constitute just cause for discharge of the agent. Restatement, Section 8.01, comment d.

## DUTIES OF PRINCIPAL TO AGENT

Although both principal and agent have rights and duties arising out of the agency relationship, more emphasis is placed on the duties of the agent. This is necessarily so because of the nature of the agency relationship. First, the acts and services to be performed, both under the agency contract and as may be required by law, are to be performed mostly by the agent. Second, the agent is a fiduciary and as such is subject to the duties discussed earlier. Nonetheless, an agent has certain rights against the principal, both under the contract and by the operation of law. Correlative to these rights are certain duties, based in contract and tort law, which the principal owes to the agent.

◆ SEE FIGURE 19-1: **Duties of Principal and Agent**

### CONTRACTUAL DUTIES

An agency relationship may exist in the absence of a contract between the principal and agent. However, many principals and agents do enter into contracts, in which case a principal has a duty to act in accordance with the express and implied terms of any contract between the principal and the agent. Restatement, Section 8.13. The contractual duties owed by a principal to an agent are the duties of compensation, reimbursement, and indemnification; each may be excluded or modified by agreement between the principal and agent. Although a gratuitous agent is not owed a duty of compensation, she is entitled to reimbursement and indemnification.

As with any party to a contract, a principal is under a duty to perform his part of the contract according to its terms. The most important duty of the principal, from the standpoint of the agent, is to compensate the agent as specified in the contract. It is also the duty of the principal not to terminate the agency wrongfully. Whether the principal must furnish the agent with the means of employment or the opportunity for work will depend upon the particular case. For example, a principal who employs an agent to sell his goods must supply the agent with conforming goods, whereas in other cases, the agent must create his own opportunity for work, as in the case of a broker employed to procure a buyer for his principal's house. How far, if at all, the principal must assist or cooperate with the agent will depend on the particular agency. Usually, cooperation on the part of the principal is more necessary where the agent's compensation is contingent upon the success of his efforts than where the agent is paid a fixed salary regularly over a period of permanent employment.

**Compensation** A principal has a duty to compensate her agent unless the agent has agreed to serve gratuitously. If the agreement does not specify a definite compensation, a principal is under a duty to pay the reasonable value of the authorized services her agent has performed. Restatement, Section 8.13, comment d. An agent loses the right to compensation by (1) breaching the duty of obedience, (2) breaching the duty of loyalty, or (3) willfully and deliberately breaching the agency contract. Furthermore, an agent whose compensation depends upon her accomplishing a specific result is entitled to the agreed compensation only if she achieves the result within the time specified or within a reasonable time, if no time is stated. A common example is a listing agreement between a seller and a real estate broker providing for a commission to the broker if he finds a buyer ready, willing, and able to buy the property on the terms specified in the agreement. A principal also has a duty to maintain and provide to the agent a true and complete account of the money or property due to her.

◆ FIGURE 19-1: **Duties of Principal and Agent**

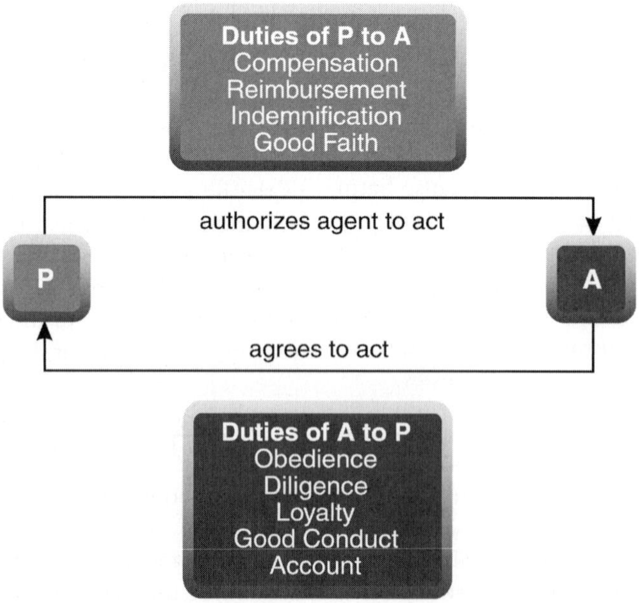

**Indemnification and Reimbursement** In general, a principal has an obligation to **indemnify** (compensate for a loss) an agent whenever the agent makes a payment or incurs an expense or other loss while acting as authorized on behalf of the principal. The contract between the principal and agent may specify the extent of this duty. In the absence of any contractual provisions, a principal has a duty to **reimburse** the agent when the agent makes a payment within the scope of the agent's actual authority. Restatement, Section 8.14. For example, an agent who reasonably and properly pays a fire insurance premium for the protection of her principal's property is entitled to reimbursement for the payment.

A principal also has a duty to indemnify the agent when the agent suffers a loss that fairly should be borne by the principal in light of their relationship. Restatement, Section 8.14. For example, suppose that Perry, the principal, has in his possession goods belonging to Margot. Perry directs Alma, his agent, to sell these goods. Alma, believing Perry to be the owner, sells the goods to Turner. Margot then sues Alma for the conversion of her goods and recovers a judgment, which Alma pays to Margot. Alma is entitled to indemnification from Perry for her loss, including the amount she reasonably expended in defense of the action brought by Margot.

**Tort and Other Duties** A principal owes to any agent the same duties under tort law that the principal owes to all parties. Moreover, a principal has a duty to deal with the agent fairly and in good faith. This duty requires that the principal provide the agent with information about risks of physical harm or monetary loss that the principal knows, has reason to know, or should know are present in the agent's work but are unknown to the agent. Restatement, Section 8.15. For instance, in directing his agent to collect rent from a tenant who is known to have assaulted rent collectors, the principal has a duty to warn the agent of the risk involved.

Where the agent is an employee, the principal owes the agent additional duties. Among these is the duty to provide reasonably safe conditions of employment and to warn the employee of any unreasonable risk involved in the employment. A negligent employer is also liable to her employees for injury caused by the negligence of other employees and of other agents doing work for her. The duties an employer owes to an employee are discussed more fully in *Chapter 43*.

## TERMINATION OF AGENCY

Because the authority of an agent is based upon the consent of the principal, the agency is terminated when such consent is withdrawn or otherwise ceases to exist. Upon termination of the agency, the agent's actual authority ends, and he is not entitled to compensation for services subsequently rendered. However, some of the agent's fiduciary duties may continue. The termination of *apparent* authority will be discussed in the next chapter. Termination may take place by the acts of the parties or by operation of law.

### ACTS OF THE PARTIES

Termination by the acts of the parties may occur by the provisions of the original agreement, by the subsequent acts of both principal and agent, or by the subsequent act of either one of them.

**Lapse of Time** An agent's actual authority terminates as agreed by the agent and the principal. Restatement, Section 3.09. Authority conferred upon an agent for a specified time terminates when that period expires. If no time is specified, authority terminates at the end of a reasonable period. Restatement, Section 3.09, comment d. For example, Palmer authorizes Avery to sell a tract of land for him. After ten years pass without communication between Palmer and Avery, though Avery purports to have sold the tract, his authorization has terminated due to lapse of time.

**Mutual Agreement of the Parties** The agency relationship is created by agreement and may be terminated at any time by mutual agreement of the principal and the agent. Restatement, Section 3.09(1).

**Revocation of Authority** A principal may revoke an agent's authority at any time by notifying the agent. Restatement, Section 3.10. If, however, such revocation constitutes a breach of contract, the agent may recover damages from the principal. For example, Patrick, in consideration of Alice's agreement to advertise and give her best energies to the sale of Patrick's property, Blackacre, grants to Alice "a power of attorney, irrevocable for one year." Alice advertises and spends time trying to sell Blackacre. At the end of three months, Patrick informs Alice that he is revoking the power of attorney. Although her authority is terminated, Alice may recover damages from Patrick. Restatement, Section 3.10, Illustration 2. Nonetheless, where the agent has seriously breached the agency contract, willfully disobeyed, or violated the fiduciary duty, the principal is not liable for terminating the agency relationship. In addition, a principal ordinarily may revoke a gratuitous agency without liability to the agent.

**Renunciation by the Agent** The agent also has the power to end the agency by notifying the principal that she renounces the authority given her. Restatement, Section 3.10. If the parties have contracted for the agency to continue for a specified time, an unjustified renunciation prior to the expiration of that time is a breach of contract. If the agency is gratuitous, however, the agent ordinarily may renounce it without liability to the principal.

## OPERATION OF LAW

The occurrence of certain events will automatically terminate an agency relationship by the operation of law. These events either make it impossible for the agent to perform or unlikely that the principal would want the agent to act. As a matter of law, the occurrence of any of the following events ordinarily terminates agency.

**DEATH** Because the authority given to an agent by a principal is strictly personal, the death of an individual agent terminates the agent's actual authority. The death of an individual principal also terminates the actual authority of the agent when the agent has notice of the principal's death. Restatement, Section 3.07. This is contrary to the Second Restatement, which took the position that the principal's death terminated the agent's actual authority whether the agent had notice or not. Section 120. For example, Polk employs Allison to sell Polk's line of goods under a contract specifying Allison's commission and the one-year period for which the employment is to continue. Without Allison's knowledge, Polk dies. Under the Second Restatement Allison no longer has authority to sell Polk's goods, even though the contract specified that she would be employed for one year. The death of Polk, the principal, terminated the authority of Allison the agent. Under the Third Restatement, on the other hand, Allison would continue to have actual authority until she received notice of Polk's death. A person has **notice** of a fact if the person knows the fact, has reason to know the fact, has received an effective notification of the fact, or should know the fact to fulfill a duty owed to another person. Restatement, Section 1.04(4). Moreover, the Uniform Durable Power of Attorney Act allows the holder of *any* power of attorney, durable or otherwise, to exercise it on the death of the principal, if its exercise is in good faith and without knowledge of the principal's death. Almost all of the States have adopted this act.

When an agent or principal is not an individual, the organizational statutes typically determine when authority terminates upon the cessation of the existence of that organization. (This will be discussed further in *Parts 6* and *7* of this book.) When the organizational statute does not specify, the Restatement provides the agent's actual authority terminates when the nonindividual principal or agent ceases to exist or begins a process that will lead to the cessation of its existence. Restatement, Section 3.07.

**INCAPACITY** Incapacity of the principal that occurs after the formation of the agency terminates the agent's actual authority when the agent has notice of the principal's incapacity. Restatement, Section 3.08. This is contrary to the Second Restatement, which took the position that the principal's incapacity terminated the agent's actual authority without notice to the agent. Section 122. To illustrate, Powell authorizes Anna to sell in the next ten months an apartment complex for not less than $2 million. Without Anna's knowledge, Powell is adjudicated incompetent two months later. Under the Second Restatement Anna's authority to sell the apartment complex is terminated. Under the Third Restatement Anna would continue to have actual authority until she received notice of Powell's incapacity.

If an agent is appointed under a durable power of attorney, the authority of an agent survives, or is triggered by, the incapacity or disability of the principal. Moreover, the Uniform Durable Power of Attorney Act allows the holder of a power of attorney that is *not* durable to exercise it on the incapacity of the principal, if its exercise is in good faith and without knowledge of the principal's incapacity.

◆ **SEE CASE 19-4**

**CHANGE IN CIRCUMSTANCES** An agent's actual authority terminates whenever the agent should reasonably conclude that the principal no longer would assent to the agent's taking action on the principal's behalf. Restatement, Section 3.09(2). Thus, Patricia authorizes Aaron to sell her eighty acres of farmland for $800 per acre. Subsequently, oil is discovered on nearby land, which causes Patricia's land to increase greatly in value. Because Aaron knows of this, but Patricia does not, Aaron's authority to sell the land is terminated.

The Second Restatement specified a number of subsequent changes in circumstances that would terminate an agent's actual authority, including accomplishment of authorized act, bankruptcy of principal or agent, change in business conditions, loss or destruction of subject matter, disloyalty of agent, change in law, and outbreak of war. The Third Restatement takes a different approach by providing a basic rule that an agent acts with actual authority "when, *at the time of taking action* that has legal consequences for the principal, the agent reasonably believes, in accordance with the principal's manifestations to the agent, that the principal wishes the agent so to act." Section 2.01 (emphasis added). Thus, if circumstances have changed such that, at the time the agent takes action, it is not reasonable for the agent to believe that the principal at that time consents to the action being taken on the principal's behalf, then the agent lacks actual authority so to act even though she would have had actual authority prior to the change in circumstances.

## IRREVOCABLE POWERS

A **power given as security** "is a power to affect the legal relations of its creator that is created in the form of a manifestation of actual authority and held for the benefit of the holder or a third person." Restatement, Section 3.12. A power given as security creates neither a relationship of agency nor actual authority, although the power enables its holder to affect the legal relations of the creator of the power. Restatement, Section 3.12, comment b. The power arises from a manifestation of assent by its creator that the holder of the power may, for example, dispose of property or other interests of the creator. To illustrate: Pillsbury owns Blackacre, which is situated next to Whiteacre, on which Pillsbury operates a restaurant. To finance renovations and expansions, Pillsbury borrows money from Ashton. A written agreement between Pillsbury and Ashton provides that Ashton shall irrevocably have Pillsbury's authority to transfer ownership of Blackacre to Ashton in the event Pillsbury defaults on the loan. Ashton has a power given as security. Restatement, Section 3.12, Illustration 1.

The Restatement's definition includes, but is more extensive than, the rule in some States regarding an **agency coupled with an interest**, in which the holder (agent) has a security interest in the power conferred upon him by the creator (principal). For example, an agency coupled with an interest would arise where an agent has advanced funds on behalf of the principal and the agent's power to act is given as security for the loan.

Unless otherwise agreed, a power given as security may *not* be revoked. In addition, the incapacity of the creator or of the holder of the power does not terminate the power. Nor will the death of the creator terminate the power, unless the duty for which the power was given terminates with the death of the creator. Restatement, Section 3.13(2). A power given as security *is* terminated by an event that discharges the obligation secured by it or that makes execution of the power illegal or impossible. Restatement, Section 3.13(1). Thus, in the example above, when the creator repays the loan, the power is terminated.

## CHAPTER SUMMARY

| | |
|---|---|
| NATURE OF AGENCY | **Definition of Agency** consensual relationship authorizing one party (the agent) to act on behalf of the other party (the principal) subject to the principal's control<br>**Scope of Agency Purposes** generally, whatever business activity a person may accomplish personally he may do through an agent<br>**Other Legal Relationships**<br>• ***Employment Relationship*** one in which the employer has the right to control the manner and means of the employee's performance of work<br>• ***Independent Contractor*** a person who contracts with another to do a particular job and who is not subject to the other's control over the manner and means of conducting the work |
| CREATION OF AGENCY | **Formalities** though agency is a consensual relationship that may be formed by contract or agreement between the principal and agent, agency may exist without consideration<br>• ***Requirements*** no particular formality usually is required in a contract of agency, although appointments of agents for a period of more than one year must be in writing<br>• ***Power of Attorney*** written, formal appointment of an agent<br>**Capacity**<br>• ***Principal*** if the principal is a minor or an incompetent not under a guardianship, his appointment of another to act as an agent is voidable, as are any resulting contracts with third parties<br>• ***Agent*** any person able to act may act as an agent, as the act of the agent is considered the act of the principal |
| DUTIES OF AGENT TO PRINCIPAL | **Duty of Obedience** an agent must act in the principal's affairs only as actually authorized by the principal and must obey all lawful instructions and directions of the principal<br>**Duty of Good Conduct** within the scope of the agency relationship, an agent must act reasonably and refrain from conduct that is likely to damage the principal's interests<br>**Duty of Diligence** an agent must act with reasonable care, competence, and diligence in performing the work for which he is employed<br>**Duty to Inform** an agent must use reasonable efforts to give the principal information material to the affairs entrusted to her<br>**Duty to Account** an agent must maintain and provide the principal with an accurate account of money or other property that the agent has received or expended on |

behalf of the principal; an agent must not mingle the principal's property with any other person's property

**Fiduciary Duty** an agent owes a duty of utmost loyalty and good faith to the principal; it includes:

- ***Conflicts of Interest***
- ***Self-dealing***
- ***Duty Not to Compete***
- ***Misappropriation***
- ***Confidential Information***
- ***Duty to Account for Financial Benefits***

**DUTIES OF PRINCIPAL TO AGENT**

**Contractual Duties**

- ***Compensation*** a principal must compensate the agent as specified in the contract, or for the reasonable value of the services provided, if no amount is specified
- ***Reimbursement*** the principal must pay back to the agent authorized payments the agent has made on the principal's behalf
- ***Indemnification*** the principal must pay the agent for losses the agent incurred while acting as directed by the principal

**Tort and Other Duties** include (1) the duty to provide an employee with reasonably safe conditions of employment and (2) the duty to deal with the agent fairly and in good faith

**TERMINATION OF AGENCY**

**Acts of the Parties**

- ***Lapse of Time***
- ***Mutual Agreement of the Parties***
- ***Revocation of Authority***
- ***Renunciation by the Agent***

**Operation of Law**

- ***Death*** of either the principal or the agent
- ***Incapacity*** of either the principal or the agent
- ***Change in Circumstances***

**Irrevocable Powers** a power given as security—including an agency coupled with an interest—is irrevocable

# CASES

## CASE 19-1 Other Legal Relationships: Employment versus Independent Contractors
## DEL PILAR v. DHL GLOBAL CUSTOMER SOLUTIONS (USA), INC.

District Court of Appeal of Florida, First District, 2008
993 So.2d 142
caselaw.findlaw.com/data2/floridastatecases/app/app1_10_2008/07-5140.pdf

**Kahn, J.**

Appellant sustained injuries when his car collided with a delivery van painted in the widely recognized DHL livery, driven by a driver clad in DHL uniform and laden with packages destined for DHL customers in Duval County [Florida] and beyond. Discovery in the negligence lawsuit stemming from the accident, revealed the van was owned not by DHL, but by Johnny Boyd, a driver for Silver Ink, Inc., a local company that was responsible at the time for picking up, sorting, and delivering all DHL packages in metropolitan Jacksonville. DHL, whose primary business focuses on shipping packages via air around the world, represented to both this court and the trial court that it has no capability to pick up or deliver local packages in Duval County and that, at the time of the accident, it relied exclusively on Silver Ink to provide such local services.

Accordingly, appellee's agreement with Silver Ink essentially delegated to Silver Ink the responsibility to service DHL customers in the Jacksonville area. The contract identified Silver Ink as an "independent contractor" and provided that "the manner and means by which Contractor performs the services shall be at Contractor's sole discretion and control and are Contractor's sole responsibility."The agreement also, however, recited an exhaustive and detailed list of procedures that Silver Ink employees were to follow in processing, picking up, and delivering packages, and contained an indemnity provision pursuant to which Silver Ink would indemnify DHL in the event Silver Ink lost or damaged packages bound for DHL's customers. The agreement conferred upon either party the power to terminate in the event of the other party's breach.

Silver Ink employees were contractually required to "wear a DHL uniform and properly display the DHL Marks (sic) and uniform in a clean, professional, and businesslike manner"; the contract specified the particular articles of clothing and accessories considered part of the DHL uniform, the purchase of which was funded by DHL. Silver Ink was required to submit to unannounced operational inspections and audits at DHL's sole discretion and was required to maintain a fleet of delivery vans operated in DHL livery, designed and placed on the vehicles in strict accordance with specifications established by DHL. Deposition testimony filed with the trial court established that Silver Ink's operational hub was co-located with DHL's Duval County facility and that DHL employees monitored and reviewed Silver Ink operations on a daily basis.

* * *

[Danny Del Pilar sued DHL for his personal injuries arising from the auto accident. The trial court granted summary judgment for DHL after concluding that Silver Ink was an independent contractor for whose alleged negligence DHL is not vicariously liable. Danny Del Pilar appealed.]

* * *

Generally, a principal is not vicariously liable for the negligence of its independent contractor, but the principal is liable for the negligence of its agent. [Citation.] Whether one laboring on behalf of another is a mere agent or an independent contractor "is a question of fact … not controlled by descriptive labels employed by the parties themselves." [Citations.]

A particularly significant factor in the determination of status is "the degree of control exercised by the employer or owner over the agent. More particularly, it is the *right* of control, and not *actual* control, which determines the relationship between the parties." [Citations.]

In most cases, the terms of a contract between the parties is a pertinent index of the principal's right of control and should factor heavily into the inquiry, "unless other provisions of the agreement, or the parties' actual practice, demonstrate that it is not a valid indicator of status [or] … belie the creation of the status agreed to by the parties." [Citation.] In that case, "the actual practice and relationship of the parties should control." [Citation.]

Elements of control that tend to suggest a relationship in which the principal is vicariously liable for the agent's negligence include, but are not limited to, (1) the principal's right to control the agent's use of the principal's trademarks, [citation]; (2) reservation to the principal of the unilateral right to prohibit the agent from working on behalf of competitors, [citations]; (3) a requirement that the agent's employees must undergo training before they work on the principal's behalf, [citation]; (4) a requirement that the agent perform services using only equipment selected pursuant to the principal's specifications, [citation]; (5) a requirement that the agent, when working on behalf of the principal, use a vehicle with the principal's logo, placed according to parameters established by the principal, [citation]; (6) a requirement that the agent adhere to customer-service procedures established by the principal, [citation]; and (7) a requirement that the agent submit to inspections conducted at the principal's discretion, [citation].

* * *

Here, the contract between appellee and Silver Ink certainly recites in conclusory terms the status of independent contractor; it identifies Silver Ink as an independent contractor and provides that "the manner and means by which Contractor performs the services shall be at Contractor's sole discretion and control and are Contractor's sole responsibility." This observation does not conclude the matter.

When we look, as we must, more deeply than the agreement's conclusory language, we find that, like provisions of the franchise agreement at issue in [citation], the balance of DHL's contract with Silver Ink "leaves nothing to chance." [Citation.] Somewhat inconsistently with the conclusory language purporting to confer broad discretion upon Silver Ink to fulfill its operational obligations, subsequent provisions list specific procedures and protocols that Silver Ink employees are to follow when picking up, sorting, and delivering DHL packages; everything from the process of scanning packages into DHL's tracking system to procedures for redelivery after unsuccessful delivery attempts is set out in detail in the agreement. Shippers and recipients are "DHL customers," and the agreement contains an indemnity provision requiring Silver Ink to indemnify DHL for damages stemming from packages lost or damaged due to Silver Ink's negligence, suggesting that DHL intends, in the first instance, to answer directly to its customers. The contract requires Silver Ink employees to "wear a DHL uniform and properly display the DHL Marks and uniform in a clean, professional, and businesslike manner," with further specification of the particular apparel considered part of the DHL uniform. Silver Ink must operate delivery vehicles painted in the DHL livery and must submit to unannounced operational inspections and audits at DHL's sole discretion. Silver Ink must pick up and deliver packages at times requested by DHL's customers pursuant to DHL's advertised guarantees.

* * * The trial court erred in concluding, as a matter of law, that Silver Ink was appellee's independent contractor. The question of DHL's control over Silver Ink operations should go to the jury. [Citations.]

* * *

Because the factual issue of Silver Ink's status presents a jury question, the summary judgment for appellee is REVERSED.

CASE 19-2

## Creation of Agency
## MILLER v. McDONALD'S CORPORATION

Court of Appeals of Oregon, 1997
150 Or.App. 274, 945 P.2d 1107

**Warren, J.**

Plaintiff seeks damages from defendant McDonald's Corporation for injuries that she suffered when she bit into a heart-shaped sapphire stone while eating a Big Mac sandwich that she had purchased at a McDonald's restaurant in Tigard. The trial court granted summary judgment to defendant on the ground that it did not own or operate the restaurant; rather, the owner and operator was a nonparty, 3K Restaurants (3K), that held a franchise from defendant. Plaintiff appeals, and we reverse.

Most of the relevant facts are not in dispute. * * * 3K owned and operated the restaurant under a License Agreement (the Agreement) with defendant that required it to operate in a manner consistent with the "McDonald's System." The Agreement described that system as including proprietary rights in trade names, service marks and trade marks, as well as "designs and color schemes for restaurant buildings, signs, equipment layouts, formulas and specifications for certain food products, methods of inventory and operation control, bookkeeping and accounting, and manuals covering business practices and policies."

The manuals contain "detailed information relating to operation of the Restaurant," including food formulas and specifications, methods of inventory control, bookkeeping procedures, business practices, and other management, advertising, and personnel policies. 3K, as the licensee, agreed to adopt and exclusively use the formulas, methods, and policies contained in the manuals, including any subsequent modifications, and to use only advertising and promotional materials that defendant either provided or approved in advance in writing.

The Agreement described the way in which 3K was to operate the restaurant in considerable detail. It expressly required 3K to operate in compliance with defendant's prescribed standards, policies, practices, and procedures, including serving only food and beverage products that defendant designated. 3K had to follow defendant's specifications and blueprints for the equipment and layout of the restaurant, including adopting subsequent reasonable changes that defendant made, and to maintain the restaurant building in compliance with defendant's standards. 3K could not make any changes in the basic design of the building without defendant's approval.

The Agreement required 3K to keep the restaurant open during the hours that defendant prescribed, including maintaining adequate supplies and employing adequate personnel to operate at maximum capacity and efficiency during those hours. 3K also had to keep the restaurant similar in appearance to all other McDonald's restaurants. 3K's employees had to wear McDonald's uniforms, to have a neat and clean appearance, and to provide competent and courteous service. 3K could use only containers and other packaging that bore McDonald's trademarks. The ingredients for the foods and beverages had to meet defendant's standards, and 3K had to use "only those methods of food handling and preparation that [defendant] may designate from time to time." In order to obtain the franchise, 3K had to represent that the franchisee had worked at a McDonald's restaurant; the Agreement did not distinguish in this respect between a company-run or a franchised restaurant. The manuals gave further details that expanded on many of these requirements.

In order to ensure conformity with the standards described in the Agreement, defendant periodically sent field consultants to the restaurant to inspect its operations. 3K trained its employees in accordance with defendant's materials and recommendations and sent some of them to training programs that defendant administered. Failure to comply with the agreed standards could result in loss of the franchise.

Despite these detailed instructions, the Agreement provided that 3K was not an agent of defendant for any purpose. Rather, it was an independent contractor and was responsible for all obligations and liabilities, including claims based on injury, illness, or death, directly or indirectly resulting from the operation of the restaurant.

Plaintiff went to the restaurant under the assumption that defendant owned, controlled, and managed it. So far as she could tell, the restaurant's appearance was similar to that of other McDonald's restaurants that she had patronized. Nothing disclosed to her that any entity other than defendant was involved in its operation. The only signs that were visible and obvious to the public had the name "McDonald's," the employees wore uniforms with McDonald's insignia, and the menu was the same that plaintiff had seen in other McDonald's restaurants. The general appearance of the restaurant and the food products that it sold were similar to the restaurants and products that plaintiff had seen in national print and television advertising that defendant had run. To the best of plaintiff's knowledge, only McDonald's sells Big Mac hamburgers.

* * *

Under these facts, 3K would be directly liable for any injuries that plaintiff suffered as a result of the restaurant's negligence. The issue on summary judgment is whether there is evidence that would permit a jury to find defendant vicariously liable for those injuries because of its relationship with 3K. Plaintiff asserts two theories of vicarious liability, actual agency and apparent agency. We hold that there is sufficient evidence to raise a jury issue under both theories. We first discuss actual agency.

The kind of actual agency relationship that would make defendant vicariously liable for 3K's negligence requires that defendant have the right to control the method by which 3K performed its obligations under the Agreement. The common context for that test is a normal master-servant (or employer-employee) relationship. [Citations.] The relationship between two business entities is not precisely an employment relationship, but the Oregon Supreme Court, in common with most if not all other courts that have considered the issue, has applied the right to control test for vicarious liability in that context as well. [Citation.] We therefore apply that test to this case.

* * *

A number of other courts have applied the right to control test to a franchise relationship. The Delaware Supreme Court, in [citation], stated the test as it applies to that context:

> If, in practical effect, the franchise agreement goes beyond the stage of setting standards, and allocates to the franchisor the right to exercise control over the daily operations of the franchise, an agency relationship exists. [Citation.]

* * *

* * * we believe that a jury could find that defendant retained sufficient control over 3K's daily operations that an actual agency relationship existed. The Agreement did not simply set standards that 3K had to meet. Rather, it required 3K to use the precise methods that defendant established, both in the Agreement and in the detailed manuals that the Agreement incorporated. Those methods included the ways in which 3K was to handle and prepare food. Defendant enforced the use of those methods by regularly sending inspectors and by its retained power to cancel the Agreement. That evidence would support a finding that defendant had the right to control the way in which 3K performed at least food handling and preparation. In her complaint, plaintiff alleges that 3K's deficiencies in those functions resulted in the sapphire being in the Big Mac and thereby caused her injuries. * * *

Plaintiff next asserts that defendant is vicariously liable for 3K's alleged negligence because 3K was defendant's apparent agent. The relevant standard is in Restatement (Second) of Agency, § 267, which we adopted in [citation]:

> One who represents that another is his servant or other agent and thereby causes a third person justifiably to rely upon the care or skill of such apparent agent is subject to liability to the third person for harm caused by the lack of care or skill of the one appearing to be a servant or other agent as if he were such. [Citation.]

We have not applied § 267 to a franchisor/franchisee situation, but courts in a number of other jurisdictions have done so in ways that we find instructive. In most cases the courts have found that there was a jury issue of apparent agency. The crucial issues are whether the putative principal held the third party out as an agent and whether the plaintiff relied on that holding out.

* * *

In this case * * * there is an issue of fact about whether defendant held 3K out as its agent. Everything about the appearance and operation of the Tigard McDonald's identified it with defendant and with the common image for all McDonald's restaurants that defendant has worked to create through national advertising, common signs and uniforms, common menus, common appearance, and common standards. The possible existence of a sign identifying 3K as the operator does not alter the conclusion that there is an issue of apparent agency for the jury. There are issues of fact of whether that sign was sufficiently visible to the public, in light of plaintiff's apparent failure to see it, and of whether one sign by itself is sufficient to remove the impression that defendant created through all of the other indicia of its control that it, and 3K under the requirements that defendant imposed, presented to the public.

Defendant does not seriously dispute that a jury could find that it held 3K out as its agent. Rather, it argues that there is insufficient evidence that plaintiff justifiably relied on that holding out. It argues that it is not sufficient for her to prove that she went to the Tigard McDonald's because it was a McDonald's restaurant. Rather, she also had to prove that she went to it because she believed that McDonald's Corporation operated both it and the other McDonald's restaurants that she had previously patronized. * * *

* * *

* * * in this case plaintiff testified that she relied on the general reputation of McDonald's in patronizing the Tigard restaurant and in her expectation of the quality of the food and service that she would receive. Especially in light of defendant's efforts to create a public perception of a common McDonald's system at all McDonald's restaurants, whoever operated them, a jury could find that plaintiff's reliance was objectively reasonable. The trial court erred in granting summary judgment on the apparent agency theory.

Reversed and remanded.

CASE 19-3

## Fiduciary Duty
## DETROIT LIONS, INC. v. ARGOVITZ

United States District Court, Eastern District of Michigan, 1984
580 F. Supp. 542, affirmed, 767 F. 2d 919

**Demascio, J.**

The plot for this Saturday afternoon serial began when Billy Sims, having signed a contract with the Houston Gamblers on July 1, 1983, signed a second contract with the Detroit Lions on December 16, 1983. On December 18, 1983, the Detroit Lions, Inc. (Lions) and Billy R. Sims filed a complaint in the Oakland County Circuit Court seeking a judicial determination that the July 1, 1983, contract between Sims and the Houston Gamblers, Inc. (Gamblers) is invalid because the defendant Jerry Argovitz (Argovitz) breached his fiduciary duty when negotiating the Gamblers' contract and because the contract was otherwise tainted by fraud and misrepresentation. * * *

For the reasons that follow, we have concluded that Argovitz's breach of his fiduciary duty during negotiations for the Gamblers' contract was so pronounced, so egregious, that to deny recision would be unconscionable.

Sometime in February or March 1983, Argovitz told Sims that he had applied for a Houston franchise in the newly formed United States Football League (USFL). In May 1983, Sims attended a press conference in Houston at which Argovitz announced that his application for a franchise had been approved. The evidence persuades us that Sims did not know the extent of Argovitz's interest in the Gamblers. He did not know the amount of Argovitz's original investment, or that Argovitz was obligated for 29 percent of a $1.5 million letter of credit, or that Argovitz was the president of the Gamblers' Corporation at an annual salary of $275,000 and 5 percent [of] the yearly cash flow. The defendants could not justifiably expect Sims to comprehend the ramifications of Argovitz's interest in the Gamblers or the manner in which that interest would create an untenable conflict of interest, a conflict that would inevitably breach Argovitz's fiduciary duty to Sims. Argovitz knew, or should have known, that he could not act as Sims' agent under any circumstances when dealing with the Gamblers. Even the USFL Constitution itself prohibits a holder of any interest in a member club from acting "as the contracting agent or representative for any player."

Pending the approval of his application for a USFL franchise in Houston, Argovitz continued his negotiations with the Lions on behalf of Sims. On April 5, 1983, Argovitz offered Sims' services to the Lions for $6 million over a four-year period. The offer included a demand for a $1 million interest-free loan to be repaid over 10 years, and for skill and injury guarantees for three years. The Lions quickly responded with a counter offer on April 7, 1983, in the face amount of $1.5 million over a five-year period with additional incentives not relevant here. The negotiating process was working. The Lions were trying to determine what Argovitz really believed the market value for Sims really was. On May 3, 1983, with his Gamblers franchise assured, Argovitz significantly reduced his offer to the Lions. He now offered Sims to the Lions for $3 million over a four-year period, one-half of the amount of his April 5, 1983, offer. Argovitz's May 3rd offer included a demand for $50,000 to permit Sims to purchase an annuity. Argovitz also dropped his previous demand for skill guarantees. The May 10, 1983 offer submitted by the Lions brought the parties much closer.

On May 30, 1983, Argovitz asked for $3.5 million over a five-year period. This offer included an interest-free loan and injury protection insurance but made no demand for skill guarantees. The May 30 offer now requested $400,000 to allow Sims to purchase an annuity. On June 1, 1983, Argovitz and the Lions were only $500,000 apart. We find that the negotiations between the Lions and Argovitz were progressing normally, not laterally as Argovitz represented to Sims. The Lions were not "dragging their feet." * * * The evidence establishes that on June 22, 1983, the Lions and Argovitz were very close to reaching an agreement on the value of Sims' services.

Apparently, in the midst of his negotiations with the Lions and with his Gamblers' franchise in hand, Argovitz decided that he would seek an offer from the Gamblers. Mr. Bernard Lerner, one of Argovitz's partners in the Gamblers agreed to negotiate a contract with Sims. Since Lerner admitted that he had no knowledge whatsoever about football, we must infer that Argovitz at the very least told Lerner the amount of money required to sign Sims and further pressed upon Lerner the Gamblers' absolute need to obtain Sims' services. In the Gamblers' organization, only Argovitz knew the value of Sims' services and how critical it was for the Gamblers to obtain Sims. In Argovitz's words, Sims would make the Gamblers' franchise.

On June 29, 1983, at Lerner's behest, Sims and his wife went to Houston to negotiate with a team that was partially owned by his own agent. When Sims arrived in Houston, he believed that the Lions organization was not negotiating in good faith; that it was not really interested in his services. His ego was bruised and his emotional outlook toward the Lions was visible to Burrough and Argovitz. Clearly, virtually all the information that Sims had up to that date came from Argovitz. * * * The negotiations began on the morning of June 30, 1983, and ended that afternoon. At the morning meeting, Lerner offered Sims a $3.5 million five-year contract, which included three years of skill and injury guarantees. The offer included a $500,000 loan at an interest rate of 1 percent over prime. It was from this loan that Argovitz planned to receive the $100,000 balance of his fee for acting as an agent in negotiating a contract with his own team. Burrough testified that Sims would have accepted that offer on the spot because he was finally receiving the guarantee that he had been requesting from the Lions, guarantees that Argovitz dropped without too much quarrel. Argovitz and Burrough took Sims and his wife into another room to discuss the offer. Argovitz did tell Sims that he thought the Lions would match the Gamblers' financial package and asked Sims whether he (Argovitz) should telephone the Lions. But, it is clear from the evidence that neither Sims nor Burrough believed that the Lions would match the offer. * * * Sims * * * agreed to become a Gambler on the terms offered. At that moment, Argovitz irreparably breached his fiduciary duty. As agent for Sims he had the duty to telephone the Lions, receive its final offer, and present the terms of both offers to Sims. Then and only then could it be said that Sims made an intelligent and knowing decision to accept the Gamblers' offer.

During these negotiations at the Gamblers' office, Mr. Nash of the Lions telephoned Argovitz, but even though Argovitz was at his office, he declined to accept the telephone call. Argovitz tried to return Nash's call after Sims had accepted the Gamblers' offer, but it was after 5 P.M. and Nash had left for the July 4th weekend. When he declined to accept Mr. Nash's call, Argovitz's breach of his fiduciary duty became even more pronounced. * * *

During the evening of June 30, 1983, Burrough struggled with the fact that they had not presented the Gamblers' offer to the Lions. He knew, as does the court, that Argovitz now had the wedge that he needed to bring finality to the Lions' negotiations. Burrough was acutely aware of the fact that Sims' actions were emotionally motivated and realized that the responsibility for Sims' future rested with him. We view with some disdain the fact that Argovitz had, in effect, delegated his entire fiduciary responsibility on the eve of his principal's most important career decision. On July 1, 1983, it was Lerner who gave lip service to Argovitz's conspicuous conflict of interest. It was Lerner, not Argovitz, who advised Sims that Argovitz's position with the Gamblers presented a conflict of interest and that Sims could, if he wished, obtain an attorney or another agent. Argovitz, upon whom Sims had relied for the past four years, was not even there. Burrough, conscious of Sims' emotional responses, never advised Sims to wait until he had talked with the Lions before making a final decision. Argovitz's conflict of interest and self-dealing put him in the position where he would not even use the wedge he now had to negotiate with the Lions, a wedge that is the dream of every agent. Two expert witnesses testified that an agent should telephone a team that he has been negotiating with once he has an offer in hand. * * * The evidence here convinces us that Argovitz's negotiations with the

Lions were ongoing and it had not made its final offer. Argovitz did not follow the common practice described by both expert witnesses. He did not do this because he knew that the Lions would not leave Sims without a contract and he further knew that if he made that type of call Sims would be lost to the Gamblers, a team he owned.

On November 12, 1983, when Sims was in Houston for the Lions game with the Houston Oilers, Argovitz asked Sims to come to his home and sign certain papers. He represented to Sims that certain papers of his contract had been mistakenly overlooked and now needed to be signed. Included among those papers he asked Sims to sign was a waiver of any claim that Sims might have against Argovitz for his blatant breach of his fiduciary duty brought on by his glaring conflict of interest. Sims did not receive independent advice with regard to the wisdom of signing such a waiver. Despite having sold his agency business in September, Argovitz did not even tell Sims' new agent of his intention to have Sims sign a waiver. Nevertheless, Sims, an unsophisticated young man, signed the waiver. This is another example of the questionable conduct on the part of Argovitz who still had business management obligations to Sims. In spite of his fiduciary relationship he had Sims sign a waiver without advising him to obtain independent counseling.

* * *

The relationship between a principal and agent is fiduciary in nature, and as such imposes a duty of loyalty, good faith, and fair and honest dealing on the agent. [Citation.]

A fiduciary relationship arises not only from a formal principal-agent relationship, but also from informal relationships of trust and confidence. [Citations.]

In light of the express agency agreement, and the relationship between Sims and Argovitz, Argovitz clearly owed Sims the fiduciary duties of an agent at all times relevant to this lawsuit.

An agent's duty of loyalty requires that he not have a personal stake that conflicts with the principal's interest in a transaction in which he represents his principal. As stated in [citation]:

> (T)he principal is entitled to the best efforts and unbiased judgment of his agent. * * * (T)he law denies the right of an agent to assume any relationship that is antagonistic to his duty to his principal, and it has many times been held that the agent cannot be both buyer and seller at the same time nor connect his own interests with property involved in his dealings as an agent for another.

A fiduciary violates the prohibition against self-dealing not only by dealing with himself on his principal's behalf, but also by dealing on his principal's behalf with a third party in which he has an interest, such as a partnership in which he is a member. * * *

Where an agent has an interest adverse to that of his principal in a transaction in which he purports to act on behalf of his principal, the transaction is voidable by the principal unless the agent disclosed all material facts within the agent's knowledge that might affect the principal's judgment. [Citation.]

The mere fact that the contract is fair to the principal does not deny the principal the right to rescind the contract when it was negotiated by an agent in violation of the prohibition against self-dealing. * * *

Once it has been shown that an agent had an interest in a transaction involving his principal antagonistic to the principal's interest, fraud on the part of the agent is presumed. The burden of proof then rests upon the agent to show that his principal had full knowledge, not only of the fact that the agent was interested, but also of every material fact known to the agent which might affect the principal and that having such knowledge, the principal freely consented to the transaction.

It is not sufficient for the agent merely to inform the principal that he has an interest that conflicts with the principal's interest. Rather, he must inform the principal "of all facts that come to his knowledge that are or may be material or which might affect his principal's rights or interests or influence the action he takes." [Citation.]

Argovitz clearly had a personal interest in signing Sims with the Gamblers that was adverse to Sims' interest—he had an ownership interest in the Gamblers and thus would profit if the Gamblers were profitable, and would incur substantial personal liabilities should the Gamblers not be financially successful. Since this showing has been made, fraud on Argovitz's part is presumed, and the Gamblers' contract must be rescinded unless Argovitz has shown by a preponderance of the evidence that he informed Sims of every material fact that might have influenced Sims' decision whether or not to sign the Gamblers' contract.

We conclude that Argovitz has failed to show by a preponderance of the evidence either: (1) that he informed Sims of the [material] facts, or (2) that these facts would not have influenced Sims' decision whether to sign the Gamblers' contract. * * *

As a court sitting in equity, we conclude that recision is the appropriate remedy. We are dismayed by Argovitz's egregious conduct. The careless fashion in which Argovitz went about ascertaining the highest price for Sims' service convinces us of the wisdom of the maxim: no man can faithfully serve two masters whose interests are in conflict.

Judgment will be entered for the plaintiffs rescinding the Gamblers' contract with Sims.

# CASE 19-4

## Termination by Incapacity/Durable Power of Attorney
## GADDY v. DOUGLASS

Court of Appeals of South Carolina, 2004
359 S.C. 329, 597 S.E.2d 12
http://caselaw.lp.findlaw.com/scripts/getcase.pl?court=sc&vol=3797&invol=1

**Kittredge, J.**

Ms. M was born in 1918 and grew up in Fairfield County [South Carolina]. She moved to Greenville, where she majored in sociology at Furman University and later worked for the South Carolina Department of Social Services. After retiring, Ms. M returned to Fairfield where she lived on her family farm with her brother, a dentist, until his death in the early 1980s. Ms. M never married.

Dr. Gaddy was Ms. M's physician and a close family friend. * * *

Conversely, Ms. M had little contact with many of her relatives, including Appellants [third cousins of Ms. M].

In 1988, * * * Ms. M then executed a durable general power of attorney (1988 durable power of attorney) designating Dr. Gaddy as her attorney-in-fact. * * *

* * * Concerns about Ms. M's progressively worsening mental condition prompted Dr. Gaddy to file the 1988 durable power of attorney in November 1995. Pursuant to the 1988 durable power of attorney, Dr. Gaddy began to act as Ms. M's attorney-in-fact and assumed control of her finances, farm, and health care. His responsibilities included paying her bills, tilling her garden, repairing fences, and hiring caregivers.

In March 1996, Dr. Gaddy discovered Ms. M had fallen in her home and fractured a vertebra. Ms. M was hospitalized for six weeks. During the hospitalization, Dr. Gaddy fumigated and cleaned her home, which had become flea-infested and unclean to the point where rat droppings were found in the house. Finding that Ms. M was not mentally competent to care for herself, he arranged for full-time caretakers to attend to her after she recovered from the injuries she sustained in her fall. He made improvements in her home, including replacing moth-eaten area rugs with new rugs and upgraded her kitchen to enable caretakers to prepare her meals. Dr. Gaddy also made plumbing repairs to the house, and took steps to adapt a bathroom to make it safer for caretakers to bathe Ms. M, who was incapable of doing so unassisted. During Ms. M's hospitalization, neither of the Appellants visited her in the hospital or sought to assist her in any manner.

Dr. Gaddy had Ms. M examined and evaluated by Dr. James E. Carnes, a neurologist, in December 1996. After examining Ms. M, Dr. Carnes found that she suffered from dementia and confirmed she was unable to handle her affairs.

As Ms. M's Alzheimer's disease progressed and her faculties deteriorated, Dr. Gaddy managed her financial affairs, oversaw maintenance of her properties, and ensured that she received constant care including food, clothing, bathing, and housekeeping. * * *

Ms. M's long-standing distant relationship with some members of her family, including Appellants, changed in March of 1999.

On March 12, 1999, Appellants visited Ms. M, and with the help of disgruntled caretaker Lil Heller, took her to an appointment with Columbia attorney Douglas N. Truslow to "get rid of Dr. Gaddy." On the drive to Truslow's office, Heller had to remind Ms. M several times of their destination and purpose. At Truslow's office, Ms. M signed a document revoking the 1988 Will and the 1988 durable power of attorney. She also signed a new durable power of attorney (1999 durable power of attorney) naming Appellants as her attorneys-in-fact. Appellants failed to disclose Ms. M's dementia to Truslow. David Byrd, a witness to the execution of the March 12 documents, was likewise not informed of Ms. M's dementia.

Armed with the revocation of the 1988 power of attorney and recently executed power of attorney in their favor, Appellants prohibited Dr. Gaddy from contacting Ms. M. Dr. Gaddy was even threatened with arrest if he tried to visit Ms. M.

On March 15, 1999, three days after Ms. M purportedly revoked the 1988 documents and executed the 1999 durable power of attorney, Dr. Gaddy initiated the present action as her attorney-in-fact pursuant to the 1988 durable power of attorney. He alleged, among other things, that the purported revocation of the 1988 durable power of attorney and the execution of the 1999 durable power of attorney were invalid because "on March 12, 1999, the date on which Ms. M purportedly signed the 1999 power of attorney and the revocation, she was not mentally competent" due to "senile dementia of the Alzheimer's type." The action sought declaratory judgment to render the 1999 durable power of attorney invalid and declare the 1988 durable power of attorney valid.

* * *

Medical testimony was presented from five physicians who had examined Ms. M. * * * [They concluded that Ms. M. (1) was "unable to handle her financial affairs" and "would need help managing her daily activities," and

(2) would not "ever have moments of lucidity" to "understand legal documents."]

* * *

The trial court concluded that Ms. M lacked contractual * * * capacity "from March 12, 1999 and continuously thereafter." As a result, he invalidated the 1999 revocation of the 1988 durable power of attorney and * * * the 1999 durable power of attorney, and declared valid the 1988 durable power of attorney. Finally, he awarded Dr. Gaddy litigation expenses to be paid from Ms. M's assets.

Since 1986, the South Carolina Legislature has expressly authorized and sanctioned the use and efficacy of *durable* powers of attorneys. * * *

Upon the execution of a durable power of attorney, the attorney-in-fact retains authority to act on the principal's behalf notwithstanding the subsequent physical disability or mental incompetence of the principal. To honor this unmistakable legislative intent, it is incumbent on courts to uphold a durable power of attorney unless the principal retains contractual capacity to revoke the then existing durable power of attorney or to execute a new power of attorney. Otherwise, the very purpose of [the statute] would be undermined.

* * *

"In order to execute or revoke a valid power of attorney, the principal must possess contractual capacity." [Citation.] Contractual capacity is generally defined as a person's ability to understand in a meaningful way, at the time the contract is executed, the nature, scope and effect of the contract. [Citation.] Where, as here, the mental condition of the principal is of a chronic nature, evidence of the principal's prior or subsequent condition is admissible as bearing upon his or her condition at the time the contract is executed. [Citation.] * * *

Here, the credible medical * * * testimony presented compellingly indicates that Ms. M suffered from at least moderate to severe dementia caused by Alzheimer's Disease, a chronic and permanent organic disease, on March 12, 1999. We are firmly persuaded that Ms. M's dementia, chronic and progressive in nature, clearly rendered her incapable of possessing contractual capacity to revoke the 1988 durable power of attorney or execute the 1999 power of attorney. We find this conclusion inescapable based on the record before us.

* * *

The very idea of a durable power of attorney is to protect the principal should he or she become incapacitated. This case is precisely the type of situation for which the durable power of attorney is intended. On March 12, 1999, Ms. M, due to her chronic and severe dementia, lacked capacity to revoke the 1988 durable power of attorney and execute the 1999 power of attorney, and the evidence in this regard is overwhelming. In so holding, we return to Dr. Gaddy his fiduciary obligations to Ms. M, which he faithfully discharged prior to Appellants' regrettable involvement. The decision of the trial court is

AFFIRMED IN PART AND VACATED IN PART.

## QUESTIONS

1. Distinguish among the following relationships: (a) agency, (b) employment, and (c) independent contractor.
2. Discuss the requirements for creating an agency relationship.
3. Discuss the duties owed by an agent to her principal.
4. Discuss the duties owed by a principal to his agent.
5. Identify the ways in which an agency relationship may be terminated.

## PROBLEMS

**1.** Parker, the owner of certain unimproved real estate in Chicago, employed Adams, a real estate agent, to sell the property for a price of $250,000 or more and agreed to pay Adams a commission of 6 percent for making a sale. Adams negotiated with Turner, who was interested in the property and willing to pay as much as $280,000 for it. Adams made an agreement with Turner that if Adams could obtain Parker's signature to a contract to sell the property to Turner for $250,000, Turner would pay Adams a bonus of $10,000. Adams prepared and Parker and Turner signed a contract for the sale of the property to Turner for $250,000. Turner refuses to pay Adams the $10,000 as promised. Parker refuses to pay Adams the 6 percent commission. In an action by Adams against Parker and Turner, what judgment?

**2.** Perry employed Alice to sell a parcel of real estate at a fixed price without knowledge that David had previously employed Alice to purchase the same property for him. Perry gave Alice no discretion as to price or terms, and Alice entered into a contract of sale with David upon the exact terms authorized by Perry. After accepting a partial payment, Perry discovered that Alice was employed by David and brought an action to rescind. David resisted on the ground that Perry had suffered no damage for the reason that Alice had been given no discretion and the sale was made upon the exact basis authorized by Perry. Discuss whether Perry will prevail.

**3.** Packer owned and operated a fruit cannery in Southton, Illinois. He stored a substantial amount of finished canned goods in a warehouse in East St. Louis, Illinois, owned and operated by Alden, in order to have goods readily available for the St. Louis market. On March 1, he had ten thousand cans of peaches and five thousand cans of apples in storage with Alden. On the day named, he borrowed $5,000 from Alden, giving Alden his promissory note for this amount due June 1 together with a letter authorizing Alden, in the event the note was not paid at maturity, to sell any or all of his goods in storage, pay the indebtedness, and account to him for any surplus. Packer died on June 2 without having paid the note. On June 8, Alden told Taylor, a wholesale food distributor, that he had for sale as agent of the owner ten thousand cans of peaches and five thousand cans of apples. Taylor said he would take the peaches and would decide later about the apples. A contract for the sale of ten thousand cans of peaches for $6,000 was thereupon signed "Alden, agent for Packer, seller; Taylor, buyer." Both Alden and Taylor knew of the death of Packer. Delivery of the peaches and payment were made on June 10. On June 11, Alden and Taylor signed a similar contract covering the five thousand cans of apples, delivery and payment to be made June 30. On June 23, Packer's executor, having learned of these contracts, wrote Alden and Taylor stating that Alden had no authority to make the contracts, demanding that Taylor return the peaches, and directing Alden not to deliver the apples. Discuss the correctness of the contentions of Packer's executor.

**4.** Western Rivers Fly Fisher (Western) operates under license of the U.S. Forest Service as an "outfitter," a corporation in the business of arranging fishing expeditions on the Green River, Utah. Michael D. Petragallo is licensed by the Forest Service as a guide to conduct fishing expeditions but cannot do so by himself, because the Forest Service licenses only outfitters to float patrons down the Green River. Western and several other licensed outfitters contact Petragallo to guide clients on fishing trips. Because the Forest Service licenses only outfitters to sponsor fishing expeditions, every guide must display on the boat and vehicle he uses the insignia of the outfitter sponsoring the particular trip. Petragallo may agree or refuse to take individuals Western refers to him, and Western does not restrict him from guiding expeditions for other outfitters. Western pays Petragallo a certain sum per fishing trip and does not make any deductions from his compensation. Petragallo's responsibilities include transporting patrons to the Green River, using his own boat for fishing trips, providing food and overnight needs for patrons, assisting patrons in fly fishing, and transporting them from the river to their vehicles. Robert McMaster contacted Western and arranged for a fishing trip for himself and two others. Jaeger was a member of McMaster's fishing party. McMaster paid Western, which set the price for the trip, planned the itinerary for the McMaster party, rented fishing rods to them, and arranged for Petragallo to be their guide. When Petragallo met the McMaster party, he answered affirmatively when Jaeger asked him if he worked for Western. While driving the McMaster party back to town at the conclusion of the fishing trip, Petragallo lost control of his vehicle, injuring Jaeger, who brought suit against Western, Petragallo, and others. Western claims that because Petragallo is an independent contractor and was never its employee, it is not liable for Petragallo's acts in causing Jaeger's injuries. Is Petragallo an independent contractor? Explain.

**5.** Palmer made a valid contract with Ames under which Ames was to sell Palmer's goods on commission from January 1 to June 30. Ames made satisfactory sales up to May 15 and was then about to close an unusually large order when Palmer suddenly and without notice revoked Ames's authority to sell. Can Ames continue to sell Palmer's goods during the unexpired term of her contract?

**6.** Piedmont Electric Co. gave a list of delinquent accounts to Alexander, an employee, with instructions to discontinue electric service to delinquent customers. Among those listed was Todd Hatchery, which was then in the process of hatching chickens in a large, electrically heated incubator. Todd Hatchery told Alexander that it did not consider its account delinquent, but Alexander nevertheless cut the wires leading to the hatchery. Subsequently, Todd Hatchery recovered a judgment of $5,000 in an action brought against Alexander for the loss resulting from the interruption of the incubation process. Alexander has paid the judgment and brings a cause of action against Piedmont Electric Co. What may he recover? Explain.

**7.** In October 2006, Black, the owner of the Grand Opera House, and Harvey entered into a written agreement leasing the Opera House to Harvey for five years at a rental of $300,000 per year. Harvey engaged Day as manager of the theatre at a salary of $1,175 per week plus 10 percent of the profits. One of Day's duties was to determine the amount of money taken in each night and, after deducting expenses, to divide the profits between Harvey and the manager of the particular attraction that was playing at the theater. In September 2011, Day went to Black and offered to rent the opera house from Black at a rental of $375,000 per year, whereupon Black entered into a lease with Day for five years at this figure. When Harvey learned of and objected to this transaction, Day offered to assign the lease to him for $600,000 per year. Harvey refused and brought an appropriate action against Day. Should Harvey recover? If so, on what basis and to what relief is he entitled?

**8.** Timothy retains Cynthia, an attorney, to bring a lawsuit upon a valid claim against Vincent. Cynthia fails to make herself aware of recently enacted legislation that shortens the statute of limitations for this type of legal action, and, consequently, she files the complaint after the statute of limitations has run. As a result, the lawsuit is dismissed. What rights, if any, does Timothy have against Cynthia?

**9.** Wilson engages Ruth to sell Wilson's antique walnut chest to Harold for $2,500. The next day, Ruth learns that Sandy is willing to pay $3,000 for Wilson's chest. Ruth nevertheless sells the chest to Harold. Wilson then discovers these facts. What are Wilson's rights, if any, against Ruth?

**10.** Morris, a salesperson for Acme, Inc., a manufacturer of household appliances, receives a commission on all sales made and no further compensation. He drives his own automobile, pays his own expenses, and calls on whom he pleases. While driving to make a call on a potential customer, Morris negligently collides with Hudson, who sues (a) Acme and (b) Morris. Who should be held liable?

**11.** Sierra Pacific Industries purchased various areas of timber and six other pieces of real property, including a ten-acre parcel on which five duplexes and two single-family units were located. Sierra Pacific requested the assistance of Joseph Carter, a licensed real estate broker, in selling the nontimberland properties. It commissioned him to sell the property for an asking price of $850,000, of which Sierra Pacific would receive $800,000 and Carter would receive $50,000 as a commission. Unable to find a prospective buyer, Carter finally sold the property to his daughter and son-in-law for $850,000 and retained the $50,000 commission without informing Sierra Pacific of his relationship to the buyers. After learning of these facts, Sierra Pacific brought an action for breach of fiduciary duty against Carter. To what relief, if any, is Sierra Pacific entitled?

**12.** Murphy, while a guest at a motel operated by the Betsy-Len Motor Hotel Corporation, sustained injuries from a fall allegedly caused by negligence in maintaining the premises. At that time, Betsy-Len was under a license agreement with Holiday Inns, Inc. The license contained provisions permitting Holiday Inns to regulate the architectural style of the buildings as well as the type and style of the furnishings and equipment. The contract, however, did not grant Holiday Inns the power to control the day-to-day operations of Betsy-Len's motel, to fix customer rates, or to demand a share of the profits. Betsy-Len could hire and fire its employees, determine wages and working conditions, supervise the employee work routine, and discipline its employees. In return, Betsy-Len used the trade name, "Holiday Inns," and paid a fee for use of the license and Holiday Inns's national advertising. Murphy sued Holiday Inns, claiming Betsy-Len was its agent. Is Murphy correct?

**13.** Tube Art was involved in moving a reader board sign to a new location. Tube Art's service manager and another employee went to the proposed site and took photographs and measurements. Later, a Tube Art employee laid out the exact size and location for the excavation by marking a four-by-four-foot-square on the asphalt surface with yellow paint. The dimensions of the hole, including its depth of six feet, were indicated with spray paint inside the square. After the layout was painted on the asphalt, Tube Art engaged a backhoe operator, Richard F. Redford, to dig the hole. Redford began digging in the early evening hours at the location designated by Tube Art. At approximately 9:30 P.M., the bucket of Redford's backhoe struck a small natural gas pipeline. After examining the pipe and finding no indication of a break or leak, he concluded that the line was not in use and left the site. Shortly before 2:00 A.M. on the following day, an explosion and fire occurred in the building serviced by that gas pipeline. As a result, two people in the building were killed, and most of its contents were destroyed. Massey and his associates, as tenants of the building, brought an action against Tube Art and Richard Redford for the total destruction of their property. Will the plaintiff prevail? Explain.

**14.** Brian Hanson sustained a paralyzing injury while playing in a lacrosse match between Ohio State University and Ashland University. Hanson had interceded in a fight between one of his teammates and an Ashland player, William Kynast. Hanson grabbed Kynast in a bear hug, but Kynast threw Hanson off his back. Hanson's head struck the ground, resulting in serious injuries. An ambulance was summoned, and after several delays Hanson was transported to a local hospital where he underwent surgery. Doctors determined that Hanson suffered a compression fracture of his sixth spinal vertebrae. Hanson, now an incomplete quadriplegic, subsequently filed suit against Ashland University, maintaining that because Kynast was acting as the agent of Ashland, the university was therefore liable for Kynast's alleged wrongful acts. Was Kynast an agent of Ashland?

**15.** Tony Wilson was a member of Troop 392 of the Boy Scouts of America (BSA) and of the St. Louis Area Council (Council). Tony went on a trip with the troop to Fort Leonard Wood, Missouri. Five adult volunteer leaders accompanied the troop. The troop stayed in a building that had thirty-foot aluminum pipes stacked next to it. At approximately 10:00 P.M., Tony and other scouts were outside the building, and the leaders were inside. Tony and two other scouts picked up a pipe and raised it so that it came into contact with 7,200-volt power lines that ran over the building. All three scouts were electrocuted, and Tony died.

His parents brought a suit for wrongful death against the Council, claiming that the volunteer leaders were agents or servants of the Council and that it was vicariously liable for their negligence. The Council filed a motion for summary judgment, arguing as follows: The BSA chartered local councils in certain areas, and councils in turn granted charters to local sponsors such as schools, churches, or civic organizations. Local councils did not administer the scouting program for the sponsor, did not select volunteers, did not prescribe training for volunteers, and did not direct or control the activities of troops. Troops were not required to get permission from local councils before participating in an activity. Are the troop leaders agents of the Council? Explain.

**16.** Harvey Hilgendorf was a licensed real estate broker acting as the agent of the Hagues in the sale of eighty acres of farmland. The Hagues, however, terminated Hilgendorf's agency before the expiration of the listing contract when they encountered financial difficulties and decided to liquidate their entire holdings of land at one time. Hilgendorf brought this action for breach of the listing contract. The Hagues maintain that Hilgendorf's duty of loyalty required him to give up the listing contract. Are the Hagues correct in their assertion?

**17.** Hunter Farms contracted with Petrolia Grain & Feed Company, a Canadian company, to purchase a large supply of the farm herbicide Sencor from Petrolia for resale. Petrolia learned from the U.S. Customs Service that the import duty for the Sencor would be 5 percent but that the final rate could be determined only upon an inspection of the Sencor at the time of importation. Petrolia forwarded this information to Hunter. Meanwhile, Hunter employed F. W. Myers & Company, an import broker, to assist in moving the herbicide through customs. When customs later determined that certain chemicals in the herbicide, not listed on its label, would increase the customs duty from $30,000 to $128,000, Myers paid the additional amount under protest and turned to Hunter for indemnification. Hunter refused to pay Myers, claiming that Myers breached its duty of care as an import broker in failing to inform Hunter that the 5 percent duty rate was subject to increase. Myers brought an action against Hunter, arguing that it was not employed to give advice to Hunter on matters of importation. Explain whether Myers had the duty to inform Hunter.

# CHAPTER 20
# Relationship with Third Parties

The purpose of an agency relationship is to allow the principal to extend his business activities by authorizing agents to enter into contracts with third persons on the principal's behalf. Accordingly, it is important that the law balance the competing interests of principals and third persons. The principal wants to be liable *only* for those contracts he actually authorizes the agent to make for him. The third party, on the other hand, wishes the principal bound on *all* contracts that the agent negotiates on the principal's behalf. As this chapter discusses, the law has adopted an intermediate outcome: the principal and the third party are bound to those contracts the principal *actually* authorizes *plus* those the principal has *apparently* authorized.

While pursuing her principal's business, an agent may tortiously injure third parties, who then may seek to hold the principal personally liable. Under what circumstances should the principal be held liable? Similar questions arise concerning a principal's criminal liability for an agent's violation of the criminal law. The law of agency has established rules to determine when the principal is liable for the torts and crimes his agents commit. These rules are discussed in this chapter.

Finally, what liability to the third party should the agent incur, and what rights should she acquire against the third party? Usually, the agent has no liability for, or rights under, the contracts she makes on behalf of her principal. As discussed in this chapter, however, in some situations the agent has contractually created obligations or rights or both.



## RELATIONSHIP OF PRINCIPAL AND THIRD PERSONS

This section will first consider the contract liability of the principal; then it will examine the principal's potential tort liability.

## CONTRACT LIABILITY OF THE PRINCIPAL

The power of an agent is his ability to change the legal status of his principal. An agent having either actual or apparent authority has the power to bind his principal. Thus, whenever an agent, acting within his authority, makes a contract for his principal, he creates new rights or liabilities for his principal, thereby changing his principal's legal status. This power of an agent to act for his principal in business transactions is the basis of agency.

A principal's contract liability also depends upon whether the principal is disclosed, unidentified, or undisclosed. The principal is a **disclosed principal** if, when an agent and a third party interact, the third party has notice that the agent is acting for a principal and also has notice of the principal's identity. The principal is an **unidentified principal** if, when an agent and a third party interact, the third party has notice that the agent is acting for a principal but does not have notice of the principal's identity. (Some courts refer to an unidentified principal as a "partially disclosed principal.") An example is an auctioneer who sells on behalf of a seller who is not identified: the seller is an unidentified principal (or a partially disclosed principal) since it is understood that the auctioneer acts as an agent. The principal is an **undisclosed principal** if, when an agent and a third party interact, the third party has no notice that the agent is acting for a principal. Restatement, Section 1.04(2).

### TYPES OF AUTHORITY

Authority is of two basic types: actual and apparent. **Actual authority** depends upon consent that the principal manifests to the agent. Section 2.01. It may be either express or implied. In either case, such authority is binding and confers upon the agent both the power and the right to create or affect the principal's legal relations with third persons. Actual express authority does not depend on the third party having knowledge of the manifestations or statements made by the principal to the agent.

**Apparent authority** is based upon acts or conduct of the principal that lead a third person to believe that the agent, or supposed agent, has actual authority, upon which belief the third person *justifiably* relies. Section 2.03. This manifestation, which confers upon the agent the power to create a legal relationship between the principal and a third party, may consist of words or actions of the principal as well as other facts and circumstances that induce the third person reasonably to rely upon the existence of an agency relationship.

**Actual Express Authority** The express authority of an agent, found in the spoken or written words the principal communicates to the agent, is actual authority stated in language directing or instructing the agent to do something specific. "As commonly used, the term 'express authority' often means actual authority that a principal has stated in very specific or detailed language." Restatement, Section 2.01, comment b. Thus, if Perkins, orally or in writing, requests his agent Abbott to sell Perkins's automobile for $6,500, Abbott's authority to sell the car for this sum is actual and express.

**Actual Implied Authority** Implied authority is not found in express or explicit words of the principal but is inferred from words or conduct that the principal manifests to the agent. An agent has implied authority to do that which she reasonably believes the principal wishes her to do, based on the agent's reasonable interpretation of the principal's manifestations to her and all other facts she knows or should know. Restatement, Section 2.02. Implied authority may arise from customs and usages of the principal's business. In addition, the authority granted to an agent to accomplish a particular purpose necessarily includes the implied authority to employ the means reasonably required to accomplish it. Restatement, Section 2.02. For example, Pearson authorizes Arlington to manage her eighty-two-unit apartment complex but says nothing about expenses. In order to manage the building, Arlington must employ a janitor, purchase fuel for heating, and arrange for ordinary maintenance. Even though Pearson has not expressly granted him the authority to incur such expenses, Arlington may, because such expenses are necessary to proper apartment management, reasonably infer the authority to incur them from the express authority to manage the building. On the other hand, suppose Paige employs Arthur, a real estate broker, to find a purchaser for her residence at a stated price. Arthur has no authority to contract for its sale.

◆ SEE FIGURE 20-1: **Contract Liability of Disclosed Principal**

**Apparent Authority** Apparent authority is power arising from words or conduct of a disclosed or unidentified principal that, when manifested to third persons, reasonably induce them to rely upon the assumption that actual authority exists. Restatement, Section 2.03. Apparent authority depends upon the principal's manifestations to the third party; an agent's own statements about the agent's authority do not by themselves create apparent authority. Apparent authority confers upon the agent, or supposed agent, the power to bind the disclosed or unidentified principal in contracts with third persons and precludes the principal from denying the existence of actual authority. Thus, when authority is apparent but not actual, the disclosed or unidentified principal is nonetheless bound by the act of the agent. By exceeding his actual authority, however, the agent violates his duty of obedience and is liable to the principal for any loss the principal suffers as a result of the agent's acting beyond his actual authority.

Common ways in which apparent authority may arise include the following:

1. When a principal appoints an agent to a position in an organization, third parties may reasonably believe that the agent has the authority to do those acts customary of an agent in such a position. (Apparent authority for agents of various business associations is discussed in *Parts 6* and *7*.)
2. If a principal has given an agent general authority to engage in a transaction, subsequently imposed limitations or restrictions will not affect the agent's apparent authority to engage in that transaction until third parties are notified of the restrictions.
3. The principal's acquiescence in prior similar transactions between the agent and a third party may create a basis for the third party reasonably to believe that the agent has apparent authority.
4. The agent shows the third party a document, such as a power of attorney, from the principal authorizing the agent to enter into such a transaction.
5. As discussed below, after many terminations of authority an agent has lingering apparent authority until the third party has actual knowledge or receives notice of the termination.

For example, Peter writes a letter to Alice authorizing her to sell his automobile and sends a copy of the letter to Thomas, a prospective purchaser. On the following day, Peter writes a letter to Alice revoking the authority to sell the car but does not send a copy of the second letter to Thomas, who is not otherwise informed of the revocation. Although Alice has no actual authority to sell the car, she continues to have apparent authority with respect to Thomas. Or suppose that Arlene, in the presence of Polly, tells Thad that Arlene is Polly's agent to buy lumber. Although this statement is not true, Polly does not deny it, as she easily could. Thad, in reliance upon the statement, ships lumber to Polly on Arlene's order. Polly is obligated to pay for the lumber because Arlene had apparent authority to act on Polly's behalf. This apparent authority of Arlene exists only with respect to Thad. If Arlene were to give David an

◆ **FIGURE 20-1: Contract Liability of Disclosed Principal**

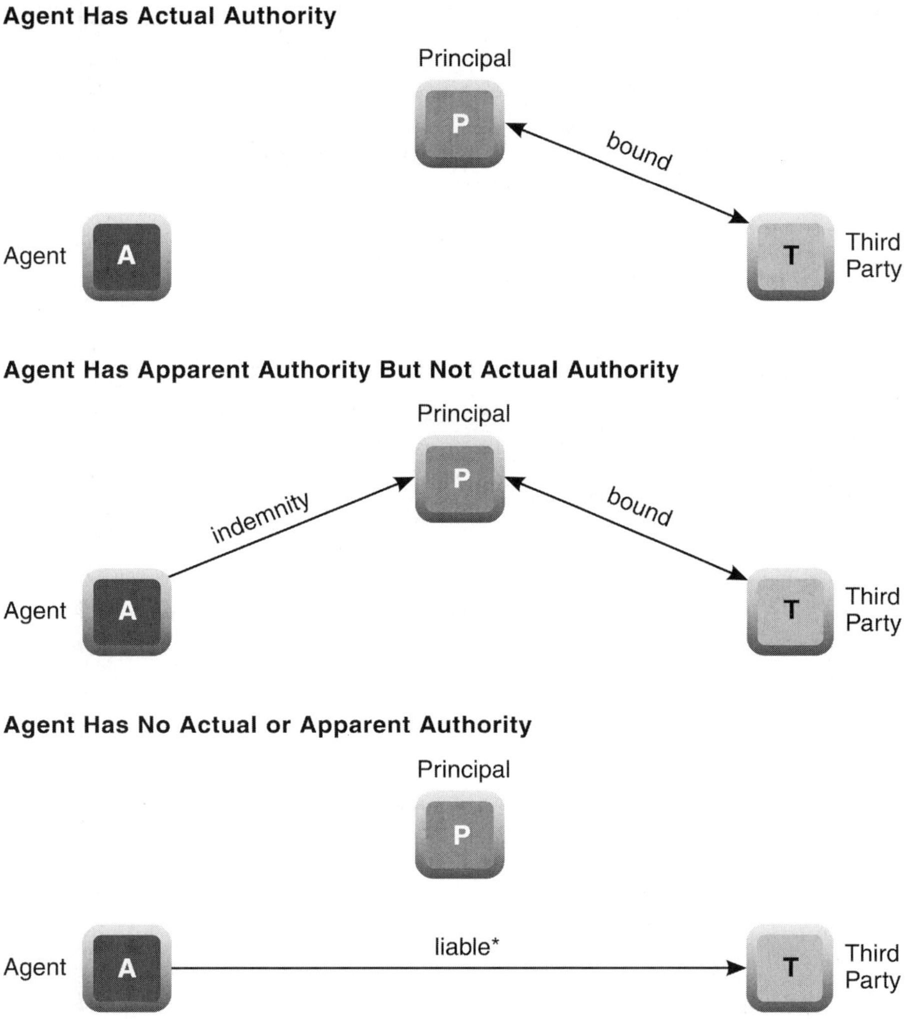


*Agent is liable for breach of implied warranty of authority or misrepresentation, as discussed later in this chapter.

order for a shipment of lumber to Polly, David would be unable to hold Polly liable. Arlene would have had neither actual authority nor, as to David, apparent authority.

Because apparent authority is the power resulting from acts that appear to the third party to be authorized by the principal, apparent authority cannot exist where the principal is undisclosed. Nor can apparent authority exist where the third party knows that the agent has no actual authority.

◆ **SEE FIGURE 20-2: Contract Liability of Unidentified Principal**

◆ **SEE FIGURE 20-3: Contract Liability of Undisclosed Principal**

◆ **SEE CASE 20-1**

## DELEGATION OF AUTHORITY

A **subagent** is a person appointed by an agent to perform functions that the agent has consented to perform on behalf of the agent's principal and for whose conduct the appointing agent is responsible to the principal. Restatement, Section 3.15(1). Because the appointment of an agent reflects the principal's confidence in and reliance upon the agent's personal skill, integrity, and other qualifications, an agent may appoint a subagent only if the agent has actual or apparent authority to do so. Restatement, Section 3.15(2).

◆ **FIGURE 20-2: Contract Liability of Unidentified Principal**

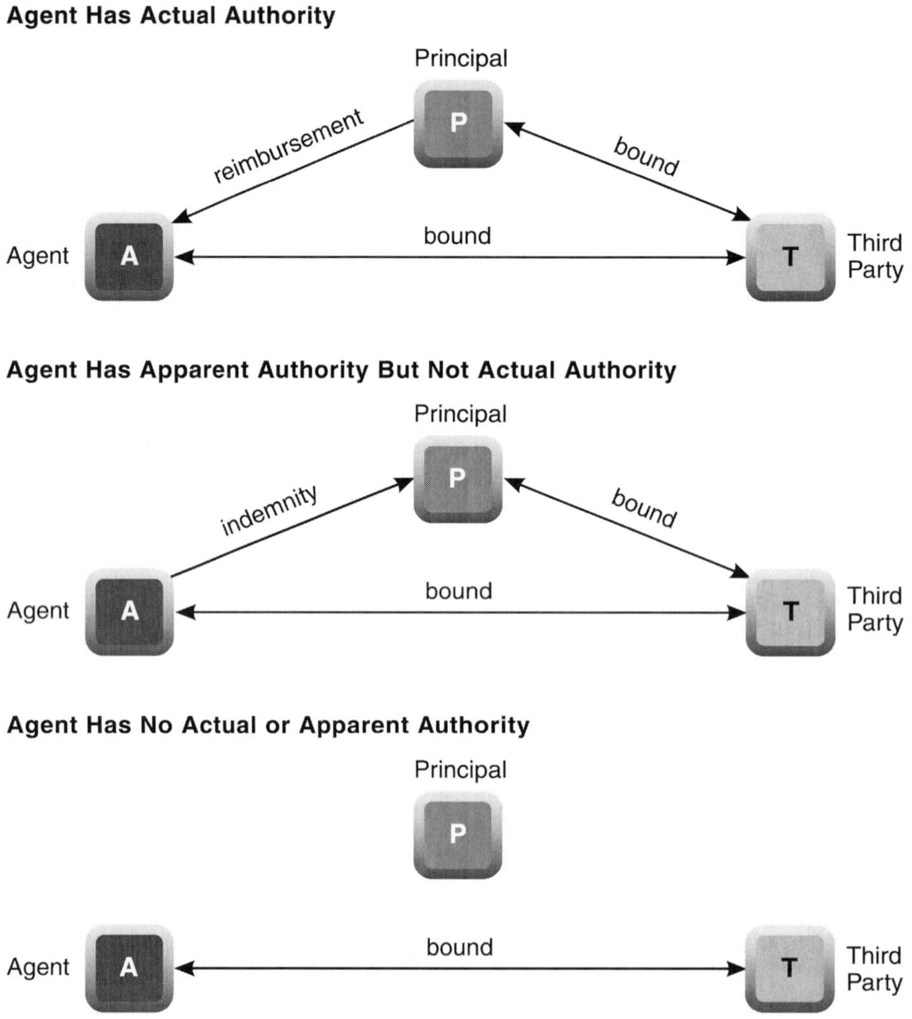


If an agent is authorized to appoint subagents, the acts of the subagent are as binding on the principal as those performed by the agent. Restatement, Section 3.15, comment b. As an agent of both the principal and the agent, the subagent owes a fiduciary duty to both. For example, P contracts with A, a real estate broker (agent), to sell P's house. P knows that A employs salespersons to show houses to prospective purchasers and to make representations about the property. The salespersons are A's employees and P's subagents.

If an agent having no authority to delegate her authority does so nevertheless, the acts of the subagent do not impose upon the principal any obligations or liability to third persons. Likewise, the principal acquires no rights against such third persons.

## EFFECT OF TERMINATION OF AGENCY ON AUTHORITY

As discussed in *Chapter 19*, when an agency terminates, the agent's *actual authority* ceases. The Second and Third Restatements differ, however, regarding when an agent's *apparent authority* ceases.

**Second Restatement** Where the performance of an authorized transaction becomes impossible, such as when the subject matter of the transaction is destroyed or the transaction is made illegal, the agent's *apparent authority* also expires and notice of such termination to third persons is *not* required. The bankruptcy of the principal terminates without notice the power of an agent to affect the principal's property, which has passed to the bankruptcy trustee.

When the termination is by the death or incapacity of the principal or agent, the Second Restatement provides that the agent's *apparent authority* also expires and notice of such termination to third persons is not required. However, with respect to the death or incapacity of the principal, this rule has been legislatively changed in more than forty States that have adopted the Uniform Durable Power of Attorney Act. This Act provides that the death of a principal, who has executed a

◆ FIGURE 20-3: **Contract Liability of Undisclosed Principal**

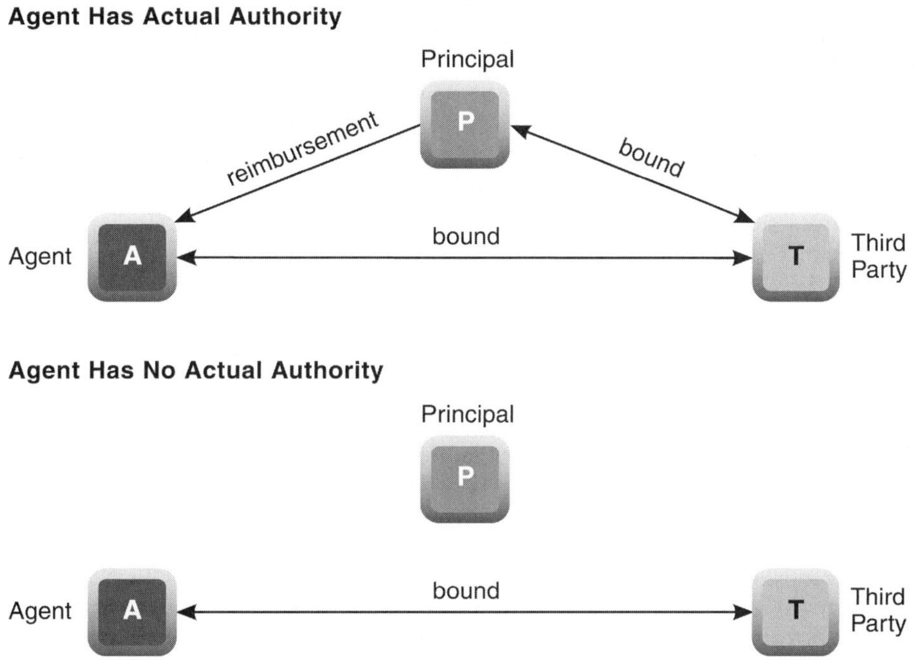


written power of attorney, whether or not it is durable, does not terminate the agency as to the attorney in fact (agent) or a third person who without actual knowledge of the principal's death acts in good faith under the power. Moreover, the Act provides that the incapacity of a principal, who has previously executed a written power of attorney that is *not* durable, does not terminate the agency as to the attorney in fact or a third person who without actual knowledge of the principal's incapacity acts in good faith under the power. If an agent is appointed under a durable power of attorney, the *actual* authority of an agent survives the incapacity of the principal.

In other cases, *apparent authority* continues until the third party has actual knowledge or receives actual notice, if that third party is one (1) with whom the agent had previously dealt on credit, (2) to whom the agent has been specially accredited, or (3) with whom the agent has begun to deal, as the principal should know. **Actual notice** requires a communication to the third party, either oral or written. If notice is given by mail, it is effective as actual notice upon delivery, not upon dispatch. All other third parties as to whom there was apparent authority must have actual knowledge or be given **constructive notice** through, for example, publication in a newspaper of general circulation in the area where the agency is regularly carried on.

**Third Restatement** Section 3.11 of the Third Restatement applies the same rule to *all* causes of termination of agency—it applies a reasonableness standard.

> (1) The termination of actual authority does not by itself end any apparent authority held by an agent.
>
> (2) Apparent authority ends when it is no longer reasonable for the third party with whom an agent deals to believe that the agent continues to act with actual authority.

The general rule of the Third Restatement is that it is reasonable for third parties to assume that an agent's actual authority continues ("lingers"), unless and until a third party has notice of circumstances that make it unreasonable to continue that assumption. These circumstances include notice that (1) the principal has revoked the agent's actual authority, (2) the agent has renounced it, or (3) circumstances otherwise have changed such that it is no longer reasonable to believe that the principal consents to the agent's act on the principal's behalf. Restatement, Section 3.11, comment c. A person has **notice** of a fact if the person knows the fact, has reason to know the fact, has received an effective notification of the fact, or should know the fact to fulfill a duty owed to another person. Restatement, Section 1.04(4).

For example, if the principal tells a third party that the agent's authority has terminated, the former agent's lingering apparent authority with respect to that third party has terminated. Moreover, if a third party has notice of facts that call the agent's authority into question, and these facts would prompt a reasonable person to make inquiry of the principal before dealing with the agent, the agent no longer acts with apparent authority. In addition, suppose that a principal has furnished an agent with a power of attorney stating the extent, nature, and duration of the agent's actual authority. Prior to the stated expiration of the power of attorney the principal terminates the agent's actual authority.

At this time the agent has a duty to return the power of attorney to the principal. If, however, the agent does not return the power of attorney to the principal, third parties to whom the agent shows the power of attorney would still be protected by apparent authority until the third parties have notice that actual authority had been terminated.

Consistent with this general rule—but contrary to the rule under the Second Restatement—a principal's death or loss of capacity does *not* automatically end the agent's apparent authority. In these instances, apparent authority terminates when the third party has (1) notice of the principal's death or (2) has notice that the principal's loss of capacity is permanent or that the principal has been adjudicated to lack capacity. Restatement, Sections 3.07 and 3.08. The Third Restatement's rule is consistent with the Uniform Durable Power of Attorney Act.

◆ **SEE CASE 20-2**

## RATIFICATION

**Ratification** is the confirmation or affirmance by one person of a prior unauthorized act performed by another who is his agent or who purports to be his agent. Restatement, Sections 4.01(1) and 4.03. The ratification of such act or contract binds the principal and the third party as if the agent or purported agent had been acting initially with actual authority. Restatement, Section 4.02(1). Once made, a valid ratification is irrevocable. Restatement, Section 4.02, comment b.

**Requirements of Ratification** Ratification may relate to acts that have exceeded the authority granted to an agent, as well as to acts that a person without any authority performs on behalf of an alleged principal. To effect a ratification, the principal must manifest an intent to do so with knowledge of all material facts concerning the transaction. Restatement, Section 4.06. The principal does not need to communicate this intent, which may be manifested by express language or implied from her conduct, such as accepting or retaining the benefits of a transaction. Thus, if Amanda, without authority, contracts in Penelope's name for the purchase of goods from Tate on credit, and Penelope, having learned of Amanda's unauthorized act, accepts the goods from Tate, she thereby impliedly ratifies the contract and is bound on it. Furthermore, a principal may ratify an unauthorized action by failing to repudiate it once the principal knows the material facts about the agent's action. Restatement, Section 4.01, comment f. If formalities are required for the authorization of an act, the same formalities apply to a ratification of that act. Restatement, Section 4.01, comment e. In any event, the principal must ratify the entire act or contract. Restatement, Section 4.07.

A person may ratify an act if the actor acted *or* purported to act as an agent on the person's behalf. Restatement, Section 4.03. Under this section and a number of relatively recent cases, an undisclosed principal may ratify an agent's unauthorized act. This is *contrary* to the Second Restatement's rule, which requires that the actor must have indicated to the third person that he was acting on a principal's behalf. Thus, under the Second Restatement there can be no ratification by an undisclosed principal. To illustrate: Archie, without any authority, contracts to sell to Tina an automobile belonging to Pierce. Archie states that the auto is his. Tina promises to pay $5,500 for the automobile. Pierce subsequently learns of the agreement and affirms. Under the Third Restatement Pierce's affirmation of Archie's action *would* be a ratification because Archie had acted on behalf of Pierce. On the other hand, under the Second Restatement it would *not* be a ratification because Archie did not indicate he was acting on behalf of a principal.

To be effective, ratification must occur before the third party gives notice of his withdrawal to the principal or agent. Restatement, Section 4.05(1). If the affirmance of a transaction occurs when the situation has so materially changed that it would be inequitable to subject the third party to liability, the third party may elect to avoid liability. Restatement, Section 4.05(2). For example, Alex has no authority, but, purporting to act for Penny, contracts to sell Penny's house to Taylor. The next day, the house burns down. Penny then affirms. Taylor is not bound. Moreover, the power to ratify is terminated by the death or loss of capacity of the third party and by the lapse of a reasonable time. Restatement, Section 4.05, comment b.

For ratification to be effective, the purported principal must have been in existence when the act was done. Restatement, Section 4.04(1)(a). For example, a promoter of a corporation not yet in existence may enter into contracts on behalf of the corporation. In the vast majority of States, however, the corporation cannot ratify these acts because it did not exist when the contracts were made. Instead, the corporation may **adopt** the contract. Adoption differs from ratification because it is not retroactive and does not release the promoter from liability. See *Chapter 34*.

If a principal's lack of capacity entitles her to avoid transactions, the principal may also avoid any ratification made when under the incapacity. Restatement, Section 4.04(2). The principal, however, may ratify a contract that is voidable because of her incapacity when the incapacity no longer exists. Thus, after she reaches majority, a principal may ratify an unauthorized contract made on her behalf during her minority. She may also avoid any ratification made prior to attaining majority.

**Effect of Ratification** Ratification retroactively creates the effects of actual authority. Restatement, Section 4.02(1). Ratification is equivalent to prior authority, which means that the effect of ratification is substantially the same as if the agent or purported agent had been actually authorized when she performed the act. The respective rights, duties, and remedies of the principal and the third party are the same as if the agent had originally possessed actual authority. Both the principal and the agent are in the same position as they would have been if the principal had actually authorized the act originally. The agent is entitled to her due compensation and, moreover, is exonerated (freed) from liability to the principal for acting as his agent without authority or for exceeding her authority, as the case may be. Between the agent and the third party, the agent is released from any liability she may have to the third party by reason of her having induced the third party to enter into the contract without the principal's authority.

### FUNDAMENTAL RULES OF CONTRACTUAL LIABILITY

The following rules summarize the contractual relations between the principal and the third party:

1. A disclosed principal and the third party are parties to the contract if the agent acts within her actual or apparent authority in making the contract on the principal's behalf. Restatement, Section 6.01(1). See *Figure 20-1.*
2. An unidentified (partially disclosed) principal and the third party are parties to the contract if the agent acts within her actual or apparent authority in making the contract on the principal's behalf. Restatement, Section 6.02(1). See *Figure 20-2.*
3. An undisclosed principal and the third party are parties to the contract if the agent acts within her actual authority in making the contract on the principal's behalf unless (a) the terms of the contract exclude the principal or (b) his existence is fraudulently concealed. Restatement, Sections 6.03 and 6.11(4). See *Figure 20-3.*
4. No principal is a party to a contract with a third party if the agent acts without any authority in making the contract on the principal's behalf, unless the principal ratifies the contract. Restatement, Section 4.02. Under the Second Restatement the principal must have been either disclosed or unidentified.

## TORT LIABILITY OF THE PRINCIPAL

In addition to being contractually liable to third persons, a principal may be liable in tort to third persons because of the acts of her agent. Tort liability may arise directly or indirectly (vicariously) from authorized or unauthorized acts of an agent. Also, a principal is liable for the unauthorized torts an agent commits in connection with a transaction that the purported principal, with full knowledge of the tort, subsequently ratifies. Restatement, Sections 4.01 and 7.04. Cases involving unauthorized but ratified torts are extremely rare. Of course, in all of these situations the wrongdoing agent is personally liable to the injured persons because he committed the tort. Restatement, Section 7.01.

◆ **SEE FIGURE 20-4: Tort Liability**

### DIRECT LIABILITY OF PRINCIPAL

A principal is liable for his own tortious conduct involving the use of agents. Such liability primarily arises in one of two ways. First, a principal is directly liable in damages for harm resulting from his directing an agent to commit a tort. Second, the principal is directly liable if he fails to exercise reasonable care in employing competent agents.

**Authorized Acts of Agent** A principal who authorizes his agent to commit a tortious act with respect to the property or person of another is liable for the injury or loss that person sustains. This liability also extends to unauthorized tortious conduct that the principal subsequently ratifies. Restatement, Section 7.04(1). The authorized act is that of the principal. Thus, if Phillip directs his agent, Anthony, to enter upon Clark's land and cut timber, which neither Phillip nor Anthony has any right to do, the cutting of the timber is a trespass, and Phillip is liable to Clark. A principal may be subject to tort liability because of an agent's conduct even though the agent is not subject to liability. Restatement, Section 7.04(2). For example, Phillip instructs his agent, Anthony, to make certain representations as to Phillip's property, which Anthony is authorized to sell. Phillip knows these representations are false, but Anthony does not know and has no reason or duty to know. Such representations by Anthony to Tammy, who buys the property in reliance on them, constitute a deceit for which Phillip is liable to Tammy. Anthony, however, would not be liable to Tammy.

**Unauthorized Acts of Agent** A principal who negligently conducts activities through an employee or other agent is liable for harm resulting from such conduct. Restatement, Section 7.05(1). For example, a principal is liable if he negligently (1) selects agents, (2) retains agents, (3) trains agents, (4) supervises agents, or (5) otherwise controls agents.

The liability of a principal under this provision—called **negligent hiring**—arises when the principal does not exercise proper care in selecting an agent for the job to be done. For example, if Patricia lends to her employee, Art, a company car with which to run a business errand knowing that Art is incapable of driving the vehicle, Patricia would be liable for her own negligence to anyone injured through Art's unsafe driving. The negligent hiring doctrine has also been used to impose liability on a principal for intentional torts committed by an agent against customers of the principal or members of the public, where the principal either knew or should have known that the agent was violent or aggressive.

◆ **FIGURE 20-4: Tort Liability**

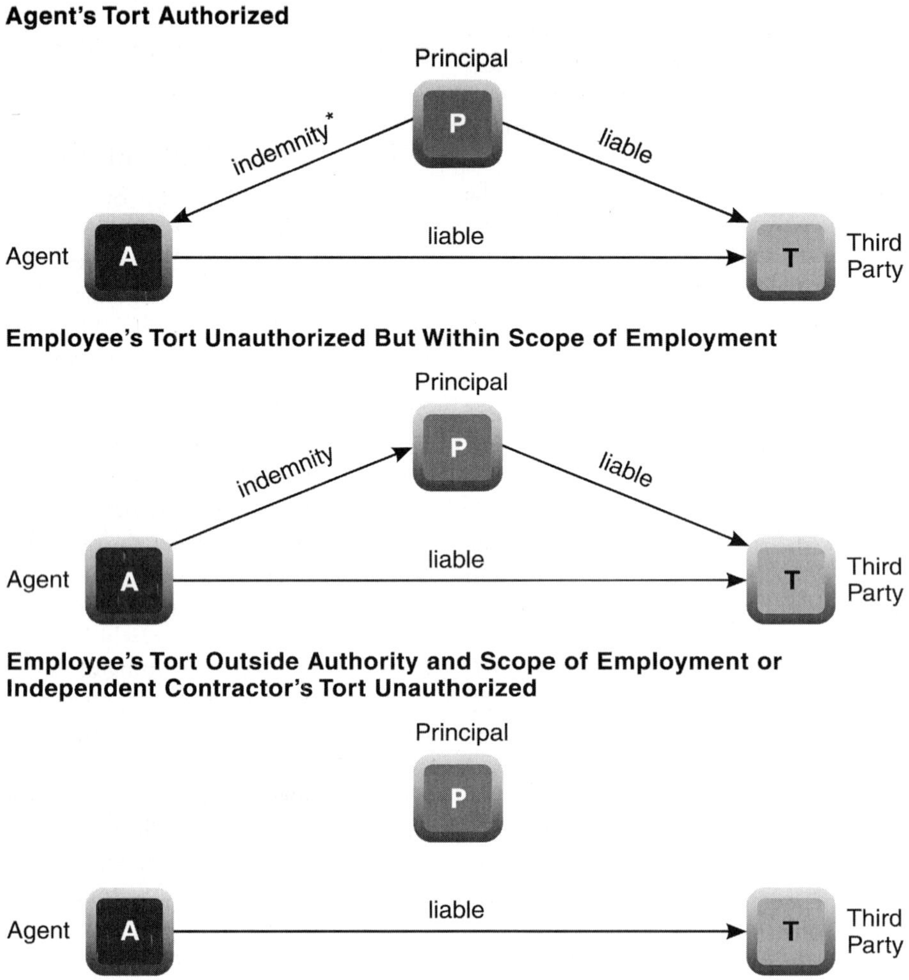


* If not illegal or known by A to be wrongful.

◆ **SEE CASE 20-3**

## VICARIOUS LIABILITY OF PRINCIPAL FOR UNAUTHORIZED ACTS OF AGENT

The vicarious liability of a principal for the unauthorized torts of an agent depends primarily on whether the agent is an employee or not. In this context, an employee is an agent whose principal controls or has the right to control the manner and means of the agent's performance of work. Restatement, Section 7.07(3)(a). By comparison, if the principal does *not* control the manner and means of the agent's performance of the work, the agent is not an employee and is often referred to as an "independent contractor." The general rule is that a principal is not liable for physical harm caused by the tortious conduct of an agent who is an independent contractor if the principal did not intend or authorize the result or the manner of performance. Conversely, a principal is liable for an unauthorized tort committed by an employee acting within the scope of his employment. Restatement, Section 7.07(1).

***Respondeat Superior*** An employer is subject to vicarious liability for an unauthorized tort committed by his employee, even one that is in flagrant disobedience of his instructions, if the employee committed the tort within the scope of his employment. This form of employer liability without fault is based upon the doctrine of *respondeat superior* (let the superior respond). It does not matter how carefully the employer selected the employee, if in fact the latter tortiously injures a third party while engaged in the scope of employment. Moreover, an *undisclosed* principal–employer is liable for the torts committed by her employee within the scope of employment. Furthermore, the principal is liable even if the work is performed gratuitously so long as the principal controls or has the right to control the manner and means of the agent's performance of work. Restatement, Section 7.07(3)(b).

The doctrine of *respondeat superior* is fundamental to the operation of tort law in the United States. The rationale for this doctrine is that a person who conducts his business activities through the use of employees should be liable for the employees' tortious conduct in carrying out those activities. The employer is more likely to insure against liability and is more likely to have the assets to satisfy a tort judgment than the employee. Moreover, *respondeat superior* creates an economic incentive for employers to exercise care in choosing, training, and supervising employees.

The liability of the principal under *respondeat superior* is vicarious or derivative and depends upon proof of wrongdoing by the employee *within the scope of his employment.* Restatement, Section 7.07. The employer's vicarious liability to the third party is in *addition* to the agent's liability to the third party. Frequently both principal and employee are joined as defendants in the same suit. Because the liability of the employer is based upon the employee's tortious conduct, if the employee is not held liable, the principal is not liable either. A principal who is held liable for her employee's tort has a right of **indemnification** against the employee, or the right to be reimbursed for the amount that she was required to pay as a result of the employee's wrongful act. Frequently, however, an employee is unable to reimburse his employer, who then must bear the brunt of the liability.

The wrongful act of the employee must be connected with his employment and within its scope if the principal is to be held liable for injuries or damage resulting to third persons. Section 7.07(2) of the Restatement provides a general rule for determining whether the conduct of an employee is within the scope of employment:

> An employee acts within the scope of employment when performing work assigned by the employer or engaging in a course of conduct subject to the employer's control. An employee's act is not within the scope of employment when it occurs within an independent course of conduct not intended by the employee to serve any purpose of the employer.

For example, Eugene, while delivering gasoline for Packer Oil Co., lights his pipe and negligently throws the blazing match into a pool of gasoline that has dripped onto the ground during the delivery. The gasoline ignites, burning Ray's filling station. Packer is subject to liability for the resulting harm because the negligence of the employee who delivered the gasoline relates directly to the manner in which he handled the goods in his custody. But if a chauffeur, while driving his employer's car on an errand for his employer, suddenly decides to shoot his pistol at pedestrians for target practice, the employer would not be liable to the pedestrians. This willful and intentional misconduct is not related to the performance of the services for which the chauffeur was employed, nor is it expectable by the employer.

To further illustrate, if Page employs Earl to deliver merchandise to Page's customers in a given city, and while driving a delivery truck to or from a place of delivery Earl negligently causes the truck to hit and injure Fred, Page is liable to Fred for the injuries he sustains. But if, after making the scheduled deliveries, Earl drives the truck to a neighboring city to visit a friend and while so doing negligently causes the truck to hit and injure Dottie, Page is not liable. In the latter case, Earl is said to be on a "frolic of his own." By using the truck to accomplish his own purposes, not those of his employer, he has deviated from serving any purpose of his employer.

A principal may be held liable for the intentional torts of his employee if the commission of the tort is so reasonably connected with the employment as to be within its scope. For example, a principal would be liable if his employee were to make fraudulent statements about the products she is selling, defame a competitor, or disparage the competitor's product.

**AGENT ACTS WITH APPARENT AUTHORITY** "A principal is subject to vicarious liability for a tort committed by an agent in dealing or communicating with a third party on or purportedly on behalf of the principal when actions taken by the agent with apparent authority constitute the tort or enable the agent to conceal its commission." Restatement, Section 7.08. This liability applies to (1) agents, whether or not they are employees, and (2) agents who are employees but whose tortious conduct is not within the scope of employment under *respondeat superior.* The torts to which this rule applies include fraudulent and negligent misrepresentations, defamation, wrongful institution of legal proceedings, and conversion of property. For example, Pillsbury engages Adams as an agent to sell some land. While negotiating with Trent, Adams states that a stream running through the property has not overflowed its banks during the past ten years. Adams knows that this is false. In reliance upon this false statement, Trent purchases the land. Pillsbury is liable to Trent for fraudulent misrepresentation.

**TORTS OF INDEPENDENT CONTRACTOR** As previously indicated, an independent contractor is not the employee of the person for whom he is performing work or rendering services. Hence, the doctrine of *respondeat superior* generally does not apply to torts committed by an independent contractor. For example, Parnell authorizes Bob, his broker, to sell land for him. Parnell, Teresa, and Bob meet in Teresa's office, where Bob arranges the sale to Teresa. While Bob is preparing the deed for Parnell to sign, he negligently knocks over an inkstand and ruins a valuable rug belonging to Teresa. Bob, but not Parnell, is liable to Teresa. Similarly, Patty employs Igor, a roofer, as an independent contractor to repair her roof. Igor drops a hammer upon Wanda, a pedestrian walking by on the public sidewalk. Igor, but not Patty, is liable to Wanda.

Nonetheless, the principal may be *directly* liable if she fails to exercise reasonable care in selecting an independent contractor. For example, Melanie employs Gordon, whom she knows to be an alcoholic, as an independent contractor to repair her roof. Gordon attempts the repairs while heavily intoxicated and negligently drops a fifty-pound bundle of shingles upon Eric, a pedestrian walking on the sidewalk. Both Gordon and Melanie are liable to Eric.

Moreover, under some circumstances a principal will be *vicariously* liable for torts committed by a carefully selected independent contractor. Certain duties imposed by law are nondelegable, and a person may not escape the consequences of their nonperformance by having entrusted them to another person, whether or not that person is an agent. Restatement, Section 7.06. For example, a landowner who permits an independent contractor to maintain a dangerous condition on his premises, such as an excavation, neither surrounded by a guardrail nor lit at night, adjoining a public sidewalk is liable to a member of the public who is injured by falling into the excavation.

A principal is also vicariously liable for an independent contractor's conduct in carrying on an abnormally dangerous activity, such as using fire or high explosives, or spraying crops.

## CRIMINAL LIABILITY OF THE PRINCIPAL

A principal is liable for the authorized criminal acts of his agents only if the principal directed, participated in, or approved of the acts. For example, if an agent, at his principal's direction or with his principal's knowledge, fixes prices with the principal's competitors, both the agent and the principal have criminally violated the antitrust laws. Otherwise, a principal ordinarily is not liable for the unauthorized criminal acts of his agents. One of the elements of a crime is mental fault, and this element is absent, so far as the criminal responsibility of the principal is concerned, in cases in which the principal did not authorize the agent's act.

An employer may, nevertheless, be subject to a criminal penalty for the act of an advisory or managerial person acting in the scope of employment. Moreover, an employer may be criminally liable under liability without fault statutes for certain unauthorized acts of an employee, whether the employee is managerial or not. These statutes, which usually are regulatory, do not require mental fault. For example, many States have statutes that punish "every person who by himself or his employee or agent sells anything at short weight," or "whoever sells liquor to a minor and any sale by an employee shall be deemed the act of the employer as well." Another example is a statute prohibiting the sale of unwholesome or adulterated food. See *Chapter 6* for a more detailed discussion of this topic.

# RELATIONSHIP OF AGENT AND THIRD PERSONS

The function of an agent is to assist in the conduct of the principal's business by carrying out his orders. Generally, the agent acquires no rights against third parties and likewise incurs no liabilities to them. There are, however, several exceptions to this general proposition. In certain instances, an agent may become personally liable to the third party for contracts she made on behalf of her principal. In some of these situations, the agent also may acquire rights against the third party. In addition, an agent who commits a tort is personally liable to the injured third party. These circumstances involving the personal liability of an agent, as well as those in which an agent may acquire rights against third persons, will be covered in this section.

## CONTRACT LIABILITY OF AGENT

The agent normally is not a party to the contract he makes with a third person on behalf of a disclosed principal. An agent who exceeds his actual and apparent authority, however, may be personally liable to the third party. In addition, an agent acting for a disclosed principal may become liable if he expressly assumes liability on the contract. When an agent enters into a contract on behalf of an unidentified (partially disclosed) principal or an undisclosed principal, the agent becomes personally liable to the third party on the contract. Furthermore, an agent who knowingly enters into a contract on behalf of a nonexistent or completely incompetent principal is personally liable to the third party on that contract.

### DISCLOSED PRINCIPAL

As explained earlier, the principal is a disclosed principal if, when an agent and a third party interact, the third party has notice that the agent is acting for a principal and also has notice of the principal's identity. The liability of an agent acting for a disclosed principal depends on whether the agent acts within her authority in making the contract or otherwise assumes liability on the contract.

**Authorized Contracts** When an agent acting with actual or apparent authority makes a contract with a third party on behalf of a disclosed principal, the agent is not a party to the contract unless she and the third party agree otherwise. Restatement, Section 6.01(2). The third person is on notice that he is transacting business with an agent who is acting for an identified principal and that the agent is not personally undertaking to perform the contract, but is simply negotiating on behalf of her principal. The resulting contract, if within the agent's actual authority, is between the third person and the principal, and the agent ordinarily incurs no liability on the contract to either party. Thus, Angela, who has actual authority to sell circuit boards manufactured by Pinter, writes to Toni, "On behalf of Pinter, I offer to sell you 5,000 circuit boards for $15,000." Toni accepts; consequently, a contract exists between Toni and Pinter. Angela is not a party to that contract and has no liability to Pinter or Toni. This is also true of unauthorized contracts that are subsequently ratified by the principal. If, however, the agent has apparent authority but no actual authority, he has no liability to the third party but is liable to the principal for any loss he causes by exceeding his actual authority.

◆ **SEE FIGURE 20-1: Contract Liability of Disclosed Principal**

**UNAUTHORIZED CONTRACTS** If an agent exceeds his actual *and* apparent authority, the principal is not bound. The fact that the principal is not bound does not, however, make the agent a party to the contract unless the agent had agreed to be a party to the contract. The agent's liability, if any, arises from express or implied representations about his authority that he makes to the third party. For example, an agent may give an **express warranty of authority** by stating that he has authority and that he will be personally liable to the third party if he does not in fact have the authority to bind his principal.

Moreover, a person who undertakes to make a contract on behalf of another gives an **implied warranty of authority** that he is in fact authorized to make the contract on behalf of the party whom he purports to represent. If the agent does not have authority to bind the principal, the agent is liable to the third party for damages unless the principal ratifies the contract or the third party knew that the agent was unauthorized. Restatement, Section 6.10. No implied warranty of authority exists, however, if the agent expressly states that the agent gives no warranty of authority or if the agent, acting in good faith, discloses to the third person all of the facts upon which his authority rests. For example, agent Larson has received an ambiguous letter of instruction from his principal, Dan. Larson shows it to Carol, stating that it represents all of the authority that he has to act, and both Larson and Carol rely upon its sufficiency. Larson has made no implied or express warranty of his authority to Carol.

The Restatement provides that breach of the implied warranty of authority subjects the agent to liability to the third party for damages caused by breach of that warranty, including loss of the benefit expected from performance by the principal. Restatement, Section 6.10. Some courts, however, limit the third party's recovery to the damage or loss the third party suffered and exclude the third party's expected gain from the contract.

If a purported agent **misrepresents** to a third person that he has authority to make a contract on behalf of a principal whom he has no power to bind, he is liable in a tort action to the third person for the loss she sustained in reliance upon the misrepresentation. If the third party knows, however, that the representation is false, then the agent is not liable.

**AGENT ASSUMES LIABILITY** An agent for a disclosed principal may agree to become liable on a contract between the principal and the third party (1) by making the contract in her own name, (2) by co-making the contract with the principal, or (3) by guaranteeing that the principal will perform the contract between the third party and the principal. In each situation, the agent's liability is separate unless the parties agree otherwise. Therefore, the third party may sue the agent separately without joining the principal and may obtain a judgment against either the principal or the agent or both. If the principal satisfies the judgment, the agent is discharged. If the agent pays the judgment, he usually will have a right of reimbursement from the principal. This right is based upon the principles of suretyship, discussed in *Chapter 38*.

### UNIDENTIFIED PRINCIPAL

As previously discussed, the principal is an unidentified principal (partially disclosed principal) if, when an agent and a third party interact, the third party has notice that the agent is acting for a principal but does not have notice of the principal's identity. The use of an unidentified principal may be helpful where, for example, the third party might inflate the price of property he was selling if he knew the principal's identity. Partial disclosure also may occur inadvertently, when the agent fails through neglect to inform the third party of the principal's identity.

Unless otherwise agreed, when an agent makes a contract with actual or apparent authority on behalf of an unidentified principal, the agent is a party to the contract. Restatement, Section 6.02. For example, Ashley writes to Terrence offering to sell a rare painting on behalf of its owner, who wishes to remain unknown. Terrence accepts. Ashley is a party to the contract.

Whether the particular transaction is authorized or not, an agent for an unidentified principal is liable to the third party. If the agent is actually or apparently authorized to make the contract, then both the agent and the unidentified principal are liable. If the agent has no actual and no apparent authority, the agent is liable either as a party to the contract or for breach of the implied warranty of authority. Restatement, Section 6.02, comment b. In any event, the agent is separately liable, and the third party may sue her individually without joining the principal and may obtain a judgment against either the principal or the agent or both. If the principal satisfies the judgment, the agent is also discharged. Restatement, Section 6.09. If the agent pays the judgment, the principal is discharged from liability to the third party, but the agent has the right to be reimbursed by the principal.

◆ SEE FIGURE 20-2: **Contract Liability of Unidentified Principal**

### UNDISCLOSED PRINCIPAL

The principal is an undisclosed principal if, when an agent and a third party interact, the third party has no notice that the agent is acting for a principal. Thus, when an agent acts for an undisclosed principal, she appears to be acting in her own behalf and the third person with whom she is dealing has no knowledge that she is acting as an agent. The principal has instructed the agent to conceal not only the principal's identity but also the agency relationship. Such concealment can also occur if the agent simply neglects to disclose the existence and identity of her principal. Thus, the third person is dealing with the agent as though she were a principal.

The agent is personally liable upon a contract she enters into with a third person on behalf of an undisclosed principal. Restatement, Section 6.03(2). The agent is liable because the third person has relied upon the agent individually and has accepted the agent's personal undertaking to perform the contract. Obviously, where the principal is undisclosed, the third person does not know of the interest of anyone in the contract other than that of himself and the agent.

The Second Restatement and many cases hold that after the third person has learned of the identity of the undisclosed principal, he may obtain performance of the contract from either the principal or the agent, but not both; and his choice, once made, binds him irrevocably. Nevertheless, to avoid the possibility that evidence at trial will fail to establish the agency relationship, the third person may bring suit against both the principal and agent. In most States following this approach, this act of bringing suit and proceeding to trial against both is not an election, but before the entry of any judgment, the third person is compelled to make an election because he is not entitled to a judgment against both. A judgment against the agent by a third party who knows the identity of the previously undisclosed principal discharges the liability of the principal. In this case, the agent would have the right to be reimbursed by the principal. If, however, the third party obtains a judgment against the agent before learning the principal's identity, the principal is not discharged. Finally, the agent is discharged from liability if the third party gets a judgment against the principal.

The Third Restatement and a number of States have recently rejected the election rule, holding that a third party's rights against the principal are *additional* and not alternative to the third party's rights against the agent. Section 6.09 provides, "When an agent has made a contract with a third party on behalf of a principal, unless the contract provides otherwise, the liability, if any, of the principal or the agent to the third party is not discharged if the third party obtains a judgment against the other." However, the liability, if any, of the principal or the agent to the third party *is* discharged to the extent a judgment against the other is satisfied.

◆ SEE FIGURE 20-3: **Contract Liability of Undisclosed Principal**

### NONEXISTENT OR INCOMPETENT PRINCIPAL

Unless the third party agrees otherwise, if a person who purports to act as an agent knows or has reason to know that the person purportedly represented does not exist or completely lacks capacity to be a party to contract, the person purporting to act as agent will become a party to the contract. Restatement, Section 6.04. Complete lack of capacity to contract includes an individual person who has been adjudicated incompetent. An example of a nonexistent principal is a corporation or limited liability corporation (LLC) that has not yet been formed. Thus, a promoter of a corporation who enters into contracts with third persons in the name of a corporation yet to be organized is personally liable on such contracts. Not yet in existence, and therefore unable to authorize the contracts, the corporation is not liable. If, after coming into existence, the corporation affirmatively adopts a preincorporation contract made on its behalf, it, in addition to the promoter, becomes bound. If the corporation enters into a new contract with such a third person, however, the prior contract between the promoter and the third person is discharged, and the liability of the promoter is terminated. This is a novation.

◆ SEE FIGURE 34-1: **Promoter's Preincorporation Contracts Made in Corporation's Name**

An agent who makes a contract for a disclosed principal whose contracts are *voidable* for lack of contractual capacity is *not* liable to the third party. Restatement, Section 6.04, comment b. There are two exceptions to this rule: (1) if the agent warrants or represents that the principal has capacity; or (2) if the agent has reason to know both of the principal's lack of capacity and of the third party's ignorance of that incapacity.

◆ SEE CASE 20-4

## TORT OF LIABILITY OF AGENT

An agent is personally liable for his tortious acts that injure third persons, whether the principal authorizes such acts or not and whether or not the principal may also be liable. Restatement, Section 7.01. For example, an agent is personally liable if he converts the goods of a third person to his principal's use. An agent is also liable for making representations that he knows to be fraudulent to a third person who in reliance sustains a loss.

## RIGHTS OF AGENT AGAINST THIRD PERSON

An agent who makes a contract with a third person on behalf of a disclosed principal usually has no right of action against the third person for breach of contract. Restatement, Section 6.01. The agent is not a party to the contract. An agent for a disclosed principal may sue on the contract, however, if it provides that the agent is a party to the contract. Furthermore, an agent for an undisclosed principal or an unidentified (partially disclosed) principal may maintain in her own name an action against the third person for breach of contract. Restatement, Sections 6.02 and 6.03.

# CHAPTER SUMMARY

## RELATIONSHIP OF PRINCIPAL AND THIRD PERSONS

### CONTRACT LIABILITY OF PRINCIPAL

**Types of Principals**
- ***Disclosed Principal*** principal whose existence and identity are known
- ***Unidentified (Partially Disclosed) Principal*** principal whose existence is known but whose identity is not known
- ***Undisclosed Principal*** principal whose existence and identity are not known

**Authority** power of an agent to change the legal status of the principal
- ***Actual Authority*** power conferred upon the agent by actual consent manifested by the principal to the agent
- ***Actual Express Authority*** actual authority derived from written or spoken words of the principal communicated to the agent
- ***Actual Implied Authority*** actual authority inferred from words or conduct manifested to the agent by the principal
- ***Apparent Authority*** power conferred upon the agent by acts or conduct of the principal that reasonably lead a third party to believe that the agent has such power

**Delegation of Authority** is usually not permitted unless actually or apparently authorized by the principal; if the agent is authorized to appoint other subagents, the acts of these subagents are as binding on the principal as those of the agent

**Effect of Termination of Agency on Authority** ends *actual* authority
- ***Second Restatement*** if the termination is by operation of law, *apparent* authority also ends without notice to third parties; if the termination is by an act of the parties, *apparent* authority ends when third parties have actual knowledge or when appropriate notice is given to third parties: actual notice must be given to third parties with whom the agent has previously dealt on credit, has been specially accredited, or has begun to deal; all other third parties as to whom there was apparent authority need be given only constructive notice
- ***Third Restatement*** termination of actual authority does not by itself end any apparent authority held by an agent; *apparent* authority ends when it is no longer reasonable for the third party with whom an agent deals to believe that the agent continues to act with actual authority

**Ratification** affirmation by one person of a prior unauthorized act that another has done as her agent or as her purported agent

**Fundamental Rules of Contractual Liability**

- ***Disclosed Principal*** is contractually bound with the third party if the agent acts within her actual or apparent authority in making the contract on the principal's behalf
- ***Partially Disclosed Principal*** is contractually bound with the third party if the agent acts within her actual or apparent authority in making the contract on the principal's behalf
- ***Undisclosed Principal*** is contractually bound with the third party if the agent acts within her actual authority in making the contract on the principal's behalf

---

**TORT LIABILITY OF PRINCIPAL**

**Direct Liability of Principal** a principal is liable for his own tortious conduct involving the use of agents

- ***Authorized Acts of Agent*** a principal is liable for torts that she authorizes another to commit or that she ratifies
- ***Unauthorized Acts of Agent*** a principal is liable for failing to exercise reasonable care in employing agents whose unauthorized acts cause harm

**Vicarious Liability of Principal for Unauthorized Acts of Agent**

- **Respondeat Superior** an employer is liable for unauthorized torts committed by an employee in the scope of his employment
- ***Agent Acts with Apparent Authority*** a principal is liable for torts committed by an agent in dealing with third parties while acting within the agent's apparent authority
- ***Independent Contractor*** a principal is usually not liable for the unauthorized torts of an independent contractor

---

**CRIMINAL LIABILITY OF PRINCIPAL**

**Authorized Acts** the principal is liable if he directed, participated in, or approved the criminal acts of his agents

**Unauthorized Acts** the principal may be liable either for a criminal act of a managerial person or under liability without fault statutes

---

## RELATIONSHIP OF AGENT AND THIRD PERSONS

**CONTRACT LIABILITY OF AGENT**

**Disclosed Principal**

- ***Authorized Contracts*** the agent is not normally a party to the contract she makes with a third person if she has actual or apparent authority or if the principal ratifies an unauthorized contract
- ***Unauthorized Contracts*** if an agent exceeds her actual and apparent authority, the principal is not bound but the agent may be liable to the third party for breach of warranty or for misrepresentation
- ***Agent Assumes Liability*** an agent may agree to become liable on a contract between the principal and the third party

**Unidentified (Partially Disclosed) Principal** an agent who acts for a partially disclosed principal is a party to the contract with the third party unless otherwise agreed

**Undisclosed Principal** an agent who acts for an undisclosed principal is personally liable on the contract to the third party

**Nonexistent or Incompetent Principal** a person who purports to act as an agent for a principal whom the agent knows to be nonexistent or completely incompetent is personally liable on a contract entered into with a third person on behalf of such a principal

---

**TORT LIABILITY OF AGENT**

**Authorized Acts** the agent is liable to the third party for his own torts

**Unauthorized Acts** the agent is liable to the third party for his own torts

| | |
|---|---|
| **RIGHTS OF AGENT AGAINST THIRD PERSON** | **Disclosed Principal** the agent usually has no rights against the third party<br>**Unidentified (Partially Disclosed) Principal** the agent may enforce the contract against the third party<br>**Undisclosed Principal** the agent may enforce the contract against the third party |

## CASES

CASE 20-1

### Types of Authority
### SCHOENBERGER v. CHICAGO TRANSIT AUTHORITY

Appellate Court of Illinois, First District, First Division, 1980
84 Ill.App.3d 1132, 39 Ill.Dec. 941, 405 N.E.2d 1076

**Campbell, J.**

The plaintiff, James Schoenberger, brought a small claims action * * * in the * * * circuit court of Cook County against the defendant, Chicago Transit Authority (hereinafter C.T.A.) to recover contract damages. The trial court ruled in favor of the defendant and against the plaintiff. The plaintiff appeals from this judgment. At issue is whether the C.T.A. may be held liable under agency principles of a promise allegedly made by an employee of the C.T.A. to the plaintiff at the time that he was hired to the effect that he would receive a $500 increase in salary within a specified period of time. We affirm.

Schoenberger was employed by the C.T.A. from August 16, 1976, to October, 1976, at a salary of $19,300. The facts surrounding his employment with the C.T.A. are controverted. The plaintiff's position at the trial was that he took the job with the C.T.A. at a salary of $19,300 upon the condition that he would receive a $500 salary increase, above and beyond any merit raises, within a year. Schoenberger testified at trial that, after filling out a job application and undergoing an initial interview with a C.T.A. Placement Department interviewer, he met several times with Frank ZuChristian, who was in charge of recruiting for the Data Center. At one of the meetings with ZuChristian, the Director of Data Center Operations, John Bonner, was present. At the third meeting held between ZuChristian and the plaintiff, ZuChristian informed the plaintiff that he desired to employ him at $19,800 and that he was making a recommendation to this effect. Schoenberger told ZuChristian that he would accept the offer. ZuChristian informed him that a formal offer would come from the Placement Department within a few days. However, when the offer was made, the salary was stated at $19,300. Schoenberger did not accept the offer immediately. Rather, he called ZuChristian for an explanation of the salary difference. After making inquiries, ZuChristian informed Schoenberger that a clerical error had been made and that it would take a number of weeks to have the necessary paperwork reapproved because several people were on vacation. To expedite matters, ZuChristian suggested Schoenberger take the job at the $19,300 figure and that he would see that the $500 would be made up to him at the April, 1976, October, 1976, or at the latest, the April, 1977, performance and salary review. The $500 increase was to be prospective and not retroactive in nature. John Hogan, the head of the Data Center, was aware of this promise, ZuChristian informed Schoenberger. Because the defendant was found to be ineligible for the October, 1976 performance evaluation and the April, 1976 review was cancelled, the April, 1977 evaluation was the first evaluation at which the issue of the salary increase was raised. When the increase was not given at that time, the plaintiff resigned and filed this suit.

* * *

The trial court, after hearing the evidence and reviewing the exhibits, ruled in favor of the defendant. The trial court ruled: (1) that it was inconceivable that the plaintiff thought ZuChristian had final authority in regard to employment contracts; and (2) that it was not shown that a commitment or promise was made to the plaintiff by an authorized agent of the C.T.A.

* * *

The main question before us is whether ZuChristian, acting as an agent of the C.T.A., orally contracted with Schoenberger for $500 in compensation in addition to his $19,300 salary. The authority of an agent may only come from the principal and it is therefore necessary to trace the source of an agent's authority to some word or act of the alleged principal. [Citations.] The authority to bind a principal will not be presumed, but rather, the person alleging authority must prove its source unless the act of the agent has been ratified.

[Citations.] Moreover, the authority must be founded upon some word or act of the principal, not on the acts or words of the agent. [Citations.]

* * * Both Hogan and Bonner, ZuChristian's superiors, testified that ZuChristian had no actual authority to either make an offer of a specific salary to Schoenberger or to make any promise of additional compensation. Furthermore, ZuChristian's testimony corroborated the testimony that he lacked the authority to make formal offers. From this evidence, it is clear that the trial court properly determined that ZuChristian lacked the actual authority to bind the C.T.A. for the additional $500 in compensation to Schoenberger.

Nor can it be said that the C.T.A. clothed ZuChristian with the apparent authority to make Schoenberger a promise of compensation over and above that formally offered by the Placement Department. The general rule to consider in determining whether an agent is acting within the apparent authority of his principal was stated in [citation] in this way:

> Apparent authority in an agent is such authority as the principal knowingly permits the agent to assume or which he holds his agent out as possessing—it is such authority as a reasonably prudent man, exercising diligence and discretion, in view of the principal's conduct, would naturally suppose the agent to possess.

* * *

Here, Schoenberger's initial contact with the C.T.A. was with the Placement Department where he filled out an application and had his first interview. There is no evidence that the C.T.A. did anything to permit ZuChristian to assume authority nor did they do anything to hold him out as having the authority to hire and set salaries. ZuChristian was not at a management level in the C.T.A. nor did his job title of Principal Communications Analyst suggest otherwise. The mere fact that he was allowed to interview prospective employees does not establish that the C.T.A. held him out as possessing the authority to hire employees or set salaries. Moreover, ZuChristian did inform Schoenberger that the formal offer of employment would be made by the Placement Department.

* * *

Our final inquiry concerns the plaintiff's contention that irrespective of ZuChristian's actual or apparent authority, the C.T.A. is bound by ZuChristian's promise because it ratified his acts. Ratification may be express or inferred and occurs where "the principal, with knowledge of the material facts of the unauthorized transaction, takes a position inconsistent with nonaffirmation of the transaction." [Citations.] Ratification is the equivalent to an original authorization and confirms that which was originally unauthorized. [Citation.] Ratification occurs where a principal attempts to seek or retain the benefits of the transaction. [Citations.]

Upon review of the evidence, we are not convinced that the C.T.A. acted to ratify ZuChristian's promise. * * *

* * *

For the reasons we have indicated, the judgment of the circuit court of Cook County granting judgment in favor of the defendant, C.T.A., is affirmed.

---

## CASE 20-2

## Effect of Termination of Agency on Authority
## PARLATO v. EQUITABLE LIFE ASSURANCE SOCIETY OF THE UNITED STATES

Supreme Court of New York, Appellate Division, First Department, 2002
299 A.D.2d 108, 749 N.Y.S.2d 216

**Friedman, J.**

Plaintiffs, who are sisters, were defrauded by Kenneth Soule, an agent of defendant Equitable Life Assurance Society of the United States (Equitable), beginning while Soule was employed by Equitable and continuing after Equitable terminated him in July 1992. Soule actually opened an Equitable account for one plaintiff, but he did not do so for the other, instead stealing all the funds that plaintiff entrusted to him. * * *

* * * Equitable hired Soule on or about April 1, 1990, as an agent authorized to sell Equitable financial products, such as insurance policies and annuities, to the public. Before becoming an Equitable agent, Soule from 1986 onward had been plaintiff Parlato's accountant and financial advisor. Parlato, a resident of Queens, began investing in Equitable financial products through Soule in May 1990, and Soule actually opened several Equitable accounts in Parlato's name while he was an Equitable agent. In the spring of 1992, however, Soule began criminally defrauding Parlato. Between March and May of 1992, Parlato, at Soule's urging, liquidated certain of her non-Equitable investments, and entrusted the proceeds to Soule for investment in Equitable financial products. Soule converted these funds, and all additional funds that Parlato subsequently entrusted to him, to his personal use.

In 1991, Soule began soliciting plaintiff Perry, Parlato's sister and a resident of Hawaii, to invest in Equitable products. In May 1992, Perry began entrusting funds to Soule to be used to open investment accounts for her at Equitable. Unlike Parlato, however, Perry alleges that Soule never opened any Equitable account for her, and that, from the start, he misappropriated every penny she ever entrusted to him. Thus, prior to the instant litigation, Perry was unknown to Equitable.

Equitable terminated Soule's employment in July 1992. Although Parlato allegedly still had an account with Equitable at that time, Equitable did not notify her of the termination. For approximately four years after his termination, Soule allegedly continued to represent himself to plaintiffs as an Equitable agent and to solicit their further investment in purported Equitable financial products. Plaintiffs do not allege, however, that they were exposed to any manifestations by Equitable of a continuing connection between Soule and Equitable after July 1992.

In August 1996, plaintiffs contacted Equitable to verify the status of their investments. At that time, Equitable informed plaintiffs that Soule had been terminated by Equitable in July 1992. This allegedly was the first time plaintiffs became aware that Soule's relationship with Equitable had been severed. Plaintiffs then alerted law enforcement authorities to Soule's misconduct. Ultimately, Soule pleaded guilty to a federal charge of mail fraud, and was sentenced to 27 months in prison and three years of supervised release, conditioned on his promise to make restitution in the amount of $ 416,000.

Plaintiffs commenced this action against Equitable in December 1999. Each plaintiff asserted a cause of action for fraud, based on the contention that she entrusted her money to Soule in reliance on the appearance of authority to act for Equitable with which the company had clothed him. [The trial court granted the defendant's motion to dismiss the complaint], and plaintiffs have appealed.

* * *

* * * [I]t is well established that a principal may be held liable in tort for the misuse by its agent of his apparent authority to defraud a third party who reasonably relies on the appearance of authority, even if the agent commits the fraud solely for his personal benefit, and to the detriment of the principal [citations]; Restatement [Second] of Agency §§261, 262, 265 [1]; [citations]. The reason for this rule is that the principal, by virtue of its ability to select its agents and to exercise control over them (*see* Restatement [Second] of Agency §1 [1]), is in a better position than third parties to prevent the perpetration of fraud by such agents through the misuse of their positions. Thus, the principal should not escape liability when an innocent third person suffers a loss as the result of an agent's abuse, for his own fraudulent purposes, of the third person's reasonable reliance on the apparent authority with which the principal has invested the agent. * * *

* * *

[The plaintiffs' claims based on frauds perpetrated during Soule's employment by Equitable are barred by the statute of limitations.]

* * * The final question before us, therefore, is whether, under these circumstances, Equitable's termination of Soule's employment in July 1992 had the effect, as a matter of law, of immediately cutting off his apparent authority to act for Equitable vis-à-vis the two plaintiffs. This question cannot be answered in the abstract. Rather, since the two plaintiffs are situated differently, the question must be addressed separately as to each plaintiff.

We hold that Parlato's claim, to the extent it is not time-barred, should not have been dismissed on a motion addressed to her pleading. The Court of Appeals has held that a third party who, like Parlato, is known by a principal to have previously dealt with the principal through the principal's authorized agent, is entitled to assume that the agent's authority continues until the third party receives notice the principal has revoked the agent's authority [citations]. The law of other states appears to be similar (*see* Restatement [Second] of Agency §§124A, 125, 127, 135, 136 [1], [2]; [citations]). In recognizing this duty of a principal to give notice of the revocation of an agent's authority, we are simply applying established principles.

In this case, Parlato alleges that Soule opened actual Equitable investment accounts for her while he was still an authorized agent of Equitable. If this is proven to be so, Parlato will be entitled to the benefit of the above-described rule permitting her, as a person known to have done business with Equitable through Soule in the past, to presume that Soule remained authorized to act for Equitable in the absence of either (1) notice that his authority had been revoked or (2) other circumstances that would have rendered it unreasonable to believe that Soule had authority to act for Equitable in the transactions he proposed [citation]; Restatement [Second] of Agency §125, Comment *b*; [citation]. Before any determination can be made as to whether it was reasonable for Parlato to believe that Soule had authority to act for Equitable in the transactions for which her claims are not time-barred, the particular facts of this case must be developed through discovery. Therefore, it was error to dismiss Parlato's claim on this pleading motion.

This brings us to the question of the viability of Perry's claim against Equitable. Perry alleges that Soule stole all of the money she entrusted to him, and that he never opened any Equitable account in her name. Thus, Perry's own allegations establish that Equitable had no way of notifying her of Soule's termination in July 1992. Under these circumstances, we hold that any apparent authority Soule may have had vis-à-vis Perry terminated along with his actual authority when his employment by Equitable came to an end.

Considerations of fairness, practicality and sound public policy lead us to this conclusion. Even in the case of a third party unknown to the principal, it seems fair to hold the principal responsible for the agent's misuse of his apparent authority while the principal-agent relationship continues to exist, bringing benefits to the principal and giving the principal a measure of control over the agent's conduct (*see* Restatement [Second] of Agency §1 [1] [an agent acts on behalf of the principal subject to the principal's control]). It seems unfair, however, to hold the principal responsible for torts its former agent commits after termination against an unknown third party, even if the former agent facilitates his wrongdoing by misrepresenting to the victim that the agency relationship is still in existence. Once the agent's employment has been terminated, the principal no longer has any power to control the agent's conduct. Moreover, the principal obviously cannot give notice of the agent's termination to a third party that is totally unknown to it. The law, of course, "does not require the impossible …" [Citation.] Further, allowing claims against a principal based on a former agent's posttermination torts against unknown third parties would subject the principal to potentially unlimited liability.

* * *

Finally, the amended complaint alleges that Equitable "made no effort to alert the public in general that Soule was no longer its agent…." It is true that section 136 (3) of the Restatement (Second) of Agency (published in 1958) takes the position that, absent public notice (as by advertisement in a newspaper of general circulation) of revocation of an agent's authority in the area in which he formerly acted for the principal, apparent authority continues to exist after such revocation as to persons who previously knew of the agency and do not receive actual notice of the revocation, even if such persons never previously did business with the agent and thus are unknown to the principal. While this rule (hereinafter, the "public notice rule") finds support in a number of very old New York cases [citation], we do not regard the public notice rule as binding at this late date, at least under the particular facts alleged by plaintiffs. There is no statutory or regulatory mandate for public notice in this context * * * and the most recent New York cases giving support to the rule appear to be from the era when the telephone was a relatively new and uncommon device. Today, a person dealing with an individual known to have represented a company in the past can easily verify that the individual is still an agent for the company by contacting the company by telephone. Moreover, there is no reason to believe that the newspaper advertisements contemplated by the public notice rule would actually be read by customers such as plaintiffs in this action. This is particularly so in the case of plaintiff Perry, who, as a resident of Hawaii, would have been highly unlikely to come across a newspaper advertisement announcing Soule's termination in the New York area (*see* Restatement [Second] of Agency §136 [3] [a] [public notice rule is satisfied by publication "in a newspaper of general circulation in the place where the agency is regularly carried on"]). We therefore decline to ascribe legal significance to Equitable's alleged failure to give public notice of Soule's termination.

[Judgment modified in part and affirmed in part.]

## CASE 20-3

## Direct Liability of Principal: Negligent Hiring
## CONNES v. MOLALLA TRANSPORT SYSTEM, INC.

Supreme Court of Colorado, 1992
831 P.2d 1316

**Quinn, J.**

[Terry Taylor was an employee of Molalla Transport. In hiring Taylor, Molalla followed its standard hiring procedure, which includes a personal interview with each applicant and requires the applicant to fill out an extensive job application form and to produce a current driver's license and a medical examiner's certificate. Molalla also contacts prior employers and other references about the applicant's qualifications and conducts an investigation of the applicant's driving record in the state where the applicant obtained the driver's license. Although applicants are asked whether they have been convicted of a crime, Molalla does not conduct an independent investigation to determine whether an applicant has been convicted of a crime. Approximately three months

after Taylor began working for Molalla, he was assigned to transport freight from Kansas to Oregon. While traveling through Colorado, Taylor left the highway and drove by a hotel where Grace Connes was working as a night clerk. Observing that Connes was alone in the lobby, Taylor pulled his truck into the parking lot and entered the lobby. Once inside, Taylor sexually assaulted Connes at knifepoint. Although Taylor denied any prior criminal convictions on his application and during his interview, police and court records obtained since these events show that Taylor had been convicted of three felonies in Colorado and had been issued three citations for lewd conduct and another citation for simple assault in Seattle, Washington.

Connes sued Molalla on the theory of negligent hiring, claiming that Molalla knew or should have known that Taylor would come into contact with members of the public, that Molalla had a duty to hire and retain high quality employees so as not to endanger members of the public, and that Molalla had breached its duty by failing to investigate fully and adequately Taylor's criminal background. The district court granted Molalla's motion for summary judgment. The Court of Appeals upheld the lower court's ruling, holding that Molalla had no legal duty to investigate the non-vehicular criminal record of its driver prior to hiring him as an employee. Connes appealed.]

* * *

## II

The elements of a negligence claim consist of the existence of a legal duty by the defendant to the plaintiff, breach of that duty by the defendant, injury to the plaintiff, and a sufficient causal relationship between the defendant's breach and the plaintiff's injuries. [Citations.] A negligence claim will fail if it is predicated on circumstances for which the law imposes no duty of care upon the defendant. [Citations.] "A court's conclusion that a duty does or does not exist is 'an expression of the sum total of those considerations of policy which lead the law to say that the plaintiff is [or is not] entitled to protection.'" [Citations.]

The initial question in any negligence action, therefore, is whether the defendant owed a legal duty to protect the plaintiff against injury. The issue of legal duty is a question of law to be determined by the court. [Citations.]

A duty of reasonable care arises when there is a foreseeable risk of injury to others from a defendant's failure to take protective action to prevent the injury. [Citation.] While foreseeability is a prime factor in the duty calculus, a court also must weigh other factors, including the social utility of the defendant's conduct, the magnitude of the burden of guarding against the harm caused to the plaintiff, the practical consequences of placing such a burden on the defendant, and any additional elements disclosed by the particular circumstances of the case. [Citations.] "No one factor is controlling, and the question of whether a duty should be imposed in a particular case is essentially one of fairness under contemporary standards—whether reasonable persons would recognize a duty and agree that it exists." [Citation.]

The tort of negligent hiring is based on the principle that a person conducting an activity through employees is subject to liability for harm resulting from negligent conduct "in the employment of improper persons or instrumentalities in work involving risk of harm to others." Restatement (Second) of Agency §213(b)(1958). This principle of liability is not based on the rule of agency but rather on the law of torts. In [citation], the New Jersey Supreme Court offered the following distinction between the tort of negligent hiring and the agency doctrine of vicarious liability based on the rule of *respondeat superior*:

> Thus, the tort of negligent hiring addresses the risk created by exposing members of the public to a potentially dangerous individual, while the doctrine of *respondeat superior* is based on the theory that the employee is the agent or is acting for the employer. Therefore the scope of employment limitation on liability which is part of the *respondeat superior* doctrine is not implicit in the wrong of negligent hiring.

Accordingly, the negligent hiring theory has been used to impose liability in cases where the employee commits an intentional tort, an action almost invariably outside the scope of employment, against the customer of a particular employer or other member of the public, where the employer either knew or should have known that the employee was violent or aggressive, or that the employee might engage in injurious conduct toward third persons.

Several jurisdictions, in addition to New Jersey, have recognized the tort of negligent hiring, * * * and we now join those jurisdictions in formally recognizing this cause of action.

In recognizing the tort of negligent hiring, we emphasize that an employer is not an insurer for violent acts committed by an employee against a third person. On the contrary, liability is predicated on the employer's hiring of a person under circumstances antecedently giving the employer reason to believe that the person, by reason of some attribute of character or prior conduct, would create an undue risk of harm to others in carrying out his or her employment responsibilities. See Restatement (Second) of Agency §213, comment d. The scope of the employer's duty in exercising reasonable care in a hiring decision will depend largely on the anticipated degree of contact which the employee will have with other persons in performing his or her employment duties.

Where the employment calls for minimum contact between the employee and other persons, there may be no reason for an employer to conduct any investigation of the applicant's background beyond obtaining past employment information and personal data during the initial interview. [Citation.] * * *

* * *

We endorse the proposition that where an employer hires a person for a job requiring frequent contact with members of the public, or involving close contact with particular persons as a result of a special relationship between such persons and the employer, the employer's duty of reasonable care is not satisfied by a mere review of personal data disclosed by the applicant on a job application form or during a personal interview. However, in the absence of circumstances antecedently giving the employer reason to believe that the job applicant, by reason of some attribute of character or prior conduct, would constitute an undue risk of harm to members of the public with whom the applicant will be in frequent contact or to particular persons standing in a special relationship to the employer and with whom the applicant will have close contact, we decline to impose upon the employer his duty to obtain and review official records of an applicant's criminal history. To impose such a requirement would mean that an employer would be obligated to seek out and evaluate official police and perhaps court records from every jurisdiction in which a job applicant had any significant contact. We have serious doubts whether such a task could be effectively achieved. Even if it could, there would remain the significant problem of interpreting the records and relating them in a practical way to the job in question. Accordingly, in the absence of circumstances antecedently giving the employer reason to believe that a job applicant, by reason of some attribute of character or prior conduct, would constitute an undue risk of harm to members of the public with whom the applicant will be in frequent contact or to particular persons who stand in a special relationship to the employer and with whom the applicant will be in close contact, the employer's duty of reasonable care does not extend to searching for and reviewing official records of a job applicant's criminal history.

### III

In the instant case, we agree with the court of appeals' determination that Molalla had no duty to conduct an independent investigation into Taylor's non-vehicular criminal background before hiring him as a long-haul driver. Molalla had no reason to foresee that its hiring of Taylor under the circumstances of this case would create a risk that Taylor would sexually assault or otherwise endanger a member of the public by engaging in violent conduct. To be sure, Molalla had a duty to use reasonable care in hiring a safe driver who would not create a danger to the public in carrying out the duties of the job. Far from requiring frequent contact with members of the public or involving close contact with persons having a special relationship with the employer, Taylor's duties were restricted to the hauling of freight on interstate highways and, as such, involved only incidental contact with third persons having no special relationship to Molalla or to Taylor. After checking on Taylor's driving record and contacting some of his references, Molalla had no reason to believe that Taylor would not be a safe driver or a dependable employee. In addition, Molalla specifically instructed its drivers to stay on the interstate highways and, except for an emergency, to stop only in order to service the truck and to eat and to sleep. It further directed its drivers to sleep in the sleeping compartment behind the driver's seat of the truck at rest areas or truck stops located along the interstate highway system. Furthermore, Molalla required Taylor to fill out a job application and to submit to a personal interview. Taylor stated on the application form and at the interview that he had never been convicted of a crime. Nothing in the hiring process gave Molalla reason to foresee that Taylor would pose an unreasonable risk of harm to members of the public with whom he might have incidental contact during the performance of his duties.

* * * We accordingly hold that Molalla, in hiring Taylor as a long-haul truck driver, had no legal duty to conduct an independent investigation into Taylor's non-vehicular criminal background in order to protect a member of the public, such as Connes, from a sexual assault committed by Taylor in the course of making a long-haul trip over the interstate highway system. The judgment of the court of appeals is affirmed.

---

## CASE 20-4

Nonexistent or Incompetent Principal

## PLAIN DEALER PUBLISHING CO. v. WORRELL

Court of Appeals of Ohio, Ninth District, Summit County, 2008

178 Ohio App.3d 485, 898 N.E.2d 1009

http://www.sconet.state.oh.us/rod/docs/pdf/9/2008/2008-ohio-4846.pdf

**Moore, P. J.**

This case arises out of an action by appellee, the Plain Dealer Publishing Company, to collect a debt against Frederick "Rick" Worrell, doing business as WRL Advertising. The lawsuit also named Martha J. Musil, who placed advertising orders with the Plain Dealer. Musil placed orders on March 14, 2003, and March 28, 2003. The order form indicated that although the ad insertions for June, July, and September were cancelled, there was still a balance on the account. There was also a balance due the Plain Dealer for April and June.

This lawsuit was commenced in August 2005 to collect a debt for advertising placed by Worrell. Shortly thereafter, Worrell filed bankruptcy, and as a result of the automatic stay, the trial court placed

this case on the inactive docket. On January 24, 2006, the trial court granted the Plain Dealer's motion to reactivate the case as to Musil only. Subsequently, the Plain Dealer moved for summary judgment, asserting that Musil was personally liable on the contracts because WRL Advertising was a fictitious entity with no legal standing. In support of its motion for summary judgment, the Plain Dealer relied primarily on the order forms that were written when the advertising orders were placed. The forms listed Musil as the contact person and indicated that the company name was WRL Advertising, and that the bill was to be sent to WRL Advertising.

Musil filed a combined response to the Plain Dealer's summary judgment motion and filed her own summary judgment motion. In her summary judgment motion, Musil confirmed that at all the relevant times, she (1) was an employee of WRL Advertising, (2) did not have an ownership interest in the company, and (3) had placed the order for advertising at the direction of her employer, WRL Advertising, of which Worrell was the owner. Musil attached to her summary judgment motion both her own affidavit and Worrell's affidavit.

On February 26, 2008, the trial court filed an order granting the Plain Dealer's motion awarding judgment against Musil in the amount of $8,720, with statutory interest from July 2, 2004. Musil timely filed the instant appeal. * * *

* * *

In resolving this case, we must look to the law of agency. Agency law in Ohio has been summarized as follows:

> (1) *Where the agent is acting for a disclosed principal, i.e.,* where both the existence of the agency and the identity of the principal are known to the person with whom the agent deals. An agent who acts for a disclosed principal and who acts within the scope of his authority and in the name of the principal is ordinarily not liable on the contracts he makes. [Citations.] The rationale for this rule is that in this situation the third party intends to deal with the principal, not his agent.
>
> (2) *Where the principal is only partially disclosed, i.e.,* where the existence of an agency is known to the third person, but the identity of the principal is not known. Here, the agent is held to be a party to the transaction and is liable to the third party, as is the agent's principal. [Citations.] The reason for the rule is that since the identity of the principal is not known to the third party, he ordinarily will not be willing to rely wholly upon the credit and integrity of an unknown party.
>
> (3) *Where the principal is undisclosed, i.e.,* where neither the existence of an agency nor the identity of the principal is known to the third party. Here, the dealing is held to be between the agent and the third party, and the agent is liable. [Citation.] Should the identity of the principal be discovered, he may be held liable by the third party who must elect to pursue either the principal or agent-both are not liable. [Citation.] The rationale for the agent's liability is that since the third party was unaware of the agency, he intended to deal with the agent as an individual, not as an agent.
>
> (4) *Where there is a fictitious or nonexistent principal, or the principal is without legal capacity or status.* If an agent purports to act on behalf of such a "principal," the agent will be liable to the third party as a party to the transaction. [Citations.] One cannot be an agent for a nonexistent principal; there is no agency. This situation frequently arises where a corporate promoter enters into contracts prior to the time the corporation is actually incorporated. [Citation.]

[Citation.]

In the instant case, the trial court determined that although Musil communicated her agency relationship to the Plain Dealer, she did not sufficiently disclose the identity of her principal. In making this determination, the trial court noted that "[i]t is also undisputed that WRL Advertising is not a legal entity in its own right, but rather a trade name for Winfield, (*sic*) Bennett & Baer, LLC, which is owned and operated by Worrell." The trial court held that the use of a principal's trade name is insufficient to identify the principal. The trial court found that because she was acting, at best, on behalf of a partially disclosed principal, Musil was liable on the contracts.

* * *

The parties do not contest the fact that Musil communicated to the Plain Dealer that she was working on behalf of a principal. In its brief, the Plain Dealer asserts that "Musil dealt directly with [the] Plain Dealer and held herself as acting on behalf of 'WRL Advertising.' Musil executed two contracts on behalf of 'WRL Advertising [,]' an entity that does not exist in Ohio." Therefore, Musil properly notified the Plain Dealer that she was acting as an agent. In Ohio, an agent is liable to a third party when she contracts in the name of a nonexistent or fictitious principal or assumes to act as an agent for a principal who has no legal status or existence. [Citations.] We hold that Musil was not acting on behalf of a fictitious entity or an entity that does not exist in Ohio, but rather that WRL Advertising was a fictitious *name* for Wingfield, Bennett, & Baer, L.L.C.

* * *

"A corporation may use a name other than its corporate name in the conduct of its business." [Citation.] * * * In the instant case, the parties do not dispute that Wingfield, Bennett & Baer L.L.C. was registered with the Secretary of State. We find that Wingfield, Bennett & Baer is therefore not a fictitious or nonexistent principal for agency law purposes. Further * * * we note that WRL Advertising was a fictitious *name* for Wingfield, Bennett & Baer and that Musil was acting on behalf of Wingfield, Bennett & Baer, which was in turn using a fictitious name.

An agent will "avoid personal liability for debts of the corporation only if he complies with the rules which apply in all agency relationships—he must so conduct himself in dealing on behalf of the corporation with third persons that those persons are aware that he is an agent of the corporation and it is the corporation (principal) with which they are dealing, not the agent individually." [Citation.] In the instant case, Musil disclosed that she was acting on behalf of a principal, and therefore, the Plain Dealer knew that it was not dealing with Musil individually. We note that the Plain Dealer knew it was dealing with an entity, but that entity was using the fictitious name WRL Advertising. We do not find, as the Plain Dealer has urged, that the use of a name other than Wingfield, Bennett & Baer in the conduct of business would render Musil liable as an agent of a nonexistent or fictitious principal. As we find that Musil was acting on behalf of a legal entity using a fictitious *name,* we hold that the trial court erred when it granted the Plain Dealer's motion for summary judgment. Accordingly, we reverse and remand for proceedings consistent with this opinion.

* * *

Judgment reversed and cause remanded.

## QUESTIONS

1. Distinguish among actual express authority, actual implied authority, and apparent authority.
2. Discuss the contractual liability of the principal, agent, and third party when the principal is (a) disclosed, (b) partially disclosed, and (c) undisclosed.
3. Explain how apparent authority is terminated and distinguish between actual and constructive notice.
4. Discuss the tort liability of a principal for the (a) authorized acts of agents, (b) unauthorized acts of employees, and (c) unauthorized acts of independent contractors.
5. Discuss the criminal liability of a principal for the acts of agents.

## PROBLEMS

**1.** Alice was Peter's traveling salesperson and was also authorized to collect accounts. Before the agreed termination of the agency, Peter wrongfully discharged Alice. Alice then called on Tom, an old customer, and collected an account from Tom. She also called on Laura, a new prospect, as Peter's agent, secured a large order, collected the price of the order, sent the order to Peter, and disappeared with the collections. Peter delivered the goods to Laura per the order.

**(a)** What result if Peter sues Tom for his account?

**(b)** What result if Peter sues Laura for the agreed price of the goods?

**2.** Paula instructed Alvin, her agent, to purchase a quantity of hides. Alvin ordered the hides from Ted in his own (Alvin's) name and delivered the hides to Paula. Ted, learning later that Paula was the principal, sends the bill to Paula, who refuses to pay Ted. Ted sues Paula and Alvin. What are Ted's rights against Paula and Alvin?

**3.** Stan sold goods to Bill in good faith, believing him to be a principal. Bill in fact was acting as agent for Nancy and was within the scope of his authority. The goods were charged to Bill, and on his refusal to pay, Stan sued Bill for the purchase price. While this action was pending, Stan learned of Bill's relationship with Nancy. Nevertheless, thirty days after learning of that relationship, Stan obtained judgment against Bill and had an execution issued that was never satisfied. Three months after rendition of the judgment, Stan sued Nancy for the purchase price of the goods. Is Nancy liable? Explain.

**4.** Green Grocery Company employed Jones as its manager. Jones was given authority by Green to purchase supplies and goods for resale and had conducted business for several years with Brown Distributing Company. Although her purchases previously had been limited to groceries, Jones contacted Brown and had it deliver a color television set to her house, informing Brown the set was to be used in promotional advertising to increase Green's business. The advertising did not develop, and Jones disappeared from the area, taking the television set with her. Brown now seeks to recover the purchase price of the set from Green. Will Brown prevail? Explain.

**5.** Stone was the agent authorized to sell stock of the Turner Company at $10 per share and was authorized in case of sale to fill in the blanks in the certificates with the name of the purchaser, the number of shares, and the date of sale. He sold one hundred shares to Barrie, and without the knowledge or consent of the company and without reporting to the company, he endorsed the back of the certificate as follows:

> It is hereby agreed that Turner Company shall, at the end of three years after the date, repurchase the stock at $13 per share on thirty days' notice. Turner Company, by Stone.

After three years, demand was made on Turner Company to repurchase. The company refused the demand and repudiated the agreement on the ground that the agent had no authority to make the agreement for repurchase. Is Turner Company liable to Barrie? Explain.

**6.** Helper, a delivery boy for Gunn, delivered two heavy packages of groceries to Reed's porch. As instructed by Gunn, Helper rang the bell to let Reed know the groceries had arrived. Mrs. Reed came to the door and asked Helper if he would deliver the groceries into the kitchen because the bags were heavy. Helper did so, and upon leaving he observed Mrs. Reed having difficulty in moving a cabinet in the dining room. He undertook to assist her, but being more interested in watching Mrs. Reed than the cabinet, he failed to observe a small, valuable antique table, which he smashed into with the cabinet and totally destroyed. Does Reed have a cause of action against Gunn for the value of the destroyed antique?

**7.** Driver picked up Friend to accompany him on an out-of-town delivery for his employer, Speedy Service. A "No Riders" sign was prominently displayed on the windshield of the truck, and Driver violated specific instructions of his employer by permitting an unauthorized person to ride in the vehicle. While discussing a planned fishing trip with Friend, Driver ran a red light and collided with an automobile driven by Motorist. Both Friend and Motorist were injured. Is Speedy Service liable to either Friend or Motorist for the injuries they sustained?

**8.** Cook's Department Store advertises that it maintains in its store a barber shop managed by Hunter. Actually, Hunter is not an employee of the store but merely rents space in it. While shaving Jordon in the barber shop, Hunter negligently puts a deep gash into one of Jordon's ears, requiring ten stitches. Should Jordon be entitled to collect damages from Cook's Department Store?

**9.** The following contract was executed on August 22:

> Ray agrees to sell and Shaw, the representative of Todd and acting on his behalf, agrees to buy 10,000 pounds of 0.32 × 1 5/8 stainless steel strip type 410.
> (signed) Ray
> (signed) Shaw

On August 26, Ray informs Shaw and Todd that the contract was in reality signed by him as agent for Upson. What are the rights of Ray, Shaw, Todd, and Upson in the event of a breach of the contract?

**10.** Harris, owner of certain land known as Red Bank, mailed a letter to Byron, a real estate broker in City X, stating, "I have been thinking of selling Red Bank. I have never met you, but a friend has advised me that you are an industrious and honest real estate broker. I therefore employ you to find a purchaser for Red Bank at a price of $350,000." Ten days after receiving the letter, Byron mailed the following reply to Harris:

> "Acting pursuant to your recent letter requesting me to find a purchaser for Red Bank, this is to advise that I have sold the property to Sims for $350,000. I enclose your copy of the contract of sale signed by Sims. Your name was signed to the contract by me as your agent."

Is Harris obligated to convey Red Bank to Sims?

**11.** While crossing a public highway in the city, Joel was struck by a horse-drawn cart driven by Morison's agent. The agent was traveling between Burton Crescent Mews and Finchley on his employer's business and was not supposed to go into the city at all. Apparently, the agent was on a detour to visit a friend when the accident occurred. Joel brought this action against Morison for the injuries sustained as a result of the agent's negligence. Morison argues that he is not liable for his agent's negligence because the agent had strayed from his assigned path. Who is correct?

**12.** Serges is the owner of a retail meat marketing business. Without authority his managing agent borrowed $3,500 from David on Serges's behalf, for use in Serges's business. Serges paid $200 on the alleged loan and on several other occasions told David that the full balance owed would eventually be paid. He then disclaimed liability on the debt, asserting that he had not authorized his agent to enter into the loan agreement. Should David succeed in an action to collect on the loan?

**13.** Sherwood negligently ran into the rear of Austen's car, which was stopped at a stoplight. As a result, Austen received bodily injuries and her car was damaged. Sherwood, arts editor for the *Mississippi Press Register*, was en route from a Louis Armstrong concert he had covered for the newspaper. When the accident occurred he was on his way to spend the night at a friend's house. Austen sued Sherwood and—under the doctrine of *respondeat superior*—Sherwood's employer, the *Mississippi Press Register*. Who is liable? Explain.

**14.** Aretta J. Parkinson owned a two-hundred-acre farm in a State that requires written authority for an agent to sell land. Prior to her death on December 23, Parkinson deeded a one-eighth undivided interest in the farm to each of her eight children as tenants in common. On January 15 of the following year, one of the daughters, Roma Funk, approached Barbara Bradshaw about selling the Parkinson farm to the Bradshaws. They orally agreed to a selling price of $800,000. After this meeting, Funk contacted Bryant Hansen, a real estate broker, to assist her in completing the transaction. Hansen prepared an earnest money agreement that was signed by the Bradshaws but by none of the Parkinson children. Hansen also prepared warranty deeds, which were signed by three of the children. Several of the children subsequently refused to convey their interests in the farm to the Bradshaws. Explain whether the Bradshaws can obtain specific performance of the oral contract of sale based on the defendants' ratification of the oral contract by their knowledge of and failure to repudiate it. Decision?

**15.** Raymond Zukaitis was a physician practicing medicine in Douglas County, Nebraska. Aetna issued a policy of professional liability insurance to Zukaitis through its agent, the Ed Larsen Insurance Agency. The policy covered the period from August 31, 2009, through August of the following year. On August 7, 2011, Dr. Zukaitis received a written notification of a claim for malpractice that occurred on September 27, 2009. Dr. Zukaitis notified the Ed Larsen Insurance Agency immediately and forwarded the written claim to them. The claim was then mistakenly referred to St. Paul Fire and Marine Insurance Company, the company that currently insured Dr. Zukaitis. Apparently without notice to Dr. Zukaitis, the agency contract between Larsen and Aetna had been canceled on August 1, 2010, and St. Paul had replaced Aetna as the insurance carrier. However, when St. Paul discovered it was not the carrier on the date of the alleged wrongdoing, it notified Aetna and withdrew from Dr. Zukaitis's defense. Aetna also refused to represent Dr. Zukaitis, contending that it was relieved of its obligation to Dr. Zukaitis because he had not notified Aetna immediately of the claim. Dr. Zukaitis then secured his own attorney to defend against the malpractice claim and brought this action against Aetna to recover attorney's fees and other expenses incurred in the defense. Should Dr. Zukaitis succeed? Explain.

**16.** Chris Zulliger was a chef at the Plaza Restaurant in the Snowbird Ski Resort in Utah. The restaurant is located at the base of a mountain. As a chef for the Plaza, Zulliger was instructed by his supervisor and the restaurant manager to make periodic trips to inspect the Mid-Gad Restaurant, which was located halfway up the mountain. Because skiing helped its employees to get to work, Snowbird preferred that its employees know how to ski and gave them ski passes as part of their compensation. Prior to beginning work at the Plaza, Zulliger went skiing. The restaurant manager asked Zulliger to stop at the Mid-Gad before beginning work that day, and Zulliger stopped at the Mid-Gad during his first run and inspected the kitchen. He then skied four runs before heading down the mountain to begin work. On the last run, Zulliger decided to take a route often taken by Snowbird employees. About midway down, Zulliger decided to jump off a crest on the side of an intermediate run. Because of the drop, a skier above the crest cannot see whether there are skiers below, and Zulliger ran into Margaret Clover, who was below the crest. The jump was well known to Snowbird; the resort's ski patrol often instructed people not to jump, and there was a sign instructing skiers to take it slow at that point. Clover sued Zulliger and, under the doctrine of *respondeat superior*, Snowbird, claiming that Zulliger had been acting within the scope of his employment. Who is liable? Explain.

**17.** Rubin, was driving on one of the city's streets when he inadvertently obstructed the path of a taxicab, causing the cab to come into contact with his vehicle. Angered by the Rubin's sudden blocking of his traffic lane, the taxi driver exited his cab, approached Rubin, and struck him about the head and shoulders with a metal pipe. Rubin filed suit against the cab driver to recover for bodily injuries resulting from the altercation. He also sued the Yellow Cab Company, asserting that the company was vicariously liable under the doctrine of *respondeat superior*. Is the Yellow Cab Company liable? Explain.

**18.** Van D. Costas, Inc. (Costas) entered into a contract to remodel the entrance of the Magic Moment Restaurant owned by Seascape Restaurants, Inc. Rosenberg, part owner and president of Seascape, signed the contract on a line under which was typed "Jeff Rosenberg, The Magic Moment." When a dispute arose over the performance and payment of the contract, Costas brought suit against Rosenberg for breach of contract. Rosenberg contended that he had no personal liability for the contract and that only Seascape, the owner of the restaurant, was liable. Costas claimed that Rosenberg signed for an undisclosed principal and, therefore, was individually liable. Is Rosenberg liable on the contract? Explain.

**19.** Virginia and her husband, Ronnie Hulbert, were involved in an accident in Mobile County when their automobile collided with another automobile, driven by Dr. Murray's nanny. The nanny's regular duties of employment included housekeeping, supervising the children, and taking the children places that they needed to go. At the time of the collision, the nanny was driving her own car and was following Dr. Murray and her family to Florida from Louisiana to accompany Dr. Murray's family on their vacation. One of Dr. Murray's daughters was in the automobile driven by the nanny. Virginia Hulbert sued Dr. Murray under the doctrine of *respondeat superior*, alleging that the nanny was acting within the scope of her employment when the automobile accident occurred. Should she be able to recover from Dr. Murray? Explain.

**20.** Sonenberg Company managed Westchester Manor Apartments through its on-site property manager, Judith. Manor Associates Limited Partnership, whose general partner is Westchester Manor, Ltd., owned the complex. The entry sign to the property did not reveal the owner's name but did disclose that Sonenberg managed the property. Judith contacted Redi-Floors and requested a proposal for installing carpet in several of the units. In preparing the proposal, Redi-Floors confirmed that Sonenberg was the managing company and that Judith was its on-site property manager. Sonenberg did not inform Redi-Floors of the owner's identity. Judith and her assistant orally ordered the carpet, and Redi-Floors installed the carpet. Redi-Floors sent invoices to the complex and received checks from "Westchester Manor Apartments." Believing Sonenberg owned the complex, Redi-Floors did not learn of the true owner's identity until after the work had been completed when a dispute arose concerning the payment of some of its later invoices. Against whom may Redi-Floors recover on the outstanding invoices? Explain.

P A R T 4

# Sales

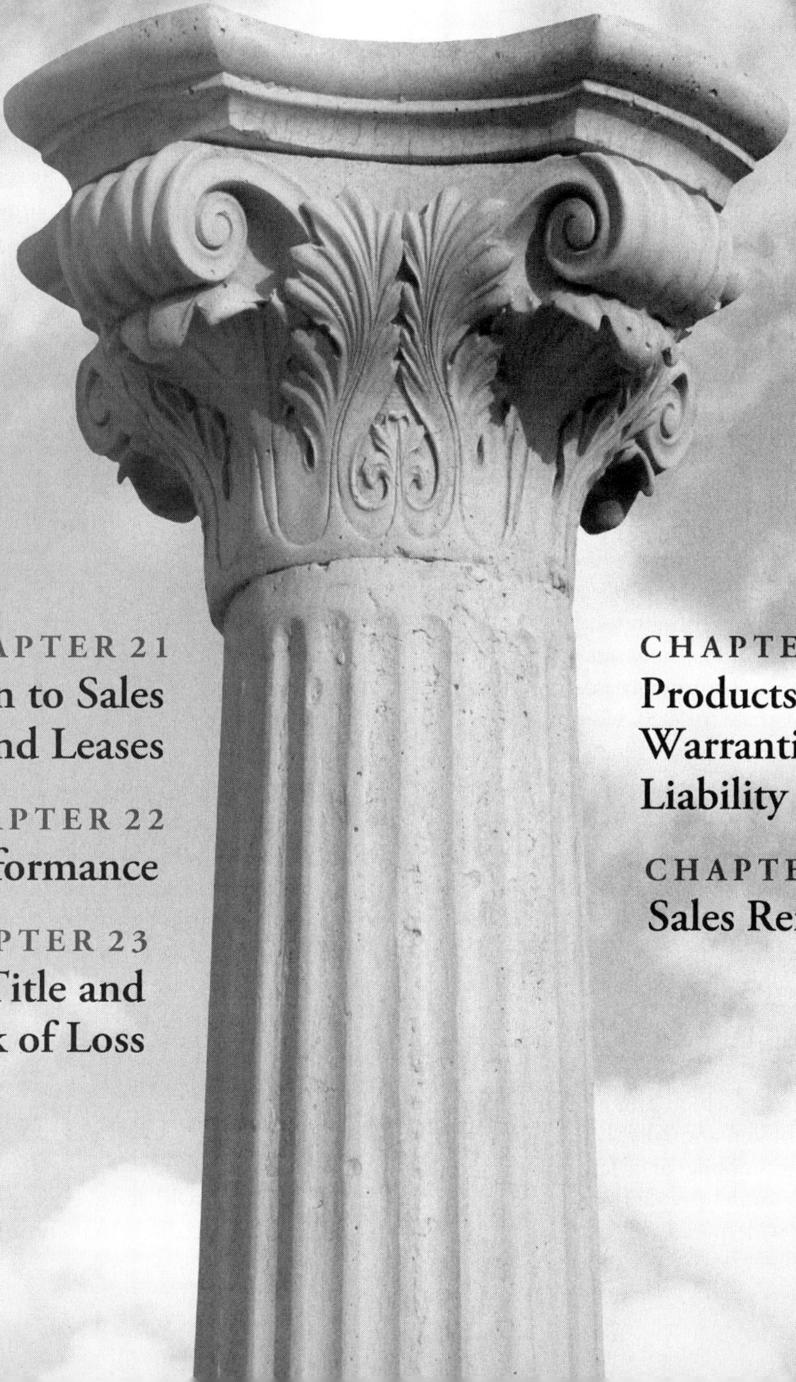

CHAPTER 21
Introduction to Sales and Leases

CHAPTER 22
Performance

CHAPTER 23
Transfer of Title and Risk of Loss

CHAPTER 24
Products Liability: Warranties and Strict Liability in Tort

CHAPTER 25
Sales Remedies

# CHAPTER 21
# Introduction to Sales and Leases

Sales are the most common and important of all commercial transactions. In an exchange economy such as ours, sales are the essential means by which the various units of production exchange their outputs, thereby providing the opportunity for specialization and enhanced productivity. An advanced, complex, industrialized economy with highly coordinated manufacturing and distribution systems requires a reliable mechanism for ensuring that *future* exchanges can be entered into today and fulfilled at a later time. Because practically everyone in our economy is a purchaser of both durable and consumable goods, the manufacture and distribution of goods involve numerous sales transactions. The law of sales establishes a framework in which these present and future exchanges may take place in a predictable, certain, and orderly fashion with a minimum of transaction costs.

Until the early 1900s, sales transactions were completely governed by general contract law. In 1906, the Uniform Sales Act was promulgated and eventually adopted by thirty-six States. By the end of the 1930s, however, dissatisfaction with this and other uniform commercial statutes brought about the development of the Uniform Commercial Code (UCC). Article 2 of the Code deals with transactions in sales and has been adopted in all of the States (except Louisiana) plus the District of Columbia and the Virgin Islands. The UCC appears in Appendix B. Amendments to Article 2 and 2A were promulgated in 2003 to accommodate electronic commerce and to reflect development of business practices, changes in other law, and interpretive difficulties of practical significance. To date no States have adopted them. However, at least thirty-seven States have adopted the 2001 Revisions to Article 1, which applies to all of the articles of the Code.

Leases of personal property, which are of great economic significance, exceed $100 billion annually. Leases range from a consumer renting an automobile or a lawn mower to a Fortune 500 corporation leasing heavy industrial machinery. Despite the frequent and widespread use of personal property leases, the law governing these transactions had been patched together from the common law of personal property, real estate leasing law, and Articles 2 and 9 of the UCC. Although containing several applicable provisions, the UCC did not directly relate to leases. Some courts have held, nevertheless, that the UCC is applicable to leases of goods because a lease is a transaction in goods; other courts have refused to apply the Code to leases because actual title to the goods never passed. Still other courts have applied the Code to lease by analogy. Even in States where Article 2 was extended to leases, which provisions were to be applied remained unclear. In any event, no unified or uniform statutory law governed leases of personal property for most of the twentieth century.

To fill this void, the drafters of the Code approved Article 2A—Leases in 1987 and subsequently amended the Article in 1990. An analogue of Article 2, the new Article adopts many of the rules contained in Article 2. Article 2A is an attempt to codify in one statute all the rules governing the leasing of personal property. South Dakota has enacted the 1987 version of Article 2A while the District of Columbia and all the other States except Louisiana have adopted the 1990 version.

This section of the book covers both the sale and the lease of goods. All of the chapters will cover Article 2A in addition to Article 2 by stating the Article 2A section number wherever Article 2A's provision is either identical to or essentially the same as the Article 2 provision. Where Article 2A significantly deviates from Article 2, both rules will generally be discussed. This chapter will discuss the nature and formation of sales and lease contracts as well as the fundamental principles of Article 2 and Article 2A.

## NATURE OF SALES AND LEASES

The law of sales, which governs contracts involving the sale of goods, is a specialized branch of both the law of contracts (discussed previously in *Chapters 9–18*) and the law of personal property (discussed later in *Chapter 48*). This section will cover the definition of sales and lease contracts and the fundamentals of Article 2 and Article 2A.

◆ SEE FIGURE 21-1: **Law of Sales and Leases**

## DEFINITIONS

### GOODS

Goods are essentially defined as movable, tangible personal property. For example, the purchase of a bicycle, CD player, or this textbook is considered a sale of goods. "Goods" also include the unborn young of animals, growing crops, and, if removed by the seller, timber, minerals, or a building attached to real property. Section 2–105(1). Under Article 2A, minerals cannot be leased prior to their extraction. Section 2A–103(1)(h).

### SALE

The Code defines a sale as the transfer of title to goods from seller to buyer for a price. Section 2–106. The price can be money, other goods, real estate, or services.

### LEASE

Article 2A defines a lease of goods as a "transfer of the right to possession and use of goods for a term in return for consideration, but … retention or creation of a security interest is not a lease." Section 2A–103(1)(j). A transaction within this definition of a lease is governed by Article 2A, but if the transaction is a security interest disguised as a lease, it is governed by Article 9. Categorizing a transaction as a lease has significant implications not only for the parties to the lease but for third parties as well. If the transaction is deemed to be a lease, then the residual interest in the goods belongs to the lessor, who need not file publicly to protect this interest. On the other hand, if the transaction is a security interest, then the provisions of Article 9 regarding enforceability, perfection, priority, and remedies apply (see *Chapter 38*). UCC Section 1–201(37) and Revised Section 1–203 provide rules that govern the determination of whether a transaction in the form of a lease creates a security interest.

**Consumer Leases** Article 2A affords special treatment for consumer leases. The definition of a consumer lease requires that (1) the transaction meet the definition of a lease under Article 2A; (2) the lessor be regularly engaged in the business of leasing *or* selling goods; (3) the lessee be an individual, not an organization; (4) the lessee take the lease interest primarily for a personal, family, or household purpose; and (5) the total payments under the lease do not exceed $25,000. Section 2A–103(1)(e). Although consumer protection for lease transactions is primarily left to other State and Federal law, Article 2A does contain a number of provisions that apply to consumer leases and that may *not* be varied by agreement of the parties.

**Finance Leases** A finance lease is a special type of lease transaction generally involving three parties instead of two. Whereas in the typical lease situation the lessor also supplies the goods, in a finance lease arrangement the lessor and the supplier are separate parties. The lessor's primary function in a finance lease is to provide financing to the lessee for a lease of goods provided by the supplier. For example, under a finance lease arrangement a manufacturer supplies goods pursuant to the lessee's instructions or specifications. The

◆ FIGURE 21-1: **Law of Sales and Leases**

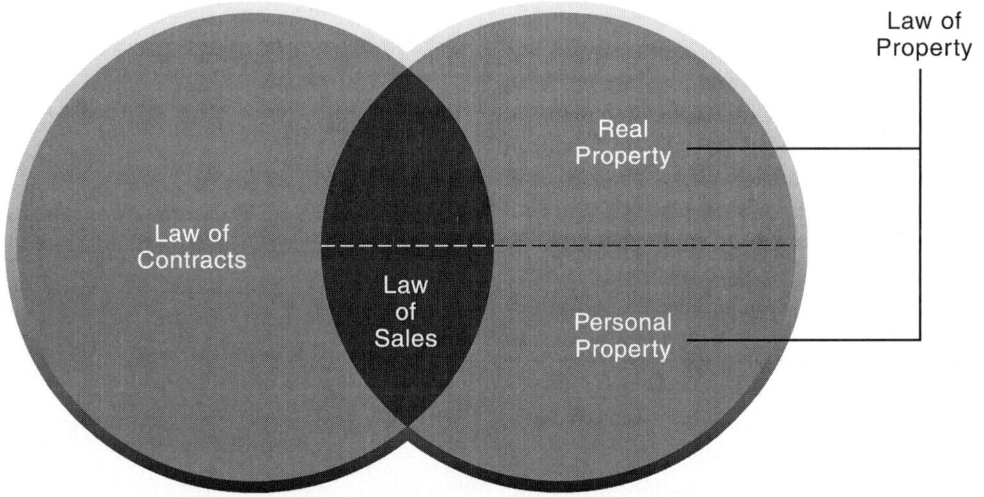

party functioning as the lessor will then either purchase those goods from the supplier or act as the prime lessee in leasing them from the supplier. In turn, the lessor will lease or sublease the goods to the lessee. Comment g to Section2A–103. Because the finance lessor functions merely as a source of credit, she typically will have no special expertise as to the goods. Due to the limited role the finance lessor usually plays, Article 2A treats finance leases differently from ordinary leases.

◆ **SEE CASE 21-1**

## GOVERNING LAW

Though sales transactions are governed by Article 2 of the Code, general contract law continues to apply where the Code has not specifically modified such law. Nevertheless, although principles of common law and equity may supplement provisions of the Code, they may not be used to supplant its provisions. Thus the law of sales is a specialized part of the general law of contracts, and the law of contracts continues to govern unless specifically displaced by the Code.

General contract law also continues to govern all contracts outside the scope of the Code. Transactions not within the scope of Article 2 include employment contracts, service contracts, insurance contracts, contracts involving real property, and contracts for the sale of intangibles such as stocks, bonds, patents, and copyrights. For an illustration of the relationship between the law of sales and the general law of contracts, see *Figure 9-1*. In determining whether a contract containing both a sale of goods and a service is a UCC contract or a general contract, the majority of States follow the predominant purpose test. This test holds that if the predominant purpose of the whole transaction is a sale of goods, then Article 2 applies to the entire transaction. If, on the other hand, the predominant purpose is the nongood or service portion, then Article 2 does not apply at all. A few States apply Article 2 to the goods part of a transaction and general contract law to the nongoods or service part of the transaction.

◆ **SEE FIGURE 9-1: Law Governing Contracts**

◆ **SEE CASES 21-2 AND 9-1**

Although Article 2 governs sales, the drafters of the Article have invited the courts to extend Code principles to nonsale transactions in goods. To date, a number of courts have accepted this invitation and have applied Code provisions by analogy to other transactions in goods not expressly included within the Act, most frequently to leases and bailments. The Code has also greatly influenced the revision of the Restatement, Second, Contracts, which, as previously discussed, has great effect upon all contracts.

Although lease transactions are governed by Article 2A of the Code, general contract law continues to apply where the Code has not specifically modified such law. In other words, the law of leases is a specialized part of the general law of contracts, and the law of contracts continues to govern unless specifically displaced by the Code.

CISG The United Nations Convention on Contracts for the International Sale of Goods (CISG), which has been ratified by the United States and more than forty other countries, governs all contracts for the international sales of goods between parties located in different nations that have ratified the CISG. Because treaties are Federal law, the CISG supersedes the UCC in any situation to which either could apply. The CISG includes provisions dealing with interpretation, trade usage, contract formation, obligations and remedies of sellers and buyers, and risk of loss. Parties to an international sales contract may, however, expressly exclude CISG governance from their contract. The CISG specifically excludes sales of (1) goods bought for personal, family, or household use; (2) ships or aircraft; and (3) electricity. In addition, it does not apply to contracts in which the primary obligation of the party furnishing the goods consists of supplying labor or services.

# FUNDAMENTAL PRINCIPLES OF ARTICLE 2 AND ARTICLE 2A

The purpose of Article 2 is to modernize, clarify, simplify, and make uniform the law of sales. Furthermore, the Article is to be interpreted in accordance with these underlying principles and not according to some abstraction such as the passage of title. The Code

> is drawn to provide flexibility so that, since it is intended to be a semi-permanent piece of legislation, it will provide its own machinery for expansion of commercial practices. It is intended to make it possible for the law embodied in this Act to be developed by the courts in the light of unforeseen and new circumstances and practices. However, the proper construction of the Act requires that its interpretation and application be limited to its reason. Section 1–102, Comment 1; Revised Section 1-103, Comment 1.

This open-ended drafting includes the following fundamental concepts.

CISG The CISG governs only the formation of the contract of sales and the rights and obligations of the seller and buyer arising from such contract. It does not cover the validity of the contract or any of its provisions. In addition, one of the purposes of the CISG is to promote uniformity of the law of sales.

## GOOD FAITH

All parties who enter into a contract or duty within the scope of the Code must perform their obligations in good faith. The Code defines **good faith** as "honesty in fact in the conduct or transaction concerned." Section 1–201(19). For a merchant (defined later), good faith also requires the observance of reasonable commercial standards of fair dealing in the trade. Section 2–103(1)(b); Section 2A–103(3). Revised Section 1–201(19) provides that "good faith means honesty in fact in the conductor transaction concerned and the observance of reasonable commercial standards of fair dealing," thus adopting the broader definition of good faith and making it applicable to both merchants and nonmerchants. For instance, if the parties agree that the seller is to set the price term, the seller must establish the price in good faith.

**CISG** The CISG is also designed to promote the observation of good faith in international trade.

## UNCONSCIONABILITY

The court may scrutinize every contract of sale to determine whether in its commercial setting, purpose, and effect it is unconscionable. The court may refuse to enforce an unconscionable contract or any part of it found to be unconscionable or may limit its application to prevent an unconscionable result. Section 2–302. Though the Code itself does not define *unconscionable*, the *New Webster's Dictionary* (Deluxe Encyclopedic Edition) defines the term as "contrary to the dictates of conscience; unscrupulous or unprincipled; exceeding that which is reasonable or customary; inordinate, unjustifiable."

The Code denies or limits enforcement of an unconscionable contract for the sale of goods to promote fairness and decency and to correct harshness or oppression in contracts resulting from inequality in the bargaining positions of the parties.

The doctrine of unconscionability has been justified on the basis that it permits the courts to resolve issues of unfairness explicitly on that basis without recourse to formalistic rules or legal fictions. In policing contracts for fairness, the courts have again demonstrated their willingness to limit freedom of contract to protect the less advantaged from overreaching by dominant contracting parties. Accordingly, most cases concerning unconscionability have involved low-income consumers.

The doctrine of unconscionability has evolved through its application by the courts to include both procedural and substantive unconscionability. **Procedural unconscionability** involves scrutiny for the presence of "bargaining naughtiness." In other words, was the negotiation process fair? Or were there procedural irregularities such as burying important terms of the agreement in fine print or obscuring the true meaning of the contract with impenetrable legal jargon?

In checking for **substantive unconscionability**, the court examines the actual terms of the contract for oppressive or grossly unfair provisions such as an exorbitant price or an unfair exclusion or limitation of contractual remedies. An all-too-common example places a necessitous buyer in an unequal bargaining position with a seller who consequently obtains an exorbitant price for his product or service. In one case, a price of $749 ($920 on time payments) for a vacuum cleaner that cost the seller $140 was held unconscionable. In another case, the buyers, welfare recipients, purchased by time payment contract a home freezer unit for $900 plus time credit charges, credit life insurance, credit property insurance, and sales tax for a total price of $1,235. The maximum retail value of the freezer unit at the time of purchase was $300. The court held the contract unconscionable and reformed it by changing the price to the total payment ($620) the buyers had managed to make. *Jones v. Star Credit Corp.*, 59 Misc.2d 189, 298 N.Y.S.2d 264 (1969).

As to leases, Article 2A provides that a court faced with an unconscionable contract or clause may refuse to enforce either the entire contract or just the unconscionable clause, or may limit the application of the unconscionable clause to avoid an unconscionable result. This is similar to Article 2's treatment of unconscionable clauses in sales contracts. A lessee under a consumer lease, however, is provided with additional protection against unconscionability. In the case of a consumer lease, if a court as a matter of law finds that any part of the lease contract has been induced by unconscionable conduct, the court is expressly empowered to grant appropriate relief. Section 2A–108(2). The same is true when unconscionable conduct occurs in the collection of a claim arising from a consumer lease contract. The explicit availability of relief for consumers subjected to unconscionable conduct (procedural unconscionability)—in addition to a provision regarding unconscionable contracts (substantive unconscionability)—represents a departure from Article 2. An additional remedy that Article 2A provides for consumers is the award of attorney's fees. If the court finds unconscionability with respect to a consumer lease, it shall award reasonable attorney's fees to the lessee. Section 2A–108(4)(a).

◆ **SEE CASES 21-3 AND 13-1**

## EXPANSION OF COMMERCIAL PRACTICES

An underlying policy of the Code is "to permit the continued expansion of commercial practices through custom, usage and agreement of the parties." Section 1–102(2)(b). In particular, the Code emphasizes the course of dealings and the usage of trade in interpreting agreements.

A **course of dealing** is a sequence of previous conduct between the parties that may fairly be regarded as establishing a common basis of understanding for interpreting their expressions and agreement. Section 1–205(1); Revised Section 1–303(b). For example, Plaza, a sugar company, enters into a written agreement with Brown, a grower of sugar beets, by which Brown agrees to raise and deliver and Plaza agrees to purchase specified quantities of beets during the coming season. No price is fixed. The agreement is on a standard form used by Plaza for Brown and many other growers in prior years. Plaza's practice is to pay all growers uniformly according to a formula based on Plaza's established accounting system. Unless otherwise agreed, the established pricing pattern is part of the agreement between Plaza and Brown as a course of dealing.

A **usage of trade** is a practice or method of dealing regularly observed and followed in a place, vocation, or trade. Section 1–205(2); Revised Section 1–303(c). To illustrate: Tamara contracts to sell Seth one thousand feet of San Domingo mahogany. By usage of dealers in mahogany, known to Tamara and Seth, good mahogany of a certain density is known as San Domingo mahogany, though it does not come from San Domingo. Unless otherwise agreed, the usage is part of the contract.

CISG The parties are bound by any usage or practices that they have agreed to or established between themselves. In addition, the parties are considered, unless otherwise agreed, to be bound by any usage of international trade that is widely known and regularly observed in the particular trade.

## SALES BY AND BETWEEN MERCHANTS

The Code establishes separate rules that apply to transactions transpiring between merchants or involving a merchant as a party. A **merchant** is defined as a person who (1) is a dealer in the type of goods the transaction involves, (2) by his occupation holds himself out as having knowledge or skill peculiar to the goods or practices involved, or (3) employs an agent or broker whom he holds out as having such knowledge or skill. Section 2–104(1); Section 2A–103(3). These rules exact a higher standard of conduct from merchants because of their knowledge of trade and commerce and because merchants as a class generally set these standards for themselves. The most significant of these merchant rules are listed in *Figure 21-2*.

◆ SEE FIGURE 21-2: **Selected Rules Applicable to Merchants**

## LIBERAL ADMINISTRATION OF REMEDIES

Section 1–106 and Revised Section 1–305 of the Code provide that its remedies shall be liberally administered to place the aggrieved party in a position as good as the one she would have occupied had the defaulting party fully

◆ FIGURE 21-2: **Selected Rules Applicable to Merchants**

| Section of UCC | Merchant Rules | Chapter in Text Where Discussed |
|---|---|---|
| **2-103(1)(b), 2-103(3)** | Good faith | 21 |
| **2-201** | Confirmation of oral contracts | 15, 21 |
| **2-205, 2A-205** | Firm offers | 10, 21 |
| **2-207(2)** | Battle of the forms | 10, 21 |
| **2-312(3), 2A-211(2)** | Warranty against infringement | 24 |
| **2-314(1), 2A-212** | Warranty of merchantability | 24 |
| **2-327(1)(c)** | Sales on approval | 23 |
| **2-402(2)** | Retention of possession of goods by seller | 23 |
| **2-403(2), 2A-304(2), 2A-305(2)** | Entrusting of goods | 23 |
| **2-509(3), 2A-219(2)(c)** | Risk of loss | 23 |
| **2-603(1), 2A-511(1)** | Duties after rightful rejection | 22 |

performed. The Code states clearly, however, that remedies are limited to compensation and do not include consequential or punitive damages, unless specifically provided by the Code. Nevertheless, the Code provides that even in cases in which it does not expressly provide a remedy for a right or obligation, the courts should provide an appropriate remedy. Remedies are discussed in *Chapter 25*.

### FREEDOM OF CONTRACT

Most of the Code's provisions are not mandatory but permit the parties by agreement to vary or displace them altogether. The parties may not, however, disclaim by agreement the obligations of good faith, diligence, reasonableness, and care the Code prescribes, though they may by agreement determine the standards by which to measure the performance of these obligations, so long as such standards are not obviously unreasonable. Section 1–102(3); Revised Sections 1–103(a)(2) and 1–302. Through this approach, the Code not only maximizes freedom of contract but also permits the continued expansion of commercial practices through private agreement.

### VALIDATION AND PRESERVATION OF SALES CONTRACTS

One of the requirements of commercial law is the establishment of rules that determine when an agreement is valid. The Code approaches this requirement by minimizing formal requisites and attempting to preserve agreements whenever the parties manifest an intent to enter into a contract.

# FORMATION OF SALES AND LEASE CONTRACTS

The Code's basic approach to validation is to recognize contracts whenever the parties manifest such an intent. This is so whether or not the parties can identify a precise moment at which the contract was formed. Section 2–204(2); Section 2A–204(2).

As already noted, the law of sales and leases is a subset of the general law of contracts and is governed by general contract law unless particular provisions of the Code displace the general law. Although the Code leaves most issues of contract formation to general contract law, it has modified the general law of contract formation in several significant respects. These modifications serve to modernize contract law, to relax the validation requirements of contract formation, and to promote fairness.

## MANIFESTATION OF MUTUAL ASSENT

For a contract to exist, there must be an objective manifestation of mutual assent: an offer and an acceptance. This section examines the UCC rules that affect offers and acceptances.

### DEFINITENESS OF AN OFFER

At common law, the terms of a contract were required to be definite and complete. The Code has rejected the strict approach of the common law by recognizing an agreement as valid, despite missing terms, if there is any reasonably certain basis for granting a remedy. Accordingly, the Code provides that even a contract from which one or more terms have been omitted need not fail for indefiniteness. Section 2–204(3); Section 2A–204(3). The Code provides standards by which the courts may ascertain and supply omitted essential terms, provided the parties intended to enter into a binding agreement. Nevertheless, the more terms the parties leave open, the less likely their intent to enter into a binding contract. Article 2A generally does not provide the same gap-filling provisions.

CISG An offer to contract is sufficiently definite if it indicates the goods and fixes or makes provision, expressly or implicitly, for determining price and quality.

**Open Price** The parties may enter into a contract for the sale of goods even though they have reached no agreement on the price (that is, left open the price term). Under the Code, the price is reasonable at the time for delivery where the agreement (1) says nothing as to price, (2) provides that the parties shall agree later as to the price and they fail to so agree, or (3) fixes the price in terms of some agreed market or other standard as set by a third person or agency, and the price is not so set. Section 2–305(1). An agreement that the price is to be fixed by the seller or buyer means that it must be fixed in good faith.

**Open Delivery** Unless otherwise agreed, the place of delivery is the seller's place of business. Moreover, in the absence of specific instructions, the delivery must be made within a reasonable time and in a single delivery. Section 2–308.

**Open Quantity: Output and Requirement Contracts** A buyer's agreement to purchase a seller's entire output for a stated period, or a seller's agreement to fulfill a buyer's need for certain goods used in her business operations, may appear to lack definiteness and mutuality of obligation. In neither case do the parties specify the exact quantity of goods, and the seller and the buyer may have some control over their respective output and requirements. Nonetheless, such agreements are enforceable by the application of an objective standard based upon the good faith of both parties, and the quantities may not be disproportionate to any stated estimate or the prior output or requirements. Section 2–306(1). For example, the seller cannot operate his factory twenty-four hours a day and insist that the buyer take all of the output when the seller operated the factory only eight hours a day at the time the agreement was made. Nor can the buyer unilaterally triple the size of her business and insist that the seller supply all of her requirements.

◆ **SEE CASE 21-3**

**Other Open Terms** The Code further provides rules, where the parties do not agree, as to the terms of payment, the duration of the contract, and the particulars of performance. Sections 2–310, 2–309, 2–307, 2–311.

### IRREVOCABLE OFFERS

An offeror generally may withdraw an offer at any time prior to its acceptance. To be effective, notice of revocation must reach the offeree before he has accepted the offer.

An **option** is a *contract* by which the offeror is bound to hold open an offer for a specified time. It must comply with all the requirements of a contract, including consideration. Option contracts apply to all types of contracts, including those for sales of goods.

The Code has made certain offers—called **firm offers**—irrevocable without any consideration being given for the promise to keep the offer open. The Code provides that a merchant who gives assurance in a signed writing that an offer will be held open is bound to keep the offer open for a maximum of three months. Section 2–205; Section 2A–205. The Code, therefore, makes a merchant's written promise not to revoke an offer for a stated time enforceable even though no consideration is given the merchant-offeror for that promise.

For example, Ben's Brewery approached Flora Flooring, Inc., to purchase tile for Ben's floor. Ben's employees would install the tile after it was delivered by Flora. On June 6, Flora sent Ben a written, signed offer to provide the tile according to Ben's specifications for $26,000 and promised that "the offer will remain open until July 17." Flora is bound by her firm offer to keep the offer open until July 17. The result would differ, however, if Flora had merely stated that the "offer terminates on July 17" or that "the offer will terminate if not accepted on or before July 17." In both of these instances, there is no assurance to keep the offer open: because it is not a firm offer, Flora could revoke it at any time prior to Ben's acceptance.

Any firm offer on a form supplied by the offeree must be separately signed by the offeror.

**CISG** An offer may not be revoked if it indicates that it is irrevocable; it need not be in writing.

### VARIANT ACCEPTANCES

The realities of modern business practices have necessitated the modification by the Code of the common law's "**mirror image**" rule, by which the acceptance cannot vary or deviate from the terms of the offer. A vast number of business transactions use standardized business forms, resulting in what has been termed the **battle of the forms**. For example, a merchant buyer sends to the merchant seller on the buyer's order form a purchase order for 1,000 dozen cotton shirts at $60 per dozen with delivery by October 1 at the buyer's place of business. On the reverse side of this standard form are twenty-five numbered paragraphs containing provisions generally favorable to the buyer. When the seller receives the buyer's order, he sends to the buyer an unequivocal acceptance of the offer on his acceptance form. Although the seller agrees to the buyer's quantity, price, and delivery terms, on the back of the form the seller utilizes in sending his unequivocal acceptance to the buyer are thirty-two numbered paragraphs generally favorable to the seller and in significant conflict with the buyer's form. Under the common law's "mirror image" rule, no contract would exist, for the seller has not in fact accepted unequivocally all of the material terms of the buyer's offer.

By comparison, Section 2–207 of the Code addresses variant acceptances by providing:

1. A definite and seasonable expression of acceptance or a written confirmation which is sent within a reasonable time operates as an acceptance even though it states terms additional to or different from those offered or agreed upon, unless acceptance is expressly made conditional on assent to the additional or different terms.
2. The additional terms are to be construed as proposals for addition to the contract. Between merchants such terms become part of the contract unless:
   (a) the offer expressly limits acceptance to the terms of the offer;
   (b) they materially alter it; or
   (c) notification of objection to them has already been given or is given within a reasonable time after notice of them is received.
3. Conduct by both parties which recognizes the existence of a contract is sufficient to establish a contract for sale although the writings of the parties do not otherwise establish a contract. In such case the terms of the particular contract consist of those terms on which the writings of the parties agree, together with any supplementary terms incorporated under any other provisions of this Act.

Thus, the Code attempts to settle the battle of the forms by focusing upon the intent of the parties. If the offeree expressly makes his acceptance conditioned upon the offeror's assent to the additional or different terms, no contract is formed. If the offeree does not expressly make his acceptance conditional upon such assent, a contract is formed. The issue then becomes whether the offeree's different or additional terms should become part of the contract. If both offeror and offeree are merchants, **additional** terms (terms the offeree proposed for the contract for the first time) will become part of the contract, provided they do not materially alter the agreement and are not objected to either in the offer itself or within a reasonable time. If either of the parties is not a merchant, or if the additional terms materially alter the offer, then the terms are merely construed as proposals for addition to the contract. **Different** terms (terms that contradict terms of the offer) proposed by the offeree generally will not become part of the contract unless specifically accepted by the offeror. The courts are divided over what terms are included when the terms conflict. The majority of courts hold that the terms cancel each other out and look to the Code to provide the missing terms; other courts hold that the offeror's terms govern. Some States follow a third alternative and apply the additional terms test to different terms.

Applying Section 2–207 to the example above: because both parties are merchants and the seller did not condition his acceptance upon the buyer's assent to the additional or different terms, (1) the contract will be formed without the *seller's different terms* unless the buyer specifically accepts them; (2) the contract will be formed without the *seller's additional terms* unless (a) the buyer specifically accepts or (b) the additional terms do not materially alter the offer and the buyer does not object to them; and (3) depending upon the jurisdiction, either (a) the conflicting (different) terms cancel each other out and the Code provides the missing terms or (b) the buyer's conflicting terms are included in the contract or (c) the additional terms test is applied.

CISG A reply to an offer that contains additions, limitations, or other modifications is a counteroffer that rejects the original offer. Nevertheless, a purported acceptance that contains additional or different terms acts as an acceptance if the terms do not materially alter the contract unless the offeror objects to the change. Changes in price, payment, quality, quantity, place and time of delivery, terms of delivery, liability of the parties, and settlement of a dispute are always considered to be material alterations.

Finally, subsection 3 of 2–207 deals with those situations in which the writings do not form a contract, but the conduct of the parties recognizes the existence of one. For instance, Ernest makes an offer to Gwen, who replies with a conditional acceptance. Although no contract has been formed, Gwen ships the ordered goods and Ernest accepts the goods. Subsection 3 provides that in this instance the contract consists of the written terms to which both parties agreed together with supplementary provisions of the Code.

◆ SEE FIGURE 21-3: **Battle of the Forms**

◆ SEE CASE 21-4

### MANNER OF ACCEPTANCE

As with the common law, the offeror may specify the manner in which the offer must be accepted. If the offeror does not and the circumstances do not otherwise clearly indicate, an offer to make a contract invites acceptance in any manner and by any medium reasonable under the circumstances. Section 2–206(1)(a); Section 2A–206(1). The Code, therefore, allows flexibility of response and the ability to keep pace with new modes of communication.

An offer to buy goods for prompt or current shipment may be accepted either by a prompt promise to ship or by prompt shipment. Section 2–206(1)(b). Acceptance by performance requires notice within a reasonable time, or the offer may be treated as lapsed. Section 2–206(2); Section 2A–206(2).

### AUCTIONS

The Code provides that if an auction sale is advertised or announced in explicit terms to be **without reserve**, the auctioneer may not withdraw the article put up for sale unless no bid is made within a reasonable time. Unless the sale is advertised as being without reserve, the sale is **with reserve**, and the auctioneer may withdraw the goods at any time until he announces completion of the sale. Whether the sale is with or without reserve, a bidder may retract his bid at anytime prior to acceptance by the auctioneer. Such retraction does not, however, revive any previous bid. Section 2–328.

If the auctioneer knowingly receives a bid by or on behalf of the seller, and notice has not been given that the seller reserves the right to bid at the auction sale, the bidder to whom the goods are sold can either avoid the sale or take the goods at the price of the last good faith bid.

CISG The CISG does not apply to sales by auctions.

## CONSIDERATION

The Code has abandoned the common law rule requiring that a modification of an existing contract be supported by consideration to be valid. The Code provides that a contract for the sale of goods can be effectively modified without new consideration, provided the modification is made in good faith. Section 2–209(1); Section 2A–208(1).

In addition, any claim of right arising out of an alleged breach of contract can be discharged in whole or in part

◆ FIGURE 21-3: **Battle of the Forms**

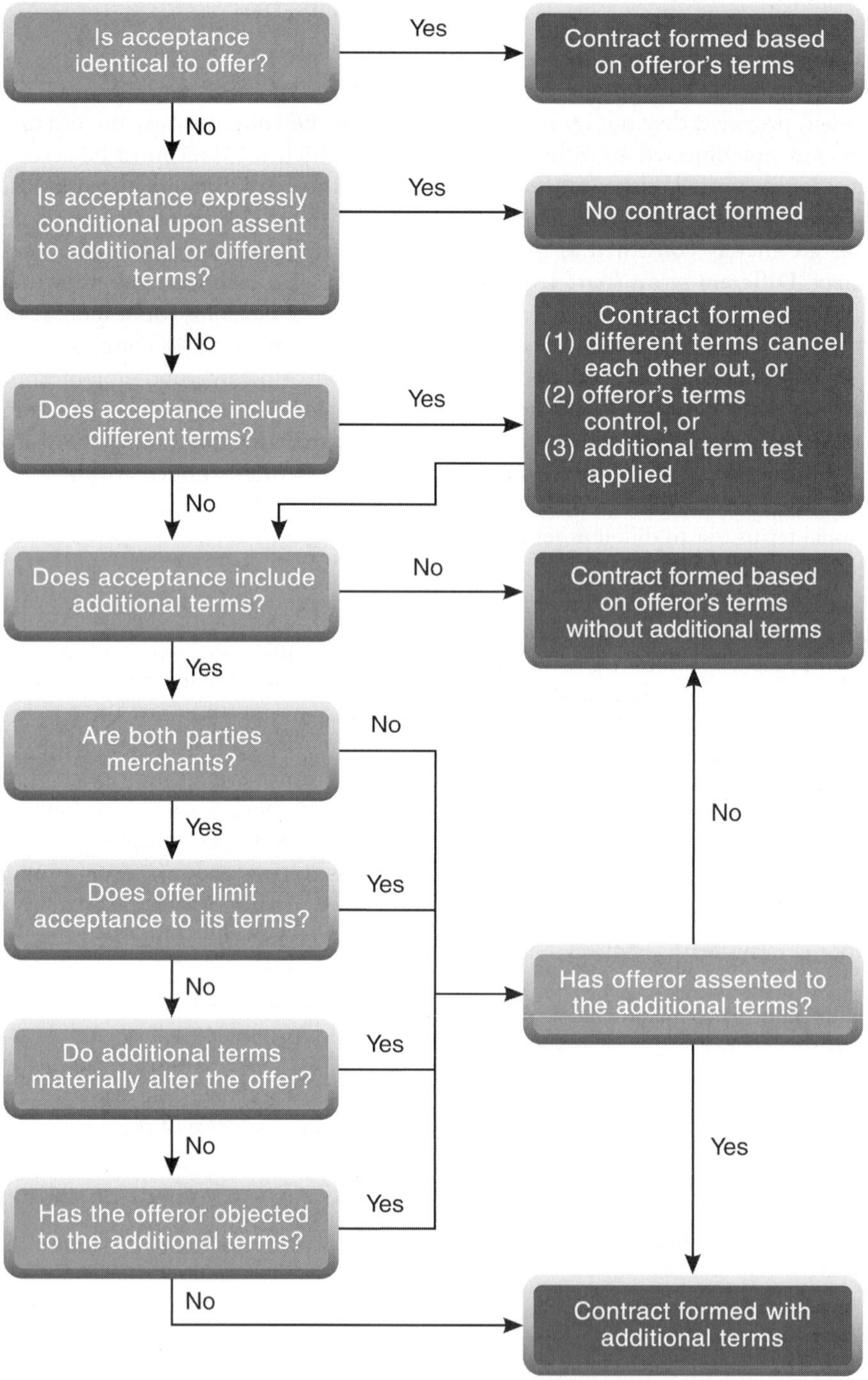


without consideration by a written waiver or renunciation signed and delivered by the aggrieved party. Section 1–107. Under the Revised UCC Article 1, a claim or right arising out of an alleged breach may be discharged in whole or in part without consideration by agreement of the aggrieved party in an authenticated record. Section 1–306. Moreover, as previously noted, a firm offer is not revocable for lack of consideration.

CISG Consideration is not needed to modify a contract.

## FORM OF THE CONTRACT

### STATUTE OF FRAUDS

The original statute of frauds, which applied to contracts for the sale of goods, has been used as a prototype for the Article 2 statute of frauds provision. Section 2–201 of the Code provides that a contract for the sale of goods costing *$500 or more* is not enforceable unless there is some writing or record sufficient to evidence the existence of a contract between the parties ($1,000 or more for leases, Section 2A–201). As discussed in *Chapter 15*, almost all of the States have adopted the **Uniform Electronic Transactions Act (UETA)**, which gives full effect to contracts formed by electronic records and signatures. The Act applies to contracts governed by Articles 2 and 2A. In addition, Congress in 2000 enacted the **Electronic Signatures in Global and National Commerce (E-Sign)**. The Act, which uses language very similar to that of UETA, makes electronic records and signatures valid and enforceable across the United States for many types of transactions in or affecting interstate or foreign commerce.

CISG A contract need not be evidenced by a writing, unless one of the parties has her place of business in a country that provides otherwise.

**Modification of Contracts** An agreement modifying a contract must be evidenced by a writing or record if the resulting contract is within the statute of frauds. Section 2–209(3) (Article 2A omits this provision). Conversely, if a contract that was previously within the statute of frauds is modified so as to no longer fall within it, the modification is enforceable even if it is oral. Thus, if the parties enter into an oral contract to sell for $450 a dining room table to be delivered to the buyer and later, prior to delivery, orally agree that the seller shall stain the table and that the buyer shall pay a price of $550, the modified contract is unenforceable. In contrast, if the parties have a written contract for the sale of 150 bushels of wheat at a price of $4.50 per bushel and later, upon oral agreement, decrease the quantity to 100 bushels at the same price per bushel, the agreement, as modified, is enforceable.

A signed agreement that requires modifications or rescissions to be in a signed writing cannot be otherwise modified or rescinded. Section 2–209(2); Section 2A–208(2). If this requirement is on a form provided by a merchant, the other party must separately sign it unless the other party is a merchant.

**Writing(s) or Record** The statute of frauds compliance provisions under the Code are more liberal than the rules under general contract law. The Code requires merely some writing or record (1) sufficient to indicate that a contract has been made between the parties, (2) signed by the party against whom enforcement is sought or by her authorized agent or broker, that (3) includes a term specifying the quantity of goods the agreement involves. Whereas general contract law requires that a writing include all essential terms, even a writing or record that omits or incorrectly states a term agreed upon may be sufficient under the Code. This is consistent with other provisions of the Code stating that contracts may be enforced despite the omission of material terms. Nevertheless, the contract is enforceable only to the extent of the quantity set forth in the writing or record. Given proof that a contract was intended and a signed writing describing the goods, their quantity, and the names of the parties, under the Code the court can supply omitted terms such as price and particulars of performance. Many courts have concluded, however, that the Code does not require a clear and precise quantity term in a requirements or output contract. Moreover, several related documents may satisfy the writing or record requirement.

Between merchants, if within a reasonable time a writing in confirmation of the contract is received, the **written merchant confirmation**, if sufficient against the sender, is also sufficient against the recipient unless he gives written notice of his objection within ten days after receiving the confirmation. Section 2–201(2). (Article 2A does not have a comparable rule.) This means that if these requirements have been met, the recipient of the writing or record is in the same position he would have assumed by signing it; and the confirmation, therefore, is enforceable against him. For example, Brown Co. and ATM Industries enter into an oral contract providing that ATM will deliver 1,000 dozen shirts to Brown at $6 per shirt. The next day, Brown sends to ATM a letter signed by Brown's president confirming the agreement. The letter contains the quantity term but does not mention the price. Brown is bound by the contract when its authorized agent sends the letter, whereas ATM is bound by the oral contract ten days after receiving the letter, unless it objects in writing within that time. Therefore, it is essential that merchants examine their mail carefully and promptly to make certain that any written confirmations conform to their understanding of their outstanding contractual agreements. Where one or both of the parties is not a merchant, however, this rule does not apply.

**Exceptions** A contract that does not satisfy the writing requirement but is otherwise valid is enforceable in the following instances.

The Code permits an oral contract for the sale of goods to be enforced against a party who in his pleading, testimony, or otherwise in court **admits** that a contract was made, but limits enforcement to the quantity of goods so admitted. Section 2–201(3)(b); Section 2A–201(4)(b). This provision recognizes that the policy behind the statute of frauds does not apply when the party seeking to avoid the oral contract admits under oath the existence of the contract.

The Code also permits enforcement of an oral contract for goods **specially manufactured** for the buyer. Section 2–201(3)(a); Section 2A–201(4)(a). Nevertheless, if the goods, although manufactured on special order, are readily marketable in the ordinary course of the seller's business, the contract is not enforceable unless in writing.

In most States, prior to the Code, delivery and acceptance of part of the goods or payment of part of the price and acceptance of the payment made the entire oral contract enforceable against the buyer who had received part delivery or against the seller who had received part payment. Under the Code such "partial performance" validates the contract only for the goods that have been **delivered and accepted** or for which **payment** has been **accepted**. Section 2–201(3)(c); Section 2A–201 (4)(c). To illustrate, Debra orally agrees to buy one thousand watches from Brian for $15,000. Brian delivers three hundred watches to Debra, who receives and accepts them. The oral contract is enforceable to the extent of three hundred watches ($4,500)—those received and accepted—but is unenforceable to the extent of seven hundred watches ($10,500).

But what if part payment under an indivisible contract, such as one for the sale of an automobile, presents a choice between not enforcing the contract or enforcing it as a whole? Presently, there is a division of authority on this issue, although the better rule appears to be that such part payment and acceptance makes the entire contract enforceable.

## PAROL EVIDENCE

Contractual terms that the parties set forth in a writing that they intend as a final expression of their agreement may not be contradicted by evidence of any prior agreement or of a contemporaneous agreement. Nevertheless, under the Code, the terms may be explained or supplemented by (1) course of dealing, usage of trade, or course of performance; and (2) evidence of consistent additional terms, unless the writing was intended as the complete and exclusive statement of the terms of the agreement. Section 2–202; Section 2A–202.

For a comparison of general contract law and the law governing sales and leases of goods, see *Figure 21-4*.

CISG The CISG permits a court to consider all relevant circumstances of the agreement, including the negotiations, any course of performance between the parties, trade usages, and any subsequent conduct.

◆ SEE FIGURE 21-4: **Contract Law Compared with Law of Sales**

◆ FIGURE 21-4: **Contract Law Compared with Law of Sales**

| Section of UCC | Contract Law | Law of Sales/Leases |
|---|---|---|
| **Definiteness** | Contract must include all material terms. | Open terms permitted if parties intend to make contract. Section 2-204; 2A-204. |
| **Counteroffers** | Acceptance must be a mirror image of offer. Counteroffer and conditional acceptance are rejections. | Battle of forms. Section 2-207. See *Figure 21-3*. |
| **Modification of Contract** | Consideration is required. | Consideration is not required. Section 2-209; 2A-208. |
| **Irrevocable Offers** | Options. | Options. Firm offers up to three months binding without consideration. Section 2-205; 2A-205. |
| **Statute of Frauds** | Writing must include all material terms. | Writing must include quantity term. Specially manufactured goods. Confirmation by merchants. Delivery or payment and acceptance. Admissions. Section 2-201; 2A-201 (except merchant confirmation). |

# CHAPTER SUMMARY

## NATURE OF SALES AND LEASES

**DEFINITIONS**

**Goods** movable personal property
**Sale** transfer of title to goods from seller to buyer for a price
**Lease** a transfer of right to possession and use of goods in return for consideration
- ***Consumer Leases*** leases by a merchant to an individual who leases for personal, family, or household purposes for no more than $25,000
- ***Finance Leases*** special type of lease transaction generally involving three parties: the lessor, the supplier, and the lessee

**Governing Law**
- ***Sales Transactions*** governed by Article 2 of the Code, but where general contract law has not been specifically modified by the Code, general contract law continues to apply
- ***Lease Transactions*** governed by Article 2A of the Code, but where general contract law has not been specifically modified by the Code, general contract law continues to apply
- ***Transactions outside the Code*** include employment contracts, service contracts, insurance contracts, contracts involving real property, and contracts for the sale of intangibles

**FUNDAMENTAL PRINCIPLES OF ARTICLE 2 AND ARTICLE 2A**

**Purpose** to modernize, clarify, simplify, and make uniform the law of sales and leases
**Good Faith** the Code requires all sales and lease contracts to be performed in good faith, which means honesty in fact in the conduct or transaction concerned; in the case of a merchant (and a nonmerchant under Revised Article 1), it also includes the observance of reasonable commercial standards
**Unconscionability** a court may refuse to enforce an unconscionable contract or any part of a contract found to be unconscionable
- ***Procedural Unconscionability*** unfairness of the bargaining process
- ***Substantive Unconscionability*** oppressive or grossly unfair contractual provisions

**Expansion of Commercial Practices**
- ***Course of Dealing*** a sequence of previous conduct between the parties establishing a common basis for interpreting their agreement
- ***Usage of Trade*** a practice or method of dealing regularly observed and followed in a place, vocation, or trade

**Sales by and between Merchants** the Code establishes separate rules that apply to transactions between merchants or involving a merchant (a dealer in goods or a person who by his occupation holds himself out as having knowledge or skill peculiar to the goods or practice involved, or who employs an agent or broker whom he holds out as having such knowledge or skill)
**Liberal Administration of Remedies**
**Freedom of Contract** most provisions of the Code may be varied by agreement
**Validation and Preservation of Sales Contract** the Code reduces formal requisites to the bare minimum and attempts to preserve agreements whenever the parties manifest an intention to enter into a contract

## FORMATION OF SALES AND LEASE CONTRACTS

**MANIFESTATION OF MUTUAL ASSENT**

**Definiteness of an Offer** the Code provides that a sales or lease contract does not fail for indefiniteness even though one or more terms may have been omitted; the Code provides standards by which missing essential terms may be supplied for sales of goods

**Irrevocable Offers**

- ***Option*** a contract to hold open an offer
- ***Firm Offer*** a signed writing by a merchant to hold open an offer for the purchase or sale of goods for a maximum of three months

**Variant Acceptances** the inclusion of different or additional terms in an acceptance is addressed by focusing on the intent of the parties

**Manner of Acceptance** an acceptance can be made in any reasonable manner and is effective upon dispatch

**Auction** auction sales are generally with reserve, permitting the auctioneer to withdraw the goods at any time prior to sale

---

**CONSIDERATION**

**Contractual Modifications** the Code provides that a contract for the sale or lease of goods may be modified without new consideration if the modification is made in good faith

**Firm Offers** are not revocable for lack of consideration

---

**FORM OF THE CONTRACT**

**Statute of Frauds** sale of goods costing $500 or more (or lease of goods for $1,000 or more) must be evidenced by a signed writing to be enforceable

- ***Writing or Record*** the Code requires some writing(s) or record sufficient to indicate that a contract has been made between the parties, signed by the party against whom enforcement is sought or by her authorized agent or broker, and including a term specifying the quantity of goods
- ***Alternative Methods of Compliance*** written confirmation between merchants, admission, specially manufactured goods, and delivery or payment and acceptance

**Parol Evidence** contractual terms that are set forth in a writing intended by the parties as a final expression of their agreement may not be contradicted by evidence of any prior agreement or of a contemporaneous oral agreement, but such terms may be explained or supplemented by course of dealing, usage of trade, course of performance, or consistent additional evidence

## CASES

## CASE 21-1

Finance Leases

### CARTER v. TOKAI FINANCIAL SERVICES, INC.

Court of Appeals of Georgia, 1998

231 Ga.App. 755, 500 S.E.2d 638

http://scholar.google.com/scholar_case?case=1919852511859232954&hl=en&as_sdt=2&as_vis=1&oi=scholarr

**Blackburn, J.**

Tokai Financial Services, Inc. brought suit against Randy P. Carter for monies owed under Carter's guaranty of a telephone equipment lease agreement. The trial court granted summary judgment to Tokai, and Carter appeals.

* * *

On January 3, 1996, Tokai's predecessor in interest, Mitel Financial, entered into a "Master Equipment Lease Agreement" (Agreement) with Applied Radiological Control, Inc. (ARC) for the lease of certain telephone equipment valued at $42,000. Carter personally guaranteed ARC's obligations under the Agreement. ARC made four rental payments and then defaulted on its obligations as of June 1, 1996. Thereafter, Tokai repossessed the telephone equipment and sold it for $5,900. * * * Tokai then brought this suit against Carter, and the trial court awarded Tokai $56,765.74.

1. In his first enumeration of error, Carter contends the Agreement is a "finance agreement" rather than a true lease. * * *

As an initial matter, we note that Paragraph 13 of the Agreement states that each lease contemplated therein is a finance lease as defined by Article 2A of the UCC. "A 'finance lease' involves three parties—the lessee/business, the finance lessor, and the equipment supplier. The lessee/business selects the equipment and negotiates particularized modifications with the equipment supplier. Instead of purchasing the equipment from the supplier, the lessee/business has a finance lessor purchase the selected equipment, and then leases the equipment from the finance lessor." [Citation.]

Carter contends, nonetheless, that the true intent of the parties was to enter into a security agreement. "Whether a transaction creates a lease or security interest is determined by the facts of each case; however, a transaction creates a security interest if the consideration the lessee is to pay the lessor for the right to possession and use of the goods is an obligation for the term of the lease not subject to termination by the lessee, and (a) [t]he original term of the lease is equal to or greater than the remaining economic life of the goods, (b) [t]he lessee is bound to renew the lease for the remaining economic life of the goods or is bound to become the owner of the goods, (c) [t]he lessee has an option to renew the lease for the remaining economic life of the goods for no additional consideration or nominal additional consideration upon compliance with the lease agreement, or (d) [t]he lessee has an option to become the owner of the goods for no additional consideration or nominal additional consideration upon compliance with the lease agreement." [UCC]1–201(37).

Here, the Agreement's initial term was for five years, ARC was not required to renew the lease or purchase the telephone equipment at the end of the term, and ARC did not have the option to renew the lease or purchase the property at the end of the term for nominal consideration. Therefore, the Agreement does not fit within the definition of a secured transaction provided by [UCC]1–201(37).

Furthermore, "it is commonly held that the 'best test' for determining the intent of an agreement which provides for an option to buy is a comparison of the option price with the market value of the equipment at the time the option is to be exercised. Such a comparison shows whether the lessee is paying actual value acquiring the property at a substantially lower price. * * * If, upon compliance with the terms of the 'lease,' the lessee has an option to become the owner of the property for no additional or for a nominal consideration, the lease is deemed to be intended for security. [Citations.] ARC was given the option to purchase the telephone equipment in this case at the end of the lease term for its fair market value. "Additional consideration is not nominal if * * * when the option to become the owner of the goods is granted to the lessee the price is stated to be the fair market value of the goods determined at the time the option is to be performed." [UCC §1–201(37)(x).] Accordingly, the agreement in this case must be considered a true lease, not a secured transaction. As a result, the procedural safeguards of Article 9 of the UCC are inapplicable to the matter at hand, and Carter's claims under this enumeration must fail. [Citations.]

* * *

"In Georgia, all lease contracts for 'goods,' including finance leases, first made or first effective on or after July 1, 1993, are governed by Article 2A of the Uniform Commercial Code." [Citations.] The Agreement was entered into by the parties on January 3, 1996; therefore, it is subject to Article 2A of the UCC. * * *

* * *

Judgment reversed.

---

CASE 21-2

## Governing Law
## PITTSLEY v. HOUSER

Idaho Court of Appeals, 1994

875 P.2d 232

http://scholar.google.com/scholar_case?case=12253852760654206938&hl=en&as_sdt=2&as_vis=1&oi=scholarr

**Swanstrom, J.**

* * *

### Facts and Procedural Background

In September of 1988, Jane Pittsley contracted with Hilton Contract Carpet Co. (Hilton) for the installation of carpet in her home. The total contract price was $4,402. Hilton paid the installers $700 to put the carpet in Pittsley's home. Following installation, Pittsley complained to Hilton that some seams were visible, that gaps appeared, that the carpet did not lay flat in all areas, and it failed to reach the wall in certain locations. Although Hilton made various attempts to fix the installation, by attempting to stretch the carpet and other methods, Pittsley was not satisfied with the work. Eventually, Pittsley refused any further efforts to fix the carpet. Pittsley initially paid Hilton $3,500 on the contract, but refused to pay the remaining balance of $902.

Pittsley later filed suit, seeking rescission of the contract, return of the $3,500 and incidental damages. Hilton answered and counterclaimed for the balance remaining on the contract. The matter was heard by a magistrate sitting without a jury. The magistrate found that there were defects in the installation and that the carpet had been installed in an unworkmanlike manner. The magistrate also found that there was a lack of evidence on damages. The trial was continued to allow the parties to procure evidence on the amount of damages incurred by Pittsley. Following this continuance, Pittsley did not introduce any further evidence of damages, though witnesses for Hilton estimated repair costs at $250.

Although Pittsley had asked for rescission of the contract and a refund of her money, the magistrate determined that rescission, as an equitable remedy, was only available when one party committed a breach so material that it destroyed the entire purpose of the contract. Because the only estimate of damages was for $250, the magistrate ruled rescission would not be a proper remedy. Instead, the magistrate awarded Pittsley $250 damages plus $150 she expended in moving furniture prior to Hilton's attempt to repair the carpet. On the counterclaim, the magistrate awarded Hilton the $902 remaining on the contract. Additionally, both parties had requested attorney fees in the action. The magistrate determined that both parties had prevailed and therefore awarded both parties their attorney fees.

Following this decision, Pittsley appealed to the district court, claiming that the transaction involved was governed by the Idaho Uniform Commercial Code (UCC), [citation]. Pittsley argued that if the UCC had been properly applied, a different result would have been reached. The district court agreed with Pittsley's argument, reversing and remanding the case to the magistrate to make additional findings of fact and to apply the UCC to the transaction. * * *

Hilton now appeals the decision of the district court. * * * Even if application of the UCC was properly raised, Hilton argues that there were no defects in the goods that were the subject of the transaction, only in the installation, making application of the UCC inappropriate. * * *

## Analysis

* * *

The single question upon which this appeal depends is whether the UCC is applicable to the subject transaction. If the underlying transaction involved the sale of "goods," then the UCC would apply. If the transaction did not involve goods, but rather was for services, then application of the UCC would be erroneous.

Idaho Code §2–105(1) defines "goods" as "all things (including specially manufactured goods) which are movable at the time of identification to the contract for sale. * * *" Although there is little dispute that carpets are "goods," the transaction in this case also involved installation, a service. Such hybrid transactions, involving both goods and services, raise difficult questions about the applicability of the UCC. Two lines of authority have emerged to deal with such situations.

The first line of authority, and the majority position, utilizes the "predominant factor" test. The Ninth Circuit, applying the Idaho Uniform Commercial Code to the subject transaction, restated the predominant factor test as:

> The test for inclusion or exclusion is not whether they are mixed, but, granting that they are mixed, whether their predominant factor, their thrust, their purpose, reasonably stated, is the rendition of service, with goods incidentally involved (e.g., contract with artist for painting) or is a transaction of sale, with labor incidentally involved (e.g., installation of a water heater in a bathroom).

[Citations.] This test essentially involves consideration of the contract in its entirety, applying the UCC to the entire contract or not at all.

The second line of authority, which Hilton urges us to adopt, allows the contract to be severed into different parts, applying the UCC to the goods involved in the contract, but not to the nongoods involved, including services as well as other nongoods assets and property. Thus, an action focusing on defects or problems with the goods themselves would be covered by the UCC, while a suit based on the service provided or some other nongoods aspect would not be covered by the UCC. * * *

We believe the predominant factor test is the more prudent rule. Severing contracts into various parts, attempting to label each as goods or nongoods and applying different law to each separate part clearly contravenes the UCC's declared purpose "to simplify, clarify and modernize the law governing commercial transactions." §1–102(2)(a). As the Supreme Court of Tennessee suggested in [citation], such a rule would, in many contexts, present "difficult and in some instances insurmountable problems of proof in segregating assets and determining their respective values at the time of the original contract and at the time of resale, in order to apply two different measures of damages."

Applying the predominant factor test to the case before us, we conclude that the UCC was applicable to the subject transaction. The record indicates that the contract between the parties called for "165 yds Masterpiece No. 2122—Installed" for a price of $4319.50. There was an additional charge for removing the existing carpet. The record indicates that Hilton paid the installers $700 for the work done in laying Pittsley's carpet. It appears that Pittsley entered into this contract for the purpose of obtaining carpet of a certain quality and color. It does not appear that the installation, either who would provide it or the nature of the work, was a factor in inducing Pittsley to choose Hilton as the carpet supplier. On these facts, we conclude that the sale of the carpet was the predominant factor in the contract, with the installation being merely incidental to the purchase. Therefore, in failing to consider the UCC, the magistrate did not apply the correct legal principles to the facts as found. We must therefore vacate the judgment and remand for further findings of fact and application of the UCC to the subject transaction.

CASE 21-3

## Unconscionability
## DJ COLEMAN, INC v. NUFARM AMERICAS, INC

United States District Court, North Dakota, 2010
___ F.Supp.2d ___, 2010 WL 890835(D.N.D.)
http://nd.findacase.com/research/wfrmDocViewer.aspx/xq/fac.%5CFDCT%5CDND%5C2010%5C20100225_0000051.DND.htm/qx

**Hovland, J.**

The plaintiff, DJ Coleman, Inc. ("DJ Coleman"), is a farm corporation that is incorporated in the State of North Dakota and conducts farming operations in Burleigh County, North Dakota. DJ Coleman's principal, Clark Coleman, is responsible for DJ Coleman's commercial farming operations. Clark Coleman is a licensed pesticide purchaser and applicator. The defendant, Nufarm Americas, Inc. ("Nufarm"), is an Illinois corporation. Between May 10, 2007 and May 24, 2007, Clark Coleman planted different varietals of sunflowers. Clark Coleman used pre-emergent chemicals, Mad Dog®, a generic glyphosate broad-spectrum herbicide, and Spartan®, a herbicide, prior to planting the sunflowers. Between June 21, 2007 and June 24, 2007, Clark Coleman sprayed his post-emergent sunflower crops with a tank mix of Assert®, Scoil®, and Asana®. Nufarm is the manufacturer of Assert® and the wholesale distributor to United Agri Products, Inc. ("UAP"), the direct North Dakota retail seller to Clark Coleman. Clark Coleman did not contact Nufarm for approval before tank mixing Assert®, Scoil®, and Asana® in 2007. DJ Coleman alleges that Assert® caused severe damage to its 2007 sunflower crop by producing stunted and deformed heads, and seeks economic and non-economic damages.

* * * DJ Coleman alleges claims of products liability, negligence, failure to warn, breach of warranties, and violations of N.D.C.C. chs. 51-12 and 51-15 for false and deceptive advertising. Nufarm now moves for summary judgment on each claim.

* * *

### (2) Application of Warranty Language Limiting Damages

Nufarm contends that the Assert® label effectively limits any damages for breach of warranties to either the purchase price or the replacement of the product. Section 41-02-94 of the North Dakota Century Code permits the recovery of consequential damages for injury to property proximately resulting from any breach of warranty. However, Section 41-02-98 of the North Dakota Century Code, which is modeled after Section 2-719 of the Uniform Commercial Code, allows the parties to an agreement to limit the remedies available upon breach and to exclude consequential damages:

41-02-98. (2-719) Contractual modification or limitation of remedy.

> **1.** Subject to the provisions of subsections 2 and 3 of this section and of section 41-02-97 on liquidation and limitation of damages:
>    (a) The agreement may provide for remedies in addition to or in substitution for those provided in this chapter and may limit or alter the measure of damages recoverable under this chapter, as by limiting the buyer's remedies to return of the goods and repayment of the price or to repair and replacement of nonconforming goods or parts; and
>    (b) Resort to a remedy as provided is optional unless the remedy is expressly agreed to be exclusive, in which case it is the sole remedy.
>
> **2.** If circumstances cause an exclusive or limited remedy to fail of its essential purpose, remedy may be had as provided in this title.
>
> **3.** Consequential damages may be limited or excluded unless the limitation or exclusion is unconscionable. Limitation of consequential damages for injury to the person in the case of consumer goods is prima facie unconscionable but limitation of damages where the loss is commercial is not.

Nufarm contends that the Assert® label limits the remedies available to the purchase price of the product. The Assert® label reads as follows:

> To the extent allowed by law, Nufarm or Seller shall not be liable for any incidental, consequential or special damages resulting from the use or handling of this product. To the extent allowed by law, THE EXCLUSIVE REMEDY OF THE USER OR BUYER, AND THE EXCLUSIVE LIABILITY OF NUFARM AND SELLER FOR ANY AND ALL CLAIMS, LOSSES, INJURIES OR DAMAGES (INCLUDING CLAIMS BASED ON BREACH OF WARRANTY, CONTRACT, NEGLIGENCE, TORTS, STRICT LIABILITY OR OTHERWISE) RESULTING FROM THE USE OR HANDLING OF THIS PRODUCT, SHALL BE THE RETURN OF THE PURCHASE PRICE OF THE PRODUCT OR AT THE ELECTION OF NUFARM OR SELLER, THE REPLACEMENT OF PRODUCT.

* * *

The doctrine of unconscionability permits a court to "'deny enforcement of a contract because of procedural abuses arising out of the contract's formation and substantive abuses relating to the terms of the contract.'" [Citation.] The determination of whether a contractual provision is unconscionable is a question of law. [Citation.] "The court is to look at the contract from the perspective of the time it was entered into, without the benefit of hindsight. The determination to be made is whether, under the circumstances presented in the particular commercial setting, the terms of the agreement are so one-sided as to be unconscionable." [Citation.]

North Dakota law provides the Court with several options when a contract, or clause of a contract, is found to be unconscionable:

1. If the court as a matter of law finds the contract or any clause of the contract to have been unconscionable at the time it was made the court may refuse to enforce the contract, or it may enforce the remainder of the contract without the unconscionable clause, or it may so limit the application of any unconscionable clause as to avoid any unconscionable result.
2. When it is claimed or appears to the court that the contract or any clause thereof may be unconscionable the parties shall be afforded a reasonable opportunity to present evidence as to its commercial setting, purpose, and effect to aid the court in making the determination.

N.D.C.C. § 41-02-19.

There is no North Dakota case that addresses whether a limitation of remedies provision is unconscionable for injury resulting from the application of agricultural chemicals. * * *

* * *

Courts from other jurisdictions vary on whether a limitation of remedies provision is unconscionable in the chemical agriculture business. * * *

In order to find that a provision is unconscionable, there must be a showing of both procedural and substantive unconscionability. "'The concept of unconscionability must necessarily be applied in a flexible manner, taking into consideration all of the facts and circumstances of a particular case.'"[Citation.]

### (a) Procedural Unconscionability

"Procedural unconscionability focuses upon formation of the contract and fairness of the bargaining process, including factors such as inequality of bargaining power, oppression, and unfair surprise." [Citation.] Courts are more likely to find unconscionability in consumer transactions than in commercial transactions involving experienced parties [Citation.] "Courts' general skepticism of unconscionability claims in purely commercial transactions stems from the presumption that businessmen possess a greater degree of commercial understanding and substantially stronger economic bargaining power than the ordinary consumer." [Citation.] Nevertheless, the North Dakota Supreme Court has stated:

> [G]eneralizations are always subject to exceptions and categorization is rarely an adequate substitution for analysis. With increasing frequency, courts have begun to recognize that experienced but legally unsophisticated businessmen may be unfairly surprised by unconscionable contract terms … and that even large business entities may have *relatively* little bargaining power, depending on the identity of the other contracting party and the commercial circumstances surrounding the agreement.

* * * It is undisputed that DJ Coleman had no bargaining power to alter the language of the limitation of remedies provision. The limitation of remedies provision contained on the Assert® label was pre-printed and was not negotiated. There is a substantial inequality in bargaining power between DJ Coleman and Nufarm. DJ Coleman is a commercial farming operation located in North Dakota, and Nufarm is part of an enormous, highly diversified, and international conglomerate. * * * the facts of this case do not demonstrate an element of unfair surprise. Clark Coleman testified that he used Assert® for ten years prior to 2007. Nonetheless, the evidence reveals that the parties had unequal bargaining power and there was no room for meaningful negotiation. The purchasers of herbicides, regardless of their experience, are not in a position to bargain for more favorable terms than those listed on the pre-printed label, nor are they in a position to test the effectiveness of a herbicide before purchasing it. The fact that Clark Coleman was an experienced farmer that had used Assert® on sunflower crops for ten years should not control whether he is entitled to consequential damages for a breach of warranty. Accordingly, the Court finds that the limitation of remedies provision was procedurally unconscionable.

### (b) Substantive Unconscionability

Substantive unconscionability focuses on the harshness or one-sidedness of the limitation of remedies provision. [Citation.] The Official Comment to Section 2-719 of the Uniform Commercial Code provides:

> However, it is of the very essence of a sales contact that at least minimum adequate remedies be available. If the parties intend to conclude a contract for sale within this Article they must accept the legal consequence that there be at least a fair quantum of remedy for breach of the obligations or duties outlined in the contract. Thus any clause purporting to modify or

> limit the remedial provisions of this Article in an unconscionable manner is subject to deletion and in that event the remedies made available by this Article are applicable as if the stricken clause had never existed.

The clause at issue here would limit DJ Coleman's remedy for a breach of an express warranty to the purchase price of Assert® or the replacement of the product. The Court finds that the limitation of remedies provision is substantively unconscionable. "[T]he farmer is required to expend large sums of money before any defect [ ] is noticeable, and once a defect is found an entire year's crop might be worthless. Once the crop has failed, the farmer's only recourse is monetary compensation to cover his lost profit and expenditures; replacement and repair are not viable options." [Citation.] It is clear that the allocation of risk for defective herbicides is better shouldered by the manufacturer of the herbicide, rather than the consumer. The consumer does not have the ability or resources to test its use, but the manufacturer does. The Court finds that the limitation of remedies provision on the Assert® label is unconscionable, both procedurally and substantively and, therefore, unenforceable. Accordingly, damages for a breach of express warranty of fitness for a particular purpose are not limited to the purchase price or replacement of the product.

* * *

* * * Summary judgment is granted on the Plaintiff's products liability, negligence, failure to warn, breach of implied warranties, and statutory violation * * * claims. Summary judgment is denied on the Plaintiff's breach of express warranties claim.

## CASE 21-4

### Variant Acceptances: Battle of the Forms

### COMMERCE & INDUSTRY INSURANCE COMPANY v. BAYER CORPORATION

Supreme Judicial Court of Massachusetts, 2001
433 Mass. 388, 742 N.E.2d 567, 44 U.C.C. Rep.Serv.2d 50
http://caselaw.lp.findlaw.com/scripts/getcase.pl?court=ma&vol=sjcslip/8358&invol=1

**Greaney, J.**

We granted the application for direct appellate review of the defendant, Bayer Corporation (Bayer), to determine the enforceability of an arbitration provision appearing in the plaintiff's, Malden Mills Industries, Inc. (Malden Mills), orders purchasing materials from Bayer. In a written decision, a judge in the Superior Court concluded that the provision was not enforceable. * * * We affirm the order.

The background of the case is as follows. Malden Mills manufactures internationally-known apparel fabrics and other textiles. On December 11, 1995, an explosion and fire destroyed several Malden Mills's buildings at its manufacturing facility. Subsequently, Malden Mills and its property insurers, the plaintiffs Commerce and Industry Insurance Company and Federal Insurance Company, commenced suit in the Superior Court against numerous defendants, including Bayer. In their complaint, the plaintiffs allege, insofar as relevant here, that the cause of the fire was the ignition, by static electrical discharge, of nylon tow (also known as bulk nylon fiber), which was sold by Bayer (but manufactured by a French business entity) to Malden Mills. * * *

Malden Mills initiated purchases of nylon tow from Bayer either by sending its standard form purchase order to Bayer, or by placing a telephone order to Bayer, followed by a standard form purchase order. Each of Malden Mills's purchase orders contained, on the reverse side, as one of its "terms and conditions," an arbitration provision stating:

> Any controversy arising out of or relating to this contract shall be settled by arbitration in the City of New York or Boston as [Malden Mills] shall determine in accordance with the Rules then obtaining of the American Arbitration Association or the General Arbitration Council of the Textile Industry, as [Malden Mills] shall determine.

Another "term and condition" appearing in paragraph one on the reverse side of each purchase order provides:

> This purchase order represents the entire agreement between both parties, not withstanding any Seller's order form, * * *, and this document cannot be modified except in writing and signed by an authorized representative of the buyer.

In response, Bayer transmitted Malden Mills's purchase orders to the manufacturer with instructions, in most instances, that the nylon tow was to be shipped directly to Malden Mills. Thereafter, Bayer prepared and sent Malden Mills an invoice. Each of the Bayer invoices contained the following language on its face, located at the bottom of the form in capital letters:

> TERMS AND CONDITIONS: NOTWITHSTANDING ANY CONTRARY OR INCONSISTENT CONDITIONS THAT MAY BE EMBODIED IN YOUR PURCHASE ORDER, YOUR ORDER IS ACCEPTED SUBJECT TO THE PRICES, TERMS AND CONDITIONS OF THE MUTUALLY EXECUTED CONTRACT BETWEEN US, OR, IF NO SUCH CONTRACT EXISTS, YOUR ORDER IS ACCEPTED SUBJECT TO OUR REGULAR SCHEDULED PRICE AND TERMS IN EFFECT AT TIME OF SHIPMENT AND SUBJECT TO THE TERMS AND CONDITIONS PRINTED ON THE REVERSE SIDE HEREOF.

The following "condition" appears in paragraph fourteen on the reverse side of each invoice:

> This document is not an Expression of Acceptance or a Confirmation document as contemplated in Section 2–207 of the Uniform Commercial Code. The acceptance of any order entered by [Malden Mills] is expressly conditioned on [Malden Mills's] assent to any additional or conflicting terms contained herein.

Malden Mills usually remitted payment to Bayer within thirty days of receiving an invoice.

Based on the arbitration provision in Malden Mills's purchase orders, Bayer demanded that Malden Mills arbitrate its claims against Bayer. After Malden Mills refused, Bayer moved to compel arbitration and to stay the litigation against it. The judge denied Bayer's motion, concluding, under §2–207 of * * * the Massachusetts enactment of the Uniform Commercial Code, that the parties' conduct, as opposed to their writings, established a contract. As to whether the arbitration provision was an enforceable term of the parties' contract, the judge concluded that subsection (3) of §2–207 governed, and, pursuant thereto, the arbitration provision was not enforceable because the parties had not agreed in their writings to arbitrate. * * *

This case presents a dispute arising from what has been styled a typical "battle of the forms" sale, in which a buyer and a seller each attempt to consummate a commercial transaction through the exchange of self-serving preprinted forms that clash, and contradict each other, on both material and minor terms. [Citation.] Here, Malden Mills's form, a purchase order, contains an arbitration provision, and Bayer's form, a seller's invoice, is silent on how the parties will resolve any disputes. Oddly enough, the buyer, Malden Mills, the party proposing the arbitration provision, and its insurers, now seek to avoid an arbitral forum.

Section 2–207 was enacted with the expectation of creating an orderly mechanism to resolve commercial disputes resulting from a "battle of the forms." The section has been characterized as "an amphibious tank that was originally designed to fight in the swamps, but was sent to fight in the desert." [Citation.] Section 2–207 sets forth rules and principles concerning contract formation and the procedures for determining the terms of a contract. As to contract formation, under §2-207, there are essentially three ways by which a contract may be formed. [Citation.] "First, if the parties exchange forms with divergent terms, yet the seller's invoice does not state that its acceptance is made 'expressly conditional' on the buyer's assent to any additional or different terms in the invoice, a contract is formed [under subsection (1) of §2–207]." "Second, if the seller does make its acceptance 'expressly conditional' on the buyer's assent to any additional or divergent terms in the seller's invoice, the invoice is merely a counteroffer, and a contract is formed [under subsection (1) of §2–207] only when the buyer expresses its affirmative acceptance of the seller's counteroffer." Third, "where for any reason the exchange of forms does not result in contract formation (e.g., the buyer 'expressly limits acceptance to the terms of [its offer]' under §2–207(2)(a), or the buyer does not accept the seller's counteroffer under the second clause of §2–207[1]), a contract nonetheless is formed [under subsection (3) of §2–207] if their subsequent conduct—for instance, the seller ships and the buyer accepts the goods—demonstrates that the parties believed that a binding agreement had been formed."

Bayer correctly concedes that its contract with Malden Mills resulted from the parties' conduct, and, thus, was formed pursuant to subsection (3) of §2–207. A contract never came into being under subsection (1) of §2–207 because (1) paragraph fourteen on the reverse side of Bayer's invoices expressly conditioned acceptance on Malden Mills's assent to "additional or different" terms, and (2) Malden Mills never expressed "affirmative acceptance" of any of Bayer's invoices. In addition, the exchange of forms between Malden Mills and Bayer did not result in a contract because Malden Mills, by means of language in paragraph one of its purchase orders, expressly limited Bayer's acceptance to the terms of Malden Mills's offers. [Citation.]

Although Bayer acknowledges that its contract with Malden Mills was formed under subsection (3) of §2–207, it nonetheless argues * * *, that the terms of the contract are determined through an application of the principles in subsection (2) of §2–207. Under this analysis, Bayer asserts that the arbitration provision became part of the parties' contract because it was not a "material alteration," and to include the provision would cause no "surprise or hardship" to the plaintiffs. This analysis is incorrect.

* * * Where a contract is formed by the parties' conduct (as opposed to writings), as is the case here, the terms of the contract are determined exclusively by subsection (3) of §2–207. [Citation.] Under subsection (3) of §2–207, "the

terms of the particular contract consist of those terms on which the writings of the parties agree, together with any supplementary terms incorporated under any other provisions of this chapter." §2–207 (3). In this respect, one commentator has aptly referred to subsection (3) of §2–207 as the "fall-back" rule. [Citation.] Under this rule, the Code accepts "common terms but rejects all the rest." While this approach "serves to leave many matters uncovered," terms may be filled by "recourse to usages of trade or course of dealing under [§]1–205 or, perhaps, the gap filling provisions of [§§]2–300s." [Citation.]

Contrary to Bayer's contentions, subsection (2) of §2–207 is not applicable for several reasons. First, subsection (2) instructs on how to ascertain the terms of a contract when the contract is formed either by the parties' writings or by a party's written confirmation of an oral contract, situations not present here (the parties' contract was formed by their conduct). [Citation.] * * *

* * *

Thus, the judge correctly concluded, under subsection (3) of §2–207, that the arbitration provision in Malden Mills's purchase orders did not become a term of the parties' contract. The arbitration provision was not common to both Malden Mills's purchase orders and Bayer's invoices. Bayer properly does not argue that any of the gap-filling provisions of [the UCC] apply. Because Bayer concedes that it never previously arbitrated a dispute with Malden Mills, we reject Bayer's claim that the parties' course of dealing requires us to enforce the arbitration provision.

* * *

Bayer may be right that the drafters of the Massachusetts version of the Code did not intend that §2–207 should provide "an avenue for a party to strike the terms of its own purchase documents." Bayer, however, cannot ignore the fact that the use of its own boilerplate invoices contributed to the result that Bayer now finds problematic. The order denying the motion to compel arbitration and to stay litigation is affirmed.

## QUESTIONS

1. Distinguish a sale and a lease from other kinds of transactions that affect goods.
2. Identify and discuss the fundamental principles of Article 2 and Article 2A.
3. Discuss the significant changes Article 2 and Article 2A have made in the need for an offer to include all material terms.
4. Distinguish between the common law's mirror image rule and the Uniform Commercial Code's (UCC's) provisions for dealing with variant acceptances.
5. Discuss (a) the UCC's approach to the requirement that certain contracts must be in writing and (b) the alternative methods of compliance.

## PROBLEMS

**1.** Adams orders one thousand widgets at $5 per widget from International Widget to be delivered within sixty days. After the contract is consummated and signed, Adams requests that International deliver the widgets within thirty days rather than sixty days. International agrees. Is the contractual modification binding?

**2.** In problem 1, what effect, if any, would the following letter have?

International Widget:

> In accordance with our agreement of this date you will deliver the one thousand previously ordered widgets within thirty days. Thank you for your cooperation in this matter.
>
> (signed) Adams

**3.** Browne & Assoc., a San Francisco company, orders from U.S. Electronics, a New York company, ten thousand electronic units. Browne & Assoc.'s order form provides that any dispute would be resolved by an arbitration panel located in San Francisco. U.S. Electronics executes and delivers to Browne & Assoc. its acknowledgment form, which accepts the order and contains the following provision: "All disputes will be resolved by the State courts of New York." A dispute arises concerning the workmanship of the parts, and Browne & Assoc. wishes the case to be arbitrated in San Francisco. What result?

**4.** Explain how the result in problem 3 might change if the U.S. Electronics form contained any of the following provisions:

**(a)** "The seller's acceptance of the purchase order to which this acknowledgment responds is expressly made conditional on the buyer's assent to any or different terms contained in this acknowledgment."

**(b)** "The seller's acceptance of the purchase order is subject to the terms and conditions on the face and reverse side hereof and which the buyer accepts by accepting the goods described herein."

**(c)** "The seller's terms govern this agreement—this acknowledgment merely constitutes a counteroffer."

**5.** Reinfort executed a written contract with Bylinski to purchase an assorted collection of shoes for $3,000. A week before the agreed shipment date, Bylinski called Reinfort and said, "We cannot deliver at $3,000; unless you agree to pay $4,000, we will cancel the order." After considerable discussion, Reinfort agreed to pay $4,000 if Bylinski would ship as agreed in the contract. After the shoes had been delivered and accepted by Reinfort, Reinfort refused to pay $4,000 and insisted on paying only $3,000. Is the contractual modification binding? Explain.

**6.** On November 23, Acorn, a dress manufacturer, mailed to Bowman a written and signed offer to sell one thousand sundresses at $50 per dress. The offer stated that it would "remain open for ten days" and that it could "not be withdrawn prior to that date."

Two days later, Acorn, noting a sudden increase in the price of sundresses, changed his mind. Acorn therefore sent Bowman a letter revoking the offer. The letter was sent on November 25 and received by Bowman on November 28.

Bowman chose to disregard the letter of November 25; instead, she happily continued to watch the price of sundresses rise. On December 1, Bowman sent a letter accepting the original offer. The letter, however, was not received by Acorn until December 9, due to a delay in the mails.

Bowman has demanded delivery of the goods according to the terms of the offer of November 23, but Acorn has refused. Does a contract exist between Acorn and Bowman? Explain.

**7.** Henry and Wilma, an elderly immigrant couple, agreed to purchase from Brown a refrigerator with fair market value of $450 for twenty-five monthly installments of $60 per month. Henry and Wilma now wish to void the contract, asserting that they did not realize the exorbitant price they were paying. Result?

**8.** Courts Distributors needed two hundred compact refrigerators on a rush basis. It contacted Eastinghouse Corporation, a manufacturer of refrigerators. Eastinghouse said it would take some time to quote a price on an order of that size. Courts replied, "Send the refrigerators immediately and bill us later." The refrigerators were delivered three days later, and the invoice ten days after that. The invoice price was $140,000. Courts believes that the wholesale market price of the refrigerators is only $120,000. Do the parties have a contract? If so, what is the price? Explain.

**9.** While adjusting a television antenna beside his mobile home and underneath a high-voltage electric transmission wire, Prince received an electric shock resulting in personal injury. He claims the high-voltage electric current jumped from the transmission wire to the antenna. The wire, which carried some 7,200 volts of electricity, did not serve his mobile home but ran directly above it. Prince sued the Navarro County Electric Co-Op, the owner and operator of the wire, for breach of implied warranty of merchantability under the Uniform Commercial Code. He contends that the Code's implied warranty of merchantability extends to the container of a product—in this instance the wiring—and that the escape of the current shows that the wiring was unfit for its purpose of transporting electricity. The electric company argues that the electricity passing through the transmission wire was not being sold to Prince and that, therefore, there was no sale of goods to Prince. Is the contract covered by the Code?

**10.** HMT, already in the business of marketing agricultural products, decided to try its hand at marketing potatoes for processing. Nine months before the potato harvest, HMT contracted to supply Bell Brand with one hundred thousand sacks of potatoes. At harvest time, Bell Brand would accept only sixty thousand sacks. HMT sues for breach of contract. Bell Brand argues that custom and usage in marketing processing potatoes allows buyers to give *estimates* in contracts, not fixed quantities, because the contracts are established so far in advance. HMT responds that the quantity term in the contract was definite and unambiguous. Can custom and trade usage be used to interpret an unambiguous contract? Discuss.

**11.** Schreiner, a cotton farmer, agreed over the telephone to sell 150 bales of cotton to Loeb & Co. Schreiner had sold cotton to Loeb & Co. for the past five years. Written confirmation of the date, parties, price, and conditions was mailed to Schreiner, who did not respond to the confirmation in any way. Four months later, when the price of cotton had doubled, Loeb & Co. sought to enforce the contract. Is the contract enforceable?

**12.** American Sand & Gravel, Inc., agreed to sell sand to Clark at a special discount if 20,000 to 25,000 tons were ordered. The discount price was $0.45 per ton, compared with the normal price of $0.55 per ton. Two years later, Clark orders, and receives, 1,600 tons of sand from American Sand & Gravel. Clark refuses to pay more than $0.45 per ton. American Sand & Gravel sues for the remaining $0.10 per ton. Decision?

**13.** In September, Auburn Plastics (defendant) submitted price quotations to CBS (plaintiff) for the manufacture of eight cavity molds to be used in making parts for CBS's toys. Each quotation specified that the offer would not be binding unless accepted within fifteen days. Furthermore, CBS would be subject to an additional 30 percent charge for engineering services upon delivery of the molds. In December, CBS sent detailed purchase orders to Auburn Plastics for cavity molds. The purchase order forms stated that CBS reserved the right to remove the molds from Auburn Plastics without an additional or "withdrawal" charge. Auburn Plastics acknowledged the purchase order and stated that the sale would be subject to all conditions contained in the price quotation. CBS paid Auburn for the molds, and Auburn began to fabricate toy parts from the molds for CBS. Later, Auburn announced a price increase, and CBS demanded delivery of the molds. Auburn refused to deliver the molds unless CBS paid the additional charge for engineering services. CBS claimed that the contract did not provide for a withdrawal charge. Who will prevail? Why?

**14.** Terminal Grain Corporation brought an action against Glen Freeman, a farmer, to recover damages for breach of an oral contract to deliver grain. According to the company, Freeman orally agreed to two sales of wheat to Terminal Grain of four thousand bushels each at $6.21 per bushel and $6.41 per bushel, respectively. Dwayne Maher, merchandising manager of Terminal Grain, sent two written confirmations of the agreements to Freeman, who never made any written objections to the confirmations. After the first transaction had occurred, the price of wheat rose to between $6.75 and $6.80 per bushel, and Freeman refused to deliver the remaining four thousand bushels at the agreed-upon price. Freeman denies entering into any agreement to sell the second four thousand bushels of wheat to Terminal Grain but admits that he received the two written confirmations sent by Maher. Decision?

**15.** Frank's Maintenance and Engineering, Inc., orally ordered steel tubing from C.A. Roberts Co. for use in the manufacture of motorcycle front fork tubes. Because these front fork tubes bear the bulk of the weight of a motorcycle, the steel used must be of high quality. Roberts Co. sent an acknowledgment with conditions of sale including one that limited consequential damages and restricted remedies available upon breach by requiring claims for defective equipment to be promptly made upon receipt. The conditions were located on the back of the acknowledgment. The legend "conditions of sale on reverse side" was stamped over so that on first appearance it read "No conditions of sale on reverse side." Roberts delivered the order in January. The steel had no visible defects; however, when Frank's Maintenance began using the steel in its manufacture in the summer, it discovered that the steel was pitted and cracked beyond repair. Frank's Maintenance informed Roberts Co. of the defects, revoked its acceptance of the steel, and sued for breach of warranty of merchantability. Is the limitation of rights enforceable?

**16.** Dorton, as a representative for The Carpet Mart, purchased carpets from Collins & Aikman that were supposedly manufactured of 100 percent Kodel polyester fiber but were, in fact, made of cheaper and inferior fibers. Dorton then brought suit for compensatory and punitive damages against Collins & Aikman for its fraud, deceit, and misrepresentation in the sale of the carpets. Collins & Aikman moved for a stay pending arbitration, claiming that Dorton was bound to an arbitration agreement printed on the reverse side of Collins & Aikman's printed sales acknowledgment form. A provision printed on the face of the acknowledgment form stated that its acceptance was "subject to all of the terms and conditions on the face and reverse side thereof, including arbitration, all of which are accepted by buyer." Is the arbitration clause enforceable?

**17.** Defendant, Gray Communications, desired to build a television tower. After a number of negotiation sessions conducted by telephone between the Defendant and Plaintiff, Kline Iron, the parties allegedly reached an oral agreement under which the Plaintiff would build a tower for the Defendant for a total price of $1,485,368. A few days later, Plaintiff sent a written document, referred to as a proposal, for execution by Defendant. The Proposal indicated that it had been prepared for immediate acceptance by Defendant and that prior to formal acceptance by Defendant it could be modified or withdrawn without notice. A few days later, without having executed the Proposal, Defendant advised Plaintiff that a competitor had provided a lower bid for construction of the tower. Defendant requested that Plaintiff explain its higher bid price, which Plaintiff failed to do. Defendant then advised Plaintiff by letter that it would not be retained to construct the tower. Plaintiff then commenced suit alleging breach of an oral contract, asserting that the oral agreement was enforceable because the common law of contracts, not the Uniform Commercial Code (UCC), governed the transaction and that under the common law a writing is not necessary to cover this type of transaction. Even if the transaction was subject to the UCC, Plaintiff alternatively argued, the contract was within the UCC "merchant's exception." Is the plaintiff correct in its assertions? Discuss.

**18.** Due to high gasoline prices, American Bakeries Company (ABC) considered converting its fleet of more than three thousand vehicles to a much less expensive propane fuel system. After negotiations with Empire Gas Corporation (Empire), ABC signed a contract for approximately three thousand converter units, "more or less depending upon requirements of Buyer," as well as agreeing to buy all propane to be used for four years from Empire. Without giving any reasons, however, ABC never ordered any converter units or propane from Empire, having apparently decided not to convert its vehicles. Empire brought suit against ABC for $3,254,963, representing lost profits on 2,242 converter units and the propane that would have been consumed during the contract period. Is ABC liable? Explain.

**19.** Emery Industries (Emery) contracted with Mechanicals, Inc. (Mechanicals), to install a pipe system to carry chemicals and fatty acids under high pressure and temperature. The system required stainless steel "stub ends" (used to connect pipe segments), which Mechanicals ordered from McJunkin Corporation (McJunkin). McJunkin in turn ordered the stub ends from the Alaskan Copper Companies, Inc. (Alaskan). McJunkin's purchase order required the seller to certify the goods and to relieve the buyer of liabilities that might arise from defective goods. After shipment of the goods to McJunkin, Alaskan sent written acknowledgment of the order, containing terms and conditions of sale different from those in McJunkin's purchase order. The acknowledgment provided a disclaimer of warranty and a requirement for inspection of the goods within ten days of receipt. The acknowledgment also contained a requirement that the buyer accept all of the seller's terms.

The stub ends were delivered to Mechanicals in several shipments over a five-month period. Each shipment included a document reciting terms the same as those on Alaskan's initial acknowledgment. Apparently, McJunkin never objected to any of the terms contained in any of Alaskan's documents.

After the stub ends were installed, they were found to be defective. Mechanicals had to remove and replace them, causing Emery to close its plant for several days. McJunkin filed a complaint alleging that Mechanicals had failed to pay $26,141.88 owed on account for the stub ends McJunkin supplied. Mechanicals filed an answer and counterclaim against McJunkin, alleging $93,586.13 in damages resulting from the replacement and repair of the defective stub ends. McJunkin filed a third-party complaint against Alaskan, alleging that Alaskan was liable for any damages Mechanicals incurred as a result of the defective stub ends. Discuss.

# CHAPTER 22
# Performance

Performance is the process of discharging contractual obligations by carrying out those obligations according to the terms of the contract. The basic obligation of the seller in a contract for the sale of goods is to transfer and deliver goods that conform to the terms of the contract. The basic obligation of the buyer is to accept and pay for conforming goods in accordance with the contract. The basic obligation of the lessor is to transfer possession of the goods for the lease term, and that of the lessee is to pay the agreed rent. Section 2A–103(1)(j). Unless the parties have agreed otherwise, a tender (offer) of performance by one party is a condition to performance by the other party. A contract of sale also requires that each party not impair the other party's expectation of having the contract performed.

The obligations of the parties are determined by their contractual agreement. For example, the contract of sale may expressly provide that the seller must deliver the goods before receiving payment of the price or that the buyer must pay the price before receiving the goods. If the contract does not sufficiently cover the particulars of performance, these terms will be supplied by the Code, common law, course of dealing, usage of trade, and course of performance. (Article 2A provides only a few gap-fillers.) In all events, both parties to the sales contract must perform their contractual obligations in good faith.

This chapter will examine the performance obligations of the seller and the buyer as well as the contractual obligations that apply to both of them.

## PERFORMANCE BY THE SELLER

Tender of conforming goods by the seller entitles him to acceptance of them by the buyer and to payment of the contractually agreed-upon price. Nonetheless, the rights of the parties may be otherwise fixed by the terms of the contract. For example, if the seller has agreed to sell goods on sixty or ninety days' credit, he is required to perform his part of the contract before the buyer performs.

**Tender** of delivery requires that the seller put and hold goods that conform to the contract at the buyer's disposition and that he give the buyer reasonable notification to enable her to take delivery. Section 2–503. Tender must also be made at a reasonable time and be kept open for a reasonable period. For example, Robert agrees to sell Barbara a home theater system composed of a speaker system (consisting of four identical, small speakers for the front and rear, a center channel speaker, and a subwoofer speaker), a Blu-Ray disc player and an audio-video receiver. Each component is specified by manufacturer and model number, and delivery is to be at Robert's store. Robert obtains the ordered equipment in accordance with the contractual specifications and notifies Barbara that she may pick up the system at her convenience. Robert has now tendered and thus has performed his obligations under the sales contract: he holds goods that conform to the contract, he has reasonably placed them at the buyer's disposal, and he has notified the buyer of their readiness.

**CISG** As specified by the contract and the CISG, the seller must deliver the goods, hand over any documents relating to them, and transfer the property in the goods.

### TIME AND MANNER OF TENDER

Tender must be at a *reasonable* time, and the goods tendered must be kept available for the period reasonably necessary to enable the buyer to take possession of them. Unless otherwise agreed, the buyer must furnish facilities reasonably suited to the receipt of the goods tendered by the seller. Section 2–503.

If the terms of the contract do not fix a definite time for delivery, the seller is allowed a reasonable time after entering into the contract within which to tender the goods to the buyer. Likewise, the buyer has a reasonable time within which to accept delivery. What length of time is reasonable depends upon the facts and circumstances of each case. If the goods can be delivered immediately, a reasonable time would be very short. Where the goods must be constructed or manufactured, however, "reasonable" would take into account the usual length of time required to make the goods.

A contract may not be performed piecemeal or in installments unless the parties specifically agree. If such performance is not so specified, all of the goods the contract specifies must be tendered in a single delivery, and payment is due on such tender.

CISG The seller must deliver the goods: (1) if a date is fixed by or determinable from the contract, on that date; (2) if a period of time is fixed by or determinable from the contract, at any time within that period unless circumstances indicate that the buyer is to choose a date; or (3) in any other case, within a reasonable time after the conclusion of the contract.

## PLACE OF TENDER

If the contract does not specify the place for delivery of the goods, the place for delivery is the *seller's place of business* or, if he has none, his residence. The seller must hold the goods for the buyer's disposition and notify her that the goods are being held for her to pick up. Section 2–308(a). If the contract is for the sale of identified goods that the parties know at the time of making the contract are located neither at the seller's place of business nor at his residence, the *location* of the goods is then the place for delivery. Section 2–308. For example, George, a boat builder in Chicago, contracts to sell to Chris a certain yacht that both parties know is anchored at Milwaukee. The place of delivery would be Milwaukee. On the other hand, if the contract provides that George shall overhaul the motor at his shipyard in Chicago, George would have to return the yacht to Chicago, and the place of delivery would be George's Chicago shipyard.

The parties frequently agree expressly upon the place of tender, typically by using one of various *delivery terms*. These terms specify whether the contract is a shipment or destination contract and determine the place where the seller must tender delivery of the goods.

CISG If the seller is not bound to deliver the goods at any other particular place and the contract of sale does not involve carriage of the goods, his obligation to deliver consists: (1) if the contract relates to specific goods, or unidentified goods to be drawn from a specific stock or to be manufactured or produced, and at the time of the conclusion of the contract the parties knew that the goods were at, or were to be manufactured or produced at, a particular place, in placing the goods at the buyer's disposal at that place; and (2) in other cases, in placing the goods at the buyer's disposal at the place where the seller had his place of business at the time of the conclusion of the contract.

**Shipment Contracts** The delivery terms *F.O.B. (free on board) place of shipment, F.A.S. (free alongside ship) port of shipment, C.I.F. (cost, insurance, and freight)*, and *C.&F. (cost and freight)* are all "shipment contracts." Under a shipment contract, the seller is required or authorized to send the goods to the buyer, but the contract does not obligate her to deliver them at a particular destination. In these cases, the seller's tender of performance occurs at the point of shipment, provided the seller meets certain specified conditions designed to protect the interests of the absent buyer. A contract is assumed to be a shipment contract unless otherwise indicated.

Under the Uniform Commercial Code (UCC), the initials "F.O.B." and "F.A.S." are delivery terms, even though they are used only in connection with a stated price. Section 2–319(1)(a). A contract providing that the sale is **F.O.B. place of shipment** or **F.A.S. port of shipment** is a shipment contract. For example, Linda, whose place of business is in New York, enters into a contract with Holly, the buyer, who is located in San Francisco. The contract calls for delivery of the goods F.O.B. New York. This would be a shipment contract. Under a **C.I.F.** ("cost, insurance, and freight") contract, in consideration for an agreed unit price for the goods, the seller agrees to pay all costs of transportation, insurance, and freight to the destination. The amount of the agreed unit price of the goods will, of course, reflect these costs. By comparison, under a **C.&F.** contract, the seller would pay "cost and freight." The unit price in such a contract is understandably less than in a C.I.F. contract as the C.&F. contract does not include the cost of insurance.

Under a shipment contract, the seller is required to (1) deliver the goods to a carrier; (2) make a contract for their transportation that is reasonable given the nature of the goods and other circumstances; (3) obtain and promptly deliver or tender to the buyer any document necessary to enable the buyer to obtain possession of the goods from the carrier; and (4) promptly notify the buyer of the shipment. Section 2–504. Failing either to make a proper contract for transportation or to notify the buyer of the shipment is a ground for rejection *only* if material loss or delay results. Section 2–504.

CISG If the seller is not bound to deliver the goods at any other particular place and if the contract of sale involves carriage of the goods, his obligation to deliver consists of handing the goods over to the first carrier for delivery to the buyer.

**Destination Contracts** The delivery terms *F.O.B. city of buyer, ex-ship*, and *no arrival, no sale* are destination contracts. Because a destination contract requires the seller to tender delivery of conforming goods at a specified destination, the seller must place the goods at the buyer's disposition and give the buyer reasonable notice to enable him to take delivery. In addition, if the destination contract involves documents of title, the seller must tender the necessary documents. Section 2–503.

Where the contract provides that the sale is **F.O.B. place of destination**, the seller must at his own expense and risk transport the goods to that place and there tender delivery of them to the buyer. Section 2–319(1)(b). For example, if the buyer is in Boston and the seller is in Chicago, a contract providing F.O.B. Boston is a destination contract under which the seller must tender the goods at the designated place in Boston at his own expense and risk. A contract that provides for delivery "**ex-ship**," or from the ship, is also a destination contract, requiring the seller to unload the goods from the carrier at the named destination. Finally, where the contract contains the terms "**no arrival, no sale**," the title and risk of loss do not pass to the buyer until the seller makes a tender of the goods after they arrive at their destination. The major significance of the "no arrival, no sale" term is that it excuses the seller from any liability to the buyer for the goods' failure to arrive, unless the seller has caused their nonarrival.

**Goods Held by Bailee** Where goods are in the possession of a bailee and are to be delivered without being moved, in most instances the seller may either tender to the buyer a document of title or obtain an acknowledgment by the bailee of the buyer's right to possess the goods. Section 2–503(4). This acknowledgment permits the buyer to obtain the goods directly from the bailee.

◆ SEE FIGURE 22-1: **Tender of Performance by the Seller**

## PERFECT TENDER RULE

The Code imposes upon the seller the obligation to conform her tender of goods *exactly* to the requirements of the contract. The seller's tender cannot deviate in any way from the terms of the contract. Thus, a buyer may rightfully reject the delivery of 110 dozen shirts under an agreement calling for delivery of 100 dozen shirts. The size or extent of the breach does not affect the right to reject.

If the goods or the tender of delivery fail in any respect to conform to the contract, the buyer may (1) reject the whole lot, (2) accept the whole lot, or (3) accept any commercial unit or units and reject the rest. Section 2–601; Section 2A–509(1). A commercial unit means such a unit of goods as by commercial usage is a single unit and which, if divided, would be materially impaired in character or value. A **commercial unit** may be a single item (such as a machine), a set of articles (such as a suite of furniture or an assortment of sizes), a quantity (such as a bale, gross, or carload), or any other unit treated in use or in the relevant market as a whole. Section 2–105(6); Section 2A–103(1)(c).

**CISG** The CISG does not follow the perfect tender rule. The buyer may declare the contract avoided if the failure by the seller to perform any of his obligations under the contract or the CISG amounts to a fundamental breach of contract. A breach of contract committed by one of the parties is fundamental if it results in such detriment to the other party as substantially to deprive her of what she is entitled to expect under the contract, unless the party in breach did not foresee and a reasonable person of the same kind in the same circumstances would not have foreseen such a result.

The buyer's right to reject the goods upon the seller's failure to comply with the perfect tender rule is subject to three basic qualifications: (1) agreement between the parties limiting the buyer's right to reject nonconforming goods, (2) cure by the seller, and (3) the existence of an installment contract. In addition, as previously discussed, the perfect tender rule does not apply to a seller's breach of her obligation under a shipment contract to make a proper contract for transportation or to give proper notice of the shipment. A failure to perform either of these obligations is a ground for rejection only if material loss or delay results. Section 2–504.

**Agreement by the Parties** The parties may contractually agree to limit the operation of the perfect tender rule. For example, they may agree that the seller shall have the right to repair or replace any defective parts or goods. Such contractual limitations are discussed in *Chapter 25*.

**Cure by the Seller** The Code recognizes two situations in which a seller may cure or correct a nonconforming tender of goods. This relaxation of the seller's obligation to make a perfect tender gives the seller an opportunity to make either a second delivery or a substitute tender. Whereas the first opportunity for cure occurs when the time for performance under the contract has not expired, the second opportunity is available after the time for performance has expired, but only if the seller had reasonable grounds to believe that the nonconforming tender would be acceptable to the buyer, with or without monetary adjustment.

Where the buyer refuses to accept a tender of goods that do not conform to the contract, the seller, by acting promptly and within the time allowed for performance, may make a proper tender or delivery of conforming goods and thereby cure his defective tender or performance. Section 2–508(1); Section 2A–513(1). Upon notice of the buyer's rightful rejection, the seller must first give the buyer reasonable notice of her intention to cure the defect and then must make a proper tender according to the *original* contract. This rule, which predates the Code, is fair to both parties. It gives the seller the full contractual period in which to perform while causing no harm to the buyer, who receives full

◆ **FIGURE 22-1: Tender of Performance by the Seller**

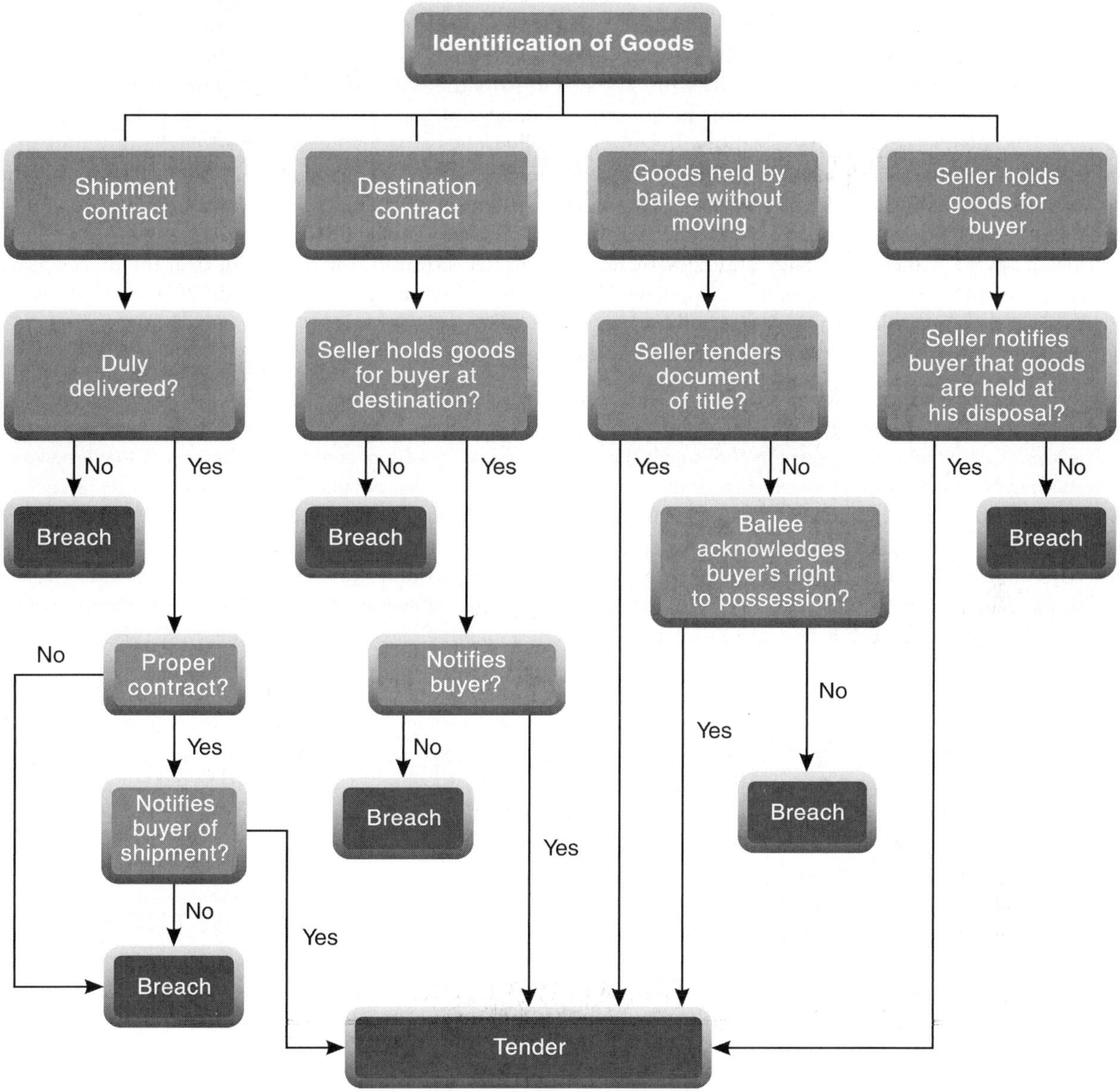


performance within the time agreed to in the contract. For example, Conroy is to deliver to Elizabeth twenty-five blue shirts and fifty white shirts by October 15. On October 1, Conroy delivers twenty-nine blue shirts and forty-six white shirts, which Elizabeth rejects as not conforming to the contract. Elizabeth notifies Conroy of her rejection and the reasons for it. Conroy has until October 15 to cure the defect by making a perfect tender, provided he seasonably notifies Elizabeth of his intention to do so.

The Code also provides the seller an opportunity after the time for performance has expired to cure a nonconforming tender, which the seller had reasonable grounds to believe would be acceptable to the buyer, with or without money allowance. Section 2–508(2); Section 2A–513(2). This Code-created opportunity to cure a nonconforming tender after the date set for performance is conditioned on the seller's satisfying the following requirements: (1) the seller had reasonable grounds for believing that the nonconforming tender would be acceptable to the buyer, (2) the seller, after being informed of the buyer's rightful rejection, seasonably notifies the buyer of his intention to cure the defect, and (3) the seller cures the defect within a reasonable time. The principal difficulty in applying this rule is whether or not the first requirement has been satisfied.

For example, Vanessa orders from Gary a model 110X S.C.A. television to be delivered on January 20. The 110X is unavailable, but Gary can obtain last year's model of the same television, a model 110, which lists for 5 percent less than the 110X. On January 20, Gary delivers to Vanessa the 110 at a discount price of 10 percent less than the contract price for the 110X. Vanessa rejects the substituted television set. Gary, who promptly notifies Vanessa that he will obtain and deliver a model 110X, will most likely have a reasonable time beyond the January 20 deadline in which to deliver the 110X television set to Vanessa, because under these facts Gary appeared to have reasonable grounds to believe the model 110 would be acceptable with the money allowance.

CISG If the seller has delivered goods before the date for delivery, the seller may, up to the delivery date, cure any deficiency, provided that the exercise of this right does not cause the buyer unreasonable inconvenience or unreasonable expense. However, the buyer retains any right to claim damages as provided for in the CISG. If the seller does not perform on time, the buyer may fix an additional period of time of reasonable length for performance by the seller of his obligations. Unless the buyer has received notice from the seller that the seller will not perform within the period so fixed, the buyer may not, during that period, resort to any remedy for breach of contract. However, the buyer retains any right he may have to claim damages for delay in performance. If the seller does not deliver the goods within the additional period of time or declares that he will not deliver within the period so fixed, the buyer may declare the contract avoided.

The seller may, even after the date for delivery, cure a defective performance, if she can do so without unreasonable delay and without causing the buyer unreasonable inconvenience. However, the buyer retains any right to claim damages for delay in performance. If the seller requests the buyer to make known whether he will accept performance and the buyer does not comply with the request within a reasonable time, the seller may perform within the time indicated in his request.

◆ **SEE CASE 22-1**

**Installment Contracts** Unless the parties have otherwise agreed, the buyer does not have to pay any part of the price of the goods until the seller has delivered or tendered the entire quantity specified in the contract. Section 2–307. An installment contract is an instance in which the parties have otherwise agreed. It expressly provides for delivery of the goods in separate lots or installments and usually provides for payment of the price in installments. If the contract is silent about payment, the Code provides that the price, if it can be apportioned, may be demanded for each lot. Section 2–307.

The buyer may reject any nonconforming installment if the nonconformity *substantially* impairs the value of that installment and cannot be cured. Section 2–612(2); Section 2A–510(1). When, however, the installment substantially impairs the value of the installment but not the value of the entire contract, the buyer cannot reject the installment if the seller gives adequate assurance of the installment's cure. Section 2–612(2); Section 2A–510(1). Whenever the nonconformity or default with respect to one or more of the installments substantially impairs the value of the whole contract, however, the buyer can treat the breach as a breach of the *whole contract*. Section 2–612(3); Section 2A–510(2).

CISG When a contract calls for delivery of goods by installments, if the seller's failure to perform any of his obligations with respect to any installment constitutes a fundamental breach of contract with respect to that installment, the buyer may declare the contract avoided with respect to that installment. A buyer who declares the contract avoided with respect to any delivery may, at the same time, declare it avoided with respect to deliveries already made or to future deliveries if, by reason of their interdependence, those deliveries could not be used for the purpose contemplated by the parties at the time of the conclusion of the contract. If the seller's failure to perform any of his obligations with respect to any installment gives the buyer good grounds to conclude that a fundamental breach of contract will occur with respect to future installments, he may declare the contract avoided for the future, provided that he does so within a reasonable time.

## PERFORMANCE BY THE BUYER

The buyer is obligated to accept conforming goods and to pay for them according to the contract terms. Section 2–301; Section 2A–103(1)(j). Payment or tender of payment by the buyer, unless otherwise agreed, is a condition to the seller's duty to tender and to complete delivery. Section 2–507(1).

The buyer is not obliged to accept a tender or delivery of goods that do not conform to the contract. Upon determining that the tender or delivery is nonconforming, the buyer has three choices. He may (1) reject all of the goods, (2) accept all of the goods, or (3) accept any commercial unit or units of the goods and reject the rest. Section 2–601; Section 2A–509(1). The buyer must pay the contract rate for the commercial units he accepts.

CISG The buyer must pay the price for the goods and take delivery of them as required by the contract and the CISG.

◆ **SEE CASE 22-2**

## INSPECTION

Unless the parties otherwise agree, the buyer has a right to inspect the goods before payment or acceptance. Section 2–513(1). (Section 2A–515(1) provides for the right to inspect before acceptance.) This **inspection** enables him to ascertain whether the goods tendered or delivered conform to the contract. If the contract requires payment before acceptance (where, for example, the contract provides for shipment C.O.D. [collect on delivery]), payment must be made prior to inspection unless the nonconformity appears without inspection. Section 2–512. Payment, however, in such a case is not an acceptance of the goods and impairs neither the buyer's right to inspect nor any of his remedies.

The buyer, allowed a reasonable time in which to inspect the goods, may lose the right to reject or revoke acceptance of nonconforming goods by failing to inspect them in a timely manner. The expenses of inspection must be borne by the buyer but may be recovered from the seller if the goods do not conform and are rejected. Section 2–513(2); Section 2A–520(1).

> CISG The buyer is not bound to pay the price until he has had an opportunity to examine the goods, unless the parties have agreed otherwise. The buyer must examine the goods within as short a period of time as is practicable in the circumstances. The buyer loses the right to rely on a lack of conformity of the goods if he does not give notice to the seller of the nonconformity within a reasonable time after he has discovered it or ought to have discovered it.

## REJECTION

**Rejection** is a manifestation by the buyer of his unwillingness to become the owner of the goods. It must be made within a reasonable time after the goods have been tendered or delivered and is not effective unless the buyer seasonably notifies the seller. Section 2–602(1); Section 2A–509(2).

The rejection of tendered or delivered goods may be rightful or wrongful, depending on whether the goods conform to the contract. The buyer's rejection of nonconforming goods or tender is rightful under the perfect tender rule. Nonetheless, if the buyer refuses a tender of goods or rejects it as nonconforming without disclosing to the seller the nature of the defect, she may not assert such defect as an excuse for not accepting the goods or as a breach of contract by the seller if the defect is curable. Section 2–605(1); Section 2A–514(1).

After the buyer has rejected the goods, any attempt she makes to exercise ownership of the goods is wrongful as against the seller. (Because the lessor retains title in a lease, this does not apply to leases.) If the buyer has possession of the rejected goods but does not have a security interest in them, she is obliged to hold them with reasonable care for a time sufficient to permit the seller to remove them. Section 2–602(2)(b); Section 2A–512(1). The buyer who is not a merchant is under no further obligation with regard to goods rightfully rejected. Section 2–602(2); Section 2A–512(1)(c). If the seller gives no instructions within a reasonable time after notification of rejection, the buyer may (1) store the goods for the seller's account, (2) reship them to the seller, or (3) resell them for the seller's account. Such action is not an acceptance or conversion of the goods. Section 2–604; Section 2A–511(2). A *merchant* buyer of goods who has rightfully rejected them has additional duties: she is obligated to follow reasonable instructions from the seller with respect to the disposition of the goods in her possession or control when the seller has no agent or business at the place of rejection. Section 2–603(1); Section 2A–511(1). If the merchant buyer receives no instructions from the seller within a reasonable time after giving notice of the rejection, and the rejected goods are perishable or threaten to decline in value speedily, she is obligated to make reasonable efforts to sell them for the seller's account. Section 2–603(1); Section 2A–511(1).

When the buyer sells the rejected goods, she is entitled to reimbursement for the reasonable expenses of caring for and selling them and a reasonable selling commission not to exceed 10 percent of the gross proceeds. Section 2–603(2); Section 2A–511(2).

> CISG If the goods do not conform to the contract and the nonconformity constitutes a fundamental breach of contract, the buyer may require delivery of substitute goods. If the buyer has received the goods and intends to exercise any right under the contract or the CISG to reject them, she must take such steps to preserve them as are reasonable in the circumstances. She is entitled to retain them until she has been reimbursed her reasonable expenses by the seller.

◆ **SEE CASE 22-2**

## ACCEPTANCE

**Acceptance** of goods means a willingness by the buyer to become the owner of the goods tendered or delivered to him by the seller. Acceptance of the goods, which includes overt acts or conduct manifesting such willingness, precludes any subsequent rejection of the goods. Section 2–607(2); Section 2A–516(2). Acceptance may be indicated by express words, by the presumed intention of the buyer through his failure to act, or by conduct of the buyer that is inconsistent with the seller's ownership of the goods. More specifically, acceptance occurs when the buyer, after a reasonable opportunity to inspect the goods, (1) signifies to the seller that the goods conform to the contract, (2) signifies to the seller that he will take the goods or retain them in spite of their nonconformity to the contract, or (3) fails to make an effective rejection of the goods. Section 2–606(1); Section 2A–515(1).

Acceptance, as previously noted, of any part of a commercial unit is acceptance of the entire unit. Section 2–606(2); Section 2A–515(2). Although the buyer must pay at the contract rate for those commercial units he accepts, he is entitled, after giving the seller timely notice of the breach, to recover from the seller or to deduct from the purchase price the amount of damages for nonconformity of the commercial units he has accepted and for nondelivery of the commercial units he has rejected. Sections 2–714 and 2–717; Sections 2A–516(1) and 2A–508(6) (except for finance leases in some situations). For example, Nancy agrees to deliver to Paul five hundred light bulbs of 100 watts each for $300 and one thousand light bulbs of 60 watts each for $500. Nancy delivers on time, but the shipment contains only four hundred of the 100-watt bulbs and eight hundred of the 60-watt bulbs. If Paul accepts the shipment, he must pay Nancy $240 for the 100-watt bulbs accepted and $400 for the 60-watt bulbs accepted, less the amount of damages Nancy's nonconforming delivery caused him.

When goods are rejected by the buyer, the burden is on the seller to establish their conformity to the contract; but the burden is on the buyer to establish any breach of contract (including warranty) with regard to goods accepted. Section 2–607(4); Section 2A–516(3)(c).

### REVOCATION OF ACCEPTANCE

A buyer might accept defective goods either because discovering the defect by inspection was difficult or because the buyer reasonably assumed that the seller would correct the defect. In either instance the buyer may revoke his acceptance of the goods if the uncorrected defect substantially impairs the value of the goods to him. With respect to the goods, **revocation of acceptance** gives the buyer rights and duties that are the same as if he had rejected them. Section 2–608(3); Section 2A–517(5).

More specifically, the buyer may revoke his acceptance of goods that do not conform to the contract when such nonconformity *substantially* impairs the value of the goods to him, provided that his acceptance was (1) premised on the reasonable assumption that the seller would cure the nonconformity, and it was not seasonably cured; or (2) made without discovery of the nonconformity, and such acceptance was reasonably induced by the difficulty of discovery before acceptance or by the seller's assurances. Section 2–608(1); Section 2A–517(1).

Revocation of acceptance is not effective until notification is given to the seller. This must be done within a reasonable time after the buyer discovers or should have discovered the grounds for revocation and before the goods have undergone any substantial change not caused by their own defects. Section 2–608(2); Section 2A–517(4).

◆ SEE CASE 22-3

### OBLIGATION OF PAYMENT

The terms of the contract may expressly state the time and place at which the buyer is obligated to pay for the goods. If so, these terms are controlling. Thus, if the buyer has agreed to pay either the seller or a carrier for the goods in advance of delivery, his duty to pay is not conditioned upon performance or a tender of performance by the seller. Furthermore, where the sale is on credit, the buyer is not obligated to pay for the goods when he receives them, as the credit provision in the contract will control the time of payment. Unless the parties agree otherwise, payment is due at the time and place at which the buyer is to receive the goods, even though the place of shipment is the place of delivery. Section 2–310(a). This rule is understandable in view of the buyer's right, in the absence of agreement to the contrary, to inspect the goods before being obliged to pay for them.

Tender of payment in the ordinary course of business is sufficient when made by any means or in any manner current, such as a check, unless the seller demands cash and allows the buyer a reasonable time within which to obtain it. Payment by personal check is defeated as between seller and buyer, however, if the check is not paid when the seller attempts to cash it. Section 2–511(3).

**CISG** Unless the buyer is bound to pay the price at any other specific time, he must pay it when the seller places either the goods or documents controlling their disposition at the buyer's disposal in accordance with the contract and the CISG. The seller may make such payment a condition for handing over the goods or documents. If the buyer is not bound to pay the price at any other particular place, he must pay it to the seller: (1) at the seller's place of business; or (2) if the payment is to be made against the handing over of the goods or of documents, at the place where the handing over takes place.

◆ SEE FIGURE 22-2: Performance by the Buyer

## OBLIGATIONS OF BOTH PARTIES

Contracts for the sale of goods necessarily involve risks concerning future events that may or may not occur. In some instances, the parties explicitly allocate these risks; in most instances, they do not. The Code contains three sections that allocate these risks when the parties fail to do so. Each provision, when applicable, relieves the parties from the obligation of full performance under the sales contract. The first

◆ FIGURE 22-2: **Performance by the Buyer**

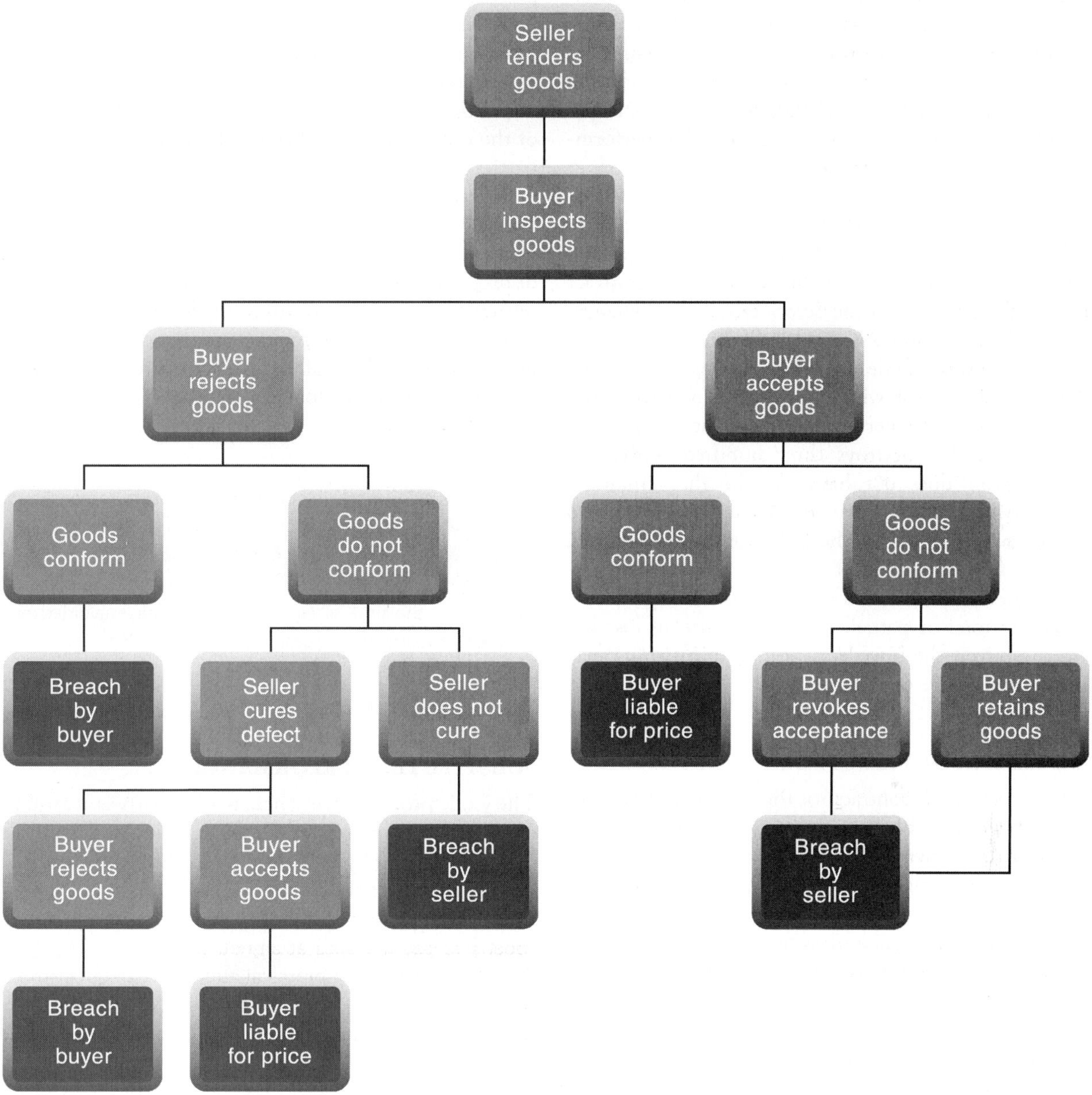


section deals with casualty to identified goods, the second with the nonhappening of presupposed conditions, and the third with substituted performance.

Related to the subject of whether the Code will excuse performance is the question of whether both parties are able and willing to perform. Should one party seem unwilling or unable, the Code allows the other party to seek reasonable assurance of the potentially defaulting party's willingness and ability to perform. In addition, if one of the parties clearly indicates an unwillingness or inability to perform, the Code protects the other party.

### CASUALTY TO IDENTIFIED GOODS

If goods are destroyed before an offer to sell or buy them is accepted, the offer is terminated by general contract law. But what if the goods are destroyed after the sales contract is formed? The rules for the passage of risk of loss (as discussed in *Chapter 23*) apply with one exception: the contract is for goods that are identified when the contract was made and the goods suffer damage without fault of either party *before* the risk of loss passes to the buyer. The outcome of this situation depends upon the degree of damage. (1) If these goods are ***totally*** lost or damaged, the contract is avoided. Section 2–613(a); Section 2A–221(a). This means that each party is excused from his performance obligation under the contract: the seller is no longer obligated to deliver and the buyer need not pay the price.

(2) In the case of a ***partial*** destruction or deterioration of the goods, the buyer may avoid the contract or may accept the goods with due allowance or deduction from the contract price sufficient to account for the deterioration or deficiency. Section 2–613(b); Section 2A–221(b) (except in a finance lease that is not a consumer lease). Thus, Adams agrees to sell to Taylor a specific lot of wheat containing one thousand bushels at a price of $4 per bushel. Without the fault of Adams or Taylor, fire destroys three hundred bushels of the wheat. Taylor does not have to take the remaining seven hundred bushels of wheat, but he has the option to do so upon paying $2,800, the price of seven hundred bushels.

On the other hand, if the destruction or damage to the goods, whether total or partial, occurs *after* risk of loss has passed to the buyer, the buyer has no option but must pay the entire contract price of the goods.

## NONHAPPENING OF PRESUPPOSED CONDITION

The ability to perform a contract for the sale of goods is subject to a number of possible hazards, such as strikes, lockouts, the unforeseen shutdown of supply sources, or the loss of a plant or machinery by fire or other casualty. Ordinarily such difficulties do not operate as an excuse on the ground of impossibility of performance, unless the contract expressly so provides. Both parties may have understood when they made the contract, however, that its performance depended upon the existence of certain facilities or that the purpose of the contract and the value of performance depended entirely upon the happening of a specific future event. In such a case, the seller is excused from her duty of performance upon the nonoccurrence of presupposed conditions which were a basic assumption of the contract, unless the seller has expressly assumed the risk. Section 2–615(a); Section 2A–405(a). Although the nonhappening of presupposed conditions may relieve the seller of her contractual duty, if the contingency affects only a part of the seller's capacity to perform, she must, to the extent of her remaining capacity, allocate delivery and production in a fair and reasonable manner among her customers. Section 2–615(b); Section 2A–405(b).

Central to the Code's approach to impossibility is the concept of **commercial impracticability**, through which the Code will excuse performance that, while not actually or literally impossible, is commercially impracticable. This, however, requires more than mere hardship or increased cost of performance. For a party to be discharged, performance must be rendered impracticable as a result of an unforeseen supervening event not within the contemplation of the parties at the time of contracting. Moreover, the nonoccurrence of the event must have been a "basic assumption" that both parties made when entering into the contract.

Increased production cost alone does not excuse performance by the seller, nor does a collapse of the market for the goods excuse the buyer. But a party to a contract for the sale of programs for a scheduled but subsequently canceled yacht regatta, or for the sale of tin horns for export, which become subject to embargo, or for the production of goods at a designated factory that suffers extensive fire damage would be excused from performance on the basis of commercial impracticability.

**CISG** A party is not liable for a failure to perform any of her obligations if she proves that the failure was due to an impediment beyond her control and that she could not reasonably be expected to have taken the impediment into account at the time of contracting or to have avoided or overcome it or its consequences.

◆ **SEE CASE 17-4**

## SUBSTITUTED PERFORMANCE

The Code provides that where neither party is at fault and the agreed manner of delivering the goods becomes commercially impracticable, as by the failure of loading or unloading facilities or the unavailability of an agreed type of carrier, a substituted manner of performance, if commercially reasonable, must be tendered and accepted. Section 2–614(1); Section 2A–404(1). Where a practical alternative or substitute exists, the Code excuses neither seller nor buyer on the ground that delivery in the express manner provided in the contract is impossible.

## RIGHT TO ADEQUATE ASSURANCE OF PERFORMANCE

A contract of sale also requires that each party not impair the other party's expectation of having the contract performed. While the essential purpose of a contract is actual performance, an important feature of such performance is a secure and continuing sense that performance will occur when due. If, after contracting but before the time for performance, either the willingness or ability of a party to perform is put in doubt, the other party is threatened with the loss of a substantial part of what he has bargained for.

Therefore, when reasonable grounds for insecurity arise regarding either party's performance, the other party may demand written assurance and suspend his own performance until he receives that assurance. The failure to provide adequate assurance of performance within a reasonable time not exceeding thirty days constitutes a repudiation of the contract. Section 2–609; Section 2A–401.

**CISG** A party may suspend the performance of his obligations if, after the conclusion of the contract, it becomes apparent that the other party will not perform a substantial part of his obligations. A party suspending performance must immediately notify the other party of the suspension and must continue with performance if the other party provides adequate assurance of his performance.

## RIGHT TO COOPERATION

Where one party's cooperation is necessary to the agreed performance but is not timely forthcoming, the other party is excused with regard to any resulting delay in her own performance. The nonbreaching party either may proceed to perform in any reasonable manner or, if the time for her performance has occurred, may treat the other's failure to cooperate as a breach. In either event, the nonbreaching party has access to any other remedies the Code may provide, as discussed in *Chapter 25*.

## ANTICIPATORY REPUDIATION

While a repudiation is a clear indication by either party that he is unwilling or unable to perform his obligations under the contract, an **anticipatory repudiation** is a repudiation made *before* the time to perform occurs. It may occur by express communication or by the repudiating party's taking an action that makes performance impossible, such as selling unique goods to a third party. A repudiation also may result from a party's failure to give timely assurance of performance after a justifiable demand. If an anticipatory repudiation substantially impairs the value of the contract, the aggrieved party may (1) await performance for a commercially reasonable time or (2) resort to any remedy for breach. In either case, he may suspend his own performance. Section 2–610; Section 2A–402. The repudiating party may retract his anticipatory repudiation and thereby reinstate the contract unless the aggrieved party has canceled the contract, materially changed his position, or otherwise indicated that she considers the anticipatory repudiation final. Section 2–611; Section 2A–403.

**CISG** If prior to the date for performance of the contract it is clear that one of the parties will commit a fundamental breach of contract, the other party may declare the contract avoided.

◆ **SEE CASE 22-4**

# CHAPTER SUMMARY

**PERFORMANCE BY THE SELLER**

**Tender of Delivery** the seller makes available to the buyer goods conforming to the contract and so notifies the buyer
- ***Buyer*** is obligated to accept conforming goods
- ***Seller*** is entitled to receive payment of the contract price

**Time and Manner of Tender** tender must be made at a reasonable time and kept open for a reasonable period of time

**Place of Tender** if none is specified, place for delivery is the seller's place of business or, if he has no such place, his residence
- ***Shipment Contracts*** seller is required to tender delivery of the goods to a carrier for delivery to buyer; shipment terms include the following: *F.O.B. place of shipment, F.A.S. port of shipment, C.I.F., C.&F.*
- ***Destination Contracts*** seller is required to tender delivery of the goods at a named destination; destination terms include the following: *F.O.B. place of destination, ex-ship*, and *no arrival, no sale*
- ***Goods Held by Bailee*** seller must either tender to the buyer a document of title or obtain an acknowledgment from the bailee

**Perfect Tender Rule** the seller's tender of performance must conform exactly to the contract, subject to the following qualifications:
- ***Agreement by the Parties*** the parties may contractually limit the operation of the perfect tender rule

- ***Cure by the Seller*** when the time for performance under the contract has not expired or when the seller has shipped nonconforming goods in the belief that the nonconforming tender would be acceptable, a seller may cure or correct her nonconforming tender
- ***Installment Contracts*** when the contract calls for the goods to be delivered in separate lots, the buyer may reject a nonconforming installment if it substantially impairs the value of that installment and cannot be cured; but if nonconformity or default of one or more of the installments substantially impairs the value of the whole contract, the buyer can treat the breach as a breach of the whole contract

---

**PERFORMANCE BY THE BUYER**

**Inspection** unless otherwise agreed, the buyer has a reasonable time in which to inspect the goods before payment or acceptance to determine whether they conform

**Rejection** buyer's manifestation of unwillingness to become the owner of the goods; must be made within a reasonable time after the goods have been tendered or delivered and gives the buyer the right to (1) reject all of the goods, (2) accept all of the goods, or (3) accept any commercial unit(s) and reject the rest

**Acceptance** buyer's express or implied manifestation of willingness to become the owner of the goods

**Revocation of Acceptance** rescission of buyer's acceptance of the goods if nonconformity of the goods substantially impairs their value, provided that the acceptance was (1) premised on the assumption that the nonconformity would be cured by the seller and it was not, or (2) the nonconformity was an undiscovered hidden defect

**Obligation of Payment** in the absence of an agreement, payment is due at the time and place the buyer is to receive the goods

---

**OBLIGATIONS OF BOTH PARTIES**

**Casualty to Identified Goods** if the contract is for goods that were identified when the contract was made and those goods are totally lost or damaged without fault of either party and before the risk of loss has passed to the buyer, the contract is avoided

**Nonhappening of Presupposed Condition** the seller is excused from the duty of performance on the nonoccurrence of presupposed conditions that were a basic assumption of the contract, unless the seller has expressly assumed the risk

**Substituted Performance** where neither party is at fault and the agreed manner of goods becomes commercially impracticable, a substituted manner of performance must be tendered and accepted

**Right to Adequate Assurance of Performance** when reasonable grounds for insecurity arise regarding either party's performance, the other party may demand written assurance and suspend his own performance until he receives that assurance

**Right to Cooperation** where one party's required cooperation is untimely, the other party is excused from any resulting delay in her own performance

**Anticipatory Repudiation** if either party clearly indicates an unwillingness or inability to perform before the performance is due, the other party may await performance for a reasonable time or resort to any remedy for breach

# CASES

## CASE 22-1

## Cure by the Seller
## WILSON v. SCAMPOLI

United States Court of Appeals, District of Columbia Circuit, 1967
228 A.2d 848

**Myers, J.**

This is an appeal from an order of the trial court granting rescission of a sales contract for a color television set and directing the return of the purchase price plus interest and costs.

Appellee [Wilson] purchased the set in question on November 4, 1965, paying the total purchase price in cash. The transaction was evidenced by a sales ticket showing the price paid and guaranteeing ninety days' free service and replacement of any defective tube and parts for a period of one year. Two days after purchase the set was delivered. * * * When the set was turned on, however, it did not function properly, the picture having a reddish tinge. Appellant's [Scampoli's] delivery man advised the buyer's daughter, Mrs. Kolley, that it was not his duty to tune in or adjust the color but that a service representative would shortly call at her house for that purpose. After the departure of the delivery men, Mrs. Kolley unplugged the set and did not use it.

On November 8, 1965, a service representative arrived, and after spending an hour in an effort to eliminate the red cast from the picture advised Mrs. Kolley that he would have to remove the chassis from the cabinet and take it to the shop as he could not determine the cause of the difficulty from his examination at the house. He also made a written memorandum of his service call, noting that the television "Needs Shop Work (Red Screen)." Mrs. Kolley refused to allow the chassis to be removed, asserting she did not want a "repaired" set but another "brand new" set. Later she demanded the return of the purchase price, although retaining the set. Appellant refused to refund the purchase price, but renewed his offer to adjust, repair, or if the set could not be made to function properly, to replace it. Ultimately, appellee instituted this suit against appellant seeking a refund of the purchase price. After a trial, the court ruled that "under the facts and circumstances the complaint is justified. Under the equity powers of the Court I will order the parties put back in their original status, let the $675 be returned, and the set returned to the defendant."

Appellant * * * contends the trial judge erred in holding that rescission here was appropriate. He argues that he was always willing to comply with the terms of the sale either by correcting the malfunction by minor repairs or, in the event the set could not be made thereby properly operative, by replacement; that as he was denied the opportunity to try to correct the difficulty, he did not breach the contract of sale or any warranty thereunder, expressed or implied.

[UCC §] 2–508 provides:

> **(1)** Where any tender or delivery by the seller is rejected because non-conforming and the time for performance has not yet expired, the seller may seasonably notify the buyer of his intention to cure and may then within the contract time make a conforming delivery.
> **(2)** Where the buyer rejects a non-conforming tender which the seller had reasonable grounds to believe would be acceptable with or without money allowance the seller may if he seasonably notifies the buyer have a further reasonable time to substitute a conforming tender.

A retail dealer would certainly expect and have reasonable grounds to believe that merchandise like color television sets, new and delivered as crated at the factory, would be acceptable as delivered and that, if defective in some way, he would have the right to substitute a conforming tender. The question then resolves itself to whether the dealer may conform his tender by adjustment or minor repair or whether he must conform by substituting brand new merchandise. The problem seems to be one of first impression. * * *

* * *

While these cases provide no mandate to require the buyer to accept patchwork goods or substantially repaired articles in lieu of flawless merchandise, they do indicate that minor repairs or reasonable adjustments are frequently the means by which an imperfect tender may be cured. In discussing the analogous question of defective title, it has been stated that:

> The seller, then, should be able to cure [the defect] under subsection 2–508(2) in those cases in which he can do so without subjecting the buyer to any great inconvenience, risk, or loss. [Citations.]

Removal of a television chassis for a short period of time in order to determine the cause of color malfunction and ascertain the extent of adjustment or correction needed to effect full operational efficiency presents no great inconvenience to the buyer. In the instant case, [Appellant's] expert witness testified that this was not infrequently necessary with new televisions. Should the set be defective in workmanship or parts, the loss would be upon the manufacturer who warranted it free from mechanical defect. Here the adamant refusal of Mrs. Kolley * * * to allow inspection essential to the determination of the cause of the excessive red tinge to the picture defeated any effort by the seller to provide timely repair or even replacement of the set if the difficulty could not be corrected. The cause of the defect might have been minor and easily adjusted or it may have been substantial and required replacement by another new set—but the seller was never given an adequate opportunity to make a determination.

We do not hold that appellant has no liability to appellee, but as he was denied access and a reasonable opportunity to repair, appellee has not shown a breach of warranty entitling him either to a brand new set or to rescission. We therefore reverse the judgment of the trial court granting rescission and directing the return of the purchase price of the set.

Reversed.

## CASE 22-2

### Performance by the Buyer
### FURLONG v. ALPHA CHI OMEGA SORORITY

Bowling Green County Municipal Court, 1993
73 Ohio Misc.2d 26, 657 N.E.2d 866

**Bachman, J.**

[Alpha Chi Omega (AXO) entered into an oral contract with Furlong to buy 168 "custom designed" sweaters for the Midnight Masquerade III. The purchase price of $3,612 was to be paid as follows: $2,000 down payment when the contract was made and $1,612 upon delivery. During phone conversations with Furlong, Emily, the AXO social chairperson, described the design to be imprinted on the sweater. She also specified the colors to be used in the lettering (hunter green on top of maroon outlined in navy blue) and the color of the mask design (hunter green). Furlong promised to have a third party imprint the sweaters as specified. Furlong later sent to Emily a sweater with maroon letters to show her the color. He then sent her a fax illustrating the sweater design with arrows indicating where each of the three colors was to appear. On the day before delivery was due, Argento, Furlong's supplier, requested design changes which Furlong approved without the consent of AXO. These changes included: deleting the navy blue outline, reducing the number of colors from three to two, changing the maroon lettering to red, and changing the color of the masks from hunter green to red. Upon delivery, AXO gave a check to Furlong's agent for the balance of the purchase price. Later that day, Emily inspected the sweaters and screamed her dismay at the design changes. AXO immediately stopped payment on the check. Amy, the president of AXO, phoned Furlong stating that the sweaters were not what AXO had ordered. She gave the specifics as to why the sweaters were not as ordered and offered to return them. Furlong refused but offered to reduce the unit price of the sweaters if AXO agreed to accept them. AXO refused this offer. Furlong then filed suit against AXO for the unpaid portion of the sweaters' purchase price ($1,612) and AXO counterclaimed for return of the down payment ($2,000).]

* * *

Furlong and Emily created an express warranty by * * * affirmation of fact (his initial phone calls); by sample (the maroon sweater); by description (the fax). This express warranty became part of the contract. Each of the three methods of showing the express warranty was not in conflict with the other two methods, and thus they are consistent and cumulative [UCC §2–317], and constitute the warranty.

The design was a "dickered" aspect of the individual bargain and went clearly to the essence of that bargain [UCC §2–313]. Thus, the express warranty was that the sweaters would be in accordance with the above design (including types of colors for the letters and the mask, and the number of colors for the same). Further, the express warranty became part of the contract. * * *

Furlong's obligation as the seller was to transfer and deliver the goods in accordance with the contract. AXO's obligation was to accept and pay in accordance with that contract [UCC §2–301]. * * *

* * *

The sweaters did not conform to the contract (specifically, the express warranty in the contract). Thus (in the words of the statute), the sweaters did "fail in any respect to conform to the contract." Actually, the sweaters failed in at least five respects [UCC §2–601]. Further, not only did they "fail in any respect," they failed in a substantial respect. In either event, they were a nonconforming tender of goods [UCC §2–601].

* * *

AXO, as the buyer, had the right to inspect the boxes of sweaters before payment or acceptance [UCC §2–513]. AXO did so at a reasonable time and place, and in a reasonable manner, on the same day that Furlong had sent the sweaters and AXO had received them [UCC §2–513]. AXO's purpose of inspection had (in the words of the statute) "to do with the buyer's check-up on whether the seller's performance is in accordance with a contract previously made. * * *" (Official Comment 9 to UCC §2–513.)

* * *

According to the statute, "if the goods * * * fail in any respect to conform to the contract, the buyer may: (A) reject the whole * * * [.]" [UCC §2–601]. As concluded above, the sweaters were nonconforming goods. Therefore, Furlong breached the contract, and AXO had the right to reject the goods (sweaters).

* * *

One [section of the] statute provides: "Rejection of goods must be within a reasonable time after their delivery. * * * It is ineffective unless the buyer seasonably notifies the seller." [UCC §2–602(1)]. AXO did what this statute requires.

That statute further provides: "[I]f the buyer has before rejection taken physical possession of goods, * * * he is under a duty after rejection to hold them with reasonable care at the seller's disposition for a time sufficient to permit the seller to remove them[.]" [UCC §2–602(2)(b).] AXO had done this, too.

Another [section of the] statute provides: "The buyer's failure to state in connection with rejection a particular defect * * * precludes him from relying on the unstated defect to justify rejection or to establish breach[.]" [UCC §2–605(1).] AXO did enough to avoid the effect of this statute also.

* * *

Thus, AXO never had an acceptance of the sweaters (as the term "acceptance" is legally defined) [UCC §2–606]. That is, AXO never did any of the following (per the statute): (1) signified to Furlong that the sweaters were conforming or that AXO would take or retain the sweaters in spite of their non-conformity; (2) failed to make an effective rejection of the sweaters; (3) did any act inconsistent with Furlong's ownership. [UCC §2–606.]

* * *

As concluded above, AXO rightfully rejected the sweaters, after having paid part of the purchase price: namely $2,000. AXO is entitled to cancel the contract and to recover the partial payment of the purchase price [UCC §2–711].

## CASE 22-3

## Revocation of Acceptance
## WADDELL v. L.V.R.V. INC.

Supreme Court of Nevada, 2006
125 P.3d 1160
http://caselaw.lp.findlaw.com/scripts/getcase.pl?court=nv&vol=122NevAdvOpNo3&invol=2

**Gibbons, J.**

L.V.R.V. Inc., D/B/A Wheeler's Las Vegas RV (Wheeler's) sold a 1996 Coachmen Santara motor home (the RV) to * * * Arthur R. Waddell and Roswitha M. Waddell (the Waddells). * * *

* * *

* * * Before they took possession of the RV, the Waddells requested that Wheeler's perform various repairs. The Waddells' request included a service on the RV's engine cooling system, new batteries, and alignment of the door frames. Wheeler's told Arthur Waddell that the repairs had been performed as requested. The Waddells took delivery of the RV on September 1, 1997.

The Waddells first noticed a problem with the RV's engine shortly after they took possession of it. They drove the RV from Las Vegas to Hemet, California. On the return trip, the RV's engine overheated while ascending a moderate grade to such a degree that Mr. Waddell had to pull over to the side of the road and wait for the engine to cool down.

When the Waddells returned from California, they took the RV back to Wheeler's for repairs. Despite Wheeler's attempts to repair the RV, the Waddells continually experienced more problems with the RV, including further episodes of engine overheating. Between September 1997 and March 1999, Wheeler's service department spent a total of seven months during different periods of time attempting to repair the RV.

On June 9, 2000, the Waddells filed a complaint in district court seeking both equitable relief and money damages. * * *

* * * The district court concluded that the RV's nonconformities substantially impaired its value to the Waddells. The district court allowed the Waddells to revoke their acceptance of the RV. * * *

* * *

[U.C.C. §2–608(1)] provides that a buyer may revoke his acceptance if the item suffers from a "nonconformity [that] substantially impairs its value *to him*" and (a) the buyer accepted the goods on the understanding that the seller would cure the nonconformity or (b) the buyer was unaware of the nonconformity and the nonconformity was concealed by the difficulty of discovery or by the seller's assurances that the good was conforming.

* * *

The Supreme Court of Oregon has established a two-part test to determine whether a nonconformity, under the totality of the circumstances, substantially impairs the value of the goods to the buyer. The test has both an objective and a subjective prong:

> Since [the statute] provides that the buyer may revoke acceptance of goods "whose nonconformity substantially impairs its value *to him*," the value of conforming goods *to the plaintiff* must first be determined. This is a subjective question in the sense that it calls for a consideration of the needs and circumstances of the plaintiff who seeks to revoke; not the needs and circumstances of an average buyer. The second inquiry is whether the nonconformity in fact substantially impairs the value of the goods to the buyer, having in mind his particular needs. This is an objective question in the sense that it calls for evidence of something more than plaintiff's assertion that the nonconformity impaired the value to him; it requires evidence from which it can be inferred that plaintiff's needs were not met because of the nonconformity. [Citation.]

* * * [W]e adopt the Supreme Court of Oregon's two-part test for determining whether a nonconformity substantially affects the good's value to the buyer under [U.C.C. §2–608(1)].

* * *

Mr. Waddell's testimony demonstrates that the RV's subjective value to the Waddells was based on their ability to spend two or three years driving the RV around the country. Thus, we must consider whether the RV's nonconformities substantially impaired the value of the RV based on the Waddells' particular needs.

Mr. Waddell testified that as a result of the RV's defects, he and his wife were unable to enjoy the RV as they had intended. Mr. Waddell further testified that the RV's engine would overheat within ten miles of embarking if the travel included any climbing. As a result of the overheating, the Waddells were forced to park on the side of the road and wait for the engine to cool down before continuing. Consequently, the RV spent a total of 213 days, or seven months and one day, at Wheeler's service department during the eighteen months immediately following the purchase. This testimony is sufficient to demonstrate an objective, substantial impairment of value.

* * *

Accordingly, we conclude that substantial evidence exists to support revocation of acceptance under [U.C.C. §2–608(1)].

Wheeler's argues that the Waddells should not have been allowed to revoke their acceptance because they did not attempt to revoke within a reasonable time after purchasing the RV. We disagree.

Under [U.C.C. §2–608(2)], "revocation of acceptance must occur within a reasonable time after the buyer discovers or should have discovered the ground for it and before any substantial change in condition of the goods which is not caused by their own defects." * * *

* * *

The seller of nonconforming goods must generally receive an opportunity to cure the nonconformity before the buyer may revoke his acceptance. * * *

Furthermore, the seller's attempts to cure do not count against the buyer regarding timely revocation. The United States District Court for the District of Nevada has held that the "time for revocation of acceptance will be tolled while the seller attempts repairs." * * *

The Waddells gave Wheeler's several opportunities to repair the defects before revoking their acceptance. Because Wheeler's was unable to repair the defects after a total of seven months, the Waddells were entitled to say "that's all" and revoke their acceptance, notwithstanding Wheeler's good-faith attempts to repair the RV. * * *

CASE 22-4

## Anticipatory Repudiation
## DONALD R. HESSLER v. CRYSTAL LAKE CHRYSLER-PLYMOUTH, INC.

Appellate Court of Illinois, Second District, 2003
788 N.E.2d 405, 273 Ill.Dec. 96, 50 U.C.C. Rep.Serv.2d 330
http://caselaw.lp.findlaw.com/scripts/getcase.pl?court=il&vol=app/2003/2020362&invol=3

**Callum, J.**

In February 1997, Chrysler Corporation introduced a new promotional vehicle called the Plymouth Prowler. However, the company did not reveal whether it would manufacture any of the vehicles. Plaintiff became aware of the vehicle and of its uncertain production, and, on February 4, 1997, contacted several dealerships to inquire about purchasing a Prowler.

On February 5, 1997, plaintiff met with Gary Rosenberg, co-owner of defendant-dealership and signed a "Retail Order for a Motor Vehicle" (hereinafter Agreement). The Agreement, which was filled out primarily by Rosenberg, stated that the order was for a 1997, V6, two-door, purple Plymouth Prowler. Moreover, it read:

> Customer to pay $5,000 00/100 over list price by manufacturer. Money refundable if can not [deliver] by 12/30/97. Dealer to keep car 2 weeks.

* * *

The order also noted that plaintiff had deposited $5,000 by check.

The Agreement contained a box labeled "TO BE DELIVERED ON OR ABOUT." Inside the box was written "ASAP" in a handwriting and ink different from that in the rest of the document. Rosenberg testified that he did not write "ASAP" on plaintiff's order himself. Rather, a salesperson wrote it in the process of "finishing up" the transaction. Rosenberg did not instruct the person to do so, but he routinely delegates to defendant's employees the processing of customer checks and the dispensing of receipts. Rosenberg stated that the term "ASAP" is used in his business "in lieu of a stock number. Just line it up in order. As soon as you can get it done, do it." He also testified that "in the literary form" it means as soon as possible. The Agreement contains another box labeled "STOCK NO.," which was left blank.

Rosenberg testified that plaintiff was the first person to place an order for a Prowler. Further, Rosenberg was "pretty sure" that plaintiff's order was the first order on which he received a deposit.

* * *

Plaintiff testified that his next contact with Rosenberg was on May 11, 1997, when he called Rosenberg to discuss the Prowler's list price. They agreed that the information they had received was that the manufacturer's list price would be $39,000.

On May 23, 1997, Salvatore Palandri entered into a contract with defendant to purchase a 1997 Plymouth Prowler. His contract reflects a purchase price of "50,000 + tax + lic + doc" and a $10,000 deposit. It further states that Palandri would receive the "first one delivered to [the] dealership." Palandri testified that he wrote a check for his deposit on the same day that he entered into the contract. Palandri stated that his initial discussions with Rosenberg about the Prowler, however, occurred about one to three months before the contract date.

Plaintiff testified that the next conversation that the parties had occurred on August 11, 1997. Plaintiff stated that Rosenberg informed plaintiff that no Prowlers would be delivered to the Midwest and that he would be returning plaintiff's check. Plaintiff requested assurance that, should defendant receive a vehicle, it would be his. Rosenberg said that it would. Plaintiff then requested assurance in writing, and Rosenberg stated that he would check with his brother. He also indicated that he was not certain that plaintiff was the first person who had a contract for a Prowler.

Rosenberg testified about this conversation as follows. Plaintiff inquired whether defendant would receive any cars and he replied that he had "no guarantees at this time." Rosenberg never understood that no Prowlers would be delivered to the Midwest. The conversation consisted of nothing more than this discussion. Rosenberg denied having stated whether the car belonged to plaintiff or that he would have to check with his brother.

Plaintiff testified that he called several dealers to check on the availability of Prowlers. He believed that he was the first customer to place an order for a Prowler because plaintiff and Rosenberg had to discuss the potential list price for the vehicle.

Plaintiff testified that he called Rosenberg on September 5 to inquire if Rosenberg had received any additional information about the Prowler. Rosenberg indicated that he had not. Plaintiff then asked for confirmation that if defendant received a car it would be allocated to plaintiff, and Rosenberg stated that it would. Plaintiff stated that Rosenberg did not mention a contract with Palandri.

Plaintiff next testified that he attended a Chrysler customer appreciation event at Great America on September 19 and spoke to a company representative about the Prowler. Two days later, the representative sent him a fax that contained a tentative list of dealers who were to receive Prowlers. Defendant's name was on the list.

Plaintiff testified that he called Rosenberg on September 22 to notify him that his dealership was on a list of dealers due to receive Prowlers. Rosenberg informed plaintiff that he would not sell plaintiff a car because plaintiff had gone behind Rosenberg's back and that contacting Chrysler would cause Rosenberg problems. Rosenberg also stated that plaintiff was not the first person with whom he contracted to sell a Prowler. Plaintiff protested and Rosenberg informed him that he did not sign the contract and would not sell plaintiff the car. Based on this and previous conversations with Rosenberg, plaintiff did not believe that he would be able to purchase a Prowler from defendant.

* * *

Beginning on September 23, 1997, plaintiff contacted 38 Chrysler-Plymouth dealerships to inquire about purchasing a 1997 Prowler, but did not obtain one. Plaintiff had "serious doubts" about whether Rosenberg would deliver to him a Prowler.

On October 24, 1997, plaintiff attended a Prowler coming-out party at the Hard Rock Cafe and saw a purple Prowler in the parking lot with a sign in its window that had defendant's name written on it. On October 25, plaintiff went to defendant's showroom and saw a Prowler parked there. He found Rosenberg and informed him that he was there to pick up his car. Rosenberg stated that he was not going to sell plaintiff the car and that he did not want to do business with him. Later that day, plaintiff purchased a Prowler from another dealer for $77,706.

On October 27, 1997, defendant sold the only Prowler it received in that year to Palandri for a total sale price of $54,859, including his $10,000 deposit.

* * *

On April 23, 1998, plaintiff sued defendant for breach of contract. * * *

Following a bench trial, the court entered judgment for plaintiff and awarded him $29,853 in damages. It concluded that defendant breached the Agreement and that plaintiff properly covered by purchasing a replacement vehicle for $29,853 more than the contract price. Further, the court found that the term "ASAP" "is not want of meaning"; that Rosenberg testified that it means "if and when a car is delivered" and "as soon as something can be done[,] do it." The court found credible plaintiff's description of at least two conversations with Rosenberg, during which Rosenberg confirmed that, if defendant took delivery of a purple Prowler, it would be sold to plaintiff. It concluded that delivery of a Prowler was to be as soon as possible and that defendant was on the road to repudiating the contract when it entered into a contract with Palandri in May 1997. The trial court also concluded that defendant repudiated its contract in September and October of 1997 when Rosenberg told plaintiff that he would not sell him a car. It found plaintiff "ready, willing, and able to perform the contract." The court found that the price plaintiff paid for the car at another dealership was the best price he could receive for a Prowler after Rosenberg's refusal to sell to him a car.

* * *

Defendant argues that the trial court erred in finding that defendant repudiated the Agreement. First, defendant takes issue with the trial court's finding that defendant was "on its way" to repudiating the Agreement when it contracted with Palandri in May 1997 to deliver to him the first Prowler. Defendant asserts that the court's reasoning was flawed because, in May, defendant did not know whether any Prowlers would be produced in that year. Thus, defendant could not have been on the road to repudiating the Agreement. Second, defendant contends that the court's finding that it repudiated the contract in September and October of 1997 also was error because it relied on plaintiff's contradictory, and therefore incredible, testimony. Defendant points to plaintiff's testimony that he had doubts that defendant would deliver to him a vehicle and to plaintiff's testimony that he was willing to purchase more than one Prowler.

Under the UCC, certain actions by a party to a contract may constitute an anticipatory repudiation of the contract if the actions are sufficiently clear manifestations of an intent not to perform under the contract. [UCC §] 2–610; [citation.]

* * *

Comment 1 to Section 2–610 provides, in relevant part:

> Anticipatory repudiation centers upon an overt communication of intention or an action which renders performance impossible or demonstrates a clear determination not to continue with performance.
>
> * * * When such a repudiation substantially impairs the value of the contract, the aggrieved party may at any time resort to his remedies for breach. * * * [UCC §] 2–610, Comment.

Comment 2 to Section 2–610 provides, in relevant part:

> It is not necessary for repudiation that performance be made literally and utterly impossible. Repudiation can result from action which reasonably indicates a rejection of the continuing obligation. [UCC §] 2–610, Comment.

* * *

Upon learning that defendant was on a tentative list to receive a Prowler, plaintiff testified that he called Rosenberg to relate the information and that Rosenberg responded that plaintiff was not the first person to contract to purchase a Prowler. Rosenberg also stated that he would not do business with plaintiff. Further, Rosenberg's testimony about this conversation corroborated plaintiff's, in that Rosenberg stated that he told plaintiff that the vehicle was already "committed." The trial court also heard both plaintiff and Rosenberg testify that, when plaintiff went to defendant's showroom on October 25 and informed Rosenberg that he was there to pick up his car, Rosenberg told plaintiff that he did not want to do business with him.

We conclude that the trial court did not err in finding that defendant's foregoing actions reasonably indicated to plaintiff that defendant would not deliver to him a Prowler under the Agreement. * * *

* * * With respect to plaintiff's actions, section 2–610(b) of the UCC provides that an aggrieved party may "resort to any remedy for breach" of the contract "even though he has notified the repudiating party that he would await the latter's performance." [UCC §] 2–610(b). One such remedy is to cover. [UCC §] 2–711(1)(a) (buyer may effect cover, upon seller's repudiation, whether or not buyer cancels the contract). The statute is clear that a buyer's willingness to proceed with performance under a contract does not excuse a repudiation. * * *

Defendant next asserts that, even if there was a repudiation in September or October of 1997, plaintiff did nothing to indicate that he thought this was the case. He took no self-help measures such as: terminating the contract; seeking to enjoin the sale to Palandri; requesting a retraction; or suspending his performance obligations. Again, we disagree. The UCC does not require a party to request assurances as a condition precedent to recovery. [Citation.]

For the foregoing reasons, we conclude that the trial court's finding of repudiation was not against the manifest weight of the evidence.

* * *

* * * [T]he judgment of the circuit court of McHenry County is affirmed.

## QUESTIONS

1. Explain the requirements of tender of delivery with respect to time, manner, and place of delivery.
2. Explain the perfect tender rule and the three limitations upon it.
3. Explain when the buyer has the right to reject the goods and what obligations the buyer has upon rejection.
4. Discuss the buyer's right to revoke acceptance.
5. Identify and discuss the excuses for nonperformance.

## PROBLEMS

**1.** Tammie contracted with Kristine to manufacture, sell, and deliver to Kristine and put in running order a certain machine. Once Tammie had set up the machine and put it in running order, however, Kristine found it unsatisfactory and notified Tammie that she rejected the machine. She continued to use it for three months but continually complained of its defective condition. At the end of the three months she notified Tammie to come and get it. Has Kristine lost her right (a) to reject the machine? (b) to revoke acceptance of the machine?

**2.** Smith, having contracted to sell to Beyer thirty tons of described fertilizer, shipped to Beyer by carrier thirty tons of fertilizer, which he stated conformed to the contract. Nothing was stated in the contract as to time of payment, but Smith demanded payment as a condition of handing over the fertilizer to Beyer. Beyer refused to pay unless he were given the opportunity to inspect the fertilizer. Who is correct? Explain.

**3.** Benny and Sheree entered into a contract for the sale of one hundred barrels of flour. No mention was made of any place of delivery. Thereafter, Sheree demanded that Benny deliver the flour at her place of business, and Benny demanded that Sheree come and take the flour from his place of business. Neither party acceded to the demand of the other. Has either one a right of action against the other?

**4.** Johnson, a manufacturer of air conditioning units, made a written contract with Maxwell to sell to Maxwell forty units at a price of $200 each and to deliver them at a certain apartment building owned by Maxwell for installation by Maxwell. Upon the arrival of Johnson's truck for delivery at the apartment building, Maxwell examined the units on the truck, counted only thirty units, and asked the driver if this was the total delivery. The driver replied that it was as far as he knew. Maxwell told the driver that she would not accept delivery of the units. The next day Johnson telephoned Maxwell and inquired why delivery was refused. Maxwell stated that the units on the truck were not what she ordered; that she ordered forty units, that only thirty were tendered, and that she was going to buy air conditioning units elsewhere. In an action by Johnson against Maxwell for breach of contract, Maxwell defends upon the ground that the tender of thirty units was improper, as the contract called for delivery of forty units. Is this a valid defense?

**5.** Edwin sells a sofa to Jack for $800. Edwin and Jack both know that the sofa is in Edwin's warehouse, located approximately ten miles from Jack's home. The contract does not specify the place of delivery, and Jack insists that the place of delivery is either his house or Edwin's store. Is Jack correct?

**6.** On November 4, Kim contracted to sell to Lynn 500 sacks of flour at $4 each to be delivered to Lynn by December 12. On November 27, Kim shipped the flour. By December 5, when the shipment arrived, containing only 450 sacks, the market price of flour had fallen. Lynn refused to accept delivery or to pay. Kim shipped 50 more sacks of flour, which arrived December 10. Lynn refused delivery. Kim resold the 500 sacks of flour for $3 per sack. What are Kim's rights against Lynn?

**7.** Farley and Trudy enter into a written contract whereby Farley agrees to sell and Trudy agrees to buy six thousand bushels of wheat at $10.33 per bushel, deliverable at the rate of one thousand bushels a month commencing June 1, the price for each installment being payable ten days after delivery thereof. Although Farley delivered and received payment for the June installment, he defaulted by failing to deliver the July and August installments. By August 15, the market price of wheat had increased to $12.00 per bushel. Trudy thereupon entered into a contract with Albert to purchase five thousand bushels of wheat at $12.00 per bushel deliverable over the ensuing four months. In late September, the market price of wheat commenced to decline and by December 1 was $9.25 per bushel. Explain whether Trudy would succeed in a legal action against Farley for breach of contract.

**8.** Bain ordered from Marcum a carload of lumber, which he intended to use in the construction of small boats for the U.S. Navy pursuant to contract. The order specified that the lumber was to be free from knots, wormholes, and defects. The lumber was shipped, and immediately upon receipt Bain looked into the door of the fully loaded car, ascertained that there was a full carload of lumber, and acknowledged to Marcum that the carload had been received. On the same day Bain moved the car to his private siding and sent to Marcum full payment in accordance with the terms of the order.

A day later, the car was moved to the work area and unloaded in the presence of the navy inspector, who refused to allow three-fourths of it to be used because of excessive knots and wormholes in the lumber. Bain then informed Marcum that he was rejecting the order and requested refund of the payment and directions on disposition of the lumber. Marcum replied that because Bain had accepted the order and unloaded it, he was not entitled to return of the purchase price. Who is correct? Explain.

**9.** Plaintiff, a seller of milk, had for ten years bid on contracts to supply milk to defendant school district and had supplied milk to other school districts in the area. On June 15, plaintiff contracted to supply defendant's requirements of milk for the next school year at a price of $0.0759 per half pint. The price of raw milk delivered from the farm had been for years controlled by the U.S. Department of Agriculture. On June 15, the department's administrator for the New York–New Jersey area had mandated a price for raw milk of $8.03 per hundredweight. By December, the mandated price had been raised to $9.31 per hundredweight, an increase of nearly 20 percent. If required to complete deliveries at the contract price, plaintiff would lose $7,350.55 on its contract with defendant and would face similar losses on contracts with two other school districts. Is the plaintiff correct in its assertion (a) that its performance had become impracticable through unforeseen events and (b) that it is entitled to relief from performance?

**10.** In April, F. W. Lang Company purchased an ice cream freezer and refrigeration compressor unit from Fleet for $2,160. Although the parties agreed to a written installment contract providing for an $850 down payment and eighteen installment payments, Lang made only one $200 payment upon receipt of the goods. One year later, Lang moved to a new location and took the equipment along without notifying Fleet. Two years after the sale, Lang disconnected the compressor from the freezer and used it to operate an air conditioner. Lang continued to use the compressor for that purpose until the sheriff seized the equipment and returned it to Fleet pursuant to a court order. Fleet then sold the equipment for $500 in what both parties conceded was a fair sale. Lang then brought an action charging that the equipment was defective and unusable for its intended purpose and sought to recover the down payment and expenses incurred in repairing the equipment. Fleet counterclaimed for the balance due under the installment contract less the proceeds from the sale. Who will prevail? Why?

**11.** Deborah McCullough bought a new car from Bill Swad Chrysler, Inc. The car was protected by both a limited warranty and an extended warranty. McCullough immediately encountered problems with the automobile's brakes, transmission, and air conditioning and discovered a number of cosmetic defects as well. She returned the car to Swad for repairs, but Swad did not fix the brakes properly or perform any of the cosmetic work. Moreover, new problems appeared with respect to the car's steering mechanism. McCullough returned the car twice more for repairs, but on each occasion, old problems persisted and new ones emerged. After the engine abruptly shut off on a short trip away from home and the brakes again failed on a more extensive excursion, McCullough presented Swad with a list of thirty-two of the car's defects and demanded their correction. When Swad failed to remedy more than a few of the problems, McCullough wrote a letter to Swad calling for rescission of the purchase agreement and a refund of the purchase price and offering to return the car upon receiving from Swad instructions regarding where to return it. Swad did not respond to the letter, and McCullough brought an action against Swad. She continued to operate the vehicle until the time of trial, some seventeen and one-half months (and twenty-three thousand miles) later. Can McCullough rescind the agreement?

**12.** On March 17, Peckham bought a new car from Larsen Chevrolet for $16,400.85. During the first one and one-half months after the purchase, Peckham discovered that the car's hood was dented, its gas tank contained no baffles, its emergency brake was inoperable, the car did not have a jack or a spare tire, and neither the clock nor the speedometer worked. Larsen claimed that Peckham knew of the defects at the time of the purchase. Peckham, on the other hand, claimed that he did not know the extent of the defects and that despite his repeated efforts the defects were not repaired until June 11. Then, on July 15, the car's dashboard caught fire, leaving the car's interior damaged and the car itself inoperable. Peckham then returned to Larsen Chevrolet and told Larsen that he had to repair the car at his own expense or that he, Peckham, would either rescind the contract or demand a new automobile. Peckham also claimed that at the end of their conversation he notified Larsen Chevrolet that he was electing to rescind the contract and demanded the return of the purchase price. Larsen denied having received that oral notification. On October

12, Peckham sent a written notice of revocation of acceptance to Larsen. What are the rights of the parties?

**13.** Joc Oil bought a cargo of fuel oil for resale. The certificate from the foreign refinery stated the sulfur content of the oil was 0.5 percent. Joc Oil entered into a written contract with Con Ed for the sale of this oil. The contract specified a sulfur content of 0.5 percent. Joc Oil knew, however, that Con Ed was authorized to buy and burn oil of up to 1 percent sulfur content and that Con Ed often bought and mixed oils of varying contents to stay within this limit. The oil under contract was delivered to Con Ed, but independent testing revealed a sulfur content of 0.92 percent. Con Ed promptly rejected the nonconforming shipment. Joc Oil immediately offered to substitute a conforming shipment of oil, although the time for performance had expired after the first shipment of oil. Con Ed refused to accept the substituted shipment. Joc Oil sues Con Ed for breach of contract. Judgment?

**14.** The plaintiff, a German wine producer and exporter, contracted to ship 620 cases of wine to the defendant, a distributor in North Carolina. The contract was silent as to the shipment destination. During the next several months, the defendant called repeatedly to find out the status of the shipment. Later, without notifying the defendant, the plaintiff delivered the wine to a shipping line in Rotterdam, destined for Wilmington, North Carolina. The ship and the wine were lost at sea en route to Wilmington. When the defendant refused to pay on the contract, the plaintiff sued. Decision?

**15.** Can-Key Industries, Inc., manufactured a turkey-hatching unit, which it sold to Industrial Leasing Corporation (ILC), which leased it to Rose-A-Linda Turkey Farms. ILC conditioned its obligation to pay on Rose-A-Linda's acceptance of the equipment. Rose-A-Linda twice notified Can-Key that the equipment was unacceptable and asked that it be removed. Over a period of fifteen months Can-Key made several unsuccessful attempts to solve the problems with the equipment. During this time, Can-Key did not instruct Rose-A-Linda to refrain from using the equipment. Rose-A-Linda indicated its dissatisfaction with the equipment, and ILC refused to perform its obligations under the contract. Can-Key then brought suit against ILC for breach of contract. It argued that Rose-A-Linda accepted the equipment, as it used it for fifteen months. ILC countered that the equipment was unacceptable and asked that it be removed. It claimed that Can-Key refused and failed to instruct Rose-A-Linda to refrain from using the equipment. Therefore, ILC argued, Rose-A-Linda effectively rejected the turkey-hatching unit, relieving ILC of its contractual obligations. Who is correct? Explain.

**16.** Frederick Manufacturing Corp. ordered 500 dozen units of Import Traders' rubber pads for $2,580. The order indicated that the pads should be "as soft as possible." Import Traders delivered the rubber pads to Frederick Manufacturing on November 19. Frederick failed to inspect the goods upon delivery, even though the parties recognized that there might be a problem with the softness. Frederick finally complained about the nonconformity of the pads in April of the following year, when Import Traders requested the contract price for the goods. Can Import Traders recover the contract price from Frederick?

**17.** Moulton Cavity & Mold, Inc., agreed to manufacture twenty-six innersole molds to be purchased by Lyn-Flex. Moulton delivered the twenty-six molds to Lyn-Flex after Lyn-Flex allegedly approved the sample molds. However, Lyn-Flex rejected the molds, claiming that the molds did not satisfy the specifications exactly, and denied that it had ever approved the sample molds. Moulton then sued, contending that Lyn-Flex wrongfully rejected the molds. Lyn-Flex argued that the Code's perfect tender rule permitted its rejection of the imperfect molds, regardless of Moulton's substantial performance. Decision?

**18.** Neptune Research & Development, Inc. (the buyer), which manufactured solar-operated valves used in scientific instruments, saw advertised in a trade journal a hole-drilling machine with a very high degree of accuracy, manufactured and sold by Teknics Industrial Systems, Inc. (the seller). As the machine's specifications met the buyer's needs, the buyer contacted the seller in late March and ordered one of the machines to be delivered in mid-June. There was no "time-of-the-essence" clause in the contract.

Although the buyer made several calls to the seller throughout the month of June, the seller never delivered the machine and never gave the buyer any reasons for the nondelivery. By late August, the buyer desperately needed the machine. The buyer went to the seller's place of business to examine the machine and discovered that the still-unbuilt machine had been redesigned, omitting a particular feature that the buyer had wanted. Nonetheless, the buyer agreed to take the machine, and the seller promised that it would be ready on September 5. The seller also agreed to call the buyer on September 3 to give the buyer two days to arrange for transportation of the machine.

The seller failed to telephone the buyer on September 3 as agreed. On September 4 the buyer called the seller to find out the status of the machine, and was told by the seller that "under no circumstances" could the seller have the machine ready by September 5. At this point, the buyer notified the seller that the order was canceled. One hour later, still on September 4, the seller called the buyer, retracted its earlier statement, and indicated that the machine would be ready by the agreed September 5 date. The buyer sued for the return of its $3,000 deposit. Should the buyer prevail? Explain.

**19.** ALPAC and Eagon are corporations that import and export raw logs. In April, Setsuo Kimura, ALPAC's president, and C. K. Ahn, Eagon's vice president, entered into a contract for ALPAC to ship about fifteen thousand cubic meters of logs between the end of July and the end of August. Eagon agreed to purchase them. Subsequently, the market for logs began to soften, making the contract less attractive to Eagon. ALPAC became concerned that Eagon would try to cancel the contract. Kimura and Ahn began a series of meetings and letters, apparently to assure ALPAC that Eagon would purchase the logs.

Eagon was troubled by the drop in timber prices and initially withheld approval of the shipment. Ahn sent numerous internal memoranda to the home office indicating that it might not wish to complete the deal, but that accepting the logs was "inevitable" under the contract.

On August 23, Eagon received a fax from ALPAC suggesting a reduction in price and volume of the contract, but Eagon did not respond. Soon after, Kimura asked Ahn whether he intended to accept the logs; Ahn admitted that he was having trouble getting approval. On August 30, Ahn informed the home office that he would attempt to avoid accepting the logs but that it would be difficult and suggested holding ALPAC responsible for shipment delay. Kimura thereafter believed that Eagon would not accept the shipment and eventually canceled the vessel reserved to ship the logs, believing that Eagon was canceling the contract. The logs were not loaded or shipped by August 31, but Ahn and Kimura continued to discuss the contract. On September 7, Ahn told Kimura that he would try to convince the firm to accept the delivery and indicated that he did not want Kimura to sell the logs to another buyer. The same day, Ahn informed Eagon that it should consider accepting the shipment in September or October.

By September 27, ALPAC had not shipped the logs and sent a final letter to Eagon stating that because it failed to take delivery of the logs, it had breached the contract. Eagon responded to the letter, stating that there was "no contract" because ALPAC's breach (not shipping by the deadline) excused Eagon's performance. Explain whether either party breached the agreement.

**20.** On February 26, 2011, William Stem purchased a used BMW from Gary Braden for $26,600. Stem's primary purpose for buying the car was to use it to transport his child. Braden indicated to Stem that the car had not been wrecked and that it was in good condition. Stem thought the car had been driven only 70,000 miles. Less than a week after the purchase, Stem discovered a disconnected plug that, when plugged in, caused the oil warning light to turn on. When Stem then took his car to a mechanic, the mechanic discovered that the front end was that of a 2003 BMW and the rear end was that of a 1999 BMW. Further investigation revealed that the front half had been driven 170,000 miles. On March 10, 2011, Stem sent a letter informing Braden that he refused the automobile and that he intended to rescind the sale. Braden refused. Stem filed an action against Braden, seeking to revoke his acceptance. Should Stem succeed?

# CHAPTER 23
# Transfer of Title and Risk of Loss

Historically, title governed nearly every aspect of the rights and duties of the buyer and seller arising out of a sales contract. In an attempt to add greater precision and certainty to sales contracts, the Uniform Commercial Code (UCC or Code) has abandoned the common law's reliance upon title. Instead, the Code approaches each legal issue arising out of a sales contract on its own merits and provides separate and specific rules to control the various transactional situations. This chapter covers the Code's approach to the transfer of title and other property rights, the passage of risk of loss, and the transfer of goods sold in bulk.

## TRANSFER OF TITLE

As previously stated, a sale of goods is defined as the transfer of title from the seller to the buyer for a price. Section 2–106. Transfer of title is, therefore, fundamental to a sale of goods. Title, however, cannot pass under a contract for sale until existing goods have been identified as those to which the contract refers. Section 2–401(1). Future goods (goods that are not both existing and identified) cannot constitute a present sale. Section 2–105. If the buyer rejects the goods, whether justifiably or not, title revests to the seller. Section 2–401(4).

In a lease, title does not pass. Instead, the lessee obtains the right to possess and use the goods for a period of time in return for consideration. Section 2A–103(1)(j).

### IDENTIFICATION

After formation of the contract, the seller normally takes steps to obtain, manufacture, prepare, or select goods with which to fulfill her obligation under the contract. At some stage in the process the seller will have identified existing goods that she intends to ship, deliver, or hold for the buyer. Identification may be made by either the seller or the buyer and can be made at any time and in any manner agreed upon by the parties. In the absence of explicit agreement, **identification** takes place as provided in Section 2–501(1) (Section 2A–217 contains similar, but not identical, provisions):

1. upon the making of the contract if it is for goods already existing and identified;
2. if the contract is for all other future goods, when the seller ships, marks, or otherwise designates existing goods as those to which the contract refers; or
3. if the contract is (a) for crops to be grown within twelve months or at the time of the next normal harvest, when the crops are planted or start growing, or (b) for the offspring of animals to be born within twelve months, when the young animals are conceived.

To illustrate, suppose Barringer contracts to purchase a particular Buick automobile from Stevenson's car lot. Identification occurs as soon as the contract is entered into. If, however, Barringer agrees to purchase a television set from Stevenson, whose storeroom is filled with such televisions, identification will not occur until either Barringer or Stevenson selects a particular television to fulfill the contract.

**Fungible goods** are goods of which any unit, by nature, agreement, or usage of trade, is the equivalent of any other like unit. Section 1–201(17); Revised Section 1–201(b)(18). If the goods are fungible, identification of a share of undivided goods occurs when the contract is entered into. Thus, if Barringer agrees to purchase one thousand gallons of gasoline from Stevenson, who owns a five-thousand-gallon tank of gasoline, identification occurs as soon as the contract is formed.

Insurable Interest For a contract or policy of insurance to be valid, the insured must have an insurable interest in the subject matter (see *Chapter 48*). At common law only a person with title or a lien (a legal claim of a creditor on property) could insure his interest in specific goods. The Code extends this right to a buyer's interest in goods that have been identified as goods to which the contract refers. Section 2–501(1); Section 2A–218(1). This **special property**

**interest** of the buyer enables her to purchase insurance protection on goods that she does not presently own but that she will own upon delivery by the seller.

So long as he has title to them or any security interest in them, the seller also has an insurable interest in the goods. Section 2–501(2). Nothing prevents both seller and buyer from simultaneously carrying insurance on goods in which they both have a property interest, whether it be title, a security interest, or a special property interest. In a lease, the lessor retains an insurable interest in the goods until an option to buy, if included in the lease, has been exercised by the lessee. Section 2A–218(3).

**Security Interest** The Code defines a security interest as an interest in personal property or fixtures that ensures payment or performance of an obligation. Section 1–201(37); Revised Section 1–201(b)(35). Any reservation by the seller of title to goods delivered to the buyer is limited in effect to a reservation of a security interest. Section 2–401(1). As mentioned above, the seller retains an insurable interest in goods for which he holds title or any security interest. Section 2–501(2). Security interests in goods are governed by Article 9 of the Code (discussed in *Chapter 38*).

## PASSAGE OF TITLE

Title passes when the parties *intend* it to pass, provided the goods are in existence and have been identified. Where the parties have no explicit agreement as to transfer of title, the Code provides rules that determine when title passes to the buyer. Section 2–401.

**Physical Movement of the Goods** When delivery is to be made by moving the goods, title passes at the time and place the seller completes his performance with reference to delivery of the goods. Section 2–401(2). When and where delivery occurs depends on whether the contract is a shipment contract or a destination contract.

A **shipment contract** requires or authorizes the seller to send the goods to the buyer but does not require the seller to deliver them to a particular destination. Under a shipment contract, title passes to the buyer at the time and place that the seller *delivers* the goods to the carrier for shipment to the buyer.

A **destination contract** requires the seller to deliver the goods to a particular destination. Under a destination contract, title passes to the buyer upon *tender* of the goods at that destination. Tender, as discussed in *Chapter 22*, requires that the seller (1) put and hold conforming goods at the buyer's disposition, (2) give the buyer reasonable notice that the goods are available, and (3) keep the goods available for a reasonable time. Section 2–503.

**No Movement of the Goods** When delivery is to be made without moving the goods, unless otherwise agreed, title passes (1) upon delivery of a document of title, if the contract calls for delivery of such document (documents of title are documents that evidence a right to receive specified goods—they are discussed more fully in *Chapter 48*); or (2) at the time and place of contracting, if the goods at the time have been identified and no documents are to be delivered. Section 2–401(3). Where the goods are not identified at the time of contracting, title passes when the goods are identified.

For a summary of passage of title in the absence of an agreement by the parties, see *Figure 23-1*.

◆ SEE FIGURE 23-1: **Passage of Title in Absence of Agreement by Parties**

## POWER TO TRANSFER TITLE

It is important to understand under what circumstances a seller has the right or power to transfer title to a buyer. If the seller is the rightful owner of goods or is authorized to sell the goods for the rightful owner, then the seller has the **right** to transfer title. But when a seller is in possession of goods that he neither owns nor has authority to sell, then the sale is not rightful. In some situations, however, these unauthorized sellers may have the **power** to transfer good title to certain buyers. This section pertains to such sales by a person in possession of goods that he neither owns nor has authority to sell.

The fundamental rule of property law protecting existing ownership of goods is the starting point for any discussion of a sale of goods by a nonowner. A basic tenet of the law is that a purchaser of goods obtains such title as his transferor had or had power to transfer, and the Code expressly so states. Section 2–403; Sections 2A–304 and 2A–305. Likewise, the purchaser of a limited interest in goods acquires rights only to the extent of the interest that he purchased. By the same token, no one can transfer what he does not have. A purported sale by a thief or finder or ordinary bailee of goods does not transfer title to the purchaser.

The principal reason underlying the policy of the law in protecting existing ownership of goods is that a person should not be required to retain possession at all times of all the goods that he owns in order to maintain his ownership of them. Incidental to the ownership of goods is the owner's freedom to make a bailment of his goods as desired; the mere possession of goods by a bailee does not authorize the bailee to sell them.

A second policy, one concerning the protection of the good faith purchaser, conflicts with the policy protecting existing ownership of goods. Protecting the expectations of good faith transactions in goods is of paramount importance in trade and commerce. To encourage and make safe good faith acquisitions of goods, *bona fide* (good faith) purchasers for value must be protected under certain circumstances. A **good faith purchaser** is defined as one who acts honestly,

◆ **FIGURE 23-1: Passage of Title in Absence of Agreement by Parties**

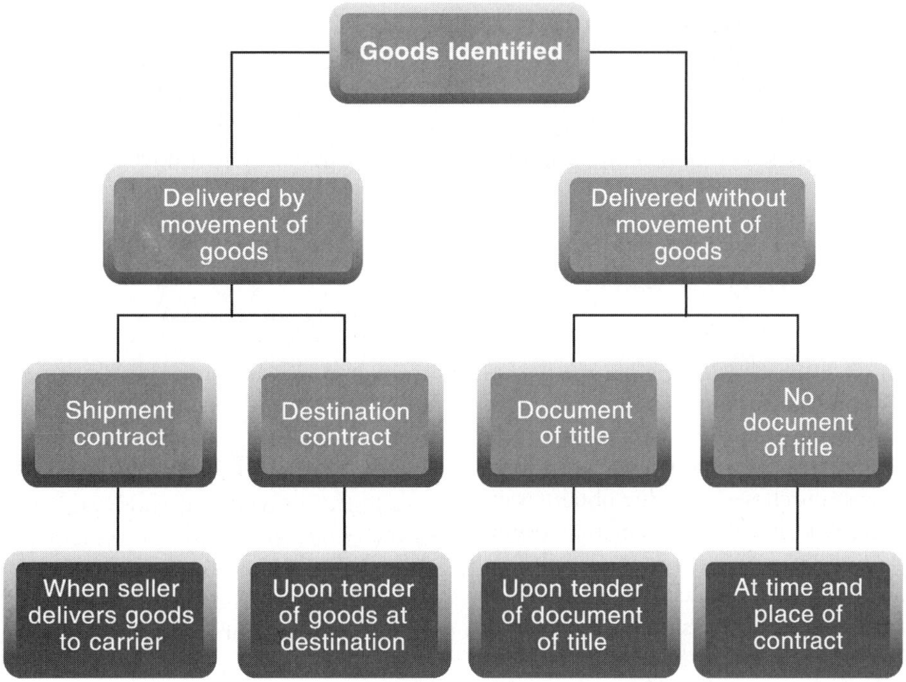


gives value, and takes the goods without notice or knowledge of any defect in the title of his transferor.

**Void and Voidable Title to Goods** A **void title** is no title. A person claiming ownership of goods by an agreement that is void obtains no title to the goods. Thus, a thief or a finder of goods or a person who acquires goods from someone under physical duress or under guardianship has no title to them and can transfer none.

A **voidable title** is one acquired under circumstances that permit the former owner to rescind the transfer and revest herself with title, as in the case of mistake, common duress, undue influence, fraud in the inducement, misrepresentation, mistake, or sale by a person without contractual capacity (other than an individual under guardianship). In these situations, the buyer has acquired legal title to the goods, which may be divested by action of the seller. If, however, before the seller has rescinded the transfer of title, the buyer were to resell the goods to a good faith purchaser for value, the right of rescission in the seller is cut off, and the good faith purchaser for value acquires good title. The Code defines good faith as "honesty in fact in the conduct or transaction concerned"; for merchants, and all parties under Revised Article 1, good faith also requires the observance of reasonable commercial standards of fair dealing. Section 1–201. The Code defines value to include a consideration sufficient to support a simple contract. Section 1–201; Revised Section 1–204.

The distinction between a void and voidable title is, therefore, extremely important in determining the rights of good faith purchasers of goods. The good faith purchaser for value always believes that she is buying the goods from the owner or from one with authority to sell. Otherwise she would not be acting in good faith. In each situation, the party selling the goods appears to be the owner whether his title is valid, void, or voidable. Given a transaction involving two innocent persons—the true owner and the good faith purchaser for value, who have done nothing wrong—the law will not disturb the *legal title* but will rule in favor of the one who has it. Thus, where A transfers possession of goods to B under such circumstances that B acquires no title or a void title, and B thereafter sells the goods to C, a good faith purchaser for value, B has nothing except possession to transfer to C. In a lawsuit between A and C involving the right to the goods, A will win because she has the legal title. C's only recourse is against B for breach of warranty of title, discussed in *Chapter 24*.

If, however, B acquired voidable title from A and resold the goods to C, in a suit between A and C over the goods, C would win. In this case, B had title, although it was voidable, which she transferred to the good faith purchaser for value. The title thus acquired by C will be protected. The voidable title in B, which is title until it has been avoided, may not be avoided after transfer to a good faith purchaser. A's only recourse is against B for restitution or damages.

◆ **FIGURE 23-2: Void Title**

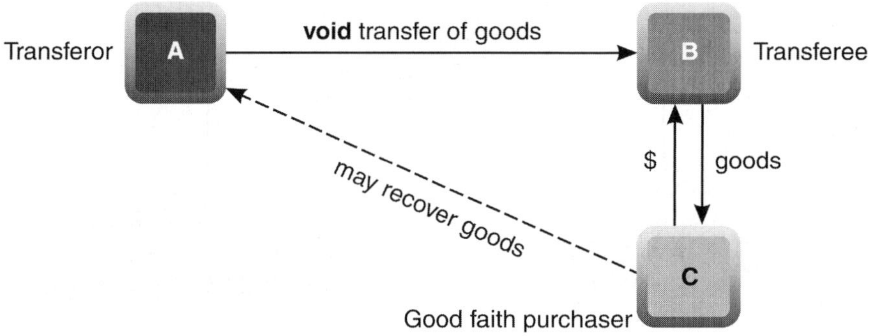


The Code has enlarged this common law doctrine by providing that a good faith purchaser for value obtains valid title from one possessing voidable title even if that person obtained voidable title by (1) fraud as to her identity; (2) exchange for a subsequently dishonored check; (3) an agreement that the transaction was to be a cash sale, and the sale price has not been paid; or (4) criminal fraud punishable as larceny. Section 2–403(1); (Sections 2A–304 and 2A–305 are similar).

In addition, the Code has expanded the rights of good faith purchasers with respect to sales by **minors**. While the common law permitted a minor seller of goods to disaffirm the sale and to recover the goods from a third person who had purchased them in good faith from the party who acquired the goods from the minor, the Code has changed this rule by no longer permitting a minor seller of goods to prevail over a good faith purchaser for value. Section 2–403.

◆ **SEE FIGURE 23-2: Void Title**

◆ **SEE FIGURE 23-3: Voidable Title**

◆ **SEE CASE 23-1**

## ENTRUSTING OF GOODS TO A MERCHANT

Frequently, an owner of goods entrusts (transfers possession of) the goods to a bailee for resale, repair, cleaning, or some other use. In some instances, the bailee violates this entrusting by selling the goods to a third party. Although the "true" owner has a right of recourse against the bailee for the value of the goods, what right, if any, should the true owner of the goods have against the third party? Once again the law must balance the right of ownership against the rights of market transactions.

The Code takes the position of protecting a buyer of goods in the ordinary course of business from a merchant who deals in goods of the kind involved in the sale, where the owner has entrusted possession of the goods to the merchant. The Code defines **buyer in ordinary course of business** as a person that buys goods in good faith, without knowledge that the sale violates the rights of another person in the goods, and in the ordinary course of business from a person, other than a pawnbroker, in the business of selling goods of that kind. Section 1–201(9); Revised Section 1–201(b)(9). Because the merchant who deals in goods of

◆ **FIGURE 23-3: Voidable Title**

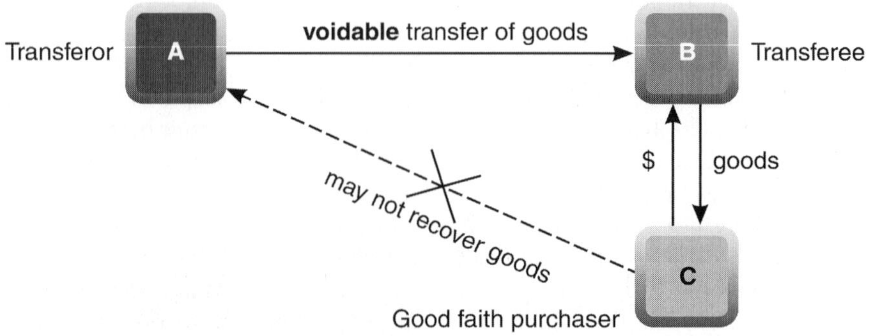

that kind is cloaked with the appearance of ownership or apparent authority to sell, the Code seeks to protect the innocent third-party purchaser. Any such entrusting of possession bestows upon the merchant the power to transfer all rights of the entruster to a buyer in the ordinary course of business. Section 2–403(2); (Sections 2A–304(2) and 2A–305(2) are similar). For example, A brings her stereo for repair to B, who also sells both new and used stereo equipment. C purchases A's stereo from B in the ordinary course of business. The Code protects the rights of C and defeats the rights of A. A's only recourse is against B.

The Code, however, does not go so far as to protect the buyer in the ordinary course of business from a merchant to whom a thief, a finder, or a completely unauthorized person has entrusted the goods. It merely grants the buyer in the ordinary course of business the rights of the entruster.

Where a buyer of goods to whom title has passed leaves the seller in possession of the goods, the buyer has "entrusted the goods" to the seller. Section 2–403(3). If that seller is a merchant and resells and delivers the goods to another buyer in the ordinary course of business, this second buyer acquires good title to the goods. Thus, Marianne sells certain goods to Martin, who pays the price but allows possession to remain with Marianne. Marianne thereafter sells the same goods to Carla, a buyer in the ordinary course of business. Carla takes delivery of the goods. Martin does not have any rights against Carla or to the goods. Martin's only remedy is against Marianne.

◆ SEE FIGURE 23-4: **Entrusting of Goods to a Merchant**

◆ SEE CASE 23-2

## RISK OF LOSS

Risk of loss, as the term is used in the law of sales, addresses the question of allocation of loss between seller and buyer where the goods have been damaged, destroyed, or lost *without the fault* of either the seller or the buyer. If the loss is placed on the buyer, he is under a duty to pay the price for the goods even though they were damaged or he never received them. If loss is placed upon the seller, he has no right to recover the purchase price from the buyer and is usually liable to the buyer for damages for nondelivery unless he tenders a performance in replacement of the lost or destroyed goods.

**CISG** Loss of or damage to the goods after the risk of loss has passed to the buyer does not discharge the buyer from his obligation to pay the purchase price.

In determining which party carries the risk of loss, the Code provides definite rules for specific situations, a sharp departure from the common law concept of risk of loss, which was determined by ownership of the goods and which depended upon the transfer of title. The transactional approach under the Code is necessarily detailed and for this reason is probably more understandable and meaningful than the common law's reliance upon the abstract concept of title. The Code has adopted rules for determining the risk of loss in the absence of breach separate from those that apply where the sales contract has been breached.

Except in a finance lease, risk of loss is retained by the lessor and does not pass to the lessee. Section 2A–219(1). In a finance lease, risk of loss passes to the lessee.

### RISK OF LOSS WHERE THERE IS A BREACH

Where one party breaches the contract, the Code places the risk of loss on the breaching party. Nevertheless, where the nonbreaching party is in control of the goods, the Code places the risk of loss on him to the extent of his insurance coverage.

**Breach by the Seller** If the seller ships nonconforming goods to the buyer, the risk of loss remains on the seller until the buyer has accepted the goods or the seller has remedied the defect. Section 2–510(1); Section 2A–220(1)(a).

◆ FIGURE 23-4: **Entrusting of Goods to a Merchant**

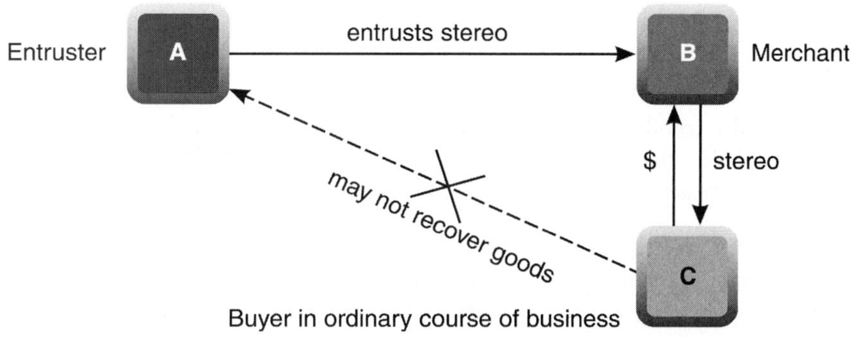

Where the buyer has accepted nonconforming goods, and thereafter by timely notice to the seller rightfully revokes his acceptance (discussed in *Chapter 22*), he may treat the risk of loss, to the extent of any deficiency in his effective insurance coverage, as resting from the beginning on the seller. Section 2–510(2); Section 2A–220(1)(b). For example, Heidi delivers to Gary nonconforming goods, which Gary accepts. Subsequently, Gary discovers a hidden defect in the goods and rightfully revokes his prior acceptance. If the goods are destroyed through no fault of either party, and Gary has insured the goods for 60 percent of their fair market value of $10,000, then the insurance company will cover $6,000 of the loss and Heidi will bear the remainder of the loss, or $4,000. Had the buyer's insurance coverage been $10,000, the seller would not bear any of the loss.

**Breach by the Buyer** Where conforming goods have been identified to a contract that the buyer repudiates or breaches before risk of loss has passed to him, the seller may treat the risk of loss as resting on the buyer "for a commercially reasonable time" to the extent of any deficiency in the seller's effective insurance coverage. Section 2–510(3); Section 2A–220(2). For example, Susan agrees to sell forty thousand pounds of plastic resin to Bernie, F.O.B. (free on board) Bernie's factory, delivery by March 1. On February 1, Bernie wrongfully repudiates the contract by telephoning Susan and telling her that he does not want the resin. Susan immediately seeks another buyer, but before she is able to locate one, and within a commercially reasonable time, the resin is destroyed by a fire through no fault of Susan's. The fair market value of the resin is $35,000. Because Susan's insurance covers only $15,000 of the loss, Bernie is liable for $20,000.

## RISK OF LOSS IN ABSENCE OF A BREACH

Where there is no breach of contract, the parties may by agreement allocate the risk of loss. Where there is no breach, and the parties have not otherwise agreed, the Code places the risk of loss, for the most part, upon the party who is more likely to have greater control over the goods, is more likely to insure the goods, or is better able to prevent their loss.

**Agreement of the Parties** The parties, by agreement, not only may shift the allocation of risk of loss but also may divide the risk between them. Section 2–303. Such agreement is controlling. Thus, the parties may agree, for example, that the seller shall retain the risk of loss even though the buyer is in possession of the goods or has title to them. Or the agreement may provide that the buyer bears 60 percent of the risk and the seller bears 40 percent.

**Trial Sales** Some sales are made with the understanding that the buyer can return the goods even though they conform to the contract. Such trial sales permit a buyer to try goods to determine whether she wishes to keep them or to try to resell them. The Code recognizes two types of trial sales, a sale on approval and a sale or return, and provides a test for distinguishing between them: unless otherwise agreed, if the goods are delivered primarily for the buyer's use, the transaction is a sale on approval; if they are delivered primarily for resale by the buyer, it is a sale or return. Section 2–326(1).

In a **sale on approval**, possession of, but not title to, the goods is transferred to the buyer for a stated time or, if no time is stated, for a reasonable time, during which the buyer may use the goods to determine whether she wishes to buy them. Both title and risk of loss remain with the *seller* until the buyer approves, or accepts, the goods. Section 2–327(1)(a). Until acceptance by the buyer, the sale is a bailment with an option to purchase.

Although use of the goods consistent with the purpose of approval is not acceptance, the buyer's failure to notify the seller within a reasonable time of her election to return the goods *is* an acceptance. The buyer also may manifest approval by exercising over the goods any dominion or control that is inconsistent with the seller's ownership. Upon approval, title and risk of loss passes to the buyer, who then becomes liable to the seller for the purchase price of the goods. If the buyer elects to return the goods and so notifies the seller, the return is at the seller's risk and expense.

In a **sale or return**, the goods are sold and delivered to the buyer with an option to return them to the seller. The risk of loss is on the *buyer*, who also has title until she revests it in the seller by returning the goods. The return of the goods is at the buyer's risk and expense.

A **consignment** is a delivery of possession of personal property to an agent for sale by the agent. Under the Code, a sale on consignment is regarded as a sale or return. Therefore, creditors of the consignee (the agent who receives the merchandise for sale) prevail over the consignor and may obtain possession of the consigned goods, provided the consignee maintains a place of business where he deals in goods of the kind involved under a name other than the name of the consignor. Nevertheless, under Section 2–326(3) the consignor will prevail if he (1) complies with applicable State law requiring a consignor's interest to be evidenced by a sign, (2) establishes that the consignee is generally known by his creditors to be substantially engaged in selling the goods of others, or (3) complies with the filing provisions of Article 9 (Secured Transactions). Section 2–326(3).

**Contracts Involving Carriers** Sales contracts frequently contain terms that indicate the agreement of the parties as to delivery by a carrier. These terms identify the contract as a shipment contract or a destination contract and, by implication, indicate when the risk of loss will pass. If the contract does not require the seller to deliver the goods to a particular destination but merely to the carrier (a **shipment contract**), risk of loss passes to the buyer upon *delivery* of the goods to the common carrier. If the seller is required to deliver them to a particular destination (a **destination contract**), risk of loss passes to the buyer at destination upon *tender* of the goods to the buyer. Section 2–509(1); Section 2A–219(2)(a).

*Windows, Inc. v. Jordan Panel Systems Corp.* deals with the question of when the risk of loss passes between parties whose contract makes no specific provision and contains no delivery term. The case demonstrates that if the contract is not clearly a destination contract or a shipment contract, the law assumes that it is a shipment contract.

CISG If the sales contract involves the carriage of the goods and the seller is not obligated to hand them over at a particular destination, the risk of loss passes to the buyer when the goods are handed over to the first carrier. If the contract requires the seller to deliver the goods to a carrier at a particular destination, the risk of loss passes when the goods are handed over to the carrier at that place.

◆ SEE CASE 23-3

### GOODS IN POSSESSION OF BAILEE

In some sales, the goods, at the time the contract is made, are held by a bailee and are to be delivered without being moved. For instance, a seller may contract with a buyer to sell grain that is located in a grain elevator and that the buyer intends to leave in the same elevator. In such situations, Sections 2–509(2) and 2A–219(2)(b) provide that the risk of loss passes to the buyer when one of the following occurs:

1. If a negotiable document of title (discussed in *Chapter 48*; 1–201(15); Revised Section 1–201(b)(16)) is involved, the risk of loss passes upon the buyer's receipt of the document.
2. If a nonnegotiable document of title is involved, the risk passes when the document is tendered to the buyer.
3. If no documents of title are employed, risk passes upon either (a) the seller's tender to the buyer of written directions to the bailee to deliver the goods to the buyer or (b) the bailee's acknowledgment of the buyer's right to possession of the goods.

In situations 2 and 3(a), if the buyer seasonably objects, the risk of loss remains upon the seller until the buyer has had a reasonable time to present the document or direction to the bailee.

CISG If the buyer is bound to take over the goods at a place other than the seller's place of business, the risk of loss passes when the buyer is aware of the fact that the goods are placed at her disposal at that location.

### ALL OTHER SALES

If the buyer possesses the goods when the contract is formed, risk of loss passes to the buyer at that time. Section 2–509(3); Section 2A–219(2)(c).

All other sales not involving breach are covered by Section 2–509(3). This catchall provision applies when the buyer picks up the goods at the seller's place of business or when the seller delivers the goods using her own transportation. In these cases, risk of loss depends on whether or not the seller is a **merchant**. If the seller is a merchant, risk of loss passes to the buyer upon the buyer's *receipt* of the goods. If the seller is **not a merchant**, it passes on *tender* of the goods from the seller to the buyer. Section 2–509(3); Section 2A–219(2)(c). The policy behind this rule is that so long as the merchant seller is making delivery at her place of business or with her own vehicle, she continues to control the goods and can be expected to insure them. The buyer, on the other hand, has no control over the goods and is not likely to have insurance on them.

Suppose Belinda goes to Sidney's furniture store, selects a particular set of dining room furniture, and pays Sidney the agreed price of $1,800 for it upon Sidney's agreement to stain the set a darker color and deliver it. Sidney stains the furniture and notifies Belinda that he will deliver it the following day. That night, the furniture is accidentally destroyed by fire. Belinda can recover from Sidney the $1,800 payment. The risk of loss is on seller Sidney as he is a merchant and the goods were not received by Belinda but were only tendered to her.

CISG If the sales contract does not involve the carriage of the goods, the risk of loss passes to the buyer when he takes over the goods, or, if the buyer does not take over the goods in due time, from the time when the goods are placed at his disposal.

On the other hand, suppose Georgia, an accountant, prior to moving to a different city, contracts to sell her household furniture to Nina for $3,000. Though Georgia notifies Nina that the furniture is available for her to pickup, Nina delays picking up the furniture for several days. In the interim, the furniture is stolen from Georgia's residence without her fault. Georgia may recover from Nina the $3,000 purchase price. The risk of loss is on the buyer (Nina), as the seller is not a merchant and tender is sufficient to transfer the risk.

◆ SEE FIGURE 23-5: **Passage of Risk of Loss in Absence of Breach**

◆ SEE CASE 23-4

◆ FIGURE 23-5: **Passage of Risk of Loss in Absence of Breach**

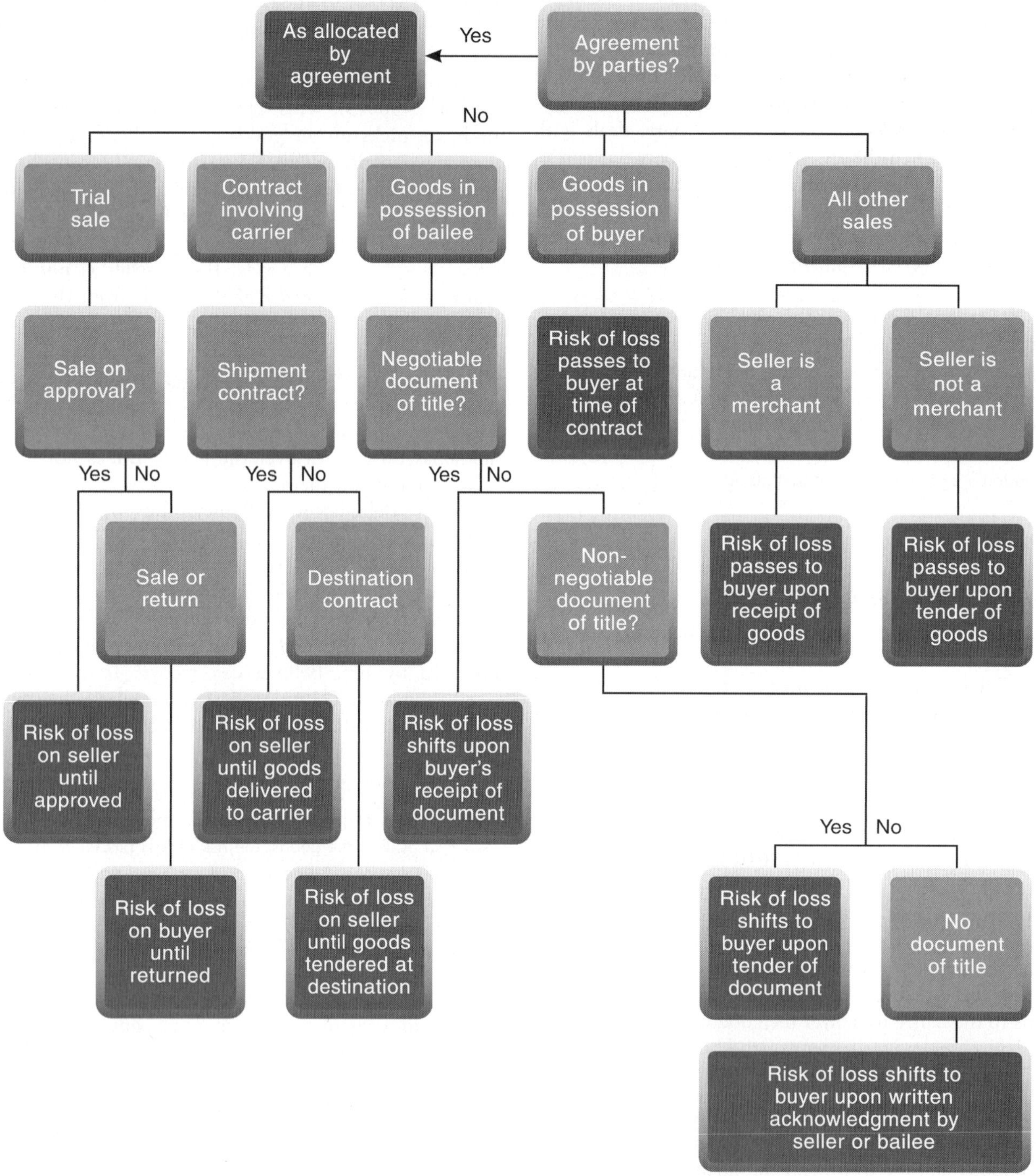


## SALES OF GOODS IN BULK

Because a debtor may secretly liquidate all or a major part of his tangible assets by a bulk sale and conceal or divert the proceeds of the sale without paying his creditors, creditors have an obvious interest in a merchant's bulk disposal of his merchandise made not in the ordinary course of business. The central purpose of bulk sales law is to deter two common forms of commercial fraud, namely (1) when the merchant, owing debts, sells out his stock in trade to a friend for a low price, pays his creditors less than he owes them, and hopes to come back into the business "through the back door" sometime in the future; and (2) when the merchant, owing debts, sells out his stock in trade to anyone for any price, pockets the proceeds, and disappears without paying his creditors.

Article 6 of the Code, which applies to such sales, defines a **bulk transfer** as "any transfer in bulk and not in the ordinary course of the transferor's business of a major part of the materials, supplies, merchandise or other inventory." Section 6–102. The transfer of a substantial part of equipment is a bulk transfer only if made in connection with a bulk transfer of inventory. Those subject to Article 6 of the Code are merchants whose principal business is the sale of merchandise from stock, including those who manufacture what they sell.

In 1988, the National Conference of Commissioners on Uniform State Laws and the American Law Institute jointly issued a recommendation stating "that changes in the business and legal contexts in which sales are conducted have made regulation of bulk sales unnecessary." They, therefore, recommended the repeal of Article 6 or, for those States that felt the need to continue the regulation of bulk sales, the adoption of a revised Article 6 designed to afford better protection to creditors while minimizing the obstacles to good faith transactions. At least forty-five States have repealed Article 6, while only a few States have adopted Revised Article 6.

## CHAPTER SUMMARY

### TRANSFER OF TITLE

**Identification** designation of specific goods as goods to which the contract of sale refers
- ***Insurable Interest*** buyer obtains an insurable interest and specific remedies in the goods by the identification of existing goods as goods to which the contract of sale refers
- ***Security Interest*** an interest in personal property or fixtures that ensures payment or performance of an obligation

**Passage of Title** title passes when the parties intend it to pass; when the parties do not specifically agree, the Code provides rules to determine when title passes
- ***Physical Movement of the Goods*** when delivery is to be made by moving the goods, title passes at the time and place where the seller completes his performance with reference to delivery
- ***No Movement of the Goods***

**Power to Transfer Title** the purchaser of goods obtains such title as her transferor either has or had the power to transfer; however, to encourage and make secure good faith acquisitions of goods, it is necessary to protect certain third parties under certain circumstances
- ***Void Title*** no title can be transferred
- ***Voidable Title*** the good faith purchaser acquires good title
- ***Entrusting of Goods to a Merchant*** buyers in the ordinary course of business acquire good title when buying from merchants

### RISK OF LOSS

**Definition** allocation of loss between seller and buyer where the goods have been damaged, destroyed, or lost without the fault of either party

**Risk of Loss Where There Is a Breach**
- ***Breach by the Seller*** if the seller ships to the buyer goods that do not conform to the contract, the risk of loss remains on the seller until the buyer has accepted the goods or until the seller has remedied the defect
- ***Breach by the Buyer*** the seller may treat the risk of loss as resting on the buyer for a commercially reasonable time to the extent of any deficiency in the seller's effective insurance coverage

**Risk of Loss in Absence of a Breach**
- ***Agreement of the Parties*** the parties may by agreement allocate the risk of loss
- ***Trial Sales*** unless otherwise agreed, if the goods are delivered primarily for the buyer's use, the transaction is a sale on approval (risk of loss remains with the

seller until "approval" or acceptance of the goods by the buyer); if they are delivered primarily for resale by the buyer, it is a sale or return (the risk of loss is on the buyer until she returns the goods)

- ***Contracts Involving Carriers*** in shipment contracts, the seller bears the risk of loss and expense until the goods are delivered to the carrier for shipment; in destination contracts, the seller bears the risk of loss and expense until tender of the goods at a particular destination
- ***Goods in Possession of Bailee***
- ***All Other Sales*** for merchant seller, risk of loss passes to buyer on the buyer's receipt of the goods; for nonmerchant seller, risk of loss passes to buyer upon tender of goods

**BULK SALES** **Definition** a transfer, not in the ordinary course of the transferor's business, of a major part of inventory
**Requirements of Article 6** transfer is ineffective against any creditor of the transferor, unless certain requirements are met

## CASES

CASE 23-1

### Void and Voidable Title to Goods
### ROBINSON v. DURHAM

Alabama Court of Civil Appeals, 1988
537 So.2d 966

**Wright, J.**

Ronald Robinson, Wyman Robinson, and Friendly Discount Auto Sales (appellants) appeal from the granting of summary judgment in favor of appellee Mike Durham (Durham).

The facts material to this appeal and dispositive of this case are undisputed. Appellants, who are in car sales, purchased a 1968 Chevrolet Camaro. At the time of the purchase, a female transferred to the appellants tag receipts in her name and in the name of the previous owner. Wyman Robinson then registered the automobile in his name. In September 1986 Durham purchased the automobile from appellants, and all prior documentation was transferred to him. Shortly thereafter, the F.B.I. seized the automobile. The automobile had been reported stolen in Florida. It was subsequently returned to the original owner.

Durham filed a suit against appellants alleging fraud, breach of contract, and breach of warranty. Durham moved for summary judgment against appellants on all counts. The trial court granted Durham's motion on the count alleging that appellants made a statement to Durham as true without knowledge of its truth and on the issue of breach of warranty of title. Durham was awarded $5,200, the amount he paid for the car. Appellants appeal.

Appellants assert that the grant of summary judgment was in error because there was "a scintilla of evidence, if not substantial evidence" from which the trial court could have concluded that appellants held good title "or at least voidable title" on the automobile, thereby conveying actual title to Durham at the time of the purchase.

Appellants' argument is without merit. It is unequivocal that "a person who has stolen goods of another cannot pass title thereto to another, whether such other knew, or did not know, that the goods were stolen." [Citations.] A thief gets only void title and without more cannot pass any title to a subsequent purchaser, even a good faith purchaser. [Citation.] It is undisputed that the automobile had been stolen. Therefore, at the time of purchase appellants obtained no title. In other words, the title was void. Appellants could not convey good title to Durham; therefore, the subsequent sale to Durham constituted a breach of warranty of good title.

Relying on §2–403(1), [UCC], appellants contend that they at least acquired a voidable title when they purchased the automobile. Section 2–403 recognizes that a person with voidable title has power to transfer a good title to a good faith purchaser for value. Voidable title can only arise from a voluntary transfer, and the rightful owner must assent to the transfer. "A possessor of goods does not have voidable title unless the true owner has consented to the transfer of title to him." [Citation.] In this case the rightful owner did not consent or assent to the transfer of the automobile. Appellants obtained no title. * * * Affirmed. All the Judges concur.

CASE 23-2

## Entrusting of Goods to a Merchant
## HEINRICH v. TITUS-WILL SALES, INC.

Court of Appeals of Washington, Division 2, 1994
73 Wash.App. 147, 868 P.2d 169

**Seinfeld, J.**

Titus-Will Ford Sales, Inc. appeals a judgment for replevin [repossession] of a 1990 Ford pickup truck that Titus-Will had previously sold to dealer/broker James Wilson. Upon consideration of the entrustment provisions of the Uniform Commercial Code, we agree that Titus-Will must bear the burden of loss of payment for the vehicle. Accordingly, we affirm the judgment in favor of Michael Heinrich, a third party bona fide purchaser for value.

In 1989 Michael Heinrich wished to buy a particular model new Ford pickup truck. James Wilson held himself out as a dealer/broker, licensed to buy and sell vehicles. Heinrich retained Wilson to make the purchase, but did not direct Wilson to any particular automobile dealer. Unbeknownst to Heinrich, Wilson had lost his Washington vehicle dealer license the previous year.

Wilson negotiated with Titus-Will for the purchase of a Ford pickup truck with Heinrich's desired options. Titus-Will had been involved in hundreds of transactions with Wilson over the years and also was unaware that Wilson was no longer licensed to act as a vehicle dealer.

Heinrich made two initial payments to Wilson: an $1,800 down payment and a $3,000 payment when Titus-Will ordered the truck. Wilson gave Heinrich a receipt using a "Used Car Wholesale Purchase Order" that displayed Wilson's alleged vehicle dealer license number. Wilson then ordered the truck from Titus-Will, using his own check to make a $7,000 down payment. The purchase order indicated the truck was being sold to Wilson. "Dealer" was written in the space on the form for tax. Wilson told the Titus-Will salesman handling the sale that he was ordering the truck for resale.

On October 13, 1989, Wilson told Heinrich the truck was ready for delivery. Heinrich paid Wilson $15,549.55 as final payment, including tax and license fees. Wilson gave Heinrich a copy of the purchase order and of an options checklist with corresponding prices. These documents indicated that Wilson was buying the truck from Titus-Will. The Titus-Will salesman had signed off on the options list; Wilson marked it "paid in full" and signed it after Heinrich paid him. On the same day, at Wilson's behest, Heinrich signed a Washington application for motor vehicle title.

Wilson agreed to deliver the truck to Heinrich at Titus-Will on Saturday, October 21, 1989. He arranged with a Titus-Will salesman to deliver a check on the morning of October 21 to a clerk in the Titus-Will office and, in return, to receive the truck keys and paperwork. The clerk accepted Wilson's check for $11,288.00, post-dated to Monday, October 23, 1989, and delivered Wilson a packet containing the keys to the truck, the owner's manual, an odometer disclosure statement, and a warranty card. The odometer statement, which Wilson and the Titus-Will salesman signed, showed Wilson as the transferor. Titus-Will did not fill out the warranty card with the name and address of the purchaser because the sale appeared to be dealer to dealer, with the warranty to benefit the ultimate purchaser.

* * *

Wilson immediately taped Heinrich's application for title in the rear window of the truck that was parked on the Titus-Will lot. When Heinrich arrived, Wilson gave him the keys and documents and Heinrich drove off in the truck.

Wilson's check did not clear. Titus-Will demanded return of the truck. On November 6, Wilson picked up the truck from Heinrich, telling him he would have Titus-Will make certain repairs under the warranty. Wilson returned the truck to Titus-Will.

On November 9, 1989, Wilson admitted to Heinrich that he did not have funds to cover his check to Titus-Will and that Titus-Will would not release the truck without payment. Heinrich then asked Titus-Will for the truck; it refused. By a pretrial arrangement, Heinrich regained possession of, but not clear title to, the truck on April 1, 1990.

Heinrich sued Titus-Will and Wilson, seeking replevin of the truck and damages for his loss of use. Heinrich obtained a default order against Wilson. After a bench trial, the court awarded Heinrich title to the truck and $3,050 in damages for loss of its use.

On appeal, Titus-Will argues that the trial court erroneously applied the entrustment doctrine of [UCC] 2–403;

* * *

### The Entrustment Doctrine

[UCC] 2–403(2) and (3) contain the entrustment provisions of the Uniform Commercial Code (UCC).

* * *

To prevail under this statute, Heinrich must show (1) Titus-Will "entrusted" the truck to Wilson and, thus, empowered Wilson subsequently to transfer all rights of Titus-Will in the truck to Heinrich; (2) Wilson was a merchant dealing in automobiles; and (3) Heinrich bought the truck from Wilson as a "buyer in ordinary course of business." [Citations.]

Three general policies support [§]2–403(2), the UCC provision placing the risk of loss on the entruster. First, it protects the innocent buyer who, based on his observation of goods in the possession of a merchant of those goods, believes that the merchant has legal title to the goods and can, therefore, pass title in the goods to another. [Citation.] The statute carries forward the pre-Uniform Commercial Code law of estoppel under which an owner, who clothes a merchant with apparent ownership of or authority to sell goods, is estopped from denying such authority as against one buying the goods from the merchant in good faith. [Citations.]

Secondly, the entrustment clause reflects the idea that the entruster is in a better position than the innocent buyer to protect against the risk that an intermediary merchant will not pay for or not deliver the goods. [Citations.]

Thirdly, the entrustment clause facilitates the flow of commerce by allowing purchasers to rely on a merchant's apparent legal right to sell the goods. [Citations.] Without the safeguards of the entrustment provision, a prudent buyer would have to delay the finalization of any sizeable sales transaction for the time necessary to research the merchant's ownership rights to the goods.

***Entrusting***

The UCC definition of "entrusting," contained in 2–403(3), is broad. [Citation.] The statute declares that "any delivery and any acquiescence in retention of possession" constitutes entrustment. 2–403(3). A person can entrust goods to a merchant by a variety of methods, such as consigning them, creating a bailment, taking a security interest in inventory, leaving them with the merchant after purchase, and delivering them for purposes of repair. [Citations.] A sale can also constitute an entrustment when some aspect of the transaction remains incomplete. [Citations.]

Titus-Will properly concedes that it entrusted the truck to Wilson. However, it argues Wilson was not a merchant and Heinrich was not a buyer in ordinary course. Further, Titus-Will contends that the timing of the entrusting deprived Wilson of the power to transfer its rights.

***Merchant***

Titus-Will argues that Wilson was not a merchant because he had no inventory. However, it is not necessary to possess an inventory to fit within the broad statutory definition of merchant. Article 2 of the UCC defines (in part) "merchant" as "a person who deals in goods of the kind or otherwise by his occupation holds himself out as having knowledge or skill peculiar to the practices or goods involved in the transaction." 2–104(1). Wilson was a merchant who dealt in automobiles; he held himself out as a dealer in automobiles and appeared to be a dealer in automobiles. Both parties treated him as one. Titus-Will processed all the documents as it would for a dealer and understood that Wilson was buying the truck for resale.

Titus-Will also argues that Wilson was not a merchant because he did not have a vehicle dealer license. However, the UCC does not require proper state licensing for merchant status. 2–104(1), 2–403(2). * * *

***Buyer in Ordinary Course***

There is also substantial evidence that Heinrich was a "buyer in ordinary course of business" although the trial court referred to him as a "good faith purchaser for value." A buyer in ordinary course of business is

> a person who in good faith and without knowledge that the sale to him is in violation of the ownership rights or security interest of a third party in the goods buys in ordinary course from a person in the business of selling goods of that kind[.] 1–201(9). "Buying" includes receiving goods * * * under a pre-existing contract for sale." 1–201(9). Good faith is "honesty in fact in the conduct or transaction concerned." 1–201(19).

The amount of the consideration is significant as evidence of good faith. [Citation.] Heinrich gave substantial value for the truck, more than Wilson agreed to pay Titus-Will. Nor did Heinrich know or have a basis to believe that Wilson's sale and delivery of the truck to him violated Titus-Will's ownership or security interest rights. There was no showing that Heinrich acted other than in good faith. * * * Wilson's illegal and fraudulent activity does not taint Heinrich's status as a buyer under 2–403(2). When Heinrich accepted delivery after previously paying Wilson, Heinrich was "buying" as defined by 1–201(9).

***Timing of Entrustment***

Titus-Will also argues that the UCC entrustment provisions should not apply because it entrusted the truck to Wilson *after* Heinrich had completely paid Wilson. This is an issue of first impression in this jurisdiction.

Before the completion of the Wilson–Heinrich sales transaction, Titus-Will entrusted Wilson not only with the truck, but also with the signed odometer disclosure statement, the owner's manual, the warranty card, and the keys. By doing so, Titus-Will clothed Wilson with additional indicia of ownership and with the apparent authority to transfer an ownership interest in the truck. It also enabled Wilson to complete the sales transaction. 2–401(2) ("Unless otherwise explicitly agreed title passes to the buyer at the time and place at which the seller completes his performance with reference to the physical delivery of the goods"). In addition, the entrustment allowed Wilson to continue to deceive Heinrich from

October 21, 1989, the date of delivery of possession, to November 9, 1989, when Wilson finally admitted the truth. We believe that under these circumstances, application of the entrustment doctrine, 2–403(2), furthers the policy of protecting the buyer who relies on the merchant's apparent legal ability to sell goods in the merchant's possession.

The second rationale for the entrustment doctrine also supports its application here. Titus-Will, in the business of selling cars, was in a better position than Heinrich to protect itself against another dealer/broker who might fail to pay for the goods. It could have insured against the loss, and it could have adopted preventive procedures. * * * The third rationale for the entrustment doctrine focuses on the flow of commerce. Here we consider the potential impact on commercial transactions of requiring purchasers to research their dealer/broker's legal title before accepting possession of the goods. Although the record contains no evidence on this issue, it seems obvious that this requirement would inevitably cause some delay. [Citation.]

Requiring the entruster to retain the burden of risk, even when the entrustment occurs after a third party purchaser gives value, supports the policies underlying the entrustment doctrine. * * * The trial court did not err in applying the entrustment doctrine and granting replevin.

* * *

We affirm the trial court's judgment.

---

CASE 23-3

## Shipment Contracts
## WINDOWS, INC. v. JORDAN PANEL SYSTEMS CORP.

United States Court of Appeals, Second Circuit, 1999
177 F.3d 114
http://laws.findlaw.com/2nd/987603.html

**Leval, C. J.**

This is an appeal by a buyer from a grant of summary judgment in favor of the seller dismissing the buyer's claim for incidental and consequential damages resulting from damage suffered by the goods during shipment. The district court found that any negligence that might have caused the damage was attributable to the carrier and not the seller. It therefore concluded that the buyer's claim for incidental and consequential damages was barred by UCC §2–613, which precludes the award of such damages when the goods are damaged "without fault of either party." We affirm, but in reliance on different provisions of the Code.

Windows, Inc. ("Windows" or "the seller") is a fabricator and seller of windows, based in South Dakota. Jordan Systems, Inc. ("Jordan" or "the buyer") is a construction subcontractor, which contracted to install window wall panels at an air cargo facility at John F. Kennedy Airport in New York City. Jordan ordered custom-made windows from Windows. The purchase contract specified that the windows were to be shipped properly packaged for cross country motor freight transit and "delivered to New York City."

Windows constructed the windows according to Jordan's specifications. It arranged to have them shipped to Jordan by a common carrier, Consolidated Freightways Corp. ("Consolidated" or "the carrier"), and delivered them to Consolidated intact and properly packaged. During the course of shipment, however, the goods sustained extensive damage. Much of the glass was broken and many of the window frames were gouged and twisted. Jordan's president signed a delivery receipt noting that approximately two-thirds of the shipment was damaged due to "load shift." Jordan, seeking to stay on its contractor's schedule, directed its employees to disassemble the window frames in an effort to salvage as much of the shipment as possible.

Jordan made a claim with Consolidated for damages it had sustained as a result of the casualty, including labor costs from its salvage efforts and other costs from Jordan's inability to perform its own contractual obligations on schedule. Jordan also ordered a new shipment from Windows, which was delivered without incident.

Jordan did not pay Windows for either the first shipment of damaged windows or the second, intact shipment. Windows filed suit to recover payment from Jordan for both shipments in the Supreme Court of the State of New York, Suffolk County. Jordan counterclaimed, seeking incidental and consequential damages resulting from the damaged shipment. * * * Windows later withdrew its claims against Jordan. The only remaining claim is Jordan's counterclaim against Windows for incidental and consequential damages.

The district court granted Windows' motion for summary judgment. * * * This appeal followed.

* * *

Jordan seeks to recover incidental and consequential damages pursuant to [the] UCC. Under that provision,

Jordan's entitlement to recover incidental and consequential damages depends on whether those damages "result[ed] from the seller's breach."

A destination contract is covered by §2–503(3); it arises where "the seller is required to deliver at a particular destination." In contrast, a shipment contract arises where "the seller is required * * * to send the goods to the buyer and the contract does not require him to deliver them at a particular destination." §2–504. Under a shipment contract, the seller must "put the goods in the possession of such a carrier and make such a contract for their transportation as may be reasonable having regard to the nature of the goods and other circumstances of the case." §2–504(a). * * *

Where the terms of an agreement are ambiguous, there is a strong presumption under the UCC favoring shipment contracts. Unless the parties "expressly specify" that the contract requires the seller to deliver to a particular destination, the contract is generally construed as one for shipment. [Citations.]

Jordan's confirmation of its purchase order, by letter to Windows dated September 22, 1993, provided, "All windows to be shipped properly crated/packaged/boxed suitable for cross country motor freight transit and delivered to New York City." We conclude that this was a shipment contract rather than a destination contract.

To overcome the presumption favoring shipment contracts, the parties must have explicitly agreed to impose on Windows the obligation to effect delivery at a particular destination. The language of this contract does not do so. Nor did Jordan use any commonly recognized industry term indicating that a seller is obligated to deliver the goods to the buyer's specified destination.

Under the terms of its contract, Windows thus satisfied its obligations to Jordan when it put the goods, properly packaged, into the possession of the carrier for shipment. Upon Windows' proper delivery to the carrier, Jordan assumed the risk of loss, and cannot recover incidental or consequential damages from the seller caused by the carrier's negligence.

This allocation of risk is confirmed by the terms of [the] UCC §2–509(1)(a), entitled "Risk of Loss in the Absence of Breach." It provides that where the contract "does not require [the seller] to deliver [the goods] at a particular destination, the risk of loss passes to the buyer when the goods are duly delivered to the carrier." UCC §2–509(1)(a). As noted earlier, Jordan does not contest the court's finding that Windows duly delivered conforming goods to the carrier. Accordingly, as Windows had already fulfilled its contractual obligations at the time the goods were damaged and Jordan had assumed the risk of loss, there was no "seller's breach" as is required for a buyer to claim incidental and consequential damages under §2–715.

* * *

The judgment of the district court is affirmed.

CASE 23-4

## Risk of Loss: Seller Not a Merchant
## MARTIN v. MELLAND'S INC.

Supreme Court of North Dakota, 1979
283 N.W.2d 76
http://scholar.google.com/scholar_case?case=2836560129405539578&hl=en&as_sdt=2&as_vis=1&oi=scholarr

**Erickstad, C. J.**

The narrow issue on this appeal is who should bear the loss of a truck and an attached haystack mover that was destroyed by fire while in the possession of the plaintiff, Israel Martin (Martin), but after certificate of title had been delivered to the defendant, Melland's Inc. (Melland's). The destroyed haymoving unit was to be used as a trade-in for a new haymoving unit that Martin ultimately purchased from Melland's. Martin appeals from a district court judgment dated September 28, 1978, that dismissed his action on the merits after it found that at the time of its destruction Martin was the owner of the unit pursuant to [UCC Section 2–401]. We hold that Section 2–401 is inapplicable to this case, but we affirm the district court judgment on the grounds that risk of loss had not passed to Melland's pursuant to [UCC Section 2–509].

On June 11, 1974, Martin entered into a written agreement with Melland's, a farm implement dealer, to purchase a truck and attached haystack mover for the total purchase price of $35,389. Martin was given a trade-in allowance of $17,389 on his old unit, leaving a balance owing of $18,000 plus sales tax of $720 or a total balance of $18,720. The agreement provided that Martin "mail or bring title" to the old unit to Melland's "this week." Martin mailed the certificate of title to Melland's pursuant to the agreement, but he was allowed to retain the use and possession of the old unit "until they had the new one ready." The new unit was not expected to be ready for two to three months because it required certain modifications. During this interim period, Melland's performed minor repairs to the trade-in unit on two occasions without charging Martin for the repairs.

Fire destroyed the truck and the haymoving unit in early August, 1974, while Martin was moving hay. The parties did not have any agreement regarding insurance or risk of loss on the unit and Martin's insurance on the trade-in unit had lapsed. Melland's refused Martin's demand for his new unit and Martin brought this suit. * * *

The district court found "that although the Plaintiff [Martin] executed the title to the * * * [haymoving unit], he did not relinquish possession of the same and therefore the Plaintiff was the owner of said truck at the time the fire occurred pursuant to Section 2–401." [Martin appealed.]

* * *

* * * the concept of title under the UCC is of decreased importance.

* * *

No longer is the question of title of any importance in determining whether a buyer or seller bears the risk of loss. [Citation.]

* * *

Thus, the question in this case is not answered by a determination of the location of title, but by the risk of loss provisions in [UCC §2–509]. Before addressing the risk of loss question in conjunction with [UCC §2–509], it is necessary to determine the posture of the parties with regard to the trade-in unit, *i.e.*, who is the buyer and the seller and how are the responsibilities allocated. It is clear that a barter or trade-in is considered a sale and is therefore subject to the Uniform Commercial Code. [Citations.] It is also clear that the party who owns the trade-in is considered the seller. [UCC §2–304] provides that the "price can be made payable in money or otherwise. If it is payable in whole or in part in goods each party is a seller of the goods which he is to transfer." [Citations.]

Martin argues that he had already sold the trade-in unit to Melland's and, although he retained possession, he did so in the capacity of a bailee (apparently pursuant to [UCC §2–509(2)]). White and Summers in their hornbook on the Uniform Commercial Code argue that the seller who retains possession should not be considered bailee within Section 2–509.

* * *

The courts that have addressed this issue have agreed with White and Summers. [Citations.]

It is undisputed that the contract did not require or authorize shipment by carrier pursuant to Section [2–509(1)]; therefore, the residue section, subsection 3, is applicable:

> In any case not within subsection 1 or 2, the risk of loss passes to the buyer on his receipt of the goods if the seller is a merchant; otherwise the risk passes to the buyer on tender of delivery.

Martin admits that he is not a merchant; therefore, it is necessary to determine if Martin tendered delivery of the trade-in unit to Melland's. * * *

It is clear that the trade-in unit was not tendered to Melland's in this case. The parties agreed that Martin would keep the old unit "until they had the new one ready."

* * *

We hold that Martin did not tender delivery of the trade-in truck and haystack mover to Melland's pursuant to [UCC §2–509]; consequently, Martin must bear the loss.

We affirm the district court judgment.

## QUESTIONS

1. Explain the relative importance of title under the common law and Article 2.
2. Distinguish between a shipment contract and a destination contract. When does title and risk of loss pass under each?
3. When does the seller have a right or power to transfer title? When is the transfer void or voidable? By whom? Against whom?
4. Discuss the rules covering (a) risk of loss in the absence of a breach, and (b) risk of loss when there is a breach.
5. What is a bulk transfer? When is it effective? What does revised Article 6 attempt to accomplish?

## PROBLEMS

1. Stein, a mechanic, and Beal, a life insurance agent, entered into a written contract for the sale of Stein's tractor to Beal for $6,800 cash. It was agreed that Stein would tune the motor on the tractor. Stein fulfilled this obligation and on the night of July 1 telephoned Beal that the tractor was ready to be picked up upon Beal's making payment. Beal responded, "I'll be there in the morning with the money." On the next morning, however, Beal was approached by an insurance prospect and decided to get the tractor at a later date. On the night of July 2, the tractor was destroyed by fire of unknown origin. Neither Stein nor Beal had any fire insurance. Who must bear the loss?

**2.** Regan received a letter from Chase, the material portion of which stated: "Chase hereby places an order with you for fifty cases of Red Top Tomatoes, ship them C.O.D." Promptly upon receipt of the letter Regan shipped the tomatoes to Chase. While en route, the railroad car carrying the tomatoes was wrecked. Upon Chase's refusal to pay for the tomatoes, Regan commenced an action to recover the purchase price. Chase defended on the ground that as the shipment was C.O.D., neither title to the tomatoes nor risk of loss passed until their delivery to Chase. Who has title? Who has risk of loss? Explain.

**3.** On May 10, the Apple Company, acting through one Brown, entered into a contract with Crane for the installation of a milking machine at Crane's farm. Following the enumeration of the articles to be furnished, together with the price of each article, the written contract provided: "This outfit is subject to thirty days' free trial and is to be installed about June 1." Within thirty days after installation the entire outfit, excepting a double utility unit, was destroyed by fire through no fault of Crane. The Apple Company sued Crane to recover the value of the articles destroyed. Explain who bears the risk of loss.

**4.** Brown, located in Knoxville, contracted to buy sixty cases of Lovely Brand canned corn from Clark in Toledo at a contract price of $1,250. Pursuant to the contract, Clark selected and set aside sixty cases of Lovely Brand canned corn and tagged them "For Brown." The contract required Clark to ship the corn to Brown via T Railroad, F.O.B. Toledo. Before Clark delivered the corn to the railroad, the sixty cases were stolen from Clark's warehouse.

**(a)** Who is liable for the loss of the sixty cases of corn, Brown or Clark?

**(b)** Suppose Clark had delivered the corn to the railroad in Toledo. After the corn had been loaded on a freight car, but before the train left the yard, the car was broken open and its contents, including the corn, stolen. As between Brown and Clark, who is liable for the loss?

**(c)** Would your answer in question (b) be the same if this was an F.O.B. Knoxville contract, all other facts remaining the same?

**5.** Gardner owned a quantity of corn, which was contained in a corncrib located on Gardner's farm. On March 12, Gardner wrote a letter to Bassett stating that he would sell to Bassett all of the corn in this crib, which he estimated at between nine hundred and one thousand bushels, for $3.90 per bushel. Bassett received this letter on March 13 and immediately wrote and mailed on the same day a letter to Gardner stating that he would buy the corn. The corncrib and its contents were accidentally destroyed by fire that broke out about 3 A.M. on March 14.

**(a)** What are the rights of the parties?

**(b)** What difference, if any, in result if Gardner were a merchant?

**6.** Anita, a New York dealer, purchased twenty-five barrels of specially graded and packed apples from a producer at Hood River, Oregon. She then resold the apples to Benji under a contract that specified an agreed price on delivery at Benji's place of business in New York. The apples were shipped to Anita from Oregon but, through no fault of either Anita or Benji, were totally destroyed before reaching New York. Does any liability rest upon Anita?

**7.** Smith was approached by a man who introduced himself as Brown of Brown & Co. Brown was not known to Smith, but Smith asked Dun & Bradstreet for a credit report and obtained a very favorable report on Brown. He thereupon sold Brown some expensive gems and billed Brown & Co. "Brown" turned out to be a clever jewel thief, who later sold the gems to Brown & Co. for valuable consideration. Brown & Co. was unaware of "Brown's" transaction with Smith. Can Smith successfully sue Brown & Co. for either the return of the gems or the price as billed to Brown & Co.?

**8.** Charlotte, the owner of a new Cadillac automobile, agreed to loan the car to Ellen for the month of February while she (Charlotte) went to Florida for a winter vacation. It was understood that Ellen, who was a small-town Cadillac dealer, would merely place Charlotte's car in her showroom for exhibition and sales promotion purposes. While Charlotte was away, Ellen sold the car to Robert. Upon Charlotte's return from Florida, she sued to recover the car from Robert. Who has title to the automobile? Explain.

**9.** Brilles offered to sell his used automobile to Nevarro for $12,600 cash. Nevarro agreed to buy the car, gave Brilles a check for $12,600, and drove away in the car. The next day Nevarro sold the car for $13,000 to Hough, a *bona fide* purchaser. The $12,600 check was returned to Brilles by the bank in which he had deposited it because of insufficient funds in Nevarro's account. Brilles brings an action against Hough to recover the automobile. What judgment?

**10.** Yount told Lewis he wished to buy Lewis's automobile. He drove the car for about ten minutes, returned to Lewis, stated he wanted to take the automobile to show it to his wife, and then left with the automobile and never returned. Yount sold the automobile in another State to Turner and gave him a bill of sale. Can Lewis recover the automobile from Turner? Explain.

**11.** On February 7, Pillsbury purchased eight thousand bushels of wheat from Landis. The wheat was being stored at the Greensville Grain Company. Pillsbury also intended to store the wheat with Greensville. On February 10, the wheat was destroyed. Landis demands payment for the wheat from Pillsbury. Who prevails? Who has title? Who has the risk of loss? Explain.

**12.** Johnson, who owned a hardware store, was indebted to Hutchinson, one of her suppliers. Johnson sold her business to Lockhart, one of Johnson's previous competitors, who combined the inventory from Johnson's store with his own and moved them to a new, larger store. Hutchinson claims that Lockhart must pay Johnson's debt because the sale of the business had been made without complying with the requirements of the bulk sales law. Discuss whether Lockhart is obligated to pay Hutchison's debt to Johnson.

**13.** Seller had manufactured forty thousands pounds of plastic resin pellets specially for the buyer, who agreed to accept them at the rate of one thousand pounds per day upon his issuance of shipping instructions. Despite numerous requests by the seller, the buyer issued no such instructions. On August 18, the seller, after warehousing the goods for forty days, demanded by letter that the buyer issue instructions. The buyer agreed to issue them beginning August 20 but never did. On September 22, a fire destroyed the seller's plant containing the goods, which were not covered by insurance. Who bears the risk of loss? Why?

**14.** Harrison, a men's clothing retailer located in Westport, Connecticut, ordered merchandise from Ninth Street East, Ltd., a Los Angeles–based clothing manufacturer. Ninth Street delivered the merchandise to Denver-Chicago Trucking Company in Los Angeles and then sent four invoices to Harrison that bore the notation "F.O.B. Los Angeles." Denver subsequently transferred the merchandise to a connecting carrier, Old Colony Transportation Company, for final delivery to Harrison's Westport store. When Old Colony tried to deliver the merchandise, Harrison's wife asked the truck driver to deliver the boxes inside the store, but the driver refused. The dispute remained unresolved, and the truck departed with Old Colony still in possession of the goods. Harrison then notified Ninth Street by letter of the nondelivery, but Ninth Street was unable to locate the shipment. Ninth Street then sought to recover the contract purchase price from Harrison. Harrison refused, contending that risk of loss remained with Ninth Street because of its refusal to deliver the merchandise to Harrison's place of business. Discuss whether the risk of loss passed from Ninth Street to Harrison.

**15.** United Road Machinery Company, a dealer in heavy road equipment (including truck scales supplied by Thurman Scale Company), received a telephone call on July 21 from James Durham, an officer of Consolidated Coal Company, seeking to acquire truck scales for his coal mining operation. United and Consolidated entered into a twenty-four-month lease-purchase arrangement. United then notified Thurman that Consolidated would take possession of the scales directly. United paid for the scales and Consolidated took possession of them, but the latter never signed or returned the contract papers forwarded to it by United. Consolidated also never made any of the rental payments ($608/month) due under the lease. On September 20, Consolidated, through its officer Durham, sold the scales to Kentucky Mobile Homes for $8,500. Kentucky's president, Ethard Jasper, checked the county records prior to the purchase and found no lien or encumbrance on the title; likewise, he denied knowledge of the dispute between Consolidated and United. On September 22, Kentucky sold the scales to Clyde Jasper, individually, for $8,500. His search also failed to disclose any lien on the title to the scales, and he denied knowledge of the dispute between Consolidated and United. Can United recover the scales from Jasper? Explain.

**16.** McCoy, an Oklahoma cattle dealer, orally agreed with Chandler, a Texas cattle broker, to ship cattle to a New Mexico feedlot for delivery to Chandler. The agreement was for six lots of cattle valued at $119,000. After McCoy delivered the cattle, he presented invoices to Chandler that described the cattle and set forth the sales price. McCoy then demanded payment, which Chandler refused. Unknown to McCoy, Chandler had obtained a loan from First National Bank and pledged the subject cattle as collateral. The bank had no knowledge of any interest that McCoy may have had in the cattle. McCoy sued to recover the cattle. The bank counterclaimed that it had a perfected security interest in the cattle that was superior to any interest of McCoy's. Who has title to the cattle? Explain.

**17.** Home Indemnity, an insurance company, paid one of its insureds after the theft of his car. The car reappeared in another State and was sold to Michael Schrier for $4,300 by a used car dealer. The dealer promised to give Mr. Schrier a certificate of title. One month later the car was seized by the police on behalf of Home Indemnity. Explain who is entitled to possession of the car.

**18.** Fred Lane, who sells boats, motors, and trailers, sold a boat, motor, and trailer to John Willis in exchange for a check for $6,285.00. The check was not honored when Lane attempted to use the funds. Willis subsequently left the boat, motor, and trailer with John Garrett, who sold the items to Jimmy Honeycutt for $2,500.00. Considering the boat's quality, Honeycutt was surprised at how inexpensive it was. He did not know where Garrett had obtained the boat, but he had dealt with Garrett before and described him as a "sly businessman." Garrett did not sell boats; normally; he sold fishing tackle and provisions. Honeycutt also received a forged certificate for the boat, on which he had observed Garrett forge the purported owner's signature. Can Lane compel Honeycutt to return the boat, motor, and trailer? Explain.

**19.** Mike Moses purchased a mobile home, including installation, from Gary Newman. Newman delivered the home to Moses's lot. Upon inspection of the home, Moses's fiancé found a broken window and water pipe. Moses also had not received keys to the front door. Before Newman corrected these problems, a windstorm destroyed the home. Who bears the risk for the loss of the home? Why?

C H A P T E R 2 4

# Products Liability: Warranties and Strict Liability in Tort

This chapter considers the liability of manufacturers and sellers of goods to buyers, users, consumers, and bystanders for damages caused by defective products. The rapidly expanding development of case law has established products liability as a distinct field of law that combines and enforces rules and principles of contracts, sales, negligence, strict liability in tort, and statutory law.

One reason for the expansion of this liability is the modern method of distributing goods. Today, retailers serve principally as conduits of prepackaged goods that are widely advertised by the manufacturer or distributor. This has brought about the extension of product liability coverage to include manufacturers and other parties along the chain of distribution. The extension of product liability to manufacturers, however, has not lessened the liability of the retailer to his immediate purchaser. Rather, it has broadened the base of liability through the development and application of new principles of law.

The entire area of products liability has attracted a great deal of public attention. According to the U.S. Consumer Product Safety Commission, deaths, injuries, and property damage from consumer product incidents cost the United States more than $800 billion annually. The resultant cost of maintaining product liability insurance has skyrocketed, causing great concern in the business community. In response to the clamor over this insurance crisis, almost all of the States have revised their tort laws to make successful tort (including product liability) lawsuits more difficult to bring. These tort reforms include legislation dealing with joint and several liability, punitive damages, noneconomic damages, and class actions. Nevertheless, repeated efforts to pass Federal product liability legislation have been unsuccessful.

The liability of manufacturers and other sellers of goods for a defective product, or for its failure to perform adequately, may be based upon one or more of the following: (1) negligence, (2) misrepresentation, (3) violation of statutory duty, (4) warranty, and (5) strict liability in tort. The first three causes of actions have been covered in *Chapters 8* and *11*. *Chapter 8* also covered traditional strict liability—where liability is imposed regardless of the defendant's negligence or intent to cause harm. In this chapter we will cover a specialized type of strict liability—strict liability in tort for products. This chapter will also explore warranty liability.

## WARRANTIES

A **warranty**, under the Uniform Commercial Code (UCC or Code), creates a duty on the part of the seller that the goods she sells will conform to certain qualities, characteristics, or conditions. A seller, however, is not required to warrant the goods; and, in general, she may, by appropriate words, disclaim, exclude, negate, or modify a particular warranty or even all warranties.

In bringing a warranty action, the buyer must prove that (1) a warranty existed, (2) the warranty has been breached, (3) the breach of the warranty proximately caused the loss suffered, and (4) notice of the breach was given to the seller. The seller has the burden of proving defenses based on the buyer's conduct. If the seller breaches his warranty, the buyer may reject or revoke acceptance of the goods. Moreover, whether he has accepted or rejected the goods, the buyer may recover a judgment against the seller for damages. Harm for which damages are recoverable include personal injury, damage to property, and economic loss. Economic loss most commonly involves damages for loss of bargain and consequential damages for lost profits. (Damages for breach of warranty are discussed in the next chapter.) This section will examine the various types of warranties as well as the obstacles to a cause of action for breach of warranty.

## TYPES OF WARRANTIES

A warranty may arise out of the mere existence of a sale (a warranty of title), any affirmation of fact or promise made by the seller to the buyer (an express warranty), or the circumstances under which the sale is made (an implied warranty). In a contract for the sale of goods, it is possible to have all three types of warranties. All warranties are construed as consistent with each other and cumulative, unless such a construction is unreasonable. A purchaser, as discussed in previous chapters, means a person who takes by sale, lease, lien, security interest, gift, or any other voluntary transaction creating an interest in property. Revised Article 1–201(b)(29), (30). (Prior Article 1 did not include leases.)

Article 2A carries over the warranty provisions of Article 2 with relatively minor revision to reflect differences in style, leasing terminology, or leasing practices. The creation of express warranties and, except for finance leases, the imposition of the implied warranties of merchantability and fitness for a particular purpose are virtually identical to their Article 2 analogues. Article 2 and Article 2A diverge somewhat in their treatment of the warranties of title and infringement as well as in their provisions for the exclusion and modification of warranties.

## WARRANTY OF TITLE

Under the Code's warranty of title, the seller implicitly warrants (1) that the title conveyed is good and its transfer rightful and (2) that the goods have no security interest or other lien (a claim on property by another for payment of debt) of which the buyer was not aware at the time of purchase. Section 2–312(1). In a lease, title does not transfer to the lessee. Accordingly, Article 2A's analogous provision protects the lessee's right to possession and use of the goods from the claims of other parties arising from an act or omission of the lessor. Section 2A–211(1).

For example, Iris acquires goods from Sherman in a transaction that is void and then sells the goods to Brenda. Sherman brings an action against Brenda and recovers the goods. Iris has breached the warranty of title: because she did not have good title to the goods, her transfer of the goods to Brenda was not rightful. Accordingly, Iris is liable to Brenda for damages.

The Code does *not* label the warranty of title as an implied warranty, even though it arises from the sale and not from any particular words or conduct. Consequently, the Code's general disclaimer provision for implied warranties does not apply to a warranty of title, which instead is subject to its own disclaimer provision. Nevertheless, a seller of goods does implicitly warrant title to those goods.

A seller who is a merchant makes an additional warranty in sales of goods of the kind in which he regularly deals: that such goods shall be delivered free of the rightful claim of any third person that the goods infringe (use without authorization) upon any existing patent. Section 2–312(3); Section 2A–211(2).

## EXPRESS WARRANTIES

An express warranty is an explicit undertaking by the seller with respect to the quality, description, condition, or performability of the goods. The undertaking may consist of an affirmation of fact or a promise that relates to the goods, a description of the goods, or a sample or model of the goods. In each of these instances, the undertaking must become or be made part of the basis of the bargain in order for an express warranty to be created. The seller need not, however, have a specific intention to make a warranty or use formal words such as "warrant" or "guarantee." Moreover, to be liable for a breach of express warranty a seller need not know that she has made a false statement; the seller may be acting in good faith. For example, if John mistakenly asserts to Sam that a rope will easily support three hundred pounds and Sam is injured when the rope breaks while supporting only two hundred pounds, John is liable for breach of an express warranty.

**Creation** The seller can create an express warranty either orally or in writing. One of the ways in which an express warranty can be created is through an **affirmation of fact** or a **promise** relating to the goods that becomes part of the basis of the bargain. Section 2–313(1)(a); Section 2A–210(1)(a). The statement can be in regard to the quality, condition, capacity, performability, or safety of the goods. For example, a statement made by a seller that an automobile will get forty-two miles to the gallon of gasoline or that a camera has automatic focus is an express warranty.

The Code further provides that a statement affirming the **value** of the goods or purporting merely to be the seller's **opinion** or recommendation of the goods does not create a warranty. Section 2–313(2); Section 2A–210(2). Such statements are not factual and do not deceive the ordinary buyer, who accepts them merely as opinions or as puffery (sales talk). For example, a statement by a salesperson that "this is one terrific deal" would likely be considered puffery. On the other hand, a statement that "this car gets thirty miles to the gallon" would be considered an express warranty, given its specificity. A statement of value may be an express warranty, however, where the seller states the price at which the goods were purchased from a former owner, or where she gives market figures relating to sales of similar goods. As statements of events, not mere opinions, these are statements of facts; and the seller is liable for breach of warranty if they are untrue. Moreover, although a statement of opinion by the seller is not ordinarily a warranty, if the seller is an expert and gives her opinion as such, she may be liable for breach of warranty. Thus, if an art expert states that a certain painting is a genuine Rembrandt, and this becomes part of the basis of the bargain, then the expert warrants the accuracy of her professional opinion.

An express warranty also can be created by the use of a **description** of the goods that becomes part of the basis of the bargain. Section 2–313(1)(b); Section 2A–210(1)(b). Under such a warranty, the seller expressly warrants that the goods shall conform to the description. Examples include statements regarding a particular brand or type of goods, technical specifications, and blueprints.

The use of a **sample** or model is another means of creating an express warranty. Section 2–313(1)(c); Section 2A–210(1)(c). If a sample or model is part of the basis of the bargain, the seller expressly warrants that the entire lot of goods sold shall conform to the sample or model. A sample is a good drawn from the bulk of goods comprising the subject matter of the sale. A model, by comparison, is offered for inspection when the subject matter is not at hand; it is not drawn from the bulk. Section 2–313, Comment 6.

◆ **SEE CASE 24-1**

CISG The seller must deliver goods that conform to quality and description required by the contract. In addition, the goods must possess the qualities of any sample or model used by the seller.

**Basis of Bargain** The Code does not require that the buyer rely on the affirmations, promises, descriptions, samples, or models the seller makes or uses but only that they constitute a part of the basis of the bargain. If they are part of the buyer's assumption underlying the sale, then reliance by the buyer is presumed. Some courts merely require that the buyer know of the affirmation or promise for it to be presumed to be part of the basis of the bargain. Relaxing the reliance requirement more often forces sellers to live up to their express warranties than does a rule requiring reliance.

Because they may constitute part of the basis of the bargain just as much as statements in advertisements or catalogs would, statements or promises the seller makes to the buyer prior to the sale may be express warranties. Furthermore, under the Code, statements or promises made by the seller subsequent to the contract of sale may become express warranties even though no new consideration is given. Sections 2–209(1) and 2A–208(1) provide that an agreement modifying a sale or lease needs no consideration to be binding. Thus, a statement, promise, or assurance with respect to the goods that the seller makes to the buyer at the time of delivery may be considered a binding modification of the prior contract of sale and held to be an express warranty basic to the bargain.

◆ **SEE CASE 24-2**

## IMPLIED WARRANTIES

An implied warranty, unlike an express warranty, is not found in the language of the sales contract or in a specific affirmation or promise by the seller. Instead, an **implied warranty** is an obligation imposed by operation of law upon the transfer of property or contract rights. This warranty, which arises out of the circumstances under which the parties enter into their contract, depends on factors such as the type of contract or sale entered into, the seller's merchant or nonmerchant status, the conduct of the parties, and the applicability of other statutes. The law has developed implied warranties not as something to which the parties must agree but as a departure from the early rule of *caveat emptor*.

**Merchantability** At early common law, a seller was not held to any implied warranty as to the quality of goods. Under the Code, however, a **merchant seller** impliedly warrants the merchantability of goods that are of the kind in which she deals. The implied warranty of **merchantability** provides that the goods are reasonably fit for the ordinary purposes for which they are used, pass without objection in the trade under the contract description, and are of fair, average quality. Section 2–314; Section 2A–212. Because the warranty arises as a matter of law, the buyer does not need to prove that she relied on the warranty or that the warranty formed a basis of the bargain. The warranty applies automatically unless disclaimed by the seller. The official Comments to the Code further provide that a contract for the sale of secondhand goods "involves only such obligation as is appropriate to such goods for that is their description."

The Code in Sections 2–314(3) and 2A–212(3) expressly provides that implied warranties may arise from course of dealing or usage of trade. Thus, where the seller of a new automobile failed to lubricate it before delivery to the buyer, and the evidence established that it was the regular custom and usage of new car dealers to do so, the seller was held liable to the buyer for the resulting damages to the automobile in an action for breach of implied warranty.

The Code further provides that the serving for value of food or drink to be consumed on the premises or elsewhere is a sale. Section 2–314(1). Where a nonedible substance in food causes an injury, however, an implied warranty may not exist if the substance is natural to the food. A minority of jurisdictions distinguish between natural objects in food, such as fish bones in fish, and foreign objects such as a pebble, a piece of wire, or glass. The modern and majority test is the reasonable expectation of the consumer. That a substance is natural to a product in one stage of preparation does not necessarily imply that the consumer will reasonably anticipate or expect it to be in the final product.

◆ **SEE CASE 24-2**

CISG The seller must deliver goods, unless otherwise agreed, that are fit for any particular purpose expressly or impliedly made known to the seller by the buyer, except where the buyer did not rely on the seller's skill and judgment or when it was unreasonable for the buyer to rely on the seller.

**Fitness for Particular Purpose** Unlike the warranty of merchantability, the implied warranty of fitness for a particular purpose applies to *any* seller, whether he is a merchant or not. The **implied warranty of fitness for a particular purpose** arises if at the time of sale the seller had reason to know the buyer's particular purpose and that the buyer was relying upon the seller's skill and judgment to select suitable goods. Section 2–315; Section 2A–213.

The implied warranty of fitness for a particular purpose does not require any specific statement by the seller. Rather, the warranty requires only that the seller know that the buyer is relying on the seller's expertise in selecting a product for the buyer's specific purpose. The buyer need not specifically inform the seller of her particular purpose; it is sufficient if the seller has reason to know it. On the other hand, the implied warranty of fitness for a particular purpose would not arise if the buyer were to insist on a particular product and the seller simply conveyed it to her.

In contrast to the implied warranty of merchantability, the implied warranty of fitness for a particular purpose pertains to the *specific* purpose of the goods. The courts disagree whether an ordinary purpose of goods can be a particular purpose. Goods that are fit for ordinary purposes, and therefore are merchantable, may nonetheless be unfit for a particular purpose. A particular purpose may be a specific use or relate to a special situation in which the buyer intends to use the goods. Thus, if Miller has reason to know that Levine is purchasing a pair of shoes for mountain climbing and that Levine is relying upon Miller's judgment to furnish shoes suitable for this purpose, an implied warranty of fitness for a particular purpose would arise in this sale. If Miller sold Levine shoes suitable only for ordinary walking purposes, Miller would breach this implied warranty. Likewise, a buyer indicates to a seller that she needs a stamping machine to stamp ten thousand packages in an eight-hour period and that she relies on the seller to select an appropriate machine. By selecting the machine, the seller impliedly warrants that the machine selected will stamp ten thousand packages in an eight-hour period.

**Reliance** is therefore required for this warranty, unlike an express warranty, which requires only that the affirmation meet the broad "basis of the bargain" test, or the implied warranty of merchantability, which requires no proof of reliance. In order to prevail in a case involving an implied warranty of fitness for a particular purpose, the buyer must be able to demonstrate specifically that she relied on the seller's skill or judgment in selecting or furnishing suitable goods.

◆ **SEE CASE 24-2**

CISG The seller must deliver goods, unless otherwise agreed, that are fit for the purposes for which goods of the same description would ordinarily be used.

## OBSTACLES TO WARRANTY ACTIONS

In certain respects, warranty claims offer injured persons many advantages. Generally, a plaintiff need only establish the existence and breach of a warranty, an injury resulting from the breach, and the giving of notice in order to recover in a warranty action. This makes warranty claims easier to bring than negligence cases, which require the plaintiff to show that the defendant failed to act with due care—often a difficult task. Nonetheless, a number of technical obstacles limit the effectiveness of warranty as a basis for recovery. These include disclaimers of warranties, limitations or modifications of warranties, privity, notice of breach, and the conduct of the plaintiff. These obstacles vary considerably from jurisdiction to jurisdiction.

### DISCLAIMER OF WARRANTIES

The Code calls for a reasonable construction of words or conduct to **disclaim** (negate) or limit warranties. Section 2–316; Section 2A–214. The Code makes clear that the seller should not rely on a time-honored formula of words and expect to obtain a disclaimer that may go unnoticed by the buyer. To be effective, disclaimers must be positive, explicit, unequivocal, and conspicuous.

**Express Exclusions** A **warranty of title** may be excluded only by specific language or by certain circumstances, including judicial sales or sales by sheriffs, executors, or foreclosing lienors. Section 2–312(2); Section 2A–214(4). In the latter cases the seller is manifestly offering to sell only such right or title as he or a third person might have in the goods, as it is apparent that the goods are not the property of the person selling them.

In general, a seller cannot provide an **express warranty** and then disclaim it. A seller can avoid making an express warranty, however, by carefully refraining from making any promise or affirmation of fact relating to the goods, refraining from making a description of the goods, or refraining from using a sample or model. Section 2–313; Section 2A–210. A seller also may be able to negate an express warranty by *clear, specific, unambiguous* language. The Code, however, provides that words or conduct relevant to the creation of an express warranty and words or conduct negating a warranty shall be construed wherever reasonable as consistent with each other and that a negation or limitation is inoperative to the extent that such construction is unreasonable. Section 2–316; Section 2A–214. For example, a seller and a buyer enter into a written contract for the sale of a camera in which the seller warrants that the camera being sold is free of defects. This express warranty renders inoperative another provision in the contract that attempts to disclaim liability for any repairs necessitated by defects in the camera. The inconsistency between the two contractual provisions makes the disclaimer ineffective. Moreover, if the seller's disclaimer attempts to negate "all express warranties," this general disclaimer would be ineffective against the specific express warranty providing that the camera is free of defects. Finally, oral warranties made prior to the execution of a written agreement that contains an express disclaimer are subject to the parol evidence rule. Thus, as discussed in *Chapter 15*, if the parties intend the written contract to be the final and complete statement of the agreement between them, oral evidence of warranties that contradict the terms of the written contract is inadmissible.

To exclude an **implied warranty of merchantability**, the language of disclaimer must mention merchantability and, in the case of a writing, must be *conspicuous*. Section 2–316(2). Article 2A requires that a disclaimer of an implied warranty of merchantability mention merchantability, be in writing, and be conspicuous. Section 2A–214(2). For example, Bart wishes to buy a used refrigerator from Ben's Used Appliances Store for $100. Given the low purchase price, Ben is unwilling to guarantee the refrigerator's performance. Bart agrees to buy it with no warranty protection. To exclude the warranty, Ben writes conspicuously on the contract, "This refrigerator carries no warranties, including no warranty of MERCHANTABILITY." Ben has effectively disclaimed the implied warranty of merchantability. Some courts, however, do not require the disclaimer to be conspicuous where a *commercial* buyer has actual knowledge of the disclaimer. The Code's test for whether a provision is *conspicuous* is whether a reasonable person against whom the disclaimer is to operate ought to have noticed it. Section 1–201(10); Revised Section 1–201(b)(10). Revised Article 1 provides that conspicuous terms include (1) a heading in capitals equal to or greater in size than the surrounding text; or in contrasting type, font, or color to the surrounding text of the same or lesser size; and (2) language in the body of a record or display in larger type than the surrounding text; or in contrasting type, font, or color to the surrounding text of the same size; or set off from surrounding text of the same size by symbols or other marks that call attention to the language. Revised Section 1–201(b)(10). Whether a term is conspicuous is an issue for the court. Revised Section 1–201, Comment.

To exclude or to modify an **implied warranty of fitness** for the particular purpose of the buyer, the disclaimer must be in *writing* and *conspicuous*. Section 2–316(2); Section 2A–214(2).

*All implied warranties*, unless the circumstances indicate otherwise, are excluded by expressions like *as is, with all faults*, or other language plainly calling the buyer's attention to the exclusion of warranties. Section 2–316(3)(a); Section 2A–214(3)(a). Most courts require the "as is" clause to be conspicuous. Implied warranties also may be excluded by course of dealing, course of performance, or usage of trade. Section 2–316(3)(c); Section 2A–214(3)(c).

The courts will invalidate disclaimers they consider unconscionable. Sections 2–302 and 2A–108 of the Code, as discussed in *Chapter 21*, permit a court to limit the application of any contract or provision of a contract that it finds unconscionable.

◆ **SEE CASE 24-3**

**Buyer's Examination or Refusal to Examine** If the buyer inspects the goods before entering into the contract, *implied warranties* do not apply to defects that are apparent upon examination. The particular buyer's skill and the normal method of examining goods in the circumstances determine what defects are excluded by examination. Section 2–316, Comment 8. Moreover, no implied warranty exists as to defects that an examination ought to have revealed, not only where the buyer has examined the goods as fully as she desired, but also where the buyer has *refused* to examine the goods. Section 2–316(3)(b); Section 2A–214(3)(b).

A mere failure or omission to examine the goods is not a refusal to examine them. It is not enough that the goods were available for inspection and the buyer did not see fit to inspect them. In order for the buyer to have "refused to examine the goods," the seller *must* first have demanded that the buyer examine them.

◆ **SEE CASE 24-3**

CISG If at the time of entering into the sales contract the buyer knew or could not have been unaware of the lack of conformity, the seller is not liable for the warranty of particular purpose, ordinary purpose, or sale by sample or model.

**Federal Legislation Relating to Warranties of Consumer Goods** To protect purchasers of consumer goods (defined as "tangible personal property normally used for personal, family, or household purposes"), Congress enacted the **Magnuson-Moss Warranty Act**. The purpose of the Act is to prevent deception and to make available to consumer purchasers adequate information with respect to warranties. Some courts have applied the Act to leases.

The Federal Trade Commission administers and enforces the Act. The commission's guidelines regarding the type of information a seller must set forth in warranties of consumer products are aimed at providing the consumer with clear and useful information. More significantly, the act provides that a seller who makes a written warranty cannot disclaim *any* implied warranty. For a complete discussion of the Act, see *Chapter 42*.

◆ **SEE FIGURE 24-1: Warranties**

## LIMITATION OR MODIFICATION OF WARRANTIES

Sometimes a seller is willing to give some warranty protection but wishes to limit the scope or type of protection she gives. For example, a seller who is willing to repair or replace

◆ **FIGURE 24-1: Warranties**

| Type of Warranty | How Created | What is Warranted | How Disclaimed |
|---|---|---|---|
| **Title (Section 2–312)/Use and Possession (2A–211)** | • Seller contracts to sell goods | • Good title<br>• Rightful transfer<br>• Not subject to lien | • Specific language<br>• Circumstances giving buyer reason to know that seller does not claim title |
| **Express (Section 2–313; Section 2A–210)** | • Affirmation of fact<br>• Promise<br>• Description<br>• Sample or model | • Conform to affirmation<br>• Conform to promise<br>• Conform to description<br>• Conform to sample or model | • Specific language (extremely difficult) |
| **Merchantability (Section 2–314; Section 2A–212*)** | • Merchant sells goods | • Fit for ordinary purpose<br>• Adequately contained, packaged, and labeled | • Must mention "merchantability"<br>• If in writing must be conspicuous/in lease must be in writing and conspicuous<br>• As-is sale<br>• Buyer examination<br>• Course of dealing, course of performance, usage of trade |
| **Fitness for a particular purpose (Section 2–315; Section 2A–213*)** | • Seller knows buyer is relying upon seller to select goods suitable for buyer's particular purpose | • Fit for particular purpose | • No buzzwords necessary<br>• Must be in writing and conspicuous<br>• As-is sale<br>• Buyer examination<br>• Course of dealing, course of performance, usage of trade |

* except in a finance lease

a defective product may not be willing to pay consequential damages, such as the buyer's lost profits, arising from any product defects. Sections 2–719 and 2A–503 of the Code permit a seller to *limit* or *modify* the buyer's remedies for breach of warranty. Two important exceptions to the seller's right are Sections 2–719(3) and 2A–503(3), which prohibit "unconscionable" limitations or exclusions of consequential damages. Specifically, the limitation of consequential damages for injury to the person in the case of consumer goods is prima facie unconscionable.

◆ **SEE CASE 21-3**

In some cases, a seller may choose not to limit the buyer's rights to seek damages for breach of warranty but to impose time limits within which the warranty is effective. Except for instances of unconscionability, the Code permits such clauses; it does not, however, permit any attempt to shorten to less than one year the time period for filing an action for personal injury.

## PRIVITY OF CONTRACT

Because of the association of warranties with contracts, a principle of law in the nineteenth century established that a plaintiff could not recover for breach of warranty unless he was in a contractual relationship with the defendant. This relationship is known as privity of contract.

**Horizontal privity** pertains to noncontracting parties who are injured by the defective goods; this group would include users, consumers, and bystanders who are not the contracting purchaser. Horizontal privity determines who benefits from a warranty and who may, therefore, sue for its breach.

Under this rule, a warranty by seller Ingrid to buyer Sylvester, who resells the goods to purchaser Lyle under a similar warranty, gives Lyle no rights against Ingrid. There is no privity of contract between Ingrid and Lyle. In the event of breach of warranty, Lyle may recover only from his seller, Sylvester, who in turn may recover from Ingrid.

The Code relaxes the requirement of horizontal privity of contract by permitting recovery on a seller's warranty, at a minimum, to members of the buyer's family or household or to guests in his home. Section 2–318 of the Code provides three alternative sections from which the States may select. *Alternative A*, the least comprehensive and most widely adopted, provides that a seller's warranty, whether express or implied, extends to any natural person who is in the family or household of the buyer or who is a guest in his home, if it is reasonable to expect that such person may use, consume, or be affected by the goods, and who is injured in person by breach of the warranty. *Alternative B* extends Alternative A to any natural person who may reasonably be expected to use, consume, or be affected by the goods. *Alternative C* further expands the coverage of the section to any person, not just natural persons, and to property damage as well as personal injury. (A natural person would not include artificial entities such as corporations.) A seller may not exclude or limit the operation of this section for injury to a person. Section 2A–216 provides the same alternatives with slight modifications.

Nonetheless, the Code merely sets a minimum standard that the States may expand through case law. Most States have judicially accepted the Code's invitation to relax the requirements of horizontal privity and, for all practical purposes, have *eliminated* horizontal privity in warranty cases.

**Vertical privity**, in determining who is liable for breach of warranty, pertains to remote sellers within the chain of distribution, such as manufacturers and wholesalers, with whom the consumer purchaser has not entered into a contract. Although the Code adopts a neutral position regarding vertical privity, the courts in most States have eliminated the requirement of vertical privity in warranty actions.

### NOTICE OF BREACH OF WARRANTY

When a buyer has accepted a tender of goods that are not as warranted by the seller, she is required to notify the seller of any breach of warranty within a reasonable time after she has discovered or should have discovered it. If the buyer fails to notify the seller of any breach within a reasonable time, she is barred from any remedy against the seller. Section 2–607(3)(a); Section 2A–516(3)(a).

The purpose of the reasonable notice requirement is (1) to enable the seller to cure the defect or to minimize the buyer's loss, (2) to provide the seller an opportunity to prepare for conflict resolution and litigation, and (3) to provide the seller with an end point to liability. In determining whether notice was provided within a reasonable time, commercial standards apply to a merchant buyer whereas standards designed to preserve a good faith consumer's right to his remedy apply to a retail consumer.

### PLAINTIFF'S CONDUCT

Because warranty liability developed in the law of sales and contracts, in most States, contributory negligence of the buyer is no defense to an action against the seller for breach of warranty. In a number of States, however, comparative negligence statutes apply to warranty actions. (Comparative negligence is discussed more fully later in this chapter.)

If the buyer discovers a defect in the goods that may cause injury and then proceeds to make use of the goods, he will not be permitted to recover damages from the seller for loss or injuries caused by such use. This is not contributory negligence but **voluntary assumption** of a known risk.

## STRICT LIABILITY IN TORT

The most recent and far-reaching development in the field of products liability is that of strict liability in tort. All but a very few States have now accepted the concept, which is embodied in **Section 402A** of the Restatement, Second, of Torts. In 1997 a new Restatement of the Law, Third, Torts: Products Liability (the Restatement Third) was promulgated. It is far more comprehensive than the second Restatement in dealing with the liability of commercial sellers and distributors of goods for harm caused by their products. (This revision will be discussed more fully later in this chapter.)

Section 402A imposes **strict liability in tort** on merchant sellers for both personal injuries and property damage resulting from selling a product in a **defective condition, unreasonably dangerous** to the user or consumer. Section 402A applies even though "the seller has exercised all possible care in the preparation and sale of his product." Thus, negligence is not the basis of liability in strict liability cases. The essential distinction between the two doctrines is that actions in strict liability do not require the plaintiff to prove that the injury-producing defect resulted from any specific act of negligence of the seller. Strict liability actions focus on the product, not on the conduct of the manufacturer. Courts in strict liability cases are interested in the fact that a product defect arose—not in how it arose. Thus, even an "innocent" manufacturer—one who has not been negligent—may be liable if his product contains a defect that injures a consumer.

The reasons asserted in support of imposing strict liability in tort upon manufacturers and assemblers of products include the following: (1) consumers should be given maximum protection against dangerous defects in products; (2) manufacturers are in the best position to prevent or reduce the hazards to life and health in defective products; (3) manufacturers, who realize the most profit from the total sales of their goods, are best able to carry the financial burden of such liability by distributing it among the public as a cost of doing business; (4) manufacturers utilize wholesalers and retailers merely as conduits in the marketing of their products and should not be permitted to avoid liability simply because they have no contract with the user or consumer; and (5) because the manufacturer is liable to his purchaser who may be a wholesaler who in turn is liable to the retailer who in turn is liable to the ultimate purchaser, time and expense is saved by making liability direct rather than a chain reaction.

Although liability for personal injuries caused by a product in an unreasonably dangerous defective condition is usually associated with sales of goods, such liability also exists with respect to **leases** and **bailments** of defective goods. The extension of liability to lessors and bailors of goods is not surprising in view of the rationale the courts have developed in imposing strict liability in tort upon manufacturers and sellers of products. The danger to which the public is exposed by defectively manufactured cars and trucks traveling on the highways, for example, does not differ greatly from the hazards of defective cars and trucks leased to operators.

## REQUIREMENTS OF STRICT LIABILITY

Section 402A imposes strict liability in tort on merchant sellers for both personal injuries and property damage that result from selling a product in a defective condition unreasonably dangerous to the user or consumer. Specifically, this section provides:

> **1.** One who sells any product in a defective condition unreasonably dangerous to the user or consumer or to his property is subject to liability for physical harm thereby caused to the ultimate user or consumer, or to his property, if (a) the seller is engaged in the business of selling such a product, and (b) it is expected to and does reach the user or consumer without substantial change in the condition in which it is sold.
>
> **2.** The rule stated in Subsection (1) applies although (a) the seller has exercised all possible care in the preparation and sale of his product, and (b) the user or consumer has not bought the product from or entered into any contractual relation with the seller.

Negligence, as previously stated, is not the basis of this liability; it applies even though "the seller has exercised all possible care in the preparation and sale of his product." The seller is not an insurer of the goods that he manufactures or sells, however; and the essential requirements for strict product liability are that (1) the defendant was engaged in the business of selling such a product; (2) the defendant sold the product in a defective condition; (3) the defective condition was one that made the product unreasonably dangerous to the user or consumer or to his property; (4) the defect in the product existed at the time it left the hands of the defendant; (5) the plaintiff sustained physical harm or property damage by use or consumption of the product; and (6) the defective condition was the proximate cause of such injury or damage.

This liability is imposed by law as a matter of public policy and does not depend upon contract, either express or implied. It does not require reliance by the injured user or consumer upon any statements made by the manufacturer or seller. The liability is not limited to persons in a buyer-seller relationship; thus, neither vertical nor horizontal privity is required. No notice of the defect is required to have been given by the injured user or consumer. The liability, furthermore, is generally not subject to disclaimer, exclusion, or modification by contractual agreement. Rather, the liability is solely in tort and arises out of the common law; it is not governed by the provisions of the UCC.

The majority of courts considering the question have held that Section 402A imposes liability for injury to person and damage to property (the economic loss doctrine) but not for commercial loss (such as loss of bargain or profits), which is recoverable in an action for breach of warranty. A minority of States have held, however, that commercial loss may be recovered in tort where the defect creates an unreasonable risk of personal injury or property damage, even though the only damage resulting is to the defective goods themselves.

### MERCHANT SELLERS

Section 402A imposes liability only upon a person who is in the *business* of selling the product involved. It does *not* apply to an occasional seller, such as a person who trades in his used car or who sells his lawn mower to a neighbor. In this respect, the section is similar to the implied warranty of merchantability, which applies only to sales by a merchant with respect to goods of the type in which he deals. A growing number of jurisdictions recognize the applicability of strict liability in tort to merchant sellers of *used* goods.

### DEFECTIVE CONDITION

In an action against a defendant manufacturer or other seller to recover damages under the rule of strict liability in tort, the plaintiff must prove a defective condition in the product, but she is not required to prove how or why the product became defective. In an action based on Section 402A, the reason for or cause of the defect is not material, although it would be in an action based on negligence. Under a strict liability approach, a manufacturer will be held liable even though it did not act negligently. For example, if the Quality Bottling Company, despite its having the most stringent quality control program in the industry, through no negligence of its own manufactures a bottle that explodes in the hands of a consumer, the company would be liable to the consumer under Section 402A. Whether or not Quality Bottling Company acted negligently is irrelevant. The plaintiff, however, must show that at the time she was injured the condition of the product was not substantially changed from the condition in which the manufacturer or seller sold it. In general, defects may arise through faulty manufacturing, faulty product design, or inadequate warning, labeling, packaging, or instructions. Some States, however, and the Restatement Third do not impose strict liability for a design defect or a failure to provide proper warnings or instructions.

**Manufacturing Defect** A manufacturing defect occurs when the product is not properly made; that is, it fails to meet its own manufacturing specifications. For instance, suppose a chair is manufactured with legs designed to be attached by four screws and glue. If such a chair were produced without the required screws, this would constitute a manufacturing defect.

**Design Defect** A product contains a design defect when, despite its being produced as specified, the product is dangerous or hazardous because of inadequate design. Design defects can result from a number of causes, including poor engineering and poor choice of materials. An example of a design defect that received great notoriety was the Ford Pinto. A number of courts found the car to be inadequately designed because its fuel tank had been placed too close to its rear axle, causing the tank to rupture upon impact from the rear.

Section 402A provides no guidance in determining which injury-producing designs should give rise to strict liability and which should not; consequently, the courts have adopted widely varying approaches in applying 402A to defective design cases.

At one extreme, a few courts have taken a very literal approach to Section 402A by ruling that a manufacturer is strictly liable for injuries caused by a design that a reasonable person would not have produced had he known of the design's harmful character at the time it was made. Whether the manufacturer did or could have known of the risk associated with the design, or of an alternative design that could have avoided the risk, is deemed irrelevant for purposes of strict liability. Manufacturers, in effect, are held liable for hazards that were unknowable at the time they manufactured their products.

A slightly larger number of courts, although still a minority, have taken the opposite approach: recognizing no difference between negligence and strict liability principles in defective design cases, they apply negligence principles to such cases. Unless the plaintiff can demonstrate that the manufacturer knew, or should have known, of a safer, cost-effective design, these courts will not hold the manufacturer liable.

The majority of courts have ostensibly adopted a middle-of-the-road approach, stating that strict liability cases should be viewed differently from negligence cases. Beyond reciting that strict liability cases focus on the product, not on the manufacturer's conduct, these courts have yet to clarify what the different view implies. Nevertheless, virtually none of them has upheld a judgment in a strict liability case in which the defendant demonstrated that the "**state of the art**" was such that the manufacturer (1) neither knew nor could have known of a product hazard, or (2) if he knew of the product hazard, could have designed a safer product given existing technology. Thus, almost all courts evaluate the design of a product on the basis of the dangers that could have been known when the product was produced or sold.

In deciding design defect cases, courts identify any government safety standards applicable to the design involved in the product liability lawsuit. If such a standard exists and the manufacturer's failure to follow it caused the plaintiff's injury, the courts tend to impose liability automatically. On the other hand, a manufacturer's compliance with safety standards does not equal automatic relief from liability. If a plaintiff can demonstrate that a safer, cost-effective design was available to the manufacturer, the plaintiff can still prevail in a product liability lawsuit even though the manufacturer complied with a government safety standard.

**Failure to Warn** A seller is under a duty to provide adequate warning of possible danger, to provide appropriate directions for safe use, and to package the product safely. Warnings do not, however, always protect sellers from liability. A seller who could have designed or manufactured a product in a safe but cost-effective manner, but who instead chooses to produce the product cheaply and to provide a warning of the product's hazards, cannot escape liability simply through the warning. Warnings usually will avoid liability only if there are no cost-effective designs or manufacturing processes available to reduce a risk of injury.

The duty to give a warning arises out of a foreseeable danger of physical harm resulting from the normal or probable use of the product and out of the likelihood that, unless warned, the user or consumer will not ordinarily be aware of such danger or hazard. For example, a seller may reasonably assume that those with allergies to products such as eggs or strawberries will know of their allergies and therefore need not be warned of this risk. On the other hand, if a product contains an ingredient to which a substantial number of persons are allergic, and the ingredient is one whose danger is not generally known or, if known, is one that the consumer would not reasonably expect to find in the product, the seller is required to give a warning about it. Under strict liability principles, sellers are generally required to provide warnings against uses for which a product is not marketed, including certain instances of consumer misuse, if such uses are foreseeable by the manufacturer and the consumer is unlikely to recognize the hazard.

Section 402A imposes liability in failure-to-warn cases only where the seller "has knowledge, or by the application of reasonable, developed human skill and foresight should have knowledge, of the … danger." Comment j. In effect, the seller is held to the knowledge and skill of an expert in the field. Some courts have ruled that this means a manufacturer not only must keep abreast of scientific knowledge, discoveries, and advances, but also must conduct research to determine whether his product contains hazards. Most courts today require proof that the manufacturer knew, or could have known, of a product hazard before imposing liability for a failure to warn.

◆ SEE CASE 24-4

### UNREASONABLY DANGEROUS

Section 402A liability applies only if the defective product is **unreasonably dangerous** to the user or consumer. An unreasonably dangerous product is one that contains a danger beyond that which the ordinary consumer, who purchases the product with common knowledge of its characteristics, would contemplate. Thus,

> good whiskey is not unreasonably dangerous merely because it will make some people drunk, and is especially dangerous to alcoholics; but bad whiskey, containing a dangerous amount of fuel oil, is unreasonably dangerous. Good tobacco is not unreasonably dangerous merely because the effects of smoking may be harmful; but tobacco containing something like marijuana may be unreasonably dangerous. Good butter is not unreasonably dangerous merely because, if such be the case, it deposits cholesterol in the arteries and leads to heart attacks; but bad butter, contaminated with poisonous fish oil, is unreasonably dangerous. Comment i to Section 402A.

Most courts have left the question of reasonable consumer expectations to the jury.

◆ SEE CASE 24-5

## OBSTACLES TO RECOVERY

Few of the obstacles to recovery in warranty cases present serious problems to plaintiffs in strict liability actions brought pursuant to Section 402A because this section was drafted largely to avoid such obstacles.

### DISCLAIMERS AND NOTICE

Comment m to Section 402A provides that the basis of strict liability rests solely in tort and therefore is not subject to contractual defenses. The comment specifically states that strict product liability is not governed by the Code, that it is not affected by contractual limitations or disclaimers, and that it is not subject to any requirement that the injured party gives notice to the seller within a reasonable time. Nevertheless, most courts have allowed clear and specific disclaimers of Section 402A liability in *commercial* transactions between merchants of relatively equal economic power.

### PRIVITY

With respect to horizontal privity, the majority of States hold that the strict liability in tort of manufacturers and other sellers extends not only to buyers, users, and consumers, but also to injured bystanders. Bystanders to whom such liability has extended include the occupants of an automobile injured in a collision with another car due to the other car's having defective brakes; a golfer killed by a runaway golf cart that started due to a faulty transmission system; a bystander injured by a runaway truck started by a short circuit; a bystander injured by the explosion of a defective beer keg; a neighbor injured by the explosion of a propane gas tank; and a bystander injured by the explosion of a shotgun barrel caused by a defective shell. Some States, however, limit liability to foreseeable purchasers or users of the product.

In terms of **vertical privity**, strict liability in tort imposes liability on any seller who is engaged in the business of selling the product, including a wholesaler or distributor as well as the manufacturer and retailer. The rule of strict liability in tort also applies to the manufacturer of a defective component that has been incorporated into a larger product where the manufacturer of the finished product has made no essential change in the component.

### PLAINTIFF'S CONDUCT

Many product liability defenses relate to the conduct of the plaintiff. The contention common to all of them is that the plaintiff's improper conduct so contributed to the plaintiff's injury that it would be unfair to blame the product or its seller.

**Contributory Negligence** Contributory negligence is conduct on the part of the plaintiff that falls below the standard to which he should conform for his own protection and that is the legal cause of the plaintiff's harm. Under traditional negligence law principles, if the negligence of the plaintiff together with that of the defendant proximately caused the plaintiff's injury, the plaintiff could not recover *any* damages from the defendant. It did not matter whether the plaintiff's contributory negligence was slight or extensive. Because strict liability is designed to assess liability without fault, Section 402A rejects contributory negligence as a defense. Thus, a seller cannot defend a strict liability lawsuit on the basis of a plaintiff's negligent failure to discover a defect or to guard against its possibility. But, as discussed below, contributory negligence in the form of an assumption of the risk can bar recovery under Section 402A.

**Comparative Negligence** The harshness of the contributory negligence doctrine has caused all but a few States to reject the all-or-nothing rule of contributory negligence and to substitute the doctrine of **comparative negligence**. Under comparative negligence, damages are apportioned between the parties in proportion to the degree of fault or negligence found against them.

Despite Section 402A's bar of contributory negligence in strict liability cases, some courts apply comparative negligence to strict liability cases. (Some courts use the term **comparative responsibility** rather than *comparative negligence.*) There are two basic types of comparative negligence or comparative responsibility. One is **pure comparative responsibility**, which simply reduces the plaintiff's recovery in proportion to her fault, whatever that may be. Thus, the recovery of a plaintiff found to be 80 percent at fault in causing an accident in which she suffered a $100,000 loss would be limited to 20 percent of her damages, or $20,000. By comparison, under **modified comparative responsibility**, the plaintiff recovers according to the general principles of comparative responsibility *unless* she is more than 50 percent responsible for her injuries, in which case she recovers nothing. The majority of comparative negligence States follow the modified comparative responsibility approach.

**Voluntary Assumption of the Risk** Under the Second Restatement of Torts, assumption of risk is a defense in an action based on strict liability in tort. Basically, **assumption of risk** is the plaintiff's express or implied consent to encounter a known danger. The user or consumer who voluntarily uses goods in an unusual, inappropriate, or improper manner for which they were not intended, such use being, under the circumstances, unreasonable, assumes the risk of injuries that result from such use. Thus, a person who drives an automobile after realizing that the brakes are not working or an employee who attempts to remove a foreign object from a high-speed roller press without shutting off the power has assumed the risk of his own injury. In a comparative negligence or comparative responsibility State, assumption of the risk would either reduce or bar recovery, depending on the degree to which it contributed to the plaintiff's injury.

To establish such a defense, the defendant must show that (1) the plaintiff actually knew and appreciated the particular risk or danger the defect created, (2) the plaintiff voluntarily encountered the risk while realizing the danger, and (3) the plaintiff's decision to encounter the known risk was unreasonable.

The Third Restatement of Torts: Apportionment of Liability has abandoned the doctrine of implied voluntary assumption of risk in tort actions generally; it is no longer a defense that the plaintiff was aware of a risk and voluntarily confronted it. This new Restatement limits the defense of assumption of risk to express assumption of risk, which consists of a contract between the plaintiff and another person to absolve the other person from liability for future harm. Section 2.

**Misuse or Abuse of the Product** Closely connected to voluntary assumption of the risk is the valid defense of misuse or abuse of the product by the injured party. **Misuse** or **abuse** occurs when the injured party knows, or should know, that he is using the product in a manner not contemplated by the seller. The major difference between misuse or abuse and assumption of the risk is that the former includes actions that the injured party does not know to be dangerous, whereas the latter does not. Instances of such misuse or abuse include standing on a rocking chair to change a light bulb or using a lawn mower to trim hedges.

The courts, however, have significantly limited this defense by requiring that the misuse or abuse not be foreseeable by the seller. If a use is foreseeable, then the seller must take measures to guard against it. For example, if William stands on a rocking chair to change a light bulb and is injured when the chair tilts and tips over, his misuse of the chair would bar his recovery. Similarly, if Jenny hammers a nail with a hair dryer and suffers an eye injury when a chip flies from the dryer, she will be unsuccessful in a claim against the manufacturer.

## SUBSEQUENT ALTERATION

Section 402A provides that liability exists only if the product reaches "the user or consumer without substantial change in the condition in which it is sold." Accordingly, most, but not all, courts would not hold a manufacturer liable for a faulty oil pump if a car dealer were to remove the part and make significant changes in it prior to reinstalling it in an automobile.

## STATUTE OF REPOSE

Numerous lawsuits have been brought against manufacturers many years after a product was first sold. In one case, a manufacturer was successfully sued twenty-two years after a defective water meter was first purchased and fourteen years after it was installed in the plaintiff's home. In another case, Volkswagen of America was ordered to pay $1.8 million in damages in an accident case centering around a missing door latch costing $0.35. The accident occurred ten years after the car had been manufactured and nine years after Volkswagen had informed its dealers about the defect.

In response, many States have adopted **statutes of repose**. These enactments limit the time period—typically to between six and twelve years—for which a manufacturer is liable for injury caused by a defective product. After the statutory period has elapsed, a manufacturer ceases to be liable for such harm.

## LIMITATIONS ON DAMAGES

More than half of the States have limited the punitive damages that a plaintiff can collect in a product liability lawsuit. They have done this by a number of means, including the following:

1. Placing caps on the amount of damages that can be awarded, with caps ranging from $50,000 to $5 million;
2. Providing for the State to receive all or a portion of any punitive damages awarded with the State's share ranging from 35 percent to 100 percent in order to reduce the plaintiff's incentive to bring products liability suits;
3. Providing for bifurcated trials; that is, separate hearings to determine liability and punitive damages;
4. Increasing the plaintiff's burden of proof for recovery of punitive damages, with most states adopting the "clear and convincing" evidence standard;
5. Requiring proportionality between compensatory and punitive damages by specifying an acceptable ratio between the two types of damages.

◆ SEE FIGURE 24-2: **Products Liabilities**

## RESTATEMENT OF TORTS (THIRD): PRODUCTS LIABILITY

The Restatement (Third) of Torts: Products Liability makes some significant changes in product liability. The adoption of the new Restatement by the States has been a slow process and the great majority of States continue to follow Section 402A of the Second Restatement of Torts.

The new Restatement expands Section 402A into an entire treatise of its own, comprising more than twenty sections. The Restatement Third does not use the term strict liability but instead defines separate liability standards for each type of defect. The new Restatement continues to cover anyone engaged in the business of selling or distributing a defective product if the defect causes harm to persons or property. Its major provision (Section 2) defines a product as defective "when, at the time of sale or distribution, it contains a manufacturing defect, is defective in design, or is defective because of inadequate instructions or warnings." Thus, Section 2 explicitly recognizes the three types of product defects discussed above: manufacturing defects, design defects, and failure to warn. However, as discussed below, strict liability is imposed

◆ FIGURE 24-2: **Products Liabilities**

| Type of Warranty | Warranty of Merchantability* | Strict Liability in Tort (§402A) |
|---|---|---|
| **Condition of Goods Creating Liability** | Not fit for ordinary purposes | Defective condition, unreasonably dangerous |
| **Type of Transaction Covered** | Sales and leases (except finance leases); some courts apply to bailments of goods | Sales, leases, and bailments of goods |
| **Disclaimer** | Must mention "merchantability"<br>If in writing, must be conspicuous (lease must be in writing)<br>Must not be unconscionable<br>Sales subject to Magnuson-Moss Act/leases may be subject | Not possible in consumer transactions; may be permitted in commercial transactions |
| **Notice to Seller** | Required within reasonable time | Not required |
| **Causation** | Required | Required |
| **Who May Sue** | In some States, buyer and the buyer's family or guests in home; in other States, any person who may be expected to use, consume, or be affected by goods | Any user or consumer of product; also, in most States, any bystander |
| **Compensable Harms** | Personal injury, property damage, economic loss | Personal injury, property damage |
| **Who May Be Sued** | Seller or lessor who is a merchant with respect to the goods sold | Seller who is a merchant with respect to the goods sold |

* The warranty of fitness for a particular purpose differs from the warranty of merchantability in the following respects: (1) the condition that triggers liability is the failure of the goods to perform according to the particular purpose of the warranty, (2) a disclaimer need not mention "fitness for a particular purpose" but must be in writing, and (3) applies to any seller.

only on the first of these, while liability for inadequate design or warning is imposed only for foreseeable risks of harm that could have been avoided by the use of an alternative *reasonable* design, warning, or instruction.

### MANUFACTURING DEFECT

Section 2(a) provides that "A product ... contains a manufacturing defect when the product departs from its intended design even though all possible care was exercised in the preparation and marketing of the product." Therefore, sellers and distributors of products remain strictly liable for manufacturing defects, although a plaintiff may seek to recover based upon allegations and proof of negligent manufacture. In actions against the manufacturer, the plaintiff ordinarily must prove that the defect existed in the product when it left the manufacturer.

### DESIGN DEFECT

Section 2(b) states:

> A product ... is defective in design when the foreseeable risks of harm posed by the product could have been reduced or avoided by the adoption of a reasonable alternative design by the seller or other distributor, or a predecessor in the commercial chain of distribution, and the omission of the reasonable alternative design renders the product not reasonably safe.

This rule pulls back from a strict liability standard and imposes a negligence-like standard by requiring that the defect be reasonably foreseeable and that it could have been avoided by a reasonable alternative design. The Comments explain that this standard involves resolving "whether a reasonable alternative design would, at a reasonable cost, have reduced the foreseeable risk of harm posed by the product and, if so, whether the omission of the alternative design by the seller ... rendered the product not reasonably safe." The burden rests upon the plaintiff to demonstrate the existence of a reasonable alternative safer design that would have reduced the foreseeable risks of harm. However, consumer expectations do not constitute an independent standard for judging the defectiveness of product designs.

### FAILURE TO WARN

Section 2(c) provides:

> A product ... is defective because of inadequate instructions or warnings when the foreseeable risks of harm posed by the product could have been reduced or avoided by the provision of reasonable instructions or warnings by the seller or other distributor, or a predecessor in the commercial chain of distribution and the omission of the instructions or warnings renders the product not reasonably safe.

Commercial product sellers must provide reasonable instructions and warnings about risks of injury associated with their products. The omission of warnings sufficient to allow informed decisions by reasonably foreseeable users or consumers renders the product not reasonably safe at time of sale. A seller, however, is under a duty to warn only if it knew or should have known of the risks involved. Moreover, warning about risks is effective only if an alternative design to avoid the risk cannot reasonably be implemented. Whenever safer products can be reasonably designed at a reasonable cost, adoption of the safer design is required rather than using a warning or instructions.

## CHAPTER SUMMARY

### WARRANTIES

**TYPES OF WARRANTIES**

**Definition of Warranty** an obligation of the seller to the buyer concerning title, quality, characteristics, or condition of goods

**Warranty of Title** the obligation of a seller to convey the right to ownership without any lien (in a lease the warranty protects the lessee's right to possess and use the goods)

**Express Warranty** an affirmation of fact or promise about the goods or a description, including a sample, of the goods that becomes part of the basis of the bargain

**Implied Warranty** a contractual obligation, arising out of certain circumstances of the sale, imposed by operation of law and not found in the language of the sales contract

- ***Merchantability*** warranty by a merchant seller that the goods are reasonably fit for the ordinary purpose for which they are manufactured or sold, pass without objection in the trade under the contract description, and are of fair, average quality

- ***Fitness for Particular Purpose*** warranty by any seller that goods are reasonably fit for a particular purpose if, at the time of contracting, the seller had reason to know the buyer's particular purpose and that the buyer was relying on the seller's skill and judgment to furnish suitable goods

---

**OBSTACLES TO WARRANTY ACTIONS**

**Disclaimers of Warranties** negations of warranties
- ***Express Warranty*** not usually possible to disclaim
- ***Warranty of Title*** may be excluded or modified by specific language or by certain circumstances, including judicial sale or a sale by a sheriff, executor, or foreclosing lienor
- ***Implied Warranty of Merchantability*** the disclaimer must mention "merchantability" and, in the case of a writing, must be conspicuous (in a lease the disclaimer must be in writing)
- ***Implied Warranty of Fitness for a Particular Purpose*** the disclaimer must be in writing and conspicuous
- ***Other Disclaimers of Implied Warranties*** the implied warranties of merchantability and fitness for a particular purpose may also be disclaimed (1) by expressions like "as is," "with all faults," or other similar language; (2) by course of dealing, course of performance, or usage of trade; or (3) as to defects an examination ought to have revealed where the buyer has examined the goods or where the buyer has refused to examine the goods
- ***Federal Legislation Relating to Warranties of Consumer Goods*** the Magnuson-Moss Warranty Act protects purchasers of consumer goods by providing that warranty information be clear and useful and that a seller who makes a written warranty cannot disclaim any implied warranty

**Limitation or Modification of Warranties** permitted as long as it is not unconscionable

**Privity of Contract** a contractual relationship between parties that was necessary at common law to maintain a lawsuit
- ***Horizontal Privity*** doctrine determining who benefits from a warranty and who therefore may bring a cause of action; the Code provides three alternatives
- ***Vertical Privity*** doctrine determining who in the chain of distribution is liable for a breach of warranty; the Code has not adopted a position on this

**Notice of Breach** if the buyer fails to notify the seller of any breach within a reasonable time, she is barred from any remedy against the seller

**Plaintiff's Conduct**
- ***Contributory Negligence*** is not a defense
- ***Voluntary Assumption of the Risk*** is a defense

---

## STRICT LIABILITY IN TORT

**NATURE**

**General Rule** imposes tort liability on merchant sellers for both personal injuries and property damage for selling a product in a defective condition unreasonably dangerous to the user or consumer

**Defective Condition**
- ***Manufacturing Defect*** by failing to meet its own manufacturing specifications, the product is not properly made
- ***Design Defect*** the product, though made as designed, is dangerous because the design is inadequate
- ***Failure to Warn*** failure to provide adequate warnings of possible danger or to provide appropriate directions for use of a product

**Unreasonably Dangerous** contains a danger beyond that which would be contemplated by the ordinary consumer

| | |
|---|---|
| **OBSTACLES TO RECOVERY** | **Contractual Defenses** defenses such as privity, disclaimers, and notice generally do not apply to tort liability<br>**Plaintiff's Conduct**<br>• ***Contributory Negligence*** not a defense in the majority of States<br>• ***Comparative Negligence*** most States have applied the rule of comparative negligence to strict liability in tort<br>• ***Voluntary Assumption of the Risk*** express assumption of risk is a defense to an action based upon strict liability; some States apply implied assumption of risk to strict liability cases<br>• ***Misuse or Abuse of the Product*** is a defense<br>**Subsequent Alteration** liability exists only if the product reaches the user or consumer without substantial change in the condition in which it is sold<br>**Statute of Repose** limits the time period for which a manufacturer is liable for injury caused by its product<br>**Limitations on Damages** many States have limited the punitive damages that a plaintiff can collect in a product liability lawsuit |
| **RESTATEMENT (THIRD) OF TORTS: PRODUCTS LIABILITY** | **General Rule** one engaged in the business of selling products who sells a defective product is subject to liability for harm to persons or property caused by the defect<br>**Manufacturing Defect** a seller is held to strict liability when the product departs from its intended design<br>**Design Defect** a product is defective when the foreseeable risks of harm posed by the product could have been reduced or avoided by the adoption of a reasonable alternative design<br>**Failure to Warn** a product is defective because of inadequate instructions or warnings when the foreseeable risks of harm posed by the product could have been reduced or avoided by the provision of reasonable instructions or warnings |

# CASES

## CASE 24-1

### Express Warranties

### BELDEN INC. v. AMERICAN ELECTRONIC COMPONENTS, INC.

Court of Appeals of Indiana, 2008

885 N.E.2d 751, 66 UCC Rep.Serv.2d 399

http://www.in.gov/judiciary/opinions/pdf/05090802mpb.pdf

**Barnes, J.**

Belden, Inc., and Belden Wire & Cable Company (collectively "Belden") * * * manufactures wire, and [American Electronic Components, Inc ] AEC manufactures automobile sensors. Since 1989, AEC, in repeated transactions, has purchased wire from Belden to use in its sensors.

In 1996 and 1997, Belden sought to comply with AEC's quality control program and provided detailed information to AEC regarding the materials it used to manufacture its wire. In its assurances, Belden indicated that it would use insulation from Quantum Chemical Corp. ("Quantum"). In June 2003, however, Belden began using insulation supplied by Dow Chemical Company ("Dow"). The Dow insulation had different physical properties than the insulation provided by Quantum.

In October 2003, Belden sold AEC wire manufactured with the Dow insulation. AEC used this wire to make its sensors, and the insulation ultimately cracked. Chrysler had installed AEC's sensors containing the faulty wire in approximately 18,000 vehicles. Chrysler recalled 14,000 vehicles and repaired the remaining 4,000 prior to sale. Pursuant to an agreement with Chrysler, AEC is required to reimburse Chrysler for expenses associated with the recall.

In 2004, AEC filed a complaint against Belden seeking consequential damages for the changes in the insulation that resulted in the recall. In 2005, AEC filed a partial motion for summary judgment. In 2006, Belden responded and filed a cross-motion for summary judgment. * * * On July 6, 2007, the trial court entered an order granting AEC's motion for partial summary judgment and denying Belden's cross-motion. Belden now appeals.

* * *

"Where an agreement is entirely in writing, the question of whether express warranties were made is one for the court." [Citation.] More specifically, if all of the representations upon which the parties rely were in writing, the existence of express warranties is a question of law. [Citation.] Because the alleged warranty is based on written exchanges, whether the writings are sufficient to create an express warranty is a question of law appropriate for summary judgment.

* * *

Belden claims that these 1996 and 1997 communications did not amount to an express warranty for purposes of the October 2003 contract. Section 2-313 of the UCC provides:

(1) Express warranties by the seller are created as follows:
  (a) any affirmation of fact or promise made by the seller to the buyer which relates to the goods and becomes part of the basis of the bargain creates an express warranty that the goods shall conform to the affirmation or promise.
  (b) any description of the goods which is made part of the basis of the bargain creates an express warranty that the goods shall conform to the description.
  (c) any sample or model which is made part of the basis of the bargain creates an express warranty that the whole of the goods shall conform to the sample or model.

(2) It is not necessary to the creation of an express warranty that the seller use formal words such as "warrant" or "guarantee" or that he have a specific intention to make a warranty, but an affirmation merely of the value of the goods or a statement purporting to be merely the seller's opinion or commendation of the goods does not create a warranty.

"An express warranty requires some representation, term or statement as to how the product is warranted." [Citation.]. There does not seem to be a dispute that in 1996 and 1997 Belden made express warranties regarding its wire. Instead, the issue is whether the 1996 and 1997 statements by Belden regarding certification created an express warranty that extended to the October 2003 contract.

Based on the designated evidence, we believe Belden's compliance with AEC's quality control program was essential to its contracts with AEC and was intended to extend to the parties' repeated contracts. First, Comment 7 to Section 2-313 provides in part, "The precise time when words of description or affirmation are made or samples are shown is not material. The sole question is whether the language or samples or models are fairly to be regarded as part of the contract." Thus, although Belden made its initial representations in 1996 and 1997, there is no indication that those representations were limited in time, that Belden subsequently disclaimed its compliance with AEC's quality control standards, or that AEC changed those standards. As the trial court observed, "it is illogical to believe that [AEC] intended to rely in this representation for only one (1) shipment of Wire and then to understand that Belden would follow whatever quality procedures it wanted as to future shipments."

Further, Comment 5 of Section 2-213 provides in part, "Past deliveries may set the description of quality, either expressly or impliedly by course of dealing. Of course, all descriptions by merchants must be read against the applicable trade usages with the general rules as to merchantability resolving any doubts." Belden claims that if the parties' course of dealing was insufficient to incorporate the limitation on damages into the parties' contract, then the course of dealing is also insufficient to establish an express warranty. We disagree. Irrespective of whether the course of dealing established that AEC assented to Belden's proposed limitation on damages, the parties' course of dealing established that Belden made an express warranty regarding its compliance with the quality control standards. The limitation on damages and the express warranty are unrelated issues-there is no correlation between the two.

A course of dealing is conduct "fairly to be regarded as establishing a common basis of understanding for interpreting their expressions and other conduct." § 1-205(1). It is undisputed that Belden's wire complied with the AEC's quality control requirements for the parties' more than 100 transactions, until October 2003, when Belden switched from Quantum insulation to the Dow insulation without informing AEC of the changes. * * *

That Belden and AEC did not repeatedly or routinely "communicate" regarding Belden's continued use of Quantum insulation does not undermine the parties' course of dealing. The very point of a course of dealing is to allow the parties' prior actions create a basis of common understanding. This is exactly what Belden's 1996 and 1997 assertions taken with its continued use of Quantum insulation did.

* * *

Affirmed.

CASE 24-2

Express Warranties/Implied Warranties

## IN RE L.B. TRUCKING, INC.

United States Bankruptcy Court, D. Del, 1994
163 BR 709, 23 U.C.C. Rep.Serv.2d 1092

**Balick, J.**

Dudley B. Durham, Jr. and Barbara L. Durham, husband and wife, and their farming and trucking corporations, Double D Farms, Inc. and L.B. Trucking, Inc. filed Chapter 11 petitions on December 20, 1983 * * *. On March 5, 1985, the Chapter 11 case of the consolidated debtors was converted to a Chapter 7 case. (James L. Patton was appointed Trustee of the Chapter 7 estate.)

At the time of trial this adversary proceeding involved a claim by Southern States Cooperative, Inc. (Southern States) for monies owed in connection with its sale and application of herbicides and other chemicals on the Durhams' farm fields. The Trustee was pursuing the Durhams' counterclaims contending that these herbicides were negligently misapplied and also breached the various UCC warranties which caused severe crop damage to the Durhams' 1983 harvest.

* * *

After consideration of the relevant facts and the applicable law, the court concludes that Southern States is not entitled to any recovery and that the Trustee, on behalf of the consolidated debtors' estate, is entitled to recover in full on its products liability claims, * * *

### Background

Dudley Durham, Jr. has been a farmer most of his life and has been farming on his own since 1972. Durham leased most of the farmland he cultivated and handled most of the planting and other farming operations himself while his wife, Barbara Durham, maintained the farm business' books and records. * * *

The facts leading to this controversy arise from the Durhams' dealings with Southern States concerning the planting of their 1983 crops. Southern States is a farmers' cooperative that engages in the business of supplying farmers with various agricultural supplies like seed, fertilizer, feed, herbicides, and other farm products as well as certain services in connection with these products * * *. Durham had done business with Southern States before switching to Flo-N-Gro, Inc. as his supplier, but due in part to the substantial debt accumulated to Flo-N-Gro and other creditors, Durham approached Southern States once again prior to planting his 1983 corn and bean crops.

In April of 1983, Durham contacted Richard Thomas, the Southern States Middletown store manager, about arranging for the application of herbicides. Durham planned to use "no-till" farming for most of his 1983 crops. The "no-till" farming procedure does not require plowing or disking of the ground like the conventional plow mode of farming; instead, the farmer kills and controls weeds through the application of herbicides and then plants the seed with a special planter machine designed to plant in untilled soil. Durham apparently had done "no-till" farming in 1980, but did not personally apply the chemicals because he feared the potential health risks * * *. In any event, Durham explained to Thomas that he wanted to use "no-till" farming for most of his 1983 corn and bean crops and discussed credit terms generally regarding the chemicals. At this initial meeting, Thomas extended to Durham a $2,000 line of credit to purchase starter fertilizer known as "10–24–0" to begin his corn planting. Nevertheless, Thomas told Durham that a crop lien would be necessary for additional credit on the rest of the needed chemicals.

Subsequently, on May 5 or 6, 1983, Durham met Thomas again, this time accompanied by his father. The elder Durham signed a credit application with Southern States so that he might guarantee any credit extended to his son. During this meeting, the younger Durham told Thomas words to the effect of "Richard, you know I'm trying to pay, get straightened around and get all my stuff straightened around. I want it done the cheapest way, the best way it can be done." In response, Thomas replied, "Will do." The two Durhams and Thomas then went into a small room of the Middletown store where Thomas outlined with some specificity the herbicidal chemicals he proposed to use on Durham's fields. Thomas stated that water would be employed as a carrier for the herbicides with nitrogen being applied by drop nozzling at a rate of 150 lbs. per acre after the crops were standing. The alternative to using a water-based carrier for the chemicals would be to use a 30% nitrogen solution which was more expensive than using water as a carrier and violated the recommendations of the University of Delaware's Department of Agriculture. The junior Durham had no experience or expertise on herbicidal chemicals and relied on Thomas' briefing on the various herbicide mixtures in choosing which ones to apply. Yet, the younger Durham did emphasize to Thomas that a large number of acres per day would require spraying in order to keep up with Durham's heavy planting schedule. Thomas answered that the 1983 season was a normal year in terms of the number of acres to be sprayed by Southern

States, and in most instances, Southern States was able to keep up with the farmers.

Durham actually began planting his crops a few days before his early May meeting with Thomas. Gilbert McClements, the principal Southern States herbicide applicator for Durham's fields, began spraying on May 8, 1983.

* * *

In sum, Durham's 1983 farming operations consisted of roughly 740 acres of corn, about 230 acres of beans, and a winter wheat crop.

As to the herbicidal chemical applications by McClements, spray tickets were issued by Southern States detailing the job date, location, approximate acreage, and the various chemicals used in each application. McClements received instructions concerning which chemicals to apply from his superiors at Southern States, namely, Mr. Thomas and Mr. Fox. McClements would mix the herbicides each day prior to spraying, but apparently did not make extensive prespraying inspections of the grass and weeds nor did he perform a "hands and knees" inspection of the planted corn prior to spraying.

After planting the corn and bean crop, Durham observed a significant number of weeds and grasses that had escaped the herbicidal treatment and the correspondingly low crop population. Durham promptly notified Southern States of these difficulties. On June 1, 1983, Thomas visited several of Durham's fields and indicated to Durham that Southern States would remedy the problem. As a result, numerous acres were resprayed by Southern States and fields with very low plant populations were replanted. Nevertheless, the 1983 corn and bean harvest was dismal and far below the County average.

* * *

## Discussion

The issues involved are: whether Southern States' herbicidal chemicals were negligently applied; [and] whether Southern States breached UCC warranties * * *. Collateral to the product liability claims, and asserted as an affirmative defense by the Trustee against Southern States' claim, is whether Southern States may recover payment for the chemicals and their application.

* * *

***Product Liability Claims Against Southern States For Alleged Harm Resulting from Use of Its Chemicals***

Delaware does not have strict products liability arising out of the sale of goods. [Citation.] (UCC warranty provisions on sales preempt judicial extension of strict liability in tort involving sale of goods.) Consequently, those claiming injury from defective products in Delaware must seek recovery under a negligence and/or warranty rubric rather than a theory premised on strict liability in tort. [Citations.]

* * *

**B. Warranty** The Delaware version of the UCC provides for three types of warranties arising from the sale of goods: (1) express warranties, UCC §2–313, (2) implied warranties of merchantability UCC §2–314, and (3) implied warranties for a particular purpose, UCC §2–315. These warranties are mutually exclusive and independent of one another but each type of warranty may arise out of the sale of goods depending on the facts surrounding the sale. See UCC §2–102.

* * *

**1. Express Warranty** An express warranty may be created by a seller through: (1) any affirmation of fact or promise to the buyer relating to the goods which becomes the basis of the bargain so that the goods conform to the affirmation or promise; (2) any description of the goods which is made part of the basis of the bargain so that the whole of the goods conform to the sample of model. UCC §2–313(1)(a)–(c). The question of whether an express warranty has been made in a particular transaction is for the trier of fact. [Citation.] In the case at bar, there are no written express warranties claimed, but instead, oral statements made principally by the Middletown store manager, Thomas, to Durham which the Trustee contends were express warranties.

The relevant testimony concerning Thomas' statements to Durham reveal several oral express warranties concerning the herbicides and their application which Southern States plainly breached. First, Thomas stated that water would be the carrier for the herbicides, especially since Durham wanted the job done inexpensively. In its application, Southern States used the nitrogen solution regardless of the University of Delaware recommendations dissuading its use and despite the fact that it is more expensive than using water as a carrier. Southern States' reference to the common trade usage of nitrogen in 1983 is inapposite in an action for breach of express warranty because it is the affirmation or promise—not the custom or trade usage—which becomes the standard against which a breach is determined. In addition, Thomas' statements were more than "seller's talk" or puffing in that they were product-specific and not overly broad or vague. Second, Thomas also made statements regarding the effectiveness of the herbicides in removing weeds and grass so as to promote successful no-till farming. The purchase of herbicides is characteristically the subject of express warranties because the buyer of the product cannot determine its effectiveness prior to use and evaluate its effectiveness in a given situation. Here, Thomas' statements in early May of 1983 were part of the basis of the bargain upon which Durham relied when purchasing the herbicides. Beyond this, Thomas had superior knowledge about the herbicides as opposed to Durham who had little or none. Consequently, Thomas' selection of herbicidal recipes combined with his statements as to their effectiveness amounted to an express warranty that the respective mixtures would do the job adequately. Thomas made at least two express warranties which formed the basis of Durham's purchase of the chemicals and were ultimately breached. The liability for breach of express warranty is a strict liability. No defect need be shown other than breach of the warranty itself which is the proximate cause of the property damage. [Citations.] Accordingly, the court finds that Southern States breached its express warranty to Durham and, thus, is liable for the Durham's crop damage. * * *

**2. Implied Warranties** There are two theories of recovery for breach of implied warranty under the Delaware UCC: breach of implied warranty of merchantability under UCC §2–314 and breach of implied warranty of fitness for a particular purpose under UCC §2–315. The implied warranty of fitness for a particular purpose may, to some degree, overlap a seller's express warranty. [Citations.] Unless there is a valid disclaimer, these implied warranties are implied in every sales transaction involving goods and run not only to those in contractual privity with the seller but to third party beneficiaries as well. UCC §2–318; [Citation.]. Obviously, Durham was in direct privity with Southern States regarding the herbicides sale.

Turning first to the implied warranty of merchantability, there are five elements which the claimant must establish: (1) that a merchant sold goods, (2) which were not merchantable at the time of sale, (3) proximately causing by the defective nature of the goods, (4) injury and damages to the claimant or his property, and (5) notice to the seller of the injury. [Citation.] As to the element requiring the seller to be a merchant, there is no doubt that Southern States was a merchant. * * *

Addressing the second element concerning whether the herbicides were "merchantable," the goods must pass without objection in the trade under the contract description be fit for the ordinary purposes for which it was intended. UCC §2–314(2)(a) and (c). The facts show that Southern States sprayed (and in some instances resprayed) the various Durham farm tracts with herbicidal and other chemicals in order to increase the crop yields. Nevertheless, the farms' respective crop yields did not improve, but rather fell dramatically as the result of the chemical applications. Specifically, the herbicidal recipes were unfit for the ordinary purpose for which they were intended to be used, chemical agents that would kill weeds without damaging the primary crops. [Citation.] The chemicals did not operate for their ordinary purpose which was to promote no-till farming which is why Durham purchased them in the first place.

There is ample evidence to support the finding that the herbicides were not merchantable. Dr. Mitchell's unrebutted expert testimony indicates that Southern States incorrectly used liquid nitrogen as the herbicidal carrier rather than a water-based carrier. As a result, this created acidic soil conditions which inhibited operation of the herbicides * * *. In this case, the herbicides did not effectively control 85% of the weeds; instead, the weeds flourished and the crops died. Dr. Mitchell cited a number of other reasons for the crop failure, including: Southern States' improper selection of herbicides needed to control weeds based on the time of the crop planting, its failure to use a sufficient volume of carrier, and its applicator's failure to perform the necessary inspections (such as the "hands and knees" examination) to determine what herbicide recipe should be applied * * *. Based on this evidence, the court concludes that the herbicide and other chemicals were not merchantable since they neither could pass in the trade without objection nor were they fit for the ordinary purpose for which they were intended.

As for proximate cause and damages, the court finds that these elements have been met. * * *

Finally, the notice requirement for a breach of implied warranty of merchantability cause of action was plainly met. Durham notified Southern States as soon as he suspected that the herbicides were failing to work just a few weeks after their application. * * *

Southern States also breached the implied warranty that the herbicides were fit for their particular purpose. * * *

The breach of this warranty is the one most apparent on the facts. As indicated earlier, Durham relied on Thomas' skill and judgment in selecting suitable herbicides to conduct no-till farming on his farms. The chemicals were mixed by Southern States' herbicide applicator, McClements, before each job based on a formula or recipe provided by Thomas or some other Southern States official. The herbicides did not effectively do their job of keeping the fields clear of weeds and the crops died. Though thoroughly familiar with till farming, Durham had no experience with the no-till farming method and, therefore, was not a "sophisticated purchaser" who might have been able to recognize mistakes made by Southern States' personnel. As a result, the herbicides' failure to do their intended task coupled with Durham's reliance on Southern States' judgment and skill in formulating, mixing, and applying the herbicidal chemicals breached the implied warranty of fitness. [Citations.] Accordingly, Southern States is found to be liable under U.C.C. §2–315.

CASE 24-3

## Disclaimer of Warranties
## WOMCO, INC. v. NAVISTAR INTERNATIONAL CORPORATION

Court of Appeals of Texas, Twelfth District, Tyler, 2002
84 S.W.3d 272, 48 U.C.C. Rep.Serv.2d 130
http://tx.findacase.com/research/wfrmDocViewer.aspx/xq/fac.%5CTX%5C2002%5C20020620_0003931.TX.htm/qx

**Griffith, J.**

* * *

Appellants, Womco, Inc. ("Womco"), C.L. Hall [(Hall)] * * * appeal the trial court's order granting summary judgment in favor of Appellees, Navistar International Corporation ("Navistar") * * *. We affirm in part, and reverse and remand in part.

### Background

In 1993, the Womco Appellants purchased thirty 1993 International model 9300 tractor trucks manufactured by Navistar through Price, a dealer. Also, in 1993, the Hall Appellants purchased sixteen 1994 International model 9300 tractor trucks also manufactured by Navistar through Mahaney, another dealer. Almost immediately after the trucks were put into service, Appellants each had problems with their respective trucks' engines overheating. As the problems occurred, Appellants took their trucks, which were still covered under warranty, to their respective dealerships for diagnoses and repairs related to the overheating problem. Although repeated attempts were made, the dealership's mechanics were unable to correct the problem.

In June 1995, Marquess, the president of Womco, had one of the trucks inspected by an independent source, Rodieck Welding & Radiator Service ("Rodieck"). Rodieck found nothing wrong with the truck's radiator, but replaced the core of the radiator to be certain. Rodieck also informed Marquess that the truck's radiator appeared to be unusually small. Despite Rodieck's efforts, the overheating problem in the Womco Appellants' trucks continued. Soon thereafter, Marquess contacted Price and spoke to Les Miller ("Miller"), informing him that he wanted to install larger radiators in his trucks. Miller responded that Price did not make a larger radiator for that particular truck and further, that the hood of the truck would not accommodate a larger radiator. Following this conversation, Marquess had an audit conducted of the cooling system of one of the trucks in July 1995 by the Tyler Truck Center, which revealed that the trucks were overheating due to insufficient radiator capacity.

The Womco Appellants filed suit on April 23, 1997. The Hall Appellants joined the suit on or about May 22, 1997 after learning of the results of the audit. In January 2000, Appellees filed a motion for summary judgment based on their affirmative defenses of * * * disclaimer of warranty. * * * The trial court granted Appellees' motion * * * for summary judgment. * * *

* * *

### Disclaimer of Warranty

It is undisputed that Appellants' breach of implied warranty claims as to nine trucks are not barred by limitations. However, * * * Appellees contend that such implied warranties were disclaimed. The Texas Uniform Commercial Code allows sellers to disclaim both the implied warranty of merchantability as well as the implied warranty of fitness for particular purpose. [UCC] §2.316(b), [citation]. In order to disclaim an implied warranty of merchantability in a sales transaction, the disclaimer must mention the word "merchantability." The disclaimer may be oral or written, but if in writing, the disclaimer must be conspicuous. [Citation]; [UCC] §2.316(b). To disclaim an implied warranty of fitness for a particular purpose, the disclaimer must be in writing and must be conspicuous. [UCC] §2.316(b); [citation]. Whether a particular disclaimer is conspicuous is a question of law to be determined by the court. [Citation.] A term or clause is conspicuous if it is written so that a reasonable person against whom it is to operate ought to have noticed it. [UCC] §1.201(10) (Vernon Supp. 2002); [citation]. Language is "conspicuous" if it is in larger type or other contrasting font or color. [Citation.] Conspicuousness is not required if the buyer has actual knowledge of the disclaimer. [Citation.]

Appellants, [UCC] section 2.316(a), argue that Appellees are also required to prove the reasonableness of the disclaimers at issue. However, section 2.316(a) concerns the disclaimer of express warranties. In the instant case, Appellants have only pleaded that Appellees breached implied warranties. Thus, section 2.316(a) and its requirement of reasonableness are inapplicable.

Further, Appellants argue that Appellees were required to offer proof of the context of the purported disclaimers, contending that in order for a disclaimer of an implied warranty to be effective, the plaintiffs must have had an opportunity to examine it prior to consummation of the contract for sale. [Citation.] * * * In *Dickenson*, [citation], the court held that a disclaimer of an express warranty was ineffective where the buyer was not given the opportunity to read the warranty or warranties made until after the contract is signed. Although the instant case concerns a converse situation to *Dickenson*, the rationale applied by the *Dickenson* court is helpful. One of the underlying purposes of [UCC] section 2.316 is to protect a buyer from surprise by permitting the exclusion of implied warranties. [UCC] §2.316, comment 1. We fail to see how section [UCC] 2–316 can fulfill such a purpose unless a disclaimer is required to be communicated to the buyer before the contract of sale has been completed, unless the buyer afterward agrees to the disclaimer as a modification of the contract. [Citations.]

In support of their motion for summary judgment, Appellees offered six disclaimers, all of which were deposition exhibits. None of these six disclaimers is probative as to the issue of whether the disclaimer was communicated prior to the completion of the contract of sale. * * * Therefore, we hold that since Appellant failed to conclusively prove that they were entitled to judgment as a matter of law on the disclaimer issue, summary judgment was not appropriate on that issue. * * *

* * *

Accordingly, the trial court's order granting summary judgment is *reversed* as to Appellants' claims for breach of warranty * * * and is *remanded* to the trial court for further proceedings. As to all other claims of Appellants, the trial court's order granting summary judgment is *affirmed.*

## CASE 24-4

### Failure to Warn
### KELSO v. BAYER CORPORATION

United States Court of Appeals, Seventh Circuit, 2005
398 F.3d 640
http://bulk.resource.org/courts.gov/c/F3/398/398.F3d.640.04-2532.html

**Manion, J.**

Ted Kelso sued Bayer Corporation for strict product liability, alleging that the warning Bayer provided on its Neo-Synephrine 12 Hour Extra Moisturizing Spray was defective. * * * Ted Kelso began using Neo-Synephrine 12 Hour Extra Moisturizing Spray in 1990. He used Neo-Synephrine continuously for more than three years. After learning that his continued use of the product caused permanent nasal tissue damage requiring multiple sinus surgeries, he sued Bayer, the manufacturer of Neo-Synephrine, alleging Bayer failed to adequately warn him of the dangers associated with Neo-Synephrine.

Bayer moved for summary judgment, arguing that the warning it provided, as follows, was adequate, as a matter of law:

> **"Do not exceed recommended dosage."**
>
> * * *
>
> "Stop use and ask a doctor if symptoms persist. Do not use this product for more than 3 days. Use only as directed. Frequent or prolonged use may cause nasal congestion to recur or worsen."

The district court agreed and granted Bayer summary judgment. Kelso appeals. * * *

Kelso argues that summary judgment was inappropriate because he presented sufficient evidence to recover in a product liability action against Bayer. "To recover in a product liability action, a plaintiff must plead and prove that the injury resulted from a condition of the product, that the condition was an unreasonably dangerous one, and that the condition existed at the time the product left the manufacturer's control." [Citation.] A product may be unreasonably dangerous because of a design defect, a manufacturing defect, "or a failure of a manufacturer to warn of a danger or instruct on the proper use of the product as to which the average consumer would not be aware." [Citation.]

Kelso claims the Neo-Synephrine was unreasonably dangerous because Bayer's warning was confusing as to whether or not the product could be used safely for more than three days, when such use was effective in relieving his congestion. * * * Kelso * * * interpreted the warning as meaning not to exceed three days use if the product failed to relieve the congestion; he only needed to see a physician if the product did not work to relieve the congestion. Also, because the container included much more than three days' dosage, Kelso insists that he had good reason to believe that he could safely use Neo-Synephrine for more than three days.

However, Kelso's personal reaction to the warning is not the test. Whether a warning is sufficient "is determined using an objective standard, i.e., the awareness of an ordinary person." [Citation.] Here, the plain, clear and unambiguous language of the warning states: "**Do not use this product for more than 3 days.**" Period. That the Neo-Synephrine container included doses sufficient to treat multiple users or multiple colds in no way takes away from the clear impact of the warning. Moreover, the warning clearly informs users to: "**Stop use and ask a physician if symptoms persist.**" The warning was clear. Yet Kelso continued using the product well beyond the three days. It is unreasonable to create an ambiguity that excuses extended use when the warning against such use is unequivocal.

Kelso also argues that the warning was inadequate because it did not warn users that the product could also cause permanent nasal tissue damage and also had a risk of habituation (meaning that users would become dependent on the product, causing them to use the product for more than three days). However, under Illinois law, a manufacturer need not warn of all possible consequences of failing to follow a primary warning. [Citation.] Here, the primary warning told consumers "**not [to] use this product for more than 3 days.**" That was sufficient under Illinois law. However, Bayer's warning went even further, informing consumers of the consequence of extended use, stating: "**[f]requent or prolonged use may cause nasal congestion to recur or worsen.**" Although Kelso believes the warning should have provided him with more detailed information, Illinois law does not require more. [Citation.] Therefore, Kelso's defective warning claim fails.

---

CASE 24-5

## Unreasonably Dangerous
## GREENE v. BODDIE-NOELL ENTERPRISES, INC.

United States District Court, W.D. Virginia, 1997
966 F.Supp. 416
http://scholar.google.com/scholar_case?case=14855332202624539345&hl=en&as_sdt=2&as_vis=1&oi=scholarr

**Jones, J.**

In this products liability case, the plaintiff contends that she was badly burned by hot coffee purchased from the drive-through window of a fast food restaurant, when the coffee spilled on her after it had been handed to her by the driver of the vehicle. The defendant restaurant operator moves for summary judgment on the ground that the plaintiff cannot show a *prima facie* case of liability. I agree, and dismiss the case.

* * *

[Plaintiff, Katherine] Greene was a passenger in a car driven by her boyfriend, Chris Blevins, on the morning of December 31, 1994, when he purchased food and drink [coffees] from the drive-through window of the Hardee's restaurant in Wise, Virginia, operated by the defendant. * * * He immediately handed the food and beverages to Greene. The food was on a plate, and the beverages were in cups. Greene placed the plate on her lap and held a cup in each hand. According to Greene, the Styrofoam coffee cup was comfortable to hold, and had a lid on the top, although she did not notice whether the lid was fully attached.

Blevins drove out of the restaurant parking lot, and over a "bad dip" at the point at which the lot meets the road. When the front tires of the car went slowly across the dip, the coffee "splashed out" on Greene, burning her legs through her clothes. Blevins remembers Greene exclaiming, "the lid came off." She did not look at the cup until the coffee burned her, and does not know whether the cup was tilted in one direction or another when the coffee spilled out.

As soon as the coffee burned her, Greene threw the food and drink to the floor of the car, and in the process stepped on the coffee cup. When the cup was later retrieved from the floor of the car, the bottom of the cup was damaged, and the lid was at least partially off of the top of the cup.

After Greene was burned by the coffee, Blevins drove her to the emergency room of a local hospital, where she was treated. She missed eleven days of work, and suffered permanent scarring to her thighs.

Both Greene and Blevins testified that they had heard of the "McDonalds' coffee case" prior to this incident and Greene testified that while she was not a coffee drinker, she had been aware that if coffee spilled on her, it would burn her. After the accident, Greene gave a recorded statement to a representative of the defendant in which she stated, "I know the lid wasn't on there good. It came off too easy."

[Court's footnote: On August 17, 1994, a state court jury in Albuquerque, New Mexico, awarded 81-year old Stella Liebeck $160,000 in compensatory damages and $2.7 million in punitive damages, after she was burned by coffee purchased from a drive-through window at a McDonalds restaurant. The trial judge later reduced the punitive damages to $480,000, and the parties settled the case before an appeal. According to news reports, Mrs. Liebeck contended that for taste reasons McDonalds served coffee about 20 degrees hotter than other fast food restaurants, and in spite of numerous complaints, had made a conscious decision not to warn customers of the possibility of serious burns. The jury's verdict received world-wide attention. See Andrea Gerlin, A Matter of Degree: How a Jury Decided That One Coffee Spill Is Worth $2.9 Million, *Wall Street Journal.*]

* * *

To prove a case of liability in Virginia, a plaintiff must show that a product had a defect which rendered it unreasonably dangerous for ordinary or foreseeable use. [Citation]. In order to meet this burden, a plaintiff must offer proof that the product violated a prevailing safety standard, whether the standard comes from business, government or reasonable consumer expectation. [Citation.]

Here the plaintiff has offered no such proof. There is no evidence that either the heat of the coffee or the security of the coffee cup lid violated any applicable standard. Do other fast food restaurants serve coffee at a lower temperature, or with lids which will prevent spills even when passing over an obstruction in the road? Do customers expect cooler coffee, which may be less tasty, or cups which may be more secure, but harder to unfasten?

In fact, the plaintiff testified that she knew, and therefore expected, that the coffee would be hot enough to burn her if it spilled. While she also expressed the opinion that the cup lid was too loose, that testimony does not substitute for evidence of a generally applicable standard or consumer expectation, since "[the plaintiff's] subjective expectations are insufficient to establish what degree of protection * * * society expects from [the product]." [Citation.]

The plaintiff argues that the mere fact that she was burned shows that the product was dangerously defective, either by being too hot or by having a lid which came off unexpectedly. But it is settled in Virginia that the happening of an accident is not sufficient proof of liability, even in products cases. [Citation.] This is not like the case of a foreign substance being found in a soft drink bottle, where a presumption of negligence arises. [Citation.]

To be merchantable, a product need not be foolproof, or perfect. As one noted treatise has expressed, "[i]t is the lawyer's challenging job to define the term 'merchantability' in [the] case in some objective way so that the court or jury can make a determination whether that standard has been breached." [Citation.]

In the present case, there has been no showing that a reasonable seller of coffee would not conclude that the beverage must be sold hot enough to be palatable to consumers, even though it is hot enough to burn other parts of the body. A reasonable seller might also conclude that patrons desire coffee lids which prevent spillage in ordinary handling, but are not tight enough to avert a spill under other circumstances, such as when driving over a bump. It was the plaintiff's obligation to demonstrate that she had proof that the defendant breached a recognizable standard, and that such proof is sufficient to justify a verdict in her favor at trial. She has not done so, and accordingly the motion for summary judgment must be granted.

## QUESTIONS

1. Identify and describe the types of warranties.
2. Discuss the various defenses that may be successfully raised to a warranty action.
3. Describe the elements of an action based upon strict liability in tort.
4. Discuss the obstacles to an action based upon strict liability in tort.
5. Compare strict liability in tort with the implied warranty of merchantability.

## PROBLEMS

**1.** At the advent of the social season, Aunt Lavinia purchased a hula skirt in Sadie's dress shop. The salesclerk told her, "This superior garment will do things for a person." Aunt Lavinia's houseguest, her niece, Florabelle, asked and obtained her aunt's permission to wear the skirt to a masquerade ball. In the midst of the festivity, at which there was much dancing, drinking, and smoking, the long skirt brushed against a glimmering cigarette butt. Unknown to Aunt Lavinia and Florabelle, its wearer, the garment was made of a fine unwoven fiber that is highly flammable. It burst into flames, and Florabelle suffered severe burns. Aunt Lavinia notified Sadie of the accident and of Florabelle's intention to recover from Sadie. Can Florabelle recover damages from Sadie, the proprietor of the dress shop, and Exotic Clothes, Inc., the manufacturer from which Sadie purchased the skirt? Explain.

**2.** The Talent Company, manufacturer of a widely advertised and expensive perfume, sold a quantity of this product to Young, a retail druggist. Dentley and Bird visited Young's store and Dentley, desiring to make a gift to Bird, purchased from Young a bottle of this perfume, asking for it by its trade name. Young wrapped up the bottle and handed it directly to Bird. The perfume contained a foreign chemical that, upon the first use of the perfume by Bird, severely burned her face and caused a permanent facial disfigurement. What are the rights of Bird, if any, against Dentley, Young, and the Talent Company, respectively?

**3.** John Doe purchased a bottle of "Bleach-All," a well-known brand, from Roe's combination service station and grocery store. When John used the "Bleach-All," his clothes deteriorated due to an error in mixing the chemicals during the detergent's manufacture. John brings an action against Roe to recover damages. Explain whether John will be successful in his lawsuit.

**4.** A route salesperson for Ideal Milk Company delivered a one-half-gallon glass jug of milk to Allen's home. The next day, when Allen grasped the milk container by its neck to take it out of his refrigerator, it shattered in his hand and caused serious injury. Allen paid Ideal on a monthly basis for the regular delivery of milk. Ideal's milk bottles each contained the legend "Property of Ideal—to be returned," and the route salesperson would pick up the empty bottles when he delivered milk. Can Allen recover damages from Ideal Milk Company? Why?

**5.** While Butler and his wife, Wanda, were browsing through Sloan's used car lot, Butler told Sloan that he was looking for a safe but cheap family car. Sloan said, "That old Cadillac hearse ain't hurt at all, and I'll sell it to you for $6,950." Butler said, "I'll have to take your word for it because I don't know a thing about cars." Butler asked Sloan whether he would guarantee the car, and Sloan replied, "I don't guarantee used cars." Then Sloan added, "But I have checked that Caddy over, and it will run another 10,000 miles without needing any repairs." Butler replied, "It has to because I won't have an extra dime for any repairs." Butler made a down payment of $900 and signed a printed form contract furnished by Sloan, which contained a provision, "Seller does not warrant the condition or performance of any used automobile."

As Butler drove the car out of Sloan's lot, the left rear wheel fell off, and Butler lost control of the vehicle. It veered over an embankment, causing serious injuries to Wanda. What is Sloan's liability to Butler and Wanda?

**6.** John purchased for cash a Revenge automobile manufactured by Japanese Motors, Ltd., from an authorized franchised dealer in the United States. The dealer told John that the car had a "24-month, 24,000-mile warranty." Two days after John accepted delivery of the car, he received an eighty-page fine print manual that stated, among other things, on page 72:

> The warranties herein are expressly in lieu of any other express or implied warranty, including any implied warranty of merchantability or fitness, and of any other obligation on the part of the company or the selling dealer.
>
> Japanese Motors, Ltd., and the selling dealer warrant to the owner each part of this vehicle to be free under use and service from defects in material and workmanship for a period of twenty-four months from the date of original retail delivery of first use, or until it has been driven for 24,000 miles, whichever first occurs.

Within nine months after the purchase, John was forced to return the car for repairs to the dealer on thirty different occasions, and the car has been in the dealer's custody for more than seventy days during these nine months. The dealer has been forced to make major repairs to the engine, transmission, and steering assembly. The car is now in the custody of the dealer for further major repairs, and John has demanded that it keep the car and refund his entire purchase price. The dealer has refused on the ground that it has not breached its contract and is willing to continue repairing the car during the remainder of the "24–24" period. What are the rights and liabilities of the dealer and John?

**7.** Fred Lyon of New York, while on vacation in California, rented a new model Home Run automobile from Hart's Drive-A-Car. The car was manufactured by the Dumars Motor Company and was purchased by Hart's from Jammer, Inc., an automobile importer. Lyon was driving the car on a street in San Jose when, due to a defect in the steering mechanism, it suddenly became impossible to steer. The speed of the car at the time was thirty miles per hour, but before Lyon could bring it to a stop, the car jumped a low curb and struck Peter Wolf, who was standing on the sidewalk, breaking both of his legs and causing other injuries. What rights does Wolf have against (a) Hart's Drive-A-Car, (b) Dumars Motor Company, (c) Jammer, and (d) Lyon?

**8.** Plaintiff brings this cause of action against a manufacturer for the loss of one leg below the hip. The leg was lost when caught in the gears of a screw auger machine sold and installed by the defendant. Shortly before the accident, plaintiff's co-employees had removed a covering panel from the machine by use of sledgehammers and crowbars in order to do repair work. After finishing the repairs, they replaced the panel with a single piece of cardboard instead of restoring the equipment to its original condition. The plaintiff stepped on the cardboard in the course of his work and fell, catching his leg in the moving parts. Explain what causes of action plaintiff may have against defendant and what defenses the defendant could raise.

**9.** The plaintiff, while driving a van manufactured by the defendant, was struck in the rear by another motor vehicle. Upon impact, the plaintiff's head was jarred backward against the rear window of the cab, causing the plaintiff serious injury. The van was not equipped with a headrest, and none was required at the time. Should the plaintiff prevail on a cause of action based upon strict liability in tort? Why?

**10.** Plaintiff, while dining at defendant's restaurant, ordered a chicken potpie. While she was eating, she swallowed a sliver of chicken bone, which became lodged in her throat, causing her serious injury. Plaintiff brings a cause of action. Should she prevail? Why?

**11.** Salem Supply Co. sells new and used gardening equipment. Ben Buyer purchased a slightly used riding lawn mower for $1,500. The price was considerably less than that of comparable used mowers. The sale was clearly indicated to be "as is." Two weeks after Ben purchased the mower, the police arrived at his house with Owen Owner, the true owner of the lawn mower, which had been stolen from his yard, and reclaimed the mower. What recourse, if any, does Ben have?

**12.** Seigel, a seventy-three-year-old man, was injured at one of Giant Food's retail food stores when a bottle of Coca-Cola exploded as he was placing a six-pack of Coke into his shopping cart. The explosion caused him to lose his balance and fall, injuring himself. Has Giant breached its implied warranty of merchantability to Seigel? Why?

**13.** Guarino and two others (plaintiffs) died of gas asphyxiation and five others were injured when they entered a sewer tunnel without masks to answer the cries for help of their crew leader, Rooney. Rooney had left the sewer shaft and entered the tunnel to fix a water leakage problem. Having corrected the problem, Rooney was returning to the shaft when he apparently was overcome by gas because of a defect in his oxygen mask, which was manufactured by Mine Safety Appliance Company (defendant). Plaintiffs brought this action against the defendant for breach of warranty, and defendant raised the defense of plaintiffs' voluntary assumption of the risk. Explain who will prevail.

**14.** Green Seed Company packaged, labeled, and marketed a quality tomato seed known as "Green's Pink Shipper" for commercial sale. Brown Seed Store, a retailer, purchased the seed from Green Seed and then sold it to Guy Jones, who was engaged in the business of growing tomato seedlings for sale to commercial tomato growers. Williams purchased the seedlings from Jones and then transplanted and raised them in accordance with accepted farming methods. The plants, however, produced not the promised "Pink Shipper" tomatoes but rather an inferior variety that spoiled in the field. Williams then brought an action against Green Seed for $900, claiming that his crop damage had been caused by Green Seed's breach of an express warranty. Green Seed argued in defense that its warranty did not extend to remote purchasers and that the company did not receive notice of the claimed breach of warranty. Who will prevail? Why?

**15.** Shell Oil Company leased to Flying Tiger Line a gasoline tank truck with a movable ladder for refueling certain types of aircraft. Under the terms of the lease, Flying Tiger was to maintain the equipment in safe operating order, but Shell was obligated to make most of the repairs at Flying Tiger's request. Four years after the lease was entered, Shell, at Flying Tiger's request, replaced the original ladder with a new one built by an undisclosed manufacturer. Both Flying Tiger and Shell inspected the new ladder. Two years later, however, Price, an aircraft mechanic employed by Flying Tiger, was seriously injured when the ladder's legs split while he was climbing onto an airplane wing. What are Price's rights against Shell and Flying Tiger?

**16.** A gasoline-powered lawn mower that had been used earlier to cut grass was left unattended next to a water heater that had been manufactured by Sears. Expert testimony was presented to demonstrate that vapors from the mower's gas tank accumulated under the water heater and resulted in an explosion. Three-year-old Shawn Toups was injured as a result. Evidence was also presented negating any claim that Shawn had been handling the gasoline can located nearby or the lawn mower. He was not burned on the soles of his feet or the palms of his hands, and, similarly, the gas can remained in an upright position even after the explosion. Is Sears liable to the Toups in strict product liability? Explain.

**17.** Mrs. Embs went into Stamper's Cash Market to buy soft drinks for her children. She removed five bottles from an upright soft drink cooler, placed them in a carton, and then turned to move away from the display when a bottle of Seven-Up in a carton at her feet exploded, cutting her leg. Apparently, several other bottles had exploded that same week. Stamper's Cash Market received its entire stock of Seven-Up from Arnold Lee Vice, the area distributor. Vice in turn received his entire stock of Seven-Up from Pepsi-Cola Bottling Co. Can Mrs. Embs recover damages from (a) Stamper, (b) Vice, or (c) Pepsi-Cola Bottling? Why?

**18.** Catania wished to paint the exterior of his house. He went to Brown, a local paint store owner, and asked him to recommend a paint for the job. Catania told Brown that the exterior walls were stucco and in a chalky, powdery condition. Brown suggested Pierce's shingle and shake paint. Brown then instructed Catania how to mix the paint and how to use a wire brush to prepare the surface. Five months later, the paint began to peel, flake, and blister. Catania brings an action against Brown. Decision?

**19.** Robinson, a truck driver for a moving company, decided to buy a used truck from the company. Branch, the owner, told Robinson that the truck was being repaired and that Robinson should wait and inspect the truck before signing the contract. Robinson, who had driven the truck before, felt that inspection was unnecessary. Again, Branch suggested Robinson wait to inspect the truck, and again Robinson declined. Branch then told Robinson he was buying the truck "as is." Robinson then signed the contract. After the truck broke down four times, Robinson sued. Will Robinson be successful? What defenses can Branch raise?

**20.** Perfect Products manufactures balloons, which are then bought and resold by wholesale novelty distributors. Mego Corp. manufactures a doll called "Bubble Yum Baby." A balloon is inserted in the doll's mouth with a mouthpiece, and the doll's arm is pumped to inflate the balloon, simulating the blowing of a bubble. Mego Corp. used Perfect Products balloons in the dolls, bought through the independent distributors. Plaintiff's infant daughter died after swallowing a balloon removed from the doll. Is Perfect Products liable to plaintiff under a theory of strict liability? Explain.

**21.** Patient was injured when the footrest of an adjustable X-ray table collapsed, causing Patient to fall to the floor. G.E. manufactured the X-ray table and the footrest. At trial, evidence was introduced that G.E. had manufactured for several years another footrest model complete with safety latches. However, there was no evidence that the footrest involved was manufactured defectively. The action is based on a theory of strict liability. Who wins? Why?

**22.** Heckman, an employee of Clark Equipment Company, severely injured his left hand when he caught it in a power press that he was operating at work. The press was manufactured by Federal Press Company and sold to Clark. It could be operated either by hand controls that required the use of both hands away from the point of operation or by an optional foot pedal. When the foot pedal was used without a guard, nothing remained to keep the operator's hands from the point of operation. Federal Press did not provide safety appliances unless the customer requested them, but when it delivered the press to Clark with the optional pedal, it suggested that Clark install a guard. The press had a similar warning embossed on it. Clark did, in fact, purchase a guard for $100, but it was not mounted on the machine at the time of the injury, nor was it believed to be an effective safety device.

Heckman argued that one type of guard, if installed, would have made the press safe in 95 percent of its customary uses. Federal, in turn, argued that the furnishing of guards was not customary in the industry; that the machine's many uses made it impracticable to design and install any one guard as standard equipment; that Clark's failure to obey Federal's warning was a superseding cause of the injury; and that state regulations placed responsibility for the safe operation of presses on employers and employees. The jury awarded Heckman $750,000, and Federal appealed. Decision?

**23.** Raymond and Sandra Duford purchased a wood-burning stove from Sears. The stove was manufactured by Preway, Inc. At trial, it was shown that Raymond had inadvertently installed the section of the chimney pipe that went through the roof upside down; and all parties agreed that such improper installation caused a fire that had destroyed the Dufords' house.

At trial, the Dufords alleged, and Preway admitted, that there were no markings on the pipe to indicate "which end was up." An expert for the Dufords then testified that the simple precaution of an embossed marking would have been satisfactory. Later, to the amazement of all the parties, a witness for Preway pointed out that the actual pipe in question had been marked with embossed letters. The pipe in fact had tiny letters spelling "UP" with two arrows pointed in the proper direction. Since no one on either side had noticed the letters except the one witness, the Dufords hastily changed their claim to that of inadequacy of the marking. Who will prevail? Why?

**24.** Vlases, a coal miner who had always raised small flocks of chickens, spent two years building a new two-story chicken coop large enough to house 4,000 chickens. After its completion, he purchased 2,200 one-day-old chicks from Montgomery Ward for the purpose of producing eggs for sale. He had selected them from Ward's catalog, which stated that these chicks, hybrid Leghorns, were noted for their excellent egg production. Vlases had equipped the coop with brand-new machinery and had taken further hygiene precautions for the chicks' health. Almost one month later, Vlases noticed that their feathers were beginning to fall off. A veterinarian's examination revealed signs of drug intoxication and hemorrhagic disease in a few of the chicks. Eight months later, it was determined that the chicks were suffering from visceral and ocular leukosis, or bird cancer, which reduced their egg-bearing capacity to zero. Avian leukosis may be transmitted either genetically or by unsanitary conditions. Subsequently, the disease infected the entire flock. Vlases then brought suit against Montgomery Ward for its breach of the implied warranties of merchantability and of fitness for a particular purpose. Ward claimed that there was no way to detect the disease in the one-day-old chicks, nor was there medication available to prevent this disease from occurring. Is Montgomery Ward liable under a warranty and/or strict liability cause of action? Explain.

**25.** For more than forty years, Rose Cipollone smoked between one and two packs of cigarettes a day. Upon her death from lung cancer, Rose's husband, Antonio Cipollone, filed suit against Liggett Group, Inc., Lorillard, Inc., and Philip Morris, Inc., three of the leading firms in the tobacco industry, for the wrongful death of his wife. Many theories of liability and defenses were asserted in this decidedly complex and protracted litigation.

One theory of liability claimed by Mr. Cipollone was breach of express warranty. It is uncontested that all three manufacturers ran multimedia ad campaigns that contained affirmations, promises, or innuendos that smoking cigarettes was safe. For example, ads for Chesterfield cigarettes boasted that a medical specialist could find no adverse health effects in subjects after six months of smoking. Chesterfields were also advertised as being manufactured with "electronic miracle" technology that made them "better and safer for you." Another ad stated that Chesterfield ingredients were tested and approved by scientists from leading universities. Another brand, L&M, publicly touted the "miracle tip" filter, claiming it was "just what the doctor ordered."

At trial, the defendant tobacco companies were not permitted to try to prove that Mrs. Cipollone disbelieved or placed no reliance on the advertisements and their safety assurances. Did the defendants breach an express warranty to the plaintiff? Explain.

**26.** Trans-Aire International, Inc. (TAI) converts ordinary automotive vans into recreational vehicles. TAI had been installing carpet and ceiling fabrics in the converted vans with an adhesive made by the 3M Company. Unfortunately, during the hot summer months, the 3M adhesive would often fail to hold the carpet and fabrics in place.

TAI contacted Northern Adhesive Company (Northern), seeking a "suitable" product to replace the 3M adhesive. Northern sent samples of several adhesives, commenting that hopefully one or more "might be applicable." Northern also informed TAI that one of the samples, Adhesive 7448, was a "match" for the 3M adhesive. After testing all the samples under cool plant conditions, TAI's chief engineer determined that Adhesive 7448 was better than the 3M adhesive. When TAI's president asked if the new adhesive should be tested under summer-like conditions, TAI's chief engineer responded that it was unnecessary to do so. The president then asked if Adhesive 7448 came with any warranties. A Northern representative stated that there were no warranties, except that the orders shipped would be identical to the sample.

After converting more than five hundred vans using Adhesive 7448, TAI became aware that high summer temperatures were causing the new adhesive to fail. Explain whether TAI should prevail against Northern in a suit claiming (a) breach of an implied warranty of fitness for a particular purpose, (b) breach of an implied warranty of merchantability, and (c) breach of express warranty.

**27.** Plaintiff's children purchased an Aero Cycle exercise bike for their mother to use in a weight-loss program. The Aero Cycle bike was manufactured by DP and purchased from Wal-Mart. The second time the plaintiff, Judy Dunne, used the bike (the first time she had used it, she used it only for a few seconds), she pedaled for three or four rotations. The rear support strut failed and the bike collapsed under plaintiff. At the time of the accident, plaintiff weighed between 450 and 500 pounds. She fell off the bike backwards, struck her head on a nearby metal file cabinet, and was knocked unconscious. When plaintiff regained consciousness, her mouth was bleeding and her neck, left shoulder, arm, leg, knee, and ankle were injured. Plaintiff was diagnosed as having a cervical strain and multiple contusions. Plaintiff filed suit against Wal-Mart and DP. Explain whether plaintiff should prevail.

**28.** Brian Felley purchased a used Ford Taurus from Thomas and Cheryl Singleton for $5,800. The car had 126,000 miles on it. After test driving the car, Felley discussed the condition of the car with Thomas Singleton, who informed Felley that the only thing known to be wrong with the car was that it had a noise in the right rear and that a grommet connecting a strut was bad or missing. Thomas told Felley that otherwise the car was in good condition. Nevertheless, Felley soon began experiencing problems with the car. On the second day that he owned the car, Felley noticed a problem with the clutch. Over the next few days, the clutch problem worsened to the point that Felley was unable to shift the gears no matter how far he pushed in the clutch pedal. Felley presented an invoice to Thomas showing that he paid $942.76 for the removal and repair of the car's clutch. In addition, the car developed serious brake problems within the first month that Felley owned it. Felley now contends that the Singletons breached their express warranty. Explain whether Felley received an express warranty and whether the Singletons are liable.

**29.** For sixteen years, Mrs. Dorothy Mae Palmer had been married to an insulator who worked with asbestos products. Mrs. Palmer was not exposed to asbestos dust in a factory setting; rather, she was exposed when her husband brought his work clothes home to be washed. Mrs. Palmer died of mesothelioma. This product liability suit was brought by Mrs. Palmer's daughters to recover for the alleged wrongful death of their mother. The daughters claim that Mrs. Palmer's mesothelioma was the result of exposure to asbestos-containing products manufactured by Owens-Corning. The daughters claim that the asbestos products were defective and unreasonably dangerous and that Owens-Corning was negligent in failing to warn of the dangers associated with its products. Explain whether the plaintiffs should prevail.

CHAPTER 25

# Sales Remedies

A contract for the sale of goods may require total performance at one time or part performance in stages, according to the agreement of the parties. At any stage, one of the parties may repudiate the contract, may become insolvent, or may breach the contract by failing to perform his obligations under it. In a sales contract, breach may consist of the seller's delivering defective goods, too few goods, the wrong goods, or no goods. The buyer may breach by not accepting conforming goods or by failing to pay for conforming goods that he has accepted. Breach may occur when the goods are in the possession of the seller, in the possession of a bailee, in transit to the buyer, or in the possession of the buyer.

Remedies, therefore, need to address not only the type of breach of contract but also the situation with respect to the goods. Consequently, the Uniform Commercial Code (UCC) provides distinct remedies for the seller and for the buyer, each specifically keyed to the factual situation.

In all events, the purpose of the Code is to put the aggrieved party in a position as good as the one he would have occupied, had the other party fully performed. To accomplish this purpose, the Code has provided that its remedies should be liberally administered. Moreover, damages do not have to be "calculable with mathematical precision": they need only be proved with "whatever definiteness and accuracy the facts permit, but no more." Comment 1 to Section 1–106. The purpose of remedies under the Code is compensation; therefore, punitive damages generally are not available.

Finally, the Code has rejected the doctrine of election of remedies, essentially providing that remedies for breach are cumulative in nature. Whether one remedy bars another depends entirely on the facts of the individual case.

**CISG** Damages for breach of contract by one party consist of a sum equal to the loss, including loss of profit, suffered by the other party as a consequence of the breach. Such damages may not exceed the loss that the party in breach foresaw or should have foreseen at the time of the conclusion of the contract as a possible consequence of the breach of contract. The aggrieved party must take such measures as are reasonable in the circumstances to mitigate the loss, including loss of profit, resulting from the breach. If he fails to take such measures, the party in breach may claim a reduction in the damages in the amount by which the loss should have been mitigated.

## REMEDIES OF THE SELLER

A buyer's default in performing any of his contractual obligations deprives the seller of the rights for which he bargained. Such default may consist of any of the following acts: wrongfully rejecting the goods, wrongfully revoking acceptance of the goods, failing to make a payment due on or before delivery, or repudiating (indicating an intention not to perform) the contract in whole or in part. Section 2–703; Section 2A–523(1). The Code catalogs the seller's remedies for each of these defaults. Section 2–703. (Section 2A–523(1) contains a comparable set of remedies for the lessor.) These remedies allow the seller to—

1. withhold delivery of the goods;
2. stop delivery of the goods by a carrier or other bailee;
3. identify to the contract conforming goods not already identified;
4. resell the goods and recover damages;
5. recover damages for nonacceptance of the goods or repudiation of the contract;
6. recover the price;
7. recover incidental damages;
8. cancel the contract; and
9. reclaim the goods on the buyer's insolvency (Section 2–702).

Under Article 2A a lessor also may recover compensation for any loss of or damage to the lessor's residual interest in the goods caused by the lessee's default. Section 2A–532.

The first three and the ninth remedies indexed above are **goods-oriented**—that is, they relate to the seller's exercising control over the goods. The fourth through seventh remedies are money-oriented because they provide the seller with the opportunity to recover monetary damages. The eighth remedy is obligation-oriented because it allows the seller to avoid his obligation under the contract.

Moreover, if the seller delivers goods on credit and the buyer fails to pay the price when due, the seller's sole remedy, unless the buyer is insolvent, is to sue for the unpaid price. If, however, the buyer received the goods on credit while insolvent, the seller may be able to reclaim the goods. The Code defines **insolvency** to include both its equity meaning and its bankruptcy meaning. Section 1–201(23); Revised Section 1–201(b)(23). The **equity** meaning of insolvency is the inability of a person to pay his debts in the ordinary course of business or as they become due. The **bankruptcy** meaning of insolvency is that total liabilities exceed the total value of all assets.

As noted above, the Code's remedies are *cumulative*. Thus, by way of example, an aggrieved seller may (1) identify goods to the contract; *and* (2) withhold delivery; *and* (3) resell or recover damages for nonacceptance or recover the price; *and* (4) recover incidental damages; *and* (5) cancel the contract.

CISG If the buyer fails to perform any of her obligations under the contract or the CISG, the seller (1) may require the buyer to pay the price or (2) may fix an additional period of time of reasonable length for performance by the buyer of his obligations. Unless the seller has received notice from the buyer that she will not perform within the period so fixed, the seller may not, during that period, resort to any remedy for breach of contract. Moreover, if the buyer's breach is fundamental or the buyer fails to perform within the additional time granted by the seller, the seller may avoid the contract. In addition to these remedies, the seller also has the right to damages.

## TO WITHHOLD DELIVERY OF THE GOODS

A seller may withhold delivery of goods to a buyer who has wrongfully rejected or revoked acceptance of the goods, who has failed to make a payment due on or before delivery, or who has repudiated the contract. Section 2–703; Section 2A–523(1). This right is essentially that of a seller to withhold or discontinue performance of her side of the contract because of the buyer's breach.

Where the contract calls for installments, any breach of an installment that impairs the value of the *whole* contract will permit the seller to withhold the entire undelivered balance of the goods. In addition, upon discovery of the buyer's insolvency, the seller may refuse to deliver the goods except for cash, including payment for all goods previously delivered under the contract. Section 2–702. (Section 2A–525(1) is similar.)

## TO STOP DELIVERY OF THE GOODS

An extension of the right to withhold delivery is the right of an aggrieved seller to stop the delivery of goods in transit to the buyer or in the possession of a bailee. A seller who discovers that the buyer is insolvent may stop *any* delivery. If the buyer is not insolvent but repudiates or otherwise breaches the contract, the seller may stop carload, truckload, planeload, or larger shipments. Section 2–705(1); Section 2A–526(1). To stop delivery, the seller must notify the carrier or other bailee soon enough for the bailee to prevent delivery of the goods. After this notification, the carrier or bailee must hold and deliver the goods according to the directions of the seller, who is liable to the carrier or bailee for any charges or damages incurred. If a negotiable document of title has been issued for the goods, the bailee need not obey a notification until the document is provided. Section 2–705(3).

The seller's right to stop delivery ceases when (1) the buyer receives the goods; (2) the bailee of the goods, except a carrier, acknowledges to the buyer that he holds them for the buyer; (3) the carrier acknowledges to the buyer that he holds them for the buyer by reshipment or as warehouseman; or (4) a negotiable document of title covering the goods is negotiated to the buyer. Section 2–705(2); Section 2A–526(2) is similar.

## TO IDENTIFY GOODS TO THE CONTRACT

Upon a breach of the contract by the buyer, the seller may proceed to identify to the contract conforming goods in her possession or control that were not so identified at the time she learned of the breach. Section 2–704(1); Section 2A–524(1). This enables the seller to exercise the remedy of resale of goods (discussed below). Furthermore, the seller may resell any unfinished goods demonstrably intended to fulfill the particular contract. The seller may either complete the manufacture of unfinished goods and identify them to the contract or cease their manufacture and resell the unfinished goods for scrap or salvage value. Section 2–704(2); Section 2A–524(2). In so deciding, the seller must exercise reasonable commercial judgment to minimize her loss.

## TO RESELL THE GOODS AND RECOVER DAMAGES

Under the same circumstances that permit the seller to withhold delivery of goods to the buyer (i.e., wrongful rejection or revocation, repudiation, or failure to make timely payment), the seller may resell the goods or the undelivered balance. If the resale is made in good faith and is commercially reasonable, the seller may recover from the buyer the difference between the contract price and the resale price, plus any incidental damages (discussed below), minus expenses saved because of the buyer's breach. Section 2–706(1). For example, Floyd agrees to sell goods to Beverly for a contract price of $8,000 due on delivery. Beverly wrongfully rejects the goods and refuses to pay Floyd anything. Floyd resells the goods in strict compliance with the Code for $6,000, incurring incidental damages for sales commissions of $500 but saving $200 in transportation costs. Floyd would recover from Beverly the difference between the contract price ($8,000) and the resale price ($6,000), plus incidental damages ($500), minus expenses saved ($200), which equals $2,300.

In a lease, the comparable recovery is the **difference between the present values** of the **old rent** due under the original lease and the **new rent** due under the new lease. More specifically, the lessor may recover (1) the accrued and unpaid rent as of the date of commencement of the new lease; (2) the present value as of that date of total rent for the then remaining term of the original lease minus the present value, as of the same date, of the rent under the new lease applicable to a comparable time period; and (3) any incidental damages, less expenses saved because of the lessee's breach. Section 2A–527(2).

The resale may be a public or private sale, and the goods may be sold as a unit or in parcels. The goods resold must be identified as those related to the contract, but where an anticipatory repudiation has occurred, for example, the goods need be neither in existence nor identified to the contract before the buyer's breach. Section 2–706(2).

Where the resale is at a private sale, the seller must give the buyer reasonable notice of his intention to resell. Section 2–706(3). The seller or a broker may carry out a private sale by negotiations or solicitations. Where the resale is at a public sale (such as an auction), only identified goods can be sold, except where a recognized market exists for a public sale of future goods of the kind involved. The public sale must be made at a usual place or market for public sale, if one is reasonably available, and the seller must give the buyer reasonable notice of the time and place of the resale unless the goods are perishable or threaten to decline in value speedily. Prospective bidders must be given an opportunity for reasonable inspection of the goods before the sale. Moreover, the seller may be a purchaser of the goods at the public sale. Section 2–706(4). In choosing between a public and private sale, the seller must observe relevant trade practices and usages and take into account the character of the goods.

The seller is not accountable to the buyer for any profit made on any resale of the goods. Section 2–706(6); Section 2A–527(5). Moreover, a *bona fide* purchaser at a resale takes the goods free of any rights of the original buyer, even if the seller has failed to comply with one or more of the requirements of the Code in making the resale. Section 2–706(5); Section 2A–524(4).

Failure to act in good faith and in a commercially reasonable manner deprives the seller of this remedy and relegates him to the remedy of recovering damages for nonacceptance or repudiation (discussed below). Section 2–706, Comment 2; Section 2A–527(3).

**CISG** If the contract is avoided and the seller has resold the goods in a reasonable manner and within a reasonable time after avoidance, he may recover the difference between the contract price and the resale price. In addition, he may recover consequential damages.

### TO RECOVER DAMAGES FOR NONACCEPTANCE OR REPUDIATION

In the event of the buyer's wrongful rejection or revocation, repudiation, or failure to make timely payment, the seller may recover damages from the buyer equal to the **difference between the unpaid contract price and the market price** at the time and place of tender of the goods, plus incidental damages, less expenses saved because of the buyer's breach. Section 2–708(1). This remedy is an alternative to the remedy of reselling the goods.

In a lease the comparable recovery is the **difference between the present values** of the **old rent due** under the original lease and the **market rent**. Section 2A–528(1).

For example, Joan in Seattle agrees to sell goods to Nelson in Chicago for $20,000 F.O.B. ("free on board") Chicago, with delivery by June 15. Nelson wrongfully rejects the goods. The market price would be ascertained as of June 15 in Chicago because F.O.B. Chicago is a destination contract in which the place of tender would be Chicago. The market price of the goods on June 15 in Chicago is $15,000. Joan, who incurred $1,000 in incidental expenses while saving $500 in expenses, would recover from Nelson the difference between the contract price ($20,000) and the market price ($15,000), plus incidental damages ($1,000), minus expenses saved ($500), which equals $5,500.

If the difference between the contract price and the market price will not place the seller in as good a position as performance would have, then the measure of damages is the **lost profit**; that is, the profit, including reasonable overhead, that the seller would have realized from full performance by the buyer, plus any incidental damages, less expenses saved because of the buyer's breach. Section 2–708(2). For example, Green, an automobile dealer, enters into a contract to sell a large, fuel-inefficient luxury car to Holland for $22,000. The price of gasoline increases 20 percent, and Holland repudiates. The market value of the car is still $22,000, but because Green cannot sell as many cars as he can obtain, his sales volume has decreased by one as a result seller an action for replevin for goods that have been identified to the contract if the buyer after a reasonable effort is unable to effect cover for such goods. Section 2–716(3); Section 2A–521(3). Article 2 also provides the buyer with the right to replevin if the goods have been shipped under reservation of a security interest in the seller and satisfaction of this security interest has been made or tendered. Section 2–716(3).

### TO SUE FOR SPECIFIC PERFORMANCE

**Specific performance** is an equitable remedy compelling the party in breach to perform the contract according to its terms. At common law, specific performance is available only if legal remedies are inadequate. For example, where the contract is for the purchase of a unique item, such as a work of art, a famous racehorse, or an heirloom, money damages may not be an adequate remedy. In such a case, a court of equity has the discretion to order the seller specifically to deliver to the buyer the goods described in the contract upon payment of the price.

The Code not only has continued the availability of specific performance but also has sought to encourage a more liberal attitude toward its use. Accordingly, it does not expressly require that the remedy at law be inadequate. Instead, the Code states that specific performance may be granted where "the goods are unique or in other proper circumstances." Section 2–716(1); Section 2A–521(1). As the Comment to Section 2–716 explains, the test of uniqueness under the Code must be made in view of the total situation that characterizes the contract.

CISG The buyer may require the seller to perform his contractual obligations. If the goods do not conform to the contract and the nonconformity constitutes a fundamental breach of contract, the buyer may require delivery of substitute goods. If the goods do not conform to the contract, the buyer may require the seller to remedy the lack of conformity by repair, unless this is unreasonable having regard to all the circumstances. Nevertheless, a court is not bound to enter a judgment for specific performance unless a court would do so under its own law in respect of similar contracts of sale not governed by the CISG.

### TO ENFORCE A SECURITY INTEREST IN THE GOODS

A buyer who has rightfully rejected or justifiably revoked acceptance of goods that remain in his possession or control has a security interest in these goods to the extent of any payment of the price that he has made and for any expenses he reasonably has incurred in their inspection, receipt, transportation, care, and custody. The buyer may hold such goods and resell them in the same manner as an aggrieved seller may resell goods. Section 2–711(3); Section 2A–508(5). In the event of resale the buyer is accountable to the seller for any amount of the net proceeds of the resale that exceeds the amount of his security interest. Section 2–706(6); Section 2A–527(5).

### TO RECOVER DAMAGES FOR BREACH IN REGARD TO ACCEPTED GOODS

Where the buyer has accepted nonconforming goods and has timely notified the seller of the breach of contract, the buyer is entitled to recover from the seller the damages resulting in the ordinary course of events from the seller's breach, as determined in any reasonable manner. Section 2–714(1); Section 2A–519(3). Where appropriate, the buyer may also recover incidental and consequential damages. Section 2–714(3); Section 2A–519(3). Nonconformity includes breaches of warranty as well as any failure of the seller to perform according to her obligations under the contract. Thus, even if a seller cures a nonconforming tender, the buyer may recover under this section for any injury he suffered because the original tender was nonconforming.

In the event of breach of warranty, the measure of damages is the **difference** at the time and place of acceptance **between** the **value of the goods that have been accepted** and the **value** that the goods would have had if they had been **as warranted**, unless special circumstances show proximate damages of a different amount. Section 2–714(2). Article 2A has a comparable provision, except the recovery is for the **present value** of the difference between the value of the use of the goods accepted and the value if they had been as warranted for the lease term. Section 2A–519(4).

The contract price of the goods does not figure in this computation because the buyer is entitled to the benefit of his bargain, which is to receive goods that are as warranted. For example, Max agrees to sell goods to Stanley for $1,000. The value of the goods accepted is only $800; had they been as warranted, their value would have been $1,200. Stanley's damages for breach of warranty are $400, which he may deduct from any unpaid balance due on the purchase price upon notice to Max of his intention to do so. Section 2–717; Section 2A–508(6).

### TO RECOVER INCIDENTAL DAMAGES

In addition to remedies such as covering, recovering damages for nondelivery or repudiation, or recovering damages for breach in regard to accepted goods, including breach of warranty, the buyer may recover **incidental damages**. A buyer's incidental damages provide reimbursement for the buyer who incurs reasonable expenses in handling rightfully rejected goods or in effecting cover. Section 2–715(1) of the Code defines the buyer's incidental damages as follows:

> Incidental damages resulting from the seller's breach include expenses reasonably incurred in inspection, receipt, transportation and care and custody of goods rightfully rejected, any commercially reasonable charges, expenses or commissions in connection with effecting cover and any other reasonable expense incident to the delay or other breach.

Article 2A has an analogous definition. Section 2A–520(1).

For example, the buyer of a racehorse who justifiably revokes acceptance because the horse does not conform to the contract will be allowed to recover as incidental damages the cost of caring for the horse from the date the horse was delivered until the buyer returns it to the seller.

### TO RECOVER CONSEQUENTIAL DAMAGES

In many cases, the remedies discussed above will not fully compensate the aggrieved buyer for her losses. For example, nonconforming goods that are accepted may in some way damage or destroy the buyer's warehouse and its contents, or undelivered goods may have been the subject of a lucrative contract of resale, the profits from which are now lost. The Code responds to this problem by providing the buyer with the opportunity to recover **consequential damages** resulting from the seller's breach, including (1) any loss resulting from the buyer's requirements and needs of which the seller at the time of contracting had reason to know and which the buyer could not reasonably prevent by cover or otherwise; and (2) injury to person or property proximately resulting from any breach of warranty. Section 2–715(2); Section 2A–520(2).

With respect to the first type of consequential damages, *particular* needs of the buyer usually must be made known to the seller, whereas *general* needs usually need not be. In the case of a buyer who is in the business of reselling goods, resale is one requirement of which the seller has reason to know. For example, Supreme Machine Co., a manufacturer, contracts to sell Allied Sales, Inc., a dealer in used machinery, a used machine that Allied plans to resell. When Supreme repudiates and Allied is unable to obtain a similar machine elsewhere, Allied's damages include the net profit that it would have made on resale of the machine. A buyer may not, however, recover consequential damages he could have prevented by cover. Section 2–715(2); Section 2A–520(2)(a). For instance, Supreme Machine Co. contracts for $10,000 to sell Capitol Manufacturing Co. a used machine to be delivered at Capitol's factory by June 1. Supreme repudiates the contract on May 1. By reasonable efforts, Capitol could buy a similar machine from United Machinery, Inc., for $11,000 in time for a June 1 delivery. Capitol fails to do so, thereby losing a $5,000 profit that it would have made from the resale of the machine. Though Capitol can recover $1,000 from Supreme, its damages do not include the loss of the $5,000 profit.

An example of the second type of consequential damages would be the following: Federal Machine Co. sells a machine to Southern Manufacturing Co., warranting its suitability for Southern's purpose. The machine is not suitable for Southern's purpose, however, and causes $10,000 in damage to Southern's property and $15,000 in personal injuries. Southern can recover the $25,000 consequential damages in addition to any other loss suffered.

◆ SEE FIGURE 25-2: **Remedies of the Buyer**

## CONTRACTUAL PROVISIONS AFFECTING REMEDIES

Within specified limits, the Code permits the parties to a sales contract to modify, exclude, or limit by agreement the remedies or damages that will be available for breach of that contract. Two basic types of contractual provisions affect remedies: (1) liquidation or limitation of damages, and (2) modification or limitation of remedy.

### LIQUIDATION OR LIMITATION OF DAMAGES

The parties may provide for liquidated damages in their contract by specifying the amount or measure of damages that either party may recover in the event of a breach by the other. The amount of such damages must be reasonable in light of the anticipated or actual loss resulting from a breach, the difficulties of proof of loss, and the inconvenience or lack of feasibility of otherwise obtaining an adequate remedy. A contractual provision fixing unreasonably large liquidated damages is void as a penalty. Section 2–718(1). An unreasonably small amount, on the other hand, might be stricken on the grounds of unconscionability. Comment 1 to Section 2–718.

To illustrate, Sterling Cabinetry Company contracts to build and install shelves and cabinets for an office building being constructed by Baron Construction Company. The contract price is $120,000, and the contract provides that Sterling would be liable for $100 per day for every day's delay beyond the completion date specified in the contract. The stipulated sum of $100 per day is reasonable and commensurate with the anticipated loss. Therefore, it is enforceable as liquidated damages. If, instead, the sum stipulated had been $5,000 per day, it would be unreasonably large and therefore would be void as a penalty.

Section 2A–504(1) authorizes liquidated damages payable by either party for default, or any other act or omission. The amount of, or formula for, liquidated damages must be reasonable in light of the then anticipated harm caused by default or other act or omission. Section 2A–504(1).

◆ FIGURE 25-2: **Remedies of the Buyer**

| | Buyer's Remedies | | |
|---|---|---|---|
| **Seller's Breach** | **Obligation-oriented** | **Goods-oriented** | **Money-oriented*** |
| **Buyer rightfully rejects goods** | Cancel | Have a security interest | • Recover payments made<br>• Cover and recover damages<br>• Recover damages for nondelivery |
| **Buyer justifiably revokes acceptance** | Cancel | Have a security interest | • Recover payments made<br>• Cover and recover damages<br>• Recover damages for nondelivery |
| **Seller fails to deliver** | Cancel | • Recover identified goods if seller is insolvent<br>• Replevy goods<br>• Obtain specific performance | • Recover payments made<br>• Cover and recover damages<br>• Recover damages for nondelivery |
| **Seller repudiates** | Cancel | • Recover identified goods if seller is insolvent<br>• Replevy goods<br>• Obtain specific performance | • Recover payments made<br>• Cover and recover damages<br>• Recover damages for nondelivery |
| **Buyer accepts nonconforming goods** | | | Recover damages for breach of warranty |

* In a lease, the lessee's recovery of damages for future rent payments is reduced to their present value.

Where the seller justifiably withholds delivery of the goods because of the buyer's breach, and the buyer has made payments on the price, the buyer is entitled to restitution of the amount by which the sum of his payments exceeds the amount of liquidated damages to which the seller is entitled under the contract. In the absence of a provision for liquidated damages, the buyer may recover the difference between the amounts that he has paid on the price and 20 percent of the value of the total performance for which he is obligated under the contract, or $500, whichever is smaller. Section 2–718(2)(b). Article 2A has a comparable provision, except the $500 provision applies only to consumer leases. Section 2A–504(3)(b). The buyer's right to restitution is offset by the seller's right to recover other damages provided in the Code and by the value of any benefits the buyer has received by reason of the contract. Section 2–718(3); Section 2A–504(4).

Thus, if a buyer, after depositing $1,500 with the seller on a $10,000 contract for goods, breaches the contract and the seller withholds delivery, in the absence of a provision for liquidated damages and in the absence of the seller's establishing greater actual damages resulting from the breach, the buyer is entitled to restitution of $1,000 ($1,500 less $500). If the deposit were $250 on a $500 contract, the buyer would be entitled to $150 ($250 less $100, which is 20 percent of the price).

◆ **SEE CASE 25-3**

## MODIFICATION OR LIMITATION OF REMEDY BY AGREEMENT

The contract between the seller and buyer may expressly provide for remedies in addition to or instead of those provided in the Code and may limit or change the measure of damages recoverable in the event of breach. Section 2–719(1); Section 2A–503(1). For instance, the contract may validly limit the buyer's remedy to a return of the goods and a refund of the price, or to the replacement of nonconforming goods or parts.

A contractual remedy is deemed optional, however, unless the parties expressly agree that it is to be exclusive of other remedies, in which event it becomes the sole remedy. Section 2–719(1)(b); Section 2A–503(2). Moreover, where circumstances cause an exclusive or limited remedy to fail in its essential purpose, the parties may resort to the remedies provided by the Code. Section 2–719(2); Section 2A–503(2).

The contract may expressly limit or exclude consequential damages unless such limitation or exclusion would be unconscionable. Limitation of consequential damages for personal injuries resulting from breach of warranty in the sale of consumer goods is *prima facie* unconscionable, whereas limitation of such damages for commercial loss is not. Section 2–719(3); Section 2A–503(3). For example, Ace Motors, Inc., sells a pickup truck to Brenda, a consumer. The contract of sale excludes liability for all consequential damages. The next day, the truck explodes, causing

Brenda serious personal injury. Brenda would recover for her personal injuries unless Ace could prove that the exclusion of consequential damages was not unconscionable.

◆ **SEE CASE 25-4**

### STATUTE OF LIMITATIONS

Any action for breach of a sales contract must be begun within four years after the cause of action has accrued. Section 2–725(1); Section 2A–506(1). The parties may reduce the period of limitation to not less than one year. Section 2–725(1); Section 2A–506(1). In a sale, they may not, however, extend the period. Article 2A does not include this limitation.

A cause of action accrues when the breach occurs without regard to the injured party's knowledge of the breach. Section 2–725(2). A breach of warranty occurs upon tender of delivery, except where the warranty extends to future performance. In that event, the cause of action occurs when the breach is or should have been discovered. In a lease, a cause of action for default accrues when the act or omission is discovered or should have been discovered by the aggrieved party, or when the default occurs, whichever is later. Section 2A–506(2).

## CHAPTER SUMMARY

**REMEDIES OF THE SELLER**

**Buyer's Default** the seller's remedies are triggered by the buyer's actions in wrongfully rejecting or revoking acceptance of the goods, in failing to make payment due on or before delivery, or in repudiating the contract

**To Withhold Delivery**

**To Stop Delivery** if the buyer is insolvent (one who is unable to pay his debts as they become due or one whose total liabilities exceed his total assets), the seller may stop any delivery; if the buyer repudiates or otherwise breaches, the seller may stop carload, truckload, planeload, or larger shipments

**To Identify Goods**

**To Resell the Goods** the seller may resell the goods concerned or the undelivered balance of the goods and recover the difference between the contract price and the resale price, together with any incidental damages, less expenses saved

- ***Type of Resale*** may be public or private
- ***Manner of Resale*** must be made in good faith and in a commercially reasonable manner

**To Recover Damages for Nonacceptance or Repudiation**

- ***Market Price Differential*** the seller may recover damages from the buyer measured by the difference between the unpaid contract price and the market price at the time and place of tender of the goods, plus incidental damages, less expenses saved
- ***Lost Profit*** in the alternative, the seller may recover the lost profit, including reasonable overhead, plus incidental damages, less expenses saved

**To Recover the Price** the seller may recover the price

- where the buyer has accepted the goods
- where the goods have been lost or damaged after the risk of loss has passed to the buyer
- where the goods have been identified to the contract and a ready market is not available for their resale

**To Recover Incidental Damages** incidental damages include any commercially reasonable charges, expenses, or commissions directly resulting from the breach

**To Cancel the Contract**

**To Reclaim the Goods upon the Buyer's Insolvency** an unpaid seller may reclaim goods from an insolvent buyer under certain circumstances

| | |
|---|---|
| **REMEDIES OF THE BUYER** | **Seller's Default** the buyer's remedies arise in cases (1) in which the seller fails to make delivery or repudiates the contract or (2) in which the buyer rightfully rejects or justifiably revokes acceptance of goods tendered or delivered<br>**To Cancel the Contract**<br>**To Recover Payments Made**<br>**To Cover** the buyer may obtain cover by proceeding in good faith and without unreasonable delay to purchase substitute goods; the buyer may recover the difference between the cost of cover and the contract price, plus any incidental and consequential damages, less expenses saved<br>**To Recover Damages for Nondelivery or Repudiation** the buyer may recover the difference between the market price at the time the buyer learned of the breach and the contract price, together with any incidental and consequential damages, less expenses saved<br>**To Recover Identified Goods on the Seller's Insolvency** for which he has paid all or part of the price<br>**To Sue for Replevin** the buyer may recover goods identified to the contract if (1) the buyer is unable to obtain cover, or (2) the goods have been shipped under reservation of a security interest in the seller<br>**To Sue for Specific Performance** the buyer may obtain specific performance in cases in which the goods are unique or in other proper circumstances<br>**To Enforce a Security Interest** a buyer who has rightfully rejected or justifiably revoked acceptance of goods that remain in her possession has a security interest in these goods for any payments that she has made on their price and for any expenses she has reasonably incurred<br>**To Recover Damages for Breach in Regard to Accepted Goods** the buyer may recover damages resulting in the ordinary course of events from the seller's breach; in the case of breach of warranty, such recovery is the difference between the value the goods would have had if they had been as warranted and the value of the nonconforming goods that have been accepted<br>**To Recover Incidental Damages** the buyer may recover incidental damages, which include any commercially reasonable expenses connected with the delay or other breach<br>**To Recover Consequential Damages** the buyer may recover consequential damages resulting from the seller's breach, including (1) any loss resulting from the buyer's requirements and needs of which the seller at the time of contracting had reason to know and which the buyer could not reasonably prevent by cover or otherwise, and (2) injury to person or property proximately resulting from any breach of warranty |
| **CONTRACTUAL PROVISIONS AFFECTING REMEDIES** | **Liquidation or Limitation of Damages** the parties may specify the amount or measure of damages that may be recovered in the event of a breach if the amount is reasonable<br>**Modification or Limitation of Remedy by Agreement** the contract between the parties may expressly provide for remedies in addition to those in the Code, or it may limit or change the measure of damages recoverable for breach |

## CASES

CASE 25-1

### Seller's Damages for Nonacceptance or Repudiation

## KENCO HOMES, INC. v. WILLIAMS

Court of Appeals of Washington, Division Two, 1999
94 Wn.App. 219, 972 P.2d 125
http://caselaw.lp.findlaw.com/scripts/getcase.pl?court=wa&vol=209071&invol=o01

**Morgan, J.**

Kenco Homes, Inc., sued Dale E. Williams and Debi A. Williams, husband and wife, for breaching a contract to purchase a mobile home. After a bench trial, the trial court ruled primarily for Williams. Kenco appealed, claiming the trial court used an incorrect measure of damages. We reverse.

Kenco buys mobile homes from the factory and sells them to the public. Sometimes, it contracts to sell a home that the factory has not yet built. It has "a virtually unlimited supply of product," * * *.

On September 27, 1994, Kenco and Williams signed a written contract whereby Kenco agreed to sell, and Williams agreed to buy, a mobile home that Kenco had not yet ordered from the factory. The contract called for a price of $39,400, with $500 down.

The contract contained two conditions pertinent here. According to the first, the contract would be enforceable only if Williams could obtain financing. According to the second, the contract would be enforceable only if Williams later approved a bid for site improvements. Financing was to cover the cost of the mobile home and the cost of the land on which the mobile home would be placed. The contract provided for damages. It stated, "I [Williams] understand that you [Kenco] shall have all the rights of a seller upon breach of contract under the Uniform Commercial Code, except the right to seek and collect 'liquidated damages' under Section 2–718." The contract provided for reasonable attorney's fees. * * * In early October, Williams accepted Kenco's bid for site improvements. As a result, the parties (a) formed a second contract and (b) fulfilled the first contract's site-improvement-approval condition. Also in early October, Williams received preliminary approval on the needed financing.

On or about October 12, Williams gave Kenco a $600 check so Kenco could order an appraisal of the land on which the mobile home would be located. Before Kenco could act, however, Williams stopped payment on the check and repudiated the entire transaction. His reason * * * was that he "had found a better deal elsewhere." When Williams repudiated, Kenco had not yet ordered the mobile home from the factory. After Williams repudiated, Kenco simply did not place the order. As a result, Kenco's only out-of-pocket expense was a minor amount of office overhead. On November 1, 1994, Kenco sued Williams for lost profits. After a bench trial, the superior court found that Williams had breached the contract; that Kenco was entitled to damages; and that Kenco had lost profits in the amount of $11,133 ($6,720 on the mobile home, and $4,413 on the site improvements). The court further found, however, that Kenco would be adequately compensated by retaining Williams' $500 down payment; that Williams was the prevailing party; and that Williams should receive reasonable attorney's fees in the amount of $1,800. Because Kenco had already received its $500, the court entered an $1,800 judgment for Williams, and Kenco filed this appeal. In this court, Williams does not contest the trial court's finding that he breached the contract. Thus, the only issues are (1) whether the superior court used the correct measure of damages, and (2) whether the superior court properly awarded attorneys' fees to Williams.

### I

Under the Uniform Commercial Code (UCC), a nonbreaching seller may recover "damages for non-acceptance" from a breaching buyer. [UCC §2–703(e)] The measure of such damages is as follows:

> **(1)** * * * the measure of damages for non-acceptance or repudiation by the buyer is the difference between the market price at the time and place for tender and the unpaid contract price together with any incidental damages provided in this Article ([UCC §] 2–710), but less expenses saved inconsequence of the buyer's breach.
>
> **(2)** If the measure of damages provided in subsection (1) is inadequate to put the seller in as good a position as performance would have done then the measure of damages is the profit (including reasonable overhead) which the seller would have made from full performance by the buyer, together with any incidental damages provided in this Article ([UCC §] 2–710), due allowance for costs reasonably incurred and due credit for payments or proceeds of resale. [UCC §] 2–708.

* * * [T]he statute's purpose is to put the nonbreaching seller in the position that he or she would have occupied if the

breaching buyer had fully performed (or, in alternative terms, to give the nonbreaching seller the benefit of his or her bargain). [UCC §] 1–106(1). A party claiming damages under subsection (2) bears the burden of showing that an award of damages under subsection (1) would be inadequate. [Citation.] In general, the adequacy of damages under subsection (1) depends on whether the nonbreaching seller has a readily available market on which he or she can resell the goods that the breaching buyer should have taken. [Citation.] When a buyer breaches before either side has begun to perform, the amount needed to give the seller the benefit of his or her bargain is the difference between the contract price and the seller's expected cost of performance. Using market price, this difference can, in turn, be subdivided into two smaller differences: (a) the difference between the contract price and the market price, and (b) the difference between the market price and the seller's expected cost of performance. So long as a nonbreaching seller can reasonably resell the breached goods on the open market, he or she can recover the difference between contract price and market price by invoking subsection (1), and the difference between market price and his or her expected cost of performance by reselling the breached goods on the open market. Thus, he or she is made whole by subsection (1), and subsection (1) damages should be deemed "adequate." But if a nonbreaching seller cannot reasonably resell the breached goods on the open market, he or she cannot recover, merely by invoking subsection (1), the difference between market price and his or her expected cost of performance. Hence, he or she is not made whole by subsection (1); subsection (1) damages are "inadequate to put the seller in as good a position as performance would have done;" and subsection (2) comes into play.

The cases illustrate at least three specific situations in which a nonbreaching seller cannot reasonably resell on the open market. In the first, the seller never comes into possession of the breached goods; although he or she plans to acquire such goods before the buyer's breach, he or she rightfully elects not to acquire them after the buyer's breach. [Citation.] In the second, the seller possesses some or all of the breached goods, but they are of such an odd or peculiar nature that the seller lacks a post-breach market on which to sell them; they are, for example, unfinished, obsolete, or highly specialized. [Citations.] In the third situation, the seller again possesses some or all of the breached goods, but because the market is already oversupplied with such goods (i.e., the available supply exceeds demand), he or she cannot resell the breached goods without displacing another sale. [Citations.] [Court's footnote: In passing, we observe that this lost volume situation can be described in several ways. Focusing on the breached unit, one can say that due to a market in which supply exceeds demand, the lost volume seller cannot resell the breached unit without sacrificing an additional sale. Focusing on the additional unit, one can say that but for the buyer's breach, the lost volume seller would have made an additional sale. Focusing on both units, one can say that but for the buyer's breach, the lost volume seller would have sold both units. Each statement is equivalent to the others.] Frequently, these sellers are labeled "jobber," "components seller," and "lost volume seller," respectively, [citation]; in our view, however, such labels confuse more than clarify.

* * * In this case, Kenco did not order the breached goods before Williams repudiated. After Williams repudiated, Kenco was not required to order the breached goods from the factory, [UCC §§2–703, 2–704(2)]; it rightfully elected not to do so; and it could not resell the breached goods on the open market. Here, then, "the measure of damages provided in subsection (1) is inadequate to put [Kenco] in as good a position as [Williams'] performance would have done;" [UCC §2-708] subsection (2) states the applicable measure of damages; and Kenco is entitled to its lost profit of $11,133.

## II

The second issue is whether Kenco is entitled to reasonable attorneys' fees. The parties' contract provided that the prevailing party would be entitled to such fees. Kenco is the prevailing party. On remand, the trial court shall award Kenco reasonable attorneys' fees incurred at trial and on appeal.

Reversed with directions to enter an amended judgment awarding Kenco its lost profit of $11,133; reasonable attorneys' fees incurred at trial and on appeal; and any ancillary amounts required by law.

CASE 25-2

## Buyer's Remedy of Cover
## BIGELOW-SANFORD, INC. v. GUNNY CORP.

United States Court of Appeals, Fifth Circuit, Unit B, 1981
649 F.2d 1060

**Kravitch, J.**

[The plaintiff, Bigelow-Sanford, Inc., contracted with defendant Gunny Corp. for the purchase of 100,000 linear yards of jute at $0.64 per yard. Gunny delivered 22,228 linear yards in January 1979. The February and March deliveries required under the contract were not made, though 8 rolls (each roll containing 66.7 linear yards) were delivered in April. With 72,265 linear yards undelivered, Gunny told Bigelow-Sanford that no more would be delivered. In mid-March, Bigelow-Sanford turned to the jute spot market to replace the balance of the order at a price of $1.21 per linear yard. Since several other companies had also defaulted on their jute contracts with Bigelow-Sanford, the plaintiff purchased a total of 164,503 linear yards on the spot market. Plaintiff sues defendant to recover losses sustained as a result of the breach of contract.]

* * *

Gunny contends that appellee's [Bigelow-Sanford] alleged cover purchases should not have been used to measure damages in that they were not made in substitution for the contract purchases, were not made seasonably or in good faith and were not shown to be due to Gunny's breach. [W]e disagree. Again, we quote UCC §2–711 providing in part for cover damages where the seller fails to make delivery or repudiates the contract:

(a) "cover" and have damages under the next section as to all the goods affected whether or not they have been identified to the contract; or
(b) recover damages for non-delivery as provided in this Article (2–713).

UCC §2–712 defines cover:

(1) After a breach within the preceding section the buyer may "cover" by making in good faith and without unreasonable delay any reasonable purchase of or contract to purchase goods in substitution for those due from the seller.
(2) The buyer may recover from the seller as damages the difference between the cost of cover and the contract price together with any incidental or consequential damages as hereinafter defined (2–715), but less expenses saved in consequence of the seller's breach.
(3) Failure of the buyer to effect cover within this section does not bar him from any other remedy.

In addition, the purchaser may recover under 2–713:

(1) Subject to the provisions of this Article with respect to proof of market price (2–723), the measure of damages for non-delivery or repudiation by the seller is the difference between the market price at the time when the buyer learned of the breach and the contract price together with any incidental and consequential damages provided in this Article (2–715), but less expenses saved in consequence of the seller's breach.
(2) Market price is to be determined as of the place for tender or, in cases of rejection after arrival or revocation of acceptance, as of the place of arrival.

Most importantly, "whether a plaintiff has made his cover purchases in a reasonable manner poses a classic jury issue." [Citation.] The district court thus acted properly in submitting the question of cover damages to the jury, which found that Gunny had breached, appellee had covered, and had done so in good faith without unreasonable delay by making reasonable purchases, and was therefore entitled to damages under §2–712. Gunny argues Bigelow is not entitled to such damages on the ground that it failed to make cover purchases without undue delay and that the jury should not have been permitted to average the cost of Bigelow's spot market purchases totalling 164,503 linear yards in order to arrive at the cost of cover for the 72,265 linear yards Gunny failed to deliver. Both arguments fail. Gunny notified Bigelow in February that no more jute would be forthcoming. Bigelow made its first spot market purchases in mid-March. Given that it is within the jury's province to decide the reasonableness of the manner in which cover purchases were made, we believe the jury could reasonably decide such purchases, made one month after the date the jury assigned to Gunny's breach, were made without undue delay. The same is true with respect to Gunny's second argument: Bigelow's spot market purchases were made to replace several vendors' shipments. Bigelow did not specifically allocate the spot market replacements to individual vendors' accounts, however, nor was there a requirement that they do so. The jury's method of averaging such costs and assigning them to Gunny in proportion to the amount of jute if [sic] failed to deliver would, therefore, seem not only fair but well within the jury's permissible bounds.

Gunny also argues that the court erroneously charged the jury regarding damages under both §§2–712 and 2–713. We disagree. Whether Bigelow covered was a question of fact submitted to the jury. In the event that it had not, alternative damages were available to Bigelow under §2–713. [Citation.] The jury found that Bigelow had covered and awarded damages under §2–712; §2–713 then became irrelevant. Since either was applicable until that time, the court's charge as to both sections was not error.

* * *

[Judgment for Bigelow is affirmed.]

## CASE 25-3

## Liquidation of Damages
## COASTAL LEASING CORPORATION v. T-BAR S CORPORATION

Court of Appeals of North Carolina, 1998
128 N.C.App. 379, 496 S.E.2d 795
http://www.aoc.state.nc.us/www/public/coa/opinions/1998/970382-1.htm

**Walker, J.**

Plaintiff entered into a lease agreement (lease) with defendant T-Bar S Corporation (T-Bar) in May of 1992, whereby plaintiff agreed to lease certain cash register equipment (equipment) to T-Bar. Under the lease, T-Bar agreed to monthly rental payments of $289.13 each for a total of 48 months. Defendants George and Sharon Talbott (appellants) were the officers of T-Bar and personally guaranteed payment of all amounts due under the lease.

After making 18 of the monthly payments, appellants and T-Bar defaulted on the lease in December of 1993. On 28 February 1994, plaintiff mailed a certified letter to appellants and T-Bar, return receipt requested, advising them that the lease was in default and, pursuant to the terms of the lease, plaintiff was accelerating the remaining payments due under the lease. They further advised appellants and T-Bar that if the entire amount due of $8,841.06 was not received within 7 days, plaintiff would seek to recover the balance due plus interest and reasonable attorneys' fees, as well as possession of the equipment. The record shows that appellants and T-Bar each received this letter on 1 March 1994.

On 10 March 1994, plaintiff mailed a certified letter and "Notice of Public Sale of Repossessed Leased Equipment" (notice of sale) to appellants and T-Bar at the same address, again return receipt requested. This letter advised appellants and T-Bar that plaintiff had taken possession of the equipment and was conducting a public sale pursuant to the terms of the lease. Although the date on the notice of sale stated that the sale was to be held on 23 March 1994, the sale was actually scheduled to be held on 25 March 1994. This letter and notice of sale were returned to plaintiffs "unclaimed" on 29 March 1994.

Plaintiffs conducted a public sale of the equipment on 25 March 1994 and no one appeared on behalf of appellants or T-Bar. There being no other bidders, plaintiff purchased the equipment at the sale for $2,000.00.

On 4 October 1994, plaintiff leased some of the same equipment to another company at a rate calculated to be $212.67 for 36 months. Plaintiff then filed this action on 6 October 1994 seeking to recover the balance due under the lease, minus the net proceeds from the 25 March 1994 public sale, plus interest and reasonable attorneys' fees. Appellants filed an answer and counterclaim on 27 July 1995. Plaintiff then filed a motion for summary judgment against appellants on 8 July 1996. * * *

After a hearing, the trial court entered summary judgment on 15 January 1997 in favor of plaintiff on its complaint and appellants' counterclaims and entered judgment against appellants for the sum of $7,223.56 plus interest and attorneys' fees of $1,083.54.

* * *

* * * Since both parties agree that the transaction at issue in this case is not a security interest, but rather is a lease, Article 2A controls.

* * *

In their appeal, appellants contend that the trial court erred by granting summary judgment in favor of plaintiff because there exists a genuine issue of material fact as to whether: (1) the liquidated damages clause contained in Paragraph 13 of the lease is reasonable in light of the then-anticipated harm caused by default; * * *.

As to appellants' first contention, the official commentary to Article 2A states that "in recognition of the diversity of the transactions to be governed [and] the sophistication of many of the parties to these transactions * * *, freedom of contract has been preserved." [UCC §] 2A–102 Official Comment. Also, under general contract principles, when the parties to a transaction deal with each other at arms length and without the exercise by one of the parties of superior bargaining power, the parties will be bound by their agreement. [Citation.]

Article 2A recognizes that "[m]any leasing transactions are predicated on the parties' ability to agree to an appropriate amount of damages or formula for damages in the event of default or other act or omission." [UCC §] 2A–504 Official Comment. [UCC §] 2A–504 states, in pertinent part:

> (1) Damages payable by either party for default, or any other act or omission * * * may be liquidated in the lease agreement but only at an amount or by a formula that is reasonable in light of the then-anticipated harm caused by the default or other act or omission.

This liquidated damages provision is more flexible than that provided by its statutory analogue under Article 2, [UCC §] 2–718. The Article 2 liquidated damages section provides, in pertinent part:

> (1) Damages for breach by either party may be liquidated in the agreement but only at an amount which is reasonable in the light of the anticipated or actual harm caused by the breach, the difficulties of proof of loss, and the inconvenience or nonfeasibility of otherwise obtaining an adequate remedy. A term fixing unreasonably large liquidated damages is void as a penalty.

[UCC §] 2–718(1). A review of these statutes reveals two major differences.

First, the drafters of Article 2A chose not to incorporate the two tests which are required by Article 2, i.e., the difficulties of proof of loss and the inconvenience or nonfeasibility of otherwise obtaining an adequate remedy. In fact, the official commentary to [UCC §] 2A–504 states that since "[t]he ability to liquidate damages is critical to modern leasing practice * * * [and] given the parties' freedom to contract at common law, the policy behind retaining these two additional requirements here was thought to be outweighed." [Citation.]

Secondly, the drafters of Article 2A recognized that in order to further promote freedom of contract, it was necessary to delete the last sentence of [UCC §] 2–718(1), which provided that unreasonably large liquidated damages provisions were void as a penalty. As such, the parties to a lease transaction are free to negotiate the amount of liquidated damages, restrained only by the rule of reasonableness.

"The basic test of the reasonableness of an agreement liquidating damages is whether the stipulated amount or amount produced by the stipulated formula represents a reasonable forecast of the probable loss." [Citation.] However, "no court should strike down a reasonable liquidated damage agreement based on foresight that has proved on hindsight to have contained an inaccurate estimation of the probable loss. * * *" [Citation.] And, "the fact that there is a difference between the actual loss, as determined at or about the time of the default, and the anticipated loss or stipulated amount or formula, as stipulated at the time the lease contract was entered into * * *," does not necessarily mean that the liquidated damage agreement is unreasonable. [Citation.] This is so because "[t]he value of a lessor's interest in leased equipment depends upon 'the physical condition of the equipment and the market conditions at that time.'" [Citation.] Further, in determining whether a liquidated damages clause is reasonable:

> [A] court should keep in mind that the clause was negotiated by the parties, who are familiar with the circumstances and practices with respect to the type of transaction involved, and the clause carries with it a consensual apportionment of the risks of the agreement that a court should be slow to overturn.

[Citation.]

In this case, Paragraph 13 of the lease (the liquidated damages clause) reads as follows:

> 13. REMEDIES If an event of default shall occur, Lessor may, at its option, at any time (a) declare the entire amount of unpaid rental for the balance of the term of this lease immediately due and payable, whereupon Lessee shall become obligated to pay to Lessor forthwith the total amount of the said rental for the balance of the said term, and (b) without demand or legal process, enter into the premises where the equipment may be found and take possession of and remove the Equipment, without liability for suit, action or other proceeding, and all rights of Lessee in the Equipment so removed shall terminate absolutely. Lessee hereby waives notice of, or hearing with respect to, such retaking. Lessor may at its option, use, ship, store, repair or lease all Equipment so removed and sell or otherwise dispose of any such Equipment at a private or public sale. In the event Lessor takes possession of the Equipment, Lessor shall give Lessee credit for any sums received by Lessor from the sale or rental of the Equipment after deduction of the expenses of sale or rental and Lessor's residual interest in the Equipment.

* * * Lessor and Lessee acknowledge the difficulty in establishing a value for the unexpired lease term and owing to such difficulty agree that the provisions of this paragraph represent an agreed measure of damages and are not to be deemed a forfeiture or penalty. * * *

* * *

After a careful review, we conclude the liquidated damages clause is a reasonable estimation of the then-anticipated damages in the event of default because it protects plaintiff's expectation interest. The liquidated damages clause places plaintiff in the position it would have occupied had the lease been fully performed by allowing it to accelerate the balance of the lease payments and repossess the equipment. Therefore, since there is no evidence that plaintiff exercised a superior bargaining position in the negotiation of the liquidated damages clause, no genuine issue of material fact exists as to its reasonableness, and the trial court did not err by enforcing its provisions.

CASE 25-4

## Limitation of Remedy by Agreement

## BOC GROUP, INC. v. CHEVRON CHEMICAL COMPANY, LLC

Superior Court of New Jersey, Appellate Division, 2003
359 N.J.Super. 135, 819 A.2d 431, 50 U.C.C. Rep.Serv.2d 489
http://lawlibrary.rutgers.edu/courts/appellate/a0338-01.opn.html

**Winkelstein, J.**

Plaintiff contracted with defendant to deliver liquid nitrogen, primarily from its Michoud, Louisiana plant, to defendant's oil refinery production facility located in Belle Chase, Louisiana. Defendant uses liquid nitrogen to ensure the safe operation of its plant. Defendant claims that plaintiff repeatedly failed to timely deliver the liquid nitrogen, dropping the liquid nitrogen to dangerously low levels, compromising the safety of plant personnel. Although the contract provided that if plaintiff failed to deliver the liquid nitrogen as required defendant's sole remedy would be to purchase the product from another supplier and charge plaintiff for the additional expenses incurred, defendant did not do so, but instead terminated plaintiff's services.

Plaintiff sued defendant for breach of contract, and defendant counterclaimed. * * * The Law Division granted plaintiff's motion for partial summary judgment on liability, * * *. After a damages trial before a jury, plaintiff was awarded a judgment in the amount of $1,200,000.

Defendant appealed, * * *. We conclude that defendant's arguments are without merit. Accordingly, we affirm.

* * *

On October 1, 1991, the parties entered into a procurement contract, whereby plaintiff would supply defendant with "all [of defendant's] requirements" for bulk nitrogen. * * * The contract, * * *, was originally effective from October 1, 1991, to September 30, 1994, and was extended until August 31, 2000.

Defendant uses liquid nitrogen to "prevent fires and explosions within process equipment and systems and to assure instrumentation and control system reliability in critical process units." The nitrogen "protects plant personnel and the public from accidental toxic material discharges and prevents product contamination [from] oxygen * * * which would reduce product quality and performance." * * *

The contract was a "requirement" contract—deliveries were based on how much liquid nitrogen defendant had in its tanks. As a result, plaintiff typically made deliveries seven days a week, and sometimes several times a day.

Under the contract's terms, defendant's exclusive remedy if plaintiff failed to timely deliver the nitrogen was "cover damages."

* * *

When the nitrogen level fell below fifty percent of the total storage capacity, the operator of defendant's plant would inform plaintiff that the levels were depleting and check on the time for the next delivery. At a twenty-five-percent level of nitrogen, defendant considered the situation "critical," and at a ten-percent level defendant could no longer maintain normal operation of the plant.

Defendant claims that from August 1997 through June 1998 plaintiff made twenty-one late deliveries. A representative of defendant stated that on "many more than two times," because of its dissipating nitrogen levels, defendant's personnel would have to call plaintiff to find out when the next delivery would arrive. Plaintiff would usually promise delivery within four hours; however, the delivery would typically not arrive for as long as twelve hours. On May 19, 1998, defendant's nitrogen supply became so low that it had to connect its own nitrogen cylinders to the hot oil surge tank to maintain operation.

That same month, Steven Earle, defendant's operations supervisor, decided to terminate the contract with plaintiff and find another liquid nitrogen supplier. He testified that he opted to terminate the contract rather than seek cover damages because he could not find alternate suppliers to deliver the required nitrogen. He claimed other suppliers were hesitant "to come in and infringe on an existing contract. * * *" He did not know, however, which suppliers interpreted the contract that way. Although he believed that Air Products, a company that delivered nitrogen to defendant's other plants, as well as other chemicals to defendant's Belle Chase plant [the plant in question], "would have been one of them," Dennis H. Boushie, an Air Products representative, testified otherwise. He said that in early 1998, when a representative of defendant told him of defendant's problems with low nitrogen inventory levels, he represented that Air Products "had the product" and could supply the product to defendant. Allen Jackson, defendant's purchasing manager, confirmed this conversation. Although no agreement materialized from the discussion, Air Products did cover defendant's liquid nitrogen supply on one occasion, in September 1998 during a hurricane.

Earle also acknowledged, however, that when he made his decision to terminate the contract in May 1998 he was not aware of the exclusive remedy provision in the contract. In fact, he had not read the contract. * * *

In July 1998, defendant advised plaintiff that because of its supply problems it intended to change suppliers. On July 15, 1998, plaintiff and defendant met to discuss plaintiff's performance under the contract. At the meeting, Earle asked plaintiff for a letter confirming that defendant could obtain nitrogen from a secondary supplier. Plaintiff agreed to do so, but never followed through.

On August 25, 1998, defendant wrote to plaintiff explaining that plaintiff's late deliveries jeopardized defendant's plant's operations. Enclosed with the letter was a proposed amendment to the contract, which essentially allowed defendant to obtain nitrogen from any supplier, not just plaintiff. The effect of the amendment would have been to terminate the contract.

Plaintiff agreed to maintain defendant's supply of liquid nitrogen at a forty-percent level, and plaintiff also offered to "provide and install [at defendant's plant] an additional 11,000 gallon vessel at no cost, to increase the present nitrogen storage from 22,000 to 33,000 gallons." Defendant declined the offer. Rather, in a September 1, 1998, letter, defendant said, "Effective October 1, 1998, Chevron's demand for liquid nitrogen from BOC will be terminated."

* * *

We * * * turn to the Law Division's entry of summary judgment on liability. The judge relied on the exclusive remedy language of the contract, limiting defendant's rights in the event plaintiff failed to deliver nitrogen at the times and in the quantities defendant required. The court found that defendant's sole remedy in the event of plaintiff's noncompliance with the contract was to purchase nitrogen from another supplier, and charge plaintiff for any additional expense defendant incurred by reason of plaintiff's untimely deliveries. The court concluded that defendant did not have the right to terminate the contract. We agree.

Under the Uniform Commercial Code (UCC) as adopted in New Jersey, parties to a contract may establish an exclusive remedy, which, if so labeled, "is the sole remedy" available to them under the terms of the contract. [UCC §] 2–719(1)(b). Yet, despite this exclusive remedy provision, "where circumstances cause an exclusive or limited remedy to fail of its essential purpose, remedy may be had as provided in [the UCC]." [UCC §] 2–719(2). The exclusive remedy provision is "'not concerned with arrangements which were oppressive at their inception, but rather with the application of an agreement to novel circumstances not contemplated by the parties.'" [Citations.] Although an arm's length contract between sophisticated commercial parties, such as in this case, should not be readily upset by a court, [citation], where a party is deprived of the substantial value of its bargain by reason of the exclusive remedy, the contract remedy will give way to the general remedy provisions of the UCC. [Citation.]

Issues concerning a contract's exclusive remedy often arise in the context of a breach of warranty. For example, when a product becomes defective, the breach of warranty provision may limit the seller's obligation to repair or replace defective equipment. [Citations.] In these types of cases—where the seller has limited the warranty to the repair or replacement of a defective part or product—before the exclusive remedy is considered to have failed in its essential purpose, the seller must be given an opportunity to repair or replace the product. [Citations.]

A remedy may also fail of its essential purpose if, "after numerous attempts to repair," the product does not operate free of defects. [Citations.]

Failure of an exclusive remedy may also come about if the buyer is required to perform an act that cannot be done, such as where a warranty calls for defective parts to be delivered to its plant, but the parts were destroyed, [citation]; or repair or replacement take an unreasonable time to complete, [citations]; or circumstances "prevent the agreed remedy from yielding its purported and expected relief." [Citation.]

When deciding whether an exclusive remedy has failed of its essential purpose, a court must examine "the facts and circumstances surrounding the contract, the nature of the basic obligations of the party, the nature of the goods involved, the uniqueness or experimental nature of the items, the general availability of the items, and the good faith and reasonableness of the provision." [Citation.] Whether an exclusive remedy fails in its essential purpose is a question of fact. [Citations.]

Here, the exclusive remedy provision of the contract limited defendant's rights in the event of plaintiff's breach. Defendant's "exclusive remedy" for the "unexcused failure on the part of [plaintiff] to deliver product to [defendant]," was defendant's right to recover from plaintiff the difference between defendant's cost to purchase nitrogen from another supplier and the price defendant would have paid plaintiff for the nitrogen under the terms of the contract. Defendant did not exercise this right because it claims it was unable to purchase nitrogen from other suppliers; therefore, defendant argues, the remedy failed in its essential purpose and may not be enforced. The proofs do not, however, support defendant's argument.

Earle testified that he believed other suppliers would not sell defendant liquid nitrogen because they did not want to "infringe" on defendant's contract with plaintiff. However, Earle was unable to point to any occasion when defendant made such a request, or to any supplier who ever turned down defendant's request. Although Earle believed Air Products may have been one of the suppliers who would not sell product to defendant, that testimony was contradicted by the testimony of Jackson and Boushie, each of whom indicated that Air Products was prepared to supply liquid nitrogen to Chevron; and, in fact, did supply liquid nitrogen to Chevron in September 1998.

Defendant's position, that the exclusive remedy failed, is further belied by Earle's testimony that at the time he decided to terminate the contract with plaintiff—May 1998—he was not even aware of the exclusive remedy provision of the contract. The clear inference being that if he did not know what the contract required if plaintiff breached, there was no reason for him to invoke the contract's exclusive remedy.

We agree with the motion judge that a rational factfinder could not find that the exclusive remedy failed in its essential purpose. On the only occasion defendant actually tried to purchase nitrogen from another supplier, it was successful. The facts paint a clear picture—defendant did not give the exclusive remedy an opportunity to work before terminating the contract. It made no attempt to purchase liquid nitrogen from other suppliers when plaintiff was delinquent in its deliveries. Instead, Earle canceled the contract despite the contract's exclusive remedy, which did not include termination.

Both plaintiff and defendant are sophisticated business entities, freely entering into a contract which limited defendant's remedies. We find no reason why the parties should not be held to the terms of their bargain. * * *

Defendant argues that the trial court did not entertain its claim that plaintiff's repeated lateness in delivering the nitrogen was tantamount to a breach of installments, impairing the value of the contract as a whole, giving defendant the right to cancel the contract. Under [UCC §] 2–612(1), an "installment contract" is a contract in which the goods are delivered in "separate lots to be separately accepted." Whenever a nonconformity or a default with respect to one or more of the installments "substantially impairs the value of the whole contract[,] there is a breach of the whole," [UCC §] 2–612(3), and the nondefaulting party may cancel the contract. [UCC §] 2–711(1). However, an "aggrieved party reinstates the contract if he accepts a non-conforming installment without seasonably notifying of cancellation or if he brings an action with respect only to past installments or demands performance as to future installments." [UCC §] 2–612(3).

Defendant points to twenty-one occasions where plaintiff was late delivering the nitrogen. Yet, defendant continued to accept delivery, without "seasonably" notifying plaintiff of its decision to cancel the contract. In fact, it was not until well after the twenty-one allegedly late deliveries that defendant told plaintiff of its intention to cancel the contract. Even after notifying plaintiff of the problems, and meeting with plaintiff in July 1998, defendant continued to accept nitrogen from plaintiff. In other words, even if plaintiff's late deliveries were deemed to substantially impair the contract, by continuing to accept the deliveries, defendant reinstated the contract. Its argument that plaintiff's repeated late deliveries permitted cancellation is therefore without merit.

* * *

Affirmed.

## QUESTIONS

1. Identify and discuss the goods-oriented remedies of the seller and the buyer.
2. Identify and discuss the obligation-oriented remedies of the seller and the buyer.
3. Identify and discuss the money-oriented damages of the seller and the buyer.
4. Identify and discuss the "specific performance" remedies of the seller and the buyer.
5. Describe the basic types of contractual provisions affecting remedies and the limitations that the Code imposes upon these provisions.

## PROBLEMS

1. Mae contracted to sell one thousand bushels of wheat to Lloyd at $5.00 per bushel. Just before Mae was to deliver the wheat, Lloyd notified her that he would not receive or accept the wheat. Mae sold the wheat for $4.60 per bushel, the market price, and later sued Lloyd for the difference of $400. Lloyd claims he was not notified by Mae of the resale and, hence, is not liable. Is Lloyd correct? Why?

**2.** On December 15, Judy wrote a letter to David stating that she would sell to David all of the mine-run coal that David might wish to buy during the next calendar year for use at David's factory, delivered at the factory at a price of $30 per ton. David immediately replied by letter to Judy, stating that he accepted the offer, that he would purchase all of his mine-run coal from Judy, and that he would need two hundred tons of coal during the first week in January. During the months of January, February, and March, Judy delivered to David a total of seven hundred tons of coal, for all of which David made payment to Judy at the rate of $30 per ton. On April 10, David ordered two hundred tons of mine-run coal from Judy, who replied to David on April 11 that she could not supply David with any more coal except at a price of $38 per ton delivered. David thereafter purchased elsewhere at the market price, namely $38 per ton, all of his factory's requirements of mine-run coal for the remainder of the year, amounting to a total of two thousand tons of coal. Can David now recover damages from Judy at the rate of $8 per ton for the coal thus purchased, amounting to $16,000?

**3.** On January 10, Betty, of Emanon, Missouri, visited the showrooms of the Forte Piano Company in St. Louis and selected a piano. A sales memorandum of the transaction signed both by Betty and by the salesperson of the Forte Piano Company read as follows: "Sold to Betty one new Andover piano, factory number 46832, price $3,300, to be shipped to the buyer at Emanon, Missouri, freight prepaid, before February 1. Prior to shipment, seller will stain the case a darker color in accordance with buyer's directions and will make the tone more brilliant." On January 15, Betty repudiated the contract by letter to the Forte Piano Company. The company subsequently stained the case, made the tone more brilliant, and offered to ship the piano to Betty on January 26. Betty persisted in her refusal to accept the piano. The Forte Piano Company sued Betty to recover the contract price. To what remedy, if any, is Forte entitled?

**4.** Sims contracted in writing to sell Blake one hundred electric motors at a price of $100 each, freight prepaid to Blake's warehouse. By the contract of sale, Sims expressly warranted that each motor would develop twenty-five-brake horsepower. The contract provided that the motors would be delivered in lots of twenty-five per week beginning January 2, and that Blake should pay for each lot of twenty-five motors as delivered, but that Blake was to have right of inspection upon delivery. Immediately upon delivery of the first lot of twenty-five motors on January 2, Blake forwarded Sims a check for $2,500, but upon testing each of the twenty-five motors Blake determined that none would develop more than fifteen-brake horsepower. State all of the remedies under the Uniform Commercial Code available to Blake.

**5.** Henry and Mary entered into a written contract whereby Henry agreed to sell and Mary agreed to buy a certain automobile for $8,500. Henry drove the car to Mary's residence and properly parked it on the street in front of her house, where he tendered it to Mary and requested payment of the price. Mary refused to take the car or pay the price. Henry informed Mary that he would hold her to the contract; but before Henry had time to enter the car and drive it away, a fire truck, answering a fire alarm and traveling at a high speed, crashed into the car and demolished it. Henry brings an action against Mary to recover the price of the car. Who is entitled to judgment? Would the result differ if Henry were a dealer in automobiles?

**6.** James sells and delivers to Gerald on June 1 certain goods and receives from Gerald at the time of delivery Gerald's check in the amount of $9,000 for the goods. The following day, Gerald is petitioned into bankruptcy, and the check is dishonored by Gerald's bank. On June 5, James serves notice upon Gerald and the trustee in bankruptcy that he reclaims the goods. The trustee is in possession of the goods and refuses to deliver them to James. What are the rights of the parties?

**7.** The ABC Company, located in Chicago, contracted to sell a carload of television sets to Dodd in St. Louis, Missouri, on sixty days' credit. ABC Company shipped the carload to Dodd. Upon arrival of the car at St. Louis, Dodd paid the freight charges and reshipped the car to Hines of Little Rock, Arkansas, to whom he had previously contracted to sell the television sets. While the car was in transit to Little Rock, Dodd went bankrupt. ABC Company was informed of this at once and immediately telephoned XYZ Railroad Company to withhold delivery of the television sets. What should the XYZ Railroad Company do?

**8.** Robert in Chicago entered into a contract to sell certain machines to Terry in New York. The machines were to be manufactured by Robert and shipped F.O.B. Chicago not later than March 25. On March 24, when Robert is about to ship the machines, he receives a letter from Terry wrongfully repudiating the contract. The machines cannot readily be resold for a reasonable price because they are a special kind used only in Terry's manufacturing processes. Robert sues Terry to recover the agreed price of the machines. What are the rights of the parties?

**9.** Calvin purchased a log home construction kit manufactured by Boone Homes, Inc., from an authorized Boone dealer. The sales contract stated that Boone would repair or replace defective materials and that this was the exclusive remedy available against Boone. The dealer assembled the house, which was defective in several respects. The knotholes in the logs caused the walls and ceiling to leak. A support beam was too small and therefore cracked, causing the floor to crack also. These defects could not be completely cured by repair. Should Calvin prevail in a lawsuit against Boone for breach of warranty to recover damages for the loss in value?

**10.** Margaret contracted to buy a particular model Rolls-Royce from Paragon Motors, Inc. Only one hundred of these models are built each year. She paid a $3,000 deposit on the car, but Paragon sold the car to Gluck. What remedy, if any, does Margaret have against Paragon?

**11.** Technical Textile agreed by written contract to manufacture and sell 20,000 pounds of yarn to Jagger Brothers at a price of $2.15 per pound. After Technical had manufactured, delivered, and been paid for 3,723 pounds of yarn, Jagger Brothers by letter informed Technical that it was repudiating the contract and that it would refuse any further yarn deliveries. On August 12, the date of the letter, the market price of yarn was $1.90 per pound. The remaining 16,277 pounds were never manufactured. Technical sued Jagger Brothers for breach of contract. To what damages, if any, is Technical entitled? Explain.

**12.** Sherman Burrus, a job printer, purchased a printing press from the Itek Corporation for a price of $7,006.08. Before making the purchase, Burrus was assured by an Itek salesperson, Mr. Nessel, that the press was appropriate for the type of printing Burrus was doing. Burrus encountered problems in operating the press almost continuously from the time he received it. Burrus, his employees, and Itek representatives spent many hours in an unsuccessful attempt to get the press to operate properly. Burrus requested that the press be replaced, but Itek refused. Burrus then brought an action against Itek for (1) damages for breach of the implied warranty of merchantability and (2) consequential damages for losses resulting from the press's defective operation. Burrus was able to prove that the actual value of the press was $1,167 and, because of the defective press, that his output decreased and he sustained a great loss of paper. Itek contends that consequential damages are not recoverable in this case since Burrus elected to keep the press and continued to use it. How much should Burrus recover in damages for breach of warranty? Is he entitled to consequential damages?

**13.** A farmer made a contract in April to sell to a grain dealer forty thousand bushels of corn to be delivered in October. On June 3, the farmer unequivocally informed the grain dealer that he was not going to plant any corn, that he would not fulfill the contract, and that, if the buyer had commitments to resell the corn, he should make other arrangements. The grain dealer waited in vain until October for performance of the repudiated contract. Then he bought corn at a greatly increased price on the market in order to fulfill commitments to his purchasers. To what damages, if any, is the grain dealer entitled? Explain.

**14.** Through information provided by S-2 Yachts, Inc., the plaintiff, Barr located a yacht to his liking at the Crow's Nest marina and yacht sales company. When Barr asked the price, he was told that, although the yacht normally sold for $102,000, Crow's Nest was willing to sell this particular one for only $80,000 to make room for a new model from the manufacturer, S-2 Yachts, Inc. Barr was assured that the yacht in question came with full manufacturer's warranties. Barr asked if the yacht was new and if anything was wrong with it. Crow's Nest told him that nothing was wrong with the yacht and that there were only twenty hours of use on the engines.

Once the yacht had been delivered and Barr had taken it for a test run, he noticed several problems associated with saltwater damage, such as rusted screws, a rusted stove, and faulty electrical wiring. Barr was assured that Crow's Nest would pay for these repairs. However, as was later discovered, the yacht was in such a damaged condition that Barr experienced great personal hazard the two times that he used the boat. Examination by a marine expert revealed clearly that the boat had been sunk in saltwater prior to Barr's purchase. The engines were severely damaged, and there was significant structural and equipment damage as well. According to the expert, not only was the yacht not new, it was worth at most only one-half of the new value of $102,000. What should Barr be able to recover from S-2 Yachts and Crow's Nest?

**15.** Lee Oldsmobile sells Rolls-Royce automobiles. Mrs. Kaiden sent Lee a $25,000 deposit on a 2001 Rolls-Royce with a purchase price of $145,500. Although Lee informed Mrs. Kaiden that the car would be delivered in November, the order form did not indicate the delivery date and contained a disclaimer for delay or failure to deliver due to circumstances beyond the dealer's control. On November 21, Mrs. Kaiden purchased another car from another dealer and canceled her car from Lee. When Lee attempted to deliver a Rolls-Royce to Mrs. Kaiden on November 29, Mrs. Kaiden refused to accept delivery. Lee later sold the car for $140,495. Mrs. Kaiden sued Lee for her $25,000 deposit plus interest. Lee counterclaims, based on the terms of the contract, for liquidated damages of $25,000 (the amount of the deposit) as a result of Mrs. Kaiden's breach of contract. What are the rights of the parties?

**16.** Servebest contracted to sell Emessee two hundred thousand pounds of 50 percent lean beef trimmings for $105,000. Upon a substantial fall in the market price, Emessee refused to pay the contract price and informed Servebest that the contract was canceled. Servebest sues Emessee for breach of contract, including (a) damages for the difference between the contract price and the resale price of the trimmings, and (b) incidental damages. Decision?

**17.** Mrs. French was the highest bidder on eight antique guns at an auction held by Sotheby & Company. Mrs. French made a down payment on the guns but subsequently refused to accept the guns and refused to pay the remaining balance of $24,886.27 owed on them. Is Sotheby's entitled to collect the price of the guns from Mrs. French?

**18.** Teledyne Industries, Inc., entered into a contract with Teradyne, Inc., to purchase a T–347A transistor test system for the list and fair market price of $98,400 less a discount of $984. After the system was packed for shipment, Teledyne canceled the order, offering to purchase a Field Effects Transistor System for $65,000. Teradyne refused the offer and sold the T–347A to another purchaser pursuant to an order that was on hand prior to the cancellation. Can Teradyne recover from Teledyne for lost profits resulting from the breach of contract? Explain.

**19.** Wilson Trading Corp. agreed to sell David Ferguson a specified quantity of yarn for use in making sweaters. The written contract provided that notice of defects, to be effective, had to be received by Wilson before knitting or within ten days of receipt of the yarn. When the knitted sweaters were washed, the color of the yarn "shaded" (i.e., variations in color from piece to piece appeared). David Ferguson immediately notified Wilson of the problem and refused to pay for the yarn, claiming that the defect made the sweaters unmarketable. Wilson brought suit against Ferguson for the contract price. What result?

**20.** Daniel Martin and John Duke contracted with J&S Distributors, Inc., to purchase a KIS Magnum Speed printer for $17,000. The parties agreed that Martin and Duke would send one half of the money as a deposit and would pay the balance upon delivery. When the machine arrived five days late, Martin and Duke refused to accept it stating that they had purchased a substitute machine elsewhere. Martin and Duke requested the return of their deposit but J&S refused. Martin and Duke sued Jeff Sheffer and J&S for breach of contract, fraud, breach of good faith, and unfair and deceptive trade practices. The defendants counterclaimed for full performance of the contract pursuant to a clause in the contract, which provides the following:

> In the event of non-payment of the balance of the purchase price reflected herein on due date and in the manner

recorded or on such extended date which may be caused by late delivery on the part of [the seller], the Customer shall be liable for:

(1) immediate payment of the full balance recorded herein; and
(2) payment of interest at the rate of 12% per annum calculated on the balance due, when due, together with any attorney's fees, collection charges and other necessary expenses incurred by [the seller].

What are the rights of the parties?

**21.** Bishop Logging Company is a large, family-owned logging contractor formed in the low country of South Carolina. Bishop Logging has traditionally harvested pine timber. However, Bishop Logging began investigating the feasibility of a fully mechanized hardwood swamp logging operation when its main customer, Stone Container Corporation, decided to expand hardwood production. In anticipating an increased demand for hardwood in conjunction with the operation of a new paper machine, Stone Container requested that Bishop Logging harvest and supply hardwood for processing at its mill. In South Carolina, most suitable hardwood is located deep in the swamplands. Because of the high accident risk in the swamp, Bishop Logging did not want to harvest hardwood by the conventional method of manual felling of trees. Because Bishop Logging had already been successful in its totally mechanized pine logging operation, it began a search for improved methods of hardwood swamp logging centered on mechanizing the process in order to reduce labor, minimize personal injury and insurance costs, and improve efficiency and productivity. Bishop Logging ultimately purchased several pieces of John Deere equipment to make up the system. The gross sales price of the machinery was $608,899. All the equipment came with a written John Deere "New Equipment Warranty," whereby John Deere agreed only to repair or replace the equipment during the warranty period and did not warrant the suitability of the equipment. In the "New Equipment Warranty," John Deere expressly provided the following: (a) John Deere would repair or replace parts that were defective in material or workmanship; (b) a disclaimer of any express warranties or implied warranties of merchantability or fitness for a particular purpose; (c) an exclusion of all incidental or consequential damages; and (d) no authority for the dealer to make any representations, promises, modifications, or limitations of John Deere's written warranty. Hoping to sell more equipment if the Bishop Logging system was successful, however, John Deere agreed to assume part of the risk of the new enterprise by extending its standard equipment warranties notwithstanding the unusual use and modifications to the equipment. Soon after being placed in operation in the swamp, the machinery began to experience numerous mechanical problems. John Deere made more than $110,000 in warranty repairs on the equipment. However, Bishop Logging contended the swamp logging system failed to operate as represented by John Deere and, as a result, it suffered a substantial financial loss. What, if any, remedies is Bishop entitled to receive? Explain.

# PART 5
# Negotiable Instruments

# CHAPTER 26
# Form and Content

In 1990, the American Law Institute and the National Conference of Commissioners on Uniform Laws approved a Revised Article 3 to the Uniform Commercial Code (UCC). Named "Negotiable Instruments," the new Article maintains the basic scope and content of prior Article 3 (Commercial Paper). In 2002, the American Law Institute and the National Conference of Commissioners on Uniform Law completed updates to Articles 3 and 4. Thirty-nine States have adopted the 1990 version of Article 3, ten States have adopted the 2002 version, and New York has retained the original version of Article 3 (Commercial Paper). This part of the text will discuss Revised Article 3 but will also point out the major changes from prior Article 3. The 1990 version of Revised Article 3 is presented in *Appendix C.*

Negotiable instruments, also referred to simply as instruments, include checks, promissory notes, drafts, and certificates of deposit. These instruments are crucial to the sale of goods and services as well as to the financing of most businesses. The use of negotiable instruments has increased to such an extent that payments made with these instruments, with checks in particular, are now many times greater than payments made with cash, which now is used primarily for smaller transactions. In the United States, approximately seventy billion checks are written each year for a total value of $42 trillion. However, the number of checks written is lower than in previous years due to the increased use of electronic payments. In addition, as of the end of 2009, in the United States $1.1 trillion of outstanding commercial paper in the form of promissory notes had been issued by corporations to fund operating expenses or current assets. Moreover, in the United States in 2007, almost $6 trillion of corporate long-term promissory notes (bonds) were outstanding. Accordingly, the vital importance of negotiable instruments and electronic transfers as methods of payment and financing cannot be overstated.

To accomplish its social and economic objectives, the payment system must be quick, sure, and efficient. The use of cash can never satisfy all of these requirements because (1) it is inconvenient to maintain large quantities of cash; (2) the risk of loss or theft is far too great; (3) the risk in sending cash is likewise too high, as is the cost of postage and insurance in shipping cash over long distances; and (4) the costs to the Federal government of maintaining an adequate supply of currency would be prohibitive. In addition, negotiable instruments used for payment provide a convenient receipt as well as a record for accounting and tax purposes. Although negotiable instruments closely approximate cash for the purpose of payment, they are not exactly equivalent because, for example, negotiable instruments may be forged, they may be drawn on insufficient funds, payment may be stopped, or the instrument may be materially altered. Nevertheless, these risks (which are real but very infrequent—more than 99 percent of all checks are paid) are slight compared with the advantages that negotiable instruments provide for payment. Consequently, a major objective of the law of negotiable instruments and the bank collection process is to reduce these risks by increasing the safety, soundness, and operating efficiency of the entire payment system.

Moreover, the credit function of negotiable instruments is indispensable. Promissory notes and drafts serve an important business purpose, not only in areas of high finance but also at the level of the small business and individual consumer. In recent years, individuals have increasingly used certificates of deposit instead of savings accounts.

## NEGOTIABILITY

Negotiability is a legal concept that makes written instruments more freely transferable and therefore a readily accepted form of payment in substitution for money.

### DEVELOPMENT OF LAW OF NEGOTIABLE INSTRUMENTS

The starting point for an understanding of negotiable instruments is recognizing that four or five centuries ago in England a contract right to the payment of money was not assignable because a contractual promise ran to the promisee. The fact that performance could be rendered only to him constituted a hardship for the owner of the right because it prevented him from selling or disposing of it. Eventually, however, the law permitted recovery upon an assignment by the assignee against the obligor.

An innocent assignee bringing an action against the obligor was subject to all defenses available to the obligor. Such an action would result in the same outcome whether it was brought by the assignee or assignor. Thus, a contract right became assignable but not very marketable because merchants had little interest in buying paper that may be subject to a defense. This remains the law of **assignments**: *the assignee stands in the shoes of his assignor.* For a discussion of assignments, see *Chapter 16.*

With the flourishing of trade and commerce, it became essential to develop a more effective means of exchanging contractual rights for money. For example, a merchant who sold goods for cash might use the cash to buy more goods for resale. If he were to make a sale on credit in exchange for a promise to pay money, why should he not be permitted to sell that promise to someone else for cash with which to carry on his business? One difficulty was that the buyer of the goods gave the seller only a promise to pay money to him. The seller was the only person to whom performance or payment was promised. If, however, the seller obtained from the buyer a promise in writing to pay money to anyone in possession (a *bearer*) of the writing (the *paper* or *instrument*) or to anyone the seller (or *payee* in this case) designated, then the duty of performance would run directly to the holder (the bearer of the paper or to the person to whom the payee ordered payment to be made). This is one of the essential distinctions between negotiable and nonnegotiable instruments. Although a negotiable instrument has other formal requirements, this particular one eliminates the limitations of a promise to pay money only to a named promisee.

Moreover, if the promise to pay were not subject to all of the defenses available against the assignor, a transferee would not only be more willing to acquire the promise but also would pay more for it. Accordingly, the law of negotiable instruments developed the concept of the **holder in due course**, whereby certain good faith transferees who gave value acquired the right to be paid, free of most of the defenses to which an assignee would be subject. By reason of this doctrine, a transferee of a negotiable instrument could acquire *greater* rights than his transferor, whereas an assignee would acquire *only* the rights of his assignor. With these basic innovations, negotiable instruments enabled merchants to sell their contractual rights more readily and thereby keep their capital working.

## ASSIGNMENT COMPARED WITH NEGOTIATION

Negotiability invests negotiable instruments with a high degree of marketability and commercial utility. It allows negotiable instruments to be freely transferable and enforceable by a person with the rights of a holder in due course against any person obligated on the instrument, subject only to a limited number of defenses. To illustrate, assume that George sells and delivers goods to Elaine for $50,000 on sixty days' credit and that, a few days later, George assigns this account to Marsha. Unless Elaine is duly notified of this assignment, she may safely pay the $50,000 to George on the due date without incurring any liability to Marsha, the assignee. Assume next that the goods were defective and that Elaine, accordingly, has a defense against George to the extent of $20,000. Assume also that Marsha duly notified Elaine of the assignment. The result is that Marsha can recover only $30,000, not $50,000, from Elaine because Elaine's defense against George is equally available against George's assignee, Marsha. In other words, an assignee of contractual rights merely "steps into the shoes" of her assignor and, hence, acquires only the same rights as her assignor—and no more.

Assume, instead, that upon the sale by George to Elaine, Elaine executes and delivers her negotiable note to George for $50,000 payable to George's order in sixty days and that, a short time later, George duly negotiates (transfers) the note to Marsha. In the first place, Marsha is not required to notify Elaine that she has acquired the note from George, because one who issues a negotiable instrument is held to know that the instrument may be negotiated and is generally obligated to pay the holder of the instrument, whoever that may be. In the second place, Elaine's defense is not available against Marsha if Marsha acquired the note in good faith and for value and had no knowledge of Elaine's defense against George and took it without reason to question its authenticity. Marsha, therefore, is entitled to hold Elaine for the full face amount of the note at maturity, namely, $50,000. In other words, Marsha, by the negotiation of the negotiable note to her, acquired rights greater than those George had, because, by keeping the note, George could have recovered only $30,000 on it because Elaine successfully could have asserted her defense in the amount of $20,000 against him.

To have the full benefit of negotiability, negotiable instruments not only must meet the requirements of negotiability but also must be acquired by a holder in due course. This chapter discusses the formal requirements instruments must satisfy to be negotiable. *Chapter 27* deals with the manner in which a negotiable instrument must be negotiated to preserve its advantages. *Chapter 28* covers the requisites and rights of a holder in due course. *Chapter 29* examines the liability of all the parties to a negotiable instrument.

◆ FIGURE 26-1: **Order to Pay: Draft or Check**

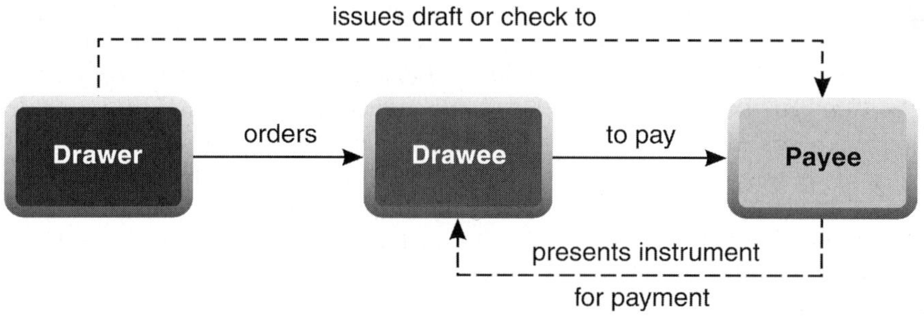


## TYPES OF NEGOTIABLE INSTRUMENTS

There are four types of negotiable instruments: drafts, checks, notes, and certificates of deposit. Section 3–104. The first two contain **orders** or directions to pay money; the last two involve **promises** to pay money.

### DRAFTS

A **draft** involves three parties, each in a distinct capacity. One party, the **drawer**, *orders* a second party, the **drawee**, to pay a fixed amount of money to a third party, the **payee**. Thus, the drawer "draws" the draft on the drawee. The drawee is ordinarily a person or entity that either is in possession of money belonging to the drawer or owes money to him. A sample draft is reproduced as *Figure 26-2*. The same party may appear in more than one capacity; for instance, the drawer may also be the payee.

Drafts may be either "time" or "sight." A **time draft** is one payable at a specified future date, whereas a **sight draft** is payable on demand (i.e., immediately upon presentation to the drawee). A form of time draft known as a trade acceptance is frequently used as a credit device in commercial transactions. A **trade acceptance** is a time draft, drawn by the seller (drawer) on the buyer (drawee), that names the seller or some third party as the payee.

◆ SEE FIGURE 26-1: **Order to Pay: Draft or Check**

◆ SEE FIGURE 26-2: **Draft**

### CHECKS

A check is a specialized form of draft, namely, an order to pay money drawn on a *bank* and payable on *demand* (i.e., upon the payee's request for payment). Section 3–104(f). Once again, parties are involved in three distinct capacities: the **drawer**, who orders the **drawee**, a bank, to pay the payee on demand. Checks are by far the most widely used form of negotiable instruments. Each year more than ten billion checks are written in the United States for a total of more than $5 trillion. The Check Clearing for the 21st Century Act (also called Check 21 or the Check Truncation Act), which went into effect in late 2004, creates a new negotiable instrument called a substitute check or image replacement document (IRD). The law permits banks to truncate original checks, to process check information electronically, and to deliver substitute checks to banks that want to continue receiving paper checks. A substitute check would be the legal equivalent of the original check and would include all the information contained on the original check. The law does not require banks to accept checks in electronic form nor does it require banks to use the new authority granted by the act to create substitute checks. This newly authorized document is more fully discussed in *Chapter 30*.

A **cashier's check** is a check drawn by a bank upon itself to the order of a named payee. Section 3–104(g).

◆ SEE FIGURE 26-3: **Check**

◆ FIGURE 26-2: **Draft**

Two years from date pay to the order of
Perry Payee
$50,000 Fifty Thousand . . . Dollars

St. Louis, Missouri
May 1, 2011

To: DEBRA DRAWEE
50 Main St.
Louisville, Kentucky

(Signed) Donald Drawer
DONALD DRAWER

◆ FIGURE 26-3: **Check**

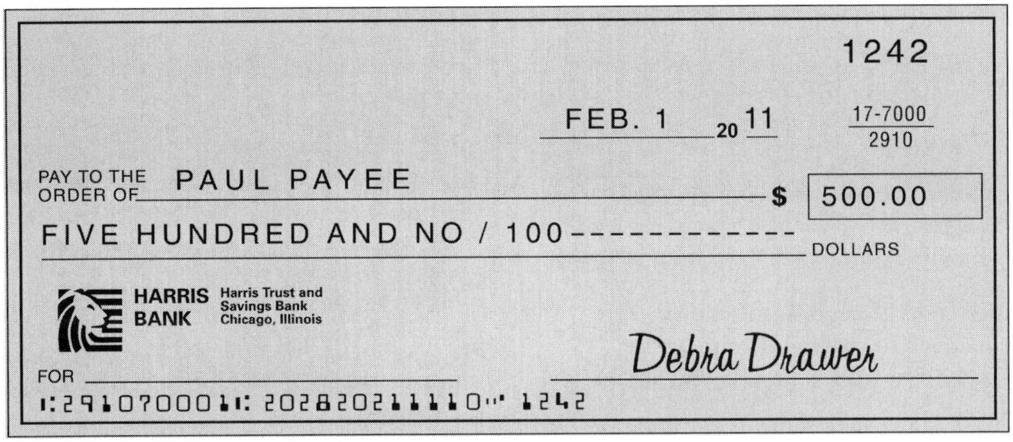


## NOTES

A **promissory note** is an instrument involving two parties in two capacities. One party, the **maker**, promises to pay a second party, the payee, a stated sum of money, either on demand or at a stated future date. The note may range from a simple "I promise to pay $X to the order of Y" form to more complex legal instruments such as installment notes, collateral notes, mortgage notes, and judgment notes. *Figure 26-5* is a note payable at a definite time—six months from the date of April 7, 2011—and hence is referred to as a **time note**. A note payable upon the request or demand of the payee or holder is a **demand note**

◆ SEE FIGURE 26-4: **Promise to Pay: Promissory Note or Certificate of Deposit**

◆ SEE FIGURE 26-5: **Note**

## CERTIFICATES OF DEPOSIT

A certificate of deposit, or CD as it is frequently called, is a specialized form of *promise* to pay money given by a *bank*. A **certificate of deposit** is a written acknowledgment by a bank of the receipt of money that it promises to repay. Section 3–104(j). The issuing party, the **maker**, which is always a bank, promises to pay a second party, the payee, who is named in the CD.

◆ SEE FIGURE 26-6: **Certificate of Deposit**

# FORMAL REQUIREMENTS OF NEGOTIABLE INSTRUMENTS

To perform its function in the business community effectively, a negotiable instrument must be able to pass freely from person to person. The fact that *negotiability* is wholly a matter of form makes such freedom possible. The instrument must contain within its "four corners" all the information required to determine whether it is negotiable. No reference to any other source is permitted. For this reason, a negotiable instrument is called a "courier without luggage." In addition, indorsements **cannot** create or destroy negotiability.

To be negotiable, the **instrument** must—

1. be in writing,
2. be signed,
3. contain a promise or order to pay,
4. be unconditional,

◆ FIGURE 26-4: **Promise to Pay: Promissory Note or Certificate of Deposit**

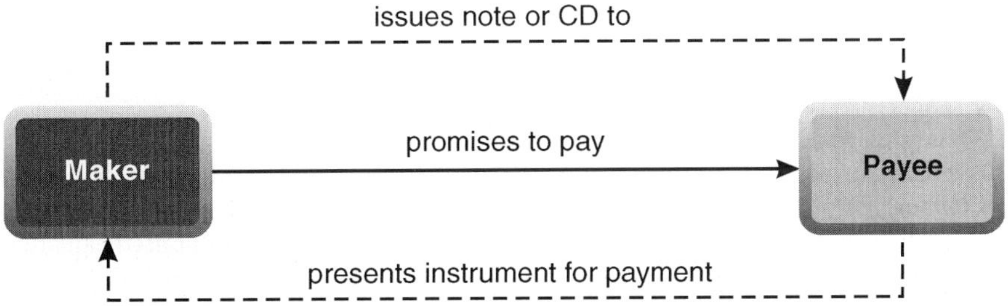

◈ **FIGURE 26-5: Note**

| | | |
|---|---|---|
| $10,000 | Albany, NY | April 7, 2011 |

Six months from date I promise to pay to the order of Pat Payee ten thousand dollars.

(signed) Matthew Maker

**5.** be for a fixed amount,
**6.** be for money,
**7.** contain no other undertaking or instruction,
**8.** be payable on demand or at a definite time, and
**9.** be payable to order or to bearer.

Section 3–104(a). If these requirements are not met, the undertaking is not negotiable (nor is it a negotiable instrument or simply an instrument), and the rights of the parties are governed by the law of contract (assignment).

◆ **SEE CASE 26-1**

## WRITING

The requirement that the instrument be a writing (Sections 3–103(a)(6), (9)) is broadly construed. Printing, typewriting, handwriting, or any other intentional tangible expression is sufficient to satisfy the requirement. Section 1–201; Revised Section 1-201. Most negotiable instruments, of course, are written on paper, but this is not required. For example, a check in one instance was reportedly written on the back of a cow and in another written on a coconut.

## SIGNED

A note or certificate of deposit must be signed by the maker; a draft or check must be signed by the drawer. As in the case of a writing, extreme latitude is granted in determining what constitutes a **signature**, which is any symbol a party executes or adopts with the present *intention* to authenticate a writing. Section 1–201(39). Revised Article 1 changes the word "authenticate" to "adopt or accept." Revised Section 1–201(b)(37). Moreover, it may consist of any word or mark used in place of a written signature, Section 3–401(b), such as initials, an X, or a thumbprint. It may be a trade name or an assumed name. Even the location of the signature on the document is unimportant. Normally, a maker or drawer signs in the lower right corner of the instrument, but this is not required. Negotiable instruments are frequently signed by an agent for her principal. For a discussion of the appropriate way in which an agent should sign a negotiable instrument, see *Chapter 29*.

## PROMISE OR ORDER TO PAY

A negotiable instrument must contain either a promise to pay money, in the case of a note or certificate of deposit, or an order to pay, in the case of a draft or check.

**Promise to Pay** A promise to pay is an undertaking and must be more than the mere acknowledgment or recognition of an existing obligation or debt. Section 3–103(a)(9). The so-called due bill or I.O.U. is not a promise but merely

◈ **FIGURE 26-6: Certificate of Deposit**

NEGOTIABLE CERTIFICATE OF DEPOSIT

The Mountain Bank

| | | |
|---|---|---|
| No. 13900 | Mountain, N.Y. | June 1, 2011 |

THIS CERTIFIES THAT THERE HAS BEEN DEPOSITED
with the undersigned the sum of $200,000.00
Two hundred thousand.................................Dollars
Payable to the order of Pablo Payee on December 1, 2011 with interest only to maturity at the rate of Seven percent (7%) per annum upon surrender of this certificate properly indorsed.

The Mountain Bank
By (Signature) Malcolm Maker, Vice President
Authorized Signature

an acknowledgment of indebtedness. Accordingly, an instrument reciting "due Adam Brown $100" or "I.O.U., Adam Brown, $100" is not negotiable because it does not contain a promise to pay.

**Order to Pay** An order to pay is an instruction to pay. It must be more than an authorization or request and must identify with reasonable certainty the person to be paid. Section 3–103(a)(6). The usual way to express an order is by use of the word *pay*: "Pay to the order of John Jones" or "Pay bearer." The addition of words of courtesy, such as "please pay" or "kindly pay," will not destroy the negotiability. Nonetheless, caution should be exercised in employing words that modify the prototypically correct "Pay." For example, the use of the words "I wish you would pay" has been held to destroy the negotiability of an instrument and to render its transfer a contractual assignment.

## UNCONDITIONAL

The requirement that the promise or order be unconditional is to prevent the inclusion of any term that could reduce the promisor's obligation to pay. Conditions limiting a promise would diminish the payment and credit functions of negotiable instruments by necessitating costly and time-consuming investigations to determine the degree of risk such conditions imposed. Moreover, if the holder (transferee) had to take an instrument subject to certain conditions, her risk factor would be substantial, and this would lead to limited transferability. Substitutes for money must be capable of rapid circulation at minimum risk.

A promise or order to pay is **unconditional** if it is absolute and not subject to any contingencies or qualifications. Thus, an instrument would not be negotiable if it stated that "ABC Corp. promises to pay $100,000 to the order of Johnson provided the helicopter sold meets all contractual specifications." On the other hand, suppose that upon delivering an instrument that provided, "ABC Corp. promises to pay $100,000 to the order of Johnson," Meeker, the president of ABC, stated that the money would be paid only if the helicopter met all contractual specifications. The instrument would be negotiable because negotiability is determined solely by examining the instrument itself and is not affected by matters beyond the instrument's face.

A promise or order is unconditional unless it states (1) that there is an express condition to payment, (2) that the promise or order is subject to or governed by another writing, or (3) that rights or obligations concerning the order or promise are stated in another writing. A mere reference to another writing, however, does not make the promise or order conditional. Section 3–106(a).

An instrument is not made conditional by the fact that it is subject to implied or constructive conditions; the condition must be expressed to destroy negotiability. Section 3–106(a). Implications of law or fact are not to be considered in deciding whether an instrument is negotiable. Thus, a statement in an instrument that it is given for an executory promise does not imply that the instrument is conditioned upon performance of that promise.

**Reference to Other Agreements** The restriction against reference to another agreement is to enable any person to determine the right to payment provided by the instrument without having to look beyond its four corners. If such right is made subject to the terms of another agreement, the instrument is nonnegotiable. Section 3–106(a)(ii).

A distinction is to be made between a mere recital of the *existence* of a separate agreement (this does not destroy negotiability) and a recital that makes the instrument *subject* to the terms of another agreement (this does destroy negotiability).

A statement in a note such as "This note is given in partial payment for a color TV set to be delivered two weeks from date in accordance with a contract of this date between the payee and the maker" does not impair negotiability. It merely describes the consideration and the transaction giving rise to the note. It does not place any restriction or condition on the maker's obligation to pay. The promise is not made subject to any other agreement.

Added words that would impair negotiability are "This note is subject to all terms of said contract." Such words make the promise to pay conditional upon the adequate performance of the television set in accordance with the terms of the contract and thus render the instrument nonnegotiable.

**The Particular Fund Doctrine** Revised Article 3 eliminates the particular fund doctrine by providing that a promise or order is not made conditional because payment is to be made only out of a particular fund. Section 3–106(b)(ii).

Under prior Article 3 an order or promise to pay only out of a particular fund was conditional and destroyed negotiability because payment depended upon the existence and sufficiency of the particular fund. On the other hand, a promise or order to pay that merely indicated a particular fund out of which reimbursement was to be made or a particular account to be debited with the amount did not impair negotiability because the promise or order relied on the drawer's or maker's general credit and the notation charging a particular account was merely a bookkeeping entry to be followed after payment.

## FIXED AMOUNT

The purpose of the requirement of a fixed amount in money is to enable the person entitled to enforce the instrument to determine from the instrument itself the amount that he is entitled to receive.

The requirement that payment be of a "fixed amount" must be considered from the point of view of the person entitled to enforce the instrument, not the maker or drawer. (Prior Article 3 used the term "sum certain," which means fundamentally the same as "fixed amount.") The holder must be assured of a determinable minimum payment, although provisions of the instrument may increase the recovery under certain circumstances. Revised Article 3, however, applies the fixed amount requirement only to the *principal.* Section 3–112, Comment 1. Thus, the fixed amount portion does not apply to interest or to other charges, such as collection fees or attorneys' fees. Moreover, negotiability of an instrument is not affected by the inclusion or omission of a stated rate of interest. If the instrument does not state a rate of interest, it is payable without interest. Section 3–112(a). If the instrument states that it is payable "with interest" but does not specify a rate, the judgment rate of interest applies.

Most significantly, Revised Article 3 provides that "Interest may be stated in an instrument as a fixed or variable amount of money or it may be expressed as a fixed or variable rate or rates." Section 3–112(b). Moreover, determination of the rate of interest "may require reference to information not contained in the instrument." Section 3–112(b). Variable rate mortgages, therefore, may be negotiable; this result is consistent with the rule that the fixed amount requirement applies only to the principal.

Under prior Article 3, both principal and interest had to be determined from the face of the instrument. Thus, courts held that variable interest rate provisions destroyed negotiability because the interest rate was tied to a published index external to the instrument.

A sum payable is a fixed amount even though it is payable in installments or payable with a fixed discount, if paid before maturity, or with a fixed addition, if paid after maturity. This is because it is always possible to use the instrument itself to compute the amount due at any given time.

## MONEY

The term **money** means a medium of exchange authorized or adopted by a sovereign government as part of its currency. Section 1–201(24). (Revised Section 1–201(b)(24) adds that the authorized or adopted currency must be the current official currency of the government.) Consequently, even though local custom may make gold or diamonds a medium of exchange, an instrument payable in such commodities would be nonnegotiable because of the lack of governmental sanction of such media as legal tender. On the other hand, an instrument paying a fixed amount in Swiss francs, English pounds, Australian dollars, Japanese yen, Nigerian naira, or other foreign currency is negotiable. Section 3–107.

## NO OTHER UNDERTAKING OR INSTRUCTION

A negotiable instrument must contain a promise or order to pay money, but it may not "state any other undertaking or instruction by the person promising or ordering payment to do any act in addition to the payment of money." Section 3–104(a)(3). Accordingly, an instrument containing an order or promise to do an act in addition to or in lieu of the payment of money is not negotiable. For example, a promise to pay $100 "and a ton of coal" would be nonnegotiable.

The Code sets out a list of terms and provisions that may be included in instruments without adversely affecting negotiability. Among these are (1) an undertaking or power to give, maintain, or protect collateral in order to secure payment, (2) an authorization or power to confess judgment (written authority by the debtor to allow the holder to enter judgment against the debtor in favor of the holder) on the instrument, (3) an authorization or power to sell or dispose of collateral upon default, and (4) a waiver of the benefit of any law intended for the advantage or protection of the obligor. It is important to note that the Code does not render any of these terms legal or effective; it merely provides that their inclusion will not affect negotiability.

## PAYABLE ON DEMAND OR AT A DEFINITE TIME

A negotiable instrument must "be payable on demand or at a definite time." Section 3–104. This requirement, like the other formal requirements of negotiability, is designed to promote certainty in determining the present value of a negotiable instrument.

**Demand** "Payable upon demand" means that the money owed under the instrument must be paid upon the holder's request. **Demand paper** always has been considered sufficiently certain as to time of payment to satisfy the requirements of negotiability because it is the person entitled to enforce the instrument who makes the demand and who thus sets the time for payment. Any instrument in which no time for payment is stated—a check, for example—is payable on demand. An instrument also qualifies as being payable on demand if it is payable at sight or on presentment. Section 3–108(a).

◆ **SEE CASE 26-2**

**Definite Time** Instruments payable at a definite time are called **time paper**. A promise or order is payable at a definite time if it is payable—

1. at a fixed date or dates,
2. at a definite period of time after sight or acceptance, or
3. at a time readily ascertainable at the time the promise or order is issued.

Section 3–108(b). An instrument is payable at a definite time if it is payable "on or before" a stated date. The person entitled to enforce the instrument is thus assured that she will have her money by the maturity date at the latest, although she may receive it sooner. This right of anticipation enables the obligor, at his option, to pay before the stated maturity date (*prepayment*) and thereby stop the further accrual of interest or, if interest rates have gone down, to refinance at a lower rate of interest. Nevertheless, it constitutes sufficient certainty so as not to impair negotiability. Section 3–108(b)(i).

Frequently, instruments are made payable at a fixed period after a stated date. For example, the instrument may be made payable "thirty days after date." This means it is payable thirty days after the date of issuance, which is recited on the instrument. Such an instrument is payable at a definite time, for its exact maturity date can be determined by simple math.

An undated instrument payable "thirty days after date" is not payable at a definite time, because the date of payment cannot be determined from its face. It is therefore nonnegotiable until it is completed.

An instrument that by its terms is otherwise payable only upon an act or event whose time of occurrence is uncertain is *not* payable at a definite time. An example would be a note providing for payment to the order "when X dies." However, as previously stated, a time that is readily ascertainable at the time the promise or order is issued is a definite time. Section 3–108(b). This changes prior Article 3 and seemingly would permit a note reading "payable on the day of the next presidential election." As long as the scheduled event is certain to happen, Revised Article 3 appears to be satisfied.

The clause "at a fixed period after sight" is frequently used in drafts. Because a fixed period after sight means a fixed period after acceptance, a simple mathematical calculation makes the maturity date certain; and the instrument is, therefore, negotiable.

An instrument payable at a fixed time subject to **acceleration** by the holder also satisfies the requirement of being payable at a definite time. Section 3–108(b)(ii). Indeed, such an instrument would seem to have a more certain maturity date than a demand instrument because it at least states a definite maturity date. In addition, the acceleration may be contingent upon the happening of some act or event.

Finally, a provision in an instrument granting the holder an option to extend the maturity of the instrument for a definite or indefinite period does not impair its negotiability. Section 3–108(b)(iii). Nor does a provision permitting the obligor of an instrument to extend the maturity date to a further definite time. Section 3–108(b)(iv). For example, a provision in a note, payable one year from date, that the maker may extend the maturity date six months does not impair negotiability. If the obligor is given an option to extend the maturity of the instrument for an indefinite period, however, his promise is illusory; and there is no certainty regarding time of payment. Such an instrument is nonnegotiable. If the obligor's right to extend is limited to a definite time, the extension clause is no more indefinite than an acceleration clause with a time limitation.

In addition, extension may be made automatic upon or after a specified act or event, provided a definite time limit is stated. An example of such an extension clause is, "I promise to pay to the order of John Doe the sum of $2,000 on December 1, 2011, but it is agreed that if the crop of sections 25 and 26 of Twp. 145 is below eight bushels per acre for the 2011 season, this note shall be extended for one year."

**At a Definite Time and On Demand** If the instrument, payable at a fixed date, *also* provides that it is payable on demand made before the fixed date, it is still a negotiable instrument. Revised Article 3 provides that the instrument is payable on demand until the fixed date and, if demand is not made prior to the specified date, becomes payable at a definite time on the fixed date. Section 3–108(c).

## PAYABLE TO ORDER OR TO BEARER

A negotiable instrument must contain words indicating that the maker or drawer intends that it may pass into the hands of someone other than the payee. Although the "magic" **words of negotiability** typically are *to the order of* or *to bearer*, other clearly equivalent words also may fulfill this requirement. The use of synonyms, however, only invites trouble. Moreover, as noted above, indorsements cannot create or destroy negotiability, which must be determined from the "face" of the instrument. Words of negotiability must be present when the instrument is issued or first comes into possession of a holder. Section 3–104(a)(1).

Revised Article 3 provides that a *check* that meets all requirements of being a negotiable instrument except that it is not payable to bearer or order is nevertheless a negotiable instrument. Section 3–104(c). This rule does *not* apply to instruments other than checks and does not exist under prior Article 3.

**Payable to Order** An instrument is payable to order if it is payable (a) to the order of an identified person or (b) to an identified person or order. Section 3–109(b). If an instrument is payable to bearer, it cannot be payable to order; an instrument that is ambiguous as to this point is payable to bearer. Prior Article 3 provided that use of the word *assigns* met the requirement of words of negotiability; Revised Article 3, however, does not so provide.

Moreover, in every instance the person to whose order the instrument is payable must be designated with reasonable certainty. Within this limitation a broad range of payees is possible, including an individual, two or more payees, an office, an estate, a trust or fund, a partnership or unincorporated association, and a corporation.

This requirement should not be confused with the requirement that the instrument contain an order or promise to pay. An order to pay is an instruction to a third party to pay the instrument as drawn. The word *order* in terms of an "order instrument," on the other hand, pertains to the transferability of the instrument rather than to instructions directing a specific party to pay.

A writing, other than a *check*, that names a specified person without indicating that it is payable to order—for example, "Pay to Justin Matthew"—is not payable to order or to bearer. Such a writing is not a negotiable instrument and is not covered by Article 3. On the other hand, a check that meets all of the requirements of a negotiable instrument, except that it does not provide the words of negotiability, is still a negotiable instrument and falls within the purview of Article 3. Section 3–104(c). Thus, a check payable to Justin Matthew is a negotiable check.

**PAYABLE TO BEARER** Section 3–109(a) of the Code states that an instrument fulfills the requirements of being **payable to bearer** if it (1) states it is payable to bearer or the order of bearer, (2) does not state a payee or (3) states it is payable to "cash" or to the order of "cash." Section 3–109(a). An instrument made payable both to order and to bearer, that is, "pay to the order of Mildred Courts or bearer," is payable to bearer. Section 3–109, Comment 2.

An instrument that does not state a payee is payable to bearer. Thus, if a drawer leaves blank the "pay to order of" line of a check or the maker of a note writes "pay to______," the instrument is a negotiable bearer instrument. Section 3–109(a)(2).

◆ **SEE CASE 26-3**

## TERMS AND OMISSIONS AND THEIR EFFECT ON NEGOTIABILITY

The negotiability of an instrument may be questioned because of an omission of certain provisions or because of ambiguity. Problems may also arise in connection with the interpretation of an instrument, whether or not negotiability is called into question. Accordingly, the Code contains rules of construction that apply to every instrument.

**DATING OF THE INSTRUMENT** The negotiability of an instrument is not affected by the fact that it is antedated, or postdated. Section 3–113(a). If the instrument is undated, its date is the date of its issuance. If it is unissued, its date is the date it first comes into the possession of a holder. Section 3–113(b).

**INCOMPLETE INSTRUMENTS** Occasionally, a party will sign a paper that clearly is intended to become an instrument but that, either by intention or through oversight, is incomplete because of the omission of a necessary element such as a promise or order, a designated payee, an amount payable, or a time for payment. Section 3–115 provides that such an instrument is not negotiable until completed.

If, for example, an undated instrument is delivered on November 1, 2011, payable "thirty days after date," the payee has implied authority to fill in "November 1, 2011." Until he does so, however, the instrument is not negotiable because it is not payable at a definite time. If the payee completes the instrument by inserting an erroneous date, the rules as to material alteration, covered in *Chapter 29*, apply.

**AMBIGUOUS INSTRUMENTS** Rather than commit the parties to the use of parol evidence to establish the interpretation of an instrument, Article 3 establishes rules to resolve common ambiguities. This promotes negotiability by providing added certainty to the holder.

Where it is doubtful whether the instrument is a draft or note, the holder may treat it as either and present it for payment to the drawee or the person signing it. Section 3–104(e). For example, an instrument reading

> To X: On demand I promise to pay $500 to the order of Y.
> Signed, Z

may be presented for payment to X as a draft or to Z as a note.

An instrument naming no drawee but stating

> On demand, pay $500 to the order of Y.
> Signed, Z

although in the form of a draft, may be treated as a note and presented to Z for payment.

If a printed form of note or draft is used and the party signing it inserts handwritten or typewritten language that is inconsistent with the printed words, the handwritten words control the typewritten and the printed words, and the typewritten words control the printed words. Section 3–114.

If the amount payable is set forth on the face of the instrument in both figures and words and the amounts differ, the words control the figures. It is presumed that the maker or drawer would be more careful with words. If the words are ambiguous, however, then the figures control. Section 3–114.

## CHAPTER SUMMARY

### NEGOTIABILITY

**Rule** invests instruments with a high degree of marketability and commercial utility by conferring upon certain good faith transferees immunity from most defenses to the instrument

**Formal Requirements** negotiability is wholly a matter of form, and all the requirements for negotiability must be met within the four corners of the instrument

### TYPES OF NEGOTIABLE INSTRUMENTS

**Orders to Pay**

- ***Drafts*** a draft involves three parties: the drawer orders the drawee to pay a fixed amount of money to the payee
- ***Checks*** a specialized form of draft that is drawn on a bank and payable on demand; the drawer orders the drawee (bank) to pay the payee on demand (upon the request of the holder)

**Promises to Pay**

- ***Notes*** a written promise by a maker (issuer) to pay a payee
- ***Certificates of Deposit*** a specialized form of note that is given by a bank or thrift association

### FORMAL REQUIREMENTS OF NEGOTIABLE INSTRUMENTS

**Writing** any intentional reduction to tangible form is sufficient

**Signed** any symbol executed or adopted by a party with the present intention to authenticate/adopt or accept a writing

**Promise or Order to Pay**

- ***Promise to Pay*** an undertaking to pay, which must be more than a mere acknowledgment or recognition of an existing debt
- ***Order to Pay*** instruction to pay

**Unconditional** an absolute promise to pay that is not subject to any contingencies

- ***Reference to Other Agreements*** does not destroy negotiability unless the recital makes the instrument subject to or governed by the terms of another agreement
- ***The Particular Fund Doctrine*** an order or promise to pay only out of a particular fund no longer is conditional and does not destroy negotiability

**Fixed Amount** the holder must be assured of a determinable minimum principal payment although provisions in the instrument may increase the amount of recovery under certain circumstances

**Money** legal tender authorized or adopted by a sovereign government as part of its currency

**No Other Undertaking or Instruction** a promise or order to do an act in addition to the payment of money destroys negotiability

**Payable on Demand or at a Definite Time** an instrument is demand paper if it must be paid upon request; an instrument is time paper if it is payable at a definite time

**Payable to Order or to Bearer** a negotiable instrument must contain words indicating that the maker or drawer intends that it pass into the hands of someone other than the payee

- ***Payable to Order*** payable to the "order of" (or other words which mean the same) a named person or anyone designated by that person
- ***Payable to Bearer*** payable to the holder of the instrument; includes instruments (1) payable to bearer or the order of bearer, (2) that do not specify a payee, or (3) payable to "cash" or to order of "cash"

# CASES

## CASE 26-1

### Formal Requirements of Negotiable Instruments
### YIN v. SOCIETY NATIONAL BANK INDIANA

Court of Appeals of Indiana, 1996
665 N.E.2d 58

**Chezem, J.**

#### Case Summary

Defendants-Appellants, Sam Yin ("Yin") and Sophia Kung ("Kung") appeal from the grant of partial summary judgment in favor of Plaintiff-Appellee, Society National Bank ("Society"). We reverse and remand for trial on the merits.

* * *

#### Facts and Procedural History

The undisputed facts are as follows. On January 2, 1991, Society agreed in a note to lend U.S.A. Diversified Products, Inc. ("USAD") up to $2,000,000.00 in the form of an operating line of credit. Paul Davis ("Davis") signed the note both personally and as the president of USAD. Yin, who jointly owns USAD with Davis, signed the note personally. Kung, who at that time was married to Yin, also signed the note personally. During negotiations regarding the note, Society directly dealt only with Davis. Once negotiations were finalized, Davis took the note, obtained Yin's and Kung's signatures, and returned it to Society. No party challenges the authenticity of any of the signatures on the 1991 note. The outstanding balance was to be paid on April 30, 1992, the note's expiration date.

* * *

Some time prior to the end of April, 1992, Davis told Society that a 60-day extension of the original payment date was needed. Society agreed to the extension. Davis represented that he would obtain Yin's and Kung's signatures as he had for the 1991 document. However, for purposes of this partial summary judgment, the parties agree that Yin's and Kung's signatures were forged on the extension document.

As a result of USAD's default on the line of credit, Society filed a complaint against USAD, Davis, Yin, and Kung on December 8, 1992. On May 27, 1994, the trial court granted partial summary judgment in favor of Society and against Yin and Kung in the amount of $2,160,331.73 including interest and attorney fees and expenses.

#### Discussion and Decision

* * *

***Is this line of credit a negotiable instrument?***

[Article 3] appl[ies] only to negotiable instruments. [Citation.] Non-negotiable agreements are governed by Indiana common law. [Citations.] Yin and Kung challenge the trial court's finding that their agreement for a line of credit is a negotiable instrument. * * * We hold that it is not.

In determining the negotiability of an agreement, we apply the law in effect at the time of the execution of the agreement [Prior Article 3.]

* * *

Yin and Kung assert that their line of credit meets neither the sum certain [fixed amount under Revised Article 3] nor the unconditional requirement. * * *

Other courts have faced the issue or a situation quite similar to it and held that such an agreement is not a negotiable instrument. For example, in [Citation] the Fifth Circuit agreed with a district court's opinion that "[t]he note in this case does not contain an obligation to pay a 'sum certain,' but rather 'the sum of TWO MILLION AND NO/100 DOLLARS ($2,000,000) or so much thereof as may be advanced. * * *'" [Citation.] The Fifth Circuit reasoned that the language employed by the note failed to disclose the exact amount to be repaid. [Citation.] That is, the amount advanced to the parties could not be determined with certainty absent an inquiry to other documents. Accordingly, the note did not facially demand payment of a sum certain [fixed amount], and hence was not negotiable. [Citations.]

The parties do not seriously dispute that the agreement in the present case is a line of credit upon which USAD could make draws of varying amounts. Indeed, the face of the note contains a notation regarding "draws." We note that although USAD did make various draws upon the line of credit, it was under no obligation to make any draws whatsoever. In fact, if USAD had never drawn upon the line of credit, it would have owed nothing when the agreement matured. The principal would have been zero. This is noteworthy because it illustrates an important feature of the line of credit: in order to ascertain the principal owed, one must look beyond the agreement itself. A current history of USAD's draws would also be necessary in order to calculate the amount USAD owed. Because of the potentially variable principal which results from such an arrangement, the line of credit contains no sum certain [fixed sum]. In addition, USAD's ability to make draws up to two million dollars was not unfettered. It was dependent upon the sufficiency of USAD's accounts receivable. That is, if USAD sold the accounts receivable (Society's security), then Society "in all likelihood * * * would put a hold on any further draws."

Society conditioned USAD's access to the line of credit by tracking the company's collateral. Lacking an unconditional promise to pay a sum certain, the line of credit falls outside the definition of a negotiable instrument. [Court's footnote: In reaching this conclusion, we distinguish between a variable principal and a variable interest rate. Unlike the former, the latter would not destroy the negotiability of an instrument. [Revised Article 3 holds] that variable interest rates do not affect negotiability. * * *] Thus, in addressing the parties' other issues regarding the line of credit, we apply Indiana common law. * * *

Because the change must be a material and binding one, we cannot agree with Yin's and Kung's assertion that the forged extension note serves to discharge them from the potential liability they incurred upon signing the original 1991 agreement. They cannot be bound by a document (here, the extension note) which does not bear their signatures. In addition, by signing the 1991 note which contained a consent to future extensions provision, they explicitly gave prior consent to an extension. [Citation.] Accordingly, the extension note has no effect on their liability.

* * *

Reversed and remanded for trial on the merits.

## CASE 26-2

### Demand
### NATIONSBANK OF VIRGINIA, N.A. v. BARNES

Virginia Circuit Court, Twentieth Circuit, 1994
33 Va.Cir. 184, 24 U.C.C. Rep.Serv.2d 782

**Horne, J.**

This matter is before the court on Plaintiff's Motion for Partial Summary Judgment. Defendants have filed a Grounds of Defense, asserting certain affirmative defenses to liability. Plaintiff argues that it is entitled to partial summary judgment. As discussed more fully below, Plaintiff's motion will be granted in part and denied in part. The court will address Defendant's affirmative defenses as they relate to each note specifically, and to both Notes in general.

* * *

The following facts are undisputed with respect to the 1991 Note which is the subject of Count II of the Motion for Judgment. Defendants Ad Barnes, Trustee, Ad Barnes and Elaine Barnes executed a * * * Note to Sovran Bank, N.A. on August 27, 1991, in the principal amount of $200,000. Plaintiff NationsBank is the successor by merger to Sovran and is now the holder of this Note. Under the terms of the Note, Plaintiff is entitled to collect all expenses, including court costs and attorney's fees, incurred in the enforcement of its rights under the Note. By letter dated February 17, 1993, NationsBank made demand on the 1991 Note.

The factual question still in dispute concerning the 1991 Note is whether it is a demand note. Plaintiff argues that the language of the note is unambiguous and is clearly a demand note. Defendants argue that the detailed enumeration of events constituting default is inconsistent with a demand note. Thus, a standard of good faith must be applied before a demand for accelerated repayment can be made.

[UCC] §1–203 establishes a general duty of good faith in every contract governed by the Commercial Code. Under any contract providing for accelerated payment at will, §1–208 states that the option is to be exercised only in the good faith belief that the prospect of payment or performance is impaired. However, the Official Comment to this section indicates that it is not applicable to a demand instrument.

[UCC] 3A–108(a) [UCC Revised §3–108(a)] states that a note is payable "on demand" if it says it is payable on demand or states no time for payment. In this case, the 1991 * * * Note is a standard form with different forms of repayment set out on the first page. The box marked payable "on demand" has been checked in this instance. There is no time set for repayment, only a provision requiring monthly payments of interest.

It is the court's opinion that the 1991 Note is unambiguous and is clearly a demand note. Thus, Plaintiff is under no obligation to show good faith before requesting payment on the note. Since demand has been made by Plaintiff, Defendants are liable. Thus, Plaintiff is entitled to summary judgment on the issue of liability under the 1991 Note.

As the question of the reasonableness of the attorney's fees and costs under the 1991 Note is still in dispute, summary judgment cannot be granted on this issue.

# CASE 26-3

## Payable to Order or to Bearer
## COOPERATIEVE CENTRALE RAIFFEISEN-BOERENLEENBANK B.A. v. BAILEY

United States District Court, Central District California, 1989
710 F.Supp. 737

**Rea, J.**

This matter comes before the court on the motion of both parties to this action for partial summary adjudication and on plaintiff's motion for summary judgment. * * *

This is an action for collection on a promissory note brought by plaintiff, Cooperatieve Centrale Raiffeisen-Boerenleenbank, B.A. ("the Bank"), against the maker of the note, William Bailey, M.D. ("Bailey"). Bailey executed the note in December, 1982, in favor of "California Dreamstreet," a joint venture which solicited investments in a cattle-breeding operation. California Dreamstreet negotiated the note in 1986 to the Bank, which in turn filed this action on August 29, 1988.

The note states in relevant part:

> DR. WILLIAM H. BAILEY * * * hereby promises to pay to the order to CALIFORNIA DREAMSTREET * * * the sum of Three Hundred Twenty Nine Thousand Eight Hundred ($329,800.00) Dollars. * * *

* * *

By this motion for partial summary adjudication, the parties seek to determine, as a threshold matter, whether the subject promissory note is a negotiable instrument. * * * [The parties] agree that the sole issue is whether the unusual language in the note obliging Bailey to "pay to the order to California Dreamstreet" renders the note non-negotiable.

Whether an instrument is negotiable is a question of law to be determined solely from the face of the instrument, without reference to the intent of the parties. [Citation.] To be negotiable, an instrument must "be payable to order or bearer." Code §3–104(1)(d) [Revised §3–104(a)(i)]. "Payable to order" is further defined by Code §3–110(1), as follows:

> (1) An instrument is payable to order when by its terms it is payable to the order or assigns of any person therein specified with reasonable certainty, or to him or his order, or when it is conspicuously designated on its face as 'exchange' or the like and names a payee.

[Compare Revised §3–109(b).]

It is well established that a promissory note is non-negotiable if it states only: "payable to (payee)," rather than "payable to the order of [payee]." [Citations.] Bailey claims that the instant note, which states "pay to the order to [payee]," falls between these two alternatives and should therefore be deemed non-negotiable.

The authorities are unhelpful. There is apparently no case on record in which a variance this small from the language of the Code has been called into question. Both parties direct the Court's attention to Official UCC Comment 5 to Code §3–104, which states:

> 5. This Article omits the original Section 10, which provided that the instrument need not follow the language of the act if it 'clearly indicates an intention to conform' to it. The provision has served no useful purpose, and it has been an encouragement to bad drafting and to liberality in holding questionable paper to be negotiable. The omission is not intended to mean that the instrument must follow the language of this section, or that one term may not be recognized as clearly the equivalent of another, as in the case of 'I undertake' instead of 'I promise,' or 'Pay to holder' instead of 'Pay to bearer.' It does mean that either the language of the section or a clear equivalent must be found, and that in doubtful cases the decision should be against negotiability.

In the court's opinion, the Comment fails to persuasively support either party's position. Rules of grammar belie the Bank's argument that the preposition "to" is an apt substitute for "of" since the resulting sentence, read literally, is not just ambiguous but incomplete. On the other hand, the Comment expressly disavows Bailey's argument that the Code drafters intended to set forth certain "magic words," the absence of which precludes negotiability.

What does emerge from the Comment is the need for certainty in determining negotiability. Though sensitive to this goal and to the potentially harsh result of such a finding, the court does not find the instant facts to present the kind of "doubtful" case which should be resolved against negotiability. In this context, the phrase "pay to the order to" can plausibly be construed only to mean "pay to the order of." While other explanations are possible, none are realistic. To hold otherwise would, in this court's opinion, set an overly technical standard that could unexpectedly frustrate legitimate expectations of negotiability in commercial transactions.

* * *

For all the above reasons, It Is Hereby Adjudged that the promissory note which is the subject of this action is a negotiable instrument. It is further Ordered that plaintiff's motion for summary judgment is denied without prejudice to its being renewed upon the completion of discovery.

## QUESTIONS

1. Discuss the concept and importance of negotiability.
2. Identify and discuss the types of negotiable instruments involving an order to pay.
3. Identify and discuss the types of negotiable instruments involving a promise to pay.
4. List and discuss the formal requirements that an instrument must meet to be negotiable.
5. Discuss the effect on the negotiability of an instrument's (a) being undated, antedated, or postdated, (b) lack of completion, and (c) ambiguity.

## PROBLEMS

**1.** State whether the following provisions impair or preclude negotiability, the instrument in each instance being otherwise in proper form. Answer each statement with either the word "Negotiable" or "Nonnegotiable" and explain why.

**(a)** A note for $2,000 payable in twenty monthly installments of $100 each that provides the following: "In case of death of maker, all payments not due at date of death are canceled."

**(b)** A note stating "This note is secured by a mortgage on personal property located at 351 Maple Street, Smithton, Illinois."

**(c)** A certificate of deposit reciting "June 6, 2011, John Jones has deposited in the Citizens Bank of Emanon, Illinois, Two Thousand Dollars, to the credit of himself, payable upon the return of this instrument properly indorsed, with interest at the rate of 6 percent per annum from date of issue upon ninety days' written notice. (Signed) Jill Crystal, President, Citizens Bank of Emanon."

**(d)** An instrument reciting "I.O.U., Mark Noble, $1,000.00."

**(e)** A note stating "In accordance with our contract of December 13, 2010, I promise to pay to the order of Sam Stone $100 on March 13, 2011."

**(f)** A draft drawn by Brown on the Acme Publishing Company for $500, payable to the order of the Sixth National Bank of Erehwon, directing the bank to "Charge this draft to my royalty account."

**(g)** A note executed by Pierre Janvier, a resident of Chicago, for $2,000, payable in Swiss francs.

**(h)** An undated note for $1,000 payable "six months after date."

**(i)** A note for $500 payable to the order of Ray Rodes six months after the death of Albert Olds.

**(j)** A note of $500 payable to the assigns of Levi Lee.

**(k)** A check made payable "to Ketisha Johnson."

**2.** State whether the following provisions in a note impair or preclude negotiability, the instrument in each instance being otherwise in proper form. Answer each statement with either the word "Negotiable" or "Nonnegotiable" and explain why.

**(a)** A note signed by Henry Brown in the trade name of the Quality Store.

**(b)** A note for $450, payable to the order of TV Products Company, "If, but only if, the color television set for which this note is given proves entirely satisfactory to me."

**(c)** A note executed by Adams, Burton, and Cady Company, a partnership, for $1,000, payable to the order of Davis, payable only out of the assets of the partnership.

**(d)** A note promising to pay $500 to the order of Leigh and to deliver ten tons of coal to Leigh.

**(e)** A note for $10,000 executed by Eaton payable to the order of the First National Bank of Emanon in which Eaton promises to give additional collateral if the bank deems itself insecure and demands additional security.

**(f)** A note reading, "I promise to pay to the order of Richard Roe $2,000 on January 31, 2011, but it is agreed that if the crop of Blackacre falls below ten bushels per acre for the 2010 season, this note shall be extended indefinitely."

**(g)** A note payable to the order of Ray Rogers fifty years from date but providing that payment shall be accelerated by the death of Silas Hughes to a point of time four months after his death.

**(h)** A note for $4,000 calling for payments of installments of $250 each and stating "In the event any installment hereof is not paid when due this note shall immediately become due at the holder's option."

**(i)** An instrument dated September 17, 2011, in the handwriting of John Henry Brown, which reads in full: "Sixty days after date, I, John Henry Brown, promise to pay to the order of William Jones $500."

**(j)** A note reciting "I promise to pay Ray Reed $100 on December 24, 2011."

**3.** On March 10, Tolliver Tolles, also known as Thomas Towle, delivered to Alonzo Craig and Abigail Craig the following instrument, written by him in pencil:

> For value received, I, Thomas Towle, promise to pay to the order of Alonzo Craig or Abigail Craig One Thousand Seventy-Five ($1,000.75) Dollars six months after my mother, Alma Tolles, dies with interest at the rate of 9 percent from date to maturity and after maturity at the rate of 9.75 percent. I hereby waive the benefit of all laws exempting real or personal property from levy or sale.

Is this instrument negotiable? Explain.

**4.** Henry Hughes, who operates a department store, executed the following instrument:

> $2,600 Chicago, March 5, 2011
>
> On July 1, 2011, I promise to pay Daniel Dalziel, or order, the sum of Twenty-Six Hundred Dollars for the privilege of one framed advertising sign, size 24 × 36 inches, at one end of each of two hundred sixty motor coaches of the

> New Omnibus Company for a term of three months from May 15, 2011.
>
> (Signed) Henry Hughes

Is this instrument negotiable? Explain.

**5.** Paul agreed to lend Marsha $500. Thereupon Marsha made and delivered her note for $500 payable to Paul or order "ten days after my marriage." Shortly thereafter Marsha was married. Is the instrument negotiable? Explain.

**6.** For the balance due on the purchase of a tractor Henry Brown executed and delivered to Jane Jones his promissory note containing the following language:

> January 1, 2011, I promise to pay to the order of Jane Jones the sum of $7,000 to be paid only out of my checking account at the XYZ National Bank in Pinckard, Illinois, in two installments of $3,500 each, payable on May 1, 2011, and on July 1, 2011, provided that if I fail to pay the first installment on the due date, the entire sum shall become immediately due.
>
> (Signed) Henry Brown

Is the note negotiable? Explain.

**7.** Sam Sharpe executed and delivered to Don Dole the following instrument:

> Knoxville, Tennessee May 29, 2011
>
> Thirty days after date I promise to pay Don Dole or order, Five Thousand Dollars. The holder of this instrument shall have the election to require the assignment and delivery to him of my 100 shares of Brookside Iron Works Corporation stock in lieu of the payment of Five Thousand Dollars in money.
>
> (Signed) Sam Sharpe

Is this instrument negotiable? Explain.

**8.** Explain whether the following instrument is negotiable.

> March 1, 2011
>
> One month from date, I, James Jimson, hereby promise to pay Edmund Edwards: Six thousand, Seven hundred Fifty ($6,750.00) dollars, plus 8 3/4% interest. Payment for cutting machines to be delivered on March 15, 2011.
>
> (Signed) James Jimson

**9.** Broadway Management Corporation obtained a judgment against Briggs. The note on which the judgment was based reads in part: "Ninety Days after date, I, we, or either of us, promise to pay to the order of Three Thousand Four Hundred Ninety Eight and 45/100 _____ Dollars." (The underlined words and symbols were typed in; the remainder was printed.) There are no blanks on the face of the instrument, any unused space having been filled in with hyphens. The note contains clauses permitting acceleration in the event the holder deems itself insecure and authorizes judgment "if this note is not paid at any stated or accelerated maturity." Explain whether the note is negotiable order paper.

**10.** Sandra and Thomas McGuire entered into a purchase and sale agreement for "Becca's Boutique" with Pascal and Rebecca Tursi. The agreement provided that the McGuires would buy the store for $75,000, with a down payment of $10,000 and the balance of $65,000 to be paid at closing on October 5, 2011. The settlement clause stated that the sale was contingent upon the McGuires' obtaining a Small Business Administration loan of $65,000. On September 4, 2011, Mrs. McGuire signed a promissory note in which the McGuires promised to pay to the order of the Tursis and the Green Mountain Inn the sum of $65,000. The note specified that interest payments of $541.66 would become due and payable on the fifth days of October, November, and December 2011. The entire balance of the note, with interest, would become due and payable at the option of the holder if any installment of interest was not paid according to that schedule.

The Tursis had for several months been negotiating with Parker Perry for the purchase of the Green Mountain Inn in Stowe, Vermont. On September 7, 2011, the Tursis delivered to Perry a $65,000 promissory note payable to the order of Green Mountain Inn, Inc. This note was secured by transfer to the Green Mountain Inn of the McGuires' note to the Tursis. Subsequently, Mrs. McGuire learned that her Small Business Administration loan had been disapproved. On December 5, 2011, the Tursis defaulted on their promissory note to the Green Mountain Inn. On June 11, 2011, PP, Inc., formerly Green Mountain Inn, Inc., brought an action against the McGuires to recover on the note held as security for the Tursis' promissory note. Discuss whether the instrument is negotiable.

**11.** On September 2, 2005, Levine executed a mortgage bond under which she promised to pay the Mykoffs a preexisting obligation of $54,000. On October 14, 2011, the Mykoffs transferred the mortgage to Bankers Trust Co., indorsing the instrument with the words "Pay to the Order of Bankers Trust Company Without Recourse." The Lincoln First Bank, N.A., brought this action asserting that the Mykoffs' mortgage is a nonnegotiable instrument because it is not payable to order or bearer; thus it is subject to Lincoln's defense that the mortgage was not supported by consideration as an antecedent debt is not consideration. Is the instrument payable to order of bearer? Discuss.

**12.** Horne executed a $100,000 note in favor of R. C. Clark. On the back of the instrument was a restriction stating that the note could not be transferred, pledged, or otherwise assigned without Horne's written consent. As part of the same transaction between Horne and Clark, Horne gave Clark a separate letter authorizing Clark to pledge the note as collateral for a loan of $50,000 that Clark intended to secure from First State Bank. Clark did secure the loan and pledged the note, which was accompanied by Horne's letter authorizing Clark to use the note as collateral. First State contacted Horne and verified the agreement between Horne and Clark as to using the note as collateral. Clark defaulted on the loan. When First State later attempted to collect on the note, Horne refused to pay, arguing that the note was not negotiable as it could not be transferred without obtaining Horne's written consent. Is the instrument negotiable? Explain.

**13.** Holly Hill Acres, Ltd. executed and delivered a promissory note and a purchase money mortgage to Rogers and Blythe. The note provided that it was secured by a mortgage on certain real estate and that the terms of that mortgage "are by this reference made a part hereof." Rogers and Blythe then assigned the note to Charter Bank, and the bank sought to foreclose on the note and mortgage. Holly Hill Acres refused to pay, claiming that it was defrauded by Rogers and Blythe. Is the note a negotiable instrument? Why?

CHAPTER 27

# Transfer

The primary advantage of negotiable instruments is their ease of transferability. Nonetheless, although both negotiable instruments and nonnegotiable undertakings are transferable by assignment, only negotiable instruments can result in the transferee becoming a holder. This distinction is highly significant. If the transferee of a negotiable instrument is entitled to payment by the terms of the instrument, he is a holder of the instrument. Only holders may be holders in due course and thus may be entitled to greater rights in the instrument than the transferor may have possessed. These rights, discussed in the next chapter, are the reason why negotiable instruments move freely in the marketplace. This chapter discusses the methods by which negotiable instruments may be transferred.

## NEGOTIATION

A holder, under the Uniform Commercial Code (UCC), is broadly defined in Section 1–201(20) as "a person who is in possession of … an instrument … drawn, issued, or indorsed to him or his order or to bearer or in blank." Revised Article 1 has a similar definition: "the person in possession of a negotiable instrument that is payable either to bearer or to an identified person that is the person in possession." Revised Section 1–201(b)(21). **Negotiation** is the transfer of possession, whether voluntary or involuntary, by a person other than the issuer of a negotiable instrument in such a manner that the transferee becomes a holder. Section 3–201(a). An instrument is transferred when a person other than its issuer delivers it for the purpose of giving the recipient the right to enforce the instrument. Section 3–203(a). Accordingly, to qualify as a holder a person must have possession of an instrument that runs to him. Thus, there are two ways in which a person can be a holder: (1) the instrument has been issued to that person, or (2) the instrument has been transferred to that person by negotiation.

The transfer of a nonnegotiable promise or order operates as an assignment, as does the transfer of a negotiable instrument by a means that does not render the transferee a holder. As discussed in *Chapter 16*, an **assignment** is the voluntary transfer to a third party of the rights arising from a contract.

Whether a transfer is by assignment or by negotiation, the transferee acquires the rights his transferor had. Section 3–203(b). The transfer need not be for value: if the instrument is transferred as a gift, the donee acquires all the rights of the donor. If the transferor was a holder in due course, the transferee acquires the rights of a holder in due course, which rights he in turn may transfer. This rule, sometimes referred to as the *shelter rule*, existed at common law and still exists under the UCC. The shelter rule is discussed more fully in *Chapter 28*.

The requirements for negotiation depend on whether the instrument is bearer paper or order paper.

### NEGOTIATION OF BEARER PAPER

If an instrument is payable to bearer, it may be negotiated by transfer of possession alone. Section 3–201(b). Because bearer paper (an instrument payable to bearer) runs to whoever is in possession of it, a finder or a thief of bearer paper would be a holder even though he did not receive possession by voluntary transfer. Section 3–201(a). For example, P loses an instrument payable to bearer that I had issued to her. F finds it and delivers it to B, who thus receives it by negotiation and is a holder. F also qualified as a holder because he was in possession of bearer paper. As a holder, F had the power to negotiate the instrument, and B, the transferee, may be a holder in due course if he meets the Code's requirements for such a holder (discussed in *Chapter 28*). See *Figure 27-1* for an illustration of this example. Because a bearer instrument is negotiated by mere *possession*, it is comparable to cash.

◆ **SEE FIGURE 27-1: Bearer Paper**

### NEGOTIATION OF ORDER PAPER

If the instrument is order paper (an instrument payable to order), both (1) transfer of its *possession* and (2) its *indorsement* (signature) by the appropriate parties are necessary for the

◆ FIGURE 27-1: **Bearer Paper**

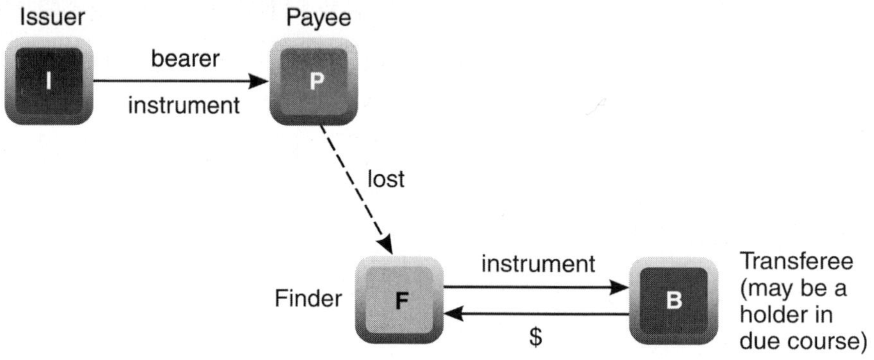


transferee to become a holder. Section 3–201(b). *Figure 27-2* compares the negotiation of bearer and order paper.

Any transfer for *value* of order paper gives the transferee the specifically enforceable right to have the unqualified indorsement of the transferor, unless the parties agree otherwise. Section 3–203(c). The parties may agree that the transfer is to be an assignment rather than a negotiation, in which case no indorsement is required. Absent such agreement, the courts presume that negotiation was intended where value is given. Where a transfer is not for value (i.e., a gift), the transaction is normally noncommercial; thus, the courts do not presume the intent to negotiate.

Until the necessary indorsement has been supplied, the transferee has nothing more than the contract rights of an assignee. Negotiation takes effect only when a proper indorsement is made, at which time the transferee becomes a holder of the instrument.

If a customer deposits a check or other instrument for collection without properly indorsing the item, the depository bank becomes a holder when it accepts the item for deposit if the depositor is a holder. Section 4–205(i). It no longer needs to supply the customer's indorsement.

◆ **SEE CASE 27-1**

◆ SEE FIGURE 27-2: **Negotiation of Bearer and Order Paper**

**The Impostor Rule** Negotiation of an order instrument requires a valid indorsement by the person to whose order the instrument is payable. The impostor rule governing unauthorized signatures is an *exception* to this general rule. Usually, the impostor rule comes into play in situations involving a confidence man who impersonates a respected citizen and who deceives a third party into delivering a negotiable instrument to the impostor in the name of the respected citizen. For instance, John Doe, falsely representing himself as Richard Roe, a prominent citizen, induces Ray Davis to loan him $10,000. Davis draws a check payable to the order of Richard Roe and delivers it to Doe, who then forges Roe's name to the check and presents it to the drawee for payment. The drawee pays it. Subsequently, Davis, the drawer, denies the drawee's right of reimbursement upon the ground that the drawee did not pay in accordance with his order: Davis ordered payment to Roe or to Roe's order. Roe did not order payment to anyone; therefore, the drawee would not acquire a right of reimbursement against Davis. The general rule governing unauthorized signatures supports this argument in favor of the drawer.

Nevertheless, Section 3–404(c) provides that the indorsement of the impostor (Doe) or of any other person in the name of the named payee is **effective** as the indorsement of the payee if the impostor has induced the maker or drawer

◆ FIGURE 27-2: **Negotiation of Bearer and Order Paper**

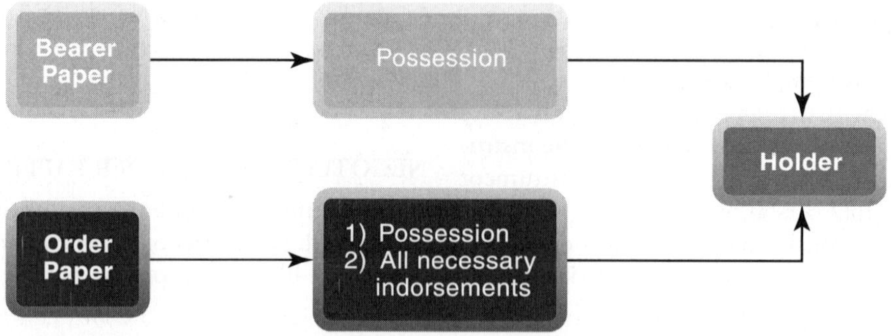

(Davis) to issue the instrument to him or his confederate using the name of the payee (Roe). It is as if the named payee had indorsed the instrument. The reason for this rule is that the drawer or maker is to blame for failing to detect the impersonation by the impostor. Thus, in the above example, the drawee would be able to debit the drawer's account. Moreover, Revised Article 3 expands the impostor rule by extending its coverage to include an impostor who is impersonating an agent. Section 3–404(a). Thus, if an impostor impersonates Jones and induces the drawer to draw a check to the order of Jones, the impostor can negotiate the check. Moreover, under the Revision, if an impostor impersonates Jones, the president of Jones Corporation, and the check is to the order of Jones Corporation, the impostor can negotiate the check. Comment 1 to Section 3–404.

If the person paying the instrument fails to exercise ordinary care, the issuer may recover from the payor to the extent the payor's negligence contributed to the loss. If the issuer is also negligent, comparative negligence would apply.

**The Fictitious Payee Rule** The rule just discussed also applies when a person who does not intend the payee to have an interest in the instrument signs as or on behalf of a maker or drawer. Section 3–404(b). In such a situation, any person's indorsement in the name of the named payee is **effective** if the person identified as the payee is a fictitious person. For instance, Palmer gives Albrecht, her employee, authority to write checks to pay Palmer's debts. Albrecht writes a check for $2,000 to Foushee, a fictitious payee, which Albrecht takes and indorses in Foushee's name to Albrecht. Albrecht cashes the check at Palmer's bank, which can debit Palmer's account because Albrecht's signature in Foushee's name is effective against Palmer. Palmer should bear the risk of her unscrupulous employees.

In a similar situation also involving a disloyal employee, a drawer's employee falsely tells the drawer that money is owed to Leon, and the drawer writes a check payable to the order of Leon and hands it to the agent for delivery to him. The agent forges Leon's name to the check and obtains payment from the drawee bank. The drawer then denies the bank's claim to reimbursement upon the ground that the bank did not comply with her order; that the drawer had ordered payment to Leon or order; that the drawee did not make payment either to Leon or as ordered by him, inasmuch as the forgery of Leon's signature is wholly inoperative; and that the drawee paid in accordance with the scheme of the faithless agent and not in compliance with the drawer's order. Under Section 3–405, an employer has liability on the instrument when one of its employees, who is entrusted with responsibility with respect to such an instrument, makes a fraudulent indorsement if (1) the instrument is payable to the employer and the employee forges the indorsement of the employer or (2) the instrument is issued by the employer and the employee forges the indorsement of the person identified as the payee. The example above falls under the second part of the rule just stated. Accordingly, the employee's indorsement is effective as that of the unintended payee, and the drawee bank will be able to debit the drawer's (employer's) account.

Section 3–405 also applies to a situation (the first part of the rule stated above) not involving a fictitious payee: a fraudulent indorsement made by an employee entrusted with responsibility with respect to an instrument payable to the employer. For example, an employee, whose job involves posting amounts of checks payable to her employer, steals some of the checks and forges her employer's indorsement. The indorsement is effective as the employer's indorsement because the employee's duties included processing checks for bookkeeping purposes.

Section 3–405 provides, however, that the employer may recover from the drawee bank to the extent the loss resulted from the bank's failure to exercise ordinary care. If the employer is also negligent, a rule of comparative negligence applies.

◆ **SEE CASE 27-2**

### NEGOTIATIONS SUBJECT TO RESCISSION

A negotiation conforming to the requirements discussed above is effective to transfer the instrument even if it is—

1. made by an infant, a corporation exceeding its powers, or a person without capacity; or
2. obtained by fraud, duress, or mistake; or
3. made in breach of a duty or as part of an illegal transaction. Section 3–202(a).

Thus, a negotiation is valid even though the transaction in which it occurs is voidable or even void. In all of these instances, the transferor loses all rights in the instrument until he regains possession of it. His right to do so, determined by State law, is valid against the immediate transferee and all subsequent holders, but not against a subsequent holder in due course or a person paying the instrument in good faith and without notice. Section 3–202(b).

## INDORSEMENTS

An **indorsement** is

> a signature, other than that of a signer as maker, drawer, or acceptor, that alone or accompanied by other words is made on an instrument for the purpose of (i) negotiating the instrument, (ii) restricting payment of the instrument, or (iii) incurring indorser's liability on the instrument, but regardless of the intent of the signer, a signature and its accompanying words

is an indorsement unless the accompanying words, terms of the instrument, place of the signature, or other circumstances unambiguously indicate that the signature was made for a purpose other than indorsement. Section 3–204(a).

An indorsement may be complex or simple. It may be dated and may indicate where it is made, but neither date nor place is required to be shown. The simplest type is merely the signature of the indorser. The indorser undertakes certain obligations, as explained later, by merely signing her name. A forged or otherwise unauthorized signature necessary to negotiation is inoperative and thus breaks the chain of title to the instrument. Section 3–403(a).

The type of indorsement used in first negotiating an instrument affects its subsequent negotiation. Every indorsement is (1) either blank or special, (2) either restrictive or nonrestrictive, and (3) either qualified or unqualified. These categories are not mutually exclusive. Indeed, each indorsement may be placed within three of these six categories because all indorsements disclose three things: (1) the method to be employed in making subsequent negotiations (this depends upon whether the indorsement is blank or special); (2) the kind of interest that is being transferred (this depends upon whether the indorsement is restrictive or nonrestrictive); and (3) the liability of the indorser (this depends upon whether the indorsement is qualified or unqualified). For instance, an indorser who merely signs her name on the back of an instrument is making a blank, nonrestrictive, unqualified indorsement. See *Figure 27-3* for further illustrations.

Revised Article 3 identifies an additional type of indorsement—an anomalous indorsement. An anomalous indorsement is "an indorsement made by a person that is not the holder of the instrument." Section 3–205(d). The only effect of an anomalous indorsement is to make the signer liable on the instrument as an indorser. Such an indorsement does not affect the manner in which the instrument may be negotiated.

The effectiveness of an indorsement as well as the rights of the transferee and transferor depend upon whether the indorsement meets certain formal requirements. This section will cover the different kinds of indorsements and the formal requirements of each.

◆ SEE FIGURE 27-3: **Indorsements**

## BLANK INDORSEMENTS

A **blank indorsement**, which specifies no indorsee, may consist solely of the signature of the indorser or her authorized agent. Section 3–205(b). Such an indorsement converts order paper into bearer paper and leaves bearer paper as bearer paper. Thus, an instrument indorsed in blank may be negotiated by delivery alone without further indorsement. Hence, the holder should treat it with the same care as cash.

◆ SEE CASE 27-3

## SPECIAL INDORSEMENTS

A **special indorsement** specifically identifies the person to whom or to whose order the instrument is to be payable. Section 3–205(a). Thus, if Peter, the payee of a note, indorses it "Pay to the order of Andrea," or even "Pay Andrea," the indorsement is special because it names the transferee. Words of negotiability—"pay to order or bearer"—are *not* required in an indorsement. Thus, an indorsement reading "Pay Edward" is interpreted as meaning "Pay to the order of Edward." Any further negotiation of the instrument would require Edward's indorsement.

Moreover, a holder of an instrument with a blank indorsement may protect himself by converting the blank indorsement to a special indorsement by writing over the signature of the indorser words identifying the person to

◆ FIGURE 27-3: **Indorsements**

| Indorsement | Type of Indorsement | Interest Transferred | Liability of Indorser |
|---|---|---|---|
| 1. "John Doe" | Blank | Nonrestrictive | Unqualified |
| 2. "Pay to Richard Roe, John Doe" | Special | Nonrestrictive | Unqualified |
| 3. "Without Recourse, John Doe" | Blank | Nonrestrictive | Qualified |
| 4. "Pay to Richard Roe in trust for John Roe, without recourse, John Doe" | Special | Restrictive | Qualified |
| 5. "For collection only, without recourse, John Doe" | Blank | Restrictive | Qualified |
| 6. "Pay to XYZ Corp., on the condition that it delivers goods ordered this date, John Doe" | Special | Nonrestrictive | Unqualified |

whom the instrument is payable. Section 3–205(c). For example, on the back of a negotiable instrument appears the blank indorsement "Sally Seller." Harry Holder, who receives the instrument from Seller, may convert this bearer instrument into order paper by inserting above Seller's signature "Pay Harry Holder" or other similar words.

◆ SEE CASE 27-3

## RESTRICTIVE INDORSEMENTS

As the term implies, a **restrictive indorsement** attempts to restrict the rights of the indorsee in some fashion. It limits the purpose for which the proceeds of the instrument can be applied. Section 3–206. The Code discusses four types of indorsements as restrictive: conditional indorsements, indorsements prohibiting further transfer, indorsements for deposit or collection, and indorsements in trust. Section 3–206. Only the last two are effective. An **unrestrictive indorsement**, in contrast, does not attempt to restrict the rights of the indorsee.

**Indorsements for Deposit or Collection** The most frequently used form of restrictive indorsement is that designed to place the instrument in the banking system for deposit or collection. Indorsements of this type, collectively referred to as "collection indorsements," include "for collection," "for deposit," and "pay any bank." Such an indorsement *effectively limits* further negotiation to those consistent with its limitation and binds (1) all nonbanking persons, (2) a depository bank that purchases the instrument or takes it for collection, and (3) a payor bank that is also the depository bank or that takes the instrument for immediate payment over the counter from a person other than a collecting bank. Section 3–206(c). Thus, a collection indorsement binds all parties except an intermediary bank (discussed in *Chapter 30*) or a payor bank that is not also the depository bank.

◆ SEE CASE 27-4

**Indorsements in Trust** Another common kind of restrictive indorsement is that in which the indorser creates a trust for the benefit of himself or others. If an instrument is indorsed "Pay Thelma in trust for Barbara," "Pay Thelma for Barbara," "Pay Thelma for account of Barbara," or "Pay Thelma as agent for Barbara," Thelma is a fiduciary, subject to liability for any breach of her obligation to Barbara. Trustees commonly and legitimately sell trust assets, and, consequently, a trustee has power to negotiate an instrument. The first taker under an indorsement to her in trust (in this case Thelma) is under a duty to pay or apply, in a manner consistent with the indorsement, all the funds she receives. Thelma's immediate transferee may safely pay Thelma for the instrument if he does not have *notice* of any breach of fiduciary duty. Section 3–206(d)(1). Subsequent indorsees or transferees are not bound by such indorsement unless they *know* that the trustee negotiated the instrument for her own benefit or otherwise in breach of her fiduciary duty. Section 3–206(d)(2).

**Indorsements with Ineffective Restrictions** A **conditional indorsement** is one by which the indorser makes the rights of the indorsee subject to the happening or nonhappening of a specified event. Suppose Marcin makes a note payable to Parker's order. Parker indorses it "Pay Rodriguez, but only if the good ship *Jolly Jack* arrives in Chicago harbor by November 15, 2011." If Marcin had used this language in the instrument itself, it would be nonnegotiable because her promise to pay must be unconditional to satisfy the formal requisites of negotiability. Revised Article 3 makes such indorsements ineffective by providing that an indorsement stating a condition to the right of a holder to receive payment does not affect the right of the indorsee to enforce the instrument. Section 3–206(b).

An indorsement may by its express terms attempt to prohibit further transfer by stating "Pay [name] only" or language to similar effect. Such an indorsement, or any other purporting to prohibit further transfer, is designed to restrict the rights of the indorsee. To remove any doubt as to the effect of such a provision, the Code provides that *no* indorsement limiting payment to a particular person or otherwise prohibiting further transfer is effective. Section 3–206(a). As a result, an indorsement that purports to prohibit further transfer of the instrument is given the same effect as an unrestricted indorsement.

## QUALIFIED AND UNQUALIFIED INDORSEMENTS

**Unqualified** indorsers promise that they will pay the instrument according to its terms at the time of their indorsement to the holder or to any subsequent indorser who paid it. Section 3–415(a). In short, an unqualified indorser guarantees payment of the instrument if certain conditions are met.

An indorser may disclaim her liability on the contract of indorsement, but only if the indorsement so declares and the disclaimer is written on the instrument. The customary manner of disclaiming an indorser's liability is to add the words "without recourse," either before or after her signature. Section 3–415(b). A "**without recourse**" indorsement, called a qualified indorsement, does not, however, eliminate all of an indorser's liability. As discussed in *Chapter 29*, a **qualified** indorsement disclaims contract liability but does not entirely remove the warranty liability of the indorser. A qualified indorsement and delivery is a negotiation and transfers legal title to the indorsee, but the indorser does not guarantee payment of the instrument. Furthermore, a qualified indorsement does not destroy negotiability or prevent further negotiation of the instrument. For example, assume that an attorney receives a check payable to her order in payment of a client's claim. She may indorse the check to the client without recourse, thereby disclaiming liability as a guarantor of payment of the check. The qualified indorsement plus delivery would transfer title to the client.

## FORMAL REQUIREMENTS OF INDORSEMENTS

**Place of Indorsement** An indorsement must be written on the instrument or on a paper, called an **allonge**, affixed to the instrument. Section 3–204(a). An allonge may be used even if the instrument contains sufficient space for the indorsement.

Customarily, indorsements are made on the back or reverse side of the instrument, starting at the top and continuing down. Under Federal Reserve Board guidelines, indorsements of checks must be in ink of an appropriate color, such as blue or black, and must be made within one and one-half inches of the trailing (left) edge of the back of the check. The remaining space is reserved for bank indorsements. Nevertheless, failure to comply with the guidelines does not destroy negotiability, and there are no penalties for violating the standard.

Occasionally, however, a signature may appear on an instrument in such a way that it is impossible to tell with certainty the nature of the liability the signer intended to undertake. In such an event, the Code specifies that the signer is to be treated as an indorser. Section 3–204(a). In keeping with the rule that a transferee must be able to determine her rights from the face of the instrument, the person who signed in an ambiguous capacity may not introduce parol evidence to establish that she intended to be something other than an indorser.

◆ SEE FIGURE 27-4: **Placement of Indorsement**

◆ FIGURE 27-4: **Placement of Indorsement**

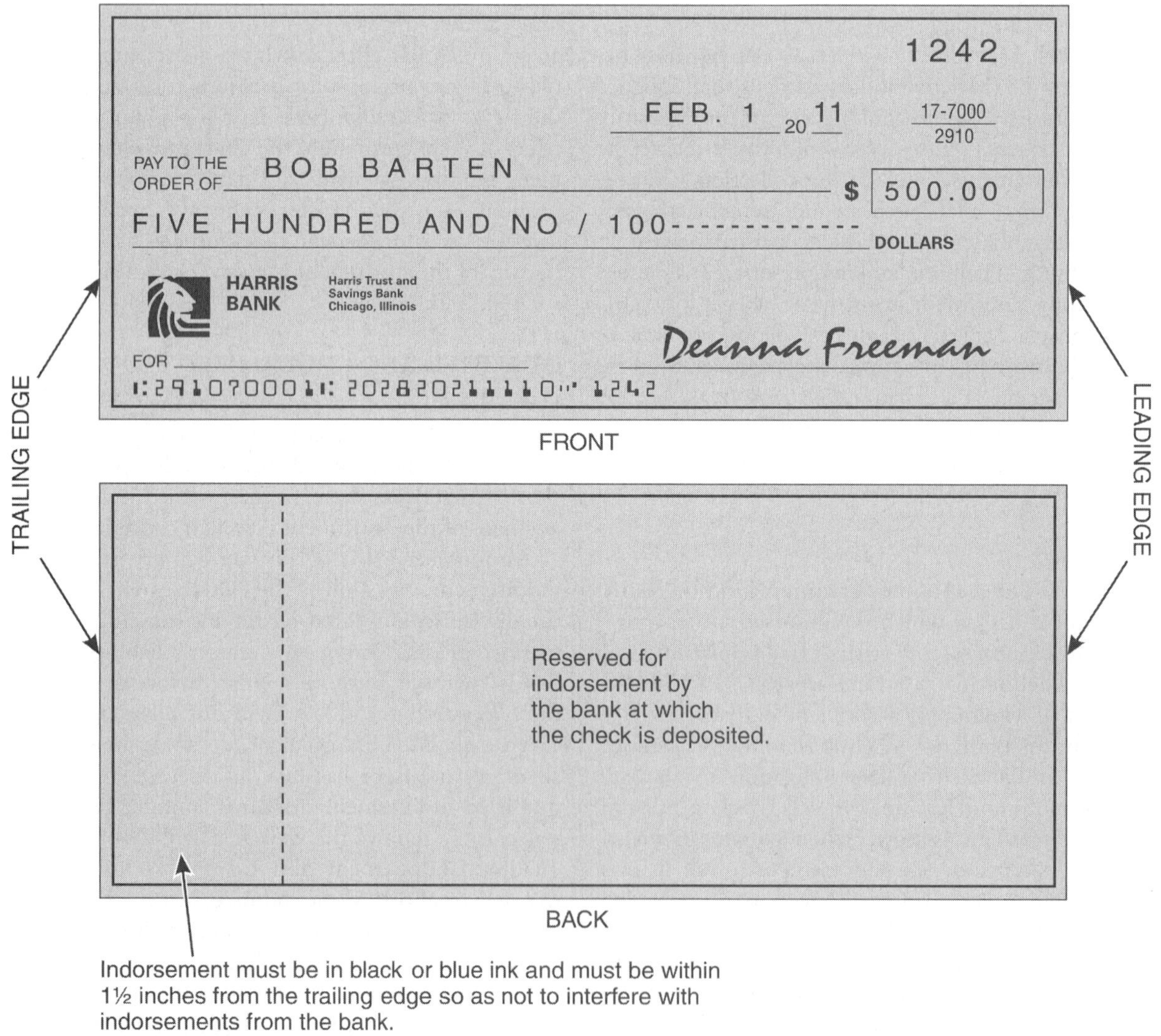

**Incorrect or Misspelled Indorsements** If an instrument is payable to a payee or indorsee under a misspelled name or a name different from that of the holder, the holder may require the indorsement in the name stated or in the holder's correct name or both. Section 3–204(d). Nevertheless, the person paying or taking the instrument for value may require the indorser to sign both names.

## CHAPTER SUMMARY

| | |
|---|---|
| NEGOTIATION | **Holder** possessor of an instrument with all necessary indorsements<br>**Shelter Rule** transferee gets rights of transferor<br>**Negotiation of Bearer Paper** transferred by mere possession<br>**Negotiation of Order Paper** transferred by possession and indorsement by all appropriate parties<br>• ***The Impostor Rule*** an indorsement of an impostor or of any other person in the name of the named payee is effective if the impostor has induced the maker or drawer to issue the instrument to him using the name of the payee<br>• ***The Fictitious Payee Rule*** an indorsement by any person in the name of the named payee is effective if an agent of the maker or drawer has supplied her with the name of the payee for fraudulent purposes<br>**Negotiations Subject to Rescission** negotiation is valid even though a transaction is void or voidable |
| INDORSEMENTS | **Definition** signature (on the instrument) of a payee, drawee, accommodation party, or holder<br>**Blank Indorsement** one specifying no indorsee and making the instrument bearer paper<br>**Special Indorsement** one identifying an indorsee to be paid and making the instrument order paper<br>**Unrestrictive Indorsement** one that does not attempt to restrict the rights of the indorsee<br>**Restrictive Indorsement** one attempting to limit the rights of the indorsee<br>• ***Indorsements for Deposit or Collection*** effectively limit further negotiation to those consistent with the indorsement<br>• ***Indorsements in Trust*** effectively require the indorsee to pay or apply all funds in accordance with the indorsement<br>• ***Indorsements with Ineffective Restrictions*** include conditional indorsements and indorsements attempting to prohibit further negotiation<br>**Unqualified Indorsement** one that imposes liability on the indorser<br>**Qualified Indorsement** without recourse, one that limits the indorser's liability<br>**Formal Requirements of Indorsements**<br>• ***Place of Indorsement***<br>• ***Incorrect or Misspelled Indorsement*** |

# CASES

## CASE 27-1

## Negotiation of Order Paper
## THE HYATT CORPORATION v. PALM BEACH NATIONAL BANK

Court of Appeal of Florida, Third District, 2003
840 So.2d 300, 49 U.C.C. Rep.Serv.2d 1039
http://www.3dca.flcourts.org/Opinions/3d02-1276.pdf

**Levy, J.**

Appellant/defendant the Hyatt Corporation appeals the lower court's Summary Final Judgment in favor of appellee/ plaintiff Palm Beach National Bank. * * * We affirm.

J&D Financial Corporation is a factoring company. Skyscraper Building Maintenance, LLC, had a contract with Hyatt to perform maintenance work for various Hyatt hotels in South Florida. Skyscraper entered into a factoring agreement with J&D. As part of the factoring agreement, J&D requested Hyatt to make checks payable for maintenance services to Skyscraper and J&D. Of the many checks issued by Hyatt to Skyscraper and J&D, two were negotiated by the bank but indorsed only by Skyscraper. They were made payable as follows:

1. Check No. 1-78671 for $22,531 payable to:
   J&D Financial Corp.
   Skyscraper Building Maint
   P.O. Box 610250
   North Miami, Florida 33261-0250
2. Check No. 1-75723 for $21,107 payable to:
   Skyscraper Building Maint
   J&D Financial Corp.
   P.O. Box 610250
   North Miami, Florida 33261-0250

Only one of the payees, Skyscraper, indorsed these two checks. The bank cashed the checks. According to J&D, it did not receive the benefit of these two payments.

J&D filed a complaint against Skyscraper and its principals on the guarantee, Hyatt and the bank. J&D sought damages against Skyscraper under the factoring agreement and separately against Hyatt and the bank for negotiation of the two checks. Hyatt answered and raised the bank's "fault" as an affirmative defense. * * * The bank, Hyatt and J&D then moved for summary judgment on the issue of whether the bank properly negotiated the checks. It was uncontested that the bank had a duty to negotiate the checks only on proper indorsement, and if it did not, it would be liable.

The bank argued that the checks were payable to J&D and Skyscraper alternatively, and thus the bank could properly negotiate the checks based upon the indorsement of either of the two payees. The bank further argued that the checks were drafted ambiguously as to whether they were payable alternatively or jointly, and thus under [UCC] Section [3–110(d)], Florida Statutes, the checks would be construed as a matter of law to be payable alternatively.

Hyatt's position was that the checks were not ambiguous, were payable jointly and not alternatively, and thus under Section [3–110], the checks could only be negotiated by indorsement of both of the payees. J&D similarly argued that the checks were payable jointly. The trial court granted Summary Judgment in favor of the bank, finding that [UCC] Section [3–110(d)] precluded the bank's liability. Hyatt appealed. J&D filed a cross-appeal.

The issue on appeal is whether or not a check payable to

J&D Financial Corporation
Skyscraper Building Maintenance

(stacked payees) is payable jointly to both payees requiring the indorsement of both, or whether it is ambiguous regarding whether the check was drafted payable alternatively, so that the bank could negotiate the check when it was indorsed by only one of the two payees.

In 1990, Article 3 of the UCC was revised, and the language of UCC Section 3–116 was added to UCC section 3–110 and became subsection (d). Revised UCC Section 3–110(d), which added language to follow former 3–116(a) and (b), states, "If an instrument payable to two or more persons is ambiguous as to whether it is payable to the persons alternatively, the instrument is payable to the persons alternatively." The net effect of the amendment was to change the presumption. What was unambiguous before is now ambiguous.

Turning to our jurisdiction, Florida has adopted the statutory revision to UCC 3–110, * * *.

The issue under review has not reached Florida's appellate courts. However, two trial courts in Florida have addressed this issue in *Bijlani v. Nationsbank of Florida, N.A.*, [citation] and *City First Mortgage Corp. v. Florida Residential Property & Casualty Joint Underwriting Ass'n.*, [citation]. We find the reasoning in both cases to be persuasive.

In *Bijlani*, the appellee paid a check which did not have Bijlani's indorsement. The check was made payable to

Bay Village Inc.
Michael Bijlani & Ron Delo & Assoc
5411 Grenada Blvd
Coral Gables, FL 33133

The trial court granted the bank's motion for summary judgment, stating that "The multiple payee designation on the check is ambiguous as to whether it is payable to 'Bay Village Inc.' "Michael Bijlani * * * jointly or alternatively." Holding that the bank was not liable, the trial court noted that the predecessor statute "provided that if an ambiguity existed as to whether multiple payees were intended as joint or alternative payees, they were deemed joint payees," while the amended statute applicable to this case "reverses the prior rule." [Citation.]

In *City First Mortgage Corp.* [citation], a Florida County Court reached the same conclusion. In *City First Mortgage Corp.*, the bank paid a check which did not have City First Mortgage Corp.'s indorsement. The check was made payable to

> BORIS LA ROSA ODALYS LA ROSA
> CITY FIRST MTG. CORP. ISAOA ATIMA

The county court granted First Union's Motion to Dismiss Complaint, stating that the Complaint failed to state a cause of action against the bank. The court found that,

> On its face, the Check is payable to two or more persons and, as a matter of law, the payee designation on the Check is ambiguous as to whether it is payable to the persons alternatively. [Citations.]

Although Florida appellate courts have not yet considered the issue at hand, other courts in the country have. [Citations.]

For example, a case which has addressed this particular issue with almost identical facts to those before us is *Allied Capital Partners, L.P. v. Bank One, Texas, N.A.*, [citation]. In *Allied*, the checks were made payable to:

> Complete Design
> Allied Capital Partners, LLP.
> 2340 E. Trinity Mills St. 300
> Carrollton, Texas 75006

The debtor indorsed the checks and deposited them into a corporate bank account. The factor then sued the bank for conversion for payment on the debtor's indorsement.

On appeal from the adverse summary judgment, the factor cited pre-revision law. The Texas appellate court affirmed the summary judgment, stating:

> While it does appear that former Section 3–116 would have required the checks in this case to be payable to and negotiable only by all of the payees listed, this is no longer the case …

[citation]. Under these facts, the court found that the check was unambiguous.

We conclude that based on the 1990 amendment to the Uniform Commercial Code, when a check lists two payees without the use of the word "and" or "or", the nature of the payee is ambiguous as to whether they are alternative payees or joint payees. Therefore, the UCC amendment prevails and they are to be treated as alternative payees, thus requiring only one of the payees' signatures. Consequently, the bank could negotiate the check when it was indorsed by only one of the two payees, thereby escaping liability.

* * *

* * * Thus, we hold that the trial court was correct in granting the Summary Final Judgment.

Affirmed.

## CASE 27-2

### Fictitious Payee Rule
### SHEARSON LEHMAN BROTHERS, INC. v. WASATCH BANK

United States District Court, D. Utah, C.D., 1992
788 F.Supp. 1184
http://scholar.google.com/scholar_case?case=4047487329373602465&hl=en&as_sdt=2&as_vis=1&oi=scholarr

**Anderson, J.**

Before the court is Defendant's Motion for Summary Judgment. The core issue presented by the motion is whether and to what extent a collecting or depository bank will be liable to the drawer or the unintended payee of a check when the drawer's faithless employee induces the drawer to issue checks, fraudulently indorses them in the name of the specified payee, and absconds with the funds. Because under the undisputed facts of the case, the "fictitious payee" defense as codified by section 3–405 [Revised §§3–404, 3–405] of the Uniform Commercial Code affords the defendant an absolute defense to all claims, summary judgment for the defendant is hereby granted.

The present litigation between plaintiff Shearson Lehman Brothers, Inc., ("Shearson") and defendant Wasatch Bank ("Wasatch") arises out of the activities of a former employee of Shearson, Stanley A. Erb ("Erb"). Erb began working as a financial consultant or broker at Shearson's Provo, Utah, branch office in 1984. By 1987, because of the volume of his sales, Erb had been given the cognomen of vice president. In 1987, Erb was contacted by McKay Matthews, the controller for the Orem, Utah, based WordPerfect

Corporation, and its sister corporation, Utah Softcopy. On Matthews' request, Erb coordinated the establishment of three separate investment accounts at Shearson. The accounts were for the benefit of WordPerfect and Utah Softcopy as corporations and one account was established for the personal benefit of the WordPerfect principals, Allen C. Ashton, Bruce W. Bastian, and Willard E. Peterson. Thereafter, Erb assumed the responsibility for managing all three of the Word Perfect accounts at Shearson.

In March 1987, Erb personally accepted from Matthews a check drawn by Utah Softcopy and payable to the order of "ABP Investments." The amount of the check was $460,150.23. At that time, there was no ABP Investment account opened at Shearson, although the WordPerfect principals maintained accounts elsewhere in that name. Notwithstanding the absence of an account in the name of the payee, Erb accepted the check for deposit at Shearson. Matthews suggested that a substitute check be correctly drawn and submitted for deposit at Shearson. Erb responded by assuring Matthews that he would personally guarantee that the check was credited to the appropriate account. However, rather than depositing the check into one of the authorized WordPerfect accounts, Erb opened a new account at Shearson in the name of "ABP Investments." Erb apparently forged the signature of Bruce Bastian on the new account documents. No evidence in the record suggests that Bastian or any other WordPerfect or Utah Softcopy representative authorized or subsequently ratified the creation of the new account. Erb listed as the address of record for the ABP Investment account a post office box number in Orem, Utah, which was unknown to WordPerfect and its principals and was different from the record address for the other three WordPerfect accounts.

Over the course of the next eleven months, Erb induced Shearson to draft checks on the ABP Investment account, payable to ABP Investments. Erb manipulated Shearson's procedure for making payments to clients by submitting to the Shearson cashier falsified payment request forms. Checks were drawn by Shearson in the requested amounts and were mailed to the Orem post office box. Erb then obtained the checks from the post office box, indorsed them in the name of ABP Investments, and took them to Wasatch for deposit into his personal account. In the course of his scheme, Erb fraudulently procured and negotiated approximately thirty-seven checks, totaling $504,295.30.

Wasatch accepted for deposit and subsequently allowed Erb to withdraw from his personal account all of the funds representing the thirty-seven checks Erb fraudulently procured from Shearson. Copies of those checks reveal that each was drawn payable to the order of ABP Investments and each was indorsed, in handwriting, in the name of ABP Investments and without Erb's personal indorsement or any other indication of Erb's authority to act on behalf of the payee. No ABP Investment account was maintained at Wasatch and therefore no signature card or other evidence on the premises of the bank could have been used to verify Erb's authority to deposit checks payable to ABP Investments. * * *

Erb's activities with respect to the ABP Investments account were not discovered until early 1989, by which time Erb had terminated his employment at Shearson. Lori Rogerson, the operations manager at the Provo Shearson office, testified that she had always been aware of the existence of the ABP Investment account, that she understood the initials "ABP" to represent the names of the WordPerfect principals, but that she also assumed the account was legitimately opened and managed by Erb. At a meeting with WordPerfect representatives in early 1989, Rogerson peripherally mentioned the ABP Investment account whereupon a WordPerfect representative informed her that neither WordPerfect nor its principals maintained such an account at Shearson. After this disclosure, Shearson requested an audit of the accounts managed by Erb and discovered the extent of his mishandling of the ABP Investment account as well as other unrelated mismanagement.

In June 1989, Shearson, WordPerfect and the WordPerfect principals entered a settlement agreement whereby all claims against Shearson arising out of Erb's mishandling of the WordPerfect and related accounts were settled for $1,208,903. Under the agreement, Shearson acquired by assignment or was subrogated to all legal rights of WordPerfect, Ashton, Bastian and Peterson. Shearson subsequently initiated the present suit against Wasatch. Shearson's complaint alleges the following causes of action: (1) common law negligence, specifically, that the deposits were suspicious, Wasatch knew Erb was employed by the drawer of the checks he deposited into his personal account, and Wasatch made no reasonable attempt to determine the authenticity of endorsements; (2) breach of warranty of good title and implied covenant of good faith and fair dealing in that Wasatch failed to follow reasonable commercial banking practices; * * *.

Wasatch subsequently moved for summary judgment and asserts as the basis for that motion the following arguments: (1) the "fictitious payee defense," UCC §3–405(1)(c) [Revised §3–405], bars all of Shearson's claims; * * *.

* * *

## Discussion

### *Whether Shearson's Claims Are Barred by the "Fictitious Payee" Defense of UCC 3–405(1)(c) [Revised §3–405]*

Wasatch acknowledges that, "[a]s a general rule, 'forged indorsements are ineffective to pass title or to authorize a drawee to pay.'" [Citations.] Consequently, when a collecting bank makes payment over a forged indorsement, it is generally liable for the amount paid. [Citations.]

Under this general rule, Wasatch clearly would be liable as the party that accepted checks over forged indorsements. Wasatch attempts to avoid such liability, however, by invoking what is known as the "fictitious payee" defense. The defense is an exception to the general rule that a party accepting or paying an instrument over a forged indorsement ultimately will be liable for the loss and is set forth in section 3–405 [Revised §3–405] of the Uniform Commercial Code:

* * *

The policy underlying section 3–405 [Revised §3–405] is thus to place the risk of loss of forgery on the party in the best position to avoid or insure against such loss. [Citations.]

As indicated by the language of section 3–405(1)(c) [Revised §3–405], if the defense applies to the facts of a given transaction, the result is to render the forged signature effective to transfer good title as if no forgery had occurred. [Citations.] * * *

For the defense to apply, an employee or agent of the drawer must "supply" the name of the payee to the drawer, and the faithless employee must intend that the payee have no interest in the instrument. [UCC] §3–405(1)(c) [Revised §3–405]. Although the defense commonly has been referred to as the "fictitious payee" defense, the payee named on the check need not be a fictitious person or entity. "It is immaterial whether a person with the name of the payee actually exists or whether the name is in fact a wholly fictitious name." [Citations.] Moreover, courts applying the defense have liberally construed the term "supply." "An employee 'supplies' the name of the payee if he 'starts the wheels of normal business procedure in motion to produce a check for a nonauthorized transaction.'" [Citations.] * * *

Thus Wasatch argues that the fictitious payee defense of section 3–405(1)(c) [Revised §3–405] applies to the undisputed facts of the present case. Erb, an employee of the drawer of the check, "supplied" the name of the payee within the meaning of the statute and obviously intended that the named payee have no interest in the checks. He then procured the checks and fraudulently indorsed them for deposit into his account at Wasatch. Wasatch accordingly argues that the effect of Erb's actions was to validate the forged indorsements and to allow good title to pass to Wasatch thereby extinguishing Wasatch's liability for the transaction.

* * *

***Conclusion***

The "fictitious payee" defense as articulated in section 3–405(1)(c) [Revised §3–405] of the Uniform Commercial Code operates under the facts of the present case to shield the collecting bank, Wasatch, from liability resulting from Erb's misconduct while in Shearson's employ. Erb deliberately induced the issuance of checks by Shearson. The payee named on those checks was never intended by Erb to take an interest in the checks. In such circumstances the mandate of the Code is clear—the drawer shall bear the loss resulting from the misdeeds of its employee. Wasatch's conduct in the relevant transactions raises serious questions about whether the bank discharged its duty to act in a commercially reasonable manner. Nevertheless, no fact has been alleged which would support the inference that Wasatch acted in bad faith so as to preclude the operation of the fictitious payee defense. [S]ummary judgment is hereby GRANTED in favor of Wasatch and all counts of Shearson's complaint are hereby dismissed with prejudice.

CASE 27-3

## Blank/Special Indorsements
## STATE OF NEW MEXICO v. HERRERA

Court of Appeals of New Mexico, 2000

130 N.M. 85, 18 P.3d 326, cert. denied, 130 N.M. 153, 20 P.3d 810

http://www.nm.net/download/n/opinion/VIEW/01ca-007.html

**Wechsler, J.**

Defendant Joshua Herrera pleaded guilty to one count of forgery * * *, reserving his right to appeal the district court's determination that Defendant's acts constituted forgery for the purpose of the indictment. We reverse.

### Facts

Defendant was the only witness at the hearing on his motion to dismiss the indictment. He testified that he found a purse in a dumpster near San Pedro and Kathryn Streets in Albuquerque. Defendant took the purse with him to a friend's house. Either Defendant or his friend called the owner of the purse and the owner retrieved the purse at some point. Defendant testified that after the purse was returned to the owner, he returned to the dumpster where he found a check and some other items. Defendant claimed that he did not know if the check or any of the other items belonged to the owner of the purse and he further claimed that he did not remember the purse owner's name at that time.

Defendant further testified that the check he found was written out to "Cash" and that he thought this meant that he "could get money for [the] check." Defendant explained that when he presented the check to the teller at a credit union to cash it, the teller instructed him to put his name on the payee line next to "Cash." Defendant followed the teller's instructions and added "to Joshua Herrera" next to the word "Cash" on the payee line of the check. Defendant also indorsed the check.

The district court ruled that "Defendant altered a writing purporting to [have] legal efficacy with intent to [defraud], [and] those acts constitute a crime of forgery." * * *

### *Whether Defendant's Acts Constitute the Crime of Forgery*

Defendant argues on appeal that his acts fail to meet the elements of forgery because (1) he signed his own name and not another's; (2) he did not alter the genuineness of the check; (3) the legislature did not intend the concept of alteration to include the addition of a genuine signature to a genuine check; and (4) he did not alter the check because he did not change the legal efficacy of the check. We address only Defendant's fourth argument because it is upon this ground that we reverse the district court's denial of Defendant's motion to dismiss.

* * *

Section 30–16–10(A) defines forgery as "falsely making or altering any signature to, or any part of, any writing purporting to have any legal efficacy with intent to injure or defraud." Section 30–16–10(B) defines forgery as the transfer of a forged document. Under Section 30–16–10(A), the State must prove that the defendant made a false document, a false signature, a false indorsement or "changed a genuine [document] so that its effect was different from the original" with an intent to deceive or cheat another. [Citation.] Under Section 30–16–10(B) the State must prove that the defendant gave or delivered a document to a victim with the intent to injure, deceive or cheat the victim or another, knowing that the document (1) was a false document; (2) contained a false signature; (3) had a false indorsement; or (4) was changed so that its effect was different from the original. [Citation.]

Defendant did not make a false signature or offer a false indorsement. Thus, a plain reading of the statute and the jury instructions indicates that under the facts of this case, Defendant could only have committed forgery by changing the legal effect of the check. [Citation.] * * * Therefore, whether Defendant changed the legal effect of the check is the dispositive question in this case. Defendant argues that the act of adding his name to the payee line next to the word "Cash" failed to alter the legal effect of the check. We look to the Uniform Commercial Code to determine whether Defendant is correct.

When a negotiable instrument is made payable to "Cash," it is a bearer instrument. [UCC] §3–109(a)(3) (1992). A bearer instrument refers to an instrument that is payable to anyone possessing the instrument and is negotiable by transfer alone. [UCC] §3–109(a)(1).

In contrast, an instrument payable to an identified person is considered an order instrument. [UCC] §3–109(b). An order instrument requires the indorsement of the identified person before it can be negotiated. [UCC] §3–201(b). The legal effect of an order instrument is different from a bearer instrument because each type of instrument has different negotiability requirements:

> Whether an instrument is an order instrument or a bearer instrument is important in determining how an instrument is negotiated. If the instrument is payable to bearer, it can be negotiated by delivery alone. If it is payable to the order of an identified person it cannot be negotiated without the indorsement of that person.

[Citations.]

At the time Defendant presented the check to the credit union teller, he possessed a bearer instrument because the check was written out to "Cash." At the direction of the teller, however, Defendant added the words "to Joshua Herrera" to the payee line after the word "Cash." By doing so, Defendant added a specific payee to what was otherwise a bearer instrument. We analyze whether Defendant changed the legal effect of the check by adding his name on the payee line of the check.

The concepts of bearer and order are mutually exclusive. [UCC] §3–109(b) states that "[a] promise or order that is not payable to bearer is payable to order if it is payable * * * to the order of an identified person." An instrument payable to bearer cannot be payable to order. [Citation.]

As a result, under the definitions in the Uniform Commercial Code, the check in this case could not have been both a bearer and an order instrument. Defendant could have changed the legal effect of the bearer instrument he possessed by adding his name only if the instrument ceased to have bearer effect. We believe that it did not.

The Official Comment to [UCC] §3–109 is instructive in this regard. The Comment addresses situations in which an instrument contains terms indicating that it is both payable to bearer and payable to order. The Comment states that when an instrument is payable both to bearer and order, the instrument states contradictory terms, but that it is nonetheless a bearer instrument. The Comment explains that an instrument that purports to be payable both to order and bearer states contradictory terms. A transferee of the instrument should be able to rely on the bearer term and acquire rights as a holder without obtaining the indorsement of the identified payee. [Citations.]

We discern from the Comment that the addition of an identified payee to a check that is otherwise a bearer instrument is insufficient to transform the legal effect of the check because it is still a bearer instrument and a transferee of the check is able to rely on the bearer term. [UCC] §3–109 Official Cmt. 2.

We do not view the fact that Defendant wrote "to Joshua Herrera" and not "or Joshua Herrera" as significant. The Official Comment to [UCC] §3–109 uses the word "or" in its example of an instrument containing bearer and order terms. [UCC] §3–109 Official Comment 2. In determining the legal status of a negotiable instrument, the significant words are those that represent either bearer or order terms.

The words "Cash" and "Bearer" have distinct legal meanings. Their presence upon the face of an instrument signifies the particular legal status of that instrument; namely, that the instrument is payable to anyone bearing it. [UCC] §3–201(b). Similarly, the presence of an identified payee such as "Joshua Herrera" on the face of an instrument signifies that the instrument is payable only to Joshua Herrera.

In this circumstance, with the check payable "to the order of Cash to Joshua Herrera," one who received it could reasonably be confused because it contains both bearer and order instructions. The Uniform Commercial Code resolves such confusion by making the bearer term prevail. [UCC] §3–109 Official Cmt. 2. We do not view the conjunction "to" in this case as sufficient to avoid confusion from the conflicting terms so as to preclude application of the principles of the commentary.

Indeed, under specific circumstances, a bearer instrument can be transformed to an order instrument. [UCC] §3–109(c) provides that when a bearer instrument is specially indorsed, it can be transformed to an order instrument. A special indorsement is one that "identifies a person to whom it makes the instrument payable." [UCC] §3–205(a). Defendant's indorsement in this case included only his name and did not include language making the check payable to an identified person. [UCC] §3–205(c). Thus, the indorsement was not a special indorsement and was not sufficient to transform the legal effect of the check from bearer to order. Instead, because Defendant's indorsement included only his signature, the indorsement qualified as an indorsement in blank. [UCC] §3–205(b). Section 3–205(b) states that when an instrument is indorsed in blank, "the instrument becomes payable to bearer and may be negotiated by transfer of possession alone." Consequently, Defendant's indorsement did not change the legal effect of the check from a bearer instrument into an order instrument under [UCC] §3–109.

Because Defendant did not change the legal effect of the check when he added his name to the payee line or when he indorsed it, Defendant did not commit the crime of forgery. * * *

* * * We reverse the district court's denial of Defendant's motion to dismiss the indictment.

## CASE 27-4

### Indorsements for Deposit or Collection
### STATE OF QATAR v. FIRST AMERICAN BANK OF VIRGINIA

United States District Court, ED Va, 1995
885 F.Supp. 849

**Ellis, J.**

At issue in this sequel to *State of Qatar v. First American Bank of Virginia* ("Qatar I") is the meaning and legal significance of the phrase "for deposit only" following an indorsement on the back of a check. More specifically, the question presented is whether a depository bank complies with the restrictive indorsement "for deposit only" when it deposits a check bearing that restriction into *any* person's account, or whether that restriction requires a depository bank to deposit the check's proceeds only into the account of the named payee. For the reasons that follow, the court holds that the unqualified language "for deposit only" following an indorsement on the back of a check requires a depository bank to place the check's proceeds into the payee's account, and the bank violates that restrictive indorsement when it credits the check to any other account.

#### I

* * *

Plaintiffs are the State of Qatar and certain of its agencies (collectively, "Qatar"). From approximately 1986 to 1992, one of Qatar's employees, Bassam Salous, defrauded his employer by having checks drawn on Qatar's account in purported payment of false or duplicated invoices that he had created. Although all of the unauthorized checks were made payable to individuals and entities other than Salous, he nonetheless successfully deposited the checks into his own personal accounts with Defendant First American Bank of Virginia ("First American") and Central Fidelity Banks, Inc.(collectively, "the depository banks").

After Qatar discovered this fraudulent scheme in 1992, it brought suit against the depository banks for conversion. * * *

Only one category of checks remains in dispute. These checks all bear the forged indorsement of the payee named on the face of the check, followed by a stamped "for deposit only" restriction.

* * *

#### II

It is now established that First American may be liable to Qatar for handling a check's proceeds in violation of a restrictive indorsement. [Citation.] Under §3–205(c) of the pre-1993 Uniform Commercial Code ("UCC" or "Code") [Virginia adopted Revised Article 3 in 1993] restrictive indorsements are defined to "include the words 'for collection,' 'for deposit,' 'pay any bank,' or like terms signifying a purpose of deposit or collection." Thus, the UCC makes clear that the phrase "for deposit only" is, in fact, a restrictive indorsement. But the Code does not define "for deposit only" or specify what bank conduct would be inconsistent with that restriction. Nor does Virginia decisional law provide any guidance on this issue. As a result, reference to decisional law from other jurisdictions is appropriate.

Not surprisingly, most courts confronted with this issue have held that the restriction "for deposit only," without additional specification or directive, instructs depository banks to deposit the funds only into the payee's account. In addition, commentators on commercial law uniformly agree that the function of such a restriction is to ensure that the checks' proceeds be deposited into the payee's account.

This construction of "for deposit only" is commercially sensible and is adopted here. The clear purpose of the restriction is to avoid the hazards of indorsing a check in blank. Pursuant to former §3–204(2), a check indorsed in blank "becomes payable to bearer." It is, essentially, cash. Thus, a payee who indorses her check in blank runs the risk of having the check stolen and freely negotiated before the check reaches its intended destination. To protect against this vulnerability, the payee can add the restriction "for deposit only" to the indorsement, and the depository bank is required to handle the check in a manner consistent with that restriction. §3–206(3). And in so adding the restriction, the payee's intent plainly is to direct that the funds be deposited into her own account, not simply that the funds be deposited into some account. [Citation.] Any other construction of the phrase "for deposit only" is illogical and without commercial justification or utility. Indeed, it is virtually impossible to imagine a scenario in which a payee cared that her check be deposited, but was indifferent with respect to the particular account to which the funds would be credited.

* * *

Finally, it is worth noting that the new revisions to the negotiable instruments provisions of the UCC, [Revised Article 3], support the result reached here. Although these revisions are inapplicable to this case, the commentary following §3–206 states that the new subdivision dealing with "for deposit only" and like restrictions "continues previous law." §3–206 comment 3. Shortly thereafter, the commentary provides an example in which a check bears the words "for deposit only" above the indorsement. In those circumstances, the commentary states, the depository bank acts inconsistently with the restrictive indorsement where it deposits the check into an account other than that of the payee. Although the restriction in that example precedes the signature, whereas the restrictions on the checks at issue here follow the signature, this distinction is immaterial. The clear meaning of the restriction in both circumstances is that the funds should be placed into the payee's account.

Therefore, First American violated the restrictive indorsements in depositing into Bassam Salous' account checks made payable to others and restrictively indorsed "for deposit only." Pursuant to the holding in Qatar I, then, First American is liable to Qatar for conversion in the amount of the total face values of these checks.

## QUESTIONS

1. Distinguish among (a) transfer, (b) negotiation, and (c) assignment.
2. Explain what is necessary to become a holder of an instrument.
3. Explain the imposter rule and the fictitious payee rule.
4. Distinguish among a blank indorsement, a special indorsement, a qualified indorsement, and an unqualified indorsement.
5. Discuss which types of restrictive indorsements are effective and ineffective.

## PROBLEMS

**1.** Roy Rand executed and delivered the following note to Sue Sims: "Chicago, Illinois, June 1, 2011; I promise to pay to Sue Sims or bearer, on or before July 1, 2011, the sum of $7,000. This note is given in consideration of Sims's transferring to the undersigned title to her 2002 Buick automobile. (signed) Roy Rand." Rand and Sims agreed to defer delivery of the car to July 1, 2011. On June 15, Sims sold and delivered the note, without indorsement, to Karl Kaye for $6,200. What rights, if any, has Kaye acquired?

**2.** Lavinia Lane received a check from Wilmore Enterprises, Inc., drawn on the Citizens Bank of Erehwon, in the sum of $10,000. Mrs. Lane indorsed the check "Mrs. Lavinia Lane for deposit only, Account of Lavinia Lane," placed it in a "Bank by Mail" envelope addressed to the First National Bank of Emanon, where she maintained a checking account, and placed the envelope over a tier of mailboxes in her apartment building along with other letters to be picked up by the postal carrier the next day. Flora Fain stole the check, went to the Bank of Omaha, where Mrs. Lane was unknown, represented herself to be Lavinia Lane, and cashed the check. Has Bank of Omaha taken the check by negotiation? Why or why not?

**3.** What types of indorsements are the following:

**(a)** "Pay to Monsein without recourse."

**(b)** "Pay to Allinore for collection."

**(c)** "I hereby assign all my rights, title, and interest in this note to Fullilove in full."

**(d)** "Pay to the Southern Trust Company."

**(e)** "Pay to the order of the Farmers Bank of Nicholasville for deposit only."

Indicate whether the indorsement is (1) blank or special, (2) restrictive or nonrestrictive, and (3) qualified or unqualified.

**4.** Explain whether each of the following transactions results in a valid negotiation:

**(a)** Arnold gives a negotiable check payable to bearer to Betsy without indorsing it.

**(b)** Golden indorses a negotiable promissory note payable to the order of Golden, "Pay to Chambers and Rambis, (signed) Golden."

**(c)** Porter lost a negotiable check payable to his order. Kersey found it and indorsed the back of the check as follows: "Pay to Drexler, (signed) Kersey."

**(d)** Thomas indorsed a negotiable promissory note payable to the order of Thomas, "(signed) Thomas," and delivered it to Sally. Sally then wrote above Thomas's signature, "Pay to Sally."

**5.** Alpha issues a negotiable check to Beta payable to the order of Beta in payment of an obligation Alpha owed Beta. Beta delivers the check to Gamma without indorsing it in exchange for one hundred shares of General Motors stock owned by Gamma. How has Beta transferred the check? What rights, if any, does Gamma have against Beta?

**6.** Melvin executed and delivered to Dawkins a negotiable promissory note payable to the order of Dawkins as payment for one hundred bushels of wheat Dawkins had sold to Melvin. Dawkins indorsed the note "Pay to Hersey only, (signed) Dawkins" and sold it to Hersey. Hersey then sold the note to Smith after indorsing it "Pay to Smith, (signed) Hersey." What rights, if any, does Smith acquire in the instrument?

**7.** Simon Sharpe executed and delivered to Ben Bates a negotiable promissory note payable to the order of Ben Bates for $500. Bates indorsed the note, "Pay to Carl Cady upon his satisfactorily repairing the roof of my house, (signed) Ben Bates," and delivered it to Cady as a down payment on the contract price of the roofing job. Cady then indorsed the note and sold it to Timothy Tate for $450. What rights, if any, does Tate acquire in the promissory note?

**8.** Debbie Dean issued a check to Betty Brown payable to the order of Cathy Cain and Betty Brown. Betty indorsed the check "Payable to Elizabeth East, (signed) Betty Brown." What rights, if any, does Elizabeth acquire in the check?

**9.** Triplett attempted to arrange a $2,850,000 loan through Meyer Rabin and his Consumer's Investment Company (CIC). CIC issued a commitment letter conditioned on the payment of a $14,250 commitment fee and the personal guarantee of C. D. Wyche. Triplett sought an additional loan from E. S. Tubin to cover the commitment fee. Tubin agreed to provide the $14,250 if the money would be "safe" pending the closing of the $2,850,000 loan and if he would receive $4,500 for the use of his money. Triplett agreed, and Tubin purchased a $14,250 cashier's check payable to Melvin Rueckhaus, his attorney. Rueckhaus typed the following indorsement on the back of the check: "PAY TO THE ORDER—CONSUMERS INVESTMENT CO. and CHARLES D. WYCHE, SR."

Rabin presented the check to Fair Park National Bank for immediate credit to CIC's account. Not knowing that Rabin had forged Wyche's signature, the bank complied, and Rabin subsequently depleted CIC's account. The loan was never closed, and the $14,250 was never returned to Tubin. Is Fair Park National Bank liable to Tubin? Discuss.

**10.** The drawer, Commercial Credit Corporation (Corporation), issued two checks payable to Rauch Motor Company. Rauch indorsed the checks in blank, deposited them to its account in University National Bank, and received a corresponding amount of money. The Bank stamped "pay any bank" on the checks and initiated collection. However, the checks were dishonored and returned to the Bank with the notation "payment stopped." Rauch, through subsequent deposits, repaid the bank. Later, to compromise a lawsuit, the Bank executed a special two-page indorsement of the two checks to Lamson. Lamson then sued the Corporation for the face value of the checks, plus interest. The Corporation contends that Lamson was not a holder of the checks because the indorsement was not in conformity with the UCC in that it was stapled to the checks. Is Lamson a holder? Why?

**11.** Edmund Jezemski, estranged and living apart from his wife, Paula, was administrator and sole heir-at-law of his deceased mother's estate, one asset of which was real estate in Philadelphia. Without Edmund's knowledge or consent, and with the assistance of John M. McAllister, an attorney, and Anthony DiBenedetto, a real estate broker, Paula arranged for a mortgage on the property through Philadelphia Title Insurance Company. Shortly before settlement, Paula represented to McAllister and DiBenedetto that her husband would be unable to attend the closing on the mortgage. She appeared at McAllister's office in advance of the closing accompanied by a man whom she introduced to McAllister and DiBenedetto as her husband. She and this man, in the presence of McAllister and DiBenedetto, executed a deed conveying the property from the estate to her husband and herself as tenants by the entireties and also executed the mortgage. McAllister and DiBenedetto were witnesses. Thereafter, McAllister, DiBenedetto, and Paula met at the office of the Title Company on the closing date, produced the signed deed and mortgage, and Paula obtained from Title Company its check for the mortgage loan proceeds of $15,640.82, payable to the order of Edmund Jezemski and Paula Jezemski individually and to Edmund as administrator.

Paula cashed the check, bearing the purported indorsements of all the payees, at Penns Grove National Bank and Trust Company. Edmund received none of the proceeds, either individually or as administrator. His purported indorsements were forgeries. In the collection process the check was presented to and paid by the drawee bank, Fidelity-Philadelphia Trust Company, and charged against the drawer Title Company's account. Upon discovery of the existence of the mortgage, Edmund brought an action which resulted in the setting aside of the deed and mortgage and the repayment of the amount advanced by the mortgagee. Title Company then sued the drawee bank (Fidelity) to recover the amount of the check, $15,640.82. Is the indorsement effective? Explain.

**12.** Cole was supervisor of the shipping department of Machine Mfg., Inc. In February, Cole found herself in need of funds and, at the end of that month, submitted to Ames, the treasurer of the corporation, a payroll listing that showed as an employee, among others, "Ben Day," to whom was allegedly owed $800 for services rendered during February. Actually, there was no employee named Day. Relying upon the word of Cole, Ames drew and delivered to her a series of corporate payroll checks, drawn upon the corporate account in the Capital Bank, one of which was made payable to the order of "Ben Day" for $800. Cole took the check, indorsed on its back "Ben Day," cashed it at the Capital Bank, and pocketed the proceeds. She repeated the same procedure at the end of March, April, and May. In mid-June, Machine Mfg., Inc., learned of Cole's fraudulent conduct, fired her, and brought an appropriate action against Capital Bank, seeking a judgment for $3,200. Is Cole's signature effective against Machine Mfg., Inc.? Explain.

**13.** While assistant treasurer of Travco Corporation, Frank Mitchell caused two checks, each payable to a fictitious company, to be drawn on Travco's account with Brown City Savings Bank. In each case, Mitchell indorsed the check in his own name and then cashed it at Citizens Federal Savings & Loan Association of Port Huron. Both checks were cleared through normal banking channels and charged against Travco's account with Brown City. Travco subsequently discovered the embezzlement, and after its demand for reimbursement was denied, it brought this suit against Citizens. Is the indorsement effective? Explain.

**14.** Arthur and Lucy Casarez contracted with Blas Garcia, who purported to be a representative of the Albuquerque Fence Company, for the construction of a new home. Blas introduced the Casarezes to Cecil Garcia, who agreed to make a loan to them to be used as a down payment on the project. Cecil then obtained a loan from Rio Grande Valley Bank in the form of a $25,000 cashier's check payable to himself, which he indorsed over to Lucy Casarez. Lucy indorsed the check with the words "Pay to the order of Albuquerque Fence Company, Lucy N. Casarez" and delivered it to Blas Garcia. Claiming he was following Cecil's instructions, Blas indorsed the check with the words "Alb. Fence Co." and gave the check to Cecil. Cecil signed his own name under "Alb. Fence Co." and presented the check to the bank in exchange for $25,000. The Casarezes soon learned that Blas and Cecil Garcia had never been in any way affiliated with or employed by the Albuquerque Fence Company. Explain whether the unauthorized signatures of Blas and Cecil Garcia invalidate the special indorsement to Albuquerque Fence Company.

**15.** Mrs. Wilson was employed as the office manager of Palmer & Ray Dental Supply of Abilene, Inc. Soon after an auditor discovered a discrepancy in the company's inventory, Mrs. Wilson confessed to cashing thirty-five checks that she was supposed to deposit on behalf of the company. Palmer & Ray Dental Supply used a rubber stamp to indorse checks. The stamp listed the company's name and address but did not read "for deposit only." The company's president, James Ray, authorized Mrs. Wilson to indorse checks with this stamp. All checks were cashed at First National Bank. Explain whether First National wrongfully cashed the checks by giving Mrs. Wilson cash instead of depositing the checks into the company's bank account.

**16.** J. R. Simplot, Inc. (d/b/a Simplot Soilbuilders) held a security interest in Richard L. Knight's 2011 crops. To protect this security interest, Simplot sent a "SECURITY INTEREST NOTICE to all potential purchasers of Knight's crops." This notice informed the buyers of Simplot's security interest and requested: "If you purchase or are involved in the sale of these farm products, please include Simplot Soilbuilders on all drafts issued to [Knight]." In 2011 Knight sold crops to George DeRuyter & Sons Dairy, which paid for the crops with a check in the amount of $32,916.79. George DeRuyter & Sons Dairy made the check payable to the order of "Rick Knight Simplot Soil Builders." Knight indorsed his name and forged the indorsement of Simplot Soilbuilders, and deposited the check into his account at Yakima Federal. Knight also sold crops to Connell Grain Growers in 2011. Connell Grain Growers paid for the crops with two checks, one in the amount of $22,494.73 and the other in the amount of $2,573.99. Connell Grain Growers made both checks payable to the order of "Rick Knight Simplot Soil Builders." Knight indorsed his name and forged the indorsement of Simplot Soilbuilders, and deposited both checks into his account at Yakima Federal.

Simplot Soilbuilders, George DeRuyter & Sons Dairy, and Connell Grain Growers did not maintain accounts at Yakima Federal, and the bank did not have a signature card for any of these businesses. Explain whether the instrument was properly indorsed.

C H A P T E R 2 8

# Holder in Due Course

The unique and most significant aspect of negotiability is the concept of the holder in due course. While a mere holder or assignee acquires a negotiable instrument subject to all claims and defenses to it, a holder in due course, except in consumer credit transactions, takes the instrument free of all claims of other parties and free of all defenses to the instrument except for a very limited number. The law has conferred this preferred position upon the holder in due course to encourage the free transferability of negotiable instruments by minimizing the risks assumed by an innocent purchaser of the instrument. The transferee of a negotiable instrument wants payment for it; he does not want to be subject to any dispute between the obligor and the obligee (generally the original payee). This chapter discusses the requirements of becoming a holder in due course and the benefits conferred upon a holder in due course.

## REQUIREMENTS OF A HOLDER IN DUE COURSE

To acquire the preferential rights of a holder in due course, a person either must meet the requirements of Section 3–302 of the Uniform Commercial Code (UCC or Code) or must "inherit" these rights under the shelter rule, Section 3–203(b) (discussed later in this chapter). To satisfy the requirements of Section 3–302, a transferee must—

**1.** be a holder of a negotiable instrument;
**2.** take it for value;
**3.** take it in good faith; and
**4.** take it without notice
  **(a)** that it is overdue or has been dishonored, or
  **(b)** that the instrument contains an unauthorized signature or an alteration, or
  **(c)** that any person has any defense against or claim to it; and
**5.** take it without reason to question its authenticity due to apparent evidence of forgery, alteration, incompleteness, or other irregularity.

*Figure 28-1* illustrates the various requirements of becoming a holder in due course and the consequence of meeting or not meeting these requirements.

◆ **SEE CASE 28-1**

◆ **SEE FIGURE 28-1: Rights of Transferees**

### HOLDER

To become a holder in due course, the transferee must first be a holder. A holder, as discussed in *Chapter 27*, is a person who is in possession of a negotiable instrument that is "payable to bearer or, in the case of an instrument payable to an identified person, if the identified person is in possession." Section 1–201(20). Revised Article 1 has a similar definition: "the person in possession of a negotiable instrument that is payable either to bearer or to an identified person that is the person in possession." Revised Section 1–201(b)(21). In other words, a holder is a person who has both possession of an instrument and all indorsements necessary to it. Whether the holder is the owner of the instrument or not, he may transfer it, negotiate it, enforce payment of it (subject to valid claims and defenses), or, with certain exceptions, discharge it.

The following factual situation, illustrated in *Figure 28-2*, defines the significance of being a holder. Poe indorsed her paycheck in blank and cashed it at a hardware store where she was a well-known customer. Shortly thereafter, a burglar stole the check from the hardware store. The owner of the hardware store immediately notified Poe's employer, who gave the drawee bank a stop payment order (an order not to pay the instrument). The burglar indorsed the check in a false name and transferred it to a grocer who took it in good faith and for value. The check was dishonored (not paid) when presented to the drawee bank. The paycheck became bearer paper when Poe indorsed it in blank. It retained this character in the hands of the owner of the hardware store, in the hands of the burglar, and in the hands of the grocer, who became a holder in due course even though he had received it from a thief who had indorsed it with a false name. Because an

◆ FIGURE 28-1: **Rights of Transferees**

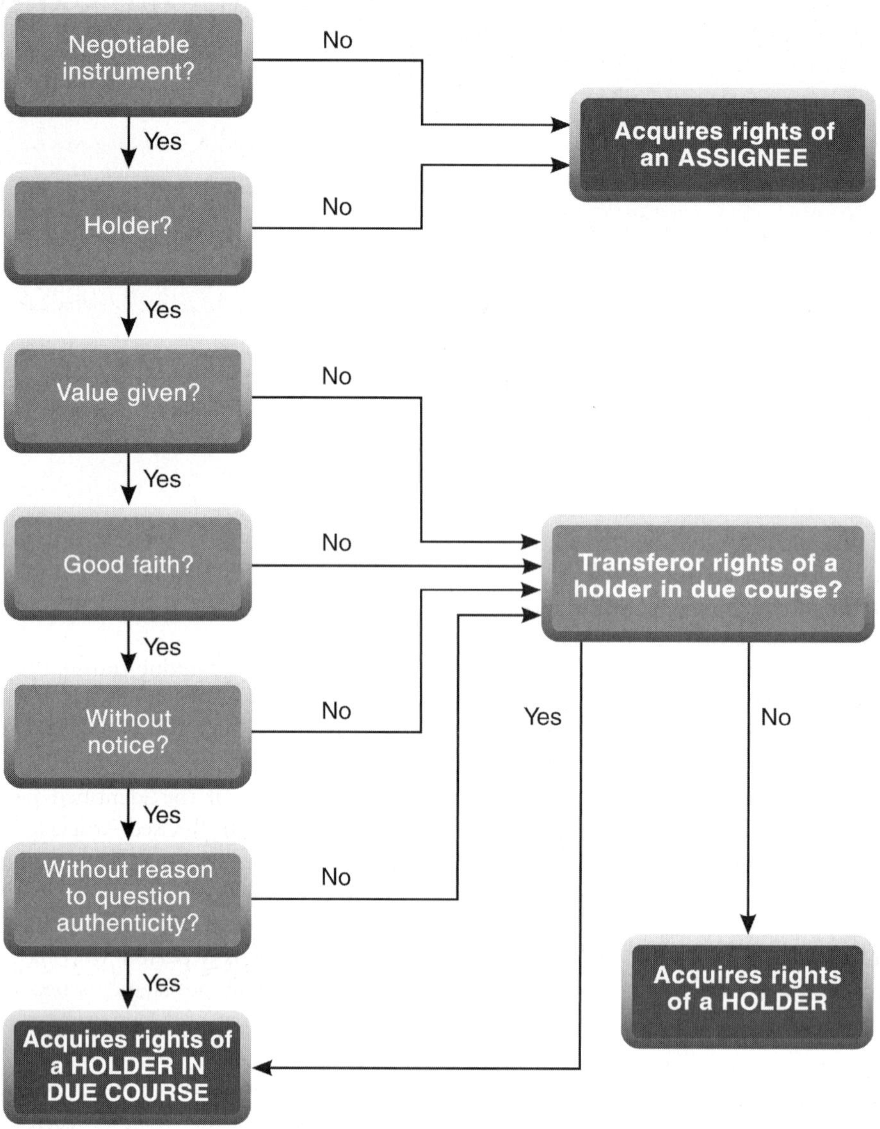


indorsement is not necessary to the negotiation of bearer paper, the fact that the indorsement was forged was immaterial. The thief was a "holder" of the check within the definition of Section 1–201 and may negotiate an instrument "whether or not he is the owner." Accordingly, one who, like the grocer, takes from a holder for value, in good faith, without notice, and without reason to question its authenticity, becomes a holder in due course. Furthermore, in the absence of a real defense, discussed later in this chapter, the grocer will be entitled to payment from the drawer.

◆ SEE FIGURE 28-2: **Stolen Bearer Paper**

This rule does not apply to a stolen order instrument. In the prior example, assume that the thief had stolen the paycheck from Poe prior to indorsement. The thief then forged Poe's signature and transferred the check to the grocer, who again took it in good faith, for value, without notice, and without reason to question its authenticity. Negotiation of an order instrument requires a valid indorsement by the person to whose order the instrument is payable, in this case Poe. A forged indorsement is not valid. Consequently, the grocer has not taken the instrument with all necessary indorsements, and, therefore, he could not be a holder and, as a result, could not be a holder in due course. The grocer's only recourse would be to collect the amount of the check from the thief. *Figure 28-3* illustrates this example.

◆ SEE FIGURE 28-3: **Stolen Order Paper**

◆ FIGURE 28-2: **Stolen Bearer Paper**

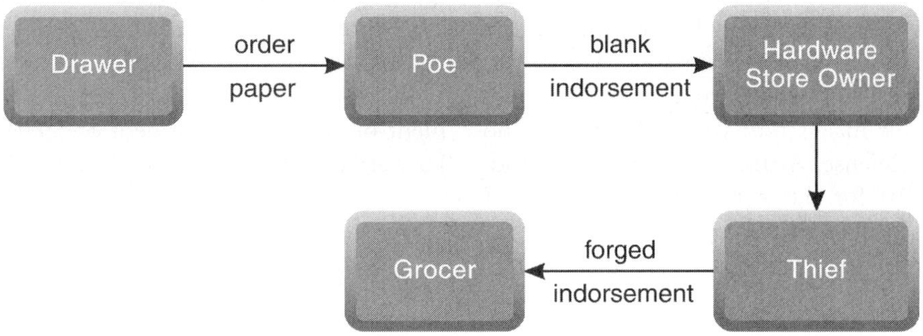


Grocer is a holder in due course because he
(1) Was a holder of a negotiable instrument,
(2) Gave value,
(3) Took in good faith,
(4) Took without notice, and
(5) Took without reason to question its authenticity.

In addition, certain other persons are entitled to enforce an instrument even though the person is not the owner of the instrument or is in wrongful possession of the instrument. Section 3–301. These other persons entitled to enforce an instrument include a nonholder in possession of the instrument who has the rights of a holder, and a person not in possession of the instrument who is entitled to enforce the instrument pursuant to special situations, such as where the instrument has been lost, destroyed, or stolen (Section 3–309) or where the instrument has been paid or accepted by mistake and the payor or acceptor has recovered the money or revoked acceptance (Section 3–418(d)).

◆ **SEE CASE 28-2**

## VALUE

The law requires a holder in due course to give value. An obvious case of the failure to do so is where the holder makes a gift of the instrument to a third person.

The concept of value in the law of negotiable instruments is not the same as that of consideration under the law of contracts. **Value**, for purposes of negotiable instruments, is defined as (1) the actual *performing* of the agreed promise (executory promises are excluded because they have not been performed); (2) the acquiring of a security interest or other lien in the instrument other than a judicial lien; (3) the taking of the instrument in payment of or as security for an antecedent debt; (4) the giving of a negotiable instrument; and (5) the giving of an irrevocable obligation to a third party. Section 3–303(a).

**Executory Promise** An executory promise, though clearly valid consideration to support a contract, is *not* the giving of value to support holder in due course status because such a promise has yet to be performed. A purchaser of a note or draft who has not yet given value may rescind the transaction if she learns of a defense to the instrument. A person who has given value, however, cannot do this; to recover value, she needs the protection accorded a holder in due course.

◆ FIGURE 28-3: **Stolen Order Paper**

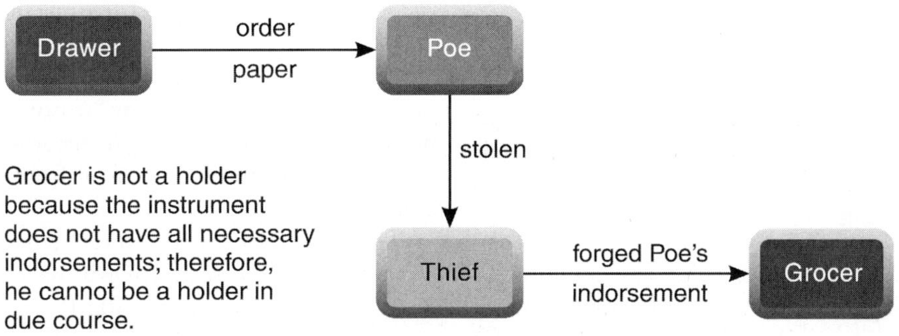

For example, Mike executes and delivers a $1,000 note payable to the order of Pat, who negotiates it to Henry, who promises to pay Pat for it a month later. During the month, Henry learns that Mike has a defense against Pat. Henry can rescind the agreement with Pat and return or tender the note back to her. Because this makes him whole, Henry has no need to cut off Mike's defense. Assume, on the other hand, that Henry has paid Pat for the note before he learns of Mike's defense. Because he may be unable to recover his money from Pat, Henry needs holder in due course protection, which permits him to recover on the instrument from Mike.

A holder therefore takes an instrument for value to the extent that the agreed promise of performance has been performed provided that performance was given prior to the holder's learning of any defense or claim to the instrument. Assume that in the previous example Henry had agreed to pay Pat $900 for the note. If Henry had paid Pat $600, he could be a holder in due course to the extent of $666.67 (600 ÷ 900 × $1000), and if a defense were available, it would be valid against him only to the extent of the balance. Section 3–302(d). When Henry paid the $300 balance to Pat, he would become a holder in due course as to the full $1,000 face value of the note, provided payment was made prior to Henry's discovery of Mike's defense. If he made the $300 payment after discovering the defense or claim, Henry would be a holder in due course only to the extent of $666.67. A holder in due course, to give value, need pay only the amount he agreed to pay, not the face amount of the instrument.

The Code provides an exception to the executory promise rule in two situations: (1) the giving of a negotiable instrument and (2) the making of an irrevocable obligation to a third party. Section 3–303(a)(4), (5).

**Security Interest** Where an instrument is given as security for an obligation, the lender is regarded as having given value to the extent of his security interest. Sections 3–302(e) and 3–303(a). For example, Pedro is the holder of a $1,000 note payable to his order, executed by Monica, and due in twelve months. Pedro uses the note as security for a $700 loan made to him by Larry. Larry has advanced $700; therefore, he has met the requirement of value to the extent of $700.

Likewise, a bank gives value when a depositor is allowed to withdraw funds against a deposited item. Sections 4–210 and 4–211. The provisional or temporary crediting of a depositor's account (discussed in *Chapter 30*) is not sufficient. If a number of checks have been deposited, and some but not all of the funds have been withdrawn, the Code traces the deposit by following the "FIFO" or "first-in, first-out" method of accounting.

**Antecedent Debt** Under general contract law, an antecedent debt (a preexisting obligation) is not consideration. Under Section 3–303(a)(3) of the Code, however, a holder gives value when she takes an instrument in payment of or as security for an antecedent debt. Thus, Martha makes and delivers a note for $1,000 to the order of Penny, who indorses the instrument and delivers it to Howard in payment of an outstanding debt of $970 which she owes him. Howard has given value.

### GOOD FAITH

Revised Article 3 defines **good faith** as "honesty in fact and the observance of reasonable commercial standards of fair dealing." Section 3–103(4). Thus, Revised Article 3 adopts a definition of good faith that has both a subjective and objective component. (This is the same definition adopted by Revised Article 1.) The subjective component ("honesty in fact") measures good faith by what the purchaser knows or believes. The objective component ("the observance of reasonable commercial standards of fair dealing") is comparable to the definition of good faith applicable to merchants under Article 2 in that it includes the requirement of the observance of reasonable commercial standards of fairness. Buying an instrument at a discounted price does not demonstrate lack of good faith.

◆ **SEE CASE 28-2**

### LACK OF NOTICE

To become a holder in due course, a holder must also take the instrument without notice that it is (1) overdue, (2) dishonored, (3) forged or altered (see discussion of these later in the chapter), or (4) subject to any claim or defense. Notice of any of these matters should alert the purchaser that she may be buying a lawsuit and consequently may not be accorded the favored position of a holder in due course. Section 1–201(25) defines *notice* as follows: "A person has 'notice' of a fact when (a) he has actual knowledge of it; or (b) he has received a notice or notification of it; or (c) from all the facts and circumstances known to him at the time in question he has reason to know that it exists." Revised Section 1–202(a) is substantially the same. Whereas the first two clauses of this definition impose a wholly subjective standard, the last clause provides a partially objective one: the presence of suspicious circumstances does not adversely affect the purchaser, unless he has reason to recognize them as suspicious. Because the applicable standard is "actual notice," "notice received," or "reason to know," constructive notice through public filing or recording is not of itself sufficient notice to prevent a person from being a holder in due course.

To be effective, notice must be received at a time and in a manner that the recipient will have a reasonable opportunity to act on it. Section 3–302(f).

**Notice an Instrument Is Overdue** To be a holder in due course, the purchaser must take the instrument without notice that it is overdue. This requirement is based on the idea that overdue paper conveys a suspicion that something is wrong. **Time paper** is due on its stated due date if the stated date is a business day or, if not, on the next business day. It "becomes overdue on the day after the due date." Section 3–304(b)(2). Thus, if an instrument is payable on July 1, a purchaser cannot become a holder in due course by buying it on July 2, provided that July 1 was a business day. In addition, in the case of an installment note or of several notes issued as part of the same transaction with successive specified maturity dates, the purchaser has notice that an instrument is overdue if he has reason to know that any part of the principal amount is overdue or that there is an uncured default in payment of another instrument of the same series. Sections 3–302(a)(2) and 3–304(b).

**Demand paper** is overdue for purposes of preventing a purchaser from becoming a holder in due course if the purchaser has notice that she is taking the instrument on a day after demand has been made or after it has been outstanding for an unreasonably long time. Section 3–304(a). The Code provides that for checks a reasonable time is ninety days after its date. For all other demand instruments the reasonable period of time varies depending upon the facts of the particular case. Thus, the particular situation, business custom, and other relevant factors must be considered in determining whether an instrument is overdue: No hard-and-fast rules are possible.

Acceleration clauses have caused problems. If an instrument's maturity date has been accelerated, the instrument becomes overdue on the day after the accelerated due date even though the holder may be unaware that it is past due. Section 3–304(b)(3).

**Notice an Instrument Has Been Dishonored** **Dishonor** is the refusal to pay or accept an instrument when it becomes due. If a transferee has notice that an instrument has been dishonored, he cannot become a holder in due course. Section 3–302(a)(2)(iii). For example, a person who takes a check stamped "NSF" (not sufficient funds) or "no account" has notice of dishonor and will not be a holder in due course.

**Notice of a Claim or Defense** A purchaser of an instrument cannot become a holder in due course if he purchases it with notice of "any claim to the instrument described in Section 3–306" or "a defense or claim in recoupment described in Section 3–305(a)." Section 3–302(a)(2). A **defense** protects a person from liability on an instrument, whereas a **claim** to an instrument asserts ownership of it.

Claims covered by Section 3–306 "include not only claims to ownership but also any other claim of a property or possessory right. It includes the claim to a lien or the claim of a person in rightful possession of an instrument who was wrongfully deprived of possession." Section 3–306, Comment. Claims to instruments may be made against thieves, finders, or possessors with void or voidable title. In many instances, both a defense and claim will be involved. For example, Donna is fraudulently induced to issue a check to Pablo. Donna has a claim to ownership of the instrument as well as a defense to Pablo's demand for payment.

Section 3–305(a), which is more fully discussed later in this chapter, provides that personal defenses are valid against a holder, while real defenses are effective against both holders and holders in due course. In addition, a person without the rights of a holder in due course is subject to an obligor's claim in recoupment "against the original payee of the instrument if the claim arose from the transaction that gave rise to the instrument." Section 3–305(a)(3). For example, Buyer gives Seller a negotiable note in exchange for Seller's promise to deliver certain goods. Seller delivers nonconforming goods that Buyer elects to accept. Buyer has a cause of action under Article 2 for breach of warranty under the contract, which "claim may be asserted against Seller ... to reduce the amount owing on the note. It is not relevant whether Seller knew or had notice that Buyer had the warranty claim." Section 3–305, Comment 3.

Buying an instrument at a discount or for a price less than face value does not mean that the buyer had notice of any defense or claim against the instrument. Nonetheless, a court may construe an unusually large discount as notice of a claim or defense.

## WITHOUT REASON TO QUESTION ITS AUTHENTICITY

Under prior Article 3, a purchaser had notice of a claim or defense if the instrument was so incomplete, contained such visible evidence of forgery or alteration, or was otherwise so irregular as to call into question its validity. Courts differed greatly as to how irregular an instrument had to be for a holder to have notice. Revised Article 3 provides that a party may become a holder in due course only if the instrument issued or negotiated to the holder "does not bear such apparent evidence of forgery or alteration or is not otherwise so irregular or incomplete as to call into question its authenticity." Section 3–302(a)(1). According to the comments to this section, the term "authenticity" clarifies the idea that the irregularity or incompleteness must indicate that the instrument may not be what it purports to be. The Revision takes the position that persons who purchase such instruments do so at their own peril and should not be protected against defenses of the obligor or claims of prior owners. In addition, the Revision takes the position that it makes no difference if the holder does not have notice of such irregularity or incompleteness; it depends only on whether the instrument's defect is apparent and whether the taker should have reason to know of the problem.

## HOLDER IN DUE COURSE STATUS

A holder who meets the requirements discussed in the previous section obtains the preferred position of holder in due course status. This section discusses whether a payee may become a holder in due course. It also addresses the rights of a transferee from a holder in due course under the shelter rule. Finally, it identifies those special circumstances that prevent a transferee from acquiring holder in due course status.

### A PAYEE MAY BE A HOLDER IN DUE COURSE

A payee may be a holder in due course. Section 3–302, Comment 4. This does not mean that a payee automatically is a holder in due course but that he *may* be one if he satisfies the requirements for such status. For example, if a seller delivers goods to a buyer and accepts a current check in payment, the seller will be a holder in due course if he acted in good faith and had no notice of defenses or claims and no reason to question its authenticity. The most common example is where the transaction involves three parties, and the defense involves the parties other than the payee. For example, after purchasing goods from Punky, Robin fraudulently obtains a check from Clem payable to the order of Punky and forwards it to Punky. Punky takes it for value and without any knowledge that Robin had defrauded Clem into issuing the check. In such a case, the payee, Punky, is a holder in due course and takes the instrument free and clear of Clem's defense of fraud in the inducement.

### THE SHELTER RULE

Through operation of the shelter rule, the transferee of an instrument acquires the *same* rights in the instrument as the transferor had. Section 3–203(b). Therefore, even a holder who does not comply fully with the requirements for being a holder in due course nevertheless acquires all the rights of a holder in due course if some previous holder of the instrument had been a holder in due course. For example, Prosser induces Mundheim, by fraud in the inducement, to make a note payable to her order and then negotiates it to Henn, a holder in due course. After the note is overdue, Henn gives it to Corbin, who has notice of the fraud. Corbin is not a holder in due course, because he took the instrument when overdue, did not pay value, and had notice of Mundheim's defense. Nonetheless, through the operation of the shelter rule, Corbin acquires Henn's rights as a holder in due course, and Mundheim cannot successfully assert his defense against Corbin. The purpose of the shelter provision is not to benefit the transferee but to assure the holder in due course of a free market for the negotiable instruments he acquires.

The shelter rule, however, provides that a transferee who has been a party to any fraud or illegality affecting the instrument cannot subsequently acquire the rights of a holder in due course. For example, Parker induces Miles, by fraud in the inducement, to make an instrument payable to the order of Parker, who subsequently negotiates the instrument to Henson, a holder in due course. If Parker later reacquires it from Henson, Parker will not succeed to Henson's rights as a holder in due course and will remain subject to the defense of fraud.

◆ **SEE CASE 28-3**

## THE PREFERRED POSITION OF A HOLDER IN DUE COURSE

In a nonconsumer transaction a holder in due course takes the instrument (1) free from all *claims* on the part of any person and (2) free from all *defenses* of any party with whom he has not dealt, except for a limited number of defenses that are available against anyone, including a holder in due course. Such defenses that are available against all parties are referred to as **real defenses**. In contrast, defenses that may not be asserted against a holder in due course are referred to as **personal** or **contractual defenses**.

### REAL DEFENSES

The real defenses available against all holders, including holders in due course, are:

1. infancy, to the extent that it is a defense to a simple contract, Section 3–305(a)(1)(i);
2. any other incapacity, duress, or illegality of the transaction that renders the obligation void, Section 3–305(a)(1)(ii);
3. fraud in the execution, Section 3–305(a)(1)(iii);
4. discharge in insolvency proceedings, Section 3–305(a)(1)(iv);
5. any other discharge of which the holder has notice when he takes the instrument, Section 3–601(b);
6. unauthorized signature, Section 3–401(a); and
7. fraudulent alteration, Section 3–407(b), (c).

**Infancy** All States have a firmly entrenched public policy of protecting minors from persons who might take advantage of them through contractual dealings. The Code does not state when minority (infancy) is available as a defense or the conditions under which it may be asserted. Rather, it provides that minority is a defense available against a holder in due course to the extent that it is a defense to a contract under the laws of the State involved. See *Chapter 14*.

**Void Obligations** Where the obligation on an instrument originates in such a way that it is *void* or null under the law of the State involved, the Code authorizes the use of this defense against a holder in due course. This follows from the idea that where the party was never obligated, it is unreasonable to permit an event over which he has no control—negotiation to a holder in due course—to convert a nullity into a valid claim against him.

Incapacity, duress, and the illegality of a transaction are defenses that may render the obligation of a party either voidable or void, depending upon the law of the State involved as applied to the facts of a given transaction. To the extent the obligation is rendered void (because of duress by physical force, because the party is a person under guardianship, or, in some cases, because the contract is illegal) the defense may be asserted against a holder in due course. To the extent it is voidable, which is generally the case, the defense (other than minority, discussed above) is not effective against a holder in due course.

◆ **SEE CASE 28-4**

**Fraud in the Execution** Fraud in the execution of the instrument renders the instrument void and therefore is a defense valid against a holder in due course. The Code describes this type of fraud as misrepresentation that induced the party to sign the instrument with neither knowledge nor reasonable opportunity to learn of its character or its essential terms. For example, Francis is asked to sign a receipt and does so without realizing or having the opportunity of learning that her signature is going on a promissory note cleverly concealed under the receipt. Because her signature has been obtained by fraud in the execution, Francis would have a valid defense against a holder in due course.

**Discharge in Insolvency Proceedings** If a party's obligation on an instrument is discharged in a proceeding for bankruptcy or for any other insolvency, he has a valid defense in any action brought against him on the instrument, including one brought by a holder in due course. Thus, a debtor whose obligation on a negotiable instrument is discharged in an insolvency proceeding (bankruptcy) is relieved of payment, even to a holder in due course.

**Discharge of Which the Holder Has Notice** Any holder, including a holder in due course, takes the instrument subject to *any* discharge of which she has notice at the time of taking. If only some, but not all, of the parties to the instrument have been discharged, the purchaser can still become a holder in due course. The discharged parties, however, have a real defense against a holder in due course who had notice of their discharge. For example, Harris, who is in possession of a negotiable instrument, strikes out the indorsement of Jones. The instrument is subsequently negotiated to Stephen, a holder in due course, against whom Jones has a real defense.

**Unauthorized Signature** A person's signature on an instrument is unauthorized when it is made without express, implied, or apparent authority. A person whose signature is unauthorized or forged cannot be held liable on the instrument in the absence of estoppel or ratification, even if the instrument is negotiated to a holder in due course. Similarly, if Joan's signature were forged on the back of an instrument, Joan could not be held as an indorser, because she has not made a contract. Thus, any unauthorized signature is totally invalid as that of the person whose name is signed unless she ratifies it or is precluded from denying it; the unauthorized signature operates only as the signature of the unauthorized signer. Section 3–403(a).

An unauthorized signature may be **ratified** and thereby become valid so far as its effect as a signature. Section 3–403(a). Thus, Kathy forges Laura's indorsement on a promissory note and negotiates it to Allison. Laura subsequently ratifies Kathy's act. As a result, Kathy is no longer liable to Allison on the note, although Laura is. Nonetheless, Laura's ratification does not relieve Kathy from civil liability to Laura; nor does it in any way affect Kathy's criminal liability for the forgery.

A party is precluded from denying the validity of his signature if his **negligence** substantially contributes to the making of the unauthorized signature. The most obvious case is that of a drawer who uses a mechanized or other automatic signing device and is negligent in safeguarding it. In such an instance, the drawer would not be permitted to assert an unauthorized signature as a defense against a holder in due course. Section 3–406(c). Under Revised Article 3, if the person seeking to enforce the instrument is also negligent, then comparative negligence applies. Section 3–406(b).

A person may also be precluded from asserting a defense by estoppel if his conduct in the matter has caused reliance by a third party to his loss or damage.

**Fraudulent Alteration** An alteration is (1) an unauthorized change that modifies the obligation of any party to the instrument or (2) an unauthorized addition or change to an incomplete instrument concerning the obligation of a party.

An alteration that is fraudulently made discharges a party whose obligation is affected by the alteration except where that party assents or is precluded by his own negligence from raising the defense. Section 3–407(b). All other alterations do not discharge any party, and the instrument may be enforced according to its original terms. Section 3–407(b). Thus, if an instrument has been nonfraudulently altered, it may be enforced, but only to the extent of its original tenor (i.e., according to its initially written terms).

A discharge under Section 3–407(b) for fraudulent alteration, however, is not effective against a holder in due course who took the instrument without notice of the alteration. Such a subsequent holder in due course may always enforce the instrument according to its original terms and, in the case of an incomplete instrument, may enforce it as completed. Section 3–407(c). (Under this section of the Code a person taking the instrument for value, in good faith, and without notice of the alteration is accorded the same protection as a holder in due course.) The following examples demonstrate the operation of these rules (*Figure 28-5* illustrates these examples).

1. M executes and delivers a note to P for $2,000, which P subsequently indorses and transfers to A for $1,900. A intentionally and skillfully changes the figure on the note to $20,000 and then negotiates it to B, who takes it, in good faith, without notice of any wrongdoing and without reason to question its authenticity, for $19,000. B is a holder in due course and, therefore, can collect the original amount of the note ($2,000) from M or P and the full amount ($20,000) from A, less any amount paid by the other parties.
2. Assume the facts in (1) except that B is not a holder in due course. M and P are both discharged by A's fraudulent alteration. B's only recourse is against A for the full amount ($20,000).
3. M issues his blank check to P, who is to complete it when the exact amount is determined. Though the correct amount is set at $2,000, P fraudulently fills in $4,000 and then negotiates the check to T. If T is a holder in due course, she can collect the amount as completed ($4,000) from either M or P. If T is not a holder in due course, however, she has no recourse against M but may recover the full amount ($4,000) from P.
4. Assume the facts in (3) except that P filled in the $4,000 amount in good faith. No party is discharged from liability on the instrument because the alteration was not

◆ FIGURE 28-4: **Effects of Alterations**

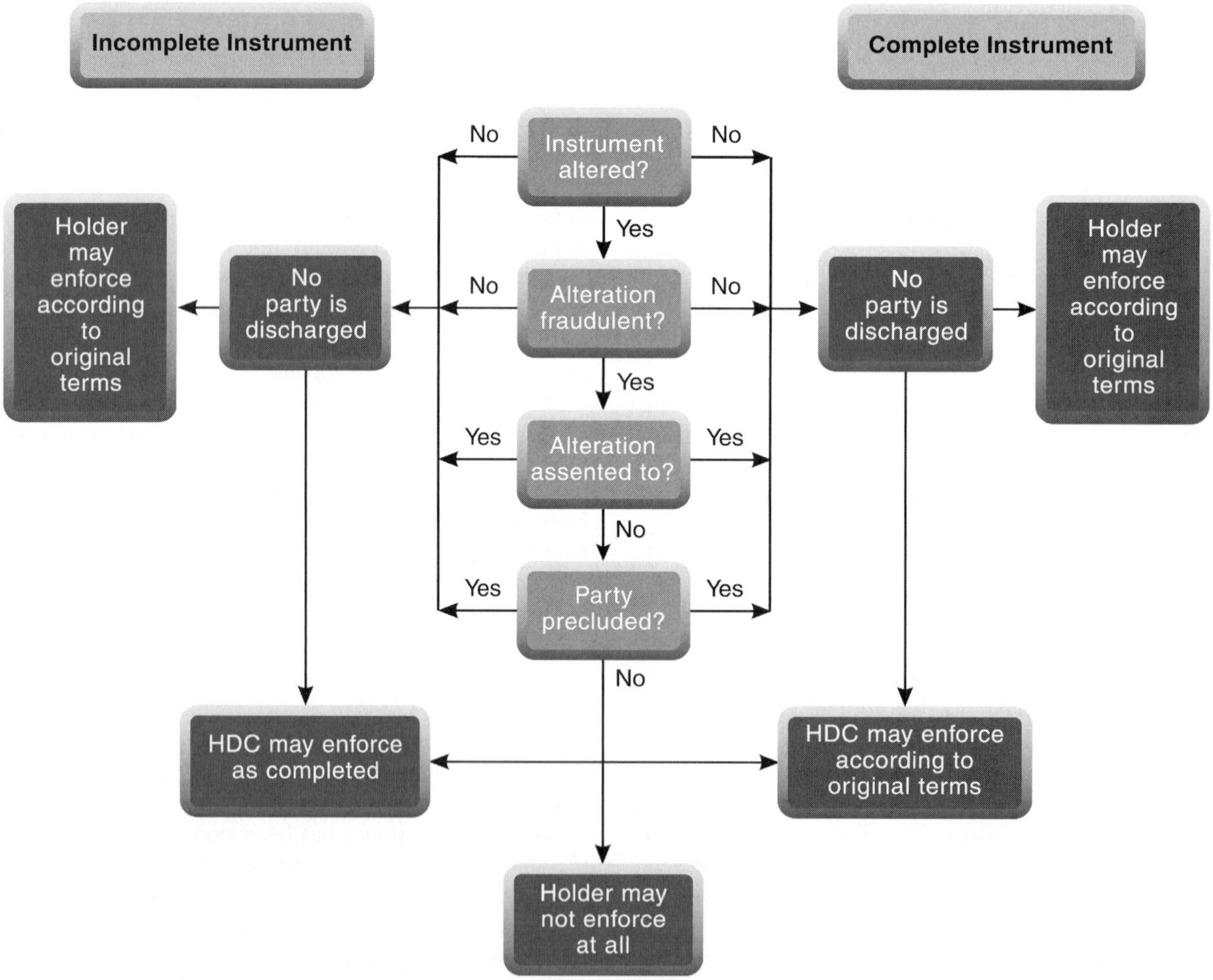

◆ **FIGURE 28-5: Material Alteration**

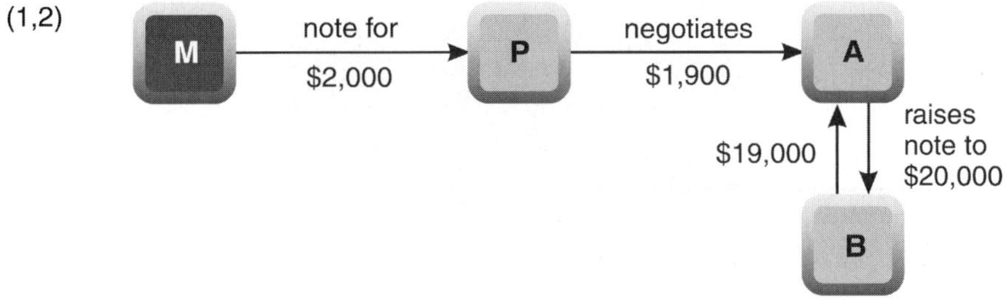


Illustration 1 / Illustration 2

| versus | M | P | A |
|---|---|---|---|
| B = HDC | $2,000 | $2,000 | $20,000 |
| B = H | 0 | 0 | $20,000 |

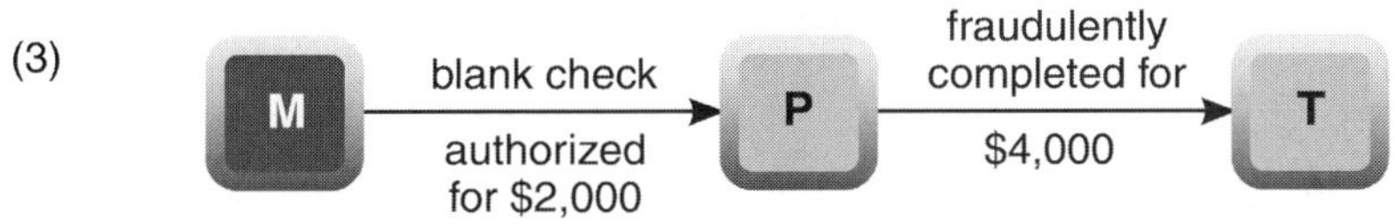


Illustration 3

| versus | M | P |
|---|---|---|
| T = HDC | $4,000 | $4,000 |
| T = H | 0 | $4,000 |

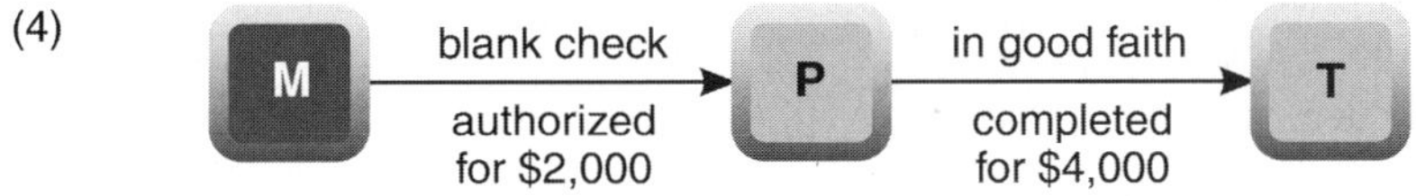


Illustration 4

| versus | M | P |
|---|---|---|
| T = HDC | $4,000 | $4,000 |
| T = H | $2,000 | $4,000 |

fraudulent. If T is not a holder in due course, M is liable for the correct amount ($2,000). If T is a holder in due course, T is entitled to receive $4,000 from M because she can enforce an incomplete instrument as completed. Whether or not T is a holder in due course, T may recover $4,000 from P.

◆ **SEE FIGURE 28-4: Effects of Alterations**

◆ **SEE FIGURE 28-5: Material Alteration**

## PERSONAL DEFENSES

Defenses to an instrument may arise in many ways, either when the instrument is issued or later. In general, the numerous defenses to liability on a negotiable instrument, which are similar to those that may be raised in an action for breach of contract, are available against any holder of the instrument unless he has the rights of a holder in due course. Among the personal defenses are (1) lack of consideration; (2) failure of consideration; (3) breach of contract; (4) fraud

◆ **FIGURE 28-6: Availability of Defenses against Holders in Due Course**

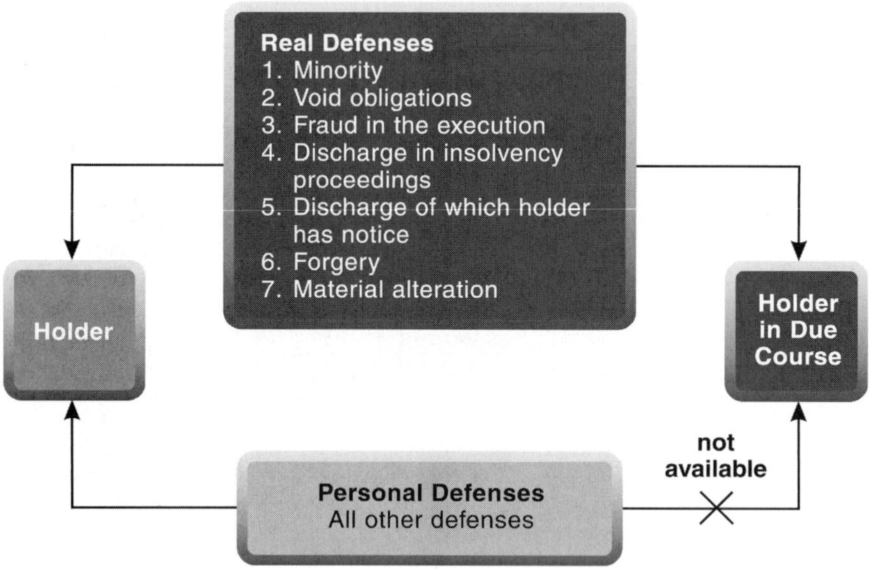


in the inducement; (5) illegality that does not render the transaction void; (6) duress, undue influence, mistake, misrepresentation, or incapacity that does not render the transaction void; (7) setoff or counterclaim; (8) discharge of which the holder in due course does not have notice; (9) nondelivery of an instrument, whether complete or incomplete; (10) unauthorized completion of an incomplete instrument; (11) payment without obtaining surrender of the instrument; (12) theft of a bearer instrument or of an instrument payable to the thief; and (13) lack of authority of a corporate officer, agent, or partner as to the particular instrument, where such officer, agent, or partner had general authority to issue negotiable paper for his principal or firm.

These situations are the most common examples, but others exist. Indeed, the Code does not attempt to detail defenses that may be cut off. It simply states that a holder in due course takes the instrument free and clear of all claims and defenses, except those listed as real defenses.

◆ **SEE FIGURE 28-6: Availability of Defenses against Holders in Due Course**

## LIMITATIONS UPON HOLDER IN DUE COURSE RIGHTS

The preferential position enjoyed by a holder in due course has been severely limited by a Federal Trade Commission (FTC) rule restricting the rights of a holder in due course of an instrument concerning a debt arising out of a consumer credit contract, which includes negotiable instruments. The rule, entitled "Preservation of Consumers' Claims and Defenses," applies to sellers and lessors of consumer goods, which are goods for personal, household, or family use. It also applies to lenders who advance money to finance a consumer's purchase of consumer goods or services. The rule is intended to prevent consumer purchase transactions from being financed in such a manner that the purchaser is legally obligated to make full payment of the price to a third party, even though the dealer from whom she bought the goods committed fraud or the goods were defective. Such obligations arise when a purchaser executes and delivers to a seller a negotiable instrument that the seller negotiates to a holder in due course. The buyer's defense that the goods were defective or that the seller committed fraud, although valid against the seller, is not valid against the holder in due course.

To correct this situation, the FTC rule preserves claims and defenses of consumer buyers and borrowers against holders in due course. The rule states that no seller or creditor can take or receive a consumer credit contract unless the contract contains this conspicuous provision:

> NOTICE: ANY HOLDER OF THIS CONSUMER CREDIT CONTRACT IS SUBJECT TO ALL CLAIMS AND DEFENSES WHICH THE DEBTOR COULD ASSERT AGAINST THE SELLER OF THE GOODS OR SERVICES OBTAINED PURSUANT HERETO OR WITH THE PROCEEDS HEREOF. RECOVERY HEREUNDER BY THE DEBTOR SHALL NOT EXCEED AMOUNTS PAID BY THE DEBTOR HEREUNDER.

◆ FIGURE 28-7: **Rights of Holder in Due Course under FTC Rule**

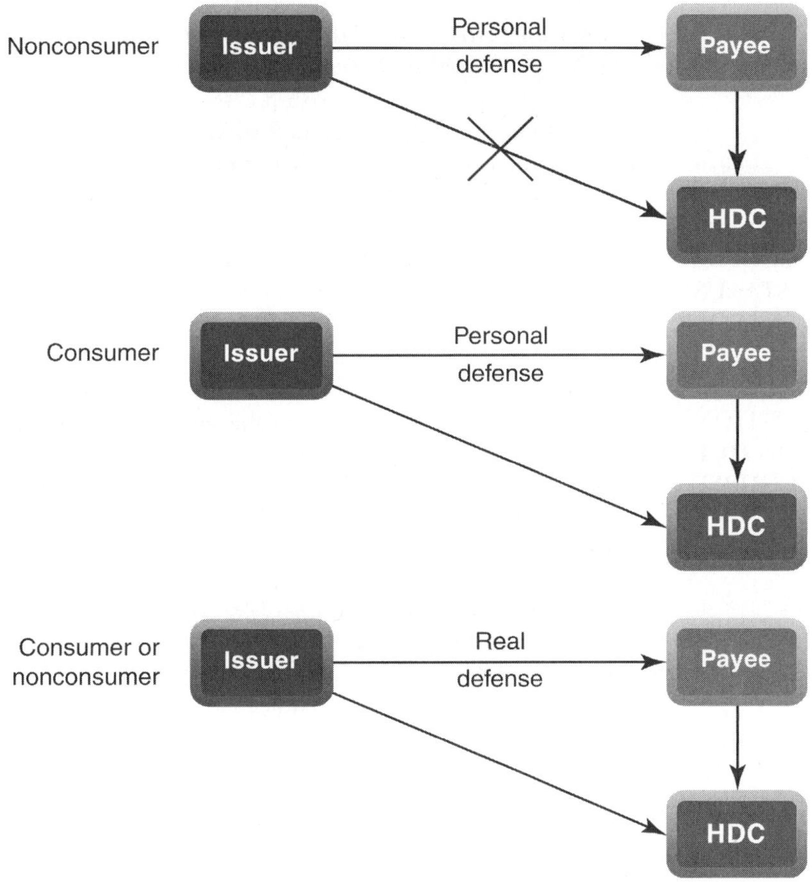


The purpose of this notice is to inform any holder in due course of a paper or negotiable instrument that he takes the instrument subject to all claims and defenses that the buyer could assert against the seller. The effect of the rule is to place the holder in due course in the position of an assignee.

◆ SEE FIGURE 28-7: **Rights of Holder in Due Course under FTC Rule**

## CHAPTER SUMMARY

**REQUIREMENTS OF A HOLDER IN DUE COURSE**

**Holder** a person who has both possession of an instrument and all indorsements necessary to it

**Value** differs from contractual consideration and consists of any of the following:

- the timely performance of legal consideration (which excludes executory promises);
- the acquisition of a security interest in or a lien on the instrument;
- taking the instrument in payment of or as security for an antecedent debt;
- the giving of a negotiable instrument; or
- the giving of an irrevocable commitment to a third party

**Good Faith** honesty in fact and the observance of reasonable commercial standards of fair dealing

**Lack of Notice**

- ***Notice an Instrument Is Overdue*** time paper is overdue after its stated date; demand paper is overdue after demand has been made or after it has been outstanding for an unreasonable period of time

- ***Notice an Instrument Has Been Dishonored*** dishonor is the refusal to pay or accept an instrument when it becomes due
- ***Notice an Instrument Has Been Forged or Altered***
- ***Notice of a Claim or Defense*** a defense protects a person from liability, while a claim is an assertion of ownership

**Without Reason to Question Its Authenticity** instrument cannot bear such apparent evidence of forgery or alteration or otherwise be so irregular or incomplete as to call into question its authenticity

**HOLDER IN DUE COURSE STATUS**

**A Payee May Be a Holder in Due Course** the payee's rights as a holder in due course are limited to defenses of persons with whom he has not dealt

**The Shelter Rule** the transferee of an instrument acquires the same rights that the transferor had in the instrument

**THE PREFERRED POSITION OF A HOLDER IN DUE COURSE**

**Real Defenses** real defenses are available against all holders, including holders in due course; such defenses are as follows:

- ***Infancy***
- ***Void Obligations***
- ***Fraud in the Execution***
- ***Discharge in Insolvency Proceedings***
- ***Discharge of Which the Holder Has Notice***
- ***Unauthorized Signature***
- ***Fraudulent Alteration***

**Personal Defenses** all other defenses that might be asserted in the case of any action for breach of contract

**Limitations upon Holder in Due Course Rights** the preferential position of a holder in due course has been severely limited by a Federal Trade Commission rule that applies to consumer credit contracts: under this rule, a transferee of consumer credit contracts cannot take as a holder in due course

## CASES

CASE 28-1

### Holder in Due Course/Holder
### GEORG v. METRO FIXTURES CONTRACTORS, INC.

Supreme Court of Colorado, En Banc, 2008
178 P.3d 1209, 66 UCC Rep.Serv.2d 477
http://scholar.google.com/scholar_case?case=17407795886687310331&q=GEORG+v.+METRO+FIXTURES+CONTRACTORS,+INC.&hl=en&as_sdt=40000000002&as_vis=1

**Hobbs, J.**

We granted certiorari in this case to address an issue of first impression in Colorado regarding whether under [UCC] § 1-201(b)(20) and [UCC] § 3-302, C.R.S. (2007), Colorado's codification of the Uniform Commercial Code ("UCC"), a person can be a holder of a negotiable instrument entitled to holder in due course status under a theory of constructive possession of a negotiable instrument. The court of appeals partially reversed the trial court's grant of summary judgment in favor of Freestyle Sports Marketing, Inc. ("Freestyle"), ruling that Freestyle was not a holder in due course because it was not a holder who had actual possession of the negotiable instrument at issue in this action.

* * *

Freestyle employed Cassandra Demery as a bookkeeper for several years before it discovered that Demery had embezzled over $200,000 for personal use and had failed to pay, on Freestyle's behalf, approximately $240,000 in state and federal employment taxes. Freestyle terminated Demery's employment, demanded that she repay Freestyle, and threatened to notify the authorities if she did not.

After leaving Freestyle, Demery went to work as a bookkeeper at Metro Fixtures Contractors, Inc. ("Metro"), a company owned by her parents. Demery's bookkeeping position at Metro included balancing the accounting books, invoicing customers, and paying outstanding bills on behalf of the company. In her position as bookkeeper, Demery wrote a check from Metro's bank account and made it payable to Freestyle in the amount of $189,000. Demery wrote "for deposit only" on the back of the check as well as Freestyle's account number, filled out a deposit form, and deposited the check in Freestyle's bank account.

Demery then informed Clinton Georg, Freestyle's president, by phone, that she had obtained a loan from her family to repay Freestyle and had deposited the funds into Freestyle's account. After Demery's phone call, Georg called his bank and confirmed the deposit of the funds into Freestyle's account. Georg subsequently used the deposited funds for payment of Freestyle's delinquent employment taxes.

After two years, Metro uncovered the transaction instigated by Demery and filed suit against Georg and Freestyle * * *. Metro alleged that it had not given Demery a loan or permission to write and deposit a check in the amount of $189,000 into Freestyle's bank account.

Freestyle moved for summary judgment, contending that it qualified as a holder in due course under [UCC] § 3-302 and [UCC] § 3-306. The trial court agreed that Freestyle was a holder in due course and granted the motion.

Metro appealed and the court of appeals partially reversed. The court of appeals held that Freestyle could not have been a holder in due course because it was not a holder with actual possession of the check. Freestyle then appealed to us arguing that it had constructive possession of the instrument when the check was deposited at its bank.

We hold, under the facts of this case, that Freestyle had constructive possession of the check and qualified as a holder in due course under [UCC] § 3-302 and [UCC] § 3-306 of Colorado's UCC.

* * *

If Freestyle is a holder in due course under [UCC] § 3-306, it takes free of Metro's claims. [Citations.]

* * *

## Holder in Due Course

* * *

A check is a negotiable instrument. [UCC] § 3-104. The holder in due course doctrine is designed to encourage the transfer and usage of checks and facilitate the flow of capital. [Citation.] An entity may qualify as a holder in due course even if the instrument at issue may have passed through the hands of a thief. [Citation.] ("The holder in due course is one of the few purchasers in Anglo-Saxon jurisprudence who may derive a good title from a chain of title that includes a thief in its links.")

A holder in due course must meet five conditions: (1) be a holder; (2) of a negotiable instrument who took it; (3) for value; (4) in good faith; (5) without notice of certain problems with the instrument. [Citation.]

To be a holder one must meet the two conditions in [UCC] § 1-201(b)(20): (1) he or she must have possession (2) of an instrument drawn, issued, or indorsed to him or her. [Citation.] Possession is an element designed to prevent two or more claimants from qualifying as holders who could take free of the other party's claim of ownership. [Citation.] With rare exceptions, those claiming to be holders have physical ownership of the instrument in question. [Citation.]

An otherwise authorized signature on a negotiable instrument is not converted into an unauthorized forgery when an agent, authorized to sign negotiable instruments in his principal's name, abuses that authority by negotiating the instrument to a holder in due course for the agent's own personal benefit. [Citations.] [UCC] § 3-402.

## Constructive Possession

Section 4-201(a), states that a collecting bank "is an agent or sub-agent of the owner of the item." Further, the statute states, "This provision applies regardless of the form of indorsement or lack of indorsement…." [Citation.] A check payable to a party and deposited in that party's account makes the party the "owner" of the check under the UCC. [Citation.] Further, the White & Summers treatise on the UCC speaks to a collecting bank as an agent for the owner's possession:

> Sometimes the one claiming to be a holder in due course will not have possession of the instrument at the time of the suit. When a collecting bank holds the check, the solution is simple, for section 4-201 makes that bank the agent of the owner of the check. *Under traditional analysis, the agent's possession would be the owner's possession and thus the owner would have "possession."*

(emphasis [in case]).

Thus, there are circumstances wherein requiring actual physical possession of the instrument would be problematic and constructive possession applies. [Citation.] Nevertheless, a determination of constructive possession should occur only when delivery is clearly for an identifiable person under circumstances excluding any other party as a holder in due course. [Citation.]

Other jurisdictions have recognized constructive possession as qualifying under the UCC for holder in due course purposes. [Citations.] * * *

Many states have not had the opportunity to address the issue of constructive possession under the UCC. * * *, decisions in six other jurisdictions, in addition to New York and Oregon, have recognized the sufficiency of constructive possession in relation to being a holder in due course. [Citations.] * * *

***Application to This Case***

In the case before us, Demery was Metro's agent, specifically its employee. As a bookkeeper for Metro, Demery's authority included the power to write checks on Metro's behalf. Despite the fact that Metro did not specifically authorize Demery to write a check to Freestyle, Metro placed her in a position to do so. Subsequently, Demery informed Freestyle that she had obtained authority from Metro's owners, her parents, to issue the check and had directly deposited the funds into Freestyle's account. Freestyle verified with its bank the deposit of these funds into its account and then, relying on the availability of those funds, paid the delinquent taxes to the state and federal authorities.

The court of appeals held that Freestyle could not be a holder in due course because it lacked possession of the check. However, this is too narrow a reading of section 3-302, which includes circumstances where the instrument does not bear apparent evidence of forgery and the person to whom the instrument is drawn took the instrument for value, in good faith, and without notice that it contained an unauthorized signature. * * *

The trial court found that Freestyle was a holder in due course based on the undisputed facts of this case. Demery delivered the check by depositing it into Freestyle's bank account. Section 1-201(b)(14), defines delivery with respect to an instrument as a voluntary transfer of possession. Two elements are required for delivery of an instrument: (1) intent of the transferor to transfer possession of an instrument, and (2) the actual transfer of the instrument. [Citation.]

However, Metro counters that the bank was not Freestyle's agent with respect to the collection of a "stolen instrument" because under the UCC, a collecting bank is only the agent for an owner of an instrument and, according to Metro, Freestyle did not own the check. But Metro's argument is contrary to prior Colorado law defining the term "owner" in relation to negotiable instruments such as checks. An otherwise authorized signature on a negotiable instrument is not converted into an unauthorized forgery when an agent, authorized to sign negotiable instruments in his principal's name, abuses that authority by negotiating the instrument to a holder in due course for the agent's own personal benefit. [Citation.] A check payable to a party and deposited in that party's account makes it the "owner" of the check under the UCC. [Citation.]

While Metro claims Freestyle was not a holder, it does not simultaneously argue that it was a competing holder. There is no other possible holder under the facts of this case. Metro's agent made out the check to Freestyle, wrote the deposit receipt to Freestyle, and delivered the check by depositing it into Freestyle's bank account. Thus, Freestyle had constructive possession of this instrument and qualifies as a holder under section 1-201(b)(20).

Freestyle was not only a holder under the facts of this case, it was a holder in due course. * * *

Freestyle argues that under section 3-303(a)(3), the instrument was issued as payment for Demery's outstanding debt to Freestyle. Metro does not contest that Demery embezzled funds from Freestyle and therefore owed Freestyle funds; rather, it asserts that it did not authorize Demery to issue the check. A pre-existing debt is sufficient consideration. [Citation.] Thus, Freestyle took the check for value.

Freestyle acted in good faith. Bad faith for the holder in due course standard means guilty knowledge or willful ignorance. [Citation.] Here, Freestyle lacked guilty knowledge or willful ignorance. The record contains no facts asserted by Metro that, if proven, would support a bad faith claim. * * *

Finally, Freestyle had no notice that Demery lacked authority to issue the check or that it was forged. The undisputed facts are that Demery was Metro's bookkeeper and had authority to issue the check. Metro simply insinuates that, because its employee stole from Freestyle, Freestyle should have been on notice that she was also stealing from Metro. However, Metro was in the best position to protect itself against Demery's action. * * *

Application of Colorado's UCC can result in loss to an innocent party in favor of a holder in due course. [Citation.] However, an important policy objective of the statute is to protect the party least able to protect himself or herself. [Citation.] "[W]here one of two innocent parties must suffer because of the wrongdoing of a third person, the loss must fall on the party who has by his conduct created the circumstances which enabled the third party to perpetuate the wrong." [Citation.]

Reasons to place the risk on the principal of an agent in commercial transactions include: (1) the increased incentive for a principal to exercise care in selecting agents; (2) the fact that the principal is in a better position to supervise the actions of the agent; and (3) the fact that the principal bears the fruit of a principal/agent relationship. [Citation.]

Applied to this case, Demery acted as a bookkeeper for Metro for several years. Metro was in the best position to have instituted internal procedures and mechanisms regarding the company's accounting. Attesting to its lack of internal procedure, Metro did not uncover the embezzlement until two years after Demery deposited the check into Freestyle's bank account. Freestyle was not in a position, as a third party, to dictate Metro's internal control procedures to prevent employee theft.

Colorado's UCC intends to promote reliability on issued instruments, not to undermine their efficacy by placing the burden on the person to whom it is issued to determine a check's validity. Metro's recourse is not against Freestyle, but rather against its agent employee for breaching her fiduciary duty to the company. [Citation.]

Having reviewed the holder in due course elements in light of the undisputed facts of the case, we determine that Freestyle was a holder with constructive possession of a negotiable instrument, which was given for value and taken in good faith without notice of a forgery or an unauthorized signature.

Accordingly, we reverse the judgment of the court of appeals and remand with directions that the court of appeals return this case to the district court for entry of judgment in favor of Freestyle.

## CASE 28-2

### Good Faith
### ANY KIND CHECKS CASHED, INC. v. TALCOTT

Court of Appeal of Florida, Fourth District, 2002
830 So.2d 160, 48 U.C.C. Rep.Serv.2d 800, rehearing denied
http://www.4dca.org/Oct2002/10-09-02/4D01-2114.pdf

**Gross, J.**

The issue in this case is whether a check cashing store qualifies as a holder in due course so that it can collect on a $10,000 check written by an elderly man who was fraudulently induced to issue the check by the person who cashed it.

We hold that the check cashing store was not a holder in due course, because the procedures it followed with the $10,000 check did not comport with reasonable commercial standards of fair dealing.

The case is the story of John G. Talcott, Jr., a ninety-three-year-old Massachusetts resident, D.J. Rivera, a "financial advisor" to Talcott, and Salvatore Guarino, a cohort of Rivera.

In the mid-1990's, Rivera sold Talcott an investment for "somewhere in the amount of $75,000." The investment produced no returns.

On December 7, 1999, Guarino established check cashing privileges at Any Kind Checks Cashed, Inc. ("Any Kind") by filling out a customer card. The card included his social security number and identification by driver's license. On the card, Guarino listed himself as a broker. That day, he cashed a $450 check without incident.

On January 10, 2000, Rivera telephoned Talcott and talked him into sending him a check for $10,000 made out to Guarino, which was to be used for travel expenses to obtain a return on the original $75,000 investment. Talcott understood that Guarino was Rivera's partner. Rivera received the check on January 11.

Talcott spoke to Rivera on the morning of January 11. Rivera indicated that $10,000 was more than what was needed for travel. He said that $5,700 would meet the travel costs. Talcott called his bank and stopped payment on the $10,000 check.

In spite of what Rivera told Talcott, Guarino appeared at Any Kind's Stuart, Florida office on January 11 and presented the $10,000 check to Nancy Michael. She was a supervisor with the company with the authority to approve checks over $2,000. Guarino showed Michael his driver's license and the Federal Express envelope from Talcott in which he received the check. She asked him the purpose of the check. Consistent with the information on the customer card, he told her that he was a broker and that the maker of the check had sent it as an investment. She was unable to contact the maker of the check by telephone. Based on her experience, Michael believed the check was good; the Federal Express envelope was "very crucial" to her decision, because it indicated that the maker of the check had sent it to the payee trying to cash the check. After deducting the 5% check cashing fee, Michael cashed the check and gave Guarino $9,500. The next day she deposited the check in the company's bank.

On January 15, 2000, Rivera called Talcott and asked about the $5,700, again promising to send him a return on his investment. The same day, Talcott sent a check for $5,700. He assumed that Rivera knew that he had stopped payment on the $10,000 check.

On January 17, 2000, Guarino went into the Stuart Any Kind store and presented the $5,700 check to the teller, Joanne Kochakian. He showed her the Federal Express envelope in which the check had come. Company policy required a supervisor to approve a check over $2,000. Kochakian noticed that Michael had previously approved the $10,000 check. She called Michael, who was working at another location, and told her about Guarino's check.

Any Kind had no written procedures that a supervisor was required to follow in deciding which checks over $2,000 to cash. Michael had the discretionary "decision-making power as a supervisor to decide whether or not the check [was] any good." She relied on "instinct and judgment" in deciding what inquiry to make before cashing a check. In the brief non-jury trial, there was no evidence concerning the general practice of the check cashing industry.

Michael instructed the cashier not to cash the check until she contacted the maker, Talcott, to obtain approval. On her first attempt, Kochakian received no answer, * * *.

On the second call, * * * Talcott approved cashing the $5,700 check. There was no discussion of the $10,000 check. Any Kind cashed the second check for Guarino, from which it deducted a 3% fee.

On January 19, Rivera called Talcott to warn him that Guarino was a cheat and a thief. Talcott immediately called his bank and stopped payment on the $5,700 check. Talcott's daughter called Any Kind and told it of the stop payment on the $5,700 check. There was no dispute at trial that Guarino and Rivera had pulled a scam on Talcott to get him to issue the checks.

Any Kind filed a two-count complaint against Guarino and Talcott, claiming that it was a holder in due course. Talcott's defense was that Any Kind was not a holder in due course and that his obligation on the checks was nullified because of Guarino's illegal acts.

The trial court entered final judgment in favor of Any Kind for only the $5,700 check. On the $10,000 check, the judge found for Talcott. The court found that the circumstances surrounding the cashing of the $10,000 check were sufficient to put [Any Kind] on notice of potential defenses and/or infirmities. The best evidence of this is that the plaintiff attempted to contact the maker but was unable to do so on the first check, and did so on the second. The circumstances of a person describing himself as a broker, receiving funds in the amount of $10,000 and negotiating the check for those funds at a $500 discount are sufficient to put [Any Kind] on inquiry notice that some confirmation or explanation should be obtained.

Using the terminology of the Uniform Commercial Code, Talcott was the maker or "drawer" of the check, the person who signed the draft "as a person ordering payment." [UCC §3–103(3)(a)] By Federal Expressing the check to Guarino, Talcott issued the check to him. See [UCC §3–105(a)] (defining "issue" as "the first delivery of an instrument by the maker or drawer * * * for the purpose of giving rights on the instrument to any person"). Guarino indorsed the check and cashed it with Any Kind. See [UCC §3–204 (a)] (defining "indorsement"). Any Kind immediately made the funds available to Guarino, less its fee. Talcott stopped payment on the check with his bank, so the check was returned to Any Kind. See [UCC §4–403(a)] (regarding a customer's right to stop payment).

When Guarino negotiated the check with Any Kind, it became a holder of the check, making it a "person entitled to enforce" the instrument. See [UCC §§3–201(a), –203(b), –301(a)]. As the drawer of the check dishonored by his bank, Talcott's obligation was to pay the draft to a person entitled to enforce the draft "according to its terms at the time it was issued. * * *" [UCC §3–414(a)].

Unless Any Kind is a holder in due course, its right to enforce Talcott's obligation to pay the draft is subject to (1) all defenses Talcott could raise "if the person entitled to enforce the instrument were enforcing a right to payment under a simple contract," and (2) a claim of "recoupment" Talcott could raise against Guarino. [UCC §3–305(a) & (b)]. Because Talcott was fraudulently induced to issue the checks, this case turns on Any Kind's entitlement to holder in due course status.

A "holder in due course" is a holder who takes an instrument without "apparent evidence of forgery or alteration" for value, in good faith, and without notice of certain claims and defenses. See [UCC §3–302(a)]. As the party claiming that it was a holder in due course, Any Kind had the burden to prove that status by a preponderance of the evidence. [Citations.]

The question for this court is whether the trial court erred in finding that Any Kind was not a holder in due course of the $10,000 check based on the findings of fact made at trial, keeping in mind that Any Kind bore the burden of proof. That question turns on whether Any Kind acted "in good faith" within the meaning of [UCC §3–302(a)(2)(ii)].

The good faith requirement of the holder in due course doctrine "has been the source of an ancient and continuing dispute." [Citation]. On the one hand, should the courts apply a so-called objective test, and ask whether a reasonably prudent person, behaving the way the alleged holder in due course behaved, would have been acting in good faith? Or should the courts instead apply a subjective test and examine the person's actual behavior, however stupid and irrespective of the reaction a reasonably prudent person would have had in the same circumstance? The legal establishment has steered a crooked course through this debate. [Citations.]

Prior to 1992, [UCC §1–201 (19)], defined "good faith" as "honesty in fact in the conduct of the transaction concerned." Florida courts interpreted this definition as creating a subjective test. [Citation.] * * * In another case, Judge Schwartz wrote that the "Florida version of the holder in due course provision of the UCC does seem to protect the objectively stupid so long as he is subjectively pure of heart." [Citation.]

Application of [old UCC's] "honesty in fact" standard to Any Kind's conduct in this case would clothe it with holder in due course status. It is undisputed that Any Kind's employees were pure of heart, that they acted without knowledge of Guarino's wrongdoing.

However, in 1992, the legislature adopted a new definition of "good faith" that applies to the [UCC §3–302] definition of a holder in due course: "'good faith' means honesty in fact and the observance of reasonable commercial standards of fair dealing." [Citation.] To the old, subjective good faith, "honesty in fact" standard, the legislature added an objective component—the "pure heart of the holder must now be accompanied by reasoning that assures conduct comporting with reasonable commercial standards of fair dealing." [Citation.] No longer may a holder of an instrument act with "a pure heart and an empty head and still obtain holder in due course status." [Citation.]

Comment 4 to section 3–103, Florida Statutes Annotated, attempts to shed light on how to interpret the new standard:

> Although fair dealing is a broad term that must be defined in context, it is clear that it is concerned with the fairness of conduct rather than the care with which an act is performed. Failure to exercise ordinary care in conducting a transaction is an entirely different concept than failure to deal fairly in conducting the transaction.

The Code does not define the term "fair dealing." * * *

> Application of holder in due course status is the law's value judgment that certain holders are worthy of protection from certain types of claims. For example, it has been argued that application of the old subjective standard facilitated the transfer of checks in the stream of commerce; arguably one would be "more willing to accept the checks if * * * she knows * * * she can be a holder in due course of that instrument and take it free of defenses that might have existed between the buyer and the seller in the underlying transaction." [Citation.] In applying the new standard, "fairness" should be measured by taking a global view of the underlying transaction and all of its participants. A holder "must act in a way that is fair according to commercial standards that are themselves reasonable." [Citation.]

To apply the law requiring "good faith" under section 3–302(a), we adopt the analysis set forth by the Supreme Court of Maine:

> The fact finder must * * * determine, first, whether the conduct of the holder comported with industry or "commercial" standards applicable to the transaction and, second, whether those standards were reasonable standards intended to result in fair dealing. Each of those determinations must be made in the context of the specific transaction at hand. If the fact finder's conclusion on each point is "yes," the holder will be determined to have acted in good faith even if, in the individual transaction at issue, the result appears unreasonable. Thus a holder may be accorded holder in due course status where it acts pursuant to those reasonable commercial standards of fair dealing—even if it is negligent—but may lose that status, even where it complies with commercial standards, if those standards are not reasonably related to achieving fair dealing.

[Citation.]

There was no evidence at trial concerning the check cashing industry's commercial standards. Even assuming that Any Kind's procedures for checks over $2,000 met the industry's gold standard, we hold that in this case the procedures followed were not reasonably related to achieve fair dealing with respect to the $10,000 check, taking into consideration all of the participants in the transaction, Talcott, Guarino, and Any Kind.

* * *

Check cashing businesses occupy a special niche in the financial industry. They are part of the "alternative financial services" or "fringe banking" sector, a part of the market that "has become a major source of traditional banking services for low-income and working poor consumers, residents of minority neighborhoods, and people with blemished credit histories." [Citations.]

Check cashing stores are often in locations where traditional banks fear to tread. * * *

In such areas, the typical check presented for cashing is not a large one—a paycheck, child support, social security, or public assistance check. [The Florida check cashing statute] contemplates that such checks will be presented at check cashing outlets; it limits the fee charged for the payment of "any kind of state public assistance or federal social security benefits payable to the bearer."

Attractions of check cashing outlets are convenience and speed. * * * Unlike banks, check cashing stores cannot place a hold on a check before releasing funds. The Florida * * * Code requires payment to be made "immediately in currency for every payment instrument received by a person engaging in the activities of a check casher." [Citation.] The statute and administrative rules also contemplate that a check cashing business will engage in various types of "verification" of a check. [Citation.]

Against this backdrop, we cannot say that the trial court erred in finding that the $10,000 check was a red flag. The $10,000 personal check was not the typical check cashed at a check cashing outlet. The size of the check, in the context of the check cashing business, was a proper factor to consider under the objective standard of good faith in deciding whether Any Kind was a holder in due course. [Citation.]

Guarino was not the typical customer of a check cashing outlet. As the trial judge observed, because of the 5% fee charged, it is unusual for a small businessman such as a broker to conduct business through a check cashing store instead of through a traditional bank. Guarino did not have a history with Any Kind of cashing checks of similar size without incident. The need for speed in a business transaction is usually less acute than for someone cashing a paycheck or welfare check to pay for life's necessities. The need for speed in cashing a large business check is consistent with a drawer who, for whatever reason, might stop payment. Fair dealing in this case required that the $10,000 check be approached with a degree of caution.

If a drawer has a right to stop payment of a check, and a traditional bank usually places a hold on uncollected funds after a payee deposits a check into an account, then the legal dispute after a stop payment will usually be between the drawer of the check and the payee, the two parties that had the dealings leading to the payment. Thus, where a check is cashed at a bank or savings and loan, the law will often place the loss on the wrongdoer in the underlying transaction. This is a desirable goal.

Where a check cashing store releases funds immediately, the holder in due course doctrine steps in, frequently putting the loss on a wronged maker, in furtherance of the policy that facilitating the transfer of checks benefits the economy. In this case, the policy reasons behind easy negotiability do not outweigh the reasons for caution. Very loose application of the objective component of "good faith" would make check cashing outlets the easy refuge of scam artists who want to take the money and run. The concept of "fair dealing" includes not being an easy, safe harbor for the dishonest.

To affirm the trial court is not to wreak havoc with the check cashing industry. Verification with the maker of a check will *not* be necessary to preserve holder in due course status in the vast majority of cases arising from check cashing outlets. This was neither the typical customer, nor the typical transaction of a check cashing outlet.

* * *

The legislature's addition of an objective standard of conduct may well have the effect of "slowing the 'wheels of commerce'" in some transactions. [Citation.] However, by adopting changes to the "good faith" standard in the holder in due course doctrine, the legislature "necessarily must have concluded that the addition of the objective requirement to the definition of 'good faith' serves an important goal. The paramount necessity of unquestioned negotiability has given way, at least in part to the desire for reasonable commercial fairness in negotiable transactions." [Citation.] In this case, reasonable commercial fairness required Any Kind to approach the $10,000 check with some caution and to verify it with the maker if it wanted to preserve its holder in due course status.

AFFIRMED.

CASE 28-3

## The Shelter Rule

## TRIFFIN v. CIGNA INSURANCE

Superior Court of New Jersey, Appellate Division, 1997

297 N.J.Super 199, 687 A.2d 1045, 31 UCC Rep.Serv.2d 1040

http://lawlibrary.rutgers.edu/decisions/appellate/a4000-95.opn.html

**Dreier, J.**

Plaintiff, Robert J. Triffin, appeals from a * * * summary judgment dismissing his complaint for payment of a draft of defendant Cigna Insurance Company transferred to plaintiff by a holder in due course after Cigna had stopped payment on the instrument.

* * * The defaulting defendant, James Mills, received a draft in the amount of $484.12, dated July 7, 1993 from one of Cigna's constituent companies, Atlantic Employers Insurance Company. The draft had been issued for workers' compensation benefits. Mills falsely indicated to the issuer that he had not received the draft due to a change in his address and requested that payment be stopped and a new draft issued by defendant. The insurer complied and stopped payment on the initial draft. Mills nevertheless negotiated the initial draft to plaintiff's assignor, Sun Corp. t/a Sun's Market, before the stop payment notation was placed on the draft. All appear to agree that Sun Corp. was a holder in due course. Sun Corp. presented the draft for payment through depositary and collecting banks. The issuer's bank dishonored the draft in accordance with its customer's direction, stamped it "Stop Payment," and returned the draft to Sun Corp. There is no question that had Sun Corp. at that point pressed its claim against the insurer as the issuer of the instrument, Sun Corp. would have been entitled to a judgment because of its status as a holder in due course.

Thereafter, plaintiff, who apparently is in the business of purchasing dishonored instruments, obtained an assignment of Sun Corp.'s interests in this instrument and proceeded with this law suit. Plaintiff does not contend that he is a holder in due course of the instrument by virtue of it being negotiated to him for value, in good faith, without notice of dishonor, under the former holder in due course statute, UCC §3–302, nor under the present statute, §3–302a(2).

Such negotiation is, of course, only one way for a holder to claim the status of a holder in due course. There exists a second method by which one may become a holder in due course. The shelter provisions of former UCC (§3–201), which was in effect when plaintiff obtained his assignment of this instrument, state clearly that "[t]ransfer of an instrument vests in the transferee such rights as the transferor has therein * * *." Official Comment 3 to that section sets to rest any question of whether this section applies to the transfer by assignment of the rights of a holder in due course. The Comment reads: "A holder in due course may transfer his rights as such * * *. [The former Negotiable Instruments Law section's] policy is to assure the holder in due course a free market for the paper, and that policy is continued in this section." Example (a) following this comment could have been drawn from this case, but is even stronger because it adds an element of fraud and posits a gratuitous transfer rather than a purchase, as in our case:

> (a) A [Mills] induces M [Cigna] by fraud to make an instrument payable to A. A negotiates it to B [Sun Corp.], who takes as a holder in due course. After the instrument is overdue B gives it to C [plaintiff], who has notice of the fraud. C succeeds to B's rights as a holder in due course, cutting off the defense.

If the 1995 amendments are to be given retroactive effect, the law governing the rights of a transferee who merely has accepted the transfer of the instrument is now found in Revised UCC [§3–203]. It restates the principle of the former Official Comment 3, example (a), as substantive law.

* * *

The Uniform Commercial Code Comment 2 to this [Revised] section similarly states:

> Under subsection (b) a holder in due course that transfers an instrument transfers those rights as a holder in due course to the purchaser. The policy is to assure the holder in due course a free market for the instrument.

* * *

Also, both the old and new sections have exceptions where the transferee participated in the fraud or where the instrument is then reconveyed to the party who originally committed the fraud. Neither exception applies to this case.

These sections could not be clearer. Plaintiff received by [negotiation] the right of a holder in due course to this instrument, which apparently had been presented and then dishonored because of defendant's stop payment order. * * *

The summary judgment appealed from is reversed, and the matter is remanded with directions to enter judgment in favor of plaintiff, with interest.

## CASE 28-4

## Void/Voidable Obligation
## FEDERAL DEPOSIT INSURANCE CORPORATION v. MEYER

United States District Court, District of Columbia, 1991
755 F.Supp. 10

**Pratt, J.**

### Background

The Federal Deposit Insurance Corporation ("FDIC") brings this action to collect on promissory notes signed by certain former partners of the law firm of Finley, Kumble, Wagner, Heine, Underberg, Manley, Myerson & Casey ("Finley Kumble"). The promissory notes secured loans that the National Bank of Washington ("NBW") made in 1986 to the Finley Partners to enable them to purchase stock in the Merchant Bank of California. After Finley Kumble declared bankruptcy, certain of the Finley Partners defaulted on their loans and NBW filed lawsuits in the Superior Court for the District of Columbia against defendants to collect on their promissory notes.

On August 10, 1990, the Office of the Comptroller of the Currency declared the NBW insolvent, closed the Bank, and appointed the Federal Deposit Insurance Corporation ("FDIC") as Receiver. The FDIC then removed these cases to federal court on September 7, 1990, and moved for summary judgment against each defendant on the grounds that the Federal Deposit Insurance Act of 1950, 12 U.S.C. §1823(e) [places the FDIC in the position of a holder in due course and thus] provides special protections for the FDIC which bar all of the Finley Partners' defenses as a matter of law.

Twenty of the Finley Partners now oppose the FDIC's motion. * * *

### Discussion

#### *Defendants' Defense of Economic Duress*

The Finley Partners argue that the FDIC's motion for summary judgment should be denied because their defense of economic duress survives the effects of §1823(e). They concede that §1823(e) operates to place the FDIC in the position of a holder in due course, making promissory notes free of personal defenses. They argue, however, that §1823(e) does not extinguish real defenses set forth in the Uniform Commercial Code ("UCC") and that their economic duress defense constitutes such a real defense.

Defendants are correct that §1823(e) bars personal defenses but not real defenses * * *. As the Supreme Court explained in *Langley v. FDIC*, a real defense renders an instrument entirely void, leaving no interest that could be "diminish[ed] or defeat[ed]." [Citations.] In contrast, personal defenses render a note voidable but not void. * * *

Thus, if the Finley Partners' economic duress defense constitutes a real defense, then their promissory notes were void from the beginning. Asserting such a real defense could not "diminish or defeat" any interest of the FDIC because the FDIC did not have any interest to start with. On the other hand, if the Finley Partners' economic duress defense is a personal defense, then the FDIC received voidable title to the promissory notes from the NBW, which [defense would be cut off by the FDIC]. * * *

The main legal question, then, is whether economic duress is a personal defense that rendered NBW's title to the promissory notes voidable, or a real defense that rendered its title entirely void. The Finley Partners suggest that duress of any nature constitutes a real defense, citing UCC §3–305 (2)(b) [Revised §3–305(a)(1)] and several cases from outside of the District of Columbia. A careful reading of the UCC and its Official Commentary reveals that it does not make such a blanket classification.

First, §3–305(2)(b) [Revised §3–305(a)(1)] provides that holders in due course take free of all defenses except for "(b) such other incapacity, or duress, or illegality of the transaction, as renders the obligation of the party a nullity." The words "such" and "as" indicate that the section is not stating that any type of duress renders an obligation to be a nullity. Rather, it suggests that only those types of duress that are so severe as to render it a nullity stand as exceptions to the rule that holders in due course take free of defenses.

Of course, the question left open is what type of duress is severe enough to render it a nullity. Neither UCC §3–305(2)(b) [Revised §3–305(a)(1)] nor the Official Comment attempt to establish a rule governing which types of duress render a transaction void as opposed to merely voidable. Instead, Official Comment 6 declares that "[a]ll such matters are therefore left to the local law." * * *

The Finley Partners do not cite any precedent from the District of Columbia that supports the view that economic duress renders a transaction void. In fact, they point out that [citation], the D.C. Court of Appeals quoted section 175 of the Restatement (Second) of Contracts which states that duress by threat (rather than by physical compulsion) renders a contract voidable rather than void. Although that case fails to distinguish between void and voidable contracts, it calls attention to the Restatement's distinction between the two categories:

> Duress takes two forms. In one, a person physically compels conduct that appears to be a manifestation of assent by a party who has no intention of engaging in that conduct. The result of this type of duress is that the conduct is not effective to create a contract (§174). In the other, a person makes an improper threat that induces a party who has no reasonable alternative to manifesting his assent. The result of this type of duress is that the contract that is created is voidable by the victim (§175). [Citation.]

* * *

The Finley Partners do not allege that they were physically compelled to sign the promissory notes in question. They themselves labeled their defense as "economic" duress, and the substance of their allegations are that they signed the notes because of the threat that their wages and standing in the firm would decrease if they refused. Such economic duress does not reach the level of physical compulsion capable of rendering a transaction entirely void. Thus, NBW held at least voidable title to the promissory notes when the FDIC took over as Receivers * * *. Thus, defendants' economic defense duress is not valid against the FDIC.

* * *

### Conclusion

For the reasons discussed above, this Court finds that neither of the defendants' arguments has merit and that the FDIC is entitled to summary judgment as a matter of law. The defendants opposing the FDIC's motion for summary judgment are liable for the obligations they accepted when they signed the promissory notes. The FDIC is entitled to recover to the full extent of those obligations, as it requests in its motion for summary judgment.

## QUESTIONS

1. Discuss the requirements for becoming a holder in due course.
2. Discuss the shelter rule and when a payee can have the rights of a holder in due course.
3. Identify, define, and discuss the real defenses.
4. Define and discuss personal defenses.
5. Discuss the limitations the Federal Trade Commission imposes upon the rights of a holder in due course.

## PROBLEMS

**1.** Moore issues a negotiable promissory note payable to the order of Parish for the amount of $3,000. Parish raises the amount to $13,000 and negotiates it to Holton for $12,000.

**(a)** If Holton is a holder in due course, how much can she recover from Moore? How much from Parish? If Moore's negligence substantially contributed to the making of the alteration, how much can Holton recover from Moore and Parish, respectively?

**(b)** If Holton is not a holder in due course, how much can she recover from Moore? How much from Parish? If Moore's negligence substantially contributed to the making of the alteration, how much can Holton recover from Moore and Parish, respectively?

**2.** On December 2, 2010, Miles executed and delivered to Proctor a negotiable promissory note for $10,000, payable to Proctor or order, due March 2, 2011, with interest at 6 percent from maturity, in partial payment of a printing press. On January 3, 2011, Proctor, in need of ready cash, indorsed and sold the note to Hughes for $8,000. Hughes paid $6,000 in cash to Proctor on January 3 and agreed to pay the balance of $2,000 one week later, namely, on January 10. On January 6, Hughes learned that Miles claimed a breach of warranty by Proctor and, for this reason, intended to refuse to pay the note when it matured. On January 10, Hughes paid Proctor $2,000, in conformity with their agreement of January 3. Following Miles's refusal to pay the note on March 2, 2011, Hughes sues Miles for $10,000. Is Hughes a holder in due course? If so, for what amount?

**3.** Thornton fraudulently represented to Daye that he would obtain for her a new car to be used in Daye's business for $17,800 from Pennek Motor Company. Daye thereupon executed her personal check for $17,800 payable to the order of Pennek Motor Company and delivered the check to Thornton, who immediately delivered it to the motor company in payment of his own prior indebtedness. The motor company had no knowledge of the representations made by Thornton to Daye. Pennek Motor Company now brings an action on the check which was not paid against Daye, who defends on the ground of failure of consideration. Is Pennek subject to this defense? Explain.

**4.** Adams, who reads with difficulty, arranged to borrow $5,000 from Bell. Bell prepared a note, which Adams read laboriously. As Adams was about to sign it, Bell diverted Adams's attention and substituted the following paper, which was identical to the note Adams had read except that the amounts were different:

> On June 1, 2011, I promise to pay Ben Bell or order Twelve Thousand Dollars with interest from date at 8 percent. This note is secured by certificate No. 13 for 100 shares of stock of Brookside Mills, Inc.

Adams did not detect the substitution, signed as maker, handed the note and stock certificate to Bell, and received from Bell $5,000. Bell indorsed and sold the paper to Fore, a holder in due course, who paid him $10,000. Fore presented the note at maturity to Adams, who refused to pay. What are Fore's rights, if any, against Adams?

**5.** On January 2, 2011, seventeen-year-old Martin paid $2,000 for a used motorboat to use in his fishing business, after Dealer's fraudulent misrepresentation of the condition of the boat. Martin signed an installment contract for $1,500, and gave Dealer the following instrument as down payment:

> Dated: 2011
>
> I promise to pay to the order of Dealer, six months after date, the sum of $500 without interest. This is given as a down payment on an installment contract for a motorboat.
>
> (signed) Martin

Dealer, on July 1, sold his business to Henry and included this note in the transaction. Dealer indorsed the note in blank and handed it to Henry, who left the note in his office safe. On July 10, Sharpie, an employee of Henry, without authority stole the note and sold it to Bert for $300, indorsing the note "Sharpie." At the time, in Bert's presence, Sharpie filled in the date on the note as February 2, 2011. Bert demanded payment from Martin, who refused to pay. What are Bert's rights against Martin?

**6.** McLaughlin borrowed $1,000 from Adler, who, apprehensive about McLaughlin's ability to pay, demanded security. McLaughlin indorsed and delivered to Adler a negotiable promissory note executed by Topping for $1,200 payable to McLaughlin's order in twelve equal monthly installments. The note did not contain an acceleration clause, but it recited that the consideration for the note was McLaughlin's promise to paint and shingle Topping's barn. At the time McLaughlin transferred the note to Adler, the first installment was overdue and unpaid. Adler was unaware that the installment had not been paid. Topping did not pay any of the installments on the note. When the last installment became due, Adler presented the note to Topping for payment. Topping refused upon the ground that McLaughlin had not painted or reshingled her barn. What are Adler's rights, if any, against Topping on the note?

**7.** McEnally purchased a refrigerator for his home from Peircault Appliance Store for $700. McEnally paid $200 in cash and signed an installment contract for $500, which in its entirety stated:

> January 15, 2011
>
> I promise to pay to the order of Peircault Appliance Store the sum of $500 in ten equal monthly installments.
>
> (Signed) McEnally

Peircault negotiated the installment contract to Hughes, who took the instrument for value, in good faith, without notice of any claim or defense of any party, and without question of the instrument's authenticity. After McEnally had paid two installments, the refrigerator ceased operating, and McEnally wishes to recover his down payment and first two monthly payments and to discontinue further payments. What outcome?

**8.** Adams, by fraudulent representations, induced Barton to purchase one hundred shares of the capital stock of the Evermore Oil Company. The shares were worthless. Barton executed and delivered to Adams a negotiable promissory note for $5,000, dated May 5, in full payment for the shares, due six months after date. On May 20, Adams indorsed and sold the note to Cooper for $4,800. On October 21, Barton, having learned that Cooper now held the note, notified Cooper of the fraud and stated he would not pay the note. On December 1, Cooper negotiated the note to Davis who, while not a party, had full knowledge of the fraud perpetrated on Barton. Upon refusal of Barton to pay the note, Davis sues Barton for $5,000. Is Davis a holder in due course or does he have the rights of a holder in due course? Explain.

**9.** Donna gives Peter a check for $2,500 in return for a laptop computer. The check is dated December 2. Peter transfers the check for value to Howard on December 14, and Howard deposits it in his bank on December 20. In the meantime, Donna has discovered that the computer is not what was promised and has stopped payment on the check. If Peter and Howard disappear, may the bank recover from Donna notwithstanding her defense of failure of consideration? What will be the bank's cause of action?

**10.** Eldon's Super Fresh Stores, Inc., is a corporation engaged in the retail grocery business. William Drexler was the attorney for and the corporate secretary of Eldon's and was also the personal attorney of Eldon Prinzing, the corporation's president and sole shareholder. From January 2010 through January 2011, Drexler maintained an active stock trading account in his name with Merrill Lynch. Eldon's had no such account. On August 12, 2010, Drexler purchased one hundred shares of Clark Oil & Refining Company stock through his Merrill Lynch stockbroker. He paid for the stock with a check drawn by Eldon's made payable to Merrill Lynch and signed by Prinzing. On August 15, 2010, Merrill Lynch accepted the check as payment for Drexler's stock purchase. There was no communication between Eldon's and Merrill Lynch until November 2011, fifteen months after the issuance of the check. At that time, Eldon's asked Merrill Lynch about the whereabouts of the stock certificate and asserted a claim to its ownership. Does Merrill Lynch qualify as a holder in due course? Why?

**11.** Consolidated Business Forms leased a Phillips business computer from Benchmark. Benchmark subsequently transferred the lease and promissory note to Exchange International Leasing Corporation. Consolidated stopped making rental payments when the computer malfunctioned, and Exchange International brought this suit to recover the payments due on the promissory note. Consolidated defends on the grounds that Benchmark prevented its agent, Mr. Spohn, from examining the contents of the agreement between the two companies and further represented that the computer would be removed with a complete refund if it failed to operate properly. Is Exchange subject to Consolidated's defense?

**12.** Litton decided to purchase photocopiers to use in its offices. Angelo Buquicchio, a Royal (a division of Litton) salesperson, recommended that Litton lease the machines from Regent. Regent was a company totally independent of Litton and had agreed to give Buquicchio "service fees" or, more appropriately, bribes. Regent borrowed money from Bankers Trust to finance purchases and transferred the Litton leases as security. A clause in the leases permitted transfer and provided that the transferee's rights would be independent of any claims or offsets of Litton as against Regent. Litton defaulted on the obligations, and Litton argues that Regent's bribery of Royal's employee rendered Litton's obligations a nullity and a defense against the banks as holders in due course. Explain whether Litton is correct in its assertion.

**13.** Supreme Radio, Inc., issued to Southern New England Distributing Corporation two notes worth $1,900. The two notes and others, all of a total face value of about $15,000, were transferred to Korzenik, an attorney, by his client Southern "as a retainer for services to be performed" by Korzenik. Although Korzenik was unaware of the fact, Southern had obtained the notes by fraud. Southern retained Korzenik on October 25 in connection with certain antitrust litigation, and the notes were transferred on October 31. The value of the services performed by Korzenik during that time is unclear. Korzenik brought this action against Supreme Radio to recover $1,900 on the notes. Will Korzenik be able to collect the funds? Explain.

**14.** Walter Duester purchased a John Deere combine from St. Paul Equipment. John Deere Co. was the lender and secured party under the agreement. The combine was pledged as collateral. Duester defaulted on his debt, and the manager of St. Paul, Hansen, was instructed to repossess the combine. Hansen went to Duester's farm to accomplish this. Duester told him that he had received some payments for custom combining and would immediately purchase a cashier's check to pay the John Deere debt. Hansen followed Duester to the Defendant, Boelus State Bank. Hansen remained outside, and Duester returned in a few minutes with a cashier's check in the amount of the balance of his indebtedness payable to John Deere. The check had been signed by an authorized bank employee. When John Deere, however, presented the check to the bank for payment shortly thereafter, the bank refused to pay. The bank claims that Duester had acquired the check by theft. Is John Deere subject to this defense? Why?

**15.** Turman executed a deed of trust note for $107,500.00 payable to Ward's Home Improvement, Inc. The note was consideration for a contract by which Ward was to construct a home on property owned by Turman, and the note was secured by a deed of trust on that property. Later that day, Ward executed a separate written assignment of the note to Pomerantz. This document specifically uses the word "assigns." Ward did not endorse the note to Pomerantz or otherwise write upon the note. Ward received $95,000.00 for the assignment from Pomerantz. Ward failed to complete the house and to do so will require the expenditure of an additional $42,000.00. Is Pomerantz a holder in due course of the $107,500.00 note? Explain.

**16.** Stephens delivered 184 bushels of corn to Aubrey, for which he was to receive $478.23. Aubrey issued a check with $478.23 typewritten in numbers, and on the line customarily used to express the amount in words appeared "$100478 and 23 cts" imprinted in red with a check-writing machine. Before Stephens cashed the check, someone crudely typed "100" in front of the typewritten $478.23. When Stephens presented this check to the State Bank of Salem, Anderson, the manager, questioned Stephens. Anderson knew that Stephens had just declared bankruptcy and was not accustomed to making such large deposits. Stephens told Anderson he had bought and sold a large quantity of corn at a great profit. Anderson accepted the explanation, applied the monies to nine promissory notes, an installment payment, and accrued interest owed by Stephens. Stephens also received $2,000 in cash, with the balance deposited in his checking account.

Later that day, Anderson reexamined the check and discovered the suspicious appearance of the typewriting. He then contacted Aubrey, who said a check in that amount was suspicious, whereupon Anderson froze the transaction. When Aubrey stopped payment on the check, the bank sustained a $28,193.91 loss because

Stephens could not be located. The bank then sued Aubrey for the loss. Explain who should bear the risk of loss.

**17.** L&M Home Health Corporation (L&M) had a checking account with Wells Fargo Bank. L&M engaged Gentner and Company, Inc. (Gentner) to provide consulting services, and paid Gentner for services rendered with a check drawn on its Wells Fargo account in the amount of $60,000, dated September 23, 2010. Eleven days later, on October 4, 2010, L&M orally instructed Wells Fargo to stop payment on the check. Eleven days after that, on October 15, 2010, Gentner presented the L&M check to Wells Fargo for payment. On the same date the teller issued a cashier's check, payable to Gentner, in the amount of $60,000. On November 5, 2010, Wells Fargo placed a "stop payment order" on the cashier's check. On January 15, 2011, Gentner deposited the cashier's check at another bank, but it was not honored and was returned stamped "Payment Stopped." Gentner sues Wells Fargo for wrongful dishonor of the cashier's check. Is Gentner a holder in due course of the check? Discuss.

**18.** Over a ten-year period, Christine Mayfield worked for Watson Coatings, Inc.—first as an accountant, then as the company controller, and finally as the company treasurer. Mayfield had authority to write checks on funds in Watson's corporate checking account. Watson placed no restrictions or dollar limitations regarding Mayfield's authority to sign checks. Mayfield was solely responsible for reconciling the company checkbook register with the bank statements. Although Watson received monthly bank statements with cancelled checks, Carol Watson, one of Watson's owners, delivered the unopened bank statements to Mayfield but never reviewed the bank statements or reconciled the checking account during Mayfield's tenure at Watson. Mayfield's husband, an American Express account holder, added Mayfield's name to his account in 2002. From August 2007 through October 2011, Mayfield wrote approximately forty-five to forty-seven checks (totaling more than $745,000) on Watson's corporate checking account payable to American Express for her or her husband's personal debt. Neither Mayfield's name nor her husband's name was printed on any of the checks. Each of the checks was made payable to the order of American Express and for credit to the American Express account of Mayfield's husband. American Express credited the Mayfield account for each of the checks. Watson informed American Express of Mayfield's fraud after Mayfield's employment with Watson ended. Can Watson recover the funds from American Express? Explain.

# CHAPTER 29
# Liability of Parties

The preceding chapters discussed the requirements of negotiability, the transfer of negotiable instruments, and the preferred position of a holder in due course. When parties issue negotiable instruments they do so with the expectation that they, either directly or indirectly, will satisfy their obligation under the instrument. Likewise, when a person accepts, indorses, or transfers an instrument, he incurs liability for the instrument under certain circumstances. This chapter examines the liability of parties arising out of negotiable instruments and the ways in which liability may be terminated.

Two types of potential liability are associated with negotiable instruments: contractual liability and warranty liability. The law imposes **contractual liability** on those who **sign**, or have a representative agent sign, a negotiable instrument. Because some parties to a negotiable instrument never sign it, they never assume contractual liability. Section 3–401(a).

Warranty liability, on the other hand, is not based on signature; thus, it may be imposed on both signers and nonsigners. **Warranty liability** applies (1) to persons who transfer an instrument and (2) to persons who obtain payment or acceptance of an instrument.

## CONTRACTUAL LIABILITY

All parties whose signatures appear on a negotiable instrument incur certain contractual obligations, unless they disclaim liability. No person is liable on an instrument unless she signs it herself or has it signed by a person whose signature binds her. Once the person signs the instrument, the person has *prima facie* liability on the instrument. The *maker* of a promissory note and the *acceptor* of a draft assume primary, or unconditional, liability, subject to valid claims and defenses, to pay according to the terms of the instrument at the time he signs it or as completed according to the rules for incomplete instruments, discussed in *Chapter 28*. **Primary liability** means that a party is legally obligated to pay without the holder's having to resort first to another party. *Indorsers* of all instruments incur secondary, or conditional, liability if the instrument is not paid. **Secondary liability** means that a party is legally obligated to pay only after another party, who is expected to pay, fails to do so. The liability of drawers of drafts and checks is also conditional because it is generally contingent upon the drawee's dishonor of the instrument. A *drawee* has *no* liability on the instrument until he accepts it.

An **accommodation party** signs the instrument to lend her credit to another party to the instrument and is a direct beneficiary of the value received. Section 3–419(a). The liability of an accommodation party, who generally signs as a comaker, or anomalous indorser, is determined by the capacity in which she signs. Section 3–419(b). If she signs as a maker, she incurs primary liability; if she signs as an anomalous indorser, she incurs secondary liability.

## SIGNATURE

The word *signature*, as discussed in *Chapter 26*, is broadly defined to include any name, word, or mark, whether handwritten, typed, printed, or in any other form, made with the intention of authenticating an instrument. Sections 3–401(b) and 1–201(39); Revised Section 1–201(b)(37). The signature may be made by the individual herself or on her behalf by the individual's authorized agent.

### AUTHORIZED SIGNATURES

A person is obligated by a signature if the signature is her own or if it is signed by an agent with authority. Authorized agents often execute negotiable instruments on behalf of their principals. The agent is not liable if she is authorized to execute the instrument and does so properly (e.g., "Prince, principal, by Adams, agent"). If these two conditions are met, then only the principal is liable on the instrument. (For a comprehensive discussion of the principal–agent relationship, see *Chapters 19* and *20*.)

Occasionally, however, the agent, although fully authorized, uses an inappropriate form of signature that may mislead holders or prospective holders as to the identity of the obligor. Although incorrect signatures by agents assume many forms, they can be conveniently sorted into three groups. In each of these instances the intention of the original parties to the instrument is that the principal is to be liable on the instrument and the agent is not.

The first type occurs when an agent signs only his own name to an instrument, neither indicating that he is signing in a representative capacity nor stating the name of the principal. For example, Adams, the agent of Prince, makes a note on behalf of Prince but signs it "Adams." The signature does not indicate that Adams has signed in a representative capacity or that he has made the instrument on behalf of Prince. The second type of incorrect form occurs when an authorized agent indicates that he is signing in a representative capacity but does not disclose the name of his principal. For example, Adams, executing an instrument on behalf of Prince, merely signs it "Adams, agent." The third type of inappropriate signature occurs when an agent reveals both her name and her principal's name, but does not indicate that she has signed in a representative capacity. For example, Adams, signing an instrument on behalf of Prince, signs it "Adams, Prince."

In all three situations, the agent is liable on the instrument only to a holder in due course without notice that Adams was not intended to be liable. Because Prince's liability on the instrument is determined by contract and agency law, Prince is liable to all holders. Under Revised Article 3, if a representative (an agent) signs his name as the drawer of a *check* without indicating his representative status and the check is payable from an account of the represented person (the principal) who is identified on the check, the representative is not liable on the check if he is an authorized agent. Some courts reached this result under prior Article 3.

◆ **SEE CASE 29-1**

### UNAUTHORIZED SIGNATURES

An unauthorized signature, with two exceptions, is totally ineffective and does not bind anybody. Unauthorized signatures include both forgeries and signatures made by an agent without authority. Though generally not binding on the person whose name appears on the instrument, the unauthorized signature is binding upon the unauthorized signer, whether her own name appears on the instrument or not, to any person who in good faith pays or gives value for the instrument. Section 3–403(a). Thus, if Adams, without authority, signed Prince's name to an instrument, Adams, not Prince, would be liable on the instrument. The rule, therefore, is an exception to the principle that only those whose names appear on a negotiable instrument can be liable on it.

**Ratification of Unauthorized Signature** An unauthorized signature may be **ratified** by the person whose name appears on the instrument. Section 3–403(a). Although the ratification may relieve the actual signer from liability on the instrument, it does not of itself affect any rights the person ratifying the signature may have against the actual signer.

**Negligence Contributing to Forged Signature** Any person who by his **negligence** substantially contributes to the making of a forged signature may *not* assert the lack of authority as a defense against a holder in due course or a person who in good faith pays the instrument or takes it for value or for collection. Section 3–406. For example, Ingrid employs a signature stamp to sign her checks and carelessly leaves it accessible to third parties. Lisa discovers the stamp and uses it to write a number of checks without Ingrid's authorization. Norman, a person who takes the instrument for value and in good faith, will not be subject to Ingrid's defense of unauthorized signature and will be able to recover the amount of the check from Ingrid, due to Ingrid's negligence in storing the signature stamp. Nevertheless, if the person asserting the preclusion also fails to exercise reasonable care, Revised Section 3–406(b) adopts a comparative negligence standard.

## LIABILITY OF PRIMARY PARTIES

There is a primary party on every note: the *maker*. The maker's commitment is unconditional. Section 3–412. No one, however, is unconditionally liable on a draft or check as issued. A *drawee* is not liable on the instrument unless he accepts it. Section 3–408. If, however, the drawee accepts the draft, after which he is known as the *acceptor*, he becomes primarily liable on the instrument. **Acceptance** or, in the case of a check, certification is the drawee's signed promise to pay a draft as presented. Section 3–409(a), (d). Presentment (i.e., a demand for payment) is not a condition to the holder's right to recover from parties with primary liability.

### MAKERS

The maker of a note is obligated to pay the instrument according to its terms at the time of issuance or, if the instrument is incomplete, according to its terms when completed, as discussed in *Chapter 28*. Section 3–412. The obligation of the maker is owed to a person entitled to enforce the instrument or to an indorser who paid the instrument.

Primary liability also applies to issuers of cashier's checks and to issuers of drafts drawn on the drawer (i.e., where the issuer is both the drawee and the drawer). Section 3–412.

### ACCEPTORS

A **drawee** has no liability on the instrument until she accepts it, at which time she becomes an acceptor and, like a maker, primarily liable. The acceptor becomes liable on the draft according to its terms at the time of acceptance or as completed according to the rules for incomplete instruments as discussed in *Chapter 28*. Section 3–413(a). Nevertheless, if the acceptor does not state the amount accepted and the amount of the draft is later raised, a subsequent holder in due course can enforce the instrument against the acceptor according to the terms at the time the holder in due course took possession. Section 3–413(b). Thus, an acceptor should always indicate on the instrument the amount that it is accepting. The acceptor owes the obligation to pay to a person entitled to enforce the instrument or to the drawer or an indorser who paid the draft under drawer's or indorser's liability. Section 3–413(a).

An acceptance must be written on the draft. Section 3–409(a). Having met this requirement, it may take many forms. It may be printed on the face of the draft, ready for the drawee's signature. It may consist of a rubber stamp, with the signature of the drawee added. It may be the drawee's signature, preceded by a word or phrase such as "Accepted," "Certified," or "Good." It may consist of nothing more than the drawee's signature. Normally, but by no means necessarily, an acceptance is written vertically across the face of the draft. It must not, however, contain any words indicating an intent to refuse to honor the draft. Furthermore, no writing separate from the draft and no oral statement or conduct of the drawee will convert the drawee into an acceptor.

Checks, when accepted, are said to be certified. **Certification** is a special type of acceptance consisting of the drawee bank's promise to pay the check when subsequently presented for payment. Section 3–409(d).

The drawee bank has no obligation to certify a check, and its refusal to certify does not constitute dishonor of the instrument. If the drawee refuses to accept or pay the instrument, he may be liable to the drawer for breach of contract.

◆ **SEE CASE 29-2**

## LIABILITY OF SECONDARY PARTIES

Parties with secondary (conditional) liability do not unconditionally promise to pay the instrument; rather, they engage to pay the instrument if the party expected to pay does not do so. The drawer is liable if the drawee dishonors the instrument. Indorsers (including the payee if he indorses) of an instrument are also conditionally liable; their liability is subject to the conditions of dishonor and notice of dishonor. If an instrument is *not* paid by the party expected to pay and the conditions precedent to the liability of a secondary party are satisfied, a secondary party is liable unless he has disclaimed his liability or he possesses a valid defense to the instrument.

### DRAWERS

A drawer of a draft orders the drawee to pay the instrument and does not expect to pay the draft personally. The drawer is obligated to pay the draft only if the drawee fails to pay the instrument. The drawer of an *unaccepted draft* is obligated to pay the instrument upon its dishonor according to its terms at the time it was issued or, in the case of an incomplete instrument, according to the rules discussed in *Chapter 28*. Under Revised Article 3, the drawer's liability is contingent only upon dishonor and does not require notice of dishonor. The drawer's obligation on an unaccepted draft is owed to a person entitled to enforce the instrument or to an indorser who paid the instrument under indorser's liability.

If the draft has been accepted and the acceptor is not a bank, the obligation of the drawer to pay the instrument is then contingent upon both dishonor of the instrument and notice of dishonor; the drawer's liability in this instance is equivalent to that of an indorser. Sections 3–414(d), 3–503.

◆ **SEE CASE 29-3**

### INDORSERS

An indorser promises that upon dishonor of the instrument *and* notice of dishonor she will pay the instrument according to the terms of the instrument at the time it was indorsed or, if an incomplete instrument when indorsed, according to its terms when completed, as discussed in *Chapter 28*. Sections 3–415, 3–503. Once again, this obligation is owed to a person entitled to enforce the instrument or to a subsequent indorser who paid the instrument under indorser's liability.

### EFFECT OF ACCEPTANCE

Where a draft is accepted by a *bank*, the drawer and all prior indorsers are discharged. Sections 3–414(c), 3–415(d). The liability of indorsers subsequent to certification is not affected. When the bank accepts a draft, it should withhold from the drawer's account funds sufficient to pay the instrument. Because the bank is primarily liable on its acceptance and has the funds, whereas the drawer does not, the discharge is reasonable.

### DISCLAIMER OF LIABILITY BY SECONDARY PARTIES

Both drawers and indorsers may disclaim their normal conditional liability by drawing or indorsing an instrument "**without recourse**." Sections 3–414(e), 3–415(b). However, drawers of checks may not disclaim contractual liability. Section 3–414(e). The use of the qualifying words *without recourse* is understood to place purchasers on notice that they may not rely on the credit of the person using this language. A person drawing or indorsing an instrument in this manner does not incur the normal contractual liability of a drawer or indorser to pay the instrument, but he may nonetheless be liable for breach of warranty.

## CONDITIONS PRECEDENT TO LIABILITY

A **condition precedent** is an event or events that must occur before liability arises. The condition precedent to the liability of the drawer of an *unaccepted* draft is dishonor. Conditions precedent to the liability of any indorser or the drawer of an *accepted* draft by a nonbank are dishonor and notice of dishonor. If the conditions to secondary liability are not met, a party's conditional obligation on the instrument is discharged, unless the conditions are excused.

**DISHONOR** **Dishonor** generally involves the refusal to pay an instrument when it is presented. **Presentment** is a demand made by or on behalf of a person entitled to enforce the instrument for (1) **payment** by the drawee or other party obligated to pay the instrument or (2) **acceptance** by the drawee of a draft. Section 3–501(a). The return of any instrument for lack of necessary indorsements or for failure of the presentment to comply with the terms of the instrument, however, is not a dishonor. Section 3–501(b)(3).

What constitutes dishonor varies depending upon the type of instrument and whether presentment is required.

1. **Note**—A *demand note* is dishonored if the maker does not pay it on the day of presentment. Section 3–502(a)(1). If the note is payable at a *definite time* and (a) the terms of the note require presentment or (b) the note is payable at or through a bank, the note is dishonored if it is not paid on the date it is presented or its due date, whichever is later. Section 3–502(a)(2). All *other time notes* need not be presented and are dishonored if they are not paid on their due dates. Section 3–502(a)(3). Nevertheless, because makers are primarily liable on their notes, their liability is not affected by failure of proper presentment.
2. **Drafts**—An *unaccepted draft* (other than a check, discussed later) that is payable on *demand* is dishonored if presentment is made and it is not paid on the date presented. Section 3–502(b)(2). A *time draft* presented for *payment* is due on the due date or presentment date, whichever is later. Section 3–502(b)(3). A *time draft* presented for *acceptance* prior to its due date is dishonored if it is not accepted on the day presented. Section 3–502(b)(3). Refusal to accept a demand instrument is not a dishonor, although acceptance may be requested. Of course, if an instrument is payable at a certain time period after acceptance or sight, a refusal to accept the draft on the day presented is a dishonor. Section 3–502(b)(4).

   An accepted demand draft is dishonored if the acceptor (who is primarily liable on the instrument) does not pay it on the day presented for payment. Section 3–502(d)(1). An accepted time draft is dishonored if it is not paid on the due date for payment or on the presentment date, whichever is later. Section 3–502(d)(2).

   Drawers, with the exception of drafts accepted by a bank, are not discharged from liability by a delay in presentment. Once an instrument has been properly presented and dishonored, a drawer becomes liable to pay the instrument. As previously indicated, drawers and prior indorsers are discharged from liability when a draft is accepted by a bank. Sections 3–414, 3–415.
3. **Checks**—If a check is presented for payment directly to the payor/drawee bank for immediate payment, a refusal to pay the check on the day presented constitutes dishonor. Section 3–502(b)(2). In the more common situation of a check being presented through the normal collection process, a check is dishonored if the payor bank makes timely return of the check, sends timely notice of dishonor or nonpayment, or becomes accountable for the amount of the check (until that payment has been made the check is dishonored, Comment 4). Section 3–502(b)(1). As more fully explained in *Chapter 30*, under Article 4 a bank in most instances has a midnight deadline (before midnight of the next banking day) in which to decide whether to honor or dishonor an instrument. Thus, depending on the number of banks involved in the collection process, the time for dishonor can greatly vary.

*Delay* in presentment discharges an *indorser* only if the instrument is a check and it is not presented for payment or given to a depositary bank for collection within thirty days after the day the indorsement was made. Section 3–415(e). The same rule does not apply, however, to a drawer. If a person entitled to enforce a check fails to present a check within thirty days after its date, the drawer will be discharged only if the delay deprives the drawer of funds because of the suspension of payments by the drawee bank such as would result from a bank failure. Section 3–414(f). This discharge is quite unlikely because of Federal bank insurance but would be available when an account is not fully insured because it exceeds $100,000 or because the account does not qualify for deposit insurance. Section 3–414, Comment 6.

◆ **SEE CASE 29-2**

## NOTICE OF DISHONOR

The obligation of an indorser of any instrument and of a drawer of a draft accepted by a nonbank is not enforceable unless the indorser or drawer is given notice of dishonor or the notice is otherwise excused. Sections 3–503(a), 3–415(c). Thus, lack of proper notice discharges the liability of an indorser; for this purpose a drawer of a draft accepted by a party other than a bank is treated as an indorser. Notice of dishonor is *not* required to retain the liability of drawers of unaccepted drafts. In addition, as previously mentioned a drawer is discharged when a draft is accepted by a *bank*. Section 3–414. In short, a drawer's liability usually is not contingent upon receiving notice of dishonor, whereas an indorser's liability is.

Notice of dishonor is normally given by the holder or by an indorser who has himself received notice. For example, Michael makes a note payable to the order of Phyllis; Phyllis indorses it to Arthur; Arthur indorses it to Bambi; and Bambi indorses it to Henry, the last holder. Henry presents it to Michael within a reasonable time, but Michael refuses to pay. Henry may give notice of dishonor to all secondary parties: Phyllis, Arthur, and Bambi. If he is satisfied that Bambi will pay him or if he does not know how to contact Phyllis or Arthur, he may notify only Bambi, who then must see to it that Arthur or Phyllis is notified, or she will have no recourse. Bambi may notify either or both. If she notifies Arthur only, Arthur will have to see to it that Phyllis is notified, or Arthur will have no recourse. When properly given, notice benefits all parties who have rights on the instrument against the party notified. Section 3–503(b). Thus, Henry's notification to Phyllis operates as notice to Phyllis by both Arthur and Bambi. Likewise, if Henry notifies only Bambi and Bambi notifies Arthur and Phyllis, then Henry has the benefit of Bambi's notification of Arthur and Phyllis. Nonetheless, it would be advisable for Henry to give notice to all prior parties because Bambi may be insolvent and thus may not bother to notify Arthur or Phyllis.

If, in the above example, Henry were to notify Phyllis alone, Arthur and Bambi would be discharged. Because she has no claim against Arthur or Bambi, who indorsed after she did, Phyllis would have no ground for complaint. It cannot matter to Phyllis that she is compelled to pay Henry rather than Arthur. Therefore, subsequent parties are permitted to skip intermediate indorsers if they want to discharge them and are willing to look solely to prior indorsers for recourse.

Any necessary notice must be given by a bank before midnight on the *next* banking day following the banking day on which it receives notice of dishonor. Any nonbank with respect to an instrument taken for collection must give notice within thirty days following the day on which it received notice. In all other situations, notice of dishonor must be within thirty days following the day on which dishonor occurred. Section 3–503(c). For instance, Donna draws a check on Youngstown Bank payable to the order of Pablo; Pablo indorses it to Andrea; Andrea deposits it to her account in Second Chicago National Bank; Second Chicago National Bank properly presents it to Youngstown Bank, the drawee; and Youngstown dishonors it because the drawer, Donna, has insufficient funds on deposit to cover it. Youngstown has until midnight of the following day to notify Second Chicago National, Andrea, or Pablo of the dishonor. Second Chicago National then has until midnight on the day after receipt of notice of dishonor to notify Andrea or Pablo. That is, if Second Chicago National received the notice of dishonor on Monday, it would have until midnight on Tuesday to notify Andrea or Pablo. If it failed to notify Andrea, it could not charge the item back to her. Andrea, in turn, has thirty days after receipt of notice of dishonor to notify Pablo. Donna, a drawer of an unaccepted draft, is not discharged from liability for failure to receive notice of dishonor.

Frequently, notice of dishonor is given by returning the unpaid instrument with an attached stamp, ticket, or memorandum stating that the item was not paid and requesting that the recipient make good on it. But because the purpose of notice is to give knowledge of dishonor and to inform the secondary party that he may be held liable on the instrument, any kind of notice which informs the recipient of his potential liability is sufficient. No formal requisites are imposed—notice may be given by any commercially reasonable means, including oral, written, or electronic communication. Section 3–503(b). An oral notice, while sufficient, is inadvisable because it may be difficult to prove. Notice of dishonor must reasonably identify the instrument. Section 3–503(b).

**PRESENTMENT AND NOTICE OF DISHONOR EXCUSED** The Uniform Commercial Code excuses *presentment* for payment or acceptance if (1) the person entitled to enforce the instrument cannot with reasonable diligence present the instrument, (2) the maker or acceptor of the instrument has repudiated the obligation to pay, is dead, or is in insolvency proceedings, (3) the terms of the instrument do not require presentment to hold the indorsers or drawer liable, (4) the drawer or indorser has waived the right of presentment, (5) the drawer instructed the drawee not to pay or accept the draft, or (6) the drawee was not obligated to the drawer to pay the draft. Section 3–504(a).

*Notice of dishonor* is excused if the terms of the instrument do not require notice to hold the party liable or if notice has been waived by the party whose obligation is being enforced. Moreover, a waiver of presentment is also a waiver of notice of dishonor. Section 3–504(b). Finally, delay in giving notice of dishonor is excused if the delay is caused by circumstances beyond the control of the person giving notice and that person exercised reasonable diligence in giving notice after the cause of the delay ceased to exist. Section 3–504(c).

◆ **SEE FIGURE 29-1: Contractual Liability**

◆ FIGURE 29-1: **Contractual Liability**

| Party | Instrument | Liability | Conditions |
|---|---|---|---|
| **Maker** | Note | Unconditional | None |
| **Acceptor** | Draft | Unconditional | None |
| **Drawer** | Unaccepted Draft | Conditional | Dishonor |
| | Draft accepted by a nonbank | Conditional | Dishonor and notice |
| | Cashier's check | Unconditional | None |
| | Draft drawn on drawer | Unconditional | None |
| | Draft accepted by a bank | None | |
| | Draft (not check) drawn without recourse | None | |
| **Indorser** | Note or draft | Conditional | Dishonor and notice |
| | Draft subsequently accepted by a bank | None | |
| | Note or draft indorsed without recourse | None | |
| **Drawee** | Draft | None | |

### LIABILITY FOR CONVERSION

**Conversion** is a tort by which a person becomes liable in damages because of his wrongful control over the personal property of another. The law applicable to conversion of personal property applies to instruments. Section 3–420(a). An instrument is so converted if the instrument "is taken by transfer, other than by negotiation, from a person not entitled to enforce the instrument or a bank makes or obtains payment with respect to the instrument for a person *not* entitled to enforce the instrument or receive payment." Section 3–420(a) (emphasis added). Examples of conversion thus would include a drawee bank that pays an instrument containing a forged indorsement or a bank that pays an instrument containing only one of two required indorsements.

## TERMINATION OF LIABILITY

Eventually, every commercial transaction must end, terminating the potential liabilities of the parties to the instrument. The Code specifies the various methods by and extent to which the liability of *any* party, primary or secondary, is discharged. "Discharge" means that the obligated individual is released from liability on the instrument due to either Article 3 or contract law. The Code also specifies when the liability of *all* parties is discharged. No discharge of a party is effective against a subsequent holder in due course, however, unless she has notice of the discharge when she takes the instrument. Section 3–601(b). In addition, discharge of liability is not always final; liability under certain circumstances (e.g., coming into possession of a subsequent holder in due course) can be revived. Discharge applies to the individual and not the instrument, and discharge of individuals may occur at different points in time. Moreover, a person's liability may be discharged with regard to one party but not to another.

### PAYMENT

The most obvious and common way for a party to discharge liability on an instrument is to pay a party entitled to enforce the instrument. Section 3–602. An instrument is paid to the extent that payment is made by or for a person obligated to pay the instrument and to a person entitled to enforce the instrument. Section 3–602(a). Subject to three exceptions, such payment results in a discharge even though it is made with knowledge of another person's claim to the instrument, unless such other person either supplies adequate indemnity or obtains an injunction in a proceeding to which the holder is made a party. It should be noted, however, that the discharge is only to the extent of the payment.

The person making payment should, of course, take possession of the instrument or have it canceled—marked "paid" or "canceled"—so that it cannot pass to a subsequent holder in due course against whom his discharge would be ineffective.

### TENDER OF PAYMENT

Any party liable on an instrument who makes proper tender of full payment to a person entitled to enforce the instrument when or after payment is due is discharged from liability for interest after the due date. Section 3–603(c). If her tender is refused, she is not discharged from liability for the face amount of the instrument or for any interest accrued until the time of tender. Moreover, if an instrument requires presentment and the obligor is ready and able to pay the instrument when it is due at the place of payment specified in the instrument, such readiness is the equivalent of tender. Section 3–603(c).

Occasionally a person entitled to enforce an instrument will refuse a tender of payment for reasons known only to himself. It may be that he believes his rights exceed the amount of the tender or that he desires to enforce payment against another party. In any event, his refusal of the tender wholly discharges to the extent of the amount of tender every party who has a right of recourse against the party making tender. Section 3–603(b).

### CANCELLATION AND RENUNCIATION

Section 3–604 provides that a person entitled to enforce an instrument may discharge the liability of any party to an instrument by an intentional voluntary act, such as by canceling the instrument or the signature of the party or parties to be discharged, by mutilating or destroying the instrument, by obliterating a signature, or by adding words indicating a discharge. Section 3–604(a). A party entitled to enforce an instrument may also renounce his rights by a writing, signed and delivered, promising not to sue or otherwise renouncing rights against the party. Like other discharges, however, a written renunciation is of no effect against a subsequent holder in due course who takes without knowledge of the renunciation. Section 3–601(b).

Cancellation or renunciation is effective even without consideration.

## LIABILITY BASED ON WARRANTY

Article 3 imposes two types of implied warranties: (1) transferor's warranties and (2) presenter's warranties. Sections 3–416 and 3–417. Although these warranties are effective whether or not the transferor or presenter signs the instrument, the extension of the transferor's warranty to subsequent holders does depend on whether one or the other has indorsed the instrument. Like other warranties, these may be disclaimed by agreement between immediate parties. In the case of an indorser, his disclaimer of transfer warranties and presentment warranties must appear in the indorsement itself and is effective, except with respect to checks. Sections 3–416(c), 3–417(e). Such disclaimers must be specific, such as "without warranty." The use of "without recourse" will disclaim only contract liability, not warranty liability.

## WARRANTIES ON TRANSFER

Any person who transfers an instrument, whether by negotiation or assignment, and receives *consideration* makes certain **transferor's warranties**. Section 3–416. Any consideration sufficient to support a contract will support transfer warranties. If transfer is by delivery alone, warranties on transfer run only to the immediate transferee. If the transfer is made by indorsement, whether qualified or unqualified, the transfer warranty runs to "any subsequent transferee." *Transfer* means that the delivery of possession is voluntary. Sections 3–201(a), 1–201(14). The warranties of the transferor are as follows.

### ENTITLEMENT TO ENFORCE

The first warranty that the Code imposes on a transferor is that the transferor is a person entitled to enforce the instrument. Section 3–416(a)(1). This warranty "is in effect a warranty that there are no unauthorized or missing indorsements that prevent the transferor from making the transferee a person entitled to enforce the instrument." Section 3–416, Comment 2. The following example illustrates this rule. Mitchell makes a note payable to the order of Penelope. A thief steals the note from Penelope, forges Penelope's indorsement, and sells the instrument to Aaron. Aaron is not entitled to enforce the instrument because the break in the indorsement chain prevents him from being a holder. If Aaron transfers the instrument to Judith for consideration, Judith can hold Aaron liable for breach of warranty. The warranty action is important to Judith because it enables her to hold Aaron liable, even if Aaron indorsed the note "without recourse."

### AUTHENTIC AND AUTHORIZED SIGNATURES

The second warranty imposed by the Code is that all signatures are authentic and authorized. In the example presented above, this warranty would also be breached. Section 3–416(a)(2). If, however, the signature of a maker, drawer, drawee, acceptor, or indorser not in the chain of title is unauthorized, there is a breach of this warranty but no breach of the warranty of entitlement to enforce.

### NO ALTERATION

The third warranty is the warranty against alteration. Section 3–416(a)(3). Suppose that Maureen makes a note payable to the order of the payee in the amount of $100. The payee, without authority, alters the note so that it appears to be drawn for $1,000 and negotiates the instrument to Lois, who buys it without knowledge of the alteration. Lois, indorsing "without recourse," negotiates the instrument to Kyle for consideration. Kyle presents the instrument to Maureen, who refuses to pay more than $100 on it. Kyle can collect the difference from Lois, for although her qualified indorsement saves Lois from liability to Kyle on the indorsement contract, she is liable to him for breach of warranty. If Lois had not qualified her indorsement, Kyle would be able to recover against her on the basis of either warranty or the indorsement contract.

### NO DEFENSES

The fourth transferor's warranty imposed by the Code is that the instrument is not subject to a defense or claim in recoupment of any party. Section 3–416(a)(4). A claim in recoupment, as discussed in *Chapter 28*, is a counterclaim that arose from the transaction that gave rise to the instrument. Suppose that Madeline, a minor and a resident of a State where minors' contracts for non-necessaries are voidable, makes a note payable to bearer in payment of a motorcycle. Pierce, the first holder, negotiates it to Iola by mere delivery. Iola indorses it and negotiates it to Justin, who unqualifiedly indorses it to Hector. All negotiations are made for consideration. Because of Madeline's minority (a real defense), Hector cannot recover upon the instrument against Madeline. Hector therefore recovers against Justin or Iola on either the breach of warranty that no valid defenses exist to the instrument or the indorsement contract. Justin, if he is forced to pay Hector, can in turn recover against Iola on either a breach of warranty or the indorsement contract. Justin, however, cannot recover against Pierce. Pierce is not liable to Justin as an indorser because he did not indorse the instrument. Although Pierce, as a transferor, warrants that there are no defenses good against him, this warranty extends only to his immediate transferee, Iola. Therefore, Justin cannot hold Pierce liable. Iola, however, can recover from Pierce on a breach of warranty.

### NO KNOWLEDGE OF INSOLVENCY

Any person who transfers a negotiable instrument warrants that he has no knowledge of any insolvency proceedings instituted with respect to the maker, acceptor, or drawer of an unaccepted instrument. Section 3–416(a)(5). Insolvency proceedings include bankruptcy and "any assignment for the benefit of creditors or other proceedings intended to liquidate or rehabilitate the estate of the person involved." Section 1–201(22). Thus, if Marcia makes a note payable to bearer, and the first holder, Taylor, negotiates it for consideration without indorsement to Ursula, who then negotiates it for consideration by qualified indorsement to Valerie, both Taylor and Ursula warrant that they do not know that Marcia is in bankruptcy. Valerie could not hold Taylor liable for breach of warranty, however, because Taylor's warranty runs only in favor of her immediate transferee, Ursula, because Taylor transferred the instrument without indorsement. If Valerie could hold Ursula liable on her warranty, Ursula could thereupon hold Taylor, her immediate transferor, liable.

◆ **SEE FIGURE 29-2: Liability on Transfer**

## WARRANTIES ON PRESENTMENT

Any party who pays or accepts an instrument must do so in strict compliance with the orders that instrument contains. For example, the payment or acceptance must be made to a person entitled to receive payment or acceptance, the amount paid or accepted must be the correct amount, and the instrument must be genuine and unaltered. If the payment or acceptance is incorrect, the payor or acceptor potentially will incur a loss. In the case of a note, a maker who pays the wrong person will not be discharged from his obligation to pay the correct person. If the maker pays too much, the excess comes out of his pocket. If a drawee pays the wrong person, he generally cannot charge the drawer's account; if he pays too much, he generally cannot charge the drawer's account for the excess. Indorsers who pay an instrument may make similar incorrect payments.

After paying or accepting an instrument to the wrong person, for the wrong amount, or in some other incorrect way, does the person who incorrectly paid or accepted have any recourse against the person who received the payment or acceptance? Section 3–418 addresses this critical question by providing that

> if an instrument has been paid or accepted by mistake ... the person paying or accepting may, to the extent permitted by the law governing mistake and restitution, (i) recover the payment from the person to whom or for whose benefit payment was made or (ii) in the case of acceptance, may revoke the acceptance. Section 3–418(b).

Nevertheless, this payment or acceptance is *final* and may not be asserted against a person who took the instrument in good faith and for value or who in good faith changed position in reliance on the payment or acceptance, unless there has been a breach of the implied **warranties on presentment**. Section 3–418(c). What warranties are given by presenters depends upon who is the payor or acceptor. The greatest protection is given to drawees of unaccepted drafts, while all other payors receive significantly less protection.

### DRAWEES OF UNACCEPTED DRAFTS

A drawee of an unaccepted draft (including uncertified checks), who pays or accepts in good faith, receives a

◆ **FIGURE 29-2: Liability on Transfer**

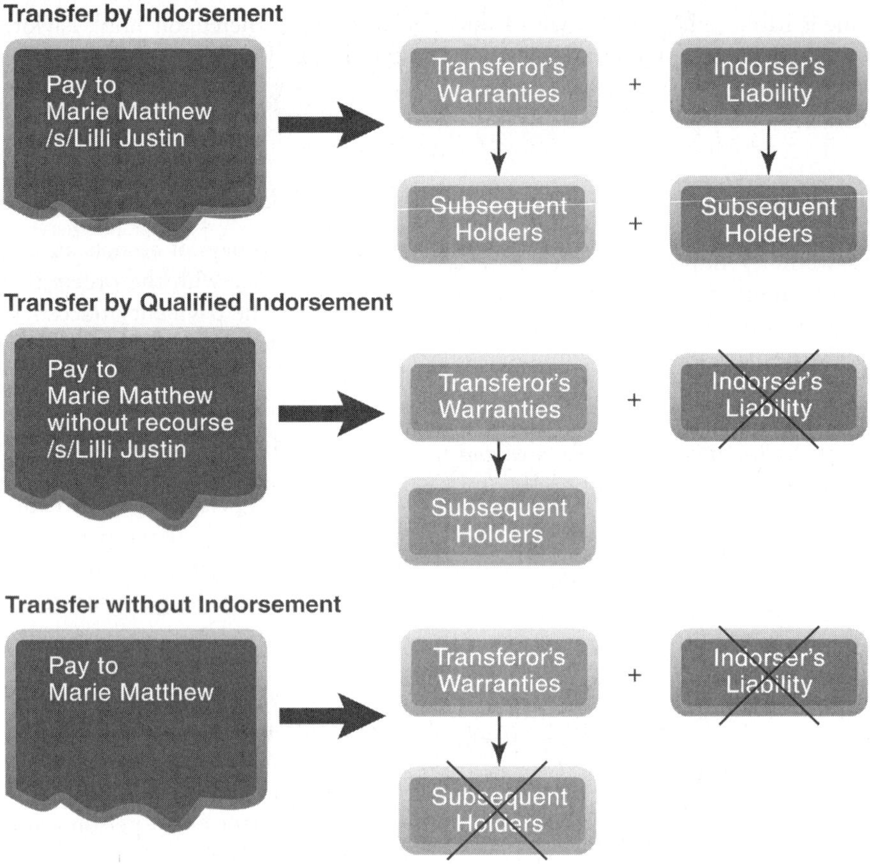


presentment warranty from the person obtaining payment or acceptance and from all prior transferors of the draft. These parties warrant to the drawee making payment or accepting the draft in good faith that (1) the warrantor is a person entitled to enforce the draft, (2) the draft has not been altered, and (3) the warrantor has no knowledge that the drawer's signature is unauthorized. Section 3–417(a).

**Entitled to Enforce** Presenters of unaccepted checks give the same warranty of entitlement to enforce to persons who pay or accept as is granted to transferees under the transferor's warranty. Thus, the presenter warrants that she is a person entitled to enforce the instrument. As explained above, this warranty extends to the genuineness and completeness of the indorser's signatures but not to the signature of the drawer or maker. It is "in effect a warranty that there are no unauthorized or missing indorsements." Section 3–417, Comment 2.

For example, if Donnese draws a check to Peter or order, and Peter's indorsement is forged, the bank does not follow Donnese's order in paying such an item and therefore cannot charge her account (except in the impostor or fictitious payee situations discussed in *Chapter 27*). The bank, however, can recover for breach of the presenter's warranty of entitlement to enforce the instrument from the person who obtained payment of the check from the bank. Although it should know the signatures of its own customers, the bank should not be expected to know the signatures of payees or other indorsers of checks; the bank, therefore, should not have to bear this loss.

**No Alteration** Presenters also give a warranty of no alteration. For example, if Dolores makes a check payable to Porter's order in the amount of $30, and the amount is fraudulently raised to $30,000, the drawee bank cannot charge to the drawer's account the $30,000 it pays out on the check. The drawee bank can charge the drawer's account only $30, because that is all the drawer ordered the drawee bank to pay. Nonetheless, because the presenter's warranty of no alteration has been breached, the drawee bank can collect the difference from all warrantors. Section 3–417(a)(2), (b).

**Genuineness of Drawer's Signature** Presenters lastly warrant that they have no knowledge that the signature of the

◆ FIGURE 29-3: **Liability Based on Warranty**

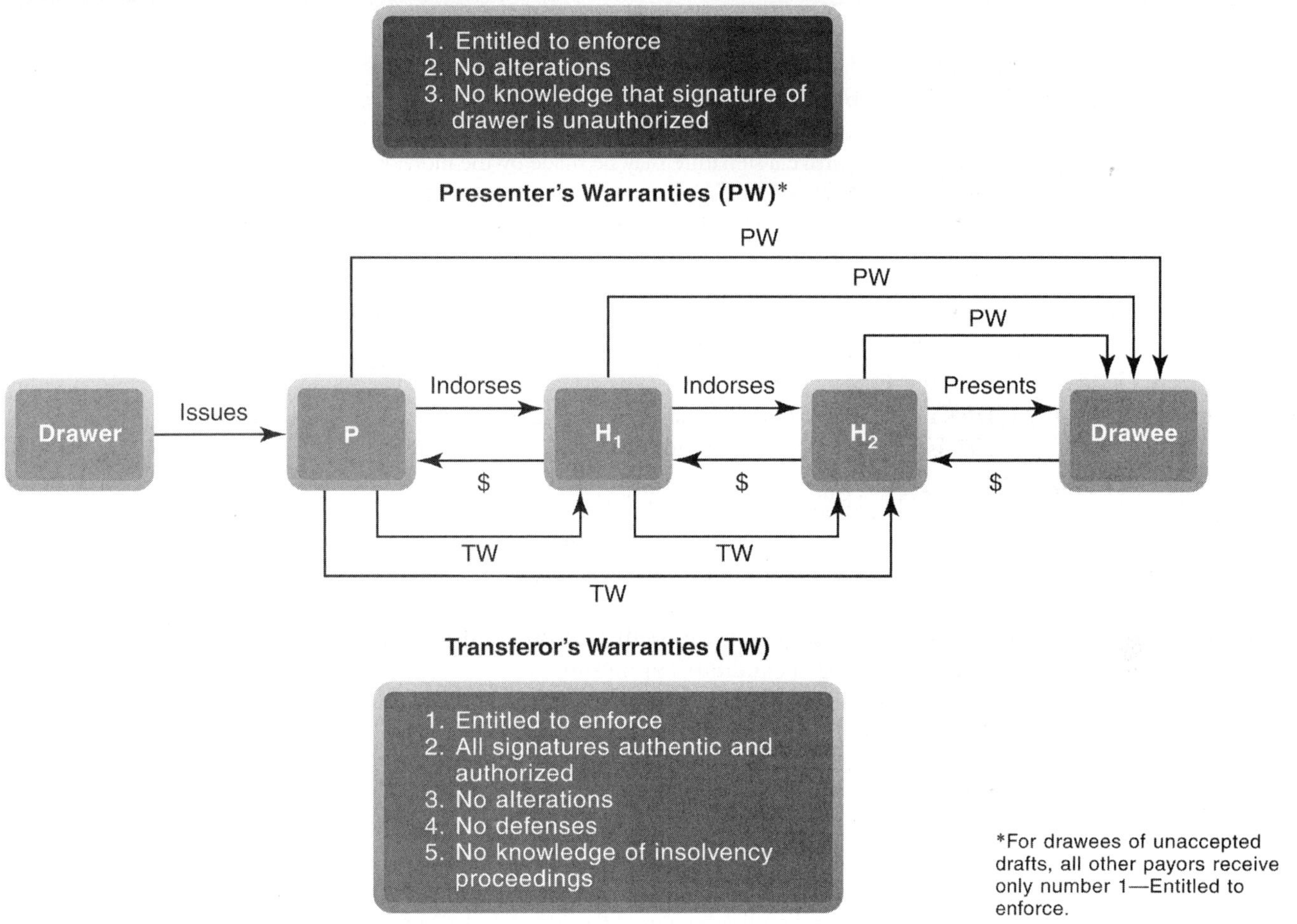


drawer is unauthorized. Thus, unless the presenter has knowledge that the drawer's signature is unauthorized, the drawee bears the risk that the drawer's signature is unauthorized.

◆ SEE FIGURE 29-3: **Liability Based on Warranty**

◆ **SEE CASES 29-2 and 29-4**

## ALL OTHER PAYORS

In all instances other than a drawee of an unaccepted draft or uncertified check, the only presentment warranty that is given is that the warrantor is a person entitled to enforce the instrument or is authorized to obtain payment on behalf of the person entitled to enforce the instrument. Section 3–417(d). This warranty is given by the person obtaining payment and prior transferors and applies to the presentment of notes and accepted drafts for the benefit of any party obliged to pay the instrument, including an indorser. It also applies to presentment of dishonored drafts if made to the drawer or an indorser.

The warranties of no alteration and authenticity of the drawer's signature are not given to all other payors. These warranties are not necessary for makers and drawers because they should know their own signature and the terms of their instruments. Similarly, indorsers have already warranted the authenticity of signatures and that the instrument was not altered. Finally, acceptors should know the terms of the instrument when they accepted it; moreover, they did receive the full presentment warranties when they as a drawee accepted the draft upon presentment.

# CHAPTER SUMMARY

## CONTRACTUAL LIABILITY

| | |
|---|---|
| **GENERAL PRINCIPLES** | **Liability on the Instrument** no person has contractual liability on an instrument unless her signature appears on it<br>**Signature** a signature may be made by the individual herself or by her authorized agent<br>• ***Authorized Signatures*** an agent who executes a negotiable instrument on behalf of his principal is not liable if the instrument is executed properly and as authorized<br>• ***Unauthorized Signatures*** include forgeries and signatures made by an agent without proper power; are generally not binding on the person whose name appears on the instrument but are binding on the unauthorized signer |
| **LIABILITY OF PRIMARY PARTIES** | **Primary Liability** absolute obligation to pay a negotiable instrument<br>**Makers** the maker guarantees that he will pay the note according to its original terms<br>**Acceptors** a drawee has no liability on the instrument until she accepts it; she then becomes primarily liable<br>• ***Acceptance*** a drawee's signed engagement to honor the instrument<br>• ***Certification*** acceptance of a check by a bank |
| **LIABILITY OF SECONDARY PARTIES** | **Secondary (Conditional) Liability** obligation to pay a negotiable instrument that is subject to conditions precedent<br>**Indorsers and Drawers** if the instrument is not paid by a primary party and if the conditions precedent to the liability of secondary parties are satisfied, indorsers and drawers are secondarily (conditionally) liable unless they have disclaimed their liability or have a valid defense to the instrument<br>**Effect of Acceptance** when a draft is accepted by a bank, the drawer and all prior indorsers are discharged from contractual liability<br>**Disclaimer by Secondary Parties** a drawer (except of a check) or indorser may disclaim liability by a qualified drawing or indorsing ("without recourse")<br>**Conditions Precedent to Liability**<br>• ***Drawer*** liability is generally only contingent upon dishonor and does not require notice<br>• ***Indorser*** liability is contingent upon dishonor and notice of dishonor |
| **LIABILITY FOR CONVERSION** | **Tort Liability** conversion occurs (1) when a drawee refuses to return a draft that was presented for acceptance, (2) when any person refuses to return an instrument after he dishonors it, or (3) when an instrument is paid on a forged indorsement |
| **TERMINATION OF LIABILITY** | **Effect of Discharge** potential liability of parties to the instrument is terminated<br>**Discharge**<br>• ***Performance***<br>• ***Tender of Payment*** for interest, costs, and attorneys' fees<br>• ***Cancellation***<br>• ***Renunciation*** |

## LIABILITY BASED ON WARRANTY

| | |
|---|---|
| **WARRANTIES ON TRANSFER** | **Parties**<br>• ***Warrantor*** any person who transfers an instrument and receives consideration gives the transferor's warranties |

- ***Beneficiary*** if the transfer is by delivery, the warranties run only to the immediate transferee; if the transfer is by indorsement, the warranties run to any subsequent holder who takes the instrument in good faith

**Warranties**
- ***Entitled to Enforce***
- ***All Signatures Are Authentic and Authorized***
- ***No Alteration***
- ***No Defenses***
- ***No Knowledge of Insolvency***

---

**WARRANTIES ON PRESENTMENT**

**Parties**
- ***Warrantor*** all people who obtain payment or acceptance of an instrument as well as all prior transferors give the presenter's warranties
- ***Beneficiary*** the presenter's warranties run to any person who in good faith pays or accepts an instrument

**Warranties**
- ***Entitled to Enforce***
- ***No Alteration***
- ***Genuineness of Drawer's Signature***

# CASES

## CASE 29-1

Signature

## COHEN v. DISNER

California Court of Appeal, Second Appellate District, 1995
36 Cal.App.4th 855, 42 Cal.Rptr.2d 782, 27 U.C.C. Rep.Serv.2d 540

**Ortega, J.**

Civil Code §1719, subdivision (a) provides in part that any person who draws a check that is dishonored due to insufficient funds shall be liable to the payee for the amount owing upon the check and treble damages of at least $100, not to exceed $500.

In this §1719 action, we conclude the [drawer] of a dishonored check may raise defenses under the Uniform Commercial Code ([UCC Revised 3] "UCC") to establish that the check is unenforceable. We affirm the summary judgment for defendants.

### Background

Attorney Eliot Disner was sued after serving as an intermediary for his clients, Irvin and Dorothea Kipnes, by tendering a check for a portion of the $961,000 settlement the Kipneses owed to Sidney and Lynne Cohen.

The Kipneses had made an initial $300,000 settlement payment to the Cohens on March 5, 1993, and their second payment of $100,100 was due on March 9, 1993. Under the settlement agreement, a missed payment would entitle the Cohens to enter judgment against the Kipneses for $1.3 million less any partial payments.

The Kipneses gave Disner checks totalling $100,100 which he deposited into his professional corporation's client trust account on March 9, 1993. After confirming with the Kipneses' bank that their account held sufficient funds, Disner wrote and delivered a trust account check for $100,100 to the Cohens' attorney, with this note: "Please find $100,100 in settlement (partial) of *Cohen v. Kipnes*, et al[.] Per our agreement, delivery to you constitutes timely delivery to your clients." Also typed on the check was a notation identifying the underlying lawsuit.

Without Disner's knowledge, the Kipneses stopped payment on their checks to him, leaving him with insufficient funds in the trust account to cover the check to the Cohens. The trust account check bounced; the Kipneses declared bankruptcy; and the Cohens served Disner and his professional corporation (jointly, Disner) with the statutory demand for payment under §1719. The Cohens sought the amount written on the check plus the $500 statutory penalty authorized under §1719.

Both sides moved for summary judgment. The trial court denied the Cohens' motion and entered summary judgment for Disner, reasoning he is not liable on the check because he was a mere conduit or agent for transferring money from the Kipneses to the Cohens. The Cohens appealed from the judgment.

### Discussion

* * *

The Cohens do not dispute on appeal that Disner was a mere conduit or agent for transferring funds. They contend his representative status and motivations for transferring the funds are irrelevant. According to the Cohens, §1719 imposes strict liability against the [drawer] of a check drawn on an account lacking sufficient funds.

Their contention of strict liability is based on legislative omission. While the UCC permits the [drawer] of a dishonored check to prove that he signed in a representative capacity and that the holder in due course took the check with notice of the representative's lack of liability (UCC, §3–402, subd. (b)(2), sometimes hereinafter referred to as the "representative capacity" defense), §1719 does not mention this defense.

* * *

The UCC recognizes the complexity of commercial transactions beyond the few good faith disputes mentioned in §1719. For example, as against a holder in due course, the UCC permits the [drawer] to assert defenses of infancy, duress, lack of legal capacity, illegality of the contract, fraud in the inducement, or discharge in bankruptcy proceedings. (UCC, §3–305 (a)). If we were to accept the Cohens' position that §1719 is a strict liability statute (with the sole exception of the stop payment defense), we would create a conflict with the preexisting law of negotiable instruments.

* * *

Nothing in §1719 affirmatively supports the Cohens' contention that the "representative capacity" and other UCC defenses were written out of §1719. On the contrary, the express language of subdivision (a) compels us to the opposite conclusion.

* * *

By acknowledging there must be an enforceable obligation to pay, §1719 echoes the UCC, which precludes recovery where the payee has no "right to enforce the obligation of a party to pay an instrument." (UCC, §3–305, subd. (a).) If the [drawer] has no enforceable obligation to pay a dishonored check, there is no amount "owing upon that check" under the plain language of §1719.

* * *

We reject the Cohens' assertion in their reply brief that the "representative capacity" defense is inapplicable here because the conditions of UCC §3–402, subdivision (c) have not been met. That subdivision provides: "If a representative signs the name of the representative as drawer of a check without indication of the representative status and the check is payable from an account of the representative person who is identified on the check, the signer is not liable on the check if the signature is an authorized signature of the represented person."

According to the official code comment on that subdivision: "Subdivision (c) is directed at the check cases. It states that if the check identifies the represented person, the agent who signs on the signature line does not have to indicate agency status. Virtually all checks used today are in personalized form which identify the person on whose account the check is drawn. In this case, nobody is deceived into thinking that the person signing the check is meant to be liable * * *." [Citation.]

As we understand it, the Cohens' assertion is that because UCC §3–402, subdivision (b)(2)'s "representative capacity" defense is "subject to" subdivision (c), Disner may not be relieved of liability unless he fulfills the requirements of the subdivision (c) defense. We do not read subdivisions (b)(2) and (c) in that restrictive manner. In our view, any finding of liability under UCC §3–402, subdivision (b)(2) is subject to subdivision (c)'s additional exception that the representative is not liable if he signed his name on a personalized check identifying the account of the represented person. Subdivision (c) expands rather than contracts the representative's defenses.

We conclude that §1719, by its clear and unambiguous language, permits the [drawer] of a dishonored check to prove he has no enforceable obligation to pay the check.

* * *

### Disposition

We affirm the summary judgment for defendants. Defendants are awarded costs on appeal.

CASE 29-2

## Acceptance/Presentment/Dishonor/Warranties
## MESSING v. BANK OF AMERICA, N.A.

Court of Appeals of Maryland, 2003
373 Md. 672, 821 A.2d 22, 50 U.C.C. Rep.Serv.2d 1
http://www.securitymanagement.com/archive/library/Messing_BankAmerica0703.pdf

**Harrell, J.**

**I**

The case * * * involves a bank check. A check is defined as a draft payable on demand and drawn on a bank. [UCC] §3–204. * * *

The case * * * arises from Petitioner's irritation with the Bank of America's Thumbprint Signature Program. Under the Thumbprint Signature Program, a bank requests non-customer presenters of checks over the counter to place an "inkless" thumbprint or fingerprint on the face of the check as part of the identification process. The program was developed, as the Court of Special Appeals informs us in its opinion in this case, by the American Bankers Association, working with the Federal Deposit Insurance Corporation (FDIC), the Federal Reserve Banks, the Office of the Comptroller of the Currency, the Federal Bureau of Investigation, and other law enforcement officials and banking trade associations across the country in response to rising instances of check fraud. [Citation.] It is undisputed that the Bank of America's Thumbprint Signature Program uses an inkless fingerprinting device that leaves no ink stains or residue.

**II**

At some point in time prior to 3 August 2000, Petitioner, as a holder, came into possession of a check in the amount of Nine Hundred Seventy-Six Dollars ($976.00) (the check) from Toyson J. Burruss, the drawer, doing business as Prestige Auto Detail Center. Instead of depositing the check into his account at his own bank, Petitioner elected to present the check for payment at a branch of Mr. Burruss' bank, Bank of America, the drawee. On 3 August 2000, Petitioner approached a teller at Bank of America's 10 Light Street Banking Center in Baltimore City and asked to cash the check. The teller, by use of a computer, confirmed the availability of funds on deposit, and placed the check into the computer's printer slot. The computer stamped certain data on the back of the check, including the time, date, amount of the check, account number, and teller number. The computer also effected a hold on the amount of $976.00 in the customer's account. The teller gave the check back to the Petitioner, who indorsed it. The teller then asked for Petitioner's identification. Petitioner presented his driver's license and a major credit card. The teller took the indorsed check from Petitioner and manually inscribed the driver's license information and certain credit card information on the back of the check.

At some point during the transaction, the teller counted out $976.00 in cash from her drawer in anticipation of completing the transaction. She asked if the Petitioner was a customer of Bank of America. The Petitioner stated that he was not. The teller returned the check to Petitioner and requested, consistent with bank policy when cashing checks for non-customers, that Petitioner place his thumbprint on the check. Petitioner refused and the teller informed him that she would be unable to complete the transaction without his thumbprint.

* * * After some additional exchanges, Petitioner left the bank with the check in his possession. The branch manager advised the teller that Petitioner had left the bank with his check. In response, the teller released the hold on the customer's funds, voided the transaction in the computer, and placed the cash back in her teller drawer.

Rather than take the check to his own bank and deposit it there, or returning it to Burruss, the drawer, as dishonored and demanding payment, Petitioner, two months later, on 10 October 2000, filed a declaratory judgment action against Bank of America (the Bank) in the Circuit Court for Baltimore City. Petitioner claimed that the Bank had violated the Maryland Uniform Commercial Code (UCC) and had violated his personal privacy when the teller asked Petitioner to place an "inkless" thumbprint on the face of the check at issue. * * *

On 15 November 2000, the Bank filed * * * for Summary Judgment. Petitioner opposed the Bank's Motion and filed a "cross" Motion for Summary Judgment. After the Circuit Court heard oral arguments on the pending motions, it * * * entered summary judgment in favor of the Bank, dismissing the Complaint with prejudice.

Petitioner appealed on 17 January 2001. The Court of Special Appeals concluded that the Circuit Court's decision in favor of the Bank was legally correct, * * *.

Petitioner petitioned this Court for a writ of certiorari. On 10 June 2002, we granted the petition. [Citation.]

* * *

### Acceptance under §3–409(a).

* * *

Under the UCC, a check is simply an order to the drawee bank to pay the sum stated, signed by the makers and payable on demand. Receipt of a check does not, however, give the recipient a right against the bank. The recipient may present the check, but if the drawee bank refuses to honor it, the recipient has no recourse against the drawee.

* * *

Absent a special relationship, a non-customer has no claim against a bank for refusing to honor a presented check. [Citation.] * * * It is also well settled that a check does not operate as an assignment of funds on deposit, [citation], and the bank only becomes obligated upon acceptance of the instrument. * * *

Once a bank accepts a check, under §3–409, it is obliged to pay on the check under §3–413. Thus, the relevant question in terms of any rights Petitioner had against the Bank turns not on the reasonableness of the thumbprint identification, but rather upon whether the Bank accepted the check when presented as defined by §3–409. As will be seen *infra*, the question of the thumbprint identification is relevant only to the issue of whether the Bank's refusal to pay the instrument constituted dishonor under §3–502, a determination which has no impact in terms of any duty allegedly owed by the Bank to the Petitioner.

Respondent Bank of America argues that the intermediate appellate court correctly found that it did not "accept" the check as that term is defined in §3–409(a). [Citation.] We agree. The mere fact that the teller's computer printed information on the back of the check does not, as Petitioner contends, amount by itself to an acceptance. * * *

The statute [UCC] clearly states that acceptance becomes effective when the presenter is notified of that fact. The facts demonstrate that at no time did the teller notify Petitioner that the Bank would pay on the check. Rather, the facts show that:

> The check was given back to [Petitioner] by the teller so that he could put his thumbprint signature on it, not to notify or give him rights on the purported acceptance. After appellant declined to put his thumbprint signature on the check, he was informed by both the teller and the branch manager that it was against bank policy to honor the check without a thumbprint signature. Indignant, [Petitioner] walked out of the bank with the check.

As the intermediate appellate court correctly pointed out, the negotiation of the check is in the nature of a contract, and there can be no agreement until notice of acceptance is received. [Citation.] As a result, there was never acceptance as defined by §3–409(a), and thus the Bank, pursuant to §3–408 never was obligated to pay the check under §3–413(a). Thus, the answer to Petitioner's second question presented is "no."

* * *

### "Reasonable Identification" under §3–501(b)(2)(ii) and "Dishonor" under §3–502

We now turn to the issue of whether the Bank's refusal to accept the check as presented constituted dishonor under §3–501 and §3–502 as Petitioner contends. Petitioner's argument that Bank of America dishonored the check under §3–502(d) fails because that section applies to dishonor of an accepted draft. We have determined * * * that Bank of America never accepted the draft. Nevertheless, the question remains as to whether Bank of America dishonored the draft under §3–502(b), * * *.

The question is whether requiring a thumbprint constitutes a request for "reasonable identification" under §3–501(b)(2)(ii). If it is "reasonable," then under §3–501(b)(3)(ii) the refusal of the Bank to accept the check from Petitioner did not constitute dishonor. If, however, requiring a thumbprint is not "reasonable" under §3–501(b)(2)(ii), then the refusal to accept the check may constitute dishonor under §3–502(b)(2). The issue of dishonor is arguably relevant because Petitioner has no cause of action against any party, including the drawer, until the check is dishonored. [Citation.]

Respondent Bank of America argues that its relationship with its customer is contractual, [citation] and that in this case, its contract with its customer, the drawer, authorizes the Bank's use of the Thumbprint Signature Program as a reasonable form of identification. * * *

According to Respondent, this contractual agreement allowed it to refuse to accept the check, without dishonoring it pursuant to §3–501(b)(3)(ii), because the Bank's refusal was based upon the presentment failing to comply with "an agreement of the parties." The intermediate appellate court agreed. [Citation.] We, however, do not.

The reason why the Bank's contract with its customer is not controlling on the issue of the reasonableness of requiring a thumbprint as identification is because the terms of §3–501 are not modified by the terms of that contract. The terms of §3–501(b) require an "agreement of the parties." The term "parties" does not refer to the parties of the Deposit Agreement, but rather, according to §3–103(a), refers to the parties to an instrument. While Petitioner is a party to the instrument, he is not a party to the Deposit Agreement, nor may he be deemed properly a third party beneficiary thereof. To be effective against the Petitioner, Messing, as the party entitled to enforce the instrument, would have to have been a party to the agreement. §3–117. Thus, while the Deposit Agreement protects the Bank from a suit for wrongful dishonor brought by its customer, the drawer, as a result of the Bank's potential dishonor of the check because the Bank's demand for a thumbprint was not met, [§4–402], the contract has no impact on the determination of the "reasonableness" of the requirement for purposes of §3–501(b), and subsequently whether the instrument was dishonored for purposes of §3–502(b)(2). In other words, the Bank and its customer cannot through their contract define the meaning of the term "reasonable" and impose it upon parties who are not in privity with that contract. Whether requiring a thumbprint constitutes "reasonable identification" within the meaning of §3–501(b)(2)(ii) is therefore a broader policy consideration, and not, as argued in this case, simply a matter of contract. * * * This also means that the Bank cannot rely on the contract as a defense against the Petitioner, on the facts presented here, to say that it did not dishonor the check.

Petitioner, as noted, argues that requiring a thumbprint violates his privacy, and further argues that a thumbprint is not a reasonable form of identification because it does not prove contemporaneously the identity of an over the counter presenter at the time presentment is made. According to Petitioner, the purpose of requiring "reasonable identification" is to allow the drawee bank to determine that the presenter is the proper person to be paid on the instrument. Because a thumbprint does not provide that information at the time presentment and payment are made, Petitioner argues that a thumbprint cannot be read to fall within the meaning of "reasonable identification" for the purposes of §3–501(b)(2)(ii).

Bank of America argues that the requirement of a thumbprint has been upheld, in other non-criminal circumstances, not to be an invasion of privacy, and is a reasonable and necessary industry response to the growing problem of check fraud. The intermediate appellate court agreed, pointing out that the form of identification was not defined by the statute, but that the Code itself recognized a thumbprint as a form of signature, §1–201(39), and observing that requiring thumbprint or fingerprint identification has been found to be reasonable and not to violate privacy rights in a number of non-criminal contexts. * * *

More compelling in terms of determining the issue of "reasonableness" is the reasoning of the intermediate appellate court in rejecting Petitioner's argument that §3–501(b)(2)(ii) implicitly contains a present tense temporal element, stating:

> We agree with [Petitioner] that a thumbprint cannot be used, in most instances, to confirm the identity of a non-account checkholder at the time that the check is presented for cashing, as his or her thumbprint is usually not on file with the drawee at that time. We disagree, however, with [Petitioner's] conclusion that a thumbprint signature is therefore not "reasonable identification" for purposes of §3–501(b)(2).

Nowhere does the language of §3–501(b)(2) suggest that "reasonable identification" is limited to information [Respondent] can authenticate at the time presentment is made. Rather, all that is required is that the "person making presentment must * * * give reasonable identification." §3–501(b)(2). While providing a thumbprint signature does not necessarily confirm identification of the checkholder at presentment—unless of course the drawee bank has a duplicate thumbprint signature on file—it does assist in the identification of the checkholder should the check later prove to be bad. It therefore serves as a powerful deterrent to those who might otherwise attempt to pass a bad check. That one method provides identification at the time of presentment and the other identification after the check may have been honored, does not prevent the latter from being "reasonable identification" for purposes of §3–501(b)(2).

[Citation.] We agree, and find this conclusion to be compelled, in fact, by our State's Commercial Law Article.

The reason has to do with warranties. The transfer of a check for consideration creates both transfer warranties (§3–416 (a)–(c)) and presentment warranties (§3–417(a)–(e)) which cannot be disclaimed. The warranties include, for example, that the payee is entitled to enforce the instrument and that there are no alterations on the check. The risk to banks is that these contractual warranties may be breached, exposing the accepting bank to a loss because the bank paid over the counter on an item which was not properly payable. *See* §4–401. [Citation.] In such an event, the bank would then incur the expense to find the presenter, to demand repayment, and legal expenses to pursue the presenter for breach of his warranties.

In short, when a bank cashes a check over the counter, it assumes the risk that it may suffer losses for counterfeit documents, forged indorsements, or forged or altered checks. Nothing in the Commercial Law Article forces a bank to assume such risks. [Citation]; §3–408. To the extent that banks are willing to cash checks over the counter, with reasonable identification, such willingness expands and facilitates the commercial activities within the State. * * *

Because the reduction of risk promotes the expansion of commercial practices, * * * we conclude that a bank's requirement of a thumbprint placed upon a check presented over the counter by a non-customer is reasonable. [Citations.] As the intermediate appellate court well documented, the Thumbprint Program is part of an industry wide response to the growing threat of check fraud. [Citation.] Prohibiting banks from taking reasonable steps to protect themselves from losses could result in banks refusing to cash checks of non-customers presented over the counter at all, a result which would be counter to the direction of [the UCC].

As a result of this conclusion, Bank of America in the present case did not dishonor the check when it refused to accept it over the counter. Under §3–501(b)(3)(ii), Bank of America "refused payment or acceptance for failure of the presentment to comply with * * * other applicable law or rule." The rule not complied with by the Petitioner-presenter was §3–502(b)(2)(ii), in that he refused to give what we have determined to be reasonable identification. Therefore, there was no dishonor of the check by Bank of America's refusal to accept it. The answer to Petitioner's third question is therefore "no," as is the answer to Petitioner's first question, though our reasoning differs somewhat from that of the Court of Special Appeals.

* * *

Judgment of the Court of Special Appeals affirmed.

CASE 29-3

## Drawer's Liability
## DAVIS v. WATSON BROTHERS PLUMBING, INC.

Court of Civil Appeals of Texas, Dallas, 1981
615 S. W.2d 844
http://scholar.google.com/scholar_case?case=16807682647541897506&hl=en&as_sdt=2&as_vis=1&oi=scholarr

**Akin, J.**

Defendant was the drawer of a check for $152.38 payable to its employee Arnett Lee. Lee, in turn, endorsed the check over to plaintiff, who operated a liquor store. After Lee endorsed the check to plaintiff and after plaintiff had placed cash on the counter, Lee stated that he wanted to buy a six-pack of beer and a bottle of scotch. When plaintiff turned to obtain the requested merchandise, a thief grabbed approximately $110.00 of the $150.88 ($152.38 less a $1.50 check cashing fee) for which plaintiff cashed the check. Lee took the remainder of the $150.88, approximately $40.88, and notified defendant of the theft. Defendant issued Lee a second check for $152.38 and stopped payment on the first check. Plaintiff sued defendant based on the dishonor of the first check.

The county court rendered judgment for plaintiff for the $40.88 that Lee actually received from plaintiff [after the robbery]. Plaintiff, as appellant, asserts that since he proved that he was the holder of the check and since defendant failed to raise any valid defenses, defendant was liable to him for the full face value of the check, $152.38. We agree.

"Holder" is defined in *Tex. Bus. & Com. Code Ann.* [UCC] §1–201(20) as: "[A] *person who is in possession of* a document of title or *an instrument* or an investment security drawn, issued or *indorsed to him* or to his order or to bearer or *in blank*." Under the undisputed facts, Lee, the payee endorsed the check in blank to plaintiff, who is now in possession of the check. Thus, as a matter of law, plaintiff is a "holder" under the code [UCC] §3–413(2), [Revised §3–414(b)] which sets forth the rights of a holder, [and] provides, in pertinent part, that: "The drawer engages that upon dishonor of the draft * * * *he will pay the amount of the draft to the holder* or to any indorser who takes it up." Thus, the defendant is liable to the holder of the dishonored check unless the defendant has raised a valid defense against the holder.

The rights of a holder not in due course are subject to the defenses specified in §3–306, [Revised §3–305] which provides:

> Unless he has the rights of a holder in due course any person takes the instrument subject to:
>
> (1) all valid claims to it on the part of any person; and
> (2) all defenses of any party which would be available in an action on a simple contract; and
> (3) *the defenses of want or failure of consideration*, nonperformance of any condition precedent, nondelivery, or delivery for a special purpose (Section 3–408); and
> (4) the defense that he or a person through whom he holds the instrument acquired it by theft, or that payment or satisfaction to such holder would be inconsistent with the terms of a restrictive indorsement. *The claim of any third person to the instrument is not otherwise available as a defense to any party liable thereon unless the third person himself defends the action for such party.*

Defendant here asserts that it may raise want or failure of consideration in the transaction between *plaintiff and Lee*, its payee, as a defense to plaintiff's enforcement of the instrument against it. We disagree.

[UCC] §3–408 [Revised §§3–303(b), 3–305] provides, in pertinent part that: "Want or failure of consideration is a defense against any person not having the rights of a holder in due course * * *." The comments to §3–408 provide that: "'Consideration' refers to what the obligor has received for his obligation, and is important only on the question of whether his obligation can be enforced against him." Thus, any holder can enforce the obligation of a draft against the drawer regardless of whether the holder gave anything in consideration for the draft to his endorser. The drawer can assert as a defense to enforcement of the draft want or failure of consideration only to the extent such defense lies against the payee of the draft. Thus, the fact that a holder remote to the drawer's transaction with the payee did not give full consideration for the draft is not a defense available to the drawer. [Citation.]

This is true because the drawer's sole obligation on the check is to pay it according to its tenor. Consequently, the fact that the transfer of the check by the payee to the transferee is without consideration is immaterial to the drawer's obligation and is not a defense available to the drawer against the holder. A similar conclusion was reached in [citation]. In that case the court held that a defendant maker was not the proper party to raise as a defense that the transfer of the note to the holder was void. Consequently, that court concluded that the maker could not assert the defense that the equitable ownership of the instrument was in someone other than the holder-plaintiff.

The rationale of this, and other decisions, reaching the same conclusion, is that the maker or drawer of an instrument admittedly owes the money and he should not be permitted to bring into the controversy equities of parties with which he has no connection. [Citation.] Furthermore, if the drawer or maker is permitted to assert the defense of another party such as the payee, the judgment on that issue would not be binding on the third party claimant who is not a party to the suit. [Citation.]

Because defendant here may not assert want or failure of consideration in the transaction between plaintiff and Lee, and because defendant has asserted no other defense against plaintiff, plaintiff is entitled to recover the full face value of the check under §3–413(b) [Revised §3–414] of the Texas Uniform Commercial Code. Accordingly, the judgment of the trial court is reversed and judgment is rendered that plaintiff recover judgment against defendant for $152.38 and all costs.

CASE 29-4

## Warranties on Presentment
## TRAVELERS INDEMNITY CO. v. STEDMAN

United States District Court, E.D. Pa., 1995
395 F.Supp. 742

**Reed, J.**

Currently pending before this court is the motion by defendant Main Line Federal Savings Bank ("Main Line") for judgment on the pleadings * * * or for partial summary judgment * * * on the crossclaim filed by codefendant Merrill, Lynch, Pierce, Fenner & Smith ("Merrill Lynch"). In dispute is the ultimate liability for pecuniary losses incurred by plaintiff The Travelers Indemnity Company ("Travelers") when defendants Main Line, as depositary and collecting bank, and Merrill Lynch, as drawee bank, honored seventeen checks unlawfully drawn on the account of the American Lung Association by codefendant Nancy Stedman. * * * In addition, Merrill Lynch advanced a claim for breach of presentment warranties against Main Line pursuant to [UCC] §3–417. The instant motion by Main Line seeks judgment in its favor with regard to twelve of the seventeen checks. Merrill Lynch concedes that Main Line is entitled to judgment on the pleadings with regard to the six checks that were neither deposited nor cashed at Main Line, but Merrill Lynch argues that Main Line is not entitled to judgment on the pleadings with regard to the other six checks at issue.

### Factual Background and Procedural History

In November 1988, plaintiff Travelers issued a comprehensive crime insurance policy to the American Lung Association (the "ALA"), thereby insuring the ALA against financial losses due to employee fraud or dishonesty. Shortly thereafter, in October of 1989, the ALA hired defendant Nancy Stedman as the Director of Bureau Affairs. In her capacity as Director of Bureau Affairs, Stedman possessed the authority to draw checks on a Working Capital Management Account (the "WCMA"), an account established by the ALA with defendant Merrill Lynch for the sole purpose of paying the ALA's operating expenses. * * *

From approximately August 12, 1990 to March 13, 1992, Stedman embarked on a scheme of defalcation, misappropriating $129,624.23 of ALA funds from the WCMA. The ALA finally discovered the scheme in late April, 1992, and subsequently received compensation for its losses under the terms of its insurance policy with Travelers. Asserting its rights as the subrogee of the ALA, Travelers filed this civil action on July 9, 1993 against defendants Nancy Stedman, Merrill Lynch, and Main Line.

Merrill Lynch and Main Line agree that the seventeen checks misappropriated by Stedman can be divided into three groups based on the combination of forged or unauthorized [drawer] and payee signatures. Group One is comprised of six checks totalling $5,343.00, each bearing a forged cosignatory's signature, or [co-drawer's] signature, and forged indorsements. Main Line and Merrill Lynch agree that the Group One checks were neither deposited at nor cashed by defendant Main Line. * * * Group Two is comprised of six checks totalling $85,241.01, each payable to either "American Lung Association" or "American Lung Association/Stedman." Each Group Two check bore two forged [drawer's] signatures and at least one forged indorsement. All Group Two checks were accepted for deposit into the personal checking account of Stedman by Main Line, and subsequently presented to and honored by Merrill Lynch. Finally, Group Three is comprised of five checks totalling $39,030.22, each payable to "American Lung Association" and bearing only a forged indorsement. * * * The Group Three checks are not the subject of the instant motion.

### Discussion

* * *

***Loss Allocation under the Uniform Commercial Code***

Liability, or loss allocation, under the Uniform Commercial Code ("UCC") for honoring negotiable instruments containing forged or unauthorized signatures is governed by whether the forgery at issue is that of a [drawer's] signature or of the indorsement of a payee or holder. [Citations.] Generally, a drawee bank is strictly liable to its customer, the drawer, for payment over either a forged [drawer's] signature or a forged indorsement. [Citation.] * * * Moreover, when a drawee bank honors an instrument bearing a forged [drawer's] signature, that payment is final in favor of a holder in due course or one who has in good faith changed his position in reliance on the payment. UCC §3–418. As a result, where the only forgery is of the signature of the [drawer] and not of the indorsement, the negligence of a holder in taking the forged instrument will not allow a drawee bank to shift liability to a prior collecting or depositary bank, unless such negligence amounts to a lack of good faith, or unless the payee bank returns the instrument or sends notice of dishonor within the limited time provided by §4–301 of the UCC. [Citation.] But where the only forged signature is an indorsement, the drawee normally may pass liability back through the collection chain to the depositary or collecting bank, or to the forger herself if she is available, by a claim for breach of presentment warranties. [Citation.]

Regrettably, the drafters of the UCC failed to address the allocation of liability for honoring instruments containing *both* a forged [drawer's] signature and a forged indorsement, so called "double forgeries." [Citation.] Nor have the state courts of Pennsylvania addressed this issue. Based on a thorough examination of the rationales behind the allocation of liability in "single forgery" cases, however, the Court of Appeals for the Fifth Circuit concluded that double forgeries should be treated as though only containing forged [drawer's] signatures. [Citations.] * * * Therefore, this court concludes that under Pennsylvania's adoption of the UCC, checks containing both a forged [drawer's] signature and a forged indorsement should be treated, for loss allocation purposes, as though bearing only a forged [drawer's] signature. As a result, the negligence of a holder in taking a double forgery will not allow a drawee bank, such as Merrill Lynch, to shift liability to a prior collecting or depositary bank, such as Main Line, unless such negligence amounts to a lack of good faith, or unless the drawee bank returns the instrument or sends notice of dishonor within the limited time provided by §4–301 of the Pennsylvania adoption of the UCC. [Citation.]

* * *

***Breach of Presentment Warranties***

The final count of the crossclaim by Merrill Lynch is a claim for an alleged breach of presentment warranties under [UCC] §3–417. As the court illustrated above, the loss allocation rules of the UCC permit a payee bank to shift liability to a depositary bank via a claim for breach of presentment warranties if, and only if, the checks at issue contain only forged indorsements. Should the checks in fact also bear forged [drawer's] signatures, then a depositary or collecting bank is immunized from liability for having honored such checks unless the depositary or collecting bank failed to meet the requirements of the final payment rule codified in [UCC] §3–418. [Citation.] Moreover, checks bearing dual forgeries are treated as though containing only forged [drawer's] signatures. Thus, because it is uncontested that all Group Two checks bear forged [drawer's] signatures, liability for honoring these checks may only be assessed under the loss allocation rules relevant to checks bearing only forged [drawer's] signatures. See discussion supra part II.B. In other words, Merrill Lynch is precluded by the operation of law from asserting a claim for breach of presentment warranties under the loss allocation scheme of the UCC. As a matter of law, therefore, Merrill Lynch can prove no set of facts in support of this claim that would entitle it to the relief demanded, and this court will accordingly also grant judgment on the pleadings to Main Line on the claim for breach of presentment warranties as it relates to the Group Two checks.

## QUESTIONS

1. Discuss contractual liability, warranty liability, and liability for conversion.
2. Discuss the liability of makers, acceptors, drawees, drawers, indorsers, and accommodation parties.
3. Discuss the conditions precedent to the liability of secondary parties.
4. Discuss the methods by which liability on an instrument may be terminated.
5. Compare the warranties on transfer with the warranties on presentment.

# PROBLEMS

1. $900.00 Smalltown, Illinois
Maker, November 15, 2011

The undersigned promises to pay to the order of John Doe Nine Hundred Dollars with interest from date of note. Payment to be made in five monthly installments of One Hundred Eighty Dollars, plus accrued interest beginning on December 1, 2011. In the event of default in the payment of any installment or interest on installment date, the holder of this instrument may declare the entire obligation due and owing and proceed forthwith to collect the balance due on this instrument.

(Signed) Acton, agent

On December 18, 2011, no payment having been made on the note, Doe indorsed and delivered the instrument to Todd to secure a preexisting debt in the amount of $800.

On January 18, 2012, Todd brought an action against Acton and Phi Corporation, Acton's principal, to collect the full amount of the instrument with interest. Acton defended on the basis that he signed the instrument in a representative capacity and that Doe had failed to deliver the consideration for which the instrument had been issued. Phi Corporation defended on the basis that it did not sign the instrument and that its name does not appear on the instrument.

For what amount, if any, are Acton and Phi Corporation liable?

2. While employed as a night security guard at the place of business of A. B. Cate Trucking Company, Fred Fain observed that the office safe had been left unlocked. It contained fifty payroll checks, which were ready for distribution to employees two days later. The checks had all been signed by the sole proprietor, Cate. Fain removed five of these checks and two blank checks that were also in the safe. Fain forged the indorsements of the payees on the five payroll checks and cashed them at local supermarkets. He then filled out one of the blank checks, making himself payee, and forged Cate's signature as drawer. After cashing that check at a supermarket, Fain departed by airplane to Jamaica. The six checks were promptly presented for payment to the drawee bank, the Bank of Emanon, which paid each one. Shortly thereafter, Cate learned about the missing payroll checks and forgeries and demanded that the Bank of Emanon credit his account with the amount of the six checks.

Must the Bank comply with Cate's demand? What are the Bank's rights, if any, against the supermarkets? You may assume that the supermarkets cashed all of the checks in good faith.

3. A negotiable promissory note executed and delivered by B to C passed in due course and was indorsed in blank by C, D, E, and F. G, the present holder, strikes out D's indorsement. What is the liability of D on her indorsement?

4. On June 15, 2006, Justin, for consideration, executed a negotiable promissory note for $10,000, payable to Reneé on or before June 15, 2011. Justin subsequently suffered financial reverses. In January 2011, Reneé on two occasions told Justin that she knew he was having a difficult time; that she, Reneé, did not need the money; and that the debt should be considered completely canceled with no other act or payment being required. These conversations were witnessed by three persons, including Larry. On March 15, 2011, Reneé changed her mind and indorsed the note for value to Larry. The note was not paid by June 15, 2011, and Larry sued Justin for the amount of the note. Justin defended upon the ground that Reneé had canceled the debt and renounced all rights against Justin and that Larry had notice of this fact. Has the debt been properly canceled? Explain.

5. Tate and Fitch were longtime friends. Tate was a man of considerable means; Fitch had encountered financial difficulties. To bolster his failing business, Fitch desired to borrow $6,000 from Farmers Bank of Erehwon. To accomplish this, he persuaded Tate to aid him in the making of a promissory note by which it would appear that Tate had the responsibility of maker, but with Fitch's agreeing to pay the instrument when due. Accordingly, they executed the following instrument:

December 1, 2011

Thirty days after date and for value received, I promise to pay to the order of Frank Fitch the sum of $6,600.

/s/ Timothy Tate

On the back of the note, Fitch indorsed, "Pay to the order of Farmers Bank of Erehwon /s/ Frank Fitch" and delivered it to the bank in exchange for $6,000.

**(a)** If the note is not paid at maturity, may the bank, without first demanding payment by Fitch, recover in an action on the note against Tate?

**(b)** If Tate voluntarily pays the note to the bank, may he then recover on the note against Fitch, who appears as an indorser?

6. Alpha orally appointed Omega as his agent to find and purchase for him a 1930 Dodge automobile in good condition, and Omega located such a car. Its owner, Roe, agreed to sell and deliver the car on January 10, 2011, for $9,000. To evidence the purchase price, Omega mailed to Roe the following instrument:

December 1, 2010 $9,000.00

We promise to pay to the order of bearer Nine Thousand Dollars with interest from date of this instrument on or before January 10, 2011. This note is given in consideration of John Roe's transferring title to and possession of his 1930 Dodge automobile.

(Signed) Omega, agent

Smith stole the note from Roe's mailbox, indorsed Roe's name on the note, and promptly discounted it with Sunset Bank for $8,700. Not having received the note, Roe sold the car to a third party. On January 10, the bank, having discovered all the facts, demanded payment of the note from Alpha and Omega. Both refused payment.

**(a)** What are Sunset Bank's rights with regard to Alpha and Omega?

**(b)** What are Sunset Bank's rights with regard to Roe and Smith?

7. In payment of the purchase price of a used motorboat that had been fraudulently misrepresented, Young signed and delivered to Armstrong his negotiable note in the amount of $2,000 due October 1, with Selby as an accommodation comaker. Young intended

to use the boat for his fishing business. Armstrong indorsed the note in blank preparatory to discounting it. Tillman stole the note from Armstrong and delivered it to McGowan on July 1 in payment of a past-due debt in the amount of $600 that he owed to McGowan, with McGowan making up the difference by giving Tillman his check for $800 and an oral promise to pay Tillman an additional $600 on October 1.

When McGowan demanded payment of the note on December 1, both Young and Selby refused to pay because the note had not been presented for payment on its due date and because Armstrong had fraudulently misrepresented the motorboat for which the note had been executed.

What are McGowan's rights, if any, against Young, Selby, Tillman, and Armstrong, respectively?

**8.** On July 1, Anderson sold D'Aveni, a jeweler, a necklace containing imitation gems, which Anderson fraudulently represented to be diamonds. In payment for the necklace, D'Aveni executed and delivered to Anderson her promissory note for $25,000 dated July 1 and payable on December 1 to Anderson's order with interest at 8 percent per annum.

The note was thereafter successively indorsed in blank and delivered by Anderson to Bylinski, by Bylinski to Conrad, and by Conrad to Shearson, who became a holder in due course on August 10. On November 1, D'Aveni discovered Anderson's fraud and immediately notified Anderson, Bylinski, Conrad, and Shearson that she would not pay the note when it became due. Bylinski, a friend of Shearson, requested that Shearson release him from liability on the note, and Shearson, as a favor to Bylinski and for no other consideration, struck out Bylinski's indorsement.

On November 15, Shearson, who was solvent and had no creditors, indorsed the note to the order of Frederick, his father, and delivered it to Frederick as a gift. At the same time, Shearson told Frederick of D'Aveni's statement that D'Aveni would not pay the note when it became due. Frederick presented the note to D'Aveni for payment on December 1, but D'Aveni refused to pay. Thereafter, Frederick gave due notice of dishonor to Anderson, Bylinski, and Conrad.

What are Frederick's rights, if any, against Anderson, Bylinski, Conrad, and D'Aveni on the note?

**9.** Saul sold goods to Bruce, warranting that the goods were of a specified quality. The goods were not of the quality warranted, however, and Saul knew this at the time of the sale. Bruce drew and delivered a check payable to Saul and drawn on Third National Bank in the amount of the purchase price. Bruce subsequently discovered the goods were faulty and stopped payment on the check. Can Saul recover payment from Bruce? Why?

**10.** R&A Concrete Contractors, Inc., executed a promissory note that identifies both R&A Concrete and Grover Roberts as its makers. On the reverse side of the note, the following appears: "X John Ament Sec. & Treas." National Bank of Georgia, the payee, now sues both R&A Concrete and Ament on the note. What rights does National Bank have against R&A and Ament?

**11.** On August 10, 2009, Theta Electronic Laboratories, Inc., executed a promissory note to George and Marguerite Thomson. Three other individuals, Gerald Exten, Emil O'Neil, and James Hane, and their wives also indorsed the note. The note was then transferred to Hane by the Thomsons on November 26, 2010. Although a default occurred at this time, it was not until April 2012, eighteen months later, that Hane gave notice of the dishonor and made a demand for payment on the Extens as indorsers. Are the Extens liable under their indorser's liability?

# CHAPTER 30

# Bank Deposits, Collections, and Funds Transfers

In today's 21st-century society, most goods and services are bought and sold without a physical transfer of "money." Credit cards, charge accounts, and various deferred payment plans have made cash sales increasingly infrequent. But even credit sales must ultimately be settled—when they are, payment is usually made by check rather than with cash. If the parties to a sales transaction happen to have accounts at the same bank, a transfer of credit is easily accomplished. In the vast majority of cases, however, the parties have accounts at different banks. Then the buyer's check must journey from the seller-payee's bank (the depositary bank), where the check is deposited by the seller for credit to his account, to the buyer-drawer's bank (the payor bank) for payment. In this collection process, the check frequently passes through one or more other banks (intermediary banks), each of which must accurately record its passing, before it may be collected. Our banking system has developed a network to handle the collection of checks and other instruments.

In recent years, payments by electronic funds transfers have increased at an astounding rate. The dollar amount of commercial payments made by wire transfer far exceeds the dollar amount made by checks or credit cards. In addition, electronic funds transfers have become exceedingly popular with consumers. Consumer electronic funds transfers are covered by the Federal Electronic Fund Transfer Act (EFTA); nonconsumer (wholesale) electronic transfers are covered by Article 4A of the Uniform Commercial Code (UCC).

This chapter will cover both the bank deposit–collection system and electronic funds transfers.



## BANK DEPOSITS AND COLLECTIONS

Article 4 of the UCC, entitled "Bank Deposits and Collections," provides the principal rules governing the bank collection process. The end result of the collection process is either the payment of the check or the dishonor (refusal to pay) of the check by the drawee bank. As items in the bank collection process are essentially those covered by Article 3, "Commercial Paper," and to a lesser extent by Article 8, "Investment Securities," these Articles often apply to a bank collection problem. In addition, Articles 3 and 4 are supplemented and, at times, preempted by Federal law: the Expedited Funds Availability Act and its implementing Federal Reserve Regulation (Regulation CC). This section will cover the collection of an item through the banking system and the relationship between the payor bank and its customer.

### COLLECTION OF ITEMS

When a person deposits a check in his bank (the depositary bank), the bank credits his account by the amount of the check. This initial crediting is **provisional**. Normally, a bank does not permit a customer to draw funds against a provisional credit; by permitting its customer to thus draw, the bank will have given *value* and, provided it meets the other requirements, will be a holder in due course. Under the customer's contract with his bank, the bank is obligated to make a reasonable effort to obtain payment of all checks deposited for collection. When the amount of the check has been collected from the payor bank (the drawee), the credit becomes a **final credit**.

The Competitive Equality Banking Act has expedited the availability of funds by establishing maximum time periods for which a bank may hold (and thereby deny a customer access to the funds represented by) various types of instruments. Under the Act, (1) cash deposits, wire transfers, government checks, the first $100 of a day's check deposits, cashier's checks, and checks deposited in one branch of a depositary institution and drawn on the same or another branch of the same institution must clear by the next business day; (2) local checks must clear within one intervening business day; and (3) nonlocal checks must clear in no more than four intervening business days.

◆ FIGURE 30-1: **Bank Collections**

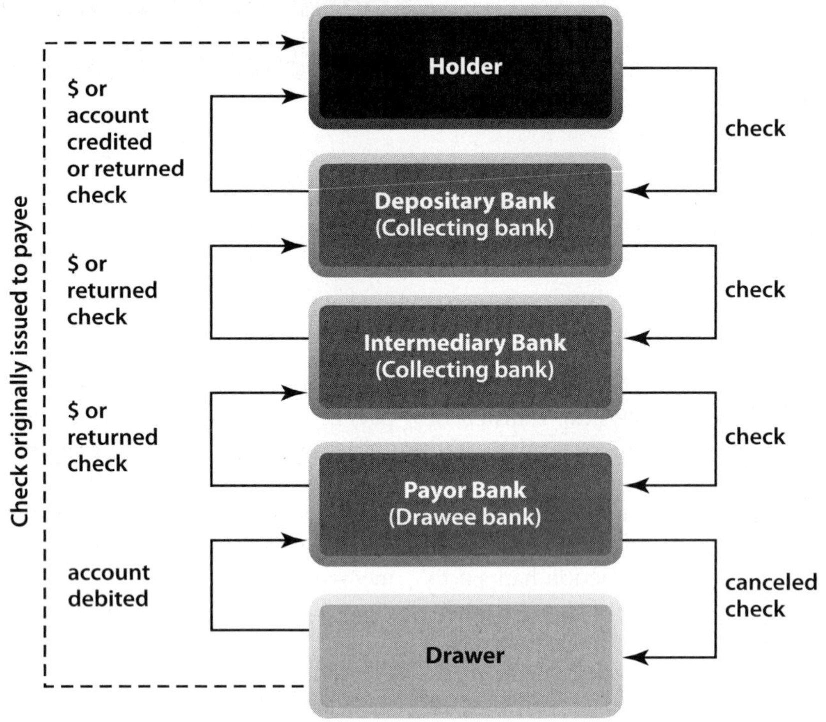


If the payor bank (the drawee bank) does not pay the check for some reason, such as a stop payment order or insufficient funds in the drawer's account, the depositary bank reverses the provisional credit to the account, debits his account for that amount, and returns the check to him with a statement of the reason for nonpayment. If, in the meantime, the customer has been permitted to draw against the provisional credit, the bank may recover the payment from him.

In some cases, the bank involved is both the depositary bank and the payor bank. In most cases, however, the depositary and payor banks are different, in which event the bank collection aspects of Article 4 come into play. Where the depositary and payor banks differ, it is necessary for the item to pass from one to the other, either directly through a clearinghouse or through one or more **intermediary banks** (banks, other than the depositary payor bank, that are involved in the collection process, such as one of the twelve Federal Reserve Banks). A **clearinghouse** is an association, composed of banks or other payors, whose members settle accounts with each other on a daily basis. Each member of the clearinghouse forwards all deposited checks drawn on other members and receives from the clearinghouse all checks drawn on it. Balances are adjusted and settled each day.

◆ SEE FIGURE 30-1: **Bank Collections**

## COLLECTING BANKS

A **collecting bank** is any bank, other than the payor bank, handling an item for payment. In the usual situation, where the depositary and payor banks are different, the depositary bank gives a provisional credit to its customer, transfers the item to the next bank in the chain, and receives a provisional credit or "settlement" from it; the process repeats until the item reaches the payor bank, which gives a provisional settlement to its transferor. When the item is paid, all the provisional settlements given by the respective banks in the chain become final, and the particular transaction has been completed. Because this procedure simplifies bookkeeping by necessitating only one entry if the item is paid, no adjustment is necessary on the books of any of the banks involved.

If, however, the payor bank does not pay the check, it returns the item, and each intermediary or collecting bank reverses the provisional settlement or credit it previously gave to its forwarding bank. Ultimately, the depositary bank will charge (remove the provisional credit from) the account of the customer who deposited the item. The customer must then seek recovery from the indorsers or the drawer.

A collecting bank is an **agent** or subagent of the owner of the item until the settlement becomes final. Section 4–201(a). Unless otherwise provided, any credit given for the item initially is provisional. Once settled, the agency relationship changes to one of **debtor-creditor**. The effects of this agency rule are that the risk of loss remains with the owner and any chargebacks go to her, not to the collecting bank.

All collecting banks have certain responsibilities and duties in collecting checks and other items. These will now be discussed.

**Duty of Care** A collecting bank must exercise ordinary care in handling an item transferred to it for collection. Section 4–202(a). The steps it takes in presenting an item or sending it for presentment are of particular importance. It must act within a reasonable time after receipt of the item and must choose a reasonable method of forwarding the item for presentment. It also is responsible for using care in routing and in selecting intermediary banks or other agents.

◆ **SEE CASE 30-1**

**Duty to Act Timely** Closely related to the collecting bank's duty of care is its duty to act in a timely manner. A collecting bank acts timely in any event if it takes proper action, such as forwarding or presenting an item before the "midnight deadline" following its receipt of the item, notice, or payment. If the bank adheres to this standard, the timeliness of its action cannot be challenged; should it, however, take a reasonably longer time, the bank bears the burden of proof in establishing timeliness. Section 4–202(b). The **midnight deadline** is the midnight of the banking day following the banking day on which the bank received the item or notice. Section 4–104(a)(10). Thus, if a bank receives a check on Monday, it must take proper action by midnight on the next banking day, or Tuesday. A banking day means the part of a day on which a bank is open to the public for carrying on substantially all of its banking functions. Section 4–104(a)(3). The midnight deadline presents a problem because it takes time to process an item through a bank—whether it be the depositary, intermediary, or payor bank. If a day's transactions are to be completed without overtime work, the bank must either close early or fix an earlier cutoff time for the day's work. Accordingly, the Code provides that for the purpose of allowing time to process items, prove balances, and make the bookkeeping entries necessary to determine its position for the day, a bank may fix an afternoon hour of 2:00 P.M. or later as a cutoff point for handling money and items and for making entries on its books. Section 4–108. Items received after the cutoff hour fixed as the close of the banking day are considered to have been received at the opening of the next banking day, and the time for taking action and for determining the bank's midnight deadline begins to run from that point.

Recognizing that everyone involved will be greatly inconvenienced if an item is not paid, Section 4–109 provides that unless otherwise instructed, a collecting bank in a good faith effort to secure payment may, in the case of a specific item drawn on a payor other than a bank, waive, modify, or extend the time limits, but not in excess of two additional banking days. This extension may be made without the approval of the parties involved and without discharging drawers or indorsers. This section does not apply to checks and other drafts drawn on a bank. The Code also authorizes delay when communications or computer facilities are interrupted as a result of blizzard, flood, hurricane, or other disaster; the suspension of payments by another bank; war; emergency conditions; failure of equipment; or other circumstances beyond the bank's control. Nevertheless, such delay will be excused only if the bank exercises such diligence as the circumstances require.

**Indorsements** An item restrictively indorsed with words such as "pay any bank" is locked into the bank collection system, and only a bank may acquire the rights of a holder. When forwarding an item for collection, a bank normally indorses the item "pay any bank," regardless of the type of indorsement, if any, that the item carried at the time of receipt. This protects the collecting bank by making it impossible for the item to stray from regular collection channels.

If the item had no indorsement when the depositary bank received it, the bank nonetheless becomes a holder of the item at the time it takes possession of the item for collection if the customer was a holder at the time of delivery to the bank and, if the bank satisfies the other requirements of a holder in due course, it will become a holder in due course in its own right. Section 4–205(1). In return, the bank warrants to the collecting banks, the payor, and the drawer that it has paid the amount of the item to the customer or deposited that amount to the customer's account. Section 4–205(2). This rule speeds up the collection process by eliminating the necessity of returning checks for indorsement when the depositary bank knows they came from its customers.

**Warranties** Customers and collecting banks give substantially the same warranties as those given by parties under Article 3 upon presentment and transfer, which were discussed in *Chapter 29*. In addition, under Article 4 customers and collecting banks may give encoding warranties. Each customer or collecting bank who transfers an item and receives a settlement or other consideration warrants to his transferee and any subsequent collecting bank that (1) he is a person entitled to enforce the item; (2) *all* signatures are authentic and authorized; (3) the item has not been altered; (4) he is not subject to any defense or claim in recoupment; and (5) he has no knowledge of any insolvency proceeding involving the maker or acceptor or the drawer of an unaccepted draft. Section 4–207(a). Moreover, each customer or collecting bank who obtains payment or acceptance from a drawee on a draft as well as each prior transferor warrants to the drawee who pays or accepts the draft in good faith that (1) she is a person entitled to enforce the draft; (2) the item has not been altered; and (3) she has no knowledge that the signature of the drawer is unauthorized. Section 4–208.

Processing of checks is now done by Magnetic Ink Character Recognition (MICR). When a check is deposited, the depositary bank magnetically encodes the check with the amount of the check (all checks are pre-encoded with the drawer's account number and the designation of the drawee bank), after which the processing occurs automatically, without further human involvement. Despite its efficiency, the magnetic encoding of checks has created several problems. The first is the problem a bank encounters when paying a postdated instrument prior to its date. The Revision changes prior law by providing that the drawee may debit the drawer's account, unless the drawer timely informs the drawee that the check is postdated. Section 4–401(c). A second difficulty arises when a depositing bank or its customer who encodes her own checks miscodes a check. Revised Article 4 provides that such an encoder **warrants** to any subsequent collecting bank and to the payor that information on a check is properly encoded. Section 4–209(a). If the customer does the encoding, the depositary bank also makes the warranty. Section 4–209(a).

**Final Payment** The provisional settlements made in the collection chain are all directed toward final payment of the item by the payor bank. From this turnaround point in the collection process, the proceeds of the item begin their return flow, and provisional settlements become final. For example, a customer of the California Country State Bank may deposit a check drawn on the State of Maine Country National Bank. The check may then take a course such as follows: from the California Country State Bank to a correspondent bank in San Francisco, to the Federal Reserve Bank of San Francisco, to the Federal Reserve Bank of Boston, to the payor bank. Provisional settlements are made at each step. When the payor bank finally pays the item, the proceeds begin to flow back over the same course.

The critical question, then, is the point at which the payor bank has **paid** the item, as this not only commences the payment process but also affects questions of priority between the payment of an item and actions such as the filing of a stop payment order against it. Under the Code, *final payment* occurs when the payor bank first does any of the following: (1) pays an item in cash; (2) settles an item and does not have the right to revoke the settlement through statute, clearinghouse rule, or agreement; or (3) makes a provisional settlement and does not revoke it within the time and in the manner permitted by statute, clearinghouse rule, or agreement. Section 4–215(a).

### PAYOR BANKS

The **payor** or drawee **bank**, under its contract of deposit with the drawer, agrees to pay to the payee or his order a check issued by the drawer, provided that the order is not countermanded and that there are sufficient funds in the drawer's account.

The tremendous increase in volume of bank collections has necessitated deferred posting procedures, whereby items are sorted and proved on the day of receipt but are not posted to customers' accounts or returned until the next banking day. The UCC not only approves such procedures but also establishes specific standards to govern their application to the actions of payor banks.

When a payor bank that is not also a depositary bank receives a demand item other than for immediate payment over the counter, it must either return the item or give its transferor a provisional settlement before **midnight** of the banking day on which the item is received. Otherwise, the bank becomes liable to its transferor for the amount of the item, unless it has a valid defense, such as breach of a presentment warranty. Section 4–302.

If the payor bank gives the provisional settlement as required, it has until the midnight deadline to return the item or, if the item is held for protest or is otherwise unavailable for return, to send written notice of dishonor or nonpayment. Section 4–301(a). After doing this, the bank is entitled to revoke the settlement and recover any payment it has made. Should it fail to return the item or send notice before its midnight deadline, the payor bank will be accountable for the amount of the item unless it has a valid defense for its inaction. If a check is for $2,500 or more, Federal law (Regulation CC) requires special notice of nonpayment—the paying bank must give notice to the depositary bank by 4:00 P.M. on the second business day following the banking day on which the check was presented to the paying bank. This regulation does not, however, relieve the paying bank of returning the check in compliance with Article 4.

A bank may dishonor an item and return it or send notice for innumerable reasons. The following situations are the most common: the drawer or maker may have no account or may have funds insufficient to cover the item, a signature on the item may be forged, or the drawer or maker may have stopped payment of the item.

If the funds in a customer's account are insufficient to pay all of the items that the bank receives on that account on any given day, the bank may charge them against the account in any order it deems convenient. The owner of the account from which the item was payable also has no basis for complaint when the bank pays one item rather than another. It is his responsibility to have enough funds on deposit to pay all of the items chargeable to his account at any time.

◆ **SEE CASE 29-2**

## RELATIONSHIP BETWEEN PAYOR BANK AND ITS CUSTOMER

The relationship between a payor bank and its checking account customer is primarily the product of their contractual arrangement. Although the parties have relatively broad latitude in establishing the terms of their agreement and in altering the provisions of the Code, a bank may not validly (1) disclaim responsibility for its lack of good faith, (2) disclaim responsibility for its failure to exercise ordinary care, or (3) limit its damages for a breach comprising such lack or failure. Section 4–103(a). The parties by agreement, however, may determine the standards by which the bank's responsibility is to be measured, if these standards are not clearly unreasonable.

### PAYMENT OF AN ITEM

A payor bank owes a duty to its customer, the drawer, to pay checks properly drawn by him on an account having funds sufficient to cover the items. A check or draft, however, is not an assignment of the drawer's funds that are in the drawee's possession. Moreover, as discussed in *Chapter 29*, the drawee is not liable on a check until it accepts the item. Section 3–408. Therefore, the *holder* of a check has no right to require the drawee bank to pay it, whether the drawer's account contains sufficient funds or not. But if a payor bank improperly refuses payment when presented with an item, it will incur a liability to the *customer* from whose account the item should have been paid. Section 4–402. If the customer has adequate funds on deposit, and there is no other valid basis for the refusal to pay, the bank is liable to its customer for damages proximately caused by the *wrongful dishonor*. Liability is limited to actual damages proved and may include damages for arrest, prosecution, or other consequential damages. Section 4–402.

When a payor bank receives an item properly payable from a customer's account but the funds in the account are insufficient to pay it, the bank may (1) dishonor the item and return it or (2) pay the item and charge its customer's account, even though the actions create an overdraft. Section 4–401(a). The item authorizes or directs the bank to make the payment and hence carries with it an enforceable implied promise to reimburse the bank. Furthermore, the customer may be liable to pay the bank a service charge for its handling of the overdraft or to pay interest on the amount of the overdraft. A customer, however, is not liable for an overdraft if the customer did not sign the item or benefit from the proceeds of the item. Section 4–401(b).

A payor bank is under no obligation to its customer to pay an uncertified check that is more than six months old. Section 4–404. This rule reflects the usual banking practice of consulting a depositor before paying a "*stale*" item (one more than six months old) on her account. The bank is not required to dishonor such an item, however; and if the bank makes payment in good faith, it may charge the amount of the item to its customers' account.

◆ **SEE CASES 30-2 and 29-2**

### SUBSTITUTE CHECK

The Check Clearing for the 21st Century Act (also called Check 21 or the Check Truncation Act) permits banks to truncate original checks, which means removing an original paper check from the check collection or return process and sending in lieu of it (1) a substitute check or, (2) *by agreement*, information relating to the original check (including data taken from the MICR line of the original check or an electronic image of the original check). The Act sets forth a statutory framework under which a substitute check is the legal equivalent of an original check for all purposes, if the substitute check (1) accurately represents all of the information on the front and back of the original check as of the time the original check was truncated; and (2) bears the legend, "This is a legal copy of your check. You can use it the same way you would use the original check." The Act defines a **substitute check** as a paper reproduction of the original check that (1) contains an image of the front and back of the original; (2) bears an MICR containing all the information appearing on the MICR line of the original check; (3) conforms, in paper stock, dimension, and otherwise, with generally applicable industry standards for substitute checks; and (4) is suitable for automated processing in the same manner as the original. Thus, a substitute check is basically a copy of the original check that shows both the front and back of the original check.

The law does not require banks to accept checks in electronic form nor does it require banks to use the new authority granted by the Act to create substitute checks. On the other hand, parties cannot refuse to accept a substitute check that meets the Act's requirements.

The Act permits banks to replace paper checks during the check collection process with either digital or paper substitutes. Thus, banks can employ digital images or image replacement documents (IRDs), which are documents that include the front, rear, and all MICR data in one image. However, the Act does not provide legal equivalence for electronic check or image presentment.

The ultimate objective of the Act is to make the collection process more efficient and much faster (transferring digital files within seconds rather than days) and to enhance fraud detection by accelerating return of dishonored checks.

### STOP PAYMENT ORDERS

A check drawn on a bank is an order to pay a sum of money and an authorization to charge the amount to the drawer's account. The customer, or any person authorized to draw on the account, may countermand this order, however, by means of a **stop payment order**. Section 4–403. If the order does not come too late, the bank is bound by it. If the bank inadvertently pays a check over a valid stop order, it is *prima facie* liable to the customer, but only to the extent of the customer's loss resulting from the payment. The burden of establishing the fact and amount of loss is on the customer.

To be effective, a stop payment order must be received in time to provide the bank a reasonable opportunity to act on it. Section 4–403(a). An oral stop order is binding on the bank for only fourteen calendar days. Section 4–403(b). If the customer confirms an oral stop order in writing within the fourteen-day period, the order is effective for six months and may be renewed in writing for additional six-month periods.

The fact that a drawer has filed a stop payment order does not automatically relieve her of liability. If the bank honors the stop payment order and returns the check, the holder may bring an action against the drawer. If the holder qualifies as a holder in due course, personal defenses that the drawer might have to such an action would be of no avail.

◆ **SEE CASE 30-2**

## BANK'S RIGHT TO SUBROGATION ON IMPROPER PAYMENT

If a payor bank pays an item over a stop payment order, after an account has been closed, or otherwise in violation of its contract with the drawer or maker, the payor bank is subrogated to (obtains) the rights of (1) any holder in due course on the item against the drawer or maker, (2) the payee or any other holder against the drawer or maker, and (3) the drawer or maker against the payee or any other holder. Section 4–407. For instance, over the drawer's stop payment order a bank pays a check presented to the bank by a holder in due course. The drawer's defense is that the check was obtained by fraud in the inducement. The drawee bank is subrogated to the rights of the holder in due course, who would not be subject to the drawer's personal defense, and thus can debit the drawer's account. Section 4–407(1). The same would be true if the presenter were the payee, against whom the drawer did not have a valid defense. Section 4–407(2).

◆ **SEE CASE 30-3**

## DISCLOSURE REQUIREMENTS

Congress enacted the Truth in Savings Act, which requires all depositary institutions (including commercial banks, savings and loan associations, savings banks, and credit unions) to disclose in great detail to consumers the terms and conditions of their deposit accounts. The stated purpose of the Act is to allow consumers to make informed decisions regarding deposit accounts by mandating standardized disclosure of rates of interest and fees to facilitate meaningful comparison of different deposit products.

More specifically, the Act provides that the disclosures must be made in a clear and conspicuous writing and must be given to the consumer when an account is opened or service is provided. These disclosures must include the following: (1) the annual percentage yield (APY) and the percentage rate; (2) how variable rates are calculated and when the rates may be changed; (3) balance information (including how the balance is calculated); (4) when and how interest is calculated and credited; (5) the amount of fees that may be charged and how they are calculated; and (6) any limitation on the number or amount of withdrawals or deposits. In addition, the Act requires the depositary institution to disclose the following information with periodic statements it sends to its customers: (1) the APY earned; (2) any fees debited during the covered period; (3) the dollar amount of the interest earned during the covered period; and (4) the dates of the covered period.

## CUSTOMER'S DEATH OR INCOMPETENCE

The general rule is that death or incompetence revokes all agency agreements. Furthermore, adjudication of incompetency by a court is regarded as notice to the world of that fact. Actual notice is not required. Section 4–405 of the Code modifies these stringent rules in several ways with respect to bank deposits and collections.

First, if either a payor or collecting bank does not know that a customer has been adjudicated incompetent, the existence of such incompetence at the time an item is issued or its collection is undertaken does not impair either bank's authority to accept, pay, or collect the item or to account for proceeds of its collection. The bank may pay the item without incurring any liability.

Second, neither death nor adjudication of incompetence of a customer revokes a payor or collecting bank's authority to accept, pay, or collect an item until the bank knows of the condition and has a reasonable opportunity to act on this knowledge.

Finally, even though a bank knows of the death of its customer, it may for ten days after the date of his death pay or certify checks drawn by the customer unless a person claiming an interest in the account, such as an heir, executor, or administrator, orders the bank to stop making such payments. Section 4–405(b).

## CUSTOMER'S DUTIES

The Code imposes certain affirmative duties on bank customers and fixes time limits within which they must assert their rights. The duties arise and the time starts to run from the point at which the bank either sends or makes available to its customer a statement of account showing payment of items against the account. The statement of account will suffice provided it describes by item the number of the item, the amount, and the date of payment. The customer must exercise reasonable promptness in examining the bank statement or the items to discover whether any payment was unauthorized due to an *unauthorized signature* on or any *alteration* of an item. Section 4–406(c). Because he is not presumed to know the signatures of payees or indorsers, this duty of prompt and careful examination applies only to alterations and the customer's own signature, both of which he should be able to detect immediately. If he discovers an unauthorized signature or an alteration, he must notify the bank promptly. Section 4–406(c). A failure to fulfill these duties of prompt examination and notice precludes the customer from asserting against the bank his unauthorized signature or any alteration if the bank establishes that it suffered a loss by reason of such failure. Section 4–406(d).

Furthermore, the customer will lose his rights in a potentially more serious situation. Occasionally a forger, possibly an employee who has access to his employer's checkbook, carries out a series of transactions involving the account of the same individual. He may forge one or more checks each month until he is finally detected. The bank, noticing nothing suspicious, might pay one or more of the customer's checks bearing the false signatures before the customer detects the forgery, months or even years later. Section 4–406(d) of the Code deals with these situations by stating that once the statement and items become available to him, the customer must examine them within a reasonable period—which in no event may exceed thirty calendar days and which may, under certain circumstances, be less—and notify the bank. Any instruments containing alterations or unauthorized signatures by the same wrongdoer that the bank pays during that period will be the bank's responsibility, but any paid thereafter but before the customer notifies the bank may not be asserted against it. This rule is based on the concept that the loss involved is directly traceable to the customer's negligence and that, as a result, he should stand the loss.

These rules depend, however, on the bank's exercising ordinary care in paying the items involved. If it does not, and that failure by the bank substantially contributed to the loss, the loss will be allocated between the bank and the customer based on their comparative negligence. Section 4–406(e). But whether the bank exercised due care or not, the customer must in all events report any alteration or his unauthorized signature within one year from the time the statement or items are made available to him or be barred from asserting them against the bank. Section 4–406(f). Any *unauthorized indorsement* must be asserted within three years under the Article's general Statute of Limitations provisions. Section 4–111.

Consistent with modern automated methods for processing checks, Articles 3 and 4 provide that "ordinary care" does not require a bank to examine every check if the failure to do so does not vary unreasonably from general banking usage. Section 3–103(7).

◆ **SEE CASE 30-4**

## ELECTRONIC FUNDS TRANSFERS

As previously mentioned, the use of negotiable instruments for payment has greatly reduced the use of *cash* in the United States. The advent and technological advances of interconnected computers have resulted in electronic fund transfer systems (EFTS) that have greatly reduced the use of *checks*. Financial institutions seek to substitute EFTS for checks for two principal reasons. The first is to eliminate the ever-increasing paperwork involved in processing the billions of checks issued annually. The second is to eliminate the "float" that a drawer of a check currently enjoys by maintaining the use of his funds during the processing period between the time at which he issues the check and final payment.

An electronic fund transfer (EFT) has been defined as "any transfer of funds, other than a transaction originated by check, draft, or similar paper instrument, which is initiated through an electronic terminal, telephonic instrument, or computer or magnetic tape so as to order, instruct or authorize a financial institution to debit or credit an account." For example, with an EFT, William in New York would be able to pay a debt he owes to Yvette in Illinois by entering into his computer an order to his bank to pay Yvette. The drawee bank would then instantly debit William's account and transfer the credit to Yvette's bank, where Yvette's account would immediately be credited in that amount. The entire transaction would be completed in minutes.

The use of EFTs generated considerable confusion concerning the legal rights of customers and financial institutions. Congress provided a partial solution to the legal issues affecting consumer EFTs by enacting the EFTA, discussed below. Transactions not covered by the EFTA—primarily wholesale electronic transfers—are covered by Article 4A—Funds Transfers of the UCC.

## TYPES OF ELECTRONIC FUNDS TRANSFERS

Although new EFTs may appear in the coming years, six main types of EFTs are currently in use: (1) automated teller machines, (2) point-of-sale systems, (3) direct deposit and withdrawal of funds, (4) pay-by-phone systems, (5) personal computer (online) banking, and (6) wholesale EFTs.

### AUTOMATED TELLER MACHINES

Automated teller machines (ATMs) permit customers to conduct various transactions with their banks through the use of electronic terminals. After activating an ATM with a plastic identification card and a personal identification number, or PIN, a customer can deposit and withdraw funds from her account, transfer funds between accounts, obtain cash advances, and make payments on loan accounts.

### POINT-OF-SALE SYSTEMS

Computerized point-of-sale (POS) systems permit consumers to transfer funds from their bank accounts to a merchant automatically. The POS machines, located within the merchant's store and activated by the consumer's identification card and code, instantaneously debit the consumer's account and credit the merchant's account.

### DIRECT DEPOSITS AND WITHDRAWALS

Another type of EFT involves deposits, authorized in advance by a customer, that are made directly to his account. Examples include direct payroll deposits, deposits of Social Security payments, and deposits of pension payments. Conversely, automatic withdrawals are preauthorized EFTs from the customer's account for regular payments to some party other than the financial institution at which the funds are deposited. Automatic withdrawals to pay insurance premiums, utility bills, or automobile loan payments are common examples of this type of EFT.

### PAY-BY-PHONE SYSTEMS

Financial institutions provide a service that permits customers to pay bills by telephoning the bank's computer system and directing a transfer of funds to a designated third party. This service also permits customers to transfer funds between accounts.

### PERSONAL COMPUTER (ONLINE) BANKING

Personal computer (online) banking enables the customer to execute many banking transactions via an Internet-connected computer. For instance, customers may view account balances, request transfers between accounts, and pay bills electronically.

### WHOLESALE ELECTRONIC FUNDS TRANSFERS

Wholesale EFTs, commonly called wholesale wire transfers, involve the movement of funds between financial institutions, between financial institutions and businesses, and between businesses. More than $1 *trillion* is transferred this way each business day over the two major transfer systems—the Federal Reserve wire transfer network system (Fedwire) and the New York Clearing House Interbank Payment System (CHIPS). In addition, a number of private wholesale wire systems exist among the large banks. Limited aspects of wholesale wire transfers are governed by uniform rules promulgated by the Federal Reserve, CHIPS, and the National Automated Clearing House Association.

## CONSUMER FUNDS TRANSFERS

Congress determined that the use of electronic systems to transfer funds provided the potential for substantial benefits to consumers. Existing consumer protection legislation failed to account for the unique characteristics of such systems, however, leaving the rights and obligations of consumers and financial institutions undefined. Accordingly, Congress enacted Title IX of the Consumer Protection Act, the EFTA, to "provide a basic framework establishing the rights, liabilities, and responsibilities of participants in electronic fund transfers" with primary emphasis on "the provision of individual consumer rights." Because the EFTA deals exclusively with the protection of **consumers**, it does not govern electronic transfers between financial institutions, between financial institutions and businesses, and between businesses. The Act is similar in many respects to the Fair Credit Billing Act (see *Chapter 42*), which applies to credit card transactions. The EFTA is administered by the Board of Governors of the Federal Reserve System, which is mandated to prescribe regulations to carry out the purposes of the Act. Pursuant to this congressional mandate, the Federal Reserve has issued Regulation E.

The Dodd-Frank Wall Street Reform and Consumer Protection Act of 2010 (CFPA), discussed in *Chapter 42*, requires that the amount of any interchange transaction fee that an issuer may receive or charge with respect to an electronic debit transaction must be reasonable and proportional to the cost incurred by the issuer, as determined by the Federal Reserve. Debit cards issued by small banks and prepaid reloadable cards are exempt from this rule.

### DISCLOSURE

The EFTA is primarily a disclosure statute and as such requires that the terms and conditions of electronic funds transfers involving a consumer's account be disclosed in readily understandable language at the time the consumer contracts for such services. Included among the required disclosure are the consumer's liability for unauthorized transfers, the kinds of EFTs allowed, the charges for transfers or for the right to make transfers, the consumer's right to stop payment of preauthorized EFTs, the consumer's right to receive documentation of EFTs, rules concerning disclosure of information to third parties, procedures for correcting account errors, and the financial institution's liability to the consumer under the Act.

### DOCUMENTATION AND PERIODIC STATEMENTS

The Act requires the financial institution to provide the consumer with written documentation of each transfer made from an electronic terminal at the time of transfer—a receipt. The receipt must clearly state the amount involved, the date, the type of transfer, the identity of the account(s) involved, the identity of any third party involved, and the location of the terminal involved.

In addition, the financial institution must provide each consumer with a periodic statement for each account of the consumer that may be accessed by means of an EFT. The statement must describe the amount, date, and location for each transfer; the fee, if any, to be charged for the transaction;

and an address and phone number for questions and information.

### PREAUTHORIZED TRANSFERS

A preauthorized transfer from a consumer's account must be authorized in advance and in writing by the consumer, and a copy of the authorization must be provided to the consumer when the transfer is made. Up to three business days before the scheduled date of the transfer, a consumer may stop payment of a preauthorized EFT by notifying the financial institution orally or in writing, though the financial institution may require the consumer to provide written confirmation of an oral notification within fourteen days.

### ERROR RESOLUTION

The consumer has sixty days after the financial institution sends a periodic statement in which to notify the institution of any errors appearing on that statement. The financial institution is required to investigate alleged errors within ten business days and to report its findings within three business days after completing the investigation. If the financial institution needs more than ten days to investigate, it may take up to forty-five days, provided it recredits the consumer's account for the amount alleged to be in error. The institution must correct an error within one business day after determining that the error has occurred. Failure to investigate in good faith makes the financial institution liable to the consumer for treble damages (three times the amount of provable damages).

### CONSUMER LIABILITY

A consumer's liability for an unauthorized electronic fund transfer is limited to a maximum of $50 if the consumer notifies the financial institution within two days after he learns of the loss or theft. If the consumer does not report the loss or theft within two days, he is liable for losses up to $500 but no more than $50 for the first two days. If the consumer fails to report the unauthorized use within sixty days of transmittal of a periodic statement, he is liable for losses resulting from any unauthorized EFT that appeared on the statement if the financial institution can show that the loss would not have occurred had the consumer reported the loss within sixty days; thus there is unlimited liability on unauthorized transfers made after sixty days following the bank's sending the periodic statement.

### LIABILITY OF FINANCIAL INSTITUTION

A financial institution is liable to a consumer for all damages proximately caused by its failure to make an EFT in accordance with the terms and conditions of an account, in the correct amount, or in a timely manner when properly instructed to do so by the consumer. There are, however, exceptions to such liability. The financial institution will not be liable if—

1. the consumer's account has insufficient funds through no fault of the financial institution,
2. the funds are subject to legal process,
3. the transfer would exceed an established credit limit,
4. an electronic terminal has insufficient cash, or
5. circumstances beyond the financial institution's control prevent the transfer.

The financial institution is also liable for failure to stop payment of a preauthorized transfer from a consumer's account when instructed to do so in accordance with the terms and conditions of the account.

## WHOLESALE FUNDS TRANSFERS

Article 4A, Funds Transfers, is designed to provide a statutory framework for payment systems that are not covered by existing Articles of the UCC or by the EFTA. The typical wholesale wire transfer involves sophisticated parties who desire great speed in transferring large sums of money. Article 4A has been universally adopted by the States and Territories. In general, "Article 4A governs a method of payment in which the person making payment (the 'originator') directly transfers an instruction to a bank to either make a payment to the person receiving the payment (the 'beneficiary') or to instruct some other bank to make payment to the beneficiary." Article 4A–102, Comment 1.

Although checks and credit cards are more common forms of payment as measured by number of transactions per day, commercial electronic transfers (commercial or wholesale wire transfers) far exceed these transactions as measured by their dollar volume, which is much greater than $1 trillion a day.

Article 4A provides that the parties to a funds transfer generally may by agreement vary their rights and obligations. Moreover, funds-transfer system rules governing banks that use the system may be effective even if such rules conflict with Article 4A. Section 4A–501. Rights and obligations under Article 4A can also be changed by Federal Reserve regulations and operating circulars of Federal Reserve Banks. Section 4A–107.

### SCOPE OF ARTICLE 4A

Article 4A, which covers wholesale funds transfers, defines a funds transfer as a

> series of transactions, beginning with the originator's payment order, made for the purpose of making payment to the beneficiary of the order. The term includes any payment order issued by the originator's bank or an intermediary bank intended to carry out

the originator's payment order. A funds transfer is completed by acceptance by the beneficiary's bank of a payment order for the benefit of the beneficiary of the originator's payment order. Section 4A– 104(a).

The Article, therefore, covers the transfers of credit that move from an originator to a beneficiary through the banking system. If any step in the process is governed by the EFTA, however, the entire transaction is excluded from the Article's coverage. Section 4A–108.

The following examples illustrate the coverage of the Article:

1. Johnson Co. instructs its bank, First National Bank (FNB), to pay $2 million to West Co., also a customer of FNB. FNB executes the payment order by crediting West's account with $2 million and notifying West that the credit has been made and is available.
2. Assume the same facts as those in the first example except that West's bank is Central Bank (CB). FNB will execute the payment order of Johnson Co. by issuing to CB its own payment order instructing CB to credit the account of West.
3. Assume the facts presented in the second example with the added fact that FNB does not have a correspondent relationship with CB. In this instance, FNB will have to issue its payment order to Northern Bank (NB), a bank that does have a correspondent relationship with CB, and NB will then issue its payment order to CB.

**Payment Order** **Payment order** is a sender's instruction to a receiving bank to pay, or to cause another bank to pay, a fixed or determinable amount of money to a beneficiary. Section 4A–103. The instruction may be communicated orally, electronically, or in writing. To be a payment order, the instruction must—

1. not contain a condition to payment other than the time of payment;
2. be sent to a receiving bank that is to be reimbursed either by debiting an account of the sender or by otherwise receiving payment from the sender; and
3. be transmitted by the sender directly to the receiving bank or indirectly through an agent, a funds-transfer system, or a communication system.

The payment order is issued when sent and, if more than one payment is to be made, each payment represents a separate payment order. Section 4A–104(b)(c). In the examples above, one payment order is issued in the first example (from Johnson Co.), two in the second example (from Johnson Co. and from First National Bank), and three in the third example (from Johnson Co., from First National Bank, and from Northern Bank).

**Parties** The **originator** is either the sender of the payment order or, in a series of payment orders, the sender of the first payment order. Section 4A–104(c). A **sender** is the party who gives an instruction to the **receiving bank**, or the bank to which the sender's instruction is addressed. Section 4A–103(4). The receiving bank may be the **originator's bank**, an intermediary bank, or the **beneficiary's bank**. The originator's bank is either the bank that receives the original payment order or the originator if the originator is a bank. Section 4A–104(d). The beneficiary's bank, the last bank in the chain of a funds transfer, is the bank instructed in the payment order to credit the beneficiary's account. Section 4A–103(a)(3). The **beneficiary** is the person to be paid by the beneficiary bank. Section 4A–103(a)(2). An **intermediary bank** is any receiving bank, other than the originator's bank or the beneficiary's bank, that receives the payment order. Section 4A–104(b). Thus, in the above examples,

1. Johnson Co. is the *originator* in all three examples;
2. Johnson Co. is a *sender* in all three examples, FNB is a sender in examples 2 and 3, and NB is a sender in example 3;
3. FNB is the *receiving bank* of Johnson Co.'s payment order in all three examples; in example 2, CB is the receiving bank of FNB's payment order; and, in example 3, CB is the receiving bank of NB's payment order and NB is the receiving bank of FNB's payment order;
4. FNB is the *originator's bank* in all three examples;
5. FNB is the *beneficiary's bank* in example 1; CB is the beneficiary's bank in examples 2 and 3;
6. West is the *beneficiary* in all three examples; and
7. NB is an *intermediary bank* in example 3.

See *Figure 30-2* for a summary of the parties in these three examples. In some instances, the originator and the beneficiary may be the same party. For example, a corporation may wish to transfer funds from one account to another account that is in the same or a different bank.

◆ **SEE FIGURE 30-2: Parties to a Funds Transfer**

**Excluded Transactions** As previously mentioned, Section 4A–108 provides that if any part of a funds transfer is governed by the EFTA, then the transfer is excluded from Article 4A coverage. In addition, Article 4A covers only credit transactions; it therefore excludes debit transactions. If the person making the payment gives the instruction, the transfer is a credit transfer. If, however, the person receiving the payment gives the instruction, the transfer is a debit transfer. For example, a seller of goods obtains authority from the purchaser to debit the purchaser's account after the seller ships the goods. Article 4A does not cover this transaction because the instructions to make payment issue from the beneficiary (the seller), not from the party whose account is to be debited (the purchaser).

◆ **SEE FIGURE 30-3: Credit Transaction**

◆ FIGURE 30-2: **Parties to a Funds Transfer**

| | Example 1 | Example 2 | Example 3 |
|---|---|---|---|
| **Originator** | Johnson Co. | Johnson Co. | Johnson Co. |
| **Sender(s)** | Johnson Co. | Johnson Co. | Johnson Co. |
| | | FNB | FNB |
| | | | NB |
| **Receiving Bank(s)** | FNB | FNB | FNB |
| | | CB | CB |
| | | | NB |
| **Originator's Bank** | FNB | FNB | FNB |
| **Beneficiary's Bank** | FNB | CB | CB |
| **Beneficiary** | West | West | West |
| **Intermediary Bank** | — | — | NB |

Note: CB = Central Bank; FNB = First National Bank; NB = Northern Bank.

## ACCEPTANCE

Rights and obligations arise as a result of a receiving bank's acceptance of a payment order. The effect of acceptance depends upon whether the payment order was issued to the beneficiary's bank or to a receiving bank other than the beneficiary's bank.

If a receiving bank is not the beneficiary's bank, the receiving bank does not subject itself to any liability until it accepts the instrument. Acceptance by a receiving bank other than the beneficiary's bank occurs when the receiving bank executes the sender's order. Section 4A–209(a). Such execution occurs when the receiving bank "issues a payment order intended to carry out" the sender's payment order. Section 4A–301(a). When the receiving bank executes the sender's payment order, the bank is entitled to payment from the sender and can debit the sender's account. Section 4A–402(c).

The beneficiary's bank may accept an order in any of three ways, and acceptance occurs at the earliest of these events: (1) when the bank (a) pays the beneficiary or (b) notifies the beneficiary that the bank has received the order or has credited the beneficiary's account with the funds; (2) when the bank receives payment of the sender's order; or (3) the opening of the next funds-transfer business day of the bank after the payment date of the order if the order was not rejected and funds are available for payment. Section 4A–209(b).

If a beneficiary's bank accepts a payment order, the bank is obliged to pay the beneficiary the amount of the order. Section 4A–404(a). The bank's acceptance of the payment order does not, however, create any obligation to either the sender or the originator.

## ERRONEOUS EXECUTION OF PAYMENT ORDERS

If a receiving bank mistakenly executes a payment order for an amount greater than the amount authorized, the bank is entitled to payment only in the amount of the sender's correct order. Section 4A–303(a). To the extent allowed by the law governing mistake and restitution, the receiving bank may then recover from the beneficiary of the erroneous order the amount in excess of the authorized amount. If the

◆ FIGURE 30-3: **Credit Transaction**

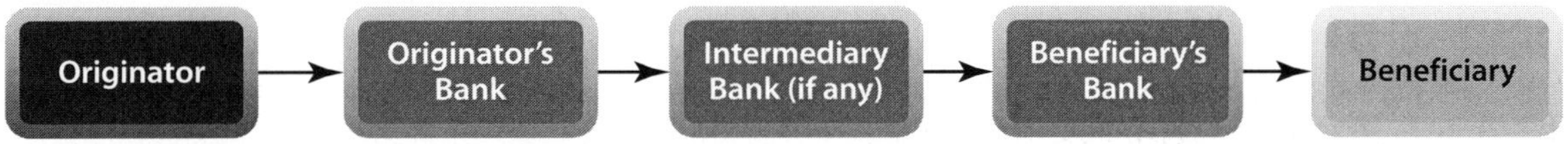

wrong beneficiary is paid, however, the bank that issued the erroneous payment order is entitled to payment neither from its sender nor from prior senders and has the burden of recovering the payment from the improper beneficiary. Section 4A–303(c).

### UNAUTHORIZED PAYMENT ORDERS

If a bank wishing to prevent unauthorized transactions establishes commercially reasonable security measures, to which a customer agrees, and the bank properly follows the process it has established, the customer must pay an order even if it was unauthorized. Section 4A–202. The customer, however, can avoid liability by showing that the unauthorized order was not caused directly or indirectly by (1) a person with access to confidential security information who was acting for the customer or (2) a person who obtained such information from a source controlled by the customer. Section 4A–203.

## CHAPTER SUMMARY

## BANK DEPOSITS AND COLLECTIONS

| | |
|---|---|
| **COLLECTION OF ITEMS** | **Depositary Bank** the bank in which the payee or holder deposits a check for credit<br>**Provisional Credit** tentative credit for the deposit of an instrument until final credit is given<br>**Final Credit** payment of the instrument by the payor bank; if the payor bank (drawee) does not pay the check, the depositary bank reverses the provisional credit<br>**Intermediary Bank** a bank, other than the depositary or payor bank, involved in the collection process<br>**Collecting Bank** any bank (other than the payor bank) handling the item for payment<br>• ***Agency*** a collecting bank is an agent or subagent of the owner of the check until the settlement becomes final<br>• ***Duty of Care*** a collecting bank must exercise ordinary care in handling an item<br>• ***Duty to Act Timely*** a collecting bank acts timely if it takes proper action before its midnight deadline (midnight of the next banking day)<br>• ***Indorsements*** if an item is restrictively indorsed "for deposit only," only a bank may be a holder<br>• ***Warranties*** customers and collecting banks give warranties on transfer, presentment, and encoding<br>• ***Final Payment*** occurs when the payor bank does any of the following, whichever happens first: (1) pays an item in cash; (2) settles and does not have the right to revoke the settlement; or (3) makes a provisional settlement and does not properly revoke it<br>**Payor Bank** under its contract with the drawer, the payor or drawee bank agrees to pay to the payee or his order checks that are issued by the drawer, provided the order is not countermanded by a stop payment order and provided there are sufficient funds in the drawer's account |
| **RELATIONSHIP BETWEEN PAYOR BANK AND ITS CUSTOMER** | **Contractual Relationship** the relationship between a payor bank and its checking account customer is primarily the product of their contractual arrangement<br>**Payment of an Item** when a payor receives an item for which the funds in the account are insufficient, the bank may either dishonor the item and return it or pay the item and charge the customer's account even though an overdraft is created |

**Substitute Check** a paper reproduction of the original check that is the legal equivalent of an original check for all purposes
**Stop Payment Orders** an oral stop payment order (a command from a drawer to a drawee not to pay an instrument) is binding for fourteen calendar days; a written order is effective for six months and may be renewed in writing
**Bank's Right to Subrogation on Improper Payment** if a payor bank pays an item over a stop payment order or otherwise in violation of its contract, the payor bank is subrogated to (obtains) the rights of (1) any holder in due course on the item against the drawer or maker; (2) the payee or any other holder against the drawer or maker; and (3) the drawer or maker against the payee or any other holder
**Disclosure Requirement** all depositary institutions must disclose in great detail to their consumers the terms and conditions of their deposit account
**Customer's Death or Incompetence** a bank may pay an item if it does not know of the customer's incompetency or death
**Customer's Duties** the customer must examine bank statements and items carefully and promptly to discover any unauthorized signatures or alterations

## ELECTRONIC FUNDS TRANSFERS

**NATURE AND TYPES OF ELECTRONIC FUNDS TRANSFERS**

**Definition** any transfer of funds, other than a transaction originated by check, draft, or similar paper instrument, which is initiated through an electronic terminal, telephonic instrument, or computer or magnetic tape so as to order, instruct, or authorize a financial institution to debit or credit an account
**Purpose** to eliminate the paperwork involved in processing checks and the "float" available to a drawer of a check
**Types of Electronic Funds Transfers**
- ***Automated Teller Machines***
- ***Point-of-Sale Systems***
- ***Direct Deposits and Withdrawals***
- ***Pay-by-Phone Systems***
- ***Personal Computer (Online) Banking***
- ***Wholesale Electronic Funds Transfers***

**CONSUMER FUNDS TRANSFERS**

**Electronic Fund Transfer Act** provides a basic framework establishing the rights, liabilities, and responsibilities of participants in consumer electronic funds transfers
**Financial Institution Responsibility** liable to a consumer for all damages proximately caused by its failure to properly handle an electronic fund transfer transaction

**WHOLESALE FUNDS TRANSFERS**

**Scope of Article 4A**
- ***Wholesale Funds Transfers*** the movement of funds through the banking system; excludes all transactions governed by the Electronic Fund Transfer Act
- ***Payment Order*** an instruction of sender to a receiving bank to pay, or to cause another bank to pay, a fixed amount of money to a beneficiary
- ***Parties*** include originator, sender, receiving bank, originator's bank, beneficiary's bank, beneficiary, and intermediary banks

**Acceptance** rights and obligations that arise as a result of a receiving bank's acceptance of a payment order

## CASES

# CASE 30-1

## Duty of Care
## HONEYCUTT v. HONEYCUTT

Court of Special Appeals of Maryland, 2002
150 Md.App. 604, 822 A.2d 551, cert. denied, 376 Md. 544, 831 A.2d 4 (2003)
http://caselaw.lp.findlaw.com/data2/marylandstatecases/cosa/2003/68s02.pdf

**Thieme, J.**

In this appeal, we review two orders entered by the Circuit Court for Baltimore City, which granted two separate Motions for Summary Judgment filed by Bank of America, N.A., appellee, against Sheldon, Inc., appellant ("Sheldon"), and Nancy Honeycutt, Personal Representative of the Estate of Ron Honeycutt, appellant ("the Estate"). Appellants' claims arose when Christine Honeycutt ("Christine Honeycutt") withdrew approximately $13,000 from the account of Sheldon maintained with the Bank. Christine Honeycutt was a former officer of Sheldon and, at the time of the withdrawal, was an authorized signatory on Sheldon's account.

On March 13, 2000, Sheldon commenced an action against Christine Honeycutt, the former vice-president and secretary of Sheldon, in the District Court of Maryland for Baltimore City in connection with her withdrawal of funds from Sheldon's account with the Bank * * *. On May 4, 2000, Sheldon amended its original Complaint in the District Court to assert additional claims against Christine Honeycutt and to add the Bank as a defendant. In its Amended Complaint, Sheldon asserted claims for conversion, breach of contract, and negligence against the Bank for permitting the allegedly unauthorized withdrawal.

* * *

On May 22, 2001, the Bank filed a Motion for Summary Judgment * * *. In its Motion, the Bank argued that * * * (ii) at the time Christine Honeycutt withdrew funds from Sheldon's account, she was an authorized signatory on the account and, therefore, the Bank committed no legal wrong when it permitted the withdrawal. * * *

* * *

Appellants' claims against Christine Honeycutt in the Circuit Court action were tried without a jury on February 15, 2002. The Honorable William D. Quarles presided and rendered a verdict in favor of the Estate and against Christine Honeycutt on the breach of contract claim.

The Estate and Sheldon filed a timely Notice of Appeal, on March 13, 2002, and now present two questions for our review:

> I. WAS THE LOWER COURT LEGALLY CORRECT IN GRANTING THE MOTION FOR SUMMARY JUDGMENT OF APPELLEE, BANK OF AMERICA, N.A. ("APPELLEE BANK") AGAINST APPELLANT SHELDON, INC. AND APPELLANT ESTATE, ON THE BASIS THAT THERE WAS NO FACTUAL EVIDENCE TO SUPPORT THE CONTENTION THAT APPELLEE BANK HAD BREACHED ITS AGREEMENT AND/OR HAD BEEN NEGLIGENT IN THIS MATTER?

* * *

For the reasons that follow, we shall affirm the judgment of the circuit court.

### Factual Background

Ron Honeycutt was the president, treasurer, and sole stockholder of Sheldon, Inc., which trades as Sheldon's Lounge, a bar located in Baltimore City. Christine Honeycutt was, at one time, Ron Honeycutt's wife and held the position of vice-president and secretary of Sheldon. On July 1, 1984, Ron Honeycutt and Christine Honeycutt opened a business checking account with Maryland National Bank, now known as Bank of America, N.A., in the name of Sheldon's Lounge. At that time, Ron Honeycutt and Christine Honeycutt executed a signature card for the account. The signature card read, in pertinent part:

> In consideration of the opening of this account and the maintenance thereof by Maryland National Bank (hereinafter "Bank), the signer(s) (hereinafter "depositor") by the signature(s) subscribed below agree(s) to the Rules and Regulations of Contract provided to depositor herewith. Bank is authorized to recognize and rely upon any of the signature(s) below on checks, drafts and orders for the payment of money, the withdrawals of funds, or the transaction of any business to this account. Depositor acknowledges receipt of a copy of the Rules and Regulations governing this account.

On the signature card, Ron Honeycutt and Christine Honeycutt checked off the box requiring only one signature to transact any business on the account. Ron Honeycutt and Christine Honeycutt were the only authorized signatories on the account and remained the only authorized signatories throughout the entire time that the Bank maintained the account.

Ron Honeycutt died February 10, 2000. On February 15, 2000, Christine Honeycutt withdrew funds in the amount of $13,066.48 from Sheldon's account. At the time of withdrawal, an employee of the Bank retrieved and reviewed the signature card on file with the Bank in order to verify Christine Honeycutt's authority to direct and conduct transactions on Sheldon's account. The Bank did not inquire as to Christine Honeycutt's status with respect to Sheldon, nor did they inquire of anyone at Sheldon as to her status. At the time, the Bank was unaware that Ron Honeycutt had died. The withdrawal took the form of a cashier's check made payable to Christine Honeycutt. According to the signature card on file at the Bank at the time Christine Honeycutt withdrew the funds, she was an authorized signatory on the account and the Bank was authorized to recognize and rely upon her signature on orders for the withdrawal of funds or the transaction of any business to the account. It was Christine Honeycutt's contention that the bank employees told her that the "money belonged to her."

### Discussion

* * *

Sheldon argues that the Bank breached its duty of care "by failing to make an adequate inquiry as to the authority of Christine Honeycutt to conduct banking on behalf of the business." We disagree.

"A bank and its customers enjoy a debtor/creditor relationship in which the rights and liabilities of each are contractual." [Citations.] "Implicit in the contract [between the bank and customer] is the duty of the bank to use ordinary care in disbursing the depositor's funds." [Citations.] * * *

A signature card may constitute a contract between a bank and its customer. [Citation.] "The signature card constituted the contract between the parties and, subject to the statutory schemes, regulates their rights and duties." [Citations.]

* * *

Here, Ron and Christine Honeycutt, on July 1, 1984, opened a business checking account in the name of Sheldon's Lounge with the Bank's predecessor. On that same day, Ron and Christine Honeycutt executed a signature card and checked off the box requiring only one signature to transact any business on the account. * * * [T]he signature card created a contractual obligation on the part of the Bank to pay the depositor's funds only as authorized by the signature card. The plain language of the signature card established that both Ron and Christine Honeycutt were authorized signatories able to transact business on Sheldon's account. Moreover, the signature card expressly and unambiguously provided that the Bank is authorized to recognize and rely upon either of Ron or Christine Honeycutt's signatures on checks, drafts and orders for the payment of money, the withdrawal of funds, or the transaction of any business to Sheldon's account.

When Christine Honeycutt withdrew funds from Sheldon's account, we find, the Bank did not breach any standard of care owed to appellants. The Bank exercised reasonable care when it inspected the signature card on file for Sheldon's account and verified that Christine Honeycutt was an authorized signatory on the account. Moreover, we are persuaded that no further inquiry was required as the Bank was legally entitled to release the funds to Christine Honeycutt based upon the express authority created by the signature card. Thus, because there was no genuine dispute as to any material fact, *i.e.*, that the 1984 signature card was the authoritative document on file with the Bank, we find that the lower court was correct to conclude, as a matter of law, that the signature card controlled the transaction and was correct to enter summary judgment in favor of appellee.

* * *

JUDGMENT AFFIRMED; * * *.

---

## CASE 30-2

## Payment of an Item/Stop Payment Order
## LEIBLING, P.C. v. MELLON PSFS (NJ) NATIONAL ASSOCIATION

Superior Court of New Jersey, Law Division, Special Civil Part, Camden County, 1998
710 A.2d 1067, 311 N.J. Super. 651, 35 UCC Rep. Serv.2d 590

**Rand, J.**

### Facts

Mr. Scott D. Liebling, P.C. (hereinafter "Plaintiff") is an attorney at law. Plaintiff maintains an attorney trust account ("Account") at Mellon Bank (NJ) National Association ("Mellon") * * *. Mellon uses a computerized system to process checks for payment.

Plaintiff represented defendant Fredy Winda Ramos ("Ramos") in a personal injury action which resulted in a settlement. On or about May 19, 1995, plaintiff issued Check No. 1031 in the amount of $8,483.06 to Ramos representing her net proceeds from the settlement. Mellon honored that check on May 26, 1995. On or about May 24, 1995, plaintiff mistakenly issued another check, Check No. 1043, to Ramos in the same amount of $8,483.06. Realizing his error, on or about May 30, 1995, Plaintiff called Ramos in Puerto Rico and advised her that the Check No. 1043 was issued by mistake and instructed her to destroy the check. Thereafter, Plaintiff called Mellon and ordered an oral stop payment on the check.

On December 21, 1996, some nineteen months after plaintiff issued the Check No. 1043, Ramos cashed the check from Puerto Rico.

Plaintiff filed this complaint against both Ramos and Mellon. Ramos was served and defaulted. Plaintiff's complaint against Mellon alleges breach of duty of good faith, negligence, breach of fiduciary duty, payment of a stale check, and breach of contract as a result of Mellon honoring the second check, Check No. 1043.

* * *

### Issue

Whether the defendant bank acted in good faith when it honored a check that was presented for payment nineteen months after it was issued and subsequent to the expiration of an oral stop payment order.

### Discussion

It is important to consider the relevant New Jersey statute sections before discussing what actions constitute "good faith." Under [UCC] 4–403(b):

> [a] stop-payment order is effective for six months, but it lapses after 14 calendar days if the original order was oral and was not confirmed in writing within that period. A stop-payment order may be renewed for additional six-month periods by a writing given to the bank within a period during which the stop-payment order is effective.

In addition, [UCC] 4–404 states:

> A bank is under no obligation to a customer having a checking account to pay a check, other than a certified check, which is presented more than six months after its date, but it may charge its customer's account for a payment made thereafter in good faith.

Thus, the issue in the present case turns on whether Mellon acted in good faith when it honored plaintiff's check. Good faith under N.J. Uniform Commercial Code has been defined in [UCC] 3–103(a)(4) as "honesty in fact and the observance of reasonable commercial standards of fair dealing." Since there is no New Jersey case law directly on point, it is necessary to consider alternate sources. One law review article [citation] addressed the present issue. Specifically, the article explained that "Article 4 of the Uniform Commercial Code imposes on all banks the responsibility to act in good faith and to exercise ordinary care. The drafters of the Code chose not to provide an explicit definition of 'ordinary' care, stating only that the term is to be used 'with its normal tort meaning and not in any special sense relating to bank collections.'" [Citation.] * * *

In addition, the Third Circuit case of [citation] appears to be analogous to the present issue. In [that case], an insurance company brought a subrogation action against a payor bank to recover on an altered check that the bank had paid. On April 17, 1984, the plaintiff placed a written stop-payment order on a certain check, and under applicable state law the stop-payment order was good for six months. On December 26, 1984, two months after the stop payment order had expired, the bank honored the check. Before concluding that the payor bank had acted in good faith, the court analyzed the definition of "good faith." The court stated that "[UCC] §1–201 defines good faith as 'honesty in fact.' This definition must be viewed subjectively; a finding of bad faith must be predicated on a showing of dishonesty. Likewise, mere negligence does not preclude a finding of good faith." [Citation.] In holding that the bank had acted in good faith, the court stated:

> [a]s a result of the expiration of the order, [the bank] cannot be said to have the actual knowledge that would deny it the status of a good faith payor * * *. The obligations which a bank incurs as a result of its customer's imposing a stop order on a check do not continue in perpetuity * * *. [The bank] was neither negligent nor reckless and certainly cannot be said to have been subjectively dishonest * * *. A finding of bad faith requires actual knowledge on the part of the payor. An objective inquiry into what the circumstances should have revealed to [the bank] is simply not germane to the analysis.

[Citation.]

* * *

In contrast, plaintiff's argument centers on the proposition that the bank's duty of good faith required it to inquire or consult with plaintiff before honoring a stale check that had a previous oral stop payment order on it. * * *

However, in the Uniform Commercial Code Treatise, Mr. Hawkland stated that the above cases are not consistent with the Uniform Commercial Code, specifically, "[t]he duty [of inquiry] is inconsistent with the provisions of subsection 4–403(2) on the expiration of the 'effectiveness' of stop orders. Such a duty is hardly practical today." Moreover: "[t]o require that a payor bank check the date of every check received via the collection process would unreasonably increase the cost of processing every check written today."

* * *

The Commercial Code was initially adopted in November, 1961 in New Jersey. In 1990, Articles III and IV of the Code were substantially revised relating to, among other things, bank deposits and collections to become effective on June 1, 1995. The court is satisfied as pointed out by the defendant that those Amendments were enacted in order to address the effect of automated systems utilized by banks with the substantial increase in check usage after the original enactment of the Code. The Official Code Comment to the 1995 Amendments for §[UCC] 4–101, states as follows:

> **1.** The great number of checks handled by banks and the country-wide nature of the bank collection process require uniformity in the law of bank collections. There is needed a uniform statement of

the principal rules of the bank collection process with ample provision for flexibility to meet the needs of the large volume handled and the changing needs and conditions that are bound to come with the years. The Article meets that need.

2. * * * An important goal of the 1990 revision of Article 4 is to promote the efficiency of the check collection process by making the provisions of Article 4 more compatible with the needs of an automated system and, by doing so, increase the speed and lower the cost of check collection for those who write and receive checks. * * *

[Citation.]

* * *

Thus, in determining whether the defendant bank in the present action acted in good faith, the above cited material must be analyzed and applied. First, it appears clear that the Uniform Commercial Code acknowledges that computerized check processing systems are common and accepted banking procedures in the United States. [Citation.] Therefore, it cannot be said that defendant bank acted in bad faith by using a computerized system when it honored plaintiff's "stale" check. Furthermore, it appears that the test for good faith is a subjective test. Thus, based on all of the foregoing material, as long as the defendant bank used an adequate computer system for processing checks (here there is no proof to the contrary), it appears to have acted in good faith even though it did not consult the Plaintiff before it honored the "stale" check that had an expired oral stop-payment order on it * * *. [T]he obligation of a bank to stop payment on a check does not continue in perpetuity once the stop payment order expires.

The bank's conduct was fair and in accordance with reasonable commercial standards. Accordingly, it appears that the defendant bank is not liable and should prevail. A finding of no liability is entered for the defendant bank.

CASE 30-3

## Bank's Right to Subrogation
## SEIGEL v. MERRILL LYNCH, PIERCE, FENNER, & SMITH, INC.

District of Columbia Court of Appeals, 2000
745 A.2d 301
http://www.dcbar.org/dcca/pdf/98cv1159.pdf

**Steadman J.**

* * *

The events giving rise to this lawsuit arose in January and February of 1997 * * *. During that time period, plaintiff/appellant Seigel, a Maryland resident, traveled to Atlantic City, New Jersey to gamble. While there, he wrote a number of checks to various casinos, and, in exchange, received gambling chips with which to wager. The checks were drawn on Seigel's cash management account with defendant/appellee, which was established through Merrill Lynch's District of Columbia offices. There were sufficient funds in the account to cover all the checks.

Seigel eventually gambled away all of the chips he had received for the checks. Upon returning to Maryland, Seigel discussed the status of the outstanding checks with Merrill Lynch, informing his broker of the gambling nature of the transactions, and his desire to avoid realizing the apparent losses. Merrill Lynch informed Seigel that it was possible to escape paying the checks by placing a stop payment order and liquidating his cash management account. Seigel took this advice and instructed Merrill Lynch to close his account, liquidate the assets, and not to honor any checks drawn on the account. Merrill Lynch agreed, and confirmed Seigel's instructions.

Many of the checks were subsequently dishonored, and are not now at issue. However, Merrill Lynch accidentally paid several of the checks totaling $143,000, despite the stop payment order and account closure. Merrill Lynch then debited Seigel's margin account to cover the payments.

Seigel brought suit in the District of Columbia against Merrill Lynch * * * demanding a return of the $143,000 plus interest * * *. Seigel filed a motion for summary judgment * * *. He argued that D.C. Code §16–1701 precluded enforcement of the checks as a void gambling debt, or in the alternative that New Jersey law prohibited the enforcement of the checks, and that therefore Merrill Lynch had no rights by way of subrogation as a defense to its payment over the stop payment order. Merrill Lynch made a cross-motion for summary judgment, denying the applicability of the D.C. statute or any relevant New Jersey law. It contended that it stood in the shoes of the casinos to whom valid and enforceable checks were given, and therefore the plaintiff had not suffered any actual loss as a result of the payment of the checks. On June 24, 1998, the trial court issued an order granting defendant's motion, and dismissing the complaint. This appeal followed.

* * *

We begin with an examination of the statutory scheme relating to stop payment orders, because we believe these provisions are determinative of this appeal. The relevant sections are found in the Uniform Commercial Code * * * §§4403 and 4407.

The basic right of the depositor to stop payment on any item drawn on the depositor's account is set forth in Section 4403(a). However, liability on the bank for payment over a stop payment order is far from automatic. On the contrary, Section 4403(c) provides: "The burden of establishing the fact and amount of loss resulting from the payment of an item contrary to a stop payment order or order to close an account is on the customer."

This provision, which places the burden on the customer to show actual loss, is reinforced by the extensive rights of subrogation given to the payor bank by Section 4407. Under that section, as to the drawer or maker (that is, the depositor), the bank is subrogated both to the rights of "any holder in due course on the item" and to the rights of "the payee or any other holder of the item against the drawer or maker either on the item or under the transaction out of which the item arose." As a leading authority on the Uniform Commercial Code has noted, this section "contemplates that the bank will use its subrogation rights primarily to defend against a suit by the customer to recover payment." [Citation.]

As applied to the facts here, then, Seigel is required to bear the burden of establishing that he in fact suffered a loss as a result of the payment of the checks. In assessing whether any such loss was actually incurred, Merrill Lynch must be treated as the subrogee of any rights of the casino payees against Seigel. As the payee of a dishonored check, the casino would have a prima facie right to recover its amount from Seigel as drawer, 3414(b), and the burden would be on Seigel to establish any defense he might assert on the instrument. 3308(b); [citation]. Seigel asserts two such defenses: duress and illegality. We turn to an examination of those defenses.

* * *

The entirety of appellant's duress argument emanates from a single sentence in his affidavit: "For years I have had [a] gambling problem." If not ambiguous, the statement is conclusory. Unlike the gambler in [citation], appellant fails to produce any evidence in the record, specific or otherwise, regarding his problem and its relation to any unconscionable duress in the transactions at issue. [Citation] (describing an abusive and bizarre "marathon gambling session," that included unsolicited credit increases from the casino, the existence of an alleged psychological disorder and defendant's concomitant use of pain killers, during which the defendant lost $285,000 in little over two days) * * *. We therefore conclude that Seigel's assertion that the checks would be unenforceable in New Jersey fails. Seigel also invokes the fact that these checks were given in order to obtain chips with which to gamble, and cites us in particular to D.C. Code * * * [which] provides that:

> A thing in action, judgment, mortgage, or other security or conveyance made and executed by a person in which any part of the consideration is for money or other valuable things won by playing at any game whatsoever, or by betting on the sides or hands of persons who play, or for the reimbursement or payment of any money knowingly lent or advanced for the purpose, or lent or advanced at the time and place of the play or bet, to a person so playing or betting or who, during the play, so plays or bets, is void.

In substance, Seigel claims that this statute would serve as a defense if the casinos were to seek to enforce the checks in the first instance in a District of Columbia court, and therefore this same statute requires that he be entitled to affirmatively recover from Merrill Lynch the amount of the checks in a District of Columbia court, regardless of the checks' enforceability elsewhere.

We may assume for present purposes that this statute would prevent direct enforcement of the checks in the District of Columbia, a somewhat dubious proposition in itself given the validity of the checks where made. But that is not this case. Rather, the question is whether under the relevant provisions of the Uniform Commercial Code, Seigel has met his burden of proof to establish actual loss. We think he has not.

As already indicated, even if payment had been stopped, the casinos could have enforced the checks in New Jersey, where the transaction was entered into. Merrill Lynch therefore, under the Code scheme, conceptually has the same right. Furthermore, even if there were a problem in asserting jurisdiction over Seigel in New Jersey, Maryland would have provided an appropriate forum for enforcing the checks. The highest Maryland court has squarely held that because there is no longer a strong public policy against gambling per se, * * * and that therefore Maryland courts will enforce gambling debts if legally incurred in a foreign jurisdiction. [Citation.] Accordingly the casinos, and hence derivatively Merrill Lynch, could enforce the checks directly against Seigel in the state of his residence—Maryland.

* * *

We conclude that Seigel failed to establish that he ultimately suffered any actual loss as a result of the payment of the checks by Merrill Lynch. * * *

*Affirmed.*

CASE 30-4

## Customer's Duties
## UNION PLANTERS BANK, NATIONAL ASSOCIATION v. ROGERS

Supreme Court of Mississippi, 2005
912 So.2d 116
http://www.mssc.state.ms.us/Images/Opinions/CO25666.pdf

**Waller, J.**

This appeal involves an issue of first impression in Mississippi—the interpretation of [UCC] 4–406 (Rev. 2002), which imposes duties on banks and their customers insofar as forgeries are concerned. The case arises from a series of forgeries made by one person on four checking accounts maintained by Helen Rogers at the Union Planters Bank. * * *

### Facts

Neal D. and Helen K. Rogers maintained four checking accounts with the Union Planters Bank in Greenville, Washington County, Mississippi. * * * The Rogers were both in their eighties when the events which gave rise to this lawsuit took place. After Neal became bedridden, Helen hired Jackie Reese to help her take care of Neal and to do chores and errands.

In September of 2000, Reese began writing checks on the Rogerses' four accounts and forged Helen's name on the signature line. Some of the checks were made out to "cash," some to "Helen K. Rogers," and some to "Jackie Reese." The following chart summarizes the forgeries to each account:

| ACCOUNT NUMBER | BEGINNING | ENDING | NUMBER OF CHECKS | AMOUNT OF CHECKS |
|---|---|---|---|---|
| 54282309 | 11/27/2000 | 6/18/2001 | 46 | $16,635.00 |
| 0039289441 | 9/27/2000 | 1/25/2001 | 10 | $ 2,701.00 |
| 6100110922 | 11/29/2000 | 8/13/2001 | 29 | $ 9,297.00 |
| 6404000343 | 11/20/2000 | 8/16/2001 | 83 | $29,765.00 |
| **TOTAL** | | | **168** | **$58,398.00** |

Neal died in late May of 2001. Shortly thereafter, the Rogerses' son, Neal, Jr., began helping Helen with financial matters. Together they discovered that many bank statements were missing and that there was not as much money in the accounts as they had thought. In June of 2001, they contacted Union Planters and asked for copies of the missing bank statements. In September of 2001, Helen was advised by Union Planters to contact the police due to forgeries made on her accounts. * * *

Subsequently, criminal charges were brought against Reese. In the meantime, Helen filed suit against Union Planters, alleging conversion (unlawful payment of forged checks) and negligence. After a trial, the jury awarded Helen $29,595 in damages, and the circuit court entered judgment accordingly. From this judgment, Union Planters appeals.

### Discussion

* * *

The relationship between Rogers and Union Planters is governed by Article 4 of the Uniform Commercial Code, [citation]. [UCC] Section 4–406(a) & (c) provide that a bank customer has a duty to discover and report "unauthorized signatures"; i.e., forgeries. Section 4–406 of the UCC reflects an underlying policy decision that furthers the UCC's "objective of promoting certainty and predictability in commercial transactions." The UCC facilitates financial transactions, benefitting both consumers and financial institutions, by allocating responsibility among the parties according to whomever is best able to prevent a loss. Because the customer is more familiar with his own signature, and should know whether or not he authorized a particular withdrawal or check, he can prevent further unauthorized activity better than a financial institution which may process thousands of transactions in a single day. Section 4–406 acknowledges that the customer is best situated to detect unauthorized transactions on his own account by placing the burden on the customer to exercise reasonable care to discover and report such transactions. The customer's duty to exercise this care is triggered when the bank satisfies its burden to provide sufficient information to the customer. As a result, if the bank provides sufficient information, the customer bears the loss when he fails to detect and notify the bank about unauthorized transactions. [Citation.]

#### *A. Union Planters' Duty to Provide Information under §4–406(a).*

The court admitted into evidence copies of all Union Planters statements sent to Rogers during the relevant time period. Enclosed with the bank statements were either the cancelled checks themselves or copies of the checks relating to the period of time of each statement. The evidence shows that all bank statements and cancelled checks were sent, via United States Mail, postage prepaid, to all customers at their "designated address" each month. Rogers introduced no evidence to the contrary. We therefore find that the bank fulfilled its duty of making the statements available to Rogers and that the remaining provisions of §4–406 are applicable to the case at bar. * * *

In defense of her failure to inspect the bank statements, Rogers claims that she never received the bank statements and cancelled checks. Even if this allegation is true, it does not excuse Rogers from failing to fulfill her duties under §4–406(a) & (c) because the statute clearly states a bank discharges its duty in providing the necessary information to a customer when it "*sends* … to a customer a statement of account showing payment of items." §4–406(a) (emphasis added). [Citation.] The word "receive" is absent. The customer's duty to inspect and report does not arise when the statement is received, as Rogers claims; the customer's duty to inspect and report arises when the bank sends the statement to the customer's address. A reasonable person who has not received a monthly statement from the bank would promptly ask the bank for a copy of the statement. Here, Rogers claims that she did not receive numerous statements. We find that she failed to act reasonably when she failed to take any action to replace the missing statements.

***B. Rogers' Duty to Report the Forgeries under §4–406(d).***

A customer who has not promptly notified a bank of an irregularity may be precluded from bringing certain claims against the bank:

> (d) If the bank proves that the customer failed, with respect to an item, to comply with the duties imposed on the customer by subsection (c), the customer is precluded from asserting against the bank:
>
> (1) The customer's unauthorized signature … on the item, if the bank also proves that it suffered a loss by reason of the failure; …

[UCC] §4–406(d)(1).

Also, when there is a series of forgeries, §4–406(d)(2) places additional duties on the customer:

> (2) The customer's unauthorized signature … by the same wrongdoer on any other item paid in good faith by the bank if the payment was made before the bank received notice from the customer of the unauthorized signature … and after the customer had been afforded a reasonable period of time, not exceeding thirty (30) days, in which to examine the item or statement of account and notify the bank.

A bank may shorten the customer's thirty-day period for notifying the bank of a series of forgeries, and here, Union Planters shortened the thirty-day period to fifteen days. The statute states that a customer must report a series of forgeries within "a reasonable period of time, *not exceeding* thirty (30) days." "The 30-day period is an outside limit only. However 30 days is presumed to be reasonable and the bank bears the burden of proving otherwise." [Citation.]

Although there is no mention of a specific date, Rogers testified that she and her son began looking for the statements in late May or early June of 2001, after her husband had died. Her son felt that it was prudent to consolidate some of the five bank accounts. When they discovered that statements were missing, they notified Union Planters in June of 2001 to replace the statements. At this time, no mention of possible forgery was made, even though Neal, Jr., thought that "something was wrong." In fact, Neal, Jr., had felt that something was wrong as far back as December of 2000, but failed to do anything. Neal, Jr., testified that neither he nor his mother knew that Reese had been forging checks until September of 2001. Courts in Louisiana and Texas have held that, under similar circumstances, a customer's claims against a bank for paying forged checks are without merit. [Citations.]

Rogers is therefore precluded from making claims against Union Planters because (1) under §4–406(a), Union Planters provided the statements to Rogers, and (2) under §4–406(d)(2), Rogers failed to notify Union Planters of the forgeries within 15 and/or 30 days of the date she should have reasonably discovered the forgeries.

* * *

* * * [U]nder §4–406, Rogers is precluded from recovering amounts paid by Union Planters on any of the forged checks because she failed to timely detect and notify the bank of the unauthorized transactions and because she failed to show that Union Planters failed to use ordinary care in its processing of the forged checks. Therefore, we reverse the circuit court's judgment and render judgment here that Rogers take nothing and that the complaint and this action are finally dismissed with prejudice.

## QUESTIONS

1. Identify and explain the various stages and parties to the collection of a check.
2. Discuss the duties of collecting banks.
3. Discuss the relationship between a payor bank and its customers.
4. Define a consumer electronic funds transfer and outline the major provisions of the Electronic Fund Transfer Act.
5. Define a wholesale funds transfer and identify the parties to such a transfer.

## PROBLEMS

**1.** On November 9, Jane Jones writes a check for $5,000 payable to Ralph Rodgers in payment for goods to be received later in the month. Before the close of business on November 9, Jane notifies the bank by telephone to stop payment on the check. On December 19, Ralph gives the check to Bill Briggs for value and without notice. On December 20, Bill deposits the check in his account at Bank A. On December 21, Bank A sends the check to its correspondent, Bank B. On December 22, Bank B presents the check through the clearinghouse to Bank C. On December 23, Bank C presents the check to Bank P, the payor bank. On December 28, the payor bank makes payment of the check final. Is Jane Jones' stop payment order effective against the payor bank? Explain.

**2.** Howard Harrison, a longtime customer of Western Bank, operates a small department store, Harrison's Store. Because his store has few experienced employees, Harrison frequently travels throughout the United States on buying trips, although he also runs the financial operations of the business. On one of his buying trips, Harrison purchased two hundred sport shirts from Well-Made Shirt Company and paid for the transaction with a check on his store account with Western Bank in the amount of $3,000. Adams, an employee of Well-Made who deposits its checks in Security Bank, sloppily raised the amount of the check to $30,000 and indorsed the check, "Pay to the order of Adams from Pension Plan Benefits, Well-Made Shirt Company by Adams." He cashed the check and cannot be found. Western Bank processed the check, paid it, and sent it to Harrison's Store with the monthly statement. After briefly examining the statement, Harrison left on another buying trip for three weeks.

**(a)** Assuming the bank acted in good faith and the alteration is not discovered and reported to the bank until an audit conducted thirteen months after the statement was received by Harrison's Store, who must bear the loss on the raised check?

**(b)** Assume that Harrison, who was unable to examine his statement promptly because of his buying trips, left instructions with the bank to carefully examine and to notify him of any item over $5,000 to be charged to his account; assume further that the bank nevertheless paid the item in his absence. Who bears the loss if the alteration is discovered one month after the statement was received by Harrison's Store? If the alteration is discovered thirteen months later?

**3.** Tom Jones owed Bank of Cleveland $10,000 on a note due November 17, with 1 percent interest due the bank for each day delinquent in payment. Jones issued a $10,000 check to Bank of Cleveland and deposited it in the night vault the evening of November 17. Several days later, he received a letter saying he owed one day's interest on the payment because of a one-day delinquency in payment. Jones refused because he said he had put the payment in the vault on November 17. Who is correct? Why?

**4.** Assume that Dinah draws a check on Oxford Bank, payable to the order of Pam; that Pam indorses it to Amy; that Amy deposits it to her account in Houston Bank; that Houston Bank presents it to Oxford Bank, the drawee; and that Oxford Bank dishonors it because of insufficient funds. Houston Bank receives notification of the dishonor on Monday but, because of an interruption of communication facilities, fails to notify Amy until Wednesday. What result?

**5.** Jones, a food wholesaler whose company has an account with City Bank in New York City, is traveling in California on business. He finds a particularly attractive offer and decides to buy a carload of oranges for delivery in New York. He gives Saltin, the seller, his company's check for $25,000 to pay for the purchase. Saltin deposits the check, with others he received that day, with his bank, the Carrboro Bank. Carrboro Bank sends the check to Downs Bank in Los Angeles, which in turn deposits it with the Los Angeles Federal Reserve Bank. The L.A. Fed sends the check, with others, to the N.Y. Fed, which forwards the check to City Bank, Jones's bank, for collection.

**(a)** Is City Bank a depositary bank? A collecting bank? A payor bank?

**(b)** Is Carrboro Bank a depositary bank? A collecting bank?

**(c)** Is the N.Y. Fed an intermediary bank?

**(d)** Is Downs Bank a collecting bank?

**6.** On April 1, Moore gave Pipkin a check properly drawn by Moore on Zebra Bank for $5,000 in payment of a painting to be framed and delivered the next day. Pipkin immediately indorsed the check and gave it to Yeager Bank as payment in full of his indebtedness to the bank on a note he previously had signed. Yeager Bank canceled the note and returned it to Pipkin.

On April 2, upon learning that the painting had been destroyed in a fire at Pipkin's studio, Moore promptly went to Zebra Bank, signed a printed form of stop payment order, and gave it to the cashier. Zebra Bank refused payment on the check upon proper presentment by Yeager Bank.

**(a)** What are the rights of Yeager Bank against Zebra Bank?

**(b)** What are the rights of Yeager Bank against Moore?

**(c)** Assuming that Zebra Bank inadvertently paid the amount of the check to Yeager Bank and debited Moore's account, what are the rights of Moore against Zebra Bank?

**7.** As payment in advance for services to be performed, Acton signed and delivered the following instrument:

> December 1, 2011
> LAST NATIONAL BANK
> MONEYVILLE, STATE X
> Pay to the order of Olaf Owen $10,500.00
> Ten Thousand Five Hundred Dollars for services to be performed by Olaf Owen starting on December 6, 2011.
> (signed) Arthur Acton

Owen requested and received Last National Bank's certification of the check even though Acton had only $9,000 on deposit. Owen indorsed the check in blank and delivered it to Dan Doty in payment of a preexisting debt.

When Owen failed to appear for work, Acton issued a written stop payment order ordering the bank not to pay the check. Doty presented the check to Last National Bank for payment. The bank refused payment.

What are the bank's rights and liabilities relating to the transactions described?

**8.** Jones drew a check for $1,000 on The First Bank and mailed it to the payee, Thrift, Inc. Caldwell stole the check from Thrift, Inc., chemically erased the name of the payee, and inserted the name of Henderson as payee. Caldwell also increased the amount of the check to $10,000 and, by using the name of Henderson, negotiated the check to Willis. Willis then took the check to The First Bank, obtained its certification on the check, and negotiated the check to Griffin, who deposited the check in The Second National Bank for collection. The Second National Bank forwarded the check to the Detroit Trust Company for collection from The First Bank, which honored the check. Griffin exhausted her account in The Second National Bank, and the account was closed. Shortly thereafter, The First Bank learned that it had paid an altered check. What are the rights of each of the parties?

**9.** Jason, who has extremely poor vision, went to an automated teller machine (ATM) to withdraw $200 on February 1. Joshua saw that Jason was having great difficulty reading the computer screen and offered to help. Joshua obtained Jason's personal identification number and secretly exchanged one of his old credit cards for Jason's ATM card. Between February 1 and February 15, Joshua withdrew $1,600 from Jason's account. On February 15, Jason discovered that his ATM card was missing and immediately notified his bank. The bank closed Jason's ATM account on February 16, by which time Joshua had withdrawn another $150. What is Jason's liability, if any, for the unauthorized use of his account?

**10.** On July 21, Boehmer, a customer of Birmingham Trust, secured a loan from that bank for the principal sum of $5,500 to purchase a boat allegedly being built for him by A.C. Manufacturing Company, Inc. After Boehmer signed a promissory note, Birmingham Trust issued a cashier's check to Boehmer and A.C. Manufacturing Company as payees. The check was given to Boehmer, who then forged A.C. Manufacturing Company's indorsement and deposited the check in his own account at Central Bank. Central Bank credited Boehmer's account and then placed the legend "P.I.G.," meaning "Prior Indorsements Guaranteed," on the check. The check was presented to and paid by Birmingham Trust on July 22. When the loan became delinquent in March of the following year, Birmingham Trust contacted A.C. Manufacturing Company to learn the location of the boat. They were informed that it had never been purchased, and they soon after learned that Boehmer had died on January 24 of that year. Can Birmingham Trust obtain reimbursement from Central Bank under Central's warranty of prior indorsements? Explain.

**11.** Advanced Alloys, Inc., issued a check in the amount of $2,500 to Sergeant Steel Corporation. The check was presented for payment fourteen months later to the Chase Manhattan Bank, which made payment on the check and charged Advanced Alloy's account. Can Advanced Alloys recover the payment made on the check? Why?

**12.** Laboratory Management deposited into its account at Pulaski Bank a check issued by Fairway Farms in the amount of $150,000. The date of deposit was February 5. Pulaski, the depositary bank, initiated the collection process immediately by forwarding the check to Worthen Bank on the sixth. Worthen sent the check on for collection to M Bank Dallas, and M Bank Dallas, still on February 6, delivered the check to M Bank Fort Worth. That same day, M Bank Fort Worth delivered the check to the Fort Worth Clearinghouse. Because TAB/West Side, the drawee/payor bank, was not a clearinghouse member, it had to rely on TAB/Fort Worth for further transmittal of the check. TASI, a processing center used by both TAB/Forth Worth and TAB/West Side, received the check on the sixth and processed it as a reject item because of insufficient funds. On the seventh, TAB/West Side determined to return the check unpaid. TASI gave M Bank Dallas telephone notice of the return on February 7 but physically misrouted the check. Because of this, M Bank Dallas did not physically receive the check until February 19. However, M Bank notified Worthen by telephone on the fifteenth of the dishonor and return of the check. Worthen received the check on the twenty-first and notified Pulaski by telephone on the twenty-second. Pulaski actually received the check from Worthen on the twenty-third. On February 22 and 23, Laboratory Management's checking account with Pulaski was $46,000. Pulaski did not freeze the account because it considered the return to be too late. The Laboratory Management account was finally frozen on April 30, 1985, when it had a balance of $1,400. Pulaski brings this suit against TAB/Fort Worth, TAB/Dallas, and TASI alleging their notice of dishonor was not timely relayed to Pulaski. Explain whether Pulaski is correct in its assertion.

**13.** On Tuesday, June 11, Siniscalchi issued a $200 check on the drawee, Valley Bank. On Saturday morning, June 15, the check was cashed. This transaction, as well as others taking place on that Saturday morning, was not recorded or processed through the bank's bookkeeping system until Monday, June 17. On that date, Siniscalchi arrived at the bank at 9:00 A.M. and asked to place a stop payment order on the check. A bank employee checked the bank records, which at that time indicated the instrument had not cleared the bank. At 9:45 A.M. she gave him a printed notice confirming his request to stop payment. Siniscalchi sought to recover the $200 paid on the check. Explain whether the stop payment order was effective.

**14.** Morvarid Kashanchi and her sister, Firoyeh Paydar, held a savings account with Texas Commerce Medical Bank. An unauthorized withdrawal of $4,900 from the account was allegedly made by means of a telephone conversation between some other unidentified individual and a bank employee. Paydar learned of the transfer of funds when she received her bank statement and notified the bank that the withdrawal was unauthorized. The bank, however, declined to recredit the account for the $4,900 transfer. Kashanchi brought an action against the bank, claiming that the bank had violated the Electronic Fund Transfer Act (EFTA). The bank defended by arguing that the Act did not apply. Is the transaction governed by the EFTA? Explain.

**15.** Tally held a savings account with American Security Bank. On seven occasions, Tally's personal secretary, who received his bank statements and had custody of his passbook, forged Tally's name on withdrawal slips that she then presented to the bank. The secretary obtained $52,825 in this manner. Three years after the secretary's last fraudulent withdrawal she confessed to Tally who promptly notified the bank of the issue. Can Tally recover the funds from American Security Bank?

**16.** For a period of sixteen months, Great Lakes Higher Education Corp. (Great Lakes), a not-for-profit student loan servicer, issued 224 student loan checks totaling $273,152.88. The checks were drawn against Great Lakes' account at First Wisconsin National Bank of Milwaukee (First Wisconsin). Each of the 224 checks was presented to Austin Bank of Chicago (Austin) without indorsement of the named payee. Austin Bank accepted each check for purposes of collection and without delay forwarded each check to First Wisconsin for that purpose. First Wisconsin paid Austin Bank the face amount of each check even though the indorsement signature of the payee was not on any of the checks. Has Austin Bank breached its warranty to First Wisconsin and Great Lakes due to the absence of proper indorsements? Explain.

**17.** Plaintiff, Mary Mansi, claims that eighteen checks on her account contain forgeries but were paid by the defendant bank, Sterling National Bank. These checks bore signatures which, according to the plaintiff's handwriting expert, were apparently "written by another person who attempted to simulate her signature" and thus were not considered obvious forgeries. The plaintiff stated at a deposition that she did not review her monthly bank statements. Sterling National Bank acknowledges that while it did honor those eighteen checks, nine of them were returned to the plaintiff more than one year prior to this action. The defendant also asserts that the plaintiff's claims on the remaining nine checks are barred due to her failure to examine her monthly bank statements. Who should prevail? Explain.

P A R T 6

# Unincorporated Business Associations

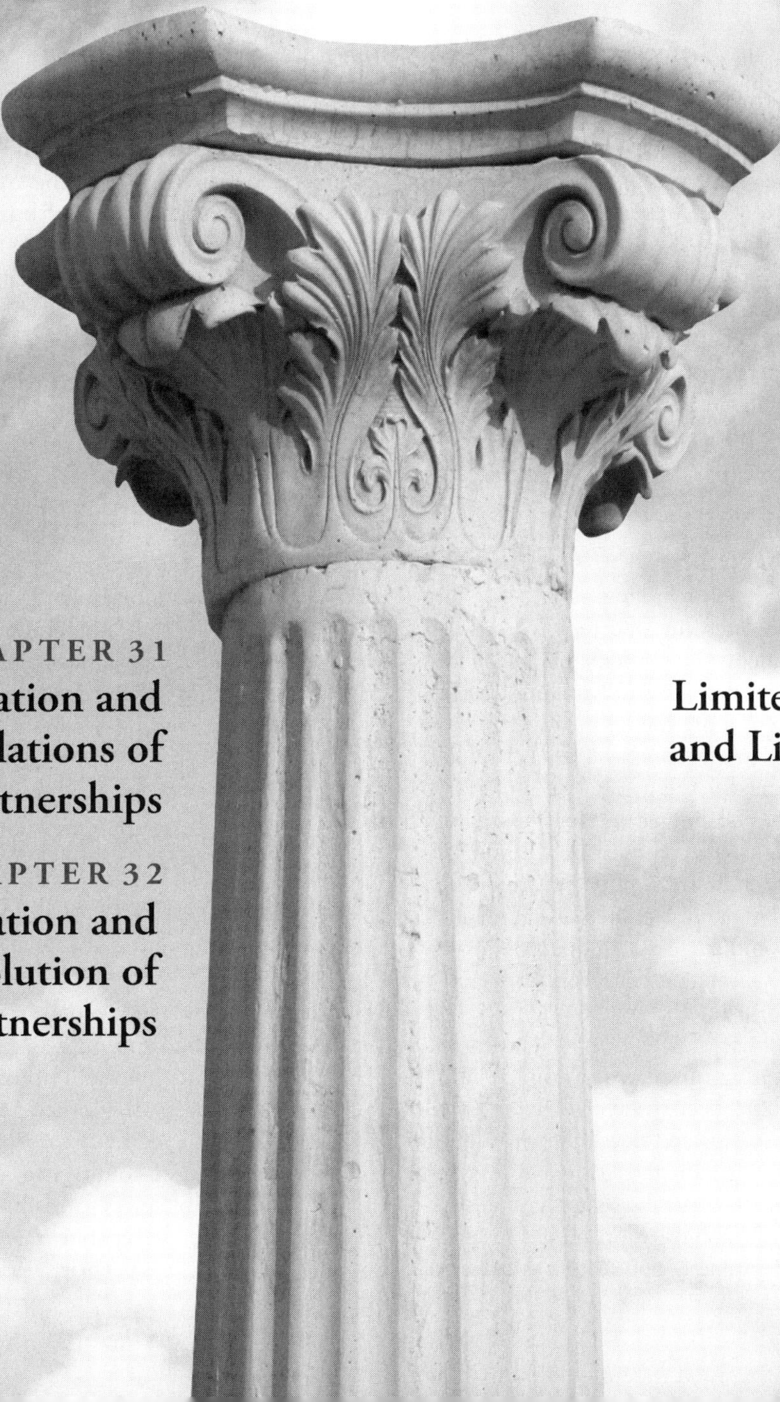

CHAPTER 31
## Formation and Internal Relations of General Partnerships

CHAPTER 32
## Operation and Dissolution of General Partnerships

CHAPTER 33
## Limited Partnerships and Limited Liability Companies

# CHAPTER 31

# Formation and Internal Relations of General Partnerships

A business enterprise may be operated or conducted as a sole proprietorship, an unincorporated business association (such as a general partnership, a limited partnership, or a limited liability company [LLC]), or a corporation. The choice of the most appropriate form cannot be determined in a general way but depends on the particular circumstances of the owners. We will begin this chapter with a brief overview of the various types of business associations and the factors that are relevant to deciding which form to use. The rest of this chapter and the next chapter will examine general partnerships. *Chapter 33* will cover other types of unincorporated business associations. *Part 7 (Chapters 34* through *37)* will address corporations.

## CHOOSING A BUSINESS ASSOCIATION

The owners of an enterprise determine the form of business unit they wish to use based upon their specific circumstances. In the United States there are more than 32 million business entities, with annual receipts of more than $34 trillion. There are approximately 23 million sole proprietorships, 5.9 million corporations, 1.8 million limited liability companies, 740,000 general partnerships, and 530,000 limited partnerships. Unincorporated business associations are common in a number of areas. General partnerships, for example, are used frequently in finance, insurance, accounting, real estate, law, and other service-related fields. Joint ventures have enjoyed popularity among major corporations planning to engage in cooperative research; in the exploitation of land and mineral rights; in the development, promotion, and sale of patents, trade names, and copyrights; and in manufacturing operations in foreign countries. Limited partnerships have been widely used for enterprises such as real estate investment and development, motion picture and theater productions, oil and gas ventures, and equipment leasing. In the last few years the States have authorized the formation of limited liability companies. This form of business organization will probably appeal to a number of businesses including real estate ventures, high-technology enterprises, businesses in which transactions involve foreign investors, professional organizations, corporate joint ventures, start-up businesses, and venture capital projects.

First to be discussed are the most important factors to consider in choosing a form of business association. This is followed by a brief description of the various forms of business associations and how they differ with respect to these factors.

◆ **SEE FIGURE 31-1: General Partnership, Limited Partnership, Limited Liability Company, and Corporation**

## FACTORS AFFECTING THE CHOICE

In choosing the form in which to conduct business the owners should consider a number of factors, including ease of formation, Federal and State income tax laws, external liability, management and control, transferability of ownership interests, and continuity. The relative importance of each factor will vary with the specific needs and objectives of the owners.

### EASE OF FORMATION

Business associations differ as to the formalities and expenses of formation. Some can be created with no formality, while others require the filing of documents with the State.

### TAXATION

Some business associations are not considered to be separate taxable entities, and taxation is on a "pass-through" basis. In these cases, the income of the business is conclusively presumed to have been distributed to the owners, who must pay taxes on that income. Losses receive comparable treatment and can be used to offset some of the owners' income. In contrast, some business forms, most significantly corporations, are considered separate tax entities and are directly taxed. When such an entity distributes income to the

◆ **FIGURE 31-1: General Partnership, Limited Partnership, Limited Liability Company, and Corporation**

| | General Partnership | Limited Partnership | Limited Liability Company | Corporation |
|---|---|---|---|---|
| **Transferability** | Financial interest may be assigned; membership requires consent of all partners | Financial interest may be assigned, and assignee may become limited partner if all partners consent | Financial interest may be assigned; membership requires consent of all members | Freely transferable unless shareholders agree otherwise |
| **Liability** | Partners have unlimited liability[1] | General partners have unlimited liability[2]; Limited partners have limited liability | All members have limited liability | Shareholders have limited liability |
| **Control** | By all partners | By general partners, not limited partners | By all members | By board of directors elected by shareholders |
| **Continuity** | RUPA: Usually unaffected by death, bankruptcy, or—in a term partnership—withdrawal of partner; UPA: Dissolved by death, bankruptcy, or withdrawal of partner | Dissolved by death, bankruptcy, or withdrawal of general partner; Unaffected by death, bankruptcy, or withdrawal of limited partner | In many States death, bankruptcy, or withdrawal of member does *not* dissolve LLC | Unaffected by death, bankruptcy, or withdrawal of shareholder |
| **Taxation** | May elect that only partners are taxed | May elect that only partners are taxed | May elect that only members are taxed | Corporation taxed unless Subchapter S applies; Shareholders taxed |

Note: RUPA = Revised Uniform Partnership Act; UPA = Uniform Partnership Act.

[1] In an LLP, the partners' liability is limited for some or all of the partnership's obligations
[2] In an LLLP, the partners' liability is limited for some or all of the partnership's obligations

owners, that income is separately taxed to the recipients. Thus, these funds are taxed twice: once to the entity and once to the owners. Unincorporated business entities can elect whether or not to be taxed as a separate entity. All businesses that have publicly traded ownership interests must be taxed as a corporation.

## EXTERNAL LIABILITY

External liability arises in a variety of ways, but the crucial and most commonly occurring are tort and contract liability. Owners of some business forms have unlimited liability for all of the obligations of the business. Thus, if the business does not have sufficient funds to pay its debts, each and every owner has personal liability to the creditors for the full amount of the debts. In brief, owners of interests in businesses with unlimited liability place their entire estates at risk. In some types of entities, the owners have unlimited liability for some but not all of the entity's obligations. Finally, in some types of business associations, the owners enjoy limited liability, which means their liability is limited to the extent of their capital contribution. It should be noted, however, that creditors often require that the owners of small businesses guarantee personally loans made to the businesses. Moreover, an owner of *any* type of business does not have limited liability for his own tortious conduct; the person is liable as an individual tortfeasor.

## MANAGEMENT AND CONTROL

In some entities, the owners can fully share in the control of the business. In other types of business associations, the owners are restricted as to their right to take part in control.

## TRANSFERABILITY

An ownership interest in a business consists of a financial interest, which is the right to share in the profits of the business, and a management interest, which is the right to participate in control of the business. In some types of business associations, the owners may freely transfer their financial interest but may not transfer their management interest without the consent of all of the other owners. In other types of business associations, the entire ownership interest is freely transferable.

### CONTINUITY

Some business associations have low continuity, which means that the death, bankruptcy, or withdrawal of an owner results in the dissolution of the association. Other types have high continuity and are not affected by the death, bankruptcy, or withdrawal of owners.

## FORMS OF BUSINESS ASSOCIATIONS

This section contains a brief description of the various types of business associations and how they differ with respect to the factors just discussed. In addition, general partnerships, limited partnerships, LLCs, limited liability partnerships (LLPs), and corporations will be discussed more extensively in this and the next part of the book.

### SOLE PROPRIETORSHIP

A sole proprietorship is an unincorporated business consisting of one person who owns and completely controls the business. It is formed without any formality, and no documents need be filed. Moreover, if one person conducts a business and does not file with the State to form an LLC or corporation, a sole proprietorship will result by default. A sole proprietorship is not a separate taxable entity and only the sole proprietor is taxed. Sole proprietors have unlimited liability for the sole proprietorship's debts. The sole proprietor's interest in the business is freely transferable. The death of a sole proprietor dissolves the sole proprietorship.

### GENERAL PARTNERSHIP

A general partnership is an unincorporated business association consisting of two or more persons who co-own a business for profit. It is formed without any formality, and no documents need be filed. Thus, if two or more people conduct a business and do not file with the State to form another type of business organization, a general partnership will result by default. A partnership may elect not to be a separate taxable entity, in which case only the partners are taxed. Partners have unlimited liability for the partnership's debts. Each partner has an equal right to control of the partnership. Partners may assign their financial interest in the partnership, but the assignee may become a member of the partnership only if all of the members consent. Under the Revised Partnership Act the death or bankruptcy of a partner usually does not dissolve a partnership; the same is also true in a term partnership for the withdrawal of a partner.

### JOINT VENTURE

A joint venture is an unincorporated business association composed of persons who combine their property, money, efforts, skill, and knowledge for the purpose of carrying out a particular business enterprise for profit. Usually, although not necessarily, it is of short duration. A joint venture, therefore, differs from a partnership, which is formed to carry on a business over a considerable or indefinite period of time. Nonetheless, except for a few differences, the law of partnerships generally governs a joint venture. An example of a joint venture is a securities underwriting syndicate or a syndicate formed to acquire a certain tract of land for subdivision and resale. Other common examples involve joint research conducted by corporations, the exploitation of mineral rights, and manufacturing operations in foreign countries.

### LIMITED PARTNERSHIP

A limited partnership is an unincorporated business association consisting of at least one general partner and at least one limited partner. It is formed by filing a certificate of limited partnership with the State. A limited partnership may elect not to be a separate taxable entity, in which case only the partners are taxed. Publicly traded limited partnerships, however, are subject to corporate income taxation. General partners have unlimited liability for the partnership's debts; limited partners have limited liability. Each general partner has an equal right to control of the partnership; limited partners have no right to participate in control. Partners may assign their financial interest in the partnership, but the assignee may become a limited partner only if all of the members consent. The death, bankruptcy, or withdrawal of a general partner dissolves a limited partnership; the limited partners have neither the right nor the power to dissolve the limited partnership.

### LIMITED LIABILITY COMPANY

An LLC is an unincorporated business association that provides limited liability to all of its owners (members) and permits all of its members to participate in management of the business. It may elect not to be a separate taxable entity, in which case only the members are taxed. As noted previously, publicly traded LLCs are subject to corporate income taxation. If an LLC has only one member, then it will be taxed as a sole proprietorship, unless separate entity tax treatment is elected. Thus, the LLC provides many of the advantages of a general partnership plus limited liability for all its members. Its benefits outweigh those of a limited partnership in that all members of an LLC not only enjoy limited liability but also may participate in management and control of the business. In most States members may assign their financial interest in the LLC, but the assignee may become a member of the LLC only if all of the members consent or the LLC's operating agreement provides otherwise. In some States the death, bankruptcy, or withdrawal of a member dissolves an LLC; in others they do not. Every State has adopted an LLC statute.

### LIMITED LIABILITY PARTNERSHIP

A registered LLP is a general partnership that, by making the statutorily required filing, limits the liability of its partners for some or all of the partnership's obligations. To become an LLP, a general partnership must file with the State an application containing specified information. All of the States have enacted LLP statutes. Except for the filing requirements and the partners' liability shield, the law governing LLPs is identical to the law governing general partnerships.

### LIMITED LIABILITY LIMITED PARTNERSHIP

A limited liability limited partnership (LLLP) is a limited partnership in which the liability of the general partners has been limited to the same extent as in an LLP. A growing number of States authorize LLLPs enabling the general partners in an LLLP to obtain the same degree of liability limitation that general partners can achieve in LLPs. Where available, a limited partnership may register as an LLLP without having to form a new organization, as would be the case in converting to an LLC.

### CORPORATION

A corporation is a legal entity separate and distinct from its owners. It is formed by filing its articles of incorporation with the State. A corporation is taxed as a separate entity, and shareholders are taxed on corporate earnings that are distributed to them. (Some corporations are eligible to elect to be taxed as Subchapter S corporations, which results in only the shareholders being taxed.) The shareholders have limited liability for the corporation's obligations. The board of directors elected by the shareholders manages the corporation. Shares in a corporation are freely transferable. The death, bankruptcy, or withdrawal of a shareholder does not dissolve the corporation.

### BUSINESS TRUSTS

The business trust, sometimes called a Massachusetts trust, was devised to avoid the burdens of corporate regulation, particularly the formerly widespread prohibition denying to corporations the power to own and deal in real estate. The business trust is used today primarily for asset securitization ventures in which income-generating assets, such as mortgages, are pooled in a trust. Like an ordinary trust between natural persons, a business trust may be created by a voluntary agreement without any authorization or consent of the State. A business trust has three distinguishing characteristics: (1) the trust estate is devoted to the conduct of a business; (2) by the terms of the agreement, each beneficiary is entitled to a certificate evidencing his ownership of a beneficial interest in the trust, which he is free to sell or otherwise transfer; and (3) the trustees have the exclusive right to manage and control the business free from control of the beneficiaries. If the third condition is not met, the trust may fail; the beneficiaries, by participating in control, would become personally liable as partners for the obligations of the business.

The trustees are personally liable for the debts of the business unless, in entering into contractual relations with others, it is expressly stated or definitely understood between the parties that the obligation is incurred solely upon the responsibility of the trust estate. To escape personal liability on the contractual obligations of the business, the trustee must obtain the agreement or consent of the other contracting party to look solely to the assets of the trust. The personal liability of the trustees for their own torts or the torts of their agents and servants employed in the operation of the business stands on a different footing. Although this liability cannot be avoided, the risk involved may be reduced substantially or eliminated altogether by insurance. In most jurisdictions, the beneficiaries of a business trust have no liability for obligations of the business trust.

## FORMATION OF GENERAL PARTNERSHIPS

The form of business association known as partnership can be traced to ancient Babylonia, classical Greece, and the Roman Empire. It was also used in Europe and England during the Middle Ages. Eventually the English common law recognized partnerships. In the nineteenth century, partnerships were widely used in England and the United States, and the common law of partnership developed considerably during this period. Partnerships are important in that they allow individuals with different expertise, backgrounds, resources, and interests to form a more competitive enterprise by combining their various skills. This part of the chapter will cover the nature of general partnerships and how they are formed. It should be recalled that except for the filing requirements and the partners' liability shield, the law governing LLPs is identical to the law governing general partnerships.

## NATURE OF PARTNERSHIP

In 1914, the National Conference of Commissioners on Uniform State Laws promulgated the Uniform Partnership Act (UPA). Since then it had been adopted in all States (except Louisiana) as well as by the District of Columbia, the Virgin Islands, and Guam. (The UPA is reprinted in Appendix C.)

In August 1986, the UPA Revision Subcommittee of the Committee on Partnerships and Unincorporated Business Organizations of the American Bar Association's Section of Corporation, Banking, and Business Law and the National Conference of Commissioners on Uniform State Laws decided to undertake a complete revision of the UPA. The revision was approved in August 1992 and was amended in 1993, 1994, 1996, and 1997. More than thirty-five States have adopted the Revised Act. This chapter will discuss the Revised Uniform Partnership Act or RUPA. (Selected provisions of the RUPA are reprinted in Appendix D.) Where the RUPA has made significant changes, the original 1914 UPA will also be discussed. (References to provisions of the RUPA will state the section number only; references to the original UPA will include the "UPA" designation.) The chapter summary reflects the RUPA.

Though fairly comprehensive, the RUPA and UPA do not cover all legal issues concerning partnerships. Accordingly, both the RUPA (Section 104) and the UPA (Section 5) provide that unless displaced by particular provisions of this Act, the principles of law and equity supplement this Act.

### DEFINITION

The RUPA defines a **partnership** as "an association of two or more persons to carry on as co-owners a business for profit." Section 101(6). The RUPA broadly defines "person" to include "individuals, partnerships, corporations, joint ventures, business trusts, estates, trusts, and any other legal or commercial entity." Section 101(10). The comments indicate that this definition would include an LLC. Also defined by Section 101, a business includes every trade, occupation, and profession. The UPA has similar definitions. UPA Sections 2 and 6.

### ENTITY THEORY

A **legal entity** is a unit capable of possessing legal rights and of being subject to legal duties. A legal entity may acquire, own, and dispose of property. It may enter into contracts, commit wrongs, sue, and be sued. For example, each business corporation is a legal entity having a legal existence separate from that of its shareholders.

A partnership was regarded by the common law as a legal aggregate, a group of individuals having no legal existence apart from that of its members. The Revised Act has greatly increased the extent to which partnerships are treated as entities. It applies aggregate treatment to very few aspects of partnerships, the most significant of which is that partners still have unlimited liability for the partnership's obligations. The UPA treats partnerships as legal entities for some purposes and as aggregates for others.

**PARTNERSHIP AS A LEGAL ENTITY** The RUPA Section 201 states: "A partnership is an entity distinct from its partners." The Revised Act embraces the entity treatment of partnerships, particularly in matters concerning title to partnership property, legal actions by and against the partnership, and continuity of existence. Examples of entity treatment include the following: (1) The assets of the firm are treated as those of the business and are considered to be distinct from the individual assets of the members. Section 203. (2) A partner is accountable as a fiduciary to the partnership. Section 404. (3) Every partner is considered an agent of the partnership. Section 301. (4) A partnership may sue and be sued in the name of the partnership. Section 307.

**PARTNERSHIP AS A LEGAL AGGREGATE** The Revised Act has retained the aggregate characteristic of a partner's unlimited liability for partnership obligations, unless the partnership has filed a statement of qualification to become an LLP. Section 306. Thus, if Meg and Mike enter into a partnership that becomes insolvent, as does Meg, Mike is fully liable for the partnership's debts. Likewise, although a partner's interest in the partnership may be assigned, the assignee does not become a partner without the consent of all the partners. Sections 401(i), 502. Moreover, a partner's dissociation results in dissolution, although only in limited circumstances. Section 801.

Under the UPA, because a partnership is considered an aggregate for some purposes, it can neither sue nor be sued in the firm name unless a statute specifically allows such an action. In addition, a partnership generally lacks continuity of existence: whenever any partner ceases to be associated with the partnership, it is dissolved. UPA Section 29.

## FORMATION OF A PARTNERSHIP

RUPA Section 202 provides that the association of two or more persons to carry on as co-owners a business for profit forms a partnership, whether or not the parties intend to form a partnership. The formation of a partnership is relatively simple and may be done consciously or unconsciously. A partnership may result from an oral or written agreement between the parties, from an informal arrangement, or from the conduct of the parties, who become partners by associating themselves in a business as co-owners. Consequently, if two or more individuals share the control and profits of a business, the law may deem them partners without regard to how they themselves characterize their relationship. Thus, associates frequently discover, to their chagrin, that they have inadvertently formed a partnership and have thereby subjected themselves to the duties and liabilities of partners. The legal existence of the relationship depends merely upon the parties' explicit or implicit agreement and their association in business as co-owners.

### PARTNERSHIP AGREEMENT

The RUPA defines a "partnership agreement" as "the agreement, whether written, oral, or implied, among the partners concerning the partnership, including amendments to the partnership agreement." Section 101(7). This definition does not include other agreements between some or all of the partners, such as a lease or a loan agreement.

Except as otherwise provided by the RUPA, the partnership agreement governs relations among the partners and between the partners and the partnership. Section 103. Thus, the RUPA gives almost total freedom to the partners to provide whatever provisions they agree upon in their partnership agreement. In essence, RUPA is primarily a set of "default rules" that apply only when the partnership agreement does not address the issue. Nevertheless, the RUPA makes some duties mandatory; these cannot be waived or varied by the partnership agreement. Section 103(b).

To render their understanding more clear, definite, and complete, partners are advised, though not usually required, to put their partnership agreement in writing. A partnership agreement can provide almost any conceivable arrangement of capital investment, control sharing, and profit distribution that the partners desire. Unless the agreement provides otherwise, the partners may amend it only by unanimous consent. Any partnership agreement should include the following:

1. The firm name and the identity of the partners;
2. The nature and scope of the partnership business;
3. The duration of the partnership;
4. The capital contributions of each partner;
5. The division of profits and sharing of losses;
6. The managerial duties of each partner;
7. A provision for salaries, if desired;
8. Restrictions, if any, upon the authority of particular partners to bind the firm;
9. Any desired variations from the partnership statute's default provisions governing dissolution; and
10. A statement of the method or formula for determining the value of a partner's interest in the partnership.

**Statute of Frauds** Because the statute of frauds does not apply expressly to a contract for the formation of a partnership, usually no writing is required to create the relationship. A contract to form a partnership to continue for a period longer than one year is within the statute, however, as is a contract for the transfer of an interest in real estate to or by a partnership; consequently, both of these contracts require a writing in order to be enforceable.

**Firm Name** In the interest of acquiring and retaining goodwill, a partnership should have a firm name. Although the name selected by the partners may not be identical or deceptively similar to the name of any other existing business concern, it may be the name of the partners or of any one of them; or the partners may decide to operate the business under a fictitious or assumed name, such as "Peachtree Restaurant," "Globe Theater," or "Paradise Laundry." A partnership may not use a name that would be likely to indicate to the public that it is a corporation. Nearly all of the States have enacted statutes that require any person or persons conducting business under an assumed or fictitious name to file in a designated public office a certificate setting forth the name under which the business is conducted and the real names and addresses of all persons conducting the business as partners or proprietors.

## TESTS OF PARTNERSHIP EXISTENCE

Partnerships can be formed without the slightest formality. Consequently, it is important that the law establish a test for determining whether or not a partnership has been formed. Two situations most often require this determination. The most common involves a creditor who has dealt only with one person but who wishes to hold another liable as well by asserting that the two were partners. Less frequently, a person seeks to share profits earned and property held by another by claiming that they are partners.

As previously mentioned, Section 202 of the UPA provides the operative rule for formation of a partnership: an association of two or more persons to carry on as co-owners a business for profit. Thus, three components are essential to the existence of a partnership: (1) an association of two or more persons, (2) conducting a business for profit, (3) which they co-own.

◆ SEE FIGURE 31-2: **Tests for Existence of a Partnership**

**Association** A partnership must consist of two or more persons who have agreed to become partners. Any natural person having full *capacity* may enter into a partnership. A corporation is defined as a "person" by Section 101 of the RUPA and is, therefore, legally capable of entering into a partnership in those States whose incorporation statutes authorize a corporation to do so. Furthermore, as previously noted, a partnership, joint venture, business trust, estate, trust, and any other legal or commercial entity may be a member of a partnership. Section 101.

**Business for Profit** The RUPA provides that co-ownership does not in itself establish a partnership, even if the co-owners share profits made by the use of the property. Section 202(c). For a partnership to exist, there must be co-ownership of a business. Thus, passive co-ownership of property by itself, as distinguished from the carrying on of a business, does not establish a partnership. Moreover, to be a partnership, the business carried on by the association of two or more persons must be "for profit." This requirement excludes unincorporated nonprofit organizations from being partnerships. State common law and statutes govern such unincorporated nonprofit organizations. These laws, however, generally do not address the issues facing nonprofit associations in a systematic or integrated fashion. Consequently, in

◆ FIGURE 31-2: **Tests for Existence of a Partnership**

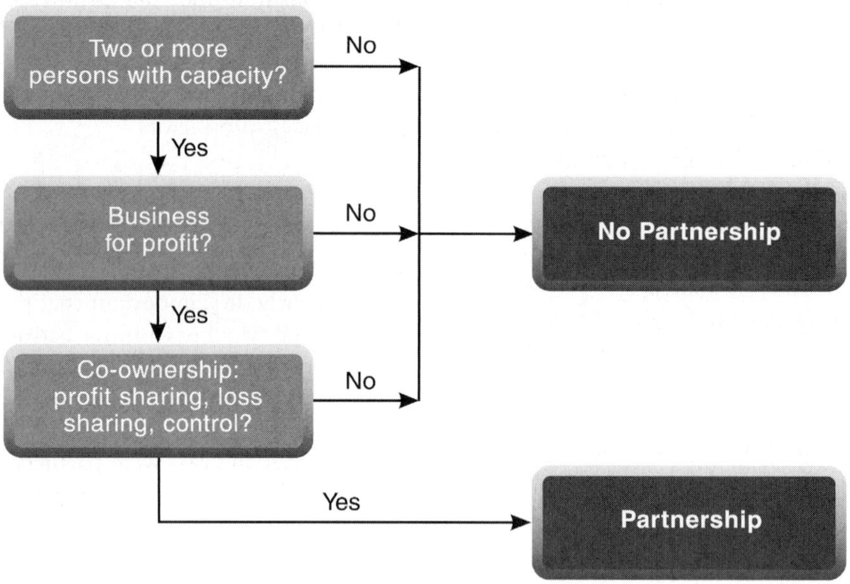


1996, the National Conference of Commissioners on Uniform State Laws promulgated a Uniform Unincorporated Nonprofit Association Act to reform the common law concerning unincorporated nonprofit associations in a limited number of major issues, including ownership of property, authority to sue and be sued, and the contract and tort liability of officers and members of the association. At least ten States have adopted the act.

Nor does a partnership exist in situations in which persons associate for mutual financial gain on a temporary or limited basis involving a single transaction or a few isolated transactions: such persons are not engaged in the continuous series of commercial activities necessary to constitute a business. Co-ownership of the means or instrumentality of accomplishing a single business transaction or a limited series of transactions may result in a joint venture but not in a general partnership.

For example, Katherine and Edith have joint ownership of shares of the capital stock of a corporation, have a joint bank account, and have inherited or purchased real estate as joint tenants or tenants in common. They share the dividends paid on the stock, the interest on the bank account, and the net proceeds from the sale or lease of the real estate. Nevertheless, Katherine and Edith are not partners. Although they are co-owners and share profits, they are not engaged in carrying on a business; hence, no partnership exists. On the other hand, if Katherine and Edith continually bought and sold real estate over a period of time and conducted a business of trading in real estate, a partnership relation would exist between them, regardless of whether they considered themselves partners or not.

To illustrate further: Alec, Laura, and Shirley each inherit an undivided one-third interest in a hotel and, instead of selling the property, decide by an informal agreement to continue operating the hotel. The operation of a hotel is a business; as co-owners of a hotel business, Alec, Laura, and Shirley are partners and are subject to all of the rights, duties, and incidents arising from the partnership relation.

**CO-OWNERSHIP** Although the co-ownership of *property* used in a business is a condition neither necessary nor sufficient for the existence of a partnership, the co-ownership of a *business* is essential. In identifying business co-ownership, the two most important factors are the sharing of profits and the right to manage and control the business.

A person who receives a share of the **profits** from a business is presumed to be a partner in the business. This means that persons who share profits are deemed to be partners unless they can prove otherwise. Section 202(c)(3) of the RUPA, however, provides that the existence of a partnership relation shall not be presumed where such profits were received in payment:

1. of a debt, by installments or otherwise;
2. for services as an independent contractor or of wages or other compensation to an employee;
3. of rent;
4. of an annuity or other retirement or health benefit to a beneficiary, representative, or designee of a deceased or retired partner;
5. of interest or other charge on a loan, even if the amount of payment varies with the profits of the business; or

**6.** for the sale of the goodwill of a business or other property by installments or otherwise.

These transactions do not give rise to a presumption that the party is a partner because the law assumes that the creditor, employee, landlord, or other recipient of such profits is unlikely to be a co-owner. It is possible, nonetheless, to establish that such a person is a partner by proof of other facts and circumstances, such as the sharing of control.

The sharing of *gross returns,* in contrast to profits, does *not* of itself establish a partnership. Section 202(c)(2). This is so whether or not the persons sharing the gross returns have a joint or common right or interest in property from which the returns are derived. Thus, two brokers who share commissions are not necessarily partners, or even presumed to be. Similarly, an author who receives royalties (a share of gross receipts from the sales of a book) is not a partner with her publisher.

By itself, evidence as to participation in the *management* or **control** of a business is not conclusive proof of a partnership relation, but it is persuasive. Limited voice in the management and control of a business may be accorded to an employee, a landlord, or a creditor. On the other hand, an actual partner may choose to take no active part in the affairs of the firm and may, by agreement with his copartners, forgo all right to exercise any control over the ordinary affairs of the business. In any event, the right to participate in control is an important factor considered by the courts in conjunction with other factors, particularly with profit sharing.

◆ SEE CASE 31-1

### PARTNERSHIP CAPITAL AND PROPERTY

The total money and property that the partners contribute and dedicate to use in the enterprise is the partnership capital. Partnership capital represents the partners' equity in the partnership. No minimum amount of capitalization is necessary before a partnership may commence business.

**Partnership property** is property acquired by a partnership. Section 203. Property acquired by the partnership is conclusively deemed to be partnership property. Property becomes partnership property if acquired in the name of the partnership, which includes a transfer to (1) the partnership in its name or (2) one or more partners in their capacity as partners in the partnership, if the name of the partnership is indicated in the instrument transferring title to the property. Section 204. Property also may be partnership property even if it is not acquired in the name of the partnership. Property is partnership property if acquired in the name of one or more of the partners with an indication in the instrument transferring title of either (1) their capacity as partners or (2) of the existence of a partnership, even if the name of the partnership is not indicated. Section 204(a)(2).

Even if the instrument transferring title to one or more of the partners does not indicate their capacity as a partner or the existence of a partnership, the property nevertheless may be partnership property. Ultimately, the partners' intention controls whether property belongs to the partnership or to one or more of the partners in their individual capacities. The RUPA sets forth two rebuttable presumptions that apply when the partners have failed to express their intent. First, under Section 204(c), property purchased with partnership funds is presumed to be partnership property, without regard to the name in which title is held. The presumption applies not only when partnership cash or property is used for payment but also when partnership credit is used to obtain financing.

Second, under Section 204(d), property acquired in the name of one or more of the partners, without an indication of their capacity as partners and without use of partnership funds or credit, is presumed to be the partners' separate property, even if used for partnership purposes. In this last case it is presumed that only the *use* of the property is contributed to the partnership.

As discussed later, who owns the property—an individual partner or the partnership—determines (1) who gets it upon dissolution of the partnership, (2) who shares in any loss or gain upon its sale, (3) who shares in income from it, and (4) who may sell it or transfer it by will.

A question may arise regarding whether property that was owned by a partner before formation of the partnership and was used in the partnership business is a capital contribution and hence an asset of the partnership. For example, a partner who owns a store building may contribute to the partnership the use of the building but not the building itself. The building is, therefore, not partnership property, and the amount of capital contributed by this partner is the reasonable value of the rental of the building.

The fact that legal title to property remains unchanged is not conclusive evidence that such property has not become a partnership asset. The intent of the partners controls the question of who owns the property. Without an express agreement, an intention to consider property as partnership property may be inferred from any of the following facts: (1) the property was improved with partnership funds; (2) the property was carried on the books of the partnership as an asset; (3) taxes, liens, or expenses, such as insurance or repairs, were paid by the partnership; (4) income or proceeds of the property were treated as partnership funds; or (5) the partners declared or admitted the property to be partnership property.

◆ SEE CASE 31-2

## RELATIONSHIPS AMONG PARTNERS

When parties enter into a partnership, the law imposes certain duties upon them and also grants them specific rights. Except as otherwise provided by the RUPA, the partnership agreement governs relations among the partners and between the partners and the partnership. Section 103. Thus, the RUPA gives almost total freedom to the partners to provide whatever provisions they agree upon in their partnership agreement. Nevertheless, the RUPA makes some duties mandatory; these cannot be waived or varied by the partnership agreement. Section 103(b).

## DUTIES AMONG PARTNERS

The principal legal duties imposed upon partners in their relations with one another are (1) the fiduciary duty (the duty of loyalty), (2) the duty of obedience, and (3) the duty of care. In addition, each partner has a duty to inform his copartners and a duty to account to the partnership. (These additional duties are discussed later, in a section covering the rights of partners.) All of these duties correspond precisely with those duties owed by an agent to his principal and reflect the fact that much of the law of partnership is the law of agency.

### FIDUCIARY DUTY

The extent of the fiduciary duty or duty of loyalty has been most eloquently expressed by the often-quoted words of Judge (later Justice) Cardozo:

> Joint adventurers, like copartners, owe to one another, while the enterprise continues, the duty of the *finest loyalty*. Many forms of conduct permissible in a workaday world for those acting at arm's length, are forbidden to those bound by fiduciary ties. A trustee is held to something stricter than the morals of the market place. *Not honesty alone, but the punctilio of an honor the most sensitive, is then the standard of behavior.* As to this there has developed a tradition that is unbending and inveterate. Uncompromising rigidity has been the attitude of courts of equity when petitioned to undermine the rule of undivided loyalty by the "disintegrating erosion" of particular exceptions. Only thus has the level of conduct for fiduciaries been kept at a level higher than that trodden by the crowd. It will not consciously be lowered by any judgment of this court. *Meinhard v. Salmon*, 249 N.Y. 458, 459, 164 N.E. 545, 546 (1928) [emphasis added].

The RUPA's provision regarding the fiduciary duty is both comprehensive and exclusive. Section 404. "In that regard, it is structurally different from the UPA which touches only sparingly on a partner's duty of loyalty and leaves any further development of the fiduciary duties of partners to the common law of agency." Comment 1 to Section 404. The RUPA completely and exclusively states the components of the duty of loyalty by specifying that a partner has a duty not to appropriate partnership benefits without the consent of her partners, to refrain from self-dealing, and to refrain from competing with the partnership. Section 404(b). More specifically, Section 404(b) of the RUPA provides that a partner's duty of loyalty to the partnership and the other partners is limited to the following:

1. to account to the partnership and hold as trustee for it any property, profit, or benefit derived by the partner in the conduct and winding up of the partnership business or derived from a use by the partner of partnership property, including the appropriation of a partnership opportunity;
2. to refrain from dealing with the partnership in the conduct or winding up of the partnership business as, or on behalf of, a party having an interest adverse to the partnership; and
3. to refrain from competing with the partnership in the conduct of the partnership business before the dissolution of the partnership.

In addition, the Revised Act provides that a partner does not violate the duty of loyalty merely because the partner's conduct furthers the partner's own interest. Section 404(e).

For example, a partner committed a breach of fiduciary duty when he retained a secret discount on purchases of petroleum that he obtained through acquisition of a bulk plant, and the partnership was entitled to the entire amount of the discount.

Within the demands of the fiduciary duty, a partner cannot acquire for herself a partnership asset or opportunity without the consent of all the partners. Thus, a partner may not renew a partnership lease in her name alone. A partner cannot, without the permission of her partners, engage in any other business within the scope of the partnership enterprise. Should she participate in a competing or similar business, the disloyal partner not only must surrender any profit she has acquired from such business but must compensate the existing partnership for any damage it may have suffered as a result of the competition. A partner, however, may enter into any business neither in competition with nor within the scope of the partnership's business. For example, a partner in a law firm may, without violating her fiduciary duty, act as an executor or administrator of an estate. Furthermore, she need not account for her fees where it cannot be shown that her service in this other capacity impaired her duty to the partnership (for example, by monopolizing her attention).

The fiduciary duty does *not* extend to the formation of the partnership, when, according to the comments to RUPA Section 404, the parties are really negotiating at arm's length. The duty not to compete terminates upon dissociation, and the dissociated partner may immediately engage in a competitive business, without any further consent. Section 603(b)(2). The partner's other fiduciary duties continue only with regard to matters arising and events occurring before the partner's dissociation, unless the partner participates in winding up the partnership's business. Section 603(b)(3). Thus, upon a partner's dissociation, a partner may appropriate to his own benefit any *new* business opportunity coming to his attention after dissociation, even if the partnership continues, and a partner may deal with the partnership as an adversary with respect to *new* matters or events. A dissociated partner is not, however, free to use confidential partnership information after dissociation.

The Revised Act imposes a duty of good faith and fair dealing when a partner discharges duties to the partnership and the other partners under the RUPA or under the partnership agreement and exercises any rights. Section 404(d). The comments to this section state:

> The obligation of good faith and fair dealing is a contract concept, imposed on the partners because of the consensual nature of a partnership. . . . It is not characterized, in RUPA, as a fiduciary duty arising out of the partners' special relationship. Nor is it a separate and independent obligation. It is an ancillary obligation that applies whenever a partner discharges a duty or exercises a right under the partnership agreement or the Act.

The partnership agreement may not eliminate the duty of loyalty or the obligation of good faith and fair dealing. However, the partnership agreement may identify specific types or categories of activities that do not violate the duty of loyalty, if not clearly unreasonable. In addition, the other partners may consent to a specific act or transaction that otherwise violates the duty of loyalty, if there has been full disclosure of all material facts regarding the act or transaction as well as the partner's conflict of interest. Similarly, the partnership agreement may prescribe the standards by which the performance of the obligation of good faith and fair dealing is to be measured, if the standards are not manifestly unreasonable. Section 103(b).

The fiduciary duty under the UPA differs in some respects from that of the RUPA. First, the partner's fiduciary duty under the UPA applies to the formation of the partnership. Second, it applies to the winding up of the partnership. The UPA states that every partner must account to the partnership for any benefit he receives and must hold as trustee for it any profits he derives without the consent of the other partners from any transaction connected with the formation, conduct, or liquidation of the partnership or from any use he makes of its property. UPA Section 21. A partner may not prefer himself over the firm, nor may he even deal at arm's length with his partners, to whom his duty is one of undivided and continuous loyalty. The fiduciary duty also applies to the purchase of a partner's interest from another partner. Each partner owes the highest duty of honesty and fair dealing to the other partners, including the obligation to disclose fully and accurately all material facts.

◆ **SEE CASE 31-3**

### DUTY OF OBEDIENCE

A partner owes his partners a duty to act in obedience to the partnership agreement and to any business decisions properly made by the partnership. Any partner who violates this duty is liable individually to his partners for any resulting loss. For example, a partner who, in violation of a specific agreement not to extend credit to relatives, advances money from partnership funds and sells goods on credit to an insolvent relative would be held personally liable to his partners for the unpaid debt.

### DUTY OF CARE

Whereas under the fiduciary duty a partner "is held to something stricter than the morals of the market place," he is held to something less than the skill of the marketplace. Each partner owes the partnership a duty of faithful service to the best of his ability. Nonetheless, he need not possess the degree of knowledge and skill of an ordinary paid agent. Under the Revised Act, a partner's duty of care to the partnership and the other partners in the conduct and winding up of the partnership business is limited to refraining from engaging in grossly negligent or reckless conduct, intentional misconduct, or a knowing violation of law. RUPA Section 404(c). For example, a partner assigned to keep the partnership books uses an overly complicated bookkeeping system and consequently produces numerous mistakes. Because these errors result simply from poor judgment, not an intent to defraud, and are not intended to and do not operate to the personal advantage of the negligent bookkeeping partner, she is *not* liable to her copartners for any resulting loss. The duty of care may not be eliminated entirely by agreement, but the standard may be reasonably reduced. Section 103(b)(4). The standard may be increased by agreement to one of ordinary care or an even higher standard of care. Comment 6 to RUPA Section 103.

## RIGHTS AMONG PARTNERS

The law provides partners with certain rights, which include (1) their right to use and possess partnership property for partnership purposes, (2) their transferable interest in the partnership, (3) their right to share in distributions (part of their transferable interest), (4) their right to participate in management, (5) their right to choose associates, and (6) their enforcement rights.

## RIGHTS IN SPECIFIC PARTNERSHIP PROPERTY

In adopting the entity theory, the Revised Act abolishes the UPA's concept of tenants in partnership: partnership property is owned by the partnership entity and not by the individual partners. Section 203. Moreover, RUPA Section 501 provides, "A partner is not a co-owner of partnership property and has no interest in partnership property which can be transferred, either voluntarily or involuntarily." A partner may use or possess partnership property only on behalf of the partnership. Section 401(g).

Under the UPA, a partner's ownership interest in any specific item of partnership property is that of a **tenant in partnership**. UPA Section 25. The UPA's tenancy in partnership reaches a similar entity result to the RUPA but states that result in aggregate terms. This type of ownership, which exists only in a partnership, has the following principal characteristics:

1. Each partner has a right equal to that of his copartners to possess partnership property for partnership purposes, but he has no right to possess it for any other purpose without his copartners' consent.
2. A partner may not make an individual assignment of his right in specific partnership property.
3. A partner's interest in specific partnership property is not subject to attachment or execution by his individual creditors. It is subject to attachment or execution only on a claim against the partnership.
4. Upon the death of a partner, his right in specific partnership property vests in the surviving partner or partners. Upon the death of the last surviving partner, his right in such property vests in his legal representative.

## PARTNER'S TRANSFERABLE INTEREST IN THE PARTNERSHIP

Each partner has an **interest in the partnership**, which is defined as "all of a partner's interests in the partnership, including the partner's transferable interest and all management and other rights." Section 101(9). A **partner's transferable interest** is a more limited concept; it is the partner's share of the profits and losses of the partnership and the partner's right to receive distributions. This interest is personal property. Section 502. A partner's transferable interest is discussed here; a partner's management and other rights are discussed later in this chapter.

**Assignability** A partner may voluntarily transfer, in whole or in part, his transferable interest in the partnership. Section 503. The transfer does not by itself cause the partner's dissociation or a dissolution and winding up of the partnership business. (Dissolution is discussed in *Chapter 32*.) The transferee, however, is not entitled to (1) participate in the management or conduct of the partnership business, (2) require access to any information concerning partnership transactions, or (3) inspect or copy the partnership books or records. She is merely entitled to receive, in accordance with the terms of the assignment, any distributions to which the assigning partner would have been entitled under the partnership agreement before dissolution. After dissolution, the transferee is entitled to receive the net amount that would have been distributed to the transferring partner upon the winding up of the business. Moreover, the assignee may apply for a court-ordered dissolution. Section 801(6). The assigning partner remains a partner with all of a partner's rights and duties other than the transferred interest in distributions.

Under Section 601(4)(ii), however, the other partners by a unanimous vote may expel a partner who has transferred substantially all of his transferable partnership interest, other than as security for a loan. The partner may be expelled, nevertheless, upon *foreclosure* of the security interest.

Under Section 103(a), the partners may agree among themselves to restrict the right to transfer their partnership interests.

**Creditors' Rights** A partner's transferable interest (the right to distributions from the partnership and the right to seek court-ordered dissolution of the partnership) is subject to the claims of that partner's creditors, who may obtain a **charging order** (a type of judicial lien) against the partner's transferable interest. Section 504. On application by a judgment creditor of a partner, a court may charge the transferable interest of the partner to satisfy the judgment. A charging order is also available to the judgment creditor of a *transferee* of a partnership interest. A charging order is the judgment creditor's exclusive remedy against a partner's transferable interest in the partnership. The court may appoint a receiver of the debtor's share of the distributions due or to become due. The court may order a foreclosure of the interest subject to the charging order at any time. The purchaser at the foreclosure sale has the rights of a transferee. At any time before foreclosure, an interest charged may be redeemed by (1) the partner who is the judgment debtor; (2) other partners with nonpartnership property; or (3) other partners with partnership property, but only with the consent of all of the remaining partners.

Neither the judgment creditor, the receiver, nor the purchaser at foreclosure becomes a partner, and thus none is entitled to participate in the partnership's management or to have access to information. Furthermore, neither the charging order nor its sale upon foreclosure causes a dissolution, though the other partners may dissolve the partnership or redeem the charged interest. Section 601(4)(ii) provides that a partner may be expelled by a unanimous vote of the other partners upon foreclosure of a judicial lien charging a partner's interest.

◆ FIGURE 31-3: **Partnership Property Compared with Partner's Interest**

| | Partnership Property | | |
|---|---|---|---|
| | **RUPA** | **UPA** | **Partner's Interest** |
| **Definition** | A partner is *not* a co-owner of partnership property | Tenant in partnership | Share of profits and surplus |
| **Possession** | For partnership purposes, not individual ones | For partnership purposes, not individual ones | Intangible, personal property right |
| **Assignability** | Partner has *no* interest in partnership property which can be transferred | If all other partners assign their rights in the property | Assignee does not become a partner |
| **Attachment** | Only for a claim against the partnership | Only for a claim against the partnership | By a charging order |
| **Inheritance** | Partner has *no* interest in partnership property which can be transferred | Goes to surviving partner(s) | Passes to the personal representative of deceased partner |

Note: RUPA = Revised Uniform Partnership Act; UPA = Uniform Partnership Act.

◆ SEE FIGURE 31-3: **Partnership Property Compared with Partner's Interest**

## RIGHT TO SHARE IN DISTRIBUTIONS

A **distribution** is a transfer of money or other partnership property from the partnership to a partner in the partner's capacity as a partner. Section 101(3). Distributions include a division of profits, a return of capital contributions, a repayment of a loan or advance made by a partner to the partnership, and a payment made to compensate a partner for services rendered to the partnership. The RUPA's rules regarding distribution are subject to contrary agreement of the partners. Section 103. A partner has no right to receive, and may not be required to accept, a distribution in kind. Section 402. The RUPA provides that each partner is deemed to have an account that is credited with the partner's contributions and share of the partnership profits and charged with distributions to the partner and the partner's share of partnership losses. Section 401.

**Right to Share in Profits** Because a partnership is an association to carry on a business for profit, each partner is entitled, unless otherwise agreed, to a share of the profits. Absent an agreement to the contrary, however, a partner does not have a right to receive a current distribution of the profits credited to his account, the timing of the distribution of profits being a matter arising in the ordinary course of business to be decided by majority vote of the partners. In the absence of an agreement regarding the division of profits, the partners share the profits *equally*, regardless of the ratio of their financial contributions or the degree of their participation in management. Thus, under this default rule, partners share profits per capita and not in proportion to their capital contributions.

Conversely, each partner is chargeable with a share of any losses the partnership sustains. Section 401(b). A partner, however, is not obligated to contribute to partnership losses before his withdrawal or the liquidation of the partnership, unless the partners agree otherwise. The partners bear losses in a proportion *identical* to that in which they share profits. Section 401(b). The partnership agreement may, however, validly provide for bearing losses in a proportion different from that in which profits are shared.

For example, Alice, Betty, and Carol form a partnership, with Alice contributing $10,000; Betty, $20,000; and Carol, $30,000. They could agree that Alice would receive 20 percent of the profits and assume 30 percent of the losses; that Betty would receive 30 percent of the profits and assume 50 percent of the losses; and that Carol would receive 50 percent of the profits and assume 20 percent of the losses. If their agreement is silent as to the sharing of profits and losses, however, each would have an equal one-third share of both profits and losses.

**Right to Return of Capital** Absent an agreement to the contrary, a partner does not have a right to receive a distribution of the capital contributions in his account before his withdrawal or the liquidation of the partnership.

Under the UPA after all the partnership's creditors have been paid, each partner is entitled to repayment of his capital contribution during the winding up of the firm. UPA Section 18(a). Unless otherwise agreed, a partner is not entitled to interest on his capital contribution; however, a delay in the return of his capital contribution entitles the partner to interest at the legal rate from the date when it should have been repaid. UPA Section 18(d).

**RIGHT TO INDEMNIFICATION** A partner who makes an advance beyond his agreed capital contribution is entitled to reimbursement from the partnership. Section 401(d). An advance is treated as a loan to the partnership that accrues interest. Section 401(e). In addition, the partnership must reimburse a partner for payments made and indemnify a partner for liabilities incurred by the partner in the ordinary course of the business of the partnership or for the protection of the partnership business or property. Section 401(c). Under the Revised Act, a loan from a partner to the partnership is treated the same as loans of a person not a partner, subject to other applicable law, such as fraudulent transfer law, the law of avoidable preferences under the Bankruptcy Act, and general debtor-creditor law. RUPA Section 404(f) and Comment 6.

◆ **SEE CASE 32-4**

Under the UPA, a partner's claim as a creditor of the firm, though subordinate to the claims of nonpartner creditors, is superior to the partners' rights to the return of capital.

**RIGHT TO COMPENSATION** The RUPA provides that, unless otherwise agreed, *no* partner is entitled to payment for services performed for the partnership. Section 401(h). Even a partner who works disproportionately harder than the others to conduct the business is entitled to no salary but only to his share of the profits. A partner may, however, by agreement among all of the partners, receive a salary. Moreover, a partner is entitled to reasonable compensation for services rendered in winding up the business of the partnership. Section 401(h).

### RIGHT TO PARTICIPATE IN MANAGEMENT

Each of the partners, unless otherwise agreed, has *equal* rights in the management and conduct of the partnership business. Section 401(f). The majority governs the actions and decisions of the partnership with respect to matters in the ordinary course of partnership business. Section 401(j). *All* the partners must consent to any act outside the ordinary course of partnership business and to any amendment of the partnership agreement. Section 401(j). In their partnership agreement, the partners may provide for unequal voting rights. For example, Jones, Smith, and Williams form a partnership, agreeing that Jones will have two votes, Smith four votes, and Williams five votes. Large partnerships commonly concentrate most or all management authority in a committee of a few partners or even in just one partner. Classes of partners with different management rights also may be created. This practice is common in accounting and law firms, which may have two classes (for example, junior and senior partners) or three classes (for example, junior, senior, and managing partners).

### RIGHT TO CHOOSE ASSOCIATES

No partner may be forced to accept as a partner any person of whom she does not approve. This is partly because of the fiduciary relationship between the partners and partly because each partner has a right to take part in the management of the business, to handle the partnership's assets for partnership purposes, and to act as an agent of the partnership. An ill-chosen partner, through negligence, poor judgment, or dishonesty, may bring financial loss or ruin to her copartners. Because of this danger and because of the close relationship among the members, partnerships must necessarily be founded on mutual trust and confidence. All this finds expression in the term *delectus personae* (literally, "choice of the person"), which indicates the right one has to choose her partners. This principle is embodied in Section 401(i) of the RUPA, which provides: "A person may become a partner only with the consent of *all* of the partners." [Emphasis added.] It is because of *delectus personae* that a purchaser (assignee) of a partner's interest does not become a partner and is not entitled to participate in management. The partnership agreement may provide, however, for admission of a new partner by a less-than-unanimous vote.

## ENFORCEMENT RIGHTS

As discussed, the partnership relationship creates a number of duties and rights among partners. Accordingly, partnership law provides partners and the partnership with the means to enforce these rights and duties.

**RIGHT TO INFORMATION AND INSPECTION OF THE BOOKS** The RUPA provides that if a partnership maintains books and records, they must be kept at its chief executive office. Section 403. A partnership must provide partners access to its books and records to inspect and copy them during ordinary business hours. Section 403(b). Former partners are given a similar right, although limited to the books and records pertaining to the period during which they were partners. A duly authorized agent on behalf of a partner may also exercise this right. A partnership may impose a reasonable charge, covering the costs of labor and material, for copies of documents furnished. The partnership agreement may *not* unreasonably restrict a partner's right of access to partnership books and records. Section 103(b)(2).

Each partner and the partnership must affirmatively disclose to a partner, *without demand*, any information concerning the partnership's business and affairs reasonably required for the proper exercise of the partner's rights and duties under the partnership agreement or the Act. Section 403(c)(1).

(In addition, under some circumstances, a disclosure duty may arise from the obligation of good faith and fair dealing.) Moreover, *on demand*, each partner and the partnership must furnish to a partner any other information concerning the partnership's business and affairs, except to the extent the demand or the information demanded is unreasonable or otherwise improper under the circumstances. The rights to receive and demand information extend also to the legal representative of a deceased partner. They may, however, be waived or varied by agreement of the partners.

**Legal Action** Under the RUPA a partner may maintain a direct suit against the partnership or another partner for legal or equitable relief, with or without an accounting as to partnership business, to enforce the partner's rights under the partnership agreement and the Revised Act. Section 405(b). Thus, under the RUPA, an accounting is not a prerequisite to the availability of the other remedies a partner may have against the partnership or the other partners. Since general partners are not passive investors, the RUPA does not authorize derivative actions. Reflecting the entity theory of partnership, the RUPA provides that the partnership itself may maintain an action against a partner for any breach of the partnership agreement or for the violation of any duty owed to the partnership, such as a breach of fiduciary duty. Section 405(a).

The UPA grants to each partner the right to an account whenever (1) his copartners wrongfully exclude him from the partnership business or possession of its property, (2) the partnership agreement so provides, (3) a partner makes a profit in violation of his fiduciary duty, or (4) other circumstances render it just and reasonable. UPA Section 22. If a partner does not receive or is dissatisfied with a requested account, she may bring an enforcement action, called an accounting. Designed to produce and evaluate all testimony relevant to the various claims of the partners, an accounting is an equitable proceeding for a comprehensive and effective settlement of partnership affairs.

# CHAPTER SUMMARY

## FORMATION OF GENERAL PARTNERSHIPS

**NATURE OF PARTNERSHIP**

**Definition** an association of two or more persons to carry on as co-owners a business for profit

**Entity Theory**

- ***Partnership as a Legal Entity*** an organization having a legal existence separate from that of its members; the Revised Act considers a partnership a legal entity for nearly all purposes
- ***Partnership as a Legal Aggregate*** a group of individuals not having a legal existence separate from that of its members; the Revised Act considers a partnership a legal aggregate for few purposes

**FORMATION OF PARTNERSHIP**

**Partnership Agreement** it is preferable, although not usually required, that the partners enter into a written partnership agreement

**Tests of Existence** the formation of a partnership requires all of the following:

- ***Association*** two or more persons with legal capacity who agree to become partners
- ***Business for Profit***
- ***Co-ownership*** includes sharing of profits and control of the business

**Partnership Capital** total money and property contributed by the partners for use by the partnership

**Partnership Property** sum of all of the partnership's assets, including all property acquired by the partnership

## RELATIONSHIPS AMONG PARTNERS

**DUTIES AMONG PARTNERS**

**Fiduciary Duty** duty of utmost loyalty, fairness, and good faith owed by partners to each other and to the partnership; includes duty not to appropriate partnership opportunities, not to compete, not to have conflicts of interest, and not to reveal confidential information

**Duty of Obedience** duty to act in accordance with the partnership agreement and any business decisions properly made by the partners

**Duty of Care** duty owed by partners to manage the partnership affairs without gross negligence, reckless conduct, intentional misconduct, or knowing violation of law

**RIGHTS AMONG PARTNERS**

**Rights in Specific Partnership Property** partners have the right to use and possess partnership property for partnership purposes

**Transferable Interest in Partnership** the partner's share of the profits and losses of the partnership and the partner's right to receive distributions

- ***Assignability*** a partner may sell or assign his transferable interest in the partnership; the new owner becomes entitled to the assigning partner's right to receive distributions but does not become a partner
- ***Creditors' Rights*** a partner's transferable interest is subject to the claims of creditors, who may obtain a charging order (judicial lien) against the partner's transferable interest

**Distributions** transfer of partnership property from the partnership to a partner

- ***Profits*** each partner is entitled to an equal share of the profits unless otherwise agreed
- ***Capital*** a partner does not have a right to receive a distribution of the capital contributions in his account before his withdrawal or the liquidation of the partnership
- ***Indemnification*** if a partner makes an advance (loan) to the partnership, he is entitled to repayment of the advance plus interest; a partner is entitled to reimbursement for payments made and indemnification for liabilities incurred by the partner in the ordinary course of the business
- ***Compensation*** unless otherwise agreed, no partner is entitled to payment for services rendered to the partnership

**Management** each partner has equal rights in management of the partnership unless otherwise agreed

**Choice of Associates** under the doctrine of *delectus personae*, no person can become a member of a partnership without the consent of all of the partners

**Enforcement Rights**

- ***Information*** each partner has the right (1) *without demand*, to any information concerning the partnership and reasonably required for the proper exercise of the partner's rights and duties and (2) *on demand*, to any other information concerning the partnership
- ***Legal Action*** a partner may maintain a direct suit against the partnership or another partner for legal or equitable relief to enforce the partner's rights; the partnership itself may maintain an action against a partner for any breach of the partnership agreement or for the violation of any duty owed to the partnership

# CASES

CASE 31-1

## Test of the Partnership Existence
## IN RE KEYTRONICS

Supreme Court of Nebraska, 2008
274 Neb. 936, 744 N.W.2d 425

**McCormack, J.**

[In 1999 King was doing business under the name of "Washco" as a sole proprietorship engaged in selling, installing, and servicing carwash systems and accessories. King offered to his customers the "QuikPay" system, a cashless vending system for carwashes that used a memory chip key that interacted with a controller at the carwash. Either a cash value can be placed on the key or the carwash usage recorded on the key is billed monthly. Washco purchased QuikPay systems for resale from Datakey Electronics Inc. (Datakey) but it was becoming unprofitable for Datakey, partly because the keys for QuikPay could only be obtained from an attendant. According to Glen Jennings, president of Datakey, since most carwashes are unattended, this reliance on the presence of the carwash owner or employee was limiting the product's market.

As QuikPay's largest distributor, King was aware that QuikPay's limitations made the product unattractive to many of his customers. King contacted Willson, an electronics technician and computer programmer, to see if Willson could develop a combined "key dispenser" and "revalue station" for the QuikPay system that would make the system self-service. King also asked Willson if he would design and install an interface between the QuikPay system and the carwash of one of King's customers. Designing such an interface was beyond King's technical expertise. Willson individually designed and installed at least four specific customer interfaces that allowed King to sell the QuikPay system to those customers, but Willson was never paid for his work.

According to King there was an oral agreement among himself, Willson, and Scott Gardeen (an employee of Datakey who was an original designer of QuikPay) to form a corporation whenever Willson developed the key dispenser-revalue station. The three parties met in the spring of 2002 to discuss the venture in which they would design and build the key dispenser-revalue station and sell it to Datakey. It was agreed that Willson would write the software and do the firmware, hardware, and any other electrical or software work; Gardeen would contribute his knowledge of the system and his contact with Datakey; and King would contribute financial resources and his experience and contacts as QuikPay's largest distributor. Together, Willson, King, and Gardeen came up with the name "Secure Data Systems" for their business. They discussed the fact that the entity's initials, "SDS," were also the initials of their first names, Scott, Don, and Scott. By the summer, Willson had built a handheld revalue station for a meeting with Jennings. Jennings indicated that if a final, marketable key dispenser-revalue station were developed, Datakey would be interested in a business relationship with Secure Data Systems.

Around October 2002, Datakey decided to discontinue its QuikPay line and referred all of its customers to King for continued support of the system. By the beginning of 2003, King had deliberately separated his QuikPay sales, maintenance, and its future development from his Washco carwash business and had moved all QuikPay business to Secure Data Systems. Around the same time, Willson developed a Web site for Secure Data Systems with e-mail accounts for King and Willson.

By the spring of 2003, Willson's work for Secure Data Systems consisted primarily of dealing with QuikPay maintenance and repair issues, although he continued to try to finish the key dispenser-revalue station whenever he had time. Willson made changes in the QuikPay software to fix problems that customers wanted fixed.

In May 2003, King and Willson went together to an international carwash convention in Las Vegas, Nevada. King suggested to Willson that he make up Secure Data Systems business cards for King and Willson. The cards presented Willson as "System Designer & Engineer" and King as "Sales." The cards described Secure Data Systems as carrying the "QuikPay Product Line."

In correspondence with clients, King often referred to Willson as the person doing technical work for QuikPay. Willson also sent e-mails communicating directly with QuikPay clients on various issues. In an e-mail dated August 12, 2003, Willson described himself as the software and hardware designer with Secure Data Systems and he referred to King as his "partner." In October 2003, King sent an e-mail to a potential customer in which King referred to Willson as "the other half of Secure Data Systems."

Willson estimated that he had put at least 2,000 hours into QuikPay sales and maintenance and in developing the key dispenser-revalue station. When Willson was asked why he invested his time and expertise into QuikPay without any remuneration, he explained, "That was my contribution to the company. I mean that was my piece." Willson contacted a law firm to draw up papers to formalize the partnership. These papers were never drafted. According to Willson, when he told King he was looking into creating a written agreement for their relationship, King "assured [him] that he was having his attorneys look at it." King and Willson had another meeting around the end of December and agreed to end their relationship and any joint QuikPay or key dispenser-revalue station activities. Approximately two weeks after this meeting, King called Willson and offered to compensate him for the time he had spent in maintaining or repairing QuikPay. Willson refused.

Willson brought an action for winding up and an accounting, alleging formation of a partnership. King denied they had formed a partnership. The trial court found that King and Willson had "pooled resources, money and labor," but found no partnership existed because there was no "specific agreement." Alternatively, the trial court found that because King did not commit his preexisting business to any specifically formed partnership, the scope of the partnership did not encompass any activity garnering profits. Willson appealed the trial court's order.]

This case is governed by the * * * revised Uniform Partnership Act. Section [202(a)] of the Act defines that a partnership is formed by "the association of two or more persons to carry on as co-owners a business for profit" and explains that this is true "whether or not the persons intend to form a partnership." [Citation.]

Obviously, the relationship between King and Willson is "of two or more persons." In addition, whether the business of QuikPay maintenance, or even the development of the never-produced key dispenser-revalue station, qualifies as a business "for profit" is not in issue. It is not essential that the business for which the association was formed ever actually be carried on, let alone that it earn a profit. Rather, a business qualifies under the "business for profit" element of [Section 202(a)] so long as the parties intended to carry on a business with the expectation of profits. [Citations.]

* * *

We first consider whether King and Willson formed an association. King correctly points out that inherent to the term "association" is the idea that the relationship between the "two or more persons" be intentional. [Citation.] King argues that no partnership was formed because he never intended to form a partnership relationship with Willson. * * *

But, as [Section 202(a)] explicitly states, the intent necessary to form an association does not refer to the intent to form a partnership per se. There is no requirement that the parties have a "specific agreement" in order to form a partnership. People do not become partners when they attain co-ownership of a business for profit through an involuntary act. [Citation.] But, if the parties' voluntary actions form a relationship in which they carry on as co-owners of a business for profit, then "they may inadvertently create a partnership despite their expressed subjective intention not to do so." [Citation.] Intent, in such cases, is still of prime concern, but it will be ascertained objectively, rather than subjectively, from all the evidence and circumstances. [Citation.]

Because of this, King's focus on his intent to form a corporation, as opposed to a partnership, does more to prove an intent to form the requisite association than to disprove it. It is, in fact, not unusual for courts to find a partnership relationship between parties that were operating with the intent to form a corporation and to specifically avoid a partnership relationship. [Citation.] * * *

In considering the parties' intent to form an association, it is generally considered relevant how the parties characterize their relationship or how they have previously referred to one another. [Citation.] The joint use of a business name is evidence of an association. [Citations.] This is especially true when the business name is composed of the parties' names or initials. [Citations.]

It is undisputed that King and Willson discussed the fact that Secure Data Systems had the initials of Scott, Don, and Scott. Granted, at its inception, Secure Data Systems was an association among three parties focused on the limited task of creating a key dispenser-revalue station. * * * King removed any QuikPay operations from his Washco business. He instead began to conduct all QuikPay business exclusively through Secure Data Systems. Willson was clearly associated with King in that venture.

* * * Business cards were created for King and Willson describing their respective positions in Secure Data Systems. King and Willson went as joint representatives of Secure Data Systems to a Las Vegas carwash convention. King and Willson worked together both in servicing the QuikPay line, assembling and repairing Datakey's old inventory, and developing the key dispenser-revalue station. Various e-mails to customers and to Datakey evidence their joint efforts in this regard. To King and to others, Willson referred to himself and King as partners. Specifically in regard to ventures involving the regular QuikPay system, King referred to Willson as "the other half of Secure Data Systems." We believe the evidence is clear that King and Willson formally associated to develop a key dispenser-revalue station and that further, this association expanded in scope to encompass all QuikPay operations.

* * * King claims that he started selling and maintaining QuikPay by himself and asserts that he maintained full control of that business line. According to King, Willson simply did what King asked him to—apparently for free.

Being "co-owners" of a business for profit does not refer to the co-ownership of property, [RUPA Section 202(c)(3)] but to the co-ownership of the business intended to garner profits. It is co-ownership that distinguishes partnerships from other commercial relationships such as creditor and debtor, employer and employee, franchisor and franchisee, and landlord and tenant. [Citation.] Co-ownership generally addresses whether the parties share the benefits, risks, and management of the enterprise such that (1) they subjectively view themselves as members of the business rather than as outsiders contracting with it and (2) they are in a better position than others dealing with the firm to monitor and obtain information about the business. [Citation.]

The objective indicia of co-ownership are commonly considered to be: (1) profit sharing, (2) control sharing, (3) loss sharing, (4) contribution, and (5) co-ownership of property. [Citation.] The five indicia of co-ownership are only that; they are not all necessary to establish a partnership relationship, and no single indicium of co-ownership is either necessary or sufficient to prove co-ownership. [Citation.]

* * * The record demonstrates that Willson contributed his time and expertise not only to the business of developing the key dispenser-revalue station, but also to the continued operations of the regular QuikPay product line. * * *

The continuing investment of one's labor without pay is generally considered a strong indicator of co-ownership. [Citations.] * * * Valid consideration for an ownership interest in a partnership may take the form of either property, capital, labor, or skill, and the law does not exalt one type of contribution over another. [Citations.]

In this case, Willson contributed his time and expertise without any compensation for approximately 1 year. Conservatively, Willson estimated his contribution as totaling over 2,000 hours. * * * that without Willson's technical assistance, King would have been unable to continue QuikPay's viability after Datakey abandoned the product. That King could have dealt with certain issues by hiring contractors or employees is irrelevant. He chose not to do so—presumably because the promise of the key dispenser-revalue station made a partnership relationship more worthwhile—and saved himself the expense of paying for this labor.

We also find that despite King's protestations to the contrary, the evidence shows that King and Willson shared control over QuikPay business. * * *

* * *

Willson also testified that he had an agreement with King to share profits, although King denies this. Of the five indicia of co-ownership, profit sharing is possibly the most important, and the presence of profit sharing is singled out in [Section 202(c)(3)] as creating a rebuttable presumption of a partnership. [Citations.] However, what is essential to a partnership is not that profits actually be distributed, but, instead, that there be an interest in the profits. [Citations.] Willson's testimony that they agreed to share in the profits of the business is, in light of all the evidence, simply more credible than King's statement that compensation "was never discussed." And even King vaguely admits that they had an understanding to share profits of the key dispenser-revalue station, if that were developed. * * *

We do not find any evidence that King and Willson had an agreement for loss sharing. But we find this of little import, since purported partners, expecting profits, often do not have any explicit understanding regarding loss sharing. [Citation.] Likewise, although King and Willson admittedly do not own any joint property, in an informal relationship, the parties may intend co-ownership of property but fail to attend to the formalities of title. [Citation.] Moreover, in this case, it is unclear that there is much QuikPay "property" at all. * * *

We conclude that the objective, as well as subjective, indicia are sufficient to prove co-ownership of the business of selling, maintaining, and developing QuikPay. Having already concluded that there was an association for the same, we conclude that Willson proved that he and King had formed a partnership for the business of selling, maintaining, and developing QuikPay.

Reversed and remanded for further proceedings.

# CASE 31-2

## Partnership Property
## THOMAS v. LLOYD

Missouri Court of Appeals, Southern District, Division One, 2000
17 S.W.3d 177
http://caselaw.findlaw.com/scripts/getcase.pl?court=mo&vol=/appeals/052000/&invol=29051600_2000

**Shrum, J.**

Plaintiff's husband of thirty years died in February 1988. In February 1989, Plaintiff met Defendant in Mobile, Alabama, while traveling. Their chance meeting quickly blossomed into a romantic relationship. When Plaintiff returned to her home in Maryland in late February 1989, Defendant accompanied her and they began living together.

Initially, Defendant told Plaintiff he worked for a major oil company, had been outside the country for the past three years, was independently wealthy, and was not married. As Plaintiff later learned, none of these statements was true. In truth, Defendant had recently been released from prison. He had multiple criminal convictions, including convictions for counterfeiting and stealing. Further, Defendant's assets at the time were no more than $2,000, and he was legally married to Patricia Lloyd.

Evidence as to when Plaintiff learned of Defendant's deceptions was contradictory. The trial court found that Plaintiff first learned of Defendant's criminal history and lack of wealth soon after she returned to Maryland in February 1989. It found that Plaintiff discovered Defendant was not single "soon after her void marriage to Defendant." The parties' "void marriage" occurred July 10, 1989, in Canada.

Except for occasional vacations, Plaintiff and Defendant resided in Plaintiff's home in Maryland from late February 1989 through October 1990. During that period, Defendant made repairs and renovations to Plaintiff's house. In October 1990, Plaintiff sold her Maryland home in an "owner-finance" arrangement.

The parties then moved to Missouri. After looking at several farm properties, they bought a 600-acre farm in Crawford County, Missouri, for $150,000. The deed was dated March 8, 1991. The grantees named in the deed and the type of tenancy created were as follows: Plaintiff, a single person, and Defendant, a single person, as joint tenants with right of survivorship. The $150,000 purchase price was paid as follows: $100,000 cash downpayment and a $50,000 purchase money note that called for 120 monthly installments of $633.38.

After buying the farm, Plaintiff and Defendant bought cattle and farm machinery, then began operating a cattle business on the property. The parties also made improvements to the farm, including remodeling an old farm house in which they lived. In June 1992, they began construction on a 4,200 square-foot house. Later, the house was expanded to 6,500 square feet. By the time of trial, Plaintiff's expenditures for labor and materials on the home exceeded $201,000.

A progressive deterioration in the parties' relationship led to the filing of this multiple-count lawsuit in October 1995. [The trial court found that the subject real estate was not a partnership asset and ordered it be sold at public auction and the net sale proceeds to be distributed ninety-eight percent to Plaintiff and two percent to Defendant. The Defendant appealed the trial court's refusal to classify farm real estate as a partnership asset. The Defendant claims he was prejudiced by this error because if the farm were properly classified as partnership property, any proceeds from its sale would be divided in accordance with the partners' interests.]

"The true method of determining whether, as between partners themselves, land standing in the names of individuals is to be treated as partnership property is to ascertain from the conduct of the parties and their course of dealing, the understanding and intention of the partners themselves, which, when ascertained, unquestionably should control." [Citations.] Whether real estate titled in the names of individual partners is partnership property is a question of fact and the burden of proof is on the one alleging that the ownership does not accord with the legal title. [Citation.]

In attempting to demonstrate that the parties intended for the real estate to be a partnership asset, Defendant points to the joint ownership of the farm and the fact that the parties operated the partnership cattle business on the farm as evidence that the two understood and intended for the farm to be a partnership asset. His reliance on those facts is misplaced, however. A joint purchase of real estate by two individuals does not, in and of itself, prove the land is a partnership asset. [Citation.] On the contrary, when land is conveyed to partnership members without any statement in the deed that the grantees hold the land as property of the firm, there is a presumption that title is in the individual grantees. [Citation.] Moreover, "[e]vidence that the land is used by the firm is of itself insufficient to rebut the presumption." [Citation.] The mere use of land by a partnership does little to show the land is owned by the partnership.

[Citation.] Standing alone, evidence of partnership usage does not compel a finding that the land is a partnership asset. [Citations.]

Defendant points to evidence that some real estate taxes and promissory note payments for the farm came from partnership funds. He argues such evidence indicates the parties intended the farm to be a partnership asset. We agree that such evidence is a factor to be considered, but it is not determinative of the issue, especially, when, as here, the partnership payment evidence is viewed in context. For instance, none of the $100,000 downpayment for the farm came from partnership funds. Instead, it all came from Plaintiff's separate funds. Plaintiff was never reimbursed by either the partnership or Defendant for her downpayment. Of eighty-four monthly farm note payments, only three were paid from the parties' joint account. Seventy-seven of the monthly farm note payments, a total of $48,770.26, were paid from Plaintiff's separate funds. Plaintiff also spent $201,927.87 of her separate money to build a new house on the farm. None of the house construction costs came from partnership funds. Of the seven years' worth of state and county real estate taxes that had been paid on the farm property, only one year was paid out of partnership funds. On the whole, the evidence is that Plaintiff invested over $350,000 of her own funds in this farm while less than $2,400 of partnership funds were used to pay the farm note and real estate taxes. Such minimal partnership expenditures is more indicative of the tendency of people—particularly in family or quasi-family businesses—to intermingle personal and partnership affairs, than it is an indication of the parties' intent to include the farm as a partnership asset. [Citation.]

Other evidence from which the parties' intent can be gleaned includes the following: (A) Plaintiff and Defendant signed as individuals on the $50,000 purchase money note and deed of trust securing the same, without a recital of partnership status; (B) neither party filed a partnership income tax return; (C) Plaintiff filed income tax returns as an individual; (D) Defendant never filed an income tax return after the farm was purchased; (E) Plaintiff wrote checks on her individual account for materials and labor for farm improvements; and (F) Plaintiff repeatedly testified she never intended nor agreed to a partnership with Defendant. We find these circumstances sufficient to support the implicit finding and judgment of the trial court that a partnership agreement did not exist regarding the land and it was not a partnership asset. The trial court did not commit reversible error when it failed to include the farm as a partnership asset.

The judgment of the trial court is affirmed.

## CASE 31-3

### Fiduciary Duty
## ENEA v. THE SUPERIOR COURT OF MONTEREY COUNTY

Court of Appeal of California, Sixth Appellate District, 2005
132 Cal.App.4th 1559, 34 Cal.Rptr. 3d 513

**Rushing, P. J.**

Defendants [William and Claudia Daniels] state that in 1980, they and other family members formed a general partnership known as 3-D. The partnership's sole asset was a building that had been converted from a residence into offices. Some portion of the property—apparently the greater part—has been rented since 1981 on a month-to-month basis by a law practice of which William Daniels is apparently the sole member. From time to time the property was rented on similar arrangements to others, including defendant Claudia Daniels. Plaintiff's counsel stipulated in the court below that "the partnership agreement has as its principal purpose the ownership, leasing and sale of the only partnership assets, which is the building." He also stipulated that the partnership agreement contained no provision that the property "[would] be leased for fair market value." Defendants also assert, as the trial court ultimately found, that there was no evidence of any agreement to maximize rental profits.

In 1993, plaintiff [Benny Enea], a client of William Daniels, purchased a one-third interest in the partnership from the latter's brother, John P. Daniels. * * * In 2001, however, plaintiff questioned William Daniels about the rents being paid for the property * * * "and in 2003, Plaintiff was 'dissociated' from the partnership."

On August 6, 2003, plaintiff brought this action "to determine partner's buyout price and for damages." Alleg[ing] that defendants had occupied the partnership property * * * [while] paying significantly less than fair rental value, "in breach of their fiduciary duty to plaintiff." In their answer, defendants denied all of these allegations except to admit that defendant Claudia Daniels had occupied a portion of the premises at one time.

* * *

[The trial court granted the defendants' motion for summary judgment, and the plaintiff appealed.]

* * *

Despite the numerous diversions offered by defendants, the case presents a very simple set of facts and issues. For present purposes it must be assumed that defendants in fact leased the property to themselves, or associated entities, at below-market rents. * * * Therefore the sole question presented is whether defendants were categorically entitled to lease partnership property to themselves, or associated entities (or for that matter, to anyone) at less than it could yield in the open market. Remarkably, we have found no case squarely addressing this precise question. We are satisfied, however, that the answer is a resounding "No."

The defining characteristic of a partnership is the combination of two or more persons to jointly conduct business. [Citation.] It is hornbook law that in forming such an arrangement the partners obligate themselves to share risks and benefits and to carry out the enterprise with the highest good faith toward one another—in short, with the loyalty and care of a fiduciary. "Partnership is a fiduciary relationship, and partners are held to the standards and duties of a trustee in their dealings with each other." "' . . . [I]n all proceedings connected with the conduct of the partnership every partner is bound to act in the highest good faith to his copartner and may not obtain any advantage over him in the partnership affairs by the slightest misrepresentation, concealment, threat or adverse pressure of any kind.' [Citations.]" [Citation.] Or to put the point more succinctly, "Partnership is a fiduciary relationship, and partners may not take advantages for themselves at the expense of the partnership." [Citations.]

Here the facts as assumed by the parties and the trial court plainly depict defendants taking advantages for themselves from partnership property *at the expense of the partnership*. The advantage consisted of occupying partnership property at below-market rates, i.e., less than they would be required to pay to an independent landlord for equivalent premises. * * *

Defendants * * * persuaded the trial court that they had no duty to collect market rents in the absence of a contract expressly requiring them to do so. This argument turns partnership law on its head. Nowhere does the law declare that partners owe each other only those duties they explicitly assume by contract. On the contrary, the fiduciary duties at issue here are *imposed by law*, and their breach sounds in tort. * * *

* * *

[Accordingly, we direct the trial court to set aside its order and deny the motion.]

## QUESTIONS

1. Identify the various types of business associations and explain the factors that are relevant to deciding which form to use.
2. Distinguish between a legal entity and a legal aggregate and identify those purposes for which a partnership is treated as a legal entity and those purposes for which it is treated as a legal aggregate.
3. Distinguish between a partner's rights in specific partnership property and a partner's interest in the partnership.
4. Discuss the duties owed by a partner to her copartners.
5. Identify and discuss the principal rights of partners.

## PROBLEMS

**1.** Lynn and Jack jointly own shares of stock of a corporation, have a joint bank account, and have purchased and own as tenants in common a piece of real estate. They share equally the dividends paid on the stock, the interest on the bank account, and the rent from the real estate. Without Lynn's knowledge, Jack makes a trip to inspect the real estate and on his way runs over Samuel. Samuel sues Lynn and Jack for his personal injuries, joining Lynn as defendant on the theory that Lynn was Jack's partner. Is Lynn a partner of Jack?

**2.** James and Suzanne engaged in the grocery business as partners. In one year they earned considerable money, and at the end of the year they invested a part of the profits in oil land, taking title to the land in their names as tenants in common. The investment was fortunate, for oil was discovered near the land, and its value increased many times. Is the oil land partnership property? Why?

**3.** Sheila owned an old roadside building that she believed could be easily converted into an antique shop. She talked to her friend Barbara, an antique fancier, and they executed the following written agreement:

**(a)** Sheila would supply the building, all utilities, and $100,000 capital for purchasing antiques.

**(b)** Barbara would supply $30,000 for purchasing antiques, Sheila would repay her when the business terminated.
**(c)** Barbara would manage the shop, make all purchases, and receive a salary of $500 per week plus 5 percent of the gross receipts.
**(d)** Fifty percent of the net profits would go into the purchase of new stock. The balance of the net profits would go to Sheila.
**(e)** The business would operate under the name "Roadside Antiques."

Business went poorly, and after one year a debt of $40,000 is owed to Old Fashioned, Inc., the principal supplier of antiques purchased by Barbara in the name of Roadside Antiques. Old Fashioned sues Roadside Antiques, and Sheila and Barbara as partners. Decision?

**4.** Clark, who owned a vacant lot, and Bird, who was engaged in building houses, entered into an oral agreement by which Bird was to erect a house on the lot. Upon the sale of the house and lot, Bird was to have his money first. Clark was then to have the agreed value of the lot, and the profits were to be equally divided. Did a partnership exist?

**5.** Grant, Arthur, and David formed a partnership for the purpose of betting on boxing matches. Grant and Arthur would become friendly with various boxers and offer them bribes to lose certain bouts. David would then place large bets, using money contributed by all three, and would collect the winnings. After David had accumulated a large sum of money, Grant and Arthur demanded their share, but David refused to make any split. Can Grant and Arthur compel David to account for the profits of the partnership? Why?

**6.** Teresa, Peter, and Walker were partners under a written agreement made in January that the partnership should continue for ten years. During the same year, Walker, being indebted to Smith, sold and conveyed his interest in the partnership to Smith. Teresa and Peter paid Smith $50,000 as Walker's share of the profits for that year but refused Smith permission to inspect the books or to come into the managing office of the partnership. Smith brings an action setting forth the above facts and asks for an account of partnership transactions and an order to inspect the books and to participate in the management of the partnership business.
**(a)** Does Walker's action dissolve the partnership?
**(b)** To what is Smith entitled with respect to (1) partnership profits, (2) inspection of partnership books, (3) an account of partnership transactions, and (4) participation in the partnership management?

**7.** Horn's Crane Service furnished supplies and services under a written contract to a partnership engaged in operating a quarry and rock-crushing business. Horn brought action against Prior and Cook, the individual members of the partnership, to recover a personal judgment against them for the partnership's liability under that contract. Horn has not sued the partnership itself, nor does he claim that the partnership property is insufficient to satisfy its debts. What result? Explain.

**8.** Cutler worked as a bartender for Bowen until they orally agreed that Bowen would have the authority and responsibility for the entire active management and operation of the tavern business known as the Havana Club. Each was to receive $300 per week plus half of the net profits. The business continued under this arrangement for four years until the building was taken over by the Salt Lake City Redevelopment Agency. The agency paid $30,000 to Bowen as compensation for disruption. The business, however, was terminated after Bowen and Cutler failed to find a new suitable location.

Cutler, alleging a partnership with Bowen, then brought this action against him to recover one-half of the $30,000. Bowen contends that he is entitled to the entire $30,000 because he was the sole owner of the business and that Cutler was merely his employee. Cutler argues that although Bowen owned the physical assets of the business, she, as a partner in the business, is entitled to one-half of the compensation that was paid for the business's goodwill and going-concern value. Who is correct? Explain.

**9.** In 2001, Gauldin and Corn entered into a partnership for the purpose of raising cattle and hogs. The two men were to share equally all costs, labor, losses, and profits. The business was started on land owned initially by Corn's parents but later acquired by Corn and his wife. No rent was ever requested or paid for use of the land. Partnership funds were used to bulldoze and clear the land, to repair and build fences, and to seed and fertilize the land. In 2005, at a cost of $2,487.50, a machine shed was built on the land. In 2010, a Cargill unit was built on the land at a cost of $8,000. When the partnership dissolved in 2011, Gauldin paid Corn $7,500 for the "removable" assets; however, the two had no agreement regarding the distribution of the barn and the Cargill unit. Is Gauldin entitled to one-half of the value of the two buildings? Explain.

**10.** Anita and Duncan had been partners for many years in a mercantile business. Their relationship deteriorated to the point at which Anita threatened to bring an action for an accounting and dissolution of the firm. Duncan then offered to buy Anita's interest in the partnership for $250,000. Anita refused the offer and told Duncan that she would take no less than $360,000. A short time later, James approached Duncan and informed him he had inside information that a proposed street change would greatly benefit the business and that he, James, would buy the entire business for $1 million or buy a one-half interest for $500,000. Duncan made a final offer of $350,000 to Anita for her interest. Anita accepted this offer, and the transaction was completed. Duncan then sold the one-half interest to James for $500,000. Several months later, Anita learned for the first time of the transaction between Duncan and James.

What rights, if any, does Anita have against Duncan?

**11.** ABCD Company is a general partnership. It consists of Dianne, Greg, Knox, and Laura, whose capital contributions were as follows: Dianne = $5,000, Greg = $7,500, Knox = $10,000, and Laura = $5,000. The partnership agreement provided that the partnership would continue for three years and that no withdrawals of capital were to be made without the consent of all the partners. The agreement also provided that all advances would be entitled to interest at 10 percent per year. Six months after the partnership was formed, Dianne advanced $10,000 to the partnership. At the end of the first year, net profits totaled $11,000 before any moneys had been distributed to partners. How should the $11,000 be allocated to Dianne, Greg, Knox, and Laura? Explain.

**12.** Donald Petersen joined his father, William Petersen, in a chicken hatchery business William had previously operated as a sole proprietorship. When the partnership was formed, William contributed the assets of the proprietorship, which included cash, equipment, and inventory having a total value of $41,000. Donald contributed nothing. They agreed to share the profits equally. For fifteen years, Donald took over the operation of the hatchery with very little help from his father. When the business was terminated William contended that he was entitled to the return of his capital investment of $41,000 before Donald could recover anything. Donald asserted that he is entitled to one-half the value of the business. Explain who is correct in his contention.

**13.** Smith, Jones, and Brown were creditors of White, who operated a grain elevator known as White's Elevator. Heavily in debt, White was about to fail when the three creditors agreed to take title to his elevator property and pay all the debts. It was also agreed that White should continue as manager of the business at a salary of $1,500 per month and that all profits of the business were to be paid to Smith, Jones, and Brown. It was further agreed that they could dispense with White's services at any time and that he was free to quit when he pleased. White accepted the proposition and continued to operate the business as before. The agreement worked successfully and for several years paid substantial profits, enough so that Smith, Jones, and Brown had received nearly all that they had originally advanced. Were Smith, Jones, and Brown partners? Explain.

**14.** Virginia, Georgia, Carolina, and Louis were partners doing business under the trade name of Morning Glory Nursery. Virginia owned a one-third interest, and Georgia, Carolina, and Louis owned two-ninths each. The partners acquired three tracts of land for the purpose of the partnership. Two of the tracts were acquired in the names of the four partners, "trading and doing business as Morning Glory Nursery." The third tract was acquired in the names of the individuals, the trade name not appearing in the deed. This third tract was acquired by the partnership out of partnership funds and for partnership purposes. Who owns each of the three tracts? Why?

**15.** Charles and L. W. Clement were brothers who had formed a partnership that lasted forty years until Charles discovered that his brother, who kept the partnership's books, had made several substantial personal investments with funds improperly withdrawn from the partnership. He then brought an action in equity seeking dissolution of the partnership, appointment of a receiver, and an accounting. Should Charles succeed? Explain.

**16.** Chaiken entered into separate but nearly identical agreements with Strazella and Spitzer to operate a barber shop. Under the terms of the "partnership" agreements, Chaiken would provide barber chairs, supplies, and licenses, while the other two would provide tools of the trade. The agreements also stated that gross returns from the partnership were to be divided on a percentage basis among the three men and that Chaiken would decide all matters of partnership policy. Finally, the agreements stated hours of work and holidays for Strazella and Spitzer and required Chaiken to hold and distribute all receipts. Are Strazella and Spitzer partners of Chaiken or are they his employees? Explain.

CHAPTER 32

# Operation and Dissolution of General Partnerships

The operation and management of a general partnership involve interactions among the partners as well as their interactions with third persons. The previous chapter covered the rights and duties of the partners among themselves. The first part of this chapter focuses on the relations among the partnership, the partners, and third persons who deal with the partnership. These relations are governed by the laws of agency, contracts, and torts as well as by the partnership statute. The second part of the chapter addresses the dissociation and dissolution of general partnerships.

## RELATIONSHIP OF PARTNERSHIP AND PARTNERS WITH THIRD PARTIES

In the course of transacting business, the partnership and the partners also may acquire rights over and incur duties to third parties. For example, under the law of agency, a principal is liable upon contracts that his duly authorized agents make on his behalf and is liable in tort for the wrongful acts his employees commit in the course of their employment. Because much of the law of partnership is the law of agency, most problems arising between partners and third persons require the application of principles of agency law. The Revised Uniform Partnership Act (RUPA) makes this relationship explicit by stating that "[e]ach partner is an agent of the partnership for the purpose of its business." Section 301(1). In addition, the RUPA provides that unless displaced by particular provisions of the RUPA, the principles of law and equity supplement the RUPA. Section 104. The law of agency is discussed in *Chapters 19* and *20*.

When a partnership becomes liable to a third party, each partner has **unlimited personal liability** for that partnership obligation.



## CONTRACTS OF PARTNERSHIP

The act of every partner binds the partnership to transactions *within* the scope of the partnership business unless the partner does not have actual or apparent authority to so act. If the partnership is bound, then each general partner has unlimited, personal liability for that partnership obligation unless the partnership is a limited liability partnership (LLP) and the LLP statute shields contract obligations. Under the Revised Act, the partners are jointly and severally liable for all contract obligations of the partnership. Section 306(a). **Joint and several liability** means that all of the partners may be sued jointly in one action or that separate actions, leading to separate judgments, may be maintained against each of them. Judgments obtained are enforceable, however, against property of only the defendant or defendants named in the suit; and payment of any one of the judgments satisfies all of them. The Revised Act, in keeping with its entity treatment of partnerships, requires the judgment creditor to exhaust the partnership's assets before enforcing a judgment against the separate assets of a partner. Section 307(d).

The Uniform Partnership Act (UPA) provides that partners are jointly liable on all debts and contract obligations of the partnership. UPA Section 15(b). Under **joint liability**, a creditor must bring suit against all of the partners as a group, and the judgment must be against all of the obligors. Therefore, any suit in contract against the partners must name all of them as defendants.

◆ **SEE FIGURE 32-1: Contract Liability**

### AUTHORITY TO BIND PARTNERSHIP

A partner may bind the partnership by her act if (1) she has actual authority, express or implied, to perform the act; or (2) she has apparent authority to perform the act. If the act is not apparently for carrying on in the ordinary course the partnership business, then the partnership is bound only where the partner has actual authority. In such a case, the third person dealing with the partner assumes the risk that such actual authority exists. Section 301(2). Where there is neither actual authority nor apparent authority, the partnership is bound only if it ratifies the act. Ratification is discussed in *Chapter 20*.

◆ FIGURE 32-1: **Contract Liability**

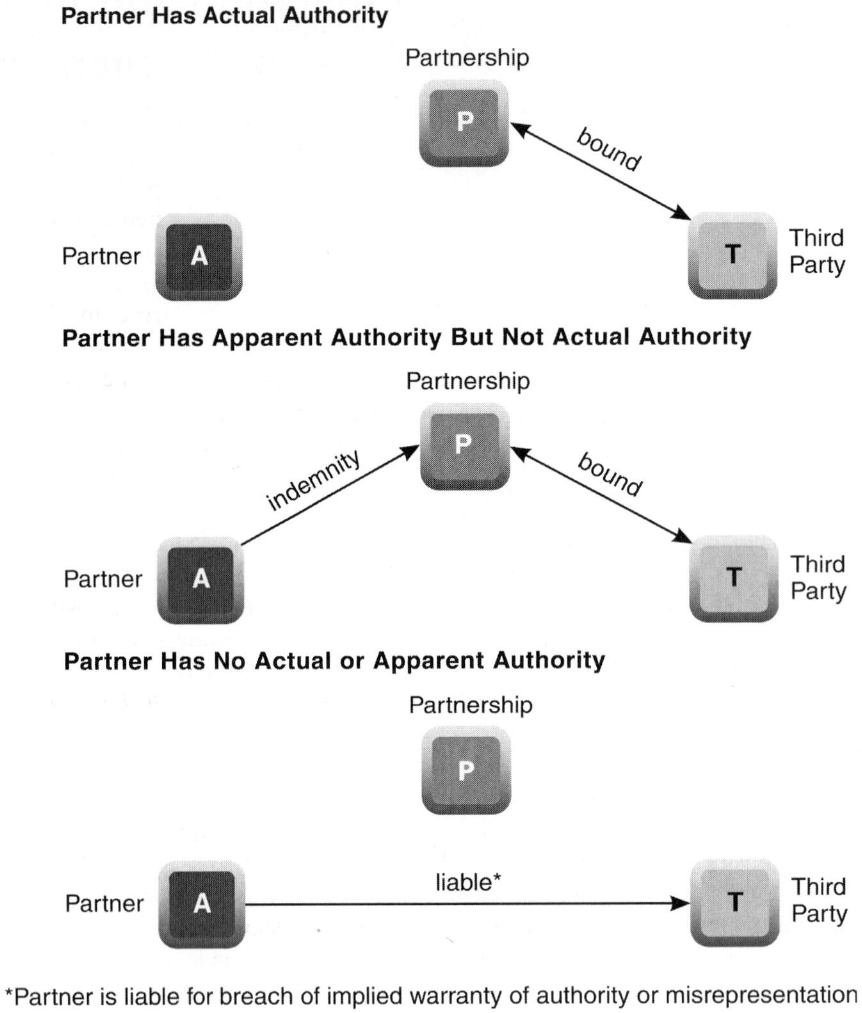


**Actual Express Authority** The actual express authority of partners may be written or oral; it may be specifically set forth in the partnership agreement or in an additional agreement between the partners. In addition, it may arise from decisions made by a majority of the partners regarding ordinary matters connected with the partnership business. Section 401(j).

A partner who does not have actual authority from *all* of her partners may not bind the partnership by any act that does not apparently carry on in the ordinary course the partnership business. Sections 301(2) and 401(j). Acts outside the ordinary course of the partnership business would include the following: (1) execution of contracts of guaranty or suretyship in the firm name, (2) sale of partnership property not held for sale in the usual course of business, and (3) payment of an individual partner's debts out of partnership assets.

The Revised Act also authorizes the optional, central filing of a statement of partnership authority specifying the names of the partners authorized to execute instruments transferring real property held in the name of the partnership. A statement may also limit the authority of a partner or partners to transfer real property. In addition, a statement may grant extraordinary authority to some or all the partners, or limit their ordinary authority, to enter into transactions on behalf of the partnership. A filed statement is effective for up to five years. Section 303. A partner, or other person named as a partner, may file a statement denying any fact asserted in a statement of partnership authority, including a denial of a person's status as a partner or of another person's authority as a partner. Section 304. A statement of denial is a limitation on authority.

Section 9(3) of the UPA provides that the following acts do **not** bind the partnership unless authorized by **all** of the partners: (1) assignment of partnership property for the benefit of its creditors; (2) disposal of the goodwill of the business; (3) any act which would make it impossible to carry on the ordinary business of the partnership; (4) confession of a judgment; or (5) submission of a partnership claim or liability to arbitration or reference.

**Actual Implied Authority** Actual implied authority is neither expressly granted nor expressly denied but is reasonably deduced from the nature of the partnership, the terms of the partnership agreement, or the relations of the partners. For example, a partner has implied authority to hire and fire employees whose services are necessary to carry on the partnership business. In addition, a partner has implied authority to purchase property necessary for the business, to receive performance of obligations due to the partnership, and to bring legal actions to enforce claims of the partnership.

**Apparent Authority** Apparent authority (which may or may not be actual) is authority that a third person, in view of the circumstances, the conduct of the parties, and a lack of knowledge or notification to the contrary, may reasonably believe to exist. Section 301(1) of the RUPA provides

> Each partner is an agent of the partnership for the purpose of its business. An act of a partner, including the execution of an instrument in the partnership name, for apparently carrying on in the ordinary course the partnership business or business of the kind carried on by the partnership binds the partnership, unless the partner had no authority to act for the partnership in the particular matter and the person with whom the partner was dealing knew or had received a notification that the partner lacked authority.

This section characterizes a partner as a general managerial agent having both actual and apparent authority within the scope of the firm's ordinary business. For example, a partner has apparent authority to indorse checks and notes, to make representations and warranties in selling goods, and to enter into contracts for advertising. A third person, however, may not rely upon apparent authority in any situation in which he already knows, or has received notification, that the partner does not have actual authority. A person knows a fact if the person has actual knowledge of it. A person receives a notification when the notification comes to the person's attention or is duly delivered at the person's place of business or at any other place held out by the person as a place for receiving communications. Section 102.

◆ **SEE CASE 32-1**

### PARTNERSHIP BY ESTOPPEL

Partnership by estoppel imposes partnership duties and liabilities upon a nonpartner who has either represented himself or consented to be represented as a partner. It extends to a third person to whom such a representation is made and who justifiably relies upon the representation. Section 308(a).

For example, Marks and Saunders are partners doing business as Marks and Company. Marks introduces Patterson to Taylor, describing Patterson as a member of the partnership. Patterson verbally confirms the statement made by Marks. Believing that Patterson is a member of the partnership and relying upon Patterson's good credit standing, Taylor sells goods on credit to Marks and Company. In an action by Taylor against Marks, Saunders, and Patterson as partners to recover the price of the goods, Patterson is liable although he is not a partner in Marks and Company. Taylor had justifiably relied upon the representation that Patterson was a partner in Marks and Company, to which Patterson actually consented. If, however, Taylor had known at the time of the sale that Patterson was not a partner, his reliance on the representation would not have been justified, and Patterson would not be liable.

Except in situations in which the representation of membership in a partnership has been made publicly, no person is entitled to rely upon a representation of partnership unless it is made directly to him. For example, Patterson falsely tells Dillon that he is a member of the partnership Marks and Company. Dillon casually relays this statement to Taylor, who in reliance sells goods on credit to Marks and Company. Taylor cannot hold Patterson liable, as he was not justified in relying on the representation made privately by Patterson to Dillon, which Patterson did not consent to have repeated to Taylor.

Where Patterson, however, knowingly consents to his name appearing publicly in the firm name or in a list of partners, or to be used in public announcements or advertisements in a manner which indicates that he is a partner in the firm, Patterson is liable to any member of the public who relies on the purported partnership, whether or not Patterson is aware of being held out as a partner to such person. Section 308(a).

## TORTS AND CRIMES OF PARTNERSHIP

As discussed in *Chapter 20*, under the doctrine of *respondeat superior* a partnership, like any employer, may be liable for an unauthorized tort committed by its employee if the employee committed the tort in the scope of his employment. With respect to a *partner's* conduct, the RUPA provides that a partnership is liable for the loss or injury any partner causes by any wrongful act or omission, or other actionable conduct, while acting within the ordinary course of the partnership business or with the authority of the partnership. Section 305(a).

Tort liability of the partnership may include not only the negligence of the partners but also trespass, fraud, defamation, and breach of fiduciary duty, so long as the tort is committed in the course of partnership business. Moreover, though the fact that a tort is intentional does not necessarily remove it from the course of business, it is a factor to be considered. The Revised Act makes the partnership liable for no-fault torts by the addition of the phrase, "or other actionable conduct." Comment to Section 305. A partnership is also liable if a partner in the course of the partnership's business or while acting with authority of the partnership breaches a trust by receiving money or property of a person not a partner, and the partner misapplies the money or property. Section 305(b).

If the partnership is liable, each partner has **unlimited, personal liability** for the partnership obligation unless the partnership is an LLP. The liability of partners for a tort or breach of trust committed by any partner or by an employee of the firm in the course of partnership business is joint and several. Section 306. As mentioned earlier, the Revised Act requires the judgment creditor to exhaust the partnership's assets before enforcing a judgment against the separate assets of a partner. RUPA Section 307(d).

The partner who commits the tort or breach of trust is directly liable to the third party and must also **indemnify** the partnership for any damages it pays to the third party. Section 405(a).

A partner is not criminally liable for the crimes of her partners unless she authorized or participated in them. Nor is a partnership criminally liable for the crimes of individual partners or employees unless a statute imposes vicarious liability. Even under such a statute, a partnership usually is liable only in those States that have adopted the entity theory or if the statute itself expressly imposes liability upon partnerships. Otherwise, the vicarious liability statute renders the partners liable as individuals.

◆ **SEE FIGURE 32-2: Tort Liability**

## NOTICE TO A PARTNER

A partner's knowledge, notice, or receipt of a notification of a fact relating to the partnership is effective immediately as knowledge by, notice to, or receipt of a notification by the partnership, except in the case of a fraud on the partnership committed by or with the consent of that partner. Section 102(f). A person has notice of a fact if the person (1) knows of it, (2) has received a notification of it, or (3) has reason to know it exists from all of the facts known to the person at the time in question. Section 102(b).

## LIABILITY OF INCOMING PARTNER

A person admitted as a partner into an existing partnership is *not* personally liable for any partnership obligations incurred before the person's admission as a partner. Section 306(b). This means that the liability of an incoming partner for **antecedent debts** and obligations of the firm is limited to his capital contribution. This restriction does not apply, of course, to **subsequent debts** (obligations arising after his admission into the partnership), for which obligations his liability is *unlimited.* For example, Nash is admitted to Higgins, Cooke, and White Co., a partnership. Nash's capital contribution is $7,500, which she paid in cash upon her

◆ **FIGURE 32-2: Tort Liability**

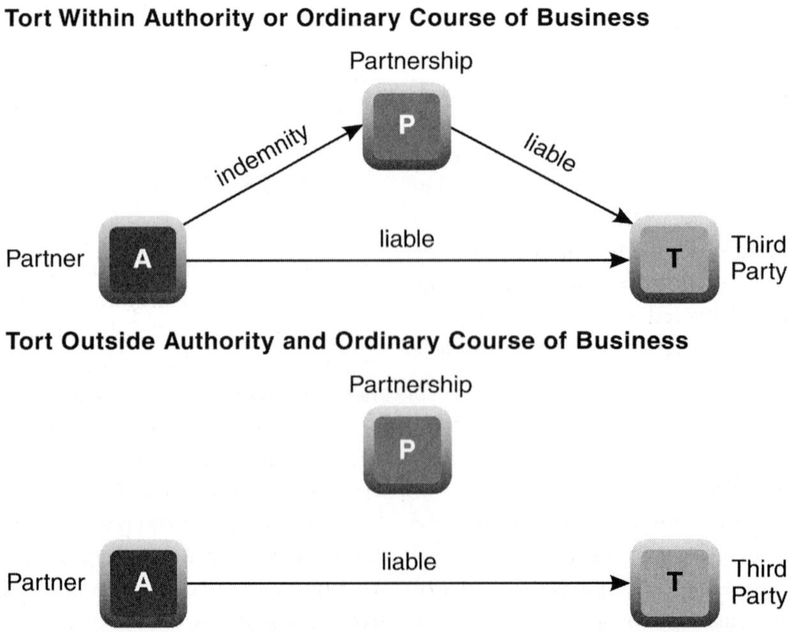

admission to the partnership. A year later, when liabilities of the firm exceed its assets by $40,000, the partnership is dissolved. Porter had lent the firm $15,000 eight months before Nash was admitted; Skinner lent the firm $20,000 two months after Nash was admitted. Nash has no liability to Porter *except* to the extent of her capital contribution, but she is *personally* liable to Skinner.

In an LLP, an incoming partner does not have personal liability for both antecedent debts *and* those subsequent debts that are shielded by that State's LLP statute.

◆ SEE CASE 32-2

# DISSOCIATION AND DISSOLUTION OF GENERAL PARTNERSHIPS UNDER RUPA

Dissociation occurs when a partner ceases to be associated in the carrying on of the business. **Dissolution** refers to those situations when the Revised Act requires a partnership to wind up and terminate. A dissociation of a partner results in dissolution only in limited circumstances. In many instances, dissociation will result merely in a buyout of the withdrawing partner's interest rather than a winding up of the partnership. When dissociation or other cause results in dissolution, the partnership *is not terminated* but continues until the winding up of its affairs is complete. During winding up, unfinished business is completed, receivables are collected, payments are made to creditors, and the remaining assets are distributed to the partners. Termination occurs when the process is finished.

## DISSOCIATION

**Dissociation** occurs when a partner ceases to be associated in the carrying on of the business. A number of events that were considered causes of dissociation or dissolution under the common law are no longer considered so under the RUPA. For example, the assignment of a partner's interest, a creditor's charging order on a partner's interest, and an accounting are not considered a dissociation or dissolution.

A partner has the *power* to dissociate at any time, rightfully or wrongfully, by expressing an intent to withdraw. Section 602(a). A partner does not, however, always have the *right* to dissociate. A partner who wrongfully dissociates is liable to the partnership for damages caused by the dissociation. Section 602(c). In addition, if the wrongful dissociation results in the dissolution of the partnership, the wrongfully dissociating partner is not entitled to participate in winding up the business.

### WRONGFUL DISSOCIATIONS

A partner's dissociation is wrongful if it breaches an express provision of the partnership agreement. In addition, dissociation is wrongful in a *term partnership* if before the expiration of the term or the completion of the undertaking (1) the partner voluntarily withdraws by express will unless the withdrawal follows within ninety days after another partner's dissociation by death, bankruptcy, or wrongful dissociation; (2) the partner is expelled for misconduct by judicial determination; (3) the partner becomes a debtor in bankruptcy; or (4) the partner is an entity (other than a trust or estate) and is expelled or otherwise dissociated because its dissolution or termination was willful. Section 602(b). A **term partnership** is a partnership for a specific term or particular undertaking. The partnership agreement may eliminate or expand the dissociations that are wrongful or modify the effects of wrongful dissociation, except for the power of a court to expel a partner for misconduct.

### RIGHTFUL DISSOCIATIONS

The RUPA provides that a partner's dissociation is wrongful only if it results from one of the events just discussed. Section 602(b). All other dissociations are rightful, including (1) in **any** partnership the death of partner, (2) in a **partnership at will** the withdrawal of a partner, (3) in **any** partnership an event occurs that was agreed to in the partnership agreement as causing dissociation, and (4) in **any** partnership a court determines that a partner has become incapable of performing the partner's duties under the partnership agreement. The RUPA defines a **partnership at will** as a partnership in which the partners have not agreed to remain partners until the expiration of a definite term or the completion of a particular undertaking. Section 101(8).

### EFFECTS OF DISSOCIATION

Upon a partner's dissociation, the partner's right to participate in the management and conduct of the partnership business terminates. Section 603(b). If, however, the dissociation results in a dissolution and winding up of the business, all of the partners who have not wrongfully dissociated may participate in winding up the business. Section 804(a). The duty not to compete terminates upon dissociation, and the dissociated partner may immediately engage in a competitive business, without any further consent. The partner's other fiduciary duties and duty of care continue only with regard to matters arising and events occurring before the partner's dissociation, unless the partner participates in winding up the partnership's business. For example, a partner who leaves a partnership providing consulting services may immediately compete with the firm for new clients, but must exercise care in completing current transactions with clients and must account to the firm for any fees received from the old clients on account of those transactions.

## DISSOLUTION

In accordance with the Revised Act's emphasis on the entity treatment of partnerships, only a limited subset of dissociations requires the dissolution of a partnership. In addition, some events other than dissociation can bring about the dissolution of a partnership under RUPA. The following sections discuss the causes and effects of dissolution.

### CAUSES OF DISSOLUTION

The basic rule under the RUPA is that a partnership is dissolved and its business must be wound up only if one of the events listed in Section 801 occur. The events causing dissolution may be brought about by (1) an act of the partners (i.e., some dissociations), (2) operation of law, or (3) court order. The provisions of Section 801 that involve an act of the parties are default provisions: the partners may by agreement modify or eliminate these grounds. The partners may *not* vary or eliminate the grounds for dissolution based on operation of law or court order. Section 103.

**Dissolution by Act of the Partners** These causes of dissolution make up a subset of dissociations. In a **partnership at will**, a partner's giving notice of intent to withdraw will result in dissolution of a partnership. Section 801. Thus, any member of a partnership at will has the right to force a liquidation of the partnership. (The death or bankruptcy of a partner does *not* dissolve a partnership at will.)

No partner by herself has the power to dissolve a term partnership. Section 801 provides for three ways in which a **term partnership** will be dissolved.

1. The term of the partnership expires or the undertaking is complete. It should be noted that if the partners continue a term partnership after the expiration of the term or completion of the undertaking, the partnership will be treated as a partnership at will. Section 406.
2. All of the partners expressly agree to dissolve. This reflects the principle that the partners can unanimously amend the partnership agreement.
3. A partner's dissociation caused by a partner's death or incapacity, bankruptcy or similar financial impairment, or wrongful dissociation will bring on a dissolution if within ninety days after dissociation at least half of the remaining partners express their will to wind up the partnership business. Thus, if a term partnership has eight partners and one of the partners wrongfully dissociates before the end of the term, the partnership will be dissolved only if four of the remaining seven partners vote in favor of liquidation.

In **all partnerships** dissolution occurs upon the happening of an event that was specified in the partnership agreement as resulting in dissolution. The partners may, however, agree to continue the business.

**Dissolution by Operation of Law** A partnership is dissolved by operation of law if an event occurs that makes it unlawful to continue all or substantially all of the partnership's business. For example, a law prohibiting the production and sale of alcoholic beverages would dissolve a partnership formed to manufacture liquor. A cure of such illegality within ninety days after notice to the partnership of the event is effective retroactively. The partnership agreement cannot vary the requirement that an uncured illegal business must be dissolved and liquidated. Section 103(b)(8).

**Dissolution by Court Order** On application by a **partner**, a court may order dissolution on grounds of another partner's misconduct or upon a finding that (1) the economic purpose of the partnership is likely to be unreasonably frustrated; (2) another partner has engaged in conduct relating to the partnership business that makes it not reasonably practicable to carry on the business in partnership with that partner; or (3) it is not otherwise reasonably practicable to carry on the partnership business in conformity with the partnership agreement. On application of a **transferee** of a partner's transferable interest or a purchaser at foreclosure of a charging order, a court may order dissolution if it determines that it is equitable to wind up the partnership business (1) at any time in a partnership at will or (2) after the term of a term partnership has expired. The partners may *not* by agreement vary or eliminate the court's power to wind up a partnership. Section 103(b)(8).

◆ **SEE CASE 32-3**

### EFFECTS OF DISSOLUTION

A partnership continues after dissolution only for the purpose of winding up its business. The partnership is terminated when the winding up of its business is completed. Section 802. The remaining partners have the right, however, to continue the business after dissolution if **all** of the partners, including any dissociating partner other than a wrongfully dissociating partner, waive the right to have the partnership's business wound up and the partnership terminated. Section 802(b). In that event the partnership resumes carrying on its business as if dissolution had not occurred.

**Authority** Upon dissolution, the *actual authority* of a partner to act for the partnership terminates, except so far as is appropriate to wind up partnership business. Section 804. Actual authority to wind up includes the authority to complete existing contracts, to collect debts, to sell partnership assets, and to pay partnership obligations. A person winding up a partnership's business also has the authority to preserve the partnership business or property as a going concern for a reasonable time, bring and defend legal actions, settle and close the partnership's business, distribute the assets of the partnership pursuant to the RUPA, settle disputes by mediation or arbitration, and perform other necessary acts. Section 803(c).

With respect to apparent authority, the partnership is bound in a transaction not appropriate for winding up only if the partner's act would have bound the partnership before dissolution and the other party to the transaction did not have notice of the dissolution. Section 804(2). A person has notice of a fact if the person (1) knows of it, (2) has received a notification of it, or (3) has reason to know it exists from all of the facts known to the person at the time in question. Section 102(b). Moreover, RUPA Section 805 provides that, after an event of dissolution, any partner who has not wrongfully dissociated may file a statement of dissolution on behalf of the partnership and that ninety days after the filing of the statement of dissolution nonpartners are deemed to have notice of the dissolution and the corresponding limitation on the authority of all partners. Thus, after ninety days the statement of dissolution operates as constructive notice conclusively limiting the apparent authority of partners to transactions that are appropriate for winding up the business.

**Liability** Partners are liable for their share of partnership liabilities incurred after dissolution. Section 806(a). That includes not only obligations that are appropriate for winding up the business, but also obligations that are inappropriate but within the partner's apparent authority. A partner, however, who, with knowledge of the dissolution nevertheless incurs a liability binding on the partnership by an act that is not appropriate for winding up the partnership business, is liable to the partnership for any damage caused to the partnership by the liability. Section 806(b).

## WINDING UP

Whenever a dissolved partnership is not to be continued, the partnership must be liquidated. The process of liquidation, called **winding up**, involves completing unfinished business, collecting debts, taking inventory, reducing assets to cash, auditing the partnership books, paying creditors, and distributing the remaining assets to the partners. During this period, the fiduciary duties of the partners continue in effect except the duty not to compete.

**Participation in Winding Up** After dissolution, a partner who has not wrongfully dissociated may participate in winding up the partnership's business. Section 803(a). On application of any partner, partner's legal representative, or transferee, the court may order judicial supervision of the winding up if good cause is shown. Any partner winding up the partnership is entitled to reasonable compensation for services rendered in the winding up. Section 401(h).

**Distribution of Assets** After all the partnership assets have been collected and reduced to cash, they are distributed to creditors and the partners. When the partnership has been profitable, the order of distribution is not critical; however, when liabilities exceed assets, the order of distribution has great importance. In winding up a partnership's business, the "assets" of the partnership include all required contributions of partners. Section 807(a).

The RUPA provides that the partnership must apply its assets first to discharge the obligations of partners who are creditors on *parity* with other creditors, subject to any other laws, such as fraudulent conveyance laws and voidable transfers under the Bankruptcy Act. Second, any surplus must be applied to pay a liquidating distribution equal to the net amount distributable to partners in accordance with their right to distributions. Section 807. (This does not distinguish between amounts owing to partners for return of capital and amounts owing to partners for profits.) The partnership agreement may vary the RUPA's rules for distributing the surplus among the partners. For example, it may distinguish between capital and operating losses, as the original UPA does.

Each partner is entitled to a settlement of all partnership accounts upon winding up. In settling accounts among the partners, profits and losses that result from the liquidation of the partnership assets must be credited and charged to the partners' accounts according to their respective shares of profits and losses. Then, the partnership must make a final liquidating distribution to those partners with a positive account balance in an amount equal to any excess of the credits over the charges in the partner's account. Any partner with a negative account balance must contribute to the partnership an amount equal to any excess of the charges over the credits in the partner's account. Section 807(b). (In an LLP a partner is *not* required to contribute for any partnership obligations for which that partner is not personally liable under the LLP statute's shield.)

Partners share proportionately in the shortfall caused by partners who fail to contribute their proportionate share. The partnership may enforce a partner's obligation to contribute. A partner is entitled to recover from the other partners any contributions in excess of that partner's share of the partnership's liabilities. After the settlement of accounts, each partner must contribute, in the proportion in which the partner shares partnership losses, the amount necessary to satisfy partnership obligations that were not known at the time of the settlement. The estate of a deceased partner is liable for the partner's obligation to contribute to the partnership.

**Marshaling of Assets** The Revised Act abolishes the marshaling of assets doctrine—which segregates and considers separately the assets and liabilities of the partnership and the respective assets and liabilities of the individual partners—

and the dual priority rule. Section 807. (These are discussed later in this chapter.) Under the RUPA, like the UPA, partnership creditors are entitled to be satisfied first out of partnership assets. Unlike the UPA, the Revised Act provides that unsatisfied partnership creditors may recover any deficiency out of the individually owned assets of the partners on equal footing with the partners' creditors.

## DISSOCIATION WITHOUT DISSOLUTION

As already mentioned, the RUPA uses the term "dissociation," instead of the UPA term "dissolution," to denote the change in the relationship caused by a partner's ceasing to be associated in the carrying on of the business. Under the RUPA, a dissociation of a partner results in dissolution only in limited circumstances, discussed previously. Thus in many instances, dissociation will result merely in a buyout of the withdrawing partner's interest rather than a winding up of the partnership.

### DISSOCIATIONS NOT CAUSING DISSOLUTION

In a **partnership at will**, a partner will be dissociated from the partnership without dissolution upon specified causes, including that partner's death, bankruptcy, or incapacity; the expulsion of that partner; or, in the case of an entity-partner, its termination. RUPA Sections 601 and 801. (As covered earlier, a partnership at will is *dissolved* upon notice of a partner's intent to withdraw.)

In a **term partnership**, if within ninety days after any specified cause of dissolution occurs, fewer than half of the remaining partners express their will to wind up the partnership business, then the partnership will not dissolve. These causes include the following: a partner's dissociation by death, bankruptcy, or incapacity; the distribution by a trust-partner of its entire partnership interest; the termination of an entity-partner; or a partner's wrongful dissociation. (A wrongful dissociation includes a partner's voluntary withdrawal in violation of the partnership agreement and the judicial expulsion of a partner.) Section 801.

With three exceptions, the partners may by agreement modify or eliminate any of the grounds for dissolution. The three exceptions are (1) carrying on an illegal business, (2) a court-ordered dissolution on application of a partner, and (3) a court-ordered dissolution on application of a transferee of a partner's interest. Section 103. Moreover, at any time after the dissolution of a partnership and before the winding up of its business is completed, all of the partners, including any dissociating partner other than a wrongfully dissociating partner, may waive the right to have the partnership's business wound up and the partnership terminated. In that event, the partnership resumes carrying on its business as if dissolution had never occurred. Section 802(b).

### CONTINUATION AFTER DISSOCIATION

If a partner is dissociated from a partnership without resulting in dissolution, the remaining partners have the right to continue the business. Creditors of the partnership remain creditors of the continued partnership. Moreover, the dissociated partner remains liable for partnership obligations incurred before dissociation. Section 703(a).

The partnership must purchase the dissociated partner's interest in the partnership. Section 701. The partnership agreement can vary these rights. Section 103. The buyout price of a dissociated partner's interest is the amount that would have been distributable to the dissociating partner in a winding up of the partnership if, on the date of dissociation, the assets of the partnership were sold at a price equal to the greater of liquidation value or going concern value without the dissociated partner. The partnership must offset against the buyout price all other amounts owing from the dissociated partner to the partnership, including damages for wrongful dissociation. RUPA Section 701. These rules, however, are merely default rules, and the partnership agreement may specify the method or formula for determining the buyout price and all of the other terms and conditions of the buyout right.

A partner in a term partnership who wrongfully dissociates before the expiration of a definite term or the completion of a particular undertaking is not entitled to payment of any portion of the buyout price until the expiration of the term or completion of the undertaking, unless the partner establishes to the satisfaction of the court that earlier payment will not cause undue hardship to the business of the partnership. Section 701(h).

A partnership must indemnify a dissociated partner whose interest is being purchased against all partnership liabilities, whether incurred before or after the dissociation, except liabilities incurred by an act of the dissociated partner after dissociation that binds the partnership, as discussed later.

◆ **SEE CASE 32-4**

◈ **SEE FIGURE 32-3: Dissociation and Dissolution under RUPA**

### DISSOCIATED PARTNER'S POWER TO BIND THE PARTNERSHIP

A dissociated partner has no actual authority to act for the partnership. Section 603(b)(1). With respect to apparent authority, Section 702 provides that for two years after a partner dissociates without resulting in a dissolution of the partnership business, the partnership is bound by an act of the dissociated partner which would have bound the partnership before dissociation but *only if* at the time of entering into the transaction the other party:

1. reasonably believed that the dissociated partner was then a partner;

◆ FIGURE 32-3: **Dissociation and Dissolution under RUPA**

| Cause | Effects | | | |
|---|---|---|---|---|
| | Partnership at Will | | Term Partnership | |
| | Dissociation | Dissolution | Dissociation | Dissolution |
| **ACTS OF PARTNERS** | | | | |
| **Assignment of partner's interest** | | | | |
| **Accounting** | | | | |
| **Withdrawal** | • | • | • | * |
| **Bankruptcy** | • | | • | * |
| **Incapacity** | • | | • | * |
| **Death** | • | | • | * |
| **Expulsion of partner** | • | | • | |
| **Expiration of term** | | | | • |
| **Event specified in partnership agreement** | • | • | • | • |
| **Unanimous agreement to dissolve** | • | • | • | • |
| **OPERATION OF LAW** | | | | |
| **Illegality** | | • | | • |
| **COURT ORDER** | | | | |
| **Judicial expulsion of partner** | • | | • | * |
| **Judicial determination of partner's incapacity to perform partnership duties** | • | | • | * |
| **Judicial determination of economic frustration or impracticability** | | • | | • |
| **Application by transferee of partner's interest if equitable** | | • | | • |

* Dissolution will occur if, within ninety days after dissociation, at least half the remaining partners express their will to wind up the partnership business.

2. did not have notice of the partner's dissociation; *and*
3. is not deemed to have had constructive notice from a filed statement of dissociation.

A dissociated partner is liable to the partnership for any damage caused to the partnership arising from an obligation improperly incurred by the dissociated partner after dissociation for which the partnership is liable. Section 702(b). The dissociated partner is also personally liable to the third party for the unauthorized obligation.

A person has *notice* of a fact if he knows or has reason to know it exists from all the facts that are known to him or he has received a notification of it. Section 102(b). The RUPA provides that ninety days after a statement of dissociation is filed, nonpartners are deemed to have constructive notice of the dissociation thereby conclusively terminating a dissociated partner's apparent authority. Section 704(c). Thus, under the RUPA a partnership should notify all known creditors of a partner's dissociation and file a statement of dissociation, which will conclusively limit a dissociated partner's continuing agency power to ninety days after filing. Conversely, third parties dealing with a partnership should check for partnership filings at least every ninety days.

### DISSOCIATED PARTNER'S LIABILITY TO THIRD PERSONS

A partner's dissociation does not of itself discharge the partner's liability for a partnership obligation incurred before dissociation. Section 703(a). A dissociated partner is not liable for a partnership obligation incurred more than two years after dissociation. For partnership obligations incurred within two years after a partner dissociates without resulting in a dissolution of the partnership business, a dissociated partner is liable for a partnership obligation if, at the time of entering into the transaction, the other party (1) reasonably believed that the dissociated partner was then a partner; (2) did not have notice of the partner's dissociation; *and* (3) is not deemed to have had constructive notice from a filed statement of dissociation. Section 703(b).

By agreement with the partnership creditor and the partners continuing the business, a dissociated partner may be released from liability for a partnership obligation. Section 703(c). Moreover, a dissociated partner is released from liability for a partnership obligation if a partnership creditor, with notice of the partner's dissociation but without the partner's consent, agrees to a material alteration in the nature or time of payment of a partnership obligation. Section 703(d).

# DISSOLUTION OF GENERAL PARTNERSHIPS UNDER UPA

The extinguishment of a partnership consists of three stages: (1) dissolution, (2) winding up or liquidation, and (3) termination. Dissolution occurs when the partners cease to carry on the business together. Upon dissolution, the partnership is not terminated but continues until the winding up of its affairs is complete. During winding up, unfinished business is completed, receivables are collected, payments are made to creditors, and the remaining assets are distributed to the partners. Termination occurs when the process is finished.

## DISSOLUTION

The UPA defines **dissolution** as the change in the relation of the partners caused by any partner's ceasing to be associated in the carrying on, as distinguished from the winding up, of the business. UPA Section 29. The following sections discuss the causes and effects of dissolution.

### CAUSES OF DISSOLUTION

Dissolution may be brought about by (1) an act of the partners, (2) operation of law, or (3) court order. UPA Section 31. A number of events that were considered causes of dissolution under the common law are no longer considered so under the UPA. For example, the assignment of a partner's interest, a creditor's charging order (judicial lien) on a partner's interest, and an accounting no longer trigger dissolution.

**Dissolution by Act of the Partners** Because a partnership is a personal relationship, a partner always has the power to dissolve it by his actions, but whether he has the right to do so is determined by the partnership agreement. A partner who has withdrawn from the partnership in violation of the partnership agreement is liable to the remaining partners for damages resulting from the **wrongful dissolution.**

A partnership is **rightfully dissolved**, that is, dissolved in such a manner that the partner's or partners' act does not violate the partnership agreement (1) when all of those partners who have not assigned their interests or permitted their interests to be charged expressly agree to dissolve the partnership; (2) when the time period provided in the agreement has ended or the purpose for which the partnership was formed has been accomplished; (3) when a partner withdraws from a partnership at will, that is, a partnership with no definite term or specific undertaking; or (4) when a partner is expelled in accordance with a power to expel conferred by the partnership agreement. UPA Section 31.

**Dissolution by Operation of Law** A partnership is dissolved by operation of law upon (1) the death of a partner, (2) the bankruptcy of a partner or of the partnership, or (3) the subsequent illegality of the partnership, which includes any event that makes it unlawful for the partnership business to be carried on or for the members to carry on the business in partnership form. Section 31.

**Dissolution by Court Order** Upon application by or for a partner, a court will order a dissolution if it finds that (1) a partner has been adjudicated mentally incompetent or suffers some other incapacity that prevents him from functioning as a partner; (2) a partner has engaged in conduct prejudicial to the business, has willfully or persistently breached the partnership agreement, or has conducted himself so that it is impracticable to carry on business; (3) the business can be carried on only at a loss; or (4) other circumstances render a dissolution equitable. UPA Section 32. An assignee of a partner's interest or a partner's personal creditor who has obtained a charging order against the partner's interest is entitled to a dissolution by court decree. If the partnership is not at will, however, the partnership will not be dissolved until the term or particular undertaking specified in the partnership agreement is complete.

### EFFECTS OF DISSOLUTION

On dissolution, the partnership is not terminated but continues until the winding up of its affairs is complete. UPA Section 30. Moreover, dissolution does not discharge the existing liability of any partner, though it does restrict her authority to act for the partnership.

Upon dissolution, the *actual authority* of a partner to act for the partnership terminates, except so far as may be necessary to wind up partnership affairs. UPA Section 33. Actual authority to wind up includes the authority to complete existing contracts, to collect debts, to sell partnership assets, and to pay partnership obligations.

Although actual authority terminates upon dissolution, *apparent authority* continues to bind the partnership for acts within the scope of the partnership business unless the third party is given notice of the dissolution. UPA Section 35. A third party who extended credit to the partnership before dissolution may hold the partnership liable for any transaction that would have bound the partnership had dissolution not occurred, unless the third party had knowledge or actual notice of the dissolution. **Actual notice** requires a verbal statement to the third party or actual delivery of a written statement. UPA Section 3(2). On the other hand, a third party who knew of or had dealt with the partnership but who had not extended credit to it before its dissolution can hold the partnership liable unless he had knowledge, actual notice, or constructive notice of the dissolution.

**Constructive notice** consists of advertising a notice of dissolution in a newspaper of general circulation in the places at which the partnership regularly conducted its business. UPA Section 35(1)(b)(II). No notice need be given to third parties who had no knowledge of the partnership before its dissolution.

## WINDING UP

Whenever a dissolved partnership is not to be continued, the partnership must be liquidated. The process of liquidation, called winding up, involves completing unfinished business, collecting debts, taking inventory, reducing assets to cash, auditing the partnership books, paying creditors, and distributing the remaining assets to the partners. During this period, the fiduciary duties of the partners continue in effect.

### THE RIGHT TO WIND UP

Upon dissolution any partner who has not wrongfully dissolved the partnership or been rightfully expelled according to the terms of the partnership agreement has the right to insist on the winding up of the partnership unless the partnership agreement provides otherwise. Unless otherwise agreed, all nonbankrupt partners who have not wrongfully dissolved the partnership have the right to wind up the partnership affairs. UPA Section 37.

### DISTRIBUTION OF ASSETS

After all the partnership assets have been collected and reduced to cash, they are distributed to creditors and the partners. When the partnership has been profitable, the order of distribution is not critical; however, when liabilities exceed assets, the order of distribution has great importance.

Section 40 of the UPA sets forth the rules for settling accounts between the parties after dissolution. It states that the liabilities of a partnership are to be paid out of partnership assets in the following order: (1) amounts owing to nonpartner creditors, (2) amounts owing to partners other than for capital and profits (loans or advances), (3) amounts owing to partners for capital, and (4) amounts owing to partners for profits. The partners may by agreement among themselves change the internal priorities of distribution (numbers 2, 3, and 4) but not the preferred position of third parties (number 1). The UPA defines partnership assets to include all partnership property as well as the contributions necessary for the payment of all partnership liabilities, which consist of numbers 1, 2, and 3. UPA Section 40(a).

In addition, the UPA provides that, in the absence of any contrary agreement, each partner shall share equally in the profits and surplus remaining after all liabilities (numbers 1, 2, and 3) are satisfied and must contribute toward the partnership's losses, capital or otherwise, according to his share in the profits. UPA Section 18(a). Thus, the proportion in which the partners bear losses depends not on their relative capital contributions but on their agreement. If no specific agreement exists, the partners bear losses in the same proportion in which they share profits.

If the partnership is insolvent, the partners individually must contribute their respective share of the losses to pay the creditors. Furthermore, if one or more of the partners is insolvent or bankrupt or is out of the jurisdiction and refuses to contribute, the other partners must contribute the additional amount necessary to pay the firm's liabilities in the relative proportions in which they share the profits. UPA Section 40(d). Any partner who pays an amount in excess of his proper share of the losses has a right of contribution against the partners who have not paid their share. UPA Section 40(f).

### MARSHALING OF ASSETS

The doctrine of marshaling of assets applies only in situations in which a court of equity is administering the assets of a partnership and of its members. **Marshaling of assets** means segregating and considering separately the assets and liabilities of the partnership and the respective assets and liabilities of the individual partners. Partnership creditors are entitled to be satisfied first out of partnership assets and may recover any deficiency out of the individually owned assets of the partners. This right is subordinate, however, to the rights of nonpartnership creditors to those assets. Conversely, the nonpartnership creditors have first claim to the individually owned assets of their respective debtors, whereas their claims to partnership assets are subordinate to the claims of partnership creditors. This approach is called the "dual priority" rule.

Finally, the assets of an insolvent partner are distributed in the following order: (1) debts and liabilities owing to her nonpartnership creditors, (2) debts and liabilities owing to partnership creditors, and (3) contributions owing to other partners who have paid more than their respective share of the firm's liabilities to partnership creditors. UPA Section 40(i).

This rule, however, is no longer followed if the partnership is a debtor under the Bankruptcy Code. In a proceeding under the Federal bankruptcy law, a trustee is appointed to administer the estate of the debtor. If the partnership property is insufficient to pay all the claims against the partnership, the statute directs the trustee to seek recovery of the deficiency first from the general partners who are not bankrupt. The trustee may then seek recovery against the estates of bankrupt partners on the same basis as other creditors of the bankrupt partner. Bankruptcy Code, Section 723. This provision, although contrary to the UPA's doctrine of marshaling of assets, governs whenever partnership assets are being administered by a bankruptcy court.

## CONTINUATION AFTER DISSOLUTION

Dissolution produces one of two outcomes: either the partnership is liquidated or the remaining partners continue the partnership. Whereas liquidation sacrifices the value of a going concern, continuation of the partnership after dissolution avoids this loss. The UPA, nonetheless, gives each partner the right to have the partnership liquidated except in a few instances in which the remaining partners have the right to continue the partnership. UPA Section 37.

### RIGHT TO CONTINUE PARTNERSHIP

After dissolution, the remaining partners have the right to continue the partnership when (1) the partnership has been dissolved in contravention of the partnership agreement, (2) a partner has been expelled in accordance with the partnership agreement, or (3) all the partners agree to continue the business. Nevertheless, the noncontinuing partner, or his legal representative, has a right to an account of his interest against the person or partnership continuing the business as of the date of dissolution, unless otherwise agreed. UPA Section 43. Moreover, when a partner dies or retires and the surviving partners continue the business, the retired partner or the legal representative of the deceased partner is entitled to be paid the value of his interest as of the date of the dissolution as an ordinary creditor of the partnership. In addition, he is entitled to receive interest on this amount or, at his option, in lieu of interest, the profits of the business attributable to the use of his right in the property of the dissolved partnership. His rights are subordinate, however, to those of creditors of the dissolved partnership. UPA Section 42.

**Continuation after Wrongful Dissolution** A partner who causes dissolution by wrongfully withdrawing cannot force the liquidation of the firm. The aggrieved partners may either liquidate the firm and recover damages for the breach of the partnership agreement or continue the partnership by buying out the withdrawing partner, who is entitled to realize his interest in the partnership less the amount of the damages that the other partners have sustained because of his breach. The withdrawing partner's interest is computed without considering the goodwill of the business. In addition, the remaining partners may use the capital contributions of the wrongdoing partner for the unexpired period of the partnership agreement. They must, however, indemnify the former partner against all present and future partnership liabilities. UPA Section 38(2).

**Continuation after Expulsion** A partner expelled pursuant to the partnership agreement cannot force the liquidation of the partnership. He is entitled only (1) to be discharged from all partnership liabilities either by payment or by a novation with the creditors, and (2) to receive in cash the net amount due him from the partnership. UPA Section 38(1).

**Continuation Agreement of the Partners** By far the best and most reliable tool for preserving a partnership business after dissolution is through a continuation agreement. Frequently used to ensure continuity in the event of a partner's death or retirement, continuation agreements permit remaining partners to keep partnership property, carry on partnership business, and specify settlements for outgoing partners.

### RIGHTS OF CREDITORS

Any change in membership dissolves a partnership and forms a new one, despite the fact that the new combination may include a majority of the old partners. The creditors of the old partnership may pursue their claims against the new partnership and also may proceed to hold all of the members of the dissolved partnership personally liable. UPA Section 41. If a withdrawing partner has made arrangements with those who continue the business whereby they assume and pay all debts and obligations of the firm, the partner is still liable to creditors whose claims arose before the dissolution. If compelled to pay such debts, the withdrawing partner nonetheless has a right of indemnity against her former partners, who agreed to pay the debts but failed to do so.

A retiring partner may be discharged from his existing liabilities by entering into a novation with the continuing partners and the creditors. A creditor must agree to a novation, although his consent may be inferred from his course of dealing with the partnership after dissolution. UPA Section 36(2). Whether such dealings with a continuing partnership constitute an implied novation is a factual question of intent.

A withdrawing partner may protect herself against liability upon contracts the firm enters subsequent to her withdrawal by giving notice that she is no longer a member of the firm. Otherwise, she will be liable for debts thus incurred to creditors who had no notice or knowledge of the partner's withdrawal. Persons who had extended credit to the partnership prior to its dissolution must receive actual notice, whereas constructive notice by newspaper publication will suffice for those who knew of the partnership but had not extended credit to it before its dissolution. UPA Section 35.

## CHAPTER SUMMARY

### RELATIONSHIP OF PARTNERSHIP AND PARTNERS WITH THIRD PARTIES

**CONTRACTS OF PARTNERSHIP**

**Partners' Liability**
- ***Personal Liability*** if the partnership is contractually bound, each partner has joint and several unlimited personal liability
- ***Joint and Several Liability*** a creditor may sue the partners jointly as a group or separately as individuals

**Authority to Bind Partnership** a partner who has actual authority (express or implied) or apparent authority may bind the partnership
- ***Actual Express Authority*** authority set forth in the partnership agreement, in additional agreements among the partners, or in decisions made by a majority of the partners regarding the ordinary business of the partnership
- ***Actual Implied Authority*** authority that is reasonably deduced from the nature of the partnership, the terms of the partnership agreement, or the relations of the partners
- ***Apparent Authority*** an act of a partner for apparently carrying on in the ordinary course the partnership business or business of the kind carried on by the partnership binds the partnership, so long as that third person has no knowledge or notice of the lack of actual authority

**Partnership by Estoppel** imposes partnership duties and liabilities on a nonpartner who has either represented himself or consented to be represented as a partner

**TORTS AND CRIMES OF PARTNERSHIP**

**Torts** the partnership is liable for loss or injury caused by any wrongful act or omission or other actionable conduct of any partner while acting within the ordinary course of the business or with the authority of her copartners; the partners are jointly and severally liable

**Breach of Trust** the partnership is liable if a partner in the course of the partnership's business or while acting with authority of the partnership breaches a trust by misapplying money or property entrusted by a third person; the partners are jointly and severally liable

**Crimes** a partner is not criminally liable for the crimes of her partners unless she authorized or participated in them

| | |
|---|---|
| **NOTICE TO A PARTNER** | **Binds Partnership** a partnership is bound by a partner's knowledge, notice, or receipt of a notification of a fact relating to the partnership<br>**Notice** a person has notice of a fact if the person (1) knows of it, (2) has received a notification of it, or (3) has reason to know it exists from all of the facts known to the person at the time in question |
| **LIABILITY OF INCOMING PARTNER** | **Antecedent Debts** the liability of an incoming partner for antecedent debts of the partnership is limited to her capital contribution<br>**Subsequent Debts** the liability of an incoming partner for subsequent debts of the partnership is unlimited |

## DISSOCIATION AND DISSOLUTION OF GENERAL PARTNERSHIPS UNDER RUPA

| | |
|---|---|
| **DISSOCIATION** | **Definition of Dissociation** change in the relation of partners caused by any partner's ceasing to be associated in carrying on of the business<br>• ***Term Partnership*** partnership for a specific term or particular undertaking<br>• ***Partnership at Will*** partnership in which the partners have not agreed to remain partners until the expiration of a definite term or the completion of a particular undertaking<br>**Wrongful Dissociation** a dissociation that breaches an express provision of the partnership agreement or in a term partnership if before the expiration of the term or the completion of the undertaking (1) the partner voluntarily withdraws by express will, (2) the partner is judicially expelled for misconduct, (3) the partner becomes a debtor in bankruptcy, or (4) the partner is an entity (other than a trust or estate) and is expelled or otherwise dissociated because its dissolution or termination was willful<br>**Rightful Dissociation** all other dissociations are rightful including the death of a partner in *any* partnership and the withdrawal of a partner in a *partnership at will*<br>**Effects of Dissociation** terminates the dissociating partner's right to participate in the management of the partnership business and duties to partnership |
| **DISSOLUTION** | **Causes of Dissolution**<br>• ***Dissolution by Act of the Partners*** **partnership at will**: withdrawal of a partner; **term partnership**: (1) the term ends, (2) all partners expressly agree to dissolve, or (3) a partner's dissociation is caused by a partner's death or incapacity, bankruptcy or similar financial impairment, or wrongful dissociation if within ninety days after dissociation at least half of the remaining partners express their will to wind up the partnership business; **any partnership**: an event occurs that was specified in the partnership agreement as resulting in dissolution<br>• ***Dissolution by Operation of Law*** a partnership is dissolved by operation of law upon the subsequent illegality of the partnership business<br>• ***Dissolution by Court Order*** a court will order dissolution of a partnership under certain conditions<br>**Effects of Dissolution** upon dissolution a partnership is not terminated but continues until the winding up is completed<br>• ***Authority*** a partner's actual authority to act for the partnership terminates, except so far as may be appropriate to wind up partnership affairs; apparent authority continues unless notice of the dissolution is given to a third party<br>• ***Liability*** dissolution does not in itself discharge the existing liability of any partner; partners are liable for their share of partnership liabilities incurred after dissolution<br>**Winding Up** completing unfinished business, collecting debts, and distributing assets to creditors and partners; also called liquidation |

- ***Winding Up Required*** a dissolved partnership must be wound up and terminated when the winding up of its business is completed unless all of the partners, including any rightfully dissociating partner, waive the right to have the partnership's business wound up and the partnership terminated
- ***Participation in Winding Up*** any partner who has not wrongfully dissociated may participate in winding up the partnership's business
- ***Distribution of Assets*** the assets of the partnership include all required contributions of partners; the liabilities of a partnership are to be paid out of partnership assets in the following order: (1) amounts owing to nonpartner and partner creditors and (2) amounts owing to partners on their partners' accounts
- ***Partnership Creditors*** are entitled to be first satisfied out of partnership assets
- ***Nonpartnership Creditors*** share on equal footing with unsatisfied partnership creditors in the individually owned assets of their respective debtor-partners

---

**DISSOCIATION WITHOUT DISSOLUTION**

**Dissociations not Causing Dissolution**

- ***Partnership at Will*** a partner's death, bankruptcy, or incapacity, the expulsion of a partner, or the termination of an entity-partner results in a dissociation of that partner but does not result in a dissolution
- ***Term Partnership*** if within ninety days after any of the following causes of dissolution occurs, fewer than half of the remaining partners express their will to wind up the partnership business, then the partnership will not dissolve: a partner's dissociation by death, bankruptcy, or incapacity, the distribution by a trust-partner of its entire partnership interest, the termination of an entity-partner, or a partner's wrongful dissociation

**Continuation after Dissociation** the remaining partners have the right to continue the partnership with a mandatory buyout of the dissociating partner; the creditors of the partnership have claims against the continued partnership

**Dissociated Partner's Power to Bind the Partnership** a dissociated partner's actual authority to act for the partnership terminates; apparent authority continues for two years unless notice of the dissolution is given to a third party

**Dissociated Partner's Liability to Third Persons** a partner's dissociation does not of itself discharge the partner's liability for a partnership obligation incurred before dissociation; a dissociated partner is liable for a partnership obligation incurred within two years after a partner dissociates unless notice of the dissolution is given to a third party

## CASES

CASE 32-1

Authority to Bind Partnership

### RNR INVESTMENTS LIMITED PARTNERSHIP v. PEOPLES FIRST COMMUNITY BANK

Court of Appeal of Florida, First District, 2002

812 So.2d 561

http://caselaw.findlaw.com/fl-district-court-of-appeal/1475046.html

**Van Nortwick, J.**

RNR is a Florida limited partnership formed * * * to purchase vacant land in Destin, Florida, and to construct a house on the land for resale. Bernard Roeger was RNR's general partner and Heinz Rapp, Claus North, and S.E. Waltz, Inc., were limited partners. The agreement of limited partnership provides for various restrictions on the authority of the general partner. Paragraph 4.1 of the agreement required the general partner to prepare a budget covering the cost of acquisition and construction of the project (defined as the "Approved Budget"). * * *

Paragraph 4.3 restricted the general partner's ability to borrow, spend partnership funds and encumber partnership assets, if not specifically provided for in the Approved Budget. Finally, with respect to the development of the partnership project, paragraph 2.2(b) provided:

> The General Partner shall not incur debts, liabilities or obligations of the Partnership which will cause any line item in the Approved Budget to be exceeded by more than ten percent (10%) or which will cause the aggregate Approved Budget to be exceed by more than five percent (5%) unless the General Partner shall receive the prior written consent of the Limited Partner.

In June 1998, RNR, through its general partner, entered into a construction loan agreement, note and mortgage in the principal amount of $990,000. From June 25, 1998 through Mar. 13, 2000, the bank disbursed the aggregate sum of $952,699, by transfers into RNR's bank account. All draws were approved by an architect, who certified that the work had progressed as indicated and that the quality of the work was in accordance with the construction contract. No representative of RNR objected to any draw of funds or asserted that the amounts disbursed were not associated with the construction of the house.

RNR defaulted under the terms of the note and mortgage by failing to make payments due in July 2000 and all monthly payments due thereafter. The Bank filed a complaint seeking foreclosure. RNR filed an answer and affirmative defenses. In its first affirmative defense, RNR alleged that the Bank had failed to review the limitations on the general partner's authority in RNR's limited partnership agreement. RNR asserted that the Bank had negligently failed to investigate and to realize that the general partner had no authority to execute notes, a mortgage and a construction loan agreement and was estopped from foreclosing. The Bank filed a motion for summary judgment with supporting affidavits attesting to the amounts due and owing and the amount of disbursements under the loan.

In opposition to the summary judgment motion, RNR filed the affidavit of Stephen E. Waltz, * * * alleg[ing] that the limited partners understood and orally agreed that the general partner would seek financing in the approximate amount of $650,000.

* * *

RNR asserts that a copy of the limited partnership agreement was maintained at its offices. Nevertheless, the record contains no copy of an Approved Budget of the partnership or any evidence that would show that a copy of RNR's partnership agreement or any partnership budget was given to the Bank or that any notice of the general partner's restricted authority was provided to the Bank.

* * * [T]he trial court entered a summary final judgment of foreclosure in favor of the Bank. The foreclosure sale has been stayed pending the outcome of this appeal.

* * *

Although the agency concept of apparent authority was applied to partnerships under the common law, [citation], in Florida the extent to which the partnership is bound by the acts of a partner acting within the apparent authority is now governed by statute. Section 301(1), [citation], a part of the Florida Revised Uniform Partnership Act (FRUPA), provides:

> Each partner is an agent of the partnership for the purpose of its business. An act of a partner, including the execution of an instrument in the partnership name, for apparently carrying on in the ordinary scope of partnership business or business of the kind carried on by the partnership, in the geographic area in which the partnership operates, binds the partnership unless the partner had no authority to act for the partnership in the particular manner and the person with whom the partner was dealing knew or had received notification that the partner lacked authority.

[Court's footnote: RNR mistakenly argues that section 301(1) has no application to a limited partnership because that section is part of the Florida Revised Uniform Partnership Act, not the Florida Revised Uniform Limited Partnership Act. Section 620.186 (comparable to Revised Uniform Limited Partnership Act Section 1105), however, provides, as follows: In any case not provided for in this act, the provisions of the Uniform Partnership Act or the Revised Uniform Partnership Act of 1995, as applicable, and the rules of law and equity shall govern.]

Thus, even if a general partner's actual authority is restricted by the terms of the partnership agreement, the general partner possesses the apparent authority to bind the partnership in the ordinary course of partnership business or in the business of the kind carried on by the partnership, unless the third party "knew or had received a notification that the partner lacked authority." [Citation.] "Knowledge" and "notice" under FRUPA are defined in section 102. That section provides that "[a] person knows a fact if the person has actual knowledge of the fact." [Citation.] Further, a third party has notice of a fact if that party "(a) knows of the fact; (b) has received notification of the fact; or (c) has reason to know the fact exists from all other facts known to the person at the time in question." [FRUPA] §102(2). Finally, under [FRUPA] section 303 a partnership may file a statement of partnership authority setting forth any restrictions in a general partner's authority.

* * *

"Absent actual knowledge, third parties have no duty to inspect the partnership agreement or inquire otherwise to ascertain the extent of a partner's actual authority in the ordinary course of business * * * even if they have some reason to question it." [Citation.] The apparent authority provisions of section 301(1), reflect a policy by the drafters that "the risk of loss from partner misconduct more appropriately belongs on the partnership than on third parties who do not knowingly participate in or take advantage of the misconduct." * * * [Citation.]

Under section 301(1), the determination of whether a partner is acting with authority to bind the partnership involves a two-step analysis. The first step is to determine whether the partner purporting to bind the partnership apparently is carrying on the partnership business in the usual way or a business of the kind carried on by the partnership. An affirmative answer on this step ends the inquiry, unless it is shown that the person with whom the partner is dealing actually knew or had received a notification that the partner lacked authority. [Citation.] Here, it is undisputed that, in entering into the loan, the general partner was carrying on the business of RNR in the usual way. The dispositive question in this appeal is whether there are issues of material fact as to whether the Bank had actual knowledge or notice of restrictions on the general partner's authority.

RNR argues that, as a result of the restrictions on the general partner's authority in the partnership agreement, the Bank had constructive knowledge of the restrictions and was obligated to inquire as to the general partner's specific authority to bind RNR in the construction loan. We cannot agree. Under section 301, the Bank could rely on the general partner's apparent authority, unless it had actual knowledge or notice of restrictions on that authority. While the RNR partners may have agreed upon restrictions that would limit the general partner to borrowing no more than $650,000 on behalf of the partnership, RNR does not contend and nothing before us would show that the Bank had actual knowledge or notice of any restrictions on the general partner's authority. Here, the partnership could have protected itself by filing a statement pursuant to section 303 or by providing notice to the Bank of the specific restrictions on the authority of the general partner.

* * *

Because there is no disputed issue of fact concerning whether the Bank had actual knowledge or notice of restrictions on the general partner's authority to borrow, summary judgment was proper.

Affirmed.

CASE 32-2

## Liability of Incoming Partner
## CONKLIN FARM v. DORIS LEIBOWITZ

Supreme Court of New Jersey, 1995
140 N.J. 417, 658 A.2d 1257
http://lawlibrary.rutgers.edu/courts/supreme/a-99-94.opn.html

**Garibaldi, J.**

This appeal addresses whether an incoming partner is personally liable for interest that accrues on a partnership debt that arose before the incoming partner's admission. Under section 17 of New Jersey's Uniform Partnership Law, [citation] (the Act), an incoming partner is liable for preexisting debt only to the extent of partnership property; the incoming partner is not personally liable for preexisting debt. The parties to this appeal differ over whether the interest on a preexisting debt that accrues after the incoming partner's admission is new debt or part of the preexisting debt.

In December 1986, Paula Hertzberg, Elliot Leibowitz, and Joel Leibowitz formed, under the Act, a general partnership, LongView Estates (LongView), to acquire from plaintiff Conklin Farm (Conklin) approximately 100 acres of land in the Township of Montville. Paula Hertzberg owned forty percent of LongView; Elliot and Joel Leibowitz owned thirty percent each. They intended to build a residential condominium complex on the property.

On the same day that Paula Hertzberg, Elliot Leibowitz, and Joel Leibowitz formed LongView, LongView executed a promissory note in favor of Conklin for $9 million. The three LongView partners signed the note as partners, and also guaranteed the note personally. The note represented a portion of the purchase price for the land, and was secured by a mortgage on the land. The note provided for monthly payments of interest only—to accrue at eight and a quarter percent annually for the first year and nine percent thereafter—with the principal and any unpaid interest due on January 15, 1992. * * * The final payment on January 15, 1992, was to include any unpaid interest and the principal amount of $9 million. * * *

* * *

On March 15, 1990, Joel Leibowitz assigned his thirty percent interest in LongView to his wife, defendant Doris Leibowitz, who "agreed to be bound by all the terms and conditions of the Partnership Agreement dated December 22, 1986." Seventeen months later, on August 30, 1991, Doris assigned the interest back to her husband. During those seventeen months, the entire principal of the Conklin note of $9 million was outstanding, and interest accrued at an annual rate of nine percent.

LongView's condominium project failed, and LongView defaulted on * * * the Conklin note. * * * In March 1991,

LongView filed a petition for bankruptcy under *Chapter 11* of the Bankruptcy Code. * * * Eventually, Paula Hertzberg, Elliot Leibowitz, and Joel Leibowitz filed for personal bankruptcy protection, and all three were discharged of any personal liability on the Conklin [note].

**II**

Conklin looked to Doris Leibowitz for payment of thirty percent of the interest that accrued on the Conklin note over the seventeen months during which she had held her husband's interest. Conklin sued her in November 1991, claiming that she was *personally* liable for $547,000: thirty percent of the interest that accrued during the seventeen months, plus interest and costs. [Court's footnote: As the opinion below noted, "It is unclear from this record why plaintiff sought only thirty percent of the interest from defendant." [Citation.] If the interest at issue is indeed new debt, Doris Leibowitz is personally liable for 100% of it under [the Partnership Act]].

* * *

* * * [T]he sole issue became whether Doris Leibowitz, as an incoming partner, was personally liable for the interest that had accrued on the preexisting debt while she had been a partner. The trial court held that the interest was part of the preexisting debt, not new debt. The trial court found that [section 17 of New Jersey's Uniform Partnership Law] therefore limited Doris Leibowitz's liability to her interest in partnership property, which, of course, was by then worthless. Holding that Doris Leibowitz was thus not personally liable for the interest, the court granted her motion for summary judgment.

Conklin filed a Notice of Appeal. * * * The Appellate Division reversed. [Citation.] Ruling that the interest on preexisting debt is new debt, the Appellate Division held that Doris Leibowitz was personally liable for the interest that accrued on the note while she was a partner of LongView.

We granted Doris Leibowitz's petition for certification, [citation], and now reverse.

**III**

We find that the plain language of section 17 of New Jersey's Uniform Partnership Law and its legislative history compel the conclusion that Doris Leibowitz, as an incoming partner, is liable for debt to Conklin only to the extent of her interest in partnership assets. Under [section 15(b) of New Jersey's Uniform Partnership Law] each partner is personally liable for the debts and obligations of a partnership. [Section 17 of New Jersey's Uniform Partnership Law] defines the liability of new partners entering an existing partnership. That statute provides:

> A person admitted as a partner into an existing partnership is liable for all the obligations of the partnership arising before his admission as though he had been a partner when such obligations were incurred, except *that this liability shall be satisfied only out of partnership property.* (Emphasis added).

Under this statute, although the original partners are personally liable for preexisting debt, the incoming partner's liability for preexisting debt is limited to partnership property.

* * *

Thus, section 17 of the Uniform Partnership Act * * * made incoming partners personally liable for preexisting debts, but only to the extent of their investment in the partnership. * * *

* * *

**IV**

The Conklin note was executed by the partnership prior to Doris Leibowitz's having any interest in LongView. She did not sign or guarantee payment of that note. Thus, the issue appears resolved by the clear language of [section 17]: Because the note was a preexisting debt, and because Doris Leibowitz was an incoming partner, she is not personally liable for the debt. The parties agree that the principal of the note was preexisting debt. However, while Doris Leibowitz argues that the interest that accrued while she was a partner was part of that preexisting debt, Conklin argues that it was new debt that arose each month as it became due. Thus, according to Conklin, Doris Leibowitz is personally liable for the interest that accrued while she was a partner. We disagree.

* * *

**V**

Conklin argues that just as a rent obligation arises for current use of property, an interest obligation arises for current use of principal. The Appellate Division described the analogy as a "sound approach," and agreed that "interest is current rent for money and also should be treated as new debt." [Citation.] We disagree, and we find the rent analogy faulty.

Contractual interest is created by the contract, and is therefore inseparable from the contractual debt. In [citation], we described contractual interest as "an integral part of the debt itself." Indeed, contractual interest does not exist absent provision for it in the debt-creating instrument. * * * The interest obligation cannot be a separate debt from the principal obligation because, independent of the contract establishing the principal obligation, there is no obligation to pay interest.

* * *

Because there is no obligation to pay interest independent of the promissory note, Conklin's rent analogy fails. Since the obligation to pay interest arises only as a result of the original loan instrument, interest, unlike rent, cannot be "new" debt. * * *

* * *

Moreover, there is no prejudice to Conklin in the fact that it may look to only the original partners for payment of the preexisting debt and interest. In executing the note, Conklin considered the personal credit of only Paula Hertzberg, Elliot Leibowitz, and Joel Leibowitz, all of whom guaranteed the loan. Conklin did not rely on the personal credit of Doris Leibowitz. When lenders loan money, they rely on the financial statements of the general partners, and not of some future, unknown general partner. * * *

**VI**

We find that contractual interest is not new debt. * * * Accordingly, LongView's obligation to pay interest arose when it executed the Conklin note, before Doris Leibowitz became a partner. Hence, the interest on the note was preexisting debt under [section 17], and Doris Leibowitz is not personally liable for its payment.

The judgment of the Appellate Division is reversed.

CASE 32-3

## Dissolution
## HORIZON/CMS HEALTHCARE CORPORATION v. SOUTHERN OAKS HEALTH CARE, INC.

Court of Appeal of Florida, Fifth District, 1999
732 So.2d 1156, petition for review denied, 744 So.2d 454

**Goshorn, J.**

Horizon is a large, publicly traded provider of both nursing home facilities and management for nursing home facilities. It wanted to expand into Osceola County in 1993. Southern Oaks was already operating in Osceola County; it owned the Southern Oaks Health Care Center and a Certificate of Need issued by the Florida Agency for Health Care Administration for a new 120-bed facility in Kissimmee. Horizon and Southern Oaks decided to form a partnership to own the proposed Kissimmee facility, which was ultimately named Royal Oaks, and agreed that Horizon would manage both the Southern Oaks facility and the new Royal Oaks facility. To that end, Southern Oaks and Horizon entered into several partnership and management contracts in 1993.

In 1996, Southern Oaks filed suit alleging numerous defaults and breaches of the twenty-year agreements. * * * The trial court found * * * that Horizon breached its obligations under two different partnership agreements * * * [and] that Horizon had breached several management contracts. Thereafter, the court ordered that the partnerships be dissolved, finding that "the parties to the various agreements which are the subject of this lawsuit are now incapable of continuing to operate in business together" and that because it was dissolving the partnerships, "there is no entitlement to future damages." * * * In its cross appeal, Southern Oaks asserts that because Horizon unilaterally and wrongfully sought dissolution of the partnerships, Southern Oaks should receive a damage award for the loss of the partnerships' seventeen remaining years' worth of future profits. We reject its argument.

* * *

* * * First, the trial court's finding that the parties are incapable of continuing to operate in business together is a finding of "irreconcilable differences," a permissible reason for dissolving the partnerships under the express terms of the partnership agreements. Thus, dissolution was not "wrongful," assuming there can be "wrongful" dissolutions, and Southern Oaks was not entitled to damages for lost future profits. Additionally, the partnership contracts also permit dissolution by "judicial decree." Although neither party cites this provision, it appears that pursuant thereto, the parties agreed that dissolution would be proper if done by a trial court for whatever reason the court found sufficient to warrant dissolution.

Second, even assuming the partnership was dissolved for a reason not provided for in the partnership agreements, damages were properly denied. Under RUPA, it is clear that wrongful dissociation triggers liability for lost future profits. See §602(3) ("A partner who wrongfully dissociates is liable to the partnership and to the other partners for damages caused by the dissociation. The liability is in addition to any other obligation of the partner to the partnership or to the other partners."). However, RUPA does not contain a similar provision for dissolution; RUPA does not refer to the dissolutions as rightful or wrongful. Section 801, "Events causing dissolution and winding up of partnership business," outlines the events causing dissolution without any provision for liability for damages. Under subsection 801(5), the statute recognizes judicial dissolution:

> A partnership is dissolved, and its business must be wound up, only upon the occurrence of any of the following events:

* * *

(5) On application by a partner, a judicial determination that:

(a) The economic purpose of the partnership is likely to be unreasonably frustrated;

(b) Another partner has engaged in conduct relating to the partnership business which makes it not reasonably practicable to carry on the business in partnership with such partner; or

(c) It is not otherwise reasonably practicable to carry on the partnership business in conformity with the partnership agreement. * * *

Paragraph (5)(c) provides the basis for the trial court's dissolution in this case. While "reasonably practicable" is not defined in RUPA, the term is broad enough to encompass the inability of partners to continue working together, which is what the court found.

Certainly the law predating RUPA allowed for recovery of lost profits upon the wrongful dissolution of a partnership. [Citations.] However, RUPA brought significant changes to partnership law, among which was the adoption of the term "dissociation." Although the term is undefined in RUPA, dissociation appears to have taken the place of "dissolution" as that word was used pre-RUPA. [Citation.] "Dissolution" under RUPA has a different meaning, although the term is undefined in RUPA. [Citation.] It follows that the pre-RUPA cases providing for future damages upon wrongful dissolution are no longer applicable to a partnership dissolution. In other words a "wrongful dissolution" referred to in the pre-RUPA case law is now, under RUPA, known as "wrongful dissociation." Simply stated, under section 602, only when a partner dissociates and the dissociation is wrongful can the remaining partners sue for damages. [Court's footnote: Dissociation is not a condition precedent to dissolution under RUPA. * * * ("Most dissolution events are dissociations. On the other hand, it is not necessary to have a dissociation to cause a dissolution and winding up.")] * * *

Southern Oaks' attempt to bring the instant dissolution under the statute applicable to dissociation is rejected. The trial court ordered dissolution of the partnership, not the dissociation of Horizon for wrongful conduct. There no longer appears to be "wrongful" dissolution—either dissolution is provided for by contract or statute or the dissolution was improper and the dissolution order should be reversed. In the instant case, because the dissolution either came within the terms of the partnership agreements or paragraph 801(5)(c) (judicial dissolution where it is not reasonably practicable to carry on the partnership business), Southern Oaks' claim for lost future profits is without merit.

---

## CASE 32-4

## Continuation after Dissociation
## WARNICK v. WARNICK

Supreme Court of Wyoming, 2003
2003 Wy 113, 76 P.3d 316
http://caselaw.findlaw.com/wy-supreme-court/1262188.html

**Golden, J.**

In August 1978, Wilbur and Dee Warnick and their son Randall Warnick contracted to purchase a ranch in Sheridan County for an agreed price of $335,000, with $90,000 down plus $245,000 in installments over ten years at 8% interest. In April 1979, they formed Warnick Ranches general partnership to operate the ranch and complete the installment purchase agreement. The partnership agreement recited that the initial capital contributions of the partners totaled $60,000, paid 36% by Wilbur, 30% by Dee, and 34% by Randall.

The partnership leased out the ranch property for the first two years. Wilbur and Dee Warnick then moved onto the ranch in 1981, living there and working the ranch up to the present time. Randall lived and worked on the ranch during the 1981 and 1982 summer haying seasons and again from 1991 to 1998.

The partners over the years each contributed additional funds to the operation of the ranch and received cash distributions from the partnership. After 1983, Randall contributed very little new money and almost all of the additional funds to pay off the mortgage came from Wilbur and Dee Warnick. Wilbur also left in the partnership account two $12,000 cash distributions that were otherwise payable to him. The net cash contributions of the partners through 1999, considering the initial contributions, payments to or on behalf of the partnership, draws not taken and distributions from the partnership were:

Wilbur $170,112.60 (51%)
Dee 138,834.63 (41%)
Randall 25,406.28 (8%)

In 1998, Randall Warnick began having discussions with his brother about the possibility of selling his interest in

Warnick Ranches. When Randall mentioned this to his father, a dispute arose between them concerning the percentage of the partnership that Randall owned. Finally, on April 14, 1999, Randall's attorney sent a letter to Warnick Ranches which stated:

> I have been asked to contact you regarding [Randall's] desire to either sell his interest in the ranch to a third party, to the partnership, or to liquidate the partnership under Paragraph 12 of the partnership agreement.
>
> * * * It would appear that it would be in the best interests of all to amicably agree to a selling price of his interest either to a third party or to the partnership as provided in the partnership agreement.

On August 11, 1999, Warnick Ranches responded in writing, treating the letter from Randall's attorney as the expressed will of a partner to dissociate. The partnership's response included a tender offer for Randall's share, as provided under [RUPA] §701(e) and (g) in the case of a dissociating partner. Randall in turn exercised his right under [RUPA] §701(j) to reject the tender and bring an action against the partnership to determine his interest in the partnership, including a buyout price if he is determined to be dissociated from the partnership.

* * * The parties stipulated to facts regarding the cash flows into and out of the partnership accounts, as well as the partnership tax returns for each year from 1979 through 1999. * * *

The district court, in granting Randall Warnick's motion for summary judgment, found that dissociation of Randall as a partner was the appropriate remedy and that the schedule of ownership recited in the partnership agreement, absent evidence of any other written agreement, controls the partners' percentage upon dissolution or dissociation. The court awarded judgment to Randall Warnick for the amount of his cash contributions, plus 34% of the partnership assets' increase in value above all partners' cash contributions. As a result of that calculation, $230,819.14, or 25.24%, of the undisputed value of the partnership was awarded to Randall, without provision of interest for any partner in the calculation.

* * *

Resolution of this matter relies almost entirely on application of the Wyoming Revised Uniform Partnership Act ("RUPA"), [citation]. * * * RUPA states in pertinent part:

> [A] partnership agreement governs relations among the partners and between the partners and the partnership. To the extent the partnership agreement does not otherwise provide, this chapter governs relations among the partners and between the partners and the partnership.

[RUPA] §103(a). "The Revised Act is, therefore, largely a series of 'default rules' that govern the relations among partners in situations they have not addressed in a partnership agreement." [Citations.]

During the existence of the partnership, each partner has authority to act on behalf of the partnership, [RUPA] §§301, 401(f), and "all partners are liable jointly and severally for all obligations of the partnership unless otherwise agreed by the claimant or provided by law." [RUPA] §306(a). "A partner may lend money to and transact other business with the partnership," [RUPA] §404(f), and "[a] partnership shall repay a partner who, in aid of the partnership, makes a payment or advance beyond the amount of capital the partner agreed to contribute." [RUPA] §401(d). Such a payment or advance by a partner constitutes a loan to the partnership which accrues interest from the date of the payment or advance. [RUPA] §401(e).

The provisions of the Warnick Ranches Partnership Agreement addressing the above subjects are paragraphs six and nine, which state:

> 6. CAPITAL CONTRIBUTION. The parties hereto hereby agree to contribute the personal property listed on Exhibit "A" attached hereto to the Partnership to be used in the Partnership business. By unanimous agreement of all Partners, additional contributions may be made to, or withdrawals may be made from, the capital of the Partnership.
>
> * * *
>
> 9. ACCOUNTING. On December 31 of each year, the accounts of the Partnership business will be closed for the year. As of that date, the Partnership income and expenses will be totaled and the difference shall be divided among the Partners on any basis which is mutually agreed upon by all Partners, giving due consideration to services rendered during the year by each Partner, drawings during the year by each Partner and the amount of capital invested by each Partner during such year.

The partnership agreement is entirely silent as to how cash advances or payments on behalf of the business are to be treated. The partners knew that additional cash would be needed to make the mortgage payments on the ranch, and perhaps assumed that paragraph six of their agreement would cover the additional funds when they would unanimously agree to adjust the capital accounts when a partner paid more money into the operation.

It is, however, undisputed that the partners never entered into a unanimous agreement to amend their partnership agreement or to reflect additional capital contributions. It is also undisputed that the advances by the partners were not anywhere documented as a loan to the partnership rather than capital contributions. The district court found these facts dispositive in granting Randall Warnick's summary judgment motion. The court specifically found that there was no documentation to support a conclusion that the payments by the elder Warnicks were a loan, so they could not be treated as a loan.

The district court's decision, however, misapplies the clear provisions of the Revised Uniform Partnership Act. RUPA operates automatically if a partnership agreement does not have contrary provisions. * * * In this sense, RUPA operates like the Uniform Probate Code, which fills in the blanks of an estate plan for those who die intestate or with a will that does not address a contingency that has occurred.

The district court's calculations in this case treat the mortgage payments as neither capital contributions nor advances, but as something else not contemplated by RUPA. The partnership agreement at paragraph ten and RUPA at [RUPA] §401(k) are consistent in requiring that the partners must unanimously consent to any amendments of the partnership agreement. Advances are not addressed in the agreement, so we must turn to RUPA's default provisions in that regard. [Citation.] Nothing in RUPA requires advances to the partnership or payment of partnership debts by partners to be memorialized in writing as a loan. In fact, the act addresses payments and advances in several places without requiring a writing or unanimous partner approval:

- [RUPA] §401(c) requires the partnership to reimburse a partner for payments made by the partner in the ordinary and proper conduct of the business of the partnership or for the preservation of its business or property;
- [RUPA] §401(d) requires the partnership to reimburse a partner for a payment or advance to the partnership beyond the amount of capital the partner agreed to contribute;
- [RUPA] §401(e) provides that a partner's cash payment on behalf of the partnership automatically constitutes a loan which accrues interest from the date of the payment;

Read [together], these provisions of the act evidence a presumption that additional amounts paid by a partner, over and above the capital contributions recited in the partnership agreement or agreed to, are presumed to be loans to the partnership, with interest payable from the date of the advance. RUPA is unequivocal on this point. The drafters' comment to §401(d) states: "Subsection (d) is based on UPA Section 18(c). It makes explicit that the partnership must reimburse a partner for an advance of funds beyond the amount of the partner's agreed capital contribution, thereby treating the advance as a loan." [Citation.]

Warnick Ranches partnership was formed "for the purpose of managing and operating a farming and ranching business" on property that was subject to a mortgage at the time the partnership was formed. It was entirely foreseeable that additional cash would be needed to meet the mortgage payments, as in fact happened. * * * The silence of the partnership agreement on [the duty to make capital contributions beyond the partnership agreement], combined with the statutory presumption in favor of advances over capital contributions, leads necessarily to the conclusion that a partner's payment of the Warnick Ranch mortgage, without the unanimous consent required for additional capital contributions, would be an advance and a loan to the partnership.

* * *

We turn then to the consequences of this dispute. RUPA, with the goal of avoiding unnecessary dissolutions of partnerships, contains a significant change from prior partnership law. Again in the words of the drafters:

> RUPA dramatically changes the law governing partnership breakups and dissolution. An entirely new concept, "dissociation," is used in lieu of the UPA term "dissolution" to denote the change in the relationship caused by a partner's ceasing to be associated in the carrying on of the business. * * *
>
> Under RUPA, unlike the UPA, the dissociation of a partner does not necessarily cause a dissolution and winding up of the business of the partnership. Section 801 identifies the situations in which the dissociation of a partner causes a winding up of the business. Section 701 provides that in all other situations there is a buyout of the partner's interest in the partnership, rather than a windup of the partnership business. In those other situations, the partnership entity continues, unaffected by the partner's dissociation.

[Revised] Uniform Partnership Act §601, cmt. 1, [citation].

The Warnick Ranch Partnership Agreement is again silent as to dissociation, addressing only liquidation. RUPA states that a partner has the power to dissociate at any time by express will, [RUPA] §602(a), and that:

> (a) A partner is dissociated from a partnership upon:
>
> (i) Receipt by the partnership of notice of the partner's express will to withdraw as a partner or upon any later date specified in the notice; * * *

* * *

Under these circumstances, the record supports the district court's conclusion that there was no genuine issue as to the material fact that a dissociation occurred. Considering the April 1999 letter from Randall's attorney to the partnership, in the context of deposition testimony regarding allegations of physical violence and misappropriation of partnership funds, we determine that the date of the letter is the date of dissociation.

However, the court erred in its calculation of the judgment. RUPA states that a dissociated partner's interest in the partnership shall be purchased by the partnership for a buyout price. [RUPA] §§603(a), 701(a), (b). The buyout price is equal to the amount that would have been distributable to the dissociating partner under [RUPA] §808(b) if, on the date of the dissociation, the partnership's assets had been sold. [RUPA] §701(b). However, §808(a) provides that partnership assets must first be applied to discharge partnership liabilities to creditors, including partners who are creditors. As noted above, as each partner advanced funds to pay the mortgage or other partnership expenses, that partner became a creditor of the partnership for the amount advanced, and is entitled to interest on each amount from the date of the advance. In calculating Randall's buyout price, it is therefore necessary to first calculate the amount that the partnership owes to each partner for advances to the partnership, with interest accrued from the date of each advance at the rate specified in [RUPA] §104(b).

Next, there is the matter of two $12,000 draws, or "guaranteed payments," that Wilbur Warnick was entitled to in 1998 and 1999, but actually left in the partnership account and did not receive. The guaranteed payment arrangement was at Randall's request and agreed among the partners in order to provide Randall an income and to avoid the partnership showing a taxable profit. Randall received his draw as agreed in 1998 and 1999 but Wilbur did not, even though he reported it as personal income and paid taxes on it. At the time he became entitled to the "guaranteed payment," the $12,000 was Wilbur's personal money and his leaving it with the partnership was the functional equivalent of another advance to the partnership. [RUPA] §401(d); [citation]. Upon remand, therefore, in calculating the buyout price for Randall Warnick's share, it is necessary to first calculate the amount the partnership owes Wilbur Warnick for the two $12,000 draws he left with the partnership, with interest from the date he was entitled to the payments.

* * *

A partnership agreement governs relations among general partners and between partners and their partnership. To the extent the agreement is silent or ambiguous, the Revised Uniform Partnership Act provisions apply. Review of the entire record leads us to conclude that there is no genuine issue regarding the fact that a partner dissociation occurred, and that the Plaintiff is entitled to a judgment as a matter of law for the buyout price of his interest. However, the district court's calculation of the dissociated partner's buyout price is reversed and the case remanded for a calculation of that price after repayment of partner advances as loans, in accord with the statute and this decision.

## QUESTIONS

1. Discuss the contract liability of a partnership and the partners.
2. Discuss the tort liability of a partnership and the partners.
3. Distinguish between the liability of an incoming partner for debts arising before his admission and those arising after his admission.
4. Identify the causes of dissolution of a partnership and the conditions under which partners have the right to continue the partnership after dissociation.
5. Explain the effect of dissolution upon the authority and liability of the partners and the order in which the assets of a partnership are distributed to creditors and partners.

## PROBLEMS

**1.** Albert, Betty, and Carol own and operate the Roy Lumber Company. Each contributed one-third of the capital, and they share equally in the profits and losses. Their partnership agreement provides that two partners must authorize all purchases over $2,500 in advance and that only Albert is authorized to draw checks. Unknown to Albert or Carol, Betty purchases on the firm's account a $5,500 diamond bracelet and a $5,000 forklift and orders $5,000 worth of logs, all from Doug, who operates a jewelry store and is engaged in various activities connected with the lumber business. Before Betty made these purchases, Albert told Doug that Betty is not the log buyer. Albert refuses to pay Doug for Betty's purchases. Doug calls at the mill to collect, and Albert again refuses to pay him. Doug calls Albert an unprintable name, and Albert then punches Doug in the nose, knocking him out. While Doug is lying unconscious on the ground, an employee of Roy Lumber Company negligently drops a log on Doug's leg, breaking three bones. The firm and the three partners are completely solvent.

What are the rights of Doug against Roy Lumber Company, Albert, Betty, and Carol?

**2.** Paula, Fred, and Stephanie agree that Paula and Fred will form and conduct a partnership business and that Stephanie will become a partner in two years. Stephanie agrees to lend the firm $50,000 and take 10 percent of the profits in lieu of interest. Without Stephanie's knowledge, Paula and Fred tell Harold that Stephanie is a partner, and Harold, relying on Stephanie's sound financial status, gives the firm credit. The firm later becomes insolvent, and Harold seeks to hold Stephanie liable as a partner. Should Harold succeed?

**3.** Simmons, Hoffman, and Murray were partners doing business under the firm name of Simmons & Co. The firm borrowed money from a bank and gave the bank the firm's note for the loan. In addition, each partner guaranteed the note individually. The firm became insolvent, and a receiver was appointed. The bank claims that it has a right to file its claim as a firm debt and also that it has a right to participate in the distribution of the assets of the individual partners before partnership creditors receive any payment from such assets.

**(a)** Explain the principle involved in this case.

**(b)** Is the bank correct?

**4.** Anthony and Karen were partners doing business as the Petite Garment Company. Leroy owned a dye plant that did much of the processing for the company. Anthony and Karen decided to offer Leroy an interest in their company, in consideration for which Leroy would contribute his dye plant to the partnership. Leroy accepted the offer and was duly admitted as a partner. At the time he was admitted as a partner, Leroy did not know that the partnership was on the verge of insolvency. About three months after Leroy was admitted to the partnership, a textile firm obtained a judgment against the partnership in the amount of $50,000. This debt represented an unpaid balance that had existed before Leroy was admitted as a partner.

The textile firm brought an action to subject the partnership property, including the dye plant, to the satisfaction of its judgment. The complaint also requested that, in the event the judgment was unsatisfied by sale of the partnership property, Leroy's home be sold and the proceeds applied to the balance of the judgment. Anthony and Karen own nothing but their interest in the partnership property.

What should be the result (a) with regard to the dye plant and (b) with regard to Leroy's home?

**5.** Jones and Ray formed a partnership on January 1, known as JR Construction Co., to engage in the construction business, each partner owning a one-half interest. On February 10, while conducting partnership business, Jones negligently injured Ware, who brought an action against Jones, Ray, and JR Construction Co. and obtained judgment for $250,000 against them on March 1. On April 15, Muir joined the partnership by contributing $100,000 cash, and by agreement each partner was entitled to a one-third interest. In July, the partners agreed to purchase new construction equipment for the partnership, and Muir was authorized to obtain a loan from XYZ Bank in the partnership name for $200,000 to finance the purchase. On July 10, Muir signed a $200,000 note on behalf of the partnership, and the equipment was purchased. In November, the partnership was in financial difficulty, its total assets amounting to $50,000. The note was in default, with a balance of $150,000 owing to XYZ Bank. Muir has substantial resources, while Jones and Ray each individually have assets of $20,000.

What is the extent of Muir's personal liability and the personal liability of Jones and Ray as to (a) the judgment obtained by Ware and (b) the debt owing to XYZ Bank?

**6.** Lauren, Matthew, and Susan form a partnership, with Lauren contributing $100,000; Matthew $50,000; and Susan her time and skill. Nothing is said regarding the division of profits. The firm later dissolves. No distributions to partners have been made since the partnership was formed. The partnership sells its assets for a loss of $90,000. After payment of all firm debts, $60,000 is left. Lauren claims that she is entitled to the entire $60,000. Matthew contends that the distribution should be $40,000 to Lauren and $20,000 to Matthew. Susan claims the $60,000 should be divided equally among the partners. Who is correct? Explain.

**7.** Adams, a consulting engineer, entered into a partnership with three others for the practice of their profession. The only written partnership agreement is a brief document specifying that Adams is entitled to 55 percent of the profits and the others to 15 percent each. The venture is a total failure. Creditors are pressing for payment, and some have filed suit. The partners cannot agree on a course of action.

How many of the partners must agree to achieve each of the following objectives?

**(a)** To add Jones, also an engineer, as a partner, Jones being willing to contribute a substantial amount of new capital.

**(b)** To sell a vacant lot held in the partnership name, which had been acquired as a future office site for the partnership.

**(c)** To move the partnership's offices to less expensive quarters.

**(d)** To demand a formal accounting.

**(e)** To dissolve the partnership.

**(f)** To agree to submit certain disputed claims to arbitration, which Adams believes will prove less expensive than litigation.

**(g)** To sell all of the partnership's personal property, with Adams having what he believes to be a good offer for the property from a newly formed engineering firm.

**(h)** To alter the respective interests of the parties in the profits and losses by decreasing Adams's share to 40 percent and increasing the others' shares accordingly.

**(i)** To assign all the partnership's assets to a bank in trust for the benefit of creditors, hoping to work out satisfactory arrangements without filing for bankruptcy.

**8.** Charles and Jack orally agreed to become partners in a tool and die business. Charles, who had experience in tool and die work, was to operate the business. Jack was to take no active part but was to contribute the entire $500,000 capitalization. Charles worked ten hours a day at the plant, for which he was paid nothing. Nevertheless, despite Charles's best efforts, the business failed. The $500,000 capital was depleted, and the partnership owed $500,000 in debts. Prior to the failure of the partnership business, Jack became personally insolvent; consequently, the creditors of the partnership collected the entire $500,000 indebtedness from Charles, who was forced to sell his home and farm to satisfy the indebtedness. Jack later regained his financial responsibility, and Charles brought an appropriate action against Jack for (a) one-half of the $500,000 he had paid to partnership creditors and (b) one-half of $80,000, the reasonable value of Charles's services during the operation of the partnership. Who will prevail and why?

**9.** Glenn refuses an invitation to become a partner of Dorothy and Cynthia in a retail grocery business. Nevertheless, Dorothy inserts an advertisement in the local newspaper representing Glenn as their partner. Glenn takes no steps to deny the existence of a partnership between them. Ron, who extended credit to the firm, seeks to hold Glenn liable as a partner. Is Glenn liable? Explain.

**10.** Hanover leased a portion of his farm to Brown and Black, doing business as the Colorite Hatchery. Brown went upon the premises to remove certain chicken sheds that he and Black had placed there for hatchery purposes. Thinking that Brown intended to remove certain other sheds, which were Hanover's property, Hanover accosted Brown, who willfully struck Hanover and knocked him down. Brown then ran to the Colorite truck, which he had previously loaded with chicken coops, and drove back to the hatchery. On the way, he picked up George, who was hitchhiking to the city to look for a job. Brown was driving at seventy miles an hour down the highway. At an open intersection with another highway, Brown in his hurry ran a stop sign, striking another vehicle. The collision caused severe injuries to George. Immediately thereafter, the partnership was dissolved, and Brown was insolvent. Hanover and George each bring separate actions against Black as copartner for the alleged tort committed by Brown against each. What judgments as to each?

**11.** Phillips and Harris are partners in a used car business. Under their oral partnership, each has an equal voice in the conduct and management of the business. Because of their irregular business hours, the two further agreed that they could use any partnership vehicle as desired. This use includes transportation to and from work, even though the vehicles are for sale at all times. Harris conducted partnership business both at the used car lot and from his home. He was on call by Phillips or customers at his home, and he went back to the lot two or three times after going home. While driving a partnership vehicle home from the used car lot, Harris negligently hit a car driven by Cook, who brought this action against Harris and Phillips individually and as copartners for his injuries. Who is liable?

**12.** Stroud and Freeman are general partners in Stroud's Food Center, a grocery store. Nothing in the articles of partnership restricts the power or authority of either partner to act in respect to the ordinary and legitimate business of the Food Center. In November, however, Stroud informed National Biscuit that he would not be personally responsible for any more bread sold to the partnership. Then, in the following February, at the request of Freeman, National Biscuit sold and delivered more bread to the Food Center. Explain whether National Biscuit will be able to recover the value of the bread delivered to the Food Center from Stroud and the partnership.

**13.** Voeller, the managing partner of the Pay-Out Drive-In Theater, signed a contract to sell to Hodge a small parcel of land belonging to the partnership. Except for the last twenty feet, which were necessary for the theater's driveway, the parcel was not used in theater operations. The agreement stated that it was between Hodge and the partnership, with Voeller signing for the partnership. Voeller claims that he told Hodge before signing that a plot plan would have to be approved by the other partners before the sale. Hodge denies this and sues for specific performance, claiming that Voeller had actual and apparent authority to bind the partnership. The partners argue that Voeller had no such authority and that Hodge knew this. Who is correct? Explain.

**14.** L. G. and S. L. Patel, husband and wife, owned and operated the City Center Motel in Eureka. On April 16, Rajeshkumar, the son of L. G. and S. L., formed a partnership with his parents and became owner of 35 percent of the City Center Motel. The partnership agreement required that Rajeshkumar approve any sale of the motel. Record title to the motel was not changed, however, to reflect his interest. On April 21, L. G. and S. L. listed their motel for sale with a real estate broker. On May 2, P. V. and Kirit Patel made an offer on the motel, which L. G. and S. L. accepted. Neither the broker nor the purchasers knew of the son's interest in the motel. When L. G. and S. L. notified Rajeshkumar of their plans, to their surprise, he refused to sell his 35 percent of the motel. On May 4, L. G. and S. L. notified P. V. and Kirit that they wished to withdraw their acceptance. They offered to pay $10,000 in damages and to give the purchasers a right of first refusal for five years. Rather than accept the offer, on May 29, P. V. and Kirit filed an action for specific performance and incidental damages. L. G., S. L., and Rajeshkumar responded that the contract could not lawfully be enforced. Discuss who will prevail and why.

**15.** Martin, Mark, and Marvin formed a retail clothing partnership named M Clothiers and conducted a business for many years, buying most of their clothing from Hill, a wholesaler. On January 15, Marvin retired from the business, but Martin and Mark decided to continue it. As part of the retirement agreement, Martin and Mark agreed in writing with Marvin that Marvin would not be responsible for any of the partnership debts, either past or future. On January 15 the partnership published a notice of Marvin's retirement in a newspaper of general circulation where the partnership carried on its business.

Before January 15, Hill was a creditor of M Clothiers to the extent of $10,000, and on January 30, he extended additional credit of $5,000. Hill was not advised and did not in fact know of Marvin's retirement and the change of the partnership. On January 30, Ray, a competitor of Hill, extended credit for the first time to M Clothiers in the amount of $3,000. Ray also was not advised and did not in fact know of Marvin's retirement and the change of the partnership.

On February 1, Martin and Mark departed for parts unknown, leaving no partnership assets with which to pay the described debts. What is Marvin's liability, if any, (a) to Hill and (b) to Ray?

**16.** Ben, Dan, and Lilli were partners sharing profits in proportions of one-fourth, one-third, and five-twelfths, respectively. Their business failed, and the firm was dissolved. At the time of dissolution, no financial adjustments between the partners were necessary with reference to their respective partners' accounts, but the firm's liabilities to creditors exceeded its assets by $24,000. Without contributing any amount toward the payment of the liabilities, Dan moved to a destination unknown. Ben and Lilli are financially responsible. How much must each contribute?

**17.** Ames, Bell, and Cole were equal partners in the ABC Construction Company. Their written partnership agreement provided that the partnership would dissolve upon the death of any partner. Cole died on June 30, and his widow, Cora Cole, qualified as executor of his will. Ames and Bell wound up the business of the partnership and on December 31 they completed the sale of all of the partnership's assets. After paying all partnership debts, they distributed the balance equally among themselves and Mrs. Cole as executor.

Subsequently, Mrs. Cole learned that Ames and Bell had made and withdrawn a net profit of $200,000 from July 1 to December 31. The profit was made through new contracts using the partnership name and assets. Ames and Bell had concealed such contracts and profit from Mrs. Cole, and she learned about them from other sources. Immediately after acquiring this information, Mrs. Cole made demand upon Ames and Bell for one-third of the profit of

$200,000. They rejected her demand. What are the rights and remedies, if any, of Cora Cole as executor?

**18.** The articles of partnership of the firm of Wilson and Company provide the following:

> William Smith to contribute $50,000; to receive interest thereon at 13 percent per annum and to devote such time as he may be able to give; to receive 30 percent of the profits.
>
> John Jones to contribute $50,000; to receive interest on same at 13 percent per annum; to give all of his time to the business and to receive 30 percent of the profits.
>
> Henry Wilson to contribute all of his time to the business and to receive 20 percent of the profits.
>
> James Brown to contribute all of his time to the business and to receive 20 percent of the profits.

There is no provision for sharing losses. After six years of operation, the firm is dissolved and wound up. No distributions to partners have been made since the partnership was formed. The partnership assets are sold for $400,000 with a loss of $198,000. Liabilities to creditors total $420,000. What are the rights and liabilities of the respective parties?

**19.** Adam, Stanley, and Rosalind formed a partnership in State X to distribute beer and wine. Their agreement provided that the partnership would continue until December 31, 2014. Which of the following events would cause the ABC partnership to dissolve? If so, when would the partnership be dissolved?

**(a)** Rosalind assigns her interest in the partnership to Mary on April 1, 2012.

**(b)** Stanley dies on June 1, 2014.

**(c)** Adam withdraws from the partnership on September 15, 2013.

**(d)** A creditor of Stanley obtains a charging order against Stanley's interest on October 9, 2011.

**(e)** In 2012, the legislature of State X enacts a statute making the sale or distribution of alcoholic beverages illegal.

**(f)** Stanley has a formal accounting of partnership affairs on September 19, 2013.

**20.** Davis and Shipman founded a partnership under the name of Shipman & Davis Lumber Company. Four years later, the partnership was dissolved by written agreement. Notice of the dissolution was published in a newspaper of general circulation in Merced County, where the business was conducted. No actual notice of dissolution was given to firms that previously had extended credit to the partnership. By the dissolution agreement, Shipman, who was to continue the business, was to pay all of the partnership's debts. He continued the business as a sole proprietorship for a short time until he formed a successor corporation, Shipman Lumber Servaes Co. After the partnership's dissolution, two firms that previously had done business with the partnership extended credit to Shipman for certain repair work and merchandise. The partnership also had a balance due to Valley Company for a prior purchase. Five months later, two checks were drawn by Shipman Lumber Servaes Co. and accepted by Valley as partial payment on this debt. Credit Bureaus of Merced County, as assignee of these three accounts, sued the partnership as well as Shipman and Davis individually. Does the dissolution of the partnership relieve Davis of personal liability for the accounts? Explain.

**21.** In August Victoria Air Conditioning, Inc. (VAC), entered into a subcontract for insulation services with Southwest Texas Mechanical Insulation Company (SWT), a partnership comprising Charlie Jupe and Tommy Nabors. In February of the following year, Jupe and Nabors dissolved the partnership, but VAC did not receive notice of the dissolution at that time. Sometime later, insulation was removed from Nabors's premises to Jupe's possession and Jupe continued the insulation project with VAC. From then on, Nabors had no more involvement with SWT. One month later, Nabors informed VAC's project manager, Von Behrenfeld, that Nabors was no longer associated with SWT, had formed his own insulation company, and was interested in bidding on new jobs. Subsequently, SWT failed to perform the subcontract and Jupe could not be found. VAC brought suit for breach of contract against SWT, Jupe, and Nabors. Nabors claims that several letters and change orders introduced by both parties show that VAC knew of the dissolution and impliedly agreed to discharge Nabors from liability. These documents indicated that VAC had dealt with Jupe, but had not dealt with Nabors, after the dissolution. VAC denies that the course of dealings between VAC and Jupe was the type from which an agreement to discharge Nabors could be inferred. Who is correct? Explain.

C H A P T E R 3 3

# Limited Partnerships and Limited Liability Companies

This chapter will consider other types of unincorporated business associations: limited partnerships, limited liability companies, limited liability partnerships, and limited liability limited partnerships. These organizations have developed to meet special business and investment needs. Consequently, each has characteristics that make it appropriate for certain purposes.

## LIMITED PARTNERSHIPS

The limited partnership has proved to be an attractive vehicle for a variety of investments because of its tax advantages and the limited liability it confers upon limited partners. Unlike general partnerships, limited partnerships are statutory creations. Before 1976, the governing statute in all States except Louisiana was the Uniform Limited Partnership Act (ULPA), which was promulgated in 1916. At that time, most limited partnerships were small and had only a few limited partners. But over time, limited partnerships became much larger, typically involving a small number of major investors and a relatively large group of widely distributed investors who purchase limited partnership interests. This type of organization has evolved to attract substantial amounts of investment capital. As a result, limited partnerships have been used to muster the sizable investments necessary in areas such as real estate, oil and gas, motion pictures, professional sports, and research and development. The large scale and multistate operations of the modern limited partnership, however, have severely burdened the framework established by the ULPA.

These shortcomings prompted the National Conference of Commissioners on Uniform State Laws to develop a Revised Uniform Limited Partnership Act (RULPA), which was promulgated in 1976. According to its preface, the RULPA is "intended to modernize the prior uniform law while retaining the special character of limited partnerships as compared with corporations." In 1985, the National Conference revised the RULPA "for the purpose of more effectively modernizing, improving and establishing uniformity in the law of limited partnerships." The 1985 Act is substantially similar to the 1976 RULPA, preserving the philosophy of the older Act and making almost no change in its basic structure. All of the States except Louisiana had adopted either the 1976 Act or the 1985 Act with a large majority of these States adopting the 1985 version.

In 2001 the National Conference of Commissioners on Uniform State Laws promulgated a new revision of the 1985 Revised Uniform Limited Partnership Act (the 2001 ReRULPA). The new Act has been drafted to reflect that limited liability partnerships and limited liability companies can meet many of the needs formerly met by limited partnerships. Accordingly, the 2001 ReRULPA adopts as default rules provisions that strongly favor current management and treat limited partners as passive investors with little control over or right to exit the limited partnership. To date, at least fifteen States have adopted the 2001 ReRULPA.

This chapter will discuss the 1985 RULPA. The ULPA, the 1976 RULPA, and the 1985 RULPA are supplemented by the Uniform Partnership Act, which applies to limited partnerships in any case for which the Limited Partnership Act does not provide. The 2001 ReRULPA is a stand-alone statute and is not linked to the Uniform Partnership Act.

◆ **SEE FIGURE 31-1: General Partnership, Limited Partnership, Limited Liability Company, and Corporation**

In addition, limited partnership interests are almost always considered to be securities, and their sale is therefore subject to State and Federal securities regulation, as discussed in *Chapter 44*.

### DEFINITION

A **limited partnership** is a partnership formed by two or more persons under the laws of a State and having one or more general partners and one or more limited partners. Section 101(7). A *person* includes a natural person, partnership, limited partnership, trust, estate, association, or corporation. Section 101(11). A limited partnership differs from a general partnership in several respects, three of which are fundamental:

1. a statute providing for the formation of limited partnerships must be in effect;
2. the limited partnership must substantially comply with the requirements of that statute; and
3. the liability of a limited partner for partnership debts or obligations is limited to the extent of the capital he has contributed or has agreed to contribute.

## FORMATION

Although the formation of a general partnership calls for no special procedures, the formation of a limited partnership requires substantial compliance with the limited partnership statute. Failure to so comply may result in the limited partners' not obtaining limited liability.

**Filing of Certificate** Section 201 of the RULPA provides that two or more persons desiring to form a limited partnership shall file in the office of the Secretary of State of the State in which the limited partnership is to have its principal office a signed certificate of limited partnership. The certificate must include the following information:

1. the name of the limited partnership;
2. the address of the office and the name and address of the agent for service of process;
3. the name and the business address of each general partner;
4. the latest date upon which the limited partnership is to dissolve; and
5. any other matters the general partners decide to include in the certificate.

The certificate of limited partnership must be amended if a new general partner is admitted, a general partner withdraws, or a general partner becomes aware that any statement in the certificate was or has become false. Section 202. In addition, the certificate may be amended at any time for any other purpose the general partners deem proper. As discussed later, false statements in a certificate or amendment that cause loss to third parties who rely on the statements may result in liability for the general partners.

**Name** The inclusion of the surname of a limited partner in the partnership name is prohibited unless it is also the name of a general partner or unless the business had operated under that name before the admission of the limited partner. A limited partner who knowingly permits his name to be used in violation of this provision is liable to any creditor who did not know that he was a limited partner. Section 303(d). In addition, a limited partnership cannot use a name that is the same as, or deceptively similar to, the name of any corporation or other limited partnership. Section 102. Finally, the name of the limited partnership must contain the unabbreviated words "limited partnership."

**Contributions** The contribution of a partner may be cash, property, services rendered, or a promissory note or other obligation to contribute cash or property or to perform services. Section 501. A promise by a limited partner to contribute to the limited partnership is not enforceable unless it is in a signed writing. Should a partner fail to make a required capital contribution described in a signed writing, the limited partnership may hold her liable to contribute the cash value of the stated contribution.

**Defective Formation** A limited partnership is formed when a certificate of limited partnership that substantially complies with the requirements of the statute is filed. Therefore, the formation is defective if no certificate is filed or if the certificate filed does not substantially meet the statutory requirements. In either case, the limited liability of limited partners is jeopardized. The RULPA provides that a person who has contributed to the capital of a business (an "equity participant"), erroneously and in good faith believing that he has become a limited partner in a limited partnership, is not liable as a general partner, provided that on ascertaining the mistake he either (1) withdraws from the business and renounces future profits or (2) files a certificate or an amendment curing the defect. Section 304. The equity participant will be liable, however, to any third party who transacted business with the enterprise before the withdrawal or amendment and who in good faith believed that the equity participant was a general partner at the time of the transaction.

The 1985 RULPA does not require that the limited partners be named in the certificate. This greatly reduces the risk that an inadvertent omission of such information will expose a limited partner to liability.

**Foreign Limited Partnerships** A limited partnership is considered "foreign" in any State other than the one in which it was formed. The laws of the State in which a foreign limited partnership is organized govern its organization, its internal affairs, and the liability of its limited partners. Section 901. In addition, the RULPA requires all foreign limited partnerships to register with the Secretary of State before transacting any business in a State. Section 902. Any foreign limited partnership transacting business without so registering may not bring enforcement actions in the State's courts until it registers, although it may defend itself in the State's courts. Section 907.

## RIGHTS

Because limited partnerships are organized pursuant to statute, the rights of the parties are usually set forth in the certificate of limited partnership and the limited partnership agreement. Unless otherwise agreed or provided in the Act, a general partner of a limited partnership has all the rights and powers of a partner in a partnership without limited partners. Section 403. A general partner also may be a limited partner; as such, he shares in profits, losses, and distributions both as a general partner and as a limited one. Section 404.

**Control** The general partners of a limited partnership have almost exclusive control and management of the limited partnership. A limited partner, on the other hand, is not permitted to share in this management or control; if he does, he may forfeit his limited liability. A limited partner who participates in the control of the business is liable only to those persons who transact business with the limited partnership reasonably believing, based upon the limited partner's conduct, that the limited partner is a general partner. Section 303(a).

In addition, Section 303(b) of the RULPA provides a "safe harbor" by enumerating activities that a limited partner may perform without being deemed to have taken part in control of the business. They are the following:

1. being a contractor for, or an agent or employee of, the limited partnership or of a general partner or being an officer, director, or shareholder of a general partner that is a corporation;
2. consulting with and advising a general partner with respect to the business of the limited partnership;
3. acting as surety for the limited partnership;
4. bringing a derivative action in the right of the limited partnership;
5. requesting or attending a meeting of partners;
6. voting on one or more of the following matters:
   (a) the dissolution and winding up of the limited partnership;
   (b) the sale, exchange, lease, mortgage, pledge, or other transfer of all or substantially all of the assets of the limited partnership;
   (c) the incurrence of indebtedness by the limited partnership other than in the ordinary course of its business;
   (d) a change in the nature of the business;
   (e) the admission or removal of a general partner;
   (f) the admission or removal of a limited partner;
   (g) a transaction involving an actual or potential conflict of interest between a general partner and the limited partnership or the limited partners;
   (h) an amendment to the partnership agreement or certificate of limited partnership; or
   (i) other matters related to the business of the limited partnership which the partnership agreement states in writing may be subject to the approval or disapproval of limited partners;
7. winding up the limited partnership; or
8. exercising any other right or power permitted to limited partners under the Act.

◆ **SEE CASE 33-1**

**Voting Rights** The partnership agreement may grant to all or a specified group of general or limited partners the right to vote on any matter. Sections 302 and 405. If, however, the agreement grants limited partners voting powers beyond the safe harbor of Section 303, a court may hold that the limited partners have participated in control of the business. The RULPA does not require that limited partners have the right to vote on matters as a class separate from the general partners, although the partnership agreement may provide such a right.

**Choice of Associates** After the formation of a limited partnership, the admission of additional limited partners requires the written consent of all partners, unless the partnership agreement provides otherwise. Section 301. The admission of the new limited partner is not effective until the records of the limited partnership have been amended to reflect that fact. Regarding the admission of additional general partners, the written partnership agreement determines the procedure for authorizing their admission. The written consent of all partners is required only if the partnership agreement fails to deal with this issue. Section 401.

**Withdrawal** A general partner may withdraw from a limited partnership at any time by giving written notice to the other partners. Section 602. If the withdrawal violates the partnership agreement, the limited partnership may recover damages from the withdrawing general partner. A limited partner may withdraw as provided in the written partnership agreement. If the agreement does not specify when a limited partner may withdraw or a definite time for the limited partnership's dissolution, a limited partner may withdraw upon giving at least six months' prior written notice to each general partner. Section 603. Upon withdrawal, a withdrawing partner is entitled to receive any distribution to which she is entitled under the partnership agreement, subject to the restrictions on amount discussed below. If the partnership agreement makes no provision, the partner is entitled to receive the fair value of her interest in the limited partnership as of the date of withdrawal, based upon her right to share in distributions from the limited partnership. Section 604.

**Assignment of Partnership Interest** A partnership interest is a partner's share of the profits and losses of a limited partnership and the right to receive distributions of partnership assets. Section 101(10). A partnership interest is personal property. Section 701. Unless otherwise provided in the partnership agreement, a partner may assign his partnership interest. An assignment does not dissolve the limited partnership. The assignee, who does not become a partner, may exercise none of the rights of a partner: the assignment entitles the assignee only to receive, to the extent of the assignment, the assigning partner's share of distributions. Except as otherwise provided in the partnership agreement, a partner ceases to be a partner upon assignment of all his partnership interest. Section 702.

An assignee of a partnership interest, including an assignee of a general partner, may, however, become a *limited* partner if all the other partners consent or if the assigning partner, having such power provided in the partnership agreement, grants the assignee this right. Section 704. An assignee who becomes a limited partner is liable for the obligation of his assignor to make or return contributions, except for those liabilities unknown to the assignee at the time he became a limited partner. Section 704(b). Upon the death of a partner, her executor or administrator has all the rights of the partner for the purpose of settling her estate, including any power the deceased partner had to make her assignee a substituted limited partner. Section 705.

A creditor of a partner may obtain a charging order against a partner's interest in the partnership. To the extent of the charging order, the creditor has the rights of an assignee of the partnership interest. Section 703.

**Profit and Loss Sharing** Profits and losses are allocated among the partners as provided in the partnership agreement. If the agreement makes no such provision in writing, then the profits and losses are allocated on the basis of the value of the contributions each partner actually has made. Section 503. Nonetheless, limited partners usually are not liable for losses beyond their capital contribution. Section 303(a).

**Distributions** The partners share distributions of cash or other assets of the limited partnership as provided in writing in the partnership agreement. The RULPA allows partners to share in distributions in a proportion different from that in which they share in profits. If the partnership agreement does not provide for allocation in writing, then distributions are based on the value of contributions each partner actually made. Section 504. Unless otherwise provided in writing, a partner has no right to demand a distribution in any form other than cash. Once a partner becomes entitled to a distribution, he has the status of a creditor with respect to that distribution. Section 606. A partner may not receive a distribution from a limited partnership unless the assets remaining after the distribution are sufficient to pay all partnership liabilities other than liabilities to partners on account of their partnership interests. Section 607.

**Loans** Both general and limited partners may be secured or unsecured creditors of the partnership with the same rights as a person who is not a partner, subject to applicable State and Federal bankruptcy and fraudulent conveyance statutes. Section 107.

**Information** The partnership must continuously maintain within the State an office at which it keeps basic organizational and financial records. Section 105. Each partner has the right to inspect and copy any of the partnership records. Each limited partner may obtain from the general partners upon reasonable demand (1) complete and accurate information regarding the business and financial condition of the limited partnership, (2) copies of the limited partnership's Federal, State, and local income tax returns for each year, and (3) any other reasonable information regarding the affairs of the limited partnership. Section 305.

**Derivative Actions** A limited partner has the right to bring an action on behalf of a limited partnership to recover a judgment in its favor if the general partners having authority to bring the action have refused to do so. Section 1001. The Act also establishes standing and pleading requirements similar to those imposed in shareholder's derivative actions and permits the court to award reasonable expenses, including attorneys' fees, to a successful plaintiff. Section 1002.

## DUTIES AND LIABILITIES

The duties and liabilities of general partners in a limited partnership are quite different from those of limited partners. A general partner is subject to all the duties and restrictions of a partner in a partnership without limited partners, whereas a limited partner is subject to few, if any, duties and enjoys limited liability.

**Duties** A *general partner* of a limited partnership owes a **fiduciary** duty to her general and limited partners. The existence of this duty is extremely important to the limited partners because of their circumscribed role in the control and management of the business enterprise. Conversely, whether a limited partner owes a fiduciary duty either to his general partners or to the limited partnership remains unclear. The very limited judicial authority on this question seems to indicate that the limited partner does not.

The RULPA does not distinguish between the duty of care owed by a general partner to a general partnership and that owed by a general partner to a limited partnership. Thus, although a general partner owes her partners a duty not to be grossly negligent (as discussed in *Chapter 31*), some courts have imposed upon general partners a higher duty of care toward *limited partners*. On the other hand, a limited partner owes no duty of care to a limited partnership as long as she remains a limited partner.

◆ **SEE CASE 33-2**

**Liabilities** One of the most appealing features of a limited partnership is the limited personal liability it offers limited partners. **Limited liability** means that a limited partner who has paid her contribution has no further liability to the limited partnership or its creditors. Thus, if a limited partner buys a 25 percent share of a limited partnership for $50,000 and does not forfeit her limited liability, her liability is limited to the $50,000 she contributed, even if the limited partnership suffers losses of $500,000. This protection is subject to three conditions discussed earlier:

1. that the partnership has substantially complied in good faith with the requirement that a certificate of limited partnership be filed;
2. that the surname of the limited partner does not appear in the partnership name; and
3. that the limited partner does not participate in control of the business.

In addition, if the certificate contains a false statement, anyone who suffers loss by reliance on that statement may hold liable any party to the certificate who knew the statement to be false when the certificate was executed. Section 207. As long as the limited partner abides by these conditions, his liability for any and all obligations of the partnership is limited to his capital contribution.

At the same time, the general partners of a limited partnership have unlimited external liability, unless the limited partnership is a limited liability limited partnership discussed later in this chapter. Also, any general partner who knew or should have known that the limited partnership certificate contained a false statement is liable to anyone who suffers loss by reliance on that statement. Moreover, a general partner is liable if he knows or should know that a statement has become false and he does not amend the certificate within a reasonable time. Accordingly, it has become a common practice for limited partnerships to be formed with a corporation or other limited liability entity as the sole general partner.

Any partner to whom any part of her contribution has been returned without violation of the partnership agreement or of the limited partnership act is liable for one year to the limited partnership, to the extent necessary to pay creditors who extended credit during the period the partnership held the contribution. Section 608. In contrast, any partner to whom any part of her contribution was returned in violation of the partnership agreement or the limited partnership act is liable to the limited partnership for six years for the amount of the contribution wrongfully returned.

◆ **SEE FIGURE 33-1: Comparison of General and Limited Partners**

## DISSOLUTION

As with a general partnership, extinguishing a limited partnership involves three steps: (1) dissolution, (2) winding up or liquidation, and (3) termination. The causes of dissolution and the priorities for distributing the assets, however, differ somewhat from those in a general partnership.

**Causes** In a limited partnership, the limited partners have no right or power to dissolve the partnership, except by court decree. The death or bankruptcy of a limited partner does not dissolve the partnership. Section 801 of the RULPA specifies those events that will trigger a dissolution, after which the affairs of the partnership must be liquidated:

1. the expiration of the time period specified in the certificate;
2. the happening of events specified in writing in the partnership agreement;
3. the unanimous written consent of all the partners;
4. the withdrawal of a general partner unless either (a) there is at least one other general partner and the written provisions of the partnership agreement permit the remaining general partners to continue the business or (b) within ninety days all partners agree in writing to continue the business; or

◆ **FIGURE 33-1: Comparison of General and Limited Partners**

| | General Partner | Limited Partner |
|---|---|---|
| **Control** | Has all the rights and powers of a partner in a partnership without limited partners | Has no right to take part in management or control |
| **Liability** | Unlimited | Limited, unless partner takes part in control or partner's name is used |
| **Agency** | Is an agent of the partnership | Is not an agent of the partnership |
| **Fiduciary Duty** | Yes | No |
| **Duty of Care** | Yes | No |

5. a decree of judicial dissolution, which may be granted whenever it is not reasonably practicable to carry on the business in conformity with the partnership agreement.

A general partner's withdrawal occurs upon his retirement, assignment of all his general partnership interest, removal, bankruptcy, death, or adjudication of incompetency.

A certificate of cancellation must be filed when the limited partnership dissolves and winding up commences. Section 203.

**Winding Up** Unless otherwise provided in the partnership agreement, the general partners who have not wrongfully dissolved the limited partnership may wind up its affairs. Section 803. The limited partners may wind up the limited partnership if all the general partners have wrongfully dissolved the partnership. But any partner, his legal representative, or his assignee may obtain a winding up by court order if cause is shown.

**Distribution of Assets** Section 804 sets forth the priorities in distributing the assets of a limited partnership:

1. to creditors, including partners who are creditors, except with respect to liabilities for distributions;
2. to partners and ex-partners in satisfaction of liabilities for unpaid distributions;
3. to partners for the return of their contributions, except as otherwise agreed; and
4. to partners for their partnership interests in the proportions in which they share in distributions, except as otherwise agreed.

General and limited partners rank equally unless the partnership agreement provides otherwise.

## LIMITED LIABILITY COMPANIES

A limited liability company (LLC) is another form of unincorporated business association. Prior to 1990, only two States had statutes permitting LLCs. Now all States have enacted LLC statutes. Until 1995, there was no uniform statute on which States might base their LLC legislation, and since its promulgation twelve States have adopted the Uniform Limited Liability Company Act (ULLCA), which was amended in 1996. (In 2006 the Revised ULLCA was completed but to date only four States have adopted it. The Revised ULLCA will *not* be covered in this chapter.) Therefore, the enabling legislation varies from State to State. Nevertheless, the LLC statutes generally share certain characteristics.

A **limited liability company** is a noncorporate business organization that provides limited liability to *all* of its owners (members) and permits all of its members to participate in management of the business. It may elect not to be a separate taxable entity, in which case only the members are taxed. (Publicly traded LLCs, however, are subject to corporate income taxation.) If an LLC has only one member, then it will be taxed as a sole proprietorship, unless separate entity tax treatment is elected. Thus, the LLC provides many of the advantages of a general partnership plus limited liability for all its members. Its benefits outweigh those of a limited partnership in that all members of an LLC not only enjoy limited liability but also may participate in management and control of the business. LLCs have become the most popular and widely used unincorporated business form that provides limited liability for its members. The most frequent use of LLCs has been in real estate transactions (about one-half of all LLCs), professional services, construction, finance, and retail. Ownership interests in an LLC may be considered to be securities, especially interests in those LLCs operated by managers. If a particular LLC interest is considered a security, its sale would be subject to State and Federal securities regulation, as discussed in *Chapter 44.*

◆ **SEE FIGURE 31-1: General Partnership, Limited Partnership, Limited Liability Company, and Corporation**

### FORMATION

The formation of an LLC requires substantial compliance with a State's LLC statute. All States permit an LLC to have only one member. Once formed, an LLC is a separate legal entity that is distinct from its members, who are normally not liable for its debts and obligations. An LLC can contract in its own name and is generally permitted to carry on any lawful purpose, although some statutes restrict the permissible activities of LLCs.

**Filing** The LLC statutes generally require the central public filing of articles of organization in a designated State office. The States vary regarding the information they require the articles to include, but all require at least the following: (1) the name of the firm, (2) the address of the principal place of business or registered office, and (3) the name and address of the agent for service of process. Most LLC statutes provide that the acceptance for filing is conclusive evidence that the LLC has been properly formed, except against the State in an involuntary dissolution or certificate revocation proceeding. Most LLC statutes require the articles to state whether the LLC will be managed by managers. Most States provide that LLCs have perpetual existence unless the members agree otherwise. The articles of organization may be amended by filing articles of amendment. In most States LLCs must file annual reports with the State.

**Name** LLC statutes generally require the name of the LLC to include the words *limited liability company* or the abbreviation

*LLC.* A number of States also permit the use of the name *limited company* and the abbreviation *LC.* The name of each LLC must be distinguishable from other firms doing business within the State.

**Contribution** The contribution of a member to an LLC may be cash, property, services rendered, a promissory note, or other obligation to contribute cash, property, or to perform services. Most LLC statutes require both a written agreement to make a contribution and a written record of contributions. Members are liable to the LLC for failing to make an agreed contribution.

**Operating Agreement** The members of most LLCs adopt an **operating agreement**, which is the basic contract among the members governing the affairs of an LLC and stating the various rights and duties of the members and any managers. The operating agreement is subordinate to Federal and State law. LLC statutes generally do not require the operating agreement to be in writing, although some statutes permit modification of certain statutory rules to be only by written provision in an operating agreement. Unless the operating agreement provides otherwise, the members may amend it only by unanimous consent.

**Foreign Limited Liability Companies** An LLC is considered "foreign" in any State other than that in which it was formed. LLC statutes typically provide that the laws of the State in which a foreign LLC is organized govern its organization, its internal affairs, and the liability of its members and managers. Foreign LLCs must register with the Secretary of State before transacting any business in a State. Any foreign LLC transacting business without so registering may not bring enforcement actions in the State's courts until it registers, although it may defend itself in the State's courts.

### RIGHTS OF MEMBERS

A member has no property interest in property owned by the LLC. On the other hand, a member does have an interest in the LLC, which is personal property. A member's interest in the LLC includes two components:

1. the **financial interest**, which is the right to share profits and losses and to receive distributions, and
2. the **management interest**, which consists of all other rights granted to a member by the LLC operating agreement and the LLC statute. The management interest typically includes the right to manage, vote, obtain information, and bring enforcement actions.

**Profit and Loss Sharing** The LLC's operating agreement determines how the partners allocate the profits and losses. If the LLC's operating agreement makes no such provision, the profits and losses are typically allocated on the basis of the value of the members' contributions. The ULLCA's default rule and a few States follow the partnership model under which profits are divided equally. Section 405.

**Distributions** LLC statutes do not provide LLC members the right to distributions before withdrawal from the LLC. Therefore, the members share distributions of cash or other assets of an LLC as provided in the operating agreement. If the LLC's operating agreement does not allocate distributions, they are typically made on the basis of the contributions each member made. Almost all LLC statutes give creditors a remedy against members who receive wrongful distributions and many also impose liability on members and managers who approved the wrongful distributions. The statutes vary in defining what constitutes a wrongful distribution, but most make a distribution wrongful if the LLC is insolvent or if the distribution would make the LLC insolvent.

**Withdrawal** Some statutes permit a member to withdraw and demand payment of her interest upon giving the notice specified in the statute or the LLC's operating agreement. Some of the statutes permit the operating agreement to deny members the right to withdraw from the LLC.

**Management** Nearly all LLC statutes provide that, in the absence of a contrary agreement, each member has equal rights in the management of the LLC. All LLC statutes permit LLCs to be managed by one or more managers who may, but need not, be members. In a member-managed LLC, the members have actual and apparent authority to bind the LLC. In a manager-managed LLC, the managers have this authority, while the members have no actual or apparent authority to bind the manager-managed LLC. Most statutes require a publicly filed document to elect a manager-managed structure; a few statutes permit the operating agreement to make that election.

◆ **SEE CASE 33-3**

**Voting** Most of the LLC statutes specify the voting rights of members, subject to a contrary provision in an LLC's operating agreement. In some States the default rule for voting follows a partnership approach (each member has equal voting rights), while the other States take a corporate approach (voting is based on the financial interests of members). Typically, members have the right to vote on proposals to (1) adopt or amend the operating agreement, (2) admit any person as a member, (3) sell all or substantially all of the LLC's assets prior to dissolution, and (4) merge the LLC with another LLC or other business entity. Some LLC statutes authorize voting by proxy. A **proxy** is a member's authorization to an agent to vote for the member.

**Information** The LLC must keep basic organizational and financial records. Each member has the right to inspect the LLC records.

**Derivative Actions** A member has the right to bring an action on behalf of an LLC to recover a judgment in its favor if the managers or members with authority to bring the action have refused to do so.

**Assignment of LLC Interest** Unless otherwise provided in the LLC's operating agreement, a member may assign his financial interest in the LLC. An assignment does not dissolve the LLC. The assignment only entitles the assignee to receive, to the extent of the assignment, the assigning member's share of distributions. A judgment creditor of a member may obtain a charging order against the member's financial interest in the LLC. The charging order gives the creditor the same rights as an assignee to the extent of the interest charged.

The assignee does not become a member and may not exercise any management rights of a member. However, an assignee of a financial interest in an LLC may acquire the other rights by being admitted as a member of the company by all the remaining members. (Some States allow admission by majority vote.) In most States this unanimous acceptance rule is now a default rule, and the operating agreement may eliminate or modify it. For example, the ULLCA provides, "A transferee of a [financial] interest may become a member of a limited liability company if and to the extent that the transferor gives the transferee the right in accordance with authority described in the operating agreement or all other members consent." Section 503(a).

## DUTIES

As with general partnerships and limited partnerships, the duties of care and loyalty also apply to LLCs. In a number of States, the LLC statute expressly imposes these duties. In other States, the common law imposes these duties. Some statutes also expressly impose an obligation of good faith and fair dealing. Who has these duties in an LLC depends upon whether the LLC is a manager-managed LLC (analogous to a limited partnership) or a member-managed LLC (analogous to a partnership).

**Manager-Managed LLCs** Most LLC statutes impose upon the managers of an LLC a duty of care. In some States, this is a duty to refrain from grossly negligent, reckless, or intentional conduct; in other States, it is a duty to act in good faith and as a prudent person would in similar circumstances. Managers also have a fiduciary duty, although the statutes vary in how they specify that duty. Usually, members of manager-managed LLCs have no duties to the LLC or its members by reason of being a member.

**Member-Managed LLCs** Members of member-managed LLCs have the same duties of care and loyalty that managers have in manager-managed LLCs.

◆ **SEE FIGURE 33-2: Comparison of Member-Managed and Manager-Managed LLCs**

## LIABILITIES

One of the most appealing features of an LLC is the limited personal liability it offers to all its members and managers. Statutes typically provide that no member or manager of an LLC shall be obligated personally for any debt, obligation, or liability of the LLC solely by reason of being a member or acting as a manager of the LLC. The limitation on liability, however, will not affect the liability of a member or manager who committed the wrongful act. A member or manager is also personally liable for any LLC obligations guaranteed by the member or manager.

As mentioned earlier, a member who fails to make an agreed contribution is liable to the LLC for the deficiency.

◆ **FIGURE 33-2: Comparison of Member-Managed and Manager-Managed LLCs**

| | Member of Member-Managed LLC<br>Manager of Manager-Managed LLC | Member of Manager-Managed LLC |
|---|---|---|
| **Control** | Full | None |
| **Liability** | Limited | Limited |
| **Agency** | Is an agent of the LLC | Is not an agent of the LLC |
| **Fiduciary Duty** | Yes | No |
| **Duty of Care** | Yes | No |

Note: LLC = limited liability company.

Moreover, under the great majority of statutes, any member who receives a distribution or return of her contribution in violation of the LLC's operating agreement or the LLC statute is liable to the LLC for the amount of the contribution wrongfully returned. Under a few of the statutes, even members who receive a return of their capital contribution without violating the LLC agreement or the LLC statute remain liable to the LLC for a specified time to the extent necessary to pay creditors.

◆ **SEE CASE 33-4**

### DISSOLUTION

LLC statutes generally provide that an LLC will automatically dissolve upon the following:

1. the expiring of the LLC's agreed duration or the happening of any of the events specified in the articles,
2. the written consent of all the members, or
3. a decree of judicial dissolution typically on the grounds that "it is not reasonably practicable to carry on the LLC's activities in conformity with the articles of organization and the operating agreement" or, under some statutes, the members or managers have acted illegally, fraudulently, or oppressively.

LLC statutes require a public filing in connection with dissolution. For example, after winding up the company, the ULLCA and some LLC statutes provide for the filing of articles of termination stating (1) the name of the company, (2) the date of the dissolution, and (3) that the company's business has been wound up and the legal existence of the company has been terminated. Other statutes require either (1) a public filing of the intent to dissolve at the time of dissolution or (2) filings at both the time of dissolution and after winding up.

**Dissociation** Dissociation means that a member has ceased to be associated with the company through voluntary withdrawal, death, incompetence, expulsion, or bankruptcy. Initially, many LLC statutes required an LLC to be dissolved upon the dissociation of a member. Most statutes permitted the nondissociating members by unanimous consent to continue the LLC after a member dissociates. Some allowed continuation by majority vote. Although some States still retain these provisions, an increasing number of States (currently about half of the States) and the amended ULLCA have eliminated a member's dissociation as a mandatory cause of dissolution.

**Winding Up** An LLC continues after dissolution only for the purpose of winding up its business, which involves completing unfinished business, collecting debts, disposing of inventory, reducing assets to cash, paying creditors, and distributing the remaining assets to the members. During this period, the fiduciary duties of members and managers continue.

**Authority** Upon dissolution, the *actual authority* of a member or manager to act for the LLC terminates, except so far as is appropriate to wind up LLC business. Actual authority to wind up includes the authority to complete existing contracts, to collect debts, to sell LLC assets, and to pay LLC obligations. In addition, some statutes expressly provide that after dissolution, members and managers continue to have *apparent* authority to bind the company that they had prior to dissolution provided that the third party did not have notice of the dissolution.

**Distribution of Assets** Most statutes provide default rules for distributing the assets of an LLC as follows:

1. to creditors, including members and managers who are creditors, except with respect to liabilities or distributions;
2. to members and former members in satisfaction of liabilities for unpaid distributions, except as otherwise agreed;
3. to members for the return of their contributions, except as otherwise agreed; and
4. to members for their LLC interests in the proportions in which members share in distributions, except as otherwise agreed.

**Protection of Creditors** Many LLC statutes establish procedures to safeguard the interests of the LLC's creditors. Such procedures typically include the required mailing of notice of dissolution to known creditors, a general publication of notice, and the preservation of claims against the LLC for a specified time. For example, the ULLCA provides that a claim against the LLC is barred unless a proceeding to enforce the claim is commenced within five years after publication of the notice of dissolution.

### MERGERS AND CONVERSIONS

Most LLC statutes expressly provide for mergers. A **merger** of two or more entities is the combination of all of their assets. One of the entities, known as the ***surviving entity***, receives title to all the assets. The other party or parties to the merger, known as the ***merged entity*** or entities, is merged into the surviving entity and ceases to exist as a separate entity. Thus, if Alpha LLC and Beta LLC combine into the Alpha LLC, Alpha is the surviving LLC and Beta is the merged LLC. The ULLCA provides that an LLC may be merged with or into one or more limited liability companies, corporations, partnerships, limited partnerships, or other entities.

The LLC statutes vary with respect to the voting rights of the members regarding approval of a merger. Some provide for a majority or unanimous vote; others leave it to the operating agreement. Some statutes require the filing of articles of merger; others require a merged LLC to file articles of dissolution. Upon the required filing the merger is effective, and the separate existence of each merged entity terminates. All property owned by each of the merged entities vests in the surviving entity, and all debts, liabilities, and other obligations of each merged entity become the obligations of the surviving entity.

Many LLC statutes provide for the conversion of another business entity into an LLC. LLC statutes and other business association statutes also provide for an LLC to be converted into another business entity. The converted entity remains the same entity that existed before the conversion.

## OTHER TYPES OF UNINCORPORATED BUSINESS ASSOCIATIONS

### LIMITED LIABILITY PARTNERSHIPS

All of the States have enacted statutes enabling the formation of limited liability partnerships (LLPs). Until 1997 there was no uniform LLP statute, so the enabling statutes vary from State to State. In 1997 the Revised Uniform Partnership Act (RUPA) was amended to add provisions enabling general partnerships to elect to become LLPs, and more than thirty States have adopted this version of the RUPA. A registered **LLP** is a general partnership that, by making the statutorily required filing, limits the liability of its partners for some or all of the partnership's obligations.

**Formalities** To become an LLP, a general partnership must file with the Secretary of State an application containing specified information. The RUPA requires the partnership to file a statement of qualification. RUPA Section 1001(c). Most of the statutes require only a majority of the partners to authorize registration as an LLP; others require unanimous approval. The RUPA requires unanimity unless the partnership agreement provides otherwise. RUPA Section 1001(b). Some statutes require renewal of registrations annually; other statutes require periodic reports; and a few require no renewal. The RUPA requires filing annual reports. RUPA Section 1003. Some statutes require a new filing after any change in membership of the partnership, but a few of the statutes do not. The RUPA does not.

**Designation** All statutes require LLPs to designate themselves as such. Most statutes require the name of the LLP to include the words *limited liability partnership* or *registered limited liability partnership*, or the abbreviation *LLP* or *RLLP*. Most statutes provide that the laws of the jurisdiction under which a foreign LLP is registered shall govern its organization, internal affairs, and the liability and authority of its partners. Many, but not all, of the statutes require a foreign LLP to register or obtain a certificate of authenticity. The RUPA requires a foreign LLP to qualify and file annual reports. RUPA Sections 1102 and 1003.

**Liability Limitation** LLP statutes have taken three different approaches to limiting the liability of partners for the partnership's obligations. The earliest statutes limited liability for negligent acts only; they retained unlimited liability for all other obligations. The next generation of statutes extended limited liability to any partnership tort or contract obligation that arose from negligence, malpractice, wrongful acts, or misconduct committed by any partner, employee, or agent of the partnership. Unlimited liability remained for ordinary contract obligations, such as those owed to suppliers, lenders, and landlords. The first two generations of LLP statutes are called "partial shield" statutes. Many of the more recent statutes (called "full shield" statutes) have provided limited liability for all debts and obligations of the partnership, including Section 306(c) of the RUPA. Most States have now adopted full shield statutes although some States still provide only a partial shield.

The statutes, however, generally provide that the limitation on liability will not affect the liability of (1) a partner who committed the wrongful act giving rise to the liability and (2) a partner who supervised the partner, employee, or agent of the partnership who committed the wrongful act. A partner is also personally liable for any partnership obligations guaranteed by the partner. The statutes also provide that the limitations on liability will apply only to claims that arise while the partnership was a registered LLP. Accordingly, partners would have unlimited liability for obligations that either arose before registration or after registration lapses.

**SEE FIGURE 33-3: Liability Limitations in LLPs**

### LIMITED LIABILITY LIMITED PARTNERSHIPS

A **limited liability limited partnership** (LLLP) is a limited partnership in which the liability of the general partners has been limited to the same extent as in an LLP. A growing number of States allow limited partnerships to become LLLPs. A number of States have statutes expressly providing for LLLPs. In other States, by operation of the provision in the RULPA that a general partner in a limited partnership assumes the liabilities of a general partner in a general partnership, the LLP statute may provide limited liability to general partners in a limited partnership that registers as an LLLP under the LLP statute. Where authorized, the general partners in an LLLP will obtain the same degree of liability limitation that general partners can achieve in LLPs. Where available, a limited partnership may register as an LLLP without having to form a new organization, as would be the case in converting to an LLC.

FIGURE 33-3: **Liability Limitations in LLPs**

| LLP Statutes | Limited Liability | Unlimited Liability |
|---|---|---|
| **First Generation** | Negligent acts | • All other obligations<br>• Wrongful partner<br>• Supervising partner |
| **Second Generation** | Tort and contract obligations arising from wrongful acts | • All other obligations<br>• Wrongful partner<br>• Supervising partner |
| **Third Generation** | All obligations | • Wrongful partner<br>• Supervising partner |

Note: LLP = limited liability partnership.

The new revision of the RULPA promulgated in 2001, which has been adopted by at least fifteen States, provides that an LLLP "means a limited partnership whose certificate of limited partnership states that the limited partnership is a limited liability limited partnership." Section 102(9). The revision provides a full shield for general partners in LLLPs:

> An obligation of a limited partnership incurred while the limited partnership is a limited liability limited partnership, whether arising in contract, tort, or otherwise, is solely the obligation of the limited partnership. A general partner is not personally liable . . . for such an obligation solely by reason of being or acting as a general partner.

Section 404(c). Moreover, under the revision, a *limited* partner cannot be held liable for the partnership debts even if he participates in the management and control of the limited partnership.

## CHAPTER SUMMARY

**LIMITED PARTNERSHIPS**

**Definition of a Limited Partnership** a partnership formed by two or more persons under the laws of a State and having one or more general partners and one or more limited partners

**Formation** a limited partnership can be formed only by substantial compliance with a State limited partnership statute

- ***Filing of Certificate*** two or more persons must file a signed certificate of limited partnership
- ***Name*** inclusion of a limited partner's surname in the partnership name in most instances will result in the loss of the limited partner's limited liability
- ***Contributions*** may be cash, property, services, or a promise to contribute cash, property, or services
- ***Defective Formation*** if no certificate is filed or if the one filed does not substantially meet the statutory requirements, the formation is defective and the limited liability of the limited partners is jeopardized
- ***Foreign Limited Partnerships*** a limited partnership is considered "foreign" in any State other than that in which it was formed

**Rights** a general partner in a limited partnership has all the rights and powers of a partner in a general partnership

- ***Control*** the general partners have almost exclusive control and management of the limited partnerships; a limited partner who participates in the control of the limited partnership may lose limited liability

- ***Voting Rights*** the partnership agreement may grant to all or a specified group of general or limited partners the right to vote on any matter
- ***Choice of Associates*** no person may be added as a general partner or a limited partner without the consent of all partners
- ***Withdrawal*** a general partner may withdraw from a limited partnership at any time by giving written notice to the other partners; a limited partner may withdraw as provided in the limited partnership certificate
- ***Assignment of Partnership Interest*** unless otherwise provided in the partnership agreement, a partner may assign his partnership interest; an assignee may become a substituted limited partner if all other partners consent
- ***Profit and Loss Sharing*** profits and losses are allocated among the partners as provided in the partnership agreement; if the partnership agreement has no such provision, then profits and losses are allocated on the basis of the contributions each partner actually made
- ***Distributions*** the partners share distributions of cash or other assets of a limited partnership as provided in the partnership agreement
- ***Loans*** both general and limited partners may be secured or unsecured creditors of the partnership
- ***Information*** each partner has the right to inspect and copy the partnership records
- ***Derivative Actions*** a limited partner may sue on behalf of a limited partnership if the general partners refuse to bring the action

**Duties and Liabilities**

- ***Duties*** general partners owe a duty of care and loyalty (fiduciary duty) to the general partners, the limited partners, and the limited partnership; limited partners do not
- ***Liabilities*** the general partners have unlimited liability; the limited partners have limited liability (liability for partnership obligations only to the extent of the capital that they contributed or agreed to contribute)

**Dissolution**

- ***Causes*** the limited partners have neither the right nor the power to dissolve the partnership, except by decree of the court; the following events trigger a dissolution: (1) the expiration of the time period; (2) the withdrawal of a general partner, unless all partners agree to continue the business; or (3) a decree of judicial dissolution
- ***Winding Up*** unless otherwise provided in the partnership agreement, the general partners who have not wrongfully dissolved the partnership may wind up its affairs
- ***Distribution of Assets*** the priorities for distribution are as follows: (1) creditors, including partners who are creditors; (2) partners and ex-partners in satisfaction of liabilities for unpaid distributions; (3) partners for the return of contributions, except as otherwise agreed; and (4) partners for their partnership interests in the proportions in which they share in distributions, except as otherwise agreed

---

**LIMITED LIABILITY COMPANIES**

**Definition** a limited liability company is a noncorporate business organization that provides limited liability to all of its owners (members) and permits all of its members to participate in management of the business

**Formation** the formation of an LLC requires substantial compliance with a State's LLC statute

- ***Filing*** the LLC statutes generally require the central filing of articles of organization in a designated State office
- ***Name*** LLC statutes generally require the name of the LLC to include the words *limited liability company* or the abbreviation *LLC*

- ***Contribution*** the contribution of a member to an LLC may be cash, property, services rendered, a promissory note, or other obligation to contribute cash, property, or to perform services
- ***Operating Agreement*** the basic contract governing the affairs of an LLC and stating the various rights and duties of the members
- ***Foreign Limited Liability Companies*** an LLC is considered "foreign" in any State other than that in which it was formed

**Rights of Members** a member's interest in the LLC includes the financial interest (the right to distributions) and the management interest (which consists of all other rights granted to a member by the LLC operating agreement and the LLC statute)

- ***Profit and Loss Sharing*** the LLC's operating agreement determines how the partners allocate the profits and losses; if the LLC's operating agreement makes no such provision, the profits and losses are typically allocated on the basis of the value of the members' contributions
- ***Distributions*** the members share distributions of cash or other assets of an LLC as provided in the operating agreement; if the LLC's operating agreement does not allocate distributions, they are typically made on the basis of the contributions each member made
- ***Withdrawal*** a member may withdraw and demand payment of her interest upon giving the notice specified in the statute or the LLC's operating agreement
- ***Management*** in the absence of a contrary agreement, each member has equal rights in the management of the LLC, but LLCs may be managed by one or more managers who may be members
- ***Voting*** LLC statutes usually specify the voting rights of members, subject to a contrary provision in an LLC's operating agreement
- ***Information*** LLCs must keep basic organizational and financial records; each member has the right to inspect the LLC records
- ***Derivative Actions*** a member has the right to bring an action on behalf of an LLC to recover a judgment in its favor if the managers or members with authority to bring the action have refused to do so
- ***Assignment of LLC Interest*** Unless otherwise provided in the LLC's operating agreement, a member may assign his financial interest in the LLC; an assignee of a financial interest in an LLC may acquire the other rights by being admitted as a member of the company if all the remaining members consent or the operating agreement so provides

**Duties**

- ***Manager-Managed LLCs*** The managers of a manager-managed LLC have a duty of care and loyalty; usually, members of a manager-managed LLC have no duties to the LLC or its members by reason of being members
- ***Member-Managed LLCs*** members of member-managed LLCs have the same duties of care and loyalty that managers have in manager-managed LLCs

**Liabilities** no member or manager of an LLC is obligated personally for any debt, obligation, or liability of the LLC solely by reason of being a member or acting as a manager of the LLC

**Dissolution** an LLC will automatically dissolve upon (1) in some States, the dissociation of a member, (2) the expiration of the LLC's agreed duration or the happening of any of the events specified in the articles, (3) the written consent of all the members, or (4) a decree of judicial dissolution

- ***Dissociation*** means that a member has ceased to be associated with the company through voluntary withdrawal, death, incompetence, expulsion, or bankruptcy
- ***Winding Up*** completing unfinished business, collecting debts, and distributing assets to creditors and members; also called liquidation

- ***Authority*** the actual authority of a member or manager to act for the LLC terminates, except so far as may be appropriate to wind up LLC affairs; apparent authority continues unless notice of the dissolution is given to a third party
- ***Distribution of Assets*** the default rules for distributing the assets of an LLC are (1) to creditors, including members and managers who are creditors, except with respect to liabilities for distributions; (2) to members and former members in satisfaction of liabilities for unpaid distributions, except as otherwise agreed; (3) to members for the return of their contributions, except as otherwise agreed; and (4) to members for their LLC interests in the proportions in which members share in distributions, except as otherwise agreed

**Mergers**

- ***Definition*** the combination of the assets of two or more business entities into one of the entities
- ***Effect*** the surviving entity receives title to all of the assets of the merged entities and assumes all of their liabilities; the merged entities cease to exist

**OTHER TYPES OF UNINCORPORATED BUSINESS ASSOCIATIONS**

**Limited Liability Partnership** a general partnership that, by making the statutorily required filing, limits the liability of its partners for some or all of the partnership's obligations

- ***Formalities*** most statutes require only a majority of the partners to authorize registration as an LLP; others require unanimous approval
- ***Designation*** the name of the LLP must include the words *limited liability partnership* or *registered limited liability partnership* or the abbreviation *LLP*
- ***Liability Limitation*** some statutes limit liability only for negligent acts; others limit liability to any partnership tort or contract obligation that arose from negligence, malpractice, wrongful acts, or misconduct committed by any partner, employee, or agent of the partnership; most provide limited liability for all debts and obligations of the partnership

**Limited Liability Limited Partnership** a limited partnership in which the liability of the general partners has been limited to the same extent as in an LLP

# CASES

## CASE 33-1

### Control
### ALZADO v. BLINDER, ROBINSON & CO., INC.

Supreme Court of Colorado, 1988
752 P.2d 544

**Kirshbaum, J.**

In the spring of 1979, Alzado, Alzado's former accountant, Tinter, and Alzado's former agent, Ronald Kauffman (Kauffman), formed Combat Promotions, Inc. to promote an eight-round exhibition boxing match in Denver, Colorado, between Alzado and Ali. Alzado, Tinter and Kauffman were the directors and sole shareholders of the corporation. Ali had agreed to engage in the match on the condition that prior to the event his attorneys would receive an irrevocable letter of credit guaranteeing payment of $250,000 to Ali.

Combat Promotions, Inc. initially encountered difficulties in obtaining the letter of credit. Ultimately, however, Meyer Blinder (Blinder), President of Blinder-Robinson, expressed an interest in the event. Blinder anticipated that his company's participation would result in a positive public relations image for its recently opened Denver office. Blinder-Robinson ultimately agreed to provide the $250,000 letter of credit.

Blinder-Robinson insisted on several conditions to protect its investment. It required the formation of a limited partnership with specific provisions governing repayment to Blinder-Robinson of any sums drawn against the letter of credit. It also required Alzado's personal secured guarantee to reimburse Blinder-Robinson for any losses it might suffer. Alzado and Combat Promotions, Inc. accepted these conditions.

On June 25, 1979, an agreement was executed by Combat Promotions, Inc. and Blinder-Robinson creating a limited partnership, Combat Associates. Under the terms of the agreement, Combat Promotions, Inc. was the general partner and Blinder-Robinson was the sole limited partner. Blinder-Robinson contributed a $250,000 letter of credit to Combat Associates, and the partnership agreement provided expressly that the letter of credit was to be paid off as a partnership expense.

On the same day, June 25, 1979, Alzado executed a separate guaranty agreement with Blinder-Robinson. This agreement provided that if Ali drew the letter of credit, Alzado personally would reimburse Blinder-Robinson for any amount Blinder-Robinson was unable to recover from Combat Associates under the terms of the limited partnership agreement. As security for his agreement, Alzado placed a general warranty deed to his residence, an assignment of an investment account and a confession of judgment in escrow for the benefit of Blinder-Robinson. Thereafter, a separate agreement was apparently executed by Alzado and Combat Associates providing that Alzado would receive $100,000 in compensation for the exhibition match but subordinating any payment of that sum to the payment of expenses of the match, including, if drawn, the letter of credit.

Approximately one week before the date of the match, Alzado announced that he might not participate because he feared he might lose the assets he had pledged as security for the guaranty agreement. Alzado informed Blinder of this concern, and the two met the next day in Blinder-Robinson's Denver office. Tinter, Kauffman and Ali's representative, Greg Campbell, were also present. Subsequently, on July 14, 1979, the event occurred as scheduled.

Few tickets were sold, and the match proved to be a financial debacle. Ali drew the letter of credit and collected the $250,000 to which he was entitled. Combat Associates paid Blinder-Robinson only $65,000; it did not pay anything to Alzado or, apparently, to other creditors.

In January of 1980, Blinder-Robinson filed this civil action seeking $185,000 in damages plus costs and attorney fees from Alzado pursuant to the terms of the June 25, 1979, guaranty agreement. Alzado denied any liability to Blinder-Robinson and * * * also filed two counterclaims against Blinder-Robinson. The first alleged that because of its conduct Blinder-Robinson must be deemed a general partner of Combat Associates and, therefore, liable to Alzado under the agreement between Alzado and the partnership for Alzado's participation in the match. * * * [The jury returned a verdict of $92,500 in favor of Alzado on this counterclaim. The court of appeals reversed.]

* * *

Alzado next contends that the Court of Appeals erred in concluding that Blinder-Robinson's conduct in promoting the match did not constitute sufficient control of Combat Associates to justify the conclusion that the company must be deemed a general rather than a limited partner. We disagree.

A limited partner may become liable to partnership creditors as a general partner if the limited partner assumes control of partnership business. [Citations]; *see also* [RULPA] §303, which provides that a limited partner does not participate in the control of partnership business solely by doing one or more of the following:

> (a) Being a contractor for or an agent or employee of the limited partnership or of a general partner;
> (b) Being an officer, director, or shareholder of a corporate general partner;
> (c) Consulting with and advising a general partner with respect to the business of the limited partnership;
>
> * * *

* * * Any determination of whether a limited partner's conduct amounts to control over the business affairs of the partnership must be determined by consideration of several factors, including the purpose of the partnership, the administrative activities undertaken, the manner in which the entity actually functioned, and the nature and frequency of the limited partner's purported activities.

* * * The record here reflects that Blinder-Robinson used its Denver office as a ticket outlet, gave two parties to promote the exhibition match and provided a meeting room for many of Combat Associates' meetings. Blinder personally appeared on a television talk show and gave television interviews to promote the match. Blinder-Robinson made no investment, accounting or other financial decisions for the partnership; all such fiscal decisions were made by officers or employees of Combat Promotions, Inc., the general partner. The evidence established at most that Blinder-Robinson engaged in a few promotional activities. It does not establish that it took part in the management or control of the business affairs of the partnership. Accordingly, we agree with the Court of Appeals that the trial court erred in denying Blinder-Robinson's motion for judgment notwithstanding the verdict with respect to Alzado's first counterclaim.

* * *

We * * * affirm the judgment of the Court of Appeals insofar as it reverses the judgments entered at trial in favor of Alzado on his first counterclaim against Blinder-Robinson.

CASE 33-2

## Duties of General Partner
## WYLER v. FEUER

California Court of Appeal, Second District, Division 2, 1978
85 Cal.App.3d 392, 149 Cal.Rptr. 626

**Fleming, J.**

Defendants Cy Feuer and Ernest Martin, associated as Feuer and Martin Productions, Inc. (FMPI), have been successful producers of Broadway musical comedies since 1948. Their first motion picture, "Cabaret," produced by Feuer in conjunction with Allied Artists and American Broadcasting Company, received eight Academy Awards in 1973. Plaintiff Wyler is president and largest shareholder of Tool Research and Engineering Corporation, a New York Stock Exchange Company based in Beverly Hills. Prior to 1972 Wyler had had no experience in the entertainment industry.

[In 1972, FMPI bought the motion picture and television rights to Simone Berteaut's best-selling books about her life with her half-sister Edith Piaf. To finance a movie based on this novel, FMPI sought a substantial private investment from Wyler. In July 1973, Wyler signed a final limited partnership agreement with FMPI. The agreement stated that Wyler would provide, interest free, 100 percent financing for the proposed $1.6 million project, in return for a certain portion of the profits, not to exceed 50 percent. In addition, FMPI would obtain $850,000 in production financing by September 30, 1973. The contract specifically provided that FMPI's failure to raise this amount by September 30, 1973, "shall not be deemed a breach of this agreement" and that Wyler's sole remedy would be a reduction in the producer's fee.]

Despite their acclaimed success in "Cabaret," defendants at the time of execution of the limited partnership agreement were experiencing difficulties in obtaining distributor commitments and knew it would be unlikely they could obtain any production financing by the September 30 deadline. Their difficulties arose from their overestimation of the attractiveness of the Piaf subject-matter, from the unknown leading actress, and from the scheduling of photography during the summer months when most Europeans go on vacation.

Filming of the motion picture began July 23 and ended October 9. By that time Wyler had advanced $1.25 million and defendants had failed to obtain any production financing. The completed cost of the picture was $1,512,000.

Early in October, Feuer met Wyler in Paris and requested an extension of the deadline for production financing to December 30, so that defendants could take advantage of distributor negotiations in process and recoup their profit percentage and their producer's fee. Wyler said he had already financed the picture and refused to extend the deadline, thereby maintaining his profit percentage at 50 percent.

[A year after its release in 1974, the motion picture proved less than an overwhelming success—costing $1.5 million but making only $478,000 in total receipts. From the receipts, Wyler received $313,500 for his investment. FMPI had failed to obtain an amount even close to the $850,000 required for production financing. Wyler then sued Feuer, Martin, and FMPI for mismanagement of the business of the limited partnership and to recover his $1.5 million as damages.]

A limited partnership affords a vehicle for capital investment whereby the limited partner restricts his liability to the amount of his investment in return for surrender of any right to manage and control the partnership business. [Citation.] In a limited partnership the general partner manages and controls the partnership business. [Citation.] In exercising his management functions the general partner comes under a fiduciary duty of good faith and fair dealing toward other members of the partnership. [Citations.]

These characteristics—limited investor liability, delegation of authority to management, and fiduciary duty owed by management to investors—are similar to those existing in corporate investment, where it has long been the rule that directors are not liable to stockholders for mistakes made in the exercise of honest business judgment [citations], or for losses incurred in the good faith performance of their duties when they have used such care as an ordinarily prudent person would use. [Citation.] By this standard a general partner may not be held liable for mistakes made or losses incurred in the good faith exercise of reasonable business judgment.

According all due inferences to plaintiff's evidence, as we do on review of a nonsuit, we agree with the trial court that plaintiff did not produce sufficient evidence to hold defendants liable for bad business management. Plaintiff's evidence showed that the Piaf picture did not make money, was not sought after by distributors, and did not live up to its producers' expectations. The same could be said of the majority of motion pictures made since the invention of cinematography. No evidence showed that defendants' decisions and efforts failed to conform to the general duty of care demanded of an ordinarily prudent person in like position under similar circumstances. The good faith business judgment and management of a general partner need only satisfy the standard of care demanded of an ordinarily prudent person, and will not be scrutinized by the courts with the cold clarity of hindsight.

[Judgment for Feuer, Martin, and FMPI affirmed.]

CASE 33-3

## Management of Limited Liability Companies
## TAGHIPOUR v. JEREZ

Supreme Court of Utah, 2002
2002 UT 74, 52 P.3d 1252
http://caselaw.findlaw.com/ut-supreme-court/1340164.html

**Russon, J.**

Namvar Taghipour, Danesh Rahemi, and Edgar Jerez ("Jerez") formed a limited liability company known as Jerez, Taghipour and Associates, LLC (the "LLC"), on August 30, 1994, to purchase and develop a particular parcel of real estate pursuant to a joint venture agreement. The LLC's articles of organization designated Jerez as the LLC's manager. In addition, the operating agreement between the members of the LLC provided: "No loans may be contracted on behalf of the [LLC] * * * unless authorized by a resolution of the members."

On August 31, 1994, the LLC acquired the intended real estate. Then, on January 10, 1997, Jerez, unbeknownst to the LLC's other members or managers, entered into a loan agreement on behalf of the LLC with Mt. Olympus. According to the agreement, Mt. Olympus lent the LLC $25,000 and, as security for the loan, Jerez executed and delivered a trust deed that conveyed the LLC's real estate property to a trustee with the power to sell the property in the event of default. Mt. Olympus then dispensed $20,000 to Jerez and retained the $5,000 balance to cover various fees. In making the loan, Mt. Olympus did not investigate Jerez's authority to effectuate the loan agreement beyond determining that Jerez was the manager of the LLC.

After Mt. Olympus dispersed the funds pursuant to the agreement, Jerez apparently misappropriated and absconded with the $20,000. Jerez never remitted a payment on the loan, and because the other members of the LLC were unaware of the loan, no loan payments were ever made by anyone, and consequently, the LLC defaulted. Therefore, Mt. Olympus foreclosed on the LLC's property. The members of the LLC, other than Jerez, were never notified of the default or pending foreclosure sale.

On June 18, 1999, Namvar Taghipour, Danesh Rahemi, and the LLC (collectively, "Taghipour") filed suit against Mt. Olympus and Jerez. Taghipour [sought] against Mt. Olympus [a] declaratory judgment that the loan agreement and subsequent foreclosure on the LLC's property were invalid because Jerez lacked the authority to bind the LLC under the operating agreement. * * * Mt. Olympus moved to dismiss * * * asserting that pursuant to Utah Code Section 48–2b–127(2), the loan agreement documents are valid and binding on the LLC since they were signed by the LLC's manager. This section provides:

> Instruments and documents providing for the acquisition, mortgage, or disposition of property of the limited liability company shall be valid and binding upon the limited liability company if they are executed by one or more managers of a limited liability company having a manager or managers or if they are executed by one or more members of a limited liability company in which management has been retained by the members.

[Citation.] The trial court granted Mt. Olympus' motion and dismissed Taghipour's claims against Mt. Olympus, ruling * * * that the complaint alleges that Jerez is the manager of the LLC, and that therefore the loan documents Jerez executed are valid and binding on the LLC.

Taghipour appealed to the Utah Court of Appeals. Taghipour argued that the trial court's interpretation of Section 48–2b–127(2) was in error, inasmuch as it failed to read it in conjunction with Utah Code Section 48–2b–125(2)(b), which provides that a manager's authority to bind a limited liability company can be limited by the operating agreement. * * *

[Citation.] The Utah Court of Appeals affirmed the trial court, concluding that the plain language of section 48–2b–127(2) provided no limitation on a manager's authority to execute certain documents and bind a limited liability company * * * if executed by one or more managers. [Citation.] Further, the court of appeals concluded that this specific statute prevailed over the general statute, Section 48–2b–125(2)(b), and that the loan documents executed by Jerez were therefore binding upon the LLC in this case. [Citation.] * * * Taghipour petitioned this court for certiorari, which we granted.

* * *

To determine whether the loan agreement in this case is valid and binding on the LLC, it must first be determined whether this case is governed by Section 48–2b–127(2), which makes certain kinds of documents binding on a limited liability company when executed by a manager, or Section 48–2b–125(2)(b), which provides that a manager's authority to bind a limited liability company can be limited or eliminated by an operating agreement.

* * * "[W]hen two statutory provisions conflict in their operation, the provision more specific in application governs over the more general provision." [Citations.]

* * *

Section 48–2b–127(2) is the more specific statute because it applies only to documents explicitly enumerated in the statute, i.e., the section expressly addresses "instruments and documents" that provide "for the acquisition, mortgage, or disposition of property of the limited liability company." [Citations.] Thus, this section is tailored precisely to address the documents and instruments Jerez executed, e.g., the trust deed and trust deed note. * * * Conversely, Section 48–2b–125(2)(b) is more general because it addresses every situation in which a manager can bind a limited liability company.

* * *

In this case * * * Jerez was designated as the LLC's manager in the articles of organization. Jerez, acting in his capacity as manager, executed loan agreement documents, e.g., the trust deed and trust deed note, on behalf of the LLC that are specifically covered by the above statute. [Citation.] As such, these documents are valid and binding on the LLC. * * *

* * * Accordingly, we affirm.

## CASE 33-4

### Liabilities
## ESTATE OF COUNTRYMAN v. FARMERS COOP. ASS'N

Supreme Court of Iowa, 2004

679 N.W.2d 598

http://www.judicial.state.ia.us/supreme_court/recent_opinions/20040512/02-0906.asp

**Cady, J.**

In the afternoon of September 6, 1999, an explosion leveled the home of Jerry Usovsky (Usovsky) in Richland, Iowa. Tragically, seven people who had gathered in the home to celebrate the Labor Day holiday died from the explosion. Six others were injured, some seriously. The likely cause of the explosion was stray propane gas. The survivors and executors of the estates of those who died eventually filed a lawsuit seeking monetary damages against a host of defendants. The legal theories of recovery included negligence, breach of warranty, and strict liability. The defendants included Iowa Double Circle, L.C. (Double Circle) and Farmers Cooperative Association of Keota (Keota).

Double Circle is an Iowa limited liability company. It is a supplier of propane, and delivered propane to Usovsky's home prior to the explosion. Keota is one of two members in Double Circle. It owns a ninety-five percent interest in the company. The other member is Farmland Industries, Inc. (Farmland Industries), a regional cooperative. Keota and Farmland Industries formed Double Circle in 1996 from an existing operation.

Keota is a farm cooperative that provides a variety of farm products and services to area farmers. It is a member of Farmland Industries and is managed by Dave Hopscheidt (Hopscheidt). The executive committee of Keota's board of directors serves as the board of directors of Double Circle, along with a representative of Farmland Industries. Keota provides managerial services to Double Circle, pursuant to a management agreement between Keota and Double Circle. Keota's duties under the agreement include "human resource and safety management." Hopscheidt oversees the daily operations of both Keota and Double Circle. However, Keota and Double Circle operate as separate entities and maintain separate finances.

Keota moved for summary judgment. * * *

The plaintiffs resisted the motion by pointing to allegations in their petition indicating Keota participated in the claims of wrongdoing through the management decisions it made in consumer safety matters. For example, plaintiffs claimed Keota, through Hopscheidt, was negligent in failing to provide proper warnings to propane users, including the failure to warn users to install a gas detector, and to properly design the odorant added to the propane. * * *

The district court granted summary judgment for Keota. It found plaintiffs failed to produce any facts to show that Keota engaged in conduct separate from its duties as director or manager of Double Circle. Consequently, it concluded Keota was protected as a matter of law from personal liability for claims of wrongful conduct attributable to Double Circle. * * *

* * *

Plaintiffs filed their notice of appeal from the summary judgment. * * * They claimed the district court erred by finding that Keota was insulated from liability as a matter of law. * * *

* * *

The limited liability company, "LLC" as it is now known, is a hybrid business entity that is considered to have the attributes of a partnership for federal income tax purposes and the limited liability protections of a corporation. [Citation.] As such, it provides for the operational advantages of a partnership by allowing the owners, called members, to participate in the management of the business.

[Citation.] Yet, the members and managers are protected from liability in the same manner shareholders, officers, and directors of a corporation are protected. [Citation.]

The LLC * * * has now been adopted by statute in every state in the nation. [Citation.] Iowa joined the trend in 1992 with the passage of the Iowa Limited Liability Company Act (ILLCA). [Citation.] The ILLCA, among other features, permits the owners or members to centralize management in one or more managers or reserve all management powers to themselves. [Citations.]

Although the tax treatment of an LLC has been largely resolved, the contours of the limited liability of an LLC are less certain. [Citation.] Only a few courts have specifically addressed the issue of tort liability. * * *

* * *

The[se] rules of liability derived from [the ILLCA] have been summarized as follows:

> Sections * * * of the Act generally provide that a member or manager of a limited liability company is not personally liable for acts or debts of the company solely by reason of being a member or manager, except in the following situations: (1) the ILLCA expressly provides for the person's liability; (2) the articles of organization provide for the person's liability; (3) the person has agreed in writing to be personally liable; (4) the person participates in tortious conduct; or (5) a shareholder of a corporation would be personally liable in the same situation, except that the failure to hold meetings and related formalities shall not be considered.

[Citation.]

* * * While liability of members and managers is limited, the statute clearly imposes liability when they participate in tortious conduct. [Citation.] This approach is compatible with the longstanding approach to liability in corporate settings, where, under general agency principles, corporate officers and directors can be liable for their torts even when committed in their capacity as an officer. [Citations.] * * *.

Keota suggests that liability of an LLC member or manager for tortious conduct is limited to conduct committed outside the member or manager role. Yet, this approach is contrary to the corporate model and agency principles upon which the liability of LLC members and managers is based, and cannot be found in the language of the statute. We acknowledge that the "participation in tortious conduct" standard would not impose tort liability on a manager for merely performing a general administrative duty. [Citations.] There must be some participation. [Citation.] The participation standard is consistent with the principle that members or managers are not liable based only on their status as members or managers. [Citation.] Instead, liability is derived from individual activities. Yet, a manager who takes part in the commission of a tort is liable even when the manager acts on behalf of a corporation. [Citation.] The ILLCA does not insulate a manager from liability for participation in tortious conduct merely because the conduct occurs within the scope and role as a manager. * * * The limit on liability created for members and managers of LLCs in [citation] means members and managers are not liable for company torts "solely by reason of being a member or manager" of an LLC. [Citation.] The phrase "solely by reason of" refers to liability based upon membership or management status. It does not distinguish between conduct of a member or manager that may be separate and independent from the member or management role. Thus, it is not inconsistent to protect a member or manager from vicarious liability, while imposing liability when the member or manager participates in a tort. Liability of members of an LLC is limited, but not to the extent claimed by Keota.

* * *

We conclude that Keota is not protected from liability if it participated in tortious conduct in performing its duties as manager of Double Circle. Consequently, the district court improperly granted summary judgment based on the limited liability provisions of [citation]. A trial is necessary to develop the facts relating to allegations of Keota's participation in the alleged torts.

We reverse the summary judgment ruling of the district court on the issue of liability under [citation], and remand for further proceedings.

## QUESTIONS

1. Distinguish between a general partnership and a limited partnership.
2. Identify those activities in which a limited partner may engage without forfeiting limited liability.
3. Distinguish between a limited partnership and a limited liability company.
4. Distinguish between a member-managed limited liability company and a manager-managed limited liability company.
5. Distinguish between a limited liability partnership and a limited liability limited partnership.

## PROBLEMS

**1.** John Palmer and Henry Morrison formed the limited partnership of Palmer & Morrison for the management of the Huntington Hotel and filed an appropriate certificate in compliance with the limited partnership statute. The limited partnership agreement provided that Palmer would contribute $400,000 and be a general partner and that Morrison would contribute $300,000 and be a limited partner. Palmer was to manage the dining and cocktail rooms, and Morrison was to manage the rest of the hotel. Nanette, a popular French singer, who knew nothing of the limited partnership's affairs, appeared for four weeks in the Blue Room at the hotel and was not paid her fee of $8,000. Subsequently, the limited partnership became insolvent. Nanette sued Palmer and Morrison for $8,000.

**(a)** For how much, if anything, are Palmer and Morrison liable?

**(b)** If Palmer and Morrison had formed a limited liability limited partnership, for how much, if anything, would Palmer and Morrison be liable?

**(c)** If Palmer and Morrison had formed a limited liability company with each as members, for how much, if anything, would Palmer and Morrison be liable?

**(d)** If Palmer and Morrison had formed a limited liability partnership with each as general partners, for how much, if anything, would Palmer and Morrison be liable?

**2.** A limited partnership was formed consisting of Webster as general partner and Stevens and Stewart as the limited partners. The limited partnership was organized in strict compliance with the limited partnership statute. Stevens was employed by the partnership as a purchasing agent. Stewart personally guaranteed a loan made to the partnership. Both Stevens and Stewart consulted with Webster with respect to partnership business, voted on a change in the nature of the partnership business, and disapproved an amendment to the partnership agreement proposed by Webster. The partnership experienced serious financial difficulties, and its creditors seek to hold Webster, Stevens, and Stewart personally liable for the debts of the partnership. Who, if anyone, is personally liable?

**3.** Fox, Dodge, and Gilbey agreed to become limited partners in Palatine Ventures, a limited partnership. In a signed writing each agreed to contribute $20,000. Fox's contribution consisted entirely of cash; Dodge contributed $12,000 in cash and gave the partnership her promissory note for $8,000; and Gilbey's contribution was his promise to perform two hundred hours of legal services for the partnership.

**(a)** What liability, if any, do Fox, Dodge, and Gilbey have to the partnership by way of capital contribution?

**(b)** If Palatine Ventures had been formed as a limited liability company (LLC) with Fox, Dodge, and Gilbey as members, what liability, if any, would Fox, Dodge, and Gilbey have to the LLC by way of capital contribution?

**4.** Madison and Tilson agree to form a limited partnership with Madison as general partner and Tilson as the limited partner, each to contribute $12,500 as capital. No papers are ever filed, and after ten months the enterprise fails, its liabilities exceeding its assets by $30,000. Creditors of the partnership seek to hold Madison and Tilson personally liable for the $30,000. Explain whether the creditors will prevail.

**5.** Kraft is a limited partner of Johnson Enterprises, a limited partnership. As provided in the limited partnership agreement, Kraft decided to leave the partnership and demanded that her capital contribution of $20,000 be returned. At this time, the partnership assets were $150,000 and liabilities to all creditors totaled $140,000. The partnership returned to Kraft her capital contribution of $20,000.

**(a)** What liability, if any, does Kraft have to the creditors of Johnson Enterprises?

**(b)** If Johnson Enterprises had been formed as a limited liability company, what liability, if any, would Kraft have to the creditors of Johnson Enterprises?

**6.** Gordon is the only limited partner in Bushmill Ventures, a limited partnership whose general partners are Daniels and McKenna. Gordon contributed $10,000 for his limited partnership interest and loaned the partnership $7,500. Daniels and McKenna each contributed $5,000 by way of capital. After a year, the partnership is dissolved, at which time it owes $12,500 to its only creditor, Dickel, and has assets of $30,000.

**(a)** How should these assets be distributed?

**(b)** If Bushmill Ventures had been formed as a limited liability company with Gordon, Daniels, and McKenna as members, how should these assets be distributed?

**7.** Discuss when a limited partner does or does not have the following rights or powers: (a) to assign his interest in the limited partnership, (b) to receive repayment of loans made to the partnership on a *pro rata* basis with general creditors, (c) to manage the affairs of the limited partnership, (d) to receive his share of the profits before the general partners receive their shares of the profits, and (e) to dissolve the partnership upon his withdrawing from the partnership.

**8.** In January, Dr. Vidricksen contributed $250,000 to become a limited partner in a Chevrolet car agency business with Thom, the general partner. Articles of limited partnership were drawn up, but no effort was made to comply with the State's statutory requirement of recording the certificate of limited partnership. In March, Vidricksen learned that because of the failure to file, he might not have formed a limited partnership. At this time, the business developed financial difficulties and went into bankruptcy on September 11. Eight days later, Vidricksen filed a renunciation of the business's profits. Is Dr. Vidricksen a general partner?

**9.** Dale Fullerton was chairman of the board of Envirosearch and the sole stockholder in Westover Hills Management. James Anderson was president of AGFC. Fullerton and Anderson agreed to form a limited partnership to purchase certain property from WYORCO, a joint venture of which Fullerton was a member. The parties intended to form a limited partnership with Westover Hills Management as the sole general partner and AGFC and Envirosearch as limited partners. The certificate filed with the Wyoming Secretary of State, however, listed all three companies as both general and limited partners of Westover Hills Ltd. Anderson and Fullerton later became aware of this error and filed an amended certificate of limited partnership, which correctly named Envirosearch and AGFC as limited partners only. Subsequently Westover Hills Ltd. Became insolvent. What is the liability of Envirosearch and AGFC to creditors of the limited partnership?

**10.** Discuss when a member of a limited liability company does or does not have the following rights or powers: (a) to assign her interest in the LLC, (b) to receive repayment of loans made to the LLC on a *pro rata* basis with general creditors, (c) to manage the affairs of the LLC, and (d) to dissolve the LLC upon her withdrawing from the LLC.

**11.** Albert, Betty, and Carol own and operate the Roy Lumber Company, a limited liability partnership (LLP). Each contributed one-third of the capital, and they share equally in the profits and losses. Their LLP agreement provides that all purchases more than $2,500 must be authorized in advance by two partners and that only Albert is authorized to draw checks. Unknown to Albert or Carol, Betty purchases on the firm's account a $5,500 diamond bracelet and a $5,000 forklift and orders $5,000 worth of logs, all from Doug, who operates a jewelry store and is engaged in various activities connected with the lumber business. Before Betty made these purchases, Albert told Doug that Betty is not the log buyer. Albert refuses to pay Doug for Betty's purchases. Doug calls at the mill to collect, and Albert again refuses to pay him. Doug calls Albert an unprintable name, and Albert then punches Doug in the nose, knocking him out. While Doug is lying unconscious on the ground, an employee of Roy Lumber Company negligently drops a log on Doug's leg, breaking three bones. The firm and the three partners are completely solvent.

What are the rights of Doug against Roy Lumber Company, Albert, Betty, and Carol?

P A R T 7

# Corporations

# CHAPTER 34
# Nature, Formation, and Powers

A corporation is an entity created by law whose existence is distinct from that of the individuals whose initiative, property, and control enable it to function. In the opinion of the Supreme Court in *Dartmouth College v. Woodward*, 17 U.S. (4 Wheat.) 518, 4 L.Ed. 629 (1819), Chief Justice Marshall stated,

> A corporation is an artificial being, invisible, intangible, and existing only in contemplation of law. Being the mere creature of law, it possesses only those properties which the charter of its creation confers upon it, either expressly or as incidental to its very existence. These are such as are supposed best calculated to effect the object for which it was created. Among the most important are immortality, and, if the expression may be allowed, individuality; properties by which a perpetual succession of many persons are considered as the same, so that they may act as a single individual. A corporation manages its own affairs, and holds property without the hazardous and endless necessity of perpetual conveyances for the purpose of transmitting it from hand to hand.

The corporation is the dominant form of business organization in the United States, accounting for 85 percent of the gross revenues of all business entities. Approximately 6 million domestic corporations, with annual revenues approaching $30 trillion and assets exceeding $50 trillion, are currently doing business in the United States. Approximately 50 percent of American households own stock directly or indirectly through institutional investors, such as mutual funds, pension funds, banks, and insurance companies. Corporations have achieved this dominance because their attributes of limited liability, free transferability of shares, and continuity have attracted great numbers of widespread investors. Moreover, the centralized management of corporations has facilitated the development of large organizations that employ great quantities of invested capital, thereby utilizing economies of scale.

Use of the corporation as an instrument of commercial enterprise has made possible the vast concentrations of wealth and capital that have largely transformed this country's economy from an agrarian to an industrial one. Due to its size, power, and impact, the business corporation is a key institution not only in the American economy but also in the world power structure.

In 1946, a committee of the American Bar Association, after careful study and research, submitted a draft of a Model Business Corporation Act (MBCA). The MBCA has been amended frequently since then. Although the provisions of the Act do not become law until enacted by a State, its influence has been widespread; and a majority of the States had adopted it in whole or in part.

In 1984, the Committee on Corporate Laws of the Section of Corporation, Banking, and Business Law of the American Bar Association approved a Revised Model Business Corporation Act (RMBCA). The Revised Act is the first complete revision of the Model Act in more than thirty years, although the Act had been amended frequently since it was first published. More than half of the States have adopted it in whole or in part. The Revised Act is "designed to be a convenient guide for revision of state business corporation statutes, reflecting current views as to the appropriate accommodation of the various commercial and social interests involved in modern business corporations." One of the tasks of the revision was to organize the provisions of the Model Act more logically and to revise the language to make the Act more consistent. In addition, substantive changes were made in a number of areas. More than half of the States have adopted the Revised Act in whole or in part, although Delaware and seven of the ten most populous States have *not* adopted either the Model Act or the Revised Act. Moreover, many States have adopted selected provisions of the Revised Act. Since 1984, a number of sections of the Revised Act have been amended. The Revised Act as amended will be used throughout the chapters on corporations in this text and will be referred to as the Revised

Act or the RMBCA. Appendix E contains the RMBCA as amended.

## NATURE OF CORPORATIONS

To understand corporations, it is helpful to examine their common attributes and their various types. Both of these topics will be discussed in this section.

## CORPORATE ATTRIBUTES

The principal attributes of a corporation are as follows: (1) it is a legal entity; (2) it owes its existence to a State, which also regulates it; (3) it provides limited liability to its shareholders; (4) its shares of stock are freely transferable; (5) its existence may be perpetual; (6) its management is centralized; and it is considered, for some purposes, (7) a person and (8) a citizen.

◆ **SEE FIGURE 31-1: General Partnership, Limited Partnership, Limited Liability Company, and Corporation**

### LEGAL ENTITY

A corporation is a legal entity separate from its shareholders, with rights and liabilities entirely distinct from theirs. It may sue or be sued by, as well as contract with, any other party, including any one of its shareholders. A transfer of stock in the corporation from one individual to another has no effect upon the legal existence of the corporation. Title to corporate property belongs not to the shareholders but to the corporation. Even where a single individual owns all of the stock of a corporation, the existence of the shareholder is distinct from that of the corporation.

### CREATURE OF THE STATE

A corporation may be formed only by substantial compliance with a State incorporation statute. Every State has a general incorporation statute authorizing the Secretary of State to issue a certificate of incorporation or charter upon compliance with its provisions.

A corporation's charter and the provisions of the statute under which it is formed constitute a contract between it and the State. Article I, Section 10, of the U.S. Constitution provides that no State shall pass any law "impairing the obligation of contracts," and this prohibition applies to contracts between a State and a corporation. See *Chapter 4*.

To avoid the impact of this provision, incorporation statutes reserve to the State the power to establish such regulations, provisions, and limitations as it deems advisable and to amend or repeal the statute at its pleasure. Section 1.02. This reservation is a material part of the contract between the State and a corporation formed under the statute; consequently, because the contract expressly permits them, amendments or modifications regulating or altering the structure of the corporation do not impair the obligation of contract.

### LIMITED LIABILITY

A corporation is a legal entity and therefore is liable out of its own assets for its debts. Generally, the shareholders have **limited liability** for the corporation's debts—their liability does not extend beyond the amount of their investment—although, as discussed later in this chapter, under certain circumstances a shareholder may be personally liable. The limitation on liability, however, will not affect the liability of a shareholder who committed the wrongful act. A shareholder is also liable for any corporate obligations personally guaranteed by the individual member or manager.

### FREE TRANSFERABILITY OF CORPORATE SHARES

In the absence of contractual restrictions, shares in a corporation may be freely transferred by way of sale, gift, or pledge. The ability to transfer shares is a valuable right and may enhance their market value. Article 8 of the Uniform Commercial Code, Investment Securities, governs transfers of shares of stock.

### PERPETUAL EXISTENCE

A corporation's existence is perpetual unless otherwise stated in its articles of incorporation. Section 3.02. Consequently, the death, withdrawal, or addition of a shareholder, director, or officer does not terminate the existence of a corporation. A corporation's existence will terminate upon its dissolution or merger into another business.

### CENTRALIZED MANAGEMENT

The shareholders of a corporation elect a board of directors to manage the business of the corporation. The board in turn appoints officers to run the day-to-day operations of the business. As neither the directors nor the officers (collectively referred to as *management*) need be shareholders, it is entirely possible, and in large corporations quite typical, for ownership and management to be separate. The management structure of corporations is discussed in *Chapter 36*.

### AS A PERSON

Whether a corporation is a "person" within the meaning of a constitution or statute is a matter of construction based upon the intent of the lawmakers in using the word. For example, a corporation is considered a person within the provision in the Fifth and Fourteenth Amendments to the U.S. Constitution that no "person" shall be "deprived of life, liberty, or property without due process of law"; and in the provision in the Fourteenth Amendment that no State shall "deny to any person within its jurisdiction the equal protection of the laws." A corporation also enjoys the right of a person to be secure against unreasonable searches and seizures, as provided for in the Fourth Amendment. On the other hand, a corporation is not considered to be a person within the Fifth Amendment's clause that protects a "person" against self-incrimination.

### AS A CITIZEN

A corporation is considered a citizen for some purposes but not for others. A corporation is not deemed to be a citizen as the term is used in the Fourteenth Amendment, which provides, "No State shall make or enforce any law which shall abridge the privileges or immunities of citizens of the United States."

A corporation is, however, regarded as a citizen of the State of its incorporation and of the State in which it has its principal office for the purpose of identifying diversity of citizenship between the parties to a lawsuit and thereby providing a basis for Federal court jurisdiction.

## CLASSIFICATION OF CORPORATIONS

Corporations may be classified as public or private, profit or nonprofit, domestic or foreign, publicly held or closely held, Subchapter S, and professional. As will be seen, these classifications are not mutually exclusive. For example, a corporation may be a closely held, professional, private, profit, domestic corporation.

### PUBLIC OR PRIVATE

A **public corporation** is one that is created to administer a unit of local civil government, such as a county, city, town, village, school district or park district, or one created by the United States to conduct public business, such as the Tennessee Valley Authority or the Federal Deposit Insurance Corporation. A public corporation usually is created by specific legislation, which determines the corporation's purpose and powers. Many public corporations are also referred to as municipal corporations.

A **private corporation** is founded by and composed of private persons for private purposes and has no governmental duties. A private corporation may be for profit or nonprofit.

### PROFIT OR NONPROFIT

A **profit corporation** is one founded for the purpose of operating a business for profit from which payments are made to the corporation's shareholders in the form of dividends.

Although a **nonprofit** (or not-for-profit) **corporation** may make a profit, the profit may not be distributed to members, directors, or officers but must be used exclusively for the charitable, educational, or scientific purpose for which the corporation was organized. Examples of nonprofit corporations include private schools, library clubs, athletic clubs, fraternities, sororities, and hospitals. Most States have special incorporation statutes governing nonprofit corporations, most of which are patterned after the Model Nonprofit Corporation Act.

### DOMESTIC OR FOREIGN

A corporation is a **domestic corporation** in the State in which it is incorporated. It is a **foreign corporation** in every other State or jurisdiction. A corporation may not do business, except for acts in interstate commerce, in a State other than the State of its incorporation without the permission and authorization of the other State. Every State, however, provides for the issuance of certificates of authority that allow foreign corporations to do business within its borders and for the taxation of such foreign businesses. Obtaining a certificate (called "qualifying") usually involves filing certain information with the Secretary of State, paying prescribed fees, and designating a resident agent. Doing or transacting business within a particular State makes the corporation subject to local litigation, regulation, and taxation.

**Doing Business** The Revised Act does not attempt to fully define what constitutes the transaction of business. Instead, the Act provides a definition by exclusion by listing activities that do *not* constitute the transaction of business. Section 15.01. Generally, any conduct more regular, systematic, or extensive than that described in this section constitutes the transaction of business and requires a corporation to obtain a certificate of authority. Conduct typically requiring a certificate of authority includes maintaining an office to conduct local intrastate business, selling personal property not in interstate commerce, entering into contracts relating to local business or sales, and owning or using real estate for general corporate purposes. Section 15.01, Comment.

The Revised Act, as stated, provides a *nonexclusive* list of "safe harbors," that is, activities in which a foreign corporation may engage without being considered to have transacted intrastate business. The list includes the following:

1. maintaining bank accounts;
2. selling through independent contractors;
3. soliciting or obtaining orders, whether by mail or through employees or agents or otherwise, if such orders require acceptance outside the State before they become contracts;
4. owning, without more, real or personal property;

5. conducting an isolated transaction that is completed within thirty days and that is not one of a number of repeated transactions of like nature; and
6. transacting business in interstate commerce.

◆ **SEE CASE 34-1**

**Scope of Regulation** It is a common and accepted principle that local courts will not interfere with the internal affairs of a foreign corporation. To this end, the Revised Act states that "this Act does not authorize this state to regulate the organization or internal affairs of a foreign corporation." Section 15.05(c). Nevertheless, subjecting foreign corporations to reasonable regulation need not violate due process or constitute a burden on interstate commerce. A few States—most notably California and New York—regulate some of the internal affairs of foreign corporations that conduct a majority of their business in those States.

**Sanctions** A foreign corporation that transacts business without having first qualified may be subject to a number of penalties. Statutes in many States provide that an unlicensed foreign corporation doing business in a State shall not be entitled to maintain a suit in the State's courts until such corporation obtains a certificate of authority to transact business in that State. Failure to obtain such a certificate does not, however, impair the validity of a contract entered into by the corporation or prevent such corporation from defending any action or proceeding brought against it in the State. Section 15.02. In addition, most States impose fines upon an unqualified corporation, while a few States also impose fines upon the corporation's officers and directors, as well as holding them personally liable on contracts made within the State.

## PUBLICLY HELD OR CLOSELY HELD

A **publicly held corporation** is one whose shares are owned by a large number of people and are widely traded. There is no accepted minimum number of shareholders, but any corporation required to register under the Federal Securities and Exchange Act of 1934 is considered to be publicly held. In addition, corporations that have issued securities subject to a registered public distribution under the Federal Securities Act of 1933 usually are also considered publicly held. The Federal securities laws are discussed in *Chapter 44*. To distinguish publicly held corporations from other corporations, the Revised Act was amended to define the term "public corporation" as "a corporation that has shares listed on a national securities exchange or regularly traded in a market maintained by one or more members of a national securities association." Section 1.40(18A).

A **corporation** is described as **closely held** or **close** when its outstanding shares of stock are held by a small number of persons who often are family, relatives, or friends. In most closely held corporations, the shareholders are active in the management and control of the business. Accordingly, they are concerned about the identities of their fellow shareholders, a concern that frequently leads shareholders to restrict the transfer of shares to prevent "outsiders" from obtaining stock in a closely held corporation. See the discussion of *Galler v. Galler* in *Chapter 36*. Although a vast majority of corporations in the United States are closely held, they account for only a small fraction of corporate revenues and assets.

In most States, closely held corporations are subject to the general incorporation statute that governs all corporations. The Revised Act includes a number of liberalizing provisions for closely held corporations. In addition, about twenty States have enacted special legislation to accommodate the needs of such corporations, and a Statutory Close Corporation Supplement to the Model and Revised Acts was promulgated. The Supplement applies only to those eligible corporations that elect statutory close corporation status. To be eligible, a corporation must have fewer than fifty shareholders. A corporation may voluntarily terminate statutory close corporation status. Other provisions of the Supplement will be discussed in this and other chapters.

In 1991 the Revised Act was amended to authorize shareholders in closely held corporations to adopt unanimous shareholders' agreements that depart from the statutory norms by altering (1) the governance of the corporation, (2) the allocation of the economic return from the business, and (3) other aspects of the relationship among shareholders, directors, and the corporation. Section 7.32. Such a shareholder agreement is valid for ten years unless the agreement provides otherwise but terminates automatically if the corporation's shares become publicly traded. Shareholder agreements validated by Section 7.32 bind only the shareholders and the corporation; they do not bind the State, creditors, or other third parties. The provisions of Section 7.32 will be discussed in this and other chapters.

## SUBCHAPTER S CORPORATION

Subchapter S of the Internal Revenue Code permits a corporation meeting specified requirements to elect to be taxed essentially as though it were a partnership. (Approximately two-thirds of all corporations in the United States are Chapter S corporations, but they account for only 20 percent of total corporate revenues and less than 5 percent of total corporate assets.) Under subchapter S, a corporation's income is taxed only once at the individual shareholder level. The requirements for a corporation to elect subchapter S treatment are (1) it must be a domestic corporation; (2) it must have no more than one hundred shareholders; (3) each shareholder must be an individual, or an estate, or certain types of trusts;

(4) no shareholder may be a nonresident alien; and (5) it may have only one class of stock, although classes of common stock differing only in voting rights are permitted.

### PROFESSIONAL CORPORATIONS

All of the States have professional association or corporation statutes that permit duly licensed individuals to practice their professions within the corporate form. Some statutes apply to all professions licensed to practice within the State, while others apply only to specified professions. There is a Model Professional Corporation Supplement to the MBCA.

## FORMATION OF A CORPORATION

The formation of a corporation under a general incorporation statute requires the action of various groups, individuals, and State officials. The procedure to organize a corporation begins with the promotion of the proposed corporation by its organizers, also known as promoters, who procure offers by interested persons, known as subscribers, to buy stock in the corporation, once created, and who prepare the necessary incorporation papers. The incorporators then execute the articles of incorporation and file them with the Secretary of State, who issues the charter or certificate of incorporation. Finally, an organizational meeting is held.

## ORGANIZING THE CORPORATION

### PROMOTERS

A **promoter** is a person who brings about the "birth" of a corporation by arranging for capital and financing; assembling the necessary assets, equipment, licenses, personnel, leases, and services; and attending to the actual legal formation of the corporation. Upon incorporation, the promoter's organizational task is finished.

**Promoters' Contracts** In addition to procuring subscriptions and preparing the incorporation papers, promoters often enter into contracts in anticipation of the creation of the corporation. The contracts may be ordinary agreements necessary for the eventual operation of the business, such as leases, purchase orders, employment contracts, sales contracts, or franchises. If the promoter executes these contracts in her own name and there is no further action, the promoter is liable on such contracts; the corporation, when created, is not liable. Moreover, a preincorporation contract made by a promoter in the name of the corporation and on its behalf does not bind the corporation. The promoter, in executing such contracts, may do so in the corporate name even if incorporation has yet to occur. Before its formation, a corporation has no capacity to enter into contracts or to employ agents or representatives. After its formation, it is not liable at common law upon any prior contract, even one made in its name, unless it adopts the contract expressly, impliedly, or by knowingly accepting benefits under it.

A promoter who enters into a preincorporation contract in the name of the corporation usually remains liable on that contract even if the corporation adopts it. This liability results from the rule of agency law stating that to be able to ratify a contract, a principal must be in existence at the time the contract is made. A promoter will be relieved of liability, however, if the contract provides that adoption shall terminate the promoter's liability or if the promoter, the third party, and the corporation enter into a novation substituting the corporation for the promoter.

◈ **SEE FIGURE 34-1: Promoter's Preincorporation Contracts Made in Corporation's Name**

◆ **SEE CASE 34-2**

**Promoters' Fiduciary Duty** The promoters of a corporation owe a fiduciary duty to one another as well as to the corporation, its subscribers, and its initial shareholders. This duty requires good faith, fair dealing, and full disclosure to an independent board of directors. If an independent board has not been elected, then full disclosure must be made to all shareholders. Accordingly, the promoters are under a duty to account for any *secret* profit they realize. Failure to disclose also may constitute a violation of Federal or State securities laws.

### SUBSCRIBERS

A **preincorporation subscription** is an offer to purchase capital stock in a corporation yet to be formed. The offeror is called a "subscriber." Courts traditionally have viewed subscriptions in one of two ways. The majority regard a subscription as a continuing offer to purchase stock from a nonexisting entity, incapable of accepting the offer until it exists. Under this view, a subscription may be revoked at any time prior to its acceptance. In contrast, a minority of jurisdictions treat a subscription as a contract among the various subscribers, rendering the subscription irrevocable except with the subscribers' unanimous consent. Most incorporation statutes have adopted an intermediate position making preincorporation subscriptions irrevocable for a stated period without regard to whether they are supported by consideration. For example, the Revised Act provides that a preincorporation subscription is irrevocable for six months, unless the subscription agreement provides a different period or all of the subscribers consent to the revocation. Section 6.20. If the corporation accepts the subscription during the period of

◆ FIGURE 34-1: **Promoter's Preincorporation Contracts Made in Corporation's Name**

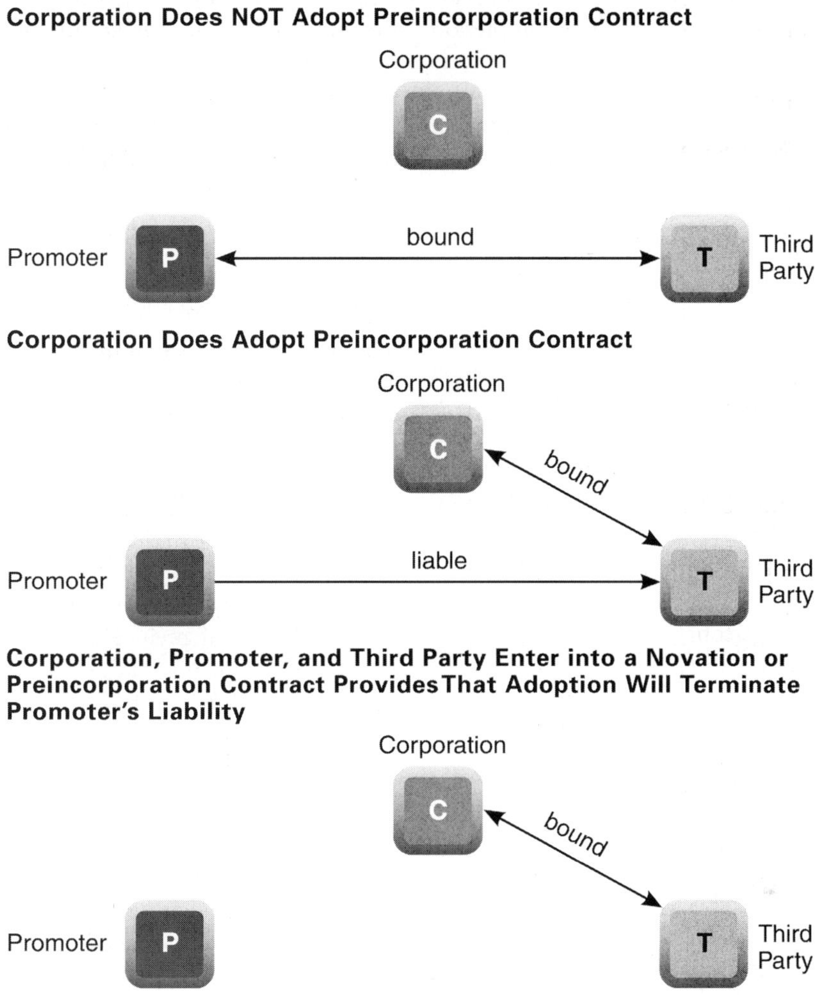


irrevocability, the subscription becomes a contract binding on both the subscriber and the corporation.

A **postincorporation subscription** is a subscription agreement entered into after incorporation. It is treated as a contract between the subscriber and the corporation. RMBCA Section 6.20(e). Unlike preincorporation subscriptions, the subscriber may withdraw her offer to enter into a postincorporation subscription anytime before the corporation accepts it. She cannot, however, withdraw the offer after the corporation has accepted it as the acceptance forms a contract.

### SELECTION OF STATE FOR INCORPORATION

A corporation is usually incorporated in the State in which it intends to be located and to transact all or the principal part of its business. Nevertheless, a corporation may be formed in one State and have its principal place of business and conduct all or most of its operations in another State or States by duly qualifying and obtaining a certificate of authority to transact business in those States. The principal criteria in selecting a State for incorporation include the flexibility accorded management, the rights granted to shareholders, the protection provided against takeovers, the limitations imposed upon the issuance of shares, the restrictions placed upon the payment of dividends, and organizational costs such as fees and taxes.

## FORMALITIES OF INCORPORATION

Although the procedure involved in organizing a corporation varies somewhat from State to State, typically the incorporators execute and deliver articles of incorporation to the Secretary of State or another designated official. The Revised Act provides that after incorporation, the board of directors named in the articles of incorporation shall hold an organizational meeting for the purpose of adopting bylaws, appointing officers, and carrying on any other business brought before the meeting. Section 2.05. After completion of these organizational details, the corporation's officers and board of directors manage its business and affairs. Several States require that a corporation have a minimum amount of capital, usually $1,000, before doing any business. The Revised Act and most States have eliminated this requirement.

### SELECTION OF NAME

Most general incorporation laws require that a corporate name contain a word or words that clearly identify the organization as a corporation, such as *corporation, company, incorporated, limited, Corp., Co., Inc.*, or *Ltd.* Section 4.01. Furthermore, the name must be distinguishable from the name of any domestic corporation or any foreign corporation authorized to do business within the State. Section 4.01.

### INCORPORATORS

The **incorporators** are the persons who sign the articles of incorporation, which are filed with the Secretary of State of the State of incorporation. Although they perform a necessary function, in many States their services as incorporators are perfunctory and short-lived, ending with the organizational meeting. Furthermore, modern statutes have greatly relaxed the qualifications of incorporators and also have reduced the number required. The Revised Act and all States provide that only one person need act as the incorporator or incorporators, though more may do so. Section 2.01. The Revised Act and most States permit artificial entities to serve as incorporators. For example, the Revised Act defines a person to include individuals and entities, with an entity defined to include domestic and foreign corporations, not-for-profit corporations, profit and not-for-profit unincorporated associations, business trusts, estates, partnerships, and trusts. Section 1.40.

### ARTICLES OF INCORPORATION

The articles of incorporation, or **charter**, is generally a rather simple document that under the Revised Act must include the name of the corporation, the number of authorized shares, the street address of the registered office and the name of the registered agent, and the name and address of each incorporator. Section 2.02(a). The Act also permits the charter to include optional information such as the identities of the corporation's initial directors, corporate purposes, procedures for managing internal affairs, powers of the corporation, the par value of shares, and any provision required or permitted to be set forth in the bylaws. Some optional provisions may be elected *only* in the charter, including cumulative voting, supermajority voting requirements, preemptive rights, and limitations on the personal liability of directors for breach of their duty of care.

To form a corporation, the charter, once it is drawn up, must be executed and filed with the Secretary of State. The articles of incorporation then become the basic governing document of the corporation, so long as its provisions are consistent with State and Federal law.

◆ **SEE FIGURE 34-2: Sample Articles of Incorporation**

### ORGANIZATIONAL MEETING

The Revised Act and most States require that an organizational meeting be held to adopt the new corporation's bylaws, appoint officers, and carry on any other business brought before it. If the articles do not name the corporation's initial directors, the incorporators hold the organizational meeting to elect directors, after which either the incorporators or the directors complete the organization of the corporation. Section 2.05. Additional business that may be brought before the meeting typically includes authorization to issue shares of stock, approval of preincorporation contracts made by promoters, selection of a bank, and approval of a corporate seal and the form of stock certificates.

### BYLAWS

The **bylaws** of a corporation are the rules and regulations that govern its internal management. Because bylaws are necessary to the organization of the corporation, their adoption is one of the first items of business at the organizational meeting held promptly after incorporation. Under the Revised Act, either the incorporators or the board of directors may adopt the bylaws. Section 2.06.

The bylaws may contain any provision for managing the business and regulating the affairs of the corporation that is not inconsistent with law or the articles of incorporation. Section 2.06. In contrast to the articles of incorporation, the bylaws do not have to be publicly filed. Under the Revised Act, the shareholders may amend or repeal the bylaws, as may the board of directors, unless (1) the articles of incorporation or other sections of the RMBCA reserve that power exclusively to the shareholders in whole or in part, or (2) the shareholders in amending, repealing, or adopting a bylaw expressly provide that the board of directors may not amend, repeal, or reinstate that bylaw. Section 10.20.

The Statutory Close Corporation Supplement (Section 22) permits close corporations to avoid the adoption of bylaws by including either in a shareholder agreement or in the articles of incorporation all information required in corporate bylaws.

◆ **SEE FIGURE 34-3: Comparison of Charter and Bylaws**

## FIGURE 34-2: Sample Articles of Incorporation

**ARTICLES OF INCORPORATION OF [CORPORATE NAME]**

The undersigned, acting as incorporator(s) of a corporation under the ____________ Business Corporation Act, adopt(s) the following Articles of Incorporation for such corporation:

*First:* The name of the corporation is ____________________________________________

____________________________________________

*Second:* The period of its duration is ____________________________________________

____________________________________________

*Third:* The purpose or purposes for which the corporation is organized are ______________________

____________________________________________

*Fourth:* The aggregate number of shares which the corporation shall have authority to issue is ____________

____________________________________________

*Fifth:* Provisions granting preemptive rights are ______________________________

____________________________________________

*Sixth:* Provisions for the regulation of the internal affairs of the corporation are ______________________

____________________________________________

*Seventh:* The address of the initial registered office of the corporation is ______________________

and the name of its initial registered agent at such address is ______________________________

*Eighth:* The number of directors constituting the initial board of directors of the corporation is ____________, and the names and addresses of the persons who are to serve as directors until the first annual meeting of shareholders or until their successors are elected and shall qualify are

| Name | Address |
|---|---|
| ____________________ | ____________________ |
| ____________________ | ____________________ |
| ____________________ | ____________________ |

*Ninth:* The name and address of each incorporator is

| Name | Address |
|---|---|
| ____________________ | ____________________ |
| ____________________ | ____________________ |
| ____________________ | ____________________ |

Dated ____________, 20 ________. ____________________

____________________

____________________

Source: Reprinted from *Corporations*, 3rd ed., by Henn & Alexander, copyright 1983 with permission of the West Group.

## RECOGNITION OR DISREGARD OF CORPORATENESS

Business associates choose to incorporate to obtain one or more corporate attributes—primarily limited liability and perpetual existence. Because a corporation is a creature of the State, such attributes are recognized when the enterprise complies with the State's requirements for incorporation. Although the formal procedures are relatively simple, errors or omissions sometimes occur. In some cases the mistakes may be trivial, such as incorrectly stating an incorporator's address; in other instances the error may be more significant, such as a complete failure to file the articles of incorporation. The consequences of procedural noncompliance depend upon the seriousness of the error. Conversely, even when a corporation has been formed in strict compliance with the incorporation statute, a court may disregard the corporateness of the enterprise if justice requires. This section addresses these two complementary issues.

## DEFECTIVE INCORPORATION

Although modern incorporation statutes have greatly simplified incorporation procedures, defective incorporations do occur. The possible consequences of a defective incorporation include the following: (1) the State brings an action against the association for involuntary dissolution, (2) the associates are held personally liable to a third party, (3) the association asserts that it is not liable on an obligation, or (4) a third party asserts that it is not liable to the association. Corporate statutes addressing this issue have taken an approach considerably different from that of the common law.

### COMMON LAW APPROACH

Under the common law, a defectively formed corporation was, under certain circumstances, accorded corporate attributes. The courts developed a set of doctrines granting corporateness to *de jure* (of right) corporations, *de facto* (of fact) corporations, and corporations by estoppel but denying corporateness to corporations that were too defectively formed.

**CORPORATION *DE JURE*** A corporation *de jure* is one that has been formed in substantial compliance with the incorporation statute and the required organizational procedure. Once such a corporation is formed, its existence may not be challenged by anyone, even by the State in a direct proceeding for this purpose.

**CORPORATION *DE FACTO*** Though it fails to comply substantially with the incorporation statute (and therefore is not *de jure*), a corporation *de facto* nevertheless is recognized for most purposes as a corporation. A failure to form a *de jure* corporation may result in the formation of a *de facto* corporation if the following requirements are met: (1) the existence of a general corporation statute, (2) a *bona fide* attempt to comply with that law in organizing a corporation under the statute, and (3) the actual exercise of corporate power by conducting business in the belief that a corporation has been formed. If the corporation sues to collect a debt, the fact that the corporation is not *de jure* is not a defense. Furthermore, the existence of the *de facto* corporation can be challenged only by the State, though not even the State can question its existence collaterally (in a proceeding involving some other issue). The State must bring an independent suit against the corporation for this express purpose, known as an action of *quo warranto* ("by what right").

**CORPORATION BY ESTOPPEL** The doctrine of corporation by estoppel is distinct from that of corporation *de facto*. Estoppel does not create a corporation. It operates only to prevent a person or persons under the facts and circumstances of a particular case from questioning a corporation's existence or its capacity to act or to own property. Corporation by estoppel requires a holding out by a purported corporation or its

◆ FIGURE 34-3: **Comparison of Charter and Bylaws**

| | Charter | Bylaws |
|---|---|---|
| **Filing** | Publicly | Not publicly |
| **Amendment** | Requires board and shareholder approval | Requires only board approval |
| **Availability** | Must include certain mandatory provisions; may include optional provisions although some optional provisions may be elected only in the charter | Must include certain provisions unless they are included in the charter |
| **Validity** | May include any provision not inconsistent with law | May include any provision not inconsistent with law and the charter |

associates and reliance by a third party. In addition, application of the doctrine depends on equitable considerations. A person who has dealt with a defectively organized corporation may be precluded or estopped from denying its corporate existence where the necessary elements of holding out and reliance are present. The doctrine can be applied not only to third parties but also to the purported corporation and to the associates who held themselves out as a corporation.

**Defective Corporation** If the associates who purported to form a corporation so fail to comply with the requirements of the incorporation statute that neither a *de jure* nor a *de facto* corporation is formed and the circumstances do not justify applying the corporation by estoppel doctrine, the courts generally deny the associates the benefits of incorporation. This results in some or all of the associates being held unlimitedly liable for the obligations of the business.

### STATUTORY APPROACH

While the common law approach to defective incorporation is cumbersome both in theory and in application, incorporation statutes now address the issue more simply. All States provide that corporate existence begins either upon the filing of the articles of incorporation or their acceptance by the Secretary of State. Moreover, the Revised Act and most States provide the *filing* or acceptance of the articles of incorporation by the Secretary of State is conclusive proof that the incorporators have satisfied all conditions precedent to incorporation, except in a proceeding brought by the State. Section 2.03(b). This applies even if the articles of incorporation contain mistakes or omissions.

With respect to the attribute of limited liability, the original Model Act and a few States provide that "[a]ll persons who assume to act as a corporation without authority so to do shall be jointly and severally liable for all debts and liabilities incurred or arising as a result thereof." Section 146. The Revised Act, however, imposes liability *only* on persons who purport to act as or on behalf of a corporation, knowing that there was no incorporation. Section 2.04.

Consider the following two illustrations: First, Smith had been shown executed articles of incorporation some months before he invested in the corporation and became an officer and director. He was also told by the corporation's attorney that the articles had been filed; however, because of confusion in the attorney's office, the filing had not in fact occurred. Under the Revised Act and many court decisions, Smith would not be held personally liable for the obligations of the defective corporation. Second, Jones represents that a corporation exists and enters into a contract in the corporate name when she knows that no corporation has been formed because no attempt has been made to file articles of incorporation. Jones would be held liable for the obligations of the defective corporation under the Model Act, the Revised Act, and most court decisions involving similar situations. RMBCA Section 2.04 and Comment.

◆ **SEE CASE 34-3**

## PIERCING THE CORPORATE VEIL

If substantial compliance with the incorporation statute results in a *de jure* or *de facto* corporation, the courts generally will recognize corporateness and its attendant attributes, including limited liability. Nonetheless, the courts will disregard the corporate entity when it is used to defeat public convenience, commit a wrongdoing, protect fraud, or circumvent the law. Going behind the corporate entity to confront those seeking to insulate themselves from personal accountability and the consequences of their wrongdoing is known as piercing the corporate veil. Courts will pierce the corporate veil where they deem such action necessary to remedy wrongdoing. However, there is no commonly accepted test used by the courts. They have done so most frequently in regard to closely held corporations and parent-subsidiary relationships. It should be noted that piercing the corporate veil is the exception, and in most cases courts uphold the separateness of corporations.

### CLOSELY HELD CORPORATIONS

The joint and active management by all the shareholders of closely held corporations frequently results in a tendency to forgo corporate formalities, such as holding meetings of the board and shareholders, while the small size of close corporations often renders creditors unable to fully satisfy their claims against the corporation. Such frustrated creditors often ask the court to disregard an organization's corporateness and to impose personal liability for the corporate obligations upon the shareholders. Courts have responded by piercing the corporate veil in cases in which the shareholders (1) have not conducted the business on a corporate basis, (2) have not provided an adequate financial basis for the business, or (3) have used the corporation to defraud. For example, *in D.I. Felsenthal Co. v. Northern Assurance Co.* 284 Ill. 343,120 N.E. 268 (1918), Felsenthal Company sued the Northern Assurance Company to collect on its fire insurance policy. Northern claimed that it was not liable under the policy because Felsenthal's property had been destroyed by a fire instigated by Fox, the president, director, creditor, and principal shareholder of Felsenthal. The court ruled in favor of Northern Assurance because the instigator of the fire, Fox, was the beneficial owner of almost all of Felsenthal's stock as well as the corporation's president and director. Under those circumstances, the corporation could not recover because to allow such a recovery would allow a wrongdoer to benefit from his own illegal act. The corporate form could not be used in this case to protect Fox and to aid him in his plan to defraud the insurance company.

Conducting the business on a corporate basis involves separately maintaining the corporation's funds and the shareholders' funds, maintaining separate financial records, holding regular directors' meetings, and generally observing corporate formalities. Adequate capitalization requires that the shareholders invest capital or purchase liability insurance sufficient to meet the reasonably anticipated requirements of the enterprise.

The Revised Act validates unanimous shareholder agreements by which the shareholders may relax traditional corporate formalities. Section 7.32. The Revised Act further provides that the existence or performance of an agreement authorized by Section 7.32

> shall not be grounds for imposing personal liability on any shareholder for the acts or the debts of the corporation even if the agreement or its performance treats the corporation as if it were a partnership or results in failure to observe the corporate formalities otherwise applicable to the matters governed by the agreement.

Thus, this section narrows the grounds for imposing personal liability on shareholders for the liabilities of a corporation for acts or omissions authorized by a shareholder agreement validated by Section 7.32.

The Statutory Close Corporation Supplement validates several arrangements whereby the shareholders may relax traditional corporate formalities. Section 25 of the Supplement provides: "The failure of a statutory close corporation to observe the usual corporate formalities or requirements relating to the exercise of its corporate powers or management of its business and affairs is not a ground for imposing personal liability on the shareholders for liabilities of the corporation." Courts may still pierce the corporate veil of a statutory close corporation if the same circumstances would justify imposing personal liability on the shareholders of a general business corporation. The Supplement simply prevents a court from piercing the corporate veil just because the corporation is a statutory close corporation.

### PARENT-SUBSIDIARY CORPORATIONS

A corporation wishing to risk only a portion of its assets in a particular enterprise may choose to form a **subsidiary corporation**. A subsidiary corporation is one in which another corporation, the **parent corporation**, owns at least a majority of the shares and over which the other corporation therefore has control. Courts may pierce the corporate veil and hold the parent liable for the debts of its subsidiary if any of the following criteria are met:

1. both corporations are not adequately capitalized, *or*
2. the formalities of separate corporate procedures are not observed, *or*
3. each corporation is not held out to the public as a separate enterprise, *or*
4. the funds of the two corporations are commingled, *or*
5. the parent corporation completely dominates the subsidiary solely to advance its own interests.

So long as a parent and a subsidiary avoid these pitfalls, the courts generally will recognize the subsidiary as a separate entity, even if the parent owns all the subsidiary's stock and the two corporations share facilities, employees, directors, and officers.

◆ **SEE CASE 34-4**

## CORPORATE POWERS

Because a corporation derives its existence and all of its powers from its State of incorporation, it possesses only those powers that the State confers on it. These powers consist of those expressly set forth in the statute unless limited by the articles of incorporation.

## SOURCES OF CORPORATE POWERS

### STATUTORY POWERS

Typical of the general corporate powers granted by incorporation statutes are those provided by Section 3.02 of the Revised Act, which include the following:

1. to have perpetual succession;
2. to sue and be sued in the corporate name;
3. to have a corporate seal;
4. to make and amend bylaws for managing the business and regulating the affairs of the corporation;
5. to acquire, own, improve, use, and dispose of real or personal property;
6. to own, vote, and dispose of shares or other interests in, or obligations of, any other entity;
7. to make contracts and guarantees; incur liabilities; borrow money; issue notes, bonds, and other obligations; and secure any corporate obligations;
8. to lend money, invest and reinvest funds, and receive and hold real and personal property as security for repayment;
9. to be a promoter, partner, member, associate, or manager of any partnership, joint venture, trust, or other entity;
10. to conduct business, locate offices, and exercise the powers granted by the Act within or without the State of incorporation;
11. to elect directors and appoint officers, employees, and agents; define their duties; fix their compensation; and lend them money and credit;

12. to pay pensions and establish pension plans, pension trusts, profit sharing plans, share bonus plans, share option plans, and benefit or incentive plans for any or all current or former directors, officers, employees, and agents;
13. to make donations for the public welfare or for charitable, scientific, or educational purposes;
14. to transact any lawful business that will aid governmental policy; and
15. to make payments or donations or do any other act, not inconsistent with law, that furthers the business and affairs of the corporation.

In most States this list is not exclusive. Moreover, the Revised Act also grants to all corporations the same powers as individuals have to do all things necessary or convenient to carry out their business and affairs. Section 3.02.

### PURPOSES

All State incorporation statutes provide that a corporation may be formed for any lawful purposes. The Revised Act permits a corporation's articles of incorporation to state a more limited purpose. Many State statutes, but not the RMBCA, require that the articles of incorporation specify the corporation's purposes although they usually permit a general statement that the corporation is formed to engage in any lawful purpose.

## *ULTRA VIRES* ACTS

Because a corporation has authority to act only within its powers, any action or contract that is not within the scope and type of acts which the corporation is legally empowered to perform is *ultra vires*. The doctrine of *ultra vires* is less significant today because modern statutes permit incorporation for any lawful purpose, and most articles of incorporation do not limit corporate powers. Consequently, far fewer acts are *ultra vires*.

### EFFECT OF *ULTRA VIRES* ACTS

Traditionally, *ultra vires* contracts were unenforceable as null and void. Under the modern approach, courts allow the *ultra vires* defense where the contract is wholly executory on both sides. A corporation having received full performance from the other party to the contract is not permitted to escape liability by a plea of *ultra vires*. Conversely, the defense of *ultra vires* is unavailable to a corporation suing for breach of a contract which has been fully performed on its side.

Almost all statutes have abolished the defense of *ultra vires* in an action by or against a corporation. The Revised Act provides that "the validity of corporate action may not be challenged on the ground that the corporation lacks or lacked the power to act." Section 3.04. This section extends beyond contract actions to encompass any corporate action, including conveyances of property. Thus, under this section, persons dealing with a corporation need not examine its articles of incorporation for limitations upon its purposes or powers. The section does not, however, validate illegal corporate actions.

### REMEDIES FOR *ULTRA VIRES* ACTS

Although *ultra vires* under modern statutes may no longer be used as a shield against liability, corporate activities that are *ultra vires* may be redressed in any of three ways, as provided by Section 3.04(b) of the Revised Act:

1. in a proceeding by a shareholder against the corporation to enjoin the unauthorized act, if such an injunction is equitable and if all affected persons are parties to the proceeding, and the court may award damages for losses suffered by the corporation or another party because of enjoining the unauthorized act;
2. in a proceeding by the corporation, or a shareholder derivatively (in a representative capacity), against the incumbent or former directors or officers for exceeding their authority; or
3. in a proceeding by the Attorney General of the State of incorporation to dissolve the corporation or to enjoin it from transacting unauthorized business.

## LIABILITY FOR TORTS AND CRIMES

A corporation is liable for the torts its agents commit in the course of their employment. The doctrine of *ultra vires*, even in those jurisdictions where it is permitted as a defense, does not apply to wrongdoing by the corporation. The doctrine of *respondeat superior* imposes full liability upon a corporation for the torts its agents and employees commit during the course of their employment. For example, Robert, a truck driver employed by the Webster Corporation, negligently runs over Pamela, a pedestrian, while on a business errand. Both Robert and the Webster Corporation are liable to Pamela in her action to recover damages for the injuries she sustained. A corporation also may be found liable for fraud, false imprisonment, malicious prosecution, libel, and other torts, though some States hold the corporation liable for *punitive* damages only if it authorized or ratified the agent's act.

Historically, corporations were not held criminally liable because, under the traditional view, a corporation could not possess the criminal intent requisite to committing a crime. Dramatic growth in the size and importance of corporations has changed this view. Under the modern approach, a corporation may be liable for violating statutes that impose liability without fault. In addition, a corporation may be liable for an offense perpetrated by a high corporate officer or by its board of directors. Punishment of a corporation for crimes is necessarily by fine, not imprisonment.

# CHAPTER SUMMARY

## NATURE OF CORPORATIONS

### CORPORATE ATTRIBUTES

**Legal Entity** a corporation is an entity apart from its shareholders, with entirely distinct rights and liabilities
**Creature of the State** a corporation may be formed only by substantial compliance with a State incorporation statute
**Limited Liability** a shareholder's liability is limited to the amount invested in the business enterprise
**Free Transferability of Corporate Shares** unless otherwise specified in the charter
**Perpetual Existence** unless the charter provides otherwise
**Centralized Management** shareholders of a corporation elect the board of directors to manage its business affairs; the board appoints officers to run the day-to-day operations of the business
**As a Person** a corporation is considered a person for some but not all purposes
**As a Citizen** a corporation is considered a citizen for some but not all purposes

### CLASSIFICATION OF CORPORATIONS

**Public or Private**
- ***Public Corporation*** one created to administer a unit of local civil government or one created by the United States to conduct public business
- ***Private Corporation*** one founded by and composed of private persons for private purposes; has no governmental duties

**Profit or Nonprofit**
- ***Profit Corporation*** one founded to operate a business for profit
- ***Nonprofit Corporation*** one whose profits must be used exclusively for charitable, educational, or scientific purposes

**Domestic or Foreign**
- ***Domestic Corporation*** one created under the laws of a given State
- ***Foreign Corporation*** one created under the laws of any other State or jurisdiction; it must obtain a certificate of authority from each State in which it does intrastate business

**Publicly Held or Closely Held**
- ***Publicly Held Corporation*** one whose shares are owned by a large number of people and are widely traded
- ***Closely Held Corporation*** one that is owned by few shareholders and whose shares are not actively traded

**Subchapter S Corporation** eligible corporation electing to be taxed as a partnership under the Internal Revenue Code
**Professional Corporations** corporate form under which duly licensed individuals may practice their professions

## FORMATION OF A CORPORATION

### ORGANIZING THE CORPORATION

**Promoter** person who takes the preliminary steps to organize a corporation
- ***Promoters' Contracts*** promoters remain liable on preincorporation contracts made in the name of the corporation unless the contract provides otherwise or unless a novation is effected

- ***Promoters' Fiduciary Duty*** promoters owe a fiduciary duty among themselves and to the corporation, its subscribers, and its initial shareholders

**Subscribers** persons who agree to purchase the initial stock in a corporation

- ***Preincorporation Subscription*** an offer to purchase capital stock in a corporation yet to be formed which under many incorporation statutes is irrevocable for a specified time period
- ***Postincorporation Subscription*** a subscription agreement entered into after incorporation; an offer to enter into such a subscription is revocable anytime before the corporation accepts it

---

**FORMALITIES OF INCORPORATION**

**Selection of Name** the name must clearly designate the entity as a corporation

**Incorporators** the persons who sign the articles of incorporation

**Articles of Incorporation** the charter or basic organizational document of a corporation

**Organizational Meeting** the first meeting, held to adopt the bylaws and appoint officers

**Bylaws** rules governing a corporation's internal management

---

## RECOGNITION OR DISREGARD OF CORPORATENESS

**DEFECTIVE INCORPORATION**

**Common Law Approach**

- ***Corporation* de Jure** one formed in substantial compliance with the incorporation statute and having all corporate attributes
- ***Corporation* de Facto** one not formed in compliance with the statute but recognized for most purposes as a corporation
- ***Corporation by Estoppel*** prevents a person from raising the question of a corporation's existence
- ***Defective Corporation*** the associates are denied the benefits of incorporation

**Statutory Approach** the filing or acceptance of the articles of incorporation is generally conclusive proof of proper incorporation

- ***Revised Model Business Corporation Act (RMBCA)*** liability is imposed only on persons who act on behalf of a defectively formed corporation knowing that there was no incorporation
- ***Model Business Corporation Act (MBCA)*** unlimited personal liability is imposed on all persons who act on behalf of a defectively formed corporation

---

**PIERCING THE CORPORATE VEIL**

**General Rule** the courts may disregard the corporate entity when it is used to defeat public convenience, commit a wrongdoing, protect fraud, or circumvent the law

**Application** most frequently applied to

- ***Closely Held Corporations***
- ***Parent-Subsidiary Corporations***

---

## CORPORATE POWERS

**SOURCES OF CORPORATE POWERS**

**Statutory Powers** typically include perpetual existence, right to hold property in the corporate name, and all powers necessary or convenient to effect the corporation's purposes

**Purposes** a corporation may be formed for any lawful purposes unless its articles of incorporation state a more limited purpose

| | |
|---|---|
| ***ULTRA VIRES* ACTS** | **Definition of *Ultra Vires* Acts** any action or contract that goes beyond a corporation's express and implied powers<br>**Effect of *Ultra Vires* Acts** under RMBCA, *ultra vires* acts and conveyances are not invalid<br>**Remedies for *Ultra Vires* Acts** the RMBCA provides three possible remedies |
| **LIABILITY FOR TORTS AND CRIMES** | **Torts** under the doctrine of *respondeat superior*, a corporation is liable for torts committed by its employees within the course of their employment<br>**Crimes** a corporation may be criminally liable for violations of statutes imposing liability without fault or for an offense perpetrated by a high corporate officer or its board of directors |

# CASES

## CASE 34-1

### Foreign Corporation
### HAROLD LANG JEWELERS, INC. v. JOHNSON

Court of Appeals of North Carolina, 2003
156 N.C.App. 187, 576 S.E.2d 360; review denied, 357 N.C. 458, 585 S.E.2d 765
http://www.aoc.state.nc.us/www/public/coa/opinions/2003/020429-1.htm

**Hudson, J.**

[Harold Lang Jewelers, Inc. ("Lang")] filed suit * * * alleging that Johnson owed it $160,322.90 plus interest for jewelry sold or consigned. Johnson answered * * * asserting as one of its eight affirmative defenses that Lang could not sue in a North Carolina court because Lang had failed to obtain a certificate of authority to transact business in the state. * * * [T]he district court granted the motion and dismissed Lang's action. Lang now appeals.

* * *

* * * Lang argues that the trial court did not find sufficient facts to support its conclusion that Lang was, in fact, transacting business in the state of North Carolina. * * *

* * *

Our courts have interpreted transacting business in the state to "require the engaging in, carrying on or exercising, in North Carolina, some of the functions for which the corporation was created." [Citation.] The business done by the corporation must be of such nature and character "as to warrant the inference that the corporation has subjected itself to the local jurisdiction and is, by its duly authorized officers and agents, present within the State." [Citation.] In other words, the activities carried on by the corporation in North Carolina must be substantial, continuous, systematic, and regular. [Citation.]

Here, the trial court concluded that Lang's business activity in North Carolina was regular, continuous, and substantial such that it was transacting business in the state. We uphold this conclusion only if it is supported by the findings of fact, and, contrary to Lang's assertion, we hold that it is. [Citation.] Specifically, the court found that Lang, through its single employee, had sold and consigned merchandise to jewelry stores in Franklin, Asheville, and Highlands, North Carolina, since 1970. The court also found that Lang's employee came to North Carolina at least twice every six weeks during the year and at least twice every four weeks during the summer months for the purpose of transacting business. Sometime he came to North Carolina to transact business as often as three times a month. The court found that when the employee came to North Carolina, he always brought jewelry with him for delivery. When he visited jewelry stores in the state, he would either (1) make a direct sale on the spot without any confirmation from any other person or entity in any other place or (2) consign the jewelry, also without any further confirmation or approval from any other person or entity anywhere. When the employee took orders, he either shipped the ordered items to the business in North Carolina or personally delivered the merchandise. He also took returns of merchandise from customers in the state. The court further found that the business that Lang conducted in North Carolina did not require it to communicate with any other person or seek any authority from any other person.

In sum, we conclude that the trial court's conclusions of law are adequately supported by the facts found in this case. There is ample evidence that Lang's business in this state has been regular, systematic, and extensive. Lang has been coming to North Carolina since about 1970 to sell

Richard and O. Ahlborg. Accordingly, we are of the opinion that CSI was dominated and controlled by Richard as an alter ego of O. Ahlborg, all to the detriment of NHA, its victim and judgment creditor.

In her decision, the trial justice failed to consider the totality of the evidentiary circumstances that support a finding that O. Ahlborg is responsible for the corporate debt of CSI. The evidence that Richard Ahlborg dominated the affairs of each entity was overwhelming; not only did he declare, whenever it was expedient to do so, that he was CSI and he was O. Ahlborg, he unhesitatingly deployed the resources of one corporation in favor of the other whenever the circumstances warranted, including steering NHA to CSI, financing the undercapitalized CSI, completing its contract with NHA, and attempting to collect CSI's indebtedness on O. Ahlborg's behalf by financing a meritless arbitration followed by a clandestine war of hide the assets.

* * *

Additionally, the evidence that CSI was undercapitalized from its inception and was insolvent for this entire period, including when it was retained by NHA * * * demonstrates undercapitalization and is damning proof that CSI was operated as a shell corporation for defendants' benefit. [Citation.]

Thus, as Richard so often proclaimed, at least for financial operations, O. Ahlborg was CSI. Accordingly, the corporate form that otherwise would shield O. Ahlborg from liability is unavailing and O. Ahlborg is liable for CSI's judgment debt.

* * *

For the reasons set forth herein, the plaintiff's appeal is sustained and the judgment is vacated.

## QUESTIONS

1. Identify the principal attributes and classifications of a corporation.
2. Discuss how a corporation is formed and the role, liability, and duties of promoters.
3. Distinguish between the statutory and common law approaches to defective formation of a corporation.
4. Explain how the doctrine of piercing the corporate veil applies to (a) closely held corporations and (b) parent-subsidiary corporations.
5. Identify the sources of corporate powers and explain the legal consequences of a corporation's exceeding its powers.

## PROBLEMS

**1.** After part of the shares of a proposed corporation had been successfully subscribed, one of the promoters hired a carpenter to repair a building that was to be conveyed to the proposed corporation. The promoters subsequently secured subscriptions to the balance of the shares and completed the organization, but the corporation, finding the building to be unsuitable for its purposes, declined to use the building or pay the carpenter. The carpenter brought suit against the corporation and the promoter for the amount that the promoter agreed would be paid to him. Who, if anyone, is liable?

**2.** C. A. Nimocks was a promoter engaged in organizing the Times Printing Company. On September 12, on behalf of the proposed corporation, he made a written contract with McArthur for her services as comptroller for a one-year period beginning October 1. The Times Printing Company was incorporated October 16, and on that date McArthur commenced her duties as comptroller. Neither the board of directors nor any officer took formal action on her employment, but all the shareholders, directors, and officers knew of the contract made by Nimocks. On December 1, McArthur was discharged without cause.

**(a)** Has she a cause of action against the Times Printing Company?

**(b)** Has she a cause of action against Nimocks?

**3.** Todd and Elaine purchased for $300,000 a building that was used for manufacturing pianos. Then as promoters, they formed a new corporation and resold the building to the new corporation for $500,000 worth of stock. After discovering the actual purchase price paid by the promoters, the other shareholders desire to have $200,000 of the common stock canceled. Can they succeed in this action?

**4.** Wayne signed a subscription agreement to purchase one hundred shares of stock of the proposed ABC Company, at a price of $18 per share in a State that has adopted the Revised Act. Two weeks later, the company was incorporated. A certificate was duly tendered to Wayne, but he refused to accept it. He was notified of all shareholders' meetings, but he never attended. A dividend check was sent to him, but he returned it. ABC Company brings a legal action against Wayne to recover $1,800. He defends upon the ground that his subscription agreement was an unaccepted offer and that he had done nothing to ratify it and was therefore not liable upon it. Is he correct? Explain.

**5.** Julian, Cornelia, and Sheila petitioned for a corporate charter for the purpose of conducting a retail shoe business. They met all of the statutory provisions, with the exception of having their charter recorded. This was simply an oversight on their part, and they felt that they had fully complied with the law. They operated the business for three years, after which time it became insolvent. The creditors desire to hold the members personally and individually liable. May they do so?

**6.** Arthur, Barbara, Carl, and Debra decided to form a corporation for bottling and selling apple cider. Arthur, Barbara, and Carl were to operate the business, and Debra was to supply the necessary capital but was to have no voice in the management. They went to Jane, a lawyer, who agreed to organize a corporation for them under the name A–B–C Inc., and paid her funds sufficient to accomplish the incorporation. Jane promised that the corporation would definitely be formed by May 3. On April 27, Arthur telephoned Jane to inquire how the incorporation was progressing, and Jane said she had drafted the articles of incorporation and would send them to the Secretary of State that very day. She assured Arthur that incorporation would occur before May 3.

Relying on Jane's assurance, Arthur, with the approval of Barbara and Carl, on May 4 entered into a written contract with Grower for the latter's entire apple crop. The contract was executed by Arthur on behalf of "A–B–C Inc." Grower delivered the apples as agreed. Unknown to Arthur, Barbara, Carl, Debra, or Grower, the articles of incorporation were never filed, through Jane's negligence. The business subsequently failed.

What are Grower's rights, if any, against Arthur, Barbara, Carl, and Debra as individuals?

**7.** The Pyro Corporation has outstanding twenty thousand shares of common stock, of which nineteen thousand are owned by Peter B. Arson, five hundred shares are owned by Elizabeth Arson, his wife, and five hundred shares are owned by Joseph Q. Arson, his brother. These three individuals are the officers and directors of the corporation. The Pyro Corporation obtained a $750,000 fire insurance policy to cover a certain building it owned. Thereafter, Peter B. Arson set fire to the building, and it was totally destroyed. Can the corporation recover from the fire insurance company on the $750,000 fire insurance policy? Why?

**8.** A corporation formed for the purpose of manufacturing, buying, selling, and dealing in drugs, chemicals, and similar products contracted to purchase, under authority of its board of directors, the land and building it occupied as a factory and store. Collins, a shareholder, sues in equity to restrain the corporation from completing the contract, claiming that as the certificate of incorporation contained no provision authorizing the corporation to purchase real estate, the contract was *ultra vires*. Can Collins prevent the contract from being executed?

**9.** Amalgamated Corporation, organized under the laws of State S, sends several traveling salespersons into State M to solicit orders, which are accepted only at the home office of Amalgamated Corporation in State S. Riley, a resident of State M, places an order which is accepted by Amalgamated Corporation in State S. The Corporation Act of State M provides that "no foreign corporation transacting business in this state without a certificate of authority shall be permitted to maintain an action in any court of this state until such corporation shall have obtained a certificate of authority." Riley fails to pay for the goods, and when Amalgamated Corporation sues Riley in a court of State M, Riley defends on the ground that Amalgamated Corporation does not possess a certificate of authority from State M. Result?

**10.** Dr. North, a surgeon practicing in Georgia, engaged an Arizona professional corporation consisting of twenty lawyers to represent him in a dispute with a Georgia hospital. West, a member of the law firm, flew to Atlanta and hired local counsel with Dr. North's approval. West represented Dr. North in two hearings before the hospital and in one court proceeding, as well as negotiating a compromise between Dr. North and the hospital. The total bill for the law firm's travel costs and professional services was $21,000, but Dr. North refused to pay $6,000 of it. When the law firm brought an action against Dr. North for the balance owed, he argued that the action should be dismissed because the law firm failed to register as a foreign corporation in accordance with the Georgia Corporation Statute. Will the law firm be prevented from collecting on the contract? Explain.

**11.** An Arkansas statute provides that if any foreign corporation authorized to do business in the State should remove to the Federal court any suit brought against it by an Arkansas citizen or initiate any suit in the Federal court against a local citizen, without the consent of the other party, Arkansas's Secretary of State should revoke all authority of the corporation to do business in the State. The Burke Construction Company, a Missouri corporation authorized to do business in Arkansas, has brought a suit in Federal court and has removed to a Federal court a State suit brought against it. Burke now seeks to enjoin the Secretary of State from revoking its authority to do business in Arkansas. Should the injunction be issued? Explain.

**12.** Little Switzerland Brewing Company was incorporated on January 28. On February 18, Ellison and Oxley were made directors of the company after they purchased some stock. Then, on September 25, Ellison and Oxley signed stock subscription agreements to purchase five thousand shares each. Under the agreement, they both issued a note that indicated that they would pay for the stock "at their discretion." Two years later in March, the board of directors passed a resolution canceling the stock subscription agreements of Ellison and Oxley. The creditors of Little Switzerland brought suit against Ellison and Oxley to recover the money owed under the subscription agreements. Are Ellison and Oxley liable? Why?

**13.** Oahe Enterprises was formed by the efforts of Emmick, who acted as a promoter and contributed shares of Colonial Manors, Inc. (CM), stock in exchange for stock in Oahe. The CM stock had been valued by CM's directors for internal stock option purposes at $19 per share. One month prior to Emmick's incorporation of Oahe Enterprises, however, CM's board reduced the stock value to $9.50 per share. Although Emmick knew of this reduction before the meeting to form Oahe Enterprises, he did not disclose this information to the Morrises, the other shareholders of the new corporation. Can Oahe Enterprises recover the shortfall?

**14.** Healthwin-Midtown Convalescent Hospital, Inc. (Healthwin), was incorporated in California for the purpose of operating a health-care facility. For three years thereafter, it participated as a provider of services under the Federal Medicare Act and received periodic payments from the U.S. Department of Health, Education and Welfare. Undisputed audits revealed that a series of overpayments had been made to Healthwin. The United States brought an action to recover this sum from the defendants, Healthwin and Israel Zide. Zide was a member of the board of directors of Healthwin, the administrator of its health-care facility, its president, and owner of 50 percent of its stock. Only Zide could sign the corporation's checks without prior approval of another corporate officer. Board meetings were not regularly held. In addition, Zide had a 50 percent interest in a partnership that owned both the realty in which Healthwin's health-care facility was located and the furnishings used at that facility. Healthwin consistently had outstanding liabilities in excess of $150,000, and its initial capitalization was only $10,000. Zide exercised control over Healthwin, causing its finances to become inextricably intertwined with both his personal finances and his other business holdings. The United States contends that the corporate veil should be pierced and that Zide should be held personally liable for the Medicare overpayments made to Healthwin. Is the United States correct in its assertion? Why?

**15.** MPL Leasing Corporation is a California corporation that provides financing plans to dealers of Saxon Business Products. MPL invited Jay Johnson, a Saxon dealer in Alabama, to attend a sales seminar in Atlanta. MPL and Johnson entered into an agreement under which Johnson was to lease Saxon copiers with an option to buy. MPL shipped the equipment into Alabama and filed a financing statement with the Secretary of State. When Johnson became delinquent with his payments to MPL, MPL brought an action against Johnson in an Alabama court. Johnson moved to dismiss the action, claiming that MPL was not qualified to conduct business in Alabama and was thus barred from enforcing its contract with Johnson in an Alabama court. Alabama law prevents foreign corporations not qualified to do business in Alabama from enforcing their intrastate contracts in the Alabama court system. Is Johnson correct?

**16.** In April, Cranson was asked to invest in a new business corporation that was about to be created. He agreed to purchase stock and to become an officer and director. After his attorney advised him that the corporation had been formed under the laws of Maryland, Cranson paid for and received a stock certificate evidencing his ownership of shares. The business of the new venture was conducted as if it were a corporation. Cranson was elected president, and he conducted all of his corporate actions, including those with IBM, as an officer of the corporation. At no time did he assume any personal obligation or pledge his individual credit to IBM. As a result of an oversight of the attorney, of which Cranson was unaware, the certificate of incorporation, which had been signed and acknowledged prior to May 1, was not filed until November 24. Between May 1 and November 8, the "corporation" purchased eight computers from IBM. The corporation made only partial payment. Can IBM hold Cranson personally liable for the balance due?

**17.** Berger was planning to produce a fashion show in Las Vegas. In April 1965, Berger entered into a written licensing agreement with CBS Films, Inc., a wholly owned subsidiary of CBS, for presentation of the show. In 1966, Stewart Cowley decided to produce a fashion show similar to Berger's and entered into a contract with CBS. CBS broadcast Cowley's show, but not Berger's; and Berger brought an action against CBS to recover damages for breach of his contract with CBS Films. Berger claimed that CBS was liable because CBS Films was not operated as a separate entity, and that the court should disregard the parent-subsidiary form. In support of this claim, Berger showed that CBS Films' directors were employees of CBS, that CBS's organizational chart included CBS Films, and that all lines of employee authority from CBS Films passed through CBS employees to the CBS chairman of the board. CBS, in turn, argued that Berger had failed to justify piercing the corporate veil and disregarding the corporate identity of CBS Films in order to hold CBS liable. Decision?

**18.** Frank McAnarney and Joseph Lemon entered into an agreement to promote a corporation to engage in the manufacture of farm implements. Before the corporation was organized, McAnarney and Lemon solicited subscriptions to the stock of the corporation and presented a written agreement for the subscribers to sign. The agreement provided that the subscribers would pay $100 per share for stock in the corporation in consideration of McAnarney and Lemon's agreement to organize the corporation and advance the preincorporation expenses. Thomas Jordan signed the agreement, making application for one hundred shares of stock. After the articles of incorporation were filed with the Secretary of State, but before the charter was issued to the corporation, Jordan died. The administrator of Jordan's estate notified McAnarney and Lemon that the estate would not honor Jordan's subscription.

After the formation of the corporation, Franklin Adams signed a subscription agreement making application for one hundred shares of stock. Before the corporation accepted the subscription, Adams informed the corporation that he was canceling it.

**(a)** Can the corporation enforce Jordan's stock subscription against Jordan's estate?

**(b)** Can the corporation enforce Adams's stock subscription?

**19.** Green & Freedman Baking Company (Green & Freedman) was a family-owned Massachusetts corporation that produced and sold baked goods. The terms of a collective bargaining agreement required Green & Freedman Baking Company to make periodic payments on behalf of its unionized drivers to the New England Teamsters and Baking Industry Health Benefits and Insurance Fund (Health Fund). After sixty years of operation Green & Freedman experienced financial difficulties and ceased to make the agreed-upon contributions. They mixed their own finances with those of Green & Freedman's. The Elmans, through their domination of Green & Freedman, caused the corporation to make payments to themselves and their relatives at a time when the corporation was known to be failing and could be expected to default, or was already in default, on its obligations to the Health Fund. It then transferred all remaining assets to a successor entity named Boston Bakers, Inc. (Boston Bakers). Boston Bakers operated essentially the same business as Green & Freedman until its demise two years later. The Health Fund sued Green & Freedman, Boston Bakers, and the two corporations' principals, Richard Elman and Stanley Elman, to recover the payments owed by Green & Freedman with interest, costs, and penalties. There was no evidence of financial self-dealing in the case of Boston Bakers. Both corporate defendants conceded liability for the delinquent contributions owed by Green & Freedman to the Health Fund. The suit against the Elmans was based on piercing the corporate veil with respect to Green & Freedman and Boston Bakers. The Elmans, however, denied they were personally liable for these corporate debts. Are the Elmans liable? Explain.

**20.** Ronald Nadler was a resident of Maryland and the CEO of Glenmar Cinestate, Inc., a Maryland corporation, as well as its principal stockholder. Glenmar leased certain space in the Westridge Square Shopping Center, located in Frederick, Maryland, and in Cranberry Mall, located in Westminster, Maryland. Tiller Construction Corporation and Nadler entered into two contracts for the construction of movie theaters at these locations, one calling for Tiller to do "the work" for Nadler at Westridge for $637,000, and the other for Tiller to do "the work" for Nadler at Cranberry for $688,800. Ronald Nadler requested that Tiller send all bills to Glenmar, the lessee at both shopping malls, but agreed to be personally liable to Tiller for the payment of both contracts. All inventory was bought and paid for locally, and Tiller paid sales tax in Maryland. Although there was no formal office in the state, Tiller leased a motel room for a considerable period of time, posted a sign at the job site, and maintained telephone numbers listed in information. In addition, Tiller engaged in fairly pervasive management functions, and the value of the projects comprised a substantial part of Tiller's revenues during the period. At the time of the suit, there was a net balance due for the Cranberry project in the amount of $229,799.46, and on the Westridge project for the sum of $264,273.85, which Nadler refused to pay, even though he had approved all work and the work had been performed in a timely, good, and workmanlike manner. Tiller Construction Corporation sued Ronald Nadler and Glenmar Cinestate, Inc., for breach of contract. Nadler filed a motion to dismiss based on Maryland's business corporation statute, which prohibits a foreign corporation that conducts intrastate business in Maryland from maintaining a suit in Maryland courts if the corporation fails to register or qualify under Maryland law. Nadler asserted that Tiller was a New York corporation that has never qualified to transact business in the state of Maryland. Tiller conceded that the corporation had not qualified to do business in Maryland but argued that Tiller was not required to qualify because its activities did not constitute, in the contemplation of the statute, doing business in the state as Tiller just had occasional business in Maryland. Discuss whether Tiller could bring suit in Maryland.

# CHAPTER 35
# Financial Structure

Capital is necessary for any business to function. Two principal sources for corporate financing involve debt and equity investment securities. While equity securities represent an ownership interest in the corporation and include both common and preferred stock, corporations finance most of their operations through debt securities. Debt securities, which include notes and bonds, do not represent an ownership interest in the corporation but rather create a debtor-creditor relationship between the corporation and the bondholder. The third principal way in which a corporation may meet its financial needs is through retained earnings.

All States have statutes regulating the issuance and sale of corporate shares and other securities. Popularly known as **blue-sky laws**, these statutes typically have provisions prohibiting fraud in the sale of securities. In addition, a number of States require the registration of securities, and some States also regulate brokers, dealers, and others who engage in the securities business.

In 1933, Congress passed the first Federal statute for the regulation of securities offered for sale and sold through the use of the mails or otherwise in interstate commerce. The statute requires a corporation to disclose certain information about a proposed security in a registration statement and in its **prospectus** (an offer a corporation makes to interest people in buying securities). Although the Securities and Exchange Commission (SEC) does not examine the merits of the proposed security and although registration does not guarantee the accuracy of the facts presented in the registration statement or prospectus, the law does prohibit false and misleading statements under penalty of fine or imprisonment or both.

Under certain conditions, a corporation may receive an exemption from the requirement of registration under the blue-sky laws of most States and the Securities Act of 1933. If no exemption is available, a corporation offering for sale or selling its shares of stock or other securities, as well as any person selling such securities, is subject to court injunction, possible criminal prosecution, and civil liability in damages to the persons to whom securities are sold in violation of the regulatory statute. A discussion of Federal regulation of securities appears in *Chapter 44*.

An investor has the right to transfer her investment securities by sale, gift, or pledge. The right to transfer is a valuable one, and easy transferability augments the value and marketability of investment securities. The availability of a ready market for any security affords liquidity and makes the security both attractive to investors and useful as collateral. The Uniform Commercial Code (UCC), Article 8, Investment Securities, contains the statutory rules applicable to transfers of investment securities; these rules are similar to those in Article 3, which concern negotiable instruments. In 1994 a revision to Article 8 was promulgated, and all of the States have adopted the revision. The Federal securities laws also regulate several aspects of the transfer of investment securities, as discussed in *Chapter 44*.

This chapter will discuss debt and equity securities as well as the payment of dividends and other distributions to shareholders.

## DEBT SECURITIES

Corporations frequently find it advantageous to use debt as a source of funds. **Debt securities** (also called **bonds**) generally involve the corporation's promise to repay the principal amount of a loan at a stated time and to pay interest, usually at a fixed rate, while the debt is outstanding. Thus, a debt security creates a debtor-creditor relationship between the corporation and the holder of the security. In addition to bonds, a corporation may finance its operations through other forms of debt, such as credit extended by its suppliers and short-term commercial paper. Some State statutes, but not the Revised Act, permit the articles of incorporation to confer voting rights on debt security holders; a few States allow other shareholder rights to be conferred on bondholders.

## AUTHORITY TO USE DEBT SECURITIES

The Revised Act provides that every corporation has the power "to make contracts and guarantees, incur liabilities, borrow money, issue its notes, bonds, and other obligations (which may be convertible into or include the option to purchase other securities of the corporation), and secure any of its obligations by mortgage or pledge of any of its property, franchises, or income." Section 3.02. The board of directors may issue bonds without the authorization or consent of the shareholders.

## TYPES OF DEBT SECURITIES

Debt securities can be classified into various types according to their characteristics. The variants and combinations possible within each type are limited only by a corporation's ingenuity. Debt securities are typically issued under an **indenture** or debt agreement, which specifies in great detail the terms of the loan. The Federal Trust Indenture Act of 1939 applies to indentures covering bonds issued for $10 million or more.

In addition, a **high-yield bond** (**non-investment-grade bond** or **junk bond**) is a bond that is rated below investment grade at the time of purchase. These bonds have a greater risk of default than investment-grade bonds but typically pay higher yields than higher grade bonds to make them attractive to investors.

◆ **SEE CASE 35-1**

### UNSECURED BONDS

Unsecured bonds, usually called **debentures**, have only the obligation of the corporation behind them. Debenture holders are thus unsecured creditors and rank equally with other general creditors. To protect the unsecured bondholders, indentures frequently impose limitations on the corporation's borrowing, its payment of dividends, and its redemption and reacquisition of its own shares. They also may require the corporation to maintain specified minimum reserves.

### SECURED BONDS

A secured creditor is one whose claim not only is enforceable against the general assets of the corporation but also is a lien upon specific property. Thus, **secured** or mortgage **bonds** provide the security of specific corporate property in addition to the general obligation of the corporation. After resorting to the specified security, the holder of secured bonds becomes a general creditor for any unpaid amount of the debt.

### INCOME BONDS

Traditionally, debt securities bear a fixed interest rate that is payable without regard to the financial condition of the corporation. **Income bonds**, on the other hand, condition the payment of interest to some extent upon corporate earnings. This provision lessens the burden of the debt upon the issuer during periods of financial adversity. **Participating bonds** call for a stated percentage of return regardless of earnings, with additional payments dependent upon earnings.

### CONVERTIBLE BONDS

**Convertible bonds** may be exchanged, usually at the option of the holder, for other securities of the corporation at a specified ratio. For example, a convertible bond may provide that the bondholder shall have the right for a specified time to exchange each bond for twenty shares of common stock.

### CALLABLE BONDS

**Callable bonds** are bonds subject to a redemption provision that permits the corporation to redeem or call (pay off) all or part of the issue before maturity at a specified redemption price. This provision enables the corporation to reduce fixed costs, to improve its credit rating, to refinance at a lower interest rate, to free mortgaged property, or to reduce its proportion of debt.

## EQUITY SECURITIES

An **equity security** is a source of capital creating an ownership interest in the corporation. The holders of equity security, as owners of the corporation, occupy a position financially riskier than that of creditors; they, more than any other class of investor, bear the impact of changes in the corporation's fortunes and general economic conditions.

Though **shares** of equity securities describe a proportionate proprietary interest in a corporate enterprise, they do not in any way vest their owner with title to any of the corporation's property. Shares do, however, confer on their owner a threefold interest in the corporation: (1) the right to participate in control, (2) the right to participate in the earnings of the corporation, and (3) the right to participate in the residual assets of the corporation upon dissolution. The shareholder's interest is usually evidenced by a certificate of ownership and is recorded by the corporation.

## ISSUANCE OF SHARES

The State of incorporation regulates the issuance of shares by determining the type of shares that may be issued, the kinds and amount of consideration for which shares may be issued, and the rights of shareholders to purchase a proportionate part of additionally issued shares. Moreover, the

Federal government and each State in which the shares are issued or sold regulate the issuance and sale of shares.

### AUTHORITY TO ISSUE

The initial amount of shares to be issued is determined by the promoters or incorporators and is generally governed by practical business considerations and financial needs. A corporation is limited, however, to selling only the amount of shares that has been authorized in its articles of incorporation. Section 6.03. Unauthorized shares of stock that a corporation purportedly issues are void. The rights of parties entitled to these overissued shares are governed by Article 8 of the UCC, which provides that the corporation must either obtain an identical security, if it is reasonably available, for the person entitled to the security or pay that person the price he (or the last purchaser for value) paid for it, with interest from the date of that person's demand. UCC Section 8–210.

Once the amount of shares that the corporation is authorized to issue has been specified in the charter, it cannot be increased or decreased without amending the articles of incorporation. This means that the shareholders, who must approve any amendment to the articles of incorporation, have residual authority over increases in the amount of authorized capital stock. Consequently, articles of incorporation commonly specify more shares than are to be issued initially.

### PREEMPTIVE RIGHTS

A shareholder's proportionate interest in a corporation can be changed by either a disproportionate issuance of additional shares or a disproportionate reacquisition of outstanding shares. In either transaction, management owes both the shareholder and the corporation a fiduciary duty. Moreover, when additional shares are issued, a shareholder may have the **preemptive right** to purchase a proportionate part of the new issue. Preemptive rights are used far more frequently in closely held corporations than in publicly traded corporations. Without such rights, a shareholder may be unable to prevent a dilution of his ownership interest in the corporation. For example, Leonard owns two hundred shares of stock of the Fordham Company, which has a total of one thousand shares outstanding. The company decides to increase its capital stock by issuing one thousand additional shares of stock. If Leonard has preemptive rights, he and every other shareholder will be offered one share of the newly issued stock for every share they own. If he accepts the offer and buys the stock, he will have four hundred shares out of a total of two thousand outstanding, and his relative interest in the corporation will be unchanged. Without preemptive rights, however, he would have only two hundred out of the two thousand shares outstanding; instead of owning 20 percent of the stock, he would own 10 percent.

Most statutes expressly authorize articles of incorporation to deny or limit preemptive rights to the issuance of additionally authorized shares. In about half of the States, preemptive rights exist unless denied by the charter (**opt-out**); in about half of the States, they do not exist unless the charter so provides (**opt-in**).

Certain shares are not subject to preemptive rights. In some States preemptive rights do not apply to the reissue of previously issued shares. In addition, preemptive rights generally do not apply to shares issued for noncash consideration or shares issued in connection with a merger or consolidation. Moreover, preemptive rights do not apply to the issuance of unissued shares that were originally authorized if the shares represent part of the initial capitalization.

The Revised Act adopts the opt-in approach: preemptive rights are nonexistent unless the charter provides for them. Section 6.30. If the charter simply states that "the corporation elects to have preemptive rights," then the shareholders have a preemptive right to acquire proportional amounts of the corporation's unissued shares, but they have no preemptive rights with respect to (1) shares issued as compensation to directors, officers, and employees; (2) shares issued within six months of incorporation; and (3) shares issued for consideration other than money. In addition, holders of nonvoting preferred stock have no preemptive rights with respect to *any* class of shares, and holders of voting common shares have no preemptive rights with respect to preferred stock unless the preferred stock is convertible into common stock. Section 6.30(b). The articles of incorporation may expressly modify any or all of these limitations.

### AMOUNT OF CONSIDERATION FOR SHARES

The board of directors usually determines the price for which the corporation will issue shares, although the charter may reserve this power to the shareholders. Section 6.21. Shares are deemed fully paid and nonassessable when the corporation receives the consideration for which the board of directors authorized their issuance. Section 6.21(d). The amount of that consideration depends upon the kind of shares being issued.

**PAR VALUE STOCK** In some States a corporation must specify in the articles of incorporation either a par value for its shares or that the shares are no par. Par value shares may be issued for any amount, not less than par, set by the board of directors or shareholders. The par value of a share of stock can be an arbitrary value selected by the corporation and may or may not reflect either the actual value of the share or the actual price paid to the corporation. It indicates only the *minimum price* that the corporation must receive for the share. The par value of stock must be stated in the articles of incorporation. The consideration received constitutes *stated capital* to the extent of the par value of the shares; any consideration in excess of par value constitutes *capital surplus.* It is common practice to authorize *low* or *nominal* par shares, such as $1 per share, and issue these shares at a considerably higher price, thereby providing ample capital surplus. By doing so the corporation, in some jurisdictions, obtains greater flexibility in declaring subsequent distributions to shareholders.

The Revised Act, the 1980 amendments to the Model Business Corporation Act (MBCA), and at least twenty-eight States have eliminated the concepts of par value, stated capital, and capital surplus. Under these acts, all shares may be issued for such consideration as authorized by the board of directors or, if the charter so provides, the shareholders. Section 6.21. A corporation, however, may elect to issue shares with par value. Section 2.02(b).

**No Par Value Stock** Shares without par value may be issued for any amount set by the board of directors or shareholders. Under incorporation statutes recognizing par value, stated value, and capital surplus, the entire consideration the corporation receives for such stock constitutes stated capital unless the board of directors allocates a portion of the consideration to capital surplus. MBCA Section 21, repealed in 1980. (As noted above, the Revised Act and the 1980 amendments to the MBCA eliminated the concepts of par value, stated capital, and capital surplus.) The directors are free to allocate any or all of the consideration received, unless the no par stock has a liquidation preference. In that event, only the consideration in excess of the amount of liquidation preference may be allocated to capital surplus. No par shares provide the directors with great latitude in establishing capital surplus, which can, in some jurisdictions, provide greater flexibility in declaring subsequent distributions to shareholders.

**Treasury Stock** Treasury stock consists of shares that the corporation has issued and subsequently reacquired. Treasury shares are issued *but not* outstanding, in contrast to shares owned by shareholders, which are issued *and* outstanding. A corporation may sell treasury shares for any amount the board of directors determines, even if the shares have a par value that is more than the sale price. Treasury shares provide neither voting rights nor preemptive rights; furthermore, no dividend may be paid upon them.

The Revised Act advances the 1980 amendments to the MBCA, which eliminated the concept of treasury shares. Under the Revised Act, all shares reacquired by a corporation constitute authorized but unissued shares, unless the articles of incorporation prohibit reissue, in which event the authorized shares are reduced by the number of shares reacquired. Section 6.31.

◆ **SEE FIGURE 35-1: Issuance of Shares**

## PAYMENT FOR SHARES

Two major issues arise regarding payment for shares. First, what type of consideration may the corporation validly accept in payment for shares? Second, who shall determine the value to be placed upon the consideration the corporation receives in payment for shares?

**Type of Consideration** In terms of the issuance of capital stock, consideration receives a more limited definition than it does under contract law. In about twenty-five States, cash, property, and services actually rendered to the corporation are generally acceptable as valid consideration, but promissory notes and promises regarding the performance of future services are not. Some States permit shares to be issued for preincorporation services; other States do not.

The Revised Act greatly liberalized these rules by specifically validating for the issuance of shares consideration consisting of any tangible or intangible property or *benefit* to the corporation, including cash, services performed, *contracts for future services*, and *promissory notes.* Section 6.21(b). To guard against possible abuse, the corporation may place the shares in escrow or otherwise restrict their transfer until the services are performed, the note is paid, or the benefits are received. If the services are not performed, the note is not paid, or the benefits are not received, the shares escrowed or restricted may be canceled. Section 6.21(e). Moreover, the Revised Act requires that corporations annually inform their shareholders in writing of all shares issued during the previous year for promissory notes or promises of future services. Section 16.21.

**Valuation of Consideration** Determining the value to be placed on the consideration that stock purchasers will exchange for shares is the responsibility of the directors. Many jurisdictions hold that this valuation is a matter of opinion and that, in the absence of fraud in the transaction, the judgment of the board of directors as to the value of the consideration actually or to be received for shares shall be conclusive. For example, assume that the directors of Elite Corporation authorize the issuance of two thousand shares of common stock for $10 per share to Kramer for property that the directors purportedly value at $20,000. The valuation is fraudulent, however, and the property is actually worth only $10,000. Kramer is liable to Elite Corporation and its creditors for $10,000. If, on the other hand, the directors had made the valuation without fraud and in good faith, Kramer would not be liable, even though the property is actually worth less than $20,000.

Under the Revised Act, the directors simply determine whether or not the consideration received (or to be received) for shares is *adequate.* Their determination is "conclusive insofar as the adequacy of consideration for the issuance of shares relates to whether the shares are validly issued, fully

◆ **FIGURE 35-1: Issuance of Shares**

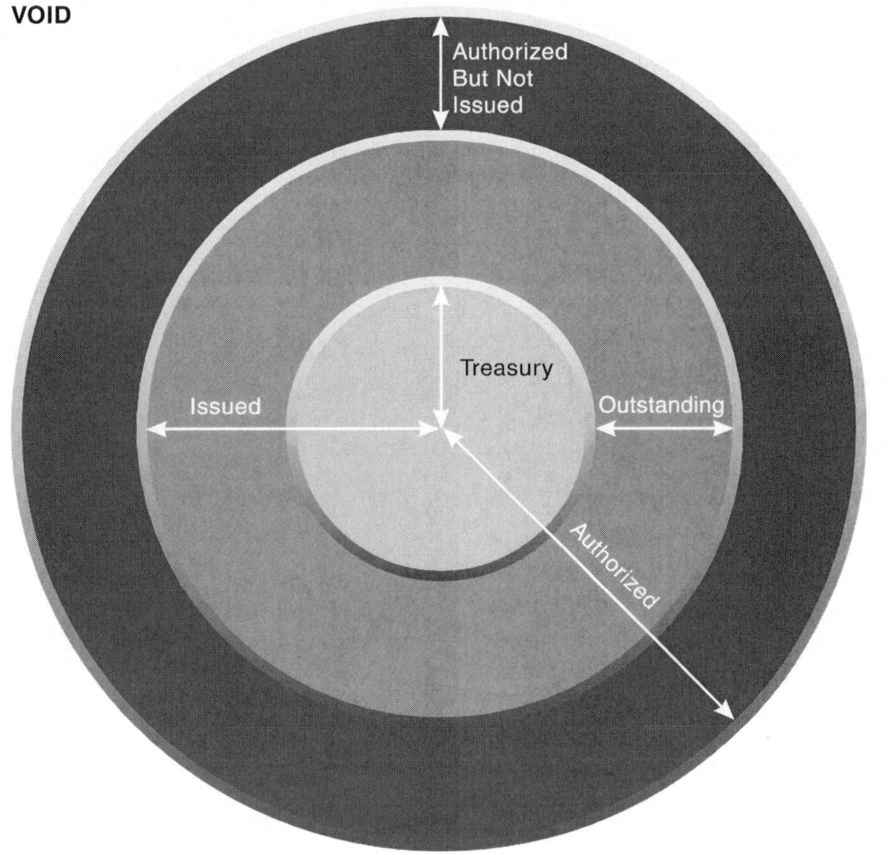


paid, and nonassessable." Section 6.21(c). Under the Revised Act, the articles of incorporation may reserve to the shareholders the powers granted to the board regarding the issuance of shares. Section 6.21(a).

### LIABILITY FOR SHARES

A purchaser of shares has no liability to the corporation or its creditors with respect to the shares except to pay the corporation either the consideration for which the shares were authorized to be issued or the consideration specified in the preincorporation stock subscription. Section 6.22(a). When the corporation receives that consideration, the shares are fully paid and nonassessable. Section 6.21(d). A transferee who acquires these shares in good faith and without knowledge or notice that the full consideration had not been paid is not personally liable to the corporation or its creditors for the unpaid portion of the consideration.

## CLASSES OF SHARES

Corporations are generally authorized by statute to issue different classes of stock, which may vary with respect to their rights to dividends, their voting rights, and their right to share in the assets of the corporation upon liquidation. The usual classifications of stock are common and preferred shares. Although the Revised Act has eliminated the terms *preferred* and *common*, it permits the issuance of shares with different preferences, limitations, and relative rights. Section 6.01. The Revised Act explicitly requires that the charter authorize "(1) one or more classes of shares that together have unlimited voting rights, and (2) one or more classes of shares (which may be the same class or classes as those with voting rights) that together are entitled to receive the net assets of the corporation upon dissolution." Section 6.01(b). In most States, however, even nonvoting shares may vote on certain mergers, share exchanges, and other fundamental changes which affect that class of shares as a class. See *Chapter 37*.

### COMMON STOCK

**Common stock** does not have any special contract rights or preferences. Often the only class of stock outstanding, it generally represents the greatest proportion of the corporation's capital structure and bears the greatest risk of loss should the enterprise fail.

Common stock may be divided into one or more classes bearing designations, limitations, or relative rights stated in the articles of incorporation. Section 6.01. The Revised Act and some States permit common stock to be redeemable or convertible. Section 6.01(c)(2). The articles also may limit or deny the voting rights of classes of common shares, but at least one or more classes of shares must together have unlimited voting rights. Section 6.01(b). For example, Class A common may be entitled to three times the dividends per share to which Class B common is entitled. Or Class A common may be entitled to elect six directors while Class B common elects three directors. Or Class A common may have two votes per share while Class B common has no votes per share.

## PREFERRED STOCK

Stock generally is considered preferred stock if it has contractual rights superior to those of common stock with regard to dividends, assets upon liquidation, or both. (Most preferred stock has both dividend and liquidation preferences.) Other special rights or privileges generally do not remove stock from the common stock classification. The articles of incorporation must provide for the contractual rights and preferences of an issue of preferred stock. Section 6.01(c).

Notwithstanding the special rights and preferences that distinguish preferred from common stock, both represent a contribution of capital. Preferred stock is no more a debt than common, and until a dividend is declared, the holder of preferred shares is not a creditor of the corporation. Furthermore, the rights of preferred shareholders are subordinate to the rights of the corporation's creditors.

**Dividend Preferences** Though the holders of an issue of preferred stock with a dividend preference will receive full dividends before any dividend may be paid to holders of common stock, no dividend is payable upon any class of stock, common or preferred, unless such dividend has been declared by the board of directors. The dividend preference may be described in terms of dollars per share ("$3.00 preferred") or as a percentage of par value ("10 percent preferred").

Preferred stock may provide that dividends are cumulative, noncumulative, or cumulative to the extent earned. For **cumulative** stock, if the board does not declare regular dividends on the preferred stock, such omitted dividends cumulate, and no dividend may be declared on common stock until all dividend arrearages on the preferred stock are declared and paid. For **noncumulative** stock, regular dividends do not cumulate upon the board's failure to declare them, and all rights to a dividend for the period omitted are gone forever. Accordingly, noncumulative stock has a priority over common only during a fiscal period in which a dividend on common stock is declared. Unless the charter expressly makes the dividends on preferred stock noncumulative, the courts generally hold them to be cumulative. **Cumulative-to-the-extent-earned** stock cumulates unpaid dividends only to the extent that funds were legally available to pay such dividends during that fiscal period.

Preferred stock also may be participating, although generally it is not. **Participating preferred** shares are entitled to their original dividend, and after the common shares receive a specified amount, the participating preferred stock shares with the common stock in any additional dividends. The manner in which preferred stock participates in dividends with common stock must be specified in the articles of incorporation. For example, a class of participating preferred stock could be entitled to share at the same rate with the common stock in any additional distribution of earnings for a given year *after* provision has been made for paying the prior preferred dividend and for paying dividends on the common at a rate equal to the fixed rate of the preferred.

**Liquidation Preferences** After a corporation has been dissolved, its assets liquidated, and the claims of its creditors satisfied, the remaining assets are distributed *pro rata* among the shareholders according to their priority as provided in the articles of incorporation. In the event that a class of stock with a dividend preference does not expressly provide for a preference of any kind upon dissolution and liquidation, its holders share *pro rata* with the common shareholders.

When the articles provide a liquidation preference, preferred stock has priority over common stock to the extent the articles state. In addition, if specified, preferred shares may participate beyond the liquidation preference in a stated ratio with other classes of shares. Such shares are said to be participating preferred with reference to liquidation. Preferred shares not so specified do not participate beyond the liquidation preference.

**Additional Rights and Limitations** Preferred stock may have additional rights, designations, and limitations. For instance, it may be expressly denied voting rights if the incorporation statute so permits, or it may be redeemable by the corporation or convertible into shares of another class. Sections 6.01(c) and 7.21(a). Preferred stock is typically nonvoting.

## STOCK OPTIONS

A corporation may issue **stock options** entitling their holders to purchase from the corporation shares of a specified class or classes. A **stock warrant** is a type of stock option that typically has a longer term and is freely transferable. A **stock right** is a short-term warrant. The board of directors determines the terms upon which stock rights, options, or warrants are issued; their form and content; and the consideration for which the shares are to be issued. Section 6.24. Stock options or warrants are used in incentive compensation plans for directors, officers, and employees. Corporations also use them in raising capital to make one class of securities more attractive by including in it the right to purchase shares in another class immediately or at a later date.

◆ SEE FIGURE 35-2: **Debt and Equity Securities**

## DIVIDENDS AND OTHER DISTRIBUTIONS

The board of directors, in its discretion, determines when and in what amount to declare distributions and dividends. The corporation's working capital requirements, shareholder expectations, tax consequences, and other factors influence the board as it creates distribution policy. In addition, the conditions under which the earnings of a business may be paid out in the form of dividends or other distributions of corporate assets will depend upon the contractual rights of those who hold the particular shares involved or shares having superior rights, provisions in the charter and bylaws of the corporation, and provisions of the State incorporation statute that are designed to protect creditors and shareholders from the dissipation of corporate assets. Creditors receive more significant protection under contractual restrictions typically included in their loan agreements, as well as under State fraudulent conveyance laws and Federal bankruptcy law.

### TYPES OF DIVIDENDS AND OTHER DISTRIBUTIONS

The Revised Act defines a **distribution** as

> a direct or indirect transfer of money or other property (except its own shares) or incurrence of indebtedness by a corporation to or for the benefit of its shareholders in respect of any of its shares. A distribution may be in the form of a declaration or payment of a dividend; a purchase, redemption, or other acquisition of shares; a distribution of indebtedness; or otherwise. Section 1.40(6).

The comments to this section explain that the term *indirect* is intended to include any other transaction the substance of which is clearly the same as that of a typical dividend or share repurchase, without regard to how the transaction is labeled or structured. Stock dividends and stock splits, which are not included in this definition, will also be covered in this section.

The Revised Act validates in close corporations unanimous shareholder agreements by which the shareholders

◆ FIGURE 35-2: **Debt and Equity Securities**

| | | Equity | |
|---|---|---|---|
| | **Debt** | **Preferred** | **Common** |
| **Ownership Interest** | No | Yes | Yes |
| **Obligation to Repay Principal** | Yes | No | No |
| **Fixed Maturity** | Yes | No | No |
| **Obligation to Pay Income** | Yes | No | No |
| **Preference on Income** | Yes | Yes | No |
| **Preference on Liquidation** | Yes | Yes | No |
| **Voting Rights** | Some States | Yes, unless denied | Yes, unless denied |
| **Redeemable** | Yes | Yes | In some States |
| **Convertible** | Yes | Yes | In some States |

may relax traditional corporate formalities. Section 7.32. This section, for example, expressly authorizes shareholder agreements that permit making distributions not in proportion to share ownership.

### CASH DIVIDENDS

The most customary type of dividend is a cash dividend, declared and paid at regular intervals from legally available funds. These dividends may vary in amount, depending upon the policy of the board of directors and the earnings of the enterprise.

### PROPERTY DIVIDENDS

Although dividends are almost always paid in cash, shareholders occasionally receive a property dividend, a distribution of earnings in the form of property. On one occasion, a distillery declared and paid a dividend in bonded whiskey.

### STOCK DIVIDENDS

A stock or share dividend is a proportional distribution of additional shares of the capital stock of a corporation to its shareholders. The practical and legal significance of a stock dividend differs greatly from that of a dividend payable in cash or property. Following the payment of a stock dividend, the assets of the corporation are no less than they were before, and the shareholder's relative interest in the net worth of the corporation is no greater than it was before, except possibly where the dividend is paid in shares of a different class. His shares will each represent a smaller proportionate interest in the corporation's assets, but by reason of the increase in the number of shares, his total investment will remain the same. Accordingly, a stock dividend is *not* considered a distribution. Under incorporation statutes recognizing par value and stated capital, a stock dividend results in the transfer from surplus to stated capital of an amount equal to the par value of the stock dividend.

### STOCK SPLITS

In a stock split, the corporation simply breaks each of the issued and outstanding shares into a greater number of shares, each representing a proportionately smaller interest in the corporation. Under incorporation statutes recognizing par value and stated capital, the par value of the shares to be split is divided among the new shares. The usual purpose of a stock split is to lower the price per share to a more marketable price and thus increase the number of potential shareholders. Like a stock dividend, a stock split is not a distribution; unlike a stock dividend, a split entails no transfer of surplus to stated capital.

### LIQUIDATING DIVIDENDS

Although dividends ordinarily are identified with the distribution of profits, a distribution of capital assets to shareholders is referred to as a liquidating dividend in some jurisdictions. Incorporation statutes usually require that the shareholder be informed when a distribution is a liquidating dividend.

### REDEMPTION OF SHARES

Redemption is the repurchase by the corporation of its own shares, usually at its own option. The Model Act and the statutes of many States permit corporations to redeem preferred shares but not common stock; the Revised Act, in contrast, does not prohibit redeemable common stock. The articles of incorporation must expressly provide for the power of redemption.

### ACQUISITION OF SHARES

A corporation may acquire its own shares. Such shares, unless canceled, are referred to as treasury shares. Under the Revised Act, such shares are considered authorized but unissued. Section 6.31. As with redemption, the acquisition of shares constitutes a distribution to shareholders and has an effect similar to a dividend.

## LEGAL RESTRICTIONS ON DIVIDENDS AND OTHER DISTRIBUTIONS

Several legal restrictions limit the amount of distributions a board of directors may declare. Though all States have statutes restricting the funds that are legally available for dividends and other distributions of corporate assets, lender-imposed contractual restrictions often limit the declaration of dividends and distributions even more stringently.

States restrict the payment of dividends and other distributions to protect creditors. All States impose the **equity insolvency test**, which prohibits the payment of any dividend or other distribution when the corporation either is insolvent or would become so through the payment of the dividend or distribution. **Insolvent** in the equity sense indicates the inability of a corporation to pay its debts as they become due in the usual course of business. In addition, almost all States impose further restrictions regarding the funds that are legally available to pay dividends and other distributions. These additional restrictions are based upon the corporation's assets or balance sheet, whereas the equity insolvency test is based upon the corporation's cash flow.

### DEFINITIONS

The legal, asset-based restrictions upon the payment of dividends or other distributions involve the concepts of earned surplus, surplus, net assets, stated capital, and capital surplus.

**Earned surplus** consists of the corporation's undistributed net profits, income, gains, and losses, computed from its date of incorporation.

**Surplus** is the amount by which the net assets of a corporation exceed its stated capital.

**Net assets** equal the amount by which the total assets of a corporation exceed its total debts.

**Stated capital** is the sum of the consideration the corporation has received for its issued stock, excepting the consideration properly allocated to capital surplus but including any amount transferred to stated capital when a stock dividend is declared. In the case of par value shares, the amount of stated capital is the total par value of all the issued shares. In the case of no par stock, it is the consideration the corporation has received for all the no par shares that it has issued, except that amount allocated to capital surplus or paid-in surplus.

**Capital surplus** means the entire surplus of a corporation other than its earned surplus. It may result from an allocation of part of the consideration received for no par shares, from any consideration in excess of par value received for par shares, or from a higher reappraisal of certain corporate assets.

◆ SEE FIGURE 35-3: **Key Concepts in Legal Restrictions upon Distributions**

## LEGAL RESTRICTIONS ON CASH DIVIDENDS

Each State imposes an equity insolvency test on the payment of dividends. The States differ regarding the asset-based or balance sheet test they apply. Some apply the earned surplus test, others use the surplus test, and the Revised Act adopts a net assets test.

**EARNED SURPLUS TEST** Unreserved and unrestricted earned surplus is available for dividends in all jurisdictions. Many States permit dividends to be paid *only* from earned surplus; corporations in these jurisdictions may not pay dividends out of capital surplus or stated capital. In addition, the corporation may not pay dividends if it is or would be rendered insolvent in the equity sense by the payment. The MBCA used this test until 1980.

**SURPLUS TEST** A number of less-restrictive States permit dividends to be paid out of any surplus—earned or capital. Some of these States express this test by prohibiting dividends that impair stated capital. Moreover, dividends may not be paid if the corporation is or would be rendered insolvent in the equity sense by the payment.

**NET ASSETS TEST** The MBCA, as amended in 1980, and the Revised Act have adopted a net assets test. Section 6.40 of the Revised Act as amended states,

> (c) No distribution may be made if, after giving it effect:
>
> (1) the corporation would not be able to pay its debts as they become due in the usual course of business; or
> (2) the corporation's total assets would be less than the sum of its total liabilities plus (unless the articles of incorporation permit otherwise) the amount that would be needed, if the corporation were to be dissolved at the time of the distribution, to satisfy the preferential rights upon dissolution of shareholders

◆ FIGURE 35-3: **Key Concepts in Legal Restrictions upon Distributions**

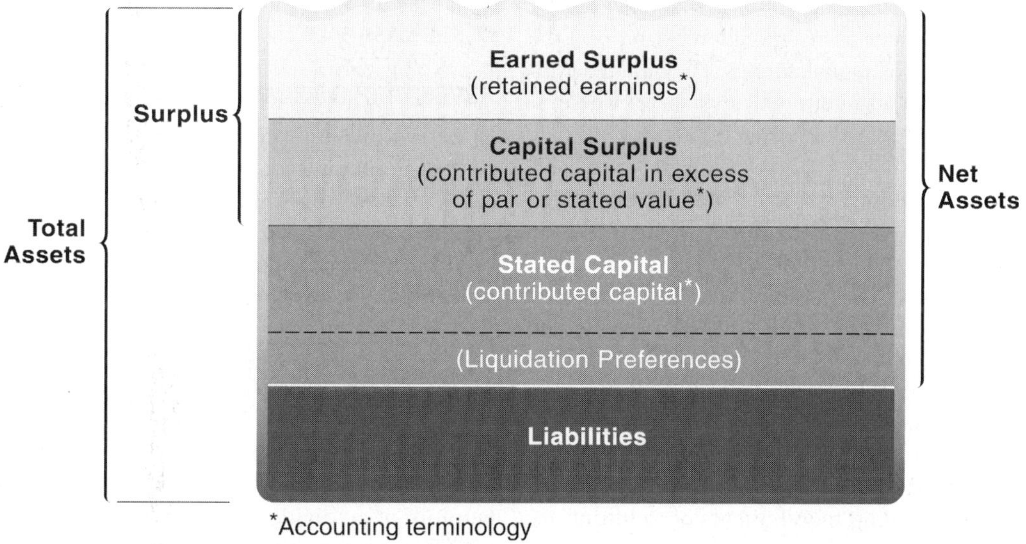

whose preferential rights are superior to those receiving the distribution.

### LEGAL RESTRICTIONS ON LIQUIDATING DISTRIBUTIONS

Even those States that do not permit cash dividends to be paid from capital surplus usually will permit distributions, or dividends, in partial liquidation from that source. Before 1980, the Model Act had such a provision. A distribution paid out of such surplus is a return to the shareholders of part of their investment.

The corporation may make no such distribution, however, when it is insolvent or when the distribution would render it so. Distributions from capital surplus are also restricted to protect the liquidation preference and cumulative dividend arrearages of preferred shareholders. Unless provided for in the articles of incorporation, a liquidating dividend must be authorized not only by the board of directors but also by the affirmative vote of the holders of a majority of the outstanding shares of stock of each class.

Because the Revised Act does not distinguish between cash and liquidating dividends, it therefore imposes upon liquidating dividends the same limitations it imposes upon cash dividends, discussed above. Section 6.40.

### LEGAL RESTRICTIONS ON REDEMPTION AND ACQUISITION OF SHARES

To protect creditors and holders of other classes of shares, most States place statutory restrictions upon redemption. A corporation may not redeem or purchase its redeemable shares when insolvent or when such redemption or purchase would render it insolvent or would reduce its net assets below the aggregate amount payable upon shares having prior or equal rights to the assets of the corporation upon involuntary dissolution.

A corporation may purchase its own shares only out of earned surplus or, if the articles of incorporation permit or if the shareholders approve, out of capital surplus. As with redemption, the corporation may make no purchase of shares when insolvent or when such purchase would make it insolvent.

The Revised Act permits a corporation to purchase, redeem, or otherwise acquire its own shares unless (1) the corporation's total assets after the distribution would be less than the sum of its total liabilities and the maximum amount that then would be payable for all outstanding shares having preferential rights in liquidation, or (2) the corporation would be unable to pay its debts as they become due in the usual course of its business. Section 6.40.

Additional restrictions may apply to a corporation's acquisition of its own shares. In close corporations, for example, courts may scrutinize acquisitions for compliance with the good faith and fair dealing requirements of the fiduciary duty.

◆ SEE CASES 35-2 AND 36-3

## DECLARATION AND PAYMENT OF DISTRIBUTIONS

The declaration of dividends and other distributions is within the discretion of the board of directors and may not be delegated. If the charter clearly and expressly provides for mandatory dividends, however, the board must comply with the provision. Nonetheless, such provisions are extremely infrequent, and shareholders cannot usurp the board's power in any other way, although it is in their power to elect a new board. Moreover, the board cannot discriminate in its declaration of dividends among shareholders of the same class.

### SHAREHOLDERS' RIGHT TO COMPEL A DIVIDEND

Should the directors fail to declare a dividend, a shareholder may bring a suit in equity against them and the corporation to seek a mandatory injunction requiring the directors to declare a dividend. Courts of equity are reluctant to order an injunction of this kind, which involves substituting the business judgment of the court for that of the directors elected by the shareholders. Where the evidence shows noncorporate motives or personal animosity as the basis for a refusal to declare dividends, however, a court may require the directors to distribute an apparently reasonable portion of the earnings. This is not a frequent occurrence; *Dodge v. Ford Motor Co.* is a landmark example.

With respect to the directors' discretion regarding the declaration of dividends, a preferred shareholder having prior rights with respect to dividends occupies a position identical to that of a holder of common shares. In the absence of special contractual or statutory rights, the holder of preferred shares, like the holder of common ones, must abide by the directors' decision.

◆ SEE CASE 35-3

### EFFECT OF DECLARATION

Once lawfully and properly declared, a cash dividend is considered a debt the corporation owes to the shareholders. It follows from this debtor-creditor relationship that, once declared, a dividend cannot be rescinded without the shareholders' consent; a stock dividend, however, may be revoked unless actually distributed.

## LIABILITY FOR IMPROPER DIVIDENDS AND DISTRIBUTIONS

The Revised Act imposes personal liability upon the directors of a corporation who vote for or assent to the declaration of a dividend or other distribution of corporate assets contrary to the incorporation statute or the articles of

◆ FIGURE 35-4: **Liability for Improper Distributions**

| | Corporation Solvent | Corporation Insolvent |
|---|---|---|
| **Nonbreaching Director** | No | No |
| **Breaching Director** | Yes | Yes |
| **Knowing Shareholder** | Yes | Yes |
| **Innocent Shareholder** | No | Yes |

incorporation. Section 8.33(a). The measure of damages is the amount of the dividend or distribution in excess of the amount that the corporation lawfully may have paid.

A director is not liable if she acted in accordance with the relevant standard of conduct: in good faith, with reasonable care, and in a manner she reasonably believed to be in the best interests of the corporation. Sections 8.30 and 8.33. (This standard of conduct is discussed in the next chapter.) In discharging this duty, a director is entitled to rely in good faith upon financial statements presented by the corporation's officers, public accountants, or finance committee. Such statements must be prepared on the basis of "accounting practices and principles that are reasonable in the circumstances or on a fair valuation or other method that is reasonable in the circumstances." Section 6.40(d). According to the Comments to this section, generally accepted accounting principles are *always* reasonable in the circumstances; other accounting principles *may* be acceptable under a general standard of reasonableness.

A shareholder's obligation to repay an illegally declared dividend depends upon a variety of factors, which may include the good or bad faith in which the shareholder accepted the dividend, his knowledge of the facts, the solvency or insolvency of the corporation, and, in some instances, special statutory provisions. Statutory liability on the part of directors does not relieve shareholders of the duty to make repayment.

A shareholder who receives illegal dividends with knowledge of their illegality is under a duty to refund them. See Section 8.33(b). Where the corporation is insolvent, the shareholder may retain not even a dividend he received in good faith, as the assets of an insolvent corporation are regarded as a trust fund for its creditors. Where an unsuspecting shareholder receives an illegal dividend from a solvent corporation, however, the majority rule is that the corporation cannot compel a refund.

◆ SEE FIGURE 35-4: **Liability for Improper Distributions**

## CHAPTER SUMMARY

### DEBT SECURITIES

**AUTHORITY TO ISSUE DEBT SECURITIES**

**Definitions**
- ***Debt Security*** source of capital creating no ownership interest and involving the corporation's promise to repay funds lent to it
- ***Bond*** a debt security

**Rule** each corporation has the power to issue debt securities as determined by the board of directors

**TYPES OF DEBT SECURITIES**

**Unsecured Bonds** called debentures; have only the obligation of the corporation behind them

**Secured Bonds** are claims against a corporation's general assets and also liens on specific property

**Income Bonds** condition to some extent the payment of interest on corporate earnings

**Participating Bonds** call for a stated percentage of return regardless of earnings, with additional payments dependent upon earnings
**Convertible Bonds** may be exchanged for other securities
**Callable Bonds** bonds subject to redemption

## EQUITY SECURITIES

**ISSUANCE OF SHARES**

**Definitions**
- ***Equity Security*** source of capital creating an ownership interest in the corporation
- ***Share*** a proportionate ownership interest in a corporation
- ***Treasury Stock*** shares reacquired by a corporation

**Authority to Issue** only those shares authorized in the articles of incorporation may be issued
**Preemptive Rights** right to purchase a *pro rata* share of new stock offerings
**Amount of Consideration for Shares** shares are deemed fully paid and nonassessable when a corporation receives the consideration for which the board of directors authorized the issuance of the shares, which in the case of par value stock must be at least par
**Payment for Newly Issued Shares** may be cash, property, and services actually rendered, as determined by the board of directors; under the Revised Act, promises to contribute cash, property, or services are also permitted

**CLASSES OF SHARES**

**Common Stock** stock not having any special contract rights
**Preferred Stock** stock having contractual rights superior to those of common stock
- ***Dividend Preferences*** must receive full dividends before any dividend may be paid on common stock
- ***Liquidation Preferences*** priority over common stock in corporate assets upon liquidation

**Stock Options** contractual right to purchase stock from a corporation

## DIVIDENDS AND OTHER DISTRIBUTIONS

**TYPES OF DIVIDENDS AND OTHER DISTRIBUTIONS**

**Distributions** transfers of property by a corporation to any of its shareholders with respect to its shares
**Cash Dividends** the most common type of distribution
**Property Dividends** distribution in the form of property
**Stock Dividends** a proportional distribution of additional shares of stock
**Stock Splits** each of the outstanding shares is broken into a greater number of shares
**Liquidating Dividends** a distribution of capital assets to shareholders
**Redemption of Shares** a corporation's exercise of the right to purchase its own shares
**Acquisition of Shares** a corporation's repurchase of its own shares

**LEGAL RESTRICTIONS ON DIVIDENDS AND OTHER DISTRIBUTIONS**

**Legal Restrictions on Cash Dividends** dividends may be paid only if the cash flow and applicable balance sheet tests are satisfied
- ***Cash Flow Test*** a corporation must not be or become insolvent (unable to pay its debts as they become due in the usual course of business)
- ***Balance Sheet Test*** varies among the States and includes the earned surplus test (available in all States), the surplus test, and the net assets test (used by the Model and Revised Acts)

**Legal Restrictions on Liquidating Distributions** States usually permit distribution in partial liquidation from capital surplus unless the company is insolvent

| | |
|---|---|
| | **Legal Restrictions on Redemptions of Shares** in most States, a corporation may not redeem shares when insolvent or when such redemption would render it insolvent<br>**Legal Restrictions on Acquisition of Shares** restrictions similar to those on cash dividends usually apply |
| **DECLARATION AND PAYMENT OF DISTRIBUTIONS** | **Shareholders' Right to Compel a Distribution** the declaration of distributions is within the discretion of the board of directors, and only rarely will a court substitute its business judgment for that of the board's<br>**Effect of Declaration** once properly declared, a distribution is considered a debt the corporation owes to the shareholders |
| **LIABILITY FOR IMPROPER DIVIDENDS AND DISTRIBUTIONS** | **Directors** the directors who assent to an improper dividend are liable for the unlawful amount of the dividend<br>**Shareholders** a shareholder must return illegal dividends if he knew of the illegality, if the dividend resulted from his fraud, or if the corporation is insolvent |

# CASES

## CASE 35-1 Debt Securities
## METROPOLITAN LIFE INSURANCE COMPANY v. RJR NABISCO, INC.

United States District Court, S.D. New York, 1989
716 F.Supp. 1504

**Walter, J.**

### Introduction

The corporate parties to this action are among the country's most sophisticated financial institutions, as familiar with the Wall Street investment community and the securities market as American consumers are with the Oreo cookies and Winston cigarettes made by defendant RJR Nabisco, Inc. (sometimes "the company" or "RJR Nabisco"). The present action traces its origins to October 20, 1988, when F. Ross Johnson, then the Chief Executive Officer of RJR Nabisco, proposed a $17 billion leveraged buy-out ("LBO") of the company's shareholders, at $75 per share. (Court's footnote: "A leveraged buy-out occurs when a group of investors, usually including members of a company's management team, buy the company under financial arrangements that include little equity and significant new debt. The necessary debt financing typically includes mortgages or high risk/high yield bonds, popularly known as "junk bonds." Additionally, a portion of this debt is generally secured by the company's assets. Some of the acquired company's assets are usually sold after the transaction is completed in order to reduce the debt incurred in the acquisition." [See *Chapter 37*.]) Within a few days, a bidding war developed among the investment group led by Johnson and the investment firm of Kohlberg Kravis Roberts & Co. ("KKR"), and others. On December 1, 1988, a special committee of RJR Nabisco directors, established by the company specifically to consider the competing proposals, recommended that the company accept the KKR proposal, a $24 billion LBO that called for the purchase of the company's outstanding stock at roughly $109 per share.

* * *

Plaintiffs * * * allege, in short, that RJR Nabisco's actions have drastically impaired the value of bonds previously issued to plaintiffs by, in effect, misappropriating the value of those bonds to help finance the LBO and to distribute an enormous windfall to the company's shareholders. As a result, plaintiffs argue, they have unfairly suffered a multimillion dollar loss in the value of their bonds.

* * *

Although the numbers involved in this case are large, and the financing necessary to complete the LBO unprecedented, the legal principles nonetheless remain discrete and familiar. Yet while the instant motions thus primarily require the Court to evaluate and apply traditional rules of equity and contract interpretation, plaintiffs do raise issues of first impression in the context of an LBO. At the heart of the present motions lies plaintiffs' claim that RJR Nabisco violated a restrictive covenant—not an explicit covenant found within the four corners of the relevant bond indentures, but rather an *implied* covenant of good faith and fair dealing—not to incur the debt necessary to facilitate the LBO and thereby betray what plaintiffs claim was the fundamental basis of their bargain with the company. The company, plaintiffs assert, consistently reassured its bondholders that it had a "mandate" from its Board of Directors to maintain RJR Nabisco's preferred credit rating. Plaintiffs ask this Court first to imply a covenant of good faith and fair dealing that would prevent the recent transaction, then to hold that this covenant has been breached, and finally to require RJR Nabisco to redeem their bonds.

RJR Nabisco defends the LBO by pointing to express provisions in the bond indentures that * * * permit mergers and the assumption of additional debt. These provisions, as well as others that could have been included but were not, were known to the market and to plaintiffs, sophisticated investors who freely bought the bonds and were equally free to sell them at any time. Any attempt by this Court to create contractual terms *post hoc*, defendants contend, not only finds no basis in the controlling law and undisputed facts of this case, but also would constitute an impermissible invasion into the free and open operation of the marketplace.

For the reasons set forth below, this Court agrees with defendants. There being no express covenant between the parties that would restrict the incurrence of new debt, and no perceived direction to that end from covenants that are express, this Court will not imply a covenant to prevent the recent LBO and thereby create an indenture term that, while bargained for in other contexts, was not bargained for here and was not even within the mutual contemplation of the parties.

## Background

* * *

### *The Parties*

Metropolitan Life Insurance Co. ("MetLife"), incorporated in New York, is a life insurance company that provides pension benefits for 42 million individuals. According to its most recent annual report, MetLife's assets exceed $88 billion and its debt securities holdings exceed $49 billion. [Citation.] MetLife alleges that it owns $340,542,000 in principal amount of six separate RJR Nabisco debt issues, bonds allegedly purchased between July 1975 and July 1988. Some bonds become due as early as this year; others will not become due until 2017. The bonds bear interest rates of anywhere from 8 to 10.25 percent. MetLife also owned 186,000 shares of RJR Nabisco common stock at the time this suit was filed. [Citation.]

Jefferson–Pilot Life Insurance Co. ("Jefferson–Pilot") is a North Carolina company that has more than $3 billion in total assets, $1.5 billion of which are invested in debt securities. Jefferson–Pilot alleges that it owns $9.34 million in principal amount of three separate RJR Nabisco debt issues, allegedly purchased between June 1978 and June 1988. Those bonds, bearing interest rates of anywhere from 8.45 to 10.75 percent, become due in 1993 and 1998. [Citation.]

RJR Nabisco, a Delaware corporation, is a consumer products holding company that owns some of the country's best known product lines, including LifeSavers candy, Oreo cookies, and Winston cigarettes. The company was formed in 1985, when R.J. Reynolds Industries, Inc. ("R.J. Reynolds") merged with Nabisco Brands, Inc. ("Nabisco Brands"). In 1979, and thus before the R.J. Reynolds–Nabisco Brands merger, R.J. Reynolds acquired the Del Monte Corporation ("Del Monte"), which distributes canned fruits and vegetables. From January 1987 until February 1989, codefendant Johnson served as the company's CEO. KKR, a private investment firm, organizes funds through which investors provide pools of equity to finance LBOs. [Citation.]

### *The Indentures*

The bonds implicated by this suit are governed by long, detailed indentures, which in turn are governed by New York contract law. No one disputes that the holders of public bond issues, like plaintiffs here, often enter the market after the indentures have been negotiated and memorialized. Thus, those indentures are often not the product of face-to-face negotiations between the ultimate holders and the issuing company. What remains equally true, however, is that underwriters ordinarily negotiate the terms of the indentures with the issuers. Since the underwriters must then sell or place the bonds, they necessarily negotiate in part with the interests of the buyers in mind. Moreover, these indentures were not secret agreements foisted upon unwitting participants in the bond market. No successive holder is required to accept or to continue to hold the bonds, governed by their accompanying indentures; indeed, plaintiffs readily admit that they could have sold their bonds right up until the announcement of the LBO. [Citation.] Instead, sophisticated investors like plaintiffs are well aware of the indenture terms and, presumably, review them carefully before lending hundreds of millions of dollars to any company.

* * *

Further, as plaintiffs themselves note, the contracts at issue "[do] not impose debt limits, since debt is assumed to be used for productive purposes." [Citation.]

## Discussion

* * *

The indentures at issue clearly address the eventuality of a merger. They impose certain related restrictions not at issue in this suit, but no restriction that would prevent the recent RJR Nabisco merger transaction. * * *

* * *

In contracts like bond indentures, "an implied covenant * * * derives its substance directly from the language of the Indenture, and 'cannot give the holders of Debentures any rights inconsistent with those set out in the Indenture.' *[Where] plaintiffs' contractual rights [have not been] violated, there can have been no breach of an implied covenant."* [Citation.] (emphasis added).

* * *

It is not necessary to decide that indentures like those at issue could never support a finding of additional benefits, under different circumstances with different parties. Rather, for present purposes, it is sufficient to conclude what obligation is not covered, either explicitly or implicitly, by these contracts held by these plaintiffs. Accordingly, this Court holds that the "fruits" of these indentures do not include an implied restrictive covenant that would prevent the incurrence of new debt to facilitate the recent LBO. To hold otherwise would permit these plaintiffs to straightjacket the company in order to guarantee their investment. These plaintiffs do not invoke an implied covenant of good faith to protect a legitimate, mutually contemplated benefit of the indentures; rather, they seek to have this Court create an additional benefit for which they did not bargain.

* * *

The sort of unbounded and one-sided elasticity urged by plaintiffs would interfere with and destabilize the market. * * * The Court has no reason to believe that the market, in evaluating bonds such as those at issue here, did not discount for the possibility that any company, even one the size of RJR Nabisco, might engage in an LBO heavily financed by debt. That the bonds did not lose any of their value until the October 20, 1988 announcement of a possible RJR Nabisco LBO only suggests that the market had theretofore evaluated the risks of such a transaction as slight.

* * *

[Judgment for defendant on count of breach of implied covenant.]

---

CASE 35-2

## Legal Restrictions on Distributions

## KLANG v. SMITH'S FOOD & DRUG CENTERS, INC.

Supreme Court of Delaware, 1997

702 A.2d 150

**Veasey, C. J.**

This appeal calls into question the actions of a corporate board in carrying out a merger and self-tender offer. Plaintiff in this purported class action alleges that a corporation's repurchase of shares violated the statutory prohibition against the impairment of capital * * *.

No corporation may repurchase or redeem its own shares except out of "surplus," as statutorily defined, or except as expressly authorized by provisions of the statute not relevant here. Balance sheets are not, however, conclusive indicators of surplus or a lack thereof. Corporations may revalue assets to show surplus, but perfection in that process is not required. Directors have reasonable latitude to depart from the balance sheet to calculate surplus, so long as they evaluate assets and liabilities in good faith, on the basis of acceptable data, by methods that they reasonably believe reflect present values, and arrive at a determination of the surplus that is not so far off the mark as to constitute actual or constructive fraud.

We hold that, on this record, the Court of Chancery was correct in finding that there was no impairment of capital * * *. Accordingly, we affirm.

Smith's Food & Drug Centers, Inc. ("SFD") is a Delaware corporation that owns and operates a chain of supermarkets in the Southwestern United States. Slightly more than three years ago, Jeffrey P. Smith, SFD's Chief Executive Officer, began to entertain suitors with an interest in acquiring SFD. At the time, and until the transactions at issue, Mr. Smith and his family held common and preferred stock constituting 62.1% voting control of SFD. Plaintiff and the class he purports to represent are holders of common stock in SFD. On January 29, 1996, SFD entered into an agreement with The Yucaipa Companies ("Yucaipa"), a California partnership also active in the supermarket industry. Under the agreement, the following would take place:

(1) Smitty's Supermarkets, Inc. ("Smitty's"), a wholly-owned subsidiary of Yucaipa that operated a supermarket chain in Arizona, was to merge into Cactus Acquisition, Inc. ("Cactus"), a subsidiary of SFD, in exchange for which SFD would deliver to Yucaipa slightly over 3 million newly-issued shares of SFD common stock;

(2) SFD was to undertake a recapitalization, in the course of which SFD would assume a sizable amount of new debt, retire old debt, and offer to repurchase

up to fifty percent of its outstanding shares (other than those issued to Yucaipa) for $36 per share; and (3) SFD was to repurchase 3 million shares of preferred stock from Jeffrey Smith and his family.

SFD hired the investment firm of Houlihan Lokey Howard & Zukin ("Houlihan") to examine the transactions and render a solvency opinion. Houlihan eventually issued a report to the SFD Board replete with assurances that the transactions would not endanger SFD's solvency, and would not impair SFD's capital in violation of 8 Del.C. §160. On May 17, 1996, in reliance on the Houlihan opinion, SFD's Board determined that there existed sufficient surplus to consummate the transactions, and enacted a resolution proclaiming as much. On May 23, 1996, SFD's stockholders voted to approve the transactions, which closed on that day. The self-tender offer was oversubscribed, so SFD repurchased fully fifty percent of its shares at the offering price of $36 per share.

* * *

A corporation may not repurchase its shares if, in so doing, it would cause an impairment of capital. [Citation.] A repurchase impairs capital if the funds used in the repurchase exceed the amount of the corporation's "surplus," defined by 8 Del.C. §154 to mean the excess of net assets over the par value of the corporation's issued stock. [Citation.]

Plaintiff asked the Court of Chancery to rescind the transactions in question as violative of Section 160. * * * First, he contends that SFD's balance sheets constitute conclusive evidence of capital impairment. He argues that the negative net worth that appeared on SFD's books following the repurchase compels us to find a violation of Section 160. Second, he suggests that even allowing the Board to "go behind the balance sheet" to calculate surplus does not save the transactions from violating Section 160. In connection with this claim, he attacks the SFD Board's off-balance-sheet method of calculating surplus on the theory that it does not adequately take into account all of SFD's assets and liabilities * * *. We hold that each of these claims is without merit.

* * *

Plaintiff advances an erroneous interpretation of Section 160. We understand that the books of a corporation do not necessarily reflect the current values of its assets and liabilities. Among other factors, unrealized appreciation or depreciation can render book numbers inaccurate. It is unrealistic to hold that a corporation is bound by its balance sheets for purposes of determining compliance with Section 160. Accordingly, we adhere to the principles of [citation] allowing corporations to revalue properly its assets and liabilities to show a surplus and thus conform to the statute.

It is helpful to recall the purpose behind Section 160. The General Assembly enacted the statute to prevent boards from draining corporations of assets to the detriment of creditors and the long-term health of the corporation. [Citation.] That a corporation has not yet realized or reflected on its balance sheet the appreciation of assets is irrelevant to this concern. Regardless of what a balance sheet that has not been updated may show, an actual, though unrealized, appreciation reflects real economic value that the corporation may borrow against or that creditors may claim or levy upon. Allowing corporations to revalue assets and liabilities to reflect current realities complies with the statute and serves well the policies behind this statute.

* * *

On May 17, 1996, Houlihan released its solvency opinion to the SFD Board, expressing its judgment that the merger and self-tender offer would not impair SFD's capital. Houlihan reached this conclusion by comparing SFD's "Total Invested Capital" of $1.8 billion—a figure Houlihan arrived at by valuing SFD's assets under the "market multiple" approach—with SFD's long-term debt of $1.46 billion. This comparison yielded an approximation of SFD's "concluded equity value" equal to $346 million, a figure clearly in excess of the outstanding par value of SFD's stock. Thus, Houlihan concluded, the transactions would not violate 8 Del.C. §160.

* * *

The record contains, in the form of the Houlihan opinion, substantial evidence that the transactions complied with Section 160. Plaintiff has provided no reason to distrust Houlihan's analysis. In cases alleging impairment of capital under Section 160, the trial court may defer to the board's measurement of surplus unless a plaintiff can show that the directors "failed to fulfill their duty to evaluate the assets on the basis of acceptable data and by standards which they are entitled to believe reasonably reflect present values." [Citation.] In the absence of bad faith or fraud on the part of the board, courts will not "substitute [our] concepts of wisdom for that of the directors." [Citation.] Here, plaintiff does not argue that the SFD Board acted in bad faith. Nor has he met his burden of showing that the methods and data that underlay the board's analysis are unreliable or that its determination of surplus is so far off the mark as to constitute actual or constructive fraud. [Court's footnote: We interpret 8 Del.C. §172 to entitle boards to rely on experts such as Houlihan to determine compliance with 8 Del.C. §160. Plaintiff has not alleged that the SFD Board failed to exercise reasonable care in selecting Houlihan, nor that rendering a solvency opinion is outside Houlihan's realm of competence. Compare 8 Del.C. §141(e) (providing that directors may rely in good faith on records, reports, experts, etc.).] Therefore, we defer to the board's determination of surplus, and hold that SFD's self-tender offer did not violate 8 Del.C. §160.

* * *

The judgment of the Court of Chancery is affirmed.

CASE 35-3

## Declaration of Dividends
## DODGE v. FORD MOTOR CO.

Supreme Court of Michigan, 1919
204 Mich. 459, 170 N.W. 668

**Ostrander, J.**

[Action in equity by John F. and Horace E. Dodge, plaintiffs, against the Ford Motor Company and its directors to compel the declaration of dividends and for an injunction restraining a contemplated expansion of the business. The complaint was filed in November 1916. Since 1909, the capital stock of the company has been $2,000,000, divided into 20,000 shares of a par value of $100 each, of which plaintiffs held 2,000. As of the close of business on July 31, 1916, the end of the company's fiscal year, the surplus above capital was $111,960,907.53 and the assets included cash on hand of $52,550,771.92.

For a number of years the company had regularly paid quarterly dividends equal to sixty percent annually on the capital stock of $2,000,000. In addition, from December 1911 to October 1915, inclusive, eleven special dividends totaling $41,000,000 had been paid, and in November 1916, after this action was commenced, a special dividend of $2,000,000 was paid.

Plaintiffs' complaint alleged that Henry Ford, president of the company and a member of its board of directors, had declared it to be the settled policy of the company not to pay any special dividends in the future but to put back into the business all future earnings in excess of the regular quarterly dividend. Plaintiffs sought an injunction restraining the carrying out of the alleged declared policy of Henry Ford and a decree requiring the directors to pay a dividend of at least seventy-five percent of the accumulated cash surplus.

In December 1917, the trial court entered a decree requiring the directors to declare and pay a dividend of $19,275,385.96 and enjoining the corporation from using its funds for a proposed smelting plant and certain other planned projects. From this decree, defendants have appealed.]

* * *

The case for plaintiffs must rest upon the claim, and the proof in support of it, that the proposed expansion of the business of the corporation involving the further use of profits as capital, ought to be enjoined because inimical to the best interests of the company and its shareholders, and upon the further claim that in any event the withholding of the special dividend asked for by plaintiffs is arbitrary action of the directors requiring judicial interference.

The rule which will govern courts in deciding these questions is not in dispute * * *. In [citation], it is stated:

> Profits earned by a corporation may be divided among its shareholders; but it is not a violation of the charter if they are allowed to accumulate and remain invested in the company's business. The managing agents of a corporation are impliedly invested with a discretionary power with regard to the time and manner of distributing its profits. They may apply profits in payment of floating or funded debts, or in development of the company's business; and so long as they do not abuse their discretionary powers, or violate the company's charter, the courts cannot interfere.
>
> But it is clear that the agents of a corporation, and even the majority, cannot arbitrarily withhold profits earned by the company, or apply them to any use which is not authorized by the company's charter. The nominal capital of a company does not necessarily limit the scope of its operations; a corporation may borrow money for the purpose of enlarging its business, and in many instances it may use profits for the same purpose * * *.

When plaintiffs made their complaint and demand for further dividends the Ford Motor Company had concluded its most prosperous year of business. The demand for its cars at the price of the preceding year continued. It could make and could market in the year beginning August 1, 1916, more than 500,000 cars. Sales of parts and repairs would necessarily increase. The cost of materials was likely to advance, and perhaps the price of labor, but it reasonably might have expected a profit for the year of upwards of $60,000,000. It had assets of more than $132,000,000, a surplus of almost $112,000,000, and its cash on hand and municipal bonds were nearly $54,000,000. Its total liabilities, including capital stock, was a little over $20,000,000. It had declared no special dividend during the business year except the October, 1915, dividend. It had been the practice, under similar circumstances, to declare larger dividends. Considering only these facts, a refusal to declare and pay further dividends appears to be not an exercise of discretion on the part of the directors, but an arbitrary refusal to do what the circumstances required to be done. These facts and others call upon the directors to justify their action, or failure or refusal to act. In justification, the defendants have offered testimony tending to prove, and which does prove, the following facts. It had been the policy of the corporation for a considerable time to annually reduce the selling price of cars, while keeping up, or improving their quality. As early as in June 1915 a general plan for the expansion of the productive capacity of the concern by a practical duplication of its plant had been talked over by the executive officers and directors and agreed upon, not all of the details having been settled and no formal action of directors having been taken. The erection of a smelter was considered, and engineering and other data in connection therewith secured. In consequence, it was determined not to reduce the selling price of cars for the year beginning August 1, 1915, but to maintain the price and to accumulate a large surplus to pay for the proposed expansion of plant and equipment, and perhaps to build a plant for smelting ore. It is hoped, by Mr. Ford, that eventually 1,000,000 cars will be annually produced. The contemplated changes will permit the increased output.

The plan, as affecting the profits of the business for the year beginning August 1, 1916, and thereafter, calls for a reduction in the selling price of cars * * *. In short, the plan does not call for and is not intended to produce immediately a more profitable business but a less profitable one; not only less profitable than formerly but less profitable than it is admitted it might be made. The apparent immediate effect will be to diminish the value of shares and the return to shareholders.

It is the contention of plaintiffs that the apparent effect of the plan is intended to be the continued and continuing effect of it and that it is deliberately proposed, not of record and not by official corporate declaration, but nevertheless proposed, to continue the corporation henceforth as a semi-eleemosynary institution and not as a business institution. In support of this contention they point to the attitude and to the expressions of Mr. Henry Ford.

Mr. Henry Ford is the dominant force in the business of the Ford Motor Company. No plan of operations could be adopted unless he consented, and no board of directors can be elected whom he does not favor. One of the directors of the company has no stock. One share was assigned to him to qualify him for the position, but it is not claimed that he owns it. A business, one of the largest in the world, and one of the most profitable, has been built up. It employs many men, at good pay.

"My ambition," said Mr. Ford, "is to employ still more men, to spread the benefits of this industrial system to the greatest possible number, to help them build up their lives and their homes. To do this we are putting the greatest share of our profits back in the business." * * *

The record, and especially the testimony of Mr. Ford, convinces that he has to some extent the attitude towards shareholders of one who has dispensed and distributed to them large gains and that they should be content to take what he chooses to give. His testimony creates the impression, also, that he thinks the Ford Motor Company has made too much money, has had too large profits, and that although large profits might still be earned, a sharing of them with the public, by reducing the price of the output of the company, ought to be undertaken. We have no doubt that certain sentiments, philanthropic and altruistic, creditable to Mr. Ford, had large influence in determining the policy to be pursued by the Ford Motor Company—the policy which has been herein referred to. * * *

These cases, after all, like all others in which the subject is treated, turn finally upon the point, the question, whether it appears that the directors were not acting for the best interest of the corporation * * *. The difference between an incidental humanitarian expenditure of corporate funds for the benefit of the employees, like the building of a hospital for their use and the employment of agencies for the betterment of their condition, and a general purpose and plan to benefit mankind at the expense of others, is obvious * * *. A business corporation is organized and carried on primarily for the profit of the stockholders. The powers of the directors are to be employed for that end. The discretion of directors is to be exercised in the choice of means to attain that end and does not extend to a change in the end itself, to the reduction of profits or to the nondistribution of profits among stockholders in order to devote them to other purposes. * * *

We are not, however, persuaded that we should interfere with the proposed expansion of the business of the Ford Motor Company. In view of the fact that the selling price of products may be increased at any time, the ultimate results of the larger business cannot be certainly estimated. The judges are not business experts. It is recognized that plans must often be made for a long future, for expected competition, for a continuing as well as an immediately profitable venture. The experience of the Ford Motor Company is evidence of capable management of its affairs. * * *

Defendants say, and it is true, that a considerable cash balance must be at all times carried by such a concern. But, as has been stated, there was a large daily, weekly, monthly, receipt of cash. The output was practically continuous and was continuously, and within a few days, turned into cash. Moreover, the contemplated expenditures were not to be immediately made. The large sum appropriated for the smelter plant was payable over a considerable period of time. So that, without going further, it would appear that, accepting and approving the plan of the directors, it was their duty to distribute on or near the first of August, 1916, a very large sum of money to stockholders. * * *

The decree of the court below fixing and determining the specific amount to be distributed to stockholders is affirmed. In other respects, except as to the allowance of costs, the said decree is reversed.

## QUESTIONS

1. Distinguish between equity and debt securities.
2. Identify and describe the principal kinds of debt securities.
3. Identify and describe the principal kinds of equity securities.
4. Explain what type and amount of consideration a corporation may validly receive for the shares it issues.
5. Explain the legal restrictions imposed upon dividends and other distributions.

## PROBLEMS

**1.** Olympic National Agencies was organized with an authorized capitalization of preferred stock and common stock. The articles of incorporation provided for a 7 percent annual dividend for the preferred stock. The articles further stated that the preferred stock would be given priority interests in the corporation's assets up to the par value of the stock. Subsequently, the shareholders voted to dissolve Olympic. Olympic's assets greatly exceeded its liabilities. The liquidating trustee petitioned the court for instructions on the respective rights of the shareholders in the assets of the corporation upon dissolution. The court ordered the trustee to distribute the corporate assets remaining after the preference of the preferred stock is satisfied to the common and preferred stockholders on a *pro rata* basis. Was the court correct in rendering this decision? Explain.

**2.** The XYZ Corporation was duly organized on July 10. Its certificate of incorporation provides for total authorized capital of $1 million, consisting of ten thousand shares of common stock with a par value of $100 per share. The corporation issues for cash a total of 500 certificates, numbered 1 to 500 inclusive, representing various amounts of shares in the names of various individuals. The shares were all paid for in advance, so the certificates are all dated and mailed on the same day. The 500 certificates of stock represent a total of 10,500 shares. Certificate 499 for 300 shares was issued to Jane Smith. Certificate 500 for 250 shares was issued to William Jones. Is the validity of the stock thus issued in any way questionable? What are the rights of Smith and Jones?

**3.** Doris subscribed for two hundred shares of 12 percent cumulative, participating, redeemable, convertible, preferred shares of the Ritz Hotel Company with a par value of $100 per share. The subscription agreement provided that she was to receive a bonus of one share of common stock of $100 par value for each share of preferred stock. Doris fully paid her subscription agreement of $20,000 and received the two hundred shares of preferred stock and the bonus stock of two hundred shares of the par value common. The Ritz Hotel Co. later becomes insolvent. Ronald, the receiver of the corporation, brings suit for $20,000, the par value of the common stock. What judgment?

**4.** The Hyperion Company has an authorized capital stock of one thousand shares with a par value of $100 per share, of which nine hundred shares, all fully paid, were outstanding. Having an ample surplus, the Hyperion Company purchased from its shareholders one hundred shares at par. Subsequently, the Hyperion Company, needing additional working capital, issued two hundred shares to Alexander at $80 per share. Two years later, the Hyperion Company was forced into bankruptcy. How much, if any, may the trustee in bankruptcy recover from Alexander?

**5.** For five years, Henry and James had been engaged as partners in building houses. They owned the equipment necessary to conduct the business and had an excellent reputation. In March, Joyce, who had previously been in the same kind of business, proposed that Henry, James, and Joyce form a corporation for the purpose of constructing medium-priced houses. They engaged attorney Portia, who did all the work required to incorporate the business under the name of Libra Corp.

The certificate of incorporation authorized 1,000 shares of $100 par value stock. At the organizational meeting of the incorporators, Henry, James, and Joyce were elected directors, and Libra Corp. issued a total of 650 shares for its stock. Henry and James each received 200 shares in consideration of transferring to Libra Corp. the equipment and goodwill of their partnership, which had a combined value of more than $40,000. Joyce received 200 shares in consideration for promising to work for Libra Corp. in the future, and Portia received 50 shares as compensation for the legal services she rendered in forming Libra Corp.

Later that year, Libra Corp. suffered several financial setbacks and in December ceased operations. What rights, if any, does Libra Corp. have against Henry, James, Joyce, and Portia in connection with the original issuance of its shares?

**6.** Paul Bunyan is the owner of noncumulative 8 percent preferred stock in the Broadview Corporation, which had no earnings or profits in 2009. In 2010, the corporation had large profits and a surplus from which it might properly have declared dividends. The directors refused to do so, however, instead using the surplus to purchase goods necessary for the corporation's expanding business. The corporation earned a small profit in 2011. The directors at the end of 2011 declared a 10 percent dividend on the common stock and an 8 percent dividend on the preferred stock without paying preferred dividends for 2010.

**(a)** Is Bunyan entitled to dividends for 2009? For 2010?

**(b)** Is Bunyan entitled to a dividend of 10 percent rather than 8 percent in 2011?

**7.** Alpha Corporation has outstanding four hundred shares of $100 par value common stock, which has been issued and sold at $105 per share for a total of $42,000. Alpha is incorporated in State X, which has adopted the earned surplus test for all distributions. At a time when the assets of the corporation amount to $65,000 and the liabilities to creditors total $10,000, the directors learn that Rachel, who holds one hundred of the four hundred shares of stock, is planning to sell her shares on the open market for $10,500. Believing that this will not be in the best interest of the corporation, the directors enter into an agreement with Rachel to buy the shares for $10,500 from her. About six months later, when the assets of the corporation have decreased to $50,000 and its liabilities, not including its liability to Rachel, have increased to $20,000, the directors use $10,000 to pay a dividend to all of the shareholders. The corporation later becomes insolvent.

(a) Does Rachel have any liability to the corporation or its creditors in connection with the reacquisition by the corporation of the one hundred shares?

(b) Was the payment of the $10,000 dividend proper?

**8.** Almega Corporation, organized under the laws of State S, has outstanding twenty thousand shares of $100 par value nonvoting preferred stock calling for noncumulative dividends of $5 per year; ten thousand shares of voting preferred stock with $50 par value, calling for cumulative dividends of $2.50 per year; and ten thousand shares of no par common stock. State S has adopted the earned surplus test for all distributions. As of the end of 2003, the corporation had no earned surplus. In 2007, the corporation had net earnings of $170,000; in 2008, $135,000; in 2009, $60,000; in 2010, $210,000; and in 2011, $120,000. The board of directors passed over all dividends during the four years from 2007 through 2010, because the company needed working capital for expansion purposes. In 2011, however, the directors declared on the noncumulative preferred shares a dividend of $5 per share, on the cumulative preferred stock a dividend of $12.50 per share, and on the common stock a dividend of $30 per share. The board submitted its declaration to the voting shareholders, and they ratified it. Before the dividends were paid, Payne, the record holder of five hundred shares of the noncumulative preferred stock, brought an appropriate action to restrain any payment to the cumulative preferred or common shareholders until the company paid to noncumulative preferred shareholders a full dividend for the period from 2007 to 2010. Decision? What is the maximum lawful dividend that may be paid to the owner of each share of common stock?

**9.** Sayre learned that Adams, Boone, and Chase were planning to form a corporation for the purpose of manufacturing and marketing a line of novelties to wholesale outlets. Sayre had patented a self-locking gas tank cap but lacked the financial backing to market it profitably. He negotiated with Adams, Boone, and Chase, who agreed to purchase the patent rights for $5,000 in cash and two hundred shares of $100 par value preferred stock in a corporation to be formed.

The corporation was formed and Sayre's stock issued to him, but the corporation has refused to make the cash payment. It has also refused to declare dividends, although the business has been very profitable because of Sayre's patent and has a substantial earned surplus with a large cash balance on hand. It is selling the remainder of the originally authorized issue of preferred shares, ignoring Sayre's demand to purchase a proportionate number of these shares. What are Sayre's rights, if any?

**10.** Wood, the receiver of Stanton Oil Company, sued Stanton's shareholders to recover dividends paid to them for three years, claiming that at the time these dividends were declared, Stanton was in fact insolvent. Wood did not allege that the present creditors were also creditors when the dividends were paid. Were the dividends wrongfully paid? Explain.

**11.** International Distributing Export Company (I.D.E.) was organized as a corporation on September 7, 2004, under the laws of New York and commenced business on November 1, 2004. I.D.E. formerly had been in existence as a sole proprietorship. On October 31, 2004, the newly organized corporation had liabilities of $64,084. Its only assets, in the sum of $33,042, were those of the former sole proprietorship. The corporation, however, set up an asset on its balance sheet in the amount of $32,000 for goodwill. As a result of this entry, I.D.E. had a surplus at the end of each of its fiscal years from 2005 until 2010. Cano, a shareholder, received $7,144 in dividends from I.D.E. during the period from 2006 to 2011. May Fried, the trustee in bankruptcy of I.D.E., recover the amount of these dividends from Cano on the basis that they had been paid when I.D.E. was insolvent or when its capital was impaired?

**12.** GM Sub Corporation (GM Sub), a subsidiary of Grand Metropolitan Limited, acquired all outstanding shares of Liggett Group, Inc., a Delaware corporation. Rothschild International Corporation (Rothschild) was the owner of 650 shares of the 7 percent cumulative preferred stock of Liggett Group, Inc. According to Liggett's certificate of incorporation, the holders of the 7 percent preferred were to receive $100 per share "in the event of any liquidation of the assets of the Corporation." GM Sub had offered $70 per share for the 7 percent preferred, $158.63 for another class of preferred stock, and $69 for each common stock share. Liggett's board of directors approved the offer as fair and recommended acceptance by Liggett's shareholders. As a result, 39.8 percent of the 7 percent preferred shares was sold to GM Sub. In addition, GM Sub acquired 75.9 percent of the other preferred stock and 87.4 percent of the common stock. The acquisition of the overwhelming majority of these classes of stock—coupled with the fact that the 7 percent preferred shareholders could not vote as a class on the merger proposal—gave GM Sub sufficient voting power to approve a follow-up merger. As a result, all remaining shareholders other than GM Sub were eliminated in return for payment of cash for their shares. These shareholders received the same consideration ($70 per share) offered in the tender offer.

Rothschild brought suit against Liggett and Grand Metropolitan, charging each with a breach of its duty of fair dealing owed to the 7 percent preferred shareholders. Rothschild based both claims on the contention that the merger was a liquidation of Liggett insofar as the rights of the 7 percent preferred stockholders were concerned and that those preferred shareholders therefore were entitled to the liquidation preference of $100 per share, not $70 per share. Are the preferred shareholders entitled to a liquidation preference? Why?

# CHAPTER 36
# Management Structure

The corporate management structure, as required by State incorporation statutes, is pyramidal. At the base of the pyramid are the *shareholders*, who are the residual owners of the corporation. Basic to their role in controlling the corporation is the right to elect representatives to manage the ordinary business matters of the corporation and the right to approve all extraordinary matters.

The *board of directors*, as the shareholders' elected representatives, are delegated the power to manage the business of the corporation. Directors exercise dominion and control over the corporation, hold positions of trust and confidence, and determine questions of operating policy. Because they are not expected to devote their time completely to the affairs of the corporation, directors have broad authority to delegate power to agents and to *officers* who hold their offices at the will of the board and who, in turn, hire and fire all necessary operating personnel and run the day-to-day affairs of the corporation.

◆ **SEE FIGURE 36-1: Management Structure of Corporations: The Statutory Model**

## CORPORATE GOVERNANCE

The statutory model of corporate management, although required by most States, accurately describes the actual governance of only a few corporations. A great majority of corporations are closely held; they have a small number of stockholders and no ready market for their shares, and most of the shareholders actively participate in the management of the business. Typically, the shareholders of a closely held corporation are also its directors and officers.

Although the statutory model and the actual governance of closely held corporations diverge, in most States **closely held corporations** must adhere to the general corporate statutory model. One of the greatest burdens conventional general business corporation statutes impose on closely held corporations is a set of rigid corporate formalities. Although these formalities may be necessary and desirable in publicly held corporations, where management and ownership are separate, in a closely held corporation, where the owners are usually the managers, many of these formalities are unnecessary and meaningless. Consequently, shareholders in closely held corporations tend to disregard corporate formalities, sometimes forfeiting their limited liability as a result. In response to this problem, the 1969 Amendments to the Model Business Corporation Act (MBCA) included several liberalizing provisions for closely held corporations. The amendments were carried over to the Revised Act. Moreover, about twenty States have enacted special legislation to accommodate the needs of closely held corporations. These statutes vary considerably but they are all optional and must be specifically elected by eligible corporations. Eligibility is generally based on the corporation having fewer than a specified maximum number of shareholders. These special close corporation statutes permit operation without a board of directors and authorize broad use of shareholder agreements, including their use in place of bylaws. Some prohibit courts from denying limited liability simply because an electing corporation engages in informal conduct.

As noted in *Chapter 34*, a Statutory Close Corporation Supplement (the Supplement) to the Model and Revised Acts has been promulgated. The Supplement relaxes the most nonessential corporate formalities by permitting operation without a board of directors, authorizing broad use of shareholder agreements (including their use in place of bylaws), making annual meetings optional, and authorizing one person to execute documents in more than one capacity. Most important, it prevents courts from denying limited liability simply because the corporation is a statutory close corporation. The general incorporation statute applies to closely held corporations except to the extent that it is inconsistent with the Supplement.

The Revised Act was amended to authorize shareholders in closely held corporations to adopt unanimous shareholders' agreements that depart from the statutory norms. Section 7.32. The section requires that the agreement is set forth either (1) in the articles of incorporation or bylaws and approved by all persons who are shareholders at the time of the agreement or (2) in a written agreement that is signed by all persons who are shareholders at the time of the agreement and is made known to the corporation. Section 7.32(b). Under this section, shareholder agreements are valid for ten years unless the agreement provides otherwise. The section *specifically* validates a number of provisions, including those (1) eliminating or restricting the powers of the board of directors; (2) establishing who shall be directors or officers; (3) specifying how directors or officers will be selected or removed; (4) governing the exercise or division of voting power by or between the shareholders and directors; (5) permitting the use of weighted voting rights or director proxies; and (6) transferring the authority of the board of directors to one or more shareholders or other persons. The section also *generally* authorizes any provision that governs the exercise of the corporate powers or the management of the business and affairs of the corporation or the relationship among the shareholders, the directors and the corporation, or among any of them, so long as it is not contrary to public policy. There are limits, however, and a shareholder agreement that provides that the directors of the corporation have no duties of care or loyalty to the corporation or the shareholders would be beyond the authorization of Section 7.32. To the extent that an agreement authorized by this section limits the discretion or powers of the board of directors, it relieves the directors of liability while imposing that liability upon the person or persons in whom such discretion or powers are vested.

In sharp contrast is the large, **publicly held corporation** with a vast market for its shares. These shares typically are widely dispersed, and very few are owned by management. Approximately two-thirds are held by institutional investors, such as insurance companies, pension and retirement funds, mutual funds, and university endowments; the remaining shares are owned directly by individual investors. Whereas a great majority of institutional investors exercise their right to vote their shares, most individual investors do not. Nonetheless, virtually all shareholders who vote for the directors do so through the use of a **proxy**—an authorization by a shareholder to an agent (usually the chief executive officer [CEO] of the corporation) to vote his shares. The majority of shareholders who return their proxies vote as management advises. As a result, the nominating committee of the board of directors actually determines the board's membership.

Thus, the 500 to 1,000 largest, publicly held corporations—which own the great bulk of the industrial wealth of the United States—are controlled by a small group of corporate officers. This great concentration of control over wealth, and the power that results from it, raises social, policy, and ethical issues concerning the governance of these corporations and the accountability of their management. The actions (or inactions) of these powerful corporations greatly affect the national economy, employment policies, the health and safety of the workplace and the environment, product quality, and the effects of overseas operations.

Accordingly, the accountability of management is a critical issue. In particular, what obligations should the large, publicly held corporation and its management have to (1) the corporation's shareholders, (2) its employees, (3) its customers, (4) its suppliers, (5) the communities in which the corporation is located, and (6) the rest of society? These critical questions remain mostly unanswered. Some corporate statutes now provide that the board of directors, committees of the board, individual directors, and individual officers *may*, in determining the corporation's best interests, consider the effects of any action upon employees, suppliers, creditors, and customers of the corporation; the communities in which the corporation maintains offices or other establishments; the economy of the State and nation; societal considerations; and all other pertinent factors.

In response to the business scandals involving companies such as Enron, WorldCom, Global Crossing, Adelphia, and Arthur Andersen, in 2002 Congress passed the Sarbanes-Oxley Act, which is further discussed in *Chapter 44*, Securities Regulation, as well as in *Chapters 6* and *45*. The legislation seeks to prevent these types of scandals by increasing corporate responsibility; adding new financial disclosure requirements; creating new criminal offenses; increasing the penalties for existing federal crimes; and creating a five-person Accounting Oversight Board with authority to review and discipline auditors. Several provisions of the Act impose governance requirements on publicly held corporations and will be discussed in this chapter.

In July 2010, President Obama signed into law the Dodd-Frank Wall Street Reform and Consumer Protection Act (CFPA), the most significant change to U.S. financial regulation since the New Deal. One of the many stand-alone statutes included in the CFPA is the Investor Protection and Securities Reform Act of 2010, which imposes new corporate governance rules on publicly held companies. These corporate governance provisions of the CFPA will be discussed in this chapter, *Chapter 37*, and *Chapter 44*.

The structure and governance of corporations must adhere to incorporation statute requirements. Therefore, this chapter will discuss the rights, duties, and liabilities of shareholders, directors, and officers under these statutes.

◆ SEE FIGURE 36-2: **Management Structure of Typical Closely Held Corporation**

◆ SEE FIGURE 36-3: **Management Structure of Typical Publicly Held Corporation**

## ROLE OF SHAREHOLDERS

The role of the shareholders in managing the corporation is generally restricted to the election of directors, the approval of certain extraordinary matters, the approval of corporate transactions that are void or voidable unless ratified, and the right to bring suits to enforce these rights.

## VOTING RIGHTS OF SHAREHOLDERS

The shareholder's right to vote is fundamental both to the corporate concept and to the corporation's management structure. In most States, a shareholder is entitled to one vote for each share of stock that she owns, unless the articles of incorporation provide otherwise. In addition, incorporation

◆ FIGURE 36-1: **Management Structure of Corporations: The Statutory Model**

◆ FIGURE 36-2: **Management Structure of Typical Closely Held Corporation**

◆ FIGURE 36-3: **Management Structure of Typical Publicly Held Corporation**

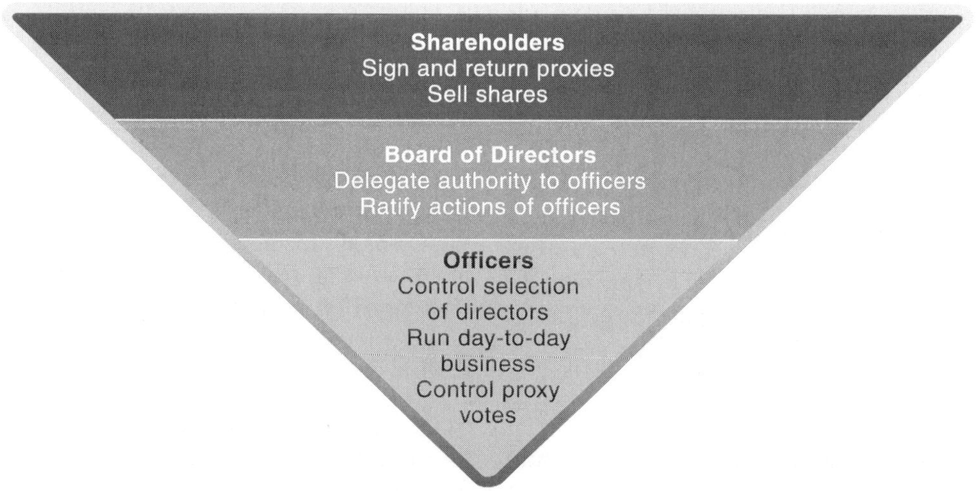

statutes generally permit the issuance of one or more classes of nonvoting stock, so long as at least one class of shares has voting rights. Section 6.01. The articles of incorporation may provide for more or less than one vote for any share. For example, in *Providence & Worcester Co. v. Baker*, 378 A.2d 121 (Del. 1977), the court upheld articles of incorporation which provided that each shareholder was entitled to one vote per share for each of fifty or fewer shares that he owned and one vote for every twenty shares in excess of fifty, but no shareholder was entitled to vote more than one-fourth of the whole number of outstanding shares.

## SHAREHOLDER MEETINGS

Shareholders may exercise their voting rights at both annual and special shareholder meetings. **Annual meetings** are required and must be held at a time fixed by the bylaws. Section 7.01. If the annual shareholder meeting is not held within the earlier of six months after the end of the corporation's fiscal year or fifteen months after its last annual meeting, any shareholder may petition and obtain a court order requiring such meeting to be held. Section 7.03. The Revised Act further provides that the failure to hold an annual meeting does not affect the validity of any corporate action. Section 7.01(c). In contrast, the Close Corporation Supplement provides that no annual meeting of shareholders need be held unless a shareholder makes a written request at least thirty days in advance of the date specified for the meeting. The date may be established in the articles of incorporation, the bylaws, or a shareholders' agreement.

**Special meetings** may be called by the board of directors, by holders of at least 10 percent of the shares, or by other persons authorized to do so in the articles of incorporation. Section 7.02. As amended, the Revised Act permits a corporation's articles of incorporation to lower or raise the 10 percent requirement, but the corporation cannot raise the requirement to more than 25 percent of the shares.

Written notice, stating the date, time, and place of the meeting and, in the case of a special meeting, the purposes for which it is called, must be given in advance of the meeting. Section 7.05. Notice, however, may be waived in writing by any shareholder entitled to notice. Section 7.06.

A number of States permit shareholders to conduct business without a meeting if they consent unanimously in writing to the action taken. Section 7.04. Some States have further relaxed the formalities of shareholder action by permitting shareholders to act without a meeting simply by obtaining the written consent of the number of shares required to act on the matter.

## QUORUM AND VOTING

To effectuate corporate business, a quorum of shares must be represented at the meeting, either in person or by proxy. Unissued shares and treasury stock may not be voted or counted in determining whether a quorum exists. The majority view is that once a quorum is present at a meeting, it is deemed present for the rest of the meeting, even if shareholders withdraw in an effort to break it. Unless the articles of incorporation otherwise provide, a majority of shares entitled to vote constitutes a quorum. In most States and under the Model Act, a quorum may not consist of less than one-third of the shares entitled to vote; the Revised Act and some States do not provide a statutory minimum for a quorum. State statutes do not impose an upper limit upon a quorum, so it may be set higher than a majority and may even require *all* the outstanding shares.

Most States require shareholder actions to be approved by a majority of shares represented at the meeting and entitled to vote if a quorum exists. The Revised Act and some States, however, provide a different rule: if a quorum exists, a shareholder action (other than the election of directors) is approved if the votes cast for the action exceed the votes cast against it. Section 7.25(c). Moreover, virtually all States permit the articles of incorporation to increase the percentage of shares required to take any action that is subject to shareholder approval. Section 7.27. A provision that increases voting requirements is commonly called a "supermajority provision." Close corporations frequently have used supermajority shareholder voting requirements to protect minority shareholders from oppression by the majority, while some publicly held corporations recently have used them to defend against hostile takeover bids.

## ELECTION OF DIRECTORS

Directors are elected each year at the annual meeting of the shareholders. Most States provide that where a corporation's board consists of nine or more directors, the charter or bylaws may provide for a **classification** or staggering of directors, that is, a division into two or three classes to be as nearly equal in number as possible and to serve for staggered terms. Under the Revised Act as amended there is no minimum-size board required. Section 8.06. If the directors are divided into two classes, the members of each class are elected once a year in alternate years for a two-year term; if divided into three classes, they are elected for three-year terms. This permits one-half of the board to be elected every two years or one-third to be elected every three years, thus lending continuity to the board's membership. Moreover, where there are two or more classes of shares, the courts generally have held that each class may elect a specified number of directors, if the articles of incorporation so provide. The Revised Act makes this explicit. Section 8.04.

**Straight Voting** Normally, each shareholder has one vote for each share owned, and under the Revised Act and many State statutes directors are elected by a *plurality* of the votes.

Section 7.28(a). In other States directors are elected by a *majority* of the votes. The charter may increase the percentage of shares required for the election of directors. Thus, under straight voting shareholders owning a majority of the voting shares can always elect the *entire* board of directors.

**Cumulative Voting** In certain States shareholders have the right of cumulative voting when electing directors. In most of these States and under the Revised Act, cumulative voting is permissive, not mandatory. Section 7.28(b). **Cumulative voting** entitles the shareholders to multiply the number of votes they are entitled to cast by the number of directors for whom they are entitled to vote and to cast the product for a single candidate or distribute the product among two or more candidates. Cumulative voting permits a minority shareholder, or a group of minority shareholders acting together, to obtain minority representation on the board if they own a certain minimum number of shares. In the absence of cumulative voting, the holder or holders of 51 percent of the voting shares can elect all of the members of the board.

The formula for determining how many shares a minority shareholder with cumulative voting rights must own, or have proxies to vote, to secure representation on the board is as follows:

$$X = \frac{ac}{b + 1} + 1$$

where

$a$ = number of shares voting
$b$ = number of directors to be elected
$c$ = number of directors desired to be elected
$X$ = number of shares necessary to elect the number of directors desired to be elected

For example, Gray Corporation has two shareholders, Stephanie with sixty-four shares and Thomas with thirty-six shares. The board of directors of Gray Corporation consists of three directors. Under "straight" or noncumulative voting, Stephanie could cast sixty-four votes for each of her three candidates, and Thomas could cast thirty-six votes for his three candidates. As a result, all three of Stephanie's candidates would be elected. On the other hand, if cumulative voting were in force, Thomas could elect one director:

$$X = \frac{ac}{b + 1} + 1$$

$$X = \frac{100(1)}{3 + 1} + 1 = 26 \text{ shares}$$

This result indicates that Thomas would need at least twenty-six shares to elect one director. Because Thomas has the right to vote thirty-six shares, he would be able to elect one director. Stephanie, of course, with her sixty-four shares, could elect the remaining two directors.

The effect of cumulative voting for directors may be diluted by classification, by staggering elections, or by reducing the size of the board. For example, if nine directors are each elected annually, only 11 percent of the shares are needed to elect one director; if the nine directors' elections are staggered and three are elected annually, 26 percent of the shares are required to elect one director.

## REMOVAL OF DIRECTORS

By a majority vote, shareholders may remove any director or the entire board of directors, with or without cause, in a meeting called for that purpose. In the case of a corporation having cumulative voting, however, a director may be removed only if the number of votes opposing his removal would be insufficient to elect him. Section 8.08(c). Removal of directors is discussed more fully later in this chapter.

## APPROVAL OF FUNDAMENTAL CHANGES

The board of directors manages the ordinary business affairs of the corporation. Extraordinary matters involving fundamental changes in the corporation require shareholder approval; such matters include amendments to the articles of incorporation, a sale or lease of all or substantially all of the corporate assets not in the regular course of business, most mergers, consolidations, compulsory share exchanges, and dissolution. Fundamental changes are discussed in *Chapter 37*.

## CONCENTRATIONS OF VOTING POWER

Certain devices enable groups of shareholders to combine their voting power for purposes such as obtaining or maintaining control or maximizing the impact of cumulative voting. The most important methods of concentrating voting power are proxies, voting trusts, and shareholder voting agreements.

◆ SEE FIGURE 36-4: **Concentrations of Voting Power**

**Proxies** A shareholder may vote either in person or by written proxy. Section 7.22(a). As mentioned earlier, a proxy is simply a shareholder's authorization to an agent to vote his shares at a particular meeting or on a particular question. Generally, proxies must be in writing to be effective; furthermore, statutes typically limit the duration of proxies to no more than eleven months, unless the proxy specifically provides otherwise. Section 7.22(c). Some States limit all proxy appointments to a period of eleven months. Because a proxy is the appointment of an agent, it is revocable, as all agencies are, unless conspicuously stated to be irrevocable *and* coupled with an interest, such as shares held as collateral. Section 7.22(d). The solicitation of proxies by publicly held corporations is also regulated by the Securities Exchange Act of 1934, as discussed in *Chapter 44*.

**FIGURE 36-4: Concentrations of Voting Power**

| | Proxy | Voting Trust | Shareholder Agreement |
|---|---|---|---|
| **Definition** | Authorization of an agent to vote shares | Conferral of voting rights on trustee | Agreement among shareholders on voting of shares |
| **Formalities** | Signed writing delivered to corporation | Signed writing delivered to corporation | Signed writing |
| **Duration** | Eleven months, unless otherwise agreed | Ten years; may be extended | No limit |
| **Revocability** | Yes, unless coupled with an interest | No | Only by unanimous agreement |
| **Prevalence** | Publicly held | Publicly and closely held | Closely held |

As discussed above, in large, publicly held corporations, virtually all shareholders who vote for the directors do so through the use of proxies. Because the majority of shareholders who return their proxies vote as management advises, the nominating committee of the board of directors almost always determines the board's membership. In 2009, the Revised Model Business Corporation Act (RMBCA) was amended to authorize the directors or shareholders of corporations to establish procedures in the corporate bylaws that (1) require the corporation to include in the corporation's proxy statement one or more individuals nominated by a shareholder in addition to individuals nominated by the board of directors and (2) require the corporation to reimburse shareholders for reasonable expenses incurred in soliciting proxies in an election of directors. Section 2.06(c).

Moreover, the CFPA authorizes the Securities and Exchange Commission (SEC) to issue rules requiring that a publicly held company's proxy solicitation include nominations for the board of directors submitted by shareholders. The SEC has issued a new such rule. See *Chapter 44*.

**Voting Trusts** Voting trusts, which are designed to concentrate corporate control in one or more persons, have been used in both publicly held and closely held corporations. A voting trust is a device by which one or more shareholders separate the voting rights of their shares from the ownership of those shares. Under a voting trust, one or more shareholders confer on a trustee the right to vote or otherwise act for them by signing a written agreement setting out the provisions of the trust and transferring their shares to the trustee. Section 7.30(a). In most States, voting trusts are permitted by statute but usually are limited in duration to ten years. The Revised Act and many States permit all or some of the parties to a voting trust to extend it for an additional term of up to ten years by signing an extension agreement and obtaining the voting trustee's written consent. Section 7.30(c). The extension runs from the time the first shareholder signs the agreement but binds only those shareholders who consent to it.

**Shareholder Voting Agreements** In most jurisdictions, shareholders may agree in writing to vote in a specified manner for the election or removal of directors or on any other matter subject to shareholder approval. Section 7.31(a). The Revised Act and some State statutes expressly provide that shareholder voting agreements are enforceable by a decree of specific performance. Section 7.31(b). Unlike voting trusts, shareholder voting agreements are usually not limited in duration. Shareholder voting agreements are used frequently in closely held corporations, especially in conjunction with restrictions on the transfer of shares, to provide each shareholder with greater control and *delectus personae* (the right to choose those who will become shareholders).

*Galler v. Galler*, 32 Ill.2d 16, 203 N.E.2d 577 (1964), provides a well-known example of the effect a shareholder agreement may have within a close corporation. In 1927, two brothers, Benjamin and Isadore Galler, incorporated the Galler Drug Co., a wholesale drug business that they had operated as equal partners since 1919. The company continued to grow, and in 1955 the two brothers and their wives, Emma and Rose Galler, entered into a written shareholder agreement to leave the corporation in equal control of each family after the death of either brother. Specifically, the agreement provided that the corporation would continue to provide income for the support and maintenance of their immediate families and that the parties would vote for directors so as to give the estate and heirs of a deceased shareholder the same representation as before. Benjamin died in 1957, and shortly thereafter his widow, Emma, requested that Isadore, the surviving brother, comply with the terms of the agreement. When he refused, instead proposing that certain changes be made in the agreement, Emma brought an action seeking specific performance of the agreement.

Isadore and his wife, Rose, defended on the ground that the shareholder agreement was against public policy and the State's corporation law. The court decided in favor of Emma Galler, explaining that a close corporation is one in which the stock is held in a few hands and is rarely traded. In contrast to a shareholder in a public corporation, who may easily trade his shares on the open market when he disagrees with management over corporate policy, the shareholder of a closely held corporation often has no ready market in which to sell his shares should he wish to do so. Moreover, the shareholder in a closely held corporation often has most of his capital invested in the corporation and, therefore, views himself not only as an investor but also as a participant in the management of the business. Without a shareholder agreement subject to specific performance by the courts, the minority shareholder might find himself at the mercy of the controlling majority shareholder. In short, the detailed shareholder voting agreement is the only sound means by which the minority shareholder can protect himself. Therefore, the court concluded, because the agreement was reasonable in its scope and purpose of providing continuing support for the Galler brothers' families, it should be enforced.

### RESTRICTIONS ON TRANSFER OF SHARES

In the absence of a specific agreement, shares of stock are freely transferable. Although free transferability of shares is usually considered an advantage of the corporate form, in some situations the shareholders may prefer to restrict the transfer of shares. In closely held corporations, for example, stock transfer restrictions are used to control who may become shareholders, thereby achieving the corporate equivalent of *delectus personae* (choice of the person). They are also used to maintain statutory close corporation status or S Corporation status by restricting the number of persons who may become shareholders. In publicly held corporations, restrictions on the transfer of shares are used to preserve exemptions under State and Federal securities laws. (These are discussed in *Chapter 44*.)

Most incorporation statutes have no provisions governing share transfer restrictions. The common law validates such restrictions if they are adopted for a lawful purpose and do not unreasonably restrain or prohibit transferability. In addition, the Uniform Commercial Code provides that an otherwise valid share transfer restriction is ineffective against a person without actual knowledge of it unless the restriction is conspicuously noted on the share certificate. Section 8–204.

The Revised Act and the statutes of several States permit the articles of incorporation, bylaws, or a shareholder agreement to impose transfer restrictions but require that the restriction be noted conspicuously on the stock certificate. The Revised Act authorizes restrictions for any reasonable purpose, including maintaining statutory close corporation status and preserving exemptions under Federal and State securities law. Section 6.27.

## ENFORCEMENT RIGHTS OF SHAREHOLDERS

To protect a shareholder's interests in the corporation, the law provides shareholders with certain enforcement rights, including the right to obtain information, the right to sue the corporation directly or to sue on the corporation's behalf, and the right to dissent.

### RIGHT TO INSPECT BOOKS AND RECORDS

Most States have enacted statutory provisions granting shareholders the right to inspect for a *proper purpose* books and records in person or through an agent and to make extracts from them. The right generally covers all records relevant to the shareholder's legitimate interest. The Revised Act extends the right to copy records to include, if reasonable, the right to receive copies made by photographic, xerographic, or other means. Section 16.03. The Act provides that every shareholder is entitled to examine *specified* corporate records upon prior written request if the demand is made in good faith, for a proper purpose, and during regular business hours at the corporation's principal office. Section 16.02. Many States, however, limit this right to shareholders who own a minimum number of shares or to those who have been shareholders for a specified minimum time. For example, the MBCA requires that a shareholder either must own 5 percent of the outstanding shares or must have owned his shares for at least six months; a court, however, may order an inspection even when neither condition is met.

A **proper purpose** for inspection is one that is reasonably relevant to a shareholder's interest in the corporation. Proper purposes include determining the financial condition of the corporation, the value of shares, the existence of mismanagement or improper transactions, or the names of other shareholders in order to communicate with them about corporate affairs. The right of inspection is subject to abuse and will be denied a shareholder who is seeking information for an improper purpose. Examples of improper purposes include obtaining proprietary information for use by a competing company or obtaining a list of shareholders in order to offer it for sale.

The Revised Act requires that a voting list of shareholders be prepared and that it be made available to shareholders upon request. Section 7.20. In addition, unlike many States, the Act requires every corporation to prepare and submit to its shareholders annual financial statements. Section 16.20.

◆ **SEE CASE 36-1**

## SHAREHOLDER SUITS

The ultimate recourse of a shareholder, short of selling her shares, is to bring suit against or on behalf of the corporation. Shareholder suits are essentially of two kinds: direct suits or derivative suits.

◆ SEE FIGURE 36-5: **Shareholder Suits**

**Direct Suits** A shareholder may bring a direct suit to enforce a claim that he has *against* the corporation, based upon his ownership of shares. Any recovery in a direct suit goes to the shareholder plaintiff. Examples of direct suits include shareholder actions to compel payment of dividends properly declared, to enforce the right to inspect corporate records, to enforce the right to vote, to protect preemptive rights, and to compel dissolution. Shareholders also may bring a class suit or class action. A **class suit** is a direct suit in which one or more shareholders purport to represent a class of shareholders in order to recover for injuries to the entire class. Such a suit is a direct suit because the representative claims that all similarly situated shareholders were injured by an act that did not injure the corporation.

**Derivative Suits** A derivative suit is a cause of action brought by one or more shareholders *on behalf* of the corporation to enforce a right belonging to the corporation. Shareholders may bring such an action when the board of directors refuses to so act on the corporation's behalf. Recovery usually goes to the corporation's treasury, so that all shareholders can benefit proportionately. Examples of derivative suits are actions to recover damages from management for an *ultra vires* act, to recover damages for a managerial breach of duty, and to recover improper dividends. In such situations, the board of directors may well be hesitant to bring suit against the corporation's officers or directors. Consequently, a shareholder derivative suit is the only recourse.

In most States, a shareholder must have owned his shares at the time the complained-of transaction occurred in order to bring a derivative suit. Section 7.41. In addition, under the Revised Act and some State statutes, the shareholder must first make demand upon the board of directors to enforce the corporate right. Section 7.42. In a number of States demand is excused in limited situations. The statutes of some States require a plaintiff to give security for reasonable expenses, including attorneys' fees, if his holdings of shares are not of a specified size or value. The Revised Act does not have this requirement.

◆ **SEE CASE 36-2**

## SHAREHOLDER'S RIGHT TO DISSENT

A shareholder has the right to dissent from certain corporate actions that require shareholder approval. These actions include most mergers, consolidations, compulsory share exchanges, and a sale or exchange of all or substantially all the assets of the corporation not in the usual and regular

◆ FIGURE 36-5: **Shareholder Suits**

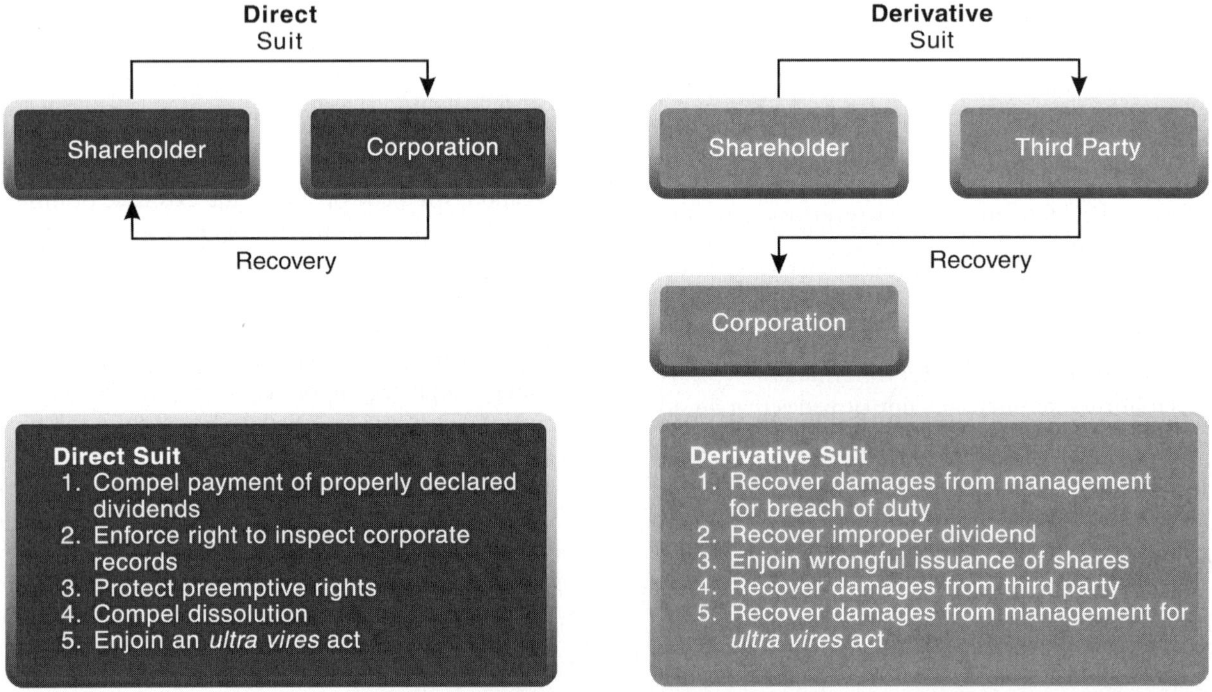

course of business. The shareholder's right to dissent is discussed in *Chapter 37*.

## ROLE OF DIRECTORS AND OFFICERS

Management of a corporation is vested by statute in its board of directors, which determines general corporate policy and appoints officers to execute that policy and to administer day-to-day corporate operations. Both the directors and the officers owe certain duties to the corporate entity as well as to the corporation's shareholders and are liable for breaching these duties.

The following sections will discuss the roles of corporate directors and officers. In some instances, controlling shareholders, or those owning a number of shares sufficient to allow them effective control over the corporation, are held to duties the same as those of directors and officers, which are discussed later in this chapter. Moreover, in close corporations, many courts impose upon *all* the shareholders a fiduciary duty similar to that imposed upon partners.

◆ **SEE CASE 36-3**

## FUNCTION OF THE BOARD OF DIRECTORS

Although the directors are elected by the shareholders to manage the corporation, the directors are neither trustees nor agents of the shareholders or the corporation. The directors are, however, fiduciaries who must perform their duties in good faith, in the best interests of the corporation, and with due care.

The Revised Act and the statutes of many States provide that "[a]ll corporate powers shall be exercised by or under the authority of, and the business and affairs of the corporation managed under the direction of, its board of directors, subject to any limitation set forth in the articles of incorporation." Section 8.01(b). In some corporations, the members of the board all are actively involved in the management of the business. In these cases, the corporate powers are exercised *by* the board of directors. On the other hand, in publicly held corporations, most board members are unlikely to be actively involved in management. Here, the corporate powers are exercised *under* the authority of the board, which formulates major management policy and monitors management's performance but does not involve itself in day-to-day management.

In publicly held corporations, the directors who are also officers or employees of the corporation are **inside directors**, while the directors who are not officers or employees are **outside directors**. Outside directors who have no business contacts with the corporation are **unaffiliated directors**; outside directors who do have such contacts with the corporation—such as investment bankers, lawyers, or suppliers—are **affiliated directors**. Historically, the boards of many publicly held corporations consisted mainly or entirely of inside directors. During the past two decades, however, the number and influence of outside directors have increased substantially, and now boards of the great majority of publicly held corporations consist primarily of outside directors.

Under the CFPA, the SEC must issue rules requiring publicly held companies to disclose in annual proxy statements the reasons why the company has chosen to separate or combine the positions of chairman of the board of directors and CEO.

In those States with special close corporation statutes, electing corporations can operate without a board of directors. Moreover, under the Revised Act as originally enacted, a corporation having fifty or fewer shareholders may dispense with or limit the authority of a board of directors by describing in its articles of incorporation those who will perform some or all of the duties of a board. The Revised Act as amended permits any corporation to dispense with a board of directors by a written agreement executed by all of the shareholders. Sections 7.32 and 8.01.

Under incorporation statutes the board has the responsibility for determining corporate policy in a number of areas, including (1) selecting and removing officers, (2) determining the corporation's capital structure, (3) initiating fundamental changes, (4) declaring dividends, and (5) setting management compensation.

### SELECTION AND REMOVAL OF OFFICERS

In most States, the board of directors is responsible for choosing the corporation's officers and may remove any officer at any time. Sections 8.40 and 8.43. Officers are corporate agents who are delegated their responsibilities by the board of directors.

### CAPITAL STRUCTURE

The board of directors determines the capital structure and financial policy of the corporation. For example, the board of directors has the power to—

1. fix the selling price of newly issued shares unless the articles reserve this power to the shareholders;
2. determine the value of the consideration the corporation will receive in payment for the shares it issues;
3. purchase, redeem, or otherwise acquire shares of the corporation's equity securities;
4. borrow money; issue notes, bonds, and other obligations; and secure any of the corporation's obligations by mortgage or pledge of any or all of the corporation's property; and
5. sell, lease, or exchange assets of the corporation in the usual and regular course of business.

### FUNDAMENTAL CHANGES

The board of directors has the power to amend or repeal the bylaws, unless the articles of incorporation reserve this power exclusively to the shareholders. Section 10.20. In a few States directors may not repeal or amend bylaws adopted by the shareholders. In addition, the board initiates certain actions that require shareholder approval. For instance, the board initiates proceedings to amend the articles of incorporation; to effect a merger, consolidation, compulsory share exchange, or the sale or lease of all or substantially all of the assets of the corporation other than in the usual and regular course of business; and to dissolve the corporation.

### DIVIDENDS

The board of directors declares the amount and type of dividends, subject to restrictions in the State incorporation statute, the articles of incorporation, and corporate loan and preferred stock agreements. Section 6.40. The board also fixes a record date for the purpose of determining the shareholders who are entitled to receive dividends. Section 6.40(b).

### MANAGEMENT COMPENSATION

The board of directors usually determines the compensation of officers. Moreover, a number of States allow the board to fix the compensation of its members. Section 8.11. In addition to fixed salaries, executive compensation may include (1) cash bonuses, (2) share bonuses, (3) share options, (4) share purchase plans, (5) insurance benefits, (6) deferred compensation, (7) retirement plans, and (8) a variety of other fringe benefits.

The CFPA requires that, at least once every three years, publicly held companies include a provision in certain proxy statements for a nonbinding shareholder vote on the compensation of executives. In a separate resolution, shareholders determine whether this "say on pay" vote should be held every one, two, or three years.

Under the Sarbanes-Oxley Act, if a publicly held company is required to issue an accounting restatement due to a material violation of securities law, the CEO and the chief financial officer must forfeit certain bonuses and compensation received, as well as any profit realized from the sale of the company's securities, during the twelve-month period following the original issuance of the noncomplying financial document.

These "clawback" requirements of the Sarbanes-Oxley Act have been greatly expanded by the CFPA. Under the CFPA, the SEC must issue rules directing the national securities exchanges to require each listed company to disclose and implement a policy regarding any incentive-based compensation that is based on financial information that must be reported under the securities laws. In the event that a company is required to prepare an accounting restatement due to the material noncompliance with any financial reporting requirement under the securities laws, the company must recover from any current or former executive officers who received excess incentive-based compensation (including stock options awarded as compensation) during the three-year period preceding the date on which the company is required to prepare an accounting restatement. The amount of the recovery is the incentive-based compensation in excess of what would have been paid to the CEO under the accounting restatement.

## ELECTION AND TENURE OF DIRECTORS

The incorporation statute, articles of incorporation, and bylaws determine the qualifications essential for those who would be directors of the corporation. They also determine the election, number, tenure, and compensation of directors. Only individuals may serve as directors. Section 8.03(a).

### ELECTION, NUMBER, AND TENURE OF DIRECTORS

The initial board of directors generally is named in the articles of incorporation and serves until the first meeting of the shareholders at which directors are elected. Section 8.05(a). Thereafter, directors are elected at annual meetings of the shareholders and hold office for one year unless their terms are staggered. If the shares represented at a meeting in person or by proxy are insufficient to constitute a quorum, however, or if the shareholders are deadlocked and unable to elect a new board, the incumbent directors continue in office as "holdover" directors until their successors are duly elected and qualified. Section 8.05(e). Although State statutes traditionally required each corporation to have three or more directors, most States permit the board to consist of one or more members. Section 8.03(a). Moreover, the number of directors may be increased or decreased, within statutory limits, by amendment to the bylaws or charter.

### VACANCIES AND REMOVAL OF DIRECTORS

The Revised Act provides that a vacancy in the board may be filled either by the shareholders or by the affirmative vote of a majority of the remaining directors, even if they constitute less than a quorum of the board. Section 8.10(a). When shareholders fill a vacant office which was held by a director elected by a class of shares, only the holders of that class of shares have the right to vote to fill that vacancy. The term of a director elected to fill a vacancy expires at the next shareholders' meeting at which directors are elected. Section 8.05(d).

Some States have no statutory provision for the removal of directors, although a common law rule permits removal for cause by action of the shareholders. The Revised Act and an increasing number of other statutes permit the shareholders to remove one or more directors or the entire board, with or without cause, at a special meeting called for that purpose, subject to cumulative voting rights, if applicable. Section 8.08. Nevertheless, the Revised Act permits the articles of incorporation to provide that directors may be removed only for cause. Section 8.08(a). In addition, however, the Revised Act and a number of States authorize a court to remove a director in a proceeding brought by the corporation or by shareholders who own at least 10 percent of the outstanding shares of any class of shares, if the court finds that (1) the director engaged in fraudulent or dishonest conduct or gross abuse of authority or discretion and (2) removal is in the best interests of the corporation. Section 8.09.

### COMPENSATION OF DIRECTORS

Traditionally, directors did not receive salaries for their directorial services, although they usually collected a fee or honorarium for attendance at meetings. The Revised Act and many incorporation statutes now specifically authorize the board of directors to fix the compensation of directors unless there is a contrary provision in the articles of incorporation or bylaws. Section 8.11.

## EXERCISE OF DIRECTORS' FUNCTIONS

Although they are powerless to bind the corporation when acting individually, directors can exert this power when acting as a board. Nevertheless, the board may act only through a meeting of the directors or with the written, unanimously signed consent of the directors, if written consent without a meeting is authorized by the statute and not contrary to the charter or bylaws. Section 8.21.

Meetings either are held at a regular time and place fixed in the bylaws or are called at special times. Notice of meetings must be given as prescribed in the bylaws. A director's attendance at any meeting is a waiver of such notice, unless the director attends only to object to the holding of the meeting or to the transacting of business at it and does not vote for or assent to action taken at the meeting. Section 8.23(b). Waiver of notice also may be given in a signed writing. Most modern statutes provide that meetings of the board may be held either in or outside the State of incorporation. Section 8.20(a).

### QUORUM AND VOTING

A majority of board members constitutes a quorum (the minimum number of members that must be present at a meeting in order to transact business). Although most States do not permit a quorum to be set at less than a majority, the Revised Act and some States allow the articles of incorporation or the bylaws to authorize a quorum consisting of as few as one-third of a board's members. Section 8.24(b). In contrast, however, in all States the articles of incorporation or bylaws may require a number greater than a simple majority. Section 8.24(a). If a quorum is present at any meeting, the act of a majority of the directors in attendance is the act of the board, unless the articles of incorporation or bylaws require the act of a greater number. Section 8.24(c).

Closely held corporations sometimes impose supermajority or unanimous quorum requirements. In addition, they may require a supermajority or unanimous vote of the board for some or all matters. The use of either or both of these provisions, however, creates the possibility of deadlock at the director level.

By requiring a quorum to be present when "a vote is taken," the Revised Act makes it clear that the board may act only when a quorum is present. Section 8.24(c) and Comment 2. This rule is in contrast to the rule governing shareholder meetings: once obtained, a quorum of shareholders cannot be broken by the withdrawal of shareholders. Many State statutes, however, do not have this provision. In any event, directors may not vote by proxy, although most States permit directors to participate in meetings through teleconference. See Section 8.20.

A director who is present at a board meeting at which action on any corporate matter is taken is deemed to have assented to such action unless, in addition to dissenting or abstaining from it, he (1) has his dissent or abstention entered in the minutes of the meeting, (2) files his written dissent or abstention to such action with the presiding officer before the meeting adjourns, or (3) delivers his written dissent or abstention to the corporation immediately after adjournment. Section 8.24(d).

### ACTION TAKEN WITHOUT A MEETING

The Revised Act and most States provide that, unless the articles of incorporation or bylaws provide otherwise, any action the statute requires or permits to be taken at a meeting of the board may be taken without a meeting if consent in writing is signed by all of the directors. Section 8.21. Such consent has the same effect as a unanimous vote.

### DELEGATION OF BOARD POWERS

Unless otherwise provided by the articles of incorporation or bylaws, the board of directors may, by majority vote of the full board, appoint one or more committees, all of whose members must be directors. Section 8.25. Many State statutes, however, permit the board to form committees only if the charter expressly authorizes such action; furthermore, the Revised Act and many States require that the creation of a committee and appointment of members to it must be approved by the greater of (1) a majority of all the directors in office when the action is taken or (2) the number of directors required by the articles of incorporation or bylaws to take action. Section 8.25(b). The Revised Act as amended and some statutes permit a committee to have as few as one member, whereas the statutes of many States require that a committee consist of at least two directors.

Committees may exercise all of the authority of the board, except with regard to certain matters specified in the incorporation statute, such as declaring dividends and other distributions, filling vacancies in the board or in any of its committees, amending the bylaws, or proposing actions that require approval by shareholders. Section 8.25(e). Delegating authority to a committee does not relieve any board member of his duties to the corporation. Commonly used committees include executive committees, audit committees (to recommend and oversee independent public accountants), compensation committees, finance committees, nominating committees, and investment committees.

The Sarbanes-Oxley Act confers on the audit committee of every publicly held corporation direct responsibility for the appointment, compensation, and oversight of the work of the public accounting firm employed by the company to perform audit services. Moreover, the public accounting firm must report directly to the audit committee, and the lead auditor must rotate every five years. Each member of the audit committee must be independent, and at least one member must qualify as a financial expert. The Act requires that the company provide appropriate funding for the audit committee to compensate the auditors, independent counsel, and other advisers. The audit committee is responsible for resolving disagreements between management and the auditor regarding the company's financial reporting. The audit committee must establish procedures for addressing complaints regarding accounting, internal accounting controls, or auditing matters.

Under the CFPA, the SEC must issue rules directing the national securities exchanges to require that each member of a listed company's compensation committee be an independent director.

### DIRECTORS' INSPECTION RIGHTS

So that they can perform their duties competently and fully, directors have the right to inspect corporate books and records. This right is considerably broader than a shareholder's right to inspect. Nevertheless, it is subject to limitations.

## OFFICERS

In most States, the officers of a corporation are appointed by the board of directors to hold the offices provided in the bylaws, which set forth the respective duties of each officer. Statutes generally require as a minimum that the officers consist of a president, one or more vice presidents as prescribed by the bylaws, a secretary, and a treasurer. A person may hold more than one office, with the exception that the same person may not hold the office of president and secretary at the same time.

The Revised Act and other modern statutes permit every corporation to designate whatever officers it wants. Although the Act specifies no particular number of officers, one of them must be delegated responsibility for preparing the minutes of directors' and shareholders' meetings and authenticating corporate records. The Revised Act permits the same individual to hold *all* of the offices of a corporation. Section 8.40(d).

### SELECTION AND REMOVAL OF OFFICERS

Most State statutes provide that officers be appointed by the board of directors and that they serve at the pleasure of the board. Accordingly, the board may remove officers with or without cause. Section 8.43(b). Of course, if the officer has an employment contract that is valid for a specified time, removing the officer without cause before that time expires would constitute a breach of the employment contract. The board also determines the compensation of officers.

### ROLE OF OFFICERS

The officers are, like the directors, fiduciaries to the corporation. On the other hand, unlike the directors, they are agents of the corporation. The roles of officers are set forth in the corporate bylaws.

### AUTHORITY OF OFFICERS

The Revised Act provides that each officer has the authority provided in the bylaws or prescribed by the board of directors, to the extent that such prescribed authority is consistent with the bylaws. Section 8.41. Like that of other agents, the authority of an officer to bind the corporation may be (1) actual express, (2) actual implied, or (3) apparent.

**Actual Express Authority** Actual express authority results when the corporation manifests its assent to the officer that the officer should act on its behalf. Actual express authority arises from the incorporation statute, the articles of incorporation, the bylaws, and resolutions of the board of directors. The last represent the principal source of such authority. The Revised Act further provides that the board of directors may authorize an officer to prescribe the duties of other officers. Section 8.41. This provision empowers officers to delegate authority to subordinates.

**Actual Implied Authority** Officers, as agents of the corporation, have actual implied authority to do what is reasonably necessary to perform their actual, delegated authority.

In addition, a common question is whether officers possess implied authority merely by virtue of their positions. The courts have been circumspect in granting such implied or inherent authority. Traditionally, the courts tended to hold that the president had no implied authority by virtue of his office, although more recent decisions tend to recognize his authority to bind the corporation in ordinary business transactions. Any act requiring board approval, such as issuing stock, however, is clearly beyond the implied authority of the president or any other officer. In most jurisdictions, implied authority of position does not extend to any officer other than the president.

**Apparent Authority** Apparent authority arises from acts of the corporation that lead third parties to believe reasonably and in good faith that an officer has the required authority. Apparent authority might arise when a third party relies on the fact that an officer has exercised the same authority in the past with the consent of the board of directors.

**Ratification** A corporation may ratify the unauthorized acts of its officers. Equivalent to the corporation's having granted the officer prior authority, ratification relates back to the original transaction and may either be express or implied from the corporation's acceptance of contractual benefits with full knowledge of the facts.

## DUTIES OF DIRECTORS AND OFFICERS

Generally, directors and officers owe the duties of obedience, diligence, and loyalty to the corporation. These duties are for the most part judicially imposed. State and Federal statutes supplement the common law by imposing liability upon directors and officers for specific acts, but the common law remains the most significant source of duties.

A corporation may not recover damages from its directors and officers for losses resulting from their poor business judgment or honest mistakes of judgment. Directors and officers are not insurers of business success. They are required only to be obedient, reasonably diligent, and completely loyal. In 1999 an amendment to the Revised Act was adopted refining the Act's standards of conduct and liability for directors.

### DUTY OF OBEDIENCE

Directors and officers must act within their respective authority. For any loss the corporation suffers because of their unauthorized acts, they are in some jurisdictions held strictly liable; in others, they are held liable only if they exceeded their authority intentionally or negligently.

### DUTY OF DILIGENCE

In discharging their duties, directors and officers must exercise ordinary care and prudence. Some States interpret this standard to mean that directors and officers must exercise "the same degree of care and prudence that [those] promoted by self-interest generally exercise in their own affairs." *Hun v. Cary*, 82 N.Y. 65 (1880). The great majority of States and the Revised Act, however, hold that the test requires a director or officer to discharge her duties—

1. in good faith;
2. with the care an ordinarily prudent person in a like position would exercise under similar circumstances; and
3. in a manner she reasonably believes to be in the best interests of the corporation.

Sections 8.30 and 8.42. A director or officer who has performed the duties of his office in compliance with these requirements is liable neither for any action he has taken as a director or officer nor for any failure to act. Sections 8.30(d) and 8.42(d).

So long as the directors and officers act in good faith and with due care, the courts will not substitute their judgment for that of the board or officer—the so-called **business judgment** rule. Directors and officers will, nonetheless, be held liable for bad faith or negligent conduct. Moreover, they may be liable for failing to act. In one instance, a bank director, who in the five-and-one-half years that he had been on the board had never attended a board meeting or made any examination of the books and records, was held liable for losses resulting from the unsupervised acts of the president and cashier, who had made various improper loans and had permitted large overdrafts.

In 1999 an amendment to the Revised Act was adopted refining the Act's standards of conduct and liability for directors. It substituted a different duty of care standard for the second point above (prudent person): When becoming informed in connection with their decision-making function or devoting attention to their oversight function, directors shall discharge their duties with the care that a person in a like position would reasonably believe appropriate under similar circumstances. Section 8.30(b) as amended. While some aspects of a director's role will be performed individually, such as preparing for meetings, this reformulation explicitly recognizes that directors perform most of their functions as a unit.

**Reliance upon Others** Directors and officers are, nevertheless, permitted to entrust important work to others, and if they have selected employees with care, they are not personally liable for the negligent acts or willful wrongs of those selected. A reasonable amount of supervision is required, however; and an officer or director who knew or should have known or suspected that an employee was incurring losses through carelessness, theft, or embezzlement will be held liable for such losses.

A director also may rely in good faith upon *information* provided him by officers and employees of the corporation;

legal counsel, public accountants, or other persons as to matters the director reasonably believes are within the person's professional or expert competence; and a committee of the board of directors of which the director is not a member if the director reasonably believes the committee merits confidence. Section 8.30 of the Revised Act. A director is not acting in good faith if he has knowledge concerning the matter in question that makes reliance unwarranted. The 1999 amendments to the Revised Act added a provision entitling a director to rely on the *performance* of board functions properly delegated by the board to officers, employees, or a committee of the board of directors of which the director is not a member unless the director has knowledge that makes reliance unwarranted. Section 8.30(c) as amended.

An officer is also entitled to rely upon this information, but this right may, in many circumstances, be more limited than a director's right to so rely because of the officer's greater familiarity with the corporation's affairs. Section 8.42 and Comment.

**Business Judgment Rule** Directors and officers are continually called upon to make decisions that require balancing benefits and risks to the corporation. Although hindsight may reveal that some of these decisions were less than optimal, the business judgment rule precludes imposing liability upon the directors or officers for honest mistakes of judgment. To subsequently benefit from the business judgment rule, a director or officer must make an informed decision, in good faith without any conflict of interests, and have a rational basis for believing it was in the best interests of the corporation. (With respect to *directors*, the 1999 amendments to the Revised Act added a new Section 8.31 codifying much of the business judgment rule and providing guidance as to its application.) Moreover, when a director or officer fails to satisfy this standard of conduct, it must be shown that her action (or inaction) is the proximate cause of damage to the corporation.

Hasty or ill-advised action also can render directors liable. The Supreme Court of Delaware has held directors liable for approving the terms of a cash-out merger because the directors did not adequately inform themselves of the company's intrinsic value and were grossly negligent in approving the terms of the merger upon two hours' consideration and without prior notice. *Smith v. Van Gorkom*, 488 A.2d 858 (1985).

◆ **SEE CASE 36-4**

## DUTY OF LOYALTY

The officers and directors of a corporation owe a duty of loyalty (a **fiduciary duty**) to the corporation and to its shareholders. The essence of a fiduciary duty is the subordination of self-interest to the interest of the person or persons to whom the duty is owing. It requires officers and directors to be constantly loyal to the corporation, which they both serve and control.

An officer or director is required to disclose fully to the corporation any financial interest that he may have in any contract or transaction to which the corporation is a party. (This is a corollary to the rule that forbids fiduciaries from making secret profits.) He must eschew self-interest in his business conduct, and he may not advance his personal interests at the corporation's expense. Moreover, he may not represent conflicting interests; his duty is one of strict allegiance to the corporation.

The remedy for breach of fiduciary duty is a suit in equity by the corporation, or more often a derivative suit instituted by a shareholder, to require the fiduciary to pay to the corporation the profits that he obtained through breach of his fiduciary duty. It need not be shown that the corporation could otherwise have made the profits that the fiduciary has realized. The object of the rule is to discourage breaches of duty by taking from the fiduciary all of the profits he has made. Though enforcing the rule may result in a windfall to the corporation, this is incidental to the rule's deterrent objective. Whenever a director or officer breaches his fiduciary duty, he forfeits his right to compensation during the period he engaged in the breach.

**Conflict of Interests** A contract or other transaction between an officer or a director and the corporation inherently involves a conflict of interest. Contracts between officers and the corporation are covered under the law of agency. (See *Chapter 19*.) Early on, the common law viewed all director–corporation transactions as automatically void or voidable but eventually regarded this rule as unreasonable because it would prevent directors from entering into contracts beneficial to the corporation. Now, therefore, if such a contract is honest and fair, the courts will uphold it. In the case of contracts between corporations having an interlocking directorate (corporations whose boards of directors share one or more members), the courts subject the contracts to scrutiny and will set them aside unless the transaction is shown to have been entirely fair and entered in good faith.

Most States and the original version of the Revised Act address these related problems by providing that such transactions are neither void nor voidable if, after full disclosure, they are approved by either the board of disinterested directors or the shareholders, or if they are fair and reasonable to the corporation.

The Revised Act was amended in 1988 to adopt a more specific approach to a director's conflict-of-interest transactions, which it defines as transactions between a corporation (or a subsidiary of it or an entity controlled by it) and one of the corporation's directors, a close relative of the director, or a person to whom the director owes a fiduciary duty. Section 8.60. The Revised Act establishes more clearly prescribed safe harbors to validate conflict-of-interest transactions. Section 8.61. The Revised Act provides two alternative safe harbors, each of which is available before or after the transaction: approval by "qualified" (disinterested) directors or approval by the shareholders. In either case, the interested director must make full disclosure to the approving group. Full disclosure requires the director to disclose both the existence of the conflicting interest and all material facts known to her regarding the subject matter of the transaction.

If neither of the safe harbor provisions is satisfied, then the transaction is subject to appropriate judicial action unless the transaction is fair to the corporation. The comments to Section 8.61 explain that fairness requires that (1) the terms of the transaction, including the price, are fair; (2) the transaction benefits the corporation; and (3) the course of dealing or process of the transaction is fair.

**Loans to Directors and Officers** The Model Act and some States permit a corporation to lend money to its directors only with its shareholders' authorization for each loan. The statutes in most States permit such loans either on a general or on a limited basis. The Revised Act initially permitted such loans if each was approved (1) by a majority of disinterested shareholders or (2) by the board of directors after its determination that the loan would benefit the corporation. Section 8.32. The 1988 amendments to the Revised Act deleted this section, instead subjecting director loans to the procedure that applies to a director's conflict-of-interest transactions.

The Sarbanes-Oxley Act prohibits any publicly held corporation from making personal loans to its directors or its executive officers, although it does provide certain limited exceptions.

**Corporate Opportunity** Directors and officers may not usurp any corporate opportunity that in all fairness should belong to the corporation. A corporate opportunity is one in which the corporation has a right, property interest, or expectancy; whether or not such an opportunity exists depends on the facts and circumstances of each case.

A corporate opportunity should be promptly offered to the corporation, which, in turn, should promptly accept or reject it. Rejection may be based on one or more of several factors, such as the corporation's lack of interest in the opportunity, its financial inability to acquire the opportunity, legal restrictions on its ability to accept the opportunity, or a third party's unwillingness to deal with the corporation. Section 8.70 was added to the Revised Act to deal with business opportunities and to provide safe-harbor protection for directors considering involvement with a business opportunity that might be considered a corporate opportunity.

For instance, a party proposes a business arrangement to a corporation through its vice president, who personally accepts the arrangement without offering it to the corporation. The vice president has usurped a corporate opportunity. On the other hand, a corporate opportunity generally would not include one that the corporation was unable to accept or one that the corporation expressly rejected by a vote of disinterested directors after full disclosure. In both of these instances, a director or officer is free to take personal advantage of the opportunity.

◆ **SEE CASE 36-5**

**Transactions in Shares** The issuance of shares at favorable prices to management by excluding other shareholders normally will constitute a violation of the fiduciary duty. So might the issuance of shares to a director at a fair price if the purpose of the issuance is to perpetuate corporate control rather than to raise capital or to serve some other interest of the corporation.

Officers and directors have access to inside advance information, unavailable to the public, which may affect the future market value of the corporation's shares. Federal statutes have attempted to deal with this trading advantage by prohibiting officers and directors from purchasing or selling shares of their corporation's stock without adequately disclosing all material facts in their possession that may affect the stock's actual or potential value. See *Chapter 44* for a discussion of these matters.

Although the imposition of liability upon officers and directors for secret, profitable use of inside information has been inconsistent under State law, the trend is toward holding them liable for breach of fiduciary duty to shareholders from whom they purchase stock without disclosing facts that give the stock added potential value. They are also held liable to the corporation for profits realized upon a sale of the stock when undisclosed conditions of the corporation make a substantial decline in value practically inevitable.

**Duty Not to Compete** As fiduciaries, directors and officers owe to the corporation the duty of undivided loyalty, which means they may not compete with the corporation. A director or officer who breaches his fiduciary duty by competing with the corporation is liable for the damages he thus causes to the corporation. Although directors and officers may engage in their own business interests, courts will closely scrutinize any interest that competes with the corporation's business. Moreover, an officer or director may not use corporate personnel, facilities, or funds for her own benefit nor disclose trade secrets of the corporation to others.

## INDEMNIFICATION OF DIRECTORS AND OFFICERS

Directors and officers incur personal liability for breaching any of the duties they owe to the corporation and its shareholders. Under many modern incorporation statutes, a corporation *may* indemnify a director or officer for liability incurred if he acted in good faith and in a manner he reasonably believed to be in the best interests of the corporation, so long as he has not been adjudged negligent or liable for misconduct. The Revised Act provides for *mandatory* indemnification of directors and officers for reasonable expenses they incur in the wholly successful defense of any proceeding brought against them because they are or were directors or officers. Sections 8.52 and 8.56. These provisions, however, may be limited by the articles of incorporation. In addition, a corporation may purchase insurance to indemnify officers and directors for liability arising out of their corporate activities, including liabilities against which the corporation is not empowered to indemnify directly. Section 8.57.

### LIABILITY LIMITATION STATUTES

Virtually all States have enacted legislation limiting the liability of directors. Most of these States, including Delaware, have authorized corporations—with shareholder approval—to limit or eliminate the liability of directors for some breaches of duty. (A few States permit shareholders to limit the liability of officers.) The Delaware statute provides that the articles of incorporation may contain a provision eliminating or limiting the personal liability of a director to the corporation or its stockholders for monetary damages for breach of her directorial duty, provided that such provision does not eliminate or limit the liability of a director (1) for any breach of the director's duty of loyalty to the corporation or its stockholders, (2) for acts or omissions lacking good faith or involving intentional misconduct or a knowing violation of law, (3) for liability for unlawful dividend payments or redemptions, or (4) for any transaction from which the director derived an improper personal benefit.

A few States have directly limited personal liability for directors, subject to certain exceptions, without requiring an amendment to the articles of incorporation. Other States adopt a third approach by limiting the amount of money damages that may be assessed against a director or officer.

The Revised Act authorizes the articles of incorporation to include a provision eliminating or limiting—with certain exceptions—the liability of a director to the corporation or its shareholders for any action that he, as a director, has taken or has failed to take. The exceptions, for which liability would be unaffected, are (1) the amount of any financial benefit the director receives to which he is not entitled, such as a bribe, kickback, or profits from a usurped corporate opportunity; (2) an intentional infliction of harm on the corporation or the shareholders; (3) liability under Section 8.33 for unlawful distributions; and (4) an intentional violation of the criminal law. Section 2.02(b)(4).

# CHAPTER SUMMARY

## ROLE OF SHAREHOLDERS

**VOTING RIGHTS OF SHAREHOLDERS**

**Management Structure of Corporations** see *Figures 36-1, 36-2,* and *36-3* for illustrations of the statutory model of corporate governance, the structure of the typical closely held corporation, and the structure of the typical publicly held corporation

**Shareholder Meetings** shareholders may exercise their voting rights at both annual and special shareholder meetings

**Quorum** minimum number necessary to be present at a meeting in order to transact business

**Election of Directors** the shareholders elect the board at the annual meeting of the corporation

- ***Straight Voting*** directors are elected by a plurality of votes
- ***Cumulative Voting*** entitles shareholders to multiply the number of votes they are entitled to cast by the number of directors for whom they are entitled to vote and to cast the product for a single candidate or to distribute the product among two or more candidates

**Removal of Directors** the shareholders may by majority vote remove directors with or without cause, subject to cumulative voting rights

**Approval of Fundamental Changes** shareholder approval is required for charter amendments, most acquisitions, and dissolution

| | |
|---|---|
| | **Concentrations of Voting Power**<br>• ***Proxy*** authorization to vote another's shares at a shareholder meeting<br>• ***Voting Trust*** transfer of corporate shares' voting rights to a trustee<br>• ***Shareholder Voting Agreement*** used to provide shareholders with greater control over the election and removal of directors and other matters<br>• ***Restrictions on Transfer of Shares*** must be reasonable and conspicuously noted on stock certificate |
| ENFORCEMENT RIGHTS OF SHAREHOLDERS | **Right to Inspect Books and Records** if the demand is made in good faith and for a proper purpose<br>**Shareholder Suits**<br>• ***Direct Suits*** brought by a shareholder or a class of shareholders against the corporation based upon the ownership of shares<br>• ***Derivative Suits*** brought by a shareholder on behalf of the corporation to enforce a right belonging to the corporation<br>• ***Shareholder's Right to Dissent*** a shareholder has the right to dissent from certain corporate actions that require shareholder approval |

## ROLE OF DIRECTORS AND OFFICERS

| | |
|---|---|
| FUNCTION OF THE BOARD OF DIRECTORS | **Selection and Removal of Officers**<br>**Capital Structure**<br>**Fundamental Changes** the directors have the power to make, amend, or repeal the bylaws, unless this power is exclusively reserved to the shareholders<br>**Dividends** directors declare the amount and type of dividends<br>**Management Compensation**<br>**Vacancies in the Board** may be filled by the vote of a majority of the remaining directors |
| EXERCISE OF DIRECTORS' FUNCTIONS | **Meeting** directors have the power to bind the corporation only when acting as a board<br>**Action Taken without a Meeting** permitted if a consent in writing is signed by all of the directors<br>**Delegation of Board Powers** committees may be appointed to perform some but not all of the board's functions<br>**Directors' Inspection Rights** directors have the right to inspect corporate books and records |
| OFFICERS | **Role of Officers** officers are agents of the corporation<br>**Authority of Officers**<br>• ***Actual Express Authority*** arises from the incorporation statute, the charter, the bylaws, and resolutions of the directors<br>• ***Actual Implied Authority*** authority to do what is reasonably necessary to perform actual authority<br>• ***Apparent Authority*** acts of the principal that lead a third party to believe reasonably and in good faith that an officer has the required authority<br>• ***Ratification*** a corporation may ratify the unauthorized acts of its officers |
| DUTIES OF DIRECTORS AND OFFICERS | **Duty of Obedience** must act within respective authority<br>**Duty of Diligence** must exercise ordinary care and prudence<br>**Duty of Loyalty** requires undeviating loyalty to the corporation<br>**Business Judgment Rule** precludes imposing liability on directors and officers for honest mistakes in judgment if they act with due care, in good faith, and in a manner reasonably believed to be in the best interests of the corporation |

**Indemnification** a corporation may indemnify a director or officer for liability incurred if he acted in good faith and was not adjudged negligent or liable for misconduct
**Liability Limitation Statutes** many States now authorize corporations—with shareholder approval—to limit or eliminate the liability of directors for some breaches of duty

## CASES

## CASE 36-1

### Right to Inspect Books and Records
### COMPAQ COMPUTER CORPORATION v. HORTON

Supreme Court of Delaware, 1993
631 A.2d 1

**Moore, J.**

This is a stocklist case arising under §220(b) of our [Delaware] General Corporation Law. The issue is whether a shareholder states a proper purpose for inspection under our statute in seeking to solicit the participation of other shareholders in legitimate nonderivative litigation against the defendant corporation. The Court of Chancery found that the litigation concerned alleged corporate wrongdoing that affected the value of the plaintiff's stock. Accordingly, the trial court concluded that plaintiff's desire to contact other stockholders, and solicit their involvement in the litigation, was a purpose reasonably related to one's interest as a stockholder. We agree and affirm.

**I**

Compaq Computer Corporation ("Compaq") refused to permit Charles E. Horton ("Horton"), a Compaq stockholder, to inspect its stock ledger and other related materials. Horton has beneficially owned 112 shares of Compaq common stock continuously since December 6, 1990. * * *

On July 22, 1991, Horton and seventy-eight other parties sued Compaq, fifteen of its advisors and certain management personnel (the "Texas litigation"). Horton and the other plaintiffs allege that Compaq and its co-defendants violated the Texas Security Act and the Texas Deceptive Trade Practices Consumer Protection Act. Plaintiffs also charge defendants with a continuing pattern of misconduct involving common law fraud, conspiracy, aiding and abetting, fraudulent concealment and breach of fiduciary duty. All these claims arise from the contention that Compaq misled the public as to the true value of its stock at a time when members of management were selling their own shares. The plaintiffs seek individual damages.

On September 22, 1992, Horton, through counsel, delivered a letter demanding to inspect Compaq's stock ledger and related information for the period from October 1, 1990, to June 30, 1991, to the extent such information is available and in the possession or control of Compaq. The demand letter stated that the purpose of the request was:

> [T]o enable Mr. Horton to communicate with other Compaq shareholders to inform them of the pending shareholders' suit of Charles E. Horton, *et al.* v. Compaq Computer Corporation and Joseph R. Canion and to ascertain whether any of them would desire to become associated with that suit or bring similar actions against Compaq, and assume a pro rata share of the litigated expenses.

On September 30, 1992, Compaq refused the demand, stating that the purpose described in the letter was not a "proper purpose" under Section 220(b) of the General Corporation Law of the State of Delaware * * *. Compaq conceded that Horton had met all of the technical requirements for making a demand under 8 Del. C. §220, and that the only issue remaining for the trial court to resolve was whether Horton stated a proper purpose for inspecting the various documents.

On November 12, 1992, the Court of Chancery ordered Compaq to permit Horton * * * to inspect and copy the stockholder lists and related stockholder information requested in their demand letter. The Vice Chancellor ruled that even though the Texas litigation is neither derivative, nor brought for the benefit of Compaq, it concerns alleged corporate wrongdoing that affected the value of Horton's Compaq stock. [Citation.] Accordingly, Horton stated a proper purpose reasonably related to his interest as a Compaq stockholder.

**II**

The question of a "proper purpose" under Section 220(b) of our General Corporation Law is an issue of law and equity which this Court reviews de novo. [Citations.]

* * * §220(b) * * * provides in pertinent part:

> Any stockholder * * * shall, upon written demand under oath stating the purpose thereof, have the right during the usual hours for business to inspect for any proper purpose the corporation's stock ledger * * *. A proper purpose shall mean a purpose reasonably related to such person's interest as a stockholder. [Citation.]

Under Section 220, when a stockholder complies with the statutory requirements as to form and manner of making a demand, then the corporation bears the burden of proving that the demand is for an improper purpose. [Citation.] If there is any doubt, it must be resolved in favor of the statutory right of the stockholder to have an inspection. [Citation.]

Horton contends that this purpose is not only proper, but was earlier approved in *State ex rel. Foster v. Standard Oil Co. of Kansas* [citation]. The holding in *Standard Oil* has been interpreted by a number of authoritative treatises for the proposition Horton advances—that shareholders may inspect stocklists for the purpose of communicating with fellow shareholders, not only about pending litigation, but to solicit their interest in joining it. [Citations.] * * *

Essentially, Horton alleges that it is in the interests of Compaq's shareholders to know that acts of mismanagement and fraud are continuing and cannot be overlooked. Thus, it is assumed that the resultant filing of a large number of individual damage claims might well discourage further acts of misconduct by the defendants. In this specific context, the antidotal effect of the Texas litigation may indeed serve a purpose reasonably related to Horton's current interest as a Compaq stockholder.

We recognize that even though a purpose may be reasonably related to one's interest as a stockholder, it cannot be adverse to the interests of the corporation. [Citations.] In this respect, it becomes clear that a stockholder's right to inspect and copy a stockholder list is not absolute. Rather, it is a qualified right depending on the facts presented. [Citation.]

Horton's ultimate objective, to solicit additional parties to the Texas litigation, may impose substantial expenses upon the company. Compaq argues, therefore, that such a purpose is per se improper as adverse to the interests of the corporation. Significantly, however, Compaq conceded at oral argument that it could cite no authority in support of its proposition that the purpose behind a demand must benefit the defendant corporation.

Horton, as a current stockholder of Compaq, has nothing to gain by harming the legitimate interests of the company. Moreover, as he argues, the prospect of the Texas litigation poses no legitimate threat to Compaq's interests. The Texas litigation is already pending with seventy-nine plaintiffs. The inclusion of more plaintiffs will not substantially increase Compaq's costs of defending the action. The real risk to Compaq is that any additional plaintiffs, who may join the suit, potentially increase the damage award against the company. Yet, insofar as law and policy require corporations and their agents to answer for the breaches of their duties to shareholders, Compaq has no legitimate interest in avoiding the payment of compensatory damages which it, its management or advisors may owe to those who own the enterprise. [Citation.] Thus, common sense and public policy dictate that a proper purpose may be stated in these circumstances, notwithstanding the lack of a direct benefit flowing to the corporation.

Equally important is the fact that if damages are assessed against Compaq in the Texas litigation, the company is entitled to seek indemnification from its co-defendant managers and advisors or to pursue its own claims against them. The availability of this diminishes the possibility that Compaq will suffer any harm at all. It is well-settled that the mere prospect of harm to a corporate defendant is insufficient to deny relief under Section 220. [Citation.] * * * Accordingly, we are satisfied that the purpose for which Horton seeks to inspect the stock ledger and related materials is not adverse to the legitimate interests of the company.

This conclusion does not suggest that Compaq's burden of showing an improper purpose is impossible to bear. Previous cases provide valuable examples of the degree to which a stated purpose is so indefinite, doubtful, uncertain or vexatious as to warrant denial of the right of inspection. In [citation], the trial court held that instituting annoying or harassing litigation against the corporation was an improper purpose. In [citation], the court ruled improper the stockholder's plan to use a stocklist in furtherance of a scheme to bring pressure on a third corporation. In [citation], it was recognized that obtaining a list for purposes of selling the stockholders' names was also improper. Finally, in [citation], the Court stated that neither conducting a "fishing expedition" nor satisfying idle curiosity were proper purposes to justify inspection. On the whole, a fair reading of these cases leads to the conclusion that where the person making demand is acting in bad faith or for reasons wholly unrelated to his or her role as a stockholder, access to the ledger will be denied. That simply is not the case here.

* * *

The judgment of the Court of Chancery is AFFIRMED.

## CASE 36-2

## Shareholder Suits
## STROUGO v. BASSINI

United States Court of Appeals for the Second Circuit, 2002
282 F.3d 162
http://caselaw.lp.findlaw.com/scripts/getcase.pl?court=2nd&navby=case&no=009303v3&exact=1

**Sack, J.**

* * * The plaintiff is a shareholder of the Brazilian Equity Fund, Inc. (the "Fund"), a non-diversified, publicly traded, closed-end investment company incorporated under the laws of Maryland * * *. As its name implies, the Fund invests primarily in the securities of Brazilian companies. The term "closed-end" indicates that the Fund has a fixed number of outstanding shares, so that investors who wish to acquire shares in the Fund ordinarily must purchase them from a shareholder rather than, as in open-end funds, directly from the Fund itself. Shares in closed-end funds are thus traded in the same manner as are other shares of corporate stock. Indeed, shares in the Fund are listed and traded on the New York Stock Exchange. The number of outstanding shares in the Fund is described as "fixed" because it does not change on a daily basis as it would were the Fund open-end, in which case the number of outstanding shares would change each time an investor invested new money in the fund, causing issuance of new shares, and each time a shareholder divested and thereby redeemed shares.

Although closed-end funds do not sell their shares to the public in the ordinary course of their business, there are methods available to them to raise new capital after their initial public offering. One such device is a "rights offering," by which a fund offers shareholders the opportunity to purchase newly issued shares. Rights so offered may be transferable, allowing the current shareholder to sell them in the open market, or non-transferable, requiring the current shareholder to use them him- or herself or lose their value when the rights expire. It was the Fund's employment of a non-transferable rights offering that generated the claims at issue on this appeal.

On June 6, 1996, the Fund announced that it would issue one "right" per outstanding share to every shareholder, and that every three rights would enable the shareholder to purchase one new share in the Fund. The subscription price per share was set at ninety percent of the lesser of (1) the average of the last reported sales price of a share of the Fund's common stock on the New York Stock Exchange on August 16, 1996, the date on which the rights expired, and the four business days preceding, and (2) the per-share net asset value at the close of business on August 16.

The plaintiff asserts that this sort of rights offering is coercive because it penalizes shareholders who do not participate. Under the Fund's pricing formula for its rights offering, the subscription price could not have been higher than ninety percent of the Fund's per-share net asset value. Thus, the introduction of new shares at a discount diluted the value of old shares. Because the rights could not be sold on the open market, a shareholder could avoid a consequent reduction in the value of his or her net equity position in the Fund only by purchasing new shares at the discounted price. This put pressure on every shareholder to "pony up" and purchase more shares, enabling the Fund to raise new capital and thereby increase its asset holdings. Such purchases would, in turn, have tended to increase the management fee paid to defendant BEA Associates, the Fund's investment advisor, because that fee is based on the Fund's total assets.

At the close of business on August 16, 1996, the last day of the rights offering, the closing market price for the Fund's shares was $12.38, and the Fund's per-share net asset value was $17.24. The Fund's shareholders purchased 70.3 percent of the new shares available at a subscription price set at $11.09 per share, ninety percent of the average closing price for the Fund on that and the preceding four days. Through the rights offering, the Fund raised $20.6 million in new capital, net of underwriting fees and other transaction costs.

On May 16, 1997, the plaintiff brought this action against the Fund's directors, senior officers, and investment advisor. The plaintiff's complaint includes three direct class-action claims on behalf of all shareholders. It alleges that the defendants, by approving the rights offering, breached their duties of loyalty and care at common law. * * * It asserts that these breaches of duty resulted in four kinds of injury to shareholders: (1) loss of share value resulting from the underwriting and other transaction costs associated with the rights offering; (2) downward pressure on share prices resulting from the supply of new shares; (3) downward pressure on share prices resulting from the offering of shares at a discount; and (4) injury resulting from coercion, in that "shareholders were forced to either invest additional monies in the Fund or suffer a substantial dilution." [Citation.]

On April 6, 1998, the district court dismissed the direct claims on the ground that the injuries alleged "applied to the shareholders as a whole." * * *

The district court entered judgment for the defendants on September 15, 2000. The plaintiff now appeals.

* * *

In deciding whether a shareholder may bring a direct suit, the question the Maryland courts ask is not whether the shareholder suffered injury; if a corporation is injured those who own the corporation are injured too. The inquiry, instead, is whether the shareholders' injury is "distinct" from that suffered by the corporation. [Citation.]

* * *

Thus, under Maryland law, when the shareholders of a corporation suffer an injury that is distinct from that of the corporation, the shareholders may bring direct suit for redress of that injury; there is shareholder standing. When the corporation is injured and the injury to its shareholders derives from that injury, however, only the corporation may bring suit; there is no shareholder standing. The shareholder may, at most, sue derivatively, seeking in effect to require the corporation to pursue a lawsuit to compensate for the injury to the corporation, and thereby ultimately redress the injury to the shareholders.

* * * To sue directly under Maryland law, a shareholder must allege an injury distinct from an injury to the corporation, not from that of other shareholders.

* * *

Applying Maryland's law of shareholder standing to the plaintiff's four alleged injuries, we conclude that one that he alleges does not support direct claims under Maryland law. The remaining alleged injuries, however—describing the set of harms arising from the alleged coercion—do.

The plaintiff alleges a loss in share value resulting from the "substantial underwriting and other transactional costs associated with the Rights Offering." * * * Underwriter fees, advisory fees, and other transaction costs incurred by a corporation decrease share price primarily because they deplete the corporation's assets, precisely the type of injury to the corporation that can be redressed under Maryland law only through a suit brought on behalf of the corporation. [Citation.]

The plaintiff's remaining alleged injuries can be read to describe the set of harms resulting from the coercive nature of the rights offering. The particular harm allegedly suffered by an individual shareholder as a result of the coercion depends on whether or not that shareholder participated in the rights offering. For example, when read in the light most favorable to the plaintiff, the alleged injury of "substantial downward pressure on the price of the Fund's shares" resulting from the issuance of new shares describes the reduction in the net equity value of the shares owned by non-participating shareholders. [Citation.] Similarly, the alleged injury from the downward pressure on share prices resulting from the setting of the "exercise price of the rights * * * at a steep discount from the pre-rights offering net asset value" can be read to refer to the involuntary dilution in equity value suffered by the non-participating shareholders. [Citation.]

* * *

* * * On the other hand, participating shareholders may have suffered harm in the form of transaction costs in liquidating other assets to purchase the new shares, and the impairment of their right to dispose of their assets as they prefer if they purchased new shares to avoid dilution.

* * *

Thus, in the case of both the participating and non-participating shareholders, it would appear that the alleged injuries were to the shareholders alone and not to the Fund. These harms therefore constitute "distinct" injuries supporting direct shareholder claims under Maryland law. The corporation cannot bring the action seeking compensation for these injuries because they were suffered by its shareholders, not itself.

* * *

For the foregoing reasons, the judgment of the district court is vacated insofar as it dismisses the plaintiff's class action claims. The case is remanded for further proceedings consistent with this opinion.

## CASE 36-3

## Duties of Controlling Shareholders
## DONAHUE v. RODD ELECTROTYPE CO., INC.

Massachusetts Supreme Court, 1974
367 Mass. 578, 328 N.E.2d 505

**Tauro, C. J.**

The plaintiff, Euphemia Donahue, a minority stockholder in the Rodd Electrotype Company of New England, Inc. (Rodd Electrotype), a Massachusetts corporation, brings this suit against the directors of Rodd Electrotype, Charles H. Rodd, Frederick I. Rodd and Mr. Harold E. Magnuson, against Harry C. Rodd, a former director, officer, and controlling stockholder of Rodd Electrotype and against Rodd Electrotype (hereinafter called defendants).

The plaintiff seeks to rescind Rodd Electrotype's purchase of Harry Rodd's shares in Rodd Electrotype and to compel Harry Rodd "to repay to the corporation the purchase price of said shares, $36,000, together with interest from the date of purchase." The plaintiff alleges that the defendants caused the corporation to purchase the shares in violation of their fiduciary duty to her, a minority stockholder of Rodd Electrotype.

* * * We deem a close corporation to be typified by: (1) a small number of stockholders; (2) no ready market for the corporate stock; and (3) substantial majority stockholder participation in the management, direction and operations of the corporation.

As thus defined, the close corporation bears striking resemblance to a partnership. Commentators and courts have noted that the close corporation is often little more than an "incorporated" or "chartered" partnership * * *. Just as in a partnership, the relationship among the stockholders must be one of trust, confidence and absolute loyalty if the enterprise is to succeed. Close corporations with substantial assets and with more numerous stockholders are no different from smaller close corporations in this regard. All participants rely on the fidelity and abilities of those stockholders who hold office. Disloyalty and self-seeking conduct on the part of any stockholder will engender bickering, corporate stalemates, and, perhaps, efforts to achieve dissolution. * * *

* * *

Although the corporate form provides * * * advantages for the stockholders (limited liability, perpetuity, and so forth), it also supplies an opportunity for the majority stockholders to oppress or disadvantage minority stockholders. The minority is vulnerable to a variety of oppressive devices, termed "freeze-outs," which the majority may employ. [Citation.] An authoritative study of such "freeze-outs" enumerates some of the possibilities: "The squeezers [those who employ the freeze-out techniques] may refuse to declare dividends; they may drain off the corporation's earnings in the form of exorbitant salaries and bonuses to the majority shareholder-officers and perhaps to their relatives, or in the form of high rent by the corporation for property leased from majority shareholders * * *; they may deprive minority shareholders of corporate offices and of employment by the company; they may cause the corporation to sell its assets at an inadequate price to the majority shareholders * * *." [Citation.] In particular, the power of the board of directors, controlled by the majority, to declare or withhold dividends and to deny the minority employment is easily converted to a device to disadvantage minority stockholders. * * *

The minority can, of course, initiate suit against the majority and their directors. Self-serving conduct by directors is proscribed by the director's fiduciary obligation to the corporation. [Citation.] However, in practice, the plaintiff will find difficulty in challenging dividend or employment policies. Such policies are considered to be within the judgment of the directors. This court has said: "The courts prefer not to interfere * * * with the sound financial management of the corporation by its directors, but declare as a general rule that the declaration of dividends rests within the sound discretion of the directors, refusing to interfere with their determination unless a plain abuse of discretion is made to appear." * * *

Thus, when these types of "freeze-outs" are attempted by the majority stockholders, the minority stockholders, cut off from all corporation-related revenues, must either suffer their losses or seek a buyer for their shares. Many minority stockholders will be unwilling or unable to wait for an alteration in majority policy. Typically, the minority stockholder in a close corporation has a substantial percentage of his personal assets invested in the corporation. [Citation.] The stockholder may have anticipated that his salary from his position with the corporation would be his livelihood. Thus, he cannot afford to wait passively. He must liquidate his investment in the close corporation in order to reinvest the funds in income-producing enterprises.

At this point, the true plight of the minority stockholder in a close corporation becomes manifest. He cannot easily reclaim his capital. In a large public corporation, the oppressed or dissident minority stockholder could sell his stock in order to extricate some of his invested capital. By definition, this market is not available for shares in the close corporation. In a partnership, a partner who feels abused by his fellow partners may cause dissolution by his "express will * * * at any time" [citation] and recover his share of partnership assets and accumulated profits * * *. To secure dissolution of the ordinary close corporation subject to [citation], the stockholder, in the absence of corporate deadlock, must own at least fifty per cent of the shares [citation] or have the advantage of a favorable provision in the articles of organization [citation]. The minority stockholder, by definition lacking fifty per cent of the corporate shares, can never "authorize" the corporation to file a petition for dissolution under [citation], by his own vote. He will seldom have at his disposal the requisite favorable provision in the articles of organization.

Thus, in a close corporation, the minority stockholders may be trapped in a disadvantageous situation. No outsider would knowingly assume the position of the disadvantaged minority. The outsider would have the same difficulties. To cut losses, the minority stockholder may be compelled to deal with the majority. This is the capstone of the majority plan. Majority "freeze-out" schemes which withhold dividends are designed to compel the minority to relinquish stock at inadequate prices * * *. When the minority stockholder agrees to sell out at less than fair value, the majority has won.

Because of the fundamental resemblance of the close corporation to the partnership, the trust and confidence which are essential to this scale and manner of enterprise, and the inherent danger to minority interests in the close corporation, we hold that stockholders in the close corporation owe one another substantially the same fiduciary duty in the operation of the enterprise that partners owe to one another. In our previous decisions, we have defined the standard of duty owed by partners to one another as the "utmost good faith and loyalty." [Citations.] Stockholders in close corporations must discharge their management and stockholder responsibilities in conformity with this strict good faith standard. They may not act out of avarice, expediency or self-interest in derogation of their duty of loyalty to the other stockholders and to the corporation.

We contrast this strict good faith standard with the somewhat less stringent standard of fiduciary duty to which directors and stockholders of all corporations must adhere in the discharge of their corporate responsibilities. Corporate directors are held to a good faith and inherent fairness standard of conduct [citation] and are not "permitted to serve two masters whose interests are antagonistic." [Citation.] "Their paramount duty is to the corporation, and their personal pecuniary interests are subordinate to that duty." [Citation.]

The more rigorous duty of partners and participants in a joint adventure, here extended to stockholders in a close corporation, was described by then Chief Judge Cardozo of the New York Court of Appeals in [citation]: "Joint adventurers, like co-partners, owe to one another, while the enterprise continues, the duty of the finest loyalty. Many forms of conduct permissible in a workaday world for those acting at arm's length, are forbidden to those bound by fiduciary ties * * *. Not honesty alone, but the punctilio of an honor the most sensitive, is then the standard of behavior."

* * *

Under settled Massachusetts law, a domestic corporation, unless forbidden by statute, has the power to purchase its own shares. When the corporation reacquiring its own stock is a close corporation, the purchase is subject to the additional requirement, in the light of our holding in this opinion, that the stockholders, who, as directors or controlling stockholders, caused the corporation to enter into the stock purchase agreement, must have acted with the utmost good faith and loyalty to the other stockholders.

To meet this test, if the stockholder whose shares were purchased was a member of the controlling group, the controlling stockholders must cause the corporation to offer each stockholder an equal opportunity to sell a ratable number of his shares to the corporation at an identical price. * * *

The benefits conferred by the purchase are two-fold: (1) provision of a market for shares; (2) access to corporate assets for personal use. By definition, there is no ready market for shares of a close corporation. The purchase creates a market for shares which previously had been unmarketable. It transforms a previously illiquid investment into a liquid one. If the close corporation purchases shares only from a member of the controlling group, the controlling stockholder can convert his shares into cash at a time when none of the other stockholders can. Consistent with its strict fiduciary duty, the controlling group may not utilize its control of the corporation to establish an exclusive market in previously unmarketable shares from which the minority stockholders are excluded. * * *

The purchase also distributes corporate assets to the stockholder whose shares were purchased. Unless an equal opportunity is given to all stockholders, the purchase of shares from a member of the controlling group operates as a *preferential* distribution of assets. In exchange for his shares, he receives a percentage of the contributed capital and accumulated profits of the enterprise. The funds he so receives are available for his personal use. The other stockholders benefit from no such access to corporate property and cannot withdraw their shares of the corporate profits and capital in this manner unless the controlling group acquiesces. Although the purchase price for the controlling stockholder's shares may seem fair to the corporation and other stockholders under the tests established in the prior case law, the controlling stockholder whose stock has been purchased has still received a relative advantage over his fellow stockholders, inconsistent with his strict fiduciary duty—an opportunity to turn corporate funds to personal use.

The rule of equal opportunity in stock purchases by close corporations provides equal access to these benefits for all stockholders. We hold that, in any case in which the controlling stockholders have exercised their power over the corporation to deny the minority such equal opportunity, the minority shall be entitled to appropriate relief. * * *

* * *

On its face, then, the purchase of Harry Rodd's shares by the corporation is a breach of the duty which the controlling stockholders, the Rodds, owed to the minority stockholders, the plaintiff and her son. The purchase distributed a portion of the corporate assets to Harry Rodd, a member of the controlling group, in exchange for his shares. The plaintiff and her son were not offered an equal opportunity to sell their shares to the corporation. In fact, their efforts to obtain an equal opportunity were rebuffed by the corporate representative. As the trial judge found, they did not, in any manner, ratify the transaction with Harry Rodd.

Because of the foregoing, we hold that the plaintiff is entitled to relief.

# CASE 36-4

## Duty of Diligence
## BREHM v. EISNER

Supreme Court of Delaware, 2000
746 A.2d 244
http://caselaw.lp.findlaw.com/data2/delawarestatecases/469-1998.pdf

**Veasey, C. J.**

[On October 1, 1995, Disney hired as its president Michael S. Ovitz, who was a long-time friend of Disney Chairman and CEO Michael Eisner. At the time, Ovitz was an important talent broker in Hollywood. Although he lacked experience managing a diversified public company, other companies with entertainment operations had been interested in hiring him for high-level executive positions. The employment agreement approved by the board of directors then in office (Old Board) had an initial term of five years and required that Ovitz "devote his full time and best efforts exclusively to the Company," with exceptions for volunteer work, service on the board of another company, and managing his passive investments. In return, Disney agreed to give Ovitz a base salary of $1 million per year, a discretionary bonus, and two sets of stock options (the "A" options and the "B" options) that collectively would enable Ovitz to purchase 5 million shares of Disney common stock. The "A" options were scheduled to vest in three annual increments of 1 million shares each, beginning at the end of the third full year of employment and continuing for the following two years. The agreement specifically provided that the "A" options would vest immediately if Disney granted Ovitz a non-fault termination of the employment agreement. The "B" options, consisting of 2 million shares, were scheduled to vest annually starting the year after the last "A" option would vest and were conditioned on Ovitz and Disney first having agreed to extend his employment beyond the five-year term of the employment agreement. In addition, Ovitz would forfeit the "B" options if his initial employment term of five years ended prematurely for any reason, even if from a non-fault termination.

The employment agreement provided three ways for Ovitz' employment to end. He might serve his five years and Disney might decide against offering him a new contract. If so, Disney would owe Ovitz a $10 million termination payment. Before the end of the initial term, Disney could terminate Ovitz for "good cause" only if Ovitz committed gross negligence or malfeasance, or if Ovitz resigned voluntarily. Disney would owe Ovitz no additional compensation if it terminated him for "good cause." Termination without cause (non-fault termination) would entitle Ovitz to the present value of his salary payments remaining under the agreement, a $10 million severance payment, an additional $7.5 million for each fiscal year remaining under the agreement, and the immediate vesting of the first 3 million stock options (the "A" Options).

Soon after Ovitz began work, problems surfaced and the situation continued to deteriorate during the first year of his employment. The deteriorating situation led Ovitz to begin seeking alternative employment and expressing his desire to leave the Company. On December 11, 1996, Eisner and Ovitz agreed to arrange for Ovitz to leave Disney on the non-fault basis provided for in the 1995 employment agreement. The board of directors then in office (New Board) approved this by authorizing a "non-fault termination" agreement with cash payments to Ovitz of almost $39 million and the immediate vesting of 3 million stock options with a value of $101 million.

Shareholders brought a derivative suit alleging that: (a) the Old Board had breached its fiduciary duty in approving an extravagant and wasteful employment agreement of Michael S. Ovitz as president of Disney and (b) the New Board had breached its fiduciary duty in agreeing to an extravagant and wasteful "non-fault" termination of the Ovitz employment agreement. The plaintiffs alleged that the Old Board had failed properly to inform itself about the total costs and incentives of the Ovitz employment agreement, especially the severance package, and failed to realize that the contract gave Ovitz an incentive to find a way to exit the Company via a non-fault termination as soon as possible because doing so would permit him to earn more than he could by fulfilling his contract. They alleged that the corporate compensation expert, Graef Crystal, who had advised Old Board in connection with its decision to approve the Ovitz employment agreement, stated two years later that the Old Board failed to consider the incentives and the total cost of the severance provisions. The defendants moved to dismiss, and the Court of Chancery granted the motion. The shareholders appealed.]

This is potentially a very troubling case on the merits. On the one hand, it appears from the Complaint that: (a) the compensation and termination payout for Ovitz were exceedingly lucrative, if not luxurious, compared to Ovitz' value to the Company; and (b) the processes of the boards of directors in dealing with the approval and termination of the Ovitz Employment Agreement were casual, if not sloppy and perfunctory. [T]he processes of the Old Board and the New Board were hardly paradigms of good corporate governance practices. Moreover, the sheer size of the payout to Ovitz, as alleged, pushes the envelope of judicial respect for the business judgment of directors in making compensation decisions. Therefore, both as to the processes of the two Boards and the waste test, this is a close case.

* * *

This is a case about whether there should be personal liability of the directors of a Delaware corporation to the corporation for lack of due care in the decisionmaking process and for waste of corporate assets. This case is not about the failure of the directors to establish and carry out ideal corporate governance practices.

All good corporate governance practices include compliance with statutory law and case law establishing fiduciary duties. But the law of corporate fiduciary duties and remedies for violation of those duties are distinct from the aspirational goals of ideal corporate governance practices. Aspirational ideals of good corporate governance practices for boards of directors that go beyond the minimal legal requirements of the corporation law are highly desirable, often tend to benefit stockholders, sometimes reduce litigation and can usually help directors avoid liability. But they are not required by the corporation law and do not define standards of liability. [Citation.]

The inquiry here is not whether we would disdain the composition, behavior and decisions of Disney's Old Board or New Board as alleged in the Complaint if we were Disney stockholders. In the absence of a legislative mandate, [citation], that determination is not for the courts. That decision is for the stockholders to make in voting for directors, urging other stockholders to reform or oust the board, or in making individual buy-sell decisions involving Disney securities. The sole issue that this Court must determine is whether the particularized facts alleged in this Complaint provide a reason to believe that the conduct of the Old Board in 1995 and the New Board in 1996 constituted a violation of their fiduciary duties.

Plaintiffs claim that the Court of Chancery erred when it concluded that a board of directors is "not required to be informed of every fact, but rather is required to be reasonably informed." [Citation.] * * * The "reasonably informed" language used by the Court of Chancery here may have been a short-hand attempt to paraphrase the Delaware jurisprudence that, in making business decisions, directors must consider all material information reasonably available, and that the directors' process is actionable only if grossly negligent. [Citation.] The question is whether the trial court's formulation is consistent with our objective test of reasonableness, the test of materiality and concepts of gross negligence. We agree with the Court of Chancery that the standard for judging the informational component of the directors' decisionmaking does not mean that the Board must be informed of every fact. The Board is responsible for considering only material facts that are reasonably available, not those that are immaterial or out of the Board's reasonable reach. [Citation.]

Certainly in this case the economic exposure of the corporation to the payout scenarios of the Ovitz contract was material, particularly given its large size, for purposes of the directors' decisionmaking process. [Court's footnote: The term "material" is used in this context to mean relevant and of a magnitude to be important to directors in carrying out their fiduciary duty of care in decisionmaking.] And those dollar exposure numbers were reasonably available because the logical inference from plaintiffs' allegations is that Crystal or the New Board could have calculated the numbers. Thus, the objective tests of reasonable availability and materiality were satisfied by this Complaint. But that is not the end of the inquiry for liability purposes.

* * *

* * * The Complaint, fairly construed, admits that the directors were advised by Crystal as an expert and that they relied on his expertise. Accordingly, the question here is whether the directors are to be "fully protected" (i.e., not held liable) on the basis that they relied in good faith on a qualified expert [citation]. * * *

* * * Plaintiffs must rebut the presumption that the directors properly exercised their business judgment, including their good faith reliance on Crystal's expertise. * * *

* * * [T]he complaint must allege particularized facts (not conclusions) that, if proved, would show, for example, that: (a) the directors did not in fact rely on the expert; (b) their reliance was not in good faith; (c) they did not reasonably believe that the expert's advice was within the expert's professional competence; (d) the expert was not selected with reasonable care by or on behalf of the corporation, and the faulty selection process was attributable to the directors; (e) the subject matter (in this case the cost calculation) that was material and reasonably available was so obvious that the board's failure to consider it was grossly negligent regardless of the expert's advice or lack of advice; or (f) that the decision of the Board was so unconscionable as to constitute waste or fraud. This Complaint includes no particular allegations of this nature, and therefore it was subject to dismissal as drafted.

* * *

We conclude that * * * the Complaint * * * as drafted, fails to create a reasonable doubt that the Old Board's decision in approving the Ovitz Employment Agreement was protected by the business judgment rule. * * *

* * *

Plaintiffs' principal theory is that the 1995 Ovitz Employment Agreement was a "wasteful transaction for Disney *ab initio*" because it was structured to "incentivize" Ovitz to seek an early non-fault termination. The Court of

Chancery correctly dismissed this theory as failing to meet the stringent requirements of the waste test, i.e., "'an exchange that is so one sided that no business person of ordinary, sound judgment could conclude that the corporation has received adequate consideration.'" Moreover, the Court concluded that a board's decision on executive compensation is entitled to great deference. It is the essence of business judgment for a board to determine if "a 'particular individual warrant[s] large amounts of money, whether in the form of current salary or severance provisions.'" [Citation.]

* * *

* * * Irrationality is the outer limit of the business judgment rule. Irrationality may be the functional equivalent of the waste test or it may tend to show that the decision is not made in good faith, which is a key ingredient of the business judgment rule. [Court's footnote: The business judgment rule has been well formulated by *Aronson* and other cases. ("It is a presumption that in making a business decision the directors * * * acted on an informed basis, in good faith and in the honest belief that the action taken was in the best interests of the corporation.") Thus, directors' decisions will be respected by courts unless the directors are interested or lack independence relative to the decision, do not act in good faith, act in a manner that cannot be attributed to a rational business purpose or reach their decision by a grossly negligent process that includes the failure to consider all material facts reasonably available.]

The plaintiffs contend in this Court that Ovitz resigned or committed acts of gross negligence or malfeasance that constituted grounds to terminate him for cause. In either event, they argue that the Company had no obligation to Ovitz and that the directors wasted the Company's assets by causing it to make an unnecessary and enormous payout of cash and stock options when it permitted Ovitz to terminate his employment on a "non-fault" basis. We have concluded, however, that the Complaint currently before us does not set forth particularized facts that he resigned or unarguably breached his Employment Agreement.

* * *

Construed most favorably to plaintiffs, the facts in the Complaint (disregarding conclusory allegations) show that Ovitz' performance as president was disappointing at best, that Eisner admitted it had been a mistake to hire him, that Ovitz lacked commitment to the Company, that he performed services for his old company, and that he negotiated for other jobs (some very lucrative) while being required under the contract to devote his full time and energy to Disney.

All this shows is that the Board had arguable grounds to fire Ovitz for cause. But what is alleged is only an argument—perhaps a good one—that Ovitz' conduct constituted gross negligence or malfeasance. * * *

The Complaint, in sum, contends that the Board committed waste by agreeing to the very lucrative payout to Ovitz under the non-fault termination provision because it had no obligation to him, thus taking the Board's decision outside the protection of the business judgment rule. Construed most favorably to plaintiffs, the Complaint contends that, by reason of the New Board's available arguments of resignation and good cause, it had the leverage to negotiate Ovitz down to a more reasonable payout than that guaranteed by his Employment Agreement. But the Complaint fails on its face to meet the waste test because it does not allege with particularity facts tending to show that no reasonable business person would have made the decision that the New Board made under these circumstances.

* * *

To rule otherwise would invite courts to become super-directors, measuring matters of degree in business decision-making and executive compensation. Such a rule would run counter to the foundation of our jurisprudence.

* * *

One can understand why Disney stockholders would be upset with such an extraordinarily lucrative compensation agreement and termination payout awarded a company president who served for only a little over a year and who under-performed to the extent alleged. That said, there is a very large—though not insurmountable—burden on stockholders who believe they should pursue the remedy of a derivative suit instead of selling their stock or seeking to reform or oust these directors from office.

[Dismissal affirmed in part, reversed in part, and case remanded.]

# CASE 36-5

## Duty of Loyalty
## BEAM v. STEWART

Court of Chancery of Delaware, New Castle, 2003
833 A.2d 961, affirmed, 845 A.2d 1040
http://courts.delaware.gov/opinions/(3trtgh55j1s2xv45plxhzp55)/download.aspx?ID=13450

**Chandler, Chancellor**

Monica A. Beam, a shareholder of Martha Stewart Living Omnimedia, Inc. ("MSO"), brings this derivative action against the defendants, all current directors and a former director of MSO, and against MSO as a nominal defendant. * * *

* * *

Plaintiff Monica A. Beam is a shareholder of MSO and has been since August 2001. Derivative plaintiff and nominal defendant MSO is a Delaware corporation that operates in the publishing, television, merchandising, and internet industries marketing products bearing the "Martha Stewart" brand name.

Defendant Martha Stewart ("Stewart") is a director of the company and its founder, chairman, chief executive officer, and by far its majority shareholder. * * * [S]he controls roughly 94.4% of the shareholder vote. Stewart, a former stockbroker, has in the past twenty years become a household icon, known for her advice and expertise on virtually all aspects of cooking, decorating, entertaining, and household affairs generally.

* * *

The market for MSO products is uniquely tied to the personal image and reputation of its founder, Stewart. MSO retains "an exclusive, worldwide, perpetual royalty-free license to use [Stewart's] name, likeness, image, voice and signature for its products and services." In its initial public offering prospectus, MSO recognized that impairment of Stewart's services to the company, including the tarnishing of her public reputation, would have a material adverse effect on its business. The prospectus distinguished Stewart's importance to MSO's business success from that of other executives of the company noting that, "Martha Stewart remains the personification of our brands as well as our senior executive and primary creative force." In fact, under the terms of her employment agreement, Stewart may be terminated for gross misconduct or felony conviction that results in harm to MSO's business or reputation but is permitted discretion over the management of her personal, financial, and legal affairs to the extent that Stewart's management of her own life does not compromise her ability to serve the company.

Stewart's alleged misadventures with ImClone arise in part out of a longstanding personal friendship with Samuel D. Waksal ("Waksal"). Waksal is the former chief executive officer of ImClone as well as a former suitor of Stewart's daughter. More pertinently, with respect to the allegations of the amended complaint, Waksal and Stewart have provided one another with reciprocal investment advice and assistance, and they share a stockbroker, Peter E. Bacanovic ("Bacanovic") of Merrill Lynch. Bacanovic, coincidentally, is a former employee of ImClone. * * * The speculative value of ImClone stock was tied quite directly to the likely success of its application for FDA approval to market the cancer treatment drug Erbitux. On December 26, Waksal received information that the FDA was rejecting the application to market Erbitux. The following day, December 27, he tried to sell his own shares and tipped his father and daughter to do the same. Stewart also sold her shares on December 27. * * * After the close of trading on December 28, ImClone publicly announced the rejection of its application to market Erbitux. The following day the trading price closed slightly more than 20% lower than the closing price on the date that Stewart had sold her shares. By mid-2002, this convergence of events had attracted the interest of the *New York Times* and other news agencies, federal prosecutors, and a committee of the United States House of Representatives. Stewart's publicized attempts to quell any suspicion were ineffective at best because they were undermined by additional information as it came to light and by the other parties' accounts of the events. Ultimately Stewart's prompt efforts to turn away unwanted media and investigative attention failed. Stewart eventually had to discontinue her regular guest appearances on CBS' *The Early Show* because of questioning during the show about her sale of ImClone shares. After barely two months of such adverse publicity, MSO's stock price had declined by slightly more than 65%. * * *

In January 2002, Stewart and the Martha Stewart Family Partnership sold 3,000,000 shares of Class A stock to [an investor group] "ValueAct." * * *

* * *

* * * [T]he amended complaint alleges that the director defendants * * * breached their fiduciary duties by failing to ensure that Stewart would not conduct her personal, financial, and legal affairs in a manner that would harm the Company, its intellectual property, or its business. The "duty to monitor" has been litigated in other circumstances, generally where directors were alleged to have been negligent in monitoring the activities of the corporation, activities that led to corporate liability. Plaintiff's allegation, however, that the Board has a duty to monitor the personal

affairs of an officer or director is quite novel. That the Company is "closely identified" with Stewart is conceded, but it does not necessarily follow that the Board is required to monitor, much less control, the way Stewart handles her *personal* financial and legal affairs.

* * *

* * * Regardless of Stewart's importance to MSO, she is not the corporation. And it is unreasonable to impose a duty upon the Board to monitor Stewart's personal affairs because such a requirement is neither legitimate nor feasible. Monitoring Stewart by, for example, hiring a private detective to monitor her behavior is more likely to generate liability *to* Stewart under some tort theory than to protect the Company from a decline in its stock price as a result of harm to Stewart's public image.

* * * [This count] is dismissed for failure to state a claim.

* * * [T]he amended complaint alleges that Stewart * * * breached [her] fiduciary duty of loyalty, usurping a corporate opportunity by selling large blocks of MSO stock to ValueAct. * * * The basic requirements for establishing usurpation of a corporate opportunity were articulated by the Delaware Supreme Court in *Broz v. Cellular Information Systems, Inc.*:

> [A] corporate officer or director may not take a business opportunity for his own if: (1) the corporation is financially able to exploit the opportunity; (2) the opportunity is within the corporation's line of business; (3) the corporation has an interest or expectancy in the opportunity; and (4) by taking the opportunity for his own, the corporate fiduciary will thereby be placed in a position [inimical] to his duties to the corporation.

In this analysis, no single factor is dispositive. Instead the Court must balance all factors as they apply to a particular case. For purposes of the present motion, I assume that the sales of stock to ValueAct could be considered to be a "business opportunity." I now address each of the four factors articulated in *Broz.*

The amended complaint asserts that MSO was able to exploit this opportunity because the Company's certificate of incorporation had sufficient authorized, yet unissued, shares of Class A common stock to cover the sale to ValueAct. Defendants do not deny that the Company could have sold previously unissued shares to ValueAct. I therefore conclude that the first factor has been met.

An opportunity is within a corporation's line of business if it is "an activity as to which [the corporation] has fundamental knowledge, practical experience and ability to pursue." * * *

* * * MSO is a consumer products company, not an investment company. Simply stated, selling stock is not the same line of business as selling advice to homemakers. * * * For the foregoing reasons, * * * the sale of stock by Stewart * * * was not within MSO's line of business.

A corporation has an interest or expectancy in an opportunity if there is "some tie between that property and the nature of the corporate business." * * * Here, plaintiff does not allege any facts that would imply that MSO was in need of additional capital, seeking additional capital, or even remotely interested in finding new investors. * * *

* * *

"The corporate opportunity doctrine is implicated only in cases where the fiduciary's seizure of an opportunity results in a conflict between the fiduciary's duties to the corporation and the self-interest of the director as actualized by the exploitation of the opportunity." Given that * * * MSO had no interest or expectancy in the issuance of new stock to ValueAct, I fail to see, based on the allegations before me, how Stewart's * * * sales placed [her] in a position inimical to their duties to the Company. * * *

Additionally, Delaware courts have recognized a policy that allows officers and directors of corporations to buy and sell shares of that corporation at will so long as they act in good faith. * * *

* * *

On balancing the four factors, I conclude that plaintiff has failed to plead facts sufficient to state a claim that Stewart * * * usurped a corporate opportunity for [herself] in violation of [her] fiduciary duty of loyalty to MSO. [This count] is dismissed in its entirety * * * for failure to state a claim upon which relief can be granted.

* * *

IT IS SO ORDERED.

## QUESTIONS

1. Compare the actual governance of closely held corporations, the actual governance of publicly held corporations, and the statutory model of corporate governance.
2. Explain the role of shareholders in the management of a corporation.
3. Explain the role of the board of directors in the management of a corporation.
4. Explain the role of officers in the management of a corporation.
5. Explain management's duties of loyalty, obedience, and diligence.

## PROBLEMS

**1.** Brown, the president and director of a corporation engaged in owning and operating a chain of motels, was advised, upon what seemed to be good authority, that a superhighway was to be constructed through the town of X, which would be a most desirable location for a motel. Brown presented these facts to the board of directors of the motel corporation and recommended that the corporation build a motel in the town of X at the location described. The board of directors agreed, and the new motel was constructed. The superhighway plans were changed, however, after the motel was constructed, and the highway was never built. Later, a packinghouse was built on property adjoining the motel, and the corporation sustained a considerable loss as a result. The shareholders brought an appropriate action against Brown, charging that his proposal had caused a substantial loss to the corporation and seeking recovery of that loss from Brown. What result?

**2.** A, B, C, D, and E constituted the board of directors of the X Corporation. While D and E were out of town, A, B, and C held a special meeting of the board. Just as the meeting began, C became ill. He then gave a proxy to A and went home. A resolution was then adopted directing and authorizing X Corporation's purchase of an adjoining piece of land owned by S as a site for an additional factory building. As was known by S, the purchase required approval by the board of directors. A and B voted for the resolution, and A, as C's proxy, cast C's vote in favor of the resolution. X Corporation then made a contract with S for the purchase of the land. After the return of D and E, another special meeting of the board was held with all five directors present. A resolution was then unanimously adopted to cancel the contract with S. So notified, may S recover damages for breach of contract from X Corporation?

**3.** Bernard Koch was president of United Corporation, a closely held corporation. Koch, James Trent, and Henry Phillips made up the three-person board of directors. At a meeting of the board, Trent was elected president, replacing Koch. At the same meeting, Trent attempted to have the salary of the president increased. He was unable to obtain board approval of the increase because, although Phillips voted for the increase, Koch voted against it. Trent was disqualified from voting by the corporation's charter. As a result, the directors, by a two-to-one vote, amended the bylaws to provide for the appointment of an executive committee composed of three reputable businesspersons to pass upon and fix all matters of salary for employees of the corporation. Subsequently, the executive committee, consisting of Jane Jones, James Black, and William Johnson, increased the salary of the president.

Will Koch succeed in an appropriate action against the corporation, Trent, and Phillips to enjoin them from paying compensation to the president above that amount fixed by the board of directors? Explain.

**4.** Zenith Steel Company operates a prosperous business. In January, Zenith's chief executive officer (CEO) and president, Roe, who is also a member of the board, was voted a $1 million bonus by the board of directors for the valuable services he provided to the company during the previous year. Roe receives an annual salary of $850,000 from the company. Black, Inc., a minority shareholder in Zenith Steel Company, brings an appropriate action to enjoin the company from paying the $1 million bonus. Explain whether Black will succeed in its attempt.

**5.** **(a)** Smith, a director of the Sample Corporation, sells a piece of vacant land to the Sample Corporation for $500,000. The land cost him $200,000.

**(b)** Jones, a shareholder of the Sample Corporation, sells a used truck to the Sample Corporation for $8,400, although the truck is worth $6,000.

Raphael, a minority shareholder of the Sample Corporation, claims that these sales are void and should be annulled. Is he correct? Why?

**6.** The X Corporation manufactures machine tools. The five directors of X Corporation are Black, White, Brown, Green, and Crimson. At a duly called meeting of the board of directors of X Corporation in January, all five directors were present. A contract for the purchase of $10 million worth of steel from the D Company, of which Black, White, and Brown are directors, was discussed and approved by a unanimous vote. The board also discussed at length entering into negotiations for the purchase of Q Corporation, which allegedly was about to be sold for around $150 million. By a three-to-two vote, it was decided not to open such negotiations.

Three months later, Green purchased Q Corporation for $150 million. Shortly thereafter, a new board of directors for X Corporation took office. X Corporation now brings actions to rescind its contract with D Company and to compel Green to assign to X Corporation his contract for the purchase of Q Corporation. Decisions as to each action?

**7.** Gore had been the owner of 1 percent of the outstanding shares of the Webster Company, a corporation, since its organization ten years ago. Ratliff, the president of the company, was the owner of 70 percent of the outstanding shares. Ratliff used the shareholders' list to submit to the shareholders an offer of $50 per share for their stock. Gore, upon receiving the offer, called Ratliff and told him that the offer was inadequate and advised that she was willing to offer $60 per share, and for that purpose demanded a shareholders' list. Ratliff knew that Gore was willing and able to supply the funds necessary to purchase the stock, but he nevertheless refused to supply the list to Gore. Further, he did not offer to transmit Gore's offer to the shareholders of record. Gore then brought an action to compel the corporation to make the shareholders' list available to her. Will Gore be able to obtain a copy of the shareholders' list? Why?

**8.** Mitchell, Nelson, Olsen, and Parker, experts in manufacturing baubles, each owned fifteen out of one hundred authorized shares of Baubles, Inc., a corporation of State X, which does not permit cumulative voting. On July 7, 2004, the corporation sold forty shares to Quentin, an investor, for $1.5 million, which it used to purchase a factory building for $1.5 million. On July 8, 2004, Mitchell, Nelson, Olsen, and Parker contracted as follows:

> All parties will act jointly in exercising voting rights as shareholders. In the event of a failure to agree, the question shall be submitted to George Yost, whose decision shall be binding upon all parties.

Until a meeting of shareholders on April 17, 2011, when a dispute arose, all parties to the contract had voted consistently and regularly for Nelson, Olsen, and Parker as directors. At that meeting, Yost considered the dispute and decided and directed that Mitchell, Nelson, Olsen, and Parker vote their shares for the latter three as directors. Nelson, Olsen, and Parker so voted. Mitchell and Quentin voted for themselves and Mrs. Quentin as directors.

**(a)** Is the contract of July 8, 2004, valid? If so, what is its effect?

**(b)** Who were elected directors of Baubles, Inc., at the meeting of its shareholders on April 17, 2011?

**9.** Acme Corporation's articles of incorporation require cumulative voting for the election of its directors. The board of directors of Acme Corporation consists of nine directors, each elected annually.

**(a)** Smith owns 24 percent of the outstanding shares of Acme Corporation. How many directors can he elect with his votes?

**(b)** If Acme Corporation were to classify its board into three classes, each consisting of three directors elected every three years, how many directors would Smith be able to elect?

**10.** Neese, trustee in bankruptcy for First Trust Company, brings a suit against the directors of the company for losses the company sustained as a result of the directors' failure to use due care and diligence in the discharge of their duties. The specific acts of negligence alleged are (a) failure to give as much time and attention to the affairs of the company as its business interests required; (b) abdication of their control of the corporation by turning its management entirely over to its president, Brown; (c) failure to keep informed as to the affairs, condition, and management of the corporation; (d) taking no action to direct or control the corporation's affairs; (e) permitting large, open, unsecured loans to affiliated but financially unsound companies that were owned and controlled by Brown; (f) failure to examine financial reports that would have shown illegal diversions and waste of the corporation's funds; and (g) failure to supervise properly the corporation's officers and directors. Which, if any, of these allegations can constitute a breach of the duty of diligence?

**11.** Minority shareholders of Midwest Technical Institute Development Corporation, a closed-end investment company owning assets consisting principally of securities of companies in technological fields, brought a shareholder derivative suit against officers and directors of Midwest, seeking to recover on Midwest's behalf profits that the officers and directors realized through dealings in stock held in Midwest's portfolio in breach of their fiduciary duty. Approximately three years after commencement of the action, a new corporation, Midtex, was organized to acquire Midwest's assets. May the shareholders now add Midtex as a party defendant to their suit? Why?

**12.** Riffe, while serving as an officer of Wilshire Oil Company, received a secret commission for work he did on behalf of a competing corporation. Can Wilshire Oil recover these secret profits and, in addition, recover the compensation paid to Riffe by Wilshire Oil during the period that he acted on behalf of the competitor? Explain.

**13.** Muller, a shareholder of SCM, brought an action against SCM over his unsuccessful negotiations to purchase some of SCM's assets overseas. He then formed a shareholder committee to challenge the position of SCM's management in that suit. To conduct a proxy battle for management control at the next election of directors, the committee sought to obtain the list of shareholders who would be eligible to vote. At the time, however, no member of the committee had owned stock in SCM for the six-month period required to gain access to such information. Then Lopez, a former SCM executive and a shareholder for more than one year, joined the committee and demanded to be allowed to inspect the minutes of SCM shareholder proceedings and to gain access to the current shareholder list. His stated reason for making the demand was to solicit proxies in support of those the committee had nominated for positions as directors. Lopez brought this action after SCM rejected this demand. Will Lopez succeed?

**14.** A bylaw of Betma Corporation provides that no shareholder can sell his shares unless he first offers them for sale to the corporation or its directors. The bylaw also states that this restriction shall be printed or stamped upon each stock certificate and shall bind all present or future owners or holders. Betma Corporation did not comply with this latter provision. Shaw, having knowledge of the bylaw restriction, nevertheless purchased twenty shares of the corporation's stock from Rice, without having Rice first offer them for sale to the corporation or its directors. When Betma Corporation refused to effectuate a transfer of the shares to her, Shaw sued to compel a transfer and the issuance of a new certificate to her. What result?

**15.** Pritchard & Baird was a reinsurance broker. A reinsurance broker arranges contracts between insurance companies so that companies that have sold large policies may sell participations in these policies to other companies in order to share the risks. Charles Pritchard, who died in December 2008, controlled Pritchard & Baird for many years. Prior to his death, he brought his two sons, Charles Jr. and William, into the business. The pair assumed an increasingly dominant role in the affairs of the business during the elder Charles's later years. Starting in 2005, Charles Jr. and William began to withdraw from the corporate account ever-increasing sums that were designated as "loans" on the balance sheet. These "loans," however, represented a significant misappropriation of funds belonging to the corporation's clients. By late 2010, Charles Jr. and William had plunged the corporation into hopeless bankruptcy. A total of $12,333,514.47 in "loans" had accumulated by October of that year. Mrs. Lillian Pritchard, the widow of the elder Charles, was a member of the corporation's board of directors until her resignation on December 3, 2010, the day before the corporation filed for bankruptcy. Francis, as trustee in the bankruptcy proceeding, brought suit against United Jersey Bank, the administrator of the estate of Charles Sr. He also charged that Lillian Pritchard, as a director of the corporation, was personally liable for the misappropriated funds on the basis of negligence in discharging her duties as director. Is Francis correct? Why?

**16.** Donald J. Richardson, Grove L. Cook, and Wayne Weaver were stockholders of Major Oil. They brought a direct action, individually and on behalf of all other stockholders of Major, against certain directors and other officers of the corporation. The complaint stated twelve causes of action. The first eight causes alleged some misappropriation of Major's assets by the defendants and sought to require the defendants to return the assets to Major. Three of the remaining four causes alleged breaches of fiduciary duty implicit in those fraudulent acts and sought compensatory or punitive damages for the injury that resulted. The final cause sought the appointment of a receiver. Richardson, Cook, and Weaver moved for an order certifying the suit as a class action. Decision?

**17.** Klinicki and Lundgren, both furloughed Pan Am pilots stationed in West Germany, decided to start their own charter airline company. They formed Berlinair, Inc., a closely held Oregon corporation. Lundgren was president and a director in charge of developing the business. Klinicki was vice president and a director in charge of operations and maintenance. Klinicki, Lundgren, and Lelco, Inc. (Lundgren's family business), each owned one-third of the stock. Klinicki and Lundgren, as representatives of Berlinair, met with BFR, a consortium of Berlin travel agents, to negotiate a lucrative air transportation contract. When Lundgren learned of the likelihood of actually obtaining the BFR contract, he formed his own solely owned company, Air Berlin Charter Company (ABC). Although he continued to negotiate for the BFR contract, he did so on behalf of ABC, not Berlinair. Eventually BFR awarded the contract to ABC. Klinicki commenced a derivative action on behalf of Berlinair and a suit against Lundgren individually for usurping a corporate opportunity of Berlinair. Lundgren claimed that Berlinair was not financially able to undertake the BFR contract and therefore no usurpation of corporate opportunity could occur. Who is correct? Explain.

C H A P T E R 37

# Fundamental Changes

Certain extraordinary changes exert such a fundamental effect on a corporation by altering the corporation's basic structure that they fall outside the authority of the board of directors and require shareholder approval. Such fundamental changes include charter amendments, mergers, consolidations, compulsory share exchanges, dissolution, and the sale or lease of all or substantially all of the corporation's assets, other than those in the regular course of business. Although each of these actions is authorized by State incorporation statutes, which impose specific procedural requirements, they are also subject to equitable limitations imposed by the courts. In 1999 substantial revisions were made to the Revised Act's treatment of fundamental changes.

Because shareholder approval for fundamental changes usually does not need to be unanimous, such changes frequently will be approved despite opposition by minority shareholders. Shareholder approval means a majority (or some other specified fraction) of *all votes entitled* to be cast, rather than a majority (or other fraction) of votes represented at a shareholders' meeting at which a quorum is present. (The 1999 amendments to the Revised Act significantly changed the voting rule: fundamental changes need only be approved by a majority of the shares present at a meeting at which a quorum is present.) In some instances, minority shareholders have the right to dissent and to recover the fair value of their shares if they follow the prescribed procedure for doing so. This right is called the appraisal remedy. The legal aspects of fundamental changes will be discussed in this chapter.

## CHARTER AMENDMENTS

Shareholders do not have a vested property right resulting from any provision in the articles of incorporation. Section 10.01(b). Accordingly, corporate charters may be amended if proper procedures are followed. The amended articles of incorporation, however, may contain only those provisions that the articles of incorporation might lawfully contain at the time of the amendment. Section 10.01(a).

### APPROVAL BY DIRECTORS AND SHAREHOLDERS

Under the Revised Act and most statutes, the typical procedure for amending the articles of incorporation requires the board of directors to adopt a resolution setting forth the proposed amendment, which must then be approved by a majority vote of the shareholders entitled to vote, although some older statutes require a two-thirds shareholder vote. Moreover, a class of shares is entitled to vote as a class on certain proposed amendments, whether the articles of incorporation provide such entitlement or not. In some States shareholders may approve charter amendments without a prior board of directors' resolution.

After the shareholders approve the amendment, the corporation executes articles of amendment and delivers them to the Secretary of State for filing. Section 10.06. The amendment does not affect the existing rights of nonshareholders. Section 10.09.

Under Section 13.02(a)(4) of the Revised Act, dissenting shareholders may obtain the appraisal remedy only if an amendment materially and adversely affects their rights by—

1. altering or abolishing a preferential right of the shares;
2. creating, altering, or abolishing a right involving the redemption of the shares;
3. altering or abolishing a preemptive right of the holder of the shares;
4. excluding or limiting the shareholder's right to vote on any matter or to cumulate his votes; or
5. reducing to a fraction of a share the number of shares the shareholder owns, if the fractional share is to be acquired for cash.

The 1999 amendments to the Revised Act eliminate the appraisal remedy for virtually all charter amendments.

Under the Revised Act, the shareholder approval required for an amendment depends upon the nature of the amendment. An amendment that would give rise to dissenters' rights must be approved by a majority of all votes entitled to be cast on the amendment, unless the act, the charter, or the board of directors requires a greater vote. All other amendments must be approved by a majority of all votes cast on the amendment at a meeting where a quorum exists, unless the act, the charter, or the board of directors requires a greater vote. Sections 10.03, 7.25.

### APPROVAL BY DIRECTORS

The Revised Act permits the board of directors to adopt certain amendments without shareholder action, unless the articles of incorporation provide otherwise. Section 10.02. These amendments include (1) extending the duration of the corporation if it was incorporated when limited duration was required by law, (2) changing each issued and unissued authorized share of an outstanding class into a greater number of whole shares if the corporation has only one class of shares, and (3) making minor name changes.

## COMBINATIONS

Acquiring all or substantially all of the assets of another corporation or corporations may be both desirable and profitable. A corporation may accomplish this through (1) purchase or lease of other corporations' assets, (2) purchase of a controlling stock interest in other corporations, (3) merger with other corporations, or (4) consolidation with other corporations. A few States have and the 1999 amendments to the Revised Act contain provisions authorizing a corporation to merge into another type of business organization, such as a limited partnership (LP), limited liability company (LLC), or a limited liability partnership (LLP).

Any method of combination that involves the issuance of shares, proxy solicitations, or tender offers may be subject to Federal securities regulation, as discussed in *Chapter 44*. Moreover, a combination that is potentially detrimental to competition may be subject to Federal antitrust laws, as discussed in *Chapter 41*.

In July 2010, President Obama signed into law the Dodd-Frank Wall Street Reform and Consumer Protection Act (CFPA), the most significant change to U.S. financial regulation since the New Deal. One of the many standalone statutes included in the CFPA is the Investor Protection and Securities Reform Act of 2010, which imposes new corporate governance rules on publicly held companies. (This Act is also discussed in *Chapters 36*, *44*, and *47*.) One of these provisions of the CFPA applies to proxy solicitations asking shareholders to approve an acquisition, merger, consolidation, or proposed sale or other disposition of all or substantially all the assets of a publicly held company issuer. In these proxy solicitations, publicly held companies must disclose, and provide shareholders with a nonbinding vote to approve, any type of compensation that is based on or relates to these specified combinations.

### PURCHASE OR LEASE OF ALL OR SUBSTANTIALLY ALL OF THE ASSETS

When one corporation purchases or leases all or substantially all of the assets of another corporation, the legal personality of neither corporation changes. The purchaser or lessee corporation simply acquires ownership or control of additional physical assets. The selling or lessor corporation, in exchange for its physical properties, receives cash, other property, or a stipulated rental. Having altered only the form or extent of its assets, each corporation continues its separate existence.

Generally, a corporation that purchases the assets of another corporation does not assume the other's liabilities unless (1) the purchaser expressly or impliedly agrees to assume the seller's liabilities; (2) the transaction amounts to a consolidation or merger of the two corporations; (3) the purchaser is a mere continuation of the seller; or (4) the sale is for the fraudulent purpose of avoiding the liabilities of the seller. Some courts recognize a fifth exception (called the "product line" exception), which imposes strict tort liability upon the purchaser for defects in products manufactured and distributed by the seller corporation when the purchaser corporation continues the product line.

**Regular Course of Business** If the sale or lease of all or substantially all of its assets is in the selling or lessor corporation's usual and regular course of business, approval by its board of directors is required but shareholder authorization is not. Similarly, a mortgage or pledge of any or all of a corporation's property and assets—whether or not in the usual or regular course of business—requires only the approval of the board of directors. Section 12.01. The Revised Act considers a transfer of any or all of a corporation's assets to a wholly owned subsidiary to be a sale in the regular course of business. Section 12.01(a)(3). Under the Revised Act, a sale of assets in the regular course of business does not require shareholder approval unless the articles of incorporation provide otherwise. Section 12.01(b).

**Other Than in Regular Course of Business** Shareholder approval is necessary *only if* a sale or lease of all or substantially all of its assets is *not* in the corporation's usual and regular course of business. (The 1999 amendments to the Revised Act adopt an objective test for determining when shareholder approval is required.) The selling corporation, by liquidating its assets, or the lessor corporation, by placing its physical assets beyond its control, has significantly changed its position and perhaps its ability to carry on the type of business contemplated in its charter. For this reason, such sale or lease must be approved not only by action of the directors but also by the affirmative vote of the holders of a majority of the corporation's shares entitled to vote at a shareholders' meeting called for this purpose. Section 12.02. In most States, dissenting shareholders of the selling corporation are given an appraisal remedy. Section 13.02(a)(3).

## PURCHASE OF SHARES

An alternative to purchasing another corporation's assets is to purchase its stock. When one corporation acquires all of, or a controlling interest in, the stock of another corporation, the legal existence of neither corporation changes. The acquiring corporation acts through its board of directors, whereas the corporation that becomes a subsidiary does not act at all, because the decision to sell stock is made not by the corporation but by its individual shareholders. The capital structure of the subsidiary remains unchanged, and that of the parent is usually not altered unless financing the acquisition of the stock necessitates a change in capital. Because the action of neither corporation requires formal shareholder approval, there is no appraisal remedy.

**SALE OF CONTROL** When a controlling interest is owned by one or a few shareholders, a privately negotiated transaction is possible, though the courts require that these sales be made with due care. The controlling shareholders must make a reasonable investigation so as not to transfer control to purchasers who wrongfully plan to steal or "loot" the corporation's assets or to act against its best interests. In addition, purchasers frequently are willing to pay a premium for a block of shares that conveys control. Although historically some courts required that this so-called control premium inure to the benefit of the corporation, virtually all courts now permit the controlling shareholders to retain the full amount of the control premium.

**TENDER OFFER** When a controlling interest is not held by one or a few shareholders, the acquisition of a corporation through the purchase of shares may take the form of a tender offer. A tender offer is a general invitation to all the shareholders of a target company to tender their shares for sale at a specified price. The offer may be for all of the target company's shares or for just a controlling interest. Tender offers for publicly held companies, which are subject to Federal securities regulation, are discussed in *Chapter 44*.

## COMPULSORY SHARE EXCHANGE

The Revised Act and some State statutes provide different procedures for which a corporation to acquire shares through a **compulsory share exchange**, a transaction by which the corporation becomes the owner of *all* the outstanding shares of one or more classes of another corporation by an exchange that is compulsory on all owners of the acquired shares. Section 11.02. The corporation may acquire the shares with its or any other corporation's shares, obligations, or other securities or for cash or other property. For example, if A corporation acquires all of the outstanding shares of B corporation through a compulsory exchange, then B becomes a wholly owned subsidiary of A. A compulsory share exchange affects the separate existence of neither corporate party to the transaction. Although they produce results similar to mergers, as discussed below, compulsory share exchanges are used instead of mergers where preserving the existence of the acquired corporation is essential or desirable, as, for example, in the formation of holding company systems for insurance companies and banks.

A compulsory share exchange requires approval from the board of directors of each corporation and from the shareholders of the corporation whose shares are being acquired. Sections 11.02 and 11.03. Each included class of shares must vote separately on the exchange. The shareholders of the acquiring corporation need not approve the transaction. Once the shareholders of the corporation whose shares are to be acquired have adopted and approved a compulsory share exchange plan, it is binding on all who hold shares of the class to be acquired. Dissenting shareholders are given an appraisal remedy. Section 13.02(a)(2).

## MERGER

A **merger** of two or more corporations is the combination of all of their assets. One of the corporations, known as the **surviving corporation**, receives title to the combined assets. The other party or parties to the merger, known as the **merged corporation** or corporations, are merged into the surviving corporation and cease their separate existence. Thus, if A Corporation and B Corporation combine into the A Corporation, A is the surviving corporation and B is the merged corporation. Under the Revised Act and most statutes, the shareholders of the merged corporation may receive stock or other securities issued by the surviving corporation or other consideration *including cash*, as provided in the merger agreement. Moreover, the surviving corporation assumes all debts and other liabilities of the merged corporation. Section 11.06.

A merger requires the approval of each corporation's board of directors, as well as the affirmative vote of the holders of a majority of the shares of each corporation that are entitled to vote. Sections 11.01 and 11.03. A dissenting shareholder of any corporate party to the merger has an appraisal remedy if shareholder approval is required and the shareholder is entitled to vote on the merger. Section 13.02(a)(1). Many States and the 1999 amendments to the Revised Act permit the vote of the shareholders of the surviving corporation to be eliminated when a merger increases the number of outstanding shares by no more than 20 percent.

In a **short-form merger**, a corporation that owns a statutorily specified percentage of the outstanding shares of each class of a subsidiary may merge the subsidiary into itself without approval by the shareholders of either corporation. The Revised Act and most States specify 90 percent. Section 11.04. Obtaining approval from the subsidiary's shareholders or from the subsidiary's board of directors is unnecessary because the parent's 90 percent ownership ensures approval of the merger plan. All the merger requires is a resolution by the board of directors of the parent corporation. The dissenting shareholders of the subsidiary have the right to obtain payment from the parent for their shares. Section 13.02(a)(1). The shareholders of the parent do not have this appraisal remedy because the transaction has not materially changed their rights. Instead of indirectly owning 90 percent of the subsidiary's assets, the parent now directly owns 100 percent of the same assets.

## CONSOLIDATION

A consolidation of two or more corporations is the combination of all of their assets, the title to which is taken by a newly created corporation known as the **consolidated corporation**. Each constituent corporation ceases to exist, and all of its debts and liabilities are assumed by the new corporation. The shareholders of the constituent corporations receive stock or other securities, not necessarily of the same class, issued to them by the new corporation or other consideration provided in the plan of consolidation. A consolidation requires the approval of each corporation's board of directors, as well as the affirmative vote of the holders of a majority of the shares of each corporation that are entitled to vote. Dissenting shareholders have an appraisal remedy.

The Revised Act has deleted all references to consolidations, as explained by the comment to Section 11.01: "In modern corporate practice consolidation transactions are obsolete since it is nearly always advantageous for one of the parties in the transaction to be the surviving corporation."

## DOMESTICATION AND CONVERSION

The Revised Act was amended in 2002 to provide for domestication and conversion into other entities without a merger. The **domestication** procedures permit a corporation to change its State of incorporation, thus allowing a domestic business corporation to become a foreign business corporation or a foreign business corporation to become a domestic business corporation. The **conversion** procedures permit a domestic business corporation to become a domestic or foreign partnership, LLC, or other entity, and also permit a domestic or foreign partnership, LLC, or other entity to become a domestic business corporation. In both of these transactions a domestic business corporation must be present immediately before or after the transaction.

## GOING PRIVATE TRANSACTIONS

Corporate combinations are sometimes used to take a publicly held corporation private in order to eliminate minority interests, to reduce the burdens of certain provisions of the Federal securities laws, or both. One method of going private is for the corporation or its majority shareholder to acquire the corporation's shares through purchases on the open market or through a tender offer for the shares. Other methods include a cash-out combination, a merger with or sale of assets to a corporation controlled by the majority shareholder. If the majority shareholder is a corporation, it may arrange a cash-out combination with itself or, if it owns enough shares, use a short-form merger. In recent years, a new type of going private transaction—a management buyout—has become much more frequent. This section will examine cash-out combinations and management buyouts.

**CASH-OUT COMBINATIONS** Cash-out combinations are used to eliminate minority shareholders by forcing them to accept cash or property for their shares. A cash-out combination often follows the acquisition, by a person, group, or company, of a large interest in a target company (T) through a tender offer. The tender offeror (TO) then seeks to eliminate all other shareholders, thereby achieving complete control of T. To do so, TO might form a new corporation (Corporation N) and take 100 percent of its stock. A cash-out merger of T into N is then arranged, with all the shareholders of T other than TO to receive cash for their shares. Because TO owns all the stock of N and a controlling interest in T, the shareholders of both companies will approve the merger. Alternatively, TO could purchase for cash or notes the assets of T, leaving the minority shareholders with only an interest in the proceeds of the sale. The use of cash-out combinations has raised questions concerning their purpose and their fairness to minority shareholders. Some States require that cash-out combinations have a valid business purpose and that they be fair to all concerned. Fairness, in this context, includes both fair dealing (which involves the procedural aspects of the transaction) and fair price (which involves the financial considerations of the merger). Other States require only the transaction to be fair.

◆ **SEE CASE 37-1**

**MANAGEMENT BUYOUT** A management buyout is a transaction by which existing management increases its ownership of a corporation while eliminating the entity's public shareholders. The typical procedure is as follows. The management of an existing company (Corporation A) forms a new corporation (Corporation B) in which the management owns some of the stock and institutional investors own the rest. Corporation B issues bonds to institutional investors to raise cash, with which it purchases the assets or stock of Corporation A. The assets of Corporation A are used as security for the bonds issued by Corporation B. (Because of the extensive use of borrowed funds, a management buyout is commonly called a **leveraged buyout** [LBO].) The result of this transaction is twofold: the public shareholders of Corporation A no longer have any proprietary interest in the assets of Corporation A, and management's equity interest in Corporation B is greater than its interest was in Corporation A.

A critical issue is the fairness of the management buyout to the shareholders of Corporation A. The transaction inherently presents a potential conflict of interest to those in management, who owe a fiduciary duty to represent the interests of the shareholders of Corporation A. As substantial shareholders of Corporation B, however, those in management are apt to have personal and probably adverse financial interests in the transaction.

### DISSENTING SHAREHOLDERS

The shareholder's right to dissent, a statutory right to obtain payment for shares, is accorded to shareholders who object to certain fundamental changes in the corporation. The Introductory Comment to Chapter 13 of the Revised Act explains the purpose of dissenters' rights:

> Chapter 13 deals with the tension between the desire of the corporate leadership to be able to enter new fields, acquire new enterprises, and rearrange investor rights and the desire of investors to adhere to the rights and the risks on the basis of which they invested. Most contemporary corporation codes in the United States attempt to resolve this tension through a combination of two devices. On the one hand, the majority is given an almost unlimited power to change the nature and shape of the enterprise and the rights of its members. On the other hand, the members who dissent from these changes are given a right to withdraw their investment at a fair value.

**Transactions Giving Rise to Dissenters' Rights** States vary considerably with respect to which transactions give rise to dissenters' rights. Some include transactions not covered by the Revised Act, and other States omit transactions included in the Revised Act.

The Revised Act grants dissenters' rights to (1) dissenting shareholders of a corporation selling or leasing all or substantially all of its property or assets not in the usual or regular course of business; (2) dissenting shareholders of each corporate party to a merger, except in a short-form merger, where only the dissenting shareholders of the subsidiary have dissenters' rights; (3) any plan of compulsory share exchange in which their corporation is to be the one acquired; (4) any amendment to the articles of incorporation that materially and adversely affects a dissenter's rights regarding her shares; and (5) any other corporate action taken pursuant to a shareholder vote with respect to which the articles of incorporation, the bylaws, or a resolution of the board of directors provides that shareholders shall have a right to dissent and obtain payment for their shares. Section 13.02. The 1999 amendments to the Revised Act narrowed the scope of the appraisal remedy: in a merger, only shareholders whose shares have been exchanged have dissenters' rights, and the appraisal remedy for virtually all charter amendments has been eliminated.

Many States have a stock market exception to the appraisal remedy. Under these statutes, a shareholder has no right to dissent if an established market, such as the New York Stock Exchange, exists for the shares. The Revised Act does not contain this exception but the 1999 amendments to the Revised Act have added it.

**Procedure** The corporation must notify the shareholders of the existence of dissenters' rights before taking the vote on the corporate action. A dissenting shareholder who strictly complies with the provisions of the statute is entitled to receive the fair value of his shares. Unless he makes written demand within the prescribed time, however, the dissenting shareholder is not entitled to payment for his shares.

**Appraisal Remedy** A dissenting shareholder who complies with all applicable requirements is entitled to an appraisal remedy, which is payment by the corporation of the **fair value** of his shares, plus accrued interest. The fair value is the value immediately preceding the effectuation of the corporate action to which the dissenter objects, excluding any appreciation or depreciation that occurs in anticipation of such corporate action, unless such exclusion would be inequitable.

A shareholder who has a right to obtain payment for his shares does not have the right to attack the validity of the corporate action that gives rise to his right to obtain payment or to have the action set aside or rescinded, except when the corporate action is unlawful or fraudulent with regard to the complaining shareholder or to the corporation. Section 13.02(b). Where the corporate action is not unlawful or fraudulent, the appraisal remedy is usually exclusive, and the shareholder may not challenge the action. Some States, however, make the appraisal remedy exclusive in all cases; others make it nonexclusive in certain cases.

◆ **SEE CASE 37-2**

## DISSOLUTION

Although a corporation may have perpetual existence, its life may be terminated in a number of ways. Incorporation statutes usually provide for both voluntary dissolution and involuntary dissolution. Dissolution does not in itself terminate the corporation's existence but does require that the corporation wind up its affairs and liquidate its assets.

### VOLUNTARY DISSOLUTION

Voluntary dissolution may be brought about through a board resolution approved by the affirmative vote of the holders of a majority of the corporation's shares entitled to vote at a shareholders' meeting duly called for this purpose. Section 14.02. Although shareholders who object to dissolution usually have no right to dissent and recover the fair value of their shares, the Revised Act grants dissenters' rights in connection with a sale or exchange of all or substantially all of a corporation's assets not made in the usual or regular course of business, including a sale in dissolution. Nevertheless, the Act excludes such rights in sales by court order and sales for cash on terms requiring that all or substantially all of the net proceeds be distributed to the shareholders within one year. Section 13.02(a)(3). In addition, in many States, but not the Revised Act, dissolution without action by the directors may be effected by unanimous consent of the shareholders.

The Revised Act authorizes shareholders in closely held corporations to adopt unanimous shareholders' agreements requiring dissolution of the corporation at the request of one or more shareholders or upon the occurrence of a specified event or contingency.

The Statutory Close Corporation Supplement gives the shareholders, if they elect such a right in the articles of incorporation, the power to dissolve the corporation. Unless the charter specifies otherwise, an amendment to include, modify, or delete a power to dissolve must be approved by all of the shareholders. The power to dissolve may be conferred upon any shareholder or holders of a specified number or percentage of shares of any class and may be exercised either at will or upon the occurrence of a specified event or contingency.

◆ SEE FIGURE 37-1: **Fundamental Changes under Pre-1999 RMBCA**

## INVOLUNTARY DISSOLUTION

A corporation may be involuntarily dissolved by administrative dissolution or by judicial dissolution.

**Administrative Dissolution** The Secretary of State may commence an administrative proceeding to dissolve a corporation if (1) the corporation does not pay within sixty days after they are due any franchise taxes or penalties; (2) the corporation does not deliver its annual report to the Secretary of State within sixty days after it is due; (3) the corporation is without a registered agent or registered office in the State for sixty days or more; (4) the corporation does not notify the Secretary of State within sixty days that it has changed its registered agent or registered office, that its registered agent has resigned, or that it has discontinued its registered office; or (5) the corporation's period of duration stated in its articles of incorporation expires. Section 14.20.

**Judicial Dissolution** The State, a shareholder, or a creditor may bring a proceeding seeking judicial dissolution. A court may dissolve a corporation in a proceeding brought by the Attorney General if it is proved that the corporation obtained its charter through fraud or has continued to exceed or abuse the authority conferred upon it by law. Section 14.30(1).

A court may dissolve a corporation in a proceeding brought by a shareholder if it is established that (1) the directors are deadlocked in the management of the corporate affairs, the shareholders are unable to break the deadlock, and the corporation is threatened with or suffering irreparable injury; (2) the acts of the directors or those in control of the corporation are illegal, oppressive, or fraudulent; (3) the corporate assets are being misapplied or wasted; or (4) the shareholders are deadlocked and have failed to elect directors for at least two consecutive annual meetings. Section 14.30(2). The Revised Act as amended provides a *closely held* corporation or the remaining shareholders a limited right to purchase at fair value the shares of a shareholder who has brought a proceeding for involuntary dissolution. Section 14.34.

A creditor may bring a court action for dissolution upon a showing that the corporation has become unable to pay its debts and obligations as they mature in the regular course of its business and that either (1) the creditor has reduced his claim to a judgment and an execution issued on it has been returned unsatisfied or (2) the corporation has admitted in writing that the claim of the creditor is due and owing. Section 14.30(3).

◆ **SEE CASE 37-3**

## LIQUIDATION

Dissolution, as mentioned earlier, requires that the corporation devote itself to winding up its affairs and liquidating its assets. After dissolution, the corporation must cease carrying on its business except as is necessary to wind up. Section 14.05. When a corporation is dissolved, its assets are liquidated and used first to pay the expenses of liquidation and its creditors according to their respective contract or lien rights. Any remainder is distributed proportionately to shareholders according to their respective contract rights; stock with a liquidation preference has priority over common stock. Voluntary liquidation is carried out by the board of directors, who serve as trustees; a court-appointed receiver may conduct involuntary liquidation. Section 14.32.

## PROTECTION OF CREDITORS

The statutory provisions governing dissolution and liquidation usually prescribe procedures to safeguard the interests of the corporation's creditors. Such procedures typically include a required mailing of notice to known creditors, a general publication of notice, and the preservation of claims

◆ FIGURE 37-1: **Fundamental Changes under Pre-1999 RMBCA**

| Change | Board of Directors Resolution Required | Shareholder Approval Required | Shareholder's Appraisal Remedy Available |
|---|---|---|---|
| **A amends its articles of incorporation** | A: Yes | A: Yes | A: No, unless amendment materially and adversely affects rights of shares |
| **B sells its assets in usual and regular course of business to A** | B: Yes | B: No | B: No |
| **B sells its assets not in usual and regular course of business to A** | B: Yes | B: Yes | B: Yes |
| **A voluntarily purchases shares of B** | A: Yes<br>B: No | A: No<br>B: No, individual shareholders decide | A: No<br>B: No |
| **A acquires shares of B through a compulsory exchange** | A: Yes<br>B: Yes | A: No<br>B: Yes | A: No<br>B: Yes |
| **A and B merge** | A: Yes<br>B: Yes | A: Yes<br>B: Yes | A: Yes<br>B: Yes |
| **A merges its 90 percent subsidiary B into A** | A: Yes<br>B: No | A: No<br>B: No | A: No<br>B: Yes |
| **A and B consolidate** | A: Yes<br>B: Yes | A: Yes<br>B: Yes | A: Yes<br>B: Yes |
| **A voluntarily dissolves** | A: Yes | A: Yes | A: No (usually) |

Note: RMBCA = Revised Model Business Corporation Act.

against the corporation. The Revised Act provides a three-year period within which an otherwise barred claim may be enforced for (1) a claimant who did not receive notice, (2) a claimant on whose timely claim the corporation failed to act, or (3) a claimant whose claim is contingent on an event occurring after dissolution. Section 14.07.

## CHAPTER SUMMARY

**CHARTER AMENDMENTS**

**Authority to Amend** statutes permit charters to be amended
**Procedure** the board of directors adopts a resolution that must be approved by a majority vote of the shareholders

---

**COMBINATIONS**

**Purchase or Lease of All or Substantially All of the Assets** results in no change in the legal personality of either corporation

- ***Regular Course of Business*** approval by the selling corporation's board of directors is required, but shareholder authorization is not
- ***Other Than in Regular Course of Business*** approval by the board of directors and shareholders of selling corporation is required

**Purchase of Shares** a transaction by which one corporation acquires all of or a controlling interest in the stock of another corporation; no change occurs in the legal existence of either corporation, and no formal shareholder approval of either corporation is required

**Compulsory Share Exchange** a transaction by which a corporation becomes the owner of all of the outstanding shares of one or more classes of stock of another corporation by an exchange that is compulsory on all owners of the acquired shares; the board of directors of each corporation and the shareholders of the corporation whose shares are being acquired must approve

**Merger** the combination of the assets of two or more corporations into one of the corporations

- ***Procedure*** requires approval by the board of directors and shareholders of each corporation
- ***Short-Form Merger*** a corporation that owns at least 90 percent of the outstanding shares of a subsidiary may merge the subsidiary into itself without approval by the shareholders of either corporation
- ***Effect*** the surviving corporation receives title to all of the assets of the merged corporation and assumes all of its liabilities; the merged corporation ceases to exist

**Consolidation** the combination of two or more corporations into a new corporation

- ***Procedure*** requires approval of the board of directors and shareholders of each corporation
- ***Effect*** each constituent corporation ceases to exist; the new corporation assumes all of their debts and liabilities

**Domestication** Revised Act permits a corporation to change its State of incorporation

**Conversion** Revised Act permits (1) a domestic business corporation to become a domestic or foreign partnership, LLC, or other entity; and (2) a domestic or foreign partnership, LLC, or other entity to become a domestic business corporation

**Going Private Transactions** a combination that makes a publicly held corporation a private one; includes cash-out combinations and management buyouts

**Dissenting Shareholder** one who opposes a fundamental change and has the right to receive the fair value of her shares

- ***Availability*** dissenters' rights arise in (1) mergers, (2) consolidations, (3) sales or leases of all or substantially all of the assets of a corporation not in the regular course of business, (4) compulsory share exchanges, and (5) amendments that materially and adversely affect the rights of shares
- ***Appraisal Remedy*** the right to receive the fair value of one's shares (the value of shares immediately before the corporate action to which the dissenter objects takes place, excluding any appreciation or depreciation in anticipation of such corporate action unless such exclusion would be inequitable)

---

**DISSOLUTION**

**Voluntary Dissolution** may be brought about by a resolution of the board of directors that is approved by the shareholders

**Involuntary Dissolution** may occur by administrative or judicial action taken (1) by the Attorney General, (2) by shareholders under certain circumstances, or (3) by a creditor on a showing that the corporation has become unable to pay its debts and obligations as they mature in the regular course of its business

**Liquidation** when a corporation is dissolved, its assets are liquidated and used first to pay its liquidation expenses and its creditors according to their respective contract or lien rights; any remainder is proportionately distributed to shareholders according to their respective contract rights

# CASES

CASE 37-1

## Cash-Out Combinations
## ALPERT v. 28 WILLIAMS ST. CORP.

New York Court of Appeals, 1984
63 N.Y.2d 557, 483 N.Y.S.2d 667, 473 N.E.2d 19

**Cooke, C. J.**

The subject of contention in this litigation is a valuable 17-story office building, located at 79 Madison Avenue in Manhattan. In dispute is the propriety of a complex series of transactions that had the net effect of permitting defendants, who were outside investors, to gain ownership of the property and to eliminate the ownership interests of plaintiffs, who were minority shareholders of the corporation that formerly owned the building. This was achieved through what is commonly known as a "two-step" merger: (1) an outside investor purchases control of the majority shares of the target corporation by tender offer or through private negotiations; (2) this newly acquired control is used to arrange for the target and a second corporation controlled by the outside investor to merge, with one condition being the "freeze-out" of the minority shareholders of the target corporation by the forced cancellation of their shares, generally through a cash purchase. This accomplishes the investor's original goal of complete ownership of the target corporation.

Since 1955, the office building was owned by 79 Realty Corporation (Realty Corporation), which had no other substantial assets. About two-thirds of Realty Corporation's outstanding shares were held by two couples, the Kimmelmans and the Zauderers, who were also the company's sole directors and officers. Plaintiffs owned 26% of the outstanding shares. The remaining shares were owned by persons who are not parties to this litigation.

Defendants, a consortium of investors, formed a limited partnership, known as Madison 28 Associates (Madison Associates), for the purpose of purchasing the building. * * *

Madison Associates formed a separate, wholly owned company, 28 Williams Street Corporation (Williams Street), to act as the nominal purchaser and owner of the Kimmelman and Zauderer interests. * * *

[T]he partners of Madison Associates approved a plan to merge Realty Corporation with Williams Street, Realty Corporation being the surviving corporation. Together with a notice for a shareholders' meeting to vote on the proposed merger, a statement of intent was sent to all shareholders of Realty Corporation, explaining the procedural and financial aspects of the merger, as well as defendants' conflict of interest and the intended exclusion of the minority shareholders from the newly constituted Realty Corporation through a cash buy-out. Defendants also disclosed that they planned to dissolve Realty Corporation after the merger and thereafter to operate the business as a partnership. The merger plan did not require approval by any of the minority shareholders.

The merger proposed by the directors was approved at the shareholders meeting, held on November 7, 1980. As a result, the office building was owned by the "new" Realty Corporation, which, in turn, was wholly owned by Madison Associates. In accordance with the merger plan, Realty Corporation was dissolved within a month of the merger and its principal asset, title to the building, devolved to Madison Associates.

* * *

The plaintiffs instituted this action * * * [seeking] rescission of the merger.

The propriety of the merger was contested on several grounds. It was contended that the merger was unlawful because its sole purpose was to personally benefit the partners of Madison Associates and that the alleged purposes had no legitimate business benefit inuring to the corporation. Plaintiffs argue that the "business judgment" of the directors in assigning various purposes for the merger was indelibly tainted by a conflict of interest because they were committed to the merger prior to becoming directors and were on both sides of the merger transaction when consummated. Further, they assert that essential financial information was not disclosed and that the value offered for the minority's shares was understated and determined in an unfair manner.

* * *

On this appeal, the principal task facing this court is to prescribe a standard for evaluating the validity of a corporate transaction that forcibly eliminates minority shareholders by means of a two-step merger. It is concluded that the analysis employed by the courts below was correct: the majority shareholders' exclusion of minority interests through a two-step merger does not violate the former's fiduciary obligations so long as the transaction viewed as a whole is fair to the minority shareholders and is justified by an independent corporate business purpose. Accordingly, this court now affirms.

* * *

In New York, two or more domestic corporations are authorized to "merge into a single corporation which shall be one of the constituent corporations," known as the "surviving corporation" [citation]. The statute does not delineate substantive justifications for mergers, but only requires compliance with certain procedures: the adoption by the boards of each corporation of a plan of merger setting forth, among other things, the terms and conditions of the merger; a statement of any changes in the certificate of incorporation of the surviving corporation; the submission of the plan to a vote of shareholders pursuant to notice to all shareholders; and adoption of the plan by a vote of two-thirds of the shareholders entitled to vote on it [citation].

Generally, the remedy of a shareholder dissenting from a merger and the offered "cash-out" price is to obtain the fair value of his or her stock through an appraisal proceeding [citation]. This protects the minority shareholder from being forced to sell at unfair values imposed by those dominating the corporation while allowing the majority to proceed with its desired merger [citations]. The pursuit of an appraisal proceeding generally constitutes the dissenting stockholder's exclusive remedy [citations]. An exception exists, however, when the merger is unlawful or fraudulent as to that shareholder, in which event an action for equitable relief is authorized [citations]. Thus, technical compliance with the Business Corporation Law's requirements alone will not necessarily exempt a merger from further judicial review.

* * *

* * * In reviewing a freeze-out merger, the essence of the judicial inquiry is to determine whether the transaction, viewed as a whole, was "fair" as to all concerned. This concept has two principal components: the majority shareholders must have followed "a course of fair dealing toward minority holders" * * * and they must also have offered a fair price for the minority's stock. * * *

* * *

Fair dealing is also concerned with the procedural fairness of the transaction, such as its timing, initiation, structure, financing, development, disclosure to the independent directors and shareholders, and how the necessary approvals were obtained * * *. Basically, the courts must look for complete and candid disclosure of all the material facts and circumstances of the proposed merger known to the majority or directors, including their dual roles and events leading up to the merger proposal. * * *

The fairness of the transaction cannot be determined without considering the component of the financial remuneration offered the dissenting shareholders. * * *

In determining whether there was a fair price, the court need not ascertain the precise "fair value" of the shares as it would be determined in an appraisal proceeding. It should be noted, however, that the factors used in an appraisal proceeding are relevant here. * * * This would include but would not be limited to net asset value, book value, earnings, market value, and investment value * * *. Elements of future value arising from the accomplishment or expectation of the merger which are known or susceptible of proof as of the date of the merger and not the product of speculation may also be considered. * * *

* * *

In the context of a freeze-out merger, variant treatment of the minority shareholders—i.e., causing their removal—will be justified when related to the advancement of a general corporate interest. The benefit need not be great, but it must be for the corporation. For example, if the sole purpose of the merger is reduction of the number of profit sharers—in contrast to increasing the corporation's capital or profits, or improving its management structure—there will exist no "independent corporate interest" [citation]. All of these purposes ultimately seek to increase the individual wealth of the remaining shareholders. What distinguishes a proper corporate purpose from an improper one is that, with the former, removal of the minority shareholders furthers the objective of conferring some general gain upon the corporation. Only then will the fiduciary duty of good and prudent management of the corporation serve to override the concurrent duty to treat all shareholders fairly [citation]. We further note that a finding that there was an independent corporate purpose for the action taken by the majority will not be defeated merely by the fact that the corporate objective could have been accomplished in another way, or by the fact that the action chosen was not the best way to achieve the bona fide business objective.

In sum, in entertaining an equitable action to review a freeze-out merger, a court should view the transaction as a whole to determine whether it was tainted with fraud, illegality, or self-dealing, whether the minority shareholders were dealt with fairly, and whether there exists any independent corporate purpose for the merger.

* * *

Without passing on all of the business purposes cited by [the trial court] as underlying the merger, it is sufficient to note that at least one justified the exclusion of plaintiff's interests: attracting additional capital to effect needed repairs of the building. There is proof that there was a good-faith belief that additional, outside capital was required. Moreover, this record supports the conclusion that this capital would not have been available through the merger had not plaintiffs' interest in the corporation been eliminated. Thus, the approval of the merger, which would extinguish plaintiffs' stock, was supported by a bona fide business purpose to advance this general corporate interest of obtaining increased capital.

Accordingly, the order of the Appellate Division should be affirmed.

CASE 37-2

## Dissenting Shareholders
## COHEN v. MIRAGE RESORTS, INC.

Supreme Court of Nevada, 2003
62 P.3d 720, petition for rehearing denied, 2003
http://caselaw.lp.findlaw.com/scripts/getcase.pl?court=nv&vol=119NevAdvOpNo1&invol=2

**Becker, J.**
Appellant Harvey Cohen was a minority shareholder in the Boardwalk, a small, publicly held casino on Las Vegas Boulevard, "The Strip." The Boardwalk had 1,200 feet of Strip frontage located between the Bellagio and the Monte Carlo, large casinos in which the Mirage Resorts had an interest. Mirage also owned twenty-three acres of land adjacent to the Boardwalk.

Mirage wished to acquire the Boardwalk as well as three parcels of land surrounding the Boardwalk. The three parcels were either owned by entities connected with the Boardwalk's majority shareholders and directors or were subject to options to purchase in favor of the Boardwalk. Mirage sought to negate the Boardwalk's options and acquire the adjacent properties for purposes of expansion.

Mirage made an offer to acquire the Boardwalk's shares through a merger with a Mirage subsidiary, Acquisition. Prior to or contemporaneous with the merger, Mirage acquired the surrounding parcels.

On May 27, 1998, the Boardwalk convened a special shareholder meeting to consider the offer. A majority of the shareholders approved the merger. The merger was consummated on June 30, 1998. Cohen and other members of the class tendered their shares without challenging the merger's validity or claiming dissenters' rights pursuant to NRS 92A.380-92A.500, setting forth the procedures for challenging the valuation of shares in a merger.

On September 28, 1999, Cohen filed suit for damages, alleging breach of fiduciary duty and/or loyalty by the Boardwalk's majority shareholders, board of directors and financial advisors, * * *. Cohen asserts Mirage conspired with the Boardwalk's majority shareholders and directors to purchase the Boardwalk at an artificially low price by offering special transactions to majority shareholders and/or members of the Boardwalk's board of directors. Cohen claims that Mirage bought land or rights owned or controlled by majority shareholders or directors in properties around or involving the Boardwalk at inflated prices. Cohen contends that these shareholders and directors then agreed to approve or recommend the merger for an amount per share that was less than the fair value of the Boardwalk's stock. Finally, Cohen asserts that the directors mismanaged the Boardwalk, causing decreased profits, and that they or majority shareholders usurped corporate opportunities.

* * *

Respondents moved to dismiss for failure to state a claim upon which relief could be granted, denying any wrongdoing. Respondents argued that, even assuming the truth of the allegations, Cohen had no standing to sue for breach of fiduciary duty because he failed to exercise his statutory rights to dissent to the merger and tendered his shares pursuant to the merger. Respondents further asserted that the provisions of NRS 92A.300-92A.500 are the exclusive method for a dissenting shareholder to challenge the value of a merged corporation's stock, * * *. Respondents also contended that because Cohen and the class were no longer shareholders, they could not bring derivative claims for lost profits and usurpation of corporate opportunities.

* * * Cohen contended, however, that the complaint asserted that the merger was approved unlawfully or as a result of wrongful conduct and therefore the time frames set forth for an appraisal proceeding did not apply. * * *

Cohen claimed that if the merger was accomplished through wrongful conduct, then he had the right to seek monetary damages, including any difference in value between the merger price and the fair value of his stock. Because he was seeking monetary damages arising from an allegedly invalid merger, Cohen contended the claims were individual and not derivative in nature and the motion to dismiss should be denied. * * *

* * *

* * * The district court granted respondents' motion to dismiss, * * *. Cohen then filed this appeal.

* * * Under Nevada law, a corporate merger must be approved by a majority of the corporation's shareholders. The existing shareholders then substitute their stock ownership in the old corporation for stock ownership in the new merged corporation. [Citation.] Shareholders who oppose the merger are not forced to become stockholders in the new corporation. Instead, the statutes give such shareholders three choices: (1) accept the terms of the merger and exchange their existing shares for new shares; (2) dissent from the merger, compelling the merged corporation to purchase their shares pursuant to a judicial appraisal proceeding; and/or (3) challenge the validity of the merger based on unlawful or wrongful conduct committed during the merger process. [Citation.] * * *

* * *

[T]he states and the Model Act * * * recognize two circumstances when minority shareholders should be able to challenge the merger process. [Citation.] A merger may be challenged if it is unlawful, that is, procedurally deficient. * * * In addition, minority shareholders may seek to stop a merger if fraud or material misrepresentation affected the shareholder vote on the merger; that is, the shareholders approved the merger based upon materially incorrect information. [Citation.] Under either theory, minority shareholders may bring suit to enjoin or rescind the merger or to recover monetary damages attributable to the loss of their shareholder interest caused by an invalid merger. They may also allege that the merger was accomplished through the wrongful conduct of majority shareholders, directors, or officers of the corporation and attempt to hold those individuals liable for monetary damages under theories of breach of fiduciary duty or loyalty. [Citation.]

Challenges to the validity of a merger based on fraud usually encompass either or both of the following: (1) lack of fair dealing or (2) lack of fair price. [Citation.] Both involve corporate directors' general duties to make independent, fully informed decisions when recommending a merger and to fully disclose material information to the shareholders before a vote is taken on a proposed merger. [Citation.] * * *

Lack of fair dealing involves allegations that the board of directors did not make an independent, informed decision to recommend approval of the merger, [citation] or that the majority shareholders approved the merger at the expense of the minority shareholders. [Citation.] * * *

Lack of fair price may involve similar allegations plus claims that the price per share was deliberately undervalued, but it can also include negligent conduct. [Citation.] For example, the directors may have hired incompetent or inexperienced persons to determine if the merger price was fair or to evaluate the fair value of the corporation's stock. [Citation.]

* * *

Shareholders who vote in favor of the merger generally have no standing to contest the validity of the merger. [Citations.] * * * Misinformed shareholders [, however,] retain their right to challenge the merger regardless of their vote on the merger and a tender of their shares. [Citation.]

* * *

Former shareholders, however, cannot simply seek more money for their stock. They must assert and prove in an equitable action that the merger was improper. [Citation.] If this is proven, then they are entitled to any monetary damages they are able to prove were proximately caused by the improper merger. [Citation.] Moreover, damages are not limited to the surviving corporation. They may also be levied against the individuals whose wrongful conduct led to the approval of the merger or the unfair stock evaluation. [Citation.]

* * *

* * * A claim brought by a dissenting shareholder that questions the validity of a merger as a result of wrongful conduct on the part of majority shareholders or directors is properly classified as an individual or direct claim. The shareholder has lost unique personal property—his or her interest in a specific corporation. [Citations.] Therefore, if the complaint alleges damages resulting from an improper merger, it should not be dismissed as a derivative claim. [Citations.] On the other hand, if it seeks damages for wrongful conduct that caused harm to the corporation, it is derivative and should be dismissed. [Citation.] * * *

* * *

We further conclude that the district court was correct in dismissing all of the derivative claims in the complaint, but erred in not permitting Cohen to amend the complaint to clarify that he was seeking rescission of the merger and/or monetary damages based upon the invalidity of the merger.

We affirm the order to the extent that it dismissed the derivative causes of action * * *. We reverse the order to the extent that it dismissed the allegations supporting claims for rescission, breach of loyalty, breach of fiduciary duty, and conspiracy involving the validity of the merger, specifically, allegations that improper incentives were paid to approve the merger at a below-market price per share. * * *

# CASE 37-3

## Involuntary Judicial Dissolution
## COOKE v. FRESH EXPRESS FOODS CORPORATION, INC.

Court of Appeals of Oregon, 2000
169 Ore.App. 101, 7 P.3d 717
http://caselaw.lp.findlaw.com/scripts/getcase.pl?court=or&vol=A101185&invol=1

**Armstrong, J.**

Terry J. Cooke (plaintiff) is the former husband of defendant, Joni Quicker (Joni); defendant Allen John Quicker (John) is Joni's father. In the early 1980s John and Joni began a business distributing fresh produce. Plaintiff soon left his job and began working with John and Joni full time. The business was originally a partnership, with John having a half interest and Joni and plaintiff together having the other half interest. The business grew throughout the 1980s. In June 1990 John, Joni, and plaintiff incorporated the business as Fresh Express Foods Corporation, Inc. (Fresh Express). John received 50 percent of the stock, and Joni and plaintiff each received 25 percent. John was the president of the corporation, Joni was the vice-president, and plaintiff was the secretary and treasurer. They also constituted the three members of the board of directors.

Fresh Express was the primary source of income for all three parties. Part of that income came from their salaries, but substantial additional amounts came as loans that the corporation made to them for various purposes, including paying their individual taxes on their portions of the corporation's retained earnings. Because Fresh Express elected to be a subchapter S corporation, which for tax purposes does not pay taxes itself but passes its income through to its shareholders, plaintiff and defendants were liable for taxes on those retained earnings whether or not the corporation actually distributed them. Without the loans, they would have had no corporate money to pay the taxes on that corporate income.

Joni and plaintiff separated at about the time of the incorporation. The tension between them increased significantly beginning in June 1993 when, after starting a relationship with a Fresh Express employee, plaintiff filed for dissolution of the marriage.

Plaintiff managed the company's delivery system, which included supervising the operation of its trucks. In December 1993, while plaintiff was on vacation, John discovered a notice on plaintiff's desk from the Public Utilities Commission (PUC) that showed deficiencies resulting in a fine of $6,000 and additional penalties of $4,000. Plaintiff had not paid those amounts, and that failure threatened Fresh Express with the loss of its PUC authority to operate. When plaintiff returned from vacation, John, acting as president of the company, gave plaintiff a written notice of termination that included the statement that "Fresh Express Foods Corporation has suffered monetary loss associated with [plaintiff's] position and this constitutes a Breach of Fiduciary Responsibility to the Corporation." It did not refer to a threatened loss of PUC operating authority. After the termination, plaintiff received his unpaid wages and two weeks' severance pay. Before the termination, the corporation distributed money to all of its shareholders that it treated as shareholder loans. It continued to make those distributions to John and Joni, but it did not make them to plaintiff after his termination. Although plaintiff remained a corporate officer and director for almost two years, he was never again informed of or consulted about corporate business.

The court entered a judgment dissolving plaintiff's and Joni's marriage in August 1994, awarding Joni approximately $27,000. Because the corporation had never issued any stock certificates, Joni was unable to use plaintiff's ownership interest in the corporation to satisfy the court judgment. In order to provide Joni a stock certificate to garnish, John called a directors' meeting for November 2, 1995, for the purpose of electing officers. At the meeting John and Joni first reelected John as president and Joni as vice-president; then they also elected Joni as secretary and treasurer. Plaintiff abstained from all three votes. A few days later Joni issued a stock certificate to plaintiff. Instead of sending the certificate to plaintiff, she immediately delivered it to the sheriff under a writ of garnishment on her judgment against plaintiff.

In September 1996, defendants called a special shareholders' meeting, at which they reduced the number of directors to two, over plaintiff's dissenting vote, and elected John and Joni to those positions. During an informal discussion, plaintiff asked John's attorney if the company intended to pay the considerable amount of money it owed to him. After consulting with John, the attorney responded that John had decided not to make any more distributions to shareholders at that time. After the shareholders' meeting ended and plaintiff left the room at their request, John and Joni held a directors' meeting at which they first removed plaintiff "from all of his positions as an officer, employee and agent of the corporation." John and Joni then agreed, despite the attorney's statement to plaintiff, to distribute the corporation's entire accumulated adjustment account to the shareholders by using it to reduce the outstanding shareholder loans. Finally, they agreed to purchase automobiles for John and Joni, and to increase John's salary from $54,000 per year to $120,000.

[The plaintiff brought suit against the corporation, John, and Joni. The trial court found that John would not have terminated Joni for a comparable error. It concluded that the purpose for firing plaintiff was to exclude him from participating in the corporate business or receiving any benefits from the corporation. The court found that the reason for the exclusion was the breakdown of the marriage and the animosities that followed. The trial court found that the defendants had acted oppressively toward plaintiff in the management and control of defendant Fresh Express. As a remedy, the court ordered defendants to purchase plaintiff's interest in Fresh Express at a price set by the court. The defendants appealed.]

Plaintiff argues that these actions together constituted a course of oppressive conduct and that defendants breached their fiduciary duties to him by freezing him out of all participation in the corporation and depriving him of all of the benefits of being a stockholder. ORS 60.661(2)(b) provides that a court may dissolve a corporation when the directors or those in control "have acted, are acting or will act in a manner that is illegal, oppressive, or fraudulent[.]" Although there is not, and probably cannot be, a definitive definition of oppressive conduct under the statute, at least in a closely held corporation conduct that violates the majority's fiduciary duties to the minority is likely to be oppressive. [Citations.] Cases that discuss either oppressive conduct or the majority's fiduciary duties are, thus, relevant to this question.

A number of cases make it clear that when

> the majority shareholders of a closely held corporation use their control over the corporation to their own advantage and exclude the minority from the benefits of participating in the corporation, [in the absence of] a legitimate business purpose, the actions constitute a breach of their fiduciary duties of loyalty, good faith and fair dealing.

[Citation.] A finding that the majority shareholders have engaged in oppressive conduct under ORS 60.661 permits the court either to order a dissolution of the corporation or to award lesser appropriate relief, including requiring the majority to buy out the minority's interest at a price that the court fixes. [Citation.] Because many things can constitute oppressive conduct or a breach of fiduciary duties, what matters is not so much matching the specific facts of one case to those of another but examining the pattern and intent of the majority and the effect on the minority of those specific facts. [Citation.]

The facts of this case show a classic squeeze-out. * * * Defendants withheld dividends and other benefits from plaintiff while preserving benefits for themselves.

> * * * [W]ithholding dividends can be especially devastating in an S corporation as all corporate income is passed through to the shareholders for tax purposes and shareholders are required to pay taxes on that income, but if no dividends are declared, the shareholders will have no cash from the enterprise with which to pay those taxes.

[Citation.] * * * In addition, the "abrupt removal of a minority shareholder from positions of employment and management can be a devastatingly effective squeeze-out technique." [Citation.] Finally, majority shareholders may siphon off corporate wealth by causing a corporation to pay the majority shareholders excessively high compensation, not only in salaries but in generous expense accounts and other fringe benefits. * * *

The existence of one or more of these characteristic signs of oppression does not necessarily mean that the majority has acted oppressively within the meaning of ORS 60.661(2)(b). Courts give significant deference to the majority's judgment in the business decisions that it makes, at least if the decisions appear to be genuine business decisions. * * * The court must evaluate the majority's actions, keeping in mind that, even if some actions may be individually justifiable, the actions in total may show a pattern of oppression that requires the court to provide a remedy to the minority.

The background of this case is a corporation that consisted of a father, a daughter, and a son-in-law and that came into existence at the very time that the marriage between the daughter and son-in-law began to dissolve. The events that we have described can best be understood as steps in a pattern whose ultimate goal was to eliminate plaintiff from all participation in what John and Joni saw as a family business. As plaintiff suggests in his brief, after firing him as an employee they tried also to fire him as a shareholder. That, however, is not as easy to achieve.

Although there were some previous signs of tension, the first action that might fit into a pattern of oppression was John's termination of plaintiff's employment with the company. Plaintiff does not challenge the dismissal as a matter of employment law. However, it is unusual for a close corporation to terminate the employment of a 25-percent shareholder and corporate director for a mistake of the sort that John described, particularly in the absence of evidence of previous problems and accompanying warnings. The written notice of termination appears to be more an attempt to create a paper justification for the termination than a statement of the actual reasons. After the termination, defendants excluded plaintiff from all involvement in the corporation and its business and all participation in its profits, things that relate to his continuing status as a shareholder and a director, not to his terminated status as an employee. Those actions suggest that the purpose of the termination was not to remove an unsatisfactory employee but, rather, to exclude plaintiff from participation in the corporation.

Defendants nominally recognized plaintiff's continuing status after his termination only when they had to follow corporate forms in order to benefit themselves at his expense. The sole purpose for the directors' meeting in November 1995 was to produce a stock certificate that Joni could garnish * * *.

Finally, in September 1996 defendants acted to ensure that they would permanently receive all benefits of the corporation. They began by replacing plaintiff as a director and reducing the number of directors to two. Although that was not necessarily improper in itself, their first actions as the sole directors of Fresh Express showed their purpose to exclude plaintiff from any share in the corporation other than his tax liabilities. They first removed defendant from any office or agency with the corporation and then took a number of actions to direct all corporate income to themselves. Despite having told plaintiff that there would be no corporate distributions, defendants distributed the entire retained earnings through a paper transaction that ensured that the corporate books would show no source for making any cash distribution to plaintiff. They then more than doubled John's salary, with the result that he received his income from the corporation as an expense that would reduce its profits rather than as a distribution of profits. Finally, they had the corporation pay for their recently purchased automobiles, again adding to the corporation's expenses and reducing its profits for their benefit.

* * *

In summary, we conclude that defendants consistently acted to further their individual interests, not the interests of the corporation, and without regard to their fiduciary duties to plaintiff. They did so either knowing or intending that their actions would harm plaintiff, among other ways by excluding him from any benefits of his ownership of one quarter of the corporate stock. They thereby violated their fiduciary duties to him and engaged in oppressive conduct.

Under ORS 60.661, the trial court had the authority to choose a remedy for defendants' actions; we agree with it that requiring defendants to purchase plaintiff's shares is the preferable option. A purchase will disentangle the parties' affairs while keeping the corporation a going concern; dissolution would not benefit anyone, and plaintiff did not seek it at trial. Defendants, however, raise some issues concerning the court's determination of the price that defendants must pay.

Plaintiff presented extensive testimony from an expert appraiser concerning the value of plaintiff's shares in the context of a judicial remedy for oppressive conduct. In doing so, the appraiser determined the value of the company as a profitable going business, made certain adjustments for excessive expenses, and determined plaintiff's one-quarter share of the total. The expert then added plaintiff's unpaid wages since his termination as a way of reflecting the benefits that he did not receive after that date. The only directly contradictory evidence that defendants presented came from the company's accountant, who calculated plaintiff's proportionate share of its liquidation value. In this case, however, the issue is the fair value of plaintiff's shares in a profitable going concern, which is not necessarily tied to the company's liquidation value; that evidence, thus, has limited relevance. The court ordered defendants to purchase plaintiff's shares at the price that the expert recommended.

* * * [B]ecause defendants must purchase plaintiff's shares as a remedy for their misconduct, and the price for plaintiff's shares is therefore based on their fair value rather than their fair market value, either a minority or marketability discount would be inappropriate. [Citation.]

Affirmed.

## QUESTIONS

1. Explain the procedure for amending the charter and identify which charter amendments give dissenting shareholders an appraisal remedy.
2. Which combinations (a) do not require shareholder approval and (b) give dissenting shareholders an appraisal remedy?
3. Distinguish between a tender offer and a compulsory share exchange.
4. Compare and contrast a cash-out combination and a management buyout.
5. Identify the ways by which involuntary and voluntary dissolution may occur.

# PROBLEMS

**1.** The stock in Hotel Management, Inc., a hotel management corporation, was divided equally between two families. For several years, the two families had been unable to agree on or cooperate in the management of the corporation. As a result, no meeting of shareholders or directors had been held for five years. There had been no withdrawal of profits for five years, and last year the hotel operated at a loss. Although the corporation was not insolvent, such a state was imminent because the business was poorly managed and its properties were in need of repair. As a result, the owners of half the stock brought an action in equity for dissolution of the corporation. Will they succeed? Explain.

**2.** **(a)** When may a corporation sell, lease, exchange, mortgage, or pledge all or substantially all of its assets in the usual and regular course of its business?

**(b)** When may a corporation sell, lease, exchange, mortgage, or pledge all or substantially all of its assets other than in the usual and regular course of its business?

**(c)** What are the rights of a shareholder who dissents from a proposed sale or exchange of all or substantially all of the assets of a corporation other than in the usual and regular course of its business?

**3.** The Cutler Company was duly merged into the Stone Company. Yetta, a shareholder of the former Cutler Company, having paid only one-half of her subscription, is now sued by the Stone Company for the balance of the subscription. Yetta, who took no part in the merger proceedings, denies liability on the ground that, inasmuch as the Cutler Company no longer exists, all her rights and obligations in connection with the Cutler Company have been terminated. Explain whether she is correct.

**4.** Smith, while in the course of his employment with the Bee Corporation, negligently ran the company's truck into Williams, injuring him severely. Subsequently, the Bee Corporation and the Sea Corporation consolidated, forming the SeaBee Corporation. Williams filed suit against the SeaBee Corporation for damages, and the SeaBee Corporation asserted the defense that the injuries Williams sustained were not caused by any of SeaBee's employees, that SeaBee did not even exist at the time of the injury, and that the SeaBee Corporation was, therefore, not liable. What decision?

**5.** The Johnson Company, a corporation organized under the laws of State X, after proper authorization by the shareholders, sold its entire assets to the Samson Company, also a State X corporation. Ellen, an unpaid creditor of the Johnson Company, sues the Samson Company upon her claim. Is Samson liable? Explain.

**6.** Zenith Steel Company operates a prosperous business. The board of directors voted to spend $20 million of the company's surplus funds to purchase a majority of the stock of two other companies—the Green Insurance Company and the Blue Trust Company. The Green Insurance Company is a thriving business whose stock is an excellent investment at the price at which it will be sold to Zenith Steel Company. The principal reasons for Zenith's purchase of the Green Insurance stock are to invest surplus funds and to diversify its business. The Blue Trust Company owns a controlling interest in Zenith Steel Company. The Blue Trust Company is subject to special governmental controls. The main purpose for Zenith's purchase of the Blue Trust Company stock is to enable the present management and directors of Zenith Steel Company to perpetuate their management of the company. Jones, a minority shareholder in Zenith Steel Company, brings an appropriate action to enjoin the purchase by Zenith Steel Company of the stock of either the Green Insurance Company or of the Blue Trust Company. What decision as to each purchase?

**7.** Mildred, Deborah, and Bob each own one-third of the stock of Nova Corporation. On Friday, Mildred received an offer to merge Nova into Buyer Corporation. Mildred, who agreed to call a shareholders' meeting to discuss the offer on the following Tuesday, telephoned Deborah and Bob and informed them of the offer and the scheduled meeting. Deborah agreed to attend. Bob, however, was unable to attend because he was leaving on a trip on Saturday and asked if the three of them could meet on Friday night instead. Mildred and Deborah agreed. The three shareholders met informally Friday night and agreed to accept the offer only if they received preferred stock of Buyer Corporation for their shares. Bob then left on his trip. On Tuesday, at the time and place appointed by Mildred, Mildred and Deborah convened the shareholders' meeting. After discussion, they concluded that the preferred stock payment limitation was unwise and passed a formal resolution to accept Buyer Corporation's offer without any such condition. Bob files suit to enjoin Mildred, Deborah, and the Nova Corporation from implementing this resolution. Explain whether the injunction should be issued.

**8.** Tretter alleged that his exposure over the years to asbestos products manufactured by Philip Carey Manufacturing Corporation caused him to contract asbestosis. Tretter brought an action against Rapid American Corporation, which was the surviving corporation of a merger between Philip Carey and Rapid American. Rapid American denied liability, claiming that immediately after the merger it had transferred its asbestos operations to a newly formed subsidiary corporation. Can Rapid avoid liability by such transfer? Explain.

**9.** Wilcox was chief executive officer, chairman of the board of directors, and owner of 60 percent of the shares of Sterling Corporation. When the market price of Sterling's shares was $22 per share, Wilcox sold all of his shares in Sterling to Conrad for $29 per share. The minority shareholders of Sterling brought suit against Wilcox to demand a portion of the amount Wilcox received in excess of the market price. What result?

**10.** All Steel Pipe and Tube is a closely held corporation engaged in the business of selling steel pipes and tubes. Leo and Scott Callier are its two equal shareholders. Scott, Leo's uncle, is one of the company's two directors and is president of the corporation. Scott is the general manager. Scott's father and Leo's grandfather, Felix, is the other director. Over the years, Scott and Leo have had differences of opinion regarding the operation of the business. Nevertheless, despite their deteriorating relationship, the company has flourished. When negotiations aimed at Leo's redemption of Scott's shares began, however, the parties could not reach an agreement. The discussion then turned to voluntary dissolution and liquidation of the corporation, but still no agreement could be reached. Finally, Leo fired Scott and began to wind down All Steel's business and to form a new corporation, Callier Steel Pipe and Tube. Leo then brought an action seeking a dissolution and liquidation of All Steel. Should the court order dissolution? Explain.

**11.** The shareholders of Endicott Johnson who had dissented from a proposed merger of Endicott with McDonough Corporation brought a proceeding to fix the fair value of their stock. At issue was the proper weight to be given to the market price of the stock in fixing its fair value. The shareholders argued that the market value should not be considered because McDonough controlled 70 percent of Endicott's stock and the stock had been delisted from the New York Stock Exchange. Are the shareholders correct?

**12.** Ray fell from a defective ladder while working for his employer. Ray brought suit in strict tort liability against the Alad Corporation (Alad II), which neither manufactured nor sold the ladder to Ray's employer. Prior to the accident, Alad II succeeded to the business of the ladder's manufacturer, the now-dissolved "Alad Corporation" (Alad I), through a purchase of Alad I's assets for an adequate cash consideration. Alad II acquired Alad I's plant, equipment, inventory, trade name, and goodwill, and continued to manufacture the same line of ladders under the "Alad" name, using the same equipment, designs, and personnel. In addition, Alad II solicited through the same sales representatives with no outward indication of any change in the ownership of the business. The parties had no agreement, however, concerning Alad II's assumption of Alad I's tort liabilities. Decision?

**13.** Kemp & Beatley was a company incorporated under the laws of New York. Eight shareholders held the corporation's outstanding 1,500 shares of stock. Petitioners Dissin and Gardstein together owned 20.33 percent of the stock, and each had been a longtime employee of the corporation. Kemp & Beatley had a long-standing practice of awarding compensation bonuses based upon stock ownership. However, when the policy was changed in 2008 to compensation based on service to the corporation, not on stock ownership, Dissin resigned. Gardstein was terminated in 2009. They commenced suit in 2010, seeking involuntary dissolution of the corporation and alleging that the corporation's board of directors had acted in a "fraudulent and oppressive" manner toward them, rendering their stock virtually worthless and frustrating their "reasonable expectations" regarding this business venture. What result?

**14.** In early 1984, Royal Dutch Petroleum Company (Royal Dutch), through various subsidiaries, controlled approximately 70 percent of the outstanding common shares of Shell Oil Co. (Shell). On January 24, 1984, Royal Dutch announced its intention to merge Shell into SPNV Holdings, Inc. (Holdings), which is now Shell Petroleum, Inc., by offering the minority shareholders $55 per share. Shell's board of directors, however, rejected the offer as inadequate. Royal Dutch then withdrew the merger proposal and initiated a tender offer at $58 per share. As a result of the tender offer, Holdings' ownership interest increased to 94.6 percent of Shell's outstanding stock. Holdings then initiated a short-form merger. Under the terms of the merger, Shell's minority stockholders were to receive $58 per share. However, if before July 1, 1985, a shareholder waived his right to seek an appraisal, he would receive an extra $2 per share. In conjunction with the short-form merger, Holdings distributed several documents to the minority, including a document entitled "Certain Information About Shell" (CIAS).

The CIAS included a table of discounted future net cash flows (DCF) for Shell's oil and gas reserves. However, due to a computer programming error, the DCF failed to account for the cash flows from approximately 295 million barrel equivalents of U.S. proved oil and gas reserves. Shell's failure to include the reserves in its calculations resulted in an understatement of its DCF of approximately $993 million to $1.1 billion or $3.00 to $3.45 per share. Moreover, as a result of the error, Shell stated in the CIAS that there had been a slight decline in the value of its oil and gas reserves from 1984 to 1985. When properly calculated, the value of the reserves had actually increased over that time period.

Shell's minority shareholders sued in the Court of Chancery, asserting that the error in the DCF along with other alleged disclosure violations constituted a breach of Holdings' fiduciary "duty of candor." Was the error in the DCF material and misleading?

PART 8

# Debtor and Creditor Relations

CHAPTER 38
**Secured Transactions and Suretyship**

CHAPTER 39
**Bankruptcy**

# CHAPTER 38

# Secured Transactions and Suretyship

"Neither a borrower nor a lender be"—Shakespeare's well-known line in *Hamlet*—reflects an earlier view of debt, for today borrowed funds are both essential and honorable under our economic system. In fact, the absence of loans would severely restrict the availability of goods and services and would greatly limit consumers in the quantities they would be able to purchase.

The public policy and social issues created by today's enormous use of debt center on certain tenets; among them are the following:

1. The means by which debt is created and transferred should be as simple and as inexpensive as possible.
2. The risks to lenders should be minimized.
3. Lenders should have a way to collect unpaid debts.

A lender typically incurs two basic collection risks: the borrower may be unwilling to repay the loan even though he is able to, or the borrower may prove to be unable to repay the loan. In addition to the remedies dealing with the first of these risks, the law has developed several devices to maximize the likelihood of repayment. These devices, which we will discuss in this chapter, include consensual security interests (also called secured transactions) and suretyships.

In addition, debtors of all sorts—wage earners, sole proprietorships, partnerships, unincorporated associations, and corporations—sometimes accumulate debts far in excess of their assets or suffer financial reverses that make it impossible for them to meet their obligations. In such an event, it is an important policy of the law to treat all creditors fairly and equitably and to provide the debtor with relief from these debts so that he may continue to contribute to society. These are the two basic purposes of the federal bankruptcy law, which we will briefly discuss in this chapter and discuss more fully in *Chapter 39*.

## SECURED TRANSACTIONS IN PERSONAL PROPERTY

An obligation or debt can exist without security if the creditor deems adequate the integrity, reputation, and net worth of the debtor. Often, however, businesses or individuals cannot obtain credit without giving adequate security, or, in some cases, even if the borrower can obtain an unsecured loan, he can negotiate more favorable terms by giving security.

Transactions involving security in personal property are governed by Article 9 of the Uniform Commercial Code (UCC). This chapter will cover revised Article 9, which is in effect in all the States. This article provides a simple and unified structure within which a tremendous variety of secured financing transactions can take place with less cost and with greater certainty than was possible before the article's enactment. Moreover, the article's flexibility and simplified formalities allow new forms of secured financing to fit comfortably under its provisions. In addition, the revised article recognizes and provides coverage for electronic commerce.

## ESSENTIALS OF SECURED TRANSACTIONS

Article 9 governs a secured transaction in personal property in which the debtor *consents* to provide a security interest in personal property to secure the payment of a debt. A security interest in property cannot exist apart from the debt it secures, and discharging the debt in any manner terminates the security interest in the property. Article 9 also applies to the *sales* of certain types of collateral (accounts, chattel paper, payment intangibles, and promissory notes). Article 9 does *not* apply to nonconsensual security interests that arise by operation of law, such as mechanics' or landlords' liens, although it does cover nonpossessory statutory agricultural liens.

A common type of consensual secured transaction covered by Article 9 occurs when a person wanting to buy goods has neither the cash nor a sufficient credit standing to obtain the goods on open credit, and the seller, to secure payment of all or part of the price, obtains a security interest in the goods. Alternatively, the buyer may borrow the purchase price from a third party and pay the seller in cash. The third-party lender may then take a security interest in the goods to secure repayment of the loan.

Every consensual secured transaction involves a debtor, a secured party, collateral, a security agreement, and a security interest. Some Article 9 definitions follow:

A **security interest** is "an interest in personal property or fixtures which secures payment or performance of an obligation." Section 1–201.

A **security agreement** is an agreement that creates or provides for a security interest. Section 9–102(a)(73).

**Collateral** is the property subject to a security interest or agricultural lien. Section 9–102(a)(12).

A **secured party** is the person in whose favor a security interest in the collateral is created or provided for under a security agreement. Section 9–102(a)(72). The definition of a secured party includes lenders, credit sellers, consignors, purchasers of certain types of collateral (accounts, chattel paper, payment intangibles, or promissory notes), and other specified persons.

A **debtor** is a person (1) having an interest in the collateral other than a security interest or lien, whether or not the person is an obligor; (2) a seller of accounts, chattel paper, payment intangibles, or promissory notes; or (3) a consignee. Section 9–102(a)(28).

An **obligor** is a person who, with respect to an obligation secured by a security interest in or an agricultural lien on the collateral, (1) owes payment or other performance, (2) has provided property other than the collateral to secure payment or performance, or (3) is otherwise accountable for payment or performance. Section 9–102(a)(59).

A **secondary obligor** is usually a guarantor or surety of the debt. Section 9–102(a)(71).

A **purchase money security interest** (PMSI) is created in goods when a seller retains a security interest in the goods sold on credit by a security agreement. Similarly, a third-party lender who advances funds to enable the debtor to purchase goods has a PMSI in goods if she has a security agreement and the debtor in fact uses the funds to purchase the goods.

In most secured transactions, the debtor is an obligor with respect to the obligation secured by the security interest. Thus, a security interest is created when an automobile dealer sells and delivers a car to an individual (the *debtor*) under a retail installment contract (a *security agreement*) that provides that the dealer (the *secured party*) obtains a *security interest* (a *PMSI*) in the car (the *collateral*) until the price is paid.

◆ SEE FIGURE 38-1: **Fundamental Rights of Secured Party and Debtor**

## CLASSIFICATION OF COLLATERAL

Although most of the provisions of Article 9 apply to all kinds of personal property, some provisions state special rules that apply only to particular kinds of collateral. Under the Code, collateral is classified according to its nature and its use. The classifications according to nature are (1) goods, (2) indispensable paper, and (3) intangibles.

### GOODS

**Goods** are all things that are movable when a security interest attaches and include fixtures, standing timber to be cut, the unborn young of animals, crops grown, growing, or to be grown, and manufactured homes. Section 9–102(a)(44). The Revised Act also includes computer programs embedded in goods if the software becomes part of the goods. (When software maintains its separate state it is considered a general intangible.) Goods are further classified according to their use.

Goods are subdivided into (1) consumer goods, (2) farm products, (3) inventory, (4) equipment, (5) fixtures, and (6) accessions. Depending on its primary use or purpose, the

◆ FIGURE 38-1: **Fundamental Rights of Secured Party and Debtor**

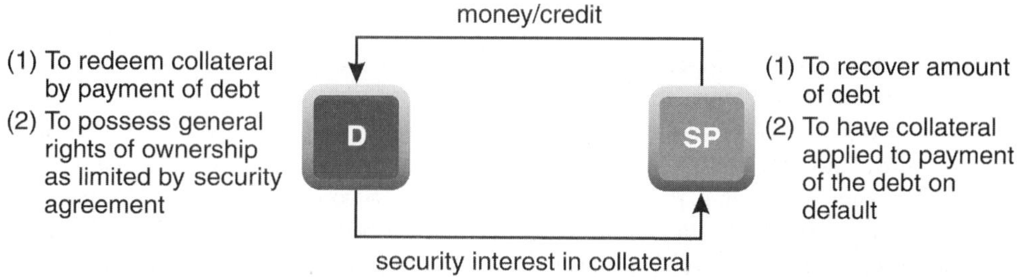

same item of goods may fall into different classifications. For example, a refrigerator purchased by a physician to store medicines in his office is classified as equipment, while the same refrigerator would be classified as consumer goods if the physician purchased it for home use. In the hands of a refrigerator dealer or manufacturer, the refrigerator would be classified as inventory. If goods are used for multiple purposes, such as by a physician in both her office and her home, their classification is dependent upon their predominant use.

**Consumer Goods** Goods used or bought primarily for personal, family, or household purposes are consumer goods. Section 9–102(a)(23).

**Farm Products** The Code defines farm products as goods, other than standing timber, which are part of a farming operation and which are crops grown, growing, or to be grown, including crops produced on trees, vines, and bushes, and aquatic goods. In addition, farm products include livestock, born or unborn, including aquatic goods such as fish raised on a fish farm as well as supplies used or produced in a farming operation. Section 9–102(a)(34). Thus, farm products would include wheat growing on the farmer's land; the farmer's pigs, cows, and hens; and the hens' eggs. When such products become the possessions of a person not engaged in farming operations, they cease to be farm products.

**Inventory** The term inventory includes nonfarm product goods (1) held for sale, held for lease, or to be furnished under a service contract; or (2) that consist of raw materials, work in process, or materials used or consumed in a business. Section 9–102(a)(33). Thus, a retailer's or a wholesaler's merchandise, as well as a manufacturer's raw materials, are inventory.

**Equipment** Goods not included in the definition of inventory, farm products, or consumer goods are classified as equipment. Section 9–102(a)(33). This category is broad enough to include a lawyer's library, a physician's office furniture, or a factory's machinery.

**Fixtures** Goods and personal property that have become so related to particular *real property* that an interest in them arises under real estate law are called fixtures. Section 9–102 (a)(41). Thus, State law other than the Code determines whether and when goods become fixtures. In general terms, fixtures are goods so firmly affixed to real estate that they are considered part of such real estate. Examples are furnaces, central air-conditioning units, and plumbing fixtures. See *Chapter 48* for a further discussion of fixtures. A security interest in fixtures may arise under Article 9, and, under certain circumstances, a perfected security interest in fixtures will have priority over a conflicting security interest or mortgage in the real property to which the goods are attached.

**Accession** Goods installed in or firmly affixed to *personal property* are accessions if the identity of the original goods is not lost. Section 9–102(a)(1). Thus, a new engine placed in an old car automobile is an accession.

## INDISPENSABLE PAPER

Four kinds of collateral involve rights evidenced by indispensable paper: (1) chattel paper, (2) instruments, (3) documents, and (4) investment property.

**Chattel Paper** Chattel paper is a record or records that evidence both a monetary obligation and a security interest in or a lease of specific goods. Section 9–102(a)(11). A record is information inscribed on a tangible medium (written on paper) or stored in an electronic or other medium and retrievable in perceivable form (electronically stored). Section 9–102(a)(69). Thus, chattel paper can be either tangible chattel paper or electronic chattel paper.

For example, Dealer sells goods on credit to Buyer who uses the goods as equipment. Dealer retains a PMSI in the goods. Dealer then borrows against (or sells) the security agreement of Buyer along with Dealer's security interest in the collateral. The collateral provided by Dealer to his lender in this type of transaction (consisting of the security agreement and the security interest) is chattel paper.

**Instruments** The definition of an instrument includes negotiable instruments (drafts, checks, promissory notes, and certificate of deposits) as well as any other writing that evidences a right to payment of money that is transferable by delivery with any necessary indorsement or assignment and that is not of itself a security agreement or lease. Section 9–102(a)(47). Negotiable instruments are covered in *Chapters 26* through *30*. An instrument does not include an investment property, a letter of credit, or writings evidencing a right to payment from a credit or charge card.

**Documents** The term document includes documents of title, such as bills of lading and warehouse receipts, which may be either negotiable or nonnegotiable. Section 9–102(a)(30). A document of title is negotiable if by its terms the goods it covers are deliverable to the bearer or to the order of a named person. Any other document is nonnegotiable. Documents of title are covered in *Chapter 48*.

**Investment Property** The term investment property means an investment security, such as stocks and bonds, as well as securities accounts, commodity contracts, and commodity accounts. Section 9–102(a)(49). A **certificated security** is an investment security that is represented by a certificate.

Section 8–102(a)(4). An **uncertificated security** is not represented by a certificate. Section 8–102(a)(18). **A security entitlement** means the rights and property interests of a person who holds securities or other financial assets through a securities intermediary such as a bank, broker, or clearing house, which in the ordinary course of business maintains security accounts for others. A security entitlement thus includes both the rights against the securities intermediary and an interest in the property held by the securities intermediary. Section 8–102(7), (14), (17).

### INTANGIBLES

The Code also recognizes two kinds of collateral that are neither goods nor indispensable paper, namely, accounts and general intangibles. These types of intangible collateral are not evidenced by any indispensable paper, such as a stock certificate or a negotiable bill of lading.

**Accounts** The term account includes the right to monetary payment, whether or not such right has been earned by performance, for (1) goods sold, leased, licensed, or otherwise disposed of, or (2) services rendered. Section 9–102(a)(2). Accounts include credit card receivables and health-care-insurance receivables. Section 9–102(a)(2). An example of an account is a business's accounts receivable.

**General Intangibles** The term general intangibles applies to any personal property *other than* goods, accounts, chattel paper, commercial tort claims, deposit accounts, documents, instruments, investment property, letter-of-credit rights, money, and oil, gas, and other minerals before extraction. Section 9–102(a)(42). Included in the definition are software, goodwill, literary rights, and interests in patents, trademarks, and copyrights to the extent they are not regulated by Federal statute. Also included is a payment intangible, which is a general intangible under which the account debtor's principal obligation is the payment of money. Section 9–102(a)(61).

### OTHER KINDS OF COLLATERAL

**Proceeds** include whatever is received upon the sale, lease, license, exchange, or other disposition of collateral; whatever is collected on, or distributed on account of, collateral; or other rights arising out of collateral. Section 9–102(a)(64). For example, an automobile dealer grants a security interest in its inventory to the automobile manufacturer that sold the inventory. When the dealer sells a car to Henry and receives from Henry a used car and the remainder of the purchase price in a monetary payment, the used car and the money are both proceeds from the sale of the new car. Unless otherwise agreed, a security agreement gives the secured party (the manufacturer in this example) the rights to proceeds. Section 9–203(f).

Additional types of collateral include timber to be cut, minerals, motor vehicles, mobile goods (goods used in more than one jurisdiction), and money. Revised Article 9 also adds the following kinds of collateral: commercial tort claim, letter-of-credit rights, and deposit accounts (a demand, savings, time, or similar account maintained with a bank). In consumer transactions, however, deposit accounts may not be taken as *original* collateral. Section 9–109(d)(13).

## ATTACHMENT

**Attachment** is the Code's term to describe the creation of a security interest that is enforceable against the *debtor*. Attachment is also a prerequisite to rendering a security interest enforceable against third parties, though in some instances attachment in itself is sufficient to create such enforceability. Perfection, which provides the greatest enforceability against third parties who assert competing interests in the collateral, is discussed later.

Until a security interest "attaches," it is *ineffective* against the debtor. Under Section 9–203 of the Code, the security interest created by a security agreement attaches to the described collateral once the following events have occurred:

1. the secured party has given value;
2. the debtor has acquired rights in the collateral or has the power to transfer such rights to a secured party; and
3. the debtor and secured party have an agreement, which in most instances must be authenticated by the debtor, although in some cases alternative evidence, such as possession by the secured party pursuant to agreement, will suffice.

The parties may, however, by explicit agreement postpone the time of attachment. Section 9–203(a).

### VALUE

The term **value** is broadly defined and includes consideration under contract law, a binding commitment to extend credit, and an antecedent debt. Section 1–201(44) and Revised Section 1–204. For example, Buyer purchases equipment from Seller on credit. When Buyer fails to make timely payment, Seller and Buyer enter into a security agreement that grants Seller a security interest in the equipment. By entering into the agreement, Seller has given value, even though he relies upon an antecedent debt—the original transfer of goods to Buyer—instead of providing new consideration. Moreover, Seller is not limited to acquiring a security interest in the equipment he sold to Buyer but also may obtain a security interest in other personal property of Buyer.

## DEBTOR'S RIGHTS IN COLLATERAL

The elusive concept of the debtor's rights in collateral is not specifically defined by the Code. As a general rule, the debtor is deemed to have **rights in collateral** that she owns or is in possession of as well as in those items that she is in the process of acquiring from the seller. Section 9–203(b)(2). For example, if Adrien borrows money from Richard and grants him a security interest in corporate stock that she owns, then Adrien had rights in the collateral before entering into the secured transaction. Likewise, if Sally sells goods to Benjamin on credit and he provides Sally a security interest in the goods, Benjamin will acquire rights in the collateral upon identification of the goods to the contract. In addition, Section 9–203(b)(2) adds the words "or the power to transfer rights in the collateral to a secured party." The comments to this section state "[h]owever, in accordance with basic personal property conveyancing principles, the baseline rule is that a security interest attaches only to whatever rights a debtor may have, broad or limited as those rights may be." Comment 6.

**Security Agreement** A security interest cannot attach unless an agreement (contract) between the debtor and creditor creates or provides the creditor with a security interest in the debtor's collateral. Sections 9–203, 9–102(a)(73). With certain exceptions (discussed below), the agreement must (1) be authenticated by the debtor and (2) contain a reasonable description of the collateral. Section 9–203(b)(3)(A). In addition, if the collateral is timber to be cut, the agreement must contain a reasonable description of the land concerned. A description of personal or real property is sufficient if it reasonably identifies what is described. Section 9–108(a). A description of personal property may identify the collateral by specific listing, category, or in most cases a type of collateral defined in the Code (e.g., inventory or farm equipment). Section 9–108(b). The description, however, may not be a super generic description, such as "all my personal property." Section 9–108(c).

The Code provides the parties with a great deal of freedom to draft the security agreement, although this freedom is limited by good faith, diligence, reasonableness, and care. Section 1–102(3) and Revised Section 1–302(b). Moreover, security agreements frequently contain a provision for acceleration at the secured party's option of all payments upon the default in any payment by the debtor, the debtor's bankruptcy or insolvency, or the debtor's failure to meet other requirements of the agreement. Sometimes security agreements require the debtor to furnish additional collateral if the secured party becomes insecure about the prospects of future payments.

**Authenticating Record** In most instances there must be a record of the security agreement authenticated by the debtor. Section 9–203(b)(3)(A). Authentication can occur in one of two ways. First, the debtor can sign a written security agreement. Section 9–102(a)(7)(A). A writing can include any printing, typewriting, or other intentional reduction to tangible form. Section 1–201. To sign includes any symbol executed or adopted by a party with the present intention to authenticate a writing. Section 1–201(39). Revised Article 1 substitutes "adopt or accept" for "authenticate." Revised Section 1-201(b)(37).

Second, in recognition of e-commerce and electronic security agreements, Revised Article 9 provides that a debtor can authenticate a security agreement by executing or otherwise adopting a symbol, or by encrypting or similarly processing a record in whole or in part, with the present intent of the authenticating party to adopt or accept the record. Section 9–102(a)(7)(B). As already mentioned, a record means information (1) on a tangible medium or (2) that is stored in an *electronic* or other medium and is retrievable in perceivable form. According to the Code "[e]xamples of current technologies commercially used to communicate or store information include, but are not limited to, magnetic media, optical discs, digital voice messaging systems, electronic mail, audio tapes, and photographic media, as well as paper. 'Record' is an inclusive term that includes all of these methods." Section 9–102, Comment 9. It does not, however, include any oral or other communication that is not stored or preserved.

**Authenticating Record Not Required** Under the Code, a record of a security agreement is not mandated in some situations. A record of a security agreement is not required when some types of collateral are pledged or are in the possession of the secured party pursuant to an agreement. Sections 9–203(b)(3)(B), 9–310(b)(6), 9–313. This rule applies to a security interest in negotiable documents, goods, instruments, money, and tangible chattel paper. A **pledge** is the delivery of personal property to a creditor as security for the payment of a debt. A pledge requires that the secured party (the pledgee) and the debtor agree to the pledge of the collateral and that the collateral be *delivered* to the pledgee. Other situations in which a secured party does not need a record authenticated by the debtor include the following: (1) The collateral is a certificated security in registered form which has been delivered to the secured party. Section 9–203(b)(3)(C). (2) The collateral is a deposit account, electronic chattel paper, investment property, or letter-of-credit rights, and the secured party has control over the collateral. Section 9–203(b)(3)(D). Control is discussed below.

◆ **SEE CASE 38-1**

**Consumer Goods** Federal regulation prohibits a credit seller or lender from obtaining a consumer's grant of a nonpossessory security interest in household goods. This rule does not apply to PMSIs or to pledges. Rather, it prevents a lender or seller from obtaining a nonpurchase money security interest covering the consumer's household goods, which are defined to include clothing, furniture, appliances, kitchenware, personal effects, wedding rings, one radio, and one television. (These hard-to-sell items are also referred to as "junk" collateral.) The definition of household goods specifically excludes works of art, other electronic entertainment equipment, antiques, and jewelry.

**After-Acquired Property** "[A] security agreement may create or provide for a security interest in after-acquired collateral." Section 9–204(a). After-acquired property is property that the debtor presently does not own or have rights to but may acquire at some time. For example, an after-acquired property clause in a security agreement may include all present and subsequently acquired inventory, accounts, or equipment of the debtor. This clause would provide the secured party with a valid security interest not only in the typewriter, desk, and file cabinet that the debtor currently owns, but also in a personal computer she purchases later. Article 9 therefore accepts the concept of a "continuing general lien," or a *floating lien*, though the Code limits the operation of an after-acquired property clause against consumers by providing that no such interest can be claimed as additional security in consumer goods, except accessions, if the goods are acquired more than ten days after the secured party gives value. Section 9–204(b)(1).

**Future Advances** The obligations covered by a security agreement may include future advances. Section 9–204(c). Frequently, a debtor obtains a line of credit from a creditor for advances to be made at some later time. For instance, a manufacturer may provide a retailer with a $60,000 line of credit, only $20,000 of which the retailer initially uses. Nevertheless, the manufacturer and the retailer may enter a security agreement granting to the manufacturer a security interest in the retailer's inventory that covers not only the initial $20,000 advance but also any future advances.

## PERFECTION

To be effective against third parties who assert competing interests in the collateral (including other creditors of the debtor, the debtor's trustee in bankruptcy, and transferees of the debtor), the security interest must be perfected. **Perfection** of a security interest occurs when it has attached *and* when all the applicable steps required for perfection have been satisfied. Section 9–308(a). If these steps precede attachment, the security interest is perfected at the time it attaches. Once a security interest becomes perfected, it "may still be or become subordinate to other interests... [h]owever, in general, after perfection the secured party is protected against creditors and transferees of the debtor and, in particular, against any representative of creditors in insolvency proceedings instituted by or against the debtor." Section 9–308, Comment 2. Thus, in most instances a perfected secured party will prevail over a subsequent perfected security interest, a subsequent lien creditor or a representative of creditors (e.g., a trustee in bankruptcy), and subsequent buyers of the collateral.

Depending on the type of collateral, a security interest may be perfected:

1. by the secured party filing a financing statement in the designated public office;
2. by the secured party taking or retaining possession of the collateral;
3. automatically, on the attachment of the security interest;
4. temporarily, for a period specified by the Code; or
5. by the secured party taking control of the collateral.

A security interest or agricultural lien is perfected continuously if it is originally perfected by one method and is later perfected by another if there is no period when it was unperfected. Section 9–308(c).

Many States have adopted certificate of title statutes for automobiles, trailers, mobile homes, boats, and farm tractors. A **certificate of title** is an official representation of ownership. In these States, Article 9's filing requirements do not apply to perfecting a security interest in such collateral except when the collateral is inventory held by a dealer for sale. Section 9–311(a),(d).

◆ SEE FIGURE 38-2: **Requisites for Enforceability of Security Interests**

### FILING A FINANCING STATEMENT

Filing a financing statement is the most common method of perfecting a security interest under Article 9. Filing is *required* to perfect a security interest in general intangibles and accounts except for assignments of isolated accounts. Filing *may* be used to perfect a security interest in any other kind of collateral, with the general *exception* of deposit accounts, letter-of-credit rights, and money. Section 9–312(b). A financing statement may be filed before or after the security interest attaches. The form of the **financing statement**, which is filed to give public notice of the security interest, may vary from State to State.

**What to File** The Revised Act continues to adopt a system of "notice filing": it indicates merely that a person may have a security interest in the collateral. It also authorizes and encourages filing financing statements electronically. Though it need not be highly detailed, the financing statement must include the name of the debtor, the name of the secured party or a representative of the secured party, and an

### FIGURE 38-2: Requisites for Enforceability of Security Interests

| Attachment | Perfection |
|---|---|
| **A.** Value given by secured party | **A.** Secured party files a financing statement |
| **B.** Debtor has rights in collateral | **B.** Secured party takes possession |
| **C.** Agreement | **C.** Automatically |
| **1.** record authenticated by debtor (except for most pledges) | **D.** Temporarily, or |
| **2.** providing a security interest | **E.** Control |
| **3.** in described collateral | |

indication of the collateral covered by the financing statement. Section 9–502(a). If the financing statement substantially complies with these requirements, minor errors that do not seriously mislead will not render the financing statement ineffective. Section 9–506(a). Significantly, the Revised Act no longer requires the debtor's signature on the financing statement in order to facilitate **paperless or electronic filing**. Section 9–502, Comment 3. Since a signature is not required, the Revised Act attempts to deter unauthorized filings by imposing statutory damages of $500 in addition to damages for any loss caused. Section 9–625(b),(e)(3).

Financing statements are indexed under the debtor's name so it is particularly important that the financing statement provide the debtor's name. Section 9–503 provides rules for what names must appear for registered organizations (such as corporations, limited partnerships, and limited liability companies), trusts, and other organizations. If the organization does not have a name, the names of the partners, members, associates, or other persons comprising the debtor must appear on the financing statement. Section 9–503(a)(4). A financing statement that includes only the trade name is insufficient. Section 9–503(c). A financing statement that does not comply with these requirements is considered to be seriously misleading. Section 9–506(b).

The description of the collateral is sufficient if it meets the requirements for a security agreement discussed above or if it indicates that the financing statement covers all assets or all personal property. Section 9–504(1),(2). Thus, the use of super generic descriptions is permitted in financing statements but is *not* permitted in security agreements. In **real-property-related filings** (collateral involving fixtures, timber to be cut, or minerals to be extracted), a description of the real property must be included sufficient to reasonably identify the real property. Section 9–502(b).

Section 9–516(b) further provides a list of grounds upon which the filing officer rejects a record of the financing statement. These reasons include the following: (1) if the statement does not indicate whether the debtor is an individual or an organization, (2) the statement does not include the addresses of the debtor and secured party, (3) the record is not communicated by a method or medium authorized, and (4) the record does not provide a sufficient description of the real property. None of these reasons, however, render an accepted financing statement ineffective, unlike those listed in Section 9–502(a) above. If the filing officer rejects the financing statement, the secured interest is not perfected; if the filing officer accepts the statement, the security interest is perfected.

SEE FIGURE 38-3: Sample Financing Statement

**Duration of Filing** A financing statement is generally effective for five years from the date of filing. Section 9–515(a). A continuation statement filed by the secured party within six months prior to expiration will extend the effectiveness of the filing for another five years. Section 9–515(d),(e). If the financing statement lapses, the security interest is no longer perfected unless it is perfected by another method. Section 9–515(c).

In many States, security interests in motor vehicles and other specified collateral must be perfected by making a notation on the certificate of title rather than by filing a financing statement. Nevertheless, as previously indicated, certificate of title laws do not apply if the collateral is held as inventory for sale by a dealer.

**Place of Filing** Revised Article 9 greatly simplifies the place or places of filing: except for real-estate-related collateral financing, statements must be filed in a central location designated by the State. Section 9–501(a)(2). With respect to real-estate-related collateral, the financing statement is to be filed in the office designated for the filing or recording of mortgages on the related real property, which is usually local. Section 9–501(a)(1). If the debtor is an individual, the financing statement is to be filed in the State of the individual's principal residence; for a registered organization, the place of filing is the State where the debtor is organized.

## FIGURE 38-3: Sample Financing Statement

[redacted]

**UCC FINANCING STATEMENT**

FOLLOW INSTRUCTIONS (front and back) CAREFULLY

A. NAME & PHONE OF CONTACT AT FILER [optional]

B. SEND ACKNOWLEDGMENT TO: (Name and Address)

THE ABOVE SPACE IS FOR FILING OFFICE USE ONLY

1. DEBTOR'S EXACT FULL LEGAL NAME - insert only one debtor name (1a or 1b) - do not abbreviate or combine names

| | | | | |
|---|---|---|---|---|
| 1a. ORGANIZATION'S NAME | | | | |
| OR 1b. INDIVIDUAL'S LAST NAME | FIRST NAME | MIDDLE NAME | | SUFFIX |
| 1c. MAILING ADDRESS | CITY | STATE | POSTAL CODE | COUNTRY |
| 1d. TAX ID #: SSN OR EIN / ADD'L INFO RE ORGANIZATION DEBTOR / 1e. TYPE OF ORGANIZATION | 1f. JURISDICTION OF ORGANIZATION | 1g. ORGANIZATIONAL ID #, if any | | NONE |

2. ADDITIONAL DEBTOR'S EXACT FULL LEGAL NAME - insert only one debtor name (2a or 2b) - do not abbreviate or combine names

| | | | | |
|---|---|---|---|---|
| 2a. ORGANIZATION'S NAME | | | | |
| OR 2b. INDIVIDUAL'S LAST NAME | FIRST NAME | MIDDLE NAME | | SUFFIX |
| 2c. MAILING ADDRESS | CITY | STATE | POSTAL CODE | COUNTRY |
| 2d. TAX ID #: SSN OR EIN / ADD'L INFO RE ORGANIZATION DEBTOR / 2e. TYPE OF ORGANIZATION | 2f. JURISDICTION OF ORGANIZATION | 2g. ORGANIZATIONAL ID #, if any | | NONE |

3. SECURED PARTY'S NAME (or NAME of TOTAL ASSIGNEE of ASSIGNOR S/P) - insert only one secured party name (3a or 3b)

| | | | | |
|---|---|---|---|---|
| 3a. ORGANIZATION'S NAME | | | | |
| OR 3b. INDIVIDUAL'S LAST NAME | FIRST NAME | MIDDLE NAME | | SUFFIX |
| 3c. MAILING ADDRESS | CITY | STATE | POSTAL CODE | COUNTRY |

4. This FINANCING STATEMENT covers the following collateral:

5. ALTERNATIVE DESIGNATION [if applicable]: ☐ LESSEE/LESSOR ☐ CONSIGNEE/CONSIGNOR ☐ BAILEE/BAILOR ☐ SELLER/BUYER ☐ AG. LIEN ☐ NON-UCC FILING

6. ☐ This FINANCING STATEMENT is to be filed [for record] (or recorded) in the REAL ESTATE RECORDS. Attach Addendum [if applicable]

7. Check to REQUEST SEARCH REPORT(S) on Debtor(s) [ADDITIONAL FEE] [optional] ☐ All Debtors ☐ Debtor 1 ☐ Debtor 2

8. OPTIONAL FILER REFERENCE DATA

**FILING OFFICE COPY** — NATIONAL UCC FINANCING STATEMENT (FORM UCC1) (REV. 07/29/98)

**Subsequent Change of Debtor's Location** After a secured party has properly filed a financing statement, the debtor may change the place of his residence or business or the location or use of the collateral and thus render the information in the filing incorrect. A change in the use of the collateral or a move within the State (intrastate) does not impair the effectiveness of the original filing. If the debtor moves to another State after the initial filing, the security interest remains perfected until the earliest of (1) the time the security interest would have terminated in the State in which perfection occurred; (2) four months after the debtor moved to the new State; or (3) the expiration of one year after the debtor transfers the collateral to a person, who becomes the debtor, in another State. Section 9–316(a).

### POSSESSION

Possession by the secured party perfects a security interest in goods (e.g., those in the possession of pawnbrokers), instruments, money, negotiable documents, or tangible chattel paper. Section 9–313(a). Moreover, a secured party may perfect a security interest in a certificated security by taking delivery of it. Sections 8–301 and 9–313(a). Possession is *not* available, however, as a means of perfecting a security interest in accounts, general intangibles, commercial tort claims, deposit accounts, other types of investment property, letter-of-credit rights, or oil, gas, and other minerals before extraction. Section 9–313, Comment 2.

A **pledge**, which is a possessory security interest, is the delivery of personal property to a creditor, or to a third party acting as an agent or bailee for the creditor, as security for the payment of a debt. No pledge occurs where the debtor retains possession of the collateral. In making a pledge, the debtor is not legally required to sign a written security agreement; an oral agreement granting the secured party a security interest is sufficient. In any situation not involving a pledge, however, the Code requires an authenticated record of the security agreement. Section 9–203(b)(3)(B).

One type of pledge is the **field warehouse**. This common arrangement for financing inventory allows the debtor access to the pledged goods and provides the secured party with control over the pledged property at the same time. In this arrangement, a professional warehouseman generally establishes a warehouse on the debtor's premises—usually by enclosing a portion of those premises and posting appropriate signs—to store the debtor's unsold inventory. The warehouseman then typically issues nonnegotiable receipts for the goods to the secured party, who may then authorize the warehouseman to release a portion of the goods to the debtor as the goods are sold, at a specified quantity per week, or at any rate on which the parties agree. Thus, the secured party legally possesses the goods while allowing the debtor easy access to her inventory.

### AUTOMATIC PERFECTION

In some situations, a security interest is automatically perfected on attachment. The most important situation to which automatic perfection applies is a PMSI in consumer goods. A partial or isolated assignment of accounts that transfers a less-than-significant portion of the assignor's outstanding accounts is also automatically perfected. Sections 9–309(2), 9–310(b)(2).

A PMSI in consumer goods, with the exception of motor vehicles, is perfected automatically upon attachment; filing a financing statement is unnecessary. Sections 9–309(1), 9–310(b)(2). For example, Doris purchases a refrigerator from Carol on credit for Doris's personal, family, or household use. Doris takes possession of the refrigerator and then grants Carol a security interest in the refrigerator pursuant to a written security agreement. Upon Doris's granting Carol the security interest, Carol's security interest attaches and is automatically perfected. The same would be true if Doris purchased the refrigerator for cash but borrowed the money from Logan, to whom Doris granted a security interest in the refrigerator pursuant to a written security agreement. Logan's security interest would attach and would be automatically perfected when she received the security agreement from Doris. Nevertheless, because an automatically perfected PMSI in consumer goods protects the secured party less fully than a filed PMSI, secured parties frequently file a financing statement, rather than rely solely on automatic perfection.

◆ **SEE CASE 38-2**

### TEMPORARY PERFECTION

Security interests in certain types of collateral are automatically, but only temporarily, perfected. Section 9–312(e) provides that a security interest in a certificated security, negotiable document, or instrument is perfected upon attachment for a period of twenty days. This provision, however, is applicable only to the extent that the security interest arises for new value given under an authenticated security agreement. Section 9–312(e). A perfected security interest in a certificated security or an instrument also remains perfected for twenty days if the secured party delivers the security certificate or instrument to the debtor for the purpose of (1) sale or exchange or (2) presentation, collection, enforcement, renewal, or registration of transfer. Section 9–312(g). After the temporary period expires, the security interest becomes unperfected unless it is perfected by other means. Section 9–312(h).

### PERFECTION BY CONTROL

A security interest in investment property, deposit accounts (not including consumer deposit accounts), electronic chattel paper, and letter-of-credit rights may be perfected by control of the collateral. Section 9–314. A security interest in deposit accounts and letter-of-credit rights may be perfected *only* by control. What constitutes control varies with the type of collateral involved. For example, control of a commercial deposit account (e.g., a checking account) is acquired if (1) the secured party is the bank with which the checking account is maintained or (2) the debtor, secured party, and bank agree in an authenticated record that the bank will comply with the secured party's instructions. Section 9–104. The rules for control for other collateral are somewhat different as provided in the following sections: investment property (Section 9–106), electronic chattel paper (Section 9–105), and letter-of-credit rights (Section 9–107).

◆ SEE FIGURE 38-4: **Methods of Perfecting Security Interests**

## PRIORITIES AMONG COMPETING INTERESTS

Revised Article 9 makes only minor changes to old Article 9 concerning the priorities of competing interests. As previously noted, a security interest must be perfected to be most effective against the debtor's other creditors, her trustee in bankruptcy, and her transferees. Nonetheless, perfection of a security interest does *not* provide the secured party with a **priority** over *all* third parties with an interest in the collateral. On the other hand, even an unperfected but attached security interest has priority over a limited number of third parties and is enforceable against the debtor. Article 9 establishes a complex set of rules that determine the relative priorities among these parties.

### AGAINST UNSECURED CREDITORS

Once a security interest *attaches*, it has priority over claims of other creditors who do not have a security interest or a lien. This priority does not depend upon perfection. If a security interest does not attach, the creditor is merely an unsecured or general creditor of the debtor.

### AGAINST OTHER SECURED CREDITORS

The rights of a secured creditor against other secured creditors depend upon the security interests perfected, when they are perfected, and the type of collateral. Notwithstanding the rules of priority, a secured party entitled to priority may subordinate her interest to that of another secured creditor. The parties may do this by agreement, and nothing need be filed.

◆ FIGURE 38-4: **Methods of Perfecting Security Interests**

| | Applicable Method of Perfection | | | | |
|---|---|---|---|---|---|
| **Collateral** | **Filing** | **Possession** | **Automatic** | **Temporary (for twenty days)** | **Control** |
| **Goods** | | | | | |
| Consumer goods | • | • | PMSI | | |
| Farm products | • | • | | | |
| Inventory | • | • | | | |
| Equipment | • | • | | | |
| Fixtures | • | • | | | |
| **Indispensable Paper** | | | | | |
| Chattel paper | • | Tangible | | | Electronic |
| Instruments | • | • | | • | |
| Documents | Negotiable | Negotiable | | Negotiable | |
| Investment property | • | Certificated | | Certificated | • |
| **Intangibles** | | | | | |
| Accounts | • | | Isolated assignment | | |
| General intangibles | • | | | | |
| **Deposit Accounts** | | | | | Commercial |
| **Letter of Credit Accounts** | | | | | • |
| **Money** | | • | | | |

Note: PMSI = purchase money security interest.

**Perfected versus Unperfected** A creditor with a perfected security interest or agricultural lien has superior rights in the collateral over a creditor with an unperfected security interest or agricultural lien, whether or not the unperfected security interest has attached. Section 9–322(a)(2).

**Perfected versus Perfected** Two parties each having a perfected security interest or agricultural lien rank according to priority in *time of filing or perfection*. This general rule is stated in Section 9–322(a)(1), which provides:

> Conflicting perfected security interests and agricultural liens rank according to priority in time of filing or perfection. Priority dates from the earlier of the time a filing covering the collateral is first made or the security interest or agricultural lien is first perfected, if there is no period thereafter when there is neither filing nor perfection.

This rule favors filing, as it can occur prior to attachment and thus grant priority from a time that may precede perfection. Generally, the original time for filing or perfection of a security interest in collateral is also the time of filing or perfection for a security interest in proceeds from that collateral. Section 9–322(b)(1).

For example, Debter Store and Leynder Bank enter into a loan agreement (assume there is no binding commitment to extend credit) under the terms of which Leynder agrees to lend $5,000 on the security of Debter's existing store equipment. A security agreement is executed and a financing statement is filed, but no funds are advanced. One week later, Debter enters into a loan agreement with Reserve Bank, and Reserve agrees to lend $5,000 on the security of the same store equipment. The funds are advanced, a security agreement is executed, and a financing statement is filed. One week later, Leynder Bank advances the agreed sum of $5,000. Debter Store defaults on both loans. Between Leynder Bank and Reserve Bank, Leynder has priority, because priority among security interests perfected by filing is determined by the order in which they were filed. Reserve Bank should have checked the financing statements on file. Had it done so, it would have discovered that Leynder Bank claimed a security interest in the equipment. Conversely, after filing its financing statement, with no prior secured party of record, Leynder had no need to check the files before advancing funds to Debter Store in accordance with its loan commitment.

To further illustrate, assume that Marc grants a security interest in a Chagall painting to Miro Bank and that the bank advances funds to Marc in accordance with the loan agreement. A financing statement is filed. Later, Marc wants more money and goes to Brague, an art dealer, who advances funds to Marc upon a pledge of the painting. Marc defaults on both loans. As between Miro and Brague, Miro has priority because its financing statement was filed before Brague's perfection by possession. By checking the financing statement on file, Brague would have discovered that Miro had a prior security interest in the painting.

There are several exceptions to the general rules just discussed:

1. A **PMSI in noninventory goods** (except livestock) takes priority over a conflicting security interest if the PMSI is perfected when the debtor receives possession of the collateral *or* within twenty days of receiving possession. Section 9–324(a). Thus, the secured party has a twenty-day grace period in which to perfect.

   For example, Dawkins Manufacturing Co. enters into a loan contract with Larkin Bank, which loans money to Dawkins on the security (as provided in the security agreement) of Dawkins's existing and future equipment and files a financing statement stating that the collateral is "all equipment presently owned and subsequently acquired" by Dawkins. At a later date, Dawkins buys new equipment from Parker Supply Co., paying 25 percent of the purchase price, with Parker retaining a security interest (as provided in the security agreement) in the equipment to secure the remaining balance. If Parker files a financing statement within ten days of Dawkins's obtaining possession of the equipment, Parker's PMSI in the new equipment purchased from Parker has priority over Larkin's interest. If, however, Parker files one day beyond the statutory grace period, Parker's interest is subordinate to Larkin's.
2. A **PMSI in inventory** has priority over earlier-filed security interests in inventory if the following requirements are met. The purchase money security holder must perfect his interest in the inventory at the time the debtor receives the inventory and send an authenticated notification to the holder of a conflicting security interest. The holder of the conflicting security interest must receive the notification within five years before the debtor receives possession of the inventory, and the notification must state that the person sending the notification has or will acquire a PMSI in the debtor's inventory and must describe the inventory. Section 9–324(b).

   For example, Dodger Store and Lyons Bank enter into a loan agreement in which Lyons agrees to finance Dodger's entire inventory of stoves, refrigerators, and other kitchen appliances. A security agreement is executed and a financing statement is filed, and Lyons advances funds to Dodger. Subsequently, Dodger enters into an agreement under which Rodger Stove Co. will supply Dodger with stoves, retaining a PMSI in this inventory. Rodger will have priority as to the inventory it supplies to Dodger, provided that Rodger files a financing statement by the time Dodger receives the goods and notifies Lyons that it is going to engage in this purchase money financing of the described stoves. If Rodger fails either to give the required notice or to file timely a financing statement, Lyons will have priority over Rodger as to the stoves Rodger supplies to Dodger. As noted, the Code adopts a system of notice filing, and secured parties who fail to check the financing statements on file proceed at their peril.

3. A **security interest perfected by control** in deposit accounts, letter-of-credit rights, or investment property has priority over a conflicting perfected security interest held by a secured party who does not have control. Sections 9–327(1), 9–328(1), 9–329(1). If both conflicting security interests are perfected by control, they rank according to priority in time of obtaining control.

**Unperfected versus Unperfected** If neither security interest or agricultural lien is perfected, then the first to attach has priority. Section 9–322(a)(3). If neither attach, both of the creditors are general, unsecured creditors.

## AGAINST BUYERS

A security interest or agricultural lien continues even in collateral that is sold, leased, licensed, exchanged, or otherwise disposed of unless the secured party authorizes the sale. Section 9–315. Thus, following a sale, lease, license, exchange, or other disposition of collateral, a secured party who did not authorize the transaction does not have to file a new financing statement to continue her perfected interest. The security interest also attaches to any identifiable proceeds from the sale, including proceeds in consumer deposit accounts. Sections 9–315(a)(2), 9–109(d)(13).

In many instances, however, buyers of collateral sold without the secured party's authorization take it free of an **unperfected** security interest. A buyer of goods, tangible chattel paper, documents, instruments, or certificated securities who gives value and receives delivery of the collateral without knowledge of the security interest *before* it is perfected takes free of the security interest. Section 9–317(b). Similarly, a buyer of accounts, electronic chattel paper, general intangibles, or investment property other than certificated securities takes free of a security interest if the buyer gives value without knowledge of the security interest and does so *before* it is perfected. Section 9–317(d). Thus, with respect to all of these types of collateral, an unperfected security interest prevails over a buyer who does *not* give value or has *knowledge* of the security interest.

In addition, in some instances, purchasers take the collateral free of a **perfected** security interest. The most significant of these instances are as follows:

**Buyers in the Ordinary Course of Business** A buyer in the ordinary course of business takes collateral (other than farm products) free of any security interest created by *the buyer's* seller, even if the security interest is perfected and the buyer *knows* of its existence. Section 9–320(a). A buyer in the ordinary course of business is a person who, without knowledge that the sale violates a security interest of a third party, buys in good faith and in ordinary course from a person in the business of selling goods of that kind. Section 1–201(9); Revised Section 1-201(b)(9). Thus, this rule applies primarily to purchasers of inventory. For example, a consumer who purchases a sofa from a furniture dealer and the dealer who purchases the sofa from another dealer are both buyers in the ordinary course of business. On the other hand, a person who purchases a sofa from a dentist who used the sofa in his waiting room or from an individual who used the sofa in his home is not a buyer in the ordinary course of business.

To illustrate further, a person who in the ordinary course of business buys an automobile from an automobile dealership will take free and clear of a security interest created by the dealer from whom she purchased the car. That same buyer in the ordinary course of business will not, however, take clear of a security interest created by any person who owned the automobile prior to the dealer. A leading case on this point is *National Shawmut Bank of Boston v. Jones,* 108 N.H. 386, 236 A.2d 484 (1967). In that case, Wever bought a 1964 Dodge Dart from Wentworth Motor Company for his own personal use and granted a security interest in the car to Wentworth. Wentworth later assigned the security interest to National Shawmut Bank, which properly perfected it. Without Shawmut's consent, Wever sold the car to Hanson-Rock, another automobile dealer. Hanson-Rock then sold the car to Jones. Even though Jones was a buyer in the ordinary course of business from Hanson-Rock, he took the automobile subject to Shawmut's security interest, as that interest had not been created by Jones's seller, Hanson-Rock.

**Buyers of Farm Products** Buyers in the ordinary course of business of **farm products**, although not protected by Section 9–320, may be protected by the Federal Food Security Act. This Act defines a buyer in the ordinary course of business as "a person who, in the ordinary course of business, buys farm products from a person engaged in farming operations who is in the business of selling farm products." The Act provides that such a buyer shall take free of most security interests created by the seller, even if the security interest is perfected and the buyer knows of its existence.

**Buyers of Consumer Goods** In the case of consumer goods, a buyer who buys without knowledge of a security interest, for value, and primarily for personal, family, or household purposes takes the goods free of any PMSI *automatically* perfected, but takes the goods subject to a security interest perfected by filing. Section 9–320(b). For example,

Ann purchases on credit a refrigerator from Sean for use in her home and grants Sean a security interest in the refrigerator. Sean does not file a financing statement but has a security interest perfected by attachment. Ann subsequently sells the refrigerator to her neighbor, Juwan, for use in his home. Juwan does not know of Sean's security interest and therefore takes the refrigerator free of that interest. If Sean had filed a financing statement, however, his security interest would continue in the collateral, even in Juwan's hands.

**Buyers of Other Collateral** To the extent provided by UCC Articles 3, 7, and 8, a secured party who has a perfected security interest in a negotiable instrument, a negotiable document of title, or a security has a *subordinate* interest to a purchaser of (1) the instrument who has the rights of a holder in due course, (2) the document of title to whom it has been duly negotiated, or (3) the security who is a protected purchaser. Section 9–331. In addition, in certain instances a secured party who has a perfected security interest in chattel paper also may have subordinate rights to a purchaser of such collateral. Section 9–330.

## AGAINST LIEN CREDITORS

A **lien creditor** is a creditor who has acquired a lien in the property by judicial decree ("attachment garnishment, or the like"), an assignee for the benefit of creditors, a receiver in equity, or a **trustee in bankruptcy**. Section 9–102(a)(52). (A trustee in bankruptcy is a representative of an estate in bankruptcy who is responsible for collecting, liquidating, and distributing the debtor's assets.) Whereas a **perfected** security interest or agricultural lien has priority over lien creditors who acquire their liens after perfection, an **unperfected** security interest or agricultural lien is subordinate to the rights of one who becomes a lien creditor before (1) its perfection or (2) a financing statement covering the collateral is filed and either (a) the debtor has authenticated a properly drawn security agreement, (b) if the collateral is a certificated security, the certificate has been delivered to the secured party, or (c) if the collateral is an uncertificated security, it is in possession of the secured party. Section 9–317(a)(2). If a secured party files with respect to a *PMSI* within twenty days after the debtor receives possession of the collateral, however, the secured party takes priority over the rights of a lien creditor that arise between the time the security interest attaches and the time of filing. Section 9–317(e). Nonetheless, a lien securing claims arising from services or materials furnished in the ordinary course of a person's business with respect to goods (an artisan's or mechanic's lien) has priority over a security interest in the goods unless the lien is created by a statute that expressly provides otherwise. Section 9–333.

## AGAINST TRUSTEE IN BANKRUPTCY

The Bankruptcy Act empowers a trustee in bankruptcy to invalidate secured claims in certain instances. It also imposes some limitations on the rights of secured parties. This section will examine the power of a trustee in bankruptcy to (1) take priority over an unperfected security interest and (2) avoid preferential transfers.

**Priority over Unperfected Security Interest** A trustee in bankruptcy may invalidate any security interest that is voidable by a creditor who obtained a judicial lien on the date the bankruptcy petition was filed. Bankruptcy Act, Section 544. Under the Code and the Bankruptcy Act, the trustee, as a hypothetical **lien creditor**, has priority over a creditor whose security interest was not perfected when the bankruptcy petition was filed. A creditor with a PMSI interest who files within the Code's statutory grace period of twenty days after the debtor receives the collateral will defeat the trustee, even if the bankruptcy petition is filed before the creditor perfects and after the security interest is created. For example, David borrowed $5,000 from Cynthia on September 1 and gave her a security interest in the equipment he purchased with the borrowed funds. On October 3, before Cynthia perfected her security interest, David filed for bankruptcy. The trustee in bankruptcy can invalidate Cynthia's security interest because it was unperfected when the bankruptcy petition was filed. If, however, David had filed for bankruptcy on September 8 and Cynthia had perfected the security interest within the Code's statutory grace period of twenty days, Cynthia would prevail.

**Avoidance of Preferential Transfers** Section 547 of the Bankruptcy Act provides that a trustee in bankruptcy may invalidate any transfer of property—including the granting of a security interest—from the debtor, provided that the transfer (1) was to or for the benefit of a creditor; (2) was made on account of an antecedent debt; (3) was made when the debtor was insolvent; (4) was made on the date of or within ninety days before the filing of the bankruptcy petition or, if made to an insider, was made within one year before the date of the filing; and (5) enabled the transferee to receive more than he would have received in bankruptcy. (An insider includes a relative or general partner of a debtor, as well as a partnership in which the debtor is a general partner or a corporation of which the debtor is a director, officer, or person in control.) In determining whether the debtor is insolvent, the Act establishes a rebuttable presumption of insolvency for the ninety days prior to the filing of the bankruptcy petition. To avoid a transfer to an insider that occurred more than one year before bankruptcy, the trustee must prove that the debtor was insolvent when the transfer was made. If a security interest is invalidated as a preferential transfer, the creditor may still make a claim for the unpaid debt, but the creditor's claim is unsecured.

To illustrate the operation of this rule, consider the following. On May 1, Debra bought and received merchandise from Stuart and gave him a security interest in the goods for the unpaid price of $20,000. On June 5, Stuart filed a financing statement. On August 1, Debra filed a petition for bankruptcy. The trustee in bankruptcy may avoid the perfected security interest as a preferential transfer because (1) the transfer of the perfected security interest on June 5 was to benefit a creditor (Stuart); (2) the transfer was on account of an antecedent debt (the $20,000 owed from the sale of the merchandise); (3) the debtor was insolvent at the time (the Act presumes that the debtor is insolvent for the ninety days preceding the date the bankruptcy petition was filed—August 1); (4) the transfer was made within ninety days of bankruptcy (June 5 is less than ninety days before August 1); and (5) the transfer enabled the creditor to receive more than he would have received in bankruptcy (Stuart would have a secured claim on which he would recover more than he would on an unsecured claim).

Nevertheless, not all transfers made within ninety days of bankruptcy are voidable. As amended in 2005, the Bankruptcy Code makes exceptions for certain prebankruptcy transfers. If the creditor gives the debtor new value which the debtor uses to acquire property in which he grants the creditor a security interest, the resulting PMSI is not voidable if the creditor perfects it within thirty days after the debtor receives possession of the property. For example, if within ninety days of the filing of the petition, the debtor purchases a refrigerator on credit and grants the seller or lender a PMSI in the refrigerator, the transfer of that interest is not voidable if the secured party perfects within thirty days after the debtor receives possession of the property.

◆ SEE FIGURE 38-5: **Priorities**

## DEFAULT

Because the Code does not define or specify what constitutes default, general contract law or the agreement between the parties will determine when a default occurs. After default, the security agreement and the applicable provisions of the Code govern the rights and remedies of the parties. In general, the secured party may reduce his claim to judgment, foreclose, or otherwise enforce the claim, security interest, or

◆ FIGURE 38-5: **Priorities**

| Versus | Unsecured creditor | Creditor with unperfected security interests | Creditor with perfected security interest | Creditor with perfected money security interest |
|---|---|---|---|---|
| **Unsecured creditor** | = | ↑ | ↑ | ↑ |
| **Creditor with unperfected security interest** | ← | first to attach | ↑ | ↑ |
| **Creditor with perfected security interest** | ← | ← | first to file or perfect | ↑ if PMSI perfected within grace period |
| **Creditor with perfected PMSI** | ← | ← | first to file or perfect | ↑ if PMSI gives notice and perfects by time debtor gets possession |
| **Buyer in ordinary course of business** | ← | ← | ← if created by immediate seller | ← |
| **Consumer buyer of consumer goods** | ← | ← | ↑ | ← if not filed |
| **Lien creditor (including trustee in bankruptcy)** | ← | ← | first in time | first in time but PMSI has grace period |
| **Trustee in bankruptcy—voidable preferences** | ← | ← | ↑ if secured party perfects within grace period | ↑ if PMSI perfects within grace period |

Note: PMSI = purchase money security interest.

agricultural lien by any available judicial procedure. Section 9–601(a)(1). If the collateral consists of documents, the secured party may proceed against the documents or the goods they cover. Section 9–601(a)(2). These rights and remedies of the creditor are cumulative. Section 9–601(c).

Unless the debtor has waived his rights in the collateral after default, he has a right of **redemption** (to free the collateral of the security interest by fulfilling all obligations securing the collateral and paying reasonable expenses and attorneys' fees) at any time before the secured party has collected the collateral, has disposed of the collateral, has entered a contract to dispose of it, or has discharged the obligation by accepting the collateral. Section 9–623.

### REPOSSESSION

Unless the parties have agreed otherwise, the secured party may take possession of the collateral on default. If it can be done without a breach of the peace, such taking may occur without judicial process. Section 9–609. The Code leaves the term *breach of the peace* for the courts to define. Some States have defined such a breach to require either the use of violence or the threat of violence, while others require merely an entry without consent. Most States require permission for entry to a residence or garage. On the other hand, the courts do permit the repossession of motor vehicles from driveways or streets. Some courts, however, do not permit a creditor to repossess if the debtor has orally protested the repossession.

After default, instead of removing the collateral, the secured party may render it unusable and leave it on the debtor's premises until disposing of it. It also may be done without judicial process if accomplished without a breach of peace. Section 9–609.

◆ **SEE CASE 38-3**

### SALE OF COLLATERAL

The secured party may sell, lease, license, or otherwise dispose of any collateral in its existing condition at the time of default or following any commercially reasonable preparation or processing. Section 9–610(a). A secured party's disposition of the collateral after default (1) transfers to a transferee for value all of the debtor's rights in the collateral, (2) discharges the security interest under which the disposition occurred, and (3) discharges any subordinate security interests and liens. Section 9–617(a).

The collateral may be disposed of at public sale (auction) or private sale, so long as all aspects of the disposition, including its method, manner, time, place, and other terms, are "commercially reasonable." Section 9–610(b). The secured party may buy at a public sale and at a private sale if the collateral is customarily sold in a recognized market or is the subject of widely distributed standard price quotations. Section 9–610(c). The collateral, if it is commercially reasonable, may be disposed of by one or more contracts or as a unit or in parcels. Section 9–610(b). The Code favors private sales since they generally garner a higher price for the collateral. Section 9–610, Comment 2. The fact that the secured party could have received a greater amount is not of itself sufficient to establish that the sale was not made in a commercially reasonable manner. Section 9–627(a). Unless the collateral is perishable or threatens to decline speedily in value or is of a type customarily sold on a recognized market, the secured party must send a reasonable authenticated notification of disposition to the debtor, any secondary obligor (surety or guarantor) and, except in the case of consumer goods, other parties who have sent an authenticated notice of a claim or any secured party or lien holder who has filed a financing statement at least ten days before the notification date. Section 9–611.

Section 9–615(a) provides that the proceeds from the sale of the collateral are to be applied in the following order:

1. paying the reasonable expenses of retaking and disposing of the collateral,
2. paying the debt owed to the secured party,
3. paying any subordinate interests in the collateral, and
4. paying a secured party that is a consignor.

The debtor is entitled to any *surplus* and is liable for any *deficiency*, except in the case of a sale of accounts, chattel paper, payment intangibles, or promissory notes for which he is neither entitled nor liable unless the security agreement so provides. Section 9–615(d)(e). If the goods are consumer goods, the secured party must give the debtor an explanation of how the surplus or deficiency was calculated. Section 9–616.

### ACCEPTANCE OF COLLATERAL

Acceptance of collateral (strict foreclosure) is a way for a secured party to acquire the debtor's interests without the need for a sale or other disposition. The secured party may, after default and repossession if the debtor consents in a record authenticated after default, keep the collateral in full or partial satisfaction of the obligation. Section 9–620(a)(1)(c). In addition, the secured party may accept the collateral in *full* satisfaction of the obligation if she sends an unconditional proposal to the debtor to accept the collateral in full satisfaction of the obligation and she does not receive a notice of objection authenticated by the debtor within twenty days. Section 9–620(c)(2). If there is an objection, however, the secured party must dispose of the collateral as provided in the Code. Section 9–620. Silence is not consent to a *partial* satisfaction of the obligation. The debtor's consent, however, will not permit the secured party to accept the collateral in satisfaction of the obligation if a person holding a junior interest (secured party or lien holder) lodges a proper objection to the proposal. Section 9–620(a)(2), Comment 3.

In the case of *consumer goods*, if the debtor has paid 60 percent or more of the obligation, the secured party who has taken possession of the collateral must dispose of it by sale within ninety days after repossession unless the debtor and all secondary obligors have agreed in a record authenticated after default to a longer period of time. Section 9–620(e),(f). Additionally, with a consumer debt, the secured party may not accept collateral in *partial* satisfaction of the obligation it secures. Section 9–620(g).

The acceptance of collateral in full or partial satisfaction discharges the obligation to the extent consented to by the debtor, transfers all of the debtor's rights to the secured party, and terminates all subordinate interests in the collateral. Section 9–622.

# SURETYSHIP

In many business transactions involving the extension of the credit, the creditor will require that someone in addition to the debtor promise to fulfill the obligation. This promisor generally is known as a surety. In a contract involving a minor, a surety commonly will act as a party with full contractual capacity who can be held responsible for the obligations arising from the contract. Sureties are often used in addition to security to further reduce the risks involved in the extension of credit and are used instead of security interests when security is unavailable or when the use of a secured transaction is too expensive or inconvenient. Employers frequently use sureties to protect against losses caused by employees' embezzlement, while property owners use sureties to bond the performance of contracts for the construction of commercial buildings. Similarly, statutes commonly require that contracts for work to be done for governmental entities have the added protection of a surety. Premiums for compensated sureties exceed $1 billion annually in the United States.

## NATURE AND FORMATION

A **surety** promises to answer for the payment of a debt or the performance of a duty owed to one person (called the **creditor**) by another (the **principal debtor**) upon the *failure* of the principal debtor to make payment or otherwise perform the obligation. Thus, the suretyship relationship involves three parties—the principal debtor, the creditor, and the surety—and three contractual obligations. Two or more persons bound for the same debt of a principal debtor are **cosureties**.

The creditor's rights against the principal debtor are determined by the contract between them. The creditor also may realize upon any collateral securing the principal debtor's performance that the creditor or the surety holds. In addition, the creditor may proceed against the surety if the principal debtor defaults. If the surety is an **absolute surety**, then the creditor may hold the surety liable as soon as the principal debtor defaults. The creditor need *not* proceed first against the principal debtor. In contrast, a surety who is a **conditional guarantor of collection** is liable only upon the creditor's first exhausting his legal remedies against the principal debtor. Thus, a conditional guarantor of collection is liable if the creditor first obtains, but is unable to collect, a judgment against the principal debtor.

A surety who is required to pay the creditor for the principal debtor's obligation is entitled to be exonerated (relieved of liability) and reimbursed by the principal debtor. In addition, the surety is subrogated to (assumes) the rights of the creditor and has a right of contribution from cosureties. These rights of sureties are discussed more fully later in this chapter.

Although in theory a surety and a guarantor are distinct entities, the two terms are nearly synonymous in common usage. Strictly speaking, a surety is bound with the principal debtor as a primary obligor, usually, although not necessarily, on the same instrument, whereas the guarantor is separately or collaterally bound to pay if the principal debtor does not. For convenience, and because the rights and duties of a surety are almost indistinguishable from those of a guarantor, the term surety will be used to include both terms.

◆ SEE FIGURE 38-6: **Suretyship Relationship**

◆ SEE CASE 38-4

### TYPES OF SURETIES

Creditors seeking to reduce the risk of default by their debtors frequently use a suretyship arrangement. For example, Philco Developers, a closely held corporation, applies to Caldwell Bank, a lending institution, for a loan. After scrutinizing the assets and financial prospects of Philco, the lender refuses to extend credit unless Simpson, the sole shareholder of Philco, promises to repay the loan if Philco does not. Simpson agrees, and Caldwell Bank makes the loan. Simpson's undertaking is that of a surety. Similarly, Philco wishes to purchase goods on credit from Bird Enterprises, the seller, who agrees to extend credit only if Philco obtains an acceptable surety. Simpson agrees to pay Bird Enterprises for the goods if Philco does not. Simpson is a surety. In each of these examples, the surety's promise gives the creditor recourse for payment against two persons—the principal debtor and the surety—instead of one, thereby reducing the creditor's risk of loss.

Another common suretyship relation arises when an owner of property subject to a mortgage sells the property to a purchaser who expressly **assumes the mortgage**. Although by assuming the obligation the purchaser becomes the principal debtor and therefore personally obligated to pay the seller's

◆ FIGURE 38-6: **Suretyship Relationship**

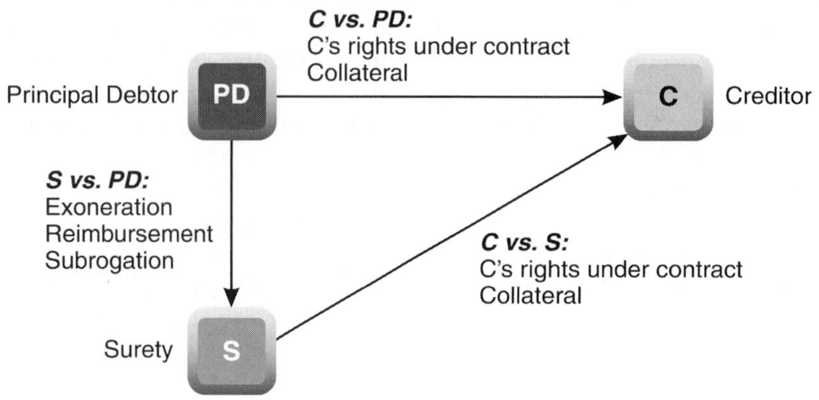


debt to the lender, the seller nevertheless remains liable to the lender and is a surety on the obligation the purchaser has assumed. If, however, the purchaser does not assume the mortgage but simply takes the property "**subject to**" the mortgage, he is neither personally liable for the mortgage nor a surety for the mortgage obligation. In this case, the purchaser's potential loss is limited to the value of the property; for although the mortgagee creditor may foreclose against the property, he may not hold the purchaser personally liable for the debt.

In addition to the more general types of sureties, there are numerous specialized kinds of suretyship, the most important of which are (1) fidelity, (2) performance, (3) official, and (4) judicial. A surety undertakes a **fidelity bond** to protect an employer against employee dishonesty. **Performance bonds** guarantee the performance of the terms and conditions of a contract. These bonds are used frequently in the construction industry to protect an owner from losses that may result from a contractor's failure to perform under a building contract. **Official bonds** arise from a common statutory requirement that public officers furnish bonds for the faithful performance of their duties. Such bonds obligate a surety for all losses that an officer causes through negligence or through nonperformance of her duties. Judicial bonds are provided on behalf of a party to a judicial proceeding to cover losses caused by delay or by deprivation of the use of property resulting from the institution of the action. In criminal proceedings, the purpose of a judicial bond, called a bail bond, is to ensure the appearance of the defendant in court.

◆ SEE FIGURE 38-7: **Assumption of Mortgage**

## FORMATION

The suretyship relationship is contractual and must satisfy all the usual elements of a contract, including offer and acceptance, consideration, capacity of the parties, and legality of object. No particular words are required to constitute a contract of suretyship or guaranty.

As discussed in *Chapter 15*, the contractual promise of a surety to the creditor must be in writing to be enforceable under the statute of frauds. This requirement, which applies only to collateral promises, is subject to the exception

◆ FIGURE 38-7: **Assumption of Mortgage**

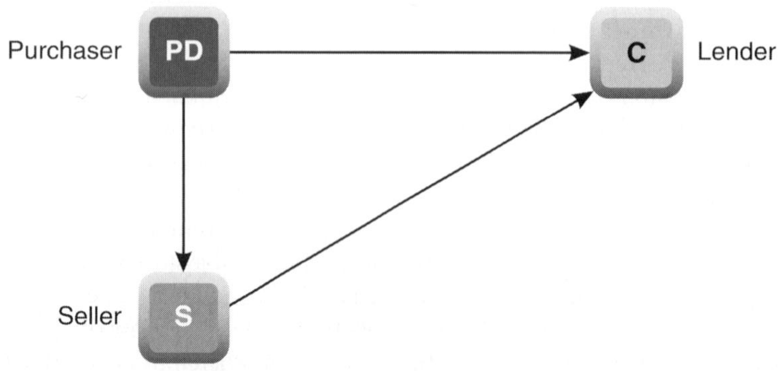

known as the *main purpose doctrine*. Under this doctrine, if the leading object (main purpose) of the promisor (surety) is to obtain an economic benefit that he did not previously enjoy, the promise is not within the statute of frauds.

The promise of a surety is *not* binding without consideration. Because the surety generally makes her promise to induce the creditor to confer a benefit upon the principal debtor, the same consideration that supports the principal debtor's promise usually supports the surety's promise as well. Thus, if Constance lends money to Philip upon Sally's promise to act as a surety, Constance's extension of credit is the consideration to support not only Philip's promise to repay the loan but also Sally's suretyship undertaking. In contrast, a surety's promise made *subsequent* to the principal debtor's receipt of the creditor's consideration must be supported by new consideration. Accordingly, if Constance has already sold goods on credit to Philip, a subsequent guaranty by Sally will not be binding unless new consideration is given.

## RIGHTS OF SURETY

Upon the principal debtor's default, the surety has a number of rights against the principal debtor, third parties, and cosureties. These rights include (1) exoneration, (2) reimbursement, (3) subrogation, and (4) contribution. As discussed above, a surety or absolute guarantor has *no* right to compel the creditor to collect from the principal debtor or to realize upon collateral provided by the principal debtor. Nor is the creditor required to give the surety notice of the principal debtor's default unless the contract of suretyship provides otherwise. A conditional guarantor of collection, on the other hand, faces no liability until the creditor first exhausts his legal remedies of collection against the principal debtor.

### EXONERATION

The ordinary expectation in a suretyship relation is that the principal debtor will perform the obligation and the surety will not be required to perform. Therefore, the surety has the right to require that her principal debtor pay the creditor when the obligation is due. This right of the surety against the principal debtor, called the right of **exoneration**, is enforceable at equity. If the principal debtor fails to pay the creditor when the debt is due, the surety may obtain a decree ordering the principal debtor to pay the creditor. The remedy of exoneration against the principal debtor does not, however, impair the creditor's right to proceed against the surety.

A surety also has a right of exoneration against his cosureties. When the principal debtor's obligation becomes due, each surety owes every other cosurety the duty to pay her proportionate share of the principal debtor's obligation to the creditor. Accordingly, a surety may bring an action in equity to obtain an order requiring his cosureties to pay their share of the debt to the creditor.

### REIMBURSEMENT

When a surety pays the creditor upon the default of the principal debtor, the surety has the right of **reimbursement** (repayment) against the principal debtor. The surety, however, has no right to reimbursement until he actually has made payment, and then only to the extent of the payment. Thus, a surety who advantageously negotiates a defaulted obligation down to a compromise figure less than the original sum may recover from the principal debtor only the sum he actually paid, not the sum before negotiation.

### SUBROGATION

Upon payment of the principal debtor's *entire* obligation, the surety "steps into the shoes" of the creditor. This process of substitution, called **subrogation**, confers upon the surety all the rights the creditor has against or through the principal debtor. These include the creditor's rights:

1. against the principal debtor, including the creditor's priorities in a bankruptcy proceeding;
2. in security of the principal debtor;
3. against third parties, such as co-makers, who are also obligated on the principal debtor's obligation; and
4. against cosureties.

### CONTRIBUTION

Up to the amount of their individual undertakings, cosureties are jointly and severally liable for the principal debtor's default. The creditor may proceed against any or all of the cosureties and collect from any of them the amount that the surety has agreed to guarantee, which may be the entire amount of the principal debtor's obligation.

A surety who pays her principal debtor's obligation may require her cosureties to pay her their proportionate shares of the obligation she has paid. This right of **contribution** arises when a surety has paid more than her proportionate share of a debt, even if the cosureties originally were unaware of each other or were bound on separate instruments. They need only be sureties for the same principal debtor and the same obligation. The right and extent of contribution is determined by contractual agreement among the cosureties. If no agreement exists, sureties obligated for equal amounts share equally; where they are obligated for varying amounts, the proportion of the debt that each surety must contribute is determined by proration according to each surety's undertaking. For example, if X, Y, and Z are cosureties for PD to C in the amounts of $5,000, $10,000, and $15,000, respectively, which totals $30,000, then X's contributive share is one-sixth ($5,000/$30,000), Y's share is one-third

($10,000/$30,000), and Z's share is one-half ($15,000/$30,000).

## DEFENSES OF SURETY AND PRINCIPAL DEBTOR

The obligations the principal debtor and the surety owe to the creditor arise out of contracts. Accordingly, those in surety relationships can assert the usual contractual defenses, such as those resulting from (1) the nonexistence of the principal debtor's obligation, (2) a discharge of the principal debtor's obligation, (3) a modification of the principal debtor's contract, or (4) a variation of the surety's risk. Some of these defenses are available only to the principal debtor, some only to the surety, and others are available to both parties.

◆ SEE FIGURE 38-8: **Defenses of Surety and Principal Debtor**

### PERSONAL DEFENSES OF PRINCIPAL DEBTOR

The defenses available only to a principal debtor are known as the personal defenses of the principal debtor. For example, the principal debtor's **incapacity** due to infancy or mental incompetency may serve as a defense for the principal debtor but not for the surety. If, however, the principal debtor disaffirms the contract and returns the consideration he received from the creditor, then the surety is discharged from his liability. In contrast, a discharge of the principal debtor's obligation in **bankruptcy** does not in turn discharge the surety's liability to the creditor on that obligation. In addition, the surety may not use as a **setoff** any claim that the principal debtor has against the creditor.

### PERSONAL DEFENSES OF SURETY

Those defenses that *only* the surety may assert are called personal defenses of the surety. The surety may use as a defense his own **incapacity**, noncompliance with the **statute of frauds**, and the absence of mutual assent or consideration to support his obligation. **Fraud** or **duress** practiced by the creditor upon the surety also is a defense. Although, as a general rule, nondisclosure of material facts by the creditor to the surety is not fraud, there are two important exceptions. First, if a prospective surety requests information, the creditor must disclose it; and the concealment of material

◆ FIGURE 38-8: **Defenses of Surety and Principal Debtor**

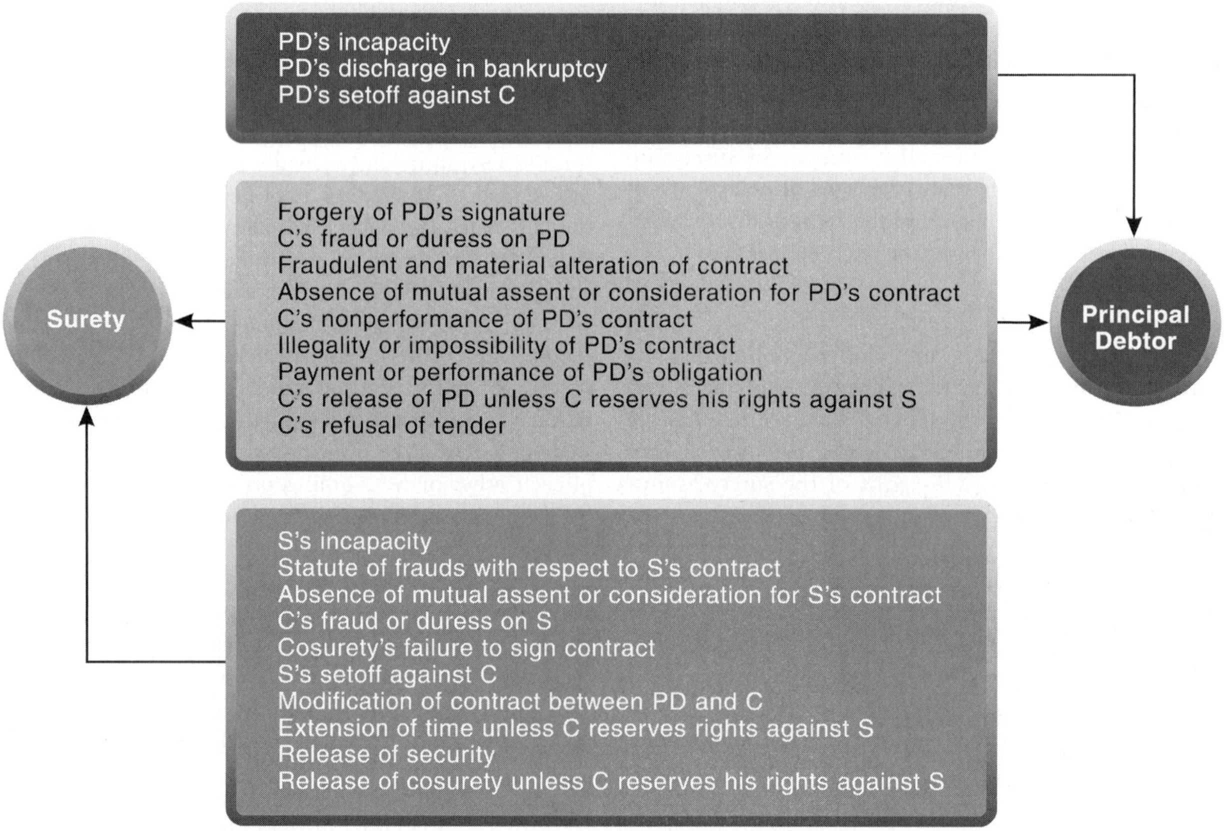

facts will constitute fraud. Second, if the creditor knows, or should know, that the surety is being deceived, the creditor is under a duty to disclose this information; and nondisclosure is considered fraud on the surety. Fraud on the part of the principal debtor may not be asserted against the creditor if the creditor is unaware of such fraud. Similarly, duress exerted by the principal debtor upon the surety is not a defense against the creditor.

A surety is not liable if an intended cosurety, as named in the contract instrument, does not sign. Furthermore, a surety may **set off** his claims against a solvent creditor. Against an insolvent creditor, however, the surety may use his claim only if the principal debtor is also insolvent.

If the principal debtor and the creditor enter into a binding **modification** of their contract, the surety may be discharged unless he assents to the modification. The courts vary in their approach to modifications made without the surety's assent. Often, the courts will discharge an uncompensated surety (an **accommodation surety**) for any material modification, even one that does not prejudice his rights. In contrast, when contemplating the discharge of a compensated surety, a number of courts require the alteration to be both material and prejudicial to the interests of the surety.

Such modifications include valid and binding extensions of the time of payment unless the creditor expressly reserves his rights against the surety. An extension of time with reservation is construed only as an agreement by the creditor not to sue the principal debtor for the period of the extension. Accordingly, the surety's rights of exoneration, reimbursement, and subrogation are not postponed. Thus, the surety's risk is not changed, and he is not discharged.

If the creditor releases or impairs the value of the security, the surety is discharged to the extent of the value of the security released or impaired. Similarly, if the creditor releases a cosurety, the other cosureties are discharged to the extent of the contributive share of the surety released. If the creditor reserves his rights against the remaining cosureties, however, the release is considered a promise not to sue. As a result, the remaining cosureties are not discharged.

## DEFENSES OF BOTH SURETY AND PRINCIPAL DEBTOR

A number of defenses are available to both the surety and the principal debtor. If the principal debtor's signature on an instrument is **forged** or if the creditor has exerted **fraud** or **duress** upon the principal debtor, neither the principal debtor nor the surety is liable. Likewise, if the creditor has fraudulently and **materially altered** the contract instrument, both the principal debtor and the surety are discharged.

The absence of mutual assent or consideration to support the principal debtor's obligation is a defense for both the principal debtor and the surety. In addition, both may assert as defenses the **illegality** and **impossibility** of performance of the principal debtor's contract.

Payment or **performance** of the principal debtor's obligation discharges both the principal debtor and the surety. If the principal debtor owes several debts to the creditor and makes a payment to the creditor without specifying the debt to which the payment should apply, the creditor is free to apply it to any one of them. For example, Pam owes Charles two debts, one for $5,000 and another for $10,000. Susan is a surety on the $10,000 debt. Pam sends Charles a payment in the amount of $3,500. If Pam directs Charles to apply the payment to the $10,000 debt, Charles must apply it accordingly. Otherwise, Charles may, if he pleases, apply the payment to the $5,000 debt.

If the creditor **releases** the principal debtor, then the surety is also discharged unless the surety consents to the release. If the creditor reserves his rights against the surety, however, the surety is not discharged, as the release with reservation is construed as a promise not to sue, which leaves the surety's rights against the principal debtor unimpaired.

The creditor's refusal to accept **tender** of payment or performance by either the principal debtor or the surety completely discharges the surety. The creditor's refusal of tender of payment by the principal debtor does not, however, discharge the principal debtor. Rather, such refusal stops further accrual of interest on the debt and deprives the creditor of court costs on a subsequent suit by him to recover the amount due.

# CHAPTER SUMMARY

## SECURED TRANSACTIONS IN PERSONAL PROPERTY

**ESSENTIALS OF SECURED TRANSACTIONS**

**Definition of Secured Transaction** an agreement by which one party obtains a security interest in the personal property of another to secure the payment of a debt

- ***Debtor*** person who has an interest in the collateral other than a security interest; typically is the person obligated on the debt secured by the security interest
- ***Secured Party*** person in whose favor a security interest in the collateral is created or provided for under the security agreement
- ***Collateral*** property subject to a security interest

- ***Security Agreement*** agreement that creates or provides for a security interest
- ***Security Interest*** right in personal property that secures payment or performance of an obligation
- ***Purchase Money Security Interest*** security interest in goods purchased; interest is retained either by the seller of the goods or by a lender who advances the purchase price

**Fundamental Rights of Debtor**

- To redeem collateral by payment of the debt
- To possess general rights of ownership

**Fundamental Rights of Secured Party**

- To recover amount of debt
- To have collateral applied to payment of debt upon default

---

**CLASSIFICATION OF COLLATERAL**

**Goods** things that are movable when a security interest attaches

- ***Consumer Goods*** goods bought or used primarily for personal, family, or household purposes
- ***Farm Products*** goods that are part of a farming operation, including crops, livestock, or supplies used or produced in farming
- ***Inventory*** includes nonfarm product goods (1) held for sale, lease, or to be furnished under a service contract, or (2) consisting of raw materials, work in process, or materials used or consumed in a business
- ***Equipment*** goods not included in the definition of consumer goods, inventory, or farm products
- ***Fixtures*** goods that are so related to real property that they are considered part of the real estate
- ***Accession*** goods installed in or firmly affixed to personal property

**Indispensable Paper**

- ***Chattel Paper*** tangible or electronic record that evidences both a debt and a security interest in specific goods
- ***Instruments*** negotiable instruments or any other writing that evidences a right to payment of money that is transferable by delivery with any necessary indorsement
- ***Documents*** documents of title
- ***Investment Property*** investment security (stocks and bonds), security accounts, commodity contracts, and commodity accounts

**Intangibles**

- ***Account*** right to payment for (1) goods sold, leased, licensed, or otherwise disposed of or (2) services rendered
- ***General Intangibles*** catchall category of collateral not otherwise covered; includes software, goodwill, literary rights, and interests in patents, trademarks, and copyrights

**Other Types of Collateral**

- ***Proceeds*** whatever is received upon sale, lease, license, exchange, or other disposition of collateral; the secured party, unless the security agreement states otherwise, has rights to the proceeds
- ***Deposit Accounts*** a demand, savings, time, or similar account maintained with a bank

---

**ATTACHMENT**

**Definition** security interest that is enforceable against the debtor

**Value** consideration under contract law, a binding commitment to extend credit, or an antecedent debt

**Debtor's Rights in Collateral** a debtor is deemed to have rights in personal property the debtor owns, possesses, is in the process of acquiring, or has the power to transfer rights to a secured party

| | |
|---|---|
| | **Security Agreement** agreement between debtor and creditor creating a security interest; must be in a record authenticated by the debtor, unless, in the case of most types of collateral, the secured party has possession of the collateral, and must contain a reasonable description of the collateral<br>• ***Consumer Goods*** Federal regulation prohibits a credit seller or lender from obtaining a consumer's grant of a nonpossessory security interest in household goods<br>• ***After-Acquired Property*** a security agreement may cover property the debtor may acquire in the future<br>• ***Future Advances*** a security agreement may include future advances |
| **PERFECTION** | **Definition** attachment plus any steps required for perfection<br>**Effect** enforceable against most third parties |
| **METHODS OF PERFECTING** | **Filing a Financing Statement** may be used for all collateral except deposit accounts, letter-of-credit rights, and money<br>• ***Financing Statement*** document filed to provide notice of a security interest<br>• ***Duration*** filing is effective for five years but may be continued by filing a continuation statement<br>• ***Place of Filing*** statements, except for real-estate-related collateral, must be filed in a central location designated by the State.<br>• ***Subsequent Change of Debtor's Location***<br>**Possession** by the secured party (a pledge); may be used for goods, instruments, money, negotiable documents, tangible chattel paper, or certificated securities<br>**Automatic Perfection** perfection upon attachment; applies to a purchase money security interest in consumer goods and isolated assignments of accounts<br>**Temporary Perfection** a security interest in certificated securities, instruments, and negotiable documents is automatically perfected for twenty days<br>**Control** may be used to perfect a security interest in electronic chattel paper, investment property, nonconsumer deposit accounts, and letter-of-credit rights |
| **PRIORITIES AMONG COMPETING INTERESTS** | See *Figure 38-5* for a summary of the priority rules |
| **DEFAULT** | **Repossession of Collateral** the secured party may take possession of the collateral on default without judicial process if it can be done without a breach of the peace<br>**Sale of Collateral** the secured party may sell, lease, license, or otherwise dispose of any collateral<br>**Acceptance of Collateral** the secured party, unless the debtor objects, may retain the collateral in full or partial satisfaction of the obligation (with the exception of the compulsory disposition of some consumer goods) |

## SURETYSHIP

| | |
|---|---|
| **NATURE AND FORMATION** | **Definition of Surety** a person who promises to answer for the payment of a debt or the performance of a duty owed to the creditor by the principal debtor, upon the principal debtor's failure to perform<br>• ***Principal Debtor*** the party primarily liable on the obligation<br>• ***Cosurety*** each of two or more sureties who are liable for the same debt of the principal debtor<br>• ***Absolute Surety*** surety liable to a creditor immediately upon the default of a principal debtor |

- ***Conditional Guarantor of Collection*** surety liable to a creditor only after the creditor has exhausted the legal remedies against the principal debtor

**Types of Sureties**

- ***Party Assuming a Mortgage***
- ***Fidelity Bonds***
- ***Performance Bonds***
- ***Official Bonds***
- ***Judicial Bonds***

**Formation** the promise of the surety must satisfy all the elements of a contract and must also be in writing

---

**RIGHTS OF SURETY**

**Exoneration** the right of a surety to be relieved of his obligation to the creditor by having the principal debtor perform the obligation
**Reimbursement** the right of a surety who has paid the creditor to be repaid by the principal debtor
**Subrogation** the right of a surety who has paid the creditor to assume all the rights the creditor has against the principal debtor
**Contribution** the right to payment from each cosurety of his proportionate share of the amount paid to the creditor

---

**DEFENSES OF SURETY AND PRINCIPAL DEBTOR**

**Personal Defenses of Principal Debtor** defenses available only to the principal debtor, including her incapacity, discharge in bankruptcy, and setoff
**Personal Defenses of Surety** defenses available only to the surety, including her own incapacity, the statute of frauds, contract defenses to her suretyship undertaking, setoff, modification of the contract between the creditor and the principal debtor, and the creditor's release of security or a cosurety
**Defenses of Both Surety and Principal Debtor** include contract defenses to the contract between the creditor and the principal debtor

# CASES

## CASE 38-1

Security Agreement

## BORDER STATE BANK OF GREENBUSH v. BAGLEY LIVESTOCK EXCHANGE, INC.

Court of Appeals of Minnesota, 2004
690 N.W.2d 326
http://caselaw.lp.findlaw.com/scripts/getcase.pl?court=mn&vol=apppub\0412\opa031973-1214&invol=1

**Lansing, J.**

Bert Johnson, doing business as Johnson Farms, and Hal Anderson entered into an oral cattle-sharing contract in December 1997. Approximately one month later, they memorialized the oral contract in written form. Under the written instrument, Anderson agreed to care for and breed cattle owned by Johnson and Johnson would receive a "guaranteed" percentage of the annual calf crop. The contract further provided that the cattle Johnson placed with Anderson were "considered to be owned by Johnson Farms and any offspring is to be sold under Johnson Farms' name." The contract required Johnson Farms and Anderson mutually to agree when the calves would be sold and within thirty days of receiving money for the sale, Johnson Farms to pay the "remainder" to Anderson "for his keeping of [the] cattle."

In the fall of 1998 and 1999, calves bred under the contract were sold under the provisions of the written contract. Anderson testified that in October 1999, Johnson asked him to care for additional cattle on the same terms. Anderson initially declined, explaining to Johnson that he was ending his cattle business because of adverse personal circumstances. Anderson said that his father had died, his mother was in a nursing home, his partner, Linda

Peterson, was caring for an ill family member, he had no additional help at his farm, he had insufficient feed for the cattle, and he had not planted hay for the coming winter. Nevertheless, according to Anderson, they continued to discuss their cattle-sharing contract, and he eventually agreed to continue based on certain modifications: (1) the share percentage would be a straight 40/60 split, without Johnson's "guaranteed" percentage; (2) Johnson would provide feed, including beet tailings; (3) Johnson would provide additional pasture; and (4) the agreement would include approximately 500 cattle, instead of the original 151 cattle.

Johnson testified that he discussed the cattle-sharing agreement with Anderson in October 1999 and that he agreed to send Anderson beet tailings, which were free to him, so long as Anderson paid the cost of shipping. Johnson also testified that he and Anderson agreed that approximately 500 cattle would be cared for under the cattle-sharing agreement, rather than the original 151 cattle. But Johnson denied that he had agreed to provide feed, other than the beet tailings, and denied that he had agreed to change the provision that "guaranteed" that his percentage of the calf crop would be calculated on the initial number of cows regardless of whether each produced a calf that survived.

In March 2000, Anderson negotiated with Border State Bank for loans totaling $155,528. To secure these loans, Anderson granted Border State Bank a security interest in, among other things, all of Anderson's "rights, title and interest" in all "livestock" then owned or thereafter acquired.

After the modification of the cattle-sharing contract, Johnson made a number of shipments of beet tailings to Anderson. When Johnson stopped the shipments, he sent checks totaling $55,000 to Anderson for the purchase of feed. In November 2000, Anderson encountered difficulty caring for the cattle due to heavy rainfall and lack of feed. The cattle were reclaimed by Johnson, but the calves remained with Anderson for sale. At trial, Anderson testified that some of the cattle that Johnson reclaimed were actually Anderson's cattle or were cattle that belonged to Evonne Stephens, another person with whom Anderson had a cattle-sharing contract.

In December 2000, 289 calves that had remained with Anderson were sold at Bagley Livestock Exchange. The livestock exchange knew of Border State's security interest in Anderson's livestock but, after discussing the agreement with Johnson, determined the security interest did not attach to the calves. The livestock exchange issued a check to Johnson Farms in the amount of $119,403. Thereafter, Johnson gave Anderson a check for $19,404, representing Anderson's share of the sale proceeds, less $55,000 that Johnson claimed as repayment for money advanced to Anderson to purchase feed.

Border State Bank sued Bagley Livestock Exchange and Johnson, contending that they had converted Border State Bank's perfected security interest in the calves sold in December 2000. In a third-party complaint, Johnson sought indemnity from Anderson, in the event that Border State Bank was successful on its conversion claim. Anderson served a counterclaim against Johnson, asserting breach of contract.

These claims were tried to a jury in September 2003. Following Border State Bank's case-in-chief, Johnson and Bagley Livestock Exchange moved for a directed verdict. The district court granted the motion, finding that, under the cattle-sharing agreement, Johnson did not "grant" Anderson an "ownership interest" in the calves. Border State Bank appeals from the directed verdict on its conversion claim.

Following the directed verdict, Anderson presented evidence on his breach-of-contract counterclaim against Johnson, and the counterclaim was submitted to the jury. In response to special-verdict questions, the jury determined that the written contract between Anderson and Johnson had been modified, Johnson breached the contract, and Johnson's breach directly caused damages to Anderson in the amount of $92,360. Johnson moved for judgment notwithstanding the verdict (JNOV), or, in the alternative, a new trial or remittitur. The district court denied Johnson's posttrial motions. Johnson appeals from that denial.

* * *

Article 9 of the Uniform Commercial Code, incorporated into Minnesota law, provides that a security interest attaches to collateral, and is enforceable against the debtor or third parties, when (1) value has been given; (2) the debtor "has rights in the collateral or the power to transfer rights"; and (3) the debtor has signed a security agreement that contains a description of the collateral. [UCC] 9–203(b). To perfect the security interest, both the security agreement and financing statement must contain an adequate description of the collateral. [Citation.] We liberally construe descriptions in the security agreement and financing statement because their essential purpose is to provide notice, not to definitively describe each item of collateral. [Citation.]

The parties do not dispute that Anderson signed a security agreement and that value was given. The security agreement stated that the collateral included, in part, "all livestock owned or hereafter acquired" and Anderson's "rights, title and interest" in such livestock. The financing statements covered "all livestock," whether "now owned or hereafter acquired, together with the proceeds from the sale thereof." The parties also do not dispute the validity of these descriptions or the assertion that "livestock" includes cattle and calves. What is disputed is whether the bank's security interest attached to the 289 calves sold in December 2000 under Anderson and Johnson's cattle-sharing agreement. [Citation.]

* * * The district court stated on the record that the cattle-sharing contract had not "granted" Anderson an "ownership interest" in the calves, specifically finding that "the modifications testified to by Mr. Anderson in the light most favorable to Border State Bank do not modify the terms of the agreement such that an ownership interest is granted." Based on the arguments presented, the district court apparently determined that, for Border State Bank's security interest to attach, Johnson would have had to grant Anderson an interest equivalent to ownership.

The provisions of the Uniform Commercial Code's Article 9, incorporated into Minnesota law, refer to "rights in the collateral," not solely the "ownership" of the collateral. [UCC] §9–203(b)(2) (stating security interest may attach to collateral if "the debtor has rights in the collateral or the power to transfer rights in the collateral"). Rights in the collateral, as the term is used in Article 9, include full ownership and limited rights that fall short of full ownership. [UCC]§9–203 U.C.C. cmt., para. 6. [Citations.] Simply stated, the UCC "does not require that collateral be owned by the debtor." [Citation.]

* * * For purposes of the UCC, "sufficient rights" arise with far less than full ownership. [Citation.] Ownership or title is not the relevant concern under Article 9; "the issue is whether the debtor has acquired sufficient rights in the collateral so that the security interest would attach." [Citation.] The "rights in the collateral" language is a "gateway through which one looks to other law to determine the extent of the debtor's rights." [Citation.] Thus, "[a]ll or some of owner's rights can be transferred by way of sale, lease, or license [and a] person with transferable rights can grant an enforceable security interest in those rights." [Citation.] A "security interest will attach to the collateral only to the extent of the debtor's rights in the collateral"; mere possession of the collateral is insufficient to support an attachment, but the debtor need not have full ownership. [Citation.] * * *

The district court did not analyze the modified cattle-sharing contract to determine the nature of Anderson's rights in the calves or whether Anderson's interests or rights were sufficient to permit attachment of a security interest. We conclude that the standard relied on by the district court is inconsistent with Minnesota law. The application of the incorrect standard prematurely terminated the analysis of the cattle-sharing agreement, which is necessary to determine whether Anderson's rights in the collateral were sufficient for the bank's security interest to attach. * * * Because the district court applied a standard of ownership that is inconsistent with Minnesota law, its finding that the security interest did not attach was influenced by an error of law.

* * * On remand, the district court shall consider the cattle-sharing agreement to determine whether Anderson had "rights" in the calves, to which the bank's security interest attached.

CASE 38-2

## Automatic Perfection
## KIMBRELL'S OF SANFORD, INC. v. KPS, INC.

Court of Appeals of North Carolina, 1994
113 N.C.App 830, 440 S.E.2d 329
http://scholar.google.com/scholar_case?case=5950766689451603162&hl=en&as_sdt=2&as_vis=1&oi=scholarr

**McCrodden, J.**

This action arises out of plaintiff's attempt to recover from defendant KPS, Inc. a VCR which plaintiff had sold to defendant Burns and which Burns had immediately pawned at the Kendale Pawn Shop. Plaintiff filed a complaint in small claims court, and the magistrate, after a hearing on 17 February 1992, entered judgment denying plaintiff recovery of the VCR. Plaintiff appealed to the district court. Judge William A. Christian, sitting without a jury, entered judgment denying plaintiff recovery and dismissing the action. From this judgment, plaintiff appeals.

Plaintiff offers one argument raising the issue of whether it was entitled to recover from defendant pawn shop a VCR plaintiff had sold to defendant Burns under a purchase money security agreement. * * *

Plaintiff argues that the judgment denying it recovery of the VCR contravened Article 9 of the Uniform Commercial Code, [citation]. We agree.

At the time defendant Burns purchased the VCR from plaintiff, he signed a purchase money security agreement, thereby granting plaintiff a purchase money security interest in the VCR. [UCC] §9–107 [Revised §9–103]. Since a VCR is a consumer good, [UCC] §9–109(1) [Revised §9–102(a)(23)], plain-tiff did not have to file a financing statement in order to perfect its purchase money security interest in the VCR. [UCC] §9–302(1)(d) [Revised §9–309]. Defendant Burns failed to make any further payments for the VCR and defaulted on the security agreement. Therefore, plaintiff was entitled to recover possession of the VCR when it filed its action in small claims court. [UCC] §9–501 [Revised §9–601], 9–503 [Revised 9–609]. Accordingly, we hold that the trial court erred in dismissing plaintiff's claim to recover possession of the VCR.

* * *

For the foregoing reasons, we reverse the judgment of the trial court and remand for entry of judgment in favor of plaintiff.

Reversed.

CASE 38-3

## Repossession
## CHAPA v. TRACIERS & ASSOCIATES

Court of Appeals of Texas, Houston (14th Dist.), 2008
267 S.W.3d 386, 66 UCC Rep.Serv.2d 451
http://www.14thcoa.courts.state.tx.us/opinions/HTMLopinion.asp?OpinionID=84777

**Guzman, J.**

In this appeal, we must determine whether appellants, the parents of two young children, have legally cognizable claims for mental anguish allegedly sustained when a repossession agent towed their vehicle out of sight before he realized their children were inside. The parents filed suit against the financing company, the repossession company it hired, and the repossession agent who towed the vehicle. They asserted claims for mental anguish and its physical manifestations under (a) [UCC] section 9.609 * * *

Ford Motor Credit Corp. ("FMCC") hired Traciers & Associates ("Traciers") to repossess a white 2002 Ford Expedition owned by Marissa Chapa, who was in default on the associated promissory note. Traciers assigned the job to its field manager, Paul Chambers, and gave him an address where the vehicle could be found. FMCC, Traciers, and Chambers were unaware that the address was that of Marissa's brother, Carlos Chapa. Coincidentally, Carlos and his wife Maria Chapa also had purchased a white Ford Expedition financed by FMCC. Their vehicle, however, was a 2003 model, and the Chapas were not in default.

On the night of February 6, 2003, Chambers went to the address and observed a white Ford Expedition. The license number of the vehicle did not match that of the vehicle he was told to repossess, and he did not see the vehicle's vehicle identification number ("VIN"), which was obscured. Chambers returned early the next morning and still could not see the Expedition's VIN. He returned to his own vehicle, which was parked two houses away.

Unseen by Chambers, Maria Chapa left the house and helped her two sons, ages ten and six, into the Expedition for the trip to school. Her mother-in-law's vehicle was parked behind her, so Maria backed her mother-in-law's vehicle into the street, then backed her Expedition out of the driveway and parked on the street. She left the keys to her truck in the ignition with the motor running while she parked her mother-in-law's car back in the driveway and reentered the house to return her mother-in-law's keys.

After Chambers saw Maria park the Expedition on the street and return to the house, it took him only thirty seconds to back his tow truck to the Expedition, hook it to his truck, and drive away. Chambers did not leave his own vehicle to perform this operation, and it is undisputed that he did not know the Chapa children were inside. When Maria emerged from the house, the Expedition, with her children, was gone. Maria began screaming, telephoned 911, and called her husband at work to tell him the children were gone.

Meanwhile, on an adjacent street, Chambers noticed that the Expedition's wheels were turning, indicating to him that the vehicle's engine was running. He stopped the tow truck and heard a sound from the Expedition. Looking inside, he discovered the two Chapa children. After he persuaded one of the boys to unlock the vehicle, Chambers drove the Expedition back to the Chapas' house. He returned the keys to Maria, who was outside her house, crying. By the time emergency personnel and Carlos Chapa arrived, the children were back home and Chambers had left the scene.

Maria testified that the incident caused her to have an anxiety attack, including chest pain and numbness in her arm. She states she has continued to experience panic attacks and has been diagnosed with an anxiety disorder. In addition, both Carlos and Maria have been diagnosed with post-traumatic stress disorder.

* * *

The Chapas first argue that the trial court erred in granting summary judgment against them on their claim that appellees are liable under [UCC] section 9.609. This statute provides in pertinent part:

(a) After default, a secured party:
(1) may take possession of the collateral;
(b) A secured party may proceed under Subsection (a):
* * *
(2) without judicial process, if it proceeds without breach of the peace. [Citation.]

The Chapas correctly point out that this statute imposes a duty on secured creditors to take precautions for public safety when repossessing property. [Citation.] Thus, the creditor who elects to pursue nonjudical repossession assumes the risk that a breach of the peace might occur. [Citation.] A secured creditor "remains liable for breaches of the peace committed by its independent contractor." [Citation.] Thus, a creditor cannot escape liability by hiring an independent contractor to repossess secured property.

The Chapas assert that FMCC and Traciers, who employed Chambers as a repossession agent, are liable for any physical or mental injuries sustained by Carlos and Maria as a result of Chambers's breach of the peace. But this argument presupposes that a breach of peace occurred. * * *

* * *

Most frequently, the expression "breach of the peace" as used in the Uniform Commercial Code "connotes conduct that incites or is likely to incite immediate public turbulence, or that leads to or is likely to lead to an immediate loss of public order and tranquility." [Citations.] ("[S]ecured creditor, in exercising privilege to enter upon premises of another to repossess collateral, may not perpetrate '[a]ny act or action manifesting force or violence, or naturally calculated to provide a breach of peace') [[Citations.] ("[A]lthough actual violence is not required to find 'breach of the peace,' within meaning of self-help repossession statute, disturbance or violence must be reasonably likely, and not merely a remote possibility."); [Citation.] (no breach of peace when vehicle repossessed from public street while debtor inside house). In addition, "[b]reach of the peace … refers to conduct at or near and/or incident to seizure of property." [Citations.] ("[E]ven in attempted repossession of a chattel off a street, parking lot or unenclosed space, if repossession is verbally or otherwise contested at actual time of and in immediate vicinity of attempted repossession by defaulting party or other person in control of chattel, secured party must desist and pursue his remedy in court.")

Here, there is no evidence that Chambers proceeded with the attempted repossession over an objection communicated to him at, near, or incident to the seizure of the property. To the contrary, Chambers immediately "desisted" repossession efforts and peaceably returned the vehicle and the children when he learned of their presence. Moreover, Chambers actively avoided confrontation. By removing an apparently unoccupied vehicle from a public street when the driver was not present, he reduced the likelihood of violence or other public disturbance.

In sum, the Chapas have not identified and we have not found any case in which the repossession of a vehicle from a public street, without objection or confrontation, has been held to constitute a breach of the peace. [Citation.] (deputy sheriff did not breach the peace when he repossessed debtor's truck because, even if he violated traffic regulation when he drove away, he did so before debtor had an opportunity to confront him); [Citation.] (no breach of the peace occurred when repossession from parking lot was not verbally or otherwise contested). We therefore conclude that Chambers's conduct did not violate a duty imposed by [UCC] section 9.609.

* * *

We therefore affirm the judgment of the trial court.

## CASE 38-4

### Nature and Formation/Personal Defenses of Surety
### AMERICAN MANUFACTURING MUTUAL INSURANCE COMPANY v. TISON HOG MARKET, INC.

United States Court of Appeals, Eleventh Circuit, 1999
182 F.3d 1284, cert. denied, 531 U.S. 819, 121 S.Ct. 59, 148 L.Ed.2d 26 (2000)
http://www.law.emory.edu/11circuit/aug99/98-8506.man.html

**Cox, J.**

Plaintiff American Manufacturing Mutual Insurance Company ("American") filed this action seeking a declaratory judgment that it was not liable to the defendant creditors on two surety bonds. The district court entered summary judgment in American's favor and the defendants appeal. For the reasons that follow, we vacate and remand.

The Packers and Stockyards Act of 1921, [citation], (the "PSA") and its implementing regulations require that every livestock dealer execute and maintain a reasonable bond to secure the performance of its obligations. [Citation.] The PSA's bonding requirement was designed "to safeguard the farmers and ranchers who produce cattle against the losses they would suffer if they sold their livestock to insolvent or defaulting purchasers." [Citation.]

Two livestock dealers, Thurston Paulk, d/b/a Paulk Livestock Company ("Paulk Livestock"), and Coffee County Stockyard, Incorporated ("Coffee County Livestock"), applied to American to serve as a surety and issue bonds for them to meet the PSA's requirements. The applications for both bonds contained agreements to indemnify American for any losses that it might incur as a result of their issuance. The principal on the first bond was Thurston Paulk, d/b/a Paulk Livestock. The application was signed by Thurston Paulk in his role as the sole proprietor of Paulk Livestock. The indemnification agreement contained the purported signatures of Thurston Paulk, Betty Paulk, and a witness. The principal on the second bond was Coffee County Livestock. The application contained the signature of Thurston Paulk in his role as president of Coffee County Livestock. The indemnification agreement contained the purported signatures of Thurston Paulk, Betty Paulk, Ashley Paulk, and a witness. American relied upon the information contained in the forms and the alleged genuineness of the signatures in making the decision to issue the bonds.

After the bonds were issued, Paulk Livestock and Coffee County Livestock purchased numerous hogs from defendants Tison Hog Market, Inc.; Gainesville Livestock Market, Inc.; Madison Hog Market, Inc., d/b/a Townsend Livestock Market; South Carolina Farm Bureau Marketing Association; and Georgia Farm Bureau Marketing Association, Inc. When the defendant hog sellers did not receive payment for the hogs, they made claims against the surety bonds for the purchase money that they were due. * * *

American conducted an investigation and learned that the bonds' indemnification agreements contained forged signatures. In particular, American discovered evidence suggesting that: (1) Ashley Paulk had not signed or authorized anyone to sign his name to the Coffee County Livestock bond indemnification agreement; and (2) Betty Paulk had not signed or authorized anyone to sign her name to either bond's indemnification agreement. American claimed that it would not have issued the bonds had it known that Betty and Ashley Paulk had not agreed to indemnify it, and it declared the bonds rescinded and returned all the premiums.

American then brought this action seeking a declaratory judgment relieving it from liability to the defendants on the ground that the bonds were void * * * under Georgia insurance law due to the fraudulent and material misrepresentations of the bonds' principals. American argued that the principals had forged the signatures of Betty and Ashley Paulk on the indemnification agreements in order to induce it into issuing the bond * * *. [The defendants] argued that Georgia insurance law did not apply to the surety contracts at issue in this case and that under both federal and Georgia surety law, American was still liable on the bonds.

Cross motions for summary judgment were filed. The district court granted American's motion for summary judgment and denied those filed by the defendants * * *. Then, applying Georgia insurance law, it concluded that the bonds were void * * *.

The ultimate issue presented by this appeal is whether a surety in Georgia is liable on its bond to creditors when the principal fraudulently induces the surety to issue the bond. The defendants argue that American is still liable on the bonds under general surety law because fraud committed by a principal alone in inducing a surety to issue a surety bond does not release the surety from liability. * * *

* * *

It is well established under the common law of suretyship that "fraud or misrepresentation practiced by the principal alone on the surety, without any knowledge or participation on the part of the creditor or obligee, in inducing the surety to enter into the suretyship contract will not affect the liability of the surety." [Citations.] From a practical standpoint, this common law treatment of a principal's fraud is the only one that makes sense. A creditor does business with a principal in reliance upon the existence of a bond. The bond provides security for the creditor because normally the creditor would have no way of knowing whether the principal is insolvent or otherwise an unreliable party with which to engage in business. [Citation.] If the creditor's ability to recover on a bond was dependent on the accuracy of the principal's representations to the surety, then the value of the bond to the creditor would be greatly lessened because the creditor would have no way of knowing what representations were made in the procurement of the bond. More importantly for the case at bar, this common law approach * * * enables a livestock seller to deal freely with livestock dealers knowing that the required bond will protect them in the event of a default even if the principal hid facts from the surety when obtaining the bond.

* * *

Instead of applying * * * insurance law, however, the district court should have applied Georgia surety law. The surety bonds in this case are surety contracts that are not governed exclusively by the insurance law of Georgia. * * *

The Georgia Code contains an entirely separate title that applies to suretyship contracts. [Citation.] The chapter defines a contract of suretyship as one "whereby a person obligates himself to pay the debt of another in consideration of a benefit flowing to the surety * * * " [citation]. This is the commonly understood definition of a surety relationship and describes the situation that we have in the case at bar. The Georgia Code does not contain a statement as to the effect of a principal's fraud on a surety's liability to the creditor. Georgia courts, however, have applied the common law and held that a surety is still liable to a creditor even if the principal commits fraud so long as the creditor does not participate in the fraud. [Citation.] * * *

Applying the common law to the case at bar, there is no evidence that the defendants participated in any fraud. The fraud was committed solely by the principals. Under these circumstances, American is not relieved of liability on the bonds.

[Citation.] * * *

## QUESTIONS

1. Name and define the various kinds of collateral.
2. Explain the purpose, methods, and requirements of attachment and perfection.
3. Discuss the priorities among the various parties who may have competing interests in collateral and the rights and remedies of the parties to a security agreement after default by the debtor.
4. Explain the requirements for the formation of a suretyship relationship.
5. Explain the rights of a creditor against a surety and the rights of a surety, including those of a cosurety.

## PROBLEMS

**1.** Victor sells to Bonnie a refrigerator for $600 payable in monthly installments of $30 for twenty months. Bonnie signs a security agreement granting Victor a security interest in the refrigerator. The refrigerator is installed in the kitchen of Bonnie's apartment. There is no filing of any financing statement. Assume that after Bonnie has made the first three monthly payments:

**(a)** Bonnie moves from her apartment and sells the refrigerator in place to the new occupant for $350 cash. What are the rights of Victor?

**(b)** Bonnie is adjudicated bankrupt, and her trustee in bankruptcy claims the refrigerator. What are the rights of the parties?

**2.** On January 2, Burt asked Logan to loan him money "against my diamond ring." Logan agreed to do so. To guard against intervening liens, Logan received permission to file a financing statement, and Burt and Logan signed a security agreement giving Logan an interest in the ring. Burt also signed a financing statement, which Logan properly filed on January 3. On January 4, Burt borrowed money from Tillo, pledging his ring to secure the debt. Tillo took possession of the ring and paid Burt the money on the same day. The next day, January 5, Logan loaned Burt the money under the assumption that Burt still had the ring. Who has priority, Logan or Tillo? Explain.

**3.** Joanna takes a security interest in the equipment in Jason Store and files a financing statement claiming "equipment and all after-acquired equipment." Berkeley later sells Jason Store a cash register taking a security interest in the register and (a) files nine days after Jason receives the register, or (b) files twenty-five days after Jason receives the register. If Jason fails to pay both Joanna and Berkeley and they foreclose their security interests, who has priority on the cash register? Explain.

**4.** Finley Motor Company sells an automobile to Sara and retains a security interest in it. The automobile is insured, and Finley is named beneficiary. Three days after the automobile is totally destroyed in an accident, Sara files a petition in bankruptcy. As between Finley and Sara's trustee in bankruptcy, who is entitled to the insurance proceeds?

**5.** On September 5, Wanda, a widow who occasionally teaches piano and organ in her home, purchased an electric organ from Murphy's music store for $4,800, trading in her old organ for $1,200 and promising in writing to pay the balance at $120 per month and granting to Murphy a security interest in the property in terms consistent with and incorporating provisions of the Uniform Commercial Code. A financing statement covering the transaction was also properly filled out and signed, and Murphy properly filed it. After Wanda failed to make the December or January payments, Murphy went to her home to collect the payments or take the organ. Finding no one home and the door unlocked, he went in and took the organ. Two hours later, Tia, a third party and the present occupant of the house, who had purchased the organ for her own use, stormed into Murphy's store, demanding the return of the organ. She showed Murphy a bill of sale from Wanda to her, dated December 15, that listed the organ and other furnishings in the house.

**(a)** What are the rights of Murphy, Tia, and Wanda?

**(b)** Would your answer change if Murphy had not filed a financing statement? Why?

**(c)** Would your answer change if the organ had been principally used to give lessons?

**6.** On May 1, Lincoln lends Donaldson $200,000 and receives from Donaldson his agreement to pay this amount in two years and takes a security interest in the machinery and equipment in

Donaldson's factory. A proper financing statement is filed with respect to the security agreement. On August 1, upon Lincoln's request, Donaldson executes an addendum to the security agreement covering after-acquired machinery and equipment in Donaldson's factory. A second financing statement covering the addendum is filed. In September, Donaldson acquires $50,000 worth of new equipment from Thompson, which Donaldson installs in his factory. In December, Carter, a judgment creditor of Donaldson, causes an attachment to issue against the new equipment. What are the rights of Lincoln, Donaldson, Carter, and Thompson? What can the parties do to best protect themselves?

**7.** Anita bought a television set from Bertrum for her personal use. Bertrum, who was out of security agreement forms, showed Anita a form he had executed with Nathan, another consumer. Anita and Bertrum orally agreed to the terms of the form. Anita subsequently defaulted on payment, and Bertrum sought to repossess the television.

**(a)** Explain who would prevail.

**(b)** Explain whether the result would differ if Bertrum had filed a financing statement.

**(c)** Explain whether the result would differ if Anita had subsequently sent Bertrum an e-mail that met all the requirements of an effective security agreement.

**8.** Aaron bought a television set for personal use from Penny. Aaron properly signed a security agreement and paid Penny $125 down, as their agreement required. Penny did not file, and subsequently Aaron sold the television for $800 to Clark, his neighbor, for use in Clark's hotel lobby.

**(a)** When Aaron fails to make the January and February payments, may Penny repossess the television from Clark?

**(b)** What if, instead of Aaron's selling the television set to Clark, a judgment creditor levied (sought possession) on the television? Who would prevail?

**(c)** What if Clark intended to use the television set in his home? Who would prevail?

**9.** Jones bought a used car from the A–Herts Car Rental System, which regularly sold its used equipment at the end of its fiscal year. First National Bank of Roxboro had previously obtained a perfected security interest in the car based upon its financing of A–Herts's automobiles. Upon A–Herts's failure to pay, First National is seeking to repossess the car from Jones. Does First National have an enforceable security interest in the car against Jones? Explain.

**10.** Standridge purchased a Chevrolet automobile from Billy Deavers, an agent of Walker Motor Company. According to the sales contract, the balance due after the trade-in allowance was $282.50, to be paid in twelve weekly installments. Standridge claims that he was unable to make the second payment and that Billy Deavers orally agreed that he could make two payments the next week. The day after the double payment was due, Standridge still had not paid. That day, Ronnie Deavers, Billy's brother, went to Standridge's place of employment to repossess the car, which the Walker Motor contract permitted. Rather than consenting to the repossession, Standridge drove the car to the Walker Motor Company's place of business and tendered the overdue payments. The Deaverses refused to accept the late payment and instead demanded the entire unpaid balance. Standridge could not pay it. The Deaverses then blocked Standridge's car with another car and told him he could just "walk his home." Standridge brought suit, seeking damages for the Deavers's wrongful repossession of his car. The Deaverses deny that they granted Standridge permission to make a double payment, that Standridge tendered the double payment, and that they rejected it. They claim that he made no payment and that, therefore, they were entitled to repossess the car. Discuss whether the car was properly repossessed.

**11.** National Cash Register Company (NCR), a manufacturer of cash registers, entered into a sales contract for a cash register with Edmund Carroll. On November 18, Firestone and Company made a loan to Carroll, who conveyed certain property to Firestone as collateral under a security agreement. The property outlined in the security agreement included "[a]ll contents of luncheonette including equipment such as … 'twenty-five different listed items,' … together with all property and articles now, and which may hereafter be, used … with, [or] added … to … any of the foregoing described property." A similarly detailed description of the property conveyed as collateral appeared in Firestone's financing statement, but the financing statement made no mention of property to be acquired thereafter, and neither document made a specific reference to a cash register. NCR delivered the cash register to Carroll in Canton between November 19 and November 25 and filed a financing statement with the town clerk of Canton on December 20 and with the Secretary of State on December 21. Carroll subsequently defaulted both on the contract with NCR and on the security agreement with Firestone. Firestone took possession of the cash register and sold it at auction. Discuss whether Firestone has a security interest in the cash register.

**12.** National Acceptance Company loaned Ultra Precision Industries $692,000, and to secure repayment of the loan Ultra executed a chattel mortgage security agreement on National's behalf on March 7, 2008. National perfected the security interest by timely filing a financing statement. Although the security interest covered specifically described equipment of Ultra, both the security agreement and the financing statement contained an after-acquired property clause that did not refer to any specific equipment.

Later in 2008 and in 2009, Ultra placed three separate orders for machines from Wolf Machinery Company. In each case it was agreed that after the machines had been shipped to Ultra and installed, Ultra would be given an opportunity to test them in operation for a reasonable period. If the machines passed inspection, Wolf would then provide financing that was satisfactory to Ultra. In all three cases, financing was arranged with Community Bank (Bank) and accepted, and a security interest was given in the machines. Furthermore, in each case a security agreement was entered into, and a financing statement was then filed by the secured parties within ten days. Ultra became bankrupt on October 7, 2011. National claimed that its security interest in the after-acquired machines should take priority over those of Wolf and Bank because their interests were not perfected by timely filed financing statements. Discuss who has priority in the disputed collateral.

**13.** Allen, Barker, and Cooper are cosureties on a $750,000 loan by Durham National Bank to Kingston Manufacturing Co., Inc. The maximum liability of the sureties is as follows: Allen, $750,000; Barker, $300,000; and Cooper, $150,000. If Kingston defaults on the entire $750,000 loan, what are the liabilities of Allen, Barker, and Cooper?

**14.** Peter Diamond owed Carter $500,000 secured by a first mortgage on Diamond's plant and land. Stephens was a surety on this obligation in the amount of $250,000. After Diamond defaulted on the debt, Carter demanded and received payment of $250,000 from Stephens. Carter then foreclosed upon the mortgage and sold the property for $375,000. What rights, if any, does Stephens have in the proceeds from the sale of the property?
**15.** Paula Daniels purchased an automobile from Carey on credit. At the time of the sale, Scott agreed to be a surety for Paula, who is sixteen years old. The automobile's odometer stated fifty-two thousand miles, but Carey had turned it back from seventy-two thousand miles. Paula refuses to make any payments due on the car. Carey proceeds against Paula and Scott. What defenses, if any, are available to (a) Paula and (b) Scott?
**16.** Stafford Surety Co. agreed to act as the conditional guarantor of collection on a debt owed by Preston Decker to Cole. Stafford was paid a premium by Preston to serve as surety. Preston defaults on the obligation. What are Cole's rights against Stafford Surety Co.?
**17.** Campbell loaned Perry Dixon $7,000, which was secured by a possessory security interest in stock owned by Perry. The stock had a market value of $4,000. In addition, Campbell insisted that Perry obtain a surety. For a premium, Sutton Surety Co. agreed to act as a surety for the full amount of the loan. Prior to the due date of the loan, Perry convinced Campbell to return the stock because its value had increased and he wished to sell it to realize the gain. Campbell released the stock and Perry subsequently defaulted. Is Sutton released from his liability?
**18.** Pamela Darden owed Clark $5,000 on an unsecured loan. On May 1, Pamela approached Clark for an additional loan of $3,000. Clark agreed to make the loan only if Pamela could obtain a surety. On May 5, Simpson agreed to be a surety on the $3,000 loan, which was granted that day. Both loans were due on October 1. On June 15, Pamela sent $1,000 to Clark but did not provide any instructions.

**(a)** What are Clark's rights?
**(b)** What are Simpson's rights?

**19.** Patrick Dillon applied for a $10,000 loan from Carlton Savings & Loan. Carlton required him to obtain a surety. Patrick approached Sinclair Surety Co., which insisted that Patrick provide it with a financial statement. Patrick did so, but the statement was materially false. In reliance upon the financial statement and in return for a premium, Sinclair agreed to act as surety. Upon Sinclair's commitment to act as surety, Carlton loaned Patrick the $10,000. After one payment of $400, Patrick defaulted. He then filed a voluntary petition in bankruptcy. Does Sinclair have any valid defense against Carlton?
**20.** On June 1, Smith contracted with Martin doing business as Martin Publishing Company to distribute Martin's newspapers and to account for the proceeds. As part of the contract, Smith agreed to furnish Martin a bond in the amount of $10,000 guaranteeing the payment of the proceeds. At the time the contract was executed and the credit extended, the bond was not furnished, and no mention was made as to the prospective sureties. On July 1, Smith signed the bond with Black and Blue signing as sureties. The bond recited the awarding of the contract for distribution of the newspapers as consideration for the bond.

On December 1, payment was due from Smith to Martin for the sum of $3,600 under the distributor's contract. Demand for payment was made, but Smith failed to make payment. As a result, Martin brought an appropriate action against Black and Blue to recover the $3,600. What result?
**21.** Diggitt Construction Company was the low bidder on a well-digging job for the Village of Drytown. On April 15, Diggitt signed a contract with Drytown for the job at a price of $40,000. At the same time, pursuant to the notice of bidding, Diggitt prevailed upon Ace Surety Company to execute a performance bond indemnifying Drytown on the contract. On May 1, after Diggitt had put in three days on the job, the president of the company refigured his bid and realized that if his company were to complete the job it would lose $10,000. Accordingly, Diggitt notified Drytown that it was canceling the contract, effective immediately. What are the rights and duties of Ace Surety Company?
**22.** Elizabeth Tilleraas received three student loans totaling $3,500 under the Federal Insured Student Loan Program (FISLP) of the Higher Education Act. These loans were secured by three promissory notes executed in favor of Dakota National Bank & Trust Co., Fargo, North Dakota. Under the terms of these student loans, periodic payments were required beginning twelve months after Tilleraas ceased to carry at least one-half of a full-time academic workload at an eligible institution. Her student status terminated on January 28, 2007, and the first installment payment thus became due January 28, 2008. She never made any payment on any of her loans. Under the provisions of the FISLP, the United States assured the lender bank repayment in the event of any failure to pay by the borrower. The first payment due on the loans was in "default" on July 27, 2008, 180 days after the failure to make the first installment payment. On December 17, 2009, Dakota National Bank & Trust sent notice of its election under the provisions of the loan to accelerate the maturity of the note. The bank demanded payment in full by December 27, 2009. It then filed FISLP insurance claims against the United States on May 6, 2010, and assigned the three Tilleraas notes to the United States on May 10, 2010. The government, in turn, paid the bank's claim in full on July 5, 2010. The government subsequently filed suit against Tilleraas. Discuss whether the United States will prevail.
**23.** New West Fruit Corporation (New West) and Coastal Berry Corporation are both brokers of fresh strawberries. In the second half of 2009, New West's predecessor, Monc's Consolidated Produce, Inc., loaned money and strawberry plants to a group of strawberry growers known as Cooperativa La Paz (La Paz). In September 2009, Monc's and La Paz signed a "Sales and Marketing Agreement" to allow Monc's the exclusive right to market the strawberries grown by La Paz during the 2009–2011 season. The agreement did not mention the advances of money or plants, but did give Monc's a security interest in all crops and proceeds on specified property in the 2010–2011 season. The financing statement was properly signed and filed. Monc's closed down in January 2011, and its assets were assigned to New West. In April, New West learned that La Paz had agreed to market its 2011 crop through Coastal Berry. New West immediately arranged a meeting to advise the Coastal Berry officers of its contract with the growers. New West requested that Coastal Berry either pay New West the amounts owed by the growers or allow New West to market the

berries to recover the money. Coastal Berry did not respond. After Coastal Berry began marketing the berries, New West sent letters demanding payment of the proceeds. In August 2011, New West filed suit against Coastal Berry, La Paz, the individual growers, and a berry freezing company that its security interest was valid and that it had duly notified Coastal Berry both through the financing statement on file and through the letters it had sent to Coastal Berry directly. Coastal Berry claimed that the security agreement was not effective because it did not specifically identify the debt (money and plants) being secured. Discuss.

**24.** James Koontz purchased a Plymouth Sundance from Chrysler Credit Corporation (Chrysler) in exchange for sixty payments of $185.92. Koontz soon defaulted, and Chrysler notified Koontz that, unless he made the payments, it would repossess the vehicle. Koontz responded by notifying Chrysler that he would make every effort to make up missed payments, that he did not want the car repossessed, and that Chrysler was not to enter his private property to repossess the vehicle. A few weeks later, Chrysler sent the M & M Agency to repossess the vehicle. Koontz, dressed only in his underwear, came outside and yelled, "Don't take it!" The repossessor ignored him and took the car anyway. Koontz did not physically challenge or threaten the repossessor. Discuss whether Chrysler legally repossessed the automobile.

# CHAPTER 39
# Bankruptcy

A debt is an obligation to pay money owed by a debtor to a creditor. Debts are created daily by countless purchasers of goods at the consumer level; by retailers of goods in buying merchandise from a manufacturer, wholesaler, or distributor; by borrowers of funds from various lending institutions; and through the issuance and sale of bonds and other types of debt securities. Multitudes of business transactions are entered into daily on a credit basis. Commercial activity would be restricted greatly if credit were not readily obtainable or if needed funds were unavailable for lending.

Fortunately, most debts are paid when due, thus justifying the extension of credit and encouraging its continuation. Although defaults may create credit and collection problems, the total amount in default normally represents a very small percentage of the total amount of outstanding indebtedness. Nevertheless, financial crises and business misfortune confront both individuals and businesses. Both may accumulate debts that exceed their total assets. Conversely, their assets may exceed their total indebtedness but be in such nonliquid form that these debtors are unable to pay their debts as they become due. For businesses as well as individuals, relief from overly burdensome debt and from the threat of impending lawsuits by creditors is frequently necessary for economic survival.

The conflict between creditor rights and debtor relief has engendered various solutions, such as voluntary adjustments and compromises requiring installment payments to creditors over a period of time during which they agree to withhold legal action. Other voluntary methods include compositions and assignments of assets by a debtor to a trustee or assignee for the benefit of creditors, who sometimes also file for equity receiverships or insolvency proceedings in a State court, pursuant to statute. Nonetheless, the most adaptable and frequently employed method of debtor relief—one that also affords protection to creditors—is a proceeding in a Federal court under Federal bankruptcy law.

## FEDERAL BANKRUPTCY LAW

The most important method of protecting creditor rights and granting debtor relief is Federal bankruptcy law, which is largely statutory and involves court supervision. U.S. bankruptcy law serves a dual purpose: (1) to effect a quick, equitable distribution of the debtor's property among her creditors, and (2) to discharge the debtor from her debts, enabling her to rehabilitate herself and start afresh. Other purposes are to provide uniform treatment of similarly situated creditors, preserve existing business relations, and stabilize commercial usages.

The Constitution of the United States provides that "the Congress shall have power … to establish … uniform Laws on the subject of Bankruptcies throughout the United States." Article I, Section 8, clause 4. Federal bankruptcy law has generally superseded State insolvency laws.

The U.S. Bankruptcy Abuse Prevention and Consumer Protection Act of 2005 (2005 Act) contains the most extensive amendments to Federal bankruptcy law since 1978. The U.S. Bankruptcy Code consists of eight odd-numbered chapters and one even-numbered chapter. Chapters 7, 9, 11, 12, and 13 provide five different types of proceedings; Chapters 1, 3, and 5 apply to all of those proceedings unless otherwise specified. **Straight**, or ordinary, **bankruptcy** (Chapter 7) provides for the liquidation of the debtor's property, whereas the other proceedings provide for the **reorganization** and adjustment of the debtor's debts and, in the case of a business debtor, the continuance of the debtor's business. In reorganization cases the creditors usually look to the debtor's future earnings, whereas in liquidation cases the creditors look to the debtor's property at the commencement of the bankruptcy proceeding. Chapters 7, 11, 12, and 13 have provisions governing conversion of a case under that chapter to another chapter. The 2005 Act added Chapter 15 to the Bankruptcy Code for cross-border insolvency cases. Chapter 1 and certain sections of Chapters 3 and 5 apply to proceedings under Chapter 15.

1. Chapter 7 applies to *all* debtors, with the exception of railroads, insurance companies, banks, savings and loan associations, homestead associations, licensed small business investment companies, and credit unions. (In the past several years, 60 to 75 percent of bankruptcies have been filed under Chapter 7.) Moreover, Chapter 7 has special provisions for liquidating the estates of stockbrokers and commodity brokers.
2. Chapter 11 applies to railroads and any person who may be a debtor under Chapter 7 (except a stockbroker or a commodity broker). (Less than 1 percent of bankruptcies are filed under Chapter 11.)
3. Chapter 9 applies only to municipalities that are generally authorized to be debtors under that chapter, that are insolvent, and that desire to effect plans to adjust their debts.
4. Chapter 12 applies to individuals, or individuals and their spouses, who are engaged in farming if 50 percent of their gross income is from farming, their aggregate debts do not exceed $3,792,650, and at least 50 percent of their debts arise out of farming operations. (Less than one-tenth of 1 percent of bankruptcies are filed under Chapter 12.) Corporations or partnerships also may qualify for Chapter 12. The 2005 Act made Chapter 12 permanent and extended its coverage to certain family fishermen if 50 percent of their gross income is from commercial fishing, their aggregate debts do not exceed $1,757,475, and at least 80 percent of their debts arise out of commercial fishing operations.
5. Chapter 13 applies to individuals with regular income who owe liquidated unsecured debts of less than $360,475 and secured debts of less than $1,081,400. (In the past several years, 25 to 39 percent of bankruptcies have been filed under Chapter 13.)
6. Chapter 15 covers cross-border (transnational) insolvencies and incorporates the Model Law on Cross-Border Insolvency, promulgated by the United Nations Commission on International Trade Law (UNCITRAL). These changes are intended to make cross-border filings easier to accomplish and provide greater predictability. Chapter 15 encourages cooperation between the United States and foreign countries with respect to transnational insolvency cases.

This text will not further cover Chapters 9, 12, and 15.

The 1994 amendments to the Bankruptcy Code require that every three years, beginning in 1998, the U.S. Judicial Conference adjust for inflation the dollar amounts of certain provisions, including eligibility for Chapters 12 and 13, requirements for filing involuntary cases, priorities, exemptions, and exceptions to discharge. Section 104.

The Bankruptcy Code grants to U.S. district courts original and exclusive jurisdiction over all bankruptcy cases and original, but not exclusive, jurisdiction over civil proceedings arising under bankruptcy cases. The district court must, however, abstain from related matters that, except for their relationship to a bankruptcy, could not have been brought in a Federal court. The district court in which a bankruptcy case is commenced has exclusive jurisdiction over all of the debtor's property. In addition, within each Federal district court the Bankruptcy Code establishes a bankruptcy court staffed by bankruptcy judges. Bankruptcy courts are authorized to hear certain matters specified by the Bankruptcy Code and to enter appropriate orders and judgments subject to review by the district court or, where established, by a panel of three bankruptcy judges. The Federal Circuit Court of Appeals has jurisdiction over appeals from the district court or panel. In all other matters, unless the parties agree otherwise, only the district court may issue final order or judgment based upon proposed findings of fact and conclusions of law submitted to the court by the bankruptcy judge.

The U.S. trustees are government officials appointed by the U.S. Attorney General with administrative responsibilities in bankruptcy cases in almost all of the districts. For example, the U.S. trustee selects bankruptcy trustees and, in Chapter 11 proceedings, appoints the members of the unsecured creditors' committee. The 2005 Act gives the U.S. trustees added responsibilities in a number of areas.

## CASE ADMINISTRATION—CHAPTER 3

Chapter 3 of the Bankruptcy Code contains provisions dealing with the commencement of a case in bankruptcy, the meetings of creditors, the officers who administer the case, and the administrative powers of those officers.

### COMMENCEMENT OF THE CASE

The filing of a voluntary or involuntary petition commences a bankruptcy case, thereby beginning the jurisdiction of the bankruptcy court and the operation of the bankruptcy laws.

**Voluntary Petitions** More than 99 percent of all bankruptcy petitions are filed voluntarily. Any person eligible to be a debtor under a given bankruptcy proceeding may file a voluntary petition under that chapter and need *not* be insolvent to do so. Commencing a voluntary case by filing a petition constitutes an automatic **order for relief**. The petition must include a list of all creditors (secured and unsecured), a list of all property the debtor owns, a list of property that the debtor claims to be exempt, and a statement of the debtor's affairs.

The 2005 Act added a requirement that all individual debtors receive credit counseling from an approved nonprofit budget and credit counseling agency within the 180-day period *before* filing the petition. This requirement does not apply to a debtor who (1) is exempted by the court, or (2) resides in a district for which the U.S. trustee or the bankruptcy administrator determines that approved nonprofit budget and credit counseling agencies are not reasonably able to provide adequate services to the additional individuals who would seek required credit counseling. The role of the credit counseling agencies is to analyze the client's current financial condition, the factors that caused the financial distress, and how the client can develop a plan to respond to these problems. Section 109(h).

**Involuntary Petitions** An involuntary petition in bankruptcy may be filed only under Chapter 7 (liquidation) or Chapter 11 (reorganization). It may be filed (1) by three or more creditors who have undisputed unsecured claims that total $14,425 or more, or (2) if the debtor has fewer than twelve creditors, by one or more creditors whose total unsecured claims equal $14,425 or more. Section 303(b). An involuntary petition may not be filed against a farmer or against a banking, insurance, or nonprofit corporation. Section 303(a).

Like a voluntary petition, the filing of an involuntary petition commences a case, but unlike a voluntary petition, it does *not* operate as an order for relief. The debtor has the right to answer. If the debtor does not timely contest the involuntary petition, the court will enter an order for relief against the debtor. If the debtor timely opposes the petition, however, the court may enter an order of relief only (1) if the debtor is generally not paying his undisputed debts as they become due, or (2) if, within 120 days before the filing of the petition, a custodian assignee or general receiver was appointed or took possession of substantially all of the debtor's property. Section 303(h).

If an involuntary petition is contested successfully by the debtor and dismissed by the court, Section 303(i) empowers the court to grant a judgment in favor of the debtor against the petitioning creditors for (1) costs, (2) reasonable attorneys' fees, and (3) damages proximately caused by the trustee's taking possession of the debtor's property. Moreover, if the petition was filed in bad faith, the court may award damages proximately caused by the filing or punitive damages.

If the court orders relief, the debtor must provide the court with schedules the same as those provided by a voluntary petitioner.

## DISMISSAL

The court may dismiss a Chapter 7 case for cause after notice and a hearing. Section 707(a). In a case filed by an individual debtor whose debts are primarily consumer debts, the court may dismiss the case, or with the debtor's consent, convert the case to one under Chapter 11 or 13, if the court finds that granting relief would be an abuse of the provisions of Chapter 7. Section 707(b). A court can find abuse in one of two ways: (1) on general grounds based on whether the debtor filed the petition in bad faith or the totality of the circumstances of the debtor's financial situation demonstrates abuse, or (2) on an unrebutted presumption of abuse based on the means test established by the 2005 Act. The means test will be discussed later in this chapter.

Under Chapter 11, the court may dismiss a case for cause after notice and a hearing. Section 1112(b). Under Chapter 13, the debtor has an absolute right to have his case dismissed. Under Chapter 13, if a motion to dismiss is filed by an interested party other than the debtor, the court may dismiss the case only for cause after notice and a hearing.

## AUTOMATIC STAYS

The filing of a voluntary or involuntary petition operates as a **stay** (i.e., restraint against) all creditors beginning or continuing to recover claims against the debtor, or creating, perfecting, or enforcing liens against property of the debtor. Section 362. This stay applies to both secured and unsecured creditors, although a secured creditor may petition the court to terminate the stay as to her security upon showing that she lacks adequate protection in the secured property. An automatic stay ends when the bankruptcy case is closed or dismissed or when the debtor receives a discharge.

## TRUSTEES

In a bankruptcy proceeding, the trustee represents the debtor's estate and has the capacity to sue and be sued on behalf of the estate. In proceedings under Chapter 7, trustees are selected by a vote of the creditors. The 1994 amendments allow the creditors to elect a trustee in a Chapter 11 proceeding if the court orders the appointment of a trustee for cause. In Chapter 13, the trustee is appointed. Under Chapter 7, the trustee is responsible for collecting, liquidating, and distributing the debtor's estate. Her duties and powers in fulfilling these responsibilities include the following: (1) to collect the property of the estate; (2) to challenge certain transfers of property of the estate; (3) to use, sell, or lease property of the estate; (4) to deposit or invest money of the estate; (5) to employ attorneys, accountants, appraisers, or auctioneers; (6) to assume or reject any executory contract or unexpired lease of the debtor; (7) to object to creditors' claims that are improper; and (8) to oppose, if advisable, the debtor's discharge. Trustees under Chapters 11 and 13 perform some but not all of the duties of a Chapter 7 trustee.

## MEETINGS OF CREDITORS

Within a reasonable time after relief is ordered, a meeting of creditors must be held. The court may not attend this meeting. The debtor must appear and submit to an examination by creditors and the trustee with respect to his financial situation. In a proceeding under Chapter 7, qualified creditors at this meeting elect a permanent trustee.

## CREDITORS, THE DEBTOR, AND THE ESTATE—CHAPTER 5

### CREDITORS

The Bankruptcy Code defines a **creditor** as any entity having a claim against the debtor that arose at the time of or before the order for relief. A **claim** means a "right to payment whether or not such right is reduced to judgment, liquidated, unliquidated, fixed, contingent, matured, unmatured, disputed, undisputed, legal, equitable, secured, or unsecured." Section 101(5).

**Proof of Claims** Creditors wishing to participate in the distribution of the debtor's estate may file a proof of claim. If a creditor does not do so in a timely manner, then the debtor or trustee may file a proof of such claim. Section 501. The debtor thereby may prevent a claim from becoming nondischargeable. Filed claims are allowed unless a party in interest objects. If an objection is made, the court determines, after a hearing, the amount and validity of the claim. The court may not allow any claim that (1) is unenforceable against the debtor or his property, (2) is for unmatured interest, or (3) is for insider or attorney services in excess of the reasonable value of such services. Section 502. An **insider** includes a relative or general partner of a debtor as well as a partnership in which the debtor is a general partner or a corporation of which the debtor is a director, officer, or person in control. Section 101(31).

**Secured and Unsecured Claims** A **lien** is a charge or interest in property to secure payment of a debt or performance of an obligation and must be satisfied before the property is available to satisfy the claims of unsecured creditors. An allowed claim of a creditor who has a lien on property of the estate is a *secured* claim to the extent of the value of the creditor's interest in the property. The creditor's claim is *unsecured* to the extent of the difference between the value of his secured interest and the allowed amount of his claim. Thus, if Andrew has an allowed claim of $5,000 against the estate of debtor Barbara and has a security interest in property of the estate that is valued at $3,000, Andrew has a secured claim in the amount of $3,000 and an unsecured claim for $2,000.

A lien or secured claim can arise by agreement, judicial proceeding, common law, or statute. Consensual security interests in personal property are governed by Article 9 of the Uniform Commercial Code (UCC) and are discussed in *Chapter 38*. Consensual security interests in real property, called mortgages or deeds of trust, are covered in *Chapter 50*. A **judicial lien** is obtained by a judgment, a levy, or some other legal or equitable process. The common law grants to certain creditors, including innkeepers and common carriers, a possessory lien on property of their debtors that is in the creditor's possession or on the creditor's premises. Finally, a number of Federal and State statutes grant liens to specified creditors.

**Priority of Claims** After secured claims have been satisfied, the remaining assets are distributed among creditors with unsecured claims. Certain classes of unsecured claims, however, have a **priority**, which means that they must be paid in full before any distribution is made to claims of lesser rank. Each claimant within a priority class shares *pro rata* if the assets are not sufficient to satisfy all claims in that class. The claims having a priority and the order of their priority, as provided in Section 507, are as follows:

1. *Domestic support obligations* (debts owed to a spouse, former spouse, or child of the debtor in the nature of alimony, maintenance, or support) subject to the expenses of a trustee in administering assets that otherwise can be used to pay support obligation.
2. *Expenses of administration* of the debtor's estate, including the filing fees paid by creditors in involuntary cases; the expenses of creditors in recovering concealed assets for the benefit of the bankrupt's estate; the trustee's necessary expenses; and reasonable compensation to receivers, trustees, and their attorneys, as allowed by the court.
3. Unsecured claims of *"gap" creditors*. These are claims in an involuntary case arising in the ordinary course of the debtor's business after the commencement of the case but before the earlier of either the appointment of the trustee or the entering of the order for relief.
4. Allowed, unsecured claims up to $11,725 for *wages, salaries, or commissions* earned within 180 days before the filing of the petition or before the date on which the debtor's business ceases, whichever comes first.
5. Allowed, unsecured claims for contributions to *employee benefit plans* arising from services rendered within 180 days before the filing of the petition or the cessation of the debtor's business, whichever occurs first, but limited to $11,725 multiplied by the number of employees covered by the plan, less the aggregate amount paid to such employees under number 3 above.
6. Allowed, unsecured claims up to $5,775 for *grain* or *fish producers* against a storage facility.
7. Allowed, unsecured claims up to $2,600 for *consumer deposits*; that is, moneys deposited in connection with the purchase, lease, or rental of property or the purchase of services for personal, family, or household use.
8. Specified income, property, employment, or excise *taxes* owed to governmental units.
9. Allowed claims for death or personal injuries resulting from the debtor's operation of a motor vehicle or vessel while legally intoxicated from using alcohol, a drug, or other substance.

After creditors with secured claims and creditors with claims having a priority have been satisfied, creditors with allowed, unsecured claims share proportionately in any remaining assets.

**Subordination of Claims** A subordination agreement is enforceable under the Bankruptcy Code to the same extent that it is enforceable under nonbankruptcy law. Section 510. In addition to statutory and contract priorities, the bankruptcy court can, at its discretion in proper cases, apply equitable priorities. Section 510. The court accomplishes this through the doctrine of subordination of claims, whereby, assuming two claims of equal statutory priority, the court declares that one claim must be paid in full before the other claim can be paid anything. Subordination is applied in cases in which allowing a claim in full would be unfair and inequitable to other creditors. (Allowing the inflated salary claims of officers in a closely held corporation would be an example.) In such cases, the court does not disallow the claim but merely orders that it be paid after all other claims are paid in full. For example, the claim of a parent corporation against its bankrupt subsidiary may be subordinated to the claims of other creditors of the subsidiary if the parent has so mismanaged the subsidiary to the detriment of its innocent creditors that this unconscionable conduct precludes the parent from seeking the aid of a bankruptcy court.

## DEBTORS

As previously indicated, the purpose of the Bankruptcy Code is to bring about an equitable distribution of the debtor's assets and to provide him a discharge. Accordingly, the Code explicitly subjects the debtor to specified duties while exempting some of his property and discharging most of his debts.

**Debtor's Duties** Under the Bankruptcy Code, the debtor must file a list of creditors, a schedule of assets and liabilities, a schedule of current income and expenditures, and a statement of her financial affairs. In any case in which a trustee is serving, the debtor must cooperate with the trustee and surrender to the trustee all property of the estate and all records relating to such property.

**Debtor's Exemptions** Section 522 of the Bankruptcy Code exempts specified property of an individual debtor from bankruptcy proceedings, including the following:

1. up to $21,625 in equity in property used as a residence or burial plot;
2. up to $3,450 in equity in one motor vehicle;
3. up to $550 for any particular item, and not to exceed $11,525 in aggregate value, of household furnishings, household goods, wearing apparel, appliances, books, animals, crops, or musical instruments that are primarily for personal, family, or household use;
4. up to $1,450 in jewelry;
5. any property up to $1,150 plus up to $10,825 of any unused amount of the first exemption;
6. up to $2,175 in implements, professional books, or tools of the debtor's trade;
7. unmatured life insurance contracts owned by the debtor, other than a credit life insurance contract;
8. professionally prescribed health aids;
9. social security, veteran's, and disability benefits;
10. unemployment compensation;
11. alimony and support payments, including child support;
12. payments from pension, profit-sharing, and annuity plans;
13. tax exempt retirement funds; and
14. payments from an award under a crime victim's reparation law, a wrongful death award, and up to $21,625, not including compensation for pain and suffering or for actual pecuniary loss, from a personal injury award.

In addition, the debtor may avoid judicial liens on any exempt property and nonpossessory, nonpurchase money security interests on certain household goods, tools of the trade, and professionally prescribed health aids.

The debtor has the option of using either the exemptions provided by the Bankruptcy Code or those available under State law. Nevertheless, a State may by specific legislative action limit its citizens to the exemptions provided by State law. More than three-quarters of the States have enacted such "opt out" legislation. The 2005 Act specifies that a debtor's exemption is governed by the law of the State where the debtor was domiciled for 730 days immediately before filing. If the debtor did not maintain a domicile in a single State for the 730-day period, then the governing law is of the State where the debtor was domiciled for 180 days immediately preceding the 730-day period (or for a longer portion of such 180-day period than in any other State).

Whether or not Federal or State exemptions apply, the 2005 Act provides that tax-exempt retirement accounts are exempt. Individual retirement accounts (IRAs) are subject to a $1,171,650 cap periodically adjusted for inflation. Nevertheless, the 2005 Act makes exempt property liable for nondischargeable domestic support obligations.

The 2005 Act also imposes limits on the use of State homestead exemptions. First, to the extent that the homestead was obtained through fraudulent conversion of nonexempt assets during the ten-year period before filing the petition, the exemption is reduced by that amount. Second, regardless of the level of the State exemption, a debtor may only exempt up to $146,450 of an interest in a homestead that was acquired during the 1,215-day period prior to the filing, but this limitation does not apply to any equity that has been transferred from the debtor's principal residence acquired more than 1,215 days before filing to the debtor's current principal residence if both residences are located in the same State. Third, a debtor may not exempt more than $146,450 if (1) the debtor has been convicted of a felony, which under the circumstances demonstrates that the filing of the case was an abuse of the Bankruptcy Code; or (2) the debtor owes a debt arising from (a) any violation of State or Federal securities laws; (b) fraud, deceit, or manipulation in a fiduciary capacity or in connection with the purchase or sale of securities registered under the Securities Exchange Act of 1934; or (c) any criminal act, intentional tort, or willful or reckless misconduct that caused serious physical injury or death to another individual in the preceding five years. The $146,450 limitation is to be adjusted periodically for inflation.

**Discharge** Discharge relieves the debtor from liability for all her dischargeable debts. Certain debts, however, are nondischargeable under the Code. A discharge of a debt voids any judgment obtained at any time with respect to that debt and operates as an injunction against commencing or continuing any action to recover that debt. Section 524. A discharge does not, however, affect a secured creditor to the extent of his security.

No private employer may terminate the employment of, or discriminate with respect to employment against, an individual who is or has been a debtor under the Bankruptcy Code solely because such debtor (1) is or has been such a debtor; (2) has been insolvent before the commencement of a case or during the case; or (3) has not paid a debt that is dischargeable in a case under the Bankruptcy Code. Section 525(b).

A reaffirmation agreement between a debtor and a creditor permitting the creditor to enforce a discharged debt is enforceable to the extent State law permits but only if (1) the agreement was made before the discharge has been granted; (2) the debtor received the required disclosures, which must be written, clear, and conspicuous, at or before the time at which the debtor signed the agreement; (3) the agreement has been filed with the court, accompanied, if applicable, by a declaration or an affidavit of the attorney who represented the debtor during the course of negotiating the agreement, which states that such agreement represents a fully informed and voluntary agreement by the debtor and imposes no undue hardship on her; (4) the debtor has not rescinded the agreement at any time prior to discharge or within sixty days after the agreement is filed with the court, whichever occurs later; (5) the court has informed a debtor who is an individual that he is not required to enter into such an agreement and has explained the legal effect of the agreement; and (6) in a case concerning an individual who was not represented by an attorney during the course of negotiating the agreement, the court has approved such agreement as imposing no undue hardship on the debtor and being in her best interests. Section 524.

Section 523 provides that certain debts of an individual are not dischargeable in bankruptcy. This section applies to individuals receiving discharges under Chapters 7, 11, and, as discussed later in this chapter, the "hardship discharge" provision of Chapter 13. (The 2005 Act makes *most* of these apply to the standard discharge provision of Chapter 13.) The nondischargeable debts include the following:

1. certain taxes and customs duties and debt incurred to pay such taxes or customs duties;
2. legal liabilities for obtaining money, property, or services by false pretenses, false representations, or actual fraud;
3. legal liability for willful and malicious injuries to the person or property of another;
4. domestic support obligations and property settlements arising from divorce or separation proceedings;
5. debts not scheduled, unless the creditor knew of the bankruptcy;
6. debts the debtor created by fraud or defalcation while acting in a fiduciary capacity, embezzlement, or larceny;
7. student loans unless excluding the debt from discharge would impose undue hardship;
8. debts that were or could have been listed in a previous bankruptcy in which the debtor waived or was denied a discharge;
9. consumer debts for luxury goods or services in excess of $600 per creditor, if incurred by an individual debtor on or within ninety days before the order for relief, are presumed to be nondischargeable;
10. cash advances aggregating more than $875 obtained by an individual debtor under an open-ended credit plan within seventy days before the order for relief are presumed to be nondischargeable;
11. liability for death or personal injury based upon the debtor's operation of a motor vehicle, vessel, or aircraft while legally intoxicated;
12. fines, penalties, or forfeitures owed to a governmental entity; and
13. certain debts incurred for violations of securities fraud law. (This provision was added by the Sarbanes-Oxley Act.)

The following illustrates the operation of discharge: Donaldson files a petition in bankruptcy. Donaldson owes Anders $1,500, Boynton $2,500, and Conroy $3,000. Assume that Anders's claim is not dischargeable in bankruptcy, whereas Boynton's and Conroy's claims are. Anders receives $180 from the liquidation of Donaldson's bankruptcy estate, Boynton receives $300, and Conroy receives $360. If Donaldson receives a bankruptcy discharge, Boynton and Conroy will be precluded from pursuing Donaldson for the remainder of their claims ($2,200 and $2,640, respectively). Anders, on the other hand, because his debt is not dischargeable, may pursue Donaldson for the remaining $1,320, subject to the applicable statute of limitations. If Donaldson does not receive a discharge, Anders, Boynton, and Conroy may all pursue Donaldson for the unpaid portions of their claims.

## THE ESTATE

The commencement of a bankruptcy case creates an estate, which is treated as a separate legal entity, distinct from the debtor. The estate consists of all legal and equitable interests of the debtor in nonexempt property at that time. The estate also includes property that the debtor acquires within 180 days after the filing of the petition by inheritance, by a property settlement, by a divorce decree, or as a beneficiary of a life insurance policy. In addition, the estate includes proceeds, rents, and profits from property of the estate and any interest in property that the estate acquires after the case commences. Section 541. The 2005 Act *excludes* from the estate savings for postsecondary education through education IRAs and 529 plans if certain criteria are met. Finally, the estate includes property that the trustee recovers under her powers (1) as a lien creditor, (2) to avoid voidable preferences, (3) to avoid fraudulent transfers, and (4) to avoid statutory liens. While in a Chapter 7 case the estate does not include earnings from services an *individual* debtor performs after the case commences, in a Chapter 13 case, it does include wages an *individual* debtor earns and property she acquires after the case commences.

**Trustee as Lien Creditor** The trustee has, as of the commencement of the case, the rights and powers of any creditor with a judicial lien against the debtor or an execution that is returned unsatisfied, whether or not such a creditor exists. Section 544(a). The trustee is made an ideal creditor possessing every right and power that the State confers by law upon its most favored creditor who has acquired a lien through legal or equitable proceedings. By assuming the rights and powers of a purely hypothetical lien creditor, the trustee has no need to locate an actual existing lien creditor.

Thus, under the UCC and the Bankruptcy Code, the trustee, as a hypothetical lien creditor, has priority over a creditor with a security interest that was not perfected when the bankruptcy petition was filed. A creditor with a purchase money security interest who files within the grace period allowed under State law, which in most States is twenty days after the debtor receives the collateral, however, will defeat the trustee, even if the creditor gap-files the petition before perfecting and after the security interest is created. For example, Donald borrows $5,000 from Cathy on September 1 and gives her a security interest in the equipment he purchases with the borrowed funds. On October 3, before Cathy perfects her security interest, Donald files for bankruptcy. The trustee in bankruptcy can invalidate Cathy's security interest because it was unperfected when the bankruptcy petition was filed. Cathy would be able to assert a claim only as an unsecured creditor. If, however, Donald had filed for bankruptcy on September 18 and Cathy had perfected the security interest on September 19, Cathy would prevail because she perfected her purchase money security interest within twenty days after Donald received the equipment.

**Voidable Preferences** The Bankruptcy Code invalidates certain preferential transfers from the debtor to favored creditors before the date of bankruptcy. A creditor who has received a transfer invalidated as preferential still may make a claim for the unpaid debt, but the property he received under the preferential transfer becomes a part of the debtor's estate to be shared by all creditors. Under Section 547 the trustee may recover any transfer of the debtor's property:

1. to or for the benefit of a creditor;
2. for or on account of an antecedent debt the debtor owed before such transfer was made;
3. made while the debtor was insolvent;
4. made on or within ninety days before the date of the filing of the petition or, if the creditor was an "insider" (as previously defined), made within one year of the date of the filing of the petition; *and*
5. that enables such creditor to receive more than he would have received under Chapter 7.

A **transfer** is any mode, direct or indirect, voluntary or involuntary, of disposing of property or an interest in property, including the retention of title as a security interest. Section 101(54). The debtor is presumed to have been insolvent on and during the ninety days immediately preceding the date on which the petition was filed. **Insolvency** is a financial condition of a debtor such that the sum of her debts exceeds the sum of all her property at fair valuation.

The policy behind the voidable preference provision is explained by the House of Representatives report as follows:

> The purpose of the preference section is two-fold. First, by permitting the trustee to avoid prebankruptcy transfers that occur within a short period before bankruptcy, creditors are discouraged from racing to the courthouse to dismember the debtor during his slide into bankruptcy. The protection thus afforded the debtor often enables him to work his way out of a difficult financial situation through cooperation with all of his creditors. Second, and more important, the preference provisions facilitate the prime bankruptcy policy of equality of distribution among creditors of the debtor. Any creditor that received a greater payment than others of his class is required to disgorge so that

all may share equally. *House of Representatives Report* 95–595 at 177–78 (1977).

For example, on March 3, David borrows $15,000 from Carla, promising to repay the loan on April 3. David repays Carla on April 3 as he promised. Then, on June 1, David files a petition in bankruptcy. His assets are sufficient to pay general creditors only forty cents on the dollar. David's repayment of the loan is a voidable preference, which the trustee may recover from Carla. The transfer (repayment) on April 3 (1) was to a creditor (Carla); (2) was on account of an antecedent debt (the $15,000 loan made on March 3); (3) was made while the debtor was insolvent (a debtor is presumed insolvent for the ninety days preceding the filing of the bankruptcy petition—June 1); (4) was made within ninety days of bankruptcy (April 3 is less than ninety days before June 1); and (5) enabled the creditor to receive more than she would have received under Chapter 7 (Carla received $15,000; she would have received 0.40 × $15,000 = $6,000 in bankruptcy). After returning the property to the trustee, Carla would have an unsecured claim of $15,000 against David's estate in bankruptcy, for which she would receive $6,000.

To illustrate further, consider the following example. On May 1, Debra buys and receives merchandise from Stuart and gives him a security interest in the goods for the unpaid price of $20,000. On May 25, Stuart files a financing statement. On August 1, Debra files a petition for bankruptcy. The trustee in bankruptcy may avoid the perfected security interest as a preferential transfer because (1) the transfer of the perfected security interest on May 25 was to benefit a creditor (Stuart); (2) it was on account of an antecedent debt (the $20,000 owed from the sale of the merchandise); (3) the debtor was insolvent at the time (the debtor's insolvency is presumed for the ninety days preceding the filing of the bankruptcy petition—August 1); (4) the transfer was made within ninety days of bankruptcy (May 25 is less than ninety days before August 1); and (5) the transfer enabled the creditor to receive more than he would have received in bankruptcy (on his secured claim, Stuart would recover more than he would on an unsecured claim).

Nevertheless, not all transfers made within ninety days of bankruptcy are voidable. The Bankruptcy Code makes exceptions for certain prebankruptcy transfers, including the following:

1. *Exchanges for new value.* If, for example, within ninety days before the petition is filed, the debtor purchases an automobile for $9,000, this transfer of property (i.e., the $9,000) is not voidable because it was not made for an antecedent debt but rather as a substantially contemporaneous exchange for new value.
2. *Enabling security interests.* If the creditor gives the debtor new value which the debtor uses to acquire property in which he grants the creditor a security interest, the security interest is not voidable if the creditor perfects it within thirty days after the debtor receives possession of the property. For example, if within ninety days of the filing of the petition, the debtor purchases a refrigerator on credit and grants the seller or lender a security interest in the refrigerator, the transfer of that interest is not voidable if the secured party perfects within thirty days after the debtor receives possession of the property.
3. *Payments in ordinary course.* The trustee may *not* avoid a transfer in payment of a debt incurred in the ordinary course of business or financial affairs of the debtor and the transferee and either (a) made in the ordinary course of business or financial affairs of the debtor and transferee, or (b) made according to ordinary business terms.
4. *Consumer debts.* This exception provides that if the debtor is an individual whose debts are primarily consumer debts, the trustee may not avoid any transfer of property valued at less than $600.
5. *Nonconsumer debts.* In a case filed by a debtor whose debts are not primarily consumer debts, the trustee may not avoid any transfer of property valued at less than $5,850.
6. *Domestic support obligations.* The trustee may not avoid any transfer that is a *bona fide* payment of a debt for a domestic support obligation. Section 547(c).

**Fraudulent Transfers** The trustee may avoid fraudulent transfers made on or within two years before the date of the filing of the petition. Section 548. One type of fraudulent transfer consists of the debtor's transferring property with the actual intent to hinder, delay, or defraud any of her creditors. Another type of fraudulent transfer involves the debtor's transfer of property for less than a reasonably equivalent consideration when she is insolvent or when the transfer would render her so. For example, Dale, who is in debt, transfers title to her house to Tony, her father, without any payment by Tony to Dale and with the understanding that when the house is no longer in danger of seizure by creditors, Tony will reconvey it to Dale. The transfer of the house by Dale to Tony is a fraudulent transfer. The 2005 Act specifies that a fraudulent transfer includes a payment to an insider under an employment contract that is not in the ordinary course of business. A 1998 amendment to the Bankruptcy Code provides that a transfer of a charitable contribution to a qualified religious or charitable entity or organization will not be considered a fraudulent transfer if the amount of that contribution does not exceed 15 percent of the gross annual income of the debtor for the year in which the transfer is made. Transfers that exceed 15 percent are protected if they are "consistent with the practices of the debtor in making charitable contributions."

In addition, the trustee may avoid transfers of the debtor's property if the transfer is voidable under State law by a creditor with an allowable, unsecured claim. Section 544(b). This section empowers a trustee to avoid transfers that violate State fraudulent conveyance statutes, which make it illegal to transfer property to another party in order to defer, hinder, or defraud creditors. These statutes generally provide a three- to six-year limitations period, which the trustee can utilize under Section 544(b). At least forty-three States have adopted the Uniform Fraudulent Transfer Act, which has a four-year statute of limitations.

**Statutory Liens** A **statutory lien** arises solely by force of a statute and does not include a security interest or judicial lien. Section 101(53). The trustee may avoid a statutory lien on property of the debtor if the lien (1) first becomes effective when the debtor becomes insolvent, (2) is not perfected or enforceable on the date of the commencement of the case against a *bona fide* purchaser, or (3) is for rent. Section 545.

## LIQUIDATION—CHAPTER 7

To accomplish its dual goals of equitably distributing the debtor's property and providing the debtor with a fresh start, the Bankruptcy Code has established two approaches: liquidation and adjustment of debts. Chapter 7 uses liquidation, whereas Chapters 11 and 13, discussed below, take the second approach, that of adjusting debts. Liquidation involves terminating the business of the debtor, distributing his nonexempt assets, and, usually, discharging all of his dischargeable debts.

### PROCEEDINGS

Proceedings under Chapter 7 apply to all debtors except railroads, insurance companies, banks, savings and loan associations, homestead associations, and credit unions. A petition commencing a case under Chapter 7 may be either voluntary or involuntary. After the order for relief, an interim trustee is appointed to serve until the creditors select a permanent trustee. If the creditors do not elect a trustee, the interim trustee becomes the permanent trustee. Under Chapter 7, the trustee collects and reduces to money the property of the estate; accounts for all property received; investigates the financial affairs of the debtor; examines and, if appropriate, challenges proofs of claims; opposes, if advisable, the discharge of the debtor; and makes a final report of the administration of the estate.

The creditors may also elect a committee of not fewer than three and not more than eleven unsecured creditors to consult with the trustee, to make recommendations to him, and to submit questions to the court.

### CONVERSION

The debtor may convert a case under Chapter 7 to Chapter 11 or 13; however, any waiver of this right is unenforceable. Moreover, on request of a party in interest and after notice and a hearing, the court may convert a case under Chapter 7 to Chapter 11. The court may also convert a case under Chapter 7 to Chapter 13, but this can occur only upon the debtor's request. Any conversion to another chapter can only occur if the debtor may also be a debtor under that chapter. Section 706.

◆ **SEE CASE 39-1**

### DISMISSAL

The court may dismiss a Chapter 7 case for cause after notice and a hearing. In a case filed by an individual debtor whose debts are primarily consumer debts, the court may dismiss a case or, with the debtor's consent, convert the case to one under Chapter 11 or 13, if the court finds that granting relief would be an abuse of the provisions of Chapter 7. A court can find abuse (1) on general grounds based on whether the debtor filed the petition in bad faith or the totality of the circumstances of the debtor's financial situation demonstrates abuse, *or* (2) on an unrebutted presumption of abuse based on a new means test established by the 2005 Act.

Under the **means test** abuse is presumed (i.e., the debtor is not eligible for Chapter 7 unless the debtor can prove special circumstances) for an individual debtor whose net current monthly income is greater than the State median income *and* if either (1) the debtor has available net income (income after deducting allowed expenses) for repayment to creditors over five years totaling at least $11,725, or (2) the available net income for repayment to creditors over five years is between $7,025 and $11,725 and such available net income is at least 25 percent of nonpriority unsecured claims. Section 707. The means test can be explained by the following scenarios:

1. If the debtor's net current monthly income is less than or equal to the State median income, no presumption of abuse arises.
2. If the debtor's net current monthly income is greater than the State median income *and* the debtor's current monthly income less allowed expenses is less than $117.08 per month, no presumption of abuse arises.
3. If the debtor's net current monthly income is greater than the State median income *and* the debtor's current monthly income less allowed expenses is at least $117.08 per month, a presumption of abuse arises *if* the current monthly income less allowed expenses is sufficient to pay 25 percent of the debtor's nonpriority unsecured claims over sixty months.
4. If the debtor's net current monthly income is greater than the State median income *and* the debtor's current monthly income less allowed expenses is at least $195.42 per month, a presumption of abuse arises without regard to the amount of nonpriority unsecured claims.

For example, Debra's net current monthly income is greater than the State median income. After deducting allowed expenses her monthly income is $150, which places her in the third situation. If her nonpriority unsecured claims are $35,000, a presumption of abuse will arise because $150 multiplied by sixty equals $9,000, which is greater than 25 percent of $35,000, which equals $8,750. On the other hand, Debra would be eligible to file under Chapter 7 if her nonpriority unsecured claims are $36,100, because $150 multiplied by sixty equals $9,000, which is less than 25 percent of $36,100, which equals $9,025.

## DISTRIBUTION OF THE ESTATE

After the trustee has collected all the assets of the debtor's estate, she distributes them to the creditors and, if any assets remain, to the debtor, in the following order:

1. Secured creditors are paid on their security interests.
2. Creditors entitled to a priority are paid in the order provided.
3. Unsecured creditors who filed their claims on time (or tardily, if they did not have notice or actual knowledge of the bankruptcy) are paid.
4. Unsecured creditors who filed their claims late are paid.
5. Claims for fines and multiple, exemplary, or punitive damages are paid.
6. Interest at the legal rate from the date of the filing of the petition is paid to all of the above claimants.
7. Whatever property remains is distributed to the debtor.

Claims of the same rank are paid *pro rata*. For example: Donley has filed a petition for a Chapter 7 proceeding. The total value of Donley's estate after paying the expenses of administration is $25,000. Evans, who is owed $15,000, has a security interest in property valued at $10,000. Fishel has an unsecured claim of $6,000, which is entitled to a priority of $2,000. The United States has a claim for income taxes of $4,000. Green has an unsecured claim of $9,000 that was filed on time. Hiller has an unsecured claim of $12,000 that was filed on time. Jerdee has a claim of $8,000 that was filed late. The distribution would be as follows:

1. Evans receives $11,500
2. Fishel receives $3,200
3. United States receives $4,000
4. Green receives $2,700
5. Hiller receives $3,600
6. Jerdee receives $0

To analyze this distribution: Evans receives $10,000 as a secured creditor and has an unsecured claim of $5,000. Fishel receives $2,000 on the portion of his claim entitled to a priority and has an unsecured claim of $4,000. The United States has a priority of $4,000. After paying $10,000 to Evans, $2,000 to Fishel, and $4,000 to the United States, there remains $9,000 ($25,000 – $10,000 – $2,000 – $4,000) to be distributed *pro rata* to unsecured creditors who filed on time. Their claims total $30,000 (Evans = $5,000, Fishel = $4,000, Green = $9,000, and Hiller = $12,000). Therefore, each will receive $9,000/$30,000, or thirty cents on the dollar. Accordingly, Evans receives an additional $1,500, Fishel receives an additional $1,200, Green receives $2,700, and Hiller receives $3,600. Because the assets were insufficient to pay all unsecured claimants who filed on time, Jerdee, who filed tardily, receives nothing. If, however, Jerdee's late filing resulted from Donley's failure to schedule Jerdee's claim, then Donley's debts to Jerdee would not be discharged unless Jerdee knew or had notice of the bankruptcy.

◆ SEE FIGURE 39-1: **Collection and Distribution of the Debtor's Estate**

## DISCHARGE

A discharge under Chapter 7 relieves the debtor of all dischargeable debts that arose before the date of the order for relief. The discharge does not include those debts that are not dischargeable. After distribution of the estate, the court will grant the debtor a discharge unless the debtor:

1. is not an individual (partnerships and corporations may not receive a discharge under Chapter 7);
2. has destroyed, falsified, concealed, or failed to keep records and account books;
3. has knowingly and fraudulently made a false oath or account, presented or used a false claim, or given or received bribes;
4. has transferred, removed, destroyed, or concealed any (a) of his property with intent to hinder, delay, or defraud his creditors within twelve months preceding the filing of the bankruptcy petition, or (b) property of the estate after the date of filing of the petition;
5. has within eight years prior to bankruptcy been granted a discharge under Chapter 7 or 11. A debtor also will be denied a discharge under Chapter 7 if she received a discharge under Chapter 13 within the past six years, unless payments under that chapter's plan totaled at least (1) 100 percent of the allowed unsecured claims or (2) 70 percent of such claims and the plan was the debtor's best effort;
6. refused to obey any lawful order of the court or to answer any question approved by the court;
7. has failed to explain satisfactorily, in terms of meeting his liabilities, any loss or deficiency of assets; or
8. has executed a written waiver of discharge approved by the court. Section 727.

The 2005 Act denies a discharge to an individual debtor who fails to complete a personal financial management course. This provision, however, does not apply if the debtor resides in a district for which the U.S. trustee or the

◆ FIGURE 39-1: **Collection and Distribution of the Debtor's Estate**

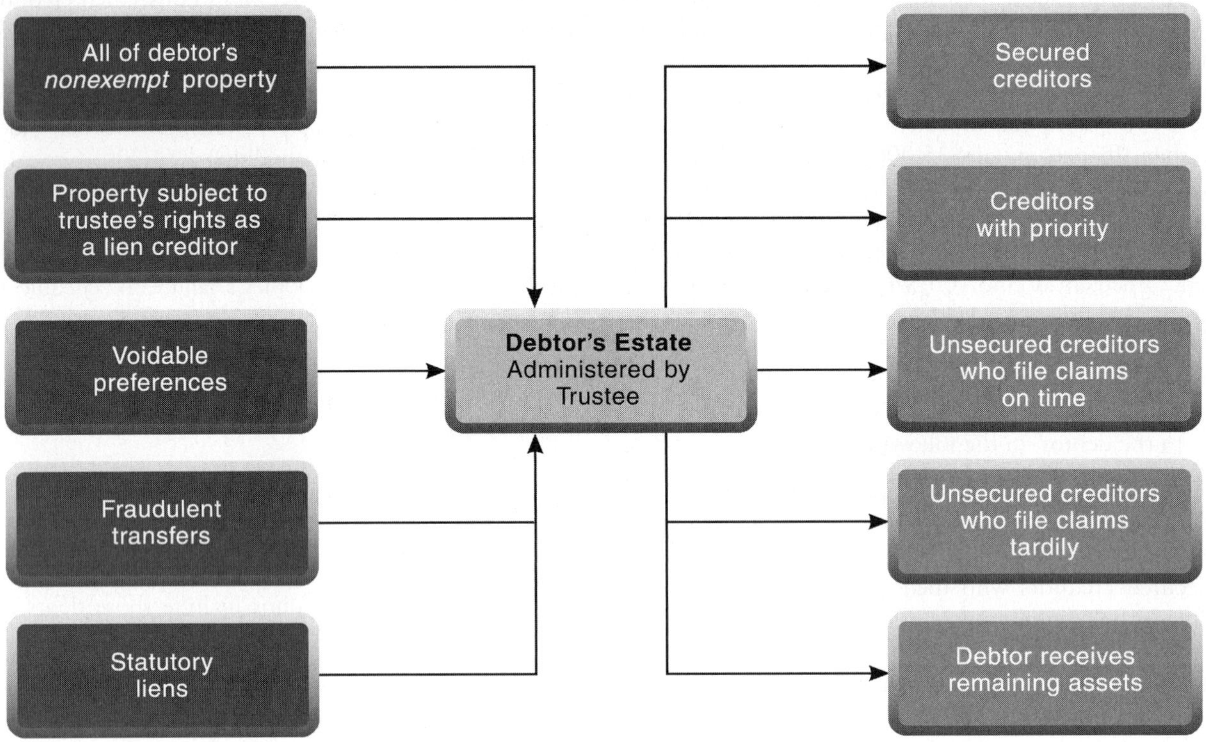


bankruptcy administrator has determined that the approved instructional courses are not adequate to service the additional individuals who would be required to complete these instructional courses.

On the request of the trustee or a creditor and after notice and a hearing, the court may revoke within one year a discharge the debtor obtained through fraud.

## REORGANIZATION—CHAPTER 11

Reorganization is the process of correcting or eliminating factors responsible for the distress of a business enterprise, thereby preserving both the enterprise and its value as a going concern. Chapter 11 of the Bankruptcy Code governs reorganization of eligible debtors, including individuals, partnerships, and corporations, and permits the restructuring of their finances. A number of large corporations have made use of Chapter 11, including WorldCom, Enron, Kmart, Texaco, AH Robins, Johns-Manville, Allied Stores, Global Crossing, Pacific Gas and Electric, CIT, Conseco, Lehman Brothers, General Motors, and Chrysler. The main objective of a reorganization proceeding is to develop and carry out a fair, equitable, and feasible plan of reorganization.

After a plan has been prepared and filed, a hearing held before the court determines whether or not it will be confirmed. Chapter 11 permits but does not require a sale of assets. Rather, it contemplates that the debtor will keep its assets and use them to generate earnings that will pay creditors under the terms of the plan confirmed by the court.

The 1994 and 2005 amendments provide for streamlined and more flexible procedures in a small business case, which is any case under Chapter 11 filed by a small business. The amendments define *small business* to include (1) persons engaged in commercial or business activities whose aggregate, noncontingent, liquidated debts do not exceed $2,343,300 (subject to periodic adjustments for inflation); and (2) cases in which the U.S. trustee has not appointed a committee of unsecured creditors or the court has determined that the committee of unsecured creditors is not sufficiently active and representative to provide effective oversight of the debtor. Under a small business case, the U.S. trustee has additional oversight duties and the debtor has additional reporting requirements, while the plan process can be simpler and the time periods and deadlines are different.

### PROCEEDINGS

Any person who may be a debtor under Chapter 7 (except stockbrokers and commodity brokers) and railroads may be a debtor under Chapter 11. Petitions may be voluntary or involuntary.

As soon as practicable after the order for relief, a committee of unsecured creditors is appointed. This committee usually consists of persons holding the seven largest unsecured claims against the debtor. In addition, the court may order the appointment of additional committees of creditors or of equity security holders, if necessary, to ensure adequate representation. Section 1102. The committee may, with the court's approval, employ attorneys, accountants, and other agents to represent or perform services for the committee. The committee may consult with the debtor or trustee concerning the administration of the case and may investigate the debtor's affairs and participate in formulating a reorganization plan. Section 1103.

The debtor will manage and remain in possession of the property of the estate unless the court orders the appointment of a trustee, who may then operate the debtor's business. The court will order the appointment of a trustee *only for cause* (including fraud, dishonesty, incompetence, or gross mismanagement of the debtor's affairs) or if the appointment is in the interests of creditors or equity security holders. Section 1104. The 1994 amendments allow the creditors to elect the trustee. If the court does not order the appointment of a trustee upon the request of a party in interest, the court will order the appointment of an examiner to investigate allegations of fraud, dishonesty, incompetence, misconduct, or mismanagement if (1) such appointment is in the interests of creditors or equity security holders or (2) the debtor's fixed, liquidated, unsecured debts exceed $5 million.

The duties of a trustee in a case under Chapter 11 include the following:

1. to be accountable for all property received;
2. to examine proofs of claims;
3. to furnish information to all parties in interest;
4. to provide the court and taxing authorities with financial reports of the debtor's business operations;
5. to make a final report and account of the administration of the estate;
6. to investigate the financial condition of the debtor and determine the desirability of continuing the debtor's business; and
7. to file a plan, to file a report explaining why there will be no plan, or to recommend that the case be converted to Chapter 7.

At any time before confirmation of a plan, the court may terminate the trustee's appointment and restore the debtor to possession and management of the property of the estate and operation of the debtor's business. Section 1105.

When a trustee has not been appointed, which is usually the case, the debtor in possession performs many of the functions and duties of a trustee, with the principal exception of investigating the debtor. Section 1107.

The Bankruptcy Code (Section 1113) deals with the rejection of collective bargaining agreements. Subsection (b)(1) provides that subsequent to filing and prior to seeking such rejection, the trustee or debtor-in-possession must propose the labor contract modifications that are necessary to enable the debtor to reorganize and that will provide for the fair and equitable treatment of all parties concerned. Subsection (b)(2) requires that good faith meetings to reach a mutually satisfactory agreement be held between management and the union. Subsection (c) authorizes the court to approve rejection of the collective bargaining agreement only if the court finds that the proposal for rejection was made in accordance with these conditions, that the union refused the proposal without good cause, and that the balance of equities clearly favors rejection.

◆ SEE FIGURE 39-2: **Comparison of Bankruptcy Proceedings**

◆ SEE CASE 39-2

◆ FIGURE 39-2: **Comparison of Bankruptcy Proceedings**

| | Chapter 7 | Chapter 11 | Chapter 12 | Chapter 13 |
|---|---|---|---|---|
| **Objective** | Liquidation | Reorganization | Adjustment | Adjustment |
| **Eligible Debtors** | Most debtors | Most debtors, including railroads | Family farmer who meets certain debt limitations | Individual with regular income who meets certain debt limitations |
| **Type of Petition** | Voluntary or involuntary | Voluntary or involuntary | Voluntary | Voluntary |
| **Trustee** | Usually selected by creditors; otherwise appointed | Only if court orders appointment for cause; creditors then may select trustee | Appointed | Appointed |

## PLAN OF REORGANIZATION

The debtor may file a plan at any time and has the exclusive right to file a plan during the 120 days after the order for relief, unless a trustee has been appointed. If the debtor has not filed a plan within 120 days or the plan has not been accepted within 180 days, then other parties in interest, including an appointed trustee or a creditors' committee, may file a plan. Section 1121. On request of an interested party and after notice and a hearing, the court may for cause reduce or increase the 120-day or 180-day periods. The 2005 Act provides, however, that the 120-day period may not be extended beyond eighteen months and the 180-day period may not be extended beyond twenty months.

A plan of reorganization must divide creditors' claims and shareholders' interests into classes, specify how each class will be treated, deal with claims within each class equally, and provide adequate means for implementing the plan. After a plan has been filed, the plan and a written disclosure statement approved by the court as containing adequate information must be transmitted to each holder of a claim before seeking acceptance or rejection of the plan. **Adequate information** is that which would enable a hypothetical, reasonable investor to make an informed judgment about the plan. Section 1125.

## ACCEPTANCE OF PLAN

Each class of claims and interests has the opportunity to accept or reject the proposed plan. To be accepted by a **class of claims**, a plan must be accepted by creditors that hold at least two-thirds in amount and more than one-half in number of the allowed claims of such class that actually voted on the plan. Acceptance of a plan by a **class of interests**, such as shareholders, requires acceptance by holders of at least two-thirds in amount of the allowed interests of such class that actually voted on the plan.

A class that is not impaired under a plan is conclusively presumed to have accepted the plan. Basically, a class is unimpaired if the plan leaves unaltered the legal, equitable, and contractual rights to which the holder of such claim or interest is entitled. Section 1124. A class that will receive no distribution under a plan is deemed not to have accepted the plan.

## CONFIRMATION OF PLAN

Before a plan is binding on any parties, the court, after notice and a hearing, must confirm such plan. To be confirmed, the plan must meet all the requirements of Section 1129 of the Bankruptcy Code. The most important of these requirements are the following.

**Good Faith** The plan must have been proposed in good faith and not by any means forbidden by law. Section 1129(a)(3).

**Feasibility** The court must find that confirmation of the plan is not likely to be followed by the debtor's liquidation or by its need for further financial reorganization. Section 1129(a)(11).

**Cash Payments** Unless the claim holder agrees otherwise, certain priority creditors must have their allowed claims paid in full in cash immediately or, in some instances, on a deferred basis. Section 1129(a)(9). These priority claims include the expenses of administration, gap creditors, claims for wages and salaries, and employee benefits and consumer deposits.

In the case of a debtor who is an individual, the 2005 Act requires that the plan provide for payments to be made out of the debtor's future earnings from personal services or other future income. It also imposes an additional requirement for confirmation if an unsecured creditor objects to confirmation of the plan: the value of property distributed on account of that claim must not be less than (1) the amount of that claim, or (2) the debtor's projected disposable income to be received during the longer of (a) the five-year period beginning on the first payment due date, or (b) the plan's term. Section 1129(a)(15).

**Acceptance by Creditors** To be confirmed, the plan must be accepted by at least *one* class of claims, and with respect to *each* class, each holder must either accept the plan *or* receive not less than the amount he would have received under Chapter 7. In addition, each class must accept the plan or be unimpaired by it. Nonetheless, under certain circumstances, the court may confirm a plan that is not accepted by all impaired classes, upon determining that the plan does not discriminate unfairly and that it is fair and equitable. Section 1129(b)(1). Under these circumstances, a class of claims or interests may, despite objections by that class, be subjected to the provisions of a plan.

"Fair and equitable" with respect to secured creditors requires that (1) they either retain their security interest and receive deferred cash payments, the present value of which is at least equal to their claims, or (2) they realize the "indubitable equivalent" of their claims. Fair and equitable with respect to unsecured creditors means that such creditors are to receive property of value equivalent to the full amount of their claim or that no junior claim or interest is to receive anything. With respect to a class of interests, a plan is fair and equitable if the holders receive full value or if no junior interest receives anything at all.

## EFFECT OF CONFIRMATION

Once confirmed, the plan governs the debtor's performance obligations. The plan binds the debtor and any creditor, equity security holder, or general partner of the debtor. Upon the entry of a final decree closing the proceedings, a debtor that is *not* an individual is discharged from all of its debts and liabilities that arose before the date the plan was confirmed, except as otherwise provided in the plan, the order of confirmation, or the Bankruptcy Code. Section 1141. Unlike under Chapter 7, under Chapter 11, partnerships and corporations may receive a discharge unless the plan calls for the liquidation of the business entity's property and termination of its business. The 2005 Act excepts from the discharge of any corporate debtor any debt (1) owed to the government as a result of fraud, or (2) arising from a fraudulent tax return or willful evasion of taxes.

An *individual* debtor is not discharged until all plan payments have been made. However, if the debtor fails to make all payments, the court may, after a hearing, grant a "hardship discharge" if the value of property actually distributed is not less than what the creditors would have received under Chapter 7 and modification of the plan is not practicable. A discharge under Chapter 11 does not discharge an *individual* debtor from debts that are not dischargeable under Section 523.

## ADJUSTMENTS OF DEBTS OF INDIVIDUALS—CHAPTER 13

To encourage debtors to pay their debts wherever possible, Congress enacted Chapter 13 of the Bankruptcy Code. This chapter permits an individual debtor to file a repayment plan which, if confirmed by the court, will discharge him from almost all of his debts when he completes his payments under the plan. If, as occurs in many cases, the debtor does not make the required payments under the plan, the case will be converted to Chapter 7 or dismissed.

### PROCEEDINGS

Chapter 13 provides a procedure for adjusting the debts of an individual with regular income who owes liquidated, unsecured debts of less than $360,475 and secured debts of less than $1,081,400. Sole proprietorships meeting these debt limitations are also eligible; partnerships and corporations are not eligible. Only a voluntary petition may initiate a case under Chapter 13, and a trustee is appointed in every Chapter 13 case. Property of the estate in Chapter 13 includes wages earned and other property acquired by the debtor after the Chapter 13 filing. Section 1306.

### CONVERSION OR DISMISSAL

The debtor may convert a case under Chapter 13 to Chapter 7. On request of the debtor, if the case has not been previously converted from Chapter 7 or 11, the court shall dismiss a case under Chapter 13. On request of a party in interest or the U.S. trustee, and after notice and a hearing, the court may convert a case under Chapter 13 to Chapter 7 *or* may dismiss a case under Chapter 13, whichever is in the best interests of creditors and the estate, for cause, including (1) unreasonable delay by the debtor; (2) failure of the debtor to file a plan timely; (3) denial of confirmation of a plan; or (4) material default by the debtor with respect to a term of a confirmed plan. Before the confirmation of a plan, on request of a party in interest or the U.S. trustee and after notice and a hearing, the court may convert a case under Chapter 13 to Chapter 11. Nonetheless, a case may *not* be converted to another chapter unless the debtor may be a debtor under that chapter. Section 1307.

◆ **SEE CASE 39-1**

### THE PLAN

The debtor files the plan and may modify it at any time before confirmation. The plan must meet three requirements under Section 1322:

1. It must require the debtor to submit all or any portion of her future earnings or income, as is necessary for the execution of the plan, to the trustee's supervision and control.
2. It must provide for full payment on a deferred basis of all claims entitled to a priority unless a holder of a claim agrees to a different treatment of such claim.
3. If the plan classifies claims, it must provide the same treatment for each claim in the same class.

In addition, the plan may modify the rights of unsecured and secured creditors, except those secured only by a security interest in the debtor's principal residence. The plan also may provide for payments on any unsecured claim to be made concurrently with payments on any secured claim. If the debtor's net current monthly income is equal to or greater than the State median income, the plan may not provide for payments over a period longer than five years. If the debtor's net current monthly income is less than the State median income, the plan may not provide for payments over a period longer than three years, unless the court approves, for cause, a longer period not to exceed five years.

### CONFIRMATION

To be confirmed by the court, the plan must meet certain requirements. Section 1325. First, the filing of the case must have been in good faith, and the plan must comply with applicable law and be proposed in good faith. Second, the present value of the property to be distributed to unsecured creditors must be not less than the amount they would receive under Chapter 7. Third, either the secured creditors must accept the plan, the plan must provide that the debtor will surrender the collateral to the secured creditors, *or* the plan must permit the secured creditors to retain their security interest and the present value of the property to be distributed to them is not less than the allowed amount of their claim. Fourth, the debtor must be able to make all payments and comply with the plan. Fifth, if the trustee or the holder of an unsecured claim objects to the plan's confirmation, then the plan must either provide for payments the present value of which is not less than the amount of that claim or provide that all of the debtor's disposable income for three years be paid to unsecured creditors under the plan. If, however, the debtor's net current monthly income is equal to or greater than the State median income, the debtor's disposable income for not less than five years must be committed to pay unsecured creditors. For purposes of this provision, *disposable income* means current monthly income received by the debtor that is not reasonably necessary for the maintenance or support of the debtor or a dependent of the debtor, for domestic support obligations, or, if the debtor is engaged in business, for the payment of expenditures necessary for continuing, preserving, and operating the business. Sixth, if a debtor is required by judicial or administrative order or statute to pay a domestic support obligation, then the debtor must pay all such obligations that became payable after the filing.

◆ SEE CASE 39-3

### EFFECT OF CONFIRMATION

The provisions of a confirmed plan bind the debtor and all of her creditors. The confirmation of a plan vests in the debtor all property of the estate free and clear of any creditor's claim or interest for which the plan provides, except as otherwise provided in the plan or in the order confirming the plan. Section 1327. A plan may be modified after confirmation at the request of the debtor, the trustee, or a holder of an unsecured claim. The modification may increase or decrease the amount of payments on claims of a particular class or extend or reduce the time for such payments. Section 1329.

### DISCHARGE

Before the 2005 Act, the discharge under Chapter 13 was considerably more extensive than that granted under Chapter 7. The 2005 Act, however, made the discharge of debts under Chapter 13 less extensive than it was previously. As a result, Chapter 13 discharges only a few types of debts that are not also discharged under Chapter 7.

After a debtor completes all payments under the plan and of certain postpetition domestic support obligations, the court will grant him a discharge of all debts provided for by the plan, with the exception of nondischargeable debts for (1) unfiled, late-filed, and fraudulent tax returns; (2) legal liabilities resulting from obtaining money, property, or services by false pretenses, false representations, or actual fraud; (3) legal liability for willful *or* malicious conduct that caused personal injury to an individual; (4) domestic support obligations; (5) debts not scheduled unless the creditor knew of the bankruptcy; (6) debts the debtor created by fraud or embezzlement while acting in a fiduciary capacity; (7) most student loans; (8) consumer debts for luxury goods or services in excess of $600 per creditor if incurred by an individual debtor on or within ninety days before the order for relief; (9) cash advances aggregating more than $875 obtained by an individual debtor under an open-ended credit plan within seventy days before the order for relief; (10) liability for death or personal injury based upon the debtor's operation of a motor vehicle, vessel, or aircraft while legally intoxicated; (11) restitution or criminal fine included in a sentence for a criminal conviction; and (12) certain long-term obligations on which payments extend beyond the term of the plan.

Even if the debtor fails to make all payments, the court may, after a hearing, grant a "hardship discharge" if the debtor's failure is due to circumstances for which the debtor is not justly accountable, the value of property actually distributed is not less than what the creditors would have received under Chapter 7, and modification of the plan is impracticable. Section 1328(b). This discharge is subject, however, to the same exceptions for nondischargeable debts as a discharge under Chapter 7.

The 2005 Act denies a discharge under Chapter 13 to a debtor who has received a discharge (1) in a prior Chapter 7 or 11 case filed during the four-year period preceding the filing of the Chapter 13 case, or (2) in a prior Chapter 13 case filed during the two-year period preceding the date of filing the subsequent Chapter 13 case. It also denies a discharge to a debtor who fails to complete a personal financial management course. This provision, however, does not apply if the debtor resides in a district for which the U.S. trustee or the bankruptcy administrator has determined that the approved instructional courses are not adequate to service the additional individuals who would be required to complete these required instructional courses. Sections 1328(f), (g).

◆ SEE FIGURE 39-2: **Comparison of Bankruptcy Proceedings**

## CREDITORS' RIGHTS AND DEBTOR'S RELIEF OUTSIDE OF BANKRUPTCY

The rights and remedies of debtors and creditors outside of bankruptcy are governed mainly by State law. Because of the expense and notoriety associated with bankruptcy, resolving claims outside of a bankruptcy proceeding is often in the best interests of both debtor and creditor. Accordingly, bankruptcy usually is considered a last resort.

The rights and remedies of creditors outside of bankruptcy are varied. The first part of this section examines the basic right of all creditors to pursue their overdue claims to judgment and to satisfy that judgment out of property belonging to the debtor. Other rights and remedies are discussed elsewhere in this book. The rights under Article 2 of the UCC of an unpaid credit seller to reclaim the goods sold are covered in *Chapter 25*. The right of a secured creditor to enforce a security interest in personal property is the subject of *Chapter 38*. Likewise, the right of a creditor to foreclose a mortgage on real property is discussed in *Chapter 50*. In addition, the right of a creditor to proceed against a surety on the debt is addressed in *Chapter 38*.

At the same time, the law attempts to protect debtors against overreaching by creditors. This goal has been pursued by a number of means. States have enacted usury laws, as discussed in *Chapter 13*. The Federal Trade Commission has limited the rights of a holder in due course against consumer debtors, as explained in *Chapter 28*. Congress has prohibited abusive, deceptive, and unfair debt collection practices employed by debt collection agencies, as discussed in *Chapter 42*. That chapter also covers other legal protection offered to *consumer* debtors. The second part of this section describes the various forms of nonbankruptcy compromises that provide relief to debtors who have become overextended and who are unable to pay all of their creditors.

## CREDITORS' RIGHTS

When a debtor fails to pay a debt, the creditor may file suit to collect the debt owed. The objective is to obtain a judgment against the debtor and ultimately to collect on that judgment.

### PREJUDGMENT REMEDIES

Because litigation takes time, a creditor attempting to collect on a claim through the judicial process will almost always experience delay in obtaining judgment. To prevent the debtor from meanwhile disposing of his assets, the creditor may use, when available, certain prejudgment remedies. The most important of these is **attachment**, the process of seizing property, by virtue of a writ, summons, or other judicial order, and bringing the property into the custody of the court to secure satisfaction of the judgment ultimately to be entered in the action. At common law, the main objective of attachment was to coerce the defendant debtor into appearing in court; today the writ of attachment is statutory and is used primarily to seize the debtor's property in the event a judgment is rendered. Most States limit attachment to specified grounds and provide the debtor an opportunity for a hearing before a judge prior to the issuance of a writ of execution. Generally, attachment is limited to situations in which (1) the defendant cannot be personally served; (2) the claim is based upon fraud or the equivalent; or (3) the defendant has or is likely to transfer his property. In addition, the plaintiff generally must post a bond to compensate the defendant for loss should the plaintiff not prevail in the cause of action.

Similar in purpose is the remedy of prejudgment **garnishment**, which is a statutory proceeding directed at a third person who owes a debt to the debtor or who has property belonging to the debtor. Garnishment is most commonly used against the employer of the debtor and the bank in which the debtor has a savings or checking account. Property garnished remains in the hands of the third party pending the outcome of the suit. For example, Calvin brings an action against Daisy to collect a debt that is past due. Alvin has property belonging to Daisy. Calvin might garnish this property so that if he is successful in his action against Daisy, his judgment could be satisfied out of that property held by Alvin. If Alvin no longer had the property when Calvin obtained judgment, Calvin could recover from Alvin.

### POSTJUDGMENT REMEDIES

If the debtor still has not paid the claim, the creditor may proceed to trial and try to obtain a court judgment against the debtor. Though necessary, obtaining a judgment is, nevertheless, only the first step in collecting the debt. If the debtor does not voluntarily pay the judgment, the creditor will have to take additional steps to collect on it. These steps are called "postjudgment remedies."

First, the judgment creditor will have the court clerk issue a **writ of execution** demanding payment of the judgment, which is served by the sheriff upon the defendant/debtor. Upon return of the writ "unsatisfied," the judgment creditor may post bond or other security and order a levy on and sale of specified nonexempt property belonging to the defendant/debtor, which is then seized by the sheriff, advertised for sale, and sold at public sale under the writ of execution.

The writ of execution is limited to nonexempt property of the debtor. All States restrict creditors from recourse to certain property, the type and amount of which varies greatly from State to State.

If the proceeds of the sale do not produce funds sufficient to pay the judgment, the creditor may institute a **supplementary proceeding** in an attempt to locate money or other property belonging to the defendant. He also may proceed by **garnishment** against the debtor's employer or against a bank in which the debtor has an account. As discussed in Chapter 42, State and Federal statutes contain exemption provisions which limit the amount of wages subject to garnishment.

## DEBTOR'S RELIEF

The creditor's pursuit of a judgment on which she can collect and the debtor's quest for relief inherently give rise to conflicts among (1) the right of diligent creditors to pursue their claims to judgment and to satisfy their judgments by sale of property of the debtor; (2) the right of unsecured creditors who have refrained from suing the debtor; and (3) the social policy of affording relief to a debtor who has contracted debts beyond his ability to pay and who therefore may bear a lifetime burden.

Various nonbankruptcy compromises provide relief to debtors. Certain compromises, such as those offered by credit agencies and adjustment bureaus, are relatively informal. Some, such as compositions and assignments, are founded in common law and involve simple contract and trust principles; others, such as statutory assignments, are statutory. Some, such as equity receiverships, involve the intervention of a court and its officers, while others do not.

## COMPOSITIONS

A common law or nonstatutory **composition** (or "workout") is an ordinary contract or agreement between the debtor and two or more of her creditors, under which the creditors receive *pro rata* a part of their claims and the debtor is discharged from the balance of the claims. A composition is the State law analogue of Chapter 11 of the Bankruptcy Act. As a contract, it requires contractual formalities, such as offer, acceptance, and consideration. For example, debtor D, owing debts of $5,000 to A, $2,000 to B, and $1,000 to C, offers to settle these claims by paying a total of $4,000 to A, B, and C. If A, B, and C accept the offer, a composition results, with A receiving $2,500, B $1,000, and C $500. The consideration for the promise of A to forgive the balance of his claim consists of the promises of B and C to forgive the balance of their claims. By avoiding a race among themselves to obtain the debtor's limited assets, all the creditors benefit.

It should be noted, however, that the debtor in a composition is discharged from liability only regarding the claims of those creditors who voluntarily consent to the composition. If, in the illustration above, C had refused to accept the offer of composition and had refused to take the $500, he could attempt to collect his full $1,000 claim. Likewise, if D owed additional debts to X, Y, and Z, these creditors would not be bound by the agreement between D and A, B, and C. Another disadvantage of the composition is the fact that any creditor can attach the assets of the debtor during the negotiation period that usually precedes the execution of the composition agreement. For instance, once D advised A, B, and C that he was offering to compose the claims, any one of the creditors could seize D's property.

A variation of the composition is an extension agreement, developed by the debtor and two or more of her creditors, that provides an extended period of time for payment of her debts either in full or proportionately reduced.

## ASSIGNMENTS FOR BENEFIT OF CREDITORS

A common law or nonstatutory assignment for the benefit of creditors, sometimes called a general assignment, is a voluntary transfer by the debtor of his property to a trustee who applies the property to the payment of all the debtor's debts. For instance, debtor D transfers title to his property to trustee T, who converts the property into money and pays it to all of the creditors on a *pro rata* basis. An assignment for the benefit of creditors is a State law analogue of Chapter 7 of the Bankruptcy Act.

In most States, statutes now govern assignments for the benefit of creditors. These statutes typically require recording of the assignment, filing schedules of assets and liabilities, and providing notice to the creditors. Almost all of the statutes require that all creditors be treated equally except those with liens or statutorily created priorities.

The advantages of an assignment over a composition are that it protects the debtor's assets from attachment and execution and that it halts diligent creditors in their race to attach. An assignment does not require the creditors' consent, and payment by the trustee of part of the claims does not discharge the debtor from the balance of them. Thus, in the previous example, even after T pays A $2,500, B $1,000, and C $500 (and makes appropriate payments to all other creditors), A, B, and C and the other creditors still may attempt to collect the balance of their claims. Moreover, an assignment for the benefit of creditors is a ground for sustaining an involuntary petition for bankruptcy.

Because assignments benefit creditors by protecting the debtor's assets from attachment, some statutory enactments have endeavored to combine the idea of the assignment with a corresponding benefit that would discharge the debtor from the balance of his debts. But because the U.S. Constitution prohibits a State from impairing the contractual obligation between private citizens, it is impossible for a State to force all creditors to discharge a debtor upon a *pro rata* distribution of assets, although, as previously discussed, the Federal government *does* have such power and exercises it in the Bankruptcy Code. Accordingly, the States generally have enacted assignment statutes permitting the debtor to obtain *voluntary* releases of the balance of claims from creditors who accept partial payments, thus combining the advantages of common law compositions and assignments.

## EQUITY RECEIVERSHIPS

One of the oldest remedies in equity is the appointment of a receiver by the court. The receiver is a disinterested person who collects and preserves the debtor's assets and income and disposes of them at the direction of the court which appointed her. The court may instruct her (1) to liquidate the assets by public or private sale; (2) to operate the business as a going concern temporarily; or (3) to conserve the assets until final disposition of the matter before the court.

The court will appoint a receiver upon the petition (1) of a secured creditor seeking foreclosure of his security; (2) of a judgment creditor who has exhausted legal remedies to satisfy the judgment; or (3) of a shareholder of a corporate debtor whose assets will likely be dissipated by fraud or mismanagement. The appointment of a receiver always rests within the sound discretion of the court. Insolvency, in the equity sense of inability by the debtor to pay his debts as they mature, is one of the factors the court considers in appointing a receiver.

## CHAPTER SUMMARY

### FEDERAL BANKRUPTCY LAW

| | |
|---|---|
| **CASE ADMINISTRATION—CHAPTER 3** | **Commencement of the Case** the filing of a voluntary or involuntary petition begins jurisdiction of the bankruptcy court<br>• ***Voluntary Petitions*** available to any eligible debtor even if solvent<br>• ***Involuntary Petitions*** may be filed only under Chapter 7 or 11 if the debtor is generally not paying his debts as they become due<br>**Dismissal** the court may dismiss a case for cause after notice and a hearing; under Chapter 13 the debtor has an absolute right to have his case dismissed<br>**Automatic Stay** prevents attempts by creditors to recover claims against the debtor<br>**Trustee** responsible for collecting, liquidating, and distributing the debtor's estate<br>**Meeting of Creditors** debtor must appear and submit to an examination of her financial situation |
| **CREDITORS, THE DEBTOR, AND THE ESTATE—CHAPTER 5** | **Creditor** any entity that has a claim against the debtor<br>• ***Claim*** a right to payment<br>• ***Lien*** charge or interest in property to secure payment of a debt or performance of an obligation<br>• ***Secured Claim*** claim with a lien on property of the debtor<br>• ***Unsecured Claim*** portion of a claim that exceeds the value of any property securing that claim<br>• ***Priority of Claims*** the right of certain claims to be paid before claims of lesser rank<br>**Debtors**<br>• ***Debtor's Duties*** the debtor must file specified information, cooperate with the trustee, and surrender all property of the estate<br>• ***Debtor's Exemptions*** determined by State or Federal law, depending upon the State<br>• ***Discharge*** relief from liability for all debts except those the Bankruptcy Code specifies as not dischargeable<br>**The Estate** all legal and equitable interests of the debtor in nonexempt property<br>• ***Trustee as Lien Creditor*** trustee gains the rights and powers of creditor with judicial lien (an interest in property, obtained by court action, to secure payment of a debt)<br>• ***Voidable Preferences*** Bankruptcy Code invalidates certain preferential transfers made before the date of bankruptcy from the debtor to favored creditors<br>• ***Fraudulent Transfers*** trustee may avoid fraudulent transfers made on or within two years before the date of bankruptcy<br>• ***Statutory Liens*** trustee may avoid statutory liens which first become effective on insolvency, are not perfected at commencement of case, or are for rent |
| **LIQUIDATION—CHAPTER 7** | **Purpose** to distribute equitably the debtor's nonexempt assets and usually to discharge all dischargeable debts of the debtor |

| | |
|---|---|
| | **Proceedings** apply to most debtors<br>**Conversion** a case may be voluntarily converted to Chapter 11 or Chapter 13; it may be involuntarily converted by the court to Chapter 11<br>**Dismissal** the court may dismiss a case on general grounds *and* in a case filed by an individual debtor based on a means test<br>**Distribution of the Estate** in the following order: (1) secured creditors, (2) creditors entitled to a priority, (3) unsecured creditors, and (4) the debtor<br>**Discharge** granted by the court unless the debtor has committed an offense under the Bankruptcy Code or has received a discharge (1) within eight years under Chapter 7 or 11, or (2) subject to exceptions within six years under Chapter 13 |
| **REORGANIZATION—CHAPTER 11** | **Purpose** to preserve a distressed entity and its value as a going concern<br>**Proceedings** debtor usually remains in possession of the property of the estate<br>**Acceptance of Plan** requires a specified proportion of creditors to approve the plan<br>**Confirmation of Plan** requires (1) good faith, (2) feasibility, (3) cash payments to certain priority creditors, and (4) usually acceptance by creditors<br>**Effect of Confirmation** binds the debtor and creditors and discharges the debtor |
| **ADJUSTMENT OF DEBTS OF INDIVIDUALS—CHAPTER 13** | **Purpose** to permit an individual debtor to file a repayment plan that will discharge her from most debts<br>**Conversion or Dismissal** a Chapter 13 case may be voluntarily or involuntarily dismissed or converted to Chapter 7 or 11<br>**Confirmation of Plan** requires (1) good faith, (2) that the present value of property distributed to unsecured creditors be not less than the amount that would be paid them under Chapter 7, (3) that secured creditors accept the plan, keep their collateral, or retain their security interest and the present value of the property to be distributed to them is not less than the allowed amount of their claim, and (4) that the debtor be able to make all payments and comply with the plan<br>**Discharge** after a debtor completes all payments under the plan |

## CREDITORS' RIGHTS AND DEBTOR'S RELIEF OUTSIDE OF BANKRUPTCY

| | |
|---|---|
| **CREDITORS' RIGHTS** | **Prejudgment Remedies** include attachment and garnishment<br>**Postjudgment Remedies** include writ of execution and garnishment |
| **DEBTOR'S RELIEF** | **Compositions** agreement between debtor and two or more of her creditors that each will take a portion of his claim as full payment<br>**Assignment for Benefit of Creditors** voluntary transfer by the debtor of his property to a trustee, who applies the property to the payment of all the debtor's debts<br>**Equity Receivership** receiver is a disinterested person appointed by the court to collect and preserve the debtor's assets and income and to dispose of them at the direction of the court |

## CASES

# CASE 39-1

## Conversion
## MARRAMA v. CITIZENS BANK

Supreme Court of the United States, 2007
549 U.S. 365, 127 S.Ct. 1105, 166 L.Ed.2d 956
http://www.supremecourtus.gov/opinions/06pdf/05-996.pdf

**Stevens, J.**

The principal purpose of the Bankruptcy Code is to grant a "'fresh start'" to the "'honest but unfortunate debtor.'" [Citation.] Both Chapter 7 and Chapter 13 of the Code permit an insolvent individual to discharge certain unpaid debts toward that end. Chapter 7 authorizes a discharge of prepetition debts following the liquidation of the debtor's assets by a bankruptcy trustee, who then distributes the proceeds to creditors. Chapter 13 authorizes an individual with regular income to obtain a discharge after the successful completion of a payment plan approved by the bankruptcy court. Under Chapter 7 the debtor's non-exempt assets are controlled by the bankruptcy trustee; under Chapter 13 the debtor retains possession of his property. A proceeding that is commenced under Chapter 7 may be converted to a Chapter 13 proceeding and vice versa. §§706(a), 1307(a) and (c).

An issue that has arisen with disturbing frequency is whether a debtor who acts in bad faith prior to, or in the course of, filing a Chapter 13 petition by, for example, fraudulently concealing significant assets, thereby forfeits his right to obtain Chapter 13 relief. The issue may arise at the outset of a Chapter 13 case in response to a motion by creditors or by the United States trustee either to dismiss the case or to convert it to Chapter 7, see §1307(c). It also may arise in a Chapter 7 case when a debtor files a motion under §706(a) to convert to Chapter 13. In the former context, despite the absence of any statutory provision specifically addressing the issue, the federal courts are virtually unanimous that prepetition bad-faith conduct may cause a forfeiture of any right to proceed with a Chapter 13 case. In the latter context, however, some courts have suggested that even a bad-faith debtor has an absolute right to convert at least one Chapter 7 proceeding into a Chapter 13 case even though the case will thereafter be dismissed or immediately returned to Chapter 7. We granted certiorari to decide whether the Code mandates that procedural anomaly. [Citation.]

On March 11, 2003, petitioner, Robert Marrama, filed a voluntary petition under Chapter 7, thereby creating an estate consisting of all his property "wherever located and by whomever held." §541(a). Respondent Mark DeGiacomo is the trustee of that estate. Respondent Citizens Bank of Massachusetts (hereinafter Bank) is the principal creditor.

In verified schedules attached to his petition, Marrama made a number of statements about his principal asset, a house in Maine, that were misleading or inaccurate. For instance, while he disclosed that he was the sole beneficiary of the trust that owned the property, he listed its value as zero. He also denied that he had transferred any property other than in the ordinary course of business during the year preceding the filing of his petition. Neither statement was true. In fact, the Maine property had substantial value, and Marrama had transferred it into the newly created trust for no consideration seven months prior to filing his Chapter 13 petition. Marrama later admitted that the purpose of the transfer was to protect the property from his creditors.

After Marrama's examination at the meeting of creditors, see §341, the trustee advised Marrama's counsel that he intended to recover the Maine property as an asset of the estate. Thereafter, Marrama filed * * * a motion to convert [to Chapter 13], to which both the trustee and the Bank filed objections. Relying primarily on Marrama's attempt to conceal the Maine property from his creditors, the trustee contended that the request to convert was made in bad faith and would constitute an abuse of the bankruptcy process. The Bank opposed the conversion on similar grounds.

* * * The Bankruptcy Judge rejected [the debtor's] arguments, ruling that * * * the facts established a "bad faith" case. [Citation.] The judge denied the request for conversion.

Marrama's principal argument on appeal to the Bankruptcy Appellate Panel for the First Circuit was that he had an absolute right to convert his case from Chapter 7 to Chapter 13 under the plain language of §706(a) of the Code. The panel affirmed the decision of the Bankruptcy Court. * * *

On appeal from the panel, the Court of Appeals for the First Circuit also rejected the argument that §706(a) gives a Chapter 7 debtor an absolute right to convert to Chapter 13. * * *

While other Courts of Appeals and bankruptcy appellate panels have refused to recognize any "bad faith" exception to the conversion right created by §706(a), we conclude that the courts in this case correctly held that Marrama forfeited his right to proceed under Chapter 13.

* * *

The class of honest but unfortunate debtors who do possess an absolute right to convert their cases from Chapter 7 to Chapter 13 includes the vast majority of the hundreds of thousands of individuals who file Chapter 7 petitions each year. Congress sought to give these individuals the chance to repay their debts should they acquire the means to do so. Moreover, as the Court of Appeals observed, the reference in §706(a) to the unenforceability of a waiver of the right to convert functions "as a consumer protection provision against adhesion contracts, whereby a debtor's creditors might be precluded from attempting to prescribe a waiver of the debtor's right to convert to chapter 13 as a non-negotiable condition of its contractual agreements." [Citation.]

A statutory provision protecting a borrower from waiver is not a shield against forfeiture. Nothing in the text of either §706 or §1307(c) (or the legislative history of either provision) limits the authority of the court to take appropriate action in response to fraudulent conduct by the atypical litigant who has demonstrated that he is not entitled to the relief available to the typical debtor. On the contrary, the broad authority granted to bankruptcy judges to take any action that is necessary or appropriate "to prevent an abuse of process" described in §105(a) of the Code, is surely adequate to authorize an immediate denial of a motion to convert filed under §706 in lieu of a conversion order that merely postpones the allowance of equivalent relief and may provide a debtor with an opportunity to take action prejudicial to creditors.

* * *

Accordingly, the judgment of the Court of Appeals is affirmed.

It is so ordered.

CASE 39-2

## Proceedings in Chapter 11
## IN RE JOHNS MANVILLE CORPORATION

United States Bankruptcy Court, Southern District of New York, 1984
36 B.R. 727, appeal denied, 39 B.R. 234

**Lifland, Bkrtcy. J.**

Whether an industrial enterprise in the United States is highly successful is often gauged by its "membership" in what has come to be known as the "Fortune 500." Having attained this measure of financial achievement, Johns Manville Corp. and its affiliated companies (collectively referred to as "Manville") were deemed a paradigm of success in corporate America by the financial community. Thus, Manville's filing for protection under Chapter 11 * * * of the United States Code ("the Code or the Bankruptcy Code") on August 26, 1982 ("the filing date") was greeted with great surprise and consternation on the part of some of its creditors and other corporations that were being sued along with Manville for injuries caused by asbestos exposure. As discussed at length herein, Manville submits that the sole factor necessitating its filing is the mammoth problem of uncontrolled proliferation of asbestos health suits brought against it because of its substantial use for many years of products containing asbestos which injured those who came into contact with the dust of this lethal substance. According to Manville, this current problem of approximately 16,000 lawsuits pending as of the filing date is compounded by the crushing economic burden to be suffered by Manville over the next 20–30 years by the filing of an even more staggering number of suits by those who had been exposed but who will not manifest the asbestos-related diseases until some time during this future period ("the future asbestos claimants"). Indeed, approximately 6,000 asbestos health claims are estimated to have arisen in only the first 16 months since the filing date. This burden is further compounded by the insurance industry's general disavowal of liability to Manville on policies written for this very purpose. * * *

It is the propriety of the filing by Manville which is the subject of the instant decision. Four separate motions to dismiss the petition * * * have been lodged before this Court.

* * *

Preliminarily, it must be stated that there is no question that Manville is eligible to be a debtor under the Code's statutory requirements.

* * *

Moreover, it should also be noted that [no] * * * provision relating to voluntary petitions by companies contains any insolvency requirement.

* * *

A "principal goal" of the Bankruptcy Code is to provide "open access" to the "bankruptcy process." [Citation.] The rationale behind this "open access" policy is to provide access to bankruptcy relief which is as "open" as "access to the credit economy." [Citation.] Thus, Congress intended that "there should be no legal barrier to voluntary petitions." [Citation.] Another major goal of the Code, that of "rehabilitation of debtors," requires that relief for debtors must be "timely." [Citation.] * * *

Accordingly, the drafters of the Code envisioned that a financially beleaguered debtor with real debt and real creditors should not be required to wait until the economic situation is beyond repair in order to file a reorganization petition. The "Congressional purpose" in enacting the Code was to encourage resort to the bankruptcy process. [Citation.] This philosophy not only comports with the elimination of an insolvency requirement, but also is a corollary of the key aim of Chapter 11 of the Code, that of avoidance of liquidation. The drafters of the Code announced this goal, declaring that reorganization is more efficient than liquidation because "assets that are used for production in the industry for which they were designed are more valuable than those same assets sold for scrap." [Citation.] Moreover, reorganization also fosters the goals of preservation of jobs in the threatened entity. [Citation.]

In the instant case, not only would liquidation be wasteful and inefficient in destroying the utility of valuable assets of the companies as well as jobs, but, more importantly, liquidation would preclude just compensation of some present asbestos victims and all future asbestos claimants. This unassailable reality represents all the more reason for this Court to adhere to this basic potential liquidation avoidance aim of Chapter 11 and deny the motions to dismiss. Manville must not be required to wait until its economic picture has deteriorated beyond salvation to file for reorganization.

* * *

In [this case] it is undeniable that there has been no sham or hoax perpetrated on the Court in that Manville is a real business with real creditors in pressing need of economic reorganization. Indeed, the Asbestos Committee has belied its own contention that Manville has no debt and no real creditors by quantifying a benchmark settlement demand approaching one billion dollars for compensation of approximately 15,500 pre-petition asbestos claimants, during the course of negotiations pitched toward achieving a consensual plan. This huge asserted liability does not even take into account the estimated 6,000 new asbestos health claims which have arisen in only the first 16 months since the filing date. The number of post-filing claims increases each day as "future claims back into the present." * * *

Moreover, asbestos related property damage claims present another substantial contingent and unliquidated liability. Prior to the filing date, various schools initiated litigation seeking compensatory and punitive damages from * * * Manville for their unknowing use of asbestos-containing products in ceilings, walls, structural members, piping, ductwork and boilers in school buildings.

* * *

In short, there was justification for Manville to elect a course contemplating a viable court-supervised rehabilitation of the real debt owed by Manville to its real creditors. Manville's filing did not in the appropriate sense abuse the jurisdiction of this Court and it is indeed, like the debtor in (citation), a "once viable business supporting employees and unsecured creditors (which) has more recently been burdened with judgments (and suits) that threaten to put it out of existence." * * * [Citation.] Thus, its petition must be sustained.

* * *

In sum, Manville is a financially besieged enterprise in desperate need of reorganization of its crushing real debt, both present and future. The reorganization provisions of the Code were drafted with the aim of liquidation avoidance by great access to Chapter 11. Accordingly, Manville's filing does not abuse the jurisdictional integrity of this Court, but rather presents the same kinds of reasons that were present in [citation], for awaiting the determination of Manville's good faith until it is considered * * * as a prerequisite to confirmation or as a part of the cadre of motions before me which are scheduled to be heard subsequently.

[Motions to dismiss the Manville petition denied.]

CASE 39-3

## Confirmation of Chapter 13 Plan
## HAMILTON v. LANNING

Supreme Court of the United States, 2010
___ U.S.___, 130 S.Ct. 2464, 177 L.Ed.2d 23
http://www.law.cornell.edu/supct/html/08-998.ZO.html

**Alito, J.**

Chapter 13 of the Bankruptcy Code provides bankruptcy protection to "individual[s] with regular income" whose debts fall within statutory limits. [Citation.] Unlike debtors who file under Chapter 7 and must liquidate their nonexempt assets in order to pay creditors, [citation], Chapter 13 debtors are permitted to keep their property, but they must agree to a court-approved plan under which they pay creditors out of their future income, [citation]. A bankruptcy trustee oversees the filing and execution of a Chapter 13 debtor's plan. [Citations.]

Section 1325 of the [Bankruptcy Code] specifies circumstances under which a bankruptcy court "shall" and "may not" confirm a plan. §1325(a), (b). If an unsecured creditor or the bankruptcy trustee objects to confirmation, §1325(b)(1) requires the debtor either to pay unsecured creditors in full or to pay all "projected disposable income" to be received by the debtor over the duration of the plan.

We granted certiorari to decide how a bankruptcy court should calculate a debtor's "projected disposable income." Some lower courts have taken what the parties term the "mechanical approach," while most have adopted what has been called the "forward-looking approach." We hold that the "forward-looking approach" is correct.

### I

* * * Before the enactment of the Bankruptcy Abuse Prevention and Consumer Protection Act of 2005 (BAPCPA), [citation], the Bankruptcy Code (Code) loosely defined "disposable income" as "income which is received by the debtor and which is not reasonably necessary to be expended" for the "maintenance or support of the debtor," for qualifying charitable contributions, or for business expenditures. §1325(b)(2)(A), (B).

The Code did not define the term "projected disposable income," and in most cases, bankruptcy courts used a mechanical approach in calculating projected disposable income. That is, they first multiplied monthly income by the number of months in the plan and then determined what portion of the result was "excess" or "disposable." [Citation.]

In exceptional cases, however, bankruptcy courts took into account foreseeable changes in a debtor's income or expenses. [Citations.]

BAPCPA left the term "projected disposable income" undefined but specified in some detail how "disposable income" is to be calculated. "Disposable income" is now defined as "current monthly income received by the debtor" less "amounts reasonably necessary to be expended" for the debtor's maintenance and support, for qualifying charitable contributions, and for business expenditures. [Citation.] "Current monthly income," in turn, is calculated by averaging the debtor's monthly income during what the parties refer to as the 6-month look-back period, which generally consists of the six full months preceding the filing of the bankruptcy petition. [Citation.] The phrase "amounts reasonably necessary to be expended" in §1325(b)(2) is also newly defined. For a debtor whose income is below the median for his or her State, the phrase includes the full amount needed for "maintenance or support," [citation], but for a debtor with income that exceeds the state median, only certain specified expenses are included, [citations.]

### II

### A

Respondent had $36,793.36 in unsecured debt when she filed for Chapter 13 bankruptcy protection in October 2006. In the six months before her filing, she received a one-time buyout from her former employer, and this payment greatly inflated her gross income for April 2006 (to $11,990.03) and for May 2006 (to $15,356.42). [Citation.] As a result of these payments, respondent's current monthly income, as averaged from April through October 2006, was $5,343.70—a figure that exceeds the median income for a family of one in Kansas. [Citation.] Respondent's monthly expenses, calculated pursuant to [citation] were $4,228.71. [Citation.] She reported a monthly "disposable income" of $1,114.98 on Form 22C. [Citation.]

On the form used for reporting monthly income (Schedule I), she reported income from her new job of $1,922 per month—which is below the state median. [Citations.] On the form used for reporting monthly expenses (Schedule J), she reported actual monthly expenses of $1,772.97. [Citation.] Subtracting the Schedule J figure from the Schedule I figure resulted in monthly disposable income of $149.03.

Respondent filed a plan that would have required her to pay $144 per month for 36 months. [Citation.]

Petitioner, a private Chapter 13 trustee, objected to confirmation of the plan because the amount respondent proposed to pay was less than the full amount of the claims against her, [citation], and because, in petitioner's view, respondent was not committing all of her "projected disposable income" to the repayment of creditors, [citation]. According to petitioner, the proper way to calculate projected disposable income was simply to multiply disposable income, as calculated on Form 22C, by the number of months in the commitment period. Employing this mechanical approach, petitioner calculated that creditors would be paid in full if respondent made monthly payments of $756 for a period of 60 months. [Citation.] There is no dispute that respondent's actual income was insufficient to make payments in that amount. [Citation.]

### B

The Bankruptcy Court endorsed respondent's proposed monthly payment of $144 but required a 60-month plan period. [Citation.] The court agreed with the majority view that the word "projected" in §1325(b)(1)(B) requires courts "to consider at confirmation the debtor's *actual* income as it was reported on Schedule I." [Citation] (emphasis added [by court]). This conclusion was warranted by the text of §1325(b)(1), the Bankruptcy Court reasoned, and was necessary to avoid the absurd result of denying bankruptcy protection to individuals with deteriorating finances in the six months before filing. [Citation.]

Petitioner appealed to the Tenth Circuit Bankruptcy Appellate Panel, which affirmed. [Citation.] * * *

The Tenth Circuit affirmed. * * *

This petition followed, and we granted certiorari. [Citation.]

## III

### A

The parties differ sharply in their interpretation of §1325's reference to "projected disposable income." Petitioner, advocating the mechanical approach, contends that "projected disposable income" means past average monthly disposable income multiplied by the number of months in a debtor's plan. Respondent, who favors the forward-looking approach, agrees that the method outlined by petitioner should be determinative in most cases, but she argues that in exceptional cases, where significant changes in a debtor's financial circumstances are known or virtually certain, a bankruptcy court has discretion to make an appropriate adjustment. Respondent has the stronger argument.

First, respondent's argument is supported by the ordinary meaning of the term "projected." "When terms used in a statute are undefined, we give them their ordinary meaning." [Citation.] Here, the term "projected" is not defined, and in ordinary usage future occurrences are not "projected" based on the assumption that the past will necessarily repeat itself. For example, projections concerning a company's future sales or the future cash flow from a license take into account anticipated events that may change past trends. * * * While a projection takes past events into account, adjustments are often made based on other factors that may affect the final outcome. [Citation.]

Second, the word "projected" appears in many federal statutes, yet Congress rarely has used it to mean simple multiplication. * * *

By contrast, we need look no further than the Bankruptcy Code to see that when Congress wishes to mandate simple multiplication, it does so unambiguously-most commonly by using the term "multiplied." [Citations.]

Third, pre-BAPCPA case law points in favor of the "forward-looking" approach. Prior to BAPCPA, the general rule was that courts would multiply a debtor's current monthly income by the number of months in the commitment period as the first step in determining projected disposable income. [Citations.] But courts also had discretion to account for known or virtually certain changes in the debtor's income. * * * Indeed, petitioner concedes that courts possessed this discretion prior to BAPCPA. [Citation.]

Pre-BAPCPA bankruptcy practice is telling because we "'will not read the Bankruptcy Code to erode past bankruptcy practice absent a clear indication that Congress intended such a departure.'" [Citation.] Congress did not amend the term "projected disposable income" in 2005, and pre-BAPCPA bankruptcy practice reflected a widely acknowledged and well-documented view that courts may take into account known or virtually certain changes to debtors' income or expenses when projecting disposable income. In light of this historical practice, we would expect that, had Congress intended for "projected" to carry a specialized—and indeed, unusual—meaning in Chapter 13, Congress would have said so expressly. [Citation.]

### B

The mechanical approach also clashes repeatedly with the terms of 11 U.S.C. §1325.

First, §1325(b)(1)(B)'s reference to projected disposable income "to be received in the applicable commitment period" strongly favors the forward-looking approach. There is no dispute that respondent would in fact receive far less than $756 per month in disposable income during the plan period, so petitioner's projection does not accurately reflect "income to be received" during that period. [Citation.] The mechanical approach effectively reads this phrase out of the statute when a debtor's current disposable income is substantially higher than the income that the debtor predictably will receive during the plan period. [Citation.]

Second, §1325(b)(1) directs courts to determine projected disposable income "as of the effective date of the plan," which is the date on which the plan is confirmed and becomes binding, see §1327(a). Had Congress intended for projected disposable income to be nothing more than a multiple of disposable income in all cases, we see no reason why Congress would not have required courts to determine that value as of the *filing* date of the plan. [Citation.] * * * Congress' decision to require courts to measure projected disposable income "as of the *effective* date of the plan" is more consistent with the view that Congress expected courts to consider postfiling information about the debtor's financial circumstances. [Citation.]

Third, the requirement that projected disposable income "will be applied to make payments" is most naturally read to contemplate that the debtor will actually pay creditors in the calculated monthly amounts. §1325(b)(1)(B). But when, as of the effective date of a plan, the debtor lacks the means to do so, this language is rendered a hollow command.

### C

The arguments advanced in favor of the mechanical approach are unpersuasive. Noting that the Code now provides a detailed and precise definition of "disposable income," proponents of the mechanical approach maintain that any departure from this method leaves that definition " 'with no apparent purpose.' " [Citation.] This argument overlooks the important role that the statutory formula for calculating "disposable income" plays under the forward-looking approach. * * *

* * *

### D

In cases in which a debtor's disposable income during the 6-month look-back period is either substantially lower or higher than the debtor's disposable income during the plan period, the mechanical approach would produce senseless results that we do not think Congress intended. In cases in which the debtor's disposable income is higher during the plan period, the mechanical approach would deny creditors payments that the debtor could easily make. And where, as in the present case, the debtor's disposable income during the plan period is substantially lower, the mechanical approach would deny the protection of Chapter 13 to debtors who meet the chapter's main eligibility requirements. Here, for example, respondent is an "individual whose income is sufficiently stable and regular" to allow her "to make payments under a plan," §101(30), and her debts fall below the limits set out in §109(e). But if the mechanical approach were used, she could not file a confirmable plan. Under §1325(a)(6), a plan cannot be confirmed unless "the debtor will be able to make all payments under the plan and comply with the plan." And as petitioner concedes, respondent could not possibly make the payments that the mechanical approach prescribes.

* * *

### IV

* * * Consistent with the text of §1325 and pre-BAPCPA practice, we hold that when a bankruptcy court calculates a debtor's projected disposable income, the court may account for changes in the debtor's income or expenses that are known or virtually certain at the time of confirmation. We therefore affirm the decision of the Court of Appeals.

## QUESTIONS

1. Explain (a) the requirements for voluntary and involuntary cases, (b) the priorities of creditors' claims, (c) the debtor's exemptions, and (d) the debts that are not dischargeable in bankruptcy.
2. Discuss the duties of a trustee and his rights (a) as a lien creditor, (b) to avoid preferential transfers, (c) to avoid fraudulent transfers, and (d) to avoid statutory liens.
3. Explain the procedure involved in distributing the debtor's estate under Chapter 7.
4. Compare the adjustment of debt proceedings under Chapters 11 and 13.
5. Identify and define the nonbankruptcy compromises between debtors and creditors.

# PROBLEMS

1. **(a)** Benson goes into bankruptcy. His estate is not sufficient to pay all taxes owed. Explain whether Benson's taxes are discharged by the proceedings.
**(b)** Benson obtained property from Anderson on credit by representing that he was solvent when in fact he knew he was insolvent. Is Benson's debt to Anderson discharged by Benson's discharge in bankruptcy?

2. Bradley goes into bankruptcy under Chapter 7 owing $5,000 as wages to his four employees. There is enough in his estate to pay all costs of administration and enough to pay his employees, but nothing will be left for general creditors. Do the employees take all the estate? If so, under what conditions? If the general creditors received nothing, would these debts be discharged?

3. Jessica sold goods to Stacy for $2,500 and retained a security interest in them. Two months later, Stacy filed a voluntary petition in bankruptcy under Chapter 7. At this time, Stacy still owed Jessica $2,000 for the purchase price of the goods, the value of which was $1,500.
**(a)** May the trustee invalidate Jessica's security interest? If so, under what provision?
**(b)** If the security interest is invalidated, what is Jessica's status in the bankruptcy proceeding?
**(c)** If the security interest is *not* invalidated, what is Jessica's status in the bankruptcy proceeding?

4. A debtor went through bankruptcy under Chapter 7 and received his discharge. Which of the following debts were completely discharged, and which will remain as future debts against him?
**(a)** A claim of $9,000 for wages earned within five months immediately prior to bankruptcy.
**(b)** A judgment of $3,000 against the debtor for breach of contract.
**(c)** $1,000 for domestic support obligations.
**(d)** A judgment of $4,000 for injuries received because of the debtor's negligent operation of an automobile.

5. Rosinoff and his wife, who were business partners, entered bankruptcy. A creditor, Baldwin, objected to their discharge in bankruptcy on the grounds that
**(a)** the partners had obtained credit from Baldwin on the basis of a false financial statement;
**(b)** the partners had failed to keep books of account and records from which their financial condition could be ascertained; and
**(c)** Rosinoff had falsely sworn that he had taken $70 from the partnership account when the amount he took was actually $700.
Were the debtors entitled to a discharge?

6. Ross Corporation is a debtor in a reorganization proceeding under Chapter 11 of the Bankruptcy Code. By fair and proper valuation, its assets are worth $100,000. The indebtedness of the corporation is $105,000, and it has outstanding $100 par value preferred stock in the amount of $20,000 and $30 par value common stock in the amount of $75,000. The plan of reorganization submitted by the trustees would give nothing to the common shareholders and would issue new bonds in the face amount of $5,000 to the creditors and new common stock in the ratio of 84 percent to the creditors and 16 percent to the preferred shareholders. Should this plan be confirmed?

7. Alex is a wage earner with a regular income. He has unsecured debts of $42,000 and secured debts owing to Betty, Connie, David, and Eunice totaling $120,000. Eunice's debt is secured only by a mortgage on Alex's house. Alex files a petition under Chapter 13 and a plan providing payment as follows: (a) 60 percent of all taxes owed; (b) 35 percent of all unsecured debts; and (c) $100,000 in total to Betty, Connie, David, and Eunice. Should the court confirm the plan? If not, how must the plan be modified and/or what other conditions must be satisfied?

8. John Bunker has assets of $130,000 and liabilities of $185,000 owed to nine creditors. Nonetheless, his cash flow is positive, and he is making payment on all of his obligations as they become due. I. M. Flintheart, who is owed $22,000 by Bunker, files an involuntary petition in bankruptcy under Chapter 7 against Bunker. Bunker contests the petition. What result? Explain.

9. Karen has filed a voluntary petition for a Chapter 7 proceeding. The total value of her estate is $35,000. Ben, who is owed $18,000, has a security interest in property valued at $12,000. Lauren has an unsecured claim of $9,000, which is entitled to a priority of $2,000. The United States has a claim for income taxes of $7,000. Steve has an unsecured claim of $10,000 that was filed on time. Sarah has an unsecured claim of $17,000 that was filed on time. Wally has a claim of $14,000 that he filed late, even though he was aware of the bankruptcy proceedings. What should each of the creditors receive in a distribution under Chapter 7?

10. Landmark at Plaza Park, Ltd., filed a plan of reorganization under Chapter 11 of the Bankruptcy Code. Landmark is a limited partnership whose only substantial asset is a two-hundred-unit garden apartment complex. City Federal holds the first mortgage on the property in the face amount of $2,250,000. The mortgage is due and payable six years from now.

Landmark has proposed a plan of reorganization under which the property now in possession of City Federal would be returned. Landmark will then deliver a nonrecourse note, payable in three years, in the face amount of $2,705,820.31 to City Federal in substitution of all of the partnership's existing liabilities. On the sixteenth month through the thirty-sixth month after the effective date of the plan, Landmark will make monthly interest payments computed on a property value of $2,260,000 at a rate 3 percent above the original mortgage rate but 2.5 percent below the market rate for loans of similar risk. Finally, the note will be secured by the existing mortgage. Landmark's theory is that the note will be paid off at the end of thirty-six months by a combination of refinancing and accumulation of cash from the project. The key is Landmark's proposal to obtain a new first mortgage in three years in the face amount of $2,400,000.

City Federal is a first mortgagee without recourse that has been collecting rents pursuant to a rent assignment agreement since the default on the mortgage eleven months ago. City Federal is impaired by the plan and has rejected the plan. May it complete its foreclosure action? Explain.

**11.** Freelin Conn filed a voluntary petition under Chapter 7 of the Bankruptcy Code on September 30, 2011. Conn listed BancOhio National Bank as having a claim incurred in October 2010 in the amount of $4,000 secured by a 2003 Oldsmobile. The car is listed as having a market value of $3,500. During the period from June 30, 2011, to September 30, 2011, Conn made three payments totaling $439.17 to BancOhio. May the trustee in bankruptcy set aside those three payments as voidable preferences? Explain.

**12.** David files a bankruptcy petition under Chapter 13. After the claims of secured and priority creditors have been satisfied, David's remaining bankruptcy estate has a value of $100,000. David's creditors with allowed unsecured claims are owed $250,000 in total. Chris, an unsecured creditor, is owed $13,500. David's Chapter 13 plan proposes to pay Chris $150 per month for three years. Should the bankruptcy court confirm David's plan? Explain.

**13.** Yolanda Christophe filed a bankruptcy petition under Chapter 13. Her scheduled debts consist of $11,100 of secured debt, $9,300 owed on an unsecured student loan, and $6,960 of other unsecured debt. Christophe asserts that the student loan is nondischargeable, and that assertion has not been questioned. Christophe's proposed amended Chapter 13 Plan calls for fifty-six monthly payments of $440 a month. The questioned provision in that Plan is the division of the unsecured creditors into two classes. The general unsecured creditors would receive 32 percent, while the separately classified student loan creditor would receive 100 percent. Should this plan be confirmed?

**14.** On December 17, ZZZZ Best Co., Inc. (the debtor), borrowed $7 million from Union Bank (the bank). On July 8 of the following year, the debtor filed a voluntary petition for bankruptcy under Chapter 7. During the preceding ninety days, the debtor had made interest payments of $100,000 to the bank on the loan. The trustee of the debtor's estate files a complaint against the bank to recover those payments as a voidable preference. The bank argues that the payments were not voidable because they came within the ordinary course of business exception. The trustee maintains that the exception applies only to short-term, not long-term, debt. Who is correct? Explain.

**15.** A landlord owned several residential properties, one of which was subject to a local rent control ordinance. The local rent control administrator determined that the landlord had been charging rents above the levels permitted by the ordinance and ordered him to refund the wrongfully collected rents to the affected tenants. The landlord did not comply with the order. The landlord subsequently filed for relief under Chapter 7 of the Bankruptcy Code, seeking to discharge his debts. The tenants filed an adversary proceeding against the landlord in the bankruptcy court, arguing that the debt owed to them arose from rent payments obtained by "actual fraud" and that the debt was therefore nondischargeable under §523(a)(2)(A) of the Bankruptcy Code. They also sought treble damages and attorneys' fees and costs pursuant to the State Consumer Fraud Act. The bankruptcy court ruled in favor of the tenants, finding that the landlord had committed "actual fraud" within the meaning of §523(a)(2)(A) and that his conduct violated State law. The court therefore awarded the tenants treble damages totaling $94,147.50. Does the Bankruptcy Code bar the discharge of treble damages awarded on account of the debtor's fraud? Explain.

**16.** Leonard and Arlene Warner sold the Warner Manufacturing Company to Elliott and Carol Archer for $610,000. A few months later the Archers sued the Warners in a State court for fraud connected with the sale. The parties settled the lawsuit for $300,000. The Warners paid the Archers $200,000 and executed a promissory note for the remaining $100,000. After the Warners failed to make the first payment on the $100,000 promissory note, the Archers sued for the payment in State court. The Warners then filed for bankruptcy under Chapter 7 of the Bankruptcy Code. The Archers asked the bankruptcy court to find the $100,000 debt nondischargeable, arguing that the promissory note debt was nondischargeable because it was for "money obtained by fraud." Arlene Warner argued that the $100,000 debt was dischargeable in bankruptcy because it was a new debt for money promised in a settlement contract and that it was not a debt for money obtained by fraud. Explain whether the debt is dischargeable in bankruptcy.

# CHAPTER 44
# Securities Regulation

The primary purpose of Federal securities regulation is to foster public confidence in the securities market by preventing fraudulent practices in the sale of securities. Federal securities law consists principally of two statutes: the Securities Act of 1933, which focuses on the issuance of securities, and the Securities Exchange Act of 1934, which deals mainly with trading in issued securities. These "secondary" transactions greatly exceed in number and dollar value the original offerings by issuers.

Both statutes are administered by the Securities and Exchange Commission (SEC), an independent, quasi-judicial agency consisting of five commissioners. The responsibilities of the SEC include interpreting Federal securities laws; issuing new rules and amending existing rules; and coordinating U.S. securities regulation with Federal, State, and foreign authorities. In 1996 Congress enacted legislation requiring the SEC, when making rules under either of the securities statutes, to consider, in addition to the protection of investors, whether its action will promote efficiency, competition, and capital formation.

In July 2010, President Obama signed into law the Dodd-Frank Wall Street Reform and Consumer Protection Act (CFPA), the most significant change to U.S. financial regulation since the New Deal. One of the many standalone statutes included in the CFPA is the Investor Protection and Securities Reform Act of 2010, which imposes new corporate governance and investor protection rules on publicly held companies. Corporate governance and investor protection provisions of the CFPA are discussed in this chapter as well as in *Chapters 36*, *37*, and *47*.

The SEC has the power to seek, in a Federal district court, civil injunctions against violations of the statutes; to recommend that the Justice Department bring criminal prosecutions; and to issue orders censuring, suspending, or expelling broker-dealers, investment advisers, and investment companies. The Securities Enforcement Remedies and Penny Stock Reform Act of 1990 granted the SEC the power to issue cease-and-desist orders and to impose administrative, civil penalties up to the current inflation-adjusted amount of $725,000. Congress enacted the Private Securities Litigation Reform Act of 1995 (Reform Act), which amends both the 1933 Act and the 1934 Act. One of its provisions grants authority to the SEC to bring civil actions for specified violations of the 1934 Act against aiders and abettors (those who knowingly provide substantial assistance to a person who violates the statute). The CFPA has extended this authority in two ways: (1) the CFPA empowers the SEC to bring enforcement actions under the 1933 Act against aiders and abettors and (2) the CFPA amends the 1933 and 1934 Acts to allow *recklessness* as well as knowledge to satisfy the mental state required for the SEC to bring aiding and abetting cases.

The Reform Act sought to prevent abuses in private securities fraud lawsuits. To prevent certain State private securities class action lawsuits alleging fraud from being used to frustrate the objectives of the Reform Act, Congress enacted the Securities Litigation Uniform Standards Act of 1998. The Act sets national standards for securities class action lawsuits involving nationally traded securities, while preserving the appropriate enforcement powers of State securities regulators and leaving unchanged the current treatment of individual lawsuits. The Act amends both the 1933 Act and the 1934 Act by prohibiting any private class action suit in State or Federal court by any private party based upon State statutory or common law alleging: (1) an untrue statement or omission in connection with the purchase or sale of a covered security; or (2) that the defendant used any manipulative or deceptive device in connection with such a transaction.

In response to the business scandals involving companies such as Enron, WorldCom, Global Crossing, Adelphia, and Arthur Andersen, in 2002 Congress passed the Sarbanes-Oxley Act, which amends the securities acts in a number of significant respects. The Act allows the SEC to add civil penalties to a disgorgement fund for the benefit of victims of violations of the 1933 Act or the 1934 Act. Other provisions of the Act are discussed later in this chapter, as well as in *Chapters 6*, *36*, and *45*. In addition, the CFPA requires the SEC to make an award to whistleblowers who voluntarily provide original information that leads to a successful enforcement action in which the SEC imposes monetary sanctions in excess of $1 million. The amount of the award must be between 10 percent and 30 percent of funds collected as monetary sanctions, as determined by the SEC.

The 1933 Act has two basic objectives: (1) to provide investors with material information concerning securities offered for sale to the public and (2) to prohibit misrepresentation, deceit, and other fraudulent acts and unfair practices in the sale of securities generally, whether or not they are required to be registered.

The 1934 Act extends protection to investors trading in securities that are already issued and outstanding. The 1934 Act also imposes disclosure requirements on publicly held corporations and regulates tender offers and proxy solicitations.

The SEC has recognized that the "use of electronic media also enhances the efficiency of the securities markets by allowing for the rapid dissemination of information to investors and financial markets in a more cost-efficient, widespread, and equitable manner than traditional paper-based methods." The SEC has provided interpretative guidance for the use of electronic media for the delivery of information required by the Federal securities laws. The SEC defined *electronic media* to include audiotapes, videotapes, facsimiles, CD-ROM, electronic mail, bulletin boards, Internet Web sites, and computer networks. Basically, electronic delivery must provide notice, access, and evidence of delivery comparable to that provided by paper delivery.

The SEC has established the EDGAR (Electronic Data Gathering, Analysis, and Retrieval) computer system, which performs automated collection, validation, indexing, acceptance, and dissemination of reports required to be filed with the SEC. Its primary purpose is to increase the efficiency and fairness of the securities market for the benefit of investors, corporations, and the economy by speeding up the receipt, acceptance, dissemination, and analysis of corporate information filed with the SEC. The SEC now requires all public domestic companies to make their filings on EDGAR, except filings exempted for hardship. EDGAR filings are posted at the SEC's Web site twenty-four hours after the date of filing.

In addition to the Federal laws regulating the sale of securities, each State has its own laws regulating such sales within its borders. Commonly called **blue sky laws**, these statutes all contain provisions prohibiting fraud in the sale of securities. In addition, most States require the registration of securities and also regulate brokers and dealers. The Uniform Securities Act of 1956 has been adopted at one time or another, in whole or in part, by thirty-seven jurisdictions, whereas the Revised Uniform Securities Act of 1985 has been adopted in only a few States. Both Acts, however, have been preempted in part by the National Securities Markets Improvement Act of 1996 and the Securities Litigation Uniform Standards Act of 1998. In 2002 the National Conference of Commissioners on Uniform State Laws promulgated a new Uniform Securities Act, which has been adopted by at least seventeen States. The 2002 Uniform Securities Act seeks to give States regulatory and enforcement authority that minimizes duplication of regulatory resources and that blends with Federal regulation and enforcement.

Any person who sells securities must comply with the Federal securities laws as well as with the securities laws of each State in which he intends to offer his securities. However, in 1996 Congress enacted the National Securities Markets Improvements Act, preempting State regulation of many offerings of securities. Because the State securities laws vary greatly, this chapter will discuss only the 1933 Act and the 1934 Act.

# SECURITIES ACT OF 1933

The 1933 Act, also called the "Truth in Securities Act," requires that a registration statement be filed with the SEC and that it become effective before any securities may be offered for sale to the public, unless either the securities or the transaction in which they are offered is exempt from registration. The purpose of registration is to disclose financial and other information about the issuer and those who control it, so that potential investors may appraise the merits of the securities. The 1933 Act also requires that potential investors be furnished with a **prospectus** (a document offering the securities for sale) containing the important data set forth in the registration statement. The 1933 Act prohibits fraud in all sales of securities involving interstate commerce or the mails, even if the securities are exempt from the registration and disclosure requirements of the 1933 Act. Civil and criminal liability may be imposed for violations of the 1933 Act.

The National Securities Markets Improvements Act of 1996 broadly authorized the SEC to issue regulations or rules exempting any person, security, or transaction from any of the provisions of the 1933 Act or the SEC's rules promulgated under that Act. This authorization extends so far as such exemption is necessary or appropriate in the public interest and is consistent with the protection of investors.

## DEFINITION OF A SECURITY

Section 2(1) of the 1933 Act defines a security as

> any note, stock, treasury stock, bond, debenture, evidence of indebtedness, certificate of interest or participation in any profit-sharing agreement, collateral-trust

> certificate, preorganization certificate or subscription, transferable share, investment contract, voting-trust certificate, certificate of deposit for a security, fractional undivided interest in oil, gas, or other mineral rights, any put, call, straddle, option, or privilege on any security … or, in general, any interest or instrument commonly known as a "security," or any certificate of interest or participation in, temporary or interim certificate for, receipt for, guarantee of, or warrant or right to subscribe to or purchase, any of the foregoing.

This definition broadly incorporates the many types of instruments that fall within the concept of a security. Furthermore, the courts generally have interpreted the statutory definition to include nontraditional forms of investments. In *Landreth Timber Co. v. Landreth*, 471 U.S. 681 (1985), the Supreme Court adopted a two-tier analysis of what constitutes a security. Under this analysis, the Court will presumptively treat as a security a financial instrument designated as a note, stock, bond, or other instrument specifically named in the Act.

On the other hand, if a financial transaction lacks the traditional characteristics of an instrument specifically named in the statute, the Court has used a three-part test, derived from *Securities and Exchange Commission v. W.J. Howey Co.*, 328 U.S. 293 (1946), to determine whether that financial transaction constitutes an investment contract and thus a security. Under the *Howey* test, a financial instrument or transaction that involves (1) an investment in a common venture (2) premised on a reasonable expectation of profit (3) to be derived from the entrepreneurial or managerial efforts of others constitutes an investment contract. Thus, limited partnership interests are usually considered securities because limited partners may not participate in management or control of the limited partnership. On the other hand, general partnership interests are usually held not to be securities because general partners have the right to participate in management of the general partnership. Similarly, interests in limited liability companies (LLCs) are considered securities when the members do not take part in management (manager-managed LLCs) but are not deemed securities when the members exercise control of the company (member-managed LLCs). In certain circumstances, investments in citrus groves, whiskey warehouse receipts, real estate condominiums, cattle, franchises, and pyramid schemes have been held to be securities under the *Howey* test.

◆ **SEE CASE 44-1**

## REGISTRATION OF SECURITIES

The 1933 Act prohibits the offer or sale of any security through the use of the mails or any means of interstate commerce unless a registration statement for the securities being offered is in effect or the issuer secures an exemption from registration. Section 5. The purpose of registration is to adequately and accurately disclose financial and other information upon which investors may appraise the merits of the securities. Registration does not, however, insure investors against loss—the SEC does not judge the financial merits of any security. Moreover, the SEC does not guarantee the accuracy of the information presented in a registration statement.

### DISCLOSURE REQUIREMENTS

In general, registration (Form S–1) calls for disclosure of such information as (1) a description of the registrant's properties, business, and competition; (2) a description of the significant provisions of the security to be offered for sale and its relationship to the registrant's other capital securities; (3) information about the management of the registrant; and (4) financial statements certified by independent public accountants. In 1992, the SEC imposed new disclosure requirements regarding compensation paid to senior executives and directors. In 2006 the SEC amended these rules to mandate clearer and more complete disclosure of compensation paid to directors, the chief executive officer (CEO), the chief financial officer (CFO), and the three other highest-paid executive officers. The registration statement must be signed by the issuer, its CEO, its CFO, its chief accounting officer, and a majority of its board of directors.

A registration statement and the prospectus become public immediately on filing with the SEC, and investors can access them using EDGAR. The effective date of a registration statement is the twentieth day after filing, although the commission, at its discretion, may advance the effective date or require an amendment to the filing, which will begin a new twenty-day period. After the effective date, the issuer may make sales, provided the purchaser has received a final prospectus. The SEC has also adopted rules to provide for an "access equals delivery" prospectus delivery model: the final prospectus delivery obligations are satisfied without printing and actually delivering final prospectuses if the issuer timely filed a final prospectus with the SEC.

In 1998 the SEC issued a rule requiring issuers to write and design the cover page, summary, and risk factors section of their prospectuses in plain English. In these sections issuers must use short sentences; definite, concrete, everyday language; tabular presentation of complex information; no legal or business jargon; and no multiple negatives. Issuers will also have to design these sections to make them inviting to the reader and free from legalese and repetition that blur important information.

### INTEGRATED DISCLOSURE

The disclosure system under the 1933 Act developed independently of that required by the 1934 Act, which is discussed later in this chapter. As a result, issuers subject to both statutes were compelled to provide duplicative or overlapping disclosure. In an effort to reduce or eliminate unnecessary duplication of corporate reporting, the SEC in 1982 adopted an integrated system that provides for different levels of disclosure, depending on the issuer's reporting history and market following. All issuers may use the detailed form (S–1) described previously. The SEC has amended these rules to recognize four categories of issuers: nonreporting issuers, unseasoned issuers, seasoned issuers, and well-known seasoned issuers.

1. A nonreporting issuer is an issuer that is not required to file reports under the 1934 Act. Such an issuer must use Form S–1.
2. An unseasoned issuer is an issuer that has reported continuously under the 1934 Act for at least three years. Such an issuer must use Form S–1, but is permitted to disclose less detailed information and to incorporate some information by reference to reports filed under the 1934 Act.
3. A seasoned issuer is an issuer that has filed continuously under the 1934 Act for at least one year and has a minimum market value of publicly held voting and nonvoting stock of $75 million. Such an issuer is permitted to use Form S–3, thus disclosing even less detail in the 1933 Act registration and incorporating even more information by reference to 1934 Act reports. An issuer that does not meet the $75 million "public float" requirement can use Form S-3 if it (a) has a class of common equity securities listed and registered on a national securities exchange, (b) has a class of securities registered under the 1934 Act, (c) has filed continuously under the 1934 Act for at least one year, and (d) does not sell more than the equivalent of one-third of its public float in primary offerings over any period of twelve calendar months. "Public float" means the value of a company's outstanding shares that is in the hands of public investors, as opposed to company officers, directors, or controlling-interest investors.
4. A well-known seasoned issuer is an issuer that has filed continuously under the 1934 Act for at least one year and has either (a) a minimum worldwide market value of its outstanding publicly held voting and nonvoting stock of $700 million, or (b) $1 billion of nonconvertible debt or preferred stock that has been issued for cash in a registered offering within the preceding three years. A well-known seasoned issuer is also eligible to use Form S–3.

In 1992, the SEC established an integrated registration and reporting system for small business issuers. These rules are intended to facilitate access to the public financial markets for start-up and developing companies and to reduce costs for small business issuers wishing to have their securities traded in public markets. As amended in 2008, the rules define a small business issuer as a noninvestment company with less than $75 million in public float. When a company is unable to calculate public float, however, the standard is less than $50 million in revenue in the last fiscal year. Small business issuers may use Form SB–2, which has no dollar limit, or Form SB–1, which permits sales of up to $10 million of securities in any twelve-month period. Form SB–1 is a streamlined disclosure document permitting either a narrative or a question-and-answer format.

## SHELF REGISTRATIONS

As amended in 2005, shelf registrations permit seasoned and well-known seasoned issuers to register unlimited amounts of securities that are to be offered and sold "off the shelf" on a delayed or continuous basis in the future. This is a departure from the requirement that an issuer must file a registration for *every* new distribution of nonexempt securities. The information in the original registration must be kept accurate and current, and the issuer must reasonably expect that the securities will be sold within three years of the effective date of the registration. Well-known seasoned issuers are eligible for a more streamlined shelf-registration process and automatic effectiveness of shelf-registration statements upon filing. Shelf registrations allow issuers to respond more quickly to market conditions such as changes in stock prices and interest rates.

## COMMUNICATIONS

The SEC's 2005 revisions greatly liberalize the rules regarding written communications before and during registered securities offerings. These rules create a new type of written communication, called a "free-writing prospectus," which is any written offer, including electronic communications, other than a statutory prospectus. The flexibility provided under the new rules depends upon the characteristics of the issuer, including the type of issuer, the issuer's history of reporting, and the issuer's market capitalization.

1. Well-known seasoned issuers may engage at any time in oral and written communications, including a free-writing prospectus, subject to certain conditions.
2. All reporting issuers (unseasoned issuers, seasoned issuers, and well-known seasoned issuers) may at any time continue to publish regularly released factual business information and forward-looking information (predictions).
3. Nonreporting issuers may at any time continue to publish factual business information that is regularly released and intended for use by persons other than in their capacity as investors or potential investors.
4. Communications by issuers more than thirty days before filing a registration statement are permitted so long as they do not refer to a securities offering that is the subject of a registration statement.
5. All issuers may use a free-writing prospectus after the filing of the registration statement, subject to certain conditions.

## EXEMPT SECURITIES

The 1933 Act exempts a number of specific securities from its registration requirements. Because these exemptions apply to the securities themselves, the securities also may be resold without registration.

### SHORT-TERM COMMERCIAL PAPER

The Act exempts any note, draft, or bankers' acceptance (a draft accepted by a bank) issued for working capital that has a maturity of not more than nine months when issued. Section 3(a)(3). This exemption is not available, however, if the proceeds are to be used for permanent purposes, such as the acquisition of a plant, or if the paper is of a type not ordinarily purchased by the general public.

### OTHER EXEMPT SECURITIES

The 1933 Act also exempts the following kinds of securities from registration:

1. securities issued or guaranteed by domestic governmental organizations, such as municipal bonds;
2. securities of domestic banks and savings and loan associations;
3. securities of not-for-profit, charitable organizations;
4. certain securities issued by Federally regulated common carriers; and
5. insurance policies and annuity contracts issued by State-regulated insurance companies.

## EXEMPT TRANSACTIONS FOR ISSUERS

In addition to exempting specific types of securities, the 1933 Act also exempts *issuers* from the registration requirements for certain kinds of transactions. These exempt transactions include (1) private placements (Rule 506), (2) limited offers not exceeding $5 million (Rule 505), (3) limited offers not exceeding $1 million (Rule 504), and (4) limited offers solely to accredited investors (Section 4(6)). Except for some issuances under Rule 504, these exemptions from registration apply only to the transaction in which the securities are issued; therefore, any resale must be made by registration, unless the resale qualifies as an exempt transaction.

In addition, the 1933 Act provides a number of securities exemptions that are in effect transaction exemptions. These include intrastate issues, exchanges between an issuer and its security holders, and reorganization securities issued and exchanged with court or other governmental approval. Moreover, the Bankruptcy Act exempts securities issued by a debtor if they are offered under a reorganization plan in exchange for a claim or interest in the debtor. Bankruptcy Act, Section 1145(a). These exemptions apply only to the original issuance; resales may be made only by registration unless the resale qualifies as an exempt transaction.

Another transaction exemption is Regulation A, which permits an issuer to sell a limited amount of securities in an unregistered public offering if certain conditions are met. Unlike other transaction exemptions, Regulation A places no restrictions upon the resale of securities issued pursuant to it.

◆ SEE FIGURE 44-1: **Registration and Exemptions under the 1933 Act**

### LIMITED OFFERS

The 1933 Act exempts, or authorizes the SEC to exempt, transactions that do not require the protection of registration because they either involve a small amount of money or are made in a limited manner. Sections 3(b) and 4(2). Promulgated in 1982 to simplify and clarify the transaction exemptions relating to small issues and small issuers, Regulation D contains three separate exemptions (Rules 504, 505, and 506), each involving limited offers. Section 4(6), also aimed at small issues, is a companion section to the exemptions under Regulation D. Each of these exemptions requires the issuer to file a Form D with the SEC online within fifteen days after the first sale of securities in the offering. Moreover, the CFPA requires the SEC to issue rules disqualifying offerings and sales of securities made under Regulation D when the person offering the securities has been convicted of any felony or misdemeanor (1) in connection with the purchase or sale of any security or (2) involving the making of any false filing with the SEC.

Securities sold pursuant to these exemptions (with the exception of some sold pursuant to Rule 504) are considered **restricted securities** and may be resold only by registration or in another transaction exempt from registration. An issuer who uses these exemptions must take reasonable care to prevent nonexempt, unregistered resales of restricted securities. Reasonable care includes, but is not limited to, the following: (1) making a reasonable inquiry to determine whether the purchaser is acquiring the securities for herself or for other persons; (2) providing written disclosure prior to the sale to each purchaser that the securities have not been registered and therefore cannot be resold unless they are registered or unless an exemption from registration is available; and (3) placing a legend on the securities certificate stating that the securities have not been registered and that they are restricted securities.

**Private Placements** The most important transaction exemption for issuers is the so-called private placement provision of the Act, which exempts "transactions by an issuer not involving any public offering." Section 4(2). SEC **Rule**

◆ FIGURE 44-1: **Registration and Exemptions under the 1933 Act**

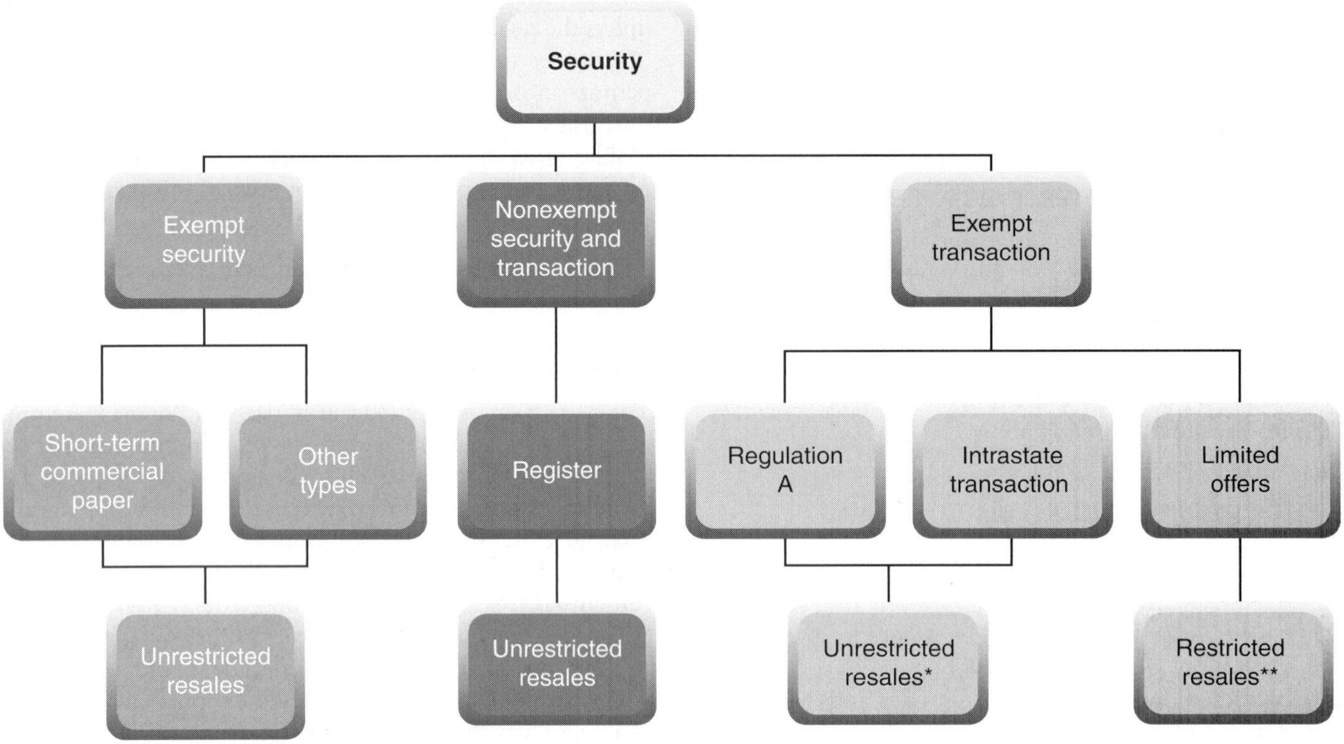


* Under intrastate exemption, resales to nonresidents may only be made nine months after the last sale in the initial issuance.
** Except some issuances under Rule 504.

**506** establishes for all issuers a nonexclusive safe harbor for limited offers and sales without regard to the dollar amount of the offering. While compliance with the rule ensures the exemption, the exemption is not presumed to be unavailable for noncomplying transactions.

Securities sold under this exemption are restricted securities and may be resold only by registration or in a transaction exempt from registration. General advertising or general solicitation is not permitted. The issue may be purchased by an unlimited number of "accredited investors" and by no more than thirty-five other purchasers. **Accredited investors** include banks, insurance companies, investment companies, executive officers or directors of the issuer, savings and loan associations, registered broker-dealers, certain employee benefit plans with total assets in excess of $5 million, any person whose net worth exceeds $1 million, and any person whose income exceeded $200,000 in each of the two preceding years and who reasonably expects an income in excess of $200,000 in the current year. Before a sale involving any nonaccredited investors, such purchasers must receive specified material information about the issuer, its business, and the securities being offered. If the sale involves only accredited investors, such disclosure is not mandatory. The issuer must reasonably believe that each purchaser who is not an accredited investor has sufficient knowledge regarding and experience in financial and business matters to evaluate capably the merits and risks of the investment or has the services of a representative possessing such knowledge and experience. The issuer must notify the SEC of sales made under the exemption and must take precautions against nonexempt, unregistered resales.

**Limited Offers Not Exceeding $5 Million** SEC **Rule 505** exempts from registration those offerings by noninvestment company issuers that do not exceed $5 million over twelve months. Securities sold under this exemption are restricted securities and may be resold only by registration or in a transaction exempt from registration. General advertising or general solicitation is not permitted. The issue may be purchased by an unlimited number of accredited investors and by no more than thirty-five other purchasers. Before a sale involving any nonaccredited investors, such purchasers must receive specified material information about the issuer, its business, and the securities being offered; in the absence of nonaccredited investors, such disclosure is unnecessary. Unlike the issuer under Rule 506, however, the issuer under

Rule 505 is *not* required to believe reasonably that each nonaccredited investor, either alone or with his representative, has sufficient knowledge and experience regarding financial matters to be capable of evaluating the merits and risks of the investment. Like its counterpart under Rule 506, the issuer must take precautions against nonexempt, unregistered resales and must notify the SEC of sales made under the exemption.

**LIMITED OFFERS NOT EXCEEDING $1 MILLION** As amended in 1999, SEC **Rule 504** provides private, noninvestment company issuers with an exemption from registration for issues not exceeding $1 million within twelve months. Issuers required to report under the 1934 Act and investment companies may not use Rule 504. The issuer is to notify the SEC of sales under the rule, which permits sales to an unlimited number of investors and does not require the issuer to furnish any information to them.

If the issuance meets certain conditions, Rule 504 permits general solicitations, and acquired shares are freely transferable. The conditions are that the issuance is either (1) registered under State law requiring public filing and delivery of a disclosure document to investors before sale or (2) exempted under State law permitting general solicitation and advertising so long as sales are made only to accredited investors.

If the issuance does not meet these conditions, general solicitation and advertising is not permitted. Moreover, the securities issued are restricted, and the issuer must take precautions against nonexempt, unregistered resales.

**LIMITED OFFERS SOLELY TO ACCREDITED INVESTORS** In 1980, Congress added **Section 4(6)**, which provides an exemption for offers and sales of $5 million made by an issuer solely to accredited investors. General advertising or public solicitation is not permitted. As with Rules 505 and 506, an unlimited number of accredited investors may purchase the issue; however, unlike these rules, Section 4(6) allows no unaccredited investors to purchase. No information is required to be furnished to the purchasers. Securities sold under this exemption are restricted securities and may be resold only by registration or in a transaction exempt from registration. The issuer must notify the SEC of sales made under the exemption and must take precautions against nonexempt, unregistered resales.

### REGULATION A

As amended in 1992, Regulation A permits an issuer to offer up to $5 million of securities in any twelve-month period without registering them, provided that the issuer files an offering statement with the SEC prior to the sale of the securities. An offering circular must also be provided to offerees and purchasers. The issuer may make offers upon filing the offering statement but may make sales only after the SEC has qualified it. Issuers required to report under the 1934 Act and investment companies may not use Regulation A. Regulation A filings are less detailed and time-consuming than full registration statements, and the required financial statements are simpler and need not be audited unless the issuer has audited financial statements prepared for other purposes. Issuers now may use an optional, simplified question-and-answer disclosure document.

Regulation A sets no restrictions regarding the number or qualifications of investors who may purchase securities under its provisions. Furthermore, securities sold under Regulation A may be resold freely after they are issued.

### INTRASTATE ISSUES

The 1933 Act also exempts from registration any security that is part of an issue offered and sold only to persons resident within a single State where the issuer of such security is resident and doing business. Section 3(a)(11). This exemption is intended to apply to local issues representing local financing carried out by local persons through local investments. The exemption does not apply if *any* offeree, who need not become a purchaser, is not a resident of the State in which the issuer is resident.

The courts and the SEC have interpreted the exemption narrowly. **Rule 147**, promulgated by the SEC, provides a nonexclusive safe harbor for securing the intrastate exemption. While compliance with the rule ensures the exemption, the exemption is not presumed to be unavailable for noncomplying transactions. Rule 147 requires that

1. the issuer be incorporated or organized in the State in which the issuance occurs;
2. the issuer be principally doing business in that State, which means that the issuer must derive 80 percent of its gross revenues from that State, 80 percent of its assets must be located in that State, and 80 percent of its net proceeds from the issue must be used in that State;
3. all of the *offerees* and purchasers be residents of that State;
4. no resales to nonresidents be made during the period of sale and for nine months after the last sale; and
5. the issuer take precautions against interstate distributions. Such precautions include (a) placing on the security certificate a legend stating that the securities have not been registered and that resales can be made only to residents of the State and (b) obtaining a written statement of residence from each purchaser.

◆ **SEE FIGURE 44-2: Exempt Transactions for Issuers under the 1933 Act**

## EXEMPT TRANSACTIONS FOR NONISSUERS

The 1933 Act requires registration for any sale by any person (including nonissuers) of any nonexempt security unless a statutory exemption can be found for the transaction. The

◆ **FIGURE 44-2: Exempt Transactions for Issuers under the 1933 Act**

| Exemption | Price Limitation | Information Required | Limitations on Purchasers | Resales |
|---|---|---|---|---|
| **Regulation A** | $5 million | Offering circular | None | Unrestricted |
| **Intrastate Rule 147** | None | None | Intrastate only | Only to residents before nine months |
| **Rule 506** | None | Material information to unaccredited purchasers | Unlimited accredited; 35 unaccredited | Restricted |
| **Rule 505** | $5 million | Material information to unaccredited purchasers | Unlimited accredited; 35 unaccredited | Restricted |
| **Rule 504** | $1 million | None | None | Restricted* |
| **Section 4(6)** | $5 million | None | Only accredited | Restricted |

* Unrestricted if under State law the issuance is either (1) registered or (2) exempted with sales only to accredited investors.

Act, however, provides a transaction exemption for any person other than an issuer, underwriter, or dealer. Section 4(1). In addition, the Act exempts most transactions by dealers and brokers. Sections 4(3) and 4(4). These three provisions exempt from the registration requirements of the 1933 Act most secondary transactions; that is, the numerous resales that occur on an exchange or in the over-the-counter market. Nevertheless, these exemptions do not extend to some situations involving resales by nonissuers, in particular to (1) resales of restricted securities acquired under Regulation D (Rules 506, 505, or 504) or Sections 4(6) and (2) sales of restricted or nonrestricted securities by affiliates. Such sales must be made pursuant to registration, Rule 144, or Regulation A, subject to the limited exception provided to some issuances by Rule 504. An **affiliate** is a person who controls, is controlled by, or is under common control with the issuer. **Control** is the direct or indirect possession of the power to direct the management and policies of a person through ownership of securities, by contract, or otherwise. Rule 405.

## RULE 144

Rule 144 of the SEC sets forth conditions that, if met by an affiliate or any person selling restricted securities, exempt her from registering those securities. As amended in 2008, the rule imposes less strict requirements on resales of securities of issuers that are subject to the reporting requirements of the 1934 Act than on resales of securities of nonreporting issuers.

**Nonreporting Issuers** Amended Rule 144 requires for an affiliate selling *restricted* securities that there be adequate current public information about the issuer, that the affiliate selling under the rule have owned the restricted securities for at least one year, that she sell them only in limited amounts in unsolicited brokers' transactions, and that notice of the sale be provided to the SEC. An affiliate selling *nonrestricted* securities is subject to the same require-ments except that the one-year holding period does not apply.

A person who is not an affiliate of the issuer when the restricted securities are sold and who has owned the restricted securities for at least one year may sell them in unlimited amounts and is not subject to any of the other requirements of Rule 144.

**Reporting Issuers** Amended Rule 144 requires for an affiliate selling *restricted* securities that there be adequate current public information about the issuer, that the affiliate selling under the rule have owned the restricted securities for at least six months, that she sell them only in limited amounts in unsolicited brokers' transactions, and that notice of the sale be provided to the SEC. An affiliate selling *nonrestricted* securities is subject to the same requirements except for the one-year holding period.

If there is adequate current public information about the issuer, a person who is *not* an affiliate of the issuer when the *restricted* securities are sold and has owned the restricted securities for at least six months may sell them in unlimited amounts and is not subject to any of the other requirements of Rule 144. After one year, the nonaffiliate selling *restricted* securities need not comply with the current information requirement of Rule 144.

## RULE 144A

While Rule 144 permits sales of restricted securities, the requirements of the rule have hampered the liquidity of privately placed securities. To improve the liquidity of such securities, in 1990 the SEC adopted Rule 144A, which provides an additional, nonexclusive safe harbor from registration for resales of restricted securities. Only securities that at the time of issue are not of the same class as securities listed on a national securities exchange or quoted in a U.S. automated interdealer quotation system ("nonfungible securities") may be sold under Rule 144A. Such nonfungible securities may be sold only to a qualified institutional buyer, defined generally as an institution that in the aggregate owns and invests on a discretionary basis at least $100 million in securities. Rule 144A also requires the seller of the nonfungible securities to take reasonable steps to ensure that the buyer knows that the seller is relying on Rule 144A. In addition, special requirements apply to securities issued by foreign companies. Securities acquired pursuant to Rule 144A are restricted securities.

### REGULATION A

In addition to providing issuers an exemption from registration for securities up to $5 million, Regulation A provides an exemption for nonissuers. Use of this exemption, which places a $1.5 million limit on the total amount of securities sold in any twelve-month period by all nonissuers, requires compliance with all of the conditions Regulation A imposes upon issuers, as discussed above.

## LIABILITY

To implement the statutory objectives of providing full disclosure and preventing fraud in the sale of securities, the 1933 Act imposes a number of sanctions for noncompliance with its requirements. These sanctions include administrative remedies by the SEC, civil liability to injured investors, and criminal penalties.

The Reform Act provides "forward-looking" statements (predictions) a "safe harbor" under the 1933 Act from civil liability based on an untrue statement of material fact or an omission of a material fact necessary to make the statement not misleading. The safe harbor applies only to issuers required to report under the 1934 Act. The safe harbor eliminates civil liability if a forward-looking statement is (1) immaterial, (2) made without actual knowledge that it was false or misleading, or (3) identified as a forward-looking statement and is accompanied by meaningful cautionary statements identifying important factors that could cause actual results to differ materially from those predicted. "Forward-looking statements" include projections of revenues, income, earnings per share, capital expenditures, dividends, or capital structure; management's plans and objectives for future operations; and statements of future economic performance. The safe harbor provision, however, does not cover statements made in connection with an initial public offering, a tender offer, a going private transaction, or offerings by a partnership or an LLC.

### UNREGISTERED SALES

The Act imposes express civil liability for the sale of an unregistered security that is required to be registered, the sale of a registered security without delivery of a prospectus, the sale of a security by use of an outdated prospectus, or the offer of a sale prior to the filing of the registration statement. **Section 12(a)(1)**. Liability is strict or absolute because there are no defenses. The person who purchases a security sold in violation of this provision has the right to tender it back to the seller and recover the purchase price. If the purchaser no longer owns the security, he may recover monetary damages from the seller.

### FALSE REGISTRATION STATEMENTS

When securities have been sold subject to a registration statement, **Section 11** of the Act imposes express liability upon those who have included any untrue statement in the registration statement or who omit from the statement any material fact. **Material** matters are those to which a reasonable investor would be substantially likely to attach importance in determining whether to purchase the security registered. SEC Rule 405. Usually, proof of reliance upon the misstatement or omission is not required. The section imposes liability upon (1) the issuer; (2) all persons who signed the registration statement, including the principal executive officer, principal financial officer, and principal accounting officer; (3) every person who was a director or partner; (4) every accountant, engineer, appraiser, or expert who prepared or certified any part of the registration statement; and (5) all underwriters. These persons generally are jointly and severally liable for the amount paid for the security, less either its value at the time of suit or the price for which it was sold, to any person who acquires the security without knowledge of the untruth or omission. A defendant is not liable for any or the entire amount otherwise recoverable under Section 11 that the defendant proves was caused by something other than the defective disclosure. The court may award attorneys' fees against any party who brings suit or asserts a defense without merit.

An expert is liable only for misstatements or omissions in the portion of the registration that he prepared or certified. Moreover, any defendant, other than the issuer (who has strict liability), may assert the affirmative defense of due diligence. This **due diligence** defense generally requires the defendant to show that she had reasonable grounds to believe, and did believe, that there were no untrue statements or material omissions. In some instances, due diligence requires a reasonable investigation to determine grounds for belief. The standard of reasonableness for such investigation and such grounds is that required of a prudent person in the management of his own property. Section 11(c).

◆ SEE CASE 44-2

## ANTIFRAUD PROVISIONS

The 1933 Act also contains two antifraud provisions: Section 12(a)(2) and Section 17(a). In addition, Rule 10b–5 of the 1934 Act applies to the issuance or sale of all securities, even those exempted by the 1933 Act. Rule 10b–5 is discussed later in this chapter.

**SECTION 12(A)(2)** Section 12(a)(2) imposes express liability upon any person who offers or sells a security by means of a prospectus or oral communication that contains an untrue statement of material fact or omits a material fact. That liability extends only to the immediate purchaser, provided she did not know of the untruth or omission. The seller may avoid liability by proving that he did not know and in the exercise of reasonable care could not have known of the untrue statement or omission. The seller is liable to the purchaser for the amount paid upon tender of the security. If the purchaser no longer owns the security, she may recover damages from the seller. A defendant is not liable for any portion of or the entire amount otherwise recoverable under Section 12(a)(2) that the defendant proves was caused by something other than the defective disclosure.

**SECTION 17(A)** Section 17(a) makes it unlawful for any person in the offer or sale of any securities, whether registered or not, to do any of the following when using any means of transportation or communication in interstate commerce or the mails:

1. employ any device, scheme, or artifice to defraud;
2. obtain money or property by means of any untrue statement of a material fact or any statement that omits a material fact, without which the information is misleading; or
3. engage in any transaction, practice, or course of business that operates or would operate as a fraud or deceit upon the purchaser.

There is considerable doubt whether the courts may imply a private right of action for persons injured by violations of

◆ FIGURE 44-3: **Registration and Liability Provisions of the 1933 Act**

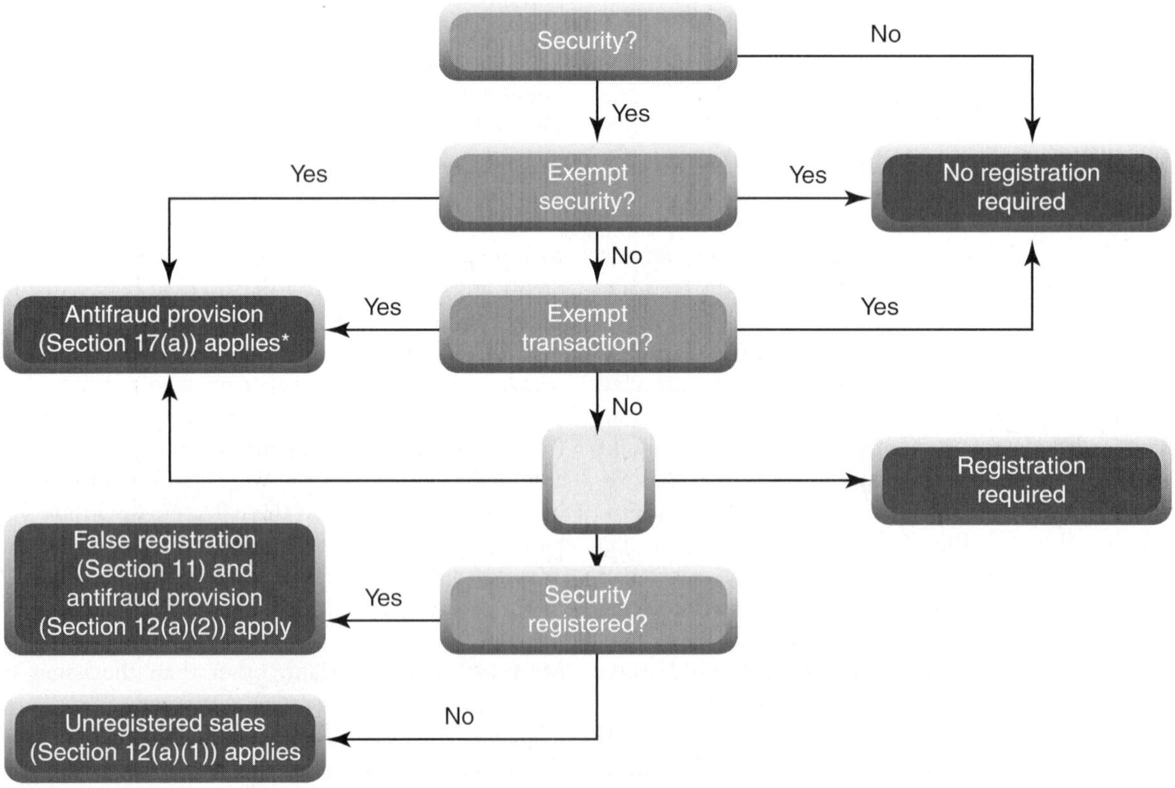


* Section 12 (a)(2) *may* apply to some of these issuances.

this section. The Supreme Court has reserved this question, and most lower courts have denied the existence of a private remedy. The SEC may, however, bring enforcement actions under Section 17(a).

### CRIMINAL SANCTIONS

The 1933 Act imposes criminal sanctions upon any person who willfully violates any of its provisions or the rules and regulations the SEC promulgates pursuant to the Act. Section 24. Conviction may carry a fine of not more than $10,000 or imprisonment of not more than five years, or both.

◆ SEE FIGURE 44-3: **Registration and Liability Provisions of the 1933 Act**

## SECURITIES EXCHANGE ACT OF 1934

The Securities Exchange Act of 1934 deals principally with the secondary distribution (resale) of securities. The definition of a security in the 1934 Act is substantially the same as the definition in the 1933 Act. The 1934 Act seeks to ensure fair and orderly securities markets by prohibiting fraudulent and manipulative practices and by establishing rules for market operations. It provides protection for holders of all securities listed on national exchanges, as well as for those holders of equity securities of companies traded over the counter whose corporate assets exceed $10 million and whose equity securities include a class with five hundred or more shareholders. Companies must register such securities and are also subject to the 1934 Act's periodic reporting requirements, short-swing profits provision, tender offer provisions, and proxy solicitation provisions, as well as the internal control and recordkeeping requirements of the Foreign Corrupt Practices Act. An over-the-counter issuer may terminate its registration when the holders of its registered equity securities number fewer than three hundred or when the issuer has had fewer than five hundred shareholders *and* assets totaling less than $10 million on the last day of each of the past three years. In addition, issuers of securities, whether registered under the 1934 Act or not, must comply with the antifraud and antibribery provisions of the Act.

◆ SEE CASE 44-1

◆ SEE FIGURE 44-4: **Applicability of the 1934 Act**

The National Securities Markets Improvements Act of 1996 broadly authorized the SEC to issue regulations, rules, or orders exempting any person, security, or transaction from any of the provisions of the 1934 Act or the SEC's rules promulgated under that Act. This authorization extends so far as such exemption is necessary or appropriate in the public interest and is consistent with the protection of investors. This exemptive authority does not, however, extend to the regulation of government securities broker-dealers.

### DISCLOSURE

The 1934 Act imposes significant disclosure requirements upon reporting companies. These include the filing of

◆ FIGURE 44-4: **Applicability of the 1934 Act**

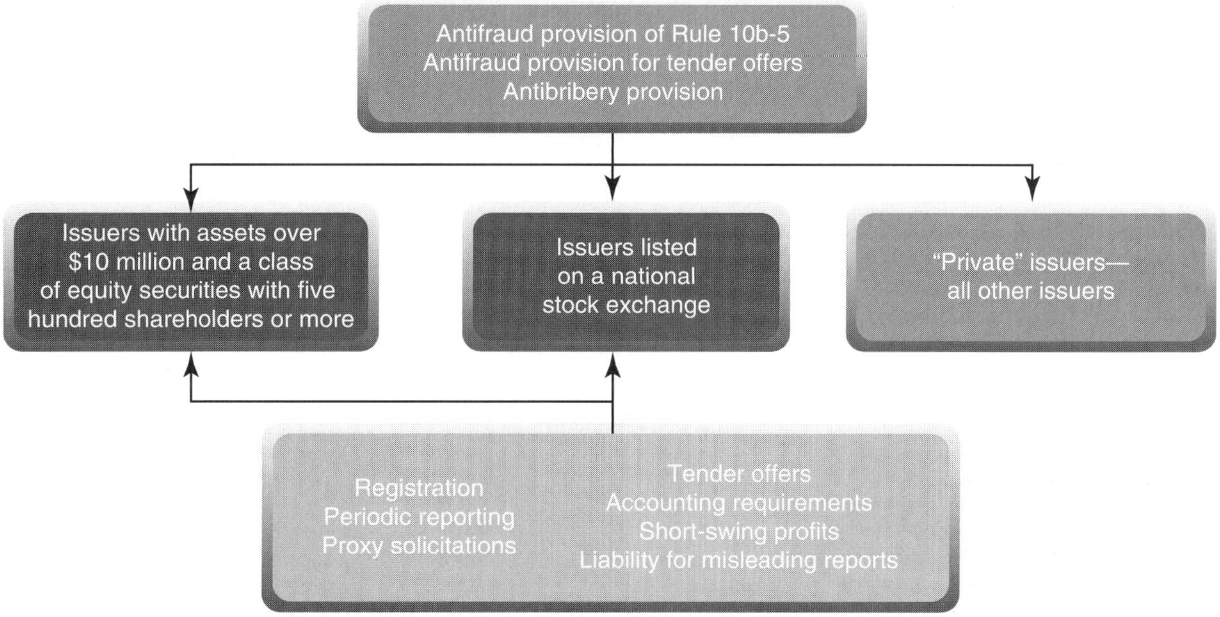

securities registrations, periodic reports, disclosure statements for proxy solicitations, and disclosure statements for tender offers, as well as compliance with the accounting requirements imposed by the Foreign Corrupt Practices Act. As part of its integrated registration and reporting system for small business issuers, in 1992 the SEC developed a new series of forms for qualifying issuers to use for registration and periodic reporting under the 1934 Act. Also in 1992, the SEC imposed new disclosure requirements for registration statements, periodic reports, and proxy statements that contain information regarding the compensation paid to senior executives and directors. As previously noted, in 2006 the SEC amended these rules to mandate clearer and more complete disclosure of compensation paid to directors, the CEO, the CFO, and the three other highest-paid executive officers. The issuer must disclose executive compensation over the past three years including salary, bonus, a dollar value for stock and option awards, amount of compensation under nonequity incentive plans, annual change in present value of accumulated pension benefits and above-market earnings on nonqualified deferred compensation, and all other compensation including perquisites. Similar disclosure is required for director compensation for the last fiscal year. Effective in 2000, a plain English summary term sheet is required in all tender offers, mergers, and going private transactions.

◆ SEE FIGURE 44-5: **Disclosure under the 1934 Act**

◆ FIGURE 44-5: **Disclosure under the 1934 Act**

| | Initial Registration | Periodic Reporting | Insider Reporting | Proxy Statement | Tender Offer |
|---|---|---|---|---|---|
| **Registrant** | Issuer if regulated, publicly held company | Issuer if regulated, publicly held company | Statutory insiders (directors, officers, and principal stockholders) | Issuer and other persons soliciting proxies | 5 percent stockholder, tender offeror, or issuer |
| **Information** | Nature of business; Financial structure; Directors and executive officers; Financial statements | Annual, quarterly, or current report updating information in initial registration | Initial statement of beneficial ownership of equity securities; Changes in beneficial ownership | Details of solicitation; Legal terms of proxy; Annual report (if directors to be elected) | Identity and background; Terms of transaction; Source of funds; Intentions |
| **Filing Date** | Within 120 days after becoming a reporting company | Annual: within 90 days* after year's end; Quarterly: within 45 days** after quarter's end; Current: within 15 days after any material change | Within 10 days of becoming a statutory insider; Within 2 days after a change in ownership takes place | 10 days before final proxy statement is distributed | 5 percent stockholder: within 10 days after acquiring more than 5 percent of a class of registered securities; Tender offeror: before tender offer is made; Issuer: before offer to repurchase |
| **Purpose of Disclosure** | Adequate and accurate disclosure of material facts regarding securities listed on a national exchange or traded publicly over the counter | Update information contained in initial registration | Prevent unfair use of information that may have been obtained by a statutory insider | Full disclosure of material information; Facilitation of shareholder proposals | Adequate and accurate disclosure of material facts; Opportunity to reach uncoerced decision |

*Certain issuers must file within sixty or seventy-five days.
**Certain issuers must file within forty days.

## REGISTRATION REQUIREMENTS FOR SECURITIES

The 1934 Act requires all regulated publicly held companies to register with the SEC. Section 12. These one-time registrations apply to an entire class of securities. Thus, they differ from registrations under the Securities Act of 1933, which relate only to the securities involved in a specific offering. Registration requires disclosure of information such as the organization, financial structure, and nature of the business; the terms, positions, rights, and privileges of the different classes of outstanding securities; the names of the directors, officers, and underwriters and of each security holder owning more than 10 percent of any class of nonexempt equity security; bonus and profit-sharing arrangements; and balance sheets and profit-and-loss statements for the three preceding fiscal years.

## PERIODIC REPORTING REQUIREMENTS

Following registration, an issuer must file specified annual (10–K) and periodic (10–Q and 8–K) reports to update the information contained in the original registration. Also subject to the periodic reporting requirements are issuers who have filed a 1933 Act registration statement with respect to any security. Section 15. This duty is suspended, however, in any subsequent year during which the securities registered under the 1933 Act are held by fewer than three hundred persons.

Effective in early 2010, the SEC adopted new requirements to improve the disclosure shareholders of public companies receive regarding compensation and corporate governance. These new rules require disclosure of (1) the qualifications of directors and nominees for director, and the reasons why that person should serve as a director of the issuer; (2) any directorships held by each director and nominee at any time during the past five years at any public company or registered investment company; (3) the consideration of diversity in the process by which candidates for director are considered for nomination by an issuer's nominating committee; (4) an issuer's board leadership structure and the board's role in the oversight of risk; (5) the aggregate grant date fair value of stock awards and option awards granted in the fiscal year computed in accordance with Financial Accounting Standards Board Accounting Standards; and (6) to the extent that risks arising from an issuer's compensation policies and practices for employees are reasonably likely to have a material adverse effect on the issuer, discussion of the issuer's compensation policies or practices as they relate to risk management and risk-taking incentives that can affect the issuer's risk and management of that risk.

The SEC has adopted rules under the Sarbanes-Oxley Act requiring an issuer's CEO and CFO to *certify* the financial and other information contained in the issuer's annual and quarterly reports. Moreover, the Act requires that each periodic report shall be *accompanied* by a written statement by the CEO and CFO of the issuer certifying that the periodic report fully complies with the requirements of the 1934 Act and that information contained in the periodic report fairly presents, in all material respects, the financial condition and results of operations of the issuer. A CEO or CFO who certifies while *knowing* that the report does not comply with the Act is subject to a fine of not more than $1 million or imprisonment of not more than ten years, or both. A CEO or CFO who *willfully* certifies a statement knowing it does not comply with the Act shall be fined not more than $5 million or imprisoned not more than twenty years, or both.

The Sarbanes-Oxley Act requires that issuers disclose in plain English to the public on a rapid and current basis such additional information concerning material changes in the financial condition or operations of the issuer as the SEC determines is necessary or useful for the protection of investors and in the public interest.

The Act, as amended by the CFPA, requires that each director, each officer, and any person who owns more than 10 percent of a registered equity security file reports with the SEC within ten days after he or she becomes such beneficial owner, director, or officer, or within such shorter time as the SEC may establish by rule. The 1934 Act also requires that each director, each officer, and any person who owns more than 10 percent of a registered equity security file reports with the SEC for any month during which changes in his ownership of such equity securities have occurred. Previously, such changes in ownership were required to be reported within ten days after the end of that month. The Sarbanes-Oxley Act requires that these reports be filed before the end of the second business day following the day on which the transaction was executed, unless the SEC establishes a different deadline. The 1934 Act also requires that these filings reporting changes in ownership be made electronically on EDGAR, that the SEC make them publicly available on its Internet site, and that the issuers make them available on their corporate Web sites, if they maintain one.

## PROXY SOLICITATIONS

A **proxy** is a writing signed by a shareholder authorizing a named person to vote his shares of stock at a specified shareholders' meeting. To ensure that shareholders have adequate information with which to vote and an opportunity to participate effectively at shareholder meetings, the 1934 Act regulates the proxy solicitation process. The Act makes it unlawful for any person to solicit any proxy with respect to any registered security "in contravention of such rules and regulations as the Commission may prescribe." Section 14. **Solicitation** includes any request for a proxy, any request not to execute a proxy, or any request to revoke a proxy. The SEC has issued comprehensive and detailed rules prescribing the solicitation process and the disclosure of information about the issuer.

**Proxy Statements** Rule 14a–3 prohibits the solicitation of a proxy unless each person solicited has been furnished with a written proxy statement containing specified information. An issuer making solicitations must furnish security holders with a *proxy statement* describing all material facts concerning the matters being submitted to their vote, together with a *proxy form* on which the security holders can indicate their approval or disapproval of each proposal to be presented. Even a company that submits a matter to a shareholder vote rather than solicits proxies must provide its shareholders with information substantially equivalent to what would appear in a proxy statement. With few exceptions, the issuer must file preliminary copies of a proxy statement and proxy form with the SEC at least ten days prior to the first date they are to be sent. In addition, in an election of directors, solicitations of proxies by a person other than the issuer are subject to similar disclosure requirements. The issuer in such an election also must include an annual report with the proxy statement. Effective in early 2010, the SEC requires in proxy materials relating to election of directors that the issuer disclose the qualifications of nominees for director, and the reasons why that person should serve as a director of the issuer. The same information is required in the proxy materials prepared with respect to nominees for director nominated by others. Moreover, the CFPA authorizes the SEC to issue rules requiring that an issuer's proxy solicitation include nominations for the board of directors submitted by shareholders. Under the CFPA, the SEC must issue rules requiring issuers to disclose in annual proxy statements the reasons why the issuer has chosen to separate or combine the positions of chairman of the board of directors and CEO.

The CFPA contains several provisions regarding executive compensation. First, at least once every three years, issuers must include a provision in certain proxy statements for a nonbinding shareholder vote on the compensation of executives. In a separate resolution, shareholders determine whether this "say on pay" vote should be held every one, two, or three years. Second, the SEC must issue rules requiring issuers to describe clearly in annual proxy statements information that shows the relationship between executive compensation actually paid and the financial performance of the issuer, taking into account any change in the value of the shares of stock and dividends of the issuer and any distributions. Third, the SEC must issue rules requiring the disclosure of (1) the median of the annual total compensation of all issuer's employees except the CEO, (2) the annual total compensation of the CEO, and (3) the ratio of the amount described in (1) to the amount described in (2).

Effective March 30, 2007, the SEC amended its proxy rules to provide an alternative method for issuers and other persons to furnish proxy materials to shareholders: posting them on an Internet Web site and providing shareholders with notice of the availability of the proxy materials. Issuers must make paper or e-mail copies of the proxy materials available without charge to shareholders on request.

**Shareholder Proposals** Where management makes a solicitation, any security holder entitled to vote has the opportunity to communicate with other security holders. Upon written request, the corporation must mail the communication at the security holder's expense or, at its option, promptly furnish to that security holder a current list of security holders.

If an eligible security holder entitled to vote submits a timely and appropriate proposal for action at a forthcoming meeting, management must include the proposal in its proxy statement and provide security holders with an opportunity to vote for or against it. To be eligible, the holder must own the lesser of 1 percent or $2,000 in market value of the security for at least one year prior to submitting the proposal. If management opposes the proposal, it must include in its proxy materials a statement by the security holder in support of the proposal. The aggregate length of the proposal and the supporting statement may not exceed five hundred words. A security holder is limited to submitting one proposal to an issuer each year.

Management may omit a proposal if, among other things, (1) under State law it is not a proper subject for shareholder action, (2) it would require the company to violate any law, (3) it is beyond the issuer's power or authority to effectuate, (4) it relates to the conduct of the ordinary business operations of the issuer, or (5) it relates to a nomination or an election for membership on the issuer's board of directors or to a procedure for such nomination or election. However, in 2010, the SEC amended the last exclusion by providing shareholders, under certain circumstances, the power to include in an issuer's proxy materials a shareholder proposal to establish in the issuer's governing documents a procedure for the inclusion in the proxy materials of director nominees selected by a shareholder or group of shareholders. Such a proposal must be consistent with the following new rule.

Under a new SEC rule issued in 2010, an issuer will be required at its own expense to include (1) on the issuer's proxy card, director nominees selected by a shareholder or a group of shareholders that meet certain eligibility requirements; and (2) in the issuer's proxy statement, information about such nominees. To use the new rule, a nominating shareholder or group of shareholders must have continuously owned for at least three years at least 3 percent of the voting power of the issuer's securities entitled to be voted at the meeting. Under the new rule, an issuer will not be required to include more than the greater of one shareholder nominee or the number of nominees that represents up to 25 percent of the issuer's board of directors. (When an issuer has a classified or staggered board, the 25 percent limit is based on the total number of directors on the board.) If more than one nominating shareholder or group of shareholders is eligible, the nominating shareholder or group with the highest percentage of the issuer's voting power will have its nominees included in the issuer's proxy materials. For smaller reporting issuers—generally, those with market capitalization of less than $75 million—the effectiveness of the new rule is deferred for three years.

## TENDER OFFERS

A **tender offer** is a general invitation by a buyer (bidder) to the shareholders of a target company to tender their shares for sale at a specified price for a specified time. In 1968, Congress enacted the Williams Act, which amended the 1934 Act to extend reporting and disclosure requirements to tender offers and other block acquisitions. The purpose of the Williams Act is to provide public shareholders with full disclosure by both the bidder and the target company, so that the shareholders may make an informed decision.

**Disclosure Requirements** The 1934 Act imposes disclosure requirements in three situations: (1) when a person or group acquires more than 5 percent of a class of voting securities registered under the 1934 Act, (2) when a person makes a tender offer for more than 5 percent of a class of registered equity securities, or (3) when the issuer makes an offer to repurchase its own registered shares. Although each situation is governed by different rules, the disclosure required is substantially the same. A statement must be filed with the SEC containing (1) the acquisitor's background; (2) the source of the funds used to acquire the securities; (3) the purpose of the acquisition, including any plans to liquidate the company or to make major changes in the corporate structure; (4) the number of shares owned; (5) the terms of the transaction; and (6) any relevant contracts, arrangements, or understandings. Sections 13(d) and 14(d). This disclosure is also required of anyone soliciting shareholders to accept or reject a tender offer. A copy of the statement must be furnished to each offeree and sent to the issuer. The target company has ten days in which to respond to the bidder's tender offer by (1) recommending acceptance or rejection, (2) expressing no opinion and remaining neutral, or (3) stating that it is unable to take a position. The target company's response must include the reasons for the position taken.

**Required Practices** A tender offer by either a third party or the issuer is subject to the following rules. The initial tender offer must be kept open for at least twenty business days and for at least ten days after any change in terms. Shareholders who tender their shares may withdraw them at any time during the offering period. The tender offer must be open to all holders of the class of shares subject to the offer, and all shares tendered must be purchased for the same price; thus, if an offering price is increased, both those who have tendered and those who have yet to tender will receive the benefit of the increase. A tender offeror who offers to purchase less than all of the outstanding securities of the target must accept, on a *pro rata* basis, securities tendered during the offer. During the tender offer, the bidder may buy shares of the target only through that tender offer. Effective in 2000, in a tender offer for all outstanding shares of a class, a tender offeror may provide a subsequent offering period of three to twenty days after completion of a tender offer, during which time security holders can tender shares without withdrawal rights.

**Defensive Tactics** When confronted by an uninvited takeover bid—or by a potential, uninvited bid—management of the target company may decide either to oppose the bid or seek to prevent it. The defensive tactics management employs to prevent or defend against undesired tender offers have developed (and are still evolving) into a highly ingenious, and metaphorically named, set of maneuvers, some of which require considerable planning and several of which are of questionable legality.

**State Regulation** More than forty States have enacted statutes regulating tender offers. Although they vary greatly, most of these statutes tend to protect a target company from an unwanted tender offer. Some empower the State to review the merits of an offer or the adequacy of disclosure. Many impose waiting periods before the tender offer becomes effective. The State statutes generally require disclosures more detailed than those the Williams Act requires, and many of them exempt tender offers supported by the target company's management. A number of States have adopted fair price statutes, which require the acquisitor to pay to all shareholders the highest price paid to any shareholder. Some States have enacted business combination statutes prohibiting transactions with an acquisitor for a specified time after change in control, unless disinterested shareholders approve.

## FOREIGN CORRUPT PRACTICES ACT

In 1977, Congress enacted the Foreign Corrupt Practices Act (FCPA) as an amendment to the 1934 Act. Amended in 1988, the Act imposes internal control requirements upon companies with securities registered under the 1934 Act and, as discussed later in this chapter, prohibits all domestic concerns from bribing foreign governmental or political officials.

The accounting requirements of the FCPA reflect the ideas that accurate recordkeeping is essential to managerial responsibility and that investors should be able to rely on the financial reports they receive. Accordingly, the accounting requirements were enacted (1) to assure that an issuer's books accurately reflect financial transactions, (2) to protect the integrity of independent audits of financial statements, and (3) to promote the reliability of financial information required by the 1934 Act.

The FCPA requires every issuer that has a class of registered securities to

1. make and keep books, records, and accounts which, in reasonable detail, accurately and fairly reflect the transactions and disposition of the assets of the issuer; and
2. devise and maintain a system of internal controls to assure that transactions are executed as authorized and recorded in conformity with generally accepted accounting principles, thereby establishing accountability with regard to assets and assuring that access to those assets is permitted only with management's authorization. Section 13(b).

## LIABILITY

To implement its objectives, the 1934 Act imposes a number of sanctions for noncompliance with its disclosure and antifraud requirements. These sanctions include civil liability to injured investors and issuers, civil penalties, and criminal penalties.

The Reform Act contains several provisions that affect civil liability under the 1934 Act. First, the Reform Act imposes on a plaintiff in any private action under the 1934 Act the burden of proving that the defendant's alleged violation of the 1934 Act caused the loss for which the plaintiff seeks to recover damages. Second, the Reform Act imposes a limit on the amount of damages a plaintiff can recover in any private action under the 1934 Act based on a material misstatement or omission in which she seeks to establish damages by reference to the market price of a security. The plaintiff may not recover damages in excess of the difference between the purchase or sale price she paid or received for the security and the mean trading price of that security during the ninety-day period beginning on the date when the information correcting the misstatement or omission is disseminated to the market. Third, the Reform Act provides a "safe harbor" under the 1934 Act from civil liability based on an untrue statement of material fact or an omission of a material fact necessary to make the statement not misleading. The safe harbor applies to issuers required to report under the 1934 Act and who make "forward-looking" statements (predictions) if the statements meet specified requirements. The requirements of the safe harbor and the transactions to which it does not apply were discussed earlier in this chapter.

### MISLEADING STATEMENTS IN REPORTS

Section 18 imposes express civil liability upon any person who makes or causes to be made any false or misleading statement with respect to any material fact in any application, report, document, or registration filed with the SEC under the 1934 Act. Any person who purchased or sold a security in reliance upon a false or misleading statement without knowing that it was false or misleading may recover under Section 18. Nevertheless, a person who made such a statement or who caused one to be made is not liable if she proves that she acted in good faith and had no knowledge that such statement was false or misleading. The court may award attorneys' fees against either the plaintiff or the defendant.

### SHORT-SWING PROFITS

**Section 16(b)** of the 1934 Act imposes express liability upon insiders—directors, officers, and any person owning more than 10 percent of the stock of a corporation listed on a national stock exchange or registered with the SEC—for all profits resulting from their "short-swing" trading in such stock. If any insider sells such stock within six months from the date of its purchase or purchases such stock within six months from the date of a sale of the stock, the corporation is entitled to recover any and all profit the insider realizes from these transactions. The "profit" recoverable is calculated by matching the highest sale price against the lowest purchase price within the relevant six-month period. Losses cannot be offset against profits. Suit to recover such profit may be brought by the issuer or by the owner of any security of the issuer in the name and on behalf of the issuer if the issuer fails or refuses to bring such suit within sixty days of the owner's request.

### ANTIFRAUD PROVISION

**Section 10(b)** of the 1934 Act and SEC **Rule 10b–5** make it unlawful for any person to do any of the following when using the mails or facilities of interstate commerce in connection with the purchase or sale of any security

1. employ any device, scheme, or artifice to defraud;
2. make any untrue statement of a material fact;
3. omit to state a material fact necessary to make the statements made not misleading; or
4. engage in any act, practice, or course of business that operates or would operate as a fraud or deceit upon any person.

Rule 10b–5 applies to any purchase or sale of any security, whether it is registered under the 1934 Act or not, whether it is publicly traded or closely held, whether it is listed on an exchange or sold over the counter, or whether it is part of an initial issuance or a secondary distribution.

There are *no* exemptions. The implied liability under Rule 10b–5 applies to purchaser as well as seller misconduct and allows both defrauded sellers and buyers to recover.

**Requisites of Rule 10b–5** Recovery of damages under Rule 10b–5 requires proof of (1) a misstatement or omission (2) that is material, (3) made with *scienter*, and (4) relied upon (5) in connection with the purchase or sale of a security, and (6) that causes economic loss. This rule differs from common law fraud in that Rule 10b–5 imposes an affirmative duty of disclosure. A misstatement or omission is **material** if there is a substantial likelihood that a reasonable investor would consider it important in deciding whether to purchase or sell the security. Examples of material facts include substantial changes in dividends or earnings, significant misstatements of asset value, and the fact that the issuer is about to become a target of a tender offer. In an action for damages under Rule 10b–5, it must be shown that the violation was committed with **scienter**, or intentional misconduct. Negligence is not sufficient. Although the Supreme Court has yet to decide whether reckless conduct is sufficient to satisfy the requirement of *scienter*, the vast majority of circuit and district courts have held recklessness to be sufficient.

Direct reliance may be difficult to prove in a 10b–5 action because the buyer and seller usually do not negotiate their deal face to face. Recognizing the special nature of securities market transactions, the Supreme Court adopted the fraud-on-the-market theory, which establishes a rebuttable presumption of reliance based on the premise that the market price of a stock reflects any misstatement or omission and that the fraudulently affected market price has injured the plaintiff.

Remedies for violations of Rule 10b–5 include rescission, damages, and injunctions. The courts are divided over the measure of damages to impose.

◆ SEE CASE 44-3

**Insider Trading** Rule 10b–5 applies to sales or purchases of securities made by an "insider" who possesses material information that is not available to the general public. An insider who fails to disclose the material, nonpublic information before trading on the information will be liable under Rule 10b–5 unless he waits for the information to become public. Under SEC Rule 10b5-1, a purchase or sale of an issuer's security is based on material nonpublic information about that security or issuer if the person making the purchase or sale was *aware* of the information when the person entered into the transaction. **Insiders**, for the purpose of Rule 10b–5, include directors, officers, employees, and agents of the security issuer, as well as those with whom the issuer has entrusted information solely for corporate purposes, such as underwriters, accountants, lawyers, and consultants. In some instances, the rule also precludes persons who receive material, nonpublic information from insiders—tippees—from trading on that information. A tippee who knows or should know that an insider has breached his fiduciary duty to the shareholders by disclosing inside information to the tippee is under a duty not to trade on such information.

◆ SEE FIGURE 44-6: **Parties Forbidden to Trade on Inside Information**

The U.S. Supreme Court has upheld the misappropriation theory as an additional and complementary basis for

◆ FIGURE 44-6: **Parties Forbidden to Trade on Inside Information**

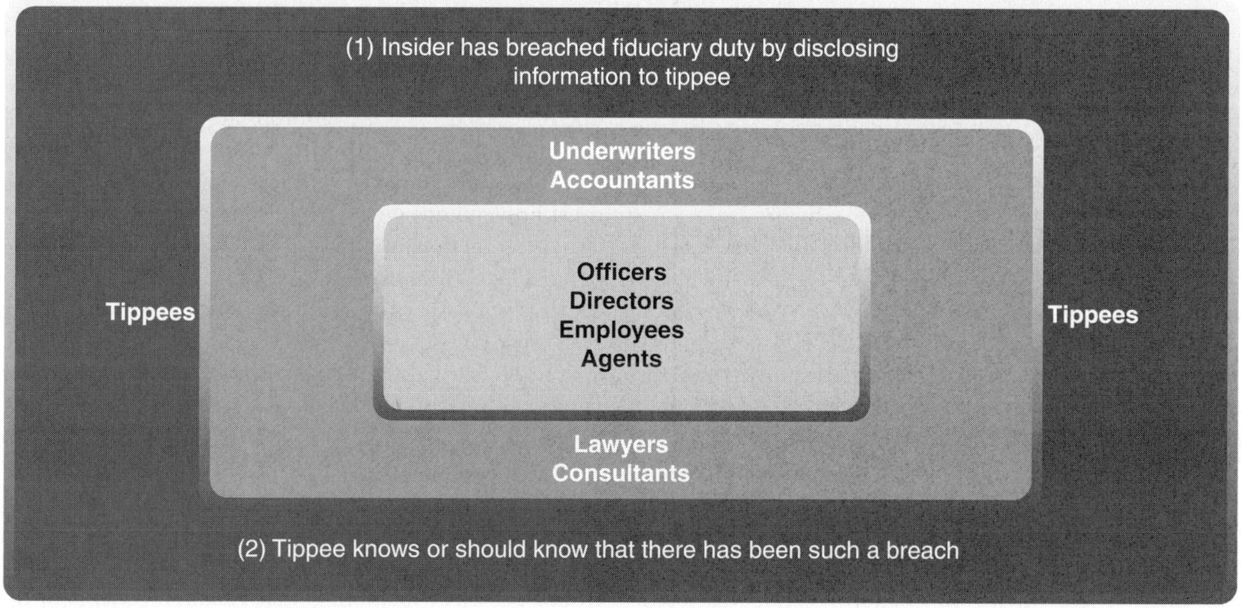

imposing liability for insider trading. Under this theory, a person may be held liable for insider trading under Rule 10b–5 if she trades in securities for personal profit using confidential information misappropriated in breach of a fiduciary duty to the source of the information. This liability applies even though the source of information is not the issuer of the securities that were traded. SEC Rule 10b5-2 adopts the misappropriation theory of liability: A violation of Section 10(b) includes the purchase or sale of a security of an issuer on the basis of material nonpublic information about that security or issuer in breach of trust or confidence that is owed to the issuer, the shareholders of that issuer, *or any other person who is the source of the material nonpublic information.* Under SEC Rule 10b5-2, a person has a duty of trust or confidence for purposes of the misappropriation theory of liability when (1) a person agrees to maintain information in confidence; (2) two people have a history, pattern, or practice of sharing confidences such that the recipient of the information knows or reasonably should know that the person communicating the material nonpublic information expects that the recipient will maintain its confidentiality; *or* (3) a person receives or obtains material nonpublic information from his or her spouse, parent, child, or sibling.

Under SEC Regulation FD (for "fair disclosure"), regulated issuers who disclose material nonpublic information to specified persons (primarily securities market professionals such as analysts and mutual fund managers) must make public disclosure of that information. If the selective disclosure was intentional or reckless, the issuer must make public disclosure simultaneously; for a nonintentional disclosure, the issuer must make public disclosure promptly, usually within twenty-four hours. With a few exceptions, Regulation FD does not apply to disclosures made in connection with a securities offering registered under the 1933 Act. The SEC can enforce this rule by bringing an administrative action seeking a cease-and-desist order or a civil action seeking an injunction and/or civil money penalties.

◆ **SEE CASE 44-4**

Although both Section 16(b) and Rule 10b–5 address the problem of insider trading and both may apply to the same transaction, they differ in several respects. First, Section 16(b) applies only to transactions involving registered equity securities; Rule 10b–5 applies to all securities. Second, the definition of *insider* under Rule 10b–5 extends beyond directors, officers, and owners of more than 10 percent of a company's stock, whereas the definition under Section 16(b) is limited to these persons. Third, Section 16(b) does not require that the insider possess material, nonpublic information; liability is strict. Rule 10b–5 applies to insider trading only where such information is not disclosed. Fourth, Section 16(b) applies only to transactions occurring within six months of each other; Rule 10b–5 has no such limitation. Fifth, under Rule 10b–5, injured investors may recover damages on their own behalf; under Section 16(b), although shareholders may bring suit, any recovery is on behalf of the corporation.

### EXPRESS INSIDER TRADING LIABILITY

In 1988, Congress amended the 1934 Act by adding **Section 20A**, which imposes express civil liability upon any person who violates the Act by purchasing or selling a security while in possession of material, nonpublic information. Any person who contemporaneously sold or purchased securities of the same class as those improperly traded may bring a private action against the traders to recover damages for the violation. The total amount of damages may not exceed the profit gained or loss avoided by the violation, diminished by any amount the violator disgorges to the SEC pursuant to a court order. The action must be brought within five years after the date of the last transaction that is the subject of the violation. Tippers are jointly and severally liable with tippees who commit a violation by trading on the inside information.

### CIVIL PENALTIES FOR INSIDER TRADING

In addition to the remedies discussed above, the SEC is authorized by legislation enacted in 1984 and 1988 to bring an action in a U.S. district court to have a civil penalty imposed upon any person who purchases or sells a security while in possession of material, nonpublic information. Liability also extends to any person who by communicating material, nonpublic information aids and abets another in committing such a violation. Liability may also be imposed on any person who directly or indirectly controlled a person who ultimately committed a violation if the controlling person knew or recklessly disregarded the fact that the controlled person was likely to commit a violation and consequently failed to take appropriate steps to prevent the transgression. Under this provision law firms, accounting firms, issuers, financial printers, news media, and others must implement policies to prevent insider trading. The violating transaction must be on or through the facilities of a national securities exchange or from or through a broker or dealer. Purchases that are part of a public offering by an issuer of securities are not subject to this provision.

The civil penalty for a person who trades on inside information is determined by the court in light of the facts and circumstances but may not exceed three times the profit gained or loss avoided as a result of the unlawful purchase or sale. The maximum amount that may be imposed upon a controlling person is the greater of $1,425,000 or three times the profit gained or loss avoided as a result of the controlled person's violation. If that violation consists of tipping inside information, the court measures the controller's liability by the profit gained or loss avoided by the person to whom the controlled person directed the tip. For the purpose of this provision, "profit gained" or "loss avoided" is "the difference between the purchase or sale price of the security and the value of that security as measured by the trading price of the security a reasonable period after public dissemination of the nonpublic information."

Civil penalties for insider trading are payable into the U.S. Treasury. An action to recover a penalty must be brought within five years after the date of the purchase or sale. The SEC is authorized to award bounties of up to 10 percent of a recovered penalty to informants who provide information leading to the imposition of the penalty. However, the CFPA has expanded whistleblower awards: the SEC now must award whistleblowers who voluntarily provide original information that leads to *any* successful enforcement action in which the SEC imposes monetary sanctions in excess of $1 million. The amount of the award must be between 10 percent and 30 percent of funds collected as monetary sanctions, as determined by the SEC.

## MISLEADING PROXY STATEMENTS

Any person who distributes a materially false or misleading proxy statement may be liable to a shareholder who relies upon the statement in purchasing or selling a security and thereby suffers a loss. In this context, a misstatement or omission is material if there is a substantial likelihood that a reasonable shareholder would consider it important in deciding how to vote. A number of courts have held that negligence is sufficient for an action under the proxy rule's antifraud provisions. In addition, when the proxy disclosure or filing requirement has been violated, a court may, if appropriate, enjoin a shareholder meeting or any action taken at that meeting. Other remedies are rescission, damages, and attorneys' fees. Since a proxy statement is filed with the SEC, a materially false or misleading proxy statement may also give rise to liability under Section 18, discussed above.

In addition, Rule 10b–5 also applies to misstatements in proxy statements. Moreover, most proxy statements used with mergers and sales of assets are also considered 1933 registration statements subject to civil liability under Section 11of the 1933 Act.

## FRAUDULENT TENDER OFFERS

It is unlawful for any person to make any untrue statement of material fact, to omit to state any material fact, or to engage in any fraudulent, deceptive, or manipulative practices in connection with any tender offer. Section 14(e). This provision applies even if the target company is not subject to the 1934 Act's reporting requirements. Insider trading during a tender offer is prohibited by Rule 14e–3, which has been upheld by the U.S. Supreme Court in *United States v. O'Hagan* (see Case 44-4).

Some courts have implied civil liability for violations of Section 14(e). Because relatively few cases have involved such violations, however, the requirements for such an action are not entirely clear. At present, a target company may seek an injunction, and a shareholder of the target may be able to recover damages or obtain rescission. Furthermore, it appears likely that the courts will require *scienter*.

◆ **SEE CASE 44-5**

◆ **SEE FIGURE 44-7: Civil Liability under the 1933 and 1934 Acts**

## ANTIBRIBERY PROVISION OF FCPA

The FCPA makes it unlawful for any domestic concern or any of its officers, directors, employees, or agents to offer or give anything of value directly or indirectly to any foreign official, political party, or political official for the purpose of (1) influencing any act or decision of that person or party in his or its official capacity, (2) inducing an act or omission in violation of his or its lawful duty, or (3) inducing such person or party to use his or its influence to affect a decision of a foreign government in order to assist the domestic concern in obtaining or retaining business. An offer or promise to make a prohibited payment is a violation even if the offer is not accepted or the promise is not performed. The 1988 amendments to the Act explicitly excluded routine governmental actions not involving the official's discretion, such as obtaining permits or processing applications. They also added an affirmative defense for payments that are lawful under the written laws or regulations of the foreign official's country.

Violations can result in fines of up to $2 million for companies; individuals may be fined a maximum of $100,000 or be imprisoned for up to five years, or both. Section 32(c). Fines imposed upon individuals may not be paid directly or indirectly by the domestic concern on whose behalf they acted. In addition, the courts may impose civil penalties of up to $16,000.

In 1997 the United States and thirty-three other nations signed the Organisation for Economic Co-operation and Development Convention on Combating Bribery of Foreign Public Officials in International Business Transactions (OECD Convention). Since then, four additional nations have signed the treaty. In 1998 Congress enacted the International Anti-Bribery and Fair Competition Act of 1998 to conform the FCPA to the Convention. The 1998 Act expands the FCPA to include (1) payments made to "secure any improper advantage" from foreign officials, (2) all

## ◆ FIGURE 44-7: Civil Liability under the 1933 and 1934 Acts

| Provision | Conduct | Plaintiffs | Defendants | Standard of Culpability | Reliance Required | Type of Liability | Remedies |
|---|---|---|---|---|---|---|---|
| **Section 12(a)(1) 1933 Act** | Unregistered sale or sale without prospectus | Purchasers from a violator | Sellers in violation | Strict liability | No | Express | Rescission<br>Damages |
| **Section 11 1933 Act** | Registration statement containing material misstatement or omission | Purchasers of registered security | Issuer;<br>Directors;<br>Signers;<br>Underwriters;<br>Experts | Strict liability for issuer; Negligence for others | No | Express | Damages<br>Attorneys' fees |
| **Section 12(a)(2) 1933 Act** | Material misstatement or omission | Purchasers from a violator | Sellers in violation | Negligence | No | Express | Rescission<br>Damages |
| **Section 18 1934 Act** | False or misleading statements in a document filed with SEC | Purchasers or sellers | Persons making filing in violation | Knowledge or bad faith | Yes | Express | Damages<br>Attorneys' fees |
| **Section 16(b) 1934 Act** | Short-swing profit by insider | Issuer;<br>Shareholder of issuer | Directors;<br>Officers;<br>10 percent shareholders | Strict liability | No | Express | Damages |
| **Rule 10b–5 1934 Act** | Deception or material misstatement or omission | Purchasers or sellers | Purchasers or sellers in violation | *Scienter* | Yes | Implied | Rescission<br>Damages<br>Injunction |
| **Section 20A 1934 Act** | Insider trading | Contemporaneous purchasers or sellers | Inside traders | *Scienter* | No | Express | Damages |
| **Section 14(a) 1934 Act** | Materially false or misleading proxy solicitation | Shareholders | Persons making proxy solicitation in violation | Negligence (probably) | Probably | Implied | Rescission<br>Damages<br>Injunction<br>Attorneys' fees |
| **Section 14(e) 1934 Act** | Tender offer with deception or manipulation or material misstatement or material omission | Target company;<br>Shareholders of target | Persons making tender offer in violation | *Scienter* (probably) | Probably | Implied | Rescission<br>Damages<br>Injunction |

Note: SEC = Securities and Exchange Commission.

foreign persons who commit an act in furtherance of a foreign bribe while in the United States, and (3) officials of public international organizations within the definition of a "foreign official." A public international organization is defined as either an organization designated by executive order pursuant to the International Organizations Immunities Act, or any other international organization designated by executive order of the president.

### CRIMINAL SANCTIONS

Section 32 of the 1934 Act imposes criminal sanctions on any person who willfully violates any provision of the Act (except the antibribery provision) or the rules and regulations the SEC promulgates pursuant to the Act. As amended by the Sarbanes-Oxley Act, for individuals, conviction may carry a fine of not more than $5 million or imprisonment for not more than twenty years, or both, with one exception: a person who proves she had no knowledge of the rule or regulation is not subject to imprisonment. If the person, however, is not a natural person (e.g., a corporation), a fine not exceeding $25 million may be imposed.

## CHAPTER SUMMARY

### SECURITIES ACT OF 1933

| | |
|---|---|
| **DEFINITION OF A SECURITY** | **Security** includes any note, stock, bond, preorganization subscription, and investment contract<br>**Investment Contract** any investment of money or property made in expectation of receiving a financial return solely from the efforts of others |
| **REGISTRATION OF SECURITIES** | **Disclosure Requirements** disclosure of accurate material information required in all public offerings of nonexempt securities unless offering is an exempt transaction<br>**Integrated Disclosure and Shelf Registrations** permitted for certain qualified issuers |
| **EXEMPT SECURITIES** | **Definition** securities not subject to the registration requirements of the 1933 Act<br>**Types** exempt securities include short-term commercial paper, municipal bonds, and certain insurance policies and annuity contracts |
| **EXEMPT TRANSACTIONS FOR ISSUERS** | **Definition** issuance of securities not subject to the registration requirements of the 1933 Act<br>**Types** exempt transactions include limited offers under Regulation D and Section 4(6), Regulation A, and intrastate issues |
| **EXEMPT TRANSACTIONS FOR NONISSUERS** | **Definition** resales by persons other than the issuer that are exempted from the registration requirements of the 1933 Act<br>**Types** exempt transactions include Rule 144 for reporting and nonreporting issuers, Regulation A, and Rule 144A |
| **LIABILITY** | **Unregistered Sales** Section 12(a)(1) imposes absolute civil liability as there are no defenses<br>**False Registration Statements** Section 11 imposes liability on the issuer, all persons who signed the statement, every director or partner, experts who prepared or certified any part of the statement, and all underwriters; defendants other than issuer may assert the defense of due diligence<br>**Antifraud Provisions** Section 12(a)(2) imposes liability upon the seller to the immediate purchaser, provided the purchaser did not know of the untruth or omission, but the seller is not liable if he did not know and, in the exercise of |

reasonable care could not have known, of the untrue statement or omission; Section 17(a) broadly prohibits fraud in the sale of securities
**Criminal Sanctions** willful violations are subject to a fine of not more than $10,000 and/or imprisonment of not more than five years

## SECURITIES EXCHANGE ACT OF 1934

**DISCLOSURE**

**Registration and Periodic Reporting Requirements** apply to all regulated publicly held companies and include one-time registration as well as annual, quarterly, and monthly reports
**Proxy Solicitations**
- ***Definition of a Proxy*** a signed writing by a shareholder authorizing a named person to vote her stock at a specified meeting of shareholders
- ***Proxy Statements*** proxy disclosure statements are required when proxies are solicited or an issuer submits a matter to a shareholder vote

**Tender Offers**
- ***Definition of a Tender Offer*** a general invitation to shareholders to purchase their shares at a specified price for a specified time
- ***Disclosure Requirements*** a statement disclosing specified information must be filed with the Securities and Exchange Commission and furnished to each offeree

**Foreign Corrupt Practices Act** imposes internal control requirements on companies with securities registered under the 1934 Act

**LIABILITY**

**Misleading Statements in Reports** Section 18 imposes civil liability for any false or misleading statement made in a registration or report filed with the Securities and Exchange Commission
**Short-Swing Profits** Section 16(b) imposes liability on certain insiders (directors, officers, and shareholders owning more than 10 percent of the stock of a corporation) for all profits made on sales and purchases within six months of each other, with any recovery going to the issuer
**Antifraud Provision** Rule 10b–5 makes it unlawful to (1) employ any device, scheme, or artifice to defraud; (2) make any untrue statement of a material fact; (3) omit to state a material fact; or (4) engage in any act that operates as a fraud
- ***Requisites of Rule 10b–5*** recovery requires (1) a misstatement or omission, (2) materiality, (3) *scienter* (intentional and knowing conduct), (4) reliance, and (5) connection with the purchase or sale of a security
- ***Insider Trading*** "insiders" are liable under Rule 10b–5 for failing to disclose material, nonpublic information before trading on the information

**Express Insider Trading Liability** is imposed on any person who sells or buys a security while in possession of inside information
**Civil Penalties for Inside Trading** may be imposed on inside traders in an amount up to three times the gains they made or losses they avoided
**Misleading Proxy Statements** any person who distributes a false or misleading proxy statement is liable to injured investors
**Fraudulent Tender Offers** Section 14(e) imposes civil liability for false and material statements or omissions or fraudulent, deceptive, or manipulative practices in connection with any tender offer
**Antibribery Provision of FCPA** prohibited bribery can result in fines and imprisonment
**Criminal Sanctions** individuals who willfully violate the 1934 Act are subject to a fine of not more than $5 million and/or imprisonment of not more than twenty years

## CASES

CASE 44-1

## Definition of a Security
## SEC v. EDWARDS

Supreme Court of the United States, 2004
540 U.S. 389, 124 S.Ct. 892, 157 L.Ed.2d 813
http://caselaw.lp.findlaw.com/cgi-bin/getcase.pl?court=US&navby=case&vol=000&invol=02-1196

**O'Connor, J.**

"Opportunity doesn't always knock * * * sometimes it rings." [Citation.] And sometimes it hangs up. So it did for the 10,000 people who invested a total of $300 million in the payphone sale-and-leaseback arrangements touted by respondent under that slogan. The Securities and Exchange Commission (SEC) argues that the arrangements were investment contracts, and thus were subject to regulation under the federal securities laws. In this case, we must decide whether a moneymaking scheme is excluded from the term "investment contract" simply because the scheme offered a contractual entitlement to a fixed, rather than a variable, return.

### I

Respondent Charles Edwards was the chairman, chief executive officer, and sole shareholder of ETS Payphones, Inc. (ETS). ETS, acting partly through a subsidiary also controlled by respondent, sold payphones to the public via independent distributors. The payphones were offered packaged with a site lease, a 5-year leaseback and management agreement, and a buyback agreement. All but a tiny fraction of purchasers chose this package, although other management options were offered. The purchase price for the payphone packages was approximately $7,000. Under the leaseback and management agreement, purchasers received $82 per month, a 14% annual return. Purchasers were not involved in the day-to-day operation of the payphones they owned. ETS selected the site for the phone, installed the equipment, arranged for connection and long-distance service, collected coin revenues, and maintained and repaired the phones. Under the buyback agreement, ETS promised to refund the full purchase price of the package at the end of the lease or within 180 days of a purchaser's request.

In its marketing materials and on its website, ETS trumpeted the "incomparable pay phone" as "an exciting business opportunity," in which recent deregulation had "open[ed] the door for profits for individual pay phone owners and operators." According to ETS, "[v]ery few business opportunities can offer the potential for ongoing revenue generation that is available in today's pay telephone industry." [Citation.]

The payphones did not generate enough revenue for ETS to make the payments required by the leaseback agreements, so the company depended on funds from new investors to meet its obligations. In September 2000, ETS filed for bankruptcy protection. The SEC brought this civil enforcement action the same month. It alleged that respondent and ETS had violated the registration requirements of §§5(a) and (c) of the Securities Act of 1933, [citation], the antifraud provisions of both §17(a) of the Securities Act of 1933, [citation], and §10(b) of the Securities Exchange Act of 1934, [citation], and Rule 10b–5 thereunder, [citation]. The District Court concluded that the payphone sale-and-leaseback arrangement was an investment contract within the meaning of, and therefore was subject to, the federal securities laws. [Citation.] The Court of Appeals reversed. [Citation.] It held that respondent's scheme was not an investment contract, on two grounds. First, it read this Court's opinions to require that an investment contract offer either capital appreciation or a participation in the earnings of the enterprise, and thus to exclude schemes, such as respondent's, offering a fixed rate of return. [Citation.] Second, it held that our opinions' requirement that the return on the investment be "derived solely from the efforts of others" was not satisfied when the purchasers had a contractual entitlement to the return. [Citation.] We conclude that it erred on both grounds.

### II

"Congress' purpose in enacting the securities laws was to regulate *investments*, in whatever form they are made and by whatever name they are called." [Citation.] To that end, it enacted a broad definition of "security," sufficient "to encompass virtually any instrument that might be sold as an investment." [Citation.] * * * [The 1993 Act and the 1934 Act] define "security" to include "any note, stock, treasury stock, security future, bond, debenture, * * * investment contract, * * * [or any] instrument commonly known as a 'security'." "Investment contract" is not itself defined.

The test for whether a particular scheme is an investment contract was established in our decision in *SEC v.*

*W. J. Howey Co.*, [citation]. We look to "whether the scheme involves an investment of money in a common enterprise with profits to come solely from the efforts of others." [Citation.] This definition "embodies a flexible rather than a static principle, one that is capable of adaptation to meet the countless and variable schemes devised by those who seek the use of the money of others on the promise of profits." [Citation.]

* * * Thus, when we held that "profits" must "come solely from the efforts of others," we were speaking of the profits that investors seek on their investment, not the profits of the scheme in which they invest. We used "profits" in the sense of income or return, to include, for example, dividends, other periodic payments, or the increased value of the investment.

There is no reason to distinguish between promises of fixed returns and promises of variable returns for purposes of the test, so understood. In both cases, the investing public is attracted by representations of investment income, as purchasers were in this case by ETS' invitation to "'watch the profits add up.'" [Citation.] Moreover, investments pitched as low-risk (such as those offering a "guaranteed" fixed return) are particularly attractive to individuals more vulnerable to investment fraud, including older and less sophisticated investors. [Citation.] Under the reading respondent advances, unscrupulous marketers of investments could evade the securities laws by picking a rate of return to promise. We will not read into the securities laws a limitation not compelled by the language that would so undermine the laws' purposes.

Respondent protests that including investment schemes promising a fixed return among investment contracts conflicts with our precedent. We disagree. * * *

* * *

Given that respondent's position is supported neither by the purposes of the securities laws nor by our precedents, it is no surprise that the SEC has consistently taken the opposite position, and maintained that a promise of a fixed return does not preclude a scheme from being an investment contract. * * *

The Eleventh Circuit's perfunctory alternative holding, that respondent's scheme falls outside the definition because purchasers had a contractual entitlement to a return, is incorrect and inconsistent with our precedent. We are considering investment *contracts*. The fact that investors have bargained for a return on their investment does not mean that the return is not also expected to come solely from the efforts of others. * * *

We hold that an investment scheme promising a fixed rate of return can be an "investment contract" and thus a "security" subject to the federal securities laws. The judgment of the United States Court of Appeals for the Eleventh Circuit is reversed, and the case is remanded for further proceedings consistent with this opinion.

It is so ordered.

CASE 44-2

## Liability for False Registration Statements
## ESCOTT v. BARCHRIS CONSTRUCTION CORP.

United States District Court, Southern District of New York, 1968

283 F.Supp. 643

http://scholar.google.com/scholar_case?case=13642266152052517214&hl=en&as_sdt=2&as_vis=1&oi=scholarr

**McLean, J.**

This is an action by purchasers of 5½ percent convertible subordinated fifteen year debentures of BarChris Construction Corporation (BarChris). * * *

The action is brought under Section 11 of the Securities Act of 1933. Plaintiffs allege that the registration statement with respect to these debentures filed with the Securities and Exchange Commission, which became effective on May 16, 1961, contained material false statements and material omissions.

Defendants fall into three categories: (1) the persons who signed the registration statement; (2) the underwriters, consisting of eight investment banking firms, led by Drexel & Co. (Drexel); and (3) BarChris's auditors, Peat, Marwick, Mitchell & Co. (Peat, Marwick).

* * *

Defendants, in addition to denying that the registration statement was false, have pleaded the defense open to them under Section 11 of the Act, * * *.

* * * On the main issue of liability, the questions to be decided are (1) did the registration statement contain false statements of fact, or did it omit to state facts which should have been stated in order to prevent it from being misleading; (2) if so, were the facts which were falsely stated or omitted "material" within the meaning of the Act; (3) if so, have defendants established their affirmative defenses?

* * *

In December 1959, BarChris sold 560,000 shares of common stock to the public at $3.00 per share. This issue was underwritten by Peter Morgan & Company, one of the present defendants.

By early 1961, BarChris needed additional working capital. The proceeds of the sale of the debentures involved in this action were to be devoted, in part at least, to fill that need.

The registration statement of the debentures, in preliminary form, was filed with the Securities and Exchange Commission on March 30, 1961. A first amendment was filed on May 11 and a second on May 16. The registration statement became effective on May 16. The closing of the financing took place on May 24. On that day BarChris received the net proceeds of the financing.

By that time BarChris was experiencing difficulties in collecting amounts due from some of its customers. Some of them were in arrears in payments due to factors on their discounted notes. As time went on those difficulties increased. Although BarChris continued to build [bowling] alleys in 1961 and 1962, it became increasingly apparent that the industry was overbuilt. Operators of alleys, often inadequately financed, began to fail. Precisely when the tide turned is a matter of dispute, but at any rate, it was painfully apparent in 1962.

In May of that year BarChris made an abortive attempt to raise more money by the sale of common stock. It filed with the Securities and Exchange Commission a registration statement for the stock issue which it later withdrew. In October 1962 BarChris came to the end of the road. On October 29, 1962, it filed in this court a petition for an arrangement under Chapter XI of the Bankruptcy Act.

[The court found that the registration statement contained material false statements.]

* * *

### *The "Due Diligence" Defenses*

Section 11(b)of the Act provides that:

> * * * no person, other than the issuer, shall be liable * * * who shall sustain the burden of proof—
>
> * * *
>
> (3) that (A) as regards any part of the registration statement not purporting to be made on the authority of an expert * * * he had, after reasonable investigation, reasonable ground to believe and did believe, at the time such part of the registration statement became effective, that the statements therein were true and that there was no omission to state a material fact required to be stated therein or necessary to make the statements therein not misleading; * * * and (C) as regards any part of the registration statement purporting to be made on the authority of an expert (other than himself) * * * he had no reasonable ground to believe and did not believe, at the time such part of the registration statement became effective, that the statements therein were untrue or that there was an omission to state a material fact required to be stated therein or necessary to make the statements therein not misleading. * * *

Section 11(c) defines "reasonable investigation" as follows:

> In determining, for the purposes of paragraph (3) of subsection (b) of this section, what constitutes reasonable investigation and reasonable ground for belief, the standard of reasonableness shall be that required of a prudent man in the management of his own property.

Every defendant, except BarChris itself, to whom, as the issuer, these defenses are not available, and except Peat, Marwick, whose position rests on a different statutory provision, has pleaded these affirmative defenses. * * *

* * *

I turn now to the question of whether defendants have proved their due diligence defenses. The position of each defendant will be separately considered.

* * *

***Kircher*** Kircher was treasurer of BarChris and its chief financial officer. He is a certified public accountant and an intelligent man. He was thoroughly familiar with BarChris's financial affairs. * * *

Moreover, as a member of the executive committee, Kircher was kept informed as to those branches of the business of which he did not have direct charge.

* * *

Knowing the facts, Kircher had reason to believe that the expertised portion of the prospectus, *i.e.*, the 1960 figures, was in part incorrect. He could not shut his eyes to the facts and rely on Peat, Marwick for that portion.

As to the rest of the prospectus, knowing the facts, he did not have a reasonable ground to believe it to be true. On the contrary, he must have known that in part it was untrue. * * *

Kircher has not proved his due diligence defenses.

* * *

***Birnbaum*** Birnbaum was a young lawyer, admitted to the bar in 1957, who, after brief periods of employment by two different law firms and an equally brief period of practicing in his own firm, was employed by BarChris as house counsel and assistant secretary in October 1960. Unfortunately for him, he became secretary and a director of BarChris on April 17, 1961, after the first version of the registration statement had been filed with the Securities and Exchange Commission. He signed the later amendments, thereby becoming responsible for the accuracy of the prospectus in its final form.

Although the prospectus, in its description of "management," lists Birnbaum among the "executive officers" and devotes several sentences to a recital of his career, the fact seems to be that he was not an executive officer in any real sense. He did not participate in the management of the company. As house counsel, he attended to legal matters of a routine nature.

* * *

One of Birnbaum's more important duties, first as assistant secretary and later as full-fledged secretary, was to keep the corporate minutes of BarChris and its subsidiaries. This necessarily informed him to a considerable extent about the company's affairs. * * *

It seems probable that Birnbaum did not know of many of the inaccuracies in the prospectus. He must, however, have appreciated some of them. In any case, he made no investigation and relied on the others to get it right * * *. As a lawyer, he should have known his obligations under the statute. He should have known that he was required to make a reasonable investigation of the truth of all the statements in the unexpertised portion of the document which he signed. Having failed to make such an investigation, he did not have reasonable ground to believe that all these statements were true. Birnbaum has not established his due diligence defenses except as to the audited 1960 figures.

***Auslander*** Auslander was an "outside" director, *i.e.*, one who was not an officer of BarChris. He was chairman of the board of Valley Stream National Bank. * * *

* * *

In considering Auslander's due diligence defenses, a distinction is to be drawn between the expertised and non-expertised portions of the prospectus. As to the former, Auslander knew that Peat, Marwick had audited the 1960 figures. He believed them to be correct because he had confidence in Peat, Marwick. He had no reasonable ground to believe otherwise.

As to the non-expertised portions, however, Auslander is in a different position. He seems to have been under the impression that Peat, Marwick was responsible for all the figures. This impression was not correct, as he would have realized if he had read the prospectus carefully. Auslander made no investigation of the accuracy of the prospectus. * * *

It is true that Auslander became a director on the eve of the financing. He had little opportunity to familiarize himself with the company's affairs. The question is whether, under such circumstances, Auslander did enough to establish his due diligence defense with respect to the non-expertised portions of the prospectus.

* * *

Section 11 imposes liability in the first instance upon a director, no matter how new he is. He is presumed to know his responsibility when he becomes a director. He can escape liability only by using that reasonable care to investigate the facts which a prudent man would employ in the management of his own property. In my opinion, a prudent man would not act in an important matter without any knowledge of the relevant facts, in sole reliance upon representations of persons who are comparative strangers and upon general information which does not purport to cover the particular case. To say that such minimal conduct measures up to the statutory standard would to all intents and purposes, absolve new directors from responsibility merely because they are new. This is not a sensible construction of Section 11, when one bears in mind its fundamental purpose of requiring full and truthful disclosures for the protection of investors.

* * *

***The Underwriters*** The underwriters other than Drexel made no investigation of the accuracy of the prospectus * * *. They all relied upon Drexel as the "lead" underwriter.

Drexel did make an investigation. The work was in charge of Coleman, a partner of the firm, assisted by Casperson, an associate. Drexel's attorneys acted as attorneys for the entire group of underwriters. Ballard did the work, assisted by Stanton.

* * *

The underwriters say that the prospectus is the company's prospectus, not theirs. Doubtless this is the way they customarily regard it. But the Securities Act makes no such distinction. The underwriters are just as responsible as the company if the prospectus is false. And prospective investors rely upon the reputation of the underwriters in deciding whether to purchase the securities.

* * *

The purpose of Section 11 is to protect investors. To that end the underwriters are made responsible for the truth of the prospectus. If they may escape that responsibility by taking at face value representations made to them by the company's management, then the inclusion of underwriters among those liable under Section 11 affords the investors no additional protection. To effectuate the statute's purpose, the phrase "reasonable investigation" must be construed to require more effort on the part of the underwriters than the mere accurate reporting in the prospectus of "data presented" to them by the company. It should make no difference that this data is elicited by questions addressed to the company officers by the underwriters, or that the underwriters at the time believe that the company's officers are truthful and reliable. In order to make the underwriters' participation in this enterprise of any value to the investors, the underwriters must make some reasonable attempt to verify the data submitted to them. They may not rely solely on the company's officers or on the company's counsel. A prudent man in the management of his own property would not rely on them.

It is impossible to lay down a rigid rule suitable for every case defining the extent to which such verification must go. It is a question of degree, a matter of judgment in each case. In the present case, the underwriters' counsel made almost no attempt to verify management's representations. I hold that that was insufficient.

On the evidence in this case, I find that the underwriters' counsel did not make a reasonable investigation of the truth of those portions of the prospectus which were not made on the authority of Peat, Marwick as an expert. Drexel is bound by their failure. It is not a matter of relying upon counsel for legal advice. Here the attorneys were dealing with matters of fact. Drexel delegated to them, as its agent, the business of examining the corporate minutes and contracts. It must bear the consequences of their failure to make an adequate examination.

The other underwriters, who did nothing and relied solely on Drexel and on the lawyers, are also bound by it. It follows that although Drexel and the other underwriters believed that those portions of the prospectus were true, they had no reasonable ground for that belief, within the meaning of the statute. Hence, they have not established their due diligence defense, except as to the 1960 audited figures.

## CASE 44-3 Rule10b–5 STONERIDGE INV. PARTNERS, LLC v. SCIENTIFIC-ATLANTA

Supreme Court of the United States, 2008
552 U.S. 148, 128 S.Ct. 761, 169 L.Ed.2d 627
http://caselaw.lp.findlaw.com/scripts/getcase.pl?court=US&vol=000&invol=06-43

**Kennedy, J.**

We consider the reach of the private right of action the Court has found implied in §10(b) of the Securities Exchange Act of 1934, [citation], and SEC Rule 10b–5, [citation]. In this suit investors alleged losses after purchasing common stock. They sought to impose liability on entities who, acting both as customers and suppliers, agreed to arrangements that allowed the investors' company to mislead its auditor and issue a misleading financial statement affecting the stock price. * * *

This class-action suit by investors was filed against Charter Communications, Inc., in the United States District Court for the Eastern District of Missouri. Stoneridge Investment Partners, LLC, a limited liability company organized under the laws of Delaware, was the lead plaintiff and is petitioner here.

Charter issued the financial statements and the securities in question. It was a named defendant along with some of its executives and Arthur Andersen LLP, Charter's independent auditor during the period in question. We are concerned, though, with two other defendants, respondents here. Respondents are Scientific-Atlanta, Inc., and Motorola, Inc. They were suppliers, and later customers, of Charter.

* * * Charter, a cable operator, engaged in a variety of fraudulent practices so its quarterly reports would meet Wall Street expectations for cable subscriber growth and operating cash flow. The fraud included misclassification of its customer base; delayed reporting of terminated customers; improper capitalization of costs that should have been shown as expenses; and manipulation of the company's billing cutoff dates to inflate reported revenues. In late 2000, Charter executives realized that, despite these efforts, the company would miss projected operating cash flow numbers by $15 to $20 million. To help meet the shortfall, Charter decided to alter its existing arrangements with respondents, Scientific-Atlanta and Motorola. * * *

Respondents supplied Charter with the digital cable converter (set top) boxes that Charter furnished to its customers. Charter arranged to overpay respondents $20 for each set top box it purchased until the end of the year, with the understanding that respondents would return the overpayment by purchasing advertising from Charter. The transactions, it is alleged, had no economic substance; but, because Charter would then record the advertising purchases as revenue and capitalize its purchase of the set top boxes, in violation of generally accepted accounting principles, the transactions would enable Charter to fool its auditor into approving a financial statement showing it met projected revenue and operating cash flow numbers. Respondents agreed to the arrangement.

So that Arthur Andersen would not discover the link between Charter's increased payments for the boxes and the advertising purchases, the companies drafted documents to make it appear the transactions were unrelated and conducted in the ordinary course of business. Following a request from Charter, Scientific-Atlanta sent documents to Charter stating—falsely—that it had increased production costs. It raised the price for set top boxes for the rest of 2000 by $20 per box. As for Motorola, in a written contract Charter agreed to purchase from Motorola a specific number of set top boxes and pay liquidated damages of $20 for each unit it did not take. The contract was made with the expectation Charter would fail to purchase all the units and pay Motorola the liquidated damages.

To return the additional money from the set top box sales, Scientific-Atlanta and Motorola signed contracts with Charter to purchase advertising time for a price higher than fair value. The new set top box agreements were backdated to make it appear that they were negotiated a month before the advertising agreements. The backdating was important to convey the impression that the negotiations were unconnected, a point Arthur Andersen considered necessary for separate treatment of the transactions. Charter recorded the advertising payments to inflate revenue and operating cash flow by approximately $17 million. The inflated number was shown on financial statements filed with the Securities and Exchange Commission (SEC) and reported to the public.

Respondents had no role in preparing or disseminating Charter's financial statements. And their own financial statements booked the transactions as a wash, under generally accepted accounting principles. It is alleged respondents knew or were in reckless disregard of Charter's intention to use the transactions to inflate its revenues and knew the resulting financial statements issued by Charter would be relied upon by research analysts and investors.

Petitioner filed a securities fraud class action on behalf of purchasers of Charter stock alleging that, by participating in the transactions, respondents violated §10(b) of the Securities Exchange Act of 1934 and SEC Rule 10b–5.

The District Court granted respondents' motion to dismiss for failure to state a claim on which relief can be granted. The United States Court of Appeals for the Eighth Circuit affirmed. * * *

* * * We granted *certiorari*.

* * *

* * * Though the text of the Securities Exchange Act does not provide for a private cause of action for §10(b) violations, the Court has found a right of action implied in the words of the statute and its implementing regulation. [Citation.] In a typical §10(b) private action a plaintiff must prove (1) a material misrepresentation or omission by the defendant; (2) scienter; (3) a connection between the misrepresentation or omission and the purchase or sale of a security; (4) reliance upon the misrepresentation or omission; (5) economic loss; and (6) loss causation. [Citation.]

* * *

The §10(b) implied private right of action does not extend to aiders and abettors. The conduct of a secondary actor must satisfy each of the elements or preconditions for liability; and we consider whether the allegations here are sufficient to do so.

* * *

Reliance by the plaintiff upon the defendant's deceptive acts is an essential element of the §10(b) private cause of action. It ensures that, for liability to arise, the "requisite causal connection between a defendant's misrepresentation and a plaintiff's injury" exists as a predicate for liability. [Citations.] We have found a rebuttable presumption of reliance in two different circumstances. First, if there is an omission of a material fact by one with a duty to disclose, the investor to whom the duty was owed need not provide specific proof of reliance. [Citation.] Second, under the fraud-on-the-market doctrine, reliance is presumed when the statements at issue become public. The public information is reflected in the market price of the security. Then it can be assumed that an investor who buys or sells stock at the market price relies upon the statement. [Citation.]

Neither presumption applies here. Respondents had no duty to disclose; and their deceptive acts were not communicated to the public. No member of the investing public had knowledge, either actual or presumed, of respondents' deceptive acts during the relevant times. Petitioner, as a result, cannot show reliance upon any of respondents' actions except in an indirect chain that we find too remote for liability.

* * *

As stated above, reliance is tied to causation, leading to the inquiry whether respondents' acts were immediate or remote to the injury. * * * In all events we conclude respondents' deceptive acts, which were not disclosed to the investing public, are too remote to satisfy the requirement of reliance. It was Charter, not respondents, that misled its auditor and filed fraudulent financial statements; nothing respondents did made it necessary or inevitable for Charter to record the transactions as it did.

* * *

The judgment of the Court of Appeals is affirmed, and the case is remanded for further proceedings consistent with this opinion.

CASE 44-4

## Insider Trading
## UNITED STATES v. O'HAGAN

Supreme Court of the United States, 1997
521 U.S. 642, 117 S.Ct. 2199, 138 L.Ed.2d 724
http://laws.findlaw.com/US/000/96-842.html

**Ginsburg, J.**

Respondent James Herman O'Hagan was a partner in the law firm of Dorsey & Whitney in Minneapolis, Minnesota. In July 1988, Grand Metropolitan PLC (Grand Met), a company based in London, England, retained Dorsey & Whitney as local counsel to represent Grand Met regarding a potential tender offer for the common stock of the Pillsbury Company, headquartered in Minneapolis. Both Grand Met and Dorsey & Whitney took precautions to protect the confidentiality of Grand Met's tender offer plans. O'Hagan did no work on the Grand Met representation. Dorsey & Whitney withdrew from representing Grand Met on September 9, 1988. Less than a month later, on October 4, 1988, Grand Met publicly announced its tender offer for Pillsbury stock.

On August 18, 1988, while Dorsey & Whitney was still representing Grand Met, O'Hagan began purchasing call options for Pillsbury stock. Each option gave him the right to purchase 100 shares of Pillsbury stock by a specified date in September 1988. Later in August and in September, O'Hagan made additional purchases of Pillsbury call options. By the end of September, he owned 2,500 unexpired Pillsbury options, apparently more than any other individual investor. [Citation.] O'Hagan also purchased, in September 1988, some 5,000 shares of Pillsbury common stock, at a price just under $39 per share. When Grand Met announced its tender offer in October, the price of Pillsbury stock rose to nearly $60 per share. O'Hagan then sold his Pillsbury call options and common stock, making a profit of more than $4.3 million.

[The Securities and Exchange Commission initiated an investigation into O'Hagan's transactions, culminating in an indictment alleging that O'Hagan defrauded his law firm and its client, Grand Met, by using for his own trading purposes material, nonpublic information regarding Grand Met's planned tender offer in violation of §10(b) of the Securities Exchange Act of 1934 and SEC Rule 10b–5. A jury convicted O'Hagan and he was sentenced to a 41-month term of imprisonment. A divided panel of the Court of Appeals for the Eighth Circuit reversed O'Hagan's conviction holding that liability under §10(b) and Rule 10b–5 may not be grounded on the "misappropriation theory" of securities fraud on which the prosecution relied.]

We address * * * the Court of Appeals' reversal of O'Hagan's convictions under §10(b) and Rule 10b–5. Following the Fourth Circuit's lead, see [citation], the Eighth Circuit rejected the misappropriation theory as a basis for §10(b) liability. We hold, in accord with several other Courts of Appeals, that criminal liability under §10(b) may be predicated on the misappropriation theory.

Under the "traditional" or "classical theory" of insider trading liability, §10(b) and Rule 10b–5 are violated when a corporate insider trades in the securities of his corporation on the basis of material, nonpublic information. Trading on such information qualifies as a "deceptive device" under §10(b), we have affirmed, because "a relationship of trust and confidence [exists] between the shareholders of a corporation and those insiders who have obtained confidential information by reason of their position with that corporation." [Citation.] That relationship, we recognized, "gives rise to a duty to disclose [or to abstain from trading] because of the 'necessity of preventing a corporate insider from * * * tak[ing] unfair advantage of * * * uninformed * * * stockholders.'" [Citation.] The classical theory applies not only to officers, directors, and other permanent insiders of a corporation, but also to attorneys, accountants, consultants, and others who temporarily become fiduciaries of a corporation. [Citation.]

The "misappropriation theory" holds that a person commits fraud "in connection with" a securities transaction, and thereby violates §10(b) and Rule 10b–5, when he misappropriates confidential information for securities trading purposes, in breach of a duty owed to the source of the information. [Citation.] Under this theory, a fiduciary's undisclosed, self-serving use of a principal's information to purchase or sell securities, in breach of a duty of loyalty and confidentiality, defrauds the principal of the exclusive use of that information. In lieu of premising liability on a fiduciary relationship between company insider and purchaser or seller of the company's stock, the misappropriation theory premises liability on a fiduciary-turned-trader's deception of those who entrusted him with access to confidential information.

The two theories are complementary, each addressing efforts to capitalize on nonpublic information through the purchase or sale of securities. The classical theory targets a corporate insider's breach of duty to shareholders with whom the insider transacts; the misappropriation theory outlaws trading on the basis of nonpublic information by a corporate "outsider" in breach of a duty owed not to a trading party, but to the source of the information. The misappropriation theory is thus designed to "protec[t] the integrity of the securities markets against abuses by 'outsiders' to a corporation who have access to confidential information that will affect th[e] corporation's security price when revealed, but who owe no fiduciary or other duty to that corporation's shareholders." [Citation.]

In this case, the indictment alleged that O'Hagan, in breach of a duty of trust and confidence he owed to his law firm, Dorsey & Whitney, and to its client, Grand Met, traded on the basis of nonpublic information regarding Grand Met's planned tender offer for Pillsbury common stock. [Citation.] This conduct, the Government charged, constituted a fraudulent device in connection with the purchase and sale of securities. [Court's footnote: The Government could not have prosecuted O'Hagan under the classical theory, for O'Hagan was not an "insider" of Pillsbury, the corporation in whose stock he traded. * * *]

We agree with the Government that misappropriation, as just defined, satisfies §10(b)'s requirement that chargeable conduct involve a "deceptive device or contrivance" used "in connection with" the purchase or sale of securities. We observe, first, that misappropriators, as the Government describes them, deal in deception. A fiduciary who "[pretends] loyalty to the principal while secretly converting the principal's information for personal gain," [citation], "dupes" or defrauds the principal. [Citation.]

* * *

* * * Because the deception essential to the misappropriation theory involves feigning fidelity to the source of information, if the fiduciary discloses to the source that he plans to trade on the nonpublic information, there is no "deceptive device" and thus no §10(b) violation—although the fiduciary-turned-trader may remain liable under state law for breach of a duty of loyalty.

We turn next to the §10(b) requirement that the misappropriator's deceptive use of information be "in connection with the purchase or sale of [a] security." This element is satisfied because the fiduciary's fraud is consummated, not when the fiduciary gains the confidential information, but when, without disclosure to his principal, he uses the information to purchase or sell securities. The securities transaction and the breach of duty thus coincide. This is so even though the person or entity defrauded is not the other party to the trade, but is, instead, the source of the nonpublic information. [Citation.] A misappropriator who trades on the basis of material, nonpublic information, in short, gains his advantageous market position through deception; he deceives the source of the information and simultaneously harms members of the investing public. [Citation.]

* * *

The misappropriation theory comports with §10(b)'s language, which requires deception "in connection with the purchase or sale of any security," not deception of an identifiable purchaser or seller. The theory is also well-tuned to an animating purpose of the Exchange Act: to insure honest securities markets and thereby promote investor confidence. [Citation.] Although informational disparity is inevitable in the securities markets, investors likely would hesitate to venture their capital in a market where trading based on misappropriated nonpublic information is unchecked by law. An investor's informational disadvantage vis-à-vis a misappropriator with material, nonpublic information stems from contrivance, not luck; it is a disadvantage that cannot be overcome with research or skill. [Citation.]

In sum, considering the inhibiting impact on market participation of trading on misappropriated information, and the congressional purposes underlying §10(b), it makes scant sense to hold a lawyer like O'Hagan a §10(b) violator if he works for a law firm representing the target of a tender offer, but not if he works for a law firm representing the bidder. The text of the statute requires no such result. The misappropriation at issue here was properly made the subject of a §10(b) charge because it meets the statutory requirement that there be "deceptive" conduct "in connection with" securities transactions.

* * *

The judgment of the Court of Appeals for the Eighth Circuit is reversed, and the case is remanded for further proceedings consistent with this opinion.

CASE 44-5

## Fraudulent Tender Offers
## SCHREIBER v. BURLINGTON NORTHERN, INC.

Supreme Court of the United States, 1985
472 U.S. 1, 105 S.Ct. 2458, 86 L.Ed.2d 1
http://laws.findlaw.com/US/472/1.html

**Burger, C. J.**

On December 21, 1982, Burlington Northern, Inc., made a hostile tender offer for El Paso Gas Co. Through a wholly owned subsidiary, Burlington proposed to purchase 25.1 million El Paso shares at $24 per share. Burlington reserved the right to terminate the offer if any of several specified events occurred. El Paso management initially opposed the takeover, but its shareholders responded favorably, fully subscribing the offer by the December 30, 1982 deadline.

Burlington did not accept those tendered shares; instead, after negotiations with El Paso management, Burlington announced on January 10, 1983, the terms of a new and friendly takeover agreement. Pursuant to the new agreement, Burlington undertook, *inter alia*, to (1) rescind the December tender offer, (2) purchase 4,166,667 shares from El Paso at $24 per share, (3) substitute a new tender offer for only 21 million shares at $24 per share, (4) provide procedural protections against a squeeze-out merger of the remaining El Paso shareholders, and (5) recognize "golden parachute" contracts between El Paso and four of its senior officers. By February 8, more than 40 million shares were tendered in response to Burlington's January offer, and the takeover was completed.

The rescission of the first tender offer caused a diminished payment to those shareholders who had tendered during the first offer. The January offer was greatly oversubscribed and consequently those shareholders who retendered were subject to substantial proration. Petitioner Barbara Schreiber filed suit on behalf of herself and similarly situated shareholders, alleging that Burlington, El Paso, and members of El Paso's board violated §14(e)'s prohibition of "fraudulent, deceptive or manipulative acts or practices * * * in connection with any tender offer." [Citation.] She claimed that Burlington's withdrawal of the December tender offer coupled with the substitution of the January tender offer was a "manipulative" distortion of the market for El Paso stock. Schreiber also alleged that Burlington violated §14(e) by failing in the January offer to disclose the "golden parachutes" offered to four of El Paso's managers. She claims that this January non-disclosure was a deceptive act forbidden by §14(e).

The District Court dismissed the suit for failure to state a claim. * * *

* * *

We are asked in this case to interpret §14(e) of the Securities Exchange Act, [citation]. The starting point is the language of the statute. Section 14(e) provides:

> It shall be unlawful for any person to make any untrue statement of a material fact or omit to state any material fact necessary in order to make the statements made, in the light of the circumstances under which they are made, not misleading, or to engage in any fraudulent, deceptive or manipulative acts or practices, in connection with any tender offer or request or invitation for tenders, or any solicitation of security holders in opposition to or in favor of any such offer, request, or invitation. The Commission shall, for the purposes of this subsection, by rules and regulations define, and prescribe means reasonably designed to prevent, such acts and practices as are fraudulent, deceptive, or manipulative. [Citation.]

* * * Petitioner reads the phrase "fraudulent, deceptive or manipulative acts or practices" to include acts which, although fully disclosed, "artificially" affect the price of the takeover target's stock. Petitioner's interpretation relies on the belief that §14(e) is directed at purposes broader than providing full and true information to investors.

Petitioner's reading of the term "manipulative" conflicts with the normal meaning of the term. We have held in the context of an alleged violation of §10(b) of the Securities Exchange Act:

> Use of the word "manipulative" is especially significant. It is and was virtually a term of art when used in connection with the securities markets. It connotes intentional or willful conduct designed to deceive or defraud investors by controlling or artificially affecting the price of securities.

*Ernst & Ernst v. Hochfelder* [see *Chapter 45*].

* * * The meaning the Court has given the term "manipulative" is consistent with the use of the term at common law, and with its traditional dictionary definition.

* * *

Our conclusion that "manipulative" acts under §14(e) require misrepresentation or nondisclosure is buttressed by the purpose and legislative history of the provision. Section 14(e) was originally added to the Securities Exchange Act as part of the Williams Act, [citation]. "The purpose of the Williams Act is to insure that public shareholders who are confronted by a cash tender offer for their stock will not be required to respond without adequate information." [Citation.]

* * *

Nowhere in the legislative history is there the slightest suggestion that §14(e) serves any purpose other than disclosure, or that the term "manipulative" should be read as an invitation to the courts to oversee the substantive fairness of tender offers; the quality of any offer is a matter for the marketplace.

* * *

We hold that the term "manipulative" as used in §14(e) requires misrepresentation or nondisclosure. It connotes "conduct designed to deceive or defraud investors by controlling or artificially affecting the price of securities." *Ernst & Ernst v. Hochfelder* [see *Chapter 45*]. Without misrepresentation or nondisclosure, §14(e) has not been violated.

Applying that definition to this case, we hold that the actions of respondents were not manipulative. The amended complaint fails to allege that the cancellation of the first tender offer was accompanied by any misrepresentation, nondisclosure or deception. The District Court correctly found, "All activity of the defendants that could have conceivably affected the price of El Paso shares was done openly." [Citation.]

* * *

The judgment of the Court of Appeals is affirmed.

## QUESTIONS

1. Explain the disclosure requirements of the 1933 Act, including which securities and transactions are exempt from these disclosure requirements.
2. Discuss the potential civil liabilities under the 1933 Act.
3. Distinguish between publicly held companies under the 1934 Act and those that are not publicly held. Which provisions of the 1934 Act apply only to publicly held companies and which apply to all companies?
4. Discuss the disclosure requirements of the 1934 Act.
5. Discuss the potential civil liabilities under the 1934 Act.

## PROBLEMS

**1.** Acme Realty, a real estate development company, is a limited partnership organized in Georgia. It is planning to develop a two-hundred-acre parcel of land for a regional shopping center and needs to raise $1,250,000. As part of its financing, Acme plans to offer $1,250,000 worth of limited partnership interests to about one hundred prospective investors in the southeastern United States. It anticipates that about forty to fifty private investors will purchase the limited partnership interests.

**(a)** Must Acme register this offering? Why or why not?

**(b)** If Acme must register but fails to do so, what are the legal consequences?

**2.** Bigelow Corporation has total assets of $850,000, sales of $1,350,000, and one class of common stock with 375 shareholders, and a class of preferred stock with 250 shareholders, both of which are traded over the counter. Which provisions of the Securities Exchange Act of 1934 apply to Bigelow Corporation?

**3.** Capricorn, Inc., is planning to "go public" by offering its common stock, which previously had been owned by only three shareholders. The company intends to limit the number of purchasers to twenty-five persons resident in the State of its incorporation. All of Capricorn's business and all of its assets are located in its State of incorporation. Based upon these facts, what exemptions from registration, if any, are available to Capricorn, and what conditions would each of these available exemptions impose upon the terms of the offer?

**4.** The boards of directors of DuMont Corp. and Epsot, Inc., agreed to enter into a friendly merger, with DuMont to be the surviving entity. The stock of both corporations was listed on a national stock exchange. In connection with the merger, both corporations distributed to their shareholders proxy statements seeking approval of the proposed merger. The shareholders of both corporations voted to approve the merger. About three weeks after the merger was consummated, the price of DuMont stock fell from $25 to $13 as a result of the discovery that Epsot had entered into several unprofitable long-term contracts two months before the merger had been proposed. The contracts will result in substantial losses from Epsot's operations for at least the next four years. The existence and effect of these contracts, although known to both corporations at the time of the proposed merger, were not disclosed in the proxy statements of either corporation. Can the shareholders of DuMont recover in a suit against DuMont under the 1934 Act? Explain.

**5.** Farthing is a director and vice president of Garp, Inc., whose common stock is listed on the New York Stock Exchange. Farthing engaged in the following transactions in the same calendar year: on January 1, Farthing sold five hundred shares at $30 per share; on January 15, she purchased three hundred shares at $30 per share; on February 1, she purchased two hundred shares at $45 per share; on March 1, she purchased three hundred shares at $60 per share; on March 15, she sold two hundred shares at $55 per share; and on April 1, she sold one hundred shares at $40 per share. Howell brings suit on behalf of Garp, alleging that Farthing has violated the Securities Exchange Act of 1934. Farthing defends on the ground that she lost money on the transactions in question. Is Farthing liable? If so, under which provisions and for what amount of money?

**6.** Intercontinental Widgets, Inc., had applied for a patent for a new state-of-the-art widget, which, if patented, would significantly increase the value of Intercontinental's shares. On September 1, the Patent Office notified Jackson, the attorney for Intercontinental, that the patent application had been approved. After informing Kingsley, the president of Intercontinental, of the good news, Jackson called his broker and purchased one thousand shares of Intercontinental at $18 per share. He also told his partner, Lucas, who immediately proceeded to purchase five hundred shares at $19 per share. Lucas then called his brother-in-law, Mammon, and told him the news. On September 3, Mammon bought four thousand shares at $21 per share. On September 4, Kingsley issued a press release which accurately reported that a patent had been granted to Intercontinental. The next day Intercontinental's stock soared to $38 per share. A class action suit is brought against Jackson, Lucas, Mammon, and Intercontinental for violations of Rule 10b–5. Who, if anyone, is liable?

**7.** Nova, Inc., sought to sell a new issue of common stock. It registered the issue with the Securities and Exchange Commission but included false information in both the registration statement and the prospectus. The issue was underwritten by Omega & Sons and was sold in its entirety by Periwinkle, Ramses, and Sheffield, Inc., a securities broker-dealer. Telford, who was unaware of the falsity of this information, purchased five hundred shares at $6 per share. Three months later, the falsity of the information contained in the prospectus was made public, and the price of the shares fell to $1 per share. The following week Telford brought suit against Nova, Inc., Omega & Sons, and Periwinkle, Ramses and Sheffield, Inc., under the Securities Act of 1933.

**(a)** Who, if anyone, is liable under the Act? If liable, under which provisions?

**(b)** What defenses, if any, are available to the various defendants?

**8.** Tanaka, a director and officer of Deep Hole Oil Company, telephoned Romani for the purpose of buying two hundred shares of Deep Hole Company stock owned by Romani. During the period of negotiations, Tanaka concealed his identity and did not disclose the fact that earlier in the day he had received a report of two rich oil strikes on the oil company's property. Romani sold his two hundred shares to Tanaka for $10 per share. Taking into consideration the new strikes, the fair value of the stock was approximately $20 per share. Romani sues Tanaka to recover damages. Is Tanaka liable? If so, under which provisions and for what amount of money?

**9.** Venable Corporation has 750,000 shares of common stock outstanding, which are owned by 640 shareholders. The assets of Venable Corporation are valued at more than $10 million. In March, Underhill began purchasing shares of Venable's common stock in the open market. By April, he had acquired 40,000 shares at prices ranging from $12 to $14. Upon discovering Underhill's activities in late April, the directors of Venable had the corporation purchase the 40,000 shares from Underhill for $18 per share. Which provisions of the 1934 Act, if any, have been violated?

**10.** Dirks was an officer of a New York broker-dealer firm that specialized in providing investment analysis of insurance company securities to institutional investors. On March 6, Dirks received information from Ronald Secrist, a former officer of Equity Funding of America. Secrist alleged that the assets of Equity Funding, a diversified corporation primarily engaged in selling life insurance and mutual funds, were vastly overstated as the result of fraudulent corporate practices. Dirks decided to investigate the allegations. He visited Equity Funding's headquarters in Los Angeles and interviewed several officers and employees of the corporation. The senior management denied any wrongdoing, but certain corporation employees corroborated the charges of fraud. Neither Dirks nor his firm owned or traded any Equity Funding stock, but throughout his investigation he openly discussed the information he had obtained with a number of clients and investors. Some of these persons sold their holdings of Equity Funding securities, including five investment advisers who liquidated holdings of more than $16 million.

While Dirks was in Los Angeles, he was in touch regularly with William Blundell, *The Wall Street Journal*'s Los Angeles bureau chief. Dirks urged Blundell to write a story on the fraud allegations. Blundell did not believe, however, that such a massive fraud could go undetected and declined to write the story. He feared that publishing such damaging hearsay might be libelous.

During the two-week period in which Dirks pursued his investigation and spread word of Secrist's charges, the price of Equity Funding stock fell from $26 per share to less than $15 per share. This led the New York Stock Exchange to halt trading on March 27. Shortly thereafter, California insurance authorities impounded Equity Funding's records and uncovered evidence of the fraud. Only then did the Securities and Exchange Commission (SEC) file a complaint against Equity Funding.

The SEC began an investigation into Dirks's role in the exposure of the fraud. After a hearing by an administrative law judge, the SEC found that Dirks had aided and abetted violations of Section 10(b) of the Securities Exchange Act of 1934 and SEC Rule 10b–5 by repeating the allegations of fraud to members of the investment community who later sold their Equity Funding stock. Has Dirks violated Section 10(b) and Rule 10b–5? Explain.

**11.** Texas Gulf Sulphur Company (TGS) was a corporation engaged in exploring for and mining certain minerals. A particular tract of Canadian land looked very promising as a source of desired minerals, and TGS drilled a test hole on November 8. Because the core sample of the hole contained minerals of amazing quality, TGS began to acquire surrounding tracts of land. Stevens, the president of TGS, instructed all on-site personnel to keep the find a secret. Because subsequent test drillings were performed, the amount of activity surrounding the drilling gave rise to rumors regarding the size and quality of the find. To counteract these rumors, Stevens authorized a press release denying the validity of the rumors and describing them as excessively optimistic. The release was issued on April 12 of the following year, though drilling continued through April 15. In the meantime, several officers, directors, and employees had purchased or accepted options to purchase additional TGS stock on the basis of the information concerning the drilling. They also recommended similar purchases to outsiders without divulging the inside information to the public. At 10:00 A.M. on April 16, an accurate report on the find was finally released to the American financial press. The Securities and Exchange Commission brought an action against TGS and several of its officers, directors, and employees to enjoin conduct alleged to violate Section 10(b) of the Securities Act of 1934 and to compel rescission by the individual defendants of securities transactions assertedly conducted in violation of Rule 10b–5. Have any of the defendants violated Section 10(b)? Explain.

**12.** W. J. Howey Company and Howey-in-the-Hills Service, Inc., were Florida corporations under direct common control and management. Howey Company owned large tracts of citrus acreage in Florida. The service company cultivated, harvested, and marketed the crops. For several years, Howey Company offered one-half of its planted acreage to the public to help it "finance additional development." Each prospective customer was offered both a land sales contract and a service contract with Howey-in-the-Hills after being told that it was not feasible to invest in the grove without a service arrangement. Upon payment of the purchase price, the land was conveyed by warranty deed. The service company was given full discretion over cultivating and marketing the crop. The purchaser had no right of entry to market the crop. The service company also was accountable only for an allocation of the net profits after the companies pooled the produce. The purchasers were predominantly nonresident businesspersons attracted by the expectation of substantial profits. Contending that this arrangement was an investment contract within the coverage of the Securities Act of 1933, the Securities and Exchange Commission (SEC) brought an action against the two companies to restrain them from using the mails and instrumentalities of interstate commerce in the offer and sale of unregistered and nonexempt securities. Should the SEC succeed?

**13.** Basic, Inc., was a publicly traded company engaged in the business of manufacturing chemical refractories for the steel industry. Beginning in September, Combustion Engineering, Inc., and Basic began discussions concerning the possibility of a merger of the two companies. Nevertheless, during the next two years, Basic made three public statements denying that it was engaged in merger negotiations. On December 18 of the second year, Basic asked the New York Stock Exchange to suspend trading in its shares and issued a statement saying that it had been "approached" by another company concerning a merger. On December 20, Basic publicly announced its approval of Combustion's offer for all its outstanding shares. Plaintiffs were former owners of Basic stock who sold their shares after Basic publicly denied that it was engaged in merger negotiations. The plaintiffs brought a class action suit against Basic and its directors, alleging that they had released false or misleading information in violation of Section 10(b) of the 1934 Act and in violation of Rule 10b–5. The plaintiffs claimed that they were injured by selling their shares at prices that were artificially depressed as a consequence of Basic's misleading public statements. The defendants claimed that the plaintiffs had not proven that they had, in fact, relied upon the misleading statements in selling their stock. Should the plaintiffs be able to recover?

# PART 10

# Property

## CHAPTER 48
Introduction to Property, Property Insurance, Bailments, and Documents of Title

## CHAPTER 49
Interests in Real Property

## CHAPTER 50
Transfer and Control of Real Property

## CHAPTER 51
Trusts and Decedents' Estates

CHAPTER 48

# Introduction to Property, Property Insurance, Bailments, and Documents of Title

In our democratic and free enterprise society, the importance of the concept of property is second only to that of the idea of liberty. Although many of our rules of property stem directly from English law, in the United States property occupies a unique status because of the protection expressly granted it by the U.S. Constitution and by most State constitutions as well. The Fifth Amendment to the Federal Constitution provides that "No person shall be … deprived of life, liberty, or property, without due process of law; nor shall private property be taken for public use, without just compensation." The Fourteenth Amendment contains a similar requirement: "No State shall … deprive any person of life, liberty, or property, without due process of law." Under the police power, however, this protection afforded to property owners is subject to regulation for the public good.

In the first part of this chapter, we will provide a general introduction to the law governing real and personal property. The second part of this chapter deals specifically with personal property; the third part covers property insurance. The fourth part of the chapter covers bailments and the last part of the chapter discusses documents of title.

## INTRODUCTION TO PROPERTY AND PERSONAL PROPERTY

**Property** is a legally protected interest or group of interests. It is valuable only because our law provides that certain consequences follow from the ownership of it. The right to use property, to sell it, and to control to whom it shall pass on the death of the owner are all included within the term *property*. Thus, a person who speaks of "owning property" may have one of two separate ideas in mind: (1) the *physical thing itself*, as when a homeowner says, "I just bought a piece of property in Oakland," meaning complete ownership of a physically identifiable parcel of land, or (2) a *right or interest* in a physical object (for example, with respect to land, a tenant under a lease has a property interest in the leased land, although he does not own the land).

### KINDS OF PROPERTY

Property may be classified as (1) tangible or intangible and (2) real or personal, but these classifications are not mutually exclusive.

◆ SEE FIGURE 48-1: **Kinds of Property**

#### TANGIBLE AND INTANGIBLE

A forty-acre farm, a chair, and a household pet are tangible property. Each of these *physical* objects embodies the group of rights or interests known as "title" to or "ownership" of **tangible property**. **Intangible property**, in contrast, does not exist in a physical form. For example, the rights represented by a stock certificate, a promissory note, and a deed granting Jones a right-of-way over Smith's land are intangible property. Each represents certain rights that defy reduction to physical possession but have a legal reality in that the courts will protect them.

The same item may be the object of both tangible and intangible property rights. Suppose Ann purchases a book published by Brown & Sons. On the first page is the statement "Copyright 2011 by Brown & Sons." Ann owns the volume she has purchased. She has the right to exclusive physical possession and use of that particular copy. It is a tangible piece of property of which she is the owner. Brown & Sons, however, has the exclusive right to publish copies of the book, a right granted the publisher by the copyright laws. The courts will protect this intangible property of Brown & Sons, as well as Ann's right to her particular volume.

#### REAL AND PERSONAL

The most significant practical distinction between types of property is the classification into real and personal property. To define this distinction simply, land and all interests in it

◆ FIGURE 48-1: **Kinds of Property**

| | Personal | Real |
|---|---|---|
| **Tangible** | Goods | Land<br>Buildings<br>Fixtures |
| **Intangible** | Negotiable instruments<br>Stock certificates<br>Contract rights<br>Copyrights<br>Patents | Leases<br>Easements<br>Mortgages |

are **real property** (also called **realty**), and every other thing or interest identified as property is **personal property** (also called **chattel**). This easy description encompasses most property, with the exception of certain physical objects that are personal property under most circumstances but that may, because of their attachment to land or their use in connection with land, become a form of real property called fixtures.

## FIXTURES

As we noted above, a **fixture** is an article or piece of property that was formerly treated as personal property but has been attached in such a manner to land or a building that it is now designated as real property even though it retains its original identity. The intent of the parties to convert the property to real property from personal property is usually shown by the permanent manner of affixation or the adaptation of the affixed object to the property. For example, building materials are clearly personal property; however, when worked into a building as its construction progresses, such materials become real property, as buildings are a part of the land they occupy. Thus, clay in its natural state is, of course, real property; when made into bricks, it becomes personal property; and if the bricks are then built into the wall of a house, the "clay" once again becomes real property.

Although doing so may be difficult, determining whether various items are personal property or real property may be the only way to settle certain conflicting ownership claims. Unless otherwise provided by agreement, personal property remains the property of the person who placed it on the real estate. On the other hand, property that has been affixed so as to become a fixture (an actual part of the real estate) becomes the property of the real estate owner.

In determining whether personal property has become a fixture, the intention of the parties, as expressed in their agreement, will control the settlement of conflicting claims. In the absence of an agreement, the following factors are relevant in determining whether any particular item is a fixture:

1. the physical relationship of the item to the land or building;
2. the intention of the person who attached the item to the land or building;
3. the purpose the item serves in relation to the land or building and in relation to the person who brought it there; and
4. the interest of that person in the land or building at the time of the item's attachment.

Although physical attachment is significant, a more important test is whether the item can be removed without causing material injury to the land or building on the land. If it *cannot* be so removed, the item is generally held to have become part of the realty.

By comparison, the test of purpose or use applies only if the item (1) is affixed to the realty in some way but (2) can be removed without material injury to the realty. In such a situation, if the use or purpose of the item is peculiar to a particular owner or occupant of the premises, the courts will tend to let him remove the item when he leaves. Accordingly, in the law of landlord and tenant, the tenant may remove trade fixtures (that is, items used in connection with a trade but not intended to become part of the realty), provided that she can accomplish this without material injury to the realty. On the other hand, doors may be removed without injury to the structure; yet, because they are necessary to the ordinary use of the building and are not peculiar to the use of the occupant, they are considered to be fixtures and thus part of the real property.

◆ SEE CASE 48-1

## TRANSFER OF TITLE TO PERSONAL PROPERTY

The transfer of title to real property typically is a formal affair. In contrast, title to personal property may be acquired and transferred with relative ease and little formality. Such facility with regard to the transfer of personal property is essential within a society whose trade and industry are based principally on transactions in personal property. In a free economy, stocks, bonds, merchandise, and intellectual property must be sold with minimal delay. It is only natural that the law will reflect these needs.

Accordingly, the law concerning personal property has been largely codified. The Uniform Commercial Code (UCC or the Code) includes the law of sales of goods (Article 2), as well as the law governing the transfer and negotiation of negotiable instruments (Article 3) and of investment securities (Article 8). Nonetheless, the Code does not cover a number of issues (addressed in this chapter) involving the ownership and transfer of title to personal property. In addition, personal property may be, and often is, acquired by producing the item, rather than by selling or transferring it.

### BY SALE

By definition, a **sale** of *tangible* personal property (goods) is transfer of title to specified existing goods for a consideration known as the price. Title passes when the parties intend it to pass, and transfer of possession is not required for a transfer of title. For a discussion of transfer of title, see *Chapter 21*.

Sales of *intangible* personal property also involve the transfer of title. Many of these sales also are governed by UCC provisions, while some, such as sales of copyrights and patents, are governed by specialized Federal legislation.

### BY GIFT

A **gift** is a transfer of title to property from one person to another without consideration. This lack of consideration is the basic distinction between a gift and a sale. Because a gift involves no consideration or compensation, it must be completed by delivery of the gift to be effective. A gratuitous promise to make a gift is not binding. In addition, there must be intent on the part of the maker (the **donor**) of the gift to make a present transfer, and there must be acceptance by the recipient (the **donee**) of the gift.

**Delivery** Delivery is essential to a valid gift. The term *delivery* has a very special meaning that includes, but is not limited to, the manual transfer of the item to the donee. A donor may effect an irrevocable delivery by, for example, turning an item over to a third person with instructions to give it to the donee. Frequently, an item, because of its size, location, or intangibility, is incapable of immediate manual delivery. In such cases, an irrevocable gift may be effected through the delivery of something that symbolizes dominion over the item. This is referred to as **constructive delivery**. For example, if Joanne declares that she gives an antique desk and all its contents to Barry and hands Barry the key to the desk, in many states a valid gift has been made.

**Intent** The law also provides clearly that the donor must intend to make a gift of the property. Thus, if Jack leaves a packet of stocks and bonds with Joan, her acquiring good title to them depends on whether Jack intended to make a gift of them or simply intended to place them in Joan's hands for safekeeping. A voluntary, uncompensated delivery made with the intent to give the recipient title constitutes a gift when the donee accepts the delivery. If these conditions are met, the donor has no further claim to the property.

Gifts, therefore, cannot be conditional. There is, however, one major exception to this rule: an engagement gift given in anticipation of marriage. If the marriage does not take place, the donor usually can recover the gift unless the donor broke the engagement without justification. But the courts will not apply the exception when a marriage is called off due to the death of one of the engaged parties.

**Acceptance** The final requirement of a valid gift is acceptance by the donee. In most instances, of course, the donee will accept the gift gratefully. Accordingly, the law usually presumes that the donee has accepted. But certain circumstances may render acceptance objectionable, such as when a gift would impose a burden upon the donee. In such cases, the law will not require the recipient to accept an unwanted gift. For example, a donee may prudently reject a gift of an elephant or a wrecked car in need of extensive repairs.

◆ **SEE CASE 48-2**

**Classification** Gifts may be either *inter vivos* or *causa mortis*. An *inter vivos* gift is a gift made by a donor during her lifetime. A gift *causa mortis* is a gift made by a donor in contemplation of her imminent death. A gift *causa mortis* is a conditional gift, contingent upon (1) the donor's death as she anticipated, (2) the donor's not revoking the gift prior to her death, and (3) the donee's surviving the donor.

### BY WILL OR DESCENT

Title to personal property frequently is acquired by inheritance from a person who dies, either with or without a will. We will discuss this method of acquiring title in *Chapter 51*.

### BY ACCESSION

Many of the practical problems surrounding the right to title to personal property stem from its principal characteristic—movability. The phrase "title by accession" denotes one general solution to the movability problem. **Accession**, in its strict sense, means the right of the owner of property to any increase in it, whether natural or human-made. For example, the owner of a cow acquires title by accession to any calves born to that cow.

### BY CONFUSION

The basic problem of confusion is somewhat similar to problems involving title by accession. **Confusion** arises when identical goods belonging to different people become so *commingled* (mixed) that the owners cannot identify their own property. For example, Hereford cattle belonging to Benton become mixed with Hereford cattle belonging to Armstrong, and neither can specifically identify his herd as a result; or grain owned by Courts is combined inseparably with similar grain owned by Reichel. Confusion may result from accident, mistake, willful act, or agreement of the parties. If the goods can be apportioned, each owner who can prove his proportion of the whole is entitled to receive his share. If, however, the confusion results from the willful and wrongful act of one of the parties, he will lose his entire interest if unable to prove his share. Frequently, problems arise not because the owners cannot prove their original interests but because there is not enough left to distribute a full share to each. In such cases, if the confusion was due to mistake, accident, or agreement, each owner will bear the loss in proportion to his share. If the confusion resulted from an intentional and unauthorized act, the wrongdoer will first bear any loss.

### BY POSSESSION

Sometimes a person may acquire title to movable personal property by taking possession of it. If the property has been intentionally **abandoned** (intentionally disposed of), a finder is entitled to the property. Moreover, under the general rule, a *finder* is entitled to **lost** (unintentionally left) **property** against everyone except the true *owner*. Suppose Zenner, the owner of an apartment complex, leases a kitchenette apartment to Terrell. One night, Waters, Terrell's mother-in-law, is invited to sleep in the convertible bed in the living room. In the course of preparing the bed, Waters finds an emerald ring caught on the springs under the mattress. She turns the ring over to the police, but diligent inquiry fails to ascertain the true owner. As the finder, Waters will be entitled to the ring.

A different rule applies when the lost property is in the ground. Here, the owner of the land has a claim superior to that of the finder. For example, Josephs employs Kasarda to excavate a lateral sewer. Kasarda uncovers ancient Native American artifacts. Josephs, not Kasarda, has the superior claim.

A further exception to the rule gives the finder first claim against all but the true owner. If property is intentionally placed somewhere by the owner, who then unintentionally leaves it, it becomes **mislaid property**. Most courts hold that if property has been mislaid, not lost, then the owner of the premises, not the finder, has first claim if the true owner is not discovered. This doctrine is frequently invoked in cases involving items found in restaurants or on trains, buses, or airplanes.

Another category of property is the **treasure trove**, which consists of coins or currency concealed by the owner. To be classified as treasure trove, the property must have been hidden or concealed for such a length of time that the owner is probably dead or undiscoverable. Treasure trove belongs to the finder as against all but the true owner.

Many States now have statutes that provide a means of vesting title to lost property in the finder where a prescribed search for the owner proves fruitless.

## PROPERTY INSURANCE

Insurance covers a vast range of contracts, each of which distributes risk among a large number of members (the insureds) through an insurance company (the insurer). **Insurance** is a contractual undertaking by the insurer to pay a sum of money or give something of value to the insured or a beneficiary upon the happening of a contingency or fortuitous event that is beyond the control of the contracting parties.

Insurance coverage of one form or another affects every commercial activity. Through insurance, a business can safeguard its tangible assets against almost any form of damage or destruction, whether resulting from natural causes or from the accidental or improper actions of people. Insurance may also protect a business from tort liability, including assertions involving strict liability, negligence, or the intentional acts of its representatives. A business may procure credit insurance to guard against losses from poor credit risks and fidelity bonds to secure it against losses incurred through employee defalcations. If a business hires a famous pianist, it may insure the latter's hands; if it decides to present an outdoor concert, it may insure against the possibility of rain. A business may purchase life insurance on its key executives to reimburse it for financial losses arising from their deaths, or it may purchase such life insurance payable to the families of executives as part of their compensation. An additional, increasingly important use of insurance is to carry out pension commitments arising from agreements with employees. Nonetheless, the remaining sections of this chapter will focus on the insurance of property.

The McCarran-Ferguson Act, enacted by Congress in 1945, left insurance regulation to the States. Statutes in each State regulate domestic insurance companies and establish standards for foreign (out-of-state) insurance companies wishing to do business within the State. Most State legislation relates to the incorporation, licensing, supervision, and liquidation of insurers and to the licensing and supervision of agents and brokers.

Because the insurance relationship arises from a contract of insurance between the insurer and the insured, the law of insurance is a branch of contract law. For this reason, the doctrines of offer and acceptance, consideration, and other rules applicable to contracts in general are equally applicable to insurance contracts. Beyond that, however, insurance law, like the law of sales, bailments, negotiable instruments, or other specialized types of contracts, contains numerous modifications of fundamental contract law, which we will examine in the following sections.

## FIRE AND PROPERTY INSURANCE

**Fire and property insurance** protects the owner (or another person with an insurable interest, such as a secured creditor or mortgagee) of real or personal property against loss resulting from damage to or destruction of the property by fire and certain related perils. Most fire insurance policies also cover damage caused by lightning, explosion, earthquake, water, wind, rain, collision, and riot.

Fire insurance policies are standardized in the United States, either by statute or by order of the State insurance departments, but their coverage is frequently enlarged through an "endorsement" or "rider" to include other perils or to benefit the insured in ways the provisions in the standard form do not. These policies normally are written for periods of one or three years.

### TYPES OF FIRE

Fire insurance policies usually are held to cover damage from "hostile" fires, but they do not cover losses caused by "friendly" fires. A **friendly fire** is one contained in its intended location (for instance, a fire in a fireplace, furnace, or stove). A **hostile fire** is any other fire—all fires outside their intended or usual locales. Thus, a friendly fire becomes hostile if it escapes from its usual confines.

A standard insurance policy therefore will not cover heat or soot damage to a fireplace resulting from its continual use or damage done to personal property accidentally thrown into a stove. Damages caused by smoke, soot, water, and heat from a hostile fire are covered by the standard fire insurance policy, whereas such damages caused by a friendly fire generally are not. Moreover, most policies do not cover recovery for business interruption, unless they contain endorsements specifically covering such loss.

### CO-INSURANCE CLAUSES

An arrangement common in property insurance, **co-insurance** is a means of sharing the risk between insurer and insured. For example, under the typical 80 percent co-insurance clause, the insured may recover the full amount of loss, not to exceed the face amount of the policy, provided the policy is for an amount not less than 80 percent of the property's insurable value. If the policy is for less than 80 percent, the insured recovers that proportion of the loss that the amount of the policy bears, up to 80 percent of the insurable value. The formula for recovery is as follows:

$$\text{Recovery} = \frac{\text{Face Value of Policy}}{\text{Fair Market Value of Property} \times \text{Co-insurance \%}} \times \text{Loss}$$

Thus, if the co-insurance percentage is 80 percent, the value of the property is $100,000, and the policy is for $80,000 or more, the insured is fully protected against loss not to exceed the policy amount. If the policy amount is less than 80 percent of the property value, however, the insured receives only the proportion of the loss amount as determined in the formula above. Thus, in the above example, if the fire policy was for $60,000 and the property was 50 percent destroyed, the loss would be $50,000, of which the insurer would pay $37,500, which is $60,000/($100,000 × 80%) of $50,000. On a total loss, the recovery could not, of course, exceed the face amount of the policy. Some States do not favor co-insurance clauses and strictly construe the applicable statute against their validity. In addition, property insurance is not held to be co-insurance unless the policy specifically so provides.

### OTHER INSURANCE CLAUSES

Recovery under property insurance policies typically is also limited by **other insurance clauses**, which generally require that liability be distributed *pro rata* among the various insurers. For example, Alexander insures his $120,000 building with Hamilton Insurance Co. for $60,000 and Jefferson Insurance Co. for $90,000. Alexander's building is partially destroyed by fire, causing Alexander $20,000 in damages. Alexander will collect two-fifths ($60,000/$150,000) of his damages from Hamilton ($8,000) and three-fifths ($90,000/$150,000) from Jefferson ($12,000).

### TYPES OF POLICIES

Property insurance may be either a valued policy or an open policy. A **valued policy** is one providing for the full value of the property, upon which value the insured and the insurer specifically agree at the time the policy is issued. Should total loss occur, the insurer must pay this amount, not the actual or fair market value of the property. By comparison, no agreement in an **open policy** specifies the property's value; instead, the insurer pays the fair market value of the property calculated immediately prior to its loss. Thus, if Latrisha insures her building for $650,000 and at the time of its loss the property is valued at $600,000, under an open policy Latrisha would recover $600,000, while under a valued policy she would recover $650,000. If she insured the building for $700,000, and it was valued at that amount just prior to being blown apart by a tornado, under both types of policies Latrisha would recover $700,000. Insurance of property under a marine policy (insurance covering marine vessels and cargo) is generally considered to be valued, whereas nonmarine property insurance is presumed to be unvalued or open.

## NATURE OF INSURANCE CONTRACTS

The basic principles of **contract** law apply to insurance policies. Furthermore, because insurance companies engage in a large volume of business over wide areas, they tend to standardize their policies. In some States, standardization is required by statute. This usually means that the insured must accept a given policy or do without the desired insurance.

### OFFER AND ACCEPTANCE

No matter how many stories tell of insurance agents aggressively soliciting would-be insureds to take out policies, the applicant usually makes the offer, and the contract is created when the insurance company accepts that offer. The company may condition its acceptance—upon payment of the premium, for instance. It also may write a policy that differs from the application, thereby making a counteroffer that the applicant may or may not choose to accept.

In fire and casualty insurance, agents often have authority to make the insurance effective immediately, when needed, by means of a **binder**. Should a loss occur before the company actually issues a policy, the binder will be effective on the same terms and conditions the policy would have had if it had been issued.

In general, insurance contracts have not been held to be subject to the statute of frauds; thus, courts have held oral contracts for insurance to be enforceable. As a practical matter, however, oral contracts for insurance are very infrequent.

### INSURABLE INTEREST

The concept of insurable interest has been developed over many years, primarily to eliminate gambling and to lessen the moral hazard. If a person could obtain an enforceable fire insurance policy on property that he did not own or in which he had no interest, he would be in a position to profit unfairly by the destruction of such property. An **insurable interest** is a relationship a person has with respect to certain property such that the happening of a possible, specific, damage-causing contingency would result in direct loss or injury to her. The purpose of insurance is protection against the risk of loss that would result from such a happening, not the realization of gain or profit.

Whether sole or concurrent, ownership obviously creates an insurable interest in property. Moreover, a right deriving from a contract concerning the property also gives rise to an insurable interest. For instance, shareholders in a closely held corporation have been held to have an insurable interest in the corporation's property to the extent of their interest. Likewise, lessees of property have insurable interests, as do holders of security interests, such as mortgagees or sellers with a purchase money security interest. Most courts have gone beyond the requirement of a legally recognized interest and apply a factual expectancy test. Under this test, the determinative question is whether the insured will obtain a benefit from the continued existence of the property or suffer a loss from its destruction. Thus, an individual who buys and insures a stolen automobile without knowledge that the automobile is stolen has an insurable interest in the automobile.

The insurable interest must exist at the time the property *loss* occurs, although some courts speak in terms of having the insurable interest at the time of insuring *and* at the time of loss. Property insurance policies are freely assignable after, but not before, a loss occurs.

### PREMIUMS

**Premiums** are the consideration paid for an insurance policy. Property insurance policies are written only for periods lasting a few years at most. Long, continued liability on this type of policy is the exception rather than the rule. State law regulates the rates that may be charged for fire and various kinds of casualty insurance. The regulatory authorities are under a duty to require that the companies' rates be reasonable, not unfairly discriminatory, and neither excessively high nor inordinately low.

### DEFENSES OF THE INSURER

An insurer may assert the ordinary defenses available to any contract. In addition, the terms of the insurance contract may provide specific defenses, such as the subject matter of the policy, types of perils covered, amount of coverage, and period of coverage. Moreover, the insurer may assert the closely related defenses of misrepresentation, breach of warranty, and concealment.

**MISREPRESENTATION** A representation is a statement made by or on behalf of an applicant for insurance to induce an insurer to enter into a contract. The representation is not a part of the insurance contract, but if the application containing the representation is incorporated by reference into the contract, the representation becomes a warranty. For a **misrepresentation** to have legal consequences, it must be material, the insurer must have relied on it as an inducement to enter into the contract, and it must either have been substantially false when the insured made it or have become so, to the insured's knowledge, before the contract was created. The principal remedy of the insurer on discovery of the material misrepresentation is rescission of the contract. To rescind the contract, the insurer must tender to the insured all premiums that have been paid, unless the misrepresentation was fraudulent. To be effective, rescission must be made as soon as possible after discovery of the misrepresentation.

**Breach of Warranty** Warranties are of great importance in insurance contracts because they operate as conditions that must exist before the contract is effective or before the insurer's promise to pay is enforceable. If such is the case, the insurer does not merely have a defense against payment of the policy but can void the policy.

Failure of the condition to exist or to occur relieves the insurer from any obligation to perform its promise. Broadly speaking, a condition is simply an event whose happening or failure to happen either precedes the existence of a legal relationship or terminates one previously existing. Conditions are either precedent or subsequent. For example, payment of the premium is a condition precedent to the enforcement of the insurer's promise, as is the happening of the insured event. A condition subsequent is an operative event the happening of which terminates an existing, matured legal obligation. A provision in a policy to the effect that the insured shall not be liable unless suit is brought within twelve months from the date on which the loss occurs is an example of a condition subsequent.

To be a warranty, the provision must be expressly included in the insurance contract or clearly incorporated by reference. Usually, the policy statements that the insurer considers to be express warranties are characterized by words such as *warrant, on condition that, provided that*, or words of similar import. Other statements important to the risk assumed, such as the address of a building in a case in which personal property at a particular location is insured against fire, are sometimes held to be informal warranties.

Generally, it is becoming more difficult for an insurer to avoid liability on a policy when an insured breaches a warranty. For example, a number of States now require a breach to be material before the insurer may avoid liability.

**Concealment** **Concealment** is the failure of an applicant for insurance to disclose material facts that the insurer does not know. The nondisclosure normally must be fraudulent as well as material to invalidate the policy; the applicant must have had reason to believe the fact was material; and its disclosure must have affected the insurer's acceptance of the risk.

### WAIVER AND ESTOPPEL

In certain instances, an insurer who normally would be entitled to deny liability under a policy because of a misrepresentation, breach of condition, or concealment is "estopped" from taking advantage of the defense or else is said to have "waived" the right to rely on it because of other facts.

The terms *waiver* and *estoppel* are used interchangeably, although by definition they are not synonymous. As generally defined, **waiver** is the intentional relinquishment of a known right; and **estoppel** means that a person is prevented by his own conduct from asserting a position inconsistent with such conduct, on which another person has justifiably relied.

Because a corporation such as an insurance company can act only through agents, situations involving waiver invariably are based on an agent's conduct. The higher the agent's position in the company's organization, the more likely his conduct is to bind the company, as an agent acting within the scope of his authority binds his principal. Insureds have the right to rely on representations made by the insurer's employees, and when such representations reasonably induce or cause the insured to change her position or prevent her from causing a condition to occur, the insurer may not assert as a defense the condition's failure to occur, whether the term applied to her situation be waiver or estoppel. Companies have tried with little success to limit the authority of local selling agents to bind the company through waiver or estoppel.

### TERMINATION

Most insurance contracts are performed according to their terms, and due **performance** terminates the insurer's obligation. Normally, the insurer pays the principal sum due and the contract is thereby performed and discharged.

**Cancellation** by mutual consent is another way of terminating an insurance contract. Cancellation by the insurer alone means that the insurer remains liable, according to the terms of the policy, until such time as the cancellation is effective. To cancel a policy, the insurer must tender the unearned portion of the premium to the insured.

# BAILMENTS AND DOCUMENTS OF TITLE

## BAILMENTS

A **bailment** is the relationship created when one person (the bailor) transfers the possession of personal property by delivery, without transfer of title, to another (the **bailee**) for the accomplishment of a certain purpose, after which the bailee is to return the property to the bailor or dispose of it according to the bailor's directions. One of the most common occurrences in everyday life, bailments are of great commercial importance. Bailments include the transportation, storage, repair, and rental of goods, which together involve billions of dollars in transactions each year. The following are common examples of bailments: keeping a car in a public garage; leaving a car, a watch, or any other article to be repaired; renting a car or truck; checking a hat or coat at a theater or restaurant; leaving clothes to be laundered; delivering jewelry, stocks, bonds, or other valuables to secure the payment of a debt; storing goods in a warehouse; and shipping goods by public or private transportation. The benefit of a bailment may, by its terms, accrue solely to the bailor, solely to the bailee, or to both parties. A bailment may be with or without compensation. On these bases, bailments are classified as follows:

1. ***Bailments for the bailor's sole benefit*** include the gratuitous custody of personal property and the gratuitous services that involve custody of personal property, such as repairs or transportation. For example, if Sherry stores, repairs, or transports Tim's goods without compensation, this is a bailment for the sole benefit of the bailor, Tim.
2. ***Bailments for the bailee's sole benefit*** are usually limited to the gratuitous loan of personal property for use by the bailee, as where Tim, without compensation, lends his car, lawn mower, or book to Sherry for her use.
3. ***Bailments for the mutual benefit*** of both parties include ordinary commercial bailments, such as the delivery of goods to a person for repair, jewels to a pawnbroker, or an automobile to a parking lot attendant.

◆ SEE CASE 48-3

## ESSENTIAL ELEMENTS OF A BAILMENT

The basic elements of a bailment are (1) the delivery of possession from a bailor to a bailee; (2) the delivery of personal property, not real property; (3) possession without ownership by the bailee for a determinable period; and (4) an absolute duty on the bailee to return the property to the bailor or to dispose of it according to the bailor's directions.

In most cases, two simple elements determine the existence of a bailment: (1) a separation of ownership and possession of the property (possession without ownership) and (2) a duty on the party in possession to redeliver the identical property to the owner or to dispose of it according to the owner's directions. Since a bailment need not be a contract, consideration is not required. A bailment may be created by operation of law from the facts of a particular situation; thus, a bailment may be **implied** or **constructive**.

**Delivery of Possession** Possession by a bailee involves (1) the bailee's power to control the personal property and (2) either the bailee's intention to control the property or her awareness that the rightful possessor has given up physical control of it. Thus, for example, when a restaurant customer hangs his hat or coat on a hook furnished for that purpose, the hat or coat is within an area under the restaurant owner's physical control. But the restaurant owner is not a bailee of the hat or coat unless he clearly signifies an intention to exercise control over the hat or coat. On the other hand, when a clerk in a store helps a customer to remove his coat to try on a new one, the owner of the store usually is held to have become a bailee of the old coat through the clerk, her employee. Here, the clerk has signified an intention to control the coat by taking it from the customer, and a bailment results.

**Personal Property** The bailment relationship can exist only with respect to personal property. The delivery of possession of real property by the owner to another is covered by real property law. Bailed property need not be tangible. Intangible property, such as the rights represented by promissory notes, corporate bonds, shares of stock, documents of title, and life insurance policies that are evidenced by written instruments and are thus capable of delivery, may be and frequently are the subject matter of bailments.

**Possession for a Determinable Time** To establish a bailment relationship, the person receiving possession must be under a duty to return the personal property and must not obtain title to it. If the identical property transferred is to be returned, even in an altered form, the transaction is a bailment; however, if other property of equal value or the money value of the original property may be returned, a transfer of title has occurred, and the transaction is a sale.

**Restoration of Possession to the Bailor** The bailee is legally obligated to restore the property to the bailor's possession when the bailment period ends. Normally, the bailee is required to return the identical goods bailed, although their condition may be changed because of the work that the bailee was required to perform on them. An exception to this rule concerns **fungible goods**, such as grain, which, for all practical purposes, consist of particles that are the equivalent of every other particle and are expected to be mingled with other like goods during a bailment. Given such goods, a bailee obviously cannot be required to return the identical goods bailed. His obligation is simply to return goods of the same quality and quantity.

A bailee has a duty to return the property to the right person. Her mistake in delivering property to the wrong person does not excuse her, even when the bailor's negligence induces the mistake. A bailee who, through mistake or intention, misdelivers the property to a third person who has no right to its possession is guilty of conversion and is liable to the bailor.

## RIGHTS AND DUTIES OF BAILOR AND BAILEE

The bailment relationship creates rights and duties on the part of the bailor and the bailee. The bailee is under a duty to exercise due care for the safety of the property and to return it to the right person; conversely, the bailee has the exclusive right to possess the property for the term of the bailment. In addition, depending on the nature of the transaction, a bailee may have the right to limit his liability, as well as to receive compensation and reimbursement of expenses. The bailor, in turn, has certain duties with respect to the condition of the bailed goods.

**Bailee's Duty to Exercise Due Care** The bailee must exercise due care not to permit injury to or destruction of the property by the bailee or by third parties. The degree of care depends on the nature of the bailment relationship and the character of the property. In the context of a **commercial bailment**, from which the parties derive a mutual benefit, the law requires the bailee to exercise the care that a reasonably prudent person would exercise under the same circumstances. When the bailment benefits the bailee alone (Tim's borrowing Michael's truck without payment would be an example), the law requires more-than-reasonable care of the bailee. On the other hand, where the bailee accepts the property for the bailor's sole benefit, the law requires a lesser degree of care. Nevertheless, the amount of care required to satisfy any of the standards will vary with the character of the property.

When the property is lost, damaged, or destroyed while in the bailee's possession, it is often impossible for the bailor to obtain enough information to show that the loss or damage was due to the bailee's failure to exercise required care. The law aids the bailor in this respect by *presuming* that the bailee was at fault. The bailor is merely required to show that certain property was delivered by way of bailment and that the bailee either has failed to return it or has returned it in a damaged condition. The burden is then on the bailee to prove that he exercised the degree of care required.

◆ SEE FIGURE 48-2: Duties in a Bailment

◆ SEE CASE 48-3

**Bailee's Absolute Liability to Return Property** As discussed, the bailee is free from liability if she exercised the degree of care required of her under the particular bailment while the property was within her control. This general rule has certain important exceptions that impose an absolute duty on the bailee to return the property undamaged to the proper person.

When the bailee has an obligation by express agreement with the bailor or by custom to insure the property against certain risks but fails to do so, and the property is destroyed or damaged through such risks, she is liable for the damage or nondelivery, even if she has exercised due care.

When the bailee uses the bailed property in a manner not authorized by the bailor or by the character of the bailment, and during the course of such use the property is damaged or destroyed, without fault on the bailee's part, the bailee is nonetheless absolutely (strictly) liable for the damage or destruction. The wrongful use by the bailee automatically terminates her lawful possession: she becomes a trespasser as to the property and, as such, is absolutely liable for whatever harm befalls it.

**Bailee's Right to Limit Liability** Certain bailees—namely, common carriers, public warehousers, and innkeepers—may limit their liability for breach of their duties to the bailor only as provided by statute. Other bailees, however, may vary their duties and liabilities by contract with the bailor. When liability may be limited by contract, the law requires that any such limitation be properly brought to the bailor's attention before he bails the property. This is especially true in the case of "professional bailees," such as repair garages, who make it their business to act as bailees and who deal with the public on a uniform, rather than on an individual, basis. Thus, a variation or limitation in writing, contained, for example, in a claim check or stub given to the bailor or posted on the walls of the bailee's place of business, ordinarily will *not* bind the bailor unless (1) the bailee draws the bailor's attention to the writing, (2) the bailee informs the bailor that it contains a limitation or variation of liability, and (3) the limitation is not the result of unequal bargaining power. Some States do not permit professional bailees (who

◆ FIGURE 48-2: **Duties in a Bailment**

| Type of Bailment | Bailor's Duty | Bailee's Duty of Care |
|---|---|---|
| **For sole benefit of bailor** | Slight care | To warn of defects of which she knew or should have known |
| **For sole benefit of bailee** | Utmost care | To warn of known defects |
| **For mutual benefit** | Ordinary care | To warn of defects of which she knew or should have known |

commonly include warehousers, garagers, and parking lot owners) to disclaim liability for their own negligence.

**Bailee's Right to Compensation** A bailee who by express or implied agreement undertakes to perform work on or render services in connection with the bailed goods is entitled to reasonable compensation for those services or that work. In most cases, the agreement between bailor and bailee fixes the amount of compensation and provides how it shall be paid. In the absence of a contrary agreement, the compensation is payable when the bailee completes the work or performs the services. If, after such completion or performance but before the redelivery of the goods to the bailor, the goods are lost or damaged through no fault of the bailee, the bailee is still entitled to compensation for his work and services.

Most bailees who are entitled to compensation for work and services performed in connection with bailed goods acquire a possessory lien on the goods to secure the payment of such compensation. In most jurisdictions, the bailee has a statutory right to obtain a judicial foreclosure of his lien and a sale of the goods. Many statutes also provide that the bailee does not lose his lien on redelivery of the goods to the bailor, as was the case at common law. Instead, the lien will continue for a specified period after redelivery, if the bailee timely records with the proper authorities an instrument claiming such a lien.

**Bailor's Duties** In a bailment for the sole benefit of the bailee, the bailor warrants that she is unaware of any defects in the bailed property. In all other instances, the bailor has a duty to warn the bailee of all defects she knows of or should have discovered upon a reasonable inspection of the bailed property. A number of courts have extended strict liability in tort and the implied warranties under Article 2 of the UCC to leases and bailments. Article 2A imposes implied warranties on the lease of goods.

## SPECIAL TYPES OF BAILMENTS

Although the general principles that apply to all bailees govern pledgees, warehousers, and safe deposit companies, certain special features about the transactions in which they respectively engage subject them to extraordinary duties of care and liability. Innkeepers and common carriers may also be said to be *extraordinary* bailees, whereas all other bailees are *ordinary* bailees. This distinction is based on the character and extent of the liability of these two classes of bailees for the loss of or injury to bailed goods. As we have seen, an **ordinary bailee** is liable only for the loss or injury that results from his failure to exercise ordinary or reasonable care. The liability of the **extraordinary bailee**, on the other hand, is, in general, *absolute*. Just as an insurer, in general, becomes automatically liable to the insured on the happening of the hazard insured against, regardless of the cause, the extraordinary bailee becomes liable to the bailor for any loss or injury to the goods, regardless of the cause and without regard to the question of his care or negligence. Thus, he insures the safety of the goods.

**Pledges** A **pledge** is a bailment for security in which the owner gives possession of her personal property to another (the secured party) to secure a debt or the performance of some obligation. The secured party does not have title to the property involved but merely a possessory security interest. Pledges of most types of personal property for security purposes are governed by Article 9 of the UCC, which we discussed in *Chapter 38*. In most respects, the secured party's duties and liabilities are the same as those of a bailee for compensation.

**Warehousing** A **warehouser** is a bailee who, for compensation, receives goods to be stored in a warehouse. Under the common law, his duties and liabilities were identical to those of the ordinary bailee for compensation. Today, because a strong public interest affects their activities, warehousers are subject to extensive State and Federal regulation. Warehousers also must be distinguished from ordinary bailees in that the receipts they issue for storage have acquired a special status in commerce. Regarded as documents of title, these receipts are governed by Article 7 of the UCC. (We will discuss documents of title later in this chapter.)

**Safe Deposit Boxes** A majority of States hold that a person who rents a safe deposit box from a bank enters into a bailment relationship. As this constitutes a bailment for the parties' mutual benefit, the bailee bank owes the customer the duty to act with ordinary due care and is liable only if negligent.

**Carriers of Goods** In the broadest sense, anyone who transports goods from one place to another, either gratuitously or for compensation, is a **carrier**. Carriers are classified primarily as common carriers and private carriers. A **common carrier** offers its services and facilities to the public on terms and under circumstances indicating that the offering is made to all persons. Stated somewhat differently, the criteria that define common carriers are as follows: (1) the carriage must be part of its business; (2) the carriage must be for remuneration; and (3) the carrier must represent to the general public that it is willing to serve the public in the transportation of property. Common carriers of goods include railroad, steamship, aircraft, public trucking, and pipeline companies. In contrast, a **private** or **contract carrier** is one who carries the goods of another on isolated occasions or who serves a limited number of customers under individual contracts without offering the same or similar contracts to the public at large.

The person who delivers goods to a carrier for shipment is known as the **consignor** or shipper. The person to whom the carrier is to deliver the goods is known as the **consignee**. The instrument containing the terms of the contract of transportation, which the carrier issues to the shipper, is called a **bill of lading** (discussed later in this chapter).

A common carrier is under a duty to serve the public to the limits of its capacity and, within those limits, to accept for carriage goods of the kind that it normally transports. A private carrier, by comparison, has no duty to accept goods for carriage, except where it agrees by contract to do so. Whether common or private, the carrier is under an absolute duty to deliver the goods to the person to whom the shipper has consigned them.

A private carrier, in the absence of special contract terms, is liable as a bailee for the goods it undertakes to carry. The liability of a common carrier, on the other hand, approaches that of an insurer of the safety of the goods, except when loss or damage is caused by an act of God, an act of a public enemy, the acts or fault of the shipper, the inherent nature of or a defect in the goods, or an act of public authority. The carrier, however, is permitted, through its contract with the shipper, to limit its liability, provided the carrier gives the shipper notice of this limitation and the opportunity to declare a higher value for the goods.

**Innkeepers** At common law, **innkeepers** (better known as hotel and motel owners or operators) are held to the same **strict** or **absolute liability** for their guests' belongings as are common carriers for the goods they carry. This rule of strict liability applies only to those who furnish lodging to the public for compensation as a regular business and extends only to the belongings of lodgers who are guests. In almost all jurisdictions, case law and statute have substantially modified the innkeeper's strict liability under common law.

## DOCUMENTS OF TITLE

A **document of title**, which includes warehouse receipts and bills of lading, is a record evidencing a right to receive, control, hold, and dispose of the record *and* the goods it covers. Documents of title thus represent title to goods. To be a document of title, a document must be issued by or addressed to a bailee and must cover goods in the bailee's possession that are either identified or are fungible portions of an identified mass.

Briefly, a document of title symbolizes ownership of the goods it describes. Because of the document's legal characteristics, its ownership is equivalent to the ownership or control of the goods it represents, without the necessity of actual or physical possession of the goods. Likewise, it transfers the ownership or control of the goods without necessitating the physical transfer of the goods themselves. For these reasons, documents of title are a convenient means of handling the billions of dollars' worth of goods that are transported by carriers or are stored with warehousers. Documents of title also facilitate the transfer of title to goods and the creation of a security interest in goods. Article 7 of the UCC governs documents of title. In 2003 a revision of UCC Article 7 was promulgated to update the original Article 7 and provide a framework for the further development of electronic documents of title. At least thirty-nine States have adopted Revised Article 7. This chapter will cover both original Article 7 and Revised Article 7.

### TYPES OF DOCUMENTS OF TITLE

To facilitate electronic documents of title, several definitions in Article 1 have been revised, including "bearer," "bill of lading," "delivery," "document of title," "holder," and "warehouse receipt." The term "electronic document of title" means "a document of title evidenced by a record consisting of information stored in an electronic medium." Revised Section 1–201(b)(16). The term "tangible document of title" means "a document of title evidenced by a record consisting of information that is inscribed in a tangible medium." Revised Section 1–201(b)(16). "Record" means "information that is inscribed on a tangible medium or that is stored in an electronic or other medium and is retrievable in perceivable form." Revised Article 7–102(10). The concept of an electronic document of title allows for commercial practice to determine whether records issued by bailees are "in the regular course of business or financing" and are "treated as adequately evidencing that the person in possession or control of the record is entitled to receive, control, hold, and dispose of the record and the goods the record covers." Preface to Revised Article 7.

**Warehouse Receipts** A warehouse receipt is a document of title issued by a person engaged in the business of storing goods for hire. A warehouser is liable for damages for loss or injury to the goods caused by his failure to exercise such care in regard to them as a reasonably careful person would exercise under the circumstances. The warehouser must deliver the goods to the person entitled to receive them under the terms of the warehouse receipt. Though a warehouser may limit his liability through a provision in the warehouse receipt fixing a specific maximum liability per article or item or unit of weight, this limitation does not apply when a warehouser converts goods to his own use.

To enforce the payment of her charges and necessary expenses in connection with keeping and handling the goods, a warehouser has a lien on the goods that enables her to sell them at public or private sale after notice and to apply the net proceeds of the sale to the amount of her charges. The Code, moreover, provides the warehouser a definite procedure for enforcing her lien against the goods stored and in her possession.

**Bills of Lading** A **bill of lading** is a document of title evidencing the receipt of goods issued by a person engaged in the business of directly or indirectly transporting or forwarding goods. It serves a threefold function: (1) as a receipt for the goods, (2) as evidence of the contract of carriage, and (3) as a document of title. A bill of lading is negotiable if, by its terms, the goods are deliverable to bearer or to the order of a named person. Any other document is nonnegotiable.

Under the Code, bills of lading may be issued not only by common carriers but also by contract carriers, freight forwarders, or any person engaged in the business of transporting or forwarding goods.

The carrier must deliver the goods to the person entitled to receive them under the terms of the bill of lading. Common carriers are extraordinary bailees under the law and are subject to greater liability than are ordinary bailees, such as warehousers.

The Code allows a carrier to limit its liability by contract in all cases in which its rates depend on the value of the goods and the carrier allows the shipper an opportunity to declare a higher value. The limitation does not apply, however, when the carrier converts goods to its own use.

On goods in its possession that are covered by a bill of lading, the carrier has a lien for the charges and expenses necessary for its preservation of such goods. Against a purchaser for value of a negotiable bill of lading, this lien is limited to charges stated in the bill or in the applicable published tariff or, if no charges are so stated, to a reasonable charge.

The carrier may enforce its lien by public or private sale of the goods after notice to all persons known by the carrier to claim an interest in them. The sale must be on terms that are "commercially reasonable," and the carrier must conduct it in a "commercially reasonable manner."

A purchaser in good faith of goods sold to enforce the lien takes those goods free of any rights of persons against whom the lien was valid, even if the enforcement of the lien does not comply with Code requirements. This rule applies both to carrier's and to warehouser's liens. Good faith, as indicated in previous chapters, has been revised to mean "honesty in fact and the observance of reasonable commercial standards of fair dealing." Revised Section 7–102(6); Revised Section 1–201(b)(20).

## NEGOTIABILITY OF DOCUMENTS OF TITLE

The concept of negotiability has long been established in law. It is important not only in connection with documents of title but also in connection with commercial paper and investment securities, topics treated in other chapters of this book.

The Code provides that a warehouse receipt, bill of lading, or other document of title is negotiable if, by its terms, the goods are to be delivered to bearer or to the order of a named person or in situations, in overseas trade, in which the document runs to a named person or assigns. Revised Article 7 provides that a document of title is negotiable if, by its terms, the goods are to be delivered to bearer or to the order of a named person. Revised Section 7–104(a). Any other document is nonnegotiable. The negotiability of a document is determined at its time of issue. Revised Section 7–104, Comment 2. Revised Article 7 provides for the integration of electronic documents of title and, to the extent possible, applies the same rules for electronic and tangible documents of title.

A nonnegotiable document, such as a straight bill of lading or a warehouse receipt under which the goods are deliverable only to a person named in the bill, not to the order of any person or to bearer, may be transferred by assignment but may not be negotiated. Only a negotiable document or instrument may be negotiated.

An individual has "control" of an **electronic document of title** "if a system employed for evidencing the transfer of interests in the electronic document reliably establishes that person as the person to which the electronic document was issued or transferred." Revised Section 7–106(a). Control of an electronic document of title replaces the concept of possession and indorsement applicable to a tangible document of title. Thus, a person with a tangible document of title delivers the document by voluntarily transferring *possession* while a person with an electronic document of title delivers the document by voluntarily transferring *control.* Revised Section 7–106, Comment 2. The key to having a system of control under Revised Article 7 is the ability to show at any point in time the one person entitled to the goods under the electronic document. Revised Section 7–106, Comment 3. Revised Article 7 leaves to the marketplace the creation of systems that meet this standard.

## DUE NEGOTIATION

The Code sets forth the manner in which a negotiable document of title may be negotiated and the requirements of due negotiation. An order form negotiable *tangible* document of title running to the order of a named person is negotiated by her indorsement and delivery. Revised Section 7–501(a). Delivery of a tangible document of title means voluntary transfer of possession. Revised Article 1–201(b)(15). After such indorsement in blank or to bearer, the document may be negotiated by delivery alone. A special indorsement, by which the document is indorsed over to a specified person, requires the indorsement of the special indorsee as well as delivery to accomplish a further negotiation.

A negotiable *electronic* document of title running to the order of a named person *or* to bearer is negotiated by delivery. Indorsement by the named person is not required to negotiate an electronic document of title. Revised Section 7–501(b). Delivery of an electronic document of title means voluntary transfer of control. Revised Article 1–201(b)(15).

**Due negotiation**, a term peculiar to Article 7, requires not only that the purchaser of the negotiable document take it in good faith, without notice of any adverse claim or defense, and pay value, but also that she take it in the regular course of business or financing, not in settlement or payment of a money obligation (in essence, a holder by due negotiation). Thus, a transfer for value of a negotiable document of title to a nonbanker or to a person not in business, such as a college professor or student, would not be a due negotiation.

Due negotiation creates new rights in the holder of the document. The transferee does not stand in the shoes of his transferor; in other words, the defects and defenses available against the transferor are not available against the new holder. Newly created by the negotiation, his rights are free of such defects and defenses. This enables bankers and businesspersons to extend credit on documents of title without concern about possible adverse claims or the rights of third parties.

The rights of a holder of a negotiable document of title to whom it has been duly negotiated include (1) title to the document; (2) title to the goods; (3) all rights accruing under the law of agency or estoppel, including rights to goods delivered to the bailee after the document was issued; and (4) the issuer's direct obligation to hold or deliver the goods according to the document's terms.

### WARRANTIES

A person, other than a collecting bank or other intermediary, who either negotiates or delivers a document of title for value incurs certain warranty obligations, unless otherwise agreed. Such transferor warrants to her immediate purchaser (1) that the document is genuine, (2) that she had no knowledge of any fact that would impair its validity or worth, and (3) that her negotiation or delivery is rightful and fully effective with respect to the title to the document and the goods it represents. Revised Article 7 makes it clear that these warranties only arise in the case of voluntary transfer of possession or control for value. Revised Section 7–507.

### INEFFECTIVE DOCUMENTS OF TITLE

For a person to obtain title to goods through the negotiation of a document to him, the goods must have been delivered to the document's issuer by their owner or by either one to whom the owner has delivered the goods or one whom the owner has entrusted with actual or apparent authority to ship, store, or sell them. A warehouser or carrier, however, may deliver goods according to the terms of the document that it has issued or otherwise dispose of the goods as provided in the Code without incurring liability, even if the document did not represent title to the goods. The warehouser or carrier need only have acted in good faith and complied with reasonable commercial standards in both the receipt and delivery or other disposition of the goods. Such a bailee has no liability even though the person from whom the bailee received the goods had no authority to obtain the issuance of the document or to dispose of the goods, and the person to whom it delivered the goods had no authority to receive them.

Thus, a carrier or warehouser who receives goods from a thief or finder and later delivers them to a person to whom the thief or finder ordered them to be delivered is not liable to the true owner of the goods. Even a sale of the goods by the carrier or warehouser to enforce a lien for transportation or storage charges and expenses would not subject it to liability.

# CHAPTER SUMMARY

## INTRODUCTION TO PROPERTY AND PERSONAL PROPERTY

**KINDS OF PROPERTY**

**Definition** interest, or group of interests, that is legally protected
**Tangible Property** physical objects
**Intangible Property** property that does not exist in a physical form
**Real Property** land and interests in land
**Personal Property** all property that is not real property
**Fixture** personal property so firmly attached to real property that an interest in it arises under real property law

**TRANSFER OF TITLE TO PERSONAL PROPERTY**

**Sale** transfer of property for consideration (price)
**Gift** transfer of property without consideration

- ***Delivery*** includes both manual transfer of the item and constructive delivery (delivery of something that symbolizes control over the item)
- ***Intent***
- ***Acceptance***
- ***Classification***

**Will** right to property acquired upon death of the owner
**Accession** right of a property owner to any increase in such property
**Confusion** intermixing of goods belonging to two or more owners such that they can identify their individual property only as part of a mass of like goods

- If due to mistake, accident, or agreement, loss shared proportionately
- If caused by an intentional or unauthorized act, wrongdoer bears loss

**Possession** a person may acquire title by taking possession of property

- ***Abandoned Property*** intentionally disposed of by the owner; the finder is entitled to the property
- ***Lost Property*** unintentionally left by the owner; the finder is generally entitled to the property
- ***Mislaid Property*** intentionally placed by the owner but unintentionally left; the owner of the premises is generally entitled to the property
- ***Treasure Trove*** coins or currency concealed by the owner for such a length of time that the owner is probably dead or undiscoverable; the finder is entitled to the property

## PROPERTY INSURANCE

**FIRE AND PROPERTY INSURANCE**

**General Definition of Insurance** contractual arrangement that distributes risk of loss among a large number of members (the insureds) through an insurance company (the insurer)
**Coverage** of fire and property insurance provides protection against loss due to fire or related perils
**Types of Fire**

- ***Friendly Fire*** fire contained in its intended location
- ***Hostile Fire*** any fire outside its intended or usual location

**Co-insurance** insurance in which a person insures property for less than its full or stated value and agrees to share the risk of loss
**Other Insurance Clauses** if multiple insurers are involved, liability is distributed *pro rata*
**Types of Policies**

- ***Valued Policy*** covers full value of property as agreed upon by the parties at the time the policy is issued
- ***Open Policy*** covers fair market value of property as calculated immediately prior to the loss

**NATURE OF INSURANCE CONTRACTS**

**General Contract Law** basic principles of contract law apply
**Insurable Interest** a financial interest or a factual expectancy in someone's property that justifies insuring the property; the interest must exist at the time the property loss occurs
**Premiums** amount to be paid for an insurance policy

**Defenses of the Insurer**

- ***Misrepresentation*** false representation of a material fact made by the insured that is justifiably relied upon by the insurer; enables the insurer to rescind the contract within a specified time
- ***Breach of Warranty*** the failure of a required condition; generally an insurer may avoid liability for a breach of warranty only if the breach is material
- ***Concealment*** fraudulent failure of an applicant for insurance to disclose material facts that the insurer does not know; allows the insurer to rescind the contract
- ***Waiver*** an insurer intentionally relinquishes the right to deny liability
- ***Estoppel*** an insurer is prevented by its own conduct from asserting a defense

**Termination** an insurance contract may be terminated by due performance or cancellation

## BAILMENTS AND DOCUMENTS OF TITLE

### BAILMENTS

**Definition** the temporary transfer of personal property by one party (the bailor) to another (the bailee)

**Classification of Bailments**

- ***For the Bailor's Sole Benefit***
- ***For the Bailee's Sole Benefit***
- ***For Mutual Benefit*** includes ordinary commercial bailments

**Essential Elements**

- ***Delivery of Possession***
- ***Personal Property***
- ***Possession, but Not Ownership, for a Determinable Time***
- ***Restoration of Possession to the Bailor***

**Rights and Duties**

- ***Bailee's Duty to Exercise Due Care*** the bailee must exercise reasonable care to protect the safety of the property and to return it to the proper person
- ***Bailee's Absolute Liability*** occurs when (1) the parties so agree; (2) the custom of the industry requires the bailee to insure the property against the risk in question, but he fails to do so; or (3) the bailee uses the bailed property in an unauthorized manner
- ***Bailee's Right to Limit Liability*** certain bailees are not permitted to limit their liability for breach of their duties, except as provided by statute
- ***Bailee's Right to Compensation*** entitled to reasonable compensation for work or services performed on the bailed goods
- ***Bailor's Duties*** in bailment for sole benefit of bailee, the bailor warrants that she is unaware of any defects; in all other bailments, the bailor has a duty to warn of all known defects and all defects she should discover upon a reasonable inspection

**Special Types**

- ***Pledge*** security interest by possession
- ***Warehouser*** storer of goods for compensation; warehouser must exercise reasonable care to protect the safety of the stored goods and to deliver them to the proper person
- ***Carrier of Goods*** transporter of goods; a common carrier is an extraordinary bailee, and a private carrier is an ordinary bailee
- ***Innkeeper*** hotel or motel operator; is an extraordinary bailee except as limited by statute or case law

**DOCUMENTS OF TITLE**

**Definition** an instrument evidencing ownership of the record and the goods it covers

**Types**

- ***Warehouse Receipt*** receipt issued by person storing goods
- ***Bill of Lading*** document issued to the shipper by the carrier (1) as a receipt for the goods, (2) as evidence of their carriage contract, and (3) as a document of title

**Negotiability** a document of title is negotiable if, by its terms, the goods are to be delivered to bearer or to the order of a named person

**Due Negotiation** delivery of a negotiable document in the regular course of business to a holder, who takes in good faith, for value, and without notice of any defense or claim

**Warranties** a person who negotiates or delivers a document of title for value, other than a collecting bank or other intermediary, incurs certain warranty obligations unless otherwise agreed

**Ineffective Documents** for a person to obtain title to goods by negotiation of a document, the goods must have been delivered to the issuer of the document by their owner or by one to whom the owner has entrusted actual or apparent authority

# CASES

## CASE 48-1

Fixtures

## FREEMAN v. BARRS

Missouri Court of Appeals, Southern District, Division One, 2007

237 S.W.3d 285

http://caselaw.lp.findlaw.com/scripts/getcase.pl?court=mo&vol=/appeals/112007/&invol=5411107

**Parrish, P. J.**

Francis B. Freeman, Jr., (plaintiff) appeals a judgment for Mary Ann Barrs (defendant) in an action plaintiff brought to replevy [recover] a cattle scale. * * *

In 2005, defendant purchased a tract of real estate consisting of approximately 4,000 acres from plaintiff for a price of $3,500,000. There were four residences on the property, two barns, and a covered pole barn with open sides. The pole barn houses the cattle scale that was the subject of plaintiff's replevin action and an enclosed veterinarian office.

The contract between the parties was a form contract. Its paragraph 2 states:

### Inclusions, Exclusions and Exceptions

The Property *includes* any and all rights, privileges and easements appurtenant thereto, together with all existing buildings and improvements and all affixed equipment now located thereon, *if any,* including all mechanical, HVAC, electrical and plumbing systems, fixtures and equipment, fencing and other attached fixtures, trees, bushes, shrubs and plants, feed bunks in the fence, installed fences and gates, propane tanks not under lease, water association rights and telephone rights where applicable, hog and cattle waterers in the fence or permanently installed, grain storage buildings and hog and cattle shades on permanent foundations, auger and conveyor systems. All grain, crops, livestock, hay, silage, and non-affixed personal property on the real estate are reserved by Seller or Seller's tenant....

* * *

The Plaintiff purchased the present scale in June 2001 for Eleven thousand dollars ($11,000). The scale was sold as a portable model. Plaintiff placed the scale in a pole-type barn on a concrete pad poured for the scale, then poured concrete ramps which would allow cattle to enter and exit the scale. Plaintiff further welded iron fence into place to help funnel the cattle through the scale area. * * *

The scale was designed to be portable, and 70% of the scales he sold were installed in the present manner. He further stated that he could move the present scales by cutting away a welded metal fence and lifting the scale with heavy machinery, and [sic] process which he often performs. McFadden further stated that the removal of the fence would take approximately one hour with use of a cutting torch, and thereafter the scale could be moved within fifteen minutes....

* * *

Judgment was entered for defendant on plaintiff's replevin claim. * * *

* * *

Paragraph 2 of the real estate contract between the parties unambiguously provides that the sale included all affixed equipment located on the property. Courts do not rewrite unambiguous contracts but construe them as written. [Citation.] Thus, as defendant suggests, if the scale constitutes a fixture, the judgment will be affirmed.

A fixture is an article in the nature of personal property which has been so annexed to the realty that it is regarded as part of the land and partakes of the legal incidents of the freehold and belongs to the person owning the land. [Citation.] The test for determining whether property has become a fixture is three-fold, consisting of: (1) the annexation to the realty; (2) the adaptation to the use to which the realty is devoted; and (3) the intent that the object become a permanent accession to the land. [Citation.] These elements or tests all present questions of fact and are not ordinarily resolvable by law. [Citation.] Whether or not an article is a fixture depends upon the facts and circumstances of a particular case. [Citation.]

* * *

* * * The * * * two elements, adaptation and intent, are more important in determining whether a chattel became a fixture than the method by which the chattel is affixed to a freehold. [Citation.] Annexation that may be slight and easily displaced does not prevent an article from becoming a fixture when the other elements are found. [Citation.]

***Annexation***

Plaintiff purchased the scale and printer in 2001. The scale was purchased by plaintiff to "start selling cattle from the ranch and not sending them to the sale barn to keep the price up a little." It was placed in a roofed structure that housed cattle-working pens and a small veterinary office. The scale weighs approximately 6,500 pounds. A fence and gates within the structure had to be cut off in order to install the scale. A concrete slab was poured in the structure for placement of the scale. The size and shape of the slab were designed to accommodate the scale. Metal cleats were welded to the bottom of the scale before it was placed on the slab. The scale was placed on pipes on the ground and pushed with a tractor across the pipes onto the slab. Concrete ramps were installed on two sides of the scale and fencing was constructed to direct cattle onto the scale. The concrete construction (other than the slab) and the metal pipe fencing were completed after the scale was placed on the slab in the pole barn. The metal posts for the fence were set in the concrete. The scale has remained in place since its installation.

***Adaptation***

Ray Stone had been ranch manager for plaintiff. At the time of trial he had an agreement with defendant that permitted him to run cattle on the property. He was running 200 head of cows and 90 calves on the property. He "just kind of [saw] after the place" for her. He told the court that the scale was integral to a cattle-working facility. The scale was used to weigh cattle for sale and to determine required dosages of medicine administered to cattle.

***Intent***

The scale was described as portable by its manufacturer. The manufacturer sold peripheral items that permitted the scale to be moved. This included a trailer and an inverter. Plaintiff did not buy that equipment. Ray Stone told the court that the scale was purchased "to be stationary whether it was portable or not."

This court concludes that the scale was a fixture; that, therefore, the sale of the real estate on which it was situate included the sale of the scale. A 6,500-pound scale placed on a specially sized concrete pad and surrounded by metal pole fencing set in the concrete is annexed to the real estate on which the concrete pad is poured. The permanency of the installation is emphasized by the fact the facility is covered * * *. The scale was put in place to facilitate the cattle operation on the premises. It had been used for that purpose since its purchase. Its adaptation for that purpose enhanced the operation of the cattle ranch.

Mindful that "[i]n determining the intention of the person making the annexation the court … is not bound by [that person's] testimony on this point, nor by his secret or undisclosed purpose but may decide this issue from his acts and conduct and the surrounding facts and circumstances," [Citation], this court holds that the evidence in this case demonstrates that it was plaintiff's intent for the scale to be a permanent installation; that the scale is a fixture and, therefore, part of the real estate.

* * *

The trial court's finding for defendant on plaintiff's claim for replevin was the correct result for the reasons heretofore stated. Plaintiff's point is denied. The judgment is affirmed.

CASE 48-2

## Delivery of Gift
## O'FALLON v. O'FALLON

Supreme Court of Arkansas, 2000
341 Ark. 138, 14 S.W.3d 506
http://caselaw.lp.findlaw.com/scripts/getcase.pl?court=ar&vol=supreme/2000a/20000420/99-806&invol=2

**Imber, J.**

Barney Laron "Ronnie" O'Fallon died intestate on May 3, 1997, and was survived by three children. His oldest son, appellant William Martin O'Fallon, was appointed administrator of the estate * * * and, proceeded to collect the assets of the estate. One of those assets was a 1996 Chevrolet Camaro automobile that had been purchased by the decedent two weeks prior to his death and delivered to his seventeen-year-old son, appellee Ronnie O'Fallon. After the administrator of the estate took possession of the vehicle, Ronnie O'Fallon filed a motion in the probate court for return of the property. He alleged that the "vehicle was intended to be a gift to [him] and from and after the purchase of the vehicle the Decedent never had possession of same." * * * The administrator denied that the decedent made a gift of the 1996 Chevrolet Camaro to Ronnie O'Fallon, * * *. After a hearing, the probate court found "by clear and convincing evidence" that the vehicle was a gift from the decedent to Ronnie O'Fallon * * *. From that decision, the administrator appealed * * *. We reversed and remanded because the probate court was without jurisdiction to adjudicate Ronnie O'Fallon's claim to the car as an alleged donee of a gift made prior to the decedent's death. We further held that the appropriate jurisdiction for the matter was chancery court.

Pursuant to our decision, the matter was transferred to the Desha County Chancery Court. Ronnie O'Fallon then filed a motion for judgment on the record and asked the chancery court to enter judgment based upon the record of the probate court, where the matter had been fully tried before the same judge. The chancellor granted the motion, finding that the 1996 Chevrolet Camaro purchased by the decedent prior to his death was a gift to Ronnie O'Fallon and ordering the estate to pay the sales tax, registration fees, and all other charges necessary for proper licensing and registration of the vehicle. * * *

For his first point on appeal, the administrator challenges the chancellor's finding that the decedent made an *inter vivos* gift of the vehicle to Ronnie O'Fallon. Our law determining a valid *inter vivos* gift is clear and well established. We have stated that a valid *inter vivos* gift is effective when the following requirements are proven by clear and convincing evidence: (1) the donor was of sound mind; (2) an actual delivery of the property took place; (3) the donor clearly intended to make an immediate, present, and final gift; (4) the donor unconditionally released all future dominion and control over the property; and (5) the donee accepted the gift. [Citation.]

In the case at hand, it is undisputed on appeal that the donor, Barney O'Fallon, was of sound mind, that there was actual delivery, and that the donee, Ronnie O'Fallon, accepted the car. The administrator's argument focuses instead on the evidence that pertains to the other two requirements for a valid *inter vivos* gift; that is, whether Barney O'Fallon intended to make the automobile a gift and whether he relinquished dominion and control over the automobile.

The administrator first points out that Barney O'Fallon retained title to the automobile. We have held, however, that the intent of the donor can negate the fact that actual title was not transferred. [Citation.] Here, Ronnie O'Fallon's mother, Linda Ngar, testified that Barney O'Fallon told her he "was going to buy" the car for Ronnie O'Fallon. Later, he told her that he "had bought" the car for Ronnie. Similar testimony was elicited from Mike Gorman, a loan officer with the Potlatch Credit Union where Barney O'Fallon applied for a loan to purchase the automobile. According to Mr. Gorman, Mr. O'Fallon told him that he was buying the car for his son who was getting ready to go to college. It should be noted that Ronnie O'Fallon was a minor at the time of the alleged gift and, therefore, could not acquire title to the automobile. [Citation.] With regard to the fact that Barney O'Fallon insured the vehicle in his name and listed himself as the only driver, Mr. O'Fallon's insurance agent, Sammy Mullis, testified that the children of a named insured may be covered as occasional drivers. Mr. Mullis further confirmed that parents do not always list their children as drivers on the family's car insurance policy because the premium would be significantly higher.

The record reflects additional evidence regarding Mr. O'Fallon's intent to make a gift and to relinquish all dominion and control over the automobile. Ms. Ngar testified that she drove Barney O'Fallon to Warren, where he picked up the 1996 Chevrolet Camaro from the dealership. He then drove it to Gillett, where Ronnie lived with his mother. After Ronnie got home from school, Mr. O'Fallon delivered the car and one set of car keys to Ronnie and gave the other set of keys to Ms. Ngar. According to Ms. Ngar, Mr. O'Fallon did not retain a set of keys to the car. Ronnie then drove his father back to his home in Arkansas City and returned to Gillett that same day in the 1996 Chevrolet

Camaro. Ronnie testified that the keys and paperwork on the car were given to him by his father and that the car stayed with him in Gillett. Furthermore, Ronnie stated that his father may have driven the car one other time prior to his death "because of his truck [being] in a bad position, like blocking the driveway or something, to go to the store." * * *

Affirmed.

---

CASE 48-3

Bailments: Classification/Essentials/Duties of Bailee

## HADFIELD v. GILCHRIST

Court of Appeals of South Carolina, 2000
343 S.C. 88, 538 S.E.2d 268
http://www.law.sc.edu/ctapp/3246.htm

**Anderson, J.**

Mark Hadfield filed this action against Sam Gilchrist, d/b/a Gilchrist's Service Center, and d/b/a Gilchrist Towing Company (Gilchrist) for damages sustained by Hadfield's vehicle while impounded on Gilchrist's lot. * * *

### *Facts/Procedural Background*

Gilchrist owns a motor vehicle towing service and maintains a storage facility for the retention of the towed vehicles. Gilchrist operates under a license issued by the City of Charleston.

Hadfield, a medical student at MUSC, went to retrieve his 1988 Lincoln Continental from the parking spot where his wife parked the vehicle. The parking spot, located near MUSC, was on private property owned by Allen Saffer. Hadfield's wife parked the vehicle on Saffer's property without Saffer's permission. The vehicle was not in the parking spot when Hadfield arrived as Saffer had called Gilchrist to have the vehicle removed.

Gilchrist towed Hadfield's car to his storage facility. Gilchrist maintained a chain link fence around the storage area, and had an employee on the lot around the clock. The employee's duties included periodically leaving the office to check on the storage area, which was some distance away from the office.

Hadfield called to retrieve his vehicle, but was informed he would have to wait until the next morning and pay towing and storage fees. Upon Hadfield's arrival to pick up his car the following morning, he paid the fees. When he went to the storage area to collect his vehicle, Hadfield discovered the vehicle had been extensively vandalized. The vandals stole the radio/compact disc player, smashed windows, and pulled many electrical wires out of the dashboard. The vehicle depended heavily upon computers and never functioned properly after the incident. The vandals entered the storage area by cutting a hole in the fence. They vandalized between six and eight vehicles on the lot that night.

The magistrate, in summarizing Hadfield's testimony, concluded Hadfield's attempts to persuade Gilchrist to pay for the damages were futile. Hadfield secured estimates for the damage to the automobile * * * at $4,021.43. * * * After more than 60 days elapsed, Hadfield sold the vehicle for $1,000.00.

The magistrate found Gilchrist liable for the damages as a bailee, and entered judgment in favor of Hadfield for $4,035.00. Gilchrist appealed to the Circuit Court, which affirmed the decision of the magistrate.

* * *

### *Issues*

I Did the Circuit Court err in applying the law of bailments?

II Did the Circuit Court err in finding Gilchrist was responsible for damages?

### *Law/Analysis*

Neither the magistrate nor the Circuit Court judge made a finding as to the type of bailment created in this case. The type of bailment created may determine the standard of care the bailee, Gilchrist, must meet. Therefore, we review the law of bailments.

### *Bailments*

A bailment is created by the delivery of personal property by one person to another in trust for a specific purpose, pursuant to an express or implied contract to fulfill that trust. [Citations.]

Bailments are generally classified as being for (1) the sole benefit of the bailor; (2) the sole benefit of the bailee; or (3) the mutual benefit of both. [Citation.] Bailments which benefit only one of the parties, the first and second classifications, are often described as gratuitous. [Citation.]

#### *A. Gratuitous Bailment*

"A gratuitous bailment is, by definition, one in which the transfer of possession or use of the bailed property is without compensation." [Citation.] For instance, a gratuitous bailment arises if the bailment is undertaken as a personal favor or is involuntary. [Citations.]

A "gratuitous bailee" acts without expectation of reward or compensation. [Citation.] To show the bailment was for the sole benefit of the bailor, the bailee must establish that it was not expecting compensation. * * *

***B. Bailment for Mutual Benefit***

By contrast, a bailment for the mutual benefit of the parties arises when one party takes the personal property of another into his or her care or custody in exchange for payment or other benefit. [Citations.]

***C. Constructive Bailment***

Although a bailment is ordinarily created by the agreement of the parties, the agreement of the parties may be implied or constructive, and the bailment may arise by operation of law. [Citation.] Such a constructive bailment arises when one person has lawfully acquired possession of another's personal property, other than by virtue of a bailment contract, and holds it under such circumstances that the law imposes on the recipient of the property the obligation to keep it safely and redeliver it to the owner. [Citations.] A constructive bailment may occur even in the absence of the voluntary delivery and acceptance of the property which is usually necessary to create a bailment relationship.

Gilchrist argues he towed the vehicle pursuant to the Charleston Municipal Ordinances, and the ordinances are for the sole benefit of the vehicle owners. Accordingly, he contends, the relationship created is a gratuitous bailment. We disagree. * * *

Clearly, the [applicable Charleston] ordinances provide for the payment to the city or its agent, the towing service, for the costs of towing and storage. Gilchrist charged Hadfield towing and storage fees.

The vehicle owned by Hadfield was plucked by Gilchrist from the private property of Saffer. Gilchrist acted pursuant to and by virtue of the licensing authority under the city ordinance. Quintessentially, the factual scenario encapsulated in this case is a paradigm of a "constructive bailment." We conclude a constructive bailment, for the mutual benefit of Hadfield and Gilchrist, was created.

***Bailment Action/Nature of Theory***

Although contractual in nature, and involving the conveyance of personal property, an action for breach of the duty of care by a bailor sounds in tort. [Citations.] Concomitantly, after finding a bailment for mutual benefit exists in this case, we must determine whether Hadfield is entitled to damages, relying on the application of tort principles rather than contract principles.

***Bailee's Degree of Care/Burden of Proof***

The degree of care required of a bailee for mutual benefit is defined as ordinary care, or due care, or the degree of care which would be exercised by a person of ordinary care in the protection of his own property. [Citations.]

In a bailment action alleging a breach of the duty of care, the bailor is entitled to be compensated for all losses that are the natural consequence and proximate result of the bailee's negligence. [Citation.] * * * The Supreme Court, in *Shoreland Freezers*, [citation], discussed a bailee's liability under a bailment for mutual benefit:

> Under the decided cases in this State, liability of a bailee under a bailment for mutual benefit arises upon a showing that (1) the goods were delivered to the bailee in good condition, (2) they were lost or returned in a damaged condition, and (3) the loss or damage to the goods was due to the failure of the bailee to exercise ordinary care in the safekeeping of the property. The burden of proof in such cases, in the first instance, rests upon the bailor to make out a prima facie case. This has been done when the bailor proves that he delivered the goods to the bailee in good condition and their loss or return in a damaged condition. When the bailor has so proven, the burden is then shifted to the bailee to show that he has used ordinary care in the storage and safekeeping of the property. [Citations.]

[Citation.]

* * *

Hadfield testified before the magistrate regarding the "nice" condition of the vehicle prior to being towed, and the damage to his vehicle, and the other vehicles on the lot. In addition, he introduced photographs depicting the damage. Thus, Hadfield made out his *prima facie* case * * *. The burden then shifted to Gilchrist to show that he used ordinary care in protecting the vehicle while in his care.

Gilchrist impounded the cars in a storage lot surrounded by a chain link fence. There was an individual on the clock at all times. The person on duty spent time in the office and only visited the storage lot to check on it. The vandal cut a hole in the fence and broke into six to eight cars on the night in question. The fact the guard was not on duty at the impound lot and, considering the only other security for the vehicles was the chain link fence, the magistrate and Circuit Court judge could have concluded Gilchrist failed to exercise ordinary care. * * *

* * *

Accordingly, the order of the Circuit Court is AFFIRMED.

## QUESTIONS

1. Define (a) tangible and intangible property, (b) real and personal property, and (c) a fixture.
2. Explain (a) the ways to transfer title to personal property, (b) the three elements of a valid gift, and (c) the difference in the law's treatment of abandoned property, lost property, and mislaid property.
3. With respect to property insurance, explain (a) the different types of fires, (b) co-insurance clauses, (c) other insurance clauses, (d) insurable interest, (e) valued and open policies, and (f) the defenses of misrepresentation, breach of warranty, concealment, waiver, and estoppel.
4. Define the essential elements of a bailment and describe the rights and duties of the bailor and bailee.
5. (a) Explain what a document of title is, and (b) identify and describe the various types of documents of title.

## PROBLEMS

1. In January, Roger Burke loaned his favorite nephew, Jimmy White, his valuable Picasso painting. Knowing that Jimmy would celebrate his twenty-first birthday on May 15, Burke sent a letter to Jimmy on April 14 stating:

   Dear Jimmy,

   Tomorrow I leave on my annual trip to Europe, and I want to make you a fitting birthday gift, which I do by sending you my enclosed promissory note. Also I want you to keep the Picasso that I loaned you last January, and you may now consider it yours. Happy birthday!

   Affectionately,
   /s/ Uncle Roger

   The negotiable promissory note for $5,000 sent with the letter was signed by Roger Burke, payable to Jimmy White or bearer, and dated May 15. On May 21, Burke was killed in an automobile accident while motoring in France.

   First Bank was appointed administrator of Burke's estate. Jimmy presented the note to the administrator and demanded payment, which was refused. Jimmy brought an action against First Bank as administrator, seeking recovery on the note. The administrator in turn brought an action against Jimmy, seeking the return of the Picasso.

   **(a)** What decision in the action on the note?
   **(b)** What decision in the action to recover the painting?
2. Several years ago, Pierce purchased a tract of land on which stood an old, vacant house. Recently, Pierce employed Fried, a carpenter, to repair and remodel the house. While Fried was tearing out a partition to enlarge one of the rooms, he found a metal box hidden in the wall. After breaking open the box and discovering that it contained $2,000 in gold and silver coins and old-style bills, Fried took the box and its contents to Pierce and told her where he had found it. When Fried handed the box and the money over to Pierce, he said, "If you do not find the owner, I claim the money." Pierce placed the money in an envelope and deposited it in her safe deposit box, where it presently remains. No one has ever claimed the money, but Pierce refuses to give it to Fried.

   Will Fried be able to recover the money from Pierce? Why?
3. Gable, the owner of a lumber company, was cutting trees over the boundary line between his property and property owned by Lane. Although he realized he had crossed onto Lane's property, Gable continued to cut trees of the same kind as those he had cut on his own land. While on Lane's property, he found a diamond ring on the ground, which he took home. All of the timber Gable cut that day was commingled.

   What are Lane's rights, if any (a) in the timber and (b) in the ring?
4. Decide each of the following problems.

   **(a)** A chimney sweep found a jewel and took it to a goldsmith, whose apprentice removed the stone and refused to return it. The chimney sweep sues the goldsmith.
   **(b)** One of several boys walking along a railroad track found an old stocking. All started playing with it until it burst in the hands of its discoverer, revealing several hundred dollars. The original discoverer claims all of the money; the other boys claim it should be divided equally.
   **(c)** A traveling salesperson leaving a store notices a parcel of bank notes on the floor. He picks them up and gives them to the owner of the store to keep for the true owner. After three years, they have not been reclaimed, and the salesperson sues the storekeeper.
   **(d)** Frank is hired to clean the swimming pool at the country club. He finds a diamond ring on the bottom of the pool. The true owner cannot be found. The country club sues Frank for possession of the ring.
   **(e)** A customer found a pocketbook lying on a barber's table. He gave it to the barber to hold for the true owner, who failed to appear. The customer sues the barber.
5. Jones had fifty crates of oranges equally divided between grades A, B, and C, grade A being the highest quality and C being the lowest. Smith had one thousand crates of oranges, about 90 percent of which were grade A, but some of which were grades B and C, the exact percentage of each being unknown. Smith willfully mixed Jones's crates with his own so that it was impossible to identify any particular crate. Jones seized the whole lot. Smith demanded nine hundred crates of grade A and fifty crates each of grades B and C. Jones refused to give them up unless Smith could identify particular crates. This Smith could not do. Smith brought an action against Jones to recover what he demanded or its value. Judgment for whom, and why?

**6.** Barnes, the owner and operator of Blackacre, decided to cease farming operations and liquidate his holdings. Barnes sold fifty head of yearling Merino sheep to Billing and then sold Blackacre to Clifton. He executed and delivered to Billing a bill of sale for the sheep and was paid for them. It was understood that Billing would send a truck for the sheep within a few days. At the same time, Barnes executed a warranty deed conveying Blackacre to Clifton. Clifton took possession of the farm and brought along one hundred head of his yearling Merino sheep and turned them into the pasture, not knowing the sheep Barnes sold Billing were still in the pasture. After the sheep were mixed, it was impossible to identify the fifty head belonging to Billing. Explain whether Billing will recover the fifty head of sheep from Clifton.

**7.** Susan permitted Kevin to take her very old grandfather clock on the basis of Kevin's representations that he was skilled at repairing such clocks and restoring them to their original condition and could do the job for $60. The clock had been badly damaged for years. Kevin immediately sold the clock to Fixit Shop for $30. Fixit Shop was in the business of repairing a large variety of items and also sold used articles. Three months later, Susan was in the Fixit Shop and clearly identified a grandfather clock Fixit Shop had for sale as the one she had given Kevin to repair. Fixit Shop had replaced more than half of the moving parts by having exact duplicates custom-made; the clock's exterior had been restored by a skilled cabinetmaker; and the clock's face had been replaced by a duplicate. All materials belonged to Fixit Shop, and its employees accomplished the work. Fixit Shop asserts it bought the clock in the normal course of business from Kevin, who represented that it belonged to him. The fair market value of the clock in its damaged condition was $30, and the value of repairs made is $220.

Susan sued Fixit Shop for return of the clock. Fixit Shop defended that it then had title to the clock and, in the alternative, that Susan must pay the value of the repairs if she is entitled to regain possession. Who will prevail? Why?

**8.** Under an oral agreement, Hyer rented from Bateman a vacant lot for a filling station. Hyer placed on the lot a lightly constructed building bolted to a concrete slab and several storage tanks laid on the ground in a shallow excavation. Later, Hyer prepared a lease which contained a provision allowing him to remove the equipment at the termination of the lease. This lease was not executed, having been rejected by Bateman due to a renewal clause it contained. Several years later, another lease was prepared, which both Hyer and Bateman did sign. This lease did not mention removal of the equipment. At the termination of this lease, Hyer removed the equipment, and Bateman brought an action to recover possession of the equipment. What judgment?

**9.** Elvers sold a parcel of real estate, describing it by its legal description and making no mention of any improvements or fixtures on it. The land had upon it a residence, a barn, a rail fence, a stack of hay, some growing corn, and a windmill. The residence had a mirror built into the west wall of the living room and a heating system consisting of a furnace, steam pipes, and coils. In the house were chairs, beds, tables, and other furniture. On the house was a lightning rod. In the basement were screens for the windows. Which of these things passed by the deed and which did not?

**10.** John Swan rented a safe deposit box at the Tenth Citizens Bank of Emanon, State of X. On December 17, 2008, Swan went to the bank with stock certificates to place in the safe deposit box. After he was admitted to the vault and had placed the stock certificates in the box, Swan found lying on a chair in the privacy booth of the vault a $5,000 negotiable bearer bond issued by the State of Wisconsin with coupons attached, due June 30, 2015. Swan picked up the bond and, observing that it did not carry the name of the owner, left the vault and went to the office of the president of the bank. He told the president what had occurred and delivered the bond to the president only after obtaining his promise that, should the owner not call for the bond or become known to the bank by June 30, 2009, the bank would redeliver the bond to Swan. On July 1, 2009, Swan learned that the owner of the bond had not called for it, nor was his identity known to the bank. Swan then asked that the bond be returned to him. The bank refused, stating that it would continue to hold the bond until the owner claimed it. Explain whether Swan will prevail in his action to recover possession of the bond.

**11.** Lile, an insurance broker who handled all insurance for Tempo Co., purchased a fire policy from Insurance Company insuring Tempo Co.'s factory against fire in the amount of $1.5 million. Before the policy was delivered to Tempo and while it was still in Lile's hands, Tempo advised Lile to cancel the policy. Prior to cancellation, however, Tempo suffered a loss. Tempo now makes a claim against Insurance Company on the policy. The premium had been billed to Lile but was unpaid at the time of loss. In an action by Tempo Co. against Insurance Company, what judgment?

**12.** On July 15, Adler purchased in Chicago a Buick sedan, intending to drive it that day to St. Louis, Missouri. He telephoned a friend, Maruchek, who was in the insurance business, and told him that he wanted liability insurance on the automobile, limited in amount to $50,000 for injuries to one person and to $100,000 for any one accident. Maruchek took the order and told Adler over the telephone that he was covered and that his policy would be written by the Young Insurance Company. Later that same day and before Maruchek had informed the Young Insurance Company of Adler's application, Adler negligently operated the automobile and seriously injured Brown, who brings suit against Adler. Is Adler covered by liability insurance?

**13.** Graham owns a building having a fair market value of $120,000. She takes out a fire insurance policy from the Bentley Insurance Company for $72,000; the policy contains an 80 percent co-insurance clause. The building is damaged by fire to the extent of $48,000. How much insurance is Graham entitled to collect?

**14.** Phil was the owner of a herd of twenty highly bred dairy cows. He was a prosperous farmer, but his health was very poor. On the advice of his doctor, Phil decided to winter in Arizona. Before he left, he made an agreement with Freya under which Freya was to keep the cows on Freya's farm through the winter, be paid the sum of $800 by Phil, and return to Phil the twenty cows at the close of the winter. For reasons that Freya thought made good farming sense, Freya sold six of the cows and replaced them with six other cows. After winter was over, Phil returned from Arizona. Is Freya liable for conversion of the original six cows? Why?

**15.** Hines stored her furniture, including a grand piano, in Arnett's warehouse. Needing more space, Arnett stored Hines's piano in Butler's warehouse next door. As a result of a fire, which occurred without any fault of Arnett or Butler, both warehouses and their contents were destroyed. Is Arnett liable to Hines for the value of her piano and furniture? Explain.

**16.** Curtis rented a safe deposit box from Reliable Safe Deposit Company, in which he deposited valuable securities and $4,000 in cash. Later, after opening the box and discovering $1,000 missing, Curtis brought an action against Reliable. At the trial, the company showed that its customary procedure was as follows: that there were two keys for each box furnished to each renter; that if a key was lost, the lock was changed; that new keys were provided for each lock each time a box was rented; that there were two clerks in charge of the vault; and that one of the clerks was always present to open the box. Reliable Safe Deposit Company also proved that two keys were given to Curtis at the time he rented his box; that his box could not be opened without the use of one of the keys in his possession; and that the company had issued no other keys to Curtis's box. Explain whether Reliable is obligated to pay Curtis for the missing $1,000.

**17.** A, B, and C each stored five thousand bushels of yellow corn in the same bin in X's warehouse. X wrongfully sold ten thousand bushels of this corn to Y. A contends that inasmuch as his five thousand bushels of corn were placed in the bin first, the remaining five thousand bushels belong to him. What are the rights of the parties?

**18.** **(a)** On April 1, Mary Rich, at the solicitation of Super Fur Company, delivered a $3,000 mink coat to the company at its place of business for storage in its vaults until November 1. On the same day, she paid the company its customary charge of $20 for such storage. After Mary left the store, the general manager of the company, on finding that its storage vaults were already filled to capacity, delivered Mary's coat to Swift Trucking Company for shipment to Fur Storage Company. En route, the truck in which Mary's coat was being transported was badly damaged by fire caused by the driver's negligence, and Mary's coat was totally destroyed. Is Super Fur Company liable to Mary for the value of her coat? Why?

**(b)** Would your answer be the same if Mary's coat had been safely delivered to Fur Storage Company and had been stolen from the company's storage vaults without negligence on its part? Why?

**19.** Rich, a club member, left his golf clubs with Bogan, the pro at the Happy Hours Country Club, to be refinished at Bogan's pro shop. The refinisher employed by Bogan suddenly left town, taking Rich's clubs with him. The refinisher had previously been above suspicion, although Bogan had never checked on the man's character references. A valuable sand wedge that Bogan had borrowed from another member, Smith, for his own use in an important tournament was also stolen by the refinisher, as well as several pairs of golf shoes that Bogan had checked for members without charge as an accommodation. The club members concerned each made claims against Bogan for their losses. Can (a) Rich, (b) Smith, and (c) the other members compel Bogan to make good their respective losses?

**20.** Donna drove an automobile into Terry's garage and requested him to make repairs for which the charge would be $125. Donna, however, never returned to get the automobile. Two months later, Carla saw the automobile in Terry's garage and claimed it as her own, asserting that it had been stolen from her. Terry told Carla that she could have the automobile if she paid for the repairs and storage. One week later, Molly appeared and proved that the automobile was hers, that it had been stolen from her, and that neither Donna nor Carla had any rights in it. Discuss whether Terry is liable for conversion of the automobile.

**21.** On June 1, Cain delivered his 2007 automobile to Barr, the operator of a repair shop, for necessary repairs. Barr put the car in his lot on Main Street. The lot, which is fenced on all sides except along Main Street, holds one hundred cars and is unguarded at night, although the police make periodic checks. The lot is well lighted. The cars do not have the keys in them when left out overnight. At some time during the night of June 4, the hood, starter, alternator, and gearshift were stolen from Cain's car. The car remained on the lot, and during the evening of June 5, the transmission was stolen from the car. The cost to replace the parts stolen in the first theft was $1,900 and in the second theft $4,800. Did Barr exercise due care in taking care of the automobile?

**22.** Seton in Phoenix, according to a contract with Rider in New York, ships to Rider goods conforming to the contract and takes from the carrier a shipper's order bill of lading that Seton indorses in blank and forwards by mail to Clemson, his agent in New York, with instructions to deliver the bill of lading to Rider on receipt of payment of the price for the goods. Forest, a thief, steals the bill of lading from Clemson and transfers it for value to Pace, a *bona fide* purchaser. Before the goods arrive in New York, Rider is insolvent. What are the rights of the parties?

**23.** Scarola purchased an automobile for value and without knowledge that it was stolen. After he insured the car with Insurance Company of North America (INA) the car was stolen once again. When INA refused to reimburse Scarola for the loss, contending that he did not have an insurable interest in the car, Scarola brought an action. Did Scarola have an insurable interest in the automobile? Why?

**24.** Sears had sold to and installed in the Seven Palms Motor Inn a number of furnishings, including drapes and bedspreads, in connection with the construction of a motel on land Seven Palms owned. Sears did not receive payment in full for the materials and labor and brought suit to recover $8,357.49, with interest, and to establish a mechanic's lien on the motel and land for the unpaid portion of the furnishings. Seven Palms asserted that neither the drapes nor bedspreads were fixtures and that, thus, Sears could not obtain a mechanic's lien on them. Explain whether the drapes and bedspreads are fixtures.

**25.** David E. Ross, his two brothers, and their families operated and owned the entire stock of five businesses. Ross had three children: Rod, David II, and Betsy. David II and Betsy were not involved in the operation of the companies, but Rod began working for one of the firms, Equitable Life and Casualty

Insurance Company, in 2004. Between 2006 and 2010, the elder Ross informed a number of persons of his desire to reward Rod for his work with Equitable Life by giving him stock in addition to the stock he would inherit. He subsequently executed several stock transfers to Rod, representing shares in various family businesses, which were reflected by appropriate entries on the corporate books. Certificates were issued in Rod's name and placed in an envelope identified with the name Rod Ross, but they were kept with the other family stock certificates in an office safe to which Rod did not have access. In all, one-fourth of the stock holdings of David E. Ross were transferred to Rod in this manner. This fact is consistent with the elder Ross's expressed intention that Rod should ultimately receive a total of one-half of the stock upon his father's death. David E. died in April 2010. His will divided the estate equally among the three children and made no reference to prior gifts of stock to Rod. David II and Betsy brought an action contesting the validity of the stock transfers. Are the *inter vivos* gifts of the stock valid? Explain.

**26.** Mrs. Laval was a patient of Dr. Leopold, a practicing psychiatrist. Dr. Leopold shared an office with two associates practicing in the same field. No receptionist or other employee attended the office. Mrs. Laval placed her coat in the clothes closet in the office reception room. Later, when she returned to retrieve the coat to leave, she found it missing. Is Dr. Leopold liable to Mrs. Laval for the value of her coat? Explain.

**27.** Mr. Sewall left his car in a parking lot owned by Fitz-Inn Auto Parks, Inc. The lot was approximately one hundred by two hundred feet in size and had a chain link fence along the rear boundary to separate the lot from a facility of the Massachusetts Bay Transportation Authority. Although the normal entrance and exit were located at the front of the lot, it was also possible to leave by way of small side streets on either side of the lot. Upon entering the lot, the driver would pay the attendant on duty a fee of $0.25 to park. The attendant's duties were limited to collecting money from patrons and directing them to parking spaces. Ordinarily, the attendant remained on duty until 11:00 A.M., after which time the lot was left unattended. Furthermore, a patron could remove his car from the lot at any time without interference by any employee of the parking lot.

On the morning of April 15, Sewall entered the lot, paid the $0.25 fee, parked his car in a space designated by the attendant, locked it, and took the keys with him. This was a routine he had followed for several years. When he returned to the unattended lot that evening, however, he found that his car was gone, apparently having been stolen by an unidentified third person. Is Fitz-Inn, the owner of the lot, liable for the value of the car? Why?

**28.** Mrs. Mieske delivered thirty-two fifty-foot reels of developed movie film to the Bartell Drug Company to be spliced together into four reels for viewing convenience. She placed the films, which contained irreplaceable pictures of her family's activities over a period of years, into the order in which they were to be spliced and then delivered them to the manager of Bartell. The manager placed a film processing packet on the bag of films and gave Mrs. Mieske a receipt that stated, "We assume no responsibility beyond retail cost of film unless otherwise agreed to in writing." Although the disclaimer was not discussed, Mrs. Mieske's parting words to the store manager were, "Don't lose these. They are my life."

Bartell sent the film to its processing agent, GAF Corporation, which intended to send them to another processing lab for splicing. While at the GAF laboratory, however, the film was accidentally placed in the garbage dumpster and was never recovered. Upon learning of the loss of their film, the Mieskes brought action to recover damages from Bartell and GAF. The defendants argued that their liability was limited to the cost of the unexposed film. Are GAF or Bartell liable to the Mieskes? If so, for how much?

**29.** Plaintiff, Heath Benjamin (Benjamin), found more than $18,000 in currency inside the wing of an airplane. At the time of this discovery, State Central Bank (State) owned the plane and it was being serviced by Lindner Aviation, Inc. (Lindner). Benjamin at the time was employed by Lindner and was conducting a routine annual inspection of the plane.

As part of the inspection, Benjamin removed panels from the underside of the wings. Although these panels were to be removed annually as part of the routine inspection, a couple of the screws holding the panel on the left wing were so rusty that Benjamin had to use a drill to remove them. Benjamin testified that the panel probably had not been removed for several years. Inside the left wing Benjamin discovered two packets approximately four inches high and wrapped in aluminum foil. He removed the packets from the wing and took off the foil wrapping. Inside the foil was approximately $18,000, tied in string and wrapped in handkerchiefs. The money was eventually turned over to the Keokuk police department.

No one came forward within twelve months claiming to be the true owner of the money. Explain who is entitled to receive the money.

**30.** Calvin Klein, Ltd. (Calvin Klein), a New York clothing company, had used the services of Trylon Trucking Corporation (Trylon) for more than three years, involving hundreds of shipments, prior to the lost shipment at issue. After completing each carriage, Trylon would forward to Calvin Klein an invoice that contained a limitation of liability provision. The provision stated, "In consideration of the rate charged, the shipper agrees that the carrier shall not be liable for more than $50.00 on any shipment accepted for delivery to one consignee unless a greater value is declared, in writing, upon receipt at time of shipment and charge for such greater value paid, or agreed to be paid, by shipper."

On April 2, Trylon dispatched its driver Jamahl Jefferson to the J.F.K. International Airport to pick up 2,833 blouses sent from Hong Kong, China, to Calvin Klein. The driver disappeared, stealing both the truck and the blouses. Calvin Klein sued Trylon for the full value of the blouses. Does the limitation of liability provision extend to the shipment? Explain.

# APPENDICES

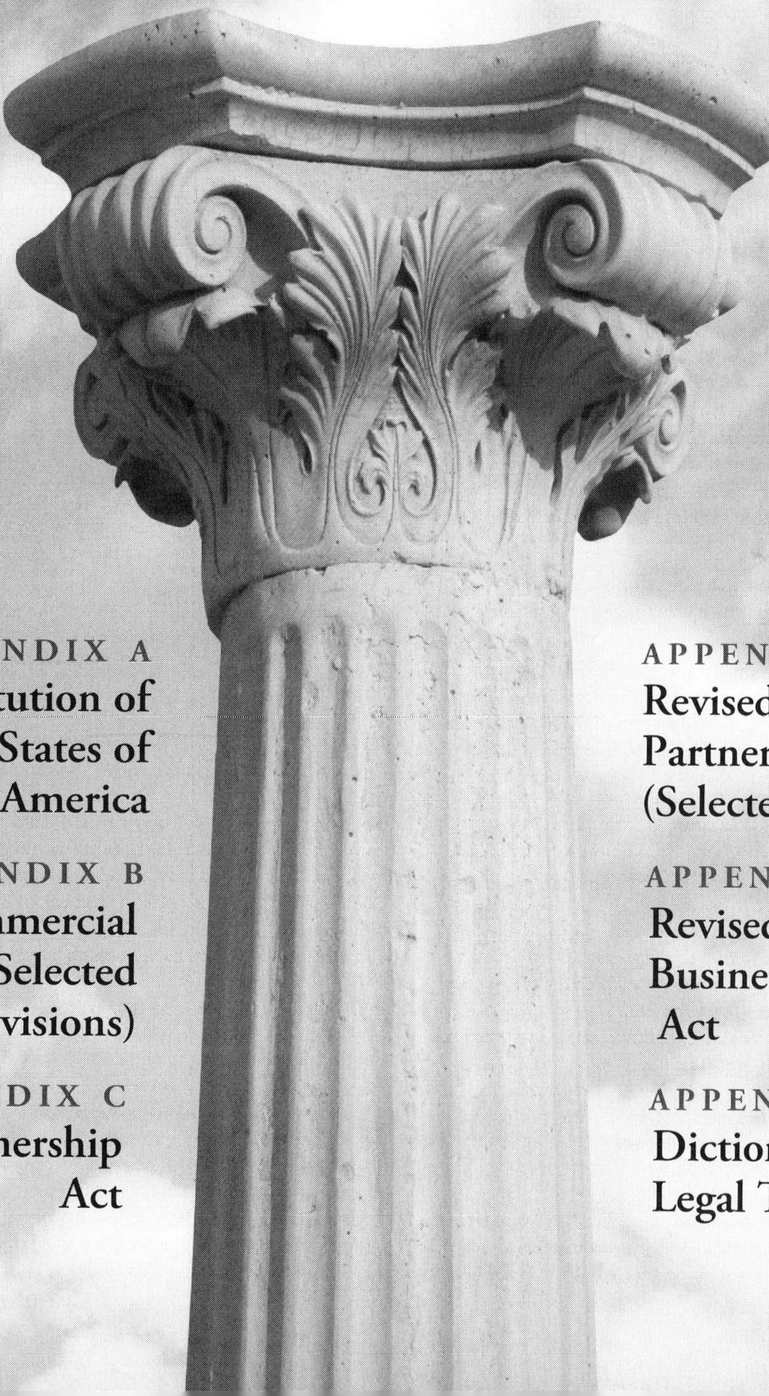

**APPENDIX A**
The Constitution of the United States of America

**APPENDIX B**
Uniform Commercial Code (Selected Provisions)

**APPENDIX C**
Uniform Partnership Act

**APPENDIX D**
Revised Uniform Partnership Act (Selected Provisions)

**APPENDIX E**
Revised Model Business Corporation Act

**APPENDIX F**
Dictionary of Legal Terms

APPENDIX A

# The Constitution of the United States of America

We the People of the United States, in Order to form a more perfect Union, establish Justice, insure domestic Tranquility, provide for the common defense, promote the general Welfare, and secure the Blessings of Liberty to ourselves and our Posterity, do ordain and establish this Constitution for the United States of America.

## ARTICLE I

### *Section 1*

All legislative Powers herein granted shall be vested in a Congress of the United States, which shall consist of a Senate and House of Representatives.

### *Section 2*

The House of Representatives shall be composed of Members chosen every second Year by the People of the several States, and the Electors in each State shall have the Qualifications requisite for Electors of the most numerous Branch of the State Legislature.

No Person shall be a Representative who shall not have attained to the Age of twenty five Years, and been seven Years a Citizen of the United States, and who shall not, when elected, be an Inhabitant of that State in which he shall be chosen.

Representatives and direct Taxes shall be apportioned among the several States which may be included within this Union, according to their respective Numbers, which shall be determined by adding to the whole Number of free Persons, including those bound to Service for a Term of Years, and excluding Indians not taxed, three fifths of all other Persons. The actual Enumeration shall be made within three Years after the first Meeting of the Congress of the United States, and within every subsequent Term of ten Years, in such Manner as they shall by Law direct. The number of Representatives shall not exceed one for every thirty Thousand, but each State shall have at Least one Representative; and until such enumeration shall be made, the State of New Hampshire shall be entitled to chuse three, Massachusetts eight, Rhode Island and Providence Plantations one, Connecticut five, New-York six, New Jersey four, Pennsylvania eight, Delaware one, Maryland six, Virginia ten, North Carolina five, South Carolina five, and Georgia three.

When vacancies happen in the Representation from any State, the Executive Authority thereof shall issue Writs of Election to fill such vacancies.

The House of Representatives shall chuse their Speaker and other Officers; and shall have the sole Power of Impeachment.

### *Section 3*

The Senate of the United States shall be composed of two Senators from each State, chosen by the Legislature thereof, for six Years; and each Senator shall have one Vote.

Immediately after they shall be assembled in Consequence of the first Election, they shall be divided as equally as may be into three Classes. The Seats of the Senators of the first Class shall be vacated at the Expiration of the second Year, of the second Class at the Expiration of the fourth Year, and of the third Class at the Expiration of the sixth Year, so that one third may be chosen every second Year; and if Vacancies happen by Resignation or otherwise, during the Recess of the Legislature of any State, the Executive thereof may make temporary Appointments until the next Meeting of the Legislature, which shall then fill such Vacancies.

No Person shall be a Senator who shall not have attained to the Age of thirty Years, and been nine Years a Citizen of the United States, and who shall not, when elected, be an Inhabitant of that State for which he shall be chosen.

The Vice President of the United States shall be President of the Senate, but shall have no Vote, unless they be equally divided.

The Senate shall chuse their other Officers, and also a President pro tempore, in the Absence of the Vice President, or when he shall exercise the Office of President of the United States.

The Senate shall have the sole power to try all Impeachments. When sitting for that Purpose, they shall be an Oath or Affirmation. When the President of the United States is tried, the Chief Justice shall preside: And no Person shall be convicted without the Concurrence of two thirds of the Members present.

Judgment in Cases of Impeachment shall not extend further than to removal from Office, and disqualification to hold and enjoy any Office of honor, Trust or Profit under the United States: but the Party convicted shall nevertheless be liable and subject to Indictment, Trial, Judgment and Punishment, according to Law.

### *Section 4*

The Times, Places and Manner of holding Elections for Senators and Representatives, shall be prescribed in each State by the Legislature thereof: but the Congress may at any time by Law make or alter such Regulations, except as to the Places of chusing Senators.

The Congress shall assemble at least once in every Year, and such Meeting shall be on the first Monday in December, unless they shall by Law appoint a different Day.

### *Section 5*

Each House shall be the Judge of the Elections, Returns and Qualifications of its own Members, and a Majority of each shall constitute a Quorum to do Business; but a smaller Number may adjourn from day to day, and may be authorized to compel the Attendance of absent Members, in such Manner, and under such Penalties as each House may provide.

Each House may determine the Rules of its Proceedings, punish its Members for disorderly Behaviour, and, with the Concurrence of two thirds, expel a Member.

Each House shall keep a Journal of its Proceedings, and from time to time publish the same, excepting such Parts as may in their Judgment require Secrecy; and the Yeas and Nays of the Members of either House on any question shall, at the Desire of one fifth of those Present, be entered on the Journal.

Neither House, during the Session of Congress, shall, without the Consent of the other, adjourn for more than three days, nor to any other Place than that in which the two Houses shall be sitting.

***Section 6***

The Senators and Representatives shall receive a Compensation for their Services, to be ascertained by Law, and paid out of the Treasury of the United States. They shall in all Cases, except Treason, Felony and Breach of the Peace, be privileged from Arrest and Breach of the Peace, be privileged from Arrest during their Attendance at the Session of their respective Houses, and in going to and returning from the same; and for any Speech or Debate in either House, they shall not be questioned in any other Place.

No Senator or Representative shall, during the Time for which he was elected, be appointed to any civil Office under the Authority of the United States, which shall have been created, or the Emoluments whereof shall have been encreased during such time; and no Person holding any Office under the United States, shall be a Member of either House during his Continuance in Office.

***Section 7***

All Bills for raising Revenue shall originate in the House of Representatives; but the Senate may propose or concur with Amendments as on other Bills.

Every Bill which shall have passed the House of Representatives and the Senate, shall, before it become a Law, be presented to the President of the United States; If he approve he shall sign it, but if not he shall return it, with his Objections to that House in which it shall have originated, who shall enter the Objections at large on their Journal, and proceed to reconsider it. If after such Reconsideration two thirds of that House shall agree to pass the Bill, it shall be sent, together with the Objections, to the other House, by which it shall likewise be reconsidered, and if approved by two thirds of that House, it shall become a Law. But in all such Cases the Votes of both Houses shall be determined by Yeas and Nays, and the Names of the Persons voting for and against the Bill shall be entered on the Journal of each House respectively. If any Bill shall not be returned by the President within ten Days (Sundays excepted) after it shall have been presented to him, the Same shall be a Law, in like Manner as if he had signed it, unless the Congress by their Adjournment prevent its Return, in which Case it shall not be a Law.

Every Order, Resolution, or Vote to which the Concurrence of the Senate and House of Representatives may be necessary (except on a question of Adjournment) shall be presented to the President of the United States; and before the Same shall take Effect, shall be approved by him, or being disapproved by him, shall be repassed by two thirds of the Senate and House of Representatives, according to the Rules and Limitations prescribed in the Case of a Bill.

***Section 8***

The Congress shall have Power to lay and collect Taxes, Duties, Imposts and Excises, to pay the Debts and provide for the common Defense and general Welfare of the United States; but all Duties, Imposts and Excises shall be uniform throughout the United States;

To borrow Money on the credit of the United States;

To regulate Commerce with foreign Nations, and among the several States, and with the Indian Tribes;

To establish an uniform Rule of Naturalization, and uniform Laws on the subject of Bankruptcies throughout the United States;

To coin Money, regulate the Value thereof, and of foreign Coin, and fix the Standard of Weights and Measures;

To provide for the Punishment of counterfeiting the Securities and current Coin of the United States;

To establish Post Offices and post Roads;

To promote the Progress of Science and useful Arts, by securing for limited Times to Authors and Inventors the exclusive Right to their respective Writings and Discoveries;

To constitute Tribunals inferior to the supreme Court;

To define and punish Piracies and Felonies committed on the high Seas, and Offenses against the Law of Nations;

To declare War, grant Letters of Marque and Reprisal, and make Rules concerning Captures on Land and Water;

To raise and support Armies, but no Appropriation of Money to that Use shall be for a longer Term than two Years;

To provide and maintain a Navy;

To make Rules for the Government and Regulation of the land and naval Forces;

To provide for calling forth the Militia to execute the Laws of the Union, suppress Insurrections and repel Invasions;

To provide for organizing, arming, and disciplining, the Militia, and for governing such Part of them as may be employed in the Service of the United States, reserving to the States respectively, the Appointment of the Officers, and the Authority of training the Militia according to the discipline described by Congress;

To exercise exclusive Legislation in all Cases whatsoever, over such District (not exceeding ten Miles square) as may, by Cession of particular States, and the Acceptance of Congress, become the Seat of the Government of the United States, and to exercise like Authority over all Places purchased by the Consent of the Legislature of the State in which the Same shall be, for the Erection of Forts, Magazines, Arsenals, dock-Yards, and other needful Buildings;—And

To make all Laws which shall be necessary and proper for carrying into Execution the foregoing Powers, and all other Powers vested by this Constitution in the Government of the United States, or in any Department or Officer thereof.

***Section 9***

The Migration or Importation of such Persons as any of the States now existing shall think proper to admit, shall not be prohibited by the Congress prior to the Year one thousand eight hundred and eight, but a Tax of Duty may be imposed on such Importation, not exceeding ten dollars for each Person.

The Privilege of the Writ of Habeas Corpus shall not be suspended, unless when in Cases of Rebellion or Invasion the public Safety may require it.

No Bill of Attainder or ex post facto Law shall be passed.

No Capitation, or other direct, Tax shall be laid, unless in Proportion to the Census or Enumeration herein before directed to be taken.

No Tax or Duty shall be laid on Articles exported from any State.

No Preference shall be given by any Regulation of Commerce or Revenue to the Ports of one State over those of another; nor shall Vessels bound to, or from, one State, be obliged to enter, clear, or pay Duties in another.

No Money shall be drawn from the Treasury, but in Consequence of Appropriations made by Laws; and a regular Statement and Account of the Receipts and Expenditures of all public Money shall be published from time to time.

No Title of Nobility shall be granted by the United States: And no Person holding any Office of Profit or Trust under them, shall, without the Consent of the Congress, accept of any present, Emolument, Office, or Title, of any kind whatever, from any King, Prince, or foreign State.

***Section 10***

No State shall enter into any Treaty, Alliance, or Confederation; grant Letters of Marque and Reprisal; coin Money; emit Bills of Credit; make any Thing but gold and silver Coin a Tender in Payment of Debts; pass any Bill of Attainder, ex post facto Law, or Law impairing the Obligation of Contracts, or grant any Title of Nobility.

No State shall, without the Consent of the Congress, lay any Imposts or Duties on Imports or Exports, except what may be absolutely necessary for executing its inspection Laws: and the net Produce of all Duties and Imposts, laid by any State on Imports or Exports, shall be for the Use of the Treasury of the United States; and all such Laws shall be subject to the Revision and Controul of the Congress.

No State shall, without the Consent of Congress, lay any Duty of Tonnage, keep Troops, or Ships of War in time of Peace, enter into any Agreement or Compact with another State, or with a foreign Power, or engage in War, unless actually invaded, or in such imminent Danger as will not admit of delay.

## ARTICLE II

### *Section 1*

The executive Power shall be vested in a President of the United States of America. He shall hold his Office during the Term of four Years, and, together with the Vice President, chosen for the same Term, be elected, as follows:

Each State shall appoint, in such Manner as the Legislature thereof may direct, a Number of Electors, equal to the whole Number of Senators and Representatives to which the State may be entitled in the Congress: but no Senator or Representative, or Person holding an Office of Trust or Profit under the United States, shall be appointed an Elector.

The Electors shall meet in their respective States, and vote by Ballot for two Persons, of whom one at least shall not be an Inhabitant of the same State with themselves. And they shall make a list of all the Persons voted for, and of the Number of Votes for each; which List they shall sign and certify, and transmit sealed to the Seat of the Government of the United States, directed to the President of the Senate. The President of the Senate shall, in the presence of the Senate and House of Representatives, open all the Certificates, and the Votes shall be counted. The Person having the greatest Number of Votes shall be the President, if such Number be a Majority of the whole Number of Electors appointed; and if there be more than one who have such Majority, and have an equal Number of Votes, then the House of Representatives shall immediately chuse by Ballot one of them for President; and if no Person have a Majority, then from the five highest on the List the said House shall in like Manner chuse the President. But in chusing the President, the Votes shall be taken by States, the Representation from each State having one Vote; A quorum for this Purpose shall consist of a Member or Members from two thirds of the States, and a Majority of all the States shall be necessary to a Choice. In every Case, after the Choice of the President, the Person having the Greatest Number of Votes of the Electors shall be the Vice President. But if there should remain two or more who have equal Votes, the Senate shall chuse from them by Ballot the Vice President.

The Congress may determine the Time of Chusing the Electors, and the Day on which they shall give their Votes; which Day shall be the same throughout the United States.

No Person except a natural born Citizen, or a Citizen of the United States, at the time of the Adoption of this Constitution, shall be eligible to the Office of President; neither shall any Person be eligible to that Office who shall not have attained to the Age of thirty five Years, and been fourteen Years a Resident within the United States.

In Case of the Removal of the President from Office, or of his Death, Resignation, or Inability to discharge the Powers and Duties of the said Office, the Same shall devolve on the Vice President, and the Congress may by Law provide for the Case of Removal, Death, Resignation or Inability, both of the President and Vice President, declaring what Officer shall then act as President, and such Officer shall act accordingly, until the Disability be removed, or a President shall be elected.

The President shall, at stated Times, receive for his Services, a Compensation, which shall neither be encreased nor diminished during the Period for which he shall have been elected, and he shall not receive within that Period any other Emolument from the United States, or any of them.

Before he enter on the Execution of his Office, he shall take the following Oath or Affirmation:—"I do solemnly swear (or affirm) that I will faithfully execute the Office of President of the United States, and will to the best of my Ability, preserve, protect and defend the Constitution of the United States."

### *Section 2*

The President shall be Commander in Chief of the Army and Navy of the United States, and of the Militia of the several States, when called into the actual Service of the United States; he may require the Opinion, in writing, of the principal Officer in each of the executive Departments, upon any Subject relating to the Duties of their respective Offices, and he shall have Power to grant Reprieves and Pardons for Offences against the United States, except in Cases of Impeachment.

He shall have Power, by and with the Advice and Consent of the Senate, to make Treaties, providing two thirds of the Senators present concur; and he shall nominate, and by and with the Advice and Consent of the Senate, shall appoint Ambassadors, other public Ministers and Consuls, Judges of the supreme Court, and all other Officers of the United States, whose Appointments are not herein otherwise provided for, and which shall be established by Law: but the Congress may by Law vest the Appointment of such inferior Officers, as they think proper, in the President alone, in the Courts of Law, or in the Heads of Departments.

The President shall have Power to fill up all Vacancies that may happen during the Recess of the Senate, by granting Commissions which shall expire at the End of their next Session.

### *Section 3*

He shall from time to time give to the Congress Information of the State of the Union, and recommend to their Consideration such Measures as he shall judge necessary and expedient; he may, on extraordinary Occasions, convene both Houses, or either of them, and in Case of Disagreement between them, with Respect to the Time of Adjournment, he may adjourn them to such Time as he shall think proper, he shall receive Ambassadors and other public Ministers; he shall take Care that the Laws be faithfully executed, and shall Commission all the Offices of the United States.

### *Section 4*

The President, Vice President and all civil Officers of the United States, shall be removed from Office on Impeachment for, and Conviction of, Treason, Bribery, or other high Crimes and Misdemeanors.

## ARTICLE III

### *Section 1*

The judicial Power of the United States, shall be vested in one supreme Court, and in such inferior Courts as the Congress may from time to time ordain and establish. The Judges, both of the supreme and inferior Courts, shall hold their Offices during good Behaviour, and shall, at Times, receive for their Services, a Compensation, which shall not be diminished during their Continuance in Office.

### *Section 2*

The judicial Power shall extend to all Cases, in Law and Equity, arising under this Constitution, the Laws of the United States, and Treaties made, or which shall be made, under their Authority;—to all Cases affecting Ambassadors, other public Ministers and Consuls;—to all Cases of admiralty and maritime Jurisdiction;—to Controversies to which the United States shall be a Party;—to controversies between two or more States;—between a State and Citizens of another State;— between Citizens of different States;—between Citizens of the same State claiming Lands under Grants of different States; and between a State, or the Citizens thereof, and foreign States, Citizens or Subjects.

In all Cases affecting Ambassadors, other public Ministers and Consuls, and those in which a State shall be Party, the supreme Court shall have original Jurisdiction. In all the other Cases before mentioned, the supreme Court shall have appellate Jurisdiction, both as to Law and Fact, with such Exceptions, and under such Regulations as the Congress shall make.

The Trial of all Crimes, except in Cases of Impeachment, shall be by Jury; and such Trial shall be held in the State where the said Crimes shall have been committed; but when not committed within any State, the Trial shall be at such Place or Places as the Congress may by Law have directed.

***Section 3***

Treason against the United States, shall consist only in levying War against them, or in adhering to their Enemies, giving them Aid and Comfort. No Person shall be convicted of Treason unless on the Testimony of two Witnesses to the same overt Act, or on Confession in open Court.

The Congress shall have Power to declare the Punishment of Treason, but no Attainder of Treason shall work Corruption of Blood, or Forfeiture except during the Life of the Person attainted.

## ARTICLE IV

***Section 1***

Full Faith and Credit shall be given in each State to the public Acts, Records, and judicial Proceedings of every other State. And the Congress may by general Laws prescribe the Manner in which such Arts, Records and Proceedings shall be proved, and the Effect thereof.

***Section 2***

The Citizens of each State shall be entitled to all Privileges and Immunities of Citizens in the several States.

A Person charged in any State with Treason, Felony, or other Crime, who shall flee from Justice, and be found in another State, shall on Demand of the executive Authority of the State from which he fled, be delivered up, to be removed to the State having Jurisdiction of the Crime.

No Person held to Service or Labour in one State, under the Laws thereof, escaping into another, shall, in Consequence of any Law or Regulation therein, be discharged from such Service or Labour, but shall be delivered up on Claim of the Party to whom such Service or Labour may be due.

***Section 3***

New States may be admitted by the Congress into this Union; but no new State shall be formed or erected within the Jurisdiction of any other State; nor any State be formed by the Junction of two or more States, or Parts of States, without the Consent of the Legislatures of the States concerned as well as the Congress.

The Congress shall have Power to dispose of and make all needful Rules and Regulations respecting the Territory or other Property belonging to the United States; and nothing in this Constitution shall be so construed as to Prejudice any Claims of the United States, or of any particular State.

***Section 4***

The United States shall guarantee to every State in this Union a Republican Form of Government, and shall protect each of them against Invasion; and on Application of the Legislature, or of the Executive (when the Legislature cannot be convened) against domestic Violence.

## ARTICLE V

The Congress, whenever two thirds of both Houses shall deem it necessary, shall propose Amendments to this Constitution, or, on the Application of the Legislatures of two thirds of the several States, shall call a Convention for proposing Amendments, which, in either Case, shall be valid to all Intents and Purposes, as Part of this Constitution, when ratified by the Legislatures of three fourths of the several States, or by Conventions in three fourths thereof, as the one or the other Mode of Ratification may be proposed by the Congress; Provided that no Amendment which may be made prior to the Year One thousand eight hundred and eight shall in any Manner affect the first and fourth Clauses in the Ninth Section of the first Article; and that no State, without its Consent, shall be deprived of its equal Suffrage in the Senate.

## ARTICLE VI

All Debts contracted and Engagements entered into, before the Adoption of this Constitution, shall be as valid against the United States under this Constitution, as under the Confederation.

This Constitution, and the Laws of the United States which shall be made in Pursuance thereof; and all Treaties made, or which shall be made, under the Authority of the United States, shall be the supreme Law of the Land; and the Judges in every State shall be bound thereby, any Thing in the Constitution or Laws of any State to the Contrary notwithstanding.

The Senators and Representatives before mentioned, and the Members of the several State Legislatures, and all executive and judicial Officers, both of the United States and of the Several States, shall be bound by Oath or Affirmation, to support this Constitution; but no religious Test shall ever be required as a Qualification to any Office or public Trust under the United States.

## ARTICLE VII

The Ratification of the Conventions of nine States, shall be sufficient for the Establishment of this Constitution between the States so ratifying the Same.

***Amendment I [1791]***

Congress shall make no law respecting an establishment of religion, or prohibiting the free exercise thereof; or abridging the freedom of speech, or the press; or the right of the people peaceably to assemble, and to petition the Government for a redress of grievances.

***Amendment II [1791]***

A well regulated Militia, being necessary to the security for a free State, the right of the people to keep and bear Arms, shall not be infringed.

***Amendment III [1791]***

No Soldier shall, in time of peace be quartered in any house, without the consent of the Owner, nor in time of war, but in a manner to be prescribed by law.

***Amendment IV [1791]***

The right of the people to be secure in their persons, houses, papers, and effects, against unreasonable searches and seizures, shall not be violated, and no Warrants shall issue, but upon probable cause, supported by Oath or Affirmation, and particularly describing the place to be searched, and the persons or things to be seized.

***Amendment V [1791]***

No person shall be held to answer for a capital, or otherwise infamous crime, unless on a presentment or indictment of a Grand Jury, except in cases arising in the land or naval forces, or in the Militia, when in actual service in time of War or public danger; nor shall any person be subject for the same offense to be twice put in jeopardy of life or limb; nor shall be compelled in any criminal case to be a witness against himself, nor be deprived of life, liberty, or property, without due process of law; nor shall private property be taken for public use, without just compensation.

***Amendment VI [1791]***

In all criminal prosecutions, the accused shall enjoy the right to a speedy and public trial, by an impartial jury of the State and district wherein the crime shall have been committed, which district shall have been previously ascertained by law, and to be informed of the nature and cause of the accusation; to be confronted with the Witnesses against him; to have compulsory process for obtaining witnesses in his favor, and to have the Assistance of counsel for his defense.

***Amendment VII [1791]***

In suits at common law, where the value in controversy shall exceed twenty dollars, the right of trial by jury shall be preserved, and no fact tried by a jury, shall be otherwise re-examined in any Court of the United States, than according to the rules of the common law.

***Amendment VIII [1791]***
Excessive bail shall not be required, no excessive fines imposed, nor cruel and unusual punishments inflicted.

***Amendment IX [1791]***
The enumeration in the Constitution, of certain rights, shall not be construed to deny or disparage others retained by the people.

***Amendment X [1791]***
The powers not delegated to the United States by the Constitution, nor prohibited by it to the States, are reserved to the States respectively, or to the people.

***Amendment XI [1798]***
The judicial power of the United States shall not be construed to extend to any suit in law or equity, commenced or prosecuted against one of the United States by Citizens of another State, or by Citizens or Subjects of any Foreign State.

***Amendment XII [1804]***
The Electors shall meet in their respective states and vote by ballot for President and Vice-President, one of whom, at least, shall not be an inhabitant of the same state with themselves; they shall name in their ballots the person voted for as President, and in distinct ballots the person voted for as Vice-President, and they shall make distinct lists of all persons voted for as President, and of all persons voted for as Vice-President, and of the number of votes for each, which lists they shall sign and certify, and transmit sealed to the seat of the government of the United States, directed to the President of the Senate;—The President of the Senate shall, in the presence of the Senate and House of Representatives, open all the certificates and the votes shall then be counted;—The person having the greatest number of votes for President, shall be the President, if such a number be a majority of the whole number of Electors appointed; and if no person have such majority, then from the persons having the highest numbers not exceeding three on the list of those voted for as President, the House of Representatives shall choose immediately, by ballot, the President. But in choosing the President, the votes shall be taken by states, the representation from each state having one vote; a quorum for this purpose shall consist of a member or members from two-thirds of the states, and a majority of all the states shall be necessary to a choice. And if the House of Representatives shall not choose a President whenever the right of choice shall devolve upon them, before the fourth day of March next following, then the Vice-President shall act as President, as in the case of the death or other constitutional disability of the President. The person having the greatest number of votes as Vice-President, shall be the Vice-President, if such number be a majority of the whole number of Electors appointed, and if no person have a majority, then from the two highest numbers on the list, the Senate shall choose the Vice-President; a quorum for the purpose shall consist of two-thirds of the whole number of Senators, and a majority of the whole number shall be necessary to a choice. But no person constitutionally ineligible to the office of President shall be eligible to that of the Vice-President of the United States.

***Amendment XIII [1865]***
**Section 1.** Neither slavery nor involuntary servitude, except as a punishment for crime whereof the party shall have been duly convicted, shall exist within the United States, or any place subject to their jurisdiction.
**Section 2.** Congress shall have power to enforce this article by appropriate legislation.

***Amendment XIV [1868]***
**Section 1.** All persons born or naturalized in the United States, and subject to the jurisdiction thereof, are citizens of the United States and of the State wherein they reside. No State shall make or enforce any law which shall abridge the privileges or immunities of citizens of the United States; nor shall any State deprive any person of life, liberty, or property, without due process of law; nor deny to any person within its jurisdiction the equal protection of the laws.
**Section 2.** Representatives shall be appointed among the several States according to their respective numbers, counting the whole number of persons in each State, excluding Indians not taxed. But when the right to vote at any election for the choice of electors for President and Vice President of the United States, Representatives in Congress, the Executive and Judicial officers of a State, or the members of the Legislature thereof, is denied to any of the male inhabitants of such State, being twenty-one years of age, and citizens of the United States, or in any way abridged, except for participation in rebellion, or other crime, the basis of representation therein shall be reduced in the proportion which the number of such male citizens shall bear the whole number of male citizens twenty-one years of age in such State.
**Section 3.** No person shall be a Senator or Representative in Congress, or elector of President and Vice President, or hold any office, civil or military, under the United States, or under any State, who, having previously taken an oath, as a member of Congress, or as an officer of the United States, or as a member of any State legislature, or as an executive or judicial officer of any State, to support the Constitution of the United States, shall have engaged in insurrection or rebellion against the same, or given aid or comfort to the enemies thereof. But Congress may by a vote of two-thirds of each House, remove such disability.
**Section 4.** The validity of the public debt of the United States, authorized by law, including debts incurred for payment of pensions and bounties for services in suppressing insurrection or rebellion, shall not be questioned. But neither the United States nor any State shall assume or pay any debt or obligation incurred in aid of insurrection of rebellion against the United States, or any claim for the loss or emancipation of any slave; but all such debts, obligations and claims shall be held illegal and void.
**Section 5.** The Congress shall have power to enforce, by appropriate legislation, the provisions of this article.

***Amendment XV [1870]***
**Section 1.** The right of citizens of the United States to vote shall not be denied or abridged by the United States or by any State on account of race, color, or previous condition of servitude.
**Section 2.** The Congress shall have power to enforce this article by appropriate legislation.

***Amendment XVI [1913]***
The Congress shall have power to lay and collect taxes on incomes, from whatever source derived, without apportionment among the several States, and without regard to any census or enumeration.

***Amendment XVII [1913]***
The Senate of the United States shall be composed of two Senators from each State, elected by the people thereof, for six years; and each Senator shall have one vote. The electors in each State shall have the qualifications requisite for electors of the most numerous branch of the State legislatures.

When vacancies happen in the representation of any State in the Senate, the executive authority of each State shall issue writs of election to fill such vacancies; Provided, That the legislature of any State may empower the executive thereof to make temporary appointments until the people fill the vacancies by election as the legislature may direct.

This amendment shall not be construed as to affect the election or term of any Senator chosen before it becomes valid as part of the Constitution.

***Amendment XVIII [1919]***
**Section 1.** After one year from the ratification of this article the manufacture, sale, or transportation of intoxicating liquors within, the importation thereof into, or the exportation thereof from the United States and all territory subject to the jurisdiction thereof for beverage purposes is hereby prohibited.
**Section 2.** The Congress and the several States shall have concurrent power to enforce this article by appropriate legislation.
**Section 3.** This article shall be inoperative unless it shall have been ratified as an amendment to the Constitution by the legislatures of the several States, as provided in the Constitution, within seven years from the date of the submission hereof to the States by the Congress.

*Amendment XIX [1920]*

The right of citizens of the United States to vote shall not be denied or abridged by the United States or by any State on account of sex.

Congress shall have power to enforce this article by appropriate legislation.

*Amendment XX [1933]*

**Section 1.** The terms of the President and Vice President shall end at noon on the 20th day of January, and the terms of Senators and Representatives at noon on the 3d day of January, of the years in which such terms would have ended if this article had not been ratified; and the terms of their successors shall then begin.

**Section 2.** The Congress shall assemble at least once in every year, and such meeting shall begin at noon on the 3d day of January, unless they shall by law appoint a different day.

**Section 3.** If, at the time fixed for the beginning of the term of the President, the President elect shall have died, the Vice President elect shall become President. If a President shall not have been chosen before the time fixed for the beginning of his term, or if the President elect shall have failed to qualify, then the Vice President elect shall act as President until a President shall have qualified; and the Congress may by law provide for the case wherein neither a President elect nor a Vice President elect shall have qualified, declaring who shall then act as President, or the manner in which one who is to act shall be selected, and such person shall act accordingly until a President or Vice President shall have qualified.

**Section 4.** The Congress may by law provide for the case of the death of any of the persons from whom the House of Representatives may choose a President whenever the right of choice shall have devolved upon them, and for the case of the death of any of the persons from whom the Senate may choose a Vice President whenever the right of choice shall have devolved upon them.

**Section 5.** Sections 1 and 2 shall take effect on the 15th day of October following the ratification of this article.

**Section 6.** This article shall be inoperative unless it shall have been ratified as an amendment to the Constitution by the legislatures of three-fourths of the several States within seven years from the date of its submission.

*Amendment XXI [1933]*

**Section 1.** The eighteenth article of amendment to the Constitution of the United States is hereby repealed.

**Section 2.** The transportation or importation into any State, Territory, or possession of the United States for delivery or use therein of intoxicating liquors, in violation of the laws thereof, is hereby prohibited.

**Section 3.** This article shall be inoperative unless it shall have been ratified as an amendment to the Constitution by conventions in the several States, as provided in the Constitution, within seven years from the date of the submission hereof to the States by the Congress.

*Amendment XXII [1951]*

**Section 1.** No person shall be elected to the office of the President more than twice, and no person who has held the office of President, or acted as President, for more than two years of a term to which some other person was elected President shall be elected to the office of the President more than once. But this Article shall not apply to any person holding the office of President when this Article was proposed by the Congress, and shall not prevent any person who may be holding the office of President, or acting as President, during the term within which this Article becomes operative from holding the office of President, or acting as President during the remainder of such term.

**Section 2.** This article shall be inoperative unless it shall have been ratified as an amendment to the Constitution by the legislatures of three-fourths of the several States within seven years from the date of its submission to the States by the Congress.

*Amendment XXIII [1961]*

**Section 1.** The District constituting the seat of Government of the United States shall appoint in such manner as the Congress may direct:

A number of electors of President and Vice President equal to the whole number of Senators and Representatives in Congress to which the District would be entitled if it were a State, but in no event more than the least populous State; they shall be in addition to those appointed by the States, but they shall be considered, for the purposes of the election of President and Vice President, to be electors appointed by a State; and they shall meet in the District and perform such duties as provided by the twelfth article of amendment.

**Section 2.** The Congress shall have power to enforce this article by appropriate legislation.

*Amendment XXIV [1964]*

**Section 1.** The right of citizens of the United States to vote in any primary or other election for President or Vice President, for electors for President or Vice President or for Senator or Representative in Congress, shall not be denied or abridged by the United States or any State by reason of failure to pay any poll tax or other tax.

**Section 2.** The Congress shall have power to enforce this article by appropriate legislation.

*Amendment XXV [1967]*

**Section 1.** In case of the removal of the President from office or of his death or resignation, the Vice President shall become President.

**Section 2.** Whenever there is a vacancy in the office of the Vice President, the President shall nominate a Vice President who shall take office upon confirmation by a majority vote of both Houses of Congress.

**Section 3.** Whenever the President transmits to the President pro tempore of the Senate and the Speaker of the House of Representatives his written declaration that he is unable to discharge the powers and duties of his office, and until he transmits to them a written declaration to the contrary, such powers and duties shall be discharged by the Vice President as Acting President.

**Section 4.** Whenever the Vice President and a majority of either the principal officers of the executive departments or of such other body as Congress may by law provide, transmit to the President pro tempore of the Senate and the Speaker of the House of Representatives their written declaration that the President is unable to discharge the powers and duties of his office, the Vice President shall immediately assume the powers and duties of the office as Acting President.

Thereafter, when the President transmits to the President pro tempore of the Senate and the Speaker of the House of Representatives his written declaration that no inability exists, he shall resume the powers and duties of his office unless the Vice President and a majority of either the principal officers of the executive department or of such other body as Congress may by law provide, transmit within four days to the President pro tempore of the Senate and the Speaker of the House of Representatives their written declaration that the President is unable to discharge the powers and duties of his office. Thereupon Congress shall decide the issue, assembling within forty-eight hours for that purpose if not in session. If the Congress, within twenty-one days after receipt of the latter written declaration, or, if Congress is not in session, within twenty-one days after Congress is required to assemble, determines by two-thirds vote of both Houses that the President is unable to discharge the powers and duties of his office, the Vice President shall continue to discharge the same as Acting President; otherwise, the President shall resume the powers and duties of his office.

*Amendment XXVI [1971]*

**Section 1.** The right of citizens of the United States, who are eighteen years of age or older, to vote shall not be denied or abridged by the United States or by any State on account of age.

**Section 2.** The Congress shall have power to enforce this article by appropriate legislation.

*Amendment XXVII [1992]*

No law, varying the compensation for the services of the Senators and Representatives, shall take effect, until an election of Representatives shall have intervened.

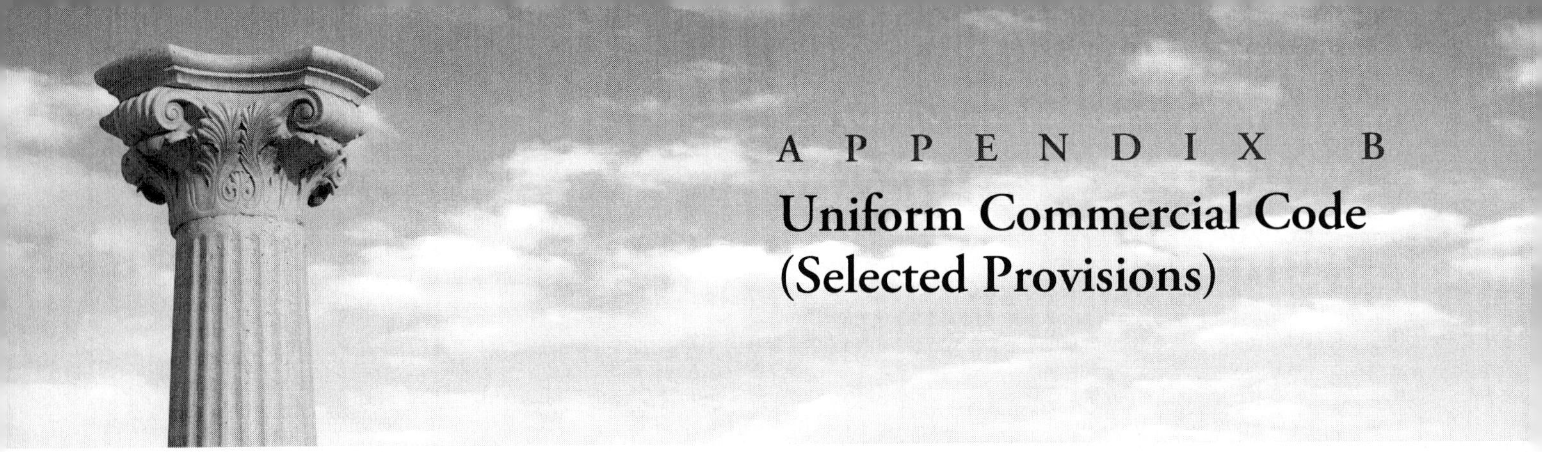

# APPENDIX B
# Uniform Commercial Code (Selected Provisions)

The Code consists of the following Articles:

1. General Provisions
2. Sales

2A. Leases

3. Negotiable Instruments
4. Bank Deposits and Collections

4A. Funds Transfers

5. Letters of Credit
6. Bulk Transfers
7. Warehouse Receipts, Bills of Lading and Other Documents of Title
8. Investment Securities
9. Secured Transactions
10. Effective Date and Repealer
11. Effective Date and Transition Provisions

**REVISION OF UNIFORM COMMERCIAL CODE**
**ARTICLE 1—GENERAL PROVISIONS**

## Part 1—General Provisions

**§1-101. Short Titles.**
(a) This [Act] may be cited as the Uniform Commercial Code.
(b) This article may be cited as Uniform Commercial Code—General Provisions.

**§1-102. Scope of Article.**
This article applies to a transaction to the extent that it is governed by another article of [the Uniform Commercial Code].

**§1-103. Construction of [Uniform Commercial Code] to Promote Its Purposes and Policies; Applicability of Supplemental Principles of Law.**
(a) [The Uniform Commercial Code] must be liberally construed and applied to promote its underlying purposes and policies, which are:
(1) to simplify, clarify, and modernize the law governing commercial transactions;
(2) to permit the continued expansion of commercial practices through custom, usage, and agreement of the parties; and
(3) to make uniform the law among the various jurisdictions.
(b) Unless displaced by the particular provisions of [the Uniform Commercial Code], the principles of law and equity, including the law merchant and the law relative to capacity to contract, principal and agent, estoppel, fraud, misrepresentation, duress, coercion, mistake, bankruptcy, and other validating or invalidating cause supplement its provisions.



**§1-104. Construction Against Implied Repeal.**
[The Uniform Commercial Code] being a general act intended as a unified coverage of its subject matter, no part of it shall be deemed to be impliedly repealed by subsequent legislation if such construction can reasonably be avoided.

**§1-105. Severability.**
If any provision or clause of [the Uniform Commercial Code] or its application to any person or circumstance is held invalid, the invalidity does not affect other provisions or applications of [the Uniform Commercial Code] which can be given effect without the invalid provision or application, and to this end the provisions of [the Uniform Commercial Code] are severable.

**§1-106. Use of Singular and Plural; Gender.**
In [the Uniform Commercial Code], unless the statutory context otherwise requires:
(1) words in the singular number include the plural, and those in the plural include the singular; and
(2) words of any gender also refer to any other gender.

**§1-107. Section Captions.**
Section captions are part of [the Uniform Commercial Code].

**§1-108. Relation to Electronic Signatures in Global and National Commerce Act.**
This article modifies, limits, and supersedes the federal Electronic Signatures in Global and National Commerce Act, 15 U.S.C. Section 7001 *et seq.*, except that nothing in this article modifies, limits, or supersedes Section 7001(c) of that Act or authorizes electronic delivery of any of the notices described in Section 7003(b) of that Act.

## Part 2—General Definitions and Principles of Interpretation

**§1-201. General Definitions.**
(a) Unless the context otherwise requires, words or phrases defined in this section, or in the additional definitions contained in other articles of [the Uniform Commercial Code] that apply to particular articles or parts thereof, have the meanings stated.
(b) Subject to definitions contained in other articles of [the Uniform Commercial Code] that apply to particular articles or parts thereof:
(1) "Action", in the sense of a judicial proceeding, includes recoupment, counterclaim, set-off, suit in equity, and any other proceeding in which rights are determined.
(2) "Aggrieved party" means a party entitled to pursue a remedy.
(3) "Agreement", as distinguished from "contract", means the bargain of the parties in fact, as found in their language or inferred from other circumstances, including course of performance, course of dealing, or usage of trade as provided in Section 1-303.

(4) "Bank" means a person engaged in the business of banking and includes a savings bank, savings and loan association, credit union, and trust company.
(5) "Bearer" means a person in possession of a negotiable instrument, document of title, or certificated security that is payable to bearer or indorsed in blank.
(6) "Bill of lading" means a document evidencing the receipt of goods for shipment issued by a person engaged in the business of transporting or forwarding goods.
(7) "Branch" includes a separately incorporated foreign branch of a bank.
(8) "Burden of establishing" a fact means the burden of persuading the trier of fact that the existence of the fact is more probable than its nonexistence.
(9) "Buyer in ordinary course of business" means a person that buys goods in good faith, without knowledge that the sale violates the rights of another person in the goods, and in the ordinary course from a person, other than a pawnbroker, in the business of selling goods of that kind. A person buys goods in the ordinary course if the sale to the person comports with the usual or customary practices in the kind of business in which the seller is engaged or with the seller's own usual or customary practices. A person that sells oil, gas, or other minerals at the wellhead or minehead is a person in the business of selling goods of that kind. A buyer in ordinary course of business may buy for cash, by exchange of other property, or on secured or unsecured credit, and may acquire goods or documents of title under a preexisting contract for sale. Only a buyer that takes possession of the goods or has a right to recover the goods from the seller under Article 2 may be a buyer in ordinary course of business. "Buyer in ordinary course of business" does not include a person that acquires goods in a transfer in bulk or as security for or in total or partial satisfaction of a money debt.
(10) "Conspicuous", with reference to a term, means so written, displayed, or presented that a reasonable person against which it is to operate ought to have noticed it. Whether a term is "conspicuous" or not is a decision for the court. Conspicuous terms include the following:
 (A) a heading in capitals equal to or greater in size than the surrounding text, or in contrasting type, font, or color to the surrounding text of the same or lesser size; and
 (B) language in the body of a record or display in larger type than the surrounding text, or in contrasting type, font, or color to the surrounding text of the same size, or set off from surrounding text of the same size by symbols or other marks that call attention to the language.
(11) "Consumer" means an individual who enters into a transaction primarily for personal, family, or household purposes.
(12) "Contract", as distinguished from "agreement", means the total legal obligation that results from the parties' agreement as determined by [the Uniform Commercial Code] as supplemented by any other applicable laws.
(13) "Creditor" includes a general creditor, a secured creditor, a lien creditor, and any representative of creditors, including an assignee for the benefit of creditors, a trustee in bankruptcy, a receiver in equity, and an executor or administrator of an insolvent debtor's or assignor's estate.
(14) "Defendant" includes a person in the position of defendant in a counterclaim, cross-claim, or third-party claim.
(15) "Delivery", with respect to an instrument, document of title, or chattel paper, means voluntary transfer of possession.
(16) "Document of title" includes bill of lading, dock warrant, dock receipt, warehouse receipt or order for the delivery of goods, and also any other document which in the regular course of business or financing is treated as adequately evidencing that the person in possession of it is entitled to receive, hold, and dispose of the document and the goods it covers. To be a document of title, a document must purport to be issued by or addressed to a bailee and purport to cover goods in the bailee's possession which are either identified or are fungible portions of an identified mass.
(17) "Fault" means a default, breach, or wrongful act or omission.
(18) "Fungible goods" means:
 (A) goods of which any unit, by nature or usage of trade, is the equivalent of any other like unit; or
 (B) goods that by agreement are treated as equivalent.
(19) "Genuine" means free of forgery or counterfeiting.
(20) "Good faith," except as otherwise provided in Article 5, means honesty in fact and the observance of reasonable commercial standards of fair dealing.
(21) "Holder" means:
 (A) the person in possession of a negotiable instrument that is payable either to bearer or to an identified person that is the person in possession; or
 (B) the person in possession of a document of title if the goods are deliverable either to bearer or to the order of the person in possession.
(22) "Insolvency proceeding" includes an assignment for the benefit of creditors or other proceeding intended to liquidate or rehabilitate the estate of the person involved.
(23) "Insolvent" means:
 (A) having generally ceased to pay debts in the ordinary course of business other than as a result of bona fide dispute;
 (B) being unable to pay debts as they become due; or
 (C) being insolvent within the meaning of federal bankruptcy law.
(24) "Money" means a medium of exchange currently authorized or adopted by a domestic or foreign government. The term includes a monetary unit of account established by an intergovernmental organization or by agreement between two or more countries.
(25) "Organization" means a person other than an individual.
(26) "Party", as distinguished from "third party", means a person that has engaged in a transaction or made an agreement subject to [the Uniform Commercial Code].
(27) "Person" means an individual, corporation, business trust, estate, trust, partnership, limited liability company, association, joint venture, government, governmental subdivision, agency, or instrumentality, public corporation, or any other legal or commercial entity.
(28) "Present value" means the amount as of a date certain of one or more sums payable in the future, discounted to the date certain by use of either an interest rate specified by the parties if that rate is not manifestly unreasonable at the time the transaction is entered into or, if an interest rate is not so specified, a commercially reasonable rate that takes into account the facts and circumstances at the time the transaction is entered into.
(29) "Purchase" means taking by sale, lease, discount, negotiation, mortgage, pledge, lien, security interest, issue or reissue, gift, or any other voluntary transaction creating an interest in property.
(30) "Purchaser" means a person that takes by purchase.
(31) "Record" means information that is inscribed on a tangible medium or that is stored in an electronic or other medium and is retrievable in perceivable form.
(32) "Remedy" means any remedial right to which an aggrieved party is entitled with or without resort to a tribunal.
(33) "Representative" means a person empowered to act for another, including an agent, an officer of a corporation or association, and a trustee, executor, or administrator of an estate.
(34) "Right" includes remedy.

(35) "Security interest" means an interest in personal property or fixtures which secures payment or performance of an obligation. "Security interest" includes any interest of a consignor and a buyer of accounts, chattel paper, a payment intangible, or a promissory note in a transaction that is subject to Article 9. "Security interest" does not include the special property interest of a buyer of goods on identification of those goods to a contract for sale under Section 2-401, but a buyer may also acquire a "security interest" by complying with Article 9. Except as otherwise provided in Section 2-505, the right of a seller or lessor of goods under Article 2 or 2A to retain or acquire possession of the goods is not a "security interest", but a seller or lessor may also acquire a "security interest" by complying with Article 9. The retention or reservation of title by a seller of goods notwithstanding shipment or delivery to the buyer under Section 2-401 is limited in effect to a reservation of a "security interest." Whether a transaction in the form of a lease creates a "security interest" is determined pursuant to Section 1-203.

(36) "Send" in connection with a writing, record, or notice means:

(A) to deposit in the mail or deliver for transmission by any other usual means of communication with postage or cost of transmission provided for and properly addressed and, in the case of an instrument, to an address specified thereon or otherwise agreed, or if there be none to any address reasonable under the circumstances; or

(B) in any other way to cause to be received any record or notice within the time it would have arrived if properly sent.

(37) "Signed" includes using any symbol executed or adopted with present intention to adopt or accept a writing.

(38) "State" means a State of the United States, the District of Columbia, Puerto Rico, the United States Virgin Islands, or any territory or insular possession subject to the jurisdiction of the United States.

(39) "Surety" includes a guarantor or other secondary obligor.

(40) "Term" means a portion of an agreement that relates to a particular matter.

(41) "Unauthorized signature" means a signature made without actual, implied, or apparent authority. The term includes a forgery.

(42) "Warehouse receipt" means a receipt issued by a person engaged in the business of storing goods for hire.

(43) "Writing" includes printing, typewriting, or any other intentional reduction to tangible form. "Written" has a corresponding meaning.

**§1-202. Notice; Knowledge.**

(a) Subject to subsection (f), a person has "notice" of a fact if the person:

(1) has actual knowledge of it;

(2) has received a notice or notification of it; or

(3) from all the facts and circumstances known to the person at the time in question, has reason to know that it exists.

(b) "Knowledge" means actual knowledge. "Knows" has a corresponding meaning.

(c) "Discover", "learn", or words of similar import refer to knowledge rather than to reason to know.

(d) A person "notifies" or "gives" a notice or notification to another person by taking such steps as may be reasonably required to inform the other person in ordinary course, whether or not the other person actually comes to know of it.

(e) Subject to subsection (f), a person "receives" a notice or notification when:

(1) it comes to that person's attention; or

(2) it is duly delivered in a form reasonable under the circumstances at the place of business through which the contract was made or at another location held out by that person as the place for receipt of such communications.

(f) Notice, knowledge, or a notice or notification received by an organization is effective for a particular transaction from the time it is brought to the attention of the individual conducting that transaction and, in any event, from the time it would have been brought to the individual's attention if the organization had exercised due diligence. An organization exercises due diligence if it maintains reasonable routines for communicating significant information to the person conducting the transaction and there is reasonable compliance with the routines. Due diligence does not require an individual acting for the organization to communicate information unless the communication is part of the individual's regular duties or the individual has reason to know of the transaction and that the transaction would be materially affected by the information.

**§1-203. Lease Distinguished from Security Interest.**

(a) Whether a transaction in the form of a lease creates a lease or security interest is determined by the facts of each case.

(b) A transaction in the form of a lease creates a security interest if the consideration that the lessee is to pay the lessor for the right to possession and use of the goods is an obligation for the term of the lease and is not subject to termination by the lessee, and:

(1) the original term of the lease is equal to or greater than the remaining economic life of the goods;

(2) the lessee is bound to renew the lease for the remaining economic life of the goods or is bound to become the owner of the goods;

(3) the lessee has an option to renew the lease for the remaining economic life of the goods for no additional consideration or for nominal additional consideration upon compliance with the lease agreement; or

(4) the lessee has an option to become the owner of the goods for no additional consideration or for nominal additional consideration upon compliance with the lease agreement.

(c) A transaction in the form of a lease does not create a security interest merely because:

(1) the present value of the consideration the lessee is obligated to pay the lessor for the right to possession and use of the goods is substantially equal to or is greater than the fair market value of the goods at the time the lease is entered into;

(2) the lessee assumes risk of loss of the goods;

(3) the lessee agrees to pay, with respect to the goods, taxes, insurance, filing, recording, or registration fees, or service or maintenance costs;

(4) the lessee has an option to renew the lease or to become the owner of the goods;

(5) the lessee has an option to renew the lease for a fixed rent that is equal to or greater than the reasonably predictable fair market rent for the use of the goods for the term of the renewal at the time the option is to be performed; or

(6) the lessee has an option to become the owner of the goods for a fixed price that is equal to or greater than the reasonably predictable fair market value of the goods at the time the option is to be performed.

(d) Additional consideration is nominal if it is less than the lessee's reasonably predictable cost of performing under the lease agreement if the option is not exercised. Additional consideration is not nominal if:

(1) when the option to renew the lease is granted to the lessee, the rent is stated to be the fair market rent for the use of the goods for the term of the renewal determined at the time the option is to be performed; or

(2) when the option to become the owner of the goods is granted to the lessee, the price is stated to be the fair market value of the goods determined at the time the option is to be performed.

(e) The "remaining economic life of the goods" and "reasonably predictable" fair market rent, fair market value, or cost of performing under the lease agreement must be determined with reference to the facts and circumstances at the time the transaction is entered into.

**§1-204. Value.**
Except as otherwise provided in Articles 3, 4, [and] 5, [and 6], a person gives value for rights if the person acquires them:
(1) in return for a binding commitment to extend credit or for the extension of immediately available credit, whether or not drawn upon and whether or not a charge-back is provided for in the event of difficulties in collection;
(2) as security for, or in total or partial satisfaction of, a preexisting claim;
(3) by accepting delivery under a preexisting contract for purchase; or
(4) in return for any consideration sufficient to support a simple contract.

**§1-205. Reasonable Time; Seasonableness.**
(a) Whether a time for taking an action required by [the Uniform Commercial Code] is reasonable depends on the nature, purpose, and circumstances of the action.
(b) An action is taken seasonably if it is taken at or within the time agreed or, if no time is agreed, at or within a reasonable time.

**§1-206. Presumptions.**
Whenever [the Uniform Commercial Code] creates a "presumption" with respect to a fact, or provides that a fact is "presumed," the trier of fact must find the existence of the fact unless and until evidence is introduced that supports a finding of its nonexistence.

## Part 3—Territorial Applicability and General Rules

**§1-301. Territorial Applicability; Parties' Power to Choose Applicable Law.**
(a) In this section:
(1) "Domestic transaction" means a transaction other than an international transaction.
(2) "International transaction" means a transaction that bears a reasonable relation to a country other than the United States.
(b) This section applies to a transaction to the extent that it is governed by another article of the [Uniform Commercial Code].
(c) Except as otherwise provided in this section:
(1) an agreement by parties to a domestic transaction that any or all of their rights and obligations are to be determined by the law of this State or of another State is effective, whether or not the transaction bears a relation to the State designated; and
(2) an agreement by parties to an international transaction that any or all of their rights and obligations are to be determined by the law of this State or of another State or country is effective, whether or not the transaction bears a relation to the State or country designated.
(d) In the absence of an agreement effective under subsection (c), and except as provided in subsections (e) and (g), the rights and obligations of the parties are determined by the law that would be selected by application of this State's conflict of laws principles.
(e) If one of the parties to a transaction is a consumer, the following rules apply:
(1) An agreement referred to in subsection (c) is not effective unless the transaction bears a reasonable relation to the State or country designated.
(2) Application of the law of the State or country determined pursuant to subsection (c) or (d) may not deprive the consumer of the protection of any rule of law governing a matter within the scope of this section, which both is protective of consumers and may not be varied by agreement:
(A) of the State or country in which the consumer principally resides, unless subparagraph (B) applies; or
(B) if the transaction is a sale of goods, of the State or country in which the consumer both makes the contract and takes delivery of those goods, if such State or country is not the State or country in which the consumer principally resides.
(f) An agreement otherwise effective under subsection (c) is not effective to the extent that application of the law of the State or country designated would be contrary to a fundamental policy of the State or country whose law would govern in the absence of agreement under subsection (d).
(g) To the extent that [the Uniform Commercial Code] governs a transaction, if one of the following provisions of [the Uniform Commercial Code] specifies the applicable law, that provision governs and a contrary agreement is effective only to the extent permitted by the law so specified:
(1) Section 2-402;
(2) Sections 2A-105 and 2A-106;
(3) Section 4-102;
(4) Section 4A-507;
(5) Section 5-116;
[(6) Section 6-103;]
(7) Section 8-110;
(8) Sections 9-301 through 9-307.

**§1-302. Variation by Agreement.**
(a) Except as otherwise provided in subsection (b) or elsewhere in [the Uniform Commercial Code], the effect of provisions of [the Uniform Commercial Code] may be varied by agreement.
(b) The obligations of good faith, diligence, reasonableness, and care prescribed by [the Uniform Commercial Code] may not be disclaimed by agreement. The parties, by agreement, may determine the standards by which the performance of those obligations is to be measured if those standards are not manifestly unreasonable. Whenever [the Uniform Commercial Code] requires an action to be taken within a reasonable time, a time that is not manifestly unreasonable may be fixed by agreement.
(c) The presence in certain provisions of [the Uniform Commercial Code] of the phrase "unless otherwise agreed", or words of similar import, does not imply that the effect of other provisions may not be varied by agreement under this section.

**§1-303. Course of Performance, Course of Dealing, and Usage of Trade.**
(a) A "course of performance" is a sequence of conduct between the parties to a particular transaction that exists if:
(1) the agreement of the parties with respect to the transaction involves repeated occasions for performance by a party; and
(2) the other party, with knowledge of the nature of the performance and opportunity for objection to it, accepts the performance or acquiesces in it without objection.
(b) A "course of dealing" is a sequence of conduct concerning previous transactions between the parties to a particular transaction that is fairly to be regarded as establishing a common basis of understanding for interpreting their expressions and other conduct.
(c) A "usage of trade" is any practice or method of dealing having such regularity of observance in a place, vocation, or trade as to justify an expectation that it will be observed with respect to the transaction in question. The existence and scope of such a usage must be proved as facts. If it is established that such a usage is embodied in a trade code or similar record, the interpretation of the record is a question of law.
(d) A course of performance or course of dealing between the parties or usage of trade in the vocation or trade in which they are engaged or of which they are or should be aware is relevant in ascertaining the meaning of the parties' agreement, may give particular meaning to specific terms of the agreement, and may supplement or qualify the terms of the agreement. A usage of trade applicable in the place in which part of the performance under the agreement is to occur may be so utilized as to that part of the performance.
(e) Except as otherwise provided in subsection (f), the express terms of an agreement and any applicable course of performance, course of dealing, or

usage of trade must be construed whenever reasonable as consistent with each other. If such a construction is unreasonable:

(1) express terms prevail over course of performance, course of dealing, and usage of trade;

(2) course of performance prevails over course of dealing and usage of trade; and

(3) course of dealing prevails over usage of trade.

(f) Subject to Section 2-209, a course of performance is relevant to show a waiver or modification of any term inconsistent with the course of performance.

(g) Evidence of a relevant usage of trade offered by one party is not admissible unless that party has given the other party notice that the court finds sufficient to prevent unfair surprise to the other party.

**§1-304. Obligation of Good Faith.**

Every contract or duty within [the Uniform Commercial Code] imposes an obligation of good faith in its performance and enforcement.

**§1-305. Remedies to be Liberally Administered.**

(a) The remedies provided by [the Uniform Commercial Code] must be liberally administered to the end that the aggrieved party may be put in as good a position as if the other party had fully performed but neither consequential or special damages nor penal damages may be had except as specifically provided in [the Uniform Commercial Code] or by other rule of law.

(b) Any right or obligation declared by [the Uniform Commercial Code] is enforceable by action unless the provision declaring it specifies a different and limited effect.

**§1-306. Waiver or Renunciation of Claim or Right After Breach.**

A claim or right arising out of an alleged breach may be discharged in whole or in part without consideration by agreement of the aggrieved party in an authenticated record.

**§1-307. Prima Facie Evidence by Third-party Documents.**

A document in due form purporting to be a bill of lading, policy or certificate of insurance, official weigher's or inspector's certificate, consular invoice, or any other document authorized or required by the contract to be issued by a third party is prima facie evidence of its own authenticity and genuineness and of the facts stated in the document by the third party.

**§1-308. Performance or Acceptance Under Reservation of Rights.**

(a) A party that with explicit reservation of rights performs or promises performance or assents to performance in a manner demanded or offered by the other party does not thereby prejudice the rights reserved. Such words as "without prejudice," "under protest," or the like are sufficient.

(b) Subsection (a) does not apply to an accord and satisfaction.

**§1-309. Option to Accelerate at Will.**

A term providing that one party or that party's successor in interest may accelerate payment or performance or require collateral or additional collateral "at will" or when the party "deems itself insecure," or words of similar import, means that the party has power to do so only if that party in good faith believes that the prospect of payment or performance is impaired. The burden of establishing lack of good faith is on the party against which the power has been exercised.

**§1-310. Subordinated Obligations.**

An obligation may be issued as subordinated to performance of another obligation of the person obligated, or a creditor may subordinate its right to performance of an obligation by agreement with either the person obligated or another creditor of the person obligated. Subordination does not create a security interest as against either the common debtor or a subordinated creditor.

## ARTICLE 1: GENERAL PROVISIONS

### Part 1—Short Title, Construction, Application and Subject Matter of the Act

**§1-101. Short Title.**

This Act shall be known and may be cited as Uniform Commercial Code.

**§1-102. Purposes; Rules of Construction; Variation by Agreement.**

(1) This Act shall be liberally construed and applied to promote its underlying purposes and policies.

(2) Underlying purposes and policies of this Act are

(a) to simplify, clarify and modernize the law governing commercial transactions;

(b) to permit the continued expansion of commercial practices through custom, usage and agreement of the parties;

(c) to make uniform the law among the various jurisdictions.

(3) The effect of provisions of this Act may be varied by agreement, except as otherwise provided in this Act and except that the obligations of good faith, diligence, reasonableness and care prescribed by this Act may not be disclaimed by agreement but the parties may by agreement determine the standards by which the performance of such obligations is to be measured if such standards are not manifestly unreasonable.

(4) The presence in certain provisions of this Act of the words "unless otherwise agreed" or words of similar import does not imply that the effect of other provisions may not be varied by agreement under subsection (3).

(5) In this Act unless the context otherwise requires

(a) words in the singular number include the plural, and in the plural include the singular;

(b) words of the masculine gender include the feminine and the neuter, and when the sense so indicates words of the neuter gender may refer to any gender.

**§1-103. Supplementary General Principles of Law Applicable.**

Unless displaced by the particular provisions of this Act, the principles of law and equity, including the law merchant and the law relative to capacity to contract, principal and agent, estoppel, fraud, misrepresentation, duress, coercion, mistake, bankruptcy, or other validating or invalidating cause shall supplement its provisions.

**§1-104. Construction Against Implicit Repeal.**

This Act being a general act intended as a unified coverage of its subject matter, no part of it shall be deemed to be impliedly repealed by subsequent legislation if such construction can reasonably be avoided.

**§1-105. Territorial Application of the Act; Parties' Power to Choose Applicable Law.**

(1) Except as provided hereafter in this section, when a transaction bears a reasonable relation to this state and also to another state or nation the parties may agree that the law either of this state or of such other state or nation shall govern their rights and duties. Failing such agreement this Act applies to transactions bearing an appropriate relation to this state.

(2) Where one of the following provisions of this Act specifies the applicable law, that provision governs and a contrary agreement is effective only to the extent permitted by the law (including the conflict of laws rules) so specified:

Rights of creditors against sold goods. Section 2-402.

Applicability of the Article on Bank Deposits and Collections. Section 4-102.

Bulk transfers subject to the Article on Bulk Transfers. Section 6-102.

Applicability of the Article on Investment Securities. Section 8-106.

Perfection provisions of the Article on Secured Transactions. Section 9-103.

**§1-106. Remedies to Be Liberally Administered.**
(1) The remedies provided by this Act shall be liberally administered to the end that the aggrieved party may be put in as good a position as if the other party had fully performed but neither consequential or special nor penal damages may be had except as specifically provided in this Act or by other rule of law.
(2) Any right or obligation declared by this Act is enforceable by action unless the provision declaring it specifies a different and limited effect.

**§1-107. Waiver or Renunciation of Claim or Right After Breach.**
Any claim or right arising out of an alleged breach can be discharged in whole or in part without consideration by a written waiver or renunciation signed and delivered by the aggrieved party.

**§1-108. Severability.**
If any provision or clause of this Act or application thereof to any person or circumstances is held invalid, such invalidity shall not affect other provisions or applications of the Act which can be given effect without the invalid provision or application, and to this end the provisions of this Act are declared to be severable.

**§1-109. Section Captions.**
Section captions are parts of this Act.

## Part 2—General Definitions and Principles of Interpretation

**§1-201. General Definitions.**
Subject to additional definitions contained in the subsequent Articles of this Act which are applicable to specific Articles or Parts thereof, and unless the context otherwise requires, in this Act:
(1) "Action" in the sense of a judicial proceeding includes recoupment, counterclaim, set-off, suit in equity and any other proceedings in which rights are determined.
(2) "Aggrieved party" means a party entitled to resort to a remedy.
(3) "Agreement" means the bargain of the parties in fact as found in their language or by implication from other circumstances including course of dealing or usage of trade or course of performance as provided in this Act (Sections 1-205 and 2-208). Whether an agreement has legal consequences is determined by the provisions of this Act, if applicable; otherwise by the law of contracts (Section 1-103). (Compare "Contract".)
(4) "Bank" means any person engaged in the business of banking.
(5) "Bearer" means the person in possession of an instrument, document of title, or certificated security payable to bearer or indorsed in blank.
(6) "Bill of lading" means a document evidencing the receipt of goods for shipment issued by a person engaged in the business of transporting or forwarding goods, and includes an airbill. "Airbill" means a document serving for air transportation as a bill of lading does for marine or rail transportation, and includes an air consignment note or air waybill.
(7) "Branch" includes a separately incorporated foreign branch of a bank.
(8) "Burden of establishing" a fact means the burden of persuading the triers of fact that the existence of the fact is more probable than its non-existence.
(9) "Buyer in ordinary course of business" means a person who in good faith and without knowledge that the sale to him is in violation of the ownership rights or security interest of a third party in the goods buys in ordinary course from a person in the business of selling goods of that kind but does not include a pawnbroker. All persons who sell minerals or the like (including oil and gas) at wellhead or minehead shall be deemed to be persons in the business of selling goods of that kind. "Buying" may be for cash or by exchange of other property or on secured or unsecured credit and includes receiving goods or documents of title under a pre-existing contract for sale but does not include a transfer in bulk or as security for or in total or partial satisfaction of a money debt.
(10) "Conspicuous": A term or clause is conspicuous when it is so written that a reasonable person against whom it is to operate ought to have noticed it. A printed heading in capitals (as: NON-NEGOTIABLE BILL OF LADING) is conspicuous. Language in the body of a form is "conspicuous" if it is in larger or other contrasting type or color. But in a telegram any stated term is "conspicuous". Whether a term or clause is "conspicuous" or not is for decision by the court.
(11) "Contract" means the total legal obligation which results from the parties' agreement as affected by this Act and any other applicable rules of law. (Compare "Agreement".)
(12) "Creditor" includes a general creditor, a secured creditor, a lien creditor and any representative of creditors, including an assignee for the benefit of creditors, a trustee in bankruptcy, a receiver in equity and an executor or administrator of an insolvent debtor's or assignor's estate.
(13) "Defendant" includes a person in the position of defendant in a cross-action or counterclaim.
(14) "Delivery" with respect to instruments, documents of title, chattel paper, or certificated securities means voluntary transfer of possession.
(15) "Document of title" includes bill of lading, dock warrant, dock receipt, warehouse receipt or order for the delivery of goods, and also any other document which in the regular course of business or financing is treated as adequately evidencing that the person in possession of it is entitled to receive, hold and dispose of the document and the goods it covers. To be a document of title a document must purport to be issued by or addressed to a bailee and purport to cover goods in the bailee's possession which are either identified or are fungible portions of an identified mass.
(16) "Fault" means wrongful act, omission or breach.
(17) "Fungible" with respect to goods or securities means goods or securities of which any unit is, by nature or usage of trade, the equivalent of any other like unit. Goods which are not fungible shall be deemed fungible for the purposes of this Act to the extent that under a particular agreement or document unlike units are treated as equivalents.
(18) "Genuine" means free of forgery or counterfeiting.
(19) "Good faith" means honesty in fact in the conduct or transaction concerned.
(20) "Holder" means a person who is in possession of a document of title or an instrument or a certificated investment security drawn, issued, or indorsed to him or his order or to bearer or in blank.
(21) To "honor" is to pay or to accept and pay, or where a credit so engages to purchase or discount a draft complying with the terms of the credit.
(22) "Insolvency proceedings" includes any assignment for the benefit of creditors or other proceedings intended to liquidate or rehabilitate the estate of the person involved.
(23) A person is "insolvent" who either has ceased to pay his debts in the ordinary course of business or cannot pay his debts as they become due or is insolvent within the meaning of the federal bankruptcy law.
(24) "Money" means a medium of exchange authorized or adopted by a domestic or foreign government as a part of its currency.
(25) A person has "notice" of a fact when
(a) he has actual knowledge of it; or
(b) he has received a notice or notification of it; or
(c) from all the facts and circumstances known to him at the time in question he has reason to know that it exists.
A person "knows" or has "knowledge" of a fact when he has actual knowledge of it. "Discover" or "learn" or a word or phrase of similar import refers to knowledge rather than to reason to know. The time and circumstances under which a notice or notification may cease to be effective are not determined by this Act.
(26) A person "notifies" or "gives" a notice or notification to another by taking such steps as may be reasonably required to inform the other in ordinary course whether or not such other actually comes to know of it. A person "receives" a notice or notification when
(a) it comes to his attention; or

(b) it is duly delivered at the place of business through which the contract was made or at any other place held out by him as the place for receipt of such communications.

(27) Notice, knowledge or a notice or notification received by an organization is effective for a particular transaction from the time when it is brought to the attention of the individual conducting that transaction, and in any event from the time when it would have been brought to his attention if the organization had exercised due diligence. An organization exercises due diligence if it maintains reasonable routines for communicating significant information to the person conducting the transaction and there is reasonable compliance with the routines. Due diligence does not require an individual acting for the organization to communicate information unless such communication is part of his regular duties or unless he has reason to know of the transaction and that the transaction would be materially affected by the information.

(28) "Organization" includes a corporation, government or governmental subdivision or agency, business trust, estate, trust, partnership or association, two or more persons having a joint or common interest, or any other legal or commercial entity.

(29) "Party", as distinct from "third party", means a person who has engaged in a transaction or made an agreement within this Act.

(30) "Person" includes an individual or an organization (See Section 1-102).

(31) "Presumption" or "presumed" means that the trier of fact must find the existence of the fact presumed unless and until evidence is introduced which would support a finding of its non-existence.

(32) "Purchase" includes taking by sale, discount, negotiation, mortgage, pledge, lien, or re-issue, gift or any other voluntary transaction creating an interest in property.

(33) "Purchaser" means a person who takes by purchase.

(34) "Remedy" means any remedial right to which an aggrieved party is entitled with or without resort to a tribunal.

(35) "Representative" includes an agent, an officer of a corporation or association, and a trustee, executor or administrator of an estate, or any other person empowered to act for another.

(36) "Rights" includes remedies.

(37) "Security interest" means an interest in personal property or fixtures which secures payment or performance of an obligation. The retention or reservation of title by a seller of goods notwithstanding shipment or delivery to the buyer (Section 2-401) is limited in effect to a reservation of a "security interest". The term also includes any interest of a buyer of accounts or chattel paper which is subject to Article 9. The special property interest of a buyer of goods on identification of such goods to a contract for sale under Section 2-401 is not a "security interest", but a buyer may also acquire a "security interest" by complying with Article 9. Unless a lease or consignment is intended as security, reservation of title thereunder is not a "security interest" but a consignment is in any event subject to the provisions on consignment sales (Section 2-326). Whether a lease is intended as security is to be determined by the facts of each case; however, (a) the inclusion of an option to purchase does not of itself make the lease one intended for security, and (b) an agreement that upon compliance with the terms of the lease the leasee shall become or has the option to become the owner of the property for no additional consideration or for a nominal consideration does make the lease one intended for security.

(38) "Send" in connection with any writing or notice means to deposit in the mail or delivery for transmission by any other usual means of communication with postage or cost of transmission provided for and properly addressed and in the case of an instrument to an address specified thereon or otherwise agreed, or if there be none to any address reasonable under the circumstances. The receipt of any writing or notice within the time at which it would have arrived if properly sent has the effect of a proper sending.

(39) "Signed" includes any symbol executed or adopted by a party with present intention to authenticate a writing.

(40) "Surety" includes guarantor.

(41) "Telegram" includes a message transmitted by radio, teletype, cable, any mechanical method of transmission, or the like.

(42) "Term" means that portion of an agreement which relates to a particular matter.

(43) "Unauthorized" signature or indorsement means one made without actual, implied or apparent authority and includes a forgery.

(44) "Value". Except as otherwise provided with respect to negotiable instruments and bank collections (Sections 3-303, 4-208 and 4-209) a person gives "value" for rights if he acquires them

(a) in return for a binding commitment to extend credit or for the extension of immediately available credit whether or not drawn upon or whether or not a chargeback is provided for in the event of difficulties in collection; or

(b) as security for or in total or partial satisfaction of a pre-existing claim; or

(c) by accepting delivery pursuant to a pre-existing contract for purchase; or

(d) generally, in return for any consideration sufficient to support a simple contract.

(45) "Warehouse receipt" means a receipt issued by a person engaged in the business of storing goods for hire.

(46) "Written" or "writing" includes printing, typewriting or any other intentional reduction to tangible form. Amended in 1962, 1972 and 1977.

**§1-202. Prima Facie Evidence by Third Party Documents.**

A document in due form purporting to be a bill of lading, policy or certificate of insurance, official weigher's or inspector's certificate, consular invoice, or any other document authorized or required by the contract to be issued by a third party shall be prima facie evidence of its own authenticity and genuineness and of the facts stated in the document by the third party.

**§1-203. Obligation of Good Faith.**

Every contract or duty within this Act imposes an obligation of good faith in its performance or enforcement.

**§1-204. Time; Reasonable Time; "Seasonably".**

(1) Whenever this Act requires any action to be taken within a reasonable time, any time which is not manifestly unreasonable may be fixed by agreement.

(2) What is a reasonable time for taking any action depends on the nature, purpose and circumstances of such action.

(3) An action is taken "seasonably" when it is taken at or within the time agreed or if no time is agreed at or within a reasonable time.

**§1-205. Course of Dealing and Usage of Trade.**

(1) A course of dealing is a sequence of previous conduct between the parties to a particular transaction which is fairly to be regarded as establishing a common basis of understanding for interpreting their expressions and other conduct.

(2) A usage of trade is any practice or method of dealing having such regularity of observance in a place, vocation or trade as to justify an expectation that it will be observed with respect to the transaction in question. The existence and scope of such a usage are to be proved as facts. If it is established that such a usage is embodied in a written trade code or similar writing the interpretation of the writing is for the court.

(3) A course of dealing between parties and any usage of trade in the vocation or trade in which they are engaged or of which they are or should be aware give particular meaning to and supplement or qualify terms of an agreement.

(4) The express terms of an agreement and an applicable course of dealing or usage of trade shall be construed wherever reasonable as consistent with each other, but when such construction is unreasonable express terms

control both course of dealing and usage of trade and course of dealing controls usage of trade.
(5) An applicable usage of trade in the place where any part of performance is to occur shall be used in interpreting the agreement as to that part of the performance.
(6) Evidence of a relevant usage of trade offered by one party is not admissible unless and until he has given the other party such notice as the court finds sufficient to prevent unfair surprise to the latter.

**§1-206. Statute of Frauds for Kinds of Personal Property Not Otherwise Covered.**
(1) Except in the cases described in subsection (2) of this section a contract for the sale of personal property is not enforceable by way of action or defense beyond five thousand dollars in amount or value of remedy unless there is some writing which indicates that a contract for sale has been made between the parties at a defined or stated price, reasonably identifies the subject matter, and is signed by the party against whom enforcement is sought or by his authorized agent.
(2) Subsection (1) of this section does not apply to contracts for the sale of goods (Section 2-201) nor of securities (Section 8-319) nor to security agreements (Section 9-203).

**§1-207. Performance or Acceptance Under Reservation of Rights.**
A party who with explicit reservation of rights performs or promises performance or assents to performance in a manner demanded or offered by the other party does not thereby prejudice the rights reserved. Such words as "without prejudice", "under protest" or the like are sufficient.

**§1-208. Option to Accelerate at Will.**
A term providing that one party or his successor in interest may accelerate payment or performance or require collateral or additional collateral "at will" or "when he deems himself insecure" or in words of similar import shall be construed to mean that he shall have power to do so only if he in good faith believes that the prospect of payment or performance is impaired. The burden of establishing lack of good faith is on the party against whom the power has been exercised.

**§1-209. Subordinated Obligations.**
An obligation may be issued as subordinated to payment of another obligation of the person obligated, or a creditor may subordinate his right to payment of an obligation by agreement with either the person obligated or another creditor of the person obligated. Such a subordination does not create a security interest as against either the common debtor or a subordinated creditor. This section shall be construed as declaring the law as it existed prior to the enactment of this section and not as modifying it. Added 1966.

Note: *This new section is proposed as an optional provision to make it clear that a subordination agreement does not create a security interest unless so intended.*

## ARTICLE 2: SALES

### Part 1—Short Title, Construction and Subject Matter

**§2-101. Short Title.**
This Article shall be known and may be cited as Uniform Commercial Code—Sales.

**§2-102. Scope; Certain Security and Other Transactions Excluded From This Article.**
Unless the context otherwise requires, this Article applies to transactions in goods; it does not apply to any transaction which although in the form of an unconditional contract to sell or present sale is intended to operate only as a security transaction nor does this Article impair or repeal any statute regulating sales to consumers, farmers or other specified classes of buyers.

**§2-103. Definitions and Index of Definitions.**
(1) In this Article unless the context otherwise requires
(a) "Buyer" means a person who buys or contracts to buy goods.
(b) "Good faith" in the case of a merchant means honesty in fact and the observance of reasonable commercial standards of fair dealing in the trade.
(c) "Receipt" of goods means taking physical possession of them.
(d) "Seller" means a person who sells or contracts to sell goods.
(2) Other definitions applying to this Article or to specified Parts thereof, and the sections in which they appear are:
"Acceptance". Section 2-606.
"Banker's credit". Section 2-325.
"Between merchants". Section 2-104.
"Cancellation". Section 2-106(4).
"Commercial unit". Section 2-105.
"Confirmed credit". Section 2-325.
"Conforming to contract". Section 2-106.
"Contract for sale". Section 2-106.
"Cover". Section 2-712.
"Entrusting". Section 2-403.
"Financing agency". Section 2-104.
"Future goods". Section 2-105.
"Goods". Section 2-105.
"Identification". Section 2-501.
"Installment contract". Section 2-612.
"Letter of Credit". Section 2-325.
"Lot". Section 2-105.
"Merchant". Section 2-104.
"Overseas". Section 2-323.
"Person in position of seller". Section 2-707.
"Present sale". Section 2-106.
"Sale". Section 2-106.
"Sale on approval". Section 2-326.
"Sale or return". Section 2-326.
"Termination". Section 2-106.
(3) The following definitions in other Articles apply to this Article:
"Check". Section 3-104.
"Consignee". Section 7-102.
"Consignor". Section 7-102.
"Consumer goods". Section 9-109.
"Dishonor". Section 3-507. "Draft". Section 3-104.
(4) In addition Article 1 contains general definitions and principles of construction and interpretation applicable throughout this Article.

**§2-104. Definitions: "Merchant"; "Between Merchants"; "Financing Agency".**
(1) "Merchant" means a person who deals in goods of the kind or otherwise by his occupation holds himself out as having knowledge or skill peculiar to the practices or goods involved in the transaction or to whom such knowledge or skill may be attributed by his employment of an agent or broker or other intermediary who by his occupation holds himself out as having such knowledge or skill.
(2) "Financing agency" means a bank, finance company or other person who in the ordinary course of business makes advances against goods or documents of title or who by arrangement with either the seller or the buyer intervenes in ordinary course to make or collect payment due or claimed under the contract for sale, as by purchasing or paying the seller's draft or making advances against it or by merely taking it for collection whether or not documents of title accompany the draft. "Financing agency" includes also a bank or other person who similarly intervenes

between persons who are in the position of seller and buyer in respect to the goods (Section 2-707).
(3) Between merchants" means in any transaction with respect to which both parties are chargeable with the knowledge or skill of merchants.

**§2-105. Definitions: Transferability; "Goods"; "Future" Goods; "Lot"; "Commercial Unit".**
(1) "Goods" means all things (including specially manufactured goods) which are movable at the time of identification to the contract for sale other than the money in which the price is to be paid, investment securities (Article 8) and things in action. "Goods" also includes the unborn young of animals and growing crops and other identified things attached to realty as described in the section on goods to be severed from realty (Section 2-107).
(2) Goods must be both existing and identified before any interest in them can pass. Goods which are not both existing and identified are "future" goods. A purported present sale of future goods or of any interest therein operates as a contract to sell.
(3) There may be a sale of a part interest in existing identified goods.
(4) An undivided share in an identified bulk of fungible goods is sufficiently identified to be sold although the quantity of the bulk is not determined. Any agreed proportion of such a bulk or any quantity thereof agreed upon by number, weight or other measure may to the extent of the seller's interest in the bulk be sold to the buyer who then becomes an owner in common.
(5) "Lot" means a parcel or a single article which is the subject matter of a separate sale or delivery, whether or not it is sufficient to perform the contract.
(6) "Commercial unit" means such a unit of goods as by commercial usage is a single whole for purposes of sale and division of which materially impairs its character or value on the market or in use. A commercial unit may be a single article (as a machine) or a set of articles (as a suite of furniture or an assortment of sizes) or a quantity (as a bale, gross, or carload) or any other unit treated in use or in the relevant market as a single whole.

**§2-106. Definitions: "Contract"; "Agreement"; "Contract for Sale"; "Sale"; "Present Sale"; "Conforming" to Contract; "Termination"; "Cancellation".**
(1) In this Article unless the context otherwise requires "contract" and "agreement" are limited to those relating to the present or future sale of goods. "Contract for sale" includes both a present sale of goods and a contract to sell goods at a future time. A "sale" consists in the passing of title from the seller to the buyer for a price (Section 2-401). A "present sale" means a sale which is accomplished by the making of the contract.
(2) Goods or conduct including any part of a performance are "conforming" or conform to the contract when they are in accordance with the obligations under the contract.
(3) "Termination" occurs when either party pursuant to a power created by agreement or law puts an end to the contract otherwise than for its breach. On "termination" all obligations which are still executory on both sides are discharged but any right based on prior breach or performance survives.
(4) "Cancellation" occurs when either party puts an end to the contract for breach by the other and its effect is the same as that of "termination" except that the cancelling party also retains any remedy for breach of the whole contract or any unperformed balance.

**§2-107. Goods to Be Severed From Realty: Recording.**
(1) A contract for the sale of minerals or the like (including oil and gas) or a structure or its materials to be removed from realty is a contract for the sale of goods within this Article if they are to be severed by the seller but until severance a purported present sale thereof which is not effective as a transfer of an interest in land is effective only as a contract to sell.
(2) A contract for the sale apart from the land of growing crops or other things attached to realty and capable of severance without material harm thereto but not described in subsection (1) or of timber to be cut is a contract for the sale of goods within this Article whether the subject matter is to be severed by the buyer or by the seller even though it forms part of the realty at the time of contracting, and the parties can by identification effect a present sale before severance.
(3) The provisions of this section are subject to any third party rights provided by the law relating to realty records, and the contract for sale may be executed and recorded as a document transferring an interest in land and shall then constitute notice to third parties of the buyer's rights under the contract for sale.

## Part 2—Form, Formation and Readjustment of Contract

**§2-201. Formal Requirements; Statute of Frauds.**
(1) Except as otherwise provided in this section a contract for the sale of goods for the price of $500 or more is not enforceable by way of action or defense unless there is some writing sufficient to indicate that a contract for sale has been made between the parties and signed by the party against whom enforcement is sought or by his authorized agent or broker. A writing is not insufficient because it omits or incorrectly states a term agreed upon but the contract is not enforceable under this paragraph beyond the quantity of goods shown in such writing.
(2) Between merchants if within a reasonable time a writing in confirmation of the contract and sufficient against the sender is received and the party receiving it has reason to know its contents, it satisfies the requirements of subsection (1) against such party unless written notice of objection to its contents is given within ten days after it is received.
(3) A contract which does not satisfy the requirements of subsection (1) but which is valid in other respects is enforceable
(a) if the goods are to be specially manufactured for the buyer and are not suitable for sale to others in the ordinary course of the seller's business and the seller, before notice of repudiation is received and under circumstances which reasonably indicate that the goods are for the buyer, has made either a substantial beginning of their manufacture or commitments for their procurement; or
(b) if the party against whom enforcement is sought admits in his pleading, testimony or otherwise in court that a contract for sale was made, but the contract is not enforceable under this provision beyond the quantity of goods admitted; or
(c) with respect to goods for which payment has been made and accepted or which have been received and accepted (Sec. 2-606).

**§2-202. Final Written Expression: Parol or Extrinsic Evidence.**
Terms with respect to which the confirmatory memoranda of the parties agree or which are otherwise set forth in a writing intended by the parties as a final expression of their agreement with respect to such terms as are included therein may not be contradicted by evidence of any prior agreement or of a contemporaneous oral agreement but may be explained or supplemented
(a) by course of dealing or usage of trade (Section 1-205) or by course of performance (Section 2-208); and
(b) by evidence of consistent additional terms unless the court finds the writing to have been intended also as a complete and exclusive statement of the terms of the agreement.

**§2-203. Seals Inoperative.**
The affixing of a seal to a writing evidencing a contract for sale or an offer to buy or sell goods does not constitute the writing a sealed instrument and the law with respect to sealed instruments does not apply to such a contract or offer.

**§2-204. Formation in General.**
(1) A contract for sale of goods may be made in any manner sufficient to show agreement, including conduct by both parties which recognizes the existence of such a contract.
(2) An agreement sufficient to constitute a contract for sale may be found even though the moment of its making is undetermined.
(3) Even though one or more terms are left open a contract for sale does not fail for indefiniteness if the parties have intended to make a contract and there is a reasonably certain basis for giving an appropriate remedy.

**§2-205. Firm Offers.**
An offer by a merchant to buy or sell goods in a signed writing which by its terms gives assurance that it will be held open is not revocable, for lack of consideration, during the time stated or if no time is stated for reasonable time, but in no event may such period of irrevocability exceed three months; but any such term of assurance on a form supplied by the offeree must be separately signed by the offeror.

**§2-206. Offer and Acceptance in Formation of Contract.**
(1) Unless other unambiguously indicated by the language or circumstances
(a) an offer to make a contract shall be construed as inviting acceptance in any manner and by any medium reasonable in the circumstances;
(b) an order or other offer to buy goods for prompt or current shipment shall be construed as inviting acceptance either by a prompt promise to ship or by the prompt or current shipment of conforming or nonconforming goods, but such a shipment of nonconforming goods does not constitute an acceptance if the seller seasonably notifies the buyer that the shipment is offered only as an accommodation to the buyer.
(2) Where the beginning of a requested performance is a reasonable mode of acceptance an offeror who is not notified of acceptance within a reasonable time may treat the offer as having lapsed before acceptance.

**§2-207. Additional Terms in Acceptance or Confirmation.**
(1) A definite and seasonable expression of acceptance or a written confirmation which is sent within a reasonable time operates as an acceptance even though it states terms additional to or different from those offered or agreed upon, unless acceptance is expressly made conditional on assent to the additional or different terms.
(2) The additional terms are to be construed as proposals for addition to the contract. Between merchants such terms become part of the contract unless:
(a) the offer expressly limits acceptance to the terms of the offer;
(b) they materially alter it; or
(c) notification of objection to them has already been given or is given within a reasonable time after notice of them is received.
(3) Conduct by both parties which recognizes the existence of a contract is sufficient to establish a contract for sale although the writings of the parties do not otherwise establish a contract. In such case the terms of the particular contract consist of those terms on which the writings of the parties agree, together with any supplementary terms incorporated under any other provisions of this Act.

**§2-208. Course of Performance or Practical Construction.**
(1) Where the contract for sale involves repeated occasions for performance by either party with knowledge of the nature of the performance and opportunity for objection to it by the other, any course of performance accepted or acquiesced in without objection shall be relevant to determine the meaning of the agreement.
(2) The express terms of the agreement and any such course of performance, as well as any course of dealing and usage of trade, shall be construed whenever reasonable as consistent with each other; but when such construction is unreasonable, express terms shall control course of performance and course of performance shall control both course of dealing and usage of trade (Section 1-205).
(3) Subject to the provisions of the next section on modification and waiver, such course of performance shall be relevant to show a waiver or modification of any term inconsistent with such course of performance.

**§2-209. Modification, Rescission and Waiver.**
(1) An agreement modifying a contract within this Article needs no consideration to be binding.
(2) A signed agreement which excludes modification or rescission except by a signed writing cannot be otherwise modified or rescinded, but except as between merchants such a requirement on a form supplied by the merchant must be separately signed by the other party.
(3) The requirements of the statute of frauds section of this Article (Section 2-201) must be satisfied if the contract as modified is within its provisions.
(4) Although an attempt at modification or rescission does not satisfy the requirements of subsection (2) or (3) it can operate as a waiver.
(5) A party who has made a waiver affecting an executory portion of the contract may retract the waiver by reasonable notification received by the other party that strict performance will be required of any term waived, unless the retraction would be unjust in view of a material change of position in reliance on the waiver.

**§2-210. Delegation of Performance; Assignment of Rights.**
(1) A party may perform his duty through a delegate unless otherwise agreed or unless the other party has a substantial interest in having his original promisor perform or control the acts required by the contract. No delegation of performance relieves the party delegating of any duty to perform or any liability for breach.
(2) Unless otherwise agreed all rights of either seller or buyer can be assigned except where the assignment would materially change the duty of the other party, or increase materially the burden or risk imposed on him by his contract, or impair materially his chance of obtaining return performance. A right to damages for breach of the whole contract or a right arising out of the assignor's due performance of his entire obligation can be assigned despite agreement otherwise.
(3) Unless the circumstances indicate the contrary a prohibition of assignment of "the contract" is to be construed as barring only the delegation to the assignee of the assignor's performance.
(4) An assignment of "the contract" or of "all my rights under the contract" or an assignment in similar general terms is an assignment of rights and unless the language or the circumstances (as in an assignment for security) indicate the contrary, it is a delegation of performance of the duties of the assignor and its acceptance by the assignee constitutes a promise by him to perform those duties. This promise is enforceable by either the assignor or the other party to the original contract.
(5) The other party may treat any assignment which delegates performance as creating reasonable grounds for insecurity and may without prejudice to his rights against the assignor demand assurances from the assignee (Section 2-609).

## Part 3—General Obligation and Construction of Contract

**§2-301. General Obligations of Parties.**
The obligation of the seller is to transfer and deliver and that of the buyer is to accept and pay in accordance with the contract.

**§2-302. Unconscionable Contract or Clause.**
(1) If the court as a matter of law finds the contract or any clause of the contract to have been unconscionable at the time it was made the court may refuse to enforce the contract, or it may enforce the remainder of the contract without the unconscionable clause, or it may so limit the application of any unconscionable clause as to avoid any unconscionable result.

(2) When it is claimed or appears to the court that the contract or any clause thereof may be unconscionable the parties shall be afforded a reasonable opportunity to present evidence as to its commercial setting, purpose and effect to aid the court in making the determination.

**§2-303. Allocation or Division of Risks.**
Where this Article allocates a risk or a burden as between the parties "unless otherwise agreed", the agreement may not only shift the allocation, but may also divide the risk or burden.

**§2-304. Price Payable in Money, Goods, Realty, or Otherwise.**
(1) The price can be made payable in money or otherwise. If it is payable in whole or in part in goods each party is a seller of the goods which he is to transfer.
(2) Even though all or part of the price is payable in an interest in realty the transfer of the goods and the seller's obligations with reference to them are subject to this Article, but not the transfer of the interest in realty or the transferor's obligations in connection therewith.

**§2-305. Open Price Term.**
(1) The parties if they so intend can conclude a contract for sale even though the price is not settled. In such a case the price is a reasonable price at the time for delivery if
(a) nothing is said as to price; or
(b) the price is left to be agreed by the parties and they fail to agree; or
(c) the price is to be fixed in terms of some agreed market or other standard as set or recorded by a third person or agency and it is not so set or recorded.
(2) A price to be fixed by the seller or by the buyer means a price for him to fix in good faith.
(3) When a price left to be fixed otherwise than by agreement of the parties fails to be fixed through fault of one party the other may at his option treat the contract as cancelled or himself fix a reasonable price.
(4) Where, however, the parties intend not to be bound unless the price be fixed or agreed and it is not fixed or agreed there is no contract. In such a case the buyer must return any goods already received or if unable so to do must pay their reasonable value at the time of delivery and the seller must return any portion of the price paid on account.

**§2-306. Output, Requirements and Exclusive Dealings.**
(1) A term which measures the quantity by the output of the seller or the requirements of the buyer means such actual output or requirements as may occur in good faith, except that no quantity unreasonably disproportionate to any stated estimate or in the absence of a stated estimate to any normal or otherwise comparable prior output or requirements may be tendered or demanded.
(2) A lawful agreement by either the seller or the buyer for exclusive dealing in the kind of goods concerned imposes unless otherwise agreed an obligation by the seller to use best efforts to supply the goods and by the buyer to use best efforts to promote their sale.

**§2-307. Delivery in Single Lot or Several Lots.**
Unless otherwise agreed all goods called for by a contract for sale must be tendered in a single delivery and payment is due only on such tender but where the circumstances give either party the right to make or demand delivery in lots the price if it can be apportioned may be demanded for each lot.

**§2-308. Absence of Specified Place for Delivery.**
Unless otherwise agreed
(a) the place for delivery of goods is the seller's place of business or if he has none his residence; but
(b) in a contract for sale of identified goods which to the knowledge of the parties at the time of contracting are in some other place, that place is the place for their delivery; and
(c) documents of title may be delivered through customary banking channels.

**§2-309. Absence of Specific Time Provisions; Notice of Termination.**
(1) The time for shipment or delivery or any other action under a contract if not provided in this Article or agreed upon shall be a reasonable time.
(2) Where the contract provides for successive performances but is indefinite in duration it is valid for a reasonable time but unless otherwise agreed may be terminated at any time by either party.
(3) Termination of a contract by one party except on the happening of an agreed event requires that reasonable notification be received by the other party and an agreement dispensing with notification is invalid if its operation would be unconscionable.

**§2-310. Open Time for Payment or Running of Credit; Authority to Ship Under Reservation.**
Unless otherwise agreed
(a) payment is due at the time and place at which the buyer is to receive the goods even though the place of shipment is the place of delivery; and
(b) if the seller is authorized to send the goods he may ship them under reservation, and may tender the documents of title, but the buyer may inspect the goods after their arrival before payment is due unless such inspection is inconsistent with the terms of the contract (Section 2-513); and
(c) if delivery is authorized and made by way of documents of title otherwise than by subsection (b) then payment is due at the time and place at which the buyer is to receive the documents regardless of where the goods are to be received; and
(d) where the seller is required or authorized to ship the goods on credit the credit period runs from the time of shipment but post-dating the invoice or delaying its dispatch will correspondingly delay the starting of the credit period.

**§2-311. Options and Cooperation Respecting Performance.**
(1) An agreement for sale which is otherwise sufficiently definite (subsection (3) of Section 2-204) to be a contract is not made invalid by the fact that it leaves particulars of performance to be specified by one of the parties. Any such specification must be made in good faith and within limits set by commercial reasonableness.
(2) Unless otherwise agreed specifications relating to assortment of the goods are at the buyer's option and except as otherwise provided in subsections (1)(c) and (3) of Section 2-319 specifications or arrangements relating to shipment are at the seller's option.
(3) Where such specification would materially affect the other party's performance but is not seasonably made or where one party's cooperation is necessary to the agreed performance of the other but is not seasonably forthcoming, the other party in addition to all other remedies
(a) is excused for any resulting delay in his own performance; and
(b) may also either proceed to perform in any reasonable manner or after the time for a material part of his own performance treat the failure to specify or to cooperate as a breach by failure to deliver or accept the goods.

**§2-312. Warranty of Title and Against Infringement; Buyer's Obligation Against Infringement.**
(1) Subject to subsection (2) there is in a contract for sale a warranty by the seller that
(a) the title conveyed shall be good, and its transfer rightful; and
(b) the goods shall be delivered free from any security interest or other lien or encumbrance of which the buyer at the time of contracting has no knowledge.
(2) A warranty under subsection (1) will be excluded or modified only by specific language or by circumstances which give the buyer reason to know that the person selling does not claim title in himself or that he is

purporting to sell only such right or title as he or a third person may have.
(3) Unless otherwise agreed a seller who is a merchant regularly dealing in goods of the kind warrants that the goods shall be delivered free of the rightful claim of any third person by way of infringement or the like but a buyer who furnishes specifications to the seller must hold the seller harmless against any such claim which arises out of compliance with the specifications.

**§2-313. Express Warranties by Affirmation, Promise, Description, Sample.**
(1) Express warranties by the seller are created as follows:
(a) Any affirmation of fact or promise made by the seller to the buyer which relates to the goods and becomes part of the basis of the bargain creates an express warranty that the goods shall conform to the affirmation or promise.
(b) Any description of the goods which is made part of the basis of the bargain creates an express warranty that the goods shall conform to the description.
(c) Any sample or model which is made part of the basis of the bargain creates an express warranty that the whole of the goods shall conform to the sample or model.
(2) It is not necessary to the creation of an express warranty that the seller use formal words such as "warrant" or "guarantee" or that he have a specific intention to make a warranty, but an affirmation merely of the value of the goods or a statement purporting to be merely the seller's opinion or commendation of the goods does not create a warranty.

**§2-314. Implied Warranty: Merchantability; Usage of Trade.**
(1) Unless excluded or modified (Section 2-316), a warranty that the goods shall be merchantable is implied in a contract for their sale if the seller is a merchant with respect to goods of that kind. Under this section the serving for value of food or drink to be consumed either on the premises or elsewhere is a sale.
(2) Goods to be merchantable must be at least such as
(a) pass without objection in the trade under the contract description; and
(b) in the case of fungible goods, are of fair average quality within the description; and
(c) are fit for the ordinary purpose for which such goods are used; and
(d) run, within the variations permitted by the agreement, of even kind, quality and quantity within each unit and among all units involved; and
(e) are adequately contained, packaged, and labeled as the agreement may require; and
(f) conform to the promises or affirmations of fact made on the container or label if any.
(3) Unless excluded or modified (Section 2-316) other implied warranties may arise from course of dealing or usage of trade.

**§2-315. Implied Warranty: Fitness for Particular Purpose.**
Where the seller at the time of contracting has reason to know any particular purpose for which the goods are required and that the buyer is relying on the seller's skill or judgment to select or furnish suitable goods, there is unless excluded or modified under the next section an implied warranty that the goods shall be fit for such purpose.

**§2-316. Exclusion or Modification of Warranties.**
(1) Words or conduct relevant to the creation of an express warranty and words or conduct tending to negate or limit warranty shall be construed wherever reasonable as consistent with each other, but subject to the provisions of this Article on parol or extrinsic evidence (Section 2-202) negation or limitation is inoperative to the extent that such construction is unreasonable.
(2) Subject to subsection (3), to exclude or modify the implied warranty of merchantability or any part of it the language must mention merchantability and in case of a writing must be conspicuous, and to exclude or modify any implied warranty of fitness the exclusion must be by a writing and conspicuous. Language to exclude all implied warranties of fitness is sufficient if it states, for example, that "There are no warranties which extend beyond the description on the face hereof."
(3) Notwithstanding subsection (2)
(a) unless the circumstances indicate otherwise, all implied warranties are excluded by expressions like "as is", "with all faults" or other language which in common understanding calls the buyer's attention to the exclusion of warranties and makes plain that there is no implied warranty; and
(b) when the buyer before entering into the contract has examined the goods or the sample or model as fully as he desired or has refused to examine the goods there is no implied warranty with regard to defects which an examination ought in the circumstances to have revealed to him; and
(c) an implied warranty can also be excluded or modified by course of dealing or course of performance or usage of trade.
(4) Remedies for breach of warranty can be limited in accordance with the provisions of this Article on liquidation or limitation of damages and on contractual modification of remedy (Sections 2-718 and 2-719).

**§2-317. Cumulation and Conflict of Warranties Express or Implied.**
Warranties whether express or implied shall be construed as consistent with each other and as cumulative, but if such construction is unreasonable the intention of the parties shall determine which warranty is dominant. In ascertaining that intention the following rules apply:
(a) Exact or technical specifications displace an inconsistent sample or model or general language of description.
(b) A sample from an existing bulk displaces inconsistent general language of description.
(c) Express warranties displace inconsistent implied warranties other than an implied warranty of fitness for a particular purpose.

**§2-318. Third Party Beneficiaries of Warranties Express or Implied.**
Note: *If this Act is introduced in the Congress of the United States this section should be omitted. (States to select one alternative.)*
***Alternative A*** A seller's warranty whether express or implied extends to any natural person who is in the family or household of his buyer or who is a guest in his home if it is reasonable to expect that such person may use, consume or be affected by the goods and who is injured in person by breach of the warranty. The seller may not exclude or limit the operation of this section.
***Alternative B*** A seller's warranty whether express or implied extends to any natural person who may reasonably be expected to use, consume or be affected by the goods and who is injured in person by breach of the warranty. A seller may not exclude or limit the operation of this section.
***Alternative C*** A seller's warranty whether express or implied extends to any person who may reasonably be expected to use, consume or be affected by the goods and who is injured by breach of the warranty. A seller may not exclude or limit the operation of this section with respect to injury to the person of an individual to whom the warranty extends. As amended 1966.

**§2-319. F.O.B. and F.A.S. Terms.**
(1) Unless otherwise agreed the term F.O.B. (which means "free on board") at a named place, even though used only in connection with the stated price, is a delivery term under which

(a) when the term is F.O.B. the place of shipment, the seller must at that place ship the goods in the manner provided in this Article (Section 2-504) and bear the expense and risk of putting them into the possession of the carrier; or

(b) when the term is F.O.B. the place of destination, the seller must at his own expense and risk transport the goods to that place and there tender delivery of them in the manner provided in this Article (Section 2-503);

(c) when under either (a) or (b) the term is also F.O.B. vessel, car or other vehicle, the seller must in addition at his own expense and risk load the goods on board. If the term is F.O.B. vessel the buyer must name the vessel and in an appropriate case the seller must comply with the provisions of this Article on the form of bill of lading (Section 2-323).

(2) Unless otherwise agreed the term F.A.S. vessel (which means "free alongside") at a named port, even though used only in connection with the stated price, is a delivery term under which the seller must

(a) at his own expense and risk deliver the goods alongside the vessel in the manner usual in that port or on a dock designated and provided by the buyer; and

(b) obtain and tender a receipt for the goods in exchange for which the carrier is under a duty to issue a bill of lading.

(3) Unless otherwise agreed in any case falling within subsection (1)(a) or (c) or subsection (2) the buyer must seasonably give any needed instructions for making delivery, including when the term is F.A.S. or F.O.B. the loading berth of the vessel and in an appropriate case its name and sailing date. The seller may treat the failure of needed instructions as a failure of cooperation under this Article (Section 2-311). He may also at his option move the goods in any reasonable manner preparatory to delivery or shipment.

(4) Under the term F.O.B. vessel or F.A.S. unless otherwise agreed the buyer must make payment against tender of the required documents and the seller may not tender nor the buyer demand delivery of the goods in substitution for the documents.

**§2-320. C.I.F. and C. & F. Terms.**

(1) The term C.I.F. means that the price includes in a lump sum the cost of the goods and the insurance and freight to the named destination. The term C. & F. or C.F. means that the price so includes cost and freight to the named destination.

(2) Unless otherwise agreed and even though used only in connection with the stated price and destination, the term C.I.F. destination or its equivalent requires the seller at his own expense and risk to

(a) put the goods into the possession of a carrier at the port for shipment and obtain a negotiable bill or bills of lading covering the entire transportation to the named destination; and

(b) load the goods and obtain a receipt from the carrier (which may be contained in the bill of lading) showing that the freight has been paid or provided for; and

(c) obtain a policy or certificate of insurance, including any war risk insurance, of a kind and on terms then current at the port of shipment in the usual amount, in the currency of the contract, shown to cover the same goods covered by the bill of lading and providing for payment of loss to the order of the buyer or for the account of whom it may concern; but the seller may add to the price the amount of premium for any such war risk insurance; and

(d) prepare an invoice of the goods and procure any other documents required to effect shipment or to comply with the contract; and

(e) forward and tender with commercial promptness all the documents in due form and with any indorsement necessary to perfect the buyer's rights.

(3) Unless otherwise agreed the term C. & F. or its equivalent has the same effect and imposes upon the seller the same obligations and risks as a C.I.F. term except the obligation as to insurance.

(4) Under the term C.I.F. or C. & F. unless otherwise agreed the buyer must make payment against tender of the required documents and the seller may not tender nor the buyer demand delivery of the goods in substitution for the documents.

**§2-321. C.I.F. or C. & F.: "Net Landed Weights"; "Payment on Arrival"; Warranty of Condition on Arrival.**

Under a contract containing a term C.I.F. or C. & F.

(1) Where the price is based on or is to be adjusted according to "net landed weights", "delivered weights", "out turn" quantity or quality or the like, unless otherwise agreed the seller must reasonably estimate the price. The payment due on tender of the documents called for by the contract is the amount so estimated, but after final adjustment of the price a settlement must be made with commercial promptness.

(2) An agreement described in subsection (1) or any warranty of quality or condition of the goods on arrival places upon the seller the risk of ordinary deterioration, shrinkage and the like in transportation but has no effect on the place or time of identification to the contract for sale or delivery or on the passing of the risk of loss.

(3) Unless otherwise agreed where the contract provides for payment on or after arrival of the goods the seller must before payment allow such preliminary inspection as is feasible; but if the goods are lost delivery of the documents and payment are due when the goods should have arrived.

**§2-322. Delivery "Ex-Ship".**

(1) Unless otherwise agreed a term for delivery of goods "ex-ship" (which means from the carrying vessel) or in equivalent language is not restricted to a particular ship and requires delivery from a ship which has reached a place at the named port of destination where goods of the kind are usually discharged.

(2) Under such a term unless otherwise agreed

(a) the seller must discharge all liens arising out of the carriage and furnish the buyer with a direction which puts the carrier under a duty to deliver the goods; and

(b) the risk of loss does not pass to the buyer until the goods leave the ship's tackle or are otherwise properly unloaded.

**§2-323. Form of Bill of Lading Required in Overseas Shipment; "Overseas".**

(1) Where the contract contemplates overseas shipment and contains a term C.I.F. or C. & F. or F.O.B. vessel, the seller unless otherwise agreed must obtain a negotiable bill of lading stating that the goods have been loaded on board or, in the case of a term C.I.F. or C. & F., received for shipment.

(2) Where in a case within subsection (1) a bill of lading has been issued in a set of parts, unless otherwise agreed if the documents are not to be sent from abroad the buyer may demand tender of the full set; otherwise only one part of the bill of lading need be tendered. Even if the agreement expressly requires a full set

(a) due tender of a single part is acceptable within the provisions of this Article on cure of improper delivery (subsection (1) of Section 2-508); and

(b) even though the full set is demanded, if the documents are sent from abroad the person tendering an incomplete set may nevertheless require payment upon furnishing an indemnity which the buyer in good faith deems adequate.

(3) A shipment by water or by air or a contract contemplating such shipment is "overseas" insofar as by usage of trade or agreement it is subject to the commercial, financing or shipping practices characteristic of international deep water commerce.

**§2-324. "No Arrival, No Sale" Term.**

Under a term "no arrival, no sale" or terms of like meaning, unless otherwise agreed,

(a) the seller must properly ship conforming goods and if they arrive by any means he must tender them on arrival but he assumes no obligation that the goods will arrive unless he has caused the non-arrival; and
(b) where without fault of the seller the goods are in part lost or have so deteriorated as no longer to conform to the contract or arrive after the contract time, the buyer may proceed as if there had been casualty to identified goods (Section 2-613).

**§2-325. "Letter of Credit" Term; "Confirmed Credit".**
(1) Failure of the buyer seasonably to furnish an agreed letter of credit is a breach of the contract for sale.
(2) The delivery to seller of a proper letter of credit suspends the buyer's obligation to pay. If the letter of credit is dishonored, the seller may on seasonable notification to the buyer require payment directly from him.
(3) Unless otherwise agreed the term "letter of credit" or "banker's credit" in a contract for sale means an irrevocable credit issued by a financing agency of good repute and, where the shipment is overseas, of good international repute. The term "confirmed credit" means that the credit must also carry the direct obligation of such an agency which does business in the seller's financial market.

**§2-326. Sale on Approval and Sale or Return; Consignment Sales and Rights of Creditors.**
(1) Unless otherwise agreed, if delivered goods may be returned by the buyer even though they conform to the contract, the transaction is
(a) a "sale on approval" if the goods are delivered primarily for use, and
(b) a "sale or return" if the goods are delivered primarily for resale.
(2) Except as provided in subsection (3), goods held on approval are not subject to the claims of the buyer's creditors until acceptance; goods held on sale or return are subject to such claims while in the buyer's possession.
(3) Where goods are delivered to a person for sale and such person maintains a place of business at which he deals in goods of the kind involved, under a name other than the name of the person making delivery, then with respect to claims of creditors of the person conducting the business the goods are deemed to be on sale or return. The provisions of this subsection are applicable even though an agreement purports to reserve title to the person making delivery until payment or resale or uses such words as "on consignment" or "on memorandum". However, this subsection is not applicable if the person making delivery
(a) complies with an applicable law providing for a consignor's interest or the like to be evidenced by a sign, or
(b) establishes that the person conducting the business is generally known by his creditors to be substantially engaged in selling the goods of others, or
(c) complies with the filing provisions of the Article on Secured Transactions (Article 9).
(4) Any "or return" term of a contract for sale is to be treated as a separate contract for sale within the statute of frauds section of this Article (Section 2-201) and as contradicting the sale aspect of the contract within the provisions of this Article on parol or extrinsic evidence (Section 2-202).

**§2-327. Special Incidents of Sale on Approval and Sale or Return.**
(1) Under a sale on approval unless otherwise agreed
(a) although the goods are identified to the contract the risk of loss and the title do not pass to the buyer until acceptance; and
(b) use of the goods consistent with the purpose of trial is not acceptance but failure seasonably to notify the seller of election to return the goods is acceptance, and if the goods conform to the contract acceptance of any part is acceptance of the whole; and
(c) after due notification of election to return, the return is at the seller's risk and expense but a merchant buyer must follow any reasonable instructions.
(2) Under a sale or return unless otherwise agreed
(a) the option to return extends to the whole or any commercial unit of the goods while in substantially their original condition, but must be exercised seasonably; and
(b) the return is at the buyer's risk and expense.

**§2-328. Sale by Auction.**
(1) In a sale by auction if goods are put up in lots each lot is the subject of a separate sale.
(2) A sale by auction is complete when the auctioneer so announces by the fall of the hammer or in other customary manner. Where a bid is made while the hammer is falling in acceptance of a prior bid the auctioneer may in his discretion reopen the bidding or declare the goods sold under the bid on which the hammer was falling.
(3) Such a sale is with reserve unless the goods are in explicit terms put up without reserve. In an auction with reserve the auctioneer may withdraw the goods at any time until he announces completion of the sale. In an auction without reserve, after the auctioneer calls for bids on an article or lot, that article or lot cannot be withdrawn unless no bid is made within a reasonable time. In either case a bidder may retract his bid until the auctioneer's announcement of completion of the sale, but a bidder's retraction does not revive any previous bid.
(4) If the auctioneer knowingly receives a bid on the seller's behalf or the seller makes or procures such a bid, and notice has not been given that liberty for such bidding is reserved, the buyer may at his option avoid the sale or take the goods at the price of the last good faith bid prior to the completion of the sale. This subsection shall not apply to any bid at a forced sale.

## Part 4—Title, Creditors and Good Faith Purchasers

**§2-401. Passing of Title; Reservation for Security; Limited Application of This Section.**
Each provision of this Article with regard to the rights, obligations and remedies of the seller, the buyer, purchasers or other third parties applies irrespective of title to the goods except where the provision refers to such title. Insofar as situations are not covered by the other provisions of this Article and matters concerning title became material the following rules apply:
(1) Title to goods cannot pass under a contract for sale prior to their identification to the contract (Section 2-501), and unless otherwise explicitly agreed the buyer acquires by their identification a special property as limited by this Act. Any retention or reservation by the seller of the title (property) in goods shipped or delivered to the buyer is limited in effect to a reservation of a security interest. Subject to these provisions and to the provisions of the Article on Secured Transactions (Article 9), title to goods passes from the seller to the buyer in any manner and on any conditions explicitly agreed on by the parties.
(2) Unless otherwise explicitly agreed title passes to the buyer at the time and place at which the seller completes his performance with reference to the physical delivery of the goods, despite any reservation of a security interest and even though a document of title is to be delivered at a different time or place; and in particular and despite any reservation of a security interest by the bill of lading
(a) if the contract requires or authorizes the seller to send the goods to the buyer but does not require him to deliver them at destination, title passes to the buyer at the time and place of shipment; but
(b) if the contract requires delivery at destination, title passes on tender there.
(3) Unless otherwise explicitly agreed where delivery is to be made without moving the goods,
(a) if the seller is to deliver a document of title, title passes at the time when and the place where he delivers such documents; or

(b) if the goods are at the time of contracting already identified and no documents are to be delivered, title passes at the time and place of contracting.

(4) A rejection or other refusal by the buyer to receive or retain the goods, whether or not justified, or a justified revocation of acceptance revests title to the goods in the seller. Such revesting occurs by operation of law and is not a "sale".

**§2-402. Rights of Seller's Creditors Against Sold Goods.**

(1) Except as provided in subsections (2) and (3), rights of unsecured creditors of the seller with respect to goods which have been identified to a contract for sale are subject to the buyer's rights to recover the goods under this Article (Sections 2-502 and 2-716).

(2) A creditor of the seller may treat a sale or an identification of goods to a contract for sale as void if as against him a retention of possession by the seller is fraudulent under any rule of law of the state where the goods are situated, except that retention of possession in good faith and current course of trade by a merchant-seller for a commercially reasonable time after a sale or identification is not fraudulent.

(3) Nothing in this Article shall be deemed to impair the rights of creditors of the seller

(a) under the provisions of the Article on Secured Transactions (Article 9); or

(b) where identification to the contract or delivery is made not in current course of trade but in satisfaction of or as security for a pre-existing claim for money, security or the like and is made under circumstances which under any rule of law of the state where the goods are situated would apart from this Article constitute the transaction a fraudulent transfer or voidable preference.

**§2-403. Power to Transfer; Good Faith Purchase of Goods; "Entrusting".**

(1) A purchaser of goods acquires all title which his transferor had or had power to transfer except that a purchaser of a limited interest acquires rights only to the extent of the interest purchased. A person with voidable title has power to transfer a good title to a good faith purchaser for value. When goods have been delivered under a transaction of purchase the purchaser has such power even though

(a) the transferor was deceived as to the identity of the purchaser, or

(b) the delivery was in exchange for a check which is later dishonored, or

(c) it was agreed that the transaction was to be a "cash sale", or

(d) the delivery was procured through fraud punishable as larcenous under the criminal law.

(2) Any entrusting of possession of goods to a merchant who deals in goods of that kind gives him power to transfer all rights of the entruster to a buyer in ordinary course of business.

(3) "Entrusting" includes any delivery and any acquiescence in retention of possession regardless of any condition expressed between the parties to the delivery or acquiescence and regardless of whether the procurement of the entrusting or the possessor's disposition of the goods have been such as to be larcenous under the criminal law.

(4) The rights of other purchasers of goods and of lien creditors are governed by the Articles on Secured Transactions (Article 9), Bulk Transfers (Article 6) and Documents of Title (Article 7).

## Part 5—Performance

**§2-501. Insurable Interest in Goods; Manner of Identification of Goods.**

(1) The buyer obtains a special property and an insurable interest in goods by identification of existing goods as goods to which the contract refers even though the goods so identified are nonconforming and he has an option to return or reject them. Such identification can be made at any time and in any manner explicitly agreed to by the parties. In the absence of explicit agreement identification occurs

(a) when the contract is made if it is for the sale of goods already existing and identified;

(b) if the contract is for the sale of future goods other than those described in paragraph (c), when goods are shipped, marked or otherwise designated by the seller as goods to which the contract refers;

(c) when the crops are planted or otherwise become growing crops or the young are conceived if the contract is for the sale of unborn young to be born within twelve months after contracting or for the sale of crops to be harvested within twelve months or the next normal harvest season after contracting whichever is longer.

(2) The seller retains an insurable interest in goods so long as title to or any security interest in the goods remains in him and where the identification is by the seller alone he may until default or insolvency or notification to the buyer that the identification is final substitute other goods for those identified.

(3) Nothing in this section impairs any insurable interest recognized under any other statute or rule of law.

**§2-502. Buyer's Right to Goods on Seller's Insolvency.**

(1) Subject to subsection (2) and even though the goods have not been shipped a buyer who has paid a part or all of the price of goods in which he has a special property under the provisions of the immediately preceding section may on making and keeping good a tender of any unpaid portion of their price recover them from the seller if the seller becomes insolvent within ten days after receipt of the first installment on their price.

(2) If the identification creating his special property has been made by the buyer he acquires the right to recover the goods only if they conform to the contract for sale.

**§2-503. Manner of Seller's Tender of Delivery.**

(1) Tender of delivery requires that the seller put and hold conforming goods at the buyer's disposition and give the buyer any notification reasonably necessary to enable him to take delivery. The manner, time and place for tender are determined by the agreement and this Article, and in particular

(a) tender must be at a reasonable hour, and if it is of goods they must be kept available for the period reasonably necessary to enable the buyer to take possession; but

(b) unless otherwise agreed the buyer must furnish facilities reasonably suited to the receipt of the goods.

(2) Where the case is within the next section respecting shipment tender requires that the seller comply with its provisions.

(3) Where the seller is required to deliver at a particular destination tender requires that he comply with subsection (1) and also in any appropriate case tender documents as described in subsections (4) and (5) of this section.

(4) Where goods are in the possession of a bailee and are to be delivered without being moved

(a) tender requires that the seller either tender a negotiable document of title covering such goods or procure acknowledgment by the bailee of the buyer's right to possession of the goods; but

(b) tender to the buyer of a non-negotiable document of title or of a written direction to the bailee to deliver is sufficient tender unless the buyer seasonably objects, and receipt by the bailee of notification of the buyer's rights fixes those rights as against the bailee and all third persons; but risk of loss of the goods and of any failure by the bailee to honor the non-negotiable document of title or to obey the direction remains on the seller until the buyer has had a reasonable time to present the document or direction, and a refusal by the bailee to honor the document or to obey the direction defeats the tender.

(5) Where the contract requires the seller to deliver documents

(a) he must tender all such documents in correct form, except as provided in this Article with respect to bills of lading in a set (subsection (2) of Section 2-323); and

(b) tender through customary banking channels is sufficient and dishonor of a draft accompanying the documents constitutes non-acceptance or rejection.

**§2-504. Shipment by Seller.**

Where the seller is required or authorized to send the goods to the buyer and the contract does not require him to deliver them at a particular destination, then unless otherwise agreed he must

(a) put the goods in the possession of such a carrier and make such a contract for their transportation as may be reasonable having regard to the nature of the goods and other circumstances of the case; and

(b) obtain and promptly deliver or tender in due form any document necessary to enable the buyer to obtain possession of the goods or otherwise required by the agreement or by usage of trade; and

(c) promptly notify the buyer of the shipment.

Failure to notify the buyer under paragraph (c) or to make a proper contract under paragraph (a) is a ground for rejection only if material delay or loss ensues.

**§2-505. Seller's Shipment Under Reservation.**

(1) Where the seller has identified goods to the contract by or before shipment:

(a) his procurement of a negotiable bill of lading to his own order or otherwise reserves in him a security interest in the goods. His procurement of the bill to the order of a financing agency or of the buyer indicates in addition only the seller's expectation of transferring that interest to the person named.

(b) a non-negotiable bill of lading to himself or his nominee reserves possession of the goods as security but except in a case of conditional delivery (subsection (2) of Section 2-507) a non-negotiable bill of lading naming the buyer as consignee reserves no security interest even though the seller retains possession of the bill of lading.

(2) When shipment by the seller with reservation of a security interest is in violation of the contract for sale it constitutes an improper contract for transportation within the preceding section but impairs neither the rights given to the buyer by shipment and identification of the goods to the contract nor the seller's powers as a holder of a negotiable document.

**§2-506. Rights of Financing Agency.**

(1) A financing agency by paying or purchasing for value a draft which relates to a shipment of goods acquires to the extent of the payment or purchase and in addition to its own rights under the draft and any document of title securing it any rights of the shipper in the goods including the right to stop delivery and the shipper's right to have the draft honored by the buyer.

(2) The right to reimbursement of a financing agency which has in good faith honored or purchased the draft under commitment to or authority from the buyer is not impaired by subsequent discovery of defects with reference to any relevant document which was apparently regular on its face.

**§2-507. Effect of Seller's Tender; Delivery on Condition.**

(1) Tender of delivery is a condition to the buyer's duty to accept the goods and, unless otherwise agreed, to his duty to pay for them. Tender entitles the seller to acceptance of the goods and to payment according to the contract.

(2) Where payment is due and demanded on the delivery to the buyer of goods or documents of title, his right as against the seller to retain or dispose of them is conditional upon his making the payment due.

**§2-508. Cure by Seller of Improper Tender or Delivery; Replacement.**

(1) Where any tender or delivery by the seller is rejected because non-conforming and the time for performance has not yet expired, the seller may seasonably notify the buyer of his intention to cure and may then within the contract time make a conforming delivery.

(2) Where the buyer rejects a non-conforming tender which the seller had reasonable grounds to believe would be acceptable with or without money allowance the seller may if he seasonably notifies the buyer have a further reasonable time to substitute a conforming tender.

**§2-509. Risk of Loss in the Absence of Breach.**

(1) Where the contract requires or authorizes the seller to ship the goods by carrier

(a) if it does not require him to deliver them at a particular destination, the risk of loss passes to the buyer when the goods are duly delivered to the carrier even though the shipment is under reservation (Section 2-505); but

(b) if it does require him to deliver them at a particular destination and the goods are there duly tendered while in the possession of the carrier, the risk of loss passes to the buyer when the goods are there duly so tendered as to enable the buyer to take delivery.

(2) Where the goods are held by a bailee to be delivered without being moved, the risk of loss passes to the buyer

(a) on his receipt of a negotiable document of title covering the goods; or

(b) on acknowledgment by the bailee of the buyer's right to possession of the goods; or

(c) after his receipt of a non-negotiable document of title or other written direction to deliver, as provided in subsection (4)(b) of Section 2-503.

(3) In any case not within subsection (1) or (2), the risk of loss passes to the buyer on his receipt of the goods if the seller is a merchant; otherwise, the risk passes to the buyer on tender of delivery.

(4) The provisions of this section are subject to contrary agreement of the parties and to the provisions of this Article on sale on approval (Section 2-327) and on effect of breach on risk of loss (Section 2-510).

**§2-510. Effect of Breach on Risk of Loss.**

(1) Where a tender or delivery of goods so fails to conform to the contract as to give a right of rejection the risk of their loss remains on the seller until cure or acceptance.

(2) Where the buyer rightfully revokes acceptance he may to the extent of any deficiency in his effective insurance coverage treat the risk of loss as having rested on the seller from the beginning.

(3) Where the buyer as to conforming goods already identified to the contract for sale repudiates or is otherwise in breach before risk of their loss has passed to him, the seller may to the extent of any deficiency in his effective insurance coverage treat the risk of loss as resting on the buyer for a commercially reasonable time.

**§2-511. Tender of Payment by Buyer; Payment by Check.**

(1) Unless otherwise agreed tender of payment is a condition to the seller's duty to tender and complete any delivery.

(2) Tender of payment is sufficient when made by any means or in any manner current in the ordinary course of business unless the seller demands payment in legal tender and gives any extension of time reasonably necessary to procure it.

(3) Subject to the provisions of this Act on the effect of an instrument on an obligation (Section 3-802), payment by check is conditional and is defeated as between the parties by dishonor of the check on due presentment.

**§2-512. Payment by Buyer Before Inspection.**

(1) Where the contract requires payment before inspection non-conformity of the goods does not excuse the buyer from so making payment unless

(a) the non-conformity appears without inspection; or

(b) despite tender of the required documents the circumstances would justify injunction against honor under the provisions of this Act (Section 5-114).

(2) Payment pursuant to subsection (1) does not constitute an acceptance of goods or impair the buyer's right to inspect or any of his remedies.

**§2-513. Buyer's Right to Inspection of Goods.**
(1) Unless otherwise agreed and subject to subsection (3), where goods are tendered or delivered or identified to the contract for sale, the buyer has a right before payment or acceptance to inspect them at any reasonable place and time and in any reasonable manner. When the seller is required or authorized to send the goods to the buyer, the inspection may be after their arrival.
(2) Expenses of inspection must be borne by the buyer but may be recovered from the seller if the goods do not conform and are rejected.
(3) Unless otherwise agreed and subject to the provisions of this Article on C.I.F. contracts (subsection (3) of Section 2-321), the buyer is not entitled to inspect the goods before payment of the price when the contract provides

(a) for delivery "C.O.D." or on other like terms; or
(b) for payment against documents of title, except where such payment is due only after the goods are to become available for inspection.

(4) A place or method of inspection fixed by the parties is presumed to be exclusive but unless otherwise expressly agreed it does not postpone identification or shift the place for delivery or for passing the risk of loss. If compliance becomes impossible, inspection shall be as provided in this section unless the place or method fixed was clearly intended as an indispensable condition failure of which avoids the contract.

**§2-514. When Documents Deliverable on Acceptance; When on Payment.**
Unless otherwise agreed documents against which a draft is drawn are to be delivered to the drawee on acceptance of the draft if it is payable more than three days after presentment; otherwise, only on payment.

**§2-515. Preserving Evidence of Goods in Dispute.**
In furtherance of the adjustment of any claim or dispute
(a) either party on reasonable notification to the other and for the purpose of ascertaining the facts and preserving evidence has the right to inspect, test and sample the goods including such of them as may be in the possession or control of the other; and
(b) the parties may agree to a third party inspection or survey to determine the conformity or condition of the goods and may agree that the findings shall be binding upon them in any subsequent litigation or adjustment.

## Part 6—Breach, Repudiation and Excuse

**§2-601. Buyer's Rights on Improper Delivery.**
Subject to the provisions of this Article on breach in installment contracts (Section 2-612) and unless otherwise agreed under the sections on contractual limitations of remedy (Sections 2-718 and 2-719), if the goods or the tender of delivery fail in any respect to conform to the contract, the buyer may

(a) reject the whole; or
(b) accept the whole; or
(c) accept any commercial unit or units and reject the rest.

**§2-602. Manner and Effect of Rightful Rejection.**
(1) Rejection of goods must be within a reasonable time after their delivery or tender. It is ineffective unless the buyer seasonably notifies the seller.
(2) Subject to the provisions of the two following sections on rejected goods (Sections 2-603 and 2-604),

(a) after rejection any exercise of ownership by the buyer with respect to any commercial unit is wrongful as against the seller; and
(b) if the buyer has before rejection taken physical possession of goods in which he does not have a security interest under the provisions of this Article (subsection (3) of Section 2-711), he is under a duty after rejection to hold them with reasonable care at the seller's disposition for a time sufficient to permit the seller to remove them; but
(c) the buyer has no further obligations with regard to goods rightfully rejected.

(3) The seller's rights with respect to goods wrongfully rejected are governed by the provisions of this Article on seller's remedies in general (Section 2-703).

**§2-603. Merchant Buyer's Duties as to Rightfully Rejected Goods.**
(1) Subject to any security interest in the buyer (subsection (3) of Section 2-711), when the seller has no agent or place of business at the market of rejection a merchant buyer is under a duty after rejection of goods in his possession or control to follow any reasonable instructions received from the seller with respect to the goods and in the absence of such instructions to make reasonable efforts to sell them for the seller's account if they are perishable or threaten to decline in value speedily. Instructions are not reasonable if on demand indemnity for expenses is not forthcoming.
(2) When the buyer sells goods under subsection (1), he is entitled to reimbursement from the seller or out of the proceeds for reasonable expenses of caring for and selling them, and if the expenses include no selling commission then to such commission as is usual in the trade or if there is none to a reasonable sum not exceeding ten per cent on the gross proceeds.
(3) In complying with this section the buyer is held only to good faith and good faith conduct hereunder is neither acceptance nor conversion nor the basis of an action for damages.

**§2-604. Buyer's Options as to Salvage of Rightfully Rejected Goods.**
Subject to the provisions of the immediately preceding section on perishables if the seller gives no instructions within a reasonable time after notification of rejection the buyer may store the rejected goods for the seller's account or reship them to him or resell them for the seller's account with reimbursement as provided in the preceding section. Such action is not acceptance or conversion.

**§2-605. Waiver of Buyer's Objections by Failure to Particularize.**
(1) The buyer's failure to state in connection with rejection a particular defect which is ascertainable by reasonable inspection precludes him from relying on the unstated defect to justify rejection or to establish breach

(a) where the seller could have cured it if stated seasonably; or
(b) between merchants when the seller has after rejection made a request in writing for a full and final written statement of all defects on which the buyer proposes to rely.

(2) Payment against documents made without reservation of rights precludes recovery of the payment for defects apparent on the face of the documents.

**§2-606. What Constitutes Acceptance of Goods.**
(1) Acceptance of goods occurs when the buyer

(a) after a reasonable opportunity to inspect the goods signifies to the seller that the goods are conforming or that he will take or retain them in spite of their nonconformity; or
(b) fails to make an effective rejection (subsection (1) of Section 2-602), but such acceptance does not occur until the buyer has had a reasonable opportunity to inspect them; or
(c) does any act inconsistent with the seller's ownership; but if such act is wrongful as against the seller it is an acceptance only if ratified by him.

(2) Acceptance of a part of any commercial unit is acceptance of that entire unit.

**§2-607. Effect of Acceptance; Notice of Breach; Burden of Establishing Breach After Acceptance; Notice of Claim or Litigation to Person Answerable Over.**
(1) The buyer must pay at the contract rate for any goods accepted.
(2) Acceptance of goods by the buyer precludes rejection of the goods accepted and if made with knowledge of a non-conformity cannot be

revoked because of it unless the acceptance was on the reasonable assumption that the non-conformity would be seasonably cured but acceptance does not of itself impair any other remedy provided by this Article for non-conformity.

(3) Where a tender has been accepted

(a) the buyer must within a reasonable time after he discovers or should have discovered any breach notify the seller of breach or be barred from any remedy; and

(b) if the claim is one for infringement or the like (subsection (3) of Section 2-312) and the buyer is sued as a result of such a breach he must so notify the seller within a reasonable time after he receives notice of the litigation or be barred from any remedy over for liability established by the litigation.

(4) The burden is on the buyer to establish any breach with respect to the goods accepted.

(5) Where the buyer is sued for breach of a warranty or other obligation for which his seller is answerable over

(a) he may give his seller written notice of the litigation. If the notice states that the seller may come in and defend and that if the seller does not do so he will be bound in any action against him by his buyer by any determination of fact common to the two litigations, then unless the seller after seasonable receipt of the notice does come in and defend he is so bound.

(b) if the claim is one for infringement or the like (subsection (3) of Section 2-312) the original seller may demand in writing that his buyer turn over to him control of the litigation including settlement or else be barred from any remedy over and if he also agrees to bear all expense and to satisfy any adverse judgment, then unless the buyer after seasonable receipt of the demand does turn over control the buyer is so barred.

(6) The provisions of subsections (3), (4) and (5) apply to any obligation of a buyer to hold the seller harmless against infringement or the like (subsection (3) of Section 2-312).

**§2-608. Revocation of Acceptance in Whole or in Part.**

(1) The buyer may revoke his acceptance of a lot or commercial unit whose non-conformity substantially impairs its value to him if he has accepted it

(a) on the reasonable assumption that its non-conformity would be cured and it has not been seasonably cured; or

(b) without discovery of such non-conformity if his acceptance was reasonably induced either by the difficulty of discovery before acceptance or by the seller's assurances.

(2) Revocation of acceptance must occur within a reasonable time after the buyer discovers or should have discovered the ground for it and before any substantial change in condition of the goods which is not caused by their own defects. It is not effective until the buyer notifies the seller of it.

(3) A buyer who so revokes has the same rights and duties with regard to the goods involved as if he had rejected them.

**§2-609. Right to Adequate Assurance of Performance.**

(1) A contract for sale imposes an obligation on each party that the other's expectation of receiving due performance will not be impaired. When reasonable grounds for insecurity arise with respect to the performance of either party the other may in writing demand adequate assurance of due performance and until he receives such assurance may if commercially reasonable suspend any performance for which he has not already received the agreed return.

(2) Between merchants the reasonableness of grounds for insecurity and the adequacy of any assurance offered shall be determined according to commercial standards.

(3) Acceptance of any improper delivery or payment does not prejudice the aggrieved party's right to demand adequate assurance of future performance.

(4) After receipt of a justified demand failure to provide within a reasonable time not exceeding thirty days such assurance of due performance as is adequate under the circumstances of the particular case is a repudiation of the contract.

**§2-610. Anticipatory Repudiation.**

When either party repudiates the contract with respect to a performance not yet due the loss of which will substantially impair the value of the contract to the other, the aggrieved party may

(a) for a commercially reasonable time await performance by the repudiating party; or

(b) resort to any remedy for breach (Section 2-703 or Section 2-711), even though he has notified the repudiating party that he would await the latter's performance and has urged retraction; and

(c) in either case suspend his own performance or proceed in accordance with the provisions of this Article on the seller's right to identify goods to the contract notwithstanding breach or to salvage unfinished goods (Section 2-704).

**§2-611. Retraction of Anticipatory Repudiation.**

(1) Until the repudiating party's next performance is due he can retract his repudiation unless the aggrieved party has since the repudiation cancelled or materially changed his position or otherwise indicated that he considers the repudiation final.

(2) Retraction may be by any method which clearly indicates to the aggrieved party that the repudiating party intends to perform, but must include any assurance justifiably demanded under the provisions of this Article (Section 2-609).

(3) Retraction reinstates the repudiating party's rights under the contract with due excuse and allowance to the aggrieved party for any delay occasioned by the repudiation.

**§2-612. "Installment Contract"; Breach.**

(1) An "installment contract" is one which requires or authorizes the delivery of goods in separate lots to be separately accepted, even though the contract contains a clause "each delivery is a separate contract" or its equivalent.

(2) The buyer may reject any installment which is non-conforming if the non-conformity substantially impairs the value of that installment and cannot be cured or if the non-conformity is a defect in the required documents; but if the non-conformity does not fall within subsection (3) and the seller gives adequate assurance of its cure the buyer must accept that installment.

(3) Whenever non-conformity or default with respect to one or more installments substantially impairs the value of the whole contract there is a breach of the whole. But the aggrieved party reinstates the contract if he accepts a non-conforming installment without seasonably notifying of cancellation or if he brings an action with respect only to past installments or demands performance as to future installments.

**§2-613. Casualty to Identified Goods.**

Where the contract requires for its performance goods identified when the contract is made, and the goods suffer casualty without fault of either party before the risk of loss passes to the buyer, or in a proper case under a "no arrival, no sale" term (Section 2-324) then

(a) if the loss is total the contract is avoided; and

(b) if the loss is partial or the goods have so deteriorated as no longer to conform to the contract the buyer may nevertheless demand inspection and at his option either treat the contract as avoided or accept the goods with due allowance from the contract price for the deterioration or the deficiency in quantity but without further right against the seller.

**§2-614. Substituted Performance.**

(1) Where without fault of either party the agreed berthing, loading, or unloading facilities fail or an agreed type of carrier becomes unavailable or the agreed manner of delivery otherwise becomes commercially

impracticable but a commercially reasonable substitute is available, such substitute performance must be tendered and accepted.
(2) If the agreed means or manner of payment fails because of domestic or foreign governmental regulation, the seller may withhold or stop delivery unless the buyer provides a means or manner of payment which is commercially a substantial equivalent. If delivery has already been taken, payment by the means or in the manner provided by the regulation discharges the buyer's obligation unless the regulation is discriminatory, oppressive or predatory.

**§2-615. Excuse by Failure of Presupposed Conditions.**
Except so far as a seller may have assumed a greater obligation and subject to the preceding section on substituted performance:
(a) Delay in delivery or non-delivery in whole or in part by a seller who complies with paragraphs (b) and (c) is not a breach of his duty under a contract for sale if performance as agreed has been made impracticable by the occurrence of a contingency the non-occurrence of which was a basic assumption on which the contract was made or by compliance in good faith with any applicable foreign or domestic governmental regulation or order whether or not it later proves to be invalid.
(b) Where the causes mentioned in paragraph (a) affect only a part of the seller's capacity to perform, he must allocate production and deliveries among his customers but may at his option include regular customers not then under contract as well as his own requirements for further manufacture. He may so allocate in any manner which is fair and reasonable.
(c) The seller must notify the buyer seasonably that there will be delay or non-delivery and, when allocation is required under paragraph (b), of the estimated quota thus made available for the buyer.

**§2-616. Procedure on Notice Claiming Excuse.**
(1) Where the buyer receives notification of a material or indefinite delay or an allocation justified under the preceding section he may by written notification to the seller as to any delivery concerned, and where the prospective deficiency substantially impairs the value of the whole contract under the provisions of this Article relating to breach of installment contracts (Section 2-612), then also as to the whole,
(a) terminate and thereby discharge any unexecuted portion of the contract; or
(b) modify the contract by agreeing to take his available quota in substitution.
(2) If after receipt of such notification from the seller the buyer fails so to modify the contract within a reasonable time not exceeding thirty days the contract lapses with respect to any deliveries affected.
(3) The provisions of this section may not be negated by agreement except in so far as the seller has assumed a greater obligation under the preceding section.

## Part 7—Remedies

**§2-701. Remedies for Breach of Collateral Contracts Not Impaired.**
Remedies for breach of any obligation or promise collateral or ancillary to a contract for sale are not impaired by the provisions of this Article.

**§2-702. Seller's Remedies on Discovery of Buyer's Insolvency.**
(1) Where the seller discovers the buyer to be insolvent he may refuse delivery except for cash including payment for all goods theretofore delivered under the contract, and stop delivery under this Article (Section 2-705).
(2) Where the seller discovers that the buyer has received goods on credit while insolvent he may reclaim the goods upon demand made within ten days after the receipt, but if misrepresentation of solvency has been made to the particular seller in writing within three months before delivery the ten day limitation does not apply. Except as provided in this subsection the seller may not base a right to reclaim goods on the buyer's fraudulent or innocent misrepresentation of solvency or of intent to pay.
(3) The seller's right to reclaim under subsection (2) is subject to the rights of a buyer in ordinary course or other good faith purchaser under this Article (Section 2-403). Successful reclamation of goods excludes all other remedies with respect to them.

**§2-703. Seller's Remedies in General.**
Where the buyer wrongfully rejects or revokes acceptance of goods or fails to make a payment due on or before delivery or repudiates with respect to a part or the whole, then with respect to any goods directly affected and, if the breach is of the whole contract (Section 2-612), then also with respect to the whole undelivered balance, the aggrieved seller may
(a) withhold delivery of such goods;
(b) stop delivery by any bailee as hereafter provided (Section 2-705);
(c) proceed under the next section respecting goods still unidentified to the contract;
(d) resell and recover damages as hereafter provided (Section 2-706);
(e) recover damages for non-acceptance (Section 2-708) or in a proper case the price (Section 2-709);
(f) cancel.

**§2-704. Seller's Right to Identify Goods to the Contract Notwithstanding Breach or to Salvage Unfinished Goods.**
(1) An aggrieved seller under the preceding section may
(a) identify to the contract conforming goods not already identified if at the time he learned of the breach they are in his possession or control;
(b) treat as the subject of resale goods which have demonstrably been intended for the particular contract even though those goods are unfinished.
(2) Where the goods are unfinished an aggrieved seller may in the exercise of reasonable commercial judgment for the purposes of avoiding loss and of effective realization either complete the manufacture and wholly identify the goods to the contract or cease manufacture and resell for scrap or salvage value or proceed in any other reasonable manner.

**§2-705. Seller's Stoppage of Delivery in Transit or Otherwise.**
(1) The seller may stop delivery of goods in the possession of a carrier or other bailee when he discovers the buyer to be insolvent (Section 2-702) and may stop delivery of carload, truckload, planeload or larger shipments of express or freight when the buyer repudiates or fails to make a payment due before delivery or if for any other reason the seller has a right to withhold or reclaim the goods.
(2) As against such buyer the seller may stop delivery until
(a) receipt of the goods by the buyer; or
(b) acknowledgment to the buyer by any bailee of the goods except a carrier that the bailee holds the goods for the buyer; or
(c) such acknowledgment to the buyer by a carrier by reshipment or as warehouseman; or
(d) negotiation to the buyer of any negotiable document of title covering the goods.
(3) (a) To stop delivery the seller must so notify as to enable the bailee by reasonable diligence to prevent delivery of the goods.
(b) After such notification the bailee must hold and deliver the goods according to the directions of the seller but the seller is liable to the bailee for any ensuing charges or damages.
(c) If a negotiable document of title has been issued for goods the bailee is not obliged to obey a notification to stop until surrender of the document.
(d) A carrier who has issued a non-negotiable bill of lading is not obliged to obey a notification to stop received from a person other than the consignor.

**§2-706. Seller's Resale Including Contract for Resale.**
(1) Under the conditions stated in Section 2-703 on seller's remedies, the seller may resell the goods concerned or the undelivered balance thereof.

Where the resale is made in good faith and in a commercially reasonable manner the seller may recover the difference between the resale price and the contract price together with any incidental damages allowed under the provisions of this Article (Section 2-710), but less expenses saved in consequence of the buyer's breach.

(2) Except as otherwise provided in subsection (3) or unless otherwise agreed resale may be at public or private sale including sale by way of one or more contracts to sell or of identification to an existing contract of the seller. Sale may be as a unit or in parcels and at any time and place and on any terms but every aspect of the sale including the method, manner, time, place and terms must be commercially reasonable. The resale must be reasonably identified as referring to the broken contract, but it is not necessary that the goods be in existence or that any or all of them have been identified to the contract before the breach.

(3) Where the resale is at private sale the seller must give the buyer reasonable notification of his intention to resell.

(4) Where the resale is at public sale

(a) only identified goods can be sold except where there is a recognized market for a public sale of futures in goods of the kind; and

(b) it must be made at a usual place or market for public sale if one is reasonably available and except in the case of goods which are perishable or threaten to decline in value speedily the seller must give the buyer reasonable notice of the time and place of the resale; and

(c) if the goods are not to be within the view of those attending the sale the notification of sale must state the place where the goods are located and provide for their reasonable inspection by prospective bidders; and

(d) the seller may buy.

(5) A purchaser who buys in good faith at a resale takes the goods free of any rights of the original buyer even though the seller fails to comply with one or more of the requirements of this section.

(6) The seller is not accountable to the buyer for any profit made on any resale. A person in the position of a seller (Section 2-707) or a buyer who has rightfully rejected or justifiably revoked acceptance must account for any excess over the amount of his security interest, as hereinafter defined (subsection (3) of Section 2-711).

**§2-707. "Person in the Position of a Seller".**

(1) A "person in the position of a seller" includes as against a principal an agent who has paid or become responsible for the price of goods on behalf of his principal or anyone who otherwise holds a security interest or other right in goods similar to that of a seller.

(2) A person in the position of a seller may as provided in this Article withhold or stop delivery (Section 2-705) and resell (Section 2-706) and recover incidental damages (Section 2-710).

**§2-708. Seller's Damages for Non-Acceptance or Repudiation.**

(1) Subject to subsection (2) and to the provisions of this Article with respect to proof of market price (Section 2-723), the measure of damages for non-acceptance or repudiation by the buyer is the difference between the market price at the time and place for tender and the unpaid contract price together with any incidental damages provided in this Article (Section 2-710), but less expenses saved in consequence of the buyer's breach.

(2) If the measure of damages provided in subsection (1) is inadequate to put the seller in as good a position as performance would have done then the measure of damages is the profit (including reasonable overhead) which the seller would have made from full performance by the buyer, together with any incidental damages provided in this Article (Section 2-710), due allowance for costs reasonably incurred and due credit for payments or proceeds of resale.

**§2-709. Action for the Price.**

(1) When the buyer fails to pay the price as it becomes due the seller may recover, together with any incidental damages under the next section, the price

(a) of goods accepted or of conforming goods lost or damaged within a commercially reasonable time after risk of their loss has passed to the buyer; and

(b) of goods identified to the contract if the seller is unable after reasonable effort to resell them at a reasonable price or the circumstances reasonably indicate that such effort will be unavailing.

(2) Where the seller sues for the price he must hold for the buyer any goods which have been identified to the contract and are still in his control except that if resale becomes possible he may resell them at any time prior to the collection of the judgment. The net proceeds of any such resale must be credited to the buyer and payment of the judgment entitles him to any goods not resold.

(3) After the buyer has wrongfully rejected or revoked acceptance of the goods or has failed to make a payment due or has repudiated (Section 2-610), a seller who is held not entitled to the price under this section shall nevertheless be awarded damages for non-acceptance under the preceding section.

**§2-710. Seller's Incidental Damages.**

Incidental damages to an aggrieved seller include any commercially reasonable charges, expenses or commissions incurred in stopping delivery, in the transportation, care and custody of goods after the buyer's breach, in connection with return or resale of the goods or otherwise resulting from the breach.

**§2-711. Buyer's Remedies in General; Buyer's Security Interest in Rejected Goods.**

(1) Where the seller fails to make delivery or repudiates or the buyer rightfully rejects or justifiably revokes acceptance then with respect to any goods involved, and with respect to the whole if the breach goes to the whole contract (Section 2-612), the buyer may cancel and whether or not he has done so may in addition to recovering so much of the price as has been paid

(a) "cover" and have damages under the next section as to all the goods affected whether or not they have been identified to the contract; or

(b) recover damages for non-delivery as provided in this Article (Section 2-713).

(2) Where the seller fails to deliver or repudiates the buyer may also

(a) if the goods have been identified recover them as provided in this Article (Section 2-502); or

(b) in a proper case obtain specific performance or replevy the goods as provided in this Article (Section 2-716).

(3) On rightful rejection or justifiable revocation of acceptance a buyer has a security interest in goods in his possession or control for any payments made on their price and any expenses reasonably incurred in their inspection, receipt, transportation, care and custody and may hold such goods and resell them in like manner as an aggrieved seller (Section 2-706).

**§2-712. "Cover"; Buyer's Procurement of Substitute Goods.**

(1) After a breach within the preceding section the buyer may "cover" by making in good faith and without unreasonable delay any reasonable purchase of or contract to purchase goods in substitution for those due from the seller.

(2) The buyer may recover from the seller as damages the difference between the cost of cover and the contract price together with any incidental or consequential damages as hereinafter defined (Section 2-715), but less expenses saved in consequence of the seller's breach.

(3) Failure of the buyer to effect cover within this section does not bar him from any other remedy.

**§2-713. Buyer's Damages for Non-Delivery or Repudiation.**
(1) Subject to provisions of this Article with respect to the proof of market price (Section 2-723), the measure of damages for non-delivery or repudiation by the seller is the difference between the market price at the time when the buyer learned of the breach and the contract price together with any incidental and consequential damages provided in this Article (Section 2-715), but less expenses saved in consequence of the seller's breach.
(2) Market price is to be determined as of the place for tender or, in cases of rejection after arrival or revocation of acceptance, as of the place of arrival.

**§2-714. Buyer's Damages for Breach in Regard to Accepted Goods.**
(1) Where the buyer has accepted goods and given notification (subsection (3) of Section 2-607) he may recover as damages for any non-conformity of tender the loss resulting in the ordinary course of events from the seller's breach as determined in any manner which is reasonable.
(2) The measure of damages for breach of warranty is the difference at the time and place of acceptance between the value of the goods accepted and the value they would have had if they had been as warranted, unless special circumstances show proximate damages of a different amount.
(3) In a proper case any incidental and consequential damages under the next section may be recovered.

**§2-715. Buyer's Incidental and Consequential Damages.**
(1) Incidental damages resulting from the seller's breach include expenses reasonably incurred in inspection, receipt, transportation and care and custody of goods rightfully rejected, any commercially reasonable charges, expenses or commissions in connection with effecting cover and any other reasonable expense incident to the delay or other breach.
(2) Consequential damages resulting from the seller's breach include
(a) any loss resulting from general or particular requirements and needs of which the seller at the time of contracting had reason to know and which could not reasonably be prevented by cover or otherwise; and
(b) injury to person or property proximately resulting from any breach of warranty.

**§2-716. Buyer's Right to Specific Performance or Replevin.**
(1) Specific performance may be decreed where the goods are unique or in other proper circumstances.
(2) The decree for specific performance may include such terms and conditions as to payment of the price, damages, or other relief as the court may deem just.
(3) The buyer has a right of replevin for goods identified to the contract if after reasonable effort he is unable to effect cover for such goods or the circumstances reasonably indicate that such effort will be unavailing or if the goods have been shipped under reservation and satisfaction of the security interest in them has been made or tendered.

**§2-717. Deduction of Damages From the Price.**
The buyer on notifying the seller of his intention to do so may deduct all or any part of the damages resulting from any breach of the contract from any part of the price still due under the same contract.

**§2-718. Liquidation or Limitation of Damages; Deposits.**
(1) Damages for breach by either party may be liquidated in the agreement but only at an amount which is reasonable in the light of the anticipated or actual harm caused by the breach, the difficulties of proof of loss, and the inconvenience or nonfeasibility of otherwise obtaining an adequate remedy. A term fixing unreasonably large liquidated damages is void as a penalty.
(2) Where the seller justifiably withholds delivery of goods because of the buyer's breach, the buyer is entitled to restitution of any amount by which the sum of his payments exceeds
(a) the amount to which the seller is entitled by virtue of terms liquidating the seller's damages in accordance with subsection (1), or
(b) in the absence of such terms, twenty per cent of the value of the total performance for which the buyer is obligated under the contract or $500, whichever is smaller.
(3) The buyer's right to restitution under subsection (2) is subject to offset to the extent that the seller establishes
(a) a right to recover damages under the provisions of this Article other than subsection (1), and
(b) the amount or value of any benefits received by the buyer directly or indirectly by reason of the contract.
(4) Where a seller has received payment in goods their reasonable value or the proceeds of their resale shall be treated as payments for the purposes of subsection (2); but if the seller has notice of the buyer's breach before reselling goods received in part performance, his resale is subject to the conditions laid down in this Article on resale by an aggrieved seller (Section 2-706).

**§2-719. Contractual Modification or Limitation of Remedy.**
(1) Subject to the provisions of subsection (2) and (3) of this section and of the preceding section on liquidation and limitation of damages,
(a) the agreement may provide for remedies in addition to or in substitution for those provided in this Article and may limit or alter the measure of damages recoverable under this Article, as by limiting the buyer's remedies to return of the goods and repayment of the price or to repair and replacement of non-conforming goods or parts; and
(b) resort to a remedy as provided is optional unless the remedy is expressly agreed to be exclusive, in which case it is the sole remedy.
(2) Where circumstances cause an exclusive or limited remedy to fail of its essential purpose, remedy may be had as provided in this Act.
(3) Consequential damages may be limited or excluded unless the limitation or exclusion is unconscionable. Limitation of consequential damages for injury to the person in the case of consumer goods is prima facie unconscionable but limitation of damages where the loss is commercial is not.

**§2-720. Effect of "Cancellation" or "Rescission" on Claims for Antecedent Breach.**
Unless the contrary intention clearly appears, expressions of "cancellation" or "rescission" of the contract or the like shall not be construed as a renunciation or discharge of any claim in damages for an antecedent breach.

**§2-721. Remedies for Fraud.**
Remedies for material misrepresentation or fraud include all remedies available under this Article for non-fraudulent breach. Neither rescission or a claim for rescission of the contract for sale nor rejection or return of the goods shall bar or be deemed inconsistent with a claim for damages or other remedy.

**§2-722. Who Can Sue Third Parties for Injury to Goods.**
Where a third party so deals with goods which have been identified to a contract for sale as to cause actionable injury to a party to that contract
(a) a right of action against the third party is in either party to the contract for sale who has title to or a security interest or a special property or an insurable interest in the goods; and if the goods have been destroyed or converted a right of action is also in the party who either bore the risk of loss under the contract for sale or has since the injury assumed that risk as against the other;
(b) if at the time of the injury the party plaintiff did not bear the risk of loss as against the other party to the contract for sale and there is no arrangement between them for disposition of the recovery, his suit or settlement is subject to his own interest, as a fiduciary for the other party to the contract;

(c) either party may with the consent of the other sue for the benefit of whom it may concern.

**§2-723. Proof of Market Price: Time and Place.**

(1) If an action based on anticipatory repudiation comes to trial before the time for performance with respect to some or all of the goods, any damages based on market price (Section 2-708 or Section 2-713) shall be determined according to the price of such goods prevailing at the time when the aggrieved party learned of the repudiation.

(2) If evidence of a price prevailing at the times or places described in this Article is not readily available the price prevailing within any reasonable time before or after the time described or at any other place which in commercial judgment or under usage of trade would serve as a reasonable substitute for the one described may be used, making any proper allowance for the cost of transporting the goods to or from such other place.

(3) Evidence of a relevant price prevailing at a time or place other than the one described in this Article offered by one party is not admissible unless and until he has given the other party such notice as the court finds sufficient to prevent unfair surprise.

**§2-724. Admissibility of Market Quotations.**

Whenever the prevailing price or value of any goods regularly bought and sold in any established commodity market is in issue, reports in official publications or trade journals or in newspapers or periodicals of general circulation published as the reports of such market shall be admissible in evidence. The circumstances of the preparation of such a report may be shown to affect its weight but not its admissibility.

**§2-725. Statute of Limitations in Contracts for Sale.**

(1) An action for breach of any contract for sale must be commenced within four years after the cause of action has accrued. By the original agreement the parties may reduce the period of limitation to not less than one year but may not extend it.

(2) A cause of action occurs when the breach occurs, regardless of the aggrieved party's lack of knowledge of the breach. A breach of warranty occurs when tender of delivery is made, except that where a warranty explicitly extends to future performance of the goods and discovery of the breach must await the time of such performance the cause of action accrues when the breach is or should have been discovered.

(3) Where an action commenced within the time limited by subsection (1) is so terminated as to leave available a remedy by another action for the same breach such other action may be commenced after the expiration of the time limited and within six months after the termination of the first action unless the termination resulted from voluntary discontinuance or from dismissal for failure or neglect to prosecute.

(4) This section does not alter the law on tolling of the statute of limitations nor does it apply to causes of action which have accrued before this Act becomes effective.

## ARTICLE 2A: LEASES

### Part 1—General Provisions

**§2A-101. Short Title.**

This Article shall be known and may be cited as the Uniform Commercial Code—Leases.

**§2A-102. Scope.**

This Article applies to any transaction, regardless of form, that creates a lease.

**§2A-103. Definitions and Index of Definitions.**

(1) In this Article unless the context otherwise requires:

(a) "Buyer in ordinary course of business" means a person who in good faith and without knowledge that the sale to him [or her] is in violation of the ownership rights or security interest or leasehold interest of a third party in the goods buys in ordinary course from a person in the business of selling goods of that kind but does not include a pawnbroker. "Buying" may be for cash or by exchange of other property or on secured or unsecured credit and includes receiving goods or documents of title under a pre-existing contract for sale but does not include a transfer in bulk or as security for or in total or partial satisfaction of a money debt.

(b) "Cancellation" occurs when either party puts an end to the lease contract for default by the other party.

(c) "Commercial unit" means such a unit of goods as by commercial usage is a single whole for purposes of lease and division of which materially impairs its character or value on the market or in use. A commercial unit may be a single article, as a machine, or a set of articles, as a suite of furniture or a line of machinery, or a quantity, as a gross or carload, or any other unit treated in use or in the relevant market as a single whole.

(d) "Conforming" goods or performance under a lease contract means goods or performance that are in accordance with the obligations under the lease contract.

(e) "Consumer lease" means a lease that a lessor regularly engaged in the business of leasing or selling makes to a lessee who is an individual and who takes under the lease primarily for a personal, family, or household purpose [, if the total payments to be made under the lease contract, excluding payments for options to renew or buy, do not exceed $__________].

(f) "Fault" means wrongful act, omission, breach, or default.

(g) "Finance lease" means a lease with respect to which:

(i) the lessor does not select, manufacture, or supply the goods;

(ii) the lessor acquires the goods or the right to possession and use of the goods in connection with the lease; and

(iii) one of the following occurs:

(A) the lessee receives a copy of the contract by which the lessor acquired the goods or the right to possession and use of the goods before signing the lease contract;

(B) the lessee's approval of the contract by which the lessor acquired the goods or the right to possession and use of the goods is a condition to effectiveness of the lease contract;

(C) the lessee, before signing the lease contract, receives an accurate and complete statement designating the promises and warranties, and any disclaimers of warranties, limitations or modifications of remedies, or liquidated damages, including those of a third party, such as the manufacturer of the goods, provided to the lessor by the person supplying the goods in connection with or as part of the contract by which the lessor acquired the goods or the right to possession and use of the goods; or

(D) if the lease is not a consumer lease, the lessor, before the lessee signs the lease contract, informs the lessee in writing (a) of the identity of the person supplying the goods to the lessor, unless the lessee has selected that person and directed the lessor to acquire the goods or the right to possession and use of the goods from that person, (b) that the lessee is entitled under this Article to the promises and warranties, including those of any third party, provided to the lessor by the person supplying the goods in connection with or as part of the contract by which the lessor acquired the goods or the right to possession and use of the goods, and (c) that the lessee may communicate with the person supplying the goods to the lessor and receive an accurate and complete statement of those promises and warranties, including any disclaimers and limitations of them or of remedies.

(h) "Goods" means all things that are movable at the time of identification to the lease contract, or are fixtures (Section 2A-309), but the term does not include money, documents, instruments, accounts, chattel paper, general intangibles, or minerals or the like, including oil and gas, before extraction. The term also includes the unborn young of animals.

(i) "Installment lease contract" means a lease contract that authorizes or requires the delivery of goods in separate lots to be separately accepted, even though the lease contract contains a clause "each delivery is a separate lease" or its equivalent.

(j) "Lease" means a transfer of the right to possession and use of goods for a term in return for consideration, but a sale, including a sale on approval or a sale or return, or retention or creation of a security interest is not a lease. Unless the context clearly indicates otherwise, the term includes a sublease.

(k) "Lease agreement" means the bargain, with respect to the lease, of the lessor and the lessee in fact as found in their language or by implication from other circumstances including course of dealing or usage of trade or course of performance as provided in this Article. Unless the context clearly indicates otherwise, the term includes a sublease agreement.

(l) "Lease contract" means the total legal obligation that results from the lease agreement as affected by this Article and any other applicable rules of law. Unless the context clearly indicates otherwise, the term includes a sublease contract.

(m) "Leasehold interest" means the interest of the lessor or the lessee under a lease contract.

(n) "Lessee" means a person who acquires the right to possession and use of goods under a lease. Unless the context clearly indicates otherwise, the term includes a sublessee.

(o) "Lessee in ordinary course of business" means a person who in good faith and without knowledge that the lease to him [or her] is in violation of the ownership rights or security interest or leasehold interest of a third party in the goods, leases in ordinary course from a person in the business of selling or leasing goods of that kind but does not include a pawnbroker. "Leasing" may be for cash or by exchange of other property or on secured or unsecured credit and includes receiving goods or documents of title under a pre-existing lease contract but does not include a transfer in bulk or as security for or in total or partial satisfaction of a money debt.

(p) "Lessor" means a person who transfers the right to possession and use of goods under a lease. Unless the context clearly indicates otherwise, the term includes a sublessor.

(q) "Lessor's residual interest" means the lessor's interest in the goods after expiration, termination, or cancellation of the lease contract.

(r) "Lien" means a charge against or interest in goods to secure payment of a debt or performance of an obligation, but the term does not include a security interest.

(s) "Lot" means a parcel or a single article that is the subject matter of a separate lease or delivery, whether or not it is sufficient to perform the lease contract.

(t) "Merchant lessee" means a lessee that is a merchant with respect to goods of the kind subject to the lease.

(u) "Present value" means the amount as of a date certain of one or more sums payable in the future, discounted to the date certain. The discount is determined by the interest rate specified by the parties if the rate was not manifestly unreasonable at the time the transaction was entered into; otherwise, the discount is determined by a commercially reasonable rate that takes into account the facts and circumstances of each case at the time the transaction was entered into.

(v) "Purchase" includes taking by sale, lease, mortgage, security interest, pledge, gift, or any other voluntary transaction creating an interest in goods.

(w) "Sublease" means a lease of goods the right to possession and use of which was acquired by the lessor as a lessee under an existing lease.

(x) "Supplier" means a person from whom a lessor buys or leases goods to be leased under a finance lease.

(y) "Supply contract" means a contract under which a lessor buys or leases goods to be leased.

(z) "Termination" occurs when either party pursuant to a power created by agreement or law puts an end to the lease contract otherwise than for default.

(2) Other definitions applying to this Article and the sections in which they appear are:

"Accessions". Section 2A-310(1).
"Construction mortgage". Section 2A-309(1)(d).
"Encumbrance". Section 2A-309(1)(e).
"Fixtures". Section 2A-309(1)(a).
"Fixture filing". Section 2A-309(1)(b).
"Purchase money lease". Section 2A-309(1)(c).

(3) The following definitions in other Articles apply to this Article:

"Account". Section 9-106.
"Between merchants". Section 2-104(3).
"Buyer". Section 2-103(1)(a).
"Chattel paper". Section 9-105(1)(b).
"Consumer goods". Section 9-109(1).
"Document". Section 9-105(1)(f).
"Entrusting". Section 2-403(3).
"General intangibles". Section 9-106.
"Good faith". Section 2-103(1)(b).
"Instrument". Section 9-105(1)(i).
"Merchant". Section 2-104(1).
"Mortgage". Section 9-105(1)(j).
"Pursuant to commitment". Section 9-105(1)(k).
"Receipt". Section 2-103(1)(c).
"Sale". Section 2-106(1).
"Sale on approval". Section 2-326.
"Sale or return". Section 2-326.
"Seller". Section 2-103(1)(d).

(4) In addition Article 1 contains general definitions and principles of construction and interpretation applicable throughout this Article.

As amended in 1990.

### §2A-104. Leases Subject to Other Law.

(1) A lease, although subject to this Article, is also subject to any applicable:

(a) certificate of title statute of this State: (list any certificate of title statutes covering automobiles, trailers, mobile homes, boats, farm tractors, and the like);

(b) certificate of title statute of another jurisdiction (Section 2A-105); or

(c) consumer protection statute of this State, or final consumer protection decision of a court of this State existing on the effective date of this Article.

(2) In case of conflict between this Article, other than Sections 2A-105, 2A-304(3), and 2A-305(3), and a statute or decision referred to in subsection (1), the statute or decision controls.

(3) Failure to comply with an applicable law has only the effect specified therein.

As amended in 1990.

### §2A-108. Unconscionability.

(1) If the court as a matter of law finds a lease contract or any clause of a lease contract to have been unconscionable at the time it was made the court may refuse to enforce the lease contract, or it may enforce the remainder of the lease contract without the unconscionable clause, or it may so limit the application of any unconscionable clause as to avoid any unconscionable result.

(2) With respect to a consumer lease, if the court as a matter of law finds that a lease contract or any clause of a lease contract has been induced by unconscionable conduct or that unconscionable conduct has occurred in the collection of a claim arising from a lease contract, the court may grant appropriate relief.
(3) Before making a finding of unconscionability under subsection (1) or (2), the court, on its own motion or that of a party, shall afford the parties a reasonable opportunity to present evidence as to the setting, purpose, and effect of the lease contract or clause thereof, or of the conduct.
(4) In an action in which the lessee claims unconscionability with respect to a consumer lease:
(a) If the court finds unconscionability under subsection (1) or (2), the court shall award reasonable attorney's fees to the lessee.
(b) If the court does not find unconscionability and the lessee claiming unconscionability has brought or maintained an action he [or she] knew to be groundless, the court shall award reasonable attorney's fees to the party against whom the claim is made.
(c) In determining attorney's fees, the amount of the recovery on behalf of the claimant under subsections (1) and (2) is not controlling.

## Part 2—Formation and Construction of Lease Contract

**§2A-201. Statute of Frauds.**
(1) A lease contract is not enforceable by way of action or defense unless:
(a) the total payments to be made under the lease contract, excluding payments for options to renew or buy, are less than $1,000; or
(b) there is a writing, signed by the party against whom enforcement is sought or by that party's authorized agent, sufficient to indicate that a lease contract has been made between the parties and to describe the goods leased and the lease term.
(2) Any description of leased goods or of the lease term is sufficient and satisfies subsection (1)(b), whether or not it is specific, if it reasonably identifies what is described.
(3) A writing is not insufficient because it omits or incorrectly states a term agreed upon, but the lease contract is not enforceable under subsection (1)(b) beyond the lease term and the quantity of goods shown in the writing.
(4) A lease contract that does not satisfy the requirements of subsection (1), but which is valid in other respects, is enforceable:
(a) if the goods are to be specially manufactured or obtained for the lessee and are not suitable for lease or sale to others in the ordinary course of the lessor's business, and the lessor, before notice of repudiation is received and under circumstances that reasonably indicate that the goods are for the lessee, has made either a substantial beginning of their manufacture or commitments for their procurement;
(b) if the party against whom enforcement is sought admits in that party's pleading, testimony or otherwise in court that a lease contract was made, but the lease contract is not enforceable under this provision beyond the quantity of goods admitted; or
(c) with respect to goods that have been received and accepted by the lessee.
(5) The lease term under a lease contract referred to in subsection (4) is:
(a) if there is a writing signed by the party against whom enforcement is sought or by that party's authorized agent specifying the lease term, the term so specified;
(b) if the party against whom enforcement is sought admits in that party's pleading, testimony, or otherwise in court a lease term, the term so admitted; or
(c) a reasonable lease term.

**§2A-202. Final Written Expression: Parol or Extrinsic Evidence.**
Terms with respect to which the confirmatory memoranda of the parties agree or which are otherwise set forth in a writing intended by the parties as a final expression of their agreement with respect to such terms as are included therein may not be contradicted by evidence of any prior agreement or of a contemporaneous oral agreement but may be explained or supplemented:
(a) by course of dealing or usage of trade or by course of performance; and
(b) by evidence of consistent additional terms unless the court finds the writing to have been intended also as a complete and exclusive statement of the terms of the agreement.

**§2A-204. Formation in General.**
(1) A lease contract may be made in any manner sufficient to show agreement, including conduct by both parties which recognizes the existence of a lease contract.
(2) An agreement sufficient to constitute a lease contract may be found although the moment of its making is undetermined.
(3) Although one or more terms are left open, a lease contract does not fail for indefiniteness if the parties have intended to make a lease contract and there is a reasonably certain basis for giving an appropriate remedy.

**§2A-205. Firm Offers.**
An offer by a merchant to lease goods to or from another person in a signed writing that by its terms gives assurance it will be held open is not revocable, for lack of consideration, during the time stated or, if no time is stated, for a reasonable time, but in no event may the period of irrevocability exceed 3 months. Any such term of assurance on a form supplied by the offeree must be separately signed by the offeror.

**§2A-206. Offer and Acceptance in Formation of Lease Contract.**
(1) Unless otherwise unambiguously indicated by the language or circumstances, an offer to make a lease contract must be construed as inviting acceptance in any manner and by any medium reasonable in the circumstances.
(2) If the beginning of a requested performance is a reasonable mode of acceptance, an offeror who is not notified of acceptance within a reasonable time may treat the offer as having lapsed before acceptance.

**§2A-207. Course of Performance or Practical Construction.**
(1) If a lease contract involves repeated occasions for performance by either party with knowledge of the nature of the performance and opportunity for objection to it by the other, any course of performance accepted or acquiesced in without objection is relevant to determine the meaning of the lease agreement.
(2) The express terms of a lease agreement and any course of performance, as well as any course of dealing and usage of trade, must be construed whenever reasonable as consistent with each other; but if that construction is unreasonable, express terms control course of performance, course of performance controls both course of dealing and usage of trade, and course of dealing controls usage of trade.
(3) Subject to the provisions of Section 2A-208 on modification and waiver, course of performance is relevant to show a waiver or modification of any term inconsistent with the course of performance.

**§2A-208. Modification, Rescission and Waiver.**
(1) An agreement modifying a lease contract needs no consideration to be binding.
(2) A signed lease agreement that excludes modification or rescission except by a signed writing may not be otherwise modified or rescinded, but, except as between merchants, such a requirement on a form supplied by a merchant must be separately signed by the other party.
(3) Although an attempt at modification or rescission does not satisfy the requirements of subsection (2), it may operate as a waiver.
(4) A party who has made a waiver affecting an executory portion of a lease contract may retract the waiver by reasonable notification received by the other party that strict performance will be required of any term waived, unless the retraction would be unjust in view of a material change of position in reliance on the waiver.

**§2A-209. Lessee Under Finance Lease as Beneficiary of Supply Contract.**
(1) The benefit of a supplier's promises to the lessor under the supply contract and of all warranties, whether express or implied, including those of any third party provided in connection with or as part of the supply contract, extends to the lessee to the extent of the lessee's leasehold interest under a finance lease related to the supply contract, but is subject to the terms of the warranty and of the supply contract and all defenses or claims arising therefrom.
(2) The extension of the benefit of a supplier's promises and of warranties to the lessee (Section 2A-209(1)) does not: (i) modify the rights and obligations of the parties to the supply contract, whether arising therefrom or otherwise, or (ii) impose any duty or liability under the supply contract on the lessee.
(3) Any modification or rescission of the supply contract by the supplier and the lessor is effective between the supplier and the lessee unless, before the modification or rescission, the supplier has received notice that the lessee has entered into a finance lease related to the supply contract. If the modification or rescission is effective between the supplier and the lessee, the lessor is deemed to have assumed, in addition to the obligations of the lessor to the lessee under the lease contract, promises of the supplier to the lessor and warranties that were so modified or rescinded as they existed and were available to the lessee before modification or rescission.
(4) In addition to the extension of the benefit of the supplier's promises and of warranties to the lessee under subsection (1), the lessee retains all rights that the lessee may have against the supplier which arise from an agreement between the lessee and the supplier or under other law.
As amended in 1990.

**§2A-210. Express Warranties.**
(1) Express warranties by the lessor are created as follows:
(a) Any affirmation of fact or promise made by the lessor to the lessee which relates to the goods and becomes part of the basis of the bargain creates an express warranty that the goods will conform to the affirmation or promise.
(b) Any description of the goods which is made part of the basis of the bargain creates an express warranty that the goods will conform to the description.
(c) Any sample or model that is made part of the basis of the bargain creates an express warranty that the whole of the goods will conform to the sample or model.
(2) It is not necessary to the creation of an express warranty that the lessor use formal words, such as "warrant" or "guarantee," or that the lessor have a specific intention to make a warranty, but an affirmation merely of the value of the goods or a statement purporting to be merely the lessor's opinion or commendation of the goods does not create a warranty.

**§2A-211. Warranties Against Interference and Against Infringement; Lessee's Obligation Against Infringement.**
(1) There is in a lease contract a warranty that for the lease term no person holds a claim to or interest in the goods that arose from an act or omission of the lessor, other than a claim by way of infringement or the like, which will interfere with the lessee's enjoyment of its leasehold interest.
(2) Except in a finance lease there is in a lease contract by a lessor who is a merchant regularly dealing in goods of the kind a warranty that the goods are delivered free of the rightful claim of any person by way of infringement or the like.
(3) A lessee who furnishes specifications to a lessor or a supplier shall hold the lessor and the supplier harmless against any claim by way of infringement or the like that arises out of compliance with the specifications.

**§2A-212. Implied Warranty of Merchantability.**
(1) Except in a finance lease, a warranty that the goods will be merchantable is implied in a lease contract if the lessor is a merchant with respect to goods of that kind.
(2) Goods to be merchantable must be at least such as
(a) pass without objection in the trade under the description in the lease agreement;
(b) in the case of fungible goods, are of fair average quality within the description;
(c) are fit for the ordinary purposes for which goods of that type are used;
(d) run, within the variation permitted by the lease agreement, of even kind, quality, and quantity within each unit and among all units involved;
(e) are adequately contained, packaged, and labeled as the lease agreement may require; and
(f) conform to any promises or affirmations of fact made on the container or label.
(3) Other implied warranties may arise from course of dealing or usage of trade.

**§2A-213. Implied Warranty of Fitness for Particular Purpose.**
Except in a finance lease, if the lessor at the time the lease contract is made has reason to know of any particular purpose for which the goods are required and that the lessee is relying on the lessor's skill or judgment to select or furnish suitable goods, there is in the lease contract an implied warranty that the goods will be fit for that purpose.

**§2A-214. Exclusion or Modification of Warranties.**
(1) Words or conduct relevant to the creation of an express warranty and words or conduct tending to negate or limit a warranty must be construed wherever reasonable as consistent with each other; but, subject to the provisions of Section 2A-202 on parol or extrinsic evidence, negation or limitation is inoperative to the extent that the construction is unreasonable.
(2) Subject to subsection (3), to exclude or modify the implied warranty of merchantability or any part of it the language must mention "merchantability", be by a writing, and be conspicuous. Subject to subsection (3), to exclude or modify any implied warranty of fitness the exclusion must be by a writing and be conspicuous. Language to exclude all implied warranties of fitness is sufficient if it is in writing, is conspicuous and states, for example, "There is no warranty that the goods will be fit for a particular purpose".
(3) Notwithstanding subsection (2), but subject to subsection (4),
(a) unless the circumstances indicate otherwise, all implied warranties are excluded by expressions like "as is," or "with all faults," or by other language that in common understanding calls the lessee's attention to the exclusion of warranties and makes plain that there is no implied warranty, if in writing and conspicuous;
(b) if the lessee before entering into the lease contract has examined the goods or the sample or model as fully as desired or has refused to examine the goods, there is no implied warranty with regard to defects that an examination ought in the circumstances to have revealed; and
(c) an implied warranty may also be excluded or modified by course of dealing, course of performance, or usage of trade.
(4) To exclude or modify a warranty against interference or against infringement (Section 2A-211) or any part of it, the language must be specific, be by a writing, and be conspicuous, unless the circumstances, including course of performance, course of dealing, or usage of trade, give the lessee reason to know that the goods are being leased subject to a claim or interest of any person.

**§2A-215. Cumulation and Conflict of Warranties Express or Implied.**
Warranties, whether express or implied, must be construed as consistent with each other and as cumulative, but if that construction is unreasonable, the intention of the parties determines which warranty is dominant. In ascertaining that intention the following rules apply:

(a) Exact or technical specifications displace an inconsistent sample or model or general language of description.
(b) A sample from an existing bulk displaces inconsistent general language of description.
(c) Express warranties displace inconsistent implied warranties other than an implied warranty of fitness for a particular purpose.

**§2A-216. Third-Party Beneficiaries of Express and Implied Warranties.**
***Alternative A*** A warranty to or for the benefit of a lessee under this Article, whether express or implied, extends to any natural person who is in the family or household of the lessee or who is a guest in the lessee's home if it is reasonable to expect that such person may use, consume, or be affected by the goods and who is injured in person by breach of the warranty. This section does not displace principles of law and equity that extend a warranty to or for the benefit of a lessee to other persons. The operation of this section may not be excluded, modified, or limited, but an exclusion, modification, or limitation of the warranty, including any with respect to rights and remedies, effective against the lessee is also effective against any beneficiary designated under this section.
***Alternative B*** A warranty to or for the benefit of a lessee under this Article, whether express or implied, extends to any natural person who may reasonably be expected to use, consume, or be affected by the goods and who is injured in person by breach of the warranty. This section does not displace principles of law and equity that extend a warranty to or for the benefit of a lessee to other persons. The operation of this section may not be excluded, modified, or limited, but an exclusion, modification, or limitation of the warranty, including any with respect to rights and remedies, effective against the lessee is also effective against the beneficiary designated under this section.
***Alternative C*** A warranty to or for the benefit of a lessee under this Article, whether express or implied, extends to any person who may reasonably be expected to use, consume, or be affected by the goods and who is injured by breach of the warranty. The operation of this section may not be excluded, modified, or limited with respect to injury to the person of an individual to whom the warranty extends, but an exclusion, modification, or limitation of the warranty, including any with respect to rights and remedies, effective against the lessee is also effective against the beneficiary designated under this section.

**§2A-219. Risk of Loss.**
(1) Except in the case of a finance lease, risk of loss is retained by the lessor and does not pass to the lessee. In the case of a finance lease, risk of loss passes to the lessee.
(2) Subject to the provisions of this Article on the effect of default on risk of loss (Section 2A-220), if risk of loss is to pass to the lessee and the time of passage is not stated, the following rules apply:
(a) If the lease contract requires or authorizes the goods to be shipped by carrier
(i) and it does not require delivery at a particular destination, the risk of loss passes to the lessee when the goods are duly delivered to the carrier; but
(ii) if it does require delivery at a particular destination and the goods are there duly tendered while in the possession of the carrier, the risk of loss passes to the lessee when the goods are there duly so tendered as to enable the lessee to take delivery.
(b) If the goods are held by a bailee to be delivered without being moved, the risk of loss passes to the lessee on acknowledgment by the bailee of the lessee's right to possession of the goods.
(c) In any case not within subsection (a) or (b), the risk of loss passes to the lessee on the lessee's receipt of the goods if the lessor, or, in the case of a finance lease, the supplier, is a merchant; otherwise the risk passes to the lessee on tender of delivery.

## Part 3—Effect of Lease Contract

**§2A-302. Title to and Possession of Goods.**
Except as otherwise provided in this Article, each provision of this Article applies whether the lessor or a third party has title to the goods, and whether the lessor, the lessee, or a third party has possession of the goods, notwithstanding any statute or rule of law that possession or the absence of possession is fraudulent.

**§2A-303. Alienability of Party's Interest Under Lease Contract or of Lessor's Residual Interest in Goods; Delegation of Performance; Transfer of Rights.**
(1) As used in this section, "creation of a security interest" includes the sale of a lease contract that is subject to Article 9, Secured Transactions, by reason of Section 9-102(1)(b).
(2) Except as provided in subsections (3) and (4), a provision in a lease agreement which (i) prohibits the voluntary or involuntary transfer, including a transfer by sale, sublease, creation or enforcement of a security interest, or attachment, levy, or other judicial process, of an interest of a party under the lease contract or of the lessor's residual interest in the goods, or (ii) makes such a transfer an event of default, gives rise to the rights and remedies provided in subsection (5), but a transfer that is prohibited or is an event of default under the lease agreement is otherwise effective.
(3) A provision in a lease agreement which (i) prohibits the creation or enforcement of a security interest in an interest of a party under the lease contract or in the lessor's residual interest in the goods, or (ii) makes such a transfer an event of default, is not enforceable unless, and then only to the extent that, there is an actual transfer by the lessee of the lessee's right of possession or use of the goods in violation of the provision or an actual delegation of a material performance of either party to the lease contract in violation of the provision. Neither the granting nor the enforcement of a security interest in (i) the lessor's interest under the lease contract or (ii) the lessor's residual interest in the goods is a transfer that materially impairs the prospect of obtaining return performance by, materially changes the duty of, or materially increases the burden or risk imposed on, the lessee within the purview of subsection (5) unless, and then only to the extent that, there is an actual delegation of a material performance of the lessor.
(4) A provision in a lease agreement which (i) prohibits a transfer of a right to damages for default with respect to the whole lease contract or of a right to payment arising out of the transferor's due performance of the transferor's entire obligation, or (ii) makes such a transfer an event of default, is not enforceable, and such a transfer is not a transfer that materially impairs the prospect of obtaining return performance by, materially changes the duty of, or materially increases the burden or risk imposed on, the other party to the lease contract within the purview of subsection
(5) Subject to subsections (3) and (4):
(a) if a transfer is made which is made an event of default under a lease agreement, the party to the lease contract not making the transfer, unless that party waives the default or otherwise agrees, has the rights and remedies described in Section 2A-501(2);
(b) if paragraph (a) is not applicable and if a transfer is made that (i) is prohibited under a lease agreement or (ii) materially impairs the prospect of obtaining return performance by, materially changes the duty of, or materially increases the burden or risk imposed on, the other party to the lease contract, unless the party not making the transfer agrees at any time to the transfer in the lease contract or otherwise, then, except as limited by contract, (i) the transferor is liable to the party not making the transfer for damages caused by the transfer to the extent that the damages could not reasonably be prevented by the party not making the transfer and (ii) a court having jurisdiction may grant other appropriate relief, including cancellation of the lease contract or an injunction against the transfer.

(6) A transfer of "the lease" or of "all my rights under the lease", or a transfer in similar general terms, is a transfer of rights and, unless the language or the circumstances, as in a transfer for security, indicate the contrary, the transfer is a delegation of duties by the transferor to the transferee. Acceptance by the transferee constitutes a promise by the transferee to perform those duties. The promise is enforceable by either the transferor or the other party to the lease contract.
(7) Unless otherwise agreed by the lessor and the lessee, a delegation of performance does not relieve the transferor as against the other party of any duty to perform or of any liability for default.
(8) In a consumer lease, to prohibit the transfer of an interest of a party under the lease contract or to make a transfer an event of default, the language must be specific, by a writing, and conspicuous.

As amended in 1990.

**§2A-304. Subsequent Lease of Goods by Lessor.**
(1) Subject to Section 2A-303, a subsequent lessee from a lessor of goods under an existing lease contract obtains, to the extent of the leasehold interest transferred, the leasehold interest in the goods that the lessor had or had power to transfer, and except as provided in subsection (2) and Section 2A-527(4), takes subject to the existing lease contract. A lessor with voidable title has power to transfer a good leasehold interest to a good faith subsequent lessee for value, but only to the extent set forth in the preceding sentence. If goods have been delivered under a transaction of purchase, the lessor has that power even though:

(a) the lessor's transferor was deceived as to the identity of the lessor;
(b) the delivery was in exchange for a check which is later dishonored;
(c) it was agreed that the transaction was to be a "cash sale"; or
(d) the delivery was procured through fraud punishable as larcenous under the criminal law.

(2) A subsequent lessee in the ordinary course of business from a lessor who is a merchant dealing in goods of that kind to whom the goods were entrusted by the existing lessee of that lessor before the interest of the subsequent lessee became enforceable against that lessor obtains, to the extent of the leasehold interest transferred, all of that lessor's and the existing lessee's rights to the goods, and takes free of the existing lease contract.
(3) A subsequent lessee from the lessor of goods that are subject to an existing lease contract and are covered by a certificate of title issued under a statute of this State or of another jurisdiction takes no greater rights than those provided both by this section and by the certificate of title statute.

As amended in 1990.

**§2A-307. Priority of Liens Arising by Attachment or Levy on, Security Interests in, and Other Claims to Goods.**
(1) Except as otherwise provided in Section 2A-306, a creditor of a lessee takes subject to the lease contract.
(2) Except as otherwise provided in subsections (3) and (4) and in Sections 2A-306 and 2A-308, a creditor of a lessor takes subject to the lease contract unless:

(a) the creditor holds a lien that attached to the goods before the lease contract became enforceable;
(b) the creditor holds a security interest in the goods and the lessee did not give value and receive delivery of the goods without knowledge of the security interest; or
(c) the creditor holds a security interest in the goods which was perfected (Section 9-303) before the lease contract became enforceable.

(3) A lessee in the ordinary course of business takes the leasehold interest free of a security interest in the goods created by the lessor even though the security interest is perfected (Section 9-303) and the lessee knows of its existence.
(4) A lessee other than a lessee in the ordinary course of business takes the leasehold interest free of a security interest to the extent that it secures future advances made after the secured party acquires knowledge of the lease or more than 45 days after the lease contract becomes enforceable, whichever first occurs, unless the future advances are made pursuant to a commitment entered into without knowledge of the lease and before the expiration of the 45-day period.

As amended in 1990.

**§2A-308. Special Rights of Creditors.**
(1) A creditor of a lessor in possession of goods subject to a lease contract may treat the lease contract as void if as against the creditor retention of possession by the lessor is fraudulent under any statute or rule of law, but retention of possession in good faith and current course of trade by the lessor for a commercially reasonable time after the lease contract becomes enforceable is not fraudulent.
(2) Nothing in this Article impairs the rights of creditors of a lessor if the lease contract (a) becomes enforceable, not in current course of trade but in satisfaction of or as security for a pre-existing claim for money, security, or the like, and (b) is made under circumstances which under any statute or rule of law apart from this Article would constitute the transaction a fraudulent transfer or voidable preference.
(3) A creditor of a seller may treat a sale or an identification of goods to a contract for sale as void if as against the creditor retention of possession by the seller is fraudulent under any statute or rule of law, but retention of possession of the goods pursuant to a lease contract entered into by the seller as lessee and the buyer as lessor in connection with the sale or identification of the goods is not fraudulent if the buyer bought for value and in good faith.

## Part 4—Performance of Lease Contract: Repudiated, Substituted and Excused

**§2A-407. Irrevocable Promises: Finance Leases.**
(1) In the case of a finance lease that is not a consumer lease the lessee's promises under the lease contract become irrevocable and independent upon the lessee's acceptance of the goods.
(2) A promise that has become irrevocable and independent under subsection (1):

(a) is effective and enforceable between the parties, and by or against third parties including assignees of the parties; and
(b) is not subject to cancellation, termination, modification, repudiation, excuse, or substitution without the consent of the party to whom the promise runs.

(3) This section does not affect the validity under any other law of a covenant in any lease contract making the lessee's promises irrevocable and independent upon the lessee's acceptance of the goods.

As amended in 1990.

## Part 5—Default

**A. IN GENERAL**

**§2A-503. Modification or Impairment of Rights and Remedies.**
(1) Except as otherwise provided in this Article, the lease agreement may include rights and remedies for default in addition to or in substitution for those provided in this Article and may limit or alter the measure of damages recoverable under this Article.
(2) Resort to a remedy provided under this Article or in the lease agreement is optional unless the remedy is expressly agreed to be exclusive. If circumstances cause an exclusive or limited remedy to fail of its essential purpose, or provision for an exclusive remedy is unconscionable, remedy may be had as provided in this Article.
(3) Consequential damages may be liquidated under Section 2A-504, or may otherwise be limited, altered, or excluded unless the limitation, alteration, or exclusion is unconscionable. Limitation, alteration, or exclusion of consequential damages for injury to the person in the case of consumer goods is prima facie unconscionable but limitation, alteration, or exclusion of damages where the loss is commercial is not prima facie unconscionable.

(4) Rights and remedies on default by the lessor or the lessee with respect to any obligation or promise collateral or ancillary to the lease contract are not impaired by this Article.

As amended in 1990.

**§2A-504. Liquidation of Damages.**

(1) Damages payable by either party for default, or any other act or omission, including indemnity for loss or diminution of anticipated tax benefits or loss or damage to lessor's residual interest, may be liquidated in the lease agreement but only at an amount or by a formula that is reasonable in light of the then anticipated harm caused by the default or other act or omission.

(2) If the lease agreement provides for liquidation of damages, and such provision does not comply with subsection (1), or such provision is an exclusive or limited remedy that circumstances cause to fail of its essential purpose, remedy may be had as provided in this Article.

(3) If the lessor justifiably withholds or stops delivery of goods because of the lessee's default or insolvency (Section 2A-525 or 2A-526), the lessee is entitled to restitution of any amount by which the sum of his [or her] payments exceeds:

(a) the amount to which the lessor is entitled by virtue of terms liquidating the lessor's damages in accordance with subsection (1); or

(b) in the absence of those terms, 20 percent of the then present value of the total rent the lessee was obligated to pay for the balance of the lease term, or, in the case of a consumer lease, the lesser of such amount or $500.

(4) A lessee's right to restitution under subsection (3) is subject to offset to the extent the lessor establishes:

(a) a right to recover damages under the provisions of this Article other than subsection (1); and

(b) the amount or value of any benefits received by the lessee directly or indirectly by reason of the lease contract.

**§2A-507. Proof of Market Rent: Time and Place.**

(1) Damages based on market rent (Section 2A-519 or 2A-528) are determined according to the rent for the use of the goods concerned for a lease term identical to the remaining lease term of the original lease agreement and prevailing at the times specified in Sections 2A-519 and 2A-528.

(2) If evidence of rent for the use of the goods concerned for a lease term identical to the remaining lease term of the original lease agreement and prevailing at the times or places described in this Article is not readily available, the rent prevailing within any reasonable time before or after the time described or at any other place or for a different lease term which in commercial judgment or under usage of trade would serve as a reasonable substitute for the one described may be used, making any proper allowance for the difference, including the cost of transporting the goods to or from the other place.

(3) Evidence of a relevant rent prevailing at a time or place or for a lease term other than the one described in this Article offered by one party is not admissible unless and until he [or she] has given the other party notice the court finds sufficient to prevent unfair surprise.

(4) If the prevailing rent or value of any goods regularly leased in any established market is in issue, reports in official publications or trade journals or in newspapers or periodicals of general circulation published as the reports of that market are admissible in evidence. The circumstances of the preparation of the report may be shown to affect its weight but not its admissibility.

As amended in 1990.

**B. Default by Lessor**

**§2A-508. Lessee's Remedies.**

(1) If a lessor fails to deliver the goods in conformity to the lease contract (Section 2A-509) or repudiates the lease contract (Section 2A-402), or a lessee rightfully rejects the goods (Section 2A-509) or justifiably revokes acceptance of the goods (Section 2A-517), then with respect to any goods involved, and with respect to all of the goods if under an installment lease contract the value of the whole lease contract is substantially impaired (Section 2A-510), the lessor is in default under the lease contract and the lessee may:

(a) cancel the lease contract (Section 2A-505(1));

(b) recover so much of the rent and security as has been paid and is just under the circumstances;

(c) cover and recover damages as to all goods affected whether or not they have been identified to the lease contract (Sections 2A-518 and 2A-520), or recover damages for nondelivery (Sections 2A-519 and 2A-520);

(d) exercise any other rights or pursue any other remedies provided in the lease contract.

(2) If a lessor fails to deliver the goods in conformity to the lease contract or repudiates the lease contract, the lessee may also:

(a) if the goods have been identified, recover them (Section 2A-522); or

(b) in a proper case, obtain specific performance or replevy the goods (Section 2A-521).

(3) If a lessor is otherwise in default under a lease contract, the lessee may exercise the rights and pursue the remedies provided in the lease contract, which may include a right to cancel the lease, and in Section 2A-519(3).

(4) If a lessor has breached a warranty, whether express or implied, the lessee may recover damages (Section 2A-519(4)).

(5) On rightful rejection or justifiable revocation of acceptance, a lessee has a security interest in goods in the lessee's possession or control for any rent and security that has been paid and any expenses reasonably incurred in their inspection, receipt, transportation, and care and custody and may hold those goods and dispose of them in good faith and in a commercially reasonable manner, subject to Section 2A-527(5).

(6) Subject to the provisions of Section 2A-407, a lessee, on notifying the lessor of the lessee's intention to do so, may deduct all or any part of the damages resulting from any default under the lease contract from any part of the rent still due under the same lease contract.

As amended in 1990.

**§2A-509. Lessee's Rights on Improper Delivery; Rightful Rejection.**

(1) Subject to the provisions of Section 2A-510 on default in installment lease contracts, if the goods or the tender or delivery fail in any respect to conform to the lease contract, the lessee may reject or accept the goods or accept any commercial unit or units and reject the rest of the goods.

(2) Rejection of goods is ineffective unless it is within a reasonable time after tender or delivery of the goods and the lessee seasonably notifies the lessor.

**§2A-510. Installment Lease Contracts: Rejection and Default.**

(1) Under an installment lease contract a lessee may reject any delivery that is nonconforming if the nonconformity substantially impairs the value of that delivery and cannot be cured or the nonconformity is a defect in the required documents; but if the nonconformity does not fall within subsection (2) and the lessor or the supplier gives adequate assurance of its cure, the lessee must accept that delivery.

(2) Whenever nonconformity or default with respect to one or more deliveries substantially impairs the value of the installment lease contract as a whole there is a default with respect to the whole. But, the aggrieved party reinstates the installment lease contract as a whole if the aggrieved party accepts a nonconforming delivery without seasonably notifying of cancellation or brings an action with respect only to past deliveries or demands performance as to future deliveries.

**§2A-511. Merchant Lessee's Duties as to Rightfully Rejected Goods.**

(1) Subject to any security interest of a lessee (Section 2A-508(5)), if a lessor or a supplier has no agent or place of business at the market of

rejection, a merchant lessee, after rejection of goods in his [or her] possession or control, shall follow any reasonable instructions received from the lessor or the supplier with respect to the goods. In the absence of those instructions, a merchant lessee shall make reasonable efforts to sell, lease, or otherwise dispose of the goods for the lessor's account if they threaten to decline in value speedily. Instructions are not reasonable if on demand indemnity for expenses is not forthcoming.
(2) If a merchant lessee (subsection (1)) or any other lessee (Section 2A-512) disposes of goods, he [or she] is entitled to reimbursement either from the lessor or the supplier or out of the proceeds for reasonable expenses of caring for and disposing of the goods and, if the expenses include no disposition commission, to such commission as is usual in the trade, or if there is none, to a reasonable sum not exceeding 10 percent of the gross proceeds.
(3) In complying with this section or Section 2A-512, the lessee is held only to good faith. Good faith conduct hereunder is neither acceptance or conversion nor the basis of an action for damages.
(4) A purchaser who purchases in good faith from a lessee pursuant to this section or Section 2A-512 takes the goods free of any rights of the lessor and the supplier even though the lessee fails to comply with one or more of the requirements of this Article.

**§2A-512. Lessee's Duties as to Rightfully Rejected Goods.**
(1) Except as otherwise provided with respect to goods that threaten to decline in value speedily (Section 2A-511) and subject to any security interest of a lessee (Section 2A-508(5)):

(a) the lessee, after rejection of goods in the lessee's possession, shall hold them with reasonable care at the lessor's or the supplier's disposition for a reasonable time after the lessee's seasonable notification of rejection;

(b) if the lessor or the supplier gives no instructions within a reasonable time after notification of rejection, the lessee may store the rejected goods for the lessor's or the supplier's account or ship them to the lessor or the supplier or dispose of them for the lessor's or the supplier's account with reimbursement in the manner provided in Section 2A-511; but

(c) the lessee has no further obligations with regard to goods rightfully rejected.

(2) Action by the lessee pursuant to subsection (1) is not acceptance or conversion.

**§2A-513. Cure by Lessor of Improper Tender or Delivery; Replacement.**
(1) If any tender or delivery by the lessor or the supplier is rejected because nonconforming and the time for performance has not yet expired, the lessor or the supplier may seasonably notify the lessee of the lessor's or the supplier's intention to cure and may then make a conforming delivery within the time provided in the lease contract.
(2) If the lessee rejects a nonconforming tender that the lessor or the supplier had reasonable grounds to believe would be acceptable with or without money allowance, the lessor or the supplier may have a further reasonable time to substitute a conforming tender if he [or she] seasonably notifies the lessee.

**§2A-515. Acceptance of Goods.**
(1) Acceptance of goods occurs after the lessee has had a reasonable opportunity to inspect the goods and

(a) the lessee signifies or acts with respect to the goods in a manner that signifies to the lessor or the supplier that the goods are conforming or that the lessee will take or retain them in spite of their nonconformity; or

(b) the lessee fails to make an effective rejection of the goods (Section 2A-509(2)).

(2) Acceptance of a part of any commercial unit is acceptance of that entire unit.

**§2A-517. Revocation of Acceptance of Goods.**
(1) A lessee may revoke acceptance of a lot or commercial unit whose nonconformity substantially impairs its value to the lessee if the lessee has accepted it:

(a) except in the case of a finance lease, on the reasonable assumption that its nonconformity would be cured and it has not been seasonably cured; or

(b) without discovery of the nonconformity if the lessee's acceptance was reasonably induced either by the lessor's assurances or, except in the case of a finance lease, by the difficulty of discovery before acceptance.

(2) Except in the case of a finance lease that is not a consumer lease, a lessee may revoke acceptance of a lot or commercial unit if the lessor defaults under the lease contract and the default substantially impairs the value of that lot or commercial unit to the lessee.
(3) If the lease agreement so provides, the lessee may revoke acceptance of a lot or commercial unit because of other defaults by the lessor.
(4) Revocation of acceptance must occur within a reasonable time after the lessee discovers or should have discovered the ground for it and before any substantial change in condition of the goods which is not caused by the nonconformity. Revocation is not effective until the lessee notifies the lessor.
(5) A lessee who so revokes has the same rights and duties with regard to the goods involved as if the lessee had rejected them.
As amended in 1990.

**§2A-518. Cover; Substitute Goods.**
(1) After a default by a lessor under the lease contract of the type described in Section 2A-508(1), or, if agreed, after other default by the lessor, the lessee may cover by making any purchase or lease of or contract to purchase or lease goods in substitution for those due from the lessor.
(2) Except as otherwise provided with respect to damages liquidated in the lease agreement (Section 2A-504) or otherwise determined pursuant to agreement of the parties (Sections 1-102(3) and 2A-503), if a lessee's cover is by a lease agreement substantially similar to the original lease agreement and the new lease agreement is made in good faith and in a commercially reasonable manner, the lessee may recover from the lessor as damages (i) the present value, as of the date of the commencement of the term of the new lease agreement, of the rent under the new lease agreement applicable to that period of the new lease term which is comparable to the then remaining term of the original lease agreement minus the present value as of the same date of the total rent for the then remaining lease term of the original lease agreement, and (ii) any incidental or consequential damages, less expenses saved in consequence of the lessor's default.
(3) If a lessee's cover is by lease agreement that for any reason does not qualify for treatment under subsection (2), or is by purchase or otherwise, the lessee may recover from the lessor as if the lessee had elected not to cover and Section 2A-519 governs.
As amended in 1990.

**§2A-519. Lessee's Damages for Non-delivery, Repudiation, Default, and Breach of Warranty in Regard to Accepted Goods.**
(1) Except as otherwise provided with respect to damages liquidated in the lease agreement (Section 2A-504) or otherwise determined pursuant to agreement of the parties (Sections 1-102(3) and 2A-503), if a lessee elects not to cover or a lessee elects to cover and the cover is by lease agreement that for any reason does not qualify for treatment under Section 2A-518(2), or is by purchase or otherwise, the measure of damages for non-delivery or repudiation by the lessor or for rejection or revocation of acceptance by the lessee is the present value, as of the date of the default, of the then market rent minus the present value as of the same date of the original rent, computed for the remaining lease term of the original lease agreement, together with incidental and consequential damages, less expenses saved in consequence of the lessor's default.

(2) Market rent is to be determined as of the place for tender or, in cases of rejection after arrival or revocation of acceptance, as of the place of arrival.

(3) Except as otherwise agreed, if the lessee has accepted goods and given notification (Section 2A-516(3)), the measure of damages for non-conforming tender or delivery or other default by a lessor is the loss resulting in the ordinary course of events from the lessor's default as determined in any manner that is reasonable together with incidental and consequential damages, less expenses saved in consequence of the lessor's default.

(4) Except as otherwise agreed, the measure of damages for breach of warranty is the present value at the time and place of acceptance of the difference between the value of the use of the goods accepted and the value if they had been as warranted for the lease term, unless special circumstances show proximate damages of a different amount, together with incidental and consequential damages, less expenses saved in consequence of the lessor's default or breach of warranty.

As amended in 1990.

**§2A-520. Lessee's Incidental and Consequential Damages.**

(1) Incidental damages resulting from a lessor's default include expenses reasonably incurred in inspection, receipt, transportation, and care and custody of goods rightfully rejected or goods the acceptance of which is justifiably revoked, any commercially reasonable charges, expenses or commissions in connection with effecting cover, and any other reasonable expense incident to the default.

(2) Consequential damages resulting from a lessor's default include:

(a) any loss resulting from general or particular requirements and needs of which the lessor at the time of contracting had reason to know and which could not reasonably be prevented by cover or otherwise; and

(b) injury to person or property proximately resulting from any breach of warranty.

**§2A-521. Lessee's Right to Specific Performance or Replevin.**

(1) Specific performance may be decreed if the goods are unique or in other proper circumstances.

(2) A decree for specific performance may include any terms and conditions as to payment of the rent, damages, or other relief that the court deems just.

(3) A lessee has a right of replevin, detinue, sequestration, claim and delivery, or the like for goods identified to the lease contract if after reasonable effort the lessee is unable to effect cover for those goods or the circumstances reasonably indicate that the effort will be unavailing.

**§2A-522. Lessee's Right to Goods on Lessor's Insolvency.**

(1) Subject to subsection (2) and even though the goods have not been shipped, a lessee who has paid a part or all of the rent and security for goods identified to a lease contract (Section 2A-217) on making and keeping good a tender of any unpaid portion of the rent and security due under the lease contract may recover the goods identified from the lessor if the lessor becomes insolvent within 10 days after receipt of the first installment of rent and security.

(2) A lessee acquires the right to recover goods identified to a lease contract only if they conform to the lease contract.

**C. Default by Lessee**

**§2A-523. Lessor's Remedies.**

(1) If a lessee wrongfully rejects or revokes acceptance of goods or fails to make a payment when due or repudiates with respect to a part or the whole, then, with respect to any goods involved, and with respect to all of the goods if under an installment lease contract the value of the whole lease contract is substantially impaired (Section 2A-510), the lessee is in default under the lease contract and the lessor may:

(a) cancel the lease contract (Section 2A-505(1));

(b) proceed respecting goods not identified to the lease contract (Section 2A-524);

(c) withhold delivery of the goods and take possession of goods previously delivered (Section 2A-525);

(d) stop delivery of the goods by any bailee (Section 2A-526);

(e) dispose of the goods and recover damages (Section 2A-527), or retain the goods and recover damages (Section 2A-528), or in a proper case recover rent (Section 2A-529);

(f) exercise any other rights or pursue any other remedies provided in the lease contract.

(2) If a lessor does not fully exercise a right or obtain a remedy to which the lessor is entitled under subsection (1), the lessor may recover the loss resulting in the ordinary course of events from the lessee's default as determined in any reasonable manner, together with incidental damages, less expenses saved in consequence of the lessee's default.

(3) If a lessee is otherwise in default under a lease contract, the lessor may exercise the rights and pursue the remedies provided in the lease contract, which may include a right to cancel the lease. In addition, unless otherwise provided in the lease contract:

(a) if the default substantially impairs the value of the lease contract to the lessor, the lessor may exercise the rights and pursue the remedies provided in subsections (1) or (2); or

(b) if the default does not substantially impair the value of the lease contract to the lessor, the lessor may recover as provided in subsection (2).

As amended in 1990.

**§2A-524. Lessor's Right to Identify Goods to Lease Contract.**

(1) After default by the lessee under the lease contract of the type described in Section 2A-523(1) or 2A-523(3)(a) or, if agreed, after other default by the lessee, the lessor may:

(a) identify to the lease contract conforming goods not already identified if at the time the lessor learned of the default they were in the lessor's or the supplier's possession or control; and

(b) dispose of goods (Section 2A-527(1)) that demonstrably have been intended for the particular lease contract even though those goods are unfinished.

(2) If the goods are unfinished, in the exercise of reasonable commercial judgment for the purposes of avoiding loss and of effective realization, an aggrieved lessor or the supplier may either complete manufacture and wholly identify the goods to the lease contract or cease manufacture and lease, sell, or otherwise dispose of the goods for scrap or salvage value or proceed in any other reasonable manner.

As amended in 1990.

**§2A-525. Lessor's Right to Possession of Goods.**

(1) If a lessor discovers the lessee to be insolvent, the lessor may refuse to deliver the goods.

(2) After a default by the lessee under the lease contract of the type described in Section 2A-523(1) or 2A-523(3)(a) or, if agreed, after other default by the lessee, the lessor has the right to take possession of the goods. If the lease contract so provides, the lessor may require the lessee to assemble the goods and make them available to the lessor at a place to be designated by the lessor which is reasonably convenient to both parties. Without removal, the lessor may render unusable any goods employed in trade or business, and may dispose of goods on the lessee's premises (Section 2A-527).

(3) The lessor may proceed under subsection (2) without judicial process if it can be done without breach of the peace or the lessor may proceed by action.

As amended in 1990.

**§2A-526. Lessor's Stoppage of Delivery in Transit or Otherwise.**

(1) A lessor may stop delivery of goods in the possession of a carrier or other bailee if the lessor discovers the lessee to be insolvent and may stop delivery of carload, truckload, planeload, or larger shipments of express or freight if the lessee repudiates or fails to make a payment due before delivery, whether for

rent, security or otherwise under the lease contract, or for any other reason the lessor has a right to withhold or take possession of the goods.

(2) In pursuing its remedies under subsection (1), the lessor may stop delivery until

(a) receipt of the goods by the lessee;

(b) acknowledgment to the lessee by any bailee of the goods, except a carrier, that the bailee holds the goods for the lessee; or

(c) such an acknowledgment to the lessee by a carrier via reshipment or as warehouseman.

(3) (a) To stop delivery, a lessor shall so notify as to enable the bailee by reasonable diligence to prevent delivery of the goods.

(b) After notification, the bailee shall hold and deliver the goods according to the directions of the lessor, but the lessor is liable to the bailee for any ensuing charges or damages.

(c) A carrier who has issued a nonnegotiable bill of lading is not obliged to obey a notification to stop received from a person other than the consignor.

**§2A-527. Lessor's Rights to Dispose of Goods.**

(1) After a default by a lessee under the lease contract of the type described in Section 2A-523(1) or 2A-523(3)(a) or after the lessor refuses to deliver or takes possession of goods (Section 2A-525 or 2A-526), or, if agreed, after other default by a lessee, the lessor may dispose of the goods concerned or the undelivered balance thereof by lease, sale, or otherwise.

(2) Except as otherwise provided with respect to damages liquidated in the lease agreement (Section 2A-504) or otherwise determined pursuant to agreement of the parties (Sections 1-102(3) and 2A-503), if the disposition is by lease agreement substantially similar to the original lease agreement and the new lease agreement is made in good faith and in a commercially reasonable manner, the lessor may recover from the lessee as damages (i) accrued and unpaid rent as of the date of the commencement of the term of the new lease agreement, (ii) the present value, as of the same date, of the total rent for the then remaining lease term of the original lease agreement minus the present value, as of the same date, of the rent under the new lease agreement applicable to that period of the new lease term which is comparable to the then remaining term of the original lease agreement, and (iii) any incidental damages allowed under Section 2A-530, less expenses saved in consequence of the lessee's default.

(3) If the lessor's disposition is by lease agreement that for any reason does not qualify for treatment under subsection (2), or is by sale or otherwise, the lessor may recover from the lessee as if the lessor had elected not to dispose of the goods and Section 2A-528 governs.

(4) A subsequent buyer or lessee who buys or leases from the lessor in good faith for value as a result of a disposition under this section takes the goods free of the original lease contract and any rights of the original lessee even though the lessor fails to comply with one or more of the requirements of this Article.

(5) The lessor is not accountable to the lessee for any profit made on any disposition. A lessee who has rightfully rejected or justifiably revoked acceptance shall account to the lessor for any excess over the amount of the lessee's security interest (Section 2A-508(5)).

As amended in 1990.

**§2A-528. Lessor's Damages for Non-acceptance, Failure to Pay, Repudiation, or Other Default.**

(1) Except as otherwise provided with respect to damages liquidated in the lease agreement (Section 2A-504) or otherwise determined pursuant to agreement of the parties (Sections 1-102(3) and 2A-503), if a lessor elects to retain the goods or a lessor elects to dispose of the goods and the disposition is by lease agreement that for any reason does not qualify for treatment under Section 2A-527(2), or is by sale or otherwise, the lessor may recover from the lessee as damages for a default of the type described in Section 2A-523(1) or 2A-523(3)(a), or, if agreed, for other default of the lessee, (i) accrued and unpaid rent as of the date of default if the lessee has never taken possession of the goods, or, if the lessee has taken possession of the goods, as of the date the lessor repossesses the goods or an earlier date on which the lessee makes a tender of the goods to the lessor, (ii) the present value as of the date determined under clause (i) of the total rent for the then remaining lease term of the original lease agreement minus the present value as of the same date of the market rent at the place where the goods are located computed for the same lease term, and (iii) any incidental damages allowed under Section 2A-530, less expenses saved in consequence of the lessee's default.

(2) If the measure of damages provided in subsection (1) is inadequate to put a lessor in as good a position as performance would have, the measure of damages is the present value of the profit, including reasonable overhead, the lessor would have made from full performance by the lessee, together with any incidental damages allowed under Section 2A-530, due allowance for costs reasonably incurred and due credit for payments or proceeds of disposition.

As amended in 1990.

**§2A-529. Lessor's Action for the Rent.**

(1) After default by the lessee under the lease contract of the type described in Section 2A-523(1) or 2A-523(3)(a) or, if agreed, after other default by the lessee, if the lessor complies with subsection (2), the lessor may recover from the lessee as damages:

(a) for goods accepted by the lessee and not repossessed by or tendered to the lessor, and for conforming goods lost or damaged within a commercially reasonable time after risk of loss passes to the lessee (Section 2A-219), (i) accrued and unpaid rent as of the date of entry of judgment in favor of the lessor, (ii) the present value as of the same date of the rent for the then remaining lease term of the lease agreement, and (iii) any incidental damages allowed under Section 2A-530, less expenses saved in consequence of the lessee's default; and

(b) for goods identified to the lease contract if the lessor is unable after reasonable effort to dispose of them at a reasonable price or the circumstances reasonably indicate that effort will be unavailing, (i) accrued and unpaid rent as of the date of entry of judgment in favor of the lessor, (ii) the present value as of the same date of the rent for the then remaining lease term of the lease agreement, and (iii) any incidental damages allowed under Section 2A-530, less expenses saved in consequence of the lessee's default.

(2) Except as provided in subsection (3), the lessor shall hold for the lessee for the remaining lease term of the lease agreement any goods that have been identified to the lease contract and are in the lessor's control.

(3) The lessor may dispose of the goods at any time before collection of the judgment for damages obtained pursuant to subsection (1). If the disposition is before the end of the remaining lease term of the lease agreement, the lessor's recovery against the lessee for damages is governed by Section 2A-527 or Section 2A-528, and the lessor will cause an appropriate credit to be provided against a judgment for damages to the extent that the amount of the judgment exceeds the recovery available pursuant to Section 2A-527 or 2A-528.

(4) Payment of the judgment for damages obtained pursuant to subsection (1) entitles the lessee to the use and possession of the goods not then disposed of for the remaining lease term of and in accordance with the lease agreement.

(5) After default by the lessee under the lease contract of the type described in Section 2A-523(1) or Section 2A-523(3)(a) or, if agreed, after other default by the lessee, a lessor who is held not entitled to rent under this section must nevertheless be awarded damages for non-acceptance under Section 2A-527 or Section 2A-528.

As amended in 1990.

**§2A-530. Lessor's Incidental Damages.**

Incidental damages to an aggrieved lessor include any commercially reasonable charges, expenses, or commissions incurred in stopping delivery, in the transportation, care and custody of goods after the lessee's default, in connection with return or disposition of the goods, or otherwise resulting from the default.

## ARTICLE 3: NEGOTIABLE INSTRUMENTS

### Part 1—General Provisions and Definitions

**§3-101. Short Title.**
This Article may be cited as Uniform Commercial Code—Negotiable Instruments.

**§3-102. Subject Matter.**
(a) This Article applies to negotiable instruments. It does not apply to money or to payment orders governed by Article 4A. A negotiable instrument that is also a certificated security under Section 8-102(1)(a) is subject to Article 8 and to this Article.
(b) In the event of conflict between the provisions of this Article and those of Article 4, Article 8, or Article 9, the provisions of Article 4, Article 8, and Article 9 prevail over those of this Article.
(c) Regulations of the Board of Governors of the Federal Reserve System and operating circulars of the Federal Reserve Banks supersede any inconsistent provision of this Article to the extent of the inconsistency.

**§3-103. Definitions.**
(a) In this Article:
(1) "Acceptor" means a drawee that has accepted a draft.
(2) "Drawee" means a person ordered in a draft to make payment.
(3) "Drawer" means a person that signs a draft as a person ordering payment.
(4) "Good faith" means honesty in fact and the observance of reasonable commercial standards of fair dealing.
(5) "Maker" means a person that signs a note as promisor of payment.
(6) "Order" means a written instruction to pay money signed by the person giving the instruction. The instruction may be addressed to any person, including the person giving the instruction, or to one or more persons jointly or in the alternative but not in succession. An authorization to pay is not an order unless the person authorized to pay is also instructed to pay.
(7) "Ordinary care" in the case of a person engaged in business means observance of reasonable commercial standards, prevailing in the area in which that person is located, with respect to the business in which that person is engaged. In the case of a bank that takes an instrument for processing for collection or payment by automated means, reasonable commercial standards do not require the bank to examine the instrument if the failure to examine does not violate the bank's prescribed procedures and the bank's procedures do not vary unreasonably from general banking usage not disapproved by this Article or Article 4.
(8) "Party" means party to an instrument.
(9) "Promise" means a written undertaking to pay money signed by the person undertaking to pay. An acknowledgment of an obligation by the obligor is not a promise unless the obligor also undertakes to pay the obligation.
(10) "Prove" with respect to a fact means to meet the burden of establishing the fact (Section 1-201(8)).
(11) "Remitter" means a person that purchases an instrument from its issuer if the instrument is payable to an identified person other than the purchaser.
(b) Other definitions applying to this Article and the sections in which they appear are:
"Acceptance" Section 3-409.
"Accommodated party" Section 3-419.
"Accommodation indorsement" Section 3-205.
"Accommodation party" Section 3-419.
"Alteration" Section 3-407.
"Blank indorsement" Section 3-205.
"Cashier's check" Section 3-104.
"Certificate of deposit" Section 3-104.
"Certified check" Section 3-409.
"Check" Section 3-104.
"Consideration" Section 3-303.
"Draft" Section 3-104.
"Fiduciary" Section 3-307.
"Guarantor" Section 3-417.
"Holder in due course" Section 3-302.
"Incomplete instrument" Section 3-115.
"Indorsement" Section 3-204.
"Indorser" Section 3-204.
"Instrument" Section 3-104.
"Issue" Section 3-105.
"Issuer" Section 3-105.
"Negotiable instrument" Section 3-104.
"Negotiation" Section 3-201.
"Note" Section 3-104.
"Payable at a definite time" Section 3-108.
"Payable on demand" Section 3-108.
"Payable to bearer" Section 3-109.
"Payable to order" Section 3-110.
"Payment" Section 3-603.
"Person entitled to enforce" Section 3-301.
"Presentment" Section 3-501.
"Reacquisition" Section 3-207.
"Represented person" Section 3-307.
"Special indorsement" Section 3-205.
"Teller's check" Section 3-104.
"Traveler's check" Section 3-104.
"Value" Section 3-303.
(c) The following definitions in other Articles apply to this Article:
"Bank" Section 4-105.
"Banking day" Section 4-104.
"Clearing house" Section 4-104.
"Collecting bank" Section 4-105.
"Customer" Section 4-104.
"Depositary bank" Section 4-105.
"Documentary draft" Section 4-104.
"Intermediary bank" Section 4-105.
"Item" Section 4-104.
"Midnight deadline" Section 4-104.
"Payor bank" Section 4-105.
"Suspends payments" Section 4-104.
(d) In addition, Article 1 contains general definitions and principles of construction and interpretation applicable throughout this Article.

**§3-104. Negotiable Instrument.**
(a) "Negotiable instrument" means an unconditional promise or order to pay a fixed amount of money, with or without interest or other charges described in the promise or order, if it:
(1) is payable to bearer or to order at the time it is issued or first comes into possession of a holder;
(2) is payable on demand or at a definite time; and
(3) does not state any other undertaking or instruction by the person promising or ordering payment to do any act in addition to the payment of money except that the promise or order may contain (i) an undertaking or power to give, maintain, or protect collateral to secure payment, (ii) an authorization or power to the holder to confess judgment or realize on or dispose of collateral, or (iii) a waiver of the benefit of any law intended for the advantage or protection of any obligor.
(b) "Instrument" means negotiable instrument.

(c) An order that meets all of the requirements of subsection (a) except subparagraph (1) and otherwise falls within the definition of "check" in subsection (f) is a negotiable instrument and a check.
(d) Notwithstanding subsection (a), a promise or order other than a check is not an instrument if, at the time it is issued or first comes into possession of a holder, it contains a conspicuous statement, however expressed, indicating that the writing is not an instrument governed by this Article.
(e) An instrument is a "note" if it is a promise, and is a "draft" if it is an order. If an instrument falls within the definition of both "note" and "draft," the person entitled to enforce the instrument may treat it as either.
(f) "Check" means (i) a draft, other than a documentary draft, payable on demand and drawn on a bank or (ii) a cashier's check or teller's check. An instrument may be a check even though it is described on its face by another term such as "money order."
(g) "Cashier's check" means a draft with respect to which the drawer and drawee are the same bank or branches of the same bank.
(h) "Teller's check" means a draft drawn by a bank (i) on another bank, or (ii) payable at or through a bank.
(i) "Traveler's check" means an instrument that (i) is payable on demand, (ii) is drawn on or payable at or through a bank, (iii) is designated by the term "traveler's check" or by a substantially similar term, and (iv) requires, as a condition to payment, a countersignature by a person whose specimen signature appears on the instrument.
(j) "Certificate of deposit" means an instrument containing an acknowledgment by a bank that a sum of money has been received by the bank, and a promise by the bank to repay the sum of money. A certificate of deposit is a note of the bank.

**§3-105. Issue of Instrument.**
(a) "Issue" means the first delivery of an instrument by the maker or drawer, whether to a holder or nonholder, for the purpose of giving rights on the instrument to any person.
(b) An unissued instrument, or an unissued incomplete instrument (Section 3-115) that is completed, is binding on the maker or drawer, but nonissuance is a defense. An instrument that is conditionally issued or is issued for a special purpose is binding on the maker or drawer, but failure of the condition or special purpose to be fulfilled is a defense.
(c) "Issuer" applies to issued and unissued instruments and means any person that signs an instrument as maker or drawer.

**§3-106. Unconditional Promise or Order.**
(a) Except as provided in subsections (b) and (c), for the purposes of Section 3-104(a), a promise or order is unconditional unless it states (i) an express condition to payment or (ii) that the promise or order is subject to or governed by another writing, or that rights or obligations with respect to the promise or order are stated in another writing; however, a mere reference to another writing does not make the promise or order conditional.
(b) A promise or order is not made conditional (i) by a reference to another writing for a statement of rights with respect to collateral, prepayment, or acceleration, or (ii) because payment is limited to resort to a particular fund or source.
(c) If a promise or order requires, as a condition to payment, a countersignature by a person whose specimen signature appears on the promise or order, the condition does not make the promise or order conditional for the purposes of Section 3-104(a). If the person whose specimen signature appears on an instrument fails to countersign the instrument, the failure to countersign is a defense to the obligation of the issuer, but the failure does not prevent a transferee of the instrument from becoming a holder of the instrument.
(d) If a promise or order at the time it is issued or first comes into possession of a holder contains a statement, required by applicable statutory or administrative law, to the effect that the rights of a holder or transferee are subject to claims or defenses that the issuer could assert against the original payee, the promise or order is not thereby made conditional for the purposes of Section 3-104(a), but there cannot be a holder in due course of the promise or order.

**§3-107. Instrument Payable in Foreign Money.**
Unless the instrument otherwise provides, an instrument that states the amount payable in foreign money may be paid in the foreign money or in an equivalent amount in dollars calculated by using the current bank-offered spot rate at the place of payment for the purchase of dollars on the day on which the instrument is paid.

**§3-108. Payable on Demand or at a Definite Time.**
(a) A promise or order is "payable on demand" if (i) it states that it is payable on demand or at sight, or otherwise indicates that it is payable at the will of the holder, or (ii) it does not state any time of payment.
(b) A promise or order is "payable at a definite time" if it is payable on elapse of a definite period of time after sight or acceptance or at a fixed date or dates or at a time or times readily ascertainable at the time the promise or order is issued, subject to rights of (i) prepayment, (ii) acceleration, or (iii) extension at the option of the holder or (iv) extension to a further definite time at the option of the maker or acceptor or automatically upon or after a specified act or event.
(c) If an instrument, payable at a fixed date, is also payable upon demand made before the fixed date, the instrument is payable on demand until the fixed date and, if demand for payment is not made before that date, becomes payable at a definite time on the fixed date.

**§3-109. Payable to Bearer or to Order.**
(a) A promise or order is payable to bearer if it:
(1) states that it is payable to bearer or to the order of bearer or otherwise indicates that the person in possession of the promise or order is entitled to payment,
(2) does not state a payee, or
(3) states that it is payable to or to the order of cash or otherwise indicates that it is not payable to an identified person.
(b) A promise or order that is not payable to bearer is payable to order if it is payable (i) to the order of an identified person or (ii) to an identified person or order. A promise or order that is payable to order is payable to the identified person.
(c) An instrument payable to bearer may become payable to an identified person if it is specially indorsed as stated in Section 3-205(a). An instrument payable to an identified person may become payable to bearer if it is indorsed in blank as stated in Section 3-205(b).

**§3-110. Identification of Person to Whom Instrument Is Payable.**
(a) A person to whom an instrument is payable is determined by the intent of the person, whether or not authorized, signing as, or in the name or behalf of, the maker or drawer. The instrument is payable to the person intended by the signer even if that person is identified in the instrument by a name or other identification that is not that of the intended person. If more than one person signs in the name or behalf of the maker or drawer and all the signers do not intend the same person as payee, the instrument is payable to any person intended by one or more of the signers.
(b) If the signature of the maker or drawer of an instrument is made by automated means such as a check-writing machine, the payee of the instrument is determined by the intent of the person who supplied the name or identification of the payee, whether or not authorized to do so.
(c) A person to whom an instrument is payable may be identified in any way including by name, identifying number, office, or account number. For the purpose of determining the holder of an instrument, the following rules apply:
(1) If an instrument is payable to an account and the account is identified only by number, the instrument is payable to the person to whom the account is payable. If an instrument is payable to an account identified by number and by the name of a person, the instrument is payable

to the named person, whether or not that person is the owner of the account identified by number.

(2) If an instrument is payable to:

(i) a trust, estate, or a person described as trustee or representative of a trust or estate, the instrument is payable to the trustee, the representative, or a successor of either, whether or not the beneficiary or estate is also named;

(ii) a person described as agent or similar representative of a named or identified person, the instrument is payable either to the represented person, the representative, or a successor of the representative;

(iii) a fund or organization that is not a legal entity, the instrument is payable to a representative of the members of the fund or organization; or

(iv) an office or to a person described as holding an office, the instrument is payable to the named person, the incumbent of the office, or a successor to the incumbent.

(d) If an instrument is payable to two or more persons alternatively, it is payable to any of them and may be negotiated, discharged, or enforced by any of them in possession of the instrument. If an instrument is payable to two or more persons not alternatively, it is payable to all of them and may be negotiated, discharged, or enforced only by all of them. If an instrument payable to two or more persons is ambiguous as to whether it is payable to the persons alternatively, the instrument is payable to the persons alternatively.

**§3-111. Place of Payment.**

Except as otherwise provided for items in Article 4, an instrument is payable at the place of payment stated in the instrument. If no place of payment is stated, an instrument is payable at the address of the drawee or maker stated in the instrument. If no address is stated, the place of payment is the place of business of the drawee or maker. If a drawee or maker has more than one place of business, the place of payment is any place of business of the drawee or maker chosen by the person entitled to enforce the instrument. If the drawee or maker has no place of business, the place of payment is the residence of the drawee or maker.

**§3-112. Interest.**

(a) Unless otherwise provided in the instrument, (i) an instrument is not payable with interest, and (ii) interest on an interest-bearing instrument is payable from the date of the instrument.

(b) Interest may be stated in an instrument as a fixed or variable amount of money or it may be expressed as a fixed or variable rate or rates. The amount or rate of interest may be stated or described in the instrument in any manner and may require reference to information not contained in the instrument. If an instrument provides for interest but the amount of interest payable cannot be ascertained from the description, interest is payable at the judgment rate in effect at the place of payment of the instrument and at the time interest first accrues.

**§3-113. Date of Instrument.**

(a) An instrument may be antedated or postdated. The date stated determines the time of payment if the instrument is payable at a fixed period after date. Except as provided in Section 4-401(3), an instrument payable on demand is not payable before the date of the instrument.

(b) If an instrument is undated, its date is the date of its issue or, in the case of an unissued instrument, the date it first comes into possession of a holder.

**§3-114. Contradictory Terms of Instrument.**

If an instrument contains contradictory terms, typewritten terms prevail over printed terms, handwritten terms prevail over both, and words prevail over numbers.

**§3-115. Incomplete Instrument.**

(a) "Incomplete instrument" means a signed writing, whether or not issued by the signer, the contents of which show at the time of signing that it is incomplete but that the signer intended it to be completed by the addition of words or numbers.

(b) Subject to subsection (c), if an incomplete instrument is an instrument under Section 3-104, it may be enforced (i) according to its terms if it is not completed, or (ii) according to its terms as augmented by completion. If an incomplete instrument is not an instrument under Section 3-104 but, after completion, the requirements of Section 3-104 are met, the instrument may be enforced according to its terms as augmented by completion.

(c) If words or numbers are added to an incomplete instrument without authority of the signer, there is an alteration of the incomplete instrument governed by Section 3-407.

(d) The burden of establishing that words or numbers were added to an incomplete instrument without authority of the signer is on the person asserting the lack of authority.

**§3-116. Joint and Several Liability; Contribution.**

(a) Except as otherwise provided in the instrument, two or more persons who have the same liability on an instrument as makers, drawers, acceptors, indorsers who are indorsing joint payees, or anomalous indorsers, are jointly and severally liable in the capacity in which they sign.

(b) Except as provided in Section 3-417(e) or by agreement of the affected parties, a party with joint and several liability that pays the instrument is entitled to receive from any party with the same joint and several liability contribution in accordance with applicable law.

(c) Discharge of one party with joint and several liability by a person entitled to enforce the instrument does not affect the right under subsection (b) of a party with the same joint and several liability to receive contribution from the party discharged.

**§3-117. Other Agreements Affecting an Instrument.**

Subject to applicable law regarding exclusion of proof of contemporaneous or prior agreements, the obligation of a party to an instrument to pay the instrument may be modified, supplemented, or nullified by a separate agreement of the obligor and a person entitled to enforce the instrument if the instrument is issued or the obligation is incurred in reliance on the agreement or as part of the same transaction giving rise to the agreement. To the extent an obligation is modified, supplemented, or nullified by an agreement under this section, the agreement is a defense to the obligation.

**§3-118. Statute of Limitations.**

(a) Except as provided in subsection (e), an action to enforce the obligation of a party to pay a note payable at a definite time must be commenced within six years after the payment date or dates stated in the note or, if a payment date is accelerated, within six years after the accelerated payment date.

(b) Except as provided in subsection (d) or (e), if demand for payment is made to the maker of a note payable on demand, an action to enforce the obligation of a party to pay the note must be commenced within six years after the demand. If no demand for payment is made to the maker, an action to enforce the note is barred if neither principal nor interest on the note has been paid for a continuous period of 10 years.

(c) Except as provided in subsection (d), an action to enforce the obligation of a party to an unaccepted draft to pay the draft must be commenced within six years after dishonor of the draft or 10 years after the date of the draft, whichever period expires first.

(d) An action to enforce the obligation of the acceptor of a certified check or the issuer of a teller's check, cashier's check, or traveler's check must be commenced within six years after demand for payment is made to the acceptor or issuer, as the case may be.

(e) An action to enforce the obligation of a party to a certificate of deposit to pay the instrument must be commenced within six years after demand for payment is made to the maker, but if the instrument states a maturity date and the maker is not required to pay before that date, the six-year period begins when a demand for payment is in effect and the maturity date has passed.

(f) This subsection applies to an action to enforce the obligation of a party to pay an accepted draft, other than a certified check. If the obligation of the acceptor is payable at a definite time, the action must be commenced within six years after the payment date or dates stated in the draft or acceptance. If the obligation of the acceptor is payable on demand, the action must be commenced within six years after the date of the acceptance.
(g) Unless governed by other law regarding claims for indemnity or contribution, an action (i) for conversion of an instrument, for money had and received, or like action based on conversion, (ii) for breach of warranty, or (iii) to enforce an obligation, duty, or right arising under this Article and not governed by this section must be commenced within three years after the cause of action accrues.

**§3-119. Notice of Right to Defend Action.**
In an action for breach of an obligation for which a third person is answerable over pursuant to this Article or Article 4, the defendant may give the third person written notice of the litigation, and the person notified may then give similar notice to any other person who is answerable over. If the notice states (i) that the person notified may come in and defend and (ii) that failure to do so will bind the person notified in an action later brought by the person giving the notice as to any determination of fact common to the two litigations, the person notified is so bound unless after seasonable receipt of the notice the person notified does come in and defend.

## Part 2—Negotiation, Transfer and Indorsement

**§3-201. Negotiation.**
(a) "Negotiation" means a transfer of possession, whether voluntary or involuntary, of an instrument to a person who thereby becomes its holder if possession is obtained from a person other than the issuer of the instrument.
(b) Except for a negotiation by a remitter, if an instrument is payable to an identified person, negotiation requires transfer of possession of the instrument and its indorsement by the holder. If an instrument is payable to bearer, it may be negotiated by transfer of possession alone.

**§3-202. Negotiation Subject to Rescission.**
(a) Negotiation is effective even if obtained (i) from an infant, a corporation exceeding its powers, or a person without capacity, or (ii) by fraud, duress, or mistake, or in breach of duty or as part of an illegal transaction.
(b) To the extent permitted by law, negotiation may be rescinded or may be subject to other remedies, but those remedies may not be asserted against a subsequent holder in due course or a person paying the instrument in good faith and without knowledge of facts that are a basis for rescission or other remedy.

**§3-203. Rights Acquired by Transfer.**
(a) An instrument is transferred when it is delivered by a person other than its issuer for the purpose of giving to the person receiving delivery the right to enforce the instrument.
(b) Transfer of an instrument, regardless of whether the transfer is a negotiation, vests in the transferee any right of the transferor to enforce the instrument, including any right as a holder in due course, but the transferee cannot acquire rights of a holder in due course by a transfer, directly or indirectly, from a holder in due course if the purchaser engaged in fraud or illegality affecting the instrument.
(c) Unless otherwise agreed, if an instrument is transferred for value and the transferee does not become a holder because of lack of indorsement by the transferor, the transferee has a specifically enforceable right to the unqualified indorsement of the transferor, but negotiation of the instrument does not occur until the indorsement is made.
(d) If a transferor purports to transfer less than the entire instrument, negotiation of the instrument does not occur. The transferee obtains no rights under this Article and has only the rights of a partial assignee.

**§3-204. Indorsement.**
(a) "Indorsement" means a signature, other than that of a maker, drawer, or acceptor, that alone or accompanied by other words, is made on an instrument for the purpose of (i) negotiating the instrument, (ii) restricting payment of the instrument, or (iii) incurring indorser's liability on the instrument, but regardless of the intent of the signer, a signature and its accompanying words is an indorsement unless the accompanying words, the terms of the instrument, the place of the signature, or other circumstances unambiguously indicate that the signature was made for a purpose other than indorsement. For the purpose of determining whether a signature is made on an instrument, a paper affixed to the instrument is a part of the instrument.
(b) "Indorser" means a person who makes an indorsement.
(c) For the purpose of determining whether the transferee of an instrument is a holder, an indorsement that transfers a security interest in the instrument is effective as an unqualified indorsement of the instrument.
(d) If an instrument is payable to a holder under a name that is not the name of the holder, indorsement may be made by the holder in the name stated in the instrument or in the holder's name or both, but signature in both names may be required by a person paying or taking the instrument for value or collection.

**§3-205. Special Indorsement; Blank Indorsement; Anomalous Indorsement.**
(a) If an indorsement is made by the holder of an instrument, whether payable to an identified person or payable to bearer, and the indorsement identifies a person to whom it makes the instrument payable, it is a "special indorsement." When specially indorsed, an instrument becomes payable to the identified person and may be negotiated only by the indorsement of that person. The principles stated in Section 3-110 apply to special indorsements.
(b) If an indorsement is made by the holder of an instrument and it is not a special indorsement, it is a "blank indorsement." When indorsed in blank, an instrument becomes payable to bearer and may be negotiated by transfer of possession alone until specially indorsed.
(c) The holder may convert a blank indorsement that consists only of a signature into a special indorsement by writing, above the signature of the indorser, words identifying the person to whom the instrument is made payable.
(d) "Anomalous indorsement" means an indorsement made by a person that is not the holder of the instrument. An anomalous indorsement does not affect the manner in which the instrument may be negotiated.

**§3-206. Restrictive Indorsement.**
(a) An indorsement limiting payment to a particular person or otherwise prohibiting further transfer or negotiation of the instrument is not effective to prevent further transfer or negotiation of the instrument.
(b) An indorsement stating a condition to the right of the indorsee to receive payment does not affect the right of the indorsee to enforce the instrument. A person paying the instrument or taking it for value or collection may disregard the condition, and the rights and liabilities of that person are not affected by whether the condition has been fulfilled.
(c) The following rules apply to an instrument bearing an indorsement (i) described in Section 4-201(2), or (ii) in blank or to a particular bank using the words "for deposit," "for collection," or other words indicating a purpose of having the instrument collected for the indorser or for a particular account:

(1) A person, other than a bank, that purchases the instrument when so indorsed converts the instrument unless the proceeds of the instrument are received by the indorser or are applied consistently with the indorsement.

(2) A depositary bank that purchases the instrument or takes it for collection when so indorsed converts the instrument unless the proceeds of the instrument are received by the indorser or applied consistently with the indorsement.

(3) A payor bank that is also the depositary bank or that takes the instrument for immediate payment over the counter from a person other than a collecting bank converts the instrument unless the proceeds of the instrument are received by the indorser or applied consistently with the indorsement.

(4) Except as otherwise provided in paragraph (3), a payor bank or intermediary bank may disregard the indorsement and is not liable if the proceeds of the instrument are not received by the indorser or applied consistently with the indorsement.

(d) Except for an indorsement covered by subsection (c), the following rules apply to an instrument bearing an indorsement using words to the effect that payment is to be made to the indorsee as agent, trustee, or other fiduciary for the benefit of the indorser or another person.

(1) Unless there is notice of breach of fiduciary duty as provided in Section 3-307, a person that purchases the instrument from the indorsee or takes the instrument from the indorsee for collection or payment may pay the proceeds of payment or the value given for the instrument to the indorsee without regard to whether the indorsee violates a fiduciary duty to the indorser.

(2) A later transferee of the instrument or person that pays the instrument is neither given notice nor otherwise affected by the restriction in the indorsement unless the transferee or payor knows that the fiduciary dealt with the instrument or its proceeds in breach of fiduciary duty.

(e) Purchase of an instrument bearing an indorsement to which this section applies does not prevent the purchaser from becoming a holder in due course of the instrument unless the purchaser is a converter under subsection (c).

(f) In an action to enforce the obligation of a party to pay the instrument, the obligor has a defense if payment would violate an indorsement to which this section applies and the payment is not permitted by this section.

**§3-207. Reacquisition.**

Reacquisition of an instrument occurs if it is transferred, by negotiation or otherwise, to a former holder. A former holder that reacquires the instrument may cancel indorsements made after the reacquirer first became a holder of the instrument. If the cancellation causes the instrument to be payable to the reacquirer or to bearer, the reacquirer may negotiate the instrument. An indorser whose indorsement is canceled is discharged, and the discharge is effective against any later holder.

## Part 3—Enforcement of Instruments

**§3-301. Person Entitled to Enforce Instrument.**

"Person entitled to enforce" an instrument means (i) the holder of the instrument, (ii) a nonholder in possession of the instrument who has the rights of a holder, or (iii) a person not in possession of the instrument who is entitled to enforce the instrument pursuant to Section 3-309. A person may be a person entitled to enforce the instrument even though the person is not the owner of the instrument or is in wrongful possession of the instrument.

**§3-302. Holder in Due Course.**

(a) Subject to subsection (c) and Section 3-106(d), "holder in due course" means the holder of an instrument if:

(1) the instrument when issued or negotiated to the holder does not bear such apparent evidence of forgery or alteration or is not otherwise so irregular or incomplete as to call into question its authenticity, and

(2) the holder took the instrument (i) for value, (ii) in good faith, (iii) without notice that the instrument is overdue or has been dishonored or that there is an uncured default with respect to payment of another instrument issued as part of the same series, (iv) without notice that the instrument contains an unauthorized signature or has been altered, (v) without notice of any claim to the instrument stated in Section 3-306, and (vi) without notice that any party to the instrument has any defense or claim in recoupment stated in Section 3-305(a).

(b) Notice of discharge of a party to the instrument, other than discharge in an insolvency proceeding, is not notice of a defense under subsection (a), but discharge is effective against a person who became a holder in due course with notice of the discharge. Public filing or recording of a document does not of itself constitute notice of a defense, claim in recoupment, or claim to the instrument.

(c) Except to the extent a transferor or predecessor in interest has rights as a holder in due course, a person does not acquire rights of a holder in due course of an instrument taken (i) by legal process or by purchase at an execution, bankruptcy, or creditor's sale or similar proceeding, (ii) by purchase as part of a bulk transaction not in ordinary course of business of the transferor, or (iii) as the successor in interest to an estate or other organization.

(d) If, under Section 3-303(a)(1), the promise of performance that is the consideration for an instrument has been partially performed, the holder may assert rights as a holder in due course of the instrument only to the fraction of the amount payable under the instrument equal to the value of the partial performance divided by the value of the promised performance.

(e) If (i) the person entitled to enforce an instrument has only a security interest in the instrument and (ii) the person obliged to pay the instrument has a defense, claim in recoupment or claim to the instrument that may be asserted against the person who granted the security interest, the person entitled to enforce the instrument may assert rights as a holder in due course only to an amount payable under the instrument which, at the time of enforcement of the instrument, does not exceed the amount of the unpaid obligation secured.

(f) To be effective, notice must be received at such time and in such manner as to give a reasonable opportunity to act on it.

(g) This section is subject to any law limiting status as a holder in due course in particular classes of transactions.

**§3-303. Value and Consideration.**

(a) An instrument is issued or transferred for value if:

(1) the instrument is issued or transferred for a promise of performance, to the extent the promise has been performed;

(2) the transferee acquires a security interest or other lien in the instrument other than a lien obtained by judicial proceedings;

(3) the instrument is issued or transferred as payment of, or as security for, an existing obligation of any person, whether or not the obligation is due;

(4) the instrument is issued or transferred in exchange for a negotiable instrument; or

(5) the instrument is issued or transferred in exchange for the incurring of an irrevocable obligation to a third party by the person taking the instrument.

(b) "Consideration" means any consideration sufficient to support a simple contract. The drawer or maker of an instrument has a defense if the instrument is issued without consideration. If an instrument is issued for a promise of performance, the drawer or maker has a defense to the extent performance of the promise is due and the promise has not been performed. If an instrument is issued for value as stated in subsection (a), the instrument is also issued for consideration.

**§3-304. Overdue Instrument.**

(a) An instrument payable on demand becomes overdue at the earliest of the following times:

(1) on the day after the day demand for payment is duly made;

(2) if the instrument is a check, 90 days after its date; or

(3) if the instrument is not a check, when the instrument has been outstanding for a period of time after its date which is unreasonably long under the circumstances of the particular case in light of the nature of the instrument and trade usage.

(b) With respect to an instrument payable at a definite time the following rules apply: (1) If the principal is payable in installments and a due date has not been accelerated, the instrument becomes overdue upon default under the instrument for nonpayment of an installment, and the instrument remains overdue until the default is cured. (2) If the principal is not payable in installments and the due date has not been accelerated, the instrument becomes overdue on the day after the due date. (3) If a due date with respect to principal has been accelerated, the instrument becomes overdue on the day after the accelerated due date.

(c) Unless the due date of principal has been accelerated, an instrument does not become overdue if there is default in payment of interest but no default in payment of principal.

**§3-305. Defenses and Claims in Recoupment.**

(a) Except as stated in subsection (b), the right to enforce the obligation of a party to pay the instrument is subject to the following:

(1) A defense of the obligor based on (i) infancy of the obligor to the extent it is a defense to a simple contract, (ii) duress, lack of legal capacity, or illegality of the transaction that nullifies the obligation of the obligor, (iii) fraud that induced the obligor to sign the instrument with neither knowledge nor reasonable opportunity to learn of its character or its essential terms, or (iv) discharge of the obligor in insolvency proceedings.

(2) A defense of the obligor stated in another section of this Article or a defense of the obligor that would be available if the person entitled to enforce the instrument were enforcing a right to payment under a simple contract.

(3) A claim in recoupment of the obligor against the original payee of the instrument if the claim arose from the transaction that gave rise to the instrument. The claim of the obligor may be asserted against a transferee of the instrument only to reduce the amount owing on the instrument at the time the action is brought.

(b) The right of a holder in due course to enforce the obligation of a party to pay the instrument is subject to defenses of the obligor stated in subsection (a)(1), but is not subject to defenses of the obligor stated in subsection (a)(2) or claims in recoupment stated in subsection (a)(3) against a person other than the holder.

(c) Except as stated in subsection (d), in an action to enforce the obligation of a party to pay the instrument, the obligor may not assert against the person entitled to enforce the instrument a defense, claim in recoupment, or claim to the instrument (Section 3-306) of another person, but the other person's claim to the instrument may be asserted by the obligor if the other person is joined in the action and personally asserts the claim against the person entitled to enforce the instrument. An obligor is not obliged to pay the instrument if the person seeking enforcement of the instrument does not have rights of a holder in due course and the obligor proves that the instrument is a lost or stolen instrument.

(d) In an action to enforce the obligation of an accommodation party to pay an instrument, the accommodation party may assert against the person entitled to enforce the instrument any defense or claim in recoupment under subsection (a) that the accommodated party could assert against the person entitled to enforce the instrument, except the defenses of discharge in insolvency proceedings, infancy, or lack of legal capacity.

**§3-306. Claims to an Instrument.**

A person taking an instrument, other than a person having rights of a holder in due course, is subject to a claim of a property or possessory right in the instrument or its proceeds, including a claim to rescind a negotiation and to recover the instrument or its proceeds. A person having rights of a holder in due course takes free of the claim to the instrument.

**§3-307. Notice of Breach of Fiduciary Duty.**

(a) This section applies if (i) an instrument is taken from a fiduciary for payment or collection or for value, (ii) the taker has knowledge of the fiduciary status of the fiduciary, and (iii) the represented person makes a claim to the instrument or its proceeds on the basis that the transaction of the fiduciary is a breach of fiduciary duty. Notice of breach of fiduciary duty by the fiduciary is notice of the claim of the represented person. "Fiduciary" means an agent, trustee, partner, corporation officer or director, or other representative owing a fiduciary duty with respect to the instrument. "Represented person" means the principal, beneficiary, partnership, corporation, or other person to whom the duty is owed.

(b) If the instrument is payable to the fiduciary, as such, or to the represented person, the taker has notice of the breach of fiduciary duty if the instrument is (i) taken in payment of or as security for a debt known by the taker to be the personal debt of the fiduciary, (ii) taken in a transaction known by the taker to be for the personal benefit of the fiduciary, or (iii) deposited to an account other than an account of the fiduciary, as such, or an account of the represented person.

(c) If the instrument is made or drawn by the fiduciary, as such, payable to the fiduciary personally, the taker does not have notice of the breach of fiduciary duty unless the taker knows of the breach of fiduciary duty.

(d) If the instrument is made or drawn by or on behalf of the represented person to the taker as payee, the taker has notice of the breach of fiduciary duty if the instrument is (i) taken in payment of or as security for a debt known by the taker to be the personal debt of the fiduciary, (ii) taken in a transaction known by the taker to be for the personal benefit of the fiduciary, or (iii) deposited to an account other than an account of the fiduciary, as such, or an account of the represented person.

**§3-308. Proof of Signatures and Status as Holder in Due Course.**

(a) In an action with respect to an instrument, the authenticity of, and authority to make, each signature on the instrument is admitted unless specifically denied in the pleadings. If the validity of a signature is denied in the pleadings, the burden of establishing validity is on the person claiming validity, but the signature is presumed to be authentic and authorized unless the action is to enforce the liability of the purported signer and the signer is dead or incompetent at the time of trial of the issue of validity of the signature. If an action to enforce the instrument is brought against a person as the undisclosed principal of a person who signed the instrument as a party to the instrument, the plaintiff has the burden of establishing that the defendant is liable on the instrument as a represented person pursuant to Section 3-402(a).

(b) If the validity of signatures is admitted or proved and there is compliance with subsection (a), a plaintiff producing the instrument is entitled to payment if the plaintiff proves entitlement to enforce the instrument under Section 3-301, unless the defendant proves a defense or claim in recoupment. If a defense or claim in recoupment is proved, the right to payment of the plaintiff is subject to the defense or claim except to the extent the plaintiff proves that the plaintiff has rights of a holder in due course which are not subject to the defense or claim.

**§3-309. Enforcement of Lost, Destroyed, or Stolen Instrument.**

(a) A person not in possession of an instrument is entitled to enforce the instrument if (i) that person was in rightful possession of the instrument and entitled to enforce it when loss of possession occurred, (ii) the loss of possession was not the result of a voluntary transfer by that person or a lawful seizure, and (iii) that person cannot reasonably obtain possession of the instrument because the instrument was destroyed, its whereabouts cannot be determined, or it is in the wrongful possession of an unknown person or a person that cannot be found or is not amenable to service of process.

(b) A person seeking enforcement of an instrument pursuant to subsection (a) must prove the terms of the instrument and the person's right to enforce the instrument. If that proof is made, Section 3-308 applies to the case as though the person seeking enforcement had produced the instrument. The court may not enter judgment in favor of the person seeking enforcement unless it finds that the person required to pay the instrument is adequately protected against loss that might occur by reason of a claim by another person to enforce the instrument. Adequate protection may be provided by any reasonable means.

**§3-310. Effect of Instrument on Obligation for Which Taken.**

(a) Unless otherwise agreed, if a certified check, cashier's check, or teller's check is taken for an obligation, the obligation is discharged to the same extent discharge would result if an amount of money equal to the amount of the instrument were taken in payment of the obligation. Discharge of the obligation does not affect any liability that the obligor may have as an indorser of the instrument.

(b) Unless otherwise agreed and except as provided in subsection (a), if a note or an uncertified check is taken for an obligation, the obligation is suspended to the same extent the obligation would be discharged if an amount of money equal to the amount of the instrument were taken.

(1) In the case of an uncertified check, suspension of the obligation continues until dishonor of the check or until it is paid or certified. Payment or certification of the check results in discharge of the obligation to the extent of the amount of the check.

(2) In the case of a note, suspension of the obligation continues until dishonor of the note or until it is paid. Payment of the note results in discharge of the obligation to the extent of the payment.

(3) If the check or note is dishonored and the obligee of the obligation for which the instrument was taken has possession of the instrument, the obligee may enforce either the instrument or the obligation. In the case of an instrument of a third person which is negotiated to the obligee by the obligor, discharge of the obligor on the instrument also discharges the obligation.

(4) If the person entitled to enforce the instrument taken for an obligation is a person other than the obligee, the obligee may not enforce the obligation to the extent the obligation is suspended. If the obligee is the person entitled to enforce the instrument but no longer has possession of it because it was lost, stolen, or destroyed, the obligation may not be enforced to the extent of the amount payable on the instrument, and to that extent the obligee's rights against the obligor are limited to enforcement of the instrument.

(c) If an instrument other than one described in subsection (a) or (b) is taken for an obligation, the effect is (i) that stated in subsection (a) if the instrument is one on which a bank is liable as maker or acceptor, or (ii) that stated in subsection (b) in any other case.

**§3-311. Accord and Satisfaction by Use of Instrument.**

(a) This section applies if a person against whom a claim is asserted proves that (i) that person in good faith tendered an instrument to the claimant as full satisfaction of the claim, (ii) the amount of the claim was unliquidated or subject to a bona fide dispute, and (iii) the claimant obtained payment of the instrument.

(b) Unless subsection (c) applies, the claim is discharged if the person against whom the claim is asserted proves that the instrument or an accompanying written communication contained a conspicuous statement to the effect that the instrument was tendered as full satisfaction of the claim.

(c) Subject to subsection (d), a claim is not discharged under subsection (b) if the claimant is an organization and proves that within a reasonable time before the tender, the claimant sent a conspicuous statement to the person against whom the claim is asserted that communications concerning disputed debts, including an instrument tendered as full satisfaction of a debt, are to be sent to a designated person, office or place, and the instrument or accompanying communication was not received by that designated person, office, or place.

(d) Notwithstanding subsection (c), a claim is discharged under subsection (b) if the person against whom the claim is asserted proves that within a reasonable time before collection of the instrument was initiated, an agent of the claimant having direct responsibility with respect to the disputed obligation knew that the instrument was tendered in full satisfaction of the claim, or received the instrument and any accompanying written communication.

## Part 4—Liability of Parties

**§3-401. Signature.**

(a) A person is not liable on an instrument unless (i) the person signed the instrument, or (ii) the person is represented by an agent or representative who signed the instrument and the signature is binding on the represented person under Section 3-402.

(b) A signature may be made (i) manually or by means of a device or machine, and (ii) by the use of any name, including any trade or assumed name, or by any word, mark, or symbol executed or adopted by a person with present intention to authenticate a writing.

**§3-402. Signature by Representative.**

(a) If a person acting, or purporting to act, as a representative signs an instrument by signing either the name of the represented person or the name of the signer, the represented person is bound by the signature to the same extent the represented person would be bound if the signature were on a simple contract. If the represented person is bound, the signature of the representative is the "authorized signature of the represented person" and the represented person is liable on the instrument, whether or not identified in the instrument.

(b) If a representative signs the name of the representative to an instrument and that signature is an authorized signature of the represented person, the following rules apply:

(1) If the form of the signature shows unambiguously that the signature is made on behalf of the represented person who is identified in the instrument, the representative is not liable on the instrument.

(2) Subject to subsection (c), if (i) the form of the signature does not show unambiguously that the signature is made in a representative capacity or (ii) the represented person is not identified in the instrument, the representative is liable on the instrument to a holder in due course that took the instrument without notice that the representative was not intended to be liable on the instrument. With respect to any other person, the representative is liable on the instrument unless the representative proves that the original parties to the instrument did not intend the representative to be liable on the instrument.

(c) If a representative signs the name of the representative as drawer of a check without indication of the representative status and the check is payable from an account of the represented person who is identified on the check, the signer is not liable on the check if the signature is an authorized signature of the represented person.

**§3-403. Unauthorized Signature.**

(a) Except as otherwise provided in this Article, an unauthorized signature is ineffective except as the signature of the unauthorized signer in favor of a person who in good faith pays the instrument or takes it for value. An unauthorized signature may be ratified for all purposes of this Article.

(b) If the signature of more than one person is required to constitute the authorized signature of an organization, the signature of the organization is unauthorized if one of the required signatures is missing.

(c) The civil or criminal liability of a person who makes an unauthorized signature is not affected by any provision of this Article that makes the unauthorized signature effective for the purposes of this Article.

**§3-404. Impostors; Fictitious Payees.**

(a) If an impostor by use of the mails or otherwise induces the maker or drawer of an instrument to issue the instrument to the impostor, or to a person acting in concert with the impostor, by impersonating the payee of the instrument or a person authorized to act for the payee, an indorsement of the instrument by any person in the name of the payee is effective as the indorsement of the payee in favor of any person that in good faith pays the instrument or takes it for value or for collection.

(b) If (i) a person whose intent determines to whom an instrument is payable (Section 3-110(a) or (b)) does not intend the person identified as payee to have any interest in the instrument, or (ii) the person identified as payee of the instrument is a fictitious person, the following rules apply until the instrument is negotiated by special indorsement:

(1) Any person in possession of the instrument is its holder.

(2) An indorsement by any person in the name of the payee stated in the instrument is effective as the indorsement of the payee in favor of any person that in good faith pays the instrument or takes it for value or for collection.

(c) Under subsection (a) or (b) an indorsement is made in the name of a payee if (i) it is made in a name substantially similar to that of the payee or (ii) the instrument, whether or not indorsed, is deposited in a depositary bank to an account in a name substantially similar to that of the payee.

(d) With respect to an instrument to which subsection (a) or (b) applies, if a person paying the instrument or taking it for value or for collection fails to exercise ordinary care in paying or taking the instrument and that failure substantially contributes to loss resulting from payment of the instrument, the person bearing the loss may recover from the person failing to exercise ordinary care to the extent the failure to exercise ordinary care contributed to the loss.

**§3-405. Employer Responsibility for Fraudulent Indorsement by Employee.**

(a) This section applies to fraudulent indorsements of instruments with respect to which an employer has entrusted an employee with responsibility as part of the employee's duties. The following definitions apply to this section:

(1) "Employee" includes, in addition to an employee of an employer, an independent contractor and employee of an independent contractor retained by the employer.

(2) "Fraudulent indorsement" means (i) in the case of an instrument payable to the employer, a forged indorsement purporting to be that of the employer, or (ii) in the case of an instrument with respect to which the employer is drawer or maker, a forged indorsement purporting to be that of the person identified as payee.

(3) "Responsibility" with respect to instruments means authority (i) to sign or indorse instruments on behalf of the employer, (ii) to process instruments received by the employer for bookkeeping purposes, for deposit to an account, or for other disposition, (iii) to prepare or process instruments for issue in the name of the employer, (iv) to supply information determining the names or addresses of payees of instruments to be issued in the name of the employer, (v) to control the disposition of instruments to be issued in the name of the employer, or (vi) to otherwise act with respect to instruments in a responsible capacity. "Responsibility" does not include the assignment of duties that merely allow an employee to have access to instruments or blank or incomplete instrument forms that are being stored or transported or are part of incoming or outgoing mail, or similar access.

(b) For the purpose of determining the rights and liabilities of a person who, in good faith, pays an instrument or takes it for value or for collection, if an employee entrusted with responsibility with respect to the instrument or a person acting in concert with the employee makes a fraudulent indorsement to the instrument, the indorsement is effective as the indorsement of the person to whom the instrument is payable if it is made in the name of that person. If the person paying the instrument or taking it for value or for collection fails to exercise ordinary care in paying or taking the instrument and that failure substantially contributes to loss resulting from the fraud, the person bearing the loss may recover from the person failing to exercise ordinary care to the extent the failure to exercise ordinary care contributed to the loss.

(c) Under subsection (b) an indorsement is made in the name of the person to whom an instrument is payable if (i) it is made in a name substantially similar to the name of that person or (ii) the instrument, whether or not indorsed, is deposited in a depositary bank to an account in a name substantially similar to the name of that person.

**§3-406. Negligence Contributing to Forged Signature or Alteration of Instrument.**

(a) A person whose failure to exercise ordinary care substantially contributes to an alteration of an instrument or to the making of a forged signature on an instrument is precluded from asserting the alteration or the forgery against a person that, in good faith, pays the instrument or takes it for value.

(b) If the person asserting the preclusion fails to exercise ordinary care in paying or taking the instrument and that failure substantially contributes to loss, the loss is allocated between the person precluded and the person asserting the preclusion according to the extent to which the failure of each to exercise ordinary care contributed to the loss.

(c) Under subsection (a) the burden of proving failure to exercise ordinary care is on the person asserting the preclusion. Under subsection (b) the burden of proving failure to exercise ordinary care is on the person precluded.

**§3-407. Alteration.**

(a) "Alteration" means (i) an unauthorized change in an instrument that purports to modify in any respect the obligation of a party to the instrument, or (ii) an unauthorized addition of words or numbers or other change to an incomplete instrument relating to the obligation of any party to the instrument.

(b) Except as provided in subsection (c), an alteration fraudulently made by the holder discharges any party to whose obligation the alteration applies unless that party assents or is precluded from asserting the alteration. No other alteration discharges any party, and the instrument may be enforced according to its original terms.

(c) If an instrument that has been fraudulently altered is acquired by a person having rights of a holder in due course, it may be enforced by that person according to its original terms. If an incomplete instrument is completed and is then acquired by a person having rights of a holder in due course, it may be enforced by that person as completed, whether or not the completion is a fraudulent alteration.

**§3-408. Drawee Not Liable on Unaccepted Draft.**

A check or other draft does not of itself operate as an assignment of funds in the hands of the drawee available for its payment, and the drawee is not liable on the instrument until the drawee accepts it.

**§3-409. Acceptance of Draft; Certified Check.**

(a) "Acceptance" means the drawee's signed agreement to pay a draft as presented. It must be written on the draft and may consist of the drawee's signature alone. Acceptance may be made at any time and becomes effective when notification pursuant to instructions is given or the accepted draft is delivered for the purpose of giving rights on the acceptance to any person.

(b) A draft may be accepted although it has not been signed by the drawer, is otherwise incomplete, is overdue, or has been dishonored.

(c) If a draft is payable at a fixed period after sight and the acceptor fails to date the acceptance, the holder may complete the acceptance by supplying a date in good faith.

(d) "Certified check" means a check accepted by the bank on which it is drawn. Acceptance may be made as stated in subsection (a) or by a writing on the check which indicates that the check is certified. The drawee of a check has no obligation to certify the check, and refusal to certify is not dishonor of the check.

**§3-410. Acceptance Varying Draft.**

(a) If the terms of a drawee's acceptance vary from the terms of the draft as presented, the holder may refuse the acceptance and treat the draft as dishonored. In that case, the drawee may cancel the acceptance.

(b) The terms of a draft are not varied by an acceptance to pay at a particular bank or place in the United States, unless the acceptance states that the draft is to be paid only at that bank or place.

(c) If the holder assents to an acceptance varying the terms of a draft, the obligation of each drawer and indorser that does not expressly assent to the acceptance is discharged.

**§3-411. Refusal to Pay Cashier's Checks, Teller's Checks, and Certified Checks.**
(a) In this section, "obligated bank" means the acceptor of a certified check or the issuer of a cashier's check or teller's check bought from the issuer.
(b) If the obligated bank wrongfully (i) refuses to pay a cashier's check or certified check, (ii) stops payment of a teller's check, or (iii) refuses to pay a dishonored teller's check, the person asserting the right to enforce the check is entitled to compensation for expenses and loss of interest resulting from the nonpayment and may recover consequential damages if the obligated bank refused to pay after receiving notice of particular circumstances giving rise to the damages.
(c) Expenses or consequential damages under subsection (b) are not recoverable if the refusal of the obligated bank to pay occurs because (i) the bank suspends payments, (ii) the obligated bank is asserting a claim or defense of the bank that it has reasonable grounds to believe is available against the person entitled to enforce the instrument, (iii) the obligated bank has a reasonable doubt whether the person demanding payment is the person entitled to enforce the instrument, or (iv) payment is prohibited by law.

**§3-412. Obligation of Maker.**
A maker of a note is obliged to pay the note (i) according to its terms at the time it was issued or, if not issued, at the time it first came into possession of a holder, or (ii) if the maker signed an incomplete instrument, according to its terms when completed as stated in Sections 3-115 and 3-407. The obligation is owed to a person entitled to enforce the note or to an indorser that paid the note pursuant to Section 3-415.

**§3-413. Obligation of Acceptor.**
(a) An acceptor of a draft is obliged to pay the draft (i) according to its terms at the time it was accepted, even though the acceptance states that the draft is payable "as originally drawn" or equivalent terms, (ii) if the acceptance varies the terms of the draft, according to the terms of the draft as varied, or (iii) if the acceptance is of a draft that is an incomplete instrument, according to its terms when completed as stated in Sections 3-115 and 3-407. The obligation is owed to a person entitled to enforce the draft or to the drawer or an indorser that paid the draft pursuant to Section 3-414 or 3-415.
(b) If the certification of a check or other acceptance of a draft states the amount certified or accepted, the obligation of the acceptor is that amount. If (i) the certification or acceptance does not state an amount, (ii) the instrument is subsequently altered by raising its amount, and (iii) the instrument is then negotiated to a holder in due course, the obligation of the acceptor is the amount of the instrument at the time it was negotiated to the holder in due course.

**§3-414. Obligation of Drawer.**
(a) If an unaccepted draft is dishonored, the drawer is obliged to pay the draft (i) according to its terms at the time it was issued or, if not issued, at the time it first came into possession of a holder, or (ii) if the drawer signed an incomplete instrument, according to its terms when completed as stated in Sections 3-115 and 3-407. The obligation is owed to a person entitled to enforce the draft or to an indorser that paid the draft pursuant to Section 3-415.
(b) If a draft is accepted by a bank and the acceptor dishonors the draft, the drawer has no obligation to pay the draft because of the dishonor, regardless of when or by whom acceptance was obtained.
(c) If a draft is accepted and the acceptor is not a bank, the obligation of the drawer to pay the draft if the draft is dishonored by the acceptor is the same as the obligation of an indorser stated in Section 3-415(a) and (c).
(d) Words in a draft indicating that the draft is drawn without recourse are effective to disclaim all liability of the drawer to pay the draft if the draft is not a check or a teller's check, but they are not effective to disclaim the obligation stated in subsection (a) if the draft is a check or a teller's check.
(e) If (i) a check is not presented for payment or given to a depositary bank for collection within 30 days after its date, (ii) the drawee suspends payments after expiration of the 30-day period without paying the check, and (iii) because of the suspension of payments the drawer is deprived of funds maintained with the drawee to cover payment of the check, the drawer to the extent deprived of funds may discharge its obligation to pay the check by assigning to the person entitled to enforce the check the rights of the drawer against the drawee with respect to the funds.

**§3-415. Obligation of Indorser.**
(a) Subject to subsections (b), (c) and (d) and to Section 3-419(d), if an instrument is dishonored, an indorser is obliged to pay the amount due on the instrument (i) according to the terms of the instrument at the time it was indorsed, or (ii) if the indorser indorsed an incomplete instrument, according to its terms when completed as stated in Sections 3-115 and 3-407. The obligation of the indorser is owed to a person entitled to enforce the instrument or to a subsequent indorser that paid the instrument pursuant to this section.
(b) If an indorsement states that it is made "without recourse" or otherwise disclaims liability of the indorser, the indorser is not liable under subsection (a) to pay the instrument.
(c) If notice of dishonor of an instrument is required by Section 3-503 and notice of dishonor complying with that section is not given to an indorser, the liability of the indorser under subsection (a) is discharged.
(d) If a draft is accepted by a bank after an indorsement was made and the acceptor dishonors the draft, the indorser is not liable under subsection (a) to pay the instrument.
(e) If an indorser of a check is liable under subsection (a) and the check is not presented for payment, or given to a depositary bank for collection, within 30 days after the day the indorsement was made, the liability of the indorser under subsection (a) is discharged.

**§3-416. Transfer Warranties.**
(a) A person that transfers an instrument for consideration warrants to the transferee and, if the transfer is by indorsement, to any subsequent transferee that:
(1) the warrantor is a person entitled to enforce the instrument,
(2) all signatures on the instrument are authentic and authorized,
(3) the instrument has not been altered,
(4) the instrument is not subject to a defense or claim in recoupment stated in Section 3-305(a) of any party that can be asserted against the warrantor, and
(5) the warrantor has no knowledge of any insolvency proceeding commenced with respect to the maker or acceptor or, in the case of an unaccepted draft, the drawer.
(b) A person to whom the warranties under subsection (a) are made and who took the instrument in good faith may recover from the warrantor as damages for breach of warranty an amount equal to the loss suffered as a result of the breach, but not more than the amount of the instrument plus expenses and loss of interest incurred as a result of the breach.
(c) The warranties stated in subsection (a) cannot be disclaimed with respect to checks. Unless notice of a claim for breach of warranty is given to the warrantor within 30 days after the claimant has reason to know of the breach and the identity of the warrantor, the warrantor is discharged to the extent of any loss caused by the delay in giving notice of the claim.
(d) A cause of action for breach of warranty under this section accrues when the claimant has reason to know of the breach.

**§3-417. Presentment Warranties.**
(a) If an unaccepted draft is presented to the drawee for payment or acceptance and the drawee pays or accepts the draft, (i) the person obtaining payment or acceptance, at the time of presentment, and (ii) a previous transferor of the draft, at the time of transfer, warrant to the drawee making payment or accepting the draft in good faith that:
(1) the warrantor is or was, at the time the warrantor transferred the draft, a person entitled to enforce the draft or authorized to obtain

payment or acceptance of the draft on behalf of a person entitled to enforce the draft;

(2) the draft has not been altered; and

(3) the warrantor has no knowledge that the signature of the purported drawer of the draft is unauthorized.

(b) A drawee making payment may recover from any warrantor damages for breach of warranty equal to the amount paid by the drawee less the amount the drawee received or is entitled to receive from the drawer because of payment of the draft. In addition the drawee is entitled to compensation for expenses and loss of interest resulting from the breach. The right of the drawee to recover damages under this subsection is not affected by any failure of the drawee to exercise ordinary care in making payment. If the drawee accepts the draft (i) breach of warranty is a defense to the obligation of the acceptor, and (ii) if the acceptor makes payment with respect to the draft, the acceptor is entitled to recover from any warrantor for breach of warranty the amounts stated in the first two sentences of this subsection.

(c) If a drawee asserts a claim for breach of warranty under subsection (a) based on an unauthorized indorsement of the draft or an alteration of the draft, the warrantor may defend by proving that the indorsement is effective under Section 3-404 or 3-405 or the drawer is precluded under Section 3-406 or 4-406 from asserting against the drawee the unauthorized indorsement or alteration.

(d) This subsection applies if (i) a dishonored draft is presented for payment to the drawer or an indorser or (ii) any other instrument is presented for payment to a party obliged to pay the instrument, and payment is received. The person obtaining payment and a prior transferor of the instrument warrant to the person making payment in good faith that the warrantor is or was, at the time the warrantor transferred the instrument, a person entitled to enforce the instrument or authorized to obtain payment on behalf of a person entitled to enforce the instrument. The person making payment may recover from any warrantor for breach of warranty an amount equal to the amount paid plus expenses and loss of interest resulting from the breach.

(e) The warranties stated in subsections (a) and (d) cannot be disclaimed with respect to checks. Unless notice of a claim for breach of warranty is given to the warrantor within 30 days after the claimant has reason to know of the breach and the identity of the warrantor, the warrantor is discharged to the extent of any loss caused by the delay in giving notice of the claim.

(f) A cause of action for breach of warranty under this section accrues when the claimant has reason to know of the breach.

**§3-418. Payment or Acceptance by Mistake.**

(a) Except as provided in subsection (c), if the drawee of a draft pays or accepts the draft and the drawee acted on the mistaken belief that (i) payment of the draft had not been stopped under Section 4-403, (ii) the signature of the purported drawer of the draft was authorized, or (iii) the balance in the drawer's account with the drawee represented available funds, the drawee may recover the amount paid from the person to whom or for whose benefit payment was made or, in the case of acceptance, may revoke the acceptance. Rights of the drawee under this subsection are not affected by failure of the drawee to exercise ordinary care in paying or accepting the draft.

(b) Except as provided in subsection (c), if an instrument has been paid or accepted by mistake and the case is not covered by subsection (a), the person paying or accepting may recover the amount paid or revoke acceptance to the extent allowed by the law governing mistake and restitution.

(c) The remedies provided by subsection (a) or (b) may not be asserted against a person who took the instrument in good faith and for value. This subsection does not limit remedies provided by Section 3-417 for breach of warranty.

**§3-419. Instruments Signed for Accommodation.**

(a) If an instrument is issued for value given for the benefit of a party to the instrument ("accommodated party") and another party to the instrument ("accommodation party") signs the instrument for the purpose of incurring liability on the instrument without being a direct beneficiary of the value given for the instrument, the instrument is signed by the accommodation party "for accommodation."

(b) An accommodation party may sign the instrument as maker, drawer, acceptor, or indorser and, subject to subsection (d), is obliged to pay the instrument in the capacity in which the accommodation party signs. The obligation of an accommodation party may be enforced notwithstanding any statute of frauds and regardless of whether the accommodation party receives consideration for the accommodation.

(c) A person signing an instrument is presumed to be an accommodation party and there is notice that the instrument is signed for accommodation if the signature is an anomalous indorsement or is accompanied by words indicating that the signer is acting as surety or guarantor with respect to the obligation of another party to the instrument. Except as provided in Section 3-606, the obligation of an accommodation party to pay the instrument is not affected by the fact that the person enforcing the obligation had notice when the instrument was taken by that person that the accommodation party signed the instrument for accommodation.

(d) If the signature of a party to an instrument is accompanied by words indicating unambiguously that the party is guaranteeing collection rather than payment of the obligation of another party to the instrument, the signer is obliged to pay the amount due on the instrument to a person entitled to enforce the instrument only if (i) execution of judgment against the other party has been returned unsatisfied, (ii) the other party is insolvent or in an insolvency proceeding, (iii) the other party cannot be served with process, or (iv) it is otherwise apparent that payment cannot be obtained from the party whose obligation is guaranteed.

(e) An accommodation party that pays the instrument is entitled to reimbursement from the accommodated party and is entitled to enforce the instrument against the accommodated party. An accommodated party that pays the instrument has no right of recourse against, and is not entitled to contribution from, an accommodation party.

**§3-420. Conversion of Instrument.**

(a) The law applicable to conversion of personal property applies to instruments. An instrument is also converted if the instrument lacks an indorsement necessary for negotiation and it is purchased or taken for collection or the drawee takes the instrument and makes payment to a person not entitled to receive payment. An action for conversion of an instrument may not be brought by (i) the maker, drawer, or acceptor of the instrument or (ii) a payee or indorsee who did not receive delivery of the instrument either directly or through delivery to an agent or a co-payee.

(b) In an action under subsection (a), the measure of liability is presumed to be the amount payable on the instrument, but recovery may not exceed the amount of the plaintiff's interest in the instrument.

(c) A representative, other than a depositary bank, that has in good faith dealt with an instrument or its proceeds on behalf of one who was not the person entitled to enforce the instrument is not liable in conversion to that person beyond the amount of any proceeds that it has not paid out.

## Part 5—Dishonor

**§3-501. Presentment.**

(a) "Presentment" means a demand (i) to pay an instrument made to the maker, drawee, or acceptor or, in the case of a note or accepted draft payable at a bank, to the bank, or (ii) to accept a draft made to the drawee, by a person entitled to enforce the instrument.

(b) Subject to Article 4, agreement of the parties, clearing house rules and the like,

(1) presentment may be made at the place of payment of the instrument and must be made at the place of payment if the instrument is payable at a bank in the United States; may be made by any commercially reasonable means, including an oral, written, or electronic communication; is effective when the demand for payment or acceptance is

received by the person to whom presentment is made; is effective if made to any one of two or more makers, acceptors, drawees or other payors; and (2) without dishonoring the instrument, the party to whom presentment is made may (i) treat presentment as occurring on the next business day after the day of presentment if the party to whom presentment is made has established a cut-off hour not earlier than 2 P.M. for the receipt and processing of instruments presented for payment or acceptance and presentment is made after the cut-off hour, (ii) require exhibition of the instrument, (iii) require reasonable identification of the person making presentment and evidence of authority to make it if made on behalf of another person, (iv) require a signed receipt on the instrument for any payment made or surrender of the instrument if full payment is made, (v) return the instrument for lack of a necessary indorsement, or (vi) refuse payment or acceptance for failure of the presentment to comply with the terms of the instrument, an agreement of the parties, or other law or applicable rule.

**§3-502. Dishonor.**

(a) Dishonor of a note is governed by the following rules:

(1) If the note is payable on demand, the note is dishonored if presentment is duly made and the note is not paid on the day of presentment.

(2) If the note is not payable on demand and is payable at or through a bank or the terms of the note require presentment, the note is dishonored if presentment is duly made and the note is not paid on the day it becomes payable or the day of presentment, whichever is later.

(3) If the note is not payable on demand and subparagraph (2) does not apply, the note is dishonored if it is not paid on the day it becomes payable.

(b) Dishonor of an unaccepted draft other than a documentary draft is governed by the following rules:

(1) If a check is presented for payment otherwise than for immediate payment over the counter, the check is dishonored if the payor bank makes timely return of the check or sends timely notice of dishonor or nonpayment under Section 4-301 or 4-302, or becomes accountable for the amount of the check under Section 4-302.

(2) If the draft is payable on demand and subparagraph (1) does not apply, the draft is dishonored if presentment for payment is duly made and the draft is not paid on the day of presentment.

(3) If the draft is payable on a date stated in the draft, the draft is dishonored if (i) presentment for payment is duly made and payment is not made on the day the draft becomes payable or the day of presentment, whichever is later, or (ii) presentment for acceptance is duly made before the day the draft becomes payable and the draft is not accepted on the day of presentment.

(4) If the draft is payable on elapse of a period of time after sight or acceptance, the draft is dishonored if presentment for acceptance is duly made and the draft is not accepted on the day of presentment.

(c) Dishonor of an unaccepted documentary draft occurs according to the rules stated in subparagraphs (2), (3), and (4) of subsection (b) except that payment or acceptance may be delayed without dishonor until no later than the close of the third business day of the drawee following the day on which payment or acceptance is required by those subparagraphs.

(d) Dishonor of an accepted draft is governed by the following rules:

(1) If the draft is payable on demand, the draft is dishonored if presentment for payment is duly made and the draft is not paid on the day of presentment.

(2) If the draft is not payable on demand, the draft is dishonored if presentment for payment is duly made and payment is not made on the day it becomes payable or the day of presentment, whichever is later.

(e) In any case in which presentment is otherwise required for dishonor under this section and presentment is excused under Section 3-504, dishonor occurs without presentment if the instrument is not duly accepted or paid.

(f) If a draft is dishonored because timely acceptance of the draft was not made and the person entitled to demand acceptance consents to a late acceptance, from the time of acceptance the draft is treated as never having been dishonored.

**§3-503. Notice of Dishonor.**

(a) The obligation of an indorser stated in Section 3-415(a) and the obligation of a drawer stated in Section 3-414(c) may not be enforced unless (i) the indorser or drawer is given notice of dishonor of the instrument complying with this section or (ii) notice of dishonor is excused under Section 3-504(c).

(b) Notice of dishonor may be given by any person; may be given by any commercially reasonable means including an oral, written, or electronic communication; is sufficient if it reasonably identifies the instrument and indicates that the instrument has been dishonored or has not been paid or accepted. Return of an instrument given to a bank for collection is a sufficient notice of dishonor.

(c) Subject to Section 3-504(d), with respect to an instrument taken for collection by a collecting bank, notice of dishonor must be given (i) by the bank before midnight of the next banking day following the banking day on which the bank receives notice of dishonor of the instrument, and (ii) by any other person within 30 days following the day on which the person receives notice of dishonor. With respect to any other instrument, notice of dishonor must be given within 30 days following the day on which dishonor occurs.

**§3-504. Excused Presentment and Notice of Dishonor.**

(a) Presentment for payment or acceptance of an instrument is excused if (i) the person entitled to present the instrument cannot with reasonable diligence make presentment, (ii) the maker or acceptor has repudiated an obligation to pay the instrument or is dead or in insolvency proceedings, (iii) by the terms of the instrument presentment is not necessary to enforce the obligation of indorsers or the drawer, or (iv) the drawer or indorser whose obligation is being enforced waived presentment or otherwise had no reason to expect or right to require that the instrument be paid or accepted.

(b) Presentment for payment or acceptance of a draft is also excused if the drawer instructed the drawee not to pay or accept the draft or the drawee was not obligated to the drawer to pay the draft.

(c) Notice of dishonor is excused if (i) by the terms of the instrument notice of dishonor is not necessary to enforce the obligation of a party to pay the instrument, or (ii) the party whose obligation is being enforced waived notice of dishonor. A waiver of presentment is also a waiver of notice of dishonor.

(d) Delay in giving notice of dishonor is excused if the delay was caused by circumstances beyond the control of the person giving the notice and the person giving the notice exercised reasonable diligence after the cause of the delay ceased to operate.

**§3-505. Evidence of Dishonor.**

(a) The following are admissible as evidence and create a presumption of dishonor and of any notice of dishonor stated:

(1) a document regular in form as provided in subsection (b) which purports to be a protest;

(2) a purported stamp or writing of the drawee, payor bank, or presenting bank on or accompanying the instrument stating that acceptance or payment has been refused unless reasons for the refusal are stated and the reasons are not consistent with dishonor;

(3) a book or record of the drawee, payor bank, or collecting bank, kept in the usual course of business which shows dishonor, even if there is no evidence of who made the entry.

(b) A protest is a certificate of dishonor made by a United States consul or vice consul, or a notary public or other person authorized to administer oaths by the law of the place where dishonor occurs. It may be made upon information satisfactory to that person. The protest must identify the instrument and certify either that presentment has been made or, if not made, the reason why it was not made, and that the instrument has been dishonored by nonacceptance or nonpayment. The protest may also certify that notice of dishonor has been given to some or all parties.

## Part 6—Discharge and Payment

**§3-601. Discharge and Effect of Discharge.**

(a) The obligation of a party to pay the instrument is discharged as stated in this Article or by an act or agreement with the party which would discharge an obligation to pay money under a simple contract.

(b) Discharge of the obligation of a party is not effective against a person acquiring rights of a holder in due course of the instrument without notice of the discharge.

**§3-602. Payment.**

(a) Subject to subsection (b), an instrument is paid to the extent payment is made (i) by or on behalf of a party obliged to pay the instrument, and (ii) to a person entitled to enforce the instrument. To the extent of the payment, the obligation of the party obliged to pay the instrument is discharged even though payment is made with knowledge of a claim to the instrument under Section 3-306 by another person.

(b) The obligation of a party to pay the instrument is not discharged under subsection (a) if:

(1) a claim to the instrument under Section 3-306 is enforceable against the party receiving payment and (i) payment is made with knowledge by the payor that payment is prohibited by injunction or similar process of a court of competent jurisdiction, or (ii) in the case of an instrument other than a cashier's check, teller's check, or certified check, the party making payment accepted, from the person having a claim to the instrument, indemnity against loss resulting from refusal to pay the person entitled to enforce the instrument, or

(2) the person making payment knows that the instrument is a stolen instrument and pays a person that it knows is in wrongful possession of the instrument.

**§3-603. Tender of Payment.**

(a) If tender of payment of an obligation of a party to an instrument is made to a person entitled to enforce the obligation, the effect of tender is governed by principles of law applicable to tender of payment of an obligation under a simple contract.

(b) If tender of payment of an obligation to pay the instrument is made to a person entitled to enforce the instrument and the tender is refused, there is discharge, to the extent of the amount of the tender, of the obligation of an indorser or accommodation party having a right of recourse against the obligor making the tender.

(c) If tender of payment of an amount due on an instrument is made by or on behalf of the obligor to the person entitled to enforce the instrument, the obligation of the obligor to pay interest after the due date on the amount tendered is discharged. If presentment is required with respect to an instrument and the obligor is able and ready to pay on the due date at every place of payment stated in the instrument, the obligor is deemed to have made tender of payment on the due date to the person entitled to enforce the instrument.

**§3-604. Discharge by Cancellation or Renunciation.**

(a) A person entitled to enforce an instrument may, with or without consideration, discharge the obligation of a party to pay the instrument (i) by an intentional voluntary act such as surrender of the instrument to the party, destruction, mutilation, or cancellation of the instrument, cancellation or striking out of the party's signature, or the addition of words to the instrument indicating discharge, or (ii) by agreeing not to sue or otherwise renouncing rights against the party by a signed writing.

(b) Cancellation or striking out of an indorsement pursuant to subsection (a) does not affect the status and rights of a party derived from the indorsement.

**§3-605. Discharge of Indorsers and Accommodation Parties.**

(a) For the purposes of this section, the term "indorser" includes a drawer having the obligation stated in Section 3-414(c).

(b) Discharge of the obligation of a party to the instrument under Section 3-605 does not discharge the obligation of an indorser or accommodation party having a right of recourse against the discharged party.

(c) If a person entitled to enforce an instrument agrees, with or without consideration, to a material modification of the obligation of a party to the instrument, including an extension of the due date, there is discharge of the obligation of an indorser or accommodation party having a right of recourse against the person whose obligation is modified to the extent the modification causes loss to the indorser or accommodation party with respect to the right of recourse. The indorser or accommodation party is deemed to have suffered loss as a result of the modification equal to the amount of the right of recourse unless the person enforcing the instrument proves that no loss was caused by the modification or that the loss caused by the modification was less than the amount of the right of recourse.

(d) If the obligation of a party to an instrument is secured by an interest in collateral and impairment of the value of the interest is caused by a person entitled to enforce the instrument, there is discharge of the obligation of an indorser or accommodation party having a right of recourse against the obligor to the extent of the impairment. The value of an interest in collateral is impaired to the extent (i) the value of the interest is reduced to an amount less than the amount of the right of recourse of the party asserting discharge, or (ii) the reduction in value of the interest causes an increase in the amount by which the amount of the right of recourse exceeds the value of the interest. The burden of proving impairment is on the party asserting discharge.

(e) If the obligation of a party to an instrument is secured by an interest in collateral not provided by an accommodation party and the value of the interest is impaired by a person entitled to enforce the instrument, the obligation of any party who is jointly and severally liable with respect to the secured obligation is discharged to the extent the impairment causes the party asserting discharge to pay more than that party would have been obliged to pay, taking into account rights of contribution, if impairment had not occurred. If the party asserting discharge is an accommodation party not entitled to discharge under subsection (d), the party is deemed to have a right to contribution based on joint and several liability rather than a right to reimbursement. The burden of proving impairment is on the party asserting discharge.

(f) Under subsection (d) or (e) causation of impairment includes (i) failure to obtain or maintain perfection or recordation of the interest in collateral, (ii) release of collateral without substitution of collateral of equal value, (iii) failure to perform a duty to preserve the value of collateral owed, under Article 9 or other law, to a debtor or surety or other person secondarily liable, or (iv) failure to comply with applicable law in disposing of collateral.

(g) An accommodation party is not discharged under subsection (c) or (d) unless the person agreeing to the modification or causing the impairment knows of the accommodation or has notice under Section 3-419(c) that the instrument was signed for accommodation. There is no discharge of any party under subsection (c), (d), or (e) if (i) the party asserting discharge consents to the event or conduct that is the basis of the discharge, or (ii) the instrument or a separate agreement of the party provides for waiver of discharge under this section either specifically or by general language indicating that parties to the instrument waive defenses based on suretyship or impairment of collateral.

# ARTICLE 4: BANK DEPOSITS AND COLLECTIONS

## Part 1—General Provisions and Definitions

**§4-101. Short Title.**

This Article shall be known and may be cited as Uniform Commercial Code—Bank Deposits and Collections.

**§4-102. Applicability.**

(1) To the extent that items within this Article are also within the scope of Articles 3 and 8, they are subject to the provisions of those Articles. In the

event of conflict the provisions of this Article govern those of Article 3 but the provisions of Article 8 govern those of this Article.
(2) The liability of a bank for action or non-action with respect to any item handled by it for purposes of presentment, payment or collection is governed by the law of the place where the bank is located. In the case of action or non-action by or at a branch or separate office of a bank, its liability is governed by the law of the place where the branch or separate office is located.

**§4-103. Variation by Agreement; Measure of Damages; Certain Action Constituting Ordinary Care.**
(1) The effect of the provisions of this Article may be varied by agreement except that no agreement can disclaim a bank's responsibility for its own lack of good faith or failure to exercise ordinary care or can limit the measure of damages for such lack or failure; but the parties may by agreement determine the standards by which such responsibility is to be measured if such standards are not manifestly unreasonable.
(2) Federal Reserve regulations and operating letters, clearing house rules, and the like, have the effect of agreements under subsection (1), whether or not specifically assented to by all parties interested in items handled.
(3) Action or non-action approved by this Article or pursuant to Federal Reserve regulations or operating letters constitutes the exercise of ordinary care and, in the absence of special instructions, action or non-action consistent with clearing house rules and the like or with a general banking usage not disapproved by this Article, prima facie constitutes the exercise of ordinary care.
(4) The specification or approval of certain procedures by this Article does not constitute disapproval of other procedures which may be reasonable under the circumstances.
(5) The measure of damages for failure to exercise ordinary care in handling an item is the amount of the item reduced by an amount which could not have been realized by the use of ordinary care, and where there is bad faith it includes other damages, if any, suffered by the party as a proximate consequence.

**§4-104. Definitions and Index of Definitions.**
(1) In this Article unless the context otherwise requires
(a) "Account" means any account with a bank and includes a checking, time, interest or savings account;
(b) "Afternoon" means the period of a day between noon and midnight;
(c) "Banking day" means that part of any day on which a bank is open to the public for carrying on substantially all of its banking functions;
(d) "Clearing house" means any association of banks or other payors regularly clearing items;
(e) "Customer" means any person having an account with a bank or for whom a bank has agreed to collect items and includes a bank carrying an account with another bank;
(f) "Documentary draft" means any negotiable or non-negotiable draft with accompanying documents, securities or other papers to be delivered against honor of the draft;
(g) "Item" means any instrument for the payment of money even though it is not negotiable but does not include money;
(h) "Midnight deadline" with respect to a bank is midnight on its next banking day following the banking day on which it receives the relevant item or notice or from which the time for taking action commences to run, whichever is later;
(i) "Properly payable" includes the availability of funds for payment at the time of decision to pay or dishonor;
(j) "Settle" means to pay in cash, by clearing house settlement, in a charge or credit or by remittance, or otherwise as instructed. A settlement may be either provisional or final;
(k) "Suspends payments" with respect to a bank means that it has been closed by order of the supervisory authorities, that a public officer has been appointed to take it over or that it ceases or refuses to make payments in the ordinary course of business.
(2) Other definitions applying to this Article and the sections in which they appear are:
"Collecting bank" Section 4-105.
"Depositary bank" Section 4-105.
"Intermediary bank" Section 4-105.
"Payor bank" Section 4-105.
"Presenting bank" Section 4-105.
"Remitting bank" Section 4-105. (3)
(3) The following definitions in other Articles apply to this Article:
"Acceptance" Section 3-410.
"Certificate of deposit" Section 3-104.
"Certification" Section 3-411.
"Check" Section 3-104.
"Draft" Section 3-104.
"Holder in due course" Section 3-302.
"Notice of dishonor" Section 3-508.
"Presentment" Section 3-504.
"Protest" Section 3-509.
"Secondary party" Section 3-102.
(4) In addition Article 1 contains general definitions and principles of construction and interpretation applicable throughout this Article.

**§4-105. "Depositary Bank"; "Intermediary Bank"; "Collecting Bank"; "Payor Bank"; "Presenting Bank"; "Remitting Bank".**
In this Article unless the context otherwise requires:
(a) "Depositary bank" means the first bank to which an item is transferred for collection even though it is also the payor bank;
(b) "Payor bank" means a bank by which an item is payable as drawn or accepted;
(c) "Intermediary bank" means any bank to which an item is transferred in course of collection except the depositary or payor bank;
(d) "Collecting bank" means any bank handling the item for collection except the payor bank;
(e) "Presenting bank" means any bank presenting an item except a payor bank;
(f) "Remitting bank" means any payor or intermediary bank remitting for an item.

**§4-106. Separate Office of a Bank.**
A branch or separate office of a bank [maintaining its own deposit ledgers] is a separate bank for the purpose of computing the time within which and determining the place at or to which action may be taken or notices or orders shall be given under this Article and under Article 3.

Note: *The brackets are to make it optional with the several states whether to require a branch to maintain its own deposit ledgers in order to be considered to be a separate bank for certain purposes under Article 4. In some states "maintaining its own deposit ledgers" is a satisfactory test. In others branch banking practices are such that this test would not be suitable.*

**§4-107. Time of Receipt of Items.**
(1) For the purpose of allowing time to process items, prove balances and make the necessary entries on its books to determine its position for the day, a bank may fix an afternoon hour of two P.M. or later as a cut-off hour for the handling of money and items and the making of entries on its books.
(2) Any item or deposit of money received on any day after a cut-off hour so fixed or after the close of the banking day may be treated as being received at the opening of the next banking day.

**§4-108. Delays.**
(1) Unless otherwise instructed, a collecting bank in a good faith effort to secure payment may, in the case of specific items and with or without the approval of any person involved, waive, modify or extend time limits imposed or permitted by this Act for a period not in excess of an additional

banking day without discharge of secondary parties and without liability to its transferor or any prior party.
(2) Delay by a collecting bank or payor bank beyond time limits prescribed or permitted by this Act or by instructions is excused if caused by interruption of communication facilities, suspension of payments by another bank, war, emergency conditions or other circumstances beyond the control of the bank provided it exercises such diligence as the circumstances require.

**§4-109. Process of Posting.**
The "process of posting" means the usual procedure followed by a payor bank in determining to pay an item and in recording the payment including one or more of the following or other steps as determined by the bank:
(a) verification of any signature;
(b) ascertaining that sufficient funds are available;
(c) affixing a "paid" or other stamp;
(d) entering a charge or entry to a customer's account;
(e) correcting or reversing an entry or erroneous action with respect to the item.

## Part 2—Collection of Items: Depositary and Collecting Banks

**§4-201. Presumption and Duration of Agency Status of Collecting Banks and Provisional Status of Credits; Applicability of Article; Item Indorsed "Pay Any Bank".**
(1) Unless a contrary intent clearly appears and prior to the time that a settlement given by a collecting bank for an item is or becomes final (subsection (3) of Section 4-211 and Sections 4-212 and 4-213) the bank is an agent or sub-agent of the owner of the item and any settlement given for the item is provisional. This provision applies regardless of the form of indorsement or lack of indorsement and even though credit given for the item is subject to immediate withdrawal as of right or is in fact withdrawn; but the continuance of ownership of an item by its owner and any rights of the owner to proceeds of the item are subject to rights of a collecting bank such as those resulting from outstanding advances on the item and valid rights of setoff. When an item is handled by banks for purposes of presentment, payment and collection, the relevant provisions of this Article apply even though action of parties clearly establishes that a particular bank has purchased the item and is the owner of it.
(2) After an item has been indorsed with the words "pay any bank" or the like, only a bank may acquire the rights of a holder
(a) until the item has been returned to the customer initiating collection; or
(b) until the item has been specially indorsed by a bank to a person who is not a bank.

**§4-202. Responsibility for Collection; When Action Seasonable.**
(1) A collecting bank must use ordinary care in
(a) presenting an item or sending it for presentment; and
(b) sending notice of dishonor or non-payment or returning an item other than a documentary draft to the bank's transferor [or directly to the depositary bank under subsection (2) of Section 4-212] (*see note to Section 4-212*) after learning that the item has not been paid or accepted as the case may be; and
(c) settling for an item when the bank receives final settlement; and
(d) making or providing for any necessary protest; and
(e) notifying its transferor of any loss or delay in transit within a reasonable time after discovery thereof.
(2) A collecting bank taking proper action before its midnight deadline following receipt of an item, notice or payment acts seasonably; taking proper action within a reasonably longer time may be seasonable but the bank has the burden of so establishing.
(3) Subject to subsection (1)(a), a bank is not liable for the insolvency, neglect, misconduct, mistake or default of another bank or person or for loss or destruction of an item in transit or in the possession of others.

**§4-203. Effect of Instructions.**
Subject to the provisions of Article 3 concerning conversion of instruments (Section 3-419) and the provisions of both Article 3 and this Article concerning restrictive indorsements only a collecting bank's transferor can give instructions which affect the bank or constitute notice to it and a collecting bank is not liable to prior parties for any action taken pursuant to such instructions or in accordance with any agreement with its transferor.

**§4-204. Methods of Sending and Presenting; Sending Direct to Payor Bank.**
(1) A collecting bank must send items by reasonably prompt method taking into consideration any relevant instructions, the nature of the item, the number of such items on hand, and the cost of collection involved and the method generally used by it or others to present such items.
(2) A collecting bank may send
(a) any item direct to the payor bank;
(b) any item to any non-bank payor if authorized by its transferor; and
(c) any item other than documentary drafts to any non-bank payor, if authorized by Federal Reserve regulation or operating letter, clearing house rule or the like.
(3) Presentment may be made by a presenting bank at a place where the payor bank has requested that presentment be made.

**§4-205. Supplying Missing Indorsement; No Notice from Prior Indorsement.**
(1) A depositary bank which has taken an item for collection may supply any indorsement of the customer which is necessary to title unless the item contains the words "payee's indorsement required" or the like. In the absence of such a requirement a statement placed on the item by the depositary bank to the effect that the item was deposited by a customer or credited to his account is effective as the customer's indorsement.
(2) An intermediary bank, or payor bank which is not a depositary bank, is neither given notice nor otherwise affected by a restrictive indorsement of any person except the bank's immediate transferor.

**§4-206. Transfer Between Banks.**
Any agreed method which identifies the transferor bank is sufficient for the item's further transfer to another bank.

**§4-207. Warranties of Customer and Collecting Bank on Transfer or Presentment of Items; Time for Claims.**
(1) Each customer or collecting bank who obtains payment or acceptance of an item and each prior customer and collecting bank warrants to the payor bank or other payor who in good faith pays or accepts the item that
(a) he has a good title to the item or is authorized to obtain payment or acceptance on behalf of one who has a good title; and
(b) he has no knowledge that the signature of the maker or drawer is unauthorized, except that this warranty is not given by any customer or collecting bank that is a holder in due course and acts in good faith
(i) to a maker with respect to the maker's own signature; or
(ii) to a drawer with respect to the drawer's own signature, whether or not the drawer is also the drawee; or
(iii) to an acceptor of an item if the holder in due course took the item after the acceptance or obtained the acceptance without knowledge that the drawer's signature was unauthorized; and
(c) the item has not been materially altered, except that this warranty is not given by any customer or collecting bank that is a holder in due course and acts in good faith
(i) to the maker of a note; or
(ii) to the drawer of a draft whether or not the drawer is also the drawee; or
(iii) to the acceptor of an item with respect to an alteration made prior to the acceptance if the holder in due course took the item after the acceptance, even though the acceptance provided "payable as originally drawn" or equivalent terms; or

(iv) to the acceptor of an item with respect to an alteration made after the acceptance.

(2) Each customer and collecting bank who transfers an item and receives a settlement or other consideration for it warrants to his transferee and to any subsequent collecting bank who takes the item in good faith that

(a) he has a good title to the item or is authorized to obtain payment or acceptance on behalf of one who has a good title and the transfer is otherwise rightful; and

(b) all signatures are genuine or authorized; and

(c) the item has not been materially altered; and

(d) no defense of any party is good against him; and

(e) he has no knowledge of any insolvency proceeding instituted with respect to the maker or acceptor or the drawer of an unaccepted item.

In addition each customer and collecting bank so transferring an item and receiving a settlement or other consideration engages that upon dishonor and any necessary notice of dishonor and protest he will take up the item.

(3) The warranties and the engagement to honor set forth in the two preceding subsections arise notwithstanding the absence of indorsement or words of guaranty or warranty in the transfer or presentment and a collecting bank remains liable for their breach despite remittance to its transferor. Damages for breach of such warranties or engagement to honor shall not exceed the consideration received by the customer or collecting bank responsible plus finance charges and expenses related to the item, if any.

(4) Unless a claim for breach of warranty under this section is made within a reasonable time after the person claiming learns of the breach, the person liable is discharged to the extent of any loss caused by the delay in making claim.

**§4-208. Security Interest of Collecting Bank in Items, Accompanying Documents and Proceeds.**

(1) A bank has a security interest in an item and any accompanying documents or the proceeds of either

(a) in case of an item deposited in an account to the extent to which credit given for the item has been withdrawn or applied;

(b) in case of an item for which it has given credit available for withdrawal as of right, to the extent of the credit given whether or not the credit is drawn upon and whether or not there is a right of charge-back; or

(c) if it makes an advance on or against the item.

(2) When credit which has been given for several items received at one time or pursuant to a single agreement is withdrawn or applied in part the security interest remains upon all the items, any accompanying documents or the proceeds of either. For the purpose of this section, credits first given are first withdrawn.

(3) Receipt by a collecting bank of a final settlement for an item is a realization on its security interest in the item, accompanying documents and proceeds. To the extent and so long as the bank does not receive final settlement for the item or give up possession of the item or accompanying documents for purposes other than collection, the security interest continues and is subject to the provisions of Article 9 except that

(a) no security agreement is necessary to make the security interest enforceable (subsection (1)(b) of Section 9-203); and

(b) no filing is required to perfect the security interest; and

(c) the security interest has priority over conflicting perfected security interests in the item, accompanying documents or proceeds.

**§4-209. When Bank Gives Value for Purposes of Holder in Due Course.**

For purposes of determining its status as a holder in due course, the bank has given value to the extent that it has a security interest in an item provided that the bank otherwise complies with the requirements of Section 3-302 on what constitutes a holder in due course.

**§4-210. Presentment by Notice of Item Not Payable by, Through or at a Bank; Liability of Secondary Parties.**

(1) Unless otherwise instructed, a collecting bank may present an item not payable by, through or at a bank by sending to the party to accept or pay a written notice that the bank holds the item for acceptance or payment. The notice must be sent in time to be received on or before the day when presentment is due and the bank must meet any requirement of the party to accept or pay under Section 3-505 by the close of the bank's next banking day after it knows of the requirement.

(2) Where presentment is made by notice and neither honor nor request for compliance with a requirement under Section 3-505 is received by the close of business on the day after maturity or in the case of demand items by the close of business on the third banking day after notice was sent, the presenting bank may treat the item as dishonored and charge any secondary party by sending him notice of the facts.

**§4-211. Media of Remittance; Provisional and Final Settlement in Remittance Cases.**

(1) A collecting bank may take in settlement of an item

(a) a check of the remitting bank or of another bank on any bank except the remitting bank; or

(b) a cashier's check or similar primary obligation of a remitting bank which is a member of or clears through a member of the same clearing house or group as the collecting bank; or

(c) appropriate authority to charge an account of the remitting bank or of another bank with the collecting bank; or

(d) if the item is drawn upon or payable by a person other than a bank, a cashier's check, certified check or other bank check or obligation.

(2) If before its midnight deadline the collecting bank properly dishonors a remittance check or authorization to charge on itself or presents or forwards for collection a remittance instrument of or on another bank which is of a kind approved by subsection (1) or has not been authorized by it, the collecting bank is not liable to prior parties in the event of the dishonor of such check, instrument or authorization.

(3) A settlement for an item by means of a remittance instrument or authorization to charge is or becomes a final settlement as to both the person making and the person receiving the settlement

(a) if the remittance instrument or authorization to charge is of a kind approved by subsection (1) or has not been authorized by the person receiving the settlement and in either case the person receiving the settlement acts seasonably before its midnight deadline in presenting, forwarding for collection or paying the instrument or authorization,—at the time the remittance instrument or authorization is finally paid by the payor by which it is payable;

(b) if the person receiving the settlement has authorized remittance by a non-bank check or obligation or by a cashier's check or similar primary obligation of or a check upon the payor or other remitting bank which is not of a kind approved by subsection (1)(b),—at the time of the receipt of such remittance check or obligation; or

(c) if in a case not covered by sub-paragraphs (a) or (b) the person receiving the settlement fails to seasonably present, forward for collection, pay or return a remittance instrument or authorization to it to charge before its midnight deadline,—at such midnight deadline.

**§4-212. Right of Charge-Back or Refund.**

(1) If a collecting bank has made provisional settlement with its customer for an item and itself fails by reason of dishonor, suspension of payments by a bank or otherwise to receive a settlement for the item which is or becomes final, the bank may revoke the settlement given by it, charge-back the amount of any credit given for the item to its customer's account or obtain refund from its customer whether or not it is able to return the items if by its midnight deadline or within a longer reasonable time after it learns the facts it returns the item or sends notification of the facts. These rights to revoke, charge-back and obtain refund terminate if and when a settlement for the item received by the bank is or becomes final (subsection (3) of Section 4-211 and subsections (2) and (3) of Section 4-213).

[(2) Within the time and manner prescribed by this section and Section 4-301, an intermediary or payor bank, as the case may be, may return an unpaid item directly to the depositary bank and may send for collection a draft on the depositary bank and obtain reimbursement. In such case, if the depositary bank has received provisional settlement for the item, it must reimburse the bank drawing the draft and any provisional credits for the item between banks shall become and remain final.]

Note: *Direct returns is recognized as an innovation that is not yet established bank practice, and therefore, Paragraph 2 has been bracketed. Some lawyers have doubts whether it should be included in legislation or left to development by agreement.*

(3) A depositary bank which is also the payor may charge-back the amount of an item to its customer's account or obtain refund in accordance with the section governing return of an item received by a payor bank for credit on its books (Section 4-301).

(4) The right to charge-back is not affected by

(a) prior use of the credit given for the item; or

(b) failure by any bank to exercise ordinary care with respect to the item but any bank so failing remains liable.

(5) A failure to charge-back or claim refund does not affect other rights of the bank against the customer or any other party.

(6) If credit is given in dollars as the equivalent of the value of an item payable in a foreign currency the dollar amount of any charge-back or refund shall be calculated on the basis of the buying sight rate for the foreign currency prevailing on the day when the person entitled to the charge-back or refund learns that it will not receive payment in ordinary course.

**§4-213. Final Payment of Item by Payor Bank; When Provisional Debits and Credits Become Final; When Certain Credits Become Available for Withdrawal.**

(1) An item is finally paid by a payor bank when the bank has done any of the following, whichever happens first:

(a) paid the item in cash; or

(b) settled for the item without reserving a right to revoke the settlement and without having such right under statute, clearing house rule or agreement; or

(c) completed the process of posting the item to the indicated account of the drawer, maker or other person to be charged therewith; or

(d) made a provisional settlement for the item and failed to revoke the settlement in the time and manner permitted by statute, clearing house rule or agreement.

Upon a final payment under subparagraphs (b), (c), or (d) the payor bank shall be accountable for the amount of the item.

(2) If provisional settlement for an item between the presenting and payor banks is made through a clearing house or by debits or credits in an account between them, then to the extent that provisional debits or credits for the item are entered in accounts between the presenting and payor banks or between the presenting and successive prior collecting banks seriatim, they become final upon final payment of the item by the payor bank.

(3) If a collecting bank receives a settlement for an item which is or becomes final (subsection (3) of Section 4-211, subsection (2) of Section 4-213) the bank is accountable to its customer for the amount of the item and any provisional credit given for the item in an account with its customer becomes final.

(4) Subject to any right of the bank to apply the credit to an obligation of the customer, credit given by a bank for an item in an account with its customer becomes available for withdrawal as of right

(a) in any case where the bank has received a provisional settlement for the item,—when such settlement becomes final and the bank has had a reasonable time to learn that the settlement is final;

(b) in any case where the bank is both a depositary bank and a payor bank and the item is finally paid,—at the opening of the bank's second banking day following receipt of the item.

(5) A deposit of money in a bank is final when made but, subject to any right of the bank to apply the deposit to an obligation of the customer, the deposit becomes available for withdrawal as of right at the opening of the bank's next banking day following receipt of the deposit.

**§4-214. Insolvency and Preference.**

(1) Any item in or coming into the possession of a payor or collecting bank which suspends payment and which item is not finally paid shall be returned by the receiver, trustee or agent in charge of the closed bank to the presenting bank or the closed bank's customer.

(2) If a payor bank finally pays an item and suspends payments without making a settlement for the item with its customer or the presenting bank which settlement is or becomes final, the owner of the item has a preferred claim against the payor bank.

(3) If a payor bank gives or a collecting bank gives or receives a provisional settlement for an item and thereafter suspends payments, the suspension does not prevent or interfere with the settlement becoming final if such finality occurs automatically upon the lapse of certain time or the happening of certain events (subsection (3) of Section 4-211, subsections (1)(d), (2) and (3) of Section 4-213).

(4) If a collecting bank receives from subsequent parties settlement for an item which settlement is or becomes final and suspends payments without making a settlement for the item with its customer which is or becomes final, the owner of the item has a preferred claim against such collecting bank.

## Part 3—Collection of Items: Payor Banks

**§4-301. Deferred Posting; Recovery of Payment by Return of Items; Time of Dishonor.**

(1) Where an authorized settlement for a demand item (other than a documentary draft) received by a payor bank otherwise than for immediate payment over the counter has been made before midnight of the banking day of receipt the payor bank may revoke the settlement and recover any payment if before it has made final payment (subsection (1) of Section 4-213) and before its midnight deadline it

(a) returns the item; or

(b) sends written notice of dishonor or nonpayment if the item is held for protest or is otherwise unavailable for return.

(2) If a demand item is received by a payor bank for credit on its books it may return such item or send notice of dishonor and may revoke any credit given or recover the amount thereof withdrawn by its customer, if it acts within the time limit and in the manner specified in the preceding subsection.

(3) Unless previous notice of dishonor has been sent an item is dishonored at the time when for purposes of dishonor it is returned or notice sent in accordance with this section.

(4) An item is returned:

(a) as to an item received through a clearing house when it is delivered to the presenting or last collecting bank or to the clearing house or is sent or delivered in accordance with its rules; or

(b) in all other cases, when it is sent or delivered to the bank's customer or transferor or pursuant to his instructions.

**§4-302. Payor Bank's Responsibility for Late Return of Item.**

In the absence of a valid defense such as breach of a presentment warranty (subsection (1) of Section 4-207), settlement effected or the like, if an item is presented on and received by a payor bank the bank is accountable for the amount of

(a) a demand item other than a documentary draft whether properly payable or not if the bank, in any case where it is not also the depositary bank, retains the item beyond midnight of the banking day of receipt without settling for it or, regardless of whether it is also the depositary bank, does not pay or return the item or send notice of dishonor until after its midnight deadline; or

(b) any other properly payable item unless within the time allowed for acceptance or payment of that item the bank either accepts or pays the item or returns it and accompanying documents.

**§4-303. When Items Subject to Notice, Stop-Order, Legal Process or Setoff; Order in Which Items May Be Charged or Certified.**
(1) Any knowledge, notice or stop-order received by, legal process served upon or setoff exercised by a payor bank, whether or not effective under other rules of law to terminate, suspend or modify the bank's right or duty to pay an item or to charge its customer's account for the item, comes too late to so terminate, suspend or modify such right or duty if the knowledge, notice, stop-order or legal process is received or served and a reasonable time for the bank to act thereon expires or the setoff is exercised after the bank has done any of the following:

(a) accepted or certified the item;

(b) paid the item in cash;

(c) settled for the item without reserving a right to revoke the settlement and without having such right under statute, clearing house rule or agreement;

(d) completed the process of posting the item to the indicated account of the drawer, maker, or other person to be charged therewith or otherwise has evidenced by examination of such indicated account and by action its decision to pay the item; or

(e) become accountable for the amount of the item under subsection (1)(d) of Section 4-213 and Section 4-302 dealing with the payor bank's responsibility for late return of items.

(2) Subject to the provisions of subsection (1) items may be accepted, paid, certified or charged to the indicated account of its customer in any order convenient to the bank.

## Part 4—Relationship Between Payor Bank and its Customer

**§4-401. When Bank May Charge Customer's Account.**
(1) As against its customer, a bank may charge against his account any item which is otherwise properly payable from that account even though the charge creates an overdraft.
(2) A bank which in good faith makes payment to a holder may charge the indicated account of its customer according to

(a) the original tenor of his altered item; or

(b) the tenor of his completed item, even though the bank knows the item has been completed unless the bank has notice that the completion was improper.

**§4-402. Bank's Liability to Customer for Wrongful Dishonor.**
A payor bank is liable to its customer for damages proximately caused by the wrongful dishonor of an item. When the dishonor occurs through mistake liability is limited to actual damages proved. If so proximately caused and proved damages may include damages for an arrest or prosecution of the customer or other consequential damages. Whether any consequential damages are proximately caused by the wrongful dishonor is a question of fact to be determined in each case.

**§4-403. Customer's Right to Stop Payment; Burden of Proof of Loss.**
(1) A customer may by order to his bank stop payment of any item payable for his account but the order must be received at such time and in such manner as to afford the bank a reasonable opportunity to act on it prior to any action by the bank with respect to the item described in Section 4-303.
(2) An oral order is binding upon the bank only for fourteen calendar days unless confirmed in writing within that period. A written order is effective for only six months unless renewed in writing.
(3) The burden of establishing the fact and amount of loss resulting from the payment of an item contrary to a binding stop payment order is on the customer.

**§4-404. Bank Not Obligated to Pay Check More Than Six Months Old.**
A bank is under no obligation to a customer having a checking account to pay a check, other than a certified check, which is presented more than six months after its date, but it may charge its customer's account for a payment made thereafter in good faith.

**§4-405. Death or Incompetence of Customer.**
(1) A payor or collecting bank's authority to accept, pay or collect an item or to account for proceeds of its collection if otherwise effective is not rendered ineffective by incompetence of a customer of either bank existing at the time the item is issued or its collection is undertaken if the bank does not know of an adjudication of incompetence. Neither death nor incompetence of a customer revokes such authority to accept, pay, collect or account until the bank knows of the fact of death or of an adjudication of incompetence and has reasonable opportunity to act on it.
(2) Even with knowledge a bank may for ten days after the date of death pay or certify checks drawn on or prior to that date unless ordered to stop payment by a person claiming an interest in the account.

**§4-406. Customer's Duty to Discover and Report Unauthorized Signature or Alteration.**
(1) When a bank sends to its customer a statement of account accompanied by items paid in good faith in support of the debit entries or holds the statement and items pursuant to a request or instructions of its customer or otherwise in a reasonable manner makes the statement and items available to the customer, the customer must exercise reasonable care and promptness to examine the statement and items to discover his unauthorized signature or any alteration on an item and must notify the bank promptly after discovery thereof.
(2) If the bank establishes that the customer failed with respect to an item to comply with the duties imposed on the customer by subsection (1) the customer is precluded from asserting against the bank

(a) his unauthorized signature or any alteration on the item if the bank also establishes that it suffered a loss by reason of such failure; and

(b) an unauthorized signature or alteration by the same wrongdoer on any other item paid in good faith by the bank after the first item and statement was available to the customer for a reasonable period not exceeding fourteen calendar days and before the bank receives notification from the customer of any such unauthorized signature or alteration.

(3) The preclusion under subsection (2) does not apply if the customer establishes lack of ordinary care on the part of the bank in paying the item(s).
(4) Without regard to care or lack of care of either the customer or the bank a customer who does not within one year from the time the statement and items are made available to the customer (subsection (1)) discover and report his unauthorized signature or any alteration on the face or back of the item or does not within three years from that time discover and report any unauthorized indorsement is precluded from asserting against the bank such unauthorized signature or indorsement or such alteration.
(5) If under this section a payor bank has a valid defense against a claim of a customer upon or resulting from payment of an item and waives or fails upon request to assert the defense the bank may not assert against any collecting bank or other prior party presenting or transferring the item a claim based upon the unauthorized signature or alteration giving rise to the customer's claim.

**§4-407. Payor Bank's Right to Subrogation on Improper Payment.**
If a payor bank has paid an item over the stop payment order of the drawer or maker or otherwise under circumstances giving a basis for objection by the drawer or maker, to prevent unjust enrichment and only to the extent necessary to prevent loss to the bank by reason of its payment of the item, the payor bank shall be subrogated to the rights.

(a) of any holder in due course on the item against the drawer or maker; and

(b) of the payee or any other holder of the item against the drawer or maker either on the item or under the transaction out of which the item arose; and

(c) of the drawer or maker against the payee or any other holder of the item with respect to the transaction out of which the item arose.

## Part 5—Collection of Documentary Drafts

### §4-501. Handling of Documentary Drafts; Duty to Send for Presentment and to Notify Customer of Dishonor.

A bank which takes a documentary draft for collection must present or send the draft and accompanying documents for presentment and upon learning that the draft has not been paid or accepted in due course must seasonably notify its customer of such fact even though it may have discounted or bought the draft or extended credit available for withdrawal as of right.

### §4-502. Presentment of "On Arrival" Drafts.

When a draft or the relevant instructions require presentment "on arrival", "when goods arrive" or the like, the collecting bank need not present until in its judgment a reasonable time for arrival of the goods has expired. Refusal to pay or accept because the goods have not arrived is not dishonor; the bank must notify its transferor of such refusal but need not present the draft again until it is instructed to do so or learns of the arrival of the goods.

### §4-503. Responsibility of Presenting Bank for Documents and Goods; Report of Reasons for Dishonor; Referee in Case of Need.

Unless otherwise instructed and except as provided in Article 5 a bank presenting a documentary draft

(a) must deliver the documents to the drawee on acceptance of the draft if it is payable more than three days after presentment; otherwise, only on payment; and

(b) upon dishonor, either in the case of presentment for acceptance or presentment for payment, may seek and follow instructions from any referee in case of need designated in the draft or if the presenting bank does not choose to utilize his services it must use diligence and good faith to ascertain the reason for dishonor, must notify its transferor of the dishonor and of the results of its effort to ascertain the reasons therefor and must request instructions.

But the presenting bank is under no obligation with respect to goods represented by the documents except to follow any reasonable instructions seasonably received; it has a right to reimbursement for any expense incurred in following instructions and to prepayment of or indemnity for such expenses.

### §4-504. Privilege of Presenting Bank to Deal With Goods; Security Interest for Expenses.

(1) A presenting bank which, following the dishonor of a documentary draft, has seasonably requested instructions but does not receive them within a reasonable time may store, sell, or otherwise deal with the goods in any reasonable manner.

(2) For its reasonable expenses incurred by action under subsection (1) the presenting bank has a lien upon the goods or their proceeds, which may be foreclosed in the same manner as an unpaid seller's lien.

# ARTICLE 4A: FUNDS TRANSFERS

## Part 1—Subject Matter and Definitions

### §4A-101. Short Title.

This Article may be cited as Uniform Commercial Code—Funds Transfers.

### §4A-102. Subject Matter.

Except as otherwise provided in Section 4A-108, this Article applies to funds transfers defined in Section 4A-104.

### §4A-103. Payment Order—Definitions.

(a) In this Article:

(1) "Payment order" means an instruction of a sender to a receiving bank, transmitted orally, electronically, or in writing, to pay, or to cause another bank to pay, a fixed or determinable amount of money to a beneficiary if:

(i) the instruction does not state a condition to payment to the beneficiary other than time of payment,

(ii) the receiving bank is to be reimbursed by debiting an account of, or otherwise receiving payment from, the sender, and

(iii) the instruction is transmitted by the sender directly to the receiving bank or to an agent, funds-transfer system, or communication system for transmittal to the receiving bank.

(2) "Beneficiary" means the person to be paid by the beneficiary's bank.

(3) "Beneficiary's bank" means the bank identified in a payment order in which an account of the beneficiary is to be credited pursuant to the order or which otherwise is to make payment to the beneficiary if the order does not provide for payment to an account.

(4) "Receiving bank" means the bank to which the sender's instruction is addressed.

(5) "Sender" means the person giving the instruction to the receiving bank.

(b) If an instruction complying with subsection (a)(1) is to make more than one payment to a beneficiary, the instruction is a separate payment order with respect to each payment.

(c) A payment order is issued when it is sent to the receiving bank.

### §4A-104. Funds Transfer—Definitions.

In this Article:

(a) "Funds transfer" means the series of transactions, beginning with the originator's payment order, made for the purpose of making payment to the beneficiary of the order. The term includes any payment order issued by the originator's bank or an intermediary bank intended to carry out the originator's payment order. A funds transfer is completed by acceptance by the beneficiary's bank of a payment order for the benefit of the beneficiary of the originator's payment order.

(b) "Intermediary bank" means a receiving bank other than the originator's bank or the beneficiary's bank.

(c) "Originator" means the sender of the first payment order in a funds transfer.

(d) "Originator's bank" means (i) the receiving bank to which the payment order of the originator is issued if the originator is not a bank, or (ii) the originator if the originator is a bank.

### §4A-105. Other Definitions.

(a) In this Article:

(1) "Authorized account" means a deposit account of a customer in a bank designated by the customer as a source of payment of payment orders issued by the customer to the bank. If a customer does not so designate an account, any account of the customer is an authorized account if payment of a payment order from that account is not inconsistent with a restriction on the use of that account.

(2) "Bank" means a person engaged in the business of banking and includes a savings bank, savings and loan association, credit union, and trust company. A branch or separate office of a bank is a separate bank for purposes of this Article.

(3) "Customer" means a person, including a bank, having an account with a bank or from whom a bank has agreed to receive payment orders.

(4) "Funds-transfer business day" of a receiving bank means the part of a day during which the receiving bank is open for the receipt, processing, and transmittal of payment orders and cancellations and amendments of payment orders.

(5) "Funds-transfer system" means a wire transfer network, automated clearing house, or other communication system of a clearing house or other association of banks through which a payment order by a bank may be transmitted to the bank to which the order is addressed.

(6) "Good faith" means honesty in fact and the observance of reasonable commercial standards of fair dealing.

(7) "Prove" with respect to a fact means to meet the burden of establishing the fact (Section 1-201(8)).

(b) Other definitions applying to this Article and the sections in which they appear are:

"Acceptance" Section 4A-209
"Beneficiary" Section 4A-103
"Beneficiary's bank" Section 4A-103
"Executed" Section 4A-301
"Execution date" Section 4A-301
"Funds transfer" Section 4A-104
"Funds-transfer system rule" Section 4A-501
"Intermediary bank" Section 4A-104
"Originator" Section 4A-104
"Originator's bank" Section 4A-104
"Payment by beneficiary's bank to beneficiary" Section 4A-405
"Payment by originator to beneficiary" Section 4A-406
"Payment by sender to receiving bank" Section 4A-403
"Payment date" Section 4A-401
"Payment order" Section 4A-103
"Receiving bank" Section 4A-103
"Security procedure" Section 4A-201
"Sender" Section 4A-103

(c) The following definitions in Article 4 apply to this Article:

"Clearing house" Section 4-104
"Item" Section 4-104
"Suspends payments" Section 4-104

(d) In addition Article 1 contains general definitions and principles of construction and interpretation applicable throughout this Article.

**§4A-106. Time Payment Order Is Received.**

(a) The time of receipt of a payment order or communication cancelling or amending a payment order is determined by the rules applicable to receipt of a notice stated in Section 1-201(27). A receiving bank may fix a cut-off time or times on a funds-transfer business day for the receipt and processing of payment orders and communications cancelling or amending payment orders. Different cut-off times may apply to payment orders, cancellations, or amendments, or to different categories of payment orders, cancellations, or amendments. A cut-off time may apply to senders generally or different cut-off times may apply to different senders or categories of payment orders. If a payment order or communication cancelling or amending a payment order is received after the close of a funds-transfer business day or after the appropriate cut-off time on a funds-transfer business day, the receiving bank may treat the payment order or communication as received at the opening of the next funds-transfer business day.

(b) If this Article refers to an execution date or payment date or states a day on which a receiving bank is required to take action, and the date or day does not fall on a funds-transfer business day, the next day that is a funds-transfer business day is treated as the date or day stated, unless the contrary is stated in this Article.

**§4A-107. Federal Reserve Regulations and Operating Circulars.**

Regulations of the Board of Governors of the Federal Reserve System and operating circulars of the Federal Reserve Banks supersede any inconsistent provision of this Article to the extent of the inconsistency.

**§4A-108. Exclusion of Consumer Transactions Governed by Federal Law.**

This Article does not apply to a funds transfer any part of which is governed by the Electronic Fund Transfer Act of 1978 (Title XX, Public Law 95-630, 92 Stat. 3728, 15 U.S.C. §1693 et seq.) as amended from time to time.

## Part 2—Issue and Acceptance of Payment Order

**§4A-201. Security Procedure.**

"Security procedure" means a procedure established by agreement of a customer and a receiving bank for the purpose of (i) verifying that a payment order or communication amending or cancelling a payment order is that of the customer, or (ii) detecting error in the transmission or the content of the payment order or communication. A security procedure may require the use of algorithms or other codes, identifying words or numbers, encryption, callback procedures, or similar security devices. Comparison of a signature on a payment order or communication with an authorized specimen signature of the customer is not by itself a security procedure.

**§4A-202. Authorized and Verified Payment Orders.**

(a) A payment order received by the receiving bank is the authorized order of the person identified as sender if that person authorized the order or is otherwise bound by it under the law of agency.

(b) If a bank and its customer have agreed that the authenticity of payment orders issued to the bank in the name of the customer as sender will be verified pursuant to a security procedure, a payment order received by the receiving bank is effective as the order of the customer, whether or not authorized, if (i) the security procedure is a commercially reasonable method of providing security against unauthorized payment orders, and (ii) the bank proves that it accepted the payment order in good faith and in compliance with the security procedure and any written agreement or instruction of the customer restricting acceptance of payment orders issued in the name of the customer. The bank is not required to follow an instruction that violates a written agreement with the customer or notice of which is not received at a time and in a manner affording the bank a reasonable opportunity to act on it before the payment order is accepted.

(c) Commercial reasonableness of a security procedure is a question of law to be determined by considering the wishes of the customer expressed to the bank, the circumstances of the customer known to the bank, including the size, type, and frequency of payment orders normally issued by the customer to the bank, alternative security procedures offered to the customer, and security procedures in general use by customers and receiving banks similarly situated. A security procedure is deemed to be commercially reasonable if (i) the security procedure was chosen by the customer after the bank offered, and the customer refused, a security procedure that was commercially reasonable for that customer, and (ii) the customer expressly agreed in writing to be bound by any payment order, whether or not authorized, issued in its name and accepted by the bank in compliance with the security procedure chosen by the customer.

(d) The term "sender" in this Article includes the customer in whose name a payment order is issued if the order is the authorized order of the customer under subsection (a), or it is effective as the order of the customer under subsection (b).

(e) This section applies to amendments and cancellations of payment orders to the same extent it applies to payment orders.

(f) Except as provided in this section and in Section 4A-203(a)(1), rights and obligations arising under this section or Section 4A-203 may not be varied by agreement.

**§4A-203. Unenforceability of Certain Verified Payment Orders.**

(a) If an accepted payment order is not, under Section 4A-202(a), an authorized order of a customer identified as sender, but is effective as an order of the customer pursuant to Section 4A-202(b), the following rules apply:

(1) By express written agreement, the receiving bank may limit the extent to which it is entitled to enforce or retain payment of the payment order.

(2) The receiving bank is not entitled to enforce or retain payment of the payment order if the customer proves that the order was not caused, directly or indirectly, by a person (i) entrusted at any time with duties to act for the customer with respect to payment orders or the security procedure, or (ii) who obtained access to transmitting facilities of the customer or who obtained, from a source controlled by the customer and without authority of the receiving bank, information facilitating breach of the security procedure, regardless of how the

information was obtained or whether the customer was at fault. Information includes any access device, computer software, or the like.

(b) This section applies to amendments of payment orders to the same extent it applies to payment orders.

**§4A-204. Refund of Payment and Duty of Customer to Report with Respect to Unauthorized Payment Order.**

(a) If a receiving bank accepts a payment order issued in the name of its customer as sender which is (i) not authorized and not effective as the order of the customer under Section 4A-202, or (ii) not enforceable, in whole or in part, against the customer under Section 4A-203, the bank shall refund any payment of the payment order received from the customer to the extent the bank is not entitled to enforce payment and shall pay interest on the refundable amount calculated from the date the bank received payment to the date of the refund. However, the customer is not entitled to interest from the bank on the amount to be refunded if the customer fails to exercise ordinary care to determine that the order was not authorized by the customer and to notify the bank of the relevant facts within a reasonable time not exceeding 90 days after the date the customer received notification from the bank that the order was accepted or that the customer's account was debited with respect to the order. The bank is not entitled to any recovery from the customer on account of a failure by the customer to give notification as stated in this section.

(b) Reasonable time under subsection (a) may be fixed by agreement as stated in Section 1-204(1), but the obligation of a receiving bank to refund payment as stated in subsection (a) may not otherwise be varied by agreement.

**§4A-205. Erroneous Payment Orders.**

(a) If an accepted payment order was transmitted pursuant to a security procedure for the detection of error and the payment order (i) erroneously instructed payment to a beneficiary not intended by the sender, (ii) erroneously instructed payment in an amount greater than the amount intended by the sender, or (iii) was an erroneously transmitted duplicate of a payment order previously sent by the sender, the following rules apply:

(1) If the sender proves that the sender or a person acting on behalf of the sender pursuant to Section 4A-206 complied with the security procedure and that the error would have been detected if the receiving bank had also complied, the sender is not obliged to pay the order to the extent stated in paragraphs (2) and (3).

(2) If the funds transfer is completed on the basis of an erroneous payment order described in clause (i) or (iii) of subsection (a), the sender is not obliged to pay the order and the receiving bank is entitled to recover from the beneficiary any amount paid to the beneficiary to the extent allowed by the law governing mistake and restitution.

(3) If the funds transfer is completed on the basis of a payment order described in clause (ii) of subsection (a), the sender is not obliged to pay the order to the extent the amount received by the beneficiary is greater than the amount intended by the sender. In that case, the receiving bank is entitled to recover from the beneficiary the excess amount received to the extent allowed by the law governing mistake and restitution.

(b) If (i) the sender of an erroneous payment order described in subsection (a) is not obliged to pay all or part of the order, and (ii) the sender receives notification from the receiving bank that the order was accepted by the bank or that the sender's account was debited with respect to the order, the sender has a duty to exercise ordinary care, on the basis of information available to the sender, to discover the error with respect to the order and to advise the bank of the relevant facts within a reasonable time, not exceeding 90 days, after the bank's notification was received by the sender. If the bank proves that the sender failed to perform that duty, the sender is liable to the bank for the loss the bank proves it incurred as a result of the failure, but the liability of the sender may not exceed the amount of the sender's order.

(c) This section applies to amendments to payment orders to the same extent it applies to payment orders.

**§4A-209. Acceptance of Payment Order.**

(a) Subject to subsection (d), a receiving bank other than the beneficiary's bank accepts a payment order when it executes the order.

(b) Subject to subsections (c) and (d), a beneficiary's bank accepts a payment order at the earliest of the following times:

(1) when the bank (i) pays the beneficiary as stated in Section 4A-405(a) or 4A-405(b), or (ii) notifies the beneficiary of receipt of the order or that the account of the beneficiary has been credited with respect to the order unless the notice indicates that the bank is rejecting the order or that funds with respect to the order may not be withdrawn or used until receipt of payment from the sender of the order;

(2) when the bank receives payment of the entire amount of the sender's order pursuant to Section 4A-403(a)(1) or 4A-403(a)(2); or

(3) the opening of the next funds-transfer business day of the bank following the payment date of the order if, at that time, the amount of the sender's order is fully covered by a withdrawable credit balance in an authorized account of the sender or the bank has otherwise received full payment from the sender, unless the order was rejected before that time or is rejected within (i) one hour after that time, or (ii) one hour after the opening of the next business day of the sender following the payment date if that time is later. If notice of rejection is received by the sender after the payment date and the authorized account of the sender does not bear interest, the bank is obliged to pay interest to the sender on the amount of the order for the number of days elapsing after the payment date to the day the sender receives notice or learns that the order was not accepted, counting that day as an elapsed day. If the withdrawable credit balance during that period falls below the amount of the order, the amount of interest payable is reduced accordingly.

(c) Acceptance of a payment order cannot occur before the order is received by the receiving bank. Acceptance does not occur under subsection (b)(2) or (b)(3) if the beneficiary of the payment order does not have an account with the receiving bank, the account has been closed, or the receiving bank is not permitted by law to receive credits for the beneficiary's account.

(d) A payment order issued to the originator's bank cannot be accepted until the payment date if the bank is the beneficiary's bank, or the execution date if the bank is not the beneficiary's bank. If the originator's bank executes the originator's payment order before the execution date or pays the beneficiary of the originator's payment order before the payment date and the payment order is subsequently canceled pursuant to Section 4A-211(b), the bank may recover from the beneficiary any payment received to the extent allowed by the law governing mistake and restitution.

## Part 3—Execution of Sender's Payment Order by Receiving Bank

**§4A-301. Execution and Execution Date.**

(a) A payment order is "executed" by the receiving bank when it issues a payment order intended to carry out the payment order received by the bank. A payment order received by the beneficiary's bank can be accepted but cannot be executed.

(b) "Execution date" of a payment order means the day on which the receiving bank may properly issue a payment order in execution of the sender's order. The execution date may be determined by instruction of the sender but cannot be earlier than the day the order is received and, unless otherwise determined, is the day the order is received. If the sender's instruction states a payment date, the execution date is the payment date or an earlier date on which execution is reasonably necessary to allow payment to the beneficiary on the payment date.

**§4A-302. Obligations of Receiving Bank in Execution of Payment Order.**

(a) Except as provided in subsections (b) through (d), if the receiving bank accepts a payment order pursuant to Section 4A-209(a), the bank has the following obligations in executing the order:

(1) The receiving bank is obliged to issue, on the execution date, a payment order complying with the sender's order and to follow the sender's instructions concerning (i) any intermediary bank or funds-transfer system to be used in carrying out the funds transfer, or (ii) the means by which payment orders are to be transmitted in the funds transfer. If the originator's bank issues a payment order to an intermediary bank, the originator's bank is obliged to instruct the intermediary bank according to the instruction of the originator. An intermediary bank in the funds transfer is similarly bound by an instruction given to it by the sender of the payment order it accepts.

(2) If the sender's instruction states that the funds transfer is to be carried out telephonically or by wire transfer or otherwise indicates that the funds transfer is to be carried out by the most expeditious means, the receiving bank is obliged to transmit its payment order by the most expeditious available means, and to instruct any intermediary bank accordingly. If a sender's instruction states a payment date, the receiving bank is obliged to transmit its payment order at a time and by means reasonably necessary to allow payment to the beneficiary on the payment date or as soon thereafter as is feasible.

(b) Unless otherwise instructed, a receiving bank executing a payment order may (i) use any funds-transfer system if use of that system is reasonable in the circumstances, and (ii) issue a payment order to the beneficiary's bank or to an intermediary bank through which a payment order conforming to the sender's order can expeditiously be issued to the beneficiary's bank if the receiving bank exercises ordinary care in the selection of the intermediary bank. A receiving bank is not required to follow an instruction of the sender designating a funds-transfer system to be used in carrying out the funds transfer if the receiving bank, in good faith, determines that it is not feasible to follow the instruction or that following the instruction would unduly delay completion of the funds transfer.

(c) Unless subsection (a)(2) applies or the receiving bank is otherwise instructed, the bank may execute a payment order by transmitting its payment order by first class mail or by any means reasonable in the circumstances. If the receiving bank is instructed to execute the sender's order by transmitting its payment order by a particular means, the receiving bank may issue its payment order by the means stated or by any means as expeditious as the means stated.

(d) Unless instructed by the sender, (i) the receiving bank may not obtain payment of its charges for services and expenses in connection with the execution of the sender's order by issuing a payment order in an amount equal to the amount of the sender's order less the amount of the charges, and (ii) may not instruct a subsequent receiving bank to obtain payment of its charges in the same manner.

**§4A-303. Erroneous Execution of Payment Order.**

(a) A receiving bank that (i) executes the payment order of the sender by issuing a payment order in an amount greater than the amount of the sender's order, or (ii) issues a payment order in execution of the sender's order and then issues a duplicate order, is entitled to payment of the amount of the sender's order under Section 4A-402(c) if that subsection is otherwise satisfied. The bank is entitled to recover from the beneficiary of the erroneous order the excess payment received to the extent allowed by the law governing mistake and restitution.

(b) A receiving bank that executes the payment order of the sender by issuing a payment order in an amount less than the amount of the sender's order is entitled to payment of the amount of the sender's order under Section 4A-402(c) if (i) that subsection is otherwise satisfied and (ii) the bank corrects its mistake by issuing an additional payment order for the benefit of the beneficiary of the sender's order. If the error is not corrected, the issuer of the erroneous order is entitled to receive or retain payment from the sender of the order it accepted only to the extent of the amount of the erroneous order. This subsection does not apply if the receiving bank executes the sender's payment order by issuing a payment order in an amount less than the amount of the sender's order for the purpose of obtaining payment of its charges for services and expenses pursuant to instruction of the sender.

(c) If a receiving bank executes the payment order of the sender by issuing a payment order to a beneficiary different from the beneficiary of the sender's order and the funds transfer is completed on the basis of that error, the sender of the payment order that was erroneously executed and all previous senders in the funds transfer are not obliged to pay the payment orders they issued. The issuer of the erroneous order is entitled to recover from the beneficiary of the order the payment received to the extent allowed by the law governing mistake and restitution.

**§4A-304. Duty of Sender to Report Erroneously Executed Payment Order.**

If the sender of a payment order that is erroneously executed as stated in Section 4A-303 receives notification from the receiving bank that the order was executed or that the sender's account was debited with respect to the order, the sender has a duty to exercise ordinary care to determine, on the basis of information available to the sender, that the order was erroneously executed and to notify the bank of the relevant facts within a reasonable time not exceeding 90 days after the notification from the bank was received by the sender. If the sender fails to perform that duty, the bank is not obliged to pay interest on any amount refundable to the sender under Section 4A-402(d) for the period before the bank learns of the execution error. The bank is not entitled to any recovery from the sender on account of a failure by the sender to perform the duty stated in this section.

**§4A-305. Liability for Late or Improper Execution or Failure to Execute Payment Order.**

(a) If a funds transfer is completed but execution of a payment order by the receiving bank in breach of Section 4A-302 results in delay in payment to the beneficiary, the bank is obliged to pay interest to either the originator or the beneficiary of the funds transfer for the period of delay caused by the improper execution. Except as provided in subsection (c), additional damages are not recoverable.

(b) If execution of a payment order by a receiving bank in breach of Section 4A-302 results in (i) noncompletion of the funds transfer, (ii) failure to use an intermediary bank designated by the originator, or (iii) issuance of a payment order that does not comply with the terms of the payment order of the originator, the bank is liable to the originator for its expenses in the funds transfer and for incidental expenses and interest losses, to the extent not covered by subsection (a), resulting from the improper execution. Except as provided in subsection (c), additional damages are not recoverable.

(c) In addition to the amounts payable under subsections (a) and (b), damages, including consequential damages, are recoverable to the extent provided in an express written agreement of the receiving bank.

(d) If a receiving bank fails to execute a payment order it was obliged by express agreement to execute, the receiving bank is liable to the sender for its expenses in the transaction and for incidental expenses and interest losses resulting from the failure to execute. Additional damages, including consequential damages, are recoverable to the extent provided in an express written agreement of the receiving bank, but are not otherwise recoverable.

(e) Reasonable attorney's fees are recoverable if demand for compensation under subsection (a) or (b) is made and refused before an action is brought on the claim. If a claim is made for breach of an agreement under subsection (d) and the agreement does not provide for damages, reasonable attorney's fees are recoverable if demand for compensation under subsection (d) is made and refused before an action is brought on the claim.

(f) Except as stated in this section, the liability of a receiving bank under subsections (a) and (b) may not be varied by agreement.

## Part 4—Payment

**§4A-401. Payment Date.**
"Payment date" of a payment order means the day on which the amount of the order is payable to the beneficiary by the beneficiary's bank. The payment date may be determined by instruction of the sender but cannot be earlier than the day the order is received by the beneficiary's bank and, unless otherwise determined, is the day the order is received by the beneficiary's bank.

**§4A-402. Obligation of Sender to Pay Receiving Bank.**
(a) This section is subject to Sections 4A-205 and 4A-207.
(b) With respect to a payment order issued to the beneficiary's bank, acceptance of the order by the bank obliges the sender to pay the bank the amount of the order, but payment is not due until the payment date of the order.
(c) This subsection is subject to subsection (e) and to Section 4A-303. With respect to a payment order issued to a receiving bank other than the beneficiary's bank, acceptance of the order by the receiving bank obliges the sender to pay the bank the amount of the sender's order. Payment by the sender is not due until the execution date of the sender's order. The obligation of that sender to pay its payment order is excused if the funds transfer is not completed by acceptance by the beneficiary's bank of a payment order instructing payment to the beneficiary of that sender's payment order.
(d) If the sender of a payment order pays the order and was not obliged to pay all or part of the amount paid, the bank receiving payment is obliged to refund payment to the extent the sender was not obliged to pay. Except as provided in Sections 4A-204 and 4A-304, interest is payable on the refundable amount from the date of payment.
(e) If a funds transfer is not completed as stated in subsection (c) and an intermediary bank is obliged to refund payment as stated in subsection (d) but is unable to do so because not permitted by applicable law or because the bank suspends payments, a sender in the funds transfer that executed a payment order in compliance with an instruction, as stated in Section 4A-302(a)(1), to route the funds transfer through that intermediary bank is entitled to receive or retain payment from the sender of the payment order that it accepted. The first sender in the funds transfer that issued an instruction requiring routing through that intermediary bank is subrogated to the right of the bank that paid the intermediary bank to refund as stated in subsection (d).
(f) The right of the sender of a payment order to be excused from the obligation to pay the order as stated in subsection (c) or to receive refund under subsection (d) may not be varied by agreement.

**§4A-403. Payment by Sender to Receiving Bank.**
(a) Payment of the sender's obligation under Section 4A-402 to pay the receiving bank occurs as follows:
(1) If the sender is a bank, payment occurs when the receiving bank receives final settlement of the obligation through a Federal Reserve Bank or through a funds-transfer system.
(2) If the sender is a bank and the sender (i) credited an account of the receiving bank with the sender, or (ii) caused an account of the receiving bank in another bank to be credited, payment occurs when the credit is withdrawn or, if not withdrawn, at midnight of the day on which the credit is withdrawable and the receiving bank learns of that fact.
(3) If the receiving bank debits an account of the sender with the receiving bank, payment occurs when the debit is made to the extent the debit is covered by a withdrawable credit balance in the account.
(b) If the sender and receiving bank are members of a funds-transfer system that nets obligations multilaterally among participants, the receiving bank receives final settlement when settlement is complete in accordance with the rules of the system. The obligation of the sender to pay the amount of a payment order transmitted through the funds-transfer system may be satisfied, to the extent permitted by the rules of the system, by setting off and applying against the sender's obligation the right of the sender to receive payment from the receiving bank of the amount of any other payment order transmitted to the sender by the receiving bank through the funds-transfer system. The aggregate balance of obligations owed by each sender to each receiving bank in the funds-transfer system may be satisfied, to the extent permitted by the rules of the system, by setting off and applying against that balance the aggregate balance of obligations owed to the sender by other members of the system. The aggregate balance is determined after the right of setoff stated in the second sentence of this subsection has been exercised.
(c) If two banks transmit payment orders to each other under an agreement that settlement of the obligations of each bank to the other under Section 4A-402 will be made at the end of the day or other period, the total amount owed with respect to all orders transmitted by one bank shall be set off against the total amount owed with respect to all orders transmitted by the other bank. To the extent of the setoff, each bank has made payment to the other.
(d) In a case not covered by subsection (a), the time when payment of the sender's obligation under Section 4A-402(b) or 4A-402(c) occurs is governed by applicable principles of law that determine when an obligation is satisfied.

**§4A-404. Obligation of Beneficiary's Bank to Pay and Give Notice to Beneficiary.**
(a) Subject to Sections 4A-211(e), 4A-405(d), and 4A-405(e), if a beneficiary's bank accepts a payment order, the bank is obliged to pay the amount of the order to the beneficiary of the order. Payment is due on the payment date of the order, but if acceptance occurs on the payment date after the close of the funds-transfer business day of the bank, payment is due on the next funds-transfer business day. If the bank refuses to pay after demand by the beneficiary and receipt of notice of particular circumstances that will give rise to consequential damages as a result of nonpayment, the beneficiary may recover damages resulting from the refusal to pay to the extent the bank had notice of the damages, unless the bank proves that it did not pay because of a reasonable doubt concerning the right of the beneficiary to payment.
(b) If a payment order accepted by the beneficiary's bank instructs payment to an account of the beneficiary, the bank is obliged to notify the beneficiary of receipt of the order before midnight of the next funds-transfer business day following the payment date. If the payment order does not instruct payment to an account of the beneficiary, the bank is required to notify the beneficiary only if notice is required by the order. Notice may be given by first class mail or any other means reasonable in the circumstances. If the bank fails to give the required notice, the bank is obliged to pay interest to the beneficiary on the amount of the payment order from the day notice should have been given until the day the beneficiary learned of receipt of the payment order by the bank. No other damages are recoverable. Reasonable attorney's fees are also recoverable if demand for interest is made and refused before an action is brought on the claim.
(c) The right of a beneficiary to receive payment and damages as stated in subsection (a) may not be varied by agreement or a funds-transfer system rule. The right of a beneficiary to be notified as stated in subsection (b) may be varied by agreement of the beneficiary or by a funds-transfer system rule if the beneficiary is notified of the rule before initiation of the funds transfer.

**§4A-405. Payment by Beneficiary's Bank to Beneficiary.**
(a) If the beneficiary's bank credits an account of the beneficiary of a payment order, payment of the bank's obligation under Section 4A-404(a) occurs when and to the extent (i) the beneficiary is notified of the right to withdraw the credit, (ii) the bank lawfully applies the credit to a debt of the beneficiary, or (iii) funds with respect to the order are otherwise made available to the beneficiary by the bank.

(b) If the beneficiary's bank does not credit an account of the beneficiary of a payment order, the time when payment of the bank's obligation under Section 4A-404(a) occurs is governed by principles of law that determine when an obligation is satisfied.
(c) Except as stated in subsections (d) and (e), if the beneficiary's bank pays the beneficiary of a payment order under a condition to payment or agreement of the beneficiary giving the bank the right to recover payment from the beneficiary if the bank does not receive payment of the order, the condition to payment or agreement is not enforceable.
(d) A funds-transfer system rule may provide that payments made to beneficiaries of funds transfers made through the system are provisional until receipt of payment by the beneficiary's bank of the payment order it accepted. A beneficiary's bank that makes a payment that is provisional under the rule is entitled to refund from the beneficiary if (i) the rule requires that both the beneficiary and the originator be given notice of the provisional nature of the payment before the funds transfer is initiated, (ii) the beneficiary, the beneficiary's bank and the originator's bank agreed to be bound by the rule, and (iii) the beneficiary's bank did not receive payment of the payment order that it accepted. If the beneficiary is obliged to refund payment to the beneficiary's bank, acceptance of the payment order by the beneficiary's bank is nullified and no payment by the originator of the funds transfer to the beneficiary occurs under Section 4A-406.
(e) This subsection applies to a funds transfer that includes a payment order transmitted over a funds-transfer system that (i) nets obligations multilaterally among participants, and (ii) has in effect a loss-sharing agreement among participants for the purpose of providing funds necessary to complete settlement of the obligations of one or more participants that do not meet their settlement obligations. If the beneficiary's bank in the funds transfer accepts a payment order and the system fails to complete settlement pursuant to its rules with respect to any payment order in the funds transfer, (i) the acceptance by the beneficiary's bank is nullified and no person has any right or obligation based on the acceptance, (ii) the beneficiary's bank is entitled to recover payment from the beneficiary, (iii) no payment by the originator to the beneficiary occurs under Section 4A-406, and (iv) subject to Section 4A-402(e), each sender in the funds transfer is excused from its obligation to pay its payment order under Section 4A-402 (c) because the funds transfer has not been completed.

**§4A-406. Payment by Originator to Beneficiary; Discharge of Underlying Obligation.**
(a) Subject to Sections 4A-211(e), 4A-405(d), and 4A-405(e), the originator of a funds transfer pays the beneficiary of the originator's payment order (i) at the time a payment order for the benefit of the beneficiary is accepted by the beneficiary's bank in the funds transfer and (ii) in an amount equal to the amount of the order accepted by the beneficiary's bank, but not more than the amount of the originator's order.
(b) If payment under subsection (a) is made to satisfy an obligation, the obligation is discharged to the same extent discharge would result from payment to the beneficiary of the same amount in money, unless (i) the payment under subsection (a) was made by a means prohibited by the contract of the beneficiary with respect to the obligation, (ii) the beneficiary, within a reasonable time after receiving notice of receipt of the order by the beneficiary's bank, notified the originator of the beneficiary's refusal of the payment, (iii) funds with respect to the order were not withdrawn by the beneficiary or applied to a debt of the beneficiary, and (iv) the beneficiary would suffer a loss that could reasonably have been avoided if payment had been made by a means complying with the contract. If payment by the originator does not result in discharge under this section, the originator is subrogated to the rights of the beneficiary to receive payment from the beneficiary's bank under Section 4A-404(a).
(c) For the purpose of determining whether discharge of an obligation occurs under subsection (b), if the beneficiary's bank accepts a payment order in an amount equal to the amount of the originator's payment order less charges of one or more receiving banks in the funds transfer, payment to the beneficiary is deemed to be in the amount of the originator's order unless upon demand by the beneficiary the originator does not pay the beneficiary the amount of the deducted charges.
(d) Rights of the originator or of the beneficiary of a funds transfer under this section may be varied only by agreement of the originator and the beneficiary.

## ARTICLE 7: WAREHOUSE RECEIPTS, BILLS OF LADING AND OTHER DOCUMENTS OF TITLE

### Part 1—General

**§7-101. Short Title.**
This Article shall be known and may be cited as Uniform Commercial Code—Documents of Title.

**§7-102. Definitions and Index of Definitions.**
(1) In this Article, unless the context otherwise requires:
(a) "Bailee" means the person who by a warehouse receipt, bill of lading or other document of title acknowledges possession of goods and contracts to deliver them.
(b) "Consignee" means the person named in a bill to whom or to whose order the bill promises delivery.
(c) "Consignor" means the person named in a bill as the person from whom the goods have been received for shipment.
(d) "Delivery order" means a written order to deliver goods directed to a warehouseman, carrier or other person who in the ordinary course of business issues warehouse receipts or bills of lading.
(e) "Document" means document of title as defined in the general definitions in Article 1 (Section 1-201).
(f) "Goods" means all things which are treated as movable for the purposes of a contract of storage or transportation.
(g) "Issuer" means a bailee who issues a document except that in relation to an unaccepted delivery order it means the person who orders the possessor of goods to deliver. Issuer includes any person for whom an agent or employee purports to act in issuing a document if the agent or employee has real or apparent authority to issue documents, notwithstanding that the issuer received no goods or that the goods were misdescribed or that in any other respect the agent or employee violated his instructions.
(h) "Warehouseman" is a person engaged in the business of storing goods for hire.
(2) Other definitions applying to this Article or to specified Parts thereof, and the sections in which they appear are:
"Duly negotiate". Section 7-501.
"Person entitled under the document". Section 7- 403(4).
(3) Definitions in other Articles applying to this Article and the sections in which they appear are:
"Contract for sale". Section 2-106.
"Overseas". Section 2-323.
"Receipt" of goods. Section 2-103.
(4) In addition Article 1 contains general definitions and principles of construction and interpretation applicable throughout this Article.

**§7-104. Negotiable and Non-Negotiable Warehouse Receipt, Bill of Lading or Other Document of Title.**
(1) A warehouse receipt, bill of lading or other document of title is negotiable
(a) if by its terms the goods are to be delivered to bearer or to the order of a named person; or
(b) where recognized in overseas trade, if it runs to a named person or assigns.
(2) Any other document is non-negotiable. A bill of lading in which it is stated that the goods are consigned to a named person is not made negotiable by a provision that the goods are to be delivered only against a written order signed by the same or another named person.

## Part 2—Warehouse Receipts: Special Provisions

### §7-201. Who May Issue a Warehouse Receipt; Storage Under Government Bond.

(1) A warehouse receipt may be issued by any warehouseman.
(2) Where goods including distilled spirits and agricultural commodities are stored under a statute requiring a bond against withdrawal or a license for the issuance of receipts in the nature of warehouse receipts, a receipt issued for the goods has like effect as a warehouse receipt even though issued by a person who is the owner of the goods and is not a warehouseman.

### §7-202. Form of Warehouse Receipt; Essential Terms; Optional Terms.

(1) A warehouse receipt need not be in any particular form.
(2) Unless a warehouse receipt embodies within its written or printed terms each of the following, the warehouseman is liable for damages caused by the omission to a person injured thereby:
(a) the location of the warehouse where the goods are stored;
(b) the date of issue of the receipt;
(c) the consecutive number of the receipt;
(d) a statement whether the goods received will be delivered to the bearer, to a specified person, or to a specified person or his order;
(e) the rate of storage and handling charges, except that where goods are stored under a field warehousing arrangement a statement of that fact is sufficient on a non-negotiable receipt;
(f) a description of the goods or of the packages containing them;
(g) the signature of the warehouseman, which may be made by his authorized agent;
(h) if the receipt is issued for goods of which the warehouseman is owner, either solely or jointly or in common with others, the fact of such ownership; and
(i) a statement of the amount of advances made and of liabilities incurred for which the warehouseman claims a lien or security interest (Section 7-209). If the precise amount of such advances made or of such liabilities incurred is, at the time of the issue of the receipt, unknown to the warehouseman or to his agent who issues it, a statement of the fact that advances have been made or liabilities incurred and the purpose thereof is sufficient.
(3) A warehouseman may insert in his receipt any other terms which are not contrary to the provisions of this Act and do not impair his obligation of delivery (Section 7-403) or his duty of care (Section 7-204). Any contrary provisions shall be ineffective.

### §7-204. Duty of Care; Contractual Limitation of Warehouseman's Liability.

(1) A warehouseman is liable for damages for loss of or injury to the goods caused by his failure to exercise such care in regard to them as a reasonably careful man would exercise under like circumstances but unless otherwise agreed he is not liable for damages which could not have been avoided by the exercise of such care.
(2) Damages may be limited by a term in the warehouse receipt or storage agreement limiting the amount of liability in case of loss or damage, and setting forth a specific liability per article or item, or value per unit of weight, beyond which the warehouseman shall not be liable; provided, however, that such liability may on written request of the bailor at the time of signing such storage agreement or within a reasonable time after receipt of the warehouse receipt be increased on part or all of the goods thereunder, in which event increased rates may be charged based on such increased valuation, but that no such increase shall be permitted contrary to a lawful limitation of liability contained in the warehouseman's tariff, if any. No such limitation is effective with respect to the warehouseman's liability for conversion to his own use.
(3) Reasonable provisions as to the time and manner of presenting claims and instituting actions based on the bailment may be included in the warehouse receipt or tariff.
(4) This section does not impair or repeal …

Note: *Insert in subsection (4) a reference to any statute which imposes a higher responsibility upon the warehouseman or invalidates contractual limitations which would be permissible under this Article.*

### §7-206. Termination of Storage at Warehouseman's Option.

(1) A warehouseman may on notifying the person on whose account the goods are held and any other person known to claim an interest in the goods require payment of any charges and removal of the goods from the warehouse at the termination of the period of storage fixed by the document, or, if no period is fixed, within a stated period not less than thirty days after the notification. If the goods are not removed before the date specified in the notification, the warehouseman may sell them in accordance with the provisions of the section on enforcement of a warehouseman's lien (Section 7-210).
(2) If a warehouseman in good faith believes that the goods are about to deteriorate or decline in value to less than the amount of his lien within the time prescribed in subsection (1) for notification, advertisement and sale, the warehouseman may specify in the notification any reasonable shorter time for removal of the goods and in case the goods are not removed, may sell them at public sale held not less than one week after a single advertisement or posting.
(3) If as a result of a quality or condition of the goods of which the warehouseman had no notice at the time of deposit the goods are a hazard to other property or to the warehouse or to persons, the warehouseman may sell the goods at public or private sale without advertisement on reasonable notification to all persons known to claim an interest in the goods. If the warehouseman after a reasonable effort is unable to sell the goods he may dispose of them in any lawful manner and shall incur no liability by reason of such disposition.
(4) The warehouseman must deliver the goods to any person entitled to them under this Article upon due demand made at any time prior to sale or other disposition under this section.
(5) The warehouseman may satisfy his lien from the proceeds of any sale or disposition under this section but must hold the balance for delivery on the demand of any person to whom he would have been bound to deliver the goods.

### §7-207. Goods Must Be Kept Separate; Fungible Goods.

(1) Unless the warehouse receipt otherwise provides, a warehouseman must keep separate the goods covered by each receipt so as to permit at all times identification and delivery of those goods except that different lots of fungible goods may be commingled.
(2) Fungible goods so commingled are owned in common by the persons entitled thereto and the warehouseman is severally liable to each owner for that owner's share. Where because of overissue a mass of fungible goods is insufficient to meet all the receipts which the warehouseman has issued against it, the persons entitled include all holders to whom overissued receipts have been duly negotiated.

### §7-209. Lien of Warehouseman.

(1) A warehouseman has a lien against the bailor on the goods covered by a warehouse receipt or on the proceeds thereof in his possession for charges for storage or transportation (including demurrage and terminal charges), insurance, labor, or charges present or future in relation to the goods, and for expenses necessary for preservation of the goods or reasonably incurred in their sale pursuant to law. If the person on whose account the goods are held is liable for like charges or expenses in relation to other goods whenever deposited and it is stated in the receipt that a lien is claimed for charges and expenses in relation to other goods, the warehouseman also has a lien against him for such charges and expenses whether or not the other goods have been delivered by the warehouseman. But against a person to whom a negotiable warehouse receipt is duly negotiated a warehouseman's lien is limited to charges in an amount or at a rate specified on

the receipt or if no charges are so specified then to a reasonable charge for storage of the goods covered by the receipt subsequent to the date of the receipt.

(2) The warehouseman may also reserve a security interest against the bailor for a maximum amount specified on the receipt for charges other than those specified in subsection (1), such as for money advanced and interest. Such a security interest is governed by the Article on Secured Transactions (Article 9).

(3) (a) A warehouseman's lien for charges and expenses under subsection (1) or a security interest under subsection (2) is also effective against any person who so entrusted the bailor with possession of the goods that a pledge of them by him to a good faith purchaser for value would have been valid but is not effective against a person as to whom the document confers no right in the goods covered by it under Section 7-503.

(b) A warehouseman's lien on household goods for charges and expenses in relation to the goods under subsection (1) is also effective against all persons if the depositor was a legal possessor of the goods at the time of deposit. "Household goods" means furniture, furnishings and personal effects used by the depositor in a dwelling.

(4) A warehouseman loses his lien on any goods which he voluntarily delivers or which he unjustifiably refuses to deliver.

## Part 3—Bills of Lading: Special Provisions

### §7-301. Liability for Non-Receipt or Misdescription; "Said to Contain"; "Shipper's Load and Count"; Improper Handling.

(1) A consignee of a non-negotiable bill who has given value in good faith or a holder to whom a negotiable bill has been duly negotiated relying in either case upon the description therein of the goods, or upon the date therein shown, may recover from the issuer damages caused by the misdating of the bill or the non-receipt or misdescription of the goods, except to the extent that the document indicates that the issuer does not know whether any part of all of the goods in fact were received or conform to the description, as where the description is in terms of marks or labels or kind, quantity, or condition or the receipt or description is qualified by "contents or condition of contents of packages unknown", "said to contain", "shipper's weight, load and count" or the like, if such indication be true.

(2) When goods are loaded by an issuer who is a common carrier, the issuer must count the packages of goods if package freight and ascertain the kind and quantity if bulk freight. In such cases "shipper's weight, load and count" or other words indicating that the description was made by the shipper are ineffective except as to freight concealed by packages.

(3) When bulk freight is loaded by a shipper who makes available to the issuer adequate facilities for weighing such freight, an issuer who is a common carrier must ascertain the kind and quantity within a reasonable time after receiving the written request of the shipper to do so. In such cases "shipper's weight" or other words of like purport are ineffective.

(4) The issuer may by inserting in the bill the words "shipper's weight, load and count" or other words of like purport indicate that the goods were loaded by the shipper; and if such statement be true the issuer shall not be liable for damages caused by the improper loading. But their omission does not imply liability for such damages.

(5) The shipper shall be deemed to have guaranteed to the issuer the accuracy at the time of shipment of the description, marks, labels, number, kind, quantity, condition and weight, as furnished by him; and the shipper shall indemnify the issuer against damage caused by inaccuracies in such particulars. The right of the issuer to such indemnity shall in no way limit his responsibility and liability under the contract of carriage to any person other than the shipper.

### §7-302. Through Bills of Lading and Similar Documents.

(1) The issuer of a through bill of lading or other document embodying an undertaking to be performed in part by persons acting as its agents or by connecting carriers is liable to anyone entitled to recover on the document for any breach by such other persons or by a connecting carrier of its obligation under the document but to the extent that the bill covers an undertaking to be performed overseas or in territory not contiguous to the continental United States or an undertaking including matters other than transportation this liability may be varied by agreement of the parties.

(2) Where goods covered by a through bill of lading or other document embodying an undertaking to be performed in part by persons other than the issuer are received by any such person, he is subject with respect to his own performance while the goods are in his possession to the obligation of the issuer. His obligation is discharged by delivery of the goods to another such person pursuant to the document, and does not include liability for breach by any other such persons or by the issuer.

(3) The issuer of such through bill of lading or other document shall be entitled to recover from the connecting carrier or such other person in possession of the goods when the breach of the obligation under the document occurred, the amount it may be required to pay to anyone entitled to recover on the document therefor, as may be evidenced by any receipt, judgment, or transcript thereof, and the amount of any expense reasonably incurred by it in defending any action brought by anyone entitled to recover on the document therefor.

### §7-307. Lien of Carrier.

(1) A carrier has a lien on the goods covered by a bill of lading for charges subsequent to the date of its receipt of the goods for storage or transportation (including demurrage and terminal charges) and for expenses necessary for preservation of the goods incident to their transportation or reasonably incurred in their sale pursuant to law. But against a purchaser for value of a negotiable bill of lading a carrier's lien is limited to charges stated in the bill or the applicable tariffs, or if no charges are stated then to a reasonable charge.

(2) A lien for charges and expenses under subsection (1) on goods which the carrier was required by law to receive for transportation is effective against the consignor or any person entitled to the goods unless the carrier had notice that the consignor lacked authority to subject the goods to such charges and expenses. Any other lien under subsection (1) is effective against the consignor and any person who permitted the bailor to have control or possession of the goods unless the carrier had notice that the bailor lacked such authority.

(3) A carrier loses his lien on any goods which he voluntarily delivers or which he unjustifiably refuses to deliver.

### §7-308. Enforcement of Carrier's Lien.

(1) A carrier's lien may be enforced by public or private sale of the goods, in bloc or in parcels, at any time or place and on any terms which are commercially reasonable, after notifying all persons known to claim an interest in the goods. Such notification must include a statement of the amount due, the nature of the proposed sale and the time and place of any public sale. The fact that a better price could have been obtained by a sale at a different time or in a different method from that selected by the carrier is not of itself sufficient to establish that the sale was not made in a commercially reasonable manner. If the carrier either sells the goods in the usual manner in any recognized market therefor or if he sells at the price current in such market at the time of his sale or if he has otherwise sold in conformity with commercially reasonable practices among dealers in the type of goods sold he has sold in a commercially reasonable manner. A sale of more goods than apparently necessary to be offered to ensure satisfaction of the obligation is not commercially reasonable except in cases covered by the preceding sentence.

(2) Before any sale pursuant to this section any person claiming a right in the goods may pay the amount necessary to satisfy the lien and the reasonable expenses incurred under this section. In that event the goods must not be sold, but must be retained by the carrier subject to the terms of the bill and this Article.

(3) The carrier may buy at any public sale pursuant to this section.

(4) A purchaser in good faith of goods sold to enforce a carrier's lien takes the goods free of any rights of persons against whom the lien was valid, despite noncompliance by the carrier with the requirements of this section.
(5) The carrier may satisfy his lien from the proceeds of any sale pursuant to this section but must hold the balance, if any, for delivery on demand to any person to whom he would have been bound to deliver the goods.
(6) The rights provided by this section shall be in addition to all other rights allowed by law to a creditor against his debtor.
(7) A carrier's lien may be enforced in accordance with either subsection (1) or the procedure set forth in subsection (2) of Section 7-210.
(8) The carrier is liable for damages caused by failure to comply with the requirements for sale under this section and in case of willful violation is liable for conversion.

**§7-309. Duty of Care; Contractual Limitation of Carrier's Liability.**
(1) A carrier who issues a bill of lading whether negotiable or non-negotiable must exercise the degree of care in relation to the goods which a reasonably careful man would exercise under like circumstances. This subsection does not repeal or change any law or rule of law which imposes liability upon a common carrier for damages not caused by its negligence.
(2) Damages may be limited by a provision that the carrier's liability shall not exceed a value stated in the document if the carrier's rates are dependent upon value and the consignor by the carrier's tariff is afforded an opportunity to declare a higher value or a value as lawfully provided in the tariff, or where no tariff is filed he is otherwise advised of such opportunity; but no such limitation is effective with respect to the carrier's liability for conversion to its own use.
(3) Reasonable provisions as to the time and manner of presenting claims and instituting actions based on the shipment may be included in a bill of lading or tariff.

## Part 4—Warehouse Receipts and Bills of Lading: General Obligations

**§7-401. Irregularities in Issue of Receipt or Bill or Conduct of Issuer.**
The obligations imposed by this Article on an issuer apply to a document of title regardless of the fact that
(a) the document may not comply with the requirements of this Article or of any other law or regulation regarding its issue, form or content; or
(b) the issuer may have violated laws regulating the conduct of his business; or
(c) the goods covered by the document were owned by the bailee at the time the document was issued; or
(d) the person issuing the document does not come within the definition of warehouseman if it purports to be a warehouse receipt.

**§7-402. Duplicate Receipt or Bill; Overissue.**
Neither a duplicate nor any other document of title purporting to cover goods already represented by an outstanding document of the same issuer confers any right in the goods, except as provided in the case of bills in a set, overissue of documents for fungible goods and substitutes for lost, stolen or destroyed documents. But the issuer is liable for damages caused by his overissue or failure to identify a duplicate document as such by conspicuous notation on its face.

**§7-403. Obligation of Warehouseman or Carrier to Deliver; Excuse.**
(1) The bailee must deliver the goods to a person entitled under the document who complies with subsections (2) and (3), unless and to the extent that the bailee establishes any of the following:
(a) delivery of the goods to a person whose receipt was rightful as against the claimant;
(b) damage to or delay, loss or destruction of the goods for which the bailee is not liable [, but the burden of establishing negligence in such cases is on the person entitled under the document];
Note: *The brackets in (1)(b) indicate that State enactments may differ on this point without serious damage to the principle of uniformity.*
(c) previous sale or other disposition of the goods in lawful enforcement of a lien or on warehouseman's lawful termination of storage;
(d) the exercise by a seller of his right to stop delivery pursuant to the provisions of the Article on Sales (Section 2-705);
(e) a diversion, reconsignment or other disposition pursuant to the provisions of this Article (Section 7-303) or tariff regulating such right;
(f) release, satisfaction or any other fact affording a personal defense against the claimant;
(g) any other lawful excuse.
(2) A person claiming goods covered by a document of title must satisfy the bailee's lien where the bailee so requests or where the bailee is prohibited by law from delivering the goods until the charges are paid.
(3) Unless the person claiming is one against whom the document confers no right under Sec. 7-503(1), he must surrender for cancellation or notation of partial deliveries any outstanding negotiable document covering the goods, and the bailee must cancel the document or conspicuously note the partial delivery thereon or be liable to any person to whom the document is duly negotiated.
(4) "Person entitled under the document" means holder in the case of a negotiable document, or the person to whom delivery is to be made by the terms of or pursuant to written instructions under a non-negotiable document.

**§7-404. No Liability for Good Faith Delivery Pursuant to Receipt or Bill.**
A bailee who in good faith including observance of reasonable commercial standards has received goods and delivered or otherwise disposed of them according to the terms of the document of title or pursuant to this Article is not liable therefor. This rule applies even though the person from whom he received the goods had no authority to procure the document or to dispose of the goods and even though the person to whom he delivered the goods had no authority to receive them.

## Part 5—Warehouse Receipts and Bills of Lading: Negotiation and Transfer

**§7-501. Form of Negotiation and Requirements of "Due Negotiation".**
(1) A negotiable document of title running to the order of a named person is negotiated by his indorsement and delivery. After his indorsement in blank or to bearer any person can negotiate it by delivery alone.
(2) (a) A negotiable document of title is also negotiated by delivery alone when by its original terms it runs to bearer.
(b) When a document running to the order of a named person is delivered to him the effect is the same as if the document had been negotiated.
(3) Negotiation of a negotiable document of title after it has been indorsed to a specified person requires indorsement by the special indorsee as well as delivery.
(4) A negotiable document of title is "duly negotiated" when it is negotiated in the manner stated in this section to a holder who purchases it in good faith without notice of any defense against or claim to it on the part of any person and for value, unless it is established that the negotiation is not in the regular course of business or financing or involves receiving the document in settlement or payment of a money obligation.
(5) Indorsement of a non-negotiable document neither makes it negotiable nor adds to the transferee's rights.
(6) The naming in a negotiable bill of a person to be notified of the arrival of the goods does not limit the negotiability of the bill nor constitute notice to a purchaser thereof of any interest of such person in the goods.

**§7-502. Rights Acquired by Due Negotiation.**
(1) Subject to the following section and to the provisions of Section 7-205 on fungible goods, a holder to whom a negotiable document of title has been duly negotiated acquires thereby:
(a) title to the document;
(b) title to the goods;

(c) all rights accruing under the law of agency or estoppel, including rights to goods delivered to the bailee after the document was issued; and

(d) the direct obligation of the issuer to hold or deliver the goods according to the terms of the document free of any defense or claim by him except those arising under the terms of the document or under this Article. In the case of a delivery order the bailee's obligation accrues only upon acceptance and the obligation acquired by the holder is that the issuer and any indorser will procure the acceptance of the bailee.

(2) Subject to the following section, title and rights so acquired are not defeated by any stoppage of the goods represented by the document or by surrender of such goods by the bailee, and are not impaired even though the negotiation or any prior negotiation constituted a breach of duty or even though any person has been deprived of possession of the document by misrepresentation, fraud, accident, mistake, duress, loss, theft or conversion, or even though a previous sale or other transfer of the goods or document has been made to a third person.

**§7-503. Document of Title to Goods Defeated in Certain Cases.**

(1) A document of title confers no right in goods against a person who before issuance of the document had a legal interest or a perfected security interest in them and who neither

(a) delivered or entrusted them or any document of title covering them to the bailor or his nominee with actual or apparent authority to ship, store or sell or with power to obtain delivery under this Article (Section 7-403) or with power of disposition under this Act (Sections 2-403 and 9-307) or other statute or rule of law; nor

(b) acquiesced in the procurement by the bailor or his nominee of any document of title.

(2) Title to goods based upon an unaccepted delivery order is subject to the rights of anyone to whom a negotiable warehouse receipt or bill of lading covering the goods has been duly negotiated. Such a title may be defeated under the next section to the same extent as the rights of the issuer or a transferee from the issuer.

(3) Title to goods based upon a bill of lading issued to a freight forwarder is subject to the rights of anyone to whom a bill issued by the freight forwarder is duly negotiated; but delivery by the carrier in accordance with Part 4 of this Article pursuant to its own bill of lading discharges the carrier's obligation to deliver.

**§7-504. Rights Acquired in the Absence of Due Negotiation; Effect of Diversion; Seller's Stoppage of Delivery.**

(1) A transferee of a document, whether negotiable or non-negotiable, to whom the document has been delivered but not duly negotiated, acquires the title and rights which his transferor had or had actual authority to convey.

(2) In the case of a non-negotiable document, until but not after the bailee receives notification of the transfer, the rights of the transferee may be defeated

(a) by those creditors of the transferor who could treat the sale as void under Section 2-402; or

(b) by a buyer from the transferor in ordinary course of business if the bailee has delivered the goods to the buyer or received notification of his rights; or

(c) as against the bailee by good faith dealings of the bailee with the transferor.

(3) A diversion or other change of shipping instructions by the consignor in a non-negotiable bill of lading which causes the bailee not to deliver to the consignee defeats the consignee's title to the goods if they have been delivered to a buyer in ordinary course of business and in any event defeats the consignee's rights against the bailee.

(4) Delivery pursuant to a non-negotiable document may be stopped by a seller under Section 2-705, and subject to the requirement of due notification there provided. A bailee honoring the seller's instructions is entitled to be indemnified by the seller against any resulting loss or expense.

**§7-505. Indorser Not a Guarantor for Other Parties.**

The indorsement of a document of title issued by a bailee does not make the indorser liable for any default by the bailee or by previous indorsers.

**§7-506. Delivery Without Indorsement: Right to Compel Indorsement.**

The transferee of a negotiable document of title has a specifically enforceable right to have his transferor supply any necessary indorsement but the transfer becomes a negotiation only as of the time the indorsement is supplied.

**§7-507. Warranties on Negotiation or Transfer of Receipt or Bill.**

Where a person negotiates or transfers a document of title for value otherwise than as a mere intermediary under the next following section, then unless otherwise agreed he warrants to his immediate purchaser only in addition to any warranty made in selling the goods

(a) that the document is genuine; and

(b) that he has no knowledge of any fact which would impair its validity or worth; and

(c) that his negotiation or transfer is rightful and fully effective with respect to the title to the document and the goods it represents.

**§7-508. Warranties of Collecting Bank as to Documents.**

A collecting bank or other intermediary known to be entrusted with documents on behalf of another or with collection of a draft of other claim against delivery of documents warrants by such delivery of the documents only its own good faith and authority. This rule applies even though the intermediary has purchased or made advances against the claim or draft to be collected.

## Part 6—Warehouse Receipts and Bills of Lading: Miscellaneous Provisions

**§7-601. Lost and Missing Documents.**

(1) If a document has been lost, stolen or destroyed, a court may order delivery of the goods or issuance of a substitute document and the bailee may without liability to any person comply with such order. If the document was negotiable the claimant must post security approved by the court to indemnify any person who may suffer loss as a result of non-surrender of the document. If the document was not negotiable, such security may be required at the discretion of the court. The court may also in its discretion order payment of the bailee's reasonable costs and counsel fees.

(2) A bailee who without court order delivers goods to a person claiming under a missing negotiable document is liable to any person injured thereby, and if the delivery is not in good faith becomes liable for conversion. Delivery in good faith is not conversion if made in accordance with a filed classification or tariff or, where no classification or tariff is filed, if the claimant posts security with the bailee in an amount at least double the value of the goods at the time of posting to indemnify any person injured by the delivery who files a notice of claim within one year after the delivery.

# REVISED ARTICLE 9: SECURED TRANSACTIONS

## Part 1—General Provisions

**§9-101. Short Title.**

This article may be cited as Uniform Commercial Code—Secured Transactions.

**§9-102. Definitions and Index of Definitions.**

(a) **[Article 9 definitions.]** In this article:

(1) "Accession" means goods that are physically united with other goods in such a manner that the identity of the original goods is not lost.

(2) "Account", except as used in "account for", means a right to payment of a monetary obligation, whether or not earned by performance, (i) for property that has been or is to be sold, leased, licensed, assigned, or otherwise disposed of, (ii) for services rendered or to be rendered,

(iii) for a policy of insurance issued or to be issued, (iv) for a secondary obligation incurred or to be incurred, (v) for energy provided or to be provided, (vi) for the use or hire of a vessel under a charter or other contract, (vii) arising out of the use of a credit or charge card or information contained on or for use with the card, or (viii) as winnings in a lottery or other game of chance operated or sponsored by a State, governmental unit of a State, or person licensed or authorized to operate the game by a State or governmental unit of a State. The term includes health-care-insurance receivables. The term does not include (i) rights to payment evidenced by chattel paper or an instrument, (ii) commercial tort claims, (iii) deposit accounts, (iv) investment property, (v) letter-of-credit rights or letters of credit, or (vi) rights to payment for money or funds advanced or sold, other than rights arising out of the use of a credit or charge card or information contained on or for use with the card.

(3) "Account debtor" means a person obligated on an account, chattel paper, or general intangible. The term does not include persons obligated to pay a negotiable instrument, even if the instrument constitutes part of chattel paper.

(4) "Accounting", except as used in "accounting for", means a record:
(A) authenticated by a secured party;
(B) indicating the aggregate unpaid secured obligations as of a date not more than 35 days earlier or 35 days later than the date of the record; and
(C) identifying the components of the obligations in reasonable detail.

(5) "Agricultural lien" means an interest, other than a security interest, in farm products:
(A) which secures payment or performance of an obligation for:
(i) goods or services furnished in connection with a debtor's farming operation; or
(ii) rent on real property leased by a debtor in connection with its farming operation;
(B) which is created by statute in favor of a person that:
(i) in the ordinary course of its business furnished goods or services to a debtor in connection with a debtor's farming operation; or
(ii) leased real property to a debtor in connection with the debtor's farming operation; and
(C) whose effectiveness does not depend on the person's possession of the personal property.

(6) "As-extracted collateral" means:
(A) oil, gas, or other minerals that are subject to a security interest that:
(i) is created by a debtor having an interest in the minerals before extraction; and
(ii) attaches to the minerals as extracted; or
(B) accounts arising out of the sale at the wellhead or minehead of oil, gas, or other minerals in which the debtor had an interest before extraction.

(7) "Authenticate" means:
(A) to sign; or
(B) to execute or otherwise adopt a symbol, or encrypt or similarly process a record in whole or in part, with the present intent of the authenticating person to identify the person and adopt or accept a record.

(8) "Bank" means an organization that is engaged in the business of banking. The term includes savings banks, savings and loan associations, credit unions, and trust companies.

(9) "Cash proceeds" means proceeds that are money, checks, deposit accounts, or the like.

(10) "Certificate of title" means a certificate of title with respect to which a statute provides for the security interest in question to be indicated on the certificate as a condition or result of the security interest's obtaining priority over the rights of a lien creditor with respect to the collateral.

(11) "Chattel paper" means a record or records that evidence both a monetary obligation and a security interest in specific goods, a security interest in specific goods and software used in the goods, a security interest in specific goods and license of software used in the goods, a lease of specific goods, or a lease of specific goods and license of software used in the goods. In this paragraph, "monetary obligation" means a monetary obligation secured by the goods or owed under a lease of the goods and includes a monetary obligation with respect to software used in the goods. The term does not include (i) charters or other contracts involving the use or hire of a vessel or (ii) records that evidence a right to payment arising out of the use of a credit or charge card or information contained on or for use with the card. If a transaction is evidenced by records that include an instrument or series of instruments, the group of records taken together constitutes chattel paper.

(12) "Collateral" means the property subject to a security interest or agricultural lien. The term includes:
(A) proceeds to which a security interest attaches;
(B) accounts, chattel paper, payment intangibles, and promissory notes that have been sold; and
(C) goods that are the subject of a consignment.

(13) "Commercial tort claim" means a claim arising in tort with respect to which:
(A) the claimant is an organization; or
(B) the claimant is an individual and the claim:
(i) arose in the course of the claimant's business or profession; and
(ii) does not include damages arising out of personal injury to or the death of an individual.

(14) "Commodity account" means an account maintained by a commodity intermediary in which a commodity contract is carried for a commodity customer.

(15) "Commodity contract" means a commodity futures contract, an option on a commodity futures contract, a commodity option, or another contract if the contract or option is:
(A) traded on or subject to the rules of a board of trade that has been designated as a contract market for such a contract pursuant to federal commodities laws; or
(B) traded on a foreign commodity board of trade, exchange, or market, and is carried on the books of a commodity intermediary for a commodity customer.

(16) "Commodity customer" means a person for which a commodity intermediary carries a commodity contract on its books.

(17) "Commodity intermediary" means a person that:
(A) is registered as a futures commission merchant under federal commodities law; or
(B) in the ordinary course of its business provides clearance or settlement services for a board of trade that has been designated as a contract market pursuant to federal commodities law.

(18) "Communicate" means:
(A) to send a written or other tangible record;
(B) to transmit a record by any means agreed upon by the persons sending and receiving the record; or
(C) in the case of transmission of a record to or by a filing office, to transmit a record by any means prescribed by filing-office rule.

(19) "Consignee" means a merchant to which goods are delivered in a consignment.

(20) "Consignment" means a transaction, regardless of its form, in which a person delivers goods to a merchant for the purpose of sale and:
(A) the merchant:
(i) deals in goods of that kind under a name other than the name of the person making delivery;

(ii) is not an auctioneer; and
(iii) is not generally known by its creditors to be substantially engaged in selling the goods of others;
(B) with respect to each delivery, the aggregate value of the goods is $1,000 or more at the time of delivery;
(C) the goods are not consumer goods immediately before delivery; and
(D) the transaction does not create a security interest that secures an obligation.

(21) "Consignor" means a person that delivers goods to a consignee in a consignment.
(22) "Consumer debtor" means a debtor in a consumer transaction.
(23) "Consumer goods" means goods that are used or bought for use primarily for personal, family, or household purposes.
(24) "Consumer-goods transaction" means a consumer transaction in which:
(A) an individual incurs an obligation primarily for personal, family, or household purposes; and
(B) a security interest in consumer goods secures the obligation.
(25) "Consumer obligor" means an obligor who is an individual and who incurred the obligation as part of a transaction entered into primarily for personal, family, or household purposes.
(26) "Consumer transaction" means a transaction in which (i) an individual incurs an obligation primarily for personal, family, or household purposes, (ii) a security interest secures the obligation, and (iii) the collateral is held or acquired primarily for personal, family, or household purposes. The term includes consumer-goods transactions.
(27) "Continuation statement" means an amendment of a financing statement which:
(A) identifies, by its file number, the initial financing statement to which it relates; and
(B) indicates that it is a continuation statement for, or that it is filed to continue the effectiveness of, the identified financing statement.
(28) "Debtor" means:
(A) a person having an interest, other than a security interest or other lien, in the collateral, whether or not the person is an obligor;
(B) a seller of accounts, chattel paper, payment intangibles, or promissory notes; or
(C) a consignee.
(29) "Deposit account" means a demand, time, savings, passbook, or similar account maintained with a bank. The term does not include investment property or accounts evidenced by an instrument.
(30) "Document" means a document of title or a receipt of the type described in Section 7-201(2).
(31) "Electronic chattel paper" means chattel paper evidenced by a record or records consisting of information stored in an electronic medium.
(32) "Encumbrance" means a right, other than an ownership interest, in real property. The term includes mortgages and other liens on real property.
(33) "Equipment" means goods other than inventory, farm products, or consumer goods.
(34) "Farm products" means goods, other than standing timber, with respect to which the debtor is engaged in a farming operation and which are:
(A) crops grown, growing, or to be grown, including:
(i) crops produced on trees, vines, and bushes; and
(ii) aquatic goods produced in aquacultural operations;
(B) livestock, born or unborn, including aquatic goods produced in aquacultural operations;
(C) supplies used or produced in a farming operation; or
(D) products of crops or livestock in their unmanufactured states.
(35) "Farming operation" means raising, cultivating, propagating, fattening, grazing, or any other farming, livestock, or aquacultural operation.
(36) "File number" means the number assigned to an initial financing statement pursuant to Section 9-519(a).
(37) "Filing office" means an office designated in Section 9-501 as the place to file a financing statement.
(38) "Filing-office rule" means a rule adopted pursuant to Section 9-526.
(39) "Financing statement" means a record or records composed of an initial financing statement and any filed record relating to the initial financing statement.
(40) "Fixture filing" means the filing of a financing statement covering goods that are or are to become fixtures and satisfying Section 9-502(a) and (b). The term includes the filing of a financing statement covering goods of a transmitting utility which are or are to become fixtures.
(41) "Fixtures" means goods that have become so related to particular real property that an interest in them arises under real property law.
(42) "General intangible" means any personal property, including things in action, other than accounts, chattel paper, commercial tort claims, deposit accounts, documents, goods, instruments, investment property, letter-of-credit rights, letters of credit, money, and oil, gas, or other minerals before extraction. The term includes payment intangibles and software.
(43) "Good faith" means honesty in fact and the observance of reasonable commercial standards of fair dealing.
(44) "Goods" means all things that are movable when a security interest attaches. The term includes (i) fixtures, (ii) standing timber that is to be cut and removed under a conveyance or contract for sale, (iii) the unborn young of animals, (iv) crops grown, growing, or to be grown, even if the crops are produced on trees, vines, or bushes, and (v) manufactured homes. The term also includes a computer program embedded in goods and any supporting information provided in connection with a transaction relating to the program if (i) the program is associated with the goods in such a manner that it customarily is considered part of the goods, or (ii) by becoming the owner of the goods, a person acquires a right to use the program in connection with the goods. The term does not include a computer program embedded in goods that consist solely of the medium in which the program is embedded. The term also does not include accounts, chattel paper, commercial tort claims, deposit accounts, documents, general intangibles, instruments, investment property, letter-of-credit rights, letters of credit, money, or oil, gas, or other minerals before extraction.
(45) "Governmental unit" means a subdivision, agency, department, county, parish, municipality, or other unit of the government of the United States, a State, or a foreign country. The term includes an organization having a separate corporate existence if the organization is eligible to issue debt on which interest is exempt from income taxation under the laws of the United States.
(46) "Health-care-insurance receivable" means an interest in or claim under a policy of insurance which is a right to payment of a monetary obligation for health-care goods or services provided.
(47) "Instrument" means a negotiable instrument or any other writing that evidences a right to the payment of a monetary obligation, is not itself a security agreement or lease, and is of a type that in ordinary course of business is transferred by delivery with any necessary indorsement or assignment. The term does not include (i) investment property, (ii) letters of credit, or (iii) writings that evidence a right to payment arising out of the use of a credit or charge card or information contained on or for use with the card.
(48) "Inventory" means goods, other than farm products, which:
(A) are leased by a person as lessor;
(B) are held by a person for sale or lease or to be furnished under a contract of service;
(C) are furnished by a person under a contract of service; or
(D) consist of raw materials, work in process, or materials used or consumed in a business.

(49) "Investment property" means a security, whether certificated or uncertificated, security entitlement, securities account, commodity contract, or commodity account.
(50) "Jurisdiction of organization", with respect to a registered organization, means the jurisdiction under whose law the organization is organized.
(51) "Letter-of-credit right" means a right to payment or performance under a letter of credit, whether or not the beneficiary has demanded or is at the time entitled to demand payment or performance. The term does not include the right of a beneficiary to demand payment or performance under a letter of credit.
(52) "Lien creditor" means:
(A) a creditor that has acquired a lien on the property involved by attachment, levy, or the like;
(B) an assignee for benefit of creditors from the time of assignment;
(C) a trustee in bankruptcy from the date of the filing of the petition; or
(D) a receiver in equity from the time of appointment.
(53) "Manufactured home" means a structure, transportable in one or more sections, which, in the traveling mode, is eight body feet or more in width or 40 body feet or more in length, or, when erected on site, is 320 or more square feet, and which is built on a permanent chassis and designed to be used as a dwelling with or without a permanent foundation when connected to the required utilities, and includes the plumbing, heating, air-conditioning, and electrical systems contained therein. The term includes any structure that meets all of the requirements of this paragraph except the size requirements and with respect to which the manufacturer voluntarily files a certification required by the United States Secretary of Housing and Urban Development and complies with the standards established under Title 42 of the United States Code.
(54) "Manufactured-home transaction" means a secured transaction:
(A) that creates a purchase-money security interest in a manufactured home, other than a manufactured home held as inventory; or
(B) in which a manufactured home, other than a manufactured home held as inventory, is the primary collateral.
(55) "Mortgage" means a consensual interest in real property, including fixtures, which secures payment or performance of an obligation.
(56) "New debtor" means a person that becomes bound as debtor under Section 9-203(d) by a security agreement previously entered into by another person.
(57) "New value" means (i) money, (ii) money's worth in property, services, or new credit, or (iii) release by a transferee of an interest in property previously transferred to the transferee. The term does not include an obligation substituted for another obligation.
(58) "Noncash proceeds" means proceeds other than cash proceeds.
(59) "Obligor" means a person that, with respect to an obligation secured by a security interest in or an agricultural lien on the collateral, (i) owes payment or other performance of the obligation, (ii) has provided property other than the collateral to secure payment or other performance of the obligation, or (iii) is otherwise accountable in whole or in part for payment or other performance of the obligation. The term does not include issuers or nominated persons under a letter of credit.
(60) "Original debtor", except as used in Section 9-310(c), means a person that, as debtor, entered into a security agreement to which a new debtor has become bound under Section 9-203(d).
(61) "Payment intangible" means a general intangible under which the account debtor's principal obligation is a monetary obligation.
(62) "Person related to", with respect to an individual, means:
(A) the spouse of the individual;
(B) a brother, brother-in-law, sister, or sister-in-law of the individual;
(C) an ancestor or lineal descendant of the individual or the individual's spouse; or
(D) any other relative, by blood or marriage, of the individual or the individual's spouse who shares the same home with the individual.
(63) "Person related to", with respect to an organization, means:
(A) a person directly or indirectly controlling, controlled by, or under common control with the organization;
(B) an officer or director of, or a person performing similar functions with respect to, the organization;
(C) an officer or director of, or a person performing similar functions with respect to, a person described in subparagraph (A);
(D) the spouse of an individual described in subparagraph (A), (B), or (C); or
(E) an individual who is related by blood or marriage to an individual described in subparagraph (A), (B), (C), or (D) and shares the same home with the individual.
(64) "Proceeds", except as used in Section 9-609(b), means the following property:
(A) whatever is acquired upon the sale, lease, license, exchange, or other disposition of collateral;
(B) whatever is collected on, or distributed on account of, collateral;
(C) rights arising out of collateral;
(D) to the extent of the value of collateral, claims arising out of the loss, nonconformity, or interference with the use of, defects or infringement of rights in, or damage to, the collateral; or
(E) to the extent of the value of collateral and to the extent payable to the debtor or the secured party, insurance payable by reason of the loss or nonconformity of, defects or infringement of rights in, or damage to, the collateral.
(65) "Promissory note" means an instrument that evidences a promise to pay a monetary obligation, does not evidence an order to pay, and does not contain an acknowledgment by a bank that the bank has received for deposit a sum of money or funds.
(66) "Proposal" means a record authenticated by a secured party which includes the terms on which the secured party is willing to accept collateral in full or partial satisfaction of the obligation it secures pursuant to Sections 9-620, 9-621, and 9-622.
(67) "Public-finance transaction" means a secured transaction in connection with which:
(A) debt securities are issued;
(B) all or a portion of the securities issued have an initial stated maturity of at least 20 years; and
(C) the debtor, obligor, secured party, account debtor or other person obligated on collateral, assignor or assignee of a secured obligation, or assignor or assignee of a security interest is a State or a governmental unit of a State.
(68) "Pursuant to commitment", with respect to an advance made or other value given by a secured party, means pursuant to the secured party's obligation, whether or not a subsequent event of default or other event not within the secured party's control has relieved or may relieve the secured party from its obligation.
(69) "Record", except as used in "for record", "of record", "record or legal title", and "record owner", means information that is inscribed on a tangible medium or which is stored in an electronic or other medium and is retrievable in perceivable form.
(70) "Registered organization" means an organization organized solely under the law of a single State or the United States and as to which the State or the United States must maintain a public record showing the organization to have been organized.
(71) "Secondary obligor" means an obligor to the extent that:
(A) the obligor's obligation is secondary; or
(B) the obligor has a right of recourse with respect to an obligation secured by collateral against the debtor, another obligor, or property of either.

(72) "Secured party" means:

(A) a person in whose favor a security interest is created or provided for under a security agreement, whether or not any obligation to be secured is outstanding;

(B) a person that holds an agricultural lien;

(C) a consignor;

(D) a person to which accounts, chattel paper, payment intangibles, or promissory notes have been sold;

(E) a trustee, indenture trustee, agent, collateral agent, or other representative in whose favor a security interest or agricultural lien is created or provided for; or

(F) a person that holds a security interest arising under Section 2-401, 2-505, 2-711(3), 2A-508(5), 4-210, or 5-118.

(73) "Security agreement" means an agreement that creates or provides for a security interest.

(74) "Send", in connection with a record or notification, means:

(A) to deposit in the mail, deliver for transmission, or transmit by any other usual means of communication, with postage or cost of transmission provided for, addressed to any address reasonable under the circumstances; or

(B) to cause the record or notification to be received within the time that it would have been received if properly sent under subparagraph (A).

(75) "Software" means a computer program and any supporting information provided in connection with a transaction relating to the program. The term does not include a computer program that is included in the definition of goods.

(76) "State" means a State of the United States, the District of Columbia, Puerto Rico, the United States Virgin Islands, or any territory or insular possession subject to the jurisdiction of the United States.

(77) "Supporting obligation" means a letter-of-credit right or secondary obligation that supports the payment or performance of an account, chattel paper, a document, a general intangible, an instrument, or investment property.

(78) "Tangible chattel paper" means chattel paper evidenced by a record or records consisting of information that is inscribed on a tangible medium.

(79) "Termination statement" means an amendment of a financing statement which:

(A) identifies, by its file number, the initial financing statement to which it relates; and

(B) indicates either that it is a termination statement or that the identified financing statement is no longer effective.

(80) "Transmitting utility" means a person primarily engaged in the business of:

(A) operating a railroad, subway, street railway, or trolley bus;

(B) transmitting communications electrically, electromagnetically, or by light;

(C) transmitting goods by pipeline or sewer; or

(D) transmitting or producing and transmitting electricity, steam, gas, or water.

(b) **[Definitions in other articles.]** The following definitions in other articles apply to this article:

"Applicant" Section 5-102.
"Beneficiary" Section 5-102.
"Broker" Section 8-102.
"Certificated security" Section 8-102.
"Check" Section 3-104.
"Clearing corporation" Section 8-102.
"Contract for sale" Section 2-106.
"Customer" Section 4-104.
"Entitlement holder" Section 8-102.
"Financial asset" Section 8-102.
"Holder in due course" Section 3-302.
"Issuer" (with respect to a letter of credit or letter-of-credit right) Section 5-102.
"Issuer" (with respect to a security) Section 8-201.
"Lease" Section 2A-103.
"Lease agreement" Section 2A-103.
"Lease contract" Section 2A-103.
"Leasehold interest" Section 2A-103.
"Lessee" Section 2A-103.
"Lessee in ordinary course of business" Section 2A-103.
"Lessor" Section 2A-103.
"Lessor's residual interest" Section 2A-103.
"Letter of credit" Section 5-102.
"Merchant" Section 2-104.
"Negotiable instrument" Section 3-104.
"Nominated person" Section 5-102.
"Note" Section 3-104.
"Proceeds of a letter of credit" Section 5-114.
"Prove" Section 3-103.
"Sale" Section 2-106.
"Securities account" Section 8-501.
"Securities intermediary" Section 8-102.
"Security" Section 8-102.
"Security certificate" Section 8-102.
"Security entitlement" Section 8-102.
"Uncertificated security" Section 8-102.

(c) **[Article 1 definitions and principles.]** Article 1 contains general definitions and principles of construction and interpretation applicable throughout this article.

**§9-103. Purchase-Money Security Interest; Application of Payments; Burden of Establishing.**

(a) **[Definitions.]** In this section:

(1) "purchase-money collateral" means goods or software that secures a purchase-money obligation incurred with respect to that collateral; and

(2) "purchase-money obligation" means an obligation of an obligor incurred as all or part of the price of the collateral or for value given to enable the debtor to acquire rights in or the use of the collateral if the value is in fact so used.

(b) **[Purchase-money security interest in goods.]** A security interest in goods is a purchase-money security interest:

(1) to the extent that the goods are purchase-money collateral with respect to that security interest;

(2) if the security interest is in inventory that is or was purchase-money collateral, also to the extent that the security interest secures a purchase-money obligation incurred with respect to other inventory in which the secured party holds or held a purchase-money security interest; and

(3) also to the extent that the security interest secures a purchase-money obligation incurred with respect to software in which the secured party holds or held a purchase-money security interest.

(c) **[Purchase-money security interest in software.]** A security interest in software is a purchase-money security interest to the extent that the security interest also secures a purchase-money obligation incurred with respect to goods in which the secured party holds or held a purchase-money security interest if:

(1) the debtor acquired its interest in the software in an integrated transaction in which it acquired an interest in the goods; and

(2) the debtor acquired its interest in the software for the principal purpose of using the software in the goods.

(d) **[Consignor's inventory purchase-money security interest.]** The security interest of a consignor in goods that are the subject of a consignment is a purchase-money security interest in inventory.

(e) **[Application of payment in non-consumer-goods transaction.]** In a transaction other than a consumer-goods transaction, if the extent to which a security interest is a purchase-money security interest depends on the application of a payment to a particular obligation, the payment must be applied:

(1) in accordance with any reasonable method of application to which the parties agree;

(2) in the absence of the parties' agreement to a reasonable method, in accordance with any intention of the obligor manifested at or before the time of payment; or

(3) in the absence of an agreement to a reasonable method and a timely manifestation of the obligor's intention, in the following order:

(A) to obligations that are not secured; and

(B) if more than one obligation is secured, to obligations secured by purchase-money security interests in the order in which those obligations were incurred.

(f) **[No loss of status of purchase-money security interest in non-consumer-goods transaction.]** In a transaction other than a consumer-goods transaction, a purchase-money security interest does not lose its status as such, even if:

(1) the purchase-money collateral also secures an obligation that is not a purchase-money obligation;

(2) collateral that is not purchase-money collateral also secures the purchase-money obligation; or

(3) the purchase-money obligation has been renewed, refinanced, consolidated, or restructured.

(g) **[Burden of proof in non-consumer-goods transaction.]** In a transaction other than a consumer-goods transaction, a secured party claiming a purchase-money security interest has the burden of establishing the extent to which the security interest is a purchase-money security interest.

(h) **[Non-consumer-goods transactions; no inference.]** The limitation of the rules in subsections (e), (f), and (g) to transactions other than consumer-goods transactions is intended to leave to the court the determination of the proper rules in consumer-goods transactions. The court may not infer from that limitation the nature of the proper rule in consumer-goods transactions and may continue to apply established approaches.

**§9-104. Control of Deposit Account.**

(a) **[Requirements for control.]** A secured party has control of a deposit account if:

(1) the secured party is the bank with which the deposit account is maintained;

(2) the debtor, secured party, and bank have agreed in an authenticated record that the bank will comply with instructions originated by the secured party directing disposition of the funds in the deposit account without further consent by the debtor; or

(3) the secured party becomes the bank's customer with respect to the deposit account.

(b) **[Debtor's right to direct disposition.]** A secured party that has satisfied subsection (a) has control, even if the debtor retains the right to direct the disposition of funds from the deposit account.

**§9-105. Control of Electronic Chattel Paper.**

A secured party has control of electronic chattel paper if the record or records comprising the chattel paper are created, stored, and assigned in such a manner that:

(1) a single authoritative copy of the record or records exists which is unique, identifiable and, except as otherwise provided in paragraphs (4), (5), and (6), unalterable;

(2) the authoritative copy identifies the secured party as the assignee of the record or records;

(3) the authoritative copy is communicated to and maintained by the secured party or its designated custodian;

(4) copies or revisions that add or change an identified assignee of the authoritative copy can be made only with the participation of the secured party;

(5) each copy of the authoritative copy and any copy of a copy is readily identifiable as a copy that is not the authoritative copy; and

(6) any revision of the authoritative copy is readily identifiable as an authorized or unauthorized revision.

**§9-106. Control of Investment Property.**

(a) **[Control under Section 8-106.]** A person has control of a certificated security, uncertificated security, or security entitlement as provided in Section 8-106.

(b) **[Control of commodity contract.]** A secured party has control of a commodity contract if:

(1) the secured party is the commodity intermediary with which the commodity contract is carried; or

(2) the commodity customer, secured party, and commodity intermediary have agreed that the commodity intermediary will apply any value distributed on account of the commodity contract as directed by the secured party without further consent by the commodity customer.

(c) **[Effect of control of securities account or commodity account.]** A secured party having control of all security entitlements or commodity contracts carried in a securities account or commodity account has control over the securities account or commodity account.

**§9-107. Control of Letter-of-Credit Right.**

A secured party has control of a letter-of-credit right to the extent of any right to payment or performance by the issuer or any nominated person if the issuer or nominated person has consented to an assignment of proceeds of the letter of credit under Section 5-114(c) or otherwise applicable law or practice.

**§9-108. Sufficiency of Description.**

(a) **[Sufficiency of description.]** Except as otherwise provided in subsections (c), (d), and (e), a description of personal or real property is sufficient, whether or not it is specific, if it reasonably identifies what is described.

(b) **[Examples of reasonable identification.]** Except as otherwise provided in subsection (d), a description of collateral reasonably identifies the collateral if it identifies the collateral by:

(1) specific listing;

(2) category;

(3) except as otherwise provided in subsection (e), a type of collateral defined in [the Uniform Commercial Code];

(4) quantity;

(5) computational or allocational formula or procedure; or

(6) except as otherwise provided in subsection (c), any other method, if the identity of the collateral is objectively determinable.

(c) **[Supergeneric description not sufficient.]** A description of collateral as "all the debtor's assets" or "all the debtor's personal property" or using words of similar import does not reasonably identify the collateral.

(d) **[Investment property.]** Except as otherwise provided in subsection (e), a description of a security entitlement, securities account, or commodity account is sufficient if it describes:

(1) the collateral by those terms or as investment property; or

(2) the underlying financial asset or commodity contract.

(e) **[When description by type insufficient.]** A description only by type of collateral defined in [the Uniform Commercial Code] is an insufficient description of:

(1) a commercial tort claim; or

(2) in a consumer transaction, consumer goods, a security entitlement, a securities account, or a commodity account.

**§9-109. Scope.**

(a) **[General scope of article.]** Except as otherwise provided in subsections (c) and (d), this article applies to:

(1) a transaction, regardless of its form, that creates a security interest in personal property or fixtures by contract;

(2) an agricultural lien;

(3) a sale of accounts, chattel paper, payment intangibles, or promissory notes;
(4) a consignment;
(5) a security interest arising under Section 2-401, 2-505, 2-711(3), or 2A-508(5), as provided in Section 9-110; and
(6) a security interest arising under Section 4-210 or 5-118.

(b) **[Security interest in secured obligation.]** The application of this article to a security interest in a secured obligation is not affected by the fact that the obligation is itself secured by a transaction or interest to which this article does not apply.

(c) **[Extent to which article does not apply.]** This article does not apply to the extent that:
(1) a statute, regulation, or treaty of the United States preempts this article;
(2) another statute of this State expressly governs the creation, perfection, priority, or enforcement of a security interest created by this State or a governmental unit of this State;
(3) a statute of another State, a foreign country, or a governmental unit of another State or a foreign country, other than a statute generally applicable to security interests, expressly governs creation, perfection, priority, or enforcement of a security interest created by the State, country, or governmental unit; or
(4) the rights of a transferee beneficiary or nominated person under a letter of credit are independent and superior under Section 5-114.

(d) **[Inapplicability of article.]** This article does not apply to:
(1) a landlord's lien, other than an agricultural lien;
(2) a lien, other than an agricultural lien, given by statute or other rule of law for services or materials, but Section 9-333 applies with respect to priority of the lien;
(3) an assignment of a claim for wages, salary, or other compensation of an employee;
(4) a sale of accounts, chattel paper, payment intangibles, or promissory notes as part of a sale of the business out of which they arose;
(5) an assignment of accounts, chattel paper, payment intangibles, or promissory notes which is for the purpose of collection only;
(6) an assignment of a right to payment under a contract to an assignee that is also obligated to perform under the contract;
(7) an assignment of a single account, payment intangible, or promissory note to an assignee in full or partial satisfaction of a preexisting indebtedness;
(8) a transfer of an interest in or an assignment of a claim under a policy of insurance, other than an assignment by or to a health-care provider of a health-care-insurance receivable and any subsequent assignment of the right to payment, but Sections 9-315 and 9-322 apply with respect to proceeds and priorities in proceeds;
(9) an assignment of a right represented by a judgment, other than a judgment taken on a right to payment that was collateral;
(10) a right of recoupment or set-off, but:
(A) Section 9-340 applies with respect to the effectiveness of rights of recoupment or set-off against deposit accounts; and
(B) Section 9-404 applies with respect to defenses or claims of an account debtor;
(11) the creation or transfer of an interest in or lien on real property, including a lease or rents thereunder, except to the extent that provision is made for:
(A) liens on real property in Sections 9-203 and 9-308;
(B) fixtures in Section 9-334;
(C) fixture filings in Sections 9-501, 9-502, 9-512, 9-516, and 9-519; and
(D) security agreements covering personal and real property in Section 9-604;
(12) an assignment of a claim arising in tort, other than a commercial tort claim, but Sections 9-315 and 9-322 apply with respect to proceeds and priorities in proceeds; or
(13) an assignment of a deposit account in a consumer transaction, but Sections 9-315 and 9-322 apply with respect to proceeds and priorities in proceeds.

**§9-110. Security Interests Arising under Article 2 or 2A.**
A security interest arising under Section 2-401, 2-505, 2-711(3), or 2A-508(5) is subject to this article. However, until the debtor obtains possession of the goods:
(1) the security interest is enforceable, even if Section 9-203(b)(3) has not been satisfied;
(2) filing is not required to perfect the security interest;
(3) the rights of the secured party after default by the debtor are governed by Article 2 or 2A; and
(4) the security interest has priority over a conflicting security interest created by the debtor.

## Part 2—Effectiveness of Security Agreement; Attachment of Security Interest; Rights of Parties to Security Agreement

**§9-201. General Effectiveness of Security Agreement.**
(a) **[General effectiveness.]** Except as otherwise provided in [the Uniform Commercial Code], a security agreement is effective according to its terms between the parties, against purchasers of the collateral, and against creditors.

(b) **[Applicable consumer laws and other law.]** A transaction subject to this article is subject to any applicable rule of law which establishes a different rule for consumers and [insert reference to (i) any other statute or regulation that regulates the rates, charges, agreements, and practices for loans, credit sales, or other extensions of credit and (ii) any consumer-protection statute or regulation].

(c) **[Other applicable law controls.]** In case of conflict between this article and a rule of law, statute, or regulation described in subsection (b), the rule of law, statute, or regulation controls. Failure to comply with a statute or regulation described in subsection (b) has only the effect the statute or regulation specifies.

(d) **[Further deference to other applicable law.]** This article does not:
(1) validate any rate, charge, agreement, or practice that violates a rule of law, statute, or regulation described in subsection (b); or
(2) extend the application of the rule of law, statute, or regulation to a transaction not otherwise subject to it.

**§9-202. Title to Collateral Immaterial.**
Except as otherwise provided with respect to consignments or sales of accounts, chattel paper, payment intangibles, or promissory notes, the provisions of this article with regard to rights and obligations apply whether title to collateral is in the secured party or the debtor.

**§9-203. Attachment and Enforceability of Security Interest; Proceeds; Supporting Obligations; Formal Requisites.**
(a) **[Attachment.]** A security interest attaches to collateral when it becomes enforceable against the debtor with respect to the collateral, unless an agreement expressly postpones the time of attachment.

(b) **[Enforceability.]** Except as otherwise provided in subsections (c) through (i), a security interest is enforceable against the debtor and third parties with respect to the collateral only if:
(1) value has been given;
(2) the debtor has rights in the collateral or the power to transfer rights in the collateral to a secured party; and
(3) one of the following conditions is met:
(A) the debtor has authenticated a security agreement that provides a description of the collateral and, if the security interest covers timber to be cut, a description of the land concerned;
(B) the collateral is not a certificated security and is in the possession of the secured party under Section 9-313 pursuant to the debtor's security agreement;

(C) the collateral is a certificated security in registered form and the security certificate has been delivered to the secured party under Section 8-301 pursuant to the debtor's security agreement; or

(D) the collateral is deposit accounts, electronic chattel paper, investment property, or letter-of-credit rights, and the secured party has control under Section 9-104, 9-105, 9-106, or 9-107 pursuant to the debtor's security agreement.

(c) **[Other UCC provisions.]** Subsection (b) is subject to Section 4-210 on the security interest of a collecting bank, Section 5-118 on the security interest of a letter-of-credit issuer or nominated person, Section 9-110 on a security interest arising under Article 2 or 2A, and Section 9-206 on security interests in investment property.

(d) **[When person becomes bound by another person's security agreement.]** A person becomes bound as debtor by a security agreement entered into by another person if, by operation of law other than this article or by contract:

(1) the security agreement becomes effective to create a security interest in the person's property; or

(2) the person becomes generally obligated for the obligations of the other person, including the obligation secured under the security agreement, and acquires or succeeds to all or substantially all of the assets of the other person.

(e) **[Effect of new debtor becoming bound.]** If a new debtor becomes bound as debtor by a security agreement entered into by another person:

(1) the agreement satisfies subsection (b)(3) with respect to existing or after-acquired property of the new debtor to the extent the property is described in the agreement; and

(2) another agreement is not necessary to make a security interest in the property enforceable.

(f) **[Proceeds and supporting obligations.]** The attachment of a security interest in collateral gives the secured party the rights to proceeds provided by Section 9-315 and is also attachment of a security interest in a supporting obligation for the collateral.

(g) **[Lien securing right to payment.]** The attachment of a security interest in a right to payment or performance secured by a security interest or other lien on personal or real property is also attachment of a security interest in the security interest, mortgage, or other lien.

(h) **[Security entitlement carried in securities account.]** The attachment of a security interest in a securities account is also attachment of a security interest in the security entitlements carried in the securities account.

(i) **[Commodity contracts carried in commodity account.]** The attachment of a security interest in a commodity account is also attachment of a security interest in the commodity contracts carried in the commodity account.

### §9-204. After-Acquired Property; Future Advances.

(a) **[After-acquired collateral.]** Except as otherwise provided in subsection (b), a security agreement may create or provide for a security interest in after-acquired collateral.

(b) **[When after-acquired property clause not effective.]** A security interest does not attach under a term constituting an after-acquired property clause to:

(1) consumer goods, other than an accession when given as additional security, unless the debtor acquires rights in them within 10 days after the secured party gives value; or

(2) a commercial tort claim.

(c) **[Future advances and other value.]** A security agreement may provide that collateral secures, or that accounts, chattel paper, payment intangibles, or promissory notes are sold in connection with, future advances or other value, whether or not the advances or value are given pursuant to commitment.

### §9-205. Use or Disposition of Collateral Permissible.

(a) **[When security interest not invalid or fraudulent.]** A security interest is not invalid or fraudulent against creditors solely because:

(1) the debtor has the right or ability to:

(A) use, commingle, or dispose of all or part of the collateral, including returned or repossessed goods;

(B) collect, compromise, enforce, or otherwise deal with collateral;

(C) accept the return of collateral or make repossessions; or

(D) use, commingle, or dispose of proceeds; or

(2) the secured party fails to require the debtor to account for proceeds or replace collateral.

(b) **[Requirements of possession not relaxed.]** This section does not relax the requirements of possession if attachment, perfection, or enforcement of a security interest depends upon possession of the collateral by the secured party.

### §9-206. Security Interest Arising in Purchase or Delivery of Financial Asset.

(a) **[Security interest when person buys through securities intermediary.]** A security interest in favor of a securities intermediary attaches to a person's security entitlement if:

(1) the person buys a financial asset through the securities intermediary in a transaction in which the person is obligated to pay the purchase price to the securities intermediary at the time of the purchase; and

(2) the securities intermediary credits the financial asset to the buyer's securities account before the buyer pays the securities intermediary.

(b) **[Security interest secures obligation to pay for financial asset.]** The security interest described in subsection (a) secures the person's obligation to pay for the financial asset.

(c) **[Security interest in payment against delivery transaction.]** A security interest in favor of a person that delivers a certificated security or other financial asset represented by a writing attaches to the security or other financial asset if:

(1) the security or other financial asset:

(A) in the ordinary course of business is transferred by delivery with any necessary indorsement or assignment; and

(B) is delivered under an agreement between persons in the business of dealing with such securities or financial assets; and

(2) the agreement calls for delivery against payment.

(d) **[Security interest secures obligation to pay for delivery.]** The security interest described in subsection (c) secures the obligation to make payment for the delivery.

### §9-207. Rights and Duties of Secured Party Having Possession Or Control of Collateral.

(a) **[Duty of care when secured party in possession.]** Except as otherwise provided in subsection (d), a secured party shall use reasonable care in the custody and preservation of collateral in the secured party's possession. In the case of chattel paper or an instrument, reasonable care includes taking necessary steps to preserve rights against prior parties unless otherwise agreed.

(b) **[Expenses, risks, duties, and rights when secured party in possession.]** Except as otherwise provided in subsection (d), if a secured party has possession of collateral:

(1) reasonable expenses, including the cost of insurance and payment of taxes or other charges, incurred in the custody, preservation, use, or operation of the collateral are chargeable to the debtor and are secured by the collateral;

(2) the risk of accidental loss or damage is on the debtor to the extent of a deficiency in any effective insurance coverage;

(3) the secured party shall keep the collateral identifiable, but fungible collateral may be commingled; and

(4) the secured party may use or operate the collateral:

(A) for the purpose of preserving the collateral or its value;

(B) as permitted by an order of a court having competent jurisdiction; or

(C) except in the case of consumer goods, in the manner and to the extent agreed by the debtor.

(c) **[Duties and rights when secured party in possession or control.]** Except as otherwise provided in subsection (d), a secured party having possession of collateral or control of collateral under Section 9-104, 9-105, 9-106, or 9-107:

(1) may hold as additional security any proceeds, except money or funds, received from the collateral;

(2) shall apply money or funds received from the collateral to reduce the secured obligation, unless remitted to the debtor; and

(3) may create a security interest in the collateral.

(d) **[Buyer of certain rights to payment.]** If the secured party is a buyer of accounts, chattel paper, payment intangibles, or promissory notes or a consignor:

(1) subsection (a) does not apply unless the secured party is entitled under an agreement:

(A) to charge back uncollected collateral; or

(B) otherwise to full or limited recourse against the debtor or a secondary obligor based on the nonpayment or other default of an account debtor or other obligor on the collateral; and

(2) subsections (b) and (c) do not apply.

**§9-208. Additional Duties of Secured Party Having Control of Collateral.**

(a) **[Applicability of section.]** This section applies to cases in which there is no outstanding secured obligation and the secured party is not committed to make advances, incur obligations, or otherwise give value.

(b) **[Duties of secured party after receiving demand from debtor.]** Within 10 days after receiving an authenticated demand by the debtor:

(1) a secured party having control of a deposit account under Section 9-104(a)(2) shall send to the bank with which the deposit account is maintained an authenticated statement that releases the bank from any further obligation to comply with instructions originated by the secured party;

(2) a secured party having control of a deposit account under Section 9-104(a)(3) shall:

(A) pay the debtor the balance on deposit in the deposit account; or

(B) transfer the balance on deposit into a deposit account in the debtor's name;

(3) a secured party, other than a buyer, having control of electronic chattel paper under Section 9-105 shall:

(A) communicate the authoritative copy of the electronic chattel paper to the debtor or its designated custodian;

(B) if the debtor designates a custodian that is the designated custodian with which the authoritative copy of the electronic chattel paper is maintained for the secured party, communicate to the custodian an authenticated record releasing the designated custodian from any further obligation to comply with instructions originated by the secured party and instructing the custodian to comply with instructions originated by the debtor; and

(C) take appropriate action to enable the debtor or its designated custodian to make copies of or revisions to the authoritative copy which add or change an identified assignee of the authoritative copy without the consent of the secured party;

(4) a secured party having control of investment property under Section 8-106(d)(2) or 9-106(b) shall send to the securities intermediary or commodity intermediary with which the security entitlement or commodity contract is maintained an authenticated record that releases the securities intermediary or commodity intermediary from any further obligation to comply with entitlement orders or directions originated by the secured party; and

(5) a secured party having control of a letter-of-credit right under Section 9-107 shall send to each person having an unfulfilled obligation to pay or deliver proceeds of the letter of credit to the secured party an authenticated release from any further obligation to pay or deliver proceeds of the letter of credit to the secured party.

**§9-209. Duties of Secured Party if Account Debtor Has Been Notified of Assignment.**

(a) **[Applicability of section.]** Except as otherwise provided in subsection (c), this section applies if:

(1) there is no outstanding secured obligation; and

(2) the secured party is not committed to make advances, incur obligations, or otherwise give value.

(b) **[Duties of secured party after receiving demand from debtor.]** Within 10 days after receiving an authenticated demand by the debtor, a secured party shall send to an account debtor that has received notification of an assignment to the secured party as assignee under Section 9-406(a) an authenticated record that releases the account debtor from any further obligation to the secured party.

(c) **[Inapplicability to sales.]** This section does not apply to an assignment constituting the sale of an account, chattel paper, or payment intangible.

**§9-210. Request for Accounting; Request Regarding List of Collateral or Statement of Account.**

(a) **[Definitions.]** In this section:

(1) "Request" means a record of a type described in paragraph (2), (3), or (4).

(2) "Request for an accounting" means a record authenticated by a debtor requesting that the recipient provide an accounting of the unpaid obligations secured by collateral and reasonably identifying the transaction or relationship that is the subject of the request.

(3) "Request regarding a list of collateral" means a record authenticated by a debtor requesting that the recipient approve or correct a list of what the debtor believes to be the collateral securing an obligation and reasonably identifying the transaction or relationship that is the subject of the request.

(4) "Request regarding a statement of account" means a record authenticated by a debtor requesting that the recipient approve or correct a statement indicating what the debtor believes to be the aggregate amount of unpaid obligations secured by collateral as of a specified date and reasonably identifying the transaction or relationship that is the subject of the request.

(b) **[Duty to respond to requests.]** Subject to subsections (c), (d), (e), and (f), a secured party, other than a buyer of accounts, chattel paper, payment intangibles, or promissory notes or a consignor, shall comply with a request within 14 days after receipt:

(1) in the case of a request for an accounting, by authenticating and sending to the debtor an accounting; and

(2) in the case of a request regarding a list of collateral or a request regarding a statement of account, by authenticating and sending to the debtor an approval or correction.

(c) **[Request regarding list of collateral; statement concerning type of collateral.]** A secured party that claims a security interest in all of a particular type of collateral owned by the debtor may comply with a request regarding a list of collateral by sending to the debtor an authenticated record including a statement to that effect within 14 days after receipt.

(d) **[Request regarding list of collateral; no interest claimed.]** A person that receives a request regarding a list of collateral, claims no interest in the collateral when it receives the request, and claimed an interest in the collateral at an earlier time shall comply with the request within 14 days after receipt by sending to the debtor an authenticated record:

(1) disclaiming any interest in the collateral; and

(2) if known to the recipient, providing the name and mailing address of any assignee of or successor to the recipient's interest in the collateral.

(e) **[Request for accounting or regarding statement of account; no interest in obligation claimed.]** A person that receives a request for an accounting or a request regarding a statement of account, claims no interest in the obligations when it receives the request, and claimed an interest in the obligations at an earlier time shall comply with the request within 14 days after receipt by sending to the debtor an authenticated record:

(1) disclaiming any interest in the obligations; and

(2) if known to the recipient, providing the name and mailing address of any assignee of or successor to the recipient's interest in the obligations.

(f) **[Charges for responses.]** A debtor is entitled without charge to one response to a request under this section during any six-month period. The secured party may require payment of a charge not exceeding $25 for each additional response.

## Part 3—Perfection and Priority

**§9-301. Law Governing Perfection and Priority of Security Interests.** Except as otherwise provided in Sections 9-303 through 9-306, the following rules determine the law governing perfection, the effect of perfection or nonperfection, and the priority of a security interest in collateral:

(1) Except as otherwise provided in this section, while a debtor is located in a jurisdiction, the local law of that jurisdiction governs perfection, the effect of perfection or nonperfection, and the priority of a security interest in collateral.

(2) While collateral is located in a jurisdiction, the local law of that jurisdiction governs perfection, the effect of perfection or nonperfection, and the priority of a possessory security interest in that collateral.

(3) Except as otherwise provided in paragraph (4), while negotiable documents, goods, instruments, money, or tangible chattel paper is located in a jurisdiction, the local law of that jurisdiction governs:

(A) perfection of a security interest in the goods by filing a fixture filing;

(B) perfection of a security interest in timber to be cut; and

(C) the effect of perfection or nonperfection and the priority of a nonpossessory security interest in the collateral.

(4) The local law of the jurisdiction in which the wellhead or minehead is located governs perfection, the effect of perfection or nonperfection, and the priority of a security interest in as-extracted collateral.

**§9-302. Law Governing Perfection and Priority of Agricultural Liens.** While farm products are located in a jurisdiction, the local law of that jurisdiction governs perfection, the effect of perfection or nonperfection, and the priority of an agricultural lien on the farm products.

**§9-303. Law Governing Perfection and Priority of Security Interests in Goods Covered by a Certificate of Title.**

(a) **[Applicability of section.]** This section applies to goods covered by a certificate of title, even if there is no other relationship between the jurisdiction under whose certificate of title the goods are covered and the goods or the debtor.

(b) **[When goods covered by certificate of title.]** Goods become covered by a certificate of title when a valid application for the certificate of title and the applicable fee are delivered to the appropriate authority. Goods cease to be covered by a certificate of title at the earlier of the time the certificate of title ceases to be effective under the law of the issuing jurisdiction or the time the goods become covered subsequently by a certificate of title issued by another jurisdiction.

(c) **[Applicable law.]** The local law of the jurisdiction under whose certificate of title the goods are covered governs perfection, the effect of perfection or nonperfection, and the priority of a security interest in goods covered by a certificate of title from the time the goods become covered by the certificate of title until the goods cease to be covered by the certificate of title.

**§9-304. Law Governing Perfection and Priority of Security Interests in Deposit Accounts.**

(a) **[Law of bank's jurisdiction governs.]** The local law of a bank's jurisdiction governs perfection, the effect of perfection or nonperfection, and the priority of a security interest in a deposit account maintained with that bank.

(b) **[Bank's jurisdiction.]** The following rules determine a bank's jurisdiction for purposes of this part:

(1) If an agreement between the bank and the debtor governing the deposit account expressly provides that a particular jurisdiction is the bank's jurisdiction for purposes of this part, this article, or [the Uniform Commercial Code], that jurisdiction is the bank's jurisdiction.

(2) If paragraph (1) does not apply and an agreement between the bank and its customer governing the deposit account expressly provides that the agreement is governed by the law of a particular jurisdiction, that jurisdiction is the bank's jurisdiction.

(3) If neither paragraph (1) nor paragraph (2) applies and an agreement between the bank and its customer governing the deposit account expressly provides that the deposit account is maintained at an office in a particular jurisdiction, that jurisdiction is the bank's jurisdiction.

(4) If none of the preceding paragraphs applies, the bank's jurisdiction is the jurisdiction in which the office identified in an account statement as the office serving the customer's account is located.

(5) If none of the preceding paragraphs applies, the bank's jurisdiction is the jurisdiction in which the chief executive office of the bank is located.

**§9-305. Law Governing Perfection and Priority of Security Interests in Investment Property.**

(a) **[Governing law: general rules.]** Except as otherwise provided in subsection (c), the following rules apply:

(1) While a security certificate is located in a jurisdiction, the local law of that jurisdiction governs perfection, the effect of perfection or nonperfection, and the priority of a security interest in the certificated security represented thereby.

(2) The local law of the issuer's jurisdiction as specified in Section 8-110(d) governs perfection, the effect of perfection or nonperfection, and the priority of a security interest in an uncertificated security.

(3) The local law of the securities intermediary's jurisdiction as specified in Section 8-110(e) governs perfection, the effect of perfection or nonperfection, and the priority of a security interest in a security entitlement or securities account.

(4) The local law of the commodity intermediary's jurisdiction governs perfection, the effect of perfection or nonperfection, and the priority of a security interest in a commodity contract or commodity account.

(b) **[Commodity intermediary's jurisdiction.]** The following rules determine a commodity intermediary's jurisdiction for purposes of this part:

(1) If an agreement between the commodity intermediary and commodity customer governing the commodity account expressly provides that a particular jurisdiction is the commodity intermediary's jurisdiction for purposes of this part, this article, or [the Uniform Commercial Code], that jurisdiction is the commodity intermediary's jurisdiction.

(2) If paragraph (1) does not apply and an agreement between the commodity intermediary and commodity customer governing the commodity account expressly provides that the agreement is governed by the law of a particular jurisdiction, that jurisdiction is the commodity intermediary's jurisdiction.

(3) If neither paragraph (1) nor paragraph (2) applies and an agreement between the commodity intermediary and commodity customer governing the commodity account expressly provides that the commodity account is maintained at an office in a particular jurisdiction, that jurisdiction is the commodity intermediary's jurisdiction.

(4) If none of the preceding paragraphs applies, the commodity intermediary's jurisdiction is the jurisdiction in which the office identified in an account statement as the office serving the commodity customer's account is located.

(5) If none of the preceding paragraphs applies, the commodity intermediary's jurisdiction is the jurisdiction in which the chief executive office of the commodity intermediary is located.

(c) **[When perfection governed by law of jurisdiction where debtor located.]** The local law of the jurisdiction in which the debtor is located governs:

(1) perfection of a security interest in investment property by filing;

(2) automatic perfection of a security interest in investment property created by a broker or securities intermediary; and

(3) automatic perfection of a security interest in a commodity contract or commodity account created by a commodity intermediary.

**§9-306. Law Governing Perfection and Priority of Security Interests in Letter-of-Credit Rights.**

(a) **[Governing law: issuer's or nominated person's jurisdiction.]** Subject to subsection (c), the local law of the issuer's jurisdiction or a nominated person's jurisdiction governs perfection, the effect of perfection or nonperfection, and the priority of a security interest in a letter-of-credit right if the issuer's jurisdiction or nominated person's jurisdiction is a State.

(b) **[Issuer's or nominated person's jurisdiction.]** For purposes of this part, an issuer's jurisdiction or nominated person's jurisdiction is the jurisdiction whose law governs the liability of the issuer or nominated person with respect to the letter-of-credit right as provided in Section 5-116.

(c) **[When section not applicable.]** This section does not apply to a security interest that is perfected only under Section 9-308(d).

**§9-307. Location of Debtor.**

(a) **["Place of business."]** In this section, "place of business" means a place where a debtor conducts its affairs.

(b) **[Debtor's location: general rules.]** Except as otherwise provided in this section, the following rules determine a debtor's location:

(1) A debtor who is an individual is located at the individual's principal residence.

(2) A debtor that is an organization and has only one place of business is located at its place of business.

(3) A debtor that is an organization and has more than one place of business is located at its chief executive office.

(c) **[Limitation of applicability of subsection (b).]** Subsection (b) applies only if a debtor's residence, place of business, or chief executive office, as applicable, is located in a jurisdiction whose law generally requires information concerning the existence of a nonpossessory security interest to be made generally available in a filing, recording, or registration system as a condition or result of the security interest's obtaining priority over the rights of a lien creditor with respect to the collateral. If subsection (b) does not apply, the debtor is located in the District of Columbia.

(d) **[Continuation of location: cessation of existence, etc.]** A person that ceases to exist, have a residence, or have a place of business continues to be located in the jurisdiction specified by subsections (b) and (c).

(e) **[Location of registered organization organized under State law.]** A registered organization that is organized under the law of a State is located in that State.

(f) **[Location of registered organization organized under federal law; bank branches and agencies.]** Except as otherwise provided in subsection (i), a registered organization that is organized under the law of the United States and a branch or agency of a bank that is not organized under the law of the United States or a State are located:

(1) in the State that the law of the United States designates, if the law designates a State of location;

(2) in the State that the registered organization, branch, or agency designates, if the law of the United States authorizes the registered organization, branch, or agency to designate its State of location; or

(3) in the District of Columbia, if neither paragraph (1) nor paragraph (2) applies.

(g) **[Continuation of location: change in status of registered organization.]** A registered organization continues to be located in the jurisdiction specified by subsection (e) or (f) notwithstanding:

(1) the suspension, revocation, forfeiture, or lapse of the registered organization's status as such in its jurisdiction of organization; or

(2) the dissolution, winding up, or cancellation of the existence of the registered organization.

(h) **[Location of United States.]** The United States is located in the District of Columbia.

(i) **[Location of foreign bank branch or agency if licensed in only one state.]** A branch or agency of a bank that is not organized under the law of the United States or a State is located in the State in which the branch or agency is licensed, if all branches and agencies of the bank are licensed in only one State.

(j) **[Location of foreign air carrier.]** A foreign air carrier under the Federal Aviation Act of 1958, as amended, is located at the designated office of the agent upon which service of process may be made on behalf of the carrier.

(k) **[Section applies only to this part.]** This section applies only for purposes of this part.

**§9-308. When Security Interest or Agricultural Lien Is Perfected; Continuity of Perfection.**

(a) **[Perfection of security interest.]** Except as otherwise provided in this section and Section 9-309, a security interest is perfected if it has attached and all of the applicable requirements for perfection in Sections 9-310 through 9-316 have been satisfied. A security interest is perfected when it attaches if the applicable requirements are satisfied before the security interest attaches.

(b) **[Perfection of agricultural lien.]** An agricultural lien is perfected if it has become effective and all of the applicable requirements for perfection in Section 9-310 have been satisfied. An agricultural lien is perfected when it becomes effective if the applicable requirements are satisfied before the agricultural lien becomes effective.

(c) **[Continuous perfection; perfection by different methods.]** A security interest or agricultural lien is perfected continuously if it is originally perfected by one method under this article and is later perfected by another method under this article, without an intermediate period when it was unperfected.

(d) **[Supporting obligation.]** Perfection of a security interest in collateral also perfects a security interest in a supporting obligation for the collateral.

(e) **[Lien securing right to payment.]** Perfection of a security interest in a right to payment or performance also perfects a security interest in a security interest, mortgage, or other lien on personal or real property securing the right.

(f) **[Security entitlement carried in securities account.]** Perfection of a security interest in a securities account also perfects a security interest in the security entitlements carried in the securities account.

(g) **[Commodity contract carried in commodity account.]** Perfection of a security interest in a commodity account also perfects a security interest in the commodity contracts carried in the commodity account.

**§9-309. Security Interest Perfected Upon Attachment.**

The following security interests are perfected when they attach:

(1) a purchase-money security interest in consumer goods, except as otherwise provided in Section 9-311(b) with respect to consumer goods that are subject to a statute or treaty described in Section 9-311(a);

(2) an assignment of accounts or payment intangibles which does not by itself or in conjunction with other assignments to the same assignee transfer a significant part of the assignor's outstanding accounts or payment intangibles;

(3) a sale of a payment intangible;

(4) a sale of a promissory note;

(5) a security interest created by the assignment of a health-care-insurance receivable to the provider of the health-care goods or services;

(6) a security interest arising under Section 2-401, 2-505, 2-711(3), or 2A-508(5), until the debtor obtains possession of the collateral;

(7) a security interest of a collecting bank arising under Section 4-210;
(8) a security interest of an issuer or nominated person arising under Section 5-118;
(9) a security interest arising in the delivery of a financial asset under Section 9-206(c);
(10) a security interest in investment property created by a broker or securities intermediary;
(11) a security interest in a commodity contract or a commodity account created by a commodity intermediary;
(12) an assignment for the benefit of all creditors of the transferor and subsequent transfers by the assignee thereunder; and
(13) a security interest created by an assignment of a beneficial interest in a decedent's estate.

**§9-310. When Filing Required to Perfect Security Interest or Agricultural Lien; Security Interests and Agricultural Liens to Which Filing Provisions Do Not Apply.**

(a) **[General rule: perfection by filing.]** Except as otherwise provided in subsection (b) and Section 9-312(b), a financing statement must be filed to perfect all security interests and agricultural liens.

(b) **[Exceptions: filing not necessary.]** The filing of a financing statement is not necessary to perfect a security interest:
(1) that is perfected under Section 9-308(d), (e), (f), or (g);
(2) that is perfected under Section 9-309 when it attaches;
(3) in property subject to a statute, regulation, or treaty described in Section 9-311(a);
(4) in goods in possession of a bailee which is perfected under Section 9-312(d)(1) or (2);
(5) in certificated securities, documents, goods, or instruments which is perfected without filing or possession under Section 9-312(e), (f), or (g);
(6) in collateral in the secured party's possession under Section 9-313;
(7) in a certificated security which is perfected by delivery of the security certificate to the secured party under Section 9-313;
(8) in deposit accounts, electronic chattel paper, investment property, or letter-of-credit rights which is perfected by control under Section 9-314;
(9) in proceeds which is perfected under Section 9-315; or
(10) that is perfected under Section 9-316.

(c) **[Assignment of perfected security interest.]** If a secured party assigns a perfected security interest or agricultural lien, a filing under this article is not required to continue the perfected status of the security interest against creditors of and transferees from the original debtor.

**§9-311. Perfection of Security Interests in Property Subject to Certain Statutes, Regulations, and Treaties.**

(a) **[Security interest subject to other law.]** Except as otherwise provided in subsection (d), the filing of a financing statement is not necessary or effective to perfect a security interest in property subject to:
(1) a statute, regulation, or treaty of the United States whose requirements for a security interest's obtaining priority over the rights of a lien creditor with respect to the property preempt Section 9-310(a);
(2) [list any certificate-of-title statute covering automobiles, trailers, mobile homes, boats, farm tractors, or the like, which provides for a security interest to be indicated on the certificate as a condition or result of perfection, and any non-Uniform Commercial Code central filing statute]; or
(3) a certificate-of-title statute of another jurisdiction which provides for a security interest to be indicated on the certificate as a condition or result of the security interest's obtaining priority over the rights of a lien creditor with respect to the property.

(b) **[Compliance with other law.]** Compliance with the requirements of a statute, regulation, or treaty described in subsection (a) for obtaining priority over the rights of a lien creditor is equivalent to the filing of a financing statement under this article. Except as otherwise provided in subsection (d) and Sections 9-313 and 9-316(d) and (e) for goods covered by a certificate of title, a security interest in property subject to a statute, regulation, or treaty described in subsection (a) may be perfected only by compliance with those requirements, and a security interest so perfected remains perfected notwithstanding a change in the use or transfer of possession of the collateral.

(c) **[Duration and renewal of perfection.]** Except as otherwise provided in subsection (d) and Section 9-316(d) and (e), duration and renewal of perfection of a security interest perfected by compliance with the requirements prescribed by a statute, regulation, or treaty described in subsection (a) are governed by the statute, regulation, or treaty. In other respects, the security interest is subject to this article.

(d) **[Inapplicability to certain inventory.]** During any period in which collateral subject to a statute specified in subsection (a)(2) is inventory held for sale or lease by a person or leased by that person as lessor and that person is in the business of selling goods of that kind, this section does not apply to a security interest in that collateral created by that person.

**§9-312. Perfection of Security Interests in Chattel Paper, Deposit Accounts, Documents, Goods Covered by Documents, Instruments, Investment Property, Letter-of-Credit Rights, and Money; Perfection by Permissive Filing; Temporary Perfection Without Filing or Transfer of Possession.**

(a) **[Perfection by filing permitted.]** A security interest in chattel paper, negotiable documents, instruments, or investment property may be perfected by filing.

(b) **[Control or possession of certain collateral.]** Except as otherwise provided in Section 9-315(c) and (d) for proceeds:
(1) a security interest in a deposit account may be perfected only by control under Section 9-314;
(2) and except as otherwise provided in Section 9-308(d), a security interest in a letter-of-credit right may be perfected only by control under Section 9-314; and
(3) a security interest in money may be perfected only by the secured party's taking possession under Section 9-313.

(c) **[Goods covered by negotiable document.]** While goods are in the possession of a bailee that has issued a negotiable document covering the goods:
(1) a security interest in the goods may be perfected by perfecting a security interest in the document; and
(2) a security interest perfected in the document has priority over any security interest that becomes perfected in the goods by another method during that time.

(d) **[Goods covered by nonnegotiable document.]** While goods are in the possession of a bailee that has issued a nonnegotiable document covering the goods, a security interest in the goods may be perfected by:
(1) issuance of a document in the name of the secured party;
(2) the bailee's receipt of notification of the secured party's interest; or
(3) filing as to the goods.

(e) **[Temporary perfection: new value.]** A security interest in certificated securities, negotiable documents, or instruments is perfected without filing or the taking of possession for a period of 20 days from the time it attaches to the extent that it arises for new value given under an authenticated security agreement.

(f) **[Temporary perfection: goods or documents made available to debtor.]** A perfected security interest in a negotiable document or goods in possession of a bailee, other than one that has issued a negotiable document for the goods, remains perfected for 20 days without filing if the secured party makes available to the debtor the goods or documents representing the goods for the purpose of:
(1) ultimate sale or exchange; or
(2) loading, unloading, storing, shipping, transshipping, manufacturing, processing, or otherwise dealing with them in a manner preliminary to their sale or exchange.

(g) **[Temporary perfection: delivery of security certificate or instrument to debtor.]** A perfected security interest in a certificated security or instrument remains perfected for 20 days without filing if the secured party delivers the security certificate or instrument to the debtor for the purpose of:

(1) ultimate sale or exchange; or

(2) presentation, collection, enforcement, renewal, or registration of transfer.

(h) **[Expiration of temporary perfection.]** After the 20-day period specified in subsection (e), (f), or (g) expires, perfection depends upon compliance with this article.

**§9-313. When Possession by or Delivery to Secured Party Perfects Security Interest Without Filing.**

(a) **[Perfection by possession or delivery.]** Except as otherwise provided in subsection (b), a secured party may perfect a security interest in negotiable documents, goods, instruments, money, or tangible chattel paper by taking possession of the collateral. A secured party may perfect a security interest in certificated securities by taking delivery of the certificated securities under Section 8-301.

(b) **[Goods covered by certificate of title.]** With respect to goods covered by a certificate of title issued by this State, a secured party may perfect a security interest in the goods by taking possession of the goods only in the circumstances described in Section 9-316(d).

(c) **[Collateral in possession of person other than debtor.]** With respect to collateral other than certificated securities and goods covered by a document, a secured party takes possession of collateral in the possession of a person other than the debtor, the secured party, or a lessee of the collateral from the debtor in the ordinary course of the debtor's business, when:

(1) the person in possession authenticates a record acknowledging that it holds possession of the collateral for the secured party's benefit; or

(2) the person takes possession of the collateral after having authenticated a record acknowledging that it will hold possession of collateral for the secured party's benefit.

(d) **[Time of perfection by possession; continuation of perfection.]** If perfection of a security interest depends upon possession of the collateral by a secured party, perfection occurs no earlier than the time the secured party takes possession and continues only while the secured party retains possession.

(e) **[Time of perfection by delivery; continuation of perfection.]** A security interest in a certificated security in registered form is perfected by delivery when delivery of the certificated security occurs under Section 8-301 and remains perfected by delivery until the debtor obtains possession of the security certificate.

(f) **[Acknowledgment not required.]** A person in possession of collateral is not required to acknowledge that it holds possession for a secured party's benefit.

(g) **[Effectiveness of acknowledgment; no duties or confirmation.]** If a person acknowledges that it holds possession for the secured party's benefit:

(1) the acknowledgment is effective under subsection (c) or Section 8-301(a), even if the acknowledgment violates the rights of a debtor; and

(2) unless the person otherwise agrees or law other than this article otherwise provides, the person does not owe any duty to the secured party and is not required to confirm the acknowledgment to another person.

(h) **[Secured party's delivery to person other than debtor.]** A secured party having possession of collateral does not relinquish possession by delivering the collateral to a person other than the debtor or a lessee of the collateral from the debtor in the ordinary course of the debtor's business if the person was instructed before the delivery or is instructed contemporaneously with the delivery:

(1) to hold possession of the collateral for the secured party's benefit; or

(2) to redeliver the collateral to the secured party.

(i) **[Effect of delivery under subsection (h); no duties or confirmation.]** A secured party does not relinquish possession, even if a delivery under subsection (h) violates the rights of a debtor. A person to which collateral is delivered under subsection (h) does not owe any duty to the secured party and is not required to confirm the delivery to another person unless the person otherwise agrees or law other than this article otherwise provides.

**§9-314. Perfection by Control.**

(a) **[Perfection by control.]** A security interest in investment property, deposit accounts, letter-of-credit rights, or electronic chattel paper may be perfected by control of the collateral under Section 9-104, 9-105, 9-106, or 9-107.

(b) **[Specified collateral: time of perfection by control; continuation of perfection.]** A security interest in deposit accounts, electronic chattel paper, or letter-of-credit rights is perfected by control under Section 9-104, 9-105, or 9-107 when the secured party obtains control and remains perfected by control only while the secured party retains control.

(c) **[Investment property: time of perfection by control; continuation of perfection.]** A security interest in investment property is perfected by control under Section 9-106 from the time the secured party obtains control and remains perfected by control until:

(1) the secured party does not have control; and

(2) one of the following occurs:

(A) if the collateral is a certificated security, the debtor has or acquires possession of the security certificate;

(B) if the collateral is an uncertificated security, the issuer has registered or registers the debtor as the registered owner; or

(C) if the collateral is a security entitlement, the debtor is or becomes the entitlement holder.

**§9-315. Secured Party's Rights on Disposition of Collateral and in Proceeds.**

(a) **[Disposition of collateral: continuation of security interest or agricultural lien; proceeds.]** Except as otherwise provided in this article and in Section 2-403(2):

(1) a security interest or agricultural lien continues in collateral notwithstanding sale, lease, license, exchange, or other disposition thereof unless the secured party authorized the disposition free of the security interest or agricultural lien; and

(2) a security interest attaches to any identifiable proceeds of collateral.

(b) **[When commingled proceeds identifiable.]** Proceeds that are commingled with other property are identifiable proceeds:

(1) if the proceeds are goods, to the extent provided by Section 9-336; and

(2) if the proceeds are not goods, to the extent that the secured party identifies the proceeds by a method of tracing, including application of equitable principles, that is permitted under law other than this article with respect to commingled property of the type involved.

(c) **[Perfection of security interest in proceeds.]** A security interest in proceeds is a perfected security interest if the security interest in the original collateral was perfected.

(d) **[Continuation of perfection.]** A perfected security interest in proceeds becomes unperfected on the 21st day after the security interest attaches to the proceeds unless:

(1) the following conditions are satisfied:

(A) a filed financing statement covers the original collateral;

(B) the proceeds are collateral in which a security interest may be perfected by filing in the office in which the financing statement has been filed; and

(C) the proceeds are not acquired with cash proceeds;

(2) the proceeds are identifiable cash proceeds; or

(3) the security interest in the proceeds is perfected other than under subsection (c) when the security interest attaches to the proceeds or within 20 days thereafter.

(e) **[When perfected security interest in proceeds becomes unperfected.]** If a filed financing statement covers the original collateral, a security interest in proceeds which remains perfected under subsection (d)(1) becomes unperfected at the later of:

(1) when the effectiveness of the filed financing statement lapses under Section 9-515 or is terminated under Section 9-513; or

(2) the 21st day after the security interest attaches to the proceeds.

**§9-316. Continued Perfection of Security Interest Following Change in Governing Law.**

(a) **[General rule: effect on perfection of change in governing law.]** A security interest perfected pursuant to the law of the jurisdiction designated in Section 9-301(1) or 9-305(c) remains perfected until the earliest of:

(1) the time perfection would have ceased under the law of that jurisdiction;

(2) the expiration of four months after a change of the debtor's location to another jurisdiction; or

(3) the expiration of one year after a transfer of collateral to a person that thereby becomes a debtor and is located in another jurisdiction.

(b) **[Security interest perfected or unperfected under law of new jurisdiction.]** If a security interest described in subsection (a) becomes perfected under the law of the other jurisdiction before the earliest time or event described in that subsection, it remains perfected thereafter. If the security interest does not become perfected under the law of the other jurisdiction before the earliest time or event, it becomes unperfected and is deemed never to have been perfected as against a purchaser of the collateral for value.

(c) **[Possessory security interest in collateral moved to new jurisdiction.]** A possessory security interest in collateral, other than goods covered by a certificate of title and as-extracted collateral consisting of goods, remains continuously perfected if:

(1) the collateral is located in one jurisdiction and subject to a security interest perfected under the law of that jurisdiction;

(2) thereafter the collateral is brought into another jurisdiction; and

(3) upon entry into the other jurisdiction, the security interest is perfected under the law of the other jurisdiction.

(d) **[Goods covered by certificate of title from this state.]** Except as otherwise provided in subsection (e), a security interest in goods covered by a certificate of title which is perfected by any method under the law of another jurisdiction when the goods become covered by a certificate of title from this State remains perfected until the security interest would have become unperfected under the law of the other jurisdiction had the goods not become so covered.

(e) **[When subsection (d) security interest becomes unperfected against purchasers.]** A security interest described in subsection (d) becomes unperfected as against a purchaser of the goods for value and is deemed never to have been perfected as against a purchaser of the goods for value if the applicable requirements for perfection under Section 9-311(b) or 9-313 are not satisfied before the earlier of:

(1) the time the security interest would have become unperfected under the law of the other jurisdiction had the goods not become covered by a certificate of title from this State; or

(2) the expiration of four months after the goods had become so covered.

(f) **[Change in jurisdiction of bank, issuer, nominated person, securities intermediary, or commodity intermediary.]** A security interest in deposit accounts, letter-of-credit rights, or investment property which is perfected under the law of the bank's jurisdiction, the issuer's jurisdiction, a nominated person's jurisdiction, the securities intermediary's jurisdiction, or the commodity intermediary's jurisdiction, as applicable, remains perfected until the earlier of:

(1) the time the security interest would have become unperfected under the law of that jurisdiction; or

(2) the expiration of four months after a change of the applicable jurisdiction to another jurisdiction.

(g) **[Subsection (f) security interest perfected or unperfected under law of new jurisdiction.]** If a security interest described in subsection (f) becomes perfected under the law of the other jurisdiction before the earlier of the time or the end of the period described in that subsection, it remains perfected thereafter. If the security interest does not become perfected under the law of the other jurisdiction before the earlier of that time or the end of that period, it becomes unperfected and is deemed never to have been perfected as against a purchaser of the collateral for value.

**§9-317. Interests That Take Priority over or Take Free of Security Interest or Agricultural Lien.**

(a) **[Conflicting security interests and rights of lien creditors.]** A security interest or agricultural lien is subordinate to the rights of:

(1) a person entitled to priority under Section 9-322; and

(2) except as otherwise provided in subsection (e), a person that becomes a lien creditor before the earlier of the time:

(A) the security interest or agricultural lien is perfected; or

(B) one of the conditions specified in Section 9-203(b)(3) is met and a financing statement covering the collateral is filed.

(b) **[Buyers that receive delivery.]** Except as otherwise provided in subsection (e), a buyer, other than a secured party, of tangible chattel paper, documents, goods, instruments, or a security certificate takes free of a security interest or agricultural lien if the buyer gives value and receives delivery of the collateral without knowledge of the security interest or agricultural lien and before it is perfected.

(c) **[Lessees that receive delivery.]** Except as otherwise provided in subsection (e), a lessee of goods takes free of a security interest or agricultural lien if the lessee gives value and receives delivery of the collateral without knowledge of the security interest or agricultural lien and before it is perfected.

(d) **[Licensees and buyers of certain collateral.]** A licensee of a general intangible or a buyer, other than a secured party, of accounts, electronic chattel paper, general intangibles, or investment property other than a certificated security takes free of a security interest if the licensee or buyer gives value without knowledge of the security interest and before it is perfected.

(e) **[Purchase-money security interest.]** Except as otherwise provided in Sections 9-320 and 9-321, if a person files a financing statement with respect to a purchase-money security interest before or within 20 days after the debtor receives delivery of the collateral, the security interest takes priority over the rights of a buyer, lessee, or lien creditor which arise between the time the security interest attaches and the time of filing.

**§9-318. No Interest Retained in Right to Payment That Is Sold; Rights and Title of Seller of Account or Chattel Paper with Respect to Creditors and Purchasers.**

(a) **[Seller retains no interest.]** A debtor that has sold an account, chattel paper, payment intangible, or promissory note does not retain a legal or equitable interest in the collateral sold.

(b) **[Deemed rights of debtor if buyer's security interest unperfected.]** For purposes of determining the rights of creditors of, and purchasers for value of an account or chattel paper from, a debtor that has sold an account or chattel paper, while the buyer's security interest is unperfected, the debtor is deemed to have rights and title to the account or chattel paper identical to those the debtor sold.

**§9-319. Rights and Title of Consignee with Respect to Creditors and Purchasers.**

(a) **[Consignee has consignor's rights.]** Except as otherwise provided in subsection (b), for purposes of determining the rights of creditors of, and purchasers for value of goods from, a consignee, while the goods are in the possession of the consignee, the consignee is deemed to have rights and title to the goods identical to those the consignor had or had power to transfer.

(b) **[Applicability of other law.]** For purposes of determining the rights of a creditor of a consignee, law other than this article determines the rights and title of a consignee while goods are in the consignee's possession if, under this part, a perfected security interest held by the consignor would have priority over the rights of the creditor.

**§9-320. Buyer of Goods.**
(a) **[Buyer in ordinary course of business.]** Except as otherwise provided in subsection (e), a buyer in ordinary course of business, other than a person buying farm products from a person engaged in farming operations, takes free of a security interest created by the buyer's seller, even if the security interest is perfected and the buyer knows of its existence.
(b) **[Buyer of consumer goods.]** Except as otherwise provided in subsection (e), a buyer of goods from a person who used or bought the goods for use primarily for personal, family, or household purposes takes free of a security interest, even if perfected, if the buyer buys:
(1) without knowledge of the security interest;
(2) for value;
(3) primarily for the buyer's personal, family, or household purposes; and
(4) before the filing of a financing statement covering the goods.
(c) **[Effectiveness of filing for subsection (b).]** To the extent that it affects the priority of a security interest over a buyer of goods under subsection (b), the period of effectiveness of a filing made in the jurisdiction in which the seller is located is governed by Section 9-316(a) and (b).
(d) **[Buyer in ordinary course of business at wellhead or minehead.]** A buyer in ordinary course of business buying oil, gas, or other minerals at the wellhead or minehead or after extraction takes free of an interest arising out of an encumbrance.
(e) **[Possessory security interest not affected.]** Subsections (a) and (b) do not affect a security interest in goods in the possession of the secured party under Section 9-313.

**§9-321. Licensee of General Intangible and Lessee of Goods in Ordinary Course of Business.**
(a) **["Licensee in ordinary course of business."]** In this section, "licensee in ordinary course of business" means a person that becomes a licensee of a general intangible in good faith, without knowledge that the license violates the rights of another person in the general intangible, and in the ordinary course from a person in the business of licensing general intangibles of that kind. A person becomes a licensee in the ordinary course if the license to the person comports with the usual or customary practices in the kind of business in which the licensor is engaged or with the licensor's own usual or customary practices.
(b) **[Rights of licensee in ordinary course of business.]** A licensee in ordinary course of business takes its rights under a nonexclusive license free of a security interest in the general intangible created by the licensor, even if the security interest is perfected and the licensee knows of its existence.
(c) **[Rights of lessee in ordinary course of business.]** A lessee in ordinary course of business takes its leasehold interest free of a security interest in the goods created by the lessor, even if the security interest is perfected and the lessee knows of its existence.

**§9-322. Priorities among Conflicting Security Interests in and Agricultural Liens on Same Collateral.**
(a) **[General priority rules.]** Except as otherwise provided in this section, priority among conflicting security interests and agricultural liens in the same collateral is determined according to the following rules:
(1) Conflicting perfected security interests and agricultural liens rank according to priority in time of filing or perfection. Priority dates from the earlier of the time a filing covering the collateral is first made or the security interest or agricultural lien is first perfected, if there is no period thereafter when there is neither filing nor perfection.
(2) A perfected security interest or agricultural lien has priority over a conflicting unperfected security interest or agricultural lien.
(3) The first security interest or agricultural lien to attach or become effective has priority if conflicting security interests and agricultural liens are unperfected.
(b) **[Time of perfection: proceeds and supporting obligations.]** For the purposes of subsection (a)(1):
(1) the time of filing or perfection as to a security interest in collateral is also the time of filing or perfection as to a security interest in proceeds; and
(2) the time of filing or perfection as to a security interest in collateral supported by a supporting obligation is also the time of filing or perfection as to a security interest in the supporting obligation.
(c) **[Special priority rules: proceeds and supporting obligations.]** Except as otherwise provided in subsection (f), a security interest in collateral which qualifies for priority over a conflicting security interest under Section 9-327, 9-328, 9-329, 9-330, or 9-331 also has priority over a conflicting security interest in:
(1) any supporting obligation for the collateral; and
(2) proceeds of the collateral if:
(A) the security interest in proceeds is perfected;
(B) the proceeds are cash proceeds or of the same type as the collateral; and
(C) in the case of proceeds that are proceeds of proceeds, all intervening proceeds are cash proceeds, proceeds of the same type as the collateral, or an account relating to the collateral.
(d) **[First-to-file priority rule for certain collateral.]** Subject to subsection (e) and except as otherwise provided in subsection (f), if a security interest in chattel paper, deposit accounts, negotiable documents, instruments, investment property, or letter-of-credit rights is perfected by a method other than filing, conflicting perfected security interests in proceeds of the collateral rank according to priority in time of filing.
(e) **[Applicability of subsection (d).]** Subsection (d) applies only if the proceeds of the collateral are not cash proceeds, chattel paper, negotiable documents, instruments, investment property, or letter-of-credit rights.
(f) **[Limitations on subsections (a) through (e).]** Subsections (a) through (e) are subject to:
(1) subsection (g) and the other provisions of this part;
(2) Section 4-210 with respect to a security interest of a collecting bank;
(3) Section 5-118 with respect to a security interest of an issuer or nominated person; and
(4) Section 9-110 with respect to a security interest arising under Article 2 or 2A.
(g) **[Priority under agricultural lien statute.]** A perfected agricultural lien on collateral has priority over a conflicting security interest in or agricultural lien on the same collateral if the statute creating the agricultural lien so provides.

**§9-323. Future Advances.**
(a) **[When priority based on time of advance.]** Except as otherwise provided in subsection (c), for purposes of determining the priority of a perfected security interest under Section 9-322(a)(1), perfection of the security interest dates from the time an advance is made to the extent that the security interest secures an advance that:
(1) is made while the security interest is perfected only:
(A) under Section 9-309 when it attaches; or
(B) temporarily under Section 9-312(e), (f), or (g); and
(2) is not made pursuant to a commitment entered into before or while the security interest is perfected by a method other than under Section 9-309 or 9-312(e), (f), or (g).
(b) **[Lien creditor.]** Except as otherwise provided in subsection (c), a security interest is subordinate to the rights of a person that becomes a lien creditor to the extent that the security interest secures an advance made more than 45 days after the person becomes a lien creditor unless the advance is made:
(1) without knowledge of the lien; or
(2) pursuant to a commitment entered into without knowledge of the lien.

(c) **[Buyer of receivables.]** Subsections (a) and (b) do not apply to a security interest held by a secured party that is a buyer of accounts, chattel paper, payment intangibles, or promissory notes or a consignor.
(d) **[Buyer of goods.]** Except as otherwise provided in subsection (e), a buyer of goods other than a buyer in ordinary course of business takes free of a security interest to the extent that it secures advances made after the earlier of:
(1) the time the secured party acquires knowledge of the buyer's purchase; or
(2) 45 days after the purchase.
(e) **[Advances made pursuant to commitment: priority of buyer of goods.]** Subsection (d) does not apply if the advance is made pursuant to a commitment entered into without knowledge of the buyer's purchase and before the expiration of the 45-day period.
(f) **[Lessee of goods.]** Except as otherwise provided in subsection (g), a lessee of goods, other than a lessee in ordinary course of business, takes the leasehold interest free of a security interest to the extent that it secures advances made after the earlier of:
(1) the time the secured party acquires knowledge of the lease; or
(2) 45 days after the lease contract becomes enforceable.
(g) **[Advances made pursuant to commitment: priority of lessee of goods.]** Subsection (f) does not apply if the advance is made pursuant to a commitment entered into without knowledge of the lease and before the expiration of the 45-day period.

**§9-324. Priority of Purchase-Money Security Interests.**
(a) **[General rule: purchase-money priority.]** Except as otherwise provided in subsection (g), a perfected purchase-money security interest in goods other than inventory or livestock has priority over a conflicting security interest in the same goods, and, except as otherwise provided in Section 9-327, a perfected security interest in its identifiable proceeds also has priority, if the purchase-money security interest is perfected when the debtor receives possession of the collateral or within 20 days thereafter.
(b) **[Inventory purchase-money priority.]** Subject to subsection (c) and except as otherwise provided in subsection (g), a perfected purchase-money security interest in inventory has priority over a conflicting security interest in the same inventory, has priority over a conflicting security interest in chattel paper or an instrument constituting proceeds of the inventory and in proceeds of the chattel paper, if so provided in Section 9-330, and, except as otherwise provided in Section 9-327, also has priority in identifiable cash proceeds of the inventory to the extent the identifiable cash proceeds are received on or before the delivery of the inventory to a buyer, if:
(1) the purchase-money security interest is perfected when the debtor receives possession of the inventory;
(2) the purchase-money secured party sends an authenticated notification to the holder of the conflicting security interest;
(3) the holder of the conflicting security interest receives the notification within five years before the debtor receives possession of the inventory; and
(4) the notification states that the person sending the notification has or expects to acquire a purchase-money security interest in inventory of the debtor and describes the inventory.
(c) **[Holders of conflicting inventory security interests to be notified.]** Subsections (b)(2) through (4) apply only if the holder of the conflicting security interest had filed a financing statement covering the same types of inventory:
(1) if the purchase-money security interest is perfected by filing, before the date of the filing; or
(2) if the purchase-money security interest is temporarily perfected without filing or possession under Section 9-312(f), before the beginning of the 20-day period thereunder.
(d) **[Livestock purchase-money priority.]** Subject to subsection (e) and except as otherwise provided in subsection (g), a perfected purchase-money security interest in livestock that are farm products has priority over a conflicting security interest in the same livestock, and, except as otherwise provided in Section 9-327, a perfected security interest in their identifiable proceeds and identifiable products in their unmanufactured states also has priority, if:
(1) the purchase-money security interest is perfected when the debtor receives possession of the livestock;
(2) the purchase-money secured party sends an authenticated notification to the holder of the conflicting security interest;
(3) the holder of the conflicting security interest receives the notification within six months before the debtor receives possession of the livestock; and
(4) the notification states that the person sending the notification has or expects to acquire a purchase-money security interest in livestock of the debtor and describes the livestock.
(e) **[Holders of conflicting livestock security interests to be notified.]** Subsections (d)(2) through (4) apply only if the holder of the conflicting security interest had filed a financing statement covering the same types of livestock:
(1) if the purchase-money security interest is perfected by filing, before the date of the filing; or
(2) if the purchase-money security interest is temporarily perfected without filing or possession under Section 9-312(f), before the beginning of the 20-day period thereunder.
(f) **[Software purchase-money priority.]** Except as otherwise provided in subsection (g), a perfected purchase-money security interest in software has priority over a conflicting security interest in the same collateral, and, except as otherwise provided in Section 9-327, a perfected security interest in its identifiable proceeds also has priority, to the extent that the purchase-money security interest in the goods in which the software was acquired for use has priority in the goods and proceeds of the goods under this section.
(g) **[Conflicting purchase-money security interests.]** If more than one security interest qualifies for priority in the same collateral under subsection (a), (b), (d), or (f):
(1) a security interest securing an obligation incurred as all or part of the price of the collateral has priority over a security interest securing an obligation incurred for value given to enable the debtor to acquire rights in or the use of collateral; and
(2) in all other cases, Section 9-322(a) applies to the qualifying security interests.

**§9-325. Priority of Security Interests in Transferred Collateral.**
(a) **[Subordination of security interest in transferred collateral.]** Except as otherwise provided in subsection (b), a security interest created by a debtor is subordinate to a security interest in the same collateral created by another person if:
(1) the debtor acquired the collateral subject to the security interest created by the other person;
(2) the security interest created by the other person was perfected when the debtor acquired the collateral; and
(3) there is no period thereafter when the security interest is unperfected.
(b) **[Limitation of subsection (a) subordination.]** Subsection (a) subordinates a security interest only if the security interest:
(1) otherwise would have priority solely under Section 9-322(a) or 9-324; or
(2) arose solely under Section 2-711(3) or 2A-508(5).

**§9-326. Priority of Security Interests Created by New Debtor.**
(a) **[Subordination of security interest created by new debtor.]** Subject to subsection (b), a security interest created by a new debtor which is perfected by a filed financing statement that is effective solely under Section 9-508 in collateral in which a new debtor has or acquires rights is subordinate to a security interest in the same collateral which is perfected other

than by a filed financing statement that is effective solely under Section 9-508.

(b) **[Priority under other provisions; multiple original debtors.]** The other provisions of this part determine the priority among conflicting security interests in the same collateral perfected by filed financing statements that are effective solely under Section 9-508. However, if the security agreements to which a new debtor became bound as debtor were not entered into by the same original debtor, the conflicting security interests rank according to priority in time of the new debtor's having become bound.

**§9-327. Priority of Security Interests in Deposit Account.**
The following rules govern priority among conflicting security interests in the same deposit account:

(1) A security interest held by a secured party having control of the deposit account under Section 9-104 has priority over a conflicting security interest held by a secured party that does not have control.

(2) Except as otherwise provided in paragraphs (3) and (4), security interests perfected by control under Section 9-314 rank according to priority in time of obtaining control.

(3) Except as otherwise provided in paragraph (4), a security interest held by the bank with which the deposit account is maintained has priority over a conflicting security interest held by another secured party.

(4) A security interest perfected by control under Section 9-104(a)(3) has priority over a security interest held by the bank with which the deposit account is maintained.

**§9-328. Priority of Security Interests in Investment Property.**
The following rules govern priority among conflicting security interests in the same investment property:

(1) A security interest held by a secured party having control of investment property under Section 9-106 has priority over a security interest held by a secured party that does not have control of the investment property.

(2) Except as otherwise provided in paragraphs (3) and (4), conflicting security interests held by secured parties each of which has control under Section 9-106 rank according to priority in time of:

(A) if the collateral is a security, obtaining control;

(B) if the collateral is a security entitlement carried in a securities account and:

(i) if the secured party obtained control under Section 8-106(d)(1), the secured party's becoming the person for which the securities account is maintained;

(ii) if the secured party obtained control under Section 8-106(d)(2), the securities intermediary's agreement to comply with the secured party's entitlement orders with respect to security entitlements carried or to be carried in the securities account; or

(iii) if the secured party obtained control through another person under Section 8-106(d)(3), the time on which priority would be based under this paragraph if the other person were the secured party; or

(C) if the collateral is a commodity contract carried with a commodity intermediary, the satisfaction of the requirement for control specified in Section 9-106(b)(2) with respect to commodity contracts carried or to be carried with the commodity intermediary.

(3) A security interest held by a securities intermediary in a security entitlement or a securities account maintained with the securities intermediary has priority over a conflicting security interest held by another secured party.

(4) A security interest held by a commodity intermediary in a commodity contract or a commodity account maintained with the commodity intermediary has priority over a conflicting security interest held by another secured party.

(5) A security interest in a certificated security in registered form which is perfected by taking delivery under Section 9-313(a) and not by control under Section 9-314 has priority over a conflicting security interest perfected by a method other than control.

(6) Conflicting security interests created by a broker, securities intermediary, or commodity intermediary which are perfected without control under Section 9-106 rank equally.

(7) In all other cases, priority among conflicting security interests in investment property is governed by Sections 9-322 and 9-323.

**§9-329. Priority of Security Interests in Letter-of-Credit Right.**
The following rules govern priority among conflicting security interests in the same letter-of-credit right:

(1) A security interest held by a secured party having control of the letter-of-credit right under Section 9-107 has priority to the extent of its control over a conflicting security interest held by a secured party that does not have control.

(2) Security interests perfected by control under Section 9-314 rank according to priority in time of obtaining control.

**§9-330. Priority of Purchaser of Chattel Paper or Instrument.**
(a) **[Purchaser's priority: security interest claimed merely as proceeds.]** A purchaser of chattel paper has priority over a security interest in the chattel paper which is claimed merely as proceeds of inventory subject to a security interest if:

(1) in good faith and in the ordinary course of the purchaser's business, the purchaser gives new value and takes possession of the chattel paper or obtains control of the chattel paper under Section 9-105; and

(2) the chattel paper does not indicate that it has been assigned to an identified assignee other than the purchaser.

(b) **[Purchaser's priority: other security interests.]** A purchaser of chattel paper has priority over a security interest in the chattel paper which is claimed other than merely as proceeds of inventory subject to a security interest if the purchaser gives new value and takes possession of the chattel paper or obtains control of the chattel paper under Section 9-105 in good faith, in the ordinary course of the purchaser's business, and without knowledge that the purchase violates the rights of the secured party.

(c) **[Chattel paper purchaser's priority in proceeds.]** Except as otherwise provided in Section 9-327, a purchaser having priority in chattel paper under subsection (a) or (b) also has priority in proceeds of the chattel paper to the extent that:

(1) Section 9-322 provides for priority in the proceeds; or

(2) the proceeds consist of the specific goods covered by the chattel paper or cash proceeds of the specific goods, even if the purchaser's security interest in the proceeds is unperfected.

(d) **[Instrument purchaser's priority.]** Except as otherwise provided in Section 9-331(a), a purchaser of an instrument has priority over a security interest in the instrument perfected by a method other than possession if the purchaser gives value and takes possession of the instrument in good faith and without knowledge that the purchase violates the rights of the secured party.

(e) **[Holder of purchase-money security interest gives new value.]** For purposes of subsections (a) and (b), the holder of a purchase-money security interest in inventory gives new value for chattel paper constituting proceeds of the inventory.

(f) **[Indication of assignment gives knowledge.]** For purposes of subsections (b) and (d), if chattel paper or an instrument indicates that it has been assigned to an identified secured party other than the purchaser, a purchaser of the chattel paper or instrument has knowledge that the purchase violates the rights of the secured party.

**§9-331. Priority of Rights of Purchasers of Instruments, Documents, and Securities under Other Articles; Priority of Interests in Financial Assets and Security Entitlements under Article 8.**
(a) **[Rights under Articles 3, 7, and 8 not limited.]** This article does not limit the rights of a holder in due course of a negotiable instrument, a

holder to which a negotiable document of title has been duly negotiated, or a protected purchaser of a security. These holders or purchasers take priority over an earlier security interest, even if perfected, to the extent provided in Articles 3, 7, and 8.
(b) **[Protection under Article 8.]** This article does not limit the rights of or impose liability on a person to the extent that the person is protected against the assertion of a claim under Article 8.
(c) **[Filing not notice.]** Filing under this article does not constitute notice of a claim or defense to the holders, or purchasers, or persons described in subsections (a) and (b).

**§9-332. Transfer of Money; Transfer of Funds from Deposit Account.**
(a) **[Transferee of money.]** A transferee of money takes the money free of a security interest unless the transferee acts in collusion with the debtor in violating the rights of the secured party.
(b) **[Transferee of funds from deposit account.]** A transferee of funds from a deposit account takes the funds free of a security interest in the deposit account unless the transferee acts in collusion with the debtor in violating the rights of the secured party.

**§9-333. Priority of Certain Liens Arising by Operation of Law.**
(a) **["Possessory lien."]** In this section, "possessory lien" means an interest, other than a security interest or an agricultural lien:
(1) which secures payment or performance of an obligation for services or materials furnished with respect to goods by a person in the ordinary course of the person's business;
(2) which is created by statute or rule of law in favor of the person; and
(3) whose effectiveness depends on the person's possession of the goods.
(b) **[Priority of possessory lien.]** A possessory lien on goods has priority over a security interest in the goods unless the lien is created by a statute that expressly provides otherwise.

**§9-334. Priority of Security Interests in Fixtures and Crops.**
(a) **[Security interest in fixtures under this article.]** A security interest under this article may be created in goods that are fixtures or may continue in goods that become fixtures. A security interest does not exist under this article in ordinary building materials incorporated into an improvement on land.
(b) **[Security interest in fixtures under real-property law.]** This article does not prevent creation of an encumbrance upon fixtures under real property law.
(c) **[General rule: subordination of security interest in fixtures.]** In cases not governed by subsections (d) through (h), a security interest in fixtures is subordinate to a conflicting interest of an encumbrancer or owner of the related real property other than the debtor.
(d) **[Fixtures purchase-money priority.]** Except as otherwise provided in subsection (h), a perfected security interest in fixtures has priority over a conflicting interest of an encumbrancer or owner of the real property if the debtor has an interest of record in or is in possession of the real property and:
(1) the security interest is a purchase-money security interest;
(2) the interest of the encumbrancer or owner arises before the goods become fixtures; and
(3) the security interest is perfected by a fixture filing before the goods become fixtures or within 20 days thereafter.
(e) **[Priority of security interest in fixtures over interests in real property.]** A perfected security interest in fixtures has priority over a conflicting interest of an encumbrancer or owner of the real property if:
(1) the debtor has an interest of record in the real property or is in possession of the real property and the security interest:
(A) is perfected by a fixture filing before the interest of the encumbrancer or owner is of record; and
(B) has priority over any conflicting interest of a predecessor in title of the encumbrancer or owner;
(2) before the goods become fixtures, the security interest is perfected by any method permitted by this article and the fixtures are readily removable:
(A) factory or office machines;
(B) equipment that is not primarily used or leased for use in the operation of the real property; or
(C) replacements of domestic appliances that are consumer goods;
(3) the conflicting interest is a lien on the real property obtained by legal or equitable proceedings after the security interest was perfected by any method permitted by this article; or
(4) the security interest is:
(A) created in a manufactured home in a manufactured-home transaction; and
(B) perfected pursuant to a statute described in Section 9-311(a)(2).
(f) **[Priority based on consent, disclaimer, or right to remove.]** A security interest in fixtures, whether or not perfected, has priority over a conflicting interest of an encumbrancer or owner of the real property if:
(1) the encumbrancer or owner has, in an authenticated record, consented to the security interest or disclaimed an interest in the goods as fixtures; or
(2) the debtor has a right to remove the goods as against the encumbrancer or owner.
(g) **[Continuation of paragraph (f)(2) priority.]** The priority of the security interest under paragraph (f)(2) continues for a reasonable time if the debtor's right to remove the goods as against the encumbrancer or owner terminates.
(h) **[Priority of construction mortgage.]** A mortgage is a construction mortgage to the extent that it secures an obligation incurred for the construction of an improvement on land, including the acquisition cost of the land, if a recorded record of the mortgage so indicates. Except as otherwise provided in subsections (e) and (f), a security interest in fixtures is subordinate to a construction mortgage if a record of the mortgage is recorded before the goods become fixtures and the goods become fixtures before the completion of the construction. A mortgage has this priority to the same extent as a construction mortgage to the extent that it is given to refinance a construction mortgage.
(i) **[Priority of security interest in crops.]** A perfected security interest in crops growing on real property has priority over a conflicting interest of an encumbrancer or owner of the real property if the debtor has an interest of record in or is in possession of the real property.
(j) **[Subsection (i) prevails.]** Subsection (i) prevails over any inconsistent provisions of the following statutes:

**§9-335. Accessions.**
(a) **[Creation of security interest in accession.]** A security interest may be created in an accession and continues in collateral that becomes an accession.
(b) **[Perfection of security interest.]** If a security interest is perfected when the collateral becomes an accession, the security interest remains perfected in the collateral.
(c) **[Priority of security interest.]** Except as otherwise provided in subsection (d), the other provisions of this part determine the priority of a security interest in an accession.
(d) **[Compliance with certificate-of-title statute.]** A security interest in an accession is subordinate to a security interest in the whole which is perfected by compliance with the requirements of a certificate-of-title statute under Section 9-311(b).
(e) **[Removal of accession after default.]** After default, subject to Part 6, a secured party may remove an accession from other goods if the security interest in the accession has priority over the claims of every person having an interest in the whole.
(f) **[Reimbursement following removal.]** A secured party that removes an accession from other goods under subsection (e) shall promptly reimburse any holder of a security interest or other lien on, or owner of, the

whole or of the other goods, other than the debtor, for the cost of repair of any physical injury to the whole or the other goods. The secured party need not reimburse the holder or owner for any diminution in value of the whole or the other goods caused by the absence of the accession removed or by any necessity for replacing it. A person entitled to reimbursement may refuse permission to remove until the secured party gives adequate assurance for the performance of the obligation to reimburse.

**§9-336. Commingled Goods.**
(a) **["Commingled goods."]** In this section, "commingled goods" means goods that are physically united with other goods in such a manner that their identity is lost in a product or mass.
(b) **[No security interest in commingled goods as such.]** A security interest does not exist in commingled goods as such. However, a security interest may attach to a product or mass that results when goods become commingled goods.
(c) **[Attachment of security interest to product or mass.]** If collateral becomes commingled goods, a security interest attaches to the product or mass.
(d) **[Perfection of security interest.]** If a security interest in collateral is perfected before the collateral becomes commingled goods, the security interest that attaches to the product or mass under subsection (c) is perfected.
(e) **[Priority of security interest.]** Except as otherwise provided in subsection (f), the other provisions of this part determine the priority of a security interest that attaches to the product or mass under subsection (c).
(f) **[Conflicting security interests in product or mass]** If more than one security interest attaches to the product or mass under subsection (c), the following rules determine priority:
(1) A security interest that is perfected under subsection (d) has priority over a security interest that is unperfected at the time the collateral becomes commingled goods.
(2) If more than one security interest is perfected under subsection (d), the security interests rank equally in proportion to the value of the collateral at the time it became commingled goods.

**§9-337. Priority of Security Interests in Goods Covered by Certificate of Title.**
If, while a security interest in goods is perfected by any method under the law of another jurisdiction, this State issues a certificate of title that does not show that the goods are subject to the security interest or contain a statement that they may be subject to security interests not shown on the certificate:
(1) a buyer of the goods, other than a person in the business of selling goods of that kind, takes free of the security interest if the buyer gives value and receives delivery of the goods after issuance of the certificate and without knowledge of the security interest; and
(2) the security interest is subordinate to a conflicting security interest in the goods that attaches, and is perfected under Section 9-311(b), after issuance of the certificate and without the conflicting secured party's knowledge of the security interest.

**§9-338. Priority of Security Interest or Agricultural Lien Perfected by Filed Financing Statement Providing Certain Incorrect Information.**
If a security interest or agricultural lien is perfected by a filed financing statement providing information described in Section 9-516(b)(5) which is incorrect at the time the financing statement is filed:
(1) the security interest or agricultural lien is subordinate to a conflicting perfected security interest in the collateral to the extent that the holder of the conflicting security interest gives value in reasonable reliance upon the incorrect information; and
(2) a purchaser, other than a secured party, of the collateral takes free of the security interest or agricultural lien to the extent that, in reasonable reliance upon the incorrect information, the purchaser gives value and, in the case of chattel paper, documents, goods, instruments, or a security certificate, receives delivery of the collateral.

**§9-339. Priority Subject to Subordination.**
This article does not preclude subordination by agreement by a person entitled to priority.

**§9-340. Effectiveness of Right of Recoupment or Set-Off Against Deposit Account.**
(a) **[Exercise of recoupment or set-off.]** Except as otherwise provided in subsection (c), a bank with which a deposit account is maintained may exercise any right of recoupment or set-off against a secured party that holds a security interest in the deposit account.
(b) **[Recoupment or set-off not affected by security interest.]** Except as otherwise provided in subsection (c), the application of this article to a security interest in a deposit account does not affect a right of recoupment or set-off of the secured party as to a deposit account maintained with the secured party.
(c) **[When set-off ineffective.]** The exercise by a bank of a set-off against a deposit account is ineffective against a secured party that holds a security interest in the deposit account which is perfected by control under Section 9-104(a)(3), if the set-off is based on a claim against the debtor.

**§9-341. Bank's Rights and Duties with Respect to Deposit Account.**
Except as otherwise provided in Section 9-340(c), and unless the bank otherwise agrees in an authenticated record, a bank's rights and duties with respect to a deposit account maintained with the bank are not terminated, suspended, or modified by:
(1) the creation, attachment, or perfection of a security interest in the deposit account;
(2) the bank's knowledge of the security interest; or
(3) the bank's receipt of instructions from the secured party.

**§9-342. Bank's Right to Refuse to Enter into or Disclose Existence of Control Agreement.**
This article does not require a bank to enter into an agreement of the kind described in Section 9-104(a)(2), even if its customer so requests or directs. A bank that has entered into such an agreement is not required to confirm the existence of the agreement to another person unless requested to do so by its customer.

## Part 4—Rights of Third Parties

**§9-401. Alienability of Debtor's Rights.**
(a) **[Other law governs alienability; exceptions.]** Except as otherwise provided in subsection (b) and Sections 9-406, 9-407, 9-408, and 9-409, whether a debtor's rights in collateral may be voluntarily or involuntarily transferred is governed by law other than this article.
(b) **[Agreement does not prevent transfer.]** An agreement between the debtor and secured party which prohibits a transfer of the debtor's rights in collateral or makes the transfer a default does not prevent the transfer from taking effect.

**§9-402. Secured Party Not Obligated on Contract of Debtor or in Tort.**
The existence of a security interest, agricultural lien, or authority given to a debtor to dispose of or use collateral, without more, does not subject a secured party to liability in contract or tort for the debtor's acts or omissions.

**§9-403. Agreement Not to Assert Defenses Against Assignee.**
(a) **["Value."]** In this section, "value" has the meaning provided in Section 3-303(a).
(b) **[Agreement not to assert claim or defense.]** Except as otherwise provided in this section, an agreement between an account debtor and an assignor not to assert against an assignee any claim or defense that the

account debtor may have against the assignor is enforceable by an assignee that takes an assignment:

(1) for value;

(2) in good faith;

(3) without notice of a claim of a property or possessory right to the property assigned; and

(4) without notice of a defense or claim in recoupment of the type that may be asserted against a person entitled to enforce a negotiable instrument under Section 3-305(a).

(c) **[When subsection (b) not applicable.]** Subsection (b) does not apply to defenses of a type that may be asserted against a holder in due course of a negotiable instrument under Section 3-305(b).

(d) **[Omission of required statement in consumer transaction.]** In a consumer transaction, if a record evidences the account debtor's obligation, law other than this article requires that the record include a statement to the effect that the rights of an assignee are subject to claims or defenses that the account debtor could assert against the original obligee, and the record does not include such a statement:

(1) the record has the same effect as if the record included such a statement; and

(2) the account debtor may assert against an assignee those claims and defenses that would have been available if the record included such a statement.

(e) **[Rule for individual under other law.]** This section is subject to law other than this article which establishes a different rule for an account debtor who is an individual and who incurred the obligation primarily for personal, family, or household purposes.

(f) **[Other law not displaced.]** Except as otherwise provided in subsection (d), this section does not displace law other than this article which gives effect to an agreement by an account debtor not to assert a claim or defense against an assignee.

### §9-404. Rights Acquired by Assignee; Claims and Defenses Against Assignee.

(a) **[Assignee's rights subject to terms, claims, and defenses; exceptions.]** Unless an account debtor has made an enforceable agreement not to assert defenses or claims, and subject to subsections (b) through (e), the rights of an assignee are subject to:

(1) all terms of the agreement between the account debtor and assignor and any defense or claim in recoupment arising from the transaction that gave rise to the contract; and

(2) any other defense or claim of the account debtor against the assignor which accrues before the account debtor receives a notification of the assignment authenticated by the assignor or the assignee.

(b) **[Account debtor's claim reduces amount owed to assignee.]** Subject to subsection (c) and except as otherwise provided in subsection (d), the claim of an account debtor against an assignor may be asserted against an assignee under subsection (a) only to reduce the amount the account debtor owes.

(c) **[Rule for individual under other law.]** This section is subject to law other than this article which establishes a different rule for an account debtor who is an individual and who incurred the obligation primarily for personal, family, or household purposes.

(d) **[Omission of required statement in consumer transaction.]** In a consumer transaction, if a record evidences the account debtor's obligation, law other than this article requires that the record include a statement to the effect that the account debtor's recovery against an assignee with respect to claims and defenses against the assignor may not exceed amounts paid by the account debtor under the record, and the record does not include such a statement, the extent to which a claim of an account debtor against the assignor may be asserted against an assignee is determined as if the record included such a statement.

(e) **[Inapplicability to health-care-insurance receivable.]** This section does not apply to an assignment of a health-care-insurance receivable.

### §9-405. Modification of Assigned Contract.

(a) **[Effect of modification on assignee.]** A modification of or substitution for an assigned contract is effective against an assignee if made in good faith. The assignee acquires corresponding rights under the modified or substituted contract. The assignment may provide that the modification or substitution is a breach of contract by the assignor. This subsection is subject to subsections (b) through (d).

(b) **[Applicability of subsection (a).]** Subsection (a) applies to the extent that:

(1) the right to payment or a part thereof under an assigned contract has not been fully earned by performance; or

(2) the right to payment or a part thereof has been fully earned by performance and the account debtor has not received notification of the assignment under Section 9-406(a).

(c) **[Rule for individual under other law.]** This section is subject to law other than this article which establishes a different rule for an account debtor who is an individual and who incurred the obligation primarily for personal, family, or household purposes.

(d) **[Inapplicability to health-care-insurance receivable.]** This section does not apply to an assignment of a health-care-insurance receivable.

### §9-406. Discharge of Account Debtor; Notification of Assignment; Identification and Proof of Assignment; Restrictions on Assignment of Accounts, Chattel Paper, Payment Intangibles, and Promissory Notes Ineffective.

(a) **[Discharge of account debtor; effect of notification.]** Subject to subsections (b) through (i), an account debtor on an account, chattel paper, or a payment intangible may discharge its obligation by paying the assignor until, but not after, the account debtor receives a notification, authenticated by the assignor or the assignee, that the amount due or to become due has been assigned and that payment is to be made to the assignee. After receipt of the notification, the account debtor may discharge its obligation by paying the assignee and may not discharge the obligation by paying the assignor.

(b) **[When notification ineffective.]** Subject to subsection (h), notification is ineffective under subsection (a):

(1) if it does not reasonably identify the rights assigned;

(2) to the extent that an agreement between an account debtor and a seller of a payment intangible limits the account debtor's duty to pay a person other than the seller and the limitation is effective under law other than this article; or

(3) at the option of an account debtor, if the notification notifies the account debtor to make less than the full amount of any installment or other periodic payment to the assignee, even if:

(A) only a portion of the account, chattel paper, or payment intangible has been assigned to that assignee;

(B) a portion has been assigned to another assignee; or

(C) the account debtor knows that the assignment to that assignee is limited.

(c) **[Proof of assignment.]** Subject to subsection (h), if requested by the account debtor, an assignee shall seasonably furnish reasonable proof that the assignment has been made. Unless the assignee complies, the account debtor may discharge its obligation by paying the assignor, even if the account debtor has received a notification under subsection (a).

(d) **[Term restricting assignment generally ineffective.]** Except as otherwise provided in subsection (e) and Sections 2A-303 and 9-407, and subject to subsection (h), a term in an agreement between an account debtor and an assignor or in a promissory note is ineffective to the extent that it:

(1) prohibits, restricts, or requires the consent of the account debtor or person obligated on the promissory note to the assignment or transfer of, or the creation, attachment, perfection, or enforcement of a security interest in, the account, chattel paper, payment intangible, or promissory note; or

(2) provides that the assignment or transfer or the creation, attachment, perfection, or enforcement of the security interest may give rise to a

default, breach, right of recoupment, claim, defense, termination, right of termination, or remedy under the account, chattel paper, payment intangible, or promissory note.

(e) **[Inapplicability of subsection (d) to certain sales.]** Subsection (d) does not apply to the sale of a payment intangible or promissory note.

(f) **[Legal restrictions on assignment generally ineffective.]** Except as otherwise provided in Sections 2A-303 and 9-407 and subject to subsections (h) and (i), a rule of law, statute, or regulation that prohibits, restricts, or requires the consent of a government, governmental body or official, or account debtor to the assignment or transfer of, or creation of a security interest in, an account or chattel paper is ineffective to the extent that the rule of law, statute, or regulation:

(1) prohibits, restricts, or requires the consent of the government, governmental body or official, or account debtor to the assignment or transfer of, or the creation, attachment, perfection, or enforcement of a security interest in the account or chattel paper; or

(2) provides that the assignment or transfer or the creation, attachment, perfection, or enforcement of the security interest may give rise to a default, breach, right of recoupment, claim, defense, termination, right of termination, or remedy under the account or chattel paper.

(g) **[Subsection (b)(3) not waivable.]** Subject to subsection (h), an account debtor may not waive or vary its option under subsection (b)(3).

(h) **[Rule for individual under other law.]** This section is subject to law other than this article which establishes a different rule for an account debtor who is an individual and who incurred the obligation primarily for personal, family, or household purposes.

(i) **[Inapplicability to health-care-insurance receivable.]** This section does not apply to an assignment of a health-care-insurance receivable.

(j) **[Section prevails over specified inconsistent law.]** This section prevails over any inconsistent provisions of the following statutes, rules, and regulations:

### §9-407. Restrictions on Creation or Enforcement of Security Interest in Leasehold Interest or in Lessor's Residual Interest.

(a) **[Term restricting assignment generally ineffective.]** Except as otherwise provided in subsection (b), a term in a lease agreement is ineffective to the extent that it:

(1) prohibits, restricts, or requires the consent of a party to the lease to the assignment or transfer of, or the creation, attachment, perfection, or enforcement of a security interest in, an interest of a party under the lease contract or in the lessor's residual interest in the goods; or

(2) provides that the assignment or transfer or the creation, attachment, perfection, or enforcement of the security interest may give rise to a default, breach, right of recoupment, claim, defense, termination, right of termination, or remedy under the lease.

(b) **[Effectiveness of certain terms.]** Except as otherwise provided in Section 2A-303(7), a term described in subsection (a)(2) is effective to the extent that there is:

(1) a transfer by the lessee of the lessee's right of possession or use of the goods in violation of the term; or

(2) a delegation of a material performance of either party to the lease contract in violation of the term.

(c) **[Security interest not material impairment.]** The creation, attachment, perfection, or enforcement of a security interest in the lessor's interest under the lease contract or the lessor's residual interest in the goods is not a transfer that materially impairs the lessee's prospect of obtaining return performance or materially changes the duty of or materially increases the burden or risk imposed on the lessee within the purview of Section 2A-303(4) unless, and then only to the extent that, enforcement actually results in a delegation of material performance of the lessor.

### §9-408. Restrictions on Assignment of Promissory Notes, Health-Care-Insurance Receivables, and Certain General Intangibles Ineffective.

(a) **[Term restricting assignment generally ineffective.]** Except as otherwise provided in subsection (b), a term in a promissory note or in an agreement between an account debtor and a debtor which relates to a health-care-insurance receivable or a general intangible, including a contract, permit, license, or franchise, and which term prohibits, restricts, or requires the consent of the person obligated on the promissory note or the account debtor to, the assignment or transfer of, or creation, attachment, or perfection of a security interest in, the promissory note, health-care-insurance receivable, or general intangible, is ineffective to the extent that the term:

(1) would impair the creation, attachment, or perfection of a security interest; or

(2) provides that the assignment or transfer or the creation, attachment, or perfection of the security interest may give rise to a default, breach, right of recoupment, claim, defense, termination, right of termination, or remedy under the promissory note, health-care-insurance receivable, or general intangible.

(b) **[Applicability of subsection (a) to sales of certain rights to payment.]** Subsection (a) applies to a security interest in a payment intangible or promissory note only if the security interest arises out of a sale of the payment intangible or promissory note.

(c) **[Legal restrictions on assignment generally ineffective.]** A rule of law, statute, or regulation that prohibits, restricts, or requires the consent of a government, governmental body or official, person obligated on a promissory note, or account debtor to the assignment or transfer of, or creation of a security interest in, a promissory note, health-care-insurance receivable, or general intangible, including a contract, permit, license, or franchise between an account debtor and a debtor, is ineffective to the extent that the rule of law, statute, or regulation:

(1) would impair the creation, attachment, or perfection of a security interest; or

(2) provides that the assignment or transfer or the creation, attachment, or perfection of the security interest may give rise to a default, breach, right of recoupment, claim, defense, termination, right of termination, or remedy under the promissory note, health-care-insurance receivable, or general intangible.

(d) **[Limitation on ineffectiveness under subsections (a) and (c).]** To the extent that a term in a promissory note or in an agreement between an account debtor and a debtor which relates to a health-care-insurance receivable or general intangible or a rule of law, statute, or regulation described in subsection (c) would be effective under law other than this article but is ineffective under subsection (a) or (c), the creation, attachment, or perfection of a security interest in the promissory note, health-care-insurance receivable, or general intangible:

(1) is not enforceable against the person obligated on the promissory note or the account debtor;

(2) does not impose a duty or obligation on the person obligated on the promissory note or the account debtor;

(3) does not require the person obligated on the promissory note or the account debtor to recognize the security interest, pay or render performance to the secured party, or accept payment or performance from the secured party;

(4) does not entitle the secured party to use or assign the debtor's rights under the promissory note, health-care-insurance receivable, or general intangible, including any related information or materials furnished to the debtor in the transaction giving rise to the promissory note, health-care-insurance receivable, or general intangible;

(5) does not entitle the secured party to use, assign, possess, or have access to any trade secrets or confidential information of the person obligated on the promissory note or the account debtor; and

(6) does not entitle the secured party to enforce the security interest in the promissory note, health-care-insurance receivable, or general intangible.

(e) **[Section prevails over specified inconsistent law.]** This section prevails over any inconsistent provisions of the following statutes, rules, and regulations:

**§9-409. Restrictions on Assignment of Letter-of-Credit Rights Ineffective.**
(a) **[Term or law restricting assignment generally ineffective.]** A term in a letter of credit or a rule of law, statute, regulation, custom, or practice applicable to the letter of credit which prohibits, restricts, or requires the consent of an applicant, issuer, or nominated person to a beneficiary's assignment of or creation of a security interest in a letter-of-credit right is ineffective to the extent that the term or rule of law, statute, regulation, custom, or practice:
(1) would impair the creation, attachment, or perfection of a security interest in the letter-of-credit right; or
(2) provides that the assignment or the creation, attachment, or perfection of the security interest may give rise to a default, breach, right of recoupment, claim, defense, termination, right of termination, or remedy under the letter-of-credit right.
(b) **[Limitation on ineffectiveness under subsection (a).]** To the extent that a term in a letter of credit is ineffective under subsection (a) but would be effective under law other than this article or a custom or practice applicable to the letter of credit, to the transfer of a right to draw or otherwise demand performance under the letter of credit, or to the assignment of a right to proceeds of the letter of credit, the creation, attachment, or perfection of a security interest in the letter-of-credit right:
(1) is not enforceable against the applicant, issuer, nominated person, or transferee beneficiary;
(2) imposes no duties or obligations on the applicant, issuer, nominated person, or transferee beneficiary; and
(3) does not require the applicant, issuer, nominated person, or transferee beneficiary to recognize the security interest, pay or render performance to the secured party, or accept payment or other performance from the secured party.

## Part 5—Filing

**§9-501. Filing Office.**
(a) **[Filing offices.]** Except as otherwise provided in subsection (b), if the local law of this State governs perfection of a security interest or agricultural lien, the office in which to file a financing statement to perfect the security interest or agricultural lien is:
(1) the office designated for the filing or recording of a record of a mortgage on the related real property, if:
(A) the collateral is as-extracted collateral or timber to be cut; or
(B) the financing statement is filed as a fixture filing and the collateral is goods that are or are to become fixtures; or
(2) the office of [Ê] [or any office duly authorized by [Ê]], in all other cases, including a case in which the collateral is goods that are or are to become fixtures and the financing statement is not filed as a fixture filing.
(b) **[Filing office for transmitting utilities.]** The office in which to file a financing statement to perfect a security interest in collateral, including fixtures, of a transmitting utility is the office of [Ê]. The financing statement also constitutes a fixture filing as to the collateral indicated in the financing statement which is or is to become fixtures.

**§9-502. Contents of Financing Statement; Record of Mortgage as Financing Statement; Time of Filing Financing Statement.**
(a) **[Sufficiency of financing statement.]** Subject to subsection (b), a financing statement is sufficient only if it:
(1) provides the name of the debtor;
(2) provides the name of the secured party or a representative of the secured party; and
(3) indicates the collateral covered by the financing statement.
(b) **[Real-property-related financing statements.]** Except as otherwise provided in Section 9-501(b), to be sufficient, a financing statement that covers as-extracted collateral or timber to be cut, or which is filed as a fixture filing and covers goods that are or are to become fixtures, must satisfy subsection (a) and also:
(1) indicate that it covers this type of collateral;
(2) indicate that it is to be filed [for record] in the real property records;
(3) provide a description of the real property to which the collateral is related [sufficient to give constructive notice of a mortgage under the law of this State if the description were contained in a record of the mortgage of the real property]; and
(4) if the debtor does not have an interest of record in the real property, provide the name of a record owner.
(c) **[Record of mortgage as financing statement.]** A record of a mortgage is effective, from the date of recording, as a financing statement filed as a fixture filing or as a financing statement covering as-extracted collateral or timber to be cut only if:
(1) the record indicates the goods or accounts that it covers;
(2) the goods are or are to become fixtures related to the real property described in the record or the collateral is related to the real property described in the record and is as-extracted collateral or timber to be cut;
(3) the record satisfies the requirements for a financing statement in this section other than an indication that it is to be filed in the real property records; and
(4) the record is [duly] recorded.
(d) **[Filing before security agreement or attachment.]** A financing statement may be filed before a security agreement is made or a security interest otherwise attaches.

**§9-503. Name of Debtor and Secured Party.**
(a) **[Sufficiency of debtor's name.]** A financing statement sufficiently provides the name of the debtor:
(1) if the debtor is a registered organization, only if the financing statement provides the name of the debtor indicated on the public record of the debtor's jurisdiction of organization which shows the debtor to have been organized;
(2) if the debtor is a decedent's estate, only if the financing statement provides the name of the decedent and indicates that the debtor is an estate;
(3) if the debtor is a trust or a trustee acting with respect to property held in trust, only if the financing statement:
(A) provides the name specified for the trust in its organic documents or, if no name is specified, provides the name of the settlor and additional information sufficient to distinguish the debtor from other trusts having one or more of the same settlors; and
(B) indicates, in the debtor's name or otherwise, that the debtor is a trust or is a trustee acting with respect to property held in trust; and
(4) in other cases:
(A) if the debtor has a name, only if it provides the individual or organizational name of the debtor; and
(B) if the debtor does not have a name, only if it provides the names of the partners, members, associates, or other persons comprising the debtor.
(b) **[Additional debtor-related information.]** A financing statement that provides the name of the debtor in accordance with subsection (a) is not rendered ineffective by the absence of:
(1) a trade name or other name of the debtor; or
(2) unless required under subsection (a)(4)(B), names of partners, members, associates, or other persons comprising the debtor.
(c) **[Debtor's trade name insufficient.]** A financing statement that provides only the debtor's trade name does not sufficiently provide the name of the debtor.
(d) **[Representative capacity.]** Failure to indicate the representative capacity of a secured party or representative of a secured party does not affect the sufficiency of a financing statement.

(e) **[Multiple debtors and secured parties.]** A financing statement may provide the name of more than one debtor and the name of more than one secured party.

**§9-504. Indication of Collateral.**
A financing statement sufficiently indicates the collateral that it covers if the financing statement provides:

(1) a description of the collateral pursuant to Section 9-108; or

(2) an indication that the financing statement covers all assets or all personal property.

**§9-505. Filing and Compliance with Other Statutes and Treaties for Consignments, Leases, Other Bailments, and Other Transactions.**
(a) **[Use of terms other than "debtor" and "secured party."]** A consignor, lessor, or other bailor of goods, a licensor, or a buyer of a payment intangible or promissory note may file a financing statement, or may comply with a statute or treaty described in Section 9-311(a), using the terms "consignor", "consignee", "lessor", "lessee", "bailor", "bailee", "licensor", "licensee", "owner", "registered owner", "buyer", "seller", or words of similar import, instead of the terms "secured party" and "debtor".
(b) **[Effect of financing statement under subsection (a).]** This part applies to the filing of a financing statement under subsection (a) and, as appropriate, to compliance that is equivalent to filing a financing statement under Section 9-311(b), but the filing or compliance is not of itself a factor in determining whether the collateral secures an obligation. If it is determined for another reason that the collateral secures an obligation, a security interest held by the consignor, lessor, bailor, licensor, owner, or buyer which attaches to the collateral is perfected by the filing or compliance.

**§9-506. Effect of Errors or Omissions.**
(a) **[Minor errors and omissions.]** A financing statement substantially satisfying the requirements of this part is effective, even if it has minor errors or omissions, unless the errors or omissions make the financing statement seriously misleading.
(b) **[Financing statement seriously misleading.]** Except as otherwise provided in subsection (c), a financing statement that fails sufficiently to provide the name of the debtor in accordance with Section 9-503(a) is seriously misleading.
(c) **[Financing statement not seriously misleading.]** If a search of the records of the filing office under the debtor's correct name, using the filing office's standard search logic, if any, would disclose a financing statement that fails sufficiently to provide the name of the debtor in accordance with Section 9-503(a), the name provided does not make the financing statement seriously misleading.
(d) **["Debtor's correct name."]** For purposes of Section 9-508(b), the "debtor's correct name" in subsection (c) means the correct name of the new debtor.

**§9-507. Effect of Certain Events on Effectiveness of Financing Statement.**
(a) **[Disposition.]** A filed financing statement remains effective with respect to collateral that is sold, exchanged, leased, licensed, or otherwise disposed of and in which a security interest or agricultural lien continues, even if the secured party knows of or consents to the disposition.
(b) **[Information becoming seriously misleading.]** Except as otherwise provided in subsection (c) and Section 9-508, a financing statement is not rendered ineffective if, after the financing statement is filed, the information provided in the financing statement becomes seriously misleading under Section 9-506.
(c) **[Change in debtor's name.]** If a debtor so changes its name that a filed financing statement becomes seriously misleading under Section 9-506:

(1) the financing statement is effective to perfect a security interest in collateral acquired by the debtor before, or within four months after, the change; and

(2) the financing statement is not effective to perfect a security interest in collateral acquired by the debtor more than four months after the change, unless an amendment to the financing statement which renders the financing statement not seriously misleading is filed within four months after the change.

**§9-508. Effectiveness of Financing Statement if New Debtor Becomes Bound by Security Agreement.**
(a) **[Financing statement naming original debtor.]** Except as otherwise provided in this section, a filed financing statement naming an original debtor is effective to perfect a security interest in collateral in which a new debtor has or acquires rights to the extent that the financing statement would have been effective had the original debtor acquired rights in the collateral.
(b) **[Financing statement becoming seriously misleading.]** If the difference between the name of the original debtor and that of the new debtor causes a filed financing statement that is effective under subsection (a) to be seriously misleading under Section 9-506:

(1) the financing statement is effective to perfect a security interest in collateral acquired by the new debtor before, and within four months after, the new debtor becomes bound under Section 9-203(d); and

(2) the financing statement is not effective to perfect a security interest in collateral acquired by the new debtor more than four months after the new debtor becomes bound under Section 9-203(d) unless an initial financing statement providing the name of the new debtor is filed before the expiration of that time.

(c) **[When section not applicable.]** This section does not apply to collateral as to which a filed financing statement remains effective against the new debtor under Section 9-507(a).

**§9-509. Persons Entitled to File A Record.**
(a) **[Person entitled to file record.]** A person may file an initial financing statement, amendment that adds collateral covered by a financing statement, or amendment that adds a debtor to a financing statement only if:

(1) the debtor authorizes the filing in an authenticated record or pursuant to subsection (b) or (c); or

(2) the person holds an agricultural lien that has become effective at the time of filing and the financing statement covers only collateral in which the person holds an agricultural lien.

(b) **[Security agreement as authorization.]** By authenticating or becoming bound as debtor by a security agreement, a debtor or new debtor authorizes the filing of an initial financing statement, and an amendment, covering:

(1) the collateral described in the security agreement; and

(2) property that becomes collateral under Section 9-315(a)(2), whether or not the security agreement expressly covers proceeds.

(c) **[Acquisition of collateral as authorization.]** By acquiring collateral in which a security interest or agricultural lien continues under Section 9-315(a)(1), a debtor authorizes the filing of an initial financing statement, and an amendment, covering the collateral and property that becomes collateral under Section 9-315(a)(2).
(d) **[Person entitled to file certain amendments.]** A person may file an amendment other than an amendment that adds collateral covered by a financing statement or an amendment that adds a debtor to a financing statement only if:

(1) the secured party of record authorizes the filing; or

(2) the amendment is a termination statement for a financing statement as to which the secured party of record has failed to file or send a termination statement as required by Section 9-513(a) or (c), the debtor authorizes the filing, and the termination statement indicates that the debtor authorized it to be filed.

(e) **[Multiple secured parties of record.]** If there is more than one secured party of record for a financing statement, each secured party of record may authorize the filing of an amendment under subsection (d).

**9-510. Effectiveness of Filed Record.**
(a) **[Filed record effective if authorized.]** A filed record is effective only to the extent that it was filed by a person that may file it under Section 9-509.

(b) **[Authorization by one secured party of record.]** A record authorized by one secured party of record does not affect the financing statement with respect to another secured party of record.
(c) **[Continuation statement not timely filed.]** A continuation statement that is not filed within the six-month period prescribed by Section 9-515(d) is ineffective.

**§9-511. Secured Party of Record.**
(a) **[Secured party of record.]** A secured party of record with respect to a financing statement is a person whose name is provided as the name of the secured party or a representative of the secured party in an initial financing statement that has been filed. If an initial financing statement is filed under Section 9-514(a), the assignee named in the initial financing statement is the secured party of record with respect to the financing statement.
(b) **[Amendment naming secured party of record.]** If an amendment of a financing statement which provides the name of a person as a secured party or a representative of a secured party is filed, the person named in the amendment is a secured party of record. If an amendment is filed under Section 9-514(b), the assignee named in the amendment is a secured party of record.
(c) **[Amendment deleting secured party of record.]** A person remains a secured party of record until the filing of an amendment of the financing statement which deletes the person.

**§9-512. Amendment of Financing Statement.**

**[Alternative A]**
(a) **[Amendment of information in financing statement.]** Subject to Section 9-509, a person may add or delete collateral covered by, continue or terminate the effectiveness of, or, subject to subsection (e), otherwise amend the information provided in, a financing statement by filing an amendment that:
(1) identifies, by its file number, the initial financing statement to which the amendment relates; and
(2) if the amendment relates to an initial financing statement filed [or recorded] in a filing office described in Section 9-501(a)(1), provides the information specified in Section 9-502(b).

**[Alternative B]**
(a) **[Amendment of information in financing statement.]** Subject to Section 9-509, a person may add or delete collateral covered by, continue or terminate the effectiveness of, or, subject to subsection (e), otherwise amend the information provided in, a financing statement by filing an amendment that:
(1) identifies, by its file number, the initial financing statement to which the amendment relates; and
(2) if the amendment relates to an initial financing statement filed [or recorded] in a filing office described in Section 9-501(a)(1), provides the date [and time] that the initial financing statement was filed [or recorded] and the information specified in Section 9-502(b).

**[End of Alternatives]**
(b) **[Period of effectiveness not affected.]** Except as otherwise provided in Section 9-515, the filing of an amendment does not extend the period of effectiveness of the financing statement.
(c) **[Effectiveness of amendment adding collateral.]** A financing statement that is amended by an amendment that adds collateral is effective as to the added collateral only from the date of the filing of the amendment.
(d) **[Effectiveness of amendment adding debtor.]** A financing statement that is amended by an amendment that adds a debtor is effective as to the added debtor only from the date of the filing of the amendment.
(e) **[Certain amendments ineffective.]** An amendment is ineffective to the extent it:
(1) purports to delete all debtors and fails to provide the name of a debtor to be covered by the financing statement; or
(2) purports to delete all secured parties of record and fails to provide the name of a new secured party of record.

**§9-513. Termination Statement.**
(a) **[Consumer goods.]** A secured party shall cause the secured party of record for a financing statement to file a termination statement for the financing statement if the financing statement covers consumer goods and:
(1) there is no obligation secured by the collateral covered by the financing statement and no commitment to make an advance, incur an obligation, or otherwise give value; or
(2) the debtor did not authorize the filing of the initial financing statement.
(b) **[Time for compliance with subsection (a).]** To comply with subsection (a), a secured party shall cause the secured party of record to file the termination statement:
(1) within one month after there is no obligation secured by the collateral covered by the financing statement and no commitment to make an advance, incur an obligation, or otherwise give value; or
(2) if earlier, within 20 days after the secured party receives an authenticated demand from a debtor.
(c) **[Other collateral.]** In cases not governed by subsection (a), within 20 days after a secured party receives an authenticated demand from a debtor, the secured party shall cause the secured party of record for a financing statement to send to the debtor a termination statement for the financing statement or file the termination statement in the filing office if:
(1) except in the case of a financing statement covering accounts or chattel paper that has been sold or goods that are the subject of a consignment, there is no obligation secured by the collateral covered by the financing statement and no commitment to make an advance, incur an obligation, or otherwise give value;
(2) the financing statement covers accounts or chattel paper that has been sold but as to which the account debtor or other person obligated has discharged its obligation;
(3) the financing statement covers goods that were the subject of a consignment to the debtor but are not in the debtor's possession; or
(4) the debtor did not authorize the filing of the initial financing statement.
(d) **[Effect of filing termination statement.]** Except as otherwise provided in Section 9-510, upon the filing of a termination statement with the filing office, the financing statement to which the termination statement relates ceases to be effective. Except as otherwise provided in Section 9-510, for purposes of Sections 9-519(g), 9-522(a), and 9-523(c), the filing with the filing office of a termination statement relating to a financing statement that indicates that the debtor is a transmitting utility also causes the effectiveness of the financing statement to lapse.

**§9-514. Assignment of Powers of Secured Party of Record.**
(a) **[Assignment reflected on initial financing statement.]** Except as otherwise provided in subsection (c), an initial financing statement may reflect an assignment of all of the secured party's power to authorize an amendment to the financing statement by providing the name and mailing address of the assignee as the name and address of the secured party.
(b) **[Assignment of filed financing statement.]** Except as otherwise provided in subsection (c), a secured party of record may assign of record all or part of its power to authorize an amendment to a financing statement by filing in the filing office an amendment of the financing statement which:
(1) identifies, by its file number, the initial financing statement to which it relates;
(2) provides the name of the assignor; and
(3) provides the name and mailing address of the assignee.
(c) **[Assignment of record of mortgage.]** An assignment of record of a security interest in a fixture covered by a record of a mortgage which is effective as a financing statement filed as a fixture filing under Section 9-502(c) may be made only by an assignment of record of the mortgage in the manner provided by law of this State other than [the Uniform Commercial Code].

**§9-515. Duration and Effectiveness of Financing Statement; Effect of Lapsed Financing Statement.**

(a) **[Five-year effectiveness.]** Except as otherwise provided in subsections (b), (e), (f), and (g), a filed financing statement is effective for a period of five years after the date of filing.

(b) **[Public-finance or manufactured-home transaction.]** Except as otherwise provided in subsections (e), (f), and (g), an initial financing statement filed in connection with a public-finance transaction or manufactured-home transaction is effective for a period of 30 years after the date of filing if it indicates that it is filed in connection with a public-finance transaction or manufactured-home transaction.

(c) **[Lapse and continuation of financing statement.]** The effectiveness of a filed financing statement lapses on the expiration of the period of its effectiveness unless before the lapse a continuation statement is filed pursuant to subsection (d). Upon lapse, a financing statement ceases to be effective and any security interest or agricultural lien that was perfected by the financing statement becomes unperfected, unless the security interest is perfected otherwise. If the security interest or agricultural lien becomes unperfected upon lapse, it is deemed never to have been perfected as against a purchaser of the collateral for value.

(d) **[When continuation statement may be filed.]** A continuation statement may be filed only within six months before the expiration of the five-year period specified in subsection (a) or the 30-year period specified in subsection (b), whichever is applicable.

(e) **[Effect of filing continuation statement.]** Except as otherwise provided in Section 9-510, upon timely filing of a continuation statement, the effectiveness of the initial financing statement continues for a period of five years commencing on the day on which the financing statement would have become ineffective in the absence of the filing. Upon the expiration of the five-year period, the financing statement lapses in the same manner as provided in subsection (c), unless, before the lapse, another continuation statement is filed pursuant to subsection (d). Succeeding continuation statements may be filed in the same manner to continue the effectiveness of the initial financing statement.

(f) **[Transmitting utility financing statement.]** If a debtor is a transmitting utility and a filed financing statement so indicates, the financing statement is effective until a termination statement is filed.

(g) **[Record of mortgage as financing statement.]** A record of a mortgage that is effective as a financing statement filed as a fixture filing under Section 9-502(c) remains effective as a financing statement filed as a fixture filing until the mortgage is released or satisfied of record or its effectiveness otherwise terminates as to the real property.

**§9-516. What Constitutes Filing; Effectiveness of Filing.**

(a) **[What constitutes filing.]** Except as otherwise provided in subsection (b), communication of a record to a filing office and tender of the filing fee or acceptance of the record by the filing office constitutes filing.

(b) **[Refusal to accept record; filing does not occur.]** Filing does not occur with respect to a record that a filing office refuses to accept because:

(1) the record is not communicated by a method or medium of communication authorized by the filing office;

(2) an amount equal to or greater than the applicable filing fee is not tendered;

(3) the filing office is unable to index the record because:

(A) in the case of an initial financing statement, the record does not provide a name for the debtor;

(B) in the case of an amendment or correction statement, the record:

(i) does not identify the initial financing statement as required by Section 9-512 or 9-518, as applicable; or

(ii) identifies an initial financing statement whose effectiveness has lapsed under Section 9-515;

(C) in the case of an initial financing statement that provides the name of a debtor identified as an individual or an amendment that provides a name of a debtor identified as an individual which was not previously provided in the financing statement to which the record relates, the record does not identify the debtor's last name; or

(D) in the case of a record filed [or recorded] in the filing office described in Section 9-501(a)(1), the record does not provide a sufficient description of the real property to which it relates;

(4) in the case of an initial financing statement or an amendment that adds a secured party of record, the record does not provide a name and mailing address for the secured party of record;

(5) in the case of an initial financing statement or an amendment that provides a name of a debtor which was not previously provided in the financing statement to which the amendment relates, the record does not:

(A) provide a mailing address for the debtor;

(B) indicate whether the debtor is an individual or an organization; or

(C) if the financing statement indicates that the debtor is an organization, provide:

(i) a type of organization for the debtor;

(ii) a jurisdiction of organization for the debtor; or

(iii) an organizational identification number for the debtor or indicate that the debtor has none;

(6) in the case of an assignment reflected in an initial financing statement under Section 9-514(a) or an amendment filed under Section 9-514(b), the record does not provide a name and mailing address for the assignee; or

(7) in the case of a continuation statement, the record is not filed within the six-month period prescribed by Section 9-515(d).

(c) **[Rules applicable to subsection (b).]** For purposes of subsection (b):

(1) a record does not provide information if the filing office is unable to read or decipher the information; and

(2) a record that does not indicate that it is an amendment or identify an initial financing statement to which it relates, as required by Section 9-512, 9-514, or 9-518, is an initial financing statement.

(d) **[Refusal to accept record; record effective as filed record.]** A record that is communicated to the filing office with tender of the filing fee, but which the filing office refuses to accept for a reason other than one set forth in subsection (b), is effective as a filed record except as against a purchaser of the collateral which gives value in reasonable reliance upon the absence of the record from the files.

**§9-517. Effect of Indexing Errors.**

The failure of the filing office to index a record correctly does not affect the effectiveness of the filed record.

**§9-518. Claim Concerning Inaccurate or Wrongfully Filed Record.**

(a) **[Correction statement.]** A person may file in the filing office a correction statement with respect to a record indexed there under the person's name if the person believes that the record is inaccurate or was wrongfully filed.

**[Alternative A]**

(b) **[Sufficiency of correction statement.]** A correction statement must:

(1) identify the record to which it relates by the file number assigned to the initial financing statement to which the record relates;

(2) indicate that it is a correction statement; and

(3) provide the basis for the person's belief that the record is inaccurate and indicate the manner in which the person believes the record should be amended to cure any inaccuracy or provide the basis for the person's belief that the record was wrongfully filed.

**[Alternative B]**

(b) **[Sufficiency of correction statement.]** A correction statement must:

(1) identify the record to which it relates by:

(A) the file number assigned to the initial financing statement to which the record relates; and

(B) if the correction statement relates to a record filed [or recorded] in a filing office described in Section 9-501(a)(1), the date [and time] that the initial financing statement was filed [or recorded] and the information specified in Section 9-502(b);

(2) indicate that it is a correction statement; and

(3) provide the basis for the person's belief that the record is inaccurate and indicate the manner in which the person believes the record should be amended to cure any inaccuracy or provide the basis for the person's belief that the record was wrongfully filed.

**[End of Alternatives]**

(c) **[Record not affected by correction statement.]** The filing of a correction statement does not affect the effectiveness of an initial financing statement or other filed record.

**§9-519. Numbering, Maintaining, and Indexing Records; Communicating Information Provided in Records.**

(a) **[Filing office duties.]** For each record filed in a filing office, the filing office shall:

(1) assign a unique number to the filed record;

(2) create a record that bears the number assigned to the filed record and the date and time of filing;

(3) maintain the filed record for public inspection; and

(4) index the filed record in accordance with subsections (c), (d), and (e).

(b) **[File number.]** A file number [assigned after January 1, 2002,] must include a digit that:

(1) is mathematically derived from or related to the other digits of the file number; and

(2) aids the filing office in determining whether a number communicated as the file number includes a single-digit or transpositional error.

(c) **[Indexing: general.]** Except as otherwise provided in subsections (d) and (e), the filing office shall:

(1) index an initial financing statement according to the name of the debtor and index all filed records relating to the initial financing statement in a manner that associates with one another an initial financing statement and all filed records relating to the initial financing statement; and

(2) index a record that provides a name of a debtor which was not previously provided in the financing statement to which the record relates also according to the name that was not previously provided.

(d) **[Indexing: real-property-related financing statement.]** If a financing statement is filed as a fixture filing or covers as-extracted collateral or timber to be cut, [it must be filed for record and] the filing office shall index it:

(1) under the names of the debtor and of each owner of record shown on the financing statement as if they were the mortgagors under a mortgage of the real property described; and

(2) to the extent that the law of this State provides for indexing of records of mortgages under the name of the mortgagee, under the name of the secured party as if the secured party were the mortgagee thereunder, or, if indexing is by description, as if the financing statement were a record of a mortgage of the real property described.

(e) **[Indexing: real-property-related assignment.]** If a financing statement is filed as a fixture filing or covers as-extracted collateral or timber to be cut, the filing office shall index an assignment filed under Section 9-514(a) or an amendment filed under Section 9-514(b):

(1) under the name of the assignor as grantor; and

(2) to the extent that the law of this State provides for indexing a record of the assignment of a mortgage under the name of the assignee, under the name of the assignee.

**[Alternative A]**

(f) **[Retrieval and association capability.]** The filing office shall maintain a capability:

(1) to retrieve a record by the name of the debtor and by the file number assigned to the initial financing statement to which the record relates; and

(2) to associate and retrieve with one another an initial financing statement and each filed record relating to the initial financing statement.

**[Alternative B]**

(f) **[Retrieval and association capability.]** The filing office shall maintain a capability:

(1) to retrieve a record by the name of the debtor and:

(A) if the filing office is described in Section 9-501(a)(1), by the file number assigned to the initial financing statement to which the record relates and the date [and time] that the record was filed [or recorded]; or

(B) if the filing office is described in Section 9-501(a)(2), by the file number assigned to the initial financing statement to which the record relates; and

(2) to associate and retrieve with one another an initial financing statement and each filed record relating to the initial financing statement.

**[End of Alternatives]**

(g) **[Removal of debtor's name.]** The filing office may not remove a debtor's name from the index until one year after the effectiveness of a financing statement naming the debtor lapses under Section 9-515 with respect to all secured parties of record.

(h) **[Timeliness of filing office performance.]** The filing office shall perform the acts required by subsections (a) through (e) at the time and in the manner prescribed by filing-office rule, but not later than two business days after the filing office receives the record in question.

(i) **[Inapplicability to real-property-related filing office.]** Subsection[s] [(b)] [and] [(h)] do[es] not apply to a filing office described in Section 9-501(a)(1).]

**§9-520. Acceptance and Refusal to Accept Record.**

(a) **[Mandatory refusal to accept record.]** A filing office shall refuse to accept a record for filing for a reason set forth in Section 9-516(b) and may refuse to accept a record for filing only for a reason set forth in Section 9-516(b).

(b) **[Communication concerning refusal.]** If a filing office refuses to accept a record for filing, it shall communicate to the person that presented the record the fact of and reason for the refusal and the date and time the record would have been filed had the filing office accepted it. The communication must be made at the time and in the manner prescribed by filing-office rule but [, in the case of a filing office described in Section 9-501(a)(2),] in no event more than two business days after the filing office receives the record.

(c) **[When filed financing statement effective.]** A filed financing statement satisfying Section 9-502(a) and (b) is effective, even if the filing office is required to refuse to accept it for filing under subsection (a). However, Section 9-338 applies to a filed financing statement providing information described in Section 9-516(b)(5) which is incorrect at the time the financing statement is filed.

(d) **[Separate application to multiple debtors.]** If a record communicated to a filing office provides information that relates to more than one debtor, this part applies as to each debtor separately.

**§9-521. Uniform Form of Written Financing Statement and Amendment.**

(a) **[Initial financing statement form.]** A filing office that accepts written records may not refuse to accept a written initial financing statement in the following form and format except for a reason set forth in Section 9-516(b):

(b) **[Amendment form.]** A filing office that accepts written records may not refuse to accept a written record in the following form and format except for a reason set forth in Section 9-516(b):

**§9-522. Maintenance and Destruction of Records.**

**[Alternative A]**

(a) **[Post-lapse maintenance and retrieval of information.]** The filing office shall maintain a record of the information provided in a filed financing statement for at least one year after the effectiveness of the financing statement has lapsed under Section 9-515 with respect to all secured parties of record. The record must be retrievable by using the name of the debtor and by using the file number assigned to the initial financing statement to which the record relates.

**[Alternative B]**

(a) **[Post-lapse maintenance and retrieval of information.]** The filing office shall maintain a record of the information provided in a filed financing statement for at least one year after the effectiveness of the financing statement has lapsed under Section 9-515 with respect to all secured parties of record. The record must be retrievable by using the name of the debtor and:

(1) if the record was filed [or recorded] in the filing office described in Section 9-501(a)(1), by using the file number assigned to the initial financing statement to which the record relates and the date [and time] that the record was filed [or recorded]; or

(2) if the record was filed in the filing office described in Section 9-501(a)(2), by using the file number assigned to the initial financing statement to which the record relates.

**[End of Alternatives]**

(b) **[Destruction of written records.]** Except to the extent that a statute governing disposition of public records provides otherwise, the filing office immediately may destroy any written record evidencing a financing statement. However, if the filing office destroys a written record, it shall maintain another record of the financing statement which complies with subsection (a).

**§9-523. Information from Filing Office; Sale or License of Records.**

(a) **[Acknowledgment of filing written record.]** If a person that files a written record requests an acknowledgment of the filing, the filing office shall send to the person an image of the record showing the number assigned to the record pursuant to Section 9-519(a)(1) and the date and time of the filing of the record. However, if the person furnishes a copy of the record to the filing office, the filing office may instead:

(1) note upon the copy the number assigned to the record pursuant to Section 9-519(a)(1) and the date and time of the filing of the record; and

(2) send the copy to the person.

(b) **[Acknowledgment of filing other record.]** If a person files a record other than a written record, the filing office shall communicate to the person an acknowledgment that provides:

(1) the information in the record;

(2) the number assigned to the record pursuant to Section 9-519(a)(1); and

(3) the date and time of the filing of the record.

(c) **[Communication of requested information.]** The filing office shall communicate or otherwise make available in a record the following information to any person that requests it:

(1) whether there is on file on a date and time specified by the filing office, but not a date earlier than three business days before the filing office receives the request, any financing statement that:

(A) designates a particular debtor [or, if the request so states, designates a particular debtor at the address specified in the request];

(B) has not lapsed under Section 9-515 with respect to all secured parties of record; and

(C) if the request so states, has lapsed under Section 9-515 and a record of which is maintained by the filing office under Section 9-522(a);

(2) the date and time of filing of each financing statement; and

(3) the information provided in each financing statement.

(d) **[Medium for communicating information.]** In complying with its duty under subsection (c), the filing office may communicate information in any medium. However, if requested, the filing office shall communicate information by issuing [its written certificate] [a record that can be admitted into evidence in the courts of this State without extrinsic evidence of its authenticity].

(e) **[Timeliness of filing office performance.]** The filing office shall perform the acts required by subsections (a) through (d) at the time and in the manner prescribed by filing-office rule, but not later than two business days after the filing office receives the request.

(f) **[Public availability of records.]** At least weekly, the [insert appropriate official or governmental agency] [filing office] shall offer to sell or license to the public on a nonexclusive basis, in bulk, copies of all records filed in it under this part, in every medium from time to time available to the filing office.

**§9-524. Delay by Filing Office.**

Delay by the filing office beyond a time limit prescribed by this part is excused if:

(1) the delay is caused by interruption of communication or computer facilities, war, emergency conditions, failure of equipment, or other circumstances beyond control of the filing office; and

(2) the filing office exercises reasonable diligence under the circumstances.

**§9-525. Fees.**

**§9-526. Filing-Office Rules.**

(a) **[Adoption of filing-office rules.]** The [insert appropriate governmental official or agency] shall adopt and publish rules to implement this article. The filing-office rules must be[:

(1)] consistent with this article[; and

(2) adopted and published in accordance with the [insert any applicable state administrative procedure act]].

(b) **[Harmonization of rules.]** To keep the filing-office rules and practices of the filing office in harmony with the rules and practices of filing offices in other jurisdictions that enact substantially this part, and to keep the technology used by the filing office compatible with the technology used by filing offices in other jurisdictions that enact substantially this part, the [insert appropriate governmental official or agency], so far as is consistent with the purposes, policies, and provisions of this article, in adopting, amending, and repealing filing-office rules, shall:

(1) consult with filing offices in other jurisdictions that enact substantially this part; and

(2) consult the most recent version of the Model Rules promulgated by the International Association of Corporate Administrators or any successor organization; and

(3) take into consideration the rules and practices of, and the technology used by, filing offices in other jurisdictions that enact substantially this part.

**§9-527. Duty to Report.**

The [insert appropriate governmental official or agency] shall report [annually on or before _________Ê] to the [Governor and Legislature] on the operation of the filing office. The report must contain a statement of the extent to which:

(1) the filing-office rules are not in harmony with the rules of filing offices in other jurisdictions that enact substantially this part and the reasons for these variations; and

(2) the filing-office rules are not in harmony with the most recent version of the Model Rules promulgated by the International Association of Corporate Administrators, or any successor organization, and the reasons for these variations.

## Part 6—Default

**§9-601. Rights after Default; Judicial Enforcement; Consignor or Buyer of Accounts, Chattel Paper, Payment Intangibles, or Promissory Notes.**

(a) **[Rights of secured party after default.]** After default, a secured party has the rights provided in this part and, except as otherwise provided in Section 9-602, those provided by agreement of the parties. A secured party:

(1) may reduce a claim to judgment, foreclose, or otherwise enforce the claim, security interest, or agricultural lien by any available judicial procedure; and

(2) if the collateral is documents, may proceed either as to the documents or as to the goods they cover.

(b) **[Rights and duties of secured party in possession or control.]** A secured party in possession of collateral or control of collateral under Section 9-104, 9-105, 9-106, or 9-107 has the rights and duties provided in Section 9-207.

(c) **[Rights cumulative; simultaneous exercise.]** The rights under subsections (a) and (b) are cumulative and may be exercised simultaneously.

(d) **[Rights of debtor and obligor.]** Except as otherwise provided in subsection (g) and Section 9-605, after default, a debtor and an obligor have the rights provided in this part and by agreement of the parties.

(e) **[Lien of levy after judgment.]** If a secured party has reduced its claim to judgment, the lien of any levy that may be made upon the collateral by virtue of an execution based upon the judgment relates back to the earliest of:

(1) the date of perfection of the security interest or agricultural lien in the collateral;

(2) the date of filing a financing statement covering the collateral; or

(3) any date specified in a statute under which the agricultural lien was created.

(f) **[Execution sale.]** A sale pursuant to an execution is a foreclosure of the security interest or agricultural lien by judicial procedure within the meaning of this section. A secured party may purchase at the sale and thereafter hold the collateral free of any other requirements of this article.

(g) **[Consignor or buyer of certain rights to payment.]** Except as otherwise provided in Section 9-607(c), this part imposes no duties upon a secured party that is a consignor or is a buyer of accounts, chattel paper, payment intangibles, or promissory notes.

**§9-602. Waiver and Variance of Rights and Duties.**

Except as otherwise provided in Section 9-624, to the extent that they give rights to a debtor or obligor and impose duties on a secured party, the debtor or obligor may not waive or vary the rules stated in the following listed sections:

(1) Section 9-207(b)(4)(C), which deals with use and operation of the collateral by the secured party;

(2) Section 9-210, which deals with requests for an accounting and requests concerning a list of collateral and statement of account;

(3) Section 9-607(c), which deals with collection and enforcement of collateral;

(4) Sections 9-608(a) and 9-615(c) to the extent that they deal with application or payment of noncash proceeds of collection, enforcement, or disposition;

(5) Sections 9-608(a) and 9-615(d) to the extent that they require accounting for or payment of surplus proceeds of collateral;

(6) Section 9-609 to the extent that it imposes upon a secured party that takes possession of collateral without judicial process the duty to do so without breach of the peace;

(7) Sections 9-610(b), 9-611, 9-613, and 9-614, which deal with disposition of collateral;

(8) Section 9-615(f), which deals with calculation of a deficiency or surplus when a disposition is made to the secured party, a person related to the secured party, or a secondary obligor;

(9) Section 9-616, which deals with explanation of the calculation of a surplus or deficiency;

(10) Sections 9-620, 9-621, and 9-622, which deal with acceptance of collateral in satisfaction of obligation;

(11) Section 9-623, which deals with redemption of collateral;

(12) Section 9-624, which deals with permissible waivers; and

(13) Sections 9-625 and 9-626, which deal with the secured party's liability for failure to comply with this article.

**§9-603. Agreement on Standards Concerning Rights and Duties.**

(a) **[Agreed standards.]** The parties may determine by agreement the standards measuring the fulfillment of the rights of a debtor or obligor and the duties of a secured party under a rule stated in Section 9-602 if the standards are not manifestly unreasonable.

(b) **[Agreed standards inapplicable to breach of peace.]** Subsection (a) does not apply to the duty under Section 9-609 to refrain from breaching the peace.

**§9-604. Procedure if Security Agreement Covers Real Property or Fixtures.**

(a) **[Enforcement: personal and real property.]** If a security agreement covers both personal and real property, a secured party may proceed:

(1) under this part as to the personal property without prejudicing any rights with respect to the real property; or

(2) as to both the personal property and the real property in accordance with the rights with respect to the real property, in which case the other provisions of this part do not apply.

(b) **[Enforcement: fixtures.]** Subject to subsection (c), if a security agreement covers goods that are or become fixtures, a secured party may proceed:

(1) under this part; or

(2) in accordance with the rights with respect to real property, in which case the other provisions of this part do not apply.

(c) **[Removal of fixtures.]** Subject to the other provisions of this part, if a secured party holding a security interest in fixtures has priority over all owners and encumbrancers of the real property, the secured party, after default, may remove the collateral from the real property.

(d) **[Injury caused by removal.]** A secured party that removes collateral shall promptly reimburse any encumbrancer or owner of the real property, other than the debtor, for the cost of repair of any physical injury caused by the removal. The secured party need not reimburse the encumbrancer or owner for any diminution in value of the real property caused by the absence of the goods removed or by any necessity of replacing them. A person entitled to reimbursement may refuse permission to remove until the secured party gives adequate assurance for the performance of the obligation to reimburse.

**§9-605. Unknown Debtor or Secondary Obligor.**

A secured party does not owe a duty based on its status as secured party:

(1) to a person that is a debtor or obligor, unless the secured party knows:

(A) that the person is a debtor or obligor;

(B) the identity of the person; and

(C) how to communicate with the person; or

(2) to a secured party or lienholder that has filed a financing statement against a person, unless the secured party knows:

(A) that the person is a debtor; and

(B) the identity of the person.

**§9-606. Time of Default for Agricultural Lien.**

For purposes of this part, a default occurs in connection with an agricultural lien at the time the secured party becomes entitled to enforce the lien in accordance with the statute under which it was created.

**§9-607. Collection and Enforcement by Secured Party.**

(a) **[Collection and enforcement generally.]** If so agreed, and in any event after default, a secured party:

(1) may notify an account debtor or other person obligated on collateral to make payment or otherwise render performance to or for the benefit of the secured party;

(2) may take any proceeds to which the secured party is entitled under Section 9-315;

(3) may enforce the obligations of an account debtor or other person obligated on collateral and exercise the rights of the debtor with respect to the obligation of the account debtor or other person obligated on collateral to make payment or otherwise render performance to the debtor, and with respect to any property that secures the obligations of the account debtor or other person obligated on the collateral;

(4) if it holds a security interest in a deposit account perfected by control under Section 9-104(a)(1), may apply the balance of the deposit account to the obligation secured by the deposit account; and

(5) if it holds a security interest in a deposit account perfected by control under Section 9-104(a)(2) or (3), may instruct the bank to pay the balance of the deposit account to or for the benefit of the secured party.

(b) **[Nonjudicial enforcement of mortgage.]** If necessary to enable a secured party to exercise under subsection (a)(3) the right of a debtor to enforce a mortgage nonjudicially, the secured party may record in the office in which a record of the mortgage is recorded:

(1) a copy of the security agreement that creates or provides for a security interest in the obligation secured by the mortgage; and

(2) the secured party's sworn affidavit in recordable form stating that:

(A) a default has occurred; and

(B) the secured party is entitled to enforce the mortgage non-judicially.

(c) **[Commercially reasonable collection and enforcement.]** A secured party shall proceed in a commercially reasonable manner if the secured party:

(1) undertakes to collect from or enforce an obligation of an account debtor or other person obligated on collateral; and

(2) is entitled to charge back uncollected collateral or otherwise to full or limited recourse against the debtor or a secondary obligor.

(d) **[Expenses of collection and enforcement.]** A secured party may deduct from the collections made pursuant to subsection (c) reasonable expenses of collection and enforcement, including reasonable attorney's fees and legal expenses incurred by the secured party.

(e) **[Duties to secured party not affected.]** This section does not determine whether an account debtor, bank, or other person obligated on collateral owes a duty to a secured party.

### §9-608. Application of Proceeds of Collection or Enforcement; Liability for Deficiency and Right to Surplus.

(a) **[Application of proceeds, surplus, and deficiency if obligation secured.]** If a security interest or agricultural lien secures payment or performance of an obligation, the following rules apply:

(1) A secured party shall apply or pay over for application the cash proceeds of collection or enforcement under Section 9-607 in the following order to:

(A) the reasonable expenses of collection and enforcement and, to the extent provided for by agreement and not prohibited by law, reasonable attorney's fees and legal expenses incurred by the secured party;

(B) the satisfaction of obligations secured by the security interest or agricultural lien under which the collection or enforcement is made; and

(C) the satisfaction of obligations secured by any subordinate security interest in or other lien on the collateral subject to the security interest or agricultural lien under which the collection or enforcement is made if the secured party receives an authenticated demand for proceeds before distribution of the proceeds is completed.

(2) If requested by a secured party, a holder of a subordinate security interest or other lien shall furnish reasonable proof of the interest or lien within a reasonable time. Unless the holder complies, the secured party need not comply with the holder's demand under paragraph (1)(C).

(3) A secured party need not apply or pay over for application noncash proceeds of collection and enforcement under Section 9-607 unless the failure to do so would be commercially unreasonable. A secured party that applies or pays over for application noncash proceeds shall do so in a commercially reasonable manner.

(4) A secured party shall account to and pay a debtor for any surplus, and the obligor is liable for any deficiency.

(b) **[No surplus or deficiency in sales of certain rights to payment.]** If the underlying transaction is a sale of accounts, chattel paper, payment intangibles, or promissory notes, the debtor is not entitled to any surplus, and the obligor is not liable for any deficiency.

### §9-609. Secured Party's Right to Take Possession after Default.

(a) **[Possession; rendering equipment unusable; disposition on debtor's premises.]** After default, a secured party:

(1) may take possession of the collateral; and

(2) without removal, may render equipment unusable and dispose of collateral on a debtor's premises under Section 9-610.

(b) **[Judicial and nonjudicial process.]** A secured party may proceed under subsection (a):

(1) pursuant to judicial process; or

(2) without judicial process, if it proceeds without breach of the peace.

(c) **[Assembly of collateral.]** If so agreed, and in any event after default, a secured party may require the debtor to assemble the collateral and make it available to the secured party at a place to be designated by the secured party which is reasonably convenient to both parties.

### §9-610. Disposition of Collateral after Default.

(a) **[Disposition after default.]** After default, a secured party may sell, lease, license, or otherwise dispose of any or all of the collateral in its present condition or following any commercially reasonable preparation or processing.

(b) **[Commercially reasonable disposition.]** Every aspect of a disposition of collateral, including the method, manner, time, place, and other terms, must be commercially reasonable. If commercially reasonable, a secured party may dispose of collateral by public or private proceedings, by one or more contracts, as a unit or in parcels, and at any time and place and on any terms.

(c) **[Purchase by secured party.]** A secured party may purchase collateral:

(1) at a public disposition; or

(2) at a private disposition only if the collateral is of a kind that is customarily sold on a recognized market or the subject of widely distributed standard price quotations.

(d) **[Warranties on disposition.]** A contract for sale, lease, license, or other disposition includes the warranties relating to title, possession, quiet enjoyment, and the like which by operation of law accompany a voluntary disposition of property of the kind subject to the contract.

(e) **[Disclaimer of warranties.]** A secured party may disclaim or modify warranties under subsection (d):

(1) in a manner that would be effective to disclaim or modify the warranties in a voluntary disposition of property of the kind subject to the contract of disposition; or

(2) by communicating to the purchaser a record evidencing the contract for disposition and including an express disclaimer or modification of the warranties.

(f) **[Record sufficient to disclaim warranties.]** A record is sufficient to disclaim warranties under subsection (e) if it indicates "There is no warranty relating to title, possession, quiet enjoyment, or the like in this disposition" or uses words of similar import.

### §9-611. Notification Before Disposition of Collateral.

(a) **["Notification date."]** In this section, "notification date" means the earlier of the date on which:

(1) a secured party sends to the debtor and any secondary obligor an authenticated notification of disposition; or

(2) the debtor and any secondary obligor waive the right to notification.

(b) **[Notification of disposition required.]** Except as otherwise provided in subsection (d), a secured party that disposes of collateral under Section 9-610 shall send to the persons specified in subsection (c) a reasonable authenticated notification of disposition.

(c) **[Persons to be notified.]** To comply with subsection (b), the secured party shall send an authenticated notification of disposition to:

(1) the debtor;

(2) any secondary obligor; and

(3) if the collateral is other than consumer goods:

(A) any other person from which the secured party has received, before the notification date, an authenticated notification of a claim of an interest in the collateral;

(B) any other secured party or lienholder that, 10 days before the notification date, held a security interest in or other lien on the collateral perfected by the filing of a financing statement that:

(i) identified the collateral;

(ii) was indexed under the debtor's name as of that date; and

(iii) was filed in the office in which to file a financing statement against the debtor covering the collateral as of that date; and

(C) any other secured party that, 10 days before the notification date, held a security interest in the collateral perfected by compliance with a statute, regulation, or treaty described in Section 9-311(a).

(d) **[Subsection (b) inapplicable: perishable collateral; recognized market.]** Subsection (b) does not apply if the collateral is perishable or threatens to decline speedily in value or is of a type customarily sold on a recognized market.

(e) **[Compliance with subsection (c)(3)(B).]** A secured party complies with the requirement for notification prescribed by subsection (c)(3)(B) if:

(1) not later than 20 days or earlier than 30 days before the notification date, the secured party requests, in a commercially reasonable manner, information concerning financing statements indexed under the debtor's name in the office indicated in subsection (c)(3)(B); and

(2) before the notification date, the secured party:

(A) did not receive a response to the request for information; or

(B) received a response to the request for information and sent an authenticated notification of disposition to each secured party or other lienholder named in that response whose financing statement covered the collateral.

### §9-612. Timelines of Notification Before Disposition of Collateral.

(a) **[Reasonable time is question of fact.]** Except as otherwise provided in subsection (b), whether a notification is sent within a reasonable time is a question of fact.

(b) **[10-day period sufficient in non-consumer transaction.]** In a transaction other than a consumer transaction, a notification of disposition sent after default and 10 days or more before the earliest time of disposition set forth in the notification is sent within a reasonable time before the disposition.

### §9-613. Contents and Form of Notification Before Disposition of Collateral: General.

Except in a consumer-goods transaction, the following rules apply:

(1) The contents of a notification of disposition are sufficient if the notification:

(A) describes the debtor and the secured party;

(B) describes the collateral that is the subject of the intended disposition;

(C) states the method of intended disposition;

(D) states that the debtor is entitled to an accounting of the unpaid indebtedness and states the charge, if any, for an accounting; and

(E) states the time and place of a public disposition or the time after which any other disposition is to be made.

(2) Whether the contents of a notification that lacks any of the information specified in paragraph (1) are nevertheless sufficient is a question of fact.

(3) The contents of a notification providing substantially the information specified in paragraph (1) are sufficient, even if the notification includes:

(A) information not specified by that paragraph; or

(B) minor errors that are not seriously misleading.

(4) A particular phrasing of the notification is not required.

(5) The following form of notification and the form appearing in Section 9-614(3), when completed, each provides sufficient information:

* * *

### §9-614. Contents and Form of Notification Before Disposition of Collateral: Consumer-Goods Transaction.

In a consumer-goods transaction, the following rules apply:

(1) A notification of disposition must provide the following information:

(A) the information specified in Section 9-613(1);

(B) a description of any liability for a deficiency of the person to which the notification is sent;

(C) a telephone number from which the amount that must be paid to the secured party to redeem the collateral under Section 9-623 is available; and

(D) a telephone number or mailing address from which additional information concerning the disposition and the obligation secured is available.

(2) A particular phrasing of the notification is not required.

(3) The following form of notification, when completed, provides sufficient information:

* * *

(4) A notification in the form of paragraph (3) is sufficient, even if additional information appears at the end of the form.

(5) A notification in the form of paragraph (3) is sufficient, even if it includes errors in information not required by paragraph (1), unless the error is misleading with respect to rights arising under this article.

(6) If a notification under this section is not in the form of paragraph (3), law other than this article determines the effect of including information not required by paragraph (1).

### §9-615. Application of Proceeds of Disposition; Liability for Deficiency and Right to Surplus.

(a) **[Application of proceeds.]** A secured party shall apply or pay over for application the cash proceeds of disposition under Section 9-610 in the following order to:

(1) the reasonable expenses of retaking, holding, preparing for disposition, processing, and disposing, and, to the extent provided for by agreement and not prohibited by law, reasonable attorney's fees and legal expenses incurred by the secured party;

(2) the satisfaction of obligations secured by the security interest or agricultural lien under which the disposition is made;

(3) the satisfaction of obligations secured by any subordinate security interest in or other subordinate lien on the collateral if:

(A) the secured party receives from the holder of the subordinate security interest or other lien an authenticated demand for proceeds before distribution of the proceeds is completed; and

(B) in a case in which a consignor has an interest in the collateral, the subordinate security interest or other lien is senior to the interest of the consignor; and

(4) a secured party that is a consignor of the collateral if the secured party receives from the consignor an authenticated demand for proceeds before distribution of the proceeds is completed.

(b) **[Proof of subordinate interest.]** If requested by a secured party, a holder of a subordinate security interest or other lien shall furnish reasonable proof of the interest or lien within a reasonable time. Unless the holder does so, the secured party need not comply with the holder's demand under subsection (a)(3).

(c) **[Application of noncash proceeds.]** A secured party need not apply or pay over for application noncash proceeds of disposition under Section 9-610 unless the failure to do so would be commercially unreasonable. A secured party that applies or pays over for application noncash proceeds shall do so in a commercially reasonable manner.

(d) **[Surplus or deficiency if obligation secured.]** If the security interest under which a disposition is made secures payment or performance of an obligation, after making the payments and applications required by subsection (a) and permitted by subsection (c):

(1) unless subsection (a)(4) requires the secured party to apply or pay over cash proceeds to a consignor, the secured party shall account to and pay a debtor for any surplus; and

(2) the obligor is liable for any deficiency.

(e) **[No surplus or deficiency in sales of certain rights to payment.]** If the underlying transaction is a sale of accounts, chattel paper, payment intangibles, or promissory notes:

(1) the debtor is not entitled to any surplus; and

(2) the obligor is not liable for any deficiency.

(f) **[Calculation of surplus or deficiency in disposition to person related to secured party.]** The surplus or deficiency following a disposition is calculated based on the amount of proceeds that would have been realized in a disposition complying with this part to a transferee other than the secured party, a person related to the secured party, or a secondary obligor if:

(1) the transferee in the disposition is the secured party, a person related to the secured party, or a secondary obligor; and

(2) the amount of proceeds of the disposition is significantly below the range of proceeds that a complying disposition to a person other than the secured party, a person related to the secured party, or a secondary obligor would have brought.

(g) **[Cash proceeds received by junior secured party.]** A secured party that receives cash proceeds of a disposition in good faith and without knowledge that the receipt violates the rights of the holder of a security interest or other lien that is not subordinate to the security interest or agricultural lien under which the disposition is made:

(1) takes the cash proceeds free of the security interest or other lien;

(2) is not obligated to apply the proceeds of the disposition to the satisfaction of obligations secured by the security interest or other lien; and

(3) is not obligated to account to or pay the holder of the security interest or other lien for any surplus.

### §9-616. Explanation of Calculation of Surplus or Deficiency.

(a) **[Definitions.]** In this section:

(1) "Explanation" means a writing that:

(A) states the amount of the surplus or deficiency;

(B) provides an explanation in accordance with subsection (c) of how the secured party calculated the surplus or deficiency;

(C) states, if applicable, that future debits, credits, charges, including additional credit service charges or interest, rebates, and expenses may affect the amount of the surplus or deficiency; and

(D) provides a telephone number or mailing address from which additional information concerning the transaction is available.

(2) "Request" means a record:

(A) authenticated by a debtor or consumer obligor;

(B) requesting that the recipient provide an explanation; and

(C) sent after disposition of the collateral under Section 9-610.

(b) **[Explanation of calculation.]** In a consumer-goods transaction in which the debtor is entitled to a surplus or a consumer obligor is liable for a deficiency under Section 9-615, the secured party shall:

(1) send an explanation to the debtor or consumer obligor, as applicable, after the disposition and:

(A) before or when the secured party accounts to the debtor and pays any surplus or first makes written demand on the consumer obligor after the disposition for payment of the deficiency; and

(B) within 14 days after receipt of a request; or

(2) in the case of a consumer obligor who is liable for a deficiency, within 14 days after receipt of a request, send to the consumer obligor a record waiving the secured party's right to a deficiency.

(c) **[Required information.]** To comply with subsection (a)(1)(B), a writing must provide the following information in the following order:

(1) the aggregate amount of obligations secured by the security interest under which the disposition was made, and, if the amount reflects a rebate of unearned interest or credit service charge, an indication of that fact, calculated as of a specified date:

(A) if the secured party takes or receives possession of the collateral after default, not more than 35 days before the secured party takes or receives possession; or

(B) if the secured party takes or receives possession of the collateral before default or does not take possession of the collateral, not more than 35 days before the disposition;

(2) the amount of proceeds of the disposition;

(3) the aggregate amount of the obligations after deducting the amount of proceeds;

(4) the amount, in the aggregate or by type, and types of expenses, including expenses of retaking, holding, preparing for disposition, processing, and disposing of the collateral, and attorney's fees secured by the collateral which are known to the secured party and relate to the current disposition;

(5) the amount, in the aggregate or by type, and types of credits, including rebates of interest or credit service charges, to which the obligor is known to be entitled and which are not reflected in the amount in paragraph (1); and

(6) the amount of the surplus or deficiency.

(d) **[Substantial compliance.]** A particular phrasing of the explanation is not required. An explanation complying substantially with the requirements of subsection (a) is sufficient, even if it includes minor errors that are not seriously misleading.

(e) **[Charges for responses.]** A debtor or consumer obligor is entitled without charge to one response to a request under this section during any six-month period in which the secured party did not send to the debtor or consumer obligor an explanation pursuant to subsection (b)(1). The secured party may require payment of a charge not exceeding $25 for each additional response.

### §9-617. Rights of Transferee of Collateral.

(a) **[Effects of disposition.]** A secured party's disposition of collateral after default:

(1) transfers to a transferee for value all of the debtor's rights in the collateral;

(2) discharges the security interest under which the disposition is made; and

(3) discharges any subordinate security interest or other subordinate lien [other than liens created under [cite acts or statutes providing for liens, if any, that are not to be discharged]].

(b) **[Rights of good-faith transferee.]** A transferee that acts in good faith takes free of the rights and interests described in subsection (a), even if the secured party fails to comply with this article or the requirements of any judicial proceeding.

(c) **[Rights of other transferee.]** If a transferee does not take free of the rights and interests described in subsection (a), the transferee takes the collateral subject to:

(1) the debtor's rights in the collateral;

(2) the security interest or agricultural lien under which the disposition is made; and

(3) any other security interest or other lien.

**§9-618. Rights and Duties of Certain Secondary Obligors.**

(a) **[Rights and duties of secondary obligor.]** A secondary obligor acquires the rights and becomes obligated to perform the duties of the secured party after the secondary obligor:

(1) receives an assignment of a secured obligation from the secured party;

(2) receives a transfer of collateral from the secured party and agrees to accept the rights and assume the duties of the secured party; or

(3) is subrogated to the rights of a secured party with respect to collateral.

(b) **[Effect of assignment, transfer, or subrogation.]** An assignment, transfer, or subrogation described in subsection (a):

(1) is not a disposition of collateral under Section 9-610; and

(2) relieves the secured party of further duties under this article.

**§9-619. Transfer of Record or Legal Title.**

(a) **["Transfer statement."]** In this section, "transfer statement" means a record authenticated by a secured party stating:

(1) that the debtor has defaulted in connection with an obligation secured by specified collateral;

(2) that the secured party has exercised its post-default remedies with respect to the collateral;

(3) that, by reason of the exercise, a transferee has acquired the rights of the debtor in the collateral; and

(4) the name and mailing address of the secured party, debtor, and transferee.

(b) **[Effect of transfer statement.]** A transfer statement entitles the transferee to the transfer of record of all rights of the debtor in the collateral specified in the statement in any official filing, recording, registration, or certificate-of-title system covering the collateral. If a transfer statement is presented with the applicable fee and request form to the official or office responsible for maintaining the system, the official or office shall:

(1) accept the transfer statement;

(2) promptly amend its records to reflect the transfer; and

(3) if applicable, issue a new appropriate certificate of title in the name of the transferee.

(c) **[Transfer not a disposition; no relief of secured party's duties.]** A transfer of the record or legal title to collateral to a secured party under subsection (b) or otherwise is not of itself a disposition of collateral under this article and does not of itself relieve the secured party of its duties under this article.

**§9-620. Acceptance of Collateral in Full or Partial Satisfaction of Obligation; Compulsory Disposition of Collateral.**

(a) **[Conditions to acceptance in satisfaction.]** Except as otherwise provided in subsection (g), a secured party may accept collateral in full or partial satisfaction of the obligation it secures only if:

(1) the debtor consents to the acceptance under subsection (c);

(2) the secured party does not receive, within the time set forth in subsection (d), a notification of objection to the proposal authenticated by:

(A) a person to which the secured party was required to send a proposal under Section 9-621; or

(B) any other person, other than the debtor, holding an interest in the collateral subordinate to the security interest that is the subject of the proposal;

(3) if the collateral is consumer goods, the collateral is not in the possession of the debtor when the debtor consents to the acceptance; and

(4) subsection (e) does not require the secured party to dispose of the collateral or the debtor waives the requirement pursuant to Section 9-624.

(b) **[Purported acceptance ineffective.]** A purported or apparent acceptance of collateral under this section is ineffective unless:

(1) the secured party consents to the acceptance in an authenticated record or sends a proposal to the debtor; and

(2) the conditions of subsection (a) are met.

(c) **[Debtor's consent.]** For purposes of this section:

(1) a debtor consents to an acceptance of collateral in partial satisfaction of the obligation it secures only if the debtor agrees to the terms of the acceptance in a record authenticated after default; and

(2) a debtor consents to an acceptance of collateral in full satisfaction of the obligation it secures only if the debtor agrees to the terms of the acceptance in a record authenticated after default or the secured party:

(A) sends to the debtor after default a proposal that is unconditional or subject only to a condition that collateral not in the possession of the secured party be preserved or maintained;

(B) in the proposal, proposes to accept collateral in full satisfaction of the obligation it secures; and

(C) does not receive a notification of objection authenticated by the debtor within 20 days after the proposal is sent.

(d) **[Effectiveness of notification.]** To be effective under subsection (a)(2), a notification of objection must be received by the secured party:

(1) in the case of a person to which the proposal was sent pursuant to Section 9-621, within 20 days after notification was sent to that person; and

(2) in other cases:

(A) within 20 days after the last notification was sent pursuant to Section 9-621; or

(B) if a notification was not sent, before the debtor consents to the acceptance under subsection (c).

(e) **[Mandatory disposition of consumer goods.]** A secured party that has taken possession of collateral shall dispose of the collateral pursuant to Section 9-610 within the time specified in subsection (f) if:

(1) 60 percent of the cash price has been paid in the case of a purchase-money security interest in consumer goods; or

(2) 60 percent of the principal amount of the obligation secured has been paid in the case of a non-purchase-money security interest in consumer goods.

(f) **[Compliance with mandatory disposition requirement.]** To comply with subsection (e), the secured party shall dispose of the collateral:

(1) within 90 days after taking possession; or

(2) within any longer period to which the debtor and all secondary obligors have agreed in an agreement to that effect entered into and authenticated after default.

(g) **[No partial satisfaction in consumer transaction.]** In a consumer transaction, a secured party may not accept collateral in partial satisfaction of the obligation it secures.

**§9-621. Notification of Proposal to Accept Collateral.**

(a) **[Persons to which proposal to be sent.]** A secured party that desires to accept collateral in full or partial satisfaction of the obligation it secures shall send its proposal to:

(1) any person from which the secured party has received, before the debtor consented to the acceptance, an authenticated notification of a claim of an interest in the collateral;

(2) any other secured party or lienholder that, 10 days before the debtor consented to the acceptance, held a security interest in or other lien on the collateral perfected by the filing of a financing statement that:

(A) identified the collateral;

(B) was indexed under the debtor's name as of that date; and

(C) was filed in the office or offices in which to file a financing statement against the debtor covering the collateral as of that date; and

(3) any other secured party that, 10 days before the debtor consented to the acceptance, held a security interest in the collateral perfected by compliance with a statute, regulation, or treaty described in Section 9-311(a).

(b) **[Proposal to be sent to secondary obligor in partial satisfaction.]** A secured party that desires to accept collateral in partial satisfaction of the obligation it secures shall send its proposal to any secondary obligor in addition to the persons described in subsection (a).

**§9-622. Effect of Acceptance of Collateral.**
(a) **[Effect of acceptance.]** A secured party's acceptance of collateral in full or partial satisfaction of the obligation it secures:

(1) discharges the obligation to the extent consented to by the debtor;
(2) transfers to the secured party all of a debtor's rights in the collateral;
(3) discharges the security interest or agricultural lien that is the subject of the debtor's consent and any subordinate security interest or other subordinate lien; and
(4) terminates any other subordinate interest.

(b) **[Discharge of subordinate interest notwithstanding noncompliance.]** A subordinate interest is discharged or terminated under subsection (a), even if the secured party fails to comply with this article.

**§9-623. Right to Redeem Collateral.**
(a) **[Persons that may redeem.]** A debtor, any secondary obligor, or any other secured party or lienholder may redeem collateral.
(b) **[Requirements for redemption.]** To redeem collateral, a person shall tender:

(1) fulfillment of all obligations secured by the collateral; and
(2) the reasonable expenses and attorney's fees described in Section 9-615(a)(1).

(c) **[When redemption may occur.]** A redemption may occur at any time before a secured party:

(1) has collected collateral under Section 9-607;
(2) has disposed of collateral or entered into a contract for its disposition under Section 9-610; or
(3) has accepted collateral in full or partial satisfaction of the obligation it secures under Section 9-622.

**§9-624. Waiver.**
(a) **[Waiver of disposition notification.]** A debtor or secondary obligor may waive the right to notification of disposition of collateral under Section 9-611 only by an agreement to that effect entered into and authenticated after default.
(b) **[Waiver of mandatory disposition.]** A debtor may waive the right to require disposition of collateral under Section 9-620(e) only by an agreement to that effect entered into and authenticated after default.
(c) **[Waiver of redemption right.]** Except in a consumer-goods transaction, a debtor or secondary obligor may waive the right to redeem collateral under Section 9-623 only by an agreement to that effect entered into and authenticated after default.

**§9-625. Remedies for Secured Party's Failure to Comply with Article.**
(a) **[Judicial orders concerning noncompliance.]** If it is established that a secured party is not proceeding in accordance with this article, a court may order or restrain collection, enforcement, or disposition of collateral on appropriate terms and conditions.
(b) **[Damages for noncompliance.]** Subject to subsections (c), (d), and (f), a person is liable for damages in the amount of any loss caused by a failure to comply with this article. Loss caused by a failure to comply may include loss resulting from the debtor's inability to obtain, or increased costs of, alternative financing.
(c) **[Persons entitled to recover damages; statutory damages in consumer-goods transaction.]** Except as otherwise provided in Section 9-628:

(1) a person that, at the time of the failure, was a debtor, was an obligor, or held a security interest in or other lien on the collateral may recover damages under subsection (b) for its loss; and
(2) if the collateral is consumer goods, a person that was a debtor or a secondary obligor at the time a secured party failed to comply with this part may recover for that failure in any event an amount not less than the credit service charge plus 10 percent of the principal amount of the obligation or the time-price differential plus 10 percent of the cash price.

(d) **[Recovery when deficiency eliminated or reduced.]** A debtor whose deficiency is eliminated under Section 9-626 may recover damages for the loss of any surplus. However, a debtor or secondary obligor whose deficiency is eliminated or reduced under Section 9-626 may not otherwise recover under subsection (b) for noncompliance with the provisions of this part relating to collection, enforcement, disposition, or acceptance.
(e) **[Statutory damages: noncompliance with specified provisions.]** In addition to any damages recoverable under subsection (b), the debtor, consumer obligor, or person named as a debtor in a filed record, as applicable, may recover $500 in each case from a person that:

(1) fails to comply with Section 9-208;
(2) fails to comply with Section 9-209;
(3) files a record that the person is not entitled to file under Section 9-509(a);
(4) fails to cause the secured party of record to file or send a termination statement as required by Section 9-513(a) or (c);
(5) fails to comply with Section 9-616(b)(1) and whose failure is part of a pattern, or consistent with a practice, of noncompliance; or
(6) fails to comply with Section 9-616(b)(2).

(f) **[Statutory damages: noncompliance with Section 9-210.]** A debtor or consumer obligor may recover damages under subsection (b) and, in addition, $500 in each case from a person that, without reasonable cause, fails to comply with a request under Section 9-210. A recipient of a request under Section 9-210 which never claimed an interest in the collateral or obligations that are the subject of a request under that section has a reasonable excuse for failure to comply with the request within the meaning of this subsection.
(g) **[Limitation of security interest: noncompliance with Section 9-210.]** If a secured party fails to comply with a request regarding a list of collateral or a statement of account under Section 9-210, the secured party may claim a security interest only as shown in the list or statement included in the request as against a person that is reasonably misled by the failure.

**§9-626. Action in Which Deficiency or Surplus Is in Issue.**
(a) **[Applicable rules if amount of deficiency or surplus in issue.]** In an action arising from a transaction, other than a consumer transaction, in which the amount of a deficiency or surplus is in issue, the following rules apply:

(1) A secured party need not prove compliance with the provisions of this part relating to collection, enforcement, disposition, or acceptance unless the debtor or a secondary obligor places the secured party's compliance in issue.
(2) If the secured party's compliance is placed in issue, the secured party has the burden of establishing that the collection, enforcement, disposition, or acceptance was conducted in accordance with this part.
(3) Except as otherwise provided in Section 9-628, if a secured party fails to prove that the collection, enforcement, disposition, or acceptance was conducted in accordance with the provisions of this part relating to collection, enforcement, disposition, or acceptance, the liability of a debtor or a secondary obligor for a deficiency is limited to an amount by which the sum of the secured obligation, expenses, and attorney's fees exceeds the greater of:

(A) the proceeds of the collection, enforcement, disposition, or acceptance; or
(B) the amount of proceeds that would have been realized had the noncomplying secured party proceeded in accordance with the provisions of this part relating to collection, enforcement, disposition, or acceptance.

(4) For purposes of paragraph (3)(B), the amount of proceeds that would have been realized is equal to the sum of the secured obligation, expenses, and attorney's fees unless the secured party proves that the amount is less than that sum.

(5) If a deficiency or surplus is calculated under Section 9-615(f), the debtor or obligor has the burden of establishing that the amount of proceeds of the disposition is significantly below the range of prices that a complying disposition to a person other than the secured party, a person related to the secured party, or a secondary obligor would have brought.

(b) **[Non-consumer transactions; no inference.]** The limitation of the rules in subsection (a) to transactions other than consumer transactions is intended to leave to the court the determination of the proper rules in consumer transactions. The court may not infer from that limitation the nature of the proper rule in consumer transactions and may continue to apply established approaches.

### §9-627. Determination of Whether Conduct Was Commercially Reasonable.

(a) **[Greater amount obtainable under other circumstances; no preclusion of commercial reasonableness.]** The fact that a greater amount could have been obtained by a collection, enforcement, disposition, or acceptance at a different time or in a different method from that selected by the secured party is not of itself sufficient to preclude the secured party from establishing that the collection, enforcement, disposition, or acceptance was made in a commercially reasonable manner.

(b) **[Dispositions that are commercially reasonable.]** A disposition of collateral is made in a commercially reasonable manner if the disposition is made:

(1) in the usual manner on any recognized market;

(2) at the price current in any recognized market at the time of the disposition; or

(3) otherwise in conformity with reasonable commercial practices among dealers in the type of property that was the subject of the disposition.

(c) **[Approval by court or on behalf of creditors.]** A collection, enforcement, disposition, or acceptance is commercially reasonable if it has been approved:

(1) in a judicial proceeding;

(2) by a bona fide creditors' committee;

(3) by a representative of creditors; or

(4) by an assignee for the benefit of creditors.

(d) **[Approval under subsection (c) not necessary; absence of approval has no effect.]** Approval under subsection (c) need not be obtained, and lack of approval does not mean that the collection, enforcement, disposition, or acceptance is not commercially reasonable.

### §9-628. Nonliability and Limitation on Liability of Secured Party; Liability of Secondary Obligor.

(a) **[Limitation of liability of secured party for noncompliance with article.]** Unless a secured party knows that a person is a debtor or obligor, knows the identity of the person, and knows how to communicate with the person:

(1) the secured party is not liable to the person, or to a secured party or lienholder that has filed a financing statement against the person, for failure to comply with this article; and

(2) the secured party's failure to comply with this article does not affect the liability of the person for a deficiency.

(b) **[Limitation of liability based on status as secured party.]** A secured party is not liable because of its status as secured party:

(1) to a person that is a debtor or obligor, unless the secured party knows:

(A) that the person is a debtor or obligor;

(B) the identity of the person; and

(C) how to communicate with the person; or

(2) to a secured party or lienholder that has filed a financing statement against a person, unless the secured party knows:

(A) that the person is a debtor; and

(B) the identity of the person.

(c) **[Limitation of liability if reasonable belief that transaction not a consumer-goods transaction or consumer transaction.]** A secured party is not liable to any person, and a person's liability for a deficiency is not affected, because of any act or omission arising out of the secured party's reasonable belief that a transaction is not a consumer-goods transaction or a consumer transaction or that goods are not consumer goods, if the secured party's belief is based on its reasonable reliance on:

(1) a debtor's representation concerning the purpose for which collateral was to be used, acquired, or held; or

(2) an obligor's representation concerning the purpose for which a secured obligation was incurred.

(d) **[Limitation of liability for statutory damages.]** A secured party is not liable to any person under Section 9-625(c)(2) for its failure to comply with Section 9-616.

(e) **[Limitation of multiple liability for statutory damages.]** A secured party is not liable under Section 9-625(c)(2) more than once with respect to any one secured obligation.

## Part 7—Transition

### §9-701. Effective Date.

This [Act] takes effect on July 1, 2001.

### §9-702. Savings Clause.

(a) **[Pre-effective-date transactions or liens.]** Except as otherwise provided in this part, this [Act] applies to a transaction or lien within its scope, even if the transaction or lien was entered into or created before this [Act] takes effect.

(b) **[Continuing validity.]** Except as otherwise provided in subsection (c) and Sections 9-703 through 9-709:

(1) transactions and liens that were not governed by [former Article 9], were validly entered into or created before this [Act] takes effect, and would be subject to this [Act] if they had been entered into or created after this [Act] takes effect, and the rights, duties, and interests flowing from those transactions and liens remain valid after this [Act] takes effect; and

(2) the transactions and liens may be terminated, completed, consummated, and enforced as required or permitted by this [Act] or by the law that otherwise would apply if this [Act] had not taken effect.

(c) **[Pre-effective-date proceedings.]** This [Act] does not affect an action, case, or proceeding commenced before this [Act] takes effect.

### §9-703. Security Interest Perfected Before Effective Date.

(a) **[Continuing priority over lien creditor: perfection requirements satisfied.]** A security interest that is enforceable immediately before this [Act] takes effect and would have priority over the rights of a person that becomes a lien creditor at that time is a perfected security interest under this [Act] if, when this [Act] takes effect, the applicable requirements for enforceability and perfection under this [Act] are satisfied without further action.

(b) **[Continuing priority over lien creditor: perfection requirements not satisfied.]** Except as otherwise provided in Section 9-705, if, immediately before this [Act] takes effect, a security interest is enforceable and would have priority over the rights of a person that becomes a lien creditor at that time, but the applicable requirements for enforceability or perfection under this [Act] are not satisfied when this [Act] takes effect, the security interest:

(1) is a perfected security interest for one year after this [Act] takes effect;

(2) remains enforceable thereafter only if the security interest becomes enforceable under Section 9-203 before the year expires; and

(3) remains perfected thereafter only if the applicable requirements for perfection under this [Act] are satisfied before the year expires.

### §9-704. Security Interest Unperfected Before Effective Date.

A security interest that is enforceable immediately before this [Act] takes effect but which would be subordinate to the rights of a person that becomes a lien creditor at that time:

(1) remains an enforceable security interest for one year after this [Act] takes effect;
(2) remains enforceable thereafter if the security interest becomes enforceable under Section 9-203 when this [Act] takes effect or within one year thereafter; and
(3) becomes perfected:
(A) without further action, when this [Act] takes effect if the applicable requirements for perfection under this [Act] are satisfied before or at that time; or
(B) when the applicable requirements for perfection are satisfied if the requirements are satisfied after that time.

**§9-705. Effectiveness of Action Taken Before Effective Date.**
(a) **[Pre-effective-date action; one-year perfection period unless reperfected.]** If action, other than the filing of a financing statement, is taken before this [Act] takes effect and the action would have resulted in priority of a security interest over the rights of a person that becomes a lien creditor had the security interest become enforceable before this [Act] takes effect, the action is effective to perfect a security interest that attaches under this [Act] within one year after this [Act] takes effect. An attached security interest becomes unperfected one year after this [Act] takes effect unless the security interest becomes a perfected security interest under this [Act] before the expiration of that period.
(b) **[Pre-effective-date filing.]** The filing of a financing statement before this [Act] takes effect is effective to perfect a security interest to the extent the filing would satisfy the applicable requirements for perfection under this [Act].
(c) **[Pre-effective-date filing in jurisdiction formerly governing perfection.]** This [Act] does not render ineffective an effective financing statement that, before this [Act] takes effect, is filed and satisfies the applicable requirements for perfection under the law of the jurisdiction governing perfection as provided in [former Section 9-103]. However, except as otherwise provided in subsections (d) and (e) and Section 9-706, the financing statement ceases to be effective at the earlier of:
(1) the time the financing statement would have ceased to be effective under the law of the jurisdiction in which it is filed; or
(2) June 30, 2006.
(d) **[Continuation statement.]** The filing of a continuation statement after this [Act] takes effect does not continue the effectiveness of the financing statement filed before this [Act] takes effect. However, upon the timely filing of a continuation statement after this [Act] takes effect and in accordance with the law of the jurisdiction governing perfection as provided in Part 3, the effectiveness of a financing statement filed in the same office in that jurisdiction before this [Act] takes effect continues for the period provided by the law of that jurisdiction.
(e) **[Application of subsection (c)(2) to transmitting utility financing statement.]** Subsection (c)(2) applies to a financing statement that, before this [Act] takes effect, is filed against a transmitting utility and satisfies the applicable requirements for perfection under the law of the jurisdiction governing perfection as provided in [former Section 9-103] only to the extent that Part 3 provides that the law of a jurisdiction other than the jurisdiction in which the financing statement is filed governs perfection of a security interest in collateral covered by the financing statement.
(f) **[Application of Part 5.]** A financing statement that includes a financing statement filed before this [Act] takes effect and a continuation statement filed after this [Act] takes effect is effective only to the extent that it satisfies the requirements of Part 5 for an initial financing statement.

**§9-706. When Initial Financing Statement Suffices to Continue Effectiveness of Financing Statement.**
(a) **[Initial financing statement in lieu of continuation statement.]** The filing of an initial financing statement in the office specified in Section 9-501 continues the effectiveness of a financing statement filed before this [Act] takes effect if:
(1) the filing of an initial financing statement in that office would be effective to perfect a security interest under this [Act];
(2) the pre-effective-date financing statement was filed in an office in another State or another office in this State; and
(3) the initial financing statement satisfies subsection (c).
(b) **[Period of continued effectiveness.]** The filing of an initial financing statement under subsection (a) continues the effectiveness of the pre-effective-date financing statement:
(1) if the initial financing statement is filed before this [Act] takes effect, for the period provided in [former Section 9-403] with respect to a financing statement; and
(2) if the initial financing statement is filed after this [Act] takes effect, for the period provided in Section 9-515 with respect to an initial financing statement.
(c) **[Requirements for initial financing statement under subsection (a).]** To be effective for purposes of subsection (a), an initial financing statement must:
(1) satisfy the requirements of Part 5 for an initial financing statement;
(2) identify the pre-effective-date financing statement by indicating the office in which the financing statement was filed and providing the dates of filing and file numbers, if any, of the financing statement and of the most recent continuation statement filed with respect to the financing statement; and
(3) indicate that the pre-effective-date financing statement remains effective.

**§9-707. Amendment of Pre-Effective-Date Financing Statement.**
(a) **["Pre-effective-date financing statement".]** In this section, "pre-effective-date financing statement" means a financing statement filed before this [Act] takes effect.
(b) **[Applicable law.]** After this [Act] takes effect, a person may add or delete collateral covered by, continue or terminate the effectiveness of, or otherwise amend the information provided in, a pre-effective-date financing statement only in accordance with the law of the jurisdiction governing perfection as provided in Part 3. However, the effectiveness of a pre-effective-date financing statement also may be terminated in accordance with the law of the jurisdiction in which the financing statement is filed.
(c) **[Method of amending: general rule.]** Except as otherwise provided in subsection (d), if the law of this State governs perfection of a security interest, the information in a pre-effective-date financing statement may be amended after this [Act] takes effect only if:
(1) the pre-effective-date financing statement and an amendment are filed in the office specified in Section 9-501;
(2) an amendment is filed in the office specified in Section 9-501 concurrently with, or after the filing in that office of, an initial financing statement that satisfies Section 9-706(c); or
(3) an initial financing statement that provides the information as amended and satisfies Section 9-706(c) is filed in the office specified in Section 9-501.
(d) **[Method of amending: continuation.]** If the law of this State governs perfection of a security interest, the effectiveness of a pre-effective-date financing statement may be continued only under Section 9-705(d) and (f) or 9-706.
(e) **[Method of amending: additional termination rule.]** Whether or not the law of this State governs perfection of a security interest, the effectiveness of a pre-effective-date financing statement filed in this State may be terminated after this [Act] takes effect by filing a termination statement in the office in which the pre-effective-date financing statement is filed, unless an initial financing statement that satisfies Section 9-706(c) has been filed in the office specified by the law of the jurisdiction governing perfection as provided in Part 3 as the office in which to file a financing statement.

**§9-708. Persons Entitled to File Initial Financing Statement or Continuation Statement.**

A person may file an initial financing statement or a continuation statement under this part if:

(1) the secured party of record authorizes the filing; and

(2) the filing is necessary under this part:

(A) to continue the effectiveness of a financing statement filed before this [Act] takes effect; or

(B) to perfect or continue the perfection of a security interest.

**§9-709. Priority.**

(a) **[Law governing priority.]** This [Act] determines the priority of conflicting claims to collateral. However, if the relative priorities of the claims were established before this [Act] takes effect, [former Article 9] determines priority.

(b) **[Priority if security interest becomes enforceable under Section 9-203.]** For purposes of Section 9-322(a), the priority of a security interest that becomes enforceable under Section 9-203 of this [Act] dates from the time this [Act] takes effect if the security interest is perfected under this [Act] by the filing of a financing statement before this [Act] takes effect which would not have been effective to perfect the security interest under [former Article 9]. This subsection does not apply to conflicting security interests each of which is perfected by the filing of such a financing statement.

# APPENDIX C
# Uniform Partnership Act

## PART I. PRELIMINARY PROVISIONS

### §1. Name of Act
This act may be cited as Uniform Partnership Act.

### §2. Definition of Terms
In this act, "Court" includes every court and judge having jurisdiction in the case.

"Business" includes every trade, occupation, or profession.

"Person" includes individuals, partnerships, corporations, and other associations.

"Bankrupt" includes bankrupt under the Federal Bankruptcy Act or insolvent under any state insolvent act.

"Conveyance" includes every assignment, lease, mortgage, or encumbrance.

"Real property" includes land and any interest or estate in land.

### §3. Interpretation of Knowledge and Notice
(1) A person has "knowledge" of a fact within the meaning of this act not only when he has actual knowledge thereof, but also when he has knowledge of such other facts as in the circumstances shows bad faith.

(2) A person has "notice" of a fact within the meaning of this act when the person who claims the benefit of the notice

(a) States the fact to such person, or

(b) Delivers through the mail, or by other means of communication, a written statement of the fact to such person or to a proper person at his place of business or residence.

### §4. Rules of Construction
(1) The rule that statutes in derogation of the common law are to be strictly construed shall have no application to this act.

(2) The law of estoppel shall apply under this act.

(3) The law of agency shall apply under this act.

(4) This act shall be so interpreted and construed as to effect its general purpose to make uniform the law of those states which enact it.

(5) This act shall not be construed so as to impair the obligations of any contract existing when the act goes into effect, nor to affect any action or proceedings begun or right accrued before this act takes effect.

### §5. Rules for Cases Not Provided for in This Act
In any case not provided for in this act the rules of law and equity, including the law merchant, shall govern.

## PART II. NATURE OF PARTNERSHIP

### §6. Partnership Defined
(1) A partnership is an association of two or more persons to carry on as co-owners a business for profit.





(2) But any association formed under any other statute of this state, or any statute adopted by authority, other than the authority of this state, is not a partnership under this act, unless such association would have been a partnership in this state prior to the adoption of this act; but this act shall apply to limited partnerships except in so far as the statutes relating to such partnerships are inconsistent herewith.

### §7. Rules for Determining the Existence of a Partnership
In determining whether a partnership exists, these rules shall apply:

(1) Except as provided by Section 16 persons who are not partners as to each other are not partners as to third persons.

(2) Joint tenancy, tenancy in common, tenancy by the entireties, joint property, common property, or part ownership does not of itself establish a partnership, whether such co-owners do or do not share any profits made by the use of the property.

(3) The sharing of gross returns does not of itself establish a partnership, whether or not the persons sharing them have a joint or common right or interest in any property from which the returns are derived.

(4) The receipt by a person of a share of the profits of a business is prima facie evidence that he is a partner in the business, but no such inference shall be drawn if such profits were received in payment:

(a) As a debt by installments or otherwise,

(b) As wages of an employee or rent to a landlord,

(c) As an annuity to a widow or representative of a deceased partner,

(d) As interest on a loan, though the amount of payment vary with the profits of the business.

(e) As the consideration for the sale of a good will of a business or other property by installments or otherwise.

### §8. Partnership Property
(1) All property originally brought into the partnership stock or subsequently acquired by purchase or otherwise, on account of the partnership, is partnership property.

(2) Unless the contrary intention appears, property acquired with partnership funds is partnership property.

(3) Any estate in real property may be acquired in the partnership name. Title so acquired can be conveyed only in the partnership name.

(4) A conveyance to a partnership in the partnership name, though without words of inheritance, passes the entire estate of the grantor unless a contrary intent appears.

## PART III. RELATIONS OF PARTNERS TO PERSONS DEALING WITH THE PARTNERSHIP

### §9. Partner Agent of Partnership as to Partnership Business
(1) Every partner is an agent of the partnership for the purpose of its business, and the act of every partner, including the execution in the partnership

name of any instrument, for apparently carrying on in the usual way the business of the partnership of which he is a member binds the partnership, unless the partner so acting has in fact no authority to act for the partnership in the particular matter, and the person with whom he is dealing has knowledge of the fact that he has no such authority.
(2) An act of a partner which is not apparently for the carrying on of the business of the partnership in the usual way does not bind the partnership unless authorized by the other partners.
(3) Unless authorized by the other partners or unless they have abandoned the business, one or more but less than all the partners have no authority to:
(a) Assign the partnership property in trust for creditors or on the assignee's promise to pay the debts of the partnership,
(b) Dispose of the good will of the business,
(c) Do any other act which would make it impossible to carry on the ordinary business of a partnership,
(d) Confess a judgment,
(e) Submit a partnership claim or liability to arbitration or reference.
(4) No act of a partner in contravention of a restriction on authority shall bind the partnership to persons having knowledge of the restriction.

**§10. Conveyance of Real Property of the Partnership**
(1) Where title to real property is in the partnership name, any partner may convey title to such property by a conveyance executed in the partnership name; but the partnership may recover such property unless the partner's act binds the partnership under the provisions of paragraph (1) of section 9 or unless such property has been conveyed by the grantee or a person claiming through such grantee to a holder for value without knowledge that the partner, in making the conveyance, has exceeded his authority.
(2) Where title to real property is in the name of the partnership, a conveyance executed by a partner, in his own name, passes the equitable interest of the partnership, provided the act is one within the authority of the partner under the provisions of paragraph (1) of section 9.
(3) Where title to real property is in the name of one or more but not all the partners, and the record does not disclose the right of the partnership, the partners in whose name the title stands may convey title to such property, but the partnership may recover such property if the partners' act does not bind the partnership under the provisions of paragraph (1) of section 9, unless the purchaser or his assignee, is a holder for value, without knowledge.
(4) Where the title to real property is in the name of one or more or all the partners, or in a third person in trust for the partnership, a conveyance executed by a partner in the partnership name, or in his own name, passes the equitable interest of the partnership, provided the act is one within the authority of the partner under the provisions of paragraph (1) of section 9.
(5) Where the title to real property is in the names of all the partners a conveyance executed by all the partners passes all their rights in such property.

**§11. Partnership Bound by Admission of Partner**
An admission or representation made by any partner concerning partnership affairs within the scope of his authority as conferred by this act is evidence against the partnership.

**§12. Partnership Charged With Knowledge of or Notice to Partner**
Notice to any partner of any matter relating to partnership affairs, and the knowledge of the partner acting in the particular matter, acquired while a partner or then present to his mind, and the knowledge of any other partner who reasonably could and should have communicated it to the acting partner, operate as notice to or knowledge of the partnership, except in the case of a fraud on the partnership committed by or with the consent of that partner.

**§13. Partnership Bound by Partner's Wrongful Act**
Where, by any wrongful act or omission of any partner acting in the ordinary course of the business of the partnership or with the authority of his co-partners, loss or injury is caused to any person, not being a partner in the partnership, or any penalty is incurred, the partnership is liable therefor to the same extent as the partner so acting or omitting to act.

**§14. Partnership Bound by Partner's Breach of Trust**
The partnership is bound to make good the loss:
(a) Where one partner acting within the scope of his apparent authority receives money or property of a third person and misapplies it; and
(b) Where the partnership in the course of its business receives money or property of a third person and the money or property so received is misapplied by any partner while it is in the custody of the partnership.

**§15. Nature of Partner's Liability**
All partners are liable
(a) Jointly and severally for everything chargeable to the partnership under sections 13 and 14.
(b) Jointly for all other debts and obligations of the partnership; but any partner may enter into a separate obligation to perform a partnership contract.

**§16. Partner by Estoppel**
(1) When a person, by words spoken or written or by conduct, represents himself, or consents to another representing him to any one, as a partner in an existing partnership or with one or more persons not actual partners, he is liable to any such person to whom such representation has been made, who has, on the faith of such representation, given credit to the actual or apparent partnership, and if he has made such representation or consented to its being made in a public manner he is liable to such person, whether the representation has or has not been made or communicated to such person so giving credit by or with the knowledge of the apparent partner making the representation or consenting to its being made.
(a) When a partnership liability results, he is liable as though he were an actual member of the partnership.
(b) When no partnership liability results, he is liable jointly with the other persons, if any, so consenting to the contract or representation as to incur liability, otherwise separately.
(2) When a person has been thus represented to be a partner in an existing partnership, or with one or more persons not actual partners, he is an agent of the persons consenting to such representation to bind them to the same extent and in the same manner as though he were a partner in fact, with respect to persons who rely upon the representation. Where all the members of the existing partnership consent to the representation, a partnership act or obligation results; but in all other cases it is the joint act or obligation of the person acting and the persons consenting to the representation.

**§17. Liability of Incoming Partner**
A person admitted as a partner into an existing partnership is liable for all the obligations of the partnership arising before his admission as though he had been a partner when such obligations were incurred, except that this liability shall be satisfied only out of partnership property.

## PART IV. RELATIONS OF PARTNERS TO ONE ANOTHER

**§18. Rules Determining Rights and Duties of Partners**
The rights and duties of the partners in relation to the partnership shall be determined, subject to any agreement between them, by the following rules:
(a) Each partner shall be repaid his contributions, whether by way of capital or advances to the partnership property and share equally in the profits and surplus remaining after all liabilities, including those to partners, are satisfied; and must contribute towards the losses, whether of capital or otherwise, sustained by the partnership according to his share in the profits.
(b) The partnership must indemnify every partner in respect of payments made and personal liabilities reasonably incurred by him in the ordinary and proper conduct of its business, or for the preservation of its business or property.

(c) A partner, who in aid of the partnership makes any payment or advance beyond the amount of capital which he agreed to contribute, shall be paid interest from the date of the payment or advance.
(d) A partner shall receive interest on the capital contributed by him only from the date when repayment should be made.
(e) All partners have equal rights in the management and conduct of the partnership business.
(f) No partner is entitled to remuneration for acting in the partnership business, except that a surviving partner is entitled to reasonable compensation for his services in winding up the partnership affairs.
(g) No person can become a member of a partnership without the consent of all the partners.
(h) Any difference arising as to ordinary matters connected with the partnership business may be decided by a majority of the partners; but no act in contravention of any agreement between the partners may be done rightfully without the consent of all the partners.

### §19. Partnership Books

The partnership books shall be kept, subject to any agreement between the partners, at the principal place of business of the partnership, and every partner shall at all times have access to and may inspect and copy any of them.

### §20. Duty of Partners to Render Information

Partners shall render on demand true and full information of all things affecting the partnership to any partner or the legal representative of any deceased partner or partner under legal disability.

### §21. Partner Accountable as a Fiduciary

(1) Every partner must account to the partnership for any benefit, and hold as trustee for it any profits derived by him without the consent of the other partners from any transaction connected with the formation, conduct, or liquidation of the partnership or from any use by him of its property.
(2) This section applies also to the representatives of a deceased partner engaged in the liquidation of the affairs of the partnership as the personal representatives of the last surviving partner.

### §22. Right to an Account

Any partner shall have the right to a formal account as to partnership affairs:

(a) If he is wrongfully excluded from the partnership business or possession of its property by his co-partners,
(b) If the right exists under the terms of any agreement,
(c) As provided by section 21,
(d) Whenever other circumstances render it just and reasonable.

### §23. Continuation of Partnership Beyond Fixed Term

(1) When a partnership for a fixed term or particular undertaking is continued after the termination of such term or particular undertaking without any express agreement, the rights and duties of the partners remain the same as they were at such termination, so far as is consistent with a partnership at will.
(2) A continuation of the business by the partners or such of them as habitually acted therein during the term, without any settlement or liquidation of the partnership affairs, is prima facie evidence of a continuation of the partnership.

## PART V. PROPERTY RIGHTS OF A PARTNER

### §24. Extent of Property Rights of a Partner

The property rights of a partner are (1) his rights in specific partnership property, (2) his interest in the partnership, and (3) his right to participate in the management.

### §25. Nature of a Partner's Right in Specific Partnership Property

(1) A partner is co-owner with his partners of specific partnership property holding as a tenant in partnership.
(2) The incidents of this tenancy are such that:

(a) A partner, subject to the provisions of this act and to any agreement between the partners, has an equal right with his partners to possess specific partnership property for partnership purposes; but he has no right to possess such property for any other purpose without the consent of his partners.
(b) A partner's right in specific partnership property is not assignable except in connection with the assignment of rights of all the partners in the same property.
(c) A partner's right in specific partnership property is not subject to attachment or execution, except on a claim against the partnership. When partnership property is attached for a partnership debt the partners, or any of them, or the representatives of a deceased partner, cannot claim any right under the homestead or exemption laws.
(d) On the death of a partner his right in specific partnership property vests in the surviving partner or partners, except where the deceased was the last surviving partner, when his right in such property vests in his legal representative. Such surviving partner or partners, or the legal representative of the last surviving partner, has no right to possess the partnership property for any but a partnership purpose.
(e) A partner's right in specific partnership property is not subject to dower, curtesy, or allowances to widows, heirs, or next of kin.

### §26. Nature of Partner's Interest in the Partnership

A partner's interest in the partnership is his share of the profits and surplus, and the same is personal property.

### §27. Assignment of Partner's Interest

(1) A conveyance by a partner of his interest in the partnership does not of itself dissolve the partnership, nor, as against the other partners in the absence of agreement, entitle the assignee, during the continuance of the partnership to interfere in the management or administration of the partnership business or affairs, or to require any information or account of partnership transactions, or to inspect the partnership books; but it merely entitles the assignee to receive in accordance with his contract the profits to which the assigning partner would otherwise be entitled.
(2) In case of a dissolution of the partnership, the assignee is entitled to receive his assignor's interest and may require an account from the date only of the last account agreed to by all the partners.

### §28. Partner's Interest Subject to Charging Order

(1) On due application to a competent court by any judgment creditor of a partner, the court which entered the judgment, order, or decree, or any other court, may charge the interest of the debtor partner with payment of the unsatisfied amount of such judgment debt with interest thereon; and may then or later appoint a receiver of his share of the profits, and of any other money due or to fall due to him in respect of the partnership, and make all other orders, directions, accounts and inquiries which the debtor partner might have made, or which the circumstances of the case may require.
(2) The interest charged may be redeemed at any time before foreclosure, or in case of a sale being directed by the court may be purchased without thereby causing a dissolution:

(a) With separate property, by any one or more of the partners, or
(b) With partnership property, by any one or more of the partners with the consent of all the partners whose interests are not so charged or sold.

(3) Nothing in this act shall be held to deprive a partner of his right, if any, under the exemption laws, as regards his interest in the partnership.

## PART VI. DISSOLUTION AND WINDING UP

### §29. Dissolution Defined

The dissolution of a partnership is the change in the relation of the partners caused by any partner ceasing to be associated in the carrying on as distinguished from the winding up of the business.

### §30. Partnership Not Terminated by Dissolution

On dissolution the partnership is not terminated, but continues until the winding up of partnership affairs is completed.

**§31. Causes of Dissolution**

Dissolution is caused:

(1) Without violation of the agreement between the partners,

(a) By the termination of the definite term or particular undertaking specified in the agreement,

(b) By the express will of any partner when no definite term or particular undertaking is specified,

(c) By the express will of all the partners who have not assigned their interests or suffered them to be charged for their separate debts, either before or after the termination of any specified term or particular undertaking,

(d) By the expulsion of any partner from the business bona fide in accordance with such a power conferred by the agreement between the partners;

(2) In contravention of the agreement between the partners, where the circumstances do not permit a dissolution under any other provision of this section, by the express will of any partner at any time;

(3) By any event which makes it unlawful for the business of the partnership to be carried on or for the members to carry it on in partnership;

(4) By the death of any partner;

(5) By the bankruptcy of any partner or the partnership;

(6) By decree of court under section 32.

**§32. Dissolution by Decree of Court**

(1) On application by or for a partner the court shall decree a dissolution whenever:

(a) A partner has been declared a lunatic in any judicial proceeding or is shown to be of unsound mind,

(b) A partner becomes in any other way incapable of performing his part of the partnership contract,

(c) A partner has been guilty of such conduct as tends to affect prejudicially the carrying on of the business,

(d) A partner wilfully or persistently commits a breach of the partnership agreement, or otherwise so conducts himself in matters relating to the partnership business that it is not reasonably practicable to carry on the business in partnership with him,

(e) The business of the partnership can only be carried on at a loss,

(f) Other circumstances render a dissolution equitable.

(2) On the application of the purchaser of a partner's interest under sections 27 or 28:

(a) After the termination of the specified term or particular undertaking,

(b) At any time if the partnership was a partnership at will when the interest was assigned or when the charging order was issued.

**§33. General Effect of Dissolution on Authority of Partner**

Except so far as may be necessary to wind up partnership affairs or to complete transactions begun but not then finished, dissolution terminates all authority of any partner to act for the partnership,

(1) With respect to the partners,

(a) When the dissolution is not by the act, bankruptcy or death of a partner; or

(b) When the dissolution is by such act, bankruptcy or death of a partner, in cases where section 34 so requires.

(2) With respect to persons not partners, as declared in section 35.

**§34. Right of Partner to Contribution From Copartners After Dissolution**

Where the dissolution is caused by the act, death or bankruptcy of a partner, each partner is liable to his copartners for his share of any liability created by any partner acting for the partnership as if the partnership had not been dissolved unless

(a) The dissolution being by act of any partner, the partner acting for the partnership had knowledge of the dissolution, or

(b) The dissolution being by the death or bankruptcy of a partner, the partner acting for the partnership had knowledge or notice of the death or bankruptcy.

**§35. Power of Partner to Bind Partnership to Third Persons After Dissolution**

(1) After dissolution a partner can bind the partnership except as provided in Paragraph (3)

(a) By any act appropriate for winding up partnership affairs or completing transactions unfinished at dissolution;

(b) By any transaction which would bind the partnership if dissolution had not taken place, provided the other party to the transaction.

(I) Had extended credit to the partnership prior to dissolution and had no knowledge or notice of the dissolution; or

(II) Though he had not so extended credit, had nevertheless known of the partnership prior to dissolution, and, having no knowledge or notice of dissolution, the fact of dissolution had not been advertised in a newspaper of general circulation in the place (or in each place if more than one) at which the partnership business was regularly carried on.

(2) The liability of a partner under paragraph (1b) shall be satisfied out of partnership assets alone when such partner had been prior to dissolution

(a) Unknown as a partner to the person with whom the contract is made; and

(b) So far unknown and inactive in partnership affairs that the business reputation of the partnership could not be said to have been in any degree due to his connection with it.

(3) The partnership is in no case bound by any act of a partner after dissolution

(a) Where the partnership is dissolved because it is unlawful to carry on the business, unless the act is appropriate for winding up partnership affairs; or

(b) Where the partner has become bankrupt; or

(c) Where the partner has no authority to wind up partnership affairs; except by a transaction with one who

(I) Had extended credit to the partnership prior to dissolution and had no knowledge or notice of his want of authority; or

(II) Had not extended credit to the partnership prior to dissolution, and, having no knowledge or notice of his want of authority, the fact of his want of authority has not been advertised in the manner provided for advertising the fact of dissolution in paragraph (1bII).

(4) Nothing in this section shall affect the liability under section 16 of any person who after dissolution represents himself or consents to another representing him as a partner in a partnership engaged in carrying on business.

**§36. Effect of Dissolution on Partner's Existing Liability**

(1) The dissolution of the partnership does not of itself discharge the existing liability of any partner.

(2) A partner is discharged from any existing liability upon dissolution of the partnership by an agreement to that effect between himself, the partnership creditor and the person or partnership continuing the business; and such agreement may be inferred from the course of dealing between the creditor having knowledge of the dissolution and the person or partnership continuing the business.

(3) Where a person agrees to assume the existing obligations of a dissolved partnership, the partners whose obligations have been assumed shall be discharged from any liability to any creditor of the partnership who, knowing of the agreement, consents to a material alteration in the nature or time of payment of such obligations.

(4) The individual property of a deceased partner shall be liable for all obligations of the partnership incurred while he was a partner but subject to the prior payment of his separate debts.

**§37. Right to Wind Up**

Unless otherwise agreed the partners who have not wrongfully dissolved the partnership or the legal representative of the last surviving partner, not bankrupt, has the right to wind up the partnership affairs; provided, however, that any partner, his legal representative or his assignee, upon cause shown, may obtain winding up by the court.

**§38. Rights of Partners to Application of Partnership Property**

(1) When dissolution is caused in any way, except in contravention of the partnership agreement, each partner as against his co-partners and all persons claiming through them in respect of their interests in the partnership, unless otherwise agreed, may have the partnership property applied to discharge its liabilities, and the surplus applied to pay in cash the net amount owing to the respective partners. But if dissolution is caused by expulsion of a partner, bona fide under the partnership agreement and if the expelled partner is discharged from all partnership liabilities, either by payment or agreement under section 36(2), he shall receive in cash only the net amount due him from the partnership.

(2) When dissolution is caused in contravention of the partnership agreement the rights of the partners shall be as follows:

(a Each partner who has not caused dissolution wrongfully shall have,

(I) All the rights specified in paragr
aph (1) of this section, and

(II) The right, as against each partner who has caused the dissolution wrongfully, to damages for breach of the agreement.

(b) The partners who have not caused the dissolution wrongfully, if they all desire to continue the business in the same name, either by themselves or jointly with others, may do so, during the agreed term for the partnership and for that purpose may possess the partnership property, provided they secure the payment by bond approved by the court, or pay to any partner who has caused the dissolution wrongfully, the value of his interest in the partnership at the dissolution, less any damages recoverable under clause (2aII) of the section, and in like manner indemnify him against all present or future partnership liabilities.

(c) A partner who has caused the dissolution wrongfully shall have:

(I) If the business is not continued under the provisions of paragraph (2b) all the rights of a partner under paragraph (1), subject to clause (2aII), of this section,

(II) If the business is continued under paragraph (2b) of this section the right as against his co-partners and all claiming through them in respect of their interests in the partnership, to have the value of his interest in the partnership, less any damages caused to his co-partners by the dissolution, ascertained and paid to him in cash, or the payment secured by bond approved by the court, and to be released from all existing liabilities of the partnership; but in ascertaining the value of the partner's interest the value of the good will of the business shall not be considered.

**§39. Rights Where Partnership Is Dissolved for Fraud or Misrepresentation**

Where a partnership contract is rescinded on the ground of the fraud or misrepresentation of one of the parties thereto, the party entitled to rescind is, without prejudice to any other right, entitled,

(a) To a lien on, or right of retention of, the surplus of the partnership property after satisfying the partnership liabilities to third persons for any sum of money paid by him for the purchase of an interest in the partnership and for any capital or advances contributed by him; and

(b) To stand, after all liabilities to third persons have been satisfied, in the place of the creditors of the partnership for any payments made by him in respect of the partnership liabilities; and

(c) To be indemnified by the person guilty of the fraud or making the representation against all debts and liabilities of the partnership.

**§40. Rules for Distribution**

In settling accounts between the partners after dissolution, the following rules shall be observed, subject to any agreement to the contrary:

(a) The assets of the partnership are:

(I) The partnership property,

(II) The contributions of the partners necessary for the payment of all the liabilities specified in clause (b) of this paragraph.

(b) The liabilities of the partnership shall rank in order of payment, as follows:

(I) Those owing to creditors other than partners,

(II) Those owing to partners other than for capital and profits,

(III) Those owing to partners in respect of capital,

(IV) Those owing to partners in respect of profits.

(c) The assets shall be applied in the order of their declaration in clause (a) of this paragraph to the satisfaction of the liabilities.

(d) The partners shall contribute, as provided by section 18(a) the amount necessary to satisfy the liabilities; but if any, but not all, of the partners are insolvent, or, not being subject to process, refuse to contribute, the other parties shall contribute their share of the liabilities, and, in the relative proportions in which they share the profits, the additional amount necessary to pay the liabilities.

(e) An assignee for the benefit of creditors or any person appointed by the court shall have the right to enforce the contributions specified in clause (d) of this paragraph.

(f) Any partner or his legal representative shall have the right to enforce the contributions specified in clause (d) of this paragraph, to the extent of the amount which he has paid in excess of his share of the liability.

(g) The individual property of a deceased partner shall be liable for the contributions specified in clause (d) of this paragraph.

(h) When partnership property and the individual properties of the partners are in possession of a court for distribution, partnership creditors shall have priority on partnership property and separate creditors on individual property, saving the rights of lien or secured creditors as heretofore.

(i) Where a partner has become bankrupt or his estate is insolvent the claims against his separate property shall rank in the following order:

(I) Those owing to separate creditors,

(II) Those owing to partnership creditors,

(III) Those owing to partners by way of contribution.

**§41. Liability of Persons Continuing the Business in Certain Cases**

(1) When any new partner is admitted into an existing partnership, or when any partner retires and assigns (or the representative of the deceased partner assigns) his rights in partnership property to two or more of the partners, or to one or more of the partners and one or more third persons, if the business is continued without liquidation of the partnership affairs, creditors of the first or dissolved partnership are also creditors of the person or partnership so continuing the business.

(2) When all but one partner retire and assign (or the representative of a deceased partner assigns) their rights in partnership property to the remaining partner, who continues the business without liquidation of partnership affairs, either alone or with others, creditors of the dissolved partnership are also creditors of the person or partnership so continuing the business.

(3) When any partner retires or dies and the business of the dissolved partnership is continued as set forth in paragraphs (1) and (2) of this section, with the consent of the retired partners or the representative of the deceased partner, but without any assignment of his right in partnership property, rights of creditors of the dissolved partnership and of the creditors of the person or partnership continuing the business shall be as if such assignment had been made.

(4) When all the partners or their representatives assign their rights in partnership property to one or more third persons who promise to pay the debts and who continue the business of the dissolved partnership, creditors of the dissolved partnership are also creditors of the person or partnership continuing the business.

(5) When any partner wrongfully causes a dissolution and the remaining partners continue the business under the provisions of section 38(2b), either alone or with others, and without liquidation of the partnership affairs, creditors of the dissolved partnership are also creditors of the person or partnership continuing the business.

(6) When a partner is expelled and the remaining partners continue the business either alone or with others, without liquidation of the partnership

affairs, creditors of the dissolved partnership are also creditors of the person or partnership continuing the business.

(7) The liability of a third person becoming a partner in the partnership continuing the business, under this section, to the creditors of the dissolved partnership shall be satisfied out of partnership property only.

(8) When the business of a partnership after dissolution is continued under any conditions set forth in this section the creditors of the dissolved partnership, as against the separate creditors of the retiring or deceased partner or the representative of the deceased partner, have a prior right to any claim of the retired partner or the representative of the deceased partner against the person or partnership continuing the business, on account of the retired or deceased partner's interest in the dissolved partnership or on account of any consideration promised for such interest or for his right in partnership property.

(9) Nothing in this section shall be held to modify any right of creditors to set aside any assignment on the ground of fraud.

(10) The use by the person or partnership continuing the business of the partnership name, or the name of a deceased partner as part thereof, shall not of itself make the individual property of the deceased partner liable for any debts contracted by such person or partnership.

### §42. Rights of Retiring or Estate of Deceased Partner When the Business Is Continued

When any partner retires or dies, and the business is continued under any of the conditions set forth in section 41(1, 2, 3, 5, 6), or section 38(2b), without any settlement of accounts as between him or his estate and the person or partnership continuing the business, unless otherwise agreed, he or his legal representative as against such persons or partnership may have the value of his interest at the date of dissolution ascertained, and shall receive as an ordinary creditor an amount equal to the value of his interest in the dissolved partnership with interest, or, at his option or at the option of his legal representative, in lieu of interest, the profits attributable to the use of his right in the property of the dissolved partnership; provided that the creditors of the dissolved partnership as against the separate creditors, or the representative of the retired or deceased partner, shall have priority on any claim arising under this section, as provided by section 41(8) of this act.

### §43. Accrual of Actions

The right to an account of his interest shall accrue to any partner, or his legal representative, as against the winding up partners or the surviving partners or the person or partnership continuing the business, at the date of dissolution, in the absence of any agreement to the contrary.

## PART VII. MISCELLANEOUS PROVISIONS

### §44. When Act Takes Effect

This act shall take effect on the __________ day of __________ one thousand nine hundred and __________.

### §45. Legislation Repealed

All acts or parts of acts inconsistent with this act are hereby repealed.

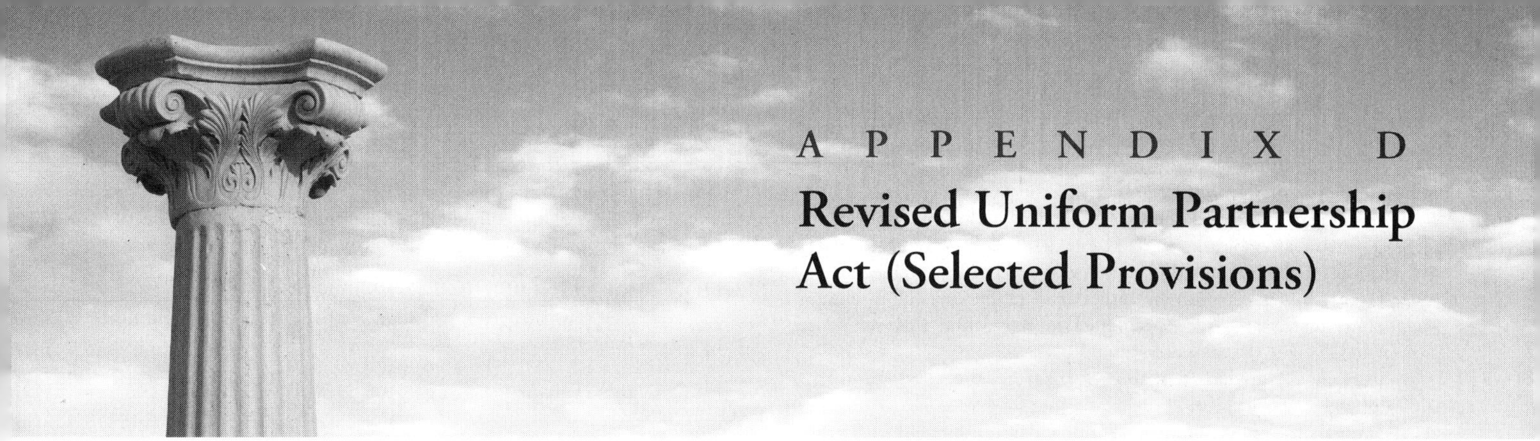

APPENDIX D

# Revised Uniform Partnership Act (Selected Provisions)

## [ARTICLE] 1

## GENERAL PROVISIONS

### SECTION 101. DEFINITIONS.

In this [Act]:

(1) "Business" includes every trade, occupation, and profession.

(2) "Debtor in bankruptcy" means a person who is the subject of:

(i) an order for relief under Title 11 of the United States Code or a comparable order under a successor statute of general application; or

(ii) a comparable order under federal, state, or foreign law governing insolvency.

(3) "Distribution" means a transfer of money or other property from a partnership to a partner in the partner's capacity as a partner or to the partner's transferee.

(4) "Foreign limited liability partnership" means a partnership that:

(i) is formed under laws other than the laws of this State; and

(ii) has the status of a limited liability partnership under those laws.

(5) "Limited liability partnership" means a partnership that has filed a statement of qualification under Section 1001 and does not have a similar statement in effect in any other jurisdiction.

(6) "Partnership" means an association of two or more persons to carry on as co-owners a business for profit formed under Section 202, predecessor law, or comparable law of another jurisdiction.

(7) "Partnership agreement" means the agreement, whether written, oral, or implied, among the partners concerning the partnership, including amendments to the partnership agreement.

(8) "Partnership at will" means a partnership in which the partners have not agreed to remain partners until the expiration of a definite term or the completion of a particular undertaking.

(9) "Partnership interest" or "partner's interest in the partnership" means all of a partner's interests in the partnership, including the partner's transferable interest and all management and other rights.

(10) "Person" means an individual, corporation, business trust, estate, trust, partnership, association, joint venture, government, governmental subdivision, agency, or instrumentality, or any other legal or commercial entity.

(11) "Property" means all property, real, personal, or mixed, tangible or intangible, or any interest therein.

(12) "State" means a State of the United States, the District of Columbia, the Commonwealth of Puerto Rico, or any territory or insular possession subject to the jurisdiction of the United States.

(13) "Statement" means a statement of partnership authority under Section 303, a statement of denial under Section 304, a statement of dissociation under Section 704, a statement of dissolution under Section 805, a statement of merger under Section 907, a statement of qualification under Section 1001, a statement of foreign qualification under Section 1102, or an amendment or cancellation of any of the foregoing.

(14) "Transfer" includes an assignment, conveyance, lease, mortgage, deed, and encumbrance.





### SECTION 102. KNOWLEDGE AND NOTICE.

(a) A person knows a fact if the person has actual knowledge of it.

(b) A person has notice of a fact if the person:

(1) knows of it;

(2) has received a notification of it; or

(3) has reason to know it exists from all of the facts known to the person at the time in question.

(c) A person notifies or gives a notification to another by taking steps reasonably required to inform the other person in ordinary course, whether or not the other person learns of it.

(d) A person receives a notification when the notification:

(1) comes to the person's attention; or

(2) is duly delivered at the person's place of business or at any other place held out by the person as a place for receiving communications.

(e) Except as otherwise provided in subsection (f), a person other than an individual knows, has notice, or receives a notification of a fact for purposes of a particular transaction when the individual conducting the transaction knows, has notice, or receives a notification of the fact, or in any event when the fact would have been brought to the individual's attention if the person had exercised reasonable diligence. The person exercises reasonable diligence if it maintains reasonable routines for communicating significant information to the individual conducting the transaction and there is reasonable compliance with the routines. Reasonable diligence does not require an individual acting for the person to communicate information unless the communication is part of the individual's regular duties or the individual has reason to know of the transaction and that the transaction would be materially affected by the information.

(f) A partner's knowledge, notice, or receipt of a notification of a fact relating to the partnership is effective immediately as knowledge by, notice to, or receipt of a notification by the partnership, except in the case of a fraud on the partnership committed by or with the consent of that partner.

### SECTION 103. EFFECT OF PARTNERSHIP AGREEMENT; NONWAIVABLE PROVISIONS.

(a) Except as otherwise provided in subsection (b), relations among the partners and between the partners and the partnership are governed by the partnership agreement. To the extent the partnership agreement does not otherwise provide, this [Act] governs relations among the partners and between the partners and the partnership.

(b) The partnership agreement may not:

(1) vary the rights and duties under Section 105 except to eliminate the duty to provide copies of statements to all of the partners;

(2) unreasonably restrict the right of access to books and records under Section 403(b);

(3) eliminate the duty of loyalty under Section 404(b) or 603(b)(3), but:

(i) the partnership agreement may identify specific types or categories of activities that do not violate the duty of loyalty, if not manifestly unreasonable; or

(ii) all of the partners or a number or percentage specified in the partnership agreement may authorize or ratify, after full disclosure of all material facts, a specific act or transaction that otherwise would violate the duty of loyalty;

(4) unreasonably reduce the duty of care under Section 404(c) or 603(b)(3);

(5) eliminate the obligation of good faith and fair dealing under Section 404(d), but the partnership agreement may prescribe the standards by which the performance of the obligation is to be measured, if the standards are not manifestly unreasonable;

(6) vary the power to dissociate as a partner under Section 602(a), except to require the notice under Section 601(1) to be in writing;

(7) vary the right of a court to expel a partner in the events specified in Section 601(5);

(8) vary the requirement to wind up the partnership business in cases specified in Section 801(4), (5), or (6);

(9) vary the law applicable to a limited liability partnership under Section 106(b); or

(10) restrict rights of third parties under this [Act].

### SECTION 104. SUPPLEMENTAL PRINCIPLES OF LAW.

(a) Unless displaced by particular provisions of this [Act], the principles of law and equity supplement this [Act].

(b) If an obligation to pay interest arises under this [Act] and the rate is not specified, the rate is that specified in [applicable statute].

## [ARTICLE] 2
## NATURE OF PARTNERSHIP

### SECTION 201. PARTNERSHIP AS ENTITY.

(a) A partnership is an entity distinct from its partners.

(b) A limited liability partnership continues to be the same entity that existed before the filing of a statement of qualification under Section 1001.

### SECTION 202. FORMATION OF PARTNERSHIP.

(a) Except as otherwise provided in subsection (b), the association of two or more persons to carry on as co-owners a business for profit forms a partnership, whether or not the persons intend to form a partnership.

(b) An association formed under a statute other than this [Act], a predecessor statute, or a comparable statute of another jurisdiction is not a partnership under this [Act].

(c) In determining whether a partnership is formed, the following rules apply:

(1) Joint tenancy, tenancy in common, tenancy by the entireties, joint property, common property, or part ownership does not by itself establish a partnership, even if the co-owners share profits made by the use of the property.

(2) The sharing of gross returns does not by itself establish a partnership, even if the persons sharing them have a joint or common right or interest in property from which the returns are derived.

(3) A person who receives a share of the profits of a business is presumed to be a partner in the business, unless the profits were received in payment:

(i) of a debt by installments or otherwise;

(ii) for services as an independent contractor or of wages or other compensation to an employee;

(iii) of rent;

(iv) of an annuity or other retirement or health benefit to a beneficiary, representative, or designee of a deceased or retired partner;

(v) of interest or other charge on a loan, even if the amount of payment varies with the profits of the business, including a direct or indirect present or future ownership of the collateral, or rights to income, proceeds, or increase in value derived from the collateral; or

(vi) for the sale of the goodwill of a business or other property by installments or otherwise.

### SECTION 203. PARTNERSHIP PROPERTY.

Property acquired by a partnership is property of the partnership and not of the partners individually.

### SECTION 204. WHEN PROPERTY IS PARTNERSHIP PROPERTY.

(a) Property is partnership property if acquired in the name of:

(1) the partnership; or

(2) one or more partners with an indication in the instrument transferring title to the property of the person's capacity as a partner or of the existence of a partnership but without an indication of the name of the partnership.

(b) Property is acquired in the name of the partnership by a transfer to:

(1) the partnership in its name; or

(2) one or more partners in their capacity as partners in the partnership, if the name of the partnership is indicated in the instrument transferring title to the property.

(c) Property is presumed to be partnership property if purchased with partnership assets, even if not acquired in the name of the partnership or of one or more partners with an indication in the instrument transferring title to the property of the person's capacity as a partner or of the existence of a partnership.

(d) Property acquired in the name of one or more of the partners, without an indication in the instrument transferring title to the property of the person's capacity as a partner or of the existence of a partnership and without use of partnership assets, is presumed to be separate property, even if used for partnership purposes.

## [ARTICLE] 3
## RELATIONS OF PARTNERS TO PERSONS DEALING WITH PARTNERSHIP

### SECTION 301. PARTNER AGENT OF PARTNERSHIP.

Subject to the effect of a statement of partnership authority under Section 303:

(1) Each partner is an agent of the partnership for the purpose of its business. An act of a partner, including the execution of an instrument in the partnership name, for apparently carrying on in the ordinary course the partnership business or business of the kind carried on by the partnership binds the partnership, unless the partner had no authority to act for the partnership in the particular matter and the person with whom the partner was dealing knew or had received a notification that the partner lacked authority.

(2) An act of a partner which is not apparently for carrying on in the ordinary course the partnership business or business of the kind carried on by the partnership binds the partnership only if the act was authorized by the other partners.

### SECTION 303. STATEMENT OF PARTNERSHIP AUTHORITY.

(a) A partnership may file a statement of partnership authority, which:

(1) must include:

(i) the name of the partnership;

(ii) the street address of its chief executive office and of one office in this State, if there is one;

(iii) the names and mailing addresses of all of the partners or of an agent appointed and maintained by the partnership for the purpose of subsection (b); and

(iv) the names of the partners authorized to execute an instrument transferring real property held in the name of the partnership; and

(2) may state the authority, or limitations on the authority, of some or all of the partners to enter into other transactions on behalf of the partnership and any other matter.

(b) If a statement of partnership authority names an agent, the agent shall maintain a list of the names and mailing addresses of all of the partners and make it available to any person on request for good cause shown.

(c) If a filed statement of partnership authority is executed pursuant to Section 105(c) and states the name of the partnership but does not contain all of the other information required by subsection (a), the statement nevertheless operates with respect to a person not a partner as provided in subsections (d) and (e).

(d) Except as otherwise provided in subsection (g), a filed statement of partnership authority supplements the authority of a partner to enter into transactions on behalf of the partnership as follows:

(1) Except for transfers of real property, a grant of authority contained in a filed statement of partnership authority is conclusive in favor of a person who gives value without knowledge to the contrary, so long as and to the extent that a limitation on that authority is not then contained in another filed statement. A filed cancellation of a limitation on authority revives the previous grant of authority.

(2) A grant of authority to transfer real property held in the name of the partnership contained in a certified copy of a filed statement of partnership authority recorded in the office for recording transfers of that real property is conclusive in favor of a person who gives value without knowledge to the contrary, so long as and to the extent that a certified copy of a filed statement containing a limitation on that authority is not then of record in the office for recording transfers of that real property. The recording in the office for recording transfers of that real property of a certified copy of a filed cancellation of a limitation on authority revives the previous grant of authority.

(e) A person not a partner is deemed to know of a limitation on the authority of a partner to transfer real property held in the name of the partnership if a certified copy of the filed statement containing the limitation on authority is of record in the office for recording transfers of that real property.

(f) Except as otherwise provided in subsections (d) and (e) and Sections 704 and 805, a person not a partner is not deemed to know of a limitation on the authority of a partner merely because the limitation is contained in a filed statement.

(g) Unless earlier canceled, a filed statement of partnership authority is canceled by operation of law five years after the date on which the statement, or the most recent amendment, was filed with the [Secretary of State].

### SECTION 305. PARTNERSHIP LIABLE FOR PARTNER'S ACTIONABLE CONDUCT.

(a) A partnership is liable for loss or injury caused to a person, or for a penalty incurred, as a result of a wrongful act or omission, or other actionable conduct, of a partner acting in the ordinary course of business of the partnership or with authority of the partnership.

(b) If, in the course of the partnership's business or while acting with authority of the partnership, a partner receives or causes the partnership to receive money or property of a person not a partner, and the money or property is misapplied by a partner, the partnership is liable for the loss.

### SECTION 306. PARTNER'S LIABILITY.

(a) Except as otherwise provided in subsections (b) and (c), all partners are liable jointly and severally for all obligations of the partnership unless otherwise agreed by the claimant or provided by law.

(b) A person admitted as a partner into an existing partnership is not personally liable for any partnership obligation incurred before the person's admission as a partner.

(c) An obligation of a partnership incurred while the partnership is a limited liability partnership, whether arising in contract, tort, or otherwise, is solely the obligation of the partnership. A partner is not personally liable, directly or indirectly, by way of contribution or otherwise, for such an obligation solely by reason of being or so acting as a partner. This subsection applies notwithstanding anything inconsistent in the partnership agreement that existed immediately before the vote required to become a limited liability partnership under Section 1001(b).

### SECTION 307. ACTIONS BY AND AGAINST PARTNERSHIP AND PARTNERS.

(a) A partnership may sue and be sued in the name of the partnership.

(b) An action may be brought against the partnership and, to the extent not inconsistent with Section 306, any or all of the partners in the same action or in separate actions.

(c) A judgment against a partnership is not by itself a judgment against a partner. A judgment against a partnership may not be satisfied from a partner's assets unless there is also a judgment against the partner.

(d) A judgment creditor of a partner may not levy execution against the assets of the partner to satisfy a judgment based on a claim against the partnership unless the partner is personally liable for the claim under Section 306 and:

(1) a judgment based on the same claim has been obtained against the partnership and a writ of execution on the judgment has been returned unsatisfied in whole or in part;

(2) the partnership is a debtor in bankruptcy;

(3) the partner has agreed that the creditor need not exhaust partnership assets;

(4) a court grants permission to the judgment creditor to levy execution against the assets of a partner based on a finding that partnership assets subject to execution are clearly insufficient to satisfy the judgment, that exhaustion of partnership assets is excessively burdensome, or that the grant of permission is an appropriate exercise of the court's equitable powers; or

(5) liability is imposed on the partner by law or contract independent of the existence of the partnership.

(e) This section applies to any partnership liability or obligation resulting from a representation by a partner or purported partner under Section 308.

### SECTION 308. LIABILITY OF PURPORTED PARTNER.

(a) If a person, by words or conduct, purports to be a partner, or consents to being represented by another as a partner, in a partnership or with one or more persons not partners, the purported partner is liable to a person to whom the representation is made, if that person, relying on the representation, enters into a transaction with the actual or purported partnership. If the representation, either by the purported partner or by a person with the purported partner's consent, is made in a public manner, the purported partner is liable to a person who relies upon the purported partnership even if the purported partner is not aware of being held out as a partner to the claimant. If partnership liability results, the purported partner is liable with respect to that liability as if the purported partner were a partner. If no partnership liability results, the purported partner is liable with respect to that liability jointly and severally with any other person consenting to the representation.

(b) If a person is thus represented to be a partner in an existing partnership, or with one or more persons not partners, the purported partner is an agent of persons consenting to the representation to bind them to the same extent and in the same manner as if the purported partner were a partner, with respect to persons who enter into transactions in reliance upon the representation. If all of the partners of the existing partnership consent to the representation, a partnership act or obligation results. If fewer than all of the partners of the existing partnership consent to the representation, the person acting and the partners consenting to the representation are jointly and severally liable.

(c) A person is not liable as a partner merely because the person is named by another in a statement of partnership authority.

(d) A person does not continue to be liable as a partner merely because of a failure to file a statement of dissociation or to amend a statement of partnership authority to indicate the partner's dissociation from the partnership.
(e) Except as otherwise provided in subsections (a) and (b), persons who are not partners as to each other are not liable as partners to other persons.

## [ARTICLE] 4

## RELATIONS OF PARTNERS TO EACH OTHER AND TO PARTNERSHIP

### SECTION 401. PARTNER'S RIGHTS AND DUTIES.

(a) Each partner is deemed to have an account that is:

(1) credited with an amount equal to the money plus the value of any other property, net of the amount of any liabilities, the partner contributes to the partnership and the partner's share of the partnership profits; and

(2) charged with an amount equal to the money plus the value of any other property, net of the amount of any liabilities, distributed by the partnership to the partner and the partner's share of the partnership losses.

(b) Each partner is entitled to an equal share of the partnership profits and is chargeable with a share of the partnership losses in proportion to the partner's share of the profits.
(c) A partnership shall reimburse a partner for payments made and indemnify a partner for liabilities incurred by the partner in the ordinary course of the business of the partnership or for the preservation of its business or property.
(d) A partnership shall reimburse a partner for an advance to the partnership beyond the amount of capital the partner agreed to contribute.
(e) A payment or advance made by a partner which gives rise to a partnership obligation under subsection (c) or (d) constitutes a loan to the partnership which accrues interest from the date of the payment or advance.
(f) Each partner has equal rights in the management and conduct of the partnership business.
(g) A partner may use or possess partnership property only on behalf of the partnership.
(h) A partner is not entitled to remuneration for services performed for the partnership, except for reasonable compensation for services rendered in winding up the business of the partnership.
(i) A person may become a partner only with the consent of all of the partners.
(j) A difference arising as to a matter in the ordinary course of business of a partnership may be decided by a majority of the partners. An act outside the ordinary course of business of a partnership and an amendment to the partnership agreement may be undertaken only with the consent of all of the partners.
(k) This section does not affect the obligations of a partnership to other persons under Section 301.

### SECTION 402. DISTRIBUTIONS IN KIND.

A partner has no right to receive, and may not be required to accept, a distribution in kind.

### SECTION 403. PARTNER'S RIGHTS AND DUTIES WITH RESPECT TO INFORMATION.

(a) A partnership shall keep its books and records, if any, at its chief executive office.
(b) A partnership shall provide partners and their agents and attorneys access to its books and records. It shall provide former partners and their agents and attorneys access to books and records pertaining to the period during which they were partners. The right of access provides the opportunity to inspect and copy books and records during ordinary business hours. A partnership may impose a reasonable charge, covering the costs of labor and material, for copies of documents furnished.
(c) Each partner and the partnership shall furnish to a partner, and to the legal representative of a deceased partner or partner under legal disability:

(1) without demand, any information concerning the partnership's business and affairs reasonably required for the proper exercise of the partner's rights and duties under the partnership agreement or this [Act]; and

(2) on demand, any other information concerning the partnership's business and affairs, except to the extent the demand or the information demanded is unreasonable or otherwise improper under the circumstances.

### SECTION 404. GENERAL STANDARDS OF PARTNER'S CONDUCT.

(a) The only fiduciary duties a partner owes to the partnership and the other partners are the duty of loyalty and the duty of care set forth in subsections (b) and (c).
(b) A partner's duty of loyalty to the partnership and the other partners is limited to the following:

(1) to account to the partnership and hold as trustee for it any property, profit, or benefit derived by the partner in the conduct and winding up of the partnership business or derived from a use by the partner of partnership property, including the appropriation of a partnership opportunity;

(2) to refrain from dealing with the partnership in the conduct or winding up of the partnership business as or on behalf of a party having an interest adverse to the partnership; and

(3) to refrain from competing with the partnership in the conduct of the partnership business before the dissolution of the partnership.

(c) A partner's duty of care to the partnership and the other partners in the conduct and winding up of the partnership business is limited to refraining from engaging in grossly negligent or reckless conduct, intentional misconduct, or a knowing violation of law.
(d) A partner shall discharge the duties to the partnership and the other partners under this [Act] or under the partnership agreement and exercise any rights consistently with the obligation of good faith and fair dealing.
(e) A partner does not violate a duty or obligation under this [Act] or under the partnership agreement merely because the partner's conduct furthers the partner's own interest.
(f) A partner may lend money to and transact other business with the partnership, and as to each loan or transaction the rights and obligations of the partner are the same as those of a person who is not a partner, subject to other applicable law.
(g) This section applies to a person winding up the partnership business as the personal or legal representative of the last surviving partner as if the person were a partner.

### SECTION 405. ACTIONS BY PARTNERSHIP AND PARTNERS.

(a) A partnership may maintain an action against a partner for a breach of the partnership agreement, or for the violation of a duty to the partnership, causing harm to the partnership.
(b) A partner may maintain an action against the partnership or another partner for legal or equitable relief, with or without an accounting as to partnership business, to:

(1) enforce the partner's rights under the partnership agreement;

(2) enforce the partner's rights under this [Act], including:

(i) the partner's rights under Sections 401, 403, or 404;

(ii) the partner's right on dissociation to have the partner's interest in the partnership purchased pursuant to Section 701 or enforce any other right under [Article] 6 or 7; or

(iii) the partner's right to compel a dissolution and winding up of the partnership business under or enforce any other right under [Article] 8; or

(3) enforce the rights and otherwise protect the interests of the partner, including rights and interests arising independently of the partnership relationship.

(c) The accrual of, and any time limitation on, a right of action for a remedy under this section is governed by other law. A right to an accounting upon a dissolution and winding up does not revive a claim barred by law.

### SECTION 406. CONTINUATION OF PARTNERSHIP BEYOND DEFINITE TERM OR PARTICULAR UNDERTAKING.

(a) If a partnership for a definite term or particular undertaking is continued, without an express agreement, after the expiration of the term or completion of the undertaking, the rights and duties of the partners remain the same as they were at the expiration or completion, so far as is consistent with a partnership at will.

(b) If the partners, or those of them who habitually acted in the business during the term or undertaking, continue the business without any settlement or liquidation of the partnership, they are presumed to have agreed that the partnership will continue.

## [ARTICLE] 5

## TRANSFEREES AND CREDITORS OF PARTNER

### SECTION 501. PARTNER NOT CO-OWNER OF PARTNERSHIP PROPERTY.

A partner is not a co-owner of partnership property and has no interest in partnership property which can be transferred, either voluntarily or involuntarily.

### SECTION 502. PARTNER'S TRANSFERABLE INTEREST IN PARTNERSHIP.

The only transferable interest of a partner in the partnership is the partner's share of the profits and losses of the partnership and the partner's right to receive distributions. The interest is personal property.

### SECTION 503. TRANSFER OF PARTNER'S TRANSFERABLE INTEREST.

(a) A transfer, in whole or in part, of a partner's transferable interest in the partnership:

(1) is permissible;

(2) does not by itself cause the partner's dissociation or a dissolution and winding up of the partnership business; and

(3) does not, as against the other partners or the partnership, entitle the transferee, during the continuance of the partnership, to participate in the management or conduct of the partnership business, to require access to information concerning partnership transactions, or to inspect or copy the partnership books or records.

(b) A transferee of a partner's transferable interest in the partnership has a right:

(1) to receive, in accordance with the transfer, distributions to which the transferor would otherwise be entitled;

(2) to receive upon the dissolution and winding up of the partnership business, in accordance with the transfer, the net amount otherwise distributable to the transferor; and

(3) to seek under (6) a judicial determination that it is equitable to wind up the partnership business.

(c) In a dissolution and winding up, a transferee is entitled to an account of partnership transactions only from the date of the latest account agreed to by all of the partners.

(d) Upon transfer, the transferor retains the rights and duties of a partner other than the interest in distributions transferred.

(e) A partnership need not give effect to a transferee's rights under this section until it has notice of the transfer.

(f) A transfer of a partner's transferable interest in the partnership in violation of a restriction on transfer contained in the partnership agreement is ineffective as to a person having notice of the restriction at the time of transfer.

### SECTION 504. PARTNER'S TRANSFERABLE INTEREST SUBJECT TO CHARGING ORDER.

(a) On application by a judgment creditor of a partner or of a partner's transferee, a court having jurisdiction may charge the transferable interest of the judgment debtor to satisfy the judgment. The court may appoint a receiver of the share of the distributions due or to become due to the judgment debtor in respect of the partnership and make all other orders, directions, accounts, and inquiries the judgment debtor might have made or which the circumstances of the case may require.

(b) A charging order constitutes a lien on the judgment debtor's transferable interest in the partnership. The court may order a foreclosure of the interest subject to the charging order at any time. The purchaser at the foreclosure sale has the rights of a transferee.

(c) At any time before foreclosure, an interest charged may be redeemed:

(1) by the judgment debtor;

(2) with property other than partnership property, by one or more of the other partners; or

(3) with partnership property, by one or more of the other partners with the consent of all of the partners whose interests are not so charged.

(d) This [Act] does not deprive a partner of a right under exemption laws with respect to the partner's interest in the partnership.

(e) This section provides the exclusive remedy by which a judgment creditor of a partner or partner's transferee may satisfy a judgment out of the judgment debtor's transferable interest in the partnership.

## [ARTICLE] 6

## PARTNER'S DISSOCIATION

### SECTION 601. EVENTS CAUSING PARTNER'S DISSOCIATION.

A partner is dissociated from a partnership upon the occurrence of any of the following events:

(1) the partnership's having notice of the partner's express will to withdraw as a partner or on a later date specified by the partner;

(2) an event agreed to in the partnership agreement as causing the partner's dissociation;

(3) the partner's expulsion pursuant to the partnership agreement;

(4) the partner's expulsion by the unanimous vote of the other partners if:

(i) it is unlawful to carry on the partnership business with that partner;

(ii) there has been a transfer of all or substantially all of that partner's transferable interest in the partnership, other than a transfer for security purposes, or a court order charging the partner's interest, which has not been foreclosed;

(iii) within 90 days after the partnership notifies a corporate partner that it will be expelled because it has filed a certificate of dissolution or the equivalent, its charter has been revoked, or its right to conduct business has been suspended by the jurisdiction of its incorporation, there is no revocation of the certificate of dissolution or no reinstatement of its charter or its right to conduct business; or

(iv) a partnership that is a partner has been dissolved and its business is being wound up;

(5) on application by the partnership or another partner, the partner's expulsion by judicial determination because:

(i) the partner engaged in wrongful conduct that adversely and materially affected the partnership business;

(ii) the partner willfully or persistently committed a material breach of the partnership agreement or of a duty owed to the partnership or the other partners under Section 404; or

(iii) the partner engaged in conduct relating to the partnership business which makes it not reasonably practicable to carry on the business in partnership with the partner;

(6) the partner's:

(i) becoming a debtor in bankruptcy;

(ii) executing an assignment for the benefit of creditors;

(iii) seeking, consenting to, or acquiescing in the appointment of a trustee, receiver, or liquidator of that partner or of all or substantially all of that partner's property; or

(iv) failing, within 90 days after the appointment, to have vacated or stayed the appointment of a trustee, receiver, or liquidator of the partner or of all or substantially all of the partner's property obtained without the partner's consent or acquiescence, or failing within 90 days after the expiration of a stay to have the appointment vacated;

(7) in the case of a partner who is an individual:

(i) the partner's death;

(ii) the appointment of a guardian or general conservator for the partner; or

(iii) a judicial determination that the partner has otherwise become incapable of performing the partner's duties under the partnership agreement;

(8) in the case of a partner that is a trust or is acting as a partner by virtue of being a trustee of a trust, distribution of the trust's entire transferable interest in the partnership, but not merely by reason of the substitution of a successor trustee;

(9) in the case of a partner that is an estate or is acting as a partner by virtue of being a personal representative of an estate, distribution of the estate's entire transferable interest in the partnership, but not merely by reason of the substitution of a successor personal representative; or

(10) termination of a partner who is not an individual, partnership, corporation, trust, or estate.

### SECTION 602. PARTNER'S POWER TO DISSOCIATE; WRONGFUL DISSOCIATION.

(a) A partner has the power to dissociate at any time, rightfully or wrongfully, by express will pursuant to Section 601(1).

(b) A partner's dissociation is wrongful only if:

(1) it is in breach of an express provision of the partnership agreement; or

(2) in the case of a partnership for a definite term or particular undertaking, before the expiration of the term or the completion of the undertaking:

(i) the partner withdraws by express will, unless the withdrawal follows within 90 days after another partner's dissociation by death or otherwise under Section 601(6) through (10) or wrongful dissociation under this subsection;

(ii) the partner is expelled by judicial determination under Section 601(5);

(iii) the partner is dissociated by becoming a debtor in bankruptcy; or

(iv) in the case of a partner who is not an individual, trust other than a business trust, or estate, the partner is expelled or otherwise dissociated because it willfully dissolved or terminated.

(c) A partner who wrongfully dissociates is liable to the partnership and to the other partners for damages caused by the dissociation. The liability is in addition to any other obligation of the partner to the partnership or to the other partners.

### SECTION 603. EFFECT OF PARTNER'S DISSOCIATION.

(a) If a partner's dissociation results in a dissolution and winding up of the partnership business, [Article] 8 applies; otherwise, [Article] 7 applies.

(b) Upon a partner's dissociation:

(1) the partner's right to participate in the management and conduct of the partnership business terminates, except as otherwise provided in Section 803;

(2) the partner's duty of loyalty under Section 404(b)(3) terminates; and

(3) the partner's duty of loyalty under Section 404(b)(1) and (2) and duty of care under Section 404(c) continue only with regard to matters arising and events occurring before the partner's dissociation, unless the partner participates in winding up the partnership's business pursuant to Section 803.

## [ARTICLE] 7

## PARTNER'S DISSOCIATION WHEN BUSINESS NOT WOUND UP

### SECTION 701. PURCHASE OF DISSOCIATED PARTNER'S INTEREST.

(a) If a partner is dissociated from a partnership without resulting in a dissolution and winding up of the partnership business under Section 801, the partnership shall cause the dissociated partner's interest in the partnership to be purchased for a buyout price determined pursuant to subsection (b).

(b) The buyout price of a dissociated partner's interest is the amount that would have been distributable to the dissociating partner under Section 807(b) if, on the date of dissociation, the assets of the partnership were sold at a price equal to the greater of the liquidation value or the value based on a sale of the entire business as a going concern without the dissociated partner and the partnership were wound up as of that date. Interest must be paid from the date of dissociation to the date of payment.

(c) Damages for wrongful dissociation under Section 602(b), and all other amounts owing, whether or not presently due, from the dissociated partner to the partnership, must be offset against the buyout price. Interest must be paid from the date the amount owed becomes due to the date of payment.

(d) A partnership shall indemnify a dissociated partner whose interest is being purchased against all partnership liabilities, whether incurred before or after the dissociation, except liabilities incurred by an act of the dissociated partner under Section 702.

(e) If no agreement for the purchase of a dissociated partner's interest is reached within 120 days after a written demand for payment, the partnership shall pay, or cause to be paid, in cash to the dissociated partner the amount the partnership estimates to be the buyout price and accrued interest, reduced by any offsets and accrued interest under subsection (c).

(f) If a deferred payment is authorized under subsection (h), the partnership may tender a written offer to pay the amount it estimates to be the buyout price and accrued interest, reduced by any offsets under subsection (c), stating the time of payment, the amount and type of security for payment, and the other terms and conditions of the obligation.

(g) The payment or tender required by subsection (e) or (f) must be accompanied by the following:

(1) a statement of partnership assets and liabilities as of the date of dissociation;

(2) the latest available partnership balance sheet and income statement, if any;

(3) an explanation of how the estimated amount of the payment was calculated; and

(4) written notice that the payment is in full satisfaction of the obligation to purchase unless, within 120 days after the written notice, the dissociated partner commences an action to determine the buyout price, any offsets under subsection (c), or other terms of the obligation to purchase.

(h) A partner who wrongfully dissociates before the expiration of a definite term or the completion of a particular undertaking is not entitled to payment of any portion of the buyout price until the expiration of the term or completion of the undertaking, unless the partner establishes to the satisfaction of the court that earlier payment will not cause undue hardship to the business of the partnership. A deferred payment must be adequately secured and bear interest.

(i) A dissociated partner may maintain an action against the partnership, pursuant to Section 405(b)(2)(ii), to determine the buyout price of that partner's interest, any offsets under subsection (c), or other terms of the obligation to purchase. The action must be commenced within 120 days after the partnership has tendered payment or an offer to pay or within one year after written demand for payment if no payment or offer to pay is tendered. The court shall determine the buyout price of the dissociated partner's interest, any offset due under subsection (c), and accrued interest, and enter judgment for any additional payment or refund. If deferred payment is authorized under subsection (h), the court shall also determine the security for payment and other terms of the obligation to purchase. The court may assess reasonable attorney's fees and the fees and expenses of appraisers or other experts for a party to the action, in amounts the court finds equitable, against a party that the court finds acted arbitrarily, vexatiously, or not in good faith. The finding may be based on the partnership's failure to tender payment or an offer to pay or to comply with subsection (g).

### SECTION 702. DISSOCIATED PARTNER'S POWER TO BIND AND LIABILITY TO PARTNERSHIP.

(a) For two years after a partner dissociates without resulting in a dissolution and winding up of the partnership business, the partnership, including a surviving partnership under [Article] 9, is bound by an act of the dissociated partner which would have bound the partnership under Section 301 before dissociation only if at the time of entering into the transaction the other party:

(1) reasonably believed that the dissociated partner was then a partner;

(2) did not have notice of the partner's dissociation; and

(3) is not deemed to have had knowledge under Section 303(e) or notice under Section 704(c).

(b) A dissociated partner is liable to the partnership for any damage caused to the partnership arising from an obligation incurred by the dissociated partner after dissociation for which the partnership is liable under subsection (a).

### SECTION 703. DISSOCIATED PARTNER'S LIABILITY TO OTHER PERSONS.

(a) A partner's dissociation does not of itself discharge the partner's liability for a partnership obligation incurred before dissociation. A dissociated partner is not liable for a partnership obligation incurred after dissociation, except as otherwise provided in subsection (b).

(b) A partner who dissociates without resulting in a dissolution and winding up of the partnership business is liable as a partner to the other party in a transaction entered into by the partnership, or a surviving partnership under [Article] 9, within two years after the partner's dissociation, only if the partner is liable for the obligation under Section 306 and at the time of entering into the transaction the other party:

(1) reasonably believed that the dissociated partner was then a partner;

(2) did not have notice of the partner's dissociation; and

(3) is not deemed to have had knowledge under Section 303(e) or notice under Section 704(c).

(c) By agreement with the partnership creditor and the partners continuing the business, a dissociated partner may be released from liability for a partnership obligation.

(d) A dissociated partner is released from liability for a partnership obligation if a partnership creditor, with notice of the partner's dissociation but without the partner's consent, agrees to a material alteration in the nature or time of payment of a partnership obligation.

### SECTION 704. STATEMENT OF DISSOCIATION.

(a) A dissociated partner or the partnership may file a statement of dissociation stating the name of the partnership and that the partner is dissociated from the partnership.

(b) A statement of dissociation is a limitation on the authority of a dissociated partner for the purposes of Section 303(d) and (e).

(c) For the purposes of Sections 702(a)(3) and 703(b)(3), a person not a partner is deemed to have notice of the dissociation 90 days after the statement of dissociation is filed.

## [ARTICLE] 8
## WINDING UP PARTNERSHIP BUSINESS

### SECTION 801. EVENTS CAUSING DISSOLUTION AND WINDING UP OF PARTNERSHIP BUSINESS.

A partnership is dissolved, and its business must be wound up, only upon the occurrence of any of the following events:

(1) in a partnership at will, the partnership's having notice from a partner, other than a partner who is dissociated under Section 601(2) through (10), of that partner's express will to withdraw as a partner, or on a later date specified by the partner;

(2) in a partnership for a definite term or particular undertaking:

(i) within 90 days after a partner's dissociation by death or otherwise under Section 601(6) through (10) or wrongful dissociation under Section 602(b), the express will of at least half of the remaining partners to wind up the partnership business, for which purpose a partner's rightful dissociation pursuant to Section 602(b)(2)(i) constitutes the expression of that partner's will to wind up the partnership business;

(ii) the express will of all of the partners to wind up the partnership business; or

(iii) the expiration of the term or the completion of the undertaking;

(3) an event agreed to in the partnership agreement resulting in the winding up of the partnership business;

(4) an event that makes it unlawful for all or substantially all of the business of the partnership to be continued, but a cure of illegality within 90 days after notice to the partnership of the event is effective retroactively to the date of the event for purposes of this section;

(5) on application by a partner, a judicial determination that:

(i) the economic purpose of the partnership is likely to be unreasonably frustrated;

(ii) another partner has engaged in conduct relating to the partnership business which makes it not reasonably practicable to carry on the business in partnership with that partner; or

(iii) it is not otherwise reasonably practicable to carry on the partnership business in conformity with the partnership agreement; or

(6) on application by a transferee of a partner's transferable interest, a judicial determination that it is equitable to wind up the partnership business:

(i) after the expiration of the term or completion of the undertaking, if the partnership was for a definite term or particular undertaking at the time of the transfer or entry of the charging order that gave rise to the transfer; or

(ii) at any time, if the partnership was a partnership at will at the time of the transfer or entry of the charging order that gave rise to the transfer.

### SECTION 802. PARTNERSHIP CONTINUES AFTER DISSOLUTION.

(a) Subject to subsection (b), a partnership continues after dissolution only for the purpose of winding up its business. The partnership is terminated when the winding up of its business is completed.

(b) At any time after the dissolution of a partnership and before the winding up of its business is completed, all of the partners, including any dissociating partner other than a wrongfully dissociating partner, may waive the right to have the partnership's business wound up and the partnership terminated. In that event:

(1) the partnership resumes carrying on its business as if dissolution had never occurred, and any liability incurred by the partnership or a partner after the dissolution and before the waiver is determined as if dissolution had never occurred; and

(2) the rights of a third party accruing under Section 804(1) or arising out of conduct in reliance on the dissolution before the third party knew or received a notification of the waiver may not be adversely affected.

### SECTION 803. RIGHT TO WIND UP PARTNERSHIP BUSINESS.

(a) After dissolution, a partner who has not wrongfully dissociated may participate in winding up the partnership's business, but on application of any partner, partner's legal representative, or transferee, the [designate the

appropriate court], for good cause shown, may order judicial supervision of the winding up.
(b) The legal representative of the last surviving partner may wind up a partnership's business.
(c) A person winding up a partnership's business may preserve the partnership business or property as a going concern for a reasonable time, prosecute and defend actions and proceedings, whether civil, criminal, or administrative, settle and close the partnership's business, dispose of and transfer the partnership's property, discharge the partnership's liabilities, distribute the assets of the partnership pursuant to Section 807, settle disputes by mediation or arbitration, and perform other necessary acts.

**SECTION 804. PARTNER'S POWER TO BIND PARTNERSHIP AFTER DISSOLUTION.**
Subject to Section 805, a partnership is bound by a partner's act after dissolution that:
(1) is appropriate for winding up the partnership business; or
(2) would have bound the partnership under Section 301 before dissolution, if the other party to the transaction did not have notice of the dissolution.

**SECTION 805. STATEMENT OF DISSOLUTION.**
(a) After dissolution, a partner who has not wrongfully dissociated may file a statement of dissolution stating the name of the partnership and that the partnership has dissolved and is winding up its business.
(b) A statement of dissolution cancels a filed statement of partnership authority for the purposes of Section 303(d) and is a limitation on authority for the purposes of Section 303(e).
(c) For the purposes of Sections 301 and 804, a person not a partner is deemed to have notice of the dissolution and the limitation on the partners' authority as a result of the statement of dissolution 90 days after it is filed.
(d) After filing and, if appropriate, recording a statement of dissolution, a dissolved partnership may file and, if appropriate, record a statement of partnership authority which will operate with respect to a person not a partner as provided in Section 303(d) and (e) in any transaction, whether or not the transaction is appropriate for winding up the partnership business.

**SECTION 806. PARTNER'S LIABILITY TO OTHER PARTNERS AFTER DISSOLUTION.**
(a) Except as otherwise provided in subsection (b) and Section 306, after dissolution a partner is liable to the other partners for the partner's share of any partnership liability incurred under Section 804.
(b) A partner who, with knowledge of the dissolution, incurs a partnership liability under Section 804(2) by an act that is not appropriate for winding up the partnership business is liable to the partnership for any damage caused to the partnership arising from the liability.

**SECTION 807. SETTLEMENT OF ACCOUNTS AND CONTRIBUTIONS AMONG PARTNERS.**
(a) In winding up a partnership's business, the assets of the partnership, including the contributions of the partners required by this section, must be applied to discharge its obligations to creditors, including, to the extent permitted by law, partners who are creditors. Any surplus must be applied to pay in cash the net amount distributable to partners in accordance with their right to distributions under subsection (b).
(b) Each partner is entitled to a settlement of all partnership accounts upon winding up the partnership business. In settling accounts among the partners, profits and losses that result from the liquidation of the partnership assets must be credited and charged to the partners' accounts. The partnership shall make a distribution to a partner in an amount equal to any excess of the credits over the charges in the partner's account. A partner shall contribute to the partnership an amount equal to any excess of the charges over the credits in the partner's account but excluding from the calculation charges attributable to an obligation for which the partner is not personally liable under Section 306.
(c) If a partner fails to contribute the full amount required under subsection (b), all of the other partners shall contribute, in the proportions in which those partners share partnership losses, the additional amount necessary to satisfy the partnership obligations for which they are personally liable under Section 306. A partner or partner's legal representative may recover from the other partners any contributions the partner makes to the extent the amount contributed exceeds that partner's share of the partnership obligations for which the partner is personally liable under Section 306.
(d) After the settlement of accounts, each partner shall contribute, in the proportion in which the partner shares partnership losses, the amount necessary to satisfy partnership obligations that were not known at the time of the settlement and for which the partner is personally liable under Section 306.
(e) The estate of a deceased partner is liable for the partner's obligation to contribute to the partnership.
(f) An assignee for the benefit of creditors of a partnership or a partner, or a person appointed by a court to represent creditors of a partnership or a partner, may enforce a partner's obligation to contribute to the partnership.

## [ARTICLE] 10
## LIMITED LIABILITY PARTNERSHIP

**SECTION 1001. STATEMENT OF QUALIFICATION.**
(a) A partnership may become a limited liability partnership pursuant to this section.
(b) The terms and conditions on which a partnership becomes a limited liability partnership must be approved by the vote necessary to amend the partnership agreement except, in the case of a partnership agreement that expressly considers obligations to contribute to the partnership, the vote necessary to amend those provisions.
(c) After the approval required by subsection (b), a partnership may become a limited liability partnership by filing a statement of qualification. The statement must contain:
(1) the name of the partnership;
(2) the street address of the partnership's chief executive office and, if different, the street address of an office in this State, if any;
(3) if the partnership does not have an office in this State, the name and street address of the partnership's agent for service of process;
(4) a statement that the partnership elects to be a limited liability partnership; and
(5) a deferred effective date, if any.
(d) The agent of a limited liability partnership for service of process must be an individual who is a resident of this State or other person authorized to do business in this State.
(e) The status of a partnership as a limited liability partnership is effective on the later of the filing of the statement or a date specified in the statement. The status remains effective, regardless of changes in the partnership, until it is canceled pursuant to Section 105(d) or revoked pursuant to Section 1003.
(f) The status of a partnership as a limited liability partnership and the liability of its partners is not affected by errors or later changes in the information required to be contained in the statement of qualification under subsection (c).
(g) The filing of a statement of qualification establishes that a partnership has satisfied all conditions precedent to the qualification of the partnership as a limited liability partnership.
(h) An amendment or cancellation of a statement of qualification is effective when it is filed or on a deferred effective date specified in the amendment or cancellation.

**SECTION 1002. NAME.**
The name of a limited liability partnership must end with "Registered Limited Liability Partnership", "Limited Liability Partnership", "R.L.L.P.", "L.L.P.", "RLLP," or "LLP".

### SECTION 1003. ANNUAL REPORT.

(a) A limited liability partnership, and a foreign limited liability partnership authorized to transact business in this State, shall file an annual report in the office of the [Secretary of State] which contains:

(1) the name of the limited liability partnership and the State or other jurisdiction under whose laws the foreign limited liability partnership is formed;

(2) the street address of the partnership's chief executive office and, if different, the street address of an office of the partnership in this State, if any; and

(3) if the partnership does not have an office in this State, the name and street address of the partnership's current agent for service of process.

(b) An annual report must be filed between [January 1 and April 1] of each year following the calendar year in which a partnership files a statement of qualification or a foreign partnership becomes authorized to transact business in this State.

(c) The [Secretary of State] may revoke the statement of qualification of a partnership that fails to file an annual report when due or pay the required filing fee. To do so, the [Secretary of State] shall provide the partnership at least 60 days' written notice of intent to revoke the statement. The notice must be mailed to the partnership at its chief executive office set forth in the last filed statement of qualification or annual report. The notice must specify the annual report that has not been filed, the fee that has not been paid, and the effective date of the revocation. The revocation is not effective if the annual report is filed and the fee is paid before the effective date of the revocation.

(d) A revocation under subsection (c) only affects a partnership's status as a limited liability partnership and is not an event of dissolution of the partnership.

(e) A partnership whose statement of qualification has been revoked may apply to the [Secretary of State] for reinstatement within two years after the effective date of the revocation. The application must state:

(1) the name of the partnership and the effective date of the revocation; and

(2) that the ground for revocation either did not exist or has been corrected.

(f) A reinstatement under subsection (e) relates back to and takes effect as of the effective date of the revocation, and the partnership's status as a limited liability partnership continues as if the revocation had never occurred.

## [ARTICLE] 11

## FOREIGN LIMITED LIABILITY PARTNERSHIP

### SECTION 1101. LAW GOVERNING FOREIGN LIMITED LIABILITY PARTNERSHIP.

(a) The law under which a foreign limited liability partnership is formed governs relations among the partners and between the partners and the partnership and the liability of partners for obligations of the partnership.

(b) A foreign limited liability partnership may not be denied a statement of foreign qualification by reason of any difference between the law under which the partnership was formed and the law of this State.

(c) A statement of foreign qualification does not authorize a foreign limited liability partnership to engage in any business or exercise any power that a partnership may not engage in or exercise in this State as a limited liability partnership.

### SECTION 1102. STATEMENT OF FOREIGN QUALIFICATION.

(a) Before transacting business in this State, a foreign limited liability partnership must file a statement of foreign qualification. The statement must contain:

(1) the name of the foreign limited liability partnership which satisfies the requirements of the State or other jurisdiction under whose law it is formed and ends with "Registered Limited Liability Partnership", "Limited Liability Partnership", "R.L.L.P.", "L.L.P.", "RLLP," or "LLP";

(2) the street address of the partnership's chief executive office and, if different, the street address of an office of the partnership in this State, if any;

(3) if there is no office of the partnership in this State, the name and street address of the partnership's agent for service of process; and

(4) a deferred effective date, if any.

(b) The agent of a foreign limited liability company for service of process must be an individual who is a resident of this State or other person authorized to do business in this State.

(c) The status of a partnership as a foreign limited liability partnership is effective on the later of the filing of the statement of foreign qualification or a date specified in the statement. The status remains effective, regardless of changes in the partnership, until it is canceled pursuant to Section 105(d) or revoked pursuant to Section 1003.

(d) An amendment or cancellation of a statement of foreign qualification is effective when it is filed or on a deferred effective date specified in the amendment or cancellation.

# APPENDIX E
# Revised Model Business Corporation Act

## CHAPTER 1. GENERAL PROVISIONS

### Subchapter A. Short Title and Reservation of Power

**§1.01 Short Title**
This Act shall be known and may be cited as the "[name of state] Business Corporation Act."

**§1.02 Reservation of Power to Amend or Repeal**
The [name of state legislature] has power to amend or repeal all or part of this Act at any time and all domestic and foreign corporations subject to this Act are governed by the amendment or repeal.

### Subchapter B. Filing Documents

**§1.20 Filing Requirements**
(a) A document must satisfy the requirements of this section, and of any other section that adds to or varies these requirements, to be entitled to filing by the secretary of state.
(b) This Act must require or permit filing the document in the office of the secretary of state.
(c) The document must contain the information required by this Act. It may contain other information as well.
(d) The document must be typewritten or printed.
(e) The document must be in the English language. A corporate name need not be in English if written in English letters or Arabic or Roman numerals, and the certificate of existence required of foreign corporations need not be in English if accompanied by a reasonably authenticated English translation.
(f) The document must be executed:
(1) by the chairman of the board of directors of a domestic or foreign corporation, by its president, or by another of its officers;
(2) if directors have not been selected or the corporation has not been formed, by an incorporator; or
(3) if the corporation is in the hands of a receiver, trustee, or other court-appointed fiduciary, by that fiduciary.
(g) The person executing the document shall sign it and state beneath or opposite his signature his name and the capacity in which he signs. The document may but need not contain: (1) the corporate seal, (2) an attestation by the secretary or an assistant secretary, (3) an acknowledgement, verification, or proof.



(h) If the secretary of state has prescribed a mandatory form for the document under section 1.21, the document must be in or on the prescribed form.
(i) The document must be delivered to the office of the secretary of state for filing and must be accompanied by one exact or conformed copy (except as provided in sections 5.03 and 15.09), the correct filing fee, and any franchise tax, license fee, or penalty required by this Act or other law.

**§1.21 Forms**
(a) The secretary of state may prescribe and furnish on request forms for: (1) an application for a certificate of existence, (2) a foreign corporation's application for a certificate of authority to transact business in this state, (3) a foreign corporation's application for a certificate of withdrawal, and (4) the annual report. If the secretary of state so requires, use of these forms is mandatory.
(b) The secretary of state may prescribe and furnish on request forms for other documents required or permitted to be filed by this Act but their use is not mandatory.

**§1.22 Filing, Service and Copying Fees**
[Text omitted.]

**§1.23 Effective Time and Date of Document**
(a) Except as provided in subsection (b) and section 1.24(c), a document accepted for filing is effective:
(1) at the time of filing on the date it is filed, as evidenced by the secretary of state's date and time endorsement on the original document; or
(2) at the time specified in the document as its effective time on the date it is filed.
(b) A document may specify a delayed effective time and date, and if it does so the document becomes effective at the time and date specified. If a delayed effective date but no time is specified, the document is effective at the close of business on that date. A delayed effective date for a document may not be later than the 90th day after the date it is filed.

**§1.24 Correcting Filed Document**
(a) A domestic or foreign corporation may correct a document filed by the secretary of state if the document (1) contains an incorrect statement or (2) was defectively executed, attested, sealed, verified, or acknowledged.
(b) A document is corrected:
(1) by preparing articles of correction that (i) describe the document (including its filing date) or attach a copy of it to the articles, (ii) specify the incorrect statement and the reason it is incorrect or the manner in which the execution was defective, and (iii) correct the incorrect statement or defective execution; and
(2) by delivering the articles to the secretary of state for filing.
(c) Articles of correction are effective on the effective date of the document they correct except as to persons relying on the uncorrected document and adversely affected by the correction. As to those persons, articles of correction are effective when filed.

**§1.25 Filing Duty of Secretary of State**

(a) If a document delivered to the office of the secretary of state for filing satisfies the requirements of section 1.20, the secretary of state shall file it.

(b) The secretary of state files a document by stamping or otherwise endorsing "Filed," together with his name and official title and the date and time of receipt, on both the original and the document copy and on the receipt for the filing fee. After filing a document, except as provided in sections 5.03 and 15.10, the secretary of state shall deliver the document copy, with the filing fee receipt (or acknowledgement of receipt if no fee is required) attached, to the domestic or foreign corporation or its representative.

(c) If the secretary of state refuses to file a document, he shall return it to the domestic or foreign corporation or its representative within five days after the document was delivered, together with a brief, written explanation of the reason for his refusal.

(d) The secretary of state's duty to file documents under this section is ministerial. His filing or refusing to file a document does not:

(1) affect the validity or invalidity of the document in whole or part;

(2) relate to the correctness or incorrectness of information contained in the document;

(3) create a presumption that the document is valid or invalid or that information contained in the document is correct or incorrect.

**§1.26 Appeal From Secretary of State's Refusal to File Document**

(a) If the secretary of state refuses to file a document delivered to his office for filing, the domestic or foreign corporation may appeal the refusal to the [name or describe] court [of the county where the corporation's principal office (or, if none in this state, its registered office) is or will be located] [of county]. The appeal is commenced by petitioning the court to compel filing the document and by attaching to the petition the document and the secretary of state's explanation of his refusal to file.

(b) The court may summarily order the secretary of state to file the document or take other action the court considers appropriate.

(c) The court's final decision may be appealed as in other civil proceedings.

**§1.27 Evidentiary Effect of Copy of Filed Document**

A certificate attached to a copy of the document filed by the secretary of state, bearing his signature (which may be in facsimile) and the seal of this state, is conclusive evidence that the original document is on file with the secretary of state.

**§1.28 Certificate of Existence**

(a) Anyone may apply to the secretary of state to furnish a certificate of existence for a domestic corporation or a certificate of authorization for a foreign corporation.

(b) A certificate of existence or authorization sets forth:

(1) the domestic corporation's corporate name or the foreign corporation's corporate name used in this state;

(2) that (i) the domestic corporation is duly incorporated under the law of this state, the date of its incorporation, and the period of its duration if less than perpetual; or (ii) that the foreign corporation is authorized to transact business in this state;

(3) that all fees, taxes, and penalties owed to this state have been paid, if (i) payment is reflected in the records of the secretary of state and (ii) nonpayment affects the existence or authorization of the domestic or foreign corporation;

(4) that its most recent annual report required by section 16.22 has been delivered to the secretary of state;

(5) that articles of dissolution have not been filed; and

(6) other facts of record in the office of the secretary of state that may be requested by the applicant.

(c) Subject to any qualification stated in the certificate, a certificate of existence or authorization issued by the secretary of state may be relied upon as conclusive evidence that the domestic or foreign corporation is in existence or is authorized to transact business in this state.

**§1.29 Penalty for Signing False Document**

(a) A person commits an offense if he signs a document he knows is false in any material respect with intent that the document be delivered to the secretary of state for filing.

(b) An offense under this section is a [______] misdemeanor [punishable by a fine of not to exceed $______].

## Subchapter C. Secretary of State

**§1.30 Powers**

The secretary of state has the power reasonably necessary to perform the duties required of him by this Act.

## Subchapter D. Definitions

**§1.40 Act Definitions**

In this Act:

(1) "Articles of incorporation" include amended and restated articles of incorporation and articles of merger.

(2) "Authorized shares" means the shares of all classes a domestic or foreign corporation is authorized to issue.

(3) "Conspicuous" means so written that a reasonable person against whom the writing is to operate should have noticed it. For example, printing in italics or boldface or contrasting color, or typing in capitals or underlined, is conspicuous.

(4) "Corporation" or "domestic corporation" means a corporation for profit, which is not a foreign corporation, incorporated under or subject to the provisions of this Act.

(5) "Deliver" includes mail.

(6) "Distribution" means a direct or indirect transfer of money or other property (except its own shares) or incurrence of indebtedness by a corporation to or for the benefit of its shareholders in respect of any of its shares. A distribution may be in the form of a declaration or payment of a dividend; a purchase, redemption, or other acquisition of shares; a distribution of indebtedness; or otherwise.

(7) "Effective date of notice" is defined in section 1.41.

(8) "Employee" includes an officer but not a director. A director may accept duties that make him also an employee.

(9) "Entity" includes corporation and foreign corporation; not-for-profit corporation; profit and not-for-profit unincorporated association; business trust, estate, partnership, trust, and two or more persons having a joint or common economic interest; and state, United States, and foreign government.

(10) "Foreign corporation" means a corporation for profit incorporated under a law other than the law of this state.

(11) "Governmental subdivision" includes authority, county, district, and municipality.

(12) "Includes" denotes a partial definition.

(13) "Individual" includes the estate of an incompetent or deceased individual.

(14) "Means" denotes an exhaustive definition.

(15) "Notice" is defined in section 1.41.

(16) "Person" includes individual and entity.

(17) "Principal office" means the office (in or out of this state) so designated in the annual report where the principal executive offices of a domestic or foreign corporation are located.

(18) "Proceeding" includes civil suit and criminal, administrative, and investigatory action.

(19) "Record date" means the date established under chapter 6 or 7 on which a corporation determines the identity of its shareholders and their shareholdings for purposes of this Act. The determinations shall be made as of the close of business on the record date unless another time for doing so is specified when the record date is fixed.

(20) "Secretary" means the corporate officer to whom the board of directors has delegated responsibility under section 8.40(c) for custody

of the minutes of the meetings of the board of directors and of the shareholders and for authenticating records of the corporation.

(21) "Share" means the unit into which the proprietary interests in a corporation are divided.

(22) "Shareholder" means the person in whose name shares are registered in the records of a corporation or the beneficial owner of shares to the extent of the rights granted by a nominee certificate on file with a corporation.

(23) "State," when referring to a part of the United States, includes a state and commonwealth (and their agencies and governmental subdivisions) and a territory, and insular possession (and their agencies and governmental subdivisions) of the United States.

(24) "Subscriber" means a person who subscribes for shares in a corporation, whether before or after incorporation.

(25) "United States" includes district, authority, bureau, commission, department, and any other agency of the United States.

(26) "Voting group" means all shares of one or more classes or series that under the articles of incorporation or this Act are entitled to vote and be counted together collectively on a matter at a meeting of shareholders. All shares entitled by the articles of incorporation or this Act to vote generally on the matter are for that purpose a single voting group.

### §1.41 Notice

(a) Notice under this Act shall be in writing unless oral notice is reasonable under the circumstances.

(b) Notice may be communicated in person; by telephone, telegraph, teletype, or other form of wire or wireless communication; or by mail or private carrier. If these forms of personal notice are impracticable, notice may be communicated by a newspaper of general circulation in the area where published; or by radio, television, or other form of public broadcast communication.

(c) Written notice by a domestic or foreign corporation to its shareholder, if in a comprehensible form, is effective when mailed, if mailed postpaid and correctly addressed to the shareholder's address shown in the corporation's current record of shareholders.

(d) Written notice to a domestic or foreign corporation (authorized to transact business in this state) may be addressed to its registered agent at its registered office or to the corporation or its secretary at its principal office shown in its most recent annual report or, in the case of a foreign corporation that has not yet delivered an annual report, in its application for a certificate of authority.

(e) Except as provided in subsections (c) and (d), written notice, if in a comprehensible form, is effective at the earliest of the following:

(1) when received;

(2) five days after its deposit in the United States Mail, as evidenced by the postmark, if mailed postpaid and correctly addressed;

(3) on the date shown on the return receipt, if sent by registered or certified mail, return receipt requested, and the receipt is signed by or on behalf of the addressee.

(f) Oral notice is effective when communicated if communicated in a comprehensible manner.

(g) If this Act prescribes notice requirements for particular circumstances, those requirements govern. If articles of incorporation or bylaws prescribe notice requirements, not inconsistent with this section or other provisions of this Act, those requirements govern.

### §1.42 Number of Shareholders

(a) For purposes of this Act, the following identified as a shareholder in a corporation's current record of shareholders constitutes one shareholder:

(1) three or fewer co-owners;

(2) a corporation, partnership, trust, estate, or other entity;

(3) the trustees, guardians, custodians, or other fiduciaries of a single trust, estate, or account.

(b) For purposes of this Act, shareholdings registered in substantially similar names constitute one shareholder if it is reasonable to believe that the names represent the same person.

## CHAPTER 2. INCORPORATION

### §2.01 Incorporators

One or more persons may act as the incorporator or incorporators of a corporation by delivering articles of incorporation to the secretary of state for filing.

### §2.02 Articles of Incorporation

(a) The articles of incorporation must set forth:

(1) a corporate name for the corporation that satisfies the requirements of section 4.01;

(2) the number of shares the corporation is authorized to issue;

(3) the street address of the corporation's initial registered office and the name of its initial registered agent at that office; and

(4) the name and address of each incorporator.

(b) The articles of incorporation may set forth:

(1) the names and addresses of the individuals who are to serve as the initial directors;

(2) provisions not inconsistent with law regarding:

(i) the purpose or purposes for which the corporation is organized;

(ii) managing the business and regulating the affairs of the corporation;

(iii) defining, limiting, and regulating the powers of the corporation, its board of directors, and shareholders;

(iv) a par value for authorized shares or classes of shares;

(v) the imposition of personal liability on shareholders for the debts of the corporation to a specified extent and upon specified conditions;

(3) any provision that under this Act is required or permitted to be set forth in the bylaws; and

(4) a provision eliminating or limiting the liability of a director to the corporation or its shareholders for money damages for any action taken, or any failure to take any action, as a director, except liability for (A) the amount of a financial benefit received by a director to which he is not entitled; (B) an intentional infliction of harm on the corporation or the shareholders; (C) a violation of section 8.33; or (D) an intentional violation of criminal law.

(c) The articles of incorporation need not set forth any of the corporate powers enumerated in this Act.

### §2.03 Incorporation

(a) Unless a delayed effective date is specified, the corporate existence begins when the articles of incorporation are filed.

(b) The secretary of state's filing of the articles of incorporation is conclusive proof that the incorporators satisfied all conditions precedent to incorporation except in a proceeding by the state to cancel or revoke the incorporation or involuntarily dissolve the corporation.

### §2.04 Liability for Preincorporation Transactions

All persons purporting to act as or on behalf of a corporation, knowing there was no incorporation under this Act, are jointly and severally liable for all liabilities created while so acting.

### §2.05 Organization of Corporation

(a) After incorporation:

(1) if initial directors are named in the articles of incorporation, the initial directors shall hold an organizational meeting, at the call of a majority of the directors, to complete the organization of the corporation by appointing officers, adopting bylaws, and carrying on any other business brought before the meeting;

(2) if initial directors are not named in the articles, the incorporator or incorporators shall hold an organizational meeting at the call of a majority of the incorporators:

(i) to elect directors and complete the organization of the corporation; or

(ii) to elect a board of directors who shall complete the organization of the corporation.

(b) Action required or permitted by this Act to be taken by incorporators at an organizational meeting may be taken without a meeting if the action taken is evidenced by one or more written consents describing the action taken and signed by each incorporator.

(c) An organizational meeting may be held in or out of this state.

### §2.06 Bylaws

(a) The incorporators or board of directors of a corporation shall adopt initial bylaws for the corporation.

(b) The bylaws of a corporation may contain any provision for managing the business and regulating the affairs of the corporation that is not inconsistent with law or the articles of incorporation.

### §2.07 Emergency Bylaws

(a) Unless the articles of incorporation provide otherwise, the board of directors of a corporation may adopt bylaws to be effective only in an emergency defined in subsection (d). The emergency bylaws, which are subject to amendment or repeal by the shareholders, may make all provisions necessary for managing the corporation during the emergency, including:

(1) procedures for calling a meeting of the board of directors;

(2) quorum requirements for the meeting; and

(3) designation of additional or substitute directors.

(b) All provisions of the regular bylaws consistent with the emergency bylaws remain effective during the emergency. The emergency bylaws are not effective after the emergency ends.

(c) Corporate action taken in good faith in accordance with the emergency bylaws:

(1) binds the corporation; and

(2) may not be used to impose liability on a corporate director, officer, employee, or agent.

(d) An emergency exists for purposes of this section if a quorum of the corporation's directors cannot readily be assembled because of some catastrophic event.

## CHAPTER 3. PURPOSES AND POWERS

### §3.01 Purposes

(a) Every corporation incorporated under this Act has the purpose of engaging in any lawful business unless a more limited purpose is set forth in the articles of incorporation.

(b) A corporation engaging in a business that is subject to regulation under another statute of this state may incorporate under this Act only if permitted by, and subject to all limitations of, the other statute.

### §3.02 General Powers

Unless its articles of incorporation provide otherwise, every corporation has perpetual duration and succession in its corporate name and has the same powers as an individual to do all things necessary or convenient to carry out its business and affairs, including without limitation power:

(1) to sue and be sued, complain and defend in its corporate name;

(2) to have a corporate seal, which may be altered at will, and to use it, or a facsimile of it, by impressing or affixing it or in any other manner reproducing it;

(3) to make and amend bylaws, not inconsistent with its articles of incorporation or with the laws of this state, for managing the business and regulating the affairs of the corporation;

(4) to purchase, receive, lease, or otherwise acquire, and own, hold, improve, use, and otherwise deal with, real or personal property, or any legal or equitable interest in property, wherever located;

(5) to sell, convey, mortgage, pledge, lease, exchange, and otherwise dispose of all or any part of its property;

(6) to purchase, receive, subscribe for, or otherwise acquire; own, hold, vote, use, sell, mortgage, lend, pledge, or otherwise dispose of; and deal in and with shares or other interests in, or obligations of, any other entity;

(7) to make contracts and guarantees, incur liabilities, borrow money, issue its notes, bonds, and other obligations, (which may be convertible into or include the option to purchase other securities of the corporation), and secure any of its obligations by mortgage or pledge of any of its property, franchises, or income;

(8) to lend money, invest and reinvest its funds, and receive and hold real and personal property as security for repayment;

(9) to be a promoter, partner, member, associate, or manager of any partnership, joint venture, trust, or other entity;

(10) to conduct its business, locate offices, and exercise the powers granted by this Act within or without this state;

(11) to elect directors and appoint officers, employees, and agents of the corporation, define their duties, fix their compensation, and lend them money and credit;

(12) to pay pensions and establish pension plans, pension trusts, profit sharing plans, share bonus plans, share option plans, and benefit or incentive plans for any or all of its current or former directors, officers, employees, and agents;

(13) to make donations for the public welfare or for charitable, scientific, or educational purposes;

(14) to transact any lawful business that will aid governmental policy;

(15) to make payments or donations, or do any other act, not inconsistent with law, that furthers the business and affairs of the corporation.

### §3.03 Emergency Powers

(a) In anticipation of or during an emergency defined in subsection (d), the board of directors of a corporation may:

(1) modify lines of succession to accommodate the incapacity of any director, officer, employee, or agent; and

(2) relocate the principal office, designate alternative principal offices or regional offices, or authorize the officers to do so.

(b) During an emergency defined in subsection (d), unless emergency bylaws provide otherwise:

(1) notice of a meeting of the board of directors need be given only to those directors whom it is practicable to reach and may be given in any practicable manner, including by publication and radio; and

(2) one or more officers of the corporation present at a meeting of the board of directors may be deemed to be directors for the meeting, in order of rank and within the same rank in order of seniority, as necessary to achieve a quorum.

(c) Corporate action taken in good faith during an emergency under this section to further the ordinary business affairs of the corporation:

(1) binds the corporation; and

(2) may not be used to impose liability on a corporate director, officer, employee, or agent.

(d) An emergency exists for purposes of this section if a quorum of the corporation's directors cannot readily be assembled because of some catastrophic event.

### §3.04 Ultra Vires

(a) Except as provided in subsection (b), the validity of corporate action may not be challenged on the ground that the corporation lacks or lacked power to act.

(b) A corporation's power to act may be challenged:

(1) in a proceeding by a shareholder against the corporation to enjoin the act;

(2) in a proceeding by the corporation, directly, derivatively, or through a receiver, trustee, or other legal representative, against an incumbent or former director, officer, employee, or agent of the corporation; or

(3) in a proceeding by the Attorney General under section 14.30.

(c) In a shareholder's proceeding under subsection (b) (1) to enjoin an unauthorized corporate act, the court may enjoin or set aside the act, if equitable and if all affected persons are parties to the proceeding, and may award damages for loss (other than anticipated profits) suffered by the corporation or another party because of enjoining the unauthorized act.

## CHAPTER 4. NAME

### §4.01 Corporate Name

(a) A corporate name:

(1) must contain the word "corporation," "incorporated," "company," or "limited," or the abbreviation "corp.," "inc.," "co.," or "ltd.," or words or abbreviations of like import in another language; and

(2) may not contain language stating or implying that the corporation is organized for a purpose other than that permitted by section 3.01 and its articles of incorporation.

(b) Except as authorized by subsections (c) and (d), a corporate name must be distinguishable upon the records of the secretary of state from:

(1) the corporate name of a corporation incorporated or authorized to transact business in this state;

(2) a corporate name reserved or registered under section 4.02 or 4.03;

(3) the fictitious name adopted by a foreign corporation authorized to transact business in this state because its real name is unavailable; and

(4) the corporate name of a not-for-profit corporation incorporated or authorized to transact business in this state.

(c) A corporation may apply to the secretary of state for authorization to use a name that is not distinguishable upon his records from one or more of the names described in subsection (b). The secretary of state shall authorize use of the name applied for if:

(1) the other corporation consents to the use in writing and submits an undertaking in form satisfactory to the secretary of state to change its name to a name that is distinguishable upon the records of the secretary of state from the name of the applying corporation; or

(2) the applicant delivers to the secretary of state a certified copy of the final judgment of a court of competent jurisdiction establishing the applicant's right to use the name applied for in this state.

(d) A corporation may use the name (including the fictitious name) of another domestic or foreign corporation that is used in this state if the other corporation is incorporated or authorized to transact business in this state and the proposed user corporation:

(1) has merged with the other corporation;

(2) has been formed by reorganization of the other corporation; or

(3) has acquired all or substantially all of the assets, including the corporate name, of the other corporation.

(e) This Act does not control the use of fictitious names.

### §4.02 Reserved Name

(a) A person may reserve the exclusive use of a corporate name, including a fictitious name for a foreign corporation whose corporate name is not available, by delivering an application to the secretary of state for filing. The application must set forth the name and address of the applicant and the name proposed to be reserved. If the secretary of state finds that the corporate name applied for is available, he shall reserve the name for the applicant's exclusive use for a nonrenewable 120-day period.

(b) The owner of a reserved corporate name may transfer the reservation to another person by delivering to the secretary of state a signed notice of the transfer that states the name and address of the transferee.

### §4.03 Registered Name

(a) A foreign corporation may register its corporate name, or its corporate name with any addition required by section 15.06, if the name is distinguishable upon the records of the secretary of state from the corporate names that are not available under section 4.01(b)(3).

(b) A foreign corporation registers its corporate name, or its corporate name with any addition required by section 15.06, by delivering to the secretary of state for filing an application:

(1) setting forth its corporate name, or its corporate name with any addition required by section 15.06, the state or country and date of its incorporation, and a brief description of the nature of the business in which it is engaged; and

(2) accompanied by a certificate of existence (or a document of similar import) from the state or country of incorporation.

(c) The name is registered for the applicant's exclusive use upon the effective date of the application.

(d) A foreign corporation whose registration is effective may renew it for successive years by delivering to the secretary of state for filing a renewal application, which complies with the requirements of subsection (b), between October 1 and December 31 of the preceding year. The renewal application renews the registration for the following calendar year.

(e) A foreign corporation whose registration is effective may thereafter qualify as a foreign corporation under that name or consent in writing to the use of that name by a corporation thereafter incorporated under this Act or by another foreign corporation thereafter authorized to transact business in this state. The registration terminates when the domestic corporation is incorporated or the foreign corporation qualifies or consents to the qualification of another foreign corporation under the registered name.

## CHAPTER 5. OFFICE AND AGENT

### §5.01 Registered Office and Registered Agent

Each corporation must continuously maintain in this state:

(1) a registered office that may be the same as any of its places of business; and

(2) a registered agent, who may be:

(i) an individual who resides in this state and whose business office is identical with the registered office;

(ii) a domestic corporation or not-for-profit domestic corporation whose business office is identical with the registered office; or

(iii) a foreign corporation or not-for-profit foreign corporation authorized to transact business in this state whose business office is identical with the registered office.

### §5.02 Change of Registered Office or Registered Agent

(a) A corporation may change its registered office or registered agent by delivering to the secretary of state for filing a statement of change that sets forth:

(1) the name of the corporation,

(2) the street address of its current registered office;

(3) if the current registered office is to be changed, the street address of the new registered office;

(4) the name of its current registered agent;

(5) if the current registered agent is to be changed, the name of the new registered agent and the new agent's written consent (either on the statement or attached to it) to the appointment; and

(6) that after the change or changes are made, the street addresses of its registered office and the business office of its registered agent will be identical.

(b) If a registered agent changes the street address of his business office, he may change the street address of the registered office of any corporation for which he is the registered agent by notifying the corporation in writing of the change and signing (either manually or in facsimile) and delivering to the secretary of state for filing a statement that complies with the requirements of subsection (a) and recites that the corporation has been notified of the change.

### §5.03 Resignation of Registered Agent

(a) A registered agent may resign his agency appointment by signing and delivering to the secretary of state for filing the signed original and two exact or conformed copies of a statement of resignation. The statement may include a statement that the registered office is also discontinued.

(b) After filing the statement the secretary of state shall mail one copy to the registered office (if not discontinued) and the other copy to the corporation at its principal office.
(c) The agency appointment is terminated, and the registered office discontinued if so provided, on the 31st day after the date on which the statement was filed.

### §5.04 Service on Corporation

(a) A corporation's registered agent is the corporation's agent for service of process, notice, or demand required or permitted by law to be served on the corporation.
(b) If a corporation has no registered agent, or the agent cannot with reasonable diligence be served, the corporation may be served by registered or certified mail, return receipt requested, addressed to the secretary of the corporation at its principal office. Service is perfected under this subsection at the earliest of:

(1) the date the corporation receives the mail;
(2) the date shown on the return receipt, if signed on behalf of the corporation; or
(3) five days after its deposit in the United States Mail, if mailed postpaid and correctly addressed.

(c) This section does not prescribe the only means, or necessarily the required means, of serving a corporation.

## CHAPTER 6. SHARES AND DISTRIBUTIONS

## Subchapter A. Shares

### §6.01 Authorized Shares

(a) The articles of incorporation must prescribe the classes of shares and the number of shares of each class that the corporation is authorized to issue. If more than one class of shares is authorized, the articles of incorporation must prescribe a distinguishing designation for each class, and prior to the issuance of shares of a class the preferences, limitations, and relative rights of that class must be described in the articles of incorporation. All shares of a class must have preferences, limitations, and relative rights identical with those of other shares of the same class except to the extent otherwise permitted by section 6.02.
(b) The articles of incorporation must authorize: (1) one or more classes of shares that together have unlimited voting rights, and (2) one or more classes of shares (which may be the same class or classes as those with voting rights) that together are entitled to receive the net assets of the corporation upon dissolution.
(c) The articles of incorporation may authorize one or more classes of shares that:

(1) have special, conditional, or limited voting rights, or no right to vote, except to the extent prohibited by this Act;
(2) are redeemable or convertible as specified in the articles of incorporation (i) at the option of the corporation, the shareholder, or another person or upon the occurrence of a designated event; (ii) for cash, indebtedness, securities, or other property; (iii) in a designated amount or in an amount determined in accordance with a designated formula or by reference to extrinsic data or events;
(3) entitle the holders to distributions calculated in any manner, including dividends that may be cumulative, noncumulative, or partially cumulative;
(4) have preference over any other class of shares with respect to distributions, including dividends and distributions upon the dissolution of the corporation.

(d) The description of the designations, preferences, limitations, and relative rights of share classes in subsection (c) is not exhaustive.

### §6.02 Terms of Class or Series Determined by Board of Directors

(a) If the articles of incorporation so provide, the board of directors may determine, in whole or part, the preferences, limitations, and relative rights (within the limits set forth in section 6.01) of (1) any class of shares before the issuance of any shares of that class or (2) one or more series within a class before the issuance of any shares of that series.
(b) Each series of a class must be given a distinguishing designation.
(c) All shares of a series must have preferences, limitations, and relative rights identical with those of other shares of the same series and, except to the extent otherwise provided in the description of the series, of those of other series of the same class.
(d) Before issuing any shares of a class or series created under this section, the corporation must deliver to the secretary of state for filing articles of amendment, which are effective without shareholder action, that set forth:

(1) the name of the corporation;
(2) the text of the amendment determining the terms of the class or series of shares;
(3) the date it was adopted; and
(4) a statement that the amendment was duly adopted by the board of directors.

### §6.03 Issued and Outstanding Shares

(a) A corporation may issue the number of shares of each class or series authorized by the articles of incorporation. Shares that are issued are outstanding shares until they are reacquired, redeemed, converted, or cancelled.
(b) The reacquisition, redemption, or conversion of outstanding shares is subject to the limitations of subsection (c) of this section and to section 6.40.
(c) At all times that shares of the corporation are outstanding, one or more shares that together have unlimited voting rights and one or more shares that together are entitled to receive the net assets of the corporation upon dissolution must be outstanding.

### §6.04 Fractional Shares

(a) A corporation may:

(1) issue fractions of a share or pay in money the value of fractions of a share;
(2) arrange for disposition of fractional shares by the shareholders;
(3) issue scrip in registered or bearer form entitling the holder to receive a full share upon surrendering enough scrip to equal a full share.

(b) Each certificate representing scrip must be conspicuously labeled "scrip" and must contain the information required by section 6.25(b).
(c) The holder of a fractional share is entitled to exercise the rights of a shareholder, including the right to vote, to receive dividends, and to participate in the assets of the corporation upon liquidation. The holder of scrip is not entitled to any of these rights unless the scrip provides for them.
(d) The board of directors may authorize the issuance of scrip subject to any condition considered desirable, including:

(1) that the scrip will become void if not exchanged for full shares before a specified date; and
(2) that the shares for which the scrip is exchangeable may be sold and the proceeds paid to the scripholders.

## Subchapter B. Issuance of Shares

### §6.20 Subscription for Shares Before Incorporation

(a) A subscription for shares entered into before incorporation is irrevocable for six months unless the subscription agreement provides a longer or shorter period or all the subscribers agree to revocation.
(b) The board of directors may determine the payment terms of subscriptions for shares that were entered into before incorporation, unless the subscription agreement specifies them. A call for payment by the board of directors must be uniform so far as practicable as to all shares of the same class or series, unless the subscription agreement specifies otherwise.
(c) Shares issued pursuant to subscriptions entered into before incorporation are fully paid and nonassessable when the corporation receives the consideration specified in the subscription agreement.

(d) If a subscriber defaults in payment of money or property under a subscription agreement entered into before incorporation, the corporation may collect the amount owed as any other debt. Alternatively, unless the subscription agreement provides otherwise, the corporation may rescind the agreement and may sell the shares if the debt remains unpaid more than 20 days after the corporation sends written demand for payment to the subscriber.
(e) A subscription agreement entered into after incorporation is a contract between the subscriber and the corporation subject to section 6.21.

**§6.21 Issuance of Shares**

(a) The powers granted in this section to the board of directors may be reserved to the shareholders by the articles of incorporation.
(b) The board of directors may authorize shares to be issued for consideration consisting of any tangible or intangible property or benefit to the corporation, including cash, promissory notes, services performed, contracts for services to be performed, or other securities of the corporation.
(c) Before the corporation issues shares, the board of directors must determine that the consideration received or to be received for shares to be issued is adequate. That determination by the board of directors is conclusive insofar as the adequacy of consideration for the issuance of shares relates to whether the shares are validly issued, fully paid, and nonassessable.
(d) When the corporation receives the consideration for which the board of directors authorized the issuance of shares, the shares issued therefor are fully paid and nonassessable.
(e) The corporation may place in escrow shares issued for a contract for future services or benefits or a promissory note, or make other arrangements to restrict the transfer of the shares, and may credit distributions in respect of the shares against their purchase price, until the services are performed, the note is paid, or the benefits received. If the services are not performed, the note is not paid, or the benefits are not received, the shares escrowed or restricted and the distributions credited may be cancelled in whole or part.

**§6.22 Liability of Shareholders**

(a) A purchaser from a corporation of its own shares is not liable to the corporation or its creditors with respect to the shares except to pay the consideration for which the shares were authorized to be issued (section 6.21) or specified in the subscription agreement (section 6.20).
(b) Unless otherwise provided in the articles of incorporation, a shareholder of a corporation is not personally liable for the acts or debts of the corporation except that he may become personally liable by reason of his own acts or conduct.

**§6.23 Share Dividends**

(a) Unless the articles of incorporation provide otherwise, shares may be issued pro rata and without consideration to the corporation's shareholders or to the shareholders of one or more classes or series. An issuance of shares under this subsection is a share dividend.
(b) Shares of one class or series may not be issued as a share dividend in respect of shares of another class or series unless (1) the articles of incorporation so authorize, (2) a majority of the votes entitled to be cast by the class or series to be issued approve the issue, or (3) there are no outstanding shares of the class or series to be issued.
(c) If the board of directors does not fix the record date for determining shareholders entitled to a share dividend, it is the date the board of directors authorizes the share dividend.

**§6.24 Share Options**

A corporation may issue rights, options, or warrants for the purchase of shares of the corporation. The board of directors shall determine the terms upon which the rights, options, or warrants are issued, their form and content, and the consideration for which the shares are to be issued.

**§6.25 Form and Content of Certificates**

(a) Shares may but need not be represented by certificates. Unless this Act or another statute expressly provides otherwise, the rights and obligations of shareholders are identical whether or not their shares are represented by certificates.
(b) At a minimum each share certificate must state on its face:
(1) the name of the issuing corporation and that it is organized under the law of this state;
(2) the name of the person to whom issued; and
(3) the number and class of shares and the designation of the series, if any, the certificate represents.
(c) If the issuing corporation is authorized to issue different classes of shares or different series within a class, the designations, relative rights, preferences, and limitations applicable to each class and the variations in rights, preferences, and limitations determined for each series (and the authority of the board of directors to determine variations for future series) must be summarized on the front or back of each certificate. Alternatively, each certificate may state conspicuously on its front or back that the corporation will furnish the shareholder this information on request in writing and without charge.
(d) Each share certificate (1) must be signed (either manually or in facsimile) by two officers designated in the bylaws or by the board of directors and (2) may bear the corporate seal or its facsimile.
(e) If the person who signed (either manually or in facsimile) a share certificate no longer holds office when the certificate is issued, the certificate is nevertheless valid.

**§6.26 Shares Without Certificates**

(a) Unless the articles of incorporation or bylaws provide otherwise, the board of directors of a corporation may authorize the issue of some or all of the shares of any or all of its classes or series without certificates. The authorization does not affect shares already represented by certificates until they are surrendered to the corporation.
(b) Within a reasonable time after the issue or transfer of shares without certificates, the corporation shall send the shareholder a written statement of the information required on certificates by section 6.25(b) and (c), and, if applicable, section 6.27.

**§6.27 Restriction on Transfer or Registration of Shares and Other Securities**

(a) The articles of incorporation, bylaws, an agreement among shareholders, or an agreement between shareholders and the corporation may impose restrictions on the transfer or registration of transfer of shares of the corporation. A restriction does not affect shares issued before the restriction was adopted unless the holders of the shares are parties to the restriction agreement or voted in favor of the restriction.
(b) A restriction on the transfer or registration of transfer of shares is valid and enforceable against the holder or a transferee of the holder if the restriction is authorized by this section and its existence is noted conspicuously on the front or back of the certificate or is contained in the information statement required by section 6.26(b). Unless so noted, a restriction is not enforceable against a person without knowledge of the restriction.
(c) A restriction on the transfer or registration of transfer of shares is authorized:
(1) to maintain the corporation's status when it is dependent on the number or identity of its shareholders;
(2) to preserve exemptions under federal or state securities law;
(3) for any other reasonable purpose.
(d) A restriction on the transfer or registration of transfer of shares may:
(1) obligate the shareholder first to offer the corporation or other persons (separately, consecutively, or simultaneously) an opportunity to acquire the restricted shares;
(2) obligate the corporation or other persons (separately, consecutively, or simultaneously) to acquire the restricted shares;
(3) require the corporation, the holders of any class of its shares, or another person to approve the transfer of the restricted shares, if the requirement is not manifestly unreasonable;

(4) prohibit the transfer of the restricted shares to designated persons or classes of persons, if the prohibition is not manifestly unreasonable.

(e) For purposes of this section, "shares" includes a security convertible into or carrying a right to subscribe for or acquire shares.

**§6.28 Expense of Issue**

A corporation may pay the expenses of selling or underwriting its shares, and of organizing or reorganizing the corporation, from the consideration received for shares.

## Subchapter C. Subsequent Acquisition of Shares by Shareholders and Corporation

**§6.30 Shareholders' Preemptive Rights**

(a) The shareholders of a corporation do not have a preemptive right to acquire the corporation's unissued shares except to the extent the articles of incorporation so provide.

(b) A statement included in the articles of incorporation that "the corporation elects to have preemptive rights" (or words of similar import) means that the following principles apply except to the extent the articles of incorporation expressly provide otherwise:

(1) The shareholders of the corporation have a preemptive right, granted on uniform terms and conditions prescribed by the board of directors to provide a fair and reasonable opportunity to exercise the right, to acquire proportional amounts of the corporation's unissued shares upon the decision of the board of directors to issue them.

(2) A shareholder may waive his preemptive right. A waiver evidenced by a writing is irrevocable even though it is not supported by consideration.

(3) There is no preemptive right with respect to:

(i) shares issued as compensation to directors, officers, agents, or employees of the corporation, its subsidiaries or affiliates;

(ii) shares issued to satisfy conversion or option rights created to provide compensation to directors, officers, agents, or employees of the corporation, its subsidiaries or affiliates;

(iii) shares authorized in articles of incorporation that are issued within six months from the effective date of incorporation;

(iv) shares sold otherwise than for money.

(4) Holders of shares of any class without general voting rights but with preferential rights to distributions or assets have no preemptive rights with respect to shares of any class.

(5) Holders of shares of any class with general voting rights but without preferential rights to distributions or assets have no preemptive rights with respect to shares of any class with preferential rights to distributions or assets unless the shares with preferential rights are convertible into or carry a right to subscribe for or acquire shares without preferential rights.

(6) Shares subject to preemptive rights that are not acquired by shareholders may be issued to any person for a period of one year after being offered to shareholders at a consideration set by the board of directors that is not lower than the consideration set for the exercise of preemptive rights. An offer at a lower consideration or after the expiration of one year is subject to the shareholders' preemptive rights.

(c) For purposes of this section, "shares" includes a security convertible into or carrying a right to subscribe for or acquire shares.

**§6.31 Corporation's Acquisition of Its Own Shares**

(a) A corporation may acquire its own shares and shares so acquired constitute authorized but unissued shares.

(b) If the articles of incorporation prohibit the reissue of acquired shares, the number of authorized shares is reduced by the number of shares acquired, effective upon amendment of the articles of incorporation.

(c) Articles of amendment may be adopted by the board of directors without shareholder action, shall be delivered to the secretary of state for filing, and shall set forth:

(1) the name of the corporation;

(2) the reduction in the number of authorized shares, itemized by class and series; and

(3) the total number of authorized shares, itemized by class and series, remaining after reduction of the shares.

## Subchapter D. Distributions

**§6.40 Distributions to Shareholders**

(a) A board of directors may authorize and the corporation may make distributions to its shareholders subject to restriction by the articles of incorporation and the limitation in subsection (c).

(b) If the board of directors does not fix the record date for determining shareholders entitled to a distribution (other than one involving a purchase, redemption, or other acquisition of the corporation's shares), it is the date the board of directors authorizes the distribution.

(c) No distribution may be made if, after giving it effect:

(1) the corporation would not be able to pay its debts as they become due in the usual course of business; or

(2) the corporation's total assets would be less than the sum of its total liabilities plus (unless the articles of incorporation permit otherwise) the amount that would be needed, if the corporation were to be dissolved at the time of the distribution, to satisfy the preferential rights upon dissolution of shareholders whose preferential rights are superior to those receiving the distribution.

(d) The board of directors may base a determination that a distribution is not prohibited under subsection (c) either on financial statements prepared on the basis of accounting practices and principles that are reasonable in the circumstances or on a fair valuation or other method that is reasonable in the circumstances.

(e) Except as provided in subsection (g), the effect of a distribution under subsection (c) is measured:

(1) in the case of distribution by purchase, redemption, or other acquisition of the corporation's shares, as of the earlier of (i) the date money or other property is transferred or debt incurred by the corporation or (ii) the date the shareholder ceases to be a shareholder with respect to the acquired shares;

(2) in the case of any other distribution of indebtedness, as of the date the indebtedness is distributed;

(3) in all other cases, as of (i) the date the distribution is authorized if the payment occurs within 120 days after the date of authorization or (ii) the date the payment is made if it occurs more than 120 days after the date of authorization.

(f) A corporation's indebtedness to a shareholder incurred by reason of a distribution made in accordance with this section is at parity with the corporation's indebtedness to its general, unsecured creditors except to the extent subordinated by agreement.

(g) Indebtedness of a corporation, including indebtedness issued as a distribution, is not considered a liability for purposes of determinations under subsection (c) if its terms provide that payment of principal and interest are made only if and to the extent that payment of a distribution to shareholders could then be made under this section. If the indebtedness is issued as a distribution, each payment of principal or interest is treated as a distribution, the effect of which is measured on the date the payment is actually made.

# CHAPTER 7. SHAREHOLDERS

## Subchapter A. Meetings

**§7.01 Annual Meeting**

(a) A corporation shall hold annually at a time stated in or fixed in accordance with the bylaws a meeting of shareholders.

(b) Annual shareholders' meetings may be held in or out of this state at the place stated in or fixed in accordance with the bylaws. If no place is stated in or fixed in accordance with the bylaws, annual meetings shall be held at the corporation's principal office.

(c) The failure to hold an annual meeting at the time stated in or fixed in accordance with a corporation's bylaws does not affect the validity of any corporate action.

**§7.02 Special Meeting**

(a) A corporation shall hold a special meeting of shareholders:

(1) on call of its board of directors or the person or persons authorized to do so by the articles of incorporation or bylaws; or

(2) if the holders of at least 10 percent of all the votes entitled to be cast on any issue proposed to be considered at the proposed special meeting sign, date, and deliver to the corporation's secretary one or more written demands for the meeting describing the purpose or purposes for which it is to be held.

(b) If not otherwise fixed under sections 7.03 or 7.07, the record date for determining shareholders entitled to demand a special meeting is the date the first shareholder signs the demand.

(c) Special shareholders' meetings may be held in or out of this state at the place stated in or fixed in accordance with the bylaws. If no place is stated or fixed in accordance with the bylaws, special meetings shall be held at the corporation's principal office.

(d) Only business within the purpose or purposes described in the meeting notice required by section 7.05(c) may be conducted at a special shareholders' meeting.

**§7.03 Court-Ordered Meeting**

(a) The [name or describe] court of the county where a corporation's principal office (or, if none in this state, its registered office) is located may summarily order a meeting to be held:

(1) on application of any shareholder of the corporation entitled to participate in an annual meeting if an annual meeting was not held within the earlier of 6 months after the end of the corporation's fiscal year or 15 months after its last annual meeting; or

(2) on application of a shareholder who signed a demand for a special meeting valid under section 7.02 if:

(i) notice of the special meeting was not given within 30 days after the date the demand was delivered to the corporation's secretary; or

(ii) the special meeting was not held in accordance with the notice.

(b) The court may fix the time and place of the meeting, determine the shares entitled to participate in the meeting, specify a record date for determining shareholders entitled to notice of and to vote at the meeting, prescribe the form and content of the meeting notice, fix the quorum required for specific matters to be considered at the meeting (or direct that the votes represented at the meeting constitute a quorum for action on those matters), and enter other orders necessary to accomplish the purpose or purposes of the meeting.

**§7.04 Action Without Meeting**

(a) Action required or permitted by this Act to be taken at a shareholders' meeting may be taken without a meeting if the action is taken by all the shareholders entitled to vote on the action. The action must be evidenced by one or more written consents describing the action taken, signed by all the shareholders entitled to vote on the action, and delivered to the corporation for inclusion in the minutes or filing with the corporate records.

(b) If not otherwise determined under sections 7.03 or 7.07, the record date for determining shareholders entitled to take action without a meeting is the date the first shareholder signs the consent under subsection (a).

(c) A consent signed under this section has the effect of a meeting vote and may be described as such in any document.

(d) If this Act requires that notice of proposed action be given to nonvoting shareholders and the action is to be taken by unanimous consent of the voting shareholders, the corporation must give its nonvoting shareholders written notice of the proposed action at least 10 days before the action is taken. The notice must contain or be accompanied by the same material that, under this Act, would have been required to be sent to nonvoting shareholders in a notice of meeting at which the proposed action would have been submitted to the shareholders for action.

**§7.05 Notice of Meeting**

(a) A corporation shall notify shareholders of the date, time, and place of each annual and special shareholders' meeting no fewer than 10 nor more than 60 days before the meeting date. Unless this Act or the articles of incorporation require otherwise, the corporation is required to give notice only to shareholders entitled to vote at the meeting.

(b) Unless this Act or the articles of incorporation require otherwise, notice of an annual meeting need not include a description of the purpose or purposes for which the meeting is called.

(c) Notice of a special meeting must include a description of the purpose or purposes for which the meeting is called.

(d) If not otherwise fixed under sections 7.03 or 7.07, the record date for determining shareholders entitled to notice of and to vote at an annual or special shareholders' meeting is the day before the first notice is delivered to shareholders.

(e) Unless the bylaws require otherwise, if an annual or special shareholders' meeting is adjourned to a different date, time, or place, notice need not be given of the new date, time, or place if the new date, time, or place is announced at the meeting before adjournment. If a new record date for the adjourned meeting is or must be fixed under section 7.07, however, notice of the adjourned meeting must be given under this section to persons who are shareholders as of the new record date.

**§7.06 Waiver of Notice**

(a) A shareholder may waive any notice required by this Act, the articles of incorporation, or bylaws before or after the date and time stated in the notice. The waiver must be in writing, be signed by the shareholder entitled to the notice, and be delivered to the corporation for inclusion in the minutes or filing with the corporate records.

(b) A shareholder's attendance at a meeting:

(1) waives objection to lack of notice or defective notice of the meeting, unless the shareholder at the beginning of the meeting objects to holding the meeting or transacting business at the meeting;

(2) waives objection to consideration of a particular matter at the meeting that is not within the purpose or purposes described in the meeting notice, unless the shareholder objects to considering the matter when it is presented.

**§7.07 Record Date**

(a) The bylaws may fix or provide the manner of fixing the record date for one or more voting groups in order to determine the shareholders entitled to notice of a shareholders' meeting, to demand a special meeting, to vote, or to take any other action. If the bylaws do not fix or provide for fixing a record date, the board of directors of the corporation may fix a future date as the record date.

(b) A record date fixed under this section may not be more than 70 days before the meeting or action requiring a determination of shareholders.

(c) A determination of shareholders entitled to notice of or to vote at a shareholders' meeting is effective for any adjournment of the meeting unless the board of directors fixes a new record date, which it must do if the meeting is adjourned to a date more than 120 days after the date fixed for the original meeting.

(d) If a court orders a meeting adjourned to a date more than 120 days after the date fixed for the original meeting, it may provide that the original record date continues in effect or it may fix a new record date.

## Subchapter B. Voting

**§7.20 Shareholders' List for Meeting**

(a) After fixing a record date for a meeting, a corporation shall prepare an alphabetical list of the names of all its shareholders who are entitled to notice of a shareholders' meeting. The list must be arranged by voting

group (and within each voting group by class or series of shares) and show the address of and number of shares held by each shareholder.
(b) The shareholders' list must be available for inspection by any shareholder, beginning two business days after notice of the meeting is given for which the list was prepared and continuing through the meeting, at the corporation's principal office or at a place identified in the meeting notice in the city where the meeting will be held. A shareholder, his agent, or attorney is entitled on written demand to inspect and, subject to the requirements of section 16.02(c), to copy the list, during regular business hours and at his expense, during the period it is available for inspection.
(c) The corporation shall make the shareholders' list available at the meeting, and any shareholder, his agent, or attorney is entitled to inspect the list at any time during the meeting or any adjournment.
(d) If the corporation refuses to allow a shareholder, his agent, or attorney to inspect the shareholders' list before or at the meeting (or copy the list as permitted by subsection (b)), the [name or describe] court of the county where a corporation's principal office (or, if none in this state, its registered office) is located, on application of the shareholder, may summarily order the inspection or copying at the corporation's expense and may postpone the meeting for which the list was prepared until the inspection or copying is complete.
(e) Refusal or failure to prepare or make available the shareholders' list does not affect the validity of action taken at the meeting.

### §7.21 Voting Entitlement of Shares

(a) Except as provided in subsections (b) and (c) or unless the articles of incorporation provide otherwise, each outstanding share, regardless of class, is entitled to one vote on each matter voted on at a shareholders' meeting. Only shares are entitled to vote.
(b) Absent special circumstances, the shares of a corporation are not entitled to vote if they are owned, directly or indirectly, by a second corporation, domestic or foreign, and the first corporation owns, directly or indirectly, a majority of the shares entitled to vote for directors of the second corporation.
(c) Subsection (b) does not limit the power of a corporation to vote any shares, including its own shares, held by it in a fiduciary capacity.
(d) Redeemable shares are not entitled to vote after notice of redemption is mailed to the holders and a sum sufficient to redeem the shares has been deposited with a bank, trust company, or other financial institution under an irrevocable obligation to pay the holders the redemption price on surrender of the shares.

### §7.22 Proxies

(a) A shareholder may vote his shares in person or by proxy.
(b) A shareholder may appoint a proxy to vote or otherwise act for him by signing an appointment form, either personally or by his attorney-in-fact.
(c) An appointment of a proxy is effective when received by the secretary or other officer or agent authorized to tabulate votes. An appointment is valid for 11 months unless a longer period is expressly provided in the appointment form.
(d) An appointment of a proxy is revocable by the shareholder unless the appointment form conspicuously states that it is irrevocable and the appointment is coupled with an interest. Appointments coupled with an interest include the appointment of:
(1) a pledgee;
(2) a person who purchased or agreed to purchase the shares;
(3) a creditor of the corporation who extended it credit under terms requiring the appointment;
(4) an employee of the corporation whose employment contract requires the appointment; or
(5) a party to a voting agreement created under section 7.31.
(e) The death or incapacity of the shareholder appointing a proxy does not affect the right of the corporation to accept the proxy's authority unless notice of the death or incapacity is received by the secretary or other officer or agent authorized to tabulate votes before the proxy exercises his authority under the appointment.
(f) An appointment made irrevocable under subsection (d) is revoked when the interest with which it is coupled is extinguished.
(g) A transferee for value of shares subject to an irrevocable appointment may revoke the appointment if he did not know of its existence when he acquired the shares and the existence of the irrevocable appointment was not noted conspicuously on the certificate representing the shares or on the information statement for shares without certificates.
(h) Subject to section 7.24 and to any express limitation on the proxy's authority appearing on the face of the appointment form, a corporation is entitled to accept the proxy's vote or other action as that of the shareholder making the appointment.

### §7.23 Shares Held by Nominees

(a) A corporation may establish a procedure by which the beneficial owner of shares that are registered in the name of a nominee is recognized by the corporation as the shareholder. The extent of this recognition may be determined in the procedure.
(b) The procedure may set forth:
(1) the types of nominees to which it applies;
(2) the rights or privileges that the corporation recognizes in a beneficial owner;
(3) the manner in which the procedure is selected by the nominee;
(4) the information that must be provided when the procedure is selected;
(5) the period for which selection of the procedure is effective; and
(6) other aspects of the rights and duties created.

### §7.24 Corporation's Acceptance of Votes

(a) If the name signed on a vote, consent, waiver, or proxy appointment corresponds to the name of a shareholder, the corporation if acting in good faith is entitled to accept the vote, consent, waiver, or proxy appointment and give it effect as the act of the shareholder.
(b) If the name signed on a vote, consent, waiver, or proxy appointment does not correspond to the name of its shareholder, the corporation if acting in good faith is nevertheless entitled to accept the vote, consent, waiver, or proxy appointment and give it effect as the act of the shareholder if:
(1) the shareholder is an entity and the name signed purports to be that of an officer or agent of the entity;
(2) the name signed purports to be that of an administrator, executor, guardian, or conservator representing the shareholder and, if the corporation requests, evidence of fiduciary status acceptable to the corporation has been presented with respect to the vote, consent, waiver, or proxy appointment;
(3) the name signed purports to be that of a receiver or trustee in bankruptcy of the shareholder and, if the corporation requests, evidence of this status acceptable to the corporation has been presented with respect to the vote, consent, waiver, or proxy appointment;
(4) the name signed purports to be that of a pledgee, beneficial owner, or attorney-in-fact of the shareholder and, if the corporation requests, evidence acceptable to the corporation of the signatory's authority to sign for the shareholder has been presented with respect to the vote, consent, waiver, or proxy appointment;
(5) two or more persons are the shareholder as cotenants or fiduciaries and the name signed purports to be the name of at least one of the coowners and the person signing appears to be acting on behalf of all the coowners.
(c) The corporation is entitled to reject a vote, consent, waiver, or proxy appointment if the secretary or other officer or agent authorized to tabulate votes, acting in good faith, has reasonable basis for doubt about the validity of the signature on it or about the signatory's authority to sign for the shareholder.
(d) The corporation and its officer or agent who accepts or rejects a vote, consent, waiver, or proxy appointment in good faith and in accordance with the standards of this section are not liable in damages to the shareholder for the consequences of the acceptance or rejection.

(e) Corporate action based on the acceptance or rejection of a vote, consent, waiver, or proxy appointment under this section is valid unless a court of competent jurisdiction determines otherwise.

**§7.25 Quorum and Voting Requirements for Voting Groups**

(a) Shares entitled to vote as a separate voting group may take action on a matter at a meeting only if a quorum of those shares exists with respect to that matter. Unless the articles of incorporation or this Act provide otherwise, a majority of the votes entitled to be cast on the matter by the voting group constitutes a quorum of that voting group for action on that matter.
(b) Once a share is represented for any purpose at a meeting, it is deemed present for quorum purposes for the remainder of the meeting and for any adjournment of that meeting unless a new record date is or must be set for that adjourned meeting.
(c) If a quorum exists, action on a matter (other than the election of directors) by a voting group is approved if the votes cast within the voting group favoring the action exceed the votes cast opposing the action, unless the articles of incorporation or this Act require a greater number of affirmative votes.
(d) An amendment of articles of incorporation adding, changing, or deleting a quorum or voting requirement for a voting group greater than specified in subsection (b) or (c) is governed by section 7.27.
(e) The election of directors is governed by section 7.28.

**§7.26 Action by Single and Multiple Voting Groups**

(a) If the articles of incorporation or this Act provide for voting by a single voting group on a matter, action on that matter is taken when voted upon by that voting group as provided in section 7.25.
(b) If the articles of incorporation or this Act provide for voting by two or more voting groups on a matter, action on that matter is taken only when voted upon by each of those voting groups counted separately as provided in section 7.25. Action may be taken by one voting group on a matter even though no action is taken by another voting group entitled to vote on the matter.

**§7.27 Greater Quorum or Voting Requirements**

(a) The articles of incorporation may provide for a greater quorum or voting requirement for shareholders (or voting groups of shareholders) than is provided for by this Act.
(b) An amendment to the articles of incorporation that adds, changes, or deletes a greater quorum or voting requirement must meet the same quorum requirement and be adopted by the same vote and voting groups required to take action under the quorum and voting requirements then in effect or proposed to be adopted, whichever is greater.

**§7.28 Voting for Directors; Cumulative Voting**

(a) Unless otherwise provided in the articles of incorporation, directors are elected by a plurality of the votes cast by the shares entitled to vote in the election at a meeting at which a quorum is present.
(b) Shareholders do not have a right to cumulate their votes for directors unless the articles of incorporation so provide.
(c) A statement included in the articles of incorporation that "[all] [a designated voting group of] shareholders are entitled to cumulate their votes for directors" (or words of similar import) means that the shareholders designated are entitled to multiply the number of votes they are entitled to cast by the number of directors for whom they are entitled to vote and cast the product for a single candidate or distribute the product among two or more candidates.
(d) Shares otherwise entitled to vote cumulatively may not be voted cumulatively at a particular meeting unless:

(1) the meeting notice or proxy statement accompanying the notice states conspicuously that cumulative voting is authorized; or
(2) a shareholder who has the right to cumulate his votes gives notice to the corporation not less than 48 hours before the time set for the meeting of his intent to cumulate his votes during the meeting, and if one shareholder gives this notice all other shareholders in the same voting group participating in the election are entitled to cumulate their votes without giving further notice.

## Subchapter C. Voting Trusts and Agreements

**§7.30 Voting Trusts**

(a) One or more shareholders may create a voting trust, conferring on a trustee the right to vote or otherwise act for them, by signing an agreement setting out the provisions of the trust (which may include anything consistent with its purpose) and transferring their shares to the trustee. When a voting trust agreement is signed, the trustee shall prepare a list of the names and addresses of all owners of beneficial interests in the trust, together with the number and class of shares each transferred to the trust, and deliver copies of the list and agreement to the corporation's principal office.
(b) A voting trust becomes effective on the date the first shares subject to the trust are registered in the trustee's name. A voting trust is valid for not more than 10 years after its effective date unless extended under subsection (c).
(c) All or some of the parties to a voting trust may extend it for additional terms of not more than 10 years each by signing an extension agreement and obtaining the voting trustee's written consent to the extension. An extension is valid for 10 years from the date the first shareholder signs the extension agreement. The voting trustee must deliver copies of the extension agreement and list of beneficial owners to the corporation's principal office. An extension agreement binds only those parties signing it.

**§7.31 Voting Agreements**

(a) Two or more shareholders may provide for the manner in which they will vote their shares by signing an agreement for that purpose. A voting agreement created under this section is not subject to the provisions of section 7.30.
(b) A voting agreement created under this section is specifically enforceable.

**§7.32 Shareholder Agreements**

(a) An agreement among the shareholders of a corporation that complies with this section is effective among the shareholders and the corporation even though it is inconsistent with one or more other provisions of this Act in that it:

(1) eliminates the board of directors or restricts the discretion or powers of the board of directors;
(2) governs the authorization or making of distributions whether or not in proportion to ownership of shares, subject to the limitations in section 6.40;
(3) establishes who shall be directors or officers of the corporation, or their terms of office or manner of selection or removal;
(4) governs, in general or in regard to specific matters, the exercise or division of voting power by or between the shareholders and directors or by or among any of them, including use of weighted voting rights or director proxies;
(5) establishes the terms and conditions of any agreement for the transfer or use of property or the provision of services between the corporation and any shareholder, director, officer or employee of the corporation or among any of them;
(6) transfers to one or more shareholders or other persons all or part of the authority to exercise the corporate powers or to manage the business and affairs of the corporation, including the resolution of any issue about which there exists a deadlock among directors or shareholders;
(7) requires dissolution of the corporation at the request of one or more of the shareholders or upon the occurrence of a specified event or contingency; or
(8) otherwise governs the exercise of the corporate powers or the management of the business and affairs of the corporation or the relationship among the shareholders, the directors and the corporation, or among any of them, and is not contrary to public policy.

(b) An agreement authorized by this section shall be:

(1) set forth (A) in the articles of incorporation or bylaws and approved by all persons who are shareholders at the time of the agreement or (B) in a written agreement that is signed by all persons who are shareholders at the time of the agreement and is made known to the corporation;

(2) subject to amendment only by all persons who are shareholders at the time of the amendment, unless the agreement provides otherwise; and

(3) valid for 10 years, unless the agreement provides otherwise.

(c) The existence of an agreement authorized by this section shall be noted conspicuously on the front or back of each certificate for outstanding shares or on the information statement required by section 6.26(b). If at the time of the agreement the corporation has shares outstanding represented by certificates, the corporation shall recall the outstanding certificates and issue substitute certificates that comply with this subsection. The failure to note the existence of the agreement on the certificate or information statement shall not affect the validity of the agreement or any action taken pursuant to it. Any purchaser of shares who, at the time of purchase, did not have knowledge of the existence of the agreement shall be entitled to rescission of the purchase. A purchaser shall be deemed to have knowledge of the existence of the agreement if its existence is noted on the certificate or information statement for the shares in compliance with this subsection and, if the shares are not represented by a certificate, the information statement is delivered to the purchaser at or prior to the time of purchase of the shares. An action to enforce the right of rescission authorized by this subsection must be commenced within the earlier of 90 days after discovery of the existence of the agreement or two years after the time of purchase of the shares.

(d) An agreement authorized by this section shall cease to be effective when shares of the corporation are listed on a national securities exchange or regularly traded in a market maintained by one or more members of a national or affiliated securities association. If the agreement ceases to be effective for any reason, the board of directors may, if the agreement is contained or referred to in the corporation's articles of incorporation or bylaws, adopt an amendment to the articles of incorporation or bylaws, without shareholder action, to delete the agreement and any references to it.

(e) An agreement authorized by this section that limits the discretion or powers of the board of directors shall relieve the directors of, and impose upon the person or persons in whom such discretion or powers are vested, liability for acts or omissions imposed by law on directors to the extent that the discretion or powers of the directors are limited by the agreement.

(f) The existence or performance of an agreement authorized by this section shall not be a ground for imposing personal liability on any shareholder for the acts or debts of the corporation even if the agreement or its performance treats the corporation as if it were a partnership or results in failure to observe the corporate formalities otherwise applicable to the matters governed by the agreement.

(g) Incorporators or subscribers for shares may act as shareholders with respect to an agreement authorized by this section if no shares have been issued when the agreement is made.

## Subchapter D. Derivative Proceedings

### §7.40 Subchapter Definitions

In this subchapter:

(1) "Derivative proceeding" means a civil suit in the right of a domestic corporation or, to the extent provided in section 7.47, in the right of a foreign corporation.

(2) "Shareholder" includes a beneficial owner whose shares are held in a voting trust or held by a nominee on the beneficial owner's behalf.

### §7.41 Standing

A shareholder may not commence or maintain a derivative proceeding unless the shareholder:

(1) was a shareholder of the corporation at the time of the act or omission complained of or became a shareholder through transfer by operation of law from one who was a shareholder at that time; and

(2) fairly and adequately represents the interests of the corporation in enforcing the right of the corporation.

### §7.42 Demand

No shareholder may commence a derivative proceeding until:

(1) a written demand has been made upon the corporation to take suitable action; and

(2) 90 days have expired from the date the demand was made unless the shareholder has earlier been notified that the demand has been rejected by the corporation or unless irreparable injury to the corporation would result by waiting for the expiration of the 90 day period.

### §7.43 Stay of Proceedings

If the corporation commences an inquiry into the allegations made in the demand or complaint, the court may stay any derivative proceeding for such period as the court deems appropriate.

### §7.44 Dismissal

(a) A derivative proceeding shall be dismissed by the court on motion by the corporation if one of the groups specified in subsections (b) or (f) has determined in good faith after conducting a reasonable inquiry upon which its conclusions are based that the maintenance of the derivative proceeding is not in the best interests of the corporation.

(b) Unless a panel is appointed pursuant to subsection (f), the determination in subsection (a) shall be made by:

(1) a majority vote of independent directors present at a meeting of the board of directors if the independent directors constitute a quorum; or

(2) a majority vote of a committee consisting of two or more independent directors appointed by majority vote of independent directors present at a meeting of the board of directors, whether or not such independent directors constituted a quorum.

(c) None of the following shall by itself cause a director to be considered not independent for purposes of this section:

(1) the nomination or election of the director by persons who are defendants in the derivative proceeding or against whom action is demanded;

(2) the naming of the director as a defendant in the derivative proceeding or as a person against whom action is demanded; or

(3) the approval by the director of the act being challenged in the derivative proceeding or demand if the act resulted in no personal benefit to the director.

(d) If a derivative proceeding is commenced after a determination has been made rejecting a demand by a shareholder, the complaint shall allege with particularity facts establishing either (1) that a majority of the board of directors did not consist of independent directors at the time the determination was made or (2) that the requirements of subsection (a) have not been met.

(e) If a majority of the board of directors does not consist of independent directors at the time the determination is made, the corporation shall have the burden of proving that the requirements of subsection (a) have been met. If a majority of the board of directors consists of independent directors at the time the determination is made, the plaintiff shall have the burden of proving that the requirements of subsection (a) have not been met.

(f) The court may appoint a panel of one or more independent persons upon motion by the corporation to make a determination whether the maintenance of the derivative proceeding is in the best interests of the corporation. In such case, the plaintiff shall have the burden of proving that the requirements of subsection (a) have not been met.

### §7.45 Discontinuance or Settlement

A derivative proceeding may not be discontinued or settled without the court's approval. If the court determines that a proposed discontinuance or settlement will substantially affect the interests of the corporation's shareholders or a class of shareholders, the court shall direct that notice be given to the shareholders affected.

### §7.46 Payment of Expenses

On termination of the derivative proceeding the court may:

(1) order the corporation to pay the plaintiff's reasonable expenses (including counsel fees) incurred in the proceeding if it finds that the proceeding has resulted in a substantial benefit to the corporation;

(2) order the plaintiff to pay any defendant's reasonable expenses (including counsel fees) incurred in defending the proceeding if it finds that the proceeding was commenced or maintained without reasonable cause or for an improper purpose; or

(3) order a party to pay an opposing party's reasonable expenses (including counsel fees) incurred because of the filing of a pleading, motion or other paper, if it finds that the pleading, motion or other paper was not well grounded in fact, after reasonable inquiry, or warranted by existing law or a good faith argument for the extension, modification or reversal of existing law and was interposed for an improper purpose, such as to harass or to cause unnecessary delay or needless increase in the cost of litigation.

### §7.47 Applicability to Foreign Corporations

In any derivative proceeding in the right of a foreign corporation, the matters covered by this subchapter shall be governed by the laws of the jurisdiction of incorporation of the foreign corporation except for sections 7.43, 7.45 and 7.46.

## CHAPTER 8. DIRECTORS AND OFFICERS

## Subchapter A. Board of Directors

### §8.01 Requirements for and Duties of Board of Directors

(a) Except as provided is section 7.32, each corporation must have a board of directors.

(b) All corporate powers shall be exercised by or under the authority of, and the business and affairs of the corporation managed under the direction of, its board of directors, subject to any limitation set forth in the articles of incorporation or in an agreement authorized under section 7.32.

### §8.02 Qualifications of Directors

The articles of incorporation or bylaws may prescribe qualifications for directors. A director need not be a resident of this state or a shareholder of the corporation unless the articles of incorporation or bylaws so prescribe.

### §8.03 Number and Election of Directors

(a) A board of directors must consist of one or more individuals, with the number specified in or fixed in accordance with the articles of incorporation or bylaws.

(b) If a board of directors has power to fix or change the number of directors, the board may increase or decrease by 30 percent or less the number of directors last approved by the shareholders, but only the shareholders may increase or decrease by more than 30 percent the number of directors last approved by the shareholders.

(c) The articles of incorporation or bylaws may establish a variable range for the size of the board of directors by fixing a minimum and maximum number of directors. If a variable range is established, the number of directors may be fixed or changed from time to time, within the minimum and maximum, by the shareholders or the board of directors. After shares are issued, only the shareholders may change the range for the size of the board or change from a fixed to a variable-range size board or vice versa.

(d) Directors are elected at the first annual shareholders' meeting and at each annual meeting thereafter unless their terms are staggered under section 8.06.

### §8.04 Election of Directors by Certain Classes of Shareholders

If the articles of incorporation authorize dividing the shares into classes, the articles may also authorize the election of all or a specified number of directors by the holders of one or more authorized classes of shares. Each class (or classes) of shares entitled to elect one or more directors is a separate voting group for purposes of the election of directors.

### §8.05 Terms of Directors Generally

(a) The terms of the initial directors of a corporation expire at the first shareholders' meeting at which directors are elected.

(b) The terms of all other directors expire at the next annual shareholders' meeting following their election unless their terms are staggered under section 8.06.

(c) A decrease in the number of directors does not shorten an incumbent director's term.

(d) The term of a director elected to fill a vacancy expires at the next shareholders' meeting at which directors are elected.

(e) Despite the expiration of a director's term, he continues to serve until his successor is elected and qualifies or until there is a decrease in the number of directors.

### §8.06 Staggered Terms for Directors

If there are nine or more directors, the articles of incorporation may provide for staggering their terms by dividing the total number of directors into two or three groups, with each group containing one-half or one-third of the total, as near as may be. In that event, the terms of directors in the first group expire at the first annual shareholders' meeting after their election, the terms of the second group expire at the second annual shareholders' meeting after their election, and the terms of the third group, if any, expire at the third annual shareholders' meeting after their election. At each annual shareholders' meeting held thereafter, directors shall be chosen for a term of two years or three years, as the case may be, to succeed those whose terms expire.

### §8.07 Resignation of Directors

(a) A director may resign at any time by delivering written notice to the board of directors, its chairman, or to the corporation.

(b) A resignation is effective when the notice is delivered unless the notice specifies a later effective date.

### §8.08 Removal of Directors by Shareholders

(a) The shareholders may remove one or more directors with or without cause unless the articles of incorporation provide that directors may be removed only for cause.

(b) If a director is elected by a voting group of shareholders, only the shareholders of that voting group may participate in the vote to remove him.

(c) If cumulative voting is authorized, a director may not be removed if the number of votes sufficient to elect him under cumulative voting is voted against his removal. If cumulative voting is not authorized, a director may be removed only if the number of votes cast to remove him exceeds the number of votes cast not to remove him.

(d) A director may be removed by the shareholders only at a meeting called for the purpose of removing him and the meeting notice must state that the purpose, or one of the purposes, of the meeting is removal of the director.

### §8.09 Removal of Directors by Judicial Proceeding

(a) The [name or describe] court of the county where a corporation's principal office (or, if none in this state, its registered office) is located may remove a director of the corporation from office in a proceeding commenced either by the corporation or by its shareholders holding at least 10 percent of the outstanding shares of any class if the court finds that (1) the director engaged in fraudulent or dishonest conduct, or gross abuse of authority or discretion, with respect to the corporation and (2) removal is in the best interest of the corporation.

(b) The court that removes a director may bar the director from reelection for a period prescribed by the court.

(c) If shareholders commence a proceeding under subsection (a), they shall make the corporation a party defendant.

### §8.10 Vacancy on Board

(a) Unless the articles of incorporation provide otherwise, if a vacancy occurs on a board of directors, including a vacancy resulting from an increase in the number of directors:

(1) the shareholders may fill the vacancy;
(2) the board of directors may fill the vacancy; or
(3) if the directors remaining in office constitute fewer than a quorum of the board, they may fill the vacancy by the affirmative vote of a majority of all the directors remaining in office.

(b) If the vacant office was held by a director elected by a voting group of shareholders, only the holders of shares of that voting group are entitled to vote to fill the vacancy if it is filled by the shareholders.

(c) A vacancy that will occur at a specific later date (by reason of a resignation effective at a later date under section 8.07(b) or otherwise) may be filled before the vacancy occurs but the new director may not take office until the vacancy occurs.

**§8.11 Compensation of Directors**

Unless the articles of incorporation or bylaws provide otherwise, the board of directors may fix the compensation of directors.

## Subchapter B. Meetings and Action of the Board

**§8.20 Meetings**

(a) The board of directors may hold regular or special meetings in or out of this state.

(b) Unless the articles of incorporation or bylaws provide otherwise, the board of directors may permit any or all directors to participate in a regular or special meeting by, or conduct the meeting through the use of, any means of communication by which all directors participating may simultaneously hear each other during the meeting. A director participating in a meeting by this means is deemed to be present in person at the meeting.

**§8.21 Action Without Meeting**

(a) Unless the articles of incorporation or bylaws provide otherwise, action required or permitted by this Act to be taken at a board of directors' meeting may be taken without a meeting if the action is taken by all members of the board. The action must be evidenced by one or more written consents describing the action taken, signed by each director, and included in the minutes or filed with the corporate records reflecting the action taken.

(b) Action taken under this section is effective when the last director signs the consent, unless the consent specifies a different effective date.

(c) A consent signed under this section has the effect of a meeting vote and may be described as such in any document.

**§8.22 Notice of Meeting**

(a) Unless the articles of incorporation or bylaws provide otherwise, regular meetings of the board of directors may be held without notice of the date, time, place, or purpose of the meeting.

(b) Unless the articles of incorporation or bylaws provide for a longer or shorter period, special meetings of the board of directors must be preceded by at least two days' notice of the date, time, and place of the meeting. The notice need not describe the purpose of the special meeting unless required by the articles of incorporation or bylaws.

**§8.23 Waiver of Notice**

(a) A director may waive any notice required by this Act, the articles of incorporation, or bylaws before or after the date and time stated in the notice. Except as provided by subsection (b), the waiver must be in writing, signed by the director entitled to the notice, and filed with the minutes or corporate records.

(b) A director's attendance at or participation in a meeting waives any required notice to him of the meeting unless the director at the beginning of the meeting (or promptly upon his arrival) objects to holding the meeting or transacting business at the meeting and does not thereafter vote for or assent to action taken at the meeting.

**§8.24 Quorum and Voting**

(a) Unless the articles of incorporation or bylaws require a greater number, a quorum of a board of directors consists of:

(1) a majority of the fixed number of directors if the corporation has a fixed board size; or
(2) a majority of the number of directors prescribed, or if no number is prescribed the number in office immediately before the meeting begins, if the corporation has a variable-range size board.

(b) The articles of incorporation or bylaws may authorize a quorum of a board of directors to consist of no fewer than one-third of the fixed or prescribed number of directors determined under subsection (a).

(c) If a quorum is present when a vote is taken, the affirmative vote of a majority of directors present is the act of the board of directors unless the articles of incorporation or bylaws require the vote of a greater number of directors.

(d) A director who is present at a meeting of the board of directors or a committee of the board of directors when corporate action is taken is deemed to have assented to the action taken unless: (1) he objects at the beginning of the meeting (or promptly upon his arrival) to holding it or transacting business at the meeting; (2) his dissent or abstention from the action taken is entered in the minutes of the meeting; or (3) he delivers written notice of his dissent or abstention to the presiding officer of the meeting before its adjournment or to the corporation immediately after adjournment of the meeting. The right of dissent or abstention is not available to a director who votes in favor of the action taken.

**§8.25 Committees**

(a) Unless the articles of incorporation or bylaws provide otherwise, a board of directors may create one or more committees and appoint members of the board of directors to serve on them. Each committee may have two or more members, who serve at the pleasure of the board of directors.

(b) The creation of a committee and appointment of members to it must be approved by the greater of (1) a majority of all the directors in office when the action is taken or (2) the number of directors required by the articles of incorporation or bylaws to take action under section 8.24.

(c) Sections 8.20 through 8.24, which govern meetings, action without meetings, notice and waiver of notice, and quorum and voting requirements of the board of directors, apply to committees and their members as well.

(d) To the extent specified by the board of directors or in the articles of incorporation or bylaws, each committee may exercise the authority of the board of directors under section 8.01.

(e) A committee may not, however:

(1) authorize distributions;
(2) approve or propose to shareholders action that this Act requires to be approved by shareholders;
(3) fill vacancies on the board of directors or on any of its committees;
(4) amend articles of incorporation pursuant to section 10.02;
(5) adopt, amend, or repeal bylaws;
(6) approve a plan of merger not requiring shareholder approval;
(7) authorize or approve reacquisition of shares, except according to a formula or method prescribed by the board of directors; or
(8) authorize or approve the issuance or sale or contract for sale of shares, or determine the designation and relative rights, preferences, and limitations of a class or series of shares, except that the board of directors may authorize a committee (or a senior executive officer of the corporation) to do so within limits specifically prescribed by the board of directors.

(f) The creation of, delegation of authority to, or action by a committee does not alone constitute compliance by a director with the standards of conduct described in section 8.30.

## Subchapter C. Standards of Conduct

**§8.30 General Standards for Directors**

(a) A director shall discharge his duties as a director, including his duties as a member of a committee:

(1) in good faith;
(2) with the care an ordinarily prudent person in a like position would exercise under similar circumstances; and
(3) in a manner he reasonably believes to be in the best interests of the corporation.

(b) In discharging his duties a director is entitled to rely on information, opinions, reports, or statements, including financial statements and other financial data, if prepared or presented by:
(1) one or more officers or employees of the corporation whom the director reasonably believes to be reliable and competent in the matters presented;
(2) legal counsel, public accountants, or other persons as to matters the director reasonably believes are within the person's professional or expert competence; or
(3) a committee of the board of directors of which he is not a member if the director reasonably believes the committee merits confidence.

(c) A director is not acting in good faith if he has knowledge concerning the matter in question that makes reliance otherwise permitted by subsection (b) unwarranted.

(d) A director is not liable for any action taken as a director, or any failure to take any action, if he performed the duties of his office in compliance with this section.

**§8.31 Director Conflict of Interest***

(a) A conflict of interest transaction is a transaction with the corporation in which a director of the corporation has a direct or indirect interest. A conflict of interest transaction is not voidable by the corporation solely because of the director's interest in the transaction if any one of the following is true:
(1) the material facts of the transaction and the director's interest were disclosed or known to the board of directors or a committee of the board of directors and the board of directors or committee authorized, approved, or ratified the transaction;
(2) the material facts of the transaction and the director's interest were disclosed or known to the shareholders entitled to vote and they authorized, approved, or ratified the transaction; or
(3) the transaction was fair to the corporation.

(b) For purposes of this section, a director of the corporation has an indirect interest in a transaction if (1) another entity in which he has a material financial interest or in which he is a general partner is a party to the transaction or (2) another entity of which he is a director, officer, or trustee is a party to the transaction and the transaction is or should be considered by the board of directors of the corporation.

(c) For purposes of subsection (a)(1), a conflict of interest transaction is authorized, approved, or ratified if it receives the affirmative vote of a majority of the directors on the board of directors (or on the committee) who have no direct or indirect interest in the transaction, but a transaction may not be authorized, approved, or ratified under this section by a single director. If a majority of the directors who have no direct or indirect interest in the transaction vote to authorize, approve, or ratify the transaction, a quorum is present for the purpose of taking action under this section. The presence of, or a vote cast by, a director with a direct or indirect interest in the transaction does not affect the validity of any action taken under subsection (a)(1) if the transaction is otherwise authorized, approved, or ratified as provided in that subsection.

(d) For purposes of subsection (a)(2), a conflict of interest transaction is authorized, approved, or ratified if it receives the vote of a majority of the shares entitled to be counted under this subsection. Shares owned by or voted under the control of a director who has a direct or indirect interest in the transaction, and shares owned by or voted under the control of an entity described in subsection (b)(1), may not be counted in a vote of shareholders to determine whether to authorize, approve, or ratify a conflict of interest transaction under subsection (a)(2). The vote of those shares, however, shall be counted in determining whether the transaction is approved under other sections of this Act. A majority of the shares, whether or not present, that are entitled to be counted in a vote on the transaction under this subsection constitutes a quorum for the purpose of taking action under this section.

*[Editors' Note: In 1989, the Revised Model Business Corporation Act was amended by deleting Sections 8.31 and 8.32 and replacing them with a new Subchapter F, consisting of Sections 8.60–8.63. Because of the relatively short period of time since the adoption of Subchapter F, this volume retains the deleted sections as well as the new material.]

**§8.32 Loans to Directors**

(a) Except as provided by subsection (c), a corporation may not lend money to or guarantee the obligation of a director of the corporation unless:
(1) the particular loan or guarantee is approved by a majority of the votes represented by the outstanding voting shares of all classes, voting as a single voting group, except the votes of shares owned by or voted under the control of the benefited director; or
(2) the corporation's board of directors determines that the loan or guarantee benefits the corporation and either approves the specific loan or guarantee or a general plan authorizing loans and guarantees.

(b) The fact that a loan or guarantee is made in violation of this section does not affect the borrower's liability on the loan.

(c) This section does not apply to loans and guarantees authorized by statute regulating any special class of corporations.

**§8.33 Liability for Unlawful Distributions**

(a) A director who votes for or assents to a distribution made in violation of section 6.40 or the articles of incorporation is personally liable to the corporation for the amount of the distribution that exceeds what could have been distributed without violating section 6.40 or the articles of incorporation if it is established that he did not perform his duties in compliance with section 8.30. In any proceeding commenced under this section, a director has all of the defenses ordinarily available to a director.

(b) A director held liable under subsection (a) for an unlawful distribution is entitled to contribution:
(1) from every other director who could be held liable under subsection (a) for the unlawful distribution; and
(2) from each shareholder for the amount the shareholder accepted knowing the distribution was made in violation of section 6.40 or the articles of incorporation.

(c) A proceeding under this section is barred unless it is commenced within two years after the date on which the effect of the distribution was measured under section 6.40(e) or (g).

## Subchapter D. Officers

**§8.40 Required Officers**

(a) A corporation has the officers described in its bylaws or appointed by the board of directors in accordance with the bylaws.

(b) A duly appointed officer may appoint one or more officers or assistant officers if authorized by the bylaws or the board of directors.

(c) The bylaws or the board of directors shall delegate to one of the officers responsibility for preparing minutes of the directors' and shareholders' meetings and for authenticating records of the corporation.

(d) The same individual may simultaneously hold more than one office in a corporation.

**§8.41 Duties of Officers**

Each officer has the authority and shall perform the duties set forth in the bylaws or, to the extent consistent with the bylaws, the duties prescribed by the board of directors or by direction of an officer authorized by the board of directors to prescribe the duties of other officers.

**§8.42 Standards of Conduct for Officers**

(a) An officer with discretionary authority shall discharge his duties under that authority:

(1) in good faith;

(2) with the care an ordinarily prudent person in a like position would exercise under similar circumstances; and

(3) in a manner he reasonably believes to be in the best interests of the corporation.

(b) In discharging his duties an officer is entitled to rely on information, opinions, reports, or statements, including financial statements and other financial data, if prepared or presented by:

(1) one or more officers or employees of the corporation whom the officer reasonably believes to be reliable and competent in the matters presented; or

(2) legal counsel, public accountants, or other persons as to matters the officer reasonably believes are within the person's professional or expert competence.

(c) An officer is not acting in good faith if he has knowledge concerning the matter in question that makes reliance otherwise permitted by subsection (b) unwarranted.

(d) An officer is not liable for any action taken as an officer, or any failure to take any action, if he performed the duties of his office in compliance with this section.

**§8.43 Resignation and Removal of Officers**

(a) An officer may resign at any time by delivering notice to the corporation. A resignation is effective when the notice is delivered unless the notice specifies a later effective date. If a resignation is made effective at a later date and the corporation accepts the future effective date, its board of directors may fill the pending vacancy before the effective date if the board of directors provides that the successor does not take office until the effective date.

(b) A board of directors may remove any officer at any time with or without cause.

**§8.44 Contract Rights of Officers**

(a) The appointment of an officer does not itself create contract rights.

(b) An officer's removal does not affect the officer's contract rights, if any, with the corporation. An officer's resignation does not affect the corporation's contract rights, if any, with the officer.

## Subchapter E. Indemnification

**§8.50 Subchapter Definitions**

In this subchapter:

(1) "Corporation" includes any domestic or foreign predecessor entity of a corporation in a merger or other transaction in which the predecessor's existence ceased upon consummation of the transaction.

(2) "Director" means an individual who is or was a director of a corporation or an individual who, while a director of a corporation, is or was serving at the corporation's request as a director, officer, partner, trustee, employee, or agent of another foreign or domestic corporation, partnership, joint venture, trust, employee benefit plan, or other enterprise. A director is considered to be serving an employee benefit plan at the corporation's request if his duties to the corporation also impose duties on, or otherwise involve services by, him to the plan or to participants in or beneficiaries of the plan. "Director" includes, unless the context requires otherwise, the estate or personal representative of a director.

(3) "Expenses" include counsel fees.

(4) "Liability" means the obligation to pay a judgment, settlement, penalty, fine (including an excise tax assessed with respect to an employee benefit plan), or reasonable expenses incurred with respect to a proceeding.

(5) "Official capacity" means: (i) when used with respect to a director, the office of director in a corporation; and (ii) when used with respect to an individual other than a director, as contemplated in section 8.56, the office in a corporation held by the officer or the employment or agency relationship undertaken by the employee or agent on behalf of the corporation. "Official capacity" does not include service for any other foreign or domestic corporation or any partnership, joint venture, trust, employee benefit plan, or other enterprise.

(6) "Party" includes an individual who was, is, or is threatened to be made a named defendant or respondent in a proceeding.

(7) "Proceeding" means any threatened, pending, or completed action, suit, or proceeding, whether civil, criminal, administrative, or investigative and whether formal or informal.

**§8.51 Authority to Indemnify**

(a) Except as provided in subsection (d), a corporation may indemnify an individual made a party to a proceeding because he is or was a director against liability incurred in the proceeding if:

(1) he conducted himself in good faith; and

(2) he reasonably believed:

(i) in the case of conduct in his official capacity with the corporation, that his conduct was in its best interests; and

(ii) in all other cases, that his conduct was at least not opposed to its best interests; and

(3) in the case of any criminal proceeding, he had no reasonable cause to believe his conduct was unlawful.

(b) A director's conduct with respect to an employee benefit plan for a purpose he reasonably believed to be in the interests of the participants in and beneficiaries of the plan is conduct that satisfies the requirement of subsection (a)(2)(ii).

(c) The termination of a proceeding by judgment, order, settlement, conviction, or upon a plea of nolo contendere or its equivalent is not, of itself, determinative that the director did not meet the standard of conduct described in this section.

(d) A corporation may not indemnify a director under this section:

(1) in connection with a proceeding by or in the right of the corporation in which the director was adjudged liable to the corporation; or

(2) in connection with any other proceeding charging improper personal benefit to him, whether or not involving action in his official capacity, in which he was adjudged liable on the basis that personal benefit was improperly received by him.

(e) Indemnification permitted under this section in connection with a proceeding by or in the right of the corporation is limited to reasonable expenses incurred in connection with the proceeding.

**§8.52 Mandatory Indemnification**

Unless limited by its articles of incorporation, a corporation shall indemnify a director who was wholly successful, on the merits or otherwise, in the defense of any proceeding to which he was a party because he is or was a director of the corporation against reasonable expenses incurred by him in connection with the proceeding.

**§8.53 Advance for Expenses**

(a) A corporation may pay for or reimburse the reasonable expenses incurred by a director who is a party to a proceeding in advance of final disposition of the proceeding if:

(1) the director furnishes the corporation a written affirmation of his good faith belief that he has met the standard of conduct described in section 8.51;

(2) the director furnishes the corporation a written undertaking, executed personally or on his behalf, to repay the advance if it is ultimately determined that he did not meet the standard of conduct; and

(3) a determination is made that the facts then known to those making the determination would not preclude indemnification under this subchapter.

(b) The undertaking required by subsection (a)(2) must be an unlimited general obligation of the director but need not be secured and may be accepted without reference to financial ability to make repayment.

(c) Determinations and authorizations of payments under this section shall be made in the manner specified in section 8.55.

**§8.54 Court-Ordered Indemnification**

Unless a corporation's articles of incorporation provide otherwise, a director of the corporation who is a party to a proceeding may apply for indemnification to the court conducting the proceeding or to another court of competent jurisdiction. On receipt of an application, the court after giving any notice the court considers necessary may order indemnification if it determines:

(1) the director is entitled to mandatory indemnification under section 8.52, in which case the court shall also order the corporation to pay the director's reasonable expenses incurred to obtain court-ordered indemnification; or

(2) the director is fairly and reasonably entitled to indemnification in view of all the relevant circumstances, whether or not he met the standard of conduct set forth in section 8.51 or was adjudged liable as described in section 8.51(d), but if he was adjudged so liable his indemnification is limited to reasonable expenses incurred.

**§8.55 Determination and Authorization of Indemnification**

(a) A corporation may not indemnify a director under section 8.51 unless authorized in the specific case after a determination has been made that indemnification of the director is permissible in the circumstances because he has met the standard of conduct set forth in section 8.51.

(b) The determination shall be made:

(1) by the board of directors by majority vote of a quorum consisting of directors not at the time parties to the proceeding;

(2) if a quorum cannot be obtained under subdivision (1), by majority vote of a committee duly designated by the board of directors (in which designation directors who are parties may participate), consisting solely of two or more directors not at the time parties to the proceeding;

(3) by special legal counsel:

(i) selected by the board of directors or its committee in the manner prescribed in subdivision (1) or (2); or

(ii) if a quorum of the board of directors cannot be obtained under subdivision (1) and a committee cannot be designated under subdivision (2), selected by majority vote of the full board of directors (in which selection directors who are parties may participate); or

(4) by the shareholders, but shares owned by or voted under the control of directors who are at the time parties to the proceeding may not be voted on the determination.

(c) Authorization of indemnification and evaluation as to reasonableness of expenses shall be made in the same manner as the determination that indemnification is permissible, except that if the determination is made by special legal counsel, authorization of indemnification and evaluation as to reasonableness of expenses shall be made by those entitled under subsection (b)(3) to select counsel.

**§8.56 Indemnification of Officers, Employees, and Agents**

Unless a corporation's articles of incorporation provide otherwise:

(1) an officer of the corporation who is not a director is entitled to mandatory indemnification under section 8.52, and is entitled to apply for court-ordered indemnification under section 8.54, in each case to the same extent as a director;

(2) the corporation may indemnify and advance expenses under this subchapter to an officer, employee, or agent of the corporation who is not a director to the same extent as to a director; and

(3) a corporation may also indemnify and advance expenses to an officer, employee, or agent who is not a director to the extent, consistent with public policy, that may be provided by its articles of incorporation, bylaws, general or specific action of its board of directors, or contract.

**§8.57 Insurance**

A corporation may purchase and maintain insurance on behalf of an individual who is or was a director, officer, employee, or agent of the corporation, or who, while a director, officer, employee, or agent of the corporation, is or was serving at the request of the corporation as a director, officer, partner, trustee, employee, or agent of another foreign or domestic corporation, partnership, joint venture, trust, employee benefit plan, or other enterprise, against liability asserted against or incurred by him in that capacity or arising from his status as a director, officer, employee, or agent, whether or not the corporation would have power to indemnify him against the same liability under section 8.51 or 8.52.

**§8.58 Application of Subchapter**

(a) A provision treating a corporation's indemnification of or advance for expenses to directors that is contained in its articles of incorporation, bylaws, a resolution of its shareholders or board of directors, or in a contract or otherwise, is valid only if and to the extent the provision is consistent with this subchapter. If articles of incorporation limit indemnification or advance for expenses, indemnification and advance for expenses are valid only to the extent consistent with the articles.

(b) This subchapter does not limit a corporation's power to pay or reimburse expenses incurred by a director in connection with his appearance as a witness in a proceeding at a time when he has not been made a named defendant or respondent to the proceeding.

## Subchapter F. Directors' Conflicting Interest Transactions*

**§8.60 Subchapter Definitions**

In this subchapter:

(1) "Conflicting interest" with respect to a corporation means the interest a director of the corporation has respecting a transaction effected or proposed to be effected by the corporation (or by a subsidiary of the corporation or any other entity in which the corporation has a controlling interest) if

(i) whether or not the transaction is brought before the board of directors of the corporation for action, the director knows at the time of commitment that he or a related person is a party to the transaction or has a beneficial financial interest in or so closely linked to the transaction and of such financial significance to the director or a related person that the interest would reasonably be expected to exert an influence on the director's judgment if he were called upon to vote on the transaction; or

(ii) the transaction is brought (or is of such character and significance to the corporation that it would in the normal course be brought) before the board of directors of the corporation for action, and the director knows at the time of commitment that any of the following persons is either a party to the transaction or has a beneficial financial interest in or so closely linked to the transaction and of such financial significance to the person that the interest would reasonably be expected to exert an influence on the director's judgment if he were called upon to vote on the transaction: (A) an entity (other than the corporation) of which the director is a director, general partner, agent, or employee; (B) a person that controls one or more of the entities specified in subclause (A) or an entity that is controlled by, or is under common

*[Editors' Note: In 1989, the Revised Model Business Corporation Act was amended by deleting Sections 8.31 and 8.32 and replacing them with a new Subchapter F, consisting of Sections 8.60–8.63. Because of the relatively short period of time since the adoption of Subchapter F, this volume retains the deleted sections as well as the new material.]

control with, one or more of the entities specified in subclause (A); or (C) an individual who is a general partner, principal, or employer of the director.

(2) "Director's conflicting interest transaction" with respect to a corporation means a transaction effected or proposed to be effected by the corporation (or by a subsidiary of the corporation or any other entity in which the corporation has a controlling interest) respecting which a director of the corporation has a conflicting interest.

(3) "Related person" of a director means (i) the spouse (or a parent or sibling thereof) of the director, or a child, grandchild, sibling, parent (or spouse of any thereof) of the director, or an individual having the same home as the director, or a trust or estate of which an individual specified in this clause (i) is a substantial beneficiary; or (ii) a trust, estate, incompetent, conservatee, or minor of which the director is a fiduciary.

(4) "Required disclosure" means disclosure by the director who has a conflicting interest of (i) the existence and nature of his conflicting interest, and (ii) all facts known to him respecting the subject matter of the transaction that an ordinarily prudent person would reasonably believe to be material to a judgment about whether or not to proceed with the transaction.

(5) "Time of commitment" respecting a transaction means the time when the transaction is consummated or, if made pursuant to contract, the time when the corporation (or its subsidiary or the entity in which it has a controlling interest) becomes contractually obligated so that its unilateral withdrawal from the transaction would entail significant loss, liability, or other damage.

**§8.61 Judicial Action**

(a) A transaction effected or proposed to be effected by a corporation (or by a subsidiary of the corporation or any other entity in which the corporation has a controlling interest) that is not a director's conflicting interest transaction may not be enjoined, set aside, or give rise to an award of damages or other sanctions, in a proceeding by a shareholder or by or in the right of the corporation, because a director of the corporation, or any person with whom or which he has a personal, economic, or other association, has an interest in the transaction.

(b) A director's conflicting interest transaction may not be enjoined, set aside, or give rise to an award of damages or other sanctions, in a proceeding by a shareholder or by or in the right of the corporation, because the director, or any person with whom or which he has a personal, economic, or other association, has an interest in the transaction, if:

(1) directors' action respecting the transaction was at any time taken in compliance with section 8.62;

(2) shareholders' action respecting the transaction was at any time taken in compliance with section 8.63; or

(3) the transaction, judged according to the circumstances at the time of commitment, is established to have been fair to the corporation.

**§8.62 Directors' Action**

(a) Directors' action respecting a transaction is effective for purposes of section 8.61(b)(1) if the transaction received the affirmative vote of a majority (but no fewer than two) of those qualified directors on the board of directors or on a duly empowered committee of the board who voted on the transaction after either required disclosure to them (to the extent the information was not known by them) or compliance with subsection (b); provided that action by a committee is so effective only if:

(1) all its members are qualified directors; and

(2) its members are either all the qualified directors on the board or are appointed by the affirmative vote of a majority of the qualified directors on the board.

(b) If a director has a conflicting interest respecting a transaction, but neither he nor a related person of the director specified in section 8.60(3)(i) is a party to the transaction, and if the director has a duty under law or professional canon, or a duty of confidentiality to another person, respecting information relating to the transaction such that the director may not make the disclosure described in section 8.60(4)(ii), then disclosure is sufficient for purposes of subsection (a) if the director (1) discloses to the directors voting on the transaction the existence and nature of his conflicting interest and informs them of the character and limitations imposed by that duty before their vote on the transaction, and (2) plays no part, directly or indirectly, in their deliberations or vote.

(c) A majority (but no fewer than two) of all the qualified directors on the board of directors, or on the committee, constitutes a quorum for purposes of action that complies with this section. Directors' action that otherwise complies with this section is not affected by the presence or vote of a director who is not a qualified director.

(d) For purposes of this section, "qualified director" means, with respect to a director's conflicting interest transaction, any director who does not have either (1) a conflicting interest respecting the transaction, or (2) a familial, financial, professional, or employment relationship with a second director who does have a conflicting interest respecting the transaction, which relationship would, in the circumstances, reasonably be expected to exert an influence on the first director's judgment when voting on the transaction.

**§8.63 Shareholders' Action**

(a) Shareholders' action respecting a transaction is effective for purposes of section 8.61(b)(2) if a majority of the votes entitled to be cast by the holders of all qualified shares were cast in favor of the transaction after (1) notice to shareholders describing the director's conflicting interest transaction, (2) provision of the information referred to in subsection (d), and (3) required disclosure to the shareholders who voted on the transaction (to the extent the information was not known by them).

(b) For purposes of this section, "qualified shares" means any shares entitled to vote with respect to the director's conflicting interest transaction except shares that, to the knowledge, before the vote, of the secretary (or other officer or agent of the corporation authorized to tabulate votes), are beneficially owned (or the voting of which is controlled) by a director who has a conflicting interest respecting the transaction or by a related person of the director, or both.

(c) A majority of the votes entitled to be cast by the holders of all qualified shares constitutes a quorum for purposes of action that complies with this section. Subject to the provisions of subsections (d) and (e), shareholders' action that otherwise complies with this section is not affected by the presence of holders, or the voting, of shares that are not qualified shares.

(d) For purposes of compliance with subsection (a), a director who has a conflicting interest respecting the transaction shall, before the shareholders' vote, inform the secretary (or other office or agent of the corporation authorized to tabulate votes) of the number, and the identity of persons holding or controlling the vote, of all shares that the director knows are beneficially owned (or the voting of which is controlled) by the director or by a related person of the director, or both.

(e) If a shareholders' vote does not comply with subsection (a) solely because of a failure of a director to comply with subsection (d), and if the director establishes that his failure did not determine and was not intended by him to influence the outcome of the vote, the court may, with or without further proceedings respecting section 8.61(b)(3), take such action respecting the transaction and the director, and give such effect, if any, to the shareholders' vote, as it considers appropriate in the circumstances.

## CHAPTER 9. [RESERVED]

## CHAPTER 10. AMENDMENT OF ARTICLES OF INCORPORATION AND BYLAWS

### Subchapter A. Amendment of Articles of Incorporation

**§10.01 Authority to Amend**

(a) A corporation may amend its articles of incorporation at any time to add or change a provision that is required or permitted in the articles of incorporation or to delete a provision not required in the articles of

incorporation. Whether a provision is required or permitted in the articles of incorporation is determined as of the effective date of the amendment.
(b) A shareholder of the corporation does not have a vested property right resulting from any provision in the articles of incorporation, including provisions relating to management, control, capital structure, dividend entitlement, or purpose or duration of the corporation.

**§10.02 Amendment by Board of Directors**
Unless the articles of incorporation provide otherwise, a corporation's board of directors may adopt one or more amendments to the corporation's articles of incorporation without shareholder action:
(1) to extend the duration of the corporation if it was incorporated at a time when limited duration was required by law;
(2) to delete the names and addresses of the initial directors;
(3) to delete the name and address of the initial registered agent or registered office, if a statement of change is on file with the secretary of state;
(4) to change each issued and unissued authorized share of an outstanding class into a greater number of whole shares if the corporation has only shares of that class outstanding;
(5) to change the corporate name by substituting the word "corporation," "incorporated," "company," "limited," or the abbreviation "corp.," "inc.," "co.," or "ltd.," for a similar word or abbreviation in the name, or by adding, deleting, or changing a geographical attribution for the name; or
(6) to make any other change expressly permitted by this Act to be made without shareholder action.

**§10.03 Amendment by Board of Directors and Shareholders**
(a) A corporation's board of directors may propose one or more amendments to the articles of incorporation for submission to the shareholders.
(b) For the amendment to be adopted:
(1) the board of directors must recommend the amendment to the shareholders unless the board of directors determines that because of conflict of interest or other special circumstances it should make no recommendation and communicates the basis for its determination to the shareholders with the amendment; and
(2) the shareholders entitled to vote on the amendment must approve the amendment as provided in subsection (e).
(c) The board of directors may condition its submission of the proposed amendment on any basis.
(d) The corporation shall notify each shareholder, whether or not entitled to vote, of the proposed shareholders' meeting in accordance with section 7.05. The notice of meeting must also state that the purpose, or one of the purposes, of the meeting is to consider the proposed amendment and contain or be accompanied by a copy or summary of the amendment.
(e) Unless this Act, the articles of incorporation, or the board of directors (acting pursuant to subsection (c)) require a greater vote or a vote by voting groups, the amendment to be adopted must be approved by:
(1) a majority of the votes entitled to be cast on the amendment by any voting group with respect to which the amendment would create dissenters' rights; and
(2) the votes required by sections 7.25 and 7.26 by every other voting group entitled to vote on the amendment.

**§10.04 Voting on Amendments by Voting Groups**
(a) The holders of the outstanding shares of a class are entitled to vote as a separate voting group (if shareholder voting is otherwise required by this Act) on a proposed amendment if the amendment would:
(1) increase or decrease the aggregate number of authorized shares of the class;
(2) effect an exchange or reclassification of all or part of the shares of the class into shares of another class;
(3) effect an exchange or reclassification, or create the right of exchange, of all or part of the shares of another class into shares of the class;
(4) change the designation, rights, preferences, or limitations of all or part of the shares of the class;
(5) change the shares of all or part of the class into a different number of shares of the same class;
(6) create a new class of shares having rights or preferences with respect to distributions or to dissolution that are prior, superior, or substantially equal to the shares of the class;
(7) increase the rights, preferences, or number of authorized shares of any class that, after giving effect to the amendment, have rights or preferences with respect to distributions or to dissolution that are prior, superior, or substantially equal to the shares of the class;
(8) limit or deny an existing preemptive right of all or part of the shares of the class; or
(9) cancel or otherwise affect rights to distributions or dividends that have accumulated but not yet been declared on all or part of the shares of the class.
(b) If a proposed amendment would affect a series of a class of shares in one or more of the ways described in subsection (a), the shares of that series are entitled to vote as a separate voting group on the proposed amendment.
(c) If a proposed amendment that entitles two or more series of shares to vote as separate voting groups under this section would affect those two or more series in the same or a substantially similar way, the shares of all the series so affected must vote together as a single voting group on the proposed amendment.
(d) A class or series of shares is entitled to the voting rights granted by this section although the articles of incorporation provide that the shares are nonvoting shares.

**§10.05 Amendment Before Issuance of Shares**
If a corporation has not yet issued shares, its incorporators or board of directors may adopt one or more amendments to the corporation's articles of incorporation.

**§10.06 Articles of Amendment**
A corporation amending its articles of incorporation shall deliver to the secretary of state for filing articles of amendment setting forth:
(1) the name of the corporation;
(2) the text of each amendment adopted;
(3) if an amendment provides for an exchange, reclassification, or cancellation of issued shares, provisions for implementing the amendment if not contained in the amendment itself;
(4) the date of each amendment's adoption;
(5) if an amendment was adopted by the incorporators or board of directors without shareholder action, a statement to that effect and that shareholder action was not required;
(6) if an amendment was approved by the share holders:
(i) the designation, number of outstanding shares, number of votes entitled to be cast by each voting group entitled to vote separately on the amendment, and number of votes of each voting group indisputably represented at the meeting;
(ii) either the total number of votes cast for and against the amendment by each voting group entitled to vote separately on the amendment or the total number of undisputed votes cast for the amendment by each voting group and a statement that the number cast for the amendment by each voting group was sufficient for approval by that voting group.

**§10.07 Restated Articles of Incorporation**
(a) A corporation's board of directors may restate its articles of incorporation at any time with or without shareholder action.
(b) The restatement may include one or more amendments to the articles. If the restatement includes an amendment requiring shareholder approval, it must be adopted as provided in section 10.03.
(c) If the board of directors submits a restatement for shareholder action, the corporation shall notify each shareholder, whether or not entitled to vote, of

the proposed shareholders' meeting in accordance with section 7.05. The notice must also state that the purpose, or one of the purposes, of the meeting is to consider the proposed restatement and contain or be accompanied by a copy of the restatement that identifies any amendment or other change it would make in the articles.

(d) A corporation restating its articles of incorporation shall deliver to the secretary of state for filing articles of restatement setting forth the name of the corporation and the text of the restated articles of incorporation together with a certificate setting forth:

(1) whether the restatement contains an amendment to the articles requiring shareholder approval and, if it does not, that the board of directors adopted the restatement; or

(2) if the restatement contains an amendment to the articles requiring shareholder approval, the information required by section 10.06.

(e) Duly adopted restated articles of incorporation supersede the original articles of incorporation and all amendments to them.

(f) The secretary of state may certify restated articles of incorporation, as the articles of incorporation currently in effect, without including the certificate information required by subsection (d).

**§10.08 Amendment Pursuant to Reorganization**

(a) A corporation's articles of incorporation may be amended without action by the board of directors or shareholders to carry out a plan of reorganization ordered or decreed by a court of competent jurisdiction under federal statute if the articles of incorporation after amendment contain only provisions required or permitted by section 2.02.

(b) The individual or individuals designated by the court shall deliver to the secretary of state for filing articles of amendment setting forth:

(1) the name of the corporation;

(2) the text of each amendment approved by the court;

(3) the date of the court's order or decree approving the articles of amendment;

(4) the title of the reorganization proceeding in which the order or decree was entered; and

(5) a statement that the court had jurisdiction of the proceeding under federal statute.

(c) Shareholders of a corporation undergoing reorganization do not have dissenters' rights except as and to the extent provided in the reorganization plan.

(d) This section does not apply after entry of a final decree in the reorganization proceeding even though the court retains jurisdiction of the proceeding for limited purposes unrelated to consummation of the reorganization plan.

**§10.09 Effect of Amendment**

An amendment to articles of incorporation does not affect a cause of action existing against or in favor of the corporation, a proceeding to which the corporation is a party, or the existing rights of persons other than shareholders of the corporation. An amendment changing a corporation's name does not abate a proceeding brought by or against the corporation in its former name.

## Subchapter B. Amendment of Bylaws

**§10.20 Amendment by Board of Directors or Shareholders**

(a) A corporation's board of directors may amend or repeal the corporation's bylaws unless:

(1) the articles of incorporation or this Act reserve this power exclusively to the shareholders in whole or part; or

(2) the shareholders in amending or repealing a particular bylaw provide expressly that the board of directors may not amend or repeal that bylaw.

(b) A corporation's shareholders may amend or repeal the corporation's bylaws even though the bylaws may also be amended or repealed by its board of directors.

**§10.21 Bylaw Increasing Quorum or Voting Requirement for Shareholders**

(a) If expressly authorized by the articles of incorporation, the shareholders may adopt or amend a bylaw that fixes a greater quorum or voting requirement for shareholders (or voting groups of shareholders) than is required by this Act. The adoption or amendment of a bylaw that adds, changes, or deletes a greater quorum or voting requirement for shareholders must meet the same quorum requirement and be adopted by the same vote and voting groups required to take action under the quorum and voting requirement then in effect or proposed to be adopted, whichever is greater.

(b) A bylaw that fixes a greater quorum or voting requirement for shareholders under subsection (a) may not be adopted, amended, or repealed by the board of directors.

**§10.22 Bylaw Increasing Quorum or Voting Requirement for Directors**

(a) A bylaw that fixes a greater quorum or voting requirement for the board of directors may be amended or repealed:

(1) if originally adopted by the shareholders, only by the shareholders;

(2) if originally adopted by the board of directors, either by the shareholders or by the board of directors.

(b) A bylaw adopted or amended by the shareholders that fixes a greater quorum or voting requirement for the board of directors may provide that it may be amended or repealed only by a specified vote of either the shareholders or the board of directors.

(c) Action by the board of directors under subsection (a)(2) to adopt or amend a bylaw that changes the quorum or voting requirement for the board of directors must meet the same quorum requirement and be adopted by the same vote required to take action under the quorum and voting requirement then in effect or proposed to be adopted, whichever is greater.

## CHAPTER 11. MERGER AND SHARE EXCHANGE

**§11.01 Merger**

(a) One or more corporations may merge into another corporation if the board of directors of each corporation adopts and its shareholders (if required by section 11.03) approve a plan of merger.

(b) The plan of merger must set forth:

(1) the name of each corporation planning to merge and the name of the surviving corporation into which each other corporation plans to merge;

(2) the terms and conditions of the merger; and

(3) the manner and basis of converting the shares of each corporation into shares, obligations, or other securities of the surviving or any other corporation or into cash or other property in whole or part.

(c) The plan of merger may set forth:

(1) amendments to the articles of incorporation of the surviving corporation; and

(2) other provisions relating to the merger.

**§11.02 Share Exchange**

(a) A corporation may acquire all of the outstanding shares of one or more classes or series of another corporation if the board of directors of each corporation adopts and its shareholders (if required by section 11.03) approve the exchange.

(b) The plan of exchange must set forth:

(1) the name of the corporation whose shares will be acquired and the name of the acquiring corporation;

(2) the terms and conditions of the exchange;

(3) the manner and basis of exchanging the shares to be acquired for shares, obligations, or other securities of the acquiring or any other corporation or for cash or other property in whole or part.

(c) The plan of exchange may set forth other provisions relating to the exchange.

(d) This section does not limit the power of a corporation to acquire all or part of the shares of one or more classes or series of another corporation through a voluntary exchange or otherwise.

**§11.03 Action on Plan**

(a) After adopting a plan of merger or share exchange, the board of directors of each corporation party to the merger, and the board of directors of the corporation whose shares will be acquired in the share exchange, shall submit the plan of merger (except as provided in subsection (g)) or share exchange for approval by its shareholders.

(b) For a plan of merger or share exchange to be approved:

(1) the board of directors must recommend the plan of merger or share exchange to the shareholders, unless the board of directors determines that because of conflict of interest or other special circumstances it should make no recommendation and communicates the basis for its determination to the shareholders with the plan; and

(2) the shareholders entitled to vote must approve the plan.

(c) The board of directors may condition its submission of the proposed merger or share exchange on any basis.

(d) The corporation shall notify each shareholder, whether or not entitled to vote, of the proposed shareholders' meeting in accordance with section 7.05. The notice must also state that the purpose, or one of the purposes, of the meeting is to consider the plan of merger or share exchange and contain or be accompanied by a copy or summary of the plan.

(e) Unless this Act, the articles of incorporation, or the board of directors (acting pursuant to subsection (c)) require a greater vote or a vote by voting groups, the plan of merger or share exchange to be authorized must be approved by each voting group entitled to vote separately on the plan by a majority of all the votes entitled to be cast on the plan by that voting group.

(f) Separate voting by voting groups is required:

(1) on a plan of merger if the plan contains a provision that, if contained in a proposed amendment to articles of incorporation, would require action by one or more separate voting groups on the proposed amendment under section 10.04;

(2) on a plan of share exchange by each class or series of shares included in the exchange, with each class or series constituting a separate voting group.

(g) Action by the shareholders of the surviving corporation on a plan of merger is not required if:

(1) the articles of incorporation of the surviving corporation will not differ (except for amendments enumerated in section 10.02) from its articles before the merger;

(2) each shareholder of the surviving corporation whose shares were outstanding immediately before the effective date of the merger will hold the same number of shares, with identical designations, preferences, limitations, and relative rights, immediately after;

(3) the number of voting shares outstanding immediately after the merger, plus the number of voting shares issuable as a result of the merger (either by the conversion of securities issued pursuant to the merger or the exercise of rights and warrants issued pursuant to the merger), will not exceed by more than 20 percent the total number of voting shares of the surviving corporation outstanding immediately before the merger; and

(4) the number of participating shares outstanding immediately after the merger, plus the number of participating shares issuable as a result of the merger (either by the conversion of securities issued pursuant to the merger or the exercise of rights and warrants issued pursuant to the merger), will not exceed by more than 20 percent the total number of participating shares outstanding immediately before the merger.

(h) As used in subsection (g):

(1) "Participating shares" means shares that entitle their holders to participate without limitation in distributions.

(2) "Voting shares" means shares that entitle their holders to vote unconditionally in elections of directors.

(i) After a merger or share exchange is authorized, and at any time before articles of merger or share exchange are filed, the planned merger or share exchange may be abandoned (subject to any contractual rights), without further shareholder action, in accordance with the procedure set forth in the plan of merger or share exchange or, if none is set forth, in the manner determined by the board of directors.

**§11.04 Merger of Subsidiary**

(a) A parent corporation owning at least 90 percent of the outstanding shares of each class of a subsidiary corporation may merge the subsidiary into itself without approval of the shareholders of the parent or subsidiary.

(b) The board of directors of the parent shall adopt a plan of merger that sets forth:

(1) the names of the parent and subsidiary; and

(2) the manner and basis of converting the shares of the subsidiary into shares, obligations, or other securities of the parent or any other corporation or into cash or other property in whole or part.

(c) The parent shall mail a copy or summary of the plan of merger to each shareholder of the subsidiary who does not waive the mailing requirement in writing.

(d) The parent may not deliver articles of merger to the secretary of state for filing until at least 30 days after the date it mailed a copy of the plan of merger to each shareholder of the subsidiary who did not waive the mailing requirement.

(e) Articles of merger under this section may not contain amendments to the articles of incorporation of the parent corporation (except for amendments enumerated in section 10.02).

**§11.05 Articles of Merger or Share Exchange**

(a) After a plan of merger or share exchange is approved by the shareholders, or adopted by the board of directors if shareholder approval is not required, the surviving or acquiring corporation shall deliver to the secretary of state for filing articles of merger or share exchange setting forth:

(1) the plan of merger or share exchange;

(2) if shareholder approval was not required, a statement to that effect;

(3) if approval of the shareholders of one or more corporations party to the merger or share exchange was required:

(i) the designation, number of outstanding shares, and number of votes entitled to be cast by each voting group entitled to vote separately on the plan as to each corporation; and

(ii) either the total number of votes cast for and against the plan by each voting group entitled to vote separately on the plan or the total number of undisputed votes cast for the plan separately by each voting group and a statement that the number cast for the plan by each voting group was sufficient for approval by that voting group.

(b) Unless a delayed effective date is specified, a merger or share exchange takes effect when the articles of merger or share exchange are filed.

**§11.06 Effect of Merger or Share Exchange**

(a) When a merger takes effect:

(1) every other corporation party to the merger merges into the surviving corporation and the separate existence of every corporation except the surviving corporation ceases;

(2) the title to all real estate and other property owned by each corporation party to the merger is vested in the surviving corporation without reversion or impairment;

(3) the surviving corporation has all liabilities of each corporation party to the merger;

(4) a proceeding pending against any corporation party to the merger may be continued as if the merger did not occur or the surviving corporation may be substituted in the proceeding for the corporation whose existence ceased;

(5) the articles of incorporation of the surviving corporation are amended to the extent provided in the plan of merger; and

(6) the shares of each corporation party to the merger that are to be converted into shares, obligations, or other securities of the surviving or any other corporation or into cash or other property are converted and the former holders of the shares are entitled only to the rights provided in the articles of merger or to their rights under chapter 13.

(b) When a share exchange takes effect, the shares of each acquired corporation are exchanged as provided in the plan, and the former holders of the shares are entitled only to the exchange rights provided in the articles of share exchange or to their rights under chapter 13.

### §11.07 Merger or Share Exchange With Foreign Corporation

(a) One or more foreign corporations may merge or enter into a share exchange with one or more domestic corporations if:

(1) in a merger, the merger is permitted by the law of the state or country under whose law each foreign corporation is incorporated and each foreign corporation complies with that law in effecting the merger;

(2) in a share exchange, the corporation whose shares will be acquired is a domestic corporation, whether or not a share exchange is permitted by the law of the state or country under whose law the acquiring corporation is incorporated;

(3) the foreign corporation complies with section 11.05 if it is the surviving corporation of the merger or acquiring corporation of the share exchange; and

(4) each domestic corporation complies with the applicable provisions of sections 11.01 through 11.04 and, if it is the surviving corporation of the merger or acquiring corporation of the share exchange, with section 11.05.

(b) Upon the merger or share exchange taking effect, the surviving foreign corporation of a merger and the acquiring foreign corporation of a share exchange is deemed:

(1) to appoint the secretary of state as its agent for service of process in a proceeding to enforce any obligation or the rights of dissenting shareholders of each domestic corporation party to the merger or share exchange; and

(2) to agree that it will promptly pay to the dissenting shareholders of each domestic corporation party to the merger or share exchange the amount, if any, to which they are entitled under chapter 13.

(c) This section does not limit the power of a foreign corporation to acquire all or part of the shares of one or more classes or series of a domestic corporation through a voluntary exchange or otherwise.

## CHAPTER 12. SALE OF ASSETS

### §12.01 Sale of Assets in Regular Course of Business and Mortgage of Assets

(a) A corporation may, on the terms and conditions and for the consideration determined by the board of directors:

(1) sell, lease, exchange, or otherwise dispose of all, or substantially all, of its property in the usual and regular course of business,

(2) mortgage, pledge, dedicate to the repayment of indebtedness (whether with or without recourse), or otherwise encumber any or all of its property whether or not in the usual and regular course of business, or

(3) transfer any or all of its property to a corporation all the shares of which are owned by the corporation.

(b) Unless the articles of incorporation require it, approval by the shareholders of a transaction described in subsection (a) is not required.

### §12.02 Sale of Assets Other Than in Regular Course of Business

(a) A corporation may sell, lease, exchange, or otherwise dispose of all, or substantially all, of its property (with or without the good will), otherwise than in the usual and regular course of business, on the terms and conditions and for the consideration determined by the corporation's board of directors, if the board of directors proposes and its shareholders approve the proposed transaction.

(b) For a transaction to be authorized:

(1) the board of directors must recommend the proposed transaction to the shareholders unless the board of directors determines that because of conflict of interest or other special circumstances it should make no recommendation and communicates the basis for its determination to the shareholders with the submission of the proposed transaction; and

(2) the shareholders entitled to vote must approve the transaction.

(c) The board of directors may condition its submission of the proposed transaction on any basis.

(d) The corporation shall notify each shareholder, whether or not entitled to vote, of the proposed shareholders' meeting in accordance with section 7.05. The notice must also state that the purpose, or one of the purposes, of the meeting is to consider the sale, lease, exchange, or other disposition of all, or substantially all, the property of the corporation and contain or be accompanied by a description of the transaction.

(e) Unless the articles of incorporation or the board of directors (acting pursuant to subsection (c)) require a greater vote or a vote by voting groups, the transaction to be authorized must be approved by a majority of all the votes entitled to be cast on the transaction.

(f) After a sale, lease, exchange, or other disposition of property is authorized, the transaction may be abandoned (subject to any contractual rights) without further shareholder action.

(g) A transaction that constitutes a distribution is governed by section 6.40 and not by this section.

## CHAPTER 13. DISSENTERS' RIGHTS

### Subchapter A. Right to Dissent and Obtain Payment for Shares

### §13.01 Definitions

In this chapter:

(1) "Corporation" means the issuer of the shares held by a dissenter before the corporate action, or the surviving or acquiring corporation by merger or share exchange of that issuer.

(2) "Dissenter" means a shareholder who is entitled to dissent from corporate action under section 13.02 and who exercises that right when and in the manner required by sections 13.20 through 13.28.

(3) "Fair value," with respect to a dissenter's shares, means the value of the shares immediately before the effectuation of the corporate action to which the dissenter objects, excluding any appreciation or depreciation in anticipation of the corporate action unless exclusion would be inequitable.

(4) "Interest" means interest from the effective date of the corporate action until the date of payment, at the average rate currently paid by the corporation on its principal bank loans or, if none, at a rate that is fair and equitable under all the circumstances.

(5) "Record shareholder" means the person in whose name shares are registered in the records of a corporation or the beneficial owner of shares to the extent of the rights granted by a nominee certificate on file with a corporation.

(6) "Beneficial shareholder" means the person who is a beneficial owner of shares held in a voting trust or by a nominee as the record shareholder.

(7) "Shareholder" means the record shareholder or the beneficial shareholder.

### §13.02 Right to Dissent

(a) A shareholder is entitled to dissent from, and obtain payment of the fair value of his shares in the event of, any of the following corporate actions:

(1) consummation of a plan of merger to which the corporation is a party (i) if shareholder approval is required for the merger by section 11.03 or the articles of incorporation and the shareholder is entitled to vote on the merger or (ii) if the corporation is a subsidiary that is merged with its parent under section 11.04;
(2) consummation of a plan of share exchange to which the corporation is a party as the corporation whose shares will be acquired, if the shareholder is entitled to vote on the plan;
(3) consummation of a sale or exchange of all, or substantially all, of the property of the corporation other than in the usual and regular course of business, if the shareholder is entitled to vote on the sale or exchange, including a sale in dissolution, but not including a sale pursuant to court order or a sale for cash pursuant to a plan by which all or substantially all of the net proceeds of the sale will be distributed to the shareholders within one year after the date of sale;
(4) an amendment of the articles of incorporation that materially and adversely affects rights in respect of a dissenter's shares because it:
(i) alters or abolishes a preferential right of the shares;
(ii) creates, alters, or abolishes a right in respect of redemption, including a provision respecting a sinking fund for the redemption or repurchase, of the shares;
(iii) alters or abolishes a preemptive right of the holder of the shares to acquire shares or other securities;
(iv) excludes or limits the right of the shares to vote on any matter, or to cumulate votes, other than a limitation by dilution through issuance of shares or other securities with similar voting rights; or
(v) reduces the number of shares owned by the shareholder to a fraction of a share if the fractional share so created is to be acquired for cash under section 6.04; or
(5) any corporate action taken pursuant to a shareholder vote to the extent the articles of incorporation, bylaws, or a resolution of the board of directors provides that voting or nonvoting shareholders are entitled to dissent and obtain payment for their shares.
(b) A shareholder entitled to dissent and obtain payment for his shares under this chapter may not challenge the corporate action creating his entitlement unless the action is unlawful or fraudulent with respect to the shareholder or the corporation.

**§13.03 Dissent by Nominees and Beneficial Owners**
(a) A record shareholder may assert dissenters' rights as to fewer than all the shares registered in his name only if he dissents with respect to all shares beneficially owned by any one person and notifies the corporation in writing of the name and address of each person on whose behalf he asserts dissenters' rights. The rights of a partial dissenter under this subsection are determined as if the shares as to which he dissents and his other shares were registered in the names of different shareholders.
(b) A beneficial shareholder may assert dissenters' rights as to shares held on his behalf only if:
(1) he submits to the corporation the record shareholder's written consent to the dissent not later than the time the beneficial shareholder asserts dissenters' rights; and
(2) he does so with respect to all shares of which he is the beneficial shareholder or over which he has power to direct the vote.

## Subchapter B. Procedure for Exercise of Dissenters' Rights

**§13.20 Notice of Dissenters' Rights**
(a) If proposed corporate action creating dissenters' rights under section 13.02 is submitted to a vote at a shareholders' meeting, the meeting notice must state that shareholders are or may be entitled to assert dissenters' rights under this chapter and be accompanied by a copy of this chapter.
(b) If corporate action creating dissenters' rights under section 13.02 is taken without a vote of shareholders, the corporation shall notify in writing all shareholders entitled to assert dissenters' rights that the action was taken and send them the dissenters' notice described in section 13.22.

**§13.21 Notice of Intent to Demand Payment**
(a) If proposed corporate action creating dissenters' rights under section 13.02 is submitted to a vote at a shareholders' meeting, a shareholder who wishes to assert dissenters' rights (1) must deliver to the corporation before the vote is taken written notice of his intent to demand payment for his shares if the proposed action is effectuated and (2) must not vote his shares in favor of the proposed action.
(b) A shareholder who does not satisfy the requirements of subsection (a) is not entitled to payment for his shares under this chapter.

**§13.22 Dissenters' Notice**
(a) If proposed corporate action creating dissenters' rights under section 13.02 is authorized at a shareholders' meeting, the corporation shall deliver a written dissenters' notice to all shareholders who satisfied the requirements of section 13.21.
(b) The dissenters' notice must be sent no later than 10 days after the corporate action was taken, and must:
(1) state where the payment demand must be sent and where and when certificates for certificated shares must be deposited;
(2) inform holders of uncertificated shares to what extent transfer of the shares will be restricted after the payment demand is received;
(3) supply a form for demanding payment that includes the date of the first announcement to news media or to shareholders of the terms of the proposed corporate action and requires that the person asserting dissenters' rights certify whether or not he acquired beneficial ownership of the shares before that date;
(4) set a date by which the corporation must receive the payment demand, which date may not be fewer than 30 nor more than 60 days after the date the subsection (a) notice is delivered; and
(5) be accompanied by a copy of this chapter.

**§13.23 Duty to Demand Payment**
(a) A shareholder sent a dissenters' notice described in section 13.22 must demand payment, certify whether he acquired beneficial ownership of the shares before the date required to be set forth in the dissenter's notice pursuant to section 13.22(b)(3), and deposit his certificates in accordance with the terms of the notice.
(b) The shareholder who demands payment and deposits his shares under section (a) retains all other rights of a shareholder until these rights are cancelled or modified by the taking of the proposed corporate action.
(c) A shareholder who does not demand payment or deposit his share certificates where required, each by the date set in the dissenters' notice, is not entitled to payment for his shares under this chapter.

**§13.24 Share Restrictions**
(a) The corporation may restrict the transfer of uncertificated shares from the date the demand for their payment is received until the proposed corporate action is taken or the restrictions released under section 13.26.
(b) The person for whom dissenters' rights are asserted as to uncertificated shares retains all other rights of a shareholder until these rights are cancelled or modified by the taking of the proposed corporate action.

**§13.25 Payment**
(a) Except as provided in section 13.27, as soon as the proposed corporate action is taken, or upon receipt of a payment demand, the corporation shall pay each dissenter who complied with section 13.23 the amount the corporation estimates to be the fair value of his shares, plus accrued interest.
(b) The payment must be accompanied by:
(1) the corporation's balance sheet as of the end of a fiscal year ending not more than 16 months before the date of payment, an income statement for that year, a statement of changes in shareholders' equity for that year, and the latest available interim financial statements, if any;
(2) a statement of the corporation's estimate of the fair value of the shares;

(3) an explanation of how the interest was calculated;
(4) a statement of the dissenter's right to demand payment under section 13.28; and
(5) a copy of this chapter.

**§13.26 Failure to Take Action**

(a) If the corporation does not take the proposed action within 60 days after the date set for demanding payment and depositing share certificates, the corporation shall return the deposited certificates and release the transfer restrictions imposed on uncertificated shares.

(b) If after returning deposited certificates and releasing transfer restrictions, the corporation takes the proposed action, it must send a new dissenters' notice under section 13.22 and repeat the payment demand procedure.

**§13.27 After-Acquired Shares**

(a) A corporation may elect to withhold payment required by section 13.25 from a dissenter unless he was the beneficial owner of the shares before the date set forth in the dissenters' notice as the date of the first announcement to news media or to shareholders of the terms of the proposed corporate action.

(b) To the extent the corporation elects to withhold payment under subsection (a), after taking the proposed corporate action, it shall estimate the fair value of the shares, plus accrued interest, and shall pay this amount to each dissenter who agrees to accept it in full satisfaction of his demand. The corporation shall send with its offer a statement of its estimate of the fair value of the shares, an explanation of how the interest was calculated, and a statement of the dissenter's right to demand payment under section 13.28.

**§13.28 Procedure if Shareholder Dissatisfied With Payment or Offer**

(a) A dissenter may notify the corporation in writing of his own estimate of the fair value of his shares and amount of interest due, and demand payment of his estimate (less any payment under section 13.25), or reject the corporation's offer under section 13.27 and demand payment of the fair value of his shares and interest due, if:

(1) the dissenter believes that the amount paid under section 13.25 or offered under section 13.27 is less than the fair value of his shares or that the interest due is incorrectly calculated;
(2) the corporation fails to make payment under section 13.25 within 60 days after the date set for demanding payment; or
(3) the corporation, having failed to take the proposed action, does not return the deposited certificates or release the transfer restrictions imposed on uncertificated shares within 60 days after the date set for demanding payment.

(b) A dissenter waives his right to demand payment under this section unless he notifies the corporation of his demand in writing under subsection (a) within 30 days after the corporation made or offered payment for his shares.

## Subchapter C. Judicial Appraisal of Shares

**§13.30 Court Action**

(a) If a demand for payment under section 13.28 remains unsettled, the corporation shall commence a proceeding within 60 days after receiving the payment demand and petition the court to determine the fair value of the shares and accrued interest. If the corporation does not commence the proceeding within the 60-day period, it shall pay each dissenter whose demand remains unsettled the amount demanded.

(b) The corporation shall commence the proceeding in the [name or describe] court of the county where a corporation's principal office (or, if none in this state, its registered office) is located. If the corporation is a foreign corporation without a registered office in this state, it shall commence the proceeding in the county in this state where the registered office of the domestic corporation merged with or whose shares were acquired by the foreign corporation was located.

(c) The corporation shall make all dissenters (whether or not residents of this state) whose demands remain unsettled parties to the proceeding as in an action against their shares and all parties must be served with a copy of the petition. Nonresidents may be served by registered or certified mail or by publication as provided by law.

(d) The jurisdiction of the court in which the proceeding is commenced under subsection (b) is plenary and exclusive. The court may appoint one or more persons as appraisers to receive evidence and recommend decision on the question of fair value. The appraisers have the powers described in the order appointing them, or in any amendment to it. The dissenters are entitled to the same discovery rights as parties in other civil proceedings.

(e) Each dissenter made a party to the proceeding is entitled to judgment (1) for the amount, if any, by which the court finds the fair value of his shares, plus interest, exceeds the amount paid by the corporation or (2) for the fair value, plus accrued interest, of his after-acquired shares for which the corporation elected to withhold payment under section 13.27.

**§13.31 Court Costs and Counsel Fees**

(a) The court in an appraisal proceeding commenced under section 13.30 shall determine all costs of the proceeding, including the reasonable compensation and expenses of appraisers appointed by the court. The court shall assess the costs against the corporation, except that the court may assess costs against all or some of the dissenters, in amounts the court finds equitable, to the extent the court finds dissenters acted arbitrarily, vexatiously, or not in good faith in demanding payment under section 13.28.

(b) The court may also assess the fees and expenses of counsel and experts for the respective parties, in amounts the court finds equitable:

(1) against the corporation and in favor of any or all dissenters if the court finds the corporation did not substantially comply with the requirements of sections 13.20 through 13.28; or
(2) against either the corporation or a dissenter, in favor of any other party, if the court finds that the party against whom the fees and expenses are assessed acted arbitrarily, vexatiously, or not in good faith with respect to the rights provided by this chapter.

(c) If the court finds that the services of counsel for any dissenter were of substantial benefit to other dissenters similarly situated, and that the fees for those services should not be assessed against the corporation, the court may award to these counsel reasonable fees to be paid out of the amounts awarded the dissenters who were benefited.

# CHAPTER 14. DISSOLUTION

## Subchapter A. Voluntary Dissolution

**§14.01 Dissolution by Incorporators or Initial Directors**

A majority of the incorporators or initial directors of a corporation that has not issued shares or has not commenced business may dissolve the corporation by delivering to the secretary of state for filing articles of dissolution that set forth:

(1) the name of the corporation;
(2) the date of its incorporation;
(3) either (i) that none of the corporation's shares has been issued or (ii) that the corporation has not commenced business;
(4) that no debt of the corporation remains unpaid;
(5) that the net assets of the corporation remaining after winding up have been distributed to the shareholders, if shares were issued; and
(6) that a majority of the incorporators or initial directors authorized the dissolution.

**§14.02 Dissolution by Board of Directors and Shareholders**

(a) A corporation's board of directors may propose dissolution for submission to the shareholders.

(b) For a proposal to dissolve to be adopted:

(1) the board of directors must recommend dissolution to the shareholders unless the board of directors determines that because of conflict

of interest or other special circumstances it should make no recommendation and communicates the basis for its determination to the shareholders; and

(2) the shareholders entitled to vote must approve the proposal to dissolve as provided in subsection (e).

(c) The board of directors may condition its submission of the proposal for dissolution on any basis.

(d) The corporation shall notify each shareholder, whether or not entitled to vote, of the proposed shareholders' meeting in accordance with section 7.05. The notice must also state that the purpose, or one of the purposes, of the meeting is to consider dissolving the corporation.

(e) Unless the articles of incorporation or the board of directors (acting pursuant to subsection (c)) require a greater vote or a vote by voting groups, the proposal to dissolve to be adopted must be approved by a majority of all the votes entitled to be cast on that proposal.

**§14.03 Articles of Dissolution**

(a) At any time after dissolution is authorized, the corporation may dissolve by delivering to the secretary of state for filing articles of dissolution setting forth:

(1) the name of the corporation;

(2) the date dissolution was authorized;

(3) if dissolution was approved by the shareholders:

(i) the number of votes entitled to be cast on the proposal to dissolve; and

(ii) either the total number of votes cast for and against dissolution or the total number of undisputed votes cast for dissolution and a statement that the number cast for dissolution was sufficient for approval.

(4) If voting by voting groups is required, the information required by subparagraph (3) shall be separately provided for each voting group entitled to vote separately on the plan to dissolve.

(b) A corporation is dissolved upon the effective date of its articles of dissolution.

**§14.04 Revocation of Dissolution**

(a) A corporation may revoke its dissolution within 120 days of its effective date.

(b) Revocation of dissolution must be authorized in the same manner as the dissolution was authorized unless that authorization permitted revocation by action by the board of directors alone, in which event the board of directors may revoke the dissolution without shareholder action.

(c) After the revocation of dissolution is authorized, the corporation may revoke the dissolution by delivering to the secretary of state for filing articles of revocation of dissolution, together with a copy of its articles of dissolution, that set forth:

(1) the name of the corporation;

(2) the effective date of the dissolution that was revoked;

(3) the date that the revocation of dissolution was authorized;

(4) if the corporation's board of directors (or incorporators) revoked the dissolution, a statement to that effect;

(5) if the corporation's board of directors revoked a dissolution authorized by the shareholders, a statement that revocation was permitted by action by the board of directors alone pursuant to that authorization; and

(6) if shareholder action was required to revoke the dissolution, the information required by section 14.03(3) or (4).

(d) Unless a delayed effective date is specified, revocation of dissolution is effective when articles of revocation of dissolution are filed.

(e) When the revocation of dissolution is effective, it relates back to and takes effect as of the effective date of the dissolution and the corporation resumes carrying on its business as if dissolution had never occurred.

**§14.05 Effect of Dissolution**

(a) A dissolved corporation continues its corporate existence but may not carry on any business except that appropriate to wind up and liquidate its business and affairs, including:

(1) collecting its assets;

(2) disposing of its properties that will not be distributed in kind to its shareholders;

(3) discharging or making provision for discharging its liabilities;

(4) distributing its remaining property among its shareholders according to their interests; and

(5) doing every other act necessary to wind up and liquidate its business and affairs.

(b) Dissolution of a corporation does not:

(1) transfer title to the corporation's property;

(2) prevent transfer of its shares or securities, although the authorization to dissolve may provide for closing the corporation's share transfer records;

(3) subject its directors or officers to standards of conduct different from those prescribed in chapter 8;

(4) change quorum or voting requirements for its board of directors or shareholders; change provisions for selection, resignation, or removal of its directors or officers or both; or change provisions for amending its bylaws;

(5) prevent commencement of a proceeding by or against the corporation in its corporate name;

(6) abate or suspend a proceeding pending by or against the corporation on the effective date of dissolution; or

(7) terminate the authority of the registered agent of the corporation.

**§14.06 Known Claims Against Dissolved Corporation**

(a) A dissolved corporation may dispose of the known claims against it by following the procedure described in this section.

(b) The dissolved corporation shall notify its known claimants in writing of the dissolution at any time after its effective date. The written notice must:

(1) describe information that must be included in a claim;

(2) provide a mailing address where a claim may be sent;

(3) state the deadline, which may not be fewer than 120 days from the effective date of the written notice, by which the dissolved corporation must receive the claim; and

(4) state that the claim will be barred if not received by the deadline.

(c) A claim against the dissolved corporation is barred:

(1) if a claimant who was given written notice under subsection (b) does not deliver the claim to the dissolved corporation by the deadline;

(2) if a claimant whose claim was rejected by the dissolved corporation does not commence a proceeding to enforce the claim within 90 days from the effective date of the rejection notice.

(d) For purposes of this section, "claim" does not include a contingent liability or a claim based on an event occurring after the effective date of dissolution.

**§14.07 Unknown Claims Against Dissolved Corporation**

(a) A dissolved corporation may also publish notice of its dissolution and request that persons with claims against the corporation present them in accordance with the notice.

(b) The notice must:

(1) be published one time in a newspaper of general circulation in the county where the dissolved corporation's principal office (or, if none in this state, its registered office) is or was last located;

(2) describe the information that must be included in a claim and provide a mailing address where the claim may be sent; and

(3) state that a claim against the corporation will be barred unless a proceeding to enforce the claim is commenced within five years after the publication of the notice.

(c) If the dissolved corporation publishes a newspaper notice in accordance with subsection (b), the claim of each of the following claimants is barred unless the claimant commences a proceeding to enforce the claim against the dissolved corporation within five years after the publication date of the newspaper notice:

(1) a claimant who did not receive written notice under section 14.06;
(2) a claimant whose claim was timely sent to the dissolved corporation but not acted on;
(3) a claimant whose claim is contingent or based on an event occurring after the effective date of dissolution.

(d) A claim may be enforced under this section:
(1) against the dissolved corporation, to the extent of its undistributed assets; or
(2) if the assets have been distributed in liquidation, against a shareholder of the dissolved corporation to the extent of his pro rata share of the claim or the corporate assets distributed to him in liquidation, whichever is less, but a shareholder's total liability for all claims under this section may not exceed the total amount of assets distributed to him.

## Subchapter B. Administrative Dissolution

### §14.20 Grounds for Administrative Dissolution

The secretary of state may commence a proceeding under section 14.21 to administratively dissolve a corporation if:
(1) the corporation does not pay within 60 days after they are due any franchise taxes or penalties imposed by this Act or other law;
(2) the corporation does not deliver its annual report to the secretary of state within 60 days after it is due;
(3) the corporation is without a registered agent or registered office in this state for 60 days or more;
(4) the corporation does not notify the secretary of state within 60 days that its registered agent or registered office has been changed, that its registered agent has resigned, or that its registered office has been discontinued; or
(5) the corporation's period of duration stated in its articles of incorporation expires.

### §14.21 Procedure for and Effect of Administrative Dissolution

(a) If the secretary of state determines that one or more grounds exist under section 14.20 for dissolving a corporation, he shall serve the corporation with written notice of his determination under section 5.04.
(b) If the corporation does not correct each ground for dissolution or demonstrate to the reasonable satisfaction of the secretary of state that each ground determined by the secretary of state does not exist within 60 days after service of the notice is perfected under section 5.04, the secretary of state shall administratively dissolve the corporation by signing a certificate of dissolution that recites the ground or grounds for dissolution and its effective date. The secretary of state shall file the original of the certificate and serve a copy on the corporation under section 5.04.
(c) A corporation administratively dissolved continues its corporate existence but may not carry on any business except that necessary to wind up and liquidate its business and affairs under section 14.05 and notify claimants under sections 14.06 and 14.07.
(d) The administrative dissolution of a corporation does not terminate the authority of its registered agent.

### §14.22 Reinstatement Following Administrative Dissolution

(a) A corporation administratively dissolved under section 14.21 may apply to the secretary of state for reinstatement within two years after the effective date of dissolution. The application must:
(1) recite the name of the corporation and the effective date of its administrative dissolution;
(2) state that the ground or grounds for dissolution either did not exist or have been eliminated;
(3) state that the corporation's name satisfies the requirements of section 4.01; and
(4) contain a certificate from the [taxing authority] reciting that all taxes owed by the corporation have been paid.

(b) If the secretary of state determines that the application contains the information required by subsection (a) and that the information is correct, he shall cancel the certificate of dissolution and prepare a certificate of reinstatement that recites his determination and the effective date of reinstatement, file the original of the certificate, and serve a copy on the corporation under section 5.04.
(c) When the reinstatement is effective, it relates back to and takes effect as of the effective date of the administrative dissolution and the corporation resumes carrying on its business as if the administrative dissolution had never occurred.

### §14.23 Appeal From Denial of Reinstatement

(a) If the secretary of state denies a corporation's application for reinstatement following administrative dissolution, he shall serve the corporation under section 5.04 with a written notice that explains the reason or reasons for denial.
(b) The corporation may appeal the denial of reinstatement to the [name or describe] court within 30 days after service of the notice of denial is perfected. The corporation appeals by petitioning the court to set aside the dissolution and attaching to the petition copies of the secretary of state's certificate of dissolution, the corporation's application for reinstatement, and the secretary of state's notice of denial.
(c) The court may summarily order the secretary of state to reinstate the dissolved corporation or may take other action the court considers appropriate.
(d) The court's final decision may be appealed as in other civil proceedings.

## Subchapter C. Judicial Dissolution

### §14.30 Grounds for Judicial Dissolution

The [name or describe court or courts] may dissolve a corporation:
(1) in a proceeding by the attorney general if it is established that:
(i) the corporation obtained its articles of incorporation through fraud; or
(ii) the corporation has continued to exceed or abuse the authority conferred upon it by law;
(2) in a proceeding by a shareholder if it is established that:
(i) the directors are deadlocked in the management of the corporate affairs, the shareholders are unable to break the deadlock, and irreparable injury to the corporation is threatened or being suffered, or the business and affairs of the corporation can no longer be conducted to the advantage of the shareholders generally, because of the deadlock;
(ii) the directors or those in control of the corporation have acted, are acting, or will act in a manner that is illegal, oppressive, or fraudulent;
(iii) the shareholders are deadlocked in voting power and have failed, for a period that includes at least two consecutive annual meeting dates, to elect successors to directors whose terms have expired; or
(iv) the corporate assets are being misapplied or wasted;
(3) in a proceeding by a creditor if it is established that:
(i) the creditor's claim has been reduced to judgment, the execution on the judgment returned unsatisfied, and the corporation is insolvent; or
(ii) the corporation has admitted in writing that the creditor's claim is due and owing and the corporation is insolvent; or
(4) in a proceeding by the corporation to have its voluntary dissolution continued under court supervision.

### §14.31 Procedure for Judicial Dissolution

(a) Venue for a proceeding by the attorney general to dissolve a corporation lies in [name the county or counties]. Venue for a proceeding brought by any other party named in section 14.30 lies in the county where a corporation's principal office (or, if none in this state, its registered office) is or was last located.

(b) It is not necessary to make shareholders parties to a proceeding to dissolve a corporation unless relief is sought against them individually.
(c) A court in a proceeding brought to dissolve a corporation may issue injunctions, appoint a receiver or custodian pendente lite with all powers and duties the court directs, take other action required to preserve the corporate assets wherever located, and carry on the business of the corporation until a full hearing can be held.
(d) Within 10 days of the commencement of a proceeding under section 14.30(2) to dissolve a corporation that has no shares listed on a national securities exchange or regularly traded in a market maintained by one or more members of a national securities exchange, the corporation must send to all shareholders, other than the petitioner, a notice stating that the shareholders are entitled to avoid the dissolution of the corporation by electing to purchase the petitioner's shares under section 14.34 and accompanied by a copy of section 14.34.

**§14.32 Receivership or Custodianship**

(a) A court in a judicial proceeding brought to dissolve a corporation may appoint one or more receivers to wind up and liquidate, or one or more custodians to manage, the business and affairs of the corporation. The court shall hold a hearing, after notifying all parties to the proceeding and any interested persons designated by the court, before appointing a receiver or custodian. The court appointing a receiver or custodian has exclusive jurisdiction over the corporation and all its property wherever located.
(b) The court may appoint an individual or a domestic or foreign corporation (authorized to transact business in this state) as a receiver or custodian. The court may require the receiver or custodian to post bond, with or without sureties, in an amount the court directs.
(c) The court shall describe the powers and duties of the receiver or custodian in its appointing order, which may be amended from time to time. Among other powers:

(1) the receiver (i) may dispose of all or any part of the assets of the corporation wherever located, at a public or private sale, if authorized by the court; and (ii) may sue and defend in his own name as receiver of the corporation in all courts of this state;

(2) the custodian may exercise all of the powers of the corporation, through or in place of its board of directors or officers, to the extent necessary to manage the affairs of the corporation in the best interests of its shareholders and creditors.

(d) The court during a receivership may redesignate the receiver a custodian, and during a custodianship may redesignate the custodian a receiver, if doing so is in the best interests of the corporation, its shareholders, and creditors.
(e) The court from time to time during the receivership or custodianship may order compensation paid and expense disbursements or reimbursements made to the receiver or custodian and his counsel from the assets of the corporation or proceeds from the sale of the assets.

**§14.33 Decree of Dissolution**

(a) If after a hearing the court determines that one or more grounds for judicial dissolution described in section 14.30 exist, it may enter a decree dissolving the corporation and specifying the effective date of the dissolution, and the clerk of the court shall deliver a certified copy of the decree to the secretary of state, who shall file it.
(b) After entering the decree of dissolution, the court shall direct the winding up and liquidation of the corporation's business and affairs in accordance with section 14.05 and the notification of claimants in accordance with sections 14.06 and 14.07.

**§14.34 Election to Purchase in Lieu of Dissolution**

(a) In a proceeding under section 14.30(2) to dissolve a corporation that has no shares listed on a national securities exchange or regularly traded in a market maintained by one or more members of a national or affiliated securities association, the corporation may elect or, if it fails to elect, one or more shareholders may elect to purchase all shares owned by the petitioning shareholder at the fair value of the shares. An election pursuant to this section shall be irrevocable unless the court determines that it is equitable to set aside or modify the election.
(b) An election to purchase pursuant to this section may be filed with the court at any time within 90 days after the filing of the petition under section 14.30(2) or at such later time as the court in its discretion may allow. If the election to purchase is filed by one or more shareholders, the corporation shall, within 10 days thereafter, give written notice to all shareholders, other than the petitioner. The notice must state the name and number of shares owned by the petitioner and the name and number of shares owned by each electing shareholder and must advise the recipients of their right to join in the election to purchase shares in accordance with this section. Shareholders who wish to participate must file notice of their intention to join in the purchase no later than 30 days after the effective date of the notice to them. All shareholders who have filed an election or notice of their intention to participate in the election to purchase thereby become parties to ownership of shares as of the date the first election was filed, unless they otherwise agree or the court otherwise directs. After an election has been filed by the corporation or one or more shareholders, the proceeding under section 14.30(2) may not be discontinued or settled, nor may the petitioning shareholder sell or otherwise dispose of his shares, unless the court determines that it would be equitable to the corporation and the shareholders, other than the petitioner, to permit such discontinuance, settlement, sale, or other disposition.
(c) If, within 60 days of the filing of the first election, the parties reach agreement as to the fair value and terms of purchase of the petitioner's shares, the court shall enter an order directing the purchase of petitioner's shares upon the terms and conditions agreed to by the parties.
(d) If the parties are unable to reach an agreement as provided for in subsection (c), the court, upon application of any party, shall stay the section 14.30(2) proceedings and determine the fair value of the petitioner's shares as of the day before the date on which the petition under section 14.30(2) was filed or as of such other date as the court deems appropriate under the circumstances.
(e) Upon determining the fair value of the shares, the court shall enter an order directing the purchase upon such terms and conditions as the court deems appropriate, which may include payment of the purchase price in installments, where necessary in the interests of equity, provision for security to assure payment of the purchase price and any additional costs, fees, and expenses as may have been awarded, and, if the shares are to be purchased by shareholders, the allocation of shares among them. In allocating petitioner's shares among holders of different classes of shares, the court should attempt to preserve the existing distribution of voting rights among holders of different classes insofar as practicable and may direct that holders of a specific class or classes shall not participate in the purchase. Interest may be allowed at the rate and from the date determined by the court to be equitable, but if the court finds that the refusal of the petitioning shareholder to accept an offer of payment was arbitrary or otherwise not in good faith, no interest shall be allowed. If the court finds that the petitioning shareholder had probable grounds for relief under paragraphs (ii) or (iv) of section 14.30(2), it may award to the petitioning shareholder reasonable fees and expenses of counsel and of any experts employed by him.
(f) Upon entry of an order under subsections (c) or (e), the court shall dismiss the petition to dissolve the corporation under section 14.30, and the petitioning shareholder shall no longer have any rights or status as a shareholder of the corporation, except the right to receive the amounts awarded to him by the order of the court which shall be enforceable in the same manner as any other judgment.
(g) The purchase ordered pursuant to subsection (e), shall be made within 10 days after the date the order becomes final unless before that time the

corporation files with the court a notice of its intention to adopt articles of dissolution pursuant to sections 14.02 and 14.03, which articles must then be adopted and filed within 50 days thereafter. Upon filing of such articles of dissolution, the corporation shall be dissolved in accordance with the provisions of sections 14.05 through 07, and the order entered pursuant to subsection (e) shall no longer be of any force or effect, except that the court may award the petitioning shareholder reasonable fees and expenses in accordance with the provisions of the last sentence of subsection (e) and the petitioner may continue to pursue any claims previously asserted on behalf of the corporation.
(h) Any payment by the corporation pursuant to an order under subsections (c) or (e), other than an award of fees and expenses pursuant to subsection (e), is subject to the provisions of section 6.40.

## Subchapter D. Miscellaneous

### §14.40 Deposit With State Treasurer

Assets of a dissolved corporation that should be transferred to a creditor, claimant, or shareholder of the corporation who cannot be found or who is not competent to receive them shall be reduced to cash and deposited with the state treasurer or other appropriate state official for safekeeping. When the creditor, claimant, or shareholder furnishes satisfactory proof of entitlement to the amount deposited, the state treasurer or other appropriate state official shall pay him or his representative that amount.

# CHAPTER 15. FOREIGN CORPORATIONS

## Subchapter A. Certificate of Authority

### §15.01 Authority to Transact Business Required

(a) A foreign corporation may not transact business in this state until it obtains a certificate of authority from the secretary of state.
(b) The following activities, among others, do not constitute transacting business within the meaning of subsection (a):

(1) maintaining, defending, or settling any proceeding;
(2) holding meetings of the board of directors or shareholders or carrying on other activities concerning internal corporate affairs;
(3) maintaining bank accounts;
(4) maintaining offices or agencies for the transfer, exchange, and registration of the corporation's own securities or maintaining trustees or depositaries with respect to those securities;
(5) selling through independent contractors;
(6) soliciting or obtaining orders, whether by mail or through employees or agents or otherwise, if the orders require acceptance outside this state before they become contracts;
(7) creating or acquiring indebtedness, mortgages, and security interests in real or personal property;
(8) securing or collecting debts or enforcing mortgages and security interests in property securing the debts;
(9) owning, without more, real or personal property;
(10) conducting an isolated transaction that is completed within 30 days and that is not one in the course of repeated transactions of a like nature;
(11) transacting business in interstate commerce.

(c) The list of activities in subsection (b) is not exhaustive.

### §15.02 Consequences of Transacting Business Without Authority

(a) A foreign corporation transacting business in this state without a certificate of authority may not maintain a proceeding in any court in this state until it obtains a certificate of authority.
(b) The successor to a foreign corporation that transacted business in this state without a certificate of authority and the assignee of a cause of action arising out of that business may not maintain a proceeding based on that cause of action in any court in this state until the foreign corporation or its successor obtains a certificate of authority.
(c) A court may stay a proceeding commenced by a foreign corporation, its successor, or assignee until it determines whether the foreign corporation or its successor requires a certificate of authority. If it so determines, the court may further stay the proceeding until the foreign corporation or its successor obtains the certificate.
(d) A foreign corporation is liable for a civil penalty of $ for each day, but not to exceed a total of $ for each year, it transacts business in this state without a certificate of authority. The attorney general may collect all penalties due under this subsection.
(e) Notwithstanding subsections (a) and (b), the failure of a foreign corporation to obtain a certificate of authority does not impair the validity of its corporate acts or prevent it from defending any proceeding in this state.

### §15.03 Application for Certificate of Authority

(a) A foreign corporation may apply for a certificate of authority to transact business in this state by delivering an application to the secretary of state for filing. The application must set forth:

(1) the name of the foreign corporation or, if its name is unavailable for use in this state, a corporate name that satisfies the requirements of section 15.06;
(2) the name of the state or country under whose law it is incorporated;
(3) its date of incorporation and period of duration;
(4) the street address of its principal office;
(5) the address of its registered office in this state and the name of its registered agent at that office; and
(6) the names and usual business addresses of its current directors and officers.

(b) The foreign corporation shall deliver with the completed application a certificate of existence (or a document of similar import) duly authenticated by the secretary of state or other official having custody of corporate records in the state or country under whose law it is incorporated.

### §15.04 Amended Certificate of Authority

(a) A foreign corporation authorized to transact business in this state must obtain an amended certificate of authority from the secretary of state if it changes:

(1) its corporate name;
(2) the period of its duration; or
(3) the state or country of its incorporation.

(b) The requirements of section 15.03 for obtaining an original certificate of authority apply to obtaining an amended certificate under this section.

### §15.05 Effect of Certificate of Authority

(a) A certificate of authority authorizes the foreign corporation to which it is issued to transact business in this state subject, however, to the right of the state to revoke the certificate as provided in this Act.
(b) A foreign corporation with a valid certificate of authority has the same but no greater rights and has the same but no greater privileges as, and except as otherwise provided by this Act is subject to the same duties, restrictions, penalties, and liabilities now or later imposed on, a domestic corporation of like character.
(c) This Act does not authorize this state to regulate the organization or internal affairs of a foreign corporation authorized to transact business in this state.

### §15.06 Corporate Name of Foreign Corporation

(a) If the corporate name of a foreign corporation does not satisfy the requirements of section 4.01, the foreign corporation to obtain or maintain a certificate of authority to transact business in this state:

(1) may add the word "corporation," "incorporated," "company," or "limited," or the abbreviation "corp.," "inc.," "co.," or "ltd.," to its corporate name for use in this state; or
(2) may use a fictitious name to transact business in this state if its real name is unavailable and it delivers to the secretary of state for filing a copy of the resolution of its board of directors, certified by its secretary, adopting the fictitious name.

(b) Except as authorized by subsections (c) and (d), the corporate name (including a fictitious name) of a foreign corporation must be distinguishable upon the records of the secretary of state from:

(1) the corporate name of a corporation incorporated or authorized to transact business in this state;

(2) a corporate name reserved or registered under section 4.02 or 4.03;

(3) the fictitious name of another foreign corporation authorized to transact business in this state; and

(4) the corporate name of a not-for-profit corporation incorporated or authorized to transact business in this state.

(c) A foreign corporation may apply to the secretary of state for authorization to use in this state the name of another corporation (incorporated or authorized to transact business in this state) that is not distinguishable upon his records from the name applied for. The secretary of state shall authorize use of the name applied for if:

(1) the other corporation consents to the use in writing and submits an undertaking in form satisfactory to the secretary of state to change its name to a name that is distinguishable upon the records of the secretary of state from the name of the applying corporation; or

(2) the applicant delivers to the secretary of state a certified copy of a final judgment of a court of competent jurisdiction establishing the applicant's right to use the name applied for in this state.

(d) A foreign corporation may use in this state the name (including the fictitious name) of another domestic or foreign corporation that is used in this state if the other corporation is incorporated or authorized to transact business in this state and the foreign corporation:

(1) has merged with the other corporation;

(2) has been formed by reorganization of the other corporation; or

(3) has acquired all or substantially all of the assets, including the corporate name, of the other corporation.

(e) If a foreign corporation authorized to transact business in this state changes its corporate name to one that does not satisfy the requirements of section 4.01, it may not transact business in this state under the changed name until it adopts a name satisfying the requirements of section 4.01 and obtains an amended certificate of authority under section 15.04.

**§15.07 Registered Office and Registered Agent of Foreign Corporation**

Each foreign corporation authorized to transact business in this state must continuously maintain in this state:

(1) a registered office that may be the same as any of its places of business; and

(2) a registered agent, who may be:

(i) an individual who resides in this state and whose business office is identical with the registered office;

(ii) a domestic corporation or not-for-profit domestic corporation whose business office is identical with the registered office; or

(iii) a foreign corporation or foreign not-for-profit corporation authorized to transact business in this state whose business office is identical with the registered office.

**§15.08 Change of Registered Office or Registered Agent of Foreign Corporation**

(a) A foreign corporation authorized to transact business in this state may change its registered office or registered agent by delivering to the secretary of state for filing a statement of change that sets forth:

(1) its name;

(2) the street address of its current registered office;

(3) if the current registered office is to be changed, the street address of its new registered office;

(4) the name of its current registered agent;

(5) if the current registered agent is to be changed, the name of its new registered agent and the new agent's written consent (either on the statement or attached to it) to the appointment; and

(6) that after the change or changes are made, the street addresses of its registered office and the business office of its registered agent will be identical.

(b) If a registered agent changes the street address of his business office, he may change the street address of the registered office of any foreign corporation for which he is the registered agent by notifying the corporation in writing of the change and signing (either manually or in facsimile) and delivering to the secretary of state for filing a statement of change that complies with the requirements of subsection (a) and recites that the corporation has been notified of the change.

**§15.09 Resignation of Registered Agent of Foreign Corporation**

(a) The registered agent of a foreign corporation may resign his agency appointment by signing and delivering to the secretary of state for filing the original and two exact or conformed copies of a statement of resignation. The statement of resignation may include a statement that the registered office is also discontinued.

(b) After filing the statement, the secretary of state shall attach the filing receipt to one copy and mail the copy and receipt to the registered office if not discontinued. The secretary of state shall mail the other copy to the foreign corporation at its principal office address shown in its most recent annual report.

(c) The agency appointment is terminated, and the registered office discontinued if so provided, on the 31st day after the date on which the statement was filed.

**§15.10 Service on Foreign Corporation**

(a) The registered agent of a foreign corporation authorized to transact business in this state is the corporation's agent for service of process, notice, or demand required or permitted by law to be served on the foreign corporation.

(b) A foreign corporation may be served by registered or certified mail, return receipt requested, addressed to the secretary of the foreign corporation at its principal office shown in its application for a certificate of authority or in its most recent annual report if the foreign corporation:

(1) has no registered agent or its registered agent cannot with reasonable diligence be served;

(2) has withdrawn from transacting business in this state under section 15.20; or

(3) has had its certificate of authority revoked under section 15.31.

(c) Service is perfected under subsection (b) at the earliest of:

(1) the date the foreign corporation receives the mail;

(2) the date shown on the return receipt, if signed on behalf of the foreign corporation; or

(3) five days after its deposit in the United States Mail, as evidenced by the postmark, if mailed postpaid and correctly addressed.

(d) This section does not prescribe the only means, or necessarily the required means, of serving a foreign corporation.

## Subchapter B. Withdrawal

**§15.20 Withdrawal of Foreign Corporation**

(a) A foreign corporation authorized to transact business in this state may not withdraw from this state until it obtains a certificate of withdrawal from the secretary of state.

(b) A foreign corporation authorized to transact business in this state may apply for a certificate of withdrawal by delivering an application to the secretary of state for filing. The application must set forth:

(1) the name of the foreign corporation and the name of the state or country under whose law it is incorporated;

(2) that it is not transacting business in this state and that it surrenders its authority to transact business in this state;

(3) that it revokes the authority of its registered agent to accept service on its behalf and appoints the secretary of state as its agent for service of process in any proceeding based on a cause of action arising during the time it was authorized to transact business in this state;

(4) a mailing address to which the secretary of state may mail a copy of any process served on him under subdivision (3); and

(5) a commitment to notify the secretary of state in the future of any change in its mailing address.

(c) After the withdrawal of the corporation is effective, service of process on the secretary of state under this section is service on the foreign corporation. Upon receipt of process, the secretary of state shall mail a copy of the process to the foreign corporation at the mailing address set forth under subsection (b).

## Subchapter C. Revocation of Certificate of Authority

### §15.30 Grounds for Revocation

The secretary of state may commence a proceeding under section 15.31 to revoke the certificate of authority of a foreign corporation authorized to transact business in this state if:

(1) the foreign corporation does not deliver its annual report to the secretary of state within 60 days after it is due;

(2) the foreign corporation does not pay within 60 days after they are due any franchise taxes or penalties imposed by this Act or other law;

(3) the foreign corporation is without a registered agent or registered office in this state for 60 days or more;

(4) the foreign corporation does not inform the secretary of state under section 15.08 or 15.09 that its registered agent or registered office has changed, that its registered agent has resigned, or that its registered office has been discontinued within 60 days of the change, resignation, or discontinuance;

(5) an incorporator, director, officer, or agent of the foreign corporation signed a document he knew was false in any material respect with intent that the document be delivered to the secretary of state for filing;

(6) the secretary of state receives a duly authenticated certificate from the secretary of state or other official having custody of corporate records in the state or country under whose law the foreign corporation is incorporated stating that it has been dissolved or disappeared as a result of a merger.

### §15.31 Procedure for and Effect of Revocation

(a) If the secretary of state determines that one or more grounds exist under section 15.30 for revocation of a certificate of authority, he shall serve the foreign corporation with written notice of his determination under section 15.10.

(b) If the foreign corporation does not correct each ground for revocation or demonstrate to the reasonable satisfaction of the secretary of state that each ground determined by the secretary of state does not exist within 60 days after service of the notice is perfected under section 15.10, the secretary of state may revoke the foreign corporation's certificate of authority by signing a certificate of revocation that recites the ground or grounds for revocation and its effective date. The secretary of state shall file the original of the certificate and serve a copy on the foreign corporation under section 15.10.

(c) The authority of a foreign corporation to transact business in this state ceases on the date shown on the certificate revoking its certificate of authority.

(d) The secretary of state's revocation of a foreign corporation's certificate of authority appoints the secretary of state the foreign corporation's agent for service of process in any proceeding based on a cause of action which arose during the time the foreign corporation was authorized to transact business in this state. Service of process on the secretary of state under this subsection is service on the foreign corporation. Upon receipt of process, the secretary of state shall mail a copy of the process to the secretary of the foreign corporation at its principal office shown in its most recent annual report or in any subsequent communication received from the corporation stating the current mailing address of its principal office, or, if none are on file, in its application for a certificate of authority.

(e) Revocation of a foreign corporation's certificate of authority does not terminate the authority of the registered agent of the corporation.

### §15.32 Appeal From Revocation

(a) A foreign corporation may appeal the secretary of state's revocation of its certificate of authority to the [name or describe] court within 30 days after service of the certificate of revocation is perfected under section 15.10. The foreign corporation appeals by petitioning the court to set aside the revocation and attaching to the petition copies of its certificate of authority and the secretary of state's certificate of revocation.

(b) The court may summarily order the secretary of state to reinstate the certificate of authority or may take any other action the court considers appropriate.

(c) The court's final decision may be appealed as in other civil proceedings.

# CHAPTER 16. RECORDS AND REPORTS

## Subchapter A. Records

### §16.01 Corporate Records

(a) A corporation shall keep as permanent records minutes of all meetings of its shareholders and board of directors, a record of all actions taken by the shareholders or board of directors without a meeting, and a record of all actions taken by a committee of the board of directors in place of the board of directors on behalf of the corporation.

(b) A corporation shall maintain appropriate accounting records.

(c) A corporation or its agent shall maintain a record of its shareholders, in a form that permits preparation of a list of the names and addresses of all shareholders, in alphabetical order by class of shares showing the number and class of shares held by each.

(d) A corporation shall maintain its records in written form or in another form capable of conversion into written form within a reasonable time.

(e) A corporation shall keep a copy of the following records at its principal office:

(1) its articles or restated articles of incorporation and all amendments to them currently in effect;

(2) its bylaws or restated bylaws and all amendments to them currently in effect;

(3) resolutions adopted by its board of directors creating one or more classes or series of shares, and fixing their relative rights, preferences, and limitations, if shares issued pursuant to those resolutions are outstanding;

(4) the minutes of all shareholders' meetings, and records of all action taken by shareholders without a meeting, for the past three years;

(5) all written communications to shareholders generally within the past three years, including the financial statements furnished for the past three years under section 16.20;

(6) a list of the names and business addresses of its current directors and officers; and

(7) its most recent annual report delivered to the secretary of state under section 16.22.

### §16.02 Inspection of Records by Shareholders

(a) Subject to section 16.03(c), a shareholder of a corporation is entitled to inspect and copy, during regular business hours at the corporation's principal office, any of the records of the corporation described in section 16.01(e) if he gives the corporation written notice of his demand at least five business days before the date on which he wishes to inspect and copy.

(b) A shareholder of a corporation is entitled to inspect and copy, during regular business hours at a reasonable location specified by the corporation, any of the following records of the corporation if the shareholder meets the requirements of subsection (c) and gives the corporation written notice of his demand at least five business days before the date on which he wishes to inspect and copy:

(1) excerpts from minutes of any meeting of the board of directors, records of any action of a committee of the board of directors while acting in place of the board of directors on behalf of the corporation, minutes of any meeting of the shareholders, and records of action taken

by the shareholders or board of directors without a meeting, to the extent not subject to inspection under section 16.02(a);
(2) accounting records of the corporation; and
(3) the record of shareholders.

(c) A shareholder may inspect and copy the records identified in subsection (b) only if:
(1) his demand is made in good faith and for a proper purpose;
(2) he describes with reasonable particularity his purpose and the records he desires to inspect; and
(3) the records are directly connected with his purpose.

(d) The right of inspection granted by this section may not be abolished or limited by a corporation's articles of incorporation or bylaws.

(e) This section does not affect:
(1) the right of a shareholder to inspect records under section 7.20 or, if the shareholder is in litigation with the corporation, to the same extent as any other litigant;
(2) the power of a court, independently of this Act, to compel the production of corporate records for examination.

(f) For purposes of this section, "shareholder" includes a beneficial owner whose shares are held in a voting trust or by a nominee on his behalf.

**§16.03 Scope of Inspection Right**

(a) A shareholder's agent or attorney has the same inspection and copying rights as the shareholder he represents.

(b) The right to copy records under section 16.02 includes, if reasonable, the right to receive copies made by photographic, xerographic, or other means.

(c) The corporation may impose a reasonable charge, covering the costs of labor and material, for copies of any documents provided to the shareholder. The charge may not exceed the estimated cost of production or reproduction of the records.

(d) The corporation may comply with a shareholder's demand to inspect the record of shareholders under section 16.02(b)(3) by providing him with a list of its shareholders that was compiled no earlier than the date of the shareholder's demand.

**§16.04 Court-Ordered Inspection**

(a) If a corporation does not allow a shareholder who complies with section 16.02(a) to inspect and copy any records required by that subsection to be available for inspection, the [name or describe court] of the county where the corporation's principal office (or, if none in this state, its registered office) is located may summarily order inspection and copying of the records demanded at the corporation's expense upon application of the shareholder.

(b) If a corporation does not within a reasonable time allow a shareholder to inspect and copy any other record, the shareholder who complies with section 16.02(b) and (c) may apply to the [name or describe court] in the county where the corporation's principal office (or, if none in this state, its registered office) is located for an order to permit inspection and copying of the records demanded. The court shall dispose of an application under this subsection on an expedited basis.

(c) If the court orders inspection and copying of the records demanded, it shall also order the corporation to pay the shareholder's costs (including reasonable counsel fees) incurred to obtain the order unless the corporation proves that it refused inspection in good faith because it had a reasonable basis for doubt about the right of the shareholder to inspect the records demanded.

(d) If the court orders inspection and copying of the records demanded, it may impose reasonable restrictions on the use or distribution of the records by the demanding shareholder.

## Subchapter B. Reports

**§16.20 Financial Statements for Shareholders**

(a) A corporation shall furnish its shareholders annual financial statements, which may be consolidated or combined statements of the corporation and one or more of its subsidiaries, as appropriate, that include a balance sheet as of the end of the fiscal year, an income statement for that year, and a statement of changes in shareholders' equity for the year unless that information appears elsewhere in the financial statements. If financial statements are prepared for the corporation on the basis of generally accepted accounting principles, the annual financial statements must also be prepared on that basis.

(b) If the annual financial statements are reported upon by a public accountant, his report must accompany them. If not, the statements must be accompanied by a statement of the president or the person responsible for the corporation's accounting records:
(1) stating his reasonable belief whether the statements were prepared on the basis of generally accepted accounting principles and, if not, describing the basis of preparation; and
(2) describing any respects in which the statements were not prepared on a basis of accounting consistent with the statements prepared for the preceding year.

(c) A corporation shall mail the annual financial statements to each shareholder within 120 days after the close of each fiscal year. Thereafter, on written request from a shareholder who was not mailed the statements, the corporation shall mail him the latest financial statements.

**§16.21 Other Reports to Shareholders**

(a) If a corporation indemnifies or advances expenses to a director under section 8.51, 8.52, 8.53, or 8.54 in connection with a proceeding by or in the right of the corporation, the corporation shall report the indemnification or advance in writing to the shareholders with or before the notice of the next shareholders' meeting.

(b) If a corporation issues or authorizes the issuance of shares for promissory notes or for promises to render services in the future, the corporation shall report in writing to the shareholders the number of shares authorized or issued, and the consideration received by the corporation, with or before the notice of the next shareholders' meeting.

**§16.22 Annual Report for Secretary of State**

(a) Each domestic corporation, and each foreign corporation authorized to transact business in this state, shall deliver to the secretary of state for filing an annual report that sets forth:
(1) the name of the corporation and the state or country under whose law it is incorporated;
(2) the address of its registered office and the name of its registered agent at that office in this state;
(3) the address of its principal office;
(4) the names and business addresses of its directors and principal officers;
(5) a brief description of the nature of its business;
(6) the total number of authorized shares, itemized by class and series, if any, within each class; and
(7) the total number of issued and outstanding shares, itemized by class and series, if any, within each class.

(b) Information in the annual report must be current as of the date the annual report is executed on behalf of the corporation.

(c) The first annual report must be delivered to the secretary of state between January 1 and April 1 of the year following the calendar year in which a domestic corporation was incorporated or a foreign corporation was authorized to transact business. Subsequent annual reports must be delivered to the secretary of state between January 1 and April 1 of the following calendar years.

(d) If an annual report does not contain the information required by this section, the secretary of state shall promptly notify the reporting domestic or foreign corporation in writing and return the report to it for correction. If the report is corrected to contain the information required by this section and delivered to the secretary of state within 30 days after the effective date of notice, it is deemed to be timely filed.

## CHAPTER 17. TRANSITION PROVISIONS

### §17.01 Application to Existing Domestic Corporations

This Act applies to all domestic corporations in existence on its effective date that were incorporated under any general statute of this state providing for incorporation of corporations for profit if power to amend or repeal the statute under which the corporation was incorporated was reserved.

### §17.02 Application to Qualified Foreign Corporations

A foreign corporation authorized to transact business in this state on the effective date of this Act is subject to this Act but is not required to obtain a new certificate of authority to transact business under this Act.

### §17.03 Saving Provisions

(a) Except as provided in subsection (b), the repeal of a statute by this Act does not affect:

(1) the operation of the statute or any action taken under it before its repeal;

(2) any ratification, right, remedy, privilege, obligation, or liability acquired, accrued, or incurred under the statute before its repeal;

(3) any violation of the statute, or any penalty, forfeiture, or punishment incurred because of the violation, before its repeal;

(4) any proceeding, reorganization, or dissolution commenced under the statute before its repeal, and the proceeding, reorganization, or dissolution may be completed in accordance with the statute as if it had not been repealed.

(b) If a penalty or punishment imposed for violation of a statute repealed by this Act is reduced by this Act, the penalty or punishment if not already imposed shall be imposed in accordance with this Act.

### §17.04 Severability

If any provision of this Act or its application to any person or circumstance is held invalid by a court of competent jurisdiction, the invalidity does not affect other provisions or applications of the Act that can be given effect without the invalid provision or application, and to this end the provisions of the Act are severable.

### §17.05 Repeal

The following laws and parts of laws are repealed: [to be inserted].

### §17.06 Effective Date

This Act takes effect _______.

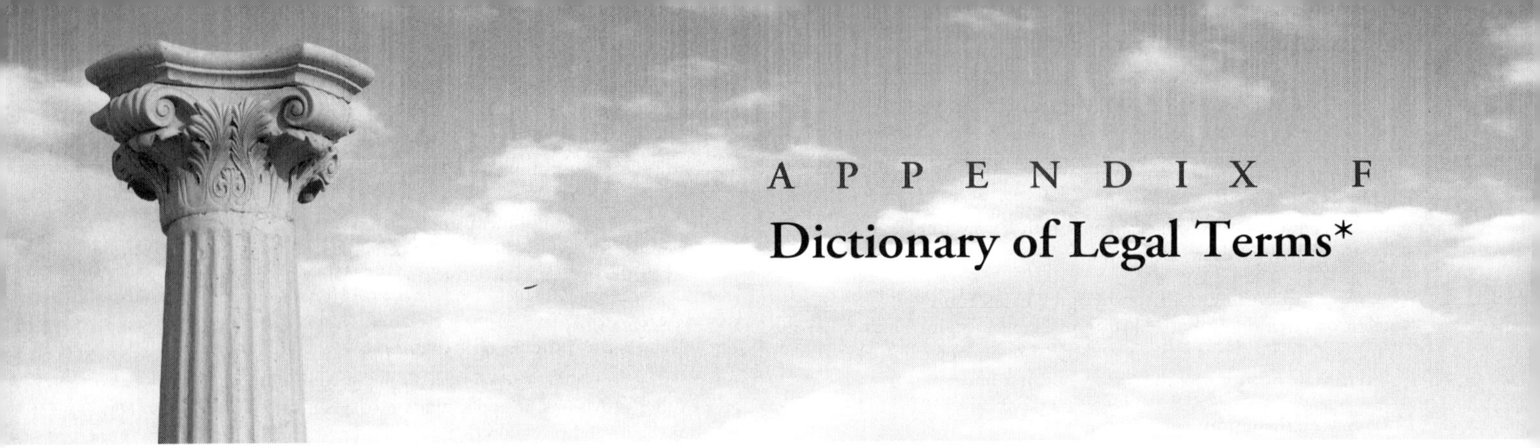

# APPENDIX F
# Dictionary of Legal Terms*

**abatement** Reduction or elimination of gifts by category upon the reduction in value of the estate.

**absolute surety** Surety liable to a creditor immediately upon the default of the principal debtor.

**acceptance**

*Commercial paper* Acceptance is the drawee's signed engagement to honor the draft as presented. It becomes operative when completed by delivery or notification. UCC §3-410.

*Contracts* Compliance by offeree with terms and conditions of offer.

*Sale of goods* UCC §2-606 provides three ways a buyer can accept goods: (1) by signifying to the seller that the goods are conforming or that he will accept them in spite of their nonconformity, (2) by failing to make an effective rejection, and (3) by doing an act inconsistent with the seller's ownership.

**acceptor** Drawee who has accepted an instrument.

**accession** An addition to one's property by increase of the original property or by production from such property. *E.g.,* A innocently converts the wheat of B into bread. UCC §9-315 changes the common law where a perfected security interest is involved.

**accident and health insurance** Provides protection from losses due to accident or sickness.

**accommodation** An arrangement made as a favor to another, usually involving a loan of money or commercial paper. While a party's intent may be to aid a maker of a note by lending his credit, if he seeks to accomplish thereby legitimate objects of his own and not simply to aid the maker, the act is not for accommodation.

**accommodation indorser** Signer not in the chain of title.

**accommodation party** A person who signs commercial paper in any capacity for the purpose of lending his name to another party to an instrument. UCC §3-415.

**accord and satisfaction** A method of discharging a claim whereby the parties agree to accept something in settlement, the "accord" being the agreement and the "satisfaction" its execution or performance. It is a new contract that is substituted for an old contract, which is thereby discharged, or for an obligation or cause of action and that must have all of the elements of a valid contract.

**account** Any account with a bank, including a checking, time, interest or savings account. UCC §4-194. Also, any right to payment, for goods or services, that is not evidenced by an instrument or chattel paper. *E.g.,* account receivable.

**accounting** Equitable proceeding for a complete settlement of all partnership affairs.

**act of state doctrine** Rule that a court should not question the validity of actions taken by a foreign government in its own country.

*Many of the definitions are abridged and adapted from *Black's Law Dictionary*, 5th edition, West Publishing Company, 1979.

**actual authority** Power conferred upon agent by actual consent given by principal.

**actual express authority** Actual authority derived from written or spoken words of principal.

**actual implied authority** Actual authority inferred from words or conduct manifested to agent by principal.

**actual notice** Knowledge actually and expressly communicated.

**actus reas** Wrongful or overt act.

**ademption** The removal or extinction of a devise by act of the testator.

**adequacy of consideration** Not required where parties have freely agreed to the exchange.

**adhesion contract** Standard "form" contract, usually between a large retailer and a consumer, in which the weaker party has no realistic choice or opportunity to bargain.

**adjudication** The giving or pronouncing of a judgment in a case; also, the judgment given.

**administrative agency** Governmental entity (other than courts and legislatures) having authority to affect the rights of private parties.

**administrative law** Law dealing with the establishment, duties, and powers of agencies in the executive branch of government.

**administrative process** Entire set of activities engaged in by administrative agencies while carrying out their rulemaking, enforcement, and adjudicative functions.

**administrator** A person appointed by the court to manage the assets and liabilities of an intestate (a person dying without a will). A person named in the will of a testator (a person dying with a will) is called the executor. Female designations are administratrix and executrix.

**adversary system** System in which opposing parties initiate and present their cases.

**adverse possession** A method of acquiring title to real property by possession for a statutory period under certain conditions. The periods of time may differ, depending on whether the adverse possessor has color of title.

**affidavit** A written statement of facts, made voluntarily, confirmed by oath or affirmation of the party making it, and taken before an authorized officer.

**affiliate** Person who controls, is controlled by, or is under common control with the issuer.

**affirm** Uphold the lower court's judgment.

**affirmative action** Active recruitment of minority applicants.

**affirmative defense** A response that attacks the plaintiff's legal right to bring an action as opposed to attacking the truth of the claim. *E.g.,* accord and satisfaction; assumption of risk; contributory negligence; duress; estoppel.

**affirmative disclosure** Requirement that an advertiser include certain information in its advertisement so that the ad is not deceptive.

**after-acquired property** Property the debtor may acquire at some time after the security interest attaches.

**agency** Relation in which one person acts for or represents another by the latter's authority.

COLUMN: © PHOTOGRAPHEROLYMPUS CLOUDS: © KERTLIS

*Actual agency* Exists where the agent is really employed by the principal.

*Agency by estoppel* One created by operation of law and established by proof of such acts of the principal as reasonably lead to the conclusion of its existence.

*Implied agency* One created by acts of the parties and deduced from proof of other facts.

**agent** Person authorized to act on another's behalf.

**allegation** A statement of a party setting out what he expects to prove.

**allonge** Piece of paper firmly affixed to the instrument.

**annuity contract** Agreement to pay periodic sums to insured upon reaching a designated age.

**annul** To annul a judgment or judicial proceeding is to deprive it of all force and operation.

**answer** The answer is the formal written statement made by a defendant setting forth the ground of his defense.

**antecedent debt** Preexisting obligation.

**anticipatory breach of contract** (or **anticipatory repudiation)** The unjustified assertion by a party that he will not perform an obligation that he is contractually obligated to perform at a future time. See UCC §§610 & 611.

**apparent authority** Such principal power that a reasonable person would assume an agent has in light of the principal's conduct.

**appeal** Resort to a superior (appellate) court to review the decision of an inferior (trial) court or administrative agency.

**appeal by right** Mandatory review by a higher court.

**appellant** A party who takes an appeal from one court to another. He may be either the plaintiff or defendant in the original court proceeding.

**appellee** The party in a cause against whom an appeal is taken; that is, the party who has an interest adverse to setting aside or reversing the judgment. Sometimes also called the "respondent."

**appropriation** Unauthorized use of another person's name or likeness for one's own benefit.

**appurtenances** Things appurtenant pass as incident to the principal thing. Sometimes an easement consisting of a right of way over one piece of land will pass with another piece of land as being appurtenant to it.

**APR** Annual percentage rate.

**arbitration** The reference of a dispute to an impartial (third) person chosen by the parties, who agree in advance to abide by the arbitrator's award issued after a hearing at which both parties have an opportunity to be heard.

**arraignment** Accused is informed of the crime against him and enters a plea.

**articles of incorporation** (or **certificate of incorporation**) The instrument under which a corporation is formed. The contents are prescribed in the particular state's general incorporation statute.

**articles of partnership** A written agreement by which parties enter into a partnership, to be governed by the terms set forth therein.

**as is** Disclaimer of implied warranties.

**assault** Unlawful attempted battery; intentional infliction of apprehension of immediate bodily harm or offensive contact.

**assignee** Party to whom contract rights are assigned.

**assignment** A transfer of the rights to real or personal property, usually intangible property such as rights in a lease, mortgage, sale agreement, or partnership.

**assignment of rights** Voluntary transfer to a third party of the rights arising from a contract.

**assignor** Party making an assignment.

**assumes** Delegatee agrees to perform the contractual obligation of the delegator.

**assumes the mortgage** Purchaser of mortgaged property becomes personally liable to pay the debt.

**assumption of risk** Plaintiff's express or implied consent to encounter a known danger.

**attachment** The process of seizing property, by virtue of a writ, summons, or other judicial order, and bringing the same into the custody of the court for the purpose of securing satisfaction of the judgment ultimately to be entered in the action. While formerly the main objective was to coerce the defendant debtor to appear in court, today the writ of attachment is used primarily to seize the debtor's property in the event a judgment is rendered.

*Distinguished from execution* See **execution**.

Also, the process by which a security interest becomes enforceable. Attachment may occur upon the taking of possession or upon the signing of a security agreement by the person who is pledging the property as collateral.

**authority** Power of an agent to change the legal status of his principal.

**authorized means** Any reasonable means of communication.

**automatic perfection** Perfection upon attachment.

**award** The decision of an arbitrator.

**bad checks** Issuing a check with funds insufficient to cover it.

**bailee** The party to whom personal property is delivered under a contract of bailment.

*Extraordinary bailee* Absolutely liable for the safety of the bailed property without regard to the cause of loss.

*Ordinary bailee* Must exercise due care.

**bailment** A delivery of personal property in trust for the execution of a special object in relation to such goods, beneficial either to the bailor or bailee or both, and upon a contract to either redeliver the goods to the bailor or otherwise dispose of the same in conformity with the purpose of the trust.

**bailor** The party who delivers goods to another in the contract of bailment.

**bankrupt** The state or condition of one who is unable to pay his debts as they are, or become, due.

**Bankruptcy Code** The Act was substantially revised in 1978, effective October 1, 1979. Straight bankruptcy is in the nature of a liquidation proceeding and involves the collection and distribution to creditors of all the bankrupt's nonexempt property by the trustee in the manner provided by the Act. The debtor rehabilitation provisions of the Act (Chapters 11 and 13) differ from straight bankruptcy in that the debtor looks to rehabilitation and reorganization, rather than liquidation, and the creditors look to future earnings of the bankrupt, rather than to property held by the bankrupt, to satisfy their claims.

**bargain** Negotiated exchange.

**bargained exchange** Mutually agreed-upon exchange.

**basis of the bargain** Part of the buyer's assumption underlying the sale.

**battery** Unlawful touching of another; intentional infliction of harmful or offensive bodily contact.

**bearer** Person in possession of an instrument.

**bearer paper** Payable to holder of the instrument.

**beneficiary** One who benefits from act of another. See also **third-party beneficiary**.

*Incidental* A person who may derive benefit from performance on contract, though he is neither the promisee nor the one to whom performance is to be rendered. Since the incidental beneficiary is not a donee or creditor beneficiary (see **third-party beneficiary**), he has no right to enforce the contract.

*Intended beneficiary* Third party intended by the two contracted parties to receive a benefit from their contract.

*Trust* As it relates to trust beneficiaries, includes a person who has any present or future interest, vested or contingent, and also includes the owner of an interest by assignment or other transfer and, as it relates to a charitable trust, includes any person entitled to enforce the trust.

**beyond a reasonable doubt** Proof that is entirely convincing and satisfying to a moral certainty; criminal law standard.

**bilateral contract** Contract in which both parties exchange promises.

**bill of lading** Document evidencing receipt of goods for shipment issued by person engaged in business of transporting or forwarding goods; includes airbill. UCC §1-201(6).

*Through bill of lading* A bill of lading which specifies at least one connecting carrier.

**bill of sale** A written agreement, formerly limited to one under seal, by which one person assigns or transfers his right to or interest in goods and personal chattels to another.

**binder** A written memorandum of the important terms of a contract of insurance which gives temporary protection to an insured pending investigation of risk by the insurance company or until a formal policy is issued.

**blue law** Prohibition of certain types of commercial activity on Sunday.

**blue sky laws** A popular name for state statutes providing for the regulation and supervision of securities offerings and sales, to protect citizen-investors from investing in fraudulent companies.

**bona fide** In good faith.

**bond** A certificate or evidence of a debt on which the issuing company or governmental body promises to pay the bondholders a specified amount of interest for a specified length of time and to repay the loan on the expiration date. In every case, a bond represents debt—its holder is a creditor of the corporation, not a part owner, as the shareholder is.

**boycott** Agreement among parties not to deal with a third party.

**breach** Wrongful failure to perform the terms of a contract.

*Material breach* Nonperformance which significantly impairs the aggrieved party's rights under the contract.

**bribery** Offering property to a public official to influence the official's decision.

**bulk transfer** Transfer not in the ordinary course of the transferor's business of a major part of his inventory.

**burglary** Breaking and entering the home of another at night with intent to commit a felony.

**business judgment rule** Protects directors from liability for honest mistakes of judgment.

**business trust** A trust (managed by a trustee for the benefit of a beneficiary) established to conduct a business for a profit.

**but for rule** Person's negligent conduct is a cause of an event if the event would not have occurred in the absence of that conduct.

**buyer in ordinary course of business** Person who buys in ordinary course, in good faith, and without knowledge that the sale to him is in violation of anyone's ownership rights or of a security interest.

**by-laws** Regulations, ordinances, rules, or laws adopted by an association or corporation for its government.

**callable bond** Bond that is subject to redemption (reacquisition) by the corporation.

**cancellation** One party's putting an end to a contract because of a breach by other party.

**capital** Accumulated goods, possessions, and assets, used for the production of profits and wealth. Owners' equity in a business. Also used to refer to the total assets of a business or to capital assets.

**capital surplus** Surplus other than earned surplus.

**carrier** Transporter of goods.

**casualty insurance** Covers property loss due to causes other than fire or the elements.

**cause of action** The ground on which an action may be sustained.

**caveat emptor** "Let the buyer beware." This maxim is more applicable to judicial sales, auctions, and the like than to sales of consumer goods, where strict liability, warranty, and other laws protect.

**certificate of deposit** A written acknowledgment by a bank or banker of a deposit with promise to pay to depositor, to his order, or to some other person or to his order. UCC §3-104(2)(c).

**certificate of title** Official representation of ownership.

**certification** Acceptance of a check by a drawee bank.

**certification of incorporation** See **articles of incorporation.**

**certification mark** Distinctive symbol, word, or design used with goods or services to certify specific characteristics.

**certiorari** "To be informed of." A writ of common law origin issued by a superior to an inferior court requiring the latter to produce a certified record of a particular case tried therein. It is most commonly used to refer to the Supreme Court of the United States, which uses the writ of certiorari as a discretionary device to choose the cases it wishes to hear.

**chancery** Equity; equitable jurisdiction; a court of equity; the system of jurisprudence administered in courts of equity.

**charging order** Judicial lien against a partner's interest in the partnership.

**charter** An instrument emanating from the sovereign power, in the nature of a grant. A charter differs from a constitution in that the former is granted by the sovereign, while the latter is established by the people themselves.

*Corporate law* An act of a legislature creating a corporation or creating and defining the franchise of a corporation. Also a corporation's constitution or organic law; that is to say, the articles of incorporation taken in connection with the law under which the corporation was organized.

**chattel mortgage** A pre-Uniform Commercial Code security device whereby the mortgagee took a security interest in personal property of the mortgagor. Such security device has generally been superseded by other types of security agreements under UCC Article 9 (Secured Transactions).

**chattel paper** Writings that evidence both a debt and a security interest.

**check** A draft drawn upon a bank and payable on demand, signed by the maker or drawer, containing an unconditional promise to pay a sum certain in money to the order of the payee. UCC §3-104(2)(b).

*Cashier's check* A bank's own check drawn on itself and signed by the cashier or other authorized official. It is a direct obligation of the bank.

**C. & F.** Cost and freight; a shipping contract.

**C.I.F.** Cost, insurance, and freight; a shipping contract.

**civil law** Laws concerned with civil or private rights and remedies, as contrasted with criminal laws.

The system of jurisprudence administered in the Roman empire, particularly as set forth in the compilation of Justinian and his successors, as distinguished from the common law of England and the canon law. The civil law (Civil Code) is followed by Louisiana.

**claim** A right to payment.

**clearinghouse** An association of banks for the purpose of settling accounts on a daily basis.

**close corporation** See **corporation.**

**closed-ended credit** Credit extended to debtor for a specific period of time.

**closed shop** Employer can only hire union members.

**C.O.D.** Collect on delivery; generally a shipping contract.

**code** A compilation of all permanent laws in force consolidated and classified according to subject matter. Many states have published official codes of all laws in force, including the common law and statutes as judicially interpreted, which have been compiled by code commissions and enacted by the legislatures.

**codicil** A supplement or an addition to a will; it may explain, modify, add to, subtract from, qualify, alter, restrain, or revoke provisions in an existing will. It must be executed with the same formalities as a will.

**cognovit judgment** Written authority by debtor for entry of judgment against him in the event he defaults in payment. Such provision in a debt instrument on default confers judgment against the debtor.

**collateral** Secondarily liable; liable only if the party with primary liability does not perform.

**collateral (security)** Personal property subject to security interest.

*Banking* Some form of security in addition to the personal obligation of the borrower.

**collateral promise** Undertaking to be secondarily liable, that is, liable if the principal debtor does not perform.

**collecting bank** Any bank, except the payor bank, handling the item for collection. UCC §4-105(d).

**collective mark** Distinctive symbol used to indicate membership in an organization.

**collision insurance** Protects the owner of an automobile against damage due to contact with other vehicles or objects.
**commerce power** Exclusive power granted by the U.S. Constitution to the federal government to regulate commerce with foreign countries and among the states.
**commercial bailment** Bailment in which parties derive a mutual benefit.
**commercial impracticability** Performance can only be accomplished with unforeseen and unjust hardship.
**commercial law** A phrase used to designate the whole body of substantive jurisprudence (*e.g.,* Uniform Commercial Code; Truth in Lending Act) applicable to the rights, intercourse, and relations of persons engaged in commerce, trade, or mercantile pursuits. See **Uniform Commercial Code**.
**commercial paper** Bills of exchange (*i.e.*, drafts), promissory notes, bank checks, and other negotiable instruments for the payment of money, which, by their form and on their face, purport to be such instruments. UCC Article 3 is the general law governing commercial paper.
**commercial reasonableness** Judgment of reasonable persons familiar with the business transaction.
**commercial speech** Expression related to the economic interests of the speaker and its audience.
**common carrier** Carrier open to the general public.
**common law** Body of law originating in England and derived from judicial decisions. As distinguished from statutory law created by the enactment of legislatures, the common law comprises the judgments and decrees of the courts recognizing, affirming, and enforcing usages and customs of immemorial antiquity.
**community property** Rights of a spouse in property acquired by the other during marriage.
**comparable worth** Equal pay for jobs of equal value to the employer.
**comparative negligence** Under comparative negligence statutes or doctrines, negligence is measured in terms of percentage, and any damages allowed shall be diminished in proportion to amount of negligence attributable to the person for whose injury, damage, or death recovery is sought.
**complainant** One who applies to the courts for legal redress by filing a complaint (*i.e.*, plaintiff).
**complaint** The pleading which sets forth a claim for relief. Such complaint (whether it be the original claim, counterclaim, cross-claim, or third-party claim) shall contain (1) a short, plain statement of the grounds upon which the court's jurisdiction depends, unless the court already has jurisdiction and the claim needs no new grounds of jurisdiction to support it, (2) a short, plain statement of the claim showing that the pleader is entitled to relief, and (3) a demand for judgment for the relief to which he deems himself entitled. Fed.R. Civil P. 8(a). The complaint, together with the summons, is required to be served on the defendant. Rule 4.
**composition** Agreement between debtor and two or more of her creditors that each will take a portion of his claim as full payment.
**compulsory arbitration** Arbitration required by statute for specific types of disputes.
**computer crime** Crime committed against or through the use of a computer or computer/services.
**concealment** Fraudulent failure to disclose a material fact.
**conciliation** Nonbinding process in which a third party acts as an intermediary between disputing parties.
**concurrent jurisdiction** Authority of more than one court to hear the same case.
**condition** An uncertain event which affects the duty of performance.
*Concurrent conditions* The parties are to perform simultaneously.
*Express condition* Performance is contingent on the happening or nonhappening of a stated event.
**condition precedent** An event which must occur or not occur before performance is due; event or events (presentment, dishonor, notice of dishonor) which must occur to hold a secondary party liable to commercial paper.
**condition subsequent** An event which terminates a duty of performance.
**conditional acceptance** An acceptance of an offer contingent upon the acceptance of an additional or different term.
**conditional contract** Obligations are contingent upon a stated event.
**conditional guarantor of collection** Surety liable to creditor only after creditor exhausts his legal remedies against the principal debtor.
**confession of judgment** Written agreement by debtor authorizing creditor to obtain a court judgment in the event debtor defaults. See also **cognovit judgment**.
**confiscation** Governmental taking of foreign-owned property without payment.
**conflict of laws** That branch of jurisprudence, arising from the diversity of the laws of different nations, states, or jurisdictions, that reconciles the inconsistencies, or decides which law is to govern in a particular case.
**confusion** Results when goods belonging to two or more owners become so intermixed that the property of any of them no longer can be identified except as part of a mass of like goods.
**consanguinity** Kinship; blood relationship; the connection or relation of persons descended from the same stock or common ancestor.
**consensual arbitration** Arbitration voluntarily entered into by the parties.
**consent** Voluntary and knowing willingness that an act should be done.
**conservator** Appointed by court to manage affairs of incompetent or to liquidate business.
**consideration** The cause, motive, price, or impelling influence which induces a contracting party to enter into a contract. Some right, interest, profit, or benefit accruing to one party or some forbearance, detriment, loss, or responsibility given, suffered, or undertaken by the other.
**consignee** One to whom a consignment is made. Person named in bill of lading to whom or to whose order the bill promises delivery. UCC §7-102(b).
**consignment** Ordinarily implies an agency; denotes that property is committed to the consignee for care or sale.
**consignor** One who sends or makes a consignment; a shipper of goods. The person named in a bill of lading as the person from whom the goods have been received for shipment. UCC §7-102(c).
**consolidation** In *corporate law*, the combination of two or more corporations into a newly created corporation. Thus, A Corporation and B Corporation consolidate to form C Corporation.
**constitution** Fundamental law of a government establishing its powers and limitations.
**constructive** That which is established by the mind of the law in its act of *construing* facts, conduct, circumstances, or instruments. That which has not in its essential nature the character assigned to it, but acquires such character in consequence of the way in which it is regarded by a rule or policy of law; hence, inferred, implied, or made out by legal interpretation; the word "legal" being sometimes used here in lieu of "constructive."
**constructive assent** An assent or consent imputed to a party from a construction or interpretation of his conduct; as distinguished from one which he actually expresses.
**constructive conditions** Conditions in contracts which are neither expressed nor implied but rather are imposed by law to meet the ends of justice.
**constructive delivery** Term comprehending all those acts which, although not truly conferring a real possession of the vendee, have been held by construction of law to be equivalent to acts of real delivery.
**constructive eviction** Failure by the landlord in any obligation under the lease that causes a substantial and lasting injury to the tenant's enjoyment of the premises.
**constructive notice** Knowledge imputed by law.
**constructive trust** Arising by operation of law to prevent unjust enrichment. See also **trustee**.
**consumer goods** Goods bought or used for personal, family, or household purposes.

**consumer product** Tangible personal property normally used for family, household, or personal purposes.
**contingent remainder** Remainder interest, conditional upon the happening of an event in addition to the termination of the preceding estate.
**contract** An agreement between two or more persons which creates an obligation to do or not to do a particular thing. Its essentials are competent parties, subject matter, a legal consideration, mutuality of agreement, and mutuality of obligation.
*Destination contract* Seller is required to tender delivery of the goods at a particular destination; seller bears the expense and risk of loss.
*Executed contract* Fully performed by all of the parties.
*Executory contract* Contract partially or entirely unperformed by one or more of the parties.
*Express contract* Agreement of parties that is expressed in words either in writing or orally.
*Formal contract* Agreement which is legally binding because of its particular form or mode or expression.
*Implied-in-fact contract* Contract where agreement of the parties is inferred from their conduct.
*Informal contract* All oral or written contracts other than formal contracts.
*Installment contract* Goods are delivered in separate lots.
*Integrated contract* Complete and total agreement.
*Output contract* A contract in which one party agrees to sell his entire output and the other agrees to buy it; it is not illusory, though it may be indefinite.
*Quasi contract* Obligation not based upon contract that is imposed to avoid injustice.
*Requirements contract* A contract in which one party agrees to purchase his total requirements from the other party; hence, such a contract is binding, not illusory.
*Substituted contract* An agreement between the parties to rescind their old contract and replace it with a new contract.
*Unconscionable contract* One which no sensible person not under delusion, duress, or in distress would make, and such as no honest and fair person would accept. A contract the terms of which are excessively unreasonable, overreaching, and one-sided.
*Unenforceable contract* Contract for the breach of which the law does not provide a remedy.
*Unilateral and bilateral* A unilateral contract is one in which one party makes an express engagement or undertakes a performance, without receiving in return any express engagement or promise of performance from the other. Bilateral (or reciprocal) contracts are those by which the parties expressly enter into mutual engagements.
**contract clause** Prohibition against the states' retroactively modifying public and private contracts.
**contractual liability** Obligation on a negotiable instrument, based upon signing the instrument.
**contribution** Payment from cosureties of their proportionate share.
**contributory negligence** An act or omission amounting to a want of ordinary care on the part of the complaining party, which, concurring with defendant's negligence, is proximate cause of injury.

The defense of contributory negligence is an absolute bar to any recovery in some states; because of this, it has been replaced by the doctrine of comparative negligence in many other states.
**conversion** Unauthorized and wrongful exercise of dominion and control over another's personal property, to exclusion of or inconsistent with rights of the owner.
**convertible bond** Bond that may be exchanged for other securities of the corporation.
**copyright** Exclusive right granted by federal government to authors of original works including literary, musical, dramatic, pictorial, graphic, sculptural, and film works.
**corporation** A legal entity ordinarily consisting of an association of numerous individuals. Such entity is regarded as having a personality and existence distinct from that of its several members and is vested with the capacity of continuous succession, irrespective of changes in its membership, either in perpetuity or for a limited term of years.
*Closely held or close corporation* Corporation that is owned by few shareholders and whose shares are not actively traded.
*Corporation de facto* One existing under color of law and in pursuance of an effort made in good faith to organize a corporation under the statute. Such a corporation is not subject to collateral attack.
*Corporation de jure* That which exists by reason of full compliance with requirements of an existing law permitting organization of such corporation.
*Domestic corporation* Corporation created under the laws of a given state.
*Foreign corporation* Corporation created under the laws of any other state, government, or country.
*Publicly held corporation* Corporation whose shares are owned by a large number of people and are widely traded.
*Subchapter S corporation* A small business corporation which, under certain conditions, may elect to have its undistributed taxable income taxed to its shareholders. I.R.C. §1371 et seq. Of major significance is the fact that Subchapter S status usually avoids the corporate income tax, and corporate losses can be claimed by the shareholders.
*Subsidiary and parent* Subsidiary corporation is one in which another corporation (called parent corporation) owns at least a majority of the shares and over which it thus has control.
**corrective advertising** Disclosure in an advertisement that previous ads were deceptive.
**costs** A pecuniary allowance, made to the successful party (and recoverable from the losing party), for his expenses in prosecuting or defending an action or a distinct proceeding within an action. Generally, "costs" do not include attorneys' fees unless such fees are by a statute denominated costs or are by statute allowed to be recovered as costs in the case.
**cosureties** Two or more sureties bound for the same debt of a principal debtor.
**co-tenants** Persons who hold title concurrently.
**counterclaim** A claim presented by a defendant in opposition to or deduction from the claim of the plaintiff.
**counteroffer** A statement by the offeree which has the legal effect of rejecting the offer and of proposing a new offer to the offeror. However, the provisions of UCC §2-207(2) modify this principle by providing that the "additional terms are to be construed as proposals for addition to the contract."
**course of dealing** A sequence of previous acts and conduct between the parties to a particular transaction which is fairly to be regarded as establishing a common basis of understanding for interpreting their expressions and other conduct. UCC §1-205(1).
**course of performance** Conduct between the parties concerning performance of the particular contract.
**court above—court below** In appellate practice, the "court above" is the one to which a cause is removed for review, whether by appeal, writ of error, or certiorari, while the "court below" is the one from which the case is being removed.
**covenant** Used primarily with respect to promises in conveyances or other instruments dealing with real estate.
*Covenants against encumbrances* A stipulation against all rights to or interests in the land which may subsist in third persons to the diminution of the value of the estate granted.
*Covenant appurtenant* A covenant which is connected with land of the grantor, not in gross. A covenant running with the land and binding heirs, executors, and assigns of the immediate parties.
*Covenant for further assurance* An undertaking, in the form of a covenant, on the part of the vendor of real estate to do such further acts for

the purpose of perfecting the purchaser's title as the latter may reasonably require.

*Covenant for possession* A covenant by which the grantee or lessee is granted possession.

*Covenant for quiet enjoyment* An assurance against the consequences of a defective title, and against any disturbances thereupon.

*Covenants for title* Covenants usually inserted in a conveyance of land, on the part of the grantor, and binding him for the completeness, security, and continuance of the title transferred to the grantee. They comprise covenants for seisin, for right to convey, against encumbrances, or quiet enjoyment, sometimes for further assurance, and almost always of warranty.

*Covenant in gross* Such as do not run with the land.

*Covenant of right to convey* An assurance by the covenantor that the grantor has sufficient capacity and title to convey the estate which he by his deed undertakes to convey.

*Covenant of seisin* An assurance to the purchaser that the grantor has the very estate in quantity and quality which he purports to convey.

*Covenant of warranty* An assurance by the grantor of an estate that the grantee shall enjoy the same without interruption by virtue of paramount title.

*Covenant running with land* A covenant which goes with the land, as being annexed to the estate, and which cannot be separated from the land or transferred without it. A covenant is said to run with the land when not only the original parties or their representatives, but each successive owner of the land, will be entitled to its benefit, or be liable (as the case may be) to its obligation. Such a covenant is said to be one which "touches and concerns" the land itself, so that its benefit or obligation passes with the ownership. Essentials are that the grantor and grantee must have intended that the covenant run with the land, the covenant must affect or concern the land with which it runs, and there must be privity of estate between the party claiming the benefit and the party who rests under the burden.

**covenant not to compete** Agreement to refrain from entering into a competing trade, profession, or business.

**cover** Buyer's purchase of goods in substitution for those not delivered by breaching seller.

**credit beneficiary** See **third-party beneficiary**.

**creditor** Any entity having a claim against the debtor.

**crime** An act or omission in violation of a public law and punishable by the government.

**criminal duress** Coercion by threat of serious bodily injury.

**criminal intent** Desired or virtually certain consequences of one's conduct.

**criminal law** The law that involves offenses against the entire community.

**cure** The right of a seller under the UCC to correct a nonconforming delivery of goods to buyer within the contract period. §2-508.

**curtesy** Husband's estate in the real property of his wife.

**cy-pres** As near (as possible). Rule for the construction of instruments in equity, by which the intention of the party is carried out *as near as may be*, when it would be impossible or illegal to give it literal effect.

**damage** Loss, injury, or deterioration caused by the negligence, design, or accident of one person, with respect to another's person or property. The word is to be distinguished from its plural, "damages," which means a compensation in money for a loss or damage.

**damages** Money sought as a remedy for breach of contract or for tortious acts.

*Actual damages* Real, substantial, and just damages, or the amount awarded to a complainant in compensation for his actual and real loss or injury, as opposed, on the one hand, to "nominal" damages and, on the other, to "exemplary" or "punitive" damages. Synonymous with "compensatory damages" and "general damages."

*Benefit-of-the-bargain damages* Difference between the value received and the value of the fraudulent party's performance as represented.

*Compensatory damages* Compensatory damages are such as will compensate the injured party for the injury sustained, and nothing more; such as will simply make good or replace the loss caused by the wrong or injury.

*Consequential damages* Such damage, loss, or injury as does not flow directly and immediately from the act of the party, but only from some of the consequences or results of such act. Consequential damages resulting from a seller's breach of contract include any loss resulting from general or particular requirements and needs of which the seller at the time of contracting had reason to know and which could not reasonably be prevented by cover or otherwise, and injury to person or property proximately resulting from any breach of warranty. UCC §2-715(2).

*Exemplary or punitive damages* Damages other than compensatory damages which may be awarded against a person to punish him for outrageous conduct.

*Expectancy damages* Calculable by subtracting the injured party's actual dollar position as a result of the breach from that party's projected dollar position had performance occurred.

*Foreseeable damages* Loss of which the party in breach had reason to know when the contract was made.

*Incidental damages* Under UCC §2-710, such damages include any commercially reasonable charges, expenses, or commissions incurred in stopping delivery, in the transportation, care, and custody of goods after the buyer's breach, in connection with the return or resale of the goods, or otherwise resulting from the breach. Also, such damages, resulting from a seller's breach of contract, include expenses reasonably incurred in inspection, receipt, transportation, and care and custody of goods rightfully rejected, any commercially reasonable charges, expenses, or commissions in connection with effecting cover, and any other reasonable expense incident to the delay or other breach. UCC §2-715(1).

*Irreparable damages* In the law pertaining to injunctions, damages for which no certain pecuniary standard exists for measurement.

*Liquidated damages and penalties* Damages for breach by either party may be liquidated in the agreement but only at an amount which is reasonable in the light of the anticipated or actual harm caused by the breach, the difficulties of proof of loss, and the inconvenience or nonfeasibility of otherwise obtaining an adequate remedy. A term fixing unreasonably large liquidated damages is void as a penalty. UCC §2-718(1).

*Mitigation of damages* A plaintiff may not recover damages for the effects of an injury which she reasonably could have avoided or substantially ameliorated. This limitation on recovery is generally denominated as "mitigation of damages" or "avoidance of consequences."

*Nominal damages* A small sum awarded where a contract has been breached but the loss is negligible or unproven.

*Out-of-pocket damages* Difference between the value received and the value given.

*Reliance damages* Contract damages placing the injured party in as good a position as he would have been in had the contract not been made.

*Treble damages* Three times actual loss.

**de facto** "In fact, in deed, actually." This phrase is used to characterize an officer, a government, a past action, or a state of affairs which must be accepted for all practical purposes but which is illegal or illegitimate. See also **corporation**, *corporation de facto*.

**de jure** Descriptive of a condition in which there has been total compliance with all requirements of law. In this sense it is the contrary of *de facto*. See also **corporation**, *corporation de jure*.

**de novo** Anew; afresh; a second time.

**debenture** Unsecured bond.

**debt security** Any form of corporate security reflected as debt on the books of the corporation in contrast to equity securities such as stock; *e.g.*, bonds, notes, and debentures are debt securities.

**debtor** Person who owes payment or performance of an obligation.
**deceit** A fraudulent and cheating misrepresentation, artifice, or device used to deceive and trick one who is ignorant of the true facts, to the prejudice and damage of the party imposed upon. See also **fraud**; **misrepresentation**.
**decree** Decision of a court of equity.
**deed** A conveyance of realty; a writing, signed by a grantor, whereby title to realty is transferred from one party to another.
**deed of trust** Interest in real property which is conveyed to a third person as trustee for the creditor.
**defamation** Injury of a person's reputation by publication of false statements.
**default judgment** Judgment against a defendant who fails to respond to a complaint.
**defendant** The party against whom legal action is sought.
**definite term** Lease that automatically expires at end of the term.
**delectus personae** Partner's right to choose who may become a member of the partnership.
**delegatee** Third party to whom the delegator's duty is delegated.
**delegation of duties** Transferring to another all or part of one's duties arising under a contract.
**delegator** Party delegating his duty to a third party.
**delivery** The physical or constructive transfer of an instrument or of goods from one person to another. See also **constructive delivery**.
**demand** Request for payment made by the holder of the instrument.
**demand paper** Payable on request.
**demurrer** An allegation of a defendant that even if the facts as stated in the pleading to which objection is taken be true, their legal consequences are not such as to require the demurring party to answer them or to proceed further with the cause.

The Federal Rules of Civil Procedure do not provide for the use of a demurrer, but provide an equivalent to a general demurrer in the motion to dismiss for failure to state a claim on which relief may be granted. Fed.R. Civil P. 12(b).

**deposition** The testimony of a witness taken upon interrogatories, not in court, but intended to be used in court. See also **discovery**.
**depository bank** The first bank to which an item is transferred for collection even though it may also be the payor bank. UCC §4-105(a).
**descent** Succession to the ownership of an estate by inheritance or by any act of law, as distinguished from "purchase."

Descents are of two sorts, *lineal* and *collateral*. Lineal descent is descent in a direct or right line, as from father or grandfather to son or grandson. Collateral descent is descent in a collateral or oblique line, that is, up to the common ancestor and then down from him, as from brother to brother, or between cousins.

**design defect** Plans or specifications inadequate to ensure the product's safety.
**devise** A testamentary disposition of land or realty; a gift of real property by the last will and testament of the donor. When used as a noun, means a testamentary disposition of real or personal property; when used as a verb, means to dispose of real or personal property by will.
**dictum** Generally used as an abbreviated form of *obiter dictum*, "a remark by the way"; that is, an observation or remark made by a judge which does not embody the resolution or determination of the court and which is made without argument or full consideration of the point.
**directed verdict** In a case in which the party with the burden of proof has failed to present a prima facie case for jury consideration, the trial judge may order the entry of a verdict without allowing the jury to consider it because, as a matter of law, there can be only one such verdict. Fed.R. Civil P. 50(a).
**disaffirmance** Avoidance of a contract.
**discharge** Termination of certain allowed claims against a debtor.
**disclaimer** Negation of warranty.
**discount** A discount by a bank means a drawback or deduction made upon its advances or loans of money, upon negotiable paper or other evidences of debt payable at a future day, which are transferred to the bank.
**discovery** The pretrial devices that can be used by one party to obtain facts and information about the case from the other party in order to assist the party's preparation for trial. Under the Federal Rules of Civil Procedure, tools of discovery include depositions upon oral and written questions, written interrogatories, production of documents or things, permission to enter upon land or other property, physical and mental examinations, and requests for admission. Rules 26–37.
**dishonor** To refuse to accept or pay a draft or to pay a promissory note when duly presented. UCC §3-507(1); §4-210. See also **protest**.
**disparagement** Publication of false statements resulting in harm to another's monetary interests.
**disputed debt** Obligation whose existence or amount is contested.
**dissenting shareholder** One who opposes a fundamental change and has the right to receive the fair value of her shares.
**dissolution** The dissolution of a partnership is the change in the relation of the partners caused by any partner's ceasing to be associated with the carrying on, as distinguished from the winding up, of the business. See also **winding up**.
**distribution** Transfer of partnership property from the partnership to a partner; transfer of property from a corporation to any of its shareholders.
**dividend** The payment designated by the board of directors of a corporation to be distributed *pro rata* among a class or classes of the shares outstanding.
**document** Document of title.
**document of title** Instrument evidencing ownership of the document and the goods it covers.
**domicile** That place where a person has his true, fixed, and permanent home and principal establishment, and to which whenever he is absent he has the intention of returning.
**dominant** Land whose owner has rights in other land.
**donee** Recipient of a gift.
**donee beneficiary** See **third-party beneficiary**.
**donor** Maker of a gift.
**dormant partner** One who is both a silent and a secret partner.
**dower** A species of life-estate which a woman is, by law, entitled to claim on the death of her husband, in the lands and tenements of which he was seised in fee during the marriage, and which her issue, if any, might by possibility have inherited.

Dower has been abolished in the majority of the states and materially altered in most of the others.

**draft** A written order by the first party, called the drawer, instructing a second party, called the drawee (such as a bank), to pay a third party, called the payee. An order to pay a sum certain in money, signed by a drawer, payable on demand or at a definite time, and to order or bearer. UCC §3-104.
**drawee** A person to whom a bill of exchange or draft is directed, and who is requested to pay the amount of money therein mentioned. The drawee of a check is the bank on which it is drawn.

When a drawee accepts, he engages that he will pay the instrument according to its tenor at the time of his engagement or as completed. UCC §3-413(1).

**drawer** The person who draws a bill or draft. The drawer of a check is the person who signs it.

The drawer engages that upon dishonor of the draft and any necessary notice of dishonor or protest, he will pay the amount of the draft to the holder or to any indorser who takes it up. The drawer may disclaim this liability by drawing without recourse. UCC §3-413(2).

**due negotiation** Transfer of a negotiable document in the regular course of business to a holder, who takes in good faith, without notice of any defense or claim, and for value.

**duress** Unlawful constraint exercised upon a person, whereby he is forced to do some act against his will.

*Physical duress* Coercion involving physical force or the threat of physical force.

**duty** Legal obligation requiring a person to perform or refrain from performing an act.

**earned surplus** Undistributed net profits, income, gains, and losses.

**earnest** The payment of a part of the price of goods sold, or the delivery of part of such goods, for the purpose of binding the contract.

**easement** A right in the owner of one parcel of land, by reason of such ownership, to use the land of another for a special purpose not inconsistent with a general property right in the owner. This right is distinguishable from a "license," which merely confers a personal privilege to do some act on the land.

*Affirmative easement* One where the servient estate must permit something to be done thereon, as to pass over it, or to discharge water on it.

*Appurtenant easement* An incorporeal right which is attached to a superior right and inheres in land to which it is attached and is in the nature of a covenant running with the land.

*Easement by necessity* Such arises by operation of law when land conveyed is completely shut off from access to any road by land retained by the grantor or by land of the grantor and that of a stranger.

*Easement by prescription* A mode of acquiring title to property by immemorial or long-continued enjoyment; refers to personal usage restricted to claimant and his ancestors or grantors.

*Easement in gross* An easement in gross is not appurtenant to any estate in land or does not belong to any person by virtue of ownership of an estate in other land but is a mere personal interest in or a right to use the land of another; it is purely personal and usually ends with death of grantee.

*Easement of access* Right of ingress and egress to and from the premises of a lot owner to a street appurtenant to the land of the lot owner.

**ejectment** An action to determine whether the title to certain land is in the plaintiff or is in the defendant.

**electronic funds transfer** A transaction with a financial institution by means of computer, telephone, or other electronic instrument.

**emancipation** The act by which an infant is liberated from the control of a parent or guardian and made his own master.

**embezzlement** The taking, in violation of a trust, of the property of one's employer.

**emergency** Sudden, unexpected event calling for immediate action.

**eminent domain** Right of the people or government to take private property for public use upon giving fair consideration.

**employment discrimination** Hiring, firing, compensating, promoting, or training of employees based on race, color, sex, religion, or national origin.

**employment relationship** One in which employer has right to control the physical conduct of employee.

**endowment contract** Agreement to pay insured a lump sum upon reaching a specified age or in event of death.

**entirety** Used to designate that which the law considers as a single whole incapable of being divided into parts.

**entrapment** Induced by a government official into committing a crime.

**entrusting** Transfer of possession of goods to a merchant who deals in goods of that kind and who may in turn transfer valid title to a buyer in the ordinary course of business.

**equal pay** Equivalent pay for the same work.

**equal protection** Requirement that similarly situated persons be treated similarly by government action.

**equipment** Goods used primarily in business.

**equitable** Just, fair, and right. Existing in equity; available or sustainable only in equity, or only upon the rules and principles of equity.

**equity** Justice administered according to fairness, as contrasted with the strictly formulated rules of common law. It is based on a system of rules and principles which originated in England as an alternative to the harsh rules of common law and which were based on what was fair in a particular situation.

**equity of redemption** The right of the mortgagor of an estate to redeem the same after it has been forfeited, at law, by a breach of the condition of the mortgage, upon paying the amount of debt, interest, and costs.

**equity securities** Stock or similar security, in contrast to debt securities such as bonds, notes, and debentures.

**error** A mistake of law, or a false or irregular application of it, such as vitiates legal proceedings and warrants reversal of the judgment.

*Harmless error* In appellate practice, an error committed in the progress of the trial below which was not prejudicial to the rights of the party assigning it and for which, therefore, the appellate court will not reverse the judgment.

*Reversible error* In appellate practice, such an error as warrants the appellate court's reversal of the judgment before it.

**escrow** A system of document transfer in which a deed, bond, or funds is or are delivered to a third person to hold until all conditions in a contract are fulfilled; *e.g.*, delivery of deed to escrow agent under installment land sale contract until full payment for land is made.

**estate** The degree, quantity, nature, and extent of interest which a person has in real and personal property. An estate in lands, tenements, and hereditaments signifies such interest as the tenant has therein.

Also, the total property of whatever kind that is owned by a decedent prior to the distribution of that property in accordance with the terms of a will or, when there is no will, by the laws of inheritance in the state of domicile of the decedent.

*Future estate* An estate limited to commence in possession at a future day, either without the intervention of a precedent estate or on the determination by lapse of time, or otherwise, of a precedent estate created at the same time. Examples include reversions and remainders.

**estoppel** A bar or impediment raised by the law which precludes a person from alleging or from denying a certain fact or state of facts, in consequence of his or her previous allegation, denial, conduct, or admission, or in consequence of a final adjudication of the matter in a court of law. See also **waiver**.

**eviction** Dispossession by process of law; the act of depriving a person of the possession of lands which he has held, pursuant to the judgment of a court.

**evidence** Any species of proof or probative matter legally presented at the trial of an issue by the act of the parties and through the medium of witnesses, records, documents, concrete objects, etc., for the purpose of inducing belief in the minds of the court or jury as to the parties' contention.

**exception** A formal objection to the action of the court, during the trial of a cause, in refusing a request or overruling an objection; implying that the party excepting does not acquiesce in the decision of the court but will seek to procure its reversal, and that he means to save the benefit of his request or objection in some future proceeding.

**exclusionary rule** Prohibition of illegally obtained evidence.

**exclusive dealing** Sole right to sell goods in a defined market.

**exclusive jurisdiction** Such jurisdiction that permits only one court (state or federal) to hear a case.

**exculpatory clause** Excusing oneself from fault or liability.

**execution** *Execution of contract* includes performance of all acts necessary to render it complete as an instrument; implies that nothing more need be done to make the contract complete and effective.

*Execution upon a money judgment* is the legal process of enforcing the judgment, usually by seizing and selling property of the debtor.

**executive order** Legislation issued by the president or a governor.

**executor** A person appointed by a testator to carry out the directions and requests in his will and to dispose of the property according to his testamentary provisions after his decease. The female designation is executrix. A person appointed by the court in an intestacy situation is called the administrator(rix).

**executory** That which is yet to be executed or performed; that which remains to be carried into operation or effect; incomplete; depending upon a future performance or event. The opposite of executed.
**executory contract** See **contracts**.
**executory promise** Unperformed obligation.
**exemplary damages** See **damages**.
**exoneration** Relieved of liability.
**express** Manifested by direct and appropriate language, as distinguished from that which is inferred from conduct. The word is usually contrasted with "implied."
**express warranty** Explicitly made contractual promise regarding property or contract rights transferred; in a sale of goods, an affirmation of fact or a promise about the goods or a description, including a sample, of goods which becomes part of the basis of the bargain.
**expropriation** Governmental taking of foreign-owned property for a public purpose and with payment.
**ex-ship** Risk of loss passes to buyer when the goods leaving the ship. See UCC §2-322. See also **F.A.S.**
**extortion** Making threats to obtain property.

**fact** An event that took place or a thing that exists.
**false imprisonment** Intentional interference with a person's freedom of movement by unlawful confinement.
**false light** Offensive publicity placing another in a false light.
**false pretenses** Intentional misrepresentation of fact in order to cheat another.
**farm products** Crops, livestock, or stock used or produced in farming.
**F.A.S.** Free alongside. Term used in sales price quotations indicating that the price includes all costs of transportation and delivery of the goods alongside the ship. See UCC §2-319(2).
**federal preemption** First right of the federal government to regulate matters within its powers to the possible exclusion of state regulation.
**federal question** Any case arising under the Constitution, statutes, or treaties of the United States.
**fee simple**

*Absolute* A fee simple absolute is an estate that is unlimited as to duration, disposition, and descendibility. It is the largest estate and most extensive interest that can be enjoyed in land.

*Conditional* Type of transfer in which grantor conveys fee simple on condition that something be done or not done.

*Defeasible* Type of fee grant which may be defeated on the happening of an event. An estate which may last forever, but which may end upon the happening of a specified event, is a "fee simple defeasible."

*Determinable* Created by conveyance which contains words effective to create a fee simple and, in addition, a provision for automatic expiration of the estate on occurrence of stated event.

**fee tail** An estate of inheritance, descending only to a certain class or classes of heirs; *e.g.*, an estate is conveyed or devised "to A. and the heirs of his body," or "to A. and the heirs male of his body," or "to A., and the heirs female of his body."
**fellow servant rule** Common law defense relieving employer from liability to an employee for injuries caused by negligence of fellow employee.
**felony** Serious crime.
**fiduciary** A person or institution who manages money or property for another and who must exercise in such management activity a standard of care imposed by law or contract; *e.g.*, executor of estate; receiver in bankruptcy; trustee.
**fiduciary duty** Duty of utmost loyalty and good faith, such as that owed by a fiduciary such as an agent to her principal.
**field warehouse** Secured party takes possession of the goods but the debtor has access to the goods.
**final credit** Payment of the instrument by the payor bank.
**financing statement** Under the Uniform Commercial Code, a financing statement is used under Article 9 to reflect a public record that there is a security interest or claim to the goods in question to secure a debt. The financing statement is filed by the security holder with the secretary of state or with a similar public body; thus filed, it becomes public record. See also **secured transaction**.
**fire (property) insurance** Provides protection against loss due to fire or other related perils.
**firm offer** Irrevocable offer to sell or buy goods by a merchant in a signed writing which gives assurance that it will not be rescinded for up to three months.
**fitness for a particular purpose** Goods are fit for a stated purpose, provided that the seller selects the product knowing the buyer's intended use and that the buyer is relying on the seller's judgment.
**fixture** An article in the nature of personal property which has been so annexed to realty that it is regarded as a part of the land. Examples include a furnace affixed to a house or other building, counters permanently affixed to the floor of a store, and a sprinkler system installed in a building. UCC §9-313(1)(a).

*Trade fixtures* Such chattels as merchants usually possess and annex to the premises occupied by them to enable them to store, handle, and display their goods, which generally are removable without material injury to the premises.

**F.O.B.** Free on board at some location (for example, F.O.B shipping point; F.O.B destination); the invoice price includes delivery at seller's expense to that location. Title to goods usually passes from seller to buyer at the F.O.B location. UCC §2-319(1).
**foreclosure** Procedure by which mortgaged property is sold on default of mortgagor in satisfaction of mortgage debt.
**forgery** Intentional falsification of a document with intent to defraud.
**four unities** Time, title, interest, and possession.
**franchise** A privilege granted or sold, such as to use a name or to sell products or services. The right given by a manufacturer or supplier to a retailer to use his products and name on terms and conditions mutually agreed upon.
**fraud** Elements include false representation; of a present or past fact; made by defendant; action in reliance thereon by plaintiff; and damage resulting to plaintiff from such misrepresentation.
**fraud in the execution** Misrepresentation that deceives the other party as to the nature of a document evidencing the contract.
**fraud in the inducement** Misrepresentation regarding the subject matter of a contract that induces the other party to enter into the contract.
**fraudulent misrepresentation** False statement made with knowledge of its falsity and intent to mislead.
**freehold** An estate for life or in fee. It must possess two qualities: (1) immobility, that is, the property must be either land or some interest issuing out of or annexed to land; and (2) indeterminate duration.
**friendly fire** Fire contained where it is intended to be.
**frustration of purpose doctrine** Excuses a promisor in certain situations when the objectives of contract have been utterly defeated by circumstances arising after formation of the agreement, and performance is excused under this rule even though there is no impediment to actual performance.
**full warranty** One under which warrantor will repair the product and, if unsuccessful, will replace it or refund its cost.
**fungibles** With respect to goods or securities, those of which any unit is, by nature or usage of trade, the equivalent of any other like unit. UCC §1-201(17); *e.g.,* a bushel of wheat or other grain.
**future estate** See **estate**.

**garnishment** A statutory proceeding whereby a person's property, money, or credits in the possession or control of another are applied to payment of the former's debt to a third person.
**general intangible** Catchall category for collateral not otherwise covered.
**general partner** Member of either a general or limited partnership with unlimited liability for its debts, full management powers, and a right to share in the profits.

**gift** A voluntary transfer of property to another made gratuitously and without consideration. Essential requisites of "gift" are capacity of donor, intention of donor to make gift, completed delivery to or for donee, and acceptance of gift by donee.
**gift causa mortis** A gift in view of death is one which is made in contemplation, fear, or peril of death and with the intent that it shall take effect only in case of the death of the giver.
**good faith** Honesty in fact in conduct or in a transaction.
**good faith purchaser** Buyer who acts honestly, gives value, and takes the goods without notice or knowledge of any defect in the title of his transferor.
**goods** A term of variable content and meaning. It may include every species of personal property, or it may be given a very restricted meaning. Sometimes the meaning of "goods" is extended to include all tangible items, as in the phrase "goods and services."

All things (including specially manufactured goods) which are movable at the time of identification to a contract for sale other than the money in which the price is to be paid, investment securities, and things in action. UCC §2-105(1).
**grantee** Transferee of property.
**grantor** A transferor of property. The creator of a trust is usually designated as the grantor of the trust.
**gratuitous promise** Promise made without consideration.
**group insurance** Covers a number of individuals.
**guaranty** A promise to answer for the payment of some debt, or the performance of some duty, in case of the failure of another person who, in the first instance, is liable for such payment or performance.

The terms *guaranty* and *suretyship* are sometimes used interchangeably; but they should not be confounded. The distinction between contract of suretyship and contract of guaranty is whether or not the undertaking is a joint undertaking with the principal or a separate and distinct contract; if it is the former, it is one of "suretyship," and if the latter, it is one of "guaranty." See also **surety**.
**guardianship** The relationship under which a person (the guardian) is appointed by a court to preserve and control the property of another (the ward).

**heir** A person who succeeds, by the rules of law, to an estate in lands, tenements, or hereditaments, upon the death of his ancestor, by descent and right of relationship.
**holder** Person who is in possession of a document of title or an instrument or an investment security drawn, issued, or indorsed to him or to his order, or to bearer, or in blank. UCC §1-201(20).
**holder in due course** A holder who takes an instrument for value, in good faith, and without notice that it is overdue or has been dishonored or of any defense against or claim to it on the part of any person.
**holograph** A will or deed written entirely by the testator or grantor with his own hand and not witnessed (attested). State laws vary with respect to the validity of the holographic will.
**homicide** Unlawful taking of another's life.
**horizontal privity** Who may bring a cause of action.
**horizontal restraints** Agreements among competitors.
**hostile fire** Any fire outside its intended or usual place.

**identified goods** Designated goods as a part of a particular contract.
**illegal per se** Conclusively presumed unreasonable and therefore illegal.
**illusory promise** Promise imposing no obligation on the promisor.
**implied-in-fact condition** Contingencies understood but not expressed by the parties.
**implied-in-law condition** Contingency that arises from operation of law.
**implied warranty** Obligation imposed by law upon the transferor of property or contract rights; implicit in the sale arising out of certain circumstances.
**implied warranty of habitability** Leased premises are fit for ordinary residential purposes.
**impossibility** Performance that cannot be done.
**in personam** "Against the person." Action seeking judgment against a person involving his personal rights and based on jurisdiction of his person, as distinguished from a judgment against property (*i.e.*, in rem).
**in personam jurisdiction** Jurisdiction based on claims against a person, in contrast to jurisdiction over his property.
**in re** In the affair; in the matter of; concerning; regarding. This is the usual method of entitling a judicial proceeding in which there are no adversary parties, but merely some res concerning which judicial action is to be taken, such as a bankrupt's estate, an estate in the probate court, a proposed public highway, etc.
**in rem** A technical term used to designate proceedings or actions instituted *against the thing*, in contradistinction to personal actions, which are said to be *in personam*.

*Quasi in rem* A term applied to proceedings which are not strictly and purely *in rem*, but are brought against the defendant personally, though the real object is to deal with particular property or subject property to the discharge of claims asserted; for example, foreign attachment, or proceedings to foreclose a mortgage, remove a cloud from title, or effect a partition.

**in rem jurisdiction** Jurisdiction based on claims against property.
**incidental beneficiary** Third party whom the two parties to a contract have no intention of benefiting by their contract.
**income bond** Bond that conditions payment of interest on corporate earnings.
**incontestability clause** The prohibition of an insurer to avoid an insurance policy after a specified period of time.
**indemnification** Duty owed by principal to agent to pay agent for losses incurred while acting as directed by principal.
**indemnify** To reimburse one for a loss already incurred.
**indenture** A written agreement under which bonds and debentures are issued, setting forth maturity date, interest rate, and other terms.
**independent contractor** Person who contracts with another to do a particular job and who is not subject to the control of the other.
**indicia** Signs; indications. Circumstances which point to the existence of a given fact as probable, but not certain.
**indictment** Grand jury charge that the defendant should stand trial.
**indispensable paper** Chattel paper, instruments, and documents.
**indorsee** The person to whom a negotiable instrument, promissory note, bill of lading, etc., is assigned by indorsement.
**indorsement** The act of a payee, drawee, accommodation indorser, or holder of a bill, note, check, or other negotiable instrument, in writing his name upon the back of the same, with or without further or qualifying words, whereby the property in the same is assigned and transferred to another. UCC §3-202 *et seq.*

*Blank indorsement* No indorsee is specified.

*Qualified indorsement* Without recourse, limiting one's liability on the instrument.

*Restrictive indorsement* Limits the rights of the indorser in some manner.

*Special indorsement* Designates an indorsee to be paid.

**infliction of emotional distress** Extreme and outrageous conduct intentionally or recklessly causing severe emotional distress.
**information** Formal accusation of a crime brought by a prosecutor.
**infringement** Unauthorized use.
**injunction** An equitable remedy forbidding the party defendant from doing some act which he is threatening or attempting to commit, or restraining him in the continuance thereof, such act being unjust and inequitable, injurious to the plaintiff, and not such as can be adequately redressed by an action at law.
**innkeeper** Hotel or motel operator.

**inquisitorial system** System in which the judiciary initiates, conducts, and decides cases.
**insider** Relative or general partner of debtor, partnership in which debtor is a partner, or corporation in which debtor is an officer, director, or controlling person.
**insiders** Directors, officers, employees, and agents of the issuer as well as those the issuer has entrusted with information solely for corporate purposes.
**insolvency** Under the UCC, a person is insolvent who either has ceased to pay his debts in the ordinary course of business or cannot pay his debts as they fall due or is insolvent within the meaning of the Federal Bankruptcy Law. UCC §1-201(23).
*Insolvency (bankruptcy)* Total liabilities exceed total value of assets.
*Insolvency (equity)* Inability to pay debts in ordinary course of business or as they become due.
**inspection** Examination of goods to determine whether they conform to a contract.
**instrument** Negotiable instruments, stocks, bonds, and other investment securities.
**insurable interest** Exists where insured derives pecuniary benefit or advantage by preservation and continued existence of property or would sustain pecuniary loss from its destruction.
**insurance** A contract whereby, for a stipulated consideration, one party undertakes to compensate the other for loss on a specified subject by specified perils. The party agreeing to make the compensation is usually called the "insurer" or "underwriter"; the other, the "insured" or "assured"; the written contract, a "policy"; the events insured against, "risks" or "perils"; and the subject, right, or interest to be protected, the "insurable interest." Insurance is a contract whereby one undertakes to indemnify another against loss, damage, or liability arising from an unknown or contingent event.
*Co-insurance* A form of insurance in which a person insures property for less than its full or stated value and agrees to share the risk of loss.
*Life insurance* Payment of a specific sum of money to a designated beneficiary upon the death of the insured.
*Ordinary life* Life insurance with a savings component that runs for the life of the insured.
*Term life* Life insurance issued for a limited number of years that does not have a savings component.
**intangible property** Protected interests that are not physical.
**intangibles** Accounts and general intangibles.
**intent** Desire to cause the consequences of an act or knowledge that the consequences are substantially certain to result from the act.
**inter alia** Among other things.
**inter se** or **inter sese** "Among or between themselves." Used to distinguish rights or duties between two or more parties from their rights or duties to others.
**interest in land** Any right, privilege, power, or immunity in real property.
**interest in partnership** Partner's share in the partnership's profits and surplus.
**interference with contractual relations** Intentionally causing one of the parties to a contract not to perform the contract.
**intermediary bank** Any bank, except the depositary or payor bank, to which an item is transferred in the course of collection. UCC §4-105(c).
**intermediate test** Requirement that legislation have a substantial relationship to an important governmental objective.
**international law** Deals with the conduct and relations of nation-states and international organizations.
**interpretation** Construction or meaning of a contract.
**interpretative rules** Statements issued by an administrative agency indicating its construction of its governing statute.
**intestate** A person is said to die intestate when he dies without making a will. The word is also often used to signify the person himself. *Compare* **testator**.
**intrusion** Unreasonable and highly offensive interference with the seclusion of another.
**inventory** Goods held for sale or lease or consumed in a business.
**invitee** A person is an "invitee" on land of another if (1) he enters by invitation, express or implied, (2) his entry is connected with the owner's business or with an activity the owner conducts or permits to be conducted on his land, and (3) there is mutual benefit or a benefit to the owner.

**joint liability** Liability where creditor must sue all of the partners as a group.
**joint and several liability** Liability where creditor may sue partners jointly as a group or separately as individuals.
**joint stock company** A general partnership with some corporate attributes.
**joint tenancy** See **tenancy**.
**joint venture** An association of two or more persons to carry on a single business transaction for profit.
**judgment** The official and authentic decision of a court of justice upon the respective rights and claims of the parties to an action or suit therein litigated and submitted to its determination.
**judgment in personam** A judgment against a particular person, as distinguished from a judgment against a thing or a right or *status*.
**judgment in rem** An adjudication pronounced upon the status of some particular thing or subject matter, by a tribunal having competent authority.
**judgment n.o.v.** Judgment *non obstante veredicto* in its broadest sense is a judgment rendered in favor of one party notwithstanding the finding of a verdict in favor of the other party.
**judgment notwithstanding the verdict** A final binding determination on the merits made by the judge after and contrary to the jury's verdict.
**judgment on the pleadings** Final binding determination on the merits made by the judge after the pleadings.
**judicial lien** Interest in property that is obtained by court action to secure payment of a debt.
**judicial review** Power of the courts to determine the constitutionality of legislative and executive acts.
**jurisdiction** The right and power of a court to adjudicate concerning the subject matter in a given case.
**jurisdiction over the parties** Power of a court to bind the parties to a suit.
**jury** A body of persons selected and summoned by law and sworn to try the facts of a case and to find according to the law and the evidence. In general, the province of the jury is to find the facts in a case, while the judge passes upon pure questions of law. As a matter of fact, however, the jury must often pass upon mixed questions of law and fact in determining the case, and in all such cases the instructions of the judge as to the law become very important.
**justifiable reliance** Reasonably influenced by a misrepresentation.

**labor dispute** Any controversy concerning terms or conditions of employment or union representation.
**laches** Based upon maxim that equity aids the vigilant and not those who slumber on their rights. It is defined as neglect to assert a right or claim which, taken together with a lapse of time and other circumstances causing prejudice to the adverse party, operates as a bar in a court of equity.
**landlord** The owner of an estate in land, or a rental property, who has leased it to another person, called the "tenant." Also called "lessor."
**larceny** Trespassory taking and carrying away of the goods of another with the intent to permanently deprive.
**last clear chance** Final opportunity to avoid an injury.
**lease** Any agreement which gives rise to relationship of landlord and tenant (real property) or lessor and lessee (real or personal property).

The person who conveys is termed the "lessor," and the person to whom conveyed, the "lessee"; and when the lessor conveys land or tenements to a lessee, he is said to lease, demise, or let them.
*Sublease,* or *underlease* One executed by the lessee of an estate to a third person, conveying the same estate for a shorter term than that for which the lessee holds it.

**leasehold** An estate in realty held under a lease. The four principal types of leasehold estates are the estate for years, periodic tenancy, tenancy at will, and tenancy at sufferance.
**leasehold estate** Right to possess real property.
**legacy** A legacy is a gift or bequest by will of personal property, whereas a devise is a testamentary disposition of real estate.
*Demonstrative legacy* A bequest of a certain sum of money, with a direction that it shall be paid out of a particular fund. It differs from a specific legacy in this respect: that, if the fund out of which it is payable fails for any cause, it is nevertheless entitled to come on the estate as a general legacy. And it differs from a general legacy in this: that it does not abate in that class, but in the class of specific legacies.
*General legacy* A pecuniary legacy, payable out of the general assets of a testator.
*Residuary legacy* A bequest of all the testator's personal estate not otherwise effectually disposed of by his will.
*Specific legacy* One which operates on property particularly designated. A legacy or gift by will of a particular specified thing, as of a horse, a piece of furniture, a term of years, and the like.
**legal aggregate** A group of individuals not having a legal existence separate from its members.
**legal benefit** Obtaining something to which one had no legal right.
**legal detriment** Doing an act one is not legally obligated to do or not doing an act one has a legal right to do.
**legal entity** An organization having a legal existence separate from that of its members.
**legal sufficiency** Benefit to promisor or detriment to promisee.
**legislative rules** Substantive rules issued by an administrative agency under the authority delegated to it by the legislature.
**letter of credit** An engagement by a bank or other person made at the request of a customer that the issuer will honor drafts or other demands for payment upon compliance with the conditions specified in the credit.
**letters of administration** Formal document issued by probate court appointing one an administrator of an estate.
**letters testamentary** The formal instrument of authority and appointment given to an executor by the proper court, empowering him to enter upon the discharge of his office as executor. It corresponds to letters of administration granted to an administrator.
**levy** To assess; raise; execute; exact; tax; collect; gather; take up; seize. Thus, to levy (assess, exact, raise, or collect) a tax; to levy an execution, *i.e.*, to levy or collect a sum of money on an execution.
**liability insurance** Covers liability to others by reason of damage resulting from injuries to another's person or property.
**liability without fault** Crime to do a specific act or cause a certain result without regard to the care exercised.
**libel** Defamation communicated by writing, television, radio, or the like.
**liberty** Ability of individuals to engage in freedom of action and choice regarding their personal lives.
**license** License with respect to real property is a privilege to go on premises for a certain purpose, but does not operate to confer on or vest in the licensee any title, interest, or estate in such property.
**licensee** Person privileged to enter or remain on land by virtue of the consent of the lawful possessor.
**lien** A qualified right of property which a creditor has in or over specific property of his debtor, as security for the debt or charge or for performance of some act.
**lien creditor** A creditor who has acquired a lien on the property by attachment.
**life estate** An estate whose duration is limited to the life of the party holding it or of some other person. Upon the death of the life tenant, the property will go to the holder of the remainder interest or to the grantor by reversion.
**limited liability** Liability limited to amount invested in a business enterprise.
**limited partner** Member of a limited partnership with liability for its debts only to the extent of her capital contribution.
**limited partnership** See **partnership**.
**limited partnership association** A partnership which closely resembles a corporation.
**liquidated** Ascertained; determined; fixed; settled; made clear or manifest. Cleared away; paid; discharged.
**liquidated damages** See **damages**.
**liquidated debt** Obligation that is certain in amount.
**liquidation** The settling of financial affairs of a business or individual, usually by liquidating (turning to cash) all assets for distribution to creditors, heirs, etc. To be distinguished from dissolution.
**loss of value** Value of promised performance minus value of actual performance.
**lost property** Property with which the owner has involuntarily parted and which she does not know where to find or recover, not including property which she has intentionally concealed or deposited in a secret place for safekeeping. Distinguishable from mislaid property, which has been deliberately placed somewhere and forgotten.

**main purpose rule** Where object of promisor/surety is to provide an economic benefit for herself, the promise is considered outside of the statute of frauds.
**maker** One who makes or executes; as the maker of a promissory note. One who signs a check; in this context, synonymous with drawer. See **draft**.
**mala in se** Morally wrong.
**mala prohibita** Wrong by law.
**mandamus** "We command." A legal writ compelling the defendant to do an official duty.
**manslaughter** Unlawful taking of another's life without malice.
*Involuntary manslaughter* Taking the life of another by criminal negligence or during the course of a misdemeanor.
*Voluntary manslaughter* Intentional killing of another under extenuating circumstances.
**manufacturing defect** Not produced according to specifications.
**mark** Trade symbol.
**market allocations** Division of market by customers, geographic location, or products.
**marketable title** Free from any defects, encumbrances, or reasonable objections to one's ownership.
**marshaling of assets** Segregating the assets and liabilities of a partnership from the assets and liabilities of the individual partners.
**master** See **principal**.
**material** Matters to which a reasonable investor would attach importance in deciding whether to purchase a security.
**material alteration** Any change that changes the contract of any party to an instrument.
**maturity** The date at which an obligation, such as the principal of a bond or a note, becomes due.
**maxim** A general legal principle.
**mechanic's lien** A claim created by state statutes for the purpose of securing priority of payment of the price or value of work performed and materials furnished in erecting or repairing a building or other structure; as such, attaches to the land as well as buildings and improvements erected thereon.
**mediation** Nonbinding process in which a third party acts as an intermediary between the disputing parties and proposes solutions for them to consider.
**mens rea** Criminal intent.
**mentally incompetent** Unable to understand the nature and effect of one's acts.
**mercantile law** An expression substantially equivalent to commercial law. It designates the system of rules, customs, and usages generally recognized

and adopted by merchants and traders that, either in its simplicity or as modified by common law or statutes, constitutes the law for the regulation of their transactions and the solution of their controversies. The Uniform Commercial Code is the general body of law governing commercial or mercantile transactions.
**merchant** A person who deals in goods of the kind involved in a transaction or who otherwise by his occupation holds himself out as having knowledge or skill peculiar to the practices or goods involved in the transaction or to whom such knowledge or skill may be attributed by his employment of an agent or broker or other intermediary who by his occupation holds himself out as having such knowledge or skill. UCC §2-104(1).
**merchantability** Merchant seller guarantees that the goods are fit for their ordinary purpose.
**merger** The fusion or absorption of one thing or right into another. In corporate law, the absorption of one company by another, the latter retaining its own name and identity and acquiring the assets, liabilities, franchises, and powers of the former, which ceases to exist as separate business entity. It differs from a consolidation, wherein all the corporations terminate their separate existences and become parties to a new one.
*Conglomerate merger* An acquisition, which is not horizontal or vertical, by one company of another.
*Horizontal merger* Merger between business competitors, such as manufacturers of the same type of products or distributors selling competing products in the same market area.
*Short-form merger* Merger of a 90 percent subsidiary into its parent.
*Vertical merger* Union with corporate customer or supplier.
**midnight deadline** Midnight of the next banking day after receiving an item.
**mining partnership** A specific type of partnership for the purpose of extracting raw minerals.
**minor** Under the age of legal majority (usually eighteen).
**mirror image rule** An acceptance cannot deviate from the terms of the offer.
**misdemeanor** Less serious crime.
**mislaid property** Property which an owner has put deliberately in a certain place that she is unable to remember, as distinguished from lost property, which the owner has left unwittingly in a location she has forgotten. See also **lost property**.
**misrepresentation** Any manifestation by words or other conduct by one person to another that, under the circumstances, amounts to an assertion not in accordance with the facts. A "misrepresentation" that justifies the rescission of a contract is a false statement of a substantive fact, or any conduct which leads to a belief of a substantive fact material to proper understanding of the matter in hand. See also **deceit**; **fraud**.
*Fraudulent misrepresentation* False statement made with knowledge of its falsity and intent to mislead.
*Innocent misrepresentation* Misrepresentation made without knowledge of its falsity but with due care.
*Negligent misrepresentation* Misrepresentation made without due care in ascertaining its falsity.
**M'Naughten Rule** Right/wrong test for criminal insanity.
**modify** Change the lower court's judgment.
**money** Medium of exchange issued by a government body.
**monopoly** Ability to control price or exclude others from the marketplace.
**mortgage** A mortgage is an interest in land created by a written instrument providing security for the performance of a duty or the payment of a debt.
**mortgagor** Debtor who uses real estate to secure an obligation.
**multinational enterprise** Business that engages in transactions involving the movement of goods, information, money, people, or services across national borders.
**multiple product order** Order requiring an advertiser to cease and desist from deceptive statements on all products it sells.
**murder** Unlawful and premeditated taking of another's life.
**mutual mistake** Where the common but erroneous belief of both parties forms the basis of a contract.

**necessaries** Items needed to maintain a person's station in life.
**negligence** The omission to do something which a reasonable person, guided by those ordinary considerations which ordinarily regulate human affairs, would do, or the doing of something which a reasonable and prudent person would not do.
*Culpable negligence* Greater than ordinary negligence but less than gross negligence.
**negligence per se** Conclusive on the issue of negligence (duty of care and breach).
**negotiable** Legally capable of being transferred by indorsement or delivery. Usually said of checks and notes and sometimes of stocks and bearer bonds.
**negotiable instrument** Signed document (such as a check or promissory note) containing an unconditional promise to pay a "sum certain" of money at a definite time to order or bearer.
**negotiation** Transferee becomes a holder.
**net assets** Total assets minus total debts.
**no arrival, no sale** A destination contract, but if goods do not arrive, seller is excused from liability unless such is due to the seller's fault.
**no-fault insurance** Compensates victims of automobile accidents regardless of fault.
**nonconforming use** Preexisting use not in accordance with a zoning ordinance.
**nonprofit corporation** One whose profits must be used exclusively for the charitable, educational, or scientific purpose for which it was formed.
**nonsuit** Action in form of a judgment taken against a plaintiff who has failed to appear to prosecute his action or failed to prove his case.
**note** See **promissory note**.
**novation** A novation substitutes a new party and discharges one of the original parties to a contract by agreement of all three parties. A new contract is created with the same terms as the original one; only the parties have changed.
**nuisance** Nuisance is that activity which arises from the unreasonable, unwarranted, or unlawful use by a person of his own property, working obstruction or injury to the right of another or to the public, and producing such material annoyance, inconvenience, and discomfort that law will presume resulting damage.

**obiter dictum** See **dictum**.
**objective fault** Gross deviation from reasonable conduct.
**objective manifestation** What a reasonable person under the circumstances would believe.
**objective satisfaction** Approval based upon whether a reasonable person would be satisfied.
**objective standard** What a reasonable person under the circumstances would reasonably believe or do.
**obligee** Party to whom a duty of performance is owed (by delegator and delegatee).
**obligor** Party owing a duty (to the assignor).
**offer** A manifestation of willingness to enter into a bargain, so made as to justify another person in understanding that his assent to that bargain is invited and will conclude it. Restatement, Second, Contracts, §24.
**offeree** Recipient of the offer.
**offeror** Person making the offer.
**open-ended credit** Credit arrangement under which debtor has rights to enter into a series of credit transactions.
**opinion** Belief in the existence of a fact or a judgment as to value.
**option** Contract providing that an offer will stay open for a specified period of time.
**order** A final disposition made by an agency.

**order paper** Payable to a named person or to anyone designated by that person.
**order to pay** Direction or command to pay.
**original promise** Promise to become primarily liable.
**output contract** See **contracts**.

**palpable unilateral mistake** Erroneous belief by one party that is recognized by the other.
**parent corporation** Corporation which controls another corporation.
**parol evidence** Literally oral evidence, but now includes prior to and contemporaneous, oral, and written evidence.
**parol evidence rule** Under this rule, when parties put their agreement in writing, all previous oral agreements merge in the writing and the contract as written cannot be modified or changed by parol evidence, in the absence of a plea of mistake or fraud in the preparation of the writing. But the rule does not forbid a resort to parol evidence not inconsistent with the matters stated in the writing. Also, as regards sales of goods, such written agreement may be explained or supplemented by course of dealing, usage of trade, or course of conduct, and by evidence of consistent additional terms, unless the court finds the writing to have been intended also as a complete and exclusive statement of the terms of the agreement. UCC §2-202.
**part performance** In order to establish part performance taking an oral contract for the sale of realty out of the statute of frauds, the acts relied upon as part performance must be of such a character that they reasonably can be naturally accounted for in no other way than that they were performed in pursuance of the contract, and they must be in conformity with its provisions. See UCC §2-201(3).
**partial assignment** Transfer of a portion of contractual rights to one or more assignees.
**partition** The dividing of lands held by joint tenants, copartners, or tenants in common into distinct portions, so that the parties may hold those lands in severalty.
**partnership** An association of two or more persons to carry on, as co-owners, a business for profit.

Partnerships are treated as a conduit and are, therefore, not subject to taxation. The various items of partnership income (gains and losses, etc.) flow through to the individual partners and are reported on their personal income tax returns.

*Limited partnership* Type of partnership comprised of one or more general partners who manage business and who are personally liable for partnership debts, and one or more limited partners who contribute capital and share in profits but who take no part in running business and incur no liability with respect to partnership obligations beyond contribution.

*Partnership at will* One with no definite term or specific undertaking.

**partnership capital** Total money and property contributed by partners for permanent use by the partnership.
**partnership property** Sum of all of the partnership's assets.
**past consideration** An act done before the contract is made.
**patent** Exclusive right to an invention.
**payee** The person in whose favor a bill of exchange, promissory note, or check is made or drawn.
**payer** or **payor** One who pays or who is to make a payment, particularly the person who is to make payment of a check, bill, or note. Correlative to "payee."
**payor bank** A bank by which an item is payable as drawn or accepted. UCC §4-105(b). Correlative to "Drawee bank."
**per capita** This term, derived from the civil law and much used in the law of descent and distribution, denotes that method of dividing an intestate estate by which an equal share is given to each of a number of persons, all of whom stand in equal degree to the decedent, without reference to their stocks or the right of representation. The opposite of *per stirpes*.
**per stirpes** This term, derived from the civil law and much used in the law of descent and distribution, denotes that method of dividing an intestate estate where a class or group of distributees takes the share to which its deceased would have been entitled, taking thus by its right of representing such ancestor and not as so many individuals. The opposite of *per capita*.
**perfect tender rule** Seller's tender of delivery must conform exactly to the contract.
**perfection of security interest** Acts required of a secured party in the way of giving at least constructive notice so as to make his security interest effective at least against lien creditors of the debtor. See UCC §§9-302 through 9-306. In most cases, the secured party may obtain perfection either by filing with the secretary of state or by taking possession of the collateral.
**performance** Fulfillment of one's contractual obligations. See also **part performance; specific performance**.
**periodic tenancy** Lease with a definite term that is to be continued.
**personal defenses** Contractual defenses which are good against holders but not holders in due course.
**personal property** Any property other than an interest in land.
**petty crime** Misdemeanor punishable by imprisonment of six months or less.
**plaintiff** The party who initiates a civil suit.
**pleadings** The formal allegations by the parties of their respective claims and defenses.

*Rules or codes of civil procedure* Unlike the rigid technical system of common law pleading, pleadings under federal and state rules or codes of civil procedure have a far more limited function, with determination and narrowing of facts and issues being left to discovery devices and pretrial conferences. In addition, the rules and codes permit liberal amendment and supplementation of pleadings. Under rules of civil procedure, the pleadings consist of a complaint, an answer, a reply to a counterclaim, an answer to a cross-claim, a third-party complaint, and a third-party answer.

**pledge** A bailment of goods to a creditor as security for some debt or engagement.

Much of the law of pledges has been replaced by the provisions for secured transactions in Article 9 of the UCC.

**possibility of reverter** The interest which remains in a grantor or testator after the conveyance or devise of a fee simple determinable and which permits the grantor to be revested automatically of his estate on breach of the condition.
**possibility test** Under the statute of frauds, asks whether performance could possibly be completed within one year.
**power of appointment** A power of authority conferred by one person by deed or will upon another (called the "donee") to appoint, that is, to select and nominate, the person or persons who is or are to receive and enjoy an estate or an income therefrom or from a fund, after the testator's death, or the donee's death, or after the termination of an existing right or interest.
**power of attorney** An instrument authorizing a person to act as the agent or attorney of the person granting it.
**power of termination** The interest left in the grantor or testator after the conveyance or devise of a fee simple on condition subsequent or conditional fee.
**precatory** Expressing a wish.
**precedent** An adjudged case or decision of a court, considered as furnishing an example or authority for an identical or similar case afterwards arising or a similar question of law. See also **stare decisis**.
**preemptive right** The privilege of a stockholder to maintain a proportionate share of ownership by purchasing a proportionate share of any new stock issues.
**preference** The act of an insolvent debtor who, in distributing his property or in assigning it for the benefit of his creditors, pays or secures to one or more creditors the full amount of their claims or a larger amount than they would be entitled to receive on a *pro rata* distribution. The treatment

of such preferential payments in bankruptcy is governed by the Bankruptcy Act, §547.
**preliminary hearing** Determines whether there is probable cause.
**premium** The price for insurance protection for a specified period of exposure.
**preponderance of the evidence** Greater weight of the evidence; standard used in civil cases.
**prescription** Acquisition of a personal right to use a way, water, light, and air by reason of continuous usage. See also **easement**.
**presenter's warranty** Warranty given to any payor or acceptor of an instrument.
**presentment** The production of a negotiable instrument to the drawee for his acceptance, or to the drawer or acceptor for payment; or of a promissory note to the party liable, for payment of the same. UCC §3-504(1).
**presumption** A presumption is a rule of law, statutory or judicial, by which a finding of a basic fact gives rise to the existence of presumed fact, until presumption is rebutted. A presumption imposes on the party against whom it is directed the burden of going forward with evidence to rebut or meet the presumption, but does not shift to such party the burden of proof in the sense of the risk of nonpersuasion, which remains throughout the trial upon the party on whom it was originally cast.
**price discrimination** Price differential.
**price fixing** Any agreement for the purpose and effect of raising, depressing, fixing, pegging, or stabilizing prices.
**prima facie** (Latin) At first sight; on the first appearance; on the face of it; so far as can be judged from the first disclosure; presumably; a fact presumed to be true unless disproved by some evidence to the contrary.
**primary liability** Absolute obligation to pay a negotiable instrument.
**principal**
*Law of agency* The term "principal" describes one who has permitted or directed another (*i.e.*, an agent or a servant) to act for his benefit and subject to his direction and control. Principal includes in its meaning the term "master" or employer, a species of principal who, in addition to other control, has a right to control the physical conduct of the species of agents known as servants or employees, as to whom special rules are applicable with reference to harm caused by their physical acts.
*Disclosed principal* One whose existence and identity are known.
*Partially disclosed principal* One whose existence is known but whose identity is not known.
*Undisclosed principal* One whose existence and identity are not known.
**principal debtor** Person whose debt is being supported by a surety.
**priority** Precedence in order of right.
**private carrier** Carrier which limits its service and is not open to the general public.
**private corporation** One organized to conduct either a privately owned business enterprise for profit or a nonprofit corporation.
**private law** The law involving relationships among individuals and legal entities.
**privilege** Immunity from tort liability.
**privity** Contractual relationship.
**privity of contract** That connection or relationship which exists between two or more contracting parties. The absence of privity as a defense in actions for damages in contract and tort actions is generally no longer viable with the enactment of warranty statutes (*e.g.*, UCC §2-318), acceptance by states of the doctrine of strict liability, and court decisions which have extended the right to sue to third-party beneficiaries and even innocent bystanders.
**probable cause** Reasonable belief of the offense charged.
**probate** Court procedure by which a will is proved to be valid or invalid, though in current usage this term has been expanded to include generally all matters and proceedings pertaining to administration of estates, guardianships, etc.
**procedural due process** Requirement that governmental action depriving a person of life, liberty, or property be done through a fair procedure.
**procedural law** Rules for enforcing substantive law.
**procedural rules** Rules issued by an administrative agency establishing its organization, method of operation, and rules of conduct for practice before it.
**procedural unconscionability** Unfair or irregular bargaining.
**proceeds** Consideration for the sale, exchange, or other disposition of collateral.
**process**
*Judicial process* In a wide sense, this term may include all the acts of a court from the beginning to the end of its proceedings in a given cause; more specifically, it means the writ, summons, mandate, or other process which is used to inform the defendant of the institution of proceedings against him and to compel his appearance, in either civil or criminal cases.
*Legal process* This term is sometimes used as equivalent to "lawful process." Thus, it is said that legal process means process not merely fair on its face but valid in fact. But properly it means a summons, writ, warrant, mandate, or other process issuing from a court.
**profit corporation** One founded for the purpose of operating a business for profit.
**profit à prendre** Right to make some use of the soil of another, such as a right to mine metals; carries with it the right of entry and the right to remove.
**promise to pay** Undertaking to pay an existing obligation.
**promisee** Person to whom a promise is made.
**promisor** Person making a promise.
**promissory estoppel** Arises where there is a promise which promisor should reasonably expect to induce action or forbearance on part of promisee and which does induce such action or forbearance, and where injustice can be avoided only by enforcement of the promise.
**promissory note** An unconditional written promise to pay a specified sum of money on demand or at a specified date. Such a note is negotiable if signed by the maker and containing an unconditional promise to pay a sum certain in money either on demand or at a definite time and payable to order or bearer. UCC §3-104.
**promoters** In the law relating to corporations, those persons who first associate themselves for the purpose of organizing a company, issuing its prospectus, procuring subscriptions to the stock, securing a charter, etc.
**property** Interest that is legally protected.
*Abandoned property* Intentionally disposed of by the owner.
*Lost property* Unintentionally left by the owner.
*Mislaid property* Intentionally placed by the owner but unintentionally left.
**prosecute** To bring a criminal proceeding.
**protest** A formal declaration made by a person interested or concerned in some act about to be done, or already performed, whereby he expresses his dissent or disapproval or affirms the act against his will. The object of such a declaration usually is to preserve some right which would be lost to the protester if his assent could be implied, or to exonerate him from some responsibility which would attach to him unless he expressly negatived his assent.
*Notice of protest* A notice given by the holder of a bill or note to the drawer or indorser that the bill has been protested for refusal of payment or acceptance. UCC §3-509.
**provisional credit** Tentative credit for the deposit of an instrument until final credit is given.
**proximate cause** Where the act or omission played a substantial part in bringing about or actually causing the injury or damage and where the injury or damage was either a direct result or a reasonably probable consequence of the act or omission.
**proxy** (Contracted from "procuracy.") Written authorization given by one person to another so that the second person can act for the first, such as that given by a shareholder to someone else to represent him and vote his shares at a shareholders' meeting.
**public corporation** One created to administer a unit of local civil government or one created by the United States to conduct public business.

**public disclosure of private facts** Offensive publicity given to private information about another person.
**public law** The law dealing with the relationship between government and individuals.
**puffery** Sales talk that is considered general bragging or overstatement.
**punitive damages** Damages awarded in excess of normal compensation to punish a defendant for a serious civil wrong.
**purchase money security interest** Security interest retained by a seller of goods in goods purchased with the loaned money.

**qualified fee** Ownership subject to its being taken away upon the happening of an event.
**quantum meruit** "As much as he deserves." Describes the extent of liability on a contract implied by law. Elements essential to recovery under quantum meruit are (1) valuable services rendered or materials furnished (2) for the person sought to be charged, (3) which services and materials such person accepted, used, and enjoyed, (4) under such circumstances as reasonably notified her that plaintiff, in performing such services, was expected to be paid by the person sought to be charged.
**quasi** As if; almost as it were; analogous to. Negatives the idea of identity but points out that the conceptions are sufficiently similar to be classed as equals of one another.
**quasi contract** Legal fiction invented by common law courts to permit recovery by contractual remedy in cases where, in fact, there is no contract, but where circumstances are such that justice warrants a recovery as though a promise had been made.
**quasi in rem** See **in rem**.
**quasi in rem jurisdiction** Jurisdiction over property not based on claims against it.
**quiet enjoyment** Right of a tenant not to have his physical possession of premises interfered with by the landlord.
**quitclaim deed** A deed of conveyance operating by way of release; that is, intended to pass any title, interest, or claim which the grantor may have in the premises but neither professing that such title is valid nor containing any warranty or covenants for title.
**quorum** When a committee, board of directors, meeting of shareholders, legislature, or other body of persons cannot act unless at least a certain number of them are present.

**rape** Unlawful, nonconsensual sexual intercourse.
**ratification** In a broad sense, the confirmation of a previous act done either by the party himself or by another; as, for example, confirmation of a voidable act.

In the law of principal and agent, the adoption and confirmation by one person, with knowledge of all material facts, of an act or contract performed or entered into in his behalf by another who at the time assumed without authority to act as his agent.
**rational relationship test** Requirement that legislation bear a rational relationship to a legitimate governmental interest.
**real defenses** Defenses that are valid against all holders, including holders in due course.
**real property** Land, and generally whatever is erected or growing upon or affixed to land. Also, rights issuing out of, annexed to, and exercisable within or about land. See also **fixture**.
**reasonable man standard** Duty of care required to avoid being negligent; one who is careful, diligent, and prudent.
**receiver** A fiduciary of the court, whose appointment is incident to other proceedings wherein certain ultimate relief is prayed. He is a trustee or ministerial officer representing the court, all parties in interest in the litigation, and the property or funds entrusted to him.
**recognizance** Formal acknowledgment of indebtedness made in court.
**redemption** The realization of a right to have the title of property restored free and clear of a mortgage, performance of the mortgage obligation being essential for such purpose. (b) Repurchase by corporation of its own shares.
**reformation** Equitable remedy used to reframe written contracts to reflect accurately real agreement between contracting parties when, either through mutual mistake or unilateral mistake coupled with actual or equitable fraud by the other party, the writing does not embody the contract as actually made.
**regulatory license** Requirement to protect the public interest.
**reimbursement** Duty owed by principal to pay back authorized payments agent has made on principal's behalf. Duty owed by a principal debtor to repay surety who pays principal debtor's obligation.
**rejection** The refusal to accept an offer; manifestation of an unwillingness to accept the goods (sales).
**release** The relinquishment, concession, or giving up of a right, claim, or privilege, by the person in whom it exists or to whom it accrues, to the person against whom it might have been demanded or enforced.
**remainder** An estate limited to take effect and be enjoyed after another estate is determined.
**remand** To send back. The sending by the appellate court of a cause back to the same court out of which it came, for the purpose of having some further action taken on it there.
**remedy** The means by which the violation of a right is prevented, redressed, or compensated. Though a remedy may be by the act of the party injured, by operation of law, or by agreement between the injurer and the injured, we are chiefly concerned with one kind of remedy, the judicial remedy, which is by action or suit.
**rent** Consideration paid for use or occupation of property. In a broader sense, it is the compensation or fee paid, usually periodically, for the use of any property, land, buildings, equipment, etc.
**replevin** An action whereby the owner or person entitled to repossession of goods or chattels may recover those goods or chattels from one who has wrongfully distrained or taken such goods or chattels or who wrongfully detains them.
**reply** Plaintiff's pleading in response to the defendant's answer.
**repudiation** Repudiation of a contract means refusal to perform duty or obligation owed to other party.
**requirements contract** See **contracts**.
**res ipsa loquitur** "The thing speaks for itself." Permits the jury to infer both negligent conduct and causation.
**rescission** An equitable action in which a party seeks to be relieved of his obligations under a contract on the grounds of mutual mistake, fraud, impossibility, etc.
**residuary** Pertaining to the residue; constituting the residue; giving or bequeathing the residue; receiving or entitled to the residue. See also **legacy, residuary legacy**.
**respondeat superior** "Let the master answer." This maxim means that a master or employer is liable in certain cases for the wrongful acts of his servant or employee, and a principal for those of his agent.
**respondent** In equity practice, the party who makes an answer to a bill or other proceeding. In appellate practice, the party who contends against an appeal; *i.e.*, the appellee. The party who appeals is called the "appellant."
**restitution** An equitable remedy under which a person who has rendered services to another seeks to be reimbursed for the costs of his acts (but not his profits) even though there was never a contract between the parties.
**restraint on alienation** A provision in an instrument of conveyance which prohibits the grantee from selling or transferring the property which is the subject of the conveyance. Many such restraints are unenforceable as against public policy and the law's policy of free alienability of land.
**restraint of trade** Agreement that eliminates or tends to eliminate competition.
**restrictive covenant** Private restriction on property contained in a conveyance.
**revenue license** Measure to raise money.

**reverse** An appellate court uses the term "reversed" to indicate that it annuls or avoids the judgment, or vacates the decree, of the trial court.
**reverse discrimination** Employment decisions taking into account race or gender in order to remedy past discrimination.
**reversion** The term reversion has two meanings. First, it designates the estate left in the grantor during the continuance of a particular estate; second, it denotes the residue left in grantor or his heirs after termination of a particular estate. It differs from a remainder in that it arises by an act of law, whereas a remainder arises by an act of the parties. A reversion, moreover, is the remnant left in the grantor, while a remainder is the remnant of the whole estate disposed of after a preceding part of the same has been given away.
**revocation** The recall of some power, authority, or thing granted, or a destroying or making void of some deed that had existence until the act of revocation made it void.
**revocation of acceptance** Rescission of one's acceptance of goods based upon a nonconformity of the goods which substantially impairs their value.
**right** Legal capacity to require another person to perform or refrain from performing an act.
**right of entry** The right to take or resume possession of land by entering on it in a peaceable manner.
**right of redemption** The right (granted by statute only) to free property from the encumbrance of a foreclosure or other judicial sale, or to recover the title passing thereby, by paying what is due, with interest, costs, etc. Not to be confounded with the "equity of redemption," which exists independently of statute but must be exercised before sale. See also **equity of redemption**.
**right to work law** State statute that prohibits union shop contracts.
**rights in collateral** Personal property the debtor owns, possesses, or is in the process of acquiring.
**risk of loss** Allocation of loss between seller and buyer where the goods have been damaged, destroyed, or lost.
**robbery** Larceny from a person by force or threat of force.
**rule** Agency statement of general or particular applicability designed to implement, interpret, or process law or policy.
**rule against perpetuities** Principle that no interest in property is good unless it must vest, if at all, not later than twenty-one years, plus period of gestation, after some life or lives in being at time of creation of interest.
**rule of reason** Balancing the anticompetitive effects of a restraint against its procompetitive effects.

**sale** Transfer of title to goods from seller to buyer for a price.
**sale on approval** Transfer of possession without title to buyer for trial period.
**sale or return** Sale where buyer has option to return goods to seller.
**sanction** Means of enforcing legal judgments.
**satisfaction** The discharge of an obligation by paying a party what is due to him (as on a mortgage, lien, or contract) or what has been awarded to him by the judgment of a court or otherwise. Thus, a judgment is satisfied by the payment of the amount due to the party who has recovered such judgment, or by his levying the amount. See also **accord and satisfaction**.
**scienter** Knowingly.
**seal** Symbol that authenticates a document.
**secondary liability** Obligation to pay is subject to the conditions of presentment, dishonor, notice of dishonor, and sometimes protest.
**secret partner** Partner whose membership in the partnership is not disclosed.
**Section 402A** Strict liability in tort.
**secured bond** A bond having a lien on specific property.
**secured claim** Claim with a lien on property of the debtor.
**secured party** Creditor who possesses a security interest in collateral.
**secured transaction** A transaction founded on a security agreement. Such agreement creates or provides for a security interest. UCC §9-105(h).
**securities** Stocks, bonds, notes, convertible debentures, warrants, or other documents that represent a share in a company or a debt owed by a company.
*Certificated security* Security represented by a certificate.
*Exempt security* Security not subject to registration requirements of 1933 Act.
*Exempt transaction* Issuance of securities not subject to the registration requirements of 1933 Act.
*Restricted securities* Securities issued under an exempt transaction.
*Uncertificated security* Security not represented by a certificate.
**security agreement** Agreement that grants a security interest.
**security interest** Right in personal property securing payment or performance of an obligation.
**seisin** Possession with an intent on the part of him who holds it to claim a freehold interest.
**self-defense** Force to protect oneself against attack.
**separation of powers** Allocation of powers among the legislative, executive, and judicial branches of government.
**service mark** Distinctive symbol, word, or design that is used to identify the services of a provider.
**servient** Land subject to an easement.
**setoff** A counterclaim demand which defendant holds against plaintiff, arising out of a transaction extrinsic to plaintiff's cause of action.
**settlor** Creator of a trust.
**severance** The destruction of any one of the unities of a joint tenancy. It is so called because the estate is no longer a joint tenancy, but is severed.
Term may also refer to the cutting of crops, such as corn, wheat, etc., or to the separation of anything from realty.
**share** A proportionate ownership interest in a corporation.
**Shelley's case, rule in** Where a person takes an estate of freehold, legally or equitably, under a deed, will, or other writing, and in the same instrument there is a limitation by way of remainder of any interest of the same legal or equitable quality to his heirs, or heirs of his body, as a class of persons to take in succession from generation to generation, the limitation to the heirs entitles the ancestor to the whole estate.
The rule was adopted as a part of the common law of this country, though it has long since been abolished by most states.
**shelter rule** Transferee gets rights of transferor.
**shipment contract** Seller is authorized or required only to bear the expense of placing goods with the common carrier and bears the risk of loss only up to such point.
**short-swing profits** Profits made by insider through sale or other disposition of corporate stock within six months after purchase.
**sight draft** An instrument payable on presentment.
**signature** Any symbol executed with intent to validate a writing.
**silent partner** Partner who takes no part in the partnership business.
**slander** Oral defamation.
**small claims courts** Inferior civil courts with jurisdiction limited by dollar amount.
**social security** Measures by which the government provides economic assistance to disabled or retired employees and their dependents.
**sole proprietorship** A form of business in which one person owns all the assets of the business, in contrast to a partnership or a corporation.
**sovereign immunity** Foreign country's freedom from a host country's laws.
**special warranty deed** Seller promises that he has not impaired title.
**specific performance** The doctrine of specific performance is that where damages would compensate inadequately for the breach of an agreement, the contractor or vendor will be compelled to perform specifically what he has agreed to do; *e.g.,* ordered to execute a specific conveyance of land.
With respect to the sale of goods, specific performance may be decreed where the goods are unique or in other proper circumstances. The decree for specific performance may include such terms and conditions as to

payment of the price, damages, or other relief as the court may deem just. UCC §§2-711(2)(b), 2–716.

**standardized business form** A preprinted contract.

**stare decisis** Doctrine that once a court has laid down a principle of law as applicable to a certain state of facts, it will adhere to that principle and apply it to all future cases having substantially the same facts, regardless of whether the parties and property are the same or not.

**state action** Actions by governments, as opposed to actions taken by private individuals.

**state-of-the-art** Made in accordance with the level of technology at the time the product is made.

**stated capital** Consideration, other than that allocated to capital surplus, received for issued stock.

**statute of frauds** A celebrated English statute, passed in 1677, which has been adopted, in a more or less modified form, in nearly all of the United States. Its chief characteristic is the provision that no action shall be brought on certain contracts unless there be a note or memorandum thereof in writing, signed by the party to be charged or by his authorized agent.

**statute of limitation** A statute prescribing limitations to the right of action on certain described causes of action; that is, declaring that no suit shall be maintained on such causes of action unless brought within a specified period after the right accrued.

**statutory lien** Interest in property, arising solely by statute, to secure payment of a debt.

**stock** "Stock" is distinguished from "bonds" and, ordinarily, from "debentures" in that it gives a right of ownership in part of the assets of a corporation and a right to interest in any surplus after the payment of debt. "Stock" in a corporation is an equity, representing an ownership interest. It is to be distinguished from obligations such as notes or bonds, which are not equities and represent no ownership interest.

*Capital stock* See **capital**.

*Common stock* Securities which represent an ownership interest in a corporation. If the company has also issued preferred stock, both common and preferred have ownership rights. Claims of both common and preferred stockholders are junior to claims of bondholders or other creditors of the company. Common stockholders assume the greater risk, but generally exercise the greater control and may gain the greater reward in the form of dividends and capital appreciation.

*Convertible stock* Stock which may be changed or converted into common stock.

*Cumulative preferred* Stock having a provision that if one or more dividends are omitted, the omitted dividends must be paid before dividends may be paid on the company's common stock.

*Preferred stock* is a separate portion or class of the stock of a corporation that is accorded, by the charter or by-laws, a preference or priority in respect to dividends, over the remainder of the stock of the corporation, which in that case is called *common stock*.

*Stock warrant* A certificate entitling the owner to buy a specified amount of stock at a specified time(s) for a specified price. Differs from a stock option only in that options are granted to employees and warrants are sold to the public.

*Treasury stock* Shares reacquired by a corporation.

**stock option** Contractual right to purchase stock from a corporation.

**stop payment** Order for a drawee not to pay an instrument.

**strict liability** A concept applied by the courts in product liability cases in which a seller is liable for any and all defective or hazardous products which unduly threaten a consumer's personal safety. This concept applies to all members involved in the manufacture and sale of any facet of the product.

**strict scrutiny test** Requirement that legislation be necessary to promote a compelling governmental interest.

**subagent** Person appointed by agent to perform agent's duties.

**subject matter jurisdiction** Authority of a court to decide a particular kind of case.

**subject to the mortgage** Purchaser is not personally obligated to pay the debt, but the property remains subject to the mortgage.

**subjective fault** Desired or virtually certain consequences of one's conduct.

**subjective satisfaction** Approval based upon a party's honestly held opinion.

**sublease** Transfer of less than all of a tenant's interest in a leasehold.

**subpoena** A subpoena is a command to appear at a certain time and place to give testimony upon a certain matter. A subpoena duces tecum requires production of books, papers, and other things.

**subrogation** The substitution of one thing for another, or of one person into the place of another with respect to rights, claims, or securities.

Subrogation denotes the putting of a third person who has paid a debt in the place of the creditor to whom he has paid it, so that he may exercise against the debtor all the rights which the creditor, if unpaid, might have exercised.

**subscribe** Literally, to write underneath, as one's name. To sign at the end of a document. Also, to agree in writing to furnish money or its equivalent, or to agree to purchase some initial stock in a corporation.

**subscriber** Person who agrees to purchase initial stock in a corporation.

**subsidiary corporation** Corporation controlled by another corporation.

**substantial performance** Equitable doctrine protects against forfeiture for technical inadvertence, trivial variations, or omissions in performance.

**substantive due process** Requirement that governmental action be compatible with individual liberties.

**substantive law** The basic law of rights and duties (contract law, criminal law, tort law, law of wills, etc.), as opposed to procedural law (law of pleading, law of evidence, law of jurisdiction, etc.).

**substantive unconscionability** Oppressive or grossly unfair contractual terms.

**sue** To begin a lawsuit in a court.

**suit** A generic term of comprehensive signification that applies to any proceeding in a court of justice in which the plaintiff pursues, in such court, the remedy which the law affords him for the redress of an injury or the recovery of a right.

*Derivative suit* Suit brought by a shareholder on behalf of a corporation to enforce a right belonging to the corporation.

*Direct suit* Suit brought by a shareholder against a corporation based upon his ownership of shares.

**summary judgment** Rule of Civil Procedure 56 permits any party to a civil action to move for a summary judgment on a claim, counterclaim, or cross-claim when he believes that there is no genuine issue of material fact and that he is entitled to prevail as a matter of law.

**summons** Writ or process directed to the sheriff or other proper officer, requiring him to notify the person named that an action has been commenced against him in the court from which the process has issued and that he is required to appear, on a day named, and answer the complaint in such action.

**superseding cause** Intervening event that occurs after the defendant's negligent conduct and relieves him of liability.

**supreme law** A law that takes precedence over all conflicting laws.

**surety** One who undertakes to pay money or to do any other act in event that his principal debtor fails therein.

**suretyship** A guarantee of debts of another.

**surplus** Excess of net assets over stated capital.

**tangible property** Physical objects.

**tariff** Duty or tax imposed on goods moving into or out of a country.

**tenancy** Possession or occupancy of land or premises under lease.

*Joint tenancy* Joint tenants have one and the same interest, accruing by one and the same conveyance, commencing at one and the same time, and held by one and the same undivided possession. The primary incident of joint tenancy is survivorship, by which the entire tenancy on the decease of any joint tenant remains to the survivors, and at length to the last survivor.

*Tenancy at sufferance* Only naked possession which continues after tenant's right of possession has terminated.

*Tenancy at will* Possession of premises by permission of owner or landlord, but without a fixed term.

*Tenancy by the entirety* A tenancy which is created between a husband and wife and by which together they hold title to the whole with right of survivorship so that, upon death of either, the other takes the whole to the exclusion of the deceased's heirs. It is essentially a "joint tenancy," modified by the common law theory that husband and wife are one person.

*Tenancy for a period* A tenancy for years or for some fixed period.

*Tenancy in common* A form of ownership whereby each tenant (*i.e.*, owner) holds an undivided interest in property. Unlike the interest of a joint tenant or a tenant by the entirety, the interest of a tenant in common does not terminate upon his or her prior death (*i.e.*, there is no right of survivorship).

**tenancy in partnership** Type of joint ownership that determines partners' rights in specific partnership property.

**tenant** Possessor of a leasehold interest.

**tender** An offer of money; the act by which one produces and offers to a person holding a claim or demand against him the amount of money which he considers and admits to be due, in satisfaction of such claim or demand, without any stipulation or condition.

Also, there may be a tender of performance of a duty other than the payment of money.

**tender of delivery** Seller makes available to buyer goods conforming to the contract and so notifies the buyer.

**tender offer** General invitation to all shareholders to purchase their shares at a specified price.

**testament** Will.

**testator** One who makes or has made a testament or will; one who dies leaving a will.

**third-party beneficiary** One for whose benefit a promise is made in a contract but who is not a party to the contract.

*Creditor beneficiary* Where performance of a promise in a contract will benefit a person other than the promisee, that person is a creditor beneficiary if no purpose to make a gift appears from the terms of the promise, in view of the accompanying circumstances, and performance of the promise will satisfy an actual, supposed, or asserted duty of the promisee to the beneficiary.

*Donee beneficiary* The person who takes the benefit of the contract even though there is no privity between him and the contracting parties. A third-party beneficiary who is not a creditor beneficiary. See also **beneficiary**.

**time paper** Payable at definite time.

**time-price doctrine** Permits sellers to have different prices for cash sales and credit sales.

**title** The means whereby the owner of lands or of personalty has the just possession of his property.

**title insurance** Provides protection against defect in title to real property.

**tort** A private or civil wrong or injury, other than breach of contract, for which a court will provide a remedy in the form of an action for damages.

Three elements of every tort action are the existence of a legal duty from defendant to plaintiff, breach of that duty, and damage as proximate result.

**tortfeasor** One who commits a tort.

**trade acceptance** A draft drawn by a seller which is presented for signature (acceptance) to the buyer at the time goods are purchased and which then becomes the equivalent of a note receivable of the seller and the note payable of the buyer.

**trade name** Name used in trade or business to identify a particular business or manufacturer.

**trade secrets** Private business information.

**trademark** Distinctive insignia, word, or design of a good that is used to identify the manufacturer.

**transferor's warranty** Warranty given by any person who transfers an instrument and receives consideration.

**treaty** An agreement between or among independent nations.

**treble damages** Three times actual loss.

**trespass** At common law, trespass was a form of action brought to recover damages for any injury to one's person or property or relationship with another.

*Trespass to chattels or personal property* An unlawful and serious interference with the possessory rights of another to personal property.

*Trespass to land* At common law, every unauthorized and direct breach of the boundaries of another's land was an actionable trespass. The present prevailing position of the courts finds liability for trespass only in the case of intentional intrusion, or negligence, or some "abnormally dangerous activity" on the part of the defendant. *Compare* **nuisance**.

**trespasser** Person who enters or remains on the land of another without permission or privilege to do so.

**trust** Any arrangement whereby property is transferred with the intention that it be administered by a trustee for another's benefit.

A trust, as the term is used in the Restatement, when not qualified by the word "charitable," "resulting," or "constructive," is a fiduciary relationship with respect to property, subjecting the person by whom the title to the property is held to equitable duties to deal with the property for the benefit of another person, which arises through a manifestation of an intention to create such benefit. Restatement, Second, Trusts §2.

*Charitable trust* To benefit humankind.

*Constructive trust* Wherever the circumstances of a transaction are such that the person who takes the legal estate in property cannot also enjoy the beneficial interest without necessarily violating some established principle of equity, the court will immediately raise a *constructive trust* and fasten it upon the conscience of the legal owner, so as to convert him into a trustee for the parties who in equity are entitled to the beneficial enjoyment.

*Inter vivos trust* Established during the settlor's lifetime.

*Resulting trust* One that arises by implication of law, where the legal estate in property is disposed of, conveyed, or transferred, but the intent appears or is inferred from the terms of the disposition, or from the accompanying facts and circumstances, that the beneficial interest is not to go or be enjoyed with the legal title.

*Spendthrift trust* Removal of the trust estate from the beneficiary's control.

*Testamentary trust* Established by a will.

*Totten trust* A tentative trust which is a joint bank account opened by the settlor.

*Voting trust* A trust which holds the voting rights to stock in a corporation. It is a useful device when a majority of the shareholders in a corporation cannot agree on corporate policy.

**trustee** In a strict sense, a "trustee" is one who holds the legal title to property for the benefit of another, while, in a broad sense, the term is sometimes applied to anyone standing in a fiduciary or confidential relation to another, such as agent, attorney, bailee, etc.

**trustee in bankruptcy** Representative of the estate in bankruptcy who is responsible for collecting, liquidating, and distributing the debtor's assets.

**tying arrangement** Conditioning a sale of a desired product (tying product) on the buyer's purchasing a second product (tied product).

**ultra vires** Acts beyond the scope of the powers of a corporation, as defined by its charter or by the laws of its state of incorporation. By the doctrine of ultra vires, a contract made by a corporation beyond the scope of its corporate powers is unlawful.

**unconscionable** Unfair or unduly harsh.

**unconscionable contract** See **contracts**.

**underwriter** Any person, banker, or syndicate that guarantees to furnish a definite sum of money by a definite date to a business or government in

return for an issue of bonds or stock. In insurance, the one assuming a risk in return for the payment of a premium.
**undisputed debt** Obligation whose existence and amount are not contested.
**undue influence** Term refers to conduct by which a person, through his power over the mind of a testator, makes the latter's desires conform to his own, thereby overmastering the volition of the testator.
**unemployment compensation** Compensation awarded to workers who have lost their jobs and cannot find other employment.
**unenforceable** Contract under which neither party can recover.
**unfair employer practice** Conduct in which an employer is prohibited from engaging.
**unfair labor practice** Conduct in which an employer or union is prohibited from engaging.
**unfair union practice** Conduct in which a union is prohibited from engaging.
**Uniform Commercial Code** One of the Uniform Laws, drafted by the National Conference of Commissioners on Uniform State Laws, governing commercial transactions (sales of goods, commercial paper, bank deposits and collections, letters of credit, bulk transfers, warehouse receipts, bills of lading, investment securities, and secured transactions).
**unilateral mistake** Erroneous belief on the part of only one of the parties to a contract.
**union shop** Employer can hire nonunion members, but such employees must then join the union.
**universal life** Ordinary life divided into two components, a renewable term insurance policy and an investment portfolio.
**unliquidated debt** Obligation that is uncertain or contested in amount.
**unqualified indorsement** (see **indorsement**) One that imposes liability upon the indorser.
**unreasonably dangerous** Danger beyond that which the ordinary consumer contemplates.
**unrestrictive indorsement** (see **indorsement**) One that does not attempt to restrict the rights of the indorsee.
**usage of trade** Any practice or method of dealing having such regularity of observance in a place, vocation, or trade as to justify an expectation that it will be observed with respect to the transaction in question.
**usury** Collectively, the laws of a jurisdiction regulating the charging of interest rates. A usurious loan is one whose interest rates are determined to be in excess of those permitted by the usury laws.

**value** The performance of legal consideration, the forgiveness of an antecedent debt, the giving of a negotiable instrument, or the giving of an irrevocable commitment to a third party. UCC §1-201(44).
**variance** A use differing from that provided in a zoning ordinance in order to avoid undue hardship.
**vendee** A purchaser or buyer; one to whom anything is sold. See also **vendor**.
**vendor** The person who transfers property by sale, particularly real estate; "seller" being more commonly used for one who sells personalty. See also **vendee**.
**venue** "Jurisdiction" of the court means the inherent power to decide a case, whereas "venue" designates the particular county or city in which a court with jurisdiction may hear and determine the case.
**verdict** The formal and unanimous decision or finding of a jury, impaneled and sworn for the trial of a cause, upon the matters or questions duly submitted to it upon the trial.
**vertical privity** Who is liable to the plaintiff.
**vertical restraints** Agreements among parties at different levels of the distribution chain.
**vested** Fixed; accrued; settled; absolute. To be "vested," a right must be more than a mere expectation based on an anticipation of the continuance of an existing law; it must have become a title, legal or equitable, to the present or future enforcement of a demand, or a legal exemption from the demand of another.
**vested remainder** Unconditional remainder that is a fixed present interest to be enjoyed in the future.
**vicarious liability** Indirect legal responsibility; for example, the liability of an employer for the acts of an employee or that of a principal for the torts and contracts of an agent.
**void** Null; ineffectual; nugatory; having no legal force or binding effect; unable, in law, to support the purpose for which it was intended.

This difference separates the words "void" and "voidable": *void* in the strict sense means that an instrument or transaction is nugatory and ineffectual, so that nothing can cure it; *voidable* exists when an imperfection or defect can be cured by the act or confirmation of the person who could take advantage of it.

Frequently, the word "void" is used and construed as having the more liberal meaning of "voidable."
**voidable** Capable of being made void. See also **void**.
**voir dire** Preliminary examination of potential jurors.
**voluntary** Resulting from free choice. The word, especially in statutes, often implies knowledge of essential facts.
**voting trust** Transfer of corporate shares' voting rights to a trustee.

**wager (gambling)** Agreement that one party will win or lose depending upon the outcome of an event in which the only interest is the gain or loss.
**waiver** Terms "estoppel" and "waiver" are not synonymous; "waiver" means the voluntary, intentional relinquishment of a known right, and "estoppel" rests upon principle that, where anyone has done an act or made a statement that would be a fraud on his part to controvert or impair, because the other party has acted upon it in belief that what was done or said was true, conscience and honest dealing require that he not be permitted to repudiate his act or gainsay his statement. See also **estoppel**.
**ward** An infant or insane person placed by authority of law under the care of a guardian.
**warehouse receipt** Receipt issued by a person storing goods.
**warehouser** Storer of goods for compensation.
**warrant, *v.*** In contracts, to engage or promise that a certain fact or state of facts, in relation to the subject matter, is, or shall be, as it is represented to be.

In conveyancing, to assure the title to property sold, by an express covenant to that effect in the deed of conveyance.
**warranty** A warranty is a statement or representation made by a seller of goods, contemporaneously with and as a part of a contract of sale, though collateral to express the object of the sale, having reference to the character, quality, or title of goods, and by which the seller promises or undertakes to ensure that certain facts are or shall be as he then represents them.

The general statutory law governing warranties on sales of goods is provided in UCC §2-312 *et seq*. The three main types of warranties are (1) express warranty; (2) implied warranty of fitness; (3) implied warranty of merchantability.
**warranty deed** Deed in which grantor warrants good clear title. The usual covenants of title are warranties of seisin, quiet enjoyment, right to convey, freedom from encumbrances, and defense of title as to all claims.

*Special warranty deed* Seller warrants that he has not impaired title.
**warranty liability** Applies to persons who transfer an instrument or receive payment or acceptance.
**warranty of title** Obligation to convey the right to ownership without any lien.
**waste** Any act or omission that does permanent injury to the realty or unreasonably changes its value.
**white-collar crime** Corporate crime.
**will** A written instrument executed with the formalities required by statutes, whereby a person makes a disposition of his property to take effect after his death.
**winding up** To settle the accounts and liquidate the assets of a partnership or corporation, for the purpose of making distribution and terminating the concern.
**without reserve** Auctioneer may not withdraw the goods from the auction.
**workers' compensation** Compensation awarded to an employee who is injured, when the injury arose out of and in the course of his employment.
**writ of certiorari** Discretionary review by a higher court. See also **certiorari**.
**writ of execution** Order served by sheriff upon debtor demanding payment of a court judgment against debtor.
**zoning** Public control over land use.

# Index

# C

# D

# E

# M



# N



# O

# P



# Q



# R

# T



# U